STAGES OF DRAMA

Classical to Contemporary Theater

Fifth Edition

STAGES OF DRAMA
Classical to Contemporary Theater

Fifth Edition

CARL H. KLAUS
University of Iowa

MIRIAM GILBERT
University of Iowa

BRADFORD S. FIELD JR.
Wayne State University

BEDFORD/ST. MARTIN'S
Boston ♦ New York

For Bedford/St. Martin's

Developmental Editor: Ellen Thibault
Senior Production Editor: Harold Chester
Senior Production Supervisor: Joe Ford
Marketing Manager: Jenna Bookin Barry
Art Direction and Cover Design: Donna Lee Dennison
Photo Research: Martha Friedman
Cover Photo: © Richard Feldman/American Repertory Theatre
Composition: Stratford Publishing Services, Inc.
Printing and Binding: RR Donnelley & Sons Company

President: Joan E. Feinberg
Editorial Director: Denise B. Wydra
Editor in Chief: Karen S. Henry
Director of Editing, Design, and Production: Marcia Cohen
Managing Editor: Erica T. Appel

Library of Congress Control Number: 2002107347

Manufactured in the United States of America.

3 2 1 0 9
f

For information, write: Bedford/St. Martin's, 75 Arlington Street, Boston, MA 02116   (617-399-4000)

ISBN-10: 0-312-39733-X
ISBN-13: 978-0-312-39733-3

Acknowledgments

Acknowledgments and copyrights appear at the back of the book on pages 1727–31, which constitute an extension of the copyright page.

PREFACE

In its fifth edition, *Stages of Drama* offers a richly varied collection of 50 outstanding plays, chronologically arranged, by major playwrights from the classical to contemporary periods. This culturally diverse and generically representative collection now features one of the most extensive selections of contemporary plays in a college anthology—22 in all—while maintaining its strong commitment to earlier periods of drama. *Stages of Drama* also provides the most extensive array of performance-oriented material, including more than 160 production shots, as well as 47 performance reviews, and 20 interviews with playwrights, directors, actors, and designers, all carefully chosen to illuminate various aspects of theatrical production for every play in the collection. And a new feature, Ideas of Drama, unique to *Stages of Drama*, offers a mini-anthology of critical works, which includes 14 selections about the nature of drama and dramatic performance by major figures from the classical to contemporary periods.

Our editorial apparatus has again been updated in this edition, so as to provide four distinctive kinds of commentary and guidance that we hope will contribute to students' understanding and enjoyment of drama:

1. An introduction on reading and witnessing a play, illustrated with a discussion of Susan Glaspell's *Trifles*.

2. Introductions to each period of drama, illustrated with detailed line drawings of the theaters typical of the period, so that each play can be seen in the context of the stage for which it was originally produced.

3. Introductions to each of the dramatists, surveying their theatrical careers and their major works, as well as discussing issues related to understanding and staging their plays.

4. An appendix on analyzing and writing about a play, which offers a detailed sample annotation of a scene from Ionesco's *The Lesson*, together with specific suggestions for kinds of papers that might develop from such analyses.

Thus from dramatist to dramatic production to ideas of drama, *Stages of Drama* offers an extensive collection of plays and supplementary material to help students experience and understand the imaginative world of theater.

NEW TO THIS EDITION

New plays: Twelve plays, embodying a broad range of dramatic styles, are new to this edition. These newly added plays include such perennially engaging and richly varied comedies as William Shakespeare's *Much Ado About Nothing*, Oscar Wilde's *The Importance of Being Earnest*, and Alan Ayckbourn's *Absurd Person Singular;* as well as such compelling naturalistic drama as J. M. Synge's *In the Shadow of the Glen*, Eugene O'Neill's *Homecoming* from *Mourning Becomes Electra*, Edward Albee's *The Zoo Story;* and contemporary plays that explore significant cultural and existential issues, such as Derek Walcott's *Pantomime*, August Wilson's *Fences*, Cherríe Moraga's *Shadow of a Man*, Tom Stoppard's *Arcadia*, Paula Vogel's *How I Learned to Drive*, and Suzan-Lori Parks's *In the Blood*.

New performance oriented material: We have included 65 new production shots and 35 new interviews, letters, reviews, and essays that shed light on the specific challenges and choices involved in writing and staging a play. Among these selections are interviews with David Mamet about the controversy surrounding *Oleanna*, and with Paula Vogel about writing *How I Learned to Drive*. Also featured are two specially commissioned interviews—one with the Nobel prize–winning Caribbean playwright Derek Walcott, in which he shares his personal ideas about the staging of *Pantomime*, the other with the distinguished actor Alvin Epstein, in which he provides candid perspectives about performing the different roles he played in two different productions of *The Bacchae* (Dionysus in the 1969 Yale production and Kadmos in the 1997 American Repertory Theatre Production). These new materials are intended to offer students numerous points of view on the staging of plays and the performance of dramatic roles, and an understanding of the theatrical experience.

New pieces about the nature of drama and dramatic performance: This distinctive section, **Ideas of Drama,** offers fourteen significant pieces of theory and criticism that deal with major genres, aspects, and elements of drama. This special mini-anthology features Aristotle on tragedy, Sir Philip Sidney on the unities, Oliver Goldsmith on comedy, Strindberg on naturalistic staging, Shaw on Ibsen's realism, Stanislavski on his revolutionary ideas of acting, Brecht and Artaud on experimental drama, Arthur Miller on tragedy and the common man, Amiri Baraka on Black theater, Martin Esslin on absurdist drama, and the contemporary playwrights Marsha Norman and Suzan-Lori Parks on the challenges of playwriting itself. This mini-collection of dramatic theory and commentary, unique to this anthology, is intended to provide students with important critical works that have shaped (and continue to shape) drama and theater.

ACKNOWLEDGMENTS

For their helpful comments on the fourth edition and suggestions for the fifth, we are grateful to Patricia Flanagan Behrendt, University of Nebraska; Karen Blansfield, University of North Carolina; Robert Brooks, Eastern Illinois University; Victor L. Cahn, Skidmore College; Keith Cushman, University of North Carolina; Rinda Frye, University of Louisville; Sister Stella Gampfer, Marian College; Diane E. Henderson, Massachusetts Institute of Technology; Joan Herrington, Western Michigan University; Woodrow Hood, High Point University; John H. Houchin, Boston College; George W. Justice, Virginia Polytechnical Institute; Gregory Kable, University of North Carolina; Michael F. Kaffer, Spring Hill College; Joyce M. Miller, Collin County Community College; Kate Musgrove, Graceland University; Patricia A. Neal, Spring Hill College; David M. Richman, University of New Hampshire; Jon D. Rossini, Texas Tech; Belinda Russell, Northeast Mississippi Community College; David K. Sauer, Spring Hill College; Terry Donovan Smith, University of South Carolina; and Kathleen Thornton, State University of New York at Albany.

For their help on the book we are grateful to many people: Ed Kahn, Lecturer in Theatre Studies at Boston College, for his research assistance; Andrew Wilson, for his work on the Walcott interview; Virginia Creeden, for clearing text permissions;

Jessica DeSpain, University of Iowa, for assistance in gathering production material; and Martha Friedman, for art research and permissions. For their expert work in bringing this fifth edition into print, we are very grateful to the staff of Bedford/St. Martin's—especially Ellen Thibault for her energetic and resourceful guidance of the revision, Harold Chester for his careful oversight of the production process, and Emily Goodall for her editorial assistance and work on the Epstein interview.

CARL H. KLAUS
MIRIAM GILBERT
BRADFORD S. FIELD JR.

CONTENTS

IDEAS OF DRAMA: CLASSICAL TO CONTEMPORARY 1655

APPENDICES

STAGES OF DRAMA

Classical to Contemporary Theater

Fifth Edition

READING AND WITNESSING A PLAY

The plays in this collection, like most works of drama, are meant to be performed on a stage and witnessed by an audience. The life of drama is, in fact, so intimately connected to stage performance that a single word—"theater"—is often used to refer both to plays and to the place where they are performed and witnessed. The theatrical nature of plays is immediately evident from the fact that they consist largely of dialogue, through which characters speak to one another rather than to us, communicate with each other rather than with us as readers. So, when reading a play, we must infer a great deal more about the plot, the characters, and the significance of their experience than we do when reading a story, when we can rely on a narrator to tell us what is happening, characterize the persons who are involved, detail their thoughts and actions, explain what is at stake, and perhaps even comment on the significance of events as they unfold.

In reading a play rather than witnessing it on stage, we also have to imagine what it might look like in performance, projecting in our mind's eye an image of the setting and the props, as well as the movements, gestures, facial expressions, and vocal intonations of the characters. In other words, we have to recognize that the text of a play is actually a script for production—but a script that contains relatively few explicit stage directions compared to the many implicit clues from which the director, set designer, costumer, and actors create the complex spectacle of a theatrical production. And we—like the director, designers, and actors—must develop our understanding of the play and our idea of the play in performance primarily from a careful reading of the dialogue, as well as from whatever stage directions and other information the dramatist might provide about the characters and the setting.

As an example of what you can discover about the imaginative world of a play through close and careful reading, consider the information that Susan Glaspell offers at the beginning of her short play, *Trifles* (1916). The cast list of five characters identifies the three men by occupation—George Henderson is the county attorney,

Henry Peters is the sheriff, and Lewis Hale is a farmer. The two women in the cast, by contrast, seem to have no first names and no occupation other than being wives, since they are identified as Mrs. Peters and Mrs. Hale. The opening stage direction may even create a brief moment of confusion for the reader, referring as it does to a character who isn't mentioned in the cast list: "Scene: *The kitchen in the now abandoned farmhouse of* John Wright, *a gloomy kitchen, and left without having been put in order.*" Readers may ask, "Who is John Wright?" and "Why is the farmhouse abandoned?"

Though Glaspell's cast list seems to offer more specific information about the men than about the women, the stage directions before anyone speaks not only describe the women more fully but even suggest their emotional states. The men are mentioned in terms of their occupations and their age: "*The Sheriff and Hale are men in middle life, the County Attorney is a young man.*" We know that they are cold because "*all are much bundled up and go at once to the stove.*" The women are more individually characterized, with the Sheriff's wife described as "*a slight wiry woman, a thin nervous face.*" Mrs. Hale is even more vividly presented: "*Mrs. Hale is larger and would ordinarily be called more comfortable looking, but she is disturbed now and looks fearfully about as she enters.*" Glaspell thus creates not only the physical temperature but also the emotional temperature, starting with the word "gloomy," and then describing Mrs. Hale's "fearful" looking about. The women, we notice, are not very eager to come into the kitchen: "*The women have come in slowly, and stand close together near the door.*" Though invited to come more fully into the room, to take advantage of the fire, they refuse, Mrs. Peters with a brief line ("I'm not—cold") and Mrs. Hale in silence. Silence is, in fact, what characterizes both women and what may well attract an audience's attention. What are these two women doing here? Why won't they come farther into the room, as a stage direction implies ("*indicating the door by which the two women are still standing*")? What are they thinking? And what does Mrs. Peters's short pause, as indicated by the dash before "cold," imply? Is there another word she would like to use?

The first section of the play is essentially one in which the audience hears—as does the County Attorney—what has happened to create the abandoned farmhouse and the disordered kitchen. Hale's recounting of his discovery of Mrs. Wright rocking back and forth in her chair, fingering her apron, looking "as if she didn't know what she was going to do next" is the prelude to his story of finding the dead body of John Wright in bed, strangled, with a rope around his neck. His repeated mention of Mrs. Wright's hand gesture, "kind of pleating at her apron," and his description of her strangely unemotional state as she answers questions seem, to any reader of detective stories, to implicate her in her husband's death. But Hale's story also characterizes her husband and the husband/wife relationship through the seemingly inconsequential detail of wanting to set up a "party telephone." Not only does this detail locate the play in the early twentieth century when a farmer might well have been able to afford only a shared phone connection, but it also suggests that Hale is willing to communicate with others, while Wright, who has turned down the idea once before, thinks that "folks talked too much anyway, and all he asked was peace and quiet." Even more telling is an almost parenthetical line, as Hale remembers that he thought he might persuade Wright to the shared line by raising the matter in front of the couple, but then adds, "though I said to Harry that I didn't know as what his wife wanted made much difference to John." The County Attorney cuts off this line—"Let's talk about that later, Mr. Hale"—and the very interruption focuses our attention on it. His unwillingness—or is it his inability?—to understand the relationship between Wright and Mrs. Wright surfaces again when he looks around the kitchen and says to the Sheriff, "You're convinced that there was nothing important here—nothing that would point to any motive?" And the Sheriff seems equally unaware, "Nothing here but kitchen things."

But is that true? Glaspell's titling of the play, her emphasis in the opening stage direction on the kitchen's disorder, and her counterpointing of the silent women with the garrulous men who see but do not understand should serve as both invitation and warning to the alert reader/audience. Why are the women so silent during the first section of the play? Why are they present at all, given that they have no "official" function in terms of investigating the murder? What did happen in the Wright household and, more importantly, *why* did it happen? We suggest that you now read Glaspell's short play, which begins on the next page. Then we will provide a brief commentary for you to compare with your own impressions and that you can use as a source of ideas for reading other plays in this collection.

TRIFLES

BY SUSAN GLASPELL

CHARACTERS

GEORGE HENDERSON, *county attorney*
HENRY PETERS, *sheriff*
LEWIS HALE, *a neighboring farmer*

MRS. PETERS
MRS. HALE

SCENE

The kitchen in the now abandoned farmhouse of John Wright, a gloomy kitchen, and left without having been put in order—the walls covered with a faded wall paper. Down right is a door leading to the parlor. On the right wall above this door is a built-in kitchen cupboard with shelves in the upper portion and drawers below. In the rear wall at right, up two steps is a door opening onto stairs leading to the second floor. In the rear wall at left is a door to the shed and from there to the outside. Between these two doors is an old-fashioned black iron stove. Running along the left wall from the shed door is an old iron sink and sink shelf, in which is set a hand pump. Downstage of the sink is an uncurtained window. Near the window is an old wooden rocker. Center stage is an unpainted wooden kitchen table with straight chairs on either side. There is a small chair down right. Unwashed pans under the sink, a loaf of bread outside the breadbox, a dish towel on the table—other signs of incompleted work. At the rear the shed door opens and the Sheriff comes in followed by the County Attorney and Hale. The Sheriff and Hale are men in middle life, the County Attorney is a young man; all are much bundled up and go at once to the stove. They are followed by the two women—the Sheriff's wife, Mrs. Peters, first: she is a slight wiry woman, a thin nervous face. Mrs. Hale is larger and would ordinarily be called more comfortable looking, but she is disturbed now and looks fearfully about as she enters. The women have come in slowly, and stand close together near the door.

COUNTY ATTORNEY (*at stove rubbing his hands*): This feels good. Come up to the fire, ladies.

MRS. PETERS (*after taking a step forward*): I'm not—cold.

SHERIFF (*unbuttoning his overcoat and stepping away from the stove to right of table as if to mark the beginning of official business*): Now, Mr. Hale, before we move things about, you explain to Mr. Henderson just what you saw when you came here yesterday morning.

COUNTY ATTORNEY (*crossing down to left of the table*): By the way, has anything been moved? Are things just as you left them yesterday?

SHERIFF (*looking about*): It's just about the same. When it dropped below zero last night I thought I'd better send Frank out this morning to make a fire for

us—(*sits right of center table*) no use getting pneumonia with a big case on, but I told him not to touch anything except the stove—and you know Frank.

COUNTY ATTORNEY: Somebody should have been left here yesterday.

SHERIFF: Oh—yesterday. When I had to send Frank to Morris Center for that man who went crazy—I want you to know I had my hands full yesterday. I knew you could get back from Omaha by today and as long as I went over everything here myself———

COUNTY ATTORNEY: Well, Mr. Hale, tell just what happened when you came here yesterday morning.

HALE (*crossing down to above table*): Harry and I had started to town with a load of potatoes. We came along the road from my place and as I got here I said, "I'm going to see if I can't get John Wright to go in with me on a party telephone." I spoke to Wright about it once before and he put me off, saying folks talked too much anyway, and all he asked was peace and quiet—I guess you know about how much he talked himself; but I thought maybe if I went to the house and talked about it before his wife, though I said to Harry that I didn't know as what his wife wanted made much difference to John———

COUNTY ATTORNEY: Let's talk about that later, Mr. Hale. I do want to talk about that, but tell now just what happened when you got to the house.

HALE: I didn't hear or see anything; I knocked at the door, and still it was all quiet inside. I knew they must be up, it was past eight o'clock. So I knocked again, and I thought I heard someone say, "Come in." I wasn't sure, I'm not sure yet, but I opened the door—this door (*indicating the door by which the two women are still standing*) and there in that rocker—(*pointing to it*) sat Mrs. Wright. (*They all look at the rocker down left.*)

COUNTY ATTORNEY: What—was she doing?

HALE: She was rockin' back and forth. She had her apron in her hand and was kind of—pleating it.

COUNTY ATTORNEY: And how did she—look?

HALE: Well, she looked queer.

COUNTY ATTORNEY: How do you mean—queer?

HALE: Well, as if she didn't know what she was going to do next. And kind of done up.

COUNTY ATTORNEY (*takes out notebook and pencil and sits left of center table*): How did she seem to feel about your coming?

HALE: Why, I don't think she minded—one way or other. She didn't pay much attention. I said, "How do, Mrs. Wright, it's cold, ain't it?" And she said, "Is it?"—and went on kind of pleating at her apron. Well, I was surprised: she didn't ask me to come up to the stove, or to set down, but just sat there, not even looking at me, so I said, "I want to see John." And then she—laughed. I guess you would call it a laugh. I thought of Harry and the team outside, so I said a little sharp: "Can't I see John?" "No," she says, kind o' dull like. "Ain't he home?" says I. "Yes," says she, "he's home." "Then why can't I see him?" I asked her, out of patience. "'Cause he's dead," says she. *Dead?* says I. She just nodded her head, not getting a bit excited, but rockin' back and forth. "Why—where is he?" says I, not knowing what to say. She just pointed upstairs—like that. (*Himself pointing to the room above.*) I started for the stairs, with the idea of going up there. I walked from there to here—then I says, "Why, what did he die of?" "He died of a rope round his neck," says she, and just went on pleatin' at her apron. Well, I went out and called Harry. I thought I might—need help. We went upstairs and there he was lyin'———

COUNTY ATTORNEY: I think I'd rather have you go into that upstairs, where you can point it all out. just go on now with the rest of the story.

HALE: Well, my first thought was to get that rope off. It looked . . . (*stops: his face twitches*) . . . but Harry, he went up to him, and he said, "No, he's dead all right, and we'd better not touch anything." So we went right back downstairs. She was still sitting that same way. "Has anybody been notified?" I asked. "No," says she, unconcerned. "Who did this, Mrs. Wright?" said Harry. He said it businesslike—and she stopped pleatin' of her apron. "I don't know," she says. "You don't *know?*" says Harry. "No," says she. "Weren't you sleepin' in the bed with him?" says Harry. "Yes," says she, "but I was on the inside." "Somebody slipped a rope round his head and strangled him and you didn't wake up?" says Harry. "I didn't wake up," she said after him. We must 'a' looked as if we didn't see how that could be, for after a minute she said, "I sleep sound." Harry was going to ask her more questions but I said maybe we ought to let her tell her story first to the coroner, or the sheriff, so Harry went fast as he could to Rivers' place, where there's a telephone.

COUNTY ATTORNEY: And what did Mrs. Wright do when she knew that you had gone for the coroner?

HALE: She moved from the rocker to that chair over there (*pointing to a small chair in the down right corner*) and just sat there with her hands held together and looking down. I got a feeling that I ought to make some conversation, so I said I had come in to see if John wanted to put in a telephone, and at that she started to laugh, and then she stopped and looked at me—scared. (*The County Attorney, who has had his notebook out, makes a note.*) I dunno, maybe it wasn't scared. I wouldn't like to say it was. Soon Harry got back, and then Dr. Lloyd came and you, Mr. Peters, and so I guess that's all I know that you don't.

COUNTY ATTORNEY (*rising and looking around*): I guess we'll go upstairs first—and then out to the barn and around there. (*To the Sheriff.*) You're convinced that there was nothing important here—nothing that would point to any motive?

SHERIFF: Nothing here but kitchen things. (*The County Attorney, after again looking around the kitchen, opens the door of a cupboard closet in right wall. He brings a small chair from right—gets on it and looks on a shelf. Pulls his hand away, sticky.*)

COUNTY ATTORNEY: Here's a nice mess. (*The women draw nearer up to center.*)

MRS. PETERS (*to the other woman*): Oh, her fruit; it did freeze. (*To the Lawyer.*) She worried about that when it turned so cold. She said the fire'd go out and her jars would break.

SHERIFF (*rises*): Well, can you beat the woman! Held for murder and worryin' about her preserves.

COUNTY ATTORNEY (*getting down from chair*): I guess before we're through she may have something more serious than preserves to worry about. (*Crosses down right center.*)

HALE: Well, women are used to worrying over trifles. (*The two women move a little closer together.*)

COUNTY ATTORNEY (*with the gallantry of a young politician*): And yet, for all their worries, what would we do without the ladies? (*The women do not unbend. He goes below the center table to the sink, takes a dipperful of water from the pail, and pouring it into a basin, washes his hands. While he is doing this the Sheriff and Hale cross to cupboard, which they inspect. The County Attorney starts to wipe his hands on the roller towel, turns it for a cleaner place.*) Dirty towels! (*Kicks his foot against the pans under the sink.*) Not much of a housekeeper, would you say, ladies?

MRS. HALE (*stiffly*): There's a great deal of work to be done on a farm.

COUNTY ATTORNEY: To be sure. And yet (*with a little bow to her*) I know there are some Dickson County farmhouses which do not have such roller towels. (*He gives it a pull to expose its full length again.*)

MRS. HALE: Those towels get dirty awful quick. Men's hands aren't always as clean as they might be.

COUNTY ATTORNEY: Ah, loyal to your sex, I see. But

you and Mrs. Wright were neighbors. I suppose you were friends, too.

MRS. HALE (*shaking her head*): I've not seen much of her of late years. I've not been in this house—it's more than a year.

COUNTY ATTORNEY (*crossing to women up center*): And why was that? You didn't like her?

MRS. HALE: I liked her all well enough. Farmers' wives have their hands full, Mr. Henderson. And then————

COUNTY ATTORNEY: Yes————?

MRS. HALE (*looking about*): It never seemed a very cheerful place.

COUNTY ATTORNEY: No—it's not cheerful. I shouldn't say she had the homemaking instinct.

MRS. HALE: Well, I don't know as Wright had, either.

COUNTY ATTORNEY: You mean that they didn't get on very well?

MRS. HALE: No, I don't mean anything. But I don't think a place'd be any cheerfuller for John Wright's being in it.

COUNTY ATTORNEY: I'd like to talk more of that a little later. I want to get the lay of things upstairs now. (*He goes past the women to up right where the steps lead to a stair door.*)

SHERIFF: I suppose anything Mrs. Peters does'll be all right. She was to take in some clothes for her, you know, and a few little things. We left in such a hurry yesterday.

COUNTY ATTORNEY: Yes, but I would like to see what you take, Mrs. Peters, and keep an eye out for anything that might be of use to us.

MRS. PETERS: Yes, Mr. Henderson. (*The men leave by up right door to stairs. The women listen to the men's steps on the stairs, then look about the kitchen.*)

MRS. HALE (*crossing left to sink*): I'd hate to have men coming into my kitchen, snooping around and criticizing. (*She arranges the pans under sink which the lawyer had shoved out of place.*)

MRS. PETERS: Of course it's no more than their duty. (*Crosses to cupboard up right.*)

MRS. HALE: Duty's all right, but I guess that deputy sheriff that came out to make the fire might have got a little of this on. (*Gives the roller towel a pull.*) Wish I'd thought of that sooner. Seems mean to talk about her for not having things slicked up when she had to come away in such a hurry. (*Crosses right to Mrs. Peters at cupboard.*)

MRS. PETERS (*who has been looking through cupboard, lifts one end of towel that covers a pan*): She had bread set. (*Stands still.*)

MRS. HALE (*eyes fixed on a loaf of bread beside the breadbox, which is on a low shelf of the cupboard*): She was going to put this in there. (*Picks up loaf, abruptly drops it. In a manner of returning to familiar things.*) It's a shame about her fruit. I wonder if it's all gone. (*Gets up on chair and looks.*) I think there's some

here that's all right, Mrs. Peters. Yes—here; (*holding it toward the window*) this is cherries, too. (*Looking again.*) I declare I believe that's the only one. (*Gets down, jar in hand. Goes to the sink and wipes it off on the outside.*) She'll feel awful bad after all her hard work in the hot weather. I remember the afternoon I put up my cherries last summer. (*She puts the jar on the big kitchen table, center of the room. With a sigh, is about to sit down in the rocking chair. Before she is seated realizes what chair it is; with a slow look at it, steps back. The chair which she has touched rocks back and forth. Mrs. Peters moves to center table and they both watch the chair rock for a moment or two.*)

MRS. PETERS (*shaking off the mood which the empty rocking chair has evoked. Now in a businesslike manner she speaks*): Well I must get those things from the front room closet. (*She goes to the door at the right but, after looking into the other room, steps back.*) You coming with me, Mrs. Hale? You could help me carry them. (*They go in the other room; reappear, Mrs. Peters carrying a dress, petticoat, and skirt, Mrs. Hale following with a pair of shoes.*) My, it's cold in there. (*She puts the clothes on the big table and hurries to the stove.*)

MRS. HALE (*right of center table examining the skirt*): Wright was close. I think maybe that's why she kept so much to herself. She didn't even belong to the Ladies' Aid. I suppose she felt she couldn't do her part, and then you don't enjoy things when you feel shabby. I heard she used to wear pretty clothes and be lively, when she was Minnie Foster, one of the town girls singing in the choir. But that—oh, that was thirty years ago. This all you want to take in?

MRS. PETERS: She said she wanted an apron. Funny thing to want, for there isn't much to get you dirty in jail, goodness knows. But I suppose just to make her feel more natural. (*Crosses to cupboard.*) She said they was in the top drawer in this cupboard. Yes, here. And then her little shawl that always hung behind the door. (*Opens stair door and looks.*) Yes, here it is. (*Quickly shuts door leading upstairs.*)

MRS. HALE (*abruptly moving toward her*): Mrs. Peters?

MRS. PETERS: Yes, Mrs. Hale? (*At up right door.*)

MRS. HALE: Do you think she did it?

MRS. PETERS (*in a frightened voice*): Oh, I don't know.

MRS. HALE: Well, I don't think she did. Asking for an apron and her little shawl. Worrying about her fruit.

MRS. PETERS (*starts to speak, glances up, where footsteps are heard in the room above. In a low voice*): Mr. Peters says it looks bad for her. Mr. Henderson is awful sarcastic in a speech and he'll make fun of her sayin' she didn't wake up.

MRS. HALE: Well, I guess John Wright didn't wake when they was slipping that rope under his neck.

MRS. PETERS (*crossing slowly to table and placing shawl and apron on table with other clothing*): No, it's strange. It must have been done awful crafty and still. They say it was such a—funny way to kill a man, rigging it all up like that.

MRS. HALE (*crossing to left of Mrs. Peters at table*): That's just what Mr. Hale said. There was a gun in the house. He says that's what he can't understand.

MRS. PETERS: Mr. Henderson said coming out that what was needed for the case was a motive: something to show anger, or—sudden feeling.

MRS. HALE (*who is standing by the table*): Well, I don't see any signs of anger around here. (*She puts her hand on the dish towel, which lies on the table, stands looking down at table, one-half of which is clean, the other half messy.*) It's wiped to here. (*Makes a move as if to finish work, then turns and looks at loaf of bread outside the breadbox. Drops towel. In that voice of coming back to familiar things.*) Wonder how they are finding things upstairs. (*Crossing below table to down right.*) I hope she had it a little more red-up° up there. You know, it seems kind of *sneaking*. Locking her up in town and then coming out here and trying to get her own house to turn against her!

MRS. PETERS: But, Mrs. Hale, the law is the law.

MRS. HALE: I s'pose 'tis. (*Unbuttoning her coat.*) Better loosen up your things, Mrs. Peters. You won't feel them when you go out. (*Mrs. Peters takes off her fur tippet, goes to hang it on chair back left of table, stands looking at the work basket on floor near down left window.*)

MRS. PETERS: She was piecing a quilt. (*She brings the large sewing basket to the center table and they look at the bright pieces, Mrs. Hale above the table and Mrs. Peters left of it.*)

MRS. HALE: It's a log cabin pattern. Pretty, isn't it? I wonder if she was goin' to quilt it or just knot it? (*Footsteps have been heard coming down the stairs. The Sheriff enters followed by Hale and the County Attorney.*)

SHERIFF: They wonder if she was going to quilt it or just knot it! (*The men laugh, the women look abashed.*)

COUNTY ATTORNEY (*rubbing his hands over the stove*): Frank's fire didn't do much up there, did it? Well, let's go out to the barn and get that cleared up. (*The men go outside by up left door.*)

MRS. HALE (*resentfully*): I don't know as there's anything so strange, our takin' up our time with little things while we're waiting for them to get the evidence. (*She sits in chair right of table smoothing out a block with decision.*) I don't see as it's anything to laugh about.

MRS. PETERS (*apologetically*): Of course they've got

awful important things on their minds. (*Pulls up a chair and joins Mrs. Hale at the left of the table.*)

MRS. HALE (*examining another block*): Mrs. Peters, look at this one. Here, this is the one she was working on, and look at the sewing! All the rest of it has been so nice and even. And look at this! It's all over the place! Why, it looks as if she didn't know what she was about! (*After she has said this they look at each other, then start to glance back at the door. After an instant Mrs. Hale has pulled at a knot and ripped the sewing.*)

MRS. PETERS: Oh, what are you doing, Mrs. Hale?

MRS. HALE (*mildly*): Just pulling out a stitch or two that's not sewed very good. (*Threading a needle.*) Bad sewing always made me fidgety.

MRS. PETERS (*with a glance at the door, nervously*): I don't think we ought to touch things.

MRS. HALE: I'll just finish up this end. (*Suddenly stopping and leaning forward.*) Mrs. Peters?

MRS. PETERS: Yes, Mrs. Hale?

MRS. HALE: What do you suppose she was so nervous about?

MRS. PETERS: Oh—I don't know. I don't know as she was nervous. I sometimes sew awful queer when I'm just tired. (*Mrs. Hale starts to say something, looks at Mrs. Peters, then goes on sewing.*) Well, I must get these things wrapped up. They may be through sooner than we think. (*Putting apron and other things together.*) I wonder where I can find a piece of paper, and string. (*Rises.*)

MRS. HALE: In that cupboard, maybe.

MRS. PETERS (*crosses right looking in cupboard*): Why, here's a bird-cage. (*Holds it up.*) Did she have a bird, Mrs. Hale?

MRS. HALE: Why, I don't know whether she did or not—I've not been here for so long. There was a man around last year selling canaries cheap, but I don't know as she took one; maybe she did. She used to sing real pretty herself.

MRS. PETERS (*glancing around*): Seems funny to think of a bird here. But she must have had one, or why would she have a cage? I wonder what happened to it?

MRS. HALE: I s'pose maybe the cat got it.

MRS. PETERS: No, she didn't have a cat. She's got that feeling some people have about cats—being afraid of them. My cat got in her room and she was real upset and asked me to take it out.

MRS. HALE: My sister Bessie was like that. Queer, ain't it?

MRS. PETERS (*examining the cage*): Why, look at this door. It's broke. One hinge is pulled apart. (*Takes a step down to Mrs. Hale's right.*)

MRS. HALE (*looking too*): Looks as if someone must have been rough with it.

MRS. PETERS: Why, yes. (*She brings the cage forward and puts it on the table.*)

---

red-up, (slang) readied (for company).

MRS. HALE (*glancing toward up left door*): I wish if they're going to find any evidence they'd be about it. I don't like this place.

MRS. PETERS: But I'm awful glad you came with me, Mrs. Hale. It would be lonesome for me sitting here alone.

MRS. HALE: It would, wouldn't it? (*Dropping her sewing.*) But I tell you what I do wish, Mrs. Peters. I wish I had come over sometimes when *she* was here. I—(*looking around the room*)—wish I had.

MRS. PETERS: But of course you were awful busy, Mrs. Hale—your house and your children.

MRS. HALE (*rises and crosses left*): I could've come. I stayed away because it weren't cheerful—and that's why I ought to have come. I—(*looking out left window*)—I've never liked this place. Maybe it's because it's down in a hollow and you don't see the road. I dunno what it is, but it's a lonesome place and always was. I wish I had come over to see Minnie Foster sometimes. I can see now—(*Shakes her head.*)

MRS. PETERS (*left of table and above it*): Well, you mustn't reproach yourself, Mrs. Hale. Somehow we just don't see how it is with other folks until—something turns up.

MRS. HALE: Not having children makes less work—but it makes a quiet house, and Wright out to work all day, and no company when he did come in. (*Turning from window.*) Did you know John Wright, Mrs. Peters?

MRS. PETERS: Not to know him; I've seen him in town. They say he was a good man.

MRS. HALE: Yes—good; he didn't drink, and kept his word as well as most, I guess, and paid his debts. But he was a hard man, Mrs. Peters. Just to pass the time of day with him—(*Shivers.*) Like a raw wind that gets to the bone. (*Pauses, her eye falling on the cage.*) I should think she would 'a' wanted a bird. But what do you suppose went with it?

MRS. PETERS: I don't know, unless it got sick and died. (*She reaches over and swings the broken door, swings it again, both women watch it.*)

MRS. HALE: You weren't raised round here, were you? (*Mrs. Peters shakes her head.*) You didn't know—her?

MRS. PETERS: Not till they brought her yesterday.

MRS. HALE: She—come to think of it, she was kind of like a bird herself—real sweet and pretty, but kind of timid and—fluttery. How—she—did—change. (*Silence: then as if struck by a happy thought and relieved to get back to everyday things. Crosses right above Mrs. Peters to cupboard, replaces small chair used to stand on to its original place down right.*) Tell you what, Mrs. Peters, why don't you take the quilt in with you? It might take up her mind.

MRS. PETERS: Why, I think that's a real nice idea, Mrs. Hale. There couldn't possibly be any objection to it could there? Now, just what would I take? I wonder if her patches are in here—and her things. (*They look in the sewing basket.*)

MRS. HALE (*crosses to right of table*): Here's some red. I expect this has got sewing things in it. (*Brings out a fancy box.*) What a pretty box. Looks like something somebody would give you. Maybe her scissors are in here. (*Opens box. Suddenly puts her hand to her nose.*) Why—— (*Mrs. Peters bends nearer, then turns her face away.*) There's something wrapped up in this piece of silk.

MRS. PETERS: Why, this isn't her scissors.

MRS. HALE (*lifting the silk*): Oh, Mrs. Peters—it's—— (*Mrs. Peters bends closer.*)

MRS. PETERS: It's the bird.

MRS. HALE: But, Mrs. Peters—look at it! Its neck! Look at its neck! It's all—other side *to*.

MRS. PETERS: Somebody—wrung—its—neck. (*Their eyes meet. A look of growing comprehension, of horror. Steps are heard outside. Mrs. Hale slips box under quilt pieces, and sinks into her chair. Enter Sheriff and County Attorney. Mrs. Peters steps down left and stands looking out of window.*)

COUNTY ATTORNEY (*as one turning from serious things to little pleasantries*): Well, ladies, have you decided whether she was going to quilt it or knot it? (*Crosses to center above table.*)

MRS. PETERS: We think she was going to—knot it. (*Sheriff crosses to right of stove, lifts stove lid, and glances at fire, then stands warming hands at stove.*)

COUNTY ATTORNEY: Well, that's interesting, I'm sure. (*Seeing the bird-cage.*) Has the bird flown?

MRS. HALE (*putting more quilt pieces over the box*): We think the—cat got it.

COUNTY ATTORNEY (*preoccupied*): Is there a cat? (*Mrs. Hale glances in a quick covert way at Mrs. Peters.*)

MRS. PETERS (*turning from window takes a step in*): Well, not *now*. They're superstitious, you know. They leave.

COUNTY ATTORNEY (*to Sheriff Peters, continuing an interrupted conversation*): No sign at all of anyone having come from the outside. Their own rope. Now let's go up again and go over it piece by piece. (*They start upstairs.*) It would have to have been someone who knew just the—— (*Mrs. Peters sits down left of table. The two women sit there not looking at one another, but as if peering into something and at the same time holding back. When they talk now it is in the manner of feeling their way over strange ground, as if afraid of what they are saying, but as if they cannot help saying it.*)

MRS. HALE: She liked the bird. She was going to bury it in that pretty box.

MRS. PETERS (*in a whisper*): When I was a girl—my kitten—there was a boy took a hatchet, and before my eyes—and before I could get there—— (*Covers her face an instant.*) If they hadn't held me back I would have—(*catches herself, looks upstairs where steps are heard, falters weakly*)—hurt him.

MRS. HALE (*with a slow look around her*): I wonder how it would seem never to have had any children around. (*Pause.*) No, Wright wouldn't like the bird—a thing that sang. She used to sing. He killed that, too.

MRS. PETERS (*moving uneasily*): We don't know who killed the bird.

MRS. HALE: I knew John Wright.

MRS. PETERS: It was an awful thing was done in this house that night, Mrs. Hale. Killing a man while he slept, slipping a rope around his neck that choked the life out of him.

MRS. HALE: His neck. Choked the life out of him. (*Her hand goes out and rests on the bird-cage.*)

MRS. PETERS (*with rising voice*): We don't know who killed him. We don't *know*.

MRS. HALE (*her own feelings not interrupted*): If there'd been years and years of nothing, then a bird to sing to you, it would be awful—still, after the bird was still.

MRS. PETERS (*something within her speaking*): I know what stillness is. When we homesteaded in Dakota, and my first baby died—after he was two years old, and me with no other then——

MRS. HALE (*moving*): How soon do you suppose they'll be through looking for the evidence?

MRS. PETERS: I know what stillness is. (*Pulling herself back.*) The law has got to punish crimes, Mrs. Hale.

MRS. HALE (*not as if answering that*): I wish you'd seen Minnie Foster when she wore a white dress with blue ribbons and stood up there in the choir and sang. (*A look around the room.*) Oh, I *wish* I'd come over here once in a while! That was a crime! That was a crime! Who's going to punish that?

MRS. PETERS (*looking upstairs*): We mustn't—take on.

MRS. HALE: I might have known she needed help! I know how things can be—for women. I tell you, it's queer, Mrs. Peters. We live close together and we live far apart. We all go through the same things—it's all just a different kind of the same thing. (*Brushes her eyes, noticing the jar of fruit, reaches out for it.*) If I was you I wouldn't tell her her fruit was gone. Tell her it *ain't*. Tell her it's all right. Take this in to prove it to her. She—she may never know whether it was broke or not.

MRS. PETERS (*takes the jar, looks about for something to wrap it in; takes petticoat from the clothes brought from the other room, very nervously begins winding this around the jar. In a false voice*): My, it's a good thing the men couldn't hear us. Wouldn't they just laugh! Getting all stirred up over a little thing like a—dead canary. As if they could have anything to

do with—with—wouldn't they *laugh!* (*The men are heard coming downstairs.*)

MRS. HALE (*under her breath*): Maybe they would—maybe they wouldn't.

COUNTY ATTORNEY: No, Peters, it's all perfectly clear except a reason for doing it. But you know juries when it comes to women. If there was some definite thing. (*Crosses slowly to above table. Sheriff crosses down right. Mrs. Hale and Mrs. Peters remain seated at either side of table.*) Something to show—something to make a story about—a thing that would connect up with this strange way of doing it——
(*The women's eyes meet for an instant. Enter Hale from outer door.*)

HALE (*remaining by door*): Well, I've got the team around. Pretty cold out there.

COUNTY ATTORNEY: I'm going to stay awhile by myself. (*To the Sheriff.*) You can send Frank out for me, can't you? I want to go over everything. I'm not satisfied that we can't do better.

SHERIFF: Do you want to see what Mrs. Peters is going to take in? (*The Lawyer picks up the apron, laughs.*)

COUNTY ATTORNEY: Oh, I guess they're not very dangerous things the ladies have picked out. (*Moves a few things about, disturbing the quilt pieces which cover the box. Steps back.*) No, Mrs. Peters doesn't need supervising. For that matter a sheriff's wife is married to the law. Ever think of it that way, Mrs. Peters?

MRS. PETERS: Not—just that way.

SHERIFF (*chuckling*): Married to the law. (*Moves to down right door to the other room.*) I just want you to come in here a minute, George. We ought to take a look at these windows.

COUNTY ATTORNEY (*scoffingly*): Oh, windows!

SHERIFF: We'll be right out, Mr. Hale. (*Hale goes outside. The Sheriff follows the County Attorney into the room. Then Mrs. Hale rises, hands tight together, looking intensely at Mrs. Peters, whose eyes make a slow turn, finally meeting Mrs. Hale's. A moment Mrs. Hale holds her, then her own eyes point the way to where the box is concealed. Suddenly Mrs. Peters throws back quilt pieces and tries to put the box in the bag she is carrying. It is too big. She opens box, starts to take bird out, cannot touch it, goes to pieces, stands there helpless. Sound of a knob turning in the other room. Mrs. Hale snatches the box and puts it in the pocket of her big coat. Enter County Attorney and Sheriff, who remains down right.*)

COUNTY ATTORNEY (*crosses to up left door facetiously*): Well, Henry, at least we found out that she was not going to quilt it. She was going to—what is it you call it, ladies?

MRS. HALE (*standing center below table facing front, her hand against her pocket*): We call it—knot it, Mr. Henderson.

The best place to begin reading closely is with the first words of a play, as we did in our commentary on the cast of characters, the opening stage directions, and the first lines. Such an approach works with any play but is especially appropriate with Glaspell's, which is about the reading—and interpreting—of visual signs. Indeed, Glaspell's play might almost serve as an instruction manual for how to read—and for how not to read—a dramatic situation. Take, for example, the first truly investigative moment we see in the play—the point at which the County Attorney *"opens the door of a cupboard closet in right wall. He brings a small chair from right—gets on it and looks on a shelf. Pulls his hand away, sticky."* So far in the play, all we've heard are reports of what someone saw or did, but now we see the beginning of the investigation process, as Henderson actually searches for evidence. In the theater, the audience may not know what he finds, although if he holds up a hand smeared with a red substance, it may guess that he's somehow stumbled onto a blood-stained clue. And his line "Here's a nice mess" doesn't reveal much more to the reader. It takes Mrs. Peters to interpret the situation, whether for reader or audience: "Oh, her fruit; it did freeze."

The difference in the two responses is noticeable. The attorney, with a brief emotional description, dismisses what he's seen; it's a "mess." Mrs. Peters, aided by her knowledge of what farm wives do in kitchens and in particular by her conversation with Mrs. Wright—"She worried about that when it turned so cold. She said the fire'd go out and her jars would break"—explains what has happened and is sympathetic to the problem. Each character is a "reader" of the same "clue," and yet Mrs. Peters is much more understanding. The same pattern repeats itself a few minutes later when the attorney washes off his sticky hands and, in reaching for the towel to dry them, notes that the towel is dirty and, kicking the pans under the sink, goes on to disparage Mrs. Wright's housekeeping, "Not much of a housekeeper, would you say, ladies?" Again he reaches for a label, "Dirty towels," and again he seems quick to evaluate (negatively) the evidence; he assumes that the dirty towels and the messy stack of pans must be the responsibility of Mrs. Wright. Mrs. Hale, a farmer's wife like Mrs. Wright, first offers two extenuating remarks, "There's a great deal of work to be done on a farm," and "Those towels get dirty awful quick. Men's hands aren't always as clean as they might be," suggesting a different view of the situation—one which recognizes the wider context of the problem. And later, when the men have gone, Mrs. Hale thinks of yet another explanation, "I guess that deputy sheriff that came out to make the fire might have got a little of this on" and *"Gives the roller towel a pull."* In her awareness of another explanation for the question "why is the roller towel so dirty?" she doesn't, like the attorney, assume only one possibility but thinks of others. In each case, the more generous explanation is also the more knowledgeable one; hasty evaluative judgments can often be so narrow as to exclude important possibilities.

Once the men leave the kitchen to continue their investigation upstairs, the women continue to look around, even though they are uncomfortably aware that they wouldn't like to have their own kitchens scrutinized. Because a kitchen is a familiar place for both women, even though neither has recently visited Mrs. Wright, they "read" its signs knowledgeably and thoughtfully. And because they continue to look—and to look with sympathetic eyes—they become our eyes and ears, our guides to the mystery with which the play began. They find the sewing basket with the half-finished quilt and recognize that the block Mrs. Wright was working on is radically different from the others: "Here, this is the one she was working on, and look at the sewing! All the rest of it has been so nice and even. And look at this! It's all over the place! Why, it looks as if she didn't know what she was about!" The look exchanged between the two women at this point is a crucial moment for the audience, since it signals—without words—an understanding that Mrs. Hale and Mrs. Peters are beginning to come to, an understanding of Mrs. Wright's pain, an understanding that they do not, or perhaps cannot, put into concrete terms.

And because they continue to look, they find what the men do not see. When Mrs. Peters goes to the cupboard for some paper and string to tie up the parcel she's planning to take to the jail, she finds a birdcage. We don't know if this is the same cupboard in which the shattered jars of preserves were stored or whether it's another one—but it's clear that the men didn't look long enough or carefully enough to find the cage. And even if they had found it, we suspect that they would not know what to make of it and would simply dismiss it as an empty birdcage with a broken door. Mrs. Hale's attempt to figure out whether it's likely that Mrs. Wright would have had a bird is instructive: "There was a man around last year selling canaries cheap, but I don't know as she took one; maybe she did. She used to sing real pretty herself." And her words remind us of her earlier description, "she used to wear pretty clothes and be lively, when she was Minnie Foster, one of the town girls singing in the choir. But that—oh, that was thirty years ago." The two speeches echo gently with the words "pretty" and "singing." Mrs. Hale expands the connection, finally making it explicit: "She—come to think of it, she was kind of like a bird herself—real sweet and pretty, but kind of timid and—fluttery. How—she—did—change." The dashes between the last few words are a clue to the actress, forcing her to slow down and give those words emphasis, as the speaker seems slowly to recognize the extent of that change.

The notion of change applies not only to Mrs. Wright, whom, after all, we never see, but, more importantly, to Mrs. Hale and Mrs. Peters, the characters we do see. One might argue that they change from audience members—silent, in the background, detached—to principal actors. And as they change, the question of the play becomes not merely "what *has* happened?" but "what *will* happen?" The more Mrs. Hale and Mrs. Peters see—the uneven sewing, the broken birdcage, and, finally, the dead bird itself—the more they are moved to action. Their decisions come gradually, almost imperceptibly. We've already mentioned the look between Mrs. Hale and Mrs. Peters after Mrs. Hale finds the piece of quilt with sewing "all over the place"; Mrs. Hale follows that speech with an action, as she begins to rip out the sewing and then continues to stitch up the square with more even stitches. When the two women find the bird, with its broken neck, again they exchange a look— "*of growing comprehension, of horror*"—and again, there is action: "*Mrs. Hale slips box under quilt pieces, and sinks into her chair.*" She is, we realize, hiding something that she now sees as evidence. And when asked a direct question about the bird—since the birdcage is on the table, the County Attorney can't help but see it—she responds with a lie, "We think the—cat got it," and with a physical covering up, "*putting more quilt pieces over the box.*" The mention of the cat is not, perhaps, the most useful way to lie, since the County Attorney asks, "Is there a cat?" and once again, there's a look between the women, and this time it is Mrs. Peters, the Sheriff's wife herself, who becomes a part of the cover-up, "Well, not *now*. They're superstitious, you know. They leave."

In the last section of the play, Mrs. Peters, linked to the forces of law and investigation by her marriage, gradually joins with Mrs. Hale to hide the signs that they see as explaining what the men see as unmotivated. There can be no doubt that the motive is cru-

cial, since they hear, as we do, the County Attorney saying to Sheriff Peters, "No, Peters, it's all perfectly clear except a reason for doing it. But you know juries when it comes to women. If there was some definite thing. Something to show—something to make a story about—a thing that would connect up with this strange way of doing it—" In his search for a motive, the County Attorney has not learned to read signs, to see how "trifles" may be important. But the women know the truth, and they tacitly share it with us as readers and audiences. We cannot be sure that the actions of Mrs. Peters and Mrs. Hale will save Mrs. Wright, but we know that they have done what they can to make that possible. The play's final line is a pun that as readers we may hear in a number of different ways: Henderson thinks he is making a little joke about quilting; Mrs. Hale's words, "We call it—knot it, Mr. Henderson" can be heard as "not it," implying that Henderson doesn't have a case, given what she's hiding in her pocket, or the word "knot" may remind us of the hangman's knot that could be waiting for the murderer.

Glaspell's play is, of course, not just a dramatized presentation of how to read signs, since this short play raises a whole series of literary, historical, and cultural questions. Literary critics have worked with the "source" of the play, the 1900 murder of an Iowa farmer and his wife's trial. They have also studied the play's reemergence as the short story "A Jury of Her Peers" that Glaspell wrote the following year (1917). The play and short story have become important texts for feminist critics who have studied, among other issues, the bleak reality of farm life at the turn of the century, the details and symbolic/social importance of quilting, and the telling irony that, in 1917, women not only couldn't vote but were allowed on juries in only four states. But all of the larger questions about gender and justice and community must begin, as the play's title suggests, with "trifles." These small objects, when viewed with respect and intelligence, reveal a complex past—not just to Mrs. Hale and Mrs. Peters, but to the audience that reads and listens and imagines. Like Glaspell herself, an Iowa newspaper reporter who wrote about the play's origins that she "never forgot going into the kitchen of a woman locked up in town," the play's characters and its audience remain fascinated by the kitchen and the absent woman whose life becomes increasingly and intensely present.

CLASSICAL THEATER

GREEK THEATER

During the fifth century B.C., the age of classical Greek drama, the theater in Athens stood empty almost 360 days a year, and yet the theater has probably never commanded quite so much attention as it did in fifth-century Athens, the home of classical Greek drama. Drama occupied a unique place in the culture of ancient Athenians, for it was intimately related to one of their most important religious celebrations and vigorously supported by their most powerful political institution. It was, in fact, produced under the auspices of the Athenian government, and during the greater part of the fifth century it was performed only once a year in connection with the *City Dionysia,* the major festival honoring Dionysus, the Greek god of fertility.

Dionysus had for centuries been worshiped in choric rituals known as *dithyrambs,* and these religious ceremonies are thought to be the principal source from which Greek tragedy emerged sometime in the mid-sixth century. It was during this period that Thespis, reputedly the first playwright, added an actor to the dithyrambic chorus, thereby bringing dramatic impersonation into ritual ceremonies that had previously consisted of narrative hymns chanted by a choric leader together with refrains sung and danced by a chorus. The Dionysian heritage of Greek tragedy probably accounts for the special status it achieved at the City Dionysia in 534 B.C., when the Athenian government established a prize, won appropriately by Thespis, for the best tragedy to be presented at the festival. By 486 B.C., when the contest was expanded to include comedy, the City Dionysia had become the most prestigious of the four annual celebrations of Dionysus. Thousands came from everywhere in the Greek world to attend the festival, which was held in late March or early April to ensure a fruitful spring. Obviously, theatrical productions constituted a major event in the rhythm of Athenian life, an event uniting the entire community in an expression of its civic pride and sacred convictions.

The magnitude of that event is revealed by the elaborate arrangements connected with the festival productions. The sole responsibility for supervising the contest was entrusted to a state official chosen by lot from the Athenian public. Dramatists who wished to enter the contest were required to submit their plays to him almost a year in advance of the festival, and he chose the three tragic as well as the three comic playwrights who had the honor of competing for each prize. This official also appointed wealthy citizens to serve as producers for each contestant, and these citizens financed the training and costuming of the chorus, the largest and most complex element of Greek theater. The balance of the costs, such as salaries for the actors and prizes for the winners, was paid by the government of Athens. This dramatic festival was the climax of nearly a year of activity on the part of hundreds of Athenian citizens.

The contest was preceded by a splendid public ceremony, featuring a lengthy procession of officials, priests, theatrical sponsors, and citizens who carried ritual offerings that they presented at the altar of Dionysus located in the theater. Once the contest began, it ran for three days, starting early in the morning and continuing throughout the afternoon. Each tragic dramatist needed almost an entire day to produce the three or four plays he was required to submit, and the remainder of each day was taken up by a single comedy each comic dramatist was required to submit. During those three days, the city of Athens became the center of a spectacular drama festival at which a total of twelve to fifteen new plays were produced.

The climax of the contest, when the prizes were awarded, was a moment of extraordinary honor for the winning dramatist and his producer. This honor was so important that the contest was judged by a panel of citizens chosen according to a very elaborate procedure that prevented bribery or any other form of unfair influence on their decision. The honor was so prestigious, in fact, that the government maintained records of all the contests, and many of the producers in turn commissioned monuments to be built as enduring records of their victories. By the middle of the fifth century, prizes had also been established for actors, and the profession of acting came to be so highly regarded that eminent actors were frequently given special public appointments and privileges. Classical Greek drama was neither a commercial enterprise as it is on Broadway, nor a coterie activity as it so often is Off-Broadway. It was a major public institution commanding the respect and support of the entire city-state.

The prestige of the dramatic contest was matched by the magnitude of the theater where it took place, the Theater of Dionysus, which was a sanctuary restricted to worship and celebration of the god. The design of this theater (see Figures 1 and 2), like the drama performed there, reflected its ritual origin. Its central element was the *orchestra* (literally, the dancing place), a circular area sixty-four feet in diameter where the dithyrambic choruses had performed their hymns to Dionysus and where the altar of Dionysus, the *thymele,* retained its focal location. The orchestra was surrounded by the *theatron* (literally, the seeing place), a semicircular sloping hillside that was terraced and equipped with benches capable of seating approximately 15,000 spectators. Facing the theatron was the *skene* (literally, the hut), which probably originated as a temporary dressing room for actors and then developed into a scenic structure possibly one hundred feet long, with three openings on to the orchestra, wings projecting toward the orchestra, and a slightly raised stage-like platform extending between the wings. Though the theater was frequently remodeled, its basic three-part structure—theatron, orchestra, and

Figure 1. The classical Greek theater.

Figure 2. The classical Greek theater at Epidaurus, in its restored state, during a production of *Agamemnon* by the National Theatre Company of Greece, 1965. (Photograph: D. A. Harissiadis.)

skene—was never altered and, in fact, served as the pattern for others in the ancient Greek world. The classical simplicity of that structure and the magnitude of its parts are unparalleled in the history of the theater.

The 15,000 people who attended the Theater of Dionysus were treated to a unique dramatic spectacle—a spectacle perfectly suited to the size, shape, and ceremonial heritage of that theater. For example, the typical Greek play, whether tragedy or comedy, contained not only units of dramatic action, known as *episodes,* but also choral odes following each episode. The performance included not only dialogue and action but also song and dance that amplified the mood and significance of the action. The chorus typically made its entrance, the *parados,* after a brief expository episode, the *prologos,* and the parados must have been a splendid event, for the members of the chorus, using either the stately rhythms of tragedy or the burlesque movements of comedy, marched into the orchestra through the passageways between the theatron and skene, then arranged themselves in a rectangular formation and began to perform their choral song and dance to the accompaniment of a flute. Once the chorus had entered the orchestra, it remained there throughout the play, performing not only during its odes but also during the episodes, sometimes exchanging dialogue with the characters through its leader, the *choragos,* sometimes making gestures and movements in sympathetic response to the action. The chorus provided a sustained point of reference, a continuous source of mediation between the audience and the actors themselves, who moved back and forth between the orchestra and the skene as their parts dictated. Although the chorus may strike modern audiences as unrealistic and undramatic, it was in keeping with the expectations of the ancient Greek audience and was totally consistent with the ceremonial form of drama required by the design and dimensions of their theater.

This theater required above all a bold and monumental form of drama—both in conception and execution. Nuances of character, complexities of plot, delicacies of gesture, subtleties of inflection—none of these qualities could have made an impact in so large a theater. Such a theater simply did not lend itself to the kinds of detail that produce a modern realistic illusion. Consequently, all the elements of staging were highly conventionalized, formalized, and stylized. Painted scenery, for example, which developed during the second quarter of the fifth century, probably consisted only of a few generalized locales, such as a palace, a temple, a cave, or a forest, represented on the areas between the entrances to the skene. Only a few props or machines were available to assist the imagination of the audience, such as a crane by which characters might be suspended as if in flight from the roof of the skene, or a tableau wheeled out of the skene to suggest offstage action, or a horse-drawn chariot wheeled into the orchestra to mark the arrival of a hero, or a torch held up to signify nighttime—props and machines, which, like the painted scenes, were capable of making a clear visual impact.

Actors also required special techniques and equipment. They made large gestures with their arms, for small movements of the hands would have been undetectable by the audience. They also delivered their lines with a clear and strong inflection; no matter how good the acoustics may have been, the actors still had to contend with sounds in the audience, and 15,000 people even when they are trying to be quiet can generate a great deal of noise. Because facial movements would have been invisible to almost everyone in the audience, the actors wore large stylized masks representing basic character types and, as their fortunes and emotions changed, they changed their masks to suit the situation. No doubt their costumes were also designed to accentuate their stature, to make them appear larger than life. In fact, after the fifth century, actors were even equipped with elevated shoes to increase the impression of their height. The chorus also wore masks and probably used lightweight costumes and shoes to facilitate the various dance movements it performed while singing choral odes. Taken as a whole—the choric singing and dancing, the simplified setting, the bold acting—dramatic productions in ancient Greece must have matched the epic dimensions of the theater and of the plays that were written for it by Aeschylus, Sophocles, Euripides, and Aristophanes.

ROMAN THEATER

Classical drama flourished in Rome from 240 B.C. to about 90 B.C., during the formation and expansion of the Roman Empire, and the theater of that age was altogether as enterprising as the community it was designed to entertain. It had to be resourceful to survive, for theatrical productions were by no means the prestigious and singular events they had been in Athens during the fifth century B.C. They took place not once a year but several times—indeed, every time the state declared a festival to honor one of the many Roman gods or to celebrate a major public event. These festivals—sometimes as many as fifteen or twenty a year—offered many kinds of amusements, such as boxing matches and chariot races, in addition to dramatic productions. Thus playwrights in Rome did not compete with one another, as they had in Athens, to win the honor of a prize for dramatic excellence; they competed instead with other forms of popular entertainment, much as modern dramatists must compete with television and the movies to attract part of a large and diverse audience.

Thousands of Romans attended the festivals, and they came from all ages, classes, and occupations. The playwrights were eager to please the audience because they were not independently wealthy but made their living or supplemented their income by writing plays that they sold for production at the festivals. Their plays were bought by directors or managers of acting groups, who in turn were paid to produce them by the organizers of the festivals—the Roman magistrates. The magistrates also catered to the audience, for they were publicly elected and knew that an entertaining festival would help keep them in office. The audience, who attended the festivals free of charge, was so influential that whenever it voiced its approval of a play, the magistrate usually paid a bonus to the author and director. Roman theater, then, was a highly commercial enterprise from which everyone who had a hand in it hoped to profit by appealing to popular tastes.

The tastes of that time favored situation comedy and melodramatic tragedy, and the dramatists met the popular demand primarily by adapting fourth-century Greek plays; this drama was perfectly suited to compete with other attractions at the Roman festivals, for it provided lively entertainment without provoking thought or raising questions about ethical, political, or religious issues. For much the same reason, comedy was preferred to tragedy—especially because later Greek comedy contented itself with poking fun at familiar social types in farcically complicated

Figure 3. The classical Roman theater, in one of its "temporary" forms.

situations. Those light situation comedies did not run the risk of being censored by the Roman authorities for attacking specific persons or problems, and they did not require many changes to make them fit the tone and style of Roman social experience. Furthermore, they were easily adaptable to the rough and ready production methods of the period. For example, the choral passages in fourth-century Greek comedy were largely incidental, so they were often eliminated by the Romans, making it possible for producers to stage plays without incurring the expenses of hiring and training a chorus. In fact, a small troupe could perform almost any comedy, for the actors used masks denoting one or another social type, thereby enabling a single performer to play two or more parts.

Staging conventions were as improvisational as the stage itself, for there were no permanent theaters during the period when drama flourished in Rome. The first permanent theater was not built, in fact, until 55 B.C., by which time regular forms of drama had lost their popular appeal, yielding the stage to a variety of other spectacles ranging from farce, mime, and pantomime to gladiator contests and mock sea battles. Before the era of permanent stone theaters, wooden stages and wooden benches were put up and taken down for each festival. Those temporary stages (see Figure 3) consisted simply of two parts: the *scaena* (literally, the scene building), which was a high wooden backdrop incorporating three doorways; and the *proscenium* (literally, the area in front of the scene building), which was a raised acting platform 100 to 200 feet long. For a typical comedy such as *The Menaechmi* of Plautus, the scaena was painted to represent a row of houses. Thus the doorways served as the entrances to the houses, and the proscenium was understood to be a public street running in front of the houses. Characters entered and exited not only through the doorways but also through the ends of the proscenium, the right side of which was conventionally taken as leading to the forum, the left as leading to the harbor or the country. In *Casina,* which takes place in front of two neighboring houses, the third door might easily have been used as a place where the slave Chalinus could "hide" and thus overhear a vital conversation at the end of the first act.

Because the stage represented a public street, it was necessarily impossible to show action taking place inside the houses, but the dramatists ingeniously overcame that theatrical limitation by using dialogue to report offstage events. Thus the characters in Roman comedy repeatedly exchange vivid, even racy, descriptions of their private affairs, informing one another—and the audience—of everything taking place behind their closed doors, from marital spats to extramarital sports. In *Casina,* for example, Olympio's description of his "wedding night" offers Plautus a chance for extended sexual double-entendre. Plenty of action also took place in front of the doors, for the actors apparently exploited the simple design and exceptional length of the stage by performing a variety of farcical routines appropriate to light social comedy; it says something about both the taste of the audience and the social realities of the period that the beating of slaves was a familiar comic routine. The actors and the dramatists thus produced a style of theater that depended not on realistic sets and costumes but on exaggerated gestures and movements. As if to accentuate the playfulness of the performance, they sang many of their lines to the accompaniment of a flute, creating an effect that must have been much like that of modern musical comedy. Indeed, a young Stephen Sondheim drew on the plays and characters of Plautus for the 1962 musical *A Funny Thing Happened on the Way to the Forum.* That musical's opening number— "Something familiar, / Something peculiar, / Something for everyone: / A comedy tonight"—speaks to contemporary audiences much as it might have spoken to Roman audiences, waiting for a hectic, buoyant play from Plautus.

The tragedies of Aeschylus are the oldest works of Greek drama, and thus of Western drama, that have survived. Although they date from the early period of Greek drama, they are by no means primitive either in conception or execution. Aeschylus, in fact, is generally credited with transforming the semidramatic elements he inherited from his predecessors into an authentically dramatic form and he is, therefore, regarded as having created the structure and style of classical Greek tragedy. He was born near Athens less than ten years after the inauguration of the dramatic contests, which he entered for the first time in 499, but did not win until 484. Subsequently, however, he was so successful and influential a dramatist in Athens that he was honored after his death by an exceptional decree of the state permitting his plays to be revived in the festival contests. He won the contest thirteen times during his life, and after his death he continued to win prizes even though his plays were competing with new works by living dramatists. He reportedly wrote more than ninety plays and, although the titles of seventy-nine have been recovered from Athenian records, only seven of his tragedies have survived.

These seven plays reveal a comprehensive vision of experience, for their action always takes into account not simply the lives of individual men and women but also the destinies of entire families, communities, nations, and sometimes even cosmic forces. In *The Persians* (472), for example, which is the earliest of his extant plays and the only one based completely on historical experience, Aeschylus shows the majestic suffering in defeat of those people who only a few years earlier had invaded Greece and threatened to replace Athenian democracy with Persian tyranny. In *Prometheus Bound* (ca. 460), he dramatizes a cosmic experience, a conflict between the gods, represented by the defiant refusal of Prometheus, though chained to a desolate mountain and threatened with endless torture, to give in to the will of Zeus.

Events and conflicts of a Promethean magnitude could not have been worked out within the limits of a single play. Thus it is not surprising that Aeschylus developed and perfected the trilogy, for its grand scope—three full-length plays joined to one another by their treatment of a single subject or theme—was ideally suited to his cosmic view of experience. His only surviving trilogy is *The Oresteia* (458), but it exemplifies the large-scale movements through time and space that are possible within the form. The three plays that make up this trilogy—*Agamemnon, The Libation Bearers,* and *The Eumenides*—dramatize a synoptic history of cultural progress, a history encompassing two generations of a family, during which time men and the gods are shown advancing from a barbaric to a civilized form of justice, from the personal vengeance enacted in *Agamemnon* and *The Libation Bearers* to the public trial by jury conducted in *The Eumenides*. Drama so large in scope had not been attempted before Aeschylus, but since his time the trilogy and other multiplay structures have been used by many dramatists, such as Shakespeare in *Henry VI,*

Eugene O'Neill in *Mourning Becomes Electra,* which is based on *The Oresteia,* and Ed Bullins in *The Twentieth Century Cycle.*

Aeschylus could never have achieved the dramatic power of his trilogies, or even of the individual plays that constitute them, had he limited himself to the rudimentary theatrical elements he inherited from Thespis: a chorus and a single actor. Given these conditions, tragedy before the time of Aeschylus must have been heavily dominated by the chorus, punctuated occasionally by the single actor impersonating a character and reciting a set speech or exchanging a few lines with the leader of the chorus. But early in his career, as early certainly as *The Persians,* Aeschylus made the revolutionary and dramatically essential innovation of using a second actor. Aeschylus thus made it possible to show characters interacting with one another, as well as with the chorus. He could then dramatize conflict and through conflict show character in action and plot in motion. In his later plays, such as *Agamemnon,* Aeschylus followed the precedent of Sophocles and used three actors.

Once it became possible to represent multiple characters, it was only a matter of time before the actors became as important as the chorus, then more important, then solely important. Aeschylus never went beyond the first stage in this process, for in his plays the chorus continues to have an important dramatic role, not only observing events and meditating on them but also interacting continuously with the characters, questioning them, prodding them, rebuking them, praising them—taking part in events as they take place. In Aeschylean drama the chorus is not a minor or detachable element. In *Agamemnon,* in fact, the chorus has nearly as many lines as the characters, and without the chorus the play would be only an abbreviated melodrama, consisting of a few sensational incidents from the aftermath of the Trojan War.

Although *Agamemnon* is the first play of a trilogy, it stands alone as a consummately tragic expression of the cultural issues resolved by the remaining two plays. Its plot, as in all the plays of Aeschylus, is remarkably spare and simple, consisting of a few bold events—the return of Agamemnon with Cassandra and the slaying of them by Clytemnestra and Aegisthus. From all the events of the Trojan War, from all the stories about Agamemnon, his ancestors, and his children, Aeschylus chooses to dramatize only the events of a single day. But through the dialogue and lyrical reflections of the chorus, these events are made to symbolize an enduring problem in the life of Agamemnon, his ancestors, his country, and his world—the problem of vengeance, that primitive form of justice, which, rather than ending crime, endlessly renews it. The cyclical nature of revenge is discovered and expressed by the chorus, which repeatedly makes the past vividly present in its recollections—of "hearts howling in boundless bloodlust," of "a war for a runaway wife," of "a virgin's blood upon the altar," of "barbarous building of hates and disloyalties grown on the family." In mingling reflection with memory, the chorus seeks both to justify revenge and to find moral alternatives to it. Through its wavering attitude, its dilemma, its repeated questionings, rememberings, and meditations, the chorus becomes a character in its own right, as dramatically compelling as Agamemnon with all his grandeur and pride, or Clytemnestra with all her bitterness and hate, or Cassandra with all her foresight and helplessness.

These characters and the stories about them were, of course, standard items of Greek legend, readily available to Aeschylus and totally familiar to all the members of his audience. Homer had told about them several hundred years earlier, and his tales had been retold by a long line of Greek poets and storytellers, but those stories took on a strikingly new meaning in the hands of Aeschylus. Just how new (and how different) can be seen by comparing the way that Agamemnon is viewed in Homer's *Odyssey* with the way he is represented in the work of Aeschylus. Whereas Homer had presented Agamemnon as a completely sympathetic character, Aeschylus shows him to be a morally ambiguous character. Their differing conceptions of Agamemnon are, at last, the consequence of their differing ideas of justice. Vengeance, which Homer takes for granted, Aeschylus calls into question.

Because it raises such large questions about the conduct of men, of families, of communities, of nations—and because neither men, nor families, nor communities, nor nations conduct themselves much differently now from the way they have for thousands of years—*Agamemnon* remains a perennially compelling play, a permanently tragic statement about the condition of things. In conjunction with the other two plays that make up *The Oresteia*, it offers actors and directors an extraordinary theatrical challenge, especially in productions that try to match its grand scope by turning to a grand style of staging involving the use of masks. Thus, when the Guthrie Theater staged the *House of Atreus* in 1967, the actors wore masks covering their hair and the top half of their faces; the stylized faces were nonetheless noticeably different from each other, so that Clytemnestra's haughty demeanor (see Figure 1) is emphasized by her upswept hairdo while Cassandra's position as a slave seems reflected by the downward slant of the mask's eyes (see Figure 2). All the leading roles were played by men throughout the trilogy including the central women's roles (Clytemnestra, Cassandra, Electra, Athena). When Peter Hall staged *The Oresteia* at London's National Theatre in 1981, he too turned to male actors for the leading roles and masks. But the masks in Hall's production, like the Greek masks represented on ancient vase paintings and marble sculptures, covered not just the hair, eyes, and nose but the entire face (see Figure 3). Hall's experience of working with contemporary actors as they learned to use the mask offers a revealing glimpse into a form of acting that may seem very distant. But as his comments suggest (see excerpts following the text), the mask is not anywhere as abstract or inhuman as it may seem. If one recognizes the powerful simplicity of a mask, and if the actor is willing to experience both the restriction and the liberation offered by the mask, then, as Hall puts it, "the masks enable an intense emotional heat to be generated that *tells* us about grief." Both of these productions, though using very different kinds of masks, present the characters as simultaneously statuesque and human, repulsive and moving, archetypes and individuals—all contradictions that the play itself explores.

AGAMEMNON

BY AESCHYLUS / TRANSLATED BY LOUIS MACNEICE

CHARACTERS*

WATCHMAN
CHORUS OF OLD MEN OF THE CITY
CLYTEMNESTRA
HERALD
AGAMEMNON
CASSANDRA
AEGISTHUS

SCENE

A space in front of the palace of Agamemnon in Argos.
Night. A WATCHMAN *on the roof of the palace.*

---

*THE FAMILY TREE

THE CHAIN OF CRIMES

The chain of crimes in this play is as follows (see Family Tree above):

Past.
   (1) Thyestes seduced Atreus' wife.
   (2) Atreus killed Thyestes' young children and gave him them as meat.
   (3) Helen forsook her husband and went to Troy with Paris.
   (4) Agamemnon, to promote the Trojan War, sacrificed his daughter Iphigeneia.

Present.
   (5) Aegisthus and Clytemnestra murder Agamemnon.

Future.
   (6) Orestes will kill Aegisthus and his mother Clytemnestra.

WATCHMAN: The gods it is I ask to release me from this watch
A year's length now, spending my nights like a dog,
Watching on my elbow on the roof of the sons of Atreus
So that I have come to know the assembly of the nightly stars
Those which bring storm and those which bring summer to men,   5
The shining Masters riveted in the sky—
I know the decline and rising of those stars.
And now I am waiting for the sign of the beacon,
The flame of fire that will carry the report from Troy,
News of her taking. Which task has been assigned me   10
By a woman of sanguine heart but a man's mind.
Yet when I take my restless rest in the soaking dew,
My night not visited with dreams—
For fear stands by me in the place of sleep
That I cannot firmly close my eyes in sleep—   15
Whenever I think to sing or hum to myself
As an antidote to sleep, then every time I groan
And fall to weeping for the fortunes of this house
Where not as before are things well ordered now.
But now may a good chance fall, escape from pain,   20
The good news visible in the midnight fire.

(Pause. A light appears, gradually increasing, the light of the beacon.)

Ha! I salute you, torch of the night whose light
Is like the day, an earnest of many dances
In the city of Argos, celebration of Peace.
I call to Agamemnon's wife; quickly to rise   25
Out of her bed and in the house to raise
Clamour of joy in answer to this torch
For the city of Troy is taken—
Such is the evident message of the beckoning flame.
And I myself will dance my solo first   30
For I shall count my master's fortune mine
Now that this beacon has thrown me a lucky throw.
And may it be when he comes, the master of this house,
That I grasp his hand in my hand.
As to the rest, I am silent. A great ox, as they say,   35
Stands on my tongue. The house itself, if it took voice,

24

Could tell the case most clearly. But I will only
    speak
To those who know. For the others I remember
    nothing.

(*Enter* CHORUS OF OLD MEN. *During the following chorus the day begins to dawn.*)

CHORUS: The tenth year it is since Priam's high
40   Adversary, Menelaus the king
    And Agamemnon, the double-throned and
        sceptred
    Yoke of the sons of Atreus
    Ruling in fee from God,
    From this land gathered an Argive army
45   On a mission of war a thousand ships,
    Their hearts howling in boundless bloodlust
    In eagles' fashion who in lonely
    Grief for nestlings above their homes hang
    Turning in cycles
50   Beating the air with the oars of their wings,
        Now to no purpose
        Their love and task of attention.

    But above there is One,
    Maybe Pan, maybe Zeus or Apollo,
55   Who cries the harsh cries of the birds
    Guests in his kingdom,
    Wherefore, though late, in requital
    He sends the Avenger.
    Thus Zeus our master
60   Guardian of guest and of host
    Sent against Paris the sons of Atreus
    For a woman of many men
    Many the dog-tired wrestlings
    Limbs and knees in the dust pressed—
65   For both the Greeks and Trojans
        An overture of breaking spears.

    Things are where they are, will finish
    In the manner fated and neither
    Fire beneath nor oil above can soothe
70   The stubborn anger of the unburnt offering.
    As for us, our bodies are bankrupt,
    The expedition left us behind
    And we wait supporting on sticks
    Our strength—the strength of a child;
75   For the marrow that leaps in a boy's body
    Is no better than that of the old
    For the War God is not in his body;
    While the man who is very old
    And his leaf withering away
80   Goes on the three-foot way
    No better than a boy, and wanders
    A dream in the middle of the day.

    But you, daughter of Tyndareus,
    Queen Clytemnestra,

What is the news, what is the truth, what have you
    learnt,   85
On the strength of whose word have you thus
Sent orders for sacrifice round?
All the gods, the gods of the town,
Of the worlds of Below and Above,
By the door, in the square,   90
Have their altars ablaze with your gifts,
From here, from there, all sides, all corners,
Sky-high leap the flame-jets fed
By gentle and undeceiving
Persuasion of sacred unguent,   95
Oil from the royal stores.
Of these things tell
That which you can, that which you may,
Be healer of this our trouble
Which at times torments with evil   100
Though at times by propitiations
A shining hope repels
The insatiable thought upon grief
Which is eating away our hearts.

Of the omen which powerfully speeded   105
That voyage of strong men, by God's grace even I
Can tell, my age can still
Be galvanized to breathe the strength of song,
To tell how the kings of all the youth of Greece
Two-throned but one in mind   110
Were launched with pike and punitive hand
Against the Trojan shore by angry birds.
Kings of the birds to our kings came,
One with a white rump, the other black,
Appearing near the palace on the spear-arm side   115
Where all could see them,
Tearing a pregnant hare with the unborn young
Foiled of their courses.
    Cry, cry upon Death; but may the good prevail.

But the diligent prophet of the army seeing the
    sons   120
Of Atreus twin in temper knew
That the hare-killing birds were the two
Generals, explained it thus—
'In time this expedition sacks the town
Of Troy before whose towers   125
By Fate's force the public
Wealth will be wasted.
Only let not some spite from the gods benight the
    bulky battalions,
The bridle of Troy, nor strike them untimely;
For the goddess feels pity, is angry   130
With the winged dogs of her father
Who killed the cowering hare with her unborn
    young;
Artemis hates the eagles' feast.'
    Cry, cry upon Death; but may the good prevail.

135 'But though you are so kind, goddess,
To the little cubs of lions
And to all the sucking young of roving beasts
In whom your heart delights,
Fulfil us the signs of these things,
140 The signs which are good but open to blame,
And I call on Apollo the Healer
That his sister raise not against the Greeks
Unremitting gales to baulk their ships,
Hurrying on another kind of sacrifice, with no
feasting
145 Barbarous building of hates and disloyalties
Grown on the family. For anger grimly returns
Cunningly haunting the house, avenging the death
of a child, never forgetting its due.'
So cried the prophet—evil and good together,
Fate that the birds foretold to the king's house.
150 In tune with this
Cry, cry upon Death; but may the good prevail.

Zeus, whoever He is, if this
Be a name acceptable,
By this name I will call him.
155 There is no one comparable
When I reckon all of the case
Excepting Zeus, if ever I am to jettison
The barren care which clogs my heart.

Not He who formerly was great
160 With brawling pride and mad for broils
Will even be said to have been.
And He who was next has met
His match and is seen no more,
But Zeus is the name to cry in your triumph-song
165 And win the prize for wisdom.

Who setting us on the road
Made this a valid law—
'That men must learn by suffering.'
Drop by drop in sleep upon the heart
170 Falls the laborious memory of pain,
Against one's will comes wisdom;
The grace of the gods is forced on us
Throned inviolably.

So at that time the elder
175 Chief of the Greek ships
Would not blame any prophet
Nor face the flail of fortune;
For unable to sail, the people
Of Greece were heavy with famine,
180 Waiting in Aulis where the tides
Flow back, opposite Chalcis.

But the winds that blew from the Strymon,
Bringing delay, hunger, evil harbourage,
Crazing men, rotting ships and cables,
185 By drawing out the time

Were shredding into nothing the flower of Argos,
When the prophet screamed a new
Cure for that bitter tempest
And heavier still for the chiefs,
Pleading the anger of Artemis so that the sons of
Atreus   190
Beat the ground with their sceptres and shed tears.

Then the elder king found voice and answered:
'Heavy is my fate, not obeying,
And heavy it is if I kill my child, the delight of my
house,
And with a virgin's blood upon the altar   195
Make foul her father's hands.
Either alternative is evil.
How can I betray the fleet
And fail the allied army?
It is right they should passionately cry for the winds
to be lulled   200
By the blood of a girl. So be it. May it be well.'

But when he had put on the halter of Necessity
Breathing in his heart a veering wind of evil
Unsanctioned, unholy, from that moment forward
He changed his counsel, would stop at nothing. 205
For the heart of man is hardened by infatuation,
A faulty adviser, the first link of sorrow.
Whatever the cause, he brought himself to slay
His daughter, an offering to promote the voyage
To a war for a runaway wife.   210

Her prayers and her cries of father,
Her life of a maiden,
Counted for nothing with those militarists;
But her father, having duly prayed, told the
attendants
To lift her, like a goat, above the altar   215
With her robes falling about her,
To lift her boldly, her spirit fainting,
And hold back with a gag upon her lovely mouth
By the dumb force of a bridle
The cry which would curse the house.   220

Then dropping on the ground her saffron dress,
Glancing at each of her appointed
Sacrificers a shaft of pity,
Plain as in a picture she wished
To speak to them by name, for often   225
At her father's table where men feasted
She had sung in celebration for her father
With a pure voice, affectionately, virginally,
The hymn for happiness at the third libation.

The sequel to this I saw not and tell not   230
But the crafts of Calchas gained their object.
To learn by suffering is the equation of Justice; the
Future
Is known when it comes, let it go till then.

235 To know in advance is sorrow in advance.
The facts will appear with the shining of the dawn.

(Enter CLYTEMNESTRA.*)*

But may good, at the least, follow after
As the queen here wishes, who stands
Nearest the throne, the only
    Defence of the land of Argos.

240 LEADER OF THE CHORUS: I have come, Clytemnestra,
    reverencing your authority.
For it is right to honour our master's wife
When the man's own throne is empty.
But you, if you have heard good news for certain,
    or if
You sacrifice on the strength of flattering hopes,
I would gladly hear. Though I cannot cavil at
245   silence.
CLYTEMNESTRA: Bearing good news, as the proverb
    says, may Dawn
Spring from her mother Night.
You will hear something now that was beyond your
    hopes.
The men of Argos have taken Priam's city.
LEADER OF THE CHORUS: What! I cannot believe it. It
250   escapes me.
CLYTEMNESTRA: Troy in the hands of the Greeks. Do
    I speak plain?
LEADER OF THE CHORUS: Joy creeps over me, calling
    out my tears.
CLYTEMNESTRA: Yes. Your eyes proclaim your loyalty.
LEADER OF THE CHORUS: But what are your grounds?
    Have you a proof of it?
CLYTEMNESTRA: There is proof indeed—unless God
255   has cheated us.
LEADER OF THE CHORUS: Perhaps you believe the
    inveigling shapes of dreams?
CLYTEMNESTRA: I would not be credited with a
    dozing brain!
LEADER OF THE CHORUS: Or are you puffed up by
    Rumour, the wingless flyer?
CLYTEMNESTRA: You mock my common sense as if I
    were a child.
LEADER OF THE CHORUS: But at what time was the city
260   given to sack?
CLYTEMNESTRA: In this very night that gave birth to
    this day.
LEADER OF THE CHORUS: What messenger could
    come so fast?
CLYTEMNESTRA: Hephaestus, launching a fine flame
    from Ida,
Beacon forwarding beacon, despatch-riders of fire,
265 Ida relayed to Hermes' cliff in Lemnos
And the great glow from the island was taken over
    third
By the height of Athos that belongs to Zeus,
And towering then to straddle over the sea
The might of the running torch joyfully tossed

270 The gold gleam forward like another sun,
Herald of light to the heights of Mount Macistus,
And he without delay, nor carelessly by sleep
Encumbered, did not shirk his intermediary role,
His farflung ray reached the Euripus' tides
275 And told Messapion's watchers, who in turn
Sent on the message further
Setting a stack of dried-up heather on fire.
And the strapping flame, not yet enfeebled, leapt
Over the plain of Asopus like a blazing moon
280 And woke on the crags of Cithaeron
Another relay in the chain of fire.
The light that was sent from far was not declined
By the look-out men, who raised a fiercer yet,
A light which jumped the water of Gorgopis
285 And to Mount Aegiplanctus duly come
Urged the reveille of the punctual fire.
So then they kindle it squanderingly and launch
A beard of flame big enough to pass
The headland that looks down upon the Saronic
    gulf,
290 Blazing and bounding till it reached at length
The Arachnaean steep, our neighbouring heights;
And leaps in the latter end on the roof of the sons
    of Atreus
Issue and image of the fire on Ida.
Such was the assignment of my torch-racers,
295 The task of each fulfilled by his successor,
And victor is he who ran both first and last.
Such is the proof I offer you, the sign
My husband sent me out of Troy.
LEADER OF THE CHORUS: To the gods, queen, I shall
    give thanks presently.
300 But I would like to hear this story further,
To wonder at it in detail from your lips.
CLYTEMNESTRA: The Greeks hold Troy upon this day.
The cries in the town I fancy do not mingle.
Pour oil and vinegar into the same jar,
305 You would say they stand apart unlovingly;
Of those who are captured and those who have
    conquered
Distinct are the sounds of their diverse fortunes,
For *these* having flung themselves about the bodies
Of husbands and brothers, or sons upon the
    bodies
310 Of aged fathers from a throat no longer
Free, lament the fate of their most loved.
But *those* a night's marauding after battle
Sets hungry to what breakfast the town offers
Not billeted duly in any barracks order
315 But as each man has drawn his lot of luck.
So in the captive homes of Troy already
They take their lodging, free of the frosts
And dews of the open. Like happy men
They will sleep all night without sentry.
320 But if they respect duly the city's gods,
Those of the captured land and the sanctuaries of
    the gods,

They need not, having conquered, fear reconquest.
But let no lust fall first upon the troops
To plunder what is not right, subdued by gain,
325 For they must still, in order to come home safe,
Get round the second lap of the doubled course.
So if they return without offence to the gods
The grievance of the slain may learn at last
A friendly talk—unless some fresh wrong falls.
330 Such are the thoughts you hear from me, a woman.
But may the good prevail for all to see.
We have much good. I only ask to enjoy it.

LEADER OF THE CHORUS: Woman, you speak with
    sense like a prudent man.
I, who have heard your valid proofs, prepare
335 To give the glory to God.
Fair recompense is brought us for our troubles.

(CLYTEMNESTRA *goes back into the palace.*)

CHORUS: O Zeus our king and Night our friend
    Donor of glories;
Night who cast on the towers of Troy
340 A close-clinging net so that neither the grown
Nor any of the children can pass
The enslaving and huge
Trap of all-taking destruction.
Great Zeus, guardian and host and guest,
345 I honour who has done his work and taken
A leisured aim at Paris so that neither
Too short nor yet over the stars
    He might shoot to no purpose.

From Zeus is the blow they can tell of,
350 This at least can be established,
They have fared according to his ruling. For some
Deny that the gods deign to consider those among
    men
Who trample on the grace of inviolate things;
It is the impious man says this,
355 For Ruin is revealed the child
Of not to be attempted actions
When men are puffed up unduly
And their houses are stuffed with riches.
Measure is the best. Let danger be distant,
360 This should suffice a man
With a proper part of wisdom.
    For a man has no protection
    Against the drunkenness of riches
    Once he has spurned from his sight
365   The high altar of Justice.

Sombre Persuasion compels him,
Intolerable child of calculating Doom;
All cure is vain, there is no glozing it over
But the mischief shines forth with a deadly light
370 And like bad coinage
By rubbings and frictions
He stands discoloured and black

Under the test—like a boy
Who chases a winged bird.
He has branded his city for ever.   375
His prayers are heard by no god.
Who makes such things his practice
The gods destroy him.
    This way came Paris
    To the house of the sons of Atreus   380
    And outraged the table of friendship
    Stealing the wife of his host.

Leaving to her countrymen clanging of
Shields and of spears and
Launching of warships   385
And bringing instead of a dowry destruction to
    Troy
Lightly she was gone through the gates daring
Things undared. Many the groans
Of the palace spokesmen on this theme—
'O the house, the house, and its princes,   390
O the bed and the imprint of her limbs;
One can see him crouching in silence
Dishonoured and unreviling.'
Through desire for her who is overseas, a ghost
Will seem to rule the household.   395
    And now her husband hates
    The grace of shapely statues;
    In the emptiness of their eyes
    All their appeal is departed.

But appearing in dreams persuasive   400
Images come bringing a joy that is vain,
Vain for when in fancy he looks to touch her—
Slipping through his hands the vision
Rapidly is gone
Following on wings the walks of sleep.   405
Such are his griefs in his house on his hearth,
Such as these and worse than these,
But everywhere through the land of Greece which
    men have left
Are mourning women with enduring hearts
To be seen in all houses; many   410
Are the thoughts which stab their hearts;
    For those they sent to war
    They know, but in place of men
    That which comes home to them
    Is merely an urn and ashes.   415

But the money-changer War, changer of bodies,
Holding his balance in the battle
Home from Troy refined by fire
Sends back to friends the dust
That is heavy with tears, stowing   420
A man's worth of ashes
In an easily handled jar.
And they wail speaking well of the men how that
    one

Was expert in battle, and one fell well in the
   carnage—
425 But for another man's wife.
Muffled and muttered words;
And resentful grief creeps up against the sons
Of Atreus and their cause.
   But others there by the wall
430   Entombed in Trojan ground
   Lie, handsome of limb,
   Holding and hidden in enemy soil.

Heavy is the murmur of an angry people
Performing the purpose of a public curse;
435 There is something cowled in the night
That I anxiously wait to hear.
For the gods are not blind to the
Murderers of many and the black
Furies in time
440 When a man prospers in sin
By erosion of life reduce him to darkness,
Who, once among the lost, can no more
Be helped. Over-great glory
Is a sore burden. The high peak
445 Is blasted by the eyes of Zeus.
   I prefer an unenvied fortune,
   Not to be a sacker of cities
   Nor to find myself living at another's
   Ruling, myself a captive.

450 AN OLD MAN: From the good news' beacon a swift
   Rumour is gone through the town.
   Who knows if it be true
   Or some deceit of the gods?
ANOTHER OLD MAN: Who is so childish or broken in
   wit
   To kindle his heart at a new-fangled message of
455   flame
   And then be downcast
   At a change of report?
ANOTHER OLD MAN: It fits the temper of a woman
   To give her assent to a story before it is proved.
ANOTHER OLD MAN: The over-credulous passion of
460   women expands
   In swift conflagration but swiftly declining is gone
   The news that a woman announced.
LEADER OF THE CHORUS: Soon we shall know about
   the illuminant torches,
   The beacons and the fiery relays,
465 Whether they were true or whether like dreams
That pleasant light came here and hoaxed our wits.
Look: I see, coming from the beach, a herald
Shadowed with olive shoots; the dust upon him,
Mud's thirsty sister and colleague, is my witness
That he will not give dumb news nor news by
470   lighting
A flame of fire with the smoke of mountain timber;
In words he will either corroborate our joy—

But the opposite version I reject with horror.
To the good appeared so far may good be added.
ANOTHER SPEAKER: Whoever makes other prayers for
   this our city,   475
May he reap himself the fruits of his wicked heart.

(Enter the HERALD, who kisses the ground before speaking.)

HERALD: Earth of my fathers, O the earth of Argos,
   In the light of the tenth year I reach you thus
   After many shattered hopes achieving one,
   For never did I dare to think that here in Argive
   land   480
   I should win a grave in the dearest soil of home;
   But now hail, land, and hail, light of the sun,
   And Zeus high above the country and the Pythian
   king—
   May he no longer shoot his arrows at us
   (Implacable long enough beside Scamander)   485
   But now be saviour to us and be healer,
   King Apollo. And all the Assembly's gods
   I call upon, and him my patron, Hermes,
   The dear herald whom all heralds adore,
   And the Heroes who sped our voyage, again with
   favour   490
   Take back the army that has escaped the spear.
   O cherished dwelling, palace of royalty,
   O august thrones and gods facing the sun,
   If ever before, now with your bright eyes
   Gladly receive your king after much time,   495
   Who comes bringing light to you in the night time,
   And to all these as well—King Agamemnon.
   Give him a good welcome as he deserves,
   Who with the axe of judgment-awarding God
   Has smashed Troy and levelled the Trojan land;   500
   The altars are destroyed, the seats of the gods,
   And the seed of all the land is perished from it.
   Having cast this halter round the neck of Troy
   The King, the elder son of Atreus, a blessed man,
   Comes, the most worthy to have honour of all   505
   Men that are now. Paris nor his guilty city
   Can boast that the crime was greater than the
   atonement.
   Convicted in a suit for rape and robbery
   He has lost his stolen goods and with consummate
   ruin
   Mowed down the whole country and his father's
   house.   510
   The sons of Priam have paid their account with
   interest.
LEADER OF THE CHORUS: Hail and be glad, herald of
   the Greek army.
HERALD: Yes. Glad indeed! So glad that at the god's
   demand
   I should no longer hesitate to die.
LEADER OF THE CHORUS: Were you so harrowed by
   desire for home?   515

HERALD: Yes. The tears come to my eyes for joy.

LEADER OF THE CHORUS: Sweet then is the fever
which afflicts you.

HERALD: What do you mean? Let me learn your drift.

LEADER OF THE CHORUS: Longing for those whose
love came back in echo.

HERALD: Meaning the land was homesick for the
520   army?

LEADER OF THE CHORUS: Yes. I would often groan
from a darkened heart.

HERALD: This sullen hatred—how did it fasten on
you?

LEADER OF THE CHORUS: I cannot say. Silence is my
stock prescription.

HERALD: What? In your masters' absence were there
some you feared?

LEADER OF THE CHORUS: Yes. In your phrase, death
525   would now be a gratification.

HERALD: Yes, for success is ours. These things have
taken time.

    Some of them we could say have fallen well,
    While some we blame. Yet who except the gods
    Is free from pain the whole duration of life?
530   If I were to tell of our labours, our hard lodging,
    The sleeping on crowded decks, the scanty
      blankets,
    Tossing and groaning, rations that never reached
      us—
    And the land too gave matter for more disgust,
    For our beds lay under the enemy's walls.
    Continuous drizzle from the sky, dews from the
535   marshes,
    Rotting our clothes, filling our hair with lice.
    And if one were to tell of the bird-destroying
      winter
    Intolerable from the snows of Ida
    Or of the heat when the sea slackens at noon
540   Waveless and dozing in a depressed calm—
    But why make these complaints? The weariness is
      over;
    Over indeed for some who never again
    Need even trouble to rise.
    Why make a computation of the lost?
    Why need the living sorrow for the spites of
545   fortune?
    I wish to say a long goodbye to disasters.
    For us, the remnant of the troops of Argos,
    The advantage remains, the pain can not outweigh
      it;
    So we can make our boast to this sun's light,
550   Flying on words above the land and sea:
    'Having taken Troy the Argive expedition
    Has nailed up throughout Greece in every temple
    These spoils, these ancient trophies.'
    Those who hear such things must praise the city
    And the generals. And the grace of God be
555   honoured

    Which brought these things about. You have the
      whole story.

LEADER OF THE CHORUS: I confess myself convinced
by your report.

    Old men are always young enough to learn.

(Enter CLYTEMNESTRA *from the palace.)*

    This news belongs by right first to the house
    And Clytemnestra—though I am enriched also.   560

CLYTEMNESTRA: Long before I shouted at joy's
command

    At the coming of the first night-messenger of fire
    Announcing the taking and capsizing of Troy.
    And people reproached me saying, 'Do mere
      beacons
    Persuade you to think that Troy is already down?   565
    Indeed a woman's heart is easily exalted.'
    Such comments made me seem to be wandering
      but yet
    I began my sacrifices and in the women's fashion
    Throughout the town they raised triumphant cries
    And in the gods' enclosures   570
    Lulling the fragrant, incense-eating flame.
    And now what need is there for you to tell me
      more?
    From the King himself I shall learn the whole story.
    But how the best to welcome my honoured lord
    I shall take pains when he comes back—For what   575
    Is a kinder light for a woman to see than this,
    To open the gates to her man come back from war
    When God has saved him? Tell this to my husband,

    To come with all speed, the city's darling;
    May he returning find a wife as loyal   580
    As when he left her, watchdog of the house,
    Good to *him* but fierce to the ill-intentioned,
    And in all other things as ever, having destroyed
    No seal or pledge at all in the length of time,
    I know no pleasure with another man, no scandal,   585
    More than I know how to dye metal red.
    Such is my boast, bearing a load of truth,
    A boast that need not disgrace a noble wife.

(Exit.)

LEADER OF THE CHORUS: Thus has she spoken; if you
take her meaning,

    Only a specious tale to shrewd interpreters.   590
    But do you, herald, tell me; I ask after Menelaus
    Whether he will, returning safe preserved,
    Come back with you, our land's loved master.

HERALD: I am not able to speak the lovely falsehood
    To profit you, my friends, for any stretch of time.   595

LEADER OF THE CHORUS: But if only the true tidings
could be also good!

    It is hard to hide a division of good and true.

HERALD: The prince is vanished out of the Greek
fleet,

Himself and ship. I speak no lie.

LEADER OF THE CHORUS: Did he put forth first in the
600   sight of all from Troy,
Or a storm that troubled all sweep him apart?

HERALD: You have hit the target like a master archer,
Told succinctly a long tale of sorrow.

LEADER OF THE CHORUS: Did the rumours current
among the remaining ships
605   Represent him as alive or dead?

HERALD: No one knows so as to tell for sure
Except the sun who nurses the breeds of earth.

LEADER OF THE CHORUS: Tell me how the storm
came on the host of ships
Through the divine anger, and how it ended.

HERALD: Day of good news should not be fouled by
610   tongue
That tells ill news. To each god his season.
When, despair in his face, a messenger brings to a
town
The hated news of a fallen army—
One general wound to the city and many men
615 Outcast, outcursed, from many homes
By the double whip which War is fond of,
Doom with a bloody spear in either hand,
One carrying such a pack of grief could well
Recite this hymn of the Furies at your asking.
But when our cause is saved and a messenger of
620   good
Comes to a city glad with festivity,
How am I to mix good news with bad, recounting
The storm that meant God's anger on the Greeks?
For they swore together, those inveterate enemies,
625 Fire and sea, and proved their alliance, destroying
The unhappy troops of Argos.
In night arose ill-waved evil,
Ships on each other the blasts from Thrace
Crashed colliding, which butting with horns in the
violence
630 Of big wind and rattle of rain were gone
To nothing, whirled all ways by a wicked shepherd.
But when there came up the shining light of the
sun
We saw the Aegean sea flowering with corpses
Of Greek men and their ships' wreckage.
635 But for us, our ship was not damaged,
Whether someone snatched it away or begged it
off,
Some god, not a man, handling the tiller;
And Saving Fortune was willing to sit upon our
ship
So that neither at anchor we took the tilt of waves
640 Nor ran to splinters on the crag-bound coast.
But then having thus escaped death on the sea,
In the white day, not trusting our fortune,
We pastured this new trouble upon our thoughts,
The fleet being battered, the sailors weary,
645 And now if any of *them* still draw breath,

They are thinking no doubt of us as being lost
And we are thinking of them as being lost.
May the best happen. As for Menelaus
The first guess and most likely is a disaster.
But still—if any ray of sun detects him   650
Alive, with living eyes, by the plan of Zeus
Not yet resolved to annul the race completely,
There is some hope then that he will return home.
So much you have heard. Know that it is the truth.

(Exit.)

CHORUS: Who was it named her thus   655
In all ways appositely
Unless it was Someone whom we do not see,
Fore-knowing fate
And plying an accurate tongue?
Helen, bride of spears and conflict's   660
Focus, who as was befitting
Proved a hell to ships and men,
Hell to her country, sailing
Away from delicately-sumptuous curtains,
Away on the wind of a giant Zephyr,   665
And shielded hunters mustered many
On the vanished track of the oars,
Oars beached on the leafy
Banks of a Trojan river
For the sake of bloody war.   670

But on Troy was thrust a marring marriage
By the Wrath that working to an end exacts
In time a price from guests
Who dishonoured their host
And dishonoured Zeus of the Hearth,   675
From those noisy celebrants
Of the wedding hymn which fell
To the brothers of Paris
To sing upon that day.
But learning this, unlearning that,   680
Priam's ancestral city now
Continually mourns, reviling
Paris the fatal bridegroom.
The city has had much sorrow,
Much desolation in life,   685
From the pitiful loss of her people.

So in his house a man might rear
A lion's cub caught from the dam
In need of suckling,
In the prelude of its life   690
Mild, gentle with children,
For old men a playmate,
Often held in the arms
Like a new-born child,
Wheedling the hand,   695
Fawning at belly's bidding.

But matured by time he showed
The temper of his stock and payed
Thanks for his fostering
700 With disaster of slaughter of sheep
Making an unbidden banquet
And now the house is a shambles,
Irremediable grief to its people,
Calamitous carnage;
705 For the pet they had fostered was sent
By God as a priest of Ruin.

So I would say there came
To the city of Troy
A notion of windless calm,
710 Delicate adornment of riches
Soft shooting of the eyes and flower
Of desire that stings the fancy.
But swerving aside she achieved
A bitter end to her marriage,
715 Ill guest and ill companion,
Hurled upon Priam's sons, convoyed
By Zeus, patron of guest and host,
Dark angel dowered with tears.

Long current among men an old saying
720 Runs that a man's prosperity
When grown to greatness
Comes to the birth, does not die childless—
His good luck breeds for his house
Distress that shall not be appeased.
725 I only, apart from the others,
Hold that the unrighteous action
Breeds true to its kind,
Leaves its own children behind it.
But the lot of a righteous house
730 Is a fair offspring always.

Ancient self-glory is accustomed
To bear to light in the evil sort of men
A new self-glory and madness,
Which sometime or sometime finds
735 The appointed hour for its birth,
And born therewith is the Spirit, intractable,
    unholy, irresistible,
The reckless lust that brings black Doom upon the
    house,
A child that is like its parents.

But Honest Dealing is clear
740 Shining in smoky homes,
Honours the god-fearing life.
Mansions gilded by filth of hands she leaves,
Turns her eyes elsewhere, visits the innocent
    house,
Not respecting the power
745 Of wealth mis-stamped with approval,
But guides all to the goal.

(Enter AGAMEMNON *and* CASSANDRA *on chariots.)*

CHORUS: Come then my King, stormer of Troy,
    Offspring of Atreus,
    How shall I hail you, how give you honour
    Neither overshooting nor falling short   750
        Of the measure of homage?
    There are many who honour appearance too much
    Passing the bounds that are right.
    To condole with the unfortunate man
    Each one is ready but the bite of the grief   755
        Never goes through to the heart.
    And they join in rejoicing, affecting to share it,
    Forcing their face to a smile.
    But he who is shrewd to shepherd his sheep
    Will not fail to notice the eyes of a man   760
    Which seem to be loyal but lie,
        Fawning with watery friendship.
    Even you, in my thought, when you marshalled the
        troops
    For Helen's sake, I will not hide it,
    Made a harsh and ugly picture,   765
    Holding badly the tiller of reason,
    Paying with the death of men
        Ransom for a willing whore.
    But now, not unfriendly, not superficially,
    I offer my service, well-doers' welcome.   770
    In time you will learn by inquiry
    Who has done rightly, who transgressed
        In the work of watching the city.

AGAMEMNON: First to Argos and the country's gods
    My fitting salutations, who have aided me   775
    To return and in the justice which I exacted
    From Priam's city. Hearing the unspoken case
    The gods unanimously had cast their vote
    Into the bloody urn for the massacre of Troy;
    But to the opposite urn   780
    Hope came, dangled her hand, but did no more.
    Smoke marks even now the city's capture.
    Whirlwinds of doom are alive, the dying ashes
    Spread on the air the fat savour of wealth.
    For these things we must pay some memorable
        return   785
    To Heaven, having exacted enormous vengeance
    For wife-rape; for a woman
    The Argive monster ground a city to powder,
    Sprung from a wooden horse, shield-wielding folk,
    Launching a leap at the setting of the Pleiads, 790
    Jumping the ramparts, a ravening lion,
    Lapped its fill of the kingly blood.
    To the gods I have drawn out this overture
    But as for your concerns, I bear them in my mind
    And say the same, you have me in agreement.   795
    To few of men does it belong by nature
    To congratulate their friends unenviously,
    For a sullen poison fastens on the heart,
    Doubling the pain of a man with this disease;

800 He feels the weight of his own griefs and when
He sees another's prosperity he groans.
I speak with knowledge, being well acquainted
With the mirror of comradeship—ghost of a
shadow
Were those who seemed to be so loyal to me.
805 Only Odysseus, who sailed against his will,
Proved, when yoked with me, a ready tracehorse;
I speak of him not knowing if he is alive.
But for what concerns the city and the gods
Appointing public debates in full assembly
810 We shall consult. That which is well already
We shall take steps to ensure it remain well.
But where there is need of medical remedies,
By applying benevolent cautery or surgery
We shall try to deflect the dangers of disease.
But now, entering the halls where stands my
815 hearth,
First I shall make salutation to the gods
Who sent me a far journey and have brought me
back.
And may my victory not leave my side.

(Enter CLYTEMNESTRA, *followed by women slaves carrying purple tapestries.)*

CLYTEMNESTRA: Men of the city, you the aged of
Argos,
820 I shall feel no shame to describe to you my love
Towards my husband. Shyness in all of us
Wears thin with time. Here are the facts first hand.
I will tell you of my own unbearable life
I led so long as this man was at Troy.
825 For first that the woman separate from her man
Should sit alone at home is extreme cruelty,
Hearing so many malignant rumours—First
Comes one, and another comes after, bad news to
worse,
Clamour of grief to the house. If Agamemnon
830 Had had so many wounds as those reported
Which poured home through the pipes of hearsay,
then—
Then he would be gashed fuller than a net has
holes!
And if only he had died . . . as often as rumour told
us,
He would be like the giant in the legend,
835 Three-bodied. Dying once for every body,
He should have by now three blankets of earth
above him—
All that above him; I care not how deep the
mattress under!
Such are the malignant rumours thanks to which
They have often seized me against my will and
undone
840 The loop of a rope from my neck.
And this is why our son is not standing here,
The guarantee of your pledges and mine,

As he should be, Orestes. Do not wonder;
He is being brought up by a friendly ally and host,
Strophius the Phocian, who warned me in advance 845
Of dubious troubles, both your risks at Troy
And the anarchy of shouting mobs that might
Overturn policy, for it is born in men
To kick the man who is down.
This is not a disingenuous excuse. 850
For me the outrushing wells of weeping are dried
up,
There is no drop left in them.
My eyes are sore from sitting late at nights
Weeping for you and for the baffled beacons,
Never lit up. And, when I slept, in dreams 855
I have been waked by the thin whizz of a buzzing
Gnat, seeing more horrors fasten on you
Than could take place in the mere time of my
dream.
Having endured all this, now, with unsorrowed
heart
I would hail this man as the watchdog of the farm, 860
Forestay that saves the ship, pillar that props
The lofty roof, appearance of an only son
To a father or of land to sailors past their hope,
The loveliest day to see after the storm,
Gush of well-water for the thirsty traveller. 865
Such are the metaphors I think befit him,
But envy be absent. Many misfortunes already
We have endured. But now, dear head, come down
Out of that car, not placing upon the ground
Your foot, O King, the foot that trampled Troy. 870
Why are you waiting, slaves, to whom the task is
assigned
To spread the pavement of his path with
tapestries?
At once, at once let his way be strewn with purple
That Justice lead him toward his unexpected
home.
The rest a mind, not overcome by sleep 875
Will arrange rightly, with God's help, as destined.
AGAMEMNON: Daughter of Leda, guardian of my
house,
You have spoken in proportion to my absence.
You have drawn your speech out long. Duly to
praise me,
That is a duty to be performed by others. 880
And further—do not by women's methods make
me
Effeminate nor in barbarian fashion
Gape ground-grovelling acclamations at me
Nor strewing my path with cloths make it invidious.
It is the gods should be honoured in this way. 885
But being mortal to tread embroidered beauty
For me is no way without fear.
I tell you to honour me as a man, not god.
Footcloths are very well—Embroidered stuffs
Are stuff for gossip. And not to think unwisely 890

Is the greatest gift of God. Call happy only him
Who has ended his life in sweet prosperity.
I have spoken. This thing I could not do with
confidence.
CLYTEMNESTRA: Tell me now, according to your
judgment.
AGAMEMNON: I tell you you shall not override my
judgment.
CLYTEMNESTRA: Supposing you had feared
something . . .
Could you have vowed to God to do this thing?
AGAMEMNON: Yes. If an expert had prescribed that
vow.
CLYTEMNESTRA: And how would Priam have acted in
your place?
AGAMEMNON: He would have trod the cloths, I think,
for certain.
CLYTEMNESTRA: Then do not flinch before the
blame of men.
AGAMEMNON: The voice of the multitude is very
strong.
CLYTEMNESTRA: But the man none envy is not
enviable.
AGAMEMNON: It is not a woman's part to love
disputing.
CLYTEMNESTRA: But it is a conqueror's part to yield
upon occasion.
AGAMEMNON: You think such victory worth fighting
for?
CLYTEMNESTRA: Give way. Consent to let me have the
mastery.
AGAMEMNON: Well, if such is your wish, let someone
quickly loose
My vassal sandals, underlings of my feet,
And stepping on these sea-purples may no god
Shoot me from far with the envy of his eye.
Great shame it is to ruin my house and spoil
The wealth of costly weavings with my feet.
But of this matter enough. This stranger woman
here
Take in with kindness. The man who is a gentle
master
God looks on from far off complacently.
For no one of his will bears the slave's yoke.
This woman, of many riches being the chosen
Flower, gift of the soldiers, has come with me.
But since I have been prevailed on by your words
I will go to my palace home, treading on purples.

(He dismounts from the chariot and begins to walk up the tapestried path. During the following speech he enters the palace.)

CLYTEMNESTRA: There is the sea and who shall drain
it dry? It breeds
Its wealth in silver of plenty of purple gushing
And ever-renewed, the dyeings of our garments.

895
900
905
910
915
920

The house has its store of these by God's grace,
King.
This house is ignorant of poverty
And I would have vowed a pavement of many
garments
Had the palace oracle enjoined that vow
Thereby to contrive a ransom for his life.
For while there is root, foliage comes to the house
Spreading a tent of shade against the Dog Star.
So now that you have reached your hearth and
home
You prove a miracle—advent of warmth in winter;
And further this—even in the time of heat
When God is fermenting wine from the bitter
grape,
Even then it is cool in the house if only
Its master walk at home, a grown man, ripe.
O Zeus the Ripener, ripen these my prayers;
Your part it is to make the ripe fruit fall.

(She enters the palace.)

CHORUS: Why, why at the doors
Of my fore-seeing heart
Does this terror keep beating its wings?
And my song play the prophet
Unbidden, unhired—
Which I cannot spit out
Like the enigmas of dreams
Nor plausible confidence
Sit on the throne of my mind?
It is long time since
The cables let down from the stern
Were chafed by the sand when the seafaring army
started for Troy.

And I learn with my eyes
And witness myself their return;
But the hymn without lyre goes up,
The dirge of the Avenging Fiend,
In the depths of my self-taught heart
Which has lost its dear
Possession of the strength of hope.
But my guts and my heart
Are not idle which seethe with the waves
Of trouble nearing its hour.
But I pray that these thoughts
May fall out not as I think
And not be fulfilled in the end.

Truly when health grows much
It respects not limit; for disease,
Its neighbour in the next door room,
Presses upon it.
A man's life, crowding sail,
Strikes on the blind reef:
But if caution in advance
Jettison part of the cargo

925
930
935
940
945
950
955
960
965
970

With the derrick of due proportion,
The whole house does not sink,
975 Though crammed with a weight of woe
The hull does not go under.
The abundant bounty of God
And his gifts from the year's furrows
Drive the famine back.

980 But when upon the ground there has fallen once
The black blood of a man's death,
Who shall summon it back by incantations?
Even Asclepius who had the art
To fetch the dead to life, even to him
985 Zeus put a provident end.
But, if of the heaven-sent fates
One did not check the other,
Cancel the other's advantage,
My heart would outrun my tongue
990 In pouring out these fears.
But now it mutters in the dark,
Embittered, no way hoping
To unravel a scheme in time
    From a burning mind.

(CLYTEMNESTRA *appears in the door of the palace.*)

CLYTEMNESTRA: Go in too, you; I speak to you,
995   Cassandra,
Since God in his clemency has put you in this house
To share our holy water, standing with many slaves
Beside the altar that protects the house,
Step down from the car there, do not be
    overproud.
1000 Heracles himself they say was once
Sold, and endured to eat the bread of slavery.
But should such a chance inexorably fall,
There is much advantage in masters who have long
    been rich.
Those who have reaped a crop they never expected
Are in all things hard on their slaves and overstep
1005   the line.
From us you will have the treatment of tradition.
LEADER OF THE CHORUS: You, it is you she has
    addressed, and clearly.
Caught as you are in these predestined toils
Obey her if you can. But should you disobey . . .
CLYTEMNESTRA: If she has more than the gibberish
1010   of the swallow,
An unintelligible barbaric speech,
I hope to read her mind, persuade her reason.
LEADER OF THE CHORUS: As things now stand for you,
    she says the best.
Obey her; leave that car and follow her.
CLYTEMNESTRA: I have no leisure to waste out here,
1015   outside the door.
Before the hearth in the middle of my house
The victims stand already, wait the knife.
You, if you will obey me, waste no time.

But if you cannot understand my language—

(*To* CHORUS LEADER)

You make it plain to her with the brute and
    voiceless hand.   1020
LEADER OF THE CHORUS: The stranger seems to need
    a clear interpreter.
She bears herself like a wild beast newly captured.
CLYTEMNESTRA: The fact is she is mad, she listens to
    evil thoughts,
Who has come here leaving a city newly captured
Without experience how to bear the bridle   1025
So as not to waste her strength in foam and blood.
I will not spend more words to be ignored.

(*She re-enters the palace.*)

CHORUS: But I, for I pity her, will not be angry.
Obey, unhappy woman. Leave this car.
Yield to your fate. Put on the untried yoke.   1030
CASSANDRA: Apollo! Apollo!
CHORUS: Why do you cry like this upon Apollo?
He is not the kind of god that calls for dirges.
CASSANDRA: Apollo! Apollo!
CHORUS: Once more her funeral cries invoke the god 1035
Who has no place at the scene of lamentation.
CASSANDRA: Apollo! Apollo!
God of the Ways! My destroyer!
Destroyed again—and this time utterly!
CHORUS: She seems about to predict her own
    misfortunes.   1040
The gift of the god endures, even in a slave's mind.
CASSANDRA: Apollo! Apollo!
God of the Ways! My destroyer!
Where? To what house? Where, where have you
    brought me?
CHORUS: To the house of the sons of Atreus. If you
    do not know it,   1045
I will tell you so. You will not find it false.
CASSANDRA: No, no, but to a god-hated, but to an
    accomplice
In much kin-killing, murdering nooses,
Man-shambles, a floor asperged with blood.
CHORUS: The stranger seems like a hound with a
    keen scent,   1050
Is picking up a trail that leads to murder.
CASSANDRA: Clues! I have clues! Look! They are
    these.
These wailing, these children, butchery of
    children;
Roasted flesh, a father sitting to dinner.
CHORUS: Of your prophetic fame we have heard
    before   1055
But in this matter prophets are not required.
CASSANDRA: What is she doing? What is she
    planning?
What is this new great sorrow?
Great crime . . . within here . . . planning

1060 Unendurable to his folk, impossible
Ever to be cured. For help
Stands far distant.
CHORUS: This reference I cannot catch. But the
children
I recognized; that refrain is hackneyed.
CASSANDRA: Damned, damned, bringing this work to
1065 completion—
Your husband who shared your bed
To bathe him, to cleanse him, and then—
How shall I tell of the end?
Soon, very soon, it will fall.
1070 The end comes hand over hand
Grasping in greed.
CHORUS: Not yet do I understand. After her former
riddles
Now I am baffled by these dim pronouncements.
CASSANDRA: Ah God, the vision! God, God, the
vision!
1075 A net, is it? Net of Hell!
But herself is the net; shared bed; shares murder.
O let the pack ever-hungering after the family
Howl for the unholy ritual, howl for the victim.
CHORUS: What black Spirit is this you call upon the
house—
To raise aloft her cries? Your speech does not
1080 lighten me.
Into my heart runs back the blood
Yellow as when for men by the spear fallen
The blood ebbs out with the rays of the setting life
And death strides quickly.
1085 CASSANDRA: Quick! Be on your guard! The bull—
Keep him clear of the cow.
Caught with a trick, the black horn's point,
She strikes. He falls; lies in the water.
Murder; a trick in a bath. I tell what I see.
1090 CHORUS: I would not claim to be expert in oracles
But these, as I deduce, portend disaster.
Do men ever get a good answer from oracles?
No. It is only through disaster
That their garrulous craft brings home
1095 The meaning of the prophet's panic.
CASSANDRA: And for me also, for me, chance ill-
destined!
My own now I lament, pour into the cup my own.
Where is this you have brought me in my misery?
Unless to die as well. What else is meant?
1100 CHORUS: You are mad, mad, carried away by the god,
Raising the dirge, the tuneless
Tune, for yourself. Like the tawny
Unsatisfied singer from her luckless heart
Lamenting 'Itys, Itys,' the nightingale
1105 Lamenting a life luxuriant with grief.
CASSANDRA: Oh the lot of the songful nightingale!
The gods enclosed her in a winged body,
Gave her a sweet and tearless passing.
But for me remains the two-edged cutting blade.

CHORUS: From whence these rushing and
God-inflicted 1110
Profitless pains?
Why shape with your sinister crying
The piercing hymn—fear-piercing?
How can you know the evil-worded landmarks
On the prophetic path? 1115
CASSANDRA: Oh the wedding, the wedding of Paris—
death to his people!
O river Scamander, water drunk by my fathers!
When I was young, alas, upon your beaches
I was brought up and cared for.
But now it is the River of Wailing and the banks of
Hell 1120
That shall hear my prophecy soon.
CHORUS: What is this clear speech, too clear?
A child could understand it.
I am bitten with fangs that draw blood
By the misery of your cries, 1125
Cries harrowing the heart.
CASSANDRA: O trouble on trouble of a city lost, lost
utterly!
My father's sacrifices before the towers,
Much killing of cattle and sheep,
No cure—availed not at all 1130
To prevent the coming of what came to Troy,
And I, my brain on fire, shall soon enter the trap.
CHORUS: This speech accords with the former.
What god, malicious, over-heavy, persistently
pressing,
Drives you to chant of these lamentable 1135
Griefs with death their burden?
But I cannot see the end.

(CASSANDRA *now steps down from the car.*)

CASSANDRA: The oracle now no longer from behind
veils
Will be peeping forth like a newly-wedded bride;
But I can feel it like a fresh wind swoop 1140
And rush in the face of the dawn and, wave-like,
wash
Against the sun a vastly greater grief
Than this one. I shall speak no more conundrums.
And bear me witness, pacing me, that I
Am trailing on the scene of ancient wrongs. 1145
For this house here a choir never deserts,
Chanting together ill. For they mean ill,
And to puff up their arrogance they have drunk
Men's blood, this band of revellers that haunts the
house,
Hard to be rid of, fiends that attend the family. 1150
Established in its rooms they hymn their hymn
Of that original sin, abhor in turn
The adultery that proved a brother's ruin.
A miss? Or do my arrows hit the mark?
Or am I a quack prophet who knocks at doors, a
babbler? 1155

Give me your oath, confess I have the facts,
The ancient history of this house's crimes.
LEADER OF THE CHORUS: And how could an oath's
assurance, however finely assured,
Turn out a remedy? I wonder, though, that you
1160 Being brought up overseas, of another tongue,
Should hit on the whole tale as if you had been
standing by.
CASSANDRA: Apollo the prophet set me to prophesy.
LEADER OF THE CHORUS: Was he, although a god,
struck by desire?
CASSANDRA: Till now I was ashamed to tell that story.
LEADER OF THE CHORUS: Yes. Good fortune keeps us
1165 all fastidious.
CASSANDRA: He wrestled hard upon me, panting
love.
LEADER OF THE CHORUS: And did you come, as they
do, to child-getting?
CASSANDRA: No. I agreed to him. And I cheated him.
LEADER OF THE CHORUS: Were you already possessed
by the mystic art?
CASSANDRA: Already I was telling the townsmen all
1170 their future suffering.
LEADER OF THE CHORUS: Then how did you escape
the doom of Apollo's anger?
CASSANDRA: I did not escape. No one ever believed
me.
LEADER OF THE CHORUS: Yet to us your words seem
worthy of belief.
CASSANDRA: Oh misery, misery!
1175 Again comes on me the terrible labour of true
Prophecy, dizzying prelude; distracts . . .
Do you see these who sit before the house,
Children, like the shapes of dreams?
Children who seem to have been killed by their
kinsfolk,
1180 Filling their hands with meat, flesh of themselves,
Guts and entrails, handfuls of lament—
Clear what they hold—the same their father tasted.
For this I declare someone is plotting vengeance—
A lion? Lion but coward, that lurks in bed,
1185 Good watchdog truly against the lord's return—
My lord, for I must bear the yoke of serfdom.
Leader of the ships, overturner of Troy,
He does not know what plots the accursed hound
With the licking tongue and the pricked-up ear will
plan
1190 In the manner of a lurking doom, in an evil hour.
A daring criminal! Female murders male.
What monster could provide her with a title?
An amphisbaena or hag of the sea who dwells
In rocks to ruin sailors—
A raving mother of death who breathes against her
1195 folk
War to the finish. Listen to her shout of triumph,
Who shirks no horrors, like men in a rout of battle.
And yet she poses as glad at their return.

If you distrust my words, what does it matter?
That which will come will come. You too will soon
stand here   1200
And admit with pity that I spoke too truly.
LEADER OF THE CHORUS: Thyestes' dinner of his
children's meat
I understood and shuddered, and fear grips me
To hear the truth, not framed in parables.
But hearing the rest I am thrown out of my course.   1205
CASSANDRA: It is Agamemnon's death I tell you you
shall witness.
LEADER OF THE CHORUS: Stop! Provoke no evil. Quiet
your mouth!
CASSANDRA: The god who gives me words is here no
healer.
LEADER OF THE CHORUS: Not if this shall be so. But
may some chance avert it.
CASSANDRA: *You* are praying. But others are busy with
murder.   1210
LEADER OF THE CHORUS: What man is he promotes
this terrible thing?
CASSANDRA: Indeed you have missed my drift by a
wide margin!
LEADER OF THE CHORUS: But I do not understand the
assassin's method.
CASSANDRA: And yet too well I know the speech of
Greece!
LEADER OF THE CHORUS: So does Delphi but the
replies are hard.   1215
CASSANDRA: Ah what a fire it is! It comes upon me.
Apollo, Wolf-Destroyer, pity, pity . . .
It is the two-foot lioness who beds
Beside a wolf, the noble lion away,
It is she will kill me. Brewing a poisoned cup   1220
She will mix my punishment too in the angry
draught
And boasts, sharpening the dagger for her
husband,
To pay back murder for my bringing here.
Why then do I wear these mockeries of myself,
The wand and the prophet's garland round my
neck?   1225
My hour is coming—but you shall perish first.
Destruction! Scattered thus you give me my
revenge;
Go and enrich some other woman with ruin.
See: Apollo himself is stripping me
Of my prophetic gear, who has looked on   1230
When in this dress I have been a laughing-stock
To friends and foes alike, and to no purpose;
They called me crazy, like a fortune-teller,
A poor starved beggar-woman—and I bore it.
And now the prophet undoing his prophetess   1235
Has brought me to this final darkness.
Instead of my father's altar the executioner's block
Waits me the victim, red with my hot blood.
But the gods will not ignore me as I die.

1240 One will come after to avenge my death,
A matricide, a murdered father's champion.
Exile and tramp and outlaw he will come back
To gable the family house of fatal crime;
His father's outstretched corpse shall lead him
home.
1245 Why need I then lament so pitifully?
For now that I have seen the town of Troy
Treated as she was treated, while her captors
Come to their reckoning thus by the god's verdict,
I will go in and have the courage to die.
Look, these gates are the gates of Death. I greet
1250 them.
And I pray that I may meet a deft and mortal
stroke
So that without a struggle I may close
My eyes and my blood ebb in easy death.
LEADER OF THE CHORUS: Oh woman very unhappy
and very wise,
1255 Your speech was long. But if in sober truth
You know your fate, why like an ox that the gods
Drive, do you walk so bravely to the altar?
CASSANDRA: There is no escape, strangers. No; not
by postponement.
LEADER OF THE CHORUS: But the last moment has the
privilege of hope.
CASSANDRA: The day is here. Little should I gain by
1260 flight.
LEADER OF THE CHORUS: This patience of yours
comes from a brave soul.
CASSANDRA: A happy man is never paid that
compliment.
LEADER OF THE CHORUS: But to die with credit graces
a mortal man.
CASSANDRA: Oh my father! You and your noble sons!

(She approaches the door, then suddenly recoils.)

LEADER OF THE CHORUS: What is it? What is the fear
1265 that drives you back?
CASSANDRA: Faugh.
LEADER OF THE CHORUS: Why faugh? Or is this some
hallucination?
CASSANDRA: These walls breathe out a death that
drips with blood.
LEADER OF THE CHORUS: Not so. It is only the smell
of the sacrifice.
1270 CASSANDRA: It is like a breath out of a charnel-house.
LEADER OF THE CHORUS: You think our palace burns
odd incense then!
CASSANDRA: But I will go to lament among the dead
My lot and Agamemnon's. Enough of life!
Strangers,
1275 I am not afraid like a bird afraid of a bush
But witness you my words after my death
When a woman dies in return for me a woman
And a man falls for a man with a wicked wife.
I ask this service, being about to die.

LEADER OF THE CHORUS: Alas, I pity you for the
death you have foretold.   1280
CASSANDRA: One more speech I have; I do not wish
to raise
The dirge for my own self. But to the sun I pray
In face of his last light that my avengers
May make my murderers pay for this my death,
Death of a woman slave, an easy victim.   1285

(She enters the palace.)

LEADER OF THE CHORUS: Ah the fortunes of men!
When they go well
A shadow sketch would match them, and in
ill-fortune
The dab of a wet sponge destroys the drawing.
It is not myself but the life of man I pity.
CHORUS: Prosperity in all men cries   1290
For more prosperity. Even the owner
Of the finger-pointed-at palace never shuts
His door against her, saying 'Come no more.'
So to our king the blessed gods had granted
To take the town of Priam, and heaven-favoured   1295
He reaches home. But now if for former bloodshed
He must pay blood
And dying for the dead shall cause
Other deaths in atonement
What man could boast he was born   1300
Secure, who heard this story?

AGAMEMNON:

(Within)

Oh! I am struck a mortal blow—within!

LEADER OF THE CHORUS: Silence! Listen. Who calls
out, wounded with a mortal stroke?

AGAMEMNON: Again—the second blow—I am struck
again.

LEADER OF THE CHORUS: You heard the king cry out.
I think the deed is done.   1305
Let us see if we can concert some sound proposal.
2ND OLD MAN: Well, I will tell you my opinion—
Raise an alarm, summon the folk to the palace.
3RD OLD MAN: I say burst in with all speed possible,
Convict them of the deed while still the sword is wet. 1310
4TH OLD MAN: And I am partner to some such
suggestion.
I am for taking some course. No time to dawdle.
5TH OLD MAN: The case is plain. This is but the
beginning.
They are going to set up dictatorship in the state.
6TH OLD MAN: We are wasting time. The assassins
tread to earth   1315
The decencies of delay and give their hands no
sleep.

7TH OLD MAN: I do not know what plan I could hit
 on to propose.
 The man who acts is in the position to plan.

8TH OLD MAN: So I think, too, for I am at a loss
1320 To raise the dead man up again with words.

9TH OLD MAN: Then to stretch out our life shall we
 yield thus
 To the rule of these profaners of the house?

10TH OLD MAN: It is not to be endured. To die is
 better.
 Death is more comfortable than tyranny.

1325 11TH OLD MAN: And are we on the evidence of groans
 Going to give oracle that the prince is dead?

12TH OLD MAN: We must know the facts for sure and
 then be angry.
 Guesswork is not the same as certain knowledge.

LEADER OF THE CHORUS: Then all of you back me
 and approve this plan—
1330 To ascertain how it is with Agamemnon.

(The doors of the palace open, revealing the bodies of
AGAMEMNON *and* CASSANDRA. CLYTEMNESTRA *stands*
above them.)

CLYTEMNESTRA: Much having been said before to fit
 the moment,
 To say the opposite now will not outface me.
 How else could one serving hate upon the hated,
 Thought to be friends, hang high the nets of doom
1335 To preclude all leaping out?
 For me I have long been training for this match,
 I tried a fall and won—a victory overdue.
 I stand here where I struck, above my victims;
 So I contrived it—this I will not deny—
1340 That he could neither fly nor ward off death;
 Inextricable like a net for fishes
 I cast about him a vicious wealth of raiment
 And struck him twice and with two groans he
 loosed
 His limbs beneath him, and upon him fallen
 I deal him the third blow to the God beneath the
1345 earth,
 To the safe keeper of the dead a votive gift,
 And with that he spits his life out where he lies
 And smartly spouting blood he sprays me with
 The sombre drizzle of bloody dew and I
1350 Rejoice no less than in God's gift of rain.
 The crops are glad when the ear of corn gives
 birth.
 These things being so, you, elders of Argos,
 Rejoice if rejoice you will. Mine is the glory.
 And if I could pay this corpse his due libation
1355 I should be right to pour it and more than right;
 With so many horrors this man mixed and filled
 The bowl—and, coming home, has drained the
 draught himself.

LEADER OF THE CHORUS: Your speech astonishes us.
 This brazen boast

Above the man who was your king and husband!

CLYTEMNESTRA: You challenge me as a woman
 without foresight   1360
But I with unflinching heart to you who know
Speak. And you, whether you will praise or blame,
It makes no matter. Here lies Agamemnon,
My husband, dead, the work of this right hand,
An honest workman. There you have the facts. 1365

CHORUS: Woman, what poisoned
 Herb of the earth have you tasted
 Or potion of the flowing sea
 To undertake this killing and the people's curses?
 You threw down, you cut off—The people will cast
 you out,   1370
 Black abomination to the town.

CLYTEMNESTRA: Now your verdict—in my case—is
 exile
And to have the people's hatred, the public curses,
Though then in no way you opposed this man
Who carelessly, as if it were a head of sheep 1375
Out of the abundance of his fleecy flocks,
Sacrificed his own daughter, to me the dearest
Fruit of travail, charm for the Thracian winds.
He was the one to have banished from this land,
Pay off the pollution. But when you hear what I 1380
Have done, you judge severely. But I warn you—
Threaten me on the understanding that I am ready
For two alternatives—Win by force the right
To rule me, but, if God brings about the contrary,
Late in time you will have to learn self-discipline. 1385

CHORUS: You are high in the thoughts,
 You speak extravagant things,
 After the soiling murder your crazy heart
 Fancies your forehead with a smear of blood.
 Unhonoured, unfriended, you must   1390
 Pay for a blow with a blow.

CLYTEMNESTRA: Listen then to this—the sanction of
 my oaths:
By the Justice totting up my child's atonement,
By the Avenging Doom and Fiend to whom I killed
 this man,
For me hope walks not in the rooms of fear 1395
So long as my fire is lit upon my hearth
By Aegisthus, loyal to me as he was before.
The man who outraged me lies here,
The darling of each courtesan at Troy,
And here with him is the prisoner clairvoyante, 1400
The fortune-teller that he took to bed,
Who shares his bed as once his bench on shipboard,
A loyal mistress. Both have their deserts.
He lies so; and she who like a swan
Sang her last dying lament   1405
Lies his lover, and the sight contributes
An appetiser to my own bed's pleasure.

CHORUS: Ah would some quick death come not
 overpainful,
 Not overlong on the sickbed,

1410 Establishing in us the ever-
Lasting unending sleep now that our guardian
Has fallen, the kindest of men,
Who suffering much for a woman
By a woman has lost his life.
1415 O Helen, insane, being one
One to have destroyed so many
And many souls under Troy,
Now is your work complete, blossomed not for
oblivion
Unfading stain of blood. Here now, if in any
home,
1420 Is Discord, here is a man's deep-rooted ruin.
CLYTEMNESTRA: Do not pray for the portion of death
Weighed down by these things, do not turn
Your anger on Helen as destroyer of men,
One woman destroyer of many
1425 Lives of Greek men,
A hurt that cannot be healed.
CHORUS: O Evil Spirit, falling on the family,
On the two sons of Atreus and using
Two sisters in heart as your tools,
1430 A power that bites to the heart—
See on the body
Perched like a raven he gloats
Harshly croaking his hymn.
CLYTEMNESTRA: Ah, now you have amended your
lips' opinion
1435 Calling upon this family's three times gorged
Genius—demon who breeds
Blood-hankering lust in the belly:
Before the old sore heals, new pus collects.
CHORUS: It is a great spirit—great—
1440 You tell of, harsh in anger,
A ghastly tale, alas,
Of unsatisfied disaster
Brought by Zeus, by Zeus,
Cause and worker of all.
1445 For without Zeus what comes to pass among us?
Which of these things is outside Providence?
O my king, my king,
How shall I pay you in tears,
Speak my affection in words?
1450 You lie in that spider's web,
In a desecrating death breathe out your life,
Lie ignominiously
Defeated by a crooked death
And the two-edged cleaver's stroke.
1455 CLYTEMNESTRA: You say this is *my* work—mine?
Do not cozen yourself that I am Agamemnon's
wife.
Masquerading as the wife
Of the corpse there the old sharp-witted Genius
Of Atreus who gave the cruel banquet
1460 Has paid with a grown man's life
The due for children dead.

CHORUS: That you are not guilty of
This murder who will attest?
No, but you may have been abetted
By some ancestral Spirit of Revenge.   1465
Wading a millrace of the family's blood
The black Manslayer forces a forward path
To make the requital at last
For the eaten children, the blood-clot cold with
time.
Oh my king, my king,   1470
How shall I pay you in tears,
Speak my affection in words?
You lie in that spider's web,
In a desecrating death breathe out your life,
Lie ignominiously   1475
Defeated by a crooked death
And the two-edged cleaver's stroke.
CLYTEMNESTRA: Did he not, too, contrive a crooked
Horror for the house? My child by him,
Shoot that I raised, much-wept-for Iphigeneia,   1480
He treated her like this;
So suffering like this he need not make
Any great brag in Hell having paid with death
Dealt by the sword for work of his own beginning.
CHORUS: I am at a loss for thought, I lack   1485
All nimble counsel as to where
To turn when the house is falling.
I fear the house-collapsing crashing
Blizzard of blood—of which these drops are
earnest.
Now is Destiny sharpening her justice   1490
On other whetstones for a new infliction.
O earth, earth, if only you had received me
Before I saw this man lie here as if in bed
In a bath lined with silver.
Who will bury him? Who will keen him?   1495
Will you, having killed your own husband,
Dare now to lament him
And after great wickedness make
Unamending amends to his ghost?
And who above this godlike hero's grave   1500
Pouring praises and tears
Will grieve with a genuine heart?
CLYTEMNESTRA: It is not your business to attend to
that.
By my hand he fell low, lies low and dead,
And I shall bury him low down in the earth,   1505
And his household need not weep him
For Iphigeneia his daughter
Tenderly, as is right,
Will meet her father at the rapid ferry of sorrows,
Put her arms round him and kiss him!   1510
CHORUS: Reproach answers reproach,
It is hard to decide,
The catcher is caught, the killer pays for his kill.
But the law abides while Zeus abides enthroned

1515 That the wrongdoer suffers. That is established.
Who could expel from the house the seed of the
Curse?
The race is soldered in sockets of Doom and
Vengeance.
CLYTEMNESTRA: In this you say what is right and the
will of God.
But for my part I am ready to make a contract
1520 With the Evil Genius of the House of Atreus
To accept what has been till now, hard though it is,
But that for the future he shall leave this house
And wear away some other stock with deaths
Imposed among themselves. Of my possessions
1525 A small part will suffice if only I
Can rid these walls of the mad exchange of
murder.

(Enter AEGISTHUS, *followed by soldiers.*)

AEGISTHUS: O welcome light of a justice-dealing day!
From now on I will say that the gods, avenging
men,
Look down from above on the crimes of earth,
1530 Seeing as I do in woven robes of the Furies
This man lying here—a sight to warm my heart—
Paying for the crooked violence of his father.
For this father Atreus, when he ruled the country,
Because his power was challenged, hounded out
1535 From state and home his own brother Thyestes.
My father—let me be plain—was this Thyestes,
Who later came back home a suppliant,
There, miserable, found so much asylum
As not to die on the spot, stain the ancestral floor.
1540 But to show his hospitality godless Atreus
Gave him an eager if not a loving welcome,
Pretending a day of feasting and rich meats
Served my father with his children's flesh.
The hands and feet, fingers and toes, he hid
1545 At the bottom of the dish. My father sitting apart
Took unknowing the unrecognizable portion
And ate of a dish that has proved, as you see,
expensive.
But when he knew he had eaten worse than poison
He fell back groaning, vomiting their flesh,
And invoking a hopeless doom on the sons of
1550 Pelops
Kicked over the table to confirm his curse—
So may the whole race perish!
Result of this—you see this man lie here.
I stitched this murder together; it was my title.
1555 Me the third son he left, an unweaned infant,
To share the bitterness of my father's exile,
But I grew up and Justice brought me back,
I grappled this man while still beyond his door,
Having pieced together the programme of his ruin.
1560 So now would even death be beautiful to me
Having seen Agamemnon in the nets of Justice.

LEADER OF THE CHORUS: Aegisthus. I cannot respect
brutality in distress.
You claim that you deliberately killed this prince
And that you alone planned this pitiful murder.
Be sure that in your turn your head shall not
escape
The people's volleyed curses mixed with stones. 1565
AEGISTHUS: Do you speak so who sit at the lower oar
While those on the upper bench control the ship?
Old as you are, you will find it is a heavy load
To go to school when old to learn the lesson of tact. 1570
For old age, too, gaol and hunger are fine
Instructors in wisdom, second-sighted doctors.
You have eyes. Cannot you see?
Do not kick against the pricks. The blow will hurt
you.
LEADER OF THE CHORUS: You woman waiting in the
house for those who return from battle 1575
While you seduce their wives! Was it you devised
The death of a master of armies?
AEGISTHUS: And these words, too, prepare the way
for tears.
Contrast your voice with the voice of Orpheus: he
Led all things after him bewitched with joy, but you 1580
Having stung me with your silly yelps shall be
Led off yourself, to prove more mild when
mastered.
LEADER OF THE CHORUS: Indeed! So you are now to
be king of Argos,
You who, when you had plotted the king's death,
Did not even dare to do that thing yourself! 1585
AEGISTHUS: No. For the trick of it was clearly
woman's work.
I was suspect, an enemy of old.
But now I shall try with Agamemnon's wealth
To rule the people. Any who is disobedient
I will harness in a heavy yoke, no tracehorse work
for him 1590
Like barley-fed colt, but hateful hunger lodging
Beside him in the dark will see his temper soften.
LEADER OF THE CHORUS: Why with your cowardly
soul did you yourself
Not strike this man but left that work to a woman
Whose presence pollutes our country and its gods? 1595
But Orestes—does he somewhere see the light
That he may come back here by favour of fortune
And kill this pair and prove the final victor?
AEGISTHUS (*summoning his guards*): Well, if such is
your design in deeds and words, you will quickly
learn—
Here my friends, here my guards, there is work for
you at hand. 1600
LEADER OF THE CHORUS: Come then, hands on hilts,
be each and all of us prepared.

(*The old men and the guards threaten each other.*)

AEGISTHUS: Very well! I too am ready to meet death
with sword in hand.

LEADER OF THE CHORUS: We are glad you speak of
dying. We accept your words for luck.

CLYTEMNESTRA: No, my dearest, do not so. Add no
more to the train of wrong.

To reap these many present wrongs is harvest
1605   enough of misery.

Enough of misery. Start no more. Our hands are
red.

But do you, and you old men, go home and yield
to fate in time,

In time before you suffer. We have tried as we had
to act.

If only our afflictions now could prove enough, we
should agree—

We who have been so hardly mauled in the heavy
1610   claws of the evil god.

So stands my word, a woman's, if any man thinks fit
to hear.

AEGISTHUS: But to think that these should thus pluck
the blooms of an idle tongue

And should throw out words like these, giving the
evil god his chance,

And should miss the path of prudence and insult
their master so!

LEADER OF THE CHORUS: It is not the Argive way to
fawn upon a cowardly man.   1615

AEGISTHUS: Perhaps. But I in later days will take
further steps with you.

LEADER OF THE CHORUS: Not if the god who rules the
family guides Orestes to his home.

AEGISTHUS: Yes. I know that men in exile feed
themselves on barren hopes.

LEADER OF THE CHORUS: Go on, grow fat defiling
justice . . . while you have your hour.

AEGISTHUS: Do not think you will not pay me a price
for your stupidity.   1620

LEADER OF THE CHORUS: Boast on in your self-
assurance, like a cock beside his hen.

CLYTEMNESTRA: Pay no heed, Aegisthus, to these
futile barkings. You and I,

Masters of this house, from now shall order all
things well.

(They enter the palace.)

Figure 1. Clytemnestra (Douglas Campbell, *left*) welcomes Agamemnon (Lee Richardson) upon his return from Troy in the Guthrie Theater Company production of *The House of Atreus,* directed by Tyrone Guthrie and designed by Tanya Moiseiwitsch, Minneapolis, 1967/68. (Photograph: the Guthrie Theater.)

Figure 2. Agamemnon (Lee Richardson, *left*) returns from the Trojan War with Cassandra (Robin Gammell) in the 1967/68 Guthrie Theater Company production of *The House of Atreus*. (Photograph: the Guthrie Theater.)

Figure 3. Clytemnestra (actor on left), her left hand covered with a red glove to symbolize blood, stands triumphant, while the corpses of Agamemnon and Cassandra are revealed to both audience and Chorus. *The Oresteia,* in a translation by Tony Harrison, was directed by Peter Hall, designed by Jocelyn Herbert, and staged at the National Theatre, London, 1981. (Photograph: Donald Cooper Photostage.)

Staging of *Agamemnon*

REVIEW OF THE GUTHRIE THEATER
PRODUCTION, 1967, BY RODERICK NORDELL

The Minnesota Theater Company's "House of Atreus" is like an ancient carving freed from stone to tell us about ourselves. Compressing Aeschylus' "Oresteia" trilogy into a single lengthy evening, it is attracting full houses to the Tyrone Guthrie Theater for a rigorous combination of spectacle, psychology, philosophy, and even a kind of God-is-alive theology.

As seen last week, the production tempted one to stay on the level of spectacle—an awesome theatrical representation of the theme familiarly translated as "Men shall learn wisdom, by affliction schooled." For Tyrone Guthrie's monumentally stylized direction is aided by the designing hand of Tanya Moiseiwitsch, as it was in "Oedipus" at Stratford, Ont., some dozen years ago. And the mythic grandeur of their work is heightened by the grotesque but tellingly differentiated masks credited to Carolyn Parker and Dahl Delu.

Cassandra's mask, for example, is vaguely reminiscent of a tragic, dark-lined Rouault portrait. Clytemnestra's is haughty, blank-eyed, with a forbidding version of the "onkos," the high hairdress Aeschylus favored.

The sleeved robes he pioneered for actors are also effectively suggested, though sometimes they seem to have been given an antiquing process recalling a painter's spattered tarpaulin. And, if history is right in saying Aeschylus raised the height of the actors' elevator shoes, "The House of Atreus" must go further than he did.

In this production, only the ordinary people, "like ourselves," are on ground level, as Guthrie has commented. The main characters, "heroic figures," are larger than life. The gods are immense.

The great rings in the massive palace gates almost overwhelm the mortal men who open them. Even the heroic figure of Orestes is dwarfed by the golden, towering Apollo who has set him on the path of vengeance—and by the enormous seated Pallas Athena who seeks to bring rational justice to the primitive situation of blood-will-have-blood.

It takes some effort to wrench oneself from the spectacle; from Dominick Argento's music with its breathy cymbal ending a spoken phrase, its tinkling triangles and more stentorian flourishes; from the sound and sight of the skilled actors, notably Douglas Campbell, who makes Clytemnestra's first silent entrance a chilling image of threat and who—without obvious feminine pitch—speaks the lines with a thoughtful, savage, womanly eloquence.

The display is marvelous in itself; it can be justified both by old tradition and by the new demands of the theater to break out of realism and into its own unique truth. Yet one has at least a passing feeling that the production could have gone in another direction— toward the sparest everyday restraint—in eliciting what Aeschylus says to today, and what is seen in him by his sensitive latter-day adapter, John Lewin, the company's resident playwright.

The feeling does not apply only to such humanizing touches as those derived from Aeschylus' own experience in the army. When a soldier returns from Troy, Mr. Lewin plausibly has him say, "You think it's cold in Greece—this was unbelievable." Is it too human to be spoken through a mask?

One also questions the apparatus when the play gets into Mr. Lewin's stated interpretation of its psychological level, with the unconscious and the "ordering intellect" in conflict and collaboration. The nightmarish Furies and the gleaming Apollo make strong images, but might they not be stronger in street clothes, so to speak? Today's dilemmas tend to be gray.

As it is, the dazzled spectator may not listen closely enough when Orestes challenges his god, Apollo: "You know what it means to do wrong. Do you know what it means to take responsibility?"

But in such lines, in the interplay between "new" and "old" gods, in the emergence of a more sophisticated form of justice, lie the issues that still exercise philosophers and theologians. In the company's "play guide," Minnesota poet Robert Bly finds Aeschylus' exploration of the "inability to forgive" pertinent to such present-day episodes as Eichmann and Vietnam. Guthrie finds a parallel to humanity's growing conception of God: "the vengeful tribal deity, the Jehovah of the earlier books of the Old Testament, becomes God the All-Merciful Father, something very different, very much more humane."

On afterthought, such themes can be pondered in relation to the sheer theater that envelops them. But in the playhouse the weight of effects, as well as that of tragedy, may contribute to the audience's laughing sigh of relief when Orestes' old nurse brings it back to earth with: "It's just one thing after another." The outer and inner drama fuse during moments such as that when the well-deployed chorus says: "The gods that give us sorrows give us tongues to mourn."

FROM *EXPOSED BY THE MASK: FORM AND LANGUAGE IN DRAMA,* 1981, BY PETER HALL, DIRECTOR OF *THE ORESTEIA*

. . . The Romans believed in absolutes: so their masks were good or bad, serious or comic. "Is he a goodie or a baddie?" says the child, seeking reassurance. So said the Romans because they wanted absolutes, not, like the Greeks, questions. The Greek mask was enigmatic, uncertain, representing the human confusion. They were soft, flexible, probably made of thin leather, and always ambiguous. Their humanity was enigmatic. They waited to be printed with the emotion of the actor. So they were neither comic nor tragic—like life itself. The Romans always needed the reassurance of caricature. Greek masks are on a human scale; Roman masks are gargantuan.

A Greek full mask can laugh or cry—it is entirely dependent on what the character wearing it is feeling. This can be as well expressed by the body as by the words that are uttered. The ambiguous mask, fully used, is often much more expressive than the human face because it is dealing with the quintessence of emotions. Its contradictions and yet its simplicity enable a range of feeling and an extremity of passion to be expressed which is often much more difficult with a naked face. The mask is an instrument of communication. The poet Tony Harrison sees it as the incandescent spot of the welder's torch, where meaning is fused and components joined. Or it can be thought of as a magnifying glass, helping us to scrutinise emotion. Uneasy attempts to explain it away are partly modern embarrassment when faced with primal feelings—or bad mask work where the passions are not strong enough to support the form. Then abstraction sets in and the mask appears dead.

The mask is *not* a device to enhance visibility in the large Greek amphitheatres; a mask of human scale is perfectly visible in Epidaurus before ten thousand people. Nor is the mask a megaphone to increase audibility. Epidaurus has no need of megaphones—only of clear consonants expressing clear thoughts. Ten thousand people can hear perfectly.

With the governance of the mask preventing overacting and telling us about grief rather than realistically crying it out, it is entirely possible to make subtle drama at Epidaurus. Precise words and eloquent actions give a clear meaning, which is in no sense ritualised. Yet the masks enable an intense emotional heat to be generated that *tells* us about grief. The same is true of the comic mask. The surrealistic extremes of Aristophanes are perfectly acceptable in this world of caricature. Without the mask, his crudity can lack grace. It runs the risk of being not life-enhancing, but just plain dirty, like an obvious seaside postcard.

Above all, the mask is the tool of the imagination. A metaphor. An audience can see on it infinite emotions. A camera will only see an immobile mask. But the camera is literal—it has no imagination. Once the mask is accepted, the work with the actor, particularly the work with the Chorus, becomes very specific. And it is here that the discoveries are biggest. . . .

It is worth considering the technique of the full mask in greater detail. A variety of masks and hats with odd bits of clothes and pieces of material are spread out on a table. The actors are asked to take any mask, any item of clothing that appeals to their imaginations and dress themselves up to make a character. There is now a traumatic moment. The actor looks for the first time into a full-length mirror. He or she must then *become* what they see. Become the character. So the look lasts for a few seconds. No more. Just a few seconds. The changed identity is then accepted by the actor and the character now follows the change wherever it may lead.

Sometimes the actor is so alarmed by the new self that he rejects it. Then he must take the mask off—immediately. He must also take it off if he feels untrue. Even the least talented actor knows when he is being untrue to his character. But then he cannot go on wearing the mask. He must always be true to it.

Sometimes the mask liberates him. Sometimes it makes the actor apprehend a whole new world. He can change his age, his bearing, his physique, even his sexuality. The change comes from using parts of himself that perhaps he did not know existed, and suppressing others irrelevant to this new person. It is the same process as the creation of a realistic character, but the mask allows the actor a much, much wider range.

When the actor first puts on the mask, he finds it almost impossible to speak. If he works honestly, he goes through a period—and it can take sometimes two to three weeks—where all he can do is make guttural sounds. He ignores everyone. Or if he looks at them, he looks belligerently. Sometimes the shock of seeing others makes him remove the mask. Sometimes he shrinks into a strange torpor. After a time, he gradually starts making sounds and words for himself. After finding his place in a social group, the hostility recedes and he begins to make sounds at others. After even more time, words may be exchanged.

This somewhat alarming process of growing up, of becoming part of a group and learning how to live in it has happened every single time I have conducted a mask workshop. On several occasions, the actors had no knowledge that our work would produce this journey. Yet it always went the same way. The actor always had to learn to speak and then to grow up. He had to take on social responsibilities, and as he did so he

became less hostile. Every time, I observed the animal learning to be human. There are truly primitive forces at work here. And the mask can have alarming consequences. I have seen an actor arrested by a policeman when in full mask he exuberantly leapt on a bicycle and pedalled out of the rehearsal room into the Chelsea crowds. I have known an actor whose incipient nervous breakdown was hastened by contemplating himself in a mask.

SOPHOCLES

496–406 B.C.

Because his life spanned almost the entire fifth century, Sophocles witnessed both the rise and the fall of Athens—a reversal of political fortune as astonishing as the one he dramatized in *Oedipus Rex*. As a young man he lived through the extraordinary growth of Athenian power and culture that followed upon the Persian Wars; as a mature man he served its power and culture in various capacities: as ambassador, dramatist, general, priest, and treasurer; and as an old man he witnessed the collapse of its power and culture under the strains of the Peloponnesian Wars, his death coming only two years before the Athenian surrender to Sparta. In many respects he seems to have been a consummate representative of the best qualities in fifth century Athenian culture, a man who not only was gifted with good looks, great wealth, and even greater talent, but who also made the most of those gifts in his public life, his religious duties, and his artistic career. Through all the distractions of public appointments and religious obligations, he somehow managed to write more than 120 plays.

Although he was a prolific writer, he wrote with great care, and his carefully wrought plays brought him great success in the festival competitions. He won first prize twenty-four times, and he never ranked lower than second. Only seven of his plays have survived, all from the mature period of his life: *Ajax* (ca. 445), *Antigone* (ca. 440), *Trachiniae* (ca. 435), *Oedipus Rex* (ca. 425), *Electra* (ca. 415), *Philoctetes* (409), and *Oedipus at Colonus* (406). All of these show him to have been a painstaking and meticulous dramatist. His plots, however complex, are always clearly worked out, with each event connected by a logic of cause and effect to every other event, so that they never contain any loose ends or improbable outcomes. His characters, though complexly motivated, are always clearly and consistently developed. Because of these qualities, his plays have always been considered the most polished examples of classical Greek tragedy—the perfection of the form.

He completely departed from Aeschylus by abandoning the trilogy, preferring instead to submit three unrelated and self-sufficient plays. Although he sacrificed the comprehensive scope of the trilogy, he was able to develop a far more intense and complete dramatic experience within the limits of a single play—an experience centering on the fate of individuals rather than on the destinies of families and nations. In developing the art of the single play, his most decisive contribution was to increase the number of actors from two to three. He was thus able to create various kinds of highly dramatic episodes out of the triangular interplay among characters that became possible with the third actor. Two such episodes occur in *Oedipus Rex:* the first, when the messenger comes to bring what he thinks is good news to Oedipus and Iocastê, but the news gradually reveals to Iocastê a horrible truth that she seeks to withhold from Oedipus; the second, when the shepherd arrives and reluctantly answers the questions of the messenger and Oedipus, providing information that finally reveals the horrible truth to Oedipus.

Once it became possible to stage such theatrically compelling episodes, it was inevitable that the actors would become more important than the chorus, and that is precisely what happened in the plays of Sophocles. Although he increased the size of the chorus from twelve to fifteen members, he actually reduced its functions, confining its activities almost exclusively to choral odes and leaving it little opportunity to interact with the characters. Its odes continued to be relevant to the mood and meaning of the action, but the chorus was no longer a dramatically integral part of that action, as it had been in the plays of Aeschylus. Thus Sophocles moved tragedy further away from its lyric origins and closer to a purely dramatic form.

Sophocles used the sophisticated form of his tragedies to represent and explore the fate of heroic individuals in a moment of moral crisis. All of his protagonists prove to be singularly heroic in their commitment to a moral principle they establish for themselves, even though their commitment brings great suffering to themselves and their loved ones. In *Antigone,* for example, the heroine opposes her uncle Creon, who as ruler of Thebes has decreed that her brother Polyneices is not to be given a burial because he led an attack on the city. Creon regards his edict as a politically necessary action, whereas Antigone believes the burial of her brother to be a sacred obligation. Although Antigone is shown to be coldly, fanatically, and inflexibly devoted to her cause, the events of the play bear out the righteousness of her action. Yet her righteous commitment is not only the source of her dignity; it is also the cause of her undoing. This paradoxical fate repeatedly besets the heroes of Sophocles, and it is one of the qualities that make his plays so compelling. Indeed, his tragedies would not be as terrifying as they are if his protagonists were as flawed as they are often considered to be.

The disaster experienced by Oedipus is often regarded as a fitting outcome of his pride, but it is difficult to see how the play justifies this interpretation of his fate. Throughout the play he is shown to be nobly unyielding in his attempt to rid Thebes of the plague by discovering and punishing the murderer of its previous king, Laïos. Even when the investigation turns into an investigation of himself, he is unflinching in his quest for truth, though he is warned against it by Teiresias and Iocastê. He relentlessly conducts his search until he discovers himself to be the criminal, the source of the city's sickness, and by exposing himself brings about the renewed health of the city. His commitment to the truth thereby proves to be at once his triumph and his disaster. *Oedipus Rex* raises haunting questions about the fate of heroic individuals—questions that it does not finally answer—except through the chorus's concluding reflections on human frailty.

Because its plot and characters are so skillfully conceived and developed, *Oedipus Rex* has come to be the most influential play ever written. The perfection of its form was recognized by Aristotle during the fourth century B.C. when he expounded his theory of tragedy in *The Poetics.* In his discussions of character and plot, Aristotle provides detailed explanations of important dramatic elements, such as "discovery" and "reversal of fortune," repeatedly citing *Oedipus Rex* as the outstanding embodiment of them. Using it as his model play, Aristotle produced a study that has come to be the most influential document in the history of dramatic theory and criticism. In choosing his model, Aristotle also had his eye on the audience, for he knew from his own experience of witnessing Greek drama just how strongly an audience can be moved to "pity and fear" by discoveries and reversals of fortune on the part of a tragic hero.

Because it is the consummate embodiment of tragic irony, *Oedipus Rex* continues to be highly successful in the modern theater, attracting major actors, directors, designers, and translators. One such production, by the Guthrie Theater in 1972, involved a new translation by the novelist Anthony Burgess, a translation that moved both director Michael Langham and composer Stanley Silverman away from the classic grandeur suggested by masks and toward a primitive world underscored by drums and ritual chants. That primitivism, visible in the costumes and setting (see Figures 1 and 2), arose after considerable discussion of the text, its background, and possible sources for the music. Letters exchanged between Burgess and Langham and Langham and Silverman reveal the creative process as one of detailed scrutiny and imaginative leaps (see excerpts following the text). Indeed, the "inspired anachronistic approach, a synoptic gospel of all ancient cultures" that finally emerged seemed to one reviewer to bring the ancient play to life, not through trendy updating but through profound immersion in ritual. The artistic eclecticism of the production stands as testimony both to the play's complexity and to its haunting enactment of the dignity and the frailty of human nature.

OEDIPUS REX

BY SOPHOCLES / TRANSLATED BY DUDLEY FITTS AND ROBERT FITZGERALD

CHARACTERS

OEDIPUS
A PRIEST
CREON
TEIRESIAS
IOCASTE
MESSENGER
SHEPHERD OF LAÏOS
SECOND MESSENGER
CHORUS OF THEBAN ELDERS

SCENE

Before the palace of Oedipus, King of Thebes. A central door and two lateral doors open onto a platform which runs the length of the façade. On the platform, right and left, are altars; and three steps lead down into the "orchestra," or chorus-ground. At the beginning of the action these steps are crowded by suppliants who have brought branches and chaplets of olive leaves and who lie in various attitudes of despair. OEDIPUS *enters.*

PROLOGUE

OEDIPUS: My children, generations of the living
In the line of Kadmos, nursed at his ancient
    hearth:
Why have you strewn yourselves before these altars
In supplication, with your boughs and garlands?
5 The breath of incense rises from the city
With a sound of prayer and lamentation.
Children,
I would not have you speak through messengers,
And therefore I have come myself to hear you—
10 I, Oedipus, who bear the famous name.

(*To a* PRIEST)

You, there, since you are eldest in the company,
Speak for them all, tell me what preys upon you,
Whether you come in dread, or crave some
    blessing:
Tell me, and never doubt that I will help you
15 In every way I can; I should be heartless
Were I not moved to find you suppliant here.
PRIEST: Great Oedipus, O powerful King of Thebes!
You see how all the ages of our people
Cling to your altar steps: here are boys
20 Who can barely stand alone, and here are priests
By weight of age, as I am a priest of God,
And young men chosen from those yet unmarried;
As for the others, all that multitude,
They wait with olive chaplets in the squares,
25 At the two shrines of Pallas, and where Apollo
Speaks in the glowing embers.
Your own eyes
Must tell you: Thebes is tossed on a murdering sea
And can not lift her head from the death surge.
30 A rust consumes the buds and fruits of the earth;
The herds are sick; children die unborn,
And labor is vain. The god of plague and pyre
Raids like detestable lightning through the city,
And all the house of Kadmos is laid waste,

All emptied, and all darkened: Death alone   35
Battens upon the misery of Thebes.

You are not one of the immortal gods, we know;
Yet we have come to you to make our prayer
As to the man surest in mortal ways
And wisest in the ways of God. You saved us   40
From the Sphinx, that flinty singer, and the tribute
We paid to her so long; yet you were never
Better informed than we, nor could we teach you;
It was some god breathed in you to set us free.

Therefore, O mighty power, we turn to you: 45
Find us our safety, find us a remedy,
Whether by counsel of the gods or men.
A king of wisdom tested in the past
Can act in a time of troubles, and act well.
Noblest of men, restore   50
Life to your city! Think how all men call you
Liberator for your boldness long ago;
Ah, when your years of kingship are remembered,
Let them not say *We rose, but later fell*—
Keep the State from going down in the storm!   55
Once, years ago, with happy augury,
You brought us fortune; be the same again!
No man questions your power to rule the land:
But rule over men, not a dead city!
Ships are only hulls, high walls are nothing,   60
When no life moves in the empty passageways.
OEDIPUS: Poor children! You may be sure I know
All that you longed for in your coming here.
I know that you are deathly sick; and yet,
Sick as you are, not one is as sick as I.   65
Each of you suffers in himself alone
His anguish, not another's; but my spirit
Groans for the city, for myself, for you.

I was not sleeping, you are not waking me.
No, I have been in tears for a long while   70

And in my restless thought walked many ways.
In all my search, I found one helpful course,
And that I have taken: I have sent Creon,
Son of Menoikeus, brother of the Queen,
75 To Delphi, Apollo's place of revelation,
To learn there, if he can,
What act or pledge of mine may save the city.
I have counted the days, and now, this very day,
I am troubled, for he has overstayed his time.
80 What is he doing? He has been gone too long.
Yet whenever he comes back, I should do ill
To scant whatever duty God reveals.
PRIEST: It is a timely promise. At this instant
They tell me Creon is here.
85 OEDIPUS: O Lord Apollo!
May his news be fair as his face is radiant!
PRIEST: It could not be otherwise: he is crowned with
bay,
The chaplet is thick with berries.
OEDIPUS: We shall soon know;
90 He is near enough to hear us now.

(Enter CREON.)

O Prince:
Brother: son of Menoikeus
What answer do you bring us from the god?
CREON: A strong one. I can tell you, great afflictions
95 Will turn out well, if they are taken well.
OEDIPUS: What was the oracle? These vague words
Leave me still hanging between hope and fear.
CREON: Is it your pleasure to hear me with all these
Gathered around us? I am prepared to speak,
100 But should we not go in?
OEDIPUS: Let them all hear it.
It is for them I suffer, more than for myself.
CREON: Then I will tell you what I heard at Delphi.
In plain words
The god commands us to expel from the land of
105 Thebes
An old defilement we are sheltering.
It is a deathly thing, beyond cure;
We must not let it feed upon us longer.
OEDIPUS: What defilement? How shall we rid
ourselves of it?
110 CREON: By exile or death, blood for blood. It was
Murder that brought the plague-wind on the
city.
OEDIPUS: Murder of whom? Surely the god has
named him?
CREON: My lord: long ago Laïos was our King,
Before you came to govern us.
115 OEDIPUS: I know;
I learned of him from others; I never saw him.
CREON: He was murdered; and Apollo commands us
now
To take revenge upon whoever killed him.

OEDIPUS: Upon whom? Where are they? Where shall
we find a clue
To solve that crime, after so many years?   120
CREON: Here in this land, he said.
If we make enquiry,
We may touch things that otherwise escape us.
OEDIPUS: Tell me: Was Laïos murdered in his house,
Or in the fields, or in some foreign country?   125
CREON: He said he planned to make a pilgrimage.
He did not come home again.
OEDIPUS: And was there no one,
No witness, no companion, to tell what happened?
CREON: They were all killed but one, and he got away 130
So frightened that he could remember one thing
only.
OEDIPUS: What was that one thing? One may be the
key
To everything, if we resolve to use it.
CREON: He said that a band of highwaymen attacked
them,
Outnumbered them, and overwhelmed the King.   135
OEDIPUS: Strange, that a highwayman should be so
daring—
Unless some faction here bribed him to do it.
CREON: We thought of that. But after Laïos' death
New troubles arose and we had no avenger.
OEDIPUS: What troubles could prevent your hunting
down the killers?   140
CREON: The riddling Sphinx's song
Made us deaf to all mysteries but her own.
OEDIPUS: Then once more I must bring what is dark
to light.
It is most fitting that Apollo shows,
As you do, this compunction for the dead.   145
You shall see how I stand by you, as I should,
To avenge the city and the city's gods,
And not as though it were for some distant friend,
But for my own sake, to be rid of evil.
Whoever killed King Laïos might—who knows?—   150
Decide at any moment to kill me as well.
By avenging the murdered King I protect myself.

Come, then, my children: leave the altar steps,
Lift up your olive boughs!
One of you go   155
And summon the people of Kadmos to gather
here.
I will do all that I can; you may tell them that.

(Exit a PAGE.)

So, with the help of God,
We shall be saved—or else indeed we are lost.
PRIEST: Let us rise, children. It was for this we came, 160
And now the King has promised it himself.
Phoibos has sent us an oracle; may he descend
Himself to save us and drive out the plague.

(Exeunt OEDIPUS *and* CREON *into the palace by the central door. The* PRIEST *and the* SUPPLIANTS *disperse right and left. After a short pause the* CHORUS *enters the orchestra.)*

PARADOS

Strophe 1

CHORUS: What is God singing in his profound
165   Delphi of gold and shadow?
        What oracle for Thebes, the sunwhipped city?

        Fear unjoints me, the roots of my heart tremble.

        Now I remember, O Healer, your power and
            wonder:
        Will you send doom like a sudden cloud, or weave
            it
170   Like nightfall of the past?

        Speak, speak to us, issue of holy sound:
        Dearest to our expectancy: be tender!

Antistrophe 1

        Let me pray to Athenê, the immortal daughter of
            Zeus,
        And to Artemis her sister
175   Who keeps her famous throne in the market ring,

        And to Apollo, bowman at the far butts of heaven—

        O gods, descend! Like three streams leap against
        The fires of our grief, the fires of darkness;
        Be swift to bring us rest!

180   As in the old time from the brilliant house
        Of air you stepped to save us, come again!

Strophe 2

        Now our afflictions have no end,
        Now all our stricken host lies down
        And no man fights off death with his mind;

185   The noble plowland bears no grain,
        And groaning mothers can not bear—

        See, how our lives like birds take wing,
        Like sparks that fly when a fire soars,
        To the shore of the god of evening.

Antistrophe 2

190   The plague burns on, it is pitiless,
        Though pallid children laden with death
        Lie unwept in the stony ways,

        And old gray women by every path
        Flock to the strand about the altars

195   There to strike their breasts and cry
        Worship of Phoibos in wailing prayers:
        Be kind, God's golden child!

Strophe 3

        There are no swords in this attack by fire,
        No shields, but we are ringed with cries.

        Send the besieger plunging from our homes   200
        Into the vast sea-room of the Atlantic
        Or into the waves that foam eastward of Thrace—

        For the day ravages what the night spares—

        Destroy our enemy, lord of the thunder!
        Let him be riven by lightning from heaven!   205

Antistrophe 3

        Phoibos Apollo, stretch the sun's bowstring,
        That golden cord, until it sing for us,
        Flashing arrows in heaven!
        Artemis, Huntress,
        Race with flaring lights upon our mountains!   210

        O scarlet god, O golden-banded brow,
        O Theban Bacchos in a storm of Maenads,

        (Enter OEDIPUS, *center.)*

        Whirl upon Death, that all the Undying hate!
        Come with blinding torches, come in joy!

SCENE I

OEDIPUS: Is this your prayer? It may be answered.
            Come,
        Listen to me act as the crisis demands,
        And you shall have relief from all these evils.

        Until now I was a stranger to this tale.
        As I had been a stranger to the crime.   5
        Could I track down the murderer without a clue?
        But now, friends,
        As one who became a citizen after the murder,
        I make this proclamation to all Thebans:

        If any man knows by whose hand Laïos, son of
            Labdakos,   10
        Met his death, I direct that man to tell me
            everything,
        No matter what he fears for having so long
            withheld it.
        Let it stand as promised that no further trouble
        Will come to him, but he may leave the land in
            safety.

        Moreover: If anyone knows the murderer to be
            foreign,   15
        Let him not keep silent: he shall have his reward
            from me.
        However, if he does conceal it; if any man

Fearing for his friend or for himself disobeys this
    edict,
Hear what I propose to do:

20 I solemnly forbid the people of this country,
Where power and throne are mine, ever to receive
    that man
Or speak to him, no matter who he is, or let him
Join in sacrifice, lustration, or in prayer.
I decree that he be driven from every house,
25 Being, as he is, corruption itself to us: the Delphic
Voice of Apollo has pronounced this revelation.
Thus I associate myself with the oracle
And take the side of the murdered king.

As for the criminal, I pray to God—
30 Whether it be a lurking thief, or one of a number—
I pray that that man's life be consumed in evil and
    wretchedness.
And as for me, this curse applies no less
If it should turn out that the culprit is my guest
    here,
Sharing my hearth.
35 You have heard the penalty.

I lay it on you now to attend to this
For my sake, for Apollo's, for the sick
Sterile city that heaven has abandoned.
Suppose the oracle had given you no command:
40 Should this defilement go uncleansed for ever?
You should have found the murderer: your king,
A noble king, had been destroyed!
Now I,
Having the power that he held before me,
45 Having his bed, begetting children there
Upon his wife, as he would have, had he lived—
Their son would have been my children's brother,
If Laïos had had luck in fatherhood!
(But surely ill luck rushed upon his reign)—
50 I say I take the son's part, just as though
I were his son, to press the fight for him
And see it won! I'll find the hand that brought
Death to Labdakos' and Polydoros' child,
Heir of Kadmos' and Agenor's line.
55 And as for those who fail me,
May the gods deny them the fruit of the earth,
Fruit of the womb, and may they rot utterly!
Let them be wretched as we are wretched, and
    worse!

For you, my loyal Thebans, and for all
60 Who find my actions right, I pray the favor
Of justice, and of all the immortal gods.
CHORAGOS: Since I am under oath, my lord, I swear
I did not do the murder, I can not name
The murderer. Might not the oracle
That has ordained the search tell where to find
65   him?

OEDIPUS: An honest question. But no man in the
    world
Can make the gods do more than the gods will.
CHORAGOS: There is one last expedient—
OEDIPUS: Tell me what it is.
Though it seem slight, you must not hold it back.   70
CHORAGOS: A lord clairvoyant to the lord Apollo,
As we all know, is the skilled Teiresias.
One might learn much about this from him,
    Oedipus.
OEDIPUS: I am not wasting time:
Creon spoke of this, and I have sent for him—   75
Twice, in fact; it is strange that he is not here.
CHORAGOS: The other matter—that old report—
    seems useless.
OEDIPUS: Tell me. I am interested in all reports.
CHORAGOS: The King was said to have been killed by
    highwaymen.
OEDIPUS: I know. But we have no witnesses to that.   80
CHORAGOS: If the killer can feel a particle of dread,
Your curse will bring him out of hiding!
OEDIPUS: No.
The man who dared that act will fear no curse.

(*Enter the blind seer* TEIRESIAS, *led by a* PAGE.)

CHORAGOS: But there is one man who may detect the
    criminal.   85
This is Teiresias, this is the holy prophet
In whom, alone of all men, truth was born.
OEDIPUS: Teiresias: seer: student of mysteries,
Of all that's taught and all that no man tells,
Secrets of Heaven and secrets of the earth: 90
Blind though you are, you know the city lies
Sick with plague; and from this plague, my lord,
We find that you alone can guard or save us.

Possibly you did not hear the messengers?
Apollo, when we sent to him,   95
Sent us back word that this great pestilence
Would lift, but only if we established clearly
The identity of those who murdered Laïos.
They must be killed or exiled.
Can you use   100
Birdflight or any art of divination
To purify yourself, and Thebes, and me
From this contagion? We are in your hands.
There is no fairer duty
Than that of helping others in distress.   105
TEIRESIAS: How dreadful knowledge of the truth can
    be
When there's no help in truth! I knew this well,
But made myself forget. I should not have come.
OEDIPUS: What is troubling you? Why are your eyes
    so cold?

TEIRESIAS: Let me go home. Bear your own fate, and
110   I'll
      Bear mine. It is better so: trust what I say.
OEDIPUS: What you say is ungracious and unhelpful
      To your native country. Do not refuse to speak.
TEIRESIAS: When it comes to speech, your own is
      neither temperate
115   Nor opportune. I wish to be more prudent.
OEDIPUS: In God's name, we all beg you—
TEIRESIAS: You are all ignorant.
      No; I will never tell you what I know.
      Now it is my misery; then it would be yours.
OEDIPUS: What! You do know something, and will
120   not tell us?
      You would betray us all and wreck the State?
TEIRESIAS: I do not intend to torture myself, or you.
      Why persist in asking? You will not persuade me.
OEDIPUS: What a wicked old man you are! You'd try a
      stone's
125   Patience! Out with it. Have you no feeling at all?
TEIRESIAS: You call me unfeeling. If you could only
      see
      The nature of your own feelings . . .
OEDIPUS: Why,
      Who would not feel as I do? Who could endure
130   Your arrogance toward the city?
TEIRESIAS: What does it matter?
      Whether I speak or not, it is bound to come.
OEDIPUS: Then, if "it" is bound to come, you are
      bound to tell me.
TEIRESIAS: No, I will not go on. Rage as you please.
135 OEDIPUS: Rage? Why not!
      And I'll tell you what I think:
      You planned it, you had it done, you all but
      Killed him with your own hands: if you had eyes,
      I'd say the crime was yours, and yours alone.
140 TEIRESIAS: So? I charge you, then,
      Abide by the proclamation you have made:
      From this day forth
      Never speak again to these men or to me;
      You yourself are the pollution of this country.
OEDIPUS: You dare say that! Can you possibly think
145   you have
      Some way of going free, after such insolence?
TEIRESIAS: I have gone free. It is the truth sustains
      me.
OEDIPUS: Who taught you shamelessness? It was not
      your craft.
TEIRESIAS: You did. You made me speak. I did not
      want to.
OEDIPUS: Speak what? Let me hear it again more
150   clearly.
TEIRESIAS: Was it not clear before? Are you tempting
      me?
OEDIPUS: I did not understand it. Say it again.
TEIRESIAS: I say that you are the murderer whom you
      seek.

OEDIPUS: Now twice you have spat out infamy. You'll
      pay for it!
TEIRESIAS: Would you care for more? Do you wish to
      be really angry?   155
OEDIPUS: Say what you will. Whatever you say is
      worthless.
TEIRESIAS: I say you live in hideous shame with those
      Most dear to you. You can not see the evil.
OEDIPUS: It seems you can go on mouthing like this
      for ever.
TEIRESIAS: I can, if there is power in truth.   160
OEDIPUS: There is:
      But not for you, not for you,
      You sightless, witless, senseless, mad old man!
TEIRESIAS: You are the madman. There is no one here
      Who will not curse you soon, as you curse me.   165
OEDIPUS: You child of total night! You can not hurt
      me
      Or any other man who sees the sun.
TEIRESIAS: True: it is not from me your fate will come.
      That lies within Apollo's competence,
      As it is his concern.   170
OEDIPUS: Tell me:
      Are you speaking for Creon, or for yourself?
TEIRESIAS: Creon is no threat. You weave your own
      doom.
OEDIPUS: Wealth, power, craft of statesmanship!
      Kingly position, everywhere admired!   175
      What savage envy is stored up against these,
      If Creon, whom I trusted, Creon my friend,
      For this great office which the city once
      Put in my hands unsought—if for this power
      Creon desires in secret to destroy me!   180

      He has bought this decrepit fortune-teller, this
      Collector of dirty pennies, this prophet fraud—
      Why, he is no more clairvoyant than I am!
      Tell us:
      Has your mystic mummery ever approached the
      truth?   185
      When that hellcat the Sphinx was performing here,
      What help were you to these people?
      Her magic was not for the first man who came
      along:
      It demanded a real exorcist. Your birds—
      What good were they? or the gods, for the matter
      of that?   190
      But I came by,
      Oedipus, the simple man, who knows nothing—
      I thought it out for myself, no birds helped me!
      And this is the man you think you can destroy,
      That you may be close to Creon when he's king!   195
      Well, you and your friend Creon, it seems to me,
      Will suffer most. If you were not an old man,
      You would have paid already for your plot.
CHORAGOS: We can not see that his words or yours
      Have been spoken except in anger, Oedipus,   200

And of anger we have no need. How can God's will
Be accomplished best? That is what most concerns
      us.
TEIRESIAS: You are a king. But where argument's
      concerned
I am your man, as much a king as you.
205 I am not your servant, but Apollo's.
I have no need of Creon to speak for me.

Listen to me. You mock my blindness, do you?
But I say that you, with both your eyes, are blind:
You can not see the wretchedness of your life,
210 Nor in whose house you live, no, nor with whom.
Who are your father and mother? Can you tell me?
You do not even know the blind wrongs
That you have done them, on earth and in the
      world below.
But the double lash of your parents' curse will whip
      you
215 Out of this land some day, with only night
Upon your precious eyes.
Your cries then—where will they not be heard?
What fastness of Kithairon will not echo them?
And that bridal-descant of yours—you'll know it
      then,
220 The song they sang when you came here to Thebes
And found your misguided berthing.
All this, and more, that you can not guess at now,
Will bring you to yourself among your children.

Be angry, then. Curse Creon. Curse my words.
225 I tell you, no man that walks upon the earth
Shall be rooted out more horribly than you.
OEDIPUS: Am I to bear this from him?—Damnation
Take you! Out of this place! Out of my sight!
TEIRESIAS: I would not have come at all if you had
      not asked me.
OEDIPUS: Could I have told that you'd talk nonsense,
      that
230 You'd come here to make a fool of yourself, and of
      me?
TEIRESIAS: A fool? Your parents thought me sane
      enough.
OEDIPUS: My parents again!—Wait: who were my
      parents?
TEIRESIAS: This day will give you a father, and break
      your heart.
OEDIPUS: Your infantile riddles! Your damned
235   abracadabra!
TEIRESIAS: You were a great man once at solving
      riddles.
OEDIPUS: Mock me with that if you like; you will find
      it true.
TEIRESIAS: It was true enough. It brought about your
      ruin.
OEDIPUS: But if it saved this town?
240 TEIRESIAS (to the PAGE): Boy, give me your hand.

OEDIPUS: Yes, boy; lead him away.
      —While you are here
We can do nothing. Go; leave us in peace.
TEIRESIAS: I will go when I have said what I have to
      say.
How can you hurt me? And I tell you again: 245
The man you have been looking for all this time,
The damned man, the murderer of Laïos,
That man is in Thebes. To your mind he is
      foreign-born,
But it will soon be shown that he is a Theban,
A revelation that will fail to please.   250
A blind man,
Who has his eyes now; a penniless man, who is rich
      now;
And he will go tapping the strange earth with his
      staff
To the children with whom he lives now he will be
Brother and father—the very same; to her   255
Who bore him, son and husband—the very same
Who came to his father's bed, wet with his father's
      blood.

Enough. Go think that over.
If later you find error in what I have said,
You may say that I have no skill in prophecy.   260

(*Exit* TEIRESIAS *led by his* PAGE. OEDIPUS *goes into the palace.*)

ODE I

Strophe 1

CHORUS: The Delphic stone of prophecies
      Remembers ancient regicide
      And a still bloody hand.
      That killer's hour of flight has come.
      He must be stronger than riderless   265
      Coursers of untiring wind,
      For the son of Zeus armed with his father's thunder
      Leaps in lightning after him;
      And the Furies follow him, the sad Furies.

Antistrophe 1

Holy Parnassos' peak of snow   270
Flashes and blinds that secret man,
That all shall hunt him down:
Though he may roam the forest shade
Like a bull gone wild from pasture
To rage through glooms of stone.   275
Doom comes down on him; flight will not avail him;
For the world's heart calls him desolate,
And the immortal Furies follow, for ever follow.

Strophe 2

But now a wilder thing is heard
From the old man skilled at hearing Fate in the
      wingbeat of a bird.   280

Bewildered as a blown bird, my soul hovers and
    can not find
Foothold in this debate, or any reason or rest of
    mind.
But no man ever brought—none can bring
Proof of strife between Thebes' royal house,
285   Labdakos' line, and the son of Polybos;
And never until now has any man brought word
Of Laïos' dark death staining Oedipus the King.

Antistrophe 2

Divine Zeus and Apollo hold
Perfect intelligence alone of all tales ever told;
And well though this diviner works, he works in his
290   own night;
No man can judge that rough unknown or trust in
    second sight,
For wisdom changes hands among the wise.
Shall I believe my great lord criminal
At a raging word that a blind old man let fall?
I saw him, when the carrion woman faced him of
295   old,
Prove his heroic mind! These evil words are lies.

SCENE II

CREON: Men of Thebes:
   I am told that heavy accusations
   Have been brought against me by King Oedipus.

   I am not the kind of man to bear this tamely.

5   If in these present difficulties
   He holds me accountable for any harm to him
   Through anything I have said or done—why, then,
   I do not value life in this dishonor.

   It is not as though this rumor touched upon
10   Some private indiscretion. The matter is grave.
   The fact is that I am being called disloyal
   To the State, to my fellow citizens, to my friends.
CHORAGOS: He may have spoken in anger, not from
   his mind.
CREON: But did you not hear him say I was the one
15   Who seduced the old prophet into lying?
CHORAGOS: The thing was said: I do not know how
   seriously.
CREON: But you were watching him! Were his eyes
   steady?
   Did he look like a man in his right mind?
CHORAGOS: I do not know.
20   I can not judge the behavior of great men.
   But here is the King himself.

   (Enter OEDIPUS.)

OEDIPUS: So you dared come back.
   Why? How brazen of you to come to my house,

You murderer!
Do you think I do not know   25
That you plotted to kill me, plotted to steal my
   throne?
Tell me, in God's name: am I coward, a fool,
That you should dream you could accomplish this?
A fool who could not see your slippery game?
A coward, not to fight back when I saw it?   30
You are the fool, Creon, are you not? hoping
Without support or friends to get a throne?
Thrones may be won or bought: you could do
   neither.
CREON: Now listen to me. You have talked; let me
   talk, too.
You can not judge unless you know the facts.   35
OEDIPUS: You speak well: there is one fact; but I find
   it hard
To learn from the deadliest enemy I have.
CREON: That above all I must dispute with you.
OEDIPUS: That above all I will not hear you deny.
CREON: If you think there is anything good in being
   stubborn   40
Against all reason, then I say you are wrong.
OEDIPUS: If you think a man can sin against his own
   kind
And not be punished for it, I say you are mad.
CREON: I agree. But tell me: what have I done to you?
OEDIPUS: You advised me to send for that wizard, did
   you not?   45
CREON: I did. I should do it again.
OEDIPUS: Very well. Now tell me:
   How long has it been since Laïos—
CREON: What of Laïos?
OEDIPUS: Since he vanished in that onset by the road?   50
CREON: It was long ago, a long time.
OEDIPUS: And this prophet,
   Was he practicing here then?
CREON: He was; and with honor, as now
OEDIPUS: Did he speak of me at that time?   55
CREON: He never did;
   At least, not when I was present.
OEDIPUS: But . . . the enquiry?
   I suppose you held one?
CREON: We did, but we learned nothing.   60
OEDIPUS: Why did the prophet not speak against me
   then?
CREON: I do not know; and I am the kind of man
   Who holds his tongue when he has no facts to go
   on.
OEDIPUS: There's one fact that you know, and you
   could tell it.
CREON: What fact is that? If I know it, you shall have it.   65
OEDIPUS: If he were not involved with you, he could
   not say
   That it was I who murdered Laïos.
CREON: If he says that, you are the one that knows
   it!—

But now it is my turn to question you.
70 OEDIPUS: Put your questions. I am no murderer.
CREON: First, then: You married my sister?
OEDIPUS: I married your sister.
CREON: And you rule the kingdom equally with her?
OEDIPUS: Everything that she wants she has from me.
75 CREON: And I am the third, equal to both of you?
OEDIPUS: That is why I call you a bad friend.
CREON: No. Reason it out, as I have done.
      Think of this first: Would any sane man prefer
      Power, with all a king's anxieties,
80   To that same power and the grace of sleep?
      Certainly not I.
      I have never longed for the king's power—only his
          rights.
      Would any wise man differ from me in this?
      As matters stand, I have my way in everything
85   With your consent, and no responsibilities.
      If I were king, I should be a slave to policy.
      How could I desire a sceptre more
      Than what is now mine—untroubled influence?
      No, I have not gone mad; I need no honors,
90   Except those with the perquisites I have now.
      I am welcome everywhere; every man salutes me,
      And those who want your favor seek my ear,
      Since I know how to manage what they ask.
      Should I exchange this ease for that anxiety?
95   Besides, no sober mind is treasonable.
      I hate anarchy
      And never would deal with any man who likes it.

      Test what I have said. Go to the priestess
      At Delphi, ask if I quoted her correctly.
100   And as for this other thing: If I am found
      Guilty of treason with Teiresias,
      Then sentence me to death! You have my word
      It is a sentence I should cast my vote for—
      But not without evidence!
105   You do wrong
      When you take good men for bad, bad men for
          good.
      A true friend thrown aside—why, life itself
      Is not more precious!
      In time you will know this well:
110   For time, and time alone, will show the just man,
      Though scoundrels are discovered in a day.
CHORAGOS: This is well said, and a prudent man
          would ponder it.
      Judgments too quickly formed are dangerous.
OEDIPUS: But is he not quick in his duplicity?
115   And shall I not be quick to parry him?
      Would you have me stand still, hold my peace, and
          let
      This man win everything, through my inaction?
CREON: And you want—what is it, then? To banish me?
OEDIPUS: No, not exile. It is your death I want,
120   So that all the world may see what treason means.

CREON: You will persist then? You will not believe
      me?
OEDIPUS: How can I believe you?
CREON: Then you are a fool.
OEDIPUS: To save myself?
CREON: In justice, think of me.   125
OEDIPUS: You are evil incarnate.
CREON: But suppose that you are wrong?
OEDIPUS: Still I must rule.
CREON: But not if you rule badly.
OEDIPUS: O city, city!   130
CREON: It is my city, too!
CHORAGOS: Now, my lords, be still. I see the Queen,
      Iocastê, coming from her palace chambers;
      And it is time she came, for the sake of you both.
      This dreadful quarrel can be resolved through her.   135

      (Enter IOCASTE.)

IOCASTE: Poor foolish men, what wicked din is this?
      With Thebes sick to death, is it not shameful
      That you should rake some private quarrel up?

      (To OEDIPUS)

      Come into the house.
      And you, Creon, go now: 140
      Let us have no more of this tumult over nothing.
CREON: Nothing? No, sister: what your husband
          plans for me
      Is one of two great evils: exile or death.
OEDIPUS: He is right.
      Why, woman I have caught him squarely   145
      Plotting against my life.
CREON: No! Let me die
      Accurst if ever I have wished you harm!
IOCASTE: Ah, believe it, Oedipus!
      In the name of the gods, respect this oath of his   150
      For my sake, for the sake of these people here!

Strophe 1

CHORAGOS: Open your mind to her, my lord. Be
      ruled by her, I beg you!
OEDIPUS: What would you have me do?
CHORAGOS: Respect Creon's word. He has never
      spoken like a fool,
      And now he has sworn an oath.   155
OEDIPUS: You know what you ask?
CHORAGOS: I do.
OEDIPUS: Speak on, then.
CHORAGOS: A friend so sworn should not be baited so,
      In blind malice, and without final proof.   160
OEDIPUS: You are aware, I hope, that what you say
      Means death for me, or exile at the least.

Strophe 2

CHORAGOS: No, I swear by Helios, first in Heaven!
      May I die friendless and accurst,
      The worst of deaths, if ever I meant that!   165

It is the withering fields
That hurt my sick heart:
Must we bear all these ills,
And now your bad blood as well?

170 OEDIPUS: Then let him go. And let me die, if I must,
Or be driven by him in shame from the land of
Thebes.
It is your unhappiness, and not his talk,
That touches me.
As for him—

175 Wherever he goes, hatred will follow him.
CREON: Ugly in yielding, as you were ugly in rage!
Natures like yours chiefly torment themselves.
OEDIPUS: Can you not go? Can you not leave me?
CREON: I can.

180 You do not know me; but the city knows me,
And in its eyes I am just, if not in yours.

(Exit CREON.*)*

Antistrophe 1

CHORAGOS: Lady Iocastê, did you not ask the King to
go to his chambers?
IOCASTE: First tell me what has happened.
CHORAGOS: There was suspicion without evidence;
yet it rankled
185 As even false charges will.
IOCASTE: On both sides?
CHORAGOS: On both.
IOCASTE: But what was said?
CHORAGOS: Oh let it rest, let it be done with!
190 Have we not suffered enough?
OEDIPUS: You see to what your decency has brought
you:
You have made difficulties where my heart saw
none.

Antistrophe 2

CHORAGOS: Oedipus, it is not once only I have told
you—
You must know I should count myself unwise
To the point of madness, should I now forsake
195 you—
You, under whose hand,
In the storm of another time,
Our dear land sailed out free.
But now stand fast at the helm!

IOCASTE: In God's name, Oedipus, inform your wife
200 as well:
Why are you so set in this hard anger?
OEDIPUS: I will tell you, for none of these men
deserves
My confidence as you do. It is Creon's work,
His treachery, his plotting against me.
205 IOCASTE: Go on, if you can make this clear to me.

OEDIPUS: He charges me with the murder of Laïos.
IOCASTE: Has he some knowledge? Or does he speak
from hearsay?
OEDIPUS: He would not commit himself to such a
charge,
But he has brought in that damnable soothsayer
To tell his story.   210
IOCASTE: Set your mind at rest.
If it is a question of soothsayers, I tell you
That you will find no man whose craft gives
knowledge
Of the unknowable.

Here is my proof: 215
An oracle was reported to Laïos once
(I will not say from Phoibos himself, but from
His appointed ministers, at any rate)
That his doom would be death at the hands of his
own son—
His son, born of his flesh and of mine!   220

Now, you remember the story: Laïos was killed
By marauding strangers where three highways
meet;
But his child had not been three days in this world
Before the King had pierced the baby's ankles
And left him to die on a lonely mountainside.   225
Thus, Apollo never caused that child
To kill his father, and it was not Laïos' fate
To die at the hands of his son, as he had feared.
This is what prophets and prophecies are worth!
Have no dread of them.   230
It is God himself
Who can show us what he wills, in his own way.
OEDIPUS: How strange a shadowy memory crossed
my mind,
Just now while you were speaking; it chilled my
heart.
IOCASTE: What do you mean? What memory do you
speak of?   235
OEDIPUS: If I understand you, Laïos was killed
At a place where three roads meet.
IOCASTE: So it was said;
We have no later story.
OEDIPUS: Where did it happen?   240
IOCASTE: Phokis, it is called: at a place where the
Theban Way
Divides into the roads toward Delphi and Daulia.
OEDIPUS: When?
IOCASTE: We had the news not long before you came
And proved the right to your succession here.   245
OEDIPUS: Ah, what net has God been weaving for me?
IOCASTE: Oedipus! Why does this trouble you?
OEDIPUS: Do not ask me yet.
First, tell me how Laïos looked, and tell me
How old he was.   250
IOCASTE: He was tall, his hair just touched

With white; his form was not unlike your own.
OEDIPUS: I think that I myself may be accurst
    By my own ignorant edict.
255 IOCASTE: You speak strangely.
    It makes me tremble to look at you, my King.
OEDIPUS: I am not sure that the blind man can not
    see.
    But I should know better if you were to tell me—
IOCASTE: Anything—though I dread to hear you ask
    it.
OEDIPUS: Was the King lightly escorted, or did he
260   ride
    With a large company, as a ruler should?
IOCASTE: There were five men with him in all: one
    was a herald,
    And a single chariot, which he was driving.
OEDIPUS: Alas, that makes it plain enough!
265   But who—
    Who told you how it happened?
IOCASTE: A household servant,
    The only one to escape.
OEDIPUS: And is he still
270   A servant of ours?
IOCASTE: No; for when he came back at last
    And found you enthroned in the place of the dead
    king,
    He came to me, touched my hand with his, and
    begged
    That I would send him away to the frontier district
275   Where only the shepherds go—
    As far away from the city as I could send him.
    I granted his prayer; for although the man was a
    slave,
    He had earned more than this favor at my hands.
OEDIPUS: Can he be called back quickly?
280 IOCASTE: Easily.
    But why?
OEDIPUS: I have taken too much upon myself
    Without enquiry; therefore I wish to consult him.
IOCASTE: Then he shall come.
285   But am I not one also
    To whom you might confide these fears of yours?
OEDIPUS: That is your right; it will not be denied you,
    Now least of all; for I have reached a pitch
    Of wild foreboding. Is there anyone
290   To whom I should sooner speak?

    Polybos of Corinth is my father.
    My mother is a Dorian: Meropê.
    I grew up chief among the men of Corinth
    Until a strange thing happened—
295   Not worth my passion, it may be, but strange.

    At a feast, a drunken man maundering in his cups
    Cries out that I am not my father's son!
    I contained myself that night, though I felt anger
    And a sinking heart. The next day I visited

My father and mother, and questioned them. They
    stormed,   300
Calling it all the slanderous rant of a fool;
And this relieved me. Yet the suspicion
Remained always aching in my mind;
I knew there was talk; I could not rest;
And finally, saying nothing to my parents,   305
I went to the shrine at Delphi.

The god dismissed my question without reply;
He spoke of other things.
Some were clear,
Full of wretchedness, dreadful, unbearable: 310
As, that I should lie with my own mother, breed
Children from whom all men would turn their
    eyes;
And that I should be my father's murderer.

I heard all this, and fled. And from that day
Corinth to me was only in the stars   315
Descending in that quarter of the sky,
As I wandered farther and farther on my way
To a land where I should never see the evil
Sung by the oracle. And I came to this country
Where, so you say, King Laïos was killed.   320

I will tell you all that happened there, my lady.

There were three highways
Coming together at a place I passed;
And there a herald came towards me, and a chariot
Drawn by horses, with a man such as you describe   325
Seated in it. The groom leading the horses
Forced me off the road at his lord's command;
But as this charioteer lurched over towards me
I struck him in my rage. The old man saw me
And brought his double goad down upon my head   330
As I came abreast.
He was paid back, and more!
Swinging my club in this right hand I knocked him
Out of his car, and he rolled on the ground.
I killed him.   335
I killed them all.
Now if that stranger and Laïos were—kin,
Where is a man more miserable than I?
More hated by the gods? Citizen and alien alike
Must never shelter me or speak to me—   340
I must be shunned by all.
And I myself
Pronounced this malediction upon myself!

Think of it: I have touched you with these hands,
These hands that killed your husband. What
    defilement!   345

Am I all evil, then? It must be so,
Since I must flee from Thebes, yet never again

See my own countrymen, my own country,
For fear of joining my mother in marriage
350 And killing Polybos, my father.
Ah,
If I was created so, born to this fate,
Who could deny the savagery of God?

355 O holy majesty of heavenly powers!
May I never see that day! Never!
Rather let me vanish from the race of men
Than know the abomination destined me!
CHORAGOS: We too, my lord, have felt dismay at this.
But there is hope: you have yet to hear the
shepherd.
360 OEDIPUS: Indeed, I fear no other hope is left me.
IOCASTE: What do you hope from him when he
comes?
OEDIPUS: This much:
If his account of the murder tallies with yours,
Then I am cleared.
365 IOCASTE: What was it that I said
Of such importance?
OEDIPUS: Why, "marauders," you said,
Killed the King, according to this man's story.
If he maintains that still, if there were several,
370 Clearly the guilt is not mine: I was alone.
But if he says one man, singlehanded, did it,
Then the evidence all points to me.
IOCASTE: You may be sure that he said there were
several;
And can he call back that story now? He can not.
375 The whole city heard it as plainly as I.
But suppose he alters some detail of it:
He can not ever show that Laïos' death
Fulfilled the oracle: for Apollo said
My child was doomed to kill him; and my child—
380 Poor baby!—it was my child that died first.

No. From now on, where oracles are concerned,
I would not waste a second thought on any.
OEDIPUS: You may be right.
But come: let someone go
For the shepherd at once. This matter must be
385 settled.
IOCASTE: I will send for him.
I would not wish to cross you in anything,
And surely not in this.—Let us go in.

(Exeunt into the palace.)

ODE II
Strophe 1

CHORUS: Let me be reverent in the ways of right,
390 Lowly the paths I journey on;
Let all my words and actions keep
The laws of the pure universe

From highest Heaven handed down.
For Heaven is their bright nurse,
Those generations of the realms of light; 395
Ah, never of mortal kind were they begot,
Nor are they slaves of memory, lost in sleep:
Their Father is greater than Time, and ages not.

Antistrophe 1

The tyrant is a child of Pride
Who drinks from his great sickening cup 400
Recklessness and vanity,
Until from his high crest headlong
He plummets to the dust of hope.
That strong man is not strong.
But let no fair ambition be denied; 405
May God protect the wrestler for the State
In government, in comely policy,
Who will fear God, and on His ordinance wait.

Strophe 2

Haughtiness and the high hand of disdain
Tempt and outrage God's holy law; 410
And any mortal who dares hold
No immortal Power in awe
Will be caught up in a net of pain:
The price for which his levity is sold.
Let each man take due earnings, then, 415
And keep his hands from holy things,
And from blasphemy stand apart—
Else the crackling blast of heaven
Blows on his head, and on his desperate heart;
Though fools will honor impious men, 420
In their cities no tragic poet sings.

Antistrophe 2

Shall we lose faith in Delphi's obscurities,
We who have heard the world's core
Discredited, and the sacred wood
Of Zeus at Elis praised no more? 425
The deeds and the strange prophecies
Must make a pattern yet to be understood.
Zeus, if indeed you are lord of all,
Throned in light over night and day,
Mirror this in your endless mind: 430
Our masters call the oracle
Words on the wind, and the Delphic vision blind!
Their hearts no longer know Apollo,
And reverence for the gods has died away.

SCENE III

(Enter IOCASTE.)

IOCASTE: Princes of Thebes, it has occurred to me
To visit the altars of the gods, bearing
These branches as a suppliant, and this incense.
Our King is not himself: his noble soul

5   Is overwrought with fantasies of dread,
    Else he would consider
    The new prophecies in the light of the old.
    He will listen to any voice that speaks disaster,
    And my advice goes for nothing.

    (She approaches the altar, right.)

10 To you, then, Apollo,
    Lycean lord, since you are nearest, I turn in prayer.

    Receive these offerings, and grant us deliverance
    From defilement. Our hearts are heavy with fear
    When we see our leader distracted, as helpless
        sailors
15 Are terrified by the confusion of their helmsman.

    (Enter MESSENGER.)

    MESSENGER: Friends, no doubt you can direct me:
        Where shall I find the house of Oedipus,
        Or, better still, where is the King himself?
    CHORAGOS: It is this very place, stranger; he is inside.
20   This is his wife and mother of his children.
    MESSENGER: I wish her happiness in a happy house,
        Blest in all the fulfillment of her marriage.
    IOCASTE: I wish as much for you: your courtesy
        Deserves a like good fortune. But now, tell me:
25   Why have you come? What have you to say to us?
    MESSENGER: Good news, my lady, for your house and
        your husband.
    IOCASTE: What news? Who sent you here?
    MESSENGER: I am from Corinth.
        The news I bring ought to mean joy for you,
30   Though it may be you will find some grief in it.
    IOCASTE: What is it? How can it touch us in both
        ways?
    MESSENGER: The word is that the people of the
        Isthmus
        Intend to call Oedipus to be their king.
    IOCASTE: But old King Polybos—is he not reigning
        still?
35 MESSENGER: No. Death holds him in his sepulchre.
    IOCASTE: What are you saying? Polybos is dead?
    MESSENGER: If I am not telling the truth, may I die
        myself.
    IOCASTE *(to a MAIDSERVANT)*: Go in, go quickly; tell
        this to your master.

    O riddlers of God's will, where are you now!
40 This was the man whom Oedipus, long ago,
    Feared so, fled so, in dread of destroying him—
    But it was another fate by which he died.

    (Enter OEDIPUS, center.)

    OEDIPUS: Dearest Iocastê, why have you sent for me?
    IOCASTE: Listen to what this man says, and then tell
        me
45 What has become of the solemn prophecies.

    OEDIPUS: Who is this man? What is his news for me?
    IOCASTE: He has come from Corinth to announce
        your father's death!
    OEDIPUS: Is it true, stranger? Tell me in your own
        words.
    MESSENGER: I can not say it more clearly: the King is
        dead.
    OEDIPUS: Was it by treason? Or by an attack of illness?   50
    MESSENGER: A little thing brings old men to their rest.
    OEDIPUS: It was sickness, then?
    MESSENGER: Yes, and his many years.
    OEDIPUS: Ah!
        Why should a man respect the Pythian hearth, or   55
        Give heed to the birds that jangle above his head?
        They prophesied that I should kill Polybos,
        Kill my own father; but he is dead and buried,
        And I am here—I never touched him, never,
        Unless he died of grief for my departure,   60
        And thus, in a sense, through me. No. Polybos
        Has packed the oracles off with him underground.
        They are empty words.
    IOCASTE: Had I not told you so?
    OEDIPUS: You had; it was my faint heart that betrayed
        me.   65
    IOCASTE: From now on never think of those things
        again.
    OEDIPUS: And yet—must I not fear my mother's bed?
    IOCASTE: Why should anyone in this world be afraid,
        Since Fate rules us and nothing can be foreseen?
        A man should live only for the present day.   70

        Have no more fear of sleeping with your mother:
        How many men, in dreams, have lain with their
        mothers!
        No reasonable man is troubled by such things.
    OEDIPUS: That is true; only—
        If only my mother were not still alive!   75
        But she is alive. I can not help my dread.
    IOCASTE: Yet this news of your father's death is
        wonderful.
    OEDIPUS: Wonderful. But I fear the living woman.
    MESSENGER: Tell me, who is this woman that you
        fear?
    OEDIPUS: It is Meropê, man; the wife of King
        Polybos.   80
    MESSENGER: Meropê? Why should you be afraid of
        her?
    OEDIPUS: An oracle of the gods, a dreadful saying.
    MESSENGER: Can you tell me about it or are you
        sworn to silence?
    OEDIPUS: I can tell you, and I will.
        Apollo said through his prophet that I was the man   85
        Who should marry his own mother, shed his
        father's blood
        With his own hands. And so, for all these years
        I have kept clear of Corinth, and no harm has
        come—

Though it would have been sweet to see my parents
again.

90 MESSENGER: And is this the fear that drove you out of
Corinth?

OEDIPUS: Would you have me kill my father?

MESSENGER: As for that
You must be reassured by the news I gave you.

OEDIPUS: If you could reassure me, I would reward
you.

95 MESSENGER: I had that in mind, I will confess: I
thought
I could count on you when you returned to
Corinth.

OEDIPUS: No: I will never go near my parents again.

MESSENGER: Ah, son, you still do not know what you
are doing—

OEDIPUS: What do you mean? In the name of God
tell me!

MESSENGER: —If these are your reasons for not going

100 home.

OEDIPUS: I tell you, I fear the oracle may come true.

MESSENGER: And guilt may come upon you through
your parents?

OEDIPUS: That is the dread that is always in my heart.

MESSENGER: Can you not see that all your fears are
groundless?

OEDIPUS: How can you say that? They are my

105 parents, surely?

MESSENGER: Polybos was not your father.

OEDIPUS: Not my father?

MESSENGER: No more your father than the man
speaking to you.

OEDIPUS: But you are nothing to me!

110 MESSENGER: Neither was he.

OEDIPUS: Then why did he call me son?

MESSENGER: I will tell you:
Long ago he had you from my hands, as a gift.

OEDIPUS: Then how could he love me so, if I was not
his?

MESSENGER: He had no children, and his heart

115 turned to you.

OEDIPUS: What of you? Did you buy me? Did you find
me by chance?

MESSENGER: I came upon you in the crooked pass of
Kithairon.

OEDIPUS: And what were you doing there?

MESSENGER: Tending my flocks.

120 OEDIPUS: A wandering shepherd?

MESSENGER: But your savior, son, that day.

OEDIPUS: From what did you save me?

MESSENGER: Your ankles should tell you that.

OEDIPUS: Ah, stranger, why do you speak of that
childhood pain?

MESSENGER: I cut the bonds that tied your ankles

125 together.

OEDIPUS: I have had the mark as long as I can
remember.

MESSENGER: That was why you were given the name
you bear.

OEDIPUS: God! Was it my father or my mother who
did it?
Tell me!

MESSENGER: I do not know. The man who gave you
to me   130
Can tell you better than I.

OEDIPUS: It was not you that found me, but another?

MESSENGER: It was another shepherd gave you to me.

OEDIPUS: Who was he? Can you tell me who he was?

MESSENGER: I think he was said to be one of Laïos'
people.   135

OEDIPUS: You mean the Laïos who was king here
years ago?

MESSENGER: Yes; King Laïos; and the man was one of
his herdsmen.

OEDIPUS: Is he still alive? Can I see him?

MESSENGER: These men here
Know best about such things.   140

OEDIPUS: Does anyone here
Know this shepherd that he is talking about?
Have you seen him in the fields, or in the town?
If you have, tell me. It is time things were made
plain.

CHORAGOS: I think the man he means is that same
shepherd   145
You have already asked to see. Iocastê perhaps
Could tell you something.

OEDIPUS: Do you know anything
About him, Lady? Is he the man we have
summoned?
Is that the man this shepherd means?   150

IOCASTE: Why think of him?
Forget this herdsman. Forget it all.
This talk is a waste of time.

OEDIPUS: How can you say that,
When the clues to my true birth are in my hands?   155

IOCASTE: For God's love, let us have no more
questioning!
Is your life nothing to you?
My own is pain enough for me to bear.

OEDIPUS: You need not worry. Suppose my mother a
slave,
And born of slaves: no baseness can touch you.   160

IOCASTE: Listen to me, I beg you: do not do this
thing!

OEDIPUS: I will not listen; the truth must be made
known.

IOCASTE: Everything that I say is for your own good!

OEDIPUS: My own good
Snaps my patience, then; I want none of it.   165

IOCASTE: You are fatally wrong! May you never learn
who you are!

OEDIPUS: Go, one of you, and bring the shepherd
here.
Let us leave this woman to brag of her royal name.

IOCASTE: Ah, miserable!
170   That is the only word I have for you now.
   That is the only word I can ever have.

   (Exit into the palace.)

CHORAGOS: Why has she left us, Oedipus? Why has
   she gone
   In such a passion of sorrow? I fear this silence:
   Something dreadful may come of it.

175 OEDIPUS: Let it come!
   However base my birth, I must know about it.
   The Queen, like a woman, is perhaps ashamed
   To think of my low origin. But I
   Am a child of Luck; I can not be dishonored.
180   Luck is my mother; the passing months, my
     brothers,
   Have seen me rich and poor.
   If this is so,
   How could I wish that I were someone else?
   How could I not be glad to know my birth?

ODE III

Strophe

185 CHORUS: If ever the coming time were known
   To my heart's pondering,
   Kithairon, now by Heaven I see the torches
   At the festival of the next full moon,
   And see the dance, and hear the choir sing
190   A grace to your gentle shade:
   Mountain where Oedipus was found,
   O mountain guard of a noble race!
   May the god who heals us lend his aid,
   And let that glory come to pass
195   For our king's cradling-ground.

Antistrophe

   Of the nymphs that flower beyond the years,
   Who bore you, royal child,
   To Pan of the hills or the timberline Apollo,
   Cold in delight where the upland clears,
200   Or Hermês for whom Kyllenê's heights are piled?
   Or flushed as evening cloud,
   Great Dionysos, roamer of mountains,
   He—was it he who found you there,
   And caught you up in his own proud
205   Arms from the sweet god-ravisher
   Who laughed by the Muses' fountains?

SCENE IV

OEDIPUS: Sirs: though I do not know the man,
   I think I see him coming, this shepherd we want:
   He is old, like our friend here, and the men
   Bringing him seem to be servants of my house.

   But you can tell, if you have ever seen him.   5

   (Enter SHEPHERD escorted by servants.)

CHORAGOS: I know him, he was Laïos' man. You can
   trust him.
OEDIPUS: Tell me first, you from Corinth: is this the
   shepherd
   We were discussing?
MESSENGER: This is the very man.
OEDIPUS *(to SHEPHERD)*: Come here. No, look at me.   10
   You must answer
   Everything I ask.—You belonged to Laïos?
SHEPHERD: Yes: born his slave, brought up in his
   house.
OEDIPUS: Tell me: what kind of work did you do for
   him?
SHEPHERD: I was a shepherd of his, most of my life.   15
OEDIPUS: Where mainly did you go for pasturage?
SHEPHERD: Sometimes Kithairon, sometimes the hills
   near-by.
OEDIPUS: Do you remember ever seeing this man out
   there?
SHEPHERD: What would he be doing there? This
   man?
OEDIPUS: This man standing here. Have you ever
   seen him before?   20
SHEPHERD: No. At least, not to my recollection.
MESSENGER: And that is not strange, my lord. But I'll
   refresh
   His memory: he must remember when we two
   Spent three whole seasons together, March to
     September,
   On Kithairon or thereabouts. He had two flocks;   25
   I had one. Each autumn I'd drive mine home
   And he would go back with his to Laïos'
     sheepfold.—
   Is this not true, just as I have described it?
SHEPHERD: True, yes; but it was all so long ago.
MESSENGER: Well, then: do you remember, back in
   those days,   30
   That you gave me a baby boy to bring up as my
     own?
SHEPHERD: What if I did? What are you trying to
   say?
MESSENGER: King Oedipus was once that little
   child.
SHEPHERD: Damn you, hold your tongue!
OEDIPUS: No more of that!   35
   It is your tongue needs watching, not this man's.
SHEPHERD: My King, my Master, what is it I have
   done wrong?
OEDIPUS: You have not answered his question about
   the boy.
SHEPHERD: He does not know . . . He is only making
   trouble . . .
OEDIPUS: Come, speak plainly, or it will go hard with
   you.   40

SHEPHERD: In God's name, do not torture an old
  man!
OEDIPUS: Come here, one of you; bind his arms
  behind him.
SHEPHERD: Unhappy king! What more do you wish
  to learn?
OEDIPUS: Did you give this man the child he speaks
  of?
45 SHEPHERD: I did.
  And I would to God I had died that very day.
OEDIPUS: You will die now unless you speak the truth.
SHEPHERD: Yet if I speak the truth, I am worse than
  dead.
OEDIPUS: Very well; since you insist upon delaying—
SHEPHERD: No! I have told you already that I gave
50 him the boy.
OEDIPUS: Where did you get him? From your house?
  From somewhere else?
SHEPHERD: Not from mine, no. A man gave him to
  me.
OEDIPUS: Is that man here? Do you know whose slave
  he was?
SHEPHERD: For God's love, my King, do not ask me
  any more!
OEDIPUS: You are a dead man if I have to ask you
55 again.
SHEPHERD: Then . . . Then the child was from the
  palace of Laïos.
OEDIPUS: A slave child? or a child of his own line?
SHEPHERD: Ah, I am on the brink of dreadful speech!
OEDIPUS: And I of dreadful hearing. Yet I must hear.
60 SHEPHERD: If you must be told, then . . .
  They said it was Laïos' child;
  But it is your wife who can tell you about that.
OEDIPUS: My wife!—Did she give it to you?
SHEPHERD: My lord, she did.
65 OEDIPUS: Do you know why?
SHEPHERD: I was told to get rid of it.
OEDIPUS: An unspeakable mother!
SHEPHERD: There had been prophecies . . .
OEDIPUS: Tell me.
SHEPHERD: It was said that the boy would kill his own
70 father.
OEDIPUS: Then why did you give him over to this old
  man?
SHEPHERD: I pitied the baby, my King,
  And I thought that this man would take him far
  away
  To his own country.
75 He saved him—but for what a fate!
  For if you are what this man says you are,
  No man living is more wretched than Oedipus.
OEDIPUS: Ah God!
  It was true!
80 All the prophecies!
  —Now,
  O Light, may I look on you for the last time!

I, Oedipus,
Oedipus, damned in his birth, in his marriage
  damned,
Damned in the blood he shed with his own hand!   85

(He rushes into the palace.)

ODE IV
Strophe 1

CHORUS: Alas for the seed of men.

What measure shall I give these generations
That breathe on the void and are void
And exist and do not exist?

Who bears more weight of joy   90
Than mass of sunlight shifting in images,
Or who shall make his thought stay on
That down time drifts away?

Your splendor is all fallen.

O naked brow of wrath and tears,   95
O change of Oedipus!
I who saw your days call no man blest—
Your great days like ghósts góne.

Antistrophe 1

That mind was a strong bow.

Deep, how deep you drew it then, hard archer,   100
At a dim fearful range,
And brought dear glory down!

You overcame the stranger—
The virgin with her hooking lion claws—
And though death sang, stood like a tower   105
To make pale Thebes take heart.

Fortress against our sorrow!

True king, giver of laws,
Majestic Oedipus!
No prince in Thebes had ever such renown,   110
No prince won such grace of power.

Strophe 2

And now of all men ever known
Most pitiful is this man's story:
His fortunes are most changed, his state
Fallen to a low slave's   115
Ground under bitter fate.

O Oedipus, most royal one!
The great door that expelled you to the light
Gave at night—ah, gave night to your glory:
As to the father, to the fathering son.   120

All understood too late.

How could that queen whom Laïos won,
The garden that he harrowed at his height,
Be silent when that act was done?

Antistrophe 2

125 But all eyes fail before time's eye,
All actions come to justice there.
Though never willed, though far down the deep
past,
Your bed, your dread sirings,
Are brought to book at last.

130 Child by Laïos doomed to die,
Then doomed to lose that fortunate little death,
Would God you never took breath in this air
That with my wailing lips I take to cry:

For I weep the world's outcast.

135 I was blind, and now I can tell why:
Asleep, for you had given ease of breath
To Thebes, while the false years went by.

EXODOS

(Enter, from the palace, SECOND MESSENGER.*)*

SECOND MESSENGER: Elders of Thebes, most honored
in this land,
What horrors are yours to see and hear, what
weight
140 Of sorrow to be endured, if, true to your birth,
You venerate the line of Labdakos!
I think neither Istros nor Phasis, those great rivers,
Could purify this place of the corruption
It shelters now, or soon must bring to light—
145 Evil not done unconsciously, but willed.

The greatest griefs are those we cause ourselves.
CHORAGOS: Surely, friend, we have grief enough
already;
What new sorrow do you mean?
SECOND MESSENGER: The Queen is dead.
150 CHORAGOS: Iocastê? Dead? But at whose hand?
SECOND MESSENGER: Her own.
The full horror of what happened you can not
know,
For you did not see it; but I, who did, will tell you
As clearly as I can how she met her death.

155 When she had left us,
In passionate silence, passing through the court,
She ran to her apartment in the house,
Her hair clutched by the fingers of both hands.
She closed the doors behind her; then, by that bed

Where long ago the fatal son was conceived— 160
That son who should bring about his father's
death—
We heard her call upon Laïos, dead so many years,
And heard her wail for the double fruit of her
marriage,
A husband by her husband, children by her child.

Exactly how she died I do not know: 165
For Oedipus burst in moaning and would not let us
Keep vigil to the end: it was by him
As he stormed about the room that our eyes were
caught.
From one to another of us he went, begging a
sword,
Cursing the wife who was not his wife, the mother 170
Whose womb had carried his own children and
himself.
I do not know: it was none of us aided him,
But surely one of the gods was in control!
For with a dreadful cry
He hurled his weight, as though wrenched out of
himself, 175
At the twin doors: the bolts gave, and he rushed in.
And there we saw her hanging, her body swaying
From the cruel cord she had noosed about her
neck.
A great sob broke from him, heartbreaking to hear,
As he loosed the rope and lowered her to the
ground. 180

I would blot out from my mind what happened
next!
For the King ripped from her gown the golden
brooches
That were her ornament, and raised them, and
plunged them down
Straight into his own eyeballs, crying, "No more,
No more shall you look on the misery about me, 185
The horrors of my own doing! Too long you have
known
The faces of those whom I should never have seen,
Too long been blind to those for whom I was
searching!
From this hour, go in darkness!" And as he spoke,
He struck at his eyes—not once, but many times; 190
And the blood spattered his beard,
Bursting from his ruined sockets like red hail.

So from the unhappiness of two this evil has
sprung,
A curse on the man and woman alike. The old
Happiness of the house of Labdakos 195
Was happiness enough: where is it today?
It is all wailing and ruin, disgrace, death—all
The misery of mankind that has a name—
And it is wholly and for ever theirs.

CHORAGOS: Is he in agony still? Is there no rest for
200   him?
SECOND MESSENGER: He is calling for someone to
    lead him to the gates
    So that all the children of Kadmos may look upon
    His father's murderer, his mother's—no,
    I can not say it!
205   And then he will leave Thebes,
    Self-exiled, in order that the curse
    Which he himself pronounced may depart from
      the house.
    He is weak, and there is none to lead him,
    So terrible is his suffering.
210   But you will see:
    Look, the doors are opening; in a moment
    You will see a thing that would crush a heart of
      stone.

    (The central door is opened; OEDIPUS, blinded, is led in.)

CHORAGOS: Dreadful indeed for men to see.
    Never have my own eyes
215   Looked on a sight so full of fear.

    Oedipus!
    What madness came upon you, what daemon
    Leaped on your life with heavier
    Punishment than a mortal man can bear?
220   No: I can not even
    Look at you, poor ruined one.
    And I would speak, question, ponder,
    If I were able. No.
    You make me shudder.
225 OEDIPUS: God.   God.
    Is there a sorrow greater?
    Where shall I find harbor in this world?
    My voice is hurled far on a dark wind.
    What has God done to me?
230 CHORAGOS: Too terrible to think of, or to see.

Strophe 1

OEDIPUS: O cloud of night,
    Never to be turned away: night coming on,
    I can not tell how: night like a shroud!

    My fair winds brought me here.
235   O God. Again
    The pain of the spikes where I had sight,
    The flooding pain
    Of memory, never to be gouged out.
CHORAGOS: This is not strange.
240   You suffer it all twice over, remorse in pain,
    Pain in remorse.

Antistrophe 1

OEDIPUS: Ah dear friend
    Are you faithful even yet, you alone?
    Are you still standing near me, will you stay here,

    Patient, to care for the blind?   245
    The blind man!
    Yet even blind I know who it is attends me,
    By the voice's tone—
    Though my new darkness hide the comforter.
CHORAGOS: Oh fearful act!   250
    What god was it drove you to rake black
    Night across your eyes?

Strophe 2

OEDIPUS: Apollo. Apollo. Dear
    Children, the god was Apollo.
    He brought my sick, sick fate upon me.   255
    But the blinding hand was my own!
    How could I bear to see
    When all my sight was horror everywhere?
CHORAGOS: Everywhere; that is true.
OEDIPUS: And now what is left?   260
    Images? Love? A greeting even,
    Sweet to the senses? Is there anything?
    Ah, no, friends: lead me away.
    Lead me away from Thebes.
    Lead the great wreck   265
    And hell of Oedipus, whom the gods hate.
CHORAGOS: Your fate is clear, you are not blind to
    that.
    Would God you had never found it out!

Antistrophe 2

OEDIPUS: Death take the man who unbound
    My feet on that hillside   270
    And delivered me from death to life! What life?
    If only I had died,
    This weight of monstrous doom
    Could not have dragged me and my darlings down.
CHORAGOS: I would have wished the same.   275
OEDIPUS: Oh never to have come here
    With my father's blood upon me! Never
    To have been the man they call his mother's
      husband!
    Oh accurst! Oh child of evil,
    To have entered that wretched bed—   280
    The selfsame one!
    More primal than sin itself, this fell to me.
CHORAGOS: I do not know how I can answer you.
    You were better dead than alive and blind.
OEDIPUS: Do not counsel me any more. This
    punishment   285
    That I have laid upon myself is just.
    If I had eyes,
    I do not know how I could bear the sight
    Of my father, when I came to the house of Death,
    Or my mother: for I have sinned against them both   290
    So vilely that I could not make my peace
    By strangling my own life.
    Or do you think my children,
    Born as they were born, would be sweet to my eyes?

295 Ah never, never! Nor this town with its high walls,
Nor the holy images of the gods.
For I,
Thrice miserable!—Oedipus, noblest of all the line
Of Kadmos, have condemned myself to enjoy
300 These things no more, by my own malediction
Expelling that man whom the gods declared
To be a defilement in the house of Laïos.
After exposing the rankness of my own guilt,
How could I look men frankly in the eyes?
305 No, I swear it,
If I could have stifled my hearing at its source,
I would have done it, and made all this body
A tight cell of misery, blank to light and sound:
So I should have been safe in a dark agony
310 Beyond all recollection.
Ah Kithairon!
Why did you shelter me? When I was cast upon you,
Why did I not die? Then I should never
Have shown the world my execrable birth.

315 Ah Polybos! Corinth, city that I believed
The ancient seat of my ancestors: how fair
I seemed, your child! And all the while this evil
Was cancerous within me!
For I am sick
320 In my daily life, sick in my origin.

O three roads, dark ravine, woodland and way
Where three roads met: you, drinking my father's blood,
My own blood, spilled by my own hand: can you remember
The unspeakable things I did there, and the things
325 I went on from there to do?
O marriage, marriage!
The act that engendered me, and again the act
Performed by the son in the same bed—
Ah, the net
330 Of incest, mingling fathers, brothers, sons,
With brides, wives, mothers: the last evil
That can be known by men: no tongue can say
How evil!
No. For the love of God, conceal me
Somewhere far from Thebes; or kill me; or hurl me
335 Into the sea, away from men's eyes for ever.
Come, lead me. You need not fear to touch me.
Of all men, I alone can bear this guilt.

(Enter CREON.*)*

CHORAGOS: We are not the ones to decide; but Creon here
340 May fitly judge of what you ask. He only
Is left to protect the city in your place.
OEDIPUS: Alas, how can I speak to him? What right have I

To beg his courtesy whom I have deeply wronged?
CREON: I have not come to mock you, Oedipus,
Or to reproach you, either.   345

(To ATTENDANTS*)*

—You, standing there:
If you have lost all respect for man's dignity,
At least respect the flame of Lord Helios:
Do not allow this pollution to show itself
Openly here, an affront to the earth   350
And Heaven's rain and the light of day. No, take him
Into the house as quickly as you can.
For it is proper
That only the close kindred see his grief.
OEDIPUS: I pray you in God's name, since your courtesy   355
Ignores my dark expectation, visiting
With mercy this man of all men most execrable:
Give me what I ask—for your good, not for mine.
CREON: And what is it that you would have me do?
OEDIPUS: Drive me out of this country as quickly as may be   360
To a place where no human voice can ever greet me.
CREON: I should have done that before now—only,
God's will had not been wholly revealed to me.
OEDIPUS: But his command is plain: the parricide
Must be destroyed. I am that evil man.   365
CREON: That is the sense of it, yes; but as things are,
We had best discover clearly what is to be done.
OEDIPUS: You would learn more about a man like me?
CREON: You are ready now to listen to the god.
OEDIPUS: I will listen. But it is to you   370
That I must turn for help. I beg you, hear me.

The woman in there—
Give her whatever funeral you think proper:
She is your sister.
—But let me go, Creon!   375
Let me purge my father's Thebes of the pollution
Of my living here, and go out to the wild hills,
To Kithairon, that has won such fame with me,
The tomb my mother and father appointed for me,
And let me die there, as they willed I should.   380
And yet I know
Death will not ever come to me through sickness
Or in any natural way: I have been preserved
For some unthinkable fate. But let that be.

As for my sons, you need not care for them.   385
They are men, they will find some way to live.
But my poor daughters, who have shared my table,
Who never before have been parted from their father—
Take care of them, Creon; do this for me.

390 And will you let me touch them with my hands
A last time, and let us weep together?
Be kind, my lord,
Great prince, be kind!
Could I but touch them.
395 They would be mine again, as when I had my eyes.

(Enter ANTIGONE and ISMENE, attended.)

Ah, God!
Is it my dearest children I hear weeping?
Has Creon pitied me and sent my daughters?
CREON: Yes, Oedipus: I knew that they were dear to
you
400 In the old days, and you must love them still.
OEDIPUS: May God bless you for this—and be a
friendlier
Guardian to you than he has been to me!

Children, where are you?
Come quickly to my hands: they are your
brother's—
Hands that have brought your father's once clear
eyes
405 To this way of seeing—
Ah dearest ones,
I had neither sight nor knowledge then, your
father
By the woman who was the source of his own life!
And I weep for you—having no strength to see
410 you—,
I weep for you when I think of the bitterness
That men will visit upon you all your lives.
What homes, what festivals can you attend
Without being forced to depart again in tears?
415 And when you come to marriageable age,
Where is the man, my daughters, who would dare
Risk the bane that lies on all my children?
Is there any evil wanting? Your father killed
His father, sowed the womb of her who bore him;
420 Engendered you at the fount of his own existence!

That is what they will say of you.

Then, whom
Can you ever marry? There are no bridegrooms for
you,
And your lives must wither away in sterile
dreaming.

425 O Creon, son of Menoikeus!
You are the only father my daughters have,

Since we, their parents, are both of us gone for
ever.
They are your own blood: you will not let them
Fall into beggary and loneliness;
You will keep them from the miseries that are
mine!
430
Take pity on them; see, they are only children,
Friendless except for you. Promise me this,
Great Prince, and give me your hand in token of it.

(CREON clasps his right hand.)

Children:
I could say much, if you could understand me,
435
But as it is, I have only this prayer for you:
Live where you can, be as happy as you can—
Happier, please God, than God has made your
father.
CREON: Enough. You have wept enough. Now go
within.
OEDIPUS: I must; but it is hard.
440
CREON: Time eases all things.
OEDIPUS: But you must promise—
CREON: Say what you desire.
OEDIPUS: Send me from Thebes!
CREON: God grant that I may!
445
OEDIPUS: But since God hates me . . .
CREON: No, he will grant your wish.
OEDIPUS: You promise?
CREON: I can not speak beyond my knowledge.
OEDIPUS: Then lead me in.
450
CREON: Come now, and leave your children.
OEDIPUS: No! Do not take them from me!
CREON: Think no longer
That you are in command here, but rather think
How, when you were, you served your own
destruction.
455

*(Exeunt into the house all but the CHORUS; the CHORA-
GOS chants directly to the audience.)*

CHORAGOS: Men of Thebes: look upon Oedipus.

This is the king who solved the famous riddle
And towered up, most powerful of men.
No mortal eyes but looked on him with envy,
Yet in the end ruin swept over him.
460

Let every man in mankind's frailty
Consider his last day; and let none
Presume on his good fortune until he find
Life, at his death, a memory without pain.

Figure 1. The Chorus of Theban Elders and Iocastê (Patricia Conolly, *rear*) plead with Oedipus (Len Cariou, *center*) to spare the life of Creon (James Blendick, *rear*) in the Guthrie Theater Company production of *Oedipus the King,* directed by Michael Langham and designed by Desmond Heeley, Minneapolis, 1972. (Photograph: the Guthrie Theater.)

Figure 2. The Corinthian Messenger (Paul Ballantyne, *left*) prods the memory of the Shepherd (Bernard Behrens, *right*) to help Oedipus (Len Cariou) discover the circumstances of his birth in the 1972 Guthrie production. (Photograph: the Guthrie Theater.)

Staging of *Oedipus Rex*

**REVIEW OF THE GUTHRIE THEATER
PRODUCTION, 1972, BY MELVIN MADDOCKS**

In the Tyrone Guthrie Theater, approximately 8,000 miles from Thebes as the Furies fly, "Oedipus the King" is being staged by an English director from a new translation written in Rome by an author also engaged on a novel about Napoleon. If all this suggests dizzy and eclectic flights in time and space, it should.

Through a rather remarkable series of letters, Michael Langham, the director, and Anthony Burgess, the translator-adaptor, have recorded their dissatisfaction with conventional approaches to Greek tragedy and their search for a style that might do justice both to Sophocles and to 1972.

Traditionally there have been two general approaches to Greek tragedy, roughly parallel to the usual approaches to Shakespeare. The low road—Sophocles without tears—has attempted to sell "Oedipus the King" as a kind of suspense thriller: the first detective story. The high road—again the comparison to Shakespearean productions seems valid—is the way of the purist: the bookman with a history of Dionysian festivals in one hand and Aristotle's "Poetics" in the other.

Not for Mr. Langham either the souped-up "Dial O for Oedipus" popularization or the stately academic pageant, complete with masks and stilts, before which audiences, recognizing a classic when they see one, simultaneously kneel and yawn. Mr. Langham—like Peter Brook and Jan Kott, to name two Shakespearean experimentalists—is trying for a new alternative.

"I have been groping," he writes, "not so much for answers that are purely Greek as for an atmosphere that is primitive in its overwhelming superstitions and timeless in its fears and hidden meanings."

The Guthrie stage is dominated by two giant pieces of steel sculpture, 23 feet high, 2½ tons. Representing portals to the palace, they appear more like the slashed entrance to a cave when Len Cariou's slightly Neanderthal Oedipus first bursts through. At the front of the stage stands an altar smothered by incense smoke. Unseen drums beat.

Mr. Langham has recreated a Thebes in the image of the sacred grove of Nemi, made famous in "The Golden Bough." It is a place where cruel ceremonies are acted out, where primal fears fill the air, where human law operates at the level of taboo.

The chorus, covered by what look like animal skins, sings its speeches as chants, dances to a sort of tom-tom, and frets with talismans and totems.

Since the translator happens to be Mr. Burgess, one is tempted to see all this as "A Clockwork Orange" run backwards through a time machine.

Here is the anthropologist's Sophocles, out of Lévi-Strauss—less contemporaneous with fifth-century B.C. Greek tragedy than with the ancient myth from which "Oedipus the King" was drawn. Here is Oedipus less as a king of a sophisticated city-state than as a tribal chieftain, or even a kind of Jungian Everyman, acting out the dark subconscious of the human race.

The drama plays less like a plot than a ritual, a primitive game of riddles and forfeits. Oedipus solves the Sphinx's riddle and saves Thebes from this monster at its gates. Then Oedipus fails to solve in time the riddle of his own identity and becomes the monster within the gates—a violator of the ultimate taboo: incest. The pattern stands out, as stark as a curse.

It is a brilliantly forceful conceit that keeps the Guthrie stage pulsing and throbbing. No pallid Greek revival could survive here—no fake plaster pillars and noble profiles posing like old coins.

But another "Oedipus the King" does fight for its place. Sophocles's play, after all, stands as one of the most subtle studies of human pride in the history of the theater—a profound inquiry into the overintoxication of power. There is nothing primitive or neo-primitive about lines like: "What was your pride must be your ruin." Or: "The shadow of success is always envy."

Inevitable contradictions result. Around that atavistic altar Oedipus and Kreon prowl, like two animals, hurling the most literate lines at one another in the most precise English repertory company accents. If Mr. Cariou's Oedipus is a savage, he is a remarkably self-aware one. Patricia Conolly's Jocasta, a collection of sensitive readings, is simply too refined for this barbaric Thebes. The better the acting, the more it is self-defeating.

Yet, finally, the raw power of Mr. Langham's vision carries the evening. He has restored to Greek tragedy the Dionysian, the religious dread that more correct productions in their fussiness neglect. He has turned his spectators into participants with the cry: "We are all Oedipus." He has brought to his "Oedipus" the one quintessential gift a classic cannot do without—he has made it of the moment, he has made it live.

AN EXCHANGE OF LETTERS ON PLANNING THE 1972 GUTHRIE PRODUCTION

FROM ANTHONY BURGESS, TRANSLATOR-ADAPTER, TO MICHAEL LANGHAM, DIRECTOR

Rome, Italy
April 11, 1972

My dear Michael,

Very many thanks for your kind letter. I note your points and enclose a couple of emendations. As for Jocasta's leavetaking ("Lost. Condemned. . . . My last word."), this is, of course, like the greater part of the play indeed, a fairly close rendering of Sophocles. I'm scared of touching it at the moment, and I feel in some ways that the paucity of words and the inner wordless struggle might be more effective with a good actress than any build-up of tragic eloquence. However, I'll think about it. The finale is a major problem. I'm scared of a bacchanal—really heretical in a tragedy according to Greek tradition, as you know, and I do need that final reference to the riddle. On the other hand, all that is needed if you want a more full-blooded choral ending is a Te Deum based on the simple words—which hence may be hidden with cymbals, etc.—"Praise to the gods." Then Oedipus could do his slow entrance, unnoticed, and the chorus cuts off for the child's comment. This is a musical matter, I feel, more than a verbal one.

I come now to music. You'll know that in English-speaking tradition, so far as the Greek tragedies are concerned, sung choruses have always been taboo. I think there should be singing. I think it should come in these places: The opening chorus—in a Greek mode, with flutes and drums only (the Phyrgian mode—E to E on the white keys of the piano). The children's farewell—in the same style, perhaps the same tune. The first main chorus should be spoken without musical accompaniment. The antistrophes require a greater rhythmical drive and should have drums. *But then:* final antistrophe beginning "Slay him, Apollo" should have the whole musical works, it should overwhelm with sonority. The Chorale ("It is enough to love the law proceeding/Out of high heaven's light . . .") should be a real Bach-type chorale, recalling one of the *Passions*. "What does it mean? . . ." not sung at all. "The night has come. . . ."—sung definitely. The very last choral commentary might be divided among individ-ual voices, except for the last few lines. I must leave this entirely to you

Again my thanks. I'll think and be in touch. Much love to all.

As ever,

Anthony

FROM MICHAEL LANGHAM TO ANTHONY BURGESS

The Guthrie Theater
Minneapolis, Minnesota
19 April 1972

My dear Anthony,

Thank you so much for your letter of April 11, in which you outline your attitude toward the kind and use of music in *Oedipus*. Both Stanley and I find your approach exciting.

However, it is a strange fact that after studying your text, Desmond Heeley (who is designing), Stanley, and I all reacted very differently from what now appears as your total conception.

Far from finding an evocation of a world suited to Bach's Passions or a Handel oratorio, the powerful directness of your writing stirred in all three of us a much more primitive feeling. And we started to work together with this in mind, with results that we feel are promising.

Speaking for myself, I have worked on your script with my imagination in much the same way as I would work on Shakespeare's *Lear*—that is, as if I were interpreting an Elizabethan writer way beyond his period, going back and searching for the essence of the pre-historic world of Lear in which the people could build Stonehenge, not because they were strong but because they were frightened.

In the case of *Oedipus,* I have been groping not so much for answers that are purely Greek as for an atmosphere that is primitive in its overwhelming superstitions and timeless in its fears and hidden meanings. I have been very conscious of the fact that no archaeological evidence of the Oedipus legend has, as you know, been discovered in Greece, but that there is a lot to be found regarding Akhaton (probably the original title figure who lived in the Mycenaean Age) in that other Thebes on the Nile.

After much study and reflection, it seemed best to all three of us not to stick to one ancient culture, but to take whatever was most helpful from all at our disposal—Egyptian, African, Tibetan, Hebraic, Cretan, and Greek. This has led us to a setting with a texture of battered, cracked, and timeworn rusty steel with only one sophisticated feature—a highly polished marble altar: and to a costume plan that would be a composite of primitive cultural sources. All male chorus, elders and lesser elders—with an assortment of symbolic headdresses, hand props, and instruments—opening the work by performing varied acts of sacrifice (possibly human)—all of which fail to produce results. There would only be three females in the play, Jocasta and the two daughters.

In terms of music, we found ourselves drawn toward Tibetan chants, the Pygmies, Hebraic influences, the Greek Orthodox Church, and Coptic chants.

We did not come by these feelings easily; they were all inspired by your text. Indeed the only conflict with your text seems to occur whenever you make reference to God as opposed to the gods.

I don't wish to be untrue to the Sophoclean pattern—as far as our understanding of it goes, which of course is limited because of the long lapse in any acting tradition. Nor do I wish to be untrue to the pre-Sophoclean myth from which he took his ingredients.

I am keen to know your reaction. If you feel it necessary, Stanley would be available to come and work with you in Rome. Please let me hear from you as soon as possible.

Much Love,

Michael

FROM ANTHONY BURGESS TO MICHAEL LANGHAM

Rome, Italy
April 22, 1972

My dear Michael,

Very many thanks for that admirable and thought-provoking letter. . . . I think you're absolutely and brilliantly right to think of a kind of inspired anachronistic approach, a synoptic gospel of all ancient cul-

tures. If this will inspire Stanley to produce music of a strangeness very remote from baroque oratorio, so much the better. But when I wrote, somewhat elliptically, of a Bach chorale, I didn't mean a straight baroque pastiche. You mentioned previously the Stravinsky-Cocteau *Oedipus,* and I had in mind probably a "wrong-note" or neurotically distorted baroque like that. . . .

My blessing, get on with it, and I know it's going to be the most astounding *Oedipus* ever to hit any stage.

Much love as always,

Anthony

FROM STANLEY SILVERMAN, COMPOSER, TO MICHAEL LANGHAM, DIRECTOR

Composer Stanley Silverman, supported by a Ford Foundation grant, went to Rome to work with Anthony Burgess on the script.

Rome, Italy
May 24, 1972

Dear Michael,

Burgess is being most cooperative and is responding favorably to the production ideas. He keeps saying that this will be a "monumental production." He's quite turned on. . . .

As for the play: He *loves* the primitive music (Pygmy, etc.) and would like to write an Indo-European chant to accompany the sacrifice you planned for the beginning, which would set the tone for the primitivism. (He is turned on to your idea for the opening.)

The following are notes answering your questions and his general comments on the text. . . .

"Listen, O King, consent . . .": Anthony thinks that if the chorus sings "Listen, O King, consent" against Oedipus speaking it could sound too "arty." What he had in mind was that it all be spoken (distributed to members of the chorus perhaps) and lyrical music should be played against it. As I write this I think I get an idea where perhaps the words could be spoken, and the musical members of the chorus could be singing or humming quietly. This way we could establish a choral "cosmos" that could encompass speech and music at the same time. Similar to the Duke's men humming a hymn at the beginning of *Taming of the Shrew.*

"King Oedipus,/Hear us once more . . .": The chorus speaks this as above.

"At a place where three roads meet": Anthony also thinks we should underline this with a sound.

"You have the first right . . .": He likes our idea of sound under Oedipus's long speech (which is why I don't particularly want to do it elsewhere).

The Chorale: Now we come to the key of the argument. It seems that the reason he liked the primitive production idea was that he meant this version to go *anywhere*, providing it underlined Oedipus's sophistication. He was reassured, for example, when the primitive music we were listening to turned out to be sophisticated. He would be genuinely delighted if you placed Oedipus anywhere that you feel fit. One of the casualties of this eclectic-universal approach is always going to be that the work will be filled with anachronisms, as they are in Shakespeare or Brecht, I suppose. Personally, I can accept them, because my music is so filled with anachronisms. This is all leading up to saying that Anthony did not mean, as we first thought, that this version was a grand Handelian oratorio. He thought we would be using elements from everywhere, and when we got here he thought we could naturally slip into a Bach-like chorale. I pointed out that we were able to achieve an "eclectic" variety of elements but keep it tightly capped under the umbrella of our primitive approach. He confessed it would place a burden on us in dealing with the "lyrics" for the chorale. I told him I would take a whack at a primitive setting of his chorale. He said a Bach-like setting would still be justified. He also said you could cut the second stanza ("Only the tyrant . . ."). . . .

As I said earlier, Anthony is excited by your production idea, and he believes his version goes with it. He wants me to throw the primitive tapes away and work from myself. In any event, he is happily prepared to leave it to you. Consequently, your idea of treating Anthony as, say, an Elizabethan writer, in order to get at the primitive core of this project, is brilliant, especially since the "Elizabethan" in question has no objections. . . .

Much love,

Stanley

EURIPIDES

484–406 B.C.

Euripides expressed more directly than any of his contemporaries the anxieties of his age: the growing skepticism in Athens about the dignity of man, the authority of the gods, and the future of Athens itself. But his view of experience was too harsh, his means of expression too unconventional, for the tastes of his audience. Although he wrote more than ninety plays, he won the festival competition only four times. While he was losing, Sophocles must have been winning, for they were nearly exact contemporaries. But they were exact opposites in both their way of life and their view of it. Whereas Sophocles was a very public and genial man, Euripides was reportedly a very private person, so unsociable that he is rumored to have spent long periods of time secluded in a cave, writing his plays in solitary confinement. Wherever he may have written them, his plays bear witness to a much darker view of human nature than those of Sophocles, for they repeatedly seem to deny it the moral heroism exhibited by the heroes and heroines of Sophocles.

Sophocles is reported to have said that Euripides shows human behavior not as it ought to be but as it is. As Euripides depicts it, human behavior is controlled primarily by emotions and passions—emotions and passions that have been crippled by nature, afflicted by circumstance, or distorted by self-indulgence. His fascination with the nature of intense feeling has also been said to explain his special interest in the experience of women, for they figure as protagonists in twelve of his eighteen surviving plays. Wherever they appear, they are either inflicting pain, or having pain inflicted on them—or both. This is the case in his two most famous studies of women in love: *Hippolytus* (428) and *Medea* (431). In *Hippolytus,* he shows the raging spectacle of a frustrated adulterous love, when Phaedra develops a consuming passion for her stepson Hippolytus, who is himself with equal passion committed to a sexless existence. Moved by both frustration and shame, she commits suicide by hanging herself, but before doing so she leaves a message for her husband Theseus accusing Hippolytus of having raped her. The result of her false accusation is that Theseus exiles his son and prays for his destruction, and his prayers are answered when Hippolytus while riding along a shore is dragged to death by his horses after they have been terrified by a bull rising from the sea. In *Medea,* Euripides represents an even more sensational spectacle, in this case the result of an abused marital love, when Medea, having been deserted by Jason, works herself up into so fierce a rage that she murders their two children and then makes her exit by flying off in a dragon-driven chariot to seek refuge in Athens. Truly, hell hath no fury like these women scorned, nor like the men who scorn them. In his study of deranged passions and human depravity, Euripides did not favor either sex.

When he was not representing the terrors of love, he was showing the horrors of war. His temperament did not permit him to remain silent about the cultural tragedy of his age. Living as he did during the Peloponnesian War, witnessing the extraordinary toll it took on Athens and Sparta during the nearly thirty years of its duration, he felt compelled to dramatize its senseless brutality in a series of antiwar plays—the tragic counterparts of the antiwar comedies written during the same period by Aristophanes. In *Hecuba* (ca. 430–415), he showed the brutality of war in its most brutalizing form, when Hecuba, driven mad by the loss of her children in the aftermath of the Trojan War, avenges their deaths by blinding Polymestor, an act whose bestiality is symbolized by her transformation into a raging dog. In *The Trojan Women* (415), the greatest of his antiwar plays, a play attacking the atrocity of his own country, he turned again to Hecuba, this time showing her to be a magnificent image of suffering as she bids farewell to each of her daughters who are being led off to slavery, then buries Hector's young son, her grandson, and then bemoans the climactic spectacle of the play: the city of Troy in flames.

Only in his tragicomedies, a dramatic form he is credited with inventing, does Euripides ever offer an optimistic view of experience. Yet even these plays, *Ion* (ca. 430–415) and *Iphigenia at Tauris* (ca. 415–410), only avoid disaster by miraculous resolutions—sisters recognizing brothers or sons recognizing mothers, moments before they are about to kill or be killed by another. Thus they offer at best an ironically comforting view of fate. In these plays, the gods are only somewhat less malign than in his tragedies, for in almost all his plays the suffering of human beings turns out to be the work of the gods. The gods themselves rarely figure among the characters in his plays, but they are almost always taken into account in the prologues and epilogues that Euripides used as a means of beginning and ending his plays. Sometimes these prologues and epilogues are spoken by gods, sometimes by human beings, but always they set the specific action of the play in a wider context that refers its events to the past, to the future, and ultimately to the gods.

Euripides has been criticized for using prologues and epilogues, as he has been criticized for a wide range of other elements distinctive to his plays, such as sensational episodes, episodic plots, elaborately rhetorical debates, irrelevant choral odes, supernatural events, and melodramatic scenes. Such elements offended Aristotle, as they later offended exponents of formal symmetry and dramatic probability. But Euripides was largely indifferent to conventions of dramatic regularity for he was committed to emotionally expressive drama and to questioning many of the established beliefs of his time. This radical combination has made him particularly attractive to dramatists such as Brian Friel, who used the central triangle from *Hippolytus* in *Living Quarters: After Hippolytus* (1977) and Suzan-Lori Parks, who chillingly evokes Medea through the actions of Hester, the protagonist of *In the Blood* (1999). These and other contemporary dramatists have turned to Euripides as the supreme playwright of irregular and convulsive experience, of passionate human beings living in an unpredictable universe.

That vision of experience is nowhere more eloquently dramatized than in *The Bacchae* (ca. 407). It is a vision at once terrifying and beautiful, as terrifying and beautiful as Dionysos, the Greek god of fertility, who stood for the mysterious and irrepressible forces working throughout nature, sustaining and renewing life in all of its abundance, all of its vitality, and all of its wild and uncontrollable energy. Just as wine, the substance with which Dionysos was most closely associated, can bring both the oblivion of sleep and the liberation of happiness, so too Dionysos seems a contradictory figure. But the play suggests that defining Dionysos is not as important as respecting his power. Those who embrace the Dionysian vision experience the joy of his followers, the chorus of Bacchantes; those who defy that vision, who seek to repudiate and, even worse, repress it, experience the suffering of Pentheus and his mother Agave. Those who neither embrace it nor deny it but nonetheless acknowledge its mystical power and meaning, as do Kadmos and Teiresias—they at least survive. Understood in this way, *The Bacchae* is a profoundly religious tragedy, as it was probably meant to be, judging from earlier Greek hymns to Dionysos, all of which stress the necessity of obedience to the god.

    The Bacchae has also been understood in other ways by other cultures. It has, for example, been seen as a dramatization of the archetypal conflict between passion and reason, symbolized in the struggle between Dionysos and Pentheus. The contemporary British playwright Peter Shaffer has drawn on that struggle, reformulating it as the conflict between Mozart and the more traditional composer Salieri in *Amadeus* (1980), or the disturbed teenager and the middle-aged psychiatrist in *Equus* (1973). The play has also been thought to be an indictment of all peoples and all cultures that forsake reason, abandoning themselves to a senseless and brutally destructive life of sensual experience. During the late 1960s, it came to be seen as a uniquely relevant statement about the countercultural activities of that decade. It has been widely performed in the United States and abroad as an expression of the conflicting lifestyles in contemporary culture. In 1969, the Yale Repertory Theatre staged the play in an ultramodern setting (see Figure 1) with the followers of Dionysos as members of the hippie subculture. Almost thirty years later, the American Repertory Theatre used a more obviously symbolic set (an all-white classical palace for Pentheus, next to which stood the blackened tomb of his aunt Semele) for a production that presented Dionysos as clearly androgynous (see Figure 2) and his female followers as both seductive in their satin tunics and dangerous in their black combat boots. The two productions were connected not only through their contemporary costuming but through the person of actor Alvin Epstein. Playing Dionysos in 1969 (see Figure 3), Epstein returned to the play in 1997 to play Kadmos, the grandfather of both Pentheus and Dionysos (see Figure 4). Though Epstein could, while playing Dionysos, believe in himself as a figure of power, and while playing Kadmos, see himself as a "silly old man" (see interview following the play), he also commented on the problems raised at the play's end when Kadmos challenges Dionysos' revenge: "And maybe like most masterpieces, a certain amount of ambiguity remains at the end." That unresolved tension, inherent in the text, makes *The Bacchae* as challenging to contemporary audiences as it must have been for audiences in the Athens of Euripides.

THE BACCHAE

BY EURIPIDES / TRANSLATED BY KENNETH CAVANDER*

CHARACTERS

DIONYSOS
CHORUS *of Asian women, followers of Dionysos*
TEIRESIAS, *a prophet*
KADMOS, *ex-King of Thebes*
PENTHEUS, *King of Thebes, grandson of Kadmos*

GUARD
HERDSMAN
SERVANT
AGAVE, *mother of Pentheus*
GUARDS, SOLDIERS, SERVANTS, PEOPLE OF THEBES

(DIONYSOS *and* CHORUS.)

DIONYSOS: Dionysos has come.
　Here, in Thebes, Zeus came swooping down and
　　took
　A woman of the earth. Lightning made
　Her labour quick, and out of her burning thighs
5　I was born.
　　Today I walk on the piece of land enclosed
　By two rivers—Dirce and Ismenos—
　The land they call . . . Thebes.
　Today I look like a man, but I am more.
　　Here was the lightning blast that killed my
　　　mother,
10　Semele, here was her room and . . .
　There's something alive! Smoke in the rubble, the
　　fire
　Of Zeus . . . still. So, something alive
　Still . . .
15　　Yes, Kadmos has said: "On this ground
　No man walks!" to remind Thebes
　Of Semele, his daughter, to keep her alive in the
　　heart
　Of Thebes. I am glad. He was right.
　The vines that cover that wall are mine. They flush,
20　And cluster . . .
　And swell . . .
　　Behind me—Lebanon and its golden plains,
　Iraq, the sun-struck steppes of Persia,
　The fortresses of Syria, the harsh country
25　Where the Afghans live, Arabia drugged,
　And all the eastern coasts, where Greece and Asia
　Merge, and towers fringe the teeming cities;
　Behind me—dance swaying bodies, intoxication,
　Life.

Here—Greece. And first in Greece—Thebes.　30
My own country, where I will be known,
Where I must be known.
There is a reason why Thebes comes first.
I made this city wild with women shrilling
My name, I slung hide on their backs, I stuck　35
Branches in their hands, spears tipped
With ivy—for a reason.
Because my mother's sisters denied I was
The son of Zeus; because they said Semele
Lost her virginity to a man here in Thebes,　40
Then blamed the result on Zeus; because they
　swore
Kadmos invented it all; because they claimed
Zeus killed Semele for lying about
Her husband.
They shouldn't have said that. They,　45
Particularly, should not have said all that.
Because now, they hurtle out of their homes,
　possessed,
Scatter to the hills, and they all wear my uniform,
They all know how to bring me to life. . . .
　I willed it, and they must.　50
Every woman in this city is mine,
Totally.
They have abandoned Thebes, and now they have
　joined
My mother's sisters in the green pine shades,
Among the cliffs and hollows. Mad. Bacchae.　55
This place must find out what it means
To be half-born, to have no
Dionysos, never to have tried me or tasted me,
This place must take account of my birth
In Semele, my descent from Zeus, my presence here,　60
And my power over man. This place
May wish it did not have to, but it must learn.
　Kadmos has given way to Pentheus, his grandson.
Authority, decision, are now all Pentheus,
Who resists me and my power, keeps me　65
Clear out of thought. When he looks outside
Himself for help, he never looks to me.
I am despised, pushed aside, stamped upon.
And therefore I'll turn him round to face me. Show
Myself in Thebes, show them they are small　70

---

* This version of The Bacchae *was originally commissioned
by the BBC and later rewritten for production at the Mermaid Theatre in London. It is an acting version. In a few
places, for the sake of a twentieth-century audience, it is
interpretative rather than literal. Nevertheless, the script
stays close to Euripides' own words at all times, and the intentions of the lines are invariably based on the suggestive power
of the original.—K.C.*

And I am great.
  This one matter set to rights I pack up
And move on, to make myself known
Elsewhere.
75 If Thebes recklessly tries to bring the women
Back from the hills and their madness by *force,* you
Will see a fight—the army versus Bacchae—
Arranged by me.
  And so I have dressed myself in flesh today.
80 I have the body and blood of a man, but
My real nature is . . . still my own.
  (To CHORUS*)* Friends, you have been loyal, you have
    followed me
From countries far across the sea, travelled
Beside me, never deserted me. Lift your drums
85 Now. Let these proud walls of Pentheus,
The king, hear the sound of the east, the creation
Of Earth, my mother, and myself. The beat!
The beat! Let the city open its eyes.
I will go to the heights of Kithairon where
90 The women are dancing on the slopes, and join
The Bacchae.

  (Exit.)

CHORUS: Look—the hills of
The East, where new life leaps—
We came from there.
95 Our work . . . !
It's easy,
It's singing work,
It's dancing labour,
It's laughing drudgery.
100 I never stop, I never tire,
Letting myself run free for Dionysos.
Clear the streets—
We're here.
Clear the streets—
105 We've come.
Room! Room! Stay at home, lips closed, because . . .
A word spilled can make a stain.
The only words allowed here are the words for
Dionysos.
110 And I sing them
Over and over,
I sing them . . .
Who is alive? Who is happy?
The one who knows . . .
115 Knows?
Knows the secret . . .
The secret?
The secret of the night
When his whole life begins again
120 And he's all one with the friends of Dionysos,
The pure lovers of the mountains,
Bedded in the earth's grasp
Plunged in forgetfulness,
Buried

. . . Living!   125
Like green leaves in winter, woodsap in snow,
Ivy crowns make you King
And from the pine tree stems your power.
Dionysos, my lord,
Dionysos, my dear harsh master.   130
Run on, run on! Bring him here, fill the streets
With the young life, the new life—
Dionysos!
Flood Greece with his fresh blood,
Beat, beat, beat him into the heart like thunder—   135
Dionysos!
  Burst from fire, gashed by thunderbolt.
He was flung into life by flame.
His mother screamed, the pain rending her,
And let him go to the lightning.   140
She died then . . .
But he lived! Hatched in a golden clasp,
In the storehouse of life in the body of Zeus.
And Hera never knew!
Then out into the world—   145
When the time was ready for him,
And he for the time.
He had bull horns empowering him.
He had snake hair crowning him.
And we will wear crowns like that—   150
We'll catch them, and tame them, and wear them—
Snakes!
  Thebes—mother land of Semele—
Wear a crown too—coiled-within-coil ivy.
Let the never-dying blossoms,   155
Flower in you, drench you in greenery, Thebes!
Oak-leaf mad,
Fir-branch crazy,
Fawn-skin clothed,
And white-wool jewelled—   160
Then you're dressed.
Hold the branch in your hand,
Power in the thick wood, feel it pulsing,
The whole land will rock,
The whole land will jump—   165
He stirs, yes, now—the power Dionysos.
And then we go up to the hills, to the hills,
Where the women who lived indoors at a loom,
Or a spindle, wait for him now
Packed, trembling, his thorn in their blood.   170
  Crete holds caves where Zeus was nursed,
And there the drum, the drum, the drum was born.
When the dance comes over you, and the strain
    drags tight,
The singing woodwind cools
The drum-beat,   175
The singing wind softens the drum
And together they make the dance, they make it,
    till . . .
The mind splits open,
The world falls in—

180 And Dionysos is glad.
Then you're tired of the running, and at last, at last
You fling yourself on the ground—
Your only cover the flakes of sunlight on the skin
of a fawn;
This is the moment, sacred and secret, in the
mountains,
185 When your hands search for the goat,
Hands grope for its blood,
And you drink,
As it comes from the goat,
The fresh red juice, the joy of . . .
190 That's the way Dionysos has led you
In the hills of the east, the morning sun . . .
          (CHORUS *makes a sound—of joy, ecstasy, praise.*)
          Earth gushing milk
Gushing wine.
Gushing rivers of honey,
195 You hold the flame
High, it smells like a scent from Syria,
Its pine wood flaring,
Smoke streaming as you hurl your body
Down through dances
200 Shouting, and raving, and reddening the torch
With your speed
Your hair floods down, the wind-gusts flourish it . . .
And among the shrilling, the shouting, the singing
a voice
Blares,
205 "Run on, run on,
My Bacchae,
Like a stream of gold from the lavish east
Sing, sing, sing!
Let the drum stamp loud,
210 Shout for him,
Throat, tongue, breath,
Blaze for him,
Let the leaping flute
Lure and tempt,
215 Calling out the powers of life
To join us, and play
In the hills,
In the hills."
Then, freedom!
220 Joy of a foal
In the meadows with its mother.
Bacchae, dart!
Bacchae, run!
Bacchae, *dance!*

          (Enter TEIRESIAS.)

225 TEIRESIAS (*knocks at door of palace*): Answer the door!
          Answer it! Call Kadmos
Out, Kadmos, the man from Phoenicia who built
A towering city here at Thebes. Go,
Someone, tell him Teiresias wants him.
230 He knows why I've come . . .

(*A* GUARD *goes.*)

We are collaborating and we have
This pact. We take branches, we twist ivy
Leaves round them, we weave more ivy in
Our hair, like crowns, but live, and then we take
Skins of young deer . . . Well, I may   235
Be old, but he is older . . .

(*Enter* KADMOS.)

KADMOS: Teiresias, my dear friend, I knew
It was you when I heard your voice.
(*To* GUARDS) Pay attention.
This is a wise, wise man.   240
(*To* TEIRESIAS) Look, I am ready. I found the
     things. We
Must give him all we can, build
Respect for him. He is a power, a wonder,
And he is the child of my own daughter.
Do we dance now? Where do we go? (*Shaking his*   245
     head.)
One—two—*back!* One—two—*back!*
Is this right, Teiresias? We are both old
But you know things, you see more.
All day and all night, I won't
Need rest—down, down—(*He thumps his stick on the*   250
     ground.)
Forget the years, we are born again, and it's
beautiful.
TEIRESIAS: Yes, do you feel it? Young again.
I'll dance too, I can, I'm ready . . .
KADMOS: We climb
To the hills, then, we don't ride there?   255
TEIRESIAS: No. We need to go *simply* into the presence
Of this being.
KADMOS: An old blind prophet
And I shall take you by the hand like a child . . .
TEIRESIAS: The one who calls us will lead us there.
     And we   260
Shall never notice the journey.
KADMOS: Are we the only
Two in Thebes to worship this way, dancing?
TEIRESIAS: We are the only two in Thebes with our
     senses left
Intact. The rest of the city has fallen apart.   265
KADMOS: I want to go. Hurry. Take my hand.
TEIRESIAS: Here, hold on to me, don't let me lose you.
KADMOS: I look at the world, the power in it, and I
Feel lost, mortal, small, small . . .
TEIRESIAS: Yes,   270
You feel those forces working in you. To them
All our intellect is a joke. There are things
Not measured in time, a birthright, an inheritance.
They exist. You can't reason them away,
You can't talk them, define them, describe them
     away,   275
Yes, I'm old, but I mean to go dancing,

Put vine leaves in my hair, and I'm not ashamed.
This power does not
Tell men apart. When they dance it can't distinguish
280 Young from old. It needs to be recognized
By everyone in the world—that is how
It lives—but it doesn't keep score. No one comes
Before anyone else . . .

KADMOS: Teiresias,
285 You have sight, but no eyes. You need
Mine to light your way for you. Listen,
Pentheus is here, the youth I gave my power to.
How he drives himself!
What's happened? What is new now?

(Enter PENTHEUS *with* SOLDIERS.*)*

290 PENTHEUS: I leave my country, I just go away,
And the result—chaos, the city in uproar. I hear
All our women have left home, and the new
Fashion is to be Bacchae, to mob
The mountains—more shadows there, of course—
295 And all in honour of someone, some moving spirit
They've just discovered—Dionysos. Who
Is he? What is Dionysos?
And this dancing . . . ? Dancing! . . . I was told
There are gatherings where they drink so much
300 You could never see the cups for the wine.
The women creep away, one here, one there,
Into the bushes—and there a man is waiting
And they copulate. They say it's all
Part of the service for this divine power.
305 Service! All they care about is being
Serviced.
I caught a few and my men have them chained
To the wall in the city gaol. The rest escaped,
They're in the hills, but I shall hunt them down.
310 Yes, that's how they'll end, in a cage,
Behind bars. No more drunken
Dancing then, no more orgies,
No more Bacchae!
    They say a stranger has come to my country—
315 Some sorcerer, hypnotist, from the East,
From Lydia or somewhere, all curly blonde
Hair stinking of scent, cheeks hot
With wine, and flashing eyes—a real seducer—
Who spends all his days—and his nights—
320 With the girls from my city. He calls it initiation.
If I get this initiator inside
My palace, I'll finish his thumping, jumping,
Hair-shaking, snaking game, I'll initiate
That head away from that body.
325 He claims Dionysos still exists,
Never died, got life from eternal
Powers. Very likely—since Dionysos was roasted
In his mother's womb, after she told
Everyone Zeus was father of her child.
330 That myth was exploded in a blast of lightning.
But this new boy has the gall

To foist it back on us. Whoever he is
He deserves a reward for that—a rope around
His neck . . . *(He sees* KADMOS *and* TEIRESIAS.*)*
No, I can't believe it! My prophet, Teiresias, 335
In a fawn skin . . . And my own grandfather
    playing
With a woolly stick. Ridiculous!
(To KADMOS*)* Grandfather, you disgust me. Look at
    you,
An old man, clowning. Throw away
That ivy, drop those toys, don't touch them . . . 340
(To TEIRESIAS*)* Teiresias, this is you. You talked him
    into it.
You want to drag this new obsession across
Our lives, so that you can squint up
At a few birds, burn a few sacrifices,
And make yourself more of a profit than ever. 345
If you weren't already mouldering in senility
You'd be rattling your chains with all the other
    Bacchae
For smuggling in this pernicious, lecherous gospel.
When women drink, and their eyes light up like
    the wine
Itself, then I say, Goodbye to decency, 350
The animals are out!
CHORUS: You—King of this place, be careful,
You, stranger, you dirty something pure,
That's dangerous.
Remember—you're born out of the earth yourself. 355
Kadmos planted dragon's teeth in soil, and
    harvested men.
To those men you are a living insult.
TEIRESIAS: Easy for some to make speeches. They're
    clever,
They pick an easy target, and the words sound
    good.
Now you—your tongue races along 360
And makes a plausible sound, which might
Almost be mistaken for sense, except
That you have none. Arrogant, self-confident, with
    a gift
For phrases—that kind of man is useless, a danger
To his fellows, while his mind stays closed. 365
This new life in our midst, which you
Sneer at, is going to be so powerful all
Over Greece, so vast, I . . . I can't
Describe it.
    You are a young man. Here are two 370
Principles for you, the two supreme principles
In life.
First the principle of earth, Demeter,
Goddess of the soil, or whatever else
You like to call it. This provides the firm 375
Solid base in man. Second, the opposite
Principle, Dionysos, who found the living
Juice in the grape, and gave it to us all,
To slake our parched, aching souls, wash us

380 In streams of wine. When living is a struggle
He is the only drug for our pain, he gives us
Sleep and oblivion. We drink him down, we
 swallow
His power, and he comes alive in us. Then
We soar, we fly, we are free, and through his
 agency

385 Man can know some happiness. You laugh at him.
You laugh at the story that he was sewn in the loins
Of Zeus. Let me show you how to interpret
That—it makes sense.
 Zeus snatched the unborn child out

390 Of the blazing thunderbolt, took him back
To where he came from, Olympos. Hera, the bride
Of Zeus, wanted her rival's child to die.
But Zeus, like the wise power he is, found
A way out of the dilemma. He broke off

395 A part of the earth's envelope, the atmosphere,
And made a *loan* of it to Hera, to protect
The real Dionysos from her jealousy.
In time people confused "loan" with "loin"—
Told some story of how he was sewn in the loins

400 Of Zeus, and made a new version.
 And there is more. The power of Dionysos can
 break
Out of time. When he invades the mind
And puts reason to sleep, we have sight
Of things to come. If he takes full possession

405 He makes those who give themselves to him
Tell the future . . . What else? . . . War! He is even
There in war, yes . . . An army is in
The field, marching into battle. Then,
Before the weapons have touched, panic! That

410 Is Dionysos . . . Delphi too, home
Of Apollo, sanctuary of reason. But look
Up at the rocks. Who do you see bounding
Over the high plateau between the peaks,
Through the pine forests, shaking winter

415 Into life with green branches?—Dionysos!
Yes, he is everywhere.
Believe me, Pentheus, never boast
That you have any power to rule your life.
You may think you do, but thought is impotent,

420 Your certainty an illusion. Dionysos is here,
In your country, at work.
 Accept him,
Pour wine for him,
Put vine leaves in your hair for him,

425 Dance for him.
 Dionysos will not restrain desire
In women. Restraint is something they must
 practise
For themselves. It cannot be imposed. But those
Who have control already will not lose it

430 Merely because they lose themselves
To Dionysos.
 Look, you are glad when crowds at the city

Gates cheer, shout, "Pentheus! Pentheus!"
Till every street rings with your name. Well,
Dionysos, too, I imagine, enjoys   435
Some recognition.
 And so Kadmos and myself—yes,
You can laugh—but we'll take our ivy branches
And we shall dance, we shall partner each other,
Old and grey as we are. Nevertheless   440
Dance we must. We shall not fight this power;
We shall not listen to your talk, which is
The most terrible madness of all. I pity you,
Pentheus. You'll get no relief from medicine,
Nor can you cure yourself.   445
CHORUS: The old man understands. He leaves reason
 where it is
Apollo has his place, and so has Dionysos . . .
You are safe. Dionysos has power—and you
Have granted it.
KADMOS: Listen to Teiresias. You are still young,   450
And he is right. Your place is here, beside us.
Don't close doors on the past. This moment
You're nowhere, suspended in a void. Your brain
Works, but only against yourself.
You may be right. Dionysos may have   455
No special powers, but even so,
Why not pretend he does? It may be a lie,
But it's a useful one. If we can say
That Semele gave birth to a superior
Being, to something undying, it will be   460
A tremendous honour to our family.
Remember how your cousin, Akteon, died.
That was a horrible end. The hounds from his own
Kennels turned man-eater and tore him apart.
He had boasted he was a greater hunter than
 Artemis   465
Herself. And so he died in a velvet glade.
It could happen to you, unless you change! Come
 here,
I'll put some leaves on your head . . . Ivy . . . Be
With us. Acknowledge him. He is a great
Power. Let me . . .   470
PENTHEUS: Don't touch me!
Go and play Bacchae, but don't smear
Your idiocy onto me! Just don't
Come near me!
 And now for your teacher, Teiresias, who fed
 you this drivel,   475
Punishment!
(To GUARD*)* One of you, here!
He has a place where he sits hoping for some
Revelation out of birdsong. Go. Take
A crowbar with you, and destroy that place.   480
Level it to the ground, all of it,
Throw his bits of wool to the winds, and let
The storms have them. *Hurry!*
 This is the one thing I can do to him
That will really hurt.   485

And you, you go into the city
And bring me this foreigner, this thing
Of doubtful gender, spreading his sick notions
Amongst our women, dragging our marriages
490   Through the filth.
When you find him, chain him up, and fetch him
Here. And then he'll have justice, because we'll
    stone him,
    (*To* GUARDS) Stone him till he's dead. He'll find
    Thebes
A hard, hard place for Bacchae!
TEIRESIAS: You fiend! Do you realise what you're
495   saying?
No, you're mad. You had little enough sense
Before, but now . . . !
    (*To* KADMOS) Kadmos, let's go. And let us pray
For him. Yes, he's a monster, but for the sake
500   Of the rest of us, let us pray this
Is overlooked. Bring your ivy branches
And follow me. Try to help me, hold me
Upright, and I'll help you. We are old
But we must stand by ourselves. Take pride in it . . .
505   Don't think of him!
We have work to do for this great power, this
    supreme
Power . . .
    Kadmos—in Greek the name Pentheus signifies
Sorrow. Does that mean anything? . . .
510   I hope not.
I don't talk of things to come—this is happening
Now (*meaning to* PENTHEUS) . . . Only a fool blurts
    out his folly!

(*Exeunt* KADMOS *and* TEIRESIAS.)

CHORUS: Back!
Keep away!
515   This is filth—stain—smear—decay—
Keep away! He turns pure gold black.
    Did you hear him?
The scorn that drips,
From his mouth, fouling Dionysos, child of his own
    city.
Doesn't know happiness, or the pure-drained drink
520   of joy.
But Dionysos is the one
Who sends you dancing out of your mind,
Flings you laughing out of yourself to the
    flute-song,
Stops your crying, stops your caring,
525   And when the bright wine dazes you
Life can't end, ivy glows on your brow
And you swallow thick sleep by the mouthful.
When reason forgets its place, wanders, and starts
    an invasion,
And words go mad and run away with their master,
530   The end has come—
The man is doomed.

Live easy, live calm, and the storm can't wreck
    you—
That way you stay whole.
There are powers in the world, who oversee life;
It's not so wise to be clever.   535
Life is short, and since it is,
Why chase more, more, more?
Can't you bear what is here?
Let others go mad, draw up the plans for
    destruction—
But don't let them take us with them!   540
I want to go back to Cyprus, island of Aphrodite,
Where desire blows warm and breathes away
    thought;
I want to lie in the fields of Paphos,
Where the distant Nile feeds a hundred wells
And gives fruit to the land without rain.   545
I want to see Pieria, because music is first there,
And the slope of Olympos leads straight to the sky.
Take me there, Dionysos, I'm calling you—
Hear me, come and lead me away. . . .
Then I can hand over my seeing,   550
Hand over my striving
And dance to my heart-beats,
And no one can say no.
Dionysos, child of the universe, comes to life in my
    laughter.
His great love is Peace,   555
Lavish with her treasures, careful of youth.
He sends the poor, he sends the rich, his one gift—
    wine.
So that the whole world can know
Where pain stops, and where joy starts.
He hates the man who says no.   560
No to the day,
No to the night,
No to life, and no to all love—
Keep away from that kind,
They are too much for you, they will consume you. 565
There is another way, never named, never
    mapped.
But the unheard-of, untalked-of people follow it.
That way I choose—I say yes to it.

(*Enter a* GUARD, *with* DIONYSOS, *chained.*)

GUARD: Pentheus, we caught him. The hunt is over,
    and here
Is the animal you sent us after . . .   570
A gentle animal, we found, made
No attempt to escape, handed himself
Over without a murmur, never went pale,
That wine-stain flush never left his cheek, and he
    smiled.
He told us to put on the chains and take him away. 575
He waited for us, making it so simple
I was embarrassed. So I said, "Stranger," I said,
"I only obey orders here. I am taking you

580 Now, on instructions from Pentheus. Pentheus
Sends for you. *Pentheus.* Not me."
But the women you captured and had locked up in
    prison,
The ones who were dancing,
They're out.
They're free, and they're away in the forest,
    running
585 Like deer, calling on Bromios—he's their master,
And governs them completely.
The chains all fell from their limbs of their own
Accord, keys turned, doors opened,
Without a hand touching them. This man
590 Is an amazing . . .
He is full of . . .
I don't understand what it is he has brought to
    Thebes
But it is your concern now, all of it.
PENTHEUS: Let him go. He is inside the cage and he
    can't
595 Escape from me now. He doesn't move
So fast.
Well, stranger, you're not at all bad-looking,
Are you? At least, to the women . . . Which is why
You have come to Thebes, I suppose . . . Long hair,
600 Crinkling down your cheeks—you've never wrestled,
I presume—very desirable . . . White
Skin—you keep out of the sun, you cultivate
The shadows, where you hunt down love
With your handsome profile. Yes?
605 Who are you? Where do you come from?
DIONYSOS: I am no one . . .
But I will give you an easier answer.
Have you heard of a river called Tmolos? It runs
Through fields of flowers . . .
610 PENTHEUS: Yes, I know that river, it circles the town
Of Sardis.
DIONYSOS: I come from there. My country is Lydia.
PENTHEUS: And these
Activities. How is it you bring them to Greece?
615 DIONYSOS: Dionysos inspired me. Dionysos . . . He
Is the son of Zeus.
PENTHEUS: So you have a Zeus
Over there, who fathers new powers
On the world.
620 DIONYSOS: No. Zeus was united
With Semele in Thebes, and gave her the child
Here.
PENTHEUS: Did this irresistible urge
Come to you at night, or were you
625 "Inspired" in the daytime?
DIONYSOS: I saw him.
He saw me. And he gave me the secret
Means to summon his presence.
PENTHEUS: And this secret—
630 What is it like? Can you tell me?
DIONYSOS: It must not

Be revealed to someone in whom Dionysos
Has not been born.
PENTHEUS: Those who share this secret—
Do they benefit—and how? 635
DIONYSOS: I am forbidden to tell.
But it is worth knowing.
PENTHEUS: You're clever, but
You're a fake! You want to make me curious.
DIONYSOS: For a man who is so sure of what he knows 640
There are no other powers, there is no other
Life. It simply escapes him.
PENTHEUS: You say you saw
Dionysos clearly . . . What did he look like?
DIONYSOS: Whatever 645
He wished. I didn't arrange it.
PENTHEUS: Very good.
But once more you evade the issue,
Your statement was meaningless.
DIONYSOS: The greatest truths often sound like
    babblings 650
Of madmen—till they are understood.
PENTHEUS: Are we
The first to be visited by you and your offer
Of supernatural aid?
DIONYSOS: No, all 655
The people of the east are awake. They dance.
They live . . .
PENTHEUS: They're out of their minds, we in Greece
Have more sense.
DIONYSOS: No, in this case, less. 660
Their way is different, that is all.
PENTHEUS: And these practices you claim are sacred—
Do they take place at night, or in the day?
DIONYSOS: Mostly at night. Darkness has dignity.
PENTHEUS: For women the night hours are
    dangerous, 665
Lascivious hours . . .
DIONYSOS: People have been known
To sin during the day.
PENTHEUS: You play with words!
You'll be punished for that. 670
DIONYSOS: You soil mysteries
With your ignorant sneers. You'll be punished
For that.
PENTHEUS: He's so sure. The drunken dancer
Has been in training—for argument. 675
DIONYSOS: Come,
Pronounce sentence. What terrible fate have you
In store for me?
PENTHEUS: First, I'll clip those flowing
Locks . . . 680
DIONYSOS: My hair must not be touched, I grow it
For Dionysos.
PENTHEUS: Next, you will hand over
Your wand, that branch you carry . . .
DIONYSOS: Take it from me 685
Yourself. I carry it for Dionysos.

PENTHEUS: Then
    We shall lock you in prison, and you will never get
      out.
DIONYSOS: Dionysos will free me, when I wish him to.
PENTHEUS: Yes, when you get your followers round
690   you and "summon
    His presence."
DIONYSOS: He sees. He's here. This minute he knows
    What is being done to me.
PENTHEUS: Where is he then?
695   I can't see him. Why doesn't he show himself?
DIONYSOS: He's here, where I stand. You, being crass
    And proud, see nothing.
PENTHEUS: You're raving.
    (To GUARDS*)* He insults me!
700   He insults you all!
DIONYSOS: I am sane. You
    Are not. I say to you, set me free.
PENTHEUS: And I say you go to prison, because
    I am master here, I have the power.
705 DIONYSOS: You don't know what your life is, what
    You are doing, who you are . . .
PENTHEUS: I am Pentheus,
    Son of Echion and Agave.
DIONYSOS: Pentheus;
710   A very convenient name for a doomed man.
PENTHEUS: Go away, go on! Go!
    (To GUARDS*)* Lock him up somewhere near—in
      the stables.
    Leave him to stare at the darkness,
    Darkness all the time.
715   *(To* DIONYSOS*)* Dance in there!
    And these creatures you have brought here, these
    Accessories,
    We'll either sell them, or we'll give their hands
      work
    To do—not this banging, thumping on pieces of
      skin,
720   But *work*. Spinning. Weaving. They'll belong to us.
DIONYSOS: I leave you now. But I shall not suffer
    What I have no need to suffer. Dionysos
    Will punish you for your gross contempt. You
    Say he does not exist. But when you send
725   Me to prison
    It is you
    Who commit the crime . . .
    Against him.

(The GUARDS *lead* DIONYSOS *away.)*

CHORUS: Gently flowing Dirce,
730   Life-stream to these fields,
    Innocent waters,
    Banks that were a cradle for the newborn Dionysos
    The day his father saved him from the blazing
      thunderbolt,
    The day Zeus shouted:
735   "Welcome, my son, welcome to the world!

My man's loins shall be your womb.
You'll have a name, and Thebes will know you by it
Because I will open their eyes."
    But now this same river they all live by here,
She doesn't want us.   740
"Don't come near," she cries,
"No ivy crowns on my banks,
No gatherings, no dancing near me!"
    Why?
Why turn away from us?   745
Why say no to us?
Some day you will long for . . . ache for . . .
  . . . *dry* . . .
Ask for . . . *parched* . . .
Wine.   750
You'll thirst! Yes, some day,
You'll thirst for Dionysos.
    Never seen such fury like the fury staring out of
Pentheus.
That's not a man. It's a beast run wild.   755
He's one of the crop, the dragon-toothed flowers.
Who gnashed the soil to get spawned in the
      world—
A snarling freak,
A monster,
A fiend, murderous to the bone.   760
He means to shut me away,
Rope me in darkness,
But I'm not his. I belong to Dionysos.
Already, in there, in a dungeon, a sightless pit,
He buries our leader . . .   765
Dionysos . . . can you see this?
We can't move,
We can't breathe,
The only ones who speak for you, crushed.
Down . . .   770
. . . With a tree in one hand . . .
Down . . .
. . . like a tower of gold
Down from Olympos . . .
DIONYSOS!   775
And tame him.
Dionysos—we are calling you
Wherever you are,
Come . . .
Come from the mountain forests,   780
Glide from the wild beasts' lairs,
Spring from a cruel snow peak,
Leap from a whirlwind dance,
Grow from a thousand branches,
Rise from a sleeping valley,   785
Descend from Olympos,
Tree-leaved and silent,
Fly on the air,
In the grass that Orpheus tamed,
Over animals silenced by his music   790
Nearer and nearer—

The drumming of feet heralds you—
Dance out of mountain torrents,
Swing over eastern rivers,
795 Surge over waves towards us,
Driving a storm of souls,
Now he's coming, he's coming into Greece!
   He's over the land now,
In the green plains alive with horses,
800 In the streams that water the fields,
He's coming.
     YES! YES!
DIONYSOS! DIONYSOS! DIONYSOS!

(As the CHORUS *ends, the voice of* DIONYSOS *comes from offstage all round.)*

DIONYSOS *(stereo)*: Aaaaaouooooooowah! Hark!
805   I got life!
I have a voice!
Hark! Aaaaoooouwah! Take me!
Aaaooouwah! Take me!
CHORUS: Has it come? . . . Hear it? . . . Feel it? . . .
810   The call! The call! . . . Where? . . . Is it here?
DIONYSOS *(stereo)*: Yes! Coming to life . . . Yes!
Coming
To life . . . Aaaooowah! . . . Born in the ground,
   born in
The sky . . . !
CHORUS: Master! Master!
Come close, come close. Come into us . . . In . . .
815   *In . . .*
NOW . . . Closer, *closer* . . .
DIONYSOS *(stereo)*: The earth—SHAKE.
The earth's floor—MOVE.
Move, nothing stand still, *move!*
CHORUS: Look, the palace of Pentheus bulges,
820   quivers . . . It will
Fall, fall . . . It's got into the palace . . . It's in,
It's *in!* . . . See, pillars melt, marble streams,
Trembles . . . It's inside now, it's taken, it's taken.
DIONYSOS *(stereo)*: Touch off the fire, flames and
   thunder!
825 Burn, burn, house of Pentheus.

(During the following speech of CHORUS, *darkness, thunder, flames, roar of collapsing masonry, triumph noise of* DIONYSOS.*)*

CHORUS: Fire! Watch the fever-fire dance round the
   grave
Of Semele, charred earth no one walks on, the
   lightning
Left a living flame there . . .
Down, down! Everyone down to the ground . . .
830 Dionysos is . . .
   . . . don't move . . .
In possession of . . .
   . . . don't look . . .

The palace
. . . don't breathe!   835
DIONYSOS: Afraid, my friends? After all our journeys
Together . . . ? Look at you, hugging the earth,
Terrorstruck . . . Yes, you saw the house
Of Pentheus split and sundered by the presence
Of Dionysos. But now . . . look up at me,   840
You're safe . . . don't flinch . . . All is well . . .
CHORUS: You're dawn for us, our life-light, and calm
   rose
In the depths of the mind . . . The sight of you is
   comfort . . .
We'd lost you, we were alone.
DIONYSOS: So you surrendered, gave in to despair.
When I was taken   845
In there you thought I would be buried in the
   death
Cells of Pentheus' darkness?
CHORUS: Yes, yes.
Who was to protect us if you were harmed?
But now you're free.   850
DIONYSOS: As always . . .
CHORUS: And safe . . .
DIONYSOS: I saved myself.
CHORUS: How? The man was in a killing mood . . .
DIONYSOS: Easy. I had no trouble with him.   855
CHORUS: But you couldn't move. He lashed your
   hands
Together.
DIONYSOS: He thought he did, but he never touched
them, never came near me. He thought he had
me, but he breakfasted on lies this morning and I   860
laughed—because I had him . . . He took me to
the stables to be locked up, and found a bull
there. This bull he loaded with chains—on its
knees, on its hooves—gasping with rage, streaming sweat all over his body, chewing his lips . . . I   865
waited close beside him, did nothing, said nothing, just sat there and watched. Meanwhile the
palace quivered. Dionysos had come, and fire
spurted from Semele's grave . . . When Pentheus
saw it he decided his house was on fire. He   870
rushed from end to end of the palace, screaming
at his servants to pump water, more water, on
the flames, till every slave was working—over
nothing. The fire existed only in his mind. All at
once he left it—snatched up a long steel sword   875
and hurled himself indoors—his prisoner, me,
had escaped. Then Dionysos—or so I think,
because I only tell you what I think—created a
phantom figure. Because Pentheus charged at
something in the courtyard, stabbing and lung-   880
ing as if it was me on the end of his blade. But
there was nothing there, only clear bright air.
More havoc followed. Dionysos shattered the
palace. Inside now is nothing but a heap of

885 rubble. My spell in prison was hard on Pentheus.
Finally, spent and limp, he threw away his sword
. . . Well, he is a man, and he fought a god. He
expected too much . . . Quietly I left his house,
and came back here to you. Pentheus never
890 troubled me . . . Listen. I hear footsteps. This
will be him . . . Watch that door. He'll come out
and say . . . but what can he say now? Let him
explode—I'll manage him easily anyhow. The
secret of life is balance, tolerance . . .

(Enter PENTHEUS.*)*

PENTHEUS: I've been cheated! I had that foreigner. I
895 had him
So trussed up he couldn't move—and still
He got away!

(Sees DIONYSOS *and gives a shout.)*

There he is! That's the man. Look,
He stands there, on the doorstep of my palace,
900 Out in the open . . .
Look at him!
DIONYSOS: Stay where you are!
Calm yourself . . .
Anger's going . . . going . . .
905 Now . . .
PENTHEUS: How did you get out? You were locked in,
chained . . .
DIONYSOS: Didn't I tell you—or didn't you hear?—
someone
Would free me?
PENTHEUS: Free you? Who? You always produce
910 A new riddle.
DIONYSOS: The grape-gardener, the wine-grower
To mankind.
PENTHEUS: The planter of all drunkenness
And disorder.
915 DIONYSOS: Insults from you would make him proud.
PENTHEUS *(to* GUARD*)*: Surround the palace. Close
every gate in the city.
Shut him in!
DIONYSOS: Come, come, if such powers
Exist, surely they move on a higher plane
920 Than your city walls.
PENTHEUS: So clever, so
Clever. All that cleverness misused!
DIONYSOS: I use it where I need it most . . . Look,
Someone is coming with a message for you. Listen
925 To him first . . . Of course we'll wait for you—
We are in no hurry to go . . . You
Hear what he has to say. He comes from the
mountains.

(Enter HERDSMAN.*)*

HERDSMAN: Pentheus, I am one of your subjects here

In Thebes. I come from Kithairon. There's still
snow
There, it dazzles you, the hills are all white . . .   930
PENTHEUS: And what is your news? How urgent is it?
HERDSMAN: I have seen
The Bacchae . . . those women, strange women,
they fling
Their white limbs like a storm of javelins across
The fields. I came to tell you and everyone here . . .   935
I want you to know, master, what marvellous things
They do . . . beyond anything you could imagine.
But first I would like your word that I can speak
Freely about what happened there. Or must I
Trim the facts a little . . . ? It's your temper, you
see,   940
Master, your very quick temper, which rules us
All so harshly . . . too harshly.
PENTHEUS: Tell me, I give my word, nothing will
happen
To you. Do your duty, and no one will be angry.
The worse you make the Bacchae sound, the more   945
Firmly shall I crush their ringmaster, as he
deserves.
HERDSMAN: Our herds of cattle are topping the rise
of the hills,
Grazing as they go, and the sun's rays are just
Beginning to warm the grass, when I see three
Circles of women—the dancers!   950
One of them is round Autonoë,
The second with Agave, your mother,
And the third is with Ino.
They are all asleep, lying every way,
Some propped against pine-tree trunks,   955
Others curled up modestly on a pile
Of oak leaves, pillowed on the earth—
None of the drunkenness you talked about,
None of the obscene abandon, or the wild
Music—no love among the bushes.   960
All at once, your mother stands up. She cries out
And wakes the rest of the women, says she can hear
The lowing of cattle. They shake the sleep petals
From their eyes, and all stand upright,
A marvel of calm and order . . . Young girls,   965
Old women, maidens who have never slept
With a man. First, they let their hair tumble
Down their shoulders. Then, the ones whose
fawn-skins
Have come loose from the brooches pinning them,
fasten them
Back on their shoulders, and belt the spotted hides   970
With snakes—
And those snakes were live—I saw their tongues
Flicker . . .
One of them might carry a fawn, cradled
In her arms, or a wild wolf cub, and give it her own   975
Milk—

You see, some had left newborn babies at home
And so their breasts were full . . .
They all weave strands of ivy, oak leaves,
980 Tendrils of flowering bryony in their hair.
Then one of them winds ivy on a branch,
Taps a rock, and out of that rock spouts
Water—running water! Fresh as dew!
Another drops her wand, a little twig,
985 On to the earth, and where she drops it some
force
Sends up a spring—a wine-spring! Some
Feel they'd like to drink fresh milk.
They scrape the tips of their fingers on the earth
And they have milk—fountains of milk! From all
990 Their ivy-covered branches sweet honey
Drips, cascades down . . . Oh, if you
Had been there and seen all this, you would have
been
On your knees, praying—not criticising—but
praying
For help and guidance.
995 All we herdsmen and shepherds hold
A meeting, we begin to talk, we compare
Stories—
Because these were fantastic things the women
were doing,
We could hardly believe our eyes . . .
1000 Someone who knows his way in the city, knows
How they make speeches there, he stands up
And makes one himself:
"You inhabitants of the majestic mountain acres,
allow me to propose to you that we hunt down
1005 Agave, mother of Pentheus, from the midst of
her Dionysiac festivities, and thereby do our
royal master in Thebes . . . a great good turn
. . ."
Applause!
We decide to lay an ambush for the women
1010 In the undergrowth,
We hide in the leaves,
We wait.
The hour for their rites approaches . . .
The sticks with ivy begin to beat out a rhythm.
1015 It gets in your blood, that rhythm.
"Iacchos!" they howl in unison,
"Bromios!"
"Son of Zeus!"
The whole mountain sways to that one beat,
beat, beat:
1020 The wild beasts join in,
Everything moves,
Everything's running, running. Agave is racing
towards me, she's coming near, nearer, almost
touches me, I leap out—I wanted to catch
1025 her, you see—I jump from my safe hiding place
and—
She gives a screech:

"Look, my swift hounds, we are being hunted
By these men. Follow me!
Follow me! 1030
Branches—get branches and arm yourselves!"
We turn and run—
If we hadn't we would have been torn to shreds
By the Bacchae . . .
As it is, they descend on our heifers grazing 1035
In the long grass. They have nothing in their
hands,
Those women—nothing metal. But imagine you
see
One of them, just with her hands, tearing a young
Well-grown heifer in two, while it screams . . .
Others have found full-grown cows and are
wrenching them 1040
Limb from limb. Ribs, hooves, toss
Up in the air, drop to the ground. Parts
Of our animals hang from the branches of pine
trees,
Dripping there, blood spattering the leaves.
Bulls with surging horns, invincible 1045
Till now, are tripped, sprawl full length
On the ground, while a mob of hands, girls'
Hands, rip them apart. Faster than you can
Blink your royal eyes the flesh is peeled
Off their bones. 1050
Then down, like flocks of birds, so fast
Their feet never touch the ground, they sweep to
the Valley
Sleeping between the hills. Here, on the banks
Of the Asopos, the grain grows deep in the
farmlands,
Little towns, Hysiai, Erythrai, snuggle 1055
Beneath the slopes of Kithairon . . .
Like an invading army those women mill
Through the valley, they tear it apart, chaos!
Children
Snatched from their beds . . . Anything they can
pick up,
And carry on their backs, stays there—nothing 1060
Holds it on, but it never slips to the ground,
Even the bronze, the iron—they put live coals
In their hair—and nothing burns them!
The people are furious, being plundered by these
women,
And rush to defend themselves. Then what
happens? 1065
—It was a terrible sight to see, master . . .
No spear, no weapon, nothing so much as
scratches
The Bacchae. But one of those wooden sticks they
carry
Draws blood at once. They throw them—and men
run
For their lives—that isn't human, there's some
other power 1070

At work . . . At last, they go, back to the mountains
Where they came from, back to the springs of
    water
Which Dionysos sent them. They wash away
The blood . . . and the snakes lick off the dirt and
    gore
1075   From the womens' cheeks with their tongues . . .
    This power, master, whoever he is, whatever
He is . . . let him into Thebes! He
Is great. And one thing above all they say
He has done, I've heard that he gave mankind
The grape . . . And the grape is the best grave—for
1080   grief.
If there were no wine
There would be no love,
There would be no joy in life.
CHORUS: In this king's company, honesty is a
    dangerous pastime
1085   Yet I must speak . . .
    . . . Say it, say it . . . !
Of all the powers in life the greatest is Dionysos.
PENTHEUS: Now, I see . . . yes! Nearer . . . nearer!
This insufferable craze is like a fire, and it's
    spreading!
1090   All Greece despises us. But we must
Be firm, not give way . . .
    (*To* GUARDS) Go to the gates of Electra, get every
    man
Under arms. I want all the cavalry, every
Spearman, every bowman, mobilised.
1095   We attack the Bacchae at once . . .
I have been too patient. But my patience
Is finished, we are being governed by a pack of
    women.
DIONYSOS: I told you, Pentheus, but you never listen.
You have not been good to me. All the same
I am going to warn you. You must not use force
1100   against
Dionysos.
End the war in yourself. He will not
Allow you to disturb his Bacchae. Leave them
In the mountains where they are happy.
1105   PENTHEUS: Don't preach
To me. You were in prison and you escaped.
Well, look after your freedom or I may remind
Myself that you have been judged and condemned.
DIONYSOS: I
1110   Would sacrifice to him . . . not rage and struggle
And kick. This is an eternal power—
You are a man.
PENTHEUS: *I'll* sacrifice to him!
A blood sacrifice, a woman sacrifice—
1115   That is all they are fit for. I will be lavish—
There will be carnage in the glades of Kithairon.
DIONYSOS: You'll lose. It will be an ignominious rout.
Your bronze shields won't hold off wooden sticks
And women's hands.

PENTHEUS: Will someone tell me how   1120
To get rid of this man? Extricate me, someone!
Whatever I do to him, whatever he does
To me, it's the same. Talk, talk, talk!
DIONYSOS: Excuse me—but you can settle all this,
No trouble . . . It is still possible.   1125
PENTHEUS: How? What
Do I do? Make myself lower than the lowest
In this country?
DIONYSOS: I will bring the women
Here, without the use of force.   1130
PENTHEUS: Yes,
I see, thank you. This is the great master
Plan—the great deception.
DIONYSOS: How can you call it
That? I want to keep you whole. I work   1135
For nothing else.
PENTHEUS: You arranged this with your friends.
Licence to dance, disorder in perpetuity.
DIONYSOS: Certainly I arranged it, quite true—
With Dionysos   1140
PENTHEUS (*to* GUARDS): Bring out my armour . . . (*To*
    DIONYSOS) You—
Keep quiet!
DIONYSOS (*to* GUARDS): Wait! (*To* PENTHEUS) Do you
    want to see them . . .
In their nests up there in the hills. See   1145
The women . . . ?
PENTHEUS: Yes, yes, I do. Yes,
I'll pay if I have to. Gold. How much? A thousand?
Ten thousand?
DIONYSOS: You've fallen in love with my idea.   1150
You can't wait. Why?
PENTHEUS: I'll see them drunk,
Hopelessly drunk. It revolts me, but . . . I . . .
DIONYSOS: But you really want to. That disgusting
    sight
Lures you there . . . ?   1155
PENTHEUS: Yes, I told you, it does.
I won't say anything, I'll be quiet, I'll stay
Among the pine trees.
DIONYSOS: You can try to hide
But they'll pick up your scent.   1160
PENTHEUS: Good point. I'd forgotten.
I'll go openly.
DIONYSOS: I'll take you there. Would you like that?
The way is before you. Will you dare?
PENTHEUS: Now!   1165
Take me there now. I hate every minute
We lose.
DIONYSOS: Then you must be covered. Find a linen
Dress to wear . . .
PENTHEUS: Wait, now what is   1170
This? I'm a man, I don't change places
With any woman. Why should 1?
DIONYSOS: In case
They kill you. Suppose you, a *man,* are discovered

1175 There—you die.
PENTHEUS: Right again. I understand.
There is some intelligence in you. I should have
    seen it
Before.
DIONYSOS: Dionysos came alive in me.
1180 All I know is him.
PENTHEUS: Yes, yes . . .
Now, this good advice of yours, how
Do we carry it out?
DIONYSOS: We go inside, and there
1185 I prepare you for your journey.
PENTHEUS: How—prepare me?
Dress me up as a woman? Oh no, no,
I would be ashamed.
DIONYSOS: Have you lost heart? The sight
Of those possessed and demented women, it no
1190   longer
Interests you?
PENTHEUS: What kind of clothing did you say
I have to wear?
DIONYSOS: Long hair to your shoulders.
1195 You must have a wig . . .
PENTHEUS: And then what else? Is there more
To this costume?
DIONYSOS: A full length robe.
And for the head—a scarf.
1200 PENTHEUS: Anything else
You want to drape me in?
DIONYSOS: We'll give you a stick
Covered with ivy to hold, and wrap a spotted
Fawn-skin round you . . .
1205 PENTHEUS: No, I could never put on
Woman's clothing.
DIONYSOS: What will you do—fight them?
It's a waste of your blood.
PENTHEUS: You're right. First we must go
1210 And watch. Nothing more yet.
DIONYSOS: That
Makes better sense than hunting down evil
With more evil.
PENTHEUS: How can I get through the streets
1215 Of Thebes and not be seen?
DIONYSOS: We'll find a secret
Way. I'll lead you.
PENTHEUS: Anything—but I will not
Be entertainment for that herd of females. Let's go
1220 Inside. I want to consider this plan.
DIONYSOS: Decide,
I'm ready for you. Nothing will be too much
    trouble . . .
PENTHEUS: No, inside . . . I may call out my army
And march up there . . . Or I may follow
1225 Your advice. We shall see.

(Exit.)

DIONYSOS (to CHORUS): Friends, the man stands in
    the gate of the trap.
He'll find the Bacchae and he'll answer to them
    with his life.
Dionysos, now your work begins.
You are not too far away, I hope. Let us
Reward this man for his attentions. First, 1230
Dislodge his thoughts, make his reason slither.
If he were sane, he would not agree to put on
Woman's clothing. But when he edges out
Of his mind then, yes, then he'll wear it.
I want him to raise a howl of derision all 1235
Through Thebes when he minces along the streets
In skirts. Once he mouthed fearsome threats,
And now . . .
Now to Pentheus, to disguise him, dress him for
His journey into death. His mother's hands 1240
Will caress him roughly to his grave, and he'll see
Dionysos face to face, know that power,
Know its nature, its ferocious gentle nature
Alive in man, an undeniable *god!*

(Exit.)

CHORUS: Night—will it ever come? 1245
And my flying feet,
Flash of white thighs in the hills,
Head flung back,
And the dew-soaked air kissing my throat—
    And running, running— 1250
Oh, when will it come?
    I want to be free and play and be happy again
Like a young deer, swathed in an emerald meadow,
When he runs in stark terror of the hunt,
And the knotted nets close in— 1255
Then he leaps up and over them,
While the hunter shrieks to his hounds to keep
    racing,
Pacing behind.
But the deer strains his flashing legs taut.
He skims and spurts across open stretches 1260
Where the river winds
Till he comes to a wood,
And the deep shade lulls him,
The green branches soothe him,
And he rests where no man is. 1265
    What does it mean to live a life?
Can you hope for better than to rise above all
    warring,
Control what threatens you,
Defeat what oppresses you?
To be strong— 1270
No, nothing is better.
I choose that.
There are forces not ruled by us,
And we obey them.
Trust them—though they travel inch by inch, 1275

They arrive.
Self-swollen and calloused,
Soul, tumoured and hard,
All the malignant growths of thought,
1280 They level, and pare, and crop,
They move in the dark with a subtle glitter
So that no one times their work,
But always the hunt goes on—
For the man who has turned his back on them.
1285 Their rules cannot be overruled—
It is your peril, and your death that follows.
But if you grant their power—what does it cost?
Nothing.
Not even a word—because
1290 These forces lack a name.
Call them whatever you like—
Spirits—
Gods—
Principles—
1295 Elements—
Currents—
Laws—
Anything, anything you like.
But they are born in your blood
1300 They have been observed and preserved since
       before time.
       What does it mean to live a life?
Can you hope for better than to rise above all
       warring,
Control what threatens you,
Defeat what oppresses you?
1305 To be strong—
No, nothing is better
I choose that.
Life is a stormy sea,
Happiness is a harbour.
1310 Finding your harbour is your life-work.
He is truly happy who succeeds in that life-work.
Some end rich, some poor,
Some are strong, some achieve nothing.
There are ten thousand hopes, ten thousand
       dreams,
1315 They may all come true—they may all vanish,
But happiness—
A man finds happiness when he lies every day
With those forces of the world on his side.
All hail to that man!

(Enter DIONYSOS.*)*

DIONYSOS *(into palace)*: You! You with a white-hot
1320   wish for a peep
At the forbidden. You, reaching out for the
       out-of-reach,
You—I'm talking to *you*—Pentheus! Come
Out here, in front of your palace, let me
See you, dressed a woman of the wild wine

Nights of Dionysos. Are you ready to spy?   1325
Your mother is there . . .
All the women are there . . .

(Enter PENTHEUS.*)*

Perfect! You are a daughter of Kadmos to the life.
PENTHEUS: No, listen. I think I see two suns,
And two Thebes. The seven-gated city   1330
Has doubled . . . and you, you look
Like a bull, leading me—horns sprout from your
       head . . .
All the time, were you that beast?
Are you the bull now . . . ?
DIONYSOS: Dionysos favours you. He is bound to us 1335
For the wine-gifts we gave him. Before he was not
Pleased. But now he is. And you see
What you ought to see.
PENTHEUS: How do I look to you?
My aunt . . . isn't this how she walks? . . . Or this . . .
       My mother   1340
Agave,—isn't it? Isn't it Agave?
DIONYSOS: It's them! When I look at you it's them I
       see . . .
Wait—a wisp of hair has come away.
It isn't lying where I set it, under the scarf.
PENTHEUS: Inside, I went this way with my head, 1345
That way—back, forward, back—I was being
A woman in a trance. And I made the hair
Come loose . . .
DIONYSOS: We must keep you groomed. I'll put it in
       place
Again. Here . . . lift your head up straight.   1350
PENTHEUS: Look . . . there . . . you do it. Make me
       pretty.
I am yours to play with. Take me.
DIONYSOS: Your sash is loose—
Look. And your dress is wrong. The pleats should
       hang
The same length round your ankles.   1355
PENTHEUS: Yes,
I see . . . a little too long by the right foot.
But on this side it seems all right, touching
My heel just there . . .
DIONYSOS: Who is your best friend?   1360
I am . . . You don't believe me? Wait till you see
Bacchae, how modest they are, how pure, how
       sane—
Astonishing.
PENTHEUS: This branch with ivy—in my right
Hand—or my left? Which makes me   1365
More like a genuine wild woman of the hills?
DIONYSOS: Hold it in your right hand, and raise it
In time with your right foot . . . Very good.
I see a change, a new mind, in you . . .
PENTHEUS: Now I could . . . I could hoist the whole
       of Kithairon   1370

On my shoulder—valleys full of women
Dancing, madness and all! . . . Yes?
DIONYSOS: Of course,
If you will it. Your mood was before most
unhealthy,
1375 Now it is all it should be.
PENTHEUS: Shall we bring iron bars, or shall I delve it
Up with my own bare hands, wedge
One shoulder or one arm under the hill-top . . . ?
DIONYSOS: And destroy the homes of the nymphs?
No, no.
1380 Pan lives there too. Let him go on playing
His pipes.
PENTHEUS: You're right. One should not coerce
women.
I shall hide myself in the boughs of a pine tree.
DIONYSOS: You find
1385 The hiding place that suits you best. You're a spy,
A secret witness of secret rites.
PENTHEUS: Yes,
Imagine, they are nestling like birds in the thick
leaves,
Locked in their lust, enjoying it . . .
1390 DIONYSOS: You must break in
And prevent them. Perhaps you will find them in
the act . . .
Unless they find you first.
PENTHEUS: Take me through Thebes,
Right through the centre. I am the only man
1395 Here who has any courage.
DIONYSOS: Yes, you alone
Make sacrifices for your people, you alone.
And so—the test. It has always been there, waiting
For you. Follow me. I am your
1400 Protector, your escort . . . as far as Kithairon—
Someone else will bring you back.
PENTHEUS: Yes, my mother . . .
DIONYSOS: In full view of everyone . . .
PENTHEUS: That's why I'm going . . .
1405 DIONYSOS: You will be borne back on high.
PENTHEUS: Yes, in triumph, you mean my great
triumph!
DIONYSOS: In the hands of your mother . . .
PENTHEUS: You'll spoil me—all this pampering!
DIONYSOS: Yes, I'll spoil you, I'll spoil you utterly.
1410 PENTHEUS: Still, I deserve it, and I shall have it!

(Exit.)

DIONYSOS: Headstrong, headstrong—you go walking
To your headlong end—which will make you
Famous, far beyond this life, beyond
This time.
1415 Agave, fling open your arms.
Prepare, you sisters, daughters of Kadmos.
I bring this young man to you—
Prepare for a great contest.

The victor shall be myself—and Dionysos.
As for the rest—wait, watch, and listen.   1420

(Exit)

CHORUS: Go, track to the mountains
Dogs of madness,
Run, dogs, run,
Find the daughters of Kadmos,
Snap at their dancing heels, sink your fangs in
their brains,   1425
Then turn them loose on the would-be woman,
The spy in the flapping skirts,
Who goes mad for the secret of the possessed.
His mother will see him first,
As he peers from a rock-wall or cliff-steeple.   1430
She'll scream to the women:
"Look! See what creeps sniffing up to our
mountain,
Our mountain, my friends—
This creature crawling across the hillside!
What mothered such a thing?   1435
Not a woman, no—it got life from a lioness
Or a beast heaved up out of African sands."
Now we shall see balance restored.
We shall see it, sharp, clear, a sword
With blood on its edge, driving deep   1440
To the gullet of Pentheus, the blossom of the
dragon's jawbone,
Who enforces his will on the forces of life,
Outlaws law,
Orders all other order out of existence.
And now—   1445
With insane and petty determination,
With intent sick passion,
All his thought corrupted,
All his mind a sewer,
He smells his way to the living heart   1450
Of the mysteries, where Dionysos is born and
re-born.
He wants to master with violence that forever-free
spirit.
The laws of all life admit no excuses,
Live by them, live as a man—
That is the way of no pain.   1455
I don't grudge man his search for knowledge,
I acclaim it, applaud it,
But there is more, there are great things
That must be brought to the daylight,
Made part of our waking and sleeping.   1460
Calmly accept them, peacefully weave them
Into your life—and it will be a good life,
Freeing you.
Now we shall see balance restored,
We shall see it, sharp, clear, a sword   1465
With blood on its edge, driving deep

To the gullet of Pentheus, the blossom of the
    dragon's jawbone,
Who enforces his will on the forces of life,
Outlaws law,
1470 Orders all other order out of existence.
    Now Dionysos, into the open!
Let him see you . . .
As a BULL!
A dragon with swarming heads!
1475 A lion, vomiting flames!
Come, Dionysos, come sweetly smiling
And string your noose round the throat of this
    hunter.
Bring the one-minded women in a pack
To trip him,
1480 Smother him,
Kill him!

(*Enter* PENTHEUS' *own* SERVANT.)

SERVANT: In this house lived people who were the
    envy
Of all Greece . . . once. A family begun
In dragon's teeth, a summer harvest reaped
1485 By Kadmos, the great traveller and merchant
Of the western seas. And I am nothing,
An obscure someone who takes orders. And yet
I pity *them.*
CHORUS: What is it? Have you news? Have you been
1490   in the hills?
SERVANT: Pentheus is dead, King Pentheus, son of
    Echion, is dead.
CHORUS: Victory! The first day of Dionysos—now
    they see you, now you live, now you face
1495   them . . .
SERVANT: What do you mean? How can you say that?
    My master is dead. Are you glad? He is dead, *dead!*
CHORUS: Not my master. I've another home. I've
    another
1500 Life . . . No more fear, no more prison, no more
    terror . . .
Free, free!
SERVANT: There are still men in Thebes who can . . .
CHORUS: Thebes can't touch me, Thebes has no
1505   power . . . Dionysos, Dionysos comes first for me.
SERVANT: I can forgive the rest, but not this. Terrible
    things have happened, and you gloat. It's ugly.
CHORUS: Terrible things? Describe them, tell us,
    how did the man die, the wrong-headed master-
1510   fool . . .
SERVANT: Behind us were the last houses of Thebes—
We had come out at the river Asopos. Then
We began to climb, mounting the slopes of
    Kithairon,
Pentheus and I—he was my master, so
1515 I followed him—and this stranger, who
Was to be the guide of our expedition.

Treading very softly, and never speaking,
So that we could see without being seen, we came
First to a glade thick with grass and rested
There . . . It was in a little valley, overhung 1520
On each side with cliffs, and fed by rills
Of water. Pine trees leant over to shade it,
And somewhere in this valley were the women,
The mad women, the Bacchae.
    Then we saw them. 1525
    They're sitting, quietly working and happy.
    Some
Are re-winding the ivy that slipped off
The tips of their branches. Others, like young
    mares
Unharnessed from their painted chariots, are
    playing.
They sing—the tunes sound strange to me, but
    they 1530
Pick them up and echo each other.
    Though they are everywhere, poor Pentheus sees
    nothing,
Not one woman. "Stranger," he says, "from where
I stand I can't get a sight of these whores
Who call themselves Bacchae. Perhaps if I went 1535
Up that slope and climbed the trunk of a pine tree
I could have a direct view of their filthy games."
And then—a miracle. There is a pine-tree there
That tickles heaven. As I watch, the stranger
Takes the topmost branch and . . . 1340
Down . . . down . . . down he draws it towards us
Out of the sunlight, into the deep shade
Where we stand. It bends like a bow—or like
A wheel, when its rim is marked out with a compass
    and traces
A full circle—that's how the stranger, with his bare 1545
Hands, made the mountain pine curve to the
    ground—
Something no man born of woman
Could have done.
He seats Pentheus on the topmost shoots, then
    gently
Lets the trunk uncoil, from his grip, being 1550
Very careful not to shake our king from his new
    throne
Among the leaves, till it towers straight in the air
Again with Pentheus perched astride it . . . Now
It is he who is in view, rather than having
A view himself . . . He is just rising into sight 1555
Above the surrounding trees, when the stranger
    vanishes,
And out of the air a voice comes—
My belief is—Dionysos spoke then.
"Young women, I bring you this man who intends
To amuse himself with me and my deepest
    mysteries. 1560
Punish him!"

While these words still echo in the hills
A pillar of fierce fire is planted between
Earth and heaven . . .
1565   The air is still now . . .
Silence.
In the cloistered trees not a leaf moves,
The noises of animals cease . . .
The women, not sure what it is they've heard, stand
1570 On tiptoe, glancing this way and that. So,
Once again, he brands the air with his voice.
This time there is no doubt. The daughters
Of Kadmos know their master, and obey.
They begin to run—they dart, they flash, like
        pigeons
1575 In flight, his mother, Agave, all her sisters,
And the rest of the women, Bacchae! Down
        through the glade,
Across the stream,
Over the rocks,
Whirled in the tempest of Dionysos' power
1580 They rush—then they see my master sitting
On the pine tree. First they clamber onto
A rock face opposite and try pelting him
With volleys of sharp stones and javelins made
From pine branches, while others fling
1585 Their ivy-covered sticks . . . Poor man,
He can only be a target . . . But they can't reach him.
Their victim is sitting too high, even for their
Terrible urgency. All the same,
He's trapped. There's nothing he can do. At last
1590 They snap off great oak boughs—a thunderbolt
Could not do it more cleanly, and using the raw
Wood as levers they try to wrench the tree
Up by its roots—and still they can't do it.
They struggle but they can't . . . they can't . . .
1595 "Here," says Agave, "make a circle and take
Hold of the stem, my friends, and we'll catch this
        agile
Beast. He must never betray the secret of our
        dancing
For Dionysos!"
        A flurry of hands reach out to the pine tree and
        tug.
1600 It comes clean out of the earth.
Down from the height where he sits, falling,
        falling,
Screaming all the time till he dashes against
The rocks, comes Pentheus.
He knows his end is near, knows it will
1605 Be hideous . . .
        His mother is first, chief priestess of the
        slaughter,
She descends on him. He rips off
The scarf around his head, hoping she'll recognize
        him,
And spare him, he touches her cheeks, he says,
        "Mother,

It's your son, Pentheus, the son   1610
You bore in the house of Echion. Mother, pity me,
Have mercy, I have sinned, but don't murder me,
Your own son for what I've . . ."
        But she can't help herself. There's froth on her
        lips,
Her eyes are rolling, staring, her mind's gone,   1615
She's been seized by a greater power, Dionysos,
And doesn't listen to her son. She grips
His left arm, just below the elbow,
Rams her foot against the poor man's ribs,
And pulls. His arm comes away at the shoulder . . .   1620
That strength didn't come from her—it came
From Dionysos.
        Meanwhile, Ino is gouging the other side,
Rending the flesh from his bones, while Autonoë
And the whole crowd of the Bacchae press down   1625
On him. His shrieking—so long as there's breath
In his lungs—and their howls of triumph merge
Into one great din. One woman carries
An arm, another, one of his feet, with a sandal
Still on it. His ribs are stripped of skin, the flesh   1630
Hangs in rags. They play with it, they toss
Pieces of Pentheus from hand to bloodstained
        hand
Like a ball, until the mountain is strewn with
        fragments
Of his body—some of it under the sheer
Rock-faces, some under the green   1635
Leaves in the depths of the wood. I don't know
How you could find it all again . . .
        His mother was left holding his destroyed head.
She impaled it on a wooden spike, as if
It was some mountain lion she had caught in the
        heart   1640
Of Kithairon, and left her sisters amongst the
        still-dancing
Women. Now, she's running this way, to the city,
Exulting in her terrible kill. She's praising
Dionysos as her fellow huntsman, the one
Who helps her in the chase, the bringer of bright   1645
Victory . . . But she'll thank him with her tears.
        I want to go. I hate suffering. I don't
Want to see Agave come home. The best
And safest thing is to keep a balance in your life,
And acknowledge the great powers around us and
        in us.   1650
I think that is the meaning of wisdom. If you have
That, and can live that way, you really are
A wise man.

        (Exit.)

CHORUS: Dance him into life!
        Move like one,   1655
        Shout like one!
        The last of the dragon is dead,
        Pentheus is dead.

He took woman's clothing,
1660 Picked up a twig, made it live with ivy,
He trusted it—
And it killed him.
And heading him into death was a bull.
Daughters of Kadmos—Bacchae—now you are
       famous.
1665 The prize—
—and the price—
Of your victory is tears, mourning.
You won the contest at a cost—
Your hands are slippery with your child's
1670 Flowing life.
       (*Looking offstage.*) Look! She's coming . . .
          Agave . . .
       . . . His mother . . .
Running home . . . her eyes, look at her eyes . . .
They're staring, they're mad . . .
Take her into our midst . . . she belongs to the
1675 god . . .
And to his happiness.

(*Enter* AGAVE, *carrying the head of* PENTHEUS.)

AGAVE: Women of the cast—Bacchae . . .
CHORUS: Why do you use that word? What do you
       want?
1680 AGAVE: I'm bringing this branch with trailing leaves, I
       cut it just now in the mountains, and look—I'm
       bringing it back home—I had to hunt—but I
       tracked it down . . . and now I'm happy . . .
CHORUS: I see . . . join us . . . become one of us . . .
1685 AGAVE: It's a lion cub. I caught it. I didn't need nets.
       You can see—look . . .
CHORUS: Where—where did it happen? Where did
       you find it?
AGAVE: Kithairon . . .
1690 CHORUS: Kithairon?
AGAVE: . . . was the killer.
CHORUS: Who struck first?
AGAVE: I struck first. I. I did it, no one else. When we
       meet in the hills, I am the one they envy—I am so
1695 lucky.
CHORUS: And who else?
AGAVE: Kadmos, Kadmos . . .
CHORUS: How, Kadmos . . . ?
AGAVE: Had children . . . those children were there,
1700 Shared the hunt—but I was first, I was first.
       Happy . . . chasing the beast . . . Come with me
       Now . . . to the meal . . .
CHORUS: How can we come . . . What meal?
AGAVE: It's a young bull . . . Here, on his
1705 Cheek, the hair is soft . . .
       Just below the crest . . . It grows . . . so sleek.
CHORUS: Yes, that hair could belong to a beast.
       It looks like an animal.
AGAVE: The hounds were whipped on by
       Dionysos . . .

He sent us hurtling after the prey . . .   1710
He knew its ways, he knows
Us all . . .
CHORUS: Yes, our prince leads the hunt.
AGAVE: You praise him?
CHORUS: I praise him.   1715
AGAVE: Then soon all Thebes will.
CHORUS: Yes . . . and Pentheus? . . . Your son?
AGAVE: Pentheus . . . Yes, he will praise his mother
       because she caught this young wild lion.
CHORUS: But think what it is.   1720
AGAVE: No! Think how I did it.
CHORUS: You're proud?
AGAVE: I'm happy. We did great, great things—as all
       the world will see—when we hunted today.
CHORUS: Then show your trophy, poor woman, show   1725
       it to everyone.
       Let people see what you brought home from the
       day's hunting.
AGAVE: Men and women of Thebes, our city of high
       Towers, so well defended, come and see
       What I brought home from the wild country for
       you.—
          A beast . . . We tracked him down, we daughters
          of Kadmos.   1730
       We used no snares, no traps,
       No spears forged in the workshops of Thessaly—
       Only our hands we used, our soft, white,
       Delicate hands—they were our spears.
       And hunters boast of their machines, their useless   1735
       Contraptions of steel and wire . . . we caught this
       beast
       And tore it limb from limb with only our hands . . .
       Where is my father? I want him here. And where
       Is Pentheus, where's my son? . . .
          Go, someone, find a ladder, and lean it   1740
       Against the palace and nail this trophy against
       The beam ends. I want everyone to see
       What I have brought home from the hunt . . .

(*Enter* KADMOS, *helping* SERVANTS *to carry the body of*
PENTHEUS.)

KADMOS: This way . . . Stay close to me . . . This
       way . . .
He seems so heavy . . . like my grief—now,   1745
Lay him down—there . . .
       Pentheus has come home.
       I searched, hoping and looking, hoping and
          looking—
It was so hard to see them, scattered among the
       trees—
No two parts together, all over Kithairon . . .   1750
Those steep paths!—I have no strength left . . .
Well, here is his body, I found it.
       I had just reached the city with Teiresias
After paying our tribute to Dionysos when

1755 I heard of the monstrous thing my daughters had
done.
Back I went, back, back to the mountainside
To bring home my grandson—or what remained
After the women . . . What was in their minds
then? . . .
1760 I saw Akteon's mother in the forest,
Autonoë, and Ino with her—it was hideous . . .
Their contorted bodies, writhing, jerking . . .
Then someone told me the same driving force
Had guided Agave here . . . Yes, they were
right . . .
There she is . . . I see . . .
1765 No, no . . . I don't want to see!
AGAVE: Father, be proud, you should be—especially
now—
The proudest man alive. You have such daughters
No one, no one in the world, could
Surpass them . . . I speak for us all, but I have gone
1770 Far beyond the others. I don't spin
And weave now. I have progressed.
Now I hunt—with my bare hands—wild beasts!
And look . . . the pickings of my success.
Here—for you—my newborn glory;
1775 Hang him against your palace wall—take him,
Father—here . . . Can't you feel the joy, the glory
Of my kill too? Tell your friends to come,
To celebrate with you—because you have much
To be thankful for, much to celebrate.
1780 Think of the great things we have done today.
KADMOS: Can I measure hurt like this . . . No, no way
of . . .
I can't even look . . . The great things you've
done—yes,
The great murders, the blood, the . . . !
Oh, fling your thanksgiving before some deity.
1785 He'll love it!
And you tell the people they must celebrate . . .
You tell me!
Celebrate! . . . (He weeps.)
For you, my child, this is for you . . .
1790 And for me. Oh, Dionysos is right,
But he is not fair!
Being so right, he has broken us . . . But then
He was born here, this is his home . . .
AGAVE: Old men! All they do is grumble.
1795 And they always look so grim. I wish my son
Was happy hunting. I wish he was like his mother.
She goes out and runs with the young women
Of Thebes till they track down an animal. But all
He can do is oppose the forces from which
1800 We draw life. You should speak to him, father,
You should advise him . . . Someone—go and fetch
him.
I want him to see me in the full flood of my joy.
KADMOS (a cry is wrenched from him): You'll know—you
must! You'll see

1805 What you've done, and the pain will wring tears
From you . . .
And yet, if you never wake from the dream you're
in . . .
Well, it won't be happiness—but you'll feel no pain.
AGAVE: Is something wrong? Are you angry with me,
father?
KADMOS: Look up at the sky.
1810 AGAVE: There . . . What do you expect me to see?
KADMOS: Does it look the same to you, or do you see
A change?
AGAVE: It looks brighter than before,
Not so blurred.
1815 KADMOS: And inside you—
Do you still feel this sense of flying?
AGAVE: I don't . . .
Understand . . . Wait. Something's happening.
My head! . . . There's a change . . . somewhere
1820 Inside, the mind shifts . . . Yes, I feel . . .
KADMOS: Listen to me.
Do you know what I'm saying? Can you answer me?
AGAVE: I've forgotten . . . What were we talking
about,
Father?
1825 KADMOS: When you were married, do you remember
whose house you came to?
AGAVE: You . . . gave me to . . .
Didn't they say his name was . . . Echion of the
Dragon's seed?
KADMOS: And you had a son.
1830 Your husband gave you a son. What was his name?
AGAVE: Pentheus—child of our true married love.
KADMOS: Now look at the face that lies between your
Hands. Whose is it?
AGAVE: It's a lion . . . You see . . . they . . . they told
me
1835 So—the hunters . . . the women.
KADMOS: Look! Look properly. It won't take long.
It's easy.
AGAVE (obeys, gives a shriek): What is it—this . . . thing!
I'm carrying?
Oh, dear God! What is this?
1840 KADMOS: Open your eyes, and see. You can't mistake
The face.
AGAVE: This foul wound, this foul . . . object!
I can't bear it . . . !
1845 KADMOS: Does it look like a lion
To you?
AGAVE: No . . . It's Pentheus . . . My son . . .
Your head . . . your poor . . .
KADMOS: My tears flowed for him long before
You knew who he was.
1850 AGAVE: Who killed him? How
Did he come here? How am I holding him?
KADMOS: You will have to hear something . . .
abominable.
Perhaps you are not ready . . .

AGAVE: Tell me! I'll choke,
1855   My heart's bursting—I *must* know!
KADMOS: You,
  And your sisters with you, murdered him.
AGAVE: Where?
1860   Where did he die? Here in the palace?
KADMOS: No.
  You remember where, long ago, Akteon
  Was savaged by his hounds . . .
AGAVE: On Kithairon!
  But why did the poor fool go there?
KADMOS: He went to jeer at Dionysos, and your
1865   dancing
  In his honour.
AGAVE: And we destroyed him . . . But what
  happened?
KADMOS: You have no minds left. The whole city
  Was convulsed. Dionysos was in possession.
1870 AGAVE: Dionysos took us and laid us waste. Now
  I see it.
KADMOS: He was displaced. He was usurped.
  You did not believe he had power.
AGAVE: Where
  Is my child's body? . . . Father, I loved him . . .
1875   Where is he?
KADMOS: I brought him home. It was hard—but I
  found him.
AGAVE: Are the limbs . . . is his body . . . a body . . .
  or . . . ?
KADMOS: He lies there.
AGAVE: Pentheus, Pentheus—my only son—my child.
1880 KADMOS: Yes, your son—*and* your heir . . .
  Heir to your madness.
AGAVE: But how could that touch Pentheus? How
  Could he inherit that from me?
KADMOS: He took
1885   From you his stubbornness. He would not open
  Himself to Dionysos—and we all suffered
  For his fault. In a sense, he united us,
  The whole family, because now we are all, like him,
  Shattered fragments.
1890   And I, who never had a son, only
  This grandson, your boy, I'm left with nothing,
  Just a carcass, a shamefully mutilated
  Corpse . . . *That* was once the hope, the new
  Life of my family . . . Pentheus, my child,
1895   You were our centre, you gave us permanence,
  Child of my child, and you were strict with them all
  In Thebes. I was an old man, but people
  Took notice of me, they respected me, so long as
  You were there. If they did not, you would pick out
1900   The culprit and punish him. But now I,
  Kadmos, Kadmos the great, I'll be banished—
  No home, no rights—and I was the man who sowed
  The seed of Thebes, and the harvest I reaped was
    the greatest
  Of our time. Child I loved best—

And now I can no longer say that. 1905
There's nothing left—never again will you touch
My beard, put your arm round me, and say,
  "Father
Of my mother, who has hurt you, who denies you
Your rights? Come, grandfather, who troubles you,
Who is unkind to you? Tell me. If anyone 1910
Has done you wrong I will have him whipped!"
  I have only my grief now, and you are a memory.
If anyone thinks that his own mind alone
Can govern the world, he should see Pentheus here
And believe, believe there are other powers, 1915
Ones he does not dominate.
CHORUS: I grieve for you, Kadmos. Your grandson
  died for a good reason, but it hurt you.
AGAVE: Father, you see how all my daylight reason
  Dawns again in me. I see, I think, 1920
I feel, and as clearly as you,
I know that I am a murderer for my sacrifice
To Dionysos. The victim is dead; the priestess
Lives polluted.
But Pentheus is my son in my heart still, 1925
The son I gave life to and watched over. I want to
Give him one last gift.
I want to arrange his body for the grave,
Though he'll never know of it—the dead feel no
Gratitude for favours to their unfeeling limbs. 1930
KADMOS: He was your child; I can't refuse you. Be
  gentle
With his body—you were not before. I have laid
  him there
As if he were asleep. Do not disturb him.
AGAVE: Pentheus, my son . . .
My baby . . . 1935
You lay in my arms so often, so helpless,
And now again you need my loving care,
My dear, dear child . . .
I killed you.
No! I will not say that. I was not there. I was . . . 1940
I was in some other place . . .
It was Dionysos. Dionysos took me, Dionysos
Used me, and Dionysos murdered you!
DIONYSOS: No! (DIONYSOS *as a god now becomes visible
  above them all.*)
Accuse yourselves, accept the guilt, 1945
You let Pentheus rule you, you were happy being
  ruled,
And for his sake you locked me out of your city.
And so Thebes will have new masters,
An army from the east will live in your homes,
Walk your streets, plough your fields. 1950
Agave—you and your sisters have no place here.
Your home now is . . . wherever a murderer
Can find rest or peace—but not in Thebes.
And you—Kadmos—you must begin again. You
  must
Forfeit your human shape, and become a dragon. 1955

Your wife, daughter of the spirit of war, Harmony
Will also be transfigured—into a snake. Then,
With your bride, you'll drive in a chariot hauled
By young bulls, at the head of an army from
1960   The east. With countless men at your command
You will plunder city after city. But once they
Have wrecked the sanctuary where Apollo speaks
Of things to come—their luck will change, they
Will be defeated, and then disperse. The war-spirit,
      however,
Will rescue you and Harmony, and keep you both
1965   alive
In the world of the undying . . .
This is the universal will of Zeus and
I tell you these things with authority from him. I
      am
Dionysos, his son—I will always return to life.
1970   If you had understood what wholeness is, you
Would now be happy, the son of Zeus would be
Helping you, a friend, an ally.
But you did not want that.
KADMOS: Dionysos, listen to us, we have been
      wrong . . .
1975   DIONYSOS: Now you understand, but now is too late.
When you should have seen, you were blind.
KADMOS: We know that.
But you are like a tide that turns and drowns us.
DIONYSOS: Because I was born with dominion over
      you
1980   And you dispossessed me.
KADMOS: Then you should not
Be like us, your subjects. You should have no
      passions.
DIONYSOS: And I don't. But these are laws of life. I
      cannot
Change them.
1985   AGAVE (weeps): It is decided, father. We must leave
And take our sorrow with us.
DIONYSOS: Why delay?
You can change nothing now. (He vanishes.)
KADMOS: My child, we have suffered cruelly, all of
      us—
1990   I did not escape . . .
I am an old man, and I must leave my home,
Go to a foreign country. And then, I am told,
My destiny is to lead this strange army
Into Greece.
1995   I shall be a dragon, my wife, a dragon; myself
And Harmony, beasts, no longer human, will bring
War to the calm altars and graves of Greece.

There will be no end to the suffering, not even in
      the country
Of the dead; I am to be allowed no peace.
AGAVE: Father, I shall lose you, never see my home
      again . . .   2000
KADMOS: No, don't hold me, my poor child . . . Why?
I'm old, a grey, dying swan—the young
Bird can't protect it . . .
AGAVE: Where shall I go?
I have no country. What will happen to me? . . .   2005
KADMOS: I don't know, my daughter, your father is
      weak.
He is tired, he is no use.
AGAVE: Goodbye, my home,
Goodbye, my city. I am leaving you. I have no
Place here. I am cursed.   2010
KADMOS: Go now, Agave . . .
AGAVE: Father! Come here! . . . I want to hold you . . .
KADMOS: Look, my tears . . . for you and for your
      sisters.
AGAVE: In our lives Dionysos has been a spirit
Of havoc, cruel, relentless . . .   2015
KADMOS: But only because
He was thrust aside, and no one let him in
Here. The cruelty was yours.
AGAVE: Goodbye, father . . .
KADMOS: Goodbye—daughter—though what is there
      good in it?   2020
AGAVE (to PEOPLE OF THEBES): Please, my friends, will
      you help me?
Take me to my sisters, who will share my exile
And the years of sorrow with me.
I want to be where Kithairon can't shadow my
      life—
Where I don't even have to see its distant slopes . . . 2025
Take me where branches wound with ivy
Can't remind me of what has happened.
Let someone else be possessed.
I have withered.
CHORUS: The forces of life are seen in disguise,   2030
A thousand disguises.
They make all things possible,
They guarantee nothing,
What you thought was forgotten, buried,
They conceive, and bring to birth again.   2035
Today you have watched their power at work—
It never ends.

CURTAIN

Figure 1. The ultramodern set designed by Santo Loquasto for the Yale Repertory Theatre production of *The Bacchae,* directed by Andre Gregory, New Haven, 1969. (Photograph: Yale Joel.)

Figure 2. Dionysos (Michael Edo Keane), as a sexually powerful figure, surrounded by his followers; though the god is in human form, the bull's head signifies his semidivine status. The 1997 production at the American Repertory Theatre, Cambridge, MA, was directed by François Rochaix. (Photograph: Richard Feldman.)

Figure 3. Dionysos (Alvin Epstein) in the 1969 Yale production. (Photograph: Sean Kernan.)

Figure 4. In the 1997 American Repertory Theatre production, Kadmos (Alvin Epstein), dressed as a follower of Dionysos, demonstrates how he will dance in honor of the god. (Photograph: Richard Feldman.)

Staging of *The Bacchae*

**REVIEW OF THE YALE REPERTORY THEATRE
PRODUCTION, 1969, BY JACK KROLL**

In a disastrous week of a disastrous and dispiriting Broadway season one's anger and depression are relieved by two trips off the Great White Way. At New Haven the Yale School of Drama Repertory Theatre, embattled in recent months by tensions, confrontations and disagreements involving students, some faculty members and its brilliant dean, Robert Brustein, has nonetheless come up with a production that commands attention, that is almost exactly the right activity for a repertory theater connected with a school of drama interested in controlled and intelligent exploration of a beleaguered art.

Kenneth Cavander has written a translation of Euripides' *The Bacchae* that is strong, spare, hard, and that seeks to capture without distorting the shape of the original, resonances of language and idea that will connect the play legitimately to the present. But this production seems in every sense to be a collaboration, a collaboration in which theatrical history itself plays a part. Director Andre Gregory and Brustein have been intensely affected by the recent visit of the Living Theatre to Yale, and this production is the first serious attempt by anybody to assimilate the implications of the Living Theatre's personality, energy and ideas into what was once called the "mainstream" of the theater.

That mainstream may indeed no longer exist. And Yale's attempt under Brustein to stabilize the headlong energies of the avant-garde, to shape them into effective form without diluting their import or impact, is a task which is currently exposing him to the exacerbations of the cultural right and left—but it is certainly the right job for him to do. "The Bacchae" shows both the point and the perils of this task. Under a decisive sculptural hand from Gregory the combined professional and student cast play Euripides' drama of Dionysiac disruption with strong overall effect and considerable fascinating detail.

Catalyzing the entire production is the remarkable set by Santo Loquasto, Yale '69. Obviously inspired by Julian Beck's wonderful design for the Living Theatre's "Frankenstein," Loquasto achieves his own success with his beautiful oval cage that structures the entire stage into levels, grades and heights that become the public places of Athens, the sequestrations of the Dionysiac forests and the hidden groins and shadows of the mind.

Euripides' play is about the explosive energy system of which human beings are the sentient parts, who forget those energies at their peril. If this description sounds mod and McLuhanesque, it is deliberately so; this "Bacchae" makes no bones about drawing parallels between the ecstatic and lethal revels of the followers of Dionysos and today's subculture of hippies and other glorious human beasts. If the parallel is sometimes too pat (the blind prophet Teiresias comes on like the Maharishi) the attempt to find dramatic shape for the historical continuum between Euripides and us is admirable—and inescapable.

The danger of this type of production is the possibility of a kind of instant academization of the energy of which the Living Theatre is the most notable example. If one questions this energy in some of its moral and esthetic implications, one must be careful not to transmute it into something not healthier but simply tamer. This production bravely confronts the dangers of transmutation and thus sets in motion a process which others must follow. The student chorus (coed) of bacchae does well, and of the professionals who play the central roles, Alvin Epstein as Dionysos—an epicene Olympian super-hoodlum with his snaky blond locks and Mick Jagger mien—and David Spielberg as the doomed Pentheus—torn apart, literally, between his drive for power and his buried passivity—are the best.

REVIEW OF AMERICAN REPERTORY THEATRE PRODUCTION, 1998, BY SCOTT CUMMINGS

The *Bacchae* is rarely mounted on American stages. All the more reason to marvel at the fact that, so far this winter, *three* productions of Euripides' masterpiece have been seen within a half-mile of each other in Cambridge: one at Cambridge Rindge and Latin School, a public high school; one sponsored by the Office of the Arts at Harvard and Radcliffe, directed by Kathryn Walker; and one at Robert Brustein's American Repertory Theatre, featuring a new translation by Paul Schmidt. What accounts for this Dionysian convergence: Millennial anxiety? The hunt for new gods in old bottles? The play's tribal dance of genders? Whatever it is, seeing this work three times in one month is an impressive reminder of its magnitude and power—not to mention the comparatively petty preoccupations of so much contemporary theater.

The A.R.T.'s *Bacchae* is of chief interest here, but it should be noted in passing that both the high school and college tries did justice to the play, handling the ever troublesome chorus with creativity and achieving moments of wonder in the process. The professional production is helmed by Swiss director François Rochaix, whose association with A.R.T. goes back three years to an epic staging of Aeschylus' *Oresteia* which ranged in style from the sublime to the ridiculous. Rochaix's approach to Greek tragedy is well-informed and precise, respectful but hardly reverent. He does not handle the plays as sacred relics or dusty museum pieces, but as down-to-earth dramas populated by characters who are more comically human than tragically heroic—the gods most of all.

Take, for example, Rochaix's Dionysos, played with hermaphroditic flair by Michael Edo Keane. Returning to his Theban birthplace to demand recognition of his divinity, he comes on with the smarmy self-assurance of a carnival pitchman or snake-oil salesman. When this likeable but untrustworthy Dionysos uses his ivy-twined thyrsus to raise the curtain and start the show, he is not only master of ceremonies but a god of theater itself. He controls the event, which means that Pentheus—the young hot-headed king of Thebes—doesn't stand a chance, especially as rendered by Benjamin Evett, who plays the character as a macho fraternity president or homophobic captain of the football team. When he strokes Dionysos' cheek for the amusement of his guards, he mocks the god's effeminacy in a way that will lead directly to his fateful (and fatal) decision to don a woman's dress and head for the hills to peep at the women's bacchanal.

Evett's overtly adolescent Pentheus keeps his transvestism at the level of a college toga party, which makes the tragedy of his dismemberment by his mother's hands all the more difficult to achieve. As Agave, Randy Danson rises to the challenge; when she enters with Pentheus' head on a stick, thinking it a lion's head, she cavorts about the stage with girlish glee as if she has just scored the winning goal in a field hockey tournament. But when Alvin Epstein's Kadmos guides her to recognize the head in her lap as that of her own son, she reacts with a cathartic scream that definitely evokes fear and pity.

This is the most Dionysian moment in a production that is otherwise cool, restrained, and Apollonian. The chorus of Asian maenads, outfitted by Catherine Zuber in fawnskins and combat boots, chants and moves in unison to a steady drumbeat that never reaches fever pitch. Jean-Claude Maret's monumental set balances the large, white palace of Thebes stage left against the smaller, gray tomb of Semele (Dionysos' mortal mother) stage right. Rochaix uses it to frame a number of memorable images: a prolonged hieroglyphic pose from Dionysos as he tempts Pentheus to spy on the women; the graffiti-like scrawling of the god's name in red spray-paint on the white palace wall; the larger-than-life bull's head which hangs from the ivy-wrapped iron fence surrounding Semele's smoldering grave; and the slow and steady rain of black ash from above, a haunting reminder of Dionysos' conception and Semele's destruction of almighty Zeus' thunderbolt.

Thus are we reminded that Dionysos has many faces, that he is everywhere, and that precisely when he seems to be out of sight he should be kept in mind. Like the play itself, Rochaix's beautiful yet oddly unmoving vision of *The Bacchae* makes it difficult to approve or disapprove of this god. He is simply a fact of life, a force of nature that can no more be denied than gravity or gender.

INTERVIEW WITH ALVIN EPSTEIN ON ACTING IN TWO PRODUCTIONS OF *THE BACCHAE*, 2002, BY EMILY GOODALL

GOODALL: What do you remember about *The Bacchae*, as an actor in the late 1960s when you played Dionysos in the production at Yale?

EPSTEIN: It was a play that I had already worked on. . . . I had an experimental group of actors in New York in the early 1960s and one of the plays that we worked on was *The Bacchae*. It was a translation by Philip Vellacott, which I liked very much. And I found the play absolutely fascinating. So by the time we did it at Yale, . . . I knew the play already.

GOODALL: Can you describe your experience acting in the 1969 production at Yale?

EPSTEIN: Well the play, when we did it at Yale—and even before when I was working on it with my workshop group in New York—seemed extremely pertinent. It's really a play about repression and the irrepressible thirst for freedom. . . . And of course it carries [those themes] to an extreme, and because it does, makes a very strong point. . . . I think that's the way I thought of the play when we were doing it at Yale, except that at Yale it was even more pertinent, you might say, because we did it there in 1969, which was the advent of . . . all the student revolts. . . . They were dealing with that at Yale too.

But of course [the play] is not a simplistic view of repression and the thirst for freedom. It really has a lot to do with self-repression, with our culture and our society, . . . with the need to censor and squelch aspects in ourselves in order to be socialized human beings. . . . It can become very personal too. Now as for playing the part—look I'm an actor and give me a good part, and I'll play it as best I can. And Dionysos is a wonderful part.

GOODALL: How did the play seem particularly relevant to you? And can you talk about the influence of the Living Theatre?*

EPSTEIN: Well I can't remember exactly the advent of the Living Theatre. . . . in one of the reviews [of *The Bacchae*, Yale, 1969], they talk about the influence of

the Living Theatre on Andre Gregory. . . . I have a feeling that [even] if the Living Theatre hadn't come back at that time, . . . that Andre Gregory still would've done pretty much the same thing.

GOODALL: Why is that?

EPSTEIN: Because it's in the nature of the play to demand that kind of ferocious . . . [behavior of] the chorus. . . . To dramatize the conflict between Dionysos and his followers, and Pentheus and his government—it's like the chorus is storming the Citadel. So rather extreme behavior is called for. But I guess that . . . the social background at that time, with all the student rebellions and the flower children and the hippies, gave an identity to the chorus that was easily recognizable by the chorus. It wasn't a line-up of ladies in togas waving their arms—not at all! They were wild kids. The influence of the Living Theatre was more in the realm of how the chorus at Yale was handled. And you know about the Santo Loquasto set?

GOODALL: The elaborate, ultra-modern set? [See Figure 1.]

EPSTEIN: Yes. It was really huge and very beautiful and it gave all the possibilities of climbing, clamoring, jumping that you get in a jungle gym. So the chorus was all over it.

GOODALL: How do you think the audience responded to the Yale production?

EPSTEIN: I think very positively. I think they were captivated by it. And I think that was just a result of the combination of the play, translation, director, set, and actors—everything gelling together. I think it was a remarkable production. And I know that a lot of attention was paid to it.

GOODALL: How would you compare the A.R.T. production in 1998 to the Yale production of 1969?

EPSTEIN: Well, that was a very different time in the life of this country. The issues that made the play very socially pertinent in 1969 were no longer there [in 1998], so it became more of a personal thing. The attention was focused more on the personalities and how [what takes place in the play] affected individuals. I mean, you know, gangs of flower children and hippies were gone. And of course the student revolt was a thing of the long-distant past. So in certain ways, I would say that it was a more traditional production. . . . the times had changed and that had a lot to

*The Living Theatre, founded by Judith Malina and Julian Beck in 1947, pioneered many experimental productions, often using audience participation and frequently stressing political and social issues.

do with it. [The audience] looked at the A.R.T. production as a theatrical event. At Yale, it was a theatrical event but also a life event. And I mean, for me, individually, the A.R.T. production was a very different kettle of fish. Playing Kadmos is not at all playing Dionysos, and vice versa. . . . I think we emphasized the comic side of Kadmos and, in a way, he is written almost as a silly old man.

GOODALL: Could you reflect on how the A.R.T. production seems to have been influenced, if at all, by the circumstances of contemporary culture?

EPSTEIN: I would say less than the Yale production. Much less.

GOODALL: Maybe now we can talk a little about the play and the characters. Can you comment on the character Dionysos and about his motives?

EPSTEIN: Well, anybody who reads the play will understand the story of the play—that he's come back to Thebes because, as he explains in the opening monologue, the Thebans under Pentheus have refused to recognize the divinity of his mother. And they are sort of spreading malicious stories. . . . Dionysos claims that [his mother] was consumed by fire because she was impregnated by Zeus, and he is the son of that. He is the child born of that union. And Pentheus and the Thebans laugh at that idea—she was just a slut. And so he comes back in order to set the record straight. I don't think he comes back in order to [take] revenge automatically. It's when he is not able to set the record straight that [he seeks] revenge. That's the story. Now what's the significance of the story? I think that even for the Greeks, they would want the story to have something to do with their lives. And I think that the play is really about the suppression of one part or a whole half of our nature. I guess the moral of the play is that if you don't express [your nature], it will destroy you.

GOODALL: How fair is Dionysos's treatment of Kadmos?

EPSTEIN: Well, the real injury that he does is not to Kadmos—Kadmos is sort of just a bystander that gets hurt by standing by. It's his grandson who is killed. It's the grandson that plays the biggest price and his mother who suffers the worst loss. So I don't think that Dionysos planned anything particularly toward Kadmos. He wasn't focused on Kadmos. Kadmos is collateral damage.

GOODALL: Could you comment on one of the last lines of the play when Kadmos says to Dionysos (in Kenneth Cavander's translation): "Then you should not/be like us, your subjects. You should have no passions." How valid is Kadmos's statement?

EPSTEIN: Well what he is saying is that a god should not have the weaknesses of humankind, should not have the thirst for revenge, should not act out of uncontrollable passion. "We are just ordinary human beings—but you are a god—you should not have those weaknesses." I think the meaning is pretty straightforward. Now is he justified? I mean we know that the Greek gods, not to mention our own, are perfectly capable of cruelty. I don't know. It's very ambiguous. The play is ambiguous. And maybe like most masterpieces, a certain amount of ambiguity remains at the end. Everybody has something right about what they're doing but the preponderance is not necessarily on one side or the other. See I don't believe in God and I don't believe in the gods. So to me, it's a fiction.

GOODALL: Is that how you felt—like it was a fiction—when you performed in the play?

EPSTEIN: No, as an actor I believed in the possibility in magic, even if it's a trick. And I certainly believed in power. Playing that role you have to assume you have the power to accomplish what you set out to accomplish, that you have the much greater power than any of the moral characters. And when [I] try to internalize that as an actor, it gives [me] strength and power so that I could believe in myself as a supernatural force, which is what I think Dionysos really is. And supernatural in the sense that he is a part of nature; he isn't outside of nature.

GOODALL: In both the Yale and A.R.T. productions, you were essentially in conflict with Pentheus—first as Dionysos, then as Kadmos. What is your sense of Pentheus and why he behaves the way he does, both with Dionysos and with Kadmos?

EPSTEIN: Well he's law and order. And my sense is that I like a lot of law and order in my life! But I guess that what happens to Pentheus is really the abuse of the power, of law and order. It's not recognizing that you have to loosen the leash. You cannot keep a tight rein all the time. And you know, modern recent history is full of Pentheuses—[Ceauşescu] in Romania, Milosevic in Yugoslavia. They were both Pentheus. And eventually, the people will not take it anymore. But they (people like Pentheus) do get away with a lot though, in the meantime.

GOODALL: Do you have any sympathy for Pentheus?

EPSTEIN: Yes. I do.

GOODALL: More in one production than in another?

EPSTEIN: That's a tough one. I'm trying to remember what I felt about Pentheus when I was Dionysos. . . . I think Dionysos does have sympathy—he can identify with the suffering that he's imposing. He would have been happy if Pentheus had given in to him at the beginning of the play, and then there would have been no play. . . .

GOODALL: And as Kadmos, did you have any sympathy for Pentheus?

EPSTEIN: As Kadmos—of course. He's my grandson, and he is the future of my family. So of course I had sympathy for him.

GOODALL: How did your perspective of the play and the characters change, if it did, when you went from playing Dionysos (1969) to Kadmos (1998)?

EPSTEIN: Had it really changed? As an actor, you personalize things as much as you can so that playing Kadmos had nothing to do with what I just described. . . . I wouldn't say that my perspective of the play had really changed. The change for me was that I was going from one role to another and had a totally different experience in doing it. I remember that there was a real sort of pleasure for the actor in that role because he goes from a sort of foolish behavior, comic behavior, to a tragic realization at the end.

So that there is a voyage to be made. And that gives you an opportunity to make that voyage, and that's exciting, of course. [The voyage of Kadmos] is a totally different voyage than that of Dionysos who really, at the very beginning of the play, says what he's come to do and then adopts all sorts of different tactics in order to get what he wants done. . . . When one thing doesn't work, he tries another and another. And then he finally gets his way. He accomplishes his task. . . . so that's a whole different kind of action you have to explore. . . . I do remember that at the end, when I was playing Dionysos, that it isn't that I felt that power. It's that I realized I had that power.

ARISTOPHANES

450–385 B.C.

The plays of Aristophanes are the only surviving examples of fifth-century Greek comedy, a form of satiric drama dominated by fantasy—fantasy so outlandish that it has never been surpassed in the history of Western drama. Its plot was not really a plot so much as a set of variations on a fantastic situation, a comic idea meant to solve a pressing social or political situation, such as the ingenious scheme of Lysistrata and her cohorts to force their Athenian husbands to make peace by refusing to make love to them until they end the war against Sparta. The fantasy was always designed to make clear the dramatist's satiric object, and what better way to show the absurdity of war than to stage a battle of the sexes—a battle in the case of *Lysistrata* that threatens to end in sexual frustration instead of fulfillment. The chorus of Greek comedy was often correspondingly fantastic, consisting, for example, of clouds, or in other situations of birds, frogs, and wasps. And even when the chorus itself was not so far-fetched, its actions were, as in the knock-down drag-out struggle that takes place between the chorus of old men and the chorus of old women in *Lysistrata*. The fantasy, moreover, was not confined to the play alone but included the audience too, for the chorus always took the liberty once during each comedy to interrupt the action and deliver a harangue directly to the spectators, as in *Lysistrata* when the chorus of women implores the citizens of Athens "to hear useful words for the state."

Precedents for these extravagant dramatic elements have never been definitely established, although one likely source seems to have been a type of festive masquerade associated with fertility rites, in which participants dressed themselves in outlandish costumes and went throughout the streets, as they do now during Halloween and Mardi Gras, singing, dancing, carousing, and jesting with bystanders. So, too, the actors in Greek comedy would not have limited themselves simply to reciting their lines but would also have performed ribald dance steps, kicking their buttocks, slapping their thighs, and possibly pummeling one another. Though ancient festivities persist in modern masquerades, ancient Greek comedy has never been matched, for later satiric dramatists have never quite escaped the bounds of ordinary experience and taken off into the free-floating world of fantasy. That is the exclusive domain of Aristophanes.

In the comedy of Aristophanes, the world is turned upside down, inside out, and every other way imaginable in a satiric universe where anything is possible. In *The Birds* (414), for example, Peithetaerus, who is disgusted with life in Athens, dreams up the bright idea of creating a new and better city in the sky. Once he is able to convince the birds that they are the original gods, he then gets them to build his Utopia, which in turn enables him to suffocate all of the ruling Greek gods by denying them the smoke of sacrificial offerings. After they give in to his power, he becomes ruler of the entire universe, equipped with his own set of wings and a wife whose thunderbolts, like those of Athena, enable him to keep the world justly under control. In *The Frogs* (405), Dionysus, the god whose festival is celebrated by the dramatic competitions, laments the fact that Sophocles and Euripides have recently died, for he fears that their deaths may lead to the death of drama itself. He thus travels to Hades, planning to bring back Euripides, whom he hopes will sustain the vitality of drama. But when Dionysus finally arrives in Hades, he comes upon Aeschylus and Euripides noisily quarreling with one another over who is to be ruler in the world of tragic theater, while Sophocles stands off to the side, reluctant to get involved in the squabble. Dionysus calms them by getting them to agree to a debate in which Aeschylus and Euripides are to criticize one another's tragedies, with the winner determined by Dionysus, and the prize a return to life in Athens. Aeschylus is judged the winner and so is triumphantly led back to Athens to begin again the great age of classical Greek drama. Thus, as in almost all of Aristophanes' plays, fantasy leads to wish fulfillment and the redemption of the world.

In the process of working out such extravagant fantasies, Aristophanes rarely directs his aim at a single target but instead scatters his satiric shots in a number of directions, picking off abuses and abusers wherever he finds them. He goes after bad government and bad rulers, bad poetry and bad poets, bad schooling and bad teachers, bad thinking and bad thinkers, freely ridiculing them all, no matter how popular, respected, or powerful they may be. Neither Socrates the philosopher nor Euripides the dramatist nor even Cleon the ruling demagogue of Athens escapes the attacks of Aristophanes. But the miraculous quality of his satiric fantasies is that they make it possible for him to solve all the problems of his world—by making a new one, as in *The Birds,* or by going back to an old and better one, as in *The Frogs.* Indeed, the fantasy life of Aristophanes' comedies not only solves all the problems of the world but also satisfies all the basic desires of men and women. In the free festive air of his plays, anything goes, no matter how lewd or obscene, just as anything went in the phallic fertility rites that gave birth to his plays. Thus, in the process of working out his fantasies, Aristophanes also satisfies the sensual desires of all men and women: for food and drink and comfort and sex.

But the fantasy, no matter how joyous it may be while it is going on, must come to an end. In its ending, as in its very being, the fantasy embodies a very poignant view of experience, for it implies that only through the most fantastic flights of the imagination is it possible, as in *The Birds,* to reclaim a fallen world, and worse still, as it turns out, the new world contains some of the very same problems—the imperial motive and the military might—that made for the misery of the old one. Even when an older and better world is reclaimed, as in *The Frogs,* it necessarily incorporates the one fact of life that is inescapable—death—that even the greatest of persons and the greatest of cultures cannot avoid.

Living as he did during the decline of Athenian culture, Aristophanes could hardly ignore the fact that it was dying, for his coming of age coincided with the beginning of the Peloponnesian Wars in 431 B.C. It is not surprising that three of his eleven surviving comedies are antiwar plays: *Acharnians* (425), *Peace* (421), and *Lysistrata* (411). And two others, *The Birds* and *The Frogs,* although not directly concerned with war, nonetheless deal with the cultural wreckage it produced. *Lysistrata* is unquestionably the most powerful of his antiwar plays, for it reveals, as none of the others do, the absurdity of the war that had gone on for more than twenty years by the time the play was produced. But *Lysistrata* transcends the particular circumstances of the struggle between Athens and Sparta, for it makes a statement about war that has been true for all times; through Lysistrata's scheme, it implicitly urges the audience to make love, not war.

Because it makes that plea more boldly than any other antiwar play ever written, *Lysistrata* was staged more often during the twentieth century than any of Aristophanes' other comedies. Most productions shy away from going all the way back to ancient Greek theatrical conventions, but Peter Hall's 1993 production blended classical and contemporary theatrical practice. Women played women and men men, but all the characters wore masks and all appeared in outrageously padded costumes. Figure 1, showing the women of Athens in Victorian bloomers, petticoats, and corsets with their breasts protruding from their underwear, stresses the timeless nature of the satire, while also alluding to the period which, for modern audiences, most clearly signifies sexual repression. The use of masks (mostly half-masks, but occasionally a full mask as can be seen in Figure 2) created characters who reminded many reviewers of British television's satirical Spitting Image puppets and allowed the actors to explore the explicit sexual references with exuberant relish. As Peter Hall indicates in his commentary on the usefulness of the mask, "the surrealistic extremes of Aristophanes are perfectly acceptable in this world of caricature" (see p. 47). Some members of the audience in Liverpool, where the production opened, were so offended by the language, costuming, and physical action that they walked out of the performance, but London audiences were delighted with the energy of both the play and the production. And, as Michael Coveney's reference to the slaughter in Bosnia in his review of the production suggests, the production's raucous farce did not hide Aristophanes' still-relevant criticism of the futility of war.

LYSISTRATA

BY ARISTOPHANES / TRANSLATED BY CHARLES T. MURPHY

CHARACTERS

LYSISTRATA, *an Athenian woman*
CALONICE, *an Athenian woman*
MYRRHINE, *an Athenian woman*
LAMPITO, *a Spartan woman*
LEADER OF CHORUS OF OLD MEN
CHORUS OF OLD MEN
LEADER OF CHORUS OF OLD WOMEN
CHORUS OF OLD WOMEN
ATHENIAN MAGISTRATE
THREE ATHENIAN WOMEN
CINESIAS, *an Athenian, husband of Myrrhine*
SPARTAN HERALD

SPARTAN AMBASSADORS
ATHENIAN AMBASSADORS
TWO ATHENIAN CITIZENS
CHORUS OF ATHENIANS
CHORUS OF SPARTANS

SCENE

In Athens, beneath the Acropolis. In the center of the stage is the Propylaea, or gate-way to the Acropolis; to one side is a small grotto, sacred to Pan. The orchestra represents a slope leading up to the gate-way. It is early in the morning. Lysistrata is pacing impatiently up and down.

LYSISTRATA: If they'd been summoned to worship the God of Wine, or Pan, or to visit the Queen of Love, why, you couldn't have pushed your way through the streets for all the timbrels. But now there's not a single woman here—except my neighbour; here she comes.

(*Enter* CALONICE.)

Good day to you, Calonice.

CALONICE: And to you, Lysistrata. (*Noticing* LYSISTRATA's *impatient air.*) But what ails you? Don't scowl, my dear; it's not becoming to you to knit your brows like that.

LYSISTRATA (*sadly*): Ah, Calonice, my heart aches; I'm so annoyed at us women. For among men we have a reputation for sly trickery—

CALONICE: And rightly too, on my word!

LYSISTRATA: —but when they were told to meet here to consider a matter of no small importance, they lie abed and don't come.

CALONICE: Oh, they'll come all right, my dear. It's not easy for a woman to get out, you know. One is working on her husband, another is getting up the maid, another has to put the baby to bed, or wash and feed it.

LYSISTRATA: But after all, there are other matters more important than all that.

CALONICE: My dear Lysistrata, just what is this matter you've summoned us women to consider! What's up? Something big?

LYSISTRATA: Very big.

CALONICE (*interested*): Is it stout, too?

LYSISTRATA (*smiling*): Yes indeed—both big and stout.

CALONICE: What? And the women still haven't come?

LYSISTRATA: It's not what you suppose; they'd have come soon enough for *that*. But I've worked up something, and for many a sleepless night I've turned it this way and that.

CALONICE (*in much disappointment*): Oh, I guess it's pretty fine and slender, if you've turned it this way and that.

LYSISTRATA: So fine that the safety of the whole of Greece lies in us women.

CALONICE: In us women? It depends on a very slender reed then.

LYSISTRATA: Our country's fortunes are in our hands; and whether the Spartans shall perish—

CALONICE: Good! Let them perish, by all means.

LYSISTRATA: —and the Boeotians shall be completely annihilated.

CALONICE: Not completely! Please spare the eels.

LYSISTRATA: As for Athens, I won't use any such unpleasant words. But you understand what I mean. But if the women will meet here—the Spartans, the Boeotians, and we Athenians—then all together we will save Greece.

CALONICE: But what could women do that's clever or distinguished? We just sit around all dolled up in silk robes, looking pretty in our sheer gowns and evening slippers.

LYSISTRATA: These are just the things I hope will save us; these silk robes, perfumes, evening slippers, rouge, and our chiffon blouses.

CALONICE: How so?

LYSISTRATA: So never a man alive will lift a spear against the foe—

CALONICE: I'll get a silk gown at once.

LYSISTRATA: —or take up his shield—

CALONICE: I'll put on my sheerest gown!

LYSISTRATA: —or sword.

CALONICE: I'll buy a pair of evening slippers.

70 LYSISTRATA: Well then, shouldn't the women have come?

CALONICE: Come? Why, they should have *flown* here.

LYSISTRATA: Well, my dear, just watch: they'll act in
75 true Athenian fashion—everything too late! And now there's not a woman here from the shore or from Salamis.

CALONICE: They're coming, I'm sure; at daybreak they were laying—to their oars to cross the straits.

80 LYSISTRATA: And those I expected would be the first to come—the women of Acharnae—they haven't arrived.

CALONICE: Yet the wife of Theagenes means to come;
85 she consulted Hecate about it. *(Seeing a group of women approaching.)* But look! Here come a few. And there are some more over here. Hurrah! Where do they come from?

LYSISTRATA: From Anagyra.

CALONICE: Yes indeed! We've raised up quite a stink
90 from Anagyra anyway.

(Enter MYRRHINE *in haste, followed by several other women.)*

MYRRHINE *(breathlessly)*: Have we come in time, Lysistrata? What do you say? Why so quiet?

LYSISTRATA: I can't say much for you, Myrrhine, coming at this hour on such important business.

95 MYRRHINE: Why, I had trouble finding my girdle in the dark. But if it's so important, we're here now; tell us.

LYSISTRATA: No. Let's wait a little for the women from Boeotia and the Peloponnesus.

100 MYRRHINE: That's a much better suggestion. Look! Here comes Lampito now.

(Enter LAMPITO *with two other women.)*

LYSISTRATA: Greetings, my dear Spartan friend. How pretty you look, my dear. What a smooth complexion and well-developed figure! You could
105 throttle an ox.

LAMPITO: Faith, yes, I think I could. I take exercises and kick my heels against my bum. *(She demonstrates with a few steps of the Spartan "bottom-kicking" dance.)*

LYSISTRATA: And what splendid breasts you have.

LAMPITO: La! You handle me like a prize steer.

110 LYSISTRATA: And who is this young lady with you?

LAMPITO: Faith, she's an Ambassadress from Boeotia.

LYSISTRATA: Oh yes, a Boeotian, and blooming like a garden too.

CALONICE *(lifting up her skirt)*: My word! How neatly
115 her garden's weeded!

LYSISTRATA: And who is the other girl?

LAMPITO: Oh, she's a Corinthian swell.

MYRRHINE *(after a rapid examination)*: Yes indeed. She swells very nicely *(pointing)* here and here.

LAMPITO: Who has gathered together this company of
120 women?

LYSISTRATA: I have.

LAMPITO: Speak up, then. What do you want?

MYRRHINE: Yes, my dear, tell us what this important
125 matter is.

LYSISTRATA: Very well, I'll tell you. But before I speak, let me ask you a little question.

MYRRHINE: Anything you like.

LYSISTRATA *(earnestly)*: Tell me: don't you yearn for the fathers of your children, who are away at the
130 wars? I know you all have husbands abroad.

CALONICE: Why, yes; mercy me! my husband's been away for five months in Thrace keeping guard on—Eucrates.

MYRRHINE: And mine for seven whole months in
135 Pylus.

LAMPITO: And mine, as soon as ever he returns from the fray, readjusts his shield and flies out of the house again.

LYSISTRATA: And as for lovers, there's not even a
140 ghost of one left. Since the Milesians revolted from us, I've not even seen an eight-inch dingus to be a leather consolation for us widows. Are you willing, if I can find a way, to help me end the
145 war?

MYRRHINE: Goodness, yes! I'd do it, even if I had to pawn my dress and—get drunk on the spot!

CALONICE: And I, even if I had to let myself be split in two like a flounder.

LAMPITO: I'd climb up Mt. Taygetus if I could catch a
150 glimpse of peace.

LYSISTRATA: I'll tell you, then, in plain and simple words. My friends, if we are going to force our men to make peace, we must do without—

MYRRHINE: Without what? Tell us.

155 LYSISTRATA: Will you do it?

MYRRHINE: We'll do it, if it kills us.

LYSISTRATA: Well then, we must do without sex altogether. *(General consternation.)* Why do you turn
160 away? Where go you? Why turn so pale? Why those tears? Will you do it or not? What means this hesitation?

MYRRHINE: I won't do it! Let the war go on.

CALONICE: Nor I! Let the war go on.

165 LYSISTRATA: So, my little flounder? Didn't you say just now you'd split yourself in half?

CALONICE: Anything else you like. I'm willing, even if I have to walk through fire. Anything rather than sex. There's nothing like it, my dear.

170 LYSISTRATA *(to* MYRRHINE*)*: What about you?

MYRRHINE *(sullenly)*: I'm willing to walk through fire, too.

LYSISTRATA: Oh vile and cursed breed! No wonder

175 they make tragedies about us: we're naught but "love-affairs and bassinets." But you, my dear Spartan friend, if you alone are with me, our enterprise might yet succeed. Will you vote with me?

180 LAMPITO: 'Tis cruel hard, by my faith, for a woman to sleep alone without her nooky; but for all that, we certainly do need peace.

LYSISTRATA: O my dearest friend! You're the only real woman here.

185 CALONICE (wavering): Well, if we do refrain from— (shuddering) what you say (God forbid!), would that bring peace?

LYSISTRATA: My goodness, yes! If we sit at home all rouged and powdered, dressed in our sheerest gowns, and neatly depilated, our men will get
190 excited and want to take us; but if you don't come to them and keep away, they'll soon make a truce.

LAMPITO: Aye; Menelaus caught sight of Helen's naked breast and dropped his sword, they say.

195 CALONICE: What if the men give us up?

LYSISTRATA: "Flay a skinned dog," as Pherecrates says.

CALONICE: Rubbish! These make-shifts are not good. But suppose they grab us and drag us into the
200 bedroom?

LYSISTRATA: Hold on to the door.

CALONICE: And if they beat us?

LYSISTRATA: Give in with a bad grace. There's no pleasure in it for them when they have to use
205 violence. And you must torment them in every possible way. They'll give up soon enough; a man gets no joy if he doesn't get along with his wife.

MYRRHINE: If this is your opinion, we agree.

210 LAMPITO: As for our men, we can persuade them to make a just and fair peace; but what about the Athenian rabble? Who will persuade them not to start any more monkey-shines?

LYSISTRATA: Don't worry. We guarantee to convince
215 them.

LAMPITO: Not while their ships are rigged so well and they have that mighty treasure in the temple of Athene.

LYSISTRATA: We've taken good care for that too: we
220 shall seize the Acropolis today. The older women have orders to do this, and while we are making our arrangements, they are to pretend to make a sacrifice and occupy the Acropolis.

LAMPITO: All will be well then. That's a very fine idea.

225 LYSISTRATA: Let's ratify this, Lampito, with the most solemn oath.

LAMPITO: Tell us what oath we shall swear.

LYSISTRATA: Well said. Where's our Policewoman? (to a Scythian slave) What are you gaping at? Set a

shield upside-down here in front of me, and give 230 me the sacred meats.

CALONICE: Lysistrata, what sort of an oath are we to take?

LYSISTRATA: What oath? I'm going to slaughter a sheep over the shield, as they do in Aeschylus. 235

CALONICE: Don't, Lysistrata! No oaths about peace over a shield.

LYSISTRATA: What shall the oath be, then?

CALONICE: How about getting a white horse some- where and cutting out its entrails for the sac- 240 rifice?

LYSISTRATA: White horse indeed!

CALONICE: Well then, how shall we swear?

MYRRHINE: I'll tell you: let's place a large black bowl upside-down and then slaughter—a flask of 245 Thasian wine. And then let's swear—not to pour in a single drop of water.

LAMPITO: Lord! How I like that oath!

LYSISTRATA: Someone bring out a bowl and a flask.

(A slave brings the utensils for the sacrifice.)

CALONICE: Look, my friends! What a big jar! Here's a 250 cup that 'twould give me joy to handle. *(She picks up the bowl.)*

LYSISTRATA: Set it down and put your hands on our victim. *(As CALONICE places her hands on the flask.)* O Lady of Persuasion and dear Loving Cup, gra- ciously vouchsafe to receive this sacrifice from us 255 women. *(She pours the wine into the bowl.)*

CALONICE: The blood has a good colour and spurts out nicely.

LAMPITO: Faith, it has a pleasant smell, too.

MYRRHINE: Oh, let me be the first to swear, ladies! 260

CALONICE: No, by our Lady! Not unless you're allot- ted the first turn.

LYSISTRATA: Place all your hands on the cup, and one of you repeat on behalf of all what I say. Then all will swear and ratify the oath. *I will suffer no man,* 265 *be he husband or lover,*

CALONICE: *I will suffer no man, be he husband or lover,*

LYSISTRATA: *To approach me all hot and horny.* (As CALONICE hesitates.) Say it!

CALONICE (slowly and painfully): *To approach me all hot* 270 *and horny.* O Lysistrata, I feel so weak in the knees!

LYSISTRATA: *I will remain at home unmated,*

CALONICE: *I will remain at home unmated,*

LYSISTRATA: *Wearing my sheerest gown and carefully* 275 *adorned,*

CALONICE: *Wearing my sheerest gown and carefully adorned,*

LYSISTRATA: *That my husband may burn with desire for me.* 280

CALONICE: *That my husband may burn with desire for me.*

LYSISTRATA: *And if he takes me by force against my will,*

CALONICE: *And if he takes me by force against my will,*

LYSISTRATA: *I shall do it badly and keep from moving.*

285 CALONICE: *I shall do it badly and keep from moving.*

LYSISTRATA: *I will not stretch my slippers toward the ceiling,*

CALONICE: *I will not stretch my slippers toward the ceiling,*

LYSISTRATA: *Nor will I take the posture of the lioness on the*
290 *knife-handle.*

CALONICE: *Nor will I take the posture of the lioness on the knife-handle.*

LYSISTRATA: *If I keep this oath, may I be permitted to drink from this cup,*

295 CALONICE: *If I keep this oath, may I be permitted to drink from this cup,*

LYSISTRATA: *But if I break it, may the cup be filled with water.*

CALONICE: *But if I break it, may the cup be filled with*
300 *water.*

LYSISTRATA: Do you all swear to this?

ALL: I do, so help me!

LYSISTRATA: Come then, I'll just consummate this offering.

(She takes a long drink from the cup.)

305 CALONICE *(snatching the cup away)*: Shares, my dear! Let's drink to our continued friendship.

(A shout is heard from off-stage.)

LAMPITO: What's that shouting?

LYSISTRATA: That's what I was telling you: the women have just seized the Acropolis. Now, Lampito, go
310 home and arrange matters in Sparta; and leave these two ladies here as hostages. We'll enter the Acropolis to join our friends and help them lock the gates.

CALONICE: Don't you suppose the men will come to
315 attack us?

LYSISTRATA: Don't worry about them. Neither threats nor fire will suffice to open the gates, except on the terms we've stated.

CALONICE: I should say not! Else we'd belie our repu-
320 tation as unmanageable pests.

(LAMPITO leaves the stage. The other women retire and enter the Acropolis through the Propylaea. Enter the CHORUS OF OLD MEN, carrying fire-pots and a load of heavy sticks.)

LEADER OF MEN: Onward, Draces, step by step, though your shoulder's aching.
Cursèd logs of olive-wood, what a load you're making!

FIRST SEMI-CHORUS OF OLD MEN *(singing)*:
Aye, many surprises await a man who lives to a ripe old age;
For who could suppose, Strymodorus my lad, that

the women we've nourished (alas!),
Who sat at home to vex our days,
Would seize the holy image here,
And occupy this sacred shrine,
With bolts and bars, with fell design,
To lock the Propylaea? [325]

LEADER OF MEN: Come with speed, Philourgus, come! to the temple hast'ning. [330]
There we'll heap these logs about in a circle round them,
And whoever has conspired, raising this rebellion,
Shall be roasted, scorched, and burnt, all without exception,
Doomed by one unanimous vote—but first the wife of Lycon.

SECOND SEMI-CHORUS *(singing)*:
No, no! by Demeter, while I'm alive, no woman shall mock at me. [335]
Not even the Spartan Cleomenes, our citadel first to seize,
Got off unscathed; for all his pride
And haughty Spartan arrogance;
He left his arms and sneaked away,
Stripped to his shirt, unkempt, unshav'd, [340]
With six years' filth still on him.

LEADER OF MEN: I besieged that hero bold, sleeping at my station,
Marshalled at these holy gates sixteen deep against him.
Shall I not these cursèd pests punish for their daring,
Burning these Euripides-and-God-detested women? [345]
Aye! or else may Marathon overturn my trophy.

FIRST SEMI-CHORUS *(singing)*: There remains of my road
Just this brow of the hill;
There I speed on my way.
Drag the logs up the hill, though we've got no ass to help. [350]
(God! my shoulder's bruised and sore!)
Onward still must we go.
Blow the fire! Don't let it go out
Now we're near the end of our road.

ALL *(blowing on the fire-pots)*: Whew! Whew! Drat the smoke! [355]

SECOND SEMI-CHORUS *(singing)*: Lord, what smoke rushing forth
From the pot, like a dog
Running mad, bites my eyes!
This must be Lemnos-fire. What a sharp and stinging smoke!
Rushing onward to the shrine [360]
Aid the gods. Once for all
Show your mettle, Laches my boy!
To the rescue hastening all!

ALL (*blowing on the fire-pots*): Whew! Whew! Drat the smoke!

(*The* CHORUS *has now reached the edge of the Orchestra nearest the stage, in front of the Propylaea. They begin laying their logs and fire-pots on the ground.*)

365 LEADER OF MEN: Thank heaven, this fire is still alive. Now let's first put down these logs here and place our torches in the pots to catch; then let's make a rush for the gates with a battering-ram. If the women don't unbar the gate at our summons,
370 we'll have to smoke them out.

Let me put down my load. Ouch! That hurts! (*To the audience.*) Would any of the generals in Samos like to lend a hand with this log? (*Throwing down a log.*) Well, *that* won't break my back any
375 more, at any rate. (*Turning to his fire-pot.*) Your job, my little pot, is to keep those coals alive and furnish me shortly with a red-hot torch.

O mistress Victory, be my ally and grant me to rout these audacious women in the Acropolis.

(*While the* MEN *are busy with their logs and fires, the* CHORUS OF OLD WOMEN *enters, carrying pitchers of water.*)

LEADER OF WOMEN: What's this I see? Smoke and
380 flames? Is that a fire ablazing?

Let's rush upon them. Hurry up! They'll find us women ready.

FIRST SEMI-CHORUS OF OLD WOMEN (*singing*):
With wingèd foot onward I fly,
Ere the flames consume Neodice;
Lest Critylla be overwhelmed
385 By a lawless, accurst herd of old men.
I shudder with fear. Am I too late to aid them?
At break of the day filled we our jars with
     water
Fresh from the spring, pushing our way straight
     through the crowds. Oh, what a din!
Mid crockery crashing, jostled by slave-girls,
390 Sped we to save them, aiding our neighbours,
Bearing this water to put out the flames.

SECOND SEMI-CHORUS OF OLD WOMEN (*singing*):
Such news I've heard; doddering fools
Come with logs, like furnace-attendants,
Loaded down with three hundred pounds,
395 Breathing many a vain, blustering threat,
That all these abhorred sluts will be burnt to
     charcoal.
O goddess, I pray never may they be kindled;
Grant them to save Greece and our men, madness
     and war help them to end.
With this as our purpose, golden-plumed Maiden,
400 Guardian of Athens, seized we thy precinct.
Be my ally, Warrior-maiden,
'Gainst these old men, bearing water with me.

(*The women have now reached their position in the Orchestra, and their* LEADER *advances toward the* LEADER *of the men.*)

LEADER OF WOMEN: Hold on there! What's this, you utter scoundrels? No decent, God-fearing citizens would act like this. 405

LEADER OF MEN: Oho! Here's something unexpected: a swarm of women have come out to attack us.

LEADER OF WOMEN: What, do we frighten you? Surely you don't think we're too many for you. And yet there are ten thousand times more of us whom 410 you haven't even seen.

LEADER OF MEN: What say, Phaedria? Shall we let these women wag their tongues? Shan't we take our sticks and break them over their backs?

LEADER OF WOMEN: Let's set our pitchers on the 415 ground; then if anyone lays a hand on us, they won't get in our way.

LEADER OF MEN: By God! If someone gave them two or three smacks on the jaw, like Bupalus, they wouldn't talk so much! 420

LEADER OF WOMEN: Go on, hit me, somebody! Here's my jaw! But no other bitch will bite a piece out of you before me.

LEADER OF MEN: Silence! or I'll knock out your— senility! 425

LEADER OF WOMEN: Just lay one finger on Stratyllis, I dare you!

LEADER OF MEN: Suppose I dust you off with this fist? What will you do?

LEADER OF WOMEN: I'll tear the living guts out of you 430 with my teeth.

LEADER OF MEN: No poet is more clever than Euripides: "There is no beast so shameless as a woman."

LEADER OF WOMEN: Let's pick up our jars of water, 435 Rhodippe.

LEADER OF MEN: Why have you come here with water, you detestable slut?

LEADER OF WOMEN: And why have you come with fire, you funeral vault? To cremate yourself? 440

LEADER OF MEN: To light a fire and singe your friends.

LEADER OF WOMEN: And I've brought water to put out your fire.

LEADER OF MEN: What? You'll put out my fire? 445

LEADER OF WOMEN: Just try and see!

LEADER OF MEN: I wonder: shall I scorch you with this torch of mine?

LEADER OF WOMEN: If you've got any soap, I'll give you a bath. 450

LEADER OF MEN: Give *me* a bath, you stinking hag?

LEADER OF WOMEN: Yes—a bridal bath!

LEADER OF MEN: Just listen to her! What crust!

LEADER OF WOMEN: Well, I'm a free citizen.

LEADER OF MEN: I'll put an end to your brawling. 455

(*The* MEN *pick up their torches.*)

LEADER OF WOMEN: You'll never do jury-duty again.

(The WOMEN *pick up their pitchers.)*

LEADER OF MEN: Singe her hair for her!
LEADER OF WOMEN: Do your duty, water!

(The WOMEN *empty their pitchers on the* MEN.*)*

LEADER OF MEN: Ow! Ow! For heaven's sake!
460 LEADER OF WOMEN: Is it too hot?
LEADER OF MEN: What do you mean "hot"? Stop! What are you doing?
LEADER OF WOMEN: I'm watering you, so you'll be fresh and green.
465 LEADER OF MEN: But I'm all withered up with shaking.
LEADER OF WOMEN: Well, you've got a fire; why don't you dry yourself?

(Enter an ATHENIAN MAGISTRATE, *accompanied by* FOUR SCYTHIAN POLICEMEN.*)*

MAGISTRATE: Have these wanton women flared up again with their timbrels and their continual
470 worship of Sabazius? Is this another Adonis-dirge upon the roof-tops—which we heard not long ago in the Assembly? That confounded Demostratus was urging us to sail to Sicily, and the whirling women shouted, "Woe for Adonis!" And
475 then Demostratus said we'd best enroll the infantry from Zacynthus, and a tipsy woman on the roof shrieked, "Beat your breasts for Adonis!" And that vile and filthy lunatic forced his measure
480 through. Such license do our women take.
LEADER OF MEN: What if you heard of the insolence of these women here? Besides their other violent acts, they threw water all over us, and we have to shake out our clothes just as if we'd leaked in
485 them.
MAGISTRATE: And rightly, too, by God! For we ourselves lead the women astray and teach them to play the wanton; from these roots such notions blossom forth. A man goes into the jeweler's shop
490 and says, "About that necklace you made for my wife, goldsmith: last night, while she was dancing, the fastening-bolt slipped out of the hole. I have to sail over to Salamis today; if you're free, do come around tonight and fit in a new bolt for
495 her." Another goes to the shoemaker, a strapping young fellow with manly parts, and says, "See here, cobbler, the sandalstrap chafes my wife's little—toe; it's so tender. Come around during the siesta and stretch it a little, so she'll be more
500 comfortable." Now we see the results of such treatment: here I'm a special Councillor and need money to procure oars for the galleys; and I'm locked out of the Treasury by these women.
But this is no time to stand around. Bring up
505 crow-bars there! I'll put an end to their insolence.

(To one of the policemen.) What are you gaping at, you wretch! What are you staring at? Got an eye out for a tavern, eh? Set your crow-bars here to the gates and force them open. *(Retiring to a safe distance.)* I'll help from over here.   510

(The gates are thrown open and LYSISTRATA *comes out followed by several other* WOMEN.*)*

LYSISTRATA: Don't force the gates; I'm coming out of my own accord. We don't need crow-bars here. What we need is good sound common-sense.
MAGISTRATE: Is that so, you strumpet? Where's my policeman? Officer, arrest her and tie her arms   515 behind her back.
LYSISTRATA: By Artemis, if he lays a finger on me, he'll pay for it, even if he is a public servant.

(The POLICEMAN *retires in terror.)*

MAGISTRATE: You there, are you afraid? Seize her round the waist—and you, too. Tie her up, both   520 of you!
FIRST WOMAN *(as the* SECOND POLICEMAN *approaches* LYSISTRATA*)*: By Pandrosus, if you but touch her with your hand, I'll kick the stuffings out of you.

(The SECOND POLICEMAN *retires in terror.)*

MAGISTRATE: Just listen to that: "kick the stuffings out." Where's another policeman? Tie *her* up first,   525 for her chatter.
SECOND WOMAN: By the Goddess of the Light, if you lay the tip of your finger on her, you'll soon need a doctor.

(The THIRD POLICEMAN *retires in terror.)*

MAGISTRATE: What's this? Where's my policeman?   530 Seize *her* too. I'll soon stop your sallies.
THIRD WOMAN: By the Goddess of Tauros, if you go near her, I'll tear out your hair until it shrieks with pain.

(The FOURTH POLICEMAN *retires in terror.)*

MAGISTRATE: Oh, damn it all! I've run out of police-   535 men. But women must never defeat us. Officers, let's charge them all together. Close up your ranks!

(The POLICEMEN *rally for a mass attack.)*

LYSISTRATA: By heaven, you'll soon find out that we have four companies of warrior-women, all fully   540 equipped within!
MAGISTRATE *(advancing)*: Twist their arms off, men!
LYSISTRATA *(shouting)*: To the rescue, my valiant women!
O sellers-of-barley-green-stuffs-and-eggs,   545
O sellers-of-garlic, ye keepers-of-taverns, and vendors-of-bread,

Grapple! Smite! Smash!

Won't you heap filth on them? Give them a tongue-lashing!

(The WOMEN beat off the POLICEMEN.)

Halt! Withdraw! No looting on the field.

550 MAGISTRATE: Damn it! My police-force has put up a very poor show.

LYSISTRATA: What did you expect? Did you think you were attacking slaves? Didn't you know that women are filled with passion?

555 MAGISTRATE: Aye, passion enough—for a good strong drink!

LEADER OF MEN: O chief and leader of this land, why spend your words in vain?

Don't argue with these shameless beasts. You know not how we've fared:

A soapless bath they've given us; our clothes are soundly soaked.

LEADER OF WOMEN: Poor fool! You never should at-
560 tack or strike a peaceful girl.

But if you do, your eyes must swell. For I am quite content

To sit unmoved, like modest maids, in peace and cause no pain;

But let a man stir up my hive, he'll find me like a wasp.

CHORUS OF MEN (singing):

O God, whatever shall we do with creatures like Womankind?

This can't be endured by any man alive. Question
565 them!

Let us try to find out what this means.

To what end have they seized on this shrine,

This steep and rugged, high and holy,

Undefiled Acropolis?

LEADER OF MEN: Come, put your questions; don't give
570 in, and probe her every statement.

For base and shameful it would be to leave this plot untested.

MAGISTRATE: Well then, first of all I wish to ask her this: for what purpose have you barred us from
575 the Acropolis?

LYSISTRATA: To keep the treasure safe, so you won't make war on account of it.

MAGISTRATE: What? Do we make war on account of the treasure?

LYSISTRATA: Yes, and you cause all our other troubles
580 for it, too. Peisander and those greedy office-seekers keep things stirred up so they can find occasions to steal. Now let them do what they like: they'll never again make off with any of this money.

585 MAGISTRATE: What will you do?

LYSISTRATA: What a question! We'll administer it ourselves.

MAGISTRATE: *You* will administer the treasure?

LYSISTRATA: What's so strange in that? Don't we administer the household money for you? 590

MAGISTRATE: That's different.

LYSISTRATA: How is it different?

MAGISTRATE: We've got to make war with this money.

LYSISTRATA: But that's the very first thing: you
mustn't make war. 595

MAGISTRATE: How else can we be saved?

LYSISTRATA: We'll save you.

MAGISTRATE: *You?*

LYSISTRATA: Yes, we!

MAGISTRATE: God forbid! 600

LYSISTRATA: We'll save you, whether you want it or not.

MAGISTRATE: Oh! This is terrible!

LYSISTRATA: You don't like it, but we're going to do it
none the less. 605

MAGISTRATE: Good God! it's illegal!

LYSISTRATA: We *will* save you, my little man!

MAGISTRATE: Suppose I don't want you to?

LYSISTRATA: That's all the more reason.

MAGISTRATE: What business have you with war and 610
peace?

LYSISTRATA: I'll explain.

MAGISTRATE (*shaking his fist*): Speak up, or you'll smart for it.

LYSISTRATA: Just listen, and try to keep your hands 615
still.

MAGISTRATE: I can't. I'm so mad I can't stop them.

FIRST WOMAN: Then you'll be the one to smart for it.

MAGISTRATE: Croak to yourself, old hag! (to LYSIS-
TRATA) Now then, speak up. 620

LYSISTRATA: Very well. Formerly we endured the war for a good long time with our usual restraint, no matter what you men did. You wouldn't let us say "boo," although nothing you did suited us. But we watched you well, and though we stayed 625 at home we'd often hear of some terribly stupid measure you'd proposed. Then, though grieving at heart, we'd smile sweetly and say, "What was passed in the Assembly today about writing on the treaty-stone?" "What's that to you?" my hus- 630 band would say. "Hold your tongue!" And I held my tongue.

FIRST WOMAN: But I wouldn't have—not I!

MAGISTRATE: You'd have been soundly smacked, if
you hadn't kept still. 635

LYSISTRATA: So I kept still at home. Then we'd hear of some plan still worse than the first; we'd say, "Hus-band, how could you pass such a stupid pro-posal!" He'd scowl at me and say, "If you don't mind your spinning, your head will be sore for 640 weeks. *War shall be the concern of men.*"

MAGISTRATE: And he was right, upon my word!

LYSISTRATA: Why right, you confounded fool, when your proposals were so stupid and we weren't allowed to make any suggestions? 645

"There's not a *man* left in the country," says one. "No, not one," says another. Therefore all we women have decided in council to make a common effort to save Greece. How long should we have waited? Now, if you're willing to listen to our excellent proposals and keep silence for us in your turn, we still may save you.

MAGISTRATE: We men keep silence for you? That's terrible; I won't endure it!

LYSISTRATA: Silence!

MAGISTRATE: Silence for *you*, you wench, when you're wearing a snood? I'd rather die!

LYSISTRATA: Well, if that's all that bothers you—here! Take my snood and tie it round your head. (*During the following words the* WOMEN *dress up the* MAGISTRATE *in women's garments.*) And *now* keep quiet! Here, take this spinning-basket, too, and card your wool with robes tucked up, munching on beans. *War shall be the concern of Women!*

LEADER OF WOMEN: Arise and leave your pitchers, girls; no time is this to falter.
We too must aid our loyal friends, our turn has come for action.

CHORUS OF WOMEN (*singing*):
I'll never tire of aiding them with song and dance;
    never may
Faintness keep my legs from moving to and fro
    endlessly.
    For I yearn to do all for my friends;
    They have charm, they have wit, they have
        grace,
    With courage, brains, and best of virtues—
        Patriotic sapience.

LEADER OF WOMEN: Come, child of manliest ancient dames, offspring of stinging nettles,
Advance with rage unsoftened; for fair breezes speed you onward.

LYSISTRATA: If only sweet Eros and the Cyprian Queen of Love shed charm over our breasts and limbs and inspire our men with amorous longing and priapic spasms, I think we may soon be called Peacemakers among the Greeks.

MAGISTRATE: What will you do?

LYSISTRATA: First of all, we'll stop those fellows who run madly about the Marketplace in arms.

FIRST WOMAN: Indeed we shall, by the Queen of Paphos.

LYSISTRATA: For now they roam about the market, amid the pots and greenstuffs, armed to the teeth like Corybantes.

MAGISTRATE: That's what manly fellows ought to do!

LYSISTRATA: But it's so silly: a chap with a Gorgon-emblazoned shield buying pickled herring.

FIRST WOMAN: Why, just the other day I saw one of those long-haired dandies who command our cavalry ride up on horseback and pour into his bronze helmet the egg-broth he'd bought from

an old dame. And there was a Thracian slinger too, shaking his lance like Tereus; he'd scared the life out of the poor fig-peddler and was gulping down all her ripest fruit.

MAGISTRATE: How can you stop all the confusion in the various states and bring them together?

LYSISTRATA: Very easily.

MAGISTRATE: Tell me how.

LYSISTRATA: Just like a ball of wool, when it's confused and snarled: we take it thus, and draw out a thread here and a thread there with our spindles; thus we'll unsnarl this war, if no one prevents us, and draw together the various states with embassies here and embassies there.

MAGISTRATE: Do you suppose you can stop this dreadful business with balls of wool and spindles, you nit-wits?

LYSISTRATA: Why, if *you* had any wits, you'd manage all affairs of state like our wool-working.

MAGISTRATE: How so?

LYSISTRATA: First you ought to treat the city as we do when we wash the dirt out of a fleece: stretch it out and pluck and thrash out of the city all those prickly scoundrels; aye, and card out those who conspire and stick together to gain office, pulling off their heads. Then card the wool, all of it, into one fair basket of goodwill, mingling in the aliens residing here, any loyal foreigners, and anyone who's in debt to the Treasury; and consider that all our colonies lie scattered round about like remnants; from all of these collect the wool and gather it together here, wind up a great ball, and then weave a good stout cloak for the democracy.

MAGISTRATE: Dreadful! Talking about thrashing and winding balls of wool, when you haven't the slightest share in the war!

LYSISTRATA: Why, you dirty scoundrel, we bear more than twice as much as you. First, we bear children and send off our sons as soldiers.

MAGISTRATE: Hush! Let bygones be bygones!

LYSISTRATA: Then, when we ought to be happy and enjoy our youth, we sleep alone because of your expeditions abroad. But never mind us married women: I grieve most for the maids who grow old at home unwed.

MAGISTRATE: Don't men grow old, too?

LYSISTRATA: For heaven's sake! That's not the same thing. When a man comes home, no matter how grey he is, he soon finds a girl to marry. But woman's bloom is short and fleeting; if she doesn't grasp her chance, no man is willing to marry her and she sits at home a prey to every fortune-teller.

MAGISTRATE (*coarsely*): But if a man can still get it up—

LYSISTRATA: See here, you: what's the matter? Aren't

you dead yet? There's plenty of room for you. Buy yourself a shroud and I'll bake you a honey-cake. *(Handing him a copper coin for his passage across the Styx.)* Here's your fare! Now get yourself a wreath.

(During the following dialogue the WOMEN *dress up the* MAGISTRATE *as a corpse.)*

755 FIRST WOMAN: Here, take these fillets.
SECOND WOMAN: Here, take this wreath.
LYSISTRATA: What do you want? What's lacking? Get moving; off to the ferry! Charon is calling you; don't keep him from sailing.
760 MAGISTRATE: Am I to endure these insults? By God! I'm going straight to the magistrates to show them how I've been treated.
LYSISTRATA: Are you grumbling that you haven't been properly laid out? Well, the day after tomorrow
765 we'll send around all the usual offerings early in the morning.

(The MAGISTRATE *goes out still wearing his funeral decorations.* LYSISTRATA *and the* WOMEN *retire into the Acropolis.)*

LEADER OF MEN: Wake, ye sons of freedom, wake! 'Tis no time for sleeping. Up and at them, like a man! Let us strip for action.

(The CHORUS OF MEN *remove their outer cloaks.)*

CHORUS OF MEN *(singing):*
770 Surely there is something here greater than meets the eye;
For without a doubt I smell Hippias' tyranny.
Dreadful fear assails me lest certain bands of Spartan men,
Meeting here with Cleisthenes, have inspired through treachery
775 All these god-detested women secretly to seize
Athens' treasure in the temple, and to stop that pay
Whence I live at my ease.
LEADER OF MEN: Now isn't it terrible for them to advise the state and chatter about shields, being mere women?
780 And they think to reconcile us with the Spartans—men who hold nothing sacred any more than hungry wolves. Surely this is a web of deceit, my friends, to conceal an attempt at tyranny. But they'll never lord it over me; I'll be on my guard
785 from now on,
"The blade I bear, A myrtle spray shall wear."
I'll occupy the market under arms and stand next to Aristogeiton.
Thus I'll stand beside him. *(He strikes the pose of the famous statue of the tyrannicides, with one arm
790 raised.)* And here's my chance to take this accurst old hag and—*(striking the* LEADER OF WOMEN*)* smack her on the jaw!

LEADER OF WOMEN: You'll go home in such a state your Ma won't recognize you!
Ladies all, upon the ground let us place these garments. 795

(The CHORUS OF WOMEN *remove their outer garments.)*

CHORUS OF WOMEN *(singing):*
Citizens of Athens, hear useful words for the state.
Rightly; for it nurtured me in my youth royally.
As a child of seven years carried I the sacred box;
Then I was a Miller-maid, grinding at Athene's shrine; 800
Next I wore the saffron robe and played Brauronia's Bear;
And I walked as a Basket-bearer, wearing chains of figs,
As a sweet maiden fair.
LEADER OF WOMEN: Therefore, am I not bound to give good advice to the city? 805
Don't take it ill that I was born a woman, if I contribute something better than our present troubles. I pay my share; for I contribute MEN. But you miserable old fools contribute nothing, and after squandering our ancestral treasure, the fruit 810 of the Persian Wars, you make no contribution in return. And now, all on account of you, we're facing ruin.
What, muttering, are you? If you annoy me, I'll take this hard, rough slipper and—*(striking the* 815 LEADER OF MEN*)* smack you on the jaw!
CHORUS OF MEN *(singing):*
This is outright insolence! Things go from bad to worse.
If you're men with any guts, prepare to meet the foe.
Let us strip our tunics off! We need the smell of male
Vigour. And we cannot fight all swaddled up in clothes. 820

(They strip off their tunics.)

Come then, my comrades, on to the battle, ye once to Leipsydrion came;
Then ye were MEN. Now call back your youthful vigour.
With light, wingèd footstep advance,
Shaking old age from your frame.
LEADER OF MEN: If any of us give these wenches the 825 slightest hold, they'll stop at nothing; such is their cunning.
They will even build ships and sail against us, like Artemisia. Or if they turn to mounting, I count our Knights as done for: a woman's such 830 a tricky jockey when she gets astraddle, with a good firm seat for trotting. Just look at those Amazons that Micon painted, fighting on horseback against men!

835　　　But we must throw them all in the pillory—
(seizing and choking the LEADER OF WOMEN*)* grabbing hold of yonder neck!

CHORUS OF WOMEN *(singing)*:
'Ware my anger! Like a boar 'twill rush upon you
men.
Soon you'll bawl aloud for help, you'll be so
soundly trimmed!
Come, my friends, let's strip with speed, and lay
840　aside these robes;
Catch the scent of women's rage. Attack with tooth
and nail!

(They strip off their tunics.)

Now then, come near me, you miserable man!
You'll never eat garlic or black beans again.
And if you utter a single hard word, in rage I will
"nurse" you as once
The beetle requited her foe.

845　LEADER OF WOMEN: For you don't worry me; no, not
so long as my Lampito lives and our Theban
friend, the noble Ismenia.
　　　You can't do anything, not even if you pass a
dozen—decrees! You miserable fool, all our
850　neighbours hate you. Why, just the other day
when I was holding a festival for Hecate, I invited
as playmate from our neighbours the Boeotians a charming, wellbred Copaic—eel. But they
refused to send me one on account of your
855　decrees.
　　　And you'll never stop passing decrees until I
grab your foot and—*(tripping up the* LEADER OF
MEN *)* toss you down and break your neck!

(Here an interval of five days is supposed to elapse. LYSIS-
TRATA *comes out from the Acropolis.)*

LEADER OF WOMEN *(dramatically)*: Empress of this great
860　emprise and undertaking,
Why come you forth, I pray, with frowning brow?

LYSISTRATA: Ah, these cursèd women! Their deeds
and female notions make me pace up and down
in utter despair.

865　LEADER OF WOMEN: Ah, what sayest thou?
LYSISTRATA: The truth, alas! the truth.
LEADER OF WOMEN: What dreadful tale hast thou to
tell thy friends?
LYSISTRATA: 'Tis shame to speak, and not to speak is
870　hard.
LEADER OF WOMEN: Hide not from me whatever woes
we suffer.
LYSISTRATA: Well then, to put it briefly, we want—
laying!
875　LEADER OF WOMEN: O Zeus, Zeus!
LYSISTRATA: Why call on Zeus? That's the way things
are. I can no longer keep them away from the
men, and they're all deserting. I caught one wrig-
gling through a hole near the grotto of Pan,

another sliding down a rope, another deserting　880
her post; and yesterday I found one getting on a
sparrow's back to fly off to Orsilochus, and had to
pull her back by the hair. They're digging up all
sorts of excuses to get home. Look, here comes
one of them now.　885

(A WOMAN *comes hastily out of the Acropolis.)*

Here you! Where are you off to in such a hurry?
FIRST WOMAN: I want to go home. My very best wool is
being devoured by moths.
LYSISTRATA: Moths? Nonsense! Go back inside.
FIRST WOMAN: I'll come back; I swear it. I just want to　890
lay it out on the bed.
LYSISTRATA: Well, you won't lay it out, and you won't
go home, either.
FIRST WOMAN: Shall I let my wool be ruined?
LYSISTRATA: If necessary, yes.　895

*(*ANOTHER WOMAN *comes out.)*

SECOND WOMAN: Oh, dear! Oh dear! My precious flax!
I left it at home all unpeeled.
LYSISTRATA: Here's another one, going home for her
"flax." Come back here!
SECOND WOMAN: But I just want to work it up a little　900
and then I'll be right back.
LYSISTRATA: No indeed! If you start this, all other
women will want to do the same.

(A THIRD WOMAN *comes out.)*

THIRD WOMAN: O Eilithyia, goddess of travail, stop my
labour till I come to a lawful spot!　905
LYSISTRATA: What's this nonsense?
THIRD WOMAN: I'm going to have a baby—right now!
LYSISTRATA: But you weren't even pregnant yesterday.
THIRD WOMAN: Well, I am today. O Lysistrata, do send　910
me home to see a midwife, right away.
LYSISTRATA: What are you talking about? *(Putting her
hand on her stomach.)* What's this hard lump here?
THIRD WOMAN: A little boy.
LYSISTRATA: My goodness, what have you got there? It　915
seems hollow; I'll just find out. *(Pulling aside her
robe.)* Why, you silly goose, you've got Athene's
sacred helmet there. And you said you were having a baby!
THIRD WOMAN: Well, I *am* having one, I swear!　920
LYSISTRATA: Then what's this helmet for?
THIRD WOMAN: If the baby starts coming while I'm
still in the Acropolis, I'll creep into this like a
pigeon and give birth to it there.
LYSISTRATA: Stuff and nonsense! It's plain enough　925
what you're up to. You just wait here for the christening of this—helmet.
THIRD WOMAN: But I can't sleep in the Acropolis since
I saw the sacred snake.

930 FIRST WOMAN: And I'm dying for lack of sleep: the hooting of owls keep me awake.

LYSISTRATA: Enough of these shams, you wretched creatures. You want your husbands, I suppose. Well, don't you think they want us? I'm sure 935 they're spending miserable nights. Hold out, my friends, and endure for just a little while. There's an oracle that we shall conquer, if we don't split up. (*Producing a roll of paper.*) Here it is.

940 FIRST WOMAN: Tell us what it says.

LYSISTRATA: Listen.

"When in the length of time the Swallows shall gather together,
Fleeing the Hoopoe's amorous flight and the Cockatoo shunning,
Then shall your woes be ended and Zeus who thunders in heaven
945 Set what's below on top—"

FIRST WOMAN: What? Are we going to be on top?

LYSISTRATA: "But if the Swallows rebel and flutter away from the temple,
Never a bird in the world shall seem more wanton and worthless."

FIRST WOMAN: That's clear enough, upon my word!

950 LYSISTRATA: By all that's holy, let's not give up the struggle now. Let's go back inside. It would be a shame, my dear friends, to disobey the oracle.

(*The* WOMEN *all retire to the Acropolis again.*)

CHORUS OF MEN (*singing*):
I have a tale to tell,
Which I know full well.
955   It was told me
        In the nursery.

Once there was a likely lad,
    Melanion they name him;
The thought of marriage made him mad,
960   For which I cannot blame him.

So off he went to mountains fair;
    (No women to upbraid him!)
A mighty hunter of the hare,
    He had a dog to aid him.

965 He never came back home to see
        Detested women's faces.
    He showed a shrewd mentality.
        With him I'd fain change places!

ONE OF THE MEN (*to* ONE OF THE WOMEN): Come here,
970   old dame; give me a kiss.

WOMAN: You'll ne'er eat garlic, if you dare!

MAN: I want to kick you—just like this!

WOMAN: Oh, there's a leg with bushy hair!

MAN: Myronides and Phormio
975   Were hairy—and they thrashed the foe.

CHORUS OF WOMEN (*singing*):
I have another tale,
With which to assail
    Your contention
    'Bout Melanion.

Once upon a time a man   980
    Named Timon left our city,
To live in some deserted land.
    (We thought him rather witty.)

He dwelt alone amidst the thorn;
    In solitude he brooded.   985
From some grim Fury he was born:
    Such hatred he exuded.

He cursed you men, as scoundrels through
    And through, till life he ended.
He couldn't stand the sight of you!   990
    But women he befriended.

WOMAN (*to* ONE OF THE MEN): I'll smash your face in, if you like.

MAN: Oh no, please don't! You frighten me.

WOMAN: I'll lift my foot—and thus I'll strike.   995

MAN: Aha! Look there! What's that I see?

WOMAN: Whate'er you see, you cannot say
That I'm not neatly trimmed today.

(LYSISTRATA *appears on the wall of the Acropolis.*)

LYSISTRATA: Hello! Hello! Girls, come here quick!

(SEVERAL WOMEN *appear beside her.*)

WOMAN: What is it? Why are you calling?   1000

LYSISTRATA: I see a man coming: he's in a dreadful state. He's mad with passion. O Queen of Cyprus, Cythera, and Paphos, just keep on this way!

WOMAN: Where is the fellow?

LYSISTRATA: There beside the shrine of Demeter.   1005

WOMAN: Oh yes, so he is. Who is he?

LYSISTRATA: Let's see. Do any of you know him?

MYRRHINE: Yes indeed. That's my husband, Cinesias.

LYSISTRATA: It's up to you, now: roast him, rack him, fool him, love him—and leave him! Do every-   1010 thing, except what our oath forbids.

MYRRHINE: Don't worry, I'll do it.

LYSISTRATA: I'll stay here to tease him and warm him up a bit. Off with you.

(*The* OTHER WOMEN *retire from the wall. Enter* CINESIAS *followed by* A SLAVE *carrying a baby.* CINESIAS *is obviously in great pain and distress.*)

CINESIAS (*groaning*): Oh-h! Oh-h-h! This is killing me!   1015
O God, what tortures I'm suffering!

LYSISTRATA (*from the wall*): Who's that within our lines?

CINESIAS: Me.

LYSISTRATA: A *man?*   1020

CINESIAS *(pointing):* A *man,* indeed!

LYSISTRATA: Well, go away!

CINESIAS: Who are you to send me away?

LYSISTRATA: The captain of the guard.

CINESIAS: Oh, for heaven's sake, call out Myrrhine for me.

LYSISTRATA: Call Myrrhine? Nonsense! Who are you?

CINESIAS: Her husband, Cinesias of Paionidai.

LYSISTRATA *(appearing much impressed):* Oh, greetings, friend. Your name is not without honour here among us. Your wife is always talking about you, and whenever she takes an egg or an apple, she says, "Here's to my dear Cinesias!"

CINESIAS *(quivering with excitement):* Oh, ye gods in heaven!

LYSISTRATA: Indeed she does! And whenever our conversations turn to men, your wife immediately says, "All others are mere rubbish compared with Cinesias."

CINESIAS *(groaning):* Oh! Do call her for me.

LYSISTRATA: Why should I? What will you give me?

CINESIAS: Whatever you want. All I have is yours—and you see what I've got.

LYSISTRATA: Well then, I'll go down and call her. *(She descends.)*

CINESIAS: And hurry up! I've had no joy of life ever since she left home. When I go in the house, I feel awful: everything seems so empty and I can't enjoy my dinner. I'm in such a state all the time!

MYRRHINE *(from behind the wall):* I *do* love him so. But he won't let me love him. No, no! Don't ask me to see him!

CINESIAS: O my darling, O Myrrhine honey, why do you do this to me?

(MYRRHINE appears on the wall.)

Come down here!

MYRRHINE: No, I won't come down.

CINESIAS: Won't you come, Myrrhine, when I call you?

MYRRHINE: No; you don't want me.

CINESIAS: *Don't want you?* I'm in agony!

MYRRHINE: I'm going now.

CINESIAS: Please don't. At least, listen to your baby. *(To the baby.)* Here you, call your mamma! *(Pinching the baby.)*

BABY: Ma-ma! Ma-ma! Ma-ma!

CINESIAS *(to* MYRRHINE*):* What's the matter with you? Have you no pity for your child, who hasn't been washed or fed for five whole days?

MYRRHINE: Oh, poor child; your father pays no attention to you.

CINESIAS: Come down then, you heartless wretch, for the baby's sake.

MYRRHINE: Oh, what it is to be a mother! I've got to come down, I suppose.

(She leaves the wall and shortly reappears at the gate.)

CINESIAS *(to himself):* She seems much younger, and she has such a sweet look about her. Oh, the way she teases me! And her pretty, provoking ways make me burn with longing.

MYRRHINE *(coming out of the gate and taking the baby):* O my sweet little angel. Naughty papa! Here, let Mummy kiss you, Mamma's little sweetheart!

(She fondles the baby lovingly.)

CINESIAS *(in despair):* You heartless creature, why do you do this? Why follow these other women and make both of us suffer so?

(He tries to embrace her.)

MYRRHINE: Don't touch me!

CINESIAS: You're letting all our things at home go to wrack and ruin.

MYRRHINE: I don't care.

CINESIAS: You don't care that your wool is being plucked to pieces by the chickens?

MYRRHINE: Not in the least.

CINESIAS: And you haven't celebrated the rites of Aphrodite for ever so long. Won't you come home?

MYRRHINE: Not on your life, unless you men make a truce and stop the war.

CINESIAS: Well, then, if that pleases you, we'll do it.

MYRRHINE: Well then, if that pleases *you,* I'll come home—afterwards! Right now I'm on oath not to.

CINESIAS: Then just lie down here with me for a moment.

MYRRHINE: No—*(in a teasing voice)* and yet I won't say I don't love you.

CINESIAS: You love me? Oh, do lie down here, Myrrhine dear!

MYRRHINE: What, you silly fool! in front of the baby?

CINESIAS *(hastily thrusting the baby at the slave):* Of course not. Here—home! Take him, Manes! *(The* SLAVE *goes off with the baby.)* See, the baby's out of the way. Now won't you lie down?

MYRRHINE: But where, my dear?

CINESIAS: Where? The grotto of Pan's a lovely spot.

MYRRHINE: How could I purify myself before returning to the shrine?

CINESIAS: Easily: just wash here in the Clepsydra.

MYRRHINE: And then, shall I go back on my oath?

CINESIAS: On my head be it! Don't worry about the oath.

MYRRHINE: All right, then. Just let me bring out a bed.

CINESIAS: No, don't. The ground's all right.

MYRRHINE: Heavens, no! Bad as you are, I won't let you lie on the bare ground.

(She goes into the Acropolis.)

CINESIAS: Why, she really loves me; it's plain to see.

MYRRHINE *(returning with a bed):* There! Now hurry up

1125 and lie down. I'll just slip off this dress. But—let's see: oh yes, I must fetch a mattress.

CINESIAS: Nonsense! No mattress for me.

MYRRHINE: Yes indeed! It's not nice on the bare springs.

1130 CINESIAS: Give me a kiss.

MYRRHINE (giving him a hasty kiss): There!

(She goes.)

CINESIAS (in mingled distress and delight): Oh-h! Hurry back!

MYRRHINE (returning with a mattress): Here's the mat-
1135 tress; lie down on it. I'm taking my things off now—but—let's see: you have no pillow.

CINESIAS: I don't want a pillow.

MYRRHINE: But I do.

(She goes.)

CINESIAS: Cheated again, just like Heracles and his
1140 dinner!

MYRRHINE (returning with a pillow): Here, lift your head. (To herself, wondering how else to tease him.) Is that all?

CINESIAS: Surely that's all! Do come here, precious!

1145 MYRRHINE: I'm taking off my girdle. But remember: don't go back on your promise about the truce.

CINESIAS: I hope to die, if I do.

MYRRHINE: You don't have a blanket.

CINESIAS (shouting in exasperation): I don't want one! I
1150 WANT TO—

MYRRHINE: Sh-h! There, there, I'll be back in a minute.

(She goes.)

CINESIAS: She'll be the death of me with these bed-clothes.

1155 MYRRHINE (returning with a blanket): Here, get up.

CINESIAS: I've got this up!

MYRRHINE: Would you like some perfume?

CINESIAS: Good heavens, no! I won't have it!

MYRRHINE: Yes, you shall, whether you want it or not.

(She goes.)

1160 CINESIAS: O lord! Confound all perfumes anyway!

MYRRHINE (returning with a flask): Stretch out your hand and put some on.

CINESIAS (suspiciously): By God, I don't much like per-fume. It smacks of shilly-shallying, and has no
1165 scent of the marriage-bed.

MYRRHINE: Oh dear! This is Rhodian perfume I've brought.

CINESIAS: It's quite all right, dear. Never mind.

MYRRHINE: Don't be silly!

(She goes out with the flask.)

1170 CINESIAS: Damn the man who first concocted per-fumes!

MYRRHINE (returning with another flask): Here, try this flask.

CINESIAS: I've got another one all ready for you. Come, you wretch, lie down and stop bringing me 117 things.

MYRRHINE: All right; I'm taking off my shoes. But, my dear, see that you vote for peace.

CINESIAS (absently): I'll consider it.

(MYRRHINE runs away to the Acropolis.)

I'm ruined! The wench has skinned me and run 118 away! (chanting, in tragic style) Alas! Alas! Deceived, deserted by this fairest of women, whom shall I— lay? Ah, my poor little child, how shall I nurture thee? Where's Cynalopex? I needs must hire a 118 nurse!

LEADER OF MEN (chanting): Ah, wretched man, in dreadful wise beguiled, bewrayed, thy soul is sore distressed. I pity thee, alas! What soul, what loins, what liver could stand this strain? How firm and unyielding he stands, with naught to aid him of a 119 morning.

CINESIAS: O lord! O Zeus! What tortures I endure!

LEADER OF MEN: This is the way she's treated you, that vile and cursèd wanton.

LEADER OF WOMEN: Nay, not vile and cursèd, but 11 sweet and dear.

LEADER OF MEN: Sweet, you say? Nay, hateful, hate-ful!

CINESIAS: Hateful indeed! O Zeus, Zeus!
Seize her and snatch her away, 12
Like a handful of dust, in a mighty,
Fiery tempest! Whirl her aloft, then let her drop
Down to the earth, with a crash, as she falls—
On the point of this waiting
Thingummybob! 12

(He goes out. Enter a SPARTAN HERALD in an obvious state of excitement, which he is doing his best to conceal.)

HERALD: Where can I find the Senate or the Prytanes? I've got an important message.

(The Athenian MAGISTRATE enters.)

MAGISTRATE: Say there, are you a man or Priapus?

HERALD (in annoyance): I'm a herald, you lout! I've come from Sparta about the truce. 12

MAGISTRATE: Is that a spear you've got under your cloak?

HERALD: No, of course not!

MAGISTRATE: Why do you twist and turn so? Why hold your cloak in front of you. Did you rupture your- 12 self on the trip?

HERALD: By gum, the fellow's an old fool.

MAGISTRATE (pointing): Why, you dirty rascal, you're excited.

HERALD: Not at all. Stop this tom-foolery. 12

MAGISTRATE: Well, what's that I see?

HERALD: A Spartan message-staff.

MAGISTRATE: Oh, certainly! That's just the kind of message-staff I've got. But tell me the honest truth: how are things going in Sparta?

HERALD: All the land of Sparta is up in arms—and our allies are up, too. We need Pellene.

MAGISTRATE: What brought this trouble on you? A sudden Panic?

HERALD: No, Lampito started it and then all the other women in Sparta with one accord chased their husbands out of their beds.

MAGISTRATE: How do you feel?

HERALD: Terrible. We walk around the city bent over like men lighting matches in a wind. For our women won't let us touch them until we all agree and make peace throughout Greece.

MAGISTRATE: This is a general conspiracy of the women; I see it now. Well, hurry back and tell the Spartans to send ambassadors here with full powers to arrange a truce. And I'll go tell the Council to choose ambassadors from here; I've got something here that will soon persuade them!

HERALD: I'll fly there; for you've made an excellent suggestion.

(The HERALD *and the* MAGISTRATE *depart on opposite sides of the stage.)*

LEADER OF MEN: No beast or fire is harder than womankind to tame,
Nor is the spotted leopard so devoid of shame.

LEADER OF WOMEN: Knowing this, you dare provoke us to attack?
I'd be your steady friend, if you'd but take us back.

LEADER OF MEN: I'll never cease my hatred keen of womankind.

LEADER OF WOMEN: Just as you will. But now just let me help you find
That cloak you threw aside. You look so silly there
Without your clothes. Here, put it on and don't go bare.

LEADER OF MEN: That's very kind, and shows you're not entirely bad.
But I threw off my things when I was good and mad.

LEADER OF WOMEN: At last you seem a man, and won't be mocked, my lad.
If you'd been nice to me, I'd take this little gnat
That's in your eye and pluck it out for you, like that.

LEADER OF MEN: So that's what bothered me and bit my eye so long!
Please dig it out for me. I own that I've been wrong.

LEADER OF WOMEN: I'll do so, though you've been a most ill-natured brat.
Ye gods! See here! A huge and monstrous little gnat!

LEADER OF MEN: Oh, how that helps! For it was digging wells in me.
And now it's out. My tears can roll down hard and free.

LEADER OF WOMEN: Here, let me wipe them off, although you're such a knave,
And kiss me.

LEADER OF MEN: No!

LEADER OF WOMEN: Whate'er you say, a kiss I'll have.

(She kisses him.)

LEADER OF MEN: Oh, confound these women! They've a coaxing way about them.
He was wise and never spoke a truer word, who said,
"We can't live with women, but we cannot live without them."
Now I'll make a truce with you. We'll fight no more; instead,
I will not injure you if you do me no wrong.
And now let's join our ranks and then begin a song.

COMBINED CHORUS *(singing)*:
Athenians, we're not prepared,
To say a single ugly word
About our fellow-citizens.
Quite the contrary: we desire but to say and to do
Naught but good. Quite enough are the ills now on hand.

Men and women, be advised:
If anyone requires
Money—minae two or three—
We've got what he desires.

My purse is yours, on easy terms:
When Peace shall reappear,
Whate'er you've borrowed will be due.
So speak up without fear.

You needn't pay me back, you see,
If you can get a cent from me!

We're about to entertain
Some foreign gentlemen;
We've soup and tender, fresh-killed pork.
Come round to dine at ten.

Come early; wash, and dress with care,
And bring the children, too.
Then step right in, no "by your leave."
We'll be expecting you.

Walk in as if you owned the place.
You'll find the door—shut in your face!

(Enter a group of SPARTAN AMBASSADORS; *they are in the same desperate condition as the* HERALD *in the previous scene.)*

LEADER OF CHORUS: Here come the envoys from Sparta, sprouting long beards and looking for the world as if they were carrying pig-pens in front of them.

1305 Greetings, gentlemen of Sparta. Tell me, in what state have you come?

SPARTAN: Why waste words? You can plainly see what state we've come in!

LEADER OF CHORUS: Wow! You're in a pretty high-strung condition, and it seems to be getting worse.

1310

SPARTAN: It's indescribable. Won't someone please arrange a peace for us—in any way you like.

LEADER OF CHORUS: Here come our own, native am-bassadors, crouching like wrestlers and holding their clothes in front of them; this seems an ath-letic kind of malady.

1315

(Enter several Athenian AMBASSADORS.*)*

ATHENIAN: Can anyone tell us where Lysistrata is? You see our condition.

1320 LEADER OF CHORUS: Here's another case of the same complaint. Tell me, are the attacks worse in the morning?

ATHENIAN: No, we're always afflicted this way. If some-one doesn't soon arrange this truce, you'd better not let me get my hands on—Cleisthenes!

1325

LEADER OF CHORUS: If you're smart, you'll arrange your cloaks so none of these fellows who smashed the Hermae can see you.

ATHENIAN: Right you are; a very good suggestion.

1330 SPARTAN: Aye, by all means. Here, let's hitch up our clothes.

ATHENIAN: Greetings, Spartan. We've suffered dread-ful things.

SPARTAN: My dear fellow, we'd have suffered still worse if one of those fellows had seen us in this condition.

1335

ATHENIAN: Well, gentlemen, we must get down to business. What's your errand here?

SPARTAN: We're ambassadors about peace.

1340 ATHENIAN: Excellent; so are we. Only Lysistrata can arrange things for us; shall we summon her?

SPARTAN: Aye, and Lysistratus too, if you like.

LEADER OF CHORUS: No need to summon her, it seems. She's coming out of her own accord.

(Enter LYSISTRATA *accompanied by a statue of a nude female figure, which represents Reconciliation.)*

1345 Hail, noblest of women; now must thou be
A judge shrewd and subtle, mild and severe,
Be sweet yet majestic: all manners employ.
The leaders of Hellas, caught by thy love-charms,
Have come to thy judgment, their charges
submitting.

1350 LYSISTRATA: This is no difficult task, if one catch them still in amorous passion, before they've re-sorted to each other. But I'll soon find out. Where's Reconciliation? Go, first bring the Spar-tans here, and don't seize them rudely and vio-lently, as our tactless husbands used to do, but as befits a woman, like an old, familiar friend; if they won't give you their hands, take them however you can. Then go fetch these Athenians here, tak-ing hold of whatever they offer you. Now then, men of Sparta, stand here beside me, and you Athenians on the other side, and listen to my words.

1355

1360

I am a woman, it is true, but I have a mind; I'm not badly off in native wit, and by listening to my father and my elders, I've had a decent schooling.

1365

Now I intend to give you a scolding which you both deserve. With one common font you wor-ship at the same altars, just like brothers, at Olympia, at Thermopylae, at Delphi—how many more might I name, if time permitted;—and the Barbarians stand by waiting with their armies; yet you are destroying the men and towns of Greece.

1370

ATHENIAN: Oh, this tension is killing me!

1375

LYSISTRATA: And now, men of Sparta,—to turn to you—don't you remember how the Spartan Pericleidas came here once as a suppliant, and sitting at our altar, all pale with fear in his crim-son cloak, begged us for an army? For all Mes-sene had attacked you and the god sent an earthquake too? Then Cimon went forth with four thousand hoplites and saved all Lacedae-mon. Such was the aid you received from Athens, and now you lay waste the country which once treated you so well.

1380

1385

ATHENIAN *(hotly)*: They're in the wrong, Lysistrata, upon my word, they are!

SPARTAN *(absently, looking at the statue of Reconciliation)*: We're in the wrong. What hips! How lovely they are!

1390

LYSISTRATA: Don't think I'm going to let you Athe-nians off. Don't you remember how the Spartans came in arms when you were wearing the rough, sheepskin cloak of slaves and slew the host of Thessalians, the comrades and allies of Hippias? Fighting with you on that day, alone of all the Greeks, they set you free and instead of a sheepskin gave your folk a handsome robe to wear.

1395

SPARTAN *(looking at* LYSISTRATA*)*: I've never seen a more distinguished woman.

1400

ATHENIAN *(looking at Reconciliation)*: I've never seen a more voluptuous body!

LYSISTRATA: Why then, with these many noble deeds to think of, do you fight each other? Why don't you stop this villainy? Why not make peace? Tell me, what prevents it?

1405

SPARTAN (*waving vaguely at Reconciliation*): We're willing, if you're willing to give up your position on
410   yonder flank.
LYSISTRATA: What position, my good man?
SPARTAN: Pylus, we've been panting for it for ever so
long.
ATHENIAN: No, by God! You shan't have it!
415 LYSISTRATA: Let them have it, my friend.
ATHENIAN: Then what shall we have to rouse things
up?
LYSISTRATA: Ask for another place in exchange.
ATHENIAN: Well, let's see: first of all (*pointing to various
420   parts of Reconciliation's anatomy*) give us Echinus
here, this Maliac Inlet in back there, and these
two Megarian legs.
SPARTAN: No, by heavens! You can't have *everything,*
you crazy fool!
425 LYSISTRATA: Let it go. Don't fight over a pair of legs.
ATHENIAN (*taking off his cloak*): I think I'll strip and do
a little planting now.
SPARTAN (*following suit*): And I'll just do a little fertil-
izing, by gosh!
430 LYSISTRATA: Wait until the truce is concluded. Now if
you've decided on this course, hold a conference
and discuss the matter with your allies.
ATHENIAN: Allies? Don't be ridiculous. They're in the
same state we are. Won't our allies want the same
435   thing we do—to jump in bed with their women?
SPARTAN: Ours will, I know.
ATHENIAN: Especially the Carystians, by God!
LYSISTRATA: Very well. Now purify yourselves, that
your wives may feast and entertain you in the
440   Acropolis; we've provisions by the basketful.
Exchange your oaths and pledges there, and then
each of you may take his wife and go home.
ATHENIAN: Let's go at once.
SPARTAN: Come on, where you will.
445 ATHENIAN: For God's sake, let's hurry!

(*They all go into the Acropolis.*)

CHORUS (*singing*):
  Whate'er I have of coverlets
    And robes of varied hue
  And golden trinkets,—without stint
    I offer them to you.

450 Take what you will and bear it home,
    Your children to delight,
  Or if your girl's a Basket-maid;
    Just choose whate'er's in sight.

  There's naught within so well secured
455   You cannot break the seal
  And bear it off; just help yourselves;
    No hesitation feel.

But you'll see nothing, though you try,
Unless you've sharper eyes than I!

If anyone needs bread to feed   1460
  A growing family,
I've lots of wheat and full-grown loaves;
  So just apply to me.

Let every poor man who desires
  Come round and bring a sack   1465
To fetch the grain; my slave is there
  To load it on his back.

But don't come near my door, I say:
Beware the dog, and stay away!

(*An* ATHENIAN *enters carrying a torch; he knocks at the
gate.*)

ATHENIAN: Open the door! (*To the* CHORUS, *which is* 1470
clustered around the gate.) Make way, won't you!
What are you hanging around for? Want me to
singe you with this torch? (*To himself.*) No; it's a
stale trick, I won't do it! (*To the audience.*) Still if
I've got to do it to please you, I suppose I'll have 1475
to take the trouble.

(*A* SECOND ATHENIAN *comes out of the gate.*)

SECOND ATHENIAN: And I'll help you.
FIRST ATHENIAN (*waving his torch at the* CHORUS): Get
out! Go bawl your heads off! Move on there,
so the Spartans can leave in peace when the 1480
banquet's over.

(*They brandish their torches until the* CHORUS *leaves the
Orchestra.*)

SECOND ATHENIAN: I've never seen such a pleasant
banquet: the Spartans are charming fellows, indeed they are! And we Athenians are very witty in
our cups.   1485
FIRST ATHENIAN: Naturally: for when we're sober
we're never at our best. If the Athenians would
listen to me, we'd always get a little tipsy on our
embassies. As things are now, we go to Sparta
when we're sober and look around to stir up 1490
trouble. And then we don't hear what they
say—and as for what they *don't* say, we have all
sorts of suspicions. And then we bring back varying reports about the mission. But this time
everything is pleasant; even if a man should 1495
sing the Telamon-song when he ought to sing
"Cleitagorus," we'd praise him and swear it was
excellent.

(*The two* CHORUSES *return, as a* CHORUS OF ATHENI-
ANS *and a* CHORUS OF SPARTANS.)

Here they come back again. Go to the devil, you
scoundrels!   1500

SECOND ATHENIAN: Get out, I say! They're coming out from the feast.

(Enter the SPARTAN *and* ATHENIAN ENVOYS, *followed by* LYSISTRATA *and all the* WOMEN.*)*

1505 SPARTAN *(to one of his fellow envoys)*: My good fellow, take up your pipes; I want to do a fancy two-step and sing a jolly song for the Athenians.

ATHENIAN: Yes, do take your pipes, by all means. I'd love to see you dance.

SPARTAN *(singing and dancing with the* CHORUS OF SPARTANS*)*:
These youths inspire
To song and dance, O Memory;
1510 Stir up my Muse, to tell how we
And Athens' men, in our galleys clashing
At Artemisium, 'gainst foemen dashing in godlike
ire,
Conquered the Persian and set Greece free.

Leonidas
1515 Led on his valiant warriors
Whetting their teeth like angry boars.
Abundant foam on their lips was flow'ring,
A stream of sweat from their limbs was show'ring.
The Persian was
Numberless as the sand on the shores.

1520 O Huntress who slayest the beasts in the glade,
O Virgin divine, hither come to our truce,
Unite us in bonds which all time will not loose.
Grant us to find in this treaty, we pray,
An unfailing source of true friendship today,
1525 And all of our days, helping us to refrain
From weaseling tricks which bring war in their
train.
Then hither, come hither! O huntress maid.

LYSISTRATA: Come then, since all is fairly done, men of Sparta, lead away your wives, and you, Atheni-
1530 ans, take yours. Let every man stand beside his wife, and every wife beside her man, and then, to celebrate our fortune, let's dance. And in the future, let's take care to avoid these misunder-standings.

CHORUS OF ATHENIANS *(singing and dancing)*:
1535 Lead on the dances, your graces revealing.
Call Artemis hither, call Artemis' twin,
Leader of dances, Apollo the Healing,
Kindly God—hither! Let's summon him in!

Nysian Bacchus call,
Who with his Maenads, his eyes flashing fire,   1540
Dances, and last of all
Zeus of the thunderbolt flaming, the Sire,
And Hera in majesty,
Queen of prosperity.
Come, ye Powers who dwell above   1545
Unforgetting, our witnesses be
Of Peace with bonds of harmonious love—
The Peace which Cypris has wrought for me.
Alleluia! Io Paean!
Leap in joy—hurrah! hurrah!   1550
'Tis victory—hurrah! hurrah!
Euoi! Euoi! Euai! Euai!

LYSISTRATA *(to the* SPARTANS*)*: Come now, sing a new song to cap ours.

CHORUS OF SPARTANS *(singing and dancing)*:
Leaving Taygetus fair and renown'd   1555
Muse of Laconia, hither come:
Amyclae's god in hymns resound.
Athene of the Brazen Home,
And Castor and Pollux, Tyndareus' sons,
Who sport where Eurotas murmuring runs.   1560

On with the dance! Heia! Ho!
All leaping along,
Mantles a-swinging as we go!
Of Sparta our song.
There the holy chorus ever gladdens,   1565
There the beat of stamping feet,
As our winsome fillies, lovely maidens,
Dance, beside Eurotas, banks a-skipping,—
Nimbly go to and fro
Hast'ning, leaping feet in measures tripping,   1570

Like the Bacchae's revels, hair a-streaming.
Leda's child, divine and mild,
Leads the holy dance, her fair face beaming.
On with the dance! as your hand
Presses the hair   1575
Streaming away unconfined.
Leap in the air
Light as the deer; footsteps resound
Aiding our dance, beating the ground.
Praise Athene, Maid divine, unrivalled in her
might,   1580
Dweller in the Brazen Home, unconquered in the
fight.

(All go out singing and dancing.)

Figure 1. In the 1993 production directed by Peter Hall, the women of Athens, with Lysistrata (Geraldine James) center (in dark corset), declare their resolve to abstain from sex until the war is over. The play was performed by the Peter Hall Company at the Old Vic Theatre, London. (Photograph: Donald Cooper, Photostage.)

Staging of *Lysistrata*

REVIEW OF THE PETER HALL COMPANY
PRODUCTION, 1993, BY MICHAEL COVENEY

In the funniest scene in Aristophanes's *Lysistrata* (Old Vic), the actress Diane Bull pops in between the erection and the hopes of her distraught spouse, who lies in a state of helpless indignity while a phallus with a mind of its own reaches for the sky. This cock and Bull story is part of the women's campaign to restore peace during the Peloponnesian War by shutting up shop in the bedroom.

The vulgar, restorative comedy has been largely forgotten in the recent enthusiastic flurry of Greek drama. Peter Hall's superb production, which might be subtitled 'Two jeers for phallocracy,' reclaims this wonderful author, not just as a virile feminist, but as a gloriously humane and still pertinent political farceur.

Hall's all-male *Oresteia* at the National used full masks and neutral costumes. Tony Harrison added the latex padding, wispy beards and dangly bits for his archaeological satyr-play *The Trackers of Oxyrynchus*. Hall's production is in a way a synthesis of those two approaches. In addition, Hall gives his cast half-masks, and women play the women.

Both strategies reap rich rewards. The chorus of old men becomes an ancient *Dad's Army* in tatty great-coats, medals and walrus moustaches. Geraldine James's Lysistrata emerges as a true voice of feminine reason, especially when Ranjit Bolt's vigorous, rhyming translation inserts a new parabasis and she removes her mask and wig to gently denounce the level of political debate in our own Parliamentary system. The women have seized the Exchequer before slamming on their chastity belts; they control the means of production, and of reproduction.

Because of its stylistic purity, and strict adherence to Aristophanes's structure of episodes and choruses, the rude excesses of dunghill imagery, priapic treaties and sex-hunger are freshly amusing, innocent, unexpected. Unlike the RSC's current Goldoni, *The Venetian Twins,* in Stratford, the show treats vulgarity with a proper respect.

The cast exhibit full vocal variety within their masks, and a corporate animation when acting in concert. Guy Woolfenden's score is generously eclectic, covering the popular waterfront from Eartha Kittenish blues to G&S patter, soft shoe shuffle and Flanagan and Allen.

I am now convinced, although I did not expect to be, that the play would be neither as effective nor as funny without masks. The visiting Greek designer Dionysis Fotopoulos throws an arc over the centuries by placing the action against a graffiti-strewn wall ('We hate Spartans'). A cut-out Acropolis suddenly floats in the sky as the Exchequer is taken, just as it does if you sit in the Herod Atticus arena in Athens.

There is no glib updating in this; the play speaks for itself, and Hall's cast, led by the luminous Ms James, step with dignity from their ancient source to its modern application. Would women still be wiping each other out in Bosnia-Herzegovina if they were in charge?

How men treat women (in thought and in speech) is another perennial theme in the play, but the beauty is that no one of either sex is ever thought to be more than imperfect. In that regard alone, the piece has something to say in the literature of sexual politics.

And, as in Hall's *Oresteia,* there is no demeaning of the actor's identity by hiding his eyes: uncompromising work here from Serena Evans and Nimmy March as the sex-strikers, with Timothy Davies, Tim Hardy and Peter Sproule providing what I suppose we must call stiff competition.

Figure 2. Reconciliation (Clare Summerfield), flanked by an Athenian soldier and looked at by the Spartan envoy (in the top hat), appears at the end of the play in the 1993 Peter Hall Company production. (Photograph: Donald Cooper, Photostage.)

According to an ancient but unverified account, Plautus began his theatrical career as a stagehand, then invested his earnings in a business that failed, after which he took up work in a flour mill and started writing plays on the side as an additional source of income. Though the story is legendary, as is every other bit of information about his life, it does suggest the vigorous and enterprising spirit that characterizes both his comedies and the dramatic traditions of his age. He wrote during that heady period when Rome was being transformed from a struggling city-state to a vast empire, controlling almost the whole of the known world from the western to the eastern Mediterranean. The political expansion of Rome brought about a corresponding cultural expansion, reflected in the theater by the development of a Greco-Roman tradition of drama, which began in 240 B.C. when a Greek slave, Livius Andronicus, turned a Greek comedy into Latin and it was successfully produced at the festival in Rome. By the time Plautus began writing during the last fifteen years of the century, the Roman practice of adapting Greek comedies was firmly established, and its practitioners were well supplied with material. They based their work on a type of Greek comedy that had been astonishingly prolific during the fourth century—Athenian social comedy, otherwise known as New Comedy to distinguish it from the Old Comedy of Aristophanes. The most popular and prolific writer of New Comedy was Menander, who wrote more than one hundred plays of which only one, *The Grumbler,* has survived intact. Still, major sections of six more plays by Menander, discoveries of texts preserved on papyrus sheets, and many brief sections quoted by other Greek and Latin writers have allowed scholars to name about sixty Greek dramatists. Trying to define a genre from fragments is risky business, but the general nature of New Comedy may be inferred through its survival in the works adapted from it by Plautus and his most famous successor, Terence (195–159 B.C.).

New Comedy was essentially a comedy of manners, incorporating stock character types from Athenian middle-class experience—eager young men and lecherous old men, cantankerous fathers and gullible fathers, parasitic friends and braggart soldiers, pimps and moneylenders, cooks and jesters, courtesans and handmaids, rich young girls and slave girls who turn out to be the long-lost daughters of rich merchants. Characters such as these and one or two ingenious servants, the masterminds of intrigue, were the staples of New Comedy, and they were combined to produce farcically complicated plots made up of love affairs, mistaken identities, and surprising discoveries—those ancient ingredients that still prevail in modern situation comedies. In adapting and translating, Plautus and Terence retained the characters and plot of a single comedy, or combined characters and plots from several comedies—always modifying the details of Athenian experience to make them fit the experience of their Roman audience, while often attributing any "immorality" to the Greek original. They also abandoned the incidental choric passages that persisted in New Comedy and thus produced a purely dramatic form of social comedy that has been profoundly influential from the Renaissance to this day. The satire on greed in Jonson's *Volpone,* on pretentiousness in Molière's *The Misanthrope,* and on love and marriage in Sheridan's *The School for Scandal* echoes, though often in more polite terms, the robust attacks of Roman comedy. In fact, virtually every comic dramatist in the Western tradition is in some way indebted to the twenty surviving plays of Plautus and the six plays of Terence. Plautus's *The Braggart Soldier,* for example, has been the inspiration for countless braggadocios, from Falstaff in Shakespeare's *Henry IV, Pts. 1 and 2* to Sergius in Shaw's *Arms and the Man.* Likewise, *The Menaechmi* is the source for innumerable comedies based on mistaken identity, the most famous being Shakespeare's *The Comedy of Errors,* which includes not one but two sets of twins and thereby doubles the comic confusion created by Plautus.

In *Casina* (retitled in this translation *A Funny Thing Happened on the Way to the Wedding*), Plautus works, as usual, from a lost Greek original by Diphilus, but makes major alterations in its plot. As the prologue makes clear, he inherits a story about a father and son who both desire the slave girl Casina. The father, already married, plans to marry her to one of his slaves so that he can go to bed with the girl, while the son, perhaps unwilling to ally himself with a slave, plans a similar ruse. But Plautus simply eliminates the son from the play (with the prologue casually explaining that the author "dropped him from our play, / by washing out a bridge that lay upon his way") and so pits husband and wife against each other, the wife supporting her son's original plan. The change thus emphasizes the struggle between Lysidamus, the foolish and sexually obsessed husband, and Cleostrata, the clever and feisty wife—a battle that Plautus evokes through mythology (the characters refer to themselves as Jupiter and Juno), through slapstick (their slaves fight it out on stage), and through aggressively humorous dialogue.

Plautus also subverts the audience's expectation through his manipulation of the play's title character, Casina. The first joke is that she never appears at all, even though the prologue hints that she will, and that she will turn out to be not a slave but a freeborn woman. But the real invention comes when the male slave, Chalinus, having lost the lot-drawing (the original name of the Greek play) that would have awarded Casina to him, reappears, disguised as Casina-the-bride. Because the role of Casina would have been played by a male actor in a mask, Plautus manages to surprise the audience and yet involve them in a joke about the nature of theater. Just as Shakespeare's Cesario/Viola in *Twelfth Night* wittily alludes to the boy-actor originally playing the role by saying "I am not what I am," so Casina boisterously reminds audiences of her actor's identity by repulsing the two men who are touching her, with a vicious foot-stamp and a hard elbow-bash. In addition, the report of the slave-groom, Olympio, about his attempts to take Casina to bed is full of elaborate sexual double-entendres.

Indeed, the language of *Casina* is highly elaborate, alternating between prose and poetry, and filled throughout with puns, metaphors, made-up words, and alliteration. The translator of the play—the classical scholar Richard C. Beacham—deliberately aimed to re-create Plautus's playful style by keeping "the language as stageworthy as possible, while preserving at all times the tone, vitality, and sense of the original, and *then,* wherever practicable, to convey as much of the literal, word-for-word meaning as these priorities would allow." When the play was produced professionally at the J. Paul Getty Museum in Los Angeles (on a double bill with Menander's *The Woman from Samos*), the director underscored the text's ribald humor by adding a chorus attending the lecherous Lysidamus, their prominent phalluses stressing his intentions (see Figure 1). The central joke of the play, the disguising of Chalinus as the title character, Casina, can be seen in the onstage appearance of the disguised slave (see Figure 2) and vividly imagined as Olympio describes his offstage "wedding night" (see Figure 3). The conflict between husband and wife, so prominent in Plautus's text, was played primarily for comedy, although reviewers noted the subversive implications created by the reversal of traditional gender power roles. Indeed, as the final tableau (see Figure 4) made clear, women *and* slaves triumph over patriarchal mastery. Laughter then is not merely the playwright's aim but also his weapon; by laughing at onstage conflicts, we end up laughing at our own desire for power and pleasure.

A FUNNY THING HAPPENED ON THE WAY TO THE WEDDING

BY PLAUTUS / TRANSLATED BY RICHARD C. BEACHAM

This translation is dedicated to Barbara Fleischman and the memory of Lawrence Fleischman. In 1994 the first public presentation of the Fleischman Collection, which included many objects relating to the ancient theater, prompted the J. Paul Getty Museum to stage Menander's Woman from Samos *and Plautus's* Casina *in conjunction with the exhibition.*

CHARACTERS

OLYMPIO, *slave and country foreman of Lysidamus*
CHALINUS, *city slave of Lysidamus and his absent son*
CLEOSTRATA, *wife of Lysidamus*
PARDALISCA, *maid to Cleostrata*
MYRRHINA, *wife of Alcesimus, neighbor to Cleostrata
and Lysidamus*
LYSIDAMUS, *an elderly Athenian*
ALCESIMUS, *friend and neighbor of Lysidamus*
COOK *and* ASSISTANTS

SCENE

A street in Athens. The setting consists of an open stage backed by a scenic façade. This has two doorways, each of which has a small porch in front of it, with steps descending to the stage. The door to the left represents the house of LYSI-DAMUS; *that to the right belongs to* ALCESIMUS. *The actor— or possibly two actors—representing the* PROLOGUE, *enter.*

PROLOGUE

Warm welcome, folks, you faithful jovial crew.
You trust in me, I'll place my trust in you.
If that seems fair, then give a little sign
to show you'll hear me with an open mind.

(Waits for applause)

5　Now wise men—men of taste, refined,
favor old farces, just like a vintage wine.
They love the works and wisdom of the good old
　　days,
and fail to see the merit of these modern plays
so faulty, feeble, flaccid, and fickle
10　with less real value than a wooden nickel.

Now rumor has it—as people have their say,
you're longing to applaud a play by Plautus here
　　today.
A titillating tale, to charm, amuse, and move;
the sort of stuff the older crowd approve.
15　You younger folks who don't remember Plautus
we'll also do our best to win your plaudits,

The Latin title of this play is *Casina*.

with such a play! The greatest glory of its age,
once more before you on a modern stage!
Those dedicated, decorated, dear-departed souls
those ancient comic playwrights shall inspire our
　　roles.　　　　　　　　　　　　　　　　　　　20

Now let me *earnest-nestly* urge you pay us close
　　attention.
Away with sorrowing, thoughts about your
　　borrowing, not to mention
work! It's fun and games, so put your cares away,
Why even bankers get a holiday!
Now all is peaceful, quiet, sunken in repose,　　25
the shops are shuttered, and the banks are
　　closed.
They're calculating, bankers—no need to hinder
　　us—
For while we take a break, they're taking interest!
So lend your ears and I'll your loan repay,
by telling you the plot and title of our play!　　30
Once known as, *Clerumenoe* by the Greeks,
'twas titled, *Sortientes* in Latin speech,
(or, let's see now, that's *Lot-Drawers* to you)
when funny, punning Plautus fashioned it anew.

(During the following passage, the characters appear "on cue" in dumb show behind the PROLOGUE*)*

35   A married gentleman, somewhat past his prime,
his son, and slave, live here, and once upon a time
—some sixteen years ago to be exact—
this slave, no knave, performed a kindly act.
A baby girl, abandoned by her mother—that's a
    fact!
40   —he saved, and gave her to the old man's wife,
begging that the baby spend its life
within this very house; the newfound foundling's
    home.
His mistress readily agreed and raised it as her own.

Now when the girl had reached that certain age,
45   when men begin to notice and to gauge
their chance for romance and to "have their way,"
the young man fell in love with her—he has it
    bad—
and strange to say, so does his dad. How *sad!*

Now each prepares his forces; summoning all
    hands,
50   while knowing nothing of his rival's plans!
The father told a slave, a rustic chap,
his farmyard foreman (something of a sap),
to make the girl his own,
so, later, his foreman having wed her, unbeknownst
55   to Mother, Dad himself can bed her.

Meanwhile, the son has told his slave, and right-
    hand man
to act for him, and seek the lady's hand
in marriage, knowing if the slave would keep his
    head,
he'll bow to master: and so to bed.

60   The old man's wife, has stumbled on the plot.
To thwart her husband, she would throw her lot
in with the son, but then, the secret's out!
Dad learns of son's infatuation, and—the lout!—
sends him abroad while wily Mother, still party to
    the plan,
65   determines to assist her son in every way she can.

Oh, a minor point and rather sad to say,
that son who went abroad won't make it back
    today.
Plautus changed his mind and dropped him from
    our play,
by washing out a bridge that lay upon his way.

Now some may mutter 'mongst themselves, no
70   doubt,
"By Hercules! But what's all this about?
Since when can slaves propose, or marriages take
    place?

Nowhere in all the world, can such things be the
    case."

And yet, *it is,* in Carthage,° and Apulia°—and the
    Greeks,
are prone, and have been known to celebrate for
    weeks   75
when slaves get wed. Who dares to disagree?
I'll bet a drink, but let the referee,
be Carthaginian, Apulian, or Greek.
Well, now's your chance. No takers? Come on,
    speak
up! Not got the nerve to bet or anything to say?   80
On second thought, I'll bet . . . you've drunk
    enough today!

Now don't forget, that foundling pet,
the girl I told you of.
The sweet young thing, whom, with a ring,
the men all long to love.   85
In fact she's free.
Well, don't blame me!
And, please, don't worry,
for she's in no hurry, to lose her . . . "way"
—not in our play at any rate. But just you wait,   90
till afterwards, to date her.
For a little money, she's anyone's honey,
and the marriage can wait till later!
That's all I know, enjoy the show,
be healthy, wise, and strong   95
to obtain what through valor you gain:
great victories, as ever.

(Exit PROLOGUE*)*

ACT I

(Enter OLYMPIO *from the right, followed closely by* CHALI-
NUS. *The scene between them should be played with a good
deal of slapstick, including physical bullying of* CHALI-
NUS *by* OLYMPIO.*)*

OLYMPIO: Can't I talk as I walk, or use my mind to
    mind my own business without being overheard,
    gallows bird, by you? Why are you following me?
CHALINUS: You might as well know: I'm resolved to go
    wherever you go. Just like your shadow, I'll follow.   5
    Even if you're strung up on the cross, I'll string
    along. So just decide for yourself, whether as
    bride for yourself, you'd descend to taking my
    intended Casina—by tricking me!
OLYMPIO: Why bother with my business?   10
CHALINUS: What's that, you creep? Why are you creep-
    ing around the town, you oversized overseer?

Carthage, ancient city of north Africa.   **Apulia,** region
in southern Italy.

OLYMPIO: I feel like it.

CHALINUS: Why aren't you back on the farm, on your
15   own turf? Why not mind your own business,
    there, and leave city affairs to city folks? You've
    come to carry off Casina, you cur! Get back to the
    outback, clodhopper!

OLYMPIO: I am perfectly mindful of my duties, Chali-
20   nus; someone's looking after the farm. And when
    I've got what I came for, and marry that girl you
    swoon over, that fellow slave of yours—that pretty,
    sweet, little Casina—when I've got her back with
    me on the farm, you can bet I'll bed down with
25   my bride, on my "own turf"!

CHALINUS: You have her, you! Hang me, by Hercules,
    I'd sooner die than let you get her!

OLYMPIO: Hang on! She's mine, my booty, baby! So
    your neck's for the noose.

30 CHALINUS: You, *d-d-dug* from a *d-d-dungheap!* She's
    your booty, booby?!

OLYMPIO: You said it; you'll see it.

CHALINUS: Damn you!

OLYMPIO: Oh, how I'll needle you at my nuptials! As
35   sure as I breathe.

CHALINUS: What'll you do to me?

OLYMPIO: What'll I do to you? First, I'll make you
    carry the torch for my new bride. Then, you'll
    go back to being your usual good-for-nothing
40   nobody. And later, when you visit the villa, I'll give
    you one pitcher, one path, one well, and eight
    enormous casks to fill. And fill you will, or you'll
    be well full of welts! I'll bend you double with
    trouble, till you look like a yoke—no joke! And
45   further, when you fancy some fodder, you'll eat
    dirt like a worm, compliments of the compost
    heap. By Pollux,° you'll eat up less than nothing;
    you'll famish on the farm. And then . . . at the
    end of the day, when you're hungry and hurting,
50   I'll see that you spend the night, just right.

CHALINUS: What'll you do?

OLYMPIO: I'll fasten you firmly in the frame of the win-
    dow, where you can listen and *stew,* while I kiss
    and . . . *"hug"* Casina. And when she murmurs to
55   me, "Oh, sweetie-pie! O Olympio, my darling, my
    little honey pot, my joy, let me kiss those cute little
    eyes of yours, my precious! Oh please, please, let
    me *love* you, light of my life, my little dickey bird,
    my lovey-dovey, my bunny-wunny!" Well then,
60   when she's cooing these things to me, you'll flut-
    ter, gallows bird, you'll shudder like a mouse shut
    up in the wall. And you can shut up now. I'm
    going in. I'm tired of talking to you.

CHALINUS: I'll follow you. By Pollux, you won't get
65   away with anything! Not while *I'm* around!

Pollux, name of one of the twin sons of Tyndarus and
Leda; the second star in the constellation Gemini.

(They exit into LYSIDAMUS's *house. Pause, then enter*
CLEOSTRATA *from the same house, speaking within to*
PARDALISCA.)

CLEOSTRATA: Lock up the pantry, and bring me the
    key. I'm going next door to the neighbor's. If my
    husband wants me, come and get me.

PARDALISCA: "Sir" is asking for his dinner.

CLEOSTRATA: Hush! Go away! Be quiet and be quick;   70
    I'll not do his dinner today! Not when he turns
    against his own dear son, and *me!* in order to
    appease his appetite, that monster of man! I'll
    wrack° that rake° with hunger and thirst, curses
    and worse. By Pollux, I'll torture him with tor-   75
    ment from my tongue! I'll give him the life
    he deserves, that dungheap dandy, the haughty
    debauchee, that sink of sin! Oh, how wretched I
    am! I think I'll just go and tell my neighbor. Ah! I
    hear her door creaking, and there she is herself,   80
    coming out. Dear me, I think I've timed this visit
    badly.

(Enter MYRRHINA *from* ALCESIMUS's *house)*

MYRRHINA: Follow me next door, girls! Hey! You! Do
    you hear what I say? I shall be there if my husband
    or anyone wants me. Somehow alone at home,   85
    I'm so drowsy I just keep drifting off. Didn't I tell
    you to fetch me my distaff?°

CLEOSTRATA: Oh, *Myrrhina!*

MYRRHINA: Why, hello! But why so miserable, Love?

CLEOSTRATA: It's the same with all unhappily married   90
    women. Indoors or out, we're always down in the
    dumps. I was just coming over for a visit.

MYRRHINA: How about that! I was on my way over
    to you! But what's on your mind? When you're
    troubled, it troubles me too.   95

CLEOSTRATA: By Castor,° but I believe it does! There's
    none of my neighbors I like more than you;
    you're always such a comfort to me.

MYRRHINA: I like you likewise, and I'm longing to
    know what's the matter.   100

CLEOSTRATA: It's simply a scandal how I'm abused in
    my own home!

MYRRHINA: Goodness, how's that again? I don't quite
    get it.

CLEOSTRATA: My husband! It's perfectly scandalous   105
    how he treats me, and as for justice, well, I can
    just forget about that.

MYRRHINA: If that's the case, it's very odd, since usu-
    ally it's the *men* who don't get what they deserve
    from their wives.   110

---

wrack, punish.   *rake,* a man of loose habits and immoral character.   *distaff,* a cleft staff about three feet long,
on which, in the ancient mode of spinning, wool or flax was
wound.   *Castor,* name of one of the twin sons of Tyndarus
and Leda; the first star in the constellation Gemini.

CLEOSTRATA: Here he is, to spite me, intending to give my maid to his foreman on the farm—the maid whom I've reared myself—because *he* fancies her!

115 MYRRHINA: Hush your mouth!

CLEOSTRATA: I'll say what I like; we're by ourselves.

MYRRHINA: So we are. Now how can she be yours? After all, a proper wife ought not to have any property apart from her husband. And if she does
120 have things, in my opinion she got them improperly; she's guilty either of stealing or stealth, or . . . *hanky-panky!* In my opinion *all* that you have is your husband's.

CLEOSTRATA: Now there you go! Accusing and abus-
125 ing your own dear friend.

MYRRHINA: Oh, do be still, you silly-billy, and listen to me! Now don't oppose your husband! Let him have his fling, and do what he wants, just so long as he looks after you properly at home.

130 CLEOSTRATA: Are you out of your mind? There you go again, speaking against me and your own interests!

MYRRHINA: You stupid woman! There's one thing you must always prevent your husband from saying.

135 CLEOSTRATA: What's that, then?

MYRRHINA: "Shove off, woman!"

CLEOSTRATA: Shh-h! Be quiet!

MYRRHINA: What's the matter?

CLEOSTRATA: Look over there! My old man's coming!
140 Go inside quickly! Hurry, love!

MYRRHINA: Already, already, I'm going!

CLEOSTRATA: Soon as we've got a moment I want to have a proper chat with you. But bye for now.

MYRRHINA: *Ciao!*

(Exit MYRRHINA *into her house;* CLEOSTRATA *withdraws; enter* LYSIDAMUS, *garlanded, pleased with himself and more than a little inebriated as he sings his love song)*

LYSIDAMUS: You can take it from me: not on land or
145 at sea
is there anything finer than love.
Nothing half so entrancing, everyday life-
enhancing
not on earth nor in heaven above.

And I do think it odd, when a cook's at his job
150 giving dishes the very best flavor,
he can't use for a spice, what is *ever* so nice,
just a sprinkling of *Love* to add savor!

Why, what more could you wish, a mouth-watering
dish
neither salty nor cloying? How handy!
Love would transform it all, making honey from
155 gall,

(Aside)
and a dirty old man to a dandy!

Now, I didn't just hear this; I speak from
experience,
for since Casina captured my heart,
quite overpowered, I have utterly flowered:
I've turned nattiness° into an art!   160

To become more alluring, I'm even procuring
the very best scent that's available.
Just a touch of perfume, to help her love bloom,
for I do think her virtue's assailable!

(Seeing his wife, glowering in the doorway)

Yet . . . I *am* at a loss. There's that old rugged cross,   165
that I bear, while she lives, called my *wife!*
And she's looking quite vile—soothing words—
mustn't rile.
Ah, how goes it, sweet light of my life?

CLEOSTRATA: Buzz off, and don't touch me!

LYSIDAMUS: Ah, now my Juno° shouldn't be cross with   170
her Jove.° Where are you going?

CLEOSTRATA: Let me go!

LYSIDAMUS: But stay!

CLEOSTRATA: I won't stay!

LYSIDAMUS: Well, then, by Pollux, I'll follow you.   175

CLEOSTRATA: Good Lord, is the man mad?

LYSIDAMUS: Yes! I'm madly in love with you.

CLEOSTRATA: I don't want any of your love.

LYSIDAMUS: You can't avoid it!

CLEOSTRATA: You shall be the death of me!   180

LYSIDAMUS *(Aside)*: If only it were true!

CLEOSTRATA *(Hearing)*: Ah, now *that* I believe!

LYSIDAMUS: Please look at me, O darling, mine!

CLEOSTRATA: Right! Just like you're mine. Excuse me,
love, but where is that smell coming from?   185

LYSIDAMUS *(Aside)*: Damnation! I'm afraid she's got me red-handed! I'd better wipe it off on my cloak. *(Looking up)* Mercury,° be a good chap and destroy that perfumer who gave me this stuff.

CLEOSTRATA: Why, you lecherous old louse! I'm almost   190
ashamed to tell you what I think of you. At your age, going about town all perfumed up, you worm!

LYSIDAMUS: Gosh, I was only assisting a certain friend of mine in choosing a scent.

CLEOSTRATA: Always ready with a smart answer! Have   195
you no shame?

LYSIDAMUS *(Humbly)*: All you could want.

CLEOSTRATA: What fleshpots° have you been stewing in lately?

---

nattiness, chic dressing. **Juno,** wife of Jupiter, goddess of marriage and childbirth. **Jove,** a poetical equivalent to Jupiter, highest deity of the ancient Romans. **Mercury,** Roman god of eloquence, skill, trading, and thieving. **fleshpots,** brothels.

200 LYSIDAMUS: *I*, in a *fleshpot?*

CLEOSTRATA: I know a lot more than you think I do.

LYSIDAMUS: How's that? What exactly do you know?

CLEOSTRATA: Of all the worthless old men, you're the worst of the worthless. Well, where were you, thick-head? Where have you been wallowing about? And, soaking it up? By Castor, you're crocked! Here, just look at the state of your cloak.

LYSIDAMUS: May the gods not love me *(Aside)*—or you either—if a single drop of wine has passed my lips today.

CLEOSTRATA: Never mind! Please yourself! Go right ahead: eat, drink, waste your life!

LYSIDAMUS: Oh now, dear wife, *please,* that's enough. Come on, get hold of yourself. And that tongue of yours. Save a bit of abuse for tomorrow's row.° Now, how about it? Instead of opposing him, can't you curb your temper long enough to do a little something nice for your husband? Hmmmm?

CLEOSTRATA: Like what?

220 LYSIDAMUS: Need you ask? Why, Casina of course. Don't you think we ought to marry her off to that fine fellow of a foreman of ours, Olympio, where she'll not want for food, fuel, warm water, or nice clothes and where she can bring up her babies? Instead of flinging her at that good-for-nothing slave, that worthless rascal, Chalinus, who hasn't got two pennies to rub together?

CLEOSTRATA: By Castor, you *disaster* of a man, you do amaze me! At your time of life, forgetting how to behave.

LYSIDAMUS: What now?

CLEOSTRATA: Well, if you acted properly and with propriety, you'd leave the maids to me; after all, they're my responsibility.

235 LYSIDAMUS: But, blast it, why do you want to give her to that lackluster lackey?

CLEOSTRATA: Because we ought to do something nice for our only son.

LYSIDAMUS: Only son be damned! He's no more my only son, than I'm his only father! *(Realizing his slip of the tongue as* CLEOSTRATA *glares)* I mean I'm as much his only father, as he's my only son, of course! He ought to want to do something nice for me.

CLEOSTRATA: By Castor, dear boy, you're pushing your luck!

LYSIDAMUS *(Aside)*: I think she's on to me! *(To* CLEOSTRATA) *M-m-m-m-eee?*

CLEOSTRATA: Yes, you. Why are you stuttering? And why are you so mad about this match?

250 LYSIDAMUS: Why, I'd like to see her go to a worthy servant instead of to a rascal.

CLEOSTRATA: Supposing I persuade Olympio as a personal favor to let Chalinus have her?

LYSIDAMUS: And supposing I persuade Chalinus to give her to Olympio? *(Aside)* Which, I believe, I *may* just be able to do.

CLEOSTRATA: It's a deal. Shall I call out Chalinus for you? You work on him, while I deal with Olympio.

LYSIDAMUS: Good idea!

CLEOSTRATA: He's on his way. Then we'll see which of us is more persuasive.

(She exits inside)

LYSIDAMUS: By Hercules, I wish the gods would do something nasty to that woman! Is that too much to ask? Here I am, aching with love, while she's doing her worst to oppose me. She's definitely got wind of what I'm up to; that's why she's so keen on helping Chalinus. May the gods do their worst to him!

(Enter CHALINUS *from* LYSIDAMUS's *house)*

CHALINUS *(Sullenly)*: Your wife says you sent for me.

LYSIDAMUS: That's right.

CHALINUS: Well, go on, tell me what you want.

LYSIDAMUS: Well, for starters, put on a happy face when you speak with me; it's ridiculous for you to scowl like that when I'm the master and you're the slave! *(Winsomely)* For some time now, I've considered you an honest and upright fellow.

CHALINUS: Oh, I quite agree. In that case, how about setting me free?

LYSIDAMUS: Oh, I'd really like to. But my wishes don't count much, unless you do your part.

CHALINUS: Well then, let me know what you have in mind.

LYSIDAMUS: Listen, I'll speak frankly. I've given my word to marry Casina off to Olympio.

CHALINUS: Yes, but your wife and son gave me their words, both of them: *two* words!

LYSIDAMUS *(Patiently)*: I know. But now, which would you really prefer? To be single and *free;* or married, with you and your kids in slavery forever and ever? The choice is yours; choose whatever you prefer!

CHALINUS: If I were free, I'd have to look after myself; as it is, I live off you. As for Casina, I'm quite determined not to give her up to any man alive.

LYSIDAMUS *(Furious)*: Go right inside and summon my wife out here at once. And bring out an urn of water and some lots.°

CHALINUS: That's okay with me.

LYSIDAMUS: By Pollux, I'll soon foil your little plot. If I can't win by persuasion, we'll draw lots. That's the way to confound you and your confederates!

CHALINUS: Fine. Except that the lots will go my way.

---

row, disturbance, fight.

lots, objects, usually made out of wood, used to make a decision or selection by chance.

LYSIDAMUS: The only way you're going, by Pollux, is toward titanic torture.

305 CHALINUS (*Teasingly*): You can curse and do your worse; the girl will marry *me!!*

LYSIDAMUS: Will you get out of my sight?

CHALINUS: Upset are we? Never mind! I'll live.

(Exits inside)

LYSIDAMUS: Was ever anyone more wretched than I?
310 Now all things do conspire against me. Now I'm worried that my wife may have talked Olympio out of marrying Casina. If so, she's made an old man very unhappy. If not, there's still hope for me in the lots. If I lose the lots, I'll just lay down
315 my life on my sword, and so, goodnight! But look! Here comes Olympio. There's hope!

(Enter OLYMPIO, speaking to CLEOSTRATA within)

OLYMPIO: By Pollux, madam, you could put me in the oven and turn me till I'm turned to toast, before I'd agree to what you're asking!
320 LYSIDAMUS: Ah! Salvation! While I hear, I hope!

OLYMPIO: Why are you trying to frighten me with threats about my freedom? Neither you nor your son, whether together or on your own, can keep me from being freed—for nothing!
325 LYSIDAMUS: Why, what's the matter, Olympio, who're you arguing with?

OLYMPIO: The same one you're always at it with.

LYSIDAMUS: My old lady.

OLYMPIO: Lady? Lady is it? You follow a real sporting
330 life with that wife of yours: day and night with a baying bloodhound.

LYSIDAMUS: What's she been going on about with you?

OLYMPIO: Screeching and beseeching me not to
335 marry Casina.

LYSIDAMUS: What'd you say?

OLYMPIO: I wouldn't give her up to Jove himself, not even if he begged me!

LYSIDAMUS: The gods preserve you! *(Aside)* For my
340 sake!

OLYMPIO: She's really on the boil now—about to explode!

LYSIDAMUS: By Pollux, if only she'd have split right down the middle!

345 OLYMPIO (*Leeringly*): Well, golly, as a good husband, you ought to know! But seriously, I've had it up to here with this love affair of yours. Your wife's turned against me, your son, the whole house-hold's turned against me.
350 LYSIDAMUS: So what's your worry? As long as old Jupiter here is on your side, these lesser deities can go flog themselves!

OLYMPIO: That's a load of litter! Don't you know how suddenly these mortal Jupiters can shuffle off?
355 Tell me this: if old Jupiter here snuffs it, and your

kingdom falls to the small fry, who's going to save my hide and cover my backside?

LYSIDAMUS: Oh, things will go better for you than you think. Just you and I cooperate, so Casina and I can . . . *(Softly)* copulate.   360

OLYMPIO: But, by Hercules, I don't see how, with your wife dead set against my getting her.

LYSIDAMUS: Here's what I plan to do. I'll put the lots in the urn, and you and Chalinus will draw. If it comes to it, we'll draw swords as well, and settle it   365
by force.

OLYMPIO: And what if the lots don't go your way?

LYSIDAMUS: Don't even think such a thing! I trust in the gods. We'll just put our faith in heaven.

OLYMPIO: I wouldn't invest a penny up there. Why   370
everyone alive trusts in heaven, but I've seen plenty of those faithful foolish folks flummoxed.

LYSIDAMUS: Shh! Just be quiet for a moment.

OLYMPIO: What's up?

LYSIDAMUS: Look over there! There's Chalinus com-   375
ing out with the urns and lots. Now's the time to close ranks and fight!

(Enter CHALINUS with urns and lots; CLEOSTRATA in the door)

CLEOSTRATA: Now, Chalinus, what is it my husband wants me to do?

CHALINUS: Gosh, what he'd *most* like is to see you   380
going up in smoke out by the crematorium!

CLEOSTRATA: By Castor, I think you're right.

CHALINUS: I don't think; I know!

LYSIDAMUS (*Aside*): It appears I have more servants than I thought: we seem to have a mind reader on   385
the staff. Well, then, shall we raise our standards and sally forth? Follow me. What are you two up to?

CHALINUS: Everything you commanded is here: wife, lots, urn, and yours truly.   390

LYSIDAMUS: I could do very well without that last item.

CHALINUS: By Pollux, I guess you could. I must really needle you. A right prick in your backside, as it were. I've got you in a real sweat, you old repro-bate.   395

LYSIDAMUS: Shut up, Chalinus!

(LYSIDAMUS pushes CHALINUS)

CHALINUS: Hey! Get hold of this fellow!

OLYMPIO: Oh, no! Get hold of him. He loves it!

LYSIDAMUS: Put the urn there. *(With the urn in the cen-ter,* LYSIDAMUS *and* OLYMPIO *stand on one side, and* CLEOSTRATA *and* CHALINUS *on the other)* Give me 400
the lots. Now concentrate, both of you. Now, my dear, I did hope, and indeed, still do hope to per-suade you, my wife, to make Casina my wife.

CLEOSTRATA: Give her to *you!?*

LYSIDAMUS: Oh, yes, please. To me . . . *(Realizing his*   405
"Freudian slip") No! I take that back! What I *meant*

to say was *me,* when I said *him.* No, that's wrong. What I wanted was for me . . . Oh dear, I seem to have become all muddled up.

410 CLEOSTRATA: Yes, indeed! You certainly are!

LYSIDAMUS: Let him . . . No, that is, on the contrary, let . . . Well now . . . uhmmm. I think I'm on the right path at last.

CLEOSTRATA: By Pollux, you're always straying from it!

415 LYSIDAMUS: Well now, that's just the way it is, when one wants something bad—uhh—*badly* enough! But, anyway, both of us—Olympio and I, recognizing your rights in the matter, appeal to you.

CLEOSTRATA: For what?

420 LYSIDAMUS: Just this, honey pot. To do a little favor for our foreman here in this Casina affair.

CLEOSTRATA: By Pollux, I won't! I wouldn't dream of it.

LYSIDAMUS: I see. Well, in that case I think we should

425 have them both draw lots at once.

CLEOSTRATA: What's stopping you?

LYSIDAMUS: That is, after all, in my considered opinion, the best and fairest thing to do. Later, if things go as we would wish, we'll celebrate; if not,

430 we'll bear it with a tranquil mind. Take this lot. What's written on it?

OLYMPIO: One.

CHALINUS: Hey! It's not fair he should get his before me!

435 LYSIDAMUS: And you may take that one.

CHALINUS: Let's have it!

OLYMPIO: Wait a minute. I just thought of something. Make sure there isn't another one in there, underwater.

440 CHALINUS: You rascal! Do you think I'm like you?

CLEOSTRATA: No, there isn't. Now calm down, everyone.

OLYMPIO: May good fortune attend my lot!

CHALINUS: Misfortune will be your lot.

445 OLYMPIO: By Pollux! I know all about your pious ways! Just wait a second. Your lot isn't made of wood, is it?

CHALINUS: What's it to you?

OLYMPIO: I just don't want it floating on top of the

450 water.

LYSIDAMUS: That's right! Be careful. Now both of you throw your lots in here. There we go. Check them, dear.

OLYMPIO: Never trust a wife!

455 LYSIDAMUS: Keep your pecker up!

OLYMPIO: By Hercules, I'm afraid if she touches them, she'll put a spell on them!

LYSIDAMUS: Be quiet.

OLYMPIO: I'm quiet. I pray the gods . . .

460 CHALINUS: . . . will fit you with a ball and chain . . .

OLYMPIO: . . . that the lots will let me . . .

CHALINUS: . . . be hung up by your heels, by Hercules!

OLYMPIO: No! Will have you blow your brains out through your nose! 465

CHALINUS: What are you worried about? The noose is all ready and waiting for you!

OLYMPIO: You're a dead man!

(They square off to fight, but are restrained)

LYSIDAMUS: Now pay attention, both of you!

OLYMPIO: I'll not say another word. 470

LYSIDAMUS: Now, Cleostrata, so you won't be suspicious or think I've tricked you, I'll let you draw the lots yourself.

OLYMPIO: You're killing me!

CHALINUS: He'll be better off for that. 475

CLEOSTRATA: Very well.

CHALINUS: I beg the gods—let your lot slip out of the urn!

OLYMPIO: You do, do you? Since you're so slippery yourself, you want everything to imitate you? 480

CHALINUS: Oh, if only your lot would dissolve, you dissolute cur!

OLYMPIO: And here's hoping you melt away yourself, soon. Warmed up with a whipping!

LYSIDAMUS: Pay attention, please, Olympio. 485

OLYMPIO: If only this outlaw would allow me!

LYSIDAMUS: May good fortune be with me!

OLYMPIO: Here here! And with me too!

CHALINUS: *No!*

OLYMPIO: Oh, yes! With *me,* by Hercules! 490

CHALINUS: Oh, no! By Hercules, *me!*

CLEOSTRATA *(To* OLYMPIO): He's going to win, and you'll always be a loser!

LYSIDAMUS: Shut that man's mouth this minute! Go on, what are you waiting for? 495

CLEOSTRATA: Don't you dare raise a hand!

OLYMPIO: Shall I sock him or slap him, sir?

LYSIDAMUS: Whichever you prefer.

OLYMPIO: Take that!!

(Hits CHALINUS)

CLEOSTRATA: How dare you strike that man!? 500

OLYMPIO: My Jupiter here gave orders.

CLEOSTRATA *(To* CHALINUS): Well, you hit him right back!

(He does so)

OLYMPIO: *Owwwwww!* He's pounding me to a pulp, Jupiter! 505

LYSIDAMUS: How dare you strike that man!?

CHALINUS: My Juno here gave orders.

LYSIDAMUS: We'll just have to put up with it. My wife's already giving the orders even though I'm still alive. 510

CLEOSTRATA: Chalinus is just as much entitled to talk as Olympio!

OLYMPIO *(Whining)*: Why did he have to go and spoil my omen?

515 LYSIDAMUS: I warn you, Chalinus. Keep an eye out for trouble!

CHALINUS: Oh, that's kind of you! After my eye's been blackened!

520 LYSIDAMUS: Get on with it, wife. Draw the lots. Both of you pay attention. Dear me, I'm so worried, I hardly know where I am! I'm afraid I've got palpitations. My heart's pumping so it's pounding me to pieces!

CLEOSTRATA: Oh, I've got a lot!

525 LYSIDAMUS: Pull it out!

CHALINUS (*Seeing the lot first*): Oh, I'm a goner!

OLYMPIO: Hold it up. Ah!! It's *mine!*

CHALINUS: Hell and damnation!

CLEOSTRATA: You've lost, Chalinus.

530 LYSIDAMUS: The gods are smiling on us, Olympio. Rejoice!

OLYMPIO: It's all due to the piety of me and my forefathers.

LYSIDAMUS: Go right inside, woman, and make way

535 for the wedding!

CLEOSTRATA: Just as you say.

LYSIDAMUS: You do understand it's a long journey out to that country villa where he's taking her.

CLEOSTRATA: I know.

540 LYSIDAMUS: Well, go on in, even though you're upset, and start getting things prepared.

CLEOSTRATA: As you wish.

(She exits)

LYSIDAMUS: Let's us go inside, too, and make sure things hurry along.

545 OLYMPIO: Who's delaying?

LYSIDAMUS: I don't wish to say anything more in present company.

(Indicating CHALINUS. They exit to LYSIDAMUS's house, leaving CHALINUS alone on stage.)

CHALINUS: If I hanged myself now from a noose the effort would serve little use.

550 Why pay out for a rope,
and thus give my foes hope
when I'm already dead from abuse?
That I've lost the lots can't be denied.
And Olympio's taken my bride.
But what rankles° me so, and I'd most like to

555 know—
why was Master so keen on his side?

How it worried and wracked the old boy!
When he won, how he capered with joy!
Wait! They're coming outside;

560 from my *kind* friends I'll hide,
and learn what I can of their ploy.

---

rankles, irritates.

(Withdraws. Enter OLYMPIO *and* LYSIDAMUS *from the house.)*

OLYMPIO: Just wait till he comes to the farm! I'll return him to you bent double like a coalman.

LYSIDAMUS: Just as you should!

565 OLYMPIO: I'll make certain of that!

LYSIDAMUS: If Chalinus were here now, I'd send him off shopping with you—to give our fallen foe even more misery and woe!

CHALINUS: I'll just creep back against this wall like a

570 crab, and listen to what they're saying. (*Conceals himself along the wall of the scenic façade*) While one of them flails me, the other one nails me! Just look at how he struts about all dressed in white. That thing with horns! That thicket of

575 thorns! That settles it. I'll postpone my passing: I won't perish till I've posted that pest off to purgatory!

OLYMPIO: I've certainly been a sensationally servile surrogate, helping you to help yourself to your

580 lady love, without your spouse suspecting!

LYSIDAMUS: Be quiet! (*Seeing* CHALINUS, *they feign the following homoerotic scene to put him off the track. Alternatively, since such an interpretation is not actually suggested by the text,* LYSIDAMUS*'s sudden passion for* OLYMPIO *may simply be an expression of his overheated state.*) May the gods not love me, if on account of it I'm able to keep myself from giving you a great big kiss, my dear!

585 CHALINUS: What's this!? "A great big kiss"? How's that again? "My dear"? Good Lord, I think Master intends to f-f-f-fondle the f-f-foreman!

OLYMPIO: You're just a little bit fond of *me* now, are you?

590 LYSIDAMUS: Oh, *no!* Far fonder than I am for myself. Won't you let me hug you?

CHALINUS: What!? "Hug" him?

OLYMPIO: Oh, I suppose so.

LYSIDAMUS: Oh, when I touch you it's like sucking

595 sugar!

*(*OLYMPIO *pulls away and* LYSIDAMUS *is left clutching him from behind)*

OLYMPIO: Hey there, lover boy! Get off my back!

CHALINUS: There you have it! That's why he made that fellow his foreman! I remember now once when I was with him he offered to make me his

600 *"butler,"* on the spot.

OLYMPIO: Ah, how I've pampered and pleased you today!

LYSIDAMUS: Ah, what a friend I'll be to you all my life—even more than I am to myself!

605 CHALINUS: I'm afraid, by Pollux, those two will soon be head over bollocks in bed! Actually the old boy always did go for anything with a beard!

(Starts to leave)

LYSIDAMUS (*Possibly having seen* CHALINUS *earlier, and now believing him to have left*): Ah, how I'll kiss and cuddle Casina today! What a life, what a lark! And
610 my wife in the dark!

CHALINUS (*Hearing this*): Ah, ha! Now, by Pollux, I'm on the right path at last! He craves Casina for himself! I've got 'em!

LYSIDAMUS: By Hercules, I'm dying to kiss and caress
615 her right now!

OLYMPIO: Not before *I've* got her! What's the rush, damn it?

LYSIDAMUS: I'm in *love.*

OLYMPIO: Well, I don't think you can bring it off
620 today.

LYSIDAMUS: Oh, yes, I can. That is, if you'd like to be off tomorrow: a *free* man.

CHALINUS (*Still concealed*): Now's the time to prick up my ears. What fun to capture two boars in one
625 bush!

LYSIDAMUS: There's a place ready for me over there at the home of my good friend and neighbor. I've told him everything about my little love affair, and he's promised to let me use his place.

630 OLYMPIO: What about his wife? Where'll she be?

LYSIDAMUS: It's neatly and completely arranged. My wife will invite Myrrhina over for the wedding where she can hang about, make herself useful, and stay the night. I've told my wife to do it, and
635 she's agreed. So Myrrhina will sleep there, (*Indicating his house*) and I can *promise* you, her husband won't be here! (*Indicating the other house*) You'll take your bride off to the farm, but the farm will be right here where Casina and I will
640 enjoy our wedding night. Tomorrow, before dawn, you'll take her away to the country. Pretty clever, huh?

OLYMPIO: Brilliant!

CHALINUS (*Concealed*): Go right ahead and plot a lot!
645 By Hercules, you two will be screwed for being so shrewd.

LYSIDAMUS: Do you know what to do now?

OLYMPIO: Tell me.

LYSIDAMUS: Take this purse, and go shopping for the
650 wedding feast. Be quick, but get something sumptuous since she's so scrumptious.

OLYMPIO: Right!

LYSIDAMUS: Get some cockles; some cuddly cuttlefish, some little octopussies, and maybe a nice piece of
655 ass.

CHALINUS (*Concealed*): You mean a bit of bass, you ass!

LYSIDAMUS: And some sole.

CHALINUS: Sole? Why not get the whole damn shoe to smash your face with, you odious old man?!

660 OLYMPIO: How about a little snapper?

LYSIDAMUS: Who needs a little snapper when we've got "Jaws," that wife of mine at home who never closes her mouth?

OLYMPIO: Once I'm there I can decide what to buy
665 from the fishmonger's stock.

LYSIDAMUS: Okay. Get on with it. But buy plenty; don't be selfish with the shellfish! Right now, I've got to meet with my neighbor to make sure he does what I've asked.

670 OLYMPIO: Can I go now?

LYSIDAMUS: You bet!

(*They exit separately, leaving* CHALINUS *on stage*)

CHALINUS: You could offer me freedom, nay offer it thrice,
but you couldn't dissuade me, whatever your price,
from cooking those two in a stew—and how?
By spilling the beans to my mistress right now.   675

Our rivals are cornered, and caught in the act.
If she does her part, then we've won—that's a fact!
We'll trap them but good; they won't get away.
We victims are victors—it's our lucky day!

How shameless our chef has cooked up his plan.   680
It's flavored and simmering inside, in the pan.
But I'll lend a hand, and give it a stir;
the seasoning I use won't satisfy, sir!

The tables are turned, so ready or not,
he'll eat what *I* serve: thus thickens the plot!   685

(*Exits*)

ACT II

(*Enter* LYSIDAMUS *and* ALCESIMUS *from the latter's house*)

LYSIDAMUS: Now we'll see whether you'll play the friend or foe, Alcesimus. The truth revealed, signed, and sealed! As for delivering lectures on my love life, you can dispense with "a man of your age!" And "with your grey hair!"—you can cut   5
that, too. And as for "and you a married man!"—
you can most certainly take that and shove it!

ALCESIMUS: I've never seen anyone more lovesick than you!

LYSIDAMUS: Get everyone out of the house.   10

ALCESIMUS: All right, by Pollux. I'm sending all the servants over to your house.

LYSIDAMUS: What a genuine genius you are! But make certain your servants bring their own provisions. Just like in the birdie's song, "to eat! to eat! to eat!   15
to eat! to eat!"

ALCESIMUS: I'll keep that in mind.

LYSIDAMUS: That's right. There never was a more generous, ingenious genius than you. Keep an eye on things. I'm off to the forum: be back soon!   20

ALCESIMUS: Have a nice day.

LYSIDAMUS: And see that you teach your house some manners.

ALCESIMUS: How's that?

25 LYSIDAMUS: So when I return it puts out a welcome (*Spelling*) M-A-T- for me, alone. Get it? *"Em-pty!"* for me!

ALCESIMUS: *Yeaccch!* You really ought to be suppressed—you and your witticisms.

30 LYSIDAMUS: What's the use of being in love, if I'm not allowed to be wise and witty? Now make sure I don't have to go looking for you.

ALCESIMUS: I'll be here at home.

(*They exit, separately. Enter* CLEOSTRATA *from her house.*)

CLEOSTRATA: By Castor, now I know the reason why
My husband's been so keen to have the neighbors by.
35 With them all here, the house next door'd be free,
where they could cuddle Casina, while conning me!
Well now, I shan't invite them, or provide a spot
for amorous rams to rut, however hot
40 they are. But wait! My neighbor's coming out.
Here comes that *bast*ion of the state, the lout!
Who panders to my husband's fatal fault.
Such men as he aren't worth a pinch of salt!

(*Enter* ALCESIMUS)

ALCESIMUS: I'm surprised no one's come to invite my
45 wife over to next door. She's been waiting ages, here, all decked out, to be asked over. Ah! There's Cleostrata, coming to invite her now, I suppose. Good day, Cleostrata!

50 CLEOSTRATA: And to you, Alcesimus! Where's your wife?

ALCESIMUS: Right inside, waiting for your invitation. Your husband beseeched me to send her over to help you out. Shall I call her?

CLEOSTRATA: No, not if she's busy.

55 ALCESIMUS: Oh, she's not!

CLEOSTRATA: Never mind! I don't want to bother her. I'll catch her later.

ALCESIMUS: Aren't you arranging a wedding over there?

60 CLEOSTRATA: That's right.

ALCESIMUS: Well, couldn't you use a hand?

CLEOSTRATA: There's plenty at home. I'll come see her after the wedding. Well, *ciao* for now! And give her my regards.

(*Moves out of sight, in her doorway*)

65 ALCESIMUS: So what do I do now? What a dastardly deed I did! On account of that ruthless, toothless old goat, I'm offering my wife's services around like some sort of scullery maid. What a lying lout he is! Saying his wife's inviting her over, and then

she says she doesn't want her! By Pollux, I wonder 70
if the woman's got wind of what's in the works?
On the other hand, on second thought, if that were the case, she'd have questioned me about it. I guess I'd better go inside and tow the old barge back to her berth. 75

(*Exits into his house*)

CLEOSTRATA (*In doorway*): Well, he's finely flummoxed! What a flutter the old fools are in! Now if only that worthless, washed-out wimp of a husband of mine would happen along, I could fix him just like I fooled the other one. I'd just love 80
to stir up a quarrel between them! And here he comes, right on cue! Goodness! Look at that solemn face. You'd almost think he was an honest man.

(*Withdraws. Enter* LYSIDAMUS, *returning from the forum.*)

LYSIDAMUS: Now it seems to my mind, really quite asinine, 85
when a lover's in service to Cupid,
with a sweetheart so pretty, to spend time in the city,
like I've done; why it's perfectly stupid!
For I've wasted my time on a kinsman of mine
who used *me* as a character witness. 90
But I'm pleased to report, he was beaten in court.
Serves him right, bothering me with his business!

Now between me and you, it is patently true,
when a man asks a friend to bear witness,
It behooves him to find, if his friend's of sound mind; 95
send him home if the witness is witless!

(*Seeing* CLEOSTRATA)

But I'm worried I'm screwed
there's the wife, looking shrewd.
And she's heard all I said, I've a hunch.

CLEOSTRATA (*Aside*): Indeed, I did hear—it'll cost the 100
rogue dear.

LYSIDAMUS (*Aside*): I'll approach. (*To her*) Well, what's up, honey bunch?

CLEOSTRATA: I've been waiting for you, by Castor!

LYSIDAMUS: Is everything prepared? Have you invited 105
our neighbor over to give you a hand?

CLEOSTRATA: Well, yes, I did invite her over as you suggested. But that good buddy and friend of yours, Alcesimus, was fuming with her about something or other. He refused to let her come 110
over when I asked.

LYSIDAMUS: That's your worst fault! You don't know how to ask nicely.

CLEOSTRATA: It's not the job of a wife, but the chore of a whore, to give pleasure, *treasure*, to another 115

wife's husband! Go invite her yourself; I've got
things to do inside that need looking after—*darling!*

LYSIDAMUS: Well, get a move on then!

120 CLEOSTRATA *(Aside)*: By Pollux, I'll give him a fright,
all right. I'll soon make this lover suffer!

(Exits. Enter ALCESIMUS *from his house.)*

ALCESIMUS: I'll just have a look to see if lover boy has
come home from the forum. Fancy that old ghoul
making a fool of my wife and me! Why, there he
125 is, right in front of the house! *(To him)* By Hercules, I was just on my way to see you!

LYSIDAMUS: Same here, by Hercules! Listen, lunch
meat!—Just what was it I asked you—nay—*begged*
you to do?

130 ALCESIMUS: Well, what?

LYSIDAMUS: Fine job you did of emptying your house
for me! Fine job of getting your wife over to our
place! Because of you, me and my affair are finished!

135 ALCESIMUS: Why don't you go hang yourself? Didn't
you tell me your very self, that your wife would
invite my wife over? *Uhmmm-mmm?*

LYSIDAMUS: Why, she says she *did* invite her, but that
you said you wouldn't let her come.

140 ALCESIMUS: Why, she told me herself that she didn't
want any help!

LYSIDAMUS: Why, she just told me herself to come
and *get* her!

ALCESIMUS: Why, I don't give a damn . . .

145 LYSIDAMUS: Why are you ruining me?

ALCESIMUS: Why, that's a blessing!

LYSIDAMUS: Why, I'll just linger a little longer.

ALCESIMUS: Why, I'd like to . . .

LYSIDAMUS: Why . . .

150 ALCESIMUS: Why, to do something *nasty!*

LYSIDAMUS: Why? I'll do the same. I'm going to have
the last "why" today, or know the reason why!

ALCESIMUS: But . . .

LYSIDAMUS: That's better!

155 ALCESIMUS: *Why?*

LYSIDAMUS *(Striking him)*: That's why!!

ALCESIMUS: Well . . . in that . . . case . . . *(Shouting) why
the hell don't you just go hang yourself once and for
all!!!*

160 LYSIDAMUS: Now, how about it? Will you send your
wife over to my place?

ALCESIMUS: Go on! Take her, and give yourself a fabulous flogging along with her, your own wife, and
that girl of yours too!! *(Cooling off)* Go away and
165 leave it to me. I'll send my wife along to yours
right away—through the back garden.

LYSIDAMUS: Now there's a real friend! *(Exit* ALCES-
IMUS*)* I wonder what omen I omitted when I
began this love affair. Or how I offended the god-
170 dess of Love. It's a clear case of *Venus-envy!* Here I

am longing to get laid, and all I get is *de*-layed!
Now what's all this unholy hubbub in the house?

(Enter MYRRHINA *from* LYSIDAMUS*'s house)*

MYRRHINA: I'm lost! Totally done for, and dead!
My heart has stopped, my limbs are trembling with
dread!
Help! Safety! Shelter! Oh, where to turn for aid?   175
Such things I saw inside, can scarcely be conveyed.
Bold and brazen badness! Turmoil and alarm!

(Calling inside)

Be careful, Cleostrata! Lest she do you harm!
The woman's lost her senses—her mind has gone
astray!
For goodness sake avoid her, but snatch the sword
away!   180

LYSIDAMUS: Now what do you suppose has frightened
our neighbor half to death, and sent her scurrying outside? *(Calls in) Pardalisca!*

(Enter PARDALISCA *onto the porch)**

PARDALISCA: Oh! I'm lost! What is this sound I hear?

LYSIDAMUS: Look over here, will you?   185

PARDALISCA: Oh, dear Master!

LYSIDAMUS: What's wrong with you? Why are you so
frightened?

PARDALISCA: I'm dead!

LYSIDAMUS: Really? Dead?   190

MYRRHINA: Dead, indeed! And you're dead, too!

LYSIDAMUS *(Checking himself)*: I'm dead? How come?

PARDALISCA: Oh, woe is you!

LYSIDAMUS: Woe is me? No, make that, "woe is you"!

PARDALISCA: That's just what I said!   195

MYRRHINA: Please help me! I . . . I . . . feel faint!

LYSIDAMUS: Look, what's going on? Tell me right now!

PARDALISCA: Please hold me—by the waist—fan me—
with your cloak!

LYSIDAMUS: You know, I'm worried about all this.   200
Unless the two of them have been knocking it
back with Bacchus.°

MYRRHINA: Oh! Hold my head!

LYSIDAMUS: Oh, get hanged, and stop hanging on
me! Go flog yourselves, waist, head, the lot! Un-   205
less you tell me this instant what's going on, I'll
bash both your brains in, you silly sluts. You've
played with me long enough!

---

* The following passage, which in the Latin text is between
Pardalisca and Lysidamus, has been altered to include
Myrrhina, in the interest of making for a more lively and
effective scene. The lines have therefore been given to two
foils for Lysidamus, instead of only one, with plural forms
used as necessary. [Translator's note]

Bacchus, god of wine.

PARDALISCA: Dear Master!

210 LYSIDAMUS: What now, dear servant?

PARDALISCA: You're too hard on us.

LYSIDAMUS: You ain't seen nothing yet! Now out with it! What the hell's going on inside? Make it snappy!

215 MYRRHINA: I'll tell you, just listen. (*Melodramatically*) Oh! It was absolutely horrible inside, just now! Your servant girl ran completely amok, and began carrying on in the most awful, most appalling, most un-Athenian manner!

220 LYSIDAMUS: What!? *Anti-attic-antics?!*

PARDALISCA: I'm so frightened, I can't speak properly . . . either.

LYSIDAMUS: Will you *please* tell me what happened?

MYRRHINA: I'll tell you. That serving girl that you

225 wanted to marry off to your foreman . . .

LYSIDAMUS: Yes??

MYRRHINA: Well, inside there, she . . .

LYSIDAMUS: *What* happened inside?

PARDALISCA: She's acting like a really nasty . . . wife.

230 LYSIDAMUS: (*Relieved*) Oh.

PARDALISCA: Threatening to *kill* her husband!

LYSIDAMUS: What the *hell!?*

MYRRHINA: AAAHHhhhh

(*Faints*)

LYSIDAMUS: What now?

235 PARDALISCA: She says she wants to kill him. She's in there with a sword.

LYSIDAMUS: A *what?*

MYRRHINA (*Revives*): A *sword!*

LYSIDAMUS: What about this sword?

240 PARDALISCA: She's got one!

LYSIDAMUS: *Mamma Mia!* Why's she got that?

MYRRHINA: She's chasing everyone all over the house and won't let a soul come near her! They're all hiding under tables and beds—struck dumb with

245 fear!

LYSIDAMUS: I'm dead and done for! But what the hell's got into her?

MYRRHINA: She's insane!

LYSIDAMUS: If I'm not the wretchedest wretch alive!

250 PARDALISCA: You should have heard what she was saying just now!

LYSIDAMUS: Yes, indeed? What did she say?

MYRRHINA: Just listen. She swore by all the gods and goddesses, that the man she sleeps with to-

255 night . . . she'll *murder!*

LYSIDAMUS: Murder *me?*

PARDALISCA (*Innocently*): What's it got to do with you, sir?

LYSIDAMUS (*Aside*): Damn!

260 MYRRHINA: Why should you be concerned about that?

LYSIDAMUS: Why, I misspoke myself. I meant to say Olympio.

MYRRHINA (*Aside*): He's good under pressure!

LYSIDAMUS: She's not threatening *me*, is she? 265

PARDALISCA: Why, you're the one she hates the very most of all!

LYSIDAMUS: What for?

MYRRHINA: Because you want to marry her to Olympio. She's sworn that neither he, nor she, nor you 270 will make it to tomorrow.

PARDALISCA: I was sent out here to tell you. So you can keep away from her.

LYSIDAMUS: By Hercules, I'm a goner!

MYRRHINA (*Aside*): You deserve it! 275

LYSIDAMUS (*Aside*): No old lover ever lived, or lives less lucky than I!

PARDALISCA (*Aside*): What fabulous foolery! It's all fantasy from first to finish! Mistress and her neighbor here set the trap, and I've been sent to 280 spring it on him!

LYSIDAMUS: Hey, Pardalisca!

PARDALISCA: Yes sir?

LYSIDAMUS: There's . . .

PARDALISCA: What? 285

LYSIDAMUS: Something I'd like to ask you.

PARDALISCA: Well, make it snappy!

LYSIDAMUS (*Aside*): I'm so unhappy! (*To her*) Look, has Casina still got the sword?

PARDALISCA: No sir. 290

LYSIDAMUS: Whewww!

MYRRHINA: She's got *two* of them.

LYSIDAMUS: Two?! Why two?

PARDALISCA: She says one's to kill Olympio with; the other's for you. This very day! 295

LYSIDAMUS: I'm the dead-deader-deadest man alive! To try and save my life, I'll put on armor! But what about my wife, couldn't *she* disarm her?

PARDALISCA: Well, she had to be very evasive.

LYSIDAMUS: The old girl can be awfully persuasive! 300

PARDALISCA: That's undoubtedly true, but I'm still telling you, how our Casina's sworn with an oath, that she won't let them go, until given to know, that she won't have to marry that oaf!

LYSIDAMUS: Well, like it or not, the ungrateful slut 305 *will* be given in marriage today. I won't change what's planned: she'll give me her hand . . .

(*Catching himself*)

To my *foreman*, I meant to say!

MYRRHINA: Seems you stumble a lot. 310

LYSIDAMUS: I'm so frightened, I'm not giving thought to the words that I say.

(*To* PARDALISCA)

But please beg my wife, if she values my life, to get Casina out of the way! 315

(To MYRRHINA*)*

And you beg her too.

PARDALISCA: And I'll beg with you!

LYSIDAMUS: Do your best, as you know how to do.
  If you hush up these scandals, I'll buy you some
    sandals,
320 a gold ring (and some other treats too!).

PARDALISCA: Well, I'll do what I may, sir.

LYSIDAMUS: Oh, please try
  to persuade her!

MYRRHINA: We'll go now, without further delay.

325 LYSIDAMUS: Yes, go right in my dear.

(They exit into the house; OLYMPIO *enters with a* COOK
and ASSISTANTS*)*

                 Oh! Olympio's
  here!
And he's gathered a crowd on his way

OLYMPIO *(To* COOK*)*: Now see to it, you crooked cook,
330 that you keep these brambles *(Indicating the assis-*
    tants) of yours under tight control.

COOK: Why, pray, do you term them "brambles"?

OLYMPIO: Because they cling to whatever they touch;
  try and get it back, and it's gone. Coming, going,
335 or standing still, they're double-trouble.

COOK: Oh dear, oh dear!

OLYMPIO: Aha! Now to dress myself in a fancy-pants
  patrician sort of way, and meet my master.

LYSIDAMUS: Ah, hello, my good man!

340 OLYMPIO: I admit it!

LYSIDAMUS: What's the latest?

OLYMPIO: You're still in love, and I'm hungry and
  thirsty.

LYSIDAMUS: You've come well-equipped!

345 OLYMPIO: Ah, yes! Today I intend to gorge myself on
  "sweet delights"!

LYSIDAMUS: Now just a minute! Don't get so uppity!

OLYMPIO: Oh, save your breath! It offends me.

LYSIDAMUS: What's this?

350 OLYMPIO: Standing around like this is a chore, and
  you're a bore!

(Starts to go inside)

LYSIDAMUS *(Restraining him)*: Unless you stand still,
  I'll more than bore you—I'll whip you as well!

OLYMPIO *(Shaking him off, and again starting to leave)*:
  Leave me alone, for the gods' sake. Do you want
355 to make me retch, wretch?

LYSIDAMUS: Wait!

OLYMPIO: Just who do you think you are?

LYSIDAMUS: I'm the master here!

OLYMPIO: Master of what?

360 LYSIDAMUS: Of *you!*

OLYMPIO: I? A slave?

LYSIDAMUS: Yes, my slave.

OLYMPIO: Am I not a free man? You do remember,
  don't you? Don't you?

LYSIDAMUS: Wait! Stop!   365

OLYMPIO: Leave me alone!

LYSIDAMUS *(On his knees)*: I'll be your slave!

OLYMPIO: That's more like it.

LYSIDAMUS: Dear, dear Olympio, my father, my patron,
  I beg . . .   370

OLYMPIO: Now you're talking sense.

LYSIDAMUS: Yes, I'm yours. Indeed I am.

OLYMPIO: What do I want with such a knave of a slave?

LYSIDAMUS: Well then, make me over. When do we
  start the *res-erection?*   375

OLYMPIO: As soon as supper's ready.

LYSIDAMUS *(Indicating* COOK *and* ASSISTANTS*)*: Well,
  let them get on with it then!

OLYMPIO *(Haughtily)*: Get on inside and hurry things
  along! Move! I'll be in in a minute. And make   380
  sure it's a super supper, with lots to drink. An elegant and dandy dinner; none of your rotten
  Roman slop! Well? What are you waiting for? Be
  off! *(They exit inside; to* LYSIDAMUS, *who lingers)*
  What's keeping you?   385

LYSIDAMUS: They say Casina's waiting inside with a
  sword. Waiting to finish us both off!

OLYMPIO: I see. Well, let her wait. What nonsense! I
  know how to deal with a bad bargain of a woman.
  Go on into the house . . . *(*LYSIDAMUS *refuses to*   390
  move) with *me.*

LYSIDAMUS: By Pollux, I fear the worst! *You* go ahead
  and reconnoiter. See what's going on.

OLYMPIO *(Thinking better of it)*: Look, I value my life as
  much as you do yours! So—*you* go in.   395

LYSIDAMUS: Well, if you insist . . . we'll go *together.*

*(They exit, each trying to get the other to go first. After
a short pause indicating a passage of time, enter* PAR-
DALISCA *from* LYSIDAMUS*'s house.)*

PARDALISCA: They never have games at Nemea,°
  nor in the Olympian arena,
  such sport of the sort as we're playing inside,
  with Master and Foreman—taking them for a ride!   400

The whole house is in turmoil and all in a flurry,
since Master is mad to make the cooks hurry;
"Don't fidgit in the kitchen, but make haste now!
Our *tempus fugits,*° so give us the chow!"

While Olympio struts in the room just outside,   405
clothed in white, wreathed and bright, as he
  grooms for his bride—
in her bedroom the bride's being dressed by her
  minions,

Nemea, a wooded district near Argos in Greece.   *tempus
fugits,* humorous version of the Latin expression tempus fugit
(time flies).

They're aware of a plot, but suppress their
　opinions!

And the cooks in their cunning are conning their
　master
410　by delaying his meal, and designing disaster;
overturning the pots right into the fire,
and contriving whatever the ladies desire!

They would like if they can, to deprive him of food,
and consume it themselves, once he's gone—very
　rude!
415　I confess that the ladies eat more than they should,
they would bloat on a boatload of food if they
　could!
But wait! I hear the door.

(She hides. Enter LYSIDAMUS.*)*

LYSIDAMUS *(Calling back inside)*: If you're wise, my dear,
　you women should go right ahead and eat as soon
420　as dinner's done. I'll consummate—*consume*—
　mine at the farm. I want to escort our new bride
　and groom there—so no one will *way-lay* her—
　knowing as I do the sort of unsavory characters
　there are around here. You two go right ahead
425　and enjoy yourselves. *(Growing impatient)* Just
　hurry up and send them out now, so we can get
　there before dark. I'll be back tomorrow and
　enjoy my piece of the party then, dear.
PARDALISCA *(Aside)*: What did I tell you? The ladies
430　are sending the old boy off, unfed!
LYSIDAMUS *(Seeing her)*: What are you doing here?
PARDALISCA: Going where Mistress sent me.
LYSIDAMUS: Really?
PARDALISCA: Yes sir!
435　LYSIDAMUS: Then why are you spying here?
PARDALISCA: I—*spy?* Not a bit of it!
LYSIDAMUS: Well, be off! Here you are hanging about
　when everyone else is rushing around inside.
PARDALISCA: I'm off!
440　LYSIDAMUS: On your way, triple-tramp! Is she gone
　yet? Now I can say what I want! By Hercules! A fel-
　low in love feels full even when he's famished!
　(Seeing OLYMPIO *approaching)* Ah, here he comes
　now! Garland on head, and torch in hand! My
445　comrade, ally, co-husband, and foreman!

(Enter OLYMPIO*)*

OLYMPIO: Come on, flautist! *(Indicating the onstage
　musician)* When they bring on the bride, make
　the whole street sound with sweet music! *(Sings)*
　"Here comes the bride! Here comes the bride!"
450　LYSIDAMUS: How are you, my savior?
OLYMPIO: Hungry, by Hercules! And there's nothing
　around to savor.
LYSIDAMUS: Yes, but I'm in love!
OLYMPIO: I don't give a flying flogging! You can feast

on love—as for me, my guts have been rumbling　455
　for hours!
LYSIDAMUS: What makes those laggards linger so long?
　The more I hurry them, the slower they go. It
　almost seems on purpose!
OLYMPIO: Well, suppose I sing the wedding song again,　460
　and see if that gets them going?
LYSIDAMUS: Good idea! And I'll sing too, since it's a
　two-some screwsome!
LYSIDAMUS and OLYMPIO: "Here comes the bride!
　Here comes the bride!"　465
LYSIDAMUS: By Hercules! I'm beat! I could sing until
　I'm flat on my back, but I'd prefer her flat on her
　back in the sack!
OLYMPIO: By Pollux, if you were a horse, you'd be a
　real champion!　470
LYSIDAMUS: Why's that?
OLYMPIO: Always champing at the bit!
LYSIDAMUS *(Suggestively)*: Ever fancy trying a *bit* with
　me?
OLYMPIO: The gods forbid! But the door's creaking—　475
　they're coming out!
LYSIDAMUS: By Hercules! The gods are looking after
　me!

(Music. Enter CHALINUS, *disguised as a bride,* PAR-
DALISCA, CLEOSTRATA, *and* MYRRHINA.*)*

PARDALISCA: Here we go, take it slow,
step over the threshold with care.　480
By his side, blushing bride,
keep the upper hand always and dare,

to hold sway, night and day.
Make him pamper you as his task.
Never cease, him to fleece.　485
Just treat him like dirt's all I ask!
OLYMPIO: By Hercules, she'll get a whopping whip-
　ping if she's guilty of even any eany meany mini-
　mischief!
LYSIDAMUS: Shut up!　490
OLYMPIO: I won't!
LYSIDAMUS: Why not?
OLYMPIO: That bawd is teaching the broad to be bad!
LYSIDAMUS: You'll unsettle what I've set up! That's
　what they'd like: to undo what I've done.　495
PARDALISCA: Go on, Olympio. If it's what you want,
　receive your bride from us.
OLYMPIO *(Impatiently)*: Well, go ahead and give her, if
　you intend doing it today!
LYSIDAMUS: Go back inside.　500
PARDALISCA *(Delaying)*: Just be kind to this innocent,
　unspoiled girl.
OLYMPIO: I will be!
PARDALISCA: Farewell!
OLYMPIO: *Go already!*　505
LYSIDAMUS: *Go!*
PARDALISCA: Well, then, farewell.

(The women exit into LYSIDAMUS*'s house)*

LYSIDAMUS: Has my wife gone!

OLYMPIO: Don't worry. She's in the house.

510 LYSIDAMUS: Hurrah! Now, by Pollux, I'm free at last! Oh, my little sweetikins, honeykins, spring chick-chickens!

OLYMPIO: Hey, you! If you're wise, you'll keep your eyes open for trouble! The girl is mine!

515 LYSIDAMUS: I know, but the firstfruits are mine!

OLYMPIO: Here! Hold this torch.

LYSIDAMUS: Oh, no! *(Caressing* CASINA*)* I'd rather hold *this* one! Almighty, mighty Aphrodite! What pleasure you gave in giving me this treasure.

520 OLYMPIO *(Holding her)*: Oh, your iddy, biddy, body, baby!—*What the hell!*

LYSIDAMUS: What's wrong?

OLYMPIO: She just stamped on my foot like an elephant!

525 LYSIDAMUS: Hush up! Never a cloud was softer than this breast!

OLYMPIO *(Fondling her)*: By Pollux, what an iddy, bitty pretty titty! *Owwww!* Good Lord!

LYSIDAMUS: What now?

530 OLYMPIO: She hit me in the chest—it wasn't an elbow; it was a battering ram!

LYSIDAMUS: Well, why are you handling her so roughly, then? Look at me. Just treat her kind and she doesn't mind!

535 OLYMPIO: *Ouch!*

LYSIDAMUS: What's the matter now?

OLYMPIO: Damnation! What a pint-sized power-house she is!! Her elbow almost laid me low!

540 LYSIDAMUS: Maybe *she'd* like to be laid low—you know?

OLYMPIO: Let's go!

LYSIDAMUS: Look lively, little, lovely lady!

(They exit into ALCESIMUS*'s house. Music. Enter* CLEOSTRATA, PARDALISCA, *and* MYRRHINA *from the other house, somewhat inebriated.)*

MYRRHINA: Nicely wined and dined, inside! Now we can come out and watch the wedding games. By

545 Castor, I've never laughed so much, or ever shall again!

PARDALISCA: I'd like to know how Chalinus is getting along—*(Making a joke)* the new *male* ordered *bride* and his new husband!

550 MYRRHINA: No playwright ever conceived a plot cleverer than this masterpiece of ours!

CLEOSTRATA: I'd like to see the old fool come out now with his face smashed! He's the nastiest old man alive. Not even that one of yours who procured

555 the place for him is worse. Pardalisca, I'd like you to stand watch here to abuse and be amused by my husband when he appears.

PARDALISCA: Gladly. Just like always.

MYRRHINA: You keep an eye on things here. Report to us inside what's happening. 560

PARDALISCA: Get thee behind me, madam!

MYRRHINA: And don't be afraid to speak up!

PARDALISCA: Shh! Your door's creaking!

(They withdraw. Enter OLYMPIO, *in great haste, from* ALCESIMUS*'s house.)*

OLYMPIO: Oh, where to run to or to hide myself from shame!

And oh, the *scandal* that it casts on Master's name, 565
and *mine!* I tremble at the shame of it and how
ridiculous we've made ourselves appear just now.
And this is something new for me to have to say;
—a *fool!*—I never felt such shame until today.

(To audience)

So listen while I tell you all, and lend an ear. 570
It's just as comical to narrate as to hear
the quite appalling mess I've made of things inside.
The moment that we went in there, I took my bride
straight to a little bedroom, which was dark as night.
Before the old man had arrived, I said, "All right, 575
get comfy on the couch." Then helped to smooth the bed,
and soon began to soothe her there, and said
a few kind words and some sweet nothings to her,
so prior to Master I could start to . . . *woo* her.

I start out slowly, but am filled with fear 580
lest turning round I find the old man there.
To get things going and begin her bliss,
I start by asking for a sloppy kiss.
She wouldn't kiss me; pushed my hand away.
That only stiffened my . . . *resolve* . . . which stayed *that* way. 585

I longed to taste in haste chaste Casina's embrace,
and let the old man come in second place!
And so, I closed the door to try and minimize
the chance that in the dark he'd take *me* by surprise.

MYRRHINA *(To the women)*: All right now. Let's go up to him. 590

CLEOSTRATA *(Approaching)*: Where is your bride, for goodness sake!

OLYMPIO *(Aside)*: *Damn!* *(Despairing)* I'm done for! It's all out! 595

MYRRHINA: In that case, you might as well tell all. What's going on inside? How's Casina? Did you find her sufficiently obliging?

OLYMPIO: I'm embarrassed to say.

CLEOSTRATA: Go right on with your story. 600

OLYMPIO: By Hercules! I'm so *ashamed!*

PARDALISCA: Stiff upper lip! That bit about the couch
   —I'd like to hear what happened next.

OLYMPIO: It's shocking.

605 CLEOSTRATA: It'll be a good lesson for our audience.

OLYMPIO: It's such a scandal!

MYRRHINA: Nonsense! Why don't you go on?

*(During the following sequence, the text of which is very
fragmentary, the characters may huddle to confer closely
among themselves, with only the occasional word uttered
aloud)*

OLYMPIO: When *(Whispers)* . . . then down below . . .

(Whispers)

CLEOSTRATA: Well!

610 OLYMPIO: . . . Wow! . . .

(Whispers)

MYRRHINA: What about it?

(Whispers)

OLYMPIO: Oh *my!*

PARDALISCA: Was it? . . .

(Whispers)

OLYMPIO: Oh, it was just *enormous!* I was afraid she
615   must still have a sword. So I started to investigate,
   and while I'm searching for the sword, checking
   to see if she's carrying one, I got hold of its hilt.
   On second thought, though, she couldn't have
   had a sword; the hilt would have felt cold . . .

620 CLEOSTRATA *(Intrigued)*: Go on.

OLYMPIO: I'm so embarrassed!

PARDALISCA: Let's see . . . was it a carrot?

(She plays charades)

OLYMPIO: No!

MYRRHINA *(Also acting charades, and suddenly thinking
   she has it)*: A cucumber!!

625 OLYMPIO: No, it wasn't any sort of vegetable. Or at
   least, if it was, it certainly was never nipped in the
   bud: whatever it was, it was full grown!

MYRRHINA: What happened next? in detail!

OLYMPIO: I appealed to her then by her name;
630   "Little wife, don't be spurning my claim!
   By Heaven above, though I crave all your love
   for myself, I'm not *really* to blame!"

   Not a word does she say, but by turning away,
   puts an end to that line of pursuit.
635   Since she's in that position, I ask her permission,
   to attempt the alternative route!

PARDALISCA *(Collapsing in laughter)*:
   What a marvelous tale!

OLYMPIO: As I tried to prevail,
   I leant over to smooch with my sweet.
640 But something was weird: she'd a bristly beard!

Then she kicked me with both of her feet!
I fell flat on the ground, and she started to pound
and beat me just as you discern.
Without a word more, I ran straight out the door,
to let the old man have his turn!   645

CLEOSTRATA: That's just *great!* But what happened to
   your cloak?

OLYMPIO: I left it inside.

PARDALISCA: Well, what do you think of our trick—
   pretty neat, huh?   650

OLYMPIO: We deserve it. But the door's creaking! She's
   not coming for me again, is she?

(They all withdraw. Enter LYSIDAMUS *from* ALCESIMUS*'s
house.)*

LYSIDAMUS: Oh! I burn with disgrace, and I'm
   dreading to face
   the awful contempt of my wife.
   The whole business is out—and this miserable lout   655
   apprehends it's the end of his life!

   The best thing, I suppose, is to suffer the blows
   that my wife will exact from my hide.
   (To the audience)
   Is there no one out there who'd be willing to share
   the fate that awaits me inside?   660

   Then I think I'll behave like a runaway slave,
   since my back's for the rack in these parts.
   I get beat black and blue. You may laugh, but it's
   true!
   It's my folly, but by *golly*, it smarts!
   I think I'd better make a run for it now!   665

(Enter CHALINUS *from* ALCESIMUS*'s house)*

CHALINUS: Hold it right there, lover boy!

LYSIDAMUS: Damnation! Someone's calling. I'll go on
   as if I didn't hear.

CHALINUS: Just where do you think you're going, you
   sneaky-Greeky lover? If you want to debauch me,   670
   now's your chance! Don't you yearn to return to
   the bedroom? You're finished, by Hercules!
   Come right this way! We don't need to go to
   court; I've a good, strong, honest judge right
   here!   675

(Brandishing a club)

LYSIDAMUS: I'm sunk! That fellow's going to tender-
   ize my slender thighs with his club! It's either
   make tracks this way, or break backs that way!

(Starts to leave in the opposite direction)

CLEOSTRATA: Greetings, lover boy!

LYSIDAMUS: *Egad!!* There's the wife! Caught between   680
   the Devil and the deep blue sea! Wolves to the
   right of me, bitches to the left! *(Indicating* CHALI-
   NUS*)* Only the wolf at *this* door, has a club! I think

I'd better change the proverb, by Hercules, and
685 hope to teach this old dog a new trick.

(Turns to face CLEOSTRATA*)*

MYRRHINA: How's the secondhand husband?
CLEOSTRATA *(Sweetly)*: Why dear, why are you going
about in this garb? What did you do with your
cane? Why, whatever's become of your cloak?
690 PARDALISCA: I think he lost them in lechery: *conjugat-
ing* with Casina.
LYSIDAMUS *(Aside)*: This is *murder!*
CHALINUS: Don't you want to go back to bed again?
(Throwing off his bridal attire) I am Casina!
695 LYSIDAMUS: Go to blazes!!
CHALINUS: Don't you love me?
CLEOSTRATA: Answer me now! What happened to
your cloak?
LYSIDAMUS: By Hercules, wife, some maenads° . . .
700 CLEOSTRATA: Maenads?
LYSIDAMUS: Lord yes, dear. Many maenads . . .
CLEOSTRATA: That's rubbish and you know it. There
aren't any maenads anymore!
LYSIDAMUS: I forgot. Well, there may not have been
705 many maenads, but there were *some!*
CLEOSTRATA: No, there weren't.
LYSIDAMUS: Well, if I'm not able to . . .
CLEOSTRATA: By Castor, you seem nervous!
LYSIDAMUS: *I?*

(All three speaking together)

710 CLEOSTRATA: Yes, by Hercules, you're lying!
MYRRHINA: Why, how pale you look!
PARDALISCA: Why, what's wrong with you?
LYSIDAMUS: Who, *me?*
OLYMPIO *(Joining in)*: Yes, *you!* Congratulations! You're
715 the dirtiest old man that ever was! And he's
brought misery and mockery on me because of
his dastardly deeds.
LYSIDAMUS *(Frantic)*: Can't you be *quiet!?*
OLYMPIO: No, by Hercules! I won't be quiet! Why, you
720 begged and egged me on to marry Casina—on
account of *your* love affair!
LYSIDAMUS *(Innocently)*: I??I did *that?*
OLYMPIO: No, Hector of Troy° did it!
LYSIDAMUS *(Aside to him)*: At least he would have
725 throttled you! You really mean to say I did all
these things?
CLEOSTRATA: You dare to ask?

(Threatening to strike him)

LYSIDAMUS: Wait, by Hercules! If I did it, then it was
wrong.

CLEOSTRATA: Just march yourself right inside. Mama 730
will limber and dismember your timber till you
remember!

(They all advance on him)

LYSIDAMUS: *Oh no, by Hercules!!* I think I'd better just
take your word for everything! But, dear wife,
please pardon your husband this once. Myrrhina, 735
beg Cleostrata! If after this, I make love to
Casina—or even *appear* to *want* to do so—let
alone *do* it—if I ever again do such a thing—well
then, dear wife, you can just suspend me and skin
me alive. 740
MYRRHINA: By Castor . . . *(Pauses)* I really think you
ought . . . *(Pauses)* to *forgive* him.
CLEOSTRATA *(After long hesitation)*: . . . Well . . . if you
say so . . . I'll do it. And the other reason I'm willing to indulge you with forgiveness—*this time!*—is 745
to keep a long play from running any longer.
LYSIDAMUS: You're really not angry?
CLEOSTRATA: No, I'm not really angry.
LYSIDAMUS: Do you promise?
CLEOSTRATA: I do. 750
LYSIDAMUS: There's not a living soul with a more lov-
ing and lovely wife than mine!
CLEOSTRATA *(To* CHALINUS*)*: Go on and give him back
his cloak and cane.
CHALINUS *(Doing so)*: If you wish, I'll surrender this
booty. 755
But, by Pollux, I've suffered acutely
For I think it's a sin to be wed to *two* men,
with neither performing his duty!

EPILOGUE

ALCESIMUS: But audience, *wait!* Learn Casina's fate.
We'll share what's discovered inside.
CLEOSTRATA: A slave no more, she's the girl from
next door!
And soon, our darling son's bride.
OLYMPIO: And now it's your right with all of your
might 5
to applaud till you bring down the house!
PARDALISCA: If you do your part, you'll get a
sweetheart!
LYSIDAMUS: To enjoy without telling *your* spouse!
MYRRHINA: Yet listen, because—if you curb your
applause—
you'll live to regret it, please note: 10
CHALINUS: *No nooky!* Instead, we'll send you to bed
with a sodden and smelly old goat!

---

maenads, female followers of Bacchus, hence possessed
by ecstatic frenzy and capable of unusual deeds. **Hector of
Troy,** heroic Trojan leader celebrated in the *Iliad.*

Figure 1. The chorus of satyrs, in costumes exaggerating the sexual organs, herald the approach of Lysidamus in the 1994 production of *Casina,* directed by Michael Hackett, at the J. Paul Getty Museum, Malibu, California. The satyrs, from left to right, are: Jeremiah Wiggins, LaJessica Mathis, Mandy Turpin, Antonia Bath, and J. Francis Aguas. (Photograph: The J. Paul Getty Museum, courtesy of Dr. Richard Beacham.)

Figure 2. "Casina" (Jon Matthews, *veiled*) is flanked by Olympio (Robert Machray) and Lysidamus (Larry Randolph), as both slave and master anticipate the wedding night in the 1994 Getty production. (Photograph: The J. Paul Getty Museum, courtesy of Dr. Richard Beacham.)

Figure 3. A disheveled and confused Olympio (Robert Machray) recounts his offstage "wedding night" adventures to Myrrhina (Loretta Devine), Cleostrata (Hope Alexander-Willis), and Pardalisca (Kathy Kinney) in the 1994 Getty production. (Photograph: The J. Paul Getty Museum, courtesy of Dr. Richard Beacham.)

Figure 4. The final tableau of *Casina* shows the entire cast about to punish Lysidamus (Larry Randolph) for his outrageous behavior in the 1994 Getty production. The columns support three projecting porches, and the neighbors' houses are thus represented by the two end porches. Background painting was taken from Pompeian frescoes. (Photograph: The J. Paul Getty Museum, courtesy of Dr. Richard Beacham.)

Staging of *A Funny Thing Happened on the Way to the Wedding (Casina)*

**REVIEW OF THE J. PAUL GETTY MUSEUM
PRODUCTION, 1994, BY DON SHIRLEY**

The J. Paul Getty Museum is hosting a rare and intoxicating event. Two ancient comedies, which are sometimes read but hardly ever played, are onstage in the Getty's inner peristyle garden.

If all this sounds serene and stately, think again. The farcical misunderstandings, low-down ribaldry and plain-spoken English adaptations of these plays are in stark contrast to the architectural majesty of the Getty.

This juxtaposition is also reflected in Nathan Birnbaum's entrancing music. Albert Vartanyan uses a variety of Armenian wind instruments to create a frenzy of orgiastic wailing (meant to suggest Aegean sounds), while solemn drummers maintain deadpan stares that are worthy of Buckingham Palace guards.

The first play, "The Woman From Samos," is by Menander, a Greek from the third century B.C. Menander's reputation far surpasses theatergoers' actual knowledge of his works, most of which aren't intact. But this one, in a translation by J. Michael Walton that confidently fills in a few of the missing passages, is fast, funny and surprisingly tender.

Before wealthy Demeas (Jay Bell) and his neighbor Nikeratos (Larry Randolph) went away on business, Demeas ordered his mistress (Tressa Scarbrough), the title character, to get rid of her pregnancy. Meanwhile, Demeas' adopted son Moschion (Jon Matthews) has impregnated Nikeratos' daughter (who remains offstage.)

Soon, complications stack up, thanks in part to the stock-character servants (Robert Machray and Kathy Kinney). But, amid the whirlwind, a few moments of genuine human feeling surface, not only in Menander's lines but also in the actors' faces—which would have been covered by masks in ancient Greece.

During breaks in the action, a chorus line entertains with simple little dances, provocative masks and outlandishly graphic outfits designed by Alex Jaeger. But these costumes are mild compared to the enlarged phalli that are carried onstage after intermission, during the bawdier, more cartoonish "Casina," by the second-century Roman playwright Plautus.

In "Casina," translated by Richard Beacham, Randolph plays a classic dirty old man, Lysidamus, who lusts after the unseen title character, a ward of his wife (Hope Alexander-Willis). The spouses try to outfox each other by setting up their respective servants (Machray and Matthews) as Casina's would-be groom, the better to control Lysidamus' access to her. Not surprisingly, the frisky old man gets his comeuppance.

This one is a rowdy, raucous party, lacking the more rounded characters of "Samos." Like many such parties, it goes on too long but it's a gas.

Michael Hackett briskly directed professional casts. UCLA, which co-produced with the Getty, provided students for the chorus.

Although this production was designed to accompany the current exhibition "A Passion for Antiquities" (open during intermission, if you can tear yourself away from the free baklava and wine), the Getty should consider keeping a permanent resident company devoted to performing classics. Judging from this production, actors can animate an era and add another dimension to the museum experience.

MEDIEVAL THEATER

During the fourteenth and fifteenth centuries—the heyday of medieval drama—permanent theaters did not exist anywhere in England or on the continent. None had been built since the fall of Rome, and none were built until the middle of the sixteenth century in France. Yet in medieval communities throughout England and Europe, theatrical productions commanded as much public attention and support as they had in Athens during the age of classical Greek drama. Drama held a privileged place in the culture of those late medieval communities because, as in ancient Greece, most of their plays were expressions of religious belief, and most of their productions were occasioned by religious events. Just as the ancient Athenians had dramatized their myths to celebrate the festival of Dionysus, so cities and towns all over England and everywhere in Europe dramatized episodes from the Old and New Testaments, from the Apocrypha, and from saints' lives to celebrate sacred events in the Christian calendar. Some towns favored saints' days, others Easter, still others Whitsuntide, which followed Easter by seven weeks, but the most popular occasion was the Feast of Corpus Christi, which took place eight and one-half weeks after Easter, between the last week in May and the third week in June—an ideal time for open-air theater.

During the tenth and eleventh centuries, when religious drama was just beginning to develop, biblical episodes were staged indoors exclusively, in cathedrals and monasteries, where they originated as an instructive but subordinate element of the church service. But by the beginning of the thirteenth century, the devotional and instructional purposes of religious drama had already stimulated a vigorous theatrical impulse that gave rise to productions outside of the church as well as inside of it. Authority over production of the plays then passed from the church to the town, from bishops and abbots to mayors and town councils. Responsibility for staging the plays likewise passed from clerics and choirboys to craft guilds, trade guilds, and religious fraternities. Theatrical productions became a very public and communal activity, involving townspeople and clergy alike. In England, for example, town councils commissioned new plays and revisions of old ones, selected plays to be performed, scheduled performances, assigned individual plays to the various guilds responsible for production, set standards for production, and even levied fines for inferior productions. Each guild in turn took care of all the other arrangements for the play it had been assigned by the council: directing, staging, costuming, rehearsing, and acting. In France, as well as other European countries, the town council and a religious fraternity that sponsored the production jointly chose a committee of supervisors who appointed a director and assistants to produce its plays. The productions were thus an expression of civic pride as well as of religious belief.

As medieval communities grew and prospered, so did religious plays; at the height of their popularity they achieved a scope and magnitude unparalleled in the history of drama. Whether they encompassed the entire biblical history of the world from creation to the last judgment, as they usually did in England, or whether they were restricted to the life of Christ, as was customary in France, they were almost always encyclopedic. Less like plays than megaplays—they are often called cycle plays—they consisted of numerous short plays (called pageants), each devoted to a separate episode or cluster of related episodes from biblical, apocryphal, or saintly experience. The length of cycles varied according to the resources of the towns where they were produced, but judging from the cycles that have survived, they were prodigious undertakings—even the shortest of them. Of the four surviving English cycles, for example, the shortest, from the city of Chester, comprises twenty-four individual pageants; Wakefield's contains thirty-two; the N-Town cycle (possibly performed in Lincolnshire or Norfolk) has forty-three pagents; and the longest, from York, has forty-eight, although with additions and revisions may have even contained fifty-seven. It seems unlikely that any of these cycles could have been staged in a few hours—or even in an entire day. The Chester cycle, according to records from the period, took three days to perform; scholars now believe that the York cycle, scheduled for a single day, may well have included selected plays rather than all that were available. The French passion cycles were just as time-consuming, usually requiring four to six days for performance, though in the exceptional case of a mid-sixteenth-century production at Valenciennes, the complete cycle required twenty-five days.

Given the extraordinary number and variety of episodes they contained, the cycles clearly called for extraordinary methods of staging. With the increasing wealth, resourcefulness, and civic pride of late medieval communities, they were able, and eager, to put on extraordinary theatrical productions, using a variety of theatrical structures. Some communities staged their cycles on fixed platforms, others in the round, and others on movable wagons. But all the methods, however different their external characteristics, embodied the same conception of theatrical space and movement that had governed the earlier staging of plays within the church. Specifically, they all combined a neutral acting area with a group of set-like structures known as "mansions" (literally, dwelling places), and as the action moved from one mansion or specific locale to the next, the acting area was understood to be an extension of one location and then another. Consequently, the various outdoor forms of staging cycle plays were all fundamentally symbolic in their use of space, and processional in their movement from one mansion or location to the next.

The procession took different forms according to the different methods of staging. In the fixed method, which prevailed in France, all the mansions for a single

Figure 1. The medieval platform stage.

day's performance were placed side by side, either in a straight line on a long platform or in a semicircle on a public square (see Figure 1). Here all of the sets—
sometimes as many as twenty to thirty on a platform 100 to 200 feet long, ranging
from heaven, which traditionally appeared at the right end, to hell, which was
located at the left—were simultaneously visible, creating a dazzling spectacle for
the audience. As the cycle unfolded, moving from one location and episode to the
next, the audience proceeded from one end of the platform, or square, to the
other. Staging in the round (the least common of the methods both in England
and on the continent) took place in circular areas 100 to 300 feet in diameter that
were designed to include spectators, sets, and actors alike (see Figure 2). The
series of mansions were arranged around the perimeter of the circle; the audience
sat or stood within the circle of sets; and the actors moved from one location to the
next around the perimeter or to the general acting area in the center of the circle.
The procession took yet another form, its most distinctive form, in the system of
movable wagons that was common both in England and Spain, for with this
method each separate pageant, staged by a different guild, was mounted on a separate wagon. The exact design and dimensions of the wagons have never been definitely established, and the conditions of performance together with the locations
implied by the texts may lead to contradictory readings. On the one hand, the
wagons had to be able to negotiate the narrow streets of a medieval city, such as
York, the one site where the route for the wagons is relatively certain. On the other
hand, the wagon had to clear the overhanging roofs of York, yet be two stories high

Figure 2. Medieval staging in the round.

to accommodate both the Hellmouth where the devils received the sinners and the elaborately draped heaven complete with twenty angels. A detailed description of the Last Judgement, as staged by Mercers of York, indicates that in addition to the devils and the angels the wagon contained two good souls, two evil souls, and eleven apostles. Even though recent actors experimented with a processional staging in York in 1988, we still cannot be sure whether the audience sat in special seats along the route, watched from upper windows, stood in front of the wagon (or on three sides, or even on four sides), or perhaps arranged themselves differently in different spaces. We do know that the medieval audiences for pageant wagons gathered in separate groups at several specified locations within a town, and at each of these points along the route the individual wagons would stop and the actors would perform their play (see Figure 3). Since plays were not all the same length, playing times would necessarily vary, and in the intervals between plays, audience members might go off in search of food or drink, or perhaps even follow the wagon on to the next playing station and watch a favorite play again.

In all these systems of staging, a rough-and-ready intimacy existed between actors and audience, quite unlike the distance that separated them in a classical Greek theater and equally unlike their separation from one another by the proscenium arches of post-Renaissance theaters. Not only the physical methods of staging but also the conventions of performance worked to bring actors and audience together. The actors, for example, were largely amateurs, members of the community, friends, and relatives of the spectators who were witnessing them from only a few feet away. Sometimes they were not even separated from one another at all. In the fixed method of staging, for example, actors might sit off to the side or actually stand among the audience before and after they performed their parts. In the

Figure 3. Medieval staging on movable wagons.

movable system, the action sometimes spilled off the wagon into the street, particularly when the situation called for action symbolizing great distances between one place and another, as when Satan and his cohorts fell from heaven to hell, or when Adam and Eve were driven out of paradise. Then the actors performed their parts by moving from the acting platform into the area of the audience. Indeed, in many places it was customary for the devils to mingle playfully with the audience. Conventions of performance were clearly not designed to create or sustain a theatrical illusion.

Instead, performance conventions emphasized the symbolic aspect of these plays. With multiple actors playing Christ—a necessity, given both the physical demands of the role and the repetition of plays—audiences would have responded to the image of the role, and its meaning, rather than to a realistic character. But since all of the characters except the devils were costumed in some kind of medieval garb—God in the imperial vestments of the pope, Jewish priests in bishops' robes, the tyrant Herod in a kingly crown, and Roman soldiers in knights' armor—the audience would also have seen biblical figures represented as contemporary ones. The devils, not surprisingly, were portrayed as fabulous beasts, their masks grotesquely elaborated as in carved gargoyles. Some costumes and props were highly symbolic such as a red-colored rib for the creation of Eve and white leather costumes for the innocent Adam and Eve. Other props were gruesomely realistic, especially in plays involving the arrest, torture, and Crucifixion of Jesus; documents from the period mention scourges, and a leather bag with blood, while in York the Crucifixion was presented by the Pinners, craftsmen who specialized in making pegs to put boards together. Special effects included dummy or live animals for Noah's Ark, barrels of water for the Flood, fire burning at Hellmouth, pulleys for bringing angels from heaven to earth, and trapdoors for the sudden appearance or disappearance of characters. All in all, the cycles must have created for medieval audiences a marvelous and miraculous spectacle. But given the visible presence in the plays of products made by the guilds, as well as the craftsmanship of the guilds involved in the production of the plays, each pageant wagon also served as an advertisement for everyday goods. The York cycle, for example, even had two plays about the Flood, so that the Shipwrights could present the building of the Ark, while the Fishers and Mariners presented the Flood itself. Thus the pageants combined the marvelous and miraculous with the spectators' everyday reality.

Cycle plays were by no means the only form of medieval drama, but they originated so early and prevailed so widely that the spatial concept governing their staging also influenced the staging of other medieval plays, such as farces and moralities. That concept of theatrical space was not only familiar to medieval audiences but was also readily adaptable to the production of both farces and moralities, whose length rarely exceeded 1,500 lines. Like a pageant in a cycle, they were short and simple in their staging requirements, ordinarily calling for only two or three mansions. Although they were staged according to the same theatrical conventions, they were not produced under the same auspices. Farces, for example, which were common largely in France during the fifteenth century, were written and performed by lawyers' guilds and student groups, who produced them to celebrate festivals such as Mardi Gras and May Day, when ribaldry and revelry were appropriate to the occasion. Morality plays, popular chiefly in England during the fifteenth and sixteenth centuries, were performed by small troupes of professional players who toured the countryside and timed their arrival in a town to coincide with a religious holiday or festival, when the spiritual message of their play was most likely to elicit contributions from their audience. Though moralities were designed primarily to exemplify Christian belief, to show the perils of sin and the rewards of virtue, they often loosened the pockets of spectators by appealing also to their sense of humor. They usually contained a few characters known as Vice figures, whose dirty jokes and slapstick stage business were meant not only to show the vulgarity of sin but also to amuse a paying audience. And to capitalize on their vulgarity, the Vice figures usually interrupted the play once or twice to collect money from the audience.

The image of the Vice figure mingling with the audience also sums up the unique qualities of medieval theater. Medieval drama encompassed a variety of plays as different as cycles, farces, and moralities, yet it persistently brought actors and spectators closer to one another than ever before or since. They were drawn together not only by the physical characteristics of the stage and the conventions of performance but also by the festive purpose of their drama. Whether the festivities were sacred or secular, the actors and spectators were joined in celebration. The plays that appear in this section are embodiments of the most communal stage in the history of Western theater.

THE WAKEFIELD MASTER

ca. 1400–1450

The unknown author of *The Second Shepherds' Play* has come to be known as the Wakefield Master, a name that fittingly identifies him with both the town for which he wrote and the consummate skill of his writing. Exactly when he lived is uncertain, but the language of his plays suggests that he probably wrote sometime during the first half of the fifteenth century. His plays also reveal that he must have received a thoroughgoing religious education, for they incorporate knowledge of biblical literature, scriptural commentary, and Latin liturgy. He was undoubtedly a member of the clergy, but he almost certainly did not lead a cloistered existence, for the five pieces he contributed to the Wakefield cycle are filled with an extraordinary array of characters and situations, some of which he must have witnessed firsthand, others that he probably picked up from current folktales, and some that he invented—but invented out of a rich storehouse of experience.

The Wakefield cycle itself originated during the second half of the fourteenth century, about fifty years before the time of the Wakefield Master, and it continued to be revised and performed until the late sixteenth century. It is, like the other surviving English cycles, a composite of plays written and rewritten by several authors at several different periods to meet the changing needs of the community. New plays were added as guilds became large and prosperous enough to mount their own productions; old plays were dropped or combined with others when a guild ran into hard times and could no longer afford its own production; or they were revised to satisfy objections of the church or the community. Although it is a patchwork of thirty-two plays, its pieces are unified by the pattern of spiritual history embodied in each play individually and all of them collectively. But the five plays written by the Wakefield Master stand out from the rest of the cycle.

His verse form is his most telling signature. The nine-line stanza he uses throughout his five plays does not occur anywhere else in the cycle except at a few points that bear the signs of his revision. In fact, his nine-line stanza is not to be found anywhere else in any of the other cycles, or anywhere else in medieval literature. Not only is it unique but it is a remarkably complex harmony of rhymes and rhythms, all of which have been reproduced in Anthony Caputi's modernized version of *The Second Shepherds' Play*. The first four lines combine not only identical end rhymes but also identical internal rhymes. The last five lines have an entirely different rhyme scheme, for the sixth, seventh, and eighth lines rhyme with one another, while the ninth line rhymes with the fifth to hold the elaborate structure of sounds together. As the rhyme scheme shifts from the first to the last part of each stanza, so does the rhythm. Each of the first four lines contains four beats; the fifth consists of only one stressed syllable; the sixth, seventh, and eighth have three stresses; and the ninth contains two stresses. The conception and execution of such an elaborate verse form is unquestionably the work of a technical virtuoso.

Even more remarkable is the fact that he sustains his verse form throughout all his plays, adapting its harmonies to widely different moods and situations, such as

God loftily giving Noah specifications for the ark, or Noah's wife peevishly refusing to board the ark, or the shepherds devoutly presenting their gifts to the newborn child, or the Jewish high priest Annas unctuously expounding legal procedure to Christ, or the tyrant Herod maniacally raging about his political power. Dramatic situations so various as these require not only a flexible verse form but also a flexibility of language, and the Wakefield Master repeatedly displays his versatility, for he draws on an extensive vocabulary, ranging from slang to colloquial to formal usage, from one medieval dialect to another, from English to Latin and back. Yet he always finds the right word or expression to suit any character in any situation.

Ultimately, his plays stand out because his characters and his plots are masterfully developed, even within the short scope of several hundred lines. *The Second Shepherds' Play,* the longest of his works, contains only 771 lines, yet it projects a vividly developed world of shepherds and sheep-stealers, a world with an imaginative life of its own as well as a relevance to the religious theme of the play. In the opening 191 lines, for example, even before the appearance of the sheep-stealer Mak, the dialogue of the three shepherds fully distinguishes them from one another. The first shepherd, Coll, is obsessed by his poverty and outraged by the gentry who exploit him and his fellows; the second shepherd, Gib, is preoccupied by the afflictions of married life; and the third shepherd, Daw, is fed up with his job of tending others' sheep while they rest and he goes hungry. Although their complaints are different, they are united by affliction, by the misery of the weather that accentuates these complaints, and by the rough but good fellowship that sustains them. And their combined suffering dramatically presents the image of a world in need of salvation, a need that anticipates the end of the play and that accounts for the joy they express on learning of the savior.

The playwright was clearly fascinated by the dramatic possibilities offered not only by the divine event but by the mortals who were summoned to witness it. In his other dramatized version of the same event (*The First Shepherds' Play*), he similarly focuses on the three shepherds, giving each a distinctive voice and creating for them a rowdy feasting scene. Perhaps it was through the writing of the first version that the Wakefield Master came to realize that the shepherds offered him even larger dramatic opportunities. So, in the second version, he substitutes for the essentially static eating and drinking scene the more active intrigue of Mak stealing a sheep from his fellow shepherds. The sheep-stealing episode is the supreme example of the playwright's skill in turning a good folk story into good theater and ultimately into good religious example.

As the farce unfolds, even before the marvelous moment of exposure, it becomes increasingly clear that Mak, his wife, and the stolen sheep disguised as a newborn child are upside-down versions of Joseph, Mary, and Christ. The make-believe birth staged by Mak and his wife provides a dramatically sharp contrast to the nativity scene that follows. Clearly, the Wakefield Master has taken enormous liberties with the brief biblical cue in the Gospel of Luke—"And there were in the same country shepherds abiding in the field, keeping watch over their flocks by night." But it is precisely those liberties that account for both the theatrical and the religious effectiveness of *The Second Shepherds' Play.*

Like all biblical plays, it is relatively easy to stage. The cast is small, the parts are short. Only two specific locations are required, one for Mak's house, the other for the stable at Bethlehem; the rest of the play takes place in the open fields. Likewise, only a few props are needed: a crib, a couple of chairs, and a bed at Mak's house; a crib and a chair at the stable; and some kind of sheep, either dummy or live. While the two locations might well be represented by different places on the stage—one on each side, with the shepherds in the "field" between them—recent stagings suggest the possibility of a different treatment. When the Royal Shakespeare Company staged the play as a special Christmas production in 1978, they not only used the company's smallest acting space, but then deliberately chose to show Mak and Gill's cottage changing into the stable, while the actors who played Mak and Gill (see Figure 1) became Joseph and Mary (see Figure 2). The doubling of the roles and the transformation of the stage space evoke two kinds of pleasure: admiration for the technical virtuosity of the actors and designers, and awareness of the symbolic connection between the two stories. The comedy of the sheep-stealing episode still remains central—one has only to look at the dubious expression on the First Shepherd's face as he holds the sheep/baby (Figure 3)—an expression which then changes to devout happiness as the same shepherd kneels before Mary (Figure 2). A 1985 production in Toronto made a similar choice, leading scholar Martin Stevens to note the appropriateness of the single setting, "such as would have been likely in a pageant-wagon performance." In both productions, as in the play itself, restriction becomes liberation, and comedy turns into piety, since the "child" so joked about in Mak's cottage is finally understood not as a lamb, but, for Christians, as the Lamb of God, the redeemer of suffering human beings.

THE SECOND SHEPHERDS' PLAY

BY THE WAKEFIELD MASTER / MODERNIZED AND EDITED BY ANTHONY CAPUTI

CHARACTERS

FIRST SHEPHERD, COLL
SECOND SHEPHERD, GIB
THIRD SHEPHERD, DAW
MAK
GILL, *his wife*
ANGEL
MARY

(Enter the FIRST SHEPHERD.*)*

FIRST SHEPHERD: Lord, but it's cold, and I'm
    wretchedly wrapped.
My hands nearly numb, so long have I napped.
My legs creak and fold, my fingers are chapped;
It is not as I would, for I am all lapped
    In sorrow.   5
In storms and tempest,
Now in the east, now in the west,
Woe is him has never rest
    Midday nor morrow!

But we poor shepherds that walk on the moor,   10
We're like, in faith, to be put out of door;
No wonder, as it stands, if we be poor,
For the tilth of our lands lies fallow as a floor,
    As ye ken.
We are so lamed,   15
So taxed and shamed,
We are made hand-tamed
    By these gentlery-men.

Thus they rob us of rest. Our Lady them harry!
These men that are lord-fast, they make the plough
    tarry.   20
Some say it's for the best; but we find it contrary.
Thus are tenants oppressed, in point to miscarry,
    In life.
Thus hold they us under;
Thus they bring us in blunder.   25
It were a great wonder
    If ever we should thrive.

'Gainst a man with painted sleeves, or a brooch,
    now-a-days,
Woe to him that shall grieve, or one word gainsay!
No man dare him reprove, what mastery he has.   30
Yet no man believes one word that he says,

No letter.
He can make purveyance,
With boast and arrogance;
And all is for maintenance   35
    Of men that are greater.

There shall come a swain as proud as a po,°
He must borrow my wain,° and my plough also,
That I am full fain to grant ere he go.
Thus live we in pain, anger, and woe   40
    By night and day.
Whatever he has willed
Must at once be fulfilled.
I were better be killed
    Than once say him nay.   45

It does me good, as I walk round alone,
Of this world for to talk in manner of groan.
To my sheep will I stalk, now as I moan;
There abide on a ridge, or sit on a stone,
    Full soon.   50
For I know, pardie,°
True men if they be,
I'll get more company
    Ere it be noon. *(Moves aside)*

(Enter the SECOND SHEPHERD.*)*
SECOND SHEPHERD: Ben'c'te° and Dominus! What
    may this bemean?   55
Why fares this world thus; the like has seldom
    been.
Lord, the weather is spiteful, and the winds bitter
    keen,
And the frosts so hideous, they water my een.°
    No lie.

---

po, peacock. **wain,** wagon. **pardie,** Pardieu; By God;
indeed. **Ben'c'te,** Benedicte. **een,** eyes.

60 Now in dry, now in wet,
Now in snow, now in sleet,
My shoes freeze to my feet,
    And all is awry.

But as far as I ken, wherever I go,
65 We poor wedded men endure much woe,
Crushed again and again, it falls oft so.
And Silly Capel, our hen, both to and fro
She cackles;
But begin she to croak,
70 To groan or to choke,
For our cock it's no joke,
    For he's in the shackles.

These men that are wed have never their will.
When they're full hard bestead,° they sigh and
    keep still.
75 God knows they are led full hard and full ill;
In bower nor in bed say they aught until
    Ebb tide.
My part have I found,
And my lesson is sound:
80 Woe to him that is bound,
    For he must abide.

But now late in our lives—a marvel to me,
That I think my heart rives such wonders to see,
What destiny drives that it should so be—
85 Some men will have two wives, and some men three
    In store.
He has woe that has any;
But so far ken I,
He has moe° that has many,
90   For he feels sore.

But young men a'wooing, before you've been
    caught,
Be well ware of wedding, and keep in your
    thought,
To moan, "Had I known," is a thing that serves
    naught.
Mickle° mourning has wedding to home often
    brought,
95   And griefs,
With many a sharp shower;
You may catch in an hour
What shall seem full sour
    As long as you live.

00 For as ever read I epistle° I've one as my dear,
As sharp as a thistle, as rough as a brere;°
She is browed like a bristle, with a sour lenten
    cheer;

Had she once wet her whistle, she could sing full
    clear
    Her paternoster.
She's as great as a whale;   105
She has a gallon of gall;
By him that died for us all
    I would I'd run till I'd lost her.

FIRST SHEPHERD: Gib, look over the row! Full deafly,
    ye stand.
SECOND SHEPHERD: Yea, the devil in your maw—ye
    blow on your hand.   110
    Saw ye anywhere Daw?
FIRST SHEPHERD: Yea, on a lea-land
    I heard him blow. He comes here at hand,
    Not far.
    Stand still.   115
SECOND SHEPHERD: Why?
FIRST SHEPHERD: I think he comes by.
SECOND SHEPHERD: He'll trick us with a lie
    Unless we beware.

(Enter the THIRD SHEPHERD, *a boy.)*

THIRD SHEPHERD: Christ's cross me speed, and Saint
    Nicholas!   120
Thereof had I need; and it's worse than it was.
Whoso can take heed and let the world pass;
It's rank as a weed and brittle as glass,
    And slides.
This world fared never so,   125
With marvels more and moe,
    Now in weal, now in woe,
        Everything writhes.

Never since Noah's flood were such floods seen,
Winds and rains so rude, and storms so keen;   130
Some stammered, some stood in doubt, as I
    ween.
Now God turn all to good! I say as I mean,
    Hereunder.
These floods so they drown,
Both in fields and in town,
And bear all down,   135
    They make you wonder.

We that walk in the nights our cattle to keep,
We see queer sights when other men sleep.
Yet methinks my heart lightens; I see my pals
    peep.   140
They are two tall wights! Now I'll give my sheep
    A turn.
O full ill am I bent,
As I walk on this land.
I may lightly repent,   145
    If my toes I spurn.

---

bestead, situated.   **moe**, more.   **mickle**, much.   **epistle**,
in the New Testament.   **brere**, briar.

(to the other two) Ah, sir, God you save, and master
    mine!
A drink would I have, and somewhat to dine.
FIRST SHEPHERD: Christ's curse, my knave, thou'rt a
    lazy swine!
SECOND SHEPHERD: The boy likes to rave! Let him
150   stand there and whine
    Till we've made it.
    Ill thrift on thy pate!
    Though the fellow came late,
    Yet is he in state
155   To dine—if he had it.

THIRD SHEPHERD: Such servants as I, that sweat and
    swink,°
Eat our bread full dry, that's what I think.
We're oft wet and weary when master men wink,°
Yet come full late both dinners and drink.
160   But neatly
Both our dame and our sire,
When we've run in the mire,
Can nip at our hire,
    And pay us full lately.

165 But hear a truth, master, for you the fare make:
I shall do, hereafter, work as I take;
I shall do a little, sir, and between times play.
For I've never had suppers that heavily weigh
    In fields.
170 And why should I bray?
I can still run away.
What sells cheap, men say,
    Never yields.

FIRST SHEPHERD: Thou are an ill lad, to ride a-wooing
175 With a man that had but little of spending.
SECOND SHEPHERD: Peace, boy! I bade; no more
    jangling,
Or I shall make thee afraid, by the Heaven's King,
    With thy frauds.
Where are the sheep, boy; lorn?
180 THIRD SHEPHERD: Sir, this same day at morn
I them left in the corn,
    When they rang lauds.°

They have pasture good; they cannot go wrong.
FIRST SHEPHERD: That's right. Oh, by the rood, these
    nights are long!
185 Yet I would, ere we go, let's have us a song.
SECOND SHEPHERD: So I thought as I stood, to cheer
    us along.
THIRD SHEPHERD: I grant.
FIRST SHEPHERD: The tenor I'll try.
SECOND SHEPHERD: And I the treble so high.

swink, toil. *wink,* doze. *lauds,* the early morning service.

THIRD SHEPHERD: Then the middle am I. 190
Let's see how ye chant. *(They sing.)*

(Enter MAK *with a cloak over his smock.)*

MAK: Now, Lord, of names seven, that made the
    moon so pale,
And more stars than I can name; Thy good will
    fails;
I am so in a whirl that my jogged brain ails
Now would God I were in heaven—where no child
    wails— 195
    Heaven so still.
FIRST SHEPHERD: Who is it that pipes so poor?
MAK: God knows what I endure,
Here a'walking on the moor,
    And not my will! 200

SECOND SHEPHERD: From where do ye come, Mak?
    What news do ye bring?
THIRD SHEPHERD: Is he come? Then everyone take
    heed to his things.

(Takes the cloak from MAK.*)*

MAK: What! I am a yeoman (hear me you) of the king,
Make way for me, the Lord's tidings I bring,
    And such. 205
Fie on you! Go hence!
This is no pretence.
I must have reverence.
    And much!

FIRST SHEPHERD: Why make ye so quaint, Mak? It's
    no good to try. 210
SECOND SHEPHERD: Why play ye the saint, Mak? We
    know that you lie.
THIRD SHEPHERD: We know you can feint, Mak, and
    give the devil the lie.
MAK: I'll make such complaint, 'lack,° I'll make you
    all fry
    At a word.
And tell what ye doth. 215
FIRST SHEPHERD: But, Mak, is that truth?
Go gild that green tooth
    With a turd.

SECOND SHEPHERD: Mak, the devil's in your eye! A
    stroke would I lend you.
THIRD SHEPHERD: Mak, know ye not me? By God, I
    could 'tend you. 220
MAK: God keep you all three! Perhaps I can mend
    you.
You're a fair company.
FIRST SHEPHERD: Can ye so bend you?
SECOND SHEPHERD: Rascal jape!°
    Thus late, as thou goes, 225

'lack, alack: an expression of surprise or dismay. *jape,* fool.

What will men suppose?
Sure thou hast an ill nose
For stealing of sheep.

MAK: And I am true as steel, all men say,
230 But a sickness I feel that takes my health away;
My belly's not well, not at all well today.
THIRD SHEPHERD: "Seldom lies the devil dead by the
way."
MAK: Therefore
Full sore am I and ill;
235 And I'll lie stone still
If I've eat even a quill
This month and more.

FIRST SHEPHERD: How fares thy wife? By my hood,
tell me true.
MAK: Lies sprawling by the fire, but that's nothing
new;
240 And a house full of brood. She drinks well, too;
Come ill or good that she'll always do
But so.
Eats as fast as she can;
And each year gives a man
245 A hungry bairn° to scan,
And some years two.

And were I more gracious and richer by far,
I were eaten still out of house and of barn.
And just look at her close, if ye come near;
250 There is none that knows what 'tis to fear
Than ken I.
Will ye see what I proffer—
I'll give all in my coffer
And masses I'll offer
255 To bid her goodbye.

SECOND SHEPHERD: I am so long wakéd, like none in
this shire,
I would sleep if I takéd less for my hire.
THIRD SHEPHERD: I am cold and near naked, and
would have a fire.
FIRST SHEPHERD: I am weary, for-rakéd,° and run in
the mire.
260 Stay awake, you!
SECOND SHEPHERD: Nay, I'll lie down by,
I must sleep must I.
THIRD SHEPHERD: I've as good need to put by
As any of you.

265 But, Mak, come hither! Between us must you be.
MAK: You're sure you don't want to talk privately?
Indeed?
From my top to my toe,

---

bairn, child. **for-rakéd,** exhausted.

Manus tuas commendo,
Pontio Pilato,° 270
Christ's cross me speed!

(*Then he rises, the shepherds being asleep, and says.*)

Now were time for a man that wants for gold
To stealthily enter into a fold,
And nimbly to work then, yet be not too bold,
For he might pay for the bargain, if it were told, 275
At the ending.
Now were time for to spell—
But he needs good counsel
That fain would fare well,
And has little spending. 280

But about you a circle as round as a moon,
Till I've done what I will, till it be noon,
Ye must lie stone still till I have done.
And I shall say thereto of words a few.
On height. 285
Over your heads my hands I lift;
Your eyes go out and senses drift
Until I make a better shift
If it be right.

Lord, how they sleep hard! That may ye all hear. 290
I never was a shepherd, but now will I learn.
If the flock be scared, when I shall creep near.
How! Draw hitherward! Now mends our cheer
From sorrow.
A fat sheep, I dare say; 295
A good fleece, dare I lay!
Pay back when I may,
But this will I borrow.

(MAK *crosses the stage to his house.*)

How, Gill, art thou in? Get us some light.
WIFE: Who makes such din this time of the night? 300
I am set for to spin; no hope that I might
Rise a penny to win. I curse them on height.
So sore
A housewife thus fares,
She always has cares 305
And all for nothing bears
All these chores.

MAK: Good wife, open the latch! Seest thou not what
I bring?
WIFE: I'll let thee draw the catch. Ah, come in my
sweeting!
MAK: Yea, thou dost not reek of my long standing. 310
WIFE: By thy bare neck for this you're like to swing.
MAK: Go away:
I'm good for something yet,

Manus . . . Pilato, "Into thy hands I commend [my spirit],
Pontius Pilate" a blasphemous echo of Christ's last words.

For in a pinch can I get
315 More than they that swink and sweat
　　All the long day.

Thus it fell to my lot, Gill, I had such grace.
WIFE: It were a foul blot to be hanged for the case.
MAK: But I have escaped, Gill, a far narrower place.
320 WIFE: Yet so long goes the pot to the water, men say,
　　At last
　　Comes it home broken.
MAK: Well know I the token,
　　But let it never be spoken;
325 　　But come and help fast.

I would he were slain; I want to eat.
This twelvemonth have I not ta'en of one sheep's
　　meat.
WIFE: Should they come ere he's slain, and hear the
　　sheep bleat—
MAK: Then might I be ta'en! That puts me in a heat!
330 　　Go bar
　　The gate door.
WIFE: Yes, Mak,
　　For if they come at thy back—
MAK: Then might I pay for the pack!
335 　　May the devil us warn.

WIFE: A good trick have I spied, since thou ken none.
Here shall we him hide till they be gone—
In my cradle abide. Let me alone,
And I shall lie beside in childbed, and groan.
340 MAK: Thou hast said;
　　And I'll say thou was light°
　　Of a male child this night.
WIFE: It's luck I was born bright,
　　And cleverly bred.

345 For shrewdness this trick can't be surpassed;
Yet a woman's advice always helps at the last!
Before they 'gin to spy, hurry thou fast.
MAK: Unless I come ere they rise, they'll blow a loud
　　blast!
　　I'll go sleep.

(MAK *returns to the shepherds and resumes his place.*)

350 Yet sleeps all this company;
　　And I shall go stalk privily,
　　As it had never been me
　　That carried their sheep.

FIRST SHEPHERD: *Resurrex a mortuis!*° Take hold of my
　　hand.
355 *Judas carnas dominus!*° I can not well stand;
　　My foot sleeps, by Jesus; and I'm dry as sand.
　　I thought we had laid us near English land.

---

　　light, delivered. **Resurrex . . .; Judas . . . dominus,** These
lines are in mock-Latin.

SECOND SHEPHERD: Ah, yea!
　　I slept so well, I feel
　　As fresh as an eel,
360 　　As light on my heel
　　As leaf on a tree.

THIRD SHEPHERD: Lord bless us all! My body's all
　　a-quake!
My heart jumps from my skin, sure and that's no
　　fake.
Who makes all this din? So my head aches.
365
I'll teach him something. Hark, fellows, awake!
We were four.
See ye aught of Mak now?
FIRST SHEPHERD: We were up ere thou.
SECOND SHEPHERD: Man, I give God a vow,
370
　　That he went nowhere.

THIRD SHEPHERD: I dreamed he was lapped in a gray
　　wolf's skin.
FIRST SHEPHERD: So many are wrapped now—
　　namely, within.
THIRD SHEPHERD: When we had so long napped,
　　methought he did begin
A fat sheep to trap; but he made no din.
375
SECOND SHEPHERD: Be still!
　　Thy dream makes thee brood;
　　It's but fancy, by the rood.
FIRST SHEPHERD: Now God turn all to good,
　　If it be his will!
380

SECOND SHEPHERD: Rise, Mak! For shame! Thou liest
　　right long.
MAK: Now Christ's holy name be us among!
　　What is this? By Saint James, I may not move
　　along!
　　I think I be the same. Ah! my neck has lain wrong
　　　Enough (*They help* MAK *up.*)
385
Mickle thanks! Since yestere'en,
Now, by Saint Stephen,
I was flayed with a dream
　　That my heart did cuff.

I thought Gill began to croak and labor full sad,
390
Indeed at the first cock had borne a young lad
To increase our flock. Guess whether I'm glad;
I am now more in hock than ever I had.
　　Ah, my head!
A house full of bairns!
395
'Devil knock out their brains!
For father is the pains,
　　And little bread!

I must go home, by your leave, to Gill, as I thought.
I pray you look in my sleeve that I steal naught;
400
I am loath you to grieve or from you take aught.

THIRD SHEPHERD: Go forth; ill might thou live! Now
would I we sought,
This morn,
That we had all our store.

405 FIRST SHEPHERD: But I will go before;
Let us meet.

SECOND SHEPHERD: Where?

THIRD SHEPHERD: At the crooked thorn.

(MAK crosses to his cottage.)

MAK: Undo this door, here! How long shall I stand?

410 WIFE: Who makes such a stir? Go walk in quicksand!

MAK: Ah, Gill, what cheer? It is I, Mak, your
husband.

WIFE: Then may we see here the devil in a band,
Sir Guile.
Lo, he comes with a knot
415 At the back of his crop.°
I'll soon to my cot
For a very long while.

MAK: Will ye hear what she makes to get her a gloze?°
She does naught but plays, and wiggles her toes.

420 WIFE: Why, who wanders? Who wakes? Who comes?
Who goes?
Who brews? Who bakes? What makes me this hose?
And then,
It's a pity to behold,
425 Now in hot, now in cold,
Full of woe is the household
That wants a woman.

But what end has thou made with the shepherds,
Mak?

MAK: The last word that they said, when I turned my
back,
430 They would look that they had their sheep, count
the pack.
I'm sure they'll not be glad to find one they lack,
Pardie.
But howsoever it goes,
They will surely suppose,
435 From me the trouble 'rose,
And cry out upon me.
But thou must do as thou hight.°

WIFE: Of course I will.
I shall swaddle him right; you trust in your Gill.
440 If it were a worse plight, yet could I help still.
I will lie down straight. Come, cover me.

MAK: I will.

WIFE: Behind!
It may be a narrow squeak.

445 MAK: Yes, if too close they peek,
Or if the sheep should speak!

WIFE: 'Tis then time to whine.

knot . . . crop, an allusion to hanging. gloze, an excuse.
hight, promised.

Hearken when they call; for they will come anon.°
Come and make ready all, and sing on thine own;
Sing lullaby thou shall, for I must groan 450
And cry out by the wall on Mary and John,
For sore.
Sing a lullaby, fast,
Like thou sang at our last;
If I play a false cast, 455
Trust me no more!

(The SHEPHERDS meet at the crooked hawthorn.)

THIRD SHEPHERD: Ah, Coll, good morn! Why sleep
thou not?

FIRST SHEPHERD: Alas, that ever I was born! We have
a foul blot.
A fat lamb have we lorn.°

THIRD SHEPHERD: Marry, God forbid! 460

SECOND SHEPHERD: Who should do us that scorne?
That were a foul spot.

FIRST SHEPHERD: Some shrew.
I have sought with my dogs
All Horbury Bogs, 465
And with fifteen hogs
Found I but one ewe.

THIRD SHEPHERD: Now trust me if ye will; by Saint
Thomas of Kent,
Either Mak or Gill was at that assent.

FIRST SHEPHERD: Peace, man, be still! I saw when he
went. 470
Thou slanders him ill. Thou ought to repent.
Good speed.

SECOND SHEPHERD: Now if ever I lie,
If I should even here die,
I would say it were he 475
That did that same deed.

THIRD SHEPHERD: Go we thither, I rede,° at a
running trot.
I shall never eat bread till the truth I've got.

FIRST SHEPHERD: Nor drink, in my heed, until we
solve this plot.

SECOND SHEPHERD: Till we know all, indeed, I will
rest no jot, 480
My brother!
One thing I will plight:
Till I see him in sight
Shall I never sleep one night
Where I do another. 485

*(At MAK's house they hear GILL groan and MAK sing a
lullaby.)*

THIRD SHEPHERD: Will ye hear how they hack? Our
sir likes to croon.

anon, soon. lorn, lost. rede, advise.

FIRST SHEPHERD: Heard I never one crack so clear
out of tune!
Call on him.

SECOND SHEPHERD: Mak! Undo your door soon.

490 MAK: Who is that spake as it were high noon
On loft?
Who is that, I say?

THIRD SHEPHERD: Good fellows, were it day.

MAK: As far as ye may,
495 Good, speak soft,

Over a sick woman's head that is ill at ease;
I had rather be dead e'er she had any dis-ease.

WIFE: Go to another place! I may not well wheeze.
Each foot that ye tread goes to make me sneeze,
500 So "he-e-e-e."

FIRST SHEPHERD: Tell us, Mak, if ye may,
How fare ye, I say?

MAK: But are ye in town today?
Now how fare ye?

505 Ye have run in the mire, and are all wet yet.
I shall make you a fire, if ye will sit.
A nurse would I hire, and never doubt it.
But at my present hire—well, I hope for a bit
In season.
510 I've more bairns than ye knew,
And sure the saying is true,
"We must drink as we brew,"
And that's but reason.

I would ye dined ere ye go. Methinks that ye sweat.

SECOND SHEPHERD: Nay, that mends not our mood,
515 neither drink nor meat.

MAK: Why, what ails you sir?

THIRD SHEPHERD: Yea, our sheep that we get
Are stolen as they go. Our loss is not sweet.

MAK: Sirs, drink!
520 Had I been there,
Someone had paid full dear.

FIRST SHEPHERD: Some men think that ye were;
And that makes us think.

SECOND SHEPHERD: Mak, some men say that it should
be ye.

THIRD SHEPHERD: Either ye or your spouse; who else
525 could it be?

MAK: Now, if ye suspect us, either Gill or me,
Come and rip our house, and then ye may see
Who had her.
If I any sheep got
530 Any cow or stott°—
And Gill, my wife, rose not
Since here she laid her.

As I am true and leal,° to God here I pray.
That this be the first meal that I shall eat this day.

FIRST SHEPHERD: Mak, as I have weal,° have a care, I
say: 535
"He learned timely to steal that could not say nay."

WIFE: I swelt!°
Out, thieves from my home!
Ye come to rob us, ye drones!

MAK: Hear ye not how she groans?   540
Your heart should melt.

WIFE: Out, thieves, from my bairn! Get out of the
door!

MAK: Knew ye what she had borne, your hearts
would be sore.
Ye do wrong, I you warn, that thus come before
To a woman that has borne. But I say no more.   545

WIFE: Ah, my middle!
I pray to God so mild,
If ever I you beguiled,
Let me eat this child
That lies in this cradle.   550

MAK: Peace, woman, for God's pain and cry not so!
Thou shalt hurt thy brain, and make me full of
woe.

SECOND SHEPHERD: I think our sheep be slain. Think
you not so?

THIRD SHEPHERD: All work we in vain; as well may we
go.
But, drat it,   555
I can find no flesh,
Hard nor nesh,°
Salt nor fresh,
But two empty platters.

There's no cattle but this, neither tame nor wild,   560
None, as have I bliss, that smells as he smelled.

WIFE: No, so God me bless, and give me joy of my
child!

FIRST SHEPHERD: We have marked amiss; I hold us
beguiled.

SECOND SHEPHERD: Sir, done.
Sir, Our Lady him save!   565
Is your child a knave?

MAK: Any lord might him crave,
This child as his son.

When he wakens, he skips, that a joy is to see.

THIRD SHEPHERD: In good time be his steps, and
happy they be!   570
Who were his godfathers, tell now to me?

MAK: So fair fall their lips!

FIRST SHEPHERD: Hark now, a lie!

MAK: So God them thank,

---

stott, bullock.

leal, loyal. *weal*, riches. *swelt*, faint. *nesh*, tender.

575 Parkin and Gibbon Waller, I say,
And gentle John Horn, in good faith,
He gave all the array
And promised a great shank.

SECOND SHEPHERD: Mak, friends will we be, for we
are all one.
580 MAK: We! Now I hold for me, from you help get I
none.
Farewell, all three! All glad were ye gone!

(*The* SHEPHERDS *go out.*)

THIRD SHEPHERD: Fair words may there be, but love
there is none
This year.
FIRST SHEPHERD: Gave ye the child anything?
585 SECOND SHEPHERD: I trow,° not one farthing!
THIRD SHEPHERD: Fast back will I fling;
Abide ye me here.

(*The* SHEPHERDS *re-enter the house.*)

Mak, take it to no grief, if I come to thy bairn.
MAK: Nay, thou does me mischief, and foul has thou
fared.
THIRD SHEPHERD: The child will not grieve, that little
590 day-star.
Mak, with your leave, let me give your bairn
But sixpence.
MAK: Nay, go 'way; he sleeps.
THIRD SHEPHERD: Methinks he peeps.
595 MAK: When he wakens he weeps!
I pray you, go hence!

THIRD SHEPHERD: Give me leave him to kiss, and lift
up the clout.°
What the devil is this? What a monstrous snout!
FIRST SHEPHERD: He is marked amiss. Let's not wait
about.
SECOND SHEPHERD: "Ill spun cloth," iwis, "aye comes
600 foul out."
Aye, so!
He is like to our sheep!
THIRD SHEPHERD: How, Gib, may I peep?
FIRST SHEPHERD: I trow, nature will creep
605 Where it may not go!

SECOND SHEPHERD: This was a quaint fraud, and a far
cast!
It should be noised abroad.
THIRD SHEPHERD: Yea, sirs, and classed.
Let's burn this bawd, and bind her fast.
610 Everyone will applaud to hang her at last,
So shall thou.
Will ye see how they swaddle
His four feet in the middle?

Saw I never in cradle
A horned lad ere now. 615

MAK: Peace, peace, I ask. You'll give the child a scare.
For I am his father, and yon woman him bare.
FIRST SHEPHERD: After what devil shall he be called?
"Mak?" Lo, Mak's heir!
SECOND SHEPHERD: Let be all that. Now God give
him care,
I say. 620
WIFE: A pretty child is he
To sit on a woman's knee;
A dilly-downe, pardie,
To make a father gay.

THIRD SHEPHERD: I know him by the ear-mark; that's
a good token. 625
MAK: I tell you, sirs, hark! His nose was broken;
Later told me a clerk that he was forespoken.°
FIRST SHEPHERD: Liar! You deserve to have your
noddle broken!
Get a weapon.
WIFE: He was taken by an elf, 630
I saw it myself;
When the clock struck twelve
He was misshapen.

SECOND SHEPHERD: Ye two are well made to lie in the
same bed.
THIRD SHEPHERD: Since they maintain their theft,
let's see them both dead. 635
MAK: If I do wrong again, cut off my head!
I'm at your will.
FIRST SHEPHERD: Sirs, take this plan, instead,
For this trespass:
We'll neither curse nor fight, 640
Quarrel nor chide,
But seize him tight
And cast him in canvas.

(*They toss* MAK *in a sheet and go back to the fields.*)

FIRST SHEPHERD: Lord, but I am sore; I feel about to
burst.
In faith, I may no more; therefore will I rest. 645
SECOND SHEPHERD: As a sheep of seven score he
weighed in my fist.
Now to sleep anywhere methinks were the best.
THIRD SHEPHERD: Now I pray you,
Let's lie down on this green.
FIRST SHEPHERD: Oh, these thieves are so keen. 650
THIRD SHEPHERD: Let's forget what has been,
So I say you. (*They sleep.*)

(*An* ANGEL *sings "Gloria in excelsis"; then let him say.*)

ANGEL: Rise, herd-men kind! For now is he born

---

trow, assert as true; admit. *clout,* cloth.

forespoken, bewitched.

That shall take from the fiend what Adam had
    lorn:
655 That devil to shame this night is he born;
God is made your friend now at this morn.
    He behests
To Bethlehem go ye,
Where lies the Free;°
660 In a manger he'll be
    Between two beasts.

FIRST SHEPHERD: This was a sweet voice as any I've
    heard.
A wonder enough to make a man scared.
SECOND SHEPHERD: To speak of God's son from on
    high he dared.
665 All the wood on the moor with lightning glared,
    Everywhere.
THIRD SHEPHERD: He said the babe lay
In Bethlehem today.
FIRST SHEPHERD: That star points the way.
670   Let us seek him there.

SECOND SHEPHERD: Say, what was his song? Heard ye
    not how he cracked it,
Three briefs to a long?°
THIRD SHEPHERD: Yea, marry, he hacked it;
Was no crotchet° wrong, nor nothing that lacked it.
FIRST SHEPHERD: For to sing us among, right as he
675   knacked it°
    I can.
SECOND SHEPHERD: Let's see how ye croon.
Can ye bark at the moon?
THIRD SHEPHERD: Hold your tongues, have done!
680 FIRST SHEPHERD: Hark after, then!

SECOND SHEPHERD: To Bethlehem he bade that we
    should go;
I am full afeared that we have been too slow.
THIRD SHEPHERD: Be merry and not sad; for sure this
    we know,
This news means joy to us men below,
685   Of no joy.
FIRST SHEPHERD: Therefore thither hie we,
Be we wet and weary,
To that child and that lady.
    We must see this boy.

SECOND SHEPHERD: We find by the prophecy—let be
690   your din!
Of David and Isaiah and others of their kin,
They prophesied by clergy that in a virgin
Should he light and lie, to slacken our sin
    And slake it,
695 Our Race from woe.

For Isaiah said so:
*"Ecce virgo
    Concipiet"°* a child that is naked.

THIRD SHEPHERD: Full glad may we be that this is
    that day
Him lovely to see, who rules for aye. 700
Lord, happy I'd be if I could say
That I knelt on my knee so that I might pray
    To that child.
But the angel said,
He was poorly arrayed, 705
And in a manger laid,
    Both humble and mild.

FIRST SHEPHERD: Patriarchs and prophets of old
    were torn
With yearning to see this child that is born.
They are gone full clean, and their trouble they've
    lorn. 710
But we shall see him, I ween,° ere it be morn,
    To token.
When I see him and feel,
Then know I full well
It is true as steel 715
    That prophets have spoken:

To so poor as we are that he would appear,
To find us and tell us by his messenger!
SECOND SHEPHERD: Go we now, let us fare, for the
    place is near.
THIRD SHEPHERD: I am ready, prepared; let us go
    with good cheer 720
    To that bright
Lord, if thy will be—
We are simple all three—
Grant us some kind of glee
    To comfort thy wight.° *(They enter the stable.)* 725

FIRST SHEPHERD: Hail, comely and clean! Hail,
    young child!
Hail, Maker, as I mean, born of maiden so mild!
Thou has cursed, I ween, the devil so wild;
The false guiler of men, now goes he beguiled.
    Lo, he merry is! 730
Look, he laughs, the sweeting!
Well, to this meeting
I bring as my greeting
    A bob of cherries!

SECOND SHEPHERD: Hail, sovereign Savior, our
    ransom thou hast bought! 735

Ecce . . . Concipiet, "Behold, a virgin shall conceive," Cf. Isaiah, 7.14; Luke, 1.31; and Matthew, 1.23. *I ween,* I imagine. *wight,* man.

---

the Free, The Divine One. *Three . . . long,* musical notes. *crotchet,* a quarter note. *knacked it,* did it cleverly.

Hail, noble child and flower, that all things has
    wrought!
Hail, full of favor, that made all of naught!
Hail! I kneel and I cower. A bird have I brought
    To my bairn.
740 Hail, little tiny mop!
Of our creed thou art crop.
I would drink of thy cup,
    Little day-star.

THIRD SHEPHERD: Hail, darling dear, thou art God
    indeed!
745 I pray thee be near when that I have need.
Hail! Sweet is thy cheer! My heart would bleed
To see thee lie here in so poor a weed,
    With no pennies.
I would give thee my all,
750 Though I bring but a ball;
Have and play thee withal,
    And go to the tennis.

MARY: The Father of Heaven, God omnipotent,
That set all in seven days, his Son has sent.

My name he has blessed with peace ere he went.   755
I conceived him through grace as God had meant;
    And now he's born.
I shall pray him so
To keep you all from woe!
Tell this wherever ye go,   760
    And mind this morn.

FIRST SHEPHERD: Farewell, lady, so fair to behold,
    With thy child on thy knee!
SECOND SHEPHERD: Still he lies full cold.
    Lord, how favored I be. Now we go forth, behold. 765
THIRD SHEPHERD: Forsooth, already this seems a
        thing told
    Full oft.
FIRST SHEPHERD: What grace we have found!
SECOND SHEPHERD: Spread the tidings around!
THIRD SHEPHERD: To sing are we bound: 770
    Let take aloft! (They sing.)

Figure 1. The shepherds (Philip McGough, David Bradley, and Hilton McRae, *left to right*) stare at Mak (Malcolm Storry) as he kneels by the cradle; Gill (Avril Carson) lies on the bed, fully covered up, pretending that she has just given birth. The 1978 Royal Shakespeare Company production, adapted by John Barton and titled *The Shepherds' Play*, was directed by David Tucker. (Photograph: Joe Cocks Studio.)

Figure 2. The bed is transformed into the manger, Mak into Joseph (Malcolm Storry), and Gill into Mary (Avril Carson), as the First Shepherd (Philip McGough) kneels in reverence in the 1978 Royal Shakespeare Company production. (Photograph: Joe Cocks Studio.)

Figure 3. Mak (Malcolm Storry) stands back while the First Shepherd (Philip McGough) looks at the swaddled sheep in disbelief; the other two shepherds (Hilton McRae and David Bradley) look on in the 1978 Royal Shakespeare Company production. (Photograph: Joe Cocks Studio.)

Staging of *The Second Shepherds' Play*

**REVIEW OF THE ROYAL SHAKESPEARE
COMPANY PRODUCTION, 1978,
BY ANN FITZGERALD**

"MAK THE SHEEP STEALER", one of the miracle plays from the Towneley cycle appears to be the main source for "The Shepherd's Play" John Barton's adaptation of a number of these mediaeval dramas telling the story of the Nativity.

The RSC Company under the direction of David Tucker present it with a tongue in cheek humour and a music hall style of connivance with the audience. It made me feel rather like a member of Duke Theseus' court watching Bottom the Weaver and the other 'rude mechanicals' taking to the stage.

That is, of course, how the plays were originally performed and the production does give a good impression of the carnival atmosphere which accompanied these early religious entertainments. But it loses sight of the fact that what is, to us, laughably simplistic in the plays was matched, originally, by an equal simplicity of faith and wonder on the part of the audience.

Ribald laughter at the antics of con-man Mak and his wife could turn instantly into breathless awe as the shepherds return to the same cottage and find it miraculously transformed into the Bethlehem stable and the characters of Mak and Gil transfigured into Joseph, Mary and the Babe, looking just like an early religious painting in Pippy Bradshaw's authentic design for the tableau.

There is plenty of audience participation with a warm-up session of old, and seldom heard, carols before and after the play, with shepherds leaping in among the audience and grabbling at sheepskin coats in the search for their lost lamb and the Angel Gabriel appearing, complete with celestial song sheet, beautifully scripted on a white silk hanging cloth.

EVERYMAN

The author of *Everyman* is unknown, but its haunting dramatization of death and redemption has a remarkable ancestry, which can be traced back at least two thousand years earlier to the well-known parables of Buddha (563–483 B.C.). Among these parables is the tale of a man who when summoned by death turns to his four wives for companionship but is refused by the three he loves most and accepted only by the one he loves least. According to Buddha, the three wives who refuse symbolize the man's friends and relatives, his worldly goods, and his bodily powers; the wife who accepts represents his moral intention. Although the parable is an expression of Buddhist faith, it could easily be revised to illustrate Christian belief, as it was thirteen hundred years later, when John Damascene, an eighth-century theologian, told about a man with three friends, two who abandon him and one who remains faithful. According to Damascene, the faithful friend represents "the company of good deeds—faith, hope, charity, alms, kindliness, and the whole band of virtues, that can go before us, when we quit the body, and may plead with the Lord on our behalf." The parable of the man and his three friends subsequently made its way throughout medieval Europe and was translated into English by the great fifteenth-century printer William Caxton, who included it in a collection of tales, *The Golden Legend,* which he published in 1483, at about the same time that *Everyman* was probably written. Caxton's version of the parable tells of a man who is summoned by death to make the ultimate pilgrimage, who seeks worldly companionship on his journey, but who discovers he can rely only on his spiritual well-being. *Everyman* may be seen as the dramatic embodiment of a universal parable about the vanity of life, the certainty of death, and the undying power of virtue.

Everyman also embodies the anxieties of its age, for the late medieval period was a time when people seemed more preoccupied with death and the afterlife than with life itself. Surely no other age before or since has been so visibly obsessed with thoughts of death. That obsession manifested itself in a wide variety of art forms—woodcuts, murals, sculptures, poems, and plays—all depicting the same morbid image: a skeletal figure who leads a group of men and women from all social stations, literally every man, in a macabre ceremony, the dance of death. That ghastly image expressed the deepest fears of the age, for it portrayed not only the inevitability but also the horror of death, and the horror was frequently emphasized by showing the skeletal figure covered with sores and pustules, grisly reminders of the bubonic plague, the Black Death, which ravaged England and the continent during the fourteenth century. Reminders of death were indeed so widespread that they were unavoidable, for if people had not witnessed the plague or seen the dance, then they heard of the agonies from traveling preachers who toured the countryside, admonishing them to think of death and exhorting them to prepare their souls for life after death. That same lesson—the lesson of how to prepare for a godly Christian death—was also the subject of innumerable handbooks, one of which, called *The Book of the Craft of Dying,* was printed by Caxton in

1490. Caxton's manual displays the same Christian view of dying that is dramatized in *Everyman*. It describes the temptation of dying human beings to turn to "temporal things" and counsels "every man, rightful and sinful, [to] bow himself and submit himself fully unto the mighty hand of God."

Everyman exemplifies that religious vision in the allegorical form of a morality play. Its characters are not particular individuals but personified abstractions—Everyman, Death, Fellowship, Good Deeds, Confession—and its plot represents not a unique experience but a paradigm of experience. In its allegorical form as in its Christian theme, *Everyman* is typical of other early morality plays, such as *The Castle of Perseverance* (ca. 1425) and *Mankind* (ca. 1475), but its plot is more focused and its tone far more somber since it concentrates exclusively on the death of Everyman, whereas the other plays portray the entire life of humankind from birth to death. *Mankind* even includes deliberately comic characters whose sacrilegious and obscene jokes were clearly intended to amuse a paying audience, but *Everyman* makes no such concessions. It has only a few comic touches in the behavior of Fellowship, Kindred, and Goods, and those few comic moments are meant less to entertain than to exemplify types of worldly temptation. *Everyman* and its contemporaneous Dutch counterpart *Elckerlijk* (literally, everyman) stand out as the most austerely unified morality plays of the medieval period.

Although *Everyman* is the product of its age—a medieval Catholic morality play—it speaks to all ages and all faiths. Its characters are abstractions, the abstractions of theology expounded in parables and sermons alike, yet those abstractions take on life through the vivid details by which they are characterized. Fellowship, for example, through his hale and hearty welcome to Everyman and his increasingly outlandish promises of assistance, immediately shows himself to be a bag of wind, even before his refusal to accompany Everyman reveals him to be a fair-weather friend. Kindred and Cousin, on the other hand, are portrayed as solicitous women of few words who have just as little to offer—not much more than the lame excuse of Cousin who claims to have a cramp in her toe. And Goods, far from offering excuses, turns out to be a cruel jester who maliciously delights in Everyman's predicament. Each of the abstractions is individualized so that they each become authentic characters whose interaction is dramatically plausible and compelling. When, for example, Everyman turns for assistance to Good Deeds, his pleading is genuinely motivated, following as it does the increasingly painful series of rejections he has received from Fellowship, Kindred, Cousin, and Goods. Similarly, when Everyman is rejected at the end of the play by Beauty, Strength, Discretion, and Five Wits, his surprise is also well motivated, for while he has been taken up with confession and penance, with the elaborate routine of his last rites, he has still not faced the inescapable facts of death: the physical decay, the loss of consciousness, the end of being in the world as he has known it.

Ultimately, all the characters derive their motivation from the logic of the human psyche, for their interaction is meant to represent the mental, emotional, and spiritual process that takes place in a representative human being during the process of dying. The stages in that process are clearly and eloquently marked out in the play—from the initial denial, to the wish for postponement, to the bargaining, to the frenzied but futile clinging to life, to the acceptance of death, to the spiritual preparation for it, to the experience itself. That is the process Everyman goes through in the play, and it is remarkably similar to the process described in modern psychological studies of dying. They reveal, as does *Everyman,* that dying is something one does alone. Friends and relatives cannot at last help anyone avoid the loneliness of death. The only possible solace is the knowledge of having lived a decent life.

Because of its timelessness, *Everyman* has been one of the most influential plays in the history of drama. In the contemporary period alone, its allegory of dying has been imitated in Beckett's *Endgame,* adapted in Geraldine Fitzgerald's *Everyman and Roach,* and parodied in Arnold Powell's *The Death of Everymom.* It has been performed often and produced variously—in modern dress, in medieval costumes, on proscenium stages, on bare platforms, and on church altars. In one sense, *Everyman* is relatively easy to stage since it requires only a few props, such as an account book, a scourge for Confession, a crucifix for Everyman, and sacks, packs, and chests for Goods; likewise, it mentions specifically only one location: the house of Salvation. But in another sense, it gives directors a challenging production problem—how to balance its abstract and concrete elements, how to make its experience at once particular and universal.

So we present two very different productions to show how directors have confronted the play's challenges. In 1973, Nicholas Rudall directed *Everyman* at the University of Chicago, and as the interview following the play makes clear, he combined realistic medieval costumes, props, and details of action within the structure of a highly ritualized performance. Using the backdrop of Rockefeller Chapel, itself based on a gothic cathedral, Rudall constructed a multilevel set with various playing areas (see Figure 1). In that large space, as he suggests, the ritual aspects of the play fit comfortably. But he also sought to create a sense of reality through the human details that enlivened the characters. By contrast the Royal Shakespeare Company's 1996 production of *Everyman* was set in the company's smallest theater, The Other Place, a simple "black box" room, and so looked very different from the medieval setting of the earlier production. Yet the RSC directors and designer also strove for a combination of realistic and ritual elements. The cracked floor of the stage reminded audiences of the cracked earth of drought-ravaged Africa, and the naked black man lying in the tin tub at the beginning of the production might have been a victim of starvation. The bathing of the body by an old woman implied that it was being prepared for burial, but then, surprisingly, the man—Everyman— turned out to be alive and the preparations were not for death but for an exuberant wedding celebration. Furthermore Death was no fearsome messenger in this production but a young and attractive woman who danced with Everyman (see Figure 2). But the production also included allegorical (if comical) versions of Strength, Beauty, and Five Wits portrayed as circus people; a symbolic version of penance as Everyman slowly walked around in a circle with a stone attached to one ankle; and a deeply moving close, in which Everyman returned to the tin tub to die (see Figure 4). Both in Stratford and in Chicago, Good Deeds was played by a woman (see Figures 3 and 4), as was Knowledge. And each production, though set in very different spaces and with very different costumes, clearly respected the play's uncompromising look at the inevitability of death.

EVERYMAN

MODERNIZED BY KATE FRANKS

CHARACTERS

MESSENGER
GOD
DEATH
EVERYMAN
FELLOWSHIP
KINDRED
COUSIN
GOODS

GOOD DEEDS
KNOWLEDGE
CONFESSION
BEAUTY
STRENGTH
DISCRETION
FIVE WITS
ANGEL
DOCTOR

*(Here beginneth a treatise how the High Father of Heaven
sendeth Death to summon every creature to come and give
account of their lives in this world, and is in manner of a
moral play.)*

(Enter MESSENGER.*)*

MESSENGER: I pray you all give your audience
And hear this matter with reverence,
By figure a moral play:
The Summoning of Everyman called it is,
5 That of our lives and ending shows
How transitory we be all day.
This matter is wondrous precious,
But the intent of it is more gracious
And sweet to bear away.
10 The story saith: Man, in the beginning
Look well, and take good heed to the ending,
Be you never so gay!
Ye think sin in the beginning full sweet,
Which in the end causeth the soul to weep,
15 When the body lieth in clay.
Here shall you see how Fellowship and Jollity
Both, Strength, Pleasure and Beauty
Will fade from thee as flower in May;
For ye shall hear how our Heaven's King
20 Calleth Everyman to a general reckoning.
Give audience, and hear what he doth say.

(Exit MESSENGER.*)*

*(*GOD *speaks.)*

GOD: I perceive, here in my majesty,
How that all creatures be to me unkind,
Living without dread in worldly prosperity.
25 Of ghostly sight° the people be so blind,
Drowned in sin, they know me not for their God.
In worldly riches is all their mind;
They fear not my righteousness, the sharp rod.
My law that I showed when I for them died

They forget clean, and shedding of my blood red.   30
I hanged between two thieves, it cannot be denied;
To get them life I suffered to be dead;
I healed their feet, with thorns hurt was my head.
I could do no more than I did, truly;
And now I see the people do clean forsake me.   35
They use the seven deadly sins damnable,
As pride, covetise, wrath, and lechery
Now in the world be made commendable;
And thus they leave of angels the heavenly
    company.
Every man liveth so after his own pleasure,   40
And yet of their life they be nothing sure.
I see the more that I them forbear
The worse they be from year to year.
All that liveth appaireth° fast;
Therefore I will, in all the haste,   45
Have a reckoning of every man's person;
For, if I leave the people thus alone
In their life and wicked tempests,
Verily they will become much worse than beasts;
For now one would by envy another up eat;   50
Charity they do all clean forget.
I hoped well that every man
In my glory should make his mansion,
And thereto I had them all elect;
But now I see, like traitors deject,   55
They thank me not for the pleasure that I to them
    meant,
Nor yet for their being that I them have lent.
I proffered the people great multitude of mercy,
And few there be that asketh it heartily.
They be so cumbered with worldly riches   60
That needs on them I must do justice,
On every man living without fear.
Where art thou, Death, thou mighty messenger?

(Enter DEATH.*)*

---

ghostly sight, spiritual sight; knowledge of God.

appaireth, worsens.

DEATH: Almighty God, I am here at your will,
65   Your commandment to fulfill.
GOD: Go thou to Everyman
      And show him, in my name,
      A pilgrimage he must on him take,
      Which he in no wise may escape;
70   And that he bring with him a sure reckoning
      Without delay or any tarrying.
DEATH: Lord, I will in the world go run over all
      And cruelly search out both great and small.
      Every man will I beset that liveth beastly
75   Out of God's laws, and dreadeth not folly.
      He that loveth riches I will strike with my dart,
      His sight to blind, and from Heaven to depart—
      Except that alms be his good friend—
      In hell for to dwell, world without end.

      (Enter EVERYMAN.)

80   Lo, yonder I see Everyman walking.
      Full little he thinketh on my coming;
      His mind is on fleshly lusts and his treasure,
      And great pain it shall cause him to endure
      Before the Lord, Heaven's King.
85   Everyman, stand still! Whither art thou going
      Thus gaily? Hast thou thy Maker forgot?
EVERYMAN: Why askest thou?
      Wouldest thou know?
DEATH: Yea, sir. I will you show:
90   In great haste I am sent to thee
      From God out of his majesty.
EVERYMAN: What, sent to me?
DEATH: Yea, certainly.
      Though thou have forgot him here,
95   He thinketh on thee in the heavenly sphere,
      As, ere we depart, thou shalt know.
EVERYMAN: What desireth God of me?
DEATH: That I shall show to thee:
      A reckoning he will needs have
100   Without any longer respite.
EVERYMAN: To give a reckoning longer leisure I
         crave;
      This blind° matter troubleth my wit.
DEATH: On thee thou must take a long journey;
      Therefore thy book of account with thee thou
         bring,
105   For turn again thou cannot, by no way.
      And look thou be sure of thy reckoning,
      For before God thou shalt answer and show
      Thy many bad deeds, and good, but a few;
      How thou hast spent thy life, and in what wise,
110   Before the Chief Lord of Paradise.
      Have ado that thou were in that way,
      For know thou well, thou shalt make no attorney.°

EVERYMAN: Full unready I am, such reckoning to
         give.
      I know thee not. What messenger art thou?
DEATH: I am Death that no man dreadeth,°   115
      For every man I rest and no man spareth;
      For it is God's commandment
      That all to me should be obedient.
EVERYMAN: O Death, thou comest when I had thee
         least in mind!
      In thy power it lieth me to save;   120
      Yet of my goods will I give thee, if thou will be
         kind—
      Yea, a thousand pound shalt thou have!—
      And defer this matter till another day.
DEATH: Everyman, it may not be, by no way.
      I set not by gold, silver, nor riches,   125
      Nor by pope, emperor, king, duke, nor princes;
      For, if I would receive gifts great,
      All the world I might get;
      But my custom is clean contrary:
      I give thee no respite. Come hence, and not tarry! 130
EVERYMAN: Alas, shall I have no longer respite?
      I may say Death giveth no warning!
      To think on thee, it maketh my heart sick,
      For all unready is my book of reckoning.
      But twelve years if I might have abiding,   135
      My accounting book I would make so clear
      That my reckoning I should not need to fear.
      Wherefore, Death, I pray thee, for God's mercy,
      Spare me till I be provided of remedy.
DEATH: Thee availeth not to cry, weep and pray;   140
      But haste thee lightly° that thou were gone that
         journey,
      And prove thy friends if thou can.
      For know thou well the tide abideth no man,
      And in the world each living creature
      For Adam's sin must die of nature.   145
EVERYMAN: Death, if I should this pilgrimage take
      And my reckoning surely make,
      Show me, for sainted charity,
      Should I not come again shortly?
DEATH: No, Everyman. If thou be once there   150
      Thou mayst never more come here,
      Trust me verily.
EVERYMAN: O gracious God in the high seat celestial,
      Have mercy on me in this most need!
      Shall I have no company from this vale terrestrial 155
      Of mine acquaintance, that way me to lead?
DEATH: Yea, if any be so hardy
      That would go with thee and bear thee company.
      Hie thee that thou were gone to God's
         magnificence,
      Thy reckoning to give before his presence. 160
      What, thinkest thou thy life is given thee

---

blind, unknown, obscure. *no attorney*, You won't be
able to plead your case.

And thy worldly goods also?

EVERYMAN: I had thought so, verily.

DEATH: Nay, nay, it was but lent thee;

165   For as soon as thou art gone,
    Another a while shall have it and then go
      therefrom,
    Even as thou hast done.
    Everyman, thou art mad! Thou hast thy wits five
    And here on earth will not amend thy life;

170   For suddenly I do come.

EVERYMAN: O wretchèd caitiff, whither shall I flee,
    That I might escape this endless sorrow?
    Now, gentle Death, spare me till tomorrow,
    That I may amend me

175   With good advisement.

DEATH: Nay, thereto I will not consent,
    Nor no man will I respite;
    But to the heart suddenly I shall smite
    Without any advisement.

180   And now out of thy sight I will me hie.
    See thou make thee ready shortly;
    For thou mayst say this is the day
    That no man living may escape away.

(Exit DEATH.)

EVERYMAN: Alas, I may well weep with sighs deep!

185   Now have I no manner of company
    To help me in my journey and me to keep;
    And also my writing is full unready.
    How shall I do now for to excuse me?
    I would to God I had never been begot!

190   To my soul a full great profit it had been;
    For now I fear pains huge and great.
    The time passeth. Lord, help, that all wrought!
    For though I mourn it availeth naught.
    The day passeth and is almost ago;

195   I know not well what for to do.
    To whom were I best my complaint to make?
    What if I to Fellowship thereof spake
    And showed him of this sudden chance?
    For in him is all mine affiance,°

200   We have in the world so many a day
    Been good friends in sport and play.

(Enter FELLOWSHIP.)

    I see him yonder, certainly.
    I trust that he will bear me company;
    Therefore to him will I speak to ease my sorrow.

205   Well met, good Fellowship, and good morrow!

FELLOWSHIP: Everyman, good morrow, by this day!
    Sir, why lookest thou so piteously?
    If anything be amiss, I pray thee me say,
    That I may help to remedy.

210 EVERYMAN: Yea, good Fellowship, yea,
    I am in great jeopardy.

FELLOWSHIP: My true friend, show to me your mind.
    I will not forsake thee to my life's end
    In the way of good company.

EVERYMAN: That was well spoken and lovingly.   215

FELLOWSHIP: Sir, I must needs know your heaviness;
    I have pity to see you in any distress.
    If any have you wronged, ye shall revenged be,
    Though I on the ground be slain for thee,
    Though that I know before that I should die.   220

EVERYMAN: Verily, Fellowship, gramercy.

FELLOWSHIP: Tush! By thy thanks I set not a straw.
    Show me your grief, and say no more.

EVERYMAN: If I my heart should to you break,
    And then you to turn your mind from me   225
    And would not me comfort when ye hear me
      speak,
    Then should I ten times sorrier be.

FELLOWSHIP: Sir, I say as I will do in deed.

EVERYMAN: Then be you a good friend in need.
    I have found you true herebefore.   230

FELLOWSHIP: And so ye shall evermore;
    For, in faith, if thou go to hell,
    I will not forsake thee by the way.

EVERYMAN: Ye speak like a good friend; I believe you
    well.
    I shall deserve it, if I may.   235

FELLOWSHIP: I speak of no deserving, by this day!
    For he that will say and nothing do
    Is not worthy with good company to go;
    Therefore show me the grief of your mind,
    As to your friend most loving and kind.   240

EVERYMAN: I shall show you how it is:
    Commanded I am to go a journey,
    A long way hard and dangerous,
    And give a straight account without delay
    Before the high judge, Adonai.°   245
    Wherefore I pray you, bear me company,
    As ye have promised, in this journey.

FELLOWSHIP: That is matter indeed! Promise is duty;
    But if I should take such a voyage on me,
    I know it well, it should be to my pain;   250
    Also it maketh me afeared, certain.
    But let us take counsel here as well as we can,
    For your words would fear a strong man.

EVERYMAN: Why, ye said if I had need
    Ye would me never forsake, quick nor dead,   255
    Though it were to hell, truly.

FELLOWSHIP: So I said, certainly,
    But such pleasures be set aside, the sooth to say;
    And also, if we took such a journey
    When should we again come?   260

EVERYMAN: Nay, never again till the day of doom.

FELLOWSHIP: In faith, then will not I come there!
    Who hath you these tidings brought?

EVERYMAN: Indeed, Death was with me here.

---

affiance, faith or trust.

Adonai, Hebrew name for God.

265 FELLOWSHIP: Now, by God that all hath bought,
   If death were the messenger,
   For no man that is living today
   I will not go that loath journey—
   Not for the father that begat me!

270 EVERYMAN: Ye promised otherwise, pardie!
   FELLOWSHIP: I know well I said so, truly;
   And yet, if thou wilt eat and drink and make good
      cheer,
   Or haunt to women the lusty company°
   I would not forsake you while the day is clear,
275   Trust me verily.
   EVERYMAN: Yea, thereto ye would be ready!
   To go to mirth, solace and play
   Your mind will sooner apply
   Than to bear me company in my long journey.

280 FELLOWSHIP: Now, in good faith, I will not that way;
   But if thou will murder or any man kill,
   In that I will help thee with a good will.
   EVERYMAN: O, that is a simple advice indeed.
   Gentle fellow, help me in my necessity!
285   We have loved long, and now I need;
   And now, gentle Fellowship, remember me.
   FELLOWSHIP: Whether ye have loved me or no,
   By Saint John, I will not with thee go!
   EVERYMAN: Yet, I pray thee, take the labor and do so
      much for me
290   To bring me forward, for sainted charity,
   And comfort me till I come within the town.
   FELLOWSHIP: Nay, if thou would give me a new gown,
   I will not a foot with thee go;
   But if thou had tarried, I would not have left thee
      so.
295   And as now, God speed thee in thy journey,
   For from thee I will depart as fast as I may.
   EVERYMAN: Wither away, Fellowship? Will thou
      forsake me?
   FELLOWSHIP: Yea, by my faith! To God I betake° thee.
   EVERYMAN: Farewell, good Fellowship! For thee my
      heart is sore.
300   Adieu forever! I shall see thee no more.
   FELLOWSHIP: In faith, Everyman, farewell now at the
      ending!
   For you I will remember that parting is mourning.

   (Exit FELLOWSHIP.)

   EVERYMAN: Alack, shall we thus depart indeed—
   Ah, Lady, help!—without any more comfort?
305   Lo, Fellowship forsaketh me in my most need.
   For help in this world whither shall I resort?
   Fellowship herebefore with me would merry make,
   And now little sorrow for me doth he take.
   It is said, "In prosperity men friends may find,
310   Which in adversity be full unkind."

   Now whither for succor shall I flee,
   Since that Fellowship hath forsaken me?
   To my kinsmen I will, truly,
   Praying them to help me in my necessity.
   I believe that they will do so,   315
   For kind will creep where it may not go.°

   (Enter KINDRED and COUSIN.)

   I will go say, for yonder I see them.
   Where be ye now, my friends and kinsmen?
   KINDRED: Here be we now at your commandment.
   Cousin, I pray you show us your intent   320
   In any wise and not spare.
   COUSIN: Yea, Everyman, and to us declare
   If ye be disposed to go anywhither;
   For know you well, we will live and die together.
   KINDRED: In wealth and woe we will with you hold, 325
   For over his kin a man may be bold.
   EVERYMAN: Gramercy, my friends and kinsmen kind.
   Now shall I show you the grief of my mind:
   I was commanded by a messenger,
   That is a high king's chief officer;   330
   He bade me go a pilgrimage, to my pain,
   And I know well I shall never come again.
   Also I must give a reckoning strait,
   For I have a great enemy that hath me in wait,
   Which intendeth me for to hinder.   335
   KINDRED: What account is that which ye must render?
   That would I know.
   EVERYMAN: Of all my works I must show
   How I have lived and my days spent;
   Also of ill deeds that I have used   340
   In my time, since life was me lent;
   And of all virtues that I have refused.
   Therefore, I pray you, go thither with me
   To help to make mine account, for saint charity.
   COUSIN: What, to go thither? Is that the matter?   345
   Nay, Everyman, I had liefer° fast bread and water
   All this five years and more.
   EVERYMAN: Alas, that ever I was born!
   For now shall I never be merry
   If that you forsake me.   350
   KINDRED: Ah, sir, but ye be a merry man!
   Take good heart to you, and make no moan.
   But one thing I warn you, by Saint Anne—
   As for me, ye shall go alone.
   EVERYMAN: My Cousin, will you not with me go?   355
   COUSIN: No, by our Lady! I have the cramp in my toe.
   Trust not to me; for, so God me speed,
   I will deceive you in your most need.
   KINDRED: It availeth not us to entice.
   Ye shall have my maid with all my heart;   360
   She loveth to go to feasts, there to be nice,
   And to dance and abroad to start.

---

   haunt . . . company, seek women's company for pleasure;
go a-whoring. **betake,** entrust.

   kind . . . go, one's kin will crawl where they may not walk;
i.e., will do what they can. **liefer,** rather.

I will give her leave to help you in that journey,
If that you and she may agree.
365 EVERYMAN: Now show me the very effect of your
mind:
Will you go with me, or abide behind?
KINDRED: Abide behind? Yea, that will I, if I may!
Therefore farewell till another day.

(*Exit* KINDRED.)

EVERYMAN: How should I be merry or glad?
370 For fair promises men to me make,
But when I have most need they me forsake.
I am deceived; that maketh me sad.
COUSIN: Cousin Everyman, farewell now,
For verily I will not go with you.
375 Also of mine own an unready reckoning
I have to account; therefore I make tarrying.
Now God keep thee, for now I go.

(*Exit* COUSIN.)

EVERYMAN: Ah, Jesus, is all come hereto?
Lo, fair words maketh fools fain;
380 They promise and nothing will do, certain.
My kinsmen promised me faithfully
For to abide with me steadfastly,
And now fast away do they flee,
Even so Fellowship promised me.
385 What friend were best me of to provide?
I lose my time here longer to abide.
Yet in my mind a thing there is:
All my life I have loved riches;
If that my Goods now help me might,
390 He would make my heart full light.
I will speak to him in this distress.
Where art thou, my Goods and riches?

(GOODS *revealed in a corner.*)

GOODS: Who calleth me? Everyman? What, hast thou
haste?
I lie here in corners, trussed and piled so high,
395 And in chests I am locked so fast,
Also sacked in bags. Thou mayst see with thine eye
I cannot stir, in packs, low I lie.
What would ye have? Lightly me say.
EVERYMAN: Come hither, Goods, in all the haste thou
may,
400 For of counsel I must desire thee.
GOODS: Sir, if ye in the world have sorrow or
adversity,
That can I help you to remedy shortly.
EVERYMAN: It is another disease that grieveth me;
In this world it is not, I tell thee so.
405 I am sent for, another way to go,
To give a strait account general
Before the highest Jupiter of all;
And all my life I have had joy and pleasure in thee.
Therefore, I pray thee, go with me;

For, peradventure, thou mayst before God
Almighty   410
My reckoning help to clean and purify;
For it is said ever among
That "money maketh all right that is wrong."
GOODS: Nay, Everyman, I sing another song.
I follow no man in such voyages;   415
For if I went with thee,
Thou shouldst fare much the worse for me.
For because on me thou did set thy mind,
Thy reckoning I have made blotted and blind,
That thine account thou cannot make truly—   420
And that hast thou for the love of me!
EVERYMAN: That would grieve me full sore,
When I should come to that fearful answer.
Up, let us go thither together.
GOODS: Nay, not so! I am too brittle, I may not
endure.   425
I will follow no man one foot, be ye sure.
EVERYMAN: Alas, I have thee loved, and had great
pleasure
All my life-days in goods and treasure.
GOODS: That is to thy damnation, without lying,
For my love is contrary to the love everlasting.   430
But if thou had loved me moderately during,
As to the poor given part of me,
Then shouldst thou not in this dolor be,
Nor in this great sorrow and care.
EVERYMAN: Lo, now was I deceived ere I was aware, 435
And all I may lay to my spending of time.
GOODS: What, thinkest thou that I am thine?
EVERYMAN: I had thought so.
GOODS: Nay, Everyman, I say no.
As for a while I was lent thee;   440
A season thou hast had me in prosperity.
My condition is a man's soul to kill;
If I save one, a thousand I do spill.
Thinkest thou that I will follow thee?
Nay, from this world not, verily.   445
EVERYMAN: I had thought otherwise.
GOODS: Therefore to thy soul Goods is a thief;
For when thou art dead, this is my guise—
Another to deceive in this same wise
As I have done thee, and all to his soul's reprief.° 450
EVERYMAN: O false Goods, cursed thou be,
Thou traitor to God, that hast deceived me
And caught me in thy snare!
GOODS: Marry, thou brought thyself in care,
Whereof I am glad.   455
I must needs laugh; I cannot be sad.
EVERYMAN: Ah, Goods, thou hast had long my hearty
love;
I gave thee that which should be the Lord's above.
But wilt thou not go with me indeed?

---

reprief, harm.

460 I pray thee truth to say.
GOODS: No, so God me speed!
Therefore farewell, and have good day.

(Exit GOODS.)

EVERYMAN: O, to whom shall I make my moan
For to go with me in that heavy journey?
465 First Fellowship said he would with me go;
His words were very pleasant and gay,
But afterward he left me alone.
Then spake I to my kinsmen, all in despair,
And also they gave me words fair;
470 They lacked no fair speaking,
But all forsook me in the ending.
Then went I to my Goods that I loved best,
In hope to have comfort; but there had I least,
For my Goods sharply did me tell
475 That he bringeth many into Hell.
Then of myself I was ashamed,
And so I am worthy to be blamed;
Thus may I well myself hate.
Of whom shall I now counsel take?
480 I think that I shall never speed
Till that I go to my Good Deeds.
But, alas, she is so weak
That she can neither go nor speak;
Yet will I venture on her now.
485 My Good Deeds, where be you?

(GOOD DEEDS revealed on the ground.)

GOOD DEEDS: Here I lie, cold in the ground.
Thy sins hath me so sore bound
That I cannot stir.
EVERYMAN: O Good Deeds, I stand in fear!
490 I must you pray of counsel,
For help now should come right well.
GOOD DEEDS: Everyman, I have understanding
That ye be summoned account to make
Before Messiah, of Jerusalem King;
495 If you do by me, that journey with you will I take.
EVERYMAN: Therefore I come to you my moan to
make.
I pray you that ye will go with me.
GOOD DEEDS: I would full fain, but I cannot stand,
verily.
EVERYMAN: Why, is there anything on you fallen?
500 GOOD DEEDS: Yea, sir, I may thank you of all.
If ye had perfectly cheered me,
Your book of account full ready would be.
Look, the books of your works and deeds eke,°
As how they lie under the feet
505 To your soul's heaviness.
EVERYMAN: Our Lord Jesus help me!
For one letter here I cannot see.

---

eke, also.

GOOD DEEDS: There is a blind reckoning in time of
distress.
EVERYMAN: Good Deeds, I pray you help me in this
need,
Or else I am forever damned indeed; 510
Therefore help me to make reckoning
Before the Redeemer of all things,
That King is, and was, and ever shall.
GOOD DEEDS: Everyman, I am sorry of your fall,
And fain would I help you if I were able. 515
EVERYMAN: Good Deeds, your counsel I pray you give
me.
GOOD DEEDS: That shall I do verily.
Though that on my feet I may not go,
I have a sister that shall with you also,
Called Knowledge, which shall with you abide 520
To help you to make that dreadful reckoning.

(Enter KNOWLEDGE.)

KNOWLEDGE: Everyman, I will go with thee and be
thy guide,
In thy most need to go by thy side.
EVERYMAN: In good condition I am now in everything
And am wholly content with this good thing; 525
Thanked be God my Creator.
GOOD DEEDS: And when she hath brought you there,
Where thou shalt heal thee of thy smart,
Then go you with your reckoning and your Good
Deeds together
For to make you joyful at heart 530
Before the Blessèd Trinity.
EVERYMAN: My Good Deeds, gramercy!
I am well content, certainly,
With your words sweet.

(EVERYMAN and KNOWLEDGE leave GOOD DEEDS.)

KNOWLEDGE: Now go we together lovingly 535
To Confession, that cleansing river.
EVERYMAN: For joy I weep; I would we were there!
But, I pray you, give me cognition
Where dwelleth that holy man, Confession.
KNOWLEDGE: In the house of salvation; 540
We shall find him in that place
That shall us comfort, by God's grace.

(KNOWLEDGE leads EVERYMAN to CONFESSION.)

Lo, this is Confession. Kneel down and ask mercy,
For he is in good esteem with God Almighty.
EVERYMAN: O glorious fountain, that all uncleanness
doth clarify, 545
Wash from me the spots of vice unclean,
That on me no sin may be seen.
I come with Knowledge for my redemption,
Redempt with hearty and full contrition;
For I am commanded a pilgrimage to take 550
And great accounts before God to make.
Now I pray you, Shrift, mother of salvation,

Help my Good Deeds for my piteous exclamation.

CONFESSION: I know your sorrow well, Everyman.
555 Because with Knowledge ye come to me,
I will you comfort as well as I can,
And a precious jewel I will give thee,
Called penance, voider of adversity;
Therewith shall your body chastised be,
With abstinence and perseverance in God's
560 servitue.
Here shall you receive that scourge of me
Which is penance strong that ye must endure,
To remember thy Saviour was scourged for thee
With sharp scourges and suffered it patiently;
So must thou, ere thou escape that painful
565 pilgrimage.

(CONFESSION *gives scourge to* KNOWLEDGE.)

Knowledge, keep him in this voyage,
And by that time Good Deeds will be with thee.
But in any wise be sure of mercy,
For your time draweth fast; if ye will saved be,
570 Ask God mercy, and he will grant truly.
When with the scourge of penance man doth him
bind,
The oil of forgiveness then shall he find.

(EVERYMAN *and* KNOWLEDGE *leave* CONFESSION.)

EVERYMAN: Thanked be God for his gracious work!
For now I will my penance begin.
575 This hath rejoiced and lighted my heart,
Though the knots be painful and hard within.
KNOWLEDGE: Everyman, look your penance that ye
fulfill,
What pain that ever it to you be;
And Knowledge shall give you counsel at will
580 How your account ye shall make clearly.
EVERYMAN: O eternal God, O heavenly figure,
O way of righteousness, O goodly vision,
Which descended down in a virgin pure
Because he would every man redeem,
585 Which Adam forfeited by his disobedience;
O blesséd Godhead, elect and high divine,
Forgive me my grievous offence!
Here I cry thee mercy in this presence.
O ghostly° treasure, O ransomer and redeemer,
590 Of all the world hope and conductor,
Mirror of joy, foundation of mercy,
Which illumineth Heaven and earth thereby,
Hear my clamorous complaint though it late be;
Receive my prayers unworthy in this heavy life!
595 Though I be a sinner most abominable,
Yet let my name be written in Moses' table.
O Mary, pray to the Maker of all things,
Me for to help at my ending;

And save me from the power of my enemy,
For Death assaileth me strongly. 600
And, Lady, that I may by means of thy prayer
Of your Son's glory to be partner,
By the means of his passion, I it crave;
I beseech you, help my soul to save.
Knowledge, give me the scourge of penance; 605
My flesh therewith shall give acquittance.
I will now begin if God give me grace.

(KNOWLEDGE *gives scourge to* EVERYMAN.)

KNOWLEDGE: Everyman, God give you time and
space!
Thus I bequeath you in the hands of our Saviour;
Now may you make your reckoning sure. 610
EVERYMAN: In the name of the Holy Trinity,
My body sore punishéd shall be:
Take this, body, for the sins of the flesh!
Also thou delightest to go gay and fresh,
And in the way of damnation thou did me bring; 615
Therefore suffer now strokes of punishing.
Now of penance I will wade the water clear
To save me from Purgatory, that sharp fire.

(GOOD DEEDS *rises from the ground.*)

GOOD DEEDS: I thank God, now I can walk and go
And am delivered of my sickness and woe. 620
Therefore with Everyman I will go and not spare;
His good works I will help him to declare.
KNOWLEDGE: Now, Everyman, be merry and glad!
Your Good Deeds cometh now; ye may not be sad
Now is your Good Deeds whole and sound, 625
Going upright upon the ground.
EVERYMAN: My heart is light and shall be evermore;
Now will I smite faster than I did before.
GOOD DEEDS: Everyman, pilgrim, my special friend,
Blessed be thou without end! 630
For thee is prepared the eternal glory.
Ye have me made whole and sound,
Therefore I will bide by thee in every stound.°
EVERYMAN: Welcome, my Good Deeds! Now I hear
thy voice
I weep for very sweetness of love. 635
KNOWLEDGE: Be no more sad, but ever rejoice;
God seeth thy living in his throne above.

(KNOWLEDGE *gives* EVERYMAN *the garment of contrition.*)

Put on this garment to thy behove,°
Which is wet with your tears,
Or else before God you may it miss 640
When you to your journey's end come shall.
EVERYMAN: Gentle Knowledge, what do ye it call?
KNOWLEDGE: It is the garment of sorrow;

---

ghostly, spiritual, as in Holy Ghost.

stound, instance, occasion. ***behove,*** benefit.

645 From pain it will you borrow.
Contrition it is
That getteth forgiveness;
It pleaseth God passing well.
GOOD DEEDS: Everyman, will you wear it for your
heal?°

(EVERYMAN *puts on the garment of contrition.*)

EVERYMAN: Now blesséd be Jesu, Mary's Son,
650 For now have I on true contrition;
And let us go now without tarrying.
Good Deeds, have we clear our reckoning?
GOOD DEEDS: Yea, indeed, I have it here.
EVERYMAN: Then I trust we need not fear.
655 Now, friends, let us not part in twain.
KNOWLEDGE: Nay, Everyman, that will we not,
certain.
GOOD DEEDS: Yet must thou lead with thee
Three persons of great might.
EVERYMAN: Who should they be?
660 GOOD DEEDS: Discretion and Strength they hight°
And thy Beauty may not abide behind.
KNOWLEDGE: Also ye must call to mind
Your Five Wits as for your counsellors.
GOOD DEEDS: You must have them ready at all hours.
665 EVERYMAN: How shall I get them hither?
KNOWLEDGE: You must call them all together,
And they will hear you incontinent.°
EVERYMAN: My friends, come hither and be present:
Discretion, Strength, my Five Wits, and Beauty.

(*Enter* DISCRETION, STRENGTH, FIVE WITS, *and*
BEAUTY.)

670 BEAUTY: Here at your will we be all ready.
What would ye that we should do?
GOOD DEEDS: That ye would with Everyman go
And help him in his pilgrimage.
Advise you, will ye with him or not in that voyage?
675 STRENGTH: We will bring him all thither
To his help and comfort, ye may believe me.
DISCRETION: So will we go with him all together.
EVERYMAN: Almighty God, loved may thou be!
I give thee laud that I have hither brought
Strength, Discretion, Beauty and Five Wits. Lack I
680 naught;
And my Good Deeds, with Knowledge clear,
All be in company at my will here.
I desire no more to my business.
STRENGTH: And I, Strength, will by you stand in
distress,
685 Though thou would in battle fight on the ground.
FIVE WITS: And though it were through the world
round,
We will not depart for sweet nor sour.

BEAUTY: No more will I unto death's hour,
Whatsoever thereof befall.
690 DISCRETION: Everyman, advise you first of all;
Go with a good advisement and deliberation.
We all give you virtuous monition
That all shall be well.
EVERYMAN: My friends, hearken what I will tell:
695 I pray God reward you in his heavenly sphere.
Now hearken, all that be here,
For I will make my testament
Here before you all present:
In alms, half of my goods I will give with my hands
twain
700 In the way of charity with good intent,
And the other half still shall remain
In queth,° to be returned where it ought to be.
This I do in despite of the fiend of hell,
To go quite out of his peril
705 Ever after and this day.
KNOWLEDGE: Everyman, hearken what I say:
Go to Priesthood, I you advise,
And receive of him in any wise
The holy sacrament and ointment together;
710 Then shortly see ye turn again hither.
We will all abide you here.
FIVE WITS: Yea, Everyman, hie you that ye ready
were.
There is no emperor, king, duke, nor baron
That of God hath commission
715 As hath the least priest in the world being;
For of the blesséd sacraments pure and benign,
He beareth the keys, and thereof hath the cure
For man's redemption—it is ever sure—
Which God for our soul's medicine
720 Gave us out of his heart with great pine.°
Here in this transitory life, for thee and me,
The blessed sacraments seven there be:
Baptism, confirmation with priesthood good,
And the sacrament of God's precious flesh and
blood,
725 Marriage, the holy extreme unction, and penance.
These seven be good to have in remembrance,
Gracious sacraments of high divinity.
EVERYMAN: Fain would I receive that holy body,
And meekly to my ghostly° father I will go.
730 FIVE WITS: Everyman, that is the best that ye can do.
God will you to salvation bring,
For priesthood exceedeth all other things:
To us holy scripture they do teach
And converteth man from sin, Heaven to reach;
735 God hath to them more power given

---

heal, salvation. *hight*, are called. *incontinent*, at once.

In queth, as a bequest; though the remainder of the line indicates that it is actually a restitution of illegally acquired property. *pine*, anguish, torment. *ghostly*, spiritual.

Than to any angel that is in Heaven.
With five words he may consecrate,
God's body in flesh and blood to make,
And handleth his Maker between his hands.
740 The priest bindeth and unbindeth all bands,
Both in earth and in Heaven.
Thou ministers all the sacraments seven;
Though we kissed thy feet, thou were worthy.
Thou art surgeon that cureth sin deadly;
745 No remedy we find under God
But all only priesthood.
Everyman, God gave priests that dignity
And setteth them in his stead among us to be;
Thus be they above angels in degree.

(Exit EVERYMAN.*)*

750 KNOWLEDGE: If priests be good, it is so, surely.
But when Jesu hanged on the cross with great
    smart,
There he gave, out of his blessèd heart,
The seven sacraments in great torment;
He sold them not to us, that Lord omnipotent;
755 Therefore Saint Peter the apostle doth say
That Jesu's curse hath all they
Which God their Saviour do buy or sell,
Or they for any money do take or tell.°
Sinful priests giveth the sinners example bad;
Their children sitteth by other men's fires, I have
760   heard;
And some haunteth women's company
With unclean life, as lusts of lechery;
These be with sin made blind.
FIVE WITS: I trust to God no such may we find;
765 Therefore let us priesthood honor
And follow their doctrine for our souls' succour.
We be their sheep, and they shepherds be
By whom we all be kept in surety.
Peace! For yonder I see Everyman come,
770 Which hath made true satisfaction.
GOOD DEEDS: Methinks it is he indeed.

(Re-enter EVERYMAN.*)*

EVERYMAN: Now Jesu be your alder speed!°
I have received the sacrament for my redemption
And then mine extreme unction.
775 Blessèd be all they that counselled me to take it!
And now, friends, let us go without longer respite.
I thank God that ye have tarried so long.
Now set each of you on this rood your hand
And shortly follow me.
780 I go before where I would be. God be our guide!

(They go toward the grave.)

STRENGTH: Everyman, we will not from you go
Till ye have done this voyage long.
DISCRETION: I, Discretion, will bide by you also.
KNOWLEDGE: And though this pilgrimage be never so
    strong,
I will never part you from. 785
STRENGTH: Everyman, I will be as sure by thee
As ever I did by Judas Maccabee.°

(They arrive at the grave.)

EVERYMAN: Alas, I am so faint I may not stand;
My limbs under me do fold.
Friends, let us not turn again to this land, 790
Not for all the world's gold;
For into this cave must I creep
And turn to earth, and thereto sleep.
BEAUTY: What, into this grave? Alas!
EVERYMAN: Yea, there shall ye consume,° more and 795
    less.
BEAUTY: And what, should I smother here?
EVERYMAN: Yea, by my faith, and never more appear.
In this world live no more we shall,
But in Heaven before the highest Lord of all.
BEAUTY: I cross out all this. Adieu, by Saint John! 800
I take my tap° in my lap and am gone.
EVERYMAN: What, Beauty, whither will ye?
BEAUTY: Peace! I am deaf. I look not behind me,
Not if thou wouldest give me all the gold in thy
    chest.

(Exit BEAUTY.*)*

EVERYMAN: Alas, whereto may I trust? 805
Beauty goeth fast away from me.
She promised with me to live and die.
STRENGTH: Everyman, I will thee also forsake and
    deny;
Thy game liketh me not at all.
EVERYMAN: Why, then, ye will forsake me all? 810
Sweet Strength, tarry a little space.
STRENGTH: Nay, sir, by the rood of grace!
I will hie me from thee fast,
Though thou weep till thy heart to-brast.°
EVERYMAN: Ye would ever bide by me, ye said. 815
STRENGTH: Yea, I have you far enough conveyed.
Ye be old enough, I understand,
Your pilgrimage to take in hand.
I repent me that I hither came.
EVERYMAN: Strength, you to displease I am to blame; 820
Yet promise is debt, this ye well wot.°

Maccabee, a Jewish leader of the second century B.C.,
known for his courage (1 Macc. 3). *shall ye consume,* the
grave devours all, both the great and the small. *tap,* an
unspun tuft of wool or flax. Hence, like a peasant housewife,
Beauty is saying, "I'm pocketing my spinning materials and
am off." *to-brast,* bursts in two. *wot,* know.

STRENGTH: In faith, I care not.
  Thou art but a fool to complain;
  You spend your speech and waste your brain.
825   Go thrust thee into the ground!

(Exit STRENGTH.*)*

EVERYMAN: I had thought surer I should you have
    found.
  He that trusteth in his Strength,
  She him deceiveth at length.
  Both Strength and Beauty forsaketh me;
830   Yet they promised me fair and lovingly.
DISCRETION: Everyman, I will after Strength be gone.
  As for me, I will leave you alone.
EVERYMAN: Why, Discretion, will ye forsake me?
DISCRETION: Yea, in faith, I will go from thee;
835   For when Strength goeth before,
  I follow after evermore.
EVERYMAN: Yet, I pray thee, for the love of the
    Trinity,
  Look in my grave once piteously.
DISCRETION: Nay, so nigh will I not come.
840   Farewell, everyone!

(Exit DISCRETION.*)*

EVERYMAN: O, all things faileth, save God alone—
  Beauty, Strength and Discretion;
  For when Death bloweth his blast,
  They all run from me full fast.
845 FIVE WITS: Everyman, my leave now of thee I take.
  I will follow the others, for here I thee forsake.
EVERYMAN: Alas, then may I wail and weep,
  For I took you for my best friend.
FIVE WITS: I will no longer thee keep.
850   Now farewell, and there an end.

(Exit FIVE WITS.*)*

EVERYMAN: O Jesu, help! All hath forsaken me.
GOOD DEEDS: Nay, Everyman, I will bide with thee.
  I will not forsake thee in deed;
  Thou shalt find me a good friend in need.
EVERYMAN: Gramercy, Good Deeds! Now may I true
855   friends see.
  They have forsaken me, every one;
  I loved them better than my Good Deeds alone.
  Knowledge, will ye forsake me also?
KNOWLEDGE: Yea, Everyman, when ye to Death shall
    go;
860   But not yet, for no manner of danger.
EVERYMAN: Gramercy, Knowledge, with all my heart.
KNOWLEDGE: Nay, yet I will not from hence depart
  Till I see where ye shall be come.
EVERYMAN: Methinks, alas, that I must be gone
865   To make my reckoning and my debts pay,
  For I see my time is nigh spent away.
  Take example, all ye that this do hear or see,
  How they that I loved best do forsake me,

  Except my Good Deeds that bideth truly.
870 GOOD DEEDS: All earthly things is but vanity:
  Beauty, Strength and Discretion do man forsake,
  Foolish friends and kinsmen that fair spake—
  All fleeth save Good Deeds, and that am I.
EVERYMAN: Have mercy on me, God most mighty,
  And stand by me, thou mother and maid, Holy
    Mary!
875 GOOD DEEDS: Fear not, I will speak for thee.
EVERYMAN: Here I cry God mercy.
GOOD DEEDS: Shorten our end, and diminish our
    pain;
  Let us go and never come again.

*(*GOOD DEEDS *leads* EVERYMAN *into grave.)*

EVERYMAN: Into thy hands, Lord, my soul I
    commend;
880   Receive it, Lord, that it be not lost.
  As thou me boughtest, so me defend
  And save me from the fiend's boast,
  That I may appear with that blessèd host
  That shall be saved at the day of doom.
885   *In manus tuas,* of might most
  Forever, *commendo spiritum meum.*°

(Exeunt EVERYMAN *and* GOOD DEEDS.*)*

KNOWLEDGE: Now hath he suffered that we all shall
    endure;
  The Good Deeds shall make all sure.
  Now hath he made ending;
890   Methinks that I hear angels sing
  And make great joy and melody
  Where Everyman's soul received shall be.

(Enter ANGEL.*)*

THE ANGEL: Come, excellent elect spouse, to Jesu!
  Here above thou shalt go
895   Because of thy singular virtue.
  Now thy soul is taken thy body from,
  Thy reckoning is crystal clear.
  Now shalt thou into the heavenly sphere,
  Unto the which all ye shall come
900   That liveth well before the day of doom.

(Exeunt ANGEL *and* KNOWLEDGE.*)*

(Enter DOCTOR.*)*

DOCTOR: This moral men may have in mind.
  Ye hearers, take it of worth, old and young,
  And forsake Pride, for he deceiveth you in the end;
  And remember Beauty, Five Wits, Strength, and
    Discretion,
905   They all at the last do Everyman forsake,
  Save his Good Deeds there doth he take.

In manus tuas . . . commendo spiritum meum, Into thy
hands I commend my spirit.

But beware, for if they be small,
Before God he hath no help at all:
910 No excuse may be there for Everyman.
Alas, how shall he do then?
For after death amends may no man make,
For them mercy and pity doth him forsake.
If his reckoning be not clear when he doth come,
915 God will say, "*Ite, maledicti, in ignem eternum.*"°

Ite . . . eternum, Go, sinners, into eternal fire.

And he that hath his account whole and sound,
High in Heaven he shall be crowned;
Unto which place God bring us all thither,
That we may live body and soul together.
Thereto help the Trinity!   920
Amen, say ye, for saint charity.

(Exit DOCTOR.*)*

(Thus endeth this moral play of Everyman.)

Figure 1. The multilevel set for the University of Chicago Theater production of *Everyman*, directed by Nicholas Rudall in the Rockefeller Chapel, 1973. (Photograph: Leslie Travis.)

Figure 2. Everyman (Joseph Mydell) and Death (Josette Bushell-Mingo) dance together at Fellowship's wedding in the 1996 Royal Shakespeare Company production of *Everyman*, directed by Kathryn Hunter and Marcello Magni. In the background are Fellowship (Edward Woodall), Cousin (Johnny Lodi), and Goods (Paul Hamilton). (Photograph: Ivan Kyncl.)

Figure 3. Good Deeds (Kelly Nespor, *left*) leads Everyman (Gordon Cameron) into his grave in the 1973 University of Chicago Theater production of *Everyman*. (Photograph: Leslie Travis.)

Figure 4. Everyman (Joseph Mydell) lies dying, attended by his faithful companion Good Deeds (Myra McFadyen), while Knowledge (Josette Bushell-Mingo) watches from upstage in the 1996 Royal Shakespeare Company production. (Photograph: Ivan Kyncl.)

Staging of *Everyman*

INTERVIEW WITH NICHOLAS RUDALL,
DIRECTOR OF THE 1973 UNIVERSITY
OF CHICAGO THEATER PRODUCTION OF
EVERYMAN, BY BRADFORD S. FIELD, JR.

FIELD: What kind of stage does a gothic cathedral like Rockefeller Chapel offer for *Everyman*? Did you do it in the round? Or at the altar?

RUDALL: We placed a large octagon with other levels attached to it right to the center of the chancel. The octagon is raised and raked. It is divided off into a main acting area, which is the octagon, with a sort of inner below at the top of the rake, through which entrances could occur, and through which this sort of tableau that I did at the beginning could be seen. At raked angles away from it, upstage, were separate areas for the individual scenes, especially at the beginning, to take place. That is, Fellowship had his own platform, Kindred had hers, Cousin had hers, Goods had his. Good Deeds was placed on a kind of sarcophagus at the very top of this structure. I conceived the play, not so much as a pilgrimage—where you'd have lots of movement to different mansions all over the church—but rather as a going away, a taking away from Everyman. All these levels were fairly close to him, but they were separate from him. When he goes to a particular area, only that area is lit. When Fellowship, for example, is finished with him, the light in that area goes out. Forever. That area of the stage is black thereafter.

FIELD: Do I get it correctly that Everyman would move to each of their positions . . .

RUDALL: That's right . . .

FIELD: . . . talk to them, and then their exit was a blackout on them, but not on him; he'd move on to the next position?

RUDALL: That's right.

FIELD: Does *Everyman* present any special kinds of problems to a director?

RUDALL: Yes, one stylistic problem, that of the very realistic details in the play, realistic characterizations, coupled with a much higher style within the play. How does one reconcile characters that have cramps in their toes with these reflections about God? How elevated a person should Everyman be? Or how colloquial? How down to earth? What's the right level? He should not be too rich, not too poor . . . not too rustic, not too aristocratic. That was a rather difficult one to solve. I think we hit upon a solution that was partially based upon the fact that it was being done in a huge, almost cathedral-like structure. The play, as it is now performed, has the feeling of a church ritual. The whole building is lit by candlelight at the beginning and there are monks chanting for the first fifteen minutes as the audience comes in. I have some cross-cutting with contemporary folk song that contrasts between the happy life and the ecclesiastical life, if you like, all before the play starts. The fact that it is in this large structure allows us to have this high-style feeling, this ritual feeling, which I don't think it would have if it were on a small stage. That high style would be impossible; you'd be forced to think of it only as "playing" at that point.

FIELD: If you put it outdoors with a cart.

RUDALL: Right.

FIELD: Or in a playground or in a supermarket parking lot . . .

RUDALL: Exactly. But on this stage it is still possible to play the humanness of Fellowship, the humanness of Kindred and Cousin. I made them very direct, human figures. Fellowship was meant to be a kind of medieval banker, richly dressed, at supper. He's eating chicken and bread and wine while he's talking to Everyman. Kindred is a sort of fifty- or sixty-year-old woman, upper bourgeois, and she's sitting there with her needlepoint, and Cousin is standing, playing with a little bird, very much a young aristocratic lady. And Goods emerges from a chest. Each character I made very specifically medieval characters, not generalizations, but very specific ones.

FIELD: The costumes then were intended to suggest a very particular social level, income level, type of business. . . .

RUDALL: Exactly that. Good Deeds is a young maiden, Knowledge is a young novice, a nun, and Strength a knight, Discretion a lawyer. One other thing, I did find that the play naturally lent itself to doubling. The first four characters to whom he goes, to Fellowship, to Kindred, Cousin and Goods, lend themselves to perfect doubling with the four parts of his personality that come back to him before he goes to the grave, Five Wits, Beauty, Discretion, and . . .

FIELD: Do they each use the same platforms, or do they come down to him?

RUDALL: I didn't want to repeat the platforms; once their light was out, they had gone forever, I didn't want to return to them. What I had intended to do was have these four characters come back on, but with a life-mask of Everyman on their faces, to show them as four extensions of his own personality. Goods and Fellowship are outside things that he goes to, but the things that he loses at the end are parts of himself—Beauty and Five Wits—so I made life-masks to be placed over their faces, so that there would be five Everymans, as it were, going down toward the grave. But because of the size of the church, that failed. They didn't look like Everyman, even though they were absolutely perfect. At a distance, that effect was lost. So I abandoned it.

FIELD: You did abandon it.

RUDALL: Yes. I did. Only because of the distance. I think in a smaller house, more intimate . . . it would have worked very well.

FIELD: I suppose if they'd all been wearing the same mask, even Everyman, they'd have matched, but then you'd have a hard time telling one from the other. Did the masks create any problem with speech?

RUDALL: Yes, one of the reasons that they failed was that we had to make too large an opening around the mouth and that made it cease to look like the person who was playing Everyman.

FIELD: Everyman was played by a man or a woman?

RUDALL: A man.

FIELD: At the turn of the century there was evidently a famous touring version of *Everyman* in which the title role was played by a—

RUDALL: A woman, yes.

FIELD: Okay . . . What kind of text did you use?

RUDALL: We took what might conveniently be called a translation. But I didn't overly modernize it, and I made adaptations for myself with a couple of professors here at Chicago and we pieced together parts which were obscure.

FIELD: What was obscure?

RUDALL: Somewhere at the beginning the medieval English says, "Thou shalt make no attournay," and we just changed that to "delay." Very simple adaptations like that. We changed many of the "and's" to "if's," where there was a modern equivalent.

FIELD: Did you make any cuts in the text?

RUDALL: No. I was sorely tempted, at one particular point. Towards the end, about three-quarters of the way through, there's a long scene about priesthood, where Five Wits talks at great length about the virtues of priesthood . . . it is self-serving, and honestly written in its time for the priests, but removed from our context. I had no way of solving it for a long, long time. And then I hit upon the idea of—while Five Wits is discoursing about priesthood—we would actually illustrate it on an upper level, by having two black-robed priest-monks set up the equipment for the last rites. While Five Wits is giving that long speech, Everyman is supposed to be off-stage getting the last rites. So instead of going off-stage, as is usually suggested, I had them do it in a kind of silhouette against the backdrop of the church, with candles and bread and oil and the chanting of Latin; while Five Wits is talking

about priesthood, we actually see them functioning, we see Everyman go to them, get the last rites, and come back down again. So that the inactivity was filled in that way.

FIELD: Were there any comic moments that you pointed for?

RUDALL: I didn't fight any of them. We pointed them up.

FIELD: Like the cramp in the toe . . .

RUDALL: And by making Kindred a dowager. She was played by a woman with a very thick English accent who sounded somewhat like Edith Evans. One could find comedy in her mere exit lines . . . She suggests too that Everyman take her maid. And that was done with a suggestion of the obscene. As was Fellowship's suggestion that if you want to go off and have fun with women, fine, he'll do that. That was the kind of thing that I didn't resist at all. Obviously the comedy is a very important part of the play.

FIELD: How did you handle Death?

RUDALL: I had Death seated at a kind of banquet. The play opened, as I said, with a chanting, a little tableau in the sort of inner below that we had at the top of the raked platform—a tableau with Death seated at a table with his back to the audience, along with Everyman, Kindred, Fellowship, and a young girl who was singing the secular song. After God spoke to them from the far end of the chapel, He calls upon Death, who just turns around from the feast. I had had Everyman enter with the girl who'd been singing, flirtatiously playing, coming from the feast. That made it very specific when Death asks, "Where are thou going thus gaily," that Everyman's mind is on fleshly lusts, specifically, coming from a feast with a woman.

FIELD: I always notice the bookkeeping imagery in the play. Did you play up any of that?

RUDALL: Yes. There are two notable instances of it. I had made a separate mansion of Everyman's house. Off the main stage, I had a little area that was a corner of his home. When Death comes to him, he runs to the house, looking for the money, the "thousand pounds I will give to you," and his book of accounts. He rifles through his books, looks to see, to offer it to Death, finds that it's not ready, and asks for twelve years . . . The second is that I had Good Deeds placed on a sarcophagus, way, way up; she was there before the audience came in. She was all white, to look like marble. Like a lady laying at rest with a book on her chest. A large pile of books nearby. And one main book, carved into the tomb at the bottom. When Everyman goes up and appeals to her she tells him to look in the book there. He takes it from the tomb and looks through it. When he says, "No letter here do I see," that's what he's talking about. And later she brings his book of accounts down to him. So I made three specific uses of the bookkeeping in the action.

FIELD: One other thing that is always interesting about this play—how did the final moment work out? It seems pretty vague when you just read the play . . .

RUDALL: At the base of this octagonal acting area, there's a very steep ramp which leads down right into the audience, and it's absolutely black out there. Whenever Everyman left Fellowship or any of those characters, he would come right to the rim of the octagon, and look out into that blackness, toward the way he was going to go.

FIELD: Toward the audience.

RUDALL: Yes. When his personal attributes leave him at the end, Five Wits and the others, when he starts to walk down that ramp, he says, "Friends, come with me," and he stumbles. "I'm too weak," he says, and he stumbles. That is the first time that the four of them, these attributes, look down into the tomb to see . . . they see him stumble, and then they are for the first time aware of the tomb. They leave him. He's left then with Good Deeds and Knowledge, in a little rim of light above this blackness. There is a line that Knowledge says that ends with the syllable, "come," . . . "where ye shall become," and at that point, I have Death, who made his exit earlier in the play down to the tomb, echo the word "come," from the back of the church.

FIELD: Wow.

RUDALL: She says ". . . become;" "Come!" he says from back there. And then for the first time, Everyman fully realizes Death. It is *the* human moment in the play. While he's acknowledged all these things that he's been going through, penance and that sort of thing, he's been busy at it. Now on these last few lines, very frightened, he asks, "Who'll come with me?" And Good Deeds comforts him. He says his last Latin words, *"In manus tuas. . . .",* and he walks down with Good Deeds, holding the cross and his book of accounts. He takes the first three steps down that ramp, and then there is a blackout. And there is Death, with a candle, all in black, but he's got an anatomical hand; he turns around and walks out; they follow him, to the chanting of monks. So it's a long death scene before Knowledge starts to speak again. The whole church is black, except for the candle in Death's hand, for about forty-five seconds. Then the lights come back up on Knowledge, and she begins to talk, with some more singing from way back up in the choir loft.

FIELD: Then the doctor comes out?

RUDALL: He's the same character, the prologue and the epilogue, is what I thought for it.

FIELD: The messenger at the beginning and the doctor at the end—

RUDALL: Right, the same character. We made him a monk. Up in the pulpit. He was the one who put out the candles in the church to get the play started. He was able to provide the . . . the solution to the problem of style . . . to acknowledge that this was a church performance. "I am the priest that is telling you to watch this play in my church"—that kind of feeling.

REVIEW OF THE ROYAL SHAKESPEARE COMPANY PRODUCTION, 1996, BY CHARLES SPENCER

The RSC's new season has got off to a tremendous start with the morality play *Everyman,* first performed in about 1500.

It is directed by those admirable Theatre de Complicité veterans Kathryn Hunter and Marcello Magni, and their distinctive, at times grotesque, imagination is well suited to this antique play.

They have set their multiracial, modern-dress production in a sun-baked peasant community. Dogs bark, cicadas chirrup and there is an inventive prologue, undreamt of by the play's anonymous author, in which we watch Everyman being bathed by a devoted servant before attending a riotous wedding, complete with rousing folk music.

Some might complain that the RSC has no right to take such liberties with a classic, rarely performed text, but I think the directors have been wise. If the play is to move an audience, it must be set in a recognisable world, and instead of coming across as a bland allegorical figure, Joseph Mydell's Everyman is a recognisable individual—a self-indulgent Jack-the-lad who fancies himself, and the pleasure of the flesh, something rotten.

But his pleasures are not to last. God, played with awesome Old Testament wrath by Paul Hamilton, has sickened of mankind's irreligious ways and sends Death to call Everyman to account. In this production Death is a stunning *femme fatale,* played with stirring sensuality by Josette Bushell-Mingo, who leads a *danse macabre* at the wedding, takes Everyman in her slinky embrace and reveals her true identity only after a passionate snog. Mydell's panicky terror at this unwelcome news is a wonder to behold.

The production is as strong on the spiritual as it is on the sexy and the comic. As Everyman is abandoned in his distress by the transient comforts of life—fellowship, worldly goods and family—Mydell movingly conveys Everyman's lonely journey from craven terror to humble repentance.

I have some niggles. The presentation of Strength, Beauty and the Five Wits (senses) as a troupe of circus freaks, for instance, seems out of place in this more serious section of the play.

But the production achieves a fine sense of solemnity and grace in its closing stages. In a lovely touch, Mydell returns to the zinc bath in which he began the play, only it has now become his coffin; and the final scene in which his soul awakes from the dead and he climbs up to heaven, to be enfolded in Christ's arms, like a *pietà* in reverse, is as beautiful as it is moving.

Everyman, with its ancient sense of ritual and repetition, not to mention the Christian certainties which will now seem obsolete to many, is a notably difficult play. There is no doubt, however, that this production succeeds in breathing new life into the neglected but still vivid text.

I will remember the evening as much for its religious profundity as for its fine sense of theatre.

RENAISSANCE ENGLISH THEATER

When James Burbage built the first permanent English public theater in 1576, he called it, simply and boldly, The Theater. Retrospectively, that name takes on emblematic force, signifying not just a single building but the beginning of the greatest period of drama since the Greeks. Burbage was the leader of the Earl of Leicester's Men, which would later become the Lord Chamberlain's Men and then the King's Men; the company's principal playwright for twenty years was William Shakespeare. Burbage's theater was so successful that it was quickly followed by others: The Curtain in 1577, The Newington Butts in 1579, The Rose in 1587, The Swan in 1595, The Globe in 1599, The Fortune in 1600, and others in the early seventeenth century.

All these public theaters, though they varied in shape from round to square to octagonal, were designed according to roughly similar principles, and they were all quite large, capable of holding between 2,000 and 3,000 spectators. The exact origin of their design has never been firmly established, but the basic plan—a yard with a stage jutting into the center of it and three levels of galleries surrounding the yard—suggests that it may well have been modeled on inn-yard or courtyard performances of an earlier period (see Figure 1). The stage itself consisted of two acting levels, and on each level there were several distinct acting areas. In the octagonally shaped Globe, for example, where many of Shakespeare's plays were performed, the primary acting surface on the ground level extended about twenty-seven feet into the yard, which was itself only about fifty-five feet in diameter. Thus the stage occupied about fifty percent of the yard. And at its widest, where it joined with the superstructure of the galleries, the stage was about forty-three feet wide. At the back of the stage on each side were doors and exits, and between the doors was an inner stage that was curtained when not in use (see Figure 1). On the second level there was another set of acting areas: windows above the doors on the lower level, a gallery between the windows, and behind the gallery another inner stage (see Figure 1). Above the second level, there may have been yet another

Figure 1. The Renaissance English theater.

gallery at the back for musicians, but the evidence for one is uncertain. Whatever the case, almost the entire stage was sheltered by a canopy that extended out from the roof of the theater.

The dimensions and design of that stage created a unique theatrical experience, unlike anything else during the Renaissance or at any other time in history. To begin with, the physical proximity of the stage to the surrounding galleries and to the spectators standing in the yard created a much more intimate relationship between actors and audience than the Greek theater provided. That physical intimacy must inevitably have aroused in the audience an immediate and personal involvement with the dramatic experience, much greater certainly than any other staging system provided, except perhaps for the medieval. At the same time, the Renaissance English theater continued to sustain a communal atmosphere, for the yard was open to the sky, and the plays were performed in daylight. Consequently, the spectators could easily see one another as they sat in the galleries or stood in the yard.

The size and design of the theater also made possible a highly flexible drama. As in the medieval period, the main acting surface was generalized, but unlike the medieval stage, it was not restricted to a limited number of locales established by set pieces. The stage could, in fact, become any number of places simply by the departure of one set of characters and the appearance of another, implying in their dialogue a new location, as in the line, "So this is the forest of Arden." The other acting areas made possible a wide variety of discovery scenes, bedroom scenes, and balcony scenes, not to mention disappearance scenes through a trapdoor on the ground level stage. Only a few props were used to suggest the location of a scene: a bed, a throne, a tree, a rock. Costuming, as in the medieval tradition, followed current rather than historically accurate styles of dress, but since Elizabethan theater managers did not spend much money on sets, they lavished their resources on costumes. The account book of Philip Henslowe, the leader of the Lord Admiral's Men and Burbage's chief competitor, records an amount of six pounds, thirteen shillings spent on a black velvet dress to be worn by the title character of *A Woman Killed with Kindness* (1603), while the same accounts tell us that the author, Thomas Heywood, received only six pounds in all for his play.

To these theaters came a rich outpouring of drama, created in part by the opportunities offered on their flexible, nonrealistic, and intimate stages, but growing also out of two different dramatic traditions. Since the mid-fifteenth century, small groups of professional actors had been touring England, setting up their show wherever they could expect to collect enough money or enough hospitality to make it worth their while. They were highly versatile performers, capable of staging any kind of play in any kind of physical situation—in a banquet room, in a town hall, in an inn-yard, or on a village green. The plays they performed were relatively short pieces known as interludes, which combined material from a wide range of sources: biblical tales, classical legends, folk stories, fables, historical events, and fictional narratives. And the range of their sources was matched by the range of activities and moods they often brought together in a single play. Much as *The Second Shepherds' Play* combines the ludicrous sheep-stealing episode with the devotional visit of the shepherds, so the interludes frequently combined comic and tragic elements, or historical and farcical elements at will. They sustained in England a highly flexible kind of drama that established important precedents for the magnificent multiplot plays that were to come into being at the end of the sixteenth century.

At the same time that the native tradition was flourishing in the early sixteenth century, the classical influence was beginning to be felt in the grammar schools and universities of England, where Roman plays were being read and performed, and English imitations were being written and performed. During the 1530s, for example, a headmaster at Eton, Nicholas Udall, wrote *Ralph Roister Doister,* which he modeled on a comedy by Plautus, *The Braggart Soldier.* Later, in the 1550s, a comedy by "Mr. S.," *Gammer Gurton's Needle,* which was performed at Cambridge, not only drew on Roman plot devices but also introduced elements from the native tradition of farce, thus anticipating that distinctive tendency of the great Renaissance drama to unite popular and classical elements in a single play. A similar kind of fusing took place in the first regular English tragedy, *Gorboduc* (1562), which dramatized the story of a legendary king of Britain who divides his kingdom and thus brings about familial dissension and political disaster. In this instance, pseudohistorical material from English chronicles was treated in the manner both of a Senecan revenge tragedy and a medieval morality play, thus anticipating the history play and the revenge tragedy that were to flourish in the late sixteenth and early seventeenth centuries. The authors of *Gorboduc,* Thomas Sackville and Thomas Norton, were students at the Inner Temple, one of the Inns of Court where young men of the period lived and studied to be lawyers. And, like the grammar schools and the universities, the Inns of Court sustained an active tradition of writing and performing plays that combined classical or Italian neoclassical precedents with native English elements. The Inns of Court performed their plays to celebrate a wide variety of occasions before an audience of the socially elite, the noble, and the educated. In Renaissance England, members of the upper class were being educated in the theater and were themselves creating a theatrical tradition that was to bear fruit in the numerous young men with university training who turned to the public theaters at the end of the sixteenth century.

Once the educated and the professional theater traditions had firmly taken hold, all that remained was for the two to be brought together—in the right way, at the right place, at the right historical moment. The right time had already come when Elizabeth I ascended to the throne in 1558. She brought religious toleration to England, calming the unrest created by her half sister Mary's attempt to restore Catholicism as the state religion. Elizabeth's political genius stimulated a heady period of exploration and expansion, marked by the voyages of Sir Francis Drake, the commerce of the merchant fleet, the defeat of the Spanish Armada, and the creation of the East India Company. England, under Elizabeth, had become a great naval power, and that power produced great wealth and national pride. The wealth rapidly turned London into a major city, the pride led quickly to a social unity ideal for the life of theater, and The Theater of Burbage gave it a place in which to live.

With the establishment of permanent theaters in London and acting troupes based in London, the golden age of English drama began. The exuberant tendencies of the period were echoed in the richness of dramatic language—for the language, on a stage without sets, had to create the world of the play for its spectators. In *Antony and Cleopatra,* for example, Shakespeare could evoke Rome in one scene and Egypt in the next simply by shifting from the austere language of Caesar to the exotic style of Cleopatra. In *Henry V,* he could evoke the battlefield at Agincourt or the palace of the French king by turning from Henry's military rhetoric to Burgundy's flowing speech of reconciliation. At the same time, the flexibility of this "bare" stage encouraged plays of every kind, and thus Polonius's definition, "comical-tragical-historical-pastoral," is more apt than he knew. Because the drama already existing in England combined so many elements, the dramatists were ready for the stage when it finally appeared, almost as if the nature of their art had called it into existence. The drama of Marlowe, Shakespeare, Jonson, Webster, and all their contemporaries was born from the wedding of fine art and commercial industry—a marriage that we still recognize in the condition of modern theater.

CHRISTOPHER MARLOWE

1564–1593

Marlowe, the earliest of the major English dramatists, wrote all of his plays, except for a youthful college piece, during an extraordinarily productive six-year period between 1587 and his death. Before he turned to the theater, Marlowe had been a scholarship student at Cambridge, where he studied for the clergy but evidently never took holy orders. Instead, he went off to London and followed the pattern of a number of other young men, most of whom had been to one of the universities and then turned to a career of writing. Usually referred to as the "University Wits," they included Robert Greene, whose double plots and comic heroines established dramatic precedents for Shakespeare's comedies; John Lyly, whose witty and ornate prose style also influenced Shakespeare; and Thomas Kyd, whose sensational revenge play, *The Spanish Tragedy,* established a theatrical precedent for such masterful revenge tragedies as *Hamlet* and John Webster's *The Duchess of Malfi.* Although the "Wits" were writing during the same period as Marlowe, when professional theater was beginning to flourish in London, none of them was so decisively and variously influential as Marlowe, and certainly none was so outstanding a dramatist. Before he was stabbed to death in a tavern quarrel, Marlowe had established the verse form and set major dramatic precedents for English tragedy, heroic drama, and the history play.

In the two parts of *Tamburlaine,* written in 1587 after he left Cambridge, Marlowe turned a fourteenth-century Mongolian warrior whom he had read about in various historical sources into the dramatic archetype of the superhero, the aspiring man of lowly birth who, by force of will and mind and strength, seeks to dominate the entire world—indeed, the entire universe. Though Tamburlaine is undone by the single force he cannot overcome—human mortality—his boldness took the Elizabethan audience by storm, calling forth a whole rash of plays with blood-and-thunder supermen. Even more influential than the character of Tamburlaine was his thundering rhetoric, which Marlowe had self-consciously announced in the prologue to the play, inviting his audience to "hear the Scythian Tamburlaine / Threatening the world with high astounding terms." In his brief but polemic prologue, Marlowe deliberately set himself off from what he called the "jigging veins of rhyming mother wits." The poetry of Tamburlaine neither jigs nor rhymes: it roars, and it roars in blank verse, heightened by rhetorical figures, rhythmical patterns, mythological allusions, dramatically suspended sentences, and dazzling imagery, the likes of which had never been heard before on the Elizabethan stage. When Marlowe proved the potency of blank verse, and, in later plays, its flexibility, it quickly became the dominant medium of Elizabethan drama, used in comedies, tragedies, and histories alike.

In subsequent plays, Marlowe continued to be preoccupied with the theme of the aspiring man, a theme that expressed the intense conflict in his own time between the medieval heritage of a divinely ordered hierarchy in religion, government, and society, and the essentially modern world developing out of Protestantism,

Machiavellian political theory, and scientific inquiry, all of which opposed medieval authority with Renaissance individualism. In *The Jew of Malta* (ca. 1589), for example, Marlowe created an extraordinarily successful merchant, Barabas the Jew, who regards the wealth he has amassed and the power it brings him as the greatest treasures in the world. Barabas is not the only villain in *The Jew of Malta:* the Christian Knights of Malta exhibit the influence of Machiavellian morality as they lie and cheat and betray their promises. Marlowe's last major play, *Edward II* (ca. 1592), also features an "aspiring man," Young Mortimer, whose opposition to Edward II, England's rightful but incompetent ruler, begins as justifiable anger and ends with an incredibly brutal murder. In true "political" fashion, Mortimer orders that murder in an unpunctuated letter—which can be read either as ordering the King's death or as sparing his life—so that he will not receive any blame if the letter is ever found.

Marlowe ultimately created his most compelling image of the aspiring man in *Doctor Faustus,* which begins with Faustus rejecting Aristotle (philosophy), Galen (medicine), Justinian (law), and the Bible (theology) as subjects of study, choosing instead to turn to magic, since he imagines that it will bring him "a world of profit and delight, / Of power, of honor, of omnipotence." He sells his soul to the devil in return for twenty-four years of power, with Mephistophilis as his servant—and seems never to hear the warnings that recur throughout the play, both before and after he makes his bargain. Not only does he ignore clear statements such as Mephistophilis' passionate outcry, "Why this is hell, nor am I out of it" but he refuses to listen to the Good Angel, who, together with the Bad Angel, appears repeatedly, urging him to repent.

The presence of characters such as the Good Angel, the Bad Angel, the Old Man, and the Seven Deadly Sins explicitly link *Dr. Faustus* with the morality play tradition of the fifteenth century. Indeed, the subject of many of those plays, the *psychomachia,* or conflict between good and evil for the human being's soul, is one of the major themes of Marlowe's play. But Marlowe internalizes that struggle as well by having Faustus frequently consider the possibility of repentance and then reject it. Even in Faustus's final soliloquy, a speech that takes him and the audience through an hour of time in less than sixty lines, Faustus knows that only one drop of Christ's blood would save his soul, but he is afraid to ask for redemption and resorts instead to bargaining, asking God for a time limit to his damnation.

Marlowe's direct source for the play was a German narrative (published in Frankfurt in 1587) that blended the historical figure of a real Faustus with legends of a scholar who sold his soul to the devil; the English translation appeared in 1592, but if, as some scholars think, the play was written as early as 1588, Marlowe might have seen the translation in manuscript. As with so many details of Marlowe's writing career, the date of *Dr. Faustus* and even the makeup of the text remain open to question, since the play exists in two noticeably different versions: the A-text, published in 1604, and the B-text, which is more than a third longer, published in 1616. The shorter version, the A-text, is quite possibly a touring version of the play, since it lacks some of the scenes requiring complicated technical tricks, which might have been difficult to produce on the road. The longer version (used here) extends the antireligious tone as well as the comic scenes. In fact, the comic elements of the play, present in both texts, are closely connected with the problematic nature of magic and how one uses its power. Faustus seems to use his power not for the grand projects he aspires to early on in the play but for playful, even cheaply funny, conjuring tricks. Whether one reads that choice as indicative of Faustus's crude impulses and limited aspirations, or as suggesting that Mephistophilis may have tricked Faustus, the fact remains that, in the words of G. B. Shand, "his puffed-up imaginings become petty and laughable realizations."

Shand's comments following the play stem not only from his teaching of *Doctor Faustus* but his work in directing it at the University of Toronto in 1984. The staging choices for that production—a relatively bare stage, an all-male cast, and frequent doubling—look both forward and backward. When the Lord Admiral's Men staged *Doctor Faustus* repeatedly in 1594 (the earliest recorded performances), they too used the bare stage of the Elizabethan theater, and male actors doubled roles. Spectacular effects may have existed, since the property lists mention a dragon for *Faustus;* a later production in 1620 featured more elaborate effects, with thunder and lightning, plus devils running across the stage with firecrackers in their mouths. Contemporary professional and university productions have experimented with doubling, so much so that, as Shand's essay suggests, the staging convention becomes a thematic commentary. A 1987 production by the Actors Touring Company (Great Britain) used just three men and assorted props, such as a white-faced puppet for Helen of Troy, with a skull visible beneath the mask emphasizing Faustus's line, "Her lips suck forth my soul." Mephistophilis played all of the Seven Deadly Sins, establishing his control through the actor's mastery. Yet another college production, at the University of Waterloo in 1985, experimented with cross-gender casting, most notably by casting a female Mephistophilis, who thus embodied the attractiveness of evil. Shand's own production had its share of stage magic (see Figure 1) and spectacle (see Figure 2), but its center of attention was clearly the relationship between Faustus and Mephistophilis. When Faustus, moved by the warnings of the Old Man, seemed ready to repent, Mephistophilis had to threaten him physically (see Figure 3), and the intensity of that moment suggested how high the stakes were for both characters. Though Faustus may believe his own flippant remark to Mephistophilis, "I think hell's a fable," and fail to hear the sardonic reply, "Ay, think so still, till experience change thy mind" (Act 2, Scene 1, lines 125–26), the play's final moments display Faustus's tragic recognition that his soul will indeed live eternally—but in hell.

THE TRAGICAL HISTORY OF THE LIFE AND DEATH OF DOCTOR FAUSTUS

BY CHRISTOPHER MARLOWE / EDITED BY IRVING RIBNER

CHARACTERS

THE CHORUS
DOCTOR FAUSTUS
WAGNER, *his student and servant*
VALDES
CORNELIUS
THREE SCHOLARS
AN OLD MAN

POPE ADRIAN
RAYMOND, *King of Hungary*
BRUNO, *the rival Pope*
TWO CARDINALS
THE ARCHBISHOP OF RHEIMS
CHARLES V, *Emperor of Germany*
MARTINO }
FREDERICK } *Gentlemen of the Emperor's court*
BENVOLIO }
DUKE OF SAXONY
DUKE OF ANHOLT
DUCHESS OF ANHOLT
ROBIN, *the clown, a hostler*
DICK
A VINTNER
A HORSE-COURSER
A CARTER

HOSTESS
GOOD ANGEL
BAD ANGEL
LUCIFER
BEELZEBUB
MEPHISTOPHILIS
PRIDE }
COVETOUSNESS }
ENVY }
WRATH } *The Seven Deadly Sins*
GLUTTONY }
SLOTH }
LECHERY }
ALEXANDER, THE GREAT
HIS PARAMOUR
DARIUS, *King of Persia*
HELEN OF TROY
TWO CUPIDS
DEVILS, BISHOPS, MONKS, FRIARS, SOLDIERS

SCENE

Wittenberg, Rome, the Emperor's court at Innsbruck, court of the Duke of Anholt, and the neighboring countryside.

PROLOGUE

(Enter CHORUS.*)*

CHORUS: Not marching in the fields of Trasimene
Where Mars° did mate° the warlike Carthagens,°
Nor sporting in the dalliance of love
In courts of kings where state° is overturned,
5   Nor in the pomp of proud audacious deeds

Intends our muse to vaunt his heavenly verse.
Only this, gentles: we must now perform
The form of Faustus' fortunes, good or bad.
And now to patient judgments we appeal,
And speak for Faustus in his infancy.   10
Now is he born, of parents base of stock,
In Germany, within a town called Rhode.
At riper years to Wittenberg he went,
Whereas his kinsmen chiefly brought him up.
So much he profits in divinity,   15
The fruitful plot of scholarism graced,°
That shortly he was graced with doctor's name,

Note: Material in brackets has been added by the editor.
Trasimene . . . Carthagens, perhaps an allusion to a lost play about the Carthaginian, Hannibal, who achieved one of his greatest victories at Lake Trasimene in 217 B.C. ***Mars,*** Roman god of war.   ***mate,*** rival, meet in battle.   ***state,*** government.

---

fruitful plot . . . graced, adorned the university.

214

Excelling all whose sweet delight disputes°
In th'heavenly matters of theology,
20　Till swoll'n with cunning of a self-conceit,
His waxen wings did mount above his reach,
And melting,° heavens conspired his overthrow;
For, falling to a devilish exercise
And glutted now with learning's golden gifts,
25　He surfeits upon cursèd necromancy.
Nothing so sweet as magic is to him,
Which he prefers before his chiefest bliss;
And this the man that in his study sits.

ACT 1 / SCENE 1

(FAUSTUS *in his study.*)

FAUSTUS: Settle thy studies, Faustus, and begin
To sound the depth of that thou wilt profess.
Having commenced,° be a divine in show;
Yet level° at the end of every art,
5　And live and die in Aristotle's works.
Sweet Analytics, 'tis thou hast ravished me!
Bene disserere est finis logices.°
Is to dispute well logic's chiefest end?
Affords this art no greater miracle?
10　Then read no more; thou hast attained that end.
A greater subject fitteth Faustus' wit!
Bid *On cay mae on*° farewell; Galen° come.
Seeing *ubi desinit philosophus ibi incipit medicus,*°
Be a physician, Faustus; heap up gold,
15　And be eternized for some wondrous cure.
Summum bonum medicinae sanitas.°
The end of physic is our body's health.
Why, Faustus, hast thou not attained that end?
Is not thy common talk sound aphorisms?
20　Are not thy bills° hung up as monuments,
Whereby whole cities have escaped the plague,
And divers desperate maladies been cured?
Yet art thou still but Faustus and a man.
Couldst thou make men to live eternally,
25　Or, being dead, raise them to life again,
Then this profession were to be esteemed.

Physic, farewell! Where is Justinian?°
Si una eademque res legatus duobus, [*He reads.*]
Alter rem, alter valorem rei, etc.°
30　A petty case of paltry legacies!
Exhaereditare filium non potest pater nisi —°[*He reads.*]
Such is the subject of the Institute
And universal body of the law.
This study fits a mercenary drudge
35　Who aims at nothing but external trash,
Too servile and illiberal for me.
When all is done, divinity is best.
Jeromè's Bible,° Faustus, view it well:
Stipendium peccati mors est.° Ha! *Stipendium, etc.* [*He reads.*]
40　The reward of sin is death. That's hard.
Si pecasse negamus, fallimur [*He reads.*]
Et nulla est in nobis veritas.°
If we say that we have no sin,
We deceive ourselves, and there's no truth in us.
45　Why then belike we must sin,
And so consequently die.
Ay, we must die an everlasting death.
What doctrine call you this? *Che serà, serà:*
What will be, shall be! Divinity, adieu!
50　These metaphysics of magicians,
And necromantic books are heavenly.
Lines, circles, signs, letters, and characters—
Ay, these are those that Faustus most desires.
O, what a world of profit and delight,
55　Of power, of honor, of omnipotence
Is promised to the studious artisan!
All things that move between the quiet poles
Shall be at my command. Emperors and kings
Are but obeyed in their several provinces,
60　Nor can they raise the wind or rend the clouds,
But his dominion that exceeds in this
Stretcheth as far as doth the mind of man.
A sound magician is a demi-god.
Here try thy brains to get a deity!
Wagner!

(*Enter* WAGNER.)

　　　Commend me to my dearest friends,
65
The German Valdes and Cornelius;
Request them earnestly to visit me.

---

whose sweet delight disputes, who takes pleasure in disputing.　*waxen wings . . . melting,* metaphor referring to Icarus's
attempt to fly with waxen wings, which melted when he
ignored his father's warning and flew too near the sun.
commenced, taken a degree.　*level,* aim.　*Bene disserere est
finis logices,* The end of logic is to dispute well. A tenet of the
anti-Aristotelian system introduced at Cambridge when Marlowe was a student there.　*On cay mae on,* from Aristotle,
being or not being.　*Galen,* Greek physician regarded
throughout the Middle Ages as a medical authority.　*ubi
desinit philosophus ibi incipit medicus,* Where the philosopher
stops, the doctor begins.　*Summum . . . sanitas,* Health is the
highest good of the practice of medicine.　*bills,* medical prescriptions.

Justinian, Roman emperor of Constantinople (527–
565), responsible for assembling the Roman law and renowned throughout the Middle Ages as a jurist.　*Si . . . rei,
etc.,* If the same object is willed to two persons, let one have
the thing itself and the other its value, etc. This is an incorrect version of one of Justinian's rules.　*Exhaereditare . . .
nisi—,* The father cannot disinherit the son except—;
another of Justinian's rules roughly paraphrased.　*Jeromè's
Bible,* St. Jerome's Vulgate [Latin] translation of the Bible.
Stipendium . . . est, translated in line 40 (Rom. 6:23).　*Si . . .
veritas,* translated in lines 43–44 (I John 1:8).

WAGNER: I will sir. (*Exit.*)

FAUSTUS: Their conference will be a greater help to me

70 Than all my labors, plod I ne'er so fast.

(*Enter the* GOOD ANGEL *and the* BAD ANGEL.)

GOOD ANGEL: O, Faustus, lay that damned book aside,
And gaze not on it, lest it tempt thy soul
And heap God's heavy wrath upon thy head.
Read, read the Scriptures. That is blasphemy.

75 BAD ANGEL: Go forward, Faustus, in that famous art
Wherein all nature's treasury is contained.
Be thou on earth as Jove is in the sky,
Lord and commander of these elements.

(*Exeunt* ° ANGELS.)

FAUSTUS: How am I glutted with conceit° of this!

80 Shall I make spirits fetch me what I please,
Resolve me of ° all ambiguities,
Perform what desperate enterprise I will?
I'll have them fly to India for gold,
Ransack the ocean for orient pearl,

85 And search all corners of the new-found world
For pleasant fruits and princely delicates.
I'll have them read me strange philosophy
And tell the secrets of all foreign kings;
I'll have them wall all Germany with brass

90 And make swift Rhine circle fair Wittenberg.°
I'll have them fill the public schools with silk
Wherewith the students shall be bravely clad.
I'll levy soldiers with the coin they bring
And chase the Prince of Parma from our land

95 And reign sole king of all the provinces.°
Yea, stranger engines for the brunt of war
Than was the fiery keel at Antwerp's bridge°
I'll make my servile spirits to invent.
Come, German Valdes and Cornelius. [*He calls
within.*]

100 And make me blessed with your sage conference!

(*Enter* VALDES *and* CORNELIUS.)

Valdes, sweet Valdes, and Cornelius,
Know that your words have won me at the last
To practice magic and concealed arts;
Yet not your words only, but mine own fantasy

105 That will receive no object, for my head
But ruminates on necromantic skill.
Philosophy is odious and obscure;
Both law and physic are for petty wits;

Divinity is basest of the three,
Unpleasant, harsh, contemptible and vile. 110
'Tis, magic, magic, that hath ravished me.
Then, gentle friends, aid me in this attempt,
And I, that have with subtle syllogisms
Gravelled° the pastors of the German church,
And made the flowering pride of Wittenberg 115
Swarm to my problems° as th'infernal spirits
On sweet Musaeus° when he came to hell,
Will be as cunning as Agrippa was,
Whose shadows° made all Europe honor him.

VALDES: Faustus, these books, thy wit, and our
experience 120
Shall make all nations to canonize us.
As Indian Moors° obey their Spanish lords,
So shall the spirits of every element
Be always serviceable to us three.
Like lions shall they guard us when we please, 125
Like Almain rutters° with their horsemen's staves
Or Lapland giants trotting by our sides,
Sometimes like women or unwedded maids,
Shadowing° more beauty in their airy brows
Than in the white breasts of the queen of love. 130
From Venice shall they drag huge argosies,
And from America the golden fleece
That yearly stuffs old Philip's treasury,
If learnèd Faustus will be resolute.

FAUSTUS: Valdes, as resolute am I in this 135
As thou to live; therefore object it not.

CORNELIUS: The miracles that magic will perform
Will make thee vow to study nothing else.
He that is grounded in astrology,
Enriched with tongues,° well seen in minerals, 140
Hath all the principles magic doth require.
Then doubt not, Faustus, but to be renowned
And more frequented for this mystery
Than heretofore the Delphian oracle.°
The spirits tell me they can dry the sea 145
And fetch the treasure of all foreign wracks,
Yea, all the wealth that our forefathers hid
Within the messy entrails of the earth.
Then tell me, Faustus, what shall we three want?

FAUSTUS: Nothing, Cornelius. O, this cheers my soul! 150
Come, show me some demonstrations magical,

Exeunt, Latin for "they go out" (plural of "exit"). *conceit,* the conception of attaining. *Resolve me of,* Explain to me. *Rhine . . . Wittenberg,* Wittenberg is actually on the Elbe River, not the Rhine. *provinces,* The Netherlands. *fiery . . . bridge,* In April 1584 the Dutch used a fireship to destroy a bridge built across a river by the Prince of Parma in an attempt to blockade Antwerp.

Gravelled, puzzled and amazed. *problems,* public disputations. *Musaeus,* a semimythical Greek poet. Following Virgil, Marlowe has him visit hell like the mythical Orpheus. *Agrippa . . . shadows,* Cornelius Agrippa (1486?–1535), a German physician and student of the occult, was said to have power to raise spirits (shadows) from the dead. *Indian Moors,* American Indians. *Almain rutters,* German cavalry. *Shadowing,* harboring, sheltering. *Enriched with tongues,* fluent in Latin, the language used for communicating with spirits. *Delphian oracle,* the high priest of Apollo at Delphi who had power to foretell the future.

That I may conjure in some lusty grove
And have these joys in full possession.

55 VALDES: Then haste thee to some solitary grove,
And bear wise Bacon's and Abanus' works,°
The Hebrew Psalter, and New Testament;
And whatsoever else is requisite
We will inform thee ere our conference cease.

CORNELIUS: Valdes, first let him know the words of
art,

60 And then, all other ceremonies learned,
Faustus may try his cunning by himself.

VALDES: First I'll instruct thee in the rudiments,
And then wilt thou be perfecter than I.

FAUSTUS: Then come and dine with me, and after
meat

65 We'll canvass every quiddity° thereof,
For ere I sleep I'll try what I can do.
This night I'll conjure, though I die therefore.

(Exeunt.)

ACT 1 / SCENE 2

(Enter two SCHOLARS.*)*

FIRST SCHOLAR: I wonder what's become of Faustus,
that was wont to make our schools ring with *sic
probo.*°

(Enter WAGNER.*)*

5 SECOND SCHOLAR: That shall we presently know; here
comes his boy.

FIRST SCHOLAR: How now sirrah! Where's thy master?

WAGNER: God in heaven knows.

SECOND SCHOLAR: Why, dost not thou know then?

WAGNER: Yes, I know, but that follows not.

10 FIRST SCHOLAR: Go to, sirrah! Leave your jesting and
tell us where he is.

WAGNER: That follows not by force of argument, which
you, being licentiates,° should stand upon; therefore acknowledge your error and be attentive.

15 SECOND SCHOLAR: Then you will not tell us?

WAGNER: You are deceived, for I will tell you. Yet if you
were not dunces, you would never ask me such a
question. For is he not *corpus naturale,* and is not
that *mobile?*° Then wherefore should you ask such

20 a question? But that I am by nature phlegmatic,
slow to wrath, and prone to lechery—to love, I
would say—it were not for you to come within forty

Bacon's . . . works, Roger Bacon (1214?–1294) and
Abanus (properly, Pietro D'Abano, 1250–1316) were famous
in the Middle Ages for their feats of magic. **quiddity,** essential element (a term from scholastic logic). **sic probo,** thus I
prove (used in scholastic argument). **licentiates,** holders of
university degrees. **corpus naturale . . . mobile,** the subject
matter of physics, in scholastic terms, was *corpus naturale seu
mobile* (natural body in motion).

---

foot of the place of execution, although I do not
doubt but to see you both hanged the next sessions. Thus having triumphed over you, I will set 25
my countenance like a precisian° and begin to
speak thus: Truly, my dear brethren, my master is
within at dinner with Valdes and Cornelius, as this
wine, if it could speak, would inform your wor-
ships. And so, the Lord bless you, preserve you, 30
and keep you, my dear brethren.

(Exit.)

FIRST SCHOLAR: O Faustus, then I fear that which I
have long suspected.
That thou art fall'n into that damnèd art
For which they two are infamous through the
world.

SECOND SCHOLAR: Were he a stranger, not allied to me, 35
The danger of his soul would make me mourn.
But come, let us go and inform the rector.°
It may be his grave counsel may reclaim him.

FIRST SCHOLAR: I fear me nothing will reclaim him
now.

SECOND SCHOLAR: Yet let us see what we can do. 40

(Exeunt.)

ACT 1 / SCENE 3

(Thunder. Enter [above] LUCIFER *and four* DEVILS.
Enter FAUSTUS *to conjure.)*

FAUSTUS: Now that the gloomy shadow of the night,
Longing to view Orion's drizzling look,
Leaps from th'Antarctic world unto the sky
And dims the welkin° with her pitchy breath,
Faustus begin thine incantations, 5
And try if devils will obey thy hest,
Seeing thou hast prayed and sacrificed to them.
Within this circle is Jehovah's name,
Forward and backward anagrammatized,
Th'abbreviated names of holy saints, 10
Figures of every adjunct to the heavens,
And characters of signs and erring° stars,
By which the spirits are enforced to rise.
Then fear not, Faustus, to be resolute,
And try the utmost magic can perform. 15

(Thunder.)

*Sint mihi Dei Acherontis propitii! Valeat numen triplex
Jehovae. Ignei, aerii, aquatani spiritus, salvete! Orientis
princeps, Beelzebub, inferni ardentis monarcha, et Demogorgon, propitiamus vos, ut appareat et surgat Mephistophilis. Quid tu moraris? Per Jehovam Gehennam, et* 20

---

precisian, Puritan. **rector,** head of the university.
welkin, sky. **erring,** wandering.

consecratam aquam quam nunc spargo, signumque
crucis quod nunc facio, et per vota nostra, ipse nunc
surgat nobis dicatus Mephistophilis.°

(Enter [MEPHISTOPHILIS,] *a* DEVIL.)

I charge thee to return and change thy shape;
25 Thou art too ugly to attend on me.
Go, and return an old Franciscan friar;
That holy shape becomes a devil best.

(Exit DEVIL.*)*

I see there's virtue in my heavenly words.
Who would not be proficient in this art?
30 How pliant is this Mephistophilis,
Full of obedience and humility.
Such is the force of magic and my spells.
Now Faustus, thou art conjurer laureate,
That canst command great Mephistophilis.
35 *Quin redis Mephistophilis fratris imagine.*°

(Enter MEPHISTOPHILIS [*dressed like a Franciscan*
friar].)

MEPHISTOPHILIS: Now Faustus, what wouldst thou
    have me do?
FAUSTUS: I charge thee wait upon me whilst I live,
    To do whatever Faustus shall command,
    Be it to make the moon drop from her sphere
40 Or the ocean to overwhelm the world.
MEPHISTOPHILIS: I am a servant to great Lucifer
    And may not follow thee without his leave.
    No more than he commands must we perform.
FAUSTUS: Did not he charge thee to appear to me?
MEPHISTOPHILIS: No, I came hither of mine own
45   accord.
FAUSTUS: Did not my conjuring speeches raise thee?
    Speak.
MEPHISTOPHILIS: That was the cause, but yet *per*
    accidens,°
    For when we hear one rack the name of God,
    Abjure the Scriptures and his Savior Christ,
50 We fly in hope to get his glorious soul;
    Nor will we come unless he use such means
    Whereby he is in danger to be damned.
    Therefore the shortest cut for conjuring

Is stoutly to abjure the Trinity
And pray devoutly to the prince of hell.   55
FAUSTUS: So Faustus hath
    Already done, and holds this principle:
    There is no chief but only Beelzebub,
    To whom Faustus doth dedicate himself.
    This word "damnation" terrifies not me,   60
    For I confound hell in Elysium.
    My ghost° be with the old philosophers!
    But leaving these vain trifles of men's souls,
    Tell me what is that Lucifer thy lord?
MEPHISTOPHILIS: Arch-regent and commander of all
    spirits.   65
FAUSTUS: Was not that Lucifer an angel once?
MEPHISTOPHILIS: Yes Faustus, and most dearly loved
    of God.
FAUSTUS: How comes it then that he is prince of
    devils?
MEPHISTOPHILIS: O, by aspiring pride and insolence,
    For which God threw him from the face of heaven.   70
FAUSTUS: And what are you that live with Lucifer?
MEPHISTOPHILIS: Unhappy spirits that fell with
    Lucifer,
    Conspired against our God with Lucifer,
    And are for ever damned with Lucifer.
FAUSTUS: Where are you damned?
MEPHISTOPHILIS: In hell.   75
FAUSTUS: How comes it then that thou art out of hell?
MEPHISTOPHILIS: Why this is hell, nor am I out of it.
    Think'st thou that I who saw the face of God
    And tasted the eternal joys of heaven
    Am not tormented with ten thousand hells   80
    In being deprived of everlasting bliss?
    O Faustus, leave these frivolous demands
    Which strike a terror to my fainting soul.
FAUSTUS: What, is great Mephistophilis so passionate
    For being deprivèd of the joys of heaven?   85
    Learn thou of Faustus' manly fortitude,
    And scorn those joys thou never shalt possess.
    Go bear these tidings to great Lucifer:
    Seeing Faustus hath incurred eternal death
    By desperate thoughts against Jove's deity,   90
    Say he surrenders up to him his soul,
    So he will spare him four and twenty years,
    Letting him live in all voluptuousness,
    Having thee ever to attend on me,
    To give me whatsoever I shall ask,   95
    To tell me whatsoever I demand,
    To slay mine enemies, and aid my friends,
    And always be obedient to my will.
    Go, and return to mighty Lucifer,
    And meet me in my study at midnight,   100
    And then resolve me of thy master's mind.
MEPHISTOPHILIS: I will, Faustus.

(Exit.)

Sint . . . Mephistophilis, May the gods of Acheron be propitious to me. Let the triple name of Jehova [the Trinity] be
gone. Hail spirits of fire, air, and water. Prince of the East,
Beelzebub, monarch of burning hell, and Demogorgon, we
petition you that Mephistophilis may appear and rise. Why
do you linger? By Jehova, Gehenna and the holy water which
I now sprinkle and the sign of the cross which I now make
and by our vows, let Mephistophilis himself now rise to serve
us. *Quin . . . imagine,* Return, Mephistophilis, in the shape
of a friar. *cause . . . per accidens,* The terms are from scholastic logic.

ghost, spirit.

FAUSTUS: Had I as many souls as there be stars,
 I'd give them all for Mephistophilis.
105 By him I'll be great emperor of the world,
 And make a bridge thorough the moving air,
 To pass the ocean with a band of men.
 I'll join the hills that bind° the Afric shore,
 And make that country continent to Spain,
110 And both contributory to my crown.
 The Emperor shall not live but by my leave,
 Nor any potentate of Germany.
 Now that I have obtained what I desire,
 I'll live in speculation of this art
115 Till Mephistophilis return again.

 (*Exit.*)

ACT 1 / SCENE 4

(Enter WAGNER *and* [ROBIN,] *the* CLOWN.*)*

WAGNER: Come hither, sirrah boy.
ROBIN: Boy! O disgrace to my person. Zounds, boy in
 your face! You have seen many boys with such
 pickedevants,° I am sure.
5 WAGNER: Sirrah, hast thou no comings in?°
ROBIN: Yes, and goings out too, you may see, sir.
WAGNER: Alas, poor slave! See how poverty jests in his
 nakedness. I know the villain's out of service, and
 so hungry that I know he would give his soul to
10 the devil for a shoulder of mutton, though it were
 blood-raw.
ROBIN: Not so neither. I had need to have it well
 roasted, and good sauce to it, if I pay so dear, I
 can tell you.
15 WAGNER: Sirrah, wilt thou be my man and wait on me,
 and I will make thee go like *Qui mihi discipulus*?°
ROBIN: What, in verse?
WAGNER: No slave; in beaten° silk and staves-acre.°
ROBIN: Staves-acre? That's good to kill vermin. Then,
20 belike, if I serve you I shall be lousy.
WAGNER: Why, so thou shalt be, whether thou dost it
 or no; for, sirrah, if thou dost not presently bind
 thyself to me for seven years, I'll turn all the lice
 about thee into familiars° and make them tear
25 thee in pieces.
ROBIN: Nay sir, you may save yourself a labor, for they
 are as familiar with me as if they paid for their
 meat and drink, I can tell you.
WAGNER: Well, sirrah, leave your jesting and take
30 these guilders.
ROBIN: Yes, marry sir, and I thank you too.
WAGNER: So, now thou art to be at an hour's warning,

---

bind, enclose. *pickedevants,* pointed beards. *comings in,* earnings. *Qui mihi discipulus,* who is my disciple (the opening words of a Latin poem by William Lyly, well known to Elizabethan schoolboys). *beaten,* embroidered with metal. *staves-acre,* a plant used for killing vermin. *familiars,* attendant evil spirits.

whensoever and wheresoever the devil shall fetch
 thee.
ROBIN: Here, take your guilders, again. I'll none of 'em. 35
WAGNER: Not I. Thou art pressed.° Prepare thyself,
 for I will presently raise up two devils to carry thee
 away. Banio! Belcher!
ROBIN: Belcher? And Belcher come here, I'll belch
 him. I am not afraid of a devil. 40

 (*Enter two* DEVILS.*)*

WAGNER: How now, sir? Will you serve me now?
ROBIN: Ay, good Wagner; take away the devil then.
WAGNER: Spirits away! Now, sirrah, follow me.

 [*Exeunt* DEVILS.]

ROBIN: I will sir. But hark you, master, will you teach
 me this conjuring occupation? 45
WAGNER: Ay, sirrah. I'll teach thee to turn thyself to a
 dog, or a cat, or a mouse, or a rat, or any thing.
ROBIN: A dog, or a cat, or a mouse, or a rat! O brave
 Wagner!
WAGNER: Villain, call me Master Wagner, and see that 50
 you walk attentively, and let your right eye be
 always diametrally° fixed upon my left heel, that
 thou may'st *quasi vestigias nostras insistere.*°
ROBIN: Well, sir, I warrant you.

 (*Exeunt.*)

ACT 2 / SCENE 1

(Enter FAUSTUS *in his study.)*

FAUSTUS: Now Faustus must thou needs be damned,
 And canst thou not be saved.
 What boots° it then to think on God or heaven?
 Away with such vain fancies, and despair;
 Despair in God, and trust in Beelzebub. 5
 Now go not backward; Faustus, be resolute.
 Why waver'st thou? O, something soundeth in
  mine ear:
 "Abjure this magic; turn to God again."
 Ay, and Faustus will turn to God again!
 To God? He loves thee not. 10
 The God thou serv'st is thine own appetite,
 Wherein is fixed the love of Beelzebub.
 To him I'll build an altar and a church,
 And offer lukewarm blood of new-born babes.

 (*Enter the two* ANGELS.*)*

BAD ANGEL: Go forward, Faustus, in that famous art. 15
GOOD ANGEL: Sweet Faustus, leave that execrable art.
FAUSTUS: Contrition, prayer, repentance—what of
 these?

---

pressed, enlisted into service in exchange for money. *diametrally,* in a straight line. *quasi . . . insistere,* as if to walk in our tracks. *boots,* avails.

GOOD ANGEL: O, they are means to bring thee unto
    heaven.
BAD ANGEL: Rather illusions, fruits of lunacy,
20   That make men foolish that do use them most.
GOOD ANGEL: Sweet Faustus, think of heaven and
    heavenly things.
BAD ANGEL: No Faustus; think of honor and wealth.

(Exeunt ANGELS.*)*

FAUSTUS: Wealth? Why, the signory of Emden° shall
    be mine.
    When Mephistophilis shall stand by me,
25   What power can hurt me? Faustus thou art safe.
    Cast no more doubts. Mephistophilis, come
    And bring glad tidings from great Lucifer.
    Is't not midnight? Come, Mephistophilis.
    Veni, veni, Mephistophile.°

(Enter MEPHISTOPHILIS.*)*

30   Now tell me what saith Lucifer, thy lord?
MEPHISTOPHILIS: That I shall wait on Faustus whilst
    he lives,
    So he will buy my service with his soul.
FAUSTUS: Already Faustus hath hazarded that for
    thee.
MEPHISTOPHILIS: But now thou must bequeath it
    solemnly
35   And write a deed of gift with thine own blood,
    For that security craves great Lucifer.
    If thou deny it, I must back to hell.
FAUSTUS: Stay, Mephistophilis! Tell me what good
    Will my soul do thy lord.
MEPHISTOPHILIS: Enlarge his kingdom.
40 FAUSTUS: Is that the reason why he tempts us thus?
MEPHISTOPHILIS: *Solamen miseris socios habuisse doloris.*°
FAUSTUS: Why, have you any pain that torture others?
MEPHISTOPHILIS: As great as have the human souls
    of men.
    But tell me, Faustus, shall I have thy soul?
45   And I will be thy slave and wait on thee
    And give thee more than thou hast wit to ask.
FAUSTUS: Ay, Mephistophilis, I'll give it him.
MEPHISTOPHILIS: Then Faustus, stab thy arm
    courageously,
    And bind thy soul that at some certain day
50   Great Lucifer may claim it as his own,
    And then be thou as great as Lucifer.
FAUSTUS: [*stabbing his arm*] Lo, Mephistophilis, for
    love of thee,
    I cut mine arm, and with my proper° blood
    Assure my soul to be great Lucifer's,
55   Chief lord and regent of perpetual night.

Emden, the chief city of East Friesland, near the mouth
of the river Ems, which had considerable trade relations
with Elizabethan England. *Veni, veni . . .* Come, come,
Mephistophilis. *Solamen . . . doloris,* It is a consolation in
misery to have a fellow sufferer. *proper,* own.

View here this blood that trickles from mine arm,
And let it be propitious for my wish.
MEPHISTOPHILIS: But Faustus,
    Write it in manner of a deed of gift.
FAUSTUS: Ay, so I do. [*He writes.*] But Mephistophilis, 60
    My blood congeals, and I can write no more.
MEPHISTOPHILIS: I'll fetch thee fire to dissolve it
    straight.

(Exit.)

FAUSTUS: What might the staying of my blood
    portend?
    Is it unwilling I should write this bill?
    Why streams it not that I may write afresh? 65
    "Faustus gives to thee his soul." Ah, there it stayed.
    Why shouldst thou not? Is not thy soul thine own?
    Then write again: "Faustus gives to thee his soul."

(Enter MEPHISTOPHILIS *with the chafer of fire.)*

MEPHISTOPHILIS: See Faustus, here is fire. Set it on.°
FAUSTUS: So. Now the blood begins to clear again. 70
    Now will I make an end immediately. [*He writes.*]
MEPHISTOPHILIS: [*Aside.*] What will not I do to
    obtain his soul?
FAUSTUS: *Consummatum est;*° this bill is ended,
    And Faustus hath bequeathed his soul to Lucifer.
    But what is this inscription on mine arm? 75
    Homo fuge!° Whither should I fly?
    If unto God, he'll throw me down to hell.
    My senses are deceived; here's nothing writ.
    O yes, I see it plain. Even here is writ
    Homo fuge! Yet shall not Faustus fly. 80
MEPHISTOPHILIS: [*Aside.*] I'll fetch him somewhat to
    delight his mind.

(Exit.)

(Enter DEVILS, *giving crowns and rich apparel to* FAUS-
TUS. *They dance and then depart. Enter* MEPHISTOPH-
ILIS.*)*

FAUSTUS: What means this show? Speak
    Mephistophilis.
MEPHISTOPHILIS: Nothing, Faustus, but to delight thy
    mind
    And let thee see what magic can perform.
FAUSTUS: But may I raise such spirits when I please? 85
MEPHISTOPHILIS: Ay Faustus, and do greater things
    than these.
FAUSTUS: Then, Mephistophilis, receive this scroll,
    A deed of gift of body and of soul,
    But yet conditionally that thou perform
    All covenants and articles between us both. 90

Set it on, Set the dish of blood on the fire. *Consummatum est,* It is completed (the words of Jesus at his Crucifixion;
John 19:30). *Homo fuge,* Fly, man.

MEPHISTOPHILIS: Faustus, I swear by hell and Lucifer
    To effect all promises between us made.
FAUSTUS: Then hear me read it Mephistophilis.

On these conditions following:
95   *First, that Faustus may be a spirit in form and substance;*
   Secondly, that Mephistophilis shall be his servant and be at his
    command;
   Thirdly, that Mephistophilis shall do for him and bring him
    whatsoever;
100 *Fourthly, that he shall be in his chamber or house invisible;*
   Lastly, that he shall appear to the said John Faustus at all
   times, in what form or shape soever he please: I, John Faustus,
   of Wittenberg, doctor, by these presents, do give both body and
   soul to Lucifer, Prince of the East, and his minister, Mephis-
105 *tophilis; and furthermore grant unto them that four and*
   twenty years being expired, the articles above written inviolate,
   full power to fetch or carry the said John Faustus, body and
   soul, flesh, blood, or goods, into their habitation wheresoever.
                     By me, John Faustus.

MEPHISTOPHILIS: Speak Faustus. Do you deliver this
110   as your deed?
FAUSTUS: Ay, take it, and the devil give thee good of
    it.
MEPHISTOPHILIS: So now, Faustus, ask me what thou
    wilt.
FAUSTUS: First will I question with thee about hell.
    Tell me, where is the place that men call hell?
115 MEPHISTOPHILIS: Under the heavens.
FAUSTUS: Ay, so are all things else. But whereabouts?
MEPHISTOPHILIS: Within the bowels of these
    elements,
    Where we are tortured and remain for ever.
    Hell hath no limits, nor is circumscribed
120   In one self place, but where we are is hell,
    And where hell is, there must we ever be.
    And, to be short, when all the world dissolves
    And every creature shall be purified,
    All places shall be hell that is not heaven.
125 FAUSTUS: I think hell's a fable.
MEPHISTOPHILIS: Ay, think so still, till experience
    change thy mind.
FAUSTUS: Why, dost thou think that Faustus shall be
    damned?
MEPHISTOPHILIS: Ay, of necessity, for here's the scroll
    In which thou hast given thy soul to Lucifer.
130 FAUSTUS: Ay, and body too. But what of that?
    Think'st thou that Faustus is so fond° to imagine
    That after this life there is any pain?
    No, these are trifles and mere old wives' tales.
MEPHISTOPHILIS: But I am an instance to prove the
    contrary,

For I tell thee I am damned and now in hell.   135
FAUSTUS: Nay, and this be hell, I'll willingly be
    damned.
    What? Sleeping, eating, walking and disputing?
    But, leaving off this, let me have a wife,
    The fairest maid in Germany,
    For I am wanton and lascivious,   140
    And cannot live without a wife.
MEPHISTOPHILIS: I prithee, Faustus, talk not of a
    wife.
FAUSTUS: Nay, sweet Mephistophilis, fetch me one,
    for I will have one.
MEPHISTOPHILIS: Well, Faustus, thou shalt have a wife.
    Sit there till I come.   145

(Enter [MEPHISTOPHILIS] *with a* DEVIL *dressed like a
woman, with fireworks.)*

FAUSTUS: What sight is this?
MEPHISTOPHILIS: Now Faustus, how dost thou like
    thy wife?
FAUSTUS: Here's a hot whore indeed! No, I'll no wife.
MEPHISTOPHILIS: Marriage is but a ceremonial toy,
    And if thou lovest me, think no more of it.   150
    I'll cull thee out the fairest courtesans
    And bring them every morning to thy bed.
    She whom thine eye shall like, thy heart shall have,
    Were she as chaste as was Penelope,°
    As wise as Saba,° or as beautiful   155
    As was bright Lucifer before his fall.
    Hold; take this book; peruse it thoroughly.
    The iterating of these lines brings gold;
    The framing of this circle on the ground
    Brings thunder, whirlwinds, storm and lightning.   160
    Pronounce this thrice devoutly to thyself,
    And men in harness° shall appear to thee,
    Ready to execute what thou command'st.
FAUSTUS: Thanks, Mephistophilis, for this sweet
    book.
    This will I keep as chary as my life.   165

(Exeunt.)

ACT 2 / SCENE 2

(Enter FAUSTUS *in his study and* MEPHISTOPHILIS.*)*

FAUSTUS: When I behold the heavens, then I repent
    And curse thee, wicked Mephistophilis,
    Because thou hast deprived me of those joys.
MEPHISTOPHILIS: 'Twas thine own seeking, Faustus;
    thank thyself.
    But think'st thou heaven is such a glorious thing?   5
    I tell thee, Faustus, 'tis not half so fair
    As thou, or any man that breathes on earth.
FAUSTUS: How prov'st thou that?

---

fond, foolish.

Penelope, the faithful wife of Ulysses in Homer's *Odyssey.*
Saba, the Queen of Sheba.   *harness,* armor.

MEPHISTOPHILIS: 'Twas made for man; then he's more excellent.

FAUSTUS: If heaven was made for man, 'twas made for me.   10
I will renounce this magic and repent.

(Enter the two ANGELS.)

GOOD ANGEL: Faustus repent; yet God will pity thee.

BAD ANGEL: Thou art a spirit;° God cannot pity thee.

FAUSTUS: Who buzzeth in mine ears I am a spirit?   15
Be I a devil, yet God may pity me;
Yea, God will pity me if I repent.

BAD ANGEL: Ay, but Faustus never shall repent.

(Exeunt ANGELS.)

FAUSTUS: My heart is hardened; I cannot repent.
Scarce can I name salvation, faith, or heaven,
But fearful echoes thunder in mine ears: 20
"Faustus, thou art damned!" Then swords and knives,
Poison, guns, halters, and envenomed steel
Are laid before me to dispatch myself;
And long ere this I should have done the deed,
Had not sweet pleasure conquered deep despair.   25
Have not I made blind Homer sing to me
Of Alexander's love and Oenone's death?°
And hath not he, that built the walls of Thebes
With ravishing sound of his melodious harp,°
Made music with my Mephistophilis?   30
Why should I die then, or basely despair?
I am resolved; Faustus shall not repent.
Come, Mephistophilis, let us dispute again
And reason of divine astrology.
Speak; are there many spheres above the moon?   35
Are all celestial bodies but one globe,
As is the substance of this centric earth?

MEPHISTOPHILIS: As are the elements, such are the heavens,
Even from the moon unto the empyreal orb,
Mutually folded in each others' spheres,   40
And jointly move upon one axle-tree.
Whose terminè° is termed the world's wide pole;
Nor are the names of Saturn, Mars, or Jupiter
Feigned, but are erring stars.°

FAUSTUS: But have they all
One motion, both *situ et tempore?*°   45

MEPHISTOPHILIS: All move from east to west in four and twenty hours upon the poles of the world, but differ in their motions upon the poles of the zodiac.

FAUSTUS: These slender questions Wagner can decide.
Hath Mephistophilis no greater skill?   50
Who knows not the double motion of the planets?
That the first is finished in a natural day?
The second thus? Saturn in thirty years?
Jupiter in twelve; Mars in four; the sun, Venus and Mercury in a year; the moon in twenty eight days   55
These are freshmen's suppositions. But tell me, hath every sphere a dominion or *intelligentia?*°

MEPHISTOPHILIS: Ay.

FAUSTUS: How many heavens or spheres are there?

MEPHISTOPHILIS: Nine—the seven planets, the firmament, and the empyreal heaven.   60

FAUSTUS: But is there not *coelum igneum, et crystallinum?*°

MEPHISTOPHILIS: No, Faustus, they be but fables.

FAUSTUS: Resolve me then in this one question: why are not conjunctions,° oppositions,° aspects,°   65
eclipses° all at one time, but in some years we have more, in some less?

MEPHISTOPHILIS: *Per inaequalem motum respectu totius.*°

FAUSTUS: Well, I am answered. Now tell me who made the world.   70

MEPHISTOPHILIS: I will not.

FAUSTUS: Sweet Mephistophilis, tell me.

MEPHISTOPHILIS: Move me not, Faustus.

FAUSTUS: Villain, have not I bound thee to tell me any thing?

MEPHISTOPHILIS: Ay, that is not against our kingdom.   75
This is. Thou art damned. Think thou of hell.

FAUSTUS: Think, Faustus, upon God that made the world.

MEPHISTOPHILIS: Remember this.

(Exit.)

FAUSTUS: Ay, go accursèd spirit to ugly hell.
'Tis thou hast damned distressèd Faustus' soul.   80
Is't not too late?

(Enter the two ANGELS.)

BAD ANGEL: Too late.

GOOD ANGEL: Never too late, if Faustus will repent.

BAD ANGEL: If thou repent, devils will tear thee in pieces.

GOOD ANGEL: Repent, and they shall never raze thy skin.   85

(Exeunt ANGELS.)

FAUSTUS: O Christ, my Savior, my Savior,
Help to save distressèd Faustus' soul.

---

spirit, devil. ***Alexander's . . . death,*** Paris (also called Alexander) loved the nymph Oenone when he lived as a shepherd on Mt. Ida. Oenone died of a broken heart when he left her. ***he . . . harp,*** Amphion, son of Zeus and Antiope, caused stones to move and the walls of Thebes to be built simply by playing on the lyre given to him by Hermes. ***terminè,*** limit. ***erring stars,*** planets. ***situ et tempore,*** in position (direction of movement) and in the time they take to revolve about the earth.

dominion or intelligentia, governing angel. ***coelum . . . crystallinum,*** the fiery heaven and crystalline sphere of Ptolemaic astronomy. ***conjunctions,*** seeming proximities of heavenly bodies. ***oppositions,*** divergences of heavenly bodies. ***aspects,*** any other relations of such bodies to one another. ***eclipses,*** the blottings out of one heavenly body by another. ***Per . . . totius,*** by their unequal movements in respect to the whole (i.e., the different speeds of the various planets within the total cosmos).

(Enter LUCIFER, BEELZEBUB, *and* MEPHISTOPHILIS.*)*

LUCIFER: Christ cannot save thy soul, for he is just.
   There's none but I have interest in the same.
90 FAUSTUS: O, what art thou that look'st so terribly?
LUCIFER: I am Lucifer,
   And this is my companion prince in hell.
FAUSTUS: O, Faustus, they are come to fetch thy soul.
BEELZEBUB: We are come to tell thee thou dost
   injure us.
LUCIFER: Thou call'st on Christ, contrary to thy
95   promise.
BEELZEBUB: Thou shouldst not think on God.
LUCIFER: Think on the devil.
BEELZEBUB: And his dam too.
FAUSTUS: Nor will I henceforth. Pardon me in this,
100   And Faustus vows never to look to heaven,
   Never to name God, or to pray to him,
   To burn his Scriptures, slay his ministers,
   And make my spirits pull his churches down.
LUCIFER: So shalt thou show thyself an obedient
     servant,
105   And we will highly gratify thee for it.
BEELZEBUB: Faustus, we are come from hell in person
   to show thee some pastime. Sit down, and thou
   shalt behold the Seven Deadly Sins appear to thee
   in their own proper shapes and likeness.
110 FAUSTUS: That sight will be as pleasant to me as Paradise was to Adam the first day of his creation.
LUCIFER: Talk not of Paradise or creation, but mark
   the show. Go, Mephistophilis, fetch them in.

[*Exit* MEPHISTOPHILIS.]

(Enter the SEVEN DEADLY SINS [*with* MEPHISTOPHILIS,
led by a PIPER].*)*

BEELZEBUB: Now Faustus, question them of their names
115   and dispositions.
FAUSTUS: That shall I soon. What art thou, the first?
PRIDE: I am Pride. I disdain to have any parents. I am
   like to Ovid's flea:° I can creep into every corner
   of a wench. Sometimes, like a periwig, I sit upon
120   her brow. Next, like a necklace, I hang about her
   neck. Then, like a fan of feathers, I kiss her lips,
   and then, turning myself to a wrought smock, do
   what I list. But fie, what a smell is here! I'll not
   speak another word unless the ground be per-
125   fumed and covered with cloth of Arras.°
FAUSTUS: Thou art a proud knave indeed. What art
   thou, the second?
COVETOUSNESS: I am Covetousness, begotten of an old
   churl in a leather bag, and might I now obtain my
130   wish, this house, you and all, should turn to gold,
   that I might lock you safe into my chest. O my
   sweet gold!
FAUSTUS: And what art thou, the third?
ENVY: I am Envy, begotten of a chimney-sweeper and
   an oyster-wife. I cannot read and therefore wish   135
   all books burned. I am lean with seeing others
   eat. O, that there would come a famine over all
   the world, that all might die, and I live alone;
   then thou shouldst see how fat I'd be. But must
   thou sit and I stand? Come down, with a ven-   140
   geance.
FAUSTUS: Out envious wretch! But what are thou, the
   fourth?
WRATH: I am Wrath. I had neither father nor mother.
   I leaped out of a lion's mouth when I was scarce   145
   an hour old, and ever since have run up and
   down the world with this case of rapiers, wounding myself when I could get none to fight withal. I
   was born in hell, and look to it, for some of you
   shall be my father.   150
FAUSTUS: And what are you, the fifth?
GLUTTONY: I am Gluttony. My parents are all dead,
   and the devil a penny they have left me but a
   small pension, and that buys me thirty meals a day
   and ten bevers°—a small trifle to suffice nature. I   155
   come of a royal pedigree. My father was a gam-
   mon of bacon, and my mother was a hogshead
   of claret wine. My godfathers were these: Peter
   Pickled-herring and Martin Martlemas-beef.° But
   my godmother, O, she was a jolly gentlewoman,   160
   and well beloved in every good town and city; her
   name was Mistress Margery March-beer.° Now
   Faustus, thou hast heard all my progeny; wilt thou
   bid me to a supper.
FAUSTUS: Not I. Thou wilt eat up all my victuals.   165
GLUTTONY: Then the devil choke thee.
FAUSTUS: Choke thyself, glutton. What art thou, the
   sixth?
SLOTH: Heigh ho! I am Sloth. I was begotten on a
   sunny bank, where I have lain ever since, and you   170
   have done me great injury to bring me from
   thence. Let me be carried thither again by Gluttony and Lechery. Heigh ho! I'll not speak a word
   more for a king's ransom.
FAUSTUS: And what are you Mistress Minx, the sev-   175
   enth and last?
LECHERY: Who, I, sir? I am one that loves an inch of raw
   mutton° better than an ell of fried stockfish,° and
   the first letter of my name begins with lechery.
LUCIFER: Away to hell! Away! On piper!   180

(Exeunt the SEVEN SINS [*and the* PIPER].*)*

---

bevers, light snacks taken between regular meals.
Martlemas-beef, salted meat hung for the winter on Mar-
tinmas, November 11. **March-beer,** a fine ale made in the
springtime and aged for two years before being drunk.
raw mutton, common slang for "whore." **stockfish,** dried cod-
fish.

Ovid's flea, The medieval poem *Carmine de Pulice* (Poem
of the Flea) was generally attributed to Ovid. **cloth of Arras,**
Flemish cloth used generally for tapestries.

FAUSTUS: O, how this sight doth delight my soul!

LUCIFER: But Faustus, in hell is all manner of delight.

FAUSTUS: O, might I see hell and return again safe, how happy were I then!

185 LUCIFER: Faustus, thou shalt. At midnight I will send for thee. Meanwhile peruse this book and view it thoroughly, and thou shalt turn thyself into what shape thou wilt.

FAUSTUS: Thanks, mighty Lucifer.

190   This will I keep as chary as my life.

LUCIFER: Now Faustus, farewell.

FAUSTUS: Farewell, great Lucifer. Come, Mephistophilis.

(Exeunt, several ways.)

ACT 2 / SCENE 3

(Enter the CLOWN *[*ROBIN, *holding a book].)*

ROBIN: What, Dick, look to the horses there till I come again. I have gotten one of Doctor Faustus' conjuring books, and now we'll have such knavery as't passes.

(Enter DICK.*)*

5 DICK: What, Robin, you must come away and walk the horses.

ROBIN: I walk the horses? I scorn't, 'faith. I have other matters in hand. Let the horses walk themselves and they will. [*He reads.*] *A per se a; t, h, e, the; o per*
10 *se o; deny orgon, gorgon.* Keep further from me, O thou illiterate and unlearned hostler.

DICK: 'Snails,° what hast thou got there? A book? Why, thou canst not tell ne'er a word on't.

ROBIN: That thou shalt see presently. Keep out of the
15 circle, I say, lest I send you into the hostry with a vengeance.

DICK: That's like, 'faith. You had best leave your foolery, for an my master come, he'll conjure you, 'faith.

ROBIN: My master conjure me? I'll tell thee what: an
20 my master come here, I'll clap as fair a pair of horns° on's head as e'er thou sawest in thy life.

DICK: Thou needst not do that, for my mistress hath done it.

ROBIN: Ay, there be of us here that have waded as
25 deep into matters as other men, if they were disposed to talk.

DICK: A plague take you! I thought you did not sneak up and down after her for nothing. But I prithee, tell me in good sadness,° Robin, is that a conjur-
30 ing book?

ROBIN: Do but speak what thou'lt have me to do, and I'll do't. If thou'lt dance naked, put off thy clothes, and I'll conjure thee about presently. Or if thou'lt go but to the tavern with me, I'll give

thee white wine, red wine, claret wine, sack, mus- 35
cadine, malmesey and whippincrust.° Hold belly, hold, and we'll not pay one penny for it.

DICK: O brave! Prithee let's to it presently, for I am as dry as a dog.

ROBIN: Come then, let's away. 40

(Exeunt.)

ACT 3 / PROLOGUE

(Enter the CHORUS.*)*

CHORUS: Learnèd Faustus,
  To find the secrets of astronomy
  Graven in the book of Jove's high firmament,
  Did mount him up to scale Olympus' top,
  Where, sitting in a chariot burning bright 5
  Drawn by the strength of yokèd dragons' necks,
  He views the clouds, the planets, and the stars,
  The tropics, zones, and quarters of the sky,
  From the bright circle of the hornèd moon
  Even to the height of *Primum Mobile.*° 10
  And whirling round with this circumference,
  Within the concave compass of the pole,
  From east to west his dragons swiftly glide
  And in eight days did bring him home again.
  Not long he stayed within his quiet house 15
  To rest his bones after his weary toil,
  But new exploits do hale him out again,
  And mounted then upon a dragon's back,
  That with his wings did part the subtle air,
  He now is gone to prove cosmography,° 20
  That measures coasts and kingdoms of the earth,
  And, as I guess, will first arrive at Rome
  To see the Pope and manner of his court
  And take some part of holy Peter's feast,
  The which this day is highly solemnized. 25

(Exit.)

ACT 3 / SCENE 1

(Enter FAUSTUS *and* MEPHISTOPHILIS.*)*

FAUSTUS: Having now, my good Mephistophilis,
  Passed with delight the stately town of Trier,
  Environed round with airy mountain tops,
  With walls of flint, and deep entrenchèd lakes,°
  Not to be won by any conquering prince; 5
  From Paris next, coasting the realm of France,
  We saw the river Main fall into Rhine,

'**Snails,** by God's nails.   **horns,** the common sign of a cuckold.   **sadness,** seriousness.

    whippincrust, possibly a corruption of "hippocras," a highly spiced and sugared wine.   **Primum Mobile,** in Ptolemaic astronomy the outermost sphere of creation, which moves the other nine spheres.   **prove cosmography,** explore the universe.   **entrenchèd lakes,** castle moats.

Whose banks are set with groves of fruitful vines;
Then up to Naples, rich Campania,
10 Whose buildings fair and gorgeous to the eye,
The streets straight forth and paved with finest
      brick,
Quarters the town in four equivalents.
There saw we learnèd Maro's° golden tomb,
The way he cut, an English mile in length,
15 Through a rock of stone in one night's space.°
From thence to Venice, Padua, and the rest,
In midst of which a sumptuous temple stands,
That threats the stars with her aspiring top,
Whose frame is paved with sundry colored stones,
20 And roofed aloft with curious work in gold.°
Thus hitherto hath Faustus spent his time.
But tell me now, what resting-place is this?
Hast thou, as erst I did command,
Conducted me within the walls of Rome?
MEPHISTOPHILIS: I have, my Faustus, and for proof
25   thereof
This is the goodly palace of the Pope;
And 'cause we are no common guests,
I choose his privy chamber for our use.
FAUSTUS: I hope his holiness will bid us welcome.
MEPHISTOPHILIS: All's one, for we'll be bold with his
30   venison.
But now, my Faustus, that thou may'st perceive
What Rome contains for to delight thine eyes,
Know that this city stands upon seven hills
That underprop the groundwork of the same.
35 Just through the midst runs flowing Tiber's stream,
With winding banks that cut it in two parts,
Over the which four stately bridges lean,
That make safe passage to each part of Rome.
Upon the bridge called Ponte Angelo
40 Erected is a castle passing strong,
Where thou shalt see such store of ordinance
As that the double cannons, forged of brass,
Do match the number of the days contained
Within the compass of one complete year;
45 Beside the gates and high pyramidès
That Julius Caesar brought from Africa.°
FAUSTUS: Now, by the kingdoms of infernal rule,
Of Styx, of Acheron, and the fiery lake
Of ever-burning Phlegethon, I swear
50 That I do long to see the monuments
And situation of bright-splendent Rome.
Come, therefore, let's away.

MEPHISTOPHILIS: Nay, stay my Faustus. I know you'd
      see the Pope
And take some part of holy Peter's feast,
The which, in state and high solemnity,   55
This day is held through Rome and Italy
In honor of the Pope's triumphant victory.
FAUSTUS: Sweet Mephistophilis, thou pleasest me.
Whilst I am here on earth, let me be cloyed
With all things that delight the heart of man.   60
My four and twenty years of liberty
I'll spend in pleasure and in dalliance,
That Faustus' name, whilst this bright frame doth
      stand,
May be admirèd through the furthest land.
MEPHISTOPHILIS: 'Tis well said, Faustus. Come then,
      stand by me   65
And thou shalt see them come immediately.
FAUSTUS: Nay, stay, my gentle Mephistophilis,
And grant me my request, and then I go.
Thou know'st within the compass of eight days
We viewed the face of heaven, of earth, and hell.   70
So high our dragons soared into the air,
That looking down, the earth appeared to me
No bigger than my hand in quantity.
There did we view the kingdoms of the world,
And what might please mine eye I there beheld.   75
Then in this show let me an actor be,
That this proud Pope may Faustus' cunning see.
MEPHISTOPHILIS: Let it be so, my Faustus. But, first
      stay
And view their triumphs° as they pass this way,
And then devise what best contents thy mind   80
By cunning in thine art to cross the Pope
Or dash the pride of this solemnity,
To make his monks and abbots stand like apes
And point like antics at his triple crown,
To beat the beads about the friars' pates   85
Or clap huge horns upon the cardinals' heads,
Or any villainy thou canst devise,
And I'll perform it, Faustus. Hark, they come.
This day shall make thee be admired in Rome.

(Enter the CARDINALS and BISHOPS, some bearing
crosiers, some the pillars; MONKS and FRIARS singing
their procession. Then the POPE and RAYMOND, King of
Hungary, with BRUNO, led in chains.)

POPE: Cast down our footstool.
RAYMOND: Saxon Bruno, stoop,   90
Whilst on thy back his holiness ascends
Saint Peter's chair and state pontifical.
BRUNO: Proud Lucifer, that state belongs to me,
But thus I fall to Peter, not to thee.
POPE: To me and Peter shalt thou groveling lie   95
And crouch before the papal dignity.
Sound trumpets then, for thus Saint Peter's heir
From Bruno's back ascends Saint Peter's chair.

Maro, Virgil. way . . . space, a tunnel between the bays
of Naples and Baiae, through Mt. Posilipo, was said to have
been cut by Virgil (regarded as a magician in the Middle
Ages) by supernatural art. In midst . . . gold, St. Mark's cathedral in Venice. gates . . . Africa, Before the gates of St.
Peter's there still stands the obelisk that was brought to
Rome from Heliopolis by the Emperor Caligula in the first
century A.D.

---

triumphs, spectacular displays.

(A flourish while he ascends.)

Thus, as the gods creep on with feet of wool
100 Long ere with iron hands they punish men,
So shall our sleeping vengeance now arise
And smite with death thy hated enterprise.
Lord Cardinals of France and Padua,
Go forthwith to our holy consistory,
105 And read amongst the Statutes Decretal°
What, by the holy council held at Trent,°
The sacred synod hath decreed for him
That doth assume the papal government
Without election and a true consent.
110 Away, and bring us word with speed.
FIRST CARDINAL: We go my Lord.

(Exeunt CARDINALS.)

POPE: Lord Raymond. [*They talk apart.*]
FAUSTUS: Go, haste thee, gentle Mephistophilis,
Follow the cardinals to the consistory,
115 And as they turn their superstitious books,
Strike them with sloth and drowsy idleness,
And make them sleep so sound that in their shapes
Thyself and I may parley with this Pope,
This proud confronter of the Emperor,
120 And in despite of all his holiness
Restore this Bruno to his liberty
And bear him to the states of Germany.
MEPHISTOPHILIS: Faustus, I go.
FAUSTUS: Dispatch it soon.
125 The Pope shall curse that Faustus came to Rome.

(Exeunt FAUSTUS and MEPHISTOPHILIS.)

BRUNO: Pope Adrian,° let me have some right of law.
I was elected by the Emperor.
POPE: We will depose the Emperor for that deed
And curse the people that submit to him.
130 Both he and thou shalt stand excommunicate
And interdict from church's privilege
And all society of holy men.
He grows too proud in his authority,
Lifting his lofty head above the clouds,
135 And like a steeple overpeers the church.
But we'll pull down his haughty insolence,
And as Pope Alexander, our progenitor,
Trod on the neck of German Frederick,°

Adding this golden sentence to our praise,
"That Peter's heirs should tread on emperors   140
And walk upon the dreadful adder's back,
Treading the lion and the dragon down
And fearless spurn the killing basilisk,"°
So will we quell that haughty schismatic,
And by authority apostolical   145
Depose him from his regal government.
BRUNO: Pope Julius swore to princely Sigismond,°
For him and the succeeding popes of Rome,
To hold the emperors their lawful lords.
POPE: Pope Julius did abuse the church's rites, 150
And therefore none of his decrees can stand.
Is not all power on earth bestowed on us?
And therefore, though we would, we cannot err.
Behold this silver belt, whereto is fixed
Seven golden keys fast sealed with seven seals   155
In token of our sevenfold power from heaven,
To bind or loose, lock fast, condemn or judge,
Resign, or seal, or whatso pleaseth us.
Then he and thou and all the world shall stoop,
Or be assurèd of our dreadful curse   160
To light as heavy as the pains of hell.

*(Enter FAUSTUS and MEPHISTOPHILIS, like the CARDI-
NALS.)*

MEPHISTOPHILIS: Now tell me, Faustus, are we not
fitted well?
FAUSTUS: Yes, Mephistophilis, and two such cardinals
Ne'er served a holy pope as we shall do.
But whilst they sleep within the consistory,   165
Let us salute his reverend fatherhood.
RAYMOND: Behold, my lord, the cardinals are
returned.
POPE: Welcome, grave fathers. Answer presently:
What have our holy council there decreed
Concerning Bruno and the Emperor,   170
In quittance of their late conspiracy
Against our state and papal dignity?
FAUSTUS: Most sacred patron of the church of Rome,
By full consent of all the synod
Of priests and prelates it is thus decreed: 175
That Bruno and the German Emperor
Be held as Lollards° and bold schismatics
And proud disturbers of the church's peace.
And if that Bruno by his own assent,
Without enforcement of the German peers,   180
Did seek to wear the triple diadem

Statutes Decretal, papal decrees concerning religious doctrine or ecclesiastical law. **council ... Trent,** The Council of Trent, held by the Church from 1545 to 1563. **Pope Adrian,** Marlowe perhaps means Pope Hadrian IV (1154–1159), who tried to assert his authority over Frederick Barbarossa, the Holy Roman Emperor. What historicity there may be in these scenes at the papal court is badly confused. **Pope Alexander ... Frederick,** Pope Alexander III (1159–1181), successor to Hadrian IV, continued the struggle against Barbarossa, forcing him to acknowledge the papal supremacy at Canossa.

---

basilisk, a mythical monster with power to kill by its looks. **Pope Julius . . . Sigismond,** None of the three popes named Julius was contemporary with the Emperor Sigismund (1368–1437). Sigismund did, however, in 1414 summon the Council of Constance (1378–1417), during which the papacy in Rome was challenged by a line of popes in Avignon. **Lollards,** followers of John Wycliffe (1320?–1384), the English reformer.

And by your death to climb Saint Peter's chair,
The Statutes Decretal have thus decreed:
He shall be straight condemned of heresy
185 And on a pile of fagots burned to death.
POPE: It is enough. Here, take him to your charge,
And bear him straight to Ponte Angelo,
And in the strongest tower enclose him fast.
Tomorrow, sitting in our consistory
190 With all our college of grave cardinals,
We will determine of his life or death.
Here, take his triple crown along with you,
And leave it in the church's treasury.
Make haste again, my good lord cardinals,
195 And take our blessing apostolical.
MEPHISTOPHILIS: So, so. Was never devil thus blessed
before.
FAUSTUS: Away, sweet Mephistophilis, be gone.
The cardinals will be plagued for this anon.

(*Exeunt* FAUSTUS *and* MEPHISTOPHILIS [*with* BRUNO].)

POPE: Go presently and bring a banquet forth,
200 That we may solemnize Saint Peter's feast,
And with Lord Raymond, King of Hungary,
Drink to our late and happy victory.

(*Exeunt.*)

ACT 3 / SCENE 2

(*A sennet* [*is sounded*] *while the banquet is brought in;
and then enter* FAUSTUS *and* MEPHISTOPHILIS *in their
own shapes.*)

MEPHISTOPHILIS: Now, Faustus, come, prepare
thyself for mirth.
The sleepy cardinals are hard at hand
To censure Bruno, that is posted hence,
And on a proud-paced steed, as swift as thought,
5 Flies o'er the Alps to fruitful Germany,
There to salute the woeful Emperor.
FAUSTUS: The Pope will curse them for their sloth
today,
That slept both Bruno and his crown away.
But now, that Faustus may delight his mind
10 And by their folly make some merriment,
Sweet Mephistophilis, so charm me here
That I may walk invisible to all
And do whate'er I please unseen of any.
MEPHISTOPHILIS: Faustus, thou shalt. Then kneel
down presently:

15 *Whilst on thy head I lay my hand*
And charm thee with this magic wand.
First wear this girdle; then appear
Invisible to all are here.
The planets seven, the gloomy air,

Hell and the Furie's° forkèd hair,   20
Pluto's blue fire, and Hecate's tree,°
With magic spells so compass thee
That no eye may thy body see.

So Faustus. Now, for all their holiness,
Do what thou wilt, thou shalt not be discerned.   25
FAUSTUS: Thanks, Mephistophilis. Now friars take
heed
Lest Faustus make your shaven crowns to bleed.
MEPHISTOPHILIS: Faustus, no more. See where the
cardinals come.

(*Enter* POPE *and all the* LORDS. *Enter the* CARDINALS
with a book.)

POPE: Welcome, lord cardinals. Come, sit down.
Lord Raymond, take your seat. Friars attend,   30
And see that all things be in readiness,
As best beseems this solemn festival.
FIRST CARDINAL: First, may it please your sacred
holiness
To view the sentence of the reverend synod
Concerning Bruno and the Emperor?   35
POPE: What needs this question? Did I not tell you
Tomorrow we would sit i' th' consistory
And there determine of his punishment?
You brought us word even now; it was decreed
That Bruno and the cursèd Emperor   40
Were by the holy council both condemned
For loathèd Lollards and base schismatics.
Then wherefore would you have me view that
book?
FIRST CARDINAL: Your grace mistakes. You gave us no
such charge.
RAYMOND: Deny it not. We all are witnesses   45
That Bruno here was late delivered you,
With his rich triple crown to be reserved
And put into the church's treasury.
BOTH CARDINALS: By holy Paul, we saw them not.
POPE: By Peter, you shall die   50
Unless you bring them forth immediately.
Hale them to prison. Lade their limbs with gyves.°
False prelates, for this hateful treachery.
Cursed be your souls to hellish misery.

[*Exeunt the two* CARDINALS *with* ATTENDANTS.]

FAUSTUS: So, they are safe. Now, Faustus, to the feast. 55
The Pope had never such a frolic guest.
POPE: Lord Archbishop of Rheims, sit down with us.
ARCHBISHOP: I thank your holiness.
FAUSTUS: Fall to. The devil choke you an you spare.°

Furies, spirits called upon to avenge crimes, especially
crimes against kin. **Hecate's tree,** Hecate is the goddess of
witchcraft. **Lade . . . gyves,** shackle their limbs. **an you
spare,** if you hold back.

60   POPE: Who's that spoke? Friars look about.
     FRIAR: Here's nobody, if it like your holiness.
     POPE: Lord Raymond, pray fall to. I am beholding
       To the Bishop of Milan for this so rare a present.
     FAUSTUS: I thank you, sir. [*He snatches the dish.*]
65   POPE: How now? Who snatched the meat from me?
       Villains, why speak you not?
       My good Lord Archbishop, here's a most dainty
         dish
       Was sent me from a cardinal in France.
     FAUSTUS: I'll have that too. [*He snatches the dish.*]
70   POPE: What Lollards do attend our holiness,
       That we receive such great indignity?
       Fetch me some wine.
     FAUSTUS: Ay, pray do, for Faustus is a-dry.
     POPE: Lord Raymond, I drink unto your grace.
75   FAUSTUS: I pledge your grace. [*He snatches the cup.*]
     POPE: My wine gone too? Ye lubbers, look about
       And find the man that doth this villainy,
       Or by our sanctitude, you all shall die.
       I pray, my lords, have patience at this
80   Troublesome banquet.
     ARCHBISHOP: Please it your holiness, I think it be
       some ghost crept out of purgatory, and now is
       come unto your holiness for his pardon.
     POPE: It may be so.
85   Go then, command our priests to sing a dirge
       To lay the fury of this same troublesome ghost.

       [*Exit an* ATTENDANT.]

       Once again, my lord, fall to.

       (*The* POPE *crosseth himself.*)

     FAUSTUS: How now?
       Must every bit be spicèd with a cross?
90   Nay then, take that. [*He strikes the* POPE.]
     POPE: O I am slain. Help me, my lords.
       O come and help to bear my body hence.
       Damned be this soul for ever for this deed.

       (*Exeunt the* POPE *and his train.*)

     MEPHISTOPHILIS: Now, Faustus, what will you do now?
95   For I can tell you you'll be cursed with bell, book,
       and candle.°
     FAUSTUS: Bell, book, and candle; candle, book, and
       bell,
       Forward and backward, to curse Faustus to hell.

       (*Enter the* FRIARS *with bell, book, and candle for the
       dirge.*)

     FIRST FRIAR: Come, brethren, let's about our business
100   with good devotion. [*They chant.*]

*Cursed be he that stole his holiness' meat from the
  table.*
    Maledicat Dominus!°
*Cursed be he that struck his holiness a blow on the
  face.*
    Maledicat Dominus!
*Cursed be he that struck Friar Sandelo a blow on the
  pate.*   105
    Maledicat Dominus!
Cursed be he that disturbeth our holy dirge.
    Maledicat Dominus!
Cursed be he that took away his holiness' wine.
    Maledicat Dominus! Et omnes sancti.°   110
Amen.

([FAUSTUS *and* MEPHISTOPHILIS] *beat the* FRIARS,
fling fireworks among them, and exeunt.)

ACT 3 / SCENE 3

    (*Enter* [ROBIN,] *the* CLOWN, *and* DICK, *with a cup.*)

  DICK: Sirrah Robin, we were best look that your devil
    can answer the stealing of this same cup, for the
    vintner's boy follows us at the hard heels.
  ROBIN: 'Tis no matter. Let him come. An he follow us,
    I'll so conjure him as he was never conjured in his   5
    life, I warrant him. Let me see the cup.

    (*Enter* VINTNER.)

  DICK: Here 'tis. Yonder he comes. Now, Robin, now or
    never show thy cunning.
  VINTNER: O, are you here? I am glad I have found
    you. You are a couple of fine companions. Pray,   10
    where's the cup you stole from the tavern?
  ROBIN: How, how? We steal a cup? Take heed what you
    say. We look not like cup stealers, I can tell you.
  VINTNER: Never deny't, for I know you have it, and I'll
    search you.   15
  ROBIN: Search me? Ay, and spare not. [*Aside to* DICK.]
    Hold the cup, Dick. Come, come, search me,
    search me.

    [*The* VINTNER *searches* ROBIN.]

  VINTNER: [*to* DICK] Come on, sirrah, let me search
    you now.   20
  DICK: Ay, ay, do, do. [*Aside to* ROBIN.] Hold the cup,
    Robin. I fear not your searching. We scorn to steal
    your cups, I can tell you.

    [*The* VINTNER *searches* DICK.]

  VINTNER: Never outface me for the matter, for sure
    the cup is between you two.   25
  ROBIN: Nay, there you lie. 'Tis beyond us both.
  VINTNER: A plague take you! I thought 'twas your
    knavery to take it away. Come, give it me again.

---

bell, book, and candle, used traditionally in the rite of
excommunication.

Maledicat Dominus, may the Lord curse him.   **Et omnes
sancti,** and all the saints.

ROBIN: Ay, much. When? Can you tell? Dick, make me
30   a circle, and stand close at my back, and stir not
       for thy life. Vintner, you shall have your cup anon.
       Say nothing, Dick, O *per se*, O Demogorgon, *Belcher
       and Mephistophilis.*

(Enter MEPHISTOPHILIS. *[Exit the* VINTNER, *in fright.])*

MEPHISTOPHILIS: Monarch of hell, under whose
       black survey
35   Great potentates do kneel with awful fear,
       Upon whose altars thousand souls do lie,
       How am I vexèd by these villains' charms!
       From Constantinople have they brought me now,
       Only for pleasure of these damnèd slaves.
40 ROBIN: By Lady, sir, you have had a shrewd journey of
       it. Will it please you to take a shoulder of mutton
       to supper and a tester° in your purse, and go back
       again?
DICK: Ay, I pray you heartily, sir, for we called you but
45   in jest, I promise you.
MEPHISTOPHILIS: To purge the rashness of this
       cursèd deed,
       First be thou turnèd to this ugly shape,
       For apish deeds transformèd to an ape.
ROBIN: O brave, an ape! I pray sir, let me have the car-
50   rying of him about to show some tricks.
MEPHISTOPHILIS: And so thou shalt. Be thou trans-
       formed to a dog, and carry him upon thy back.
       Away, be gone!
ROBIN: A dog? That's excellent. Let the maids look
55   well to their porridge pots, for I'll into the
       kitchen presently. Come, Dick, come.

*(Exeunt [*ROBIN *and* DICK,] *the two clowns.)*

MEPHISTOPHILIS: Now with the flames of ever-
       burning fire,
       I'll wing myself and forthwith fly amain
       Unto my Faustus, to the great Turk's court.

(Exit.)

ACT 4 / PROLOGUE

(Enter CHORUS.*)*

CHORUS: When Faustus had with pleasure ta'en the
       view
       Of rarest things and royal courts of kings,
       He stayed his course and so returnèd home;
       Where such as bare his absence but with grief—
5   I mean his friends and nearest companions—
       Did gratulate his safety with kind words
       And in their conference of what befell
       Touching his journey through the world and air,
       They put forth questions of astrology,
10   Which Faustus answered with such learnèd skill

As they admired and wondered at his wit.
       Now is his fame spread forth in every land.
       Amongst the rest, the Emperor is one—
       Carolus the fifth°—at whose palace now
       Faustus is feasted 'mongst his noblemen.   15
       What there he did in trial of his art
       I leave untold, your eyes shall see performed.

(Exit.)

ACT 4 / SCENE 1

(Enter MARTINO *and* FREDERICK, *at several doors.)*

MARTINO: What ho, officers, gentlemen,
       Hie to the presence° to attend the Emperor.
       Good Frederick, see the rooms be voided straight;
       His majesty is coming to the hall.
       Go back, and see the state° in readiness.   5
FREDERICK: But where is Bruno, our elected Pope,
       That on a fury's back came post from Rome?
       Will not his grace consort the Emperor?
MARTINO: O yes, and with him comes the German
       conjurer,
       The learnèd Faustus, fame of Wittenberg,   10
       The wonder of the world for magic art;
       And he intends to show great Carolus
       The race of all his stout progenitors,
       And bring in presence of his majesty
       The royal shapes and warlike semblances   15
       Of Alexander° and his beauteous paramour.
FREDERICK: Where is Benvolio?
MARTINO: Fast asleep, I warrant you.
       He took his rouse with stoups° of Rhenish wine
       So kindly yesternight to Bruno's health   20
       That all this day the sluggard keeps his bed.
FREDERICK: See, see, his window's ope. We'll call to
       him.
MARTINO: What ho, Benvolio!

(Enter BENVOLIO *above at a window, in his nightcap,
buttoning.)*

BENVOLIO: What a devil ail you two?
MARTINO: Speak softly, sir, lest the devil hear you,   25
       For Faustus at the court is late arrived,
       And at his heels a thousand furies wait
       To accomplish whatsoever the doctor please.
BENVOLIO: What of this?
MARTINO: Come, leave thy chamber first, and thou
       shalt see   30
       This conjurer perform such rare exploits

---

tester, sixpence.

Carolus the fifth, Charles V, King of Spain (as Charles I from 1516 to 1556) and Holy Roman Emperor from 1519 to 1556. ***presence,*** Emperor's chamber. ***state,*** throne. ***Alexander,*** Alexander the Great. ***took . . . stoups,*** had a drinking bout with brimming goblets.

Before the Pope° and royal Emperor
As never yet was seen in Germany.
BENVOLIO: Has not the Pope enough of conjuring yet?
35 He was upon the devil's back late enough,
And if he be so far in love with him,
I would he would post with him to Rome again.
FREDERICK: Speak, wilt thou come and see this sport?
BENVOLIO: Not I.
MARTINO: Wilt thou stand in thy window and see it
then?
40 BENVOLIO: Ay, and I fall not asleep i' th' meantime.
MARTINO: The Emperor is at hand, who comes to see
What wonders by black spells may compassed be.
BENVOLIO: Well, go you attend the Emperor. I am
content for this once to thrust my head out at a
45 window, for they say if a man be drunk overnight
the devil cannot hurt him in the morning. If that
be true, I have a charm in my head shall control
him as well as the conjurer, I warrant you.

(*Exit* [FREDERICK, *with* MARTINO. BENVOLIO *remains at the window above*].)

ACT 4 / SCENE 2

(*A sennet* [*is sounded. Enter*] CHARLES, *the German Emperor*, BRUNO, [*the Duke of*] *Saxony*, FAUSTUS, MEPHISTOPHILIS, FREDERICK, MARTINO, *and* ATTENDANTS.)

EMPEROR: Wonder of men, renowned magician,
Thrice-learnèd Faustus, welcome to our court.
This deed of thine, in setting Bruno free
From his and our professèd enemy,
5   Shall add more excellence unto thine art
Than if by powerful necromantic spells
Thou couldst command the world's obedience.
Forever be beloved of Carolus,
And if this Bruno thou hast late redeemed°
10 In peace possess the triple diadem
And sit in Peter's chair despite of chance,
Thou shalt be famous through all Italy
And honored of the German Emperor.
FAUSTUS: These gracious words, most royal Carolus,
15 Shall make poor Faustus to his utmost power
Both love and serve the German Emperor
And lay his life at holy Bruno's feet.
For proof whereof, if so your grace be pleased,
The doctor stands prepared by power of art
20 To cast his magic charms that shall pierce through
The ebon gates of ever-burning hell,
And hale the stubborn Furies from their caves
To compass whatsoe'er your grace commands.
BENVOLIO: [*above*] Blood, he speaks terribly, but for
25   all that, I do not greatly believe him. He looks as

---

the Pope, Bruno. *redeemed,* rescued.

like a conjurer as the Pope° to a costermonger.°
EMPEROR: Then, Faustus, as thou late did'st promise
us,
We would behold that famous conqueror,
Great Alexander, and his paramour
In their true shapes and state majestical,   30
That we may wonder at their excellence.
FAUSTUS: Your majesty shall see them presently.
Mephistophilis, away,
And with a solemn noise of trumpets' sound
Present before this royal Emperor,   35
Great Alexander and his beauteous paramour.
MEPHISTOPHILIS: Faustus, I will.

[*Exit.*]

BENVOLIO: Well, master doctor, an your devils come
not away quickly, you shall have me asleep presently. Zounds, I could eat myself for anger to   40
think I have been such an ass all this while, to
stand gaping after the devil's governor and can
see nothing.
FAUSTUS: I'll make you feel something anon, if my
art fail me not.
My lord, I must forewarn your majesty   45
That when my spirits present the royal shapes
Of Alexander and his paramour,
Your grace demand no questions of the king,
But in dumb silence let them come and go.
EMPEROR: Be it as Faustus please; we are content. 50
BENVOLIO: Ay, ay, and I am content too. And thou
bring Alexander and his paramour before the
Emperor, I'll be Actaeon and turn myself to a stag.
FAUSTUS: And I'll play Diana and send you the horns
presently.   55

([*A*] *sennet* [*is sounded*]. *Enter at one* [*door*] *the* EMPEROR ALEXANDER, *at the other* DARIUS.° *They meet* [*in combat*]. DARIUS *is thrown down;* ALEXANDER *kills him, takes off his crown, and, offering to go out, his paramour meets him. He embraceth her and sets* DARIUS' *crown upon her head; and coming back, both salute the* EMPEROR, *who, leaving his state, offers to embrace them, which* FAUSTUS *seeing, suddenly stays him. Then trumpets cease and music sounds.*)

My gracious lord, you do forget yourself.
These are but shadows, not substantial.
EMPEROR: O pardon me. My thoughts are so ravishèd
With sight of this renownèd emperor,
That in mine arms I would have compassed him.   60
But, Faustus, since I may not speak to them,
To satisfy my longing thoughts at full,
Let me this tell thee: I have heard it said

---

the Pope, Bruno. *costermonger,* fruit vendor; a term of
contempt. *Darius,* King Darius III of Persia (336–330 B.C.),
defeated at Granicus in 334 B.C. by the Greeks under Alexander the Great.

That this fair lady, whilst she lived on earth,
65 Had on her neck a little wart or mole;
How may I prove that saying to be true?
FAUSTUS: Your majesty may boldly go and see.
EMPEROR: Faustus, I see it plain,
And in this sight thou better pleasest me
70 Than if I gained another monarchy.
FAUSTUS: Away! Be gone!

  (*Exit show.*)

See, see, my gracious lord, what strange beast is
yon, that thrusts his head out at window?
EMPEROR: O wondrous sight! See, Duke of Saxony,
75 Two spreading horns most strangely fastenèd
Upon the head of young Benvolio.
SAXONY: What? Is he asleep or dead?
FAUSTUS: He sleeps, my lord, but dreams not of his
horns.
EMPEROR: This sport is excellent. We'll call and wake
him.
80 What ho, Benvolio!
BENVOLIO: A plague upon you! Let me sleep a while.
EMPEROR: I blame thee not to sleep much, having
such a head of thine own.
SAXONY: Look up, Benvolio; 'tis the Emperor calls.
BENVOLIO: The Emperor? Where? O zounds, my
85 head!
EMPEROR: Nay, and thy horns hold, 'tis no matter for
thy head, for that's armed sufficiently.
FAUSTUS: Why, how now, sir knight! What, hanged by
the horns? This is most horrible. Fie, fie, pull in
90 your head for shame. Let not all the world won-
der at you.
BENVOLIO: Zounds, doctor, is this your villainy?
FAUSTUS: O say not so, sir. The doctor has no skill,
No art, no cunning, to present these lords
95 Or bring before this royal Emperor
The mighty monarch, warlike Alexander.
If Faustus do it, you are straight resolved
In bold Actaeon's shape to turn a stag.
And therefore, my lord, so please your majesty,
00 I'll raise a kennel of hounds shall hunt him so
As all his footmanship shall scarce prevail
To keep his carcass from their bloody fangs.
Ho, Belimote, Argiron, Asterote!
BENVOLIO: Hold, hold! Zounds, he'll raise a kennel of
05 devils, I think, anon. Good, my lord, entreat for
me. 'Sblood, I am never able to endure these tor-
ments.
EMPEROR: Then, good master doctor,
Let me entreat you to remove his horns.
10 He has done penance now sufficiently.
FAUSTUS: My gracious lord, not so much for injury
done to me, as to delight your majesty with some
mirth, hath Faustus justly requited this injurious°

injurious, insulting.

knight; which being all I desire, I am content to
remove his horns. Mephistophilis, transform him. 115

[MEPHISTOPHILIS *removes the horns.*]

And hereafter, sir, look you speak well of scholars.
BENVOLIO: [*aside.*] Speak well of ye? 'Sblood, and
scholars be such cuckold makers to clap horns of
honest men's heads o' this order, I'll ne'er trust
smooth faces and small ruffs° more. But an I be 120
not revenged for this, would I might be turned to
a gaping oyster and drink nothing but salt water.

[*Exit* BENVOLIO *above.*]

EMPEROR: Come, Faustus. While the Emperor lives,
In recompense of this thy high desert,
Thou shalt command the state of Germany 125
And lived beloved of mighty Carolus.

  (*Exeunt.*)

ACT 4 / SCENE 3

(*Enter* BENVOLIO, MARTINO, FREDERICK, *and*
SOLDIERS.)

MARTINO: Nay, sweet Benvolio, let us sway thy
thoughts
From this attempt against the conjurer.
BENVOLIO: Away! You love me not to urge me thus.
Shall I let slip so great an injury,
When every servile groom jests at my wrongs 5
And in their rustic gambols proudly say,
"Benvolio's head was graced with horns today"?
O, may these eyelids never close again
Till with my sword I have that conjurer slain.
If you will aid me in this enterprise, 10
Then draw your weapons and be resolute.
If not, depart. Here will Benvolio die,
But Faustus' death shall quit° my infamy.
FREDERICK: Nay, we will stay with thee, betide what
may,
And kill that doctor if he come this way. 15
BENVOLIO: Then, gentle Frederick, hie thee to the
grove,
And place our servants and our followers
Close in an ambush there behind the trees.
By this, I know, the conjurer is near.
I saw him kneel and kiss the Emperor's hand 20
And take his leave, laden with rich rewards.
Then, soldiers, boldly fight. If Faustus die,
Take you the wealth; leave us the victory.
FREDERICK: Come, soldiers. Follow me unto the grove.
Who kills him shall have gold and endless love. 25

(*Exit* FREDERICK *with the* SOLDIERS.)

small ruffs, academic gowns. *quit,* pay for.

BENVOLIO: My head is lighter than it was by th' horns,
    But yet my heart's more ponderous than my head
    And pants until I see that conjurer dead.
MARTINO: Where shall we place ourselves, Benvolio?
30 BENVOLIO: Here will we stay to bide the first assault.
    O, were that damnèd hell-hound but in place,
    Thou soon shouldst see me quit my foul disgrace.

    (Enter FREDERICK.*)*

FREDERICK: Close, close, the conjurer is at hand
    And all alone comes walking in his gown.
35   Be ready then, and strike the peasant down.
BENVOLIO: Mine be that honor then. Now, sword,
    strike home.
    For horns he gave I'll have his head anon.

    (Enter FAUSTUS *with the false head.)*

MARTINO: See, see, he comes.
BENVOLIO: No words! This blow ends all.
    Hell take his soul; his body thus must fall.

    [*He stabs* FAUSTUS.]

40 FAUSTUS: [*falling*] Oh!
FREDERICK: Groan you, master doctor?
BENVOLIO: Break may his heart with groans! Dear
    Frederick, see,
    Thus will I end his griefs immediately.
MARTINO: Strike with a willing hand. His head is off.

    [BENVOLIO *strikes off* FAUSTUS' *false head.*]

BENVOLIO: The devil's dead. The Furies now may
45   laugh.
FREDERICK: Was this that stern aspèct, that awful
    frown,
    Made the grim monarch of infernal spirits
    Tremble and quake at his commanding charms?
MARTINO: Was this that damnèd head whose heart
    conspired
50   Benvolio's shame before the Emperor?
BENVOLIO: Ay, that's the head, and here the body
    lies,
    Justly rewarded for his villainies.
FREDERICK: Come, let's devise how we may add more
    shame
    To the black scandal of his hated name.
BENVOLIO: First, on his head, in quittance of my
55   wrongs,
    I'll nail huge forkèd horns and let them hang
    Within the window where he yoked° me first,
    That all the world may see my just revenge.
MARTINO: What use shall we put his beard to?
60 BENVOLIO: We'll sell it to a chimney-sweeper. It will
    wear out ten birchen brooms, I warrant you.
FREDERICK: What shall his eyes do?
BENVOLIO: We'll put out his eyes, and they shall serve

    for buttons to his lips to keep his tongue from
    catching cold.   65
MARTINO: An excellent policy! And now, sirs, having
    divided him, what shall the body do?

    [FAUSTUS *rises.*]

BENVOLIO: Zounds, the devil's alive again.
FREDERICK: Give him his head, for God's sake.
FAUSTUS: Nay, keep it. Faustus will have heads and
    hands,   70
    Ay, all your hearts, to recompense this deed.
    Knew you not, traitors, I was limited
    For four-and-twenty years to breathe on earth?
    And had you cut my body with your swords,
    Or hewed this flesh and bones as small as sand,   75
    Yet in a minute had my spirit returned,
    And I had breathed a man made free from harm.
    But wherefore do I dally my revenge?
    Asteroth, Belimoth, Mephistophilis!

    (Enter MEPHISTOPHILIS *and other* DEVILS.*)*

    Go, horse these traitors on your fiery backs,   80
    And mount aloft with them as high as heaven;
    Thence pitch them headlong to the lowest hell.
    Yet stay. The world shall see their misery,
    And hell shall after plague their treachery.
    Go, Belimoth, and take this caitiff° hence,   85
    And hurl him in some lake of mud and dirt.
    Take thou this other; drag him through the woods
    Amongst the pricking thorns and sharpest briars,
    Whilst with my gentle Mephistophilis
    This traitor flies unto some steepy rock   90
    That, rolling down, may break the villain's bones
    As he intended to dismember me.
    Fly hence. Dispatch my charge immediately.
FREDERICK: Pity us, gentle Faustus. Save our lives.
FAUSTUS: Away!   95
FREDERICK: He must needs go that the devil drives.

    (Exeunt SPIRITS [DEVILS] *with the* KNIGHTS [BENVO-
    LIO, MARTINO, FREDERICK].*)*

    (Enter the ambushed SOLDIERS.*)*

FIRST SOLDIER: Come, sirs, prepare yourselves in
    readiness.
    Make haste to help these noble gentlemen;
    I heard them parley with the conjurer.
SECOND SOLDIER: See where he comes. Dispatch and
    kill the slave.   100
FAUSTUS: What's here? An ambush to betray my life?
    Then, Faustus, try thy skill. Base peasants, stand,
    For lo, these trees remove at my command
    And stand as bulwarks 'twixt yourselves and me,
    To shield me from your hated treachery.   10
    Yet to encounter this your weak attempt,
    Behold an army comes incontinent.°

---

    yoked, placed the horns on.   **caitiff,** despicable wretch.   ***incontinent,*** at once.

(FAUSTUS *strikes the door, and enter a* DEVIL *playing on a drum, after him another bearing an ensign, and divers with weapons,* MEPHISTOPHILIS *with fireworks. They set upon the* SOLDIERS *and drive them out.* [*Exit* FAUSTUS.])

ACT 4 / SCENE 4

(*Enter at several doors* BENVOLIO, FREDERICK, *and* MARTINO, *their heads and faces bloody and besmeared with mud and dirt, all having horns on their heads.*)

MARTINO: What ho, Benvolio!

BENVOLIO: Here! What, Frederick, ho!

FREDERICK: O help me, gentle friend. Where is Martino?

MARTINO: Dear Frederick, here,

5   Half smothered in a lake of mud and dirt,
       Through which the Furies dragged me by the heels.

FREDERICK: Martino, see! Benvolio's horns again.

MARTINO: O misery! How now, Benvolio?

BENVOLIO: Defend me, heaven. Shall I be haunted° still?

MARTINO: Nay, fear not man; we have not power to

10   kill.

BENVOLIO: My friends transformèd thus! O hellish spite!
       Your heads are all set with horns.

FREDERICK: You hit it right.
       It is your own you mean. Feel on your head.

BENVOLIO: Zounds, horns again!

15 MARTINO: Nay, chafe not man. We all are sped.°

BENVOLIO: What devil attends this damned magician,
       That, spite of spite, our wrongs are doublèd?

FREDERICK: What may we do, that we may hide our shames?

BENVOLIO: If we should follow him to work revenge,

20   He'd join long asses' ears to these huge horns,
       And make us laughing-stocks to all the world.

MARTINO: What shall we then do, dear Benvolio?

BENVOLIO: I have a castle joining near these woods,
       And thither we'll repair and live obscure

25   Till time shall alter these our brutish shapes.
       Sith black disgrace hath thus eclipsed our fame,
       We'll rather die with grief than live with shame.

(*Exeunt omnes.*°)

ACT 4 / SCENE 5°

(*Enter* FAUSTUS *and* MEPHISTOPHILIS.)

---

haunted, (1) bewitched (2) hunted, pursued (since he is a stag). **sped,** provided (with horns). ***Exeunt omnes,*** Latin for "All go out." **Act 4/Scene 5,** The first eleven lines of Scene 5 do not appear in all versions of the play, but they provide a transition to the Horse-Courser episode and remind readers of Faustus's impending tragedy.

FAUSTUS: Now, Mephistophilis, the restless course
       That time doth run with calm and silent foot,
       Shortening my days and thread of vital life,
       Calls for the payment of my latest years.
       Therefore, sweet Mephistophilis, let us   5
       Make haste to Wittenberg.

MEPHISTOPHILIS: What, will you go on horseback, or on foot?

FAUSTUS: Nay, till I am past this fair and pleasant green,
       I'll walk on foot.

[*Exit* MEPHISTOPHILIS.]

(*Enter a* HORSE-COURSER.°)

HORSE-COURSER: I have been all this day seeking one   10
       Master Fustian.° Mass, see where he is. God save
       you, master doctor.

FAUSTUS: What, horse-courser! You are well met.

HORSE-COURSER: I beseech your worship, accept of
       these forty dollars.   15

FAUSTUS: Friend, thou canst not buy so good a horse
       for so small a price. I have no great need to sell
       him, but if thou likest him for ten dollars more,
       take him, because I see thou hast a good mind to
       him.   20

HORSE-COURSER: I beseech you, sir, accept of this. I am
       a very poor man and have lost very much of late by
       horse-flesh, and this bargain will set me up again.

FAUSTUS: Well, I will not stand with thee.° Give me the
       money.   25

[*The* HORSE-COURSER *gives* FAUSTUS *money.*]

       Now, sirrah, I must tell you that you may ride him
       o'er hedge and ditch, and spare him not. But, do
       you hear? In any case, ride him not into the water.

HORSE-COURSER: How sir? Not into the water? Why,
       will he not drink of all waters?°   30

FAUSTUS: Yes, he will drink of all waters, but ride him
       not into the water—o'er hedge and ditch, or
       where thou wilt, but not into the water. Go, bid
       the hostler deliver him unto you, and remember
       what I say.   35

HORSE-COURSER: I warrant you, sir. O joyful day! Now
       am I a man made forever.

(*Exit.*)

FAUSTUS: What art thou, Faustus, but a man
       condemned to die?
       Thy fatal time draws to a final end.
       Despair doth drive distrust into my thoughts.
       Confound these passions with a quiet sleep.   40

Horse-Courser, one who deals in horses. **Fustian,** the perversion of Faustus's name is a deliberate attempt at humor. **stand with thee,** bargain. **drink . . . waters,** be ready for anything (a common proverb of the time).

Tush! Christ did call the thief upon the cross;
Then rest thee, Faustus, quiet in conceit.°

(He sits to sleep [in his chair].)

(Enter the HORSE-COURSER, *wet.)*

45 HORSE-COURSER: O what a cozening doctor was this? I
riding my horse into the water, thinking some hidden mystery° had been in the horse, I had nothing
under me but a little straw and had much ado to
escape drowning. Well, I'll go rouse him and make
him give me my forty dollars again. Ho, sirrah doc-
50 tor, you cozening scab!° Master doctor, awake and
rise, and give me my money again, for your horse is
turned to a bottle° of hay. Master doctor!

(He [tries to wake FAUSTUS, *and in doing so] pulls off
his leg.)*

Alas, I am undone! What shall I do? I have pulled
off his leg.

[FAUSTUS *awakes.*]

55 FAUSTUS: O, help, help! The villain hath murdered me.
HORSE-COURSER: Murder or not murder, now he has
but one leg, I'll outrun him and cast this leg into
some ditch or other.
60 FAUSTUS: Stop him, stop him, stop him! Ha, ha, ha,
Faustus hath his leg again, and the horse-courser
a bundle of hay for his forty dollars.

(Enter WAGNER.)

How now, Wagner, what news with thee?
WAGNER: If it please you, the Duke of Anholt doth
earnestly entreat your company and hath sent
65 some of his men to attend you with provision fit
for your journey.
FAUSTUS: The Duke of Anholt's an honorable gentleman, and one to whom I must be no niggard of
my cunning. Come away.

(Exeunt.)

ACT 4 / SCENE 6

*(Enter [*ROBIN, *the]* CLOWN, DICK, *[the]* HORSE-
COURSER, *and a* CARTER.°)

CARTER: Come, my masters, I'll bring you to the best
beer in Europe. What ho, hostess! Where be
these whores?

(Enter HOSTESS.)

HOSTESS: How now, what lack you? What, my old
5 guests, welcome.

ROBIN: Sirrah, Dick, dost thou know why I stand so
mute?
DICK: No, Robin; why is't?
ROBIN: I am eighteen pence on the score.° But say
nothing; see if she have forgotten me. 10
HOSTESS: Who's this that stands so solemnly by him-
self? What, my old guest?
ROBIN: O hostess, how do you? I hope my score stands
still.°
HOSTESS: Ay, there's no doubt of that, for methinks 15
you make no haste to wipe it out.
DICK: Why, hostess, I say, fetch us some beer.
HOSTESS: You shall presently. Look up into th'hall
there, ho!

(Exit.)

DICK: Come, sirs, what shall we do now till mine host- 20
ess come?
CARTER: Marry, sir, I'll tell you the bravest tale how a
conjurer served me. You know Doctor Fauster?
HORSE-COURSER: Ay, a plague take him. Here's some
on's have cause to know him. Did he conjure thee 25
too?
CARTER: I'll tell you how he served me. As I was going
to Wittenberg t'other day with a load of hay, he
met me and asked me what he should give me for
as much hay as he could eat. Now, sir, I thinking 30
that a little would serve his turn, bade him take as
much as he would for three farthings. So he
presently gave me my money and fell to eating;
and as I am a cursen° man, he never left eating till
he had eat up all my load of hay. 35
ALL: O monstrous! Eat a whole load of hay!
ROBIN: Yes, yes, that may be, for I have heard of one
that has eat a load of logs.
HORSE-COURSER: Now, sirs, you shall hear how villain-
ously he served me. I went to him yesterday to buy 40
a horse of him, and he would by no means sell
him under forty dollars. So, sir, because I knew
him to be such a horse as would run over hedge
and ditch and never tire, I gave him his money. So
when I had my horse, Doctor Fauster bade me 45
ride him night and day and spare him no time;
but, quoth he, in any case ride him not into the
water. Now sir, I thinking the horse had had some
rare quality that he would not have me know of,
what did I but ride him into a great river, and 50
when I came just in the midst, my horse vanished
away, and I sat straddling upon a bottle of hay.
ALL: O brave doctor!
HORSE-COURSER: But you shall hear how bravely I
served him for it. I went me home to his house, 55

---

conceit, thoughts. *mystery,* quality. *cozening scab,*
deceitful, contemptible rascal. *bottle,* bundle. *Carter,* a
person who drives a cart.

---

on the score, in debt. *stands still,* does not go higher.
cursen, christened.

and there I found him asleep. I kept a hallooing and whooping in his ears, but all could not wake him. I seeing that, took him by the leg and never rested pulling till I had pulled me his leg quite off, and now 'tis at home in mine hostry.

60

ROBIN: And has the doctor but one leg then? That's excellent, for one of his devils turned me into the likeness of an ape's face.

CARTER: Some more drink, hostess.

65 ROBIN: Hark you, we'll into another room and drink a while, and then we'll go seek out the doctor.

(Exeunt.)

ACT 4 / SCENE 7

(Enter the DUKE *of Anholt, his* DUCHESS, FAUSTUS, *and* MEPHISTOPHILIS [*Servants and Attendants*].*)*

DUKE: Thanks, master doctor, for these pleasant sights. Nor know I how sufficiently to recompense your great deserts° in erecting that enchanted castle in the air, the sight whereof so delighted me, as noth-

5 ing in the world could please me more.

FAUSTUS: I do think myself, my good lord, highly recompensed in that it pleaseth your grace to think but well of that which Faustus hath performed. But, gracious lady, it may be that you have taken

10 no pleasure in those sights. Therefore, I pray you, tell me what is the thing you most desire to have; be it in the world, it shall be yours. I have heard that great-bellied women do long for things are rare and dainty.

15 DUCHESS: True, master doctor, and since I find you so kind, I will make known unto you what my heart desires to have. And were it now summer, as it is January, a dead time of the winter, I would request no better meat than a dish of ripe grapes.

20 FAUSTUS: This is but a small matter. Go, Mephistophilis, away!

(Exit MEPHISTOPHILIS.*)*

Madam, I will do more than this for your content.

(Enter MEPHISTOPHILIS *again with the grapes.)*

Here; now taste ye these. They should be good, for they come from a far country, I can tell you.

25 DUKE: This makes me wonder more than all the rest, that at this time of year, when every tree is barren of his fruit, from whence you had these ripe grapes.

FAUSTUS: Please it, your grace, the year is divided into two circles over the whole world, so that when it is

30 winter with us, in the contrary circle it is likewise summer with them, as in India, Saba,° and such countries that lie far east, where they have fruit

twice a year. From whence, by means of a swift spirit that I have, I had these grapes brought, as you see.

DUCHESS: And trust me, they are the sweetest grapes 35 that e'er I tasted.

(The CLOWN[S, ROBIN, DICK, *the* CARTER, *and the* HORSE-COURSER,] *bounce at the gate within.)*

DUKE: What rude disturbers have we at the gate? Go, pacify their fury. Set it ope, And then demand of them what they would have.

[*Exit a* SERVANT.]

(They knock again and call out to talk with FAUSTUS.*)*

[*Enter* SERVANT *to them.*]

SERVANT: Why, how now, masters, what a coil° is there?   40
What is the reason you disturb the duke.

DICK: We have no reason for it; therefore a fig for him.

SERVANT: Why, saucy varlets,° dare you be so bold?

HORSE-COURSER: I hope, sir, we have wit enough to be more bold than welcome.   45

SERVANT: It appears so. Pray be bold elsewhere, And trouble not the duke.

DUKE: What would they have?

SERVANT: They all cry out to speak with Doctor Faustus.

CARTER: Ay, and we will speak with him.

DUKE: Will you, sir? Commit the rascals.   50

DICK: Commit with us! He were as good commit with his father as commit with us.

FAUSTUS: I do beseech your grace, let them come in; They are good subject for a merriment.

DUKE: Do as thou wilt, Faustus. I give thee leave.   55

FAUSTUS: I thank your grace.

(Enter ROBIN, DICK, CARTER, *and* HORSE-COURSER.*)*

                        Why, how now, my good friends?
'Faith you are too outrageous,° but come near;
I have procured your pardons. Welcome all!

ROBIN: Nay, sir, we will be welcome for our money, and we will pay for what we take. What ho! Give's 60 half a dozen of beer here, and be hanged.

FAUSTUS: Nay, hark you; can you tell me where you are?

CARTER: Ay, marry can I: we are under heaven.

SERVANT: Ay, but sir sauce-box, know you in what 65 place?

HORSE-COURSER: Ay, ay, the house is good enough to drink in. Zouns, fill us some beer, or we'll break all the barrels in the house and dash out all your brains with your bottles.   70

---

deserts, good deeds.   **Saba,** Sheba.

coil, disturbance.   **varlets,** knaves, rascals.   **outrageous,** violent.

FAUSTUS: Be not so furious. Come, you shall have
beer.
My lord, beseech you give me leave a while:
I'll gage my credit, 'twill content your grace.
DUKE: With all my heart, kind doctor. Please thyself;
75　Our servants and our court's at thy command.
FAUSTUS: I humbly thank your grace. Then fetch
some beer.
HORSE-COURSER: Ay, marry, there spake a doctor
indeed, and 'faith, I'll drink a health to thy
80　wooden leg for that word.
FAUSTUS: My wooden leg? What dost thou mean by
that?
CARTER: Ha, ha, ha! Dost hear him, Dick? He has
forgot his leg.
85　HORSE-COURSER: Ay, ay, he does not stand much°
upon that.
FAUSTUS: No, faith; not much upon a wooden leg.
CARTER: Good lord, that flesh and blood should be so
frail with your worship! Do not you remember a
90　horse-courser you sold a horse to?
FAUSTUS: Yes, I remember I sold one a horse.
CARTER: And do you remember you bid he should
not ride into the water?
FAUSTUS: Yes, I do very well remember that.
95　CARTER: And do you remember nothing of your leg?
FAUSTUS: No, in good sooth.
CARTER: Then, I pray, remember your courtesy.°
FAUSTUS: I thank you, sir.
CARTER: 'Tis not so much worth. I pray you, tell me
100　one thing.
FAUSTUS: What's that?
CARTER: Be both your legs bedfellows every night
together?
FAUSTUS: Wouldst thou make a Colossus° of me, that
105　thou askest me such questions?
CARTER: No, truly, sir. I would make nothing of you,
but I would fain know that.

(Enter HOSTESS with drink.)

FAUSTUS: Then, I assure thee, certainly they are.
CARTER: I thank you; I am fully satisfied.
110　FAUSTUS: But wherefore dost thou ask?
CARTER: For nothing, sir. But methinks you should
have a wooden bedfellow of one of 'em.
HORSE-COURSER: Why, do you hear, sir; did not I pull
off one of your legs when you were asleep?
115　FAUSTUS: But I have it again, now I am awake. Look
you here, sir.
ALL: O horrible! Had the doctor three legs?
CARTER: Do you remember, sir, how you cozened me
and ate up my load of—

---

stand much, make much of (with a quibble). **courtesy,**
curtsy, or leg. **Colossus,** a giant statue said to have stood with
its legs astride at the entrance to the ancient harbor of
Rhodes.

(FAUSTUS charms him dumb.)

DICK: Do you remember how you made me wear an　120
ape's—

[FAUSTUS charms him dumb.]

HORSE-COURSER: You whoreson conjuring scab, do
you remember how you cozened me with a ho—

[FAUSTUS charms him dumb.]

ROBIN: Ha' you forgotten me? You think to carry it
away° with your *hey-pass* and *re-pass*; do you　125
remember the dog's fa—

[FAUSTUS charms him dumb.]

(Exeunt CLOWNS.)

HOSTESS: Who pays for the ale? Hear you, master doctor, now you have sent away my guests, I pray who
shall pay me for my a—

[FAUSTUS charms her dumb.]

(Exit HOSTESS.)

DUCHESS: My lord,　130
We are much beholding to this learnèd man.
DUKE: So are we, madam, which we will recompense
With all the love and kindness that we may.
His artful sport drives all sad thoughts away.

(Exeunt.)

ACT 5 / SCENE 1

(*Thunder and lightning. Enter* DEVILS *with covered
dishes.* MEPHISTOPHILIS *leads them into* FAUSTUS'
study. Then enter WAGNER.)

WAGNER: I think my master means to die shortly.
He has made his will and given me his wealth,
His house, his goods, and store of golden plate,
Besides two thousand ducats ready coined.
I wonder what he means. If death were nigh,　5
He would not frolic thus. He's now at supper
With the scholars, where there's such belly-cheer
As Wagner in his life ne'er saw the like.
And see where they come; belike the feast is done.

(*Exit.*)

(Enter FAUSTUS, MEPHISTOPHILIS, *and two or three*
SCHOLARS.)

FIRST SCHOLAR: Master Doctor Faustus, since our con-　10
ference about fair ladies, which was the beauti-
fulest in all the world, we have determined with
ourselves that Helen of Greece was the admir-

---

carry it away, come off best.

ablest lady that ever lived. Therefore, master doc-
15 tor, if you will do us so much favor as to let us see
that peerless dame of Greece, whom all the world
admires for majesty, we should think ourselves
much beholding unto you.
FAUSTUS: Gentlemen,
20 For that I know your friendship is unfeigned,
And Faustus' custom is not to deny
The just requests of those that wish him well,
You shall behold that peerless dame of Greece,
No otherwise for pomp and majesty
25 Than when Sir Paris crossed the seas with her
And brought the spoils to rich Dardania.°
Be silent then, for danger is in words.

(*Music sounds.* MEPHISTOPHILIS *brings in* HELEN; *she
passeth over the stage.*)

SECOND SCHOLAR: Was this fair Helen, whose
admirèd worth
Made Greece with ten years' war afflict poor Troy?
30 Too simple is my wit to tell her praise,
Whom all the world admires for majesty.
THIRD SCHOLAR: No marvel though the angry Greeks
pursued
With ten years' war the rape of such a queen,
Whose heavenly beauty passeth all compare.
FIRST SCHOLAR: Since we have seen the pride of
35 nature's works
And only paragon of excellence,
We'll take our leaves and for this blessèd sight
Happy and blest be Faustus evermore.
FAUSTUS: Gentlemen, farewell; the same wish I to you.

(*Exeunt* SCHOLARS.)

(*Enter an* OLD MAN.)

40 OLD MAN: O gentle Faustus, leave this damnèd art,
This magic that will charm thy soul to hell
And quite bereave thee of salvation.
Though thou hast now offended like a man,
Do not persevere in it like a devil.
45 Yet, yet, thou hast an amiable° soul,
If sin by custom grow not into nature.
Then, Faustus, will repentance come too late;
Then thou art banished from the sight of heaven.
No mortal can express the pains of hell.
50 It may be this my exhortation
Seems harsh and all unpleasant; let it not,
For, gentle son, I speak it not in wrath
Or envy of° thee, but in tender love
And pity of thy future misery.

And so have hope that this my kind rebuke,   55
Checking° thy body, may amend thy soul.
FAUSTUS: Where art thou, Faustus? Wretch, what hast
thou done?
Damned art thou, Faustus, damned; despair and
die!
Hell claims his right, and with a roaring voice
Says, "Faustus, come; thine hour is almost come";   60
And Faustus now will come to do thee right.

(MEPHISTOPHILIS *gives him a dagger.*)

OLD MAN: O stay, good Faustus, stay thy desperate
steps.
I see an angel hovers o'er thy head,
And with a vial full of precious grace
Offers to pour the same into thy soul.   65
Then call for mercy and avoid despair.
FAUSTUS: Ah, my sweet friend, I feel thy words
To comfort my distressèd soul.
Leave me a while to ponder on my sins.
OLD MAN: Faustus, I leave thee, but with grief of
heart,   70
Fearing the enemy of thy hapless soul. (*Exit.*)
FAUSTUS: Accursèd Faustus, where is mercy now?
I do repent, and yet I do despair.
Hell strives with grace for conquest in my breast.
What shall I do to shun the snares of death?   75
MEPHISTOPHILIS: Thou traitor, Faustus, I arrest thy
soul
For disobedience to my sovereign lord.
Revolt, or I'll in piecemeal tear thy flesh.
FAUSTUS: I do repent I e'er offended him.
Sweet Mephistophilis, entreat thy lord   80
To pardon my unjust presumption,
And with my blood again I will confirm
The former vow I made to Lucifer.
MEPHISTOPHILIS: Do it then, Faustus, with
unfeignèd° heart,
Lest greater dangers do attend thy drift.°   85

[FAUSTUS *stabs his arm and writes on a paper with his
blood.*]

FAUSTUS: Torment, sweet friend, that base and agèd
man
That durst dissuade me from thy Lucifer,
With greatest torment that our hell affords.
MEPHISTOPHILIS: His faith is great; I cannot touch
his soul,
But what I may afflict his body with   90
I will attempt, which is but little worth.
FAUSTUS: One thing, good servant, let me crave of
thee
To glut the longing of my heart's desire—

Peerless dame . . . Dardania, The Greek Helen (the
"peerless dame"), wife of Menelaus, was carried off to Troy
(Dardania) by Paris, sparking the Trojan War. *amiable,* worthy of divine love or grace. *envy of,* ill will toward.

Checking, admonishing. *unfeignèd,* honest. *drift,*
purpose.

That I may have unto my paramour
95 That heavenly Helen which I saw of late,
Whose sweet embracings may extinguish clear
Those thoughts that do dissuade me from my vow,
And keep mine oath I made to Lucifer.
MEPHISTOPHILIS: This, or what else my Faustus shall desire,
100 Shall be performed in twinkling of an eye.

(*Enter* HELEN *again, passing over* [*the stage*] *between two* CUPIDS.)

FAUSTUS: Was this the face that launched a thousand ships
And burnt the topless towers of Ilium?
Sweet Helen, make me immortal with a kiss. [*She kisses him.*]
105 Her lips suck forth my soul. See where it flies!
Come, Helen, come, give me my soul again.
Here will I dwell, for heaven is in these lips,
And all is dross that is not Helena.

[*Enter the* OLD MAN.]

I will be Paris, and for love of thee
Instead of Troy shall Wittenberg be sacked;
110 And I will combat with weak Menelaus°
And wear thy colors on my plumèd crest.
Yea, I will wound Achilles° in the heel
And then return to Helen for a kiss.
O, thou art fairer than the evening's air,
115 Clad in the beauty of a thousand stars.
Brighter art thou than flaming Jupiter°
When he appeared to hapless Semele,°
More lovely than the monarch of the sky
In wanton Arethusa's azured arms,°
120 And none but thou shalt be my paramour.

(*Exeunt* [*all but the* OLD MAN].)

OLD MAN: Accursèd Faustus, miserable man,
That from thy soul exclud'st the grace of heaven
And fliest the throne of his tribunal seat!

(*Enter the* DEVILS.)

Satan begins to sift me with his pride.
125 As in this furnace God shall try my faith,
My faith, vile hell, shall triumph over thee.
Ambitious fiends, see how the heavens smiles
At your repulse and laughs your state° to scorn.
Hence hell, for hence I fly unto my God.

(*Exeunt.*)

Menelaus, the husband of Helen of Troy. **Achilles,** the Greek hero of the Trojan War, wounded in the heel by Paris. **Jupiter,** Zeus. **Semele,** the daughter of Cadmus and Harmonia who bore Zeus the child Dionysus. **monarch . . . arms,** Arethusa was a nymph, one of the Nereids, who governed a fountain on the isle of Ortygia near Syracuse. **state,** royal power.

ACT 5 / SCENE 2

(*Thunder. Enter* [*above*] LUCIFER, BEELZEBUB, *and* MEPHISTOPHILIS.)

LUCIFER: Thus from infernal Dis° do we ascend
To view the subjects of our monarchy,
Those souls which sin seals the black sons of hell,
'Mong which as chief, Faustus, we come to thee,
Bringing with us lasting damnation   5
To wait upon thy soul. The time is come
Which makes it forfeit.
MEPHISTOPHILIS: And this gloomy night,
Here in this room will wretched Faustus be.
BEELZEBUB: And here we'll stay
To mark him how he doth demean himself.   10
MEPHISTOPHILIS: How should he, but in desperate lunacy?
Fond worldling, now his heart-blood dries with grief;
His conscience kills it, and his laboring brain
Begets a world of idle fantasies
To over-reach the devil. But all in vain;   15
His store of pleasures must be sauced° with pain.
He and his servant, Wagner, are at hand.
Both come from drawing Faustus' latest will.
See where they come.

(*Enter* FAUSTUS *and* WAGNER.)

FAUSTUS: Say, Wagner, thou has perused my will;   20
How dost thou like it?
WAGNER: Sir, so wondrous well
As in all humble duty I do yield
My life and lasting service for your love.

(*Enter the* SCHOLARS.)

FAUSTUS: Gramercies,° Wagner. Welcome, gentlemen.

[*Exit* WAGNER.]

FIRST SCHOLAR: Now, worthy Faustus, methinks your   25
looks are changed.
FAUSTUS: Ah, gentlemen!
SECOND SCHOLAR: What ails Faustus?
FAUSTUS: Ah, my sweet chamber-fellow, had I lived
with thee, then had I lived still, but now must die   30
eternally. Look, sirs; comes he not? Comes he not?
FIRST SCHOLAR: O my dear Faustus, what imports this fear?
SECOND SCHOLAR: Is all our pleasure turned to melancholy?   35
THIRD SCHOLAR: He is not well with being over-solitary.
SECOND SCHOLAR: If it be so, we'll have physicians, and Faustus shall be cured.

Dis, Hades, or hell. **sauced,** paid for. **Gramercies,** thanks.

THIRD SCHOLAR: 'Tis but a surfeit sir; fear nothing.
40 FAUSTUS: A surfeit of deadly sin that hath damned
both body and soul.
SECOND SCHOLAR: Yet Faustus, look up to heaven, and
remember mercy is infinite.
FAUSTUS: But Faustus' offence can ne'er be pardoned.
45 The serpent that tempted Eve may be saved, but
not Faustus. Ah gentlemen, hear me with patience
and tremble not at my speeches. Though my heart
pants and quivers to remember that I have been a
student here these thirty years, O, would I had
50 never seen Wittenberg, never read book. And what
wonders I have done, all Germany can witness—
yea, all the world—for which Faustus hath lost
both Germany and the world, yea heaven itself,
heaven the seat of God, the throne of the blessed,
55 the kingdom of joy, and must remain in hell for
ever. Hell, ah hell for ever! Sweet friends, what
shall become of Faustus, being in hell for ever?
SECOND SCHOLAR: Yet Faustus, call on God.
FAUSTUS: On God, whom Faustus hath abjured? On
60 God, whom Faustus hath blasphemed? Ah, my
God, I would weep, but the devil draws in my tears.
Gush forth blood instead of tears, yea life and
soul. O, he stays my tongue! I would lift up my
hands, but see, they hold 'em; they hold 'em.
65 ALL: Who, Faustus?
FAUSTUS: Why, Lucifer and Mephistophilis. Ah, gentlemen, I gave them my soul for my cunning.
ALL: God forbid!
FAUSTUS: God forbade it indeed, but Faustus hath
70 done it. For the vain pleasure of four and twenty
years hath Faustus lost eternal joy and felicity. I
writ them a bill with mine own blood. The date is
expired. This is the time, and he will fetch me.
FIRST SCHOLAR: Why did not Faustus tell us of this
75 before, that divines might have prayed for thee?
FAUSTUS: Oft have I thought to have done so, but the
devil threatened to tear me in pieces if I named
God, to fetch me, body and soul, if I once gave ear
to divinity. And now 'tis too late. Gentlemen away,
80 lest you perish with me.
SECOND SCHOLAR: O, what may we do to save Faustus?
FAUSTUS: Talk not of me, but save yourselves and
depart.
THIRD SCHOLAR: God will strengthen me; I will stay
85 with Faustus.
FIRST SCHOLAR: Tempt not God, sweet friend, but let
us into the next room and there pray for him.
FAUSTUS: Ay, pray for me, pray for me; and what noise
soever you hear, come not unto me, for nothing
90 can rescue me.
SECOND SCHOLAR: Pray thou, and we will pray that
God may have mercy upon thee.
FAUSTUS: Gentlemen, farewell. If I live till morning,
I'll visit you; if not, Faustus is gone to hell.
95 ALL: Faustus, farewell.

(Exeunt SCHOLARS.)

MEPHISTOPHILIS: [above] Ay, Faustus, now thou hast
no hope of heaven;
Therefore despair. Think only upon hell,
For that must be thy mansion, there to dwell.
FAUSTUS: O thou bewitching fiend, 'twas thy
temptation
Hath robbed me of eternal happiness. 100
MEPHISTOPHILIS: I do confess it, Faustus, and rejoice.
'Twas I, that when thou wert i' the way to heaven,
Damned up thy passage. When thou took'st the
book
To view the Scriptures, then I turned the leaves
And led thine eye. 105
What, weep'st thou? 'Tis too late. Despair!
Farewell!
Fools that will laugh on earth must weep in hell.

(Exit.)

(Enter the GOOD ANGEL and the BAD ANGEL at several
doors.)

GOOD ANGEL: Ah, Faustus, if thou hadst given ear to
me,
Innumerable joys had followed thee;
But thou didst love the world.
BAD ANGEL: Gave ear to me, 110
And now must taste hell's pains perpetually.
GOOD ANGEL: O what will all thy riches, pleasures,
pomps
Avail thee now?
BAD ANGEL: Nothing but vex thee more,
To want in hell, that had on earth such store.

(Music while the throne descends.)

GOOD ANGEL: O, thou hast lost celestial happiness, 115
Pleasures unspeakable, bliss without end.
Hadst thou affected sweet divinity,
Hell or the devil had had no power on thee.
Hadst thou kept on that way, Faustus, behold
In what resplendent glory thou hadst sat 120
In yonder throne, like those bright shining saints.
And triumphed over hell. That hast thou lost,
And now, poor soul, must thy good angel leave
thee.

[The throne ascends.]

The jaws of hell are open to receive thee.

(Exit.)

(Hell is discovered.)

BAD ANGEL: Now, Faustus, let thine eyes with horror
stare 125
Into that vast perpetual torture-house.
There are the Furies tossing damnèd souls
On burning forks; their bodies boil in lead.
There are live quarters broiling on the coals,

130   That ne'er can die. This ever-burning chair
        Is for o'er-tortured souls to rest them in.
        These that are fed with sops of flaming fire
        Were gluttons and loved only delicates
        And laughed to see the poor starve at their gates.
135   But yet all these are nothing; thou shalt see
        Ten thousand tortures that more horrid be.
FAUSTUS: O, I have seen enough to torture me.
BAD ANGEL: Nay, thou must feel them, taste the smart
        of all.
        He that loves pleasure must for pleasure fall.
140   And so I leave thee, Faustus, till anon;
        Then wilt thou tumble in confusion.

        (Exit.)

        ([Hell disappears.] The clock strikes eleven.)

FAUSTUS: Ah Faustus,
        Now hast thou but one bare hour to live,
        And then thou must be damned perpetually.
145   Stand still, you ever-moving spheres of heaven,
        That time may cease and midnight never come.
        Fair nature's eye, rise, rise again, and make
        Perpetual day; or let this hour be but
        A year, a month, a week, a natural day,
150   That Faustus may repent and save his soul.
        O lente, lente currite noctis equi!°
        The stars move still; time runs; the clock will strike;
        The devil will come, and Faustus must be damned.
        O, I'll leap up to my God! Who pulls me down?
        See, see, where Christ's blood streams in the
155   firmament!
        One drop would save my soul, half a drop! Ah, my
        Christ!
        Rend not my heart for naming of my Christ!
        Yet will I call on him. O, spare me, Lucifer!
        Where is it now? 'Tis gone. And see where God
160   Stretcheth out his arm and bends his ireful brows.
        Mountains and hills, come, come, and fall on me,
        And hide me from the heavy wrath of God.
        No, no!
        Then will I headlong run into the earth.
165   Earth, gape! O no, it will not harbor me!
        You stars that reigned at my nativity,
        Whose influence hath allotted death and hell.
        Now draw up Faustus like a foggy mist
        Into the entrails of yon laboring cloud,
170   That when you vomit forth into the air,
        My limbs may issue from your smoky mouths,
        So that my soul may but ascend to heaven.

        (The watch strikes.)

        Ah, half the hour is past; 'twill all be past anon.
        O God,

O . . . equi, O slowly, slowly; run you horses of night
(adapted from Ovid's Amores).

If thou wilt not have mercy on my soul,   175
        Yet for Christ's sake, whose blood hath ransomed
        me,
        Impose some end to my incessant pain.
        Let Faustus live in hell a thousand years,
        A hundred thousand, and at last be saved.
        O, no end is limited to damnèd souls.   180
        Why wert thou not a creature wanting soul?
        Or why is this immortal that thou hast?
        Ah, Pythagoras' metempsychosis,° were that true,
        This soul should fly from me and I be changed
        Into some brutish beast. All beasts are happy,   185
        For, when they die
        Their souls are soon dissolved in elements,
        But mine must live still to be plagued in hell.
        Cursed be the parents that engendered me!
        No, Faustus, curse thyself, curse Lucifer   190
        That hath deprived thee of the joys of heaven.

        (The clock strikes twelve.)

        O, it strikes, it strikes! Now, body, turn to air,
        Or Lucifer will bear thee quick° to hell.
        O soul, be changed to little water-drops,
        And fall into the ocean, ne'er be found!   195

        (Thunder, and enter the DEVILS.)

        My God, my God, look not so fierce on me!
        Adders and serpents, let me breathe a while!
        Ugly hell, gape not! Come not, Lucifer!
        I'll burn my books! Ah, Mephistophilis!

        (Exeunt [FAUSTUS and DEVILS].)

ACT 5 / SCENE 3

        (Enter the SCHOLARS.)

FIRST SCHOLAR: Come, gentlemen, let us go visit
        Faustus,
        For such a dreadful night was never seen
        Since first the world's creation did begin.
        Such fearful shrieks and cries were never heard.
        Pray heaven the doctor have escaped the danger.   5
SECOND SCHOLAR: O help us, heaven! See, here are
        Faustus' limbs,
        All torn asunder by the hand of death.
THIRD SCHOLAR: The devils whom Faustus served
        have torn him thus;
        For 'twixt the hours of twelve and one, methought
        I heard him shriek and call aloud for help,
        At which self time the house seemed all on fire   10
        With dreadful horror of these damnèd fiends.

---

metempsychosis, belief in the transmigration of souls,
associated with the Greek philosopher Pythagoras of Samos.
quick, alive.

SECOND SCHOLAR: Well, gentlemen, though Faustus'
    end be such
As every Christian heart laments to think on,
15   Yet for he was a scholar, once admired
For wondrous knowledge in our German schools,
We'll give his mangled limbs due burial;
And all the students clothed in mourning black,
Shall wait upon° his heavy° funeral.

(Exeunt.)

EPILOGUE

(Enter CHORUS.*)*

CHORUS: Cut is the branch that might have grown
    full straight,

---

wait upon, be present at.   *heavy,* sorrowful.

And burnèd is Apollo's laurel bough
That sometime grew within this learnèd man.
Faustus is gone. Regard his hellish fall,
Whose fiendful fortune may exhort the wise   5
Only to wonder at unlawful things,
Whose deepness doth entice such forward wits
To practice more than heavenly power permits.

[*Exit.*]

    Terminat hora diem; terminat author opus.°

    Terminat. . . opus, The hour ends the day; the author
ends his work.

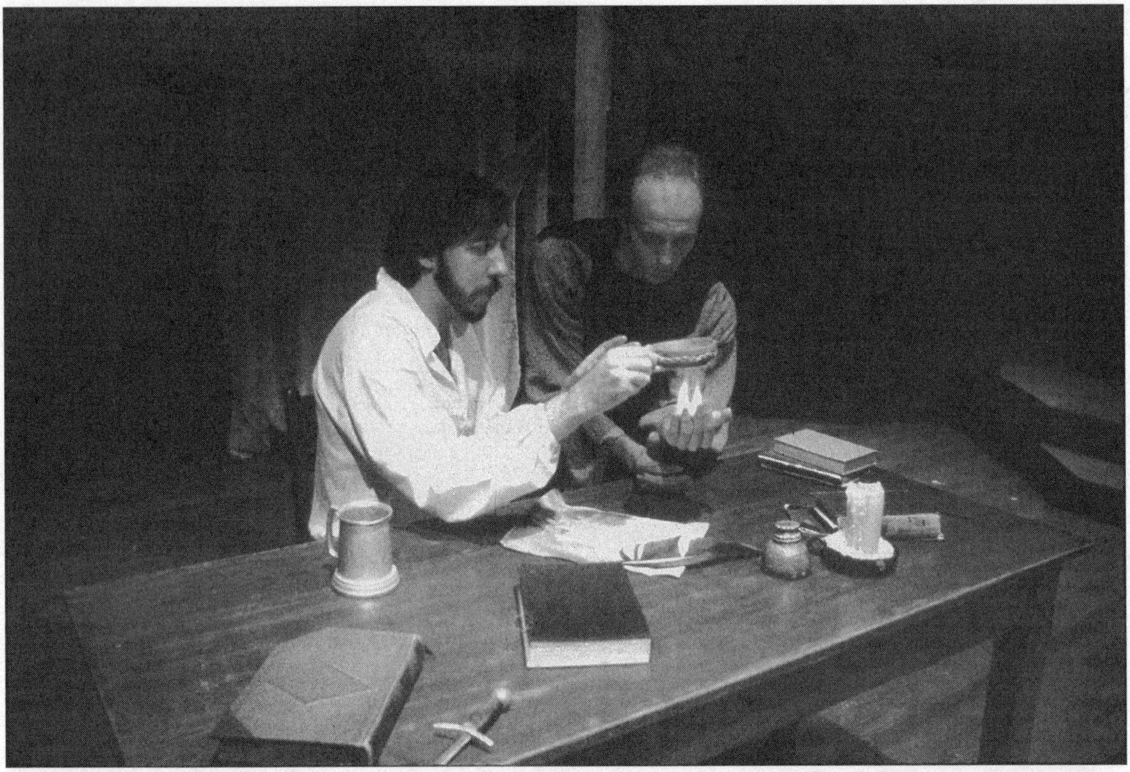

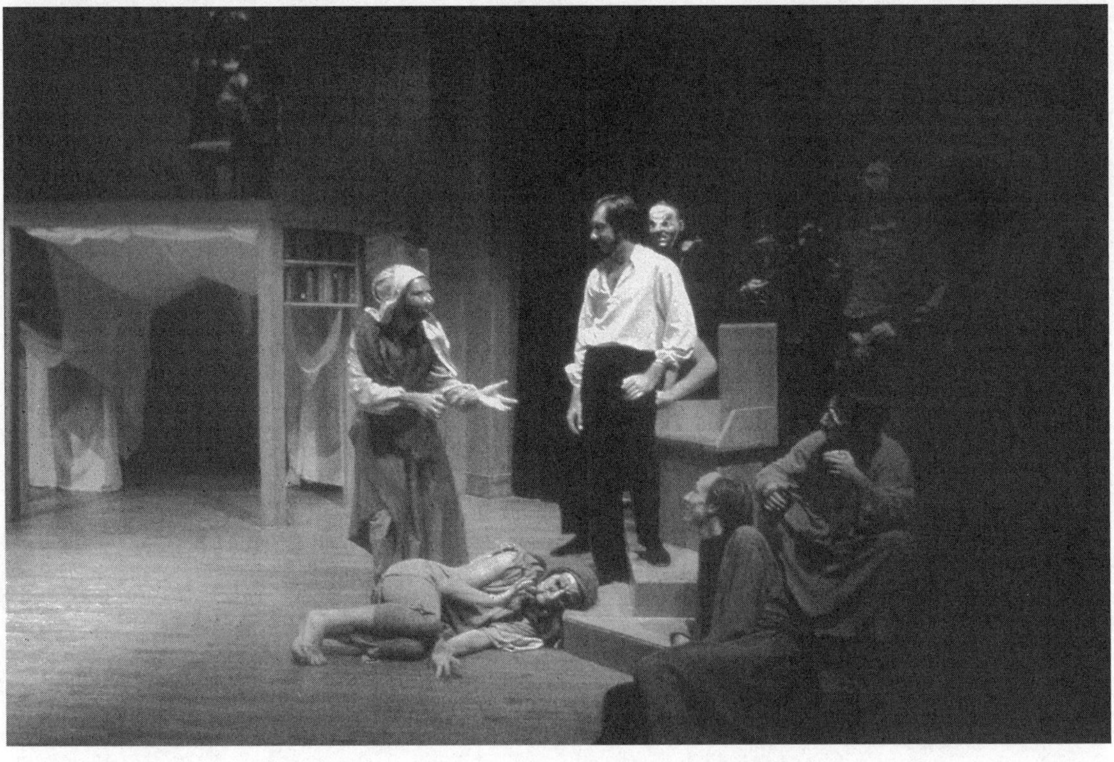

Figure 1. (facing page, top) Mephistophilis (Alex Fallis) magically produces flames in his hand so that Faustus's congealed blood will flow again and allow Faustus (Robert Bruce Latimer) to sign away his soul. G. B. Shand directed the play for Poculi Ludique Societas (The Drinking and Playing Society) at the University of Toronto, 1984. (Photograph: Courtesy of G. B. Shand.)

Figure 2. (facing page, bottom) Faustus (Robert Bruce Latimer, *center*), listens to the appeal of Lechery (David Philip), while Sloth (Frederick Omsted) sprawls on the floor in front of Faustus. Framing the scene are Mephistophilis (Alex Fallis, *on floor, right*) and, seated above, Lucifer (John Bruce Bannerman) and Beelzebub (John A. G. McKeown). From the Poculi Ludique Societas production. (Photograph: Courtesy of G. B. Shand.)

Figure 3. (above) Near the end of the play, Faustus (Robert Bruce Latimer) thinks of repentance, but Mephistophilis (Alex Fallis) holds a dagger to his throat and threatens him, "Revolt, or I'll in piecemeal tear thy flesh." From the Poculi Ludique Societas production. (Photograph: Courtesy of G. B. Shand.)

Staging of *Doctor Faustus*

G. B. SHAND ON DIRECTING THE POCULI
LUDIQUE SOCIETAS PRODUCTION OF
DOCTOR FAUSTUS AT THE UNIVERSITY
OF TORONTO, 1984

[. . .] Ours was a heavily doubled, transparently all-male production, its stylistic stress on performance, on a troupe of actors telling the story of Faustus. We consulted a magician, and together devised a series of fire-tricks and materializations, all looking ahead to hell, all effected by Mephostophilis* (Alex Fallis). The tricks were the sort any illusionist can master readily: fire in the bare palm to heat Faustus's congealed blood, a flaming book, grapes materializing from a flash of fire in an empty pan, Mephostophilis (once again a devil rather than a friar) spitting fire from the upper level at his final appearance—all part of our sense that Faustus wastes his wonder on petty yet dangerous flashiness, different not only in degree but in kind from the high imaginings of his first two scenes, and totally dependent on Mephostophilis for its accomplishing.

We used fourteen actors, one each for Faustus, Mephostophilis, and Chorus, with the remaining eleven sharing fifty-one roles. In fact, thirteen actors can cover the play comfortably in any of several doubling schemes, but we elected to have the Chorus onstage throughout. I found casting to a predetermined pattern too limiting and chose instead to assemble a company of actors around Faustus and Mephostophilis and then parcel out roles. The seven deadly sins served as a kind of core, from which I fanned out into the rest of the play. Most doubles arose from the special qualities of individual actors, of course (in our case, Good Angel and Pope, for instance, at the sacrifice of the text's invitation to double the Pope with Lucifer—B.3.1.899), but several grew interestingly from the sins themselves: Lechery became a lecherous Robin, excitedly chafing his crotch as he gloated over Faustus's conjuring book and anticipated his imminent success with the maidens of the parish; Gluttony became a series of orally fixated characters—the Duke of Anholt, transfixed by his wife's grapes, Raymond of Hungary at the papal banquet; and Sloth, with its attendant connotation of despair, became Helen of Troy. An early note to all the sin-actors was to keep their sin in mind and watch for how (if at all) it might colour any of their other roles.

*Shand refers to an alternate version of the text that uses archaic spellings.

The omnipresent Chorus was our way of staying in touch with the morality dimension of the play. He was intended as a constant reminder of Time and Death, as well as presenter of the action's exempla. He wore a ragged garment hung with odd bits of bone; he carried a tabor reminiscent of one of Holbein's Death figures; and he beat that tabor with a human arm bone to punctuate the terms of Faustus's contract, to accompany the procession of the sins, to augment the sounds of hell at the first appearance of Mephostophilis, and so on. With that same bone and a small gong he struck the hours in Faustus's final night. (And that bone, seized from him, became the wand Mephostophilis used to charm Faustus invisible before the papal banquet.) The idea grew out of the piper who, in the B-text, leads the Seven Deadly Sins (2.2.730).

The George Ignatieff Theatre has an Elizabethan-style thrust platform. Michael Crawford, the set designer, provided a booth-like structure, up centre, with an upper level on it. Faustus's study was identified with the booth, though his scenes came forward from it onto the platform. (This was of a piece with our decision to take his opening soliloquy out to the audience in large part, rather than to have him internalize it— we treated it as public rationalization and persuasion after the fact, rather than as private decision-making.) The booth also served as a hell-mouth at the end, the transformation merely suggested by lighting and smoke. Front and centre was a small frame prie-dieu, onstage throughout as a constant invitation to repentance. The usual symmetry of the Elizabethan platform was broken by a slightly raised dais stage left with an all-purpose throne on it (papal throne, Faustus's seat for the show of the seven deadlies, and so on), and by an irregular arrangement of blacks hung at the rear. There is neither trap nor fly-space in this theatre, so Mephostophilis first entered from the booth, while Faustus conjured above him, and the throne in the heavens was only suggested by a white spotlight.

The costumes, designed by Claudia Sommers, consisted of a basic loose shirt and elastic-waisted corduroy pants for all, to which identifying elements were added as the actors moved from role to role, sometimes in view of the audience (most notably when Mephostophilis transformed himself from devil into friar in the upstage shadows while Faustus descended from the upper level to meet him on the forestage). One of the advantages of the basic costume was that it drew a clear visual link between Faustus and the Good and Bad Angels—no further identifying costume was added to the angels at all. Claudia Sommers's original scheme for the angels had involved a more conventional imagery—wings and the like—but I saw them as spiritual figures of something like Temptation and Conscience.

At least one interesting convention in our production grew from our handling of the angels in rehearsal. Fairly early on, to help Robert Latimer find the real energy of Faustus's first soliloquy, I had the Bad Angel come onstage near the beginning of the speech and just remain here, unobtrusive but present, as Faustus went through the motions of his temptation to magic and necromancy. The presence of the Bad Angel made so strong and interesting a statement that we retained it, and indeed let it develop into a convention in which the Bad Angel was regularly onstage ahead of the Good Angel to start their scenes, and lingered after the Good Angel's departure as those scenes concluded. This weighted the action on the side of hell, of course, but my sense is that B's version of the damnation clearly does that in any event. We found, incidentally, something not apparent in the script: a highly playable tension between the angels, achieved through eye-contact and through the constant awareness of each angel that his audience is not merely Faustus but the other angel as well. A sharp element of contest thus informed each of their appearances, and Faustus's damnation became, at last, a clear victory for the Bad Angel, not simply over Faustus but over the Good Angel as well.

It was a more complicated and painful victory for Mephostophilis. As we watched his character grow, we listened closely to the pain in:

Why this is hel, nor am I out of it:
Thinkst thou that I who saw the face of God,

And tasted the eternal ioyes of heauen,
Am not tormented with ten thousand hels,
In being depriv'd of euerlasting blisse. (A.3.32 1-25)

We postulated that his personal hell is to be forced to relive his own fall over and over for eternity by engineering and attending the falls of others, that he knows Faustus's fall will recapitulate his own, that that is his special trap. One of the most interesting offstage moments to us, therefore, was Mephostophilis's interview with Lucifer after his first meeting with Faustus, when he must relay Faustus's proposal and receive his own orders. There are many routes to a deeply-felt and affecting Mephostophilis, but one of them is surely to plant the seed of this meeting in the actor's mind, by improvising this offstage scene, and remembering its emotional content.

All-male *Faustuses* have perhaps become commonplace, but there is good reason for casting this way, namely that, in this play at least, Marlowe not only wrote for the all-male convention but by and large failed to transcend it in his imagination and realization of female character. (I have an intuition of Shakespeare imagining his fictive women as he wrote, Marlowe imagining his male actors.) Certainly, little in *Faustus* gives any sign that Marlowe foresaw (consciously or subliminally) performance of the play's females by women. There are, of the more than fifty roles in the play, five females. Three of these (hot whore, Paramour, and Helen) are non-speaking walk-ons. The other two (Hostess and Duchess) appear together and share a total of eight lines. It is not as if women hired for the female roles in *Doctor Faustus* will get much by the way of challenging and gratifying work. But men, playing combinations of male and female roles in the piece, can be given very satisfying assignments without violating the conventions of the play. The all-male choice seemed (and seems) to me an inherent condition of the play, part and parcel of its essential anti-romantic nature. [. . .]

WILLIAM SHAKESPEARE

1564–1616

The story of Othello's life is filled with "most disastrous chances," "moving accidents," and "hair-breadth escapes," but the life of his creator was evidently far more mundane. We know from church registers that Shakespeare married in 1582, that he had a daughter in 1583, and twins, a son and daughter, in 1585. Legal documents tell us that he defaulted several times on paying his taxes, that he bought a large house in Stratford, that, like many of his contemporaries, he engaged in taking others to court. And records from the royal court show him performing for both Elizabeth I and James I. But information about his theatrical career is disappointingly fragmentary. We know that at some point between 1585 and 1592, Shakespeare left Stratford, went to London, and became an actor and playwright, yet we do not know exactly when or how he became involved with the professional theater companies. We know that he was both an actor and shareholder in one of the major theatrical companies, first called the Lord Chamberlain's Men, then the King's Men, but we have no details about the company's rehearsals and few about its performances, so we do not know anything specific about his day-to-day activities in the company. We do not even know for certain the exact order in which he composed his plays, nor do we know exactly how he occupied himself after 1611, when he appears to have retired almost completely from playwriting and the theatrical world of London.

Although little is known about his personal life in Stratford or his professional activities in London, we can begin to understand his remarkably productive career as a playwright—thirty-seven plays in a period of twenty-three years—by recognizing the numerous literary and dramatic sources that nurtured it, for Shakespeare was not an isolated genius, weaving plots and characters entirely out of the threads of his own imagination. Like his contemporaries, Marlowe, Jonson, and Webster, he was influenced by classical plays available in English translation, as well as numerous French and Italian works, not to mention the rich tradition of native English drama, including cycle plays, morality plays, folk plays from the countryside, and highly formal plays from the University writers of his own time. Throughout his career, in fact, Shakespeare drew ideas for his plays from a richly varied body of material: Roman comedies, Roman histories, English chronicles, English novellas, and French as well as Italian stories. But he always transformed the material he borrowed. He began his career, for example, by borrowing from the Roman dramatist Plautus (ca. 254–184 B.C.), turning Plautus's *Menaechmi* into his own *The Comedy of Errors* (1590), a farce far more comically confusing than its counterpart because Shakespeare added twin servants to the twin protagonists of Plautus. In history plays, such as *Richard II* (1595), *Henry IV, Part I* (1597), *Henry IV, Part II* (1598), and *Henry V* (1599), he condensed large and cumbersome bodies of material from the English chronicler Holinshed into powerful theatrical experiences, each of which can stand on its own, yet which together embody a coherent political philosophy. In *Much Ado About Nothing* (1599), he drew not only from his own earlier plays—the battle between the sexes is familiar from *The Taming of the Shrew* (1593) and *Love's Labors Lost* (1594)—but also from multiple versions of the deceived lover story, retold in Italian (Ariosto and Bandello) and English (Spenser). And in *Othello* (1604), he turned a brief but rambling story by the Italian writer Giraldi Cinthio into one of his most tightly constructed tragedies, adding events, creating new characters, such as Roderigo, and endowing the main characters with complex motivations.

In the making of plots, Shakespeare was equally resourceful and experimental. He was particularly intrigued by plots that bring together seemingly disparate groups of characters. In *A Midsummer Night's Dream* (1595), he juggles three wildly different worlds of experience by intertwining the crisscross love entanglements of four young Athenians with the love jealousy of the King and Queen of the Fairies and the comically bumbling rehearsal and production of a tragic love story by a group of Athenian workmen—and all these different lines of action are framed by the marriage festivities for Theseus, Duke of Athens, and Hippolyta, Queen of the Amazons. In *Much Ado About Nothing*, Shakespeare juxtaposes two very different couples, the easily swayed Claudio and the obedient Hero with the wittily independent Benedick and Beatrice whose arguments seem likely to continue even after the play ends. And though in *Othello* Shakespeare moves the action from the city of Venice to the island of Cyprus, he nonetheless designs the single plot so carefully that neither characters nor audience members have time to question the inexorable development of the tragedy.

Above all, Shakespeare was highly flexible in his use of language. Blank verse is the dominant form for most of his plays, but he tuned that line to the harmonies of every mood and feeling—to the strident rhythms of men at war, as in *Henry V;* to the intoxicated melodies of men and women in love, as in *A Midsummer Night's Dream;* and to the heavenly music of visionaries, as in *The Tempest.* Yet he did not hesitate to move from the harmonies of verse to the different harmonies of prose—within a play, a scene, or the dialogue of a single character—always suiting the style to the dramatic situation. In Act 3, Scene 1 of *Much Ado,* for example, Beatrice overhears Hero and Ursula talking—in a carefully staged conversation—of Benedick's love for Beatrice; after Hero and Ursula leave, Beatrice, who has only spoken in prose so far, comes forward and expresses her surprise in an abbreviated sonnet, the change from her normal language emphasizing the change in her feelings. In Act 1, Scene 3 and Act 2, Scene 1 of *Othello,* a prose scene between Roderigo and Iago is followed by a blank verse soliloquy from Iago, and here the different style subtly reinforces our sense of Iago as a wearer of masks, especially of verbal ones. Thus the shift from one form to another is not tied to specific social classes or emotions. Anyone can speak in rhymed couplets or in blank verse or in prose, and an important clue for an actor's interpretation of a character is to notice when shifts occur and why.

Whatever the form, Shakespeare's language is always tuned to the theatrical situation, implying gestures, movement, tone of voice. Beatrice's first line to Benedick, "I wonder that you will still be talking, Signior Benedick; nobody marks you," could simply state an obvious fact (Benedick is making a joke but the other people on stage aren't listening, or perhaps have moved away) or it might be a way to call herself to his attention (clearly, he hasn't "marked" her and so she makes sure that he does). And Benedick's reply, "What, my dear Lady Disdain! Are you yet living?" echoes her line ("still talking" and "yet living"), twisting it and challenging her in the first of their verbal duels. One of Othello's early lines prevents an actual fight as he speaks to the group of armed men seeking to arrest him (Act 1, Scene 2); "Keep up your bright swords, for the dew will rust them" quickly lets us know of the potential fight and of the calm, slightly ironic voice that disarms the men more surely than a blow.

Much Ado About Nothing appears near the middle of Shakespeare's career, one of the three major comedies written between 1598 and 1600 and like the other two, *As You Like It* and *Twelfth Night*, seems to say with the title that nothing really serious is going on. But the title is deceptive, just as one of the subjects of *Much Ado* is deception: romantic deception when Don Pedro woos Hero for his young friend Claudio; comic deception practiced on Benedick to make him believe that Beatrice is in love with him—and on Beatrice to make her think that Benedick is in love with her; and destructive deception created by Don John to plant doubts about Hero's fidelity in the mind of Claudio, her fiancé. Indeed, the main plot of *Much Ado*, in which Claudio comes to believe that Hero has been unfaithful to him, and so rejects her, is a story that Shakespeare turned to throughout his career. While Claudio's behavior at the wedding causes Hero to swoon, thus lending credence to the report that she has died, in later plays male jealousy is even more destructive. In *Othello*, Iago's insinuations about Othello's bride, Desdemona, finally move Othello to murder his beloved wife; in *Cymbeline* (1609), Posthumus, exiled from Britain, sees evidence that makes him believe his wife, Imogen, has been unfaithful and he tries to have her murdered; and in *The Winter's Tale* (1610), King Leontes, without any outside prompting, accuses his wife, Hermione, of infidelity, seizes and sends away her newborn daughter, and brings his wife to public trial. Each of these jealous men—Claudio, Othello, Posthumus, and Leontes—finally comes to realize his mistake, but not before the women they claim to love have been shamed, attacked, and even, as with Desdemona, killed.

Despite the pain and embarrassment associated with the story of Hero and Claudio, *Much Ado* remains for most audiences a sparkling and delightful comedy. In large part, the play's appeal grows out of the witty repartee between Benedick and Beatrice, who can't stop talking about each other, even if they do so with one verbal put-down after another. And though they are "deceived" by cunningly devised conversations into admitting their affection for each other, we recognize from their earliest interchange that each seeks the other's notice and approval. So the overhearing scenes in Act 2, Scene 3, and Act 3, Scene 1, are delightful comic mechanisms that bring both Benedick and Beatrice to admitting what we, the audience, already know. Moreover, once we see how easily Claudio and Don Pedro (and even Leonato, Hero's father) come to believe the insinuations of Don John and move from love to suspicion, we recognize the truth of Benedick's wry comment to Beatrice: "Thou and I are too wise to woo peaceably." The very smoothness of the Hero/Claudio courtship has not allowed them any time to really get to know each other, while the witty antagonism of Benedick and Beatrice has, at least, revealed their less appealing aspects to each other.

Though Benedick and Beatrice tend, in discussion and in performance, to take over as the main characters, we should remember that, for all their wit and intelligence, they are not able to prevent or even to solve the ugly situation created at the wedding. The real villains (Don John and his henchman, Borachio) are ultimately unmasked by characters who are simultaneously inept and effective. Though Dogberry, the local constable, and Verges, his partner, know that the watchmen have arrested "two aspicious persons" (Don John's servants Borachio and Conrade), they so muddle the conversation that Leonato gives up trying to figure out what they are talking about and hurries off to the wedding—the wedding that might have been saved if Dogberry had been able to get to the point directly. Fortunately the watchmen are finally able to cut through Dogberry's loquacious irrelevance and reveal the scheming of Don John.

These varied elements—the melodrama of the main plot, the wit of Benedick and Beatrice, and the comic incompetence of Dogberry—provoke questions about personal and social relationships that can be embodied in a wide range of geographical settings and historical periods. In 1976, John Barton of the Royal Shakespeare Company set the play in nineteenth-century India, with Dogberry as a Sikh officer inordinately proud of his inadequate English. The play's nominal setting, Messina, has been represented as Messina, Sicily, in Franco Zeffirelli's broadly farcical version for England's National Theatre (1965) and Messina, Texas, in Spanish Colonial America at the American Shakespeare Festival in 1957. Perhaps the major question for contemporary productions has been to find an appropriate post-war setting, one in which the camaraderie and relaxation of soldiers no longer fighting will be evident. Thus, A. J. Antoon set his 1972 production for the New York Shakespeare Festival at the beginning of the twentieth century; the Spanish-American War was over, the First World War had not yet begun, and the intervening time was, as Antoon told his actors (see Staging of *Much Ado About Nothing*) "an age of innocence and simplicity." The costumes for the women echoed those of the Gibson Girls (see Figure 1); Dogberry, Verges, and the Watch were versions of the Keystone Kops, complete with a car chase when the Watch tried to catch Borachio and Conrade; and the production rewrote Benedick's final line from "Strike up, pipers" to the familiar American phrase "Strike up the band." The success of that production—not just in Central Park for free, but then on Broadway, with a television version shown in 1973—grew not only from its exuberantly American setting (Benedick overheard the conversation about Beatrice's love for him while hiding behind a canoe, as in Figure 2, rather than while skulking in an English orchard), but from its exploration of the central characters. When Douglass Watson's Don Pedro, responding to Beatrice's self-deprecatory comment about remaining single, asked her to marry him, he wasn't entirely joking, and Kathleen Widdoes' Beatrice had to pause before finding a gentle way to say "no" (see Figure 3). And even after Benedick and Beatrice had admitted their love to each other, they still maintained their masks of detachment (see Figure 4), preserving the witty individuality that is simultaneously attractive and defensive.

Though *Much Ado* and *Othello* share a similar plot, they are nonetheless strikingly different. Shakespeare's comedies and his tragedies differ primarily in scale, since the major tragedies—*Hamlet* (1601), *Othello* (1604), *King Lear* (1605), *Macbeth* (1605), and *Antony and Cleopatra* (1606)—are all about imposing figures in extremely trying situations. This emphasis on extremes is the source of the tragedies' special power. The marriage of Othello and Desdemona joins not just a man and a woman, but a middle-aged black Moorish soldier of obscure lineage and a young white Venetian lady of noble birth. This marriage, so hated by Desdemona's father, is for its partners an emblem of perfection. Desdemona tells the senators, "My heart's subdued / Even to the very quality of my lord," and Othello repeatedly stresses the extreme value he gives to Desdemona's love, as when he meets her after a dangerous sea voyage and exclaims, "If it were now to die, / 'Twere now to be most happy." Such declarations also imply the possibility of destruction, and the task Shakespeare sets for himself is first to create the reality of this extraordinary relationship and then to destroy it. The marriage of Iago and Emilia, by contrast, with its bitter jests and spiteful remarks, as well as the casual flirtation of Cassio with Bianca, make us see more clearly the special beauty of the love between Othello and Desdemona.

Although *Othello* may be seen as a Shakespeare morality play—with all the forces for good represented by Desdemona's beauty, strength, honesty, and faith, balanced by the forces for evil embodied in Iago's hatred of beauty, his cowardice, his lying, and his cynicism—it is nonetheless strikingly contemporary in its exploration of psychological behavior. Othello seems outwardly calm when faced by swords, senators, or Turks, but inwardly he worries about his age, his blackness, his status as an outsider in Venetian society, and about his relationship to his wife. And Iago's ability to find Othello's vulnerable spots reveals to us that Iago, like Othello, is also jealous, and creates in the man he hates, and serves, the same poisonous jealousy that he feels. Both Othello and Iago are products of the male military world, a world in which women seem to have no real place, except as they dominate the thoughts and feelings of their husbands.

In addition to a series of complicated male-female relationships (see Gwyn Morgan's interview following the text), the play raises further questions for both audiences and actors with its persistent focus on race and racial prejudice. From the opening scene of the play, characters constantly refer to Othello as "the Moor" even when they claim that they respect his soldierly accomplishments; Iago, Roderigo, and Brabantio are much less complimentary. The role was for many years played only by white actors (in varying shades of makeup), and not until 1930 did the great American actor-singer Paul Robeson appear in London in a major professional production of the play. Indeed, when Laurence Olivier, considered by many the greatest Shakespearean actor of the twentieth century, played Othello in 1964 and emphasized Othello's racial otherness (see Ronald Bryden's review), some critics were appalled. But Olivier generated controversy not only with his physical presence, his blackness accentuated by costumes in white and black (see Figure 1), but also with his sense of the self-deception which informs and defines the character. Olivier's Othello was less a deluded victim than a proud lover who seemed to drag the lies out of Iago (note Kenneth Tynan's description of the rehearsal process in "Staging of *Othello*"), and Frank Finlay played Iago with an open face and slightly bent posture (see Figure 2), which seemed to suggest that Iago might, indeed, be harmless. Perhaps, since Olivier had himself played Iago (in 1938), he knew how easily an Iago could dominate the stage and wanted to make sure that his Othello was indeed the commanding figure of the play.

In contrast, the 1989 RSC production made Othello particularly vulnerable to Iago through Trevor Nunn's casting of Willard White, the Jamaican-born bass-baritone, as Othello. Experienced as an opera singer, with a deep and resonant voice (many reviewers were reminded of Paul Robeson, the only other black actor before White to play Othello at Stratford), Willard White was nonetheless new to Shakespeare. So when faced with the Iago of Ian McKellen, one of England's best-known Shakespearean actors, he seemed both dignified and naïve. Nunn's production was staged in the RSC's smallest auditorium, with the audience seated on all three sides, close enough to catch all the nuances of the complicated relationships, not just the central male-female relationships, but subsidiary relationships such as Iago's deft consoling of both Roderigo and Cassio and the conflicting feelings of Zoe Wanamaker's Emilia, at least ten years older than the Desdemona of Imogen Stubbs (see Figure 3), torn between a desire to help the young woman and resentment of Desdemona's happiness. Realistic props—the cigars Iago stole from the senate chamber, the small box of sweets that Cassio brought to Desdemona, the lemonade that Desdemona made for Othello but forgot to sweeten—helped to define the characters, and so the central importance of the handkerchief seemed utterly natural. When Iago wanted to twist Othello's thoughts, he did so while working at a table, handing military documents back and forth to him (see Figure 4), thus veiling his attack by launching it in between moments of stage business. Only when he is alone does Iago reveal his hatred to the audience, and at the play's end, he gazes in silence at the bed containing the dead Othello and Desdemona, looking with dispassionate appreciation at the destruction he has caused. Such silence—chosen by Iago when Othello tries to find out why Iago has "thus ensnared my soul and body"—may be the silence of unknowable evil, of defiant resentment, of trapped defeat, but it leaves the audience as frustrated as Othello, unable to find either answers or comfort in the play's bleak ending.

MUCH ADO ABOUT NOTHING

BY WILLIAM SHAKESPEARE / EDITED BY DAVID L. STEVENSON

CHARACTERS

DON PEDRO, *Prince of Aragon*
DON JOHN, *his bastard brother*
CLAUDIO, *a young lord of Florence*
BENEDICK, *a young lord of Padua*
LEONATO, *Governor of Messina*
ANTONIO, *an old man, his brother*
BALTHASAR, *attendant on Don Pedro*
BORACHIO ⎱
CONRADE ⎰ *followers of Don John*
FRIAR FRANCIS
DOGBERRY, *a constable*

VERGES, *a headborough*
A SEXTON
A BOY
HERO, *daughter to Leonato*
BEATRICE, *niece to Leonato*
MARGARET ⎱
URSULA ⎰ *gentlewomen attending on Hero*
MESSENGERS, WATCH, ATTENDANTS, *etc.*

SCENE
Messina

ACT 1 / SCENE 1

(Before LEONATO'*s house)*
(Enter LEONATO, *Governor of Messina,* HERO, *his daughter, and* BEATRICE, *his niece, with a* MESSENGER.*)*

LEONATO: I learn in this letter that Don Pedro of Aragon comes this night to Messina.

MESSENGER: He is very near by this. He was not three leagues off when I left him.

5 LEONATO: How many gentlemen° have you lost in this action?

MESSENGER: But few of any sort,° and none of name.°

LEONATO: A victory is twice itself when the achiever brings home full numbers. I find here that Don Pedro hath bestowed much honor on a young Florentine called Claudio.

MESSENGER: Much deserved on his part, and equally rememb'red by Don Pedro. He hath borne himself beyond the promise of his age, doing, in the figure of a lamb, the feats of a lion. He hath indeed better bett'red expectation° than you must expect of me to tell you how.

LEONATO: He hath an uncle° here in Messina will be very much glad of it.

20 MESSENGER: I have already delivered him letters, and there appears much joy in him; even so much

that joy could not show itself modest enough without a badge° of bitterness.

LEONATO: Did he break out into tears?

MESSENGER: In great measure. 25

LEONATO: A kind overflow of kindness.° There are no faces truer than those that are so washed. How much better is it to weep at joy than to joy at weeping!

BEATRICE: I pray you, is Signior Mountanto° returned 30 from the wars or no?

MESSENGER: I know none of that name, lady. There was none such in the army of any sort.

LEONATO: What is he that you ask for, niece?

HERO: My cousin means Signior Benedick of Padua. 35

MESSENGER: O, he's returned, and as pleasant° as ever he was.

BEATRICE: He set up his bills° here in Messina and challenged Cupid at the flight;° and my uncle's fool, reading the challenge, subscribed° for Cupid 40 and challenged him at the burbolt.° I pray you, how many hath he killed and eaten in these wars? But how many hath he killed? For indeed, I promised to eat all of his killing.

LEONATO: Faith, niece, you tax° Signior Benedick too 45 much; but he'll be meet° with you, I doubt it not.

---

gentlemen, men of upper class. **sort,** rank. **name,** distinguished family. **better bett'red expectation,** greatly exceeded anticipated valor. **uncle,** (does not appear in the play).

badge, emblem. **kind overflow of kindness,** natural overflow of tenderness. **Mountanto,** a fencing thrust. **pleasant,** lively. **bills,** advertising placards. **flight,** shooting contest (i.e., he thought himself a lady-killer). **subscribed,** signed up. **burbolt,** blunt arrow. **tax,** i.e., tease too hard. **meet,** even.

MESSENGER: He hath done good service, lady, in these
wars.

BEATRICE: You had musty victual, and he hath holp to
50   eat it. He is a very valiant trencherman;° he hath
an excellent stomach.

MESSENGER: And a good soldier too, lady.

BEATRICE: And a good soldier to° a lady. But what is
he to a lord?

55   MESSENGER: A lord to a lord, a man to a man; stuffed
with all honorable virtues.

BEATRICE: It is so, indeed; he is no less than a stuffed
man.° But for the stuffing—well, we are all mortal.

LEONATO: You must not, sir, mistake my niece. There
60   is a kind of merry war betwixt Signior Benedick
and her. They never meet but there's a skirmish
of wit between them.

BEATRICE: Alas, he gets nothing by that! In our last
conflict four of his five wits° went halting° off, and
65   now is the whole man governed with one; so that
if he have wit enough to keep himself warm, let
him bear it for a difference between himself and
his horse. For it is all the wealth that he hath left
to be known a reasonable creature. Who is his
70   companion now? He hath every month a new
sworn brother.

MESSENGER: Is't possible?

BEATRICE: Very easily possible. He wears his faith but
as the fashion of his hat; it ever changes with the
75   next block.°

MESSENGER: I see, lady, the gentleman is not in your
books.°

BEATRICE: No. And° he were, I would burn my study.
But I pray you, who is his companion? Is there no
80   young squarer° now that will make a voyage with
him to the devil?

MESSENGER: He is most in the company of the right
noble Claudio.

BEATRICE: O Lord, he will hang upon him like a dis-
85   ease. He is sooner caught than the pestilence,
and the taker runs presently° mad. God help the
noble Claudio if he have caught the Benedict;° it
will cost him a thousand pound ere 'a° be cured.

MESSENGER: I will hold friends with you, lady.

90   BEATRICE: Do, good friend.

LEONATO: You will never run mad,° niece.

BEATRICE: No, not till a hot January.

MESSENGER: Don Pedro is approached.

(*Enter* DON PEDRO, CLAUDIO, BENEDICK, BALTHASAR,
and JOHN *the Bastard.*)

DON PEDRO: Good Signior Leonato, are you come to
meet your trouble? The fashion of the world is to   95
avoid cost, and you encounter it.

LEONATO: Never came trouble to my house in the likeness of your Grace; for trouble being gone, comfort should remain. But when you depart from
me, sorrow abides, and happiness takes his leave.   100

DON PEDRO: You embrace your charge° too willingly. I
think this is your daughter.

LEONATO: Her mother hath many times told me so.

BENEDICK: Were you in doubt, sir, that you asked her?

LEONATO: Signior Benedick, no; for then were you a   105
child.

DON PEDRO: You have it full, Benedick. We may guess
by this what you are, being a man. Truly the lady
fathers herself.° Be happy, lady, for you are like an
honorable father.   110

BENEDICK: If Signior Leonato be her father, she
would not have his head° on her shoulders for all
Messina, as like him as she is.

BEATRICE: I wonder that you will still° be talking,
Signior Benedick; nobody marks you.   115

BENEDICK: What, my dear Lady Disdain! Are you yet
living?

BEATRICE: Is it possible Disdain should die while she
hath such meet food to feed it as Signior Benedick? Courtesy itself must convert to Disdain if   120
you come in her presence.

BENEDICK: Then is courtesy a turncoat. But it is certain I am loved of all ladies,° only you excepted;
and I would I could find in my heart that I had
not a hard heart; for truly I love none.   125

BEATRICE: A dear happiness to women! They would
else have been troubled with a pernicious suitor. I
thank God and my cold blood, I am of your
humor for that.° I had rather hear my dog bark at
a crow than a man swear he loves me.   130

BENEDICK: God keep your ladyship still in that mind,
so some gentleman or other shall scape a predestinate scratched face.

BEATRICE: Scratching could not make it worse and
'twere such a face as yours were.   135

BENEDICK: Well, you are a rare parrot-teacher.°

BEATRICE: A bird of my tongue is better than a beast
of yours.

BENEDICK: I would my horse had the speed of your

---

trencherman, eater. *to,* in comparison with. *stuffed
man,* dummy. *five wits,* common sense, imagination, fancy,
estimation, memory. *halting,* limping. *next block,* most
recent shape. *books,* favor. *And,* if. *squarer,* brawler.
presently, immediately (the usual sense in Shakespeare).
Benedict, (the change in spelling suggests a disease based on
Benedick's name). *'a,* he. *run mad,* catch the Benedict.

---

charge, burden (of my visit). *fathers herself,* shows who
her father is by resembling him. *his head,* white-haired and
bearded (?). *still,* always (the usual sense in Shakespeare).
loved of all ladies, (he had "challenged Cupid"). *of your
humor for that,* in agreement on that. *parrot-teacher,* i.e.,
monotonous speaker of nonsense.

140 tongue, and so good a continuer.° But keep your
     way, a God's name! I have done.

BEATRICE: You always end with a jade's trick.° I know
     you of old.

DON PEDRO: That is the sum of all,° Leonato. Signior
145 Claudio and Signior Benedick, my dear friend
     Leonato hath invited you all. I tell him we shall
     stay here, at the least a month, and he heartily
     prays some occasion may detain us longer. I dare
     swear he is no hypocrite, but prays from his heart.

150 LEONATO: If you swear, my lord, you shall not be for-
     sworn. [To DON JOHN] Let me bid you welcome,
     my lord; being reconciled to the Prince your
     brother, I owe you all duty.

DON JOHN: I thank you. I am not of many words, but I
155 thank you.

LEONATO: Please it your Grace lead on?

DON PEDRO: Your hand, Leonato. We will go together.

(Exeunt. Manent° BENEDICK and CLAUDIO.)

CLAUDIO: Benedick, didst thou note the daughter of
     Signior Leonato?

160 BENEDICK: I noted° her not, but I looked on her.

CLAUDIO: Is she not a modest young lady?

BENEDICK: Do you question me as an honest man
     should do, for my simple true judgment? Or would
     you have me speak after my custom, as being a
165 professed tyrant to their sex?

CLAUDIO: No, I pray thee speak in sober judgment.

BENEDICK: Why, i' faith, methinks she's too low for a
     high praise, too brown for a fair praise, and too
     little for a great praise. Only this commendation
170 I can afford her, that were she other than she is,
     she were unhandsome, and being no other but as
     she is, I do not like her.

CLAUDIO: Thou thinkest I am in sport. I pray thee tell
     me truly how thou lik'st her.

175 BENEDICK: Would you buy her, that you inquire after
     her?

CLAUDIO: Can the world buy such a jewel?

BENEDICK: Yea, and a case to put it into. But speak you
     this with a sad brow?° Or do you play the flouting
180 Jack, to tell us Cupid is a good hare-finder and
     Vulcan a rare carpenter?° Come, in what key shall
     a man take you to go in the song?

CLAUDIO: In mine eye she is the sweetest lady that ever
     I looked on.

185 BENEDICK: I can see yet without spectacles, and I see
     no such matter. There's her cousin, and she were

---

continuer, staying power. *jade's trick,* trick of a vicious
horse (i.e., a sudden stop?). *the sum of all,* the end of the
sparring match. *Manent,* remain (Latin). *noted,* (1) scrutinized (2) set to music (3) stigmatized. *with a sad brow,* seriously. *to tell us . . . carpenter,* i.e., to mock us with nonsense
(Cupid was blind, Vulcan was a blacksmith).

---

     not possessed with a fury, exceeds her as much in
     beauty as the first of May doth the last of Decem-
     ber. But I hope you have no intent to turn hus-
     band, have you?   190

CLAUDIO: I would scarce trust myself, though I had
     sworn the contrary, if Hero would be my wife.

BENEDICK: Is't come to this? In faith, hath not the
     world one man but he will wear his cap with suspi-
     cion?° Shall I never see a bachelor of threescore   195
     again? Go to, i' faith! And thou wilt needs thrust
     thy neck into a yoke, wear the print of it and sigh
     away Sundays.° Look! Don Pedro is returned to
     seek you.

(Enter DON PEDRO.)

DON PEDRO: What secret hath held you here, that you   200
     followed not to Leonato's?

BENEDICK: I would your Grace would constrain me to
     tell.

DON PEDRO: I charge thee on thy allegiance.°

BENEDICK: You hear, Count Claudio; I can be secret as   205
     a dumb man. I would have you think so. But, on
     my allegiance—mark you this—on my allegiance!
     He is in love. With who? Now that is your Grace's
     part. Mark how short his answer is—with Hero,
     Leonato's short daughter.   210

CLAUDIO: If this were so, so were it utt'red.

BENEDICK: Like the old tale, my lord: "It is not so,
     nor 'twas not so, but indeed, God forbid it should
     be so!"

CLAUDIO: If my passion change not shortly, God for-   215
     bid it should be otherwise.

DON PEDRO: Amen, if you love her, for the lady is very
     well worthy.

CLAUDIO: You speak this to fetch me in, my lord.

DON PEDRO: By my troth, I speak my thought.   220

CLAUDIO: And, in faith, my lord, I spoke mine.

BENEDICK: And, by my two faiths and troths, my lord, I
     spoke mine.

CLAUDIO: That I love her, I feel.

DON PEDRO: That she is worthy, I know.   225

BENEDICK: That I neither feel how she should be loved,
     nor know how she should be worthy, is the opin-
     ion that fire cannot melt out of me. I will die in it
     at the stake.

DON PEDRO: Thou wast ever an obstinate heretic in   230
     the despite of° beauty.

CLAUDIO: And never could maintain his part but in
     the force of his will.°

BENEDICK: That a woman conceived me, I thank her;

---

but he . . . suspicion, who (because he is unmarried) will
not fear that he has a cuckold's horns. *thrust thy neck . . .
Sundays,* i.e., enjoy the tiresome bondage of marriage. *allegiance,* solemn obligation to a prince. *in the despite of,* in
contempt of. *will,* sexual appetite.

235 that she brought me up, I likewise give her most
humble thanks. But that I will have a rechate°
winded in my forehead, or hang my bugle in an
invisible baldrick,° all women shall pardon me.
Because I will not do them the wrong to mistrust

240 any, I will do myself the right to trust none; and
the fine° is (for the which I may go the finer), I
will live a bachelor.

DON PEDRO: I shall see thee, ere I die, look pale with
love.

245 BENEDICK: With anger, with sickness, or with hunger,
my lord, not with love. Prove that ever I lose more
blood with love than I will get again with drinking, pick out mine eyes with a ballad maker's pen
and hang me up at the door of a brothel house

250 for the sign of blind Cupid.

DON PEDRO: Well, if ever thou dost fall from this faith,
thou wilt prove a notable argument.°

BENEDICK: If I do, hang me in a bottle° like a cat and
shoot at me; and he that hits me, let him be

255 clapped on the shoulder and called Adam.°

DON PEDRO: Well, as time shall try: "In time the savage
bull doth bear the yoke."

BENEDICK: The savage bull may, but if ever the sensible Benedick bear it, pluck off the bull's horns

260 and set them in my forehead, and let me be vilely
painted, and in such great letters as they write
"Here is good horse to hire," let them signify
under my sign "Here you may see Benedick the
married man."

265 CLAUDIO: If this should ever happen, thou wouldst be
horn-mad.°

DON PEDRO: Nay, if Cupid have not spent all his quiver
in Venice,° thou wilt quake for this shortly.

BENEDICK: I look for an earthquake too then.

270 DON PEDRO: Well, you will temporize with the hours.°
In the meantime, good Signior Benedick, repair
to Leonato's. Commend me to him and tell him I
will not fail him at supper; for indeed he hath
made great preparation.

275 BENEDICK: I have almost matter° enough in me for
such an embassage, and so I commit you—

CLAUDIO: To the tuition° of God. From my house, if I
had it—

DON PEDRO: The sixth of July. Your loving friend,

280 Benedick.

---

rechate, recheate, notes on a hunting horn. **baldrick,**
belt, sling (the reference here, and in *rechate,* is to the horns
of a cuckold). *fine,* finis, result. **notable argument,** famous
example. **bottle,** basket. **Adam,** i.e., Adam Bell, one of
the three superlative archers in the ballad "Adam Bell."
horn-mad, mad with jealousy (perhaps also "sexually insatiable"). **Venice,** (famous for sexual license). **temporize
with the hours,** change temper or attitude with time. **matter,**
sense. **tuition,** custody.

BENEDICK: Nay, mock not, mock not. The body of
your discourse is sometime guarded° with fragments, and the guards are but slightly basted on
neither. Ere you flout old ends° any further, examine your conscience. And so I leave you. (*Exit.*) 285

CLAUDIO: My liege, your Highness now may do me
good.

DON PEDRO: My love is thine to teach. Teach it but
how,
And thou shalt see how apt it is to learn
Any hard lesson that may do thee good.

CLAUDIO: Hath Leonato any son, my lord? 290

DON PEDRO: No child but Hero; she's his only heir.
Dost thou affect° her, Claudio?

CLAUDIO: O my lord,
When you went onward on this ended action,°
I looked upon her with a soldier's eye,
That liked, but had a rougher task in hand 295
Than to drive liking to the name of love.
But now I am returned and that° war-thoughts
Have left their places vacant, in their rooms
Come thronging soft and delicate desires,
All prompting me how fair young Hero is, 300
Saying I liked her ere I went to wars.

DON PEDRO: Thou wilt be like a lover presently
And tire the hearer with a book of words.
If thou dost love fair Hero, cherish it,
And I will break° with her and with her father, 305
And thou shalt have her. Was't not to this end
That thou began'st to twist so fine a story?

CLAUDIO: How sweetly you do minister to love,
That know love's grief by his complexion!°
But lest my liking might too sudden seem, 310
I would have salved it with a longer treatise.

DON PEDRO: What need the bridge much broader
than the flood?
The fairest grant is the necessity.°
Look, what will serve is fit. 'Tis once,° thou lovest,
And I will fit thee with the remedy. 315
I know we shall have reveling tonight.
I will assume thy part in some disguise
And tell fair Hero I am Claudio,
And in her bosom I'll unclasp my heart
And take her hearing prisoner with the force 320
And strong encounter of my amorous tale;
Then after to her father will I break,
And the conclusion is, she shall be thine.
In practice let us put it presently. (*Exeunt.*)

---

guarded, trimmed (used of clothing). *flout old ends,*
i.e., indulge in derision at my expense. *affect,* love. *ended
action,* war just concluded. *that,* because. *break,* open
negotiations. *complexion,* appearance. *The fairest grant is
the necessity,* the most attractive giving is when the receiver
really needs something. *'Tis once,* in short.

ACT 1 / SCENE 2

(LEONATO's house)

(Enter LEONATO and an old man [ANTONIO], brother to LEONATO.)

LEONATO: How now, brother? Where is my cousin° your son? Hath he provided this music?

ANTONIO: He is very busy about it. But, brother, I can tell you strange news that you yet dreamt not of.

5 LEONATO: Are they° good?

ANTONIO: As the events stamps° them. But they have a good cover, they show well outward. The Prince and Count Claudio, walking in a thick-pleached alley in mine orchard,° were thus much over-

10 heard by a man of mine. The Prince discovered° to Claudio that he loved my niece your daughter and meant to acknowledge it this night in a dance, and if he found her accordant,° he meant to take the present time by the top° and instantly break

15 with you of it.

LEONATO: Hath the fellow any wit that told you this?

ANTONIO: A good sharp fellow. I will send for him, and question him yourself.

LEONATO: No, no. We will hold it as a dream till it

20 appear itself. But I will acquaint my daughter withal, that she may be the better prepared for an answer, if peradventure this be true. Go you and tell her of it.

[Enter ATTENDANTS.]

Cousin, you know what you have to do. O, I cry

25 you mercy,° friend. Go you with me, and I will use your skill. Good cousin, have a care this busy time.

(Exeunt.)

ACT 1 / SCENE 3

(LEONATO's house)

(Enter Sir [DON] JOHN the Bastard and CONRADE, his companion.)

CONRADE: What the goodyear,° my lord! Why are you thus out of measure sad?°

DON JOHN: There is no measure in the occasion that breeds; therefore the sadness is without limit.

5 CONRADE: You should hear reason.

---

cousin, kinsman.   they, i.e., the news (plural in the six-teenth century).   As the events stamps them, as the outcome proves them to be (a plural noun, especially when felt to be singular, often has a verb ending in -s).   thick-pleached alley in mine orchard, walk or arbor fenced by interwoven branches in my garden.   discovered, disclosed.   accordant, agreeing.   top, forelock.   cry you mercy, beg your pardon. What the goodyear, (an expletive).   out of measure sad, unduly morose.

DON JOHN: And when I have heard it, what blessing brings it?

CONRADE: If not a present remedy, at least a patient sufferance.

10 DON JOHN: I wonder that thou, being (as thou say'st thou art) born under Saturn,° goest about to apply a moral medicine to a mortifying mischief.° I cannot hide what I am. I must be sad when I have cause, and smile at no man's jests; eat when I

15 have stomach, and wait for no man's leisure; sleep when I am drowsy, and tend on no man's busi-ness; laugh when I am merry, and claw no man in his humor.°

CONRADE: Yea, but you must not make the full show of this till you may do it without controlment. You

20 have of late stood out against your brother, and he hath ta'en you newly into his grace, where it is impossible you should take true root but by the fair weather that you make yourself. It is needful that you frame° the season for your own harvest.

25 DON JOHN: I had rather be a canker° in a hedge than a rose in his grace, and it better fits my blood to be disdained of all than to fashion a carriage° to rob love from any. In this, though I cannot be said to be a flattering honest man, it must not be denied

30 but I am a plain-dealing villain. I am trusted with a muzzle and enfranchised with a clog; therefore I have decreed not to sing in my cage. If I had my mouth, I would bite; if I had my liberty, I would do my liking. In the meantime let me be that I

35 am, and seek not to alter me.

CONRADE: Can you make no use of your discontent?

DON JOHN: I make all use of it, for I use it only. Who comes here?

(Enter BORACHIO.)

What news, Borachio?

40 BORACHIO: I came yonder from a great supper. The Prince your brother is royally entertained by Leonato, and I can give you intelligence° of an intended marriage.

45 DON JOHN: Will it serve for any model to build mis-chief on? What is he for a fool that betroths him-self to unquietness?

BORACHIO: Marry,° it is your brother's right hand.

DON JOHN: Who? The most exquisite Claudio?

BORACHIO: Even he.

50 DON JOHN: A proper squire!° And who? And who? Which way looks he?

---

under Saturn, i.e., naturally sullen.   mortifying mischief, killing calamity.   claw no man in his humor, i.e., flatter no man (claw = pat or scratch on the back; humor = whim).   frame, bring about.   canker, wild rose.   fashion a carriage, contrive a behavior.   intelligence, information.   Marry, (an expletive, from "by the Virgin Mary").   proper squire, fine young fellow.

BORACHIO: Marry, one Hero, the daughter and heir of Leonato.

55 DON JOHN: A very forward March-chick!° How came you to this?

BORACHIO: Being entertained for° a perfumer, as I was smoking° a musty room, comes me the Prince and Claudio, hand in hand in sad° conference. I

60 whipped me behind the arras and there heard it agreed upon that the Prince should woo Hero for himself, and having obtained her, give her to Count Claudio.

DON JOHN: Come, come, let us thither. This may prove

65 food to my displeasure. That young start-up hath all the glory of my overthrow. If I can cross him any way, I bless myself every way. You are both sure,° and will assist me?

CONRADE: To the death, my lord.

70 DON JOHN: Let us to the great supper. Their cheer is the greater that I am subdued. Would the cook were o' my mind! Shall we go prove° what's to be done?

BORACHIO: We'll wait upon your lordship.

(Exit [with others].)

ACT 2 / SCENE 1

(LEONATO's house)
(Enter LEONATO, his brother [ANTONIO], HERO, his daughter, and BEATRICE, his niece, [also MARGARET and URSULA].)

LEONATO: Was not Count John here at supper?

ANTONIO: I saw him not.

BEATRICE: How tartly that gentleman looks! I never can see him but I am heartburned an hour after.

5 HERO: He is of a very melancholy° disposition.

BEATRICE: He were an excellent man that were made just in the midway between him and Benedick. The one is too like an image and says nothing, and the other too like my lady's eldest son,° ever-

10 more tattling.

LEONATO: Then half Signior Benedick's tongue in Count John's mouth, and half Count John's melancholy in Signior Benedick's face—

BEATRICE: With a good leg and a good foot,° uncle,

15 and money enough in his purse, such a man would win any woman in the world, if 'a could get her good will.

LEONATO: By my troth, niece, thou wilt never get thee a husband if thou be so shrewd° of thy tongue.

ANTONIO: In faith, she's too curst.° 20

BEATRICE: Too curst is more than curst. I shall lessen God's sending that way, for it is said, "God sends a curst cow short horns"; but to a cow too curst he sends none.

LEONATO: So, by being too curst, God will send you no 25 horns.°

BEATRICE: Just,° if he send me no husband; for the which blessing I am at him upon my knees every morning and evening. Lord, I could not endure a husband with a beard on his face. I had rather lie 30 in the woolen!°

LEONATO: You may light on a husband that hath no beard.

BEATRICE: What should I do with him? Dress him in my apparel and make him my waiting gentle- 35 woman? He that hath a beard is more than a youth, and he that hath no beard is less than a man; and he that is more than a youth is not for me; and he that is less than a man, I am not for him. Therefore I will even take sixpence in 40 earnest° of the berrord° and lead his apes into hell.°

LEONATO: Well then, go you into hell?

BEATRICE: No; but to the gate, and there will the devil meet me like an old cuckold with horns on his 45 head, and say, "Get you to heaven, Beatrice, get you to heaven. Here's no place for you maids." So deliver I up my apes, and away to Saint Peter. For the heavens, he shows me where the bachelors° sit, and there live we as merry as the day is long. 50

ANTONIO: *[To HERO]* Well, niece, I trust you will be ruled by your father.

BEATRICE: Yes, faith. It is my cousin's duty to make cursy° and say, "Father, as it please you." But yet for all that, cousin, let him be a handsome fellow, 55 or else make another cursy, and say, "Father, as it please me."

LEONATO: *[To BEATRICE]* Well, niece, I hope to see you one day fitted° with a husband.

BEATRICE: Not till God make men of some other 60 metal° than earth. Would it not grieve a woman to be overmastered with a piece of valiant dust? To make an account of her life to a clod of wayward

---

forward March-chick, precocious fellow (i.e., born in early spring). *entertained for,* employed as. *smoking,* fumigating (or possibly merely perfuming). *sad,* serious. *sure,* reliable. *prove,* try. *melancholy,* ill-tempered. *eldest son,* i.e., overly confident (as heir presumptive). *foot,* (perhaps with a pun on French *foutre,* to copulate—i.e., a good lover).

shrewd, sharp. *curst,* shrewish. *no horns,* (i.e., horn used as phallic symbol, as Beatrice's next remark makes plain). *just,* exactly. *in the woolen,* between scratchy blankets. *in earnest* (1) advance payment (2) in all seriousness. *berrord,* bearward, animal keeper. *lead his apes into hell,* traditional punishment for dying unwed. *bachelors,* unwed persons (female as well as male). *cursy,* curtsy. *fitted,* (continues playful sexual innuendo of the scene). *metal,* substance.

marl?° No, uncle, I'll none. Adam's sons are my
65   brethren, and truly I hold it a sin to match in my
      kindred.
LEONATO: Daughter, remember what I told you. If the
      Prince do solicit you in that kind, you know your
      answer.
70 BEATRICE: The fault will be in the music, cousin, if
      you be not wooed in good time. If the Prince be
      too important,° tell him there is measure° in
      everything, and so dance out the answer. For,
      hear me, Hero: wooing, wedding, and repenting
75   is as a Scotch jig, a measure, and a cinquepace.°
      The first suit is hot and hasty like a Scotch jig
      (and full as fantastical); the wedding, mannerly
      modest, as a measure, full of state and ancientry;
      and then comes Repentance and with his bad legs
80   falls into the cinquepace faster and faster, till he
      sink into his grave.
LEONATO: Cousin, you apprehend passing shrewdly.
BEATRICE: I have a good eye, uncle; I can see a church
      by daylight.
85 LEONATO: The revelers are ent'ring, brother. Make
      good room.

      [*All put on their masks.*]
      (*Enter Prince* [DON] PEDRO, CLAUDIO, *and* BENEDICK,
      and BALTHASAR [*masked; and without masks* BORA-
      CHIO *and*] DON JOHN.)

DON PEDRO: Lady, will you walk about with your friend?°
HERO: So you walk softly and look sweetly and say
      nothing, I am yours for the walk; and especially
90   when I walk away.
DON PEDRO: With me in your company?
HERO: I may say so when I please.
DON PEDRO: And when please you to say so?
HERO: When I like your favor,° for God defend° the
95   lute should be like the case!°
DON PEDRO: My visor° is Philemon's° roof; within the
      house is Jove.
HERO: Why then, your visor should be thatched.
DON PEDRO: Speak low if you speak love.

      [*Draws her aside.*]

100 BENEDICK:° Well, I would you did like me.

MARGARET: So would not I for your own sake, for I
      have many ill qualities.
BENEDICK: Which is one?
MARGARET: I say my prayers aloud.
BENEDICK: I love you the better. The hearers may cry 105
      amen.
MARGARET: God match me with a good dancer!
BALTHASAR: [*Interposing*] Amen.
MARGARET: And God keep him out of my sight when
      the dance is done! Answer, clerk. 110
BALTHASAR: No more words. The clerk is answered.
URSULA: I know you well enough. You are Signior
      Antonio.
ANTONIO: At a word, I am not.
URSULA: I know you by the waggling° of your head. 115
ANTONIO: To tell you true, I counterfeit him.
URSULA: You could never do him so ill-well unless you
      were the very man. Here's his dry° hand up and
      down. You are he, you are he!
ANTONIO: At a word I am not. 120
URSULA: Come, come, do you think I do not know you
      by your excellent wit? Can virtue hide itself? Go
      to, mum, you are he. Graces will appear, and
      there's an end.
BEATRICE: Will you not tell me who told you so? 125
BENEDICK: No, you shall pardon me.
BEATRICE: Nor will you not tell me who you are?
BENEDICK: Not now.
BEATRICE: That I was disdainful, and that I had my
      good wit out of the "Hundred Merry Tales."° 130
      Well, this was Signior Benedick that said so.
BENEDICK: What's he?
BEATRICE: I am sure you know him well enough.
BENEDICK: Not I, believe me.
BEATRICE: Did he never make you laugh? 135
BENEDICK: I pray you, what is he?
BEATRICE: Why, he is the Prince's jester, a very dull
      fool. Only his° gift is in devising impossible slan-
      ders. None but libertines delight in him, and
      the commendation is not in his wit, but in his 140
      villainy; for he both pleases men and angers
      them, and then they laugh at him and beat him.
      I am sure he is in the fleet;° I would he had
      boarded me.
BENEDICK: When I know the gentleman, I'll tell him 145
      what you say.
BEATRICE: Do, do. He'll but break a comparison or
      two on me; which peradventure (not marked or
      not laughed at), strikes him into melancholy, and
      then there's a partridge wing saved, for the fool 150

---

marl, earth. *important,* importunate. *measure,* (1) dis-
cernible time sequence (2) moderation (the entire speech
is a light parody of Sir John Davies' *Orchestra, A Poem of Dancing* [1596]; cf. stanza 23: "Time the measure of all moving
is/And dancing is a moving all in measure"). *cinquepace,*
lively dance. *friend,* lover. *favor,* face. *defend,* forbid. *the
lute . . . case,* i.e., your face be as ugly as your mask. *visor,*
mask. *Philemon,* peasant who entertained Jove in his house.
Benedick, (many editors emend the Quarto, and give this and
Benedick's two subsequent speeches to Balthasar; but in 5.2
Benedick and Margaret spar, and they may well do so here).

---

waggling, i.e., palsy. *dry,* dried-up (with age). *Hundred Merry Tales,* a popular collection of amusing, coarse
anecdotes. *Only his,* his only. *fleet,* group (the related
meaning, group of ships, leads to *boarded me,* but perhaps
too there is an allusion to Fleet Prison).

will eat no supper that night. [*Music.*] We must follow the leaders.

BENEDICK: In every good thing.

BEATRICE: Nay, if they lead to any ill, I will leave them
155   at the next turning.

(Dance. Exeunt [all except DON JOHN, BORACHIO, *and* CLAUDIO].)*

DON JOHN: Sure my brother is amorous on Hero and hath withdrawn her father to break with him about it. The ladies follow her and but one visor remains.

160 BORACHIO: And that is Claudio. I know him by his bearing.

DON JOHN: Are not you Signior Benedick?

CLAUDIO: You know me well. I am he.

DON JOHN: Signior, you are very near my brother in
165   his love. He is enamored on Hero. I pray you dissuade him from her; she is no equal for his birth. You may do the part of an honest man in it.

CLAUDIO: How know you he loves her?

DON JOHN: I heard him swear his affection.

170 BORACHIO: So did I too, and he swore he would marry her tonight.

DON JOHN: Come, let us to the banquet.°

(Exeunt. Manet CLAUDIO.*)*

CLAUDIO: Thus answer I in name of Benedick
But hear these ill news with the ears of Claudio.
175   'Tis certain so. The Prince woos for himself.
Friendship is constant in all other things
Save in the office° and affairs of love.
Therefore all hearts in love use their own tongues;
Let every eye negotiate for itself
180   And trust no agent; for beauty is a witch
Against whose charms faith melteth into blood.°
This is an accident of hourly proof,°
Which I mistrusted not. Farewell therefore Hero!

(Enter BENEDICK.*)*

BENEDICK: Count Claudio?
185 CLAUDIO: Yea, the same.

BENEDICK: Come, will you go with me?

CLAUDIO: Whither?

BENEDICK: Even to the next° willow,° about your own business, County.° What fashion will you wear the
190   garland of? About your neck, like an usurer's chain? Or under your arm, like a lieutenant's scarf? You must wear it one way, for the Prince hath got your Hero.

CLAUDIO: I wish him joy of her.

BENEDICK: Why, that's spoken like an honest drovier.° 195
So they sell bullocks. But did you think the Prince would have served you thus?

CLAUDIO: I pray you leave me.

BENEDICK: Ho! Now you strike like the blind man!
'Twas the boy that stole your meat, and you'll beat 200
the post.°

CLAUDIO: If it will not be, I'll leave you. *(Exit.)*

BENEDICK: Alas, poor hurt fowl! Now will he creep into sedges. But, that my Lady Beatrice should know me, and not know me! The Prince's fool! 205
Ha! It may be I go under that title because I am merry. Yea, but so I am apt to do myself wrong. I am not so reputed. It is the base (though bitter) disposition of Beatrice that puts the world into her person and so gives me out.° Well, I'll be 210
revenged as I may.

(Enter the Prince [DON PEDRO], HERO, LEONATO.*)*

DON PEDRO: Now, signior, where's the Count? Did you see him?

BENEDICK: Troth, my lord, I have played the part of Lady Fame.° I found him here as melancholy as a 215
lodge in a warren.° I told him, and I think I told him true, that your Grace had got the good will of this young lady, and I off'red him my company to a willow tree, either to make him a garland, as being forsaken, or to bind him up a rod, as being 220
worthy to be whipped.

DON PEDRO: To be whipped? What's his fault?

BENEDICK: The flat transgression of a schoolboy who being overjoyed with finding a bird's nest, shows it his companion, and he steals it. 225

DON PEDRO: Wilt thou make a trust a transgression? The transgression is in the stealer.

BENEDICK: Yet it had not been amiss the rod had been made, and the garland too; for the garland he might have worn himself, and the rod he might 230
have bestowed on you, who (as I take it) have stol'n his bird's nest.

DON PEDRO: I will but teach them to sing and restore them to the owner.

BENEDICK: If their singing answer your saying, by my 235
faith you say honestly.

DON PEDRO: The Lady Beatrice hath a quarrel to you. The gentleman that danced with her told her she is much wronged by you.

BENEDICK: O, she misused me past the endurance of 240
a block! An oak but with one green leaf on it would have answered her; my very visor began to

---

banquet, light meal, or course, of fruit, wine, and dessert. *office*, business. *blood*, passion, desire. *accident of hourly proof*, common happening. *next*, nearest. *willow*, symbol of unrequited love. *County*, Count.

---

drovier, cattle dealer. *beat the post*, i.e., strike out blindly. *It is . . . gives me out*, it is the low and harsh disposition of Beatrice to assume her opinion of me is the world's opinion of me. *Lady Fame*, goddess of rumor. *in a warren*, i.e., in a lonely place.

assume life and scold with her. She told me, not thinking I had been myself, that I was the Prince's jester, that I was duller than a great thaw; huddling jest upon jest with such impossible conveyance° upon me that I stood like a man at a mark,° with a whole army shooting at me. She speaks poniards, and every word stabs. If her breath were as terrible as her terminations,° there were no living near her; she would infect to the North Star. I would not marry her though she were endowed with all that Adam had left him before he transgressed. She would have made Hercules have turned spit, yea, and have cleft his club to make the fire too. Come, talk not of her. You shall find her the infernal Ate° in good apparel. I would to God some scholar would conjure her,° for certainly, while she is here, a man may live as quiet in hell as in a sanctuary; and people sin upon purpose, because they would go thither; so indeed all disquiet, horror, and perturbation follows her.

(Enter CLAUDIO *and* BEATRICE.*)*

DON PEDRO: Look, here she comes.

BENEDICK: Will your Grace command me any service to the world's end? I will go on the slightest errand now to the Antipodes that you can devise to send me on; I will fetch you a toothpicker now from the furthest inch of Asia; bring you the length of Prester John's° foot; fetch you a hair off the great Cham's° beard; do you any embassage to the Pygmies—rather than hold three words' conference with this harpy. You have no employment for me?

DON PEDRO: None, but to desire your good company.

BENEDICK: O God, sir, here's a dish I love not! I cannot endure my Lady Tongue. *(Exit.)*

DON PEDRO: Come, lady, come; you have lost the heart of Signior Benedick.

BEATRICE: Indeed, my lord, he lent it me awhile, and I gave him use° for it, a double heart for his single one. Marry, once before he won it of me with false dice; therefore your Grace may well say I have lost it.

DON PEDRO: You have put him down, lady; you have put him down.

BEATRICE: So I would not he should do me, my lord, lest I should prove the mother of fools.° I have brought Count Claudio, whom you sent me to seek.

DON PEDRO: Why, how now, Count? Wherefore are you sad?

CLAUDIO: Not sad, my lord.

DON PEDRO: How then? Sick?

CLAUDIO: Neither, my lord.

BEATRICE: The Count is neither sad, nor sick, nor merry, nor well; but civil Count, civil° as an orange, and something of that jealous complexion.°

DON PEDRO: I' faith, lady, I think your blazon° to be true; though I'll be sworn, if he be so, his conceit° is false. Here, Claudio, I have wooed in thy name, and fair Hero is won. I have broke with her father, and his good will obtained. Name the day of marriage, and God give thee joy!

LEONATO: Count, take of me my daughter, and with her my fortunes. His Grace hath made the match, and all grace say amen to it!

BEATRICE: Speak, Count, 'tis your cue.

CLAUDIO: Silence is the perfectest herald of joy. I were but little happy if I could say how much. Lady, as you are mine, I am yours. I give away myself for you and dote upon the exchange.

BEATRICE: Speak, cousin; or (if you cannot) stop his mouth with a kiss and let not him speak neither.

DON PEDRO: In faith, lady, you have a merry heart.

BEATRICE: Yea, my lord; I thank it, poor fool, it keeps on the windy° side of care. My cousin tells him in his ear that he is in her heart.

CLAUDIO: And so she doth, cousin.

BEATRICE: Good Lord, for alliance! Thus goes every one to the world but I, and I am sunburnt.° I may sit in a corner and cry "Heigh-ho for a husband!"

DON PEDRO: Lady Beatrice, I will get you one.

BEATRICE: I would rather have one of your father's getting.° Hath your Grace ne'er a brother like you? Your father got excellent husbands, if a maid could come by them.

DON PEDRO: Will you have me, lady?

BEATRICE: No, my lord, unless I might have another for working days; your Grace is too costly to wear every day. But I beseech your Grace pardon me. I was born to speak all mirth and no matter.

DON PEDRO: Your silence most offends me, and to be merry best becomes you, for out o' question you were born in a merry hour.

BEATRICE: No, sure, my lord, my mother cried; but then there was a star danced, and under that was I born. Cousins, God give you joy!

LEONATO: Niece, will you look to those things I told you of?

---

impossible conveyance, incredible dexterity.   *mark,* target.   *terminations,* words.   *Ate,* goddess of discord.   *conjure her,* i.e., exorcise the devil out of her.   *Prester John,* legendary Christian king in remote Asia.   *Cham,* Khan.   *use,* interest. *fools,* babies.

civil, polite (with a pun on orange of Seville).   *complexion,* (1) disposition (2) color (i.e., yellowish for jealousy). *blazon,* description.   *conceit,* idea, concept.   *windy,* windward, safe.   *Good Lord . . . sunburnt,* i.e., everyone gets a husband but me, and I am ugly (*sunburnt* = tanned, and therefore ugly in the sixteenth century).   *getting,* begetting.

BEATRICE: I cry you mercy,° uncle. By your Grace's pardon.

(Exit BEATRICE.)

DON PEDRO: By my troth, a pleasant-spirited lady.

LEONATO: There's little of the melancholy element
345 in her, my lord. She is never sad but when she
sleeps, and not ever° sad then; for I have heard
my daughter say she hath often dreamt of unhappiness and waked herself with laughing.

DON PEDRO: She cannot endure to hear tell of a hus-
350 band.

LEONATO: O, by no means! She mocks all her wooers
out of suit.

DON PEDRO: She were an excellent wife for Benedick.

LEONATO: O Lord, my lord! If they were but a week
355 married, they would talk themselves mad.

DON PEDRO: County Claudio, when mean you to go to
church?

CLAUDIO: Tomorrow, my lord. Time goes on crutches
till Love have all his rites.

360 LEONATO: Not till Monday, my dear son, which is
hence a just sevennight; and a time too brief too,
to have all things answer my mind.

DON PEDRO: Come, you shake the head at so long a
breathing; but I warrant thee, Claudio, the time
365 shall not go dully by us. I will in the interim
undertake one of Hercules' labors, which is, to
bring Signior Benedick and the Lady Beatrice
into a mountain of affection th' one with th'
other. I would fain have it a match, and I doubt
370 not but to fashion it if you three will but minister
such assistance as I shall give you direction.

LEONATO: My lord, I am for you, though it cost me ten
nights' watchings.°

CLAUDIO: And I, my lord.

375 DON PEDRO: And you too, gentle Hero?

HERO: I will do any modest office, my lord, to help my
cousin to a good husband.

DON PEDRO: And Benedick is not the unhopefullest
husband that I know. Thus far can I praise him:
380 he is of a noble strain, of approved° valor and
confirmed honesty. I will teach you how to humor
your cousin, that she shall fall in love with Benedick; and I [*to LEONATO and CLAUDIO*], with your
two helps, will so practice on° Benedick that, in
385 despite of his quick wit and his queasy stomach,
he shall fall in love with Beatrice. If we can do
this, Cupid is no longer an archer; his glory shall
be ours, for we are the only love-gods. Go in with
me, and I will tell you my drift.

(Exit [with the others].)

---

cry you mercy, beg your pardon. **ever,** always. **ten nights' watchings,** ten nights awake. **approved,** tested. **practice on,** deceive.

ACT 2 / SCENE 2

(LEONATO's house)
(Enter [DON] JOHN and BORACHIO.)

DON JOHN: It is so. The Count Claudio shall marry the
daughter of Leonato.

BORACHIO: Yea, my lord; but I can cross it.

DON JOHN: Any bar, any cross, any impediment will be
medicinable to me. I am sick in displeasure to 5
him, and whatsoever comes athwart his affection
ranges evenly° with mine. How canst thou cross
this marriage?

BORACHIO: Not honestly, my lord; but so covertly that
no dishonesty shall appear in me. 10

DON JOHN: Show me briefly how.

BORACHIO: I think I told your lordship, a year since,
how much I am in the favor of Margaret, the waiting gentlewoman to Hero.

DON JOHN: I remember. 15

BORACHIO: I can, at any unseasonable instant of the
night, appoint her to look out at her lady's chamber window.

DON JOHN: What life is in that to be the death of this
marriage? 20

BORACHIO: The poison of that lies in you to temper.
Go you to the Prince your brother; spare not to
tell him that he hath wronged his honor in marrying the renowned Claudio (whose estimation do
you mightily hold up) to a contaminated stale,° 25
such a one as Hero.

DON JOHN: What proof shall I make of that?

BORACHIO: Proof enough to misuse the Prince, to vex
Claudio, to undo Hero, and kill Leonato. Look
you for any other issue? 30

DON JOHN: Only to despite them I will endeavor anything.

BORACHIO: Go then; find me a meet hour° to draw
Don Pedro and the Count Claudio alone; tell
them that you know that Hero loves me; intend° a 35
kind of zeal both to the Prince and Claudio (as in
love of your brother's honor, who hath made this
match, and his friend's reputation, who is thus
like to be cozened° with the semblance of a maid)
that you have discovered thus. They will scarcely 40
believe this without trial. Offer them instances;°
which shall bear no less likelihood than to see me
at her chamber window, hear me call Margaret
Hero, hear Margaret term me Claudio; and bring
them to see this the very night before the in- 45
tended wedding. For in the meantime I will so
fashion the matter that Hero shall be absent; and
there shall appear such seeming truth of Hero's

---

ranges evenly, goes in a straight line (i.e., suits me exactly). **stale,** prostitute. **meet hour,** suitable time. **intend,** pretend. **cozened,** cheated. **instances,** proofs.

50   disloyalty that jealousy° shall be called assurance
      and all the preparation overthrown.

DON JOHN: Grow this to what adverse issue it can, I will
      put it in practice. Be cunning in the working this,
      and thy fee is a thousand ducats.

55 BORACHIO: Be you constant in the accusation, and my
      cunning shall not shame me.

DON JOHN: I will presently go learn their day of mar-
      riage.

    (Exit [with BORACHIO]*.)*

ACT 2 / SCENE 3

*(*LEONATO*'s garden)*
(Enter BENEDICK *alone.)*

BENEDICK: Boy!

    [*Enter* BOY.]

BOY: Signior?

BENEDICK: In my chamber window lies a book. Bring
      it hither to me in the orchard.°

5 BOY: I am here already, sir.

BENEDICK: I know that, but I would have thee hence
      and here again. *(Exit [*BOY].)* I do much wonder
      that one man, seeing how much another man is a
      fool when he dedicates his behaviors to love, will,
10   after he hath laughed at such shallow follies in
      others, become the argument° of his own scorn
      by falling in love; and such a man is Claudio. I
      have known when there was no music with him
      but the drum and the fife; and now had he rather
15   hear the tabor and the pipe.° I have known when
      he would have walked ten mile afoot to see a good
      armor; and now will he lie ten nights awake carv-
      ing the fashion° of a new doublet. He was wont to
      speak plain and to the purpose, like an honest
20   man and a soldier; and now is he turned orthog-
      raphy;° his words are a very fantastical banquet—
      just so many strange dishes. May I be so converted
      and see with these eyes? I cannot tell; I think not.
      I will not be sworn but love may transform me to
25   an oyster; but I'll take my oath on it, till he have
      made an oyster of me he shall never make me
      such a fool. One woman is fair, yet I am well;
      another is wise, yet I am well; another virtuous,
      yet I am well. But till all graces be in one woman,
30   one woman shall not come in my grace. Rich she
      shall be, that's certain; wise, or I'll none; virtuous,
      or I'll never cheapen° her; fair, or I'll never look
      on her; mild, or come not near me; noble, or not

    I for an angel;° of good discourse,° an excellent
      musician, and her hair shall be of what color it   35
      please God. Ha, the Prince and Monsieur Love!
      (Retiring) I will hide me in the arbor.

    *(Enter Prince [*DON PEDRO], LEONATO, CLAUDIO, [*to
    the sound of*] *music.)*

DON PEDRO: Come, shall we hear this music?

CLAUDIO: Yea, my good lord. How still the evening is,
      As hushed on purpose to grace harmony!   40

DON PEDRO: See you where Benedick hath hid
      himself?

CLAUDIO: O, very well, my lord. The music ended,
      We'll fit the kid fox with a pennyworth.°

    (Enter BALTHASAR *with music.)*

DON PEDRO: Come, Balthasar, we'll hear that song
      again.

BALTHASAR: O, good my lord, tax not so bad a voice   45
      To slander music any more than once.

DON PEDRO: It is the witness still of excellency
      To put a strange face on his own perfection.
      I pray thee sing, and let me woo no more.

BALTHASAR: Because you talk of wooing, I will sing,   50
      Since many a wooer doth commence his suit
      To her he thinks not worthy, yet he woos,
      Yet will he swear he loves.

DON PEDRO: Nay, pray thee come;
      Or if thou wilt hold longer argument,
      Do it in notes.

BALTHASAR: Note this before my notes: 55
      There's not a note of mine that's worth the noting.

DON PEDRO: Why, these are very crotchets° that he
      speaks!
      Note notes, forsooth, and nothing!° [*Music.*]

BENEDICK: *(Aside)* Now divine air! Now is his soul rav-
      ished. Is it not strange that sheep's guts should   60
      hale souls out of men's bodies? Well, a horn for
      my money, when all's done. [BALTHASAR *sings.*]

THE SONG

Sigh no more, ladies, sigh no more,
    Men were deceivers ever,
One foot in sea, and one on shore,   65
    To one thing constant never.
      Then sigh not so,
      But let them go,
    And be you blithe and bonny,
Converting all your sounds of woe   70
    Into hey nonny, nonny.

---

jealousy, mistrust. *orchard,* garden. *argument,* subject
matter. *tabor and the pipe,* music of an unmartial sort.
carving the fashion, considering the design. *orthography,* i.e.,
into a pedant (?). *cheapen,* bargain for.

noble . . . angel, (puns: both words are Elizabethan coins).
discourse, conversation. *We'll . . . pennyworth,* i.e., we'll give
Benedick a little something (perhaps *kid fox* means "young
fox," perhaps "known fox"). *crotchets,* (1) whims (2) musical notes. *nothing,* (pronounced "noting," hence a pun).

Sing no more ditties, sing no moe,
Of dumps° so dull and heavy;
The fraud of men was ever so,
75 *Since summer first was leavy.*
Then sigh not so, &c.

DON PEDRO: By my troth, a good song.
BALTHASAR: And an ill singer, my lord.
DON PEDRO: Ha, no, no, faith! Thou sing'st well
80 enough for a shift.°
BENEDICK: [*Aside*] And he had been a dog that should
    have howled thus, they would have hanged him;
    and I pray God his bad voice bode no mischief. I
    had as live° have heard the night raven, come
85   what plague could have come after it.
DON PEDRO: Yea, marry. Dost thou hear, Balthasar? I
    pray thee get us some excellent music; for tomor-
    row night we would have it at the Lady Hero's
    chamber window.
90 BALTHASAR: The best I can, my lord.
DON PEDRO: Do so. Farewell.

  (*Exit* BALTHASAR [*with Musicians*].)

    Come hither, Leonato. What was it you told me of
    today? That your niece Beatrice was in love with
    Signior Benedick?
95 CLAUDIO: O, ay! [*In a low voice to* DON PEDRO] Stalk on,
    stalk on; the fowl sits. [*In full voice*] I did never
    think that lady would have loved any man.
LEONATO: No, nor I neither; but most wonderful that
    she should so dote on Signior Benedick, whom
100   she hath in all outward behaviors seemed ever to
    abhor.
BENEDICK: [*Aside*] Is't possible? Sits the wind in that
    corner?
LEONATO: By my troth, my lord, I cannot tell what to
105 think of it, but that she loves him with an enraged
    affection, it is past the infinite of thought.
DON PEDRO: May be she doth but counterfeit.
CLAUDIO: Faith, like enough.
LEONATO: O God, counterfeit? There was never coun-
110 terfeit of passion came so near the life of passion
    as she discovers° it.
DON PEDRO: Why, what effects of passion shows she?
CLAUDIO: [*In a low voice*] Bait the hook well! This fish
    will bite.
115 LEONATO: What effects, my lord? She will sit you, you
    heard my daughter tell you how.
CLAUDIO: She did indeed.
DON PEDRO: How, how, I pray you? You amaze me! I
    would have thought her spirit had been invincible
120   against all assaults of affection.

LEONATO: I would have sworn it had, my lord—espe-
    cially against Benedick.
BENEDICK: [*Aside*] I should think this a gull° but that
    the white-bearded fellow speaks it. Knavery can-
    not, sure, hide himself in such reverence.   125
CLAUDIO: [*In a low voice*] He hath ta'en th' infection;
    hold° it up.
DON PEDRO: Hath she made her affection known to
    Benedick?
LEONATO: No, and swears she never will. That's her   130
    torment.
CLAUDIO: 'Tis true indeed. So your daughter says.
    "Shall I," says she, "that have so oft encount'red
    him with scorn, write to him that I love him?"
LEONATO: This says she now when she is beginning to 135
    write to him; for she'll be up twenty times a night,
    and there will she sit in her smock till she have
    writ a sheet of paper. My daughter tells us all.
CLAUDIO: Now you talk of a sheet of paper, I remem-
    ber a pretty jest your daughter told us of.   140
LEONATO: O, when she had writ it, and was reading it
    over, she found "Benedick" and "Beatrice" be-
    tween the sheet?
CLAUDIO: That.
LEONATO: O, she tore the letter into a thousand half- 145
    pence,° railed at herself that she should be so
    immodest to write to one that she knew would
    flout her. "I measure him," says she, "by my own
    spirit; for I should flout him if he writ to me. Yea,
    though I love him, I should."   150
CLAUDIO: Then down upon her knees she falls, weeps,
    sobs, beats her heart, tears her hair, prays, curses—
    "O sweet Benedick! God give me patience!"
LEONATO: She doth indeed; my daughter says so, and
    the ecstasy° hath so much overborne her that my 155
    daughter is sometime afeard she will do a desper-
    ate outrage to herself. It is very true.
DON PEDRO: It were good that Benedick knew of it by
    some other, if she will not discover it.
CLAUDIO: To what end? He would make but a sport of 160
    it and torment the poor lady worse.
DON PEDRO: And he should, it were an alms° to hang
    him! She's an excellent sweet lady, and, out of all
    suspicion, she is virtuous.
CLAUDIO: And she is exceeding wise.   165
DON PEDRO: In everything but in loving Benedick.
LEONATO: O, my lord, wisdom and blood° combat-
    ing in so tender a body, we have ten proofs to
    one that blood hath the victory. I am sorry for her,
    as I have just cause, being her uncle and her   170
    guardian.
DON PEDRO: I would she had bestowed this dotage on

---
dumps, sad songs. *shift,* makeshift. *live,* lief. *discov-*
ers, reveals, betrays.

gull, trick. *hold,* keep. *halfpence,* i.e., small pieces.
ecstasy, madness. *an alms,* a charity. *blood,* passion.

me; I would have daffed all other respects° and
made her half myself. I pray you tell Benedick of
175 it and hear what'a will say.

LEONATO: Were it good, think you?

CLAUDIO: Hero thinks surely she will die; for she says
she will die if he love her not, and she will die ere
she make her love known, and she will die, if he
180 woo her, rather than she will bate° one breath of
her accustomed crossness.

DON PEDRO: She doth well. If she should make ten-
der° of her love, 'tis very possible he'll scorn it; for
the man, as you know all, hath a contemptible°
185 spirit.

CLAUDIO: He is a very proper° man.

DON PEDRO: He hath indeed a good outward happiness.

CLAUDIO: Before God, and in my mind, very wise.

190 DON PEDRO: He doth indeed show some sparks that
are like wit.°

CLAUDIO: And I take him to be valiant.

DON PEDRO: As Hector, I assure you. And in the managing of quarrels you may say he is wise, for either
195 he avoids them with great discretion, or undertakes them with a most Christianlike fear.

LEONATO: If he do fear God, 'a must necessarily keep
peace. If he break the peace, he ought to enter
into a quarrel with fear and trembling.

200 DON PEDRO: And so will he do; for the man doth fear
God, howsoever it seems not in him by some large
jests° he will make. Well, I am sorry for your niece.
Shall we go seek Benedick and tell him of her
love?

205 CLAUDIO: Never tell him, my lord; let her wear it out
with good counsel.

LEONATO: Nay, that's impossible; she may wear her
heart out first.

DON PEDRO: Well, we will hear further of it by your
210 daughter. Let it cool the while. I love Benedick
well, and I could wish he would modestly examine himself to see how much he is unworthy so
good a lady.

LEONATO: My lord, will you walk? Dinner is ready.

[*They walk away.*]

215 CLAUDIO: If he do not dote on her upon this, I will
never trust my expectation.

DON PEDRO: Let there be the same net spread for her,
and that must your daughter and her gentlewomen carry.° The sport will be, when they hold
220 one an opinion of another's dotage, and no such
matter. That's the scene that I would see, which

will be merely a dumb show.° Let us send her to
call him in to dinner.

[*Exeunt* DON PEDRO, CLAUDIO, *and* LEONATO.]

BENEDICK: [*Advancing*] This can be no trick; the conference was sadly° borne. They have the truth of   225
this from Hero. They seem to pity the lady; it
seems her affections have their full bent.° Love
me? Why, it must be requited. I hear how I am
censured. They say I will bear myself proudly if I
perceive the love come from her. They say too   230
that she will rather die than give any sign of affection. I did never think to marry; I must not seem
proud. Happy are they that hear their detractions
and can put them to mending. They say the lady
is fair—'tis a truth, I can bear them witness; and   235
virtuous—'tis so, I cannot reprove it; and wise, but
for loving me; by my troth, it is no addition to her
wit, nor no great argument of her folly; for I will
be horribly in love with her. I may chance have
some odd quirks and remnants of wit broken   240
on me because I have railed so long against marriage; but doth not the appetite alter? A man
loves the meat in his youth that he cannot endure
in his age. Shall quips and sentences° and these
paper bullets of the brain awe a man from the   245
career° of his humor? No, the world must be
peopled. When I said I would die a bachelor, I did
not think I should live till I were married. Here
comes Beatrice. By this day, she's a fair lady. I do
spy some marks of love in her.   250

(*Enter* BEATRICE.)

BEATRICE: Against my will I am sent to bid you come
in to dinner.

BENEDICK: Fair Beatrice, I thank you for your pains.

BEATRICE: I took no more pains for those thanks than
you take pains to thank me. If it had been painful,   255
I would not have come.

BENEDICK: You take pleasure then in the message?

BEATRICE: Yea, just so much as you may take upon a
knife's point, and choke a daw withal.° You have
no stomach,° signior? Fare you well. (*Exit.*)   260

BENEDICK: Ha! "Against my will I am sent to bid you
come in to dinner." There's a double meaning in
that. "I took no more pains for those thanks than
you took pains to thank me." That's as much as to
say, "Any pains that I take for you is as easy as   265
thanks." If I do not take pity of her, I am a villain;
if I do not love her, I am a Jew. I will go get her picture. (*Exit.*)

---

daffed all other respects, put aside all other considerations (i.e., of disparity in rank). **bate,** abate, give up. **tender,** offer. **contemptible,** disdainful. **proper,** handsome.
wit, intelligence. **large jests,** broad jokes. **carry,** manage.

dumb show, pantomime (because of embarrassment).
sadly, seriously. **affections have their full bent,** emotions
are tightly stretched (like a bent bow). **sentences,** maxims.
career, course. **withal,** with. **no stomach,** no wish to argue
(as well as "no appetite").

ACT 3 / SCENE 1

(LEONATO's garden)
(Enter HERO and two Gentlewomen, MARGARET and
URSULA.)

HERO: Good Margaret, run thee to the parlor.
　　There shalt thou find my cousin Beatrice
　　Proposing with° the Prince and Claudio.
　　Whisper her ear and tell her, I and Ursley
5　　Walk in the orchard, and our whole discourse
　　Is all of her. Say that thou overheard'st us;
　　And bid her steal into the pleachèd bower,
　　Where honeysuckles, ripened by the sun,
　　Forbid the sun to enter—like favorites,
10　　Made proud by princes, that advance their pride
　　Against that power that bred it.° There will she
　　　　hide her
　　To listen our propose. This is thy office;°
　　Bear thee well in it and leave us alone.
　　MARGARET: I'll make her come, I warrant you,
　　　　presently.

[Exit.]

15　HERO: Now, Ursula, when Beatrice doth come,
　　As we do trace° this alley up and down,
　　Our talk must only be of Benedick.
　　When I do name him, let it be thy part
　　To praise him more than ever man did merit.
20　　My talk to thee must be how Benedick
　　Is sick in love with Beatrice. Of this matter
　　Is little Cupid's crafty° arrow made,
　　That only° wounds by hearsay.

(Enter BEATRICE.)

　　　　　　　　　　　　　Now begin;
　　For look where Beatrice like a lapwing runs
25　　Close by the ground, to hear our conference.
　　URSULA: The pleasant'st angling is to see the fish
　　Cut with her golden oars the silver stream
　　And greedily devour the treacherous bait;
　　So angle we for Beatrice, who even now
30　　Is couchèd in the woodbine coverture.°
　　Fear you not my part of the dialogue.
　　HERO: Then go we near her, that her ear lose
　　　　nothing
　　Of the false sweet bait that we lay for it.

[They approach the bower.]

　　No, truly, Ursula, she is too disdainful.
35　　I know her spirits are as coy° and wild

As haggards° of the rock.
URSULA:　　　　　　　　But are you sure
　　That Benedick loves Beatrice so entirely?
HERO: So says the Prince, and my new-trothèd lord.
URSULA: And did they bid you tell her of it, madam?
HERO: They did entreat me to acquaint her of it;　40
　　But I persuaded them, if they loved Benedick,
　　To wish him wrestle with affection
　　And never to let Beatrice know of it.
URSULA: Why did you so? Doth not the gentleman
　　Deserve as full as fortunate a bed　　　　45
　　As ever Beatrice shall couch upon?
HERO: O god of love! I know he doth deserve
　　As much as may be yielded to a man;
　　But Nature never framed a woman's heart
　　Of prouder stuff than that of Beatrice.　　50
　　Disdain and Scorn ride sparkling in her eyes,
　　Misprizing° what they look on; and her wit
　　Values itself so highly that to her
　　All matter else seems weak. She cannot love,
　　Nor take no shape nor project° of affection,　55
　　She is so self-endeared.
URSULA:　　　　　　　　Sure I think so;
　　And therefore certainly it were not good
　　She knew his love, lest she'll make sport at it.
HERO: Why, you speak truth. I never yet saw man,
　　How wise, how noble, young, how rarely featured,　60
　　But she would spell him backward. If fair-faced,
　　She would swear the gentleman should be her
　　　　sister;
　　If black,° why, Nature, drawing of an antic,°
　　Made a foul blot; if tall, a lance ill-headed;
　　If low, an agate very vilely cut;°　　　　65
　　If speaking, why, a vane blown with all winds;
　　If silent, why, a block movèd with none.
　　So turns she every man the wrong side out
　　And never gives to truth and virtue that
　　Which simpleness and merit purchaseth.　　70
URSULA: Sure, sure, such carping is not
　　　　commendable.
HERO: No, not to be so odd, and from all fashions,°
　　As Beatrice is, cannot be commendable.
　　But who dare tell her so? If I should speak,
　　She would mock me into air; O, she would laugh me　75
　　Out of myself, press me to death with wit!
　　Therefore let Benedick, like covered fire,
　　Consume away in sighs, waste inwardly.
　　It were a better death than die with mocks,
　　Which is as bad as die with tickling.　　80
URSULA: Yet tell her of it. Hear what she will say.
HERO: No; rather I will go to Benedick

Proposing with, talking to. **Made proud . . . bred it,** (an
Elizabethan audience of c.1600 would be reminded of the Earl
of Essex). **office,** duty. **trace,** walk. **crafty,** skillfully wrought.
only, solely. **woodbine coverture,** honeysuckle thicket. **coy,**
disdainful.

---

haggards, wild and intractable hawks. **Misprizing,** de-
spising. **project,** notion. **black,** dark-complexioned. **antic,**
grotesque figure. **agate very vilely cut,** poorly done miniature. **from all fashions,** contrary.

And counsel him to fight against his passion.
And truly, I'll devise some honest° slanders
85 To stain my cousin with. One doth not know
How much an ill word may empoison liking.
URSULA: O, do not do your cousin such a wrong!
She cannot be so much without true judgment
(Having so swift and excellent a wit
90 As she is prized to have) as to refuse
So rare a gentleman as Signior Benedick.
HERO: He is the only man of Italy,
Always excepted my dear Claudio.
URSULA: I pray you be not angry with me, madam,
95 Speaking my fancy. Signior Benedick,
For shape, for bearing, argument, and valor,
Goes foremost in report through Italy.
HERO: Indeed he hath an excellent good name.
URSULA: His excellence did earn it ere he had it.
100 When are you married, madam?
HERO: Why, everyday tomorrow!° Come, go in.
I'll show thee some attires, and have thy counsel
Which is the best to furnish° me tomorrow.

[*They walk away.*]

URSULA: She's limed,° I warrant you! We have caught
her, madam.
105 HERO: If it prove so, then loving goes by haps;°
Some Cupid kills with arrows, some with traps.

[*Exeunt* HERO *and* URSULA.]

BEATRICE: [*Coming forward*] What fire is in mine ears?
Can this be true?
Stand I condemned for pride and scorn so much?
Contempt, farewell! And maiden pride, adieu!
110 No glory lives behind the back of such.
And, Benedick, love on; I will requite thee,
Taming my wild heart to thy loving hand.
If thou dost love, my kindness shall incite thee
To bind our loves up in a holy band;
115 For others say thou dost deserve, and I
Believe it better than reportingly.° (*Exit.*)

ACT 3 / SCENE 2

(LEONATO *'s house*)
(*Enter Prince* [DON PEDRO], CLAUDIO, BENEDICK, *and*
LEONATO.)

DON PEDRO: I do but stay till your marriage be consummate, and then go I toward Aragon.
CLAUDIO: I'll bring you thither, my lord, if you'll
vouchsafe° me.

DON PEDRO: Nay, that would be as great a soil in the 5
new gloss of your marriage as to show a child his
new coat and forbid him to wear it. I will only be
bold with Benedick for his company; for, from the
crown of his head to the sole of his foot, he is all
mirth. He hath twice or thrice cut Cupid's bow- 10
string,° and the little hangman dare not shoot at
him. He hath a heart as sound as a bell; and his
tongue is the clapper, for what his heart thinks,
his tongue speaks.
BENEDICK: Gallants, I am not as I have been. 15
LEONATO: So say I. Methinks you are sadder.°
CLAUDIO: I hope he be in love.
DON PEDRO: Hang him truant?° There's no true drop
of blood in him to be truly touched with love. If
he be sad, he wants money. 20
BENEDICK: I have the toothache.
DON PEDRO: Draw it.°
BENEDICK: Hang it!
CLAUDIO: You must hang it first and draw it afterwards.
DON PEDRO: What? Sigh for the toothache? 25
LEONATO: Where is but a humor or a worm.°
BENEDICK: Well, everyone cannot master a grief but
he that has it.°
CLAUDIO: Yet say I he is in love.
DON PEDRO: There is no appearance of fancy° in him, 30
unless it be a fancy that he hath to strange disguises; as to be a Dutchman today, a Frenchman
tomorrow; or in the shape of two countries at
once, as a German from the waist downward, all
slops,° and a Spaniard from the hip upward, no 35
doublet.° Unless he have a fancy to this foolery, as
it appears he hath, he is no fool for fancy, as you
would have it appear he is.
CLAUDIO: If he be not in love with some woman, there
is no believing old signs; 'a brushes his hat o' 40
mornings. What should that bode?
DON PEDRO: Hath any man seen him at the barber's?
CLAUDIO: No, but the barber's man hath been seen
with him, and the old ornament of his cheek hath
already stuffed tennis balls.° 45
LEONATO: Indeed he looks younger than he did, by
the loss of a beard.

---

honest, appropriate. **everyday tomorrow,** i.e., tomorrow
I shall be married forever. **furnish,** dress. **limed,** caught (as
a bird is caught in birdlime, a sticky substance smeared on
branches). **haps,** chance. **reportingly,** i.e., mere hearsay.
vouchsafe, permit.

cut Cupid's bowstring, i.e., avoided falling in love. **sadder,** graver. **truant,** i.e., as unfaithful to his antiromantic
stance. **Draw it,** extract it (but **draw** also means "eviscerate";
traitors were hanged, drawn, and quartered. **Draw it** thus
leads to the exclamation **Hang it**). **a humor or a worm,** (supposed causes of tooth decay, **humor** = secretion). **Well . . .
has it,** i.e., a man has to have a grief first before he can master
it (Benedick does not admit that he has a grief; but some editors emend **cannot** to "can"). **fancy,** love. **slops,** loose
breeches. **doublet,** close-fitting jacket. **the old ornament . . .
tennis balls,** (cf. Beatrice's remark, 2.1.29–30 "I could not
endure a husband with a beard on his face").

DON PEDRO: Nay, 'a rubs himself with civet.° Can you smell him out by that?

50 CLAUDIO: That's as much as to say, the sweet youth's in love.

DON PEDRO: The greatest note of it is his melancholy.

CLAUDIO: And when was he wont to wash his face?

DON PEDRO: Yea, or to paint himself?° For the which I
55 hear what they say of him.

CLAUDIO: Nay, but his jesting spirit, which is now crept into a lutestring, and now governed by stops.°

DON PEDRO: Indeed that tells a heavy tale for him. Conclude, conclude, he is in love.

60 CLAUDIO: Nay, but I know who loves him.

DON PEDRO: That would I know too. I warrant, one that knows him not.

CLAUDIO: Yes, and his ill conditions;° and in despite of all,° dies° for him.

65 DON PEDRO: She shall be buried with her face upwards.°

BENEDICK: Yet is this no charm for the toothache. Old signior, walk aside with me; I have studied eight or nine wise words to speak to you, which these
70 hobbyhorses° must not hear.

[*Exeunt* BENEDICK *and* LEONATO.]

DON PEDRO: For my life, to break with him about Beatrice!

CLAUDIO: 'Tis even so. Hero and Margaret have by this played their parts with Beatrice, and then the two
75 bears will not bite one another when they meet.

(*Enter* JOHN *the Bastard.*)

DON JOHN: My lord and brother, God save you.

DON PEDRO: Good den,° brother.

DON JOHN: If your leisure served, I would speak with you.

80 DON PEDRO: In private?

DON JOHN: If it please you. Yet Count Claudio may hear, for what I would speak of concerns him.

DON PEDRO: What's the matter?

DON JOHN: [*To* CLAUDIO] Means your lordship to be
85 married tomorrow?

DON PEDRO: You know he does.

DON JOHN: I know not that, when he knows what I know.

CLAUDIO: If there be any impediment, I pray you dis-
90 cover it.

DON JOHN: You may think I love you not; let that appear hereafter, and aim better at me° by that° I now will manifest. For my brother (I think he holds you well, and in dearness of heart) hath help to effect your ensuing marriage—surely suit 95 ill spent and labor ill bestowed!

DON PEDRO: Why, what's the matter?

DON JOHN: I came hither to tell you, and, circumstances short'ned (for she has been too long a-talking of), the lady is disloyal. 100

CLAUDIO: Who? Hero?

DON JOHN: Even she—Leonato's Hero, your Hero, every man's Hero.

CLAUDIO: Disloyal?

DON JOHN: The word is too good to paint out her 105 wickedness. I could say she were worse. Think you of a worse title, and I will fit her to it. Wonder not till further warrant. Go but with me tonight, you shall see her chamber window ent'red, even the night before her wedding day. If you love her 110 then, tomorrow wed her. But it would better fit your honor to change your mind.

CLAUDIO: May this be so?

DON PEDRO: I will not think it.

DON JOHN: If you dare not trust that you see, confess 115 not that you know. If you will follow me, I will show you enough; and when you have seen more and heard more, proceed accordingly.

CLAUDIO: If I see anything tonight why I should not marry her tomorrow, in the congregation where I 120 should wed, there will I shame her.

DON PEDRO: And, as I wooed for thee to obtain her, I will join with thee to disgrace her.

DON JOHN: I will disparage her no farther till you are my witnesses. Bear it coldly° but till midnight, and 125 let the issue show itself.

DON PEDRO: O day untowardly turned!

CLAUDIO: O mischief strangely thwarting!

DON JOHN: O plague right well prevented! So will you say when you have seen the sequel. [*Exeunt.*] 130

ACT 3 / SCENE 3

(*A street*)

(*Enter* DOGBERRY *and his compartner* [VERGES,] *with the* WATCH.)

DOGBERRY: Are you good men and true?

VERGES: Yea, or else it were pity but they should suffer salvation,° body and soul.

DOGBERRY: Nay, that were a punishment too good for them if they should have any allegiance in them, 5 being chosen for the Prince's watch.

---

civet, perfume. *to paint himself,* to use cosmetics. *stops,* frets (on the lute). *conditions,* qualities. *in despite of all,* notwithstanding. *dies,* (1) pines away (2) is willing to "die" in the act of sex. *She shall . . . upwards,* (continues sexual innuendo). *hobbyhorses,* jokers (originally an imitation horse fastened around the waist of a morris dancer). *Good den,* good evening.

aim better at me, judge better of me. *that,* that which. *coldly,* calmly. *salvation,* damnation (the beginning of the malapropisms basic to the comedy of Dogberry and Verges).

VERGES: Well, give them their charge,° neighbor Dogberry.

DOGBERRY: First, who think you the most desartless
10   man to be constable?

FIRST WATCH: Hugh Oatcake, sir, or George Seacole,
for they can write and read.

DOGBERRY: Come hither, neighbor Seacole. God hath
blessed you with a good name. To be a well-
15   favored° man is the gift of fortune, but to write
and read comes by nature.

SECOND WATCH: Both which, Master Constable—

DOGBERRY: You have; I knew it would be your answer.
Well, for your favor, sir, why, give God thanks and
20   make no boast of it; and for your writing and
reading, let that appear when there is no need of
such vanity. You are thought here to be the most
senseless and fit man for the constable of the
watch. Therefore bear you the lanthorn. This is
25   your charge: you shall comprehend all vagrom°
men; you are to bid any man stand,° in the
Prince's name.

SECOND WATCH: How if 'a will not stand?

DOGBERRY: Why then, take no note of him, but let
30   him go, and presently call the rest of the watch
together and thank God you are rid of a knave.

VERGES: If he will not stand when he is bidden, he is
none of the Prince's subjects.

DOGBERRY: True, and they are to meddle with none
35   but the Prince's subjects. You shall also make no
noise in the streets; for, for the watch to babble
and to talk is most tolerable, and not to be endured.

WATCH:° We will rather sleep than talk; we know what
40   belongs to a watch.

DOGBERRY: Why, you speak like an ancient and most
quiet watchman, for I cannot see how sleeping
should offend. Only, have a care that your bills°
be not stol'n. Well, you are to call at all the ale-
45   houses and bid those that are drunk get them to
bed.

WATCH: How if they will not?

DOGBERRY: Why then, let them alone till they are
sober. If they make you not then the better answer,
50   you may say they are not the men you took them
for.

WATCH: Well, sir.

DOGBERRY: If you meet a thief, you may suspect him,
by virtue of your office, to be no true man; and for
55   such kind of men, the less you meddle or make
with them, why, the more is for your honesty.

WATCH: If we know him to be a thief, shall we not lay
hands on him?

DOGBERRY: Truly, by your office you may; but I think
they that touch pitch will be defiled. The most   60
peaceable way for you, if you do take a thief, is to
let him show himself what he is, and steal out of
your company.

VERGES: You have been always called a merciful man,
partner.   65

DOGBERRY: Truly, I would not hang a dog by my will,
much more a man who hath any honesty in him.

VERGES: If you hear a child cry in the night, you must
call to the nurse and bid her still it.

WATCH: How if the nurse be asleep and will not   70
hear us?

DOGBERRY: Why then, depart in peace and let the
child wake her with crying; for the ewe that will
not hear her lamb when it baes will never answer
a calf when he bleats.   75

VERGES: 'Tis very true.

DOGBERRY: This is the end of the charge: you, constable, are to present the Prince's own person. If
you meet the Prince in the night, you may stay him.

VERGES: Nay, by'r lady, that I think 'a cannot.   80

DOGBERRY: Five shillings to one on't, with any man
that knows the statutes, he may stay him! Marry,
not without the Prince be willing; for indeed the
watch ought to offend no man, and it is an
offense to stay a man against his will.   85

VERGES: By'r lady, I think it be so.

DOGBERRY: Ha, ah, ha! Well, masters, good night.
And there be any matter of weight chances, call
up me. Keep your fellows' counsels and your own,
and good night. Come, neighbor.   90

WATCH: Well, masters, we hear our charge. Let us go
sit here upon the church bench till two, and then
all to bed.

DOGBERRY: One word more, honest neighbors. I pray
you watch about Signior Leonato's door; for the   95
wedding being there tomorrow, there is a great
coil° tonight. Adieu. Be vigitant, I beseech you.

(Exeunt [DOGBERRY *and* VERGES].*)*
(Enter BORACHIO *and* CONRADE.*)*

BORACHIO: What, Conrade!

WATCH: [*Aside*] Peace! Stir not!

BORACHIO: Conrade, I say!   100

CONRADE: Here, man. I am at thy elbow.

BORACHIO: Mass,° and my elbow itched; I thought
there would a scab° follow.

CONRADE: I will owe thee an answer for that; and now
forward with thy tale.   105

---

charge, instructions. *well-favored,* handsome. *compre-*
hend all vagrom, i.e., apprehend all vagrant. *stand,* halt,
stop. *Watch,* (neither the Quarto nor the Folio differentiates again between First Watch and Second Watch until the
end of this scene). *bills,* constables' pikes.

---

coil, to-do, turmoil. *Mass,* (an interjection, from "by
the Mass"). *scab,* (1) crust over a wound (2) contemptible
person.

BORACHIO: Stand thee close then under this penthouse,° for it drizzles rain, and I will, like a true
drunkard,° utter all to thee.

WATCH: [*Aside*] Some treason, masters; yet stand close.

110 BORACHIO: Therefore know I have earned of Don John
a thousand ducats.

CONRADE: Is it possible that any villainy should be so
dear?

BORACHIO: Thou shouldst rather ask if it were pos-
115 sible any villainy should be so rich; for when rich
villains have need of poor ones, poor ones may
make what price they will.

CONRADE: I wonder at it.

BORACHIO: That shows thou art unconfirmed.° Thou
120 knowest that the fashion of a doublet, or a hat, or
a cloak, is nothing to a man.°

CONRADE: Yes, it is apparel.

BORACHIO: I mean the fashion.

CONRADE: Yes, the fashion is the fashion.

125 BORACHIO: Tush! I may as well say the fool's the fool.
But seest thou not what a deformed thief this
fashion is?

WATCH: [*Aside*] I know that Deformed; 'a has been a
vile thief this seven year; 'a goes up and down like
130 a gentleman. I remember his name.

BORACHIO: Didst thou not hear somebody?

CONRADE: No; 'twas the vane on the house.

BORACHIO: Seest thou not, I say, what a deformed
thief this fashion is? How giddily 'a turns about all
135 the hotbloods between fourteen and five-and-
thirty? Sometimes fashioning them like Pharaoh's
soldiers in the reechy° painting, sometime like
god Bel's priests° in the old church window, sometime like the shaven Hercules in the smirched
140 worm-eaten tapestry, where his codpiece° seems
as massy as his club?

CONRADE: All this I see; and I see that the fashion
wears out more apparel than the man. But art not
thou thyself giddy with the fashion too, that thou
145 hast shifted out of thy tale into telling me of the
fashion?

BORACHIO: Not so neither. But know that I have tonight wooed Margaret, the Lady Hero's gentlewoman, by the name of Hero. She leans me out at
150 her mistress' chamber window, bids me a thousand times good night. I tell this tale vilely—I
should first tell thee how the Prince, Claudio, and
my master, planted and placed and possessed° by
my master Don John, saw afar off in the orchard
155 this amiable encounter.

CONRADE: And thought they Margaret was Hero?

BORACHIO: Two of them did, the Prince and Claudio;
but the devil my master knew she was Margaret;
and partly by his oaths, which first possessed
them, partly by the dark night, which did deceive 160
them, but chiefly by my villainy, which did confirm any slander that Don John had made, away
went Claudio enraged; swore he would meet her,
as he was appointed, next morning at the temple,
and there, before the whole congregation, shame 165
her with what he saw o'ernight and send her
home again without a husband.

FIRST WATCH: We charge you in the Prince's name
stand!

SECOND WATCH: Call up the right Master Constable. 170
We have here recovered the most dangerous
piece of lechery that ever was known in the commonwealth.

FIRST WATCH: And one Deformed is one of them; I
know him; 'a wears a lock.° 175

CONRADE: Masters, masters—

SECOND WATCH: You'll be made bring Deformed
forth, I warrant you.

CONRADE: Masters, never speak; we charge you let us
obey you to go with us.° 180

BORACHIO: We are like to prove a goodly commodity,
being taken up of these men's bills.°

CONRADE: A commodity in question,° I warrant you.
Come, we'll obey you. (*Exeunt.*)

ACT 3 / SCENE 4

(LEONATO's *house*)
(*Enter* HERO, *and* MARGARET, *and* URSULA.)

HERO: Good Ursula, wake my cousin Beatrice and desire her to rise.

URSULA: I will, lady.

HERO: And bid her come hither.

URSULA: Well. [*Exit.*] 5

MARGARET: Troth, I think your other rabato° were
better.

HERO: No, pray thee, good Meg, I'll wear this.

MARGARET: By my troth, 's not so good, and I warrant
your cousin will say so. 10

HERO: My cousin's a fool, and thou art another. I'll
wear none but this.

---

penthouse, shed, lean-to. drunkard, (his name is based
on the Spanish *borracho,* "drunkard"). unconfirmed, innocent.
is nothing to a man, i.e., fails to reveal his actual character.
reechy, grimy, filthy. god Bel's priests, (from the Apocrypha).
codpiece, (decorative pouch at the fly of a sixteenth-century
man's breeches). possessed, informed, deluded.

lock, lovelock, curl of hair hanging by the ear. Masters . . . with us, (Conrade is mocking the language of the Second Watch; he means, "Say no more, we will go along with
you"). We are . . . bills, (Borachio continues the mockery
with a series of puns: commodity, [1] merchandise [2] profit;
taken up, [1] arrested [2] bought on credit; bills, [1] pikes
[2] bonds or sureties). in question, (1) subject to judicial
examination (2) of doubtful value. rabato, ruff.

MARGARET: I like the new tire° within° excellently,
if the hair were a thought browner; and your
gown's a most rare fashion, i' faith. I saw the
Duchess of Milan's gown that they praise so.

HERO: O, that exceeds, they say.

MARGARET: By my troth, 's but a nightgown° in respect of yours—cloth o' gold and cuts,° and laced
with silver, set with pearls, down sleeves, side-
sleeves,° and skirts, round underborne with a
bluish tinsel. But for a fine, quaint,° graceful, and
excellent fashion, yours is worth ten on't.

HERO: God give me joy to wear it, for my heart is
exceeding heavy.

MARGARET: 'Twill be heavier soon by the weight of a
man.

HERO: Fie upon thee! Art not ashamed?

MARGARET: Of what, lady? Of speaking honorably? Is
not marriage honorable in a beggar? Is not your
lord honorable without marriage? I think you
would have me say, "saving your reverence, a husband." And bad thinking do not wrest true speaking, I'll offend nobody. Is there any harm in "the
heavier for a husband"? None, I think, and it be
the right husband and the right wife; otherwise
'tis light,° and not heavy. Ask my Lady Beatrice
else. Here she comes.

(Enter BEATRICE.*)*

HERO: Good morrow, coz.

BEATRICE: Good morrow, sweet Hero.

HERO: Why, how now? Do you speak in the sick tune?

BEATRICE: I am out of all other tune, methinks.

MARGARET: Clap's into° "Light o' love." That goes without a burden.° Do you sing it, and I'll dance it.

BEATRICE: Ye light o' love with your heels!° Then, if
your husband have stables enough, you'll see he
shall lack no barns.°

MARGARET: O illegitimate construction! I scorn that
with my heels.

BEATRICE: 'Tis almost five o'clock, cousin; 'tis time
you were ready. By my troth, I am exceeding ill.
Heigh-ho!

MARGARET: For a hawk, a horse, or a husband?

BEATRICE: For the letter that begins them all, *H.*°

MARGARET: Well, and you be not turned Turk,° there's
no more sailing by the star.

BEATRICE: What means the fool, trow?°

MARGARET: Nothing I; but God send everyone their
heart's desire!

HERO: These gloves the Count sent me, they are an
excellent perfume.

BEATRICE: I am stuffed,° cousin; I cannot smell.

MARGARET: A maid, and stuffed!° There's goodly
catching of cold.

BEATRICE: O, God help me! God help me! How long
have you professed apprehension?°

MARGARET: Ever since you left it. Doth not my wit
become me rarely?

BEATRICE: It is not seen enough. You should wear it in
your cap. By my troth, I am sick.

MARGARET: Get you some of this distilled *Carduus
Benedictus*° and lay it to your heart. It is the only
thing for a qualm.°

HERO: There thou prick'st her with a thistle.

BEATRICE: *Benedictus?* Why *Benedictus?* You have some
moral° in this *Benedictus.*

MARGARET: Moral? No, by my troth, I have no moral
meaning. I meant plain holy thistle. You may
think perchance that I think you are in love. Nay,
by'r lady, I am not such a fool to think what I list;°
nor I list not to think what I can; nor indeed I cannot think, if I would think my heart out of thinking, that you are in love, or that you will be in
love, or that you can be in love. Yet Benedick was
such another, and now is he become a man. He
swore he would never marry; and yet now in despite of his heart he eats his meat without grudging.° And how you may be converted I know not;
but methinks you look with your eyes as other
women do.

BEATRICE: What pace is this that thy tongue keeps?

MARGARET: Not a false gallop.

(Enter URSULA.*)*

URSULA: Madam, withdraw. The Prince, the Count,
Signior Benedick, Don John, and all the gallants
of the town are come to fetch you to church.

HERO: Help to dress me, good coz, good Meg, good
Ursula. [*Exeunt.*]

ACT 3 / SCENE 5

(Another room in LEONATO*'s house)*
(Enter LEONATO *and the Constable* [DOGBERRY], *and
the Headborough* [VERGES].*)*

LEONATO: What would you with me, honest neighbor?

---

tire, headdress. *within,* in the next room. *nightgown,*
dressing gown. *cuts,* slashes to show rich fabric underneath.
down sleeves, side-sleeves, long sleeves covering the arms, open
sleeves hanging from the shoulder. *quaint,* pretty, dainty.
light, (pun on "wanton"). *Clap's into,* let us sing. *burden,*
bass part (with pun on "the heavier for a husband"). *Ye ...
your heels,* (sexual innuendo). *barns,* (pun on "bairns," children). *H,* ("ache" was pronounced "aitch"). *turned Turk,*
completely changed.

---

trow, I wonder. *I am stuffed,* I have a head cold.
stuffed, filled (as with a child). *apprehension,* wit. *Carduus
Benedictus,* blessed thistle, a medicinal herb. *qualm,* sensation of sickness. *moral,* special meaning. *list,* please. *he
eats his meat without grudging,* he finds that he can still eat.

DOGBERRY: Marry, sir, I would have some confidence with you that decerns you nearly.

LEONATO: Brief, I pray you, for you see it is a busy time with me.

DOGBERRY: Marry, this is it, sir.

VERGES: Yes, in truth it is, sir.

LEONATO: What is it, my good friends?

DOGBERRY: Goodman Verges, sir, speaks a little off the matter—an old man, sir, and his wits are not so blunt as, God help, I would desire they were; but, in faith, honest as the skin between his brows.

VERGES: Yes, I thank God I am as honest as any man living that is an old man and no honester than I.

DOGBERRY: Comparisons are odorous; Palabras,° neighbor Verges.

LEONATO: Neighbors, you are tedious.

DOGBERRY: It pleases your worship to say so, but we are the poor Duke's officers; but truly, for mine own part, if I were as tedious as a king, I could find in my heart to bestow it all of your worship.

LEONATO: All thy tediousness on me, ah?

DOGBERRY: Yea, and 'twere a thousand pound more than 'tis; for I hear as good exclamation on your worship as of any man in the city, and though I be but a poor man, I am glad to hear it.

VERGES: And so am I.

LEONATO: I would fain know what you have to say.

VERGES: Marry, sir, our watch tonight, excepting your worship's presence, ha' ta'en a couple of as arrant knaves as any in Messina.

DOGBERRY: A good old man, sir; he will be talking. As they say, "When the age is in, the wit is out." God help us! It is a world to see! Well said, i' faith, neighbor Verges. Well, God's a good man. And two men ride of a horse, one must ride behind. An honest soul, i' faith, sir, by my troth he is, as ever broke bread; but God is to be worshiped; all men are not alike, alas, good neighbor!

LEONATO: Indeed, neighbor, he comes too short of you.

DOGBERRY: Gifts that God gives.

LEONATO: I must leave you.

DOGBERRY: One word, sir. Our watch, sir, have indeed comprehended two aspicious persons, and we would have them this morning examined before your worship.

LEONATO: Take their examination yourself and bring it me; I am now in great haste, as it may appear unto you.

DOGBERRY: It shall be suffigance.

LEONATO: Drink some wine ere you go. Fare you well.

[*Enter a* MESSENGER.]

MESSENGER: My lord, they stay for you to give your daughter to her husband.

LEONATO: I'll wait upon them. I am ready.   55

(*Exit* [LEONATO, *with* MESSENGER].)

DOGBERRY: Go, good partner, go get you to Francis Seacole; bid him bring his pen and inkhorn to the jail. We are now to examination these men.

VERGES: And we must do it wisely.

DOGBERRY: We will spare for no wit, I warrant you;   60
here's that shall drive some of them to a non-come.° Only get the learned writer to set down our excommunication, and meet me at the jail.
[*Exeunt.*]

ACT 4 / SCENE 1

(*A church*)
(*Enter Prince* [DON PEDRO], [DON JOHN *the*] *Bastard,* LEONATO, *Friar* [FRANCIS], CLAUDIO, BENEDICK, HERO, *and* BEATRICE [*and* ATTENDANTS].)

LEONATO: Come, Friar Francis, be brief. Only to the plain form of marriage, and you shall recount their particular° duties afterwards.

FRIAR: You come hither, my lord, to marry this lady?

CLAUDIO: No.   5

LEONATO: To be married to her; Friar, you come to marry her.

FRIAR: Lady, you come hither to be married to this count?

HERO: I do.   10

FRIAR: If either of you know any inward impediment why you should not be conjoined, I charge you on your souls to utter it.

CLAUDIO: Know you any, Hero?

HERO: None, my lord.   15

FRIAR: Know you any, Count?

LEONATO: I dare make his answer, none.

CLAUDIO: O, what men dare do! What men may do! What men daily do, not knowing what they do!

BENEDICK: How now? Interjections? Why then, some   20
be of° laughing, as, ah, ha, he!°

CLAUDIO: Stand thee by,° friar. Father, by your leave,
Will you with free and unconstrainèd soul
Give me this maid your daughter?

LEONATO: As freely, son, as God did give her me.   25

CLAUDIO: And what have I to give you back whose worth
May counterpoise this rich and precious gift?

DON PEDRO: Nothing, unless you render her again.

---

non-come, short for Latin phrase *non compos mentis* (not of sound mind). **particular,** personal. **some be of,** some are concerned with. **ah, ha, he!,** (examples of interjections). **Stand thee by,** stand aside.

CLAUDIO: Sweet Prince, you learn me noble
  thankfulness.
30 There, Leonato, take her back again.
  Give not this rotten orange to your friend.
  She's but the sign and semblance of her honor.
  Behold how like a maid she blushes here!
  O, what authority and show of truth
35 Can cunning sin cover itself withal!
  Comes not that blood, as modest evidence,
  To witness simple virtue? Would you not swear,
  All you that see her, that she were a maid,
  By these exterior shows? But she is none.
40 She knows the heat of a luxurious° bed;
  Her blush is guiltiness, not modesty.
LEONATO: What do you mean, my lord?
CLAUDIO: Not to be married,
  Not to knit my soul to an approvèd° wanton.
LEONATO: Dear my lord, if you, in your own proof,°
45 Have vanquished the resistance of her youth
  And made defeat of her virginity—
CLAUDIO: I know what you would say: if I have
  known° her,
  You will say she did embrace me as a husband,
  And so extenuate the 'forehand sin.
50 No, Leonato,
  I never tempted her with word too large,
  But, as a brother to his sister, showed
  Bashful sincerity and comely love.
HERO: And seemed I ever otherwise to you?
CLAUDIO: Out on thee, seeming! I will write against
55 it.
  You seem to me as Dian in her orb,
  As chaste as is the bud ere it be blown;°
  But you are more intemperate in your blood°
  Than Venus; or those pamp'red animals
60 That rage in savage sensuality.
HERO: Is my lord well that he doth speak so wide?°
LEONATO: Sweet Prince, why speak not you?
DON PEDRO: What should I speak?
  I stand dishonored that have gone about
  To link my dear friend to a common stale.°
65 LEONATO: Are these things spoken, or do I but
  dream?
DON JOHN: Sir, they are spoken, and these things are
  true.
BENEDICK: This looks not like a nuptial.
HERO: "True," O God!
CLAUDIO: Leonato, stand I here?
  Is this the Prince? Is this the Prince's brother?
70 Is this face Hero's? Are our eyes our own?
LEONATO: All this is so. But what of this, my lord?

CLAUDIO: Let me but move one question to your
  daughter;
  And by that fatherly and kindly° power
  That you have in her, bid her answer truly.
LEONATO: I charge thee do so, as thou art my child. 75
HERO: O, God defend me! How am I beset?
  What kind of catechizing call you this?
CLAUDIO: To make you answer truly to your name.
HERO: Is it not Hero? Who can blot that name
  With any just reproach?
CLAUDIO: Marry, that can Hero! 80
  Hero itself can blot out Hero's virtue.
  What man was he talked with you yesternight,
  Out at your window betwixt twelve and one?
  Now, if you are a maid, answer to this.
HERO: I talked with no man at that hour, my lord. 85
DON PEDRO: Why, then are you no maiden. Leonato,
  I am sorry you must hear. Upon mine honor
  Myself, my brother, and this grievèd Count
  Did see her, hear her, at that hour last night
  Talk with a ruffian at her chamber window 90
  Who hath indeed, most like a liberal° villain,
  Confessed the vile encounters they have had
  A thousand times in secret.
DON JOHN: Fie, fie! They are not to be named, my
  lord—
  Not to be spoke of; 95
  There is not chastity enough in language
  Without offense to utter them. Thus, pretty lady,
  I am sorry for thy much misgovernment.
CLAUDIO: O Hero! What a Hero hadst thou been
  If half thy outward graces had been placed 100
  About thy thoughts and counsels of thy heart!
  But fare thee well, most foul, most fair, farewell;
  Thou pure impiety and impious purity,
  For thee I'll lock up all the gates of love,
  And on my eyelids shall conjecture° hang, 105
  To turn all beauty into thoughts of harm,
  And never shall it more be gracious.
LEONATO: Hath no man's dagger here a point for
  me?

[HERO swoons.]

BEATRICE: Why, how now, cousin? Wherefore sink
  you down?
DON JOHN: Come, let us go. These things, come thus
  to light, 110
  Smother her spirits up.

[Exeunt DON PEDRO, DON JOHN, and CLAUDIO.]

BENEDICK: How doth the lady?
BEATRICE: Dead I think. Help, uncle!

---

luxurious, lustful. approvèd, tested. proof, experience.
known, had intercourse with. blown, blossomed. blood, sexual desire. so wide, so far from the truth. stale, prostitute.

---

kindly, natural. liberal, licentious. conjecture, suspicion.

Hero! Why, Hero! Uncle! Signior Benedick! Friar!
LEONATO: O Fate, take not away thy heavy hand!
115   Death is the fairest cover for her shame
       That may be wished for.
BEATRICE: How now, cousin Hero?
FRIAR: Have comfort, lady.
LEONATO: Dost thou look up?
FRIAR: Yea, wherefore should she not?
LEONATO: Wherefore? Why, doth not every earthly
       thing
120   Cry shame upon her? Could she here deny
       The story that is printed in her blood?°
       Do not live, Hero; do not ope thine eyes;
       For, did I think thou wouldst not quickly die,
       Thought I thy spirits were stronger than thy
          shames,
125   Myself would on the rearward of reproaches
       Strike at thy life. Grieved I, I had but one?
       Chid I for that at frugal nature's frame?°
       O, one too much by thee! Why had I one?
       Why ever wast thou lovely in my eyes?
130   Why had I not with charitable hand
       Took up a beggar's issue at my gates,
       Who smirchèd thus and mired with infamy,
       I might have said, "No part of it is mine;
       This shame derives itself from unknown loins"?
135   But mine, and mine I loved, and mine I praised,
       And mine that I was proud on, mine so much
       That I myself was to myself not mine,
       Valuing of her—why she, O, she is fall'n
       Into a pit of ink, that the wide sea
140   Hath drops too few to wash her clean again,
       And salt too little which may season give°
       To her foul tainted flesh!
BENEDICK: Sir, sir, be patient.
       For my part, I am so attired in wonder,
       I know not what to say.
145 BEATRICE: O, on my soul, my cousin is belied!
BENEDICK: Lady, were you her bedfellow last night?
BEATRICE: No, truly, not; although, until last night,
       I have this twelvemonth been her bedfellow.
LEONATO: Confirmed, confirmed! O, that is stronger
       made
150   Which was before barred up with ribs of iron!
       Would the two princes lie, and Claudio lie,
       Who loved her so that, speaking of her foulness,
       Washed it with tears? Hence from her! Let her die.
FRIAR: Hear me a little;
155   For I have only been silent so long,
       And given way unto this course of fortune,
       By noting of the lady. I have marked
       A thousand blushing apparitions
       To start into her face, a thousand innocent shames

In angel whiteness beat away those blushes,   16○
And in her eye there hath appeared a fire
To burn the errors that these princes hold
Against her maiden truth. Call me a fool;
Trust not my reading nor my observations,
Which with experimental seal° doth warrant   16○
The tenor° of my book; trust not my age,
My reverence, calling, nor divinity,
If this sweet lady lie not guiltless here
Under some biting error.
LEONATO: Friar, it cannot be.
Thou seest that all the grace that she hath left   17○
Is that she will not add to her damnation
A sin of perjury; she not denies it.
Why seek'st thou then to cover with excuse
That which appears in proper nakedness?
FRIAR: Lady, what man is he you are accused of?   17○
HERO: They know that do accuse me; I know none.
If I know more of any man alive
Than that which maiden modesty doth warrant,
Let all my sins lack mercy! O my father,
Prove you that any man with me conversed   18○
At hours unmeet, or that I yesternight
Maintained the change° of words with any
   creature,
Refuse me, hate me, torture me to death!
FRIAR: There is some strange misprision° in the
   princes.
BENEDICK: Two of them have the very bent° of
   honor;   18○
And if their wisdoms be misled in this,
The practice° of it lives in John the bastard,
Whose spirits toil in frame of villainies.
LEONATO: I know not. If they speak but truth of
   her,
These hands shall tear her. If they wrong her
   honor,   19○
The proudest of them shall well hear of it.
Time hath not yet so dried this blood of mine,
Nor age so eat up my invention,°
Nor fortune made such havoc of my means,
Nor my bad life reft me so much of friends,   19○
But they shall find awaked in such a kind
Both strength of limb and policy of mind,
Ability in means, and choice of friends,
To quit° me of them throughly.
FRIAR: Pause awhile
And let my counsel sway you in this case.   20○
Your daughter here the princes left for dead.
Let her awhile be secretly kept in,
And publish it that she is dead indeed;

---

printed in her blood, written in her blushes.   frame, plan.
season give, act as a preservative.

experimental seal, seal of experience.   tenor, purport.
maintained the change, held exchange.   misprision, mistaking.
bent, shape (or perhaps "inclination").   practice, scheming.
invention, inventiveness.   quit, revenge.

Maintain a mourning ostentation,°
205 And on your family's old monument
Hang mournful epitaphs, and do all rites
That appertain unto a burial.
LEONATO: What shall become of this? What will this
do?
FRIAR: Marry, this well carried shall on her behalf
210 Change slander to remorse; that is some good.
But not for that dream I on this strange course,
But on this travail look for greater birth.
She dying, as it must be so maintained,
Upon the instant that she was accused,
215 Shall be lamented, pitied, and excused
Of every hearer. For it so falls out
That what we have we prize not to the worth
Whiles we enjoy it; but being lacked and lost,
Why, then we rack° the value, then we find
220 The virtue that possession would not show us
Whiles it was ours. So will it fare with Claudio.
When he shall hear she died upon his words,
Th' idea of her life shall sweetly creep
Into his study of imagination,°
225 And every lovely organ° of her life
Shall come appareled in more precious habit,°
More moving, delicate, and full of life,
Into the eye and prospect of his soul
Than when she lived indeed. Then shall he
mourn,
230 If ever love had interest in his liver,°
And wish he had not so accusèd her,
No, though he thought his accusation true.
Let this be so, and doubt not but success°
Will fashion the event° in better shape
235 Than I can lay it down in likelihood.
But if all aim, but this, be leveled false,°
The supposition of the lady's death
Will quench the wonder of her infamy;
And if it sort° not well, you may conceal her,
240 As best befits her wounded reputation,
In some reclusive and religious life,
Out of all eyes, tongues, minds, and injuries.
BENEDICK: Signior Leonato, let the friar advise you;
And though you know my inwardness° and love
245 Is very much unto the Prince and Claudio,
Yet, by mine honor, I will deal in this
As secretly and justly as your soul
Should with your body.

LEONATO: Being that I flow in grief,
The smallest twine may lead me.
FRIAR: 'Tis well consented. Presently away; 250
For to strange sores strangely they strain the
cure.
Come, lady, die to live. This wedding day
Perhaps is but prolonged. Have patience and
endure.

(Exit [with all but BEATRICE and BENEDICK].)

BENEDICK: Lady Beatrice, have you wept all this while?
BEATRICE: Yea, and I will weep a while longer. 255
BENEDICK: I will not desire that.
BEATRICE: You have no reason. I do it freely.
BENEDICK: Surely I do believe your fair cousin is
wronged.
BEATRICE: Ah, how much might the man deserve of 260
me that would right her!
BENEDICK: Is there any way to show such friendship?
BEATRICE: A very even° way, but no such friend.
BENEDICK: May a man do it?
BEATRICE: It is a man's office, but not yours. 265
BENEDICK: I do love nothing in the world so well as
you. Is not that strange?
BEATRICE: As strange as the thing I know not. It were
as possible for me to say I loved nothing so well as
you. But believe me not; and yet I lie not. I con- 270
fess nothing, nor I deny nothing. I am sorry for
my cousin.
BENEDICK: By my sword, Beatrice, thou lovest me.
BEATRICE: Do not swear and eat it.
BENEDICK: I will swear by it that you love me, and I will 275
make him eat it that says I love not you.
BEATRICE: Will you not eat your word?
BENEDICK: With no sauce that can be devised to it. I
protest° I love thee.
BEATRICE: Why then, God forgive me! 280
BENEDICK: What offense, sweet Beatrice?
BEATRICE: You have stayed me in a happy hour.° I was
about to protest I loved you.
BENEDICK: And do it with all thy heart.
BEATRICE: I love you with so much of my heart that 285
none is left to protest.
BENEDICK: Come, bid me do anything for thee.
BEATRICE: Kill Claudio.
BENEDICK: Ha! Not for the wide world!
BEATRICE: You kill me to deny it. Farewell. 290
BENEDICK: Tarry, sweet Beatrice. [He holds her.]
BEATRICE: I am gone, though I am here; there is no
love in you. Nay, I pray you let me go!
BENEDICK: Beatrice—
BEATRICE: In faith, I will go! 295
BENEDICK: We'll be friends first. [He lets her go.]

Maintain a mourning ostentation, perform the outward show of mourning. *rack,* stretch. *study of imagination,* meditation, musing. *organ,* physical feature. *habit,* dress. *liver,* (supposed seat of love). *success,* what follows. *event,* outcome. *But if . . . false,* but if all conjecture, except this (i.e., the mere supposition of Hero's death), be aimed (*leveled*) falsely. *sort,* turn out. *inwardness,* most intimate feelings.

---

even, direct.   *protest,* avow.   *in a happy hour,* just in time.

BEATRICE: You dare easier be friends with me than fight with mine enemy.

BENEDICK: Is Claudio thine enemy?

300 BEATRICE: Is 'a not approved in the height a villain, that hath slandered, scorned, dishonored my kinswoman? O that I were a man! What, bear her in hand° until they come to take hands; and then, with public accusation, uncovered slander, unmit-
305 igated rancor—O God, that I were a man! I would eat his heart in the market place!

BENEDICK: Hear me, Beatrice—

BEATRICE: Talk with a man out at a window! A proper saying!

310 BENEDICK: Nay, but Beatrice—

BEATRICE: Sweet Hero, she is wronged, she is slan-d'red, she is undone.

BENEDICK: Beat—

BEATRICE: Princes and counties! Surely, a princely tes-
315 timony, a goodly count, Count Comfect;° a sweet gallant surely! O that I were a man for his sake! Or that I had any friend would be a man for my sake! But manhood is melted into cursies,° valor into compliment, and men are only turned into
320 tongue, and trim ones too. He is now as valiant as Hercules that only tells a lie, and swears it. I can-not be a man with wishing; therefore I will die a woman with grieving.

BENEDICK: Tarry, good Beatrice. By this hand, I love
325 thee.

BEATRICE: Use it for my love some other way than swearing by it.

BENEDICK: Think you in your soul the Count Claudio hath wronged Hero?

330 BEATRICE: Yea, as sure as I have a thought or a soul.

BENEDICK: Enough, I am engaged. I will challenge him. I will kiss your hand, and so I leave you. By this hand, Claudio shall render me a dear account. As you hear of me, so think of me. Go
335 comfort your cousin. I must say she is dead. And so farewell.

[*Exeunt.*]

ACT 4 / SCENE 2

(*A prison*)
(*Enter the Constables* [DOGBERRY *and* VERGES] *and the Town Clerk* [SEXTON] *in gowns,* BORACHIO, [CON-RADE, *and* WATCH].)

DOGBERRY: Is our whole dissembly appeared?

VERGES: O, a stool and a cushion for the sexton.

SEXTON: Which be the malefactors?

DOGBERRY: Marry, that am I and my partner.

VERGES: Nay, that's certain. We have the exhibition to 5 examine.

SEXTON: But which are the offenders that are to be ex-amined? Let them come before Master Constable.

DOGBERRY: Yea, marry, let them come before me. What is your name, friend? 10

BORACHIO: Borachio.

DOGBERRY: Pray write down Borachio. Yours, sirrah?°

CONRADE: I am a gentleman, sir, and my name is Conrade.

DOGBERRY: Write down Master Gentleman Conrade. 15 Masters, do you serve God?

BOTH: Yea, sir, we hope.

DOGBERRY: Write down that they hope they serve God; and write God first, for God defend but God should go before such villains! Masters, it is proved 20 already that you are little better than false knaves, and it will go near to be thought so shortly. How answer you for yourselves?

CONRADE: Marry, sir, we say we are none.

DOGBERRY: A marvelous witty fellow, I assure you; but 25 I will go about with him.° Come you hither, sir-rah; a word in your ear. Sir, I say to you, it is thought you are false knaves.

BORACHIO: Sir, I say to you we are none.°

DOGBERRY: Well, stand aside. 'Fore God, they are both 30 in a tale.° Have you writ down that they are none?

SEXTON: Master Constable, you go not the way to ex-amine. You must call forth the watch that are their accusers.

DOGBERRY: Yea, marry, that's the eftest° way. Let the 35 watch come forth. Masters, I charge you in the Prince's name, accuse these men.

FIRST WATCH: This man said, sir, that Don John the Prince's brother was a villain.

DOGBERRY: Write down Prince John a villain. Why, this 40 is flat perjury, to call a prince's brother villain.

BORACHIO: Master Constable!

DOGBERRY: Pray thee, fellow, peace. I do not like thy look; I promise thee.

SEXTON: What heard you him say else? 45

SECOND WATCH: Marry, that he had received a thou-sand ducats of Don John for accusing the Lady Hero wrongfully.

DOGBERRY: Flat burglary as ever was committed.

VERGES: Yea, by mass, that it is. 50

SEXTON: What else, fellow?

FIRST WATCH: And that Count Claudio did mean, upon his words, to disgrace Hero before the whole assembly, and not marry her.

---

bear her in hand, fool her. **Comfect,** sugar candy. **cur-sies,** curtsies.

sirrah, (term of address used to an inferior). **go about with him,** get the better of him. **none,** (apparently pro-nounced the same as "known," and so taken by Dogberry in his next speech). **they are both in a tale,** their stories agree. **eftest,** quickest.

55 DOGBERRY: O villain! Thou wilt be condemned into
　　everlasting redemption for this.
SEXTON: What else?
WATCH: That is all.
SEXTON: And this is more, masters, than you can deny.
60　Prince John is this morning secretly stol'n away.
　　Hero was in this manner accused, in this very
　　manner refused, and upon the grief of this sud-
　　denly died. Master Constable, let these men be
　　bound and brought to Leonato's. I will go before
65　and show him their examination. [*Exit.*]
DOGBERRY: [*To the* WATCH] Come, let them be opin-
　　ioned.°
VERGES: Let them be in the hands of Coxcomb.°
DOGBERRY: God's my life, where's the sexton? Let him
70　write down the Prince's officer Coxcomb. Come,
　　bind them. Thou naughty° varlet!
CONRADE: Away! You are an ass, you are an ass.
DOGBERRY: Dost thou not suspect my place? Dost
　　thou not suspect my years? O that he were here to
75　write me down an ass! But, masters, remember
　　that I am an ass. Though it be not written down,
　　yet forget not that I am an ass. No, thou villain,
　　thou art full of piety, as shall be proved upon thee
　　by good witness. I am a wise fellow; and which is
80　more, an officer; and which is more, a house-
　　holder; and which is more, as pretty a piece of
　　flesh as any is in Messina, and one that knows the
　　law, go to! And a rich fellow enough, go to! And
　　a fellow that hath had losses; and one that hath
85　two gowns and everything handsome about him.
　　Bring him away. O that I had been writ down an
　　ass! (*Exit* [*with the others*].)

ACT 5 / SCENE 1

(*Before* LEONATO*'s house*)
(*Enter* LEONATO *and his brother* [ANTONIO].)

ANTONIO: If you go on thus, you will kill yourself,
　　And 'tis not wisdom thus to second° grief
　　Against yourself.
LEONATO:　　　　　I pray thee cease thy counsel,
　　Which falls into mine ears as profitless
5　As water in a sieve. Give not me counsel,
　　Nor let no comforter delight mine ear
　　But such a one whose wrongs do suit with° mine.
　　Bring me a father that so loved his child,
　　Whose joy of her is overwhelmed like mine,
10　And bid him speak of patience.

Measure his woe the length and breadth of mine,
And let it answer every strain° for strain,
As thus for thus, and such a grief for such,
In every lineament, branch, shape, and form.
If such a one will smile and stroke his beard,　　15
And sorrow wag,° cry "hem" when he should
　　groan;
Patch grief with proverbs, make misfortune drunk
With candle-wasters;° bring him yet° to me,
And I of him will gather patience.
But there is no such man. For, brother, men　　20
Can counsel and speak comfort to that grief
Which they themselves not feel; but, tasting it,
Their counsel turns to passion, which before
Would give preceptial medicine° to rage,
Fetter strong madness in a silken thread,　　25
Charm ache with air and agony with words.
No, no! 'Tis all men's office to speak patience
To those that wring under the load of sorrow,
But no man's virtue nor sufficiency
To be so moral° when he shall endure　　30
The like himself. Therefore give me no counsel;
My griefs cry louder than advertisement.°
ANTONIO: Therein do men from children nothing
　　differ.
LEONATO: I pray thee peace. I will be flesh and
　　blood;
For there was never yet philosopher　　35
That could endure the toothache patiently,
However they have writ the style of gods
And made a push at chance and sufferance.°
ANTONIO: Yet bend not all the harm upon yourself.
　　Make those that do offend you suffer too.　　40
LEONATO: There thou speak'st reason. Nay, I will
　　do so.
My soul doth tell me Hero is belied;
And that shall Claudio know; so shall the Prince,
And all of them that thus dishonor her.

(*Enter Prince* [DON PEDRO] *and* CLAUDIO.)

ANTONIO: Here comes the Prince and Claudio
　　hastily.　　45
DON PEDRO: Good den, good den.
CLAUDIO:　　　　　　Good day to both of you.
LEONATO: Hear you, my lords—
DON PEDRO:　　　　We have some haste, Leonato.
LEONATO: Some haste, my lord! Well, fare you well,
　　my lord.
Are you so hasty now? Well, all is one.

---

　　opinioned, (he means "pinioned"). *Coxcomb*, (apparently Verges thinks this is an elegant name for one of the
Watch; editors commonly emend "of Coxcomb" to "off, coxcomb," and give to Conrade). *naughty*, wicked. *second*,
assist. *suit with*, accord with.

　　strain, quality, trait. *wag*, wave away. *candle-wasters*,
revelers (?) philosophers (?). *yet*, then. *preceptial medicine*, medicine of precepts (cf. line 17: "Patch grief with
proverbs"). *moral*, moralizing. *advertisement*, counsel.
made . . . sufferance, defied mischance and suffering.

DON PEDRO: Nay, do not quarrel with us, good old
50   man.

ANTONIO: If he could right himself with quarreling,
    Some of us would lie low.

CLAUDIO: Who wrongs him?

LEONATO: Marry, thou dost wrong me, thou
    dissembler, thou!
    Nay, never lay thy hand upon thy sword;
    I fear thee not.

55 CLAUDIO: Marry, beshrew° my hand
    If it should give your age such cause of fear.
    In faith, my hand meant nothing to my sword.

LEONATO: Tush, tush, man! Never fleer° and jest at
    me.
    I speak not like a dotard nor a fool,
60   As under privilege of age to brag
    What I have done being young, or what would do,
    Were I not old. Know, Claudio, to thy head,°
    Thou hast so wronged mine innocent child and me
    That I am forced to lay my reverence by
65   And, with gray hairs and bruise of many days,
    Do challenge thee to trial of a man.°
    I say thou hast belied mine innocent child.
    Thy slander hath gone through and through her
    heart,
    And she lies buried with her ancestors;
70   O, in a tomb where never scandal slept,
    Save this of hers, framed° by thy villainy!

CLAUDIO: My villainy?

LEONATO: Thine, Claudio; thine I say.

DON PEDRO: You say not right, old man.

LEONATO: My lord, my lord,
    I'll prove it on his body if he dare,
75   Despite his nice fence° and his active practice,
    His May of youth and bloom of lustihood.

CLAUDIO: Away! I will not have to do with you.

LEONATO: Canst thou so daff° me? Thou hast killed
    my child.
    If thou kill'st me, boy, thou shalt kill a man.

80 ANTONIO: He shall kill two of us, and men indeed.
    But that's no matter; let him kill one first.
    Win me and wear me! Let him answer me.
    Come, follow me, boy; come, sir boy; come, follow
    me.
    Sir boy, I'll whip you from your foining° fence!
85   Nay, as I am a gentleman, I will.

LEONATO: Brother—

ANTONIO: Content yourself. God knows I loved my
    niece;
    And she is dead, slandered to death by villains,

That dare as well answer a man indeed
    As I dare take a serpent by the tongue.   90
    Boys, apes, braggarts, Jacks,° milksops!

LEONATO: Brother Anthony—

ANTONIO: Hold you content. What, man! I know
    them, yea,
    And what they weigh, even to the utmost scruple;°
    Scambling,° outfacing, fashionmonging° boys,
    That lie and cog° and flout, deprave and slander,   95
    Go anticly,° and show outward hideousness,
    And speak off half a dozen dang'rous words,
    How they might hurt their enemies, if they durst;
    And this is all.

LEONATO: But, brother Anthony—

ANTONIO: Come, 'tis no matter.   100
    Do not you meddle; let me deal in this.

DON PEDRO: Gentlemen both, we will not wake your
    patience.°
    My heart is sorry for your daughter's death.
    But, on my honor, she was charged with nothing
    But what was true, and very full of proof.   105

LEONATO: My lord, my lord!

DON PEDRO: I will not hear you.

LEONATO: No? Come, brother, away! I will be
    heard!

ANTONIO: And shall, or some of us will smart for it.

*(Exeunt ambo° [*LEONATO *and* ANTONIO*].)*
(Enter BENEDICK.*)*

DON PEDRO: See, see! Here comes the man we went
    to seek.   110

CLAUDIO: Now, signior, what news?

BENEDICK: Good day, my lord.

DON PEDRO: Welcome, signior. You are almost come
    to part almost a fray.

CLAUDIO: We had liked to have had our two noses   115
    snapped off with two old men without teeth.

DON PEDRO: Leonato and his brother. What think'st
    thou? Had we fought, I doubt° we should have
    been too young for them.

BENEDICK: In a false quarrel there is no true valor. I   120
    came to seek you both.

CLAUDIO: We have been up and down to seek thee; for
    we are high-proof° melancholy, and would fain
    have it beaten away. Wilt thou use thy wit?

BENEDICK: It is in my scabbard. Shall I draw it?   125

DON PEDRO: Dost thou wear thy wit by thy side?

CLAUDIO: Never any did so, though very many have

---

beshrew, curse (but not a strong word). ***fleer,*** sneer.
head, face. ***trial of a man,*** manly test, i.e., a duel. ***framed,***
made. ***nice fence,*** elegant fencing. ***daff,*** put off. ***foining,***
thrusting.

Jacks, (a contemptuous term of no precise meaning).
scruple, smallest unit. ***Scambling,*** brawling. ***fashionmong-
ing,*** fashion following. ***cog,*** cheat. ***anticly,*** grotesquely
dressed. ***wake your patience,*** arouse your indulgence (heavily ironic). s.d. ***ambo,*** both (Latin). ***doubt,*** suspect. ***high-
proof,*** in the highest degree.

been beside their wit. I will bid thee draw, as we
do the minstrels: draw° to pleasure us.

DON PEDRO: As I am an honest man, he looks pale. Art 130
thou sick, or angry?

CLAUDIO: What, courage, man! What though care
killed a cat, thou hast mettle enough in thee to
kill care. 135

BENEDICK: Sir, I shall meet your wit in the career° and 135
you charge° it against me. I pray you choose another subject.

CLAUDIO: Nay then, give him another staff. This last
was broke cross.°

DON PEDRO: By this light, he changes more and more. 140
I think he be angry indeed.

CLAUDIO: If he be, he knows how to turn his girdle.°

BENEDICK: Shall I speak a word in your ear?

CLAUDIO: God bless me from a challenge!

BENEDICK: [Aside to CLAUDIO] You are a villain; I jest 145
not; I will make it good how you dare, with what
you dare, and when you dare. Do me right, or I
will protest° your cowardice. You have killed a
sweet lady, and her death shall fall heavy on you.
Let me hear from you. 150

CLAUDIO: Well, I will meet you, so I may have good
cheer.

DON PEDRO: What, a feast, a feast?

CLAUDIO: I' faith, I thank him; he hath bid me to a
calf's head and a capon; the which if I do not 155
carve most curiously,° say my knife's naught. Shall
I not find a woodcock° too?

BENEDICK: Sir, your wit ambles well; it goes easily.

DON PEDRO: I'll tell thee how Beatrice praised thy wit
the other day. I said thou hadst a fine wit. "True," 160
said she, "a fine little one." "No," said I, "a great
wit." "Right," says she, "a great gross one." "Nay,"
said I, "a good wit." "Just," said she, "it hurts nobody." "Nay," said I, "the gentleman is wise." "Certain," said she, "a wise gentleman." "Nay," said I, 165
"he hath the tongues."° "That I believe," said she,
"for he swore a thing to me on Monday night
which he forswore on Tuesday morning; there's a
double tongue; there's two tongues." Thus did
she an hour together transshape° thy particular 170
virtues. Yet at last she concluded with a sigh, thou
wast the prop'rest° man in Italy.

---

draw, i.e., draw not a sword but a fiddle bow. *in the
career*, headlong. *charge*, i.e., as in tilting with staves or
lances. *broke cross*, ineptly broken (by crossing the opponent's shield instead of striking it headlong). *turn his girdle*,
challenge me (by reaching for his dagger?). *protest*, proclaim. *curiously*, skillfully. *woodcock*, stupid bird (Claudio
reduces the duel to a carving up of symbols of stupidity—a
calf's head, a capon, and a woodcock). *hath the tongues*,
knows foreign languages. *transshape*, distort. *prop'rest*,
most handsome.

CLAUDIO: For the which she wept heartily and said she
cared not.

DON PEDRO: Yea, that she did; but yet, for all that, and 175
if she did not hate him deadly, she would love him
dearly. The old man's daughter told us all.

CLAUDIO: All, all! And moreover, God saw him when
he was hid in the garden.

DON PEDRO: But when shall we set the savage bull's 180
horns on the sensible Benedick's head?

CLAUDIO: Yea, and text underneath, "Here dwells
Benedick, the married man"?

BENEDICK: Fare you well, boy; you know my mind. I
will leave you now to your gossiplike humor; you 185
break jests as braggards do their blades, which
God be thanked hurt not. [*To* DON PEDRO] My
lord, for your many courtesies I thank you. I must
discontinue your company. Your brother the bastard is fled from Messina. You have among you 190
killed a sweet and innocent lady. For my Lord
Lackbeard there, he and I shall meet; and till
then peace be with him. [*Exit.*]

DON PEDRO: He is in earnest.

CLAUDIO: In most profound earnest; and, I'll warrant 195
you, for the love of Beatrice.

DON PEDRO: And hath challenged thee?

CLAUDIO: Most sincerely.

DON PEDRO: What a pretty thing man is when he goes
in his doublet and hose and leaves off his wit! 200

(*Enter Constables* [DOGBERRY, VERGES, *and the* WATCH,
with] CONRADE *and* BORACHIO.)

CLAUDIO: He is then a giant to an ape; but then is an
ape a doctor to such a man.°

DON PEDRO: But, soft you, let me be! Pluck up, my
heart, and be sad. Did he not say my brother was
fled? 205

DOGBERRY: Come you, sir. If justice cannot tame you,
she shall ne'er weigh more reasons in her balance. Nay, and you be a cursing hypocrite once,
you must be looked to.

DON PEDRO: How now? Two of my brother's men 210
bound? Borachio one.

CLAUDIO: Hearken after° their offense, my lord.

DON PEDRO: Officers, what offense have these men
done?

DOGBERRY: Marry, sir, they have committed false re- 215
port; moreover, they have spoken untruths; sec-
ondarily, they are slanders; sixth and lastly, they
have belied a lady; thirdly, they have verified
unjust things; and to conclude, they are lying
knaves. 220

He is then . . . a man, i.e., an ape would consider him
important, but an ape is actually a scholar (*doctor*) compared
to such a fool. *Hearken after*, inquire into.

DON PEDRO: First, I ask thee what they have done; thirdly, I ask thee what's their offense; sixth and lastly, why they are committed; and to conclude, what you lay to their charge.

225 CLAUDIO: Rightly reasoned, and in his own division; and, by my troth, there's one meaning well suited.°

DON PEDRO: Who have you offended, masters, that you are thus bound° to your answer? This learned constable is too cunning° to be understood. What's

230 your offense?

BORACHIO: Sweet Prince, let me go no farther to mine answer. Do you hear me, and let this count kill me. I have deceived even your very eyes. What your wisdoms could not discover, these shallow

235 fools have brought to light, who in the night overheard me confessing to this man, how Don John your brother incensed me to slander the Lady Hero; how you were brought into the orchard and saw me court Margaret in Hero's garments;

240 how you disgraced her when you should marry her. My villainy they have upon record, which I had rather seal with my death than repeat over to my shame. The lady is dead upon mine and my master's false accusation; and briefly, I desire

245 nothing but the reward of a villain.

DON PEDRO: Runs not this speech like iron through your blood?

CLAUDIO: I have drunk poison whiles he uttered it.

DON PEDRO: But did my brother set thee on to this?

250 BORACHIO: Yea, and paid me richly for the practice of it.

DON PEDRO: He is composed and framed of treachery,
And fled he is upon this villainy.

CLAUDIO: Sweet Hero, now thy image doth appear
255 In the rare semblance that I loved it first.

DOGBERRY: Come, bring away the plaintiffs. By this time our sexton hath reformed Signior Leonato of the matter. And, masters, do not forget to specify, when time and place shall serve, that I am

260 an ass.

VERGES: Here, here comes Master Signior Leonato, and the sexton too.

(Enter LEONATO, his brother [ANTONIO], and the SEXTON.)

LEONATO: Which is the villain? Let me see his eyes
That, when I note another man like him,
265 I may avoid him. Which of these is he?

BORACHIO: If you would know your wronger, look on me.

LEONATO: Art thou the slave that with thy breath hast killed

Mine innocent child?

BORACHIO: Yea, even I alone.

LEONATO: No, not so, villain! Thou beliest thyself.
Here stand a pair of honorable men;   270
A third is fled, that had a hand in it.
I thank you, princes, for my daughter's death.
Record it with your high and worthy deeds.
'Twas bravely done, if you bethink you of it.

CLAUDIO: I know not how to pray your patience;°   275
Yet I must speak. Choose your revenge yourself;
Impose me to what penance your invention°
Can lay upon my sin. Yet sinned I not
But in mistaking.

DON PEDRO: By my soul, nor I;
And yet, to satisfy this good old man,   280
I would bend under any heavy weight
That he'll enjoin me to.

LEONATO: I cannot bid you bid my daughter live;
That were impossible; but I pray you both,
Possess° the people in Messina here   285
How innocent she died; and if your love
Can labor aught in sad invention,
Hang her an epitaph upon her tomb,
And sing it to her bones, sing it tonight.
Tomorrow morning come you to my house;   290
And since you could not be my son-in-law,
Be yet my nephew. My brother hath a daughter,
Almost the copy of my child that's dead,
And she alone is heir to both of us.
Give her the right° you should have giv'n her
     cousin,   295
And so dies my revenge.

CLAUDIO: O noble sir!
Your overkindness doth wring tears from me.
I do embrace your offer; and dispose
For henceforth of poor Claudio.

LEONATO: Tomorrow then I will expect your coming;   300
Tonight I take my leave. This naughty man
Shall face to face be brought to Margaret,
Who I believe was packed° in all this wrong,
Hired to it by your brother.

BORACHIO: No, by my soul, she was not:
Nor knew not what she did when she spoke to me;   305
But always hath been just and virtuous
In anything that I do know by her.

DOGBERRY: Moreover, sir, which indeed is not under white and black,° this plaintiff here, the offender, did call me ass. I beseech you let it be remem-   310
b'red in his punishment. And also the watch heard them talk of one Deformed; they say he

---

well suited, well dressed out. ***bound,*** arraigned. ***cunning,*** intelligent.

pray your patience, ask your forgiveness. ***invention,*** imagination. ***Possess,*** inform. ***right,*** (Hero had a right to claim Claudio as her husband; probably there is also a pun on "rite"). ***packed,*** combined, i.e., an accomplice. ***not under white and black,*** not in the official record.

wears a key° in his ear, and a lock hanging by it, and borrows money in God's name, the which he
315　hath used so long and never paid that now men grow hard-hearted and will lend nothing for God's sake. Pray you examine him upon that point.

LEONATO: I thank thee for thy care and honest pains.

DOGBERRY: Your worship speaks like a most thankful
320　and reverent youth, and I praise God for you.

LEONATO: There's for thy pains. [*Gives money.*]

DOGBERRY: God save the foundation!°

LEONATO: Go, I discharge° thee of thy prisoner, and I thank thee.

325　DOGBERRY: I leave an arrant knave with your worship, which I beseech your worship to correct yourself, for the example of others. God keep your worship! I wish your worship well. God restore you to health! I humbly give you leave to depart; and if a
330　merry meeting may be wished, God prohibit it! Come, neighbor. [*Exeunt* DOGBERRY *and* VERGES.]

LEONATO: Until tomorrow morning, lords, farewell.

ANTONIO: Farewell, my lords. We look for you tomorrow.

DON PEDRO: We will not fail.

335　CLAUDIO:　　　　　　　　　Tonight I'll mourn with Hero.

[*Exeunt* DON PEDRO *and* CLAUDIO.]

LEONATO: [*To the* WATCH] Bring you these fellows on. We'll talk with Margaret,
How her acquaintance grew with this lewd° fellow.

(*Exeunt* [*separately*].)

ACT 5 / SCENE 2

(LEONATO's *garden*)
(*Enter* BENEDICK *and* MARGARET [*meeting*].)

BENEDICK: Pray thee, sweet Mistress Margaret, deserve well at my hands by helping me to the speech of Beatrice.

MARGARET: Will you then write me a sonnet in praise
5　of my beauty?

BENEDICK: In so high a style,° Margaret, that no man living shall come over it; for in most comely truth thou deservest it.

MARGARET: To have no man come over me!° Why,
10　shall I always keep belowstairs?°

BENEDICK: Thy wit is as quick as the greyhound's mouth; it catches.

MARGARET: And yours as blunt as the fencer's foils, which hit but hurt not.

BENEDICK: A most manly wit, Margaret; it will not hurt　15
a woman. And so, I pray thee call Beatrice. I give thee the bucklers.°

MARGARET: Give us the swords; we have bucklers of our own.

BENEDICK: If you use them, Margaret, you must put in　20
the pikes° with a vice;° and they are dangerous weapons for maids.

MARGARET: Well, I will call Beatrice to you, who I think hath legs. (*Exit* MARGARET.)

BENEDICK: And therefore will come.　25

[*Sings*]

　　　The god of love,
　　　That sits above
　And knows me, and knows me,
　　　How pitiful I deserve—

I mean in singing; but in loving, Leander the　30
good swimmer, Troilus° the first employer of panders, and a whole book full of these quondam carpetmongers,° whose names yet run smoothly in the even road of a blank verse—why, they were never so truly turned over and over as my poor　35
self in love. Marry, I cannot show it in rhyme. I have tried. I can find out no rhyme to "lady" but "baby," an innocent rhyme; for "scorn," "horn," a hard rhyme; for "school," "fool," a babbling rhyme. Very ominous endings. No, I was not born under　40
a rhyming planet, nor I cannot woo in festival terms.

(*Enter* BEATRICE.)

Sweet Beatrice, wouldst thou come when I called thee?

BEATRICE: Yea, signior, and depart when you bid me.　45

BENEDICK: O, stay but till then!

BEATRICE: "Then" is spoken. Fare you well now. And yet, ere I go, let me go with that I came, which is, with knowing what hath passed between you and Claudio.　50

BENEDICK: Only foul words; and thereupon I will kiss thee.

BEATRICE: Foul words is but foul wind, and foul wind is but foul breath, and foul breath is noisome. Therefore I will depart unkissed.　55

BENEDICK: Thou hast frighted the word out of his

---

key, ring (but perhaps Dogberry merely assumes that if a man wears a lock in his hair he must wear a key too). **the foundation,** (as if Leonato were a charitable institution). **discharge,** relieve. **lewd,** low. **style,** (pun on "stile," a set of steps for passing over a fence). **come over me,** (the beginning of an interchange of sexual innuendoes). **keep belowstairs,** dwell in the servants' quarters.

I give thee the bucklers, I yield. **pikes,** spikes in the center of bucklers. **vice,** screw. ***Leander . . . Troilus,*** (legendary lovers; Leander nightly swam the Hellespont to visit Hero, Troilus was aided in his love for Cressida by Pandarus). ***quondam carpetmongers,*** ancient boudoir knights.

right sense, so forcible is thy wit. But I must tell thee plainly, Claudio undergoes my challenge; and either I must shortly hear from him or I will
60   subscribe him° a coward. And I pray thee now tell me, for which of my bad parts didst thou first fall in love with me?

BEATRICE: For them all together, which maintained so politic a state° of evil that they will not admit
65   any good part to intermingle with them. But for which of my good parts did you first suffer love for me?

BENEDICK: Suffer love! A good epithet. I do suffer love indeed, for I love thee against my will.

70 BEATRICE: In spite of your heart, I think. Alas, poor heart! If you spite it for my sake, I will spite it for yours, for I will never love that which my friend hates.

BENEDICK: Thou and I are too wise to woo peaceably.

75 BEATRICE: It appears not in this confession. There's not one wise man among twenty that will praise himself.

BENEDICK: An old, an old instance,° Beatrice, that lived in the time of good neighbors. If a man do not
80   erect in this age his own tomb ere he dies, he shall live no longer in monument than the bell rings and the widow weeps.

BEATRICE: And how long is that, think you?

BENEDICK: Question: why, an hour in clamor and a
85   quarter in rheum;° therefore is it most expedient for the wise, if Don Worm, his conscience, find no impediment to the contrary, to be the trumpet of his own virtues, as I am to myself. So much for praising myself, who, I myself will bear witness, is
90   praiseworthy. And now tell me, how doth your cousin?

BEATRICE: Very ill.

BENEDICK: And how do you?

BEATRICE: Very ill too.

95 BENEDICK: Serve God, love me, and mend. There will I leave you too, for here comes one in haste.

(Enter URSULA.*)*

URSULA: Madam, you must come to your uncle. Yonder's old coil° at home. It is proved my Lady Hero hath been falsely accused, the Prince and Claudio
100   mightily abused, and Don John is the author of all, who is fled and gone. Will you come presently?

BEATRICE: Will you go hear this news, signior?

BENEDICK: I will live in thy heart, die in thy lap, and be buried in thy eyes; and moreover, I will go
105   with thee to thy uncle's. *(Exit* [*with* BEATRICE *and* URSULA].*)*

---

subscribe him, write him down. **politic a state,** well-ordered a community. **instance,** example. **rheum,** tears. **old coil,** plenty of confusion.

ACT 5 / SCENE 3

(A church)
(Enter CLAUDIO, *Prince* [DON PEDRO, LORD,] *and three or four with tapers* [*followed by Musicians*]*.)*

CLAUDIO: Is this the monument of Leonato?

LORD: It is, my lord.

[CLAUDIO *reads from a scroll.*]

EPITAPH

Done to death by slanderous tongues
  Was the Hero that here lies;
Death, in guerdon° of her wrongs,
  Gives her fame which never dies.   5
So the life that died with shame
Lives in death with glorious fame.

[*Hangs up the scroll.*]

Hang thou there upon the tomb,
Praising her when I am dumb.   10

CLAUDIO: Now, music, sound, and sing your solemn hymn.

SONG

Pardon, goddess of the night,°
Those that slew thy virgin knight;
For the which, with songs of woe,   15
Round about her tomb they go.
Midnight, assist our moan;
Help us to sigh and groan,
  Heavily, heavily.
Graves, yawn and yield your dead,   20
Till death be utterèd,
  Heavily, heavily.

CLAUDIO: Now unto thy bones good night!
  Yearly will I do this rite.

DON PEDRO: Good morrow, masters; put your torches out.   25
  The wolves have preyed, and look, the gentle day,
Before the wheels of Phoebus,° round about
  Dapples the drowsy east with spots of gray.
Thanks to you all, and leave us. Fare you well.

CLAUDIO: Good morrow, masters; each his several way.   30

DON PEDRO: Come, let us hence and put on other weeds,°
And then to Leonato's we will go.

---

guerdon, reward. **goddess of the night,** Diana, goddess of the moon and of chastity. **wheels of Phoebus,** wheels of the sun god's chariot. **weeds,** apparel.

CLAUDIO: And Hymen° now with luckier issue
    speeds°
    Than this for whom we rend'red up this woe.

(Exeunt.)

ACT 5 / SCENE 4

(LEONATO's house)
(Enter LEONATO, BENEDICK, [BEATRICE,] MARGARET,
URSULA, *Old Man* [ANTONIO], FRIAR [FRANCIS],
HERO.)

FRIAR: Did I not tell you she was innocent?
LEONATO: So are the Prince and Claudio, who
    accused her
    Upon the error that you heard debated.
    But Margaret was in some fault for this,
5   Although against her will, as it appears
    In the true course of all the question.°
ANTONIO: Well, I am glad that all things sorts° so
    well.
BENEDICK: And so am I, being else by faith enforced
    To call young Claudio to a reckoning for it.
10 LEONATO: Well, daughter, and you gentlewomen all,
    Withdraw into a chamber by yourselves,
    And when I send for you, come hither masked.
    The Prince and Claudio promised by this hour
    To visit me. You know your office, brother;
15   You must be father to your brother's daughter,
    And give her to young Claudio. *(Exeunt Ladies.)*
ANTONIO: Which I will do with confirmed°
    countenance.
BENEDICK: Friar, I must entreat your pains, I think.
FRIAR: To do what, signior?
20 BENEDICK: To bind me, or undo me—one of them.
    Signior Leonato, truth it is, good signior,
    Your niece regards me with an eye of favor.
LEONATO: That eye my daughter lent her; 'tis most
    true.
BENEDICK: And I do with an eye of love requite her.
LEONATO: The sight whereof I think you had from
25   me,
    From Claudio, and the Prince. But what's your will?
BENEDICK: Your answer, sir, is enigmatical.
    But, for my will, my will is, your good will
    May stand with ours, this day to be conjoined
30   In the state of honorable marriage;
    In which, good friar, I shall desire your help.
LEONATO: My heart is with your liking.
FRIAR: And my help.
    Here comes the Prince and Claudio.

(Enter Prince [DON PEDRO] *and* CLAUDIO *and two or
three other.)*

DON PEDRO: Good morrow to this fair assembly.
LEONATO: Good morrow, Prince; good morrow,
    Claudio.   35
    We here attend you. Are you yet determined
    Today to marry with my brother's daughter?
CLAUDIO: I'll hold my mind, were she an Ethiope.
LEONATO: Call her forth, brother. Here's the friar
    ready. [*Exit* ANTONIO.]   40
DON PEDRO: Good morrow, Benedick. Why, what's
    the matter
    That you have such a February face,
    So full of frost, of storm, and cloudiness?
CLAUDIO: I think he thinks upon the savage bull.°
    Tush, fear not, man! We'll tip thy horns with gold,°   45
    And all Europa° shall rejoice at thee,
    As once Europa did at lusty Jove
    When he would play the noble beast in love.
BENEDICK: Bull Jove, sir, had an amiable low,
    And some such strange bull leaped your father's
    cow   50
    And got a calf in that same noble feat
    Much like to you, for you have just his bleat.

(Enter [LEONATO's] *brother* [ANTONIO], HERO, BEAT-
RICE, MARGARET, URSULA, [*the ladies wearing masks*].)

CLAUDIO: For this I owe you.° Here comes other
    reck'nings.
    Which is the lady I must seize upon?
ANTONIO: This same is she, and I do give you her.   55
CLAUDIO: Why then, she's mine. Sweet, let me see
    your face.
LEONATO: No, that you shall not till you take her
    hand
    Before this friar and swear to marry her.
CLAUDIO: Give me your hand; before this holy friar
    I am your husband if you like of me.   60
HERO: And when I lived I was your other wife;
    [*unmasking*]
    And when you loved you were my other husband.
CLAUDIO: Another Hero!
HERO: Nothing certainer.
    One Hero died defiled; but I do live,
    And surely as I live, I am a maid.   65
DON PEDRO: The former Hero! Hero that is dead!
LEONATO: She died, my lord, but whiles° her slander
    lived.

---

savage bull, (refers to 1.1.256–57). *tip thy horns with
gold*, i.e., make your cuckolding something to be proud of.
Europa, Europe (though in the next line the word designates
the girl that Jupiter wooed in the guise of a bull). *I owe you*,
i.e., I will pay you back (for calling me a calf and a bastard).
but whiles, only while.

Hymen, god of marriage. *speeds*, succeeds. *question*,
investigation. *sorts*, turn out. *confirmed*, steady.

FRIAR: All this amazement can I qualify,°
When, after that the holy rites are ended,
70 I'll tell you largely° of fair Hero's death.
Meantime let wonder seem familiar,
And to the chapel let us presently.
BENEDICK: Soft and fair, friar. Which is Beatrice?
BEATRICE: [*Unmasking*] I answer to that name. What
is your will?
BENEDICK: Do not you love me?
75 BEATRICE: Why, no; no more than reason.
BENEDICK: Why, then your uncle, and the Prince,
and Claudio
Have been deceived—they swore you did.
BEATRICE: Do not you love me?
BENEDICK: Troth, no; no more than reason.
BEATRICE: Why, then my cousin, Margaret, and
Ursula
80 Are much deceived; for they did swear you did.
BENEDICK: They swore that you were almost sick for
me.
BEATRICE: They swore that you were well-nigh dead
for me.
BENEDICK: 'Tis no such matter. Then you do not love
me?
BEATRICE: No, truly, but in friendly recompense.
LEONATO: Come, cousin, I am sure you love the
85 gentleman.
CLAUDIO: And I'll be sworn upon't that he loves her;
For here's a paper written in his hand,
A halting° sonnet of his own pure brain,
Fashioned to Beatrice.
HERO: And here's another,
90 Writ in my cousin's hand, stol'n from her pocket,
Containing her affection unto Benedick.
BENEDICK: A miracle! Here's our own hands against
our hearts. Come, I will have thee; but, by this
light, I take thee for pity.
95 BEATRICE: I would not deny you; but, by this good day,
I yield upon great persuasion, and partly to save
your life, for I was told you were in a consumption.

---

qualify, abate. *largely,* in detail. *halting,* limping.

BENEDICK:° Peace! I will stop your mouth. [*Kisses her.*]
DON PEDRO: How dost thou, Benedick, the married   100
man?
BENEDICK: I'll tell thee what, Prince: a college of wit-
crackers cannot flout me out of my humor. Dost
thou think I care for a satire or an epigram? No. If
a man will be beaten with brains, 'a shall wear   105
nothing handsome about him. In brief, since I do
purpose to marry, I will think nothing to any purpose that the world can say against it; and therefore never flout at me for what I have said against
it; for man is a giddy thing, and this is my conclu-   110
sion. For thy part, Claudio, I did think to have
beaten thee; but in that thou art like to be my
kinsman, live unbruised, and love my cousin.
CLAUDIO: I had well hoped thou wouldst have denied
Beatrice, that I might have cudgeled thee out of   115
thy single life, to make thee a double-dealer,°
which out of question thou wilt be if my cousin do
not look exceeding narrowly to thee.
BENEDICK: Come, come, we are friends. Let's have a
dance ere we are married, that we may lighten   120
our own hearts and our wives' heels.
LEONATO: We'll have dancing afterward.
BENEDICK: First, of my word; therefore play, music.
Prince, thou art sad; get thee a wife, get thee a
wife! There is no staff more reverend than one   125
tipped with horn.°

(*Enter* MESSENGER.)

MESSENGER: My lord, your brother John is ta'en in
flight,
And brought with armèd men back to Messina.
BENEDICK: Think not on him till tomorrow. I'll devise
thee brave punishments for him. Strike up, pipers!   130

(*Dance.* [*Exeunt.*])

FINIS.

Benedick, (both Quarto and Folio assign this line to Leonato; possibly the original reading is correct, and Leonato
forces Benedick to kiss Beatrice). **double-dealer,** (1) married
man (2) unfaithful husband. **with horn,** (final reference to
the horns of a cuckold).

Figure 1. Beatrice (Kathleen Widdoes, *right*), turns away from Benedick (Sam Waterston) after their first encounter. Don Pedro (Douglass Watson, *far left*), Leonato (Mark Hammer, *behind Benedick*), Hero (April Shawhan), and Margaret (Jeanne Hepple) look on. The multi-level set designed by Ming Cho Lee for the New York Shakespeare Festival's production of *Much Ado About Nothing*, directed by A. J. Antoon, 1972, echoes the structure of the Elizabethan stage while simultaneously suggesting an elaborate gazebo. (Photograph: George E. Joseph.)

Figure 2. Benedick (Sam Waterston, *far right*) hides behind a canoe as he listens to Claudio (Glenn Walken, *left*), Leonato (Mark Hammer, *center*), and Don Pedro (Douglass Watson, *right*) talking about Beatrice's love for Benedick in the New York Shakespeare Festival production. (Photograph: George E. Joseph.)

286 / MUCH ADO ABOUT NOTHING

Figure 3. Beatrice (Kathleen Widdoes) tactfully rejects the half-joking, half-serious proposal of Don Pedro (Douglass Watson) in the New York Shakespeare Festival production. (Photograph: George E. Joseph.)

Figure 4. "But for which of my good parts did you first suffer love for me?" Beatrice (Kathleen Widdoes) asks Benedick (Sam Waterston) in the New York Shakespeare Festival production. The verbal contradiction of "suffer love" is echoed in the characters' body language, as they sit closely together, hands lightly touching, but not looking at each other. (Photograph: George E. Joseph.)

Staging of *Much Ado About Nothing*

REVIEW OF THE A. J. ANTOON PRODUCTION
AT THE JOSEPH PAPP PUBLIC THEATER,
1972, BY MEL GUSSOW

A. J. Antoon, the director, has said that theater for him is an invitation to the audience to come into his kitchen and eat. By that measure, Antoon's "Much Ado About Nothing," which opened Wednesday night at the Delacorte Theater in Central Park, is a feast.

Antoon has transposed Shakespeare's Messina to a small town in Middle America. This is a pre–World War I America—marked by chauvinism, self-confidence and suddenly requited love. The gentlemen wear spats and carry pocket flasks. The ladies sneak a shared cigarette, and clear the smoke away before the father of the house enters. Almost everyone is inhibited by social conventions—yet everyone is having a glorious time. As sparklers flare, the couples dance Donald Saddler dances by the light of Japanese lanterns—and the Central Park moon could be part of the set.

Does this sound more like "No, No, Nanette" than like "Much Ado About Nothing"? For Antoon, the nostalgia is intentional. Happily, Middle America is not a forced concept for "Much Ado," but a comfortable setting—a place in which to play the comedy, to give it more relevance to its audience. This, like "Two Gentlemen of Verona," is Shakespeare for the contemporary masses.

What makes it such an entertaining evening is not just Antoon's imaginative direction, but, of course, the play's intelligence and urbanity. In "Much Ado" Shakespeare raises persiflage and badinage to a high art.

The cast, drawn mostly from Joseph Papp's deep-welled reserve of actors who have worked with him before, is splendid—particularly Sam Waterston as Benedick.

He is a boyish—but not immature—Benedick. He is sharptongued and headstrong, never losing sight of the character's propulsively romantic nature. It is a long step from the misogyny of "What, my dear Lady Disdain! are you yet living?" to the love-sickness of "When I said I would die a bachelor, I did not think I would live till I married," but Waterston leaps it with enormous grace.

Kathleen Widdoes is a lovely foiler as Beatrice. She is a paragon for Woman's Lib—strong and acidulous but never dropping her feminity. She is not a shrew, but as Beatrice should be, a thoroughly merry woman.

Even as the two parry insults, there is never any doubt about the magnetism of the mutual attraction.

Also outstanding is Douglass Watson as Don Pedro—breezily assured and always orchestrating his followers. As Hero and Claudio, outwardly but not actually the focus of the play, April Shawhan and Glenn Walken manage to portray innocence without seeming foolish.

Before the play begins, a blue-jacketed brass band marches on stage, interspersing foot-tapping Peter Link tunes with Scott Joplin rags. Later, the band underscores the action—there are very few actual songs in this show. Love scenes, for example, are played against a background of sentimental ballads.

Insouciantly, the director shifts some of the scenes from the original settings. Waterston soliloquizes while paddling a canoe, then upturns the vessel and hides behind it as his friends discuss Beatrice's supposed love for him. He is hilarious as he flashes looks of unconcealed pleasure.

Most of the switches in time and place work, but occasionally Antoon's theatrical exuberance carries him into small errors and excesses. The play begins awkwardly—and for no reason—with a portrait photographer, instead of a messenger, bringing news of Don Pedro's return.

The bastard Don John is turned into a sneering, almost Hitlerian villain and his followers are dressed like Chicago gangsters. Dogberry and his provincial constabulary are Keystone Kops, and despite Barnard Hughes's amusing performance as Dogberry, the scenes are too farcical and too long.

But these are minor demurrers in an otherwise disarming evening. In addition to the major beneficences, this "Much Ado" is a good excuse for Theoni V. Aldredge to broaden her canvas of costumes, for Ming Cho Lee to create a set that is a bright collage of early century Americana, and for Henry (Bootsie) Normand's band to play beer-and-pretzel music loud enough to drown out the rival Schaeffer Music Festival in Central Park. Suitably, the show ends not with Shakespeare's "Strike up, pipers!" but with Antoon's "Strike up the band!"

COMMENTARY ON THE COLLABORATION OF JOSEPH PAPP AND A. J. ANTOON, 1974, BY STUART W. LITTLE

[. . .] Papp was always in on the beginning of each new production. The first conferences were with the director, and most of the artistic choices came from those initial meetings, which laid the groundwork for subsequent conferences with the set designer, the casting department, the costume designer. The final decision on casting was a prerogative Papp reserved for himself, and in some cases the original choices were entirely his: Kathleen Widdoes as Beatrice, Douglass Watson as Don Pedro, Barnard Hughes as Dogberry, Sam Waterston as Benedick. Curiously, on concept, Papp and Antoon had disagreed, and more than any one thing it was from this very disputed concept that the success of the production was to stem. Papp had imagined a middle-aged Benedick and Beatrice and a setting in Victorian England. Antoon felt that was all wrong. When he reread the play with this production in mind, the first visual image that came into his head was—Gibson Girls! Shirtwaist blouses and flowing skirts. Garden parties and broad-brimmed leghorns with streamer ribbons lifted by the breeze. Wicker picnic hampers and peppermint jackets. When Papp himself had directed a production of *Much Ado About Nothing* in 1961, he had relocated the play in time and place, setting it in a Spanish town with castanets and flashing flamenco dancing. With Nan Martin and J. D. Cannon as the lovers, the production was one of Papp's most stylish successes. But this time, as Antoon later recalled, "Joe saw it as very English, very stiff and Victorian. I felt that was all wrong. He couldn't see my Gibson Girls." Once the main artistic questions were resolved and rehearsals were under way, Papp allowed a director great latitude and scrupulously refrained from interfering. Normally, except for a few cursory looks, he would not come in again until toward the end.

Now Papp walked out of the Anspacher, leaving the stage to Antoon, and Antoon began to address his cast. "I have a concept. I don't know how it will work." In him there was this attractive blend of assurance and apology that made his work with older and more experienced actors so successful. "We are going to set the play in America in the period just before the First World War. It is the only era that can capture all the feelings of the play. It was an age of innocence and simplicity. What would happen to a country if the war was over? If there was no more war? If there was just peace? Going back, it was best to see this life in albums, so we have studied a lot of photo albums of the period."

Antoon had been studying the family albums of Sam Waterston, the actor who would play Benedick, whose own New England church-school background suggested the milieu of this era. Antoon also came from Massachusetts but was out of an Armenian shopkeeping family. "There must be an absolutely nostalgic feeling," Antoon continued. "So this play is called *Much Ado About Nothing, or the Summer of 1905*. It is not camp in any sense. There is no blood in this play, no piece of violence. The feelings are those of innocent love, feelings that love will be forever. Just to give you the style of the play. As Joe said, the important things in the play are the relationships. Everything comes from that. [. . .]

From Stuart W. Little, *Enter Joseph Papp* (New York: Coward, McGann & Geoghegan, Inc., 1974).

THE TRAGEDY OF OTHELLO
The Moor of Venice

BY WILLIAM SHAKESPEARE / EDITED BY ALVIN KERNAN

CHARACTERS

OTHELLO, *the Moor*
BRABANTIO, *father to Desdemona*
CASSIO, *an honorable lieutenant*
IAGO, *a villain*
RODERIGO, *a gulled gentleman*
DUKE OF VENICE
SENATORS
MONTANO, *Governor of Cyprus*
GENTLEMAN OF CYPRUS
LODOVICO *and* GRATIANO, *two noble Venetians*

SAILORS
CLOWN
DESDEMONA, *wife to Othello*
EMILIA, *wife to Iago*
BIANCA, *a courtesan*
MESSENGER, HERALD, OFFICERS, GENTLEMEN, MUSICIANS, ATTENDANTS

SCENE

Venice and Cyprus

ACT 1 / SCENE 1

[*Venice. A street*]
(*Enter* RODERIGO *and* IAGO.)

RODERIGO: Tush! Never tell me? I take it much
    unkindly
    That thou, Iago, who hast had my purse
    As if the strings were thine, shouldst know of this.
IAGO: 'Sblood,° but you'll not hear me! If ever I did
    dream
    Of such a matter, abhor me.
5 RODERIGO: Thou told'st me
    Thou didst hold him in thy hate.
IAGO: Despise me
    If I do not. Three great ones of the city,
    In personal suit to make me his lieutenant,
    Off-capped° to him; and, by the faith of man,
10   I know my price; I am worth no worse a place.
    But he, as loving his own pride and purposes,
    Evades them with a bombast circumstance,°
    Horribly stuffed with epithets of war;
    Nonsuits° my mediators. For, "Certes," says he,
15   "I have already chose my officer." And what was he?
    Forsooth, a great arithmetician,°
    One Michael Cassio, a Florentine,

    (A fellow almost damned in a fair wife)°
    That never set a squadron in the field,
    Nor the division of a battle knows   20
    More than a spinster; unless the bookish theoric,
    Wherein the tonguèd° consuls can propose
    As masterly as he. Mere prattle without practice
    Is all his soldiership. But he, sir, had th' election;
    And I, of whom his eyes had seen the proof   25
    At Rhodes, at Cyprus, and on other grounds
    Christian and heathen, must be belee'd and
    calmed
    By debitor and creditor. This counter-caster,°
    He, in good time, must his lieutenant be,
    And I—God bless the mark!—his Moorship's
    ancient.°   30
RODERIGO: By heaven, I rather would have been his
    hangman.
IAGO: Why, there's no remedy. 'Tis the curse of
    service:
    Preferment goes by letter and affection,°

'Sblood, by God's blood. *Off-capped,* doffed their
caps—as a mark of respect. **bombast circumstance,** stuffed,
roundabout speech. *Nonsuits,* rejects. **arithmetician,** theorist (rather than practitioner).

A . . . wife, (a much-disputed passage, which is probably
best taken as a general sneer at Cassio as a dandy and a ladies'
man. But in the story from which Shakespeare took his plot
the counterpart of Cassio is married, and it may be that at the
beginning of the play Shakespeare had decided to keep him
married but later changed his mind). *tonguèd,* eloquent.
counter-caster, i.e., a bookkeeper who *casts* (reckons up) figures
on a *counter* (abacus). *ancient,* standard-bearer; an underofficer. *letter and affection,* recommendations (from men of
power) and personal preference.

And not by old gradation,° where each second
35 Stood heir to th' first. Now, sir, be judge yourself,
Whether I in any just term am affined°
To love the Moor.
RODERIGO: I would not follow him then.
IAGO: O, sir, content you.
I follow him to serve my turn upon him.
40 We cannot all be masters, nor all masters
Cannot be truly followed. You shall mark
Many a duteous and knee-crooking° knave
That, doting on his own obsequious bondage,
Wears out his time, much like his master's ass,
For naught but provender; and when he's old,
45   cashiered.
Whip me such honest knaves! Others there are
Who, trimmed in forms and visages of duty,
Keep yet their hearts attending on themselves,
And, throwing but shows of service on their lords,
Do well thrive by them, and when they have lined
50   their coats,
Do themselves homage. These fellows have some
      soul;
And such a one do I profess myself. For, sir,
It is as sure as you are Roderigo,
Were I the Moor, I would not be Iago.
55 In following him, I follow but myself.
Heaven is my judge, not I for love and duty,
But seeming so, for my peculiar° end;
For when my outward action doth demonstrate
The native° act and figure of my heart
60 In compliment extern,° 'tis not long after
But I will wear my heart upon my sleeve
For daws to peck at; I am not what I am.
RODERIGO: What a fortune does the thick-lips owe°
If he can carry't thus!
IAGO: Call up her father,
65 Rouse him. Make after him, poison his delight,
Proclaim him in the streets, incense her kinsmen,
And though he in a fertile climate dwell,
Plague him with flies; though that his joy be joy,
Yet throw such changes of vexation on't
70 As it may lose some color.
RODERIGO: Here is her father's house. I'll call aloud.
IAGO: Do, with like timorous° accent and dire yell
As when, by night and negligence, the fire
Is spied in populous cities.
RODERIGO: What, ho, Brabantio! Signior Brabantio,
75   ho!
IAGO: Awake! What, ho, Brabantio! Thieves! Thieves!
Look to your house, your daughter, and your bags!
Thieves! Thieves!

(BRABANTIO *above*° [*at a window*].)

BRABANTIO: What is the reason of this terrible
      summons?
What is the matter there?   80
RODERIGO: Signior, is all your family within?
IAGO: Are your doors locked?
BRABANTIO: Why, wherefore ask you this?
IAGO: Zounds, sir, y'are robbed! For shame. Put on
      your gown!
Your heart is burst, you have lost half your soul.
Even now, now, very now, an old black ram   85
Is tupping your white ewe. Arise, arise!
Awake the snorting citizens with the bell,
Or else the devil will make a grandsire of you.
Arise, I say!
BRABANTIO: What, have you lost your wits?
RODERIGO: Most reverend signior, do you know my
      voice?   90
BRABANTIO: Not I. What are you?
RODERIGO: My name is Roderigo.
BRABANTIO: The worser welcome!
I have charged thee not to haunt about my doors.
In honest plainness thou hast heard me say
My daughter is not for thee; and now, in madness,   95
Being full of supper and distempr'ing draughts,°
Upon malicious knavery dost thou come
To start° my quiet.
RODERIGO: Sir, sir, sir——
BRABANTIO: But thou must needs be sure
My spirits and my place° have in their power   100
To make this bitter to thee.
RODERIGO: Patience, good sir.
BRABANTIO: What tell'st thou me of robbing? This is
      Venice;
My house is not a grange.°
RODERIGO: Most grave Brabantio,
In simple and pure soul I come to you.
IAGO: Zounds, sir, you are one of those that will not 105
serve God if the devil bid you. Because we come
to do you service and you think we are ruffians,
you'll have your daughter covered with a Bar-
bary° horse, you'll have your nephews° neigh to
you, you'll have coursers for cousins,° and gen-   110
nets for germans.°
BRABANTIO: What profane wretch art thou?
IAGO: I am one, sir, that comes to tell you your daughter and the Moor are making the beast with two
backs.   115

---

old gradation, seniority. **affined,** bound. **knee-crooking,**
bowing. **peculiar,** personal. **native,** natural, innate. **complement extern,** outward appearances. **owe,** own. **timorous,**
frightening.

above, i.e., on the small upper stage above and to the
rear of the main platform stage, which resembled the projecting upper story of an Elizabethan house. **distemp'ring
draughts,** unsettling drinks. **start,** disrupt. **place,** rank, i.e.,
of senator. **grange,** isolated house. **Barbary,** Arabian, i.e.,
Moorish. **nephews,** i.e., grandsons. **cousins,** relations. **gen-
nets for germans,** Spanish horses for blood relatives.

BRABANTIO: Thou art a villain.

IAGO: You are—a senator.

BRABANTIO: This thou shalt answer. I know thee,
    Roderigo.

RODERIGO: Sir, I will answer anything. But I beseech
    you,
    If't be your pleasure and most wise consent,
120   As partly I find it is, that your fair daughter,
    At this odd-even° and dull watch o' th' night,
    Transported, with no worse nor better guard
    But with a knave of common hire, a gondolier,
    To the gross clasps of a lascivious Moor—
125   If this be known to you, and your allowance,
    We then have done you bold and saucy wrongs;
    But if you know not this, my manners tell me
    We have your wrong rebuke. Do not believe
    That, from the sense of all civility°
130   I thus would play and trifle with your reverence.
    Your daughter, if you have not given her leave,
    I say again, hath made a gross revolt,
    Tying her duty, beauty, wit, and fortunes
    In an extravagant° and wheeling stranger
135   Of here and everywhere. Straight satisfy yourself.
    If she be in her chamber, or your house,
    Let loose on me the justice of the state
    For thus deluding you.

BRABANTIO: Strike on the tinder, ho!
    Give me a taper! Call up all my people!
140   This accident° is not unlike my dream.
    Belief of it oppresses me already.
    Light, I say! Light! *(Exit [above].)*

IAGO: Farewell, for I must leave you.
    It seems not meet, nor wholesome to my place,
    To be produced—as, if I stay, I shall—
145   Against the Moor. For I do know the State,
    However this may gall him with some check,°
    Cannot with safety cast° him; for he's embarked
    With such loud reason to the Cyprus wars,
    Which even now stands in act,° that for their
    souls
150   Another of his fathom° they have none
    To lead their business; in which regard,
    Though I do hate him as I do hell-pains,
    Yet, for necessity of present life,
    I must show out a flag and sign of love,
    Which is indeed but sign. That you shall surely find
155   him,
    Lead to the Sagittary° the raisèd search;
    And there will I be with him. So farewell. *(Exit.)*

---

    odd-even, between night and morning. **sense of all civility,** feeling of what is proper. **extravagant,** vagrant, wandering (Othello is not Venetian and thus may be considered a wandering soldier of fortune). **accident,** happening. **check,** restraint. **cast,** dismiss. **stands in act,** takes place. **fathom,** ability. **Sagittary,** (probably the name of an inn).

(Enter BRABANTIO *[in his nightgown], with* SERVANTS *and torches.)*

BRABANTIO: It is too true an evil. Gone she is;
    And what's to come of my despisèd time
    Is naught but bitterness. Now, Roderigo,   160
    Where didst thou see her?—O unhappy girl!—
    With the Moor, say'st thou?—Who would be a
    father?—
    How didst thou know 'twas she?—O, she deceives
    me
    Past thought!—What said she to you?—Get moe°
    tapers!
    Raise all my kindred!—Are they married, think
    you?   165

RODERIGO: Truly I think they are.

BRABANTIO: O heaven! How got she out? O treason
    of the blood!
    Fathers, from hence trust not your daughters'
    minds
    By what you see them act.° Is there not charms
    By which the property° of youth and maidhood   170
    May be abused? Have you not read, Roderigo,
    Of some such thing?

RODERIGO: Yes, sir, I have indeed.

BRABANTIO: Call up my brother.—O, would you had
    had her!—
    Some one way, some another.—Do you know
    Where we may apprehend her and the Moor?   175

RODERIGO: I think I can discover him, if you please
    To get good guard and go along with me.

BRABANTIO: Pray you lead on. At every house I'll
    call;
    I may command at most.—Get weapons, ho!
    And raise some special officers of might.—   180
    On, good Roderigo; I will deserve your pains.°

(Exeunt.)

ACT 1 / SCENE 2

[A street]
(Enter OTHELLO, IAGO, ATTENDANTS *with torches.)*

IAGO: Though in the trade of war I have slain men,
    Yet do I hold it very stuff° o' th' conscience
    To do no contrived murder. I lack iniquity
    Sometime to do me service. Nine or ten times
    I had thought t' have yerked° him here, under the
    ribs.   5

OTHELLO: 'Tis better as it is.

IAGO: Nay, but he prated,
    And spoke such scurvy and provoking terms

---

    moe, more. **act,** do. **property,** true nature. **deserve your pains,** be worthy of (and reward) your efforts. **stuff,** essence. **yerked,** stabbed.

Against your honor, that with the little godliness I
  have
I did full hard forbear him. But I pray you, sir,
10 Are you fast married? Be assured of this,
That the magnifico° is much beloved,
And hath in his effect a voice potential
As double as the Duke's.° He will divorce you,
Or put upon you what restraint or grievance
15 The law, with all his might to enforce it on,
Will give him cable.°
OTHELLO: Let him do his spite.
My services which I have done the Signiory°
Shall out-tongue his complaints. 'Tis yet to
  know°—
Which when I know that boasting is an honor
20 I shall promulgate—I fetch my life and being
From men of royal siege;° and my demerits°
May speak unbonneted to as proud a fortune
As this that I have reached.° For know, Iago,
But that I love the gentle Desdemona,
25 I would not my unhousèd° free condition
Put into circumscription and confine
For the sea's worth. But look, what lights come yond?

(Enter CASSIO, *with* [OFFICERS *and*] *torches.)*

IAGO: Those are the raisèd father and his friends.
  You were best go in.
OTHELLO: Not I. I must be found.
30 My parts, my title, and my perfect soul°
Shall manifest me rightly. Is it they?
IAGO: By Janus, I think no.
OTHELLO: The servants of the Duke? And my
  lieutenant?
The goodness of the night upon you, friends.
What is the news?
35 CASSIO: The Duke does greet you, general;
And he requires your haste-posthaste appearance
Even on the instant.
OTHELLO: What is the matter, think you?
CASSIO: Something from Cyprus, as I may divine.
It is a business of some heat. The galleys
40 Have sent a dozen sequent° messengers
This very night at one another's heels,
And many of the consuls, raised and met,
Are at the Duke's already. You have been hotly
  called for.
When, being not at your lodging to be found,
45 The Senate hath sent about three several° quests

To search you out.
OTHELLO: 'Tis well I am found by you.
I will but spend a word here in the house,
And go with you. [*Exit.*]
CASSIO: Ancient, what makes he here?
IAGO: Faith, he tonight hath boarded a land carack.°
If it prove lawful prize, he's made forever.°   50
CASSIO: I do not understand.
IAGO: He's married.
CASSIO: To who?

[*Enter* OTHELLO.]

IAGO: Marry,° to—Come, captain, will you go?
OTHELLO: Have with you.
CASSIO: Here comes another troop to seek for you.

(Enter BRABANTIO, RODERIGO, *with* OFFICERS *and
torches.)*

IAGO: It is Brabantio. General, be advised.
He comes to bad intent.
OTHELLO: Holla! Stand there!   55
RODERIGO: Signior, it is the Moor.
BRABANTIO: Down with him, thief!

[*They draw swords.*]

IAGO: You, Roderigo? Come, sir I am for you.
OTHELLO: Keep up your bright swords, for the dew
  will rust them.
Good signior, you shall more command with years
Than with your weapons.   60
BRABANTIO: O thou foul thief, where has thou
  stowed my daughter?
Damned as thou art, thou hast enchanted her!
For I'll refer me to all things of sense,°
If she in chains of magic were not bound,
Whether a maid so tender, fair, and happy,   65
So opposite to marriage that she shunned
The wealthy curlèd darlings of our nation,
Would ever have, t' incur a general mock,°
Run from her guardage to the sooty bosom
Of such a thing as thou—to fear, not to delight. 70
Judge me the world if 'tis not gross in sense°
That thou hast practiced° on her with foul charms,
Abused her delicate youth with drugs or minerals
That weaken motion.° I'll have't disputed on;
'Tis probable, and palpable to thinking.   75
I therefore apprehend and do attach° thee
For an abuser of the world, a practicer
Of arts inhibited and out of warrant.°

---

magnifico, nobleman. *hath . . . Duke's,* i.e., can be as
effective as the Duke. *cable,* range, scope. *Signiory,* the
rulers of Venice. *yet to know,* unknown as yet. *siege,* rank.
demerits, deserts. *May . . . reached,* i.e., are the equal of the
family I have married into. *unhousèd,* unconfined. *perfect
soul,* clear, unflawed conscience. *sequent,* successive. *several,* separate.

---

carack, treasure ship. *Marry,* By Mary (an interjection).
refer . . . sense, i.e., base (my argument) on all ordinary understanding of nature. *general mock,* public shame. *gross in
sense,* obvious. *practiced,* used tricks. *motion,* thought, i.e.,
reason. *attach,* arrest. *inhibited . . . warrant,* prohibited
and illegal (black magic).

Lay hold upon him. If he do resist,
Subdue him at his peril.

80 OTHELLO: Hold your hands,
Both you of my inclining and the rest.
Were it my cue to fight, I should have known it
Without a prompter. Where will you that I go
To answer this your charge?

BRABANTIO: To prison, till fit time
85 Of law and course of direct session
Call thee to answer.

OTHELLO: What if I do obey?
How may the Duke be therewith satisfied,
Whose messengers are here about my side
Upon some present° business of the state
To bring me to him?

90 OFFICER: 'Tis true, most worthy signior.
The Duke's in council, and your noble self
I am sure is sent for.

BRABANTIO: How? The Duke in council?
In this time of the night? Bring him away.
Mine's not an idle cause. The Duke himself,
95 Or any of my brothers° of the state,
Cannot but feel this wrong as 'twere their own;
For if such actions may have passage free,
Bondslaves and pagans shall our statesmen be.

(Exeunt.)

ACT 1 / SCENE 3

[*A council chamber*]
(Enter DUKE, SENATORS, *and* OFFICERS [*set at a table,
with lights and* ATTENDANTS].*)*

DUKE: There's no composition° in this news
That gives them credit.°

FIRST SENATOR: Indeed, they are disproportioned.
My letters say a hundred and seven galleys.

DUKE: And mine a hundred forty.

SECOND SENATOR: And mine two hundred.
5 But though they jump° not on a just accompt°—
As in these cases where the aim° reports
'Tis oft with difference—yet do they all confirm
A Turkish fleet, and bearing up to Cyprus.

DUKE: Nay, it is possible enough to judgment.°
10 I do not so secure me in the error,
But the main article I do approve
In fearful sense.°

---

present, immediate. *brothers*, i.e., the other senators.
composition, agreement. *gives them credit*, makes them believable. *jump*, agree. *just accompt*, exact counting. *aim*,
approximation. *to judgment*, when carefully considered. *I
do . . . sense*, i.e., just because the numbers disagree in the
reports, I do not doubt that the principal information (that
the Turkish fleet is out) is fearfully true.

SAILOR: *(Within)* What, ho! What, ho! What, ho!

(Enter SAILOR.*)*

OFFICER: A messenger from the galleys.

DUKE: Now? What's the business?

SAILOR: The Turkish preparation makes for Rhodes.   15
So was I bid report here to the State
By Signior Angelo.

DUKE: How say you by this change?

FIRST SENATOR: This cannot be
By no assay of reason. 'Tis a pageant°
To keep us in false gaze.° When we consider   20
Th' importancy of Cyprus to the Turk,
And let ourselves again but understand
That, as it more concerns the Turk than Rhodes,
So may he with more facile question° bear it,
For that it stands not in such warlike brace,°   25
But altogether lacks th' abilities
That Rhodes is dressed in. If we make thought of
this,
We must not think the Turk is so unskillful
To leave that latest which concerns him first,
Neglecting an attempt of ease and gain   30
To wake and wage a danger profitless.

DUKE: Nay, in all confidence he's not for Rhodes.

OFFICER: Here is more news.

(Enter a MESSENGER.*)*

MESSENGER: The Ottomites, reverend and gracious,
Steering with due course toward the isle of Rhodes,   35
Have there injointed them with an after° fleet.

FIRST SENATOR: Ay, so I thought. How many, as you
guess?

MESSENGER: Of thirty sail; and now they do restem
Their backward course, bearing with frank
appearance
Their purposes toward Cyprus. Signior Montano,   40
Your trusty and most valiant servitor,
With his free duty° recommends° you thus,
And prays you to believe him.

DUKE: 'Tis certain then for Cyprus.
Marcus Luccicos, is not he in town?   45

FIRST SENATOR: He's now in Florence.

DUKE: Write from us to him; post-posthaste dispatch.

FIRST SENATOR: Here comes Brabantio and the
valiant Moor.

(Enter BRABANTIO, OTHELLO, CASSIO, IAGO, RODE-
RIGO, *and* OFFICERS.*)*

DUKE: Valiant Othello, we must straight° employ you
Against the general° enemy Ottoman.   50

---

pageant, show, pretense. *in false gaze*, looking the wrong
way. *facile question*, easy struggle. *warlike brace*, "military
posture." *after*, following. *free duty*, unlimited respect. *recommends*, informs. *straight*, at once. *general*, universal.

[*To* BRABANTIO] I did not see you. Welcome, gentle
  signior.
We lacked your counsel and your help tonight.
BRABANTIO: So did I yours. Good your grace, pardon
  me.
Neither my place, nor aught I heard of business,
Hath raised me from my bed; nor doth the general
55 care
Take hold on me; for my particular grief
Is of so floodgate and o'erbearing nature
That it englutts and swallows other sorrows,
And it is still itself.
DUKE: Why, what's the matter?
BRABANTIO: My daughter! O, my daughter!
SENATORS: Dead?
60 BRABANTIO: Ay, to me.
She is abused, stol'n from me, and corrupted
By spells and medicines bought of mountebanks;
For nature so prepost'rously to err,
Being not deficient, blind, or lame of sense,
65 Sans° witchcraft could not.
DUKE: Whoe'er he be that in this foul proceeding
Hath thus beguiled your daughter of herself,
And you of her, the bloody book of law
You shall yourself read in the bitter letter
70 After your own sense; yea, though our proper° son
Stood in your action.°
BRABANTIO: Humbly I thank your Grace.
Here is the man—this Moor, whom now, it seems,
Your special mandate for the state affairs
Hath hither brought.
ALL: We are very sorry for't.
75 DUKE: [*To* OTHELLO] What in your own part can you
  say to this?
BRABANTIO: Nothing, but this is so.
OTHELLO: Most potent, grave, and reverend signiors,
My very noble, and approved° good masters,
That I have ta'en away this old man's daughter,
80 It is most true; true I have married her.
The very head and front° of my offending
Hath this extent, no more. Rude am I in my
  speech,
And little blessed with the soft phrase of peace,
For since these arms of mine had seven years'
  pith°
85 Till now some nine moons wasted,° they have used
Their dearest° action in the tented field;
And little of this great world can I speak
More than pertains to feats of broil and battle;
And therefore little shall I grace my cause

In speaking for myself. Yet, by your gracious
  patience,   90
I will a round° unvarnished tale deliver
Of my whole course of love—what drugs, what
  charms,
What conjuration, and what mighty magic;
For such proceeding am I charged withal,
I won his daughter—
BRABANTIO: A maiden never bold,   95
Of spirit so still and quiet that her motion
Blushed at herself;° and she, in spite of nature,
Of years, of country, credit, everything,
To fall in love with what she feared to look on!
It is a judgment maimed and most imperfect   100
That will confess perfection so could err
Against all rules of nature, and must be driven
To find out practices of cunning hell
Why this should be. I therefore vouch again
That with some mixtures pow'rful o'er the blood,   105
Or with some dram, conjured to this effect,
He wrought upon her.
DUKE: To vouch this is no proof,
Without more wider and more overt test
Than these thin habits° and poor likelihoods
Of modern° seeming do prefer against him.   110
FIRST SENATOR: But, Othello, speak.
Did you by indirect and forcèd courses
Subdue and poison this young maid's affections?
Or came it by request, and such fair question°
As soul to soul affordeth?
OTHELLO: I do beseech you,   115
Send for the lady to the Sagittary
And let her speak of me before her father.
If you do find me foul in her report,
The trust, the office, I do hold of you
Not only take away, but let your sentence   120
Even fall upon my life.
DUKE: Fetch Desdemona hither.
OTHELLO: Ancient, conduct them; you best know the
  place.

[*Exit* IAGO, *with two or three* ATTENDANTS.]

And till she come, as truly as to heaven
I do confess the vices of my blood,
So justly to your grave ears I'll present   125
How I did thrive in this fair lady's love,
And she in mine.
DUKE: Say it, Othello.
OTHELLO: Her father loved me; oft invited me;
Still° questioned me the story of my life
From year to year, the battle, sieges, fortune   130

Sans, without. **proper,** own. **Stood in your action,** were
the accused in your suit. **approved,** tested, proven by past
performance. **head and front,** extreme form (*front* = forehead). **pith,** strength. **wasted,** past. **dearest,** most important.

---

round, blunt. **her motion/Blushed at herself,** i.e., she was
so modest that she blushed at every thought (and move-
ment). **habits,** clothing. **modern,** trivial. **question,** discussion. **Still,** regularly.

That I have passed.
I ran it through, even from my boyish days
To th' very moment that he bade me tell it.
Wherein I spoke of most disastrous chances,
135 Of moving accidents by flood and field,
Of hairbreadth scapes i' th' imminent° deadly
    breach;
Of being taken by the insolent foe
And sold to slavery, of my redemption thence
And portance° in my travel's history,
140 Wherein of anters° vast and deserts idle,°
Rough quarries, rocks, and hills whose heads touch
    heaven,
It was my hint to speak. Such was my process.
And of the Cannibals that each other eat,
The Anthropophagi,° and men whose heads
145 Grew beneath their shoulders. These things to
    hear
Would Desdemona seriously incline;
But still the house affairs would draw her thence;
Which ever as she could with haste dispatch,
She'd come again, and with a greedy ear
150 Devour up my discourse. Which I observing,
Took once a pliant hour, and found good means
To draw from her a prayer of earnest heart
That I would all my pilgrimage dilate,°
Whereof by parcels she had something heard,
155 But not intentively.° I did consent,
And often did beguile her of her tears
When I did speak of some distressful stroke
That my youth suffered. My story being done,
She gave me for my pains a world of kisses.
She swore in faith, 'twas strange, 'twas passing°
160   strange;
'Twas pitiful, 'twas wondrous pitiful.
She wished she had not heard it; yet she wished
That heaven had made her such a man. She
    thanked me,
And bade me, if I had a friend that loved her,
165 I should but teach him how to tell my story,
And that would woo her. Upon this hint I spake.
She loved me for the dangers I had passed,
And I loved her that she did pity them.
This only is the witchcraft I have used.
170 Here comes the lady. Let her witness it.

(Enter DESDEMONA, IAGO, ATTENDANTS.*)*

DUKE: I think this tale would win my daughter too.
    Good Brabantio, take up this mangled matter at
    the best.°

Men do their broken weapons rather use
Than their bare hands.
BRABANTIO: I pray you hear her speak.
If she confess that she was half the wooer,   175
Destruction on my head if my bad blame
Light on the man. Come hither, gentle mistress.
Do you perceive in all this noble company
Where most you owe obedience?
DESDEMONA: My noble father,
I do perceive here a divided duty.   180
To you I am bound for life and education;
My life and education both do learn me
How to respect you. You are the lord of duty,
I am hitherto your daughter. But here's my
    husband,
And so much duty as my mother showed   185
To you, preferring you before her father,
So much I challenge° that I may profess
Due to the Moor my lord.
BRABANTIO: God be with you. I have done.
Please it your Grace, on to the state affairs.
I had rather to adopt a child than get° it.   190
Come hither, Moor.
I here do give thee that with all my heart
Which, but thou hast already, with all my heart
I would keep from thee. For your sake,° jewel,
I am glad at soul I have no other child,   195
For thy escape would teach me tyranny,
To hang clogs on them. I have done, my lord.
DUKE: Let me speak like yourself and lay a sentence°
Which, as a grise° or step, may help these lovers.
When remedies are past, the griefs are ended   200
By seeing the worst, which late on hopes
    depended.°
To mourn a mischief that is past and gone
Is the next° way to draw new mischief on.
What cannot be preserved when fortune takes,
Patience her injury a mock'ry makes.   205
The robbed that smiles, steals something from the
    thief;
He robs himself that spends a bootless° grief.
BRABANTIO: So let the Turk of Cyprus us beguile:
We lose it not so long as we can smile.
He bears the sentence well that nothing bears   210
But the free comfort which from thence he hears;
But he bears both the sentence and the sorrow
That to pay grief must of poor patience borrow.
These sentences, to sugar, or to gall,
Being strong on both sides, are equivocal.   215
But words are words. I never yet did hear

---

imminent, threatening. **portance,** manner of acting. **anters,** caves. **idle,** empty, sterile. **Anthropophagi,** man-eaters. **dilate,** relate in full. **intentively,** at length and in sequence. **passing,** surpassing. **Take . . . best,** i.e., make the best of this disaster.

challenge, claim as right. **get,** beget. **For your sake,** because of you. **lay a sentence,** provide a maxim. **grise,** step. **late on hopes depended,** was supported by hope (of a better outcome) until lately. **next,** closest, surest. **bootless,** valueless.

That the bruisèd heart was piercèd° through the
  ear.
I humbly beseech you, proceed to th' affairs of
  state.
220 DUKE: The Turk with a most mighty preparation
  makes for Cyprus. Othello, the fortitude° of the
  place is best known to you; and though we have
  there a substitute° of most allowed sufficiency,°
  yet opinion, a more sovereign mistress of effects,
225 throws a more safer voice on you.° You must
  therefore be content to slubber° the gloss of your
  new fortunes with this more stubborn and bois-
  terous° expedition.
OTHELLO: The tyrant Custom, most grave senators,
  Hath made the flinty and steel couch of war
230 My thrice-driven° bed of down. I do agnize°
  A natural and prompt alacrity
  I find in hardness and do undertake
  This present wars against the Ottomites.
  Most humbly, therefore, bending to your state,
235 I crave fit disposition for my wife,
  Due reference of place, and exhibition,°
  With such accommodation and besort
  As levels with° her breeding.
DUKE: Why, at her father's.
BRABANTIO: I will not have it so.
OTHELLO: Nor I.
DESDEMONA: Nor would I there reside,
240 To put my father in impatient thoughts
  By being in his eye. Most gracious Duke,
  To my unfolding° lend your prosperous° ear,
  And let me find a charter in your voice,
  T' assist my simpleness.
DUKE: What would you, Desdemona?
DESDEMONA: That I did love the Moor to live with
  him,
245 My downright violence, and storm of fortunes,
  May trumpet to the world. My heart's subdued
  Even to the very quality of my lord.°
  I saw Othello's visage in his mind,

And to his honors and his valiant parts   250
Did I my soul and fortunes consecrate.
So that, dear lords, if I be left behind,
A moth of peace, and he go to the war,
The rites° for why I love him are bereft me,
And I a heavy interim shall support   255
By his dear absence. Let me go with him.
OTHELLO: Let her have your voice.°
  Vouch with me, heaven, I therefore beg it not
  To please the palate of my appetite,
  Nor to comply with heat°—the young affects°   260
  In me defunct—and proper satisfaction;°
  But to be free and bounteous to her mind;
  And heaven defend° your good souls that you
    think
  I will your serious and great business scant
  When she is with me. No, when light-winged toys   265
  Of feathered Cupid seel° with wanton° dullness
  My speculative and officed instrument,°
  That my disports corrupt and taint my business,
  Let housewives make a skillet of my helm,
  And all indign° and base adversities   270
  Make head° against my estimation!°—
DUKE: Be it as you shall privately determine,
  Either for her stay or going. Th' affair cries haste,
  And speed must answer it.
FIRST SENATOR: You must away tonight.
OTHELLO: With all my heart.   275
DUKE: At nine i' th' morning here we'll meet again.
  Othello, leave some officer behind,
  And he shall our commission bring to you,
  And such things else of quality and respect
  As doth import you.
OTHELLO: So please your grace, my ancient;   280
  A man he is of honesty and trust.
  To his conveyance I assign my wife,
  With what else needful your good grace shall think
  To be sent after me.
DUKE: Let it be so.
  Good night to every one. [*To* BRABANTIO] And,
    noble signior,   285
  If virtue no delighted° beauty lack,
  Your son-in-law is far more fair than black.
FIRST SENATOR: Adieu, brave Moor. Use Desdemona
  well.
BRABANTIO: Look to her, Moor, if thou hast eyes to
  see:
  She has deceived her father, and may thee.   290

---

piercèd, (some editors emend to *pieced,* i.e., "healed."
But *pierced* makes good sense: Brabantio is saying in effect
that his heart cannot be further hurt [pierced] by the indignity of the useless, conventional advice the Duke offers him.
Pierced can also mean, however, "lanced" in the medical
sense, and would then mean "treated"). fortitude, fortification. substitute, viceroy. most allowed sufficiency, generally
acknowledged capability. opinion . . . you, i.e., the general
opinion, which finally controls affairs, is that you would be
the best man in this situation. slubber, besmear. stubborn
and boisterous, rough and violent. thrice-driven, i.e., softest.
agnize, know in myself. exhibition, grant of funds. levels
with, is suitable to. unfolding, explanation. prosperous, fa-
voring. charter, permission. My . . . lord, i.e., I have become one in nature and being with the man I married
(therefore, I too would go to the wars like a soldier).

---

rites, (may refer either to the marriage rites or to the
rites, formalities, of war). voice, consent. heat, lust. affects, passions. proper satisfaction, i.e., consummation of the
marriage. defend, forbid. seel, sew up. wanton, lascivious.
speculative . . . instrument, i.e., sight (and, by extension, the
mind). indign, unworthy. Make head, form an army, i.e.,
attack. estimation, reputation. delighted, delightful.

[*Exeunt* DUKE, SENATORS, OFFICERS, *etc.*]

OTHELLO: My life upon her faith! Honest Iago,
My Desdemona must I leave to thee.
I prithee let thy wife attend on her,
And bring them after in the best advantage.°
295   Come, Desdemona. I have but an hour
Of love, of worldly matter, and direction
To spend with thee. We must obey the time.

(*Exit* [MOOR *with* DESDEMONA].)

RODERIGO: Iago?
IAGO: What say'st thou, noble heart?
300 RODERIGO: What will I do, think'st thou?
IAGO: Why, go to bed and sleep.
RODERIGO: I will incontinently° drown myself.
IAGO: If thou dost, I shall never love thee after. Why,
thou silly gentleman?
305 RODERIGO: It is silliness to live when to live is torment;
and then have we a prescription to die when
death is our physician.
IAGO: O villainous! I have looked upon the world for
four times seven years, and since I could distin-
310 guish betwixt a benefit and an injury, I never
found man that knew how to love himself. Ere I
would say I would drown myself for the love of a
guinea hen, I would change my humanity with a
baboon.
315 RODERIGO: What should I do? I confess it is my shame
to be so fond, but it is not in my virtue° to amend
it.
IAGO: Virtue? A fig! 'Tis in ourselves that we are thus,
or thus. Our bodies are our gardens, to the which
320 our wills are gardeners; so that if we will plant
nettles or sow lettuce, set hyssop and weed up
thyme, supply it with one gender of herbs or dis-
tract° it with many—either to have it sterile with
idleness or manured with industry—why, the
325 power and corrigible° authority of this lies in our
wills. If the balance of our lives had not one scale
of reason to poise another of sensuality, the blood
and baseness of our natures would conduct us to
most prepost'rous conclusions.° But we have rea-
330 son to cool our raging motions, our carnal stings
or unbitted° lusts, whereof I take this that you call
love to be a sect or scion.°
RODERIGO: It cannot be.
IAGO: It is merely a lust of the blood and a permission
335 of the will. Come, be a man! Drown thyself?
Drown cats and blind puppies! I have professed
me thy friend, and I confess me knit to thy deserv-

ing with cables of perdurable toughness. I could
never better stead° thee than now. Put money in
thy purse. Follow thou the wars; defeat thy favor° 340
with an usurped° beard. I say, put money in thy
purse. It cannot be that Desdemona should continue her love to the Moor. Put money in thy
purse. Nor he his to her. It was a violent commencement in her and thou shalt see an answer- 345
able° sequestration°—put but money in thy
purse. These Moors are changeable in their
wills—fill thy purse with money. The food that to
him now is as luscious as locusts° shall be to him
shortly as bitter as coloquintida.° She must 350
change for youth; when she is sated with his body,
she will find the errors of her choice. Therefore,
put money in thy purse. If thou wilt needs damn
thyself, do it a more delicate way than drowning.
Make all the money thou canst. If sanctimony° 355
and a frail vow betwixt an erring° barbarian and
supersubtle Venetian be not too hard for my wits,
and all the tribe of hell, thou shalt enjoy her.
Therefore, make money. A pox of drowning thyself, it is clean out of the way. Seek thou rather to 360
be hanged in compassing° thy joy than to be
drowned and go without her.
RODERIGO: Wilt thou be fast to my hopes, if I depend
on the issue?
IAGO: Thou art sure of me. Go, make money. I have 365
told thee often, and I retell thee again and again,
I hate the Moor. My cause is hearted;° thine hath
no less reason. Let us be conjunctive° in our
revenge against him. If thou canst cuckold him,
thou dost thyself a pleasure, me a sport. There are 370
many events in the womb of time, which will be
delivered. Traverse, go, provide thy money! We
will have more of this tomorrow. Adieu.
RODERIGO: Where shall we meet i' th' morning?
IAGO: At my lodging. 375
RODERIGO: I'll be with thee betimes.
IAGO: Go to, farewell. Do you hear, Roderigo?
RODERIGO: I'll sell all my land. (*Exit.*)
IAGO: Thus do I ever make my fool my purse;
For I mine own gained knowledge° should profane 380
If I would time expend with such a snipe
But for my sport and profit. I hate the Moor,
And it is thought abroad that 'twixt my sheets
H'as done my office. I know not if't be true,
But I, for mere suspicion in that kind, 385

---

advantage, opportunity. *incontinently,* at once. *virtue,* strength (Roderigo is saying that his nature controls him). *distract,* vary. *corrigible,* corrective. *conclusions,* ends. *unbitted,* i.e., uncontrolled. *sect or scion,* offshoot.

stead, serve. *defeat thy favor,* disguise your face. *usurped,* assumed. *answerable,* similar. *sequestration,* ending. *locusts,* (a sweet fruit). *coloquintida,* (a purgative derived from a bitter apple). *sanctimony,* sacred bond (of marriage). *erring,* wandering. *compassing,* encompassing, achieving. *hearted,* deep-seated in the heart. *conjunctive,* joined. *gained knowledge,* i.e., practical, worldly wisdom.

Will do, as if for surety.° He holds me well;
The better shall my purpose work on him.
Cassio's a proper° man. Let me see now:
To get his place, and to plume up my will°
390 In double knavery. How? How? Let's see.
After some time, to abuse Othello's ears
That he is too familiar with his wife.
He hath a person and a smooth dispose°
To be suspected—framed° to make women false.
395 The Moor is of a free and open nature
That thinks men honest that but seem to be so;
And will as tenderly be led by th' nose
As asses are.
I have't! It is engendered! Hell and night
Must bring this monstrous birth to the world's
400 light.

[*Exit.*]

ACT 2 / SCENE 1

[*Cyprus*]
(*Enter* MONTANO *and two* GENTLEMEN, [*one above*].°)

MONTANO: What from the cape can you discern at
   sea?
FIRST GENTLEMAN: Nothing at all, it is a high-
   wrought flood.
I cannot 'twixt the heaven and the main
Descry a sail.
MONTANO: Methinks the wind hath spoke aloud at
5   land;
A fuller blast ne'er shook our battlements.
If it hath ruffianed so upon the sea,
What ribs of oak, when mountains melt on them,
Can hold the mortise? What shall we hear of this?
SECOND GENTLEMAN: A segregation° of the Turkish
10   fleet.
For do but stand upon the foaming shore,
The chidden billow seems to pelt the clouds;
The wind-shaked surge, with high and monstrous
   main,°
Seems to cast water on the burning Bear
15 And quench the guards of th' ever-fixèd pole.°

I never did like molestation view
On the enchafèd flood.
MONTANO: If that the Turkish fleet
Be not ensheltered and embayed, they are
   drowned;
It is impossible to bear it out.

(*Enter a* [THIRD] GENTLEMAN.)

THIRD GENTLEMAN: News, lads! Our wars are done.   20
The desperate tempest hath so banged the Turks
That their designment halts. A noble ship of
   Venice
Hath seen a grievous wrack and sufferance°
On most part of their fleet.
MONTANO: How? Is this true?
THIRD GENTLEMAN: The ship is here put in,   25
A Veronesa; Michael Cassio,
Lieutenant to the warlike Moor Othello,
Is come on shore; the Moor himself at sea,
And is in full commission here for Cyprus.
MONTANO: I am glad on't. 'Tis a worthy governor.   30
THIRD GENTLEMAN: But this same Cassio, though he
   speak of comfort
Touching the Turkish loss, yet he looks sadly
And prays the Moor be safe, for they were parted
With foul and violent tempest.
MONTANO: Pray heaven he be;
For I have served him, and the man commands   35
Like a full soldier. Let's to the seaside, ho!
As well to see the vessel that's come in
As to throw out our eyes for brave Othello,
Even till we make the main and th' aerial blue
An indistinct regard.°
THIRD GENTLEMAN: Come, let's do so;   40
For every minute is expectancy
Of more arrivancie.°

(*Enter* CASSIO.)

CASSIO: Thanks, you the valiant of this warlike isle,
That so approve° the Moor. O, let the heavens
Give him defense against the elements,   45
For I have lost him on a dangerous sea.
MONTANO: Is he well shipped?
CASSIO: His bark is stoutly timbered, and his pilot
Of very expert and approved allowance;°
Therefore my hopes, not surfeited to death,°   50
Stand in bold cure.° (*Within*) A sail, a sail, a sail!
CASSIO: What noise?

---

surety, certainty. **proper,** handsome. ***plume up my will,***
(many explanations have been offered for this crucial line,
which in Q1 reads "make up my will." The general sense is
something like "to make more proud and gratify my ego").
dispose, manner. ***framed,*** designed. ***above,*** (the Folio
arrangement of this scene requires that the First Gentleman
stand above—on the upper stage—and act as a lookout
reporting sights which cannot be seen by Montano standing
below on the main stage). **segregation,** separation. ***main,***
(both "ocean" and "strength"). ***Seems . . . pole,*** (the constellation Ursa Minor contains two stars which are the *guards,* or
companions, of the *pole,* or North Star).

---

sufferance, damage. ***the main . . . regard,*** i.e., the sea
and sky become indistinguishable. ***arrivancie,*** arrivals.
approve, ("honor" or, perhaps, "are as warlike and valiant as
your governor"). ***approved allowance,*** known and tested.
not surfeited to death, i.e., not so great as to be in danger.
Stand in bold cure, i.e., are likely to be restored.

FIRST GENTLEMAN: The town is empty; on the brow
   o' th' sea
   Stand ranks of people, and they cry, "A sail!"
55 CASSIO: My hopes do shape him for the governor.

[A shot.]

SECOND GENTLEMAN: They do discharge their shot of
   courtesy:
   Our friends at least.
CASSIO: I pray you, sir, go forth
   And give us truth who 'tis that is arrived.
SECOND GENTLEMAN: I shall. (Exit.)
MONTANO: But, good lieutenant, is your general
60   wived?
CASSIO: Most fortunately. He hath achieved a maid
   That paragons° description and wild fame;°
   One that excels the quirks of blazoning pens,°
   And in th' essential vesture of creation°
   Does tire the ingener.°

(Enter [SECOND] GENTLEMAN.)

65   How now? Who has put in?
SECOND GENTLEMAN: 'Tis one Iago, ancient to the
   general.
CASSIO: H'as had most favorable and happy speed:
   Tempests themselves, high seas, and howling
     winds,
   The guttered° rocks and congregated° sands,
70   Traitors ensteeped° to enclog the guiltless keel,
   As having sense° of beauty, do omit
   Their mortal° natures, letting go safely by
   The divine Desdemona.
MONTANO: What is she?
CASSIO: She that I spake of, our great captain's
   captain,
75   Left in the conduct of the bold Iago,
   Whose footing° here anticipates our thoughts
   A se'nnight's° speed. Great Jove, Othello guard,
   And swell his sail with thine own pow'rful breath,
   That he may bless this bay with his tall° ship,
80   Make love's quick pants in Desdemona's arms,
   Give renewed fire to our extinct spirits.

(Enter DESDEMONA, IAGO, RODERIGO, and EMILIA.)

   O, behold! The riches of the ship is come on
     shore!
   You men of Cyprus, let her have your knees.

[Kneeling.]

Hail to thee, lady! and the grace of heaven,
Before, behind thee, and on every hand,
Enwheel thee round.   85
DESDEMONA: I thank you, valiant Cassio.
   What tidings can you tell of my lord?
CASSIO: He is not yet arrived, nor know I aught
   But that he's well and will be shortly here.
DESDEMONA: O but I fear. How lost you company?   90
CASSIO: The great contention of the sea and skies
   Parted our fellowship. (Within. "A sail, a sail!")

[A shot.]

               But hark. A sail!
SECOND GENTLEMAN: They give this greeting to the
   citadel;
   This likewise is a friend.
CASSIO: See for the news.

[Exit GENTLEMAN.]

Good ancient, you are welcome. [To EMILIA]
   Welcome, mistress.   95
Let it not gall your patience, good Iago,
That I extend° my manners. 'Tis my breeding°
That gives me this bold show of courtesy. [Kisses
EMILIA.]
IAGO: Sir, would she give you so much of her lips
   As of her tongue she oft bestows on me,   100
   You would have enough.
DESDEMONA: Alas, she has no speech.
IAGO: In faith, too much.
   I find it still when I have leave to sleep.°
   Marry, before your ladyship,° I grant,
   She puts her tongue a little in her heart   105
   And chides with thinking.
EMILIA: You have little cause to say so.
IAGO: Come on, come on! You are pictures° out of
   door,
   Bells in your parlors, wildcats in your kitchens,
   Saints in your injuries,° devils being offended,
   Players in your housewifery,° and housewives in
     your beds.   110
DESDEMONA: O, fie upon thee, slanderer!

---

paragons, exceeds. wild fame, extravagant report.
quirks of blazoning pens, ingenuities of praising pens. essential vesture of creation, i.e., essential human nature as given by the Creator. tire the ingener, (a difficult line which probably means something like "outdo the human ability to imagine and picture"). guttered, jagged. congregated, gathered. ensteeped, submerged. sense, awareness. mortal, deadly. footing, landing. se'nnight's, week's. tall, brave.

extend, stretch. breeding, careful training in manners (Cassio is considerably more the polished gentleman than Iago, and aware of it). still . . . sleep, i.e., even when she allows me to sleep she continues to scold. before your ladyship, in your presence. pictures, models (of virtue). in your injuries, when you injure others. housewifery, (this word can mean "careful, economical household management," and Iago would then be accusing women of only pretending to be good housekeepers, while in bed they are either [1] economical of their favors, or more likely [2] serious and dedicated workers).

IAGO: Nay, it is true, or else I am a Turk:
  You rise to play, and go to bed to work.
EMILIA: You shall not write my praise.
IAGO: No, let me not.
DESDEMONA: What wouldst write of me, if thou
115 shouldst praise me?
IAGO: O gentle lady, do not put me to't,
  For I am nothing if not critical.
DESDEMONA: Come on, assay. There's one gone to
  the harbor?
IAGO: Ay, madam.
DESDEMONA: [*Aside*] I am not merry; but I do beguile
120 The thing I am by seeming otherwise.—
  Come, how wouldst thou praise me?
IAGO: I am about it; but indeed my invention
  Comes from my pate as birdlime° does from
    frieze°—
  It plucks out brains and all. But my Muse labors,
125 And thus she is delivered:
  If she be fair° and wise: fairness and wit,
  The one's for use, the other useth it.
DESDEMONA: Well praised. How if she be black° and
  witty?
IAGO: If she be black, and thereto have a wit,
130 She'll find a white that shall her blackness fit.
DESDEMONA: Worse and worse!
EMILIA: How if fair and foolish?
IAGO: She never yet was foolish that was fair,
  For even her folly helped her to an heir.
135 DESDEMONA: These are old fond° paradoxes to make
  fools laugh i' th' alehouse. What miserable praise
  hast thou for her that's foul and foolish?
IAGO: There's none so foul, and foolish thereunto,
  But does foul pranks which fair and wise ones do.
140 DESDEMONA: O heavy ignorance. Thou praisest the
  worst best. But what praise couldst thou bestow
  on a deserving woman indeed—one that in the
  authority of her merit did justly put on the vouch
  of very malice itself?°
145 IAGO: She that was ever fair, and never proud;
  Had tongue at will, and yet was never loud;
  Never lacked gold, and yet went never gay;
  Fled from her wish, and yet said "Now I may";
  She that being angered, her revenge being nigh,
150 Bade her wrong stay, and her displeasure fly;
  She that in wisdom never was so frail
  To change the cod's head for the salmon's tail;°
  She that could think, and nev'r disclose her mind;

See suitors following, and not look behind:
  She was a wight° (if ever such wights were)—   155
DESDEMONA: To do what?
IAGO: To suckle fools and chronicle small beer.°
DESDEMONA: O most lame and impotent conclusion.
  Do not learn of him, Emilia, though he be thy
  husband. How say you, Cassio? Is he not a most   160
  profane and liberal° counselor?
CASSIO: He speaks home,° madam. You may relish him
  more in° the soldier than in the scholar. [*Takes*
  DESDEMONA*'s hand.*]
IAGO: [*Aside*] He takes her by the palm. Ay, well said,
  whisper! With as little a web as this will I ensnare   165
  as great a fly as Cassio. Ay, smile upon her, do! I
  will gyve° thee in thine own courtship.—You say
  true; 'tis so, indeed!—If such tricks as these strip
  you out of your lieutenantry, it had been better you
  had not kissed your three fingers so oft—which   170
  now again you are most apt to play the sir° in. Very
  good! Well kissed! An excellent curtsy!° 'Tis so,
  indeed. Yet again your fingers to your lips? Would
  they were clyster pipes° for your sake! [*Trumpets*
  within.] The Moor! I know his trumpet.°   175
CASSIO: 'Tis truly so.
DESDEMONA: Let's meet him and receive him.
CASSIO: Lo, where he comes.

(*Enter* OTHELLO *and* ATTENDANTS.)

OTHELLO: O my fair warrior!
DESDEMONA: My dear Othello.
OTHELLO: It gives me wonder great as my content   180
  To see you here before me. O my soul's joy!
  If after every tempest come such calms,
  May the winds blow till they have wakened
    death.
  And let the laboring bark climb hills of seas
  Olympus-high, and duck again as low   185
  As hell's from heaven. If it were now to die,
  'Twere now to be most happy; for I fear
  My soul hath her content so absolute
  That not another comfort like to this
  Succeeds in unknown fate.
DESDEMONA: The heavens forbid   190
  But that our loves and comforts should increase
  Even as our days do grow.
OTHELLO: Amen to that, sweet powers!
  I cannot speak enough of this content;

---

birdlime, a sticky substance put on branches to catch birds. **frieze,** rough cloth. **fair,** light-complexioned. **black,** brunette. **fond,** foolish. **one . . . itself,** i.e., a woman so honest and deserving that even malice would be forced to approve of her. **To . . . tail,** i.e., to exchange something valuable for something useless.

wight, person. **chronicle small beer,** i.e., keep household accounts (the most trivial of occupations in Iago's opinion). **liberal,** licentious. **speaks home,** thrusts deeply with his speech. **relish him more in,** enjoy him more as. **gyve,** bind. **the sir,** the fashionable gentleman. **curtsy,** courtesy, i.e., bow. **clyster pipes,** enema tubes. **his trumpet,** (great men had their own distinctive calls).

It stops me here [*touches his heart*]; it is too much of
    joy.
195 And this, and this, the greatest discords be

[*They kiss.*]

That e'er our hearts shall make!
IAGO: [*Aside*] O, you are well tuned now!
But I'll set down the pegs° that make this music,
As honest as I am.
OTHELLO: Come, let us to the castle.
News, friends! Our wars are done; the Turks are
    drowned.
200 How does my old acquaintance of this isle?
Honey, you shall be well desired in Cyprus;
I have found great love amongst them. O my sweet,
I prattle out of fashion, and I dote
In mine own comforts. I prithee, good Iago,
205 Go to the bay and disembark my coffers.
Bring thou the master to the citadel;
He is a good one, and his worthiness
Does challenge° much respect. Come, Desdemona,
Once more well met at Cyprus.

(*Exit* OTHELLO *and* DESDEMONA [*and all but* IAGO
and RODERIGO].)

210 IAGO: [*To an* ATTENDANT] Do thou meet me presently
    at the harbor. [*To* RODERIGO] Come hither. If
    thou be'st valiant (as they say base men being in
    love have then a nobility in their natures more
    than is native to them), list me. The lieutenant
215   tonight watches on the court of guard.° First, I
    must tell thee this: Desdemona is directly in love
    with him.
RODERIGO: With him? Why, 'tis not possible.
IAGO: Lay thy finger thus [*puts his finger to his lips*], and
220   let thy soul be instructed. Mark me with what vio-
    lence she first loved the Moor but for bragging
    and telling her fantastical lies. To love him still for
    prating? Let not thy discreet heart think it. Her
    eye must be fed. And what delight shall she have
225   to look on the devil? When the blood is made dull
    with the act of sport, there should be a game° to
    inflame it and to give satiety a fresh appetite, love-
    liness in favor,° sympathy in years,° manners, and
    beauties; all which the Moor is defective in. Now
230   for want of these required conveniences,° her del-
    icate tenderness will find itself abused, begin to
    heave the gorge,° disrelish and abhor the Moor.
    Very nature will instruct her in it and compel her

to some second choice. Now, sir, this granted—as
it is a most pregnant° and unforced position—   235
who stands so eminent in the degree of this fortune as Cassio does? A knave very voluble; no
further conscionable° than in putting on the
mere form of civil and humane° seeming for the
better compassing of his salt° and most hidden   240
loose° affection. Why, none! Why, none! A slipper°
and subtle knave, a finder of occasion, that has an
eye can stamp and counterfeit advantages, though
true advantage never present itself. A devilish
knave. Besides, the knave is handsome, young,   245
and hath all those requisites in him that folly and
green minds look after. A pestilent complete
knave, and the woman hath found him already.
RODERIGO: I cannot believe that in her; she's full of
    most blessed condition.   250
IAGO: Blessed fig's-end! The wine she drinks is made
    of grapes. If she had been blessed, she would
    never have loved the Moor. Blessed pudding!
    Didst thou not see her paddle with the palm of his
    hand? Didst not mark that?   255
RODERIGO: Yes, that I did; but that was but courtesy.
IAGO: Lechery, by this hand! [*Extends his index finger.*]
    An index° and obscure prologue to the history of
    lust and foul thoughts. They met so near with
    their lips that their breaths embraced together.   260
    Villainous thoughts, Roderigo. When these mutu-
    alities so marshal the way, hard at hand comes the
    master and main exercise, th' incorporate° con-
    clusion. Pish! But, sir, be you ruled by me. I have
    brought you from Venice. Watch you tonight; for   265
    the command, I'll lay't upon you. Cassio knows
    you not. I'll not be far from you. Do you find
    some occasion to anger Cassio, either by speaking
    too loud, or tainting° his discipline, or from what
    other course you please which the time shall   270
    more favorably minister.
RODERIGO: Well.
IAGO: Sir, he's rash and very sudden in choler,° and
    haply may strike at you. Provoke him that he may;
    for even out of that will I cause these of Cyprus to   275
    mutiny, whose qualification shall come into no
    true taste° again but by the displanting of Cassio.
    So shall you have a shorter journey to your desires
    by the means I shall then have to prefer them;
    and the impediment most profitably removed   280
    without the which there were no expectation of
    our prosperity.

---

set down the pegs, loosen the strings (to produce discord).
challenge, require, exact. **court of guard,** guardhouse. **game,**
sport (with the added sense of "gamey," "rank"). **favor,**
countenance, appearance. **sympathy in years,** sameness of
age. **conveniences,** advantages. **heave the gorge,** vomit.

---

pregnant, likely. **no further conscionable,** having no more
conscience. **humane,** polite. **salt,** lecherous. **loose,** immoral. **slipper,** slippery. **index,** pointer. **incorporate,** carnal. **tainting,** discrediting. **choler,** anger. **qualification . . .
taste,** i.e., appeasement will not be brought about (wine was
"qualified" by adding water).

RODERIGO: I will do this if you can bring it to any
   opportunity.
285 IAGO: I warrant thee. Meet me by and by at the cita-
   del. I must fetch his necessaries ashore. Farewell.
RODERIGO: Adieu. (*Exit.*)
IAGO: That Cassio loves her, I do well believe 't;
   That she loves him, 'tis apt and of great credit.
290 The Moor, howbeit that I endure him not,
   Is of a constant, loving, noble nature,
   And I dare think he'll prove to Desdemona
   A most dear° husband. Now I do love her too;
   Not out of absolute° lust, though peradventure°
295 I stand accountant for as great a sin,
   But partly led to diet° my revenge,
   For that I do suspect the lusty Moor
   Hath leaped into my seat; the thought whereof
   Doth, like a poisonous mineral, gnaw my inwards;
300 And nothing can or shall content my soul
   Till I am evened with him, wife for wife.
   Or failing so, yet that I put the Moor
   At least into a jealousy so strong
   That judgment cannot cure. Which thing to do,
305 If this poor trash of Venice, whom I trace°
   For his quick hunting, stand the putting on,
   I'll have our Michael Cassio on the hip,
   Abuse him to the Moor in the rank garb°
   (For I fear Cassio with my nightcap too),
310 Make the Moor thank me, love me, and reward me
   For making him egregiously an ass
   And practicing upon° his peace and quiet,
   Even to madness. 'Tis here, but yet confused:
   Knavery's plain face is never seen till used. (*Exit.*)

ACT 2 / SCENE 2

[*A street*]
(*Enter* OTHELLO's HERALD, *with a proclamation.*)

HERALD: It is Othello's pleasure, our noble and valiant
   general, that upon certain tidings now arrived
   importing the mere perdition° of the Turkish
   fleet, every man put himself into triumph. Some
5 to dance, some to make bonfires, each man to
   what sport and revels his addition° leads him. For,
   besides these beneficial news, it is the celebration
   of his nuptial. So much was his pleasure should
   be proclaimed. All offices° are open, and there is

full liberty of feasting from this present hour of   10
five till the bell have told eleven. Bless the isle of
Cyprus and our noble general Othello! (*Exit.*)

ACT 2 / SCENE 3

[*The citadel of Cyprus*]
(*Enter* OTHELLO, DESDEMONA, CASSIO, *and* ATTEN-
DANTS.)

OTHELLO: Good Michael, look you to the guard
   tonight.
   Let's teach ourselves that honorable stop,
   Not to outsport discretion.
CASSIO: Iago hath direction what to do;
   But not withstanding, with my personal eye   5
   Will I look to 't.
OTHELLO: Iago is most honest.
   Michael, good night. Tomorrow with your earliest
   Let me have speech with you. [*To* DESDEMONA].
      Come, my dear love,
   The purchase made, the fruits are to ensue,
   That profit's yet to come 'tween me and you.   10
   Good night.

(*Exit* [OTHELLO *with* DESDEMONA *and* ATTENDANTS].)
(*Enter* IAGO.)

CASSIO: Welcome, Iago. We must to the watch.
IAGO: Not this hour, lieutenant; 'tis not yet ten o' th'
   clock. Our general cast° us thus early for the love
   of his Desdemona; who let us not therefore blame. 15
   He hath not yet made wanton the night with her,
   and she is sport for Jove.
CASSIO: She's a most exquisite lady.
IAGO: And, I'll warrant her, full of game.
CASSIO: Indeed, she's a most fresh and delicate crea- 20
   ture.
IAGO: What an eye she has! Methinks it sounds a parley to provocation.
CASSIO: An inviting eye; and yet methinks right modest.
IAGO: And when she speaks, is it not an alarum° to   25
   love?
CASSIO: She is indeed perfection.
IAGO: Well, happiness to their sheets! Come, lieutenant, I have a stoup° of wine, and here without
   are a brace of Cyprus gallants that would fain   30
   have a measure to the health of black Othello.
CASSIO: Not tonight, good Iago. I have very poor and
   unhappy brains for drinking; I could well wish
   courtesy would invent some other custom of
   entertainment.   35
IAGO: O, they are our friends. But one cup! I'll drink
   for you.

---

dear, expensive. *out of absolute,* absolutely out of. *per-*
adventure, perchance. *diet,* feed. *trace,* (most editors emend
to "trash," meaning to hang weights on a dog to slow his
hunting; but "trace" clearly means something like "put on
the trace" or "set on the track"). *right garb,* i.e., "proper
fashion." *practicing upon,* scheming to destroy. *mere perdi-*
tion, absolute destruction. *addition,* rank. *offices,* kitchens
and storerooms of food.

---

cast, dismissed. *alarum,* the call to action, "general
quarters." *stoup,* two-quart tankard.

CASSIO: I have drunk but one cup tonight, and that
    was craftily qualified° too; and behold what inno-
40   vation it makes here. I am unfortunate in the
    infirmity and dare not task my weakness with any
    more.
IAGO: What, man! 'Tis a night of revels, the gallants
    desire it.
45 CASSIO: Where are they?
IAGO: Here, at the door. I pray you call them in.
CASSIO: I'll do't, but it dislikes me. *(Exit.)*
IAGO: If I can fasten but one cup upon him
    With that which he hath drunk tonight already,
50   He'll be as full of quarrel and offense
    As my young mistress' dog. Now, my sick fool
      Roderigo,
    Whom love hath turned almost the wrong side out,
    To Desdemona hath tonight caroused
    Potations pottle-deep;° and he's to watch.
55   Three else° of Cyprus, noble swelling spirits,
    That hold their honors in a wary distance,°
    The very elements of this warlike isle,
    Have I tonight flustered with flowing cups,
    And they watch too. Now, 'mongst this flock of
      drunkards
60   Am I to put our Cassio in some action
    That may offend the isle. But here they come.

(Enter CASSIO, MONTANO, *and* GENTLEMEN.*)*

    If consequence do but approve my dream,
    My boat sails freely, both with wind and stream.
CASSIO: 'Fore God, they have given me a rouse° al-
65   ready.
MONTANO: Good faith, a little one; not past a pint, as I
    am a soldier.
IAGO: Some wine, ho!

    [Sings] *And let me the canakin clink, clink;*
70   *And let me the canakin clink.*
      A soldier's a man;
      O man's life's but a span,
      Why then, let a soldier drink.

    Some wine, boys!
75 CASSIO: 'Fore God, an excellent song!
IAGO: I learned it in England, where indeed they are
    most potent in potting. Your Dane, your German,
    and your swag-bellied° Hollander—Drink, ho!—
    are nothing to your English.
80 CASSIO: Is your Englishman so exquisite° in his drink-
    ing?

IAGO: Why, he drinks you with facility your Dane dead
    drunk; he sweats not to overthrow your Almain;
    he gives your Hollander a vomit ere the next
    pottle can be filled.   85
CASSIO: To the health of our general!
MONTANO: I am for it, lieutenant, and I'll do you
    justice.
IAGO: O sweet England!

    [Sings] *King Stephen was and a worthy peer;*   90
      His breeches cost him but a crown;
      He held them sixpence all too dear,
      With that he called the tailor lown.°
      He was a wight of high renown,
      And thou art but of low degree: 95
      'Tis pride that pulls the country down;
      Then take thine auld cloak about thee.

    Some wine, ho!
CASSIO: 'Fore God, this is a more exquisite song than
    the other.   100
IAGO: Will you hear't again?
CASSIO: No, for I hold him to be unworthy of his place
    that does those things. Well, God's above all; and
    there be souls must be saved, and there be souls
    must not be saved.   105
IAGO: It's true, good lieutenant.
CASSIO: For mine own part—no offense to the gen-
    eral, nor any man of quality—I hope to be saved.
IAGO: And so do I too, lieutenant.
CASSIO: Ay, but, by your leave, not before me. The 110
    lieutenant is to be saved before the ancient. Let's
    have no more of this; let's to our affairs.—God
    forgive us our sins!—Gentlemen, let's look to our
    business. Do not think, gentlemen, I am drunk.
    This is my ancient; this is my right hand, and this 115
    is my left. I am not drunk now. I can stand well
    enough, and I speak well enough.
GENTLEMEN: Excellent well!
CASSIO: Why, very well then. You must not think then
    that I am drunk. *(Exit.)*   120
MONTANO: To th' platform, masters. Come, let's set
    the watch.
IAGO: You see this fellow that is gone before.
    He's a soldier fit to stand by Caesar
    And give direction; and do but see his vice.
    'Tis to his virtue a just equinox,°   125
    The one as long as th' other. 'Tis pity of him.
    I fear the trust Othello puts him in,
    On some odd time of his infirmity,
    Will shake this island.
MONTANO: But is he often thus?

---

qualified, diluted.   **pottle-deep,** to the bottom of the cup.
else, others. **hold . . . distance,** are scrupulous in maintaining
their honor. **rouse,** drink. **swag-bellied,** hanging. **exquisite,** superb.

---

lown, lout. **just equinox,** exact balance (of dark and
light).

130 IAGO: 'Tis evermore his prologue to his sleep:
He'll watch the horologe a double set°
If drink rock not his cradle.
MONTANO: It were well
The general were put in mind of it.
135 Perhaps he sees it not, or his good nature
Prizes the virtue that appears in Cassio
And looks not on his evils. Is not this true?

(Enter RODERIGO.*)*

IAGO: [*Aside*] How now, Roderigo?
I pray you after the lieutenant, go! [*Exit*
RODERIGO.]
140 MONTANO: And 'tis great pity that the noble Moor
Should hazard such a place as his own second
With one of an ingraft° infirmity.
It were an honest action to say so
To the Moor.
IAGO: Not I, for this fair island!
145 I do love Cassio well and would do much
To cure him of this evil. (*"Help! Help!" Within.*)
But hark? What noise?

(Enter CASSIO, *pursuing* RODERIGO.*)*

CASSIO: Zounds, you rogue! You rascal!
MONTANO: What's the matter, lieutenant?
CASSIO: A knave teach me my duty? I'll beat the knave
150 into a twiggen° bottle.
RODERIGO: Beat me?
CASSIO: Dost thou prate, rogue? [*Strikes him.*]
MONTANO: Nay, good lieutenant! I pray you, sir, hold
your hand.

[*Stays him.*]

155 CASSIO: Let me go, sir, or I'll knock you o'er the maz-
zard.°
MONTANO: Come, come, you're drunk!
CASSIO: Drunk? [*They fight.*]
IAGO: [*Aside to* RODERIGO] Away, I say! Go out and cry
160 a mutiny!

[*Exit* RODERIGO.]

Nay, good lieutenant. God's will gentlemen!
Help, ho! Lieutenant. Sir. Montano.
Help, masters! Here's a goodly watch indeed!

[*A bell rung.*]

Who's that which rings the bell? Diablo, ho!
165 The town will rise. God's will, lieutenant,
You'll be ashamed forever.

(Enter OTHELLO *and* ATTENDANTS.*)*

OTHELLO: What is the matter here?
MONTANO: Zounds, I bleed still. I am hurt to death.
He dies. [*He and* CASSIO *fight again.*]
OTHELLO: Hold for your lives!
IAGO: Hold, ho! Lieutenant. Sir. Montano.
Gentlemen!   170
Have you forgot all place of sense and duty?
Hold! The general speaks to you. Hold, for shame!
OTHELLO: Why, how now, ho? From whence ariseth
this?
Are we turned Turks, and to ourselves do that
Which heaven hath forbid the Ottomites?°   175
For Christian shame put by this barbarous brawl!
He that stirs next to carve for his own rage
Holds his soul light;° he dies upon his motion.
Silence that dreadful bell! It frights the isle
From her propriety.° What's the matter, masters?   180
Honest Iago, that looks dead with grieving,
Speak. Who began this? On thy love, I charge thee.
IAGO: I do not know. Friends all, but now, even now,
In quarter° and in terms like bride and groom
Devesting them for bed; and then, but now—   185
As if some planet had unwitted men—
Swords out, and tilting one at other's breasts
In opposition bloody. I cannot speak
Any beginning to this peevish odds,°
And would in action glorious I had lost   190
Those legs that brought me to a part of it!
OTHELLO: How comes it, Michael, you are thus
forgot?
CASSIO: I pray you pardon me; I cannot speak.
OTHELLO: Worthy Montano, you were wont to be
civil;
The gravity and stillness of your youth   195
The world hath noted, and your name is great
In mouths of wisest censure.° What's the matter
That you unlace° your reputation thus
And spend your rich opinion° for the name
Of a night-brawler? Give me answer to it.   200
MONTANO: Worthy Othello, I am hurt to danger.
Your officer, Iago, can inform you,
While I spare speech, which something now
offends° me,
Of all that I do know; nor know I aught
By me that's said or done amiss this night,   205
Unless self-charity be sometimes a vice,
And to defend ourselves it be a sin
When violence assails us.

---

heaven . . . Ottomites, i.e., by sending the storm that dispersed the Turks. *Holds his soul light,* values his soul lightly. *propriety,* proper order. *In quarter,* on duty. *odds,* quarrel. *censure,* judgment. *unlace,* undo (the term refers specifically to the dressing of a wild boar killed in the hunt). *opinion,* reputation. *offends,* harms, hurts.

---

watch . . . set, stay awake twice around the clock. *ingraft,* ingrained. *twiggen,* wicker-covered. *mazzard,* head.

OTHELLO: Now, by heaven,
My blood begins my safer guides to rule,
210 And passion, having my best judgment collied,°
Assays to lead the way. If I once stir
Or do but lift this arm, the best of you
Shall sink in my rebuke. Give me to know
How this foul rout began, who set it on;
215 And he that is approved in this offense,
Though he had twinned with me, both at a birth,
Shall lose me. What? In a town of war
Yet wild, the people's hearts brimful of fear,
To manage° private and domestic quarrel?
220 In night, and on the court and guard of safety?
'Tis monstrous. Iago, who began't?
MONTANO: If partially affined, or leagued in office,°
Thou dost deliver more or less than truth,
Thou art no soldier.
IAGO: Touch me not so near.
225 I had rather have this tongue cut from my mouth
Than it should do offense to Michael Cassio.
Yet I persuade myself, to speak the truth
Shall nothing wrong him. This it is, general.
Montano and myself being in speech,
230 There comes a fellow crying out for help,
And Cassio following him with determined
    sword
To execute upon him. Sir, this gentleman
Steps in to Cassio and entreats his pause.
Myself the crying fellow did pursue,
235 Lest by his clamor—as it so fell out—
The town might fall in fright. He, swift of foot,
Outran my purpose; and I returned then rather
For that I heard the clink and fall of swords,
And Cassio high in oath; which till tonight
240 I ne'er might say before. When I came back—
For this was brief—I found them close together
At blow and thrust, even as again they were
When you yourself did part them.
More of this matter cannot I report;
245 But men are men; the best sometimes forget.
Though Cassio did some little wrong to him,
As men in rage strike those that wish them best,
Yet surely Cassio I believe received
From him that fled some strange indignity,
Which patience could not pass.°
250 OTHELLO: I know, Iago,
Thy honesty and love doth mince° this matter,
Making it light to Cassio. Cassio, I love thee;
But never more be officer of mine.

(*Enter* DESDEMONA, *attended.*)

Look if my gentle love be not raised up.
I'll make thee an example.
DESDEMONA: What is the matter, dear. 255
OTHELLO: All's well, sweeting; come away to bed.
[*To* MONTANO] Sir, for your hurts, myself will be
    your surgeon.
Lead him off. [MONTANO *led off.*]
Iago, look with care about the town
And silence those whom this vile brawl distracted. 260
Come, Desdemona: 'tis the soldiers' life
To have their balmy slumbers waked with strife.

(*Exit* [*with all but* IAGO *and* CASSIO].)

IAGO: What, are you hurt, lieutenant?
CASSIO: Ay, past all surgery.
IAGO: Marry, God forbid! 265
CASSIO: Reputation, reputation, reputation! O, I have
lost my reputation! I have lost the immortal part
of myself, and what remains is bestial. My reputation, Iago, my reputation.
IAGO: As I am an honest man, I had thought you 270
had received some bodily wound. There is more
sense° in that than in reputation. Reputation is
an idle and most false imposition,° oft got without
merit and lost without deserving. You have lost no
reputation at all unless you repute yourself such a 275
loser. What, man, there are more ways to recover
the general again. You are but now cast in his
mood°—a punishment more in policy° than in
malice—even so as one would beat his offenseless
dog to affright an imperious lion. Sue to him 280
again, and he's yours.
CASSIO: I will rather sue to be despised than to deceive so good a commander with so slight, so
drunken, and so indiscreet an officer. Drunk! And
speak parrot!° And squabble! Swagger! Swear! and 285
discourse fustian° with one's own shadow! O thou
invisible spirit of wine, if thou hast no name to be
known by, let us call thee devil!
IAGO: What was he that you followed with your sword?
What had he done to you? 290
CASSIO: I know not.
IAGO: Is't possible?
CASSIO: I remember a mass of things, but nothing distinctly: a quarrel, but nothing wherefore. O God,
that men should put an enemy in their mouths 295
to steal away their brains! that we should with
joy, pleasance, revel, and applause transform ourselves into beasts!

---

collied, darkened. **manage,** conduct. **If . . . office,** if
you are partial because you are related ("affined") or the
brother officer (of Cassio). **pass,** allow to pass. **mince,** cut
up (i.e., tell only part of).

sense, physical feeling. **imposition,** external thing. **cast
in his mood,** dismissed because of his anger. **in policy,** politically necessary. **speak parrot,** gabble without sense. **discourse fustian,** speak nonsense ("fustian" was a coarse cloth
used for stuffing).

IAGO: Why, but you are now well enough. How came
300   you thus recovered?
CASSIO: It hath pleased the devil drunkenness to give
         place to the devil wrath. One unperfectness shows
         me another, to make me frankly despise myself.
IAGO: Come, you are too severe a moraler. As the time,
305   the place, and the condition of this country stands,
         I could heartily wish this had not so befall'n; but
         since it is as it is, mend it for your own good.
CASSIO: I will ask him for my place again: he shall tell
         me I am a drunkard. Had I as many mouths as
310   Hydra, such an answer would stop them all. To
         be now a sensible man, by and by a fool, and
         presently a beast! O strange! Every inordinate
         cup is unblest, and the ingredient is a devil.
IAGO: Come, come, good wine is a good familiar crea-
315   ture if it be well used. Exclaim no more against
         it. And, good lieutenant, I think you think I love
         you.
CASSIO: I have well approved it, sir. I drunk?
IAGO: You or any man living may be drunk at a time,
320   man. I tell you what you shall do. Our general's
         wife is now the general. I may say so in this re-
         spect, for he hath devoted and given up himself
         to the contemplation, mark, and devotement of
         her parts° and graces. Confess yourself freely to
325   her; importune her help to put you in your place
         again. She is of so free, so kind, so apt, so blessed
         a disposition she holds it a vice in her goodness
         not to do more than she is requested. This bro-
         ken joint between you and her husband entreat
330   her to splinter;° and my fortunes against any lay°
         worth naming, this crack of your love shall grow
         stronger than it was before.
CASSIO: You advise me well.
IAGO: I protest, in the sincerity of love and honest
335   kindness.
CASSIO: I think it freely; and betimes in the morning I
         will beseech the virtuous Desdemona to under-
         take for me. I am desperate of my fortunes if they
         check° me.
340 IAGO: You are in the right. Good night, lieutenant; I
         must to the watch.
CASSIO: Good night, honest Iago. *(Exit* CASSIO.*)*
IAGO: And what's he then that says I play the
         villain,
         When this advice is free° I give, and honest,
345   Probal to° thinking, and indeed the course
         To win the Moor again? For 'tis most easy
         Th' inclining° Desdemona to subdue
         In any honest suit; she's framed as fruitful°

As the free elements.° And then for her
To win the Moor—were't to renounce his baptism,   350
All seals and symbols of redeemèd sin—
His soul is so enfettered to her love
That she may make, unmake, do what she list,
Even as her appetite° shall play the god
With his weak function.° How am I then a villain   355
To counsel Cassio to this parallel course,
Directly to his good? Divinity of hell!
When devils will the blackest sins put on,°
They do suggest at first with heavenly shows,°
As I do now. For whiles this honest fool   360
Plies Desdemona to repair his fortune,
And she for him pleads strongly to the Moor,
I'll pour this pestilence into his ear:
That she repeals him° for her body's lust;
And by how much she strives to do him good,   365
She shall undo her credit with the Moor.
So will I turn her virtue into pitch,
And out of her own goodness make the net
That shall enmesh them all. How now, Roderigo?

(Enter RODERIGO.*)*

RODERIGO: I do follow here in the chase, not like a   370
         hound that hunts, but one that fills up the cry.°
         My money is almost spent; I have been tonight
         exceedingly well cudgeled; and I think the issue
         will be, I shall have so much experience for my
         pains; and so, with no money at all, and a little   375
         more wit, return again to Venice.
IAGO: How poor are they that have not patience!
         What wound did ever heal but by degrees?
         Thou know'st we work by wit, and not by
         witchcraft;
         And wit depends on dilatory time.   380
         Does't not go well? Cassio hath beaten thee,
         And thou by that small hurt hast cashiered Cassio.
         Though other things grow fair against the sun,
         Yet fruits that blossom first will first be ripe.
         Content thyself awhile. By the mass, 'tis morning! 385
         Pleasure and action make the hours seem short.
         Retire thee; go where thou art billeted.
         Away, I say! Thou shalt know more hereafter.
         Nay, get thee gone! *(Exit* RODERIGO.*)*
                    Two things are to be done:
         My wife must move° for Cassio to her mistress;   390
         I'll set her on;
         Myself awhile° to draw the Moor apart
         And bring him jump° when he may Cassio find

---

          devotement of her parts, devotion to her qualities. *splin-*
ter, split. *lay,* wager. *check,* repulse. *free,* generous and
open. *Probal to,* provable by. *inclining,* inclined (to be
helpful). *framed as fruitful,* made as generous.

elements, i.e., basic nature. *appetite,* liking. *function,*
thought. *put on,* advance, further. *shows,* appearances.
repeals him, asks for (Cassio's reinstatement). *fills up the cry,*
makes up one of the hunting pack, adding to the noise but
not actually tracking. *move,* petition. *awhile,* at the same
time. *jump,* at the precise moment and place.

Soliciting his wife. Ay, that's the way!
395 Dull not device by coldness and delay. *(Exit.)*

ACT 3 / SCENE 1

[*A street*]
(Enter CASSIO [*and*] MUSICIANS.*)*

CASSIO: Masters, play here. I will content your pains.°
Something that's brief; and bid "Good morrow,
general." [*They play.*]

[*Enter* CLOWN.°]

CLOWN: Why, masters, have your instruments been in
Naples° that they speak i' th' nose thus?
5 MUSICIAN: How, sir, how?
CLOWN: Are these, I pray you, wind instruments?
MUSICIAN: Ay, marry, are they, sir.
CLOWN: O, thereby hangs a tale.
MUSICIAN: Whereby hangs a tale, sir?
10 CLOWN: Marry, sir, by many a wind instrument that I
know. But, masters, here's money for you; and the
general so likes your music that he desires you,
for love's sake, to make no more noise with it.
MUSICIAN: Well, sir, we will not.
15 CLOWN: If you have any music that may not be heard,
to 't again. But, as they say, to hear music the general does not greatly care.
MUSICIAN: We have none such, sir.
CLOWN: Then put up your pipes in your bag, for I'll
20 away. Go, vanish into air, away!

(Exit MUSICIANS.*)*

CASSIO: Dost thou hear me, mine honest friend?
CLOWN: No. I hear not your honest friend. I hear you.
CASSIO: Prithee keep up thy quillets.° There's a poor
piece of gold for thee. If the gentlewoman that at-
25 tends the general's wife be stirring, tell her there's
one Cassio entreats her a little favor of speech.
Wilt thou do this?
CLOWN: She is stirring, sir. If she will stir hither, I shall
seem to notify unto her.° *(Exit* CLOWN.*)*

(Enter IAGO.*)*

CASSIO: In happy time, Iago.
30 IAGO: You have not been abed then?
CASSIO: Why, no, the day had broke before we parted.
I have made bold, Iago, to send in to your wife;
My suit to her is that she will to virtuous Desdemona
Procure me some access.

IAGO: I'll send her to you presently,
And I'll devise a mean to draw the Moor 35
Out of the way, that your converse and business
May be more free.
CASSIO: I humbly thank you for 't. *(Exit* [IAGO].*)*
I never knew
A Florentine° more kind and honest.

(Enter EMILIA.*)*

EMILIA: Good morrow, good lieutenant. I am sorry 40
For your displeasure;° but all will sure be well.
The general and his wife are talking of it,
And she speaks for you stoutly. The Moor replies
That he you hurt is of great fame in Cyprus
And great affinity,° and that in wholesome wisdom 45
He might not but refuse you. But he protests he
loves you,
And needs no other suitor but his likings
To bring you in again.
CASSIO: Yet I beseech you,
If you think fit, or that it may be done,
Give me advantage of some brief discourse 50
With Desdemona alone.
EMILIA: Pray you come in.
I will bestow you where you shall have time
To speak your bosom° freely.
CASSIO: I am much bound to you.

[*Exeunt.*]

ACT 3 / SCENE 2

[*The citadel*]
(Enter OTHELLO, IAGO, *and* GENTLEMEN.*)*

OTHELLO: These letters give, Iago, to the pilot
And by him do my duties to the Senate.
That done, I will be walking on the works;
Repair° there to me.
IAGO: Well, my good lord, I'll do 't.
OTHELLO: This fortification, gentlemen, shall we see 't? 5
GENTLEMEN: We'll wait upon your lordship. *(Exeunt.)*

ACT 3 / SCENE 3

[*The citadel*]
(Enter DESDEMONA, CASSIO, *and* EMILIA.*)*

DESDEMONA: Be thou assured, good Cassio, I will do
All my abilities in thy behalf.
EMILIA: Good madam, do. I warrant it grieves my
husband
As if the cause were his.

---

content your pains, reward your efforts. **Clown,** fool.
Naples, (this may refer either to the Neapolitan nasal tone, or
to syphilis—rife in Naples—which breaks down the nose).
quillets, puns. **seem . . . her,** (the Clown is mocking Cassio's
overly elegant manner of speaking).

Florentine, i.e., Iago is as kind as if he were from Cassio's
home town, Florence. **displeasure,** discomforting. **affinity,**
family. **bosom,** inmost thoughts. **Repair,** go.

DESDEMONA: O, that's an honest fellow. Do not
5   doubt, Cassio,
    But I will have my lord and you again
    As friendly as you were.
CASSIO: Bounteous madam,
    Whatever shall become of Michael Cassio,
    He's never anything but your true servant.
DESDEMONA: I know't; I thank you. You do love my
10   lord.
    You have known him long, and be you well assured
    He shall in strangeness stand no farther off
    Than in a politic distance.°
CASSIO: Ay, but, lady,
    That policy may either last so long,
15   Or feed upon such nice° and waterish diet,
    Or breed itself so out of circumstances,°
    That, I being absent, and my place supplied,°
    My general will forget my love and service.
DESDEMONA: Do not doubt° that; before Emilia here
20   I give thee warrant of thy place. Assure thee,
    If I do vow a friendship, I'll perform it
    To the last article. My lord shall never rest;
    I'll watch him tame° and talk him out of patience;
    His bed shall seem a school, his board a shrift;°
25   I'll intermingle everything he does
    With Cassio's suit. Therefore be merry, Cassio,
    For thy solicitor shall rather die
    Than give thy cause away.

(Enter OTHELLO and IAGO [at a distance].)

EMILIA: Madam, here comes my lord.
30 CASSIO: Madam, I'll take my leave.
DESDEMONA: Why, stay, and hear me speak.
CASSIO: Madam, not now. I am very ill at ease,
    Unfit for mine own purposes.
DESDEMONA: Well, do your discretion. *(Exit CASSIO.)*
IAGO: Ha! I like not that.
35 OTHELLO: What dost thou say?
IAGO: Nothing, my lord; or if—I know not what.
OTHELLO: Was not that Cassio parted from my wife?
IAGO: Cassio, my lord? No, sure, I cannot think it
    That he would steal away so guilty-like,
    Seeing you coming.
40 OTHELLO: I do believe 'twas he.
DESDEMONA: *[Coming to them]* How now, my lord?
    I have been talking with a suitor here,
    A man that languishes in your displeasure.
OTHELLO: Who is't you mean?

DESDEMONA: Why, your lieutenant, Cassio. Good my
    lord,   45
    If I have any grace or power to move you,
    His present° reconciliation take.
    For if he be not one that truly loves you,
    That errs in ignorance, and not in cunning,
    I have no judgment in an honest face.   50
    I prithee call him back.
OTHELLO: Went he hence now?
DESDEMONA: I' sooth so humbled
    That he hath left part of his grief with me
    To suffer with him. Good love, call him back.
OTHELLO: Not now, sweet Desdemon; some other
    time.   55
DESDEMONA: But shall't be shortly?
OTHELLO: The sooner, sweet, for you.
DESDEMONA: Shall't be tonight at supper?
OTHELLO: No, not tonight.
DESDEMONA: Tomorrow dinner then?
OTHELLO: I shall not dine at home;
    I meet the captains at the citadel.
DESDEMONA: Why then, tomorrow night, on Tuesday
    morn,   60
    On Tuesday noon, or night, on Wednesday morn.
    I prithee name the time, but let it not
    Exceed three days. In faith, he's penitent;
    And yet his trespass, in our common reason
    (Save that, they say, the wars must make example   65
    Out of her best), is not almost a fault
    T' incur a private check.° When shall he come?
    Tell me, Othello. I wonder in my soul
    What you would ask me that I should deny
    Or stand so mamm'ring° on. What? Michael
    Cassio,   70
    That came awooing with you, and so many a time,
    When I have spoke of you dispraisingly,
    Hath ta'en your part—to have so much to do
    To bring him in? By'r Lady, I could do much—
OTHELLO: Prithee no more. Let him come when he
    will!   75
    I will deny thee nothing.
DESDEMONA: Why, this is not a boon;
    'Tis as I should entreat you wear your gloves,
    Or feed on nourishing dishes, or keep you warm,
    Or sue to you to do a peculiar profit°
    To your own person. Nay, when I have a suit   80
    Wherein I mean to touch your love indeed,
    It shall be full of poise° and difficult weight,
    And fearful to be granted.
OTHELLO: I will deny thee nothing!

He . . . distance, i.e., he shall act no more distant to you than is necessary for political reasons. *nice,* trivial. *Or . . . circumstances,* i.e., or grow so on the basis of accidental happenings and political needs. *supplied,* filled. *doubt,* imagine. *watch him tame,* (animals were tamed by being kept awake). *board a shrift,* table (seem) a confessional.

---

present, immediate. *is . . . check,* is almost not serious enough for a private rebuke (let alone a public disgrace). *mamm'ring,* hesitating. *peculiar profit,* particularly personal good. *poise,* weight.

85   Whereon I do beseech thee grant me this,
    To leave me but a little to myself.
DESDEMONA: Shall I deny you? No. Farewell, my lord.
OTHELLO: Farewell, my Desdemona: I'll come to thee
    straight.°
DESDEMONA: Emilia, come. Be as your fancies teach
    you;
    Whate'er you be, I am obedient. (*Exit* [*with*
    EMILIA].)
90 OTHELLO: Excellent wretch! Perdition catch my soul
    But I do love thee! and when I love thee not,
    Chaos is come again.
IAGO: My noble lord——
OTHELLO: What dost thou say, Iago?
IAGO: Did Michael Cassio, when you wooed my lady,
95   Know of your love?
OTHELLO: He did, from first to last. Why dost thou
    ask?
IAGO: But for a satisfaction of my thought,
    No further harm.
OTHELLO: Why of thy thought, Iago?
IAGO: I did not think he had been acquainted with
    her.
100 OTHELLO: O, yes, and went between us° very oft.
IAGO: Indeed?
OTHELLO: Indeed? Ay, indeed! Discern'st thou aught
    in that?
    Is he not honest?
IAGO: Honest, my lord?
OTHELLO: Honest? Ay, honest.
IAGO: My lord, for aught I know.
OTHELLO: What dost thou think?
IAGO: Think, my lord?
105 OTHELLO: Think, my lord?
    By heaven, he echoes me,
    As if there were some monster in thy thought
    Too hideous to be shown. Thou dost mean
    something.
    I heard thee say even now, thou lik'st not that,
110   When Cassio left my wife. What didst not like?
    And when I told thee he was of my counsel°
    Of my whole course of wooing, thou cried'st
    "Indeed?"
    And didst contract and purse thy brow together,
    As if thou then hadst shut up in thy brain
115   Some horrible conceit.° If thou dost love me,
    Show me thy thought.
IAGO: My lord, you know I love you.
OTHELLO: I think thou dost;
    And, for I know thou'rt full of love and honesty
    And weigh'st thy words before thou giv'st them
    breath,

Therefore these stops° of thine fright me the
    more;   120
For such things in a false disloyal knave
Are tricks of custom;° but in a man that's just
They're close dilations,° working from the heart
That passion cannot rule.
IAGO: For Michael Cassio,
    I dare be sworn, I think that he is honest.   125
OTHELLO: I think so too.
IAGO: Men should be what they seem;
    Or those that be not, would they might seem none!
OTHELLO: Certain, men should be what they seem.
IAGO: Why then, I think Cassio's an honest man.
OTHELLO: Nay, yet there's more in this?   130
    I prithee speak to me as to thy thinkings,
    As thou dost ruminate, and give thy worst of
    thoughts
    The worst of words.
IAGO: Good my lord, pardon me:
    Though I am bound to every act of duty,
    I am not bound to that all slaves are free to.   135
    Utter my thoughts? Why, say they are vile and false,
    As where's the palace whereinto foul things
    Sometimes intrude not? Who has that breast so
    pure
    But some uncleanly apprehensions
    Keep leets and law days,° and in sessions sit   140
    With meditations lawful?
OTHELLO: Thou dost conspire against thy friend,
    Iago,
    If thou but think'st him wronged, and mak'st his
    ear
    A stranger to thy thoughts.
IAGO: I do beseech you—
    Though I perchance am vicious in my guess   145
    (As I confess it is my nature's plague
    To spy into abuses, and of my jealousy
    Shape faults that are not), that your wisdom
    From one that so imperfectly conceits
    Would take no notice, nor build yourself a trouble   150
    Out of his scattering and unsure observance.
    It were not for your quiet nor your good,
    Nor for my manhood, honesty, and wisdom,
    To let you know my thoughts.
OTHELLO: What dost thou mean?
IAGO: Good name in man and woman, dear my lord,   155
    Is the immediate jewel of their souls.
    Who steals my purse steals trash; 'tis something,
    nothing;
    'Twas mine, 'tis his, and has been slave to
    thousands;

---

straight, at once. *between us,* i.e., as messenger. *of my counsel,* in my confidence. *conceit,* thought.

stops, interruptions. *of custom,* customary. *close dilations,* expressions of hidden thoughts. *leets and law days,* meetings of local courts.

But he that filches from me my good name
160 Robs me of that which not enriches him
And makes me poor indeed.
OTHELLO: By heaven, I'll know thy thoughts!
IAGO: You cannot, if my heart were in your hand;
Nor shall not whilst 'tis in my custody.
OTHELLO: Ha!
165 IAGO: O, beware, my lord, of jealousy!
It is the green-eyed monster, which doth mock
The meat it feeds on. That cuckold lives in bliss
Who, certain of his fate, loves not his wronger;
But O, what damnèd minutes tells° he o'er
170 Who dotes, yet doubts—suspects, yet fondly° loves!
OTHELLO: O misery.
IAGO: Poor and content is rich, and rich enough;
But riches fineless° is as poor as winter
To him that ever fears he shall be poor.
175 Good God the souls of all my tribe defend
From jealousy!
OTHELLO: Why? Why is this?
Think'st thou I'd make a life of jealousy,
To follow still° the changes of the moon
With fresh suspicions? No! To be once in doubt
180 Is once to be resolved. Exchange me for a goat
When I shall turn the business of my soul
To such exsufflicate and blown° surmises,
Matching thy inference. 'Tis not to make me jealous
To say my wife is fair, feeds well, loves company,
185 Is free of speech, sings, plays, and dances;
Where virtue is, these are more virtuous.
Nor from mine own weak merits will I draw
The smallest fear or doubt of her revolt,
For she had eyes, and chose me. No, Iago;
190 I'll see before I doubt; when I doubt, prove;
And on the proof there is no more but this:
Away at once with love or jealousy!
IAGO: I am glad of this; for now I shall have reason
To show the love and duty that I bear you
195 With franker spirit. Therefore, as I am bound,
Receive it from me. I speak not yet of proof.
Look to your wife; observe her well with Cassio;
Wear your eyes thus: not jealous nor secure.
I would not have your free and noble nature
200 Out of self-bounty° be abused. Look to't.
I know our country disposition well:
In Venice they do let heaven see the pranks
They dare not show their husbands; their best
conscience
Is not to leave't undone, but kept unknown.°

OTHELLO: Dost thou say so?   205
IAGO: She did deceive her father, marrying you;
And when she seemed to shake and fear your
looks,
She loved them most.
OTHELLO: And so she did.
IAGO: Why, go to then!
She that so young could give out such a seeming
To seel° her father's eyes up close as oak°—   210
He thought 'twas witchcraft. But I am much to
blame.
I humbly do beseech you of your pardon
For too much loving you.
OTHELLO: I am bound to thee forever.
IAGO: I see this hath a little dashed your spirits.
OTHELLO: Not a jot, not a jot.
IAGO: Trust me, I fear it has.   215
I hope you will consider what is spoke
Comes from my love. But I do see y' are moved.
I am to pray you not to strain° my speech
To grosser issues, nor to larger reach°
Than to suspicion.   220
OTHELLO: I will not.
IAGO: Should you do so, my lord,
My speech should fall into such vile success
Which my thoughts aimed not. Cassio's my worthy
friend—
My lord, I see y' are moved.
OTHELLO: No, not much moved.
I do not think but Desdemona's honest.   225
IAGO: Long live she so. And long live you to think so.
OTHELLO: And yet, how nature erring from itself—
IAGO: Ay, there's the point, as (to be bold with you)
Not to affect many proposèd matches
Of her own clime, complexion, and degree,°   230
Whereto we see in all things nature tends°—
Foh! one may smell in such a will most rank,
Foul disproportions, thoughts unnatural.
But, pardon me, I do not in position°
Distinctly° speak of her; though I may fear   235
Her will, recoiling to her better judgment,
May fall to match° you with her country forms,°
And happily° repent.
OTHELLO: Farewell, farewell!
If more thou dost perceive, let me know more.
Set on thy wife to observe. Leave me, Iago.   240
IAGO: My lord, I take my leave. [Going.]
OTHELLO: Why did I marry? This honest creature
doubtless

---

tells, counts. **fondly,** foolishly. **fineless,** infinite. **To follow still,** to change always (as the phases of the moon).
exsufflicate and blown, inflated and flyblown. **self-bounty,**
innate kindness (which attributes his own motives to others).
their . . . unknown, i.e., their morality does not forbid adultery, but it does forbid being found out.

seel, hoodwink. **oak,** (a close-grained wood). **strain,**
enlarge the meaning of. **reach,** meaning. **degree,** social station. **in . . . tends,** i.e., all things in nature seek out their own
kind. **position,** general argument. **Distinctly,** specifically.
fall to match, happen to compare. **country forms,** i.e., the
familiar appearances of her countrymen. **happily,** by chance.

Sees and knows more, much more, than he unfolds.
IAGO: [*Returns.*] My lord, I would I might entreat
    your honor
245 To scan this thing no farther. Leave it to time.
Although 'tis fit that Cassio have his place,
For sure he fills it up with great ability,
Yet, if you please to hold him off awhile,
You shall by that perceive him and his means.
250 Note if your lady strain his entertainment°
With any strong or vehement importunity;
Much will be seen in that. In the meantime
Let me be thought too busy in my fears
(As worthy cause I have to fear I am)
255 And hold her free, I do beseech your honor.
OTHELLO: Fear not my government.°
IAGO: I once more take my leave.

    (*Exit.*)

OTHELLO: This fellow's of exceeding honesty,
And knows all qualities,° with a learnèd spirit
Of human dealings. If I do prove her haggard,°
260 Though that her jesses° were my dear heartstrings,
I'd whistle her off and let her down the wind°
To prey at fortune. Haply for° I am black
And have not those soft parts° of conversation
That chamberers° have, or for I am declined
265 Into the vale of years—yet that's not much—
She's gone. I am abused, and my relief
Must be to loathe her. O curse of marriage,
That we can call these delicate creatures ours,
And not their appetites! I had rather be a toad
270 And live upon the vapor of a dungeon
Than keep a corner in the thing I love
For others' uses. Yet 'tis the plague to great ones;
Prerogatived are they less than the base.
'Tis destiny unshunnable, like death.
275 Even then this forkèd° plague is fated to us
When we do quicken.° Look where she comes.

    (*Enter* DESDEMONA *and* EMILIA.)

If she be false, heaven mocked itself!
I'll not believe 't.
DESDEMONA: How now, my dear Othello?
Your dinner, and the generous islanders
280 By you invited, do attend° your presence.

OTHELLO: I am to blame.
DESDEMONA: Why do you speak so faintly?
Are you not well?
OTHELLO: I have a pain upon my forehead, here.°
DESDEMONA: Why, that's with watching; 'twill away
    again.
Let me but bind it hard, within this hour   285
It will be well.
OTHELLO: Your napkin° is too little;

    [*He pushes the handkerchief away, and it falls.*]

Let it° alone. Come, I'll go in with you.
DESDEMONA: I am very sorry that you are not well.

    (*Exit* [*with* OTHELLO].)

EMILIA: I am glad I have found this napkin;
This was her first remembrance from the Moor.   290
My wayward husband hath a hundred times
Wooed me to steal it; but she so loves the token
(For he conjured her she should ever keep it)
That she reserves it evermore about her
To kiss and talk to. I'll have the work ta'en out°   295
And give 't Iago. What he will do with it,
Heaven knows, not I; I nothing° but to please his
    fantasy.°

    (*Enter* IAGO.)

IAGO: How now? What do you here alone?
EMILIA: Do not you chide; I have a thing for you.
IAGO: You have a thing for me? It is a common
    thing——   300
EMILIA: Ha?
IAGO: To have a foolish wife.
EMILIA: O, is that all? What will you give me now
For that same handkerchief?
IAGO: What handkerchief?
EMILIA: What handkerchief?   305
Why, that the Moor first gave to Desdemona,
That which so often you did bid me steal.
IAGO: Hast stol'n it from her?
EMILIA: No, but she let it drop by negligence,
And to th' advantage,° I, being here, took 't up.   310
Look, here 't is.
IAGO: A good wench. Give it me.
EMILIA: What will you do with 't, that you have been
    so earnest
To have me filch it?
IAGO: Why, what is that to you?

---

    strain his entertainment, urge strongly that he be reinstated. *government,* self-control. *qualities,* natures, types of people. *haggard,* a partly trained hawk that has gone wild again. *jesses,* straps that held the hawk's legs to the trainer's wrist. *I'd . . . wind,* I would release her (like an untamable hawk) and let her fly free. *Haply for,* it may be because. *soft parts,* gentle qualities and manners. *chamberers,* courtiers—or perhaps, accomplished seducers. *forkèd,* horned (the sign of the cuckold was horns). *do quicken,* are born. *attend,* wait.

---

    here, (he points to his imaginary horns). *napkin,* elaborately worked handkerchief. *it,* (it makes a considerable difference in the interpretation of later events whether this "it" refers to Othello's forehead or to the handkerchief; nothing in the text makes the reference clear). *work ta'en out,* needlework copied. *I nothing,* I wish nothing. *fantasy,* fancy, whim. *to th' advantage,* being lucky.

[Takes it.]

EMILIA: If it be not for some purpose of import,°
315　Give't me again. Poor lady, she'll run mad
　　When she shall lack° it.
IAGO:　　　　　　　　Be not acknown on't.°
　　I have use for it. Go, leave me. *(Exit* EMILIA.*)*
　　I will in Cassio's lodging lose this napkin
　　And let him find it. Trifles light as air
320　Are to the jealous confirmations strong
　　As proofs of Holy Writ. This may do something.
　　The Moor already changes with my poison:
　　Dangerous conceits are in their natures poisons,
　　Which at the first are scarce found to distaste,°
325　But, with a little,° act upon the blood,
　　Burn like the mines of sulfur. I did say so.

(Enter OTHELLO.*)*

　　Look where he comes! Not poppy nor
　　　mandragora,°
　　Nor all the drowsy syrups of the world,
　　Shall ever medicine thee to that sweet sleep
　　Which thou owedst° yesterday.
330 OTHELLO:　　　　　　Ha! ha! False to me?
IAGO: Why, how now, general? No more of that!
OTHELLO: Avaunt! be gone! Thou hast set me on the
　　　rack.
　　I swear 'tis better to be much abused
　　Than but to know't a little.
IAGO:　　　　　　　　How now, my lord?
OTHELLO: What sense had I of her stol'n hours of
335　lust?
　　I saw't not, thought it not, it harmed not me;
　　I slept the next night well, fed well, was free and
　　　merry;
　　I found not Cassio's kisses on her lips.
　　He that is robbed, not wanting° what is stol'n,
340　Let him not know't, and he's not robbed at all.
IAGO: I am sorry to hear this.
OTHELLO: I had been happy if the general camp,
　　Pioners° and all, had tasted her sweet body,
　　So I had nothing known. O now, forever
345　Farewell the tranquil mind! Farewell content!
　　Farewell the plumèd troop, and the big wars
　　That make ambition virtue! O, farewell!
　　Farewell the neighing steed and the shrill
　　　trump,
　　The spirit-stirring drum, th' ear-piercing fife,
350　The royal banner, and all quality,

　　Pride, pomp, and circumstance° of glorious war!
　　And O you mortal engines° whose rude throats
　　Th' immortal Jove's dread clamors° counterfeit,
　　Farewell! Othello's occupation's gone!
IAGO: Is't possible, my lord?　　　　　　　355
OTHELLO: Villain, be sure thou prove my love a
　　　whore!
　　Be sure of it; give me the ocular proof;
　　Or, by the worth of mine eternal soul,
　　Thou hadst been better have been born a dog
　　Than answer my waked wrath!
IAGO:　　　　　　　　Is't come to this?　360
OTHELLO: Make me to see't; or at least so prove it
　　That the probation° bear no hinge nor loop
　　To hang a doubt on—or woe upon thy life!
IAGO: My noble lord—
OTHELLO: If thou dost slander her and torture me,　365
　　Never pray more; abandon all remorse;
　　On horror's head horrors accumulate;
　　Do deeds to make heaven weep, all earth amazed;
　　For nothing canst thou to damnation add
　　Greater than that.
IAGO:　　　　O grace! O heaven forgive me!　370
　　Are you a man? Have you a soul or sense?
　　God b' wi' you! Take mine office. O wretched fool,
　　That lov'st to make thine honesty a vice!
　　O monstrous world! Take note, take note, O world,
　　To be direct and honest is not safe.　　　375
　　I thank you for this profit, and from hence
　　I'll love no friend, sith° love breeds such offense.
OTHELLO: Nay, stay. Thou shouldst be honest.
IAGO: I should be wise; for honesty's a fool
　　And loses that it works for.
OTHELLO:　　　　　　By the world,　380
　　I think my wife be honest, and think she is not;
　　I think that thou art just, and think thou art not.
　　I'll have some proof. My name, that was as fresh
　　As Dian's° visage, is now begrimed and black
　　As mine own face. If there be cords, or knives,　385
　　Poison, or fire, or suffocating streams,
　　I'll not endure it. Would I were satisfied!
IAGO: I see you are eaten up with passion.
　　I do repent me that I put it to you.
　　You would be satisfied?
OTHELLO:　　　　　Would? Nay, and I will.　390
IAGO: And may; but how? How satisfied, my lord?
　　Would you, the supervisor,° grossly gape on?
　　Behold her topped?
OTHELLO:　　　　Death and damnation! O!
IAGO: It were a tedious° difficulty, I think,

---

import, importance. **lack,** miss. **Be not acknown on't,** forget you ever saw it. **are scarce found to distaste,** scarcely can be tasted. **with a little,** in a short time. **poppy nor mandragora,** (soporifics). **owedst,** possessed. **wanting,** missing. **Pioners,** (the basest manual laborers in the army, who dug trenches and mines).

---

circumstance, pageantry. **mortal engines,** lethal weapons, i.e., cannon. **clamors,** i.e., thunder. **probation,** proof. **sith,** since. **Dian's,** Diana's (goddess of the moon and of chastity). **supervisor,** onlooker. **tedious,** hard to arrange.

To bring them to that prospect.° Damn them
395   then,
If ever mortal eyes do see them bolster°
More than their own! What then? How then?
What shall I say? Where's satisfaction?
It is impossible you should see this,
400 Were they as prime° as goats, as hot as monkeys,
As salt° as wolves in pride,° and fools as gross
As ignorance made drunk. But yet, I say,
If imputation and strong circumstances
Which lead directly to the door of truth
405 Will give you satisfaction, you may have't.
OTHELLO: Give me a living reason she's disloyal.
IAGO: I do not like the office.°
But sith I am entered in this cause so far,
Pricked° to't by foolish honesty and love,
410 I will go on. I lay with Cassio lately,
And being troubled with a raging tooth,
I could not sleep.
There are a kind of men so loose of soul
That in their sleeps will mutter their affairs.
415 One of this kind is Cassio.
In sleep, I heard him say, "Sweet Desdemona,
Let us be wary, let us hide our loves!"
And then, sir, would he gripe° and wring my
    hand,
Cry "O sweet creature!" Then kiss me hard,
420 As if he plucked up kisses by the roots
That grew upon my lips; laid his leg o'er my thigh,
And sighed, and kissed, and then cry, "Cursèd fate
That gave thee to the Moor!"
OTHELLO: O monstrous! monstrous!
IAGO: Nay, this was but his dream.
425 OTHELLO: But this denoted a foregone conclusion,°
'Tis a shrewd doubt,° though it be but a dream.
IAGO: And this may help to thicken other proofs
That do demonstrate° thinly.
OTHELLO: I'll tear her all to pieces!
IAGO: Nay, yet be wise. Yet we see nothing done;
430 She may be honest yet. Tell me but this:
Have you not sometimes seen a handkerchief
Spotted with strawberries in your wife's hand?
OTHELLO: I gave her such a one; 'twas my first gift.
IAGO: I know not that; but such a handkerchief—
435 I am sure it was your wife's—did I today
See Cassio wipe his beard with.
OTHELLO: If it be that——
IAGO: If it be that, or any that was hers,
It speaks against her with the other proofs.
OTHELLO: O, that the slave had forty thousand
    lives!

One is too poor, too weak for my revenge.   440
Now do I see 'tis true. Look here, Iago:
All my fond love thus do I blow to heaven.
'Tis gone.
Arise, black vengeance, from the hollow hell!
Yield up, O Love, thy crown and hearted° throne   445
To tyrannous hate! Swell, bosom, with thy fraught,°
For 'tis of aspics'° tongues!
IAGO: Yet be content.°
OTHELLO: O, blood, blood, blood!
IAGO: Patience, I say. Your mind may change.
OTHELLO: Never, Iago. Like to the Pontic Sea,°   450
Whose icy current and compulsive course
Nev'r keeps retiring ebb, but keeps due on
To the Propontic and the Hellespont,
Even so my bloody thoughts, with violent pace,
Shall nev'r look back, nev'r ebb to humble love,   455
Till that a capable and wide° revenge
Swallow them up. [He kneels.] Now, by yond marble
    heaven,
In the due reverence of a sacred vow
I here engage my words.
IAGO: Do not rise yet.

[IAGO kneels.]

Witness, you ever-burning lights above,   460
You elements that clip° us round about,
Witness that here Iago doth give up
The execution° of his wit, hands, heart
To wronged Othello's service! Let him command,
And to obey shall be in me remorse,°   465
What bloody business ever.° [They rise.]
OTHELLO: I greet thy love,
Not with vain thanks but with acceptance
    bounteous,°
And will upon the instant put thee to't.°
Within these three days let me hear thee say
That Cassio's not alive.   470
IAGO: My friend is dead. 'tis done at your request.
But let her live.
OTHELLO: Damn her, lewd minx! O, damn
    her! Damn her!
Come, go with me apart. I will withdraw
To furnish me with some swift means of death
For the fair devil. Now art thou my lieutenant.   475
IAGO: I am your own forever. (Exeunt.)

---

prospect, sight (where they can be seen). bolster, go to
bed. prime, salt, lustful. pride, heat. office, duty. Pricked,
spurred. gripe, seize. foregone conclusion, consummated fact.
shrewd doubt, penetrating guess. demonstrate, show, appear.

hearted, seated in the heart. fraught, burden. aspics',
asps'. content, patient, quiet. Pontic Sea, the Black Sea
(famous for the strong and constant current with which it
flows through the Bosporus into the Mediterranean, where
the water level is lower). capable and wide, sufficient and
far-reaching. clip, enfold. execution, workings, action. remorse, pity. ever, soever. bounteous, absolute. to't, i.e., to
the work you have said you are prepared to do.

ACT 3 / SCENE 4

[*A street*]
(*Enter* DESDEMONA, EMILIA, *and* CLOWN.)

DESDEMONA: Do you know, sirrah, where Lieutenant
Cassio lies?°

CLOWN: I dare not say he lies anywhere.

DESDEMONA: Why, man?

5   CLOWN: He's a soldier, and for me to say a soldier lies,
'tis stabbing.

DESDEMONA: Go to. Where lodges he?

CLOWN: To tell you where he lodges is to tell you
where I lie.

10 DESDEMONA: Can anything be made of this?

CLOWN: I know not where he lodges, and for me to
devise a lodging, and say he lies here or lies there,
were to lie in mine own throat.°

DESDEMONA: Can you enquire him out, and be edi-
15 fied° by report?

CLOWN: I will catechize the world for him; that is,
make questions, and by them answer.

DESDEMONA: Seek him, bid him come hither. Tell him
I have moved° my lord on his behalf and hope all
20 will be well.

CLOWN: To do this is within the compass° of man's
wit, and therefore I'll attempt the doing it. (*Exit*
CLOWN.)

DESDEMONA: Where should° I lose that handkerchief,
Emilia?

25 EMILIA: I know not, madam.

DESDEMONA: Believe me, I had rather have lost my
purse
Full of crusadoes.° And but my noble Moor
Is true of mind, and made of no such baseness
As jealous creatures are, it were enough
To put him to ill thinking.

30 EMILIA: Is he not jealous?

DESDEMONA: Who? He? I think the sun where he was
born
Drew all such humors° from him.

EMILIA: Look where he comes.

(*Enter* OTHELLO.)

DESDEMONA: I will not leave him now till Cassio
Be called to him. How is't with you, my lord?

OTHELLO: Well, my good lady. [*Aside*] O, hardness to
35 dissemble!°—

How do you, Desdemona?

DESDEMONA: Well, my good lord.

OTHELLO: Give me your hand. This hand is moist,°
my lady.

DESDEMONA: It hath felt no age nor known no
sorrow.

OTHELLO: This argues° fruitfulness and liberal°
heart.
Hot, hot, and moist. This hand of yours requires   40
A sequester° from liberty; fasting and prayer;
Much castigation; exercise devout;
For here's a young and sweating devil here
That commonly rebels. 'Tis a good hand,
A frank one.   45

DESDEMONA: You may, indeed, say so;
For 'twas that hand that gave away my heart.

OTHELLO: A liberal hand! The hearts of old gave
hands,
But our new heraldry° is hands, not hearts.

DESDEMONA: I cannot speak of this. Come now, your
promise!   50

OTHELLO: What promise, chuck?

DESDEMONA: I have sent to bid Cassio come speak
with you.

OTHELLO: I have a salt and sorry rheum° offends me.
Lend me thy handkerchief.

DESDEMONA: Here, my lord.

OTHELLO: That which I gave you.

DESDEMONA: I have it not about me.   55

OTHELLO: Not?

DESDEMONA: No, indeed, my lord.

OTHELLO: That's a fault.
That handkerchief
Did an Egyptian to my mother give.
She was a charmer,° and could almost read
The thoughts of people. She told her, while she
kept it,   60
'Twould make her amiable° and subdue my
father
Entirely to her love; but if she lost it
Or made a gift of it, my father's eye
Should hold her loathèd, and his spirits should
hunt
After new fancies. She, dying, gave it me,   65
And bid me, when my fate would have me wived,
To give it her. I did so; and take heed on't;
Make it a darling like your precious eye.

---

lies, lodges. **lie in mine own throat,** (to lie in the throat
is to lie absolutely and completely). **edified,** enlightened
(Desdemona mocks the Clown's overly elaborate diction).
moved, pleaded with. **compass,** reach. **should,** might. **crusadoes,** Portuguese gold coins. **humors,** characteristics. **hardness to dissemble,** (Othello may refer here either to the difficulty
he has in maintaining his appearance of composure, or to
what he believes to be Desdemona's hardened hypocrisy).

---

moist, (a moist, hot hand was taken as a sign of a lustful
nature). **argues,** suggests. **liberal,** free, open (but also with
a suggestion of "licentious"; from here on in this scene Othello's words bear a double meaning, seeming to be normal
but accusing Desdemona of being unfaithful). **sequester,**
separation. **heraldry,** heraldic symbolism. **a salt and sorry
rheum,** a heavy, running head cold. **charmer,** magician.
amiable, desirable.

To lose't or give't away were such perdition
As nothing else could match.

70 DESDEMONA: Is't possible?

OTHELLO: 'Tis true. There's magic in the web° of it.
A sibyl that had numbered in the world
The sun to course two hundred compasses,
In her prophetic fury° sewed the work;

75 The worms were hallowed that did breed the silk,
And it was dyed in mummy° which the skillful
Conserved of maidens' hearts.

DESDEMONA: Indeed? Is't true?

OTHELLO: Most veritable. Therefore look to't well.

DESDEMONA: Then would to God that I had never
seen't!

80 OTHELLO: Ha! Wherefore?

DESDEMONA: Why do you speak so startingly and
rash?

OTHELLO: Is't lost? Is't gone? Speak, is it out o' th'
way?

DESDEMONA: Heaven bless us!

OTHELLO: Say you?

85 DESDEMONA: It is not lost. But what an if it were?

OTHELLO: How?

DESDEMONA: I say it is not lost.

OTHELLO: Fetch't, let me see't!

DESDEMONA: Why, so I can; but I will not now.

90 This is a trick to put me from my suit:
Pray you let Cassio be received again.

OTHELLO: Fetch me the handkerchief! My mind
misgives.

DESDEMONA: Come, come!
You'll never meet a more sufficient° man——

OTHELLO: The handkerchief!

95 DESDEMONA: A man that all his time
Hath founded his good fortunes on your love,
Shared dangers with you——

OTHELLO: The handkerchief!

DESDEMONA: I' faith, you are to blame.

100 OTHELLO: Away! *(Exit OTHELLO.)*

EMILIA: Is not this man jealous?

DESDEMONA: I nev'r saw this before.
Sure there's some wonder in this handkerchief;
I am most unhappy in the loss of it.

105 EMILIA: 'Tis not a year or two shows us a man.
They are all but stomachs, and we all but food;
They eat us hungerly, and when they are full,
They belch us.

(Enter IAGO and CASSIO.)

           Look you, Cassio and my husband.

IAGO: There is no other way; 'tis she must do't.

110 And lo the happiness! Go and importune her.

DESDEMONA: How now, good Cassio? What's the news
with you?

CASSIO: Madam, my former suit. I do beseech you
That by your virtuous means I may again
Exist, and be a member of his love
Whom I with all the office° of my heart   115
Entirely honor. I would not be delayed.
If my offense be of such mortal kind
That nor my service past, nor present sorrows,
Nor purposed merit in futurity,
Can ransom me into his love again,   120
But to know so must be my benefit.°
So shall I clothe me in a forced content,
And shut myself up in some other course
To fortune's alms.

DESDEMONA: Alas, thrice-gentle Cassio,
My advocation° is not now in tune.   125
My lord is not my lord; nor should I know him
Were he in favor° as in humor altered.
So help me every spirit sanctified
As I have spoken for you all my best
And stood within the blank° of his displeasure   130
For my free speech. You must awhile be patient.
What I can do I will; and more I will
Than for myself I dare. Let that suffice you.

IAGO: Is my lord angry?

EMILIA: He went hence but now,
And certainly in strange unquietness.   135

IAGO: Can he be angry? I have seen the cannon
When it hath blown his ranks into the air
And, like the devil, from his very arm
Puffed his own brother. And is he angry?
Something of moment° then. I will go meet him.   140
There's matter in't indeed if he be angry.

DESDEMONA: I prithee do so. *(Exit [IAGO].)*
                Something sure of state,°
Either from Venice or some unhatched practice°
Made demonstrable here in Cyprus to him,
Hath puddled° his clear spirit; and in such cases   145
Men's natures wrangle with inferior things,
Though great ones are their object. 'Tis even so.
For let our finger ache, and it endues°
Our other, healthful members even to a sense
Of pain. Nay, we must think men are not gods,   150
Nor of them look for such observancy
As fits the bridal. Beshrew me much, Emilia,
I was, unhandsome warrior as I am,
Arraigning his unkindness with my soul;
But now I find I had suborned the witness,   155
And he's indicted falsely.

EMILIA: Pray heaven it be

---

web, weaving. **prophetic fury,** seized by the spirit and able to prophesy. **mummy,** liquid drained from embalmed bodies. **sufficient,** complete, with all proper qualities. **office,** duty. **benefit,** good. **advocation,** advocacy. **favor,** countenance. **blank,** bull's-eye of a target. **moment,** importance. **of state,** state affairs. **unhatched practice,** undisclosed plot. **puddled,** muddied. **endues,** leads.

State matters, as you think, and no conception
Nor no jealous toy° concerning you.

DESDEMONA: Alas the day! I never gave him cause.

160 EMILIA: But jealous souls will not be answered so;
They are not ever jealous for the cause,
But jealous for they're jealous. It is a monster
Begot upon itself, born on itself.

DESDEMONA: Heaven keep that monster from
Othello's mind!

165 EMILIA: Lady, amen.

DESDEMONA: I will go seek him. Cassio, walk here
about.
If I do find him fit,° I'll move your suit
And seek to effect it to my uttermost.

CASSIO: I humbly thank your ladyship.

(Exit [DESDEMONA with EMILIA].)
(Enter BIANCA.)

BIANCA: Save you, friend Cassio!

170 CASSIO: What make you from home?
How is't with you, my most fair Bianca?
I' faith, sweet love, I was coming to your house.

BIANCA: And I was going to your lodging, Cassio.
What, keep a week away? Seven days and nights?

175 Eightscore eight hours? And lovers' absent hours
More tedious than the dial eightscore times?
O weary reck'ning.°

CASSIO: Pardon me, Bianca.
I have this while with leaden thoughts been
pressed,
But I shall in a more continuate° time

180 Strike off this score° of absence. Sweet Bianca,

[Gives her DESDEMONA's handkerchief.]

Take me this work out.

BIANCA: O Cassio, whence came this?
This is some token from a newer friend.
To the felt absence now I feel a cause.
Is't come to this? Well, well.

CASSIO: Go to, woman!

185 Throw your vile guesses in the devil's teeth,
From whence you have them. You are jealous now
That this is from some mistress, some
remembrance.
No, by my faith, Bianca.

BIANCA: Why, whose is it?

CASSIO: I know not neither; I found it in my
chamber.

190 I like the work well; ere it be demanded,°
As like enough it will, I would have it copied.
Take it and do't, and leave me for this time.

BIANCA: Leave you? Wherefore?

CASSIO: I do attend here on the general
And think it no addition, nor my wish,   195
To have him see me womaned.

BIANCA: Why, I pray you?

CASSIO: Not that I love you not.

BIANCA: But that you do not love me!
I pray you bring° me on the way a little,
And say if I shall see you soon at night.

CASSIO: 'Tis but a little way that I can bring you,   200
For I attend here; but I'll see you soon.

BIANCA: 'Tis very good. I must be circumstanced.°

(Exeunt omnes.)

ACT 4 / SCENE 1

[A street]
(Enter OTHELLO and IAGO.)

IAGO: Will you think so?

OTHELLO: Think so, Iago?

IAGO: What,
To kiss in private?

OTHELLO: An unauthorized° kiss?

IAGO: Or to be naked with her friend in bed
An hour or more, not meaning any harm?

OTHELLO: Naked in bed, Iago, and not mean harm?   5
It is hypocrisy against the devil.
They that mean virtuously, and yet do so,
The devil their virtue tempts, and they tempt
heaven.

IAGO: If they do nothing, 'tis a venial slip.
But if I give my wife a handkerchief——   10

OTHELLO: What then?

IAGO: Why, then 'tis hers, my lord; and being hers,
She may, I think, bestow't on any man.

OTHELLO: She is protectress of her honor too.
May she give that?   15

IAGO: Her honor is an essence that's not seen;
They have it very oft that have it not.
But for the handkerchief——

OTHELLO: By heaven, I would most gladly have forgot
it!
Thou said'st—O, it comes o'er my memory   20
As doth the raven° o'er the infected house,
Boding to all—he had my handkerchief.

IAGO: Ay, what of that?

OTHELLO: That's not so good now.

IAGO: What if I had said I had seen him do you
wrong?
Or heard him say—as knaves be such abroad°   25
Who having, by their own importunate suit,

---

toy, trifle. *fit*, receptive. *reck'ning*, addition. **continu-
ate**, uninterrupted. ***Strike off this score***, i.e., pay this bill
(the *score* being the account of drinks kept in a tavern).
demanded, asked for (by the person who lost it).

bring, accompany. *circumstanced*, accept things as they
are. **unauthorized**, illicit. **raven**, (a harbinger of death).
abroad, i.e., in the world.

Or voluntary dotage° of some mistress,
Convincèd or supplied° them, cannot choose
But they must blab——

OTHELLO: Hath he said anything?

30 IAGO: He hath, my lord; but be you well assured,
No more than he'll unswear.

OTHELLO: What hath he said?

IAGO: Why, that he did—I know not what he did.

OTHELLO: What? what?

IAGO: Lie——

OTHELLO: With her?

35 IAGO: With her, on her; what you will.

OTHELLO: Lie with her? Lie on her?—We say lie on
her when they belie her.—Lie with her! Zounds,
that's fulsome.°—Handkerchief—confessions—
handkerchief!—To confess, and be hanged for his
40 labor—first to be hanged, and then to confess!
I tremble at it. Nature would not invest herself
in such shadowing passion without some instruction.° It is not words that shakes me thus.—Pish!
Noses, ears, and lips? Is't possible?—Confess?—
45 Handkerchief?—O devil! *(Falls in a trance.)*

IAGO: Work on,
My med'cine works! Thus credulous fools are
caught,
And many worthy and chaste dames even thus,
All guiltless, meet reproach.° What, ho! My lord!
My lord, I say! Othello!

(Enter CASSIO.*)*

50 How now, Cassio?

CASSIO: What's the matter?

IAGO: My lord is fall'n into an epilepsy.
This is his second fit; he had one yesterday.

CASSIO: Rub him about the temples.

55 IAGO: The lethargy° must have his quiet course.
If not, he foams at mouth, and by and by
Breaks out to savage madness. Look, he stirs.
Do you withdraw yourself a little while.
He will recover straight. When he is gone,
60 I would on great occasion° speak with you.

[*Exit* CASSIO.]

How is it, general? Have you not hurt your head?

OTHELLO: Dost thou mock° me?

IAGO: I mock you not, by heaven.

Would you would bear your fortune like a man.

OTHELLO: A hornèd man's a monster and a beast.

IAGO: There's many a beast then in a populous city,   65
And many a civil° monster.

OTHELLO: Did he confess it?

IAGO: Good, sir, be a man.
Think every bearded fellow that's but yoked
May draw° with you. There's millions now alive
That nightly lie in those unproper° beds   70
Which they dare swear peculiar.° Your case is
better.
O, 'tis the spite of hell, the fiend's arch-mock,
To lip a wanton in a secure couch,
And to suppose her chaste. No, let me know;
And knowing what I am, I know what she shall be.   75

OTHELLO: O, thou are wise! 'Tis certain.

IAGO: Stand you awhile apart;
Confine yourself but in a patient list.°
Whilst you were here, o'erwhelmèd with your
grief—
A passion most unsuiting such a man—
Cassio came hither. I shifted him away°   80
And laid good 'scuses upon your ecstasy;°
Bade him anon return, and here speak with me;
The which he promised. Do but encave° yourself
And mark the fleers,° the gibes, and notable°
scorns
That dwell in every region of his face.   85
For I will make him tell the tale anew:
Where, how, how oft, how long ago, and when
He hath, and is again to cope your wife.
I say, but mark his gesture. Marry patience,
Or I shall say you're all in all in spleen,°   90
And nothing of a man.

OTHELLO: Dost thou hear, Iago?
I will be found most cunning in my patience;
But—dost thou hear?—most bloody.

IAGO: That's not amiss;
But yet keep time in all. Will you withdraw?

[OTHELLO *moves to one side, where his remarks are not
audible to* CASSIO *and* IAGO.]

Now will I question Cassio of Bianca,   95
A huswife° that by selling her desires
Buys herself bread and cloth. It is a creature
That dotes on Cassio, as 'tis the strumpet's plague

---

voluntary dotage, weakness of the will. *Convincèd or supplied,* persuaded or gratified (the mistress). *fulsome,* foul,
repulsive. *Nature . . . instruction,* i.e., my mind would not
become so darkened (with anger) unless there were something in this (accusation); (it should be remembered that
Othello believes in the workings of magic and supernatural
forces). *reproach,* shame. *lethargy,* coma. *great occasion,*
very important matter. *mock,* (Othello takes Iago's comment as a reference to his horns—which it is).

---

civil, city-dwelling. *draw,* i.e., like the horned ox.
unproper, i.e., not exclusively the husband's. *peculiar,* their
own alone. *a patient list,* the bounds of patience. *shifted
him away,* got rid of him by a stratagem. *ecstasy,* trance (the
literal meaning, "outside one-self," bears on the meaning of
the change Othello is undergoing). *encave,* hide. *fleers,*
mocking looks or speeches. *notable,* obvious. *spleen,* passion, particularly anger. *huswife,* housewife (but with the
special meaning here of "prostitute").

To beguile many and be beguiled by one.
100   He, when he hears of her, cannot restrain
From the excess of laughter. Here he comes.

(Enter CASSIO.*)*

As he shall smile, Othello shall go mad;
And his unbookish° jealousy must conster°
Poor Cassio's smiles, gestures, and light behaviors
105   Quite in the wrong. How do you, lieutenant?
CASSIO: The worser that you give me the addition°
Whose want even kills me.
IAGO: Ply Desdemona well, and you are sure on't.
Now, if this suit lay in Bianca's power,
How quickly should you speed!
110   CASSIO: Alas, poor caitiff!°
OTHELLO: Look how he laughs already!
IAGO: I never knew woman love man so.
CASSIO: Alas, poor rogue! I think, i' faith, she loves
me.
OTHELLO: Now he denies it faintly, and laughs it out.
IAGO: Do you hear, Cassio?
115   OTHELLO: Now he importunes him
To tell it o'er. Go to! Well said, well said!
IAGO: She gives it out that you shall marry her.
Do you intend it?
CASSIO: Ha, ha, ha!
120   OTHELLO: Do ye triumph, Roman? Do you triumph?
CASSIO: I marry? What, a customer?° Prithee bear
some charity to my wit; do not think it so un-
wholesome. Ha, ha, ha!
OTHELLO: So, so, so, so. They laugh that win.
125   IAGO: Why, the cry goes that you marry her.
CASSIO: Prithee, say true.
IAGO: I am a very villain else.
OTHELLO: Have you scored° me? Well.
CASSIO: This is the monkey's own giving out. She is
130   persuaded I will marry her out of her own love
and flattery, not out of my promise.
OTHELLO: Iago beckons me; now he begins the story.

[OTHELLO *moves close enough to hear.*]

CASSIO: She was here even now; she haunts me in
every place. I was the other day talking on the sea
135   bank with certain Venetians, and thither comes
the bauble,° and falls me thus about my neck——
OTHELLO: Crying "O dear Cassio!" as it were. His gesture imports it.
CASSIO: So hangs, and lolls, and weeps upon me; so
140   shakes and pulls me! Ha, ha, ha!
OTHELLO: Now he tells how she plucked him to my
chamber. O, I see that nose of yours, but not that
dog I shall throw it to.

CASSIO: Well, I must leave her company.
IAGO: Before me!° Look where she comes.   145

(Enter BIANCA.*)*

CASSIO: 'Tis such another fitchew!° Marry a perfumed
one? What do you mean by this haunting of me?
BIANCA: Let the devil and his dam haunt you! What
did you mean by that same handkerchief you gave
me even now? I was a fine fool to take it. I must   150
take out the work? A likely piece of work that you
should find it in your chamber and know not who
left it there! This is some minx's token, and I must
take out the work? There! [*She throws down the
handkerchief.*] Give it your hobbyhorse.° Whereso-   155
ever you had it, I'll take out no work on't.
CASSIO: How now, my sweet Bianca? How now? how
now?
OTHELLO: By heaven, that should be my handkerchief!
BIANCA: If you'll come to supper tonight, you may; if   160
you will not, come when you are next prepared
for.° *(Exit.)*
IAGO: After her, after her!
CASSIO: Faith, I must; she'll rail in the streets else.
IAGO: Will you sup there?   165
CASSIO: Yes, I intend so.
IAGO: Well, I may chance to see you, for I would very
fain speak with you.
CASSIO: Prithee come. Will you?
IAGO: Go to, say no more. [*Exit* CASSIO.]   170
OTHELLO: [*Comes forward.*] How shall I murder him,
Iago?
IAGO: Did you perceive how he laughed at his vice?
OTHELLO: O Iago!
IAGO: And did you see the handkerchief?   175
OTHELLO: Was that mine?
IAGO: Yours, by this hand! And to see how he prizes
the foolish woman your wife! She gave it him, and
he hath giv'n it his whore.
OTHELLO: I would have him nine years a-killing!—A   180
fine woman, a fair woman, a sweet woman?
IAGO: Nay, you must forget that.
OTHELLO: Ay, let her rot, and perish, and be damned
tonight; for she shall not live. No, my heart is
turned to stone; I strike it, and it hurts my hand.   185
O, the world hath not a sweeter creature! She
might lie by an emperor's side and command him
tasks.
IAGO: Nay, that's not your way.°
OTHELLO: Hang her! I do but say what she is. So   190
delicate with her needle. An admirable musician.

---

unbookish, ignorant. **conster,** construe. **addition,** title.
caitiff, wretch. **customer,** one who sells, a merchant (here, a
prostitute). **scored,** marked, defaced. **bauble,** plaything.

Before me!, (an exclamation of surprise). **fitchew,** pole-
cat, i.e., strong-smelling creature. **hobbyhorse,** prostitute.
next prepared for, next expected—i.e., never. **way,** proper
course.

O, she will sing the savageness out of a bear! Of so
high and plenteous wit and invention°——
IAGO: She's the worse for all this.
195 OTHELLO: O, a thousand, a thousand times. And then,
of so gentle a condition?°
IAGO: Ay, too gentle.
OTHELLO: Nay, that's certain. But yet the pity of it,
Iago. O Iago, the pity of it, Iago.
200 IAGO: If you are so fond over her iniquity, give her
patent to offend; for if it touch° not you, it comes
near nobody.
OTHELLO: I will chop her into messes!° Cuckold me!
IAGO: O, 'tis foul in her.
205 OTHELLO: With mine officer!
IAGO: That's fouler.
OTHELLO: Get me some poison, Iago, this night. I'll
not expostulate with her, lest her body and beauty
unprovide my mind° again. This night, Iago!
210 IAGO: Do it not with poison. Strangle her in her bed,
even the bed she hath contaminated.
OTHELLO: Good, good! The justice of it pleases. Very
good!
IAGO: And for Cassio, let me be his undertaker.° You
215 shall hear more by midnight.
OTHELLO: Excellent good! [A trumpet.]
What trumpet is that same?
IAGO: I warrant something from Venice.

(Enter LODOVICO, DESDEMONA, and ATTENDANTS.)

'Tis Lodovico,
This comes from the Duke. See, your wife's with
him.
LODOVICO: God save you, worthy general.
OTHELLO: With° all my heart, sir.
LODOVICO: The Duke and the senators of Venice
220 greet you. [Gives him a letter.]
OTHELLO: I kiss the instrument of their pleasures.

[Opens the letter and reads.]

DESDEMONA: And what's the news, good cousin
Lodovico?
IAGO: I am very glad to see you, signior.
Welcome to Cyprus.
LODOVICO: I thank you. How does Lieutenant
Cassio?
225 IAGO: Lives, sir.
DESDEMONA: Cousin, there's fall'n between him and
my lord
An unkind° breach; but you shall make all well.
OTHELLO: Are you sure of that?

DESDEMONA: My lord?
OTHELLO: [Reads] "This fail you not to do, as you
will——"   230
LODOVICO: He did not call; he's busy in the paper.
Is there division 'twixt my lord and Cassio?
DESDEMONA: A most unhappy one. I would do much
T' atone° them, for the love I bear to Cassio.
OTHELLO: Fire and brimstone!
DESDEMONA: My lord?
OTHELLO: Are you wise?   235
DESDEMONA: What, is he angry?
LODOVICO: May be th' letter moved him;
For, as I think, they do command him home,
Deputing Cassio in his government.°
DESDEMONA: Trust me, I am glad on't.
OTHELLO: Indeed?
DESDEMONA: My lord?
OTHELLO: I am glad to see you mad.
DESDEMONA: Why, sweet Othello—   240
OTHELLO: Devil! [Strikes her.]
DESDEMONA: I have not deserved this.
LODOVICO: My lord, this would not be believed in
Venice,
Though I should swear I saw't. 'Tis very much.
Make her amends; she weeps.
OTHELLO: O devil, devil!   245
If that the earth could teem° with woman's tears,
Each drop she falls° would prove a crocodile.°
Out of my sight!
DESDEMONA: I will not stay to offend you. [Going.]
LODOVICO: Truly, an obedient lady.
I do beseech your lordship call her back.   250
OTHELLO: Mistress!
DESDEMONA: My lord?
OTHELLO: What would you with her, sir?
LODOVICO: Who? I, my lord?
OTHELLO: Ay! You did wish that I would make her
turn.
Sir, she can turn, and turn, and yet go on
And turn again; and she can weep, sir, weep;   255
And she's obedient; as you say, obedient.
Very obedient. Proceed you in your tears.
Concerning this, sir—O well-painted passion!
I am commanded home.—Get you away;
I'll send for you anon.—Sir, I obey the mandate   260
And will return to Venice.—Hence, avaunt!

[Exit DESDEMONA.]

Cassio shall have my place. And, sir, tonight
I do entreat that we may sup together.
You are welcome, sir, to Cyprus.—Goats and
monkeys! (Exit.)

---

invention, imagination. gentle a condition, (1) well born
(2) of a gentle nature. touch, affects. messes, bits. unprovide my mind, undo my resolution. undertaker, not "burier"
but "one who undertakes to do something." With, i.e., I
greet you with. unkind, unnatural.

---

atone, reconcile. government, office. teem, conceive.
falls, drops. crocodile, (the crocodile was supposed to shed
false tears to lure its victims).

LODOVICO: Is this the noble Moor whom our full
265   Senate
        Call all in all sufficient? Is this the nature
        Whom passion could not shake? whose solid virtue
        The shot of accident nor dart of chance
        Could neither graze nor pierce?
IAGO: He is much changed.
270 LODOVICO: Are his wits safe? Is he not light of brain?
IAGO: He's that he is; I may not breathe my censure.
        What he might be (if, what he might, he is not)
        I would to heaven he were!
LODOVICO: What, strike his wife?
IAGO: Faith, that was not so well; yet would I knew
        That stroke would prove the worst.
275 LODOVICO: Is it his use?°
        Or did the letter work upon his blood°
        And new-create his fault?
IAGO: Alas, alas!
        It is not honesty in me to speak
        What I have seen and known. You shall observe
           him,
280   And his own courses° will denote him so
        That I may save my speech. Do but go after
        And mark how he continues.
LODOVICO: I am sorry that I am deceived in him.

        (Exeunt.)

ACT 4 / SCENE 2

[The citadel]
(Enter OTHELLO and EMILIA.)

OTHELLO: You have seen nothing then?
EMILIA: Nor ever heard, nor ever did suspect.
OTHELLO: Yes, you have seen Cassio and she
           together.
EMILIA: But then I saw no harm, and then I heard
5   Each syllable that breath made up° between them.
OTHELLO: What, did they never whisper?
EMILIA: Never, my lord.
OTHELLO: Nor send you out o' th' way?
EMILIA: Never.
OTHELLO: To fetch her fan, her gloves, her mask, nor
           nothing?
10 EMILIA: Never, my lord.
OTHELLO: That's strange.
EMILIA: I durst, my lord, to wager she is honest,
        Lay down my soul at stake.° If you think other,
        Remove your thought. It doth abuse your bosom.
15   If any wretch have put this in your head,
        Let heaven requite it with the serpent's curse,°

For if she be not honest,° chaste, and true,
There's no man happy. The purest of their wives
Is foul as slander.
OTHELLO: Bid her come hither. Go.

(Exit EMILIA.)

She says enough; yet she's a simple bawd°   20
That cannot say as much. This is a subtle whore,
A closet lock and key of villainous secrets,
And yet she'll kneel and pray; I have seen her do't.

(Enter DESDEMONA and EMILIA.)

DESDEMONA: My lord, what is your will?
OTHELLO: Pray you, chuck, come hither.
DESDEMONA: What is your pleasure?
OTHELLO: Let me see your eyes.   25
        Look in my face.
DESDEMONA: What horrible fancy's this?
OTHELLO: [To EMILIA] Some of your function,°
        mistress:
        Leave procreants alone and shut the door;
        Cough or cry hem if anybody come.
        Your mystery,° your mystery! Nay, dispatch!   30

(Exit EMILIA.)

DESDEMONA: Upon my knee, what doth your speech
           import?
        I understand a fury in your words.°
OTHELLO: Why, what art thou?
DESDEMONA: Your wife, my lord; your true
        And loyal wife.
OTHELLO: Come, swear it, damn thyself;
        Lest, being like one of heaven, the devils
           themselves   35
        Should fear to seize thee. Therefore be double-
           damned:
        Swear thou art honest.
DESDEMONA: Heaven doth truly know it.
OTHELLO: Heaven truly knows that thou art false as
        hell.
DESDEMONA: To whom, my lord? With whom? How
        am I false?
OTHELLO: Ah, Desdemon! Away! Away! Away!   40
DESDEMONA: Alas the heavy day! Why do you weep?
        Am I the motive° of these tears, my lord?
        If haply° you my father do suspect
        An instrument of this your calling back,
        Lay not your blame on me. If you have lost him,   45
        I have lost him too.
OTHELLO: Had it pleased heaven
        To try me with affliction, had they rained

---

use, habit. *blood,* passion. *courses,* actions. ***that breath
made up,*** spoken. *at stake,* as the wager. ***serpent's curse,***
(God's curse on the serpent after the fall in Eden).

honest, chaste. *bawd,* procuress. ***Some of your function,***
do your proper work (as the operator of a brothel). ***mystery,***
trade. *words,* (Q1 adds to this line, "But not the words").
motive, cause. *haply,* by chance.

All kinds of sores and shames on my bare head,
Steeped° me in poverty to the very lips,
50 Given to captivity me and my utmost hopes,
I should have found in some place of my soul
A drop of patience. But, alas, to make me
A fixèd figure for the time of scorn°
To point his slow and moving finger at.
55 Yet could I bear that too, well, very well.
But there where I have garnered up my heart,
Where either I must live or bear no life,
The fountain from the which my current runs
Or else dries up—to be discarded thence,
60 Or keep it as a cistern for foul toads
To knot and gender° in—turn thy complexion
    there,
Patience, thou young and rose-lipped cherubin!
I here look grim as hell!°
DESDEMONA: I hope my noble lord esteems me
    honest.
OTHELLO: O, ay, as summer flies are in the
65   shambles,°
That quicken even with blowing.° O thou weed,
Who art so lovely fair, and smell'st so sweet,
That the sense aches at thee, would thou hadst
    never been born!
DESDEMONA: Alas, what ignorant° sin have I
    committed?
70 OTHELLO: Was this fair paper, this most goodly book,
Made to write "whore" upon? What committed?
Committed? O thou public commoner,°
I should make very forges of my cheeks
That would to cinders burn up modesty,
75 Did I but speak thy deeds. What committed?
Heaven stops the nose at it, and the moon winks;°
The bawdy wind that kisses all it meets
Is hushed within the hollow mine of earth
And will not hear 't. What committed?
80 DESDEMONA: By heaven, you do me wrong!
OTHELLO: Are not you a strumpet?
DESDEMONA: No, as I am a Christian!
If to preserve this vessel for my lord
From any other foul unlawful touch
Be not to be a strumpet, I am none.
OTHELLO: What, not a whore?
85 DESDEMONA: No, as I shall be saved!
OTHELLO: Is't possible?

Steeped, submerged. *The . . . scorn,* the very image of scorn in our time. *knot and gender,* twist in bunches and procreate. *turn . . . hell,* (the rough sense would seem to be, "even Patience would grow pale, turn complexion, at Desdemona's perfidy, but that Othello looks grimly on"). *shambles,* abattoirs. *quicken even with blowing,* become impregnated as soon as they lay their eggs. *ignorant,* unknowing. *commoner,* prostitute. *winks,* closes its eyes (the moon was the symbol of chastity).

DESDEMONA: O, heaven forgive us!
OTHELLO: I cry you mercy° then.
I took you for that cunning whore of Venice
That married with Othello. [*Calling*] You, mistress,

(Enter EMILIA.)

That have the office opposite to Saint Peter   90
And keep the gate of hell! You, you, ay, you!
We have done our course; there's money for your
    pains. [*Throws her some coins.*]
I pray you turn the key and keep your counsel.

(Exit.)

EMILIA: Alas, what does this gentleman conceive?
How do you, madam? How do you, my good lady?   95
DESDEMONA: Faith, half asleep.
EMILIA: Good madam, what's the matter with my
    lord?
DESDEMONA: With who?
EMILIA: Why, with my lord, madam.
DESDEMONA: Who is thy lord?
EMILIA: He that is yours, sweet lady.   100
DESDEMONA: I have none. Do not talk to me, Emilia.
I cannot weep, nor answers have I none
But what should go by water.° Prithee tonight
Lay on my bed my wedding sheets, remember;
And call thy husband hither.
EMILIA: Here's a change indeed!   105

(Exit.)

DESDEMONA: 'Tis meet I should be used so, very
    meet.
How have I been behaved, that he might stick
The small'st opinion on my least misuse?°

(Enter IAGO and EMILIA.)

IAGO: What is your pleasure, madam? How is't with
    you?
DESDEMONA: I cannot tell. Those that do teach
    young babes   110
Do it with gentle means and easy tasks.
He might have chid me so; for, in good faith,
I am a child to chiding.
IAGO: What is the matter, lady?
EMILIA: Alas, Iago, my lord hath so bewhored her,
Thrown such despite° and heavy terms upon her   115
That true hearts cannot bear it.
DESDEMONA: Am I that name, Iago?
IAGO: What name, fair lady?
DESDEMONA: Such as she said my lord did say I was.
EMILIA: He called her whore. A beggar in his drink
Could not have laid such terms upon his callet.°   120

---

cry you mercy, ask your pardon. *water,* tears. *stick . . .
misuse,* base any doubt on my smallest fault. *despite,* abuse.
callet, slut.

IAGO: Why did he so?

DESDEMONA: I do not know; I am sure I am none such.

IAGO: Do not weep, do not weep. Alas the day.

EMILIA: Hath she forsook so many noble matches,
125   Her father and her country, and her friends,
     To be called whore? Would it not make one weep?

DESDEMONA: It is my wretched fortune.

IAGO: Beshrew° him for 't!
     How comes this trick upon him?

DESDEMONA: Nay, heaven doth know.

EMILIA: I will be hanged if some eternal villain,
130   Some busy and insinuating rogue,
     Some cogging,° cozening slave, to get some office,
     Have not devised this slander. I will be hanged else.

IAGO: Fie, there is no such man! It is impossible.

DESDEMONA: If any such there be, heaven pardon him.

EMILIA: A halter pardon him! And hell gnaw his
135   bones!
     Why should he call her whore? Who keeps her company?
     What place? What time? What form? What likelihood?
     The Moor's abused by some most villainous knave,
     Some base notorious knave, some scurvy fellow.
     O heavens, that such companions° thou'dst
140   unfold,°
     And put in every honest hand a whip
     To lash the rascals naked through the world
     Even from the east to th' west!

IAGO: Speak within door.°

EMILIA: O, fie upon them! Some such squire° he was
145   That turned your wit the seamy side without
     And made you to suspect me with the Moor.

IAGO: You are a fool. Go to.

DESDEMONA: Alas, Iago,
     What shall I do to win my lord again?
     Good friend, go to him, for, by this light of heaven,
150   I know not how I lost him. Here I kneel:
     If e'er my will did trespass 'gainst his love
     Either in discourse of thought° or actual deed,
     Or that mine eyes, mine ears, or any sense
     Delighted them in any other form;
155   Or that I do not yet, and ever did,
     And ever will (though he do shake me off
     To beggarly divorcement) love him dearly,
     Comfort forswear me. Unkindness may do much,
     And his unkindness may defeat° my life,
160   But never taint my love. I cannot say "whore."
     It does abhor me now I speak the word;

To do the act that might the addition earn
Not the world's mass of vanity could make me.

IAGO: I pray you be content. 'Tis but his humor.°
     The business of the state does him offense.   165

DESDEMONA: If 'twere no other.

IAGO: It is but so, I warrant.

[*Trumpets within.*]

Hark how these instruments summon to supper.
The messengers of Venice stay the meat.°
Go in, and weep not. All things shall be well.

[*Exeunt* DESDEMONA *and* EMILIA.]
(*Enter* RODERIGO.)

How now, Roderigo?   170

RODERIGO: I do not find that thou deal'st justly with me.

IAGO: What in the contrary?

RODERIGO: Every day thou daff'st° me with some de-   175
     vice,° Iago, and rather, as it seems to me now, keep-
     'st from me all conveniency° than suppliest me
     with the least advantage of hope. I will indeed no
     longer endure it; nor am I yet persuaded to put
     up° in peace what already I have foolishly suffered.

IAGO: Will you hear me, Roderigo?   180

RODERIGO: I have heard too much, and your words
     and performance are no kin together.

IAGO: You charge me most unjustly.

RODERIGO: With naught but truth. I have wasted
     myself out of my means. The jewels you have had   185
     from me to deliver Desdemona would half have
     corrupted a votarist.° You have told me she hath
     received them, and returned me expectations and
     comforts of sudden respect° and acquaintance;
     but I find none.   190

IAGO: Well, go to; very well.

RODERIGO: Very well? Go to? I cannot go to, man; nor
     'tis not very well. Nay, I think it is scurvy, and
     begin to find myself fopped° in it.

IAGO: Very well.   195

RODERIGO: I tell you 'tis not very well. I will make
     myself known to Desdemona. If she will return
     me my jewels, I will give over my suit and repent
     my unlawful solicitation. If not, assure yourself I
     will seek satisfaction of you.   200

IAGO: You have said now?

RODERIGO: Ay, and said nothing but what I protest°
     intendment of doing.

IAGO: Why, now I see there's mettle° in thee, and even
     from this instant do build on thee a better opinion   205
     than ever before. Give me thy hand, Roderigo.

Beshrew, curse. *cogging,* cheating. *companions,* fellows,
rogues. *unfold,* disclose. *within door,* more quietly and moderately. *squire,* (a term of contempt). *discourse of thought,*
thinking. *defeat,* destroy.

humor, mood. *stay the meat,* await the meal. *daff'st,*
put off. *device,* scheme. *conveniency,* what is needful. *put
up,* accept. *votarist,* nun. *sudden respect,* immediate consideration. *fopped,* duped. *protest,* aver. *mettle,* spirit.

Thou hast taken against me a most just exception;° but yet I protest I have dealt most directly°
in thy affair.

210 RODERIGO: It hath not appeared.

IAGO: I grant indeed it hath not appeared, and your
suspicion is not without wit and judgment. But,
Roderigo, if thou hast that in thee indeed which
I have greater reason to believe now than ever—
215 I mean purpose, courage, and valor—this night
show it. If thou the next night following enjoy not
Desdemona, take me from this world with treachery and devise engines for° my life.

RODERIGO: Well, what is it? Is it within reason and
220 compass?°

IAGO: Sir, there is especial commission come from
Venice to depute Cassio in Othello's place.

RODERIGO: Is that true? Why, then Othello and Desdemona return again to Venice.

225 IAGO: O, no; he goes into Mauritania and takes away
with him the fair Desdemona, unless his abode be
lingered here by some accident; wherein none
can be so determinate° as the removing of Cassio.

RODERIGO: How do you mean, removing him?

230 IAGO: Why, by making him uncapable of Othello's
place—knocking out his brains.

RODERIGO: And that you would have me to do?

IAGO: Ay, if you dare do yourself a profit and a right.
He sups tonight with a harlotry,° and thither will
235 I go to him. He knows not yet of his honorable
fortune. If you will watch his going thence, which
I will fashion to fall out° between twelve and
one, you may take him at your pleasure. I will be
near to second° your attempt, and he shall fall
240 between us. Come, stand not amazed at it, but go
along with me. I will show you such a necessity in
his death that you shall think yourself bound to
put it on him. It is now high supper time, and the
night grows to waste. About it.

245 RODERIGO: I will hear further reason for this.

IAGO: And you shall be satisfied. *(Exeunt.)*

ACT 4 / SCENE 3

[*The citadel*]

(*Enter* OTHELLO, LODOVICO, DESDEMONA, EMILIA, *and*
ATTENDANTS.)

LODOVICO: I do beseech you, sir, trouble yourself no
further.

OTHELLO: O, pardon me; 'twill do me good to walk.

LODOVICO: Madam, good night. I humbly thank your
ladyship.

---

exception, objection. *directly*, straightforwardly. *engines for*, schemes against. *compass*, possibility. *determinate*,
effective. *harlotry*, female. *fall out*, occur. *second*, support.

DESDEMONA: Your honor is most welcome.

OTHELLO: Will you walk, sir? O, Desdemona. 5

DESDEMONA: My lord?

OTHELLO: Get you to bed on th' instant; I will be returned forthwith. Dismiss your attendant there.
Look't be done.

DESDEMONA: I will, my lord. 10

(*Exit* [OTHELLO, *with* LODOVICO *and* ATTENDANTS].)

EMILIA: How goes it now? He looks gentler than he
did.

DESDEMONA: He says he will return incontinent,°
And hath commanded me to go to bed,
And bade me to dismiss you.

EMILIA: Dismiss me?

DESDEMONA: It was his bidding; therefore, good
Emilia, 15
Give me my nightly wearing, and adieu.
We must not now displease him.

EMILIA: I would you had never seen him!

DESDEMONA: So would not I. My love doth so
approve him
That even his stubbornness, his checks,° his
frowns— 20
Prithee unpin me—have grace and favor.

EMILIA: I have laid these sheets you bade me on the
bed.

DESDEMONA: All's one.° Good faith, how foolish are
our minds!
If I do die before, prithee shroud me
In one of these same sheets.

EMILIA: Come, come! You talk. 25

DESDEMONA: My mother had a maid called Barbary.
She was in love; and he she loved proved mad
And did forsake her. She had a song of "Willow";
An old thing 'twas, but it expressed her fortune,
And she died singing it. That song tonight 30
Will not go from my mind; I have much to do
But to go hang my head all at one side
And sing it like poor Barbary. Prithee dispatch.

EMILIA: Shall I go fetch your nightgown?

DESDEMONA: No, unpin me here. 35
This Lodovico is a proper man.

EMILIA: A very handsome man.

DESDEMONA: He speaks well.

EMILIA: I know a lady in Venice would have walked
barefoot to Palestine for a touch of his nether lip. 40

DESDEMONA: [*Sings*]

> "The poor soul sat sighing by a sycamore tree,
>   Sing all a green willow;
> Her hand on her bosom, her head on her knee,
>   Sing willow, willow, willow.

---

incontinent, at once. *checks*, rebukes. *All's one*, no
matter.

45 *The fresh streams ran by her and murmured her moans;*
   Sing willow, willow, willow;
   Her salt tears fell from her, and soft'ned the stones—
   Sing willow, willow, willow—"

   Lay by these. [*Gives* EMILIA *her clothes.*]
50   "Willow, Willow"——
   Prithee hie° thee; he'll come anon.°
   "Sing all a green willow must be my garland.
   Let nobody blame him; his scorn I approve"——
   Nay, that's not next. Hark! Who is't that knocks?
55 EMILIA: It is the wind.
   DESDEMONA: [*Sings*]

   "I called my love false love; but what said he then?
   Sing willow, willow, willow:
   If I court moe° women, you'll couch with moe men."

   So, get thee gone; good night. Mine eyes do itch.
   Doth that bode weeping?
60 EMILIA: 'Tis neither here nor there.
   DESDEMONA: I have heard it said so. O, these men,
      these men.
   Dost thou in conscience think, tell me, Emilia,
   That there be women do abuse their husbands
   In such gross kind?
   EMILIA: There be some such, no question.
   DESDEMONA: Wouldst thou do such a deed for all the
65   world?
   EMILIA: Why, would not you?
   DESDEMONA: No, by this heavenly light!
   EMILIA: Nor I neither by this heavenly light.
   I might do't as well i' th' dark.
   DESDEMONA: Wouldst thou do such a deed for all the
70   world?
   EMILIA: The world's a huge thing; it is a great price
      for a small vice.
   DESDEMONA: In troth, I think thou wouldst not.
   EMILIA: In troth, I think I should; and undo't when I
      had done it. Marry, I would not do such a thing
75   for a joint-ring,° nor for measures of lawn,° nor
      for gowns, petticoats, nor caps, nor any petty ex-
      hibition,° but for all the whole world? Why, who
      would not make her husband a cuckold to make
      him a monarch? I should venture purgatory for't.
80 DESDEMONA: Beshrew me if I would do such a wrong
      for the whole world.
   EMILIA: Why, the wrong is but a wrong i' th' world;
      and having the world for your labor, 'tis a wrong
      in your own world, and you might quickly make it
85   right.
   DESDEMONA: I do not think there is any such woman.

EMILIA: Yes, a dozen; and as many to th' vantage as
   would store° the world they played for.
But I do think it is their husbands' faults
If wives do fall. Say that they slack their duties   90
And pour our treasures into foreign° laps;
Or else break out in peevish jealousies,
Throwing restraint upon us; or say they strike us,
Or scant our former having in despite°—
Why, we have galls; and though we have some
   grace,   95
Yet have we some revenge. Let husbands know
Their wives have sense like them. They see, and
   smell,
And have their palates both for sweet and sour,
As husbands have. What is it that they do
When they change° us for others? Is it sport?   100
I think it is. And doth affection° breed it?
I think it doth. Is't frailty that thus errs?
It is so too. And have not we affections?
Desires for sport? and frailty? as men have?
Then let them use us well; else let them know,   105
The ills we do, their ills instruct us so.°
DESDEMONA: Good night, good night. Heaven me
   such uses° send,
Not to pick bad from bad, but by bad mend.
   (*Exeunt.*)

ACT 5 / SCENE 1

[*A street*]
(*Enter* IAGO *and* RODERIGO.)

IAGO: Here, stand behind this bulk;° straight will he
   come.
Wear thy good rapier bare, and put it home.
Quick, quick! Fear nothing; I'll be at thy elbow.
It makes us, or it mars us, think on that,
And fix most firm thy resolution.   5
RODERIGO: Be near at hand; I may miscarry in't.
IAGO: Here, at thy hand. Be bold, and take thy stand.

[*Moves to one side.*]

RODERIGO: I have no great devotion to the deed,
And yet he hath given me satisfying reasons.
'Tis but a man gone. Forth my sword! He dies!   10
IAGO: I have rubbed this young quat° almost to the
   sense,°
And he grows angry. Now, whether he kill Cassio,
Or Cassio him, or each do kill the other,

---

hie, hurry. *anon,* at once. *moe,* more. *joint-ring,* (a ring with two interlocking halves). *lawn,* fine linen. *exhibition,* payment.

to . . . store, in addition as would fill. *foreign,* alien, i.e., other than the wife. *scant . . . despite,* reduce, in spite, our household allowance (?). *change,* exchange. *affection,* strong feeling, desire. *instruct us so,* teach us to do likewise. *uses,* practices. *bulk,* projecting stall of a shop. *quat,* pimple. *to the sense,* raw.

Every way makes my gain. Live Roderigo,
15 He calls me to a restitution large
Of gold and jewels that I bobbed° from him
As gifts to Desdemona.
It must not be. If Cassio do remain,
He hath a daily beauty in his life
20 That makes me ugly; and besides, the Moor
May unfold me to him; there stand I in much peril.
No, he must die. But so, I hear him coming.

(Enter CASSIO.)

RODERIGO: I know his gait. 'Tis he. Villain, thou diest!

[Thrusts at CASSIO.]

CASSIO: That thrust had been mine enemy indeed
25 But that my coat° is better than thou know'st.
I will make proof of thine. [*Fights with RODERIGO.*]
RODERIGO: O, I am slain!°
CASSIO: I am maimed forever. Help, ho! Murder!
Murder!

(Enter OTHELLO [to one side].)

OTHELLO: The voice of Cassio. Iago keeps his word.
RODERIGO: O, villain that I am!
OTHELLO: It is even so.
30 CASSIO: O help, ho! Light! A surgeon!
OTHELLO: 'Tis he. O brave Iago, honest and just,
That hast such noble sense of thy friend's wrong!
Thou teachest me. Minion,° your dear lies dead,
And your unblest° fate hies.° Strumpet, I come.
Forth of my heart those charms, thine eyes, are
35 blotted.
Thy bed, lust-stained, shall with lust's blood be
spotted.

(Exit OTHELLO.)
(Enter LODOVICO and GRATIANO.)

CASSIO: What, ho? No watch? No passage?° Murder!
Murder!
GRATIANO: 'Tis some mischance. The voice is very
direful.
CASSIO: O, help!
40 LODOVICO: Hark!
RODERIGO: O wretched villain!
LODOVICO: Two or three groan. 'Tis heavy night.

These may be counterfeits. Let's think't unsafe
To come into the cry without more help.
RODERIGO: Nobody come? Then shall I bleed to
death.   45
LODOVICO: Hark!

(Enter IAGO [with a light].)

GRATIANO: Here's one comes in his shirt, with light
and weapons.
IAGO: Who's there? Whose noise is this that cries on
murder?
LODOVICO: We do not know.
IAGO: Did not you hear a cry?
CASSIO: Here, here! For heaven's sake, help
me!   50
IAGO: What's the matter?
GRATIANO: This is Othello's ancient, as I take it.
LODOVICO: The same indeed, a very valiant fellow.
IAGO: What are you here that cry so grievously?
CASSIO: Iago? O, I am spoiled, undone by villains!   55
Give me some help.
IAGO: O me, lieutenant! What villains have done
this?
CASSIO: I think that one of them is hereabout
And cannot make away.
IAGO: O treacherous villains!
[*To LODOVICO and GRATIANO*] What are you there?   60
Come in, and give some help.
RODERIGO: O, help me there!
CASSIO: That's one of them.
IAGO: O murd'rous slave! O
villain! [*Stabs RODERIGO.*]
RODERIGO: O damned Iago! O inhuman dog!
IAGO: Kill men i' th' dark?—Where be these bloody
thieves?—
How silent is this town!—Ho! Murder! Murder!—   65
What may you be? Are you of good or evil?
LODOVICO: As you shall prove us, praise us.
IAGO: Signior Lodovico?
LODOVICO: He, sir.
IAGO: I cry you mercy. Here's Cassio hurt by villains.   70
GRATIANO: Cassio?
IAGO: How is't, brother?
CASSIO: My leg is cut in two.
IAGO: Marry, heaven forbid!
Light, gentlemen. I'll bind it with my shirt.

(Enter BIANCA.)

BIANCA: What is the matter, ho? Who is't that cried?   75
IAGO: Who is't that cried?
BIANCA: O my dear Cassio! My sweet Cassio!
O Cassio, Cassio, Cassio!
IAGO: O notable strumpet!—Cassio, may you suspect
Who they should be that thus have mangled you?   80
CASSIO: No.
GRATIANO: I am sorry to find you thus. I have been to
seek you.

---

bobbed, swindled.   **coat,** i.e., a mail shirt or bulletproof
vest.   **slain,** (most editors add here a stage direction which
has Iago wounding Cassio in the leg from behind, but
remaining unseen. However, nothing in the text requires
this, and Cassio's wound can be given him in the fight with
Roderigo, for presumably when Cassio attacks Roderigo the
latter would not simply accept the thrust but would parry.
Since Iago enters again at line 46, he must exit at some point
after line 22).   **Minion,** hussy, i.e., Desdemona.   **unblest,** un-
sanctified.   **hies,** approaches swiftly.   **passage,** passersby.

IAGO: Lend me a garter. So. O for a chair
  To bear him easily hence.
85 BIANCA: Alas, he faints! O Cassio, Cassio, Cassio!
IAGO: Gentlemen all, I do suspect this trash
  To be a party in this injury.—
  Patience awhile, good Cassio.—Come, come.
  Lend me a light. Know we this face or no?
90   Alas, my friend and my dear countryman
  Roderigo? No.—Yes, sure.—Yes, 'tis Roderigo!
GRATIANO: What, of Venice?
IAGO: Even he, sir. Did you know him?
GRATIANO: Know him? Ay.
IAGO: Signior Gratiano? I cry your gentle pardon.
95   These bloody accidents must excuse my manners
  That so neglected you.
GRATIANO: I am glad to see you.
IAGO: How do you, Cassio?—O, a chair, a chair!
GRATIANO: Roderigo?
IAGO: He, he, 'tis he! [*A chair brought in.*] O, that's
  well said;° the chair.
100   Some good man bear him carefully from hence.
  I'll fetch the general's surgeon. [*To* BIANCA] For
    you, mistress,
  Save you your labor. [*To* CASSIO] He that lies slain
    here, Cassio,
  Was my dear friend. What malice was between you?
CASSIO: None in the world; nor do I know the man.
IAGO: What, look you pale?—O, bear him out o' th'
105   air. [CASSIO *is carried off.*]
  Stay you, good gentlemen.—Look you pale,
    mistress?
  Do you perceive the gastness° of her eye?
  Nay, if you stare, we shall hear more anon.
  Behold her well; I pray you look upon her.
110   Do you see, gentlemen? Nay, guiltiness will speak,
  Though tongues were out of use.°

[*Enter* EMILIA.]

EMILIA: Alas, what is the matter? What is the matter,
  husband?
IAGO: Cassio hath here been set on in the dark
115   By Roderigo and fellows that are scaped.
  He's almost slain, and Roderigo quite dead.
EMILIA: Alas, good gentleman! Alas, good Cassio!
IAGO: This is the fruits of whoring. Prithee, Emilia,
  Go know of Cassio where he supped tonight.
  [*To* BIANCA] What, do you shake at that?
BIANCA: He supped at my house; but I therefore
120   shake not.
IAGO: O, did he so? I charge° you go with me.
EMILIA: Oh fie upon thee, strumpet!
BIANCA: I am no strumpet, but of life as honest
  As you that thus abuse me.

EMILIA: As I? Fie upon thee!
IAGO: Kind gentlemen, let's go see poor Cassio
  dressed.°   125
  [*To* BIANCA] Come, mistress, you must tell's
    another tale.
  Emilia, run you to the citadel
  And tell my lord and lady what hath happed.

[*Exit* EMILIA.]

  Will you go on afore? (*Exeunt* [*all but* IAGO].)
               This is the night
  That either makes me or fordoes me quite.° [*Exit.*]   130

ACT 5 / SCENE 2

[DESDEMONA*'s chamber*]
(*Enter* OTHELLO [*with a light*]*; and* DESDEMONA *in
her bed.*)

OTHELLO: It is the cause, it is the cause, my soul.
  Let me not name it to you, you chaste stars.
  It is the cause. Yet I'll not shed her blood,
  Nor scar that whiter skin of hers than snow,
  And smooth as monumental alabaster.   5
  Yet she must die, else she'll betray more men.
  Put out the light, and then put out the light.
  If I quench thee, thou flaming minister,°
  I can again thy former light restore,
  Should I repent me; but once put out thy light,   10
  Thou cunning'st° pattern of excelling nature,
  I know not where is that Promethean heat°
  That can thy light relume.° When I have plucked
    the rose,
  I cannot give it vital° growth again;
  It needs must wither. I'll smell thee on the tree.   15

[*He kisses her.*]

  O balmy breath, that dost almost persuade
  Justice to break her sword. One more, one more!
  Be thus when thou art dead, and I will kill thee,
  And love thee after. One more, and that's the last!
  So sweet was ne'er so fatal. I must weep,   20
  But they are cruel tears. This sorrow's heavenly;
  It strikes where it doth love. She wakes.
DESDEMONA: Who's there? Othello?
OTHELLO: Ay, Desdemona.
DESDEMONA: Will you come to bed, my lord?
OTHELLO: Have you prayed tonight, Desdemon?
DESDEMONA: Ay, my lord.   25
OTHELLO: If you bethink yourself of any crime

---

well said, well done. **gastness,** terror. **tongues were out
of use,** men no longer spoke. **charge,** command.

dressed, bandaged. **fordoes me quite,** completely ruins
me. **minister,** worker, servant. **cunning'st,** most intricate
and skillfully wrought (by nature excelling itself).
Promethean heat, divine fire (Prometheus is the Titan who
stole fire from heaven and gave it to man). **relume,** relight.
vital, living.

Unreconciled as yet to heaven and grace,
Solicit for it straight.

DESDEMONA: Alack, my lord, what may you mean by
that?

30 OTHELLO: Well, do it, and be brief; I will walk by.°
I would not kill thy unpreparèd spirit.
No, heavens forfend! I would not kill thy soul.

DESDEMONA: Talk you of killing?

OTHELLO: Ay, I do.

DESDEMONA: Then heaven
Have mercy on me!

OTHELLO: Amen, with all my heart.

35 DESDEMONA: If you say so, I hope you will not kill me.

OTHELLO: Humh.

DESDEMONA: And yet I fear you; for you're fatal then
When your eyes roll so. Why I should fear I know
not,
Since guiltiness I know not; but yet I feel I fear.

OTHELLO: Think on thy sins.

40 DESDEMONA: They are loves I bear to you.

OTHELLO: Ay, and for that thou diest.

DESDEMONA: That death's unnatural that kills for
loving.
Alas, why gnaw you so your nether lip?
Some bloody passion shakes your very frame.

45 These are portents; but yet I hope, I hope,
They do not point on me.

OTHELLO: Peace and be still.

DESDEMONA: I will so. What's the matter?

OTHELLO: That handkerchief which I so loved and
gave thee,
Thou gav'st to Cassio.

DESDEMONA: No, by my life and soul!
Send for the man and ask him.

50 OTHELLO: Sweet soul, take heed,
Take heed of perjury; thou art on thy deathbed.

DESDEMONA: Ay, but not yet to die.

OTHELLO: Presently.°
Therefore confess thee freely of thy sin,
For to deny each article° with oath

55 Cannot remove nor choke the strong conception
That I do groan withal. Thou art to die.

DESDEMONA: Then Lord have mercy on me.

OTHELLO: I say, amen.

DESDEMONA: And have you mercy too. I never did
Offend you in my life; never loved Cassio

60 But with such general warranty° of heaven
As I might love. I never gave him token.

OTHELLO: By heaven, I saw my handkerchief in's
hand!
O perjured woman! thou dost stone° my heart,

And mak'st me call what I intend to do
A murder, which I thought a sacrifice.   65
I saw the handkerchief.

DESDEMONA: He found it then.
I never gave it him. Send for him hither.
Let him confess a truth.

OTHELLO: He hath confessed.

DESDEMONA: What, my lord?

OTHELLO: That he hath used thee.

DESDEMONA: How? Unlawfully?

OTHELLO: Ay.   70

DESDEMONA: He will not say so.

OTHELLO: No, his mouth is stopped.
Honest Iago hath ta'en order for't.°

DESDEMONA: O, my fear interprets. What, is he dead?

OTHELLO: Had all his hairs been lives, my great
revenge
Had stomach° for them all.   75

DESDEMONA: Alas, he is betrayed, and I undone!

OTHELLO: Out, strumpet! Weep'st thou for him to
my face?

DESDEMONA: O, banish me, my lord, but kill me not!

OTHELLO: Down, strumpet!

DESDEMONA: Kill me tomorrow; let me live tonight!   80

OTHELLO: Nay, if you strive——

DESDEMONA: But half an hour!

OTHELLO: Being done, there is no pause.

DESDEMONA: But while I say one prayer!

OTHELLO: It is too late.

(Smothers her.)
(EMILIA at the door.)

EMILIA: [*Calls within.*] My lord, my lord! What, ho,
my lord, my lord!

OTHELLO: What noise is this? Not dead? Not yet quite
dead?   85
I that am cruel am yet merciful;
I would not have thee linger in thy pain.
So, so.

EMILIA: [*Within*] What, ho! My lord, my lord!

OTHELLO: Who's there?

EMILIA: [*Within*] O, good my lord, I would speak a
word with you.

OTHELLO: Yes, 'tis Emilia.—By and by.—She's
dead.—   90
'Tis like she comes to speak of Cassio's death.
The noise was high.° Ha! No more moving?
Still as the grave.—Shall she come in? Were't
good?—
I think she stirs again. No.—What's best to do?
If she come in, she'll sure speak to my wife.   95
My wife! My wife! What wife? I have no wife.

---

by, nearby. *Presently,* immediately. *article,* item (of
the charge of adultery. Othello makes heavy use of legal
terms in this scene). *warranty,* allowance. *stone,* turn to
stone.

---

ta'en order for't, make sure of it. *stomach,* appetite.
high, loud (Q1 reads "here").

O, insupportable! O heavy hour!
Methinks it should be now a huge eclipse
Of sun and moon, and that th' affrighted globe
Should yawn° at alteration.
100 EMILIA: [*Within*] I do beseech you
That I may speak with you, O good my lord!
OTHELLO: I had forgot thee. O, come in, Emilia.
Soft, by and by.—Let me the curtains draw.—

[*Draws the bed hangings and then opens the door.*]

Where art thou?

(*Enter* EMILIA.)
                              What's the matter with thee now?
105 EMILIA: O my good lord, yonder's foul murder done!
OTHELLO: What? Now?
EMILIA: But now, my lord.
OTHELLO: It is the very error° of the moon.
She comes more nearer earth than she was wont
110 And makes men mad.
EMILIA: Cassio, my lord, hath killed a young
   Venetian
Called Roderigo.
OTHELLO: Roderigo killed?
And Cassio killed?
EMILIA: No, Cassio is not killed.
OTHELLO: Not Cassio killed? Then murder's out of
   tune,
115 And sweet revenge grows harsh.
DESDEMONA: O, falsely, falsely murdered!
EMILIA: O Lord! What cry is that?
OTHELLO: That? What?
EMILIA: Out and alas! that was my lady's voice.
Help! Help, ho! Help! O lady, speak again!
120 Sweet Desdemona! O sweet mistress, speak!
DESDEMONA: A guiltless death I die.
EMILIA: O, who hath done this deed?
DESDEMONA: Nobody—I myself. Farewell.
Commend me to my kind lord. O, farewell!

[*She dies.*]

OTHELLO: Why, how should she be murd'red?
125 EMILIA: Alas, who knows?
OTHELLO: You heard her say herself, it was not I.
EMILIA: She said so. I must needs report the truth.
OTHELLO: She's like a liar gone to burning hell!
'Twas I that killed her.
EMILIA: O, the more angel she,
130 And you the blacker devil!

Methinks . . . alteration, (the Elizabethans believed that great changes in human affairs were reflected by disorders in nature). **yawn,** gape open (as in an earthquake). **error,** wandering out of the regular course (disorders in the heavens were believed by some to cause disorders on earth, as well as vice versa).

OTHELLO: She turned to folly, and she was a whore.
EMILIA: Thou dost belie her, and thou art a devil.
OTHELLO: She was false as water.
EMILIA: Thou art rash as fire to say
That she was false. O, she was heavenly true!
OTHELLO: Cassio did top her. Ask thy husband else.   135
O, I were damned beneath all depth in hell
But that I did proceed upon just grounds
To this extremity. Thy husband knew it all.
EMILIA: My husband?
OTHELLO: Thy husband.
EMILIA: That she was false to wedlock?
OTHELLO: Ay, with Cassio. Had she been true,   140
If heaven would make me such another world
Of one entire and perfect chrysolite,°
I'd not have sold her for it.
EMILIA: My husband?
OTHELLO: Ay, 'twas he that told me on her first.
An honest man he is, and hates the slime   145
That sticks on filthy deeds.
EMILIA: My husband?
OTHELLO: What needs this iterance? Woman, I say
   thy husband.
EMILIA: O mistress, villainy hath made mocks with
   love!
My husband say she was false?
OTHELLO: He, woman.
I say, thy husband. Dost understand the word?   150
My friend, thy husband; honest, honest, Iago.
EMILIA: If he say so, may his pernicious soul
Rot half a grain a day! He lies to th' heart.
She was too fond of her most filthy bargain.
OTHELLO: Hah?   155
EMILIA: Do thy worst.
This deed of thine is no more worthy heaven
Than thou wast worthy her.
OTHELLO: Peace, you were best.°
EMILIA: Thou hast not half that pow'r to do me harm
As I have to be hurt. O gull! O dolt!   160
As ignorant as dirt! Thou hast done a deed—

[OTHELLO *moves to draw his sword.*]

I care not for thy sword; I'll make thee known,
Though I lost twenty lives. Help! Help! Ho! Help!
The Moor hath killed my mistress! Murder!
   murder!

(*Enter* MONTANO, GRATIANO, *and* IAGO [*and* OTH-
ERS].)

MONTANO: What is the matter? How now, general?   165
EMILIA: O, are you come, Iago? You have done well,
That men must lay their murders on your neck.
GRATIANO: What is the matter?

---

chrysolite, topaz. **Peace, you were best,** i.e., you had better be silent.

EMILIA: Disprove this villain, if thou be'st a man.
170 He says thou told'st him that his wife was false.
    I know thou didst not; thou'rt not such a villain.
    Speak, for my heart is full.
IAGO: I told him what I thought, and told no more
    Than what he found himself was apt and true.
175 EMILIA: But did you ever tell him she was false?
IAGO: I did.
EMILIA: You told a lie, an odious damnèd lie!
    Upon my soul, a lie! A wicked lie!
    She false with Cassio? Did you say with Cassio?
IAGO: With Cassio, mistress. Go to, charm° your
180   tongue.
EMILIA: I will not charm my tongue; I am bound to
    speak:
    My mistress here lies murdered in her bed.
ALL: O heavens forfend!
EMILIA: And your reports have set the murder on.
185 OTHELLO: Nay, stare not, masters. It is true indeed.
GRATIANO: 'Tis a strange truth.
MONTANO: O monstrous act!
EMILIA: Villainy, villainy, villainy!
    I think upon't—I think I smell't!—O villainy!
    I thought so then.—I'll kill myself for grief.—
190 O villainy, villainy!
IAGO: What, are you mad? I charge you get you
    home.
EMILIA: Good gentlemen, let me have leave to speak.
    'Tis proper I obey him, but not now.
    Perchance, Iago, I will ne'er go home.
OTHELLO: O! O! O! [*Falls on the bed.*]
195 EMILIA: Nay, lay thee down and roar,
    For thou hast killed the sweetest innocent
    That e'er did lift up eye.
OTHELLO: O, she was foul! [*Rises.*]
    I scarce did know you, uncle. There lies your niece,
    Whose breath, indeed, these hands have newly
    stopped.
200 I know this act shows horrible and grim.
GRATIANO: Poor Desdemon! I am glad thy father's
    dead.
    Thy match was mortal to him, and pure grief
    Shore his old thread in twain. Did he live now,
    This sight would make him do a desperate turn;
205 Yea, curse his better angel from his side,
    And fall to reprobation.°
OTHELLO: 'Tis pitiful; but yet Iago knows
    That she with Cassio hath the act of shame
    A thousand times committed. Cassio confessed it;
210 And she did gratify his amorous works
    With that recognizance and pledge of love,
    Which I first gave her. I saw it in his hand.
    It was a handkerchief, an antique token
    My father gave my mother.

EMILIA: O God! O heavenly God!   215
IAGO: Zounds, hold your peace!
EMILIA: 'Twill out, 'twill out! I peace?
    No, I will speak as liberal as the north.°
    Let heaven and men and devils, let them all,
    All, all, cry shame against me, yet I'll speak.
IAGO: Be wise, and get you home.
EMILIA: I will not.   220

[IAGO *draws and threatens* EMILIA.]

GRATIANO: Fie! Your sword upon a woman?
EMILIA: O thou dull Moor, that handkerchief thou
    speak'st of
    I found by fortune, and did give my husband;
    For often with a solemn earnestness—
    More than indeed belonged to such a trifle—   225
    He begged of me to steal 't.
IAGO: Villainous whore!
EMILIA: She give it Cassio? No, alas, I found it,
    And I did give 't my husband.
IAGO: Filth, thou liest!
EMILIA: By heaven, I do not, I do not, gentlemen.
    O murd'rous coxcomb! What should such a fool   230
    Do with so good a wife?
OTHELLO: Are there no stones° in heaven
    But what serves for the thunder? Precious villain!

[*The* MOOR *runs at* IAGO, *but is disarmed by* MONTANO.
IAGO *kills his wife.*]

GRATIANO: The woman falls. Sure he hath killed his
    wife.
EMILIA: Ay, ay. O, lay me by my mistress' side.

[*Exit* IAGO.]

GRATIANO: He's gone, but his wife's killed.   235
MONTANO: 'Tis a notorious° villain. Take you this
    weapon,
    Which I have here recovered from the Moor.
    Come, guard the door without. Let him not pass,
    But kill him rather. I'll after the same villain,
    For 'tis a damnèd slave.

(*Exit* [*with all but* OTHELLO *and* EMILIA].)

OTHELLO: I am not valiant neither;   240
    But every puny whipster° gets my sword.
    But why should honor outlive honesty?
    Let it go all.
EMILIA: What did thy song bode, lady?
    Hark, canst thou hear me? I will play the swan,
    And die in music. [*Sings*] "Willow, willow, willow."   245
    Moor, she was chaste. She loved thee, cruel Moor,
    So come my soul to bliss as I speak true.

---

    liberal as the north, freely (and bitingly) as the north
wind blows. ***stones,*** thunderbolts. ***notorious,*** out-and-out.
puny whipster, small top-whipping boy (?).

---

    charm, control.   ***reprobation,*** damnation.

So speaking as I think, alas, I die. [*She dies.*]

OTHELLO: I have another weapon in this chamber;
250   It was a sword of Spain, the ice-brook's temper.
       O, here it is.—Uncle, I must come forth.

GRATIANO: [*Within*] If thou attempt it, it will cost
       thee dear.
       Thou hast no weapon, and perforce must suffer.

OTHELLO: Look in upon me then and speak with me,
255   Or, naked as I am, I will assault thee.

       [*Enter* GRATIANO.]

GRATIANO: What is the matter?
OTHELLO: Behold, I have a weapon;
       A better never did itself sustain
       Upon a soldier's thigh. I have seen the day
       That with this little arm and this good sword
260   I have made my way through more impediments
       Than twenty times your stop. But O vain boast!
       Who can control his fate? 'Tis not so now.
       Be not afraid, though you do see me weaponed.
       Here is my journey's end, here is my butt,°
265   And very seamark of my utmost sail.°
       Do you go back dismayed? 'Tis a lost fear.
       Man but a rush° against Othello's breast,
       And he retires. Where should Othello go?
       Now, how dost thou look now? O ill-starred
       wench!
270   Pale as thy smock! When we shall meet at compt,°
       This look of thine will hurl my soul from heaven,
       And fiends will snatch at it. Cold, cold, my girl?
       Even like thy chastity.
       O cursèd, cursèd slave! Whip me, ye devils,
275   From the possession of° this heavenly sight!
       Blow me about in the winds! roast me in sulfur!
       Wash me in steep-down gulfs of liquid fire!
       O Desdemon! Dead Desdemon; dead. O! O!

       (*Enter* LODOVICO, CASSIO, MONTANO, *and* IAGO [*as
       prisoner,*] *with* OFFICERS.)

LODOVICO: Where is this rash and most unfortunate
       man?
280 OTHELLO: That's he that was Othello; Here I am.
LODOVICO: Where is that viper? Bring the villain
       forth.
OTHELLO: I look down towards his feet°—but that's a
       fable.
       If that thou be'st a devil, I cannot kill thee.

       [*Wounds* IAGO.]

LODOVICO: Wrench his sword from him.

       [OTHELLO *is disarmed.*]

---

butt, target, stopping place. *seamark of my utmost sail,*
marker of my farthest journey. *Man but a rush,* attack with
only a reed. *compt,* Judgment Day. *the possession of,* being
possessed by. *towards his feet,* i.e., for his cloven hoofs.

IAGO: I bleed, sir, but not killed.
OTHELLO: I am not sorry neither. I'd have thee live;   285
       For in my sense, 'tis happiness to die.
LODOVICO: O thou Othello that was once so good,
       Fall'n in the practice° of a cursèd slave,
       What shall be said to thee?
OTHELLO: Why, anything:
       An honorable murderer, if you will;   290
       For naught I did in hate, but all in honor.
LODOVICO: This wretch hath part confessed his
       villainy.
       Did you and he consent in Cassio's death?
OTHELLO: Ay.
CASSIO: Dear general, I never gave you cause.   295
OTHELLO: I do believe it, and I ask your pardon.
       Will you, I pray, demand that demi-devil
       Why he hath thus ensnared my soul and body?
IAGO: Demand me nothing. What you know, you
       know.
       From this time forth I never will speak word.   300
LODOVICO: What, not to pray?
GRATIANO: Torments will ope your lips.
OTHELLO: Well, thou dost best.
LODOVICO: Sir, you shall understand what hath
       befall'n,
       Which, as I think, you know not. Here is a letter
       Found in the pocket of the slain Roderigo;   305
       And here another. The one of them imports
       The death of Cassio to be undertook
       By Roderigo.
OTHELLO: O villain!
CASSIO: Most heathenish and most gross!
LODOVICO: Now here's another discontented paper   310
       Found in his pocket too; and this, it seems,
       Roderigo meant t' have sent this damnèd villain;
       But that, belike, Iago in the interim
       Came in and satisfied him.
OTHELLO: O thou pernicious caitiff!
       How came you, Cassio, by that handkerchief   315
       That was my wife's?
CASSIO: I found it in my chamber;
       And he himself confessed it but even now
       That there he dropped it for a special purpose
       Which wrought to his desire.
OTHELLO: O fool! Fool! Fool!
CASSIO: There is besides in Roderigo's letter,   320
       How he upbraids Iago that he made him
       Brave me upon the watch; whereon it came
       That I was cast; and even but now he spake,
       After long seeming dead—Iago hurt him,
       Iago set him on.   325
LODOVICO: You must forsake this room and go with
       us.

---

practice, plotting.

Your power and your command is taken off,
And Cassio rules in Cyprus. For this slave,
If there be any cunning cruelty
330   That can torment him much and hold him long,
It shall be his. You shall close prisoner rest
Till that the nature of your fault be known
To the Venetian state. Come, bring away.
OTHELLO: Soft you, a word or two before you go.
I have done the state some service, and they
335   know't.
No more of that. I pray you, in your letters,
When you shall these unlucky deeds relate,
Speak of me as I am. Nothing extenuate,
Nor set down aught in malice. Then must you
    speak
340   Of one that loved not wisely, but too well;
Of one not easily jealous, but, being wrought,
Perplexed in the extreme; of one whose hand,
Like the base Judean,° threw a pearl away
Richer than all his tribe; of one whose subdued
    eyes,
345   Albeit unusèd to the melting mood,
Drops tears as fast as the Arabian trees
Their med'cinable gum. Set you down this.
And say besides that in Aleppo once,

Judean, (most editors use the Q1 reading, "Indian,"
here, but F is clear; both readings point toward the infidel,
the unbeliever).

Where a malignant and a turbaned Turk
Beat a Venetian and traduced the state,   350
I took by th' throat the circumcisèd dog
And smote him—thus. [*He stabs himself.*]
LODOVICO: O bloody period!°
GRATIANO: All that is spoke is marred.
OTHELLO: I kissed thee ere I killed thee. No way but
    this,
Killing myself, to die upon a kiss.   355

[*He falls over* DESDEMONA *and dies.*]

CASSIO: This did I fear, but thought he had no
    weapon;
For he was great of heart.
LODOVICO: [*To* IAGO] O Spartan dog,
More fell° than anguish, hunger, or the sea!
Look on the tragic loading of this bed.
This is thy work. The object poisons sight;   360
Let it be hid. [*Bed curtains drawn.*]
              Gratiano, keep° the house,
And seize upon the fortunes of the Moor,
For they succeed on you. To you, lord governor,
Remains the censure of this hellish villain,
The time, the place, the torture. O, enforce it!   365
Myself will straight aboard, and to the state
This heavy act with heavy heart relate. (*Exeunt.*)

FINIS

---

period, end.   **fell,** cruel.   **keep,** remain in.

Figure 1. In the 1964 National Theatre production of *Othello,* directed by John Dexter, Desdemona (Maggie Smith) appeals to Othello (Laurence Olivier) to reinstate Cassio; her intimate gesture and his amused look suggest their happiness. In the background, Emilia (Joyce Redman) looks on. (Photograph: Angus McBean, © Harvard Theatre Collection, The Houghton Library.)

Figure 2. In the 1964 National Theatre production, Othello (Laurence Olivier) listens to the insinuations of Iago (Frank Finlay); Othello's bare feet, anke and wrist bracelets, and black robe set him apart from the uniformed Iago. (Photograph: Angus McBean, © Harvard Theatre Collection, The Houghton Library.)

Figure 3. Emilia (Zoe Wanamaker) comforts a distraught Desdemona (Imogen Stubbs) after Othello has called Desdemona a whore. The 1989 Royal Shakespeare Company production was directed by Trevor Nunn. (Photograph: Joe Cocks Studio.)

Figure 4. Othello (Willard White, *seated*) looks up from his work in surprise as Iago (Ian McKellen) expresses his suspicions of Cassio. Trevor Nunn's 1989 Royal Shakespeare Company production was set in the nineteenth century, and both men wear uniforms, though Othello's shirt-sleeved appearance makes him seem much more relaxed and vulnerable than the buttoned-up Iago. (Photograph: Joe Cocks Studio.)

Staging of *Othello*

INTERVIEW WITH LAURENCE OLIVIER,
BY KENNETH TYNAN

When you came to play Othello yourself, did you feel physically equipped for it in every respect?

No, I didn't. That was another thing that had troubled me. I didn't think that I had the voice for it. But I did go through a long period of vocal training especially for it, to increase the depth of my voice, and I actually managed to attain about six more notes in the bass. I never used to be able to sing below D, but now, after a little exercising, I can get down to A, through all the semitones; and that helps at the beginning of the play, it helps the violet velvet that I felt was necessary in the timbre of the voice. And then, from the physical point of view, I went through, and I still do, a very severe physical training course.

What was there in your conception of the part that made it different from the conventional Othellos that we're used to seeing?

Well, you know that very rough estimate of the theme of Shakespearian tragedy. It's constantly said that Shakespearian tragedy is founded by Shakespeare upon the theme of a perfect statue of a man, a perfect statue; and he shows one fissure in the statue, and how that fissure makes the statue crumble and disappear into utter disorder. From that idea you get that Othello is perfect except that he's too easily jealous; that Macbeth is perfect except that he's too ambitious; that Lear is perfect except that he's too bloody-minded, too pigheaded; that Coriolanus is too proud; that Hamlet lacks resolution; and so on. But there seems to me, and there has grown in me a conviction over the last few years, that in most of the characters, not all, but in most of them, that weakness is accompanied by the weakness of self-deception, as a companion fault to whatever fault may be specified by the character in the play. It's quite easy to find in Othello, and once you've found it I think you have to go along with it; that he sees himself as this noble creature. It's so easy in the senate scene for you to present the absolutely cold-blooded man who doesn't even worry about marital relations with his wife on his honeymoon night, to reassure the senate that he's utterly perfect, pure beyond any reproach as to his character, and you can find that, and trace it, constantly throughout. He's constantly wishing to present himself in a certain light, even at the end, which is remarkable. I believe, and I've tried to show, that when he says "Not easily jealous" it's the most appalling bit of self-deception. He's the most easily jealous man that anybody's ever written about. The minute he suspects, or thinks he has the smallest grounds for suspecting, Desdemona, he wishes to think her guilty, he wishes to. And the very first thing he does, almost on top of that, is to give way to the passion, perhaps the worst temptation in the world, which is murder. He immediately wants to murder her, immediately. Therefore he's an extremely hot-blooded individual, an extremely savage creature who has kidded himself and managed to kid everybody else, all this time, that he's nothing of the kind. And if you've got that, I think you've really got the basis of the character. Lodovico says it for us: "Is this the noble Moor . . . whom passion could not shake. . . . I am sorry that I am deceived in him."

REHEARSING *OTHELLO*, BY KENNETH TYNAN

ACT 1 / SCENE 3

The Senate scene: a midnight meeting, convened in panic at the impending Turkish threat. Dexter tells the senators to chatter among themselves about what really concerns them—namely, the effect on their own pockets if the Turks seize a trading centre as important as Cyprus: "Look at the economics of the scene.

From Kenneth Tynan, *Othello: The National Theatre Production*, London, 1966.

It's not about religion, it's not about politics, it's about money."

Othello, a fully "assimilated" Moor, wears a crucifix round his neck and crosses himself when Brabantio accuses him of having won Desdemona's love with witchcraft. For the great account of the wooing, he is still and central. "Her father—loved me" is directed straight at Brabantio, in tones of wondering rebuke. There is lofty pride in the re-telling of his magical adventures; and when he reaches the line about "the Cannibals, that each other eat, / The Anthropophagi," he utters the Greek word by way of kindly parenthetical explanation, as if to say: "That, in case you didn't know, is the scholarly term for these creatures." He also manages to convey his sardonic awareness that this is just the kind of story that Europeans would expect Africans to tell. (All this in a single phrase? Yes, such is the power of inflexion when practised by a master.) "She wisht she had not heard it: yet she wisht / That heaven had made her such a man" modulates from gentle, amused reminiscence to proud, erotic self-congratulation. "Upon this hint I spake" is preceded by a smiling shrug, the actor dwelling on "hint" as a jocular understatement, and forcing the senators to share his pleasure. On "This only is the witchcraft I have used," Olivier isolates the word "witchcraft" so that you can almost hear the inverted commas, deliberately making the second vowel harsh and African, and pointedly eyeing Brabantio as he delivers it. Throughout the speech, he is at once the Duke's servant and the white man's master. Every time we rehearse it, the room is pin-still. For some of us, this is the high point of the performance.

ACT 3 / SCENE 3

The great jealousy scene, the fulcrum that thrusts the energy of the play towards tragedy. To Desdemona's pleas for the reinstatement of Cassio, Othello reacts with paternal chuckles, a man besotted by the toy white trophy he has conquered. For the duologue with Iago, Dexter deliberately makes things technically hard for both actors. Othello usually sits at a desk, riffling through military documents while Iago begins his needling; Dexter forbids the desk, thereby compelling the actors to make the scene work without recourse to props. He is swiftly proved right. With no official tasks to perform, Othello ceases to be a sitting target, and Iago must struggle to hold his attention: both actors must find reasons deeper than accidents of duty to keep them together long enough for the deadly duologue to be irrevocably launched. Stroke of genius by Olivier: no sooner has Iago mentioned Cassio than *he* takes the initiative. Iago seems to be hiding

something, so Othello determines to quiz him, in order to get a full report on Cassio's character; after all, Desdemona wants the lieutenant reinstated, and the general owes it to his wife to find out all the facts. "What dost thou *think*?," he asks with avuncular persistence, like a headmaster ordering one prefect to tell tales on another. On "By heaven, he echoes me," he is mock-severe, rebuking Iago for talking in riddles. His whole attitude is one of supreme self-confidence. (Query: will the public and critics realise that this is an egocentric Othello, not an egocentric performance?) What he expects is that Iago will disclose a story about a mess bill that Cassio left unpaid, or some similar peccadillo. At this point Othello is cat to Iago's mouse; or, to put it the other way round, Iago is a reluctant matador in danger of being dominated by his bull.

As Othello's interrogation progresses, Iago retreats and hedges, refusing to reveal his thoughts. A showdown is the last thing he wants to precipitate; he is unprepared for anything so drastic. Driven into a corner, he suddenly says: "O, beware, my lord, of jealousy." This is pure improvisation, a shot in the dark. The notion has never before crossed Othello's mind: he thought they were discussing matters of military discipline, and his immediate response is angry incomprehension. When Iago continues: "But, O, what damned minutes tells he o'er / Who dotes, yet doubts, suspects, yet strongly loves!"—he replies "O misery!" with a bewildered emphasis that implies: "Yes, it must be miserable to feel like that, but what has it to do with me?"

Next development: Othello explodes in outrage, and Iago is almost frightened by the ferocity he has inadvertently unleashed. But having gone so far, he must now go further, stressing that a girl unnatural enough to deceive her father and marry a black is capable of anything. Such is Olivier's shame that he cannot face Iago while delivering the treacherous order: "Set on thy wife to observe." Once Iago has departed, his ego reasserts itself: "Why did I marry?" is uttered with the first person singular heavily italicised, as if to say: "I—of all people."

REVIEW OF THE NATIONAL THEATRE PRODUCTION, 1964, BY RONALD BRYDEN

All posterity will want to know is how he played. John Dexter's National Theatre *Othello* is efficient and clear, if slow, and contains some intelligent minor novelties. But in the long run all that matters is that it left the stage as bare as possible for its athlete. What

requires record is how he, tackling Burbage's role for the first time at 57, created the Moor.

He came on smelling a rose, laughing softly with a private delight; barefooted, ankleted, black. He had chosen to play a Negro. The story fits a true Moor better: one of those striding hawks, fierce in a narrow range of medieval passions, whose women still veil themselves like Henry Moore sleepers against the blowing sands of Nouakchott's surrealistically modern streets. But Shakespeare muddled, giving him the excuse to turn himself into a coastal African from below the Senegal: dark, thick-lipped, open, laughing.

He sauntered downstage, with a loose, bare-heeled roll of the buttocks; came to rest feet splayed apart, hip lounging outward. For him, the great Richard III of his day, the part was too simple. He had made it difficult and interesting for himself by studying, as scrupulously as he studied the flat vowels, dead grin and hunched time-steps of Archie Rice, how an African looks, moves, sounds. The make-up, exact in pigment, covered his body almost wholly: an hour's job at least. The hands hung big and graceful. The whole voice was characterised, the o's and the a's deepened, the consonants thickened with faint, guttural deliberation. "Put up your bright swords, or de dew will rus' dem": not quite so crude, but in that direction.

It could have been caricature, an embarrassment. Instead, after the second performance, a well-known Negro actor rose in the stalls bravoing. For obviously it was done with love; with the main purpose of substituting for the dead grandeur of the Moorish empire one modern audiences could respond to: the grandeur of Africa. He was the continent, like a figure of Rubens allegory. In Cyprus, he strode ashore in a cloak and spiked helmet which brought to mind the medieval emirates of Ethiopia and Niger. Facing Doge and senators, he hooded his eyes in a pouting ebony mask: an old chief listening watchfully in tribal conclave. When he named them "my masters" it was proudly edged: he had been a slave, their inquisition recalled his slavery, he reminded them in turn of his service and generalship.

He described Desdemona's encouragement smiling down at them, easy with sexual confidence. This was the other key to the choice of a Negro: Finlay's Iago, bony, crop-haired, staring with the fanatic mule-grin of a Mississippi redneck, was to be goaded by a small white man's sexual jealousy of the black, a jealousy sliding into ambiguous fascination. Like Yeats's crowd staring, sweating, at Don Juan's mighty thigh, this Iago gazed, licking dry lips, on a black one. All he need do is teach his own disease.

Mannerisms established, they were lifted into the older, broader imagery of the part. Leading Desdemona to bed, he pretended to snap at her with playful

teeth. At Iago's first hints, he made a chuckling mock of twisting truth out of him by the ear. Then, during the temptation, he began to pace, turning his head sharply like a lion listening. The climax was his farewell to his occupation: bellowing the words as pure, wounded outcry, he hurled back his head until the ululating tongue showed pink against the roof of his mouth like a trumpeting elephant's. As he grew into a great beast, Finlay shrunk beside him, clinging to his shoulder like an ape, hugging his heels like a jackal.

He used every clue in the part, its most strenuous difficulties. Reassured by Desdemona's innocence, he bent to kiss her—and paused looking, sickened, at her lips. Long before his raging return, you knew he had found Cassio's kisses there. Faced with the lung-torturing hurdle of "Like to the Pontic sea," he found a brilliant device for breaking the period: at "Shall ne'er look back," he let the memories he was forswearing rush in and stop him, gasping with pain, until he caught breath. Then, at "By yond marble heaven," he tore the crucifix from his neck (Iago, you recall, says casually Othello'd renounce his baptism for Desdemona) and, crouching forehead to ground, made his "sacred vow" in the religion which caked Benin's altars with blood.

Possibly it was too early a climax, built to make a curtain of Iago's "I am your own for ever." In Act Four he could only repeat himself with increased volume, adding a humming animal moan as he fell into his fit, a strangler's look to the dangling hands, a sharper danger to the turns of his head as he questioned Emilia. But it gave him time to wind down to a superb returned dignity and tenderness for the murder. This became an act of love—at "I would not have thee linger in thy pain" he threw aside the pillow and, stopping her lips with a kiss, strangled her. The last speech was spoken kneeling on the bed, her body clutched upright to him as a shield for the dagger he turns on himself.

As he slumped beside her in the sheets, the current stopped. A couple of wigged actors stood awkwardly about. You could only pity them: we had seen history, and it was over. Perhaps it's as well to have seen the performance while still unripe, constructed in fragments, still knitting itself. Now you can see how it's done; later, it will be a torrent. But before it exhausts him, a film should be made. It couldn't save the whole truth, but it might save something the unborn should know.

INTERVIEW WITH IMOGEN STUBBS, MARSHA HUNT, AND ZOE WANAMAKER ON ACTING IN *OTHELLO,* 1989, BY GWYN MORGAN

'Tis not a year or two shows us a man:
They are all but stomachs, and we all but food;
They eat us hungerly, and when they are full,
They belch us.'

EMILIA'S view of relations between the sexes must be one of the most jaundiced in Shakespeare. In *Othello,* the theme of men's unkindness to women is given full tragic treatment and yet, at first glance, the three women in the play hardly seem to be worth the fuss. The clichéd image of Desdemona is reminiscent of Little Nell—a gentle, submissive victim in a white nightgown. Emilia is bracketed with Juliet's nurse as an unimaginative crude servant; and Bianca is just a local prostitute who is functional for the plot.

Trevor Nunn's massively successful production for the RSC at The Other Place and The Young Vic explodes all such ideas by the hard-won method of approaching the text with intelligence and without prejudice. 'Trevor has staged it impeccably,' says Marsha Hunt, who plays a guileless and wounded Bianca. 'I feel you go home with a sense of three women in the play rather than two. Because that's what Shakespeare wrote—he was drawing comparisons between men and women in relationships, comparing their jealousy, their passion. He shows it in Othello and Desdemona, in Emilia and Iago and in Bianca and Cassio. In all these relationships, the power of jealousy is destructive and in all of them, the men are eating the women up and spitting them out. It's very modern. It's feminist.'

Marsha Hunt first played Bianca 18 years ago in the rock musical *Catch My Soul.* Since her famous appearance in *Hair,* the American-born actress has enjoyed a career in the theatre, broadcasting and writing. 'I haven't been taking work recently because I've been finishing a book. I thought the part of Bianca was small enough to enable me to work on the book at the same time. But I've so loved rehearsals I've been coming along even when I wasn't called for them.'

Nunn's rehearsals began with a week in which the text was read and discussed. 'It was like a great lecture by someone who not only knew the text but loved it,' says Hunt. 'As ourselves, not our characters, we went through the text and decided how, as a group, we were presenting it. Before any blocking or formulation,

we'd all taken part in deciding what Shakespeare had to say.'

The company's joy in creating their parts is tangible in performance. Although set in the period of the American civil war, there is no hint of a director and designer imposing a concept. Imogen Stubbs (Desdemona) explains: 'The nineteenth century is not there to make huge statements: it's just quite a good way of setting it to let Shakespeare's effects really work.'

Stubbs is also enthusiastic about Nunn's approach: 'I haven't done much Shakespeare and sometimes I loathe it because I don't believe real people are speaking. Now, I really believe in the people and don't cheat the lines. There's a real pleasure in speaking Shakespeare and still feeling no barrier between your heart and your brain. I love being in a production which says you must find out why you say something and not cover it up with a gimmick or something in the set.'

Imogen Stubbs knows *Othello* well, having done an entire exam paper on it for her first class degree in English from Oxford. Stubbs' manner is ingenuous but her views on her part are underpinned by a deep knowledge of the text and a series of clear-witted observations. Desdemona is a puzzle because she is described by her father as gentle and obedient but her elopement with a black man is violently unconventional. 'Parents do see their children differently from how they really are. And falling in love changes everyone. In Desdemona's first scene (in the Duke's council chamber), she's trying to be kind to her father but she's saying; 'I can't be your little girl for ever.'

Desdemona's love for Othello is crucial: 'She thinks he's wonderful and extravagant and marvellous. We worked on the happiness and giddiness and laughing together. I wanted to show a hint of this huge secret love life they have together. The hardest thing in a Shakespeare play is to forget the end: the audience must believe in the possibility that their love could conquer all the hate.'

Perhaps because the audience is so close to the actors at The Other Place, there is an absurd but strong temptation to intervene in the action and stop the wickedness. And the suffering is the more unbearable because of Stubbs' charming vulnerability as a new wife. 'When she goes to Cyprus, she plays lots of different roles—being a wife, having fun or fussing over him. I like the idea that she's a chameleon. Lots of girls are like that: they try out all sorts of people . . . she does it to make herself and others laugh. She's a great 'seemer' in an innocent way, a light way. Like Scarlett O'Hara, she thinks everything will be all right . . .'

Like Stubbs' Desdemona, Zoe Wanamaker's performance as Emilia has received much admiration. From the moment she first appears, blowing her nose after a rough sea crossing to Cyprus, she seems a complete person: complicated, suffering, open to events. 'By the time we enter the play, we're halfway through a life—in the middle of a conversation,' she says. 'You bring a whole life onto the stage with you.'

Never imposing on the text, but drawing from all its hints and comments, Wanamaker has built up a meticulous picture of her character. 'She married Iago because she fell in love with him. Perhaps she married beneath her. After the first passion and a year or two's happiness, Iago wasn't climbing any further in his career and the frustrations and envies started to come in. He took it all out on her.'

Wanamaker first saw *Othello* as a child in Stratford when her father Sam played Iago opposite Paul Robeson. She has drawn widely from her own and others' experiences in order to portray Emilia's misery. 'An actor has to have a magpie intelligence and pick up from here and there. The last play I did, *Mrs Klein,* was an incredible help. Klein has a huge chapter on envy. Emilia is married to a man who's jealous of his wife and envious of everyone else's success. When you're with someone who's jealous, you live in fear. One of my first boyfriends was like that.'

This interpretation explains Emilia's response to the love of Desdemona and Othello. She doesn't like being close to so much happiness and the pain on Zoe Wanamaker's face is agonizing to watch.

But Emilia is not self-obsessed: she is the first person to realise what is going on. 'All Shakespeare's women have insights, the second women particularly—Celia, Bianca in *The Taming of the Shrew*—they're all terribly important roles. And they're always being played by blonde wimps. I felt also that Emilia was not this jolly lady. She's a locked cupboard. She's been hurt so many times, she's encased in this prison.'

Both Emilia and Desdemona grow from their relationship with each other. Only when Emilia sees Desdemona being ill-treated, undergoing the crazy jealousy that she too had endured, do the two women reach out to each other. In the willow song scene, Emilia breaks free from her emotional enslavement to Iago. She begins to make jokes and is able to comfort Desdemona. 'There's a bonding between the women, an opening of a huge window onto another person's life.'

Affection for each other radiates from the three actresses. Each of them often refers to the support and the ideas they have given and received from each other. And they are enthusiastic about working with Willard White and Ian McKellen. ('Mr and Mrs Iago probably have a dog. Ian and I have discussed this' says Zoe Wanamaker. 'It may be a shih tzu. Iago loves it and gives it a lot of affection.')

Praise for designer Bob Crowley and, above all, for Trevor Nunn, is fulsome: 'I've never seen an entire cast fall in love with a director before,' says Imogen Stubbs, 'and it makes you put something special in.'

BEN JONSON

1572–1637

"He was better versed and knew more in Greek and Latin than all the poets in England. . . ." This heady appraisal of Jonson was made by Jonson himself during a boisterous conversation with the Scottish poet William Drummond. Yet the statement should not be taken simply as a sign of Jonson's bravado or as the overflow of Drummond's plentiful liquor supply, for Jonson was a profoundly learned man, even though he never received any formal education after he finished Westminster School in 1589. At Westminster, he studied under William Camden, a scholar and historian of international reputation, from whom he received a thorough training in the classics and a reverence for them that left its mark on everything he wrote. Jonson was not only the most learned, but also the most independent-minded dramatist of his age. After finishing school, he was forced by his stepfather to apprentice himself as a bricklayer, but after a year at this trade he fled the country and hired himself out as a soldier to fight on the side of Holland in its war against Spain. From 1597 on, we hear of him as a playwright, an actor, and, intermittently, a jailbird. In 1597, for example, he was arrested and imprisoned for his part as an actor and collaborator in *The Isle of Dogs,* a lost satiric comedy that was apparently so offensive in its topical references that it prompted the authorities to close the theaters temporarily. In 1598, his killing of a fellow actor in a duel would have taken him to the gallows had he not pled "benefit of clergy" (the ability to read and write). Combat came naturally to Jonson. Indeed, two of his plays, *Cynthia's Revels* (1600) and *Poetaster* (1601), contained such fierce attacks on several of his dramatic contemporaries that they fomented a satiric war in the theaters of the time.

The spirit of attack that so marks Jonson's life found theatrical form in satire, which he explained in the prologue to his first play, *Every Man in His Humour* (1598). There Jonson defined his dramatic art as being realistic in its method and satiric in its purpose, consisting of "deeds, and language, such as men do use: / And persons, such as comedy would choose, / When she would show an image of the times, / And sport with human follies, not with crimes." In this dramatic manifesto, he was deliberately opposing himself to the romantic comedies, revenge tragedies, and English history plays that dominated the theater of his day. And in the play itself, he offers deftly drawn portraits of various Elizabethan character types—a solemn city gentleman, a plain-speaking country squire, a country bumpkin with city pretensions, a city simpleton with literary pretensions, a cowardly man with military pretensions, an ignorant water-bearer and his credulous wife, a witty young man and his ingenious servant, and a jealous husband. That gallery of portraits, which Jonson had drawn from Roman comedy and London life, was an immediate success, so much so that he quickly followed it with a companion piece, *Every Man Out of His Humour* (1599). The prologue for this play was not just a single speech but an induction of almost three hundred lines in which three characters discuss the proper bases for dramatic satire. Their conversation distinguishes between true and false behavior, between behavior resulting from a psychological and physiological condition that the Elizabethans called a person's "humour," and behavior guided by social pretensions that Jonson called "affected humour." By exposing all the affected humors of his time, Jonson aimed to drive men and women out of their false social behavior, and he did so by producing such caricatures as the vainglorious traveler, the railing courtier, the fastidious dresser, and the officious lady.

The gallery of fools he portrayed in these early comedies clearly displayed his temperament and talent for the satiric art of social comedy. And during the years from 1606 to 1614, he deliberately followed his bent, turning out a series of comedies—*Volpone* (1606), *Epicoene* (1609), *The Alchemist* (1610), and *Bartholomew Fair* (1614)—that have established his reputation as one of the major social satirists of the English dramatic tradition. Jonson's comedies, in fact, established the tradition of social comedy on the English stage. His comedies of London life directly influenced his contemporaries—Middleton, Beaumont, and Fletcher—and led in turn to the Restoration comedies of sophisticated city life by Etherege, Wycherley, and Congreve, all of whom borrowed from Jonson and regarded him as their model. And they admired him not only for his satiric portraiture but also for the perfection of his comic plots, which all depend on elaborate outwitting intrigues that are at once theatrically compelling and satirically significant. In *The Alchemist*, for example, Jonson constructs an elaborate con game in which three schemers—an Elizabethan underworld man with a smattering of alchemical jargon, a whore, and a servant with a knack for disguises—dupe a law clerk, a tobacco merchant, a gamester, a sensualist, a preacher, a deacon, and a young country gentleman. The brilliance of the play lies in the speed with which the crooks change styles and tricks to fit the next gull who enters—and in the dizzying buildup of comic situations as more and more of the characters try to claim their promised treasure at once.

Volpone also involves an elaborate con game in which a pack of scoundrels attempts to exploit a group of money-hungry fools, but it is a far grimmer work, for though Jonson claimed that his comedy sported "with human follies, not with crimes," the specimens shown to us in *Volpone* are not merely fools but, in several instances, morally despicable knaves. The names of the principal characters immediately suggest their depravity, for they are identified with the world of beasts. Thus, the lawyer Voltore is named for the vulture, the deaf old gentleman Corbaccio for the raven, the violent Corvino is a crow, while the chief schemers are Volpone, the fox, and his parasite Mosca, the fly. Even the more purely comic characters of the subplot share in the beast imagery: Sir Politic Would-be, the gullible knight who imagines messages from spies in cabbages, reduces to Sir Pol, the parrot; his wife, Lady Politic Would-be, chatters endlessly, like another parrot; and Peregrine, the young traveler, is named for a hunting falcon. The fools of the subplot, though in one sense apparently harmless, are also unwitting echoes of the knaves, and in fact they are also unwitting accomplices of the knaves, for the social pretensions of the Would-bes play directly into the hands of Volpone's schemes at several points in the plot. Only Celia and Bonario escape the animal imagery, but they, too, are morally typed by their names, for Celia literally means heavenly, while Bonario signifies good-natured.

Although the central comic trick of *Volpone*—that of a man pretending to be sick—is a fairly common comic ploy and the plot ultimately turns into the tricking of the trickster, Jonson uses a variety of means to emphasize the darker implications of the trickery that pervades *Volpone*. Volpone's pretended sickness is mortal; the gulls are clustered around him, waiting for his death and the chance to inherit his great wealth; and the extremes to which they are willing to go, such as disinheriting a son and prostituting a wife, are cruel and unnatural. The language of the play also emphasizes its darker tones. Gold is not merely the object for which all strive, but becomes in Volpone's opening speech a substitute for God. The play's emphasis on disease and physical degeneration is, of course, part of the comic plot, but it is also a metaphor for the moral illness of this gold-dominated world. At the end of the play, the false sickness of Volpone is converted to real pain and all of his money given to the incurables, of which, spiritually, he is one.

These darker aspects of *Volpone* came to life in the 1995 production at Britain's Royal National Theatre. Many reviewers commented on the added "prologue" devised by director Matthew Warchus, in which Volpone was chased around the revolving set by torch-carrying figures, a scene that revealed Volpone's nightmares of discovery and exposure. And even when Volpone "woke up" in his bed, a skeleton with an hourglass hung over him, a visible reminder of death (see Figure 1). Bright-colored costumes, such as the orange dress worn by Lady Would-be, added a sense of luxury to this decadent world, while the often grotesque headdresses— Corbaccio's ear-trumpet bizarrely fastened on top of his head (see Figure 4) or Lady Would-be's elaborately curled wig (see Figure 2)—distanced the audience from sympathy with such characters. By contrast, Celia, one of the play's two innocents, was much more simply dressed (Figure 3). The production was dominated by Volpone and Mosca—Michael Gambon's Volpone usually center stage in bed (see Figures 1 and 3), while Simon Russell Beale's Mosca roamed the revolving stage. But both were masters of pretense, as one can see in Figure 4, where Volpone feigns illness with a blank stare while Mosca adopts a look of sympathetic concern. Ultimately, of course, their pretenses lead them into seeking more than they can possibly win, but not before they have exposed the greed and folly of their world—and entertained the audience mightily as well.

VOLPONE, OR THE FOXE

BY BEN JONSON / EDITED BY PHILIP BROCKBANK*

CHARACTERS

VOLPONE,° *a Magnifico*°
MOSCA,° *his Parasite*
VOLTORE,° *an Advocate*
CORBACCIO,° *an old Gentleman*
CORVINO,° *a Merchant*
AVOCATORI,° *four Magistrates*
NOTARIO, *the Register*°
NANO,° *a Dwarf*
CASTRONE, *an Eunuch*
GREGE *(a crowd)*
SIR POLITIC WOULD-BE, *a Knight*

PEREGRINE,° *a Gentleman-traveller*
BONARIO, *a young Gentleman*
FINE MADAME WOULD-BE, *the Knight's wife*
CELIA, *the Merchant's wife*
COMMANDADORI, *Officers*
MERCATORI, *three Merchants*
ANDROGYNO,° *a Hermaphrodite*
SERVITORE, *a Servant*
WOMEN

SCENE

Venice

THE ARGUMENT°

V OLPONE, childless, rich, feigns sick, despairs,
O ffers his state° to hopes of several heirs,
L ies languishing; his Parasite receives
P resents of all, assures, deludes: then weaves
5 O ther cross-plots, which ope themselves, are told.
N ew tricks for safety are sought; they thrive; when,
   bold,
E ach tempts th'other again, and all are sold.

---

*There are two texts of the play in existence. The first is the play published on its own, in the Quarto (*Q*) of 1607; the second is the Folio (*F*) of 1616, better known as the *Works*. The texts are very similar, although the Folio has more stage directions.

   Volpone, "an old fox, an old reinard, an old craftie, slie, subtle companion, sneaking lurking wily deceiver." This definition, and others, come from the 1598 Italian/English dictionary, *A Worlde of Wordes,* prepared by John Florio (1553[?]–1625), scholar, grammarian, and eventually tutor of French and Italian at the court of James I. Jonson evidently knew and used this dictionary, since he sent a copy of *Volpone* to Florio, with an inscription to "his loving father and worthy friend, Master John Florio." *Magnifico,* magnate of Venice. *Mosca,* "any kind of flye" (Florio); Beelzebub, the "Prince of Devils," is in Hebrew "the Lord of the flies." *Voltore,* "a ravenous bird called a vultur, a geyre or grap. Also a greedie cormorant" (Florio). *Corbaccio,* "a filthie great raven" (Florio). *Corvino,* crow; "of a ravens nature or colour" (Florio, 1611 edition). *Avocatori,* state prosecutors. *Register,* clerk of the court. *Nano,* Latin *nanus,* a dwarf. *Argument,* the acrostic form is imitated from Plautus; *The Alchemist* also has one. *state,* estate.

PROLOGUE

Now, luck yet send us, and a little wit
   Will serve, to make our play hit;
According to the palates of the season,
   Here is rime, not empty of reason:
This we were bid to credit from our Poet,   5
   Whose true scope, if you would know it,
In all his poems, still, hath been this measure,
   To mix profit with your pleasure;
And not as some° (whose throats their envy failing)
   Cry hoarsely, 'All he writes, is railing.'   10
And when his plays come forth, think they can flout
      them,
   With saying, 'He was a year° about them,'
To these there needs no lie, but this his creature,
   Which was, two months since, no feature;
And though he dares give them five lives to mend it, 15
   'Tis known, five weeks fully penned it;
From his own hand, without a coadjutor,°
   Novice, journeyman,° or tutor.
Yet, thus much I can give you, as a token
   Of his play's worth: no eggs are broken,   20
Nor quaking custards° with fierce teeth affrighted,
   Wherewith your rout are so delighted;

   Peregrine, a hawk; a traveler. *Androgyno,* from Greek *andros* (man) and *gyne* (woman). **as some,** specifically Marston in *The Dutch Curtezan* (prologue). **a year,** "you nasty tortoise, you and your itchy poetry break out like Christmas, but once a year" (*Satiromastix* V.ii, 217). **coadjutor,** Jonson worked with collaborators on *Eastward Ho.* **journeyman,** qualified craftsman, more than novice but less than master. **quaking custards,** cowards; also perhaps custard-pie comedy, based on sport with huge custard at the Lord mayor's feast.

Nor hales he in a gull,° old ends° reciting,
  To stop gaps in his loose writing,
25 With such a deal of monstrous, and forced action;
  As might make Bet'lem a faction;°
Nor made he his play, for jests, stol'n from each table,
  But makes jests, to fit his fable.°
And, so presents quick° comedy, refined,
30   As best critics have designed;
The laws of time, place, persons he observeth,
  From no needful rule he swerveth.
All gall, and copperas,° from his ink, he draineth,
  Only, a little salt° remaineth,
Wherewith, he'll rub your cheeks, till, red with
35   laughter,
They shall look fresh, a week after.

ACT 1 / SCENE 1

[VOLPONE'S *house*]
([Enter] VOLPONE, MOSCA.*)*

VOLPONE: Good morning to the day; and, next, my
  gold!
  Open the shrine,° that I may see my saint.

[MOSCA *reveals the treasure.*]

  Hail the world's soul,° and mine! More glad than is
  The teeming earth to see the longed-for sun
5   Peep through the horns of the celestial Ram,°
  Am I, to view thy splendour, darkening his;
  That, lying here, amongst my other hoards,
  Show'st like a flame, by night; or like the day
  Struck out of Chaos,° when all darkness fled
10   Unto the centre. O, thou sun of Sol,°
  But brighter than thy father, let me kiss,
  With adoration, thee, and every relic°
  Of sacred treasure, in this blessed room.
  Well did wise Poets, by thy glorious name
15   Title that age,° which they would have the best;
  Thou being the best of things; and far transcending

---

gull, dupe, one who swallows anything (from gull-gorge). **ends,** tags. **make Bet'lem a faction,** either "make a party for the madhouse" or "enlist the support of the mad-house"; Bet'lem, or Bedlam, was the asylum of St. Mary of Bethlehem. **fable,** plot. **quick,** lively. **gall, and copperas,** oak galls and iron sulfate, used to make ink; rancor was attributed to the gallbladder and copperas is bitter. **salt,** not used in ink, but iron sulfate was called "salt of iron" and Jonson needs it to introduce the following joke out of Horace (*Satires* I. x, 3). **shrine,** Volpone is at his devotions and the treasure has the aspect of a holy reliquary. **world's soul,** with a pun on "sol," the sun; also perhaps the coin. **celestial Ram,** the sun enters Aries at the spring equinox. **day . . . Chaos,** the first day of creation (*Genesis* 1.2–4). **sun of Sol,** alchemy held gold to be the offspring of the sun. **relic,** i.e., the kind found in a shrine. **that age,** the Golden Age (described by Ovid, *Met.* 1.89–112).

All style of joy in children, parents, friends,
  Or any other waking dream on earth.
  Thy looks when they to Venus did ascribe,°
  They should have given her twenty thousand
    Cupids;   20
  Such are thy beauties, and our loves! Dear *saint*,
  Riches, the dumb god,° that giv'st all men tongues;
  That canst do nought, and yet mak'st men do all
    things;
  The price of souls; even hell, with thee to boot,
  Is made worth heaven! Thou art virtue, fame,   25
  Honour, and all things else! Who can get thee,
  He shall be noble, valiant, honest, wise°—
MOSCA: And what he will, sir. Riches are in fortune
  A greater good, than wisdom is in nature.°
VOLPONE: True, my beloved Mosca. Yet, I glory   30
  More in the cunning purchase° of my wealth,
  Than in the glad possession; since I gain
  No common way: I use no trade, no venture;
  I wound no earth with ploughshares; fat no beasts
  To feed the shambles;° have no mills for iron,   35
  Oil, corn, or men, to grind 'em° into poulder;
  I blow no subtle° glass; expose no ships
  To threat'nings of the furrow-faced sea;
  I turn° no moneys, in the public bank;
  Nor usure° private°—
MOSCA: No, sir, nor devour   40
  Soft prodigals. You shall ha' some will swallow
  A melting heir, as glibly as your Dutch
  Will pills of butter,° and ne'er purge for't
  Tear forth the fathers of poor families
  Out of their beds, and coffin them alive   45
  In some kind, clasping prison, where their bones
  May be forth-coming, when the flesh is rotten:
  But your sweet nature doth abhor these courses;
  You loathe, the widow's, or the orphan's tears
  Should wash your pavements; or their piteous cries   50
  Ring in your roofs; and beat the air, for vengeance—
VOLPONE: Right, Mosca, I do loathe it.
MOSCA: And besides, sir,
  You are not like the thresher,° that doth stand
  With a huge flail, watching a heap of corn,
  And, hungry, dares not taste the smallest grain,   55
  But feeds on mallows, and such bitter herbs;
  Not like the merchant, who hath filled his vaults

Venus . . . ascribe, following Homeric tradition the Latin poets often called Venus "golden" (*aurea*). **the dumb god,** "silence is golden." **Thou art . . . wise,** compare Horace, *Satires* II. iii, 94. **Riches . . . nature,** "Better to be endowed by chance with riches than by nature with wisdom." **purchase,** procurance. **shambles,** slaughterhouse. **grind 'em,** i.e., exploit the men. **subtle,** tenuous, delicate: Venice was famed for its glass. **turn,** exchange. **usure,** exchange at high interest. **private,** privately. **Dutch . . . butter,** a notorious Dutch weakness. **the thresher,** from Horace, *Satires* II. iii, 111.

With Romagnia,° and rich Candian wines,°
Yet drinks the lees of Lombard's vinegar;
60   You will not lie in straw, whilst moths, and worms
Feed on your sumptuous hangings, and soft beds.
You know the use of riches, and dare give, now,
From that bright heap, to me, your poor observer,
Or to your dwarf, or your hermaphrodite,
65   Your eunuch, or what other household trifle
Your pleasure allows maintenance—
VOLPONE: Hold thee,° Mosca,

[*Gives him money.*]

Take, of my hand; thou strik'st on truth, in all:
And they are envious term thee parasite.
Call forth my dwarf, my eunuch, and my fool,
70   And let 'em make me sport. What should I do,
But cocker up° my *genius,* and live free
To all delights, my fortune calls me to?
I have no wife, no parent, child, ally,
To give my substance to; but whom I make
75   Must be my heir: and this makes men observe° me.
This draws new clients,° daily, to my house,
Women, and men, of every sex and age,
That bring me presents, send me plate, coin, jewels,
With hope, that when I die (which they expect
80   Each greedy minute) it shall then return,
Tenfold, upon them; whilst some, covetous
Above the rest, seek to engross me, whole,
And counter-work, the one, unto the other,
Contend in gifts, as they would seem, in love:
85   All which I suffer, playing with their hopes,
And am content to coin 'em into profit,
And look upon their kindness, and take more,
And look on that; still° bearing them in hand,°
Letting the cherry° knock against their lips,
And, draw it, by their mouths, and back again. How
90   now!

ACT 1 / SCENE 2

[*Enter* MOSCA, *with* NANO, ANDROGYNO, *and* CAS-
TRONE.]
[*An entertainment follows.*]

NANO: Now, room for fresh gamesters, who do will
          you to know,
          They do bring you neither play, nor University
          show;

Romagnia, Rumney, a sweet Greek wine. *Candian
wines,* Malmsey from Candy (Crete). *Hold thee,* keep yourself. *cocker up,* pamper, indulge (Latin, *indulgere genio*).
observe, "treat with ceremonious respect or reverence"
(*OED*). *clients,* followers who wait upon the patronage of
Volpone the Magnifico (ironic). *still,* continually. *bearing
. . . hand,* leading them on. *cherry,* in the game of chop-
cherry the player tried to bite a dangling cherry.

And therefore do intreat you, that whatsoever they
          rehearse,°
          May not fare a whit the worse, for the false pace°
          of the verse.
If you wonder at this, you will wonder more, ere we
          pass,   5
          For know [*pointing to* ANDROGYNO], here is
          enclosed the Soul of Pythagoras,
That juggler divine, as hereafter shall follow;
          Which soul, fast and loose,° sir, came first from
          Apollo,
And was breathed into Aethalides,° Mercurius his
          son,
          Where it had the gift to remember all that ever
          was done.   10
From thence it fled forth, and made quick
          transmigration
          To goldy-locked Euphorbus,° who was killed, in
          good fashion,
At the siege of old Troy, by the cuckold of Sparta.°
          Hermotimus° was next (I find it in my charta)°
To whom it did pass, where no sooner it was
          missing,   15
          But with one Pyrrhus, of Delos,° it learned to go
          a-fishing:
And thence did it enter the Sophist of Greece.°
          From Pythagore, she went into a beautiful piece,
Hight° Aspasia, the meretrix;° and the next toss of
          her
          Was, again, of a whore, she became a
          philosopher,   20
Crates° the Cynic: as itself° does relate it.
          Since, kings, knights, and beggars, knaves, lords
          and fools gat it,
Besides, ox, and ass, camel, mule, goat, and brock,
          In all which it hath spoke, as in the cobbler's
          cock.°
But I come not here, to discourse of that matter,   25

rehearse, recite. *false pace,* exemplified by Nano as he
speaks; the old-fashioned loose four-stress rhythm, with
forced rhymes, falsifies the natural sense. *fast and loose,*
"slippery, hard to catch," from a betting game in which one
player guessed whether or not a dagger was held fast in a belt
intricately folded by the other. *Aethalides,* herald to the
Argonauts and heir to an omniscient memory. *Euphorbus,*
the Trojan who first wounded Patroclus (*Iliad* 17). *cuckold
of Sparta,* Menelaus. *Hermotimus,* a Greek philosopher.
charta, paper, perhaps Lucian's dialogue. *Pyrrhus, of Delos,*
a philosopher; the name and the allusion to fishing are supplied by Diogenes Laertius without explanation. *Sophist of
Greece,* Pythagoras is so styled by Lucian. *Hight,* (Old
English), named, called *Aspasia* mistress of Pericles. *meretrix,* courtesan. *Crates,* a pupil of Diogenes. *itself,* either
the cock in Lucian, or Androgyno. *cobbler's cock,* the cock
tells the story in Lucian.

Or his one, two, or three, or his great oath, 'By
    Quater!'°
His musics,° his trigon, his golden thigh,°
Or his telling how elements shift; but I
Would ask, how of late, thou has suffered translation,
    And shifted thy coat, in these days of
30   reformation?°
ANDROGYNO: Like one of the reformèd,° a fool, as
    you see,
    Counting all old doctrine heresy.
NANO: But not on thine own forbid meats° hast thou
    ventured?
ANDROGYNO: On fish, when first, a Carthusian° I
    entered.
NANO: Why, then thy dogmatical silence° hath left
35   thee?
ANDROGYNO: Of that an obstreperous° lawyer bereft
    me.
NANO: O wonderful change! when Sir Lawyer
    forsook thee,
    For Pythagore's sake, what body then took thee?
ANDROGYNO: A good dull moyle.°
NANO: And how! by that means,
40 Thou wert brought to allow of the eating of beans?
ANDROGYNO: Yes.
NANO: But, from the moyle, into whom
    did'st thou pass?
ANDROGYNO: Into a very strange beast, by some
    writers called an ass;
    By others, a precise,° pure, illuminate° brother,
    Of those devour flesh, and sometimes one
        another;
45 And will drop forth a libel, or a sanctified lie,
    Betwixt every spoonful of a nativity-pie.°
NANO: Now quit thee, for heaven, of that profane
    nation;
    And gently, report thy next transmigration.
ANDROGYNO: To the same that I am.
NANO: A creature of delight?
    And, what is more than a fool, an
50   hermaphrodite?

Now pray thee, sweet soul, in all thy variation,
    Which body would'st thou choose, to take up thy
        station?
ANDROGYNO: Troth, this I am in, even here would I
    tarry.
NANO: 'Cause here, the delight of each sex thou
    canst vary?
ANDROGYNO: Alas, those pleasures be stale, and
    forsaken;   55
    No, 'tis your fool, wherewith I am so taken;
    The only one creature, that I can call blessed,
    For all other forms I have proved most
        distressed.
NANO: Spoke true, as thou wert in Pythagoras still.
    This learned opinion we celebrate will,   60
    Fellow eunuch, as behoves us, with all our wit and
        art,
    To dignify that° whereof our selves are so great,
        and special a part.
VOLPONE: Now very, very pretty! Mosca, this
    Was thy invention?
MOSCA: If it please my patron,
    Not else.
VOLPONE: It doth, good Mosca.
MOSCA: Then it was, sir.   65

SONG°

Fools, they are the only nation°
Worth men's envy, or admiration;
Free from care, or sorrow-taking,
Selves, and others merry making: 70
All they speak, or do, is sterling.°
Your Fool, he is your great man's dearling,
And your ladies' sport, and pleasure;
Tongue, and bable° are his treasure.
E'en his face begetteth laughter,   75
And he speaks truth, free from slaughter;°
He's the grace of every feast,
And, sometimes, the chiefest guest;
Hath his trencher, and his stool,
When wit waits upon the fool.°   80
    O, who would not be
    He, he, he?

(One knocks without.)

VOLPONE: Who's that? Away!

[*Exeunt* NANO, CASTRONE.]

                                Look Mosca!

Quater, the Pythagorean trigon or triangle of four, symbol of cosmic and moral harmony. *musics,* Pythagorean theory related the spacing of the cosmic spheres to the laws of harmony. *golden thigh,* attributed to Pythagoras by his followers. *reformation,* the Protestant reformation; Jonson was still a Catholic in 1606. *reformèd,* evidently the Puritans. *forbid meats,* forbidden foods; Pythagoreans were forbidden fish and beans. *Carthusian,* an order strict in its diet but allowing fish. *dogmatical silence,* Pythagoreans were enjoined to a five-year silence, which might have been maintained among the Carthusians. *obstreperous,* vociferous. *moyle,* mule. *precise,* "strict in religious observance, puritanical" *(OED).* *illuminate,* visionary. *nativity-pie,* Christmas pie, evading the word "mass." See *The Alchemist* III. ii, 43.

that, i.e., folly. *Song,* it might be sung by the grotesques, by Mosca alone, or by all. *nation,* sect. *sterling,* capable of standing every test. *bable,* the fool's bauble or scepter; slang for phallus. *free from slaughter,* without being called to account. *wit . . . fool,* the fool dines off his host; wit waits upon the fool's words.

MOSCA: Fool, begone!

(Exit ANDROGYNO.*)*

'Tis Signior Voltore, the advocate;
I know him, by his knock.

85 VOLPONE: Fetch me my gown,
My furs,° and night caps; say, my couch is
changing:
And let him entertain himself, awhile,
Without i' th' gallery. Now, now, my clients
Begin their visitation! vulture, kite,
90 Raven, and gor-crow,° all my birds of prey,
That think me turning carcass, now they come.
I am not for 'em yet. How now? the news?

[*Enter* MOSCA.]

MOSCA: A piece of plate, sir.
VOLPONE: Of what bigness?
MOSCA: Huge,
Massy, and antique, with your name inscribed,
And arms engraven.
95 VOLPONE: Good! and not a fox
Stretched on the earth, with fine delusive sleights,
Mocking a gaping crow?° ha, Mosca?
MOSCA: Sharp, sir.
VOLPONE: Give me my furs. Why dost thou laugh so,
man?
MOSCA: I cannot choose, sir, when I apprehend
100 What thoughts he has, without, now, as he walks:
That this might be the last gift he should give;
That this would fetch you; if you died today,
And gave him all, what he should be tomorrow;
What large return would come of all his ventures;°
105 How he should worshipped be, and reverenced;
Ride, with his furs, and foot-cloths;° waited on
By herds of fools, and clients; have clear way
Made for his moyle, as lettered as himself;
Be called the great, and learned advocate:
110 And then concludes, there's nought impossible.
VOLPONE: Yes, to be learned, Mosca.
MOSCA: O, no: rich
Implies it. Hood an ass with reverend purple,°
So you can hide his two ambitious ears,
And he shall pass for a cathedral doctor.°
VOLPONE: My caps, my caps,° good Mosca. Fetch him
115 in.

MOSCA: Stay, sir, your ointment° for your eyes.
VOLPONE: That's true;
Dispatch, dispatch; I long to have possession
Of my new present.
MOSCA: That, and thousands more,
I hope to see you lord of.
VOLPONE: Thanks, kind Mosca.
MOSCA: And that, when I am lost in blended dust, 120
And hundred such as I am, in succession—
VOLPONE: Nay, that were too much, Mosca.
MOSCA: You shall live,
Still, to delude these harpies.
VOLPONE: Loving Mosca!

[*Looking into a glass.*]

'Tis well! My pillow now, and let him enter.

[*Exit* MOSCA.]

Now, my feigned cough, my phthisic,° and my
gout, 125
My apoplexy, palsie, and catarrhs,
Help, with your forced functions, this my posture,°
Wherein, this three year, I have milked their hopes.
He comes, I hear him—uh! uh! uh! uh! O—

ACT 1 / SCENE 3

[*Enter* MOSCA, *with* VOLTORE *bearing plate.* VOLPONE
in bed.]

MOSCA: You still are what you were, sir. Only you,
Of all the rest, are he, commands his love:
And you do wisely, to preserve it, thus,
With early visitation, and kind notes°
Of your good meaning° to him, which, I know, 5
Cannot but come most grateful. Patron, sir!
Here's Signior Voltore is come—
VOLPONE: What say you?
MOSCA: Sir, Signior Voltore is come, this morning,
To visit you.
VOLPONE: I thank him.
MOSCA: And hath brought
A piece of antique plate, bought of St. Mark,° 10
With which he here presents you.
VOLPONE: He is welcome.
Pray him, to come more often.
MOSCA: Yes.

---

furs, worn by the sick for warmth. **gor-crow,** carrion crow. **fox . . . crow,** for a similar application of the fable of the crow, dropping its cheese as it sings for the adulatory fox, see Horace, *Satires* II. v, 55. **ventures,** enterprising investments. **foot-cloths,** pageant drapery for a horse. **reverend purple,** crimson robes of a Doctor of Divinity. **cathedral doctor,** a Doctor of Divinity. **caps,** probably ear-caps, prompted by line 86; at this point, perhaps, Volpone gets into bed.

ointment, to make his eyes sticky and rheumy. *Now . . . posture,* a sacrilegious invocation in the epic manner to the powers of feigned disease. **phthisic,** consumption or asthma. **posture,** pose, imposture. "This and the following scenes are really a Roman *salutio,* i.e., the morning visit of clients to their patron so often referred to and described by the satirists" (Rea). **notes,** signs. **good meaning,** well-wishing. **of St. Mark,** in St. Mark's Square, celebrated for its goldsmiths' shops.

VOLTORE: What says he?

MOSCA: He thanks you, and desires you to see him
　　often.

VOLPONE: Mosca!

MOSCA: My patron?

VOLPONE: Bring him near, where is he?
　I long to feel his hand.

MOSCA [*guiding* VOLPONE*'s hand*]: The plate is here,
15　　sir.

VOLPONE: How fare you, sir?

VOLPONE: I thank you, Signior Voltore.
　Where is the plate? Mine eyes are bad.

VOLTORE [*putting it into his hand*]: I'm sorry
　To see you still thus weak.

MOSCA [*aside*]:   That he is not weaker.

VOLPONE: You are too munificent.

VOLTORE: No, sir, would to heaven,
20　I could as well give health to you, as that plate.

VOLPONE: You gave, sir, what you can. I thank you.
　Your love
　Hath taste in° this, and shall not be unanswered.
　I pray you see me often.

VOLTORE: Yes, I shall, sir.

VOLPONE: Be not far from me.

MOSCA [*to* VOLTORE]:   Do you observe that, sir?

25 VOLPONE: Hearken unto me, still: it will concern you.

MOSCA: You are a happy man, sir, know your good.

VOLPONE: I cannot now last long—

MOSCA: You are his heir, sir.

VOLTORE: Am I?

VOLPONE: I feel me going, uh! uh! uh! uh!
　I am sailing to my port, uh! uh! uh! uh!
30　And I am glad, I am so near my haven.

MOSCA: Alas, kind gentleman; well, we must all go—

VOLTORE: But, Mosca—

MOSCA: Age will conquer.

VOLTORE: Pray thee hear me.
　Am I inscribed his heir, for certain?

MOSCA: Are you?
　I do beseech you, sir, you will vouchsafe
35　To write me, i' your family.° All my hopes
　Depend upon your worship. I am lost,
　Except the rising sun do shine on me.

VOLTORE: It shall both shine, and warm thee, Mosca.

MOSCA: Sir,
　I am a man that have not done your love
40　All the worst offices: here I wear your keys,°
　See all your coffers and your caskets locked,
　Keep the poor inventory of your jewels,
　Your plate, and monies; am your steward, sir,
　Husband your goods here.

VOLTORE: But am I sole heir?

MOSCA: Without a partner, sir, confirmed this
　　morning;   45
　The wax is warm yet, and the ink scarce dry
　Upon the parchment.

VOLTORE: Happy, happy, me!
　By what good chance, sweet Mosca?

MOSCA: Your desert, sir;
　I know no second cause.

VOLTORE: Thy modesty
　Is loath to know it;° well, we shall requite it.   50

MOSCA: He ever liked your course,° sir, that first
　　took° him.
　I, oft, have heard him say, how he admired
　Men of your large° profession, that could speak
　To every cause, and things mere contraries,
　Till they were hoarse again, yet all be law;   55
　That, with most quick agility, could turn,
　And re-turn; make knots, and undo them;
　Give forkèd° counsel; take provoking gold°
　On either hand,° and put it up:° these men,
　He knew, would thrive, with their humility.   60
　And, for his part, he thought, he should be bless'd
　To have his heir of such a suffering spirit,
　So wise, so grave, of so perplexed° a tongue,
　And loud withall, that would not wag, nor scarce
　Lie still, without a fee; when every word   65
　Your worship but lets fall, is a chequeen!°

(Another knocks.)

　Who's that? one knocks; I would not have you seen,
　　sir.
　And yet—pretend you came, and went in haste;
　I'll fashion an excuse. And gentle sir,
　When you do come to swim, in golden lard,   70
　Up to the arms, in honey, that your chin
　Is born up stiff, with fatness of the flood,
　Think on your vassal; but remember me:
　I ha' not been your worst of clients.

VOLTORE: Mosca—

MOSCA: When will you have your inventory brought,
　　sir?   75
　Or see a copy of the will? [*Knocking again.*] Anon!
　I'll bring 'em to you, sir. Away, be gone
　Put business in your face.

[*Exit* VOLTORE.]

VOLPONE: Excellent, Mosca!
　Come hither, let me kiss thee.

　　Hath taste in, can be felt in.　***write . . . family,*** names of
servants were entered in a "Household Book."　***your keys,***
i.e., Voltore's because Volpone's.

　　know it, acknowledge it.　***course,*** way of doing things.
took, captivated.　***large,*** liberal, expansive, and eloquent.
forkèd, equivocal.　***provoking gold,*** court fees; ***provoke,***
"to call to a judge or court to take up one's cause" *(OED)*.
either hand, for either party.　***put it up,*** either "deposit
it" or (Mosca's real meaning) "pocket it."　***perplexed,*** involved, puzzling.　***chequeen*** (F, cecchine), Venetian gold
coin, sequin.

MOSCA: Keep you still, sir.
Here is Corbaccio.

80 VOLPONE: Set the plate away.
The vulture's gone, and the old raven's come.

ACT 1 / SCENE 4

MOSCA: Betake you to your silence, and your sleep.
[*Sets plate aside.*] Stand there, and multiply. Now we shall see
A wretch who is indeed more impotent
Than this can feign to be; yet hopes to hop
Over his grave. [*Enter* CORBACCIO.] Signior
5   Corbaccio!
You're very welcome, sir.

CORBACCIO: How does your patron?
MOSCA: Troth, as he did, sir, no amends.
CORBACCIO: What? mends he?
MOSCA: No, sir: he is rather worse.
CORBACCIO: That's well. Where is he?
MOSCA: Upon his couch, sir, newly fall'n asleep.
CORBACCIO: Does he sleep well?
10 MOSCA: No wink, sir, all this night,
Nor yesterday, but slumbers.°
CORBACCIO: Good! He should take
Some counsel of physicians; I have brought him
An opiate here, from mine own doctor—
MOSCA: He will not hear of drugs.
CORBACCIO: Why? I myself
Stood by, while 't was made; saw all th'
15   ingredients;
And know, it cannot but most gently work.
My life for his, 'tis but to make him sleep.
VOLPONE [*aside*]: Ay, his last sleep, if he would take it.
MOSCA: Sir,
He has no faith in physic.
CORBACCIO: Say you, say you?
20 MOSCA: He has no faith in physic: he does think
Most of your° doctors are the greater danger,
And worse disease t'escape. I often have
Heard him protest, that your physician
Should never be his heir.
25 CORBACCIO: Not I his heir?
MOSCA: Not your physician, sir.
CORBACCIO: O, no, no, no,
I do not mean it.
MOSCA: No, sir, nor their fees
He cannot brook: he says, they flay° a man
Before they kill him.
CORBACCIO: Right, I do conceive° you.
MOSCA: And then, they do it by experiment;°
30   For which the law not only doth absolve 'em,

But gives them great reward: and he is loath
To hire his death, so.
CORBACCIO: It is true, they kill,
With as much licence, as a judge.
MOSCA: Nay, more;
For he but kills, sir, where the law condemns,
And these can kill him, too.
CORBACCIO: Ay, or me: 35
Or any man. How does his apoplex?°
Is that strong on him still?
MOSCA: Most violent.
His speech is broken, and his eyes are set,
His face drawn longer than 't was wont—
CORBACCIO: How? How?   40
Stronger than he was wont?
MOSCA: No, sir: his face
Drawn longer, than 't was wont.
CORBACCIO: O, good.
MOSCA: His mouth
Is ever gaping, and his eyelids hang.
CORBACCIO: Good.
MOSCA: A freezing numbness stiffens all his joints,
And makes the colour of his flesh like lead.
CORBACCIO: 'Tis good.
MOSCA: His pulse beats slow, and dull.
CORBACCIO: Good symptoms, still.   45
MOSCA: And, from his brain°—
CORBACCIO: Ha? how? Not from his brain?
MOSCA: Yes, sir, and from his brain—
CORBACCIO: I conceive you, good.
MOSCA: Flows a cold sweat, with a continual rheum,
Forth the resolvèd° corners of his eyes.
CORBACCIO: Is't possible? Yet I am better, ha!   50
How does he, with the swimming of his head?
MOSCA: O, sir, 'tis past the *scotomy;*° he, now,
Hath lost his feeling, and hath left° to snort,
You hardly can perceive him, that he breathes.
CORBACCIO: Excellent, excellent, sure I shall outlast
him: 55
This makes me young again, a score of years.
MOSCA: I was a-coming for you, sir.
CORBACCIO: Has he made his will?
What has he given me?
MOSCA: No, sir.
CORBACCIO: Nothing? ha?
MOSCA: He has not made his will, sir.
CORBACCIO: Oh, oh, oh.
What then did° Voltore, the lawyer, here?   60
MOSCA: He smelt a carcass, sir, when he but heard

---

slumbers, dozes. **your**, i.e., doctors and physicians in general. **flay**, strip off skin. **conceive**, understand. **experiment**, trial upon the patient.

---

apoplex, apoplexy; Hippocrates held the "strong apoplex" incurable. **from his brain**, drainage of brain fluid was believed the last stage of strong apoplexy, and Corbaccio eagerly recognizes its significance. **resolvèd**, slackened. **scotomy**, "dizziness accompanied by dimness of sight" (*OED*). **left**, ceased. **What then did**, F (Q, But what did).

My master was about his testament;
As I did urge him to it, for your good—
CORBACCIO: He came unto him, did he? I thought so.
65 MOSCA: Yes, and presented him this piece of plate.
CORBACCIO: To be his heir?
MOSCA: I do not know, sir.
CORBACCIO: True,
I know it too.
MOSCA: By your own scale,° sir.
CORBACCIO: Well,
I shall prevent° him, yet. See, Mosca, look,
Here, I have brought a bag of bright chequeens,
Will quite weigh down° his plate.
70 MOSCA: Yea, marry, sir!
This is true physic, this your sacred medicine,
No talk of *opiates,* to this great *elixir.*°
CORBACCIO: 'Tis *aurum palpabile,* if not *potabile.*°
MOSCA: It shall be ministered to him in his bowl?
CORBACCIO: Ay, do, do, do.
75 MOSCA: Most blessed cordial!°
This will recover him.
CORBACCIO: Yes, do, do, do.
MOSCA: I think, it were not best, sir.
CORBACCIO: What?
MOSCA: To recover him.
CORBACCIO: O, no, no, no; by no means.
MOSCA: Why, sir, this
Will work some strange effect, if he but feel it.
CORBACCIO: 'Tis true, therefore forbear, I'll take my
80   venture:°
Give me 't again.
MOSCA: At no hand, pardon me;
You shall not do yourself that wrong, sir. I
Will so advise you, you shall have it all.
CORBACCIO: How?
MOSCA: All, sir, 'tis your right, your own; no man
85 Can claim a part: 'tis yours, without a rival,
Decreed by destiny.
CORBACCIO: How? how, good Mosca?
MOSCA: I'll tell you, sir. This fit he shall recover—
CORBACCIO: I do conceive you.
MOSCA: And, on first advantage°
Of his gained° sense, will I re-importune him
90 Unto the making of his testament;
And show him this.

CORBACCIO: Good, good.
MOSCA: 'Tis better yet,
If you will hear, sir.
CORBACCIO: Yes, with all my heart.
MOSCA: Now, would I counsel you, make home with
speed;
There, frame° a will: whereto° you shall inscribe
My master your sole heir.
CORBACCIO: And disinherit   95
My son?
MOSCA: O, sir, the better: for that colour°
Shall make it much more taking.°
CORBACCIO: O, but colour?
MOSCA: This will, sir, you shall send it unto me.
Now, when I come to enforce,° as I will do,
Your cares, your watchings, and your many prayers,   100
Your more than many gifts, your this day's present,
And, last, produce your will; where, without
thought,
Or least regard, unto your proper issue,°
A son so brave, and highly meriting,
The stream of your diverted love hath thrown you   105
Upon my master, and made him your heir:
He cannot be so stupid, or stone dead,
But, out of conscience, and mere gratitude—
CORBACCIO: He must pronounce me, his?
MOSCA: 'Tis true.
CORBACCIO: This plot
Did I think on before.
MOSCA: I do believe it.   110
CORBACCIO: Do you not believe it?
MOSCA: Yes, sir.
CORBACCIO: Mine own project.
MOSCA: Which when he hath done, sir—
CORBACCIO: Published me his heir?
MOSCA: And you so certain to survive him—
CORBACCIO: Ay.
MOSCA: Being so lusty a man—
CORBACCIO: 'Tis true.
MOSCA: Yes, sir.
CORBACCIO: I thought on that too. See, how he
should be°   115
The very organ,° to express my thoughts!
MOSCA: You have not only done yourself a good—
CORBACCIO: But multiplied it on my son?
MOSCA: 'Tis right, sir.
CORBACCIO: Still, my invention.
MOSCA: 'Las,° sir, heaven knows,
It hath been all my study, all my care,   120
(I e'en grow grey withal) how to work things—
CORBACCIO: I do conceive, sweet Mosca.

By . . . scale, either "by your own estimation, without my help" or "judging by your own case." *prevent,* keep in front of. *weigh down,* outweigh; perhaps suggested by Mosca's "scale." *elixir,* alchemical essence fabled to make life eternal; analogous to the "stone" thought to eternalize base metal into gold. *aurum . . . potabile,* "palpable, if not drinkable, gold." Aurum potabile was held a sovereign remedy for all diseases. *cordial,* a medicine to invigorate the heart, e.g., potable gold. *venture,* i.e., the bag of gold. *advantage,* opportunity. *gained,* regained.

frame, devise. *whereto,* to the end that. *colour,* semblance. *taking,* attractive. *enforce,* urge. *proper issue,* own true offspring. *See . . . be,* "See, if he isn't . . ." *organ,* medium, instrument. *'Las,* Alas.

MOSCA: You are he,
For whom I labour, here.
CORBACCIO: Ay, do, do, do:
I'll straight° about it. [*Begins to go.*]
MOSCA [*aside*]:   Rook go with you,° raven.
CORBACCIO: I know thee honest.
MOSCA: You do lie, sir.
125 CORBACCIO: And—
MOSCA: Your knowledge is no better than your ears,°
    sir.
CORBACCIO: I do not doubt, to be a father to thee.
MOSCA: Nor I, to gull my brother° of his blessing.
CORBACCIO: I may ha' my youth restored to me, why
    not?
MOSCA: Your worship is a precious ass—
130 CORBACCIO: What say'st thou?
MOSCA: I do desire your worship, to make haste, sir.
CORBACCIO: 'Tis done, 'tis done, I go.

  [*Exit* CORBACCIO.]

VOLPONE [*leaping up*]:   O I shall burst;
Let out my sides, let out my sides—
MOSCA: Contain
Your flux° of laughter, sir. You know this hope
135 Is such a bait, it covers any hook.
VOLPONE: O, but thy working, and thy placing it!
I cannot hold; good rascal, let me kiss thee:
I never knew thee, in so rare a humour.°
MOSCA: Alas, sir, I but do, as I am taught;
140 Follow your grave instructions; give 'em words;°
Pour oil into their ears;° and send them hence.
VOLPONE: 'Tis true, 'tis true. What a rare punishment
Is avarice, to itself!
MOSCA: Ay, with our help, sir.
VOLPONE: So many cares, so many maladies,
145 So many fears attending old age,
Yea, death so often called on, as no wish
Can be more frequent with 'em, their limbs faint,
Their senses dull, their seeing, hearing, going,°
All dead before them; yea, their very teeth,
150 Their instruments of eating, failing them:
Yet this is reckoned life! Nay, here was one,
Is now gone home, that wishes to live longer!
Feels not his gout, nor palsy, feigns himself
Younger by scores of years, flatters his age,
155 With confident belying it, hopes he may
With charms, like Aeson,° have his youth restored:

---

straight, immediately. *Rook go with you,* "may you be rooked." *Your . . . ears,* both a taunt and a strict truth. *my brother,* i.e., Corbaccio's son, with a glance at Jacob's cheating of Esau (*Genesis* 27). *flux,* flow, morbid discharge. *rare a humour,* fine and inventive mood. *give 'em words,* deceive (proverbial). *Pour . . . ears,* deceive with fulsome words (proverbial). *going,* ability to walk. *Aeson,* Jason's father, whose youth was restored by Medea's magic.

And with these thoughts so battens,° as if fate
Would be as easily cheated on, as he,
And all turns air! (*Another knocks.*) Who's that,
    there, now? a third?
MOSCA: Close, to your couch again; I hear his voice. 160
It is Corvino, our spruce merchant.
VOLPONE [*lying down*]:   Dead.
MOSCA: Another bout,° sir, with your eyes. Who's
    there?

ACT 1 / SCENE 5

  [*Enter* CORVINO.]

MOSCA: Signior Corvino! come most wished for! O,
How happy were you, if you knew it, now!
CORVINO: Why? what? wherein?
MOSCA: The tardy hour is come, sir.
CORVINO: He is not dead?
MOSCA: Not dead, sir, but as good;
He knows no man.
CORVINO: How shall I do, then?
MOSCA: Why, sir? 5
CORVINO: I have brought him, here, a pearl.
MOSCA: Perhaps he has
So much remembrance left, as to know you, sir;
He still calls on you, nothing but your name
Is in his mouth; is your pearl orient,° sir?
CORVINO: Venice was never owner of the like. 10
VOLPONE [*faintly*]: Signior Corvino.
MOSCA: Hark.
VOLPONE: Signior Corvino.
MOSCA: He calls you, step and give it him. He's here,
    sir.
And he has brought you a rich pearl.
CORVINO: How do you, sir?
Tell him it doubles the twelfth carat.°
MOSCA: Sir,
He cannot understand, his hearing's gone; 15
And yet it comforts him, to see you—
CORVINO: Say,
I have a diamant° for him, too.
MOSCA: Best show't, sir,
Put it into his hand; 'tis only there
He apprehends: he has his feeling, yet.

  [VOLPONE *seizes the pearl.*]

See, how he grasps it!
CORVINO: 'Las, good gentleman! 20
How pitiful the sight is!

---

battens, grows fat. *Another bout,* Mosca applies more ointment. *orient,* Eastern pearls were of superior value and brilliancy. *carat,* measure of weight of precious stones (then 3½ grains). *diamant,* Jonson anachronistically preferred this Middle English form.

MOSCA: Tut, forget, sir.°
  The weeping of an heir should still be laughter,
  Under a visor.°
CORVINO: Why? am I his heir?
MOSCA: Sir, I am sworn, I may not show the will,
25   Till he be dead; but, here has been Corbaccio,
  Here has been Voltore, here were others too,
  I cannot number 'em, they were so many,
  All gaping here for legacies, but I,
  Taking the vantage of his naming you,
30   'Signior Corvino, Signior Corvino',° took
  Paper, and pen, and ink, and there I asked him,
  Whom he would have his heir? 'Corvino'. Who
  Should be executor? 'Corvino'. And
  To any question he was silent to,
35   I still interpreted the nods he made,
  Through weakness, for consent; and sent home th'
    others,
  Nothing bequeathed them, but to cry, and curse.

  (They embrace.)

CORVINO: O, my dear Mosca. Does he not perceive
  us?
MOSCA: No more than a blind harper.° He knows no
  man,
40   No face of friend, nor name of any servant,
  Who 'twas that fed him last, or gave him drink:
  Not those, he hath begotten, or brought up
  Can he remember.
CORVINO: Has he children?
MOSCA: Bastards,
  Some dozen, or more, that he begot on beggars,
  Gipsies, and Jews, and black-moors, when he was
45   drunk.
  Knew you not that, sir? 'Tis the common fable,°
  The Dwarf, the Fool, the Eunuch are all his;
  He's the true father of his family,°
  In all, save me: but he has given 'em nothing.
CORVINO: That's well, that's well. Art sure he does
50   not hear us?
MOSCA: Sure, sir? Why, look you, credit your own
  sense. [*Shouts in* VOLPONE's *ear.*]
  The pox° approach, and add to your diseases,
  If it would send you hence the sooner, sir,
  For, your incontinence, it hath deserved it°
55   Throughly and throughly, and the plague to boot.
  [*to* CORVINO.] You may come near, sir.
              Would you once close
  Those filthy eyes of yours, that flow with slime,

Like two frog-pits; and those same hanging cheeks,
  Covered with hide instead of skin—Nay, help, sir—
  That look like frozen dish-clouts, set on end.   60
CORVINO: Or, like an old smoked wall, on which the
  rain
  Ran down in streaks.
MOSCA: Excellent, sir, speak out;
  You may be louder yet; a culverin°
  Dischargèd in his ear, would hardly bore it.
CORVINO: His nose is like a common sewer, still
  running.   65
MOSCA: 'Tis good! And what his mouth?
CORVINO: A very draught.°
MOSCA: O, stop it up—[*Starts to smother him.*]
CORVINO: By no means.
MOSCA: Pray you, let me.
  Faith, I could stifle him, rarely,° with a pillow,
  As well as any woman that should keep° him.
CORVINO: Do as you will, but I'll be gone.
MOSCA: Be so;   70
  It is your presence makes him last so long.
CORVINO: I pray you, use no violence.
MOSCA: No, sir? why?
  Why should you be thus scrupulous, pray you, sir?
CORVINO: Nay, at your discretion.
MOSCA: Well, good sir, be gone.
CORVINO: I will not trouble him now, to take my
  pearl?°   75
MOSCA: Puh! nor your diamant, What a needless care
  Is this afflicts you! [*Takes the jewels.*] Is not all, here,
    yours?
  Am not I here? whom you have made? your
    creature?
  That owe my being to you?
CORVINO: Grateful Mosca!
  Thou art my friend, my fellow, my companion,   80
  My partner, and shalt share in all my fortunes.
MOSCA: Excepting one.
CORVINO: What's that?
MOSCA: Your gallant° wife, sir.

[*Exit* CORVINO.]

  Now, is he gone; we had no other means
  To shoot him hence, but this.
VOLPONE: My divine Mosca!
  Thou hast today outgone thyself. *(Another knocks.)*
              Who's there?   85
  I will be troubled with no more. Prepare
  Me music, dances, banquets, all delights;
  The Turk is not more sensual in his pleasures

---

visor, a mask. ***Signior Corvino,*** Mosca mimics Volpone's feeble cry. ***blind harper,*** proverbial term for anonymous figure in a crowd. ***fable,*** story, report (not "fiction"). ***family,*** household. ***pox,*** the great pox, syphilis. ***it . . . it,*** "your incontinence hath deserved the pox."

---

culverin, hand-gun. ***draught,*** sink, cesspool. ***rarely,*** excellent. ***keep,*** keep house for, look after. ***pearl,*** this, with the diamond, is still in Volpone's fist. ***gallant,*** fine, beautiful.

354 / VOLPONE, OR THE FOXE

ACT 2 / SCENE 1

Than will Volpone. [*Exit* MOSCA.] Let me see, a
    pearl!
A diamant! plate! chequeens! Good morning's
90   purchase;°
Why, this is better than rob churches, yet;
Or fat, by eating, once a month, a man. [*Enter*
    MOSCA.]
Who is't?
MOSCA: The beauteous Lady Would-be, sir,
Wife, to the English knight, Sir Politic Would-be,
95   (This is the style, sir, is directed me)
Hath sent to know, how you have slept tonight,
And if you would be visited.
VOLPONE: Not now.
Some three hours hence—
MOSCA: I told the squire so much.
VOLPONE: When I am high with mirth, and wine:
    then, then.
100   'Fore heaven, I wonder at the desperate valour°
Of the bold English, that they dare let loose
Their wives, to all encounters!
MOSCA: Sir, this knight
Had not his name for nothing, he is politic,
And knows, how e'er his wife affect strange airs,
105   She hath not yet the face, to be dishonest.°
But, had she Signior Corvino's wife's face—
VOLPONE: Has she so rare a face?
MOSCA: O, Sir, the wonder,
The blazing star of Italy! a wench
O' the first year,° a beauty, ripe, as harvest!
110   Whose skin is whiter than a swan, all over!
Than silver, snow, or lillies! a soft lip,
Would tempt you to eternity of kissing!
And flesh that melteth, in the touch, to blood!
Bright as your gold! and lovely as your gold!
VOLPONE: Why had I not known this before?
115 MOSCA: Alas, sir,
Myself, but yesterday, discovered it.
VOLPONE: How might I see her?
MOSCA: O, not possible;
She's kept as warily as is your gold;
Never does come abroad,° never takes air
120   But at a window. All her looks are sweet,
As the first grapes, or cherries, and are watched
As near° as they are.
VOLPONE: I must see her—
MOSCA: Sir,
There is a guard, of ten spies thick, upon her;
All his whole household: each of which is set

Upon his fellow, and have all their charge,   125
When he goes out, when he comes in, examined.°
VOLPONE: I will go see her, though but at her window.
MOSCA: In some disguise, then.
VOLPONE: That is true. I must
Maintain mine own shape,° still, the same; we'll
    think.

[*Exeunt* VOLPONE, MOSCA.]

ACT 2 / SCENE 1

[*The Square, before* CORVINO'*s house*]
([*Enter*] POLITIC WOULD-BE, PEREGRINE.)

SIR POLITIC: Sir, to a wise man, all the world's his soil.
It is not Italy, nor France, nor Europe,
That must bound me, if my fates call me forth.
Yet, I protest, it is no salt° desire
Of seeing countries, shifting a religion,   5
Nor any disaffection to the state
Where I was bred (and unto which I owe
My dearest plots°) hath brought me out; much less
That idle, antique, stale, grey-headed project
Of knowing men's minds, and manners, with
    Ulysses;°   10
But a peculiar humour° of my wife's,
Laid for this height° of Venice, to observe,
To quote,° to learn the language, and so forth—
I hope you travel, sir, with licence?°
PEREGRINE: Yes.
SIR POLITIC: I dare the safelier converse—How long,
    sir,   15
Since you left England?
PEREGRINE: Seven weeks.
SIR POLITIC: So lately!
You ha' not been with my lord ambassador?°
PEREGRINE: Not yet, sir.
SIR POLITIC: Pray you, what news, sir, vents°
    our climate?
I heard, last night, a most strange thing reported
By some of my lord's followers, and I long   20
To hear, how 'twill be seconded.
PEREGRINE: What was't, sir?
SIR POLITIC: Marry, sir, of a raven, that should° build
In a ship royal of the King's.

---

purchase, haul (thieves' cant). *desperate valour*, the
English were much wondered at in Italy for the freedom they
allowed their wives; the Italians were reputed to incarcerate
them. *dishonest*, unchaste. *O' the first year*, perhaps "without blemish." *abroad*, out of the house. *near*, closely.

charge . . . examined, i.e., each is questioned about the
servant under his charge. *mine own shape*, i.e., his own
apparent shape. *salt*, wanton (used of bitches in heat).
plots, projects. *knowing . . . Ulysses*, alluding to the first
lines of the *Odyssey*. *humour*, whim, obsession. **Laid for this
height**, setting course for this latitude. *quote*, make notes.
licence, warrant from the Lords of Council. *my lord ambassador*, Sir Henry Wotton was ambassador to Venice from 1604
to 1612; Sir Politic has been thought to caricature him.
vents, "comes out of" or "publishes"; the rhetoric strains
either usage. *should*, "it is said," from an Old English usage.

PEREGRINE [*aside*]:   —This fellow
Does he gull° me, trow? or is gulled?—Your name,
   sir?
SIR POLITIC: My name is Politic Would-be.
25 PEREGRINE [*aside*]:   O, that speaks him°—
A knight, sir?
SIR POLITIC: A poor knight, sir.
PEREGRINE: Your lady
Lies° here, in Venice, for intelligence
Of tires,° and fashions, and behaviour
Among the courtesans? The fine Lady Would-be?
30 SIR POLITIC: Yes, sir, the spider, and the bee, oft-times,
Suck from one flower.
PEREGRINE: Good Sir Politic!
I cry your mercy;° I have heard much of you:
'Tis true, sir, of your raven.
SIR POLITIC: On your knowledge?°
PEREGRINE: Yes, and your lions whelping, in the
   Tower.
SIR POLITIC: Another whelp!°
PEREGRINE: Another, sir.
35 SIR POLITIC: Now, heaven!
What prodigies be these? The fires at Berwick!°
And the new star!° These things concurring,
   strange!
And full of omen! Saw you those meteors?°
PEREGRINE: I did, sir.
SIR POLITIC: Fearful! Pray you sir, confirm me,
Were there three porcpisces° seen, above the
40   bridge,
As they give out?
PEREGRINE: Six, and a sturgeon, sir.
SIR POLITIC: I am astonished!
PEREGRINE: Nay, sir, be not so;
I'll tell you a greater prodigy, than these—
SIR POLITIC: What should these things portend!
PEREGRINE: The very day
45 (Let me be sure) that I put forth from London,
There was a whale discovered, in the river,

As high as Woolwich, that had waited there,
Few know how many months, for the subversion
Of the Stode fleet.°
SIR POLITIC: Is't possible? Believe it,
'Twas either sent from Spain, or the Archdukes!°   50
Spinola's° whale, upon my life, my credit!
Will they not leave these projects? Worthy sir,
Some other news.
PEREGRINE: Faith, Stone° the fool is dead,
And they do lack a tavern fool, extremely.
SIR POLITIC: Is Mas'° Stone dead?
PEREGRINE: He's dead, sir; why? I hope   55
You thought him not immortal? [*aside*]—O, this
   knight,
Were he well known, would be a precious thing
To fit our English stage: he that should write
But such a fellow, should be thought to feign
Extremely, if not maliciously.
SIR POLITIC: Stone dead!   60
PEREGRINE: Dead. Lord! how deeply, sir, you
   apprehend° it!
He was no kinsman to you?
SIR POLITIC: That I know of.°
Well! that same fellow was an unknown° fool.
PEREGRINE: And yet you knew him, it seems?
SIR POLITIC: I did so. Sir,
I knew him one of the most dangerous heads   65
Living within the state, and so I held him.
PEREGRINE: Indeed, sir?
SIR POLITIC: While he lived, in action.
He has received weekly intelligence,
Upon my knowledge, out of the Low Countries,
For all parts of the world, in cabbages;°   70
And those dispensed, again, t'ambassadors,
In oranges, musk-melons,° apricots,
Lemons, pome-citrons,° and such-like: sometimes
In Colchester oysters, and your Selsey cockles.°

---

gull, take in, fool. **speaks him,** expresses what he is.
Lies, stays. **tires,** attires, head-dresses. **I cry your mercy,** I beg
your pardon. **On your knowledge,** "your" may be impersonal,
"This is known to be true?" **Another whelp,** Stow's *Annals*
reports the whelping of King James's lions in the Tower on 5
August 1604 and 26 February 1605. **fires at Berwick,** ghostly
battles on Halidon Hill near Berwick caused border alarms in
1604; aurora borealis has been suggested as contributory to
this and other marvels of the time. **the new star,** Kepler discovered a nova in constellation Serpens in 1604; it was
brighter than Jupiter and disappeared after two years. **meteors,** taken as ill omens, because an apparent disturbance of
the cosmos. **porcpisces,** Jonson's spelling is retained with its
correct etymology; Stow tells of "a great Porpus" taken from
the Thames, and of "a very great whale" upriver a few days
later.

Stode fleet, the English Merchant Adventurers were displaced from Hamburg and settled at Stade (Stode) at the
mouth of the Elbe. **Archdukes,** *F,* (*Q,* Arch-duke); the *F*
reading may be the possessive (Archduke's) or it may be the
correct style for Isabella and Albert, joint rulers of the Spanish Netherlands. **Spinola,** commander of the Spanish army
in the Netherlands, often credited by the gullible with monstrous ingenuity; he was said to have hired a whale to drown
London "by snuffing up the Thames and spouting it upon
the City." **Stone,** in the spring of 1605 "Stone the fool" was
whipped in Bridewell for "a blasphemous speech" in which
he called the Lord Admiral a fool. **Mas',** master. **apprehend,** both "feel" and "understand." **That I know of,** "not"
understood before "that." **unknown,** i.e., not known for what
he really was. **cabbages,** regularly imported from Holland at
this time. **musk-melons,** common melons. **pome-citrons,** cit-
rons, or limes. **Colchester oysters . . . Selsey cockles,** both delicacies in court circles.

PEREGRINE: You make me wonder!

75 SIR POLITIC: Sir, upon my knowledge.
Nay, I have observed him, at your public ordinary,°
Take his advertisement,° from a traveller
(A concealed statesman°) in a trencher of meat;
And, instantly, before the meal was done,
Convey an answer in a toothpick.

80 PEREGRINE: Strange!
How could this be, sir?

SIR POLITIC: Why, the meat was cut
So like his character,° and so laid, as he
Must easily read the cipher.

PEREGRINE: I have heard,
He could not read, sir.

SIR POLITIC: So 'twas given out,
85 In polity, by those that did employ him:
But he could read, and had your languages,
And to't, as sound a noddle°—

PEREGRINE: I have heard, sir,
That your baboons were spies; and that they were
A kind of subtle nation, near to China.

90 SIR POLITIC: Ay, ay, your *Mamuluchi.*° Faith, they had
Their hand in a French plot, or two; but they
Were so extremely given to women, as
They made discovery° of all: yet I
Had my advices° here, on Wednesday last,
95 From one of their own coat,° they were returned,
Made their relations,° as the fashion is,
And now stand fair,° for fresh employment.

PEREGRINE [*aside*]:   —'Heart!°
This Sir Pol would be ignorant of nothing—
It seems, sir, you know all?

SIR POLITIC: Not all, sir. But,
100 I have some general notions; I do love
To note, and to observe: though I live out,
Free from the active torrent, yet I'd mark
The currents, and the passages of things,
For mine own private use; and know the ebbs,
And flows of state.

105 PEREGRINE: Believe it, sir, I hold
Myself, in no small tie,° unto my fortunes
For casting me thus luckily, upon you;
Whose knowledge, if your bounty equal it,
May do me great assistance, in instruction
110 For my behaviour, and my bearing, which
Is yet so rude, and raw.

SIR POLITIC: Why? came you forth
Empty of rules for travel?

PEREGRINE: Faith, I had
Some common ones, from out that vulgar
grammar,°
Which he that cried° Italian to me, taught me.

SIR POLITIC: Why, this it is, that spoils all our brave
bloods;   115
Trusting our hopeful gentry unto pedants:
Fellows of outside, and mere bark.° You seem
To be a gentleman, of ingenuous° race—
I not profess it, but my fate hath been
To be, where I have been consulted with,   120
In this high kind,° touching some great men's
sons.
Persons of blood, and honour—

PEREGRINE [*seeing people approach*]: Who be these, sir?

ACT 2 / SCENE 2

[*Enter* MOSCA *and* NANO, *disguised, with materials for a
scaffold stage. A crowd follows.*]

MOSCA: Under that window, there't must be. The
same.

SIR POLITIC: Fellows, to mount a bank!° Did your
instructor
In the dear° tongues, never discourse to you
Of the Italian mountebanks?

PEREGRINE: Yes, sir.

SIR POLITIC: Why,
Here shall you see one.

PEREGRINE: They are quacksalvers,°   5
Fellows, that live by venting° oils and drugs?

SIR POLITIC: Was that the character he gave you of
them?

PEREGRINE: As I remember.

SIR POLITIC: Pity his ignorance.
They are the only knowing men of Europe!
Great general scholars, excellent physicians,   10
Most admired statesmen, professed favourites,
And cabinet counsellors, to the greatest princes!
The only languaged men, of all the world!

PEREGRINE: And, I have heard, they are most lewd°
impostors;
Made all of terms, and shreds;° no less beliers°   15

---

ordinary, tavern offering fixed prices. *advertisement,*
instruction or information. *concealed statesman,* disguised
agent of state. *character,* cipher, code. *noddle,* the back of
the head and seat of the mind; perhaps less playful here than
in its common use. *Mamuluchi,* a macaronic version of
mamalik, Circassian slaves who came to rule Egypt in the thirteenth century; nothing to do with baboons or China. *dis-*
covery, disclosure. *advices,* news, dispatches. *coat,* side.
relations, reports. *stand fair,* are well set. *'Heart,* i.e., God's
Heart! *tie,* obligation.

vulgar grammar, ordinary grammar book, apt to contain
phrases and precepts; Florio's grammar may be intended.
cried, called out, intoned. *bark,* shell, outward appearance;
may include pun suggested by "cried." *ingenuous,* noble; Sir
Politic pauses to weigh Peregrine's potential. *high kind,*
important capacity. *mount a bank,* from Italian *monta in
banco;* bank bench. *dear,* esteemed. *quacksalvers,* a Dutch
word for quackers about ointment; hence modern "quack."
venting, vending. *lewd,* ignorant. *terms, and shreds,* jargon,
snatches and tags. *beliers,* misreporters.

Of great men's favours, than their own vile
   medicines;
Which they will utter,° upon monstrous oaths:
Selling that drug, for twopence, ere they part,
Which they have valued at twelve crowns, before.

SIR POLITIC: Sir, calumnies are answered best with
20   silence:
Yourself shall judge. Who is it mounts, my friends?

MOSCA: Scoto of Mantua,° sir.

SIR POLITIC: Is't he? Nay, then
I'll proudly promise, sir, you shall behold
Another man, than has been phant'sied to you.
25 I wonder, yet, that he should mount his bank
Here, in this nook, that has been wont t'appear
In face of° the Piazza! Here, he comes.

[*Enter* VOLPONE, *as a mountebank; with a crowd.*]

VOLPONE [*to* NANO]: Mount, zany.°

CROWD: Follow, follow, follow, follow, follow.

SIR POLITIC: See how the people follow him! He's a
   man
May write ten thousand crowns, in bank, here.
30   Note,
Mark but his gesture: I do use to observe
The state he keeps, in getting up! [VOLPONE *mounts
stage.*]

PEREGRINE: 'Tis worth it, sir.

VOLPONE: Most noble gentlemen, and my worthy
   patrons, it may seem strange, that I, your Scoto
35   Mantuano, who was ever wont to fix my bank
   in face of the public Piazza, near the shelter of
   the Portico to the Procuratia,° should, now, after
   eight months' absence, from this illustrious city
   of Venice humbly retire myself, into an obscure
40   nook of the Piazza.

SIR POLITIC: Did not I, now, object° the same?

PEREGRINE: Peace, sir.

VOLPONE: Let me tell you: I am not, as your Lombard
   proverb saith, cold on my feet,° or content to part
   with my commodities at a cheaper rate, than I
45   accustomed: look not for it. Nor, that the calum-
   nious reports of that impudent detractor, and
   shame to our profession—Alessandro Buttone,° I
   mean—who gave out, in public, I was condemned
   a sforzato° to the galleys, for poisoning the Cardi-

nal Bembo's—cook,° hath at all attached,° much 50
less dejected me. No, no, worthy gentlemen, to
tell you true, I cannot endure, to see the rabble
of these ground *ciarlitani*,° that spread their
cloaks on the pavement, as if they meant to do
feats of activity, and then come in, lamely, with 55
their mouldy tales out of Boccaccio, like stale
Tabarine,° the fabulist: some of them discoursing
their travels, and of their tedious captivity in
the Turk's galleys, when indeed, were the truth
known, they were the Christian's galleys, where 60
very temperately, they ate bread, and drunk water,
as a wholesome penance, enjoined them by their
confessors, for base pilferies.

SIR POLITIC: Note but his bearing, and contempt of
   these. 65

VOLPONE: These turdy-facy-nasty-paty-lousy-fartical°
   rogues, with one poor groat's-worth of unprepared antimony, finely wrapped up in several°
   scartoccios,° are able, very well, to kill their twenty
   a week, and play; yet, these meagre starved spirits, 70
   who have half stopped the organs of their minds
   with earthy oppilations,° want not their favourers
   among your shrivelled, salad°-eating artisans: who
   are overjoyed, that they may have their half-
   pe'rth° of physic, though it purge 'em into 75
   another world, 't makes no matter.

SIR POLITIC: Excellent! Ha' you heard better language, sir?

VOLPONE: Well, let 'em go. And gentlemen, honourable gentlemen, know that for this time, our 80
   bank, being thus removed from the clamours of
   the *canaglia*,° shall be the scene of pleasure, and
   delight; for, I have nothing to sell, little, or nothing to sell.

SIR POLITIC: I told you, sir, his end.

PEREGRINE: You did so, sir. 85

VOLPONE: I protest, I, and my six servants, are not able
   to make of this precious liquor, so fast, as it is
   fetched away from my lodgings by gentlemen of
   your city; strangers of the Terra Firma;° worshipful merchants; ay, and senators too: who, ever 90
   since my arrival, have detained me to their uses,

    ***utter*,** sell. ***Scoto of Mantua*,** renowned Italian juggler who visited Elizabeth's court in 1576. ***In face of*,** facing on to. ***zany*,** clown and servant, comic assistant. ***Portico to the Procuratia*,** the arcaded residence of the Procurators on the north side of St. Mark's. ***object*,** possibly in archaic sense "put before the mind." ***cold on my feet*,** Italian, *aver freddo a' piedi*, i.e., to be forced by poverty to sell cheaply. ***Buttone*,** the name of this rival owes nothing to fact. ***sforzato*,** "*Sfortzati*, gallie-slaves, prisoners perforce" (Florio).

    ***Bembo's—cook*,** the pause insinuates "mistress"; Pietro Bembo (1470–1547), the great humanist, was born in Venice. ***attached*,** arrested, constrained. ***ground ciarlitani*,** charlatans working on the ground, without a bank. ***Tabarine*,** a famous zany in a touring Italian troop of the 1570s. ***turdy . . . fartical*,** an Aristophanic phrase, compounded of abusive improvisations. ***several*,** separate. ***scartoccios*,** "a coffin of paper for spice" (Florio). ***earthy oppilations*,** gross obstructions, i.e., mundane concerns. ***salad*,** probably meaning "raw vegetables." ***half-pe'rth*,** ha'p'orth. ***canaglia*,** "raskallie people onelie fit for dogs companie" (Florio). ***Terra Firma*,** name for the mainland part of Venice.

by their splendidous° liberalities. And worthily.
For, what avails your rich man to have his maga-
zines° stuffed with *moscadelli,*° or of the purest
95   grape, when his physicians prescribe him, on pain
of death, to drink nothing but water, cocted° with
aniseeds? O, health! health! the blessing of the
rich! the riches of the poor! who can buy thee at
too dear a rate, since there is no enjoying this
100   world without thee? Be not then so sparing of your
purses, honourable gentlemen, as to abridge the
natural course of life—
PEREGRINE: You see his end?
SIR POLITIC: Ay, is't not good?
VOLPONE: For, when a humid flux, or catarrh, by the
105   mutability of air, falls from your head, into an
arm, or shoulder, or any other part; take you a
ducat, or your chequeen of gold, and apply to the
place affected: see, what good effect it can work.
No, no, 'tis this blessed *unguento,*° this rare extrac-
110   tion, that hath only power to disperse all malignant humours,° that proceed, either of hot, cold,
moist, or windy causes—
PEREGRINE: I would he had put in dry too.
SIR POLITIC: Pray you, observe.
VOLPONE: To fortify the most indigest, and crude°
115   stomach, ay, were it of one that, through extreme
weakness, vomited blood, applying only a warm
napkin to the place, after the unction, and fricace;° for the *vertigine,*° in the head, putting but a
drop into your nostrils, likewise, behind the ears;
120   a most sovereign, and approved remedy: the *mal
caduco,*° cramps, convulsions, paralyses, epilep-
sies, *tremor-cordia,*° retired nerves,° ill vapours of
the spleen, stoppings of the liver, the stone, the
strangury,° *hernia ventosa,*° *iliaca passio;*° stops a
125   *disenteria* immediately; easeth the tortion of the
small guts; and cures *melancholia hypocondriaca,*°

being taken and applied, according to my printed
receipt.° *(Pointing to his bill and his glass.)* For, this
is the physician, this the medicine; this counsels,
this cures; this gives the direction, this works the   130
effect: and, in sum, both together may be termed
an abstract of the theoric, and practic in the Aes-
culapian° art. 'Twill cost you eight crowns. And,
Zan Fritada,° pray thee sing a verse, extempore,
in honour of it.   135
SIR POLITIC: How do you like him, sir?
PEREGRINE: Most strangely, I!
SIR POLITIC: Is not his language rare?
PEREGRINE: But° alchemy,
I never heard the like: or Broughton's° books.

[NANO *sings.*]

                          SONG

Had old Hippocrates, or Galen,°   140
That to their books put medicines all in,
But known this secret, they had never
(Of which they will be guilty ever)
Been murderers of so much paper,
Or wasted many a hurtless° taper: 145

No Indian drug had ere been famèd,
Tobacco, sassafras° not named,
Ne yet of guacum° one small stick, sir,
Nor Raymond Lully's° great elixir.
Ne had been known the Danish Gonswart,°   150
Or Paracelsus, with his long sword.°

PEREGRINE: All this, yet, will not do; eight crowns is
high.
VOLPONE: No more; gentlemen, if I had but time to
discourse to you the miraculous effects of this my
oil, surnamed *oglio del Scoto;* with the countless   155
catalogue of those I have cured of th'aforsaid,

splendidous, common variant of "splendid." **magazines,**
storehouses. **moscadelli,** "the wine Muscadine" (Florio), mus-
catel. **cocted,** boiled. **unguento,** ointment. **malignant humours,** According to classical and medieval medical theory
the four cardinal humors of the body were blood, phlegm,
choler and melancholy, and they corresponded with the four
elements—air (hot and moist), water (cold and moist), fire
(hot and dry) and earth (cold and dry). Both pathological
and temperamental traits were attributed to the dominance
of one humor over the others, or to "fluxes"—flowings
of humors from one part of the body to another. **crude,**
sour. **fricace,** massage. **vertigine,** dizziness. **mal caduco,**
falling sickness (epilepsy). **tremor-cordia,** heart palpitations.
retired nerves, shrunken sinews. **strangury,** painful urination.
hernia ventosa, gaseous protrusion (possibly strangulated hernia). **iliaca passio,** "pain and wringing of the small guts"
(Holland's *Pliny* II. 39). **melancholia hypocondriaca,** melancholy was supposed to be seated in the hypochondria—the
soft parts of the body below the rib cartilages.

receipt, recipe. **Aesculapian,** after Aesculapius, Greek
and Roman god of medicine. **Zan Fritada,** Volpone calls
Nano by the name of a celebrated zany (*fritada* = pancake).
But, "except for" or "pure." **Broughton,** Hugh Broughton
(1549–1612), rabbinical scholar and Puritan. **Hippocrates,
or Galen,** Hippocrates (born ca. 460 B.C.) invented the theory of humors and Galen (born ca. A.D. 130) expounded it;
their authority in all medical matters was still recognized in
Jonson's time. **hurtless,** harmless. **Tobacco, sassafras,** both
used medicinally and newly introduced from America. **gua-
cum,** drug extracted from resin of guaiacum tree. **Raymond
Lully** (1235–1315), sage, evangelist, and astrologer from Ma-
jorca; apocryphal alchemical works were ascribed to him
posthumously, hence the tradition that he discovered the
elixir of life. **Danish Gonswart,** unidentified: suggestions include a Dutch theologian (Wessel Gansfort) and a Danish
chemist (Berthold Schwarz). **Paracelsus . . . sword,** Paracelsus was supposed to have kept his quintessences in the pom-
mel of his sword.

and many more diseases; the patents and privileges of all the princes and commonwealths of Christendom; or but the depositions of those that appeared on my part, before the signiory of the *Sanita*,° and most learned college of physicians; where I was authorized, upon notice taken of the admirable virtues of my medicaments, and mine own excellency, in matter of rare, and unknown secrets, not only to dispense them publicly in this famous city, but in all the territories, that happily joy under the government of the most pious and magnificent states of Italy. But may some other gallant fellow say, 'O, there be divers that make profession to have as good, and as experimented receipts as yours.' Indeed, very many have assayed, like apes in imitation of that, which is really and essentially in me, to make of this oil; bestowed great cost in furnaces, stills, alembics,° continual fires and preparation of the ingredients (as indeed there goes to it six hundred several° simples,° besides some quantity of human fat, for the conglutination, which we buy of the anatomists) but, when these practitioners come to the last decoction,° blow, blow,° puff, puff, and all flies *in fumo*:° ha, ha, ha! Poor wretches! I rather pity their folly, and indiscretion, than their loss of time, and money; for those may be covered by industry: but to be a fool born, is a disease incurable. For my self, I always from my youth have endeavoured to get the rarest secrets, and book them; either in exchange, or for money: I spared not cost, nor labour, where anything was worthy to be learned. And gentlemen, honourable gentlemen, I will undertake, by virtue of chemical art, out of the honourable hat, that covers your head, to extract the four elements; that is to say, the fire, air, water, and earth, and return you your felt without burn, or stain. For, whilst others have been at the balloo,° I have been at my book; and am now past the craggy paths of study, and come to the flowery plains of honour, and reputation.

SIR POLITIC: I do assure you, sir, that is his aim.

VOLPONE: But, to our price—

PEREGRINE: And that withall, Sir Pol.

VOLPONE: You all know, honourable gentlemen, I never valued this *ampulla*,° or vial, at less than eight crowns, but for this time, I am content to be deprived of it for six; six crowns is the price; and less in courtesy, I know you cannot offer me: take it, or leave it, howsoever, both it, and I, am at your service. I ask you not, as the value of the thing, for then I should demand of you a thousand crowns, so the Cardinals Montalto, Fernese,° the great Duke of Tuscany,° my gossip,° with divers other princes have given me; but I despise money: only to show my affection to you, honourable gentlemen, and your illustrious state here, I have neglected the messages of these princes, mine own offices,° framed my journey hither, only to present you with the fruits of my travels. [*to* NANO *and* MOSCA] Tune your voices once more to the touch of your instruments, and give the honourable assembly some delightful recreation.

PEREGRINE: What monstrous,° and most painful circumstance
Is here, to get some three or four *gazets*!°
Some threepence, i' th' whole, for that 'twill come to.

SONG

You that would last long, list to my song,
Make no more coil,° but buy of this oil.
Would you be ever fair? and young?
Stout of teeth? and strong of tongue?
Tart° of palate? quick of ear?
Sharp of sight? of nostril clear?
Moist of hand?° and light of foot?
Or, I will come nearer to it,
Would you live free from all diseases?
Do the act, your mistress pleases;
Yet fright all aches from your bones?°
Here's a medicine, for the nones.°

VOLPONE: Well, I am in a humour, at this time, to make a present of the small quantity my coffer contains: to the rich, in courtesy, and to the poor, for God's sake. Wherefore, now mark; I asked you six crowns; and six crowns, at other times, you have paid me; you shall not give me six crowns, or

---

signiory of the Sanita, the "health masters" of Venice who licensed physicians, drug-vendors and mountebanks. *alembics,* alchemical stills. *several,* separate. *simples,* remedies made from one herb only. *decoction,* boiling down to extract essences. *blow, blow,* imitates the alchemist at his furnace. *in fumo,* (It.) in smoke. *balloo* (balloon), Venetian game. *ampulla,* "a thin viole-glasse" (Florio).

Cardinals Montalto, Fernese, Montalto became Pope Sixtus V in 1585; *Fernese* probably an allusion to the notorious Alessandro Farnese who became Pope Paul III in 1534 but there was also a later Cardinal Alessandro Farnese (1520–1589). *Duke of Tuscany,* office held by Cosimo de' Medici after 1569. *gossip,* godsib, godfather; also "familiar acquaintance." *offices,* duties. *What monstrous . . . ,* Peregrine's speech is probably aside to the audience. *gazets,* Venetian pennies, as Peregrine's explanation indicates. *coil,* pother, fuss. *Tart,* sharp, keen. *Moist of hand,* the sign of "pith and livelihood" in *Venus & Adonis* 25–26. *aches . . . bones,* probably alluding to venereal disease. *nones,* nonce, occasion.

five, nor four, nor three, nor two, nor one; nor
half a ducat; no, nor a *moccenigo:*° six-pence it will
cost you, or six hundred pound—expect no lower
245 price, for by the banner of my front,° I will not
bate° a *bagatine,*° that I will have, only, a pledge of
your loves, to carry something from amongst you,
to show, I am not contemned by you. Therefore,
now, toss your handkerchiefs,° cheerfully, cheer-
250 fully; and be advertised, that the first heroic spirit,
that deigns to grace me, with a handkerchief, I
will give it° a little remembrance of something,
beside, shall please it better, than if I had presented it with a double pistolet.°
255 PEREGRINE: Will you be that heroic spark,° Sir Pol?
O, see! the window has prevented you.

(CELIA *at the window*° *throws down her handkerchief.*)

VOLPONE: Lady, I kiss your bounty: and for this timely
grace, you have done your poor Scoto of Mantua,
I will return you, over and above my oil, a secret
260 of that high, and inestimable nature, shall make
you for ever enamoured on that minute, wherein
your eye first descended on so mean, yet not altogether to be despised, an object. Here is a poulder,° concealed in this paper, of which, if I should
265 speak to the worth, nine thousand volumes were
but as one page, that page as a line, that line as a
word; so short is this pilgrimage of man (which
some call life) to the expressing of it. Would I
reflect on the price? Why, the whole world were
270 but as an empire, that empire as a province, that
province as a bank, that bank as a private purse,
to the purchase of it. I will, only, tell you; it is the
poulder that made Venus a goddess, given her by
Apollo, that kept her perpetually young, cleared
275 her wrinkles, firmed her gums, filled her skin,
coloured her hair; from her, derived to Helen,
and at the sack of Troy, unfortunately, lost: till
now, in this our age, it was as happily recovered,
by a studious antiquary, out of some ruins of Asia,
280 who sent a moiety° of it, to the court of France
(but much sophisticated°), wherewith the ladies
there, now, colour their hair. The rest, at this

present, remains with me; extracted to a quintessence: so that, wherever it but touches, in youth it
perpetually preserves, in age restores the com-   285
plexion; seats your teeth, did they dance like virginal jacks,° firm as a wall; makes them white, as
ivory, that were black, as—

ACT 2 / SCENE 3

[*Enter* CORVINO.]

CORVINO: Spite o' the devil, and my shame! come
      down here;
   Come down! No house but mine to make your
      scene?

(*He beats away the mountebank.*)

   Signior Flaminio,° will you down, sir? down!
   What, is my wife your Franciscina,° sir?
   No windows on the whole Piazza, here,   5
   To make your properties, but mine? but mine?
   Heart! ere tomorrow, I shall be new christened,
   And called the *Pantalone di Besogniosi,*°
   About the town. [*Exit.*]
PEREGRINE: What should this mean, Sir Pol?
SIR POLITIC: Some trick of state, believe it. I will home. 10
PEREGRINE: It may be some design, on you.
SIR POLITIC: I know not.
   I'll stand upon my guard.
PEREGRINE: It is your best, sir.
SIR POLITIC: This three weeks, all my advices, all my
      letters,
   They have been intercepted.
PEREGRINE: Indeed, sir?
   Best have a care.
SIR POLITIC: Nay, so I will.
PEREGRINE: This knight,   15
   I may not lose him, for my mirth, till night.

ACT 2 / SCENE 4

[VOLPONE'*s house.*]
([*Enter*] VOLPONE, MOSCA.)

VOLPONE: O, I am wounded.
MOSCA: Where, sir?
VOLPONE: Not without;
   Those blows were nothing: I could bear them ever.

---

moccenigo, "a kind of coine in Venice" (Florio) perhaps
worth nine *gazets.* *banner of my front,* displayed upon the
scaffold, listing maladies and cures. *bate,* abate. *bagatine,*
"a little coine in Italie" (Florio) about a third of a farthing.
handkerchiefs, i.e., with the money knotted into a corner; the
usual practice. *give it,* i.e., the heroic spirit. *pistolet,* Spanish gold coin, then worth about eighteen shillings. *spark,*
gallant, brave fellow. *Celia at the window,* presumably on the
tarras (upper stage) or in the window stage; the text does not
say when she first appears. *poulder,* powder; Jonson preferred this spelling (Latin *pulvis*). *moiety,* a half, or a part.
sophisticated, adulterated.

---

virginal jacks, strictly the pieces of wood bearing the
quills of the virginals, but sometimes erroneously used for
keys (the image derives from Rabelais). *Flaminio,* Flaminio
Scala, leading figure in the *commedia,* associated with Venice.
Franciscina, stock character of maid in the *commedia.* *Pantalone di Besogniosi,* stock Venetian character in the *commedia;*
a lean old man in loose slippers, black cap and gown, and red
dress, his name derives him from a line of paupers, and it was
often his role to be cuckolded.

But angry Cupid, bolting° from her eyes,
Hath shot himself into me, like a flame;
5 Where, now, he flings about his burning heat,
As in a furnace, an ambitious fire°
Whose vent is stopped. The fight is all within me.
I cannot live, except thou help me, Mosca;
My liver° melts, and I, without the hope
10 Of some soft air, from her refreshing breath,
Am but a heap of cinders.
MOSCA: 'Las, good sir!
Would you had never seen her.
VOLPONE: Nay, would thou
Hadst never told me of her.
MOSCA: Sir, 'tis true;
I do confess, I was unfortunate,
15 And you unhappy: but I am bound in conscience,
No less than duty, to effect my best
To your release of torment, and I will, sir.
VOLPONE: Dear Mosca, shall I hope?
MOSCA: Sir, more than dear,
I will not bid you to despair of ought,
Within a human compass.
20 VOLPONE: O, there spoke
My better Angel. Mosca, take my keys,
Gold, plate and jewels, all's at thy devotion;°
Employ them, how thou wilt; nay, coin me,° too:
So thou, in this, but crown° my longings.—
Mosca?°
MOSCA: Use but your patience.
VOLPONE: So I have.
25 MOSCA: I doubt not
To bring success to your desires.
VOLPONE: Nay, then,
I not repent me of my late disguise.
MOSCA: If you can horn him,° sir, you need not.
VOLPONE: True:
Besides, I never meant him for my heir.
30 Is not the colour° o' my beard, and eyebrows,
To make me known?
MOSCA: No jot.
VOLPONE: I did it well.
MOSCA: So well, would I could follow you in mine,°
With half the happiness;° and, yet, I would
Escape your epilogue.°
VOLPONE: But, were they gulled
With a belief, that I was Scoto?

MOSCA: Sir,   35
Scoto himself could hardly have distinguished!
I have not time to flatter you, now, we'll part:
And, as I prosper, so applaud my art. [Exeunt.]

ACT 2 / SCENE 5

[CORVINO's house.]
([Enter] CORVINO, CELIA.)

CORVINO: Death of mine honour, with the city's fool?
A juggling, tooth-drawing,° prating mountebank?
And at a public window? where, whilst he,
With his strained action,° and his dole of faces,°
To his drug lectures draws your itching ears,   5
A crew of old, unmarried, noted lechers
Stood leering up, like satyrs: and you smile
Most graciously! and fan your favours forth,
To give your hot spectators satisfaction!
What, was your mountebank their call? their
whistle?°   10
Or were you enamoured on his copper rings.
His saffron jewel, with the toad-stone° in't?
Or his embroidered suit, with the cope-stitch,°
Made of a hearse-cloth?° or his old tilt-feather?°
Or his starched beard?° Well! you shall have him,
yes.   15
He shall come home, and minister unto you
The fricace, for the mother.° Or, let me see,
I think, you'd rather mount?° Would you not
mount?
Why, if you'll mount, you may; yes truly, you may:
And so, you may be seen, down to th' foot.   20
Get you a cittern,° Lady Vanity,°
And be a dealer,° with the virtuous man;°
Make one:° I'll but protest° myself a cuckold,

bolting, darting arrows (bolts). ambitious fire, rising, swelling flames, recoiling to find other outlets. liver, believed the seat of intense passions. devotion, disposal, with pun on religious sense. coin me, render me into coin. crown, perfect, with pun on coin. —Mosca? expressing impatience at Mosca's thoughtful silence. horn him, cuckold him. colour, i.e., the fox's color, red. mine, i.e., "my art" (of disguise and mimicry). happiness, felicitous aptitude. your epilogue, i.e., the beating, but may hint at the end of Mosca's plot.

tooth-drawing, the responsibility of mountebanks and barbers. strained action, extravagant gesture. dole of faces, mean repertory of expressions. call...whistle, alluding to the enticement of game-fowl. toad-stone, believed to lie between the toad's eyes and to have magical and restorative properties. cope-stitch, used to decorate a cope border. hearse-cloth, coffin drapery, here either cheap or stolen. tilt-feather, plume worn in tilting helmet; here perhaps found with the hearse-cloth. starched beard, gummed and waxed beards were high fashion. fricace, for the mother, massage for hysteria, believed to be seated in the womb; Corvino puns on suggestions of seduction and birth. mount, i.e., the mountebank's platform, or the mountebank himself; another indecent pun affecting the meaning of "down to the foot." cittern, kind of zither or guitar, often carried by a mountebank's wench. Lady Vanity, a character in some morality plays, including that acted in Sir Thomas More IV. i. be a dealer, do a deal, trade with (hinting at prostitution). virtuous man, with sneering pun on "virtuoso." Make one, make a deal; mate. protest, declare.

And save your dowry.° I am a Dutchman,° I!
25 For, if you thought me an Italian,
You would be damned, ere you did this, you whore:
Thou'dst tremble, to imagine, that the murder
Of father, mother, brother, all thy race,
Should follow, as the subject of my justice.
CELIA: Good sir, have patience!
30 CORVINO: What couldst thou purpose
Less to thyself, than, in this heat of wrath,
And stung with my dishonour, I should strike

[*Takes his sword.*]

This steel into thee, with as many stabs,
As thou wert gazed upon with goatish eyes?
35 CELIA: Alas sir, be appeased! I could not think
My being at the window should more, now,
Move your impatience, than at other times.
CORVINO: No? not to seek, and entertain a parley,°
With a known knave? before a multitude?
40 You were an actor, with your handkerchief!
Which he, most sweetly, kissed in the receipt,
And might, no doubt, return it, with a letter,
And point the place, where you might meet: your
sister's,
Your mother's, or your aunt's might serve the turn.
45 CELIA: Why, dear sir, when do I make these excuses?
Or ever stir, abroad, but to the church?
And that, so seldom—
CORVINO: Well, it shall be less;
And thy restraint, before, was liberty
To what I now decree: and therefore, mark me.
50 First, I will have this bawdy light° dammed up;
And, till't be done, some two, or three yards off,
I'll chalk a line; o'er which, if thou but chance
To set thy desp'rate foot; more hell, more horror,
More wild, remorseless rage shall seize on thee,
55 Than on a conjurer that had heedless left
His circle's° safety, ere his devil was laid.
Then, here's a lock,° which I will hang upon thee;
And, now I think on't, I will keep thee backwards;
Thy lodging shall be backwards;° thy walks
backwards;
60 Thy prospect—all be backwards; and no pleasure
That thou shalt know, but backwards. Nay, since
you force
My honest nature, know it is your own
Being too open, makes me use you thus.
Since you will not contain your subtle° nostrils
65 In a sweet room, but they must snuff the air

Of rank, and sweaty passengers°—(*Knock within.*)
One knocks.
Away, and be not seen, pain° of thy life;
Not look° toward the window, if thou dost—
Nay, stay, hear this; let me not prosper, whore,
But I will make thee an anatomy,°   70
Dissect thee mine own self, and read a lecture
Upon thee, to the city, and in public.
Away! [*Exit* CELIA.] Who's there? [*Enter* SERVANT.]
SERVANT: 'Tis Signior Mosca, sir.

ACT 2 / SCENE 6

CORVINO: Let him come in, his master's dead.
There's yet
Some good, to help the bad. [*Enter* MOSCA.] My
Mosca, welcome!
I guess your news.
MOSCA: I fear you cannot, sir.
CORVINO: Is't not his death?
MOSCA: Rather the contrary.
CORVINO: Not his recovery?
MOSCA: Yes, sir.
CORVINO: I am cursed,   5
I am bewitched, my crosses° meet to vex me.
How? how? how? how?
MOSCA: Why, sir, with Scoto's oil!
Corbaccio, and Voltore brought of it,
Whilst I was busy in an inner room—
CORVINO: Death! that damned mountebank! But for
the law,   10
Now I could kill the rascal: 't cannot be,
His oil should have that virtue. Ha' not I
Known him a common rogue, come fiddling in
To th' *osteria,*° with a tumbling whore,°
And when he has done all his forced tricks, been
glad   15
Of a poor spoonful of dead wine, with flies in 't?
It cannot be. All his ingredients
Are a sheep's gall, a roasted bitch's marrow,
Some few sod° earwigs, pounded caterpillars,
A little capon's grease, and fasting spittle:°   20
I know 'em, to a dram.
MOSCA: I know not, sir,
But some on't, there, they poured into his ears,
Some in his nostrils, and recovered him;
Applying but the fricace.
CORVINO: Pox o' that fricace.
MOSCA: And since, to seem the more officious,°   25
And flattering of his health, there, they have had,

---

save your dowry, an adulteress was deprived of all her inheritance. **Dutchman,** believed to be long-suffering and phlegmatic. **parley,** conversation. **light,** window. **circle,** the magician was supposed safe in his circle until the devil was "laid" to hell. **lock,** chastity belt. **backwards,** i.e., at the back of the house. **subtle,** insidiously acute.

passengers, passersby. **pain,** on pain. **Not look,** do not look. **anatomy,** body for anatomical demonstration; also moral analysis. **crosses,** afflictions; with a touch of ironic blasphemy. **osteria,** inn. **tumbling whore,** disreputable acrobat (with indecent pun). **sod,** boiled. **fasting spittle,** here the saliva of the starving Scoto. **officious,** dutiful, zealous.

At extreme fees,° the college of physicians
Consulting on him, how they might restore him;
Where one would have a cataplasm° of spices,
30 Another, a flayed ape clapped to his breast,
A third would ha' it a dog, a fourth an oil
With wild cats' skins: at last, they all resolved
That, to preserve him, was no other means,
But some young woman must be straight sought
    out,
35 Lusty, and full of juice, to sleep by him;
And, to this service, most unhappily
And most unwillingly, am I now employed,
Which, here, I thought to pre-acquaint you with,
For your advice, since it concerns you most,
49 Because, I would not do that thing might cross
Your ends,° on whom I have my whole
    dependence, sir:
Yet, if I do it not, they may delate°
My slackness to my patron, work me out
Of his opinion; and there, all your hopes,
45 Ventures, or whatsoever, are all frustrate.
I do but tell you, sir. Besides, they are all
Now striving, who shall first present him.°
    Therefore—°
I could entreat you, briefly, conclude somewhat:°
Prevent 'em° if you can.
CORVINO: Death to my hopes!
50 This is my villainous fortune! Best to hire
Some common courtesan?
MOSCA: Ay, I thought of that, sir.
But they are all so subtle, full of art,
And age again° doting, and flexible,
So as—I cannot tell—we may perchance
Light on a quean,° may cheat us all.
55 CORVINO: 'Tis true.
MOSCA: No, no: it must be one, that has no tricks, sir,
Some simple thing, a creature, made unto it;°
Some wench you may command. Ha' you no
    kinswoman?
God's so°—Think, think, think, think, think, think,
    think, sir.
60 One o' the doctors offered, there, his daughter.
CORVINO: How?
MOSCA: Yes, Signior Lupo,° the physician.
CORVINO: His daughter!

MOSCA: And a virgin, sir. Why, alas
He knows the state of 's body, what it is;
That nought can warm his blood, sir, but a fever;
Nor any incantation raise his spirit;   65
A long forgetfulness hath seized that part.
Besides, sir, who shall know it? some one, or
    two—
CORVINO: I pray thee give me leave. [Walks aside.] If
    any man
But I had had this luck—The thing, in 't self,
I know, is nothing—Wherefore should not I   70
As well command my blood, and my affections,
As this dull doctor? In the point of honour,
The cases are all one, of wife, and daughter.
MOSCA [aside]: I hear him coming.
CORVINO: She shall do't: 'tis done.
'Slight,° if this doctor, who is not engaged,°   75
Unless 't be for his counsel, which is nothing,
Offer his daughter, what should I, that am
So deeply in? I will prevent him: wretch!
Covetous wretch! Mosca, I have determined.
MOSCA: How, sir?
CORVINO: We'll make all sure. The party, you wot of,   80
Shall be mine own wife, Mosca.
MOSCA: Sir, the thing,
But that I would not seem to counsel you,
I should have motioned° to you, at the first:
And, make your count,° you have cut all their
    throats.
Why! 'tis directly taking a possession!°   85
And, in this next fit, we may let him go.
'Tis but to pull the pillow, from his head,
And he is throttled: 't had been done before,
But for your scrupulous doubts.
CORVINO: Ay, a plague on 't,
My conscience fools my wit.° Well, I'll be brief,°   90
And so be thou, lest they should be before us;
Go home, prepare him, tell him, with what zeal
And willingness, I do it: swear it was,
On the first hearing, as thou mayst do, truly,
Mine own free motion.
MOSCA: Sir, I warrant you,   95
I'll so possess him with it, that the rest
Of his starved clients shall be banished, all;
And only you received. But come not, sir,
Until I send, for I have something else
To ripen,° for your good; you must not know it.   100
CORVINO: But do not you forget to send, now.
MOSCA: Fear not. [Exit MOSCA.]

---

extreme fees, the greatest cost. **cataplasm,** poultice.
cross Your ends, obstruct your aims. **delate,** report. **present**
him, i.e., with the young woman. **Therefore—,** the dash
expresses an emphatic pause. **briefly, conclude somewhat,**
quickly decide something. **Prevent 'em,** beat 'em to it.
again, on the other hand. **quean,** strumpet. **made unto it,**
made for the part; or possibly "made to do it" by command.
God's so, God's soul; also corruption of *cazzo,* Italian for male
organ. **Signior Lupo,** Mr. Wolf; Mosca's invention parodies
Jonson's own.

'Slight, God's light. **engaged,** involved. **motioned,** proposed. **make your count,** count on it; or possibly "count your
gains." **taking a possession,** Mosca uses the legal phrase in a
grotesque context. **wit,** intelligence. **brief,** quick. **some-**
thing . . . ripen, i.e., the plot to disinherit Corbaccio's son.

ACT 2 / SCENE 7

CORVINO: Where are you, wife? my Celia? wife!

[*Enter* CELIA *weeping.*]

                                    What, blubbering?
Come, dry those tears, I think, thou thought'st me
   in earnest?
Ha? by this light, I talked so but to try thee.
Methinks, the lightness of the occasion
Should ha'confirmed° thee. Come, I am not
5   jealous.
CELIA: No?
CORVINO: Faith, I am not, I, nor never was:
It is a poor, unprofitable humour.
Do not I know, if women have a will,°
They'll do 'gainst all the watches° o' the world?
10 And that the fiercest spies, are tamed with gold?
Tut, I am confident in thee, thou shalt see't:
And see, I'll give thee cause too, to believe it.
Come, kiss me. Go, and make thee ready straight,
In all thy best attire, thy choicest jewels,
15 Put 'em all on, and with 'em, thy best looks:
We are invited to a solemn° feast,
At old Volpone's, where it shall appear
How far I am free, from jealousy, or fear.

ACT 3 / SCENE 1

[*A Street.*]
([*Enter*] MOSCA.)

MOSCA: I fear, I shall begin to grow in love
With my dear self, and my most prosperous parts,°
They do so spring, and burgeon; I can feel
A whimsy° i' my blood: I know not how,
5 Success hath made me wanton. I could skip
Out of my skin, now, like a subtle° snake,
I am so limber.° O! your parasite
Is a most precious thing, dropped from above,
Not bred 'mongst clods, and clotpoles, here on
   earth.
10 I muse the mystery° was not made a science,°
It is so liberally° professed! Almost
All the wise world is little else, in nature,
But parasites, or sub-parasites. And yet,
I mean not those, that have your bare town-art,°
15 To know, who's fit to feed 'em; have no house,

No family, no care, and therefore mould
Tales° for men's ears, to bait that sense; or get
Kitchen-invention,° and some stale receipts
To please the belly, and the groin;° not those,
With their court-dog-tricks, that can fawn, and
   fleer,°   20
Make their revènue out of legs and faces,°
Echo my lord, and lick away a moth:°
But your fine, elegant rascal, that can rise,
And stoop, almost together, like an arrow;
Shoot through the air, as nimbly as a star;   25
Turn short, as doth a swallow; and be here,
And there, and here, and yonder, all at once;
Present to any humour, all occasion;
And change a visor,° swifter, than a thought!
This is the creature, had the art born with him; 30
Toils not to learn it, but doth practise it
Out of most excellent nature: and such sparks,
Are the true parasites, others but their zanies.°

ACT 3 / SCENE 2

[*Enter* BONARIO.]

MOSCA: Who's this? Bonario? old Corbaccio's son?
The person I was bound° to seek. Fair sir,
You are happ'ly met.
BONARIO: That cannot be, by thee.
MOSCA: Why, sir?
BONARIO: Nay, 'pray thee know thy way, and
   leave me:
I would be loath to interchange discourse,   5
With such a mate, as thou art.
MOSCA: Courteous sir,
Scorn not my poverty.
BONARIO: Not I, by heaven:
But thou shalt give me leave to hate thy baseness.
MOSCA: Baseness?
BONARIO: Ay, answer me, is not thy sloth
Sufficient argument? thy flattery?   10
Thy means of feeding?
MOSCA: Heaven, be good to me,
These imputations are too common, sir,
And eas'ly stuck on virtue, when she's poor;
You are unequal° to me, and howe'er
Your sentence may be righteous, yet you are not, 15
That ere you know me, thus, proceed in censure:

---

confirmed, assured. *will*, sexual appetite. *watches*, watchmen, or vigilances in general. *solemn*, formal, sumptuous. *parts*, abilities. *whimsy*, vertigo, whirling. *subtle*, applied to the snake to signify its elusive movement, its texture and its traditional cunning. *limber*, pliant, supple. *mystery*, professional craft. *science*, branch of formal knowledge. *liberally*, "widely practiced by gentlemen"; Mosca puns on the sense describing the sciences "worthy of a free man" (see *OED*). *bare town-art*, the minimal skills of a street parasite.

mould Tales, concoct scandal, with suggestion of shaping traps for the ear. *Kitchen-invention*, perhaps new ways of preparing old dishes ("stale receipts"); or possibly "kitchen gossip"; invention need not imply novelty (see *OED*). *groin*, suggests that the receipts (recipes) include aphrodisiacs. *fleer*, smile obsequiously. *legs and faces*, bows and smirks. *lick . . . moth*, servile grooming; "moth" signified vermin in general. *visor*, mask, hence "expression" or "role." *zanies*, attendant clowns. *bound*, on my way. *unequal*, unjust, but with allusion to the difference of station.

St. Mark bear witness 'gainst you, 'tis inhuman.
   [*weeps.*]
BONARIO: What? does he weep? the sign is soft, and
   good!
I do repent me, that I was so harsh.
20 MOSCA: 'Tis true, that, swayed by strong necessity,
I am enforced to eat my careful° bread
With too much obsequy; 'tis true, beside,
That I am fain° to spin mine own poor raiment,
Out of my mere observance,° being not born
25 To a free fortune: but that I have done
Base offices, in rending friends asunder,
Dividing families, betraying counsels,
Whispering false lies, or mining° men with praises,
Trained° their credulity with perjuries,
30 Corrupted chastity, or am in love
With mine own tender ease, but would not rather
Prove° the most rugged, and laborious course,
That might redeem my present estimation;
Let me here perish, in all hope of goodness.
35 BONARIO: This cannot be a personated passion!
I was to blame, so to mistake thy nature;
'Pray thee forgive me: and speak out thy business.
MOSCA: Sir, it concerns you; and though I may seem,
At first, to make a main° offence, in manners,
40 And in my gratitude, unto my master,
Yet, for the pure love, which I bear all right,
And hatred of the wrong, I must reveal it.
This very hour, your father is in purpose
To disinherit you—
BONARIO: How!
MOSCA: And thrust you forth,
45 As a mere stranger to his blood; 'tis true, sir:
The work no way engageth me, but, as
I claim an interest in the general state
Of goodness, and true virtue, which I hear
T'abound in you: and, for which mere respect,°
50 Without a second aim, sir, I have done it.
BONARIO: This tale hath lost thee much of the late
   trust,
Thou hadst with me; it is impossible:
I know not how to lend it any thought,
My father should be so unnatural.
55 MOSCA: It is a confidence, that well becomes
Your piety;° and formed, no doubt, it is,
From your own simple innocence: which makes
Your wrong more monstrous, and abhorred. But, sir,
I now, will tell you more. This very minute,
60 It is, or will be doing; and, if you
Shall be but pleased to go with me, I'll bring you,
I dare not say where you shall see, but where

Your ear shall be a witness of the deed;
Hear yourself written bastard: and professed°
The common issue of the earth.°
BONARIO: I'm mazed!   65
MOSCA: Sir, if I do it not, draw your just sword,
And score° your vengeance, on my front,° and face;
Make me your villain; you have too much wrong,
And I do suffer for you, sir. My heart
Weeps blood, in anguish—
BONARIO: Lead, I follow thee.   70

ACT 3 / SCENE 3

[VOLPONE*'s house*]
[*Enter* VOLPONE, *followed by* NANO, ANDROGYNO *and*
CASTRONE.]

VOLPONE: Mosca stays long, methinks. Bring forth
   your sports
And help to make the wretched time more sweet.
NANO: Dwarf, Fool, and Eunuch, well met here we be.
A question it were now, whether° of us three,
Being all, the known delicates° of a rich man.   5
In pleasing him, claim the precedency can?
CASTRONE: I claim for myself.
ANDROGYNO: And, so doth the fool.
NANO: 'Tis foolish indeed: let me set you both to
   school.
First, for your dwarf, he's little, and witty,
And every thing, as it is little, is pretty;   10
Else, why do men say to a creature of my shape,
So soon as they see him, 'It's a pretty little ape?'
And, why a pretty ape? but for pleasing imitation
Of greater men's action, in a ridiculous fashion.
Beside, this feat° body of mine doth not crave   15
Half the meat, drink, and cloth, one of your
   bulks will have.
Admit, your fool's face be the mother of laughter,
Yet, for his brain, it must always come after:
And, though that do feed him, it's a pitiful case.
His body is beholding to such a bad face.   20

(*One knocks.*)

VOLPONE: Who's there? my couch; away, look Nano,
   see:
Give me my caps, first—go, enquire!

[*Exeunt* NANO, ANDROGYNO, CASTRONE; VOLPONE *to*
his bed.]

                        Now, Cupid
Send it be Mosca, and with fair return.°

---

careful, hard-won. **fain,** obliged. **observance,** dutiful
service. **mining,** undermining. **Trained,** taken in, led on
(see *OED*). **Prove,** undergo. **main,** major. **for . . . respect,**
for which reason alone. **piety,** filial love (Latin *pietas*).

professed, proclaimed. **common . . . earth,** of obscure or
unknown parentage (Latin *terrae filius*). **score,** mark up.
front, forehead or face. **whether,** which. **known delicates,**
acknowledged indulgences. **feat,** dainty. **fair return,** i.e.,
from a profitable venture.

NANO [*at the door*]: It is the beauteous madam—
VOLPONE: Would-be—is it?
NANO: The same.
25 VOLPONE: Now, torment on me; squire her in:
For she will enter, or dwell here for ever.
Nay, quickly, that my fit were past. I fear
A second hell too, that my loathing this
Will quite expel my appetite to the other:
30 Would she were taking, now, her tedious leave.
Lord, how it threats me, what I am to suffer!

ACT 3 / SCENE 4

[*Enter* NANO *with* LADY WOULD-BE.]

LADY WOULD-BE: I thank you, good sir. Pray you
signify
Unto your patron, I am here. This band°
Shows not my neck enough—I trouble you, sir,
Let me request you, bid one of my women
5 Come hither to me—in good faith, I am dressed
Most favourably° today, it is no matter.

[*Enter* 1st WOMAN.]

'Tis well enough. Look, see these petulant things!
How they have done this!
VOLPONE: I do feel the fever
Ent'ring, in at mine ears; O for a charm,
To fright it hence.
10 LADY WOULD-BE: Come nearer: is this curl
In his right place? or this? why is this higher
Than all the rest? you ha'not washed your eyes, yet?
Or do they not stand even i' your head?
Where's your fellow? call her. [*Exit* 1st WOMAN.]
NANO: Now, St. Mark
15 Deliver us: anon,° she'll beat her women,
Because her nose is red.

[*Enter* 1st WOMAN *with* 2nd WOMAN.]

LADY WOULD-BE: I pray you, view
This tire,° forsooth: are all things apt, or no?
1st WOMAN: One hair a little, here, sticks out,
forsooth.
LADY WOULD-BE: Does't so forsooth? and where was
your dear sight
20 When it did so, forsooth? what now? bird-eyed?°
And you, too? pray you both approach, and mend it.
Now, by that light, I muse, you're not ashamed!
I, that have preached these things, so oft, unto you,
Read you the principles, argued all the grounds,
25 Disputed every fitness, every grace,°

Called you to counsel of so frequent
dressings—
NANO [*aside*]: More carefully, than of your fame,° or
honour.
LADY WOULD-BE: Made you acquainted, what an
ample dowry
The knowledge of these things would be unto you,
Able, alone, to get you noble husbands   30
At your return: and you, thus, to neglect it?
Besides, you seeing what a curious° nation
Th' Italians are, what will they say of me?
'The English lady cannot dress herself.'—
Here's a fine imputation, to our country!   35
Well, go your ways, and stay, i'the next room.
This fucus° was too coarse too, it's no matter.
Good sir, you'll give 'em entertainment?

[*Exeunt* NANO, 1st *and* 2nd WOMEN.]

VOLPONE: The storm comes toward me.
LADY WOULD-BE: How does my Volp?
VOLPONE: Troubled with noise, I cannot sleep; I
dreamt   40
That a strange fury entered, now, my house,
And, with the dreadful tempest of her breath,
Did cleave my roof asunder.
LADY WOULD-BE: Believe me, and I
Had the most fearful dream, could I remember 't—
VOLPONE: Out on my fate; I ha'given her the occasion 45
How to torment me: she will tell me hers.
LADY WOULD-BE: Methought, the golden mediocrity°
Polite, and delicate—
VOLPONE: O, if you do love me,
No more; I sweat, and suffer, at the mention
Of any dream: feel, how I tremble yet.   50
LADY WOULD-BE: Alas, good soul! the passion of the
heart.°
Seed-pearl° were good now, boiled with syrup of
apples,
Tincture of gold, and coral,° citron-pills,
Your elecampane° root, myrobalanes°—
VOLPONE [*aside*]: Ay me, I have ta'en a grass-hopper
by the wing.   55
LADY WOULD-BE: Burnt silk,° and amber,° you have
muscadel
Good i' the house—
VOLPONE: You will not drink, and part?

---

band, ruff or collar. **favourably,** pleasingly (but ironic). **anon,** shortly. **tire,** head-dress. **bird-eyed,** probably "pop-eyed," startled; possibly "short-sighted" or "timid." **preached . . . grace,** Lady Would-be deploys the terminology of formal rhetoric.

fame, reputation. **curious,** particular about details. **fucus,** cosmetic paste. **golden mediocrity,** a travesty of the "golden mean." **passion of the heart,** heartburn. **Seed-pearl,** said by Burton to "avail to the exhilaration of the heart" (*Anatomy of Melancholy* [1632], p. 376). **coral,** hung around the neck, supposed to drive away fears, devils, and bad dreams. **elecampane,** plant with bitter aromatic leaves and root, used as stimulant. **myrobalanes,** astringent plum-like fruit prescribed for melancholy and agues. **Burnt silk,** taken in water for the small-pox. **amber,** used to perfume the air.

LADY WOULD-BE: No, fear not that. I doubt, we shall not get
    Some English saffron°—half a dram would serve—
60   Your sixteen cloves, a little musk, dried mints,
    Bugloss,° and barley-meal—
VOLPONE: She's in again,
    Before I feigned diseases, now I have one.
LADY WOULD-BE: And these applied, with a right
    scarlet cloth°—
VOLPONE: Another flood of words! a very torrent!
LADY WOULD-BE: Shall I, sir, make you a poultice?
65 VOLPONE: No, no, no;
    I'm very well: you need prescribe no more.
LADY WOULD-BE: I have, a little, studied physic; but now,
    I'm all for music: save, i'the forenoons,°
    An hour, or two, for painting. I would have
70   A lady, indeed, to have all, letters, and arts,
    Be able to discourse, to write, to paint,
    But principal, as Plato holds, your music,
    And so does wise Pythagoras, I take it,
    Is your true rapture; when there is concent°
75   In face, in voice, and clothes: and is, indeed,
    Our sex's chiefest ornament.
VOLPONE: The poet,°
    As old in time, as Plato, and as knowing,
    Says that your highest female grace is silence.
LADY WOULD-BE: Which o' your poets? Petrarch? or Tasso? or Dante?
80   Guarini? Ariosto? Aretine?
    Cieco di Hadria?° I have read them all.
VOLPONE: Is everything a cause, to my destruction?
LADY WOULD-BE: I think, I ha' two or three of 'em, about me.
VOLPONE: The sun, the sea will sooner, both, stand still,
85   Than her eternal tongue! nothing can scape it.
LADY WOULD-BE: Here's *Pastor Fido*°—
VOLPONE: Profess obstinate silence,
    That's now, my safest.
LADY WOULD-BE: All our English writers,
    I mean such, as are happy in th'Italian,
    Will deign to steal out of this author, mainly;
90   Almost as much, as from Montagnié:
    He has so modern, and facile a vein,
    Fitting the time, and catching the court-ear.
    Your Petrarch is more passionate, yet he,

    In days of sonneting, trusted 'em, with much:°
    Dante is hard, and few can understand him.   95
    But, for a desperate wit,° there's Aretine!
    Only, his pictures are a little obscene—
    You mark me not?
VOLPONE: Alas, my mind's perturb'd.
LADY WOULD-BE: Why, in such cases, we must cure ourselves,
    Make use of our philosophy—
VOLPONE: O'y me!   100
LADY WOULD-BE: And, as we find our passions do rebel,
    Encounter 'em with reason; or divert 'em,
    By giving scope unto some other humour
    Of lesser danger: as, in politic bodies,°
    There's nothing, more, doth overwhelm the judgement,   105
    And clouds the understanding, than too much
    Settling, and fixing, and (as't were) subsiding
    Upon one object. For the incorporating
    Of these same outward things, into that part,
    Which we call mental, leaves some certain faeces   110
    That stop the organs, and, as Plato says,
    Assassinates our knowledge.°
VOLPONE: Now, the spirit
    Of patience help me.
LADY WOULD-BE: Come, in faith, I must
    Visit you more a days;° and make you well:
    Laugh, and be lusty.
VOLPONE: My good angel save me!   115
LADY WOULD-BE: There was but one sole man, in all the world,
    With whom I ere could sympathize; and he
    Would lie you often, three, four hours together,
    To hear me speak: and be, sometime, so rapt,
    As he would answer me, quite from the purpose,   120
    Like you, and you are like him, just. I'll discourse,
    And't be but only, sir, to bring you asleep,
    How we did spend our time, and loves, together,
    For some six years.
VOLPONE: Oh, oh, oh, oh, oh, oh.
LADY WOULD-BE: For we were *coaetanei*,° and brought up—   125
VOLPONE [*aside*]: Some power, some fate, some fortune rescue me!

---

    saffron, then grown in England (e.g., at Saffron Walden) for medical and confectory use. **Bugloss**, recommended by Burton as a heart stimulant (*Anatomy* [1632], p. 373). **scarlet cloth**, another treatment for small-pox; the patient was wrapped in it. **forenoons**, mornings. **concent**, harmony, concord. **The poet**, i.e., Sophocles. **Cieco di Hadria**, "the blind man of Adria," Luigi Groto (1541–1585), a prolific, but minor, poet in comparison with the five first named. **Pastor Fido**, Guarini's pastoral (1590), translated into English as *The Faithful Shepherd* in 1602.

    trusted . . . much, left much in their keeping; Petrarch was imitated as a sonneteer by Wyatt, Surrey, Sidney, and Spenser, among others. **desperate wit**, outrageous poet; Aretino wrote a number of pornographic poems including the sixteen *Sonneti lussoriosi* which were published to designs by Giulio Romano in 1523. **politic bodies**, kingdom, states. **overwhelm . . . knowledge**, Lady Would-be's theories of obsession and perception are a travesty of Platonic thinking. **more a days**, on more days, more often (compare "nowadays"). **coaetanei**, of the same age (*co-aetaneus*).

ACT 3 / SCENE 5

[*Enter* MOSCA.]

MOSCA: God save you, madam!
LADY WOULD-BE: Good sir.
VOLPONE: Mosca! welcome,
   Welcome to my redemption!
MOSCA: Why, sir?
VOLPONE: Oh,
   Rid me of this my torture, quickly, there;
   My Madam, with the everlasting voice:
5   The bells, in time of pestilence,° ne'er made
   Like noise, or were in that perpetual motion;
   The cock-pit° comes not near it. All my house,
   But now, steamed like a bath, with her thick
      breath.
   A lawyer could not have been heard; nor scarce
10   Another woman, such a hail of words
   She has let fall. For hell's sake, rid her hence.
MOSCA: Has she presented?
VOLPONE: O, I do not care,
   I'll take her absence, upon any price,
   With any loss.
MOSCA: Madam—
LADY WOULD-BE: I ha'brought your patron
   A toy, a cap here, of mine own work—
15 MOSCA: 'Tis well,
   I had forgot to tell you, I saw your knight,
   Where you'd little think it—
LADY WOULD-BE: Where?
MOSCA: Marry,
   Where yet, if you make haste, you may apprehend
     him,
   Rowing upon the water in a gondola,
20   With the most cunning courtesan of Venice.
LADY WOULD-BE: Is't true?
MOSCA: Pursue 'em, and believe your eyes:
   Leave me, to make your gift. [*Exit* LADY WOULD-BE.]
     I knew 'twould take.
   For lightly,° they that use themselves most licence,
   Are still° most jealous.
VOLPONE: Mosca, hearty thanks,
25   For thy quick fiction, and delivery of me.
   Now, to my hopes, what say'st thou?

[*Enter* LADY WOULD-BE.]

LADY WOULD-BE: But do you hear, sir?—
VOLPONE: Again; I fear a paroxysm.
LADY WOULD-BE: Which way
   Rowed they together?
MOSCA: Toward the Rialto.
LADY WOULD-BE: I pray you lend me your dwarf.

---

bells . . . *pestilence,* death knells.   *cock-pit,* to be found in Venice or London; the Drury lane cockpit was enclosed and later became a theater.   *lightly,* often, usually.   *still,* always.

MOSCA: I pray you, take him.

[*Exit* LADY WOULD-BE.]

   Your hopes, sir, are like happy blossoms, fair,   30
   And promise timely fruit, if you will stay
   But the maturing; keep you, at your couch,
   Corbaccio will arrive straight, with the will:
   When he is gone, I'll tell you more.
VOLPONE: My blood,
   My spirits are returned, I am alive: 35
   And like your wanton gamester, at *primero,*°
   Whose thought had whispered to him, not go less,
   Methinks I lie, and draw—for an encounter.

[VOLPONE *draws the curtains across his bed.*]

ACT 3 / SCENE 6

[MOSCA *leads* BONARIO *in and hides him.*]

MOSCA: Sir, here concealed, you may hear all. But
     pray you
   Have patience, sir; *(One knocks)* the same's your
     father, knocks:
   I am compelled to leave you.
BONARIO: Do so. Yet,
   Cannot my thought imagine this a truth.

ACT 3 / SCENE 7

[MOSCA *admits* CORVINO *and* CELIA.]

MOSCA: Death on me! you are come too soon, what
     meant you?
   Did not I say, I would send?
CORVINO: Yes, but I feared
   You might forget it, and then they prevent us.
MOSCA: Prevent? [*aside*]—Did e'er man haste so, for
     his horns?
   A courtier would not ply it so, for a place.—   5
   Well, now there's no helping it, stay here;
   I'll presently return. [*Moves toward* BONARIO.]
CORVINO: Where are you, Celia?
   You know not wherefore I have brought you
     hither?
CELIA: Not well, except° you told me.
CORVINO: Now, I will:
   Hark hither. [*They converse apart.*]
MOSCA [*to* BONARIO]: Sir, your father hath sent word,   10
   It will be half an hour, ere he come;
   And therefore, if you please to walk, the while,
   Into that gallery—at the upper end,
   There are some books to entertain the time:
   And I'll take care, no man shall come unto you, sir.   15

---

primero, a gambling card game resembling poker; Volpone puns on its technical terms "go less," "lie," "draw" and "encounter."   *except,* except what.

BONARIO: Yes, I will stay there. [*aside*] I do doubt this
　　fellow.

　　[*Exit* BONARIO *to the gallery.*]

MOSCA: There, he is far enough; he can hear
　　nothing;
　　And, for his father, I can keep him off. [*Moves to*
　　VOLPONE.]

CORVINO: Nay, now, there is no starting back; and
　　therefore,
20　　Resolve upon it: I have so decreed.
　　It must be done. Nor, would I move't° afore,
　　Because I would avoid all shifts and tricks,
　　That might deny me.

CELIA: 　　　　　　　　　Sir, let me beseech you,
　　Affect° not these strange° trials; if you doubt
25　　My chastity, why lock me up, for ever:
　　Make me the heir of darkness. Let me live,
　　Where I may please your fears, if not your trust.

CORVINO: Believe it, I have no such humour, I.
　　All that I speak, I mean; yet I am not mad;
30　　Not horn-mad,° see you? Go to, show yourself
　　Obedient, and a wife.

CELIA: 　　　　　　　　　O heaven!

CORVINO: 　　　　　　　　　　　　I say it,
　　Do so.

CELIA: Was this the train?°

CORVINO: 　　　　　　　　　　　I've told you reasons;
　　What the physicians have set down; how much,
　　It may concern me; what my engagements are;
35　　My means;° and the necessity of those means,
　　For my recovery: wherefore, if you be
　　Loyal, and mine, be won, respect my venture.°

CELIA: Before your honour?

CORVINO: 　　　　　　　　Honour? tut, a breath;
　　There's no such thing, in nature: a mere term
40　　Invented to awe fools. What is my gold
　　The worse, for touching? clothes for being looked
　　on?
　　Why, this's no more. An old, decrepit wretch,
　　That has no sense,° no sinew; takes his meat
　　With others' fingers; only knows to gape,
45　　When you do scald his gums; a voice; a shadow;
　　And what can this man hurt you?

CELIA: 　　　　　　　　　　　Lord! what spirit
　　Is this hath entered him?

CORVINO: 　　　　　　　And for your fame,
　　That's such a jig;° as if I would go tell it,
　　Cry it, on the Piazza! who shall know it?
50　　But he, that cannot speak it; and this fellow,

Whose lips are i' my pocket: save yourself,
　　If you'll proclaim't, you may. I know no other,
　　Should come to know it.

CELIA: 　　　　　　Are heaven, and saints then nothing?
　　Will they be blind, or stupid?

CORVINO: 　　　　　　　　　How?

CELIA: 　　　　　　　　　　　　　　Good sir,
55　　Be jealous still, emulate them; and think
　　What hate they burn with, toward every sin.

CORVINO: I grant you: if I thought it were a sin,
　　I would not urge you. Should I offer this
　　To some young Frenchman, or hot Tuscan blood,
60　　That had read Aretine, conned all his prints,
　　Knew every quirk° within lust's labyrinth,
　　And were professed critic,° in lechery:
　　And° I would look upon him, and applaud him,
　　This were a sin: but here, 'tis contrary,
65　　A pious work, mere charity, for physic,
　　And honest polity, to assure mine own.°

CELIA: O heaven! canst thou suffer such a change?

VOLPONE: Thou art mine honour, Mosca, and my
　　pride,
　　My joy, my tickling, my delight! go, bring 'em.

MOSCA: Please you draw near, sir.

CORVINO: 　　　　　　　　　Come on, what—
70　　You will not be rebellious? by that light—

　　[*Drags her to the bed.*]

MOSCA: Sir, Signior Corvino, here, is come to see
　　you—

VOLPONE: Oh!

MOSCA: 　　　　　And hearing of the consultation had,
　　So lately, for your health, is come to offer,
　　Or rather, sir, to prostitute—

CORVINO: 　　　　　　　　　Thanks, sweet Mosca.
75
MOSCA: Freely, unasked, or unentreated—

CORVINO: 　　　　　　　　　　　　Well.

MOSCA: As the true, fervent instance of his love,
　　His own most fair and proper wife; the beauty,
　　Only of price,° in Venice—

CORVINO: 　　　　　　　　　'Tis well urged.

MOSCA: To be your comfortress, and to preserve
　　you.
80
VOLPONE: Alas, I'm past already! pray you, thank
　　him,
　　For his good care, and promptness, but for that,
　　'Tis a vain labour, e'en to fight 'gainst heaven;
　　Applying fire to a stone:—uh, uh, uh, uh.—
　　Making a dead leaf grow again. I take
85
　　His wishes gently, though; and, you may tell him,
　　What I've done for him: marry, my state is
　　hopeless!

---

move't, urge. *Affect,* seek (not necessarily implying pretense). *strange,* exceptional, extreme. *horn-mad,* mad at being cuckolded, mad at the prospect, or mad to be so. *train,* trick, trap. *means,* financial resources. *venture,* enterprise. *sense,* sensory awareness. *jig,* trifle.

---

quirk, sudden twist. *professed critic,* qualified expert. *And,* if. *mine own,* i.e., the inheritance. *Only of price,* of unique excellence.

Will him, to pray for me; and t'use his fortune,
With reverence, when he comes to't.
MOSCA: Do you hear, sir?
Go to him, with your wife.
90   CORVINO: Heart of my father!
Wilt thou persist thus? come, I pray thee, come.
Thou seest 'tis nothing: Celia! by this hand
I shall grow violent. Come, do't, I say.
CELIA: Sir, kill me, rather: I will take down poison,
Eat burning coals,° do anything—
95   CORVINO: Be damned!
Heart, I will drag thee hence, home, by the hair;
Cry thee a strumpet, through the streets; rip up
Thy mouth, unto thine ears; and slit thy nose,
Like a raw rotchet°—Do not tempt me, come.
100   Yield, I am loath—Death, I will buy some slave,°
Whom I will kill, and bind thee to him, alive;
And at my window, hang you forth: devising
Some monstrous crime, which I, in capital letters,
Will eat into thy flesh, with aquafortis,°
105   And burning corsives,° on this stubborn breast.
Now, by the blood, thou hast incensed, I'll do't.
CELIA: Sir, what you please, you may; I am your
      martyr.
CORVINO: Be not thus obstinate, I ha' not deserved it:
Think, who it is, entreats you. Pray thee, sweet;
110   Good faith, thou shalt have jewels, gowns, attires,
What thou wilt think, and ask—Do, but, go kiss
      him.
Or touch him, but. For my sake. At my suit.
This once. No? not? I shall remember this.
Will you disgrace me, thus? do you thirst my
      undoing?
MOSCA: Nay, gentle lady, be advised.
115   CORVINO: No, no.
She has watched her time. God's precious,° this is
      scurvy;
'Tis very scurvy: and you are—
MOSCA: Nay, good sir.
CORVINO: An errant° locust, by heaven, a locust.
      Whore,
Crocodile,° that has thy tears prepared,
Expecting,° how thou'lt bid 'em flow.
120   MOSCA: Nay, pray you, sir,
She will consider.
CELIA: Would my life would serve
To satisfy—
CORVINO: 'Sdeath, if she would but speak to him,

And save my reputation, 'twere somewhat;
But, spitefully to affect my utter ruin°—
MOSCA: Ay, now you've put your fortune in her hands.   12
Why i'faith, it is her modesty, I must quit° her;
If you were absent, she would be more coming;°
I know it: and dare undertake for her.
What woman can, before her husband? Pray you,
Let us depart, and leave her, here.
CORVINO: Sweet Celia,   13
Thou mayst redeem all, yet; I'll say no more:
If not, esteem yourself as lost. [CELIA starts to leave.]
      Nay, stay there.

[Exeunt CORVINO, MOSCA.]

CELIA: O, God, and his good angels! whither, whither
Is shame fled human breasts? that with such ease,
Men dare put off your honours, and their own?   13
Is that, which ever was a cause of life,
Now placed beneath the basest circumstance?
And modesty an exile made, for money?
VOLPONE: Ay, in Corvino, and such earth-fed minds,

(He leaps off from his couch.)

That never tasted the true heaven of love.   14
Assure thee, Celia, he that would sell thee,
Only for hope of gain, and that uncertain,
He would have sold his part of paradise
For ready money, had he met a cope-man.°
Why art thou mazed,° to see me thus revived?   14
Rather applaud thy beauty's miracle;
'Tis thy great work: that hath, not now alone,
But sundry times, raised me, in several shapes,
And, but this morning, like a mountebank,
To see thee at thy window. Ay, before   15
I would have left my practice,° for thy love,
In varying figures,° I would have contended
With the blue Proteus,° or the hornèd flood.°
Now, art thou welcome.
CELIA: Sir!
VOLPONE: Nay, fly me not.
Nor, let thy false imagination   15
That I was bedrid, make thee think, I am so:
Thou shalt not find it. I am, now, as fresh,
As hot, as high, as in as jovial° plight,°

Eat . . . coals, Brutus's wife, Portia, died in this way.
rotchet, the red gurnet (a fish).   some slave, this was Tarquin's
threat to Lucrece.   aquafortis, nitric acid, used for etching.
corsives, corrosives.   God's precious, i.e., precious blood.
errant, either "wandering" or "arrant, downright"; the senses
are related and both applicable—"arrant, promiscuous parasite."   Crocodile, believed to entice its victims with artful
tears.   Expecting, anticipating.

ruin—(F, ruin, Q, ruin:), Q indicates that the thought is
incomplete, or that Mosca interrupts it; some editors read
"ruin!"   quit, clear, acquit.   coming, forthcoming, responsive.   cope-man, chapman, dealer.   mazed, bewildered.   practice, scheming, intriguing.   figures, appearances, shapes.
blue Proteus, marine blue (Latin caeruleus); Menelaus contends with the many shapes of Proteus (Odyssey IV. 456–458).
hornèd flood, the river-God Achelous who fought Hercules in
the forms of bull, serpent, and man-bull; the shape may symbolize the river's branchings and its roar.   jovial, born under
Jupiter, and therefore apt to share Jove's convivial temperament and amorous propensities.   plight, state, trim.

As when, in that so celebrated scene,
160 At recitation of our comedy,
For entertainment of the great Valois,°
I acted young Antinous;° and attracted
The eyes, and ears of all the ladies present,
T'admire each graceful gesture, note, and footing.

165   SONG°

Come, my Celia, let us prove,°
While we can, the sports of love;
Time will not be ours, for ever,
He, at length, our good will sever;
170 *Spend not then his gifts, in vain.*
Suns, that set, may rise again:
But if, once, we lose this light,
'Tis with us perpetual night.
Why should we defer our joys?
175 *Fame, and rumour are but toys.°*
Cannot we delude the eyes
Of a few poor household spies?
Or his easier ears beguile,
Thus removèd, by our wile?
180 *'Tis no sin, love's fruits to steal;*
But the sweet thefts to reveal:
To be taken, to be seen,
These have crimes accounted been.

CELIA: Some *serene*° blast me, or dire lightning strike
This my offending face.
185 VOLPONE: Why droops my Celia?
Thou hast in place of a base husband, found
A worthy lover: use thy fortune well,
With secrecy, and pleasure. See, behold,
What thou art queen of; not in expectation,
190 As I feed others; but possessed, and crowned.
See, here, a rope of pearl; and each, more orient°
Than that the brave Egyptian queen° caroused:
Dissolve, and drink 'em. See, a carbuncle,
May put out both the eyes of our St. Mark;°
195 A diamant, would have bought Lollia Paulina,°

When she came in, like star-light, hid with jewels,
That were the spoils of provinces; take these,
And wear, and lose 'em: yet remains an ear-ring
To purchase them again, and this whole state.
A gem, but worth a private patrimony,   200
Is nothing: we will eat such at a meal.
The heads of parrots, tongues of nightingales,
The brains of peacocks, and of ostriches
Shall be our food: and, could we get the phoenix,°
Though nature lost her kind, she were our dish.   205
CELIA: Good sir, these things might move a mind
    affected
With such delights; but I, whose innocence
Is all I can think wealthy, or worth th'enjoying,
And which once lost, I have nought to lose beyond
    it,
Cannot be taken with these sensual baits: 210
If you have conscience—
VOLPONE: 'Tis the beggar's virtue,
If thou hast wisdom, hear me, Celia.
Thy baths shall be the juice of July-flowers,°
Spirit of roses, and of violets,
The milk of unicorns,° and panthers' breath°   215
Gathered in bags, and mixed with Cretan wines.°
Our drink shall be preparèd gold, and amber;
Which we will take, until my roof whirl round
With the vertigo: and my dwarf shall dance,
My eunuch sing, my fool make up the antic.°   220
Whilst we, in changed shapes, act Ovid's tales,°
Thou, like Europa now, and I like Jove,°
Then I like Mars, and thou like Erycine,°
So, of the rest, till we have quite run through
And wearied all the fables of the gods.   225
Then will I have thee in more modern forms,
Attired like some sprightly dame of France,
Brave Tuscan lady, or proud Spanish beauty;
Sometimes, unto the Persian Sophy's° wife;
Or the Grand Signor's° mistress; and, for change,   230
To one of our most artful courtesans,
Or some quick° Negro, or cold Russian;
And I will meet thee, in as many shapes:

Valois, Henry of Valois was entertained at Venice in 1574. *Antinous,* beautiful youth, minion of the Emperor Hadrian. *Song,* imitated largely from Catullus's fifth ode, *Vivamus, mea Lesbia. prove,* try. *toys,* trifles. *serene,* (French *serein*), twilight mist in hot countries; once thought noxious. *orient,* rare and fine. *Egyptian queen,* Pliny (*Naturalis Historia* IX.120) tells how Cleopatra met Antony's challenge to spend a hundred thousand sesterces at a meal by drinking a priceless pearl dissolved in vinegar. *both . . . St. Mark,* perhaps an image of St. Mark with gems for eyes, but none is recorded; possibly two famous carbuncles in Venice, one in St. Mark's treasury; possibly an extravagant sacrilegious metaphor. *Lollia Paulina,* wife of the Emperor Caligula; an heiress whose wealth was extorted from the provinces by her father; Pliny describes her clad in jewels and glittering like the sun at a betrothal party.

phoenix, the mythical Arabian bird, supposed to renew itself from its own ashes every five hundred years. *July-flowers,* gillyflowers (clove-scented pinks). *milk of unicorns,* a delicacy found only here; but powdered unicorn horn (from the rhinoceros) was used as medicine. *panthers' breath,* panthers were said to attract their prey by the sweetness of their scent. *Cretan wines,* rather rich and sweet for bathing; there is evidence that Mary Queen of Scots habitually bathed in wine. *antic,* grotesque dance. *Ovid's tales,* i.e., *Metamorphoses. Europa . . . Jove,* Zeus won Europa by playing with her in the form of a bull before bearing her to Crete on his back. *Erycine,* Venus, after her temple at Eryx in Sicily. *Sophy,* the Shah, supreme ruler. *Grand Signor,* Sultan of Turkey. *quick,* lively.

235 Where we may, so, transfuse° our wand'ring souls,
Out at our lips, and score up sums of pleasures,
[*Sings.*]

That the curious shall not know,
How to tell them, as they flow;
And the envious, when they find
What their number is, be pined.°

240 CELIA: If you have ears that will be pierced; or eyes,
That can be opened; a heart, may be touched;
Or any part, that yet sounds man,° about you:
If you have touch of holy saints, or heaven,
Do me the grace, to let me scape. If not,
245 Be bountiful, and kill me. You do know,
I am a creature, hither ill betrayed,
By one, whose shame I would forget it were.
If you will deign me neither of these graces,
Yet feed your wrath, sir, rather than your lust;
250 (It is a vice, comes nearer manliness)
And punish that unhappy crime of nature,
Which you miscall my beauty: flay my face,
Or poison it, with ointments, for seducing
Your blood to this rebellion. Rub these hands,
255 With what may cause an eating leprosy,
E'en to my bones, and marrow: anything,
That may disfavour° me, save in my honour.
And I will kneel to you, pray for you, pay down
A thousand hourly vows, sir, for your health,
Report, and think you virtuous—
260 VOLPONE: Think me cold,
Frozen, and impotent, and so report me?
That I had Nestor's hernia,° thou wouldst think.
I do degenerate,° and abuse my nation,
To play with opportunity, thus long:
265 I should have done the act, and then parleyed.
Yield, or I'll force thee.
CELIA: O! just God.
VOLPONE: In vain—

([BONARIO] *leaps out from where* MOSCA *had placed*
him.)

BONARIO: Forbear, foul ravisher, libidinous swine,
Free the forced lady, or thou diest, impostor.
But that I am loath to snatch thy punishment
270 Out of the hand of justice, thou shouldst, yet,
Be made the timely sacrifice of vengeance,

Before this altar, and this dross,° thy idol.
Lady, let's quit the place, it is the den
Of villainy; fear nought, you have a guard:
And he, ere long, shall meet his just reward. 275
VOLPONE: Fall on me, roof, and bury me in ruin,
Become my grave, that wert my shelter. O!
I am unmasked, unspirited, undone,
Betrayed to beggary, to infamy—

ACT 3 / SCENE 8

[*Enter* MOSCA, *bleeding.*]

MOSCA: Where shall I run, most wretched shame of
men,
To beat out my unlucky brains?
VOLPONE: Here, here.
What! dost thou bleed?
MOSCA: O, that his well-driven sword
Had been so courteous to have cleft me down,
Unto the navel; ere I lived to see 5
My life, my hopes, my spirits, my patron, all
Thus desperately engagèd,° by my error.
VOLPONE: Woe, on thy fortune.
MOSCA: And my follies, sir.
VOLPONE: Th'hast made me miserable.
MOSCA: And myself, sir.
Who would have thought, he would have
hearkened, so? 10
VOLPONE: What shall we do?
MOSCA: I know not, if my heart
Could expiate the mischance, I'd pluck it out.
Will you be pleased to hang me? or cut my
throat?
And I'll requite you, sir. Let's die like Romans,°
Since we have lived, like Grecians.° (*They knock*
without.)
VOLPONE: Hark, who's there? 15
I hear some footing,° officers, the Saffi°
Come to apprehend us! I do feel the brand°
Hissing already, at my forehead: now,
Mine ears are boring.°
MOSCA: To your couch, sir, you
Make that place good, however.° Guilty men 20
Suspect, what they deserve still. Signior
Corbaccio!

---

transfuse, "to cause to flow from one to another" *(OED)*; the image is from Petronius, *Satyricon* 79. **pined,** tormented. **sounds man,** proclaims you a man. **disfavour,** disfigure. **Nestor's hernia,** Nestor embodies the strengths as well as the weaknesses of age in Homer's *Iliad;* this glance at his impotence is from Juvenal, *Satires* VI, 326. **degenerate,** possibly used transitively "cause my nation (Italy) to lose its ancestral virtue," but the intransitive use is more probable.

dross, "the scum thrown off from metals in smelting" *(OED)*; a perverse dismissal of Volpone's gold. **engagèd,** entangled. **like Romans,** stoically, by suicide. **like Grecians,** dissolutely and histrionically. **footing,** footsteps. **Saffi,** "*Saffo,* a catchpole, or sergeant" (Florio); bailiffs. **brand,** Jonson himself was branded on the thumb for killing Gabriel Spencer. **boring,** this suggests earrings or ear brandings for criminals, but no other evidence has been brought to bear. **Make . . . however,** "keep up that role whatever you do."

ACT 3 / SCENE 9

[*Enter* CORBACCIO.]

CORBACCIO: Why! how now? Mosca!

[*Enter* VOLTORE *unseen.*]

MOSCA: O, undone, amazed,° sir.
  Your son, I know not by what accident,
  Acquainted with your purpose to my patron,
  Touching your will, and making him your heir;
  Entered our house with violence, his sword
5   drawn,
  Sought for you, called you wretch, unnatural,
  Vowed he would kill you.
CORBACCIO: Me?
MOSCA: Yes, and my patron.
CORBACCIO: This act, shall disinherit him indeed:°
  Here is the will.
MOSCA: 'Tis well, sir.
CORBACCIO: Right and well.
  Be you as careful° now, for me.
10 MOSCA: My life, sir,
  Is not more tendered,° I am only yours.
CORBACCIO: How does he? will he die shortly, thinkst
    thou?
MOSCA: I fear
  He'll outlast May.
CORBACCIO: Today?
MOSCA: No, last out May, sir.
CORBACCIO: Couldst thou not gi'him a dram?°
MOSCA: O, by no means, sir.
CORBACCIO: Nay, I'll not bid you.
15 VOLTORE (*aside*):   This is a knave, I see.
MOSCA (*aside*): How! Signior Voltore! did he hear me?
VOLTORE: Parasite!
MOSCA: Who's that? O, sir, most timely welcome—
VOLTORE: Scarce,
  To the discovery of your tricks, I fear.
  You are his, only? and mine, also? are you not?
MOSCA: Who? I, sir!
20 VOLTORE: You sir, what device° is this
  About a will?
MOSCA: A plot for you, sir.
VOLTORE: Come,
  Put not your foists° upon me, I shall scent 'em.
MOSCA: Did you not hear it?
VOLTORE: Yes, I hear, Corbaccio
  Hath made your patron, there, his heir.
MOSCA: 'Tis true,
25 By my device, drawn to it by my plot,
  With hope—

VOLTORE: Your patron should reciprocate?
  And, you have promised?
MOSCA: For your good, I did, sir.
  Nay more, I told his son, brought, hid him here,
  Where he might hear his father pass the deed;
  Being persuaded to it, by this thought, sir,   30
  That the unnaturalness, first, of the act,
  And then, his father's oft disclaiming in him,°
  Which I did mean t'help on, would sure enrage
    him
  To do some violence upon his parent.
  On which the law should take sufficient hold,   35
  And you be stated° in a double hope:
  Truth be my comfort, and my conscience,
  My only aim was, to dig you a fortune
  Out of these two, old rotten sepulchres—
VOLTORE: I cry thee mercy, Mosca.
MOSCA: Worth your patience,   40
  And your great merit, sir. And, see the change!
VOLTORE: Why? what success?°
MOSCA: Most hapless!° you must help, sir.
  Whilst we expected th'old raven, in comes
  Corvino's wife, sent hither, by her husband—
VOLTORE: What, with a present?
MOSCA: No, sir, on visitation: 45
  (I'll tell you how, anon) and, staying long,
  The youth, he grows impatient, rushes forth,
  Seizeth the lady, wounds me, makes me swear
  (Or he would murder her, that was his vow)
  T'affirm my patron to have° done her rape: 50
  Which how unlike it is, you see! and, hence,
  With that pretext, he's gone, t'accuse his father;
  Defame my patron; defeat you—
VOLTORE: Where's her husband?
  Let him be sent for, straight.
MOSCA: Sir, I'll go fetch him.
VOLTORE: Bring him, to the Scrutineo.°
MOSCA: Sir, I will.   55
VOLTORE: This must be stopped.
MOSCA: O, you do nobly, sir.
  Alas, 'twas laboured all, sir, for your good;
  Nor, was there any want of counsel, in the plot:
  But fortune can, at any time, o'erthrow
  The projects of a hundred learned clerks,° sir.   60
CORBACCIO: What's that?
VOLTORE: Wilt please you sir, to go along?

[*Exeunt* CORBACCIO, VOLTORE.]

MOSCA: Patron, go in, and pray for our success.
VOLPONE: Need makes devotion: heaven your labour
    bless.

---

amazed, confused. *disinherit . . . indeed,* i.e., permanently. *careful,* solicitous. *tendered,* tenderly cared for. *dram,* dose. *device,* contrivance. *foists,* rogueries; also foist, "to smell or grow musty" (*OED*).

disclaiming in him, disowning; renouncing legal claim. *stated,* instated. *success,* outcome. *hapless,* unfortunate. *to have,* F, (*Q,* would have). *Scrutineo,* law court in Senate House. *clerks,* scholars.

ACT 4 / SCENE 1

[*A street.*]

[*Enter* SIR POLITIC WOULD-BE, PEREGRINE.]

SIR POLITIC: I told you, sir, it was a plot°: you see
    What observation is. You mentioned me,°
    For some instructions: I will tell you, sir,
    Since we are met, here, in this height° of Venice,
5   Some few particulars, I have set down,
    Only for this meridian; fit to be known
    Of your crude traveller, and they are these.
    I will not touch, sir, at your° phrase,° or clothes,
    For they are old.
PEREGRINE: Sir, I have better.
SIR POLITIC: Pardon,
    I meant, as they are themes.°
10 PEREGRINE: O, sir, proceed:
    I'll slander you no more of wit,° good sir.
SIR POLITIC: First, for your garb,° it must be grave,
      and serious;
    Very reserved, and locked; not tell a secret,
    On any terms, not to your father; scarce
15   A fable,° but with caution; make sure choice
    Both of your company, and discourse; beware,
    You never speak a truth—
PEREGRINE: How!
SIR POLITIC: Not to strangers,
    For those be they you must converse with, most;
    Others I would not know,° sir, but at distance,
20   So as I still might be a saver, in 'em:°
    You shall have tricks, else, passed upon you hourly.
    And then, for your religion, profess none;
    But wonder, at the diversity of all;
    And, for your part, protest, were there no other
    But simply the laws o'the land, you could content
25   you:
    Nick Machiavel, and Monsieur Bodin,° both,
    Were of this mind. Then, must you learn the use,
    And handling of your silver fork,° at meals;
    The metal° of your glass—these are main° matters,

With your Italian—and to know the hour,   30
    When you must eat your melons, and your figs.
PEREGRINE: Is that a point of state, too?
SIR POLITIC: Here it is.
    For your Venetian, if he see a man
    Preposterous,° in the least, he has him straight;°
    He has: he strips him. I'll acquaint you, sir,   35
    I now have lived here, 'tis some fourteen months,
    Within the first week of my landing here,
    All took me for a citizen of Venice:
    I knew the forms so well—
PEREGRINE [*aside*]:   And nothing else.
SIR POLITIC: I had read Contarene,° took me a
      house,   40
    Dealt with my Jews, to furnish it with moveables°—
    Well, if I could but find one man—one man.
    To mine own heart—whom I durst trust, I would—
PEREGRINE: What? what, sir?
SIR POLITIC: Make him rich, make him a fortune:
    He should not think, again. I would command it.   45
PEREGRINE: As how?
SIR POLITIC: With certain projects, that I have,
    Which, I may not discover.°
PEREGRINE (*aside*):   If I had
    But one to wager with, I would lay odds, now,
    He tells me, instantly.
SIR POLITIC: One is (and that
    I care not greatly, who knows) to serve the state   50
    Of Venice, with red herrings, for three years,
    And at a certain rate, from Rotterdam,
    Where I have correspondence.° There's a letter,
    Sent me from one o' the States,° and to that
      purpose;
    He cannot write his name, but that's his mark.   55
PEREGRINE: He is a chandler?°
SIR POLITIC: No, a cheesemonger.
    There are some other too, with whom I treat,
    About the same negotiation;
    And, I will not undertake it: for, 'tis thus,
    I'll do 't with ease, I've cast° it all. Your hoy°   60
    Carries but three men in her, and a boy;
    And she shall make me three returns, a year:
    So, if there come but one of three, I save,
    If two, I can defalk.° But, this is now,
    If my main project fail.

---

it was a plot, i.e., the mountebank scene. ***mentioned me,*** asked me in passing (?) ***height,*** latitude. ***your,*** the impersonal, familiar use which Peregrine affects to misinterpret. ***phrase,*** manner of speaking. ***themes,*** topics. ***slander . . . wit,*** either "I'll no more misrepresent you for the sake of being witty," or "I'll no more accuse you of being quick-witted." ***garb,*** demeanor. ***fable,*** fiction. ***know,*** acknowledge. ***be . . . 'em,*** "keep myself safe in respect to them" (either from danger or from inconvenience). ***Machiavel . . . Bodin,*** the sentiments are falsely attributed, but Machiavelli did tend to subordinate religion to the state, and Jean Bodin elaborated a theory of toleration. ***fork,*** forks were not much used in England at this time. ***metal,*** "the material used for making glass, in a molten state" (*OED*); Sir Politic is exhibiting his technical knowledge. ***main,*** of primary importance.

Preposterous, back-to-front, in the wrong order. ***has him straight,*** sums him up instantly. ***Contarene,*** Cardinal Gasparo Contarini published a book on Venice, *De Magistratibus et Republica Venetorum* (1589), translated into English in 1599. ***moveables,*** at this time commonly distinguished from fixed furnishings. ***discover,*** reveal. ***correspondence,*** connections. ***one o' the States,*** a member of the Dutch assembly, the States-General. ***chandler?*** Peregrine speculates from the greasy state of the letter. ***cast,*** reckoned. ***hoy,*** Dutch coastal vessel, meant for short hauls. ***defalk,*** allow a deduction, perhaps on the price of the herrings, but the financial strategy is obscure.

65 PEREGRINE: Then, you have others?
    SIR POLITIC: I should be loath to draw the subtle air°
        Of such a place, without my thousand aims.
        I'll not dissemble sir, where'er I come
        I love to be considerative;° and, 'tis true,
70   I have, at my free hours, thought upon
        Some certain goods, unto the state of Venice,
        Which I do call my cautions:° and, sir, which
        I mean, in hope of pension, to propound
        To the Great Council, then unto the Forty,
75   So to the Ten.° My means° are made already—
    PEREGRINE: By whom?
    SIR POLITIC: Sir, one, that though his place
            be obscure,
        Yet, he can sway, and they will hear him. He's
        A commendatore.
    PEREGRINE: What, a common sergeant?°
    SIR POLITIC: Sir, such as they are, put it in their
            mouths,°
80   What they should say, sometimes: as well as greater.
        I think I have my notes, to show you—
    PEREGRINE: Good, sir.
    SIR POLITIC: But, you shall swear unto me, on your
            gentry,
        Not to anticipate—
    PEREGRINE: I, sir?
    SIR POLITIC: Nor reveal
        A circumstance—My paper is not with me.
    PEREGRINE: O, but, you can remember, sir.
85 SIR POLITIC: My first is,
        Concerning tinder-boxes. You must know,
        No family is, here, without its box.
        Now sir, it being so portable a thing,
        Put case,° that you, or I were ill affected
90   Unto the state; sir, with it in our pockets,
        Might not I go into the arsenale?°
        Or you? come out again? and none the wiser?
    PEREGRINE: Except yourself, sir.
    SIR POLITIC: Go to, then. I, therefore,
        Advertise° to the state, how fit it were,
95   That none, but such as were known patriots,
        Sound lovers of their country, should be suffered
        T'enjoy them in their houses: and, even those,
        Sealed,° at some office, and, at such a bigness,
        As might not lurk in pockets.
    PEREGRINE: Admirable!

SIR POLITIC: My next is, how t'enquire, and be
    resolved,   100
    By present demonstration,° whether a ship,
    Newly arrived from Soria,° or from
    Any suspected part of all the Levant,
    Be guilty of the plague: and, where they use,
    To lie out forty, fifty days, sometimes,   105
    About the Lazaretto,° for their trial;
    I'll save that charge, and loss unto the merchant,
    And, in an hour, clear the doubt.
PEREGRINE: Indeed, sir?
SIR POLITIC: Or—I will lose my labour.
PEREGRINE: My faith, that's much.
SIR POLITIC: Nay, sir, conceive me. 'Twill cost me, in
    onions,°   110
    Some thirty livres°—
PEREGRINE: Which is one pound sterling.
SIR POLITIC: Beside my water-works: for this I do, sir.
    First, I bring in your ship, 'twixt two brick walls;
    (But those the state shall venture°) on the one
    I strain° me a fair tarpaulin; and, in that,   115
    I stick my onions, cut in halves: the other
    Is full of loop-holes, out at which, I thrust
    The noses of my bellows; and, those bellows
    I keep, with water-works, in perpetual motion,
    (Which is the easiest matter of a hundred).   120
    Now, sir, your onion, which doth naturally
    Attract th'infection, and your bellows, blowing
    The air upon him, will show (instantly)
    By his changed colour, if there be contagion,
    Or else, remain as fair, as at the first.   125
    Now 'tis known, 'tis nothing.
PEREGRINE: You are right, sir.
SIR POLITIC: I would I had my note.°
PEREGRINE: Faith, so would I:
    But, you ha' done well, for once, sir.
SIR POLITIC: Were I false,°
    Or would be made so, I could show you reasons,
    How I could sell this state, now, to the Turk;   130
    Spite of their gallies, or their—°
PEREGRINE: Pray you, Sir Pol.
SIR POLITIC: I have 'em not, about me.
PEREGRINE: That I feared.
    They're there, sir?
SIR POLITIC: No, this is my diary.
    Wherein I note my actions of the day.
PEREGRINE: Pray you, let's see, sir. What is here?
    'Notandum,   135

---

subtle air, atmosphere of intrigue. considerative, pru-
dently deliberate. cautions, can mean "precautions," but
taken here "in hope of pension." Great . . . Ten, the ad-
ministrative hierarchy of Venice. means, means of access,
contacts. sergeant, officer charged with the arrest or summoning of offenders. their mouths, i.e., the mouths of the
great. Put case, "say for example." arsenale, Sir Politic may
use the Italian pronunciation; the Arsenal of Venice housed
all its ships and weapons. Advertise, make known. Sealed,
registered under seal.

---

present demonstration, on-the-spot proof. Soria, Syria.
Lazaretto, pest-house; two were established in islands of the
Gulf of Venice after the plagues of 1423 and 1576. onions,
supposed to protect against the plague by gathering the
infection. livre, French coin. venture, invest in. strain,
stretch. note, possibly note of patent. false, traitorous. or
their— Sir Politic breaks off as he searches for his papers.

A rat had gnawn my spur-leathers; notwithstanding,
I put on new, and did go forth: but, first,
I threw three beans over the threshold.° *Item,*
I went, and bought two tooth-picks,° whereof one
140 I burst, immediately, in a discourse
With a Dutch merchant, 'bout *ragion del stato.*°
From him I went, and paid a *moccenigo,*
For piecing my silk stockings; by the way,
I cheapened sprats:° and at St. Mark's I urined,'
Faith, these are politic notes!
145 SIR POLITIC: Sir, I do slip
No action of my life, thus, but I quote° it.
PEREGRINE: Believe me it is wise!
SIR POLITIC: Nay, sir, read forth.

ACT 4 / SCENE 2

[*Enter* LADY WOULD-BE, NANO *and two* WOMEN]

LADY WOULD-BE: Where should this loose° knight be,
    trow? sure, he's housed.
NANO: Why, then he's fast.
LADY WOULD-BE: Ay, he plays both, with me:
    I pray you, stay. This heat will do more harm
    To my complexion, than his heart is worth.
5   (I do not care to° hinder, but to take him)
    How it comes off! [*Rubbing her face*]
1st WOMAN: My master's yonder.
LADY WOULD-BE: Where?
2nd WOMAN: With a young gentleman.
LADY WOULD-BE: That same's the party!
    In man's apparel. Pray you, sir, jog my knight:
    I will be tender to his reputation,
    However he demerit.°
SIR POLITIC: My lady?
10 PEREGRINE: Where?
SIR POLITIC: 'Tis she indeed, sir, you shall know her.
    She is,
    Were she not mine, a lady of that merit,
    For fashion, and behaviour; and, for beauty
    I durst compare—
PEREGRINE: It seems, you are not jealous,
    That dare commend her.
15 SIR POLITIC: Nay, and for discourse—
PEREGRINE: Being your wife, she cannot miss° that.
SIR POLITIC [*the parties meet*]:   Madam,
    Here is a gentleman, pray you, use him, fairly,
    He seems a youth, but he is—

LADY WOULD-BE: None?
SIR POLITIC: Yes, one
    Has put his face, as soon,° into the world—
LADY WOULD-BE: You mean, as early? but today?
SIR POLITIC: How's this! 20
LADY WOULD-BE: Why in this habit, sir, you
    apprehend me.
    Well, Master Would-be, this doth not become
    you;
    I had thought, the odour, sir, of your good name,
    Had been more precious to you; that you would
    not
    Have done this dire massacre,° on your honour; 25
    One of your gravity, and rank, besides!
    But, knights, I see, care little for the oath
    They make to ladies: chiefly, their own ladies.
SIR POLITIC: Now, by my spurs, the symbol of my
    knight-hood—
PEREGRINE [*aside*]: Lord! how his brain is humbled,°
    for an oath. 30
SIR POLITIC: I reach° you not.
LADY WOULD-BE: Right, sir, your polity°
    May bear it through,° thus. [*to* PEREGRINE] Sir, a
    word with you.
    I would be loath, to contest publicly,
    With any gentlewoman; or to seem
    Froward,° or violent (as *The Courtier* says) 35
    It comes too near rusticity, in a lady,
    Which I would shun, by all means: and, however
    I may deserve from Master Would-be, yet,
    T'have one fair gentlewoman, thus, be made
    Th'unkind instrument, to wrong another, 40
    And one she knows not; ay, and to persever:
    In my poor judgment, is not warranted
    From being a solecism° in our sex,
    If not in manners.
PEREGRINE: How is this!
SIR POLITIC: Sweet madam,
    Come nearer to your aim.
LADY WOULD-BE: Marry, and will, sir. 45
    Since you provoke me, with your impudence,
    And laughter of your light land-siren, here,
    Your Sporus,° your hermaphrodite—
PEREGRINE: What's here?
    Poetic fury, and historic° storms!

A rat . . . threshold, some details here are owed to Theophrastus's Character of a Superstitious Man. *tooth-picks,* for the fashion of using toothpicks expressively see *King John* I. i., 190–193. *ragion del stato,* reasons and affairs of state. *cheapened sprats,* by haggling; Coryat tells how Venetian gentlemen did their own shopping in the market. *quote,* note. *loose,* the game of fast-and-loose. *I do not care to,* I am not anxious to. *demerit,* merits blame. *miss,* lack.

as soon, at so early an age; but the phrase is open to Lady Would-be's wilful misinterpretation. *massacre,* accented on second syllable here. *humbled,* brought low—down to his spurs; editors have here found a sneer at King James's readiness to create new knights. *reach,* understand. *polity,* policy, cunning bluff. *bear it through,* carry it off. *Froward,* refractory. *solecism,* a grammatical, not a sexual, impropriety; the word is itself a solecism here. *Sporus,* minion castrated and "married" by Nero. *historic,* perhaps "epoch-making."

50   SIR POLITIC: The gentleman, believe it, is of worth,
      And of our nation.
     LADY WOULD-BE: Ay, your Whitefriars nation!°
      Come, I blush for you, Master Would-be, I;
      And am ashamed, you should ha' no more
        forehead,°
      Than, thus, to be the patron, or St. George
55   To a lewd harlot, a base fricatrice,°
      A female devil, in a male outside.
    SIR POLITIC [*to* PEREGRINE]:   Nay,
      And you be° such a one, I must bid adieu
      To your delights! The case° appears too liquid.°

     [*Exit* SIR POLITIC.]

    LADY WOULD-BE: Ay, you may carry't clear, with your
      state-face!°
60   But, for your carnival° concupiscence,°
      Who here is fled for liberty of conscience,°
      From furious persecution of the marshal,
      Her will I disple.°
    PEREGRINE: This is fine, i' faith!
      And do you use this,° often? is this part
65   Of your wit's exercise, 'gainst you have occasion?
      Madam—
    LADY WOULD-BE: Go to, sir.
    PEREGRINE: Do you hear me, lady?
      Why, if your knight have set you to beg shirts,°
      Or to invite me home, you might have done it
      A nearer° way, by far.
    LADY WOULD-BE: This cannot work you,
      Out of my snare.
70   PEREGRINE: Why? am I in it, then?
      Indeed, your husband told me, you were fair,
      And so you are; only your nose inclines,
      That side, that's next the sun, to the queen-
        apple.°
    LADY WOULD-BE: This cannot be endured, by any
      patience.

Whitefriars nation, Whitefriars was a "liberty" under the old priory charter, inside the City of London but outside its jurisdiction; it became almost a miniature state for outcasts. *forehead,* "capacity for blushing, modesty" *(OED).* *fricatrice,* whore (Latin, *fricare,* to rub). *you be,* addressed either to Lady Would-be or to Peregrine. *case,* possibly "mask" or "disguise." *liquid,* "transparent, easily seen through" or "amorphous, hard to grasp"; and Lady Would-be may be sobbing. *state-face,* politic countenance. *carnival,* probably for "carnal." *concupiscence,* for "concupiscent (woman)." *liberty of conscience,* freedom from religious persecution; the prison marshal is conceived as the persecutor and concupiscence as the religion. *disple,* ed. (F, Q, disc'ple) "to subject to discipline; especially as a religious practice" *(OED).* *use this,* act like this. *beg shirts,* Lady Would-be is evidently tugging at Peregrine's shirt. *nearer,* more direct. *queen-apple,* perhaps a quince, or early variety of apple; Lady Would-be's nose is red on one side.

ACT 4 / SCENE 3

[*Enter* MOSCA.]

MOSCA: What's the matter, madam?
LADY WOULD-BE: If the Senate
      Right not my quest,° in this; I will protest° 'em,
      To all the world, no aristocracy.
MOSCA: What is the injury, lady?
LADY WOULD-BE: Why, the callet,
      You told me of, here I have ta'en disguised.   5
MOSCA: Who? this? what means your ladyship? the
      creature
      I mentioned to you, is apprehended, now,
      Before the Senate, you shall see her—
LADY WOULD-BE: Where?
MOSCA: I'll bring you to her. This young gentleman
      I saw him land, this morning, at the port.   10
LADY WOULD-BE: Is't possible! how has my judgement
      wandered!
      Sir, I must, blushing, say to you, I have erred:
      And plead you pardon.
PEREGRINE: What! more changes, yet?
LADY WOULD-BE: I hope, you ha'not the malice to
      remember
      A gentlewoman's passion. If you stay,   15
      In Venice, here, please you to use me,° sir—
MOSCA: Will you go, madam?
LADY WOULD-BE: Pray you, sir, use me. In faith,
      The more you see me, the more I shall conceive,°
      You have forgot our quarrel.
PEREGRINE: This is rare!
      Sir Politic Would-be? no, Sir Politic Bawd!   20
      To bring me, thus, acquainted with his wife!
      Well, wise Sir Pol: since you have practised,° thus,
      Upon my freshmanship, I'll try your salt-head,°
      What proof it is against a counter-plot.

ACT 4 / SCENE 4

[*The Scrutineo*]
([*Enter*] VOLTORE, CORBACCIO, CORVINO, MOSCA.)

VOLTORE: Well, now you see the carriage° of the
      business,
      Your constancy is all, that is required
      Unto the safety of it.
MOSCA: Is the lie
      Safely conveyed amongst us? is that sure?
      Knows every man his burden?°

---

quest, petition. *protest,* proclaim. *use me,* Lady Would-be intends to be socially useful but her rhetoric insinuates her readiness to be Peregrine's mistress. *conceive,* understand; become pregnant. *practised,* plotted; Peregrine thinks he has been gulled. *salt-head,* seasoned, experienced; salacious, bawdy. *carriage,* management. *burden,* refrain of a song; hence "part in the performance."

CORVINO: Yes.

5   MOSCA: Then, shrink not.
CORVINO [*aside to* MOSCA]: But, knows the advocate
    the truth?
MOSCA: O, sir,
By no means. I devised a formal° tale,
That salved° your reputation. But, be valiant, sir.
CORVINO: I fear no one, but him; that, this his
    pleading
Should make him stand for a co-heir—
10 MOSCA: Co-halter.
Hang him: we will but use his tongue, his noise,
As we do Croaker's here. [*Pointing to*
    CORBACCIO.]
CORVINO: Ay, what shall he do?
MOSCA: When we ha' done, you mean?
CORVINO: Yes.
MOSCA: Why, we'll think:
Sell him for mummia,° he's half dust already.
15 [*to* VOLTORE] Do not you smile, to see this buffalo,°
    [*Pointing to* CORVINO.]
How he doth sport it with his head?—[*aside*] I
    should
If all were well, and past. [*to* CORBACCIO] Sir, only
    you
Are he, that shall enjoy the crop of all,
And these not know for whom they toil.
CORBACCIO: Ay, peace.
MOSCA (*to* CORVINO): But you shall eat it.° (*Then to*
20 VOLTORE *again.*) Much! Worshipful sir,
Mercury° sit upon your thund'ring tongue,
Or the French Hercules,° and make your
    language
As conquering as his club, to beat along,
As with a tempest, flat, our adversaries:
But, much more, yours, sir.
25 VOLTORE: Here they come, ha' done.
MOSCA: I have another witness, if you need, sir,
I can produce.
VOLTORE: Who is it?
MOSCA: Sir, I have her.

---

formal, "elaborately constructed, circumstantial" (*OED*).
salved, healed, made good. *mummia,* a medicinal preparation from the substance of mummies; fake mummy was made
from baked corpses. *buffalo,* alluding to the cuckold's
horns that the "formal tale" sets upon Corvino. *eat it,* i.e.,
the crop, the legacy; Corvino may overhear the words to Corbaccio. *Mercury,* god of eloquence and of trade; also associated with trickery and theft. *French Hercules,* Hercules was
fabled to have fathered the Celts in Gaul while returning
from the Far West with the oxen of Geryon; as the Celtic Hercules he was the symbol of eloquence.

[*Enter four* AVOCATORI, BONARIO, CELIA, NOTARIO,
COMMENDATORI *and* OTHERS.]

1st AVOCATORE: The like of this the Senate never
    heard of.
2nd AVOCATORE: 'Twill come most strange to them,
    when we report it.
4th AVOCATORE: The gentlewoman has been ever
    held
Of unreprovèd name.
3rd AVOCATORE: So, the young man.
4th AVOCATORE: The more unnatural part that of his
    father.   5
2nd AVOCATORE: More of the husband.
1st AVOCATORE: I not know to give
His act a name, it is so monstrous!
4th AVOCATORE: But the impostor, he is a thing
    created
T'exceed example!°
1st AVOCATORE: And all after times!°
2nd AVOCATORE: I never heard a true voluptuary   10
Described, but him.
3rd AVOCATORE: Appear yet those were cited?°
NOTARIO: All, but the old magnifico, Volpone.
1st AVOCATORE: Why is not he here?
MOSCA: Please your fatherhoods,
Here is his advocate. Himself's, so weak,
So feeble—
4th AVOCATORE: What are you?
BONARIO: His parasite,   15
His knave, his pandar: I beseech the court,
He may be forced to come, that your grave eyes
May bear strong witness of his strange impostures.
VOLTORE: Upon my faith, and credit, with your
    virtues,
He is not able to endure the air.   20
2nd AVOCATORE: Bring him, however.
3rd AVOCATORE: We will see him.
4th AVOCATORE: Fetch him.
VOLTORE: Your fatherhoods' fit pleasures be obeyed,
Be sure, the sight will rather move your pities,
Than indignation; may it please the court,
In the meantime, he may be heard in me: 25
I know this place most void of prejudice,
And therefore crave it, since we have no reason
To fear our truth should hurt our cause.
3rd AVOCATORE: Speak free.
VOLTORE: Then know, most honoured fathers, I must
    now

---

example, precedent. *after times,* i.e., future possibilities. *cited,* summoned, called as witnesses.

30   Discover, to your strangely abused ears,
       The most prodigious, and most frontless° piece
       Of solid impudence, and treachery,
       That ever vicious nature yet brought forth
       To shame the state of Venice. This lewd woman
35   (That wants° no artificial looks, or tears,
       To help the visor,° she has now put on)
       Hath long been known a close° adulteress,
       To that lascivious youth there; not suspected,
       I say, but known; and taken, in the act,
40   With him; and by this man, the easy husband,
       Pardoned: whose timeless° bounty makes him,
          now,
       Stand here, the most unhappy, innocent person,
       That ever man's own goodness made accused.
       For these, not knowing how to owe° a gift
45   Of that dear grace,° but with their shame; being
          placed
       So above all powers of their gratitude,°
       Began to hate the benefit; and, in place
       Of thanks, devise t'extirp° the memory
       Of such an act. Wherein, I pray your fatherhoods,
50   To observe the malice, yea, the rage of creatures
       Discovered in their evils; and what heart°
       Such take, even from their crimes. But that, anon,
       Will more appear. This gentleman, the father,
       Hearing of this foul fact, with many others,
55   Which daily struck at his too-tender ears,
       And, grieved in nothing more, than that he could
          not
       Preserve himself a parent (his son's ills°
       Growing to that strange flood) at last decreed
       To disinherit him.
       1st AVOCATORE: These be strange turns!°
       2nd AVOCATORE: The young man's fame was ever
60   fair, and honest.
       VOLTORE: So much more full of danger is his vice,
       That can beguile so, under shade of virtue.
       But as I said, my honoured sires, his father
       Having this settled purpose, (by what means
65   To him betrayed, we know not) and this day
       Appointed for the deed; that parricide,
       (I cannot style him better) by confederacy°
       Preparing this his paramour to be there,
       Entered Volpone's house (who was the man
70   Your fatherhoods must understand, designed°

       For the inheritance) there sought his father:
       But, with what purpose sought he him, my lords?
       (I tremble to pronounce it, that a son
       Unto a father, and to such a father
       Should have so foul, felonious intent)   75
       It was, to murder him. When, being prevented
       By his more happy absence, what then did he?
       Not check his wicked thoughts; no, now new deeds:
       (Mischief doth ever° end, where it begins)
       An act of horror, fathers! he dragged forth   80
       The agèd gentleman, that had there lain, bed-rid,
       Three years, and more, out of his innocent couch,
       Naked, upon the floor, there left him; wounded
       His servant in the face; and, with this strumpet,
       The stale° to his forged practice,° who was glad   85
       To be so active, (I shall here desire
       Your fatherhoods to note but my collections,°
       As most remarkable) thought, at once, to stop
       His father's ends;° discredit his free choice,
       In the old gentleman;° redeem themselves,   90
       By laying infamy upon this man,
       To whom, with blushing, they should owe° their
          lives.
       1st AVOCATORE: What proofs have you of this?
       BONARIO: Most honoured fathers,
       I humbly crave, there be no credit given
       To this man's mercenary tongue.
       2nd AVOCATORE: Forbear.   95
       BONARIO: His soul moves in his fee.
       3rd AVOCATORE: O, sir.
       BONARIO: This fellow,
       For six sols° more, would plead against his maker.
       1st AVOCATORE: You do forget yourself.
       VOLTORE: Nay, nay, grave fathers,
       Let him have scope: can any man imagine
       That he will spare his accuser, that would not   100
       Have spared his parent?
       1st AVOCATORE: Well, produce your proofs.
       CELIA: I would I could forget, I were a creature.
       VOLTORE: Signior Corbaccio.
       4th AVOCATORE: What is he?
       VOLTORE: The father.
       2nd AVOCATORE: Has he had an oath?
       NOTARIO: Yes.
       CORBACCIO: What must I do now?
       NOTARIO: Your testimony's craved.
       CORBACCIO: Speak to the knave?   105

---

frontless, shameless. *wants*, lacks. *visor*, mask. *close*, secret. *timeless*, untimely. *owe*, acknowledge (= own), or "properly possess." *gift . . . grace*, "so precious and unmerited a gift (of pardon)." *So . . . gratitude*, i.e., in a position of indebtedness beyond the reach of their powers of gratitude. *extirp*, extirpate, eradicate. *heart*, hardness of heart; impudent courage. *ills*, evils. *turns*, turns of event. *confederacy*, conspiracy. *designed*, designated.

ever, the reading "never" has been proposed and followed by some editors, but "ever" means "what begins badly ends badly." *stale*, lure; "a prostitute of the lowest class employed as a decoy by thieves" *(OED)*. *forged practice*, contrived plot. *collections*, conclusions. *ends*, purposes, aims. *gentleman*, i.e., Volpone. *owe*, acknowledge as due. *sols*, French coins worth one twentieth of a livre.

I'll ha' my mouth, first, stopped with earth; my
    heart
Abhors his knowledge:° I disclaim° in him.
1st AVOCATORE: But, for what cause?
CORBACCIO: The mere portent° of nature.
    He is an utter stranger, to my loins.
BONARIO: Have they made° you to this!
110 CORBACCIO: I will not hear thee,
    Monster of men, swine, goat, wolf, parricide,
    Speak not, thou viper.
BONARIO: Sir, I will sit down,
    And rather wish my innocence should suffer,
    Than I resist the authority of a father.
VOLTORE: Signior Corvino.
2nd AVOCATORE: This is strange!
115 1st AVOCATORE: Who's this?
NOTARIO: The husband.
4th AVOCATORE: Is he sworn?
NOTARIO: He is.
3rd AVOCATORE: Speak then.
CORVINO: This woman, please your fatherhoods, is a
    whore,
    Of most hot exercise, more than a partridge,°
    Upon record—
1st AVOCATORE: No more.
CORVINO: Neighs, like a jennet.°
NOTARIO: Preserve the honour of the court.
120 CORVINO: I shall,
    And modesty of your most reverend ears.
    And yet, I hope that I may say, these eyes
    Have seen her glued unto that piece of cedar;
    That fine well-timbered° gallant: and that, here,°
125 The letters may be read, thorough the horn,°
    That makes the story perfect.°
MOSCA: Excellent! sir.
CORVINO: There is no shame in this, now, is there?
MOSCA: None.
CORVINO: Or if I said, I hoped that she were onward°
    To her damnation, if there be a hell
130 Greater than whore, and woman; a good Catholic
    May make the doubt.
3rd AVOCATORE: His grief hath made him frantic.
1st AVOCATORE: Remove him, hence.
2nd AVOCATORE: Look to the woman. *(She swoons.)*
CORVINO: Rare!
    Prettily feigned! again!

---

his knowledge, knowledge of him. *disclaim,* deny kinship. *portent,* ominous freak; suggesting unnatural birth
and leading to the denial of paternity. *made,* forced, or possibly "shaped." *partridge,* described by Pliny as the most
concupiscent of creatures (*Nat. Hist.* X. 102). *jennet,*
small Spanish horse. *well-timbered,* well-built. *here,* Corvino holds his forked fingers to his forehead to give himself
cuckold's horns. *letters . . . horn,* punning on "horn-book,"
a primer (so-called because protected by translucent horn).
perfect, complete. *onward,* well on the way.

4th AVOCATORE: Stand from about her.
1st AVOCATORE: Give her the air.
3rd AVOCATORE [*to* MOSCA]:   What can you say?
MOSCA: My wound,
    May't please your wisdoms, speaks for me,
        received   135
    In aid of my good patron, when he missed
    His sought-for father, when that well-taught dame
    Had her cue given her, to cry out a rape.
BONARIO: O, most laid° impudence! Fathers—
3rd AVOCATORE: Sir, be silent,
    You had your hearing free,° so must they theirs.   140
2nd AVOCATORE: I do begin to doubt th' imposture
        here.
4th AVOCATORE: This woman, has too many moods.
VOLTORE: Grave fathers,
    She is a creature, of a most professed,
    And prostituted lewdness.
CORVINO: Most impetuous!
    Unsatisfied, grave fathers!
VOLTORE: May her feignings   145
    Not take your wisdoms; but this day, she baited°
    A stranger, a grave knight, with her loose eyes,
    And more lascivious kisses. This man saw 'em
    Together, on the water, in a gondola.
MOSCA: Here is the lady herself, that saw 'em too,   150
    Without;° who, then, had in the open streets
    Pursued them, but for saving her knight's honour.
1st AVOCATORE: Produce that lady.
2nd AVOCATORE: Let her come. [*Exit* MOSCA.]
4th AVOCATORE: These things
    They strike, with wonder!
3rd AVOCATORE: I am turned a stone!

ACT 4 / SCENE 6

[*Enter* MOSCA *with* LADY WOULD-BE.]

MOSCA: Be resolute, madam.
LADY WOULD-BE: Ay, this same is she.
    Out, thou chameleon° harlot: now, thine eyes
    Vie tears with the hyaena:° dar'st thou look
    Upon my wrongèd face? I cry your pardons.
    I fear, I have, forgettingly, transgressed   5
    Against the dignity of the court—
2nd AVOCATORE: No, madam.
LADY WOULD-BE: And been exorbitant°—
4th AVOCATORE: You have not, lady.
    These proofs are strong.

---

laid, plotted. *free,* i.e., from interruption. *baited,* enticed. *Without,* outside. *chameleon,* its color changes made
it a symbol of fraud and treachery; Lady Would-be alludes to
the inconstant appearance of her quarry. *hyaena,* another
symbol of treachery because it attracted its victims by its
quasi-human cry (but not by its tears). *exorbitant,* beyond
bounds, outrageous.

LADY WOULD-BE: Surely, I had no purpose,
   To scandalize your honours, or my sex's.
3rd AVOCATORE: We do believe it.
10 LADY WOULD-BE: Surely, you may believe it.
2nd AVOCATORE: Madam, we do.
LADY WOULD-BE: Indeed, you may; my breeding
   Is not so coarse—
4th AVOCATORE: We know it.
LADY WOULD-BE: To offend
   With pertinacy—
3rd AVOCATORE: Lady.
LADY WOULD-BE: Such a presence:
   No, surely.
1st AVOCATORE: We well think it.
LADY WOULD-BE: You may think it.
1st AVOCATORE: Let her o'ercome.° [to BONARIO]
15   What witnesses have you,
   To make good your report?
BONARIO: Our consciences—
CELIA: And heaven, that never fails the innocent.
4th AVOCATORE: These are no testimonies.
BONARIO: Not in your courts,
   Where multitude,° and clamour, overcomes.
1st AVOCATORE: Nay, then you do wax insolent.
20 VOLTORE: Here, here,

(VOLPONE is brought in, as impotent.°)

   The testimony comes, that will convince,
   And put to utter dumbness their bold tongues.
   See here, grave fathers, here's the ravisher,
   The rider on men's wives, the great impostor,
25   The grand voluptuary! do you not think,
   These limbs should affect venery?° or these eyes
   Covet a concubine? pray you, mark these hands.
   Are they not fit to stroke a lady's breasts?
   Perhaps, he doth dissemble?
BONARIO: So he does.
VOLTORE: Would you ha'him tortured?
30 BONARIO: I would have him proved.°
VOLTORE: Best try him, then, with goads, or burning
      irons;
   Put him to the strappado:° I have heard,
   The rack had cured the gout,° faith, give it him,
   And help° him of a malady, be courteous.
35   I'll undertake, before these honoured fathers,
   He shall have, yet, as many left diseases,
   As she has known adulterers, or thou strumpets.

O, my most equal° hearers, if these deeds,
Acts, of this bold, and most exorbitant strain,°
May pass with sufferance, what one citizen,   40
But owes the forfeit of his life, yea fame,
To him that dares traduce him?° which of you
Are safe, my honoured fathers? I would ask,
With leave of your grave fatherhoods, if their plot
Have any face, or colour like to truth?   45
Or if, unto the dullest nostril, here,
It smell not rank, and most abhorred slander?
I crave your care of this good gentleman,
Whose life is much endangered, by their fable;°
And, as for them, I will conclude with this,   50
That vicious persons when they are hot, and
   fleshed°
In impious acts, their constancy° abounds:
Damned deeds are done with greatest confidence.
1st AVOCATORE: Take 'em to custody, and sever
   them.°

[CELIA and BONARIO taken out.]

2nd AVOCATORE: 'Tis pity, two such prodigies° should
   live.   55
1st AVOCATORE: Let the old gentleman be returned,
   with care:
   I'm sorry, our credulity wronged him. [VOLPONE
   borne off.]
4th AVOCATORE: These are two creatures!
3rd AVOCATORE: I have an earthquake in me!
2nd AVOCATORE: Their shame, even in their cradles,
   fled their faces.
4th AVOCATORE: You've done a worthy service to the
   state, sir,   60
   In their discovery.
1st AVOCATORE: You shall hear, ere night,
   What punishment the court decrees upon 'em.
VOLTORE: We thank your fatherhoods.

[Exeunt AVOCATORI, NOTARIO, OFFICERS.]

                            How did you like it?
MOSCA: Rare.
   I'd ha'your tongue, sir, tipped with gold, for this;
   I'd ha'you be the heir to the whole city;   65
   The earth I'd have want men, ere you want living:°
   They're bound to erect your statue, in St. Mark's.
   Signior Corvino, I would have you go,
   And show yourself, that you have conquered.
CORVINO: Yes.

---

o'ercome, prevail, have the last word. *multitude,* numbers (not necessarily a crowd). *impotent,* totally disabled; Lady Would-be may kiss Volpone at this point, or when he is borne out. *affect venery,* enjoy sexual pleasure; or "affect" may = "effect." *proved,* put to the proof, tested. *strappado,* a form of torture; the victim is hoisted by a rope binding his wrists behind his back, then dropped with a jerk. *rack . . . gout,* a common sentiment. *help,* relieve.

---

equal, just. *exorbitant strain,* outrageous nature. *what . . . traduce him,* "what single citizen would there be whose life, and indeed reputation, would not be forfeitable to any who had the impudence to slander him?" *fable,* falsehood, or plot. *fleshed,* inured. *constancy,* resolution. *sever them,* keep them apart. *prodigies,* monsters, unnatural creatures. *want living,* lack a livelihood.

70 MOSCA: It was much better, that you should profess
    Yourself a cuckold, thus; than that the other°
    Should have been proved.
CORVINO: Nay, I considered that:
    Now, it is her fault—
MOSCA: Then, it had been yours.
CORVINO: True, I do doubt this advocate, still.
MOSCA: I'faith,
75 You need not, I dare ease you of that care.
CORVINO: I trust thee, Mosca.
MOSCA: As your own soul, sir.
CORBACCIO: Mosca!
MOSCA: Now for your business, sir.
CORBACCIO: How? ha'you business?
MOSCA: Yes, yours, sir.
CORBACCIO: O, none else?
MOSCA: None else, not I.
CORBACCIO: Be careful then.
MOSCA: Rest you, with both your eyes,° sir.
CORBACCIO: Dispatch it—
MOSCA: Instantly.
80 CORBACCIO: And look, that all,
    Whatever, be put in,° jewels, plate, monies,
    Household stuff, bedding, curtains.
MOSCA: Curtain-rings, sir,
    Only, the advocate's fee must be deducted.
CORBACCIO: I'll pay him now: you'll be too prodigal.
MOSCA: Sir, I must tender it.°
85 CORBACCIO: Two chequeens is well?
MOSCA: No, six, sir.
CORBACCIO: 'Tis too much.
MOSCA: He talked a great while.
    You must consider that, sir.
CORBACCIO: Well, there's three—
MOSCA: I'll give it him.
CORBACCIO: Do so, and there's for thee.
    [*Exit* CORBACCIO.]
MOSCA: Bountiful bones!° What horrid strange offence
90 Did he commit 'gainst nature, in his youth,
    Worthy his age?° you see, sir, how I work
    Unto your ends; take you no notice.°
VOLTORE: No,
    I'll leave you.
MOSCA: All is yours; [*Exit* VOLTORE.] the devil, and all:
    Good advocate.—Madame, I'll bring you home.
LADY WOULD-BE: No, I'll go see your patron.
95 MOSCA: That you shall not:
    I'll tell you, why. My purpose is to urge

My patron to reform° his will; and, for
The zeal you've shown today, whereas before
You were but third, or fourth, you shall be now
Put in the first: which would appear as begged,   100
If you were present. Therefore—
LADY WOULD-BE: You shall sway° me.
    [*Exeunt* MOSCA, LADY WOULD-BE.]

ACT 5 / SCENE 1

[VOLPONE*'s house*]
([*Enter*] VOLPONE.°)

VOLPONE: Well, I am here; and all this brunt° is past:
    I ne'er was in dislike with my disguise,
    Till this fled° moment; here, 'twas good, in private,
    But, in your public—Cavè,° whilst I breathe. [*Gets up.*]
    'Fore God, my left leg 'gan to have the cramp;   5
    And I apprehended,° straight,° some power had struck me
    With a dead palsy: well, I must be merry,
    And shake it off. A many° of these fears
    Would put me into some villainous disease,
    Should they come thick upon me: I'll prevent 'em.   10
    Give me a bowl of lusty wine, to fright
    This humour from my heart. (*He drinks.*) Hum, hum, hum!
    'Tis almost gone, already: I shall conquer.
    Any device, now, of rare, ingenious knavery,
    That would possess me with a violent laughter,   15
    Would make me up, again! (*Drinks again.*) So, so, so, so.
    This heat is life;° 'tis blood, by this time: Mosca!

ACT 5 / SCENE 2

[*Enter* MOSCA.]

MOSCA: How now, sir? does the day look clear again?
    Are we recovered? and wrought out of error,
    Into our way?° to see our path, before us?
    Is our trade free, once more?
VOLPONE: Exquisite Mosca!
MOSCA: Was it not carried learnedly?
VOLPONE: And stoutly.   5
    Good wits are greatest in extremities.
MOSCA: It were a folly, beyond thought, to trust

---

the other, i.e., the procuration of his wife for Volpone.
Rest . . . eyes, "relax completely." *put in,* i.e., in the inventory
of the inheritance. *tender it,* give it him. *Bountiful bones!*
apt to the meanness and leanness of Corbaccio. *Worthy . . .
age,* "deserving an old age like this." *take . . . notice,* "ignore
me"; perhaps Lady Would-be is watching.

reform, recast. *sway,* rule. *Enter Volpone,* Volpone may
be carried in, discovered on his litter, or be back in his
bed. *brunt,* shock, crisis. *fled,* past. *Cavè* (Latin), beware;
Volpone may ask the audience to keep a lookout while he
relaxes, or he may address the warning to himself. *appre-
hended,* felt. *straight,* immediately. *many,* used as a noun
(compare "a great many"). *This heat is life,* Volpone identifies the response of his blood to wine with the processes by
which the body's vital heat is generated. *wrought . . . way,*
Mosca talks with mock piety.

Any grand act unto a cowardly spirit:
You are not taken with it, enough,° methinks?
10　VOLPONE: O, more, than if I had enjoyed the wench:
The pleasure of all woman-kind's not like it.
MOSCA: Why, now you speak, sir. We must, here, be
　　fixed;
Here, we must rest; this is our masterpiece:
We cannot think, to go beyond this.
VOLPONE:　　　　　　　　　　　　　　True.
Thou'st played thy prize, my precious Mosca.
15　MOSCA:　　　　　　　　　　　　　　　　　Nay, sir,
To gull the court—
VOLPONE:　　　　　　　And, quite divert the torrent
Upon the innocent.
MOSCA:　　　　　　　　　　Yes, and to make
So rare a music out of discords—
VOLPONE:　　　　　　　　　　　　Right,
That, yet, to me's the strangest!° how thou'st borne
　　it!
20　That these, being so divided 'mongst themselves,
Should not scent somewhat, or in me, or° thee,
Or doubt their own side.
MOSCA:　　　　　　　　　True, they will not see't.
Too much lights blinds 'em, I think. Each of 'em
Is so possessed,° and stuffed with his own hopes,
25　That anything, unto the contrary,
Never so true, or never so apparent,
Never so palpable, they will resist it—
VOLPONE: Like a temptation of the devil.
MOSCA:　　　　　　　　　　　　Right, sir.
Merchants may talk of trade, and your great
　　signiors
30　Of land, that yields well; but if Italy
Have any glebe,° more fruitful, than these fellows,
I am deceived. Did not your advocate rare?°
VOLPONE: O—'My most honoured fathers, my grave
　　fathers,
Under correction of your fatherhoods.
35　What face of truth, is here? If these strange deeds
May pass, most honoured fathers'—I had much
　　ado
To forbear laughing.
MOSCA:　　　　　　　'T seemed to me, you sweat,° sir.
VOLPONE: In troth, I did a little.
MOSCA:　　　　　　　　　　But confess, sir,
Were you not daunted?°

VOLPONE:　　　　　　　In good faith, I was
A little in a mist; but not dejected:　　　　　　　40
Never, but still myself.
MOSCA:　　　　　　　I think° it, sir.
Now, so truth help me, I must needs say this, sir,
And, out of conscience, for your advocate:
He's taken pains, in faith, sir, and deserved,
(In my poor judgement, I speak it, under favour,°　45
Not to contrary you, sir) very richly—
Well—to be cozened.°
VOLPONE:　　　　　　　'Troth, and I think so too,
By that I heard him, in the latter end.
MOSCA: O, but before, sir; had you heard him, first,
Draw it to certain heads,° then aggravate,°　　　　50
Then use his vehement figures°—I looked still,
When he would shift a shirt;° and, doing this
Out of pure love, no hope of gain—
VOLPONE:　　　　　　　　　　　'Tis right.
I cannot answer° him, Mosca, as I would,
Not yet; but, for thy sake, at thy entreaty,　　　　55
I will begin, even now, to vex 'em all:
This very instant.
MOSCA:　　　　　Good, sir.
VOLPONE:　　　　　　　　　Call the dwarf,
And eunuch, forth.
MOSCA:　　　　　　　Castrone, Nano!

[*Enter* CASTRONE *and* NANO.]

NANO:　　　　　　　　　　　　　　　　Here.
VOLPONE: Shall we have a jig,° now?
MOSCA:　　　　　　　　　　What you please, sir.
VOLPONE:　　　　　　　　　　　　　　Go,
Straight, give out, about the streets, you two,　　60
That I am dead; do it with constancy,°
Sadly,° do you hear? impute it to the grief
Of this late slander.

[*Exeunt* CASTRONE *and* NANO.]

MOSCA:　　　　　　　What do you mean,° sir?
VOLPONE:　　　　　　　　　　　　　　O,
I shall have, instantly, my vulture, crow,
Raven, come flying hither, on the news,　　　　　65
To peck for carrion, my she-wolf, and all,
Greedy, and full of expectation—
MOSCA: And then to have it ravished from their
　　mouths?

You . . . enough, Mosca may sense that Volpone is already thinking of the next device, towards which the dialogue now subtly moves.　*strangest,* most wonderful and ingenious; the word "strange" is important in this act.　*or . . . or,* either . . . or.　*possessed,* the sense hovers between "possessing" and "possessed by"; another key word.　*glebe,* earth, soil.　*rare,* rarely.　*sweat,* sweated; Mosca insists that Volpone was afraid.　*daunted,* "dazed" or "abashed"; Volpone's reply meets both senses, he was a little confused *(in a mist)* but not downcast *(dejected).*

think, believe.　*under favour,* "with your permission"; Mosca now parodies Voltore.　*cozened,* cheated.　*heads,* chief points of a discourse (*OED*).　*aggravate,* put weight upon, solemnly emphasize with *gravitas.*　*vehement figures,* may refer to figures of both speech and gesture.　*shift a shirt,* change a shirt; a figure for Voltore's gesticulations.　*answer,* repay.　*a jig,* a jest, "some sport"; a burlesque "jig" sometimes followed serious drama in the Elizabethan theater, which may be the point here.　*with constancy,* firmly, or perhaps "with straight faces."　*Sadly,* gravely.　*mean,* intend.

VOLPONE: 'Tis true, I will ha' thee put on a gown,
70   And take upon thee,° as thou wert mine heir;
      Show 'em a will: open that chest, and reach
      Forth one of those, that has° the blanks.° I'll
         straight
      Put in thy name.
MOSCA: It will be rare, sir.
VOLPONE: Ay,
      When they e'en° gape, and find themselves
         deluded—
MOSCA: Yes.
75 VOLPONE: And thou use them scurvily. Dispatch,
      Get on thy gown.
MOSCA: But, what, sir, if they ask
      After the body?
VOLPONE: Say, it was corrupted.
MOSCA: I'll say it stunk, sir; and was fain° t' have it
      Coffined up instantly, and sent away.
VOLPONE: Anything, what thou wilt. Hold, here's my
80   will.
      Get thee a cap, a count-book,° pen and ink,
      Papers afore thee; sit, as thou wert taking
      An inventory of parcels:° I'll get up,
      Behind the curtain, on a stool, and hearken;
85   Sometime, peep over; see, how they do look;
      With what degrees, their blood doth leave their
         faces!
      O, 'twill afford me a rare meal of laughter.
MOSCA: Your advocate will turn stark dull,° upon it.
VOLPONE: It will take off his oratory's edge.
90 MOSCA: But your *clarissimo,*° old round-back, he
      Will crump you, like a hog-louse,° with the
         touch.
VOLPONE: And what Corvino?
MOSCA: O, sir, look for him,
      Tomorrow morning, with a rope, and a dagger,°
      To visit all the streets; he must run mad.
95   My lady too, that came into the court,
      To bear false witness, for your worship—
VOLPONE: Yes,
      And kissed me 'fore the fathers; when my face
      Flowed all with oils—
MOSCA: And sweat, sir. Why, your gold
      Is such another medicine, it dries up
100   All those offensive savours! It transforms
      The most deformed, and restores 'em lovely,

As 'twere the strange poetical girdle.° Jove
Could not invent, t' himself, a shroud more subtle,
To pass Acrisius'° guards. It is the thing
Makes all the world her grace, her youth, her
   beauty.   105
VOLPONE: I think, she loves me.
MOSCA: Who? the lady,° sir?
   She's jealous of you.
VOLPONE: Do'st thou say so? [*Knocking without.*]
MOSCA: Hark,
   There's some already.
VOLPONE: Look.
MOSCA: It is the vulture:
   He has the quickest scent.
VOLPONE: I'll to my place, [*conceals himself.*]
   Thou, to thy posture.°
MOSCA: I am set.
VOLPONE: But, Mosca,   110
   Play the artificer° now, torture 'em, rarely.

ACT 5 / SCENE 3

[*Enter* VOLTORE.]

VOLTORE: How now, my Mosca?
MOSCA: Turkey carpets,° nine—
VOLTORE: Taking an inventory? that is well.
MOSCA: Two suits of bedding, tissue°—
VOLTORE: Where's the will?
   Let me read that, the while.

[*Enter* CORBACCIO *carried in a chair.*]

CORBACCIO: So, set me down:
   And get you home. [*Exeunt* PORTERS.]
VOLTORE: Is he come, now, to trouble us?   5
MOSCA: Of cloth of gold, two more—
CORBACCIO: Is it done, Mosca?
MOSCA: Of several velvets,° eight—
VOLTORE: I like his care.
CORBACCIO: Dost thou not hear?

[*Enter* CORVINO.]

CORVINO: Ha! is the hour come, Mosca?

(VOLPONE *peeps from behind a traverse.*)

---

take upon thee, assume the part. **has,** i.e., have. **blanks,** spaces for the legatee's names. **e'en,** just, doing nothing else but. **fain,** i.e., "I was fain (obliged)." **count-book,** account book. **parcels,** lots, items. **dull,** insensible; but Volpone replies to the sense "blunt." **clarissimo,** a Venetian grandee. **crump . . . hog-louse,** "curl up like a wood-louse." **rope . . . dagger,** stock properties of suicidal or homicidal madness induced by despair; compare Hieronimo's madness (once played by Jonson) in *The Spanish Tragedy* IV.iv.

poetical girdle, the Folio adds the explanation "*Cestus*" after "Jove"; it was possibly meant as a correction to replace "girdle"; Cestus, the girdle of Venus described by Homer, could transfigure ugliness and awaken passion even in old age. **Acrisius,** the father of Danae; he shut her in a tower of brass but Jove reached her in a shower of gold. **the lady,** presumably Lady Would-be, but some have supposed Celia. **posture,** pose, act. **Play the artificer,** "do a craftsman's job," with pun on the sense "trickster." **Turkey carpets,** then used as table and wall drapery. **tissue,** cloth woven with gold or silver. **velvets,** velvet hangings (several = separate).

VOLPONE *(aside)*: Ay, now they muster.
CORVINO: What does the advocate here?
    Or this Corbaccio?
CORBACCIO: What do these here?

[*Enter* LADY WOULD-BE.]

10 LADY WOULD-BE: Mosca!
    Is his thread° spun?
MOSCA: Eight chests of linen—
VOLPONE [*aside*]:
    My fine dame Would-be, too!
CORVINO: Mosca, the will,
    That I may show it these, and rid 'em hence.
MOSCA: Six chests of diaper,° four of damask—
    There. [*Gives them the will.*]
CORBACCIO: Is that the will?
MOSCA: Down-beds, and bolsters—
15 VOLPONE [*aside*]:   Rare!
    Be busy still. Now, they begin to flutter:
    They never think of me. Look, see, see, see!
    How their swift eyes run over the long deed,
    Unto the name, and to the legacies,
    What is bequeathed them, there—
20 MOSCA: Ten suits of hangings°—
VOLPONE [*aside*]: Ay, i'their garters,° Mosca. Now,
        their hopes
    Are at the gasp.°
VOLTORE: Mosca the heir!
CORBACCIO: What's that?
VOLPONE [*aside*]: My advocate is dumb, look to my
        merchant,
    He has heard of some strange storm, a ship is lost,
25 He faints: my lady will swoon. Old glazen-eyes,°
    He hath not reached his despair, yet.
CORBACCIO: All these
    Are out of hope, I am sure the man.
CORVINO: But, Mosca—
MOSCA: Two cabinets—
CORVINO: Is this in earnest?
MOSCA: One
    Of ebony—
CORVINO: Or, do you but delude me?
30 MOSCA: The other, mother of pearl—I am very busy.
    Good faith, it is a fortune thrown upon me—
    Item, one salt° of agate—not my seeking.
LADY WOULD-BE: Do you hear, sir?
MOSCA: A perfumed box—'pray you forbear,
    You see I am troubled°—made of an onyx—

LADY WOULD-BE: How!
MOSCA: Tomorrow, or next day, I shall be at leisure,   35
    To talk with you all.
CORVINO:`   Is this my large hope's issue?
LADY WOULD-BE: Sir, I must have a fairer answer.
MOSCA: Madam!
    Marry, and shall: pray you, fairly° quit my house.
    Nay, raise no tempest with your looks; but, hark
        you:
    Remember, what your ladyship offered me,   40
    To put you in, an heir; go to, think on't.
    And what you said, e'en your best madams did
    For maintenance, and why not you? enough.
    Go home, and use the poor Sir Pol, your knight,
        well;
    For fear I tell some riddles:° go, be melancholic.   45
    [*Exit* LADY WOULD-BE.]
VOLPONE [*aside*]: O, my fine devil!
CORVINO: Mosca, pray you a word.
MOSCA: Lord! will not you take your dispatch hence,
        yet?
    Methinks, of all, you should have been
        th'example.°
    Why should you stay, here? with what thought?
        what promise?
    Hear you, do not you know, I know you an ass?   50
    And that you would, most fain, have been a wittol,°
    If fortune would have let you? that you are
    A declared cuckold, on good terms?° this pearl,
    You'll say, was yours? right: this diamant?
    I'll not deny't, but thank you. Much here, else?   55
    It may be so. Why, think that these good works
    May help to hide your bad: I'll not betray you,
    Although you be but extraordinary,°
    And have it only in title, it sufficeth.
    Go home, be melancholic too, or mad. [*Exit*   60
        CORVINO.]
VOLPONE [*aside*]: Rare, Mosca! how this villainy
        becomes him!
VOLTORE: Certain, he doth delude all these, for me.
CORBACCIO: Mosca, the heir?
VOLPONE [*aside*]:   O, his four eyes have found it!
CORBACCIO: I'm cozened, cheated, by a parasite slave;
    Harlot° thou'st gulled me.
MOSCA: Yes, sir. Stop your mouth,   65
    Or I shall draw the only tooth, is left.
    Are not you he, that filthy covetous wretch,
    With the three legs,° that here, in hope of prey,

---

thread, of the Three Fates: Clothos spun the thread of life, Lachesis measured it, and Atropos cut it; but the phrase was a popular pomposity. *diaper,* fabric with diamond-like pattern. *suits of hangings,* sets for four-poster bed. *garters,* Volpone puns on the popular jibe "Hang yourself in your own garters." *gasp,* last gasp. *glazen-eyes,* Corbaccio wears spectacles. *salt,* salt-cellar. *troubled,* busy, being put to some trouble; or perhaps "vexed."

fairly, probably "well and truly," completely. *riddles,* mysteries, secrets. *example,* i.e., in leading the way when "dispatched." *wittol,* conniving cuckold. *on good terms,* i.e., outspokenly so, fair and square. *extraordinary,* in title only (as Mosca explains); used of offices held extra to the establishment. *Harlot,* base-born fellow. *three legs,* i.e., with his stick; in the riddle of the Sphinx, the child goes upon four legs, the man on two, and the old man on three.

Have, any time this three year, snuffed about,
With your most grov'ling nose; and would have
70   hired
Me to the poisoning of my patron? sir?
Are not you he, that have, today, in court,
Professed the disinheriting of your son?
Perjured yourself? Go home, and die, and stink;
75 If you but croak a syllable, all comes out:
Away and call your porters, go, go, stink. [*Exit*
    CORBACCIO.]
VOLPONE [*aside*]: Excellent varlet!
VOLTORE: Now, my faithful Mosca,
  I find thy constancy—
MOSCA: Sir?
VOLTORE: Sincere.
MOSCA: A table
  Of porphyry—I mar'l,° you'll be thus troublesome.
VOLTORE: Nay, leave off now, they are gone.
80 MOSCA: Why, who are you?
  What, who did send for you? O, cry your mercy,
  Reverend sir! good faith, I am grieved for you,
  That any chance° of mine should thus defeat
  Your, I must needs say, most deserving travails:
85 But, I protest, sir, it was cast upon me,
  And I could, almost, wish to be without it,
  But that the will o'the dead, must be observed.
  Marry, my joy is, that you need it not,
  You have a gift, sir, thank your education,
90 Will never let you want,° while there are men,
  And malice, to breed causes.° Would I had
  But half the like, for all my fortune, sir.
  If I have any suits (as I do hope,
  Things being so easy, and direct, I shall not)
95 I will make bold with your obstreperous° aid,
  Conceive me, for your fee,° sir. In meantime,
  You, that have so much law, I know ha' the
    conscience,
  Not to be covetous of what is mine.
  Good sir, I thank you for my plate:° 'twill help
100 To set up a young man. Good faith, you look
  As you were costive; best go home, and purge, sir.
    [*Exit* VOLTORE.]
VOLPONE [*coming out*]: Bid him, eat lettuce° well: my
    witty mischief,
  Let me embrace thee. O, that I could now
  Transform thee to a Venus—Mosca, go,
105 Straight, take my habit of *clarissimo;*
  And walk the streets; be seen, torment 'em more:
  We must pursue, as well as plot. Who would
  Have lost this feast?

MOSCA: I doubt it will lose them.°
VOLPONE: O, my recovery shall recover all.
  That I could now but think on some disguise,   110
  To meet 'em in: and ask 'em questions.
  How I would vex 'em still, at every turn!
MOSCA: Sir, I can fit you.
VOLPONE: Canst thou?
MOSCA: Yes, I know
  One of the *commendatori,*° sir, so like you,
  Him will I straight make drunk, can bring you his
    habit.   115
VOLPONE: A rare disguise, and answering thy
  brain!
  O, I will be a sharp disease unto 'em.
MOSCA: Sir, you must look for curses—
VOLPONE: Till they burst;
  The Fox fares ever best, when he is cursed.°

ACT 5 / SCENE 4

[SIR POLITIC WOULD-BE's *house*]
[*Enter* PEREGRINE *disguised, and three* MERCHANTS.]

PEREGRINE: Am I enough disguised?
1st MERCHANT: I warrant° you.
PEREGRINE: All my ambition is to fright him, only.
2nd MERCHANT: If you could ship him away, 'twere
    excellent.
3rd MERCHANT: To Zant,° or to Aleppo?
PEREGRINE: Yes, and ha'his
  Adventures put i'the *Book of Voyages,*°   5
  And his gulled story° registered, for truth?
  Well, gentlemen, when I am in, a while,
  And that you think us warm in our discourse,
  Know your approaches.°
1st MERCHANT: Trust it to our care. [*Exeunt*
  MERCHANTS.]

[*Enter* WAITING WOMAN.]

PEREGRINE: Save you, fair lady. Is Sir Pol within?   10
WOMAN: I do not know, sir.
PEREGRINE: Pray you, say unto him,
  Here is a merchant, upon earnest° business,
  Desires to speak with him.
WOMAN: I will see, sir.

---

    mar'l, marvel. **chance**, good fortune. **want**, be in need. **causes**, lawsuits. **obstreperous**, vociferous. **Conceive . . . fee**, "I shall expect to pay the usual fee, you understand." **plate**, i.e., that presented by Voltore. **lettuce**, a recognized treatment for constipation, and for frenzy.

    doubt . . . them, possibly "I doubt if it will get rid of them," but Volpone's reply interprets "I fear it will lose them to us as a source of income." **commendatori**, a term for the court officers, sergeants at law. **Fox . . . cursed**, a proverb; the fox is only cursed by the hunter when he gets away. **warrant**, assure. **Zant**, Zante, one of the Ionian islands, and a Venetian possession at the time. **Book of Voyages**, Hakluyt's *Principal Navigations* was published in its enlarged form in 1598–1600, but there were other books of voyages too. **gulled story**, "the story of his gulling." **Know . . . approaches**, get ready to enter (perhaps nautical jargon). **earnest**, weighty.

PEREGRINE: Pray you. [*Exit* WOMAN.]
    I see, the family is all female, here.

    [*Enter* WAITING WOMAN.]

15 WOMAN: He says, sir, he has weighty affairs of state,
        That now require him whole°—some other time
        You may possess him.°
    PEREGRINE: Pray you, may again,
        If those require him whole, these will exact him,°
        Whereof I bring him tidings. (*Exit* WOMAN.) What
            might be
20   His grave affair of state, now? how to make
        Bolognian sausages, here, in Venice, sparing°
        One o' th'ingredients.

    [*Enter* WAITING WOMAN.]

    WOMAN: Sir, he says, he knows
        By your word, tidings,° that you are no statesman,
        And therefore, wills you stay.
    PEREGRINE: Sweet, pray you return him,°
25   I have not read so many proclamations,
        And studied them, for words, as he has done;
        But—Here he deigns to come. [*Exit* WOMAN.]

    [*Enter* SIR POLITIC WOULD-BE.]

    SIR POLITIC: Sir, I must crave
        Your courteous pardon. There hath chanced, today,
        Unkind disaster, 'twixt my lady, and me:
30   And I was penning my apology
        To give her satisfaction, as you came, now.
    PEREGRINE: Sir, I am grieved, I bring you worse
            disaster;
        The gentleman, you met at the port, today,
        That told you, he was newly arrived—
    SIR POLITIC: Ay, was
        A fugitive? punk?°
35 PEREGRINE: No, sir, a spy, set on you:
        And, he has made relation° to the Senate,
        That you professed to him, to have a plot,
        To sell the state of Venice, to the Turk.
    SIR POLITIC: O me!
    PEREGRINE: For which, warrants are signed
            by this time,
40   To apprehend you, and to search your study,
        For papers—
    SIR POLITIC: Alas, sir. I have none, but notes,
        Drawn out of play-books—
    PEREGRINE: All the better, sir.
    SIR POLITIC: And some essays.° What shall I do?

PEREGRINE: Sir, best
    Convey yourself into a sugar-chest,
    Or, if you could lie round,° a frail° were rare: 45
    And I could send you, aboard.
SIR POLITIC: Sir, I but talked so,
    For discourse sake, merely. (*They knock without.*)
PEREGRINE: Hark, they are there.
SIR POLITIC: I am a wretch, a wretch.
PEREGRINE: What will you do, sir?
    H'you ne'er a currant-butt to leap into?
    They'll put you to the rack, you must be sudden.°   50
SIR POLITIC: Sir, I have an engine°—
3rd MERCHANT [*off-stage*]:   Sir Politic Would-be?
2nd MERCHANT [*off-stage*]: Where is he?
SIR POLITIC: That I have thought upon,
    before time.
PEREGRINE: What is it?
SIR POLITIC: —I shall ne'er endure the torture.—
    Marry, it is, sir, of a tortoise-shell,°
    Fitted,° for these extremities: 'pray you sir, help
        me.   55
    Here, I've a place, sir, to put back my legs,—
    Please you to lay it on, sir—with this cap,
    And my black gloves, I'll lie, sir, like a tortoise,
    Till they are gone.
PEREGRINE: And, call you this an engine?
SIR POLITIC: Mine own device°—good sir, bid my
        wife's women   60
    To burn my papers.°

    (*[*MERCHANTS*] rush in.*)

1st MERCHANT: Where's he hid?
3rd MERCHANT: We must,
    And will, sure, find him.
2nd MERCHANT: Which is his study?
1st MERCHANT: What
    Are you, sir?
PEREGRINE: I'm a merchant, that came here
    To look upon this tortoise.
3rd MERCHANT: How?
1st MERCHANT: St. Mark!
    What beast is this?
PEREGRINE: It is a fish.
2nd MERCHANT: Come out, here.   65
PEREGRINE: Nay, you may strike him, sir, and tread
        upon him:
    He'll bear a cart.
1st MERCHANT: What, to run over him?
PEREGRINE: Yes.
3rd MERCHANT: Let's jump upon him.

---

require . . . whole, require his whole attention. ***possess him,*** have his company. ***exact him,*** probably "force him out," extract him from his study (see *OED*). ***sparing,*** leaving out. ***tidings,*** Sir Politic's word is "intelligence." ***return him,*** answer him. ***punk,*** prostitute. ***made relation,*** Peregrine now uses state language. ***essays,*** a literary form that Jonson despised.

---

lie round, curl up. ***frail,*** rush basket for figs. ***sudden,*** quick. ***engine,*** device, contrivance. ***tortoise-shell,*** a feature of the Venetian market; the tortoise was a symbol of polity. ***Fitted,*** suited. ***device,*** invention (of own devising). ***burn my papers,*** Peregrine must tell the woman to do this as the merchants rush in and look around.

2nd MERCHANT: Can he not go?
PEREGRINE: He creeps, sir.
1st MERCHANT: Let's see him creep. [*Prods him.*]
PEREGRINE: No, good sir, you will hurt him.
2nd MERCHANT: Heart, I'll see him creep; or prick
70   his guts.
3rd MERCHANT: Come out, here.
PEREGRINE: Pray you sir. [*to* SIR POLITIC]
    Creep a little!
1st MERCHANT: Forth!
2nd MERCHANT: Yet further.
PEREGRINE: Good sir! [*to* SIR POLITIC] Creep!
2nd MERCHANT: We'll see his legs.

    (*They pull off the shell and discover him.*)

3rd MERCHANT: God's so—, he has garters!
1st MERCHANT: Ay, and gloves!
2nd MERCHANT: Is this
    Your fearful tortoise?
PEREGRINE [*throwing off his disguise*]: Now, Sir Pol, we
    are even;
75   For your next project, I shall be prepared:
    I am sorry for the funeral of your notes, sir.
1st MERCHANT: 'Twere a rare motion,° to be seen in
    Fleet Street!
2nd MERCHANT: Ay, i'the term.°
1st MERCHANT: Or Smithfield,° in the fair.
3rd MERCHANT: Methinks, 'tis but a melancholic
    sight!
PEREGRINE: Farewell, most politic tortoise. [*Exeunt*
    PEREGRINE, MERCHANTS.]

80   [*Enter* WAITING WOMAN.]

SIR POLITIC: Where's my lady?
    Knows she of this?
WOMAN: I know not, sir.
SIR POLITIC: Enquire. [*Exit* WOMAN.]
    O, I shall be the fable of all feasts;
    The freight of the *gazetti;*° ship-boys' tale;
    And, which is more, even talk for ordinaries.°

    [*Enter* WAITING WOMAN.]

85   WOMAN: My lady's come most melancholic, home,
    And says, sir, she will straight to sea, for physic.°
SIR POLITIC: And I, to shun, this place, and clime for
    ever;
    Creeping, with house, on back: and think it
    well,
    To shrink my poor head, in my politic shell.

ACT 5 / SCENE 5

[VOLPONE*'s house*]
([*Enter*] VOLPONE, MOSCA; *the first, in the habit*° *of a
commendatore: the other, of a clarissimo.*)

VOLPONE: Am I then like him?
MOSCA: O, sir, you are he:
    No man can sever° you.
VOLPONE: Good.
MOSCA: But, what am I?
VOLPONE: 'Fore heaven, a brave *clarissimo,* thou
    becom'st it!
    Pity, thou wert not born one.
MOSCA: If I hold°
    My made one, 'twill be well.
VOLPONE: I'll go, and see   5
    What news, first, at the court. [*Exit* VOLPONE.]
MOSCA: Do so. My Fox
    Is out on his hole,° and, ere he shall re-enter,
    I'll make him languish in his borrowed case,°
    Except° he come to composition,° with me:
    Androgyno, Castrone, Nano!

    [*Enter* ANDROGYNO, CASTRONE, NANO.]

ALL: Here.   10
MOSCA: Go recreate° yourselves, abroad;° go, sport.
    [*Exeunt the three.*]
    So, now I have the keys, and am possessed.°
    Since he will, needs, be dead, afore his time,
    I'll bury him, or gain by him. I'm his heir:
    And so will keep me,° till he share at least.   15
    To cozen him of all, were but a cheat
    Well placed; no man would construe it a sin:
    Let his sport pay for't,° this is called the Fox-trap.

    [*Exit* MOSCA.]

ACT 5 / SCENE 6

[*A street*]
[*Enter* CORBACCIO *and* CORVINO.]

CORBACCIO: They say, the court is set.
CORVINO: We must maintain
    Our first tale good, for both our reputations.

---

motion, puppet-show. **term,** the law term, when the lawyers of the Inns of Court were in residence and their clients in town. **Smithfield,** site of Bartholomew Fair; Jonson's *Bartholomew Fair* features a puppet-show. **freight . . . gazetti,** i.e., carried by the news-sheets. **ordinaries,** taverns. **physic,** medical treatment, recuperation.

habit, Gifford describes the dress as "a black stuff gown and a red cap with two gilt buttons in front." **sever,** separate, distinguish. **hold,** either "keep up" or "remain in" the assumed role; Mosca equivocates between modesty and guile. **Fox . . . hole,** alluding to the boys' game, Fox-in-the-Hole; players hop, and strike each other with gloves and light thongs. **case,** disguise. **Except,** unless. **composition,** agreement, compromise. **recreate,** refresh, amuse. **abroad,** outside. **possessed,** in possession (but the word has its other potentials). **keep me,** remain. **Let . . . for't,** "Let his amusement compensate his loss," but "sport" is also apt for the hunting and hunted fox.

CORBACCIO: Why? mine's no tale: my son would,
   there, have killed me.
CORVINO: That's true, I had forgot: mine is, I am
   sure.
   But, for your will, sir.
5 CORBACCIO: Ay, I'll come upon° him,
   For that, hereafter, now his patron's dead.

   [*Enter* VOLPONE *disguised.*]

VOLPONE: Signior Corvino! and Corbaccio! sir,
   Much joy unto you.
CORVINO: Of what?
VOLPONE: The sudden good,
   Dropped down upon you—
CORBACCIO: Where?
VOLPONE: And none knows how—
   From old Volpone, sir.
10 CORBACCIO: Out, errant° knave.
VOLPONE: Let not your too much wealth, sir, make
   you furious.
CORBACCIO: Away, thou varlet.
VOLPONE: Why sir?
CORBACCIO: Dost thou mock me?
VOLPONE: You mock the world,° sir, did you not
   change° wills?
CORBACCIO: Out, harlot.
VOLPONE: O! belike you are the man,
15 Signior Corvino? Faith, you carry it well;
   You grow not mad withal: I love your spirit.
   You are not over-leavened,° with your
      fortune.
   You should ha'some would swell,° now, like a
      wine-fat,°
   With such an autumn°—Did he gi' you all, sir?
CORVINO: Avoid,° you rascal.
20 VOLPONE: Troth, your wife has shown
   Herself a very woman:° but, you are well,
   You need not care, you have a good estate,
   To bear it out,° sir: better by this chance.
   Except Corbaccio have a share?
CORBACCIO: Hence, varlet.
VOLPONE: You will not be aknown,° sir: why, 'tis
25   wise.
   Thus do all gamesters, at all games, dissemble.
   No man will seem to win. [*Exeunt* CORBACCIO,
      CORVINO]
                        Here, comes my vulture,
   Heaving his beak up i'the air, and snuffing.

ACT 5 / SCENE 7

   [*Enter* VOLTORE *to* VOLPONE.]

VOLTORE: Outstripped thus, by a parasite? a slave?
   Would run on errands? and make legs,° for
      crumbs?
   Well, what I'll do—
VOLPONE: The court stays° for your worship.
   I e'en rejoice, sir, at your worship's happiness,
   And that it fell into so learned hands,   5
   That understand the fingering.—
VOLTORE: What do you mean?
VOLPONE: I mean to be a suitor to your worship,
   For the small tenement,° out of reparations;°
   That, at the end of your long row of houses,
   By the Piscaria:° it was, in Volpone's time,   10
   Your predecessor, ere he grew diseased,
   A handsome, pretty, customed,° bawdy-house,
   As any was in Venice (none dispraised)
   But fell with him; his body, and that house
   Decayed, together.
VOLTORE: Come, sir, leave your prating.   15
VOLPONE: Why, if your worship gave me but your
      hand,
   That I may ha'the refusal;° I have done.
   'Tis a mere toy to you, sir; candle-rents:°
   As your learn'd worship knows—
VOLTORE: What do I know?
VOLPONE: Marry, no end of your wealth, sir, God
      decrease° it!   20
VOLTORE: Mistaking knave! what, mock'st thou my
      misfortune?
VOLPONE: His blessing on your heart, sir, would
   'twere more.

   [*Exit* VOLTORE.]

            —Now, to my first, again; at the next corner.
   [*Watches, apart.*]

ACT 5 / SCENE 8

   ([*Enter*] CORBACCIO, CORVINO, [MOSCA *passant*°].)

CORBACCIO: See, in our habit! see the impudent
   varlet!
CORVINO: That I could shoot mine eyes at him, like
   gun-stones!°
VOLPONE: But, is this true, sir, of the parasite?

---

   come upon, "make a demand or claim upon" (*OED*).
errant, arrant. **mock the world,** "are laughing at everyone."
change, exchange. **over-leavened,** puffed up (as with too
much yeast). **You . . . swell,** "You'd have some swelling . . ."
wine-fat, wine-vat. **autumn,** i.e., harvest. **Avoid,** be gone!
a very woman, a woman indeed. **bear it out,** carry it off.
aknown, acknowledged (to be the heir).

   make legs, bow and scrape. **stays,** waits. **tenement,**
house. **reparations,** repair(s). **Piscaria,** fish-market. **customed,** well patronized. **refusal,** i.e., "first refusal." **candle-
rents,** rents from deteriorating property (self-consuming, like
candles). **decrease,** a calculated Dogberryism for "increase";
hence the double force of Voltore's response "Mistaking
knave." MOSCA **passant,** i.e., crosses the stage in his role of
clarissimo. **gun-stones,** stone cannon-shot.

CORBACCIO: Again, t'afflict us? monster!

VOLPONE: In good faith, sir,

5   I'm heartily grieved, a beard of your grave length°
     Should be so over-reached, I never brooked
     That parasite's hair, methought his nose should
       cozen:
     There still was somewhat, in his look, did promise
     The bane° of a *clarissimo.*

CORBACCIO: Knave—

VOLPONE: Methinks,

10   Yet you, that are so traded° i'the world,
     A witty merchant, the fine bird, Corvino,
     That have such moral emblems° on your name,
     Should not have sung your shame; and dropped
       your cheese:
     To let the Fox laugh at your emptiness.°

CORVINO: Sirrah, you think, the privilege of the

15   place,°
     And your red saucy cap, that seems, to me,
     Nailed to your jolt-head,° with those two
       chequeens,°
     Can warrant° your abuses; come you, hither?
     You shall perceive, sir, I dare beat you. Approach.

20 VOLPONE: No haste, sir, I do know your valour, well:
     Since you durst publish what you are, sir.

CORVINO: Tarry,
     I'd speak, with you.

VOLPONE: Sir, sir, another time—

CORVINO: Nay, now.

VOLPONE: O God, sir! I were a wise man,
     Would stand° the fury of a distracted cuckold.

(MOSCA walks by 'em.)

CORBACCIO: What! come again?

25 VOLPONE: Upon 'em, Mosca; save me!

CORBACCIO: The air's infected, where he breathes.

CORVINO: Let's fly him.

VOLPONE: Excellent basilisk!° turn upon the vulture.

ACT 5 / SCENE 9

[Enter VOLTORE.]

VOLTORE: Well, flesh-fly,° it is summer with you, now;
     Your winter will come on.

MOSCA: Good advocate,
     Pray thee, not rail, nor threaten out of place, thus;

---

beard . . . length, "one so old and wise," but probably literal too. **bane,** ruin, destruction. **traded,** experienced. **moral emblems,** Corvino's name recalls the crow that dropped its cheese to sing to the fox. **emptiness,** i.e., of belly and of head. **place,** station, rank (as a commendatore). **jolt-head,** block-head. **chequeens,** i.e., the coin-like buttons of his hat. **warrant,** sanction, protect by official authority. **stand,** withstand. **basilisk,** or cockatrice, a fabulous reptile hatched by a serpent from a cock's egg and capable of killing by its glance. **flesh-fly,** a blow-fly, the meaning of "Mosca."

Thou'lt make a solecism, as madam says.
     Get you a biggin° more: your brain breaks loose.   5

VOLTORE: Well, sir.

VOLPONE: Would you ha' me beat the insolent slave?
     Throw dirt, upon his first good clothes?

VOLTORE: This same
     Is, doubtless, some familiar!°

VOLPONE: Sir, the court
     In troth, stays for you. I am mad,° a mule,°
     That never read Justinian,° should get up,   10
     And ride an advocate. Had you no quirk,°
     To avoid gullage,° sir, by such a creature?
     I hope you do but jest; he has not done't:
     This's but confederacy,° to blind the rest.
     You are the heir?

VOLTORE: A strange, officious,   15
     Troublesome knave! thou dost torment me.

VOLPONE: I know—
     It cannot be, sir, that you should be cozened;
     'Tis not within the wit of man, to do it:
     You are so wise, so prudent—and, 'tis fit,
     That wealth, and wisdom still, should go together.   20

ACT 5 / SCENE 10

[The Scrutineo]

([Enter] Four AVOCATORI, NOTARIO, COMMENDATORI, BONARIO, CELIA, CORBACCIO, CORVINO.)

1st AVOCATORE: Are all the parties, here?

NOTARIO: All, but the advocate.

2nd AVOCATORE: And, here he comes.

[Enter VOLTORE, with VOLPONE disguised.]

1st AVOCATORE: Then bring 'em forth to sentence.

VOLTORE: O, my most honoured fathers, let your
     mercy
     Once win upon° your justice, to forgive—
     I am distracted—

VOLPONE *[aside]:* What will he do, now?

VOLTORE: O,   5
     I know not which t'address myself to, first,
     Whether your fatherhoods, or these innocents—

CORVINO *[aside]:* Will he betray himself?

VOLTORE: Whom, equally,
     I have abused, out of most covetous ends°—

CORVINO *[to CORBACCIO]:* The man is mad!

CORBACCIO: What's that?

CORVINO: He is possessed.°   10

---

biggin, lawyer's cap or coif. **familiar,** i.e., "some fellow of the same household." **mad,** furious (that). **mule,** mules were customarily ridden by lawyers. **Justinian,** i.e., the *Corpus Jurus Civilis,* the Roman code of law compiled under the direction of Justinian I. **quirk,** trick. **gullage,** being gulled. **confederacy,** i.e., between Mosca and Voltore. **win upon,** overcome. **ends,** purposes, motives. **possessed,** i.e., of a devil.

VOLTORE: For which, now struck in conscience, here
    I prostrate
Myself, at your offended feet, for pardon.
1st and 2nd AVOCATORI: Arise!
CELIA: O heaven, how just thou art?
VOLPONE [*aside*]:   I'm caught
    I'mine own noose—
CORVINO [*to* CORBACCIO]: Be constant,° sir, nought
    now
    Can help, but impudence.°
1st AVOCATORE: Speak forward.
15 COMMENDATORE: Silence!
VOLTORE: It is not passion° in me, reverend fathers,
    But only conscience, my good sires,
    That makes me, now, tell truth. That parasite,
    That knave hath been the instrument of all.
2nd AVOCATORE: Where is that knave? fetch him!
VOLPONE: I go. [*Exit* VOLPONE.]
20 CORVINO: Grave fathers,
    This man's distracted; he confessed it, now:°
    For, hoping to be old Volpone's heir,
    Who now is dead—
3rd AVOCATORE: How?
2nd AVOCATORE: Is Volpone dead?
CORVINO: Dead since, grave fathers—
BONARIO: O, sure vengeance!
1st AVOCATORE: Stay,
    Then, he was no deceiver?
25 VOLTORE: O no, none:
    The parasite, grave fathers—
CORVINO: He does speak,
    Out of mere envy, 'cause the servant's made°
    The thing, he gaped for;° please your fatherhoods,
    This is the truth: though, I'll not justify
30   The other, but he may° be some-deal° faulty.
VOLTORE: Ay, to your hopes, as well as mine, Corvino:
    But I'll use modesty.° Pleaseth your wisdoms
    To view these certain° notes, and but confer° them,

    [*Gives them papers.*]

    As I hope favour, they shall speak clear truth.
CORVINO: The devil has entered him!
35 BONARIO: Or bides in you.
4th AVOCATORE: We have done ill, by a public officer°
    To send for him, if he be heir.
2nd AVOCATORE: For whom?
4th AVOCATORE: Him, that they call the parasite.
3rd AVOCATORE: 'Tis true;
    He is a man, of great estate, now left.

4th AVOCATORE: Go you, and learn his name, and say,
    the court   40
    Entreats his presence, here; but, to the clearing
    Of some few doubts. [*Exit* NOTARIO.]
2nd AVOCATORE: This same's a labyrinth!
1st AVOCATORE: Stand you unto your first report?
CORVINO: My state,°
    My life, my fame—
BONARIO (*aside*):   Where is it?
CORVINO: Are at the stake.°
1st AVOCATORE: Is yours so too?
CORBACCIO: The advocate's a knave: 45
    And has a forked tongue—
2nd AVOCATORE: Speak to the point.
CORBACCIO: So is the parasite, too.
1st AVOCATORE: This is confusion.
VOLTORE: I do beseech your fatherhoods, read but
    those.
CORVINO: And credit nothing, the false spirit hath
    writ:
    It cannot be, but he is possessed, grave fathers. 50

ACT 5 / SCENE 11

[*A street*]
([*Enter*] VOLPONE.)

VOLPONE: To make a snare, for mine own neck! and
    run
    My head into it, wilfully! with laughter!
    When I had newly scaped, was free, and clear!
    Out of mere wantonness! O, the dull devil°
    Was in this brain of mine, when I devised it; 5
    And Mosca gave it second;° he must now
    Help to sear° up this vein, or we bleed dead.

[*Enter* NANO, ANDROGYNO, CASTRONE.]

    How now! who let you loose? whither go you, now?
    What? to buy ginger-bread? or to drown kitlings?°
NANO: Sir, master Mosca called us out of doors. 10
    And bid us all go play, and took the keys.
ANDROGYNO: Yes.
VOLPONE: Did master Mosca take the keys? why, so!
    I am farther in. These are my fine conceits!°
    I must be merry, with a mischief to me!°
    What a vile wretch was I, that could not bear 15
    My fortune° soberly? I must ha' my crotchets!°

---

    constant, firm, consistent. ***impudence,*** unblushing effrontery. ***passion,*** frenzy. ***now,*** just now. ***made,*** achieved, grabbed. ***gaped for,*** hungered after. ***but he may,*** "he may yet." ***some-deal,*** somewhere. ***modesty,*** moderation. ***certain,*** "particular" or perhaps "reliable." ***confer,*** either "compare" or "consult together about." ***public officer,*** describing the status of Volpone as commendatore.

    state, estate. **Are . . . stake,** "are all staked on the truth of what I have said." ***dull devil,*** "devil of stupidity." ***gave it second,*** seconded it. ***sear,*** cauterize, stem blood with hot iron. ***buy . . . kitlings,*** presumably the pastimes of self-indulgent and malicious children. ***conceits,*** notions, schemes. ***with . . . to me,*** either reflective, "with this mischievous result," or imprecatory, "a mischief take me!" ***fortune,*** i.e., good fortune in surviving the court action, or perhaps "wealth." ***crotchets,*** whimsical fancies, perverse conceits (*OED*).

And my conundrums!° well, go you, and seek him:
His meaning may be truer, than my fear.
Bid him, he straight come to me, to the court;
20   Thither will I, and, if 't be possible,
Unscrew° my advocate, upon° new hopes:
When I provoked him, then I lost myself.

ACT 5 / SCENE 12

[*The Scrutineo*]
[*Four* AVOCATORI, NOTARIO, VOLTORE, BONARIO, CE-
LIA, CORBACCIO, CORVINO, COMMENDATORI.]

1st AVOCATORE [*with* VOLTORE*'s notes*]: These things
    can ne'er be reconciled. He, here,
Professeth, that the gentleman was wronged;
And that the gentlewoman was brought thither,
Forced by her husband: and there left.
VOLTORE: Most true.
CELIA: How ready is heaven to those, that pray!
5   1st AVOCATORE: But, that
Volpone would have ravished her, he holds
Utterly false; knowing his impotence.
CORVINO: Grave fathers, he is possessed; again, I say,
Possessed: nay, if there be possession,
And obsession,° he has both.
10   3rd AVOCATORE: Here comes our officer.

    [*Enter* VOLPONE, *disguised.*]

VOLPONE: The parasite will straight be here, grave
    fathers.
4th AVOCATORE: You might invent° some other
    name, sir varlet.°
3rd AVOCATORE: Did not the notary meet him?
VOLPONE: Not that I know.
4th AVOCATORE: His coming will clear all.
2nd AVOCATORE: Yet it is misty.
VOLTORE: May 't please your fatherhoods—

    (VOLPONE *whispers to the* ADVOCATE.)

15   VOLPONE: Sir, the parasite
Willed me to tell you, that his master lives;
That you are still the man; your hopes, the same;
And this was, only a jest—
VOLTORE: How?
VOLPONE: Sir, to try
If you were firm, and how you stood affected.°
VOLTORE: Art sure he lives?

VOLPONE: Do I live, sir?°
VOLTORE: O me!   20
    I was too violent.
VOLPONE: Sir, you may redeem it—
    They said, you were possessed; fall down, and seem
    so:
    I'll help to make it good. (VOLTORE *falls.*)
                    God bless the man!
    [*aside*] Stop your wind° hard, and swell—See, see,
    see, see!
    He vomits crooked pins! his eyes are set,   25
    Like a dead hare's, hung in a poulter's° shop!
    His mouth's running away!° do you see, signior?
    Now, 'tis in his belly.
CORVINO: Ay, the devil!
VOLTORE: Now, in his throat.
CORVINO: Ay, I perceive it plain.
VOLTORE: 'Twill out, 'twill out; stand clear. See,
    where it flies!   30
    In shape of a blue toad, with a bat's wings!
    Do not you see it, sir?
CORBACCIO: What? I think I do.
CORVINO: 'Tis too manifest.
VOLTORE: Look! he comes t'himself!
VOLTORE: Where am I?
VOLPONE: Take good heart, the worst is past, sir.
    You are dispossessed.
1st AVOCATORE: What accident is this?   35
2nd AVOCATORE: Sudden, and full of wonder!
3rd AVOCATORE: If he were
    Possessed, as it appears, all this is nothing.
CORVINO: He has been, often, subject to these fits.
1st AVOCATORE: Show him that writing, do you know
    it, sir?
VOLPONE [*aside to* VOLTORE]: Deny it, sir, forswear it,
    know it not.   40
VOLTORE: Yes, I do know it well, it is my hand:°
    But all, that it contains, is false.
BONARIO: O practice!
2nd AVOCATORE: What maze is this!
1st AVOCATORE: Is he not guilty, then,
    Whom you, there, name the parasite?
VOLTORE: Grave fathers,
    No more than, his good patron, old Volpone.   45
4th AVOCATORE: Why, he is dead?
VOLTORE: O no, my honoured fathers.
    He lives—
1st AVOCATORE: How! lives?
VOLTORE: Lives.
2nd AVOCATORE: This is subtler° yet!

---

conundrums, whims, crotchets. **Unscrew,** i.e., "dislodge
him from his present course"; or perhaps "unwind him" as if
he were a loaded cross-bow. **upon,** used to indicate manner—"in" or "by." **obsession,** "actuation by the devil or an
evil spirit from without" (*OED*). **invent,** find. **varlet,** menial
or knave (here used to slight the commendatore). **how . . .
affected,** "which way you were inclined," "how you would feel
and act."

Do . . . sir? Volpone evidently discloses his identity to
Voltore, perhaps by showing his red hair, or a signet ring.
Stop your wind, hold your breath. **poulter's,** poulterers.
running away, twisting from one side to the other. **hand,**
handwriting. **subtler,** more elusive and bewildering.

3rd AVOCATORE: You said he was dead!
VOLTORE: Never.
3rd AVOCATORE [*to* CORVINO]:   You said so!
CORVINO: I heard so.
4th AVOCATORE: Here comes the gentleman, make
    him way.

    [*Enter* MOSCA *as clarissimo.*]

3rd AVOCATORE: A stool!
4th AVOCATORE [*aside*]: A proper° man! and were
50   Volpone dead,
    A fit match for my daughter.
3rd AVOCATORE: Give him way.
VOLPONE [*aside to* MOSCA]: Mosca, I was almost lost,
    the advocate
    Had betrayed all; but, now, it is recovered:°
    All's o'the hinge° again—say, I am living.
MOSCA: What busy° knave is this! most reverend
55   fathers,
    I sooner, had attended your grave pleasures,
    But that my order, for the funeral
    Of my dear patron did require me—
VOLPONE [*aside*]:   Mosca!
MOSCA: Whom I intend to bury, like a gentleman.
VOLPONE [*aside*]: Aye, quick,° and cozen me of all.
60 2nd AVOCATORE: Still stranger!
    More intricate!
1st AVOCATORE: And come about° again!
4th AVOCATORE [*aside*]: It is a match, my daughter is
    bestowed.
MOSCA [*aside to* VOLPONE]: Will you give me half?
VOLPONE [*aside to* MOSCA]: First, I'll be hanged.
MOSCA [*aside to* VOLPONE]:   I know,
    Your voice is good, cry° not so loud.
1st AVOCATORE: Demand°
65   The advocate. Sir, did you not affirm,
    Volpone was alive?
VOLPONE: Yes, and he is;
    This gent'man told me so. [*aside to* MOSCA] Thou
    shalt have half.
MOSCA: Whose drunkard is this same? speak some
    that know him:
    I never saw his face. [*aside to* VOLPONE] I cannot now
    Afford it you so cheap.
VOLPONE [*aside to* MOSCA]: No?
70 1st AVOCATORE: What say you?
VOLTORE: The officer told me.
VOLPONE: I did, grave fathers,
    And will maintain, he lives, with mine own life.
    And, that this creature told me. [*Aside*] I was born
    With all good° stars my enemies.

---

proper, handsome. *recovered,* got back again; covered
up again. *o'the hinge,* running smoothly, no longer un-
hinged (o' = on). *busy,* officious. *quick,* alive. *come about,*
turned round, reversed. *cry,* shout. *Demand,* ask. *good,*
propitious.

MOSCA: Most grave fathers,
    If such an insolence, as this, must pass°   75
    Upon me, I am silent; 'twas not this,
    For which you sent, I hope.
2nd AVOCATORE: Take him away.
VOLPONE [*aside*]: Mosca!
3rd AVOCATORE: Let him be whipped,—
VOLPONE [*aside*]:   Wilt thou betray me?
    Cozen me?
3rd AVOCATORE: And taught to bear himself
    Toward a person of his rank.
4th AVOCATORE: Away. [VOLPONE *is seized.*]   80
MOSCA: I humbly thank your fatherhoods.
VOLPONE [*aside*]:   Soft, soft: whipped?
    And lose all that I have? if I confess.
    It cannot be much more.
4th AVOCATORE [*to* MOSCA]: Sir, are you married?
VOLPONE: They'll be allied,° anon;° I must be
    resolute:

(He puts off his disguise.)

    The Fox shall, here, uncase.°
MOSCA: Patron!°
VOLPONE: Nay, now,   85
    My ruins shall not come alone; your match
    I'll hinder sure: my substance shall not glue° you,
    Nor screw° you, into a family.
MOSCA: Why, patron!
VOLPONE: I am Volpone, and this is my knave;°
    This, his own knave; this, avarice's fool;°   90
    This, a chimera° of wittol,° fool, and knave;
    And, reverend fathers, since we all can hope
    Nought, but a sentence, let's not now despair it.°
    You hear me brief.
CORVINO: May it please your fatherhoods—
COMMENDATORE: Silence!
1st AVOCATORE: The knot is now undone, by miracle!   95
2nd AVOCATORE: Nothing can be more clear.
3rd AVOCATORE: Or can more prove
    These innocent.
1st AVOCATORE: Give 'em their liberty.
BONARIO: Heaven could not, long, let such gross
    crimes be hid.
2nd AVOCATORE: If this be held the highway to get
    riches,
    May I be poor.
3rd AVOCATORE: This's° not the gain, but torment.   100

---

    pass, be allowed. *allied,* i.e., by a marriage bargain.
anon, in a moment. *uncase,* remove disguise, perhaps with a
suggestion of the fox breaking cover. *Patron!* Mosca is
apparently startled back into his servile role. *glue,* suggests
a parasitic attachment. *screw,* suggests a tortuous one.
knave, menial; rogue. *fool,* dupe. *chimera,* mythical beast
with a lion-head, goat-body and serpent-tail; hence a triple
monster. *wittol,* conniving cuckold. *let's . . . it,* "let us not
despair for want of a sentence." *This's,* i.e., riches.

1st AVOCATORE: These possess wealth, as sick men
    possess fevers,
    Which, trulier, may be said to possess them.
2nd AVOCATORE: Disrobe that parasite.
CORVINO, MOSCA: Most honoured fathers—
1st AVOCATORE: Can you plead ought to stay the
    course of justice?
    If you can, speak.
CORVINO, VOLTORE: We beg favour.
105 CELIA: And mercy.
1st AVOCATORE: You hurt your innocence, suing for
    the guilty.
    Stand forth; and first, the parasite. You appear
    T'have been the chiefest minister,° if not plotter,
    In all these lewd° impostures; and now, lastly,
110   Have, with your impudence, abused the court,
    And habit of a gentleman of Venice,
    Being a fellow of no birth, or blood:
    For which, our sentence is, first thou be whipped;
    Then live perpetual prisoner in our gallies.
VOLPONE: I thank you, for him.
115 MOSCA: Bane° to thy woolvish nature.
1st AVOCATORE: Deliver him to the Saffi.° [MOSCA *is*
    led off.] Thou, Volpone,
    By blood, and rank a gentleman, canst not fall
    Under like censure; but our judgement on thee
    Is, that thy substance all be straight confiscate
120   To the hospital, of the *Incurabili:*°
    And, since the most was gotten by imposture,
    By feigning lame, gout, palsy, and such diseases,
    Thou art to lie in prison, cramped with irons,
    Till thou be'st sick, and lame indeed. Remove him.
125 VOLPONE: This is called mortifying° of a fox.
    [VOLPONE *is led off.*]
1st AVOCATORE: Thou, Voltore, to take away the
    scandal
    Thou hast given all worthy men, of thy profession,
    Art banished from their fellowship, and our state.
    Corbaccio!—bring him near. We here possess

---

minister, agent, instrument. **lewd,** wicked, base. **Bane,**
death. **Saffi,** bailiffs. **Incurabili,** the Hospital of Incurables
was founded in Venice in 1522 for the treatment of venereal
disease; the punishment is therefore particularly appropriate. *mortifying,* several senses are relevant: humiliating; rendering dead to the world and the flesh by spiritual discipline;
hanging game to make it tender.

Thy son, of all thy state; and confine thee   130
    To the monastery of *San Spirito:*°
    Where, since thou knew'st not how to live well
    here,
    Thou shalt be learn'd to die well.
CORBACCIO: Ha! what said he?
COMMENDATORE: You shall know anon, sir.
1ST AVOCATORE: Thou, Corvino, shalt
    Be straight embarked from thine own house, and
    rowed   135
    Round about Venice, through the Grand Canal,
    Wearing a cap, with fair, long ass's ears,
    Instead of horns: and, so to mount, a paper
    Pinned on thy breast, to the berlino°—
CORVINO: Yes,
    And, have mine eyes beat out with stinking fish,   140
    Bruised fruit, and rotten eggs—'Tis well. I'm glad,
    I shall not see my shame, yet.
1st AVOCATORE: And to expiate
    Thy wrongs done to thy wife, thou art to send her
    Home, to her father, with her dowry trebled:
    And these are all your judgements—
ALL: Honoured fathers.   145
1st AVOCATORE: Which may not be revoked. Now, you
    begin,
    When crimes are done, and past, and to be
    punished,
    To think what your crimes are: away with them!
    Let all, that see these vices thus rewarded,
    Take heart, and love to study 'em. Mischiefs feed   150
    Like beasts, till they be fat, and then they bleed.
    [*Exeunt.*]

[*To speak the Epilogue.*]

VOLPONE: The seasoning of a play is the applause.
    Now, though the Fox be punished by the laws,
    He, yet, doth hope there is no suffering due,
    For any fact,° which he hath done 'gainst you;   155
    If there be, censure him: here he, doubtful, stands.
    If not, fare jovially, and clap your hands.

THE END

San Spirito, the monastery of the Holy Spirit stood on
the Giudecca canal. **berlino,** pillory. **fact,** crime (as in the
legal phrase "after the fact").

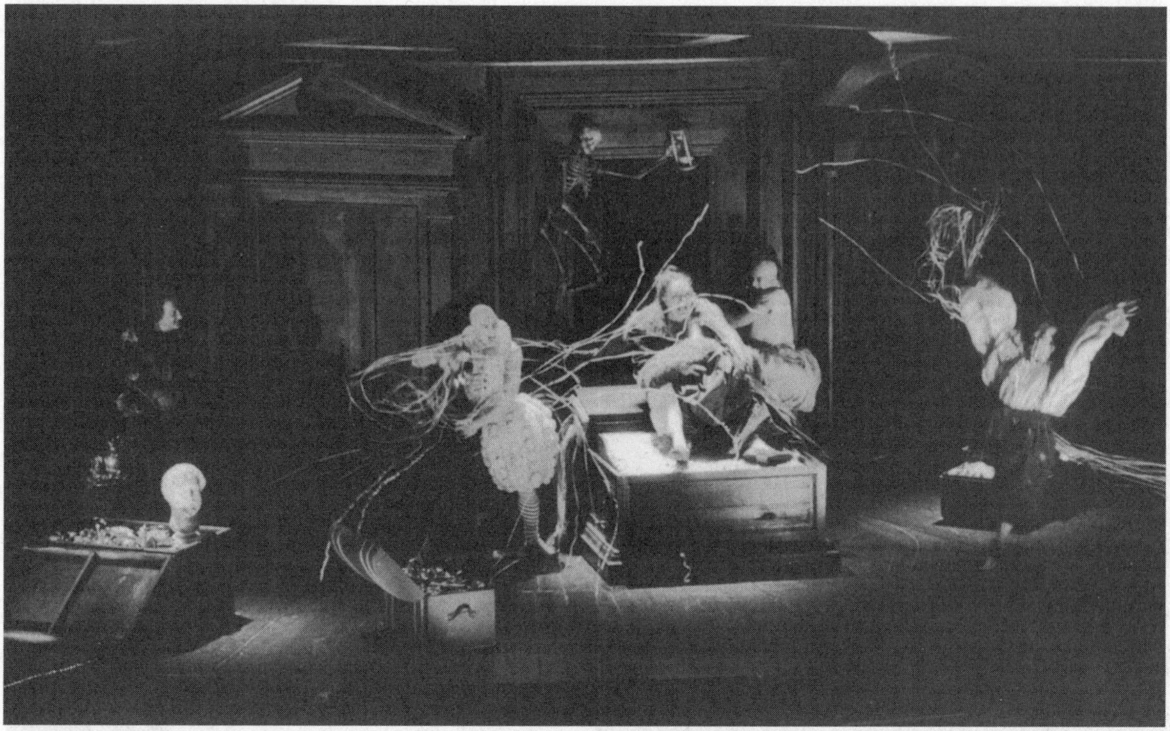

Figure 1. Volpone (Michael Gambon, *on bed*) is surrounded by his trio of freakish servants, Androgyno (Joyce Henderson, *left*), Nano (Wayne Cater, *upstage of bed*), and Castrone (Jonathan Stone, *right*) in the nightmarish opening to Matthew Warchus's production of *Volpone* at the Royal National Theatre, London, 1995. (Photograph: Ivan Kyncl.)

Figure 2. In the 1995 Royal National Theatre production, a fawning Mosca (Simon Russell Beale) tells Lady Would-be (Cheryl Campbell) that he has seen her husband with a courtesan. (Photograph: Ivan Kyncl.)

Figure 3. Volpone (Michael Gambon, *wearing his invalid's hat*) pleads his love to Celia (Matilda Ziegler) in the 1995 Royal National Theatre production. (Photograph: Ivan Kyncl.)

Figure 4. In the 1995 Royal National Theatre production, Volpone (Michael Gambon) stares blankly into space, while Mosca (Simon Russell Beale) tries to convince Voltore (Stephen Boxer, *right*) that he was trying to help Voltore's case by bringing Bonario, Corbaccio's son, to Volpone's bed-chamber. Corbaccio (Trevor Peacock, *left*) can't hear the conversation, in spite of the ear-trumpet on his cap. (Photograph: Ivan Kyncl.)

Staging of *Volpone*

REVIEW OF THE ROYAL NATIONAL THEATRE PRODUCTION, 1995, BY SARAH HEMMING

Matthew Warchus's scintillating production of *Volpone* in the Olivier Theatre opens with a coup de theatre that at once seizes your attention and creates the fevered, dangerous mood of Jonson's masterpiece. He adds an audacious prologue that pre-empts the play's ending.

Actors burst on to the stage in a confusion of light and noise and we realise we are in Volpone's nightmare: a terrifying fox hunt in which he scrabbles around the tunnels of the revolving set pursued by a pack of vicious, fire-wielding figures in swirling cloaks. When he awakes with the famous words, "Good morning to the world; and next, my gold!" it is a relief, but the pace, mood and urgency of the play have been set. With this hellish opening, Warchus reminds you of the Faustian side of the play; the import of the characters' evil behaviour. And he launches a production that captures wonderfully the scope of the drama, underpinning all the comedy with a sinister desperation.

But this opening is also superbly theatrical, and this too is canny. Jonson did not just write a vicious satire on the greed, gullibility and ugliness of human beings at their worst, he created a hymn to the craft of the actor. Volpone and Mosca are, in a sense, a fantastic double act, whom we admire despite their loathsomeness because of their cunning, energy and ability. This is wonderfully brought out here: as the first of the money grubbers arrives to visit Volpone, the face-powder that has rendered him an invalid is still settling on the ground. And Michael Gambon as Volpone and Simon Russell Beale as Mosca, revel in the theatrical inventiveness of the two.

Both Gambon and Russell Beale are superb. Their mutual admiration is almost erotically charged. Gambon is wonderfully funny and endlessly watchable: wily, stealthy, athletic even, yet driven by some desperate, empty hunger that cannot be satisfied. And despite looking like some long dead trout in a paper doily, he can still stop the laugh in your throat.

Simon Russell Beale, meanwhile, in his flyblown doublet and hose seems to reek of putrefaction. He must have been kept up many a night by mosquitos to have so perfected the peculiar resourcefulness of a fly. And yet he suggests buzzing without making a sound—just the way he rubs his hands together has your fingers itching for a rolled up newspaper. But when he does Mosca's soliloquy in praise of parasites, he holds you with a ghastly fascination—excellent, disturbing and vivid.

Throughout, the balance is kept between fable and plausibility, with the animal references beautifully done. Stephen Boxer, in particular makes a wonderful vulture. But at the same time Jonson's Venice has enough reality. On Richard Hudson's revolving set it emerges a place of gloomy corridors, dark chambers and cold hearts, where all that glistens is the gold in Volpone's lair.

The production has its longueurs—it drags with the English subplot, for instance. But it is full of delightful ideas (Corbaccio's hearing device that protrudes, periscope-like from his head) and inspired moments (Cheryl Campbell, a rasping Lady Would-be in a tangerine farthingale, who looks like a mix between Queen Bess and Sybil Fawlty, throwing open the doors to roar "I pray you lend me your dwarf"). This is a speedy, bold and exuberant reading that brings Jonson's old gold masterpiece up shining like new.

NEOCLASSICAL THEATER

In the middle of the seventeenth century, drama moved indoors and stayed there. It moved from daylight to candlelight, from large open-air theaters, some capable of seating as many as 2,000, to relatively small auditoriums, usually accommodating no more than 700. And this radical shift in the environment of drama not only produced a radically different theatrical experience but also called forth radically different changes in the conception of drama itself. This change in the theatrical environment had already been anticipated by developments dating back to the early sixteenth century, when indoor theaters began to be built in the banqueting halls of Italy and in remodeled tennis courts in France. English private theaters, located in former monasteries such as Blackfriars and Whitefriars, began in the late 1500s. In all these spaces, the stage usually occupied one end of a long hall, and the audience watched from side galleries and from the floor in front of the stage. By the last third of the seventeenth century, theaters reflecting this design had become standard throughout the major dramatic centers in Europe, and these theaters were conventionally equipped with a proscenium arch framing the stage, a design derived from Italian stage architecture of the sixteenth century. In English theaters of the later seventeenth century, a sizable forestage, recalling the platform of the Elizabethan public theater, extended beyond the proscenium, and double doors, also in front of the proscenium, gave actors ready access to this favored acting area (see Figure 1). French theaters of the same period have a much shallower forestage, no doors, and, in some cases, benches to seat members of the audience on stage behind the proscenium (see Figure 2). In both theaters, the pit, or floor area directly in front of the stage, is shared by standing and seated spectators. Earlier, this space had entirely been given to standing room or left vacant so that the royal party could have an uninterrupted view of the stage.

Just as the English and French had borrowed from the Italians in their use of a proscenium arch, so they turned to Italy for the sets they were to display behind the picture frame of the arch. Italian set design had been pioneered by Sebastian Serlio, who created in his lengthy treatise, *Architettura* (1545), a set of detailed

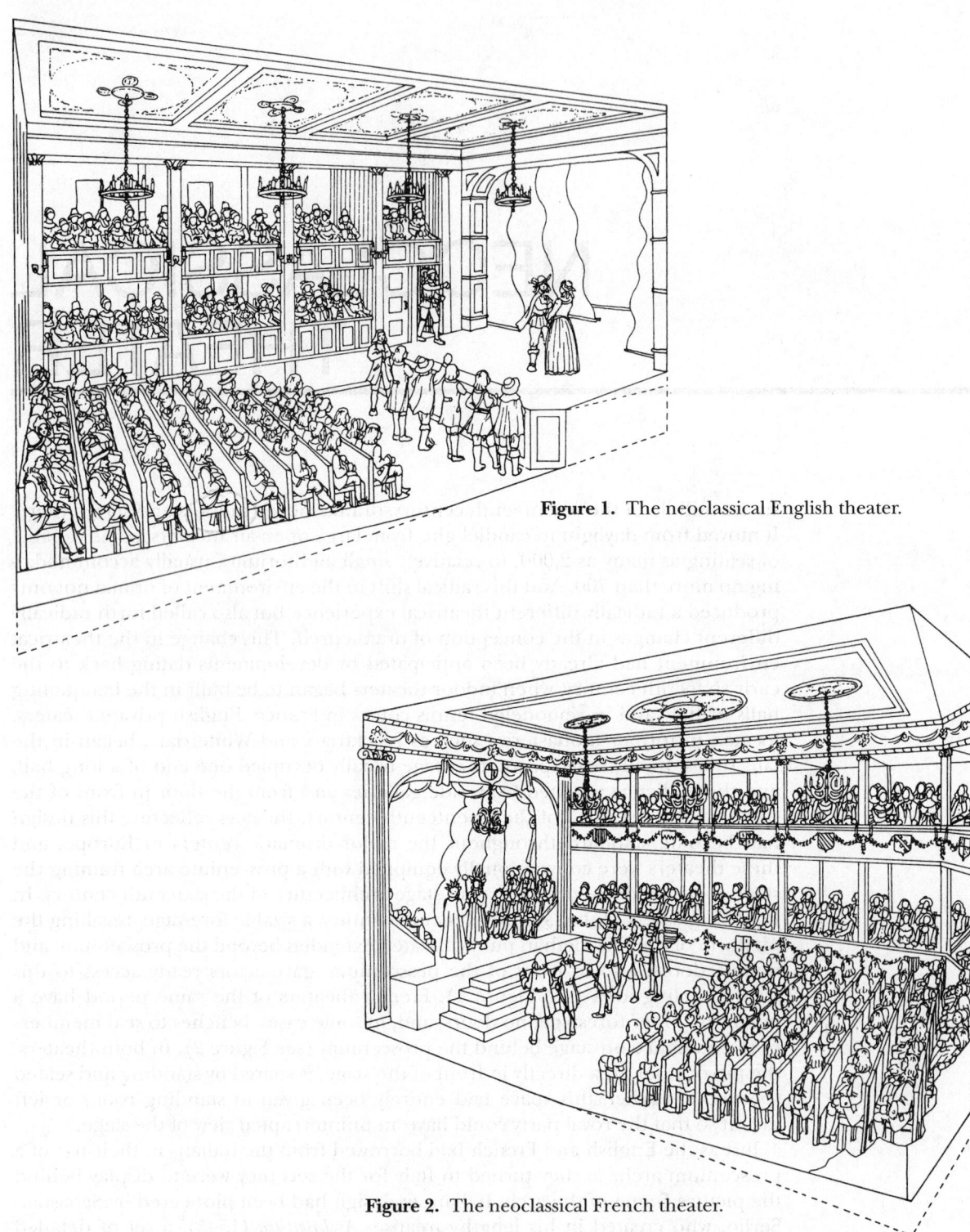

Figure 1. The neoclassical English theater.

Figure 2. The neoclassical French theater.

drawings for three typical sets, which he based on his reading of a classical Roman treatise. His dependence on a classical source is only one of the many instances that account for the term "neoclassicism." Later designers simplified his three-dimensional details into painted ones and substituted flat wings for the angle wings Serlio had used. At first, the elaborate Italianate sets were used primarily for court entertainments—masques in early-seventeenth-century England, and court ballets in mid-seventeenth-century France. But the very possibility of being able to represent different locales by changing a painted backdrop and wings (instead of saying "So this is the Forest of Arden" and expecting the audience to imagine the new locale) led to a new and crucial feature in theater architecture. Because flats that are to be shifted require machinery, stagehands, or both to move them, it became necessary to conceal such backstage efforts. Designers began by using plain flats for concealing the activity, but gradually looked for a permanent frame for the stage: the proscenium arch. While the proscenium masked backstage maneuvers, it also detached the space on stage from the space in the remainder of the theater and thus separated the actors from the audience. Lighting changes also reinforced this separation. In the drawings reproduced here, we see chandeliers with candles lighting both the audience and the stage. But in the late seventeenth century, footlights were added, and more attention was given to lighting the stage alone. And in the eighteenth century, dimming devices (such as lowering the candle footlights) were invented, lamps began to replace candles, and lamps with reflectors were placed *behind* the proscenium arch, focusing light more sharply on the acting area.

Still, the theaters of this period are nothing like the darkened auditoriums of today, and audiences then would not have wished them so, since they came to the theater to be seen as much as to see. For English audiences after 1660 (the date of the Restoration of the monarchy and the Restoration of theatrical activity), the playhouse was the place to meet friends, to talk, to flirt, to eat and drink. Prologues to Restoration plays frequently comment on the audience's behavior and especially on the attention of those in the pit (still the cheapest seats) to orange-women, prostitutes, and young men trying to be witty. The performance, it might almost be said, ran simultaneously onstage and offstage. Well-known liaisons between actresses and nobles brought performers and audience together even more closely. In a famous painting by the satiric artist William Hogarth of the final scene from Gay's *The Beggar's Opera* (1728), an actress can be seen gazing not only at the actor who should command her exclusive attention but also at the Duke of Bolton, her real-life lover, who sits in an onstage box. The costuming of most plays in contemporary dress added to the mirror effect, since people onstage looked very much like those off-stage. Paintings of the famous actor David Garrick, for example, show him wearing the standard wig and dress of the mid-eighteenth century—for Macbeth! Actors owned their own wardrobes and, like the audience members, spent lavish amounts on a single costume. The stage picture was thus likely to be highly gorgeous but not necessarily consistent, and certainly not historically accurate.

The similarities between onstage and offstage behavior can be found in the plays as well as in performance practices. Indeed, the two are closely related, particularly in the social comedies of Behn, Etherege, Wycherley, Congreve, Molière, Goldsmith, and Sheridan. In these plays the audience could easily see itself. *The Rover,* for example, though set in the more "permissive" Neapolitan society, still reflects

London society, since women attending the theater often wore masks to hide their identity, just as the women in this play disguise themselves as Gypsies when they leave the safety of their home. In France, Molière also finds a wide range of satiric targets that mirror the life of his audience—from the bourgeois who try to be upper class to the fashionable salon society obsessed with trivial affairs. But even when he comes close to satirizing his own audience directly, he is careful to leave an escape route, for his onstage characters are always highly exaggerated versions of actual experience, and their exaggeration is usually the source of his mockery.

The relation of drama to actual experience was, in fact, a central issue in critical theories of the period, most of which were derived from Italian commentaries on classical criticism. The treatises of Minturno, Scaliger, and Castelvetro, which sought to define literary art or to comment on Aristotle and Horace, argued for "verisimilitude," likeness to truth, and formulated a number of elaborate rules to bring drama closer to reality. But for them, reality was to be achieved not through having the stage life exactly like real life, but through abiding by certain normative conditions. Tragedy, for example, was to follow the norms of elevated speech, characters of high rank, and plots with unhappy endings, while comedy was to use a more colloquial style befitting its middle- or lower-class characters and was to end happily. Verisimilitude also demanded that certain events, especially violent ones, be kept offstage, since they were thought unlikely to be convincing onstage. Finally, a play was to deal only with a single series of incidents, occurring in a single locale, within a period of twenty-four hours or less. These famous, even notorious, "unities" of action, place, and time were thought to support verisimilitude, since an audience in a theater presumably knew that it had been in the same place for several hours only, and in that limited time it could not believe a multitude of actions taking place.

Such theories, called neoclassical because they are based on reinterpretations of classical texts, could not, of course, last forever. And by the end of the eighteenth century, one of England's great literary critics, Samuel Johnson, a man thoroughly steeped in neoclassical theory, offered a commonsense repudiation of the rules in his *Preface to Shakespeare:*

> The truth is, that the spectators are always in their senses, and know, from the first act to the last, that the stage is only a stage, and that the players are only players. They come to hear a certain number of lines recited with just gesture and elegant modulation. The lines relate to some action, and an action must be in some place; but the different actions that complete a story may be in places very remote from each other; and where is the absurdity of allowing that space to represent first Athens, and then Sicily, which was always known to be neither Sicily nor Athens, but a modern theater?

But by the end of the eighteenth century, staging techniques were being designed to make spectators forget they were in a theater. The development of machinery for changing sets, the elaboration of scenery painting, and the increased use of sophisticated lighting that would focus primarily on the stage were clear indications of a growing interest in making the stage picture look "real," in creating a detailed theatrical illusion. Acting styles, too, edged slightly closer to "realistic" portrayal of characters. In these ways, the theater's move indoors led eventually to drama that focused almost totally on the individual character, showing how external environment and inner emotional life together shape the destiny of the individual.

MOLIÈRE

Molière, the preeminent comic dramatist in the history of French theater, was also known in his own time as the director and the leading actor of the major theatrical company in Paris. He was, in fact, so thoroughly a man of the stage that once he became involved in it, after a brief period of studying law, he abandoned his given name, Jean-Baptiste Poquelin, and replaced it with the singular one by which he has since been known. His theatrical career began in 1643, when he formed a small company, known as the Illustre Théâtre, with a family of talented actors, the Béjarts. But their enterprise failed so badly that Molière was temporarily imprisoned for debts, and the company was forced to leave Paris. They regrouped themselves in the provinces and toured the countryside from 1645 to 1658, a period when Molière evidently trained himself in every aspect of the theater from set building to playwriting. During this time, for example, he witnessed the touring Italian companies and steeped himself in their extensive repertoire of comic techniques—techniques of the *commedia dell'arte,* such as stock characters, slapstick routines (known as *lazzi*), intrigue plots, and conventional "surprise" endings. By the end of this period, Molière had also become director of the troupe, which he had enlarged and improved by attracting some of the most accomplished actors and actresses of his day. When he took his troupe back to Paris in 1658, having arranged a special performance for the youthful Louis XIV and his court, Molière won the king's favor and was granted permission to remain in Paris and perform at the Théâtre du Petit-Bourbon, one of the few existing theaters in the city. He had won over the king, it should be noted, not by his troupe's production of a tragedy of Corneille, but by his comic performance in *The Amorous Doctor,* a farcical afterpiece he had written himself.

Molière's genius was clearly attuned to the world of comedy, and it led his troupe ultimately to be commissioned as chief entertainers to the court of Louis XIV. In 1661 he gained control of the theater in the Palais Royal, and in 1665 his group was formally designated "The King's Company." Throughout his career in Paris, Molière wrote approximately thirty theatrical pieces, some known as *comédies-ballets,* which were plays interspersed with music and dancing for presentation to the court at Versailles, and others that were purely dramatic for staging in his own theater at the Palais Royal. The *comédies-ballets* were notable not only for their music, dancing, and spectacular scenic effects, but also because the ballet sections were often performed by members of the court, including the king himself. Yet these works were conceived by Molière to be fully worked out plays as well. In fact, one of Molière's most famous comedies, *The Would-Be Gentleman* (1670), was a *comédie-ballet,* designed at the king's command to include a musical section with a Turkish theme. This material could easily be omitted from the work, as indeed it was by Molière when he produced it as an entirely dramatic work in 1671 at the Palais Royal.

Whether writing entertainments for the court or plays for the public, Molière's comic purpose was always the same: to expose through laughter the follies of society. Even so, his satiric treatment of various social types often aroused the displeasure of some members in the fashionable world who felt he was engaging in personal assaults on their reputation. In his own defense, he wrote a play about the theater itself, *The Versailles Impromptu* (1663), in which one of the characters offers a very revealing conversation he has had with Molière about the purpose of his comedies:

> His aim, he said, is to portray types and not individuals, and all the people who appear in his plays are imaginary, phantoms if you like; he invents them as he goes along, in such a way as to entertain the audience; and he would be embarrassed if they resembled actual people . . . and I agree with him. Why bother to pin such and such a trait on so-and-so when his characters have traits that could fit a hundred different people? The business of comedy is to present the flaws common to all men, and especially the men of our time.

In revealing human flaws, Molière typically designed his plays to focus on the comically absurd behavior of a single character who is controlled by a singular obsession. Arnolphe, for example, in *The School for Wives* (1662) is a forty-two-year-old man so desirous of being married yet so fearful of being cuckolded that he has contrived to raise a young girl of six in almost monastic seclusion for thirteen years, assuming that her total ignorance of other men and her rigorous instruction in the duties of a wife will make her completely obedient to him. But shortly after the play opens, the young girl Agnès is discovered by a young man, and the delicious progress of their courtship comically exposes the major weakness in Arnolphe's fanatically designed plan—he has failed to realize that a marriage can truly be secured only by love. Harpagon, on the other hand, the title character of *The Miser* (1668), is so avaricious that he is even willing to marry off his young daughter to a much older man, simply because the man is willing to marry her, as Harpagon gleefully reports, "without a dowry." And Orgon, the main character in *Tartuffe* (1669), is so fanatically devoted to the sham holy man Tartuffe that he worries more about the welfare of Tartuffe than about anyone else in his own family. When he is told that his wife is suffering from a fever, his reply is comically inappropriate: "Ah. And Tartuffe?" Indeed, Orgon is so blindly devoted to Tartuffe that he persistently refuses to see the hypocrisy of Tartuffe until he is nearly undone by it.

The obsessions of these characters are usually called to their attention—and to ours—by the presence of reasonable and sensible persons in their world. Sometimes these *raisonneurs* (rational commentators) are servants, sometimes friends, sometimes close relatives of the obsessed characters, but whatever their status, they repeatedly fail to bring them to their senses through rational appeals. Only the power of extremely painful experience seems capable of curing these characters, and thus Molière displays the extremity of their fixations. Although their obsessions are huge—and hugely funny—these characters are not only magnificent in their delusions but also intensely human in their attachments to them. And thus Molière conceives his obsessed characters so that we will not only laugh at them but also comprehend their pain. How else can an audience respond when Arnolphe finally recognizes that Agnès loves someone else and turns to the audience expressing his hurt and frustration? Moments such as these, as well as the sustained allegiance of the *raisonneurs* in their world, suggest that Molière intended us to see these misguided characters—whose roles he so often performed himself—as deserving both our judgment and our sympathy.

In *The Misanthrope* (1666), we are once again faced with an obsessed figure, Alceste, who produces conflicting reactions but for far more complicated reasons than Molière's comedies usually contain. Unlike his counterparts, Alceste is obsessed with an admirable idea—namely, a belief that honesty and integrity are the most important bases of all human relationships. Consequently, he is moved to condemn his society as being filled with shallow flirts and sycophants, with hypocrites who praise people to their faces and mock them as soon as they are gone. And surely Alceste is right in condemning these characters in his world. But surely Philinte, the *raisonneur* friend of Alceste, is also correct in recognizing that a brutally frank honesty such as Alceste recommends would be the undoing of society itself. Beyond the questions raised by Philinte, we are also forced to see that Alceste is so obsessed with his vision that he sees himself as the only sincere person in his world, and thus he appears to be a supremely self-regarding egotist. And to top off these contradictions, Alceste is in love with the most beautiful—and the most insincere—woman in his society, so that he is trapped between what he believes and what he feels.

The doubts raised by Alceste's demands for sincerity coupled with his love for Célimène find their structural analogue in the to-and-fro motion of the play. The setting, appropriately, is Célimène's house, the center of social activity, and Alceste is constantly being taken away either by his legal affairs or by his anger with Célimène, yet he repeatedly returns, always attempting to get Célimène to understand his true feelings and admit to her own. In the gathering action that brings more and more people on stage, we come to expect the comic recognition and resolution customary in the finales of Molière's other works. But in the final act, Molière reverses this pattern and our expectations. The movement instead is one of gradual dispersal. Célimène's sarcastic condemnation of her own circle alienates her admirers and they slowly leave; Alceste, in turn, asks her to flee society with him, but she refuses, so he angrily rejects her; and the play ends with only a slight note of hope as Philinte and Éliante, the two *raisonneurs,* go after Alceste, hoping to change his bitter mood. The play ends very much as it began—in a stalemate.

Still, the serious issues raised by *The Misanthrope* and the ambiguous tone of its ending are counterpointed, both on the page and on the stage, by deliciously witty speeches and comic characters. Richard Wilbur's translation has caught the epigrammatic quality and elegant formality of Molière's rhymed couplets, so much so that it is hard to imagine a production in anything other than seventeenth-century style. Indeed, the 1968 A.P.A. Repertory Company production used the elaborate costumes of the period to suggest the decorative and self-conscious society that so offended Alceste (see Figure 1). But Molière's attack on hypocritical pretentiousness can also work in a contemporary setting, as evidenced by the 1999 Classic Stage Company's production (translated by Martin Crimp) that turned Alceste into a playwright and Célimène into an American film star. The set, by Narelle Sissons, used metal and mirrors—an aluminum floor and a huge mirror upstage (see Figure 2)—to create a world simultaneously gorgeous and fake, alluring and repulsive, a world relecting the paradox that neither Alceste nor Molière can resolve.

THE MISANTHROPE

BY MOLIÈRE / TRANSLATED BY RICHARD WILBUR

CHARACTERS

ALCESTE, *in love with Célimène*
PHILINTE, *Alceste's friend*
ORONTE, *in love with Célimène*
CÉLIMÈNE, *Alceste's beloved*
ELIANTE, *Célimène's cousin*
ARSINOÉ, *a friend of Célimène's*
ACASTE, *marquess*

CLITANDRE, *marquess*
BASQUE, *Célimène's servant*
A GUARD *of the Marshalsea*
DUBOIS, *Alceste's valet*

SCENE

The scene throughout is in Célimène's house at Paris.

ACT 1

(The scene opens on PHILINTE and ALCESTE.)

PHILINTE: Now, what's got into you?
ALCESTE *(seated):*   Kindly leave me alone.
PHILINTE: Come, come, what is it? This lugubrious
  tone . . .
ALCESTE: Leave me, I said; you spoil my solitude.
PHILINTE: Oh, listen to me, now, and don't be rude.
ALCESTE: I choose to be rude, Sir, and to be hard of
5 hearing.
PHILINTE: These ugly moods of yours are not
    endearing;
  Friends though we are, I really must insist . . .
ALCESTE *(abruptly rising):* Friends? Friends, you say?
    Well, cross me off your list.
  I've been your friend till now, as you well know;
10 But after what I saw a moment ago
  I tell you flatly that our ways must part.
  I wish no place in a dishonest heart.
PHILINTE: Why, what have I done, Alceste? Is this
    quite just?
ALCESTE: My God, you ought to die of self-disgust.
15 I call your conduct inexcusable, Sir,
  And every man of honor will concur.
  I see you almost hug a man to death,
  Exclaim for joy until you're out of breath,
  And supplement these loving demonstrations
20 With endless offers, vows, and protestations;
  Then when I ask you "Who was that?", I find
  That you can barely bring his name to mind!
  Once the man's back is turned, you cease to love
    him,
  And speak with absolute indifference of him!
25 By God, I say it's base and scandalous
  To falsify the heart's affections thus;
  If I caught myself behaving in such a way,
  I'd hang myself for shame, without delay.
PHILINTE: It hardly seems a hanging matter to me;
30 I hope that you will take it graciously
  If I extend myself a slight reprieve,
  And live a little longer, by your leave.

ALCESTE: How dare you joke about a crime so grave?
PHILINTE: What crime? How else are people to
    behave?
ALCESTE: I'd have them be sincere, and never part   35
  With any word that isn't from the heart.
PHILINTE: When someone greets us with a show of
    pleasure,
  It's but polite to give him equal measure,
  Return his love the best that we know how,
  And trade him offer for offer, vow for vow.   40
ALCESTE: No, no, this formula you'd have me follow,
  However fashionable, is false and hollow,
  And I despise the frenzied operations
  Of all these barterers of protestations,
  These lavishers of meaningless embraces,   45
  These utterers of obliging commonplaces,
  Who court and flatter everyone on earth
  And praise the fool no less than the man of worth.
  Should you rejoice that someone fondles you,
  Offers his love and service, swears to be true,   50
  And fills your ears with praises of your name,
  When to the first damned fop he'll say the same?
  No, no: no self-respecting heart would dream
  Of prizing so promiscuous an esteem;
  However high the praise, there's nothing worse   55
  Than sharing honors with the universe.
  Esteem is founded on comparison:
  To honor all men is to honor none.
  Since you embrace this indiscriminate vice,
  Your friendship comes at far too cheap a price;   60
  I spurn the easy tribute of a heart
  Which will not set the worthy man apart:
  I choose, Sir, to be chosen; and in fine,
  The friend of mankind is no friend of mine.
PHILINTE: But in polite society, custom decrees   65
  That we show certain outward courtesies. . . .
ALCESTE: Ah, no! We should condemn with all our
    force
  Such false and artificial intercourse.
  Let men behave like men; let them display
  Their inmost hearts in everything they say;   70
  Let the heart speak, and let our sentiments

Not mask themselves in silly compliments.
PHILINTE: In certain cases it would be uncouth
And most absurd to speak the naked truth;
75 With all respect for your exalted notions,
It's often best to veil one's true emotions.
Wouldn't the social fabric come undone
If we were wholly frank with everyone?
Suppose you met with someone you couldn't bear;
80 Would you inform him of it then and there?
ALCESTE: Yes.
PHILINTE: Then you'd tell old Emilie it's pathetic
The way she daubs her features with cosmetic
And plays the gay coquette at sixty-four?
ALCESTE: I would.
PHILINTE: And you'd call Dorilas a bore,
85 And tell him every ear at court is lame
From hearing him brag about his noble name?
ALCESTE: Precisely.
PHILINTE: Ah, you're joking.
ALCESTE: Au contraire:°
In this regard there's none I'd choose to spare.
All are corrupt; there's nothing to be seen
90 In court or town but aggravates my spleen.°
I fall into deep gloom and melancholy
When I survey the scene of human folly,
Finding on every hand base flattery,
Injustice, fraud, self-interest, treachery. . . .
95 Ah, it's too much; mankind has grown so base,
I mean to break with the whole human race.
PHILINTE: This philosophic rage is a bit extreme;
You've no idea how comical you seem;
Indeed, we're like those brothers in the play
100 Called School for Husbands,° one of whom was
prey . . .
ALCESTE: Enough, now! None of your stupid similes.
PHILINTE: Then let's have no more tirades, if you
please.
The world won't change, whatever you say or do;
And since plain speaking means so much to you,
105 I'll tell you plainly that by being frank
You've earned the reputation of a crank,
And that you're thought ridiculous when you rage
And rant against the manners of the age.
ALCESTE: So much the better; just what I wish to hear.
110 No news could be more grateful to my ear.
All men are so detestable in my eyes,
I should be sorry if they thought me wise.
PHILINTE: Your hatred's very sweeping, is it not?
ALCESTE: Quite right: I hate the whole degraded lot.

Au contraire, "on the contrary." *spleen,* the traditional
seat of anger. *School for Husbands,* in Molière's *School for
Husbands* (1661) Sganarelle and Ariste also view human
nature in contrasting ways, one critically, the other with
philosophical indulgence.

PHILINTE: Must all poor human creatures be
embrace,   115
Without distinction, by your vast distaste?
Even in these bad times, there are surely a few . . .
ALCESTE: No, I include all men in one dim view:
Some men I hate for being rogues; the others
I hate because they treat the rogues like brothers,   120
And, lacking a virtuous scorn for what is vile,
Receive the villain with a complaisant smile.
Notice how tolerant people choose to be
Toward that bold rascal who's at law° with me.
His social polish can't conceal his nature;   125
One sees at once that he's a treacherous creature;
No one could possibly be taken in
By those soft speeches and that sugary grin.
The whole world knows the shady means by which
The low-brow's grown so powerful and rich,   130
And risen to a rank so bright and high
That virtue can but blush, and merit sigh.
Whenever his name comes up in conversation,
None will defend his wretched reputation;
Call him knave, liar, scoundrel, and all the rest,   135
Each head will nod, and no one will protest.
And yet his smirk is seen in every house,
He's greeted everywhere with smiles and bows,
And when there's any honor that can be got
By pulling strings, he'll get it, like as not.   140
My God! It chills my heart to see the ways
Men come to terms with evil nowadays;
Sometimes, I swear, I'm moved to flee and find
Some desert land unfouled by humankind.
PHILINTE: Come, let's forget the follies of the times 145
And pardon mankind for its petty crimes;
Let's have an end of rantings and of railings,
And show some leniency toward human failings.
This world requires a pliant rectitude;
Too stern a virtue makes one stiff and rude;   150
Good sense views all extremes with detestation,
And bids us to be noble in moderation.
The rigid virtues of the ancient days
Are not for us; they jar with all our ways
And ask of us too lofty a perfection.   155
Wise men accept their times without objection,
And there's no greater folly, if you ask me
Than trying to reform society.
Like you, I see each day a hundred and one
Unhandsome deeds that might be better done,   160
But still, for all the faults that meet my view,
I'm never known to storm and rave like you.
I take men as they are, or let them be,
And teach my soul to bear their frailty;
And whether in court or town, whatever the scene,   165

My phlegm's° as philosophic as your spleen.
ALCESTE: This phlegm which you so eloquently
  commend,
Does nothing ever rile it up, my friend?
Suppose some man you trust should treacherously
170 Conspire to rob you of your property,
And do his best to wreck your reputation?
Wouldn't you feel a certain indignation?
PHILINTE: Why, no. These faults of which you so
  complain
Are part of human nature, I maintain,
175 And it's no more a matter for disgust
That men are knavish, selfish and unjust,
Than that the vulture dines upon the dead,
And wolves are furious, and apes ill-bred.
ALCESTE: Shall I see myself betrayed, robbed, torn to
  bits,
180 And not . . . Oh, let's be still and rest our wits.
Enough of reasoning, now. I've had my fill.
PHILINTE: Indeed, you would do well, Sir, to be still.
Rage less at your opponent, and give some thought
To how you'll win this lawsuit that he's brought.
185 ALCESTE: I assure you I'll do nothing of the sort.
PHILINTE: Then who will plead your case before the
  court?
ALCESTE: Reason and right and justice will plead for
  me.
PHILINTE: Oh, Lord! What judges do you plan to
  see?°
ALCESTE: Why, none. The justice of my cause is clear.
PHILINTE: Of course, man; but there's politics to
190 fear. . . .
ALCESTE: No, I refuse to lift a hand. That's flat.
I'm either right, or wrong.
PHILINTE: Don't count on that.
ALCESTE: No, I'll do nothing.
PHILINTE: Your enemy's influence
Is great, you know . . .
ALCESTE: That makes no difference.
PHILINTE: It will; you'll see.
195 ALCESTE: Must honor bow to guile?
If so, I shall be proud to lose the trial.
PHILINTE: Oh, really . . .
ALCESTE: I'll discover by this case
Whether or not men are sufficiently base
And impudent and villainous and perverse
200 To do me wrong before the universe.
PHILINTE: What a man!
ALCESTE: Oh, I could wish, whatever the cost,
Just for the beauty of it, that my trial were lost.
PHILINTE: If people heard you talking so, Alceste,

---

    phlegm's, one of the four humors, or basic fluids,
thought to determine temperament. An excess of phlegm
made one slow, lazy, and complacent. **judges . . . see,** the
common practice of the time was to solicit the favor of judges
and make them gifts.

They'd split their sides. Your name would be a jest.
ALCESTE: So much the worse for jesters.
PHILINTE: May I enquire   205
Whether this rectitude you so admire,
And these hard virtues you're enamored of
Are qualities of the lady whom you love?
It much surprises me that you, who seem
To view mankind with furious disesteem   210
Have yet found something to enchant your eyes
Amidst a species which you so despise.
And what is more amazing, I'm afraid,
Is the most curious choice your heart has made.
The honest Eliante is fond of you,   215
Arsinoé, the prude, admires you too;
And yet your spirit's been perversely led
To choose the flighty Célimène instead,
Whose brittle malice and coquettish ways
So typify the manners of our days.   220
How is it that the traits you most abhor
Are bearable in this lady you adore?
Are you so blind with love that you can't find them?
Or do you contrive, in her case, not to mind them?
ALCESTE: My love for that young widow's not the kind   225
That can't perceive defects; no, I'm not blind.
I see her faults, despite my ardent love,
And all I see I fervently reprove.
And yet I'm weak; for all her falsity,
That woman knows the art of pleasing me,   230
And though I never cease complaining of her,
I swear I cannot manage not to love her.
Her charm outweighs her faults; I can but aim
To cleanse her spirit in my love's pure flame.
PHILINTE: That's no small task; I wish you all success.   235
You think then that she loves you?
ALCESTE: Heavens, yes!
I wouldn't love her did she not love me.
PHILINTE: Well, if her taste for you is plain to see,
Why do these rivals cause you such despair?
ALCESTE: True love, Sir, is possessive, and cannot bear   240
To share with all the world. I'm here today
To tell her she must send that mob away.
PHILINTE: If I were you, and had your choice to
  make,
Eliante, her cousin, would be the one I'd take;
That honest heart, which cares for you alone,   245
Would harmonize far better with your own.
ALCESTE: True, true: each day my reason tells me so;
But reason doesn't rule in love, you know.
PHILINTE: I fear some bitter sorrow is in store;
This love . . .

(Enter ORONTE.*)*

ORONTE *(to* ALCESTE*)*: The servants told me at the
  door   250
That Eliante and Célimène were out,
But when I heard, dear Sir, that you were about,
I came to say, without exaggeration,

That I hold you in the vastest admiration,
255   And that it's always been my dearest desire
To be the friend of one I so admire.
I hope to see my love of merit requited,
And you and I in friendship's bond united.
I'm sure you won't refuse—if I may be frank—
260   A friend of my devotedness—and rank. *(During this*
speech of Oronte's, ORONTE *is abstracted, and seems*
unaware that he is being spoken to. He only breaks off
his reverie when ORONTE *says:)*
It was for you, if you please, that my words were
intended.
ALCESTE: For me, Sir?
ORONTE: Yes, for you. You're not offended?
ALCESTE: By no means. But this much surprises
me. . . .
The honor comes most unexpectedly. . . .
265   ORONTE: My high regard should not astonish you;
The whole world feels the same. It is your due.
ALCESTE: Sir . . .
ORONTE: Why, in all the State there isn't one
Can match your merits; they shine, Sir, like the sun.
ALCESTE: Sir . . .
ORONTE: You are higher in my estimation
270   Than all that's most illustrious in the nation.
ALCESTE: Sir . . .
ORONTE: If I lie, may heaven strike me dead!
To show you that I mean what I have said,
Permit me, Sir, to embrace you most sincerely,
And swear that I will prize our friendship dearly.
275   Give me your hand. And now, Sir, if you choose,
We'll make our vows,
ALCESTE: Sir . . .
ORONTE: What! You refuse?
ALCESTE: Sir, it's a very great honor you extend:
But friendship is a sacred thing, my friend;
It would be profanation to bestow
280   The name of friend on one you hardly know.
All parts are better played when well-rehearsed;
Let's put off friendship, and get acquainted first.
We may discover it would be unwise
To try to make our natures harmonize.
285   ORONTE: By heaven! You're sagacious to the core;
This speech has made me admire you even more.
Let time, then, bring us closer day by day;
Meanwhile, I shall be yours in every way.
If, for example, there should be anything
290   You wish at court, I'll mention it to the King.
I have his ear, of course; it's quite well known
That I am much in favor with the throne.
In short, I am your servant. And now, dear friend,
Since you have such fine judgment, I intend
295   To please you, if I can, with a small sonnet°
I wrote not long ago. Please comment on it,

---

sonnet, during this period the term "sonnet" applied to
any lyric poem.

And tell me whether I ought to publish it.
ALCESTE: You must excuse me, Sir; I'm hardly fit
To judge such matters.
ORONTE: Why not?
ALCESTE: I am, I fear,
Inclined to be unfashionably sincere.   300
ORONTE: Just what I ask; I'd take no satisfaction
In anything but your sincere reaction.
I beg you not to dream of being kind.
ALCESTE: Since you desire it, Sir, I'll speak my mind.
ORONTE: *Sonnet.* It's a sonnet. . . ."Hope". . . The
poem's addressed   305
To a lady who wakened hopes within my breast.
"Hope". . . this is not the pompous sort of thing,
Just modest little verses, with a tender ring.
ALCESTE: Well, we shall see.
ORONTE: "Hope". . . I'm anxious to hear
Whether the style seems properly smooth and clear,   310
And whether the choice of words is good or bad.
ALCESTE: We'll see, we'll see.
ORONTE: Perhaps I ought to add
That it took me only a quarter-hour to write it.
ALCESTE: The time's irrelevant, Sir; kindly recite it.
ORONTE *(reading):* "Hope comforts us awhile, t'is true, 315
Lulling our cares with careless laughter,
And yet such joy is full of rue,
My Phyllis, if nothing follows after."
PHILINTE: I'm charmed by this already; the style's
delightful.
ALCESTE *(sotto voce, to* PHILINTE*):* How can you say
that? Why, the thing is frightful.   320
ORONTE: "Your fair face smiled on me awhile,
But was it kindness so to enchant me?
'Twould have been fairer not to smile,
If hope was all you meant to grant me."
PHILINTE: What a clever thought! How handsomely
you phrase it!   325
ALCESTE *(sotto voce, to* PHILINTE*):* You know the thing
is trash. How dare you praise it?
ORONTE: "If it's to be my passion's fate
Thus everlastingly to wait,
Then death will come to set me free:
For death is fairer than the fair;   330
Phyllis, to hope is to despair
When one must hope eternally."
PHILINTE: The close is exquisite—full of feeling and
grace.
ALCESTE *(sotto voce, aside):* Oh, blast the close; you'd
better close your face
Before you send your lying soul to hell.   335
PHILINTE: I can't remember a poem I've liked so well.
ALCESTE *(sotto voce, aside):* Good Lord!
ORONTE *(to* PHILINTE*):*   I fear you're flattering
me a bit.
PHILINTE: Oh, no!
ALCESTE *(sotto voce, aside):* What else d'you call it, you
hypocrite?

ORONTE (*to* ALCESTE): But you, Sir, keep your
    promise now: don't shrink
340   From telling me sincerely what you think.
ALCESTE: Sir, these are delicate matters; we all desire
    To be told that we've the true poetic fire.
    But once, to one whose name I shall not mention,
    I said, regarding some verse of his invention,
345   That gentlemen should rigorously control
    That itch to write which often afflicts the soul;
    That one should curb the heady inclination
    To publicize one's little avocation;
    And that in showing off one's works of art
350   One often plays a very clownish part.
ORONTE: Are you suggesting in a devious way
    That I ought not . . .
ALCESTE: Oh, that I do not say.
    Further, I told him that no fault is worse
    Than that of writing frigid, lifeless verse,
355   And that the merest whisper of such a shame
    Suffices to destroy a man's good name.
ORONTE: D'you mean to say my sonnet's dull and
    trite?
ALCESTE: I don't say that. But I went on to cite
    Numerous cases of once-respected men
360   Who came to grief by taking up the pen.
ORONTE: And am I like them? Do I write so poorly?
ALCESTE: I don't say that. But I told this person, "Surely
    You're under no necessity to compose;
    Why you should wish to publish, heaven knows.
365   There's no excuse for printing tedious rot
    Unless one writes for bread, as you do not.
    Resist temptation, then, I beg of you;
    Conceal your pastimes from the public view;
    And don't give up, on any provocation,
370   Your present high and courtly reputation,
    To purchase at a greedy printer's shop
    The name of silly author and scribbling fop."
    These were the points I tried to make him see.
ORONTE: I sense that they are also aimed at me;
375   But now—about my sonnet—I'd like to be told . . .
ALCESTE: Frankly, that sonnet should be pigeonholed.
    You've chosen the worst models to imitate.
    The style's unnatural. Let me illustrate:

    For example, "Your fair face smiled on me awhile,"
    Followed by, " 'Twould have been fairer not to
380   smile!"
    Or this: "such joy is full of rue;"
    Or this: "For death is fairer than the fair;"
    Or, "Phyllis, to hope is to despair
        When one must hope eternally!"

385   This artificial style, that's all the fashion,
    Has neither taste, nor honesty, nor passion;
    It's nothing but a sort of wordy play,
    And nature never spoke in such a way.

What, in this shallow age, is not debased?
Our fathers, though less refined, had better taste;   390
I'd barter all that men admire today
For one old love-song I shall try to say:

"If the King had given me for my own
Paris, his citadel,
And I for that must leave alone   395
Her whom I love so well,
I'd say then to the Crown,
Take back your glittering town;
My darling is more fair, I swear,
My darling is more fair."   400

The rhyme's not rich, the style is rough and old,
But don't you see that it's the purest gold
Beside the tinsel nonsense now preferred,
And that there's passion in its every word?

"If the King had given me for my own   405
Paris, his citadel,
And I for that must leave alone
Her whom I love so well,
I'd say then to the Crown,
Take back your glittering town;   410
My darling is more fair, I swear,
My darling is more fair."

There speaks a loving heart. (*to* PHILINTE) You're
    laughing, eh?
Laugh on, my precious wit. Whatever you say,
I hold that song's worth all the bibelots°   415
That people hail today with "ah's" and "oh's."
ORONTE: And I maintain my sonnet's very good.
ALCESTE: It's not at all surprising that you should.
    You have your reasons, permit me to have mine
    For thinking that you cannot write a line.   420
ORONTE: Others have praised my sonnet to the skies.
ALCESTE: I lack their art of telling pleasant lies.
ORONTE: You seem to think you've got no end of wit.
ALCESTE: To praise your verse, I'd need still more of
    it.
ORONTE: I'm not in need of your approval, Sir.   425
ALCESTE: That's good; you couldn't have it if you
    were.
ORONTE: Come now, I'll lend you the subject of my
    sonnet;
    I'd like to see you try to improve upon it.
ALCESTE: I might, by chance, write something just as
    shoddy;
    But then I wouldn't show it to everybody.   430
ORONTE: You're most opinionated and conceited.

---

bibelots, trinkets.

ALCESTE: Go find your flatterers, and be better
  treated.

ORONTE: Look here, my little fellow, pray watch your
  tone.

ALCESTE: My great big fellow, you'd better watch
  your own.

PHILINTE (*stepping between them*): Oh, please, please,
435 gentlemen! This will never do.

ORONTE: The fault is mine, and I leave the field to
  you.
  I am your servant, Sir, in every way.

ALCESTE: And I, Sir, am your most abject valet. (*Exit
  ORONTE.*)

PHILINTE: Well, as you see, sincerity in excess
440 Can get you into a very pretty mess;
  Oronte was hungry for appreciation. . . .

ALCESTE: Don't speak to me.

PHILINTE: What?

ALCESTE: No more conversation.

PHILINTE: Really, now . . .

ALCESTE: Leave me alone.

PHILINTE: If I . . .

ALCESTE: Out of my sight!

PHILINTE: But what . . .

ALCESTE: I won't listen.

PHILINTE: But . . .

ALCESTE: Silence!

445 PHILINTE: Now, is it polite . . .

ALCESTE: By heaven, I've had enough. Don't follow
  me.

PHILINTE: Ah, you're just joking. I'll keep you
  company. (*They go out.*)

ACT 2

(*Enter* ALCESTE *and* CÉLIMÈNE.)

ALCESTE: Shall I speak plainly, Madam? I confess
  Your conduct gives me infinite distress,
  And my resentment's grown too hot to smother.
  Soon, I foresee, we'll break with one another.
5 If I said otherwise, I should deceive you;
  Sooner or later, I shall be forced to leave you,
  And if I swore that we shall never part,
  I should misread the omens of my heart.

CELIMENE: You kindly saw me home, it would appear,
10 So as to pour invectives in my ear.

ALCESTE: I've no desire to quarrel. But I deplore
  Your inability to shut the door
  On all these suitors who beset you so.
  There's what annoys me, if you care to know.

CELIMENE: Is it my fault that all these men pursue
15 me?
  Am I to blame if they're attracted to me?
  And when they gently beg an audience,
  Ought I to take a stick and drive them hence?

ALCESTE: Madam, there's no necessity for a stick;
20 A less responsive heart would do the trick.

Of your attractiveness I don't complain;
But those your charms attract, you then detain
By a most melting and receptive manner,
And so enlist their hearts beneath your banner.
It's the agreeable hopes which you excite   25
That keep these lovers round you day and night;
Were they less liberally smiled upon,
That sighing troop would very soon be gone.
But tell me, Madam, why it is that lately
This man Clitandre interests you so greatly?   30
Because of what high merits do you deem
Him worthy of the honor of your esteem?
Is it that your admitting glances linger
On the splendidly long nail of his little finger?
Or do you share the general deep respect   35
For the blond wig he chooses to affect?
Are you in love with his embroidered hose?
Do you adore his ribbons and his bows?
Or is it that this paragon bewitches
Your tasteful eye with his vast German breeches?°   40
Perhaps his giggle, or his falsetto voice,
Makes him the latest gallant of your choice?

CELIMENE: You're much mistaken to resent him so.
  Why I put up with him you surely know:
  My lawsuit's very shortly to be tried,   45
  And I must have his influence on my side.

ALCESTE: Then lose your lawsuit, Madam, or let it
  drop.
  Don't torture me by humoring such a fop.

CELIMENE: You're jealous of the whole world, Sir.

ALCESTE: That's true,
  Since the whole world is well-received by you.   50

CELIMENE: That my good nature is so unconfined
  Should serve to pacify your jealous mind;
  Were I to smile on one, and scorn the rest,
  Then you might have some cause to be distressed.

ALCESTE: Well, if I mustn't be jealous, tell me, then,   55
  Just how I'm better treated than other men.

CELIMENE: You know you have my love. Will that not
  do?

ALCESTE: What proof have I that what you say is true?

CELIMENE: I would expect, Sir, that my having said it
  Might give the statement a sufficient credit.   60

ALCESTE: But how can I be sure that you don't tell
  The selfsame thing to other men as well?

CELIMENE: What a gallant speech! How flattering to
  me!
  What a sweet creature you make me out to be!
  Well then, to save you from the pangs of doubt,   65
  All that I've said I hereby cancel out;
  Now, none but yourself shall make a monkey of
  you:
  Are you content?

---

breeches, fashionable wide breeches called *rhingraves,*
after the Rhingrave Frederick, Governor of Maestricht.

ALCESTE: Why, why am I doomed to love you?
I swear that I shall bless the blissful hour
70   When this poor heart's no longer in your power!
I make no secret of it: I've done my best
To exorcise this passion from my breast;
But thus far all in vain; it will not go;
It's for my sins that I must love you so.
CELIMENE: Your love for me is matchless, Sir; that's
75   clear.
ALCESTE: Indeed, in all the world it has no peer;
Words can't describe the nature of my passion,
And no man ever loved in such a fashion.
CELIMENE: Yes, it's a brand-new fashion, I agree:
80   You show your love by castigating me,
And all your speeches are enraged and rude.
I've never been so furiously wooed.
ALCESTE: Yet you could calm that fury, if you chose.
Come, shall we bring our quarrels to a close?
85   Let's speak with open hearts, then, and begin . . .

(Enter BASQUE.)

CELIMENE: What is it?
BASQUE: Acaste is here.
CELIMENE: Well, send him in. *(Exit* BASQUE.)
ALCESTE: What! Shall we never be alone at all?
You're always ready to receive a call,
And you can't bear, for ten ticks of the clock,
90   Not to keep open house for all who knock.
CELIMENE: I couldn't refuse him: he'd be most put
out.
ALCESTE: Surely that's not worth worrying about.
CELIMENE: Acaste would never forgive me if he
guessed
That I consider him a dreadful pest.
95   ALCESTE: If he's a pest, why bother with him then?
CELIMENE: Heavens! One can't antagonize such men;
Why, they're the chartered gossips of the court,
And have a say in things of every sort.
One must receive them, and be full of charm;
100   They're no great help, but they can do you harm,
And though your influence be ever so great,
They're hardly the best people to alienate.
ALCESTE: I see, dear lady, that you could make a case
For putting up with the whole human race;
105   These friendships that you calculate so nicely . . .

*(*BASQUE *re-enters.)*

BASQUE: Madam, Clitandre is here as well.
ALCESTE: Precisely.
CELIMENE: Where are you going?
ALCESTE: Elsewhere.
CELIMENE: Stay.
ALCESTE: No, no.
CELIMENE: Stay, Sir.
ALCESTE: I can't.
CELIMENE: I wish it.
ALCESTE: No, I must go.

I beg you, Madam, not to press the matter;
You know I have no taste for idle chatter.   110
CELIMENE: Stay: I command you.
ALCESTE: No, I cannot stay.
CELIMENE: Very well; you have my leave to go away.

(Enter ELIANTE, PHILINTE, ACASTE, *and* CLITANDRE.)

ELIANTE *(to* CÉLIMÈNE): The Marquesses have kindly
come to call.
Were they announced?
CELIMENE: Yes. Basque, bring chairs for all.

*(*BASQUE *provides the chairs and exits.)*

(to ALCESTE): You haven't gone?
ALCESTE: No; and I shan't depart   115
Till you decide who's foremost in your heart.
CELIMENE: Oh, hush.
ALCESTE: It's time to choose; take them, or me.
CELIMENE: You're mad.
ALCESTE: I'm not, as you shall shortly see.
CELIMENE: Oh?
ALCESTE: You'll decide.
CELIMENE: You're joking now, dear friend.
ALCESTE: No, no; you'll choose; my patience is at an
end.   120
CLITANDRE: Madam, I come from court, where poor
Cléonte
Behaved like a perfect fool, as is his wont.
Has he no friend to counsel him, I wonder,
And teach him less unerringly to blunder?
CELIMENE: It's true, the man's a most accomplished
dunce;   125
His gauche behavior charms the eye at once;
And every time one sees him, on my word,
His manner's grown a trifle more absurd.
ACASTE: Speaking of dunces, I've just now conversed
With old Damon, who's one of the very worst;   130
I stood a lifetime in the broiling sun
Before his dreary monologue was done.
CELIMENE: Oh, he's a wondrous talker, and has the
power
To tell you nothing hour after hour:
If, by mistake, he ever came to the point,   135
The shock would put his jawbone out of joint.
ELIANTE *(to* PHILINTE): The conversation takes its
usual turn,
And all our dear friends' ears will shortly burn.
CLITANDRE: Timante's a character, Madam.
CELIMENE: Isn't he, though?
A man of mystery from top to toe,   140
Who moves about in a romantic mist
On secret missions which do not exist.
His talk is full of eyebrows and grimaces;
How tired one gets of his momentous faces;
He's always whispering something confidential   145
Which turns out to be quite inconsequential;
Nothing's too slight for him to mystify;

He even whispers when he says "good-by."
ACASTE: Tell us about Géralde.
CELIMENE: That tiresome ass.
150   He mixes only with the titled class,
And fawns on dukes and princes, and is bored
With anyone who's not at least a lord.
The man's obsessed with rank, and his discourses
Are all of hounds and carriages and horses;
155   He uses Christian names with all the great,
And the word "Milord," with him, is out of date.
CLITANDRE: He's very taken with Bélise, I hear.
CELIMENE: She is the dreariest company, poor dear.
Whenever she comes to call, I grope about
160   To find some topic which will draw her out,
But, owing to her dry and faint replies,
The conversation wilts, and droops, and dies.
In vain one hopes to animate her face
By mentioning the ultimate commonplace;
165   But sun or shower, even hail or frost
Are matters she can instantly exhaust.
Meanwhile her visit, painful though it is,
Drags on and on through mute eternities,
And though you ask the time, and yawn, and yawn,
170   She sits there like a stone and won't be gone.
ACASTE: Now for Adraste.
CELIMENE: Oh, that conceited elf
Has a gigantic passion for himself;
He rails against the court, and cannot bear it
That none will recognize his hidden merit;
175   All honors given to others give offense
To his imaginary excellence.
CLITANDRE: What about young Cléon? His house,
they say,
Is full of the best society, night and day.
CELIMENE: His cook has made him popular, not he:
180   It's Cléon's table that people come to see.
ELIANTE: He gives a splendid dinner, you must
admit.
CELIMENE: But must he serve himself along with it?
For my taste, he's a most insipid dish
Whose presence sours the wine and spoils the fish.
185 PHILINTE: Damis, his uncle, is admired no end.
What's your opinion, Madam?
CELIMENE: Why, he's my friend.
PHILINTE: He seems a decent fellow, and rather
clever.
CELIMENE: He works too hard at cleverness, however.
I hate to see him sweat and struggle so
190   To fill his conversation with bons mots.°
Since he's decided to become a wit
His taste's so pure that nothing pleases it;
He scolds at all the latest books and plays,
Thinking that wit must never stoop to praise,
195   That finding fault's a sign of intellect,

That all appreciation is abject,
And that by damning everything in sight
One shows oneself in a distinguished light.
He's scornful even of our conversations:
Their trivial nature sorely tries his patience;   200
He folds his arms, and stands above the battle,
And listens sadly to our childish prattle.
ACASTE: Wonderful, Madam! You've hit him off
precisely.
CLITANDRE: No one can sketch a character so nicely.
ALCESTE: How bravely, Sirs, you cut and thrust at all   205
These absent fools, till one by one they fall:
But let one come in sight, and you'll at once
Embrace the man you lately called a dunce,
Telling him in a tone sincere and fervent
How proud you are to be his humble servant.   210
CLITANDRE: Why pick on us? Madame's been
speaking, Sir,
And you should quarrel, if you must, with her.
ALCESTE: No, no, by God, the fault is yours, because
You lead her on with laughter and applause,
And make her think that she's the more delightful   215
The more her talk is scandalous and spiteful.
Oh, she would stoop to malice far, far less
If no such claque° approved her cleverness.
It's flatterers like you whose foolish praise
Nourishes all the vices of these days.   220
PHILINTE: But why protest when someone ridicules
Those you'd condemn, yourself, as knaves or fools?
CELIMENE: Why, Sir? Because he loves to make a fuss.
You don't expect him to agree with us,
When there's an opportunity to express   225
His heaven-sent spirit of contrariness?
What other people think, he can't abide;
Whatever they say, he's on the other side;
He lives in deadly terror of agreeing;
'Twould make him seem an ordinary being.   230
Indeed, he's so in love with contradiction,
He'll turn against his most profound conviction
And with a furious eloquence deplore it,
If only someone else is speaking for it.
ALCESTE: Go on, dear lady, mock me as you please;   235
You have your audience in ecstasies.
PHILINTE: But what she says is true: you have a way
Of bridling at whatever people say;
Whether they praise or blame, your angry spirit
Is equally unsatisfied to hear it.   240
ALCESTE: Men, Sir, are always wrong, and that's the
reason
That righteous anger's never out of season;
All that I hear in all their conversation
Is flattering praise or reckless condemnation.
CELIMENE: But . . .
ALCESTE: No, no, Madam, l am forced to state   245

---

bons mots, witty sayings.

claque, band of followers.

That you have pleasures which I deprecate,
And that these others, here, are much to blame
For nourishing the faults which are your shame.

CLITANDRE: I shan't defend myself, Sir; but I vow
250 I'd thought this lady faultless until now.

ACASTE: I see her charms and graces, which are
          many;
But as for faults, I've never noticed any.

ALCESTE: I see them, Sir; and rather than ignore
          them,
I strenuously criticize her for them.
255 The more one loves, the more one should object
To every blemish, every least defect.
Were I this lady, I would soon get rid
Of lovers who approved of all I did,
And by their slack indulgence and applause
260 Endorsed my follies and excused my flaws.

CELIMENE: If all hearts beat according to your
          measure,
The dawn of love would be the end of pleasure;
And love would find its perfect consummation
In ecstasies of rage and reprobation.

265 ELIANTE: Love, as a rule, affects men otherwise,
And lovers rarely love to criticize.
They see their lady as a charming blur,
And find all things commendable in her.
If she has any blemish, fault, or shame,
270 They will redeem it by a pleasing name.
The pale-faced lady's lily-white, perforce;
The swarthy one's a sweet brunette, of course;
The spindly lady has a slender grace;
The fat one has a most majestic pace;
275 The plain one, with her dress in disarray,
They classify as _beauté négligée_,°
The hulking one's a goddess in their eyes,
The dwarf, a concentrate of Paradise;
The haughty lady has a noble mind;
280 The mean one's witty, and the dull one's kind;
The chatterbox has liveliness and verve,
The mute one has a virtuous reserve.
So lovers manage, in their passion's cause,
To love their ladies even for their flaws.

ALCESTE: But I still say . . .

285 CELIMENE: I think it would be nice
To stroll around the gallery once or twice.
What! You're not going, Sirs?

CLITANDRE _and_ ACASTE: No, Madam, no.

ALCESTE: You seem to be in terror lest they go.
Do what you will, Sirs; leave, or linger on,
290 But I shan't go till after you are gone.

ACASTE: I'm free to linger, unless I should perceive
Madame is tired, and wishes me to leave.

CLITANDRE: And as for me, I needn't go today
Until the hour of the King's _coucher._°

CELIMENE _(to_ ALCESTE_)_: You're joking, surely?

ALCESTE: Not in the least; we'll see   295
Whether you'd rather part with them, or me.

(Enter BASQUE_.)_

BASQUE _(to_ ALCESTE_)_: Sir, there's a fellow here who
          bids me state
That he must see you, and that it can't wait.

ALCESTE: Tell him that I have no such pressing
          affairs.

BASQUE: It's a long tailcoat that this fellow wears,   300
With gold all over.

CELIMENE _(to_ ALCESTE_)_: You'd best go down and see.
Or—have him enter.

_(_ALCESTE _indicates to_ BASQUE _to show the visitor in. Exit_
BASQUE_.)_
(Enter a GUARD _of the Marshalsea._°_)_

ALCESTE _(confronting the_ GUARD_)_: Well, what do you
          want with me?
Come in, Sir.

GUARD: I've a word, Sir, for your ear.

ALCESTE: Speak it aloud, Sir; I shall strive to hear.

GUARD: The Marshals have instructed me to say   305
You must report to them without delay.

ALCESTE: Who? Me, Sir?

GUARD: Yes, Sir; you.

ALCESTE: But what do they want?

PHILINTE _(to_ ALCESTE_)_: To scotch your silly quarrel
          with Oronte.

CELIMENE _(to_ PHILINTE_)_: What quarrel?

PHILINTE: Oronte and he have fallen out
Over some verse he spoke his mind about;   310
The Marshals wish to arbitrate the matter.

ALCESTE: Never shall I equivocate or flatter!

PHILINTE: You'd best obey their summons; come,
          let's go.

ALCESTE: How can they mend our quarrel, I'd like to
          know?
Am I to make a cowardly retraction,   315
And praise those jingles to his satisfaction?
I'll not recant; I've judged that sonnet rightly.
It's bad.

PHILINTE: But you might say so more politely . . .

ALCESTE: I'll not back down; his verses make me sick.

PHILINTE: If only you could be more politic!   320
But come, let's go.

ALCESTE: I'll go, but I won't unsay
A single word.

PHILINTE: Well, let's be on our way.

ALCESTE: Till I am ordered by my lord the King
To praise that poem, I shall say the thing
Is scandalous, by God, and that the poet   325
Ought to be hanged for having the nerve to show

---

beauté négligée, "careless beauty."   _coucher,_ an evening
reception held in the King's bedchamber.

Marshalsea, The Marshalsea Tribunal handled quarrels
among members of the nobility.

it. (to CLITANDRE and ACASTE, who are laughing)
By heaven, Sirs, I really didn't know
That I was being humorous.

CELIMENE: Go, Sir, go;
Settle your business.

ALCESTE: I shall, and when I'm through,
330   I shall return to settle things with you.

(Exit ALCESTE with the GUARD. The others withdraw.)

ACT 3

(Enter CLITANDRE and ACASTE.)

CLITANDRE: Dear Marquess, how contented you
        appear;
    All things delight you, nothing mars your cheer.
    Can you, in perfect honesty, declare
    That you've a right to be so debonair?
5   ACASTE: By Jove, when I survey myself, I find
    No cause whatever for distress of mind.
    I'm young and rich; I can in modesty
    Lay claim to an exalted pedigree;
    And owing to my name and my condition
10   I shall not want for honors and position.
    Then as to courage, that most precious trait,
    I seem to have it, as was proved of late
    Upon the field of honor, where my bearing,
    They say, was very cool and rather daring.
15   I've wit, of course; and taste in such perfection
    That I can judge without the least reflection,
    And at the theater, which is my delight,
    Can make or break a play on opening night,
    And lead the crowd in hisses or bravos,
20   And generally be known as one who knows.
    I'm clever, handsome, gracefully polite;
    My waist is small, my teeth are strong and white;
    As for my dress, the world's astonished eyes
    Assure me that I bear away the prize.
25   I find myself in favor everywhere,
    Honored by men, and worshipped by the fair;
    And since these things are so, it seems to me
    I'm justified in my complacency.
    CLITANDRE: Well, if so many ladies hold you dear,
30   Why do you press a hopeless courtship here?
    ACASTE: Hopeless, you say? I'm not the sort of fool
    That likes his ladies difficult and cool.
    Men who are awkward, shy, and peasantish
    May pine for heartless beauties, if they wish,
35   Grovel before them, bear their cruelties,
    Woo them with tears and sighs and bended knees,
    And hope by dogged faithfulness to gain
    What their poor merits never could obtain.
    For men like me, however, it makes no sense
40   To love on trust, and foot the whole expense.
    Whatever any lady's merits be,
    I think, thank God, that I'm as choice as she;
    That if my heart is kind enough to burn

For her, she owes me something in return;
And that in any proper love affair   45
The partners must invest an equal share.
CLITANDRE: You think, then, that our hostess favors
        you?
ACASTE: I've reason to believe that that is true.
CLITANDRE: How did you come to such a mad
        conclusion?
    You're blind, dear fellow. This is sheer delusion.   50
ACASTE: All right, then: I'm deluded and I'm blind.
CLITANDRE: Whatever put the notion in your mind?
ACASTE: Delusion.
CLITANDRE: What persuades you that you're right?
ACASTE: I'm blind.
CLITANDRE: But have you any proofs to cite?
ACASTE: I tell you I'm deluded.
CLITANDRE: Have you, then,   55
    Received some secret pledge from Célimène?
ACASTE: Oh, no; she scorns me.
CLITANDRE: Tell me the truth, I beg.
ACASTE: She just can't bear me.
CLITANDRE: Ah, don't pull my leg.
    Tell me what hope she's given you, I pray.
ACASTE: I'm hopeless, and it's you who win the day.   60
    She hates me thoroughly, and I'm so vexed
    I mean to hang myself on Tuesday next.
CLITANDRE: Dear Marquess, let us have an armistice
    And make a treaty. What do you say to this?
    If ever one of us can plainly prove   65
    That Célimène encourages his love,
    The other must abandon hope, and yield,
    And leave him in possession of the field.
ACASTE: Now, there's a bargain that appeals to me;
    With all my heart, dear Marquess, I agree.   70
    But hush.

(Enter CÉLIMÈNE.)

CELIMENE: Still here?
CLITANDRE: T'was love that stayed our feet.
CELIMENE: I think I heard a carriage in the street.
    Whose is it? D'you know?

(Enter BASQUE.)

BASQUE: Arsinoé is here, Madame.
CELIMENE: Arsinoé, you say? Oh, dear.
BASQUE: Eliante is entertaining her below. (Exit.)   75
CELIMENE: What brings the creature here, I'd like to
        know?
ACASTE: They say she's dreadfully prudish, but in
        fact
    I think her piety . . .
CELIMENE: It's all an act.
    At heart she's worldly, and her poor success
    In snaring men explains her prudishness.   80
    It breaks her heart to see the beaux and gallants
    Engrossed by other women's charms and talents,
    And so she's always in a jealous rage

Against the faulty standards of the age.
85 She lets the world believe that she's a prude
To justify her loveless solitude,
And strives to put a band of moral shame
On all the graces that she cannot claim.
But still she'd love a lover; and Alceste
90 Appears to be the one she'd love the best.
His visits here are poison to her pride;
She seems to think I've lured him from her side;
And everywhere, at court or in the town,
The spiteful, envious woman runs me down.
95 In short, she's just as stupid as can be,
Vicious and arrogant in the last degree,
And . . .

(Enter ARSINOÉ.*)*

Ah! What happy chance has brought you here?
I've thought about you ever so much, my dear.
ARSINOE: I've come to tell you something you should
know.
100 CELIMENE: How good of you to think of doing so!

*(*CLITANDRE *and* ACASTE *go out, laughing.)*

ARSINOE: It's just as well those gentlemen didn't tarry.
CELIMENE: Shall we sit down?
ARSINOE: That won't be necessary.
Madam, the flame of friendship ought to burn
Brightest in matters of the most concern,
105 And as there's nothing which concerns us more
Than honor, I have hastened to your door
To bring you, as your friend, some information
About the status of your reputation.
I visited, last night, some virtuous folk,
110 And, quite by chance, it was of you they spoke;
There was I fear no tendency to praise
Your light behavior and your dashing ways.
The quantity of gentlemen you see
And your by now notorious coquetry
115 Were both so vehemently criticized
By everyone, that I was much surprised.
Of course, I needn't tell you where I stood;
I came to your defense as best I could,
Assured them you were harmless, and declared
120 Your soul was absolutely unimpaired.
But there are some things, you must realize,
One can't excuse, however hard one tries,
And I was forced at least into conceding
That your behavior, Madam, is misleading,
125 That it makes a bad impression, giving rise
To ugly gossip and obscene surmise,
And that if you were more *overtly* good,
You wouldn't be so much misunderstood.
Not that I think you've been unchaste.—No! No!
130 The saints preserve me from a thought so low!
But mere good conscience never did suffice;
One must avoid the outward show of vice.
Madam, you're too intelligent, I'm sure,

To think my motives anything but pure
In offering you this counsel—which I do   135
Out of a zealous interest in you.
CELIMENE: Madam, I haven't taken you amiss;
I'm very much obliged to you for this;
And I'll at once discharge the obligation
By telling you about *your* reputation.   140
You've been so friendly as to let me know
What certain people say of me, and so
I mean to follow your benign example
By offering you a somewhat similar sample.
The other day, I went to an affair   145
And found some most distinguished people there
Discussing piety, both false and true.
The conversation soon came round to you.
Alas! Your prudery and bustling zeal
Appeared to have a very slight appeal.   150
Your affectation of a grave demeanor,
Your endless talk of virtue and of honor,
The aptitude of your suspicious mind
For finding sin where there is none to find,
Your towering self-esteem, that pitying face   155
With which you contemplate the human race,
Your sermonizings and your sharp aspersions
On people's pure and innocent diversions—
All these were mentioned, Madam, and, in fact,
Were roundly and concertedly attacked.   160
"What good," they said, "are all those outward
        shows,
When everything belies her pious pose?
She prays incessantly; but then, they say,
She beats her maids and cheats them of their pay;
She shows her zeal in every holy place,   165
But still she's vain enough to paint her face;
She holds that naked statues are immoral,
But with a naked *man* she'd have no quarrel."
Of course, I said to everybody there
That they were being viciously unfair;   170
But still they were disposed to criticize you,
And all agreed that someone should advise you
To leave the morals of the world alone,
And worry rather more about your own.
They felt that one's self-knowledge should be
        great   175
Before one thinks of setting others straight;
That one should learn the art of living well
Before one threatens other men with hell.
And that the Church is best equipped, no doubt,
To guide our souls and root our vices out.   180
Madam, you're too intelligent, I'm sure,
To think my motives anything but pure
In offering you this counsel—which I do
Out of a zealous interest in you.
ARSINOE: I dared not hope for gratitude, but I   185
Did not expect so acid a reply;
I judge, since you've been so extremely tart,
That my good counsel pierced you to the heart.

CELIMENE: Far from it, Madam. Indeed, it seems to me
190   We ought to trade advice more frequently.
One's vision of oneself is so defective
That it would be an excellent corrective.
If you are willing, Madam, let's arrange
Shortly to have another frank exchange
195   In which we'll teach each other, *entre nous,*°
What you've heard tell of me, and I of you.

ARSINOE: Oh, people never censure you, my dear;
It's me they criticize. Or so I hear.

CELIMENE: Madam, I think we either blame or praise
200   According to our taste and length of days.
There is a time of life for coquetry,
And there's a season, too, for prudery.
When all one's charms are gone, it is, I'm sure,
Good strategy to be devout and pure:
205   It makes one seem a little less forsaken.
Some day, perhaps, I'll take the road you've taken:
Time brings all things. But I have time aplenty,
And see no cause to be a prude at twenty.

ARSINOE: You give your age in such a gloating tone
210   That one would think I was an ancient crone;
We're not so far apart, in sober truth,
That you can mock me with a boast of youth!
Madam, you baffle me. I wish I knew
What moves you to provoke me as you do.

215 CELIMENE: For my part, Madam, I should like to know
Why you abuse me everywhere you go.
Is it my fault, dear lady, that your hand
Is not, alas, in very great demand?
If men admire me, if they pay me court
220   And daily make me offers of the sort
You'd dearly love to have them make to you,
How can I help it? What would you have me do?
If what you want is lovers, please feel free
To take as many as you can from me.

ARSINOE: Oh, come. D'you think the world is losing
225   sleep
Over that flock of lovers which you keep,
Or that we find it difficult to guess
What price you pay for their devotedness?
Surely you don't expect us to suppose
230   Mere merit could attract so many beaux?
It's not your virtue that they're dazzled by;
Nor is it virtuous love for which they sigh.
You're fooling no one, Madam; the world's not
blind;
There's many a lady heaven has designed
235   To call men's noblest, tenderest feelings out,
Who has no lovers dogging her about;
From which it's plain that lovers nowadays
Must be acquired in bold and shameless ways,
And only pay one court for such reward

As modesty and virtue can't afford.   240
Then don't be quite so puffed up, if you please,
About your tawdry little victories;
Try, if you can, to be a shade less vain,
And treat the world with somewhat less disdain.
If one were envious of your amours,   245
One soon could have a following like yours;
Lovers are no great trouble to collect
If one prefers them to one's self-respect.

CELIMENE: Collect them then, my dear; I'd love to see
You demonstrate that charming theory;   250
Who knows, you might . . .

ARSINOE: Now, Madam, that will do;
It's time to end this trying interview.
My coach is late in coming to your door,
Or I'd have taken leave of you before.

CELIMENE: Oh, please don't feel that you must rush
away;   255
I'd be delighted, Madam, if you'd stay.
However, lest my conversation bore you,
Let me provide some better company for you;
This gentleman, who comes most apropos,
Will please you more than I could do, I know.   260

(Enter ALCESTE.*)*

Alceste, I have a little note to write
Which simply must go out before tonight;
Please entertain *Madame;* I'm sure that she
Will overlook my incivility. *(Exit.)*

ARSINOE: Well, Sir, our hostess graciously contrives   265
For us to chat until my coach arrives;
And I shall be forever in her debt
For granting me this little tête-à-tête.°
We women very rightly give our hearts
To men of noble character and parts,   270
And your especial merits, dear Alceste,
Have roused the deepest sympathy in my breast.
Oh, how I wish they had sufficient sense
At court, to recognize your excellence!
They wrong you greatly, Sir. How it must hurt you   275
Never to be rewarded for your virtue!

ALCESTE: Why, Madam, what cause have I to feel
aggrieved?
What great and brilliant thing have I achieved?
What service have I rendered to the King
That I should look to him for anything?   280

ARSINOE: Not everyone who's honored by the State
Has done great services. A man must wait
Till time and fortune offer him the chance.
Your merit, Sir, is obvious at a glance,
And . . .

ALCESTE: Ah, forget my merit; I'm not neglected.   285
The court, I think, can hardly be expected
To mine men's souls for merit, and unearth

---

entre nous, "between us."

tête-à-tête, literally head-to-head; i.e., private conversation.

Our hidden virtues and our secret worth.
ARSINOE: *Some* virtues, though, are far too bright to hide;
290 Yours are acknowledged, Sir, on every side.
Indeed, I've heard you warmly praised of late
By persons of considerable weight.
ALCESTE: This fawning age has praise for everyone,
And all distinctions, Madam, are undone.
295 All things have equal honor nowadays,
And no one should be gratified by praise.
To be admired, one only need exist,
And every lackey's on the honors list.
ARSINOE: I only wish, Sir, that you had your eye
300 On some position at court, however high;
You'd only have to hint at such a notion
For me to set the proper wheels in motion;
I've certain friendships I'd be glad to use
To get you any office you might choose.
305 ALCESTE: Madam, I fear that any such ambition
Is wholly foreign to my disposition.
The soul God gave me isn't of the sort
That prospers in the weather of a court.
It's all too obvious that I don't possess
310 The virtues necessary for success.
My one great talent is for speaking plain;
I've never learned to flatter or to feign;
And anyone so stupidly sincere
Had best not seek a courtier's career.
315 Outside the court, I know, one must dispense
With honors, privilege, and influence;
But still one gains the right, foregoing these,
Not to be tortured by the wish to please.
One needn't live in dread of snubs and slights,
320 Nor praise the verse that every idiot writes,
Nor humor silly Marquesses, nor bestow
Politic sighs on Madam So-and-So.
ARSINOE: Forget the court, then; let the matter rest.
But I've another cause to be distressed
325 About your present situation, Sir.
It's to your love affair that I refer.
She whom you love, and who pretends to love you,
Is, I regret to say, unworthy of you.
ALCESTE: Why, Madam! Can you seriously intend
330 To make so grave a charge against your friend?
ARSINOE: Alas, I must. I've stood aside too long
And let that lady do you grievous wrong;
But now my debt to conscience shall be paid:
I tell you that your love has been betrayed.
ALCESTE: I thank you, Madam; you're extremely
335 kind.
Such words are soothing to a lover's mind.
ARSINOE: Yes, though she *is* my friend, I say again
You're very much too good for Célimène.
She's wantonly misled you from the start.
ALCESTE: You may be right; who knows another's
340 heart?
But ask yourself if it's the part of charity

To shake my soul with doubts of her sincerity.
ARSINOE: Well, if you'd rather be a dupe than doubt her,
That's your affair. I'll say no more about her.
ALCESTE: Madam, you know that doubt and vague suspicion 345
Are painful to a man in my position;
It's most unkind to worry me this way
Unless you've some real proof of what you say.
ARSINOE: Sir, say no more: all doubt shall be removed,
And all that I've been saying shall be proved. 350
You've only to escort me home, and there
We'll look into the heart of this affair.
I've ocular° evidence which will persuade you
Beyond a doubt, that Célimène's betrayed you.
Then, if you're saddened by that revelation, 355
Perhaps I can provide some consolation. (*They go out.*)

ACT 4

(*Enter* ELIANTE *and* PHILINTE.)

PHILINTE: Madam, he acted like a stubborn child;
I thought they never would be reconciled;
In vain we reasoned, threatened, and appealed;
He stood his ground and simply would not yield.
The Marshals, I feel sure, have never heard 5
An argument so splendidly absurd.
"No, gentlemen," said he, "I'll not retract.
His verse is bad: extremely bad, in fact.
Surely it does the man no harm to know it.
Does it disgrace him, not to be a poet? 10
A gentleman may be respected still,
Whether he writes a sonnet well or ill.
That I dislike his verse should not offend him;
In all that touches honor, I commend him;
He's noble, brave, and virtuous—but I fear 15
He can't in truth be called a sonneteer.
I'll gladly praise his wardrobe; I'll endorse
His dancing, or the way he sits a horse;
But, gentlemen, I cannot praise his rhyme.
In fact, it ought to be a capital crime 20
For anyone so sadly unendowed
To write a sonnet, and read the thing aloud."
At length he fell into a gentler mood
And, striking a concessive attitude,
He paid Oronte the following courtesies: 25
"Sir, I regret that I'm so hard to please,
And I'm profoundly sorry that your lyric
Failed to provoke me to a panegyric."
After these curious words, the two embraced,
And then the hearing was adjourned—in haste. 30

---

ocular, visible.

ELIANTE: His conduct has been very singular lately;
　　　Still, I confess that I respect him greatly.
　　　The honesty in which he takes such pride
　　　Has—to my mind—its noble, heroic side.
35　　In this false age, such candor seems outrageous;
　　　But I could wish that it were more contagious.
PHILINTE: What most intrigues me in our friend
　　　Alceste
　　　Is the grand passion that rages in his breast.
　　　The sullen humors he's compounded of
40　　Should not, I think, dispose his heart to love;
　　　But since they do, it puzzles me still more
　　　That he should choose your cousin to adore.
ELIANTE: It does, indeed, belie the theory
　　　That love is born of gentle sympathy,
45　　And that the tender passion must be based
　　　On sweet accords of temper and of taste.
PHILINTE: Does she return his love, do you suppose?
ELIANTE: Ah, that's a difficult question, Sir. Who
　　　knows?
　　　How can we judge the truth of her devotion?
50　　Her heart's a stranger to its own emotion.
　　　Sometimes it thinks it loves, when no love's there;
　　　At other times it loves quite unaware.
PHILINTE: I rather think Alceste is in for more
　　　Distress and sorrow than he's bargained for;
55　　Were he of my mind, Madam, his affection
　　　Would turn in quite a different direction,
　　　And we would see him more responsive to
　　　The kind regard which he receives from you.
ELIANTE: Sir, I believe in frankness, and I'm inclined,
60　　In matters of the heart, to speak my mind.
　　　I don't oppose his love for her; indeed,
　　　I hope with all my heart that he'll succeed,
　　　And were it in my power, I'd rejoice
　　　In giving him the lady of his choice.
65　　But if, as happens frequently enough
　　　In love affairs, he meets with a rebuff—
　　　If Célimène should grant some rival's suit—
　　　I'd gladly play the role of substitute;
　　　Nor would his tender speeches please me less
70　　Because they'd once been made without success.
PHILINTE: Well, Madam, as for me, I don't oppose
　　　Your hopes in this affair; and heaven knows
　　　That in my conversations with the man
　　　I plead your cause as often as I can.
75　　But if those two should marry, and so remove
　　　All chance that he will offer you his love,
　　　Then I'll declare my own, and hope to see
　　　Your gracious favor pass from him to me.
　　　In short, should you be cheated of Alceste,
80　　I'd be most happy to be second best.
ELIANTE: Philinte, you're teasing.
PHILINTE:　　　　　　　　Ah, Madam, never fear;
　　　No words of mine were ever so sincere,
　　　And I shall live in fretful expectation
　　　Till I can make a fuller declaration.

(Enter ALCESTE.*)*

ALCESTE: Avenge me, Madam! I must have
　　　satisfaction,   85
　　　Or this great wrong will drive me to distraction!
ELIANTE: Why, what's the matter? What's upset you
　　　so?
ALCESTE: Madam, I've had a mortal, mortal blow
　　　If Chaos repossessed the universe,
　　　I swear I'd not be shaken any worse.   90
　　　I'm ruined. . . . I can say no more. . . . My soul . . .
ELIANTE: Do, try, Sir, to regain your self-control.
ALCESTE: Just heaven! Why were so much beauty and
　　　grace
　　　Bestowed on one so vicious and so base?
ELIANTE: Once more, Sir, tell us. . . .
ALCESTE:　　　　　　　My world has gone to wrack;   95
　　　I'm—I'm betrayed; she's stabbed me in the back:
　　　Yes, Célimène (who would have thought it of her?)
　　　Is false to me, and has another lover.
ELIANTE: Are you quite certain? Can you prove these
　　　things?
PHILINTE: Lovers are prey to wild imaginings   100
　　　And jealous fancies. No doubt there's some
　　　mistake. . . .
ALCESTE: Mind your own business, Sir, for heaven's
　　　sake.
　　　(to ELIANTE*)* Madam, I have the proof that you
　　　demand
　　　Here in my pocket, penned by her own hand.
　　　Yes, all the shameful evidence one could want   105
　　　Lies in this letter written to Oronte—
　　　Oronte! Whom I felt sure she couldn't love,
　　　And hardly bothered to be jealous of.
PHILINTE: Still, in a letter, appearances may deceive;
　　　This may not be so bad as you believe.   110
ALCESTE: Once more I beg you, Sir, to let me be;
　　　Tend to your own affairs; leave mine to me.
ELIANTE: Compose yourself; this anguish that you
　　　feel . . .
ALCESTE: Is something, Madam, you alone can heal.
　　　My outraged heart, beside itself with grief,   115
　　　Appeals to you for comfort and relief.
　　　Avenge me on your cousin, whose unjust
　　　And faithless nature has deceived my trust;
　　　Avenge a crime your pure soul must detest.
ELIANTE: But how, Sir?
ALCESTE:　　　　　　Madam, this heart within my breast   120
　　　Is yours; pray take it; redeem my heart from her,
　　　And so avenge me on my torturer.
　　　Let her be punished by the fond emotion,
　　　The ardent love, the bottomless devotion,
　　　The faithful worship which this heart of mine   125
　　　Will offer up to yours as to a shrine.
ELIANTE: You have my sympathy, Sir, in all you
　　　suffer;
　　　Nor do I scorn the noble heart you offer;

But I suspect you'll soon be mollified,
130 And this desire for vengeance will subside.
When some beloved hand has done us wrong
We thirst for retribution—but not for long;
However dark the deed that she's committed,
A lovely culprit's very soon acquitted.
135 Nothing's so stormy as an injured lover,
And yet no storm so quickly passes over.
ALCESTE: No, Madam, no—this is no lovers' spat;
I'll not forgive her; it's gone too far for that;
My mind's made up; I'll kill myself before
140 I waste my hopes upon her any more.
Ah, here she is. My wrath intensifies.
I shall confront her with her tricks and lies,
And crush her utterly, and bring you then
A heart no longer slave to Célimène. (*Exit* ELIANTE
and PHILINTE.)

(*Enter* CÉLIMÈNE.)

ALCESTE (*aside*): Sweet heaven, help me to control
145 my passion.
CELIMENE (*to* ALCESTE): Oh, Lord. Why stand there
staring in that fashion?
And what d'you mean by those dramatic sighs,
And that malignant glitter in your eyes?
ALCESTE: I mean that sins which cause the blood to
freeze
150 Look innocent beside your treacheries;
That nothing Hell's or Heaven's wrath could do
Ever produced so bad a thing as you.
CELIMENE: Your compliments were always sweet and
pretty.
ALCESTE: Madam, it's not the moment to be witty.
No, blush and hang your head; you've ample
155 reason,
Since I've the fullest evidence of your treason.
Ah, this is what my sad heart prophesied;
Now all my anxious fears are verified;
My dark suspicion and my gloomy doubt
160 Divined the truth, and now the truth is out.
For all your trickery, I was not deceived;
It was my bitter stars that I believed.
But don't imagine that you'll go scot-free;
You shan't misuse me with impunity.
165 I know that love's irrational and blind;
I know the heart's not subject to the mind,
And can't be reasoned into beating faster;
I know each soul is free to choose its master;
Therefore had you but spoken from the heart,
170 Rejecting my attentions from the start,
I'd have no grievance, or at any rate
I could complain of nothing but my fate.
Ah, but so falsely to encourage me—
That was a treason and a treachery
175 For which you cannot suffer too severely,
And you shall pay for that behavior dearly.
Yes, now I have no pity, not a shred;

My temper's out of hand; I've lost my head;
Shocked by the knowledge of your double-
dealings,
My reason can't restrain my savage feelings; 180
A righteous wrath deprives me of my senses,
And I won't answer for the consequences.
CELIMENE: What does this outburst mean? Will you
please explain?
Have you, by any chance, gone quite insane?
ALCESTE: Yes, yes, I went insane the day I fell 185
A victim to your black and fatal spell,
Thinking to meet with some sincerity
Among the treacherous charms that beckoned me.
CELIMENE: Pooh. Of what treachery can you
complain?
ALCESTE: How sly you are, how cleverly you feign! 190
But you'll not victimize me any more.
Look: here's a document you've seen before.
This evidence, which I acquired today,
Leaves you, I think, without a thing to say.
CELIMENE: Is this what sent you into such a fit? 195
ALCESTE: You should be blushing at the sight of it.
CELIMENE: Ought I to blush? I truly don't see why.
ALCESTE: Ah, now you're being bold as well as sly;
Since there's no signature, perhaps you'll claim . . .
CELIMENE: I wrote it, whether or not it bears my
name. 200
ALCESTE: And you can view with equanimity
This proof of your disloyalty to me!
CELIMENE: Oh, don't be so outrageous and extreme.
ALCESTE: You take this matter lightly, it would seem.
Was it no wrong to me, no shame to you, 205
That you should send Oronte this billet-doux?°
CELIMENE: Oronte! Who said it was for him?
ALCESTE: Why, those
Who brought me this example of your prose.
But what's the difference? If you wrote the letter
To someone else, it pleases me no better. 210
My grievance and your guilt remain the same.
CELIMENE: But need you rage, and need I blush for
shame,
If this was written to a *woman* friend?
ALCESTE: Ah! Most ingenious. I'm impressed no end;
And after that incredible evasion 215
Your guilt is clear. I need no more persuasion.
How dare you try so clumsy a deception?
D'you think I'm wholly wanting in perception?
Come, come, let's see how brazenly you'll try
To bolster up so palpable a lie: 220
Kindly construe this ardent closing section
As nothing more than sisterly affection!
Here, let me read it. Tell me, if you dare to,
That this is for a woman . . .
CELIMENE: I don't care to.

---

billet-doux, love letter.

225 What right have you to badger and berate me,
And so highhandedly interrogate me?
ALCESTE: Now, don't be angry; all I ask of you
Is that you justify a phrase or two . . .
CELIMENE: No, I shall not. I utterly refuse,
230 And you may take those phrases as you choose.
ALCESTE: Just show me how this letter could be meant
For a woman's eyes, and I shall be content.
CELIMENE: No, no, it's for Oronte; you're perfectly
right.
I welcome his attentions with delight,
235 I prize his character and his intellect,
And everything is just as you suspect.
Come, do your worst now; give your rage free rein;
But kindly cease to bicker and complain.
ALCESTE (aside): Good God! Could anything be more
inhuman?
240 Was ever a heart so mangled by a woman?
When I complain of how she has betrayed me,
She bridles, and commences to upbraid me!
She tries my tortured patience to the limit;
She won't deny her guilt; she glories in it!
245 And yet my heart's too faint and cowardly
To break these chains of passion, and be free,
To scorn her as it should, and rise above
This unrewarded, mad, and bitter love.
(to CÉLIMÈNE): Ah, traitress, in how confident a
fashion
250 You take advantage of my helpless passion,
And use my weakness for your faithless charms
To make me once again throw down my arms!
But do at least deny this black transgression;
Take back that mocking and perverse confession;
255 Defend this letter and your innocence,
And I, poor fool, will aid in your defense.
Pretend, pretend, that you are just and true,
And I shall make myself believe in you.
CELIMENE: Oh, stop it. Don't be such a jealous dunce,
260 Or I shall leave off loving you at once.
Just why should I *pretend*? What could impel me
To stoop so low as that? And kindly tell me
Why, if I loved another, I shouldn't merely
Inform you of it, simply and sincerely!
265 I've told you where you stand, and that admission
Should altogether clear me of suspicion;
After so generous a guarantee,
What right have you to harbor doubts of me?
Since women are (from natural reticence)
270 Reluctant to declare their sentiments,
And since the honor of our sex requires
That we conceal our amorous desires,
Ought any man for whom such laws are broken
To question what the oracle has spoken?
275 Should he not rather feel an obligation
To trust that most obliging declaration?
Enough, now. Your suspicions quite disgust me;
Why should I love a man who doesn't trust me?

I cannot understand why I continue,
Fool that I am, to take an interest in you.   280
I ought to choose a man less prone to doubt,
And give you something to be vexed about.
ALCESTE: Ah, what a poor enchanted fool I am;
These gentle words, no doubt, were all a sham;
But destiny requires me to entrust   285
My happiness to you, and so I must.
I'll love you to the bitter end, and see
How false and treacherous you dare to be.
CELIMENE: No, you don't really love me as you ought.
ALCESTE: I love you more than can be said or
thought;   290
Indeed, I wish you were in such distress
That I might show my deep devotedness.
Yes, I could wish that you were wretchedly poor,
Unloved, uncherished, utterly obscure;
That fate had set you down upon the earth   295
Without possessions, rank, or gentle birth;
Then, by the offer of my heart, I might
Repair the great injustice of your plight;
I'd raise you from the dust, and proudly prove
The purity and vastness of my love.   300
CELIMENE: This is a strange benevolence indeed!
God grant that I may never be in need. . . .
Ah, here's Monsieur Dubois, in quaint disguise.

(Enter MONSIEUR DUBOIS.)

ALCESTE: Well, why this costume? Why those
frightened eyes?
What ails you?
DUBOIS: Well, sir, things are most mysterious.   305
ALCESTE: What do you mean?
DUBOIS: I fear they're very serious.
ALCESTE: What?
DUBOIS: Shall I speak more loudly?
ALCESTE: Yes; speak out.
DUBOIS: Isn't there someone here, Sir?
ALCESTE: Speak, you lout!
Stop wasting time.
DUBOIS: Sir, we must slip away.
ALCESTE: How's that?
DUBOIS: We must decamp without delay.   310
ALCESTE: Explain yourself.
DUBOIS: I tell you we must fly.
ALCESTE: What for?
DUBOIS: We mustn't pause to say good-by.
ALCESTE: Now what d'you mean by all of this, you
clown?
DUBOIS: I mean, Sir, that we've got to leave this town.
ALCESTE: I'll tear you limb from limb and joint from
joint   315
If you don't come more quickly to the point.
DUBOIS: Well, Sir, today a man in a black suit,
Who wore a black and ugly scowl to boot,
Left us a document scrawled in such a hand
As even Satan couldn't understand.   320

It bears upon your lawsuit, I don't doubt;
But all hell's devils couldn't make it out.
ALCESTE: Well, well, go on. What then? I fail to see
How this event obliges us to flee.
325 DUBOIS: Well, Sir: an hour later, hardly more,
A gentleman who's often called before
Came looking for you in an anxious way.
Not finding you, he asked me to convey
(Knowing I could be trusted with the same)
The following message. . . . Now, what *was* his
330 name?
ALCESTE: Forget his name, you idiot. What did he
say?
DUBOIS: Well, it was one of your friends, Sir, anyway.
He warned you to begone, and he suggested
That if you stay, you may well be arrested.
335 ALCESTE: What? Nothing more specific? Think, man,
think!
DUBOIS: No, Sir. He had me bring him pen and ink,
And dashed you off a letter which, I'm sure,
Will render things distinctly less obscure.
ALCESTE: Well—let me have it!
CELIMENE: What *is* this all about?
ALCESTE: God knows; but I have hopes of finding
340 out.
How long am I to wait, you blitherer?
DUBOIS (*after a protracted search for the letter*): I must
have left it on your table, Sir.
ALCESTE: I ought to . . .
CELIMENE: No, no, keep your self-control;
Go find out what's behind his rigmarole.
345 ALCESTE: It seems that fate, no matter what I do,
Has sworn that I may not converse with you;
But, Madam, pray permit your faithful lover
To try once more before the day is over.

(DUBOIS *and* ALCESTE *leave, then* CÉLIMÈNE *with-draws.*)

ACT 5

(*Enter* ALCESTE *and* PHILINTE.)

ALCESTE: No, it's too much. My mind's made up, I
tell you.
PHILINTE: Why should this blow, however hard,
compel you . . .
ALCESTE: No, no, don't waste your breath in
argument;
Nothing you say will alter my intent;
5 This age is vile, and I've made up my mind
To have no further commerce with mankind.
Did not truth, honor, decency, and the laws
Oppose my enemy and approve my cause?
My claims were justified in all men's sight;
10 I put my trust in equity and right;
Yet, to my horror and the world's disgrace,
Justice is mocked, and I have lost my case!

A scoundrel whose dishonesty is notorious
Emerges from another lie victorious!
Honor and right condone his brazen fraud,   15
While rectitude and decency applaud!
Before his smirking face, the truth stands charmed,
And virtue conquered, and the law disarmed!
His crime is sanctioned by a court decree!
And not content with what he's done to me,   20
The dog now seeks to ruin me by stating
That I composed a book now circulating,
A book so wholly criminal and vicious
That even to speak its title is seditious!
Meanwhile Oronte, my rival, lends his credit   25
To the same libelous tale, and helps to spread it!
Oronte! A man of honor and of rank,
With whom I've been entirely fair and frank;
Who sought me out and forced me, willy-nilly,
To judge some verse I found extremely silly;   30
And who, because I properly refused
To flatter him, or see the truth abused,
Abets my enemy in a rotten slander!
There's the reward of honesty and candor!
The man will hate me to the end of time   35
For failing to commend his wretched rhyme!
And not this man alone, but all humanity
Do what they do from interest and vanity;
They prate of honor, truth, and righteousness,
But lie, betray, and swindle nonetheless.   40
Come then: man's villainy is too much to bear;
Let's leave this jungle and this jackal's lair.
Yes! Treacherous and savage race of men,
You shall not look upon my face again.
PHILINTE: Oh, don't rush into exile prematurely;   45
Things aren't as dreadful as you make them,
surely.
It's rather obvious, since you're still at large,
That people don't believe your enemy's charge.
Indeed, his tale's so patently untrue
That it may do more harm to him than you.   50
ALCESTE: Nothing could do that scoundrel any harm:
His frank corruption is his greatest charm,
And, far from hurting him, a further shame
Would only serve to magnify his name.
PHILINTE: In any case, his bald prevarication   55
Has done no injury to your reputation,
And you may feel secure in that regard.
As for your lawsuit, it should not be hard
To have the case reopened, and contest
This judgment . . .
ALCESTE: No, no, let the verdict rest.   60
Whatever cruel penalty it may bring.
I wouldn't have it changed for anything.
It shows the times' injustice with such clarity
That I shall pass it down to our posterity
As a great proof and signal demonstration   65
Of the black wickedness of this generation.
It may cost twenty thousand francs; but I

Shall pay their twenty thousand, and gain thereby
The right to storm and rage at human evil,
70   And send the race of mankind to the devil.
PHILINTE: Listen to me. . . .
ALCESTE: Why? What can you possibly say?
Don't argue, Sir; your labor's thrown away.
Do you propose to offer lame excuses
For men's behavior and the times' abuses?
75   PHILINTE: No, all you say I'll readily concede:
This is a low, conniving age indeed;
Nothing but trickery prospers nowadays,
And people ought to mend their shabby ways.
Yes, man's a beastly creature; but must we then
80   Abandon the society of men?
Here in the world, each human frailty
Provides occasion for philosophy,
And that is virtue's noblest exercise;
If honesty shone forth from all men's eyes,
85   If every heart were frank and kind and just,
What could our virtues do but gather dust
(Since their employment is to help us bear
The villainies of men without despair)?
A heart well-armed with virtue can endure. . . .
90   ALCESTE: Sir, you're a matchless reasoner, to be sure;
Your words are fine and full of cogency;
But don't waste time and eloquence on me.
My reason bids me go, for my own good.
My tongue won't lie and flatter as it should;
95   God knows what frankness it might next commit,
And what I'd suffer on account of it.
Pray let me wait for Célimène's return
In peace and quiet. I shall shortly learn,
By her response to what I have in view,
100   Whether her love for me is feigned or true.
PHILINTE: Till then, let's visit Eliante upstairs.
ALCESTE: No, I am too weighed down with somber
         cares.
Go to her, do; and leave me with my gloom
Here in the darkened corner of this room.
105   PHILINTE: Why, that's no sort of company, my friend;
I'll see if Eliante will not descend.

        (*Exit* PHILINTE, ALCESTE *withdraws to a corner.*)
        (*Enter* CÉLIMÈNE *and* ORONTE.)

ORONTE: Yes, Madam, if you wish me to remain
Your true and ardent lover, you must deign
To give me some more positive assurance.
110   All this suspense is quite beyond endurance.
If your heart shares the sweet desires of mine,
Show me as much by some convincing sign;
And here's the sign I urgently suggest:
That you no longer tolerate Alceste,
115   But sacrifice him to my love, and sever
All your relations with the man forever.
CELIMENE: Why do you suddenly dislike him so?
You praised him to the skies not long ago.

ORONTE: Madam, that's not the point. I'm here to find
Which way your tender feelings are inclined.   120
Choose, if you please, between Alceste and me,
And I shall stay or go accordingly.
ALCESTE (*emerging from the corner*): Yes, Madam,
      choose; this gentleman's demand
Is wholly just, and I support his stand.
I too am true and ardent; I too am here   125
To ask you that you make your feelings clear.
No more delays, now; no equivocation;
The time has come to make your declaration.
ORONTE: Sir, I've no wish in any way to be
An obstacle to your felicity.   130
ALCESTE: Sir, I've no wish to share her heart with
      you;
That may sound jealous, but at least it's true.
ORONTE: If, weighing us, she leans in your
      direction . . .
ALCESTE: If she regard you with the least
      affection . . .
ORONTE: I swear I'll yield her to you there and then.   135
ALCESTE: I swear I'll never see her face again.
ORONTE: Now, Madam, tell us what we've come to
      hear.
ALCESTE: Madam, speak openly and have no fear.
ORONTE: Just say which one is to remain your lover.
ALCESTE: Just name one name, and it will all be over.   140
ORONTE: What! Is it possible that you're undecided?
ALCESTE: What! Can your feelings possibly be
      divided?
CELIMENE: Enough: this inquisition is gone too far:
How utterly unreasonable you are!
Not that I couldn't make the choice with ease;   145
My heart has no conflicting sympathies;
I know full well which one of you I favor,
And you'd not see me hesitate or waver.
But how can you expect me to reveal
So cruelly and bluntly what I feel?   150
I think it altogether too unpleasant
To choose between two men when both are
      present;
One's heart has means more subtle and more kind
Of letting its affections be divined,
Nor need one be uncharitably plain   155
To let a lover know he loves in vain.
ORONTE: No, no, speak plainly; I for one can stand it.
I beg you to be frank.
ALCESTE: And I demand it.
The simple truth is what I wish to know,
And there's no need for softening the blow.   160
You've made an art of pleasing everyone,
But now your days of coquetry are done:
You have no choice now, Madam, but to choose,
For I'll know what to think if you refuse;
I'll take your silence for a clear admission   165
That I'm entitled to my worst suspicion.
ORONTE: I thank you for this ultimatum, Sir,

And I may say I heartily concur.

CELIMENE: Really, this foolishness is very wearing:
170 Must you be so unjust and overbearing?
Haven't I told you why I must demur?
Ah, here's Eliante; I'll put the case to her.

(Enter ELIANTE *and* PHILINTE.*)*

Cousin, I'm being persecuted here
By these two persons, who, it would appear,
175 Will not be satisfied till I confess
Which one I love the more, and which the less,
And tell the latter to his face that he
Is henceforth banished from my company.
Tell me, has ever such a thing been done?
180 ELIANTE: You'd best not turn to me, I'm not the one
To back you in a matter of this kind:
I'm all for those who frankly speak their mind.
ORONTE: Madam, you'll search in vain for a
defender.
ALCESTE: You're beaten, Madam, and may as well
surrender.
ORONTE: Speak, speak, you must; and end this awful
185 strain.
ALCESTE: Or don't, and your position will be plain.
ORONTE: A single word will close this painful scene.
ALCESTE: But if you're silent, I'll know what you
mean.

(Enter ARSINOÉ, ACASTE, *and* CLITANDRE.*)*

ACASTE *(to* CÉLIMÈNE*)*: Madam, with all due
deference, we two
190 Have come to pick a little bone with you.
CLITANDRE *(to* ORONTE *and* ALCESTE*)*: I'm glad you're
present, Sirs; as you'll soon learn,
Our business here is also your concern.
ARSINOE *(to* CÉLIMÈNE*)*: Madam, I visit you so soon
again
Only because of these two gentlemen,
195 Who came to me indignant and aggrieved
About a crime too base to be believed.
Knowing your virtue, having such confidence in it,
I couldn't think you guilty for a minute,
In spite of all their telling evidence;
200 And, rising above our little difference,
I've hastened here in friendship's name to see
You clear yourself of this great calumny.
ACASTE: Yes, Madam, let us see with what composure
You'll manage to respond to this disclosure.
205 You lately sent Clitandre this tender note.
CLITANDRE: And this one, for Acaste, you also wrote.
ACASTE *(to* ORONTE *and* ALCESTE*)*: You'll recognize
this writing, Sirs, I think;
The lady is so free with pen and ink
That you must know it all too well, I fear.
210 But listen: this is something you should hear.

"How absurd you are to condemn my light-
heartedness in society, and to accuse me of being
happiest in the company of others. Nothing could
be more unjust; and if you do not come to me
instantly and beg pardon for saying such a thing, I
shall never forgive you as long as I live. Our big
bumbling friend the Viscount . . ."

What a shame that he's not here.

"Our big bumbling friend the Viscount, whose
name stands first in your complaint, is hardly a man
to my taste; and ever since the day I watched him
spending three-quarters of an hour spitting into a
well, so as to make circles in the water, I have been
unable to think highly of him. As for the little Marquess . . ."

In all modesty, gentlemen, that is I.

"As for the little Marquess, who sat squeezing my
hand for such a long while yesterday, I find him in
all respects the most trifling creature alive; and the
only things of value about him are his cape and his
sword. As for the man with the green ribbons . . ."

(to ALCESTE*)*: It's your turn now, Sir.

"As for the man with the green ribbons, he
amuses me now and then with his bluntness and his
bearish ill-humor; but there are many times indeed
when I think him the greatest bore in the world.
And as for the sonneteer . . ."

(to ORONTE*)*: Here's your helping.

"And as for the sonneteer, who has taken it into
his head to be witty, and insists on being an author
in the teeth of opinion, I simply cannot be bothered
to listen to him, and his prose wearies me quite as
much as his poetry. Be assured that I am not always
so well-entertained as you suppose; that I long for
your company, more than I dare to say, at all these
entertainments to which people drag me; and that
the presence of those one loves is the true and perfect seasoning to all one's pleasures."

CLITANDRE: And now for me.

"Clitandre, whom you mention, and who so
pesters me with his saccharine speeches, is the last
man on earth for whom I could feel any affection.
He is quite mad to suppose that I love him, and so
are you, to doubt that you are loved. Do come to
your senses; exchange your suppositions for his;
and visit me as often as possible, to help me bear the
annoyance of his unwelcome attentions."

It's a sweet character that these letters show,
And what to call it, Madam, you well know.

260   Enough. We're off to make the world acquainted
    With this sublime self-portrait that you've painted.
ACASTE: Madam, I'll make you no farewell oration;
    No, you're not worthy of my indignation.
    Far choicer hearts than yours, as you'll discover,
265   Would like this little Marquess for a lover.

    (Exit ACASTE *and* CLITANDRE.*)*

ORONTE: So! After all those loving letters you wrote,
    You turn on me like this, and cut my throat!
    And your dissembling, faithless heart, I find,
    Has pledged itself by turns to all mankind!
270   How blind I've been! But now I clearly see;
    I thank you, Madam, for enlightening me.
    My heart is mine once more, and I'm content;
    The loss of it shall be your punishment
    (to ALCESTE*)* Sir, she is yours; I'll seek no more to
        stand
275   Between your wishes and this lady's hand. *(Exit.)*
ARSINOE *(to* CÉLIMÈNE*)*: Madam, I'm forced to speak.
      I'm far too stirred
    To keep my counsel, after what I've heard.
    I'm shocked and staggered by your want of morals.
    It's not my way to mix in others' quarrels;
280   But really, when this fine and noble spirit,
    This man of honor and surpassing merit,
    Laid down the offering of his heart before you,
    How *could* you . . .
ALCESTE: Madam, permit me, I implore you,
    To represent myself in this debate.
285   Don't bother, please, to be my advocate.
    My heart, in any case, could not afford
    To give your services their due reward;
    And if I chose, for consolation's sake,
    Some other lady, t'would not be you I'd take.
ARSINOE: What makes you think you could, Sir? And
290   how dare you
    Imply that I've been trying to ensnare you?
    If you can for a moment entertain
    Such flattering fancies, you're extremely vain.
    I'm not so interested as you suppose
295   In Célimène's discarded gigolos.
    Get rid of that absurd illusion, do.
    Women like me are not for such as you.
    Stay with this creature, to whom you're so
      attached;
    I've never seen two people better matched.

    (Exit ARSINOÉ.*)*

ALCESTE *(to* CÉLIMÈNE*)*: Well, I've been still
300   throughout this exposé,
    Till everyone but me has said his say.
    Come, have I shown sufficient self-restraint?
    And may I now . . .
CELIMENE: Yes, make your just complaint.
    Reproach me freely, call me what you will;
305   You've every right to say I've used you ill.
    I've wronged you, I confess it; and in my shame

    I'll make no effort to escape the blame.
    The anger of those others I could despise;
    My guilt toward you I sadly recognize.
    Your wrath is wholly justified, I fear;   310
    I know how culpable I must appear,
    I know all things bespeak my treachery,
    And that, in short, you've grounds for hating me.
    Do so; I give you leave.
ALCESTE: Ah, traitress—how,
    How should I cease to love you, even now?   315
    Though mind and will were passionately bent
    On hating you, my heart would not consent.
    (to ELIANTE *and* PHILINTE*)* Be witness to my
      madness, both of you;
    See what infatuation drives one to;
    But wait; my folly's only just begun,   320
    And I shall prove to you before I'm done
    How strange the human heart is, and how far
    From rational we sorry creatures are.
    (to CÉLIMÈNE*)* Woman, I'm willing to forget your
      shame,
    And clothe your treacheries in a sweeter name;   325
    I'll call them youthful errors, instead of crimes,
    And lay the blame on these corrupting times.
    My one condition is that you agree
    To share my chosen fate, and fly with me
    To that wild, trackless, solitary place   330
    In which I shall forget the human race.
    Only by such a course can you atone
    For those atrocious letters; by that alone
    Can you remove my present horror of you,
    And make it possible for me to love you.   335
CELIMENE: What! *I* renounce the world at my young
      age,
    And die of boredom in some hermitage?
ALCESTE: Ah, if you really loved me as you ought,
    You wouldn't give the world a moment's
      thought;
    Must you have me, and all the world beside?   340
CELIMENE: Alas, at twenty-one is terrified
    Of solitude. I fear I lack the force
    And depth of soul to take so stern a course.
    But if my hand in marriage will content you,
    Why, there's a plan which I might well consent to,   345
    And . . .
ALCESTE: No, I detest you now. I could excuse
    Everything else, but since you thus refuse
    To love me wholly, as a wife should do,
    And see the world in me, as I in you,
    Go! I reject your hand, and disenthrall   350
    My heart from your enchantments, once for all.
    (Exit CÉLIMÈNE.*)*
ALCESTE *(to* ELIANTE*)*: Madam, your virtuous beauty
      has no peer;
    Of all this world, you only are sincere;
    I've long esteemed you highly, as you know;
    Permit me ever to esteem you so,   355
    And if I do not now request your hand,

Forgive me, Madam, and try to understand.
I feel unworthy of it; I sense that fate
Does not intend me for the married state,
360   That I should do you wrong by offering you
My shattered heart's unhappy residue,
And that in short . . .
ELIANTE: Your argument's well taken:
Nor need you fear that I shall feel forsaken.
365   Were I to offer him this hand of mine,
Your friend Philinte, I think, would not decline.
PHILINTE: Ah, Madam, that's my heart's most
        cherished goal,

For which I'd gladly give my life and soul.
ALCESTE (to ELIANTE and PHILINTE): May you be true
        to all you now profess,
And so deserve unending happiness.
Meanwhile, betrayed and wronged in everything,   370
I'll flee this bitter world where vice is king,
And seek some spot unpeopled and apart
Where I'll be free to have an honest heart. (Exit
        ALCESTE.)
PHILINTE: Come, Madam, let's do everything we can
To change the mind of this unhappy man. (They   375
        follow him.)

Figure 1. Acaste (Brian Bedford, *left*), Eliante (Patricia Conolly, *standing*), Célimène (Christine Pickles), and Clitandre (Joseph Bird) in the A.P.A. Repertory Company production of *The Misanthrope,* directed by Stephen Porter, designed by James Tilton, and presented by the Professional Theater Program of the University of Michigan, Ann Arbor, 1968. (Photograph: University Productions of the University of Michigan.)

Figure 2. Alceste (Roger Rees), dressed in black, pleads with the glamor-
ously overdressed Célimène (Uma Thurman) in the 1999 Classic Stage
Company's production of *The Misanthrope,* directed by Barry Edelstein and
designed by Narelle Sissons. (Photograph: Dixie Sheridan.)

Staging of *The Misanthrope*

REVIEW OF THE A.P.A. REPERTORY
COMPANY-PHOENIX THEATRE
PRODUCTION, 1968, BY CLIVE BARNES

Of course, Molière's "The Misanthrope" is, as of last night, the best play in town, and gratifyingly the A.P.A. Repertory Company comes close enough to doing it justice. I only hope Broadway audiences, so thinly nurtured on what often passes for wit on our stages, will have the sense to flock to it.

The play is timely. It might be said that it is always the function of a masterpiece to be timely, but in the case of "The Misanthrope" its social attitudes find a mockingly telling echo in our society. Molière was writing of a Paris dominated by the French court of the mid-17th century. A society as mannered as a ruffle and as hypocritical as a duelist's courtesy.

Bad verse gushed out of society's faucet; manners were a comedy; comedies were manners, and all manner of bows, scrapes, bobs, bows and falsities eased the daily traffic of human intercourse and quite obviated the need for honesty. Into this society comes Alceste, who, sadness of sadness, not only has the bad taste to speak his mind but, alas and alas, also is head over rapier in love with Celimene, who is all coquetry, all wiles, all deceit and all entrancements. In short, a witch of the first water.

Celimene, who is as surrounded with lovers as a lap dog might be with cushions, is the very epitome of the age. She is a gossip who cannot bear to hear a good word about anyone, and she relates the bad word with such a pretty display of dazzling malice that her barbs go out to her victims as sharp as Cupid's arrows.

Against such a woman the bluff and honest Alceste has no defenses. He rampages through polite society telling people to their face things that should be said only behind their backs, and as a result he has become a misanthrope, determined to abandon a society he finds false and the company of men he finds abhorrent. But then, there is always Celimene to lead him back to the straight and narrow primrose path.

It is a play that mixes humor and humanity so skillfully that anyone wanting to know what a comedy really is could well study it. The characters of the play—with the ill-contrasted lovers set against a background of tittlers and tattlers—are sweetly balanced, and progress of the play is exquisite right up to the masterly conclusion, which is wittily inconclusive.

Molière provides one great scene after another as the characters pirouette round, flicking one another like fencers. Yet beyond the wit and the dazzle, the insults and the ripostes, lies a serious play of a man disgusted by the false values he finds around him. Molière is too humane to be a satirist. He never loads the battle; he never really takes sides. Alceste is not only the one completely honest man in the play, he is also the one prig, and is not a little pompous.

His very aggressiveness is comic, and he sometimes protests so much that he seems to take as much pleasure out of his protestation as out of his virtue. No, perhaps, Molière's ideal is conveyed better in the characters of his friend Philinte and Eliante, Celimene's cousin, who, in the words of Philinte, hold that "in polite society, custom decrees that we show certain outward courtesies." Celimene, faithless yet vivacious, has a lesson to learn, but then so has Alceste.

What often stands in the way of Molière in English is the incredible difficulty of translating the poet's rhymed couplets while preserving rhyme, sense, rhythm, wit and sensibility. Richard Wilbur's marvelous translation does this. It is supple and subtle, it trips affectionately off the tongue with the rise and fall of natural speech to it, and the wit shimmers at its heart like a priceless diamond on a bed of velvet.

The A.P.A. rose manfully to the challenge, helped manfully by the swiftly naturalistic staging of Stephen Porter, who let the language speak for itself and the play make its own points. Although the company is dangerously shallow in depth, Richard Easton made an excellent Alceste, bluff, comically—but never too comically—wronged and surprisingly warm, as if at times he was not only the dupe of Celimene but also of his own unbending rectitude.

The other outstanding performance came from Brian Bedford—who in only his second performance with the company is shaping up as the right kind of repertory star—as the foppish Acaste. Mr. Bedford uses both his eyes and teeth with such exceptional virtuosity that one might easily overlook his perfect period manners, in which only Mr. Easton could rival him, and his deftly accurate comic timing. Keene Curtis, yet another of Celimene's suitors, also gave a very well-judged portrayal, with one gorgeous scene in which he reads a sonnet to Mr. Easton, asks for an honest opinion and disconcertingly receives it.

The women (Rosemary Harris come home wherever you are!) do not come off so well. Christine Pickles, however, makes a very brave attempt at Celimene, and has the right looks, the right voice and even the right spirit. But at this performance they somehow failed to come together at the right time; it was a portrayal almost right, and on another night might well prove more memorable than on this.

INTERVIEW WITH NARELLE SISSONS, DESIGNER OF THE CLASSIC STAGE COMPANY PRODUCTION, 1999, BY DAVID BARBOUR

Most of the buzz surrounding the recent Classic Stage Company production of *The Misanthrope* centered around the theatrical debut of Uma Thurman, in the role of flirtatious, gossipy Celimene (here named Jennifer). But even more notable was the production's design—one of the wittiest seen Off Broadway this season. Martin Crimp's adaptation resets the action among today's London glitterati, where sex, drugs, and character assassination (not necessarily in that order) are the main entertainments. For this mordant update, scenic designer Narelle Sissons created a perfectly heartless world of reflecting surfaces, consisting of an aluminum diamond-plate floor, two sharply angled walls at stage right and left (one of copper leaf, one of aluminum leaf), with a giant, tilted mirror at the rear.

Noting that Crimp's script gives away no details about the setting, except that we're in Jennifer's hotel room in modern London, the designer probed the text for ideas. "The main idea is that all the set's surfaces are reflective—the characters can see themselves in the floor and in the mirror above and behind them. They get a 360° view of themselves." The mirror idea, she adds, tells you something about these trendy, irresponsible fame-seekers: "When you stand in front of a mirror, you see yourself in the moment. The minute you step away, you're gone. That's the idea I was going for."

Picking on a line from the script, unprintable here, about literary theory (just ask yourself what word rhymes with "deconstruct"), Sissons pursued the idea of deconstruction in her design as well: "For instance," she says, "the giant mirror has its original rusted steel frame around it. It has a chic quality in its deconstructed state. Also, all the furniture is deconstructed. There's a dentist's chair that's been pulled apart and reupholstered with fake pony skin. The couch is a psychiatrist's couch so whenever there's a moment when a character starts looking inward, it always takes place on the couch. The little telephone table is made of funnels and steel pipes from one of the Bowery kitchen supply shops; the champagne bucket is made of stainless-steel pieces from the same place."

Everywhere you looked, there were tiny, satirical visual surprises. Thurman made her first appearance standing downstage watering a tiny patch of grass. A towering glass sculpture was revealed to be nothing but cocktail tumblers. The stage left well featured little

fleur-de-lis (for Molière) and martini glasses (for modern decadence), all of which were backlit. "We actually nicknamed the hotel room 'The Versailles,' because we thought it had a touch of the baroque," Sissons says.

Things got really baroque in the final scene, which took place at a party with a 17th-century theme. Servants hung chandeliers on the sides of the walls, and scattered little candles all over the stage. "The candles," Sissons explains, "are votives stuck to kitchen pans, muffin trays—there's also a cake plate, and a sauce dish divided into three sections. It's as if they've stolen all these pieces from the hotel's kitchen to make a party." A large period painting—"Le bat" by Hugh Taraval—showing a man adoring a woman, was brought onstage sideways, a caustic comment on leading man Alceste (Roger Rees) and his obsession with Jennifer.

Naturally, the implementation of Sissons' design required considerable ingenuity, given the production's typically low budget. "The mirror frame was given to us at a very low rate by a construction company," she says; "we had it glazed and hung." The mirror was made of pieces of mirrored Plexiglas secured to a solid backing. "Everything else was just a matter of the director and me looking for the right materials," she adds. "We went to a metal shop in Queens [Typin], an extraordinary warehouse filled with every type of sheet metal."

The rest of the design team worked in unison on the production, directed by Barry Edelstein. Stephen Strawbridge's lighting blended superbly with the set's metallic surfaces, creating startling shifts of mood by switching from highly colored looks to subtle white light. Martin Pakledinaz's costumes provided witty commentary on the fashions of two centuries, especially in the final baroque party sequence (Thurman appeared in 17th-century-style dress with images of eyes and lips all over the skirt). Darron L. West's sound design provided a strong, clear setting both for Michael Torke's incidental music and the vocalizations of the Pet Shop Boys. All four designers helped to build a bridge between neo-classic France and postmodern London. Molière never seemed so modern; after this production, don't be surprised if CAA tries to sign him up to a three-picture deal. *The Misanthrope* ran at CSC through March 7.

APHRA BEHN

1640?–1689

Aphra Behn, according to Virginia Woolf, "earned [women] the right to speak their minds." "Earned" is a crucial word for Woolf, since she valued the fact that Aphra Behn wrote to make money—and, indeed, made enough from her writing to support herself. Successful as she was, her life is shrouded in mystery. Little is known about Behn's childhood—even her family name, which may have been Johnson, cannot be verified—when she married, or when her husband died. Scholars assume that, as a young woman, she traveled to Surinam in the West Indies with her family. Her stay there was probably brief, since her father died en route, but details from that visit turn up in her novella *Oronooko, or the Royal Slave* (1688), whose black protagonist is both victim and revolutionary leader, lover and murderer. Other parts of her past are similarly obscure and similarly echoed in her writing. She obviously knew both French and Spanish, since she earned money doing a number of translations. Did she learn those languages in a convent school, since her plays and short stories include a number of women either educated in a convent or, like Hellena in *The Rover,* destined for a nun's vocation? Was her marriage—to, one assumes, a Mr. Behn, whom she never mentions in her writing—an arranged one, and perhaps even an unhappy one, given the number of forced and unhappy marriages, or engagements, in her plays? How did she become a spy, as she certainly was in 1666–67, working in Antwerp? And how did she move into London's theatrical world, writing plays for the Duke's Company, one of the two theater companies licensed to produce plays?

Whatever the answers to these haunting questions, the fact remains that Aphra Behn, working at a furious pace (in part because she was deeply in debt as a result of her time in Antwerp), wrote some eighteen plays between 1670 and 1687—more than the combined output of her well-known fellow dramatists George Etherege (three plays), William Wycherley (four plays), and William Congreve (six plays). Writing at that pace, sometimes two or three plays in a single year, she often borrowed plots and characters—and sometimes whole stretches of dialogue—from other writers. Her single romantic tragedy *Abdelazar* (1676), in all its lavish spectacle (a coronation, a battle, and multiple murders), was adapted from an anonymous play; her first comedy set in London, *The Town Fop* (1676), was similarly adapted, this time from a play called *The Miseries of Enforced Marriage*; and both parts of *The Rover* (Part I in 1677, Part II in 1681) are based on an extensive reworking of Thomas Killigrew's *Thomaso*. In *Sir Patient Fancy* (1678), one can see the influence of several of Molière's comedies, including the hypochondriac title character who resembles Molière's "imaginary invalid" and the pretentious Lady Knowell whose name signals her connection to Molière's "learned ladies." Behn's borrowings did not go unnoticed, and she was often criticized for this practice.

But literary borrowing was a well-established practice, especially in the theater—Shakespeare, for example, borrowed characters or plots for almost all of his plays. So it's difficult to know whether the attacks on Behn sprang from her notorious success or from the fact that she was a woman in what was essentially a male-dominated world. Moreover, she was a woman whose plays, like those of her famous contemporaries, dealt directly with issues of sexual morality and often contained dialogue that was not merely witty but bawdy, for which she was also attacked. In a preface to her late comedy *The Lucky Chance* (1686), Behn defends herself at length, claiming that her comedy was being attacked because she was a woman, and comparing the bedroom scene where Sir Feeble approaches his new wife and "opens his night gown" to scenes in other plays, both contemporary and older, that feature explicit sexual situations, both in words and in actions. Behn's spirited defense of her own practice turns into a plea for equality: "All I ask, is the privilege for my masculine part the poet in me (if any such you will allow me) to tread in those successful paths my predecessors have so long thrived in, to take those measures that both the ancient and modern writers have set me, and by which they have pleased the world so well."

Much of Behn's work seems to be aimed at producing as lively and bawdy a theatrical experience as her male counterparts, rather than preaching a feminist agenda. But *The Rover,* her best-known work (if we consider only Part I), manages to do both, combining at least four romantic intrigues with the adventures of two strong-minded and relatively independent women, Florinda and Hellena, each seeking to escape their brother's restrictive plans for their futures, plans that would arrange a marriage for Florinda and send Hellena to a convent. By disguising themselves during Carnival time, both women become "rovers"—able to move out to the streets where they can exercise at least a measure of choice. The play's title applies most obviously to Willmore, the displaced Royalist soldier, whose penchant for women leads him into several comic as well as amorous encounters not only with Hellena but also with the courtesan Angellica Bianca.

Notable in these various relationships is the power that women sometimes hold. Angellica Bianca, though a courtesan, prices herself beyond the reach of most men (one thousand crowns a month), and Lucetta, a prostitute, ends up with the money, ornaments, and clothes of Ned Blunt, a country gentleman. Hellena, the youngest of the women, offers a sardonically vivid portrait of the woes of marriage (Act 1, Scene 1) and responds to Willmore's offer of love without marriage by pointing out that she will get "a cradle full of noise and mischief, with a pack of repentance at my back." Angellica Bianca's attack is both verbal and physical, when she assails Willmore for flirting with another woman and holds a pistol to his chest to emphasize her point. Yet Angellica's angry jealousy testifies also to the power Willmore has over her. She has tried to maintain both sexual and economic control by setting her price very high, but when she encounters Willmore, a man who can't possibly afford her, she falls in love and offers herself to him for free.

The popularity of *The Rover*—both during Behn's lifetime and even more during the first half of the eighteenth century, when London playgoers could have seen the play in almost every theater season between 1703 and 1743—must have sprung from the range and vitality of the characters. Indeed, Behn tried to capitalize on the play's success by writing a second part to give Willmore yet another chance to exert his dangerous charms. But by the late eighteenth century the play, now bowdlerized and weakened into an adaptation called *Love in Many Masks,* appeared briefly and then disappeared. Aphra Behn became almost invisible on the professional stage for close to two hundred years. Then, in July of 1984, productions of *The Rover* and *The Lucky Chance* both appeared in London. The Royal Shakespeare Company produced *The Rover* in 1986 in Stratford-upon-Avon, then in 1987 in London, and the play's exuberant stage-worthiness became even more apparent.

Just as Aphra Behn had adapted an earlier play into *The Rover,* so too the RSC director, John Barton, felt free to adapt Behn's text, changing the setting from Naples to a Spanish colony, moving sections of text, and even going back to Killigrew's *Thomaso* (Behn's source) for new lines. While some critics carped about Barton's changes or questioned Behn's originality, Stratford audiences were delighted by a production described by one critic as a "rollicking romp." Like Restoration audiences, which enjoyed the linking of offstage romance with onstage actors in a theater where everyone seemed to know which actress was the mistress of which nobleman, audiences in 1986 could also savor an offstage dimension in the Willmore/Angellica Bianca scenes (see Figure 1), since a husband-and-wife team, Jeremy Irons and Sinead Cusack, played the roles. The festivities of the Carnival pervaded the performance, from the masquerade costumes for the women (see Figure 2) to the fireworks at the end, thus underlining the change for Florinda and Hellena from their previously repressive environment (see Figure 3). Even Blunt's embarrassed discomfiture (see Figure 4) was hilarious, especially when he crawled back out of the trapdoor (representing the sewers into which he had been pitched) clad in Lucetta's underwear; the moment is not in Aphra Behn's text, but the momentary cross-dressing is certainly consistent with the disguises throughout the play. While one cannot claim too much influence for a single production, it may be worth noting that since the RSC produced the play, there has been almost an explosion of work on Behn, including a major modern scholarly edition of her work, a series of critical articles, additional productions including a multiracial version of *The Rover* in 1994, and the appearance of *The Rover* in a number of anthologies. Contemporary audiences, both as readers and as theatergoers, once more have the chance to experience the delight in social intrigue and the questioning of social values that characterize Aphra Behn's work.

THE ROVER; OR, THE BANISHED CAVALIERS

BY APHRA BEHN

CHARACTERS

[Men]

DON ANTONIO, *the Viceroy's son*
DON PEDRO, *a noble Spaniard, his friend*
BELVILE, *an English colonel in love with Florinda*
WILLMORE, *the Rover*
FREDERICK, *an English gentleman, and friend to Belvile and Blunt*
BLUNT, *an English country gentleman*
STEPHANO, *servant to Don Pedro*
PHILIPPO, *Lucetta's gallant*
SANCHO, *pimp to Lucetta*
BISKEY and SEBASTIAN, *two bravos° to Angellica*
OFFICER and SOLDIERS
[DIEGO,] *page to Don Antonio*

[Women]

FLORINDA, *sister to Don Pedro*
HELLENA, *a gay young woman designed for a nun, and sister to Florinda*
VALERIA, *a kinswoman to Florinda*
ANGELLICA BIANCA, *a famous courtesan*
MORETTA, *her woman*
CALLIS, *governess to Florinda and Hellena*
LUCETTA, *a jilting wench*
SERVANTS, *other* MASQUERADERS, MEN *and* WOMEN

SCENE

Naples, in Carnival time

PROLOGUE

Wits, like physicians, never can agree,
When of a different society.
And Rabel's drops° were never more cried down
By all the learned doctors of the town,
5 Than a new play whose author is unknown.
Nor can those doctors with more malice sue
(And powerful purses) the dissenting few,
Than those, with an insulting pride, do rail
At all who are not of their own cabal.°
10   If a young poet hit your humor right,
You judge him then out of revenge and spite.
So amongst men there are ridiculous elves,
Who monkeys hate for being too like themselves.
So that the reason of the grand debate
15 Why wit so oft is damned when good plays take,
Is that you censure as you love, or hate.
       Thus like a learned conclave poets sit,
Catholic° judges both of sense and wit,
And damn or save as they themselves think fit.
20 Yet those who to others' faults are so severe,
Are not so perfect but themselves may err.
Some write correct, indeed, but then the whole
(Bating° their own dull stuff i'th' play) is stole:
As bees do suck from flowers their honeydew,
25 So they rob others striving to please you.
       Some write their characters genteel and fine,

But then they do so toil for every line,
That what to you does easy seem, and plain,
Is the hard issue of their laboring brain.
And some th' effects of all their pains, we see,   30
Is but to mimic good extempore.°
Others, by long converse about the town,
Have wit enough to write a lewd lampoon,
But their chief skill lies in a bawdy song.
In short, the only wit that's now in fashion,   35
Is but the gleanings of good conversation.
As for the author of this coming play,
I asked him what he thought fit I should say
In thanks for your good company today:
He called me fool, and said it was well known   40
You came not here for our sakes, but your own.
New plays are stuffed with wits, and with deboches,°
That crowd and sweat like cits° in May-Day coaches.°

WRITTEN BY A PERSON OF QUALITY

ACT 1

Scene 1

(A Chamber. Enter FLORINDA *and* HELLENA.*)*

FLORINDA: What an impertinent thing is a young girl bred in a nunnery! How full of questions! Prithee no more, Hellena; I have told thee more than thou understand'st already.

---

bravos, villains, hired ruffians. **Rabel's drops,** a patent medicine. **cabal,** secret political faction. **Catholic,** widespread, therefore liberal. **Bating,** excepting.

extempore, an improvised performance. **deboches,** debauches, orgies. **cits,** citizens. **May-Day coaches,** carriages parading during a spring festival.

5 HELLENA: The more's my grief. I would fain know as much as you, which makes me so inquisitive; nor is't enough I know you're a lover, unless you tell me too who 'tis you sigh for.

FLORINDA: When you're a lover I'll think you fit for a
10 secret of that nature.

HELLENA: 'Tis true, I never was a lover yet, but I begin to have a shrewd guess what 'tis to be so, and fancy it very pretty to sigh, and sing, and blush, and wish, and dream and wish, and long and wish
15 to see the man, and when I do, look pale and tremble, just as you did when my brother brought home the fine English colonel to see you. What do you call him? Don Belvile?

FLORINDA: Fie,° Hellena.

20 HELLENA: That blush betrays you. I am sure 'tis so. Or is it Don Antonio the Viceroy's son? Or perhaps the rich old Don Vincentio, whom my father designs you for a husband? Why do you blush again?

FLORINDA: With indignation; and how near soever my
25 father thinks I am to marrying that hated object, I shall let him see I understand better what's due to my beauty, birth, and fortune, and more to my soul, than to obey those unjust commands.

HELLENA: Now hang me, if I don't love thee for that
30 dear disobedience. I love mischief strangely, as most of our sex do who are come to love nothing else. But tell me, dear Florinda, don't you love that fine *Anglese*?° For I vow, next to loving him myself, 'twill please me most that you do so, for he
35 is so gay and so handsome.

FLORINDA: Hellena, a maid designed for a nun ought not to be so curious in a discourse of love.

HELLENA: And dost thou think that ever I'll be a nun? Or at least till I'm so old I'm fit for nothing else?
40 Faith no, sister; and that which makes me long to know whether you love Belvile, is because I hope he has some mad companion or other that will spoil my devotion. Nay, I'm resolved to provide myself this Carnival,° if there be e'er a handsome
45 proper fellow of my humor above ground,° though I ask first.

FLORINDA: Prithee be not so wild.

HELLENA: Now you have provided yourself of a man you take no care of poor me. Prithee tell me, what
50 dost thou see about me that is unfit for love? Have I not a world of youth? A humor gay? A beauty passable? A vigor desirable? Well shaped? Clean limbed? Sweet breathed? And sense enough to know how all these ought to be employed to the
55 best advantage? Yes, I do and will; therefore lay aside your hopes of my fortune by my being a

devote,° and tell me how you came acquainted with this Belvile. For I perceive you knew him before he came to Naples.

FLORINDA: Yes, I knew him at the siege of Pamplona;   60
he was then a colonel of French horse,° who when the town was ransacked, nobly treated my brother and myself, preserving us from all insolences. And I must own, besides great obligations, I have I know not what that pleads kindly for him   65
about my heart, and will suffer no other to enter. But see, my brother.

(Enter DON PEDRO, STEPHANO *with a masking habit,°
and* CALLIS.)

PEDRO: Good morrow, sister. Pray when saw you your lover Don Vincentio?

FLORINDA: I know not, sir. Callis, when was he here?   70
For I consider it so little I know not when it was.

PEDRO: I have a command from my father here to tell you you ought not to despise him, a man of so vast a fortune, and such a passion for you.—
Stephano, my things.   75

(Puts on his masking habit.)

FLORINDA: A passion for me? 'Tis more than e'er I saw, or he had a desire should be known. I hate Vincentio, sir, and I would not have a man so dear to me as my brother follow the ill customs of our country and make a slave of his sister. And, sir, my   80
father's will I'm sure you may divert.

PEDRO: I know not how dear I am to you, but I wish only to be ranked in your esteem equal with the English colonel Belvile. Why do you frown and blush? Is there any guilt belongs to the name of   85
that cavalier?

FLORINDA: I'll not deny I value Belvile. When I was exposed to such dangers as the licensed lust of common soldiers threatened when rage and conquest flew through the city, then Belvile, this   90
criminal for my sake, threw himself into all dangers to save my honor. And will you not allow him my esteem?

PEDRO: Yes, pay him what you will in honor, but you must consider Don Vincentio's fortune, and the   95
jointure° he'll make you.

FLORINDA: Let him consider my youth, beauty, and fortune, which ought not to be thrown away on his age and jointure.

PEDRO: 'Tis true, he's not so young and fine a gentle-   100
man as that Belvile. But what jewels will that cavalier present you with? Those of his eyes and heart?

HELLENA: And are not those better than any Don Vincentio has brought from the Indies?

Fie, expression of disapproval. *Anglese,* Englishman, i.e., Belvile. *Carnival,* the week devoted to festivities and revelry before Lent.   *above ground,* alive.

devote, nun.   *horse,* cavalry.   *masking habit,* costume for taking part in the masquerades of Carnival.   *jointure,* estate settled on the wife in place of a dowry.

105 PEDRO: Why, how now! Has your nunnery breeding taught you to understand the value of hearts and eyes?

HELLENA: Better than to believe Vincentio's deserve value from any woman. He may perhaps increase
110 her bags,° but not her family.

PEDRO: This is fine! Go! Up to your devotion! You are not designed for the conversation of lovers.

HELLENA (aside): Nor saints yet a while, I hope.—Is't not enough you make a nun of me, but you must
115 cast my sister away too, exposing her to a worse confinement than a religious life?

PEDRO: The girl's mad! It is a confinement to be carried into the country to an ancient villa belonging to the family of the Vincentios these five hundred
120 years, and have no other prospect than that pleasing one of seeing all her own that meets her eyes: a fine air, large fields, and gardens where she may walk and gather flowers?

HELLENA: When, by moonlight? For I am sure she
125 dares not encounter with the heat of the sun; that were a task only for Don Vincentio and his Indian breeding, who loves it in the dog days.° And if these be her daily divertissements,° what are those of the night? To lie in a wide moth-eaten
130 bedchamber with furniture in fashion in the reign of King Sancho the First;° the bed, that which his forefathers lived and died in.

PEDRO: Very well.

HELLENA: This apartment, new furbrushed° and fit-
135 ted out for the young wife, he out of freedom makes his dressing room; and being a frugal and a jealous coxcomb,° instead of a valet to uncase° his feeble carcass, he desires you to do that office. Signs of favor, I'll assure you, and such as you
140 must not hope for unless your woman be out of the way.

PEDRO: Have you done yet?

HELLENA: That honor being past, the giant stretches itself, yawns and sighs a belch or two loud as a
145 musket, throws himself into bed, and expects you in his foul sheets; and ere you can get yourself undressed, calls you with a snore or two. And are not these fine blessings to a young lady?

PEDRO: Have you done yet?

150 HELLENA: And this man you must kiss, nay you must kiss none but him too, and nuzzle through his beard to find his lips. And this you must submit to for threescore years, and all for a jointure.

PEDRO: For all your character of Don Vincentio, she is
155 as like to marry him as she was before.

HELLENA: Marry Don Vincentio! Hang me, such a wedlock would be worse than adultery with another man. I had rather see her in the *Hostel de Dieu*,° to waste her youth there in vows, and be a
160 handmaid to lazars° and cripples, than to lose it in such a marriage.

PEDRO: You have considered, sister, that Belvile has no fortune to bring you to; banished his country,° despised at home, and pitied abroad.

HELLENA: What then? The Viceroy's son is better than
165 that old Sir Fifty. Don Vincentio! Don Indian! He thinks he's trading to Gambo° still, and would barter himself—that bell and bauble—for your youth and fortune.

PEDRO: Callis, take her hence and lock her up all this
170 Carnival, and at Lent she shall begin her everlasting penance in a monastery.

HELLENA: I care not; I had rather be a nun than be obliged to marry as you would have me if I were
175 designed for't.

PEDRO: Do not fear the blessing of that choice. You shall be a nun.

HELLENA (aside): Shall I so? You may chance to be mistaken in my way of devotion. A nun! Yes, I am like
180 to make a fine nun! I have an excellent humor for a grate!° No, I'll have a saint of my own to pray to shortly, if I like any that dares venture° on me.

PEDRO: Callis, make it your business to watch this wildcat.—As for you, Florinda, I've only tried you all
185 this while and urged my father's will; but mine is that you would love Antonio: He is brave and young, and all that can complete the happiness of a gallant maid. This absence of my father will give us opportunity to free you from Vincentio by mar-
190 rying here, which you must do tomorrow.

FLORINDA: Tomorrow!

PEDRO: Tomorrow, or 'twill be too late. 'Tis not my friendship to Antonio which makes me urge this, but love to thee and hatred to Vincentio; there-
195 fore resolve upon tomorrow.

FLORINDA: Sir, I shall strive to do as shall become your sister.

PEDRO: I'll both believe and trust you. Adieu.

(Exeunt PEDRO and STEPHANO.)

HELLENA: As becomes his sister! That is to be as
200 resolved your way as he is his.

---

bags, fortune. *dog days,* hot summer days. *divertissements,* entertainments. *King Sancho the First,* probably a medieval Spanish king, Sancho I of Castile (970–1035). *furbrushed,* i.e., furbished or refurbished. *coxcomb,* conceited fool. *uncase,* undress.

Hostel de Dieu, hospital or inn operated by a group of nuns. *lazars,* beggars, lepers. *banished his country,* banished from his country. *Gambo,* a British colony located in West Africa, now called Gambia. *I have an excellent humor for a grate,* I'd love to be locked in (sarcastic). *venture,* take a chance.

(HELLENA *goes to* CALLIS.)

FLORINDA: I ne'er till now perceived my ruin near.
  I've no defense against Antonio's love,
  For he has all the advantages of nature,
  The moving arguments of youth and fortune.

205 HELLENA: But hark you, Callis, you will not be so cruel
  to lock me up indeed, will you?

CALLIS: I must obey the commands I have. Besides, do
  you consider what a life you are going to lead?

HELLENA: Yes, Callis, that of a nun; and till then I'll be
210   indebted a world of prayers to you if you'll let me
  now see what I never did, the divertissements of a
  Carnival.

CALLIS: What, go in masquerade? 'Twill be a fine
  farewell to the world, I take it. Pray what would
215   you do there?

HELLENA: That which all the world does, as I am told:
  Be as mad as the rest and take all innocent free-
  doms. Sister, you'll go too, will you not? Come,
  prithee be not sad. We'll outwit twenty brothers if
220   you'll be ruled by me. Come, put off this dull
  humor with your clothes, and assume one as gay
  and as fantastic as the dress my cousin Valeria and
  I have provided, and let's ramble.°

FLORINDA: Callis, will you give us leave to go?

225 CALLIS (*aside*): I have a youthful itch of going myself.—Madam, if I thought your brother might
  not know it, and I might wait on you; for by my
  troth I'll not trust young girls alone.

FLORINDA: Thou seest my brother's gone already, and
230   thou shalt attend and watch us.

(*Enter* STEPHANO.)

STEPHANO: Madam, the habits° are come, and your
  cousin Valeria is dressed and stays for you.

FLORINDA (*aside*): 'Tis well. I'll write a note, and if I
  chance to see Belvile and want an opportunity to
235   speak to him, that shall let him know what I've
  resolved in favor of him.

HELLENA: Come, let's in and dress us. (*Exeunt.*)

Scene 2

(*A long street. Enter* BELVILE, *melancholy;* BLUNT *and*
FREDERICK.)

FREDERICK: Why, what the devil ails the colonel, in a
  time when all the world is gay to look like mere
  Lent thus?° Hadst thou been long enough in
  Naples to have been in love, I should have sworn
5   some such judgment had befallen thee.

BELVILE: No, I have made no new amours since I
  came to Naples.

FREDERICK: You have left none behind you in Paris?

BELVILE: Neither.

FREDERICK: I cannot divine the cause then, unless the 10
  old cause, the want of money.

BLUNT: And another old cause, the want of a wench.
  Would not that revive you?

BELVILE: You are mistaken, Ned.

BLUNT: Nay, 'adsheartlikins,° then thou'rt past cure. 15

FREDERICK: I have found it out: Thou hast renewed
  thy acquaintance with the lady that cost thee
  so many sighs at the siege of Pamplona—pox
  on't,° what d'ye call her—her brother's a noble
  Spaniard, nephew to the dead general. Florinda. 20
  Ay, Florinda. And will nothing serve thy turn but
  that damned virtuous woman, whom on my conscience thou lov'st in spite too, because thou seest
  little or no possibility of gaining her.

BELVILE: Thou art mistaken; I have int'rest enough in 25
  that lovely virgin's heart to make me proud and
  vain, were it not abated by the severity of a
  brother, who, perceiving my happiness—

FREDERICK: Has civilly forbid thee the house?

BELVILE: 'Tis so, to make way for a powerful rival, the 30
  Viceroy's son, who has the advantage of me in
  being a man of fortune, a Spaniard, and her
  brother's friend; which gives him liberty to make
  his court, whilst I have recourse only to letters
  and distant looks from her window, which are as 35
  soft and kind as those which heaven sends down
  on penitents.

BLUNT: Heyday! 'Adsheartlikins, simile! By this light
  the man is quite spoiled. Fred, what the devil are
  we made of that we cannot be thus concerned for 40
  a wench? 'Adsheartlikins, our Cupids are like the
  cooks of the camp: They can roast or boil a
  woman, but they have none of the fine tricks to
  set 'em off; no hogoes° to make the sauce pleasant and the stomach sharp. 45

FREDERICK: I dare swear I have had a hundred as
  young, kind, and handsome as this Florinda; and
  dogs eat me if they were not as troublesome to me
  i'th' morning as they were welcome o'er night.

BLUNT: And yet I warrant he would not touch another 50
  woman if he might have her for nothing.

BELVILE: That's thy joy, a cheap whore.

BLUNT: Why, 'adsheartlikins, I love a frank soul. When
  did you ever hear of an honest woman that took a
  man's money? I warrant 'em good ones. But gen- 55
  tlemen, you may be free; you have been kept so
  poor with parliaments and protectors that the
  little stock you have is not worth preserving. But I

---

ramble, stroll, walk around. **habits,** costumes. **to look
like mere Lent thus,** to look so solemn during a time of festivity.

    'adsheartlikins, an oath, literally God's heart likings,
slurred together. **pox on't,** an expression similar to "damn
it." **hogoes,** from *haut-goût,* high or strong flavoring.

60 thank my stars I had more grace than to forfeit my estate by cavaliering.

BELVILE: Methinks only following the court should be sufficient to entitle 'em to that.

BLUNT: 'Adsheartlikins, they know I follow it to do it no good, unless they pick a hole in my coat for lending you money now and then, which is a greater crime to my conscience, gentlemen, than to the commonwealth.

(Enter WILLMORE.*)*

WILLMORE: Ha! Dear Belvile! Noble colonel!

BELVILE: Willmore! Welcome ashore, my dear rover! What happy wind blew us this good fortune?

WILLMORE: Let me salute my dear Fred, and then command me.—How is't, honest lad?

FREDERICK: Fair, sir, the old compliment, infinitely the better to see my dear mad Willmore again. Prithee, why camest thou ashore? And where's the Prince?°

WILLMORE: He's well, and reigns still lord of the wat'ry element. I must aboard again within a day or two, and my business ashore was only to enjoy myself a little this Carnival.

BELVILE: Pray know our new friend, sir; he's but bashful, a raw traveler, but honest, stout, and one of us. *(Embraces* BLUNT.*)*

WILLMORE: That you esteem him gives him an int'rest here.

BLUNT: Your servant, sir.

WILLMORE: But well, faith, I'm glad to meet you again in a warm climate, where the kind sun has its god-like power still over the wine and women. Love and mirth are my business in Naples, and if I mistake not the place, here's an excellent market for chapmen° of my humor.

BELVILE: See, here be those kind merchants of love you look for.

(Enter several men in masking habits, some playing on music, others dancing after; women dressed like courtesans,° with papers pinned on their breasts, and baskets of flowers in their hands.)

BLUNT: 'Adsheartlikins, what have we here?

FREDERICK: Now the game begins.

WILLMORE: Fine pretty creatures! May a stranger have leave to look and love? What's here? "Roses for every month"? *(Reads the papers.)*

BLUNT: Roses for every month? What means that?

BELVILE: They are, or would have you think they're courtesans, who here in Naples are to be hired by the month.

WILLMORE: Kind and obliging to inform us, pray where do these roses grow? I would fain plant some of 'em in a bed of mine.

WOMAN: Beware such roses, sir.

WILLMORE: A pox of fear: I'll be baked with thee between a pair of sheets, and that's thy proper still; so I might but strew such roses over me and under me. Fair one, would you would give me leave to gather at your bush this idle month; I would go near to make somebody smell of it all the year after.

BELVILE: And thou hast need of such a remedy, for thou stink'st of tar and ropes' ends like a dock or pesthouse.°

(The Woman puts herself into the hands of a man and exeunt.)

WILLMORE: Nay, nay, you shall not leave me so.

BELVILE: By all means use no violence here.

WILLMORE: Death! just as I was going to be damnably in love, to have her led off! I could pluck that rose out of his hand, and even kiss the bed the bush grew in.

FREDERICK: No friend to love like a long voyage at sea.

BLUNT: Except a nunnery, Fred.

WILLMORE: Death! But will they not be kind? Quickly be kind? Thou know'st I'm no tame sigher, but a rampant lion of the forest.

(Advances from the farther end of the scenes two men dressed all over with horns° of several sorts, making grimaces at one another, with papers pinned on their backs.)

BELVILE: Oh the fantastical rogues, how they're dressed! 'Tis a satire against the whole sex.

WILLMORE: Is this a fruit that grows in this warm country?

BELVILE: Yes, 'tis pretty to see these Italians start, swell, and stab at the word cuckold, and yet stumble at horns on every threshold.

WILLMORE: See what's on their back. *(Reads.)* "Flowers of every night." Ah, rogue! And more sweet than roses of every month! This is a gardener of Adam's own breeding.

(They dance.)

BELVILE: What think you of these grave people? Is a wake in Essex half so mad or extravagant?

WILLMORE: I like their sober grave way; 'tis a kind of legal authorized fornication, where the men are

---

Prince, During England's Civil War, Charles II (1630–85) was forced into exile after his forces were defeated in Worcester (1651). In 1660 he was summoned back as king. **chapmen,** merchants or traders. **courtesans,** harlots, prostitutes.

---

pesthouse, a shelter or hospital for those infected with a contagious disease. **horns,** indicative of a man whose wife has been unfaithful and has therefore made a fool of him.

145 not chid° for't, nor the women despised, as amongst our dull English. Even the monsieurs° want that part of good manners.

BELVILE: But here in Italy, a monsieur is the humblest best-bred gentleman: Duels are so baffled by bravos that an age shows not one but between a
150 Frenchman and a hangman, who is as much too hard for him on the Piazza as they are for a Dutchman on the New Bridge. But see, another crew.

(Enter FLORINDA, HELLENA, and VALERIA, dressed like gypsies; CALLIS and STEPHANO, LUCETTA, PHILIPPO, and SANCHO in masquerade.)

HELLENA: Sister, there's your Englishman, and with
155 him a handsome proper fellow. I'll to him, and instead of telling him his fortune, try my own.

WILLMORE: Gypsies, on my life. Sure these will prattle if a man cross their hands.° *(Goes to HELLENA.)*— Dear, pretty, and, I hope, young devil, will you tell
160 an amorous stranger what luck he's like to have?

HELLENA: Have a care how you venture with me, sir, lest I pick your pocket, which will more vex your English humor than an Italian fortune will please you.

165 WILLMORE: How the devil cam'st thou to know my country and humor?

HELLENA: The first I guess by a certain forward impudence, which does not displease me at this time; and the loss of your money will vex you because I
170 hope you have but very little to lose.

WILLMORE: Egad, child, thou'rt i'th' right; it is so little I dare not offer it thee for a kindness. But cannot you divine what other things of more value I have about me that I would more willingly part with?

175 HELLENA: Indeed no, that's the business of a witch, and I am but a gypsy yet. Yet without looking in your hand, I have a parlous° guess 'tis some foolish heart you mean, an inconstant English heart, as little worth stealing as your purse.

180 WILLMORE: Nay, then thou dost deal with the devil, that's certain. Thou hast guessed as right as if thou hadst been one of that number it has languished for. I find you'll be better acquainted with it, nor can you take it in a better time; for I
185 am come from sea, child, and Venus not being propitious to me in her own element,° I have a world of love in store. Would you would be good-natured and take some on't° off my hands.

HELLENA: Why, I could be inclined that way, but for a foolish vow I am going to make to die a maid. 190

WILLMORE: Then thou art damned without redemption, and as I am a good Christian, I ought in charity to divert so wicked a design. Therefore prithee, dear creature, let me know quickly when and where I shall begin to set a helping hand to 195 so good a work.

HELLENA: If you should prevail with my tender heart, as I begin to fear you will, for you have horrible loving eyes, there will be difficulty in't that you'll hardly undergo for my sake. 200

WILLMORE: Faith, child, I have been bred in dangers, and wear a sword that has been employed in a worse cause than for a handsome kind woman. Name the danger; let it be anything but a long siege, and I'll undertake it. 205

HELLENA: Can you storm?

WILLMORE: Oh, most furiously.

HELLENA: What think you of a nunnery wall? For he that wins me must gain that first.

WILLMORE: A nun! Oh, now I love thee for't! There's 210 no sinner like a young saint. Nay, now there's no denying me; the old law had no curse to a woman like dying a maid: Witness Jeptha's daughter.°

HELLENA: A very good text this, if well handled; and I perceive, Father Captain, you would impose no 215 severe penance on her who were inclined to console herself before she took orders.°

WILLMORE: If she be young and handsome.

HELLENA: Ay, there's it. But if she be not—

WILLMORE: By this hand, child, I have an implicit 220 faith, and dare venture on thee with all faults. Besides, 'tis more meritorious to leave the world when thou hast tasted and proved the pleasure on't. Then 'twill be a virtue in thee, which now will be pure ignorance. 225

HELLENA: I perceive, good Father Captain, you design only to make me fit for heaven. But if, on the contrary, you should quite divert me from it, and bring me back to the world again, I should have a new man to seek, I find. And what a grief that will 230 be; for when I begin, I fancy I shall love like anything; I never tried yet.

WILLMORE: Egad, and that's kind! Prithee, dear creature, give me credit for a heart, for faith, I'm a very honest fellow. Oh, I long to come first to the 235 banquet of love! And such a swinging appetite I

---

chid, chided, scolded. **monsieurs,** literally gentlemen, here French gentlemen. **cross their hands,** i.e., with silver, pay for fortune-telling. **parlous,** from perilous, but here dangerously clever. **element,** Venus was born from sea foam. **on't,** contracted form "of it."

Jeptha's daughter, In exchange for victory over the Ammonites, Jeptha vowed to sacrifice the first person he saw upon returning home. His daughter and only child was the first person he met. He allowed her two months to "lament her virginity on the mountains," after which time Jeptha fulfilled his vow (Judges, 11:38–40). *took orders,* religious orders, i.e., became a nun.

bring. Oh, I'm impatient. Thy lodging, sweetheart, thy lodging, or I'm a dead man!

HELLENA: Why must we be either guilty of fornication
240   or murder if we converse with you men? And is there no difference between leave to love me, and leave to lie with me?

WILLMORE: Faith, child, they were made to go together.

LUCETTA (*pointing to* BLUNT): Are you sure this is the
245   man?

SANCHO: When did I mistake your game?

LUCETTA: This is a stranger, I know by his gazing; if he be brisk he'll venture to follow me, and then, if I understand my trade, he's mine. He's English,
250   too, and they say that's a sort of good-natured loving people, and have generally so kind an opinion of themselves that a woman with any wit may flatter 'em into any sort of fool she pleases.

(She often passes by BLUNT *and gazes on him; he struts and cocks, and walks and gazes on her.)*

BLUNT: 'Tis so, she is taken; I have beauties which my
255   false glass° at home did not discover.

FLORINDA (*aside*): This woman watches me so, I shall get no opportunity to discover myself to him, and so miss the intent of my coming.— [*To* BELVILE.] But as I was saying, sir, by this line you should be a
260   lover. (*Looking in his hand.*)

BELVILE: I thought how right you guessed: All men are in love, or pretend to be so. Come, let me go; I'm weary of this fooling. (*Walks away.*)

FLORINDA: I will not, sir, till you have confessed
265   whether the passion that you have vowed Florinda be true or false.

(She holds him; he strives to get from her.)

BELVILE: Florinda! (*Turns quick toward her.*)

FLORINDA: Softly.

BELVILE: Thou hast nam'd one will fix me here forever.

270 FLORINDA: She'll be disappointed then, who expects you this night at the garden gate. And if you fail not, as—(*Looks on* CALLIS, *who observes 'em.*) Let me see the other hand—you will go near to do, she vows to die or make you happy.

275 BELVILE: What canst thou mean?

FLORINDA: That which I say. Farewell.

(Offers to go.)

BELVILE: O charming sibyl,° stay; complete that joy which as it is will turn into distraction! Where must I be? At the garden gate? I know it. At night,
280   you say? I'll sooner forfeit heaven than disobey.

(Enter DON PEDRO *and other maskers, and pass over the stage.)*

CALLIS: Madam, your brother's here.

---

glass, mirror.   **sibyl,** prophetess, here a fortune-teller.

FLORINDA: Take this to instruct you farther.

(Gives him a letter, and goes off.)

FREDERICK: Have a care, sir, what you promise; this may be a trap laid by her brother to ruin you.

BELVILE: Do not disturb my happiness with doubts. 285

(Opens the letter.)

WILLMORE: My dear pretty creature, a thousand blessings on thee! Still in this habit, you say? And after dinner at this place?

HELLENA: Yes, if you will swear to keep your heart and not bestow it between this and that. 290

WILLMORE: By all the little gods of love, I swear; I'll leave it with you, and if you run away with it, those deities of justice will revenge me.

(Exeunt all the women [except LUCETTA].)*

FREDERICK: Do you know the hand?

BELVILE: 'Tis Florinda's. 295
   All blessings fall upon the virtuous maid.

FREDERICK: Nay, no idolatry; a sober sacrifice I'll allow you.

BELVILE: Oh friends, the welcom'st news! The softest letter! Nay, you shall all see it. And could you now 300 be serious, I might be made the happiest man the sun shines on!

WILLMORE: The reason of this mighty joy?

BELVILE: See how kindly she invites me to deliver her from the threatened violence of her brother. Will 305 you not assist me?

WILLMORE: I know not what thou mean'st, but I'll make one at any mischief where a woman's concerned. But she'll be grateful to us for the favor, will she not? 310

BELVILE: How mean you?

WILLMORE: How should I mean? Thou know'st there's but one way for a woman to oblige me.

BELVILE: Do not profane; the maid is nicely virtuous.

WILLMORE: Who, pox, then she's fit for nothing but a 315 husband. Let her e'en go, colonel.

FREDERICK: Peace, she's the colonel's mistress, sir.

WILLMORE: Let her be the devil; if she be thy mistress, I'll serve her. Name the way.

BELVILE: Read here this postscript. 320

(Gives him a letter.)

WILLMORE (*reads*): "At ten at night, at the garden gate, of which, if I cannot get the key, I will contrive a way over the wall. Come attended with a friend or two."—Kind heart, if we three cannot weave a string to let her down a garden wall, 'twere pity 325 but the hangman wove one for us all.

FREDERICK: Let her alone for that; your woman's wit, your fair kind woman, will outtrick a broker or a

Jew, and contrive like a Jesuit in chains.° But see,
330 Ned Blunt is stolen out after the lure of a damsel.

(*Exeunt* BLUNT *and* LUCETTA.)

BELVILE: So, he'll scarce find his way home again
unless we get him cried by the bellman in the
market place. And 'twould sound prettily: "A lost
English boy of thirty."
335 FREDERICK: I hope 'tis some common crafty sinner,
one that will fit him. It may be she'll sell him for
Peru:° The rogue's sturdy, and would work well in
a mine. At least I hope she'll dress him for our
mirth, cheat him of all, then have him well-
340 favoredly banged, and turned out at midnight.
WILLMORE: Prithee what humor is he of, that you wish
him so well?
BELVILE: Why, of an English elder brother's humor:
educated in a nursery, with a maid to tend him till
345 fifteen, and lies with his grandmother till he's of
age; one that knows no pleasure beyond riding to
the next fair, or going up to London with his right
worshipful father in parliament time, wearing gay
clothes, or making honorable love to his lady
350 mother's laundry maid; gets drunk at a hunting
match, and ten to one then gives some proofs of
his prowess. A pox upon him, he's our banker,
and has all our cash about him; and if he fail, we
are all broke.
355 FREDERICK: Oh, let him alone for that matter; he's of
a damned stingy quality that will secure our stock.
I know not in what danger it were indeed if the jilt
should pretend she's in love with him, for 'tis a
kind believing coxcomb; otherwise, if he part
360 with more than a piece of eight,° geld° him—for
which offer he may chance to be beaten if she be
a whore of the first rank.
BELVILE: Nay, the rogue will not be easily beaten; he's
stout enough. Perhaps if they talk beyond his
365 capacity he may chance to exercise his courage
upon some of them, else I'm sure they'll find it as
difficult to beat as to please him.
WILLMORE: 'Tis a lucky devil to light upon so kind a
wench!
370 FREDERICK: Thou hadst a great deal of talk with thy
little gypsy; couldst thou do no good upon her?
For mine was hardhearted.
WILLMORE: Hang her, she was some damned honest
person of quality, I'm sure, she was so very free
375 and witty. If her face be but answerable to her wit
and humor, I would be bound to constancy this

month to gain her. In the meantime, have you
made no kind acquaintance since you came to
town? You do not use to be honest° so long, gentlemen. 380
FREDERICK: Faith, love has kept us honest: We have
been all fir'd with a beauty newly come to town,
the famous Paduana° Angellica Bianca.
WILLMORE: What, the mistress of the dead Spanish
general? 385
BELVILE: Yes, she's now the only ador'd beauty of all
the youth in Naples, who put on all their charms
to appear lovely in her sight: Their coaches, liveries, and themselves all gay as on a monarch's
birthday to attract the eyes of this fair charmer, 390
while she has the pleasure to behold all languish
for her that see her.
FREDERICK: 'Tis pretty to see with how much love the
men regard her, and how much envy the women.
WILLMORE: What gallant has she? 395
BELVILE: None; she's exposed to sale, and four days in
the week she's yours, for so much a month.
WILLMORE: The very thought of it quenches all manner of fire in me. Yet prithee, let's see her.
BELVILE: Let's first to dinner, and after that we'll pass 400
the day as you please. But at night ye must all be
at my devotion.
WILLMORE: I will not fail you. [*Exeunt.*]

ACT 2

Scene 1

(*The long street. Enter* BELVILE *and* FREDERICK *in masking habits, and* WILLMORE *in his own clothes, with a
vizard*° *in his hand.*)

WILLMORE: But why thus disguised and muzzled?
BELVILE: Because whatever extravagances we commit
in these faces, our own may not be obliged to
answer 'em.
WILLMORE: I should have changed my eternal buff,° 5
too; but no matter, my little gypsy would not have
found me out then. For if she should change
hers, it is impossible I should know her unless I
should hear her prattle. A pox on't, I cannot get
her out of my head. Pray heaven, if ever I do see 10
her again, she prove damnably ugly, that I may
fortify myself against her tongue.
BELVILE: Have a care of love, for o' my conscience she
was not of a quality to give thee any hopes.
WILLMORE: Pox on 'em, why do they draw a man in 15
then? She has played with my heart so, that 'twill
never lie still till I have met with some kind wench

---

outtrick a broker . . . in chains, all three men (the financial dealer, the Jew, and the Jesuit) were proverbial examples
of shrewdness and dishonesty. *sell him for Peru,* sell him into
slavery; Peru was known for its mines manned by slaves.
piece of eight, Spanish dollar, or peso, that was marked with
the figure 8. *geld,* castrate.

You do not use to be honest so long, you do not usually
remain sexually inactive for so long. *Paduana,* woman born
in Padua. *vizard,* mask. *eternal buff,* customary leather
(buff) coat.

that will play the game out with me. Oh, for my arms full of soft, white, kind woman—such as I
20 fancy Angellica.

BELVILE: This is her house, if you were but in stock to get admittance. They have not dined yet; I perceive the picture is not out.°

(Enter BLUNT.)

WILLMORE: I long to see the shadow of the fair sub-
25 stance; a man may gaze on that for nothing.

BLUNT: Colonel, thy hand. And thine, Fred. I have been an ass, a deluded fool, a very coxcomb from my birth till this hour, and heartily repent my little faith.

30 BELVILE: What the devil's the matter with thee, Ned?

BLUNT: Oh, such a mistress, Fred! Such a girl!

WILLMORE: Ha! Where?

FREDERICK: Ay, where?

BLUNT: So fond, so amorous, so toying, and so fine!
35 And all for sheer love, ye rogue! Oh, how she looked and kissed! And soothed my heart from my bosom! I cannot think I was awake, and yet methinks I see and feel her charms still. Fred, try if she have not left the taste of her balmy kisses
40 upon my lips. *(Kisses him.)*

BELVILE: Ha! Ha! Ha!

WILLMORE: Death, man, where is she?

BLUNT: What a dog was I to stay in dull England so long! How have I laughed at the colonel when he
45 sighed for love! But now the little archer° has revenged him! And by this one dart I can guess at all his joys, which then I took for fancies, mere dreams and fables. Well, I'm resolved to sell all in Essex and plant here forever.

50 BELVILE: What a blessing 'tis, thou hast a mistress thou dar'st boast of; for I know thy humor is rather to have a proclaimed clap than a secret amour.°

WILLMORE: Dost know her name?

BLUNT: Her name? No, 'adsheartlikins. What care I
55 for names? She's fair, young, brisk and kind, even to ravishment! And what a pox care I for knowing her by any other title?

WILLMORE: Didst give her anything?

BLUNT: Give her? Ha! Ha! Ha! Why, she's a person of
60 quality. That's a good one! Give her? 'Adsheartlikins, dost think such creatures are to be bought? Or are we provided for such a purchase? Give her, quoth ye? Why, she presented me with this bracelet for the toy of a diamond I used to wear.
65 No, gentlemen, Ned Blunt is not everybody. She expects me again tonight.

WILLMORE: Egad, that's well; we'll all go.

BLUNT: Not a soul! No, gentlemen, you are wits; I am a dull country rogue, I.

FREDERICK: Well, sir, for all your person of quality, I 70 shall be very glad to understand your purse be secure; 'tis our whole estate at present, which we are loath to hazard in one bottom.° Come sir, unlade.°

BLUNT: Take the necessary trifle useless now to me, 75 that am beloved by such a gentlewoman. 'Adsheartlikins, money! Here, take mine too.

FREDERICK: No, keep that to be cozened,° that we may laugh.

WILLMORE: Cozened? Death! Would I could meet 80 with one that would cozen me of all the love I could spare tonight.

FREDERICK: Pox, 'tis some common whore, upon my life.

BLUNT: A whore? Yes, with such clothes, such jewels, 85 such a house, such furniture, and so attended! A whore!

BELVILE: Why yes, sir, they are whores, though they'll neither entertain you with drinking, swearing, or bawdry; are whores in all those gay clothes and 90 right° jewels; are whores with those great houses richly furnished with velvet beds, store of plate,° handsome attendance, and fine coaches; are whores, and errant ones.

WILLMORE: Pox on't, where do these fine whores live? 95

BELVILE: Where no rogues in office, ycleped° constables, dare give 'em laws, nor the wine-inspired bullies of the town break their windows; yet they are whores though this Essex calf° believe 'em persons of quality. 100

BLUNT: 'Adsheartlikins, y'are all fools. There are things about this Essex calf that shall take with the ladies, beyond all your wit and parts. This shape and size, gentlemen, are not to be despised; my waist, too, tolerably long, with other inviting signs 105 that shall be nameless.

WILLMORE: Egad, I believe he may have met with some person of quality that may be kind to him.

BELVILE: Dost thou perceive any such tempting things about him that should make a fine woman, and of 110 quality, pick him out from all mankind to throw away her youth and beauty upon; nay, and her dear heart, too? No, no, Angellica has raised the price too high.

WILLMORE: May she languish for mankind till she die, 115 and be damned for that one sin alone.

---

picture is not out, the courtesan would hang her picture outside when she was ready for business. *little archer,* Cupid. *a proclaimed clap than a secret amour,* a venereal disease rather than a secret lover. Belvile claims that Blunt is likely to be sexually promiscuous.

which we are loath to hazard in one bottom, which we hate to risk keeping in one place, here the bottom of a ship. *unlade,* unload (a ship). *cozened,* cheated. *right,* real. *plate,* objects made of silver. *ycleped,* called. *calf,* fool, simpleton.

(*Enter two Bravos and hang up a great picture of* ANGEL-LICA's *against the balcony, and two little ones at each side of the door.*)

BELVILE: See there the fair sign to the inn where a man may lodge that's fool enough to give her price.

(WILLMORE *gazes on the picture.*)

120 BLUNT: 'Adsheartlikins, gentlemen, what's this?

BELVILE: A famous courtesan, that's to be sold.

BLUNT: How? To be sold? Nay, then I have nothing to say to her. Sold? What impudence is practiced in this country; with what order and decency whor-
125 ing's established here by virtue of the Inquisi-tion!° Come, let's be gone; I'm sure we're no chapmen for this commodity.

FREDERICK: Thou art none, I'm sure, unless thou couldst have her in thy bed at a price of a coach in the street.

130 WILLMORE: How wondrous fair she is! A thousand crowns a month? By heaven, as many kingdoms were too little! A plague of this poverty, of which I ne'er complain but when it hinders my ap-proach to beauty which virtue ne'er could
135 purchase.

(*Turns from the picture.*)

BLUNT: What's this? (*Reads.*) "A thousand crowns a month"! 'Adsheartlikins, here's a sum! Sure 'tis a mistake.—[*To one of the Bravos.*] Hark you, friend, does she take or give so much by the month?

140 FREDERICK: A thousand crowns! Why, 'tis a portion for the Infanta!°

BLUNT: Hark ye, friends, won't she trust?

BRAVO: This is a trade, sir, that cannot live by credit.

(*Enter* DON PEDRO *in masquerade, followed by* STE-PHANO.)

BELVILE: See, here's more company; let's walk off a
145 while.

(*Exeunt* ENGLISH;° PEDRO *reads.*)

PEDRO: Fetch me a thousand crowns; I never wished to buy this beauty at an easier rate. (*Passes off.*)

(*Enter* ANGELLICA *and* MORETTA *in the balcony, and draw a silk curtain.*)

ANGELLICA: Prithee, what said those fellows to thee?

BRAVO: Madam, the first were admirers of beauty only,

---

but no purchasers; they were merry with your
150 price and picture, laughed at the sum, and so passed off.

ANGELLICA: No matter, I'm not displeased with their rallying; their wonder feeds my vanity, and he that wishes but to buy gives me more pride than he
155 that gives my price can make my pleasure.

BRAVO: Madam, the last I knew through all his dis-guises to be Don Pedro, nephew to the general, and who was with him in Pamplona.

ANGELLICA: Don Pedro? My old gallant's nephew?
160 When his uncle died he left him a vast sum of money; it is he who was so in love with me at Padua, and who used to make the general so jeal-ous.

MORETTA: Is this he that used to prance before our
165 window, and take such care to show himself an amorous ass? If I am not mistaken, he is the likeli-est man to give your price.

ANGELLICA: The man is brave and generous, but of a humor so uneasy and inconstant that the victory
170 over his heart is as soon lost as won; a slave that can add little to the triumph of the conqueror. But inconstancy's the sin of all mankind, there-fore I'm resolved that nothing but gold shall charm my heart.
175

MORETTA: I'm glad on't; 'tis only interest that women of our profession ought to consider, though I wonder what has kept you from that general dis-ease of our sex so long; I mean, that of being in love.
180

ANGELLICA: A kind but sullen star under which I had the happiness to be born. Yet I have had no time for love; the bravest and noblest of mankind have purchased my favors at so dear a rate, as if no coin but gold were current with our trade. But here's
185 Don Pedro again; fetch me my lute, for 'tis for him or Don Antonio the Viceroy's son that I have spread my nets.

(*Enter at one door* DON PEDRO, STEPHANO; DON ANTO-NIO *and* DIEGO [*his page*] *at the other door, with people following him in masquerade, antically attired, some with music. They both go up to the picture.*)

ANTONIO: A thousand crowns! Had not the painter flattered her, I should not think it dear.
190

PEDRO: Flattered her? By heaven, he cannot. I have seen the original, nor is there one charm here more than adorns her face and eyes; all this soft and sweet, with a certain languishing air that no artist can represent.
195

ANTONIO: What I heard of her beauty before had fired my soul, but this confirmation of it has blown it to a flame.

PEDRO: Ha!

PAGE: Sir, I have known you throw away a thousand
200 crowns on a worse face, and though y'are near

Inquisition, The Spanish Inquisition (1478–1834), origi-nally a tribunal to suppress heresy, became an instrument for state censorship and repression; in addition to persecuting Jews and Moors, the Inquisition forced prostitutes to flee Spain and take refuge in the surrounding countries. *Infanta,* Spanish princess. *English,* English characters.

your marriage, you may venture a little love here;
Florinda will not miss it.

PEDRO (*aside*): Ha! Florinda! Sure 'tis Antonio.

205 ANTONIO: Florinda! Name not those distant joys;
there's not one thought of her will check my passion here.

PEDRO [*aside*]: Florinda scorned! (*A noise of a lute
above.*) And all my hopes defeated of the possession

210 of Angellica! (ANTONIO *gazes up.*) Her injuries, by
heaven, he shall not boast of!

(*Song to a lute above.*)

SONG

I

When Damon first began to love
He languished in a soft desire,
And knew not how the gods to move,
215 *To lessen or increase his fire.*
For Caelia in her charming eyes
Wore all love's sweets, and all his cruelties.

II

But as beneath a shade he lay,
Weaving of flowers for Caelia's hair,
220 *She chanced to lead her flock that way,*
And saw the am'rous shepherd there.
She gazed around upon the place,
And saw the grove, resembling night,
To all the joys of love invite,
225 *Whilst guilty smiles and blushes dressed her face.*
At this the bashful youth all transport grew,
And with kind force he taught the virgin how
To yield what all his sighs could never do.

(ANGELLICA *throws open the curtains and bows to*
ANTONIO, *who pulls off his vizard and bows and blows*
up kisses. PEDRO, *unseen, looks in's face.* [*The curtains*
close.])

ANTONIO: By heaven, she's charming fair!
230 PEDRO (*aside*): 'Tis he, the false Antonio!
ANTONIO (*to the Bravo*): Friend, where must I pay my
off'ring of love?
My thousand crowns I mean.

PEDRO: That off'ring I have designed to make,
And yours will come too late.

235 ANTONIO: Prithee begone; I shall grow angry else,
And then thou art not safe.

PEDRO: My anger may be fatal, sir, as yours,
And he that enters here may prove this truth.

ANTONIO: I know not who thou art, but I am sure
240 thou'rt worth my killing, for aiming at Angellica.

(*They draw and fight.*)
(*Enter* WILLMORE *and* BLUNT, *who draw and part 'em.*)

BLUNT: 'Adsheartlikins, here's fine doings.

WILLMORE: Tilting° for the wench, I'm sure. Nay, gad,
if that would win her I have as good a sword as the
best of ye. Put up, put up, and take another time
and place, for this is designed for lovers only. 245
(*They all put up.*)

PEDRO: We are prevented; dare you meet me tomorrow on the Molo?°
For I've a title to a better quarrel,
That of Florinda, in whose credulous heart
Thou'st made an int'rest, and destroyed my hopes.

ANTONIO: Dare! 250
I'll meet thee there as early as the day.

PEDRO: We will come thus disguised, that whosoever
chance to get the better, he may escape unknown.

ANTONIO: It shall be so.

(*Exeunt* PEDRO *and* STEPHANO.)

—Who should this rival be? Unless the English 255
colonel, of whom I've often heard Don Pedro
speak. It must be he, and time he were removed
who lays a claim to all my happiness.

(WILLMORE, *having gazed all this while on the picture*[*s*],
pulls down a little one.)

WILLMORE: This posture's loose and negligent;
The sight on't would beget a warm desire 260
In souls whom impotence and age had chilled.
This must along with me.

BRAVO: What means this rudeness, sir? Restore the
picture.

ANTONIO: Ha! Rudeness committed to the fair Angel- 265
lica!—Restore the picture, sir.

WILLMORE: Indeed I will not, sir.

ANTONIO: By heaven, but you shall.

WILLMORE: Nay, do not show your sword; if you do, by
this dear beauty, I will show mine too. 270

ANTONIO: What right can you pretend to't?

WILLMORE: That of possession, which I will maintain.
You, perhaps, have a thousand crowns to give for
the original.

ANTONIO: No matter, sir, you shall restore the picture. 275

([*The curtains open.*] ANGELLICA *and* MORETTA
above.)

ANGELLICA: Oh, Moretta, what's the matter?

ANTONIO: Or leave your life behind.

WILLMORE: Death! You lie; I will do neither.

(*They fight. The Spaniards join with* ANTONIO, BLUNT
laying on like mad.)

ANGELLICA: Hold, I command you, if for me you fight.

(*They leave off and bow.*)

Tilting, fighting.   *Molo*, pier, waterfront.

WILLMORE [*aside*]: How heavenly fair she is! Ah, plague of her price! 280

ANGELLICA: You sir, in buff, you that appear a soldier, that first began this insolence—

WILLMORE: 'Tis true, I did so, if you call it insolence 285 for a man to preserve himself. I saw your charming picture and was wounded; quite through my soul each pointed beauty ran; and wanting a thousand crowns to procure my remedy, I laid this little picture to my bosom, which, if you can- 290 not allow me, I'll resign.

ANGELLICA: No, you may keep the trifle.

ANTONIO: You shall first ask me leave, and this.

(Fight again as before.)

(Enter BELVILE *and* FREDERICK, *who join with the English.)*

ANGELLICA: Hold! Will you ruin me?—Biskey! Sebastian! Part 'em!

(The Spaniards are beaten off.)

MORETTA: Oh, madam, we're undone. A pox upon 295 that rude fellow; he's set on to ruin us. We shall never see good days again till all these fighting poor rogues are sent to the galleys.

(Enter BELVILE, BLUNT, FREDERICK, *and* WILLMORE *with's shirt bloody.)*

BLUNT: 'Adsheartlikins, beat me at this sport and I'll ne'er wear sword more. 300

BELVILE *(to* WILLMORE*)*: The devil's in thee for a mad fellow; thou art always one at an unlucky adventure. Come, let's be gone whilst we're safe, and remember these are Spaniards, a sort of people 305 that know how to revenge an affront.

FREDERICK: You bleed! I hope you are not wounded.

WILLMORE: Not much. A plague on your dons;° if they fight no better they'll ne'er recover Flanders.° What the devil was't to them that I took down the 310 picture?

BLUNT: Took it! 'Adsheartlikins, we'll have the great one too; 'tis ours by conquest. Prithee help me up and I'll pull it down.

ANGELLICA [*to* WILLMORE]: Stay, sir, and ere you af- 315 front me farther let me know how you durst commit this outrage. To you I speak, sir, for you appear a gentleman.

WILLMORE: To me, madam?—Gentlemen, your servant.

*(*BELVILE *stays him.°)*

BELVILE: Is the devil in thee? Dost know the danger of 320 ent'ring the house of an incensed courtesan?

WILLMORE: I thank you for your care, but there are other matters in hand, there are, though we have no great temptation. Death! Let me go!

FREDERICK: Yes, to your lodging if you will, but not in 325 here. Damn these gay harlots; by this hand I'll have as sound and handsome a whore for a patacoon.° Death, man, she'll murder thee!

WILLMORE: Oh, fear me not. Shall I not venture where a beauty calls? A lovely charming beauty! For fear 330 of danger? When, by heaven, there's none so great as to long for her whilst I want money to purchase her.

FREDERICK: Therefore 'tis loss of time unless you had the thousand crowns to pay. 335

WILLMORE: It may be she may give a favor; at least I shall have the pleasure of saluting her when I enter and when I depart.

BELVILE: Pox, she'll as soon lie with thee as kiss thee, and sooner stab than do either. You shall not go. 340

ANGELLICA: Fear not, sir, all I have to wound with is my eyes.

BLUNT: Let him go. 'Adsheartlikins, I believe the gentlewoman means well.

BELVILE: Well, take thy fortune; we'll expect you in 345 the next street. Farewell, fool, farewell.

WILLMORE: 'Bye, colonel. *(Goes in.)*

FREDERICK: The rogue's stark mad for a wench.

(Exeunt.)

Scene 2

(A fine chamber. Enter WILLMORE, ANGELLICA, *and* MORETTA.*)*

ANGELLICA: Insolent sir, how durst you pull down my picture?

WILLMORE: Rather, how durst you set it up to tempt poor am'rous mortals with so much excellence, which I find you have but too well consulted by 5 the unmerciful price you set upon't. Is all this heaven of beauty shown to move despair in those that cannot buy? And can you think th'effects of that despair should be less extravagant than I have shown? 10

ANGELLICA: I sent for you to ask my pardon, sir, not to aggravate your crime. I thought I should have seen you at my feet imploring it.

WILLMORE: You are deceived. I came to rail at you, and rail such truths too, as shall let you see the 15 vanity of that pride which taught you how to set such price on sin.

___
dons, Spanish gentlemen. *ne'er recover Flanders,* a region in Belgium, given by Spain to France as part of an agreement to end a war. *stays him,* detains him.

___
patacoon, Portuguese or Spanish silver coins of small denomination.

For such it is whilst that which is love's due
Is meanly bartered for.

20 ANGELLICA: Ha! Ha! Ha! Alas, good captain, what pity
'tis your edifying doctrine will do no good upon
me. Moretta, fetch the gentleman a glass, and let
him survey himself to see what charms he has.—
(Aside, in a soft tone.) And guess my business.

25 MORETTA: He knows himself of old: I believe those
breeches and he have been acquainted ever since
he was beaten at Worcester.°

ANGELLICA: Nay, do not abuse the poor creature.

MORETTA: Good weather-beaten corporal, will you
30 march off? We have no need of your doctrine,
though you have of our charity. But at present we
have no scraps; we can afford no kindness for
God's sake. In fine, sirrah, the price is too high
i'th' mouth° for you, therefore troop,° I say.

35 WILLMORE: Here, good forewoman of the shop, serve
me and I'll be gone.

MORETTA: Keep it to pay your laundress; your linen
stinks of the gun room. For here's no selling by
retail.

40 WILLMORE: Thou hast sold plenty of thy stale ware at a
cheap rate.

MORETTA: Ay, the more silly kind heart I, but this is an
age wherein beauty is at higher rates. In fine, you
know the price of this.

45 WILLMORE: I grant you 'tis here set down, a thousand
crowns a month. Pray, how much may come to
my share for a pistole?° Bawd, take your black
lead° and sum it up, that I may have a pistole's
worth of this vain gay thing, and I'll trouble you
50 no more.

MORETTA: Pox on him, he'll fret me to death! Abominable fellow, I tell thee we only sell by the whole
piece.

WILLMORE: 'Tis very hard, the whole cargo or noth-
55 ing. Faith, madam, my stock will not reach it; I
cannot be your chapman. Yet I have countrymen
in town, merchants of love like me; I'll see if
they'll put in for a share. We cannot lose much by
it, and what we have no use for, we'll sell upon the
60 Friday's mart at "Who gives more?"—I am studying, madam, how to purchase you, though at
present I am unprovided of money.

ANGELLICA *(aside)*: Sure this from any other man
would anger me; nor shall he know the conquest
65 he has made.—Poor angry man, how I despise
this railing.

WILLMORE: Yes, I am poor. But I'm a gentleman,

And one that scorns this baseness which you
practice.
Poor as I am I would not sell myself,
No, not to gain your charming high-prized person. 70
Though I admire you strangely for your beauty,
Yet I contemn° your mind.
And yet I would at any rate enjoy you;
At your own rate; but cannot. See here
The only sum I can command on earth: 75
I know not where to eat when this is gone.
Yet such a slave I am to love and beauty
This last reserve I'll sacrifice to enjoy you.
Nay, do not frown, I know you're to be bought,
And would be bought by me. By me, 80
For a meaning trifling sum, if I could pay it down.
Which happy knowledge I will still repeat,
And lay it to my heart: It has a virtue in't,
And soon will cure those wounds your eyes have
made.
And yet, there's something so divinely powerful
there— 85
Nay, I will gaze, to let you see my strength.

(Holds her, looks on her, and pauses and sighs.)

By heav'n, bright creature, I would not for the world
Thy fame were half so fair as is thy face.

(Turns her away from him.)

ANGELLICA *(aside)*: His words go through me to the
very soul.—
If you have nothing else to say to me— 90

WILLMORE: Yes, you shall hear how infamous you are—
For which I do not hate thee—
But that secures my heart, and all the flames it feels
Are but so many lusts:
I know it by their sudden bold intrusion. 95
The fire's impatient and betrays; 'tis false.
For had it been the purer flame of love,
I should have pined and languished at your feet,
Ere found the impudence to have discovered it.
I now dare stand your scorn and your denial. 100

MORETTA: Sure she's bewitched, that she can stand
thus tamely and hear his saucy railing.—Sirrah,
will you be gone?

ANGELLICA *(to MORETTA)*: How dare you take this liberty! Withdraw!—Pray tell me, sir, are not you 105
guilty of the same mercenary crime? When a lady
is proposed to you for a wife, you never ask how
fair, discreet, or virtuous she is, but what's her fortune; which, if but small, you cry "She will not do
my business," and basely leave her, though she 110
languish for you. Say, is not this as poor?

WILLMORE: It is a barbarous custom, which I will scorn
to defend in our sex, and do despise in yours.

Worcester, location where Charles II was defeated by
Cromwell (see note to Act 1, Scene 2, line 76). **high i'th'
mouth,** roughly equivalent to high and mighty. **troop,**
march, go your way. **pistole,** from pistolet, French name
given to a Spanish gold coin. **black lead,** pencil.

---

contemn, condemn, here disapprove.

ANGELLICA: Thou'rt a brave fellow! Put up thy gold, and know,
115 That were thy fortune as large as is thy soul,
Thou shouldst not buy my love.
Couldst thou forget those mean effects of vanity
Which set me out to sale,
And as a lover prize my yielding joys.
120 Canst thou believe they'll be entirely thine,
Without considering they were mercenary?
WILLMORE: I cannot tell, I must bethink me first.
    (Aside.) Ha! Death, I'm going to believe her.
ANGELLICA: Prithee confirm that faith, or if thou canst not,
Flatter me a little: 'Twill please me from thy
125 mouth.
WILLMORE *(aside)*: Curse on thy charming tongue! Dost thou return
My feigned contempt with so much subtlety?—
Thou'st found the easiest way into my heart,
Though I yet know that all thou say'st is false.

(Turning from her in rage.)

130 ANGELLICA: By all that's good, 'tis real;
I never loved before, though oft a mistress.
Shall my first vows be slighted?
WILLMORE *(aside)*: What can she mean?
ANGELLICA *(in an angry tone)*: I find you cannot credit me.
135 WILLMORE: I know you take me for an errant ass,
An ass that may be soothed into belief,
And then be used at pleasure;
But, madam, I have been so often cheated
By perjured, soft, deluding hypocrites,
140 That I've no faith left for the cozening sex,
Especially for women of your trade.
ANGELLICA: The low esteem you have of me perhaps
May bring my heart again:
For I have pride that yet surmounts my love.

(She turns with pride; he holds her.)

145 WILLMORE: Throw off this pride, this enemy to bliss,
And show the power of love: 'Tis with those arms
I can be only vanquished, made a slave.
ANGELLICA: Is all my mighty expectation vanished?
No, I will not hear thee talk; thou hast a charm
150 In every word that draws my heart away,
And all the thousand trophies I designed
Thou hast undone. Why art thou soft?
Thy looks are bravely rough, and meant for war.
Couldst thou not storm on still?
155 I then perhaps had been as free as thou.
WILLMORE *(aside)*: Death, how she throws her fire about my soul!—
Take heed, fair creature, how you raise my hopes,
Which once assumed pretends to all dominion:
There's not a joy thou hast in store
160 I shall not then command.

For which I'll pay you back my soul, my life!
Come, let's begin th'account this happy minute!
ANGELLICA: And will you pay me then the price I ask?
WILLMORE: Oh, why dost thou draw me from an awful worship,
By showing thou art no divinity.   165
Conceal the fiend, and show me all the angel!
Keep me but ignorant, and I'll be devout
And pay my vows forever at this shrine.

(Kneels and kisses her hand.)

ANGELLICA: The pay I mean is but thy love for mine.
Can you give that?   170
WILLMORE: Entirely. Come, let's withdraw where I'll
renew my vows, and breathe 'em with such ardor
thou shalt not doubt my zeal.
ANGELLICA: Thou hast a power too strong to be resisted.   175

(Exeunt WILLMORE *and* ANGELLICA.*)*

MORETTA: Now my curse go with you! Is all our project fallen to this? To love the only enemy to our trade? Nay, to love such a shameroon;° a very beggar; nay, a pirate beggar, whose business is to rifle and be gone; a no-purchase, no-pay tatter-   180
demalion,° and English picaroon;° a rogue that fights for daily drink, and takes a pride in being loyally lousy? Oh, I could curse now, if I durst. This is the fate of most whores.

Trophies, which from believing fops we win,
Are spoils to those who cozen us again. [*Exit.*]

ACT 3

Scene 1

(A street. Enter FLORINDA, VALERIA, HELLENA, *in antic°*
different dresses from what they were in before; CALLIS
attending.)

FLORINDA: I wonder what should make my brother in so ill a humor? I hope he has not found out our ramble this morning.
HELLENA: No, if he had, we should have heard on't at both ears, and have been mewed up° this after-   5
noon, which I would not for the world should have happened. Hey ho, I'm as sad as a lover's lute.
VALERIA: Well, methinks we have learnt this trade of gypsies as readily as if we had been bred upon the   10
road to Loretto;° and yet I did so fumble when I told the stranger his fortune that I was afraid I

---

shameroon, shameful person. tatterdemalion, a ragged
or beggarly fellow. picaroon, wanderer. antic, ridiculous,
bizarre. mewed up, confined. Loretto, Italian town, site of a
shrine to the Virgin Mary and focus of many pilgrimages.

should have told my own and yours by mistake.
But methinks Hellena has been very serious ever
15 since.
FLORINDA: I would give my garters she were in love, to
be revenged upon her for abusing me. How is't,
Hellena?
HELLENA: Ah, would I had never seen my mad mon-
20 sieur. And yet, for all your laughing, I am not in
love. And yet this small acquaintance, o' my conscience, will never out of my head.
VALERIA: Ha! Ha! Ha! I laugh to think how thou art
fitted with a lover, a fellow that I warrant loves
25 every new face he sees.
HELLENA: Hum, he has not kept his word with me
here, and may be taken up. That thought is not
very pleasant to me. What the deuce should this
be now that I feel?
30 VALERIA: What is't like?
HELLENA: Nay, the Lord knows, but if I should be
hanged I cannot choose but be angry and afraid
when I think that mad fellow should be in love
with anybody but me. What to think of myself I
35 know not: Would I could meet with some true
damned gypsy, that I might know my fortune.
VALERIA: Know it! Why there's nothing so easy: Thou
wilt love this wand'ring inconstant till thou find'st
thyself hanged about his neck, and then be as
40 mad to get free again.
FLORINDA: Yes, Valeria, we shall see her bestride his
baggage horse and follow him to the campaign.
HELLENA: So, so, now you are provided for there's no
care taken of poor me. But since you have set my
45 heart a-wishing, I am resolved to know for what; I
will not die of the pip,° so I will not.
FLORINDA: Art thou mad to talk so? Who will like thee
well enough to have thee, that hears what a mad
wench thou art?
50 HELLENA: Like me? I don't intend every he that likes
me shall have me, but he that I like. I should have
stayed in the nunnery still if I had liked my lady
abbess as well as she liked me. No, I came thence
not, as my wise brother imagines, to take an eter-
55 nal farewell of the world but to love and to be
beloved; and I will be beloved, or I'll get one of
your men, so I will.
VALERIA: Am I put into the number of lovers?
HELLENA: You? Why, coz, I know thou'rt too good-
60 natured to leave us in any design; thou wouldst
venture a cast° though thou comest off a loser,
especially with such a gamester. I observed your
man, and your willing ear incline that way; and if

you are not a lover, 'tis an art soon learnt—that I
find. (Sighs.) 65
FLORINDA: I wonder how you learnt to love so easily. I
had a thousand charms to meet my eyes and ears
ere I could yield, and 'twas the knowledge of Belvile's merit, not the surprising person, took my
soul. Thou art too rash, to give a heart at first sight. 70
HELLENA: Hang your considering lover! I never
thought beyond the fancy that 'twas a very pretty,
idle, silly kind of pleasure to pass one's time with:
to write little soft nonsensical billets,° and with
great difficulty and danger receive answers in 75
which I shall have my beauty praised, my wit
admired, though little or none, and have the vanity and power to know I am desirable. Then I have
the more inclination that way because I am to be
a nun, and so shall not be suspected to have any 80
such earthly thoughts about me; but when I walk
thus—and sigh thus—they'll think my mind's
upon my monastery, and cry, "How happy 'tis
she's so resolved." But not a word of man.
FLORINDA: What a mad creature's this! 85
HELLENA: I'll warrant, if my brother hears either of
you sigh, he cries gravely, "I fear you have the
indiscretion to be in love, but take heed of the
honor of our house, and your own unspotted
fame"; and so he conjures° on till he has laid the 90
soft winged god in your hearts, or broke the bird's
nest.° But see, here comes your lover, but where's
my inconstant? Let's step aside, and we may learn
something.

(Go aside.)
(Enter BELVILE, FREDERICK, and BLUNT.)

BELVILE: What means this! The picture's taken in. 95
BLUNT: It may be the wench is good-natured, and will
be kind gratis.° Your friend's a proper handsome
fellow.
BELVILE: I rather think she has cut his throat and is
fled; I am mad he should throw himself into dan- 100
gers. Pox on't, I shall want him, too, at night. Let's
knock and ask for him.
HELLENA: My heart goes a-pit, a-pat, for fear 'tis my
man they talk of.

(Knock; MORETTA above.)

MORETTA: What would you have? 105
BELVILE: Tell the stranger that entered here about
two hours ago that his friends stay here for him.
MORETTA: A curse upon him for Moretta: Would he
were at the devil! But he's coming to you.

---

pip, bird disease, with a scale or crust forming on the tongue; loosely and humorously applied to human ailments. **venture a cast,** toss the dice.

billets, short letters. **conjures,** influences with charms. **laid . . . bird's nest,** made you fall in love (through Cupid, the soft-winged god) or broken your heart (where the love-god nests). **gratis,** free.

(Enter WILLMORE.*)*

110 HELLENA: Ay, ay 'tis he. Oh, how this vexes me!

BELVILE: And how and how, dear lad, has fortune smiled? Are we to break her windows, or raise up altars to her, hah?

WILLMORE: Does not my fortune sit triumphant on
115 my brow? Dost not see the little wanton god there all gay and smiling? Have I not an air about my face and eyes that distinguish me from the crowd of common lovers? By heaven, Cupid's quiver has not half so many darts as her eyes! Oh, such a
120 *bona roba!*° To sleep in her arms is lying *in fresco,*° all perfumed air about me.

HELLENA *(aside)*: Here's fine encouragement for me to fool on!

WILLMORE: Hark'ee, where didst thou purchase that
125 rich Canary° we drank today? Tell me, that I may adore the spigot and sacrifice to the butt.° The juice was divine; into which I must dip my rosary, and then bless all things that I would have bold or fortunate.

130 BELVILE: Well, sir, let's go take a bottle and hear the story of your success.

FREDERICK: Would not French wine do better?

WILLMORE: Damn the hungry balderdash!° Cheerful sack° has a generous virtue in't inspiring a suc-
135 cessful confidence, gives eloquence to the tongue and vigor to the soul, and has in a few hours completed all my hopes and wishes! There's nothing left to raise a new desire in me. Come, let's be gay and wanton. And, gentlemen, study; study what
140 you want, for here are friends that will supply gentlemen. [*Jingles gold.*] Hark what a charming sound they make! 'Tis he and she gold whilst here, and shall beget new pleasures every moment.

BLUNT: But hark'ee, sir, you are not married, are you?

145 WILLMORE: All the honey of matrimony but none of the sting, friend.

BLUNT: 'Adsheartlikins, thou'rt a fortunate rogue!

WILLMORE: I am so, sir: let these inform you! Ha, how sweetly they chime! Pox of poverty: It makes a
150 man a slave, makes wit and honor sneak. My soul grew lean and rusty for want of credit.

BLUNT: 'Adsheartlikins, this I like well; it looks like my lucky bargain! Oh, how I long for the approach of my squire, that is to conduct me to her house
155 again. Why, here's two provided for!

FREDERICK: By this light, y'are happy men.

BLUNT: Fortune is pleased to smile on us, gentlemen, to smile on us.

---

bona roba, a courtesan, smartly dressed. *in fresco,* outside, in the fresh air. *Canary,* sweet wine from the Canary Islands, similar to Madeira. *butt,* a large cask for wine, beer, or water. *balderdash,* mixture of liquors. *sack,* white wine imported to England from Spain and the Canary Islands.

(Enter SANCHO *and pulls down* BLUNT *by the sleeve; they go aside.)*

SANCHO: Sir, my lady expects you. She has removed all
160 that might oppose your will and pleasure, and is impatient till you come.

BLUNT: Sir, I'll attend you.—Oh the happiest rogue! I'll take no leave, lest they either dog° me or stay me.

(Exit with SANCHO.*)*

BELVILE: But then the little gypsy is forgot? 165

WILLMORE: A mischief on thee for putting her into my thoughts! I had quite forgot her else, and this night's debauch had drunk her quite down.

HELLENA: Had it so, good captain!

(Claps him on the back.)

WILLMORE *(aside)*: Ha! I hope she did not hear me! 170

HELLENA: What, afraid of such a champion?

WILLMORE: Oh, you're a fine lady of your word, are you not? To make a man languish a whole day—

HELLENA: In tedious search of me.

WILLMORE: Egad, child, thou'rt in the right. Hadst 175
thou seen what a melancholy dog I have been ever since I was a lover, how I have walked the streets like a Capuchin,° with my hands in my sleeves—faith, sweetheart, thou wouldst pity me.

HELLENA *(aside)*: Now if I should be hanged I can't be 180
angry with him, he dissembles° so heartily.—Alas, good captain, what pains you have taken; now were I ungrateful not to reward so true a servant.

WILLMORE: Poor soul, that's kindly said; I see thou barest conscience. Come then, for a beginning 185
show me thy dear face.

HELLENA: I'm afraid, my small acquaintance, you have been staying that swinging stomach you boasted of this morning. I then remember my little collation° would have gone down with you without the 190
sauce of a handsome face. Is your stomach so queasy now?

WILLMORE: Faith, long fasting, child, spoils a man's appetite. Yet if you durst treat, I could so lay about me still— 195

HELLENA: And would you fall to before a priest says grace?

WILLMORE: O fie, fie, what an old out-of-fashioned thing hast thou named? Thou couldst not dash me more out of countenance shouldst thou show 200
me an ugly face.

(Whilst he is seemingly courting HELLENA, *enter* ANGEL-LICA, MORETTA, BISKEY, *and* SEBASTIAN, *all in masquerade.* ANGELLICA *sees* WILLMORE *and stares.)*

---

dog, to chase or follow. *Capuchin,* a Franciscan friar. *dissembles,* pretends, feigns. *collation,* a light meal.

ANGELLICA: Heavens, 'tis he! And passionately fond to see another woman!

MORETTA: What could you less expect from such a swaggerer?

ANGELLICA: Expect? As much as I paid him: a heart entire,
Which I had pride enough to think when'er I gave,
It would have raised the man above the vulgar,
Made him all soul, and that all soft and constant.

HELLENA: You see, captain, how willing I am to be friends with you, till time and ill luck make us lovers; and ask you the question first rather than put your modesty to the blush by asking me. For alas, I know you captains are such strict men, and such severe observers of your vows to chastity, that 'twill be hard to prevail with your tender conscience to marry a young willing maid.

WILLMORE: Do not abuse me, for fear I should take thee at thy word and marry thee indeed, which I'm sure will be revenge sufficient.

HELLENA: O' my conscience, that will be our destiny, because we are both of one humor: I am as inconstant as you, for I have considered, captain, that a handsome woman has a great deal to do whilst her face is good. For then is our harvesttime to gather friends, and should I in these days of my youth catch a fit of foolish constancy, I were undone: 'tis loitering by daylight in our great journey. Therefore, I declare I'll allow but one year for love, one year for indifference, and one year for hate; and then go hang yourself, for I profess myself the gay, the kind, and the inconstant. The devil's in't if this won't please you!

WILLMORE: Oh, most damnably. I have a heart with a hole quite through it too; no prison mine, to keep a mistress in.

ANGELLICA (aside): Perjured man! How I believe thee now!

HELLENA: Well, I see our business as well as humors are alike: yours to cozen as many maids as will trust you, and I as many men as have faith. See if I have not as desperate a lying look as you can have for the heart of you. (Pulls off her vizard; he starts.) How do you like it, captain?

WILLMORE: Like it! By heaven, I never saw so much beauty! Oh, the charms of those sprightly black eyes! That strangely fair face, full of smiles and dimples! Those soft round melting cherry lips and small even white teeth! Not to be expressed, but silently adored! [She replaces her mask.] Oh, one look more, and strike me dumb, or I shall repeat nothing else till I'm mad.

(He seems to court her to pull off her vizard; she refuses.)

ANGELLICA: I can endure no more. Nor is it fit to interrupt him, for if I do, my jealousy has so destroyed my reason I shall undo him. Therefore I'll retire, and you, Sebastian (to one of her Bravos), follow that woman and learn who 'tis; while you (to the other Bravo) tell the fugitive I would speak to him instantly. (Exit.)

(This while FLORINDA is talking to BELVILE, who stands sullenly; FREDERICK courting VALERIA.)

VALERIA [to BELVILE]: Prithee, dear stranger, be not so sullen, for though you have lost your love you see my friend frankly offers you hers to play with in the meantime.

BELVILE: Faith, madam, I am sorry I can't play at her game.

FREDERICK [to VALERIA]: Pray leave your intercession and mind your own affair. They'll better agree apart: He's a modest sigher in company, but alone no woman 'scapes him.

FLORINDA [aside]: Sure he does but rally. Yet, if it should be true? I'll tempt him farther.—Believe me, noble stranger, I'm no common mistress. And for a little proof on't, wear this jewel.° Nay, take it, sir, 'tis right, and bills of exchange may sometimes miscarry.

BELVILE: Madam, why am I chose out of all mankind to be the object of your bounty?

VALERIA: There's another civil question asked.

FREDERICK [aside]: Pox of's modesty; it spoils his own markets and hinders mine.

FLORINDA: Sir, from my window I have often seen you, and women of my quality have so few opportunities for love that we ought to lose none.

FREDERICK [to VALERIA]: Ay, this is something! Here's a woman! When shall I be blest with so much kindness from your fair mouth?—(Aside to BELVILE.) Take the jewel, fool!

BELVILE: You tempt me strangely, madam, every way—

FLORINDA (aside): So, if I find him false, my whole repose is gone.

BELVILE: And but for a vow I've made to a very fair lady, this goodness had subdued me.

FREDERICK [aside to BELVILE]: Pox on't, be kind, in pity to me be kind. For I am to thrive here but as you treat her friend.

HELLENA: Tell me what you did in yonder house, and I'll unmask.

WILLMORE: Yonder house? Oh I went to a—to—why, there's a friend of mine lives there.

HELLENA: What, a she or a he friend?

WILLMORE: A man, upon honor, a man. A she friend? No, no, madam, you have done my business, I thank you.

HELLENA: And was't your man friend that had more

---

jewel, probably a locket containing her picture—see stage direction following line 342.

darts in's eyes than Cupid carries in's whole budget of arrows?

WILLMORE: So—

HELLENA: "Ah, such a *bona roba!* To be in her arms is lying *in fresco,* all perfumed air about me." Was this your man friend too?

WILLMORE: So—

HELLENA: That gave you the he and the she gold, that begets young pleasures?

WILLMORE: Well, well, madam, then you can see there are ladies in the world that will not be cruel. There are, madam, there are.

HELLENA: And there be men, too, as fine, wild, inconstant fellows as yourself. There be, captain, there be, if you go to that now. Therefore, I'm resolved—

WILLMORE: Oh!

HELLENA: To see your face no more—

WILLMORE: Oh!

HELLENA: Till tomorrow.

WILLMORE: Egad, you frighted me.

HELLENA: Nor then neither, unless you'll swear never to see that lady more.

WILLMORE: See her! Why, never to think of womankind again.

HELLENA: Kneel and swear.

(Kneels; she gives him her hand.)

WILLMORE: I do, never to think, to see, to love, nor lie, with any but thyself.

HELLENA: Kiss the book.

WILLMORE: Oh, most religiously. *(Kisses her hand.)*

HELLENA: Now what a wicked creature am I, to damn a proper fellow.

CALLIS *(to* FLORINDA*)*: Madam, I'll stay no longer: 'tis e'en dark.

FLORINDA [*to* BELVILE]: However, sir, I'll leave this with you, that when I'm gone you may repent the opportunity you have lost by your modesty.

(Gives him the jewel, which is her picture, and exit. He gazes after her.)

WILLMORE [*to* HELLENA]: 'Twill be an age till tomorrow, and till then I will most impatiently expect you. Adieu, my dear pretty angel.

(Exeunt all the women.)

BELVILE: Ha! Florinda's picture! 'Twas she herself. What a dull dog was I! I would have given the world for one minute's discourse with her.

FREDERICK: This comes of your modesty. Ah, pox o' your vow, 'twas ten to one but we had lost the jewel by't.

BELVILE: Willmore, the blessed'st opportunity lost! Florinda, friends, Florinda!

WILLMORE: Ah, rogue! Such black eyes! Such a face! Such a mouth! Such teeth! And so much wit!

BELVILE: All, all, and a thousand charms besides.

WILLMORE: Why, dost thou know her?

BELVILE: Know her! Ay, ay, and a pox take me with all my heart for being so modest.

WILLMORE: But hark'ee, friend of mine, are you my rival? And have I been only beating the bush all this while?

BELVILE: I understand thee not. I'm mad! See here—

(Shows the picture.)

WILLMORE: Ha! Whose picture's this? 'Tis a fine wench!

FREDERICK: The colonel's mistress, sir.

WILLMORE: Oh, oh, here. *(Gives the picture back.)* I thought't had been another prize. Come, come, a bottle will set thee right again.

BELVILE: I am content to try, and by that time 'twill be late enough for our design.

WILLMORE: Agreed.

> Love does all day the soul's great empire keep,
> But wine at night lulls the soft god° asleep.

(Exeunt.)

Scene 2

*(*LUCETTA*'s house. Enter* BLUNT *and* LUCETTA *with a light.)*

LUCETTA: Now we are safe and free: no fears of the coming home of my old jealous husband, which made me a little thoughtful when you came in first. But now love is all the business of my soul.

BLUNT: I am transported!—*(Aside.)* Pox on't, that I had but some fine things to say to her, such as lovers use. I was a fool not to learn of Fred a little by heart before I came. Something I must say.— 'Adsheartlikins, sweet soul, I am not used to compliment, but I'm an honest gentleman, and thy humble servant.

LUCETTA: I have nothing to pay for so great a favor, but such a love as cannot but be great, since at first sight of that sweet face and shape it made me your absolute captive.

BLUNT *(aside)*: Kind heart, how prettily she talks! Egad, I'll show her husband a Spanish trick: Send him out of the world and marry her; she's damnably in love with me, and will ne'er mind settlements,° and so there's that saved.

LUCETTA: Well, sir, I'll go and undress me, and be with you instantly.

BLUNT: Make haste then, for 'adsheartlikins, dear soul, thou canst not guess at the pain of a longing lover when his joys are drawn within the compass of a few minutes.

---

soft god, Cupid. *settlements,* property given to a wife after marriage.

LUCETTA: You speak my sense, and I'll make haste to prove it. *(Exit.)*

30 BLUNT: 'Tis a rare girl, and this one night's enjoyment with her will be worth all the days I ever passed in Essex. Would she would go with me into England, though to say truth, there's plenty of whores already. Put a pox on 'em, they are such merce-
35 nary prodigal whores that they want such a one as this, that's free and generous, to give 'em good examples. Why, what a house she has, how rich and fine!

(Enter SANCHO.*)*

SANCHO: Sir, my lady has sent me to conduct you to her chamber.

40 BLUNT: Sir, I shall be proud to follow.—*(Aside.)* Here's one of her servants too; 'adsheartlikins, by this garb and gravity he might be a justice of peace in Essex, and is but a pimp here.

(Exeunt.)

Scene 3

(The scene changes to a chamber with an alcove bed in't, a table, etc.; LUCETTA *in bed. Enter* SANCHO *and* BLUNT, *who takes the candle of* SANCHO *at the door.)*

SANCHO: Sir, my commission reaches no farther.
BLUNT: Sir, I'll excuse your compliment.

[*Exit* SANCHO.]

—What, in bed, my sweet mistress?
LUCETTA: You see, I still outdo you in kindness.
5 BLUNT: And thou shalt see what haste I'll make to quit scores.° Oh, the luckiest rogue!

(He undresses himself.)

LUCETTA: Should you be false or cruel now—
BLUNT: False! 'Adsheartlikins, what dost thou take me for, a Jew? An insensible heathen? A pox of thy
10 old jealous husband: An° he were dead, egad, sweet soul, it should be none of my fault if I did not marry thee.
LUCETTA: It never should be mine.
BLUNT: Good soul! I'm the fortunatest dog!
15 LUCETTA: Are you not undressed yet?
BLUNT: As much as my impatience will permit.

(Goes toward the bed in his shirt, drawers, etc.)

LUCETTA: Hold, sir, put out the light; it may betray us else.
BLUNT: Anything; I need no other light but that of
20 thine eyes.—*(Aside.)* 'Adsheartlikins, there I think I had it.

(Puts out the candle; the bed descends; he gropes about to find it.)

Why, why, where am I got? What, not yet? Where are you, sweetest?—Ah, the rogue's silent now. A pretty love-trick this; how she'll laugh at me anon!—You need not, my dear rogue, you need 25 not! I'm all on fire already; come, come, now call me, in pity.—Sure I'm enchanted! I have been round the chamber, and can find neither woman nor bed. I locked the door; I'm sure she cannot go that way, or if she could, the bed could 30 not.—Enough, enough, my pretty wanton; do not carry the jest too far! *(Lights on a trap, and is let down.)*—Ha! Betrayed! Dogs! Rogues! Pimps! Help! Help!

(Enter LUCETTA, PHILIPPO, *and* SANCHO *with a light.)*

PHILIPPO: Ha! Ha! Ha! He's dispatched finely. 35
LUCETTA: Now, sir, had I been coy, we had missed of this booty.
PHILIPPO: Nay, when I saw 'twas a substantial fool, I was mollified. But when you dote upon a serenading coxcomb, upon a face, fine clothes, and a 40 lute, it makes me rage.
LUCETTA: You know I was never guilty of that folly, my dear Philippo, but with yourself. But come, let's see what we have got by this.
PHILIPPO: A rich coat; sword and hat; these breeches, 45 too, are well lined! See here, a gold watch! A purse—Ha! Gold! At least two hundred pistoles! A bunch of diamond rings, and one with the family arms! A gold box, with a medal of his king, and his lady mother's picture! These were sacred 50 relics, believe me. See, the waistband of his breeches have a mine of gold—old queen Bess's!° We have a quarrel to her ever since eighty-eight,° and may therefore justify the theft: The Inquisition might have committed it. 55
LUCETTA: See, a bracelet of bowed gold! These his sisters tied about his arm at parting. But well, for all this, I fear his being a stranger may make a noise and hinder our trade with them hereafter.
PHILIPPO: That's our security: He is not only a 60 stranger to us, but to the country too. The common shore° into which he is descended, thou know'st, conducts him into another street, which this light will hinder him from ever finding again. He knows neither your name, nor that of the 65 street where your house is; nay, nor the way to his own lodgings.
LUCETTA: And art thou not an unmerciful rogue, not

---

quit scores, even the score. **An,** if.

Bess's, Queen Elizabeth I (1558–1603). **eighty-eight,** The English defeated the Spanish Armada in 1588. **common shore,** public sewer.

to afford him one night for all this? I should not
70   have been such a Jew.

PHILIPPO: Blame me not, Lucetta, to keep as much of
thee as I can to myself. Come, that thought makes
me wanton; let's to bed.—Sancho, lock up these.

This is the fleece which fools do bear,
Designed for witty men to shear. (Exeunt.)

Scene 4

(The scene changes, and discovers BLUNT *creeping out of
a common shore; his face, etc., all dirty.)*

BLUNT *(climbing up):* Oh, Lord, I am got out at last,
and, which is a miracle, without a clue. And now
to damning and cursing! But if that would ease
me, where shall I begin? With my fortune, myself,
5   or the quean° that cozened me? What a dog I was
to believe in woman! Oh, coxcomb! Ignorant
conceited coxcomb! To fancy she could be enamored with my person! At first sight enamored!
Oh, I'm a cursed puppy! 'Tis plain, fool was writ
10   upon my forehead! She perceived it; saw the
Essex calf there. For what allurements could there
be in this countenance, which I can endure because I'm acquainted with it. Oh dull, silly dog, to
be thus soothed into a cozening! Had I been
15   drunk, I might fondly have credited the young
quean; but as I was in my right wits to be thus
cheated, confirms it: I am a dull believing English
country fop. But my comrades! Death and the
devil, there's the worst of all! Then a ballad will
20   be sung tomorrow on the Prado,° to a lousy tune
of the enchanted squire and the annihilated
damsel. But Fred—that rogue—and the colonel
will abuse me beyond all Christian patience. Had
she left me my clothes, I have a bill of exchange at
25   home would have saved my credit. But now all
hope is taken from me. Well, I'll home, if I can
find the way, with this consolation: that I am not
the first kind believing coxcomb; but there are,
gallants, many such good natures amongst ye.

30   *And though you've better arts to hide your follies,*
'Adsheartlikins, y'are all as errant cullies.°

(Exit.)

Scene 5

(Scene: the garden in the night. Enter FLORINDA *in an
undress,° with a key and a little box.)*

FLORINDA: Well, thus far I'm in my way to happiness. I
have got myself free from Callis; my brother too, I

find by yonder light, is got into his cabinet,° and
thinks not of me; I have by good fortune got the
key of the garden back door. I'll open it to pre-   5
vent Belvile's knocking: A little noise will now
alarm my brother. Now am I as fearful as a young
thief. *(Unlocks the door.)* Hark! What noise is that?
Oh, 'twas the wind that played amongst the
boughs. Belvile stays long, methinks; it's time.   10
Stay, for fear of a surprise, I'll hide these jewels in
yonder jasmine. *(She goes to lay down the box.)*

(Enter WILLMORE, *drunk.)*

WILLMORE: What the devil is become of these fellows
Belvile and Frederick? They promised to stay at
the next corner for me, but who the devil knows   15
the corner of a full moon? Now, whereabouts am
I? Ha, what have we here? A garden! A very convenient place to sleep in. Ha! What has God sent
us here? A female! By this light, a woman! I'm a
dog if it be not a very wench!   20

FLORINDA: He's come! Ha! Who's there?

WILLMORE: Sweet soul, let me salute thy shoestring.

FLORINDA [*aside*]: 'Tis not my Belvile. Good heavens, I
know him not!—Who are you, and from whence
come you?   25

WILLMORE: Prithee, prithee, child, not so many hard
questions! Let it suffice I am here, child. Come,
come kiss me.

FLORINDA: Good gods! What luck is mine?

WILLMORE: Only good luck, child, parlous° good luck.   30
Come hither.—'Tis a delicate shining wench. By
this hand, she's perfumed, and smells like any
nosegay.°—Prithee, dear soul, let's not play the
fool and lose time—precious time. For as Gad
shall save me, I'm as honest a fellow as breathes,   35
though I'm a little disguised° at present. Come, I
say. Why, thou mayst be free with me: I'll be very
secret. I'll not boast who 'twas obliged me, not I;
for hang me if I know thy name.

FLORINDA: Heavens! What a filthy beast is this!   40

WILLMORE: I am so, and thou ought'st the sooner to
lie with me for that reason. For look you, child,
there will be no sin in't, because 'twas neither
designed nor premeditated: 'Tis pure accident
on both sides. That's a certain thing now. Indeed,   45
should I make love to you, and you vow fidelity,
and swear and lie till you believed and yielded—
that were to make it willful fornication, the crying
sin of the nation. Thou art, therefore, as thou art
a good Christian, obliged in conscience to deny   50
me nothing. Now, come be kind without any
more idle prating.

FLORINDA: Oh, I am ruined! Wicked man, unhand me!

---

quean, a hussy, harlot, or strumpet. **Prado,** a public
park in Madrid, a fashionable or popular promenade. **cullies,** plural of cully, one who is easily duped. **undress,** underwear or nightgown.

cabinet, a private chamber. **parlous,** excessively.
nosegay, small bouquet of flowers. **disguised,** intoxicated.

WILLMORE: Wicked? Egad, child, a judge, were he
55   young and vigorous, and saw those eyes of thine,
would know 'twas they gave the first blow, the first
provocation. Come, prithee let's lose no time, I
say. This is a fine convenient place.
FLORINDA: Sir, let me go, I conjure° you, or I'll call out.
60 WILLMORE: Ay, ay, you were best to call witness to see
how finely you treat me. Do!
FLORINDA: I'll cry murder, rape, or anything, if you do
not instantly let me go!
WILLMORE: A rape? Come, come, you lie, you bag-
65   gage, you lie. What! I'll warrant you would fain
have the world believe now that you are not so
forward as I. No, not you. Why at this time of
night was your cobweb door set open, dear spider,
but to catch flies? Ha! Come, or I shall be
70   damnably angry. Why, what a coil° is here!
FLORINDA: Sir, can you think—
WILLMORE: That you would do't for nothing? Oh, oh,
I find what you would be at. Look here, here's a
pistole for you. Here's a work indeed! Here, take
75   it, I say!
FLORINDA: For heaven's sake, sir, as you're a gentleman—
WILLMORE: So now, now, she would be wheedling me
for more! What, you will not take it then? You are
80   resolved you will not? Come, come, take it or I'll
put it up again, for look ye, I never give more.
Why, how now, mistress, are you so high i'th'
mouth a pistole won't down with you? Ha! Why,
what a work's here! In good time! Come, no
85   struggling to be gone. But an y'are good at a
dumb wrestle, I'm for ye. Look ye, I'm for ye.

(She struggles with him.)
(Enter BELVILE *and* FREDERICK.*)*

BELVILE: The door is open. A pox of this mad fellow!
I'm angry that we've lost him; I durst have sworn
he had followed us.
90 FREDERICK: But you were so hasty, colonel, to be gone.
FLORINDA: Help! Help! Murder! Help! Oh, I am
ruined!
BELVILE: Ha! Sure that's Florinda's voice! *(Comes up to
them.)* A man!—Villain, let go that lady!

(A noise; WILLMORE *turns and draws;* FREDERICK *interposes.)*

95 FLORINDA: Belvile! Heavens! My brother too is coming, and 'twill be impossible to escape. Belvile, I
conjure you to walk under my chamber window,
from whence I'll give you some instructions what
to do. This rude man has undone us. *(Exit.)*
100 WILLMORE: Belvile!

---

conjure, beg, beseech.   *coil,* tumult, disturbance.

(Enter PEDRO, STEPHANO, *and other servants, with
lights.)*
PEDRO: I'm betrayed! Run, Stephano, and see if Florinda be safe.

(Exit STEPHANO.*)*
(They fight, and PEDRO*'s party beats 'em out.)*

—So, whoe'er they be, all is not well. I'll to Florinda's chamber. *(Going out, meets* STEPHANO.*)*
STEPHANO: You need not, sir: The poor lady's fast 105
asleep, and thinks no harm. I would not awake
her, sir, for fear of frighting her with your danger.
PEDRO: I'm glad she's there.—Rascals, how came the
garden door open? 110
STEPHANO: That question comes too late, sir. Some of
my fellow servants masquerading, I'll warrant.
PEDRO: Masquerading! A lewd custom to debauch our
youth! There's something more in this than I
imagine. *(Exeunt.)* 115

Scene 6

(Scene changes to the street. Enter BELVILE *in rage,* FRED-
ERICK *holding him,* WILLMORE *melancholy.)*

WILLMORE: Why, how the devil should I know Florinda?
BELVILE: Ah, plague of your ignorance! If it had not
been Florinda, must you be a beast? A brute? A
senseless swine? 5
WILLMORE: Well, sir, you see I am endued° with patience: I can bear. Though egad, y'are very free
with me, methinks. I was in good hopes the quarrel would have been on my side, for so uncivilly
interrupting me. 10
BELVILE: Peace, brute, whilst thou'rt safe. Oh, I'm distracted!
WILLMORE: Nay, nay, I'm an unlucky dog, that's certain.
BELVILE: Ah, curse upon the star that ruled my birth, 15
or whatsoever other influence that makes me still
so wretched.
WILLMORE: Thou break'st my heart with these complaints. There is no star in fault, no influence but
sack, the cursed sack I drunk. 20
FREDERICK: Why, how the devil came you so drunk?
WILLMORE: Why, how the devil came you so sober?
BELVILE: A curse upon his thin skull, he was always
beforehand that way.
FREDERICK: Prithee, dear colonel, forgive him; he's 25
sorry for his fault.
BELVILE: He's always so after he has done a mischief.
A plague on all such brutes!
WILLMORE: By this light, I took her for an errant
harlot. 30

---

endued, endowed.

BELVILE: Damn your debauched opinion! Tell me, sot, hadst thou so much sense and light about thee to distinguish her woman, and couldst not see something about her face and person to strike
35   an awful reverence into thy soul?

WILLMORE: Faith no, I considered her as mere a woman as I could wish.

BELVILE: 'Sdeath, I have no patience. Draw, or I'll kill you!

40 WILLMORE: Let that alone till tomorrow, and if I set not all right again, use your pleasure.

BELVILE: Tomorrow! Damn it,
   The spiteful light will lead me to no happiness.
   Tomorrow is Antonio's, and perhaps
45   Guides him to my undoing. Oh, that I could meet
   This rival, this powerful fortunate!

WILLMORE: What then?

BELVILE: Let thy own reason, or my rage, instruct thee.

WILLMORE: I shall be finely informed then, no doubt.
50   Hear me, colonel, hear me; show me the man and I'll do his business.

BELVILE: I know him no more than thou, or if I did I should not need thy aid.

WILLMORE: This you say is Angellica's house; I prom-
55   ised the kind baggage to lie with her tonight.

(Offers to go in.)

(Enter ANTONIO *and his* PAGE. ANTONIO *knocks on the hilt of's sword.)*

ANTONIO: You paid the thousand crowns I directed?

PAGE: To the lady's old woman, sir, I did.

WILLMORE: Who the devil have we here?

BELVILE: I'll now plant myself under Florinda's win-
60   dow, and if I find no comfort there, I'll die.

(Exeunt BELVILE *and* FREDERICK.*)*
(Enter MORETTA.*)*

MORETTA: Page?

PAGE: Here's my lord.

WILLMORE: How is this? A picaroon going to board my frigate?—Here's one chase gun for you!

(Drawing his sword, justles ANTONIO, *who turns and draws. They fight;* ANTONIO *falls.)*

65 MORETTA: Oh, bless us! We're all undone!

(Runs in and shuts the door.)

PAGE: Help! Murder!

*(*BELVILE *returns at the noise of fighting.)*

BELVILE: Ha! The mad rogue's engaged in some un-lucky adventure again.

(Enter two or three MASQUERADERS.*)*

MASQUERADER: Ha! A man killed!

70 WILLMORE: How, a man killed? Then I'll go home to sleep.

(Puts up and reels out. Exeunt MASQUERADERS *another way.)*

BELVILE: Who should it be? Pray heaven the rogue is safe, for all my quarrel to him.

(As BELVILE *is groping about, enter an* OFFICER *and six* SOLDIERS.*)*

SOLDIER: Who's there?

OFFICER: So, here's one dispatched. Secure the mur- 75
derer.

BELVILE: Do not mistake my charity for murder! I came to his assistance!

(Soldiers seize on BELVILE.*)*

OFFICER: That shall be tried, sir. St. Jago!° Swords drawn in the Carnival time! *(Goes to* ANTONIO.*)* 80

ANTONIO: Thy hand, prithee.

OFFICER: Ha! Don Antonio! Look well to the villain there.—How is it, sir?

ANTONIO: I'm hurt.

BELVILE: Has my humanity made me a criminal? 85

OFFICER: Away with him!

BELVILE: What a curst chance is this!

(Exeunt soldiers with BELVILE.*)*

ANTONIO [*aside*]: This is the man that has set upon me twice.—*(To the officer.)* Carry him to my apartment till you have further orders from me. 90

(Exit ANTONIO, *led.)*

ACT 4

Scene 1

(A fine room. Discovers BELVILE *as by dark alone.)*

BELVILE: When shall I be weary of railing on fortune, who is resolved never to turn with smiles upon me? Two such defeats in one night none but the devil and that mad rogue could have contrived to have plagued me with. I am here a prisoner. But 5 where, heaven knows. And if there be murder done, I can soon decide the fate of a stranger in a nation without mercy. Yet this is nothing to the torture my soul bows with when I think of losing my fair, my dear Florinda. Hark, my door opens. 10 A light! A man, and seems of quality. Armed, too! Now shall I die like a dog, without defense.

(Enter ANTONIO *in a nightgown, with a light; his arm in a scarf, and a sword under his arm. He sets the candle on the table.)*

ANTONIO: Sir, I come to know what injuries I have done you, that could provoke you to so mean an

---

St. Jago, Spanish for St. James.

15 action as to attack me basely without allowing time for my defense?

BELVILE: Sir, for a man in my circumstances to plead innocence would look like fear. But view me well, and you will find no marks of coward on me, nor
20 anything that betrays that brutality you accuse me with.

ANTONIO: In vain, sir, you impose upon my sense. You are not only he who drew on me last night, but yesterday before the same house, that of Angel-
25 lica. Yet there is something in your face and mien, that makes me wish I were mistaken.

BELVILE: I own I fought today in the defense of a friend of mine with whom you, if you're the same, and your party were first engaged. Perhaps you
30 think this crime enough to kill me; but if you do, I cannot fear you'll do it basely.

ANTONIO: No sir, I'll make you fit for a defense with this. (Gives him the sword.)

BELVILE: This gallantry surprises me, nor know I how
35 to use this present, sir, against a man so brave.

ANTONIO: You shall not need. For know, I come to snatch you from a danger that is decreed against you: perhaps your life, or long imprisonment. And 'twas with so much courage you offended, I
40 cannot see you punished.

BELVILE: How shall I pay this generosity?

ANTONIO: It had been safer to have killed another than have attempted me. To show your danger, sir, I'll let you know my quality: And 'tis the
45 Viceroy's son whom you have wounded.

BELVILE: The Viceroy's son!—(Aside.) Death and confusion! Was this plague reserved to complete all the rest? Obliged by° him, the man of all the world I would destroy!

50 ANTONIO: You seem disordered, sir.

BELVILE: Yes, trust me, I am, and 'tis with pain that man receives such bounties who wants the power to pay 'em back again.

ANTONIO: To gallant spirits 'tis indeed uneasy, but you
55 may quickly overpay me, sir.

BELVILE (aside): Then I am well. Kind heaven, but set us even, that I may fight with him and keep my honor safe.—Oh, I'm impatient, sir, to be discounting the mighty debt I owe you. Command
60 me quickly.

ANTONIO: I have a quarrel with a rival, sir, about the maid we love.

BELVILE (aside): Death, 'tis Florinda he means! That thought destroys my reason, and I shall kill him.

65 ANTONIO: My rival, sir, is one has all the virtues man can boast of—

BELVILE (aside): Death, who should this be?

ANTONIO: He challenged me to meet him on the

Molo as soon as day appeared, but last night's quarrel has made my arm unfit to guide a sword. 70

BELVILE: I apprehend you, sir. You'd have me kill the man that lays a claim to the maid you speak of. I'll do't. I'll fly to do't!

ANTONIO: Sir, do you know her?

BELVILE: No, sir, but 'tis enough she is admired by you. 75

ANTONIO: Sir, I shall rob you of the glory on't, for you must fight under my name and dress.

BELVILE: That opinion must be strangely obliging that makes you think I can personate the brave Antonio, whom I can but strive to imitate. 80

ANTONIO: You say too much to my advantage. Come, sir, the day appears that calls you forth. Within, sir, is the habit.° (Exit ANTONIO.)

BELVILE: Fantastic fortune, thou deceitful light, That cheats the wearied traveler by night, 85 Though on a precipice each step you tread, I am resolved to follow where you lead. (Exit.)

Scene 2

(The Molo. Enter FLORINDA and CALLIS in masks, with STEPHANO.)

FLORINDA (aside): I'm dying with my fears: Belvile's not coming as I expected under my window makes me believe that all those fears are true.— Canst thou not tell with whom my brother fights? 5

STEPHANO: No, madam, they were both in masquerade. I was by when they challenged one another, and they had decided the quarrel then, but were prevented by some cavaliers; which made 'em put it off till now. But I am sure 'tis about you they 10 fight.

FLORINDA (aside): Nay, then, 'tis with Belvile, for what other lover have I that dares fight for me except Antonio, and he is too much in favor with my brother. If it be he, for whom shall I direct my 15 prayers to heaven?

STEPHANO: Madam, I must leave you, for if my master see me, I shall be hanged for being your conductor. I escaped narrowly for the excuse I made for you last night i'th' garden. 20

FLORINDA: I'll reward thee for't. Prithee, no more.

(Exit STEPHANO.)
(Enter DON PEDRO in his masking habit.)

PEDRO: Antonio's late today; the place will fill, and we may be prevented. (Walks about.)

FLORINDA (aside): Antonio? Sure I heard amiss.

PEDRO: But who will not excuse a happy lover 25 When soft fair arms confine the yielding neck, And the kind whisper languishingly breathes

---

Obliged by, shown kindness by.

habit, disguise (Antonio's clothing).

"Must you be gone so soon?"
Sure I had dwelt forever on her bosom—
30 But stay, he's here.

(Enter BELVILE *dressed in* ANTONIO'*s clothes.)*

FLORINDA [*aside*]: 'Tis not Belvile; half my fears are
      vanished.
PEDRO: Antonio!
BELVILE *(aside)*: This must be he.—You're early, sir; I
35   do not use to be outdone this way.
PEDRO: The wretched, sir, are watchful, and 'tis enough
      you've the advantage of me in Angellica.
BELVILE *(aside)*: Angellica! Or° I've mistook my man,
      or else Antonio! Can he forget his interest in
40   Florinda and fight for common prize?
PEDRO: Come, sir, you know our terms.
BELVILE *(aside)*: By heaven, not I.—No talking; I am
      ready, sir.

(Offers to fight; FLORINDA *runs in.)*

FLORINDA *(to* BELVILE*)*: Oh, hold! Whoe'er you be, I
45   do conjure you hold! If you strike here, I die!
PEDRO: Florinda!
BELVILE: Florinda imploring for my rival!
PEDRO: Away; this kindness is unseasonable.

(Puts her by; they fight; she runs in just as BELVILE *disarms* PEDRO.*)*

FLORINDA: Who are you, sir, that dares deny my
50   prayers?
BELVILE: Thy prayers destroy him; if thou wouldst preserve him, do that thou'rt unacquainted with,
      and curse him.

(She holds him.)

FLORINDA: By all you hold most dear, by her you love,
55   I do conjure you, touch him not.
BELVILE: By her I love?
      See, I obey, and at your feet resign
      The useless trophy of my victory.

(Lays his sword at her feet.)

PEDRO: Antonio, you've done enough to prove you
60   love Florinda.
BELVILE: Love Florinda! Does heaven love adoration,
      prayer, or penitence? Love her? Here, sir, your
      sword again.

(Snatches up the sword and gives it to him.)

      Upon this truth I'll fight my life away.
65 PEDRO: No, you've redeemed my sister, and my friendship.

(He gives him FLORINDA, *and pulls off his vizard to show
his face, and puts it on again.)*

Or, either.

BELVILE: Don Pedro!
PEDRO: Can you resign your claims to other women,
      and give your heart entirely to Florinda?
BELVILE: Entire, as dying saints' confessions are!   70
      I can delay my happiness no longer:
      This minute let me make Florinda mine.
PEDRO: This minute let it be. No time so proper: This
      night my father will arrive from Rome, and possibly may hinder what we purpose.   75
FLORINDA: O, heavens! This minute?

(Enter MASQUERADERS *and pass over.)*

BELVILE: Oh, do not ruin me!
PEDRO: The place begins to fill, and that we may not
      be observed, do you walk off to St. Peter's church,
      where I will meet you and conclude your happiness.   80
BELVILE: I'll meet you there.—*(Aside.)* If there be no
      more saints' churches in Naples.
FLORINDA: Oh, stay, sir, and recall your hasty doom!
      Alas, I have not yet prepared my heart   85
      To entertain so strange a guest.
PEDRO: Away; this silly modesty is assumed too late.
BELVILE: Heaven, madam, what do you do?
FLORINDA: Do? Despise the man that lays a tyrant's
      claim
      To what he ought to conquer by submission.   90
BELVILE: You do not know me. Move a little this way.

(Draws her aside.)

FLORINDA: Yes, you may force me even to the altar,
      But not the holy man that offers there
      Shall force me to be thine.

*(*PEDRO *talks to* CALLIS *this while.)*

BELVILE: Oh, do not lose so blest an opportunity!   95

(Pulls off his vizard.)

      See, 'tis your Belvile, not Antonio,
      Whom your mistaken scorn and anger ruins.
FLORINDA: Belvile!
      Where was my soul it could not meet thy voice,
      And take this knowledge in.   100

(As they are talking, enter WILLMORE, *finely dressed, and*
FREDERICK.*)*

WILLMORE: No intelligence? No news of Belvile yet?
      Well, I am the most unlucky rascal in nature. Ha!
      Am I deceived, or is it he? Look, Fred! 'Tis he, my
      dear Belvile!

(Runs and embraces him; BELVILE'*s vizard falls out on's
hand.)*

BELVILE: Hell and confusion seize thee!   105
PEDRO: Ha! Belvile! I beg your pardon, sir.

(Takes FLORINDA *from him.)*

BELVILE: Nay, touch her not. She's mine by conquest, sir;
I won her by my sword.
WILLMORE: Didst thou so? And egad, child, we'll
110 keep her by the sword.

(Draws on PEDRO; BELVILE *goes between.)*

BELVILE: Stand off!
Thou'rt so profanely lewd, so curst by heaven,
All quarrels thou espousest must be fatal.
WILLMORE: Nay, an you be so hot, my valor's coy,
115 And shall be courted when you want it next.

(Puts up his sword.)

BELVILE *(to* PEDRO*):* You know I ought to claim a
victor's right,
But you're the brother to divine Florinda,
To whom I'm such a slave. To purchase her
I durst not hurt the man she holds so dear.
120 PEDRO: 'Twas by Antonio's, not by Belvile's sword
This question should have been decided, sir.
I must confess much to your bravery's due,
Both now and when I met you last in arms;
But I am nicely punctual in my word,
125 As men of honor ought, and beg your pardon:
For this mistake another time shall clear.

(Aside to FLORINDA *as they are going out.)*

—This was some plot between you and Belvile,
But I'll prevent you.

[*Exeunt* PEDRO *and* FLORINDA.]
*(*BELVILE *looks after her and begins to walk up and down
in rage.)*

WILLMORE: Do not be modest now and lose the
130 woman. But if we shall fetch her back so—
BELVILE: Do not speak to me!
WILLMORE: Not speak to you? Egad, I'll speak to you,
and will be answered, too.
BELVILE: Will you, sir?
135 WILLMORE: I know I've done some mischief, but I'm
so dull a puppy that I'm the son of a whore if I
know how or where. Prithee inform my understanding.
BELVILE: Leave me, I say, and leave me instantly!
140 WILLMORE: I will not leave you in this humor, nor till I
know my crime.
BELVILE: Death, I'll tell you, sir—

(Draws and runs at WILLMORE; *he runs out,* BELVILE
after him; FREDERICK *interposes.)*
(Enter ANGELLICA, MORETTA, *and* SEBASTIAN.)

ANGELLICA: Ha! Sebastian, is that not Willmore?
Haste! haste and bring him back.

[*Exit* SEBASTIAN.]

FREDERICK [*aside*]: The colonel's mad: I never saw 14[5]
him thus before. I'll after 'em lest he do some
mischief, for I am sure Willmore will not draw on
him. *(Exit.)*
ANGELLICA: I am all rage! My first desires defeated!
For one for aught he knows that has no 15[0]
Other merit than her quality,
Her being Don Pedro's sister. He loves her!
I know 'tis so. Dull, dull, insensible,
He will not see me now, though oft invited,
And broke his word last night. False perjured man! 15[5]
He that but yesterday fought for my favors,
And would have made his life a sacrifice
To've gained one night with me,
Must now be hired and courted to my arms.
MORETTA: I told you what would come on't, but Mo- 16[0]
retta's an old doting fool. Why did you give him
five hundred crowns, but to set himself out
for other lovers? You should have kept him poor
if you had meant to have had any good from
him. 16[5]
ANGELLICA: Oh, name not such mean trifles! Had I
given
Him all my youth has earned from sin,
I had not lost a thought nor sigh upon't.
But I have given him my eternal rest,
My whole repose, my future joys, my heart! 17[0]
My virgin heart, Moretta! Oh, 'tis gone!
MORETTA: Curse on him, here he comes. How fine
she has made him, too.

(Enter WILLMORE *and* SEBASTIAN; ANGELLICA *turns
and walks away.)*

WILLMORE: How now, turned shadow?
Fly when I pursue, and follow when I fly? *(Sings.)* 17[5]

> Stay, gentle shadow of my dove,
>   And tell me ere I go,
> Whether the substance may not prove
>   A fleeting thing like you.

(As she turns she looks on him.)

There's a soft kind look remaining yet. 18[0]
ANGELLICA: Well, sir, you may be gay: All happiness,
all joys pursue you still. Fortune's your slave, and
gives you every hour choice of new hearts and
beauties, till you are cloyed° with the repeated
bliss which others vainly languish for. But know, 18[5]
false man, that I shall be revenged.

(Turns away in rage.)

WILLMORE: So, gad, there are of those faint-hearted
lovers, whom such a sharp lesson next their hearts

---

cloyed, sated.

190 would make as impotent as fourscore.° Pox o' this
whining; my business is to laugh and love. A pox
on't, I hate your sullen lover: A man shall lose as
much time to put you in humor now as would
serve to gain a new woman.

195 ANGELLICA: I scorn to cool that fire I cannot raise,
Or do the drudgery of your virtuous mistress.

WILLMORE: A virtuous mistress? Death, what a thing
thou hast found out for me! Why, what the devil
should I do with a virtuous woman, a sort of ill-
200 natured creatures that take a pride to torment a
lover. Virtue is but an infirmity in woman, a disease that renders even the handsome ungrateful;
whilst the ill-favored, for want of solicitations and
address, only fancy themselves so. I have lain with
a woman of quality who has all the while been
205 railing at whores.

ANGELLICA: I will not answer for your mistress's
virtue,
Though she be young enough to know no guilt;
And I could wish you would persuade my heart
'Twas the two hundred thousand crowns you
courted.

210 WILLMORE: Two hundred thousand crowns! What
story's this? What trick? What woman, ha?

ANGELLICA: How strange you make it. Have you forgot the creature you entertained on the Piazzo
last night?

215 WILLMORE (aside): Ha! My gypsy worth two hundred
thousand crowns! Oh, how I long to be with her!
Pox, I knew she was of quality.

ANGELLICA: False man! I see my ruin in thy face.
How many vows you breathed upon my bosom
220 Never to be unjust. Have you forgot so soon?

WILLMORE: Faith, no; I was just coming to repeat
'em. But here's a humor indeed would make a
man a saint.—(Aside.) Would she would be angry
enough to leave me, and command me not to
225 wait on her.

(Enter HELLENA dressed in man's clothes.)

HELLENA: This must be Angellica: I know it by her
mumping° matron here. Ay, ay, 'tis she. My mad
captain's with her, too, for all his swearing. How
this unconstant humor makes me love him!—
230 Pray, good grave gentlewoman, is not this Angellica?

MORETTA: My too young sir, it is.—[Aside.] I hope 'tis
one from Don Antonio. (Goes to ANGELLICA.)

HELLENA (aside): Well, something I'll do to vex him
235 for this.

---

as fourscore, as someone eighty years old. **mumping,**
brooding.

ANGELLICA: I will not speak with him. Am I in humor
to receive a lover?

WILLMORE: Not speak with him? Why, I'll be gone,
and wait your idler minutes. Can I show less obedience to the thing I love so fondly? (Offers to go.) 240

ANGELLICA: A fine excuse this! Stay—

WILLMORE: And hinder your advantage? Should I
repay your bounties so ungratefully?

ANGELLICA [to HELLENA]: Come hither, boy.—
[To WILLMORE.] That I may let you see   245
How much above the advantages you name
I prize one minute's joy with you.

WILLMORE (impatient to be gone): Oh, you destroy me
with this endearment.—[Aside.] Death, how shall
I get away?—Madam, 'twill not be fit I should be   250
seen with you. Besides, it will not be convenient.
And I've a friend—that's dangerously sick.

ANGELLICA: I see you're impatient. Yet you shall stay.

WILLMORE (aside): And miss my assignation with my
gypsy.   255

(Walks about impatiently; MORETTA brings HELLENA,
who addresses herself to ANGELLICA.)

HELLENA: Madam,
You'll hardly pardon my intrusion
When you shall know my business,
And I'm too young to tell my tale with art;
But there must be a wondrous store of goodness   260
Where so much beauty dwells.

ANGELLICA: A pretty advocate, whoever sent thee.
Prithee proceed.
(To WILLMORE, who is stealing off.)
—Nay, sir, you shall not go.

WILLMORE (aside): Then I shall lose my dear gypsy forever. Pox on't, she stays me out of spite.   265

HELLENA: I am related to a lady, madam,
Young, rich, and nobly born, but has the fate
To be in love with a young English gentleman.
Strangely she loves him, at first sight she loved him,
But did adore him when she heard him speak;   270
For he, she said, had charms in every word
That failed not to surprise, to wound and conquer.

WILLMORE (aside): Ha! Egad, I hope this concerns me.

ANGELLICA (aside): 'Tis my false man he means.
Would he were gone:
This praise will raise his pride, and ruin me.
(To WILLMORE.)—Well,   275
Since you are so impatient to be gone,
I will release you, sir.

WILLMORE (aside): Nay, then I'm sure 'twas me he
spoke of: This cannot be the effects of kindness
in her.—No, Madam, I've considered better on't, 280
and will not give you cause of jealousy.

ANGELLICA: But sir, I've business that—

WILLMORE: This shall not do; I know 'tis but to try me.

ANGELLICA: Well, to your story, boy.—(Aside).

285 Though 'twill undo me.
HELLENA: With this addition to his other beauties,
    He won her unresisting tender heart.
    He vowed, and sighed, and swore he loved her
        dearly;
    And she believed the cunning flatterer,
290 And thought herself the happiest maid alive.
    Today was the appointed time by both
    To consummate their bliss:
    The virgin, altar, and the priest were dressed;
    And whilst she languished for th'expected
        bridegroom,
295 She heard he paid his broken vows to you.
WILLMORE (aside): So, this is some dear rogue that's in
    love with me, and this way lets me know it. Or, if it
    be not me, he means someone whose place I may
    supply.
300 ANGELLICA: Now I perceive
    The cause of thy impatience to be gone,
    And all the business of this glorious dress.
WILLMORE: Damn the young prater;° I know not what
    he means.
305 HELLENA: Madam,
    In your fair eyes I read too much concern
    To tell my further business.
ANGELLICA: Prithee, sweet youth, talk on: Thou
        mayst perhaps
    Raise here a storm that may undo my passion,
310 And then I'll grant thee anything.
HELLENA: Madam, 'tis to entreat you (oh
        unreasonable)
    You would not see this stranger.
    For if you do, she vows you are undone;
    Though nature never made a man so excellent,
315 And sure he 'ad been a god, but for inconstancy.
WILLMORE (aside): Ah, rogue, how finely he's in-
    structed! 'Tis plain, some woman that has seen
    me en passant.°
ANGELLICA: Oh, I shall burst with jealousy! Do you
320 know the man you speak of?
HELLENA: Yes, madam, he used to be in buff and scar-
    let.
ANGELLICA (to WILLMORE): Thou false as hell, what
    canst thou say to this?
325 WILLMORE: By heaven—
ANGELLICA: Hold, do not damn thyself—
HELLENA: Nor hope to be believed.

    (He walks about; they follow.)

ANGELLICA: Oh perjured man!
    Is't thus you pay my generous passion back?
330 HELLENA: Why would you, sir, abuse my lady's faith?
ANGELLICA: And use me so unhumanely.
HELLENA: A maid so young, so innocent—

---

prater, chatter-box.   en passant, in passing.

WILLMORE: Ah, young devil!
ANGELLICA: Dost thou not know thy life is in my
    power?   335
HELLENA: Or think my lady cannot be revenged?
WILLMORE (aside): So, so, the storm comes finely on.
ANGELLICA: Now thou art silent: Guilt has struck
    thee dumb.
    Oh, hadst thou still been so, I'd lived in safety.

(She turns away and weeps.)

WILLMORE (aside to HELLENA): Sweetheart, the lady's   340
    name and house—quickly! I'm impatient to be
    with her.

(Looks toward ANGELLICA to watch her turning, and as
she comes towards them he meets her.)

HELLENA (aside): So, now is he for another woman.
WILLMORE: The impudent'st young thing in nature:
    I cannot persuade him out of his error, madam.   345
ANGELLICA: I know he's in the right; yet thou'st a
    tongue
    That would persuade him to deny his faith.

(In rage walks away.)

WILLMORE (said softly to HELLENA): Her name, her
    name, dear boy!
HELLENA: Have you forgot it, sir?   350
WILLMORE (aside): Oh, I perceive he's not to know
    I am a stranger to his lady.—Yes, yes, I do know,
    but I have forgot the—(ANGELLICA turns.)—By
    heaven, such early confidence I never saw.
ANGELLICA: Did I not charge you with this mistress,
    sir?   355
    Which you denied, though I beheld your perjury.
    This little generosity of thine has rendered back
    my heart. (Walks away.)
WILLMORE (to HELLENA): So, you have made sweet
    work here, my little mischief. Look your lady
    be kind and good-natured now, or I shall have but 360
    a cursed bargain on't. (ANGELLICA turns toward
    them.)—The rogue's bred up to mischief; art thou
    so great a fool to credit him?
ANGELLICA: Yes, I do, and you in vain impose upon
    me. Come hither, boy. Is not this he you spake of? 365
HELLENA: I think it is. I cannot swear, but I vow he has
    just such another lying lover's look.

(HELLENA looks in his face; he gazes on her.)

WILLMORE (aside): Ha! Do I not know that face? By
    heaven, my little gypsy! What a dull dog was I:
    Had I but looked that way I'd known her. Are all   370
    my hopes of a new woman banished?—Egad, if I
    do not fit thee for this, hang me.—[To ANGEL-
    LICA.] Madam, I have found out the plot.
HELLENA [aside]: Oh lord, what does he say? Am I dis-
    covered now?   375
WILLMORE: Do you see this young spark here?

HELLENA [*aside*]: He'll tell her who I am.

WILLMORE: Who do you think this is?

HELLENA [*aside*]: Ay, ay, he does know me.—Nay, dear
380   captain, I am undone if you discover me.

WILLMORE: Nay, nay, no cogging;° she shall know
    what a precious mistress I have.

HELLENA: Will you be such a devil?

WILLMORE: Nay, nay, I'll teach you to spoil sport you
385   will not make.—This small ambassador comes
    not from a person of quality, as you imagine and
    he says, but from a very errant gypsy: the talk-
    ing'st, prating'st, canting'st° little animal thou
    ever saw'st.

390 ANGELICA: What news you tell me, that's the thing I
    mean.

HELLENA (*aside*): Would I were well off the place! If
    ever I go a-captain-hunting again—

WILLMORE: Mean that thing? That gypsy thing? Thou
395   mayst as well be jealous of thy monkey or parrot as
    of her. A German motion° were worth a dozen of
    her, and a dream were a better enjoyment—a crea-
    ture of a constitution fitter for heaven than man.

HELLENA (*aside*): Though I'm sure he lies, yet this
400   vexes me.

ANGELICA: You are mistaken: she's a Spanish woman
    made up of no such dull materials.

WILLMORE: Materials? Egad, an she be made of any
    that will either dispense or admit of love, I'll be
405   bound to continence.

HELLENA (*aside to him*): Unreasonable man, do you
    think so?

WILLMORE: You may return, my little brazen head,
410   and tell your lady, that till she be handsome
    enough to be beloved, or I dull enough to be reli-
    gious, there will be small hopes of me.

ANGELICA: Did you not promise, then, to marry her?

WILLMORE: Not I, by heaven.

ANGELICA: You cannot undeceive my fears and tor-
415   ments, till you have vowed you will not marry her.

HELLENA (*aside*): If he swears that, he'll be revenged
    on me indeed for all my rogueries.

ANGELICA: I know what arguments you'll bring
    against me: fortune and honor.

420 WILLMORE: Honor! I tell you, I hate it in your sex; and
    those that fancy themselves possessed of that fop-
    pery are the most impertinently troublesome of
    all womankind, and will transgress nine com-
    mandments to keep one. And to satisfy your jeal-
425   ousy, I swear—

HELLENA (*aside to him*): Oh, no swearing, dear captain.

WILLMORE: If it were possible I should ever be in-
    clined to marry, it should be some kind young
    sinner: one that has generosity enough to give a

favor handsomely to one that can ask it discreetly, 430
one that has wit enough to manage an intrigue of
love. Oh, how civil such a wench is to a man that
does her the honor to marry her.

ANGELICA: By heaven, there's no faith in anything he
    says. 435

(*Enter* SEBASTIAN.)

SEBASTIAN: Madam, Don Antonio—

ANGELICA: Come hither.

HELLENA [*aside*]: Ha! Antonio! He may be coming
    hither, and he'll certainly discover me. I'll there-
    fore retire without a ceremony. (*Exit* HELLENA.) 440

ANGELICA: I'll see him. Get my coach ready.

SEBASTIAN: It waits you, madam.

WILLMORE [*aside*]: This is lucky.—What, madam, now
    I may be gone and leave you to the enjoyment of
    my rival? 445

ANGELICA: Dull man, that canst not see how ill, how
    poor,
That false dissimulation looks. Be gone,
And never let me see thy cozening face again,
Lest I relapse and kill thee.

WILLMORE: Yes, you can spare me now. Farewell, till 450
    you're in better humor.—[*Aside.*] I'm glad of this
    release. Now for my gypsy:
For though to worse we change, yet still we find
New joys, new charms, in a new miss that's kind.

(*Exit* WILLMORE.)

ANGELICA: He's gone, and in this ague° of my soul 455
The shivering fit returns.
Oh, with what willing haste he took his leave,
As if the longed-for minute were arrived
Of some blest assignation.
In vain I have consulted all my charms, 460
In vain this beauty prized, in vain believed
My eyes could kindle any lasting fires;
I had forgot my name, my infamy,
And the reproach that honor lays on those
That dare pretend a sober passion here. 465
Nice reputation, though it leave behind
More virtues than inhabit where that dwells,
Yet that once gone, those virtues shine no more.
Then since I am not fit to be beloved,
I am resolved to think on a revenge 470
On him that soothed me thus to my undoing.

(*Exeunt.*)

Scene 3

(*A street. Enter* FLORINDA *and* VALERIA *in habits different from what they have been seen in.*)

FLORINDA: We're happily escaped, and yet I tremble
    still.

---

cogging, wheedling, fawning.   **canting'st,** most affectedly
pious.   **motion,** puppet show.

ague, a violent fever.

VALERIA: A lover, and fear? Why, I am but half an one, and yet I have courage for any attempt. Would Hellena were here: I would fain have had her as deep in this mischief as we; she'll fare but ill else, I doubt.

FLORINDA: She pretended a visit to the Augustine nuns; but I believe some other design carried her out; pray heaven we light on her. Prithee, what didst do with Callis?

VALERIA: When I saw no reason would do good on her, I followed her into the wardrobe, and as she was looking for something in a great chest, I toppled her in by the heels, snatched the key of the apartment where you were confined, locked her in, and left her bawling for help.

FLORINDA: 'Tis well you resolve to follow my fortunes, for thou darest never appear at home again after such an action.

VALERIA: That's according as the young stranger and I shall agree. But to our business. I delivered your note to Belvile when I got out under pretense of going to mass. I found him at his lodging, and believe me it came seasonably, for never was man in so desperate a condition. I told him of your resolution of making your escape today if your brother would be absent long enough to permit you; if not, to die rather than be Antonio's.

FLORINDA: Thou should'st have told him I was confined to my chamber upon my brother's suspicion that the business on the Molo was a plot laid between him and I.

VALERIA: I said all this, and told him your brother was now gone to his devotion; and he resolves to visit every church till he find him, and not only undeceive him in that, but caress him so as shall delay his return home.

FLORINDA: Oh heavens! He's here, and Belvile with him, too.

(They put on their vizards.)
(Enter DON PEDRO, BELVILE, WILLMORE; BELVILE *and* DON PEDRO *seeming in serious discourse.)*

VALERIA: Walk boldly by them, and I'll come at a distance, lest he suspect us.

(She walks by them and looks back on them.)

WILLMORE: Ha! A woman, and of excellent mien!
PEDRO: She throws a kind look back on you.
WILLMORE: Death, 'tis a likely wench, and that kind look shall not be cast away. I'll follow her.
BELVILE: Prithee do not.
WILLMORE: Do not? By heavens, to the antipodies,° with such an invitation.

(She goes out, and WILLMORE *follows her.)*

---

antipodies, antipodes, locations on the earth's surface that are directly opposite each other, hence very far away.

BELVILE: 'Tis a mad fellow for a wench.

(Enter FREDERICK.*)*

FREDERICK: Oh, colonel, such news!
BELVILE: Prithee what?
FREDERICK: News that will make you laugh in spite of fortune.
BELVILE: What, Blunt has had some damned trick put upon him? Cheated, banged, or clapped?°
FREDERICK: Cheated, sir, rarely cheated of all but his shirt and drawers; the unconscionable whore too turned him out before consummation, so that, traversing the streets at midnight, the watch found him in this *fresco* and conducted him home. By heaven, 'tis such a sight, and yet I durst as well been hanged as laughed at him or pity him: He beats all that do but ask him a question, and is in such an humor.
PEDRO: Who is't has met with this ill usage, sir?
BELVILE: A friend of ours whom you must see for mirth's sake.—*(Aside.)* I'll employ him to give Florinda time for an escape.
PEDRO: What is he?
BELVILE: A young countryman of ours, one that has been educated at so plentiful a rate he yet ne'er knew the want of money; and 'twill be a great jest to see how simply he'll look without it. For my part, I'll lend him none: And the rogue know not how to put on a borrowing face and ask first, I'll let him see how good 'tis to play our parts whilst I play his. Prithee, Fred, do you go home and keep him in that posture till we come. *(Exeunt.)*

(Enter FLORINDA *from the farther end of the scene, looking behind her.)*

FLORINDA: I am followed still. Ha! My brother too advancing this way! Good heavens defend me from being seen by him! *(She goes off.)*

(Enter WILLMORE, *and after him* VALERIA, *at a little distance.)*

WILLMORE: Ah, there she sails! She looks back as she were willing to be boarded; I'll warrant her prize. *(He goes out,* VALERIA *following.)*

(Enter HELLENA, *just as he goes out, with a page.)*

HELLENA: Ha, is not that my captain that has a woman in chase? 'Tis not Angellica.—Boy, follow those people at a distance, and bring me an account where they go in. *(Exit* PAGE.*)* —I'll find his haunts, and plague him everywhere. Ha! My brother!

*(*BELVILE, WILLMORE, PEDRO *cross the stage;* HELLENA *runs off.)*

---

clapped, "clap" is slang for gonorrhea.

Scene 4

(Scene changes to another street. Enter FLORINDA.*)*

FLORINDA: What shall I do? My brother now pursues me. Will no kind power protect me from his tyranny? Ha! Here's a door open; I'll venture in, since nothing can be worse than to fall into his hands. My life and honor are at stake, and my necessity has no choice. *(She goes in.)*

(Enter VALERIA, HELLENA's PAGE *peeping after* FLORINDA.*)*

PAGE: Here she went in; I shall remember this house.

(Exit BOY.*)*

VALERIA: This is Belvile's lodging; she's gone in as readily as if she knew it. Ha! Here's that mad fellow again; I dare not venture in. I'll watch my opportunity. *(Goes aside.)*

(Enter WILLMORE, *gazing about him.)*

WILLMORE: I have lost her hereabouts. Pox on't, she must not 'scape me so. *(Goes out.)*

Scene 5

(Scene changes to BLUNT's *chamber, discovers him sitting on a couch in his shirt and drawers, reading.)*

BLUNT: So, now my mind's a little at peace, since I have resolved revenge. A pox on this tailor, though, for not bringing home the clothes I bespoke. And a pox of all poor cavaliers: A man can never keep a spare suit for 'em, and I shall have these rogues come in and find me naked, and then I'm undone. But I'm resolved to arm myself: The rascals shall not insult over me too much. *(Puts on an old rusty sword and buff belt.)* Now, how like a morris dancer° I am equipped! A fine ladylike whore to cheat me thus without affording me a kindness for my money! A pox light on her, I shall never be reconciled to the sex more; she has made me as faithless as a physician, as uncharitable as a churchman, and as ill-natured as a poet. Oh, how I'll use all womankind hereafter! What would I give to have one of 'em within my reach now! Any mortal thing in petticoats, kind fortune, send me, and I'll forgive thy last night's malice.—Here's a cursed book, too—a warning to all young travelers—that can instruct me how to prevent such mischiefs now 'tis too late. Well, 'tis a rare convenient thing to read a little now and then, as well as hawk and hunt. *(Sits down again and reads.)*

(Enter to him FLORINDA.*)*

---

morris dancer, a morris dance was a vigorous dance performed by men wearing fancy costumes and bells.

FLORINDA: This house is haunted, sure: 'Tis well furnished, and no living thing inhabits it. Ha! A man! Heavens, how he's attired! Sure 'tis some rope dancer, or fencing master. I tremble now for fear, and yet I must venture now to speak to him.—Sir, if I may not interrupt your meditations—

(He starts up and gazes.)

BLUNT: Ha, what's here? Are my wishes granted? And is not that a she creature? 'Adsheartlikins, 'tis.—What wretched thing art thou, ha?

FLORINDA: Charitable sir, you've told yourself already what I am: a very wretched maid, forced by a strange unlucky accident to seek a safety here, and must be ruined if you do not grant it.

BLUNT: Ruined! Is there any ruin so inevitable as that which now threatens thee? Dost thou know, miserable woman, into what den of mischiefs thou art fallen; what abyss of confusion, ha? Dost not see something in my looks that frights thy guilty soul, and makes thee wish to change that shape of woman for any humble animal, or devil? For those were safer for thee, and less mischievous.

FLORINDA: Alas, what mean you, sir? I must confess, your looks have something in 'em makes me fear, but I beseech you, as you seem a gentleman, pity a harmless virgin that takes your house for sanctuary.

BLUNT: Talk on, talk on; and weep, too, till my faith return. Do, flatter me out of my senses again. A harmless virgin with a pox; as much one as t'other, 'adsheartlikins. Why, what the devil, can I not be safe in my house for you, not in my chamber? Nay, not even being naked too cannot secure me? This is an impudence greater than has invaded me yet. Come, no resistance. *(Pulls her rudely.)*

FLORINDA: Dare you be so cruel?

BLUNT: Cruel? 'Adsheartlikins, as a galley slave, or a Spanish whore. Cruel? Yes, I will kiss and beat thee all over, kiss and see thee all over; thou shalt lie with me too, not that I care for the enjoyment, but to let thee see I have ta'en deliberated malice to thee, and will be revenged on one whore for the sins of another. I will smile and deceive thee; flatter thee, and beat thee; embrace thee and rob thee, as she did me; fawn on thee, and strip thee stark naked; then hang thee out at my window by the heels, with a paper of scurvy verses fastened to thy breast in praise of damnable women. Come, come, along.

FLORINDA: Alas, sir, must I be sacrificed for the crimes of the most infamous of my sex? I never understood the sins you name.

BLUNT: Do, persuade the fool you love him, or that one of you can be just or honest; tell me I was not an easy coxcomb, or any strange impossible tale: It will be believed sooner than thy false showers

or protestations. A generation of damned hypocrites! To flatter my very clothes from my back! Dissembling witches! Are these the returns you make an honest gentleman that trusts, believes,
85 and loves you? But if I be not even with you—Come along, or I shall —*(Pulls her again.)*

(Enter FREDERICK.*)*

FREDERICK: Ha, what's here to do?

BLUNT: 'Adsheartlikins, Fred, I am glad thou art come, to be a witness of my dire revenge.

90 FREDERICK: What's this, a person of quality too, who is upon the ramble to supply the defects of some grave impotent husband?

BLUNT: No, this has another pretense: Some very unfortunate accident brought her hither, to save a
95 life pursued by I know not who or why, and forced to take sanctuary here at fool's haven. 'Adsheartlikins, to me of all mankind for protection? Is the ass to be cajoled again, think ye? No, young one, no prayers or tears shall mitigate my rage; there-
100 fore prepare for both my pleasures of enjoyment and revenge. For I am resolved to make up my loss here on thy body: I'll take it out in kindness and in beating.

FREDERICK: Now, mistress of mine, what do you think
105 of this?

FLORINDA: I think he will not, dares not be so barbarous.

FREDERICK: Have a care, Blunt, she fetched a deep sigh; she is enamored with thy shirt and drawers.
110 She'll strip thee even of that; there are of her calling such unconscionable baggages and such dexterous thieves, they'll flea° a man and he shall ne'er miss his skin till he feels the cold. There was a country-man of ours robbed of a row of teeth
115 whilst he was a-sleeping, which the jilt made him buy again when he waked. You see, lady, how little reason we have to trust you.

BLUNT: 'Adsheartlikins, why this is most abominable!

FLORINDA: Some such devils there may be, but by all
120 that's holy, I am none such. I entered here to save a life in danger.

BLUNT: For no goodness, I'll warrant her.

FREDERICK: Faith, damsel, you had e'en confessed the plain truth, for we are fellows not to be caught
125 twice in the same trap. Look on that wreck: a tight vessel when he set out of haven, well trimmed and laden. And see how a female picaroon of this island of rogues has shattered him, and canst thou hope for any mercy?

130 BLUNT: No, no, gentlewoman, come along; 'adsheartlikins, we must be better acquainted.—We'll both lie with her, and then let me alone to bang her.

FREDERICK: I'm ready to serve you in matters of revenge that has a double pleasure in't.

135 BLUNT: Well said.—You hear, little one, how you are condemned by public vote to the bed within; there's no resisting your destiny, sweetheart.

(Pulls her.)

FLORINDA: Stay, sir. I have seen you with Belvile, an English cavalier. For his sake, use me kindly. You
140 know him, sir.

BLUNT: Belvile? Why yes, sweeting, we do know Belvile, and wish he were with us now. He's a cormorant at whore and bacon;° He'd have a limb or two of thee, my virgin pullet. But 'tis no matter;
145 we'll leave him the bones to pick.

FLORINDA: Sir, if you have any esteem for that Belvile, I conjure you to treat me with more gentleness; he'll thank you for the justice.

FREDERICK: Hark'ee, Blunt, I doubt we are mistaken
150 in this matter.

FLORINDA: Sir, if you find me not worth Belvile's care, use me as you please. And that you may think I merit better treatment than you threaten, pray take this present.

(Gives him a ring; he looks on it.)

155 BLUNT: Hum, a diamond! Why, 'tis a wonderful virtue now that lies in this ring, a mollifying virtue. 'Adsheartlikins, there's more persuasive rhetoric in't than all her sex can utter.

FREDERICK: I begin to suspect something, and 'twould
160 anger us vilely to be trussed up° for a rape upon a maid of quality, when we only believe we ruffle a harlot.

BLUNT: Thou art a credulous fellow, but 'adsheartlikins, I have no faith yet. Why, my saint prattled
165 as parlously as this does; she gave me a bracelet, too, a devil on her! But I sent my man to sell it today for necessaries, and it proved as counterfeit as her vows of love.

FREDERICK: However, let it reprieve her till we see
170 Belvile.

BLUNT: That's hard, yet I will grant it.

(Enter a SERVANT.*)*

SERVANT: Oh, sir, the colonel is just come in with his new friend and a Spaniard of quality, and talks of having you to dinner with 'em.

175 BLUNT: 'Adsheartlikins, I'm undone! I would not see 'em for the world. Hark'ee, Fred, lock up the wench in your chamber.

FREDERICK: Fear nothing, madam: Whate'er he threatens, you are safe whilst in my hands.

---

flea, i.e., flay (skin).

cormorant at whore and bacon, greedy (metaphor taken from the scavenger bird) for illicit sex. *trussed up,* tied up.

(Exeunt FREDERICK *and* FLORINDA.*)*

180   BLUNT: And sirrah, upon your life, say I am not at home, or that I'm asleep, or—or—anything. Away; I'll prevent their coming this way.

(Locks the door, and exeunt.)

ACT 5

*(*BLUNT*'s chamber. After a great knocking as at his chamber door, enter* BLUNT *softly crossing the stage, in his shirt and drawers as before.)*

[VOICES] *(call within):* Ned! Ned Blunt! Ned Blunt!

BLUNT: The rogues are up in arms. 'Adsheartlikins, this villainous Frederick has betrayed me: They have heard of my blessed fortune.

5   [VOICES] *(and knocking within):* Ned Blunt! Ned! Ned!

BELVILE [*within*]: Why, he's dead, sir, without dispute dead; he has not been seen today. Let's break open the door. Here, boy—

BLUNT: Ha, break open the door? 'Adsheartlikins, that
10   mad fellow will be as good as his word.

BELVILE [*within*]: Boy, bring something to force the door.

(A great noise within, at the door again.)

BLUNT: So, now must I speak in my own defense; I'll try what rhetoric will do.—Hold, hold! What do
15   you mean, gentlemen, what do you mean?

BELVILE *(within):* Oh, rogue, art alive? Prithee open the door and convince us.

BLUNT: Yes, I am alive, gentlemen, but at present a little busy.

20   BELVILE *(within):* How, Blunt grown a man of business? Come, come, open and let's see this miracle.

BLUNT: No, no, no, no, gentlemen, 'tis no great business. But—I am—at—my devotion. 'Adsheartlikins, will you not allow a man time to pray?

25   BELVILE *(within):* Turned religious? A greater wonder than the first! Therefore open quickly, or we shall unhinge, we shall.

BLUNT [*aside*]: This won't do.—Why hark'ee, colonel, to tell you the truth, I am about a necessary affair
30   of life: I have a wench with me. You apprehend me?—The devil's in't if they be so uncivil as to disturb me now.

WILLMORE [*within*]: How, a wench? Nay then, we must enter and partake. No resistance. Unless it be
35   your lady of quality, and then we'll keep our distance.

BLUNT: So, the business is out.

WILLMORE [*within*]: Come, come, lend's more hands to the door. Now heave, all together. *(Breaks open*
40   *the door.)* So, well done, my boys.

(Enter BELVILE [*and his* PAGE], WILLMORE, FREDERICK, *and* PEDRO. BLUNT *looks simply, they all laugh at*

him; he lays his hand on his sword, and comes up to WILLMORE.*)*

BLUNT: Hark'ee, sir, laugh out your laugh quickly, d'ye hear, and be gone. I shall spoil your sport else, 'adsheartlikins, sir. I shall. The jest has been carried on too long.—*(Aside.)* A plague upon my
45   tailor!

WILLMORE: 'Sdeath, how the whore has dressed him! Faith, sir, I'm sorry.

BLUNT: Are you so, sir? Keep't to yourself then, sir, I advise you, d'ye hear, for I can as little endure
50   your pity as his mirth.

(Lays his hand on's sword.)

BELVILE: Indeed, Willmore, thou wert a little too rough with Ned Blunt's mistress. Call a person of quality whore, and one so young, so handsome, and so eloquent? Ha, ha, he.

BLUNT: Hark'ee, sir, you know me, and know I can be
55   angry. Have a care, for 'adsheartlikins, I can fight, too, I can, sir. Do you mark me? No more.

BELVILE: Why so peevish, good Ned? Some disappointments, I'll warrant. What, did the jealous count, her husband, return just in the nick?
60

BLUNT: Or the devil, sir. *(They laugh.)* D'ye laugh? Look ye settle me a good sober countenance, and that quickly, too, or you shall know Ned Blunt is not—

BELVILE: Not everybody, we know that.
65

BLUNT: Not an ass to be laughed at, sir.

WILLMORE: Unconscionable sinner! To bring a lover so near his happiness—a vigorous passionate lover—and then not only cheat him of his movables,° but his very desires, too.
70

BELVILE: Ah, sir, a mistress is a trifle with Blunt; he'll have a dozen the next time he looks abroad. His eyes have charms not to be resisted; there needs no more than to expose that taking person to the view of the fair, and he leads 'em all in triumph.
75

PEDRO: Sir, though I'm a stranger to you, I am ashamed at the rudeness of my nation; and could you learn who did it, would assist you to make an example of 'em.

BLUNT: Why ay, there's one speaks sense now, and
80   handsomely. And let me tell you, gentlemen, I should not have showed myself like a jack pudding° thus to have made you mirth, but that I have revenge within my power. For know, I have got into my possession a female, who had better
85   have fallen under any curse than the ruin I design her. 'Adsheartlikins, she assaulted me here in my own lodgings, and had doubtless committed a rape upon me, had not this sword defended me.

---

movables, property that can be moved, as opposed to land.   **jack pudding,** a buffoon.

90 FREDERICK: I know not that, but o' my conscience thou had ravished her, had she not redeemed herself with a ring. Let's see't, Blunt.

(BLUNT *shows the ring.*)

BELVILE [*aside*]: Ha! The ring I gave Florinda when we exchanged our vows!—Hark'ee, Blunt—

(*Goes to whisper to him.*)

95 WILLMORE: No whispering, good colonel, there's a woman in the case. No whispering.

BELVILE [*aside to* BLUNT]: Hark'ee, fool, be advised, and conceal both the ring and the story for your reputation's sake. Do not let people know what 100 despised cullies we English are; to be cheated and abused by one whore, and another rather bribe thee than be kind to thee, is an infamy to our nation.

WILLMORE: Come, come, where's the wench? We'll 105 see her; let her be what she will, we'll see her.

PEDRO: Ay, ay, let us see her. I can soon discover whether she be of quality, or for your diversion.

BLUNT: She's in Fred's custody.

WILLMORE: Come, come, the key—

(*To* FREDERICK, *who gives him the key; they are going.*)

110 BELVILE [*aside*]: Death, what shall I do?—Stay, gentlemen.—[*Aside.*] Yet if I hinder 'em, I shall discover all.—Hold, let's go one at once.° Give me the key.

WILLMORE: Nay, hold there, colonel, I'll go first.

FREDERICK: Nay, no dispute, Ned and I have the pro-115 priety of her.

WILLMORE: Damn propriety! Then we'll draw cuts.° (BELVILE *goes to whisper* [*to*] WILLMORE.) Nay, no corruption, good colonel. Come, the longest sword carries her.

(*They all draw, forgetting* DON PEDRO, *being a Spaniard, had the longest.*)

120 BLUNT: I yield up my interest to you gentlemen, and that will be revenge sufficient.

WILLMORE (*to* PEDRO): The wench is yours.—[*Aside.*] Pox of his Toledo,° I had forgot that.

FREDERICK: Come, sir, I'll conduct you to the lady.

(*Exeunt* FREDERICK *and* PEDRO.)

125 BELVILE (*aside*): To hinder him will certainly discover her.—Dost know, dull beast, what mischief thou hast done?

(WILLMORE *walking up and down, out of humor.*)

WILLMORE: Ay, ay, to trust our fortune to lots! A devil on't, 'twas madness, that's the truth on't.

BELVILE: Oh, intolerable sot— 130

(Enter FLORINDA *running, masked,* PEDRO *after her;* WILLMORE *gazing round her.*)

FLORINDA (*aside*): Good heaven defend me from discovery!

PEDRO: 'Tis but in vain to fly me; you're fallen to my lot.

BELVILE [*aside*]: Sure she's undiscovered yet, but now 135 I fear there is no way to bring her off.

WILLMORE [*aside*]: Why, what a pox, is not this my woman, the same I followed but now?

(PEDRO *talking to* FLORINDA, *who walks up and down.*)

PEDRO: As if I did not know ye, and your business here.

FLORINDA (*aside*): Good heaven, I fear he does indeed! 140

PEDRO: Come, pray be kind; I know you meant to be so when you entered here, for these are proper gentlemen.

WILLMORE: But sir, perhaps the lady will not be imposed upon: She'll choose her man. 145

PEDRO: I am better bred than not to leave her choice free.

(Enter VALERIA, *and is surprised at sight of* DON PEDRO.)

VALERIA (*aside*): Don Pedro here! There's no avoiding him.

FLORINDA (*aside*): Valeria! Then I'm undone. 150

VALERIA (*to* PEDRO, *running to him*): Oh, I have found you, sir! The strangest accident—if I had breath—to tell it.

PEDRO: Speak! Is Florinda safe? Hellena well?

VALERIA: Ay, ay, sir. Florinda is safe.—[*Aside.*] From 155 any fears of you.

PEDRO: Why, where's Florinda? Speak!

VALERIA: Ay, where indeed, sir; I wish I could inform you. But to hold you no longer in doubt —

FLORINDA (*aside*): Oh, what will she say? 160

VALERIA: She's fled away in the habit—of one of her pages, sir. But Callis thinks you may retrieve her yet, if you make haste away. She'll tell you, sir, the rest.—(*Aside.*) If you can find her out.

PEDRO: Dishonorable girl, she has undone my aim.— 165 [*To* BELVILE.] Sir, you see my necessity of leaving you, and I hope you'll pardon it. My sister, I know, will make her flight to you; and if she do, I shall expect she should be rendered back.

BELVILE: I shall consult my love and honor, sir. 170

(*Exit* PEDRO.)

FLORINDA (*to* VALERIA): My dear preserver, let me embrace thee.

WILLMORE: What the devil's all this?

BLUNT: Mystery, by this light.

---

one at once, one at a time.   **draw cuts,** draw swords, to see who has the longest sword.   **Toledo,** a sword made in the Spanish city of Toledo.

175 VALERIA: Come, come, make haste and get yourselves married quickly, for your brother will return again.

BELVILE: I'm so surprised with fears and joys, so amazed to find you here in safety, I can scarce
180 persuade my heart into a faith of what I see.

WILLMORE: Hark'ee, colonel, is this that mistress who has cost you so many sighs, and me so many quarrels with you?

BELVILE: It is.—[*To* FLORINDA.] Pray give him the
185 honor of your hand.

WILLMORE: Thus it must be received, then. (*Kneels and kisses her hand.*) And with it give your pardon, too.

FLORINDA: The friend to Belvile may command me
190 anything.

WILLMORE (*aside*): Death, would I might; 'tis a surprising beauty.

BELVILE: Boy, run and fetch a father° instantly.

(*Exit* BOY.)

FREDERICK: So, now do I stand like a dog, and have
195 not a syllable to plead my own cause with. By this hand, madam, I was never thoroughly confounded before, nor shall I ever more dare look up with confidence, till you are pleased to pardon me.

200 FLORINDA: Sir, I'll be reconciled to you on one condition: that you'll follow the example of your friend in marrying a maid that does not hate you, and whose fortune, I believe, will not be unwelcome to you.

205 FREDERICK: Madam, had I no inclinations that way, I should obey your kind commands.

BELVILE: Who, Fred marry? He has so few inclinations for womankind that had he been possessed of paradise he might have continued there to this day, if
210 no crime but love could have disinherited him.

FREDERICK: Oh, I do not use to boast of my intrigues.

BELVILE: Boast! Why, thou dost nothing but boast. And I dare swear, wert thou as innocent from the sin of the grape as thou art from the apple, thou
215 might'st yet claim that right in Eden which our first parents lost by too much loving.

FREDERICK: I wish this lady would think me so modest a man.

VALERIA: She would be sorry then, and not like you
220 half so well. And I should be loath to break my word with you, which was, that if your friend and mine agreed, it should be a match between you and I. (*She gives him her hand.*)

FREDERICK: Bear witness, colonel, 'tis a bargain.

---

father, priest.

(*Kisses her hand.*)

BLUNT (*to* FLORINDA): I have a pardon to beg, too; but 225
'adsheartlikins, I am so out of countenance that I'm a dog if I can say anything to purpose.

FLORINDA: Sir, I heartily forgive you all.

BLUNT: That's nobly said, sweet lady.—Belvile, prithee present her her ring again, for I find I have not 230
courage to approach her myself.

(*Gives him the ring; he gives it to* FLORINDA.)
(*Enter* BOY.)

BOY: Sir, I have brought the father that you sent for. [*Exit* BOY.]

BELVILE: 'Tis well. And now, my dear Florinda, let's fly to complete that mighty joy we have so long wished and sighed for.—Come, Fred, you'll follow? 235

FREDERICK: Your example, sir, 'twas ever my ambition in war, and must be so in love.

WILLMORE: And must not I see this juggling° knot tied?

BELVILE: No, thou shalt do us better service and be 240
our guard, lest Don Pedro's sudden return interrupt the ceremony.

WILLMORE: Content; I'll secure this pass.

(*Exeunt* BELVILE, FLORINDA, FREDERICK, *and* VALERIA.)
(*Enter* BOY.)

BOY (*to* WILLMORE): Sir, there's a lady without would speak to you. 245

WILLMORE: Conduct her in; I dare not quit my post.

BOY [*to* BLUNT]: And sir, your tailor waits you in your chamber.

BLUNT: Some comfort yet: I shall not dance naked at the wedding. 250

(*Exeunt* BLUNT *and* BOY.)
(*Enter again the* BOY, *conducting in* ANGELLICA *in a masking habit and a vizard.* WILLMORE *runs to her.*)

WILLMORE [*aside*]: This can be none but my pretty gypsy.—Oh, I see you can follow as well as fly. Come, confess thyself the most malicious devil in nature; you think you have done my business with Angellica— 255

ANGELLICA: Stand off, base villain!

(*She draws a pistol and holds it to his breast.*)

WILLMORE: Ha, 'tis not she! Who art thou, and what's thy business?

ANGELLICA: One thou hast injured, and who comes to kill thee for't. 260

WILLMORE: What the devil canst thou mean?

ANGELLICA: By all my hopes to kill thee—

---

juggling, treacherous, deceitful.

(Holds still the pistol to his breast; he going back, she following still.)

WILLMORE: Prithee, on what acquaintance? For I know thee not.

ANGELLICA: Behold this face so lost to thy remem-
265   brance, *(Pulls off her vizard.)*
And then call all thy sins about thy soul,
And let 'em die with thee.

WILLMORE: Angellica!

ANGELLICA: Yes, traitor! Does not thy guilty blood run
270   shivering through thy veins? Hast thou no horror
at this sight, that tells thee thou hast not long to
boast thy shameful conquest?

WILLMORE: Faith, no, child. My blood keeps its old
ebbs and flows still, and that usual heat too, that
275   could oblige thee with a kindness, had I but
opportunity.

ANGELLICA: Devil! Dost wanton with my pain? Have at
thy heart!

WILLMORE: Hold, dear virago!° Hold thy hand a little;
280   I am not now at leisure to be killed. Hold and
hear me.—*(Aside.)* Death, I think she's in earnest.

ANGELLICA *(aside, turning from him)*: Oh, if I take not
heed, my coward heart will leave me to his
mercy.—What have you, sir, to say?—But should I
285   hear thee, thoud'st talk away all that is brave
about me, and I have vowed thy death by all that's
sacred.

(Follows him with the pistol to his breast.)

WILLMORE: Why then, there's an end of a proper
handsome fellow, that might 'a lived to have done
290   good service yet. That's all I can say to't.

ANGELLICA *(pausingly)*: Yet—I would give thee time
for—penitence.

WILLMORE: Faith, child, I thank God I have ever took
care to lead a good, sober, hopeful life, and am of
295   a religion that teaches me to believe I shall depart
in peace.

ANGELLICA: So will the devil! Tell me,
How many poor believing fools thou hast undone?
How many hearts thou hast betrayed to ruin?
300 Yet these are little mischiefs to the ills
Thou'st taught mine to commit: Thou'st taught it
love.

WILLMORE: Egad, 'twas shrewdly hurt the while.

ANGELLICA: Love, that has robbed it of its
unconcern,
Of all that pride that taught me how to value it.
305 And in its room
A mean submissive passion was conveyed,

---

virago, a strong woman, sometimes with implication of being unwomanly.

That made me humbly bow, which I ne'er did
To anything but heaven.
Thou, perjured man, didst this; and with thy oaths,
Which on thy knees thou didst devoutly make,   310
Softened my yielding heart, and then I was a slave.
Yet still had been content to've worn my chains,
Worn 'em with vanity and joy forever,
Hadst thou not broke those vows that put them on.
'Twas then I was undone.   315

(All this while follows him with the pistol to his breast.)

WILLMORE: Broke my vows? Why, where hast thou
lived? Amongst the gods? For I never heard of
mortal man that has not broke a thousand vows.

ANGELLICA: Oh, impudence!

WILLMORE: Angellica, that beauty has been too long   320
tempting, not to have made a thousand lovers
languish; who, in the amorous fever, no doubt
have sworn like me. Did they all die in that faith,
still adoring? I do not think they did.

ANGELLICA: No, faithless man; had I repaid their vows,   325
as I did thine, I would have killed the ingrateful
that had abandoned me.

WILLMORE: This old general has quite spoiled thee:
Nothing makes a woman so vain as being flattered. Your old lover ever supplies the defects of   330
age with intolerable dotage, vast charge, and that
which you call constancy; and attributing all this
to your own merits, you domineer, and throw
your favors in's teeth, upbraiding him still with
the defects of age, and cuckold him as often as he   335
deceives your expectations. But the gay, young,
brisk lover, that brings his equal fires, and can
give you dart for dart, you'll find will be as nice as
you sometimes.

ANGELLICA: All this thou'st made me know, for which
I hate thee.   340
Had I remained in innocent security,
I should have thought all men were born my slaves,
And worn my power like lightning in my eyes,
To have destroyed at pleasure when offended.
But when love held the mirror, the undeceiving   345
glass
Reflected all the weakness of my soul, and made
me know
My richest treasure being lost, my honor,
All the remaining spoil could not be worth
The conqueror's care or value.
Oh, how I fell, like a long-worshiped idol,   350
Discovering all the cheat.
Would not the incense and rich sacrifice
Which blind devotion offered at my altars
Have fallen to thee?
Why wouldst thou then destroy my fancied power?   355

WILLMORE: By heaven, thou'rt brave, and I admire
thee strangely.

I wish I were that dull, that constant thing
Which thou wouldst have, and nature never meant
    me.
360 I must, like cheerful birds, sing in all groves,
And perch on every bough,
Billing the next kind she that flies to meet me;
Yet, after all, could build my nest with thee,
Thither repairing when I'd loved my round,
And still reserve a tributary flame.
365 To gain your credit, I'll pay you back your charity,
And be obliged for nothing but for love.

(Offers her a purse of gold.)

ANGELLICA: Oh, that thou wert in earnest!
So mean a thought of me
Would turn my rage to scorn, and I should pity
    thee,
370 And give thee leave to live;
Which for the public safety of our sex,
And my own private injuries, I dare not do.
Prepare— *(Follows still, as before.)*
I will no more be tempted with replies.
375 WILLMORE: Sure—
ANGELLICA: Another word will damn thee! I've heard
    thee talk too long.

(She follows him with the pistol ready to shoot; he retires, still amazed. Enter DON ANTONIO, *his arm in a scarf, and lays hold on the pistol.)*

ANTONIO: Ha! Angellica!
ANGELLICA: Antonio! What devil brought thee hither?
380 ANTONIO: Love and curiosity, seeing your coach at
    door. Let me disarm you of this unbecoming in-
    strument of death. *(Takes away the pistol.)* Amongst
    the number of your slaves was there not one wor-
    thy the honor to have fought your quarrel?—[*To*
385 WILLMORE.] Who are you, sir, that are so very
    wretched to merit death from her?
WILLMORE: One, sir, that could have made a better
    end of an amorous quarrel without you, than with
    you.
390 ANTONIO: Sure 'tis some rival. Ha! The very man took
    down her picture yesterday; the very same that set
    on me last night! Blessed opportunity—

(Offers to shoot him.)

ANGELLICA: Hold, you're mistaken, sir.
ANTONIO: By heaven, the very same!—Sir, what pre-
395 tensions have you to this lady?
WILLMORE: Sir, I do not use to be examined, and am
    ill at all disputes but this—

(Draws; ANTONIO *offers to shoot.)*

ANGELLICA *(to* WILLMORE*)*: Oh, hold! You see he's
    armed with certain death.
—And you, Antonio, I command you hold,

By all the passion you've so lately vowed me.   400

(Enter DON PEDRO, *sees* ANTONIO, *and stays.)*

PEDRO *(aside)*: Ha! Antonio! And Angellica!
ANTONIO: When I refuse obedience to your will,
May you destroy me with your mortal hate.
By all that's holy, I adore you so,
That even my rival, who has charms enough   405
To make him fall a victim to my jealousy,
Shall live; nay, and have leave to love on still.
PEDRO *(aside)*: What's this I hear?
ANGELLICA *(pointing to* WILLMORE*)*: Ah thus, 'twas
    thus he talked, and I believed.
Antonio, yesterday   410
I'd not have sold my interest in his heart
For all the sword has won and lost in battle.
—But now, to show my utmost of contempt,
I give thee life; which, if thou wouldst preserve,
Live where my eyes may never see thee more.   415
Live to undo someone whose soul may prove
So bravely constant to revenge my love.

(Goes out. ANTONIO *follows, but* PEDRO *pulls him back.)*

PEDRO: Antonio, stay.
ANTONIO: Don Pedro!
PEDRO: What coward fear was that prevented thee   420
    from meeting me this morning on the Molo?
ANTONIO: Meet thee?
PEDRO: Yes, me; I was the man that dared thee to't.
ANTONIO: Hast thou so often seen me fight in war, to
    find no better cause to excuse my absence? I sent   425
    my sword and one to do thee right, finding myself
    uncapable to use a sword.
PEDRO: But 'twas Florinda's quarrel that we fought,
    and you, to show how little you esteemed her,
    sent me your rival, giving him your interest. But I 430
    have found the cause of this affront, and when
    I meet you fit for the dispute, I'll tell you my
    resentment.
ANTONIO: I shall be ready, sir, ere long, to do you rea-
    son. *(Exit* ANTONIO.*)*   435
PEDRO: If I could find Florinda, now whilst my anger's
    high, I think I should be kind, and give her to
    Belvile in revenge.
WILLMORE: Faith, sir, I know not what you would do,
    but I believe the priest within has been so kind.   440
PEDRO: How? My sister married?
WILLMORE: I hope by this time he is, and bedded too,
    or he has not my longings about him.
PEDRO: Dares he do this? Does he not fear my power?
WILLMORE: Faith, not at all; if you will go in and thank 445
    him for the favor he has done your sister, so; if
    not, sir, my power's greater in this house than
    yours: I have a damned surly crew here that will
    keep you till the next tide, and then clap you on
    board for prize. My ship lies but a league off the   450

Molo, and we shall show your donship a damned Tramontana° rover's trick.

(Enter BELVILE.*)*

BELVILE: This rogue's in some new mischief. Ha! Pedro returned!

455 PEDRO: Colonel Belvile, I hear you have married my sister.

BELVILE: You have heard truth then, sir.

PEDRO: Have I so? Then, sir, I wish you joy.

BELVILE: How?

460 PEDRO: By this embrace I do, and I am glad on't.

BELVILE: Are you in earnest?

PEDRO: By our long friendship and my obligations to thee, I am; the sudden change I'll give you reasons for anon. Come, lead me to my sister, that 465 she may know I now approve her choice.

(Exit BELVILE *with* PEDRO.*)*
*(*WILLMORE *goes to follow them. Enter* HELLENA, *as before in boy's clothes, and pulls him back.)*

WILLMORE: Ha! My gypsy! Now a thousand blessings on thee for this kindness. Egad, child, I was e'en in despair of ever seeing thee again; my friends are all provided for within, each man his kind 470 woman.

HELLENA: Ha! I thought they had served me some such trick!

WILLMORE: And I was e'en resolved to go aboard, and condemn myself to my lone cabin, and the 475 thoughts of thee.

HELLENA: And could you have left me behind? Would you have been so ill natured?

WILLMORE: Why, 'twould have broke my heart, child. But since we are met again, I defy foul weather to 480 part us.

HELLENA: And would you be a faithful friend now, if a maid should trust you?

WILLMORE: For a friend I cannot promise: Thou art of a form so excellent, a face and humor too good 485 for cold dull friendship. I am parlously afraid of being in love, child; and you have not forgotten how severely you have used me?

HELLENA: That's all one; such usage you must still look for: to find out all your haunts, to rail at you 490 to all that love you, till I have made you love only me in your own defense, because nobody else will love you.

WILLMORE: But hast thou no better quality to recommend thyself by?

495 HELLENA: Faith, none, captain. Why, 'twill be the greater charity to take me for thy mistress. I am a lone child, a kind of orphan lover; and why I

should die a maid, and in a captain's hands too, I do not understand.

WILLMORE: Egad, I was never clawed away with broad- 500 sides from any female before. Thou hast one virtue I adore—good nature. I hate a coy demure mistress, she's as troublesome as a colt; I'll break none. No, give me a mad mistress when mewed, and in flying, one I dare trust upon the wing, that 505 whilst she's kind will come to the lure.°

HELLENA: Nay, as kind as you will, good captain, whilst it lasts. But let's lose no time.

WILLMORE: My time's as precious to me as thine can be. Therefore, dear creature, since we are so well 510 agreed, let's retire to my chamber; and if ever thou wert treated with such savory love! Come, my bed's prepared for such a guest all clean and sweet as thy fair self. I love to steal a dish and a bottle with a friend, and hate long graces. Come, 515 let's retire and fall to.

HELLENA: 'Tis but getting my consent, and the business is soon done. Let but old gaffer Hymen° and his priest say amen to't, and I dare lay my mother's daughter by as proper a fellow as your 520 father's son, without fear or blushing.

WILLMORE: Hold, hold, no bug words, child. Priest and Hymen? Prithee add a hangman to 'em to make up the consort. No, no, we'll have no vows but love, child, nor witness but the lover: The 525 kind deity enjoins naught but love and enjoy. Hymen and priest wait still upon portion and jointure; love and beauty have their own ceremonies. Marriage is as certain a bane to love as lending money is to friendship. I'll neither ask 530 nor give a vow, though I could be content to turn gypsy and become a left-handed° bridegroom to have the pleasure of working that great miracle of making a maid a mother, if you durst venture. 'Tis upse gypsy° that, and if I miss I'll 535 lose my labor.

HELLENA: And if you do not lose, what shall I get? A cradle full of noise and mischief, with a pack of repentance at my back? Can you teach me to weave incle° to pass my time with? 'Tis upse gypsy 540 that, too.

WILLMORE: I can teach thee to weave a true love's knot better.

HELLENA: So can my dog.

WILLMORE: Well, I see we are both upon our guards, 545 and I see there's no way to conquer good nature

---

Tramontana, area north of the Italian Alps.

flying . . . lure, The metaphor is of the woman as a falcon, either imprisoned ("mewed") or flying free ("on the wing"), but returning to the falconer's "lure." *Hymen,* god of marriage. *left-handed,* indicative of shady or underhanded dealings. *upse gypsy,* variation of upsy, meaning in the mode of the gypsy. *incle,* linen tape.

but by yielding. Here, give me thy hand: One kiss,
and I am thine.

550 HELLENA: One kiss! How like my page he speaks! I am
resolved you shall have none, for asking such a
sneaking sum. He that will be satisfied with one
kiss will never die of that longing. Good friend
single-kiss, is all your talking come to this? A kiss,
a caudle!° Farewell, captain single-kiss.

(Going out; he stays her.)

555 WILLMORE: Nay, if we part so, let me die like a bird
upon a bough, at the sheriff's charge. By heaven,
both the Indies shall not buy thee from me. I
adore thy humor and will marry thee, and we are
so of one humor it must be a bargain. Give me thy
560 hand. *(Kisses her hand.)* And now let the blind
ones, love and fortune, do their worst.

HELLENA: Why, god-a-mercy,° captain!

WILLMORE: But hark'ee: the bargain is now made, but
is it not fit we should know each other's names,
565 that when we have reason to curse one another
hereafter, and people ask me who 'tis I give to the
devil, I may at least be able to tell what family you
came of?

HELLENA: Good reason, captain; and where I have
570 cause, as I doubt not but I shall have plentiful,
that I may know at whom to throw my—blessings,
I beseech ye your name.

WILLMORE: I am called Robert the Constant.

HELLENA: A very fine name! Pray was it your faulkner°
575 or butler that christened you? Do they not use to
whistle when they call you?

WILLMORE: I hope you have a better, that a man may
name without crossing himself—you are so merry
with mine.

580 HELLENA: I am called Hellena the Inconstant.

(Enter PEDRO, BELVILE, FLORINDA, FREDERICK, VA-
LERIA.*)*

PEDRO: Ha! Hellena!

FLORINDA: Hellena!

HELLENA: The very same. Ha! My brother! Now, captain, show your love and courage; stand to your
585 arms and defend me bravely, or I am lost forever.

PEDRO: What's this I hear? False girl, how came you
hither, and what's your business? Speak!

(Goes roughly to her.)

WILLMORE: Hold off, sir; you have leave to parley°
only. *(Puts himself between.)*

---

caudle, drink made of warm thin gruel mixed with wine
and/or ale and administered to the sick.   god-a-mercy, God
have mercy.   faulkner, falconer, one who trains hawks.   parley, speak.

HELLENA: I had e'en as good tell it, as you guess it. 590
Faith, brother, my business is the same with all living creatures of my age: to love and be beloved—
and here's the man.

PEDRO: Perfidious maid, hast thou deceived me too;
deceived thyself and heaven?   595

HELLENA: 'Tis time enough to make my peace with
that;
Be you but kind, let me alone with heaven.

PEDRO: Belvile, I did not expect this false play from
you. Was't not enough you'd gain Florinda, which
I pardoned, but your lewd friends too must be   600
enriched with the spoils of a noble family?

BELVILE: Faith, sir, I am as much surprised at this as
you can be. Yet, sir, my friends are gentlemen,
and ought to be esteemed for their misfortunes,
since they have the glory to suffer with the best of 605
men and kings. 'Tis true, he's a rover of fortune,
yet a prince aboard his little wooden world.

PEDRO: What's this to the maintenance of a woman of
her birth and quality?

WILLMORE: Faith, sir, I can boast of nothing but a   610
sword which does me right where'er I come, and
has defended a worse cause than a woman's; and
since I loved her before I either knew her birth or
name, I must pursue my resolution and marry
her.   615

PEDRO: And is all your holy intent of becoming a nun
debauched into a desire of man?

HELLENA: Why, I have considered the matter, brother,
and find the three hundred thousand crowns my
uncle left me, and you cannot keep from me, will   620
be better laid out in love than in religion, and
turn to as good an account. Let most voices carry
it: for heaven or the captain?

ALL CRY: A captain! A captain!

HELLENA: Look ye, sir, 'tis a clear case.   625

PEDRO: Oh, I am mad!—*(Aside.)* If I refuse, my life's in
danger.—Come, there's one motive induces me.
Take her; I shall now be free from fears of her
honor. Guard it you now, if you can; I have been a
slave to't long enough. *(Gives her to him.)*   630

WILLMORE: Faith, sir, I am of a nation that are of opinion a woman's honor is not worth guarding when
she has a mind to part with it.

HELLENA: Well said, captain.

PEDRO *(to* VALERIA*)*:   This was your plot, mistress, but I 635
hope you have married one that will revenge my
quarrel to you.

VALERIA: There's no altering destiny, sir.

PEDRO: Sooner than a woman's will; therefore I forgive you all, and wish you may get my father's par- 640
don as easily, which I fear.

(Enter BLUNT *dressed in a Spanish habit, looking very
ridiculous; his* MAN *adjusting his band.)*

MAN: 'Tis very well, sir.

BLUNT: Well, sir! 'Adsheartlikins, I tell you 'tis damnable ill, sir. A Spanish habit! Good Lord! Could
645 the devil and my tailor devise no other punishment for me but the mode of a nation I abomi-
nate?

BELVILE: What's the matter, Ned?

BLUNT: Pray view me round, and judge.

(Turns round.)

650 BELVILE: I must confess thou art a kind of an odd
figure.

BLUNT: In a Spanish habit with a vengeance! I had
rather be in the Inquisition for Judaism° than in
this doublet and breeches; a pillory° were an easy
655 collar to this, three handfuls high; and these
shoes, too, are worse than the stocks, with the sole
an inch shorter than my foot. In fine, gentlemen,
methinks I look like a bag of bays° stuffed full of
fool's flesh.

660 BELVILE: Methinks 'tis well, and makes thee look e'en
cavalier. Come, sir, settle your face and salute our
friends. Lady—

BLUNT *(to* HELLENA*)*: Ha! Sayst thou so, my little
rover? Lady, if you be one, give me leave to kiss
665 your hand, and tell you, 'adsheartlikins, for all I
look so, I am your humble servant. A pox of my
Spanish habit! *(Music is heard to play.)*

WILLMORE: Hark! What's this?

(Enter BOY.*)*

BOY: Sir, as the custom is, the gay people in masquer-
670 ade, who make every man's house their own, are
coming up.

*(Enter several men and women in masking habits, with
music; they put themselves in order and dance.)*

BLUNT: 'Adsheartlikins, would 'twere lawful to pull off
their false faces, that I might see if my doxy° were
not amongst 'em.

675 BELVILE *(to the maskers)*: Ladies and gentlemen, since
you are come so *a propos,*° you must take a small
collation with us.

WILLMORE *(to* HELLENA*)*: Whilst we'll to the good man
within, who stays to give us a cast of his office.°
680 Have you no trembling at the near approach?

HELLENA: No more than you have in an engagement
or a tempest.

Inquisition for Judaism, Cf. note to Act 2, Scene 1, line
124. *pillory,* wooden structure, with three holes, for impris-
oning and punishing criminals. *bag of bays,* bay leaves and
other spices wrapped together and used in cooking. *doxy,*
mistress, prostitute. *a propos,* conveniently. *who stays to
give us a cast of his office,* who waits to perform his duty (i.e., to
marry them).

WILLMORE: Egad, thou'rt a brave girl, and I admire
thy love and courage.

Lead on; no other dangers they can dread, 685
Who venture in the storms o'th' marriage bed.

(Exeunt.)

EPILOGUE

The banished cavaliers! A roving blade!
A popish carnival! A masquerade!
The devil's in't if this will please the nation
In these our blessed times of reformation,
When conventickling° is so much in fashion. 5
And yet—
That mutinous tribe less factions do beget,
Than your continual differing in wit.
Your judgment's, as your passion's, a disease:
Nor muse nor miss your appetite can please; 10
You're grown as nice as queasy consciences,
Whose each convulsion, when the spirit moves,
Damns everything that maggot° disapproves.
   With canting° rule you would the stage refine,
And to dull method all our sense confine. 15
With th'insolence of commonwealths you rule,
Where each gay fop and politic grave fool
On monarch wit impose, without control.
As for the last, who seldom sees a play,
Unless it be the old Blackfriars° way; 20
Shaking his empty noddle° o'er bamboo,°
He cries, "Good faith, these plays will never do!
Ah, sir, in my young days, what lofty wit,
What high-strained scenes of fighting there were writ.
These are slight airy toys. But tell me, pray, 25
What has the House of Commons done today?"
Then shows his politics, to let you see
Of state affairs he'll judge as notably
As he can do of wit and poetry.
The younger sparks, who hither do resort, 30
Cry,
"Pox o' your genteel things! Give us more sport!
Damn me, I'm sure 'twill never please the court."
   Such fops are never pleased, unless the play
Be stuffed with fools as brisk and dull as they. 35
Such might the half-crown spare, and in a glass
At home behold a more accomplished ass.
Where they may set their cravats, wigs, and faces,
And practice all their buffoonry grimaces:
See how this huff becomes, this damny,° stare, 40

---

conventickling, from conventicle: a secret worship meeting for religious dissenters. *maggot,* conscience. *canting,*
affectedly pious. *Blackfriars,* London theater, originally part
of a monastery. *noodle,* head. *bamboo,* a walking stick.
damny, a contraction of damn me.

Which they at home may act because they dare,
But must with prudent caution do elsewhere.
Oh that our Nokes, or Tony Lee,° could show
A fop but half so much to th' life as you.

POSTSCRIPT

    This play had been sooner in print, but for a report about the town (made by some either very malicious or very ignorant) that 'twas *Thomaso*° altered; which made the booksellers fear some trouble from the proprietor of that admirable play, which indeed has wit enough to stock a poet, and is not to be pieced or mended by any but the excellent author himself. That I have stolen some hints from it, may be a proof that I valued it more than to pretend to alter it, had I the dexterity of some poets, who are not more expert in stealing than in the art of concealing, and who even that way outdo the Spartan boys.° I might have appropriated all to myself; but I, vainly proud of my judgment, hang out the sign of Angellica (the only stolen object) to give notice where a great part of the wit dwelt; though if the *Play of the Novella*° were as well worth remembering as *Thomaso,* they might (bating° the name) have as well said I took it from thence. I will only say the plot and business (not to boast on't) is my own; as for the words and characters, I leave the reader to judge and compare 'em with *Thomaso,* to whom I recommend the great entertainment of reading it. Though had this succeeded ill, I should have had no need of imploring that justice from the critics, who are naturally so kind to any that pretend to usurp their dominion, especially of our sex: They would doubtless have given me the whole honor on't. Therefore I will only say in English what the famous Vergil does in Latin: I make verses, and others have the fame.

Nokes, or Tony Lee, well-known comedians. James Nokes usually played foolish old husbands and fops and sometimes played foolish old ladies as well. *Thomaso, Thomaso, or The Wanderer,* a play by Thomas Killigrew written around 1654 and published ten years later; Behn's source. *Spartan boys,* cf. Plutarch's *Life of Lycurgus.* The Spartan boys were deprived of food and trained to steal without getting caught. *Play of the Novella, The Novella,* a play by Richard Brome (1632). *bating,* except for.

Figure 1. Angellica Bianca (Sinead Cusack) and Willmore (Jeremy Irons) in the Royal Shakespeare Company's 1986 production of *The Rover*, directed by John Barton. (Photograph: Joe Cocks Studio.)

Figure 2. Florinda (Geraldine Fitzgerald), Hellena (Imogen Stubbs), and Valeria (Susie Fairfax), dressed as gypsies, look forward to the freedom of the carnival in the RSC production of *The Rover*. (Photograph: Joe Cocks Studio.)

Figure 3. Florinda (Geraldine Fitzgerald), Hellena (Imogen Stubbs, *reading*), and Valeria (Susie Fairfax) listen with repressed indignation while Don Pedro (Nathaniel Parker) changes his clothes for the carnival, helped by Callis (Jenni George) and watched by Stephano (Trevor Gordon) in the opening scene of *The Rover.* (Photograph: Joe Cocks Studio.)

Figure 4. Ned Blunt (David Troughton) stumbles in the dark, looking for the prostitute Lucetta (Caroline Johnson, *back to audience*) in the RSC production of *The Rover.* (Photograph: Joe Cocks Studio.)

Staging of *The Rover*

REVIEW OF THE ROYAL SHAKESPEARE
COMPANY PRODUCTION, 1986,
BY BENEDICT NIGHTINGALE

"All women together ought to let flowers fall on the tomb of Aphra Behn, for it was she who earned them the right to speak their minds." So rhapsodised Virginia Woolf, perhaps a bit less plausibly than she would have wished. After all, it wasn't until the late seventies that women playwrights began confidently and in numbers to re-enter the theatrical sanctum whose portals Mrs. Behn had penetrated three centuries before; and even today there aren't many who speak their minds as robustly as she, in any literary form.

Partly that's because she was of her period, and that was the period of Sedley and Rochester. *The Rover*, though purportedly set in Spanish territory during the Commonwealth era, plunges us into a bawdy, gaudy, post-Restoration world, where the unprincipled pursuit of female flesh is, along with drinking and fighting, the prime concern of a gentleman. Professional whores are all around, flaunting their availability and price, and an unprotected woman is liable to find herself treated with little more respect. What is the reaction of the principals, among them her own brother, when the disguised heroine seeks sanctuary in one's house? "We'll both lie with her, and then let me alone to bang her."

Those who expect Behn to respond to such conduct with moral rancour are mistaking their woman. Yet something is different, markedly different, from the run of Restoration comedies; and that "something" has everything to do with the playwright's gender. *The Rover* may be a standard tale of amorous intrigue—masks, disguises and, at the centre of the comic camouflage, a soldier yearning for the beauteous Florinda, promised by her possessive brother to another—but it is seen and told primarily from the stance of the women involved. And right from the start, when the heroine and her two sisters surreptitiously leave their domestic prison to go on sexual safari in carnival country, it's evident that some of those women are pretty bold, determined people.

Take Hellena, the sprightliest of these manhunters and played at Stratford with verve and charm by the season's major discovery, Imogen Stubbs. She fancies the roving cavalier of the title largely because she identifies with his skittishness and irresponsibility; she persistently takes the sexual initiative with him; and she claims more or less the same freedom he takes for granted. "Well, I see our business as well as our humours are alike," she concludes, "yours to cozen as many maids as will trust you, and I as many men as have faith." Theirs is less a tale of boy-gets-girl than girl-grabs-boy: the affectionate pairing, on the woman's terms, of two amiably amoral spirits.

Not that Behn fails to recognise that her world is ultimately controlled by men. Hellena herself waxes articulate about her brother's period assumption that Florinda, so far from pursuing personal preference, should become the property of a husband who "sighs a belch or two, stales in your pot, farts loud as a musket, throws himself into bed, and expects you in his foul sheets." Even the whores have voices worth hearing. The most expensive of them, Angellica Bianca, is the only character privileged to speak, not in colloquial prose, but in dignified pentameters; and she's some serious points to make, not least about double sexual standards. "Who made the laws by which you judge me?" she asks Willmore, the feckless and lustful "rover," "Men! Men who would rove and ramble, but require that women must be nice."

Actually, she becomes almost too serious for the play, falling authentically in love with Willmore and seething and pining at her inevitable rejection in Hellena's favour; and Sinead Cusack, who performs the part, deserves credit both for sustaining emotional honesty and for keeping it within the bounds of the comic. But then everyone involved has done well by Behn: Jeremy Irons, a blend of buccaneer and prototypical pop star, grinning and swaggering through the role of Willmore himself; David Troughton, Hugh Quarshie, Geraldine Fitzgerald, Nathaniel Parker; and the director, John Barton, even though (or perhaps *because*) he has trimmed and tidied the original text.

What they collectively show is that our first woman playwright, unoriginal though her raw material and unremarkable though her powers of plotting might be, was a fine entertainer with a personality all her own. "Thou hast one virtue I adore," says Willmore to Hellena, as they prepare to leap into what promises to be a lively marriage, "Good nature." He could have been speaking of their joint author.

RICHARD BRINSLEY SHERIDAN

1751–1816

By the age of twenty-six, Richard Brinsley Sheridan had achieved remarkable successes in both his personal and his professional life. He had married the beautiful Miss Linley with whom he had eloped to France to save her from an unwelcome suitor; he had survived two duels with her frustrated suitor; his first play, *The Rivals,* had been successfully presented at Covent Garden, and later in the same year, 1775, his comic opera, *The Duenna,* began a run that would stretch to an amazing seventy-five performances; he had bought the well-known Drury Lane Theatre; and *The School for Scandal,* his most famous play, opened there with great success on May 7, 1777. Sheridan's remaining years in the theater were much less noteworthy. He was constantly plagued by debts—running a theater is an expensive business— and he wrote only two more plays: *The Critic* (1779), a witty burlesque of the theatrical process itself, and *Pizarro,* a melodrama adapted from a German source. His interest subsequently turned to politics, and when he died he was given a large public funeral and buried in Westminster Abbey.

The Rivals and *The School for Scandal,* Sheridan's two masterpieces, are not only brilliant theatrical works in themselves, but mark an important moment in English comedy—the return of wit and humor to the stage. For most of the eighteenth century, reactions against the so-called "Immorality and Profaneness of the English Stage" (the words are from the title of Jeremy Collier's famous attack of 1698 on Restoration comedy) had turned comedy away from laughter into melodrama filled with moral and emotional appeals. Such drama is usually referred to as "sentimental comedy," and its characteristics were succinctly described by Oliver Goldsmith, the author of the other great comedy of the late eighteenth century, *She Stoops to Conquer* (1773), in his "Essay on the Theater; or, A Comparison between Laughing and Sentimental Comedy" (1773):

> In these plays almost all the characters are good and exceedingly generous; they are lavish enough of their *tin* money on the stage; and though they want humor, have abundance of sentiment and feeling. If they happen to have faults or foibles, the spectator is taught not only to pardon but to applaud them, in consideration of the goodness of their hearts; so that folly, instead of being ridiculed, is commended, and the comedy aims at touching our passions without the power of being truly pathetic.

As Goldsmith implies here and makes explicit elsewhere in his essay (see Ideas of Drama), the spirit of sentimental comedy runs counter to the great tradition of corrective laughter that begins in Greek comedy, finds compelling force in the comedies of Ben Jonson, and dominates the later seventeenth century both in the plays of Molière and those of the English Restoration playwrights.

Sheridan also responded to such "weeping comedy" with his own "laughing comedy," *The Rivals,* which quickly reveals his intentions in the second scene, where he introduces a young woman of markedly sentimental tendencies—so marked, indeed, that they are clearly meant to be a comic caricature. Her name, Lydia Languish, clearly denotes her sentimental excesses, as do the mawkish titles of the books in her library: *The Reward of Constancy, The Fatal Connection, The Mistakes of the Heart,* and *The Delicate Mistress.* Although Lydia is the comedy's romantic heroine, she is nonetheless an extremely silly girl, overwhelmed with romantic notions that Sheridan constantly undercuts. The play's genuine humor, however, derives not from the problems of Lydia but from the schemes of her lover, Captain Absolute, who disguises himself to woo her and then experiences the comic complications that result from his double identity. Even more memorable to most audiences are two characters whose language is a perpetual source of comic delight: Bob Acres and Mrs. Malaprop. Acres, a country gentleman, figures in the plot as a rival to Absolute for Lydia's hand, but his real stage function is to amuse the audience with his attempts at fashionable dress and speech. Again Sheridan pokes fun at the excesses of sentiment, for Acres is intent on swearing so that "the oath should be an echo to the sense; and this we call the *oath referential* or *sentimental swearing.*" Even more extreme as a figure of affectation and humor is Mrs. Malaprop, whose name has given the word "malapropism" to our language. Her expressed concern for the correct use of language makes the repeatedly garbled language of her speeches even more ludicrous: "but above all, Sir Anthony, she should be mistress of orthodoxy, that she might not mis-spell and mis-pronounce words so shamefully as girls usually do; and likewise that she might reprehend the true meaning of what she is saying."

The School for Scandal at first seems an extension of Sheridan's attack on sentimental comedy, especially considering the satiric portrayal of Joseph Surface, who is praised as a "man of sentiment," when, as his last name implies, he is actually a man of deception. But it should be noted that the moral and emotional sentiments Joseph expresses are themselves neither offensive nor necessarily false. Instead, Sheridan attacks Joseph's *pose* as a man who makes moral statements—"to smile at the jest which plants a thorn in another's breast is to become a principal in the mischief"—while actually scheming to slander his brother Charles and steal his beloved. And though Joseph Surface is the subtlest, the most cunning, of the scandalmongers because he wears the mask of moral concern, he is by no means the only one in the play. With such tag names as Lady Sneerwell, Mrs. Candour, Crabtree, Snake, and Sir Benjamin Backbite, Sheridan, like Molière in *The Misanthrope,* creates an entire gallery of malicious gossips to populate his school for scandal.

Although Sheridan attacks malice masquerading as sentiment, he also presents the value of true sentiment, of genuine feelings that prompt generous actions. In Act 4, Scene 1, when the seemingly rakish Charles refuses to sell the portrait of his uncle, Sir Oliver, because "The old fellow has been very good to me, and, egad, I'll keep his picture while I've a room to put it in," the improvident generosity of his impulse wins him the affection of the disguised Oliver. Similarly, the play's climactic and most intricately structured scene, the "screen scene," is a masterful blend of witty double-entendre, farcical maneuverings, and at the end honest feelings. The scene's tension builds slowly as Lady Teazle, then her husband Sir Peter, and finally Charles Surface enter Joseph's library, creating a situation that we hope will finally lead to the revelation of Joseph's duplicity. And when the revelation comes, with the toppling of the screen and the discovery of Lady Teazle's hiding place, we get not only the punch line to the long joke but something more. While Lady Teazle has been hiding behind the screen she has had a chance to hear Sir Peter's open confession of his love for her, his young, headstrong wife. And when she is discovered, she responds not with the expected evasion but with a frank acknowledgment of her faults and a promise to be a better wife.

Because the play encompasses so many moods, it can be performed in a variety of ways, as it has been on the contemporary stage. The customary choice has been to aim for a high style reminiscent of fashionable eighteenth-century society. But the actors in the Stratford, Ontario, production of 1970 were praised by Clive Barnes for avoiding "any preconceptions they may have about English high comedy style." And Michael Langham, that production's director, makes clear in an interview following the text that he tried to emphasize the "soiled" quality of the scandalmongers (see Figure 1), much as he tried to portray the realistic side of the relationship between Sir Peter Teazle and Lady Teazle (see Figure 2). As both the painful action of the portrait scene (see Figure 3) and the vigorous action in the screen scene suggest (see Figure 4), Langham deliberately moved away from the "icy artifice of most modern staging" so as to convey the complex world of the play. But no matter how it is staged, *The School for Scandal* remains a masterful blend of wit and true sentiment.

THE SCHOOL FOR SCANDAL

BY RICHARD BRINSLEY SHERIDAN / EDITED BY GEORGE H. NETTLETON AND ARTHUR E. CASE

CHARACTERS

SIR PETER TEAZLE
SIR OLIVER SURFACE
JOSEPH SURFACE
CHARLES SURFACE
CRABTREE
SIR BENJAMIN BACKBITE
ROWLEY
TRIP
MOSES

SNAKE
CARELESS *and other Companions to* CHARLES SURFACE
SERVANTS, *etc.*
LADY TEAZLE
MARIA
LADY SNEERWELL
MRS. CANDOUR

SCENE
London

PROLOGUE

by David Garrick, Esq.

A School for Scandal! tell me, I beseech you,
Needs there a school this modish art to teach you?
No need of lessons now, the knowing think—
We might as well be taught to eat and drink—
5 Caused by a dearth of scandal, should the vapors
Distress our fair ones—let 'em read the papers;
Their own pow'rful mixtures such disorders hit;
Crave what they will, there's *quantum sufficit.*°
    'Lord!' cries my Lady Wormwood (who loves
      tattle,
10 And puts much salt and pepper in her prattle),
Just ris'n at noon, all night at cards when threshing
Strong tea and scandal—'Bless me, how refreshing!
Give me the papers, Lisp—how bold and free! *(Sips.)*
Last night Lord L—(sips) was caught with Lady D—
15 For aching heads what charming sal volatile! *(Sips.)*
If Mrs. B—will still continue flirting,
We hope she'll DRAW, *or we'll* UNDRAW *the curtain.*
Fine satire, poz°—in public all abuse it,
But by ourselves *(sips)*, our praise we can't refuse it.
20 Now, Lisp, read *you*—there, at that dash and star.'°
'Yes, ma'am.—*A certain Lord had best beware,*
Who lives not twenty miles from Grosv'nor Square;
For should he Lady W—find willing,
WORMWOOD *is bitter*'—'Oh! that's me! the villain!
25 Throw it behind the fire, and never more
Let that vile paper come within my door.'—

---

      quantum sufficit, plenty. *poz*, positively. **dash and star,**
a frequent method of veiled reference to the names of those
involved in fashionable intrigues.

Thus at our friends we laugh, who feel the dart;
To reach our feelings, we ourselves must smart.
Is our young bard so young, to think that he
Can stop the full spring-tide of calumny?   30
Knows he the world so little, and its trade?
Alas! the devil is sooner raised than laid.
So strong, so swift, the monster there's no gagging:
Cut Scandal's head off—still the tongue is wagging.
Proud of your smiles once lavishly bestow'd,   35
Again your young Don Quixote takes the road:
To show his gratitude, he draws his pen,
And seeks this hydra, Scandal, in his den.
For your applause all perils he would through—
He'll fight—that's *write*—a cavalliero true,   40
Till every drop of blood—that's *ink*—is spilt for you.

ACT 1 / SCENE 1

    (LADY SNEERWELL'*s house*)
    (LADY SNEERWELL *at the dressing-table*—SNAKE *drinking chocolate.*)

LADY SNEERWELL: The paragraphs, you say, Mr. Snake,
    were all inserted?
SNAKE: They were madam, and as I copied them
    myself in a feigned hand, there can be no suspi-
    cion whence they came.   5
LADY SNEERWELL: Did you circulate the reports of
    Lady Brittle's intrigue with Captain Boastall?
SNAKE: That is in as fine a train as your ladyship could
    wish,—in the common course of things, I think it
    must reach Mrs. Clackit's ears within four-and-   10
    twenty hours; and then, you know, the business is
    as good as done.
LADY SNEERWELL: Why, truly, Mrs. Clackit has a very
    pretty talent, and a great deal of industry.

15 SNAKE: True, madam, and has been tolerably successful in her day:—to my knowledge, she has been
the cause of six matches being broken off, and
three sons being disinherited, of four forced
elopements, as many close confinements, nine
20 separate maintenances, and two divorces;—nay, I
have more than once traced her causing a *Tête-à-
Tête* in the *Town and Country Magazine,*° when the
parties perhaps had never seen each other's faces
before in the course of their lives.
25 LADY SNEERWELL: She certainly has talents, but her
manner is gross.
SNAKE: 'Tis very true,—she generally designs well, has
a free tongue, and a bold invention; but her col-
oring is too dark, and her outline often extrava-
30 gant. She wants that *delicacy of hint,* and *mellowness
of sneer,* which distinguish your ladyship's scandal.
LADY SNEERWELL: Ah! you are partial, Snake.
SNAKE: Not in the least; everybody allows that Lady
Sneerwell can do more with *a word* or *a look* than
35 many can with the most labored detail, even
when they happen to have a little truth on their
side to support it.
LADY SNEERWELL: Yes, my dear Snake; and I am no
hypocrite to deny the satisfaction I reap from the
40 success of my efforts. Wounded myself, in the
early part of my life, by the envenomed tongue of
slander, I confess I have since known no pleasure
equal to the reducing others to the level of my
own injured reputation.
45 SNAKE: Nothing can be more natural. But Lady Sneerwell, there is one affair in which you have lately
employed me, wherein, I confess, I am at a loss to
guess your motives.
LADY SNEERWELL: I conceive you mean with respect to
50 my neighbor, Sir Peter Teazle, and his family?
SNAKE: I do; here are two young men, to whom Sir
Peter has acted as a kind of guardian since their
father's death; the elder possessing the most amiable character, and universally well spoken of; the
55 youngest, the most dissipated and extravagant
young fellow in the kingdom, without friends or
character,—the former an avowed admirer of
your ladyship, and apparently your favorite; the
latter attached to Maria, Sir Peter's ward, and
60 confessedly beloved by her. Now, on the face of
these circumstances, it is utterly unaccountable to
me, why you, the widow of a city knight, with a
good jointure, should not close with the passion
of a man of such character and expectations as
65 Mr. Surface; and more so why you should be so

Town and Country Magazine, since 1769, this magazine
had published monthly sketches of fashionable intrigues.

uncommonly earnest to destroy the mutual attachment subsisting between his brother Charles
and Maria.
LADY SNEERWELL: Then, at once to unravel this mys- 70
tery, I must inform you that love has no share
whatever in the intercourse between Mr. Surface
and me.
SNAKE: No!
LADY SNEERWELL: His real attachment is to Maria, or 75
her fortune; but finding in his brother a favored
rival, he has been obliged to mask his pretensions, and profit by my assistance.
SNAKE: Yet still I am more puzzled why you should
interest yourself in his success.
LADY SNEERWELL: Heav'ns! how dull you are! Can- 80
not you surmise the weakness which I hitherto,
through shame, have concealed even from *you?*
Must I confess that Charles—that libertine, that
extravagant, that bankrupt in fortune and reputation—that he it is for whom I am thus anxious 85
and malicious, and to gain whom I would sacrifice everything?
SNAKE: Now, indeed, your conduct appears consistent; but how came you and Mr. Surface so confidential? 90
LADY SNEERWELL: For our mutual interest. I have
found him out a long time since—I know him to
be artful, selfish, and malicious—in short, a sentimental knave.
SNAKE: Yet, Sir Peter vows he has not his equal in 95
England—and, above all, he praises him as a man
of sentiment.
LADY SNEERWELL: True; and with the assistance of his
sentiment and hypocrisy he has brought Sir Peter
entirely into his interest with regard to Maria. 100

(Enter SERVANT.*)*

SERVANT: Mr. Surface.
LADY SNEERWELL: Show him up. *(Exit* SERVANT.*)* He
generally calls about this time. I don't wonder at
people's giving him to me for a lover.

(Enter JOSEPH SURFACE.*)*

JOSEPH SURFACE: My dear Lady Sneerwell, how do you 105
do to-day? Mr. Snake, your most obedient.
LADY SNEERWELL: Snake has just been arraigning me
on our mutual attachment, but I have informed
him of our real views; you know how useful he has
been to us; and, believe me, the confidence is not 110
ill placed.
JOSEPH SURFACE: Madam, it is impossible for me to
suspect a man of Mr. Snake's sensibility and discernment.
LADY SNEERWELL: Well, well, no compliments now;— 115
but tell me when you saw your mistress, Maria—
or, what is more material to me, your brother.

JOSEPH SURFACE: I have not seen either since I left you; but I can inform you that they never meet. Some of your stories have taken a good effect on Maria.

LADY SNEERWELL: Oh, my dear Snake! the merit of this belongs to you. But do your brother's distresses increase?

JOSEPH SURFACE: Every hour;—I am told he has had another execution in the house yesterday; in short, his dissipation and extravagance exceed anything I ever heard of.

LADY SNEERWELL: Poor Charles!

JOSEPH SURFACE: True, madam;—notwithstanding his vices, one can't help feeling for him.—Aye, poor Charles! I'm sure I wish it was in *my* power to be of any essential service to him.—For the man who does not share in the distresses of a brother, even though merited by his own misconduct, deserves—

LADY SNEERWELL: O lud! you are going to be moral, and forget that you are among friends.

JOSEPH SURFACE: Egad, that's true!—I'll keep that sentiment till I see Sir Peter. However, it is certainly a charity to rescue Maria from such a libertine, who, if he is to be reclaimed, can be so only by a person of your ladyship's superior accomplishments and understanding.

SNAKE: I believe, Lady Sneerwell, here's company coming,—I'll go and copy the letter I mentioned to you.—Mr. Surface, your most obedient. *(Exit SNAKE.)*

JOSEPH SURFACE: Sir, your very devoted.—Lady Sneerwell, I am very sorry you have put any further confidence in that fellow.

LADY SNEERWELL: Why so?

JOSEPH SURFACE: I have lately detected him in frequent conference with old Rowley, who was formerly my father's steward, and has never, you know, been a friend of mine.

LADY SNEERWELL: And do you think he would betray us?

JOSEPH SURFACE: Nothing more likely: take my word for't, Lady Sneerwell, that fellow hasn't virtue enough to be faithful even to his own villainy.—Hah! Maria!

(Enter MARIA.)

LADY SNEERWELL: Maria, my dear, how do you do?—What's the matter?

MARIA: Oh! there is that disagreeable lover of mine, Sir Benjamin Backbite, has just called at my guardian's, with his odious uncle, Crabtree; so I slipped out, and ran hither to avoid them.

LADY SNEERWELL: Is that all?

JOSEPH SURFACE: If my brother Charles had been of the party, ma'am, perhaps you would not have been so much alarmed.

LADY SNEERWELL: Nay, now you are severe; for I dare swear the truth of the matter is, Maria heard *you* were here;—but, my dear, what has Sir Benjamin done, that you should avoid him so?

MARIA: Oh, he has done nothing—but 'tis for what he has said,—his conversation is a perpetual libel on all his acquaintance.

JOSEPH SURFACE: Aye, and the worst of it is, there is no advantage in not knowing him; for he'll abuse a stranger just as soon as his best friend—and his uncle's as bad.

LADY SNEERWELL: Nay, but we should make allowance; Sir Benjamin is a wit and a poet.

MARIA: For my part, I own, madam, wit loses its respect with me, when I see it in company with malice.—What do you think, Mr. Surface?

JOSEPH SURFACE: Certainly, madam; to smile at the jest which plants a thorn in another's breast is to become a principal in the mischief.

LADY SNEERWELL: Pshaw! there's no possibility of being witty without a little ill nature: the malice of a good thing is the barb that makes it stick.—What's your opinion, Mr. Surface?

JOSEPH SURFACE: To be sure, madam, that conversation, where the spirit of raillery is suppressed, will ever appear tedious and insipid.

MARIA: Well I'll not debate how far scandal may be allowable; but in a man, I am sure, it is always contemptible.—We have pride, envy, rivalship, and a thousand motives to depreciate each other; but the male slanderer must have the cowardice of a woman before he can traduce one.

(Enter SERVANT.)

SERVANT: Madam, Mrs. Candour is below, and, if your ladyship's at leisure, will leave her carriage.

LADY SNEERWELL: Beg her to walk in. *(Exit SERVANT.)* Now Maria, however here is a character to your taste; for, though Mrs. Candour is a little talkative, everybody allows her to be the best-natured and best sort of woman.

MARIA: Yes, with a very gross affectation of good nature and benevolence, she does more mischief than the direct malice of old Crabtree.

JOSEPH SURFACE: I'faith 'tis very true, Lady Sneerwell; whenever I hear the current running against the characters of my friends, I never think them in such danger as when Candour undertakes their defence.

LADY SNEERWELL: Hush!—here she is!

(Enter MRS. CANDOUR.)

MRS. CANDOUR: My dear Lady Sneerwell, how have you been this century?—Mr. Surface, what news do you hear?—though indeed it is no matter, for I think one hears nothing else but scandal.

JOSEPH SURFACE: Just so, indeed, madam.

225 MRS. CANDOUR: Ah, Maria! child,—what, is the whole affair off between you and Charles? His extravagance, I presume—the town talks of nothing else.

MARIA: I am very sorry, ma'am, the town has so little to do.

230 MRS. CANDOUR: True, true, child: but there is no stopping people's tongues.—I own I was hurt to hear it, as indeed I was to learn, from the same quarter, that your guardian, Sir Peter, and Lady Teazle have not agreed lately so well as could be wished.

235 MARIA: 'Tis strangely impertinent for people to busy themselves so.

MRS. CANDOUR: Very true, child, but what's to be done? People will talk—there's no preventing it.—Why, it was but yesterday I was told that Miss
240 Gadabout had eloped with Sir Filigree Flirt.—But, Lord! there's no minding what one hears—though, to be sure, I had this from very good authority.

MARIA: Such reports are highly scandalous.

245 MRS. CANDOUR: So they are, child—shameful, shameful! But the world is so censorious, no character escapes.—Lord, now who would have suspected your friend, Miss Prim, of an indiscretion? Yet such is the ill-nature of people, that they say her
250 uncle stopped her last week, just as she was stepping into the York Diligence with her dancing-master.

MARIA: I'll answer for't there are no grounds for the report.

255 MRS. CANDOUR: Oh, no foundation in the world, I dare swear; no more, probably, than for the story circulated last month of Mrs. Festino's affair with Colonel Cassino;—though, to be sure, that matter was never rightly cleared up.

260 JOSEPH SURFACE: The license of invention some people take is monstrous indeed.

MARIA: 'Tis so.—But, in my opinion, those who report such things are equally culpable.

MRS. CANDOUR: To be sure, they are; tale-bearers are
265 as bad as the tale-makers—'tis an old observation, and a very true one—but what's to be done, as I said before? how will you prevent people from talking?—To-day, Mrs. Clackit assured me Mr. and Mrs. Honeymoon were at last become mere
270 man and wife, like the rest of their acquaintances.—She likewise hinted that a certain widow, in the next street, had got rid of her dropsy and recovered her shape in a most surprising manner. And at the same time Miss Tattle, who was by,
275 affirmed that Lord Buffalo had discovered his lady at a house of no extraordinary fame—and that Sir Harry Bouquet and Tom Saunter were to measure swords on a similar provocation. But, Lord, do you think I would report these things!
280 No, no! tale-bearers, as I said before, are just as bad as tale-makers.

JOSEPH SURFACE: Ah! Mrs. Candour, if everybody had your forbearance and good nature!

MRS. CANDOUR: I confess, Mr. Surface, I cannot bear to hear people attacked behind their backs, and 285 when ugly circumstances come out against one's acquaintance I own I always love to think the best.—By the bye, I hope it is not true that your brother is absolutely ruined?

JOSEPH SURFACE: I am afraid his circumstances are 290 very bad indeed, ma'am.

MRS. CANDOUR: Ah!—I heard so—but you must tell him to keep up his spirits—everybody almost is in the same way! Lord Spindle, Sir Thomas Splint, Captain Quinze, and Mr. Nickit—all up, I hear, 295 within this week; so, if Charles is undone, he'll find half his acquaintances ruined too—and that, you know, is a consolation.

JOSEPH SURFACE: Doubtless, ma'am—a very great one.

(Enter SERVANT.)

SERVANT: Mr. Crabtree and Sir Benjamin Backbite. 300 (Exit SERVANT.)

LADY SNEERWELL: So, Maria, you see your lover pursues you; positively you shan't escape.

(Enter CRABTREE and SIR BENJAMIN BACKBITE.)

CRABTREE: Lady Sneerwell, I kiss your hands. Mrs. Candour, I don't believe you are acquainted with my nephew, Sir Benjamin Backbite? Egad, 305 ma'am, he has a pretty wit, and is a pretty poet too; isn't he, Lady Sneerwell?

SIR BENJAMIN: O fie, uncle!

CRABTREE: Nay, egad it's true—I'll back him at a rebus or a charade against the best rhymer in 310 the kingdom. Has your ladyship heard the epigram he wrote last week on Lady Frizzle's feather catching fire?—Do, Benjamin, repeat it—or the charade you made last night extempore at Mrs. Drowzie's conversazione.—Come now; your first 315 is the name of a fish, your second a great naval commander, and—

SIR BENJAMIN: Uncle, now—prithee—

CRABTREE: I'faith, ma am, 'twould surprise you to hear how ready he is at these things. 320

LADY SNEERWELL: I wonder, Sir Benjamin, you never publish anything.

SIR BENJAMIN: To say truth, ma'am, 'tis very vulgar to print; and, as my little productions are mostly satires and lampoons on particular people, I 325 find they circulate more by giving copies in confidence to the friends of the parties—however, I have some love elegies, which, when favored with this lady's smiles, I mean to give to the public. 330

CRABTREE: 'Fore heav'n, ma'am, they'll immortalize

you!—you'll be handed down to posterity like Petrarch's Laura, or Waller's Sacharissa.°

SIR BENJAMIN: Yes, madam, I think you will like them, when you shall see them on a beautiful quarto page, where a neat rivulet of text shall murmur through a meadow of margin. 'Fore gad, they will be the most elegant things of their kind!

CRABTREE: But, ladies, that's true—have you heard the news?

MRS. CANDOUR: What, sir, do you mean the report of—

CRABTREE: No, ma'am, that's not it.—Miss Nicely is going to be married to her own footman.

MRS. CANDOUR: Impossible!

CRABTREE: Ask Sir Benjamin.

SIR BENJAMIN: 'Tis very true, ma'am—everything is fixed, and the wedding liveries bespoke.

CRABTREE: Yes—and they *do* say there were pressing reasons for it.

LADY SNEERWELL: Why, I *have* heard something of this before.

MRS. CANDOUR: It can't be—and I wonder any one should believe such a story of so prudent a lady as Miss Nicely.

SIR BENJAMIN: O lud! ma'am, that's the very reason 'twas believed at once. She has always been so *cautious* and so *reserved,* that everybody was sure there was some reason for it at bottom.

MRS. CANDOUR: Why, to be sure, a tale of scandal is as fatal to the credit of a prudent lady of her stamp as a fever is generally to those of the strongest constitutions; but there is a sort of puny, sickly reputation that is always ailing, yet will outlive the robuster characters of a hundred prudes.

SIR BENJAMIN: True, madam, there are valetudinarians in reputation as well as constitution, who, being conscious of their weak part, avoid the least breath of air, and supply their want of stamina by care and circumspection.

MRS. CANDOUR: Well, but this may be all a mistake. You know, Sir Benjamin, very trifling circumstances often give rise to the most injurious tales.

CRABTREE: That they do, I'll be sworn, ma'am. Did you ever hear how Miss Piper came to lose her lover and her character last summer at Tunbridge?—Sir Benjamin, you remember it?

SIR BENJAMIN: Oh, to be sure!—the most whimsical circumstance—

LADY SNEERWELL: How was it, pray?

CRABTREE: Why, one evening, at Mrs. Ponto's assembly, the conversation happened to turn on the difficulty of breeding Nova Scotia sheep in this country. Says a young lady in company, 'I have

known instances of it; for Miss Letitia Piper, a first cousin of mine, had a Nova Scotia sheep that produced her twins.' 'What!' cries the old Dowager Lady Dundizzy (who you know is as deaf as a post), 'has Miss Piper had twins?' This mistake, as you may imagine, threw the whole company into a fit of laughing. However, 'twas the next morning everywhere reported, and in a few days believed by the whole town, that Miss Letitia Piper had actually been brought to bed of a fine boy and a girl—and in less than a week there were people who could name the father, and the farm-house where the babies were put out to nurse!

LADY SNEERWELL: Strange, indeed!

CRABTREE: Matter of fact, I assure you.—O lud! Mr. Surface, pray is it true that your uncle, Sir Oliver, is coming home?

JOSEPH SURFACE: Not that I know of, indeed, sir.

CRABTREE: He has been in the East Indies a long time. You can scarcely remember him, I believe.—Sad comfort, whenever he returns, to hear how your brother has gone on!

JOSEPH SURFACE: Charles has been imprudent, sir, to be sure; but I hope no busy people have already prejudiced Sir Oliver against him,—he may reform.

SIR BENJAMIN: To be sure he may—for my part I never believed him to be so utterly void of principle as people say—and though he has lost all his friends, I am told nobody is better spoken of by the Jews.

CRABTREE: That's true, egad, nephew. If the old Jewry were a ward, I believe Charles would be an alderman; no man more popular there, 'fore gad! I hear he pays as many annuities as the Irish tontine; and that, whenever he's sick, they have prayers for the recovery of his health in the Synagogue.

SIR BENJAMIN: Yet no man lives in greater splendor.— They tell me, when he entertains his friends, he can sit down to dinner with a dozen of his own securities; have a score of tradesmen waiting in the antechamber, and an officer behind every guest's chair.

JOSEPH SURFACE: This may be entertainment to you, gentlemen, but you pay very little regard to the feelings of a brother.

MARIA: Their malice is intolerable!—Lady Sneerwell, I must wish you a good morning—I'm not very well. *(Exit* MARIA.*)*

MRS. CANDOUR: O dear! she changes color very much!

LADY SNEERWELL: Do, Mrs. Candour, follow her—she may want assistance.

MRS. CANDOUR: That I will, with all my soul, ma'am.— Poor dear girl! who knows what her situation may be! *(Exit* MRS. CANDOUR.*)*

LADY SNEERWELL: 'Twas nothing but that she could

Sacharissa, Edmund Waller's poetical name for Lady Dorothy Sidney.

not bear to hear Charles reflected on, notwithstanding their difference.

SIR BENJAMIN: The young lady's *penchant* is obvious.

445 CRABTREE: But, Benjamin, you mustn't give up the pursuit for that; follow her, and put her into good humor. Repeat her some of your own verses.—Come, I'll assist you.

SIR BENJAMIN: Mr. Surface, I did not mean to hurt
450 you; but depend upon't your brother is utterly undone. (*Going.*)

CRABTREE: O lud, aye! undone as ever man was—can't raise a guinea. (*Going.*)

SIR BENJAMIN: And everything sold, I'm told, that was
455 movable. (*Going.*)

CRABTREE: I have seen one that was at his house—not a thing left but some empty bottles that were overlooked, and the family pictures, which I believe are framed in the wainscot. (*Going.*)

460 SIR BENJAMIN: And I am very sorry to hear also some bad stories against him. (*Going.*)

CRABTREE: Oh, he has done many mean things, that's certain. (*Going.*)

SIR BENJAMIN: But, however, as he's your brother—
(*Going.*)

465 CRABTREE: We'll tell you all, another opportunity.

(*Exeunt* CRABTREE *and* SIR BENJAMIN.)

LADY SNEERWELL: Ha, ha, ha! 'tis very hard for them to leave a subject they have not quite run down.

JOSEPH SURFACE: And I believe the abuse was no more acceptable to your ladyship than to Maria.

470 LADY SNEERWELL: I doubt° her affections are farther engaged than we imagined; but the family are to be here this evening, so you may as well dine where you are, and we shall have an opportunity of observing farther;—in the meantime, I'll go
475 and plot mischief, and you shall study sentiments. (*Exeunt.*)

ACT 1 / SCENE 2

(SIR PETER TEAZLE's *house.*)
(*Enter* SIR PETER.)

SIR PETER: When an old bachelor takes a young wife, what is he to expect?—'Tis now six months since Lady Teazle made me the happiest of men—and I
5 have been the miserablest dog ever since that ever committed wedlock! We tift a little going to church, and came to a quarrel before the bells were done ringing. I was more than once nearly choked with gall during the honeymoon, and had lost all comfort in life before my friends had done
10 wishing me joy! Yet I chose with caution—a girl bred wholly in the country, who never knew lux-

---

doubt, suspect.

ury beyond one silk gown, nor dissipation above the annual gala of a race ball. Yet now she plays her part in all the extravagant fopperies of the
15 fashion and the town, with as ready a grace as if she had never seen a bush nor a grass-plat out of Grosvenor Square! I am sneered at by my old acquaintance—paragraphed in the newspapers. She dissipates my fortune, and contradicts all my
20 humors; yet the worst of it is, I doubt I love her, or I should never bear all this. However, I'll never be weak enough to own it.

(*Enter* ROWLEY.)

ROWLEY: Oh! Sir Peter, your servant,—how is it with you, sir?

SIR PETER: Very bad, Master Rowley, very bad;—I
25 meet with nothing but crosses and vexations.

ROWLEY: What can have happened to trouble you since yesterday?

SIR PETER: A good question to a married man!

ROWLEY: Nay, I'm sure your lady, Sir Peter, can't be
30 the cause of your uneasiness.

SIR PETER: Why, has anyone told you she was dead?

ROWLEY: Come, come, Sir Peter, you love her, notwithstanding your tempers don't exactly agree.

SIR PETER: But the fault is entirely hers, Master Row-
35 ley. I am, myself, the sweetest-tempered man alive, and hate a teasing temper—and so I tell her a hundred times a day.

ROWLEY: Indeed!

SIR PETER: Aye; and what is very extraordinary, in all
40 our disputes she is always in the wrong! But Lady Sneerwell, and the set she meets at her house, encourage the perverseness of her disposition. Then, to complete my vexations, Maria, my ward, whom I ought to have the power of a father over,
45 is determined to turn rebel too, and absolutely refuses the man whom I have long resolved on for her husband;—meaning, I suppose, to bestow herself on his profligate brother.

ROWLEY: You know, Sir Peter, I have always taken the
50 liberty to differ with you on the subject of these two young gentlemen. I only wish you may not be deceived in your opinion of the elder. For Charles, my life on't! he will retrieve his errors yet. Their worthy father, once my honored mas-
55 ter, was, at his years, nearly as wild a spark; yet, when he died, he did not leave a more benevolent heart to lament his loss.

SIR PETER: You are wrong, Master Rowley. On their father's death, you know, I acted as a kind of
60 guardian to them both, till their uncle Sir Oliver's Eastern liberality gave them an early independence; of course, no person could have more opportunities of judging of their hearts, and I was never mistaken in my life. Joseph is indeed a
65 model for the young men of the age. He is a man

of sentiment, and acts up to the sentiments he professes; but, for the other, take my word for't, if he had any grains of virtue by descent, he has dissipated them with the rest of his inheritance. Ah! my old friend, Sir Oliver, will be deeply mortified when he finds how part of his bounty has been misapplied.

ROWLEY: I am sorry to find you so violent against the young man, because this may be the most critical period of his fortune. I came hither with news that will surprise you.

SIR PETER: What! let me hear.

ROWLEY: Sir Oliver *is* arrived, and at this moment in town.

SIR PETER: How! you astonish me! I thought you did not expect him this month.

ROWLEY: I did not; but his passage has been remarkably quick.

SIR PETER: Egad, I shall rejoice to see my old friend,—'tis sixteen years since we met—we have had many a day together; but does he still enjoin us not to inform his nephews of his arrival?

ROWLEY: Most strictly. He means, before it is known, to make some trial of their dispositions.

SIR PETER: Ah! There needs no art to discover their merits—however, he shall have his way; but, pray, does he know I am married?

ROWLEY: Yes, and will soon wish you joy.

SIR PETER: What, as we drink health to a friend in a consumption! Ah, Oliver will laugh at me—we used to rail at matrimony together—but he has been steady to his text. Well, he must be at my house, though—I'll instantly give orders for his reception. But, Master Rowley, don't drop a word that Lady Teazle and I ever disagree.

ROWLEY: By no means.

SIR PETER: For I should never be able to stand Noll's jokes; so I'd have him think, Lord forgive me! that we are a very happy couple.

ROWLEY: I understand you—but then you must be very careful not to differ while he's in the house with you.

SIR PETER: Egad, and so we must—and that's impossible. Ah! Master Rowley, when an old bachelor marries a young wife, he deserves—no—the crime carries the punishment along with it. (*Exeunt.*)

ACT 2 / SCENE 1

(SIR PETER TEAZLE*'s house*)
(*Enter* SIR PETER *and* LADY TEAZLE.)

SIR PETER: Lady Teazle, Lady Teazle, I'll not bear it!

LADY TEAZLE: Sir Peter, Sir Peter, you may bear it or not, as you please; but I ought to have my own way in everything, and what's more, I *will* too.—

What! though I was educated in the country, I know very well that women of fashion in London are accountable to nobody after they are married.

SIR PETER: Very well, ma'am, very well,—so a husband is to have no influence, no authority?

LADY TEAZLE: Authority! No, to be sure—if you wanted authority over me, you should have adopted me, and not married me; I am sure you were old enough.

SIR PETER: Old enough!—aye, there it is!—Well, well, Lady Teazle, though my life may be made unhappy by your temper, I'll not be ruined by your extravagance.

LADY TEAZLE: My extravagance! I'm sure I'm not more extravagant than a woman of fashion ought to be.

SIR PETER: No, no, madam, you shall throw away no more sums on such unmeaning luxury. 'Slife! to spend as much to furnish your dressing room with flowers in winter as would suffice to turn the Pantheon° into a greenhouse, and give a *fête champêtre*° at Christmas!

LADY TEAZLE: Lord, Sir Peter, am I to blame because flowers are dear in cold weather? You should find fault with the climate, and not with me. For my part, I am sure I wish it was spring all the year round, and that roses grew under one's feet!

SIR PETER: Oons! madam—if you had been born to this, I shouldn't wonder at your talking thus.—But you forget what your situation was when I married you.

LADY TEAZLE: No, no, I don't; 'twas a very disagreeable one, or I should never have married *you*.

SIR PETER: Yes, yes, madam, you were then in somewhat a humbler style—the daughter of a plain country squire. Recollect, Lady Teazle, when I saw you first, sitting at your tambour,° in a pretty figured linen gown, with a bunch of keys by your side, your hair combed smooth over a roll, and your apartment hung round with fruits in worsted, of your own working.

LADY TEAZLE: O, yes! I remember it very well, and a curious life I led—my daily occupation to inspect the dairy, superintend the poultry, and make extracts from the family receipt-book, and comb my aunt Deborah's lap-dog.

SIR PETER: Yes, yes, ma'am, 'twas so indeed.

LADY TEAZLE: And then, you know, my evening amusements! To draw patterns for ruffles, which I had not the materials to make; to play Pope Joan° with the curate; to read a novel to my aunt; or to

---

Pantheon, a fashionable concert-hall in Oxford Street. *fête champêtre,* an open-air festival. *tambour,* embroidery frame. *Pope Joan,* an old-fashioned game of cards.

be stuck down to an old spinet to strum my father to sleep after a fox-chase.

SIR PETER: I am glad you have so good a memory. Yes, madam, these were the recreations I took you from; but now you must have your own coach—*vis-à-vis*—and three powdered footmen before your chair and, in summer, a pair of white cats° to draw you to Kensington Gardens.—No recollection, I suppose, when you were content to ride double, behind the butler, on a docked coach-horse?

LADY TEAZLE: No—I swear I never did that—I deny the butler and the coach-horse.

SIR PETER: This, madam, was your situation—and what have I not done for you? I have made you a woman of fashion, of fortune, of rank—in short, I have made you my wife.

LADY TEAZLE: Well, then, and there is but one thing more you can make me to add to the obligation— and that is—

SIR PETER: My widow, I suppose?

LADY TEAZLE: Hem! hem!

SIR PETER: Thank you, madam—but don't flatter yourself; for though your ill-conduct may disturb my peace, it shall never break my heart, I promise you: however, I am equally obliged to you for the hint.

LADY TEAZLE: Then why will you endeavor to make yourself so disagreeable to me, and thwart me in every little elegant expense?

SIR PETER: 'Slife, madam, I say, had you any of these elegant expenses when you married me?

LADY TEAZLE: Lud, Sir Peter! would you have me be out of fashion?

SIR PETER: The fashion, indeed! what had you to do with the fashion before you married me?

LADY TEAZLE: For my part, I should think you would like to have your wife thought a woman of taste.

SIR PETER: Aye—there again—taste! Zounds! madam, you had no taste when you married *me!*

LADY TEAZLE: That's very true, indeed, Sir Peter! and, *after* having married you, I am sure I should never pretend to taste again! But now, Sir Peter, if we have finished our daily jangle, I presume I may go to my engagement at Lady Sneerwell's?

SIR PETER: Aye—there's another precious circumstance!—a charming set of acquaintance you have made there!

LADY TEAZLE: Nay, Sir Peter, they are people of rank and fortune, and remarkably tenacious of reputation.

SIR PETER: Yes, egad, they are tenacious of reputation with a vengeance; for they don't choose anybody should have a character but themselves! Such a crew! Ah! many a wretch has rid on a hurdle° who

has done less mischief than those utterers of forged tales, coiners of scandal,—and clippers of reputation.

LADY TEAZLE: What! would you restrain the freedom of speech?

SIR PETER: Oh! they have made you just as bad as any one of the society.

LADY TEAZLE: Why, I believe I do bear a part with a tolerable grace. But I vow I have no malice against the people I abuse; when I say an ill-natured thing, 'tis out of pure good humor—and I take it for granted they deal exactly in the same manner with me. But, Sir Peter, you know you promised to come to Lady Sneerwell's too.

SIR PETER: Well, well, I'll call in just to look after my own character.

LADY TEAZLE: Then, indeed, you must make haste after me or you'll be too late.—So good-bye to ye. (*Exit* LADY TEAZLE.)

SIR PETER: So—I have gained much by my intended expostulations! Yet with what a charming air she contradicts everything I say, and how pleasingly she shows her contempt of my authority! Well, though I can't make her love me, there is a great satisfaction in quarreling with her; and I think she never appears to such advantage as when she's doing everything in her power to plague me. (*Exit.*)

ACT 2 / SCENE 2

(LADY SNEERWELL *'s*)

(LADY SNEERWELL, MRS. CANDOUR, CRABTREE, SIR BENJAMIN BACKBITE, *and* JOSEPH SURFACE.)

LADY SNEERWELL: Nay, positively, we will hear it.

JOSEPH SURFACE: Yes, yes, the epigram, by all means.

SIR BENJAMIN: Plague on't, uncle! 'tis mere nonsense.

CRABTREE: No, no; 'fore gad, very clever for an extempore!

SIR BENJAMIN: But, ladies, you should be acquainted with the circumstance,—you must know that one day last week, as Lady Betty Curricle was taking the dust in Hyde Park, in a sort of duodecimo° phaëton, she desired me to write some verses on her ponies; upon which, I took out my pocketbook, and in one moment produced the following:

'Sure never were seen two such beautiful ponies! Other horses are clowns, and these macaronies! Nay, to give 'em this title I'm sure isn't wrong— Their legs are so slim and their tails are so long.'

CRABTREE: There, ladies—done in the smack of a whip, and on horseback too!

---

cats, ponies. ***hurdle,*** rough cart on which criminals were taken to the place of execution.

duodecimo, diminutive.

JOSEPH SURFACE: A very Phœbus, mounted—indeed,
20   Sir Benjamin.
SIR BENJAMIN: O dear sir—trifles—trifles.

(*Enter* LADY TEAZLE *and* MARIA.)

MRS. CANDOUR: I must have a copy.
LADY SNEERWELL: Lady Teazle, I hope we shall see Sir
      Peter.
25 LADY TEAZLE: I believe he'll wait on your ladyship
      presently.
LADY SNEERWELL: Maria, my love, you look grave.
      Come, you shall sit down to cards with Mr. Surface.
MARIA: I take very little pleasure in cards—however,
30   I'll do as your ladyship pleases.
LADY TEAZLE (*aside*): I am surprised Mr. Surface
      should sit down with *her.*—I thought he would
      have embraced this opportunity of speaking to
      me before Sir Peter came.
35 MRS. CANDOUR: Now, I'll die but you are so scan-
      dalous, I'll forswear your society.
LADY TEAZLE: What's the matter, Mrs. Candour?
MRS. CANDOUR: They'll not allow our friend Miss Ver-
      milion to be handsome.
40 LADY SNEERWELL: Oh, surely, she's a pretty woman.
CRABTREE: I am very glad you think so, ma'am.
MRS. CANDOUR: She has a charming fresh color.
LADY TEAZLE: Yes, when it is fresh put on.
MRS. CANDOUR: O fie! I'll swear her color is natural—I
45   have seen it come and go.
LADY TEAZLE: I dare swear you have, ma'am—it goes
      of a night, and comes again in the morning.
MRS. CANDOUR: Ha! ha! ha! how I hate to hear you
      talk so! But surely, now, her sister *is,* or *was,* very
50   handsome.
CRABTREE: Who? Mrs. Evergreen?—O Lord! she's six-
      and-fifty if she's an hour!
MRS. CANDOUR: Now positively you wrong her; fifty-
      two or fifty-three is the utmost—and I don't think
55   she looks more.
SIR BENJAMIN: Ah! there is no judging by her looks,
      unless one could see her face.
LADY SNEERWELL: Well, well, if Mrs. Evergreen *does*
      take some pains to repair the ravages of time, you
60   must allow she effects it with great ingenuity; and
      surely that's better than the careless manner in
      which the widow Ochre caulks her wrinkles.
SIR BENJAMIN: Nay, now, Lady Sneerwell, you are
      severe upon the widow. Come, come, it is not that
65   she paints so ill—but, when she has finished her
      face, she joins it on so badly to her neck, that she
      looks like a mended statue, in which the connois-
      seur may see at once that the head's modern,
      though the trunk's antique!
70 CRABTREE: Ha! ha! ha! well said, nephew!
MRS. CANDOUR: Ha! ha! ha! Well, you make me laugh,
      but I vow I hate you for't.—What do you think of
      Miss Simper?

SIR BENJAMIN: Why, she has very pretty teeth.
LADY TEAZLE: Yes; and on that account, when she is 75
      neither speaking nor laughing (which very sel-
      dom happens), she never absolutely shuts her
      mouth, but leaves it always on a jar, as it were.
MRS. CANDOUR: How can you be so ill-natured?
LADY TEAZLE: Nay, I allow even that's better than the 80
      pains Mrs. Prim takes to conceal her losses in
      front. She draws her mouth till it positively resem-
      bles the aperture of a poor's-box,° and all her
      words appear to slide out edgeways.
LADY SNEERWELL: Very well, Lady Teazle; I see you can 85
      be a little severe.
LADY TEAZLE: In defence of a friend it is but justice;—
      but here comes Sir Peter to spoil our pleasantry.

(*Enter* SIR PETER TEAZLE.)

SIR PETER: Ladies, your most obedient—Mercy on
      me, here is the whole set! a character dead at 90
      every word, I suppose. (*aside*)
MRS. CANDOUR: I am rejoiced you are come, Sir Peter.
      They have been *so* censorious. They will allow
      good qualities to nobody—not even good nature
      to our friend Mrs. Pursy. 95
LADY TEAZLE: What, the fat dowager who was at Mrs.
      Codille's last night?
MRS. CANDOUR: Nay, her bulk is her misfortune; and,
      when she takes such pains to get rid of it, you
      ought not to reflect on her. 100
LADY SNEERWELL: That's very true, indeed.
LADY TEAZLE: Yes, I know she almost lives on acids
      and small whey; laces herself by pulleys; and
      often, in the hottest noon of summer, you may see
      her on a little squat pony, with her hair platted up 105
      behind like a drummer's, and puffing round the
      Ring° on a full trot.
MRS. CANDOUR: I thank you, Lady Teazle, for defend-
      ing her.
SIR PETER: Yes, a good defence, truly. 110
MRS. CANDOUR: But Sir Benjamin is as censorious as
      Miss Sallow.
CRABTREE: Yes, and she is a curious being to pretend
      to be censorious!—an awkward gawky, without
      any one good point under heaven. 115
MRS. CANDOUR: Positively you shall not be so very
      severe. Miss Sallow is a relation of mine by mar-
      riage, and, as for her person, great allowance is to
      be made; for, let me tell you, a woman labors
      under many disadvantages who tries to pass for a 120
      girl at six-and-thirty.
LADY SNEERWELL: Though, surely, she is handsome

---

poor's-box, referring to the narrow slit in the top of the
church contribution box for the poor of the parish. **Ring,**
the fashionable drive originally laid out in Hyde Park by
Charles II.

still—and for the weakness in her eyes, considering how much she reads by candle-light, it is not
to be wondered at.

MRS. CANDOUR: True; and then as to her manner,
upon my word I think it is particularly graceful,
considering she never had the least education;
for you know her mother was a Welch milliner,
and her father a sugar-baker at Bristol.

SIR BENJAMIN: Ah! you are both of you too good-
natured!

SIR PETER: Yes, damned good-natured! This their own
relation! mercy on me! *(aside)*

SIR BENJAMIN: And Mrs. Candour is of so moral a turn
she can sit for an hour to hear Lady Stucco talk
sentiment.

LADY TEAZLE: Nay, I vow Lady Stucco is very well with
the dessert after dinner; for she's just like the
French fruit one cracks for mottoes—made up of
paint and proverb.

MRS. CANDOUR: Well, I never will join in ridiculing a
friend; and so I constantly tell my cousin Ogle,
and you all know what pretensions she has to be
critical in beauty.

CRABTREE: Oh, to be sure! she has herself the oddest
countenance that ever was seen; 'tis a collection
of features from all the different countries of the
globe.

SIR BENJAMIN: So she has, indeed—an Irish front!

CRABTREE: Caledonian locks!

SIR BENJAMIN: Dutch nose!

CRABTREE: Austrian lip!

SIR BENJAMIN: Complexion of a Spaniard!

CRABTREE: And teeth *à la Chinoise!*

SIR BENJAMIN: In short, her face resembles a *table d'hôte*
at Spa—where no two guests are of a nation—

CRABTREE: Or a congress at the close of a general
war—wherein all the members, even to her eyes,
appear to have a different interest, and her nose
and chin are the only parties likely to join issue.

MRS. CANDOUR: Ha! ha! ha!

SIR PETER: Mercy on my life!—a person they dine with
twice a week! *(aside)*

LADY SNEERWELL: Go—go—you are a couple of provoking toads.

MRS. CANDOUR: Nay, but I vow you shall not carry the
laugh off so—for give me leave to say, that Mrs.
Ogle—

SIR PETER: Madam, madam, I beg your pardon—
there's no stopping these good gentlemen's
tongues. But when I tell *you*, Mrs. Candour, that
the lady they are abusing is a particular friend of
mine—I hope you'll not take her part.

LADY SNEERWELL: Well said, Sir Peter! but you are a
cruel creature—too phlegmatic yourself for a jest,
and too peevish to allow wit on others.

SIR PETER: Ah, madam, true wit is more nearly allied
to good nature than your ladyship is aware of.

LADY TEAZLE: True, Sir Peter; I believe they are so
near akin that they can never be united.

SIR BENJAMIN: Or rather, madam, suppose them man
and wife, because one so seldom sees them together.

LADY TEAZLE: But Sir Peter is such an enemy to scandal, I believe he would have it put down by parliament.

SIR PETER: 'Fore heaven, madam, if they were to consider the sporting with reputation of as much
importance as poaching on manors, and pass *An
Act for the Preservation of Fame*, I believe many
would thank them for the bill.

LADY SNEERWELL: O lud! Sir Peter; would you deprive
us of our privileges?

SIR PETER: Aye, madam; and then no person should
be permitted to kill characters or run down reputations, but qualified old maids and disappointed
widows.

LADY SNEERWELL: Go, you monster!

MRS. CANDOUR: But sure you would not be quite so
severe on those who report what they hear.

SIR PETER: Yes, madam, I would have law merchant°
for them too; and in all cases of slander currency,
whenever the drawer of the lie was not to be
found, the injured parties should have a right to
come on any of the indorsers.

CRABTREE: Well, for my part, I believe there never was
a scandalous tale without some foundation.

LADY SNEERWELL: Come, ladies, shall we sit down to
cards in the next room?

(Enter SERVANT *and whispers* SIR PETER.*)*

SIR PETER: I'll be with them directly.—*(Exit* SERVANT.*)*
I'll get away unperceived. *(aside)*

LADY SNEERWELL: Sir Peter, you are not leaving us?

SIR PETER: Your ladyship must excuse me; I'm called
away by particular business—but I leave my character behind me. *(Exit* SIR PETER.*)*

SIR BENJAMIN: Well certainly, Lady Teazle, that lord of
yours is a strange being; I could tell you some stories of him would make you laugh heartily, if he
wasn't your husband.

LADY TEAZLE: O pray don't mind that—come, do let's
hear them.

*(They join the rest of the company, all talking as they are
going into the next room.)*

JOSEPH SURFACE *(rising with* MARIA*)*: Maria, I see you
have no satisfaction in this society.

MARIA: How is it possible I should? If to raise malicious smiles at the infirmities and misfortunes of
those who have never injured us be the province

---

law merchant, mercantile law.

of wit or humor, heaven grant me a double portion of dulness!

230 JOSEPH SURFACE: Yet they appear more ill-natured than they are; they have no malice at heart.

MARIA: Then is their conduct still more contemptible; for, in my opinion, nothing could excuse the intemperance of their tongues but a natural and
235 ungovernable bitterness of mind.

JOSEPH SURFACE: But can you, Maria, feel thus for others, and be unkind to me alone? Is hope to be denied the tenderest passion?

MARIA: Why will you distress me by renewing this sub-
240 ject?

JOSEPH SURFACE: Ah, Maria! you would not treat me thus, and oppose your guardian, Sir Peter's will, but that I see that profligate Charles is still a favored rival.

245 MARIA: Ungenerously urged! But, whatever my sentiments of that unfortunate young man are, be assured I shall not feel more bound to give him up, because his distresses have lost him the regard even of a brother.

(LADY TEAZLE returns.)

250 JOSEPH SURFACE: Nay, but, Maria, do not leave me with a frown—by all that's honest, I swear—Gad's life, here's Lady Teazle. *(aside)* You must not—no, you shall not—for, though I have the greatest regard for Lady Teazle—

255 MARIA: Lady Teazle!

JOSEPH SURFACE: Yet were Sir Peter to suspect—

LADY TEAZLE *(coming forward)*: What's this, pray? Do you take her for me?—Child, you are wanted in the next room.—*(Exit MARIA.)* What is all this,
260 pray?

JOSEPH SURFACE: Oh, the most unlucky circumstance in nature! Maria has somehow suspected the tender concern I have for your happiness, and threatened to acquaint Sir Peter with her suspi-
265 cions, and I was just endeavoring to reason with her when you came.

LADY TEAZLE: Indeed! but you seemed to adopt a very tender mode of reasoning—do you *usually* argue on your knees?

270 JOSEPH SURFACE: Oh, she's a child—and I thought a little bombast—but, Lady Teazle, when are you to give me your judgment on my library, as you promised?

LADY TEAZLE: No, no—I begin to think it would be
275 imprudent, and you know I admit you as a lover no further than *fashion* requires.

JOSEPH SURFACE: True—a mere Platonic cicisbeo,° what every London wife is *entitled* to.

LADY TEAZLE: Certainly, one must not be out of the

fashion; however, I have so many of my country 280
prejudices left, that, though Sir Peter's ill humor may vex me ever so, it never shall provoke me to—

JOSEPH SURFACE: The only revenge in your power. Well, I applaud your moderation. 285

LADY TEAZLE: Go—you are an insinuating wretch! But we shall be missed—let us join the company.

JOSEPH SURFACE: But we had best not return together.

LADY TEAZLE: Well, don't stay—for Maria shan't come to hear any more of your *reasoning*, I promise you. 290
(Exit LADY TEAZLE.)

JOSEPH SURFACE: A curious dilemma, truly, my politics have run me into! I wanted, at first, only to ingratiate myself with Lady Teazle, that she might not be my enemy with Maria; and I have, I don't know how, become her serious lover. Sincerely I begin 295
to wish I had never made such a point of gaining so *very good* a character, for it has led me into so many cursed rogueries that I doubt I shall be exposed at last. *(Exit.)*

ACT 2 / SCENE 3

(SIR PETER's)
(Enter SIR OLIVER SURFACE and ROWLEY.)

SIR OLIVER: Ha! ha! ha! and so my old friend is married, hey?—a young wife out of the country.—Ha! ha! ha!—that he should have stood bluff° to old bachelor so long, and sink into a husband at last! 5

ROWLEY: But you must not rally him on the subject, Sir Oliver; 'tis a tender point, I assure you, though he has been married only seven months.

SIR OLIVER: Then he has been just half a year on the stool of repentance!—Poor Peter! But you say he 10
has entirely given up Charles—never sees him, hey?

ROWLEY: His prejudice against him is astonishing, and I am sure greatly increased by a jealousy of him with Lady Teazle, which he has been industri- 15
ously led into by a scandalous society in the neighborhood, who have contributed not a little to Charles's ill name; whereas the truth is, I believe, if the lady is partial to either of them, his brother is the favorite. 20

SIR OLIVER: Aye,—I know there are a set of malicious, prating, prudent gossips, both male and female, who murder characters to kill time, and will rob a young fellow of his good name before he has years to know the value of it,—but I am not 25
to be prejudiced against my nephew by such, I promise you! No, no;—if Charles has done

---

cicisbeo, gallant to a married woman.

stood bluff, steadfast.

nothing false or mean, I shall compound for his extravagance.—

30 ROWLEY: Then, my life on't, you will reclaim him.— Ah, sir, it gives me new life to find that *your* heart is not turned against him, and that the son of my good old master has one friend, however, left.

35 SIR OLIVER: What! shall I forget, Master Rowley, when I was at his years myself? Egad, my brother and I were neither of us very *prudent* youths—and yet, I believe, you have not seen many better men than your old master was?

ROWLEY: Sir, 'tis this reflection gives me assurance
40 that Charles may yet be a credit to his family.— But here comes Sir Peter.

SIR OLIVER: Egad so he does!—Mercy on me, he's greatly altered, and seems to have a settled married look! One may read husband in his face at
45 this distance!

(Enter SIR PETER TEAZLE.)

SIR PETER: Hah! Sir Oliver—my old friend! Welcome to England a thousand times!

SIR OLIVER: Thank you, thank you, Sir Peter! and i'faith I am glad to find you well, believe me!

50 SIR PETER: Ah! 'tis a long time since we met—sixteen years, I doubt, Sir Oliver, and many a cross accident in the time.

SIR OLIVER: Aye, I have had my share—but, what! I find you are married, hey, my old boy?—Well,
55 well, it can't be helped—and so I wish you joy with all my heart!

SIR PETER: Thank you, thank you, Sir Oliver—Yes, I have entered into the happy state—but we'll not talk of that now.

60 SIR OLIVER: True, true, Sir Peter; old friends should not begin on grievances at first meeting. No, no, no.

ROWLEY *(to SIR OLIVER)*: Take care, pray, sir.

SIR OLIVER: Well, so one of my nephews is a wild
65 rogue, hey?

SIR PETER: Wild! Ah! my old friend, I grieve for your disappointment there—he's a lost young man, indeed; however, his brother will make you amends; Joseph is, indeed, what a youth should
70 be—everybody in the world speaks well of him.

SIR OLIVER: I am sorry to hear it—he has too good a character to be an honest fellow.—Everybody speaks well of him! Psha! then he has bowed as low to knaves and fools as to the honest dignity of
75 genius or virtue.

SIR PETER: What, Sir Oliver! do you blame him for not making enemies?

SIR OLIVER: Yes, if he has merit enough to deserve them.

80 SIR PETER: Well, well—you'll be convinced when you know him. 'Tis edification to hear him converse—he professes the noblest sentiments.

SIR OLIVER: Ah, plague of his sentiments! If he salutes me with a scrap of morality in his mouth, I shall be sick directly. But, however, don't mistake me, 85 Sir Peter; I don't mean to defend Charles's errors—but, before I form my judgment of either of them, I intend to make a trial of their hearts— and my friend Rowley and I have planned something for the purpose. 90

ROWLEY: And Sir Peter shall own for once he has been mistaken.

SIR PETER: Oh, my life on Joseph's honor!

SIR OLIVER: Well, come, give us a bottle of good wine, and we'll drink the lad's health, and tell you our 95 scheme.

SIR PETER: *Allons,* then!

SIR OLIVER: And don't, Sir Peter, be so severe against your old friend's son. Odds my life! I am not sorry that he has run out of the course a little; for my 100 part, I hate to see prudence clinging to the green succors of my youth; 'tis like ivy round a sapling, and spoils the growth of the tree. *(Exeunt.)*

ACT 3 / SCENE 1

(SIR PETER's)

(SIR PETER TEAZLE, SIR OLIVER SURFACE, and ROWLEY.)

SIR PETER: Well, then—we will see this fellow first, and have our wine afterwards. But how is this, Master Rowley? I don't see the jet° of your scheme.

ROWLEY: Why, sir, this Mr. Stanley, whom I was speaking of, is nearly related to them, by their mother; 5 he was once a merchant in Dublin, but has been ruined by a series of undeserved misfortunes. He has applied, by letter, since his confinement, both to Mr. Surface and Charles—from the former he has received nothing but evasive promises of 10 future service, while Charles has done all that his extravagance has left him power to do; and he is, at this time, endeavoring to raise a sum of money, part of which, in the midst of his own distresses, I know he intends for the service of poor Stanley. 15

SIR OLIVER: Ah! he is my brother's son.

SIR PETER: Well, but how is Sir Oliver personally to—

ROWLEY: Why, sir, I will inform Charles and his brother that Stanley has obtained permission to apply in person to his friends, and, as they have 20 neither of them ever seen him, let Sir Oliver assume his character, and he will have a fair opportunity of judging at least of the benevolence of their dispositions; and believe me, sir, you will find in the youngest brother one who, in 25 the midst of folly and dissipation, has still, as our immortal bard expresses it,—

---

jet, point, gist.

'a tear for pity, and a hand
Open as day, for melting charity.'°

30 SIR PETER: Psha! What signifies his having an open
hand or purse either, when he has nothing left to
give? Well, well, make the trial, if you please; but
where is the fellow whom you brought for Sir
Oliver to examine, relative to Charles's affairs?

35 ROWLEY: Below, waiting his commands, and no one
can give him better intelligence.—This, Sir Oliver,
is a friendly Jew, who, to do him justice, had done
everything in his power to bring your nephew to a
proper sense of his extravagance.

40 SIR PETER: Pray let us have him in.
ROWLEY: Desire Mr. Moses to walk upstairs.
SIR PETER: But why should you suppose he will speak
the truth?
ROWLEY: Oh, I have convinced him that he has no
45 chance of recovering certain sums advanced to
Charles but through the bounty of Sir Oliver, who
he knows is arrived; so that you may depend on
his fidelity to his own interest. I have also another
evidence in my power, one Snake, whom I have
50 detected in a matter little short of forgery, and
shall shortly produce to remove some of *your*
prejudices, Sir Peter, relative to Charles and Lady
Teazle.
SIR PETER: I have heard too much on that subject.
55 ROWLEY: Here comes the honest Israelite.

(*Enter* MOSES.)

—This is Sir Oliver.
SIR OLIVER: Sir, I understand you have lately had great
dealings with my nephew Charles.
MOSES: Yes, Sir Oliver—I have done all I could for
60 him, but he was ruined before he came to me for
assistance.
SIR OLIVER: That was unlucky, truly—for you have had
no opportunity of showing your talents.
MOSES: None at all—I hadn't the pleasure of knowing
65 his distresses—till he was some thousands worse
than nothing.
SIR OLIVER: Unfortunate, indeed! But I suppose you
have done all in your power for him, honest
Moses?
70 MOSES: Yes, he knows that. This very evening I was to
have brought him a gentleman from the city, who
doesn't know him, and will, I believe, advance
him some money.
SIR PETER: What, one Charles has never had money
75 from before?
MOSES: Yes; Mr. Premium, of Crutched Friars°—formerly a broker.

a tear ... charity, from *Henry IV, Part II,* IV. iv. 31–32.
Crutched Friars, a street, not far from the Tower of London,
named from an old Convent of Crossed or Crouched Friars.

SIR PETER: Egad, Sir Oliver, a thought strikes me!—
Charles, you say, doesn't know Mr. Premium?
MOSES: Not at all. 80
SIR PETER: Now then, Sir Oliver, you may have a better
opportunity of satisfying yourself than by an old
romancing tale of a poor relation;—go with my
friend Moses, and represent Mr. Premium, and
then I'll answer for't, you will see your nephew in 85
all his glory.
SIR OLIVER: Egad, I like this idea better than the
other and I may visit Joseph afterwards, as old
Stanley.
SIR PETER: True—so you may. 90
ROWLEY: Well, this is taking Charles rather at a disadvantage, to be sure. However, Moses—you understand Sir Peter, and will be faithful?
MOSES: You may depend upon me,—this is near the
time I was to have gone. 95
SIR OLIVER: I'll accompany you as soon as you please,
Moses; but hold! I have forgot one thing—how
the plague shall I be able to pass for a Jew?
MOSES: There's no need—the principal is Christian.
SIR OLIVER: Is he?—I'm sorry to hear it—but, then 100
again, an't I rather too smartly dressed to look
like a money-lender?
SIR PETER: Not at all; 'twould not be out of character,
if you went in your own carriage—would it,
Moses? 105
MOSES: Not in the least.
SIR OLIVER: Well, but how must I talk? there's cer-
tainly some cant of usury, and mode of treating,
that I ought to know.
SIR PETER: Oh, there's not much to learn—the great 110
point, as I take it, is to be exorbitant enough in
your demands—hey, Moses?
MOSES: Yes, that's a very great point.
SIR OLIVER: I'll answer for't I'll not be wanting in that.
I'll ask him eight or ten per cent on the loan, at 115
least.
MOSES: If you ask him no more than that, you'll be dis-
covered immediately.
SIR OLIVER: Hey! What the plague! how much then?
MOSES: That depends upon the circumstances. If 120
he appears not very anxious for the supply, you
should require only forty or fifty per cent; but if
you find him in great distress, and want the mon-
eys very bad—you may ask double.
SIR PETER: A good honest trade you're learning, Sir 125
Oliver!
SIR OLIVER: Truly I think so—and not unprofitable.
MOSES: Then, you know, you haven't the moneys your-
self, but are forced to borrow them for him of a
friend. 130
SIR OLIVER: Oh! I borrow it of a friend, do I?
MOSES: Yes, and your friend is an unconscionable
dog, but you can't help it.
SIR OLIVER: My friend is an unconscionable dog, is he?

135 MOSES: Yes, and he himself has not the moneys by him—but is forced to sell stock at a great loss.

SIR OLIVER: He is forced to sell stock, is he, at a great loss, is he? Well, that's very kind of him.

SIR PETER: I'faith, Sir Oliver—Mr. Premium, I
140 mean—you'll soon be master of the trade. But, Moses! wouldn't you have him run out a little against the Annuity Bill?° That would be in character, I should think.

MOSES: Very much.

145 ROWLEY: And lament that a young man now must be at years of discretion before he is suffered to ruin himself?

MOSES: Aye, great pity!

SIR PETER: And abuse the public for allowing merit to
150 an act whose only object is to snatch misfortune and imprudence from the rapacious relief of usury, and give the minor a chance of inheriting his estate without being undone by coming into possession.

155 SIR OLIVER: So, so—Moses shall give me further instructions as we go together.

SIR PETER: You will not have much time, for your nephew lives hard by.

SIR OLIVER: Oh, never fear! my tutor appears so able,
160 that though Charles lived in the next street, it must be my own fault if I am not a complete rogue before I turn the corner. (*Exeunt* SIR OLIVER *and* MOSES.)

SIR PETER: So now I think Sir Oliver will be convinced;—you are partial, Rowley, and would have
165 prepared Charles for the other plot.

ROWLEY: No, upon my word, Sir Peter.

SIR PETER: Well, go bring me this Snake, and I'll hear what he has to say presently.—I see Maria, and want to speak with her.—(*Exit* ROWLEY.) I should
170 be glad to be convinced my suspicions of Lady Teazle and Charles were unjust. I have never yet opened my mind on this subject to my friend Joseph—I'm determined I will do it—*he* will give me his opinion sincerely.

(Enter MARIA.)

175 So, child, has Mr. Surface returned with you?

MARIA: No, sir—he was engaged.

SIR PETER: Well, Maria, do you not reflect, the more you converse with that amiable young man, what return his partiality for you deserves?

180 MARIA: Indeed, Sir Peter, your frequent importunity on this subject distresses me extremely—you compel me to declare, that I know no man who has ever paid me a particular attention whom I would not prefer to Mr. Surface.

SIR PETER: So,—here's perverseness! No, no, Maria, 185 'tis Charles only whom you would prefer—'tis evident his vices and follies have won your heart.

MARIA: This is unkind, sir—you know I have obeyed you in neither seeing nor corresponding with him; I have heard enough to convince me that 190 he is unworthy my regard. Yet I cannot think it culpable, if, while my understanding severely condemns his vices, my heart suggests some pity for his distresses.

SIR PETER: Well, well, pity him as much as you please, 195 but give your heart and hand to a worthier object.

MARIA: Never to his brother!

SIR PETER: Go, perverse and obstinate! But take care, madam; you have never yet known what the authority of a guardian is—don't compel me to 200 inform you of it.

MARIA: I can only say, you shall not have *just* reason. 'Tis true, by my father's will, I am for a short period bound to regard you as his substitute, but must cease to think you so, when you would com- 205 pel me to be miserable. (*Exit* MARIA.)

SIR PETER: Was ever man so crossed as I am! everything conspiring to fret me!—I had not been involved in matrimony a fortnight, before her father, a hale and hearty man, died—on purpose, 210 I believe, for the pleasure of plaguing me with the care of his daughter. But here comes my helpmate! She appears in great good humor. How happy I should be if I could tease her into loving me, though but a little! 215

(Enter LADY TEAZLE.)

LADY TEAZLE: Lud! Sir Peter, I hope you haven't been quarreling with Maria—it isn't using me well to be ill humored when I am not by.

SIR PETER: Ah, Lady Teazle, you might have the power to make me good humored at all times. 220

LADY TEAZLE: I am sure I wish I had—for I want you to be in charming sweet temper at this moment. Do be good humored now, and let me have two hundred pounds, will you?

SIR PETER: Two hundred pounds! what, an't I to be in 225 a good humor without paying for it! But speak to me thus, and i'faith there's nothing I could refuse you. You shall have it; but seal me a bond for the repayment.

LADY TEAZLE: O no—there—my note of hand will do 230 as well.

SIR PETER (*kissing her hand*): And you shall no longer reproach me with not giving you an independent settlement,—I mean shortly to surprise you; but shall we always live thus, hey? 235

LADY TEAZLE: If you please. I'm sure I don't care how

Annuity Bill, the Annuity Bill, presented in the House of Commons April 29, 1777, and passed in May (after the first performance of *The S. for S.*) was aimed to safeguard minors against grantors of life annuities.

soon we leave off quarreling, provided you'll own *you* were tired first.

240 SIR PETER: Well—then let our future contest be, who shall be most obliging.

LADY TEAZLE: I assure you, Sir Peter, good nature becomes you. You look now as you did before we were married!—when you used to walk with me 245 under the elms, and tell me stories of what a gallant you were in your youth, and chuck me under the chin, you would, and ask me if I thought I could love an old fellow, who would deny me nothing—didn't you?

250 SIR PETER: Yes, yes, and you were as kind and attentive.

LADY TEAZLE: Aye, so I was, and would always take your part, when my acquaintance used to abuse you, and turn you into ridicule.

SIR PETER: Indeed!

255 LADY TEAZLE: Aye, and when my cousin Sophy has called you a stiff, peevish old bachelor, and laughed at me for thinking of marrying one who might be my father, I have always defended you— and said I didn't think you so ugly by any means, 260 and that I dared say you'd make a very good sort of a husband.

SIR PETER: And you prophesied right—and we shall certainly now be the happiest couple—

LADY TEAZLE: And never differ again!

265 SIR PETER: No, never!—though at the same time, indeed, my dear Lady Teazle, you must watch your temper very narrowly; for all in all our little quarrels, my dear, if you recollect, my love, you always began first.

270 LADY TEAZLE: I beg your pardon, my dear Sir Peter: indeed, you always gave the provocation.

SIR PETER: Now, see, my angel! take care—*contradicting* isn't the way to keep friends.

LADY TEAZLE: Then don't *you* begin it, my love!

275 SIR PETER: There, now! you—you are going on—you don't perceive, my life, that you are just doing the very thing which you know always makes me angry.

LADY TEAZLE: Nay, you know if you will be angry without any reason—

280 SIR PETER: There now! you want to quarrel again.

LADY TEAZLE: No, I am sure I don't—but, if you will be so peevish—

SIR PETER: There now! who begins first?

LADY TEAZLE: Why, you, to be sure. I said nothing— 285 but there's no bearing your temper.

SIR PETER: No, no, madam, the fault's in your own temper.

LADY TEAZLE: Aye, you are just what my cousin Sophy said you would be.

290 SIR PETER: Your cousin Sophy is a forward, impertinent gipsy.

LADY TEAZLE: You are a great bear, I'm sure, to abuse my relations.

SIR PETER: Now may all the plagues of marriage be doubled on me, if ever I try to be friends with you 295 any more!

LADY TEAZLE: So much the better.

SIR PETER: No, no, madam; 'tis evident you never cared a pin for me, and I was a madman to marry you—a pert, rural coquette, that had refused half 300 the honest squires in the neighborhood!

LADY TEAZLE: And I am sure I was a fool to marry you—an old dangling bachelor, who was single at fifty, only because he never could meet with any one who would have him. 305

SIR PETER: Aye, aye, madam; but you were pleased enough to listen to me—*you* never had such an offer before.

LADY TEAZLE: No! didn't I refuse Sir Twivy Tarrier, who everybody said would have been a better match— 310 for his estate is just as good as yours—and he has broke his neck since we have been married.

SIR PETER: I have done with you, madam! You are an unfeeling, ungrateful—but there's an end of everything. I believe you capable of anything 315 that's bad. Yes, madam, I now believe the reports relative to you and Charles, madam—yes, madam, you and Charles—are not without grounds—

LADY TEAZLE: Take care, Sir Peter! you had better not insinuate any such thing! I'll not be suspected 320 *without cause,* I promise you.

SIR PETER: Very well, madam! very well! a separate maintenance as soon as you please. Yes, madam, or a divorce! I'll make an example of myself for the benefit of all old bachelors. Let us separate, 325 madam.

LADY TEAZLE: Agreed! agreed! And now, my dear Sir Peter, we are of a mind once more, we may be the *happiest couple,* and *never differ again,* you know: ha! ha! Well, you are going to be in a passion, I 330 see, and I shall only interrupt you.—so bye! bye! (*Exit.*)

SIR PETER: Plagues and tortures! can't I make her angry neither? Oh, I am the miserablest fellow! But I'll not bear her presuming to keep her temper—no! she may break my heart, but she shan't 335 keep her temper. (*Exit.*)

ACT 3 / SCENE 2

(CHARLES'S *house*)
(*Enter* TRIP, MOSES, *and* SIR OLIVER SURFACE.)

TRIP: Here, Master Moses! if you'll stay a moment, I'll try whether—what's the gentleman's name?

SIR OLIVER: Mr. Moses, what *is* my name? (*aside*)

MOSES: Mr. Premium.

TRIP: Premium—very well. (*Exit* TRIP, *taking snuff.*) 5

SIR OLIVER: To judge by the servants, one wouldn't believe the master was ruined. But what!—sure, this was my brother's house?

MOSES: Yes, sir; Mr. Charles bought it of Mr. Joseph,
10   with the furniture, pictures, &c., just as the old
          gentleman left it—Sir Peter thought it a great
          piece of extravagance in him.
SIR OLIVER: In my mind, the other's economy in *sell-
          ing* it to him was more reprehensible by half.

     (*Re-enter* TRIP.)

15   TRIP: My master says you must wait, gentlemen; he
          has company, and he can't speak with you yet.
     SIR OLIVER: If he knew *who* it was wanted to see him,
          perhaps he wouldn't have sent such a message.
     TRIP: Yes, yes, sir; he knows *you* are here—I didn't for-
20   get little Premium—no, no, no.
     SIR OLIVER: Very well—and I pray, sir, what may be
          your name?
     TRIP: Trip, sir—my name is Trip, at your service.
     SIR OLIVER: Well, then, Mr. Trip, you have a pleasant
25   sort of a place here, I guess.
     TRIP: Why, yes—here are three or four of us pass our
          time agreeably enough; but then our wages are
          sometimes a little in arrear—and not very great
          either—but fifty pounds a year, and find our own
30   bags and bouquets.°
     SIR OLIVER (*aside*): Bags and bouquets! halters and
          bastinadoes!
     TRIP: But *à propos*, Moses, have you been able to get
          me that little bill discounted?
35   SIR OLIVER (*aside*): Wants to raise money, too!—mercy
          on me. Has his distresses, I warrant, like a lord,—
          and affects creditors and duns.
     MOSES: 'Twas not to be done, indeed, Mr. Trip. (*Gives
          the note.*)
     TRIP: Good lack, you surprise me! My friend Brush
40   has indorsed it, and I thought when he put his
          mark on the back of a bill 'twas as good as cash.
     MOSES: No, 'twouldn't do.
     TRIP: A small sum—but twenty pounds. Hark'ee,
          Moses, do you think you couldn't get it me by way
45   of annuity?
     SIR OLIVER (*aside*): An annuity! ha! ha! ha! a footman
          raise money by way of annuity! Well done, luxury,
          egad!
     MOSES: But you must insure your place.
50   TRIP: Oh, with all my heart! I'll insure my place, and
          my life too, if you please.
     SIR OLIVER (*aside*): It's more than I would your neck.
     TRIP: But then, Moses, it must be done before this
          d—d register° takes place—one wouldn't like to
55   have one's name made public, you know.

---

bags and bouquets, footman's trappings. The back-hair of
the bagwig was enclosed in an ornamental bag. **register,**
another reference to the Annuity Bill of 1777, proposed on
April 29 and passed in May. It provided "for registering the
Grants of Life Annuities."

MOSES: No, certainly. But is there nothing you could
          deposit?
     TRIP: Why, nothing capital of my master's wardrobe
          has dropped lately; but I could give you a mort-
          gage on some of his winter clothes, with equity of   60
          redemption before November—or you shall have
          the reversion of the French velvet, or a post-obit°
          on the blue and silver;—these, I should think,
          Moses, with a few pair of point ruffles, as a collat-
          eral security—hey, my little fellow?   65
     MOSES: Well, well. (*Bell rings.*)
     TRIP: Gad, I heard the bell! I believe, gentlemen, I can
          now introduce you. Don't forget the annuity, little
          Moses! This way, gentlemen, insure my place, you
          know.   70
     SIR OLIVER (*aside*): If the man be a shadow of his mas-
          ter, this is the temple of dissipation indeed! (*Exe-
          unt.*)

ACT 3 / SCENE 3

     (CHARLES SURFACE, CARELESS, *and others at a table
     with wine, etc.*)

CHARLES SURFACE: 'Fore heaven, 'tis true!—there's the
          great degeneracy of the age. Many of our acquain-
          tance have taste, spirit, and politeness; but plague
          on't, they won't drink.
     CARELESS: It is so, indeed, Charles! they give in to all   5
          the substantial luxuries of the table, and abstain
          from nothing but wine and wit.
     CHARLES SURFACE: Oh, certainly society suffers by it
          intolerably! for now, instead of the social spirit of
          raillery that used to mantle over a glass of bright   10
          Burgundy, their conversation is become just like
          the Spa-water they drink, which has all the pert-
          ness and flatulence of champagne, without its
          spirit or flavor.
     1 GENTLEMAN: But what are *they* to do who love play   15
          better than wine?
     CARELESS: True! there's Harry diets himself for gam-
          ing, and is now under a hazard regimen.°
     CHARLES SURFACE: Then he'll have the worst of it.
          What! you wouldn't train a horse for the course   20
          by keeping him from corn! For my part, egad, I
          am now never so successful as when I am a little
          merry—let me throw on a bottle of champagne,
          and I never lose—at least I never feel my losses,
          which is exactly the same thing.   25
     2 GENTLEMAN: Aye, that I believe.
     CHARLES SURFACE: And, then, what man can pretend
          to be a believer in love, who is an abjurer of wine?
          'Tis the test by which the lover knows his own
          heart. Fill a dozen bumpers to a dozen beauties,   30

---

post-obit, future claim.   **hazard regimen,** "keeps in strict
training for gambling."

and she that floats at top is the maid that has bewitched you.

CARELESS: Now then, Charles, be honest, and give us your real favorite.

35 CHARLES SURFACE: Why, I have withheld her only in compassion to you. If I toast her, you must give a round of her peers—which is impossible—on earth.

CARELESS: Oh, then we'll find some canonised vestals

40   or heathen goddesses that will do, I warrant!

CHARLES SURFACE: Here then, bumpers, you rogues! bumpers! Maria! Maria!—*(Drink.)*

1 GENTLEMAN: Maria who?

CHARLES SURFACE: O, damn the surname!—'tis too

45   formal to be registered in Love's calendar—but now, Sir Toby Bumper, beware—we must have beauty superlative.

CARELESS: Nay, never study, Sir Toby: we'll stand to the toast, though your mistress should want an

50   eye—and you know you have a song will excuse you.

SIR TOBY: Egad, so I have! and I'll give him the song instead of the lady. *(Sings.)*

SONG AND CHORUS

Here's to the maiden of bashful fifteen;
55   *Here's to the widow of fifty;*
Here's to the flaunting extravagant quean,
And here's to the housewife that's thrifty.
Chorus. *Let the toast pass—*
       Drink to the lass—
60 *I'll warrant she'll prove an excuse for the glass.*
Here's to the charmer whose dimples we prize:
Now to the maid who has none, sir;
Here's to the girl with a pair of blue eyes,
And here's to the nymph with but one, sir.
65 Chorus. *Let the toast pass, &c.*

Here's to the maid with a bosom of snow:
Now to her that's as brown as a berry:
Here's to the wife with a face full of woe,
And now for the damsel that's merry.
70 Chorus. *Let the toast pass, &c.*

For let 'em be clumsy, or let 'em be slim,
Young or ancient, I care not a feather:
So fill a pint bumper quite up to the brim,
—And let us e'en toast 'em together.
75 Chorus. *Let the toast pass, &c.*

ALL: Bravo! Bravo!

(Enter TRIP, *and whispers* CHARLES SURFACE.*)*

CHARLES SURFACE: Gentlemen, you must excuse me a little.—Careless, take the chair, will you?

CARELESS: Nay, prithee, Charles, what now? This is

one of your peerless beauties, I suppose, has 80 dropped in by chance?

CHARLES SURFACE: No, faith! To tell you the truth, 'tis a Jew and a broker, who are come by appointment.

CARELESS: Oh, damn it! let's have the Jew in— 85

1 GENTLEMAN: Aye, and the broker too, by all means.

2 GENTLEMAN: Yes, yes, the Jew and the broker.

CHARLES SURFACE: Egad, with all my heart!—Trip, bid the gentlemen walk in.—*(Exit* TRIP.*)* Though there's one of them a stranger, I can tell you. 90

CARELESS: Charles, let us give them some generous Burgundy, and perhaps they'll grow conscientious.

CHARLES SURFACE: Oh, hang 'em, no! wine does but draw forth a man's *natural* qualities; and to make 95 *them* drink would only be to whet their knavery.

(Enter TRIP, SIR OLIVER SURFACE, *and* MOSES.*)*

CHARLES SURFACE: So, honest Moses; walk in, pray, Mr. Premium—that's the gentleman's name, isn't it, Moses?

MOSES: Yes, sir. 100

CHARLES SURFACE: Set chairs, Trip.—Sit down, Mr. Premium.—Glasses, Trip.—Sit down, Moses.— Come, Mr. Premium, I'll give you a sentiment; here's 'Success to usury!'—Moses, fill the gentleman a bumper. 105

MOSES: Success to usury!

CARELESS: Right, Moses—usury is prudence and industry, and deserves to succeed.

SIR OLIVER: Then here's—All the success it deserves!

CARELESS: No, no, that won't do! Mr. Premium, you 110 have demurred to the toast, and must drink it in a pint bumper.

1 GENTLEMAN: A pint bumper, at least.

MOSES: Oh, pray, sir, consider—Mr. Premium's a gentleman. 115

CARELESS: And therefore loves good wine.

2 GENTLEMAN: Give Moses a quart glass—this is mutiny, and a high contempt of the chair.

CARELESS: Here, now for't! I'll see justice done, to the last drop of my bottle. 120

SIR OLIVER: Nay, pray, gentlemen—I did not expect this usage.

CHARLES SURFACE: No, hang it, Careless, you shan't; Mr. Premium's a stranger.

SIR OLIVER *(aside)*: Odd! I wish I was well out of this 125 company.

CARELESS: Plague on 'em then! if they won't drink, we'll not sit down with 'em. Come, Harry, the dice are in the next room.—Charles, you'll join us— when you have finished your business with these 130 gentlemen?

CHARLES SURFACE: I will! I will!—*(Exeunt Gentlemen.)* Careless!

CARELESS *(returning)*: Well!

135 CHARLES SURFACE: Perhaps I may want *you*.

CARELESS: Oh, you know I am always ready—word, note, or bond, 'tis all the same to me. *(Exit.)*

MOSES: Sir, this is Mr. Premium, a gentleman of the strictest honor and secrecy; and always performs

140   what he undertakes. Mr. Premium, this is—

CHARLES SURFACE: Pshaw! have done! Sir, my friend Moses is a very honest fellow, but a little slow at expression; he'll be an hour giving us our titles. Mr. Premium, the plain state of the matter is

145 this—I am an extravagant young fellow who wants money to borrow; you I take to be a prudent old fellow, who has got money to lend. I am block-head enough to give fifty per cent sooner than not have it; and you, I presume, are rogue

150 enough to take a hundred if you could get it. Now, sir, you see we are acquainted at once, and may proceed to business without farther ceremony.

SIR OLIVER: Exceeding frank, upon my word. I see, sir,

155 you are not a man of many compliments.

CHARLES SURFACE: Oh, no, sir! plain dealing in business I always think best.

SIR OLIVER: Sir, I like you the better for't. However, you are mistaken in one thing—I have no money

160 to lend, but I believe I could procure some of a friend; but then he's an unconscionable dog—isn't he, Moses? And must sell stock to accommodate you—mustn't he, Moses?

MOSES: Yes, indeed! You know I always speak the

165 truth, and scorn to tell a lie!

CHARLES SURFACE: Right! People that expect truth generally do. But these are trifles, Mr. Premium. What! I know money isn't to be bought without paying for't!

170 SIR OLIVER: Well, but what security could you give? You have no land, I suppose?

CHARLES SURFACE: Not a mole-hill, nor a twig, but what's in beau-pots° out at the window!

SIR OLIVER: Nor any stock, I presume?

175 CHARLES SURFACE: Nothing but live stock—and that's only a few pointers and ponies. But pray, Mr. Premium, are you acquainted at all with any of my connections?

SIR OLIVER: Why, to say truth, I am.

180 CHARLES SURFACE: Then you must know that I have a devilish rich uncle in the East Indies, Sir Oliver Surface, from whom I have the greatest expectations.

SIR OLIVER: That you have a wealthy uncle, I have

185 heard—but how your expectations will turn out is more, I believe, than you can tell.

---

beau-pots, large ornamental flowerpots.

CHARLES SURFACE: Oh, no!—there can be no doubt—they tell me I'm a prodigious favorite—and that he talks of leaving me everything.

SIR OLIVER: Indeed! this is the first I've heard on't.   190

CHARLES SURFACE: Yes, yes, 'tis just so.—Moses knows 'tis true; don't you, Moses?

MOSES: Oh, yes! I'll swear to't.

SIR OLIVER *(aside)*: Egad, they'll persuade me presently I'm at Bengal.   195

CHARLES SURFACE: Now I propose, Mr. Premium, if it's agreeable to you, a post-obit on Sir Oliver's life; though at the same time the old fellow has been so liberal to me that I give you my word I should be very sorry to hear anything had hap-   200 pened to him.

SIR OLIVER: Not more than *I* should, I assure you. But the bond you mention happens to be just the worst security you could offer me—for I might live to a hundred and never recover the principal.   205

CHARLES SURFACE: Oh, yes, you would!—the moment Sir Oliver dies, you know, you'd come on me for the money.

SIR OLIVER: Then I believe I should be the most unwelcome dun you ever had in your life.   210

CHARLES SURFACE: What! I suppose you are afraid now that Sir Oliver is too good a life?

SIR OLIVER: No, indeed I am not—though I have heard he is as hale and healthy as any man of his years in Christendom.   215

CHARLES SURFACE: There again you are misinformed. No, no, the climate has hurt him considerably, poor uncle Oliver. Yes, he breaks apace, I'm told—and so much altered lately that his nearest relations don't know him.   220

SIR OLIVER: No! Ha! ha! ha! so much altered lately that his relations don't know him! Ha! ha! ha! that's droll, egad—ha! ha! ha!

CHARLES SURFACE: Ha! ha!—you're glad to hear that, little Premium.   225

SIR OLIVER: No, no, I'm not.

CHARLES SURFACE: Yes, yes, you are—ha! ha! ha!—you know that mends your chance.

SIR OLIVER: But I'm told Sir Oliver is coming over—nay, some say he is actually arrived.   230

CHARLES SURFACE: Pshaw! sure I must know better than you whether he's come or not. No, no, rely on't, he is at this moment at Calcutta, isn't he, Moses?

MOSES: Oh yes, certainly.   235

SIR OLIVER: Very true, as you say, you must know better than I, though I have it from pretty good authority—haven't I, Moses?

MOSES: Yes, most undoubted!

SIR OLIVER: But, sir, as I understand you want a few   240 hundreds immediately, is there nothing you would dispose of?

CHARLES SURFACE: How do you mean?

SIR OLIVER: For instance, now—I have heard—that
245 your father left behind him a great quantity of
massy old plate.

CHARLES SURFACE: O lud! that's gone long ago—
Moses can tell you how better than I can.

SIR OLIVER: Good lack! all the family race-cups and
250 corporation bowls! *(aside)* —Then it was also supposed that his library was one of the most valuable and complete.

CHARLES SURFACE: Yes, yes, so it was—vastly too much
so for a private gentleman—for my part, I
255 was always of a communicative disposition, so I
thought it a shame to keep so much knowledge to
myself.

SIR OLIVER *(aside)*: Mercy on me! learning that had
run in the family like an heirloom!—*(Aloud)* Pray,
260 what are become of the books?

CHARLES SURFACE: You must inquire of the auctioneer, Master Premium, for I don't believe even
Moses can direct you there.

MOSES: I never meddle with books.

265 SIR OLIVER: So, so, nothing of the family property left,
I suppose?

CHARLES SURFACE: Not much, indeed; unless you
have a mind to the family pictures. I have got a
room full of ancestors above—and if you have
270 a taste for old paintings, egad, you shall have 'em
a bargain!

SIR OLIVER: Hey! and the devil! sure, you wouldn't sell
your forefathers, would you?

CHARLES SURFACE: Every man of 'em, to the best bid-
275 der.

SIR OLIVER: What! your great-uncles and aunts?

CHARLES SURFACE: Aye, and my great-grandfathers
and grandmothers too.

SIR OLIVER: Now I give him up!—*(aside)* What the
280 plague, have you no vowels for your own kindred?
Odd's life! do you take me for Shylock in the play,
that you would raise money of me on your own
flesh and blood?

CHARLES SURFACE: Nay, my little broker, don't be
285 angry: what need *you* care, if you have your
money's worth?

SIR OLIVER: Well, I'll be the purchaser—I think I can
dispose of the family.—*(aside)* Oh, I'll never forgive him this! never!

(Enter CARELESS.)

290 CARELESS: Come, Charles, what keeps you?

CHARLES SURFACE: I can't come yet. I'faith! we are
going to have a sale above—here's little Premium
will buy all my ancestors!

CARELESS: Oh, burn your ancestors!

295 CHARLES SURFACE: No, he may do that afterwards, if
he pleases. Stay, Careless, we want you; egad, you
shall be auctioneer—so come along with us.

CARELESS: Oh, have with you, if that's the case.—I can
handle a hammer as well as a dice box!

SIR OLIVER: Oh, the profligates! 300

CHARLES SURFACE: Come, Moses, you shall be ap-
praiser, if we want one.—Gad's life, little Premium, you don't seem to like the business.

SIR OLIVER: Oh, yes, I do, vastly! Ha! ha! yes, yes, I
think it a rare joke to sell one's family by auc- 305
tion—ha! ha!—*(aside)* Oh, the prodigal!

CHARLES SURFACE: To be sure! when a man wants
money, where the plague should he get assistance, if he can't make free with his own relations? *(Exeunt.)* 310

ACT 4 / SCENE 1

(Picture-room at CHARLES's.)
*(Enter CHARLES SURFACE, SIR OLIVER SURFACE, MOSES,
and CARELESS.)*

CHARLES SURFACE: Walk in, gentlemen, pray walk in!
—here they are, the family of the Surfaces, up to
the Conquest.

SIR OLIVER: And, in my opinion, a goodly collection.

CHARLES SURFACE: Aye, aye, these are done in true 5
spirit of portrait-painting—no volunteer grace or
expression—not like the works of your modern
Raphael, who gives you the strongest resemblance, yet contrives to make your own portrait
independent of you; so that you may sink the 10
original and not hurt the picture. No, no; the
merit of these is the inveterate likeness—all stiff
and awkward as the originals, and like nothing in
human nature beside!

SIR OLIVER: Ah! we shall never see such figures of 15
men again.

CHARLES SURFACE: I hope not. Well, you see, Master
Premium, what a domestic character I am—here
I sit of an evening surrounded by my family. But
come, get to your pulpit, Mr. Auctioneer—here's 20
an old gouty chair of my grandfather's will answer
the purpose.

CARELESS: Aye, aye, this will do. But, Charles, I have
ne'er a hammer; and what's an auctioneer without his hammer? 25

CHARLES SURFACE: Egad, that's true. What parchment
have we here? *(Takes down a roll.)* 'Richard, heir to
Thomas'—our genealogy in full. Here, Careless,
you shall have no common bit of mahogany—
here's the family tree for you, you rogue—this 30
shall be your hammer, and now you may knock
down my ancestors with their own pedigree.

SIR OLIVER *(aside)*: What an unnatural rogue!—an *ex
post facto* parricide!

CARELESS: Yes, yes, here's a list of your generation 35
indeed;—faith, Charles, this is the most convenient thing you could have found for the business, for 'twill serve not only as a hammer, but a

40   catalogue into the bargain.—But come, begin—
     A-going, a-going, a-going!

CHARLES SURFACE: Bravo, Careless! Well, here's my
     great uncle, Sir Richard Raviline, a marvellous
     good general in his day, I assure you. He served in
     all the Duke of Marlborough's wars, and got that
45   cut over his eye at the battle of Malplaquet.° What
     say you, Mr. Premium? look at him—there's a
     hero for you! not cut out of his feathers, as your
     modern clipped captains are, but enveloped in
     wig and regimentals, as a general should be. What
50   do you bid?

MOSES: Mr. Premium would have you speak.

CHARLES SURFACE: Why, then, he shall have him for
     ten pounds, and I am sure that's not dear for a
     staff-officer.

55 SIR OLIVER: Heaven deliver me! his famous uncle
     Richard for ten pounds!—Very well, sir, I take
     him at that.

CHARLES SURFACE: Careless, knock down my uncle
     Richard.—Here, now, is a maiden sister of his, my
60   great-aunt Deborah, done by Kneller,° thought to
     be in his best manner, and a very formidable like-
     ness. There she is, you see, a shepherdess feeding
     her flock. You shall have her for five pounds
     ten—the sheep are worth the money.

65 SIR OLIVER: Ah! poor Deborah! a woman who set such
     a value on herself!—Five pound ten—she's mine.

CHARLES SURFACE: Knock down my aunt Deborah!
     Here, now, are two that were a sort of cousins of
     theirs.—You see, Moses, these pictures were done
70   some time ago, when beaux wore wigs, and the
     ladies wore their own hair.

SIR OLIVER: Yes, truly, head-dresses appear to have
     been a little lower in those days.

CHARLES SURFACE: Well, take that couple for the
75   same.

MOSES: 'Tis a good bargain.

CHARLES SURFACE: Careless!—This, now, is a grandfa-
     ther of my mother's, a learned judge, well known
     on the western circuit.—What do you rate him at,
80   Moses?

MOSES: Four guineas.

CHARLES SURFACE: Four guineas! Gad's life, you don't
     bid me the price of his wig.—Mr. Premium, *you*
     have more respect for the woolsack;° do let us
85   knock his lordship down at fifteen.

SIR OLIVER: By all means.

CARELESS: Gone!

CHARLES SURFACE: And there are two brothers of his,

William and Walter Blunt, Esquires, both members of Parliament, and noted speakers; and, 90
what's very extraordinary, I believe this is the first
time they were ever bought and sold.

SIR OLIVER: That's very extraordinary, indeed! I'll
take them at your own price, for the honor of Parliament. 95

CARELESS: Well said, little Premium! I'll knock 'em
down at forty.

CHARLES SURFACE: Here's a jolly fellow—I don't know
what relation, but he was mayor of Manchester;
take him at eight pounds. 100

SIR OLIVER: No, no—six will do for the mayor.

CHARLES SURFACE: Come, make it guineas, and I'll
throw you the two aldermen there into the bargain.

SIR OLIVER: They're mine. 105

CHARLES SURFACE: Careless, knock down the mayor
and aldermen. But, plague on't! we shall be all
day retailing in this manner; do let us deal wholesale—what say you, little Premium? Give me three
hundred pounds for the rest of the family in the 110
lump.

CARELESS: Aye, aye, that will be the best way.

SIR OLIVER: Well, well, anything to accommodate you;
they are mine. But there is one portrait which you
have always passed over. 115

CARELESS: What, that ill-looking little fellow over the
settee?

SIR OLIVER: Yes, sir, I mean that; though I don't think
him so ill-looking a little fellow, by any means.

CHARLES SURFACE: What, that? Oh, that's my uncle 120
Oliver! 'Twas done before he went to India.

CARELESS: Your uncle Oliver! Gad, then you'll never
be friends, Charles. That, now, to me, is as stern a
looking rogue as ever I saw—an unforgiving eye,
and a damned disinheriting countenance! an 125
inveterate knave, depend on't. Don't you think
so, little Premium?

SIR OLIVER: Upon my soul, sir, I do not; I think it is as
honest a looking face as any in the room, dead or
alive. But I suppose your uncle Oliver goes with 130
the rest of the lumber?

CHARLES SURFACE: No, hang it! I'll not part with poor
Noll. The old fellow has been very good to me,
and, egad, I'll keep his picture while I've a room
to put it in. 135

SIR OLIVER: The rogue's my nephew after all!
(aside)—But, sir, I have somehow taken a fancy to
that picture.

CHARLES SURFACE: I'm sorry for't, for you certainly
will not have it. Oons! haven't you got enough 140
of 'em?

SIR OLIVER: I forgive him everything! *(aside)* But, sir,
when I take a whim in my head, I don't value
money. I'll give you as much for that as for all the
rest. 145

<hr>

battle of Malplaquet, on September 11, 1709. **Kneller,**
Sir Godfrey Kneller (1648–1723), who painted many portraits of English sovereigns and nobles. **woolsack,** "for
lawyers." The reference to the Lord Chancellor's seat on the
Woolsack in the House of Lords is here meant as the symbol
of the profession of law.

CHARLES SURFACE: Don't tease me, master broker; I tell you I'll not part with it, and there's an end on't.

SIR OLIVER: How like his father the dog is!—*(Aloud)*
150 Well, well, I have done.—I did not perceive it before, but I think I never saw such a resemblance.—Well, sir—here's a draught for your sum.

CHARLES SURFACE: Why, 'tis for eight hundred pounds!
155 SIR OLIVER: You will not let Sir Oliver go?

CHARLES SURFACE: Zounds! no! I tell you, once more.

SIR OLIVER: Then never mind the difference; we'll balance another time. But give me your hand on the bargain; you are an honest fellow, Charles—I
160 beg pardon, sir, for being so free.—Come, Moses.

CHARLES SURFACE: Egad, this is a whimsical old fellow!—but hark'ee, Premium, you'll prepare lodgings for these gentlemen.

SIR OLIVER: Yes, yes, I'll send for them in a day or two.
165 CHARLES SURFACE: But hold—do now—send a genteel conveyance for them, for, I assure you, they were most of them used to ride in their own carriages.

SIR OLIVER: I will, I will, for all but—Oliver.
170 CHARLES SURFACE: Aye, all but the little honest nabob.

SIR OLIVER: You're fixed on that?

CHARLES SURFACE: Peremptorily.

SIR OLIVER: A dear extravagant rogue!—Good day!— Come, Moses,—Let me hear now who dares call
175 him profligate! *(Exeunt* SIR OLIVER *and* MOSES.*)*

CARELESS: Why, this is the oddest genius of the sort I ever saw!

CHARLES SURFACE: Egad, he's the prince of brokers, I think. I wonder how the devil Moses got ac-
180 quainted with so honest a fellow.—Ha! here's Rowley.—Do, Careless, say I'll join the company in a moment.

CARELESS: I will—but don't let that old blockhead persuade you to squander any of that money on
185 old musty debts, or any such nonsense; for tradesmen, Charles, are the most exorbitant fellows!

CHARLES SURFACE: Very true, and paying them is only encouraging them.

CARELESS: Nothing else.
190 CHARLES SURFACE: Aye, aye, never fear.—*(Exit* CARELESS.*)* So! this was an odd old fellow, indeed! Let me see, two-thirds of this is mine by right—five hundred and thirty pounds. 'Fore heaven! I find one's ancestors are more valuable relations than I
195 took 'em for!—Ladies and gentlemen, your most obedient and very grateful humble servant.

(Enter ROWLEY.*)*

Ha! old Rowley! egad, you are just come in time to take leave of your old acquaintance.

ROWLEY: Yes, I heard they were going. But I wonder
200 you can have such spirits under so many distresses.

CHARLES SURFACE: Why, there's the point—my distresses are so many, that I can't afford to part with my spirits; but I shall be rich and splenetic, all in good time. However, I suppose you are surprised that I am not more sorrowful at parting with so 205 many near relations; to be sure, 'tis very affecting; but rot 'em, you see they never move a muscle, so why should I?

ROWLEY: There's no making you serious a moment.

CHARLES SURFACE: Yes, faith: I am so now. Here, my 210 honest Rowley, here, get me this changed, and take a hundred pounds of it immediately to old Stanley.

ROWLEY: A hundred pounds! Consider only—

CHARLES SURFACE: Gad's life, don't talk about it! poor 215 Stanley's wants are pressing, and, if you don't make haste, we shall have some one call that has a better right to the money.

ROWLEY: Ah! there's the point! I never will cease dunning you with the old proverb— 220

CHARLES SURFACE: 'Be *just* before you're *generous*,' hey!—Why, so I would if I could; but Justice is an old lame hobbling beldame, and I can't get her to keep pace with Generosity, for the soul of me.

ROWLEY: Yet, Charles, believe me, one hour's reflec- 225 tion—

CHARLES SURFACE: Aye, aye, it's all very true; but, hark'ee, Rowley, while I have, by heaven I'll give—so, damn your economy! and now for hazard. *(Exit.)* 230

ACT 4 / SCENE 2

(The parlor)
(Enter SIR OLIVER SURFACE *and* MOSES.*)*

MOSES: Well, sir, I think, as Sir Peter said, you have seen Mr. Charles in high glory: 'tis great pity he's so extravagant.

SIR OLIVER: True, but he wouldn't sell my picture.

MOSES: And loves wine and women so much. 5

SIR OLIVER: But he wouldn't sell my picture!

MOSES: And games so deep.

SIR OLIVER: But he wouldn't sell my picture. Oh, here's Rowley.

(Enter ROWLEY.*)*

ROWLEY: So, Sir Oliver, I find you have made a pur- 10 chase—

SIR OLIVER: Yes, yes, our young rake has parted with his ancestors like old tapestry.

ROWLEY: And here has he commissioned me to redeliver your part of the purchase-money—I 15 mean, though, in your necessitous character of old Stanley.

MOSES: Ah! there is the pity of all: he is so damned charitable.

ROWLEY: And I left a hosier and two tailors in the hall, 20

who, I'm sure, won't be paid, and this hundred would satisfy 'em.

SIR OLIVER: Well, well, I'll pay his debts—and his benevolence too; but now I am no more a broker, and you shall introduce me to the elder brother as old Stanley.

ROWLEY: Not yet awhile; Sir Peter, I know, means to call there about this time.

(Enter TRIP.*)*

TRIP: O gentlemen, I beg pardon for not showing you out; this way—Moses, a word. *(Exeunt* TRIP *and* MOSES.*)*

SIR OLIVER: There's a fellow for you! Would you believe it, that puppy intercepted the Jew on our coming, and wanted to raise money before he got to his master!

ROWLEY: Indeed!

SIR OLIVER: Yes, they are now planning an annuity business. Ah, Master Rowley, in my days, servants were content with the follies of their masters, when they were worn a little threadbare—but now they have their vices, like their birthday clothes,° with the gloss on. *(Exeunt.)*

ACT 4 / SCENE 3

(A library in JOSEPH SURFACE*'s house)*
*(*JOSEPH SURFACE *and* SERVANT.*)*

JOSEPH SURFACE: No letter from Lady Teazle?

SERVANT: No, sir.

JOSEPH SURFACE *(aside)*: I am surprised she hasn't sent, if she's prevented from coming. Sir Peter certainly does not suspect me. Yet I wish I may not lose the heiress, through the scrape I have drawn myself in with the wife; however, Charles's imprudence and bad character are great points in my favor. *(Knocking.)*

SERVANT: Sir, I believe that must be Lady Teazle.

JOSEPH SURFACE: Hold! See whether it is or not, before you go to the door—I have a particular message for you, if it should be my brother.

SERVANT: 'Tis her ladyship, sir; she always leaves her chair at the milliner's in the next street.

JOSEPH SURFACE: Stay, stay—draw that screen before the window—that will do;—my opposite neighbor is a maiden lady of so curious a temper.— *(*SERVANT *draws the screen and exits.)* I have a difficult hand to play in this affair. Lady Teazle has lately suspected my views on Maria; but she must by no means be let into that secret,—at least, not till I have her more in my power.

(Enter LADY TEAZLE.*)*

---

birthday clothes, ceremonial dress for the king's birthday celebrations.

LADY TEAZLE: What, sentiment in soliloquy! Have you been very impatient now? O lud! don't pretend to look grave. I vow I couldn't come before.

JOSEPH SURFACE: O madam, punctuality is a species of constancy, a very unfashionable quality in a lady.

LADY TEAZLE: Upon my word, you ought to pity me. Do you know that Sir Peter is grown so ill-tempered to me of late, and so jealous of Charles too—that's the best of the story, isn't it?

JOSEPH SURFACE *(aside)*: I am glad my scandalous friends keep that up.

LADY TEAZLE: I am sure I wish he would let Maria marry him, and then perhaps he would be convinced; don't you, Mr. Surface?

JOSEPH SURFACE *(aside)*: Indeed I do not.—Oh, certainly I do! for then my dear Lady Teazle would also be convinced how wrong her suspicions were of my having any design on the silly girl.

LADY TEAZLE: Well, well, I'm inclined to believe you. But isn't it provoking, to have the most ill-natured things said to one? And there's my friend Lady Sneerwell has circulated I don't know how many scandalous tales of me! and all without any foundation, too—that's what vexes me.

JOSEPH SURFACE: Aye, madam, to be sure, that *is* the provoking circumstance—without foundation! yes, yes, there's the mortification, indeed; for when a scandalous story is believed against one, there certainly is no comfort like the consciousness of having deserved it.

LADY TEAZLE: No, to be sure—then I'd forgive their malice; but to attack me, who am really so innocent, and who never say an ill-natured thing of anybody—that is, of any friend—and then Sir Peter, too, to have him so peevish, and so suspicious, when I know the integrity of my own heart—indeed 'tis monstrous!

JOSEPH SURFACE: But, my dear Lady Teazle, 'tis your own fault if you suffer it. When a husband entertains a groundless suspicion of his wife, and withdraws his confidence from her, the original compact is broke, and she owes it to the honor of her sex to endeavor to outwit him.

LADY TEAZLE: Indeed! So that, if he suspects me without cause, it follows that the best way of curing his jealousy is to give him reason for't?

JOSEPH SURFACE: Undoubtedly—for your husband should never be deceived in you: and in that case it becomes *you* to be frail in compliment to *his* discernment.

LADY TEAZLE: To be sure, what you say is very reasonable, and when the consciousness of my own innocence—

JOSEPH SURFACE: Ah, my dear madam, there is the great mistake; 'tis this very conscious innocence that is of the greatest prejudice to you. What is it makes you negligent of forms, and careless of the

world's opinion? why, the *consciousness* of your innocence. What makes you thoughtless in your conduct, and apt to run into a thousand little imprudences? why, the *consciousness* of your innocence. What makes you impatient of Sir Peter's temper and outrageous at his suspicions? why, the *consciousness* of your own innocence!

LADY TEAZLE: 'Tis very true!

JOSEPH SURFACE: Now, my dear Lady Teazle, if you would but once make a trifling *faux pas,* you can't conceive how cautious you would grow—and how ready to humor and agree with your husband.

LADY TEAZLE: Do you think so?

JOSEPH SURFACE: Oh, I'm sure on't; and then you would find all scandal would cease at once, for—in short, your character at present is like a person in a plethora, absolutely dying of too much health.

LADY TEAZLE: So, so; then I perceive your prescription is, that I must sin in my own defence, and part with my virtue to preserve my reputation.

JOSEPH SURFACE: Exactly so, upon my credit, ma'am.

LADY TEAZLE: Well, certainly this is the oddest doctrine, and the newest receipt for avoiding calumny?

JOSEPH SURFACE: An infallible one, believe me. *Prudence,* like *experience,* must be paid for.

LADY TEAZLE: Why, if my understanding were once convinced—

JOSEPH SURFACE: Oh, certainly, madam, your understanding *should* be convinced. Yes, yes—heaven forbid I should persuade you to do anything you *thought* wrong. No, no, I have too much honor to desire it.

LADY TEAZLE: Don't you think we may as well leave honor out of the argument?

JOSEPH SURFACE: Ah, the ill effects of your country education, I see, still remain with you.

LADY TEAZLE: I doubt they do, indeed; and I will fairly own to you, that if I could be persuaded to do wrong, it would be by Sir Peter's ill-usage sooner than your honorable logic, after all.

JOSEPH SURFACE: Then, by this hand, which he is unworthy of—*(Taking her hand.)*

(Re-enter SERVANT.*)*

'Sdeath, you blockhead—what do you want?

SERVANT: I beg pardon, sir, but I thought you wouldn't choose Sir Peter to come up without announcing him.

JOSEPH SURFACE: Sir Peter!—Oons—the devil!

LADY TEAZLE: Sir Peter! O lud! I'm ruined! I'm ruined!

SERVANT: Sir, 'twasn't I let him in.

LADY TEAZLE: Oh! I'm undone! What will become of me, now, Mr. Logic?—Oh! mercy, he's on the stairs—I'll get behind here—and if ever I'm so imprudent again—*(Goes behind the screen.)*

JOSEPH SURFACE: Give me that book. *(Sits down.* SERVANT *pretends to adjust his hair.)*

(Enter SIR PETER TEAZLE.*)*

SIR PETER: Aye, ever improving himself!—Mr. Surface, Mr. Surface—

JOSEPH SURFACE: Oh, my dear Sir Peter, I beg your pardon. *(Gaping, and throws away the book.)* I have been dozing over a stupid book. Well, I am much obliged to you for this call. You haven't been here, I believe, since I fitted up this room. Books, you know, are the only things I am a coxcomb in.

SIR PETER: 'Tis very neat indeed. Well, well, that's proper; and you make even your screen a source of knowledge—hung, I perceive, with maps.

JOSEPH SURFACE: Oh, yes, I find great use in that screen.

SIR PETER: I dare say you must—certainly—when you want to find anything in a hurry.

JOSEPH SURFACE *(aside):* Aye, or to hide anything in a hurry either.

SIR PETER: Well, I have a little private business—

JOSEPH SURFACE: You needn't stay. *(to* SERVANT*)*

SERVANT: No, sir. *(Exit.)*

JOSEPH SURFACE: Here's a chair, Sir Peter—I beg—

SIR PETER: Well, now we are alone, there is a subject, my dear friend, on which I wish to unburden my mind to you—a point of the greatest moment to my peace: in short, my good friend, Lady Teazle's conduct of late has made me extremely unhappy.

JOSEPH SURFACE: Indeed! I am very sorry to hear it.

SIR PETER: Yes, 'tis but too plain she has not the least regard for me; but what's worse, I have pretty good authority to suspect she must have formed an attachment to another.

JOSEPH SURFACE: You astonish me!

SIR PETER: Yes! and, between ourselves, I think I have discovered the person.

JOSEPH SURFACE: How! you alarm me exceedingly.

SIR PETER: Aye, my dear friend, I knew you would sympathize with me!

JOSEPH SURFACE: Yes, believe me, Sir Peter, such a discovery would hurt me just as much as it would you.

SIR PETER: I am convinced of it.—Ah! it is a happiness to have a friend whom one can trust even with one's family secrets. But have you no guess who I mean?

JOSEPH SURFACE: I haven't the most distant idea. It can't be Sir Benjamin Backbite!

SIR PETER: O, no! What say you to Charles?

JOSEPH SURFACE: My brother! impossible!

SIR PETER: Ah, my dear friend, the goodness of your own heart misleads you—you judge of others by yourself.

JOSEPH SURFACE: Certainly, Sir Peter, the heart that is

190 conscious of its own integrity is ever slow to credit
another's treachery.

SIR PETER: True; but your brother has no sentiment—
you never hear him talk so.

JOSEPH SURFACE: Yet I can't but think Lady Teazle her-
195 self has too much principle—

SIR PETER: Aye; but what's her principle against the
flattery of a handsome, lively young fellow?

JOSEPH SURFACE: That's very true.

SIR PETER: And then, you know, the difference of our
200 ages makes it very improbable that she should
have any great affection for me; and if she were to
be frail, and I were to make it public, why the
town would only laugh at me, the foolish old
bachelor who had married a girl.

205 JOSEPH SURFACE: That's true, to be sure—they *would*
laugh.

SIR PETER: Laugh! aye, and make ballads, and paragraphs, and the devil knows what of me.

JOSEPH SURFACE: No, you must never make it public.

210 SIR PETER: But then again—that the nephew of my
old friend, Sir Oliver, should be the person to
attempt such a wrong, hurts me more nearly.

JOSEPH SURFACE: Aye, there's the point. When ingratitude barbs the dart of injury, the wound has
215 double danger in it.

SIR PETER: Aye—I, that was, in a manner, left his
guardian—in whose house he had been so often
entertained—who never in my life denied him—
my advice!

220 JOSEPH SURFACE: Oh, 'tis not to be credited! There
may be a man capable of such baseness, to be
sure; but, for my part, till you can give me positive
proofs, I cannot but doubt it. However, if it
should be proved on him, he is no longer a
225 brother of mine! I disclaim kindred with him—
for the man who can break through the laws of
hospitality, and attempt the wife of his friend,
deserves to be branded as the pest of society.

SIR PETER: What a difference there is between you!
230 What noble sentiments!

JOSEPH SURFACE: Yet I cannot suspect Lady Teazle's
honor.

SIR PETER: I am sure I wish to think well of her, and
to remove all ground of quarrel between us. She
235 has lately reproached me more than once with
having made no settlement on her; and, in our
last quarrel, she almost hinted that she should
not break her heart if I was dead. Now, as we
seem to differ in our ideas of expense, I have
240 resolved she shall be her own mistress in that
respect for the future; and, if I *were* to die, she
shall find that I have not been inattentive to
her interest while living. Here, my friend, are
the drafts of two deeds, which I wish to have
245 your opinion on. By one, she will enjoy eight
hundred a year independent while I live; and,

by the other, the bulk of my fortune after my
death.

JOSEPH SURFACE: This conduct, Sir Peter, is indeed
truly generous.—*(aside)* I wish it may not corrupt 250
my pupil.

SIR PETER: Yes, I am determined she shall have no
cause to complain, though I would not have her
acquainted with the latter instance of my affection yet awhile.   255

JOSEPH SURFACE: Nor I, if I could help it. *(aside)*

SIR PETER: And now, my dear friend, if you please, we
will talk over the situation of your hopes with
Maria.

JOSEPH SURFACE *(softly)*: No, no, Sir Peter; another 260
time, if you please.

SIR PETER: I am sensibly chagrined at the little progress you seem to make in her affection.

JOSEPH SURFACE: I beg you will not mention it. What
are my disappointments when your happiness is 265
in debate! *(Softly.)* —'Sdeath, I shall be ruined
every way! *(aside)*

SIR PETER: And though you are so averse to my
acquainting Lady Teazle with your passion, I am
sure she's not your enemy in the affair.   270

JOSEPH SURFACE: Pray, Sir Peter, now oblige me. I am
really too much affected by the subject we have
been speaking on to bestow a thought on my own
concerns. The man who is entrusted with his
friend's distresses can never—   275

(Enter SERVANT.*)*

Well, sir?

SERVANT: Your brother, sir, is speaking to a gentleman
in the street, and says he knows you are within.

JOSEPH SURFACE: 'Sdeath, blockhead—I'm not within
—I'm out for the day.   280

SIR PETER: Stay—hold—a thought has struck me—
you shall be at home.

JOSEPH SURFACE: Well, well, let him up.—*(Exit* SER-
VANT.*)* He'll interrupt Sir Peter—however—

SIR PETER: Now, my good friend, oblige me, I entreat 285
you. Before Charles comes, let me conceal myself
somewhere; then do you tax him on the point we
have been talking on, and his answers may satisfy
me at once.

JOSEPH SURFACE: O fie, Sir Peter! would you have me 290
join in so mean a trick?—to trepan my brother
so?

SIR PETER: Nay, you tell me you are *sure* he is innocent; if so, you do him the greatest service by giving him an opportunity to clear himself, and you 295
will set my heart at rest. Come, you shall not
refuse me; here, behind the screen will be *(Goes to
the screen.)*—Hey! what the devil! there seems to
be *one* listener here already—I'll swear I saw a petticoat!   300

JOSEPH SURFACE: Ha! ha! ha! Well, this is ridiculous

enough. I'll tell you, Sir Peter, though I hold a man of intrigue to be a most despicable character, yet you know, it doesn't follow that one is to

305 be an absolute Joseph either! Hark'ee! 'tis a little French milliner, a silly rogue that plagues me— and having some character—on your coming, she ran behind the screen.

SIR PETER: Ah, you rogue!—But, egad, she has over-
310 heard all I have been saying of my wife.

JOSEPH SURFACE: Oh, 'twill never go any further, you may depend on't!

SIR PETER: No! then, i'faith, let her hear it out.— Here's a closet will do as well.

315 JOSEPH SURFACE: Well, go in then.

SIR PETER: Sly rogue! sly rogue! *(Goes into the closet.)*

JOSEPH SURFACE: A very narrow escape, indeed! and a curious situation I'm in, to part man and wife in this manner.

320 LADY TEAZLE *(peeping from the screen)*: Couldn't I steal off?

JOSEPH SURFACE: Keep close, my angel!

SIR PETER *(peeping out)*: Joseph, tax him home.

JOSEPH SURFACE: Back, my dear friend!

325 LADY TEAZLE *(peeping)*: Couldn't you lock Sir Peter in?

JOSEPH SURFACE: Be still, my life!

SIR PETER *(peeping)*: You're sure the little milliner won't blab?

JOSEPH SURFACE: In, in, my dear Sir Peter!—'Fore
330 gad, I wish I had a key to the door.

(Enter CHARLES SURFACE.*)*

CHARLES SURFACE: Hollo! brother, what has been the matter? Your fellow would not let me up at first. What! have you had a Jew or a wench with you?

JOSEPH SURFACE: Neither, brother, I assure you.

335 CHARLES SURFACE: But what has made Sir Peter steal off? I thought he had been with you.

JOSEPH SURFACE: He was, brother; but, hearing *you* were coming, he did not choose to stay.

CHARLES SURFACE: What! was the old gentleman
340 afraid I wanted to borrow money of him!

JOSEPH SURFACE: No, sir: but I am sorry to find, Charles, that you have lately given that worthy man grounds for great uneasiness.

CHARLES SURFACE: Yes, they tell me I do that to a great
345 many worthy men. But how so, pray?

JOSEPH SURFACE: To be plain with you, brother, he thinks you are endeavoring to gain Lady Teazle's affections from him.

CHARLES SURFACE: Who, I? O lud! not I, upon my
350 word.—Ha! ha! ha! so the old fellow has found out that he has got a young wife, has he?—or, what's worse, has her ladyship discovered that she has an old husband?

JOSEPH: This is no subject to jest on, brother.—He
355 who can laugh—

CHARLES SURFACE: True, true, as you were going to

say—then, seriously, I never had the least idea of what you charge me with, upon my honor.

JOSEPH SURFACE: Well, it will give Sir Peter great satis
360 faction to hear this. *(Aloud.)*

CHARLES SURFACE: To be sure, I once thought the lady seemed to have taken a great fancy to me; but, upon my soul, I never gave her the least encouragement. Besides, you know my attachment to
365 Maria.

JOSEPH SURFACE: But sure, brother, even if Lady Teazle had betrayed the fondest partiality for you—

CHARLES SURFACE: Why, look'ee, Joseph, I hope I shall never deliberately do a dishonorable ac
370 tion—but if a pretty woman were purposely to throw herself in my way—and that pretty woman married to a man old enough to be her father—

JOSEPH SURFACE: Well!

CHARLES SURFACE: Why, I believe I should be obliged
375 to borrow a little of your morality, that's all.— But brother, do you know now that you surprise me exceedingly, by naming *me* with Lady Teazle; for, faith, I always understood *you* were her favorite.

380 JOSEPH SURFACE: Oh, for shame, Charles! This retort is foolish.

CHARLES SURFACE: Nay, I swear I have seen you exchange such significant glances—

JOSEPH SURFACE: Nay, nay, sir, this is no jest—

385 CHARLES SURFACE: Egad, I'm serious! Don't you remember—one day, when I called here—

JOSEPH SURFACE: Nay, prithee, Charles—

CHARLES SURFACE: And found you together—

JOSEPH SURFACE: Zounds, sir, I insist—

390 CHARLES SURFACE: And another time, when your servant—

JOSEPH SURFACE: Brother, brother, a word with you!— *(aside)* Gad, I must stop him.

CHARLES SURFACE: Informed me, I say, that—

395 JOSEPH SURFACE: Hush! I beg your pardon, but Sir Peter has overheard all we have been saying—I knew you would clear yourself, or I should not have consented.

CHARLES SURFACE: How Sir Peter! Where is he?

JOSEPH SURFACE: Softly, there! *(Points to the closet.)*
400 CHARLES SURFACE: Oh, 'fore heaven, I'll have him out.—Sir Peter, come forth!

JOSEPH SURFACE: No, no—

CHARLES SURFACE: I say, Sir Peter, come into court.— *(Pulls in* SIR PETER.*)* What! my old guardian!—
405 What—turn inquisitor, and take evidence, incog.?

SIR PETER: Give me your hand, Charles—I believe I have suspected you wrongfully—but you mustn't be angry with Joseph—'twas my plan!

CHARLES SURFACE: Indeed!

410 SIR PETER: But I acquit you. I promise you I don't think near so ill of you as I did. What I have heard has given me great satisfaction.

CHARLES SURFACE: Egad, then, 'twas lucky you didn't
415   hear any more. Wasn't it, Joseph? *(Half aside)*
SIR PETER: Well, well, I believe you.
JOSEPH SURFACE: Would they were both out of the
        room!
SIR PETER: And in future, perhaps, we may not be
420   such strangers.

(Enter SERVANT *who whispers* JOSEPH SURFACE.*)*

JOSEPH SURFACE: Lady Sneerwell!—stop her by all
        means—*(Exit* SERVANT.*)* Gentlemen— I beg par-
        don—I must wait on you downstairs—here's a
        person come on particular business.
425 CHARLES SURFACE: Well, you can see him in another
        room. Sir Peter and I haven't met a long time,
        and I have something to say to him.
JOSEPH SURFACE: They must not be left together.—I'll
        send Lady Sneerwell away, and return directly.—
430   *(aside)* Sir Peter, not a word on the French
        milliner. *(Exit* JOSEPH SURFACE.*)*
SIR PETER: Oh! not for the world!—Ah, Charles, if you
        associated more with your brother, one might
        indeed hope for your reformation. He is a man of
435   sentiment.—Well, there is nothing in the world so
        noble as a man of sentiment!
CHARLES SURFACE: Pshaw! he is too moral by half, and
        so apprehensive of his good name, as he calls it,
        that I suppose he would as soon let a priest into
440   his house as a girl.
SIR PETER: No, no.—come, come,—you wrong him.
        No, no, Joseph is no rake, but he is not such a
        saint in that respect either,—I have a great mind
        to tell him—we should have a laugh! *(aside)*
445 CHARLES SURFACE: Oh, hang him! he's a very an-
        chorite, a young hermit!
SIR PETER: Hark'ee—you must not abuse him; he may
        chance to hear of it again, I promise you.
CHARLES SURFACE: Why, you won't tell him?
450 SIR PETER: No—but—this way.—*(aside)* Egad, I'll tell
        him.—Hark'ee, have you a mind to have a good
        laugh at Joseph?
CHARLES SURFACE: I should like it of all things.
SIR PETER: Then, i'faith, we will!—I'll be quit with
455   him for discovering me. *(aside)*—He had a girl
        with him when I called.
CHARLES SURFACE: What! Joseph? you jest.
SIR PETER: Hush!—a little—French milliner—and
        the best of the jest is—she's in the room now.
460 CHARLES SURFACE: The devil she is!
SIR PETER: Hush! I tell you. *(Points to the screen.)*
CHARLES SURFACE: Behind the screen! 'Slife, let's un-
        veil her!
SIR PETER: No, no, he's coming:—you shan't, indeed!
465 CHARLES SURFACE: Oh, egad, we'll have a peep at the
        little milliner!
SIR PETER: Not for the world!—Joseph will never for-
        give me.

CHARLES SURFACE: I'll stand by you—
SIR PETER *(struggling with* CHARLES*)*: Odds, here he is!   470

*(*JOSEPH SURFACE *enters just as* CHARLES *throws down
the screen.)*

CHARLES SURFACE: Lady Teazle, by all that's wonder-
        ful!
SIR PETER: Lady Teazle, by all that's horrible!
CHARLES SURFACE: Sir Peter, this is one of the smartest
        French milliners I ever saw. Egad, you seem all to   475
        have been diverting yourselves here at hide and
        seek—and I don't see who is out of the secret.
        Shall I beg your ladyship to inform me?—Not a
        word!—Brother, will you please to explain this
        matter? What! Morality dumb too!—Sir Peter,   480
        though I *found* you in the dark, perhaps you are
        not so now! All mute! Well—though *I* can make
        nothing of the affair, I suppose you perfectly
        understand one another; so I'll leave you to your-
        selves.—*(Going.)* Brother, I'm sorry to find you   485
        have given that worthy man so much uneasiness.—Sir
        Peter! there's nothing *in the world so noble as a man
        of sentiment! (Exit* CHARLES.*)*

(They stand for some time looking at each other.)

JOSEPH SURFACE: Sir Peter—notwithstanding I con-
        fess that appearances are against me—if you will   490
        afford me your patience—I make no doubt but I
        shall explain everything to your satisfaction.
SIR PETER: If you please—
JOSEPH SURFACE: The fact is, sir, that Lady Teazle,
        knowing my pretensions to your ward Maria—I   495
        say, sir, Lady Teazle, being apprehensive of the
        jealousy of your temper—and knowing my friend-
        ship to the family—she, sir, I say—called here—in
        order that—I might explain those pretensions—
        but on your coming—being apprehensive—as I   500
        said—of your jealousy—she withdrew—and this,
        you may depend on't is the whole truth of the
        matter.
SIR PETER: A very clear account, upon my word; and
        I dare swear the lady will vouch for every article   505
        of it.
LADY TEAZLE *(coming forward)*: For not one word of it,
        Sir Peter!
SIR PETER: How! don't you think it worth while to
        agree in the lie?   510
LADY TEAZLE: There is not one syllable of truth in
        what that gentleman has told you.
SIR PETER: I believe you, upon my soul, ma'am!
JOSEPH SURFACE *(aside)*: 'Sdeath, madam, will you be-
        tray me?   515
LADY TEAZLE: Good Mr. Hypocrite, by your leave, I
        will speak for myself.
SIR PETER: Aye, let her alone, sir; you'll find she'll
        make out a better story than *you,* without prompt-
        ing.   520

LADY TEAZLE: Hear me, Sir Peter!—I came here on no matter relating to your ward, and even ignorant of this gentleman's pretensions to her—but I came, seduced by his insidious arguments, at least to listen to his pretended passion, if not to sacrifice *your* honor to his baseness.

SIR PETER: Now, I believe, the truth *is* coming, indeed!

JOSEPH SURFACE: The woman's mad!

LADY TEAZLE: No, sir; she's recovered her senses, and your own arts have furnished her with the means.—Sir Peter, I do not expect you to credit me—but the tenderness you expressed for me, when I am sure you could not think I was a witness to it, has penetrated to my heart, and had I left the place without the shame of this discovery, my future life should have spoken the sincerity of my gratitude. As for that smooth-tongue hypocrite, who would have seduced the wife of his too credulous friend, while he affected honorable addresses to his ward—I behold him now in a light so truly despicable, that I shall never again respect myself for having listened to him. *(Exit.)*

JOSEPH SURFACE: Notwithstanding all this, Sir Peter, heaven knows—

SIR PETER: That you are a villain!—and so I leave you to your conscience.

JOSEPH SURFACE: You are too rash, Sir Peter; you shall hear me. The man who shuts out conviction by refusing to—

SIR PETER: Oh!—

(Exeunt, JOSEPH SURFACE *following and speaking.)*

ACT 5 / SCENE 1

(The library in JOSEPH SURFACE's *house.)*
(Enter JOSEPH SURFACE *and* SERVANT.*)*

JOSEPH SURFACE: Mr. Stanley! why should you think I would see him? you *must* know he comes to ask something.

SERVANT: Sir, I should not have let him in, but that Mr. Rowley came to the door with him.

JOSEPH SURFACE: Pshaw! blockhead! to suppose that I should *now* be in a temper to receive visits from poor relations!—Well, why don't you show the fellow up?

SERVANT: I will, sir—Why sir, it was not my fault that Sir Peter discovered my lady—

JOSEPH SURFACE: Go, fool! *(Exit* SERVANT.*)* Sure, Fortune never played a man of my policy such a trick before! My character with Sir Peter, my hopes with Maria, destroyed in a moment! I'm in a rare humor to listen to other people's distresses! I shan't be able to bestow even a benevolent sentiment on Stanley.—So! here he comes, and Row-

ley with him. I must try to recover myself—and put a little charity into my face, however. *(Exit.)*

(Enter SIR OLIVER SURFACE *and* ROWLEY.*)*

SIR OLIVER: What! does he avoid us? That was he, was it not?

ROWLEY: It was, sir—but I doubt you are come a little too abruptly—his nerves are so weak, that the sight of a poor relation may be too much for him.—I should have gone first to break you to him.

SIR OLIVER: A plague of his nerves!—Yet this is he whom Sir Peter extols as a man of the most benevolent way of thinking!

ROWLEY: As to his way of thinking, I cannot pretend to decide; for, to do him justice, he appears to have as much speculative benevolence as any private gentleman in the kingdom, though he is seldom so sensual as to indulge himself in the exercise of it.

SIR OLIVER: Yet has a string of charitable sentiments, I suppose, at his fingers' ends!

ROWLEY: Or, rather, at his tongue's end, Sir Oliver; for I believe there is no sentiment he has more faith in than that 'Charity begins at home.'

SIR OLIVER: And his, I presume, is of that domestic sort which never stirs abroad at all.

ROWLEY: I doubt you'll find it so;—but he's coming—I mustn't seem to interrupt you; and you know, immediately as you leave him, I come in to announce your arrival in your real character.

SIR OLIVER: True; and afterwards you'll meet me at Sir Peter's.

ROWLEY: Without losing a moment. *(Exit* ROWLEY.*)*

SIR OLIVER: So! I don't like the complaisance of his features.

(Re-enter JOSEPH SURFACE.*)*

JOSEPH SURFACE: Sir, I beg you ten thousand pardons for keeping you a moment waiting—Mr. Stanley, I presume.

SIR OLIVER: At your service.

JOSEPH SURFACE: Sir, I beg you will do me the honor to sit down—I entreat you, sir.

SIR OLIVER: Dear sir—there's no occasion.—Too civil by half! *(aside)*

JOSEPH SURFACE: I have not the pleasure of knowing you, Mr. Stanley; but I am extremely happy to see you look so well. You were nearly related to my mother, I think, Mr. Stanley?

SIR OLIVER: I was sir—so nearly that my present poverty, I fear, may do discredit to her wealthy children—else I should not have presumed to trouble you.

JOSEPH SURFACE: Dear sir, there needs no apology: he that is in distress, though a stranger, has a right to claim kindred with the wealthy;—I am sure I wish *I* was one of that class, and had it in my power to offer you even a small relief.

SIR OLIVER: If your uncle, Sir Oliver, were here, I
75   should have a friend.

JOSEPH SURFACE: I wish he were, sir, with all my heart: you should not want an advocate with him, believe me, sir.

SIR OLIVER: I should not *need* one—my distresses
80   would recommend me; but I imagined his bounty had enabled *you* to become the agent of his charity.

JOSEPH SURFACE: My dear sir, you were strangely misinformed. Sir Oliver is a worthy man, a very wor-
85   thy sort of man; but—avarice, Mr. Stanley, is the vice of age. I will tell you, my good sir, in confidence, what he has done for me has been a mere nothing; though people, I know, have thought otherwise, and for my part, I never chose to con-
90   tradict the report.

SIR OLIVER: What! has he never transmitted you bullion! rupees!° pagodas!°

JOSEPH SURFACE: O dear sir, nothing of the kind! No, no; a few presents now and then—china
95   —shawls—Congo tea—avadavats,° and Indian crackers°—little more, believe me.

SIR OLIVER (*aside*): Here's gratitude for twelve thousand pounds!—Avadavats and Indian crackers!

JOSEPH SURFACE: Then, my dear sir, you have heard, I
100 doubt not, of the extravagance of my brother; there are very few would credit what I have done for that unfortunate young man.

SIR OLIVER: Not I, for one! (*aside*)

JOSEPH SURFACE: The sums I have lent him! Indeed I
105 have been exceedingly to blame—it was an amiable weakness: however, I don't pretend to defend it—and now I feel it doubly culpable, since it has deprived me of the pleasure of serving *you*, Mr. Stanley, as my heart dictates.

110 SIR OLIVER (*aside*): Dissembler!—Then, sir, you cannot assist me?

JOSEPH SURFACE: At present, it grieves me to say, I cannot; but, whenever I have the ability, you may depend upon hearing from me.

115 SIR OLIVER: I am extremely sorry—

JOSEPH SURFACE: Not more than I am, believe me; to pity, without the power to relieve, is still more painful than to ask and be denied.

---

rupees, silver coins of India, then valued at two shillings. *pagodas,* gold coins of India, then valued at eight shillings. *avadavats,* small singing birds of India, having red and black plumage. *Indian crackers,* firecrackers with colored wrappers.

SIR OLIVER: Kind sir, your most obedient humble ser-
     vant.   120

JOSEPH SURFACE: You leave me deeply affected, Mr. Stanley.—William, be ready to open the door.

SIR OLIVER: O dear sir, no ceremony.

JOSEPH SURFACE: Your very obedient.

SIR OLIVER: Sir, your most obsequious.   125

JOSEPH SURFACE: You may depend upon hearing from me, whenever I can be of service.

SIR OLIVER: Sweet sir, you are too good.

JOSEPH SURFACE: In the meantime I wish you health and spirits.   130

SIR OLIVER: Your ever grateful and perpetual humble servant.

JOSEPH SURFACE: Sir, yours as sincerely.

SIR OLIVER: Now I am satisfied! (*Exit.*)

JOSEPH SURFACE (*solus*): This is one bad effect of a 135
     good character; it invites applications from the unfortunate, and there needs no small degree of address to gain the reputation of benevolence without incurring the expense. The silver ore of pure charity is an expensive article in the cata- 140
     logue of a man's good qualities; whereas the sentimental French plate I use instead of it makes just as good a show, and pays no tax.

(*Enter* ROWLEY.)

ROWLEY: Mr. Surface, your servant—I was apprehensive of interrupting you—though my business   145
     demands immediate attention—as this note will inform you.

JOSEPH SURFACE: Always happy to see Mr. Rowley.— (*Reads.*) How! 'Oliver—Surface!'—My uncle arrived!

ROWLEY: He is, indeed—we have just parted—quite   150
     well, after a speedy voyage, and impatient to embrace his worthy nephew.

JOSEPH SURFACE: I am astonished!—William! stop Mr. Stanley, if he's not gone.

ROWLEY: Oh! he's out of reach, I believe.   155

JOSEPH SURFACE: Why didn't you let me know this when you came in together?

ROWLEY: I thought you had particular business. But I must be gone to inform your brother, and appoint him here to meet his uncle. He will be   160
     with you in a quarter of an hour.

JOSEPH SURFACE: So he says. Well I am strangely overjoyed at his coming.—(*aside*) Never, to be sure, was anything so damned unlucky!

ROWLEY: You will be delighted to see how well he   165
     looks.

JOSEPH SURFACE: Oh! I'm rejoiced to hear it.—(*aside*) Just at this time!

ROWLEY: I'll tell him how impatiently you expect him.   170

JOSEPH SURFACE: Do, do; pray give my best duty and affection. Indeed, I cannot express the sensations

I feel at the thought of seeing him.—*(Exit* ROW-
LEY.*)* Certainly his coming just at this time is the
cruellest piece of ill fortune. *(Exit.)*

ACT 5 / SCENE 2

(At SIR PETER's*)*
(Enter MRS. CANDOUR *and* MAID.*)*

MAID: Indeed, ma'am, my lady will see nobody at
present.

MRS. CANDOUR: Did you tell her it was her friend Mrs.
Candour?

MAID: Yes, madam; but she begs you will excuse her.

MRS. CANDOUR: Do go again; I shall be glad to see her,
if it be only for a moment, for I am sure she must
be in great distress. *(Exit* MAID.*)* Dear heart, how
provoking! I'm not mistress of half the circumstances! We shall have the whole affair in the
newspapers, with the names of the parties at
length, before I have dropped the story at a
dozen houses.

(Enter SIR BENJAMIN BACKBITE.*)*

O dear Sir Benjamin! you have heard, I suppose—

SIR BENJAMIN: Of Lady Teazle and Mr. Surface—

MRS. CANDOUR: And Sir Peter's discovery—

SIR BENJAMIN: Oh, the strangest piece of business, to
be sure!

MRS. CANDOUR: Well, I never was so surprised in my
life. I am so sorry for all parties, indeed I am.

SIR BENJAMIN: Now, I don't pity Sir Peter at all—he
was so extravagantly partial to Mr. Surface.

MRS. CANDOUR: Mr. Surface! Why, 'twas with Charles
Lady Teazle was detected.

SIR BENJAMIN: No such thing—Mr. Surface is the gallant.

MRS. CANDOUR: No, no—Charles is the man. 'Twas
Mr. Surface brought Sir Peter on purpose to discover them.

SIR BENJAMIN: I tell you I have it from one—

MRS. CANDOUR: And I have it from one—

SIR BENJAMIN: Who had it from one, who had it—

MRS. CANDOUR: From one immediately—But here's
Lady Sneerwell; perhaps she knows the whole
affair.

(Enter LADY SNEERWELL.*)*

LADY SNEERWELL: So, my dear Mrs. Candour, here's a
sad affair of our friend Lady Teazle!

MRS. CANDOUR: Aye, my dear friend, who could have
thought it—

LADY SNEERWELL: Well, there's no trusting appearances; though, indeed, she was always too lively
for me.

MRS. CANDOUR: To be sure, her manners were a little
too free—but she was very young!

LADY SNEERWELL: And had, indeed, some good qualities.

MRS. CANDOUR: So she had, indeed. But have you
heard the particulars?

LADY SNEERWELL: No; but everybody says that Mr. Surface—

SIR BENJAMIN: Aye, there, I told you—Mr. Surface was
the man.

MRS. CANDOUR: No, no, indeed—the assignation was
with Charles.

LADY SNEERWELL: With Charles! You alarm me, Mrs.
Candour.

MRS. CANDOUR: Yes, yes, he was the lover. Mr. Surface—do him justice—was only the informer.

SIR BENJAMIN: Well, I'll not dispute with you, Mrs.
Candour; but, be it which it may, I hope that Sir
Peter's wound will not—

MRS. CANDOUR: Sir Peter's wound! Oh, mercy! I didn't
hear a word of their fighting.

LADY SNEERWELL: Nor I, a syllable.

SIR BENJAMIN: No! what, no mention of the duel?

MRS. CANDOUR: Not a word.

SIR BENJAMIN: O Lord—yes, yes, they fought before
they left the room.

LADY SNEERWELL: Pray let us hear.

MRS. CANDOUR: Aye, do oblige us with the duel.

SIR BENJAMIN: 'Sir,' says Sir Peter—immediately after
the discovery—'you are a most ungrateful fellow.'

MRS. CANDOUR: Aye, to Charles—

SIR BENJAMIN: No, no—to Mr. Surface—'a most
ungrateful fellow; and old as I am, sir,' says he, 'I
insist on immediate satisfaction.'

MRS. CANDOUR: Aye, that must have been to Charles;
for 'tis very unlikely Mr. Surface should go to fight
in his house.

SIR BENJAMIN: 'Gad's life, ma'am, not at all—'giving
me immediate satisfaction.'—On this, madam,
Lady Teazle, seeing Sir Peter in such danger, ran
out of the room in strong hysterics, and Charles
after her, calling out for hartshorn and water!
Then, madam, they began to fight with swords—

(Enter CRABTREE.*)*

CRABTREE: With pistols, nephew—I have it from undoubted authority.

MRS. CANDOUR: O Mr. Crabtree, then it is all true!

CRABTREE: Too true, indeed, ma'am, and Sir Peter's
dangerously wounded—

SIR BENJAMIN: By a thrust of in *seconde*° quite through
his left side—

CRABTREE: By a bullet lodged in the thorax.

MRS. CANDOUR: Mercy on me! Poor Sir Peter!

CRABTREE: Yes, ma'am—though Charles would have
avoided the matter, if he could.

---

seconde, a term in fencing.

MRS. CANDOUR: I knew Charles was the person.

SIR BENJAMIN: Oh, my uncle, I see, knows nothing of
    the matter.

CRABTREE: But Sir Peter taxed him with the basest
    ingratitude—

SIR BENJAMIN: That I told you, you know.

CRABTREE: Do, nephew, let me speak!—and insisted
    on an immediate—

SIR BENJAMIN: Just as I said.

CRABTREE: Odds life, nephew, allow others to know
    something too! A pair of pistols lay on the bureau
    (for Mr. Surface, it seems, had come the night
    before late from Salt-Hill, where he had been to
    see the Montem° with a friend, who has a son at
    Eton), so, unluckily, the pistols were left charged.

SIR BENJAMIN: I heard nothing of this.

CRABTREE: Sir Peter forced Charles to take one, and
    they fired, it seems, pretty nearly together.
    Charles's shot took place, as I told you, and Sir
    Peter's missed; but, what is very extraordinary, the
    ball struck against a little bronze Pliny that stood
    over the chimney-piece, grazed out of the window
    at a right angle, and wounded the postman, who
    was just coming to the door with a double letter
    from Northamptonshire.

SIR BENJAMIN: My uncle's account is more circum-
    stantial, I must confess; but I believe mine is the
    true one, for all that.

LADY SNEERWELL (aside): I am more interested in this
    affair than they imagine, and must have better
    information. (Exit LADY SNEERWELL.)

SIR BENJAMIN (after a pause looking at each other): Ah!
    Lady Sneerwell's alarm is very easily accounted
    for.

CRABTREE: Yes, yes, they certainly do say—but that's
    neither here nor there.

MRS. CANDOUR: But, pray, where is Sir Peter at pres-
    ent?

CRABTREE: Oh! they brought him home, and he is
    now in the house, though the servants are or-
    dered to deny it.

MRS. CANDOUR: I believe so, and Lady Teazle, I sup-
    pose, attending him.

CRABTREE: Yes, yes; I saw one of the faculty enter just
    before me.

SIR BENJAMIN: Hey! who comes here?

CRABTREE: Oh, this is he—the physician, depend
    on't.

MRS. CANDOUR: Oh, certainly! it must be the physi-
    cian; and now we shall know.

(Enter SIR OLIVER SURFACE.)

Montem, It was formerly the custom of Eton schoolboys
to go to Salt-Hill (processus ad montem) every third year on
Whit-Tuesday, and levy salt money from the onlookers at the
ceremony.

CRABTREE: Well, doctor, what hopes?

MRS. CANDOUR: Aye, doctor, how's your patient?

SIR BENJAMIN: Now, doctor, isn't it a wound with a
    small-sword?

CRABTREE: A bullet lodged in the thorax, for a hun-
    dred!

SIR OLIVER: Doctor! a wound with a small-sword! and
    a bullet in the thorax?—Oons! are you mad, good
    people?

SIR BENJAMIN: Perhaps, sir, you are not a doctor?

SIR OLIVER: Truly, I am to thank you for my degree, if
    I am.

CRABTREE: Only a friend of Sir Peter's then, I pre-
    sume. But, sir, you must have heard of this acci-
    dent?

SIR OLIVER: Not a word!

CRABTREE: Not of his being dangerously wounded?

SIR OLIVER: The devil he is!

SIR BENJAMIN: Run through the body—

CRABTREE: Shot in the breast—

SIR BENJAMIN: By one Mr. Surface—

CRABTREE: Aye, the younger.

SIR OLIVER: Hey! what the plague! you seem to differ
    strangely in your accounts—however, you agree
    that Sir Peter is dangerously wounded.

SIR BENJAMIN: Oh, yes, we agree there.

CRABTREE: Yes, yes, I believe there can be no doubt of
    that.

SIR OLIVER: Then, upon my word, for a person in that
    situation, he is the most imprudent man alive—
    for here he comes, walking as if nothing at all
    were the matter.

(Enter SIR PETER TEAZLE.)

    Odds heart, Sir Peter! you are come in good time,
    I promise you; for we had just given you over.

SIR BENJAMIN: Egad, uncle, this is the most sudden
    recovery!

SIR OLIVER: Why, man! what do you do out of bed with
    a small-sword through your body, and a bullet
    lodged in your thorax?

SIR PETER: A small-sword and a bullet?

SIR OLIVER: Aye; these gentlemen would have killed
    you without law or physic, and wanted to dub me
    a doctor—to make me an accomplice.

SIR PETER: Why, what is all this?

SIR BENJAMIN: We rejoice, Sir Peter, that the story of
    the duel is not true, and are sincerely sorry for
    your other misfortunes.

SIR PETER: So, so; all over the town already. (aside)

CRABTREE: Though, Sir Peter, you were certainly vastly
    to blame to marry at all, at your years.

SIR PETER: Sir, what business is that of yours?

MRS. CANDOUR: Though, indeed, as Sir Peter made so
    good a husband, he's very much to be pitied.

SIR PETER: Plague on your pity, ma'am! I desire none
    of it.

SIR BENJAMIN: However, Sir Peter, you must not mind the laughing and jests you will meet with on this occasion.

SIR PETER: Sir, I desire to be master in my own house.

CRABTREE: 'Tis no uncommon case, that's one comfort.

SIR PETER: I insist on being left to myself: without ceremony, I insist on your leaving my house directly!

MRS. CANDOUR: Well, well, we are going; and depend on't, we'll make the best report of you we can.

SIR PETER: Leave my house!

CRABTREE: And tell how hardly you have been treated.

SIR PETER: Leave my house!

SIR BENJAMIN: And how patiently you bear it.

SIR PETER: Fiends! vipers! furies! Oh! that their own venom would choke them!

(Exeunt MRS. CANDOUR, SIR BENJAMIN BACKBITE, CRABTREE, *etc.)*

SIR OLIVER: They are very provoking indeed, Sir Peter.

(Enter ROWLEY.*)*

ROWLEY: I heard high words—what has ruffled you, Sir Peter?

SIR PETER: Pshaw! what signifies asking? Do I ever pass a day without my vexations?

SIR OLIVER: Well, I'm not inquisitive—I come only to tell you that I have seen both my nephews in the manner we proposed.

SIR PETER: A precious couple they are!

ROWLEY: Yes, and Sir Oliver is convinced that your judgment was right, Sir Peter.

SIR OLIVER: Yes, I find *Joseph* is indeed the man, after all.

ROWLEY: Yes, as Sir Peter says, he's a man of sentiment.

SIR OLIVER: And acts up to the sentiments he professes.

ROWLEY: It certainly is edification to hear him talk.

SIR OLIVER: Oh, he's a model for the young men of the age! But how's this, Sir Peter? you don't join in your friend Joseph's praise, as I expected.

SIR PETER: Sir Oliver, we live in a damned wicked world, and the fewer we praise the better.

ROWLEY: What! do *you* say so, Sir Peter, who were never mistaken in your life?

SIR PETER: Pshaw! plague on you both! I see by your sneering you have heard the whole affair. I shall go mad among you!

ROWLEY: Then, to fret you no longer, Sir Peter, we are indeed acquainted with it all. I met Lady Teazle coming from Mr. Surface's, so humbled that she deigned to request me to be her advocate with you.

SIR PETER: And does Sir Oliver know all too?

SIR OLIVER: Every circumstance.

SIR PETER: What, of the closet—and the screen, hey?

SIR OLIVER: Yes, yes, and the little French milliner. Oh, I have been vastly diverted with the story! ha! ha!

SIR PETER: 'Twas very pleasant.

SIR OLIVER: I never laughed more in my life, I assure you: ha! ha!

SIR PETER: O, vastly diverting! ha! ha!

ROWLEY: To be sure, Joseph with his sentiments! ha! ha!

SIR PETER: Yes, yes, his sentiments! ha! ha! A hypocritical villain!

SIR OLIVER: Aye, and that rogue Charles to pull Sir Peter out of the closet: ha! ha!

SIR PETER: Ha! ha! 'twas devilish entertaining, to be sure!

SIR OLIVER: Ha! ha! Egad, Sir Peter, I should like to have seen your face when the screen was thrown down: ha! ha!

SIR PETER: Yes, yes, my face when the screen was thrown down: ha! ha! Oh, I must never show my head again!

SIR OLIVER: But come, come, it isn't fair to laugh at you neither, my old friend—though, upon my soul, I can't help it.

SIR PETER: Oh, pray don't restrain your mirth on my account—it does not hurt me at all! I laugh at the whole affair myself. Yes, yes, I think being a standing jest for all one's acquaintances a very happy situation. O yes, and then of a morning to read the paragraphs about Mr. S—, Lady T—, and Sir P—, will be so entertaining!

ROWLEY: Without affectation, Sir Peter, you may despise the ridicule of fools. But I see Lady Teazle going towards the next room; I am sure you must desire a reconciliation as earnestly as she does.

SIR OLIVER: Perhaps my being here prevents her coming to you. Well, I'll leave honest Rowley to mediate between you; but he must bring you all presently to Mr. Surface's, where I am not returning, if not to reclaim a libertine, at least to expose hypocrisy.

SIR PETER: Ah! I'll be present at your discovering yourself there with all my heart—though 'tis a vile unlucky place for discoveries!

ROWLEY: We'll follow. *(Exit* SIR OLIVER SURFACE.*)*

SIR PETER: She is not coming here, you see, Rowley.

ROWLEY: No, but she has left the door of that room open, you perceive. See, she is in tears!

SIR PETER: Certainly a little mortification appears very becoming in a wife! Don't you think it will do her good to let her pine a little?

ROWLEY: Oh, this is ungenerous in you!

SIR PETER: Well, I know not what to think. You remember, Rowley, the letter I found of hers, evidently intended for Charles!

ROWLEY: A mere forgery, Sir Peter! laid in your way on purpose. This is one of the points which I intend *Snake* shall give you conviction on.

SIR PETER: I wish I were once satisfied of that. She looks this way. What a remarkably elegant turn of the head she has! Rowley, I'll go to her.

315 ROWLEY: Certainly.

SIR PETER: Though, when it is known that we are reconciled, people will laugh at me ten times more!

ROWLEY: Let them laugh, and retort their malice only
320 by showing them you are happy in spite of it.

SIR PETER: I'faith, so I will! and, if I'm not mistaken, we may yet be the happiest couple in the country.

ROWLEY: Nay, Sir Peter—he who once lays aside suspicion—

325 SIR PETER: Hold, my dear Rowley! if you have any regard for me, never let me hear you utter anything like a sentiment—I have had enough of them to serve me the rest of my life. (*Exeunt.*)

ACT 5 / SCENE 3

(*The library in* JOSEPH SURFACE's *house.*)
(JOSEPH SURFACE *and* LADY SNEERWELL.)

LADY SNEERWELL: Impossible! Will not Sir Peter immediately be reconciled to Charles, and of consequence no longer oppose his union with Maria? The thought is distraction to me!

5 JOSEPH SURFACE: Can passion furnish a remedy?

LADY SNEERWELL: No, nor cunning either. Oh, I was a fool, an idiot, to league with such a blunderer!

JOSEPH SURFACE: Sure, Lady Sneerwell, *I* am the greatest sufferer; yet you see I bear the accident
10 with calmness.

LADY SNEERWELL: Because the disappointment doesn't reach your *heart;* your *interest* only attached you to Maria. Had you felt for *her* what *I* have for that ungrateful libertine, neither your temper nor
15 hypocrisy could prevent your showing the sharpness of your vexation.

JOSEPH SURFACE: But why should your reproaches fall on *me* for this disappointment?

LADY SNEERWELL: Are you not the cause of it? What
20 had you to do to bate in your pursuit of Maria to pervert Lady Teazle by the way? Had you not a sufficient field for your roguery in blinding Sir Peter, and supplanting your brother? I hate such an avarice of crimes; 'tis an unfair monopoly, and
25 never prospers.

JOSEPH SURFACE: Well, I admit I have been to blame. I confess I deviated from the direct road of wrong, but I don't think we're so totally defeated neither.

LADY SNEERWELL: No!

30 JOSEPH SURFACE: You tell me you have made a trial of Snake since we met, and that you still believe him faithful to us—

LADY SNEERWELL: I do believe so.

JOSEPH SURFACE: And that he has undertaken, should
35 it be necessary, to swear and prove that Charles is

at this time contracted by vows and honor to your ladyship—which some of his former letters to you will serve to support?

LADY SNEERWELL: This, indeed, might have assisted.

JOSEPH SURFACE: Come, come; it is not too late yet.— 40
(*Knocking at the door.*) But hark! this is probably my uncle, Sir Oliver: retire to that room; we'll consult farther when he's gone.

LADY SNEERWELL: Well! but if *he* should find you out too— 45

JOSEPH SURFACE: Oh, I have no fear of that. Sir Peter will hold his tongue for his own credit's sake— and you may depend on't I shall soon discover Sir Oliver's weak side!

LADY SNEERWELL: I have no diffidence of your abili- 50
ties—only be constant to one roguery at a time. (*Exit.*)

JOSEPH SURFACE: I will, I will! So! 'tis confounded hard, after such bad fortune, to be baited by one's confederate in evil. Well, at all events, my character is so much better than Charles's, that I cer- 55
tainly—hey!—what!—this is not Sir Oliver, but old Stanley again! Plague on't! that he should return to leave me just now! We shall have Sir Oliver come and find him here—and—

(*Enter* SIR OLIVER SURFACE.)

Gad's life, Mr. Stanley, why have you come back to 60
plague me just at this time? You must not stay now, upon my word.

SIR OLIVER: Sir, I hear your uncle Oliver is expected here, and though he has been so penurious to *you,* I'll try what he'll do for *me.* 65

JOSEPH SURFACE: Sir, 'tis impossible for you to stay now, so I must beg—Come any other time, and I promise you, you shall be assisted.

SIR OLIVER: No: Sir Oliver and I must be acquainted.

JOSEPH SURFACE: Zounds, sir! then I insist on your 70
quitting the room directly.

SIR OLIVER: Nay, sir!

JOSEPH SURFACE: Sir, I insist on't!—Here, William! show this gentleman out. Since you compel me, sir—not one moment—this is such insolence! 75
(*Going to push him out.*)

(*Enter* CHARLES SURFACE.)

CHARLES SURFACE: Heyday! what's the matter now? What the devil, have you got hold of my little broker here? Zounds, brother, don't hurt little Premium. What's the matter, my little fellow?

JOSEPH SURFACE: So! he has been with you, too, has 80
he?

CHARLES SURFACE: To be sure he has! Why, 'tis as honest a little—but sure, Joseph, you have not been borrowing money too, have you?

JOSEPH SURFACE: Borrowing! no! But, brother, you 85
know here we expect Sir Oliver every—

CHARLES SURFACE: O gad, that's true! Noll mustn't find the little broker here, to be sure.

JOSEPH SURFACE: Yet, Mr. Stanley insists—

90 CHARLES SURFACE: Stanley! why his name is Premium.

JOSEPH SURFACE: No, no, Stanley.

CHARLES SURFACE: No, no, Premium.

JOSEPH SURFACE: Well, no matter which—but—

CHARLES SURFACE: Aye, aye, Stanley or Premium, 'tis
95 the same thing, as you say; for I suppose he goes by half a hundred names, besides A.B.'s° at the coffee-houses.

JOSEPH SURFACE: Death! here's Sir Oliver at the door. *(Knocking again.)* Now I beg, Mr. Stanley—

100 CHARLES SURFACE: Aye, and I beg, Mr. Premium—

SIR OLIVER: Gentlemen—

JOSEPH SURFACE: Sir, by heaven you shall go!

CHARLES SURFACE: Aye, out with him, certainly.

SIR OLIVER: This violence—

105 JOSEPH SURFACE: 'Tis your own fault.

CHARLES SURFACE: Out with him, to be sure. *(Both forcing* SIR OLIVER *out.)*

(Enter SIR PETER *and* LADY TEAZLE, MARIA, *and* ROWLEY.*)*

SIR PETER: My old friend, Sir Oliver—hey! What in the name of wonder!—Here are dutiful nephews!—assault their uncle at the first visit!

110 LADY TEAZLE: Indeed, Sir Oliver, 'twas well we came in to rescue you.

ROWLEY: Truly it was; for I perceive, Sir Oliver, the character of old Stanley was no protection to you.

SIR OLIVER: Nor of Premium either: the necessities of
115 the *former* could not extort a shilling from *that* benevolent gentleman; and now, egad, I stood a chance of faring worse than my ancestors, and being knocked down without being bid for.

(After a pause, JOSEPH *and* CHARLES *turning to each other.)*

JOSEPH SURFACE: Charles!

120 CHARLES SURFACE: Joseph!

JOSEPH SURFACE: 'Tis now complete!

CHARLES SURFACE: Very!

SIR OLIVER: Sir Peter, my friend, and Rowley too—look on that elder nephew of mine. You know
125 what he has already received from my bounty; and you know also how gladly I would have regarded half my fortune as held in trust for him—judge, then, my disappointment in discovering him to be destitute of truth—charity—and
130 gratitude!

SIR PETER: Sir Oliver, I should be more surprised at

A.B.'s, a reference to appointments at the coffeehouses made under concealed names.

this declaration, if I had not myself found him selfish, treacherous, and hypocritical!

LADY TEAZLE: And if the gentleman pleads not guilty to these, pray let him call *me* to his character. 135

SIR PETER: Then, I believe, we need add no more.—If he knows himself, he will consider it as the most perfect punishment that he is known to the world.

CHARLES SURFACE *(aside)*: If they talk this way to *Honesty*, what will they say to *me*, by and by? 140

(SIR PETER, LADY TEAZLE, and MARIA retire.)

SIR OLIVER: As for that prodigal, his brother, there—

CHARLES SURFACE *(aside)*: Aye, now comes my turn: the damned family pictures will ruin me!

JOSEPH SURFACE: Sir Oliver!—uncle!—will you honor 145 me with a hearing?

CHARLES SURFACE *(aside)*: Now if Joseph would make one of his long speeches, I might recollect myself a little.

SIR OLIVER *(to* JOSEPH SURFACE*)*: I suppose you would 150 undertake to justify yourself entirely?

JOSEPH SURFACE: I trust I could.

SIR OLIVER: Pshaw!—Well, sir! and *you (to* CHARLES*)* could justify yourself too, I suppose?

CHARLES SURFACE: Not that I know of, Sir Oliver. 155

SIR OLIVER: What!—Little Premium has been let too much into the secret I presume?

CHARLES SURFACE: True sir; but they were family secrets, and should never be mentioned again, you know. 160

ROWLEY: Come, Sir Oliver, I know you cannot speak of Charles's follies with anger.

SIR OLIVER: Odd's heart, no more I can—nor with gravity either. Sir Peter, do you know the rogue bargained with me for all his ancestors—sold me 165 judges and generals by the foot—and maiden aunts as cheap as broken china.

CHARLES SURFACE: To be sure, Sir Oliver, I did make a little free with the family canvas, that's the truth on't. My ancestors may certainly rise in evidence 170 against me, there's no denying it; but believe me sincere when I tell you—and upon my soul I would not say it if I was not—that if I do not appear mortified at the exposure of my follies, it is because I feel at this moment the warmest satis- 175 faction in seeing you, my liberal benefactor.

SIR OLIVER: Charles, I believe you. Give me your hand again; the ill-looking little fellow over the settee has made your peace.

CHARLES SURFACE: Then, sir, my gratitude to the orig- 180 inal is still increased.

LADY TEAZLE *(pointing to* MARIA*)*: Yet, I believe, Sir Oliver, here is one whom Charles is still more anxious to be reconciled to.

SIR OLIVER: Oh, I have heard of his attachment there; 185

and, with the young lady's pardon, if I construe
right—that blush—

SIR PETER: Well, child, speak your sentiments.

MARIA: Sir, I have little to say, but that I shall rejoice to
190   hear that he is happy; for me, whatever claim I
had to his affection, I willingly resign it to one
who has a better title.

CHARLES SURFACE: How, Maria!

SIR PETER: Heyday! what's the mystery now? While he
195   appeared an incorrigible rake, you would give
your hand to no one else; and now that he is likely
to reform, I warrant you won't have him.

MARIA: His own heart—and Lady Sneerwell know the
cause.

200 CHARLES SURFACE: Lady Sneerwell!

JOSEPH SURFACE: Brother, it is with great concern I am
obliged to speak on this point, but my regard to
justice compels me, and Lady Sneerwell's injuries
can no longer be concealed. (*Goes to the door.*)

(*Enter* LADY SNEERWELL.)

205 SIR PETER: So! another French milliner!—Egad, he
has one in every room in the house, I suppose!

LADY SNEERWELL: Ungrateful Charles! Well may you
be surprised, and feel for the indelicate situation
which your perfidy has forced me into.

210 CHARLES SURFACE: Pray, uncle, is this another plot of
yours? For, as I have life, I don't understand it.

JOSEPH SURFACE: I believe, sir, there is but the evidence of one person more necessary to make it
extremely clear.

215 SIR PETER: And that person, I imagine, is Mr. Snake.—
Rowley, you were perfectly right to bring him with
us, and pray let him appear.

ROWLEY: Walk in, Mr. Snake.

(*Enter* SNAKE.)

I thought his testimony might be wanted; how-
220   ever, it happens unluckily, that he comes to confront Lady Sneerwell, and not to support her.

LADY SNEERWELL: Villain! Treacherous to me at last!
(*aside*) —Speak, fellow, have *you* too conspired
against me?

225 SNAKE: I beg your ladyship ten thousand pardons: you
paid me extremely liberally for the lie in question; but I have unfortunately been offered
double to speak the truth.

SIR PETER: Plot and counterplot, egad—I wish your
230   ladyship joy of the success of your negotiation.

LADY SNEERWELL: The torments of shame and disappointment on you all!

LADY TEAZLE: Hold, Lady Sneerwell—before you go,
let me thank you for the trouble you and that
235   gentleman have taken, in writing letters to me
from Charles, and answering them yourself; and
let me also request you to make my respects to the

Scandalous College, of which you are president,
and inform them, that Lady Teazle, licentiate,
begs leave to return the diploma they granted   240
her, as she leaves off practice, and kills characters
no longer.

LADY SNEERWELL: You too, madam!—provoking—insolent! May your husband live these fifty years!
(*Exit.*)

SIR PETER: Oons! what a fury!   245

LADY TEAZLE: A malicious creature, indeed!

SIR PETER: Hey! not for her last wish?

LADY TEAZLE: Oh, no!

SIR OLIVER: Well, sir, and what have you to say now?

JOSEPH SURFACE: Sir, I am so confounded, to find that   250
Lady Sneerwell could be guilty of suborning Mr.
Snake in this manner, to impose on us all, that I
know not what to say; however, lest her revengeful
spirit should prompt her to injure my brother, I
had certainly better follow her directly. (*Exit.*)   255

SIR PETER: Moral to the last drop!

SIR OLIVER: Aye, and marry her, Joseph, if you can.—
Oil and vinegar, egad! you'll do very well together.

ROWLEY: I believe we have no more occasion for Mr.   260
Snake at present.

SNAKE: Before I go, I beg pardon once for all, for
whatever uneasiness I have been the humble instrument of causing to the parties present.

SIR PETER: Well, well, you have made atonement by a   265
good deed at last.

SNAKE: But I must request of the company, that it shall
never be known.

SIR PETER: Hey! what the plague! are you ashamed of
having done a right thing once in your life?   270

SNAKE: Ah, sir—consider I live by the badness of my
character—I have nothing but my infamy to depend on! and, if it were once known that I had
been betrayed into an honest action, I should
lose every friend I have in the world.   275

SIR OLIVER: Well, well—we'll not traduce you by saying anything in your praise, never fear. (*Exit*
SNAKE.)

SIR PETER: There's a precious rogue! yet that fellow is
a writer and a critic!

LADY TEAZLE: See, Sir Oliver, there needs no persua-   280
sion now to reconcile your nephew and Maria.
(CHARLES *and* MARIA *apart.*)

SIR OLIVER: Aye, aye, that's as it should be, and, egad,
we'll have the wedding to-morrow morning.

CHARLES SURFACE: Thank you, my dear uncle.

SIR PETER: What, you rogue! don't you ask the girl's   285
consent first?

CHARLES SURFACE: Oh, I have done that a long time—
above a minute ago—and she has looked yes.

MARIA: For shame, Charles!—I protest, Sir Peter,
there has not been a word—   290

SIR OLIVER: Well, then, the fewer the better—may your love for each other never know abatement.

SIR PETER: And may you live as happily together as Lady Teazle and I—intend to do!

295 CHARLES SURFACE: Rowley, my old friend, I am sure you congratulate me; and I suspect that I owe you much.

SIR OLIVER: You do, indeed, Charles.

ROWLEY: If my efforts to serve you had not succeeded

300 you would have been in my debt for the attempt—but deserve to be happy—and you overpay me.

SIR PETER: Aye, honest Rowley always said you would reform.

305 CHARLES SURFACE: Why as to reforming, Sir Peter, I'll make no promises, and that I take to be a proof that I intend to set about it.—But here shall be my monitor—my gentle guide.—Ah! can I leave the virtuous path those eyes illumine?

    Though thou, dear maid, shouldst waive thy
310   *beauty's* sway,
    Thou still must rule, because I *will* obey:
    An humbled fugitive from Folly view,
    No sanctuary near but *Love* and—You;

(To the audience.)

    You can, indeed, each anxious fear remove.
315   For even *Scandal* dies, if *you* approve.

FINIS

EPILOGUE

By George Colman°

(Spoken by LADY TEAZLE.)

I, who was late so volatile and gay,
Like a trade-wind must now blow all one way,
Bend all my cares, my studies, and my vows,
To one old rusty weathercock—my spouse!
5 So wills our virtuous bard—the motley Bayes°
Of crying epilogues and laughing plays!
    Old bachelors, who marry smart young wives,
Learn from our play to regulate your lives:
Each bring his dear to town, all faults upon her—
10 London will prove the very source of honor.
Plunged fairly in, like a cold bath it serves,
When principles relax, to brace the nerves.

Such is my case;—and yet I might deplore
That the gay dream of dissipation's o'er;
And say, ye fair, was ever lively wife,   15
Born with a genius for the highest life,
Like me untimely blasted in her bloom,
Like me condemned to such a dismal doom?
Save money—when I just knew how to waste it!
Leave London—just as I began to taste it!   20
Must I then watch the early crowing cock,
The melancholy ticking of a clock;
In the lone rustic hall for ever pounded,
With dogs, cats, rats, and squalling brats
    surrounded?
With humble curates can I now retire,   25
(While good Sir Peter boozes with the squire,)
And at backgammon mortify my soul,
That pants for loo,° or flutters at a vole?°
Seven's the main!° Dear sound!—that must expire,
Lost at hot cockles,° round a Christmas fire!   30
The transient hour of fashion too soon spent,
Farewell the tranquil mind, farewell content!°
Farewell the plumèd head, the cushioned tête,
That takes the cushion from its proper seat!
That spirit-stirring drum!°—card drums I mean,   35
Spadille°—odd trick—pam°—basto°—king and
    queen!
And you, ye knockers, that, with brazen throat,
The welcome visitors' approach denote;
Farewell! all quality of high renown,
Pride, pomp, and circumstance of glorious town!   40
Farewell! your revels I partake no more,
And Lady Teazle's occupation's o'er!
All this I told our bard—he smiled, and said 'twas
    clear,
I ought to play deep tragedy next year.
Meanwhile he drew wise morals from his play,   45
And in these solemn periods stalked away:—
'Blest were the fair like you; her faults who
    stopped,
And closed her follies when the curtain dropped!
No more in vice or error to engage,
Or play the fool at large on life's great stage.'   50

George Colman, author of *The Jealous Wife.*   **Bayes,** poet, dramatist (from Bayes in *The Rehearsal*).

    loo, a favorite eighteenth-century game of cards. **flutters . . . vole,** winning all the tricks. **main,** in hazard, the caster of the dice "called his *main*" by naming a number from five to nine. **hot cockles,** a game in which one kneels, and covering his eyes lays his head in another's lap and guesses who struck him. **Farewell . . . content,** these lines parody Othello's soliloquy, III, iii, l. 345. **drum,** fashionable card-party. **Spadille,** the ace of spades. **pam,** the knave of clubs. **basto,** the ace of clubs.

Figure 1. Sir Benjamin Backbite (Eric Donkin, *center foreground*) recites one of his malicious epigrams to entertain Mrs. Candour (Jane Casson, *left*), Joseph Surface (Robin Gammell, *center background*), and Lady Sneerwell (Pat Galloway, *right*) in the Stratford Festival production of *The School for Scandal*, directed by Michael Langham and designed by Leslie Hurry, Stratford, Ontario, 1970. (Photograph: Douglas Spillane. Courtesy of the Stratford Festival.)

Figure 2. Sir Peter Teazle (Stephen Murray) berates Lady Teazle (Helen Carey) for the extravagance of her fashionable inclinations. (Photograph: Douglas Spillane. Courtesy of the Stratford Festival.)

Figure 3. Charles Surface (Barry MacGregor, *left*) offers to sell the portrait of his great-aunt Deborah to Sir Oliver Surface (Mervyn Blake), here posing as the broker Mr. Premium. (Photograph: Douglas Spillane. Courtesy of the Stratford Festival.)

Figure 4. Sir Peter Teazle (Stephen Murray, *left*) tries to prevent Charles (Barry MacGregor) from pulling away the screen that purportedly conceals Joseph's mistress. (Photograph: Douglas Spillane. Courtesy of the Stratford Festival.)

Staging of *The School for Scandal*

INTERVIEW WITH MICHAEL LANGHAM, DIRECTOR OF THE STRATFORD PRODUCTION, 1970, BY BRADFORD S. FIELD JR.

FIELD: I hear that *The School for Scandal* at Stratford was very successful.

LANGHAM: It was very well received, but, like all plays written for an eighteenth century theatre, rather difficult to arrange for a thrust stage like the one at Stratford.

FIELD: From the reviews you got you seem to have had no real trouble.

LANGHAM: Only technical problems, but it was a very confident production. We had a tone pitched at about the right level. We tried to avoid the usual icy artifice of most modern staging. It is clear to anyone who reads the play that the idiom of the language is not modern, but rather a special one.

FIELD: Wit, polish, repartee . . .

LANGHAM: Like that. It was written for an audience which had not yet lost the art of conversation. And the idiom affects everything else, the way one walks, for instance, was more a matter of displaying oneself than of getting from A to B in a straight line.

FIELD: Then you strove for some type of artifice, such as that in Restoration comedy.

LANGHAM: Yes and no. In the manner of speech and movement yes. The play itself imitates that earlier dramatic style. But by Sheridan's day that style was a century old. His play is in content not nearly so, ah, bumptious.

FIELD: How do you avoid a Restoration style when you do a play that imitates a Restoration style?

LANGHAM: It wasn't a Restoration style we sought to avoid, but modern versions of it. It's become a theatrical convention, you know, to suppose that since the language is so neat and precise in plays like these, that the society is, also.

FIELD: Then your production presented a society that was dirty?

LANGHAM: Not smutty, but soiled. Characters walked about with chickenshit on their boots. Their toilet facilities were primitive. For example, we began the play with only Snake on stage. Lady Sneerwell was off stage, shouting her lines. When she came in she was carrying an armful of gossip sheets, obviously having been sitting on the john. And that was only a beginning. She entered bald. We had a bald wig on her. And in her shift. During the rest of the scene we saw her gradual transformation as she dressed, and built up this fantastic facade. It was a good visual image, heavily impressed on the audience, to show how much *The School for Scandal* is about facades.

FIELD: You especially emphasized that point?

LANGHAM: Well, that's only one theme. Did you ever notice how much reference there is in the play to the loss of the American colonies?

FIELD: None, that I can remember.

LANGHAM: None at all. It was occurring right at that time, yet the play ignores it, as, I think, the Englishman of that time tended to do. Most interest was centered in the progress of the East India Company. That is where Sir Oliver returns from, India.

FIELD: Still, there has to be something in a play to interest a modern audience.

LANGHAM: Yes, well, the play is very funny, that's timeless enough.

FIELD: But lots of plays are funny. Why choose *The School for Scandal*?

LANGHAM: In the production we did at Stratford we saw the play revealing a changeover in the leadership of the country from the old aristocrats to the new merchant classes. Sir Oliver is a representative of that old class and tries to exemplify its virtues. And in the portrait scene, where all those old ancestors are being sold off without pity, we can see that changeover in a way just as striking as Lady Sneerwell's facades. The scene, as we played it, had almost a heartbreaking quality.

FIELD: Then your appeal to the modern audience is to show them the realistic basis of the action.

LANGHAM: Yes, the Teazle-plot fits that approach quite well. Lady Teazle was revealed as really from the country, but on the make, you know . . . oh, not just a bumpkin, more of a hoyden. Sir Peter we made not ludicrous but poignant, pointing out the dangers and difficulties of that kind of marriage.

FIELD: What was the most serious problem which you had to work out in staging this play?

LANGHAM: Well, I suppose I would have to say our greatest problem was a kind of North American infelicity with language!

FIELD: Surely not actors!

LANGHAM: Yes. In England the problem is not so serious. People in fact still do enjoy a tradition of facility of words and complicated phrasing; but over here, while the language, the tone, is much more open and direct, that's not much help in projecting the delicate facades that are offered by Sheridan's language. So we had some hard work to overcome that.

FIELD: Which scenes or characters in the play gave you more trouble than others?

LANGHAM: Sneerwell's role gave us problems because she reappears after such a long absence that we had to worry about re-establishing her character. Oh, there were some little things, too. In the last scene when it seems clear that Maria has won Charles—and Lady Sneerwell had had a secret lust for him—she goes for Maria's eyes with her nails. Charles holds her back and her wig falls off, revealing the hideous bald dome again. Well, in a theatre an audience often thinks that a wig's falling off must be a mistake. So we had to add some *further* business with everyone on stage re-acting with elaborate revulsion at the sight of her—to underscore the point that it was an intended part of the play.

FIELD: Were there parts that worked out better than you expected?

LANGHAM: Yes . . . the music, and the final moments . . . we finished the play with a tableau. We had a marvelous musical score by Stanley Silverman. In tone and style it ranged from 1776 then worked its way up to 1969 in the middle, and then back again, so at the end of the play the music—and the tone of the whole production—had returned to the tone of the eighteenth century. We sang a period song among the central characters as the scandal-mongers all leaned out from the wings to discover what they might overhear, and so we brought the cast on together for a final tableau.

REVIEW OF THE STRATFORD PRODUCTION, 1970, BY CLIVE BARNES

Gossip, malice and hypocrisy, like the poor, will always be with us, and therefore every production of Sheridan's exquisite comedy, "The School for Scandal," can hardly fail to be timely. Michael Langham's new production of the play seen for the first time at the Stratford Festival last night is more than timely, it is well-timed.

The rough vigor and dramatic ambiguity of the opening night's "Merchant of Venice" could be completely forgotten in the volatile brilliance of this "School for Scandal," which showed the company off to its best advantage.

This is such a good play, with all its plots and counterplots intermeshing like the parts of a watch, with Sheridan's timeless jokes as funny as ever, and with Sheridan's insight into his fellow beings as sharp as a surgeon's scalpel.

Two brothers—one the perfect hypocrite, the other a hellbent rake—are vying for both the good will of their rich uncle and the hand of an equally rich heiress. It is 18th-century fashionable London, a world dominated by tattle, appearances, costumes and money.

The conniving hypocrite, Joseph Surface, is exposed; the good-natured rake, Charles Surface, gets fortune, bride and reformation, and Sir Peter Teazle, guardian of the young heiress, obtains reconciliation with his young, and hitherto flighty, country wife, Lady Teazle. It all works merrily and morally enough, with wit and truth enough to spare for everyone.

Mr. Langham, who was director of the Stratford Festival from 1955 until 1967, has returned for the first time, and here gives Sheridan his due. In the past I have not always numbered myself among Mr. Langham's greatest admirers. He seemed too arch a disciple of that bad old Tyrone Guthrie school of directing, where every story had to tell a picture, while gimmickeries ran riot and devil take the playwright.

This "School for Scandal," however, seems to find Mr. Langham in a most un-Guthrie-like mood of clarity and simplicity. To be sure, he feels impelled to end the piece with a tableau of piercing irrelevance. Also for some reason, the jollifications of Charles and his friends are accompanied by a kind of thinly baroque version of rock music, which might perhaps be termed "Mr. Bach Goes to Rock," and is a little vulgar and obvious. Yet, for the rest I have nothing but praise.

What it seems that Mr. Langham has achieved is to persuade his cast to forget any preconceptions they may have about English high comedy style. As a result, not only is there a much more interesting, much more alive feel to the playing, but you also get actors actually playing roles such as Joseph Surface and Sir Peter, rather than actors playing Sir John Gielgud and Sir Ralph Richardson playing Joseph Surface and Sir Peter. It is an enormous difference.

And Mr. Langham himself, if I can say this without offering offense, appears a new man. Gone are those circular dances for his actors that he once seemed to find integral to staging on a thrust stage, gone are those exaggerations of character actors blinking knowingly through inches of make-up, and gone are most of the tricks and the foibles. This was a beautiful production.

The actors have responded. Robin Gammell's unctuous yet oddly not unattractive Joseph Surface is perfect in every glance and every inflection. He plays the role as if it were farce rather than comedy—it is a very pushing, physical performance—and the result is fresh and appealing. As the honest, if wayward, brother, Barry MacGregor shows just the right hazy generosity of spirit. More than in most productions, these two contrasting brothers (rather like Hogarth's "Idle and Industrious Apprentices" seen through Sheridan's more worldly eyes) become the focal point of the play as, I suspect, the playwright intended.

As a result of this focus, the fighting Teazles quite rightly step back a little into the play's mechanism. However, Stephen Murray's natural friendly and avuncular Sir Peter is a portrayal of great quality, and is matched by the girlish flightiness of Helen Carey as Lady Teazle.

Of the rest, there are many good performances, including those of the scandalous scholastics, Jane Casson, Bernard Behrens, Eric Donkin, Pat Galloway and Robin Marshall, and I liked also the bluffness of Mervyn Blake as Sir Oliver Surface and James Blendick as the faithful Rowley.

A fine evening, then, much aided by the handsome and stylish scenery and costumes by Leslie Hurry. Incidentally, and apropos of almost nothing, in the director's note given in the program, Mr. Langham reminds us all that the phrase "the silent majority" originated with Homer. The dear old Greek used it to describe the dead. It is amazing how many gaps in an education can be filled in by assiduous theatergoing.

MODERN THEATER

Modern drama, like modern painting and other forms of modern art, developed not in the twentieth century, as might be casually assumed, but during the nineteenth century. It was born out of a widespread reaction against the subject matters, forms, and methods of staging that had prevailed in many eighteenth- and early-nineteenth-century plays—against aristocratic or exotic heroes and heroines, against the rigorous unities of a neoclassical tragedy or the flamboyant events of a romantic melodrama, against declamatory styles of acting or spectacular forms of setting, against theatrical conventions that were regarded as being too far from the truth of ordinary existence. "Reality," in turn, became a watchword among early modern dramatists, actors, directors, and set designers. Indeed, the realistic impulse in one form or another so heavily influenced theater through the first half of the twentieth century that the history of modern drama may well be understood in terms of the movements that grew out of realism, either as a refinement of it or as a reaction against it.

Realism in its most literal sense developed out of a desire to bring the stage into greater conformity with the surface details of ordinary human experience. This impulse first manifested itself in the efforts of set designers to create a full-scale visual illusion in the theater, to make the stage setting look like an interior place where ordinary people actually lived and worked—or, as one recent director has put it, to show "a real chair in a real setting." This concept of staging clearly required a set more visually plausible than the sliding wings and canvas backdrops of the neoclassical stage, which usually depicted doors and windows, sometimes even chairs, by means of perspective painting on the backdrop, instead of incorporating movable doors, windows, and furniture.

To create the illusion of a three-dimensional interior, nineteenth-century set designers devised a set composed of flats arranged to form connected walls enclosing three sides of the stage, with the fourth wall removed so that the audience could look into a stage room that spatially seemed just like a real one. The realistic illusion of this stage design, known as the *box set*, was enhanced by movable windows and doors built into the walls of the back or side flats, as well as by false thickness pieces built into the window and door openings, which gave them an air of

Figure 1. The box set decorated with wall and window hangings, as well as furniture and props, to create the illusion of an actual room.

solidity. When the interior walls of the set were decorated and hung with fixtures, and when the floor space enclosed by the walls was equipped with rugs, furniture, and other props, the stage resembled a real room in every respect (see Figure 1). By the middle of the nineteenth century, the box set had been used in theaters throughout Europe, and its subsequent importance to the history of drama may be seen in the fact that detailed interiors figure prominently in almost all the plays written in the modern realistic tradition, such as Ibsen's *A Doll's House,* Strindberg's *Miss Julie,* Chekhov's *The Cherry Orchard,* Wilde's *The Importance of Being Earnest,* Shaw's *Pygmalion,* and Williams's *Cat on a Hot Tin Roof.*

The development of the box set took place during the same period as major technological advances in lighting. Gaslights, as well as lime or calcium light, superseded oil lamps during the first half of the nineteenth century, making possible not only a greater degree of power and control in stage lighting but also a variety of realistic effects, such as the illusion of sunlight, moonlight, or lamplight coming through doors and windows. During the second half of the nineteenth century, the invention of the carbon arc lamp and finally the incandescent lamp not only freed theaters from the terrible fire hazards of gaslights but also encouraged directors and designers to invent elaborately realistic lighting effects.

Acting styles were slower to approximate the natural gestures, movements, and tones of voice appropriate to realistic staging, in part because the declamatory style of romantic acting was highly popular with audiences, but also because anything less pronounced would have been inadequate to make a clearly audible and visual impression in the cavernous theaters common during the late eighteenth century and much of the nineteenth. The auditoriums in these theaters were typically based on a design that was calculated to accommodate as large an audience as possible—sometimes as many as four thousand—with little concern for the needs of the actors or of the spectators. That design can readily be understood by first imagining a large cylinder at whose base is seated the majority of the audience, looking at a large opening that has been pierced in the cylinder to form the proscenium arch of the stage (see Figure 2). Then imagine that the builders or remodelers of such theaters, in order to fit in more paying spectators, hung balconies at four or five levels around the inside walls of the cylinder above the base (see Figure 3). Clearly, an actor or actress performing in these theaters had to develop an exaggerated style of movement, gesture, and intonation to make an impact on the audience sitting in those balconies.

But during the late nineteenth and early twentieth centuries, theater architecture began to undergo significant modifications, which were intended to create

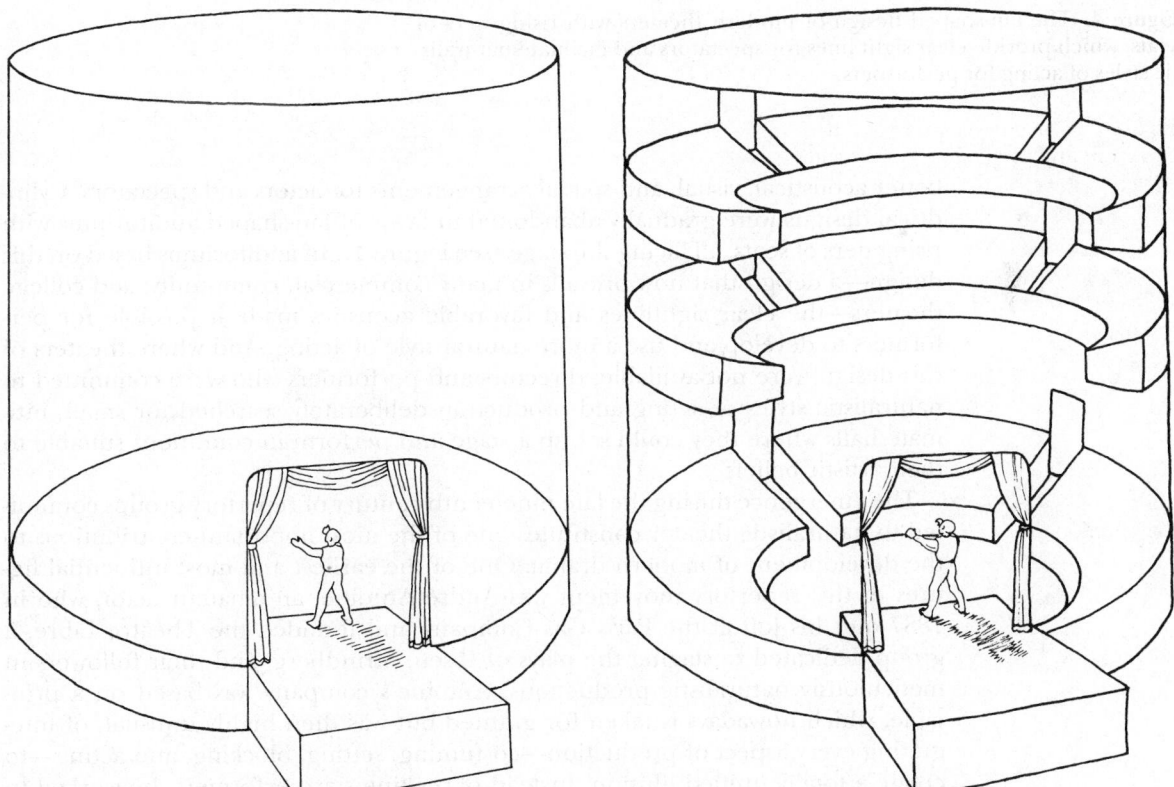

Figure 2. The cylindrical design of late-eighteenth- and early-nineteenth-century theaters.

Figure 3. The cylindrically designed theater, showing multiple balconies remote from the actor on stage.

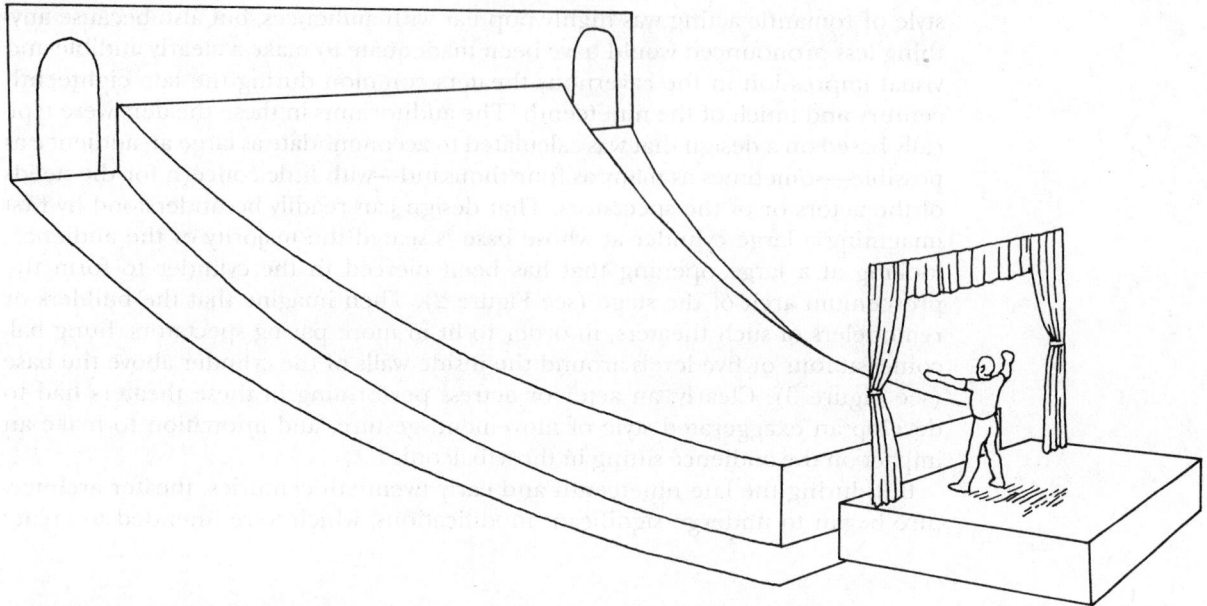

Figure 4. The fan-shaped design of modern theaters with rising tiers of seats, which provide clear sight lines for spectators and facilitate naturalistic styles of acting for performers.

better acoustical, visual, and spatial arrangements for actors and spectators. Cylindrical designs were gradually abandoned in favor of fan-shaped auditoriums with rising tiers of seats, all facing the stage (see Figure 4). In auditoriums based on this design—a design that now prevails in many commercial, community, and college theaters—the clear sightlines and favorable acoustics made it possible for performers to develop and use a more natural style of acting. And where theaters of this design were not available, directors and performers who were committed to naturalistic styles of acting and production deliberately searched for small, intimate halls where they could set up a stage and perform in conditions suitable to their artistic beliefs.

The emergence during the late nineteenth century of repertory groups committed to naturalistic theater constitutes one of the most important contributions to the development of modern drama. One of the earliest and most influential figures in this repertory movement was André Antoine, an amateur actor, who in 1887 quit his job at the Paris Gas Company and founded the Théâtre Libre, a group dedicated to staging the plays of Ibsen, Strindberg, and their followers in meticulously naturalistic productions. Antoine's company was based on a principle, which nowadays is taken for granted but was then highly unusual, of integrating every aspect of production—costuming, setting, blocking, and acting—to create a totally unified illusion. Instead of seeking star performers, he worked to develop an ensemble of actors and actresses, painstakingly rehearsing them so that each performer was responsive not only to the demands of his or her individual role but also to the needs of every other role at every moment in a production. Antoine's example quickly inspired similar companies to be formed throughout Europe and America.

The most well-known and influential organization to develop during the early repertory movement was the Moscow Art Theatre, founded in 1898 by Konstantin Stanislavsky, an amateur actor and director, and by Vladimir Nemirovich-Danchenko, a successful playwright. The Moscow Art Theatre achieved its early fame by producing the plays of Chekhov in a style that accentuated their emotional and psychological subtlety. This style entailed not only a detailed attention to elements of staging—including even the use of music to underline important emotional moments—but also a carefully defined method of acting, propounded by Stanislavsky, whose fundamental purpose was to create "the inner life of a human spirit." Stanislavsky's method, which he subsequently expounded in several highly influential books—among them *My Life in Art* (1924) and *An Actor Prepares* (1926)—required actors to think "about the inner side of a role, and how to create its spiritual life through the help of the internal process of living the part. You must live it by actually experiencing feelings that are analogous to it, each and every time you repeat the process of creating it." The illusion of reality, as Stanislavsky defined it, depended on using the theater to dramatize not simply the external but, more important, the internal condition of human experience.

Stanislavsky's emphasis on the "inner side of a role," on "living the part," would have been impossible without dramatic roles that called for such an approach, without plays that offered probing studies of psychologically complex characters in complex social, domestic, and personal situations. In this profound sense, realistic and naturalistic drama originated not from an interest in representing the surface details—the literal image—of human activity but out of a concern with reflecting the environmental and psychological conditions that account for the problematic quality of ordinary human experience. In this sense Ibsen is often considered the "father" of modern drama. Beginning in 1877, for example, Ibsen wrote a series of realistic "problem" plays, in which he systematically shattered popular illusions about such then-sacred institutions as marriage and religion—plays in which he showed the inner life of his characters as they come to recognize the painful realities of their personal situations. Chekhov dramatized a similar kind of experience in his turn-of-the-century plays, though he presented his characters as being at once comic, pitiable, and admirably human in their futile efforts to overcome both the romantic illusions and the banal necessities of their existence. Strindberg exposed even harsher realities in his naturalistic dramatizations of the sexual antagonism between men and women.

In portraying characters, the early modern dramatists relied not only on the psychological nuances of dialogue and action but also on the emblematic significances of the box set itself, for its detailed interiors may be seen as not only tangibly revealing a particular place in which the characters exist but also exposing the quality of their existence. In *A Doll's House,* for example, the setting called for in Ibsen's stage directions—a room cluttered with bric-a-brac and overstuffed chairs—is as stifling and deceiving as the marriage of Nora and Helmer. In

Chekhov's *The Cherry Orchard*, the cozy nursery where the play begins and ends is an emblem of the childish and irrepressibly romantic illusions that govern the thoughts of Lyubov and Gayev and make them incapable of coming to terms with the changing society around them. And in *Miss Julie*, the kitchen, which constitutes the setting for the entire play, is a continual reminder of the cultural and psychological servitude that Jean, the valet, is bent on overthrowing.

Though the realism of box sets and the naturalism of psychologically motivated characters was dramatically compelling, modern drama also developed along non-realistic and even antirealistic lines. As early as 1835, a young medical researcher named Georg Büchner began writing plays that challenged the romantic historical dramas of Germany's Friedrich Schiller, plays whose protagonists (Mary Stuart, William Tell, Joan of Arc) are clearly heroic figures. Though Büchner's first play, *Danton's Death*, dealt with the major political event of the eighteenth century—the French Revolution—his treatment of it was decidedly nonromantic, both in characterization and in style. Instead of blank verse and classical dramatic structure, Büchner turned to prose and an almost cinematic juxtaposition of scenes. Büchner, in fact, was so far ahead of his time that editions of his work did not even appear until the second half of the century. Indeed, the first performance of *Woyzeck*, Büchner's major work, did not take place until 1913, one hundred years after his birth.

By the late nineteenth century, various antirealistic tendencies—known as symbolism, expressionism, and surrealism—had already taken form in the critical statements and plays of *avant-garde* dramatists. Proponents of these counterrealistic movements argued that dramatic truth was not to be found in the tangible surfaces of a box set nor even in the intangible life of a psychologically complex character, but in symbols, images, legends, myths, fantasies, dreams, and other mysterious manifestations of spirituality, subjectivity, or the unconscious. Symbolists, for example, claimed the existence of a higher truth than was evident in external reality, and they aimed to create in the theater a mysterious and quasi-religious experience. Expressionists believed that truth existed not in the external appearance of reality but in the subjective perception of reality, no matter how psychologically distorted that perception might be, and they often sought to dramatize how the world appears to a disturbed and convulsive mind. Surrealists claimed that truth was to be found not in the logic of everyday events but in the irrational processes of the unconscious mind, and they tried to re-create the strange combinations of the familiar and the mysterious that often take place in dreams.

From a late-twentieth-century perspective, these various antirealistic tendencies seem commonplace, but in their own day they were revolutionary and attracted not only experimental writers but major dramatists who had already established themselves as masters of realistic and naturalistic drama. Ibsen's late plays, especially *The Lady from the Sea* (1888) and *When We Dead Awaken* (1899), are manifestly symbolic not only in their titles but also in their settings and in their action. Although Strindberg began by writing such naturalistic plays as *The Father* (1887) and *Miss Julie* (1888), he later turned to the fantasy world of *A Dream Play* (1901) and the haunting, personal symbolism of *The Ghost Sonata* (1907). Even Shaw, so thoroughly committed to a theater of intellectual and social realism, wrote a five-play parable set in the Garden of Eden, Mesopotamia, as well as in England in both his own time and the future in *Back to Methusaleh* (1920). For the American playwright O'Neill, symbolic and expressionistic drama came early in his career rather than at the end in the psychologically distorted perceptions of *The Emperor Jones* (1920), the symbolic events of *The Hairy Ape* (1922), and the expressionistic symbols of *The Great God Brown* (1926). In Italy, Luigi Pirandello dramatized the enduring struggle between appearance and reality by bringing on stage both "actors" and "characters," the latter group dizzying in their simultaneous reality and nonreality. And though the Spanish playwright García Lorca called his last play, *The House of Bernarda Alba* (1936), "a photographic document," the text begins with symbolic insistence on the "very white room" in Bernarda's house, and ends with Bernarda insisting on the spiritual whiteness of her youngest daughter: "My daughter died a virgin."

Symbolic drama of the early modern period was mirrored in a variety of staging techniques that were often intentionally designed to obliterate any hint of a realistic environment. In France, the main exponent of symbolist staging was Aurélien-Marie Lugné-Poe, who established an avant-garde repertory group known as the Théâtre de l'Oeuvre, which was dedicated to the production of symbolist plays. In Lugné-Poe's productions, scenery was often reduced to painted, abstract backdrops; props and furniture were often minimal or nonexistent; lighting was often minimal and dispersed instead of focused; and actors strived to evoke a mood rather than to reveal psychological motivation. In expressionistic stagings, which were largely developed in German theater during the 1920s, representational settings were replaced with expressively stylized backdrops, showing exterior or interior locations that had been distorted and exaggerated in color and shape; lighting was often harshly focused or nervously scattered; and actors strived through disjointed movements and telegraphic speech patterns to evoke human behavior as it might be perceived by a psychologically convulsive personality. Surrealistic stagings, which were launched by Antonin Artaud and André Breton in Parisian theaters of the 1920s, pushed productions even further toward expressive abstraction in backdrops, costumes, lighting, and acting styles.

By the end of the twenties, these counterrealistic movements, though polemically extreme in their practices, had worked substantial changes in the style of drama and theatrical production—changes that resulted in a synthesis of realistic and naturalistic methods with symbolic, expressionistic, or surrealistic techniques. The power of such a synthesis was convincingly displayed in the work of Bertolt Brecht, the major German playwright and director of the twentieth century. From the 1920s through the early 1950s, Brecht wrote an extensive series of plays that were simultaneously realistic in their depiction of human motives and values, expressionistic in their episodic structure, and politically explicit in their ideology. And he created stagings for his plays with the Berliner Ensemble, which used realistic costumes and set pieces combined with an abstract backdrop, visible lighting instruments, visible scene changing, and scene titles or other messages projected onto the backdrop. By means of this synthesis, Brecht aimed both to engage an audience in the situation of his characters and to distance them sufficiently so that they would be provoked to think about its social and political implications. Once Brecht had established the theatrical power of such a synthesis, it gradually came to be a dominant approach in serious theater of the twentieth century. Tennessee

Williams, for example, blended realism and expressionism in all of his plays, beginning with his notes on music, lighting, and pantomime for *The Glass Menagerie* (1944) and continuing with his emphasis on the bedroom and the bed in *Cat on a Hot Tin Roof* (1955). So, when Arthur Miller's *Death of a Salesman* (1949) opened on Broadway with a striking combination of naturalistic and expressionistic effects, both in the physical set (see Figure 1, p. 906) and in the play's structure, his mixture of styles evoked almost no surprise at all.

GEORG BÜCHNER

1813–1837

Though he died quite young, Georg Büchner led three distinctly different lives. His first and most successful was as a medical researcher and lecturer, a profession that came naturally to the son of a doctor. Büchner was educated at Darmstadt in his native Germany. In 1831 he went to Strasbourg to study medicine but after two years returned to Germany, conforming to a state law that required students from Hesse (the region in which Büchner lived) to study at the state university. Here he began his second life as a student revolutionary, involved in an underground society aimed at attacking the regime of Ludwig II, grand duke of Hesse. As coauthor of *The Hessian Courier* (1834), a manifesto against the extortionist tactics of the grand duke, Büchner attempted to arouse his readers by reminding them of the French Revolution and its disappointing political aftermath: France, only temporarily a republic, became again a monarchy, and Germany, frightened by the violence in France, gave its people constitutions that served to quiet revolt rather than establish true freedom. To escape possible arrest, Büchner left Germany for Strasbourg in 1835, finished his medical studies, wrote a treatise on the nervous system of the barbel (a large fish), and then on the strength of that treatise moved to Zurich in late 1836, where he was offered a lectureship. A promising career as a teacher and researcher seemed to open before him, only to close on February 19, 1837, when he died of typhoid fever.

In the last few years before his death, Büchner had also begun to lead a third life, that of a dramatist. At first, playwriting may have seemed merely a way to make money, since he composed his first work, *Danton's Death,* in 1835 and sent it to a well-known editor, together with a letter indicating that he was financially strapped. But after his return to Strasbourg, Büchner translated two plays by Victor Hugo and wrote a second play, *Leonce and Lena* (1836), in response to a competition for the best German comedy; his manuscript arrived after the deadline and so was not eligible. His third play, *Woyzeck,* must also date from 1836, but it remained in manuscript form, in several incomplete drafts. A fourth play, *Pietro Aretino,* survives only in its title.

Büchner's choice to write about the French Revolution at a time when he was desperate for money and planning to leave Germany to avoid arrest may have contributed to his distinctly unheroic portrayal of major figures from the Revolution. Set in 1794, near the end of the Reign of Terror, *Danton's Death* focuses on internal power struggles rather than the larger social context. In this play, Robespierre and Saint-Just are portrayed as coldly calculating individuals who use abstractions such as "freedom" and "humanity" to hide their manipulative search for power. But Georges Danton, rather than heroically opposing these men, seems strangely passive, refusing to leave Paris even though his friends warn him, preferring to spend his time not only with his wife, Julie, but with numerous prostitutes. Though he rouses himself during his trial to remind his accusers of his actions in the early days of the Revolution, he sinks at the play's end to a fatalistic aphorism: "The world is

529

chaos. Nothingness is the world-god yet to be born." Büchner's historical play never glorifies the Revolution. In keeping with this unglorified view of the Revolution, *Danton's Death* is written in prose rather than blank verse, and it presents the voices not only of Danton and Robespierre but of nameless citizens and powerless women. "What are we but puppets, manipulated on wires by unknown powers?" asks Danton as he muses to Julie about the rightness of his actions, a metaphor used as stage setting in Jonathan Miller's 1971 production, which featured side boxes with headless mannequins, as well as projections of Roman statues.

Büchner's vision of human beings as puppets emerges again in *Leonce and Lena*, a play that superficially seems completely different from *Danton's Death* and its specific historical context. Büchner sets up a fairy-tale world in which Prince Leonce, unwilling to accept an arranged marriage, and Princess Lena, equally unwilling to sacrifice herself, disguise themselves and run away. Of course, they meet and fall in love, but the names of their countries, Popo and Pipi, with their echoes of excrement and urination, should alert us to the darker side of the fairy-tale world. In the final scene, disguised as "two world-famous automatons," Leonce and Lena are married. When they remove their masks, they find that instead of "escaping into Paradise" they "have been deceived." Though the tone of the play is light, the story line clearly argues the inability of human beings to control their destinies.

Though *Danton's Death* and *Leonce and Lena* are strikingly different in setting and tone, though one play deals with actual figures of the French Revolution and the other with imaginary and comic royal personages, both plays are "costume dramas," requiring the creation of a world noticeably unlike the one in which Büchner actually lived. In contrast, *Woyzeck* is based on a real murder that took place in Leipzig in 1821, when Johann Christian Woyzeck stabbed his ex-mistress seven times. Woyzeck's execution did not take place until three years after the murder because of several appeals, but two investigations by a court-appointed physician, Johann Clarus, concluded that Woyzeck was legally responsible for his actions. While these reports, available to Büchner through his father, aimed at justifying Woyzeck's execution, they also included many of the details that might well have been used to argue for extenuating circumstances, particularly Woyzeck's claims that he had visions and heard voices.

Yet *Woyzeck*'s peculiar force comes not from its basis in real life but from Büchner's extraordinarily stripped-down style. Gone are the long speeches of argument that punctuate *Danton's Death*; gone are the long pseudo-meditations of *Leonce and Lena*. Instead, the characters in *Woyzeck* speak in short, choppy phrases, in allusions rather than explanations, in snatches of songs or of biblical quotations. Such a style fits the central character, who finds it difficult to express his feelings and who finally seeks refuge in violent action rather than in language. Significantly, we most mistrust the characters in this play who *can* speak freely: the Captain, who preaches a meaningless morality while driving Woyzeck mad with his insinuations about Marie, Woyzeck's common-law wife; and the Doctor, who preaches human freedom to the man he is using for his bizarre scientific experiments. Gone too is any attempt at linear development or an intrigue plot. In its place is a series of short scenes, some involving just four or six speeches. The language, the action, the motivation, the scene structure—all are fragmentary.

Fragmentary is more than a metaphor for the form and content of *Woyzeck*; it is an accurate description of the play text itself. For unlike any other work in this volume, *Woyzeck* is incomplete. It exists only in a manuscript that contains four different versions or groupings of scenes: one contains twenty-one scenes, the second has nine scenes, the third has two scenes, and the fourth has seventeen scenes. Some scenes seem to be revisions of others, while others appear only once. These different versions raise a host of questions about Büchner's unresolved intentions. Does the play begin with Woyzeck and Andres in the field (as in two sequences of the manuscript) or with the fair (Scene 3 in our text), thereby immediately introducing Woyzeck, Marie, and the Drum Major who will become her new lover? How many times does Woyzeck tell Andres he hears a voice telling him to stab only to be met with the prosaic remedy of "brandy with a painkiller in it" (Scenes 13 and 17)? The scene appears in two different forms, and one might reasonably argue that Büchner meant it to appear just once, or that he wanted the scene in twice, to emphasize Woyzeck's "voices" and Andres's lack of sympathy. Scenes 18 and 27 appear on a separate page of the manuscript and nowhere else, with no indication of where Büchner meant to put them. The choice to use Scene 27 as the final scene is also an interpretation of one of the play's unresolved questions. Does Woyzeck drown himself after throwing away the knife he used to kill Marie, perhaps because of guilt (the last lines of Scene 24 echo Lady Macbeth's famous lines), or does he merely wash himself off and return to town where his child seems to reject him (Scene 27)?

Thus, every reader of the play is, to some extent, acting as its editor, just as Henry J. Schmidt has titled his translation in this volume a "reconstruction of the text." Schmidt has worked from the most complete modern edition of the play available and has considered all the variant scenes, as well as the order that the manuscript suggests for certain scenes. But, as Mel Gussow suggests in his review of the New York Shakespeare Festival production, "the play is open to free-handed interpretation" and to various production styles. In this production, JoAnne Akalaitis draws on images from the twentieth century, such as the antiseptically white mechanical chair in which the Captain sits while Woyzeck shaves him (see Figure 1). The townspeople who surround Woyzeck after the murder wear clothes evoking the 1930s and 1940s (see Figure 2). Images of the concentration camps dominate the production: Gussow explicitly links Woyzeck to a prisoner at Dachau, while the murder of Marie (see Figure 3) takes place in what seems to be an empty shower room, evoking memories of the "shower rooms" that were really gas chambers in which so many prisoners died. These visual reminders of the prejudice and hatred of the twentieth century testify to the play's enduring power. Though the fragmentary nature of the play on the page may at times frustrate editors and readers, the play onstage shows us pieces of a life that coalesce into an emblem of contemporary pain and despair.

WOYZECK

BY GEORG BÜCHNER / A RECONSTRUCTION OF THE ORIGINAL TEXT, TRANSLATED BY HENRY J. SCHMIDT

CHARACTERS

FRANZ WOYZECK
MARIE
CAPTAIN
DOCTOR
DRUM MAJOR
SERGEANT
ANDRES
MARGRET
BARKER
ANNOUNCER } *can be played by one actor*
OLD MAN
CHILD
JEW
INNKEEPER

FIRST APPRENTICE
SECOND APPRENTICE
KARL, *an idiot*
KATEY
GRANDMOTHER
FIRST CHILD
SECOND CHILD
THIRD CHILD
FIRST PERSON
SECOND PERSON
COURT CLERK
JUDGE
SOLDIERS, STUDENTS, YOUNG MEN, GIRLS,
    CHILDREN

1

(Open field. The town in the distance.)

(WOYZECK and ANDRES are cutting branches in the bushes.)

WOYZECK: Hey, Andres! That streak across the grass—that's where heads roll at night. Once somebody picked one up, thought it was a hedgehog. Three days and three nights, and he was lying in a coffin. *(Softly.)* Andres, it was the Freemasons.° That's it—the Freemasons! Shh!

ANDRES: *(Sings.)*

> I saw two big rabbits
> Chewing up the green, green grass . . .

WOYZECK: Shh! Something's moving!

ANDRES:

> Chewing up the green, green grass
> Till it all was gone.

WOYZECK: Something's moving behind me—under me. *(Stamps on the ground.)* Hollow! You hear that? It's all hollow down there. The Freemasons!

ANDRES: I'm scared.

WOYZECK: It's so quiet—that's strange. You feel like holding your breath. Andres!

Freemasons, an international secret society.

ANDRES: What?

WOYZECK: Say something! *(Stares off into the distance.)* Andres! Look how bright it is! There's fire raging around the sky, and a noise is coming down like trumpets. It's coming closer! Let's go! Don't look back! *(Drags him into the bushes.)*

ANDRES: *(After a pause.)* Woyzeck! Do you still hear it?

WOYZECK: Quiet, everything's quiet, like the world was dead.

ANDRES: Listen! They're drumming. We've got to get back.

2

(The town.)

(MARIE with her CHILD at the window. MARGRET. A parade goes by, the DRUM MAJOR leading.)

MARIE: *(Rocking the CHILD in her arms.)* Hey, boy! Ta-ra-ra-ra! You hear it? They're coming.

MARGRET: What a man, like a tree!

MARIE: He stands on his feet like a lion. *(The DRUM MAJOR greets them.)*

MARGRET: Say, what a friendly look you gave him, neighbor. We're not used to that from you.

MARIE: *(Sings.)*

> A soldier is a handsome fellow . . .

MARGRET: Your eyes are still shining.

MARIE: So what? Why don't you take *your* eyes to the Jew and have them polished—maybe they'll shine enough to sell as two buttons.

MARGRET: What? Why, Mrs. Virgin! I'm a decent woman, but you—you can stare through seven pairs of leather pants!

MARIE: Bitch! *(Slams the window shut.)* Come on, boy. What do they want from us, anyway? You're only the son of a whore, and you make your mother happy with your bastard face. Ta-ta! *(Sings.)*

> *Maiden, how sorrow can sting,*
> *You've got a son but no ring!*
> *Oh, who cares what is right,*
> *I'll sing to you all night:*
> *Rockabye baby, my baby are you,*
> *Nobody cares what we do.*
>
> *Johnny, hitch up your six horses fleet,*
> *Go bring them something to eat.*
> *From oats they will turn,*
> *From water they'll turn,*
> *Only cool wine will be fine, hooray!*
> *Only cool wine will be fine.*

(A knock at the window.)

MARIE: Who's that? Is that you, Franz? Come on in!

WOYZECK: I can't. Have to go to roll call.

MARIE: What's the matter with you, Franz?

WOYZECK: *(Mysteriously.)* Marie, there was something out there again—a lot. Isn't it written: "And lo, the smoke of the country went up as the smoke of a furnace"?°

MARIE: Franz . . .

WOYZECK: It followed me until I reached town. What's going to happen?

MARIE: Franz!

WOYZECK: I've got to go. *(He leaves.)*

MARIE: That man! He's seeing things. He didn't even look at his own child. He'll go crazy with those thoughts of his. Why are you so quiet, son? Are you scared? It's getting so dark, you'd think you were blind. Usually there's a light shining in. I can't stand it. It frightens me. *(Goes off.)*

3

(Fair booths. Lights. People.)

(An OLD MAN sings to a barrel organ, a CHILD dances.)

OLD MAN:

> *How long we live, just time will tell,*
> *We all have got to die,*
> *We know that very well!*

MARIE: Hey! Wow!

"**And lo, . . . furnace,**" Gen. 19:28, the destruction of Sodom and Gomorrah.

WOYZECK: Poor man, old man! Poor child! Little child! Cares and fairs! Hey, Marie, should I . . . ?

MARIE: Even a fool must have some sense to be able to say: Foolish world! Beautiful world!

BARKER: *(In front of a booth, with a WOMAN wearing pants. He presents a costumed monkey. The BARKER speaks with a French accent.)* Gentlemen! Gentlemen! Look at this creature, as God made it—he's nothing, nothing at all. Now see the effect of art: he walks upright, wears coat and pants, carries a sword! Ho! Take a bow! Presto—you're a baron. Give me a kiss! *(The monkey trumpets.)* The little fellow is musical. Ladies and gentlemen, here is to be seen the astronomical horse and the little cannery-birds°—they're favorites of all potentates of Europe—they're members of all learned societies. They'll tell you everything: how old you are, how many children you have, what kind of illnesses. *(Points to the monkey.)* He shoots a pistol, stands on one leg. It's all education; he has merely a beastly reason, or rather a very reasonable beastliness—he's no dumb individual like a lot of people, present company excepted. Observe the progress of civilization. Everything progresses—a horse, a monkey, a cannery-bird! The monkey is already a soldier. That's not much—it's the lowest level of the human race. Enter! The presentation will begin. The commencement of the beginning will start immediately.

WOYZECK: Want to?

MARIE: All right. It ought to be good. Look at his tassels—and the woman's got pants on!

(SERGEANT. DRUM MAJOR.)

SERGEANT: Hold it! Over there. Look at her! What a piece!

DRUM MAJOR: Goddamn! Good enough for the propagation of cavalry regiments and the breeding of drum majors!

SERGEANT: Look how she holds her head—you'd think that black hair would pull her down like a weight. And those eyes, black . . .

DRUM MAJOR: It's like looking down a well or a chimney. Come on, after her!

MARIE: *(Entering the booth.)* Those lights! My eyes!

WOYZECK: Yeah, like a barrel of black cats with fiery eyes. Hey, what a night!

(Inside the booth.)

ANNOUNCER: *(Presenting a horse.)* Show your talent! Show your beastly wisdom. Put human society to shame. Gentlemen, this animal that you see here, with a tail on his body, with his four hoofs, is a

---

cannery-birds, the Barker says *Canaillevogel* instead of *Kanarienvogel,* meaning "canaries."

member of all learned societies, is a professor at our university with whom the students learn to ride and fight. That was simple comprehension. Now think with double *raison.*° What do you do when you think with double *raison?* Is there in the learned *société*° an ass? *(The horse shakes its head.)* Now you understand double *raison?* That is beast-iognomy.° Yes, that is no dumb animal, that's a person! A human being, a beastly human being, but still an animal, *une bête. (The horse behaves improperly.)* That's right, put *société* to shame. You see, the beast is still nature, unideal nature. Take a lesson from him. Go ask the doctor, it's very unhealthy.° All this means: Man, be natural. You were created from dust, sand, dirt. Do you want to be more than dust, sand, dirt? Observe his reason: he can add, but he can't count on his fingers. How come? He simply can't express himself, explain himself. He's a transformed person! Tell the gentlemen what time it is. Does anyone have a watch—a watch?

SERGEANT: A watch! *(Slowly and grandly he pulls a watch out of his pocket.)* There you are.

MARIE: This I've got to see. *(She climbs into the first row. The* SERGEANT *helps her.)*

4

(Room.)

*(*MARIE *sits with her* CHILD *on her lap, a piece of mirror in her hand.)*

MARIE: *(Looks at herself in the mirror.)* These stones really sparkle! What kind are they? What did he call them? Go to sleep, son! Shut your eyes tight. *(The* CHILD *covers his eyes with his hands.)* Tighter—stay quiet or he'll come get you. *(Sings.)*

Close up your shop, fair maid,
A gypsy boy's in the glade.
He'll lead you by the hand
Off into gypsyland.

(Looks in the mirror again.) It must be gold. The likes of us only have a little corner in the world and a little piece of mirror, but my mouth is just as red as the great ladies with their mirrors from top to toe, and handsome lords who kiss their hands. I'm just a poor woman. *(The* CHILD *sits up.)* Shh, son, eyes shut! Look, the sandman! He's running along the wall. *(She flashes with the mirror.)* Eyes shut, or he'll look into them, and you'll go blind.

*(*WOYZECK *enters behind her. She jumps up with her hands over her ears.)*

---

raison, reason. **société,** company. **beastiognomy,** *Vieh-sionomik:* a pun on "beast" and "physiognomy." **unhealthy,** meaning "to hold it in."

WOYZECK: What's that you got there?

MARIE: Nothing.

WOYZECK: Something's shining under your fingers.

MARIE: An earring. I found it.

WOYZECK: I've never found anything like that. Two at once.

MARIE: What am I—a whore?

WOYZECK: It's all right, Marie. Look, the boy's asleep. Lift him up under his arms, the chair's hurting him. Those shiny drops on his forehead; everything under the sun is work. Sweat, even in our sleep. Us poor people! Here's some more money, Marie, my pay and some from my captain.

MARIE: Bless you, Franz.

WOYZECK: I have to go. See you tonight, Marie. Bye.

MARIE: *(Alone, after a pause.)* What a bitch I am. I could stab myself. Oh, what a world! Everything goes to hell anyhow, man and woman alike.

5

(The CAPTAIN. WOYZECK.*)*

(The CAPTAIN *in a chair,* WOYZECK *shaves him.)*

CAPTAIN: Take it easy, Woyzeck, take it easy. One thing at a time. You're making me dizzy. You're going to finish early today—what am I supposed to do with the extra ten minutes? Woyzeck, just think, you've still got a good thirty years to live, thirty years! That's 360 months, and days, hours, minutes! What are you going to do with that ungodly amount of time? Get organized, Woyzeck.

WOYZECK: Yes, Cap'n.

CAPTAIN: I fear for the world when I think about eternity. Activity, Woyzeck, activity! Eternal—that's eternal—that is—eternal—you realize that, of course. But then again it's not eternal, it's only a moment, yes, a moment. Woyzeck, it frightens me to think that the earth rotates in one day. What a waste of time! What will come of that? Woyzeck, I can't look at a mill wheel anymore or I get melancholy.

WOYZECK: Yes, Cap'n.

CAPTAIN: Woyzeck, you always look so upset. A good man doesn't act like that, a good man with a good conscience. Say something, Woyzeck. What's the weather like?

WOYZECK: It's bad, Cap'n, bad—wind.

CAPTAIN: I can feel it, there's something rapid out there. A wind like that reminds me of a mouse. *(Cunningly.)* I believe it's coming from the south-north.

WOYZECK: Yes, Cap'n.

CAPTAIN: Ha-ha-ha! South-north! Ha-ha-ha! Oh, are you stupid, terribly stupid! *(Sentimentally.)* Woyzeck, you're a good man, a good man—*(With dignity.)* but Woyzeck, you've got no morality. Morality—that's when you are moral, you understand. It's a good word. You have a child without the blessing of the church, as our Reverend Chaplain says, without the blessing of the church. *I* didn't make that up.

WOYZECK: Cap'n, the good Lord isn't going to look at a poor worm only because amen was said over it before it was created. The Lord said: "Suffer little children to come unto me."

CAPTAIN: What's that you're saying? What kind of a crazy answer is that? You're getting me all confused. When I say *you,* I mean you—you!

WOYZECK: Us poor people. You see, Cap'n—money, money. If you don't have money . . . Just try to raise your own kind on morality in this world. After all, we're flesh and blood. The likes of us are unhappy in this world and in the next. I guess if we ever got to Heaven, we'd have to help with the thunder.

CAPTAIN: Woyzeck, you have no virtue. You're not a virtuous person. Flesh and blood? When I'm lying at the window after it has rained, and I watch the white stockings as they go tripping down the street—damn it, Woyzeck, then love comes all over me. I've got flesh and blood, too. But Woyzeck, virtue, virtue! How else could I make time go by? I always say to myself: you're a virtuous man, *(Sentimentally.)* a good man, a good man.

WOYZECK: Yes, Cap'n, virtue! I haven't figured it out yet. You see, us common people, we don't have virtue. We act like nature tells us. But if I was a gentleman, and had a hat and a watch and a topcoat and could talk refined, then I'd be virtuous, too. Virtue must be nice, Cap'n. But I'm just a poor guy.

CAPTAIN: That's fine, Woyzeck. You're a good man, a good man. But you think too much, that's unhealthy. You always look so upset. This discussion has really worn me out. You can go now—and don't run like that! Slowly, nice and slow down the street.

6

(MARIE. DRUM MAJOR.)

DRUM MAJOR: Marie!

MARIE: *(Looking at him expressively.)* Go march up and down for me. A chest like a bull and a beard like a lion. Nobody else is like that. No woman is prouder than me.

DRUM MAJOR: Sundays when I have my plumed helmet and my white gloves—goddamn, Marie! The prince always says: man, you're quite a guy!

MARIE: *(Mockingly.)* Aw, go on! *(Goes up to him.)* What a man!

DRUM MAJOR: What a woman! Hell, let's breed a race of drum majors, hey? *(He embraces her.)*

MARIE: *(Moody.)* Leave me alone!

DRUM MAJOR: You wildcat!

MARIE: *(Violently.)* Just try to touch me!

DRUM MAJOR: You've got the devil in your eyes.

MARIE: For all I care. What does it matter?

7

(On the street.)

(MARIE. WOYZECK.)

WOYZECK: *(Stares at her, shakes his head.)* Hm! I don't see anything, I don't see anything. Oh, I should be able to see it; I should be able to grab it with my fists.

MARIE: *(Intimidated.)* What's the matter, Franz? You're out of your mind, Franz.

WOYZECK: A sin so fat and so wide—it stinks enough to smoke the angels out of Heaven. You've got a red mouth, Marie. No blister on it? Good-bye, Marie. You're as beautiful as sin. Can mortal sin be so beautiful?

MARIE: Franz, you're delirious.

WOYZECK: Damn it! Was he standing here like this, like this?

MARIE: As the day is long and the world is old, lots of people can stand on one spot, one after another.

WOYZECK: I saw him.

MARIE: You can see all sorts of things if you've got two eyes and aren't blind, and the sun is shining.

WOYZECK: With my own eyes!

MARIE: *(Fresh.)* So what!

8

(At the DOCTOR's.)

(WOYZECK. *The* DOCTOR.)

DOCTOR: What is this I hear, Woyzeck? A man of honor!

WOYZECK: What is it, Doctor?

DOCTOR: I saw it, Woyzeck. You pissed on the street, you pissed on the wall like a dog. And you get two cents a day. Woyzeck, that's bad. The world's getting bad, very bad.

WOYZECK: But Doctor, the call of nature . . .

DOCTOR: The call of nature, the call of nature! Nature! Haven't I proved that the *musculus constrictor vesicae*° is subject to the will? Nature! Woyzeck, man is free. In man alone is individuality exalted to freedom. Couldn't hold it in! *(Shakes his head, puts his hands behind his back, and paces back and forth.)* Did you eat your peas already, Woyzeck? I'm revolutionizing science, I'll blow it sky-high. Urea ten per cent, ammonium chloride, hyperoxidic. Woyzeck, try pissing again. Go in there and try.

---

musculus constrictor vesicae, muscle controlling the bladder.

WOYZECK: I can't, Doctor.

DOCTOR: *(With emotion.)* But pissing on the wall! I have it in writing. Here's the contract. I saw it all—saw it with my own eyes. I was just holding my nose out the window, letting the sun's rays hit it, so as to examine the process of sneezing. *(Goes up to him.)* No, Woyzeck, I'm not getting angry. Anger is unhealthy, unscientific. I am calm, perfectly calm. My pulse is beating at its usual sixty, and I tell you this in all cold-bloodedness. Now, who would get excited about a human being, a human being? If it were a Proteus that were dying—! But you shouldn't have pissed on the wall . . .

WOYZECK: You see, Doctor, sometimes you've got a certain character, a certain structure. But with nature, that's something else, you see, with nature. *(He cracks his knuckles.)* That's like—how should I put it—for example . . .

DOCTOR: Woyzeck, you're philosophizing again.

WOYZECK: *(Confidingly.)* Doctor, have you ever seen anything of double nature? When the sun's standing high at noon and the world seems to be going up in flames, I've heard a terrible voice talking to me!

DOCTOR: Woyzeck, you've got an *aberratio!°*

WOYZECK: *(Puts his finger to his nose.)* The toadstools, Doctor. There—that's where it is. Have you seen how they grow in patterns? If only someone could read that.

DOCTOR: Woyzeck, you've got a marvelous *aberratio mentalis partialis,°* second species, beautifully developed. Woyzeck, you're getting a raise. Second species: fixed idea with a generally rational condition. You're doing everything as usual? Shaving your captain?

WOYZECK: Yes, sir.

DOCTOR: Eating your peas?

WOYZECK: Same as ever, Doctor. My wife gets the money for the household.

DOCTOR: Going on duty?

WOYZECK: Yes, sir.

DOCTOR: You're an interesting case. Subject Woyzeck, you're getting a raise. Now behave yourself. Show me your pulse! Yes.

9

(Street.)

(CAPTAIN. DOCTOR. The CAPTAIN comes panting down the street, stops, pants, looks around.)

CAPTAIN: Doctor, I feel sorry for horses when I think that the poor beasts have to go everywhere on foot. Don't run like that! Don't wave your cane around in the air like that! You'll run yourself to death that way. A good man with a good conscience doesn't go so fast. A good man . . . *(He catches the DOCTOR by the coat.)* Doctor, allow me to save a human life. You're racing . . . Doctor, I'm so melancholy. I get so emotional. I always start crying when I see my coat hanging on the wall—there it is.

DOCTOR: Hm! Bloated, fat, thick neck, apoplectic constitution. Yes, Captain, you might be stricken by an *apoplexia cerebralis.°* But you might get it just on one side and be half paralyzed, or—best of all—you might become mentally affected and just vegetate from then on. Those are approximately your prospects for the next four weeks. Moreover, I can assure you that you will be a most interesting case, and if, God willing, your tongue is partially paralyzed, we'll make immortal experiments.

CAPTAIN: Doctor, don't frighten me! People have been known to die of fright, of pure, sheer fright. I can see them now, with flowers in their hands—but they'll say, he was a good man, a good man. You damn coffin nail!

DOCTOR: *(Holds out his hat.)* What's this, Captain? That's brain-less!

CAPTAIN: *(Makes a crease.)* What's this, Doctor? That's increase!

DOCTOR: I take my leave, most honorable Mr. Drill-prick.

CAPTAIN: Likewise, dearest Mr. Coffin Nail.

(WOYZECK comes running down the street.)

CAPTAIN: Hey, Woyzeck, why are you running past us like that? Stay here, Woyzeck. You're running around like an open razor blade. You might cut someone! You're running like you had to shave a regiment of castrates and would be hanged while the last hair was disappearing. But about those long beards—what was I going to say? Woyzeck—those long beards . . .

DOCTOR: A long beard on the chin. Pliny° speaks of it. Soldiers should be made to give them up.

CAPTAIN: *(Continues.)* Hey? What about those long beards? Say, Woyzeck, haven't you found a hair from a beard in your soup bowl yet? Hey? You understand, of course, a human hair, from the beard of an engineer, a sergeant, a—drum major? Hey, Woyzeck? But you've got a decent wife. Not like others.

WOYZECK: Yes, sir! What are you trying to say, Cap'n?

---

aberratio, aberration. *aberratio mentalis partialis,* partial aberration.

apoplexia cerebralis, brain tumor. *Pliny,* Roman scholar (A.D. 23–79), although the story that Alexander the Great ordered his soldiers to shave their beards to prevent the enemy from grabbing them actually derives from the Greek historian Plutarch (A.D. 46–119).

CAPTAIN: Look at the face he's making! Now, it doesn't necessarily have to be in the soup, but if you hurry around the corner, you might find one on a pair of lips—a pair of lips, Woyzeck. I know what love is, too, Woyzeck. Say! You're as white as chalk!

WOYZECK: Cap'n, I'm just a poor devil—and that's all I have in the world. Cap'n, if you're joking . . .

CAPTAIN: Joking? Me? Who do you think you are?

DOCTOR: Your pulse, Woyzeck, your pulse—short, hard, skipping, irregular.

WOYZECK: Cap'n, the earth is hot as hell—for me it's ice cold! Ice cold—hell is cold, I'll bet. It can't be! God! God! It can't be!

CAPTAIN: Listen, fellow, how'd you like to be shot, how'd you like to have a couple of bullets in your head? You're looking daggers at me; but I only mean well, because you're a good man, Woyzeck, a good man.

DOCTOR: Facial muscles rigid, tense, occasionally twitching. Posture erect, tense.

WOYZECK: I'm going. A lot is possible. A man! A lot is possible. The weather's nice, Cap'n. Look: such a beautiful, hard, rough sky—you'd almost feel like pounding a block of wood into it and hanging yourself on it, only because of the hyphen between yes, and yes again—and no. Cap'n, yes and no? Is no to blame for yes, or yes for no? I'll have to think about that. *(Goes off with long strides, first slowly, then ever faster.)*

DOCTOR: *(Races after him.)* A phenomenon! Woyzeck! Another raise!

CAPTAIN: These people make me dizzy. Look at them go—that tall rascal takes off like the shadow before a spider, and the short one—he's trotting along. The tall one is lightning and the short one is thunder. Ha-ha! After them. Grotesque! Grotesque!

10

(The guardroom.)

(WOYZECK. ANDRES.)

ANDRES: *(Sings.)*

> Our hostess has a pretty maid,
> She's in her garden night and day,
> She sits inside her garden . . .

WOYZECK: Andres!

ANDRES: Huh?

WOYZECK: Nice weather.

ANDRES: Sunday weather. There's music outside town. All the broads are out there already, everybody's sweating—it's really moving along.

WOYZECK: *(Restlessly.)* A dance, Andres. They're dancing.

ANDRES: Yeah, at the Horse and at the Star.

WOYZECK: Dancing, dancing.

ANDRES: Big deal. *(Sings.)*

> She sits inside her garden,
> Until the bells have all struck twelve,
> And stares at all the soldiers.

WOYZECK: Andres, I can't keep still.

ANDRES: Stupid!

WOYZECK: I've got to get out of here. I can't see straight. Dancing. Dancing. With their hot hands. Damn it, Andres!

ANDRES: What do you want?

WOYZECK: I've got to go.

ANDRES: With that broad?

WOYZECK: I've got to get out. It's so hot in here.

11

(Inn.)

(The windows are open, a dance. Benches in front of the house. APPRENTICES.)

FIRST APPRENTICE:

> This shirt I've got, I don't know whose,
> My soul it stinks like booze . . .

SECOND APPRENTICE: Brother, shall I in friendship bore a hole in your nature? Onward! I want to bore a hole in your nature. I'm quite a guy, too, you know. I'm going to kill all the fleas on his body.

FIRST APPRENTICE: My soul, my soul it stinks like booze. Even money must eventually decay. Forget-me-not! Oh, is this world beautiful! Brother, I could cry a rain barrel full of tears. I wish our noses were two bottles and we could pour them down each other's throats.

OTHERS: *(In chorus.)*

> A hunter from the west
> Once went riding through the woods.
> Hip-hip, hooray! A hunter's life is always gay,
> O'er meadow and o'er stream,
> Oh, hunting is my dream!

(WOYZECK stands at the window. MARIE and the DRUM MAJOR dance past without seeing him.)

MARIE: *(Dancing by.)* On! and on, on and on!

WOYZECK: *(Chokes.)* On and on! On and on! *(Jumps up violently and sinks back on the bench.)* On and on, on and on. *(Beats his hands together.)* Spin around, roll around. Why doesn't God blow out the sun so that everything can roll around in lust, man and woman, man and beast. They'll do it in broad daylight, they'll do it on our hands, like flies. Woman! That woman is hot, hot! On and on, on and on. *(Jumps up.)* The bastard! Look how he's grabbing her, grabbing her body! He—he's got her now, like I used to have her!

FIRST APPRENTICE: *(Preaches on the table.)* Yet when a wanderer stands leaning against the stream of time and/or gives answer in the wisdom of God, asking himself: Why does Man exist? Why does Man exist? But verily I say unto you: how could the farmer, the cooper, the shoemaker, the doctor exist if God hadn't created man? How could the tailor exist if God hadn't given man a feeling of shame? How could the soldier exist, if men didn't feel the necessity of killing one another? Therefore, do not ye despair, yes, yes, life is lovely and fine, yet all that is earthly is passing, even money must eventually decay. In conclusion, my dear friends, let us piss crosswise so that a Jew will die.

12

(Open field.)

WOYZECK: On and on! On and on! Shh! Music! *(Stretches out on the ground.)* Ha—what—what are you saying? Louder, louder . . . stab—stab the bitch to death? Stab—stab the bitch to death. Should I? Must I? Do I hear it over there, is the wind saying it too? It goes on and on—stab her to death . . . to death.

13

(Night.)

(ANDRES *and* WOYZECK *in a bed.*)

WOYZECK: *(Shakes* ANDRES.*)* Andres! Andres! I can't sleep. When I close my eyes, everything starts turning, and I hear the fiddles, on and on, on and on, and then there's a voice from the wall. Don't you hear anything?

ANDRES: Oh, yeah. Let them dance! God bless us, amen. *(Falls asleep again.)*

WOYZECK: It keeps saying: stab, stab! And it floats between my eyes like a knife.

ANDRES: Drink some brandy with a painkiller in it. That'll cut your fever.

14

(Inn.)

(DRUM MAJOR. WOYZECK. ONLOOKERS.)

DRUM MAJOR: I'm a man! *(Pounds his chest.)* A man, you hear? Who wants to start something? If you're not drunk as a lord, stay away from me. I'll shove your nose up your ass. I'll . . . *(To* WOYZECK.*)* Man, have a drink. A man gotta drink. I wish the world was booze, booze.

WOYZECK: *(Whistles.)*

DRUM MAJOR: You bastard, you want me to pull your tongue out of your throat and wrap it around you? *(They wrestle,* WOYZECK *loses.)* You want me to leave you enough breath to fart with?

(WOYZECK *sits on the bench, exhausted and trembling.*)

DRUM MAJOR: He thinks he's so great. Ha!

Oh, brandy, that's my life,
Oh, brandy gives me courage!

AN ONLOOKER: He sure got his.
ANOTHER: He's bleeding.
WOYZECK: One thing after another.

15

(Shop.)

(WOYZECK. *The* JEW.)

WOYZECK: The pistol costs too much.
JEW: Well, do you want it or don't you?
WOYZECK: How much is the knife?
JEW: It's good and straight. You want to cut your throat with it? Well, how about it? I'll give it to you as cheap as anybody else. Your death'll be cheap—but not for nothing. How about it? You'll have an economical death.
WOYZECK: That can cut more than just bread.
JEW: Two cents.
WOYZECK: There! *(Goes off.)*
JEW: There! Like it was nothing. But it's money! The dog.

16

(Room.)

(MARIE, KARL, *the idiot.* CHILD.)

MARIE: *(Leafs through the Bible.)* "And no guile is found in his mouth"° . . . My God! my God! Don't look at me. *(Pages further.)* "And the scribes and Pharisees brought unto him a woman taken in adultery, and set her in the midst . . . And Jesus said unto her, 'Neither do I condemn thee: go, and sin no more'"° *(Clasps her hands together.)* My God! My God, I can't. God, just give me enough strength to pray. *(The* CHILD *snuggles up to her.)* The boy is like a knife in my heart. Karl! He's sunning himself.
KARL: *(Lies on the ground and tells himself fairy tales on his fingers.)* This one has a golden crown—he's a king.

"And no guile . . . mouth," 1 Peter 2:22. **"And the scribes . . . more,"** John 8:3–11.

Tomorrow I'll go get the queen's child. Blood sausage says, come on, liver sausage! (He takes the CHILD and is quiet.)

MARIE: Franz hasn't come, not yesterday, not today. It's getting hot in here. (She opens the window.) "And stood at his feet weeping, and began to wash his feet with tears, and did wipe them with the hairs of her head, and kissed his feet, and anointed them with ointment."° (Beats her breast.) It's all dead! Savior, Savior, I wish I could anoint your feet!

17

(Barracks.)

(ANDRES. WOYZECK rummages through his things.)

WOYZECK: This jacket isn't part of the uniform, Andres. You can use it, Andres. The crucifix is my sister's—so's the little ring. I've got an icon, too—two hearts in beautiful gold. It was in my mother's Bible, and it says:

May pain be my reward,
Through pain I love my Lord.

Lord, like Thy body, red and sore,
So be my heart forevermore.

My mother can only feel the sun shining on her hands now. That doesn't matter.

ANDRES: (Blankly, answers to everything.) Yeah.

WOYZECK: (Pulls out a piece of paper.) Friedrich Johann Franz Woyzeck, soldier, rifleman in the second regiment, second battalion, fourth company, born on the Feast of the Annunciation. Today I'm thirty years, seven months, and twelve days old.

ANDRES: Franz, you better go to the hospital. You poor guy—drink brandy with a painkiller in it. That'll kill the fever.

WOYZECK: You know, Andres, when the carpenter nails those boards together, nobody knows who's going to be lying between them.

18

(The DOCTOR's courtyard.)

(STUDENTS below, the DOCTOR at the attic window.)

DOCTOR: Gentlemen, I am on the roof like David when he saw Bathsheba,° but all I see are panties hanging in the garden of the girls' boarding house. Gentlemen, we are dealing with the important question of the relationship of subject to object. If we take only one of the things in which

the organic self-affirmation of the Divine manifests itself to such a high degree, and examine its relationship to space, to the earth, to the planetary system . . . gentlemen, if I throw this cat out of the window, how will it relate to the centrum gravitationis° and to its own instinct? Hey, Woyzeck. (Shouts.) Woyzeck! (DOCTOR comes down.)

WOYZECK: Doctor, it bites!

DOCTOR: The fellow holds the beast so tenderly, like it was his own grandmother!

WOYZECK: Doctor, I've got the shivers.

DOCTOR: (Elated.) Say, that's wonderful, Woyzeck! (Rubs his hands. He takes the cat.) What's this, gentlemen—a new species of rabbit louse, a beautiful species. (He pulls out a magnifying glass.) Gentlemen—(The cat runs off.) gentlemen, that animal has no scientific instinct. Gentlemen, instead of that you can see something else. Take note of this man—for a quarter of a year he hasn't eaten anything but peas. Notice the result. Feel how uneven his pulse is. There—and the eyes.

WOYZECK: Doctor, everything's getting black. (He sits down.)

DOCTOR: Courage! Just a few more days, Woyzeck, and then it'll be all over. Feel him, gentlemen, feel him. (STUDENTS feel his temples, pulse, and chest.) Apropos, Woyzeck, wiggle your ears for the gentlemen. I meant to show it to you before. He uses two muscles. Come on, hop to it!

WOYZECK: Oh, Doctor!

DOCTOR: You dog, do I have to wiggle them for you? Are you going to act like the cat? This, gentlemen, represents a transition to the donkey, frequently resulting from being brought up by women and from the use of the mother tongue. How much hair has your mother pulled out for a tender memory? It's gotten very thin in the last few days. Yes, the peas, gentlemen.

19

(Street.)

(MARIE with little girls in front of the house door. GRANDMOTHER. Then WOYZECK.)

GIRLS:

How bright the sun on Candlemas Day,
On fields of golden grain.
As two by two they marched along
Down the country lane.
The pipers up in front,
The fiddlers in a chain.
Their red socks . . .

"And stood at his feet . . . ointment," Luke 7:37–38. David when he saw Bathsheba, cf. 2 Sam. 11:2ff.

centrum gravitationis, center of gravity.

FIRST CHILD: I don't like it!
SECOND CHILD: What do you want, anyway?
THIRD CHILD: Why'd you start it?
SECOND CHILD: Yeah, why?
FIRST CHILD: Because!
SECOND CHILD: Why because?
THIRD CHILD: Who's going to sing—? (*Looks questioningly around the circle and points to the* FIRST CHILD.)
FIRST CHILD: I can't.
ALL THE CHILDREN: Marie, you sing to us.
MARIE: Come, you little crabs.

(*Children's games: "Ring-around-a-rosy" and "King Herod."*°)

Grandmother, tell a story.

GRANDMOTHER: Once upon a time, there was a poor little child with no father and no mother. Everything was dead, and no one was left in the whole world. Everything was dead, and the child went and cried day and night. And since nobody was left on the earth, he wanted to go up to the heavens, 'cause the moon was looking at him so friendly, and when he finally got to the moon, the moon was a piece of rotten wood, and then he went to the sun, and when he got there, the sun was a wilted sunflower, and when he got to the stars, they were little golden flies stuck up there like the shrike° sticks them on the blackthorn; and when he wanted to go back down to the earth, the earth was an upset pot, and the child was all alone, and he sat down and cried, and there he sits to this day, all alone.
WOYZECK: Marie!
MARIE: (*Startled.*) What is it?
WOYZECK: Marie, we have to go. It's time.
MARIE: Where to?
WOYZECK: How do I know?

20

(*Evening. The town in the distance.*)

(MARIE. WOYZECK.)

MARIE: That must be the town back there. It's dark.
WOYZECK: Stay here. Come on, sit down.
MARIE: But I have to get back.
WOYZECK: You won't get sore feet.
MARIE: What's gotten into you!
WOYZECK: Do you know how long it's been, Marie?

MARIE: Two years since Pentecost.°
WOYZECK: Do you know how long it's going to be?
MARIE: I've got to go make supper.
WOYZECK: Are you freezing, Marie? But you're warm. How hot your lips are! Hot—the hot breath of a whore—but I'd give heaven and earth to kiss them once more. Once you're cold, you don't freeze anymore. The morning dew won't make you freeze.
MARIE: What are you talking about?
WOYZECK: Nothing. (*Silence.*)
MARIE: Look how red the moon is.
WOYZECK: Like a bloody blade.
MARIE: What are you up to? Franz, you're so pale. (*He pulls out the knife.*) Franz—wait! For God's sake—help!
WOYZECK: Take that and that! Can't you die? There! There! Ah—she's still twitching. Not yet? Not yet? Still alive? (*Keeps on stabbing.*) Are you dead? Dead! Dead! (*People approach, he runs off.*)

21

(*Two people.*)

FIRST PERSON: Wait!
SECOND PERSON: You hear it? Shh! Over there!
FIRST PERSON: Ooh! There! What a sound!
SECOND PERSON: That's the water, it's calling. Nobody has drowned for a long time. Let's go. It's bad to hear things like that.
FIRST PERSON: Ooh! There it is again. Like someone dying.
SECOND PERSON: It's weird. It's so foggy—gray mist everywhere and the beetles humming like broken bells. Let's get out of here!
FIRST PERSON: No—it's too clear, too loud. Up this way. Come on.

22

(*Inn.*)

(WOYZECK. KATEY. KARL. INNKEEPER. *People.*)

WOYZECK: Dance, all of you, on and on. Sweat and stink. He'll get you all in the end. (*Sings.*)

> *Our hostess has a pretty maid,*
> *She's in her garden night and day,*
> *She sits inside her garden,*
> *Until the bells have all struck twelve,*
> *And stares at all the soldiers.*

"King Herod," the name of the children's game or rhyme derives from the biblical figure who ordered the massacre of children (Matt. 2). *shrike,* also known as the "butcher bird" because it impales its prey on thorns.

Pentecost, Christian festival commemorating the revelation of the Holy Spirit to the apostles.

(He dances.) Come on, Katey! Sit down! I'm hot, hot. *(He takes off his jacket.)* That's the way it is: the devil takes one and lets the other go. Katey, you're hot! Why? Katey, you'll be cold someday, too. Be reasonable. Can't you sing something?

KATEY: *(Sings.)*

> For Swabian hills I do not yearn,
> And flowing gowns I always spurn,
> For flowing gowns and pointed shoes
> A servant girl should never choose.

WOYZECK: No, no shoes. You can go to hell without shoes, too.

KATEY: *(Dances.)*

> For shame, my love, I'm not your own,
> Just keep your money and sleep alone.

WOYZECK: Yes, you're right! I don't want to make myself bloody.

KATEY: But what's that on your hand?

WOYZECK: Who? Me?

KATEY: Red . . . blood! *(People gather around.)*

WOYZECK: Blood? Blood.

INNKEEPER: Ooh. Blood.

WOYZECK: I guess I must have cut myself on my right hand.

INNKEEPER: But how'd it get on your elbow?

WOYZECK: I wiped it off.

INNKEEPER: What! With your right hand on your right elbow? You're talented.

KARL: And then the giant said: I smell, I smell, I smell human flesh. Phew! That stinks already.

WOYZECK: Damn it, what do you want? What do you care? Get away, or the first one who . . . God damn it! You think I killed someone? Am I a murderer? What are you staring at? Look at yourselves! Out of my way! *(He runs out.)*

23

(Night. The town in the distance.)

(WOYZECK alone.)

WOYZECK: The knife? Where's the knife? Here's where I left it. It'll give me away! Closer, still closer! What kind of a place is this? What's that I hear? Something's moving. Shh! Over there. Marie! Ah—Marie! Quiet. Everything's quiet! You're so pale, Marie. Why is that red thread around your neck? Who helped you earn that for your sins? They made you black, black! Now I've made you white. Your black hair looks so wild. Didn't you do your braids today? Something's lying over there! Cold, wet, still. Got to get away from here. The knife, the knife—is that it? There! People—over there. *(He runs off.)*

24

(WOYZECK at a pond.)

WOYZECK: Down it goes! *(He throws the knife in.)* It sinks like a stone in the dark water. The moon is like a bloody blade. Is the whole world going to give me away? No—it's too far in front—when people go swimming—*(He goes into the pond and throws it far out.)* All right, now—but in the summer, when they go diving for shells . . . Oh, it'll rust. Who'll recognize it? I wish I'd smashed it! Am I still bloody? I better wash myself. There's a spot—and there's another.°

25

(Street.)

(Children.)

FIRST CHILD: Come on! Marie!

SECOND CHILD: What's wrong?

FIRST CHILD: Don't you know? Everybody's gone out there already. Someone's lying there!

SECOND CHILD: Where?

FIRST CHILD: To the left through the forest, near that red cross.

SECOND CHILD: Let's go, so we can still see something. Otherwise they'll carry her away.

26

(COURT CLERK, DOCTOR, JUDGE.)

CLERK: A good murder, a real murder, a beautiful murder. As good a murder as you'd ever want to see. We haven't had one like this for a long time.

27

(KARL. The CHILD. WOYZECK.)

KARL: *(Holds the CHILD on his lap.)* He fell in the water, he fell in the water, he fell in the water.

WOYZECK: Son—Christian!

KARL: *(Stares at him.)* He fell in the water.

WOYZECK: *(Wants to caress the CHILD, who turns away and screams.)* My God!

KARL: He fell in the water.

WOYZECK: Christian, you'll get a horsey. Da-da! *(The CHILD resists. To KARL.)* Here, go buy the boy a horsey.

KARL: *(Stares at him.)*

WOYZECK: Hop-hop! Horsey!

KARL: *(Cheers.)* Hop-hop! Horsey! Horsey! *(Runs off with the CHILD.)*

(WOYZECK remains, alone.)

There's a spot . . . another, cf. *Macbeth* 5.1.

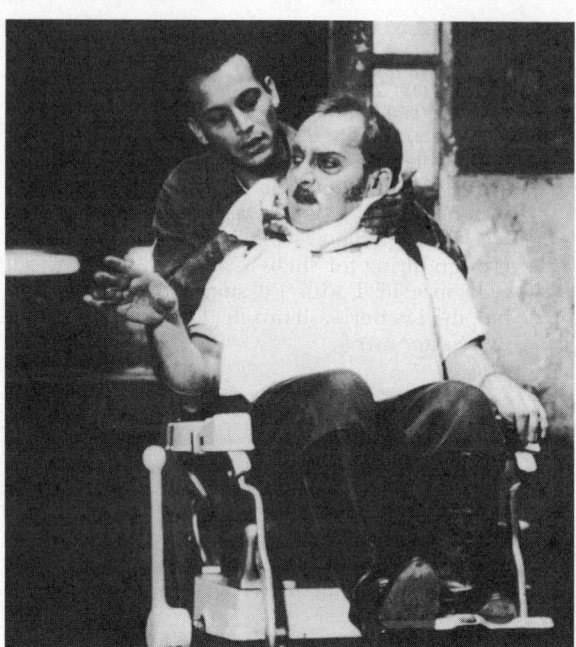

Figure 1. Woyzeck (Jesse Borrego) shaves the Captain (Zach Grenier) in the New York Shakespeare Festival production of *Woyzeck,* directed by JoAnne Akalaitis, 1992. (Photograph: Martha Swope.)

Figure 2. The townspeople stare at Woyzeck (Jesse Borrego) after the murder of Marie in the 1992 production. (Photograph: Martha Swope.)

Figure 3. In the 1992 production, the murder of Marie (Sheila Tousey) takes place in slow motion, focusing attention on Woyzeck's (Jesse Borrego) upraised hand and Marie's attempt to stop the knife's descent. (Photograph: Martha Swope.)

Staging of *Woyzeck*

REVIEW OF THE NEW YORK SHAKESPEARE
FESTIVAL PRODUCTION, 1992,
BY MEL GUSSOW

The title character in "Woyzeck" is, we are told, "running around like an open razor blade." The image, in common with the play itself, is as precise as it is terrifying. Woyzeck, a military barber and the most ordinary of common men, is overcome by dementia. He hears strange sounds, sees visions and is driven to a desperate act of murder. Along with "Danton's Death," the play certified Georg Büchner's reputation as the first modern playwright. Written in the 1830's and discovered as fragments after the author's death, the work foreshadowed explorations by Kafka, Brecht and Beckett. The modernism of Büchner is basic to JoAnne Akalaitis's compelling production at the Joseph Papp Public Theater in New York.

Because of the nonlinear style and the focus on an irrational antihero, the play is open to free-handed interpretation. In search of "Woyzeck," Ms. Akalaitis uses alternate scenes and extracts from early drafts of the play, filtering Henry J. Schmidt's translation through her fervid theatrical imagination. The difficulty this director has had in dealing with Shakespeare is not in evidence in her treatment of Büchner.

In the reordering of scenes the play gains in momentum, accruing intensity and psychological awareness as Woyzeck moves through the last stages of his calamitous life. The director has given greater centricity to the role of Marie, Woyzeck's common-law wife and the object of his homicidal impulse. But of course this is still Woyzeck's tragedy, as he is crushed by people and events beyond his control.

Ms. Akalaitis has accentuated the folk elements within the play, crucial to Büchner, for whom this was a ballad-like dramatization of an actual occurrence. Philip Glass's sizzling music is often paired with folk-style lyrics by Paul Schmidt, and martial clog dancing adds to the ritualistic background.

In contrast to the stark simplicity of Richard Foreman's version of the play several seasons ago at Hartford Stage, Ms. Akalaitis's approach has a visual richness. The productions are equally valid but they are so dissimilar in concept that they could be staged together in repertory. Naturally they share the same themes, characters and impact.

Ms. Akalaitis takes a cue from her own early work as a director and playwright with Mabou Mines, in terms of using imagery to enhance a text, as she did in "Dressed Like an Egg," her lush collage of the life of Colette. With "Woyzeck," she seems to be influenced by German Expressionist art. In scene after scene there are striking stage pictures of people caught in a frenzy or in a moment of aggrieved anticipation.

The military barracks that is the central environment of the play would need no conversion to become a concentration camp. As designed by Marina Draghici, who did the impressive settings for Caryl Churchill's "Mad Forest," the scenery simulates all the coldness and malevolence of a life in confinement. The bare plastered walls and streaked windows, evocatively lighted by Mimi Jordan Sherin, are like conjurations of the paintings of Anselm Kiefer.

Woyzeck (Jesse Borrego) tears across the stage in a fever. In his rag uniform and with a haunted look in his deep-set eyes, Mr. Borrego resembles a prisoner of Dachau suddenly released and brought into a blinding light. Repeatedly he is transfixed like an apparition in a nightmare.

Shaving his captain (Zach Grenier), Woyzeck strops his razor for so long that it seems as if he is sharpening his blade for slaughter. The autocratic officer flinches as the barber approaches his chair; still he never stops badgering his subordinate. Wherever Woyzeck turns, he is besieged, even, as it turns out, in his home, up to then his single sanctuary. In response, he tries to outrun his demons.

In those moments when things stand still, velocity is replaced by what could be called frieze frames. Townspeople sit in a line as in a pew and a grandmother tells the bleakest and most Büchnerian of fairy tales: "Once upon a time there was a poor child with no father and no mother; everything was dead, and no one was left in the whole world."

Ms. Akalaitis uses her painterly eye to illuminate motifs, but along the way there are a few questionable directorial choices. The production begins awkwardly with a film clip of Mr. Borrego climbing rocks. This is apparently a scene from Ms. Akalaitis's adaptation of other Büchner works, which she entitled "Leon and Lena (Lenz)," and presented at the Guthrie Theater. The film has no direct bearing on the play we are seeing. The carnival sequence is surprisingly mundane and a scene of soldiers showering detracts from a later, symbolic moment when Woyzeck tries to wash away his bloody deed.

Furthermore, some of the acting lacks resilience, even allowing for the fact that those characters who have no names, like the drum major, are intended to be emblematic. But the production is anchored by the actors in the three most important roles: the commandingly imperious Mr. Grenier as the captain, Sheila Tousey as Marie and Mr. Borrego, who grasps the tortured essence of Woyzeck.

When he turns against Marie, who has been his only source of stability, he attacks her as if she were the incarnation of everything that had been bedeviling him. The scene is staged with ferocity: the victim is helpless, the murderer uncontrollable. Around the time he was creating "Woyzeck," Büchner wrote a letter to his parents in which he commented on German militarism and what he considered to be the brute force of the law. He asked, "Aren't we in an eternal state of violence?" That question and its accompanying cry for help are searingly captured by the playwright and by Ms. Akalaitis as his contemporary interpreter.

HENRIK IBSEN

1828–1906

When Ibsen was born, his father was a prosperous merchant in Skien, a small town in the southeastern part of Norway, but by the time Ibsen was eight his father had gone bankrupt and the family was compelled to leave its spacious home for quarters in an attic apartment filled with the abandoned possessions of a previous tenant. Ibsen never forgot that painful reversal of fortune. In fact, he recorded its details in an unfinished autobiography that he began in 1881. That early exposure to human suffering was to leave its mark on many of his plays, not in any specific autobiographical sense, but in a general concern with the economic, social, and psychological conditions that afflict the lives of ordinary men and women.

During his early dramatic career, from 1851 to 1867, when he was still influenced by the style and subject matter of romantic theater, Ibsen wrote a series of plays in blank verse, most of them based on Norwegian myth and history. Yet even in these works, particularly *Brand* (1866) and *Peer Gynt* (1867), Ibsen revealed a concern with moral and social issues that was to characterize his later plays. In *Brand* he created a protagonist so single-mindedly committed to his religious ministry that he sacrifices first his child, then his wife, and ultimately himself to the fulfillment of his mission; then in the character of Peer Gynt, the demonic antithesis of Brand, he created a protagonist so committed to his own selfish desires that he devotes his life to a series of fanatically deceitful adventures with which he deceives even himself, until at the moment of his death he discovers his irredeemable hollowness. Although *Brand* and *Peer Gynt* made Ibsen famous and financially secure, they were the last works he was to write in the tradition of romantic drama.

Beginning with *The League of Youth* (1869), a play that attacked the hypocrisy of provincial politics and politicians, Ibsen turned from history, myth, and folklore to contemporary social problems; from romantic idealism to realistic drama; from verse to prose. In *The Pillars of Society* (1877), he continued his iconoclastic aims by exposing the disreputable behavior of a socially respectable businessman and by reforming him through the agency of a socially liberated woman. Having attacked business and politics, he then went after the most sacred of all social institutions—marriage—by making the heroine of his next play, *A Doll's House* (1879), a young wife who gradually becomes aware that she has been turned into a helpless child by her husband, whom she abandons after discovering that he is an emotional hypocrite. Ibsen's audience was shocked by the ending of *A Doll's House,* but he was unrelenting in his attack and answered their outrage with *Ghosts* (1881), whose heroine heeds the advice of her minister to remain with her husband and, therefore, must spend the rest of her life concealing her own feelings and the truth about her husband's dissolute behavior. Ibsen's frank treatment of syphilis in *Ghosts,* and his implicit attack on Norwegian social and religious values, roused even stronger criticism than *A Doll's House.* It is not surprising that Ibsen's next play, *An Enemy of the People* (1882), dealt with the difficulty of being the outsider who brings unpleasant truths to the attention of the community. Then, in a startling reversal, Ibsen made the truth-bringer in *The Wild Duck* (1884) a morally ambiguous figure, so intent on forcing long-hidden secrets into the open that he destroys an entire family. In his later, more overtly symbolic plays, particularly *Rosmersholm* (1886), *Hedda Gabler* (1890), and *The Master Builder* (1892), Ibsen moved away from his concern with social problems into a psychological exploration of emotionally and sexually driven individuals who become entangled in self-destructive personal relationships.

This body of plays quickly earned Ibsen the reputation of a fighting social realist—a description applied to him by Bernard Shaw, his Anglo-Irish contemporary, in *The Quintessence of Ibsenism* (1891). From his own time to this day, many of Ibsen's prose plays have primarily been interpreted as pieces of social criticism. *A Doll's House,* for example, is frequently celebrated nowadays as an attack on male chauvinism and an affirmation of women's rights, for there is much about the relationship of Torvald and Nora that supports this interpretation. Torvald's patronizing conception of Nora as his "little songbird" and "doll" as well as his assertion, "First and foremost you are a wife and a mother," leads ultimately to Nora's rejection of those descriptions and her decision to "think things out for myself, and try to find my own answer." Yet it is also important to recognize that *A Doll's House,* like Ibsen's other prose plays, is first and foremost a psychologically realistic work about a human being in an ordinary world, who slowly and painfully comes to an extraordinary understanding about the importance of personal integrity in human affairs. That special understanding leads Nora to assert that "I am first and foremost a human being." And that belief leads her at last to leave Torvald not because he has subjugated her but because he has profoundly disappointed her by valuing his material welfare and social status more highly than her human love. So it is that she is moved to tell Torvald "you neither think nor talk like the man I could share my life with." The implication of these remarks seems to be that she could have forgiven him everything had he finally been true to her hopeful vision of him. Her departure, then, might well be seen as the logical consequence of her shattered illusions about Torvald rather than as an assertion of her woman's rights.

Ibsen himself may well have meant to show both Nora and Torvald as being imprisoned in their relationship, even though for years the play has been read as his plea for female emancipation. Ibsen explicitly disclaimed a feminist interpretation of the play several years after its production, when speaking to a meeting of the Norwegian Association for Women's Rights: "I must decline the honor of being said to have worked for the Women's Rights movement. I am not even very sure what Women's Rights are. To me it has been a question of human rights." Given Ibsen's disclaimer, the play might well be interpreted as a skillfully constructed piece that begins as a suspense story (will Nora be able to keep Torvald from learning her guilty secret?) but develops into a painfully probing exposure of a human relationship based on misunderstanding and lack of communication—a relationship that denies both individuals their human rights. As Nora accurately observes near the end, "In eight whole years—no, longer—ever since we first met—we have never exchanged a serious word on a serious subject." The problem of the play, in this sense, appears to be less an issue of Nora's rights than the issue of what a marriage must be if it is to achieve the "miracle of miracles"—a true and lasting relationship that allows both partners their human rights.

These questions about the play ultimately lead back to questions about how to play Nora. Some readers and spectators may find themselves troubled by the plausibility of Nora's transformation from a naive young wife into a resolutely independent human being. Such a transformation provides a major problem for any actress who plays Nora, as Walter Kerr noted in his review of the 1971 production starring Claire Bloom: "How does one turn an enchanting child into a dominating adult, especially when the transition is missing?" To do so, as Kerr makes clear in his review, evidently requires an actress to convey more than mere childishness in the beginning, even as it requires her to convey something other than mere domination at the end. Photographs of Claire Bloom performing the role of Nora show that in the beginning of the play she did suggest a degree of thoughtful reservation far exceeding that of a child (see Figure 1), much as at the end of the play she expressed a sense of painful awareness and resoluteness not to be expected of a merely dominating adult (see Figures 2 and 3). In her facial expression, as in the austere clothing she wears during the final scene, Claire Bloom's Nora is clearly aware that in slamming the door on Torvald she has relinquished a set of emotional ties that still tug at her, without finding a clear sense of what will become of her.

More recently, Janet McTeer brought a physically ebullient and sensually alive Nora to the stage both in London and in New York, stressing the character's flighty energy to such an extent that audiences might genuinely be moved to wonder whether she was really the blonde airhead that she seemed to be. And by working with a tall, handsome Torvald, to whom she was evidently attracted (see Figure 4 and interview with McTeer in "Staging of *A Doll's House*"), McTeer's Nora seemed to be happy in her marriage, not trapped in it. But when Torvald turned out to be brutally angry in his response to Krogstad's letter and its revelation of Nora's forgery, McTeer's Nora first became frightened (see Figure 5) and then, slowly and tearfully, came to the realization that she had to leave the home she had loved so much. Taking with her a small silver-framed photograph of the children, she left Torvald, tentatively, even hesitantly, setting out into the night. Though offering a striking physical contrast with Claire Bloom, Janet McTeer also seemed to suggest that Nora pays a high price for the new self she hopes to find.

A DOLL'S HOUSE

BY HENRIK IBSEN / TRANSLATED BY MICHAEL MEYER

CHARACTERS

TORVALD HELMER, *a lawyer*
NORA, *his wife*
DR. RANK
MRS. LINDE
NILS KROGSTAD, *also a lawyer*
The HELMERS' *three small children*

ANNE-MARIE, *their nurse*
HELEN, *the maid*
A PORTER

SCENE

The action takes place in the Helmers' apartment.

ACT 1

(A comfortably and tastefully, but not expensively fur-nished room. Backstage right a door leads out to the hall; backstage left, another door to HELMER's study. Between these two doors stands a piano. In the middle of the left-hand wall is a door, with a window downstage of it. Near the window, a round table with armchairs and a small sofa. In the right-hand wall, slightly upstage, is a door; downstage of this, against the same wall, a stove lined with porcelain tiles, with a couple of armchairs and a rocking-chair in front of it. Between the stove and the side door is a small table. Engravings on the wall. A what-not with china and other bric-a-brac; a small bookcase with leather-bound books. A carpet on the floor; a fire in the stove. A winter day.

A bell rings in the hall outside. After a moment, we hear the front door being opened. NORA enters the room, hum-ming contentedly to herself. She is wearing outdoor clothes and carrying a lot of parcels, which she puts down on the table right. She leaves the door to the hall open; through it, we can see a PORTER carrying a Christmas tree and a bas-ket. He gives these to the MAID, who has opened the door for them.)

NORA: Hide that Christmas tree away, Helen. The chil-dren mustn't see it before I've decorated it this evening. *(to the PORTER, taking out her purse)* How much—?

PORTER: A shilling.

NORA: Here's half a crown.° No, keep it.

(The PORTER touches his cap and goes. NORA closes the door. She continues to laugh happily to herself as she removes her coat, etc. She takes from her pocket a bag con-taining macaroons and eats a couple. Then she tiptoes across and listens at her husband's door.)

NORA: Yes, he's here. *(Starts humming again as she goes over to the table, right.)*

HELMER *(from his room)*: Is that my skylark twittering out there?

---

half a crown, Nora's tip is more than twice the amount requested.

NORA *(opening some of the parcels)*: It is!

HELMER: Is that my squirrel rustling?

NORA: Yes!

HELMER: When did my squirrel come home?

NORA: Just now. *(Pops the bag of macaroons in her pocket and wipes her mouth.)* Come out here, Torvald, and see what I've bought.

HELMER: You mustn't disturb me! *(Short pause, then he opens the door and looks in, his pen in his hand.)* Bought, did you say? All that? Has my little squan-derbird been overspending again?

NORA: Oh, Torvald, surely we can let ourselves go a little this year! It's the first Christmas we don't have to scrape.

HELMER: Well, you know, we can't afford to be extrav-agant.

NORA: Oh yes, Torvald, we can be a little extravagant now. Can't we? Just a tiny bit? You've got a big salary now, and you're going to make lots and lots of money.

HELMER: Next year, yes. But my new salary doesn't start till April.

NORA: Pooh; we can borrow till then.

HELMER: Nora! *(Goes over to her and takes her playfully by the ear.)* What a little spendthrift you are! Suppose I were to borrow fifty pounds today, and you spent it all over Christmas, and then on New Year's Eve a tile fell off a roof on to my head—

NORA *(puts her hand over his mouth)*: Oh, Torvald! Don't say such dreadful things!

HELMER: Yes, but suppose something like that did happen? What then?

NORA: If anything as frightful as that happened, it wouldn't make much difference whether I was in debt or not.

HELMER: But what about the people I'd borrowed from?

NORA: Them? Who cares about them? They're strangers.

HELMER: Oh, Nora, Nora, how like a woman! No, but seriously, Nora, you know how I feel about this. No debts! Never borrow! A home that is founded on debts can never be a place of freedom and beauty. We two have stuck it out bravely up to now; and we shall continue to do so for the short time we still have to.

NORA *(goes over toward the stove)*: Very well, Torvald. As you say.

HELMER *(follows her)*: Now, now! My little songbird mustn't droop her wings. What's this? Is little squirrel sulking? *(Takes out his purse.)* Nora; guess what I've got here!

NORA *(turns quickly)*: Money!

HELMER: Look. *(Hands her some banknotes.)* I know how these small expenses crop up at Christmas.

NORA *(counts them)*: One—two—three—four. Oh, thank you, Torvald, thank you! I should be able to manage with this.

HELMER: You'll have to.

NORA: Yes, yes, of course I will. But come over here, I want to show you everything I've bought. And so cheaply! Look, here are new clothes for Ivar—and a sword. And a horse and a trumpet for Bob. And a doll and a cradle for Emmy—they're nothing much, but she'll pull them apart in a few days. And some bits of material and handkerchiefs for the maids. Old Anne-Marie ought to have had something better, really.

HELMER: And what's in that parcel?

NORA *(cries)*: No, Torvald, you mustn't see that before this evening!

HELMER: Very well. But now, tell me, you little spendthrift, what do you want for Christmas?

NORA: Me? Oh, pooh, I don't want anything.

HELMER: Oh, yes, you do. Now tell me, what, within reason, would you most like?

NORA: No, I really don't know. Oh, yes—Torvald—!

HELMER: Well?

NORA *(plays with his coat-buttons, not looking at him)*: If you really want to give me something, you could—you could—

HELMER: Come on, out with it.

NORA *(quickly)*: You could give me money, Torvald. Only as much as you feel you can afford; then later I'll buy something with it.

HELMER: But, Nora—

NORA: Oh yes, Torvald dear, please! Please! Then I'll wrap up the notes in pretty gold paper and hang them on the Christmas tree. Wouldn't that be fun?

HELMER: What's the name of that little bird that can never keep any money?

NORA: Yes, yes, squanderbird; I know. But let's do as I say, Torvald; then I'll have time to think about what I need most. Isn't that the best way? Mm?

HELMER *(smiles)*: To be sure it would be, if you could keep what I gave you and really buy yourself something with it. But you'll spend it on all sorts of useless things for the house, and then I'll have to put my hand in my pocket again.

NORA: Oh, but Torvald—

HELMER: You can't deny it, Nora dear. *(Puts his arm round her waist.)* The squanderbird's a pretty little creature, but she gets through an awful lot of money. It's incredible what an expensive pet she is for a man to keep.

NORA: For shame! How can you say such a thing? I save every penny I can.

HELMER *(laughs)*: That's quite true. Every penny you can. But you can't.

NORA *(hums and smiles, quietly gleeful)*: Hm. If you only knew how many expenses we larks and squirrels have, Torvald.

HELMER: You're a funny little creature. Just like your father used to be. Always on the look-out for some way to get money, but as soon as you have any it just runs through your fingers, and you never know where it's gone. Well, I suppose I must take you as you are. It's in your blood. Yes, yes, yes, these things are hereditary, Nora.

NORA: Oh, I wish I'd inherited more of Papa's qualities.

HELMER: And I wouldn't wish my darling little songbird to be any different from what she is. By the way, that reminds me. You look awfully—how shall I put it?—awfully guilty today.

NORA: Do I—

HELMER: Yes, you do. Look me in the eyes.

NORA *(looks at him)*: Well?

HELMER *(wags his finger)*: Has my little sweet-tooth been indulging herself in town today, by any chance?

NORA: No, how can you think of such a thing?

HELMER: Not a tiny little digression into a pastry shop?

NORA: No, Torvald, I promise—

HELMER: Not just a wee jam tart?

NORA: Certainly not.

HELMER: Not a little nibble at a macaroon?

NORA: No, Torvald—I promise you, honestly—

HELMER: There, there. I was only joking.

NORA *(goes over to the table, right)*: You know I could never act against your wishes.

HELMER: Of course not. And you've given me your word—*(Goes over to her.)* Well, my beloved Nora, you keep your little Christmas secrets to yourself. They'll be revealed this evening, I've no doubt, once the Christmas tree has been lit.

NORA: Have you remembered to invite Dr. Rank?

HELMER: No. But there's no need; he knows he'll be dining with us. Anyway, I'll ask him when he comes this morning. I've ordered some good wine. Oh, Nora, you can't imagine how I'm looking forward to this evening.

NORA: So am I. And, Torvald, how the children will love it!

HELMER: Yes, it's a wonderful thing to know that one's position is assured and that one has an ample income. Don't you agree? It's good to know that, isn't it?

NORA: Yes, it's almost like a miracle.

HELMER: Do you remember last Christmas? For three whole weeks you shut yourself away every evening to make flowers for the Christmas tree, and all those other things you were going to surprise us with. Ugh, it was the most boring time I've ever had in my life.

NORA: I didn't find it boring.

HELMER (smiles): But it all came to nothing in the end, didn't it?

NORA: Oh, are you going to bring that up again? How could I help the cat getting in and tearing everything to bits?

HELMER: No, my poor little Nora, of course you couldn't. You simply wanted to make us happy, and that's all that matters. But it's good that those hard times are past.

NORA: Yes, it's wonderful.

HELMER: I don't have to sit by myself and be bored. And you don't have to tire your pretty eyes and your delicate little hands—

NORA (claps her hands): No, Torvald, that's true, isn't it—I don't have to any longer? Oh, it's really all just like a miracle. (Takes his arm.) Now, I'm going to tell you what I thought we might do, Torvald. As soon as Christmas is over—(A bell rings in the hall.) Oh, there's the doorbell. (Tidies up one or two things in the room.) Someone's coming. What a bore.

HELMER: I'm not at home to any visitors. Remember!

MAID (in the doorway): A lady's called, madam. A stranger.

NORA: Well, ask her to come in.

MAID: And the doctor's here too, sir.

HELMER: Has he gone to my room?

MAID: Yes, sir.

(HELMER goes into his room. The MAID shows in MRS. LINDE, who is dressed in travelling clothes, and closes the door.)

MRS. LINDE (shyly and a little hesitantly): Good evening, Nora.

NORA (uncertainly): Good evening—

MRS. LINDE: I don't suppose you recognize me.

NORA: No, I'm afraid I— Yes, wait a minute—surely— (Exclaims.) Why, Christine! Is it really you?

MRS. LINDE: Yes, it's me.

NORA: Christine! And I didn't recognize you! But how could I—? (More quietly.) How you've changed, Christine!

MRS. LINDE: Yes, I know. It's been nine years—nearly ten—

NORA: Is it so long? Yes, it must be. Oh, these last eight years have been such a happy time for me! So you've come to town? All that way in winter! How brave of you!

MRS. LINDE: I arrived by the steamer this morning.

NORA: Yes, of course—to enjoy yourself over Christmas. Oh, how splendid! We'll have to celebrate! But take off your coat. You're not cold, are you? (Helps her off with it.) There! Now let's sit down here by the stove and be comfortable. No, you take the armchair. I'll sit here in the rocking-chair. (Clasps MRS. LINDE's hands.) Yes, now you look like your old self. It was just at first that—you've got a little paler, though, Christine. And perhaps a bit thinner.

MRS. LINDE: And older, Nora. Much, much older.

NORA: Yes, perhaps a little older. Just a tiny bit. Not much. (Checks herself suddenly and says earnestly.) Oh, but how thoughtless of me to sit here and chatter away like this! Dear, sweet Christine, can you forgive me?

MRS. LINDE: What do you mean, Nora?

NORA (quietly): Poor Christine, you've become a widow.

MRS. LINDE: Yes. Three years ago.

NORA: I know, I know—I read it in the papers. Oh, Christine, I meant to write to you so often, honestly. But I always put it off, and something else always cropped up.

MRS. LINDE: I understand, Nora dear.

NORA: No, Christine, it was beastly of me. Oh, my poor darling, what you've gone through! And he didn't leave you anything?

MRS. LINDE: No.

NORA: No children, either?

MRS. LINDE: No.

NORA: Nothing at all, then?

MRS. LINDE: Not even a feeling of loss or sorrow.

NORA (looks incredulously at her): But, Christine, how is that possible?

MRS. LINDE (smiles sadly and strokes NORA's hair): Oh, these things happen, Nora.

NORA: All alone. How dreadful that must be for you. I've three lovely children. I'm afraid you can't see them now, because they're out with nanny. But you must tell me everything—

MRS. LINDE: No, no, no. I want to hear about you.

NORA: No, you start. I'm not going to be selfish today. I'm just going to think about you. Oh, but there's one thing I must tell you. Have you heard of the wonderful luck we've just had?

MRS. LINDE: No. What?

NORA: Would you believe it—my husband's just been made manager of the bank!

MRS. LINDE: Your husband? Oh, how lucky—!

NORA: Yes, isn't it? Being a lawyer is so uncertain, you know, especially if one isn't prepared to touch any case that isn't—well—quite nice. And of course Torvald's been very firm about that—and I'm absolutely with him. Oh, you can imagine how happy we are! He's joining the bank in the New Year, and he'll be getting a big salary, and lots of percentages too. From now on we'll be able to live quite differently—we'll be able to do whatever we want. Oh, Christine, it's such a relief! I feel so happy! Well, I mean, it's lovely to have heaps of money and not to have to worry about anything. Don't you think?

MRS. LINDE: It must be lovely to have enough to cover one's needs, anyway.

NORA: Not just our needs! We're going to have heaps and heaps of money!

MRS. LINDE (smiles): Nora, Nora, haven't you grown up yet? When we were at school you were a terrible little spendthrift.

NORA (laughs quietly): Yes, Torvald still says that. (Wags her finger.) But "Nora, Nora" isn't as silly as you think. Oh, we've been in no position for me to waste money. We've both had to work.

MRS. LINDE: You too?

NORA: Yes, little things—fancy work, crocheting, embroidery and so forth. (Casually.) And other things too. I suppose you know Torvald left the Ministry when we got married? There were no prospects for promotion in his department, and of course he needed more money. But the first year he overworked himself quite dreadfully. He had to take on all sorts of extra jobs, and worked day and night. But it was too much for him, and he became frightfully ill. The doctors said he'd have to go to a warmer climate.

MRS. LINDE: Yes, you spent a whole year in Italy, didn't you?

NORA: Yes. It wasn't easy for me to get away, you know. I'd just had Ivar. But of course we had to do it. Oh, it was a marvelous trip! And it saved Torvald's life. But it cost an awful lot of money, Christine.

MRS. LINDE: I can imagine.

NORA: Two hundred and fifty pounds.° That's a lot of money, you know.

MRS. LINDE: How lucky you had it.

NORA: Well, actually, we got it from my father.

MRS. LINDE: Oh, I see. Didn't he die just about that time?

NORA: Yes, Christine, just about then. Wasn't it dreadful, I couldn't go and look after him. I was expecting little Ivar any day. And then I had my poor Torvald to care for—we really didn't think he'd live. Dear, kind Papa! I never saw him again, Christine. Oh, it's the saddest thing that's happened to me since I got married.

MRS. LINDE: I know you were very fond of him. But you went to Italy—?

NORA: Yes. Well, we had the money, you see, and the doctors said we mustn't delay. So we went the month after Papa died.

Two hundred and fifty pounds, in the Norwegian text, 4800 kroner, worth approximately $29,000 today.

MRS. LINDE: And your husband came back completely cured?

NORA: Fit as a fiddle!

MRS. LINDE: But—the doctor?

NORA: How do you mean?

MRS. LINDE: I thought the maid said that the gentleman who arrived with me was the doctor.

NORA: Oh yes, that's Doctor Rank, but he doesn't come because anyone's ill. He's our best friend, and he looks us up at least once every day. No, Torvald hasn't had a moment's illness since we went away. And the children are fit and healthy and so am I. (Jumps up and claps her hands.) Oh God, oh God, Christine, isn't it a wonderful thing to be alive and happy! Oh, but how beastly of me! I'm only talking about myself. (Sits on a footstool and rests her arms on MRS. LINDE's knee.) Oh, please don't be angry with me! Tell me, is it really true you didn't love your husband? Why did you marry him, then?

MRS. LINDE: Well, my mother was still alive; and she was helpless and bedridden. And I had my two little brothers to take care of. I didn't feel I could say no.

NORA: Yes, well, perhaps you're right. He was rich then, was he?

MRS. LINDE: Quite comfortably off, I believe. But his business was unsound, you see, Nora. When he died it went bankrupt, and there was nothing left.

NORA: What did you do?

MRS. LINDE: Well, I had to try to make ends meet somehow, so I started a little shop, and a little school, and anything else I could turn my hand to. These last three years have been just one endless slog for me, without a moment's rest. But now it's over, Nora. My poor dear mother doesn't need me any more; she's passed away. And the boys don't need me either; they've got jobs now and can look after themselves.

NORA: How relieved you must feel—

MRS. LINDE: No, Nora. Just unspeakably empty. No one to live for any more. (Gets up restlessly.) That's why I couldn't bear to stay out there any longer, cut off from the world. I thought it'd be easier to find some work here that will exercise and occupy my mind. If only I could get a regular job—office work of some kind—

NORA: Oh but, Christine, that's dreadfully exhausting; and you look practically finished already. It'd be much better for you if you could go away somewhere.

MRS. LINDE (goes over to the window): I have no Papa to pay for my holidays, Nora.

NORA (gets up): Oh, please don't be angry with me.

MRS. LINDE: My dear Nora, it's I who should ask you not to be angry. That's the worst thing about this kind of situation—it makes one so bitter. One has no one to work for; and yet one has to be continually sponging for jobs. One has to live; and so one becomes completely egocentric. When you told me about this luck you've just had with Torvald's new job—can you imagine?—I was happy not so much on your account, as on my own.

NORA: How do you mean? Oh, I understand. You mean Torvald might be able to do something for you?

MRS. LINDE: Yes, I was thinking that.

NORA: He will too, Christine. Just you leave it to me. I'll lead up to it so delicately, so delicately; I'll get him in the right mood. Oh, Christine, I do so want to help you.

MRS. LINDE: It's sweet of you to bother so much about me, Nora. Especially since you know so little of the worries and hardships of life.

NORA: You say I know little of—?

MRS. LINDE (smiles): Well, good heavens—those bits of fancy work of yours—well, really—! You're a child, Nora.

NORA (tosses her head and walks across the room): You shouldn't say that so patronizingly.

MRS. LINDE: Oh?

NORA: You're like the rest. You all think I'm incapable of getting down to anything serious—

MRS. LINDE: My dear—

NORA: You think I've never had any worries like the rest of you.

MRS. LINDE: Nora dear, you've just told me about all your difficulties—

NORA: Pooh—that! (Quietly.) I haven't told you about the big thing.

MRS. LINDE: What big thing? What do you mean?

NORA: You patronize me, Christine; but you shouldn't. You're proud that you've worked so long and so hard for your mother.

MRS. LINDE: I don't patronize anyone, Nora. But you're right—I am both proud and happy that I was able to make my mother's last months on earth comparatively easy.

NORA: And you're also proud at what you've done for your brothers.

MRS. LINDE: I think I have a right to be.

NORA: I think so too. But let me tell you something, Christine. I too have done something to be proud and happy about.

MRS. LINDE: I don't doubt it. But—how do you mean?

NORA: Speak quietly! Suppose Torvald should hear! He mustn't, at any price—no one must know, Christine—no one but you.

MRS. LINDE: But what is this?

NORA: Come over here. (Pulls her down on to the sofa beside her.) Yes, Christine—I too have done something to be happy and proud about. It was I who saved Torvald's life.

MRS. LINDE: Saved his—? How did you save it?

NORA: I told you about our trip to Italy. Torvald couldn't have lived if he hadn't managed to get down there—

MRS. LINDE: Yes, well—your father provided the money—

NORA (smiles): So Torvald and everyone else thinks. But—

MRS. LINDE: Yes?

NORA: Papa didn't give us a penny. It was I who found the money.

MRS. LINDE: You? All of it?

NORA: Two hundred and fifty pounds. What do you say to that?

MRS. LINDE: But Nora, how could you? Did you win a lottery or something?

NORA (scornfully): Lottery? (Sniffs.) What would there be to be proud of in that?

MRS. LINDE: But where did you get it from, then?

NORA (hums and smiles secretively): Hm; tra-la-la-la!

MRS. LINDE: You couldn't have borrowed it.

NORA: Oh? Why not?

MRS. LINDE: Well, a wife can't borrow money without her husband's consent.

NORA (tosses her head): Ah, but when a wife has a little business sense, and knows how to be clever—

MRS. LINDE: But Nora, I simply don't understand—

NORA: You don't have to. No one has said I borrowed the money. I could have got it in some other way. (Throws herself back on the sofa.) I could have got it from an admirer. When a girl's as pretty as I am—

MRS. LINDE: Nora, you're crazy!

NORA: You're dying of curiosity now, aren't you, Christine?

MRS. LINDE: Nora, dear, you haven't done anything foolish?

NORA (sits up again): Is it foolish to save one's husband's life?

MRS. LINDE: I think it's foolish if without his knowledge you—

NORA: But the whole point was that he mustn't know! Great heavens, don't you see? He hadn't to know how dangerously ill he was. I was the one they told that his life was in danger and that only going to a warm climate could save him. Do you suppose I didn't try to think of other ways of getting him down there? I told him how wonderful it would be for me to go abroad like other young wives: I cried and prayed; I asked him to remember my condition, and said he ought to be nice and tender to me; and then I suggested he might quite easily borrow the money. But then he got almost angry with me, Christine. He said I was frivolous, and that it was his duty as a husband not to pander to my moods and caprices—I think that's what he called them. Well, well, I thought, you've got to be saved somehow. And then I thought of a way—

MRS. LINDE: But didn't your husband find out from your father that the money hadn't come from him?

NORA: No, never. Papa died just then. I'd thought of letting him into the plot and asking him not to tell. But since he was so ill—! And as things turned out, it didn't become necessary.

MRS. LINDE: And you've never told your husband about this?

NORA: For heaven's sake, no! What an idea! He's frightfully strict about such matters. And besides—he's so proud of being a *man*—it'd be so painful and humiliating for him to know that he owed anything to me. It'd completely wreck our relationship. This life we have built together would no longer exist.

MRS. LINDE: Will you never tell him?

NORA (*thoughtfully, half-smiling*): Yes—some time, perhaps. Years from now, when I'm no longer pretty. You mustn't laugh! I mean of course, when Torvald no longer loves me as he does now; when it no longer amuses him to see me dance and dress up and play the fool for him. Then it might be useful to have something up my sleeve. (*Breaks off.*) Stupid, stupid, stupid! That time will never come. Well, what do you think of my big secret, Christine? I'm not completely useless, am I? Mind you, all this has caused me a frightful lot of worry. It hasn't been easy for me to meet my obligations punctually. In case you don't know, in the world of business there are things called quarterly instalments and interest, and they're a terrible problem to cope with. So I've had to scrape a little here and save a little there as best I can. I haven't been able to save much on the housekeeping money, because Torvald likes to live well, and I couldn't let the children go short of clothes—I couldn't take anything out of what he gives me for them. The poor little angels!

MRS. LINDE: So you've had to stint yourself, my poor Nora?

NORA: Of course. Well, after all, it was my problem. Whenever Torvald gave me money to buy myself new clothes, I never used more than half of it; and I always bought what was cheapest and plainest. Thank heaven anything suits me, so that Torvald's never noticed. But it made me a bit sad sometimes, because it's lovely to wear pretty clothes. Don't you think?

MRS. LINDE: Indeed it is.

NORA: And then I've found one or two other sources of income. Last winter I managed to get a lot of copying to do. So I shut myself away and wrote every evening, late into the night. Oh, I often got so tired. But it was great fun, though, sitting there working and earning money. It was almost like being a man.

MRS. LINDE: But how much have you managed to pay off like this?

NORA: Well, I can't say exactly. It's awfully difficult to keep an exact check on these kind of transactions. I only know I've paid everything I've managed to scrape together. Sometimes I really didn't know where to turn. (*Smiles.*) Then I'd sit here and imagine some rich old gentleman had fallen in love with me—

MRS. LINDE: What! What gentleman?

NORA: Silly! And that now he'd died and when they opened his will it said in big letters: "Everything I possess is to be paid forthwith to my beloved Mrs. Nora Helmer in cash."

MRS. LINDE: But, Nora dear, who was this gentleman?

NORA: Great heavens, don't you understand? There wasn't any old gentleman; he was just something I used to dream up as I sat here evening after evening wondering how on earth I could raise the money. But what does it matter? The old bore can stay imaginary as far as I'm concerned, because now I don't have to worry any longer! (*Jumps up.*) Oh, Christine, isn't it wonderful! I don't have to worry any more! No more troubles! I can play all day with the children, I can fill the house with pretty things, just the way Torvald likes. And, Christine, it'll soon be spring, and the air'll be fresh and the skies blue,—and then perhaps we'll be able to take a little trip somewhere. I shall be able to see the sun again. Oh, yes, yes, it's a wonderful thing to be alive and happy!

(*The bell rings in the hall.*)

MRS. LINDE (*gets up*): You've a visitor. Perhaps I'd better go.

NORA: No, stay. It won't be for me. It's someone for Torvald—

MAID (*in the doorway*): Excuse me, madam, a gentleman's called who says he wants to speak to the master. But I didn't know—seeing as the doctor's with him—

NORA: Who is this gentleman?

KROGSTAD (*in the doorway*): It's me, Mrs. Helmer.

(MRS. LINDE *starts, composes herself and turns away to the window.*)

NORA (*takes a step towards him and whispers tensely*): You? What is it? What do you want to talk to my husband about?

KROGSTAD: Business—you might call it. I hold a minor post in the bank, and I hear your husband is to become our new chief—

NORA: Oh—then it isn't—?

KROGSTAD: Pure business, Mrs. Helmer. Nothing more.

NORA: Well, you'll find him in his study.

(*Nods indifferently as she closes the hall door behind him. Then she walks across the room and sees to the stove.*)

MRS. LINDE: Nora, who was that man?

NORA: A lawyer called Krogstad.

MRS. LINDE: It was him, then.

NORA: Do you know that man?

MRS. LINDE: I used to know him—some years ago. He was a solicitor's clerk in our town, for a while.

NORA: Yes, of course, so he was.

MRS. LINDE: How he's changed!

NORA: He was very unhappily married, I believe.

MRS. LINDE: Is he a widower now?

NORA: Yes, with a lot of children. Ah, now it's alight.

(She closes the door of the stove and moves the rocking-chair a little to one side.)

MRS. LINDE: He does—various things now, I hear?

NORA: Does he? It's quite possible—I really don't know. But don't let's talk about business. It's so boring.

(DR. RANK enters from HELMER's study.)

RANK *(still in the doorway)*: No, no, my dear chap, don't see me out. I'll go and have a word with your wife. *(Closes the door and notices MRS. LINDE.)* Oh, I beg your pardon. I seem to be *de trop°* here too.

NORA: Not in the least. *(Introduces them.)* Dr. Rank. Mrs. Linde.

RANK: Ah! A name I have often heard in this house. I believe I passed you on the stairs as I came up.

MRS. LINDE: Yes. Stairs tire me; I have to take them slowly.

RANK: Oh, have you hurt yourself?

MRS. LINDE: No, I'm just a little run down.

RANK: Ah, is that all? Then I take it you've come to town to cure yourself by a round of parties?

MRS. LINDE: I have come here to find work.

RANK: Is that an approved remedy for being run down?

MRS. LINDE: One has to live, Doctor.

RANK: Yes, people do seem to regard it as a necessity.

NORA: Oh, really, Dr. Rank. I bet you want to stay alive.

RANK: You bet I do. However miserable I sometimes feel, I still want to go on being tortured for as long as possible. It's the same with all my patients; and with people who are morally sick, too. There's a moral cripple in with Helmer at this very moment—

MRS. LINDE *(softly)*: Oh!

NORA: Whom do you mean?

RANK: Oh, a lawyer fellow called Krogstad—you wouldn't know him. He's crippled all right; morally twisted. But even he started off by announcing, as though it were a matter of enormous importance, that he had to live.

NORA: Oh? What did he want to talk to Torvald about?

RANK: I haven't the faintest idea. All I heard was something about the bank.

NORA: I didn't know that Krog—that this man Krogstad had any connection with the bank.

---

de trop, French phrase, implying "in the way."

RANK: Yes, he's got some kind of job down there. *(to MRS. LINDE)* I wonder if in your part of the world you too have a species of human being that spends its time fussing around trying to smell out moral corruption? And when they find a case they give him some nice, comfortable position so that they can keep a good watch on him. The healthy ones just have to lump it.

MRS. LINDE: But surely it's the sick who need care most?

RANK *(shrugs his shoulders)*: Well, there we have it. It's that attitude that's turning human society into a hospital.

(NORA, lost in her own thoughts, laughs half to herself and claps her hands.)

RANK: Why are you laughing? Do you really know what society is?

NORA: What do I care about society? I think it's a bore. I was laughing at something else—something frightfully funny. Tell me, Dr. Rank—will everyone who works at the bank come under Torvald now?

RANK: Do you find that particularly funny?

NORA *(smiles and hums)*: Never mind! Never you mind! *(Walks around the room.)* Yes, I find it very amusing to think that we—I mean, Torvald—has obtained so much influence over so many people. *(Takes the paper bag from her pocket.)* Dr. Rank, would you like a small macaroon?

RANK: Macaroons! I say! I thought they were forbidden here.

NORA: Yes, well, these are some Christine gave me.

MRS. LINDE: What? I—?

NORA: All right, all right, don't get frightened. You weren't to know Torvald had forbidden them. He's afraid they'll ruin my teeth. But, dash it—for once—! Don't you agree, Dr. Rank? Here! *(Pops a macaroon into his mouth.)* You too, Christine. And I'll have one too. Just a little one. Two at the most. *(Begins to walk round again.)* Yes, now I feel really, really happy. Now there's just one thing in the world I'd really love to do.

RANK: Oh? And what is that?

NORA: Just something I'd love to say to Torvald.

RANK: Well, why don't you say it?

NORA: No, I daren't. It's too dreadful.

MRS. LINDE: Dreadful?

RANK: Well, then, you'd better not. But you can say it to us. What is it you'd so love to say to Torvald?

NORA: I've the most extraordinary longing to say: "Bloody hell!"

RANK: Are you mad?

MRS. LINDE: My dear Nora—!

RANK: Say it. Here he is.

NORA *(hiding the bag of macaroons)*: Ssh! Ssh!

(HELMER, *with his overcoat on his arm and his hat in his hand, enters from his study.*)

NORA (*goes to meet him*): Well, Torvald dear, did you get rid of him?

HELMER: Yes, he's just gone.

NORA: May I introduce you—? This is Christine. She's just arrived in town.

HELMER: Christine—? Forgive me, but I don't think—

NORA: Mrs. Linde, Torvald dear. Christine Linde.

HELMER: Ah. A childhood friend of my wife's, I presume?

MRS. LINDE: Yes, we knew each other in earlier days.

NORA: And imagine, now she's travelled all this way to talk to you.

HELMER: Oh?

MRS. LINDE: Well, I didn't really—

NORA: You see, Christine's frightfully good at office work, and she's mad to come under some really clever man who can teach her even more than she knows already—

HELMER: Very sensible, madam.

NORA: So when she heard you'd become head of the bank—it was in her local paper—she came here as quickly as she could and—Torvald, you will, won't you? Do a little something to help Christine? For my sake?

HELMER: Well, that shouldn't be impossible. You are a widow, I take it, Mrs. Linde?

MRS. LINDE: Yes.

HELMER: And you have experience of office work?

MRS. LINDE: Yes, quite a bit.

HELMER: Well then, it's quite likely I may be able to find some job for you—

NORA (*claps her hands*): You see, you see!

HELMER: You've come at a lucky moment, Mrs. Linde.

MRS. LINDE: Oh, how can I ever thank you—?

HELMER: There's absolutely no need. (*Puts on his overcoat.*) But now I'm afraid I must ask you to excuse me—

RANK: Wait. I'll come with you.

(*He gets his fur coat from the hall and warms it at the stove.*)

NORA: Don't be long, Torvald dear.

HELMER: I'll only be an hour.

NORA: Are you going too, Christine?

MRS. LINDE (*puts on her outdoor clothes*): Yes, I must start to look round for a room.

HELMER: Then perhaps we can walk part of the way together.

NORA (*helps her*): It's such a nuisance we're so cramped here—I'm afraid we can't offer to—

MRS. LINDE: Oh, I wouldn't dream of it. Goodbye, Nora dear, and thanks for everything.

NORA: Au revoir. You'll be coming back this evening, of course. And you too, Dr. Rank. What? If you're well enough? Of course you'll be well enough. Wrap up warmly, though.

(*They go out, talking, into the hall. Children's voices are heard from the stairs.*)

NORA: Here they are! Here they are!

(*She runs out and opens the door.* ANNE-MARIE, *the nurse, enters with the children.*)

NORA: Come in, come in! (*Stoops down and kisses them.*) Oh, my sweet darlings—! Look at them, Christine! Aren't they beautiful?

RANK: Don't stand here chattering in this draught!

HELMER: Come, Mrs. Linde. This is for mothers only.

(DR. RANK, HELMER, *and* MRS. LINDE *go down the stairs. The* NURSE *brings the children into the room.* NORA *follows, and closes the door to the hall.*)

NORA: How well you look! What red cheeks you've got! Like apples and roses! (*The children answer her inaudibly as she talks to them.*) Have you had fun? That's splendid. You gave Emmy and Bob a ride on the sledge? What, both together? I say! What a clever boy you are, Ivar! Oh, let me hold her for a moment, Anne-Marie! My sweet little baby doll! (*Takes the smallest child from the* NURSE *and dances with her.*) Yes, yes, Mummy will dance with Bob too. What? Have you been throwing snowballs? Oh, I wish I'd been there! No, don't—I'll undress them myself, Anne-Marie. No, please let me; it's such fun. Go inside and warm yourself; you look frozen. There's some hot coffee on the stove. (*The* NURSE *goes into the room on the left.* NORA *takes off the children's outdoor clothes and throws them anywhere while they all chatter simultaneously.*) What? A big dog ran after you? But he didn't bite you? No, dogs don't bite lovely little baby dolls. Leave those parcels alone, Ivar. What's in them? Ah, wouldn't you like to know! No, no; it's nothing nice. Come on, let's play a game. What shall we play? Hide and seek. Yes, let's play hide and seek. Bob shall hide first. You want me to? All right, let me hide first.

(NORA *and the children play around the room, and in the adjacent room to the left, laughing and shouting. At length* NORA *hides under the table. The children rush in, look, but cannot find her. Then they hear her half-stifled laughter, run to the table, lift up the cloth and see her. Great excitement. She crawls out as though to frighten them. Further excitement. Meanwhile, there has been a knock on the door leading from the hall, but no one has noticed it. Now the door is half-opened and* KROGSTAD *enters. He waits for a moment; the game continues.*)

KROGSTAD: Excuse me, Mrs. Helmer—

NORA (*turns with a stifled cry and half jumps up*): Oh! What do you want?

KROGSTAD: I beg your pardon; the front door was ajar. Someone must have forgotten to close it.

NORA (*gets up*): My husband is not at home, Mr. Krogstad.

KROGSTAD: I know.

NORA: Well, what do you want here, then?

KROGSTAD: A word with you.

NORA: With—? (*to the children, quietly*) Go inside to Anne-Marie. What? No, the strange gentleman won't do anything to hurt Mummy. When he's gone we'll start playing again.

(*She takes the children into the room on the left and closes the door behind them.*)

NORA (*uneasy, tense*): You want to speak to me?

KROGSTAD: Yes.

NORA: Today? But it's not the first of the month yet.

KROGSTAD: No, it is Christmas Eve. Whether or not you have a merry Christmas depends on you.

NORA: What do you want? I can't give you anything today—

KROGSTAD: We won't talk about that for the present. There's something else. You have a moment to spare?

NORA: Oh, yes. Yes, I suppose so; though—

KROGSTAD: Good. I was sitting in the café down below and I saw your husband cross the street—

NORA: Yes.

KROGSTAD: With a lady.

NORA: Well?

KROGSTAD: Might I be so bold as to ask: was not that lady a Mrs. Linde?

NORA: Yes.

KROGSTAD: Recently arrived in town?

NORA: Yes, today.

KROGSTAD: She is a good friend of yours, is she not?

NORA: Yes, she is. But I don't see—

KROGSTAD: I used to know her too once.

NORA: I know.

KROGSTAD: Oh? You've discovered that. Yes, I thought you would. Well then, may I ask you a straight question: is Mrs. Linde to be employed at the bank?

NORA: How dare you presume to cross-examine me, Mr. Krogstad? You, one of my husband's employees? But since you ask, you shall have an answer. Yes, Mrs. Linde is to be employed by the bank. And I arranged it, Mr. Krogstad. Now you know.

KROGSTAD: I guessed right, then.

NORA (*walks up and down the room*): Oh, one has a little influence, you know. Just because one's a woman it doesn't necessarily mean that—When one is in a humble position, Mr. Krogstad, one should think twice before offending someone who—hm—

KROGSTAD: —who has influence?

NORA: Precisely.

KROGSTAD (*changes his tone*): Mrs. Helmer, will you have the kindness to use your influence on my behalf?

NORA: What? What do you mean?

KROGSTAD: Will you be so good as to see that I keep my humble position at the bank?

NORA: What do you mean? Who is thinking of removing you from your position?

KROGSTAD: Oh, you don't need to play the innocent with me. I realize it can't be very pleasant for your friend to risk bumping into me; and now I also realize whom I have to thank for being hounded out like this.

NORA: But I assure you—

KROGSTAD: Look, let's not beat about the bush. There's still time, and I'd advise you to use your influence to stop it.

NORA: But, Mr. Krogstad, I have no influence!

KROGSTAD: Oh? I thought you just said—

NORA: But I didn't mean it like that! I? How on earth could you imagine that I would have any influence over my husband?

KROGSTAD: Oh, I've known your husband since we were students together. I imagine he has his weaknesses like other married men.

NORA: If you speak impertinently of my husband, I shall show you the door.

KROGSTAD: You're a bold woman, Mrs. Helmer.

NORA: I'm not afraid of you any longer. Once the New Year is in, I'll soon be rid of you.

KROGSTAD (*more controlled*): Now listen to me, Mrs. Helmer. If I'm forced to, I shall fight for my little job at the bank as I would fight for my life.

NORA: So it sounds.

KROGSTAD: It isn't just the money; that's the last thing I care about. There's something else—well, you might as well know. It's like this, you see. You know of course, as everyone else does, that some years ago I committed an indiscretion.

NORA: I think I did hear something—

KROGSTAD: It never came into court; but from that day, every opening was barred to me. So I turned my hand to the kind of business you know about. I had to do something; and I don't think I was one of the worst. But now I want to give up all that. My sons are growing up; for their sake, I must try to regain what respectability I can. This job in the bank was the first step on the ladder. And now your husband wants to kick me off that ladder back into the dirt.

NORA: But my dear Mr. Krogstad, it simply isn't in my power to help you.

KROGSTAD: You say that because you don't want to help me. But I have the means to make you.

NORA: You don't mean you'd tell my husband that I owe you money?

KROGSTAD: And if I did?

NORA: That'd be a filthy trick! (*Almost in tears.*) This

secret that is my pride and my joy—that he should hear about it in such a filthy, beastly way— hear about it from you! It'd involve me in the most dreadful unpleasantness—

KROGSTAD: Only—unpleasantness?

NORA (*vehemently*): All right, do it! You'll be the one who'll suffer. It'll show my husband the kind of man you are, and then you'll never keep your job.

KROGSTAD: I asked you whether it was merely domestic unpleasantness you were afraid of.

NORA: If my husband hears about it, he will of course immediately pay you whatever is owing. And then we shall have nothing more to do with you.

KROGSTAD (*Takes a step closer*): Listen, Mrs. Helmer. Either you've a bad memory or else you know very little about financial transactions. I had better enlighten you.

NORA: What do you mean?

KROGSTAD: When your husband was ill, you came to me to borrow two hundred and fifty pounds.

NORA: I didn't know anyone else.

KROGSTAD: I promised to find that sum for you—

NORA: And you did find it.

KROGSTAD: I promised to find that sum for you on certain conditions. You were so worried about your husband's illness and so keen to get the money to take him abroad that I don't think you bothered much about the details. So it won't be out of place if I refresh your memory. Well—I promised to get you the money in exchange for an I.O.U., which I drew up.

NORA: Yes, and which I signed.

KROGSTAD: Exactly. But then I added a few lines naming your father as security for the debt. This paragraph was to be signed by your father.

NORA: Was to be? He did sign it.

KROGSTAD: I left the date blank for your father to fill in when he signed this paper. You remember, Mrs. Helmer?

NORA: Yes, I think so—

KROGSTAD: Then I gave you back this I.O.U. for you to post to your father. Is that not correct?

NORA: Yes.

KROGSTAD: And of course you posted it at once; for within five or six days you brought it along to me with your father's signature on it. Whereupon I handed you the money.

NORA: Yes, well. Haven't I repaid the instalments as agreed?

KROGSTAD: Mm—yes, more or less. But to return to what we were speaking about—that was a difficult time for you just then, wasn't it, Mrs. Helmer?

NORA: Yes, it was.

KROGSTAD: Your father was very ill, if I am not mistaken.

NORA: He was dying.

KROGSTAD: He did in fact die shortly afterwards?

NORA: Yes.

KROGSTAD: Tell me, Mrs. Helmer, do you by any chance remember the date of your father's death? The day of the month, I mean.

NORA: Papa died on the twenty-ninth of September.

KROGSTAD: Quite correct; I took the trouble to confirm it. And that leaves me with a curious little problem—(*Takes out a paper.*)—which I simply cannot solve.

NORA: Problem? I don't see—

KROGSTAD: The problem, Mrs. Helmer, is that your father signed this paper three days after his death.

NORA: What? I don't understand—

KROGSTAD: Your father died on the twenty-ninth of September. But look at this. Here your father has dated his signature the second of October. Isn't that a curious little problem, Mrs. Helmer? (*Nora is silent.*) Can you suggest any explanation? (*She remains silent.*) And there's another curious thing. The words "second of October" and the year are written in a hand which is not your father's, but which I seem to know. Well, there's a simple explanation to that. Your father could have forgotten to write in the date when he signed, and someone else could have added it before the news came of his death. There's nothing criminal about that. It's the signature itself I'm wondering about. It *is* genuine, I suppose, Mrs. Helmer? It was your father who wrote his name here?

NORA (*after a short silence, throws back her head and looks defiantly at him*): No, it was not. It was I who wrote Papa's name there.

KROGSTAD: Look, Mrs. Helmer, do you realize this is a dangerous admission?

NORA: Why? You'll get your money.

KROGSTAD: May I ask you a question? Why didn't you send this paper to your father?

NORA: I couldn't. Papa was very ill. If I'd asked him to sign this, I'd have had to tell him what the money was for. But I couldn't have told him in his condition that my husband's life was in danger. I couldn't have done that!

KROGSTAD: Then you would have been wiser to have given up your idea of a holiday.

NORA: But I couldn't! It was to save my husband's life. I couldn't put it off.

KROGSTAD: But didn't it occur to you that you were being dishonest towards me?

NORA: I couldn't bother about that. I didn't care about you. I hated you because of all the beastly difficulties you'd put in my way when you knew how dangerously ill my husband was.

KROGSTAD: Mrs. Helmer, you evidently don't appreciate exactly what you have done. But I can assure you that it is no bigger nor worse a crime than the one I once committed, and thereby ruined my whole social position.

NORA: You? Do you expect me to believe that you would have taken a risk like that to save your wife's life?

KROGSTAD: The law does not concern itself with motives.

NORA: Then the law must be very stupid.

KROGSTAD: Stupid or not, if I show this paper to the police, you will be judged according to it.

NORA: I don't believe that. Hasn't a daughter the right to shield her father from worry and anxiety when he's old and dying? Hasn't a wife the right to save her husband's life? I don't know much about the law, but there must be something somewhere that says that such things are allowed. You ought to know about that, you're meant to be a lawyer, aren't you? You can't be a very good lawyer, Mr. Krogstad.

KROGSTAD: Possibly not. But business, the kind of business we two have been transacting—I think you'll admit I understand something about that? Good. Do as you please. But I tell you this. If I get thrown into the gutter for a second time, I shall take you with me.

(*He bows and goes out through the hall.*)

NORA (*stands for a moment in thought, then tosses her head*): What nonsense! He's trying to frighten me! I'm not that stupid. (*Busies herself gathering together the children's clothes; then she suddenly stops.*) But—? No, it's impossible. I did it for love, didn't I?

THE CHILDREN (*in the doorway, left*): Mummy, the strange gentleman's gone out into the street.

NORA: Yes, yes, I know. But don't talk to anyone about the strange gentleman. You hear? Not even to Daddy.

CHILDREN: No, Mummy. Will you play with us again now?

NORA: No, no. Not now.

CHILDREN: Oh but, Mummy, you promised!

NORA: I know, but I can't just now. Go back to the nursery. I've got a lot to do. Go away, my darlings, go away. (*She pushes them gently into the other room, and closes the door behind them. She sits on the sofa, takes up her embroidery, stitches for a few moments, but soon stops.*) No! (*Throws the embroidery aside, gets up, goes to the door leading to the hall and calls.*) Helen! Bring in the Christmas tree! (*She goes to the table on the left and opens the drawer in it; then pauses again.*) No, but it's utterly impossible!

MAID (*enters with the tree*): Where shall I put it, madam?

NORA: There, in the middle of the room.

MAID: Will you be wanting anything else?

NORA: No, thank you. I have everything I need.

(*The* MAID *puts down the tree and goes out.*)

NORA (*busy decorating the tree*): Now—candles here—and flowers here. That loathsome man! Non-sense, nonsense, there's nothing to be frightened about. The Christmas tree must be beautiful. I'll do everything that you like, Torvald. I'll sing for you, dance for you—

(HELMER, *with a bundle of papers under his arm, enters.*)

NORA: Oh—are you back already?

HELMER: Yes. Has anyone been here?

NORA: Here? No.

HELMER: That's strange. I saw Krogstad come out of the front door.

NORA: Did you? Oh yes, that's quite right—Krogstad was here for a few minutes.

HELMER: Nora, I can tell from your face, he's been here and asked you to put in a good word for him.

NORA: Yes.

HELMER: And you were to pretend you were doing it of your own accord? You weren't going to tell me he'd been here? He asked you to do that too, didn't he?

NORA: Yes, Torvald. But—

HELMER: Nora, Nora! And you were ready to enter into such a conspiracy? Talking to a man like that, and making him promises—and then, on top of it all, to tell me an untruth!

NORA: An untruth?

HELMER: Didn't you say no one had been here? (*Wags his finger.*) My little songbird must never do that again. A songbird must have a clean beak to sing with; otherwise she'll start twittering out of tune. (*Puts his arm around her waist.*) Isn't that the way we want things? Yes, of course it is. (*Lets go of her.*) So let's hear no more about that. (*Sits down in front of the stove.*) Ah, how cosy and peaceful it is here. (*Glances for a few moments at his papers.*)

NORA (*busy with the tree, after a short silence*): Torvald.

HELMER: Yes.

NORA: I'm terribly looking forward to that fancy dress ball at the Stenborgs on Boxing Day.°

HELMER: And I'm terribly curious to see what you're going to surprise me with.

NORA: Oh, it's so maddening.

HELMER: What is?

NORA: I can't think of anything to wear. It all seems so stupid and meaningless.

HELMER: So my little Nora's come to that conclusion, has she?

NORA (*behind his chair, resting her arms on its back*): Are you very busy, Torvald?

HELMER: Oh—

NORA: What are those papers?

HELMER: Just something to do with the bank.

NORA: Already?

HELMER: I persuaded the trustees to give me authority

Boxing Day, British phrase, December 26th.

to make certain immediate changes in the staff and organization. I want to have everything straight by the New Year.

NORA: Then that's why this poor man Krogstad—

HELMER: Hm.

NORA (*still leaning over his chair, slowly strokes the back of his head*): If you hadn't been so busy, I was going to ask you an enormous favour, Torvald.

HELMER: Well, tell me. What was it to be?

NORA: You know I trust your taste more than anyone's. I'm so anxious to look really beautiful at the fancy dress ball. Torvald, couldn't you help me to decide what I shall go as, and what kind of costume I ought to wear?

HELMER: Aha! So little Miss Independent's in trouble and needs a man to rescue her, does she?

NORA: Yes, Torvald. I can't get anywhere without your help.

HELMER: Well, well, I'll give the matter thought. We'll find something.

NORA: Oh, how kind of you! (*Goes back to the tree. Pause.*) How pretty these red flowers look! But, tell me is it so dreadful, this thing that Krogstad's done?

HELMER: He forged someone else's name. Have you any idea what that means?

NORA: Mightn't he have been forced to do it by some emergency?

HELMER: He probably just didn't think—that's what usually happens. I'm not so heartless as to condemn a man for an isolated action.

NORA: No, Torvald, of course not!

HELMER: Men often succeed in re-establishing themselves if they admit their crime and take their punishment.

NORA: Punishment?

HELMER: But Krogstad didn't do that. He chose to try and trick his way out of it, and that's what has morally destroyed him.

NORA: You think that would—?

HELMER: Just think how a man with that load on his conscience must always be lying and cheating and dissembling; how he must wear a mask even in the presence of those who are dearest to him, even his own wife and children! Yes, the children. That's the worst danger, Nora.

NORA: Why?

HELMER: Because an atmosphere of lies contaminates and poisons every corner of the home. Every breath that the children draw in such a house contains the germs of evil.

NORA (*comes closer behind him*): Do you really believe that?

HELMER: Oh, my dear, I've come across it so often in my work at the bar. Nearly all young criminals are the children of mothers who are constitutional liars.

NORA: Why do you say mothers?

HELMER: It's usually the mother; though of course the father can have the same influence. Every lawyer knows that only too well. And yet this fellow Krogstad has been sitting at home all these years poisoning his children with his lies and pretences. That's why I say that, morally speaking, he is dead. (*Stretches out his hands toward her.*) So my pretty little Nora must promise me not to plead his case. Your hand on it. Come, come, what's this? Give me your hand. There. That's settled, now. I assure you it'd be quite impossible for me to work in the same building as him. I literally feel physically ill in the presence of a man like that.

NORA (*draws her hand from his and goes over to the other side of the Christmas tree*): How hot it is in here! And I've so much to do.

HELMER (*gets up and gathers his papers*): Yes, and I must try to get some of this read before dinner. I'll think about your costume too. And I may even have something up my sleeve to hang in gold paper on the Christmas tree. (*Lays his hand on her head.*) My precious little songbird!

(*He goes into his study and closes the door.*)

NORA (*softly, after a pause*): It's nonsense. It must be. It's impossible. It *must* be impossible!

NURSE (*in the doorway, left*): The children are asking if they can come in to Mummy.

NORA: No, no, no; don't let them in! You stay with them, Anne-Marie.

NURSE: Very good, madam. (*Closes the door.*)

NORA (*pale with fear*): Corrupt my little children—! Poison my home! (*Short pause. She throws back her head.*) It isn't true! It *couldn't* be true!

ACT 2

(*The same room. In the corner by the piano the Christmas tree stands, stripped and disheveled, its candles burned to their sockets. NORA's outdoor clothes lie on the sofa. She is alone in the room, walking restlessly to and fro. At length she stops by the sofa and picks up her coat.*)

NORA (*drops the coat again*): There's someone coming! (*Goes to the door and listens.*) No, it's no one. Of course—no one'll come today, it's Christmas Day. Nor tomorrow. But perhaps—! (*Opens the door and looks out.*) No. Nothing in the letter-box. Quite empty. (*Walks across the room.*) Silly, silly. Of course he won't do anything. It couldn't happen. It isn't possible. Why, I've three small children.

(*The NURSE, carrying a large cardboard box, enters from the room on the left.*)

NURSE: I found those fancy dress clothes at last, madam.

NORA: Thank you. Put them on the table.

NURSE (*does so*): They're all rumpled up.

NORA: Oh, I wish I could tear them into a million pieces!

NURSE: Why, madam! They'll be all right. Just a little patience.

NORA: Yes, of course. I'll go and get Mrs. Linde to help me.

NURSE: What, out again? In this dreadful weather? You'll catch a chill, madam.

NORA: Well, that wouldn't be the worst. How are the children?

NURSE: Playing with their Christmas presents, poor little dears. But—

NORA: Are they still asking to see me?

NURSE: They're so used to having their Mummy with them.

NORA: Yes, but, Anne-Marie, from now on I shan't be able to spend so much time with them.

NURSE: Well, children get used to anything in time.

NORA: Do you think so? Do you think they'd forget their mother if she went away from them—for ever?

NURSE: Mercy's sake, madam! For ever!

NORA: Tell me, Anne-Marie—I've so often wondered. How could you bear to give your child away—to strangers?

NURSE: But I had to when I came to nurse my little Miss Nora.

NORA: Do you mean you wanted to?

NURSE: When I had the chance of such a good job? A poor girl what's got into trouble can't afford to pick and choose. That good-for-nothing didn't lift a finger.

NORA: But your daughter must have completely forgotten you.

NURSE: Oh no, indeed she hasn't. She's written to me twice, once when she got confirmed and then again when she got married.

NORA (hugs her): Dear old Anne-Marie, you were a good mother to me.

NURSE: Poor little Miss Nora, you never had any mother but me.

NORA: And if my little ones had no one else, I know you would—no, silly, silly, silly! (Opens the cardboard box.) Go back to them, Anne-Marie. Now I must—Tomorrow you'll see how pretty I shall look.

NURSE: Why, there'll be no one at the ball as beautiful as my Miss Nora.

(She goes into the room, left.)

NORA (begins to unpack the clothes from the box, but soon throws them down again): Oh, if only I dared go out! If I could be sure no one would come and nothing would happen while I was away! Stupid, stupid! No one will come. I just mustn't think about it. Brush this muff. Pretty gloves, pretty gloves! Don't think about it, don't think about it!

One, two, three, four, five, six—(Cries.) Ah—they're coming—!

(She begins to run towards the door, but stops uncertainly. MRS. LINDE enters from the hall, where she has been taking off her outdoor clothes.)

NORA: Oh, it's you, Christine. There's no one else out there, is there? Oh, I'm so glad you've come.

MRS. LINDE: I hear you were at my room asking for me.

NORA: Yes, I just happened to be passing. I want to ask you to help me with something. Let's sit down here on the sofa. Look at this. There's going to be a fancy dress ball tomorrow night upstairs at Consul Stenborg's, and Torvald wants me to go as a Neapolitan fisher-girl and dance the tarantella.° I learned it on Capri.

MRS. LINDE: I say, are you going to give a performance?

NORA: Yes, Torvald says I should. Look, here's the dress. Torvald had it made for me in Italy; but now it's all so torn, I don't know—

MRS. LINDE: Oh, we'll soon put that right; the stitching's just come away. Needle and thread? Ah, here we are.

NORA: You're being awfully sweet.

MRS. LINDE (sews): So you're going to dress up tomorrow, Nora? I must pop over for a moment to see how you look. Oh, but I've completely forgotten to thank you for that nice evening yesterday.

NORA (gets up and walks across the room): Oh, I didn't think it was as nice as usual. You ought to have come to town a little earlier, Christine. . . . Yes, Torvald understands how to make a home look attractive.

MRS. LINDE: I'm sure you do, too. You're not your father's daughter for nothing. But tell me. Is Dr. Rank always in such low spirits as he was yesterday?

NORA: No, last night it was very noticeable. But he's got a terrible disease; he's got spinal tuberculosis, poor man. His father was a frightful creature who kept mistresses and so on. As a result Dr. Rank has been sickly ever since he was a child—you understand—

MRS. LINDE (puts down her sewing): But, my dear Nora, how on earth did you get to know about such things?

NORA (walks about the room): Oh, don't be silly, Christine—when one has three children, one comes into contact with women who—well, who know about medical matters, and they tell one a thing or two.

---

tarantella, exuberant Italian dance whose name derives from the tarantula, a poisonous spider.

MRS. LINDE (*sews again; a short silence*): Does Dr. Rank visit you every day?

NORA: Yes, every day. He's Torvald's oldest friend, and a good friend to me too. Dr. Rank's almost one of the family.

MRS. LINDE: But, tell me—is he quite sincere? I mean, doesn't he rather say the sort of thing he thinks people want to hear?

NORA: No, quite the contrary. What gave you that idea?

MRS. LINDE: When you introduced me to him yesterday, he said he'd often heard my name mentioned here. But later I noticed your husband had no idea who I was. So how could Dr. Rank—?

NORA: Yes, that's quite right, Christine. You see, Torvald's so hopelessly in love with me that he wants to have me all to himself—those were his very words. When we were first married, he got quite jealous if I as much as mentioned any of my old friends back home. So naturally, I stopped talking about them. But I often chat with Dr. Rank about that kind of thing. He enjoys it, you see.

MRS. LINDE: Now listen, Nora. In many ways you're still a child; I'm a bit older than you and have a little more experience of the world. There's something I want to say to you. You ought to give up this business with Dr. Rank.

NORA: What business?

MRS. LINDE: Well, everything. Last night you were speaking about this rich admirer of yours who was going to give you money—

NORA: Yes, and who doesn't exist—unfortunately. But what's that got to do with—?

MRS. LINDE: Is Dr. Rank rich?

NORA: Yes.

MRS. LINDE: And he has no dependents?

NORA: No, no one. But—

MRS. LINDE: And he comes here to see you every day?

NORA: Yes, I've told you.

MRS. LINDE: But how dare a man of his education be so forward?

NORA: What on earth are you talking about?

MRS. LINDE: Oh, stop pretending, Nora. Do you think I haven't guessed who it was who lent you that two hundred pounds?

NORA: Are you out of your mind? How could you imagine such a thing? A friend, someone who comes every day! Why, that'd be an impossible situation!

MRS. LINDE: Then it really wasn't him?

NORA: No, of course not. I've never for a moment dreamed of—anyway, he hadn't any money to lend then. He didn't come into that till later.

MRS. LINDE: Well, I think that was a lucky thing for you, Nora dear.

NORA: No, I could never have dreamed of asking Dr. Rank—though I'm sure that if I ever did ask him—

MRS. LINDE: But of course you won't.

NORA: Of course not. I can't imagine that it should ever become necessary. But I'm perfectly sure that if I did speak to Dr. Rank—

MRS. LINDE: Behind your husband's back?

NORA: I've got to get out of this other business; and *that's* been going on behind his back. I've *got* to get out of it.

MRS. LINDE: Yes, well, that's what I told you yesterday. But—

NORA (*walking up and down*): It's much easier for a man to arrange these things than a woman—

MRS. LINDE: One's own husband, yes.

NORA: Oh, bosh. (*Stops walking.*) When you've completely repaid a debt, you get your I.O.U. back, don't you?

MRS. LINDE: Yes, of course.

NORA: And you can tear it into a thousand pieces and burn the filthy, beastly thing!

MRS. LINDE (*looks hard at her, puts down her sewing and gets up slowly*): Nora, you're hiding something from me.

NORA: Can you see that?

MRS. LINDE: Something has happened since yesterday morning. Nora, what is it?

NORA (*goes toward her*): Christine! (*Listens.*) Ssh! There's Torvald. Would you mind going into the nursery for a few minutes? Torvald can't bear to see sewing around. Anne-Marie'll help you.

MRS. LINDE (*gathers some of her things together*): Very well. But I shan't leave this house until we've talked this matter out.

(*She goes into the nursery, left. As she does so,* HELMER *enters from the hall.*)

NORA (*runs to meet him*): Oh, Torvald dear, I've been so longing for you to come back!

HELMER: Was that the dressmaker?

NORA: No, it was Christine. She's helping me mend my costume. I'm going to look rather splendid in that.

HELMER: Yes, that was quite a bright idea of mine, wasn't it?

NORA: Wonderful! But wasn't it nice of me to give in to you?

HELMER (*takes her chin in his hand*): Nice—to give in to your husband? All right, little silly, I know you didn't mean it like that. But I won't disturb you. I expect you'll be wanting to try it on.

NORA: Are you going to work now?

HELMER: Yes. (*Shows her a bundle of papers.*) Look at these. I've been down to the bank—(*Turns to go into his study.*)

NORA: Torvald.

HELMER (*stops*): Yes.

NORA: If little squirrel asked you really prettily to grant her a wish—

HELMER: Well?

NORA: Would you grant it to her?

HELMER: First I should naturally have to know what it was.

NORA: Squirrel would do lots of pretty tricks for you if you granted her wish.

HELMER: Out with it, then.

NORA: Your little skylark would sing in every room—

HELMER: My little skylark does that already.

NORA: I'd turn myself into a little fairy and dance for you in the moonlight, Torvald.

HELMER: Nora, it isn't that business you were talking about this morning?

NORA (comes closer): Yes, Torvald—oh, please! I beg of you!

HELMER: Have you really the nerve to bring that up again?

NORA: Yes, Torvald, yes, you must do as I ask! You must let Krogstad keep his place at the bank!

HELMER: My dear Nora, his is the job I'm giving to Mrs. Linde.

NORA: Yes, that's terribly sweet of you. But you can get rid of one of the other clerks instead of Krogstad.

HELMER: Really, you're being incredibly obstinate. Just because you thoughtlessly promised to put in a word for him, you expect me to—

NORA: No, it isn't that, Helmer. It's for your own sake. That man writes for the most beastly newspapers—you said so yourself. He could do you tremendous harm. I'm so dreadfully frightened of him—

HELMER: Oh, I understand. Memories of the past. That's what's frightening you.

NORA: What do you mean?

HELMER: You're thinking of your father, aren't you?

NORA: Yes, yes. Of course. Just think what those dreadful men wrote in the papers about Papa! The most frightful slanders. I really believe it would have lost him his job if the Ministry hadn't sent you down to investigate, and you hadn't been so kind and helpful to him.

HELMER: But my dear little Nora, there's a considerable difference between your father and me. Your father was not a man of unassailable reputation. But I am; and I hope to remain so all my life.

NORA: But no one knows what spiteful people may not dig up. We could be so peaceful and happy now, Torvald—we could be free from every worry—you and I and the children. Oh, please Torvald, please—!

HELMER: The very fact of your pleading his cause makes it impossible for me to keep him. Everyone at the bank already knows that I intend to dismiss Krogstad. If the rumor got about that the new manager had allowed his wife to persuade him to change his mind—

NORA: Well, what then?

HELMER: Oh, nothing, nothing. As long as my little Miss Obstinate gets her way—! Do you expect me to make a laughing-stock of myself before my entire staff—give people the idea that I am open to outside influence? Believe me, I'd soon feel the consequences! Besides—there's something else that makes it impossible for Krogstad to remain in the bank while I am its manager.

NORA: What is that?

HELMER: I might conceivably have allowed myself to ignore his moral obloquies—

NORA: Yes, Torvald, surely?

HELMER: And I hear he's quite efficient at his job. But we—well, we were schoolfriends. It was one of those friendships that one enters into overhastily and so often comes to regret later in life. I might as well confess the truth. We—well, we're on Christian name terms. And the tactless idiot makes no attempt to conceal it when other people are present. On the contrary, he thinks it gives him the right to be familiar with me. He shows off the whole time, with "Torvald this," and "Torvald that." I can tell you, I find it damned annoying. If he stayed, he'd make my position intolerable.

NORA: Torvald, you can't mean this seriously.

HELMER: Oh? And why not?

NORA: But it's so petty.

HELMER: What did you say? Petty? You think I am petty?

NORA: No, Torvald dear, of course you're not. That's just why—

HELMER: Don't quibble! You call my motives petty. Then I must be petty too. Petty! I see. Well, I've had enough of this. (Goes to the door and calls into the hall.) Helen!

NORA: What are you going to do?

HELMER (searching among his papers): I'm going to settle this matter once and for all. (The MAID enters.) Take this letter downstairs at once. Find a messenger and see that he delivers it. Immediately! The address is on the envelope. Here's the money.

MAID: Very good, sir. (Goes out with the letter.)

HELMER (putting his papers in order): There now, little Miss Obstinate.

NORA (tensely): Torvald—what was in that letter?

HELMER: Krogstad's dismissal.

NORA: Call her back, Torvald! There's still time. Oh, Torvald, call her back! Do it for my sake—for your own sake—for the children! Do you hear me, Torvald? Please do it! You don't realize what this may do to us all!

HELMER: Too late.

NORA: Yes. Too late.

HELMER: My dear Nora, I forgive you this anxiety. Though it is a bit of an insult to me. Oh, but it is!

Isn't it an insult to imply that I should be frightened by the vindictiveness of a depraved hack journalist? But I forgive you, because it so charmingly testifies to the love you bear me. *(Takes her in his arms.)* Which is as it should be, my own dearest Nora. Let what will happen, happen. When the real crisis comes, you will not find me lacking in strength or courage. I am man enough to bear the burden for us both.

NORA *(fearfully)*: What do you mean?

HELMER: The whole burden, I say—

NORA *(calmly)*: I shall never let you do that.

HELMER: Very well. We shall share it, Nora—as man and wife. And that is as it should be. *(Caresses her.)* Are you happy now? There, there, there; don't look at me with those frightened little eyes. You're simply imagining things. You go ahead now and do your tarantella, and get some practice on that tambourine. I'll sit in my study and close the door. Then I won't hear anything, and you can make all the noise you want. *(Turns in the doorway.)* When Dr. Rank comes, tell him where to find me. *(He nods to her, goes into his room with his papers and closes the door.)*

NORA *(desperate with anxiety, stands as though transfixed, and whispers)*: He said he'd do it. He will do it. He will do it, and nothing'll stop him. No, never that. I'd rather anything. There must be some escape—! Some way out—! *(The bell rings in the hall.)* Dr. Rank—! Anything but that! Anything, I don't care—!

(She passes her hand across her face, composes herself, walks across and opens the door to the hall. DR. RANK is standing there, hanging up his fur coat. During the following scene it begins to grow dark.)

NORA: Good evening, Dr. Rank. I recognized your ring. But you mustn't go in to Torvald yet. I think he's busy.

RANK: And—you?

NORA *(as he enters the room and she closes the door behind him)*: Oh, you know very well I've always time to talk to you.

RANK: Thank you. I shall avail myself of that privilege as long as I can.

NORA: What do you mean by that? As long as you *can*?

RANK: Yes. Does that frighten you?

NORA: Well, it's rather a curious expression. Is something going to happen?

RANK: Something I've been expecting to happen for a long time. But I didn't think it would happen quite so soon.

NORA *(seizes his arm)*: What is it? Dr. Rank, you must tell me!

RANK *(sits down by the stove)*: I'm on the way out. And there's nothing to be done about it.

NORA *(sighs with relief)*: Oh, it's you—?

RANK: Who else? No, it's no good lying to oneself. I am the most wretched of all my patients, Mrs. Helmer. These last few days I've been going through the books of this poor body of mine, and I find I am bankrupt. Within a month I may be rotting up there in the churchyard.

NORA: Ugh, what a nasty way to talk!

RANK: The facts aren't exactly nice. But the worst is that there's so much else that's nasty to come first. I've only one more test to make. When that's done I'll have a pretty accurate idea of when the final disintegration is likely to begin. I want to ask you a favor. Helmer's a sensitive chap, and I know how he hates anything ugly. I don't want him to visit me when I'm in hospital—

NORA: Oh but, Dr. Rank—

RANK: I don't want him there. On any pretext. I shan't have him allowed in. As soon as I know the worst, I'll send you my visiting card with a black cross on it, and then you'll know that the final filthy process has begun.

NORA: Really, you're being quite impossible this evening. And I did hope you'd be in a good mood.

RANK: With death on my hands? And all this to atone for someone else's sin? Is there justice in that? And in every single family, in one way or another, the same merciless law of retribution is at work—

NORA *(holds her hands to her ears)*: Nonsense! Cheer up! Laugh!

RANK: Yes, you're right. Laughter's all the damned thing's fit for. My poor innocent spine must pay for the fun my father had as a gay young lieutenant.

NORA *(at the table, left)*: You mean he was too fond of asparagus and *foie gras*?°

RANK: Yes; and truffles too.

NORA: Yes, of course, truffles, yes. And oysters too, I suppose?

RANK: Yes, oysters, oysters. Of course.

NORA: And all that port and champagne to wash them down. It's too sad that all those lovely things should affect one's spine.

RANK: Especially a poor spine that never got any pleasure out of them.

NORA: Oh yes, that's the saddest thing of all.

RANK *(looks searchingly at her)*: Hm—

NORA *(after a moment)*: Why did you smile?

RANK: No, it was you who laughed.

NORA: No, it was you who smiled, Dr. Rank!

RANK *(gets up)*: You're a worse little rogue than I thought.

NORA: Oh, I'm full of stupid tricks today.

RANK: So it seems.

NORA *(puts both her hands on his shoulders)*: Dear, dear

---

foie gras, pâté of goose liver.

Dr. Rank, you mustn't die and leave Torvald and me.

RANK: Oh, you'll soon get over it. Once one is gone, one is soon forgotten.

NORA (*looks at him anxiously*): Do you believe that?

RANK: One finds replacements, and then—

NORA: Who will find a replacement?

RANK: You and Helmer both will, when I am gone. You seem to have made a start already, haven't you? What was this Mrs. Linde doing here yesterday evening?

NORA: Aha! But surely you can't be jealous of poor Christine?

RANK: Indeed I am. She will be my successor in this house. When I have moved on, this lady will—

NORA: Ssh—don't speak so loud! She's in there!

RANK: Today again? You see!

NORA: She's only come to mend my dress. Good heavens, how unreasonable you are! (*Sits on the sofa.*) Be nice now, Dr. Rank. Tomorrow you'll see how beautifully I shall dance; and you must imagine that I'm doing it just for you. And for Torvald, of course; obviously. (*Takes some things out of the box.*) Dr. Rank, sit down here and I'll show you something.

RANK (*sits*): What's this?

NORA: Look here! Look!

RANK: Silk stockings!

NORA: Flesh-coloured. Aren't they beautiful? It's very dark in here now, of course, but tomorrow—! No, no, no; only the soles. Oh well, I suppose you can look a bit higher if you want to.

RANK: Hm—

NORA: Why are you looking so critical? Don't you think they'll fit me?

RANK: I can't really give you a qualified opinion on that.

NORA (*looks at him for a moment*): Shame on you! (*Flicks him on the ear with the stockings.*) Take that. (*Puts them back in the box.*)

RANK: What other wonders are to be revealed to me?

NORA: I shan't show you anything else. You're being naughty.

(*She hums a little and looks among the things in the box.*)

RANK (*after a short silence*): When I sit here like this being so intimate with you, I can't think—I cannot imagine what would have become of me if I had never entered this house.

NORA (*smiles*): Yes, I think you enjoy being with us, don't you?

RANK (*more quietly, looking into the middle distance*): And now to have to leave it all—

NORA: Nonsense. You're not leaving us.

RANK (*as before*): And not to be able to leave even the most wretched token of gratitude behind; hardly even a passing sense of loss; only an empty place, to be filled by the next comer.

NORA: Suppose I were to ask you to—? No—

RANK: To do what?

NORA: To give me proof of your friendship—

RANK: Yes, yes?

NORA: No, I mean—to do me a very great service—

RANK: Would you really for once grant me that happiness?

NORA: But you've no idea what it is.

RANK: Very well, tell me, then.

NORA: No, but, Dr. Rank, I can't. It's far too much—I want your help and advice, and I want you to do something for me.

RANK: The more the better. I've no idea what it can be. But tell me. You do trust me, don't you?

NORA: Oh, yes, more than anyone. You're my best and truest friend. Otherwise I couldn't tell you. Well then, Dr. Rank—there's something you must help me to prevent. You know how much Torvald loves me—he'd never hesitate for an instant to lay down his life for me—

RANK (*leans over toward her*): Nora—do you think he is the only one—?

NORA (*with a slight start*): What do you mean?

RANK: Who would gladly lay down his life for you?

NORA (*sadly*): Oh, I see.

RANK: I swore to myself I would let you know that before I go. I shall never have a better opportunity. . . . Well, Nora, now you know that. And now you also know that you can trust me as you can trust nobody else.

NORA (*rises; calmly and quietly*): Let me pass, please.

RANK (*makes room for her but remains seated*): Nora—

NORA (*in the doorway to the hall*): Helen, bring the lamp. (*Goes over to the stove.*) Oh, dear Dr. Rank, this was really horrid of you.

RANK (*gets up*): That I have loved you as deeply as anyone else has? Was that horrid of me?

NORA: No—but that you should go and tell me. That was quite unnecessary—

RANK: What do you mean? Did you know, then—?

(*The* MAID *enters with the lamp, puts it on the table and goes out.*)

RANK: Nora—Mrs. Helmer—I am asking you, did you know this?

NORA: Oh, what do I know, what did I know, what didn't I know—I really can't say. How could you be so stupid, Dr. Rank? Everything was so nice.

RANK: Well, at any rate now you know that I am ready to serve you, body and soul. So—please continue.

NORA (*looks at him*): After this?

RANK: Please tell me what it is.

NORA: I can't possibly tell you now.

RANK: Yes, yes! You mustn't punish me like this. Let me be allowed to do what I can for you.

NORA: You can't do anything for me now. Anyway, I

don't need any help. It was only my imagina-tion—you'll see. Yes, really. Honestly. (*Sits in the rocking chair, looks at him and smiles.*) Well, upon my word you *are* a fine gentleman, Dr. Rank. Aren't you ashamed of yourself, now that the lamp's been lit?

RANK: Frankly, no. But perhaps I ought to say—*adieu?*

NORA: Of course not. You will naturally continue to visit us as before. You know quite well how Tor-vald depends on your company.

RANK: Yes, but you?

NORA: Oh, I always think it's enormous fun having you here.

RANK: That was what misled me. You're a riddle to me, you know. I'd often felt you'd just as soon be with me as with Helmer.

NORA: Well, you see, there are some people whom one loves, and others whom it's almost more fun to be with.

RANK: Oh yes, there's some truth in that.

NORA: When I was at home, of course I loved Papa best. But I always used to think it was terribly amusing to go down and talk to the servants; because they never told me what I ought to do; and they were such fun to listen to.

RANK: I see. So I've taken their place?

NORA (*jumps up and runs over to him*): Oh, dear sweet Dr. Rank, I didn't mean that at all. But I'm sure you understand—I feel the same about Torvald as I did about Papa.

MAID (*enters from the hall*): Excuse me, madam. (*Whis-pers to her and hands her a visiting card.*)

NORA (*glances at the card*): Oh! (*Puts it quickly in her pocket.*)

RANK: Anything wrong?

NORA: No, no, nothing at all. It's just something that—it's my new dress.

RANK: What? But your costume is lying over there.

NORA: Oh—that, yes—but there's another—I ordered it specially—Torvald mustn't know—

RANK: Ah, so that's your big secret?

NORA: Yes, yes. Go in and talk to him—he's in his study—keep him talking for a bit—

RANK: Don't worry. He won't get away from me. (*Goes into* HELMER's *study.*)

NORA (*to the* MAID): Is he waiting in the kitchen?

MAID: Yes, madam, he came up the back way—

NORA: But didn't you tell him I had a visitor?

MAID: Yes, but he wouldn't go.

NORA: Wouldn't go?

MAID: No, madam, not until he'd spoken with you.

NORA: Very well, show him in; but quietly. Helen, you mustn't tell anyone about this. It's a surprise for my husband.

MAID: Very good, madam. I understand. (*Goes.*)

NORA: It's happening. It's happening after all. No, no, no, it can't happen, it mustn't happen.

(*She walks across and bolts the door of* HELMER's *study. The* MAID *opens the door from the hall to admit* KROGSTAD, *and closes it behind him. He is wearing an overcoat, heavy boots and a fur cap.*)

NORA (*goes toward him.*): Speak quietly. My husband's at home.

KROGSTAD: Let him hear.

NORA: What do you want from me?

KROGSTAD: Information.

NORA: Hurry up, then. What is it?

KROGSTAD: I suppose you know I've been given the sack.

NORA: I couldn't stop it, Mr. Krogstad. I did my best for you, but it didn't help.

KROGSTAD: Does your husband love you so little? He knows what I can do to you, and yet he dares to—

NORA: Surely you don't imagine I told him?

KROGSTAD: No, I didn't really think you had. It wouldn't have been like my old friend Torvald Helmer to show that much courage—

NORA: Mr. Krogstad, I'll trouble you to speak respect-fully of my husband.

KROGSTAD: Don't worry, I'll show him all the respect he deserves. But since you're so anxious to keep this matter hushed up, I presume you're better informed than you were yesterday of the gravity of what you've done?

NORA: I've learned more than you could ever teach me.

KROGSTAD: Yes, a bad lawyer like me—

NORA: What do you want from me?

KROGSTAD: I just wanted to see how things were with you, Mrs. Helmer. I've been thinking about you all day. Even duns° and hack journalists have hearts, you know.

NORA: Show some heart, then. Think of my little children.

KROGSTAD: Have you and your husband thought of mine? Well, let's forget that. I just wanted to tell you, you don't need to take this business too seri-ously. I'm not going to take any action for the present.

NORA: Oh, no—you won't, will you? I knew it.

KROGSTAD: It can all be settled quite amicably. There's no need for it to become public. We'll keep it among the three of us.

NORA: My husband must never know about this.

KROGSTAD: How can you stop him? Can you pay the balance of what you owe me?

NORA: Not immediately.

KROGSTAD: Have you any means of raising the money during the next few days?

NORA: None that I would care to use.

---

duns, noun derived from verb meaning to demand pay-ment.

KROGSTAD: Well, it wouldn't have helped anyway. However much money you offered me now I wouldn't give you back that paper.

NORA: What are you going to do with it?

KROGSTAD: Just keep it. No one else need ever hear about it. So in case you were thinking of doing anything desperate—

NORA: I am.

KROGSTAD: Such as running away—

NORA: I am.

KROGSTAD: Or anything more desperate—

NORA: How did you know?

KROGSTAD: —just give up the idea.

NORA: How did you know?

KROGSTAD: Most of us think of that at first. I did. But I hadn't the courage—

NORA (dully): Neither have I.

KROGSTAD (relieved): It's true, isn't it? You haven't the courage either?

NORA: No. I haven't. I haven't.

KROGSTAD: It'd be a stupid thing to do anyway. Once the first little domestic explosion is over. . . . I've got a letter in my pocket here addressed to your husband—

NORA: Telling him everything?

KROGSTAD: As delicately as possible.

NORA (quickly): He must never see that letter. Tear it up. I'll find the money somehow—

KROGSTAD: I'm sorry, Mrs. Helmer, I thought I'd explained—

NORA: Oh, I don't mean the money I owe you. Let me know how much you want from my husband, and I'll find it for you.

KROGSTAD: I'm not asking your husband for money.

NORA: What do you want, then?

KROGSTAD: I'll tell you. I want to get on my feet again, Mrs. Helmer. I want to get to the top. And your husband's going to help me. For eighteen months now my record's been clean. I've been in hard straits all that time; I was content to fight my way back inch by inch. Now I've been chucked back into the mud, and I'm not going to be satisfied with just getting back my job. I'm going to get to the top, I tell you. I'm going to get back into the bank, and it's going to be higher up. Your husband's going to create a new job for me—

NORA: He'll never do that!

KROGSTAD: Oh, yes he will. I know him. He won't dare to risk a scandal. And once I'm in there with him, you'll see! Within a year I'll be his right-hand man. It'll be Nils Krogstad who'll be running that bank, not Torvald Helmer!

NORA: That will never happen.

KROGSTAD: Are you thinking of—?

NORA: Now I *have* the courage.

KROGSTAD: Oh, you can't frighten me. A pampered little pretty like you—

NORA: You'll see! You'll see!

KROGSTAD: Under the ice? Down in the cold, black water? And then, in the spring to float up again, ugly, unrecognizable, hairless—?

NORA: You can't frighten me.

KROGSTAD: And you can't frighten me. People don't do such things, Mrs. Helmer. And anyway, what'd be the use? I've got him in my pocket.

NORA: But afterwards? When I'm no longer—?

KROGSTAD: Have you forgotten that then your reputation will be in my hands? (She looks at him speechlessly.) Well, I've warned you. Don't do anything silly. When Helmer's read my letter, he'll get in touch with me. And remember, it's your husband who's forced me to act like this. And for that I'll never forgive him. Goodbye, Mrs. Helmer. (He goes out through the hall.)

NORA (runs to the hall door, opens it a few inches and listens): He's going. He's not going to give him the letter. Oh, no, no, it couldn't possibly happen. (Opens the door a little wider). What's he doing? Standing outside the front door. He's not going downstairs. Is he changing his mind? Yes, he—!

(A letter falls into the letter-box. KROGSTAD's footsteps die away down the stairs.)

NORA (with a stifled cry, runs across the room toward the table by the sofa. A pause): In the letter-box. (Steals timidly over toward the hall door.) There it is! Oh, Torvald, Torvald! Now we're lost!

MRS. LINDE (enters from the nursery with NORA's costume): Well, I've done the best I can. Shall we see how it looks—?

NORA (whispers hoarsely): Christine, come here.

MRS. LINDE (throws the dress on the sofa): What's wrong with you? You look as though you'd seen a ghost!

NORA: Come here. Do you see that letter? There—look—through the glass of the letter-box.

MRS. LINDE: Yes, yes, I see it.

NORA: That letter's from Krogstad—

MRS. LINDE: Nora! It was Krogstad who lent you the money!

NORA: Yes. And now Torvald's going to discover everything.

MRS. LINDE: Oh, believe me, Nora, it'll be best for you both.

NORA: You don't know what's happened. I've committed a forgery—

MRS. LINDE: But, for heaven's sake—!

NORA: Christine, all I want is for you to be my witness.

MRS. LINDE: What do you mean? Witness what?

NORA: If I should go out of my mind—and it might easily happen—

MRS. LINDE: Nora!

NORA: Or if anything else should happen to me—so that I wasn't here any longer—

MRS. LINDE: Nora, Nora, you don't know what you're saying!

NORA: If anyone should try to take the blame, and say it was all his fault—you understand—?

MRS. LINDE: Yes, yes—but how can you think—?

NORA: Then you must testify that it isn't true, Christine. I'm not mad—I know exactly what I'm saying—and I'm telling you, no one else knows anything about this. I did it entirely on my own. Remember that.

MRS. LINDE: All right. But I simply don't understand—

NORA: Oh, how could you understand? A miracle—is—about to happen.

MRS. LINDE: Miracle?

NORA: Yes. A miracle. But it's so frightening, Christine. It *mustn't* happen, not for anything in the world.

MRS. LINDE: I'll go over and talk to Krogstad.

NORA: Don't go near him. He'll only do something to hurt you.

MRS. LINDE: Once upon a time he'd have done anything for my sake.

NORA: He?

MRS. LINDE: Where does he live?

NORA: Oh, how should I know—? Oh yes, wait a moment—! *(Feels in her pocket.)* Here's his card. But the letter, the letter—!

HELMER *(from his study, knocks on the door)*: Nora!

NORA *(cries in alarm)*: What is it?

HELMER: Now, now, don't get alarmed. We're not coming in, you've closed the door. Are you trying on your costume?

NORA: Yes, yes—I'm trying on my costume. I'm going to look so pretty for you, Torvald.

MRS. LINDE *(who has been reading the card)*: Why, he lives just round the corner.

NORA: Yes; but it's no use. There's nothing to be done now. The letter's lying there in the box.

MRS. LINDE: And your husband has the key?

NORA: Yes, he always keeps it.

MRS. LINDE: Krogstad must ask him to send the letter back unread. He must find some excuse—

NORA: But Torvald always opens the box at just about this time—

MRS. LINDE: You must stop him. Go in and keep him talking. I'll be back as quickly as I can.

(She hurries out through the hall.)

NORA *(goes over to HELMER's door, opens it and peeps in)*: Torvald!

HELMER *(offstage)*: Well, may a man enter his own drawing room again? Come on, Rank, now we'll see what—*(In the doorway.)* But what's this?

NORA: What, Torvald dear?

HELMER: Rank's been preparing me for some great transformation scene.

RANK *(in the doorway)*: So I understood. But I seem to have been mistaken.

NORA: Yes, no one's to be allowed to see me before tomorrow night.

HELMER: But, my dear Nora, you look quite worn out. Have you been practising too hard?

NORA: No, I haven't practised at all yet.

HELMER: Well, you must.

NORA: Yes, Torvald, I must, I know. But I can't get anywhere without your help. I've completely forgotten everything.

HELMER: Oh, we'll soon put that to rights.

NORA: Yes, help me, Torvald. Promise me you will? Oh, I'm so nervous. All those people—! You must forget everything except me this evening. You mustn't think of business—I won't even let you touch a pen. Promise me, Torvald?

HELMER: I promise. This evening I shall think of nothing but you—my poor, helpless little darling. Oh, there's just one thing I must see to—*(Goes toward the hall door.)*

NORA: What do you want out there?

HELMER: I'm only going to see if any letters have come.

NORA: No, Torvald, no!

HELMER: Why, what's the matter?

NORA: Torvald, I beg you. There's nothing there.

HELMER: Well, I'll just make sure.

(He moves toward the door. NORA runs to the piano and plays the first bars of the tarantella.)

HELMER *(at the door, turns)*: Aha!

NORA: I can't dance tomorrow if I don't practise with you now.

HELMER *(goes over to her)*: Are you really so frightened, Nora dear?

NORA: Yes, terribly frightened. Let me start practising now, at once—we've still time before dinner. Oh, do sit down and play for me, Torvald dear. Correct me, lead me, the way you always do.

HELMER: Very well, my dear, if you wish it.

(He sits down at the piano. NORA seizes the tambourine and a long multi-coloured shawl from the cardboard box, wraps the latter hastily around her, then takes a quick leap into the center of the room.)

NORA: Play for me! I want to dance!

(HELMER plays and NORA dances. DR. RANK stands behind HELMER at the piano and watches her.)

HELMER *(as he plays)*: Slower, slower!

NORA: I can't!

HELMER: Not so violently, Nora.

NORA: I must!

HELMER *(stops playing)*: No, no, this won't do at all.

NORA *(laughs and swings her tambourine)*: Isn't that what I told you?

RANK: Let me play for her.

HELMER *(gets up)*: Yes, would you? Then it'll be easier for me to show her.

(RANK *sits down at the piano and plays.* NORA *dances more and more wildly.* HELMER *has stationed himself by the stove and tries repeatedly to correct her, but she seems not to hear him. Her hair works loose and falls over her shoulders; she ignores it and continues to dance.* MRS. LINDE *enters.*)

MRS. LINDE (*stands in the doorway as though tongue-tied*): Ah—!

NORA (*as she dances*): Christine, we're having such fun!

HELMER: But, Nora darling, you're dancing as if your life depended on it.

NORA: It does.

HELMER: Rank, stop it! This is sheer lunacy. Stop it, I say!

(RANK *ceases playing.* NORA *suddenly stops dancing.*)

HELMER (*goes over to her*): I'd never have believed it. You've forgotten everything I taught you.

NORA (*throws away the tambourine*): You see!

HELMER: I'll have to show you every step.

NORA: You see how much I need you! You must show me every step of the way. Right to the end of the dance. Promise me you will, Torvald?

HELMER: Never fear. I will.

NORA: You mustn't think about anything but me—today or tomorrow. Don't open any letters—don't even open the letter-box—

HELMER: Aha, you're still worried about that fellow—

NORA: Oh, yes, yes, him too.

HELMER: Nora, I can tell from the way you're behaving, there's a letter from him already there.

NORA: I don't know. I think so. But you mustn't read it now. I don't want anything ugly to come between us till it's all over.

RANK (*quietly, to* HELMER): Better give her her way.

HELMER (*puts his arm around her*): My child shall have her way. But tomorrow night, when your dance is over—

NORA: Then you will be free.

MAID (*appears in the doorway, right*): Dinner is served, madam.

NORA: Put out some champagne, Helen.

MAID: Very good, madam. (*Goes.*)

HELMER: I say! What's this, a banquet?

NORA: We'll drink champagne until dawn! (*Calls.*) And, Helen! Put out some macaroons! Lots of macaroons—for once!

HELMER (*takes her hands in his*): Now, now, now. Don't get so excited. Where's my little songbird, the one I know?

NORA: All right. Go and sit down—and you too, Dr. Rank. I'll be with you in a minute. Christine, you must help me put my hair up.

RANK (*quietly, as they go*): There's nothing wrong, is there? I mean, she isn't—er—expecting—?

HELMER: Good heavens no, my dear chap. She just gets scared like a child sometimes—I told you before—

(*They go out right.*)

NORA: Well?

MRS. LINDE: He's left town.

NORA: I saw it from your face.

MRS. LINDE: He'll be back tomorrow evening. I left a note for him.

NORA: You needn't have bothered. You can't stop anything now. Anyway, it's wonderful really, in a way—sitting here and waiting for the miracle to happen.

MRS. LINDE: Waiting for what?

NORA: Oh, you wouldn't understand. Go in and join them. I'll be with you in a moment.

(MRS. LINDE *goes into the dining-room.*)

NORA (*stands for a moment as though collecting herself. Then she looks at her watch*): Five o'clock. Seven hours till midnight. Then another twenty-four hours till midnight tomorrow. And then the tarantella will be finished. Twenty-four and seven? Thirty-one hours to live.

HELMER (*appears in the doorway, right*): What's happened to my little songbird?

NORA (*runs to him with her arms wide*): Your songbird is here!

ACT 3

(*The same room. The table which was formerly by the sofa has been moved into the centre of the room; the chairs surround it as before. The door to the hall stands open. Dance music can be heard from the floor above.* MRS. LINDE *is seated at the table, absent-mindedly glancing through a book. She is trying to read, but seems unable to keep her mind on it. More than once she turns and listens anxiously toward the front door.*)

MRS. LINDE (*looks at her watch*): Not here yet. There's not much time left. Please God he hasn't—! (*Listens again.*) Ah, here he is. (*Goes out into the hall and cautiously opens the front door. Footsteps can be heard softly ascending the stairs. She whispers.*) Come in. There's no one here.

KROGSTAD (*in the doorway*): I found a note from you at my lodgings. What does this mean?

MRS. LINDE: I must speak with you.

KROGSTAD: Oh? And must our conversation take place in this house?

MRS. LINDE: We couldn't meet at my place; my room has no separate entrance. Come in. We're quite alone. The maid's asleep, and the Helmers are at the dance upstairs.

KROGSTAD (*comes into the room*): Well, well! So the

Helmers are dancing this evening? Are they indeed?

MRS. LINDE: Yes, why not?

KROGSTAD: True enough. Why not?

MRS. LINDE: Well, Krogstad. You and I must have a talk together.

KROGSTAD: Have we two anything further to discuss?

MRS. LINDE: We have a great deal to discuss.

KROGSTAD: I wasn't aware of it.

MRS. LINDE: That's because you've never really understood me.

KROGSTAD: Was there anything to understand? It's the old story, isn't it—a woman chucking a man because something better turns up?

MRS. LINDE: Do you really think I'm so utterly heartless? You think it was easy for me to give you up?

KROGSTAD: Wasn't it?

MRS. LINDE: Oh, Nils, did you really believe that?

KROGSTAD: Then why did you write to me the way you did?

MRS. LINDE: I had to. Since I had to break with you, I thought it my duty to destroy all the feelings you had for me.

KROGSTAD (clenches his fists): So that was it. And you did this for money!

MRS. LINDE: You mustn't forget I had a helpless mother to take care of, and two little brothers. We couldn't wait for you, Nils. It would have been so long before you'd had enough to support us.

KROGSTAD: Maybe. But you had no right to cast me off for someone else.

MRS. LINDE: Perhaps not. I've often asked myself that.

KROGSTAD (more quietly): When I lost you, it was just as though all solid ground had been swept from under my feet. Look at me. Now I am a shipwrecked man, clinging to a spar.

MRS. LINDE: Help may be near at hand.

KROGSTAD: It was near. But then you came, and stood between it and me.

MRS. LINDE: I didn't know, Nils. No one told me till today that this job I'd found was yours.

KROGSTAD: I believe you, since you say so. But now you know, won't you give it up?

MRS. LINDE: No—because it wouldn't help you even if I did.

KROGSTAD: Wouldn't it? I'd do it all the same.

MRS. LINDE: I've learned to look at things practically. Life and poverty have taught me that.

KROGSTAD: And life has taught me to distrust fine words.

MRS. LINDE: Then it's taught you a useful lesson. But surely you still believe in actions?

KROGSTAD: What do you mean?

MRS. LINDE: You said you were like a shipwrecked man clinging to a spar.

KROGSTAD: I have good reason to say it.

MRS. LINDE: I'm in the same position as you. No one to care about, no one to care for.

KROGSTAD: You made your own choice.

MRS. LINDE: I had no choice—then.

KROGSTAD: Well?

MRS. LINDE: Nils, suppose we two shipwrecked souls could join hands?

KROGSTAD: What are you saying?

MRS. LINDE: Castaways have a better chance of survival together than on their own.

KROGSTAD: Christine!

MRS. LINDE: Why do you suppose I came to this town?

KROGSTAD: You mean—you came because of me?

MRS. LINDE: I must work if I'm to find life worth living. I've always worked, for as long as I can remember; it's been the greatest joy of my life—my only joy. But now I'm alone in the world, and I feel so dreadfully lost and empty. There's no joy in working just for oneself. Oh, Nils, give me something—someone—to work for.

KROGSTAD: I don't believe all that. You're just being hysterical and romantic. You want to find an excuse for self-sacrifice.

MRS. LINDE: Have you ever known me to be hysterical?

KROGSTAD: You mean you really—? Is it possible? Tell me—you know all about my past?

MRS. LINDE: Yes.

KROGSTAD: And you know what people think of me here?

MRS. LINDE: You said just now that with me you might have become a different person.

KROGSTAD: I know I could have.

MRS. LINDE: Could it still happen?

KROGSTAD: Christine—do you really mean this? Yes—you do—I see it in your face. Have you really the courage—?

MRS. LINDE: I need someone to be a mother to; and your children need a mother. And you and I need each other. I believe in you, Nils. I am afraid of nothing—with you.

KROGSTAD (clasps her hands): Thank you, Christine—thank you! Now I shall make the world believe in me as you do! Oh—but I'd forgotten—

MRS. LINDE (listens): Ssh! The tarantella! Go quickly, go!

KROGSTAD: Why? What is it?

MRS. LINDE: You hear that dance? As soon as it's finished, they'll be coming down.

KROGSTAD: All right, I'll go. It's no good, Christine. I'd forgotten—you don't know what I've just done to the Helmers.

MRS. LINDE: Yes, Nils. I know.

KROGSTAD: And yet you'd still have the courage to—?

MRS. LINDE: I know what despair can drive a man like you to.

KROGSTAD: Oh, if only I could undo this!

MRS. LINDE: You can. Your letter is still lying in the box.

KROGSTAD: Are you sure?

MRS. LINDE: Quite sure. But—

KROGSTAD (looks searchingly): Is that why you're doing this? You want to save your friend at any price? Tell me the truth. Is that the reason?

MRS. LINDE: Nils, a woman who has sold herself once for the sake of others doesn't make the same mistake again.

KROGSTAD: I shall demand my letter back.

MRS. LINDE: No, no.

KROGSTAD: Of course I shall. I shall stay here till Helmer comes down. I'll tell him he must give me back my letter—I'll say it was only to do with my dismissal, and that I don't want him to read it—

MRS. LINDE: No, Nils, you mustn't ask for that letter back.

KROGSTAD: But—tell me—wasn't that the real reason you asked me to come here?

MRS. LINDE: Yes—at first, when I was frightened. But a day has passed since then, and in that time I've seen incredible things happen in this house. Helmer must know the truth. This unhappy secret of Nora's must be revealed. They must come to a full understanding; there must be an end of all these shiftings and evasions.

KROGSTAD: Very well. If you're prepared to risk it. But one thing I can do—and at once—

MRS. LINDE (listens): Hurry! Go, go! The dance is over. We aren't safe here another moment.

KROGSTAD: I'll wait for you downstairs.

MRS. LINDE: Yes, do. You can see me home.

KROGSTAD: I've never been so happy in my life before!

(He goes through the front door. The door leading from the room into the hall remains open.)

MRS. LINDE (tidies the room a little and gets her hat and coat): What a change! Oh, what a change! Someone to work for—to live for! A home to bring joy into! I won't let this chance of happiness slip through my fingers. Oh, why don't they come? (Listens.) Ah, here they are. I must get my coat on.

(She takes her hat and coat. HELMER's and NORA's voices become audible outside. A key is turned in the lock and HELMER leads NORA almost forcibly into the hall. She is dressed in an Italian costume with a large black shawl. He is in evening dress, with a black cloak.)

NORA (still in the doorway, resisting him): No, no, no—not in here! I want to go back upstairs. I don't want to leave so early.

HELMER: But my dearest Nora—

NORA: Oh, please, Torvald, please! Just another hour!

HELMER: Not another minute, Nora, my sweet. You know what we agreed. Come along, now. Into the drawing-room. You'll catch cold if you stay out here.

(He leads her, despite her efforts to resist him, gently into the room.)

MRS. LINDE: Good evening.

NORA: Christine!

HELMER: Oh, hullo, Mrs. Linde. You still here?

MRS. LINDE: Please forgive me. I did so want to see Nora in her costume.

NORA: Have you been sitting here waiting for me?

MRS. LINDE: Yes, I got here too late, I'm afraid. You'd already gone up. And I felt I really couldn't go back home without seeing you.

HELMER (takes off NORA's shawl): Well, take a good look at her. She's worth looking at, don't you think? Isn't she beautiful, Mrs. Linde?

MRS. LINDE: Oh, yes, indeed—

HELMER: Isn't she unbelievably beautiful? Everyone at the party said so. But dreadfully stubborn she is, bless her pretty little heart. What's to be done about that? Would you believe it, I practically had to use force to get her away!

NORA: Oh, Torvald, you're going to regret not letting me stay—just half an hour longer.

HELMER: Hear that, Mrs. Linde? She dances her tarantella—makes a roaring success—and very well deserved—though possibly a trifle too realistic—more so than was aesthetically necessary, strictly speaking. But never mind that. Main thing is—she had a success—roaring success. Was I going to let her stay on after that and spoil the impression? No, thank you. I took my beautiful little Capri signorina—my capricious little Capricienne, what?—under my arm—a swift round of the ballroom, a curtsey to the company, and, as they say in novels, the beautiful apparition disappeared! An exit should always be dramatic, Mrs. Linde. But unfortunately that's just what I can't get Nora to realize. I say, it's hot in here. (Throws his cloak on a chair and opens the door to his study.) What's this? It's dark in here. Ah, yes, of course—excuse me. (Goes in and lights a couple of candles.)

NORA (whispers swiftly, breathlessly): Well?

MRS. LINDE (quietly): I've spoken to him.

NORA: Yes?

MRS. LINDE: Nora—you must tell your husband everything.

NORA (dully): I knew it.

MRS. LINDE: You've nothing to fear from Krogstad. But you must tell him.

NORA: I shan't tell him anything.

MRS. LINDE: Then the letter will.

NORA: Thank you, Christine. Now I know what I must do. Ssh!

HELMER (returns): Well, Mrs. Linde, finished admiring her?

MRS. LINDE: Yes. Now I must say good night.

HELMER: Oh, already? Does this knitting belong to you?

MRS. LINDE (*takes it*): Thank you, yes. I nearly forgot it.

HELMER: You knit, then?

MRS. LINDE: Why, yes.

HELMER: Know what? You ought to take up embroidery.

MRS. LINDE: Oh? Why?

HELMER: It's much prettier. Watch me, now. You hold the embroidery in your left hand, like this, and then you take the needle in your right hand and go in and out in a slow, easy movement—like this. I am right, aren't I?

MRS. LINDE: Yes, I'm sure—

HELMER: But knitting, now—that's an ugly business—can't help it. Look—arms all huddled up—great clumsy needles going up and down—makes you look like a damned Chinaman. I say, that really was a magnificent champagne they served us.

MRS. LINDE: Well, good night, Nora. And stop being stubborn. Remember!

HELMER: Quite right, Mrs. Linde!

MRS. LINDE: Good night, Mr. Helmer.

HELMER (*accompanies her to the door*): Good night, good night! I hope you'll manage to get home all right? I'd gladly—but you haven't far to go, have you? Good night, good night. (*She goes. He closes the door behind her and returns.*) Well, we've got rid of her at last. Dreadful bore that woman is!

NORA: Aren't you very tired, Torvald?

HELMER: No, not in the least.

NORA: Aren't you sleepy?

HELMER: Not a bit. On the contrary, I feel extraordinarily exhilarated. But what about you? Yes, you look very sleepy and tired.

NORA: Yes, I am very tired. Soon I shall sleep.

HELMER: You see, you see! How right I was not to let you stay longer!

NORA: Oh, you're always right, whatever you do.

HELMER (*kisses her on the forehead*): Now my little songbird's talking just like a real big human being. I say, did you notice how cheerful Rank was this evening?

NORA: Oh? Was he? I didn't have a chance to speak with him.

HELMER: I hardly did. But I haven't seen him in such a jolly mood for ages. (*Looks at her for a moment, then comes closer.*) I say, it's nice to get back to one's home again, and be all alone with you. Upon my word, you're a distractingly beautiful young woman.

NORA: Don't look at me like that, Torvald!

HELMER: What, not look at my most treasured possession? At all this wonderful beauty that's mine, mine alone, all mine.

NORA (*goes round to the other side of the table*): You mustn't talk to me like that tonight.

HELMER (*follows her*): You've still the tarantella in your blood, I see. And that makes you even more desir-

able. Listen! Now the other guests are beginning to go. (*More quietly.*) Nora—soon the whole house will be absolutely quiet.

NORA: Yes, I hope so.

HELMER: Yes, my beloved Nora, of course you do! Do you know—when I'm out with you among other people like we were tonight, do you know why I say so little to you, why I keep so aloof from you, and just throw you an occasional glance? Do you know why I do that? It's because I pretend to myself that you're my secret mistress, my clandestine little sweetheart, and that nobody knows there's anything at all between us.

NORA: Oh, yes, yes, yes—I know you never think of anything but me.

HELMER: And then when we're about to go, and I wrap the shawl round your lovely young shoulders, over this wonderful curve of your neck— Then I pretend to myself that you are my young bride, that we've just come from the wedding, that I'm taking you to my house for the first time—that, for the first time, I am alone with you—quite alone with you, as you stand there young and trembling and beautiful. All evening I've had no eyes for anyone but you. When I saw you dance the tarantella, like a huntress, a temptress, my blood grew hot, I couldn't stand it any longer! That was why I seized you and dragged you down here with me—

NORA: Leave me, Torvald! Get away from me! I don't want all this.

HELMER: What? Now, Nora, you're joking with me. Don't want, don't want—? Aren't I your husband—?

(*There is a knock on the front door.*)

NORA (*starts*): What was that?

HELMER (*goes toward the hall*): Who is it?

RANK (*outside*): It's me. May I come in for a moment?

HELMER (*quietly, annoyed*): Oh, what does he want now? (*Calls.*) Wait a moment. (*Walks over and opens the door.*) Well! Nice of you not to go by without looking in.

RANK: I thought I heard your voice, so I felt I had to say goodbye. (*His eyes travel swiftly around the room.*) Ah, yes—these dear rooms, how well I know them. What a happy, peaceful home you two have.

HELMER: You seemed to be having a pretty happy time yourself upstairs.

RANK: Indeed I did. Why not? Why shouldn't one make the most of this world? As much as one can, and for as long as one can. The wine was excellent—

HELMER: Especially the champagne.

RANK: You noticed that too? It's almost incredible how much I managed to get down.

NORA: Torvald drank a lot of champagne too, this evening.

RANK: Oh?

NORA: Yes. It always makes him merry afterwards.

RANK: Well, why shouldn't a man have a merry evening after a well-spent day?

HELMER: Well-spent? Oh, I don't know that I can claim that.

RANK (*slaps him across the back*): I can, though, my dear fellow!

NORA: Yes, of course, Dr. Rank—you've been carrying out a scientific experiment today, haven't you?

RANK: Exactly.

HELMER: Scientific experiment! Those are big words for my little Nora to use!

NORA: And may I congratulate you on the finding?

RANK: You may indeed.

NORA: It was good, then?

RANK: The best possible finding—both for the doctor and the patient. Certainty.

NORA (*quickly*): Certainty?

RANK: Absolute certainty. So aren't I entitled to have a merry evening after that?

NORA: Yes, Dr. Rank. You were quite right to.

HELMER: I agree. Provided you don't have to regret it tomorrow.

RANK: Well, you never get anything in this life without paying for it.

NORA: Dr. Rank—you like masquerades, don't you?

RANK: Yes, if the disguises are sufficiently amusing.

NORA: Tell me. What shall we two wear at the next masquerade?

HELMER: You little gadabout! Are you thinking about the next one already?

RANK: We two? Yes, I'll tell you. You must go as the Spirit of Happiness—

HELMER: You try to think of a costume that'll convey that.

RANK: Your wife need only appear as her normal, every-day self—

HELMER: Quite right! Well said! But what are you going to be? Have you decided that?

RANK: Yes, my dear friend. I have decided that.

HELMER: Well?

RANK: At the next masquerade, I shall be invisible.

HELMER: Well, that's a funny idea.

RANK: There's a big, black hat—haven't you heard of the invisible hat? Once it's over your head, no one can see you any more.

HELMER (*represses a smile*): Ah yes, of course.

RANK: But I'm forgetting what I came for. Helmer, give me a cigar. One of your black Havanas.

HELMER: With the greatest pleasure. (*Offers him the box.*)

RANK (*takes one and cuts off the tip*): Thank you.

NORA (*strikes a match*): Let me give you a light.

RANK: Thank you. (*She holds out the match for him. He lights his cigar.*) And now—goodbye.

HELMER: Goodbye, my dear chap, goodbye.

NORA: Sleep well, Dr. Rank.

RANK: Thank you for that kind wish.

NORA: Wish me the same.

RANK: You? Very well—since you ask. Sleep well. And thank you for the light. (*He nods to them both and goes.*)

HELMER (*quietly*): He's been drinking too much.

NORA (*abstractedly*): Perhaps.

(HELMER *takes his bunch of keys from his pocket and goes out into the hall.*)

NORA: Torvald, what do you want out there?

HELMER: I must empty the letter-box. It's absolutely full. There'll be no room for the newspapers in the morning.

NORA: Are you going to work tonight?

HELMER: You know very well I'm not. Hullo, what's this? Someone's been at the lock.

NORA: At the lock—?

HELMER: Yes, I'm sure of it. Who on earth—? Surely not one of the maids? Here's a broken hairpin. Nora, it's yours—

NORA (*quickly*): Then it must have been the children.

HELMER: Well, you'll have to break them of that habit. Hm, hm. Ah, that's done it. (*Takes out the contents of the box and calls into the kitchen.*) Helen! Helen! Put out the light on the staircase. (*Comes back into the drawing room with the letters in his hand and closes the door to the hall.*) Look at this! You see how they've piled up? (*Glances through them.*) What on earth's this?

NORA (*at the window*): The letter! Oh, no, Torvald, no!

HELMER: Two visiting cards—from Rank.

NORA: From Dr. Rank?

HELMER (*looks at them*): Peter Rank, M.D. They were on top. He must have dropped them in as he left.

NORA: Has he written anything on them?

HELMER: There's a black cross above his name. Look. Rather gruesome, isn't it? It looks just as though he was announcing his death.

NORA: He is.

HELMER: What? Do you know something? Has he told you anything?

NORA: Yes. When these cards come, it means he's said goodbye to us. He wants to shut himself up in his house and die.

HELMER: Ah, poor fellow. I knew I wouldn't be seeing him for much longer. But so soon—! And now he's going to slink away and hide like a wounded beast.

NORA: When the time comes, it's best to go silently. Don't you think so, Torvald?

HELMER (*walks up and down*): He was so much a part of our life. I can't realize that he's gone. His suffering and loneliness seemed to provide a kind of dark background to the happy sunlight of our marriage. Well, perhaps it's best this way. For him, anyway. (*Stops walking.*) And perhaps for us too,

NORA. Now we have only each other. *(Embraces her.)* Oh, my beloved wife—I feel as though I could never hold you close enough. Do you know, Nora, often I wish some terrible danger might threaten you, so that I could offer my life and my blood, everything, for your sake.

NORA *(tears herself loose and says in a clear, firm voice):* Read your letters now, Torvald.

HELMER: No, no. Not tonight. Tonight I want to be with you, my darling wife—

NORA: When your friend is about to die—?

HELMER: You're right. This news has upset us both. An ugliness has come between us; thoughts of death and dissolution. We must try to forget them. Until then—you go to your room; I shall go to mine.

NORA *(throws her arms round his neck):* Good night, Torvald! Good night!

HELMER *(kisses her on the forehead):* Good night, my darling little songbird. Sleep well, Nora. I'll go and read my letters.

(He goes into the study with the letters in his hand, and closes the door.)

NORA *(wild-eyed, fumbles around, seizes* HELMER's *cloak, throws it round herself and whispers quickly, hoarsely):* Never see him again. Never. Never. Never. *(Throws the shawl over her head.)* Never see the children again. Them too. Never. Never. Oh—the icy black water! Oh—that bottomless—that—! Oh, if only it were all over! Now he's got it—he's reading it. Oh, no, no! Goodbye, Torvald! Goodbye, my darlings!

(She turns to run into the hall. As she does so, HELMER *throws open his door and stands there with an open letter in his hand.)*

HELMER: Nora!

NORA *(shrieks):* Ah—!

HELMER: What is this? Do you know what is in this letter?

NORA: Yes, I know. Let me go! Let me go!

HELMER *(holds her back):* Go? Where?

NORA *(tries to tear herself loose):* You mustn't try to save me, Torvald!

HELMER *(staggers back):* Is it true? Is it true, what he writes? Oh, my God! No, no—it's impossible, it can't be true!

NORA: It *is* true. I've loved you more than anything else in the world.

HELMER: Oh, don't try to make silly excuses.

NORA *(takes a step toward him):* Torvald—

HELMER: Wretched woman! What have you done?

NORA: Let me go! You're not going to suffer for my sake. I won't let you!

HELMER: Stop being theatrical. *(Locks the front door.)* You're going to stay here and explain yourself. Do you understand what you've done? Answer me! Do you understand?

NORA *(looks unflinchingly at him and, her expression growing colder, says):* Yes. Now I am beginning to understand.

HELMER *(walking round the room):* Oh, what a dreadful awakening! For eight whole years—she who was my joy and my pride—a hypocrite, a liar—worse, worse—a criminal! Oh, the hideousness of it! Shame on you, shame!

*(*NORA *is silent and stares unblinkingly at him.)*

HELMER *(stops in front of her):* I ought to have guessed that something of this sort would happen. I should have foreseen it. All your father's recklessness and instability—be quiet!—I repeat, all your father's recklessness and instability he has handed on to you. No religion, no morals, no sense of duty! Oh, how I have been punished for closing my eyes to his faults! I did it for your sake. And now you reward me like this.

NORA: Yes. Like this.

HELMER: Now you have destroyed all my happiness. You have ruined my whole future. Oh, it's too dreadful to contemplate! I am in the power of a man who is completely without scruples. He can do what he likes with me, demand what he pleases, order me to do anything—I dare not disobey him. I am condemned to humiliation and ruin simply for the weakness of a woman.

NORA: When I am gone from this world, you will be free.

HELMER: Oh, don't be melodramatic. Your father was always ready with that kind of remark. How would it help me if you were "gone from this world," as you put it? It wouldn't assist me in the slightest. He can still make all the facts public; and if he does, I may quite easily be suspected of having been an accomplice in your crime. People may think that I was behind it—that it was I who encouraged you! And for all this I have to thank you, you whom I have carried on my hands through all the years of our marriage! Now do you realize what you've done to me?

NORA *(coldly calm):* Yes.

HELMER: It's so unbelievable I can hardly credit it. But we must try to find some way out. Take off that shawl. Take it off, I say! I must try to buy him off somehow. This thing must be hushed up at any price. As regards our relationship—we must appear to be living together just as before. Only *appear*, of course. You will therefore continue to reside here. That is understood. But the children shall be taken out of your hands. I dare no longer entrust them to you. Oh, to have to say this to the woman I once loved so dearly—and whom I still—! Well, all that must be finished. Henceforth there can be no question of happiness; we must merely strive to save what shreds and tatters—(*The front door bell rings.* HELMER *starts.*) What can that be? At this hour? Surely not—? He wouldn't—? Hide yourself, Nora. Say you're ill.

(NORA *does not move.* HELMER *goes to the door of the room and opens it. The* MAID *is standing half-dressed in the hall.*)

MAID: A letter for madam.

HELMER: Give it me. (*Seizes the letter and shuts the door.*) Yes, it's from him. You're not having it. I'll read this myself.

NORA: Read it.

HELMER (*by the lamp*): I hardly dare to. This may mean the end for us both. No. I must know. (*Tears open the letter hastily; reads a few lines; looks at a piece of paper which is enclosed with it; utters a cry of joy.*) Nora! (*She looks at him questioningly.*) Nora! No—I must read it once more. Yes, yes, it's true! I am saved! Nora, I am saved!

NORA: What about me?

HELMER: You too, of course. We're both saved, you and I. Look! He's returning your I.O.U. He writes that he is sorry for what has happened—a happy accident has changed his life—oh, what does it matter what he writes? We are saved, Nora! No one can harm you now. Oh, Nora, Nora—no, first let me destroy this filthy thing. Let me see—! (*Glances at the I.O.U.*) No, I don't want to look at it. I shall merely regard the whole business as a dream. (*He tears the I.O.U. and both letters into pieces, throws them into the stove and watches them burn.*) There. Now they're destroyed. He wrote that ever since Christmas Eve you've been—oh, these must have been three dreadful days for you, Nora.

NORA: Yes. It's been a hard fight.

HELMER: It must have been terrible—seeing no way out except—no, we'll forget the whole sordid business. We'll just be happy and go on telling ourselves over and over again: "It's over! It's over!" Listen to me, Nora. You don't seem to realize. It's over! Why are you looking so pale? Ah, my poor little Nora, I understand. You can't believe that I have forgiven you. But I have, Nora. I swear it to you. I have forgiven you everything. I know that what you did you did for your love of me.

NORA: That is true.

HELMER: You have loved me as a wife should love her husband. It was simply that in your inexperience you chose the wrong means. But do you think I love you any the less because you don't know how to act on your own initiative? No, no. Just lean on me. I shall counsel you. I shall guide you. I would not be a true man if your feminine helplessness

did not make you doubly attractive in my eyes. You mustn't mind the hard words I said to you in those first dreadful moments when my whole world seemed to be tumbling about my ears. I have forgiven you, Nora. I swear it to you; I have forgiven you.

NORA: Thank you for your forgiveness.

(*She goes out through the door, right.*)

HELMER: No, don't go—(*Looks in.*) What are you doing there?

NORA (*offstage*): Taking off my fancy dress.

HELMER (*by the open door*): Yes, do that. Try to calm yourself and get your balance again, my frightened little songbird. Don't be afraid. I have broad wings to shield you. (*Begins to walk around near the door.*) How lovely and peaceful this little home of ours is, Nora. You are safe here; I shall watch over you like a hunted dove which I have snatched unharmed from the claws of the falcon. Your wildly beating little heart shall find peace with me. It will happen, Nora; it will take time, but it will happen, believe me. Tomorrow all this will seem quite different. Soon everything will be as it was before. I shall no longer need to remind you that I have forgiven you; your own heart will tell you that it is true. Do you really think I could ever bring myself to disown you, or even to reproach you? Ah, Nora, you don't understand what goes on in a husband's heart. There is something indescribably wonderful and satisfying for a husband in knowing that he has forgiven his wife—forgiven her unreservedly, from the bottom of his heart. It means that she has become his property in a double sense; he has, as it were, brought her into the world anew; she is now not only his wife but also his child. From now on that is what you shall be to me, my poor, helpless, bewildered little creature. Never be frightened of anything again, Nora. Just open your heart to me. I shall be both your will and your conscience. What's this? Not in bed? Have you changed?

NORA (*in her everyday dress*): Yes, Torvald. I've changed.

HELMER: But why now—so late—?

NORA: I shall not sleep tonight.

HELMER: But, my dear Nora—

NORA (*looks at her watch*): It isn't that late. Sit down here, Torvald. You and I have a lot to talk about.

(*She sits down on one side of the table.*)

HELMER: Nora, what does this mean? You look quite drawn—

NORA: Sit down. It's going to take a long time. I've a lot to say to you.

HELMER (*sits down on the other side of the table*): You alarm me, Nora. I don't understand you.

NORA: No, that's just it. You don't understand me. And

I've never understood you—until this evening. No, don't interrupt me. Just listen to what I have to say. You and I have got to face facts, Torvald.

HELMER: What do you mean by that?

NORA (*after a short silence*): Doesn't anything strike you about the way we're sitting here?

HELMER: What?

NORA: We've been married for eight years. Does it occur to you that this is the first time that we two, you and I, man and wife, have ever had a serious talk together?

HELMER: Serious? What do you mean, serious?

NORA: In eight whole years—no, longer—ever since we first met—we have never exchanged a serious word on a serious subject.

HELMER: Did you expect me to drag you into all my worries—worries you couldn't possibly have helped me with?

NORA: I'm not talking about worries. I'm simply saying that we have never sat down seriously to try to get to the bottom of anything.

HELMER: But, my dear Nora, what on earth has that got to do with you?

NORA: That's just the point. You have never understood me. A great wrong has been done to me, Torvald. First by Papa, and then by you.

HELMER: What? But we two have loved you more than anyone in the world!

NORA (*shakes her head*): You have never loved me. You just thought it was fun to be in love with me.

HELMER: Nora, what kind of a way is this to talk?

NORA: It's the truth, Torvald. When I lived with Papa, he used to tell me what he thought about everything, so that I never had any opinions but his. And if I did have any of my own, I kept them quiet, because he wouldn't have liked them. He called me his little doll, and he played with me just the way I played with my dolls. Then I came here to live in your house—

HELMER: What kind of a way is that to describe our marriage?

NORA (*undisturbed*): I mean, then I passed from Papa's hands into yours. You arranged everything the way you wanted it, so that I simply took over your taste in everything—or pretended I did—I don't really know—I think it was a little of both—first one and then the other. Now I look back on it, it's as if I've been living here like a pauper, from hand to mouth. I performed tricks for you, and you gave me food and drink. But that was how you wanted it. You and Papa have done me a great wrong. It's your fault that I have done nothing with my life.

HELMER: Nora, how can you be so unreasonable and ungrateful? Haven't you been happy here?

NORA: No; never. I used to think I was; but I haven't ever been happy.

HELMER: Not—not happy?

NORA: No. I've just had fun. You've always been very kind to me. But our home has never been anything but a playroom. I've been your doll-wife, just as I used to be Papa's doll-child. And the children have been my dolls. I used to think it was fun when you came in and played with me, just as they think it's fun when I go in and play games with them. That's all our marriage has been, Torvald.

HELMER: There may be a little truth in what you say, though you exaggerate and romanticize. But from now on it'll be different. Playtime is over. Now the time has come for education.

NORA: Whose education? Mine or the children's?

HELMER: Both yours and the children's, my dearest Nora.

NORA: Oh, Torvald, you're not the man to educate me into being the right wife for you.

HELMER: How can you say that?

NORA: And what about me? Am I fit to educate the children?

HELMER: Nora!

NORA: Didn't you say yourself a few minutes ago that you dare not leave them in my charge?

HELMER: In a moment of excitement. Surely you don't think I meant it seriously?

NORA: Yes. You were perfectly right. I'm not fitted to educate them. There's something else I must do first. I must educate myself. And you can't help me with that. It's something I must do by myself. That's why I'm leaving you.

HELMER (*jumps up*): What did you say?

NORA: I must stand on my own feet if I am to find out the truth about myself and about life. So I can't go on living here with you any longer.

HELMER: Nora, Nora!

NORA: I'm leaving you now, at once. Christine will put me up for tonight—

HELMER: You're out of your mind! You can't do this! I forbid you!

NORA: It's no use your trying to forbid me any more. I shall take with me nothing but what is mine. I don't want anything from you, now or ever.

HELMER: What kind of madness is this?

NORA: Tomorrow I shall go home—I mean, to where I was born. It'll be easiest for me to find some kind of a job there.

HELMER: But you're blind! You've no experience of the world—

NORA: I must try to get some, Torvald.

HELMER: But to leave your home, your husband, your children! Have you thought what people will say?

NORA: I can't help that. I only know that I must do this.

HELMER: But this is monstrous! Can you neglect your most sacred duties?

NORA: What do you call my most sacred duties?

HELMER: Do I have to tell you? Your duties towards your husband, and your children.

NORA: I have another duty which is equally sacred.

HELMER: You have not. What on earth could that be?

NORA: My duty towards myself.

HELMER: First and foremost you are a wife and a mother.

NORA: I don't believe that any longer. I believe that I am first and foremost a human being, like you—or anyway, that I must try to become one. I know most people think as you do, Torvald, and I know there's something of the sort to be found in books. But I'm no longer prepared to accept what people say and what's written in books. I must think things out for myself, and try to find my own answer.

HELMER: Do you need to ask where your duty lies in your own home? Haven't you an infallible guide in such matters—your religion?

NORA: Oh, Torvald, I don't really know what religion means.

HELMER: What are you saying?

NORA: I only know what Pastor Hansen told me when I went to confirmation. He explained that religion meant this and that. When I get away from all this and can think things out on my own, that's one of the questions I want to look into. I want to find out whether what Pastor Hansen said was right—or anyway, whether it is right for me.

HELMER: But it's unheard of for so young a woman to behave like this! If religion cannot guide you, let me at least appeal to your conscience. I presume you have some moral feelings left? Or—perhaps you haven't? Well, answer me.

NORA: Oh, Torvald, that isn't an easy question to answer. I simply don't know. I don't know where I am in these matters. I only know that these things mean something quite different to me from what they do to you. I've learned now that certain laws are different from what I'd imagined them to be; but I can't accept that such laws can be right. Has a woman really not the right to spare her dying father pain, or save her husband's life? I can't believe that.

HELMER: You're talking like a child. You don't understand how society works.

NORA: No, I don't. But now I intend to learn. I must try to satisfy myself which is right, society or I.

HELMER: Nora, you're ill; you're feverish. I almost believe you're out of your mind.

NORA: I've never felt so sane and sure in my life.

HELMER: You feel sure that it is right to leave your husband and your children?

NORA: Yes. I do.

HELMER: Then there is only one possible explanation.

NORA: What?

HELMER: That you don't love me any longer.

NORA: No, that's exactly it.

HELMER: Nora! How can you say this to me?

NORA: Oh, Torvald, it hurts me terribly to have to say it, because you've always been so kind to me. But I can't help it. I don't love you any longer.

HELMER (controlling his emotions with difficulty): And you feel quite sure about this too?

NORA: Yes, absolutely sure. That's why I can't go on living here any longer.

HELMER: Can you also explain why I have lost your love?

NORA: Yes, I can. It happened this evening, when the miracle failed to happen. It was then that I realized you weren't the man I'd thought you to be.

HELMER: Explain more clearly. I don't understand you.

NORA: I've waited so patiently, for eight whole years—well, good heavens, I'm not such a fool as to suppose that miracles occur every day. Then this dreadful thing happened to me, and then I *knew*: "Now the miracle will take place!" When Krogstad's letter was lying out there, it never occurred to me for a moment that you would let that man trample over you. I *knew* that you would say to him: "Publish the facts to the world." And when he had done this—

HELMER: Yes, what then? When I'd exposed my wife's name to shame and scandal—

NORA: Then I was certain that you would step forward and take all the blame on yourself, and say: "I am the one who is guilty!"

HELMER: Nora!

NORA: You're thinking I wouldn't have accepted such a sacrifice from you? No, of course I wouldn't! But what would my word have counted for against yours? That was the miracle I was hoping for, and dreading. And it was to prevent it happening that I wanted to end my life.

HELMER: Nora, I would gladly work for you night and day, and endure sorrow and hardship for your sake. But no man can be expected to sacrifice his honor, even for the person he loves.

NORA: Millions of women have done it.

HELMER: Oh, you think and talk like a stupid child.

NORA: That may be. But you neither think nor talk like the man I could share my life with. Once you'd got over your fright—and you weren't frightened of what might threaten me, but only of what threatened you—once the danger was past, then as far as you were concerned it was exactly as though nothing had happened. I was your little songbird just as before—your doll whom henceforth you would take particular care to protect from the world because she was so weak and fragile. (Gets up.) Torvald, in that moment I realized that for eight years I had been living here with a

complete stranger, and had borne him three children—! Oh, I can't bear to think of it! I could tear
myself to pieces!

HELMER *(sadly)*: I see it, I see it. A gulf has indeed
opened between us. Oh, but Nora—couldn't it be
bridged?

NORA: As I am now, I am no wife for you.

HELMER: I have the strength to change.

NORA: Perhaps—if your doll is taken from you.

HELMER: But to be parted—to be parted from you!
No, no, Nora, I can't conceive of it happening!

NORA *(goes into the room, right)*: All the more necessary
that it should happen.

*(She comes back with her outdoor things and a small trav-
eling-bag, which she puts down on a chair by the table.)*

HELMER: Nora, Nora, not now! Wait till tomorrow!

NORA *(puts on her coat)*: I can't spend the night in a
strange man's house.

HELMER: But can't we live here as brother and sister,
then—?

NORA *(fastens her hat)*: You know quite well it wouldn't
last. *(Puts on her shawl.)* Goodbye, Torvald. I don't
want to see the children. I know they're in better
hands than mine. As I am now, I can be nothing
to them.

HELMER: But some time, Nora—some time—?

NORA: How can I tell? I've no idea what will happen to
me.

HELMER: But you are my wife, both as you are and as
you will be.

NORA: Listen, Torvald. When a wife leaves her husband's house, as I'm doing now, I'm told that
according to the law he is freed of any obligations
towards her. In any case, I release you from any
such obligations. You mustn't feel bound to me in
any way, however small, just as I shall not feel
bound to you. We must both be quite free. Here is
your ring back. Give me mine.

HELMER: That too?

NORA: That too.

HELMER: Here it is.

NORA: Good. Well, now it's over. I'll leave the keys
here. The servants know about everything to do
with the house—much better than I do. Tomorrow, when I have left town, Christine will come to
pack the things I brought here from home. I'll
have them sent on after me.

HELMER: This is the end then! Nora, will you never
think of me any more?

NORA: Yes, of course. I shall often think of you and the
children and this house.

HELMER: May I write to you, Nora?

NORA: No. Never. You mustn't do that.

HELMER: But at least you must let me send you—

NORA: Nothing. Nothing.

HELMER: But if you should need help—?

NORA: I tell you, no. I don't accept things from
strangers.

HELMER: Nora—can I never be anything but a
stranger to you?

NORA *(picks up her bag)*: Oh, Torvald! Then the miracle of miracles would have to happen.

HELMER: The miracle of miracles?

NORA: You and I would both have to change so much
that—oh, Torvald, I don't believe in miracles any
longer.

HELMER: But I want to believe in them. Tell me. We
should have to change so much that—?

NORA: That life together between us two could
become a marriage. Goodbye.

(She goes out through the hall.)

HELMER *(sinks down on a chair by the door and buries his
face in his hands)*: Nora! Nora! *(Looks round and
gets up.)* Empty! She's gone! *(A hope strikes him.)*
The miracle of miracles—?

(The street door is slammed shut downstairs.)

Figure 1. Nora (Claire Bloom) shows Torvald (Donald Madden) a doll that she has bought as a Christmas present for one of their children in the Playhouse production of *A Doll's House,* directed by Patrick Garland, New York, 1971. (Photograph: Henry Grossman.)

Figure 3. Nora (Claire Bloom) prepares to leave Torvald (Donald Madden) in the final scene of the Playhouse production, 1971. The transformation of Nora that Claire Bloom sought to project through her performance of the role may be seen by comparing her facial expression and costume in this photograph with those shown in Figures 1 and 2. (Photograph: Henry Grossman.)

Figure 2. Torvald (Donald Madden) berates Nora (Claire Bloom) after reading the blackmail letter from Krogstad in the Playhouse production, 1971. (Photograph: Henry Grossman.)

Figure 4. Back in their home after the party at which Nora has danced the tarantella, Torvald (Owen Teale) tells Nora (Janet McTeer) how he thinks of her as his young bride, in the Belasco Theater production of *A Doll's House*, directed by Anthony Page, New York, 1997. (Photograph: Sara Krulwich/NYT Pictures.)

Figure 5. Torvald (Owen Teale) angrily confronts Nora (Janet McTeer) about the letter from Krogstad in the Belasco Theater production, 1997. (Photograph: Sara Krulwich/NYT Pictures.)

Staging of *A Doll's House*

REVIEW OF THE PLAYHOUSE PRODUCTION,
NEW YORK, 1971, BY WALTER KERR

The difficulty with Ibsen today is that we must try to take two separate things seriously, the playwright's ideas and the playwright's playwriting. The ideas, of course, present no particular problem. One has only to listen to Claire Bloom's last long speech in the current—and very sleek—revival of "A Doll's House," which will soon be alternating with "Hedda Gabler" at the Playhouse, or to glance at the brief excerpts from Ibsen's "Notes for a Modern Tragedy" that have been included in the program to know that the ideas were sound, advanced, on target. "A woman cannot be herself in modern society," the notes read. "It is an exclusively male society, with laws made by men and with prosecutors and judges who assess female conduct from a male standpoint." Kate Millett sounds old-fashioned beside that.

But how, how, how do you take the playwriting seriously? From what vantage point, what perch or roost or perspective in time, can you attend, without doubling up, to the spectacle of a woman so determined to keep a secret from her husband that she promptly spills it, virtually within his hearing, to the very first acquaintance who walks in the door? Add to that the fact that she hasn't seen the acquaintance in years, and doesn't even recognize her when they do meet, and you've got a rather peculiar secret-keeper on your hands.

Peculiar things are going to keep happening, peculiar and predictable. Ibsen did work by notebook, which means that he jotted down most logically all the little twists and turns of motivation he was going to need and then clipped them together to make a scene whether they precisely flowed or not. If they didn't flow, he forced them ("Tell me, is it true you didn't love your husband?").

The terrible danger in this shuffled-note method is that you are going to hear the papers rustling, the clips slipping on. You can't *help* hearing them. And so you know, infallibly, that the moment the child-wife Nora exclaims "Oh, God, it's good to be alive and happy!," a doorbell will ring and a furtive fellow will slip in who's going to bring down her doll's house in ruins. Just as you know, with a certainty close to hilarity, that when Nora's fatuous lord and master, Torvald, exclaims "I often wish you were threatened with some impending disaster so that I could risk everything!," disaster is not only impending but here. Torvald has only to go to the mailbox ("I'm going to see if there's any mail"), slit open the first letter to hand, and the fat is in the fire. (In the current production, the fat is not

only in the fire, Nora is on the floor, having been hurled there by a vigorous spouse who, it turns out, is willing to risk nothing.)

The underpinnings are all transparent, line by line and blow by blow, and we must struggle to induce in ourselves a state of mind that holds humor at bay in honor of the social proposition being so implausibly stated. It's a real battle, one that is often lost; Ibsen believed in his mechanics as well as in his creed, and we cannot. The effort isn't exacerbating, especially; we needn't come away exhausted from it. It is possible to look at the foolishness and feel fond, if not doting, as we wait for the message that is going to come of it all. But it's nip and tuck the whole way, and the thin ice of the situation poses extremely thorny problems for actors.

It's not only a matter of how the good lady doing Nora is going to try to stitch together the two parts of the role, the giddy, fawning creature who is willing to leap up and down like a puppy dog snatching at proffered bones for two acts and the serene, stern woman who lays down the new law in Act 3, having matured wonderfully during intermission. It's a matter of how everyone onstage, pompous husband, long-lost confidante, sniveling blackmailer, dying Dr. Rank who is willing to offer Nora his love with his next-to-last breath, is going to get us past the preposterous and into the ringing preachment. Do they try to steal home, eliding all that is awkward as quietly as possible? Do they rush it, pouncing upon line two before we have quite noticed line one? Do they stylize it, lifting themselves into daguerreotype postures that plainly have little to do with reality?

The present company, under Patrick Garland's direction, has tried taking it by storm, with a bit of the daguerreotype thrown in. Donald Madden, a Torvald who might well see Dr. Rank about hypertension, glides across the highly lacquered floor (this Nora has such difficulty getting money out of her husband that you feel he won't even allow the lady carpeting) to exchange his wife's swift kisses for quickly palmed coins as though the two were Harlequins giving a summer-park performance in a high wind. Robert Gerringer, the forger who has come to accuse Nora of forgery (motives do get piggy-backed in this odd way), keeps his mouth open and working so that no matter who is talking his teeth will show.

All work at a high pitch and in some fever, as though a Racinian *tirade* might spin off into space at any moment. (If you have never seen "A Doll's House," and I was stunned to discover how many first-nighters never had, this is a crystal-clear reading of it, laid out like silverware.) And there are some genuine successes within the near-stylization. Roy Shuman's Dr. Rank, for instance, is highly mannered: head thrown back, hands always on the point of clapping, eyes darting this way and that as he bluntly, briskly mocks himself and his approaching death. The effect is perfect, that of a man already halfway to the horizon waving farewell with his thumb to his nose. I have never seen the part more robustly or more persuasively played. Patricia Elliott's Kristine, so quickly privy to Nora's secrets, speaks vast amounts of exposition exquisitely, then zeroes in fiercely upon the play's point as she grips her shawl severely and remembers that her only happiness has lain in work.

But what of Nora? Claire Bloom has made, I think, an admirable choice, though a choice with a canker to it. Most Noras won't sacrifice the opportunity to charm, to be bird-like and winsome and if possible adorable, during the first two acts. And you can't entirely blame *them*. Nora is, as written in these acts, a ninny underneath, a girl who really can't feel any sympathy for creditors because, after all, they're "strangers," a girl who, though her secret debt is much on her mind, hasn't the faintest notion of how much of it she's paid off. She subsists, it would seem, on macaroons. But actresses who go for charm and a pretty mindlessness are stuck with the last act. How does one turn an enchanting child into a dominating adult, especially when the transition is missing?

Miss Bloom tries to create the transition from the beginning, which is surely an intelligent thing to do. Even as her Nora is nestling her pretty head against her husband's waistcoat while she seduces him with quick flattery into giving her old friend a job, there is a strain about the eyes, an indication of an intelligence withheld, that adds initial dimension to the role. Where most Noras seem to have an instinct for being playful, fluttering as to the cocoon born, Miss Bloom's playfulness is plainly put on, a trick she has learned, a device that does not wholly engage her.

She is constantly listening to herself make the sounds a pompous husband expects, aware of their insincerity and worried about the gulf between what she is doing and what she might be feeling. Faintly alienated from the outset, she has given us a base for the play's ending. The reserve that we felt in her was the conscience that might have been awakened at any time but is not in fact awakened until it is time to make that speech and slam that door.

The catch to doing it this way, because the part is split in the writing, is a curious sense of heartlessness that overtakes Nora en route. Being to a degree disengaged, she seems not only indifferent to her children and extremely obtuse about her friend Kristine's personal problems but horrendously cold-blooded about the devoted Dr. Rank. He announces his impending death and she scarcely looks up from her sewing. He makes a gesture of love toward her, a gesture that has to be disinterested because he will never see her again, and she recoils as though he had proposed, perhaps, another forgery. Clipping the butterfly's wings leaves us with something of a dragonfly. Or are we merely being given a bit of "Hedda" ahead of time?

Miss Bloom works honorably, looks well, arrives at her last scene logically, and doesn't seem anyone you'd care to trust your heart with (I'm not thinking of Torvald, who is an oaf, but, say, of Dr. Rank, who is not). Miss Bloom has cooled Nora to make the way for the ultimate avalanche; the move does take away anything that was ever very appealing about her.

Good try. The problem, which persists, lies in the play. Ibsen simply could not, or did not, get his meaning and his method to match up. When he speaks of "laws made by men" and "judges who assess female conduct from a male standpoint," we know exactly what he is talking about. We also know that he is right. But the technical illustration in the play proper runs like this. Nora has forged her father's signature to get money to help her ailing husband, who must not know he is being helped. Why didn't she have her father sign the document? Because he, too, was ailing; she didn't want to trouble him. Thus there are two kinds of law: male law (don't forge) and female law (don't bother father). Serious as the point is, the illustration can only make us smile.

The actors must try to make us contain the smile, which, in this revival, they occasionally do.

REVIEW OF THE BELASCO THEATER
PRODUCTION, NEW YORK, 1997,
BY BEN BRANTLEY

It just doesn't happen that often, and when it does, you sit there, open-mouthed, grateful, admiring and shaken, and think, "This is why I love the theater."

It's the response that comes when a dramatic performance is so completely and richly realized that you find yourself truly living through the character portrayed onstage, even when you want to pull back to a comfortable spectator's distance. The pulse quickens, the eyes well. And there is somehow the sense that ordinary life has been heightened to the bursting point.

The occasion for this revelation is the new production of Ibsen's "A Doll's House," a London import that opened last night at the Belasco Theater. The name of the revelation is Janet McTeer, an actress, little known in America, whose apparition on Broadway suggests the theater's timely answer to the Hale-Bopp comet.

What Ms. McTeer achieves, with the magnificent support of the director Anthony Page and a flawless supporting cast, is the sense that the landmark, century-old role of Ibsen's Nora Helmer, the childlike housewife who comes so painfully of age, was only just written, and written specifically for her. You may think you know "A Doll's House" inside out. This production is guaranteed to prove you wrong.

The 1879 classic, with its iconoclastic portrayal of a woman who leaves her marriage to find herself, assumed an instant, thundering social significance and that has clouded perceptions of the play. There was a theory, starting with George Bernard Shaw, that the drama's greatness was more historical than artistic, and that, like most things searingly topical, it was destined to become a fossil.

Still, the play has never left the international repertory, with great actresses repeatedly drawn to Nora like the proverbial moths to the flame. Very often, they have indeed been burned, provoking criticism that Nora's conversion from domestic plaything to proto-feminist requires radical jumps in psychological continuity, accompanied by the creaking of a mechanical, agenda-driven plot.

Not a single creak is heard in Mr. Page's production, Ms. McTeer's performance or Frank McGuinness's wonderfully loose-limbed adaptation. They never impose on Ibsen's text but instead mine it for an emotional consistency and logic that is very definitely there. And marvel of marvels, the most stirring part of this interpretation comes in its last 20 minutes, when Nora speaks the lines that, out of context, have become feminist rallying cries.

Ms. McTeer's Nora, confronting her husband, Torvald (the masterly Owen Teale), with the failure of their marriage, is no coolly articulate visionary, for whom a light has suddenly been turned on after a lifetime of benightedness. She is still fumbling in the dark, still struggling to find words to match her growing belief that something is very, very wrong. She seems surprised, in fact, by her own perceptions, as if they were only just taking form in her consciousness.

The entire evening builds carefully to this moment in ways you are aware of only after you've arrived there.

From the outset, Ms. McTeer's performance has suggested a struggle between willful self-delusion and a subterranean uneasiness that Nora reflexively works to suppress. She's a hard-working actress who doesn't even know she's playing a part or how tired she has grown of it.

Ms. McTeer starts off with a mannered intensity some audience members may at first find grating. There's a glow of fever about Nora as she busily trims her comfortably appointed living room for Christmas. The laughter with which she punctuates her speech has a loonlike quality; she tries on different, silly voices like an eager-to-please comedian; she flaps her wrists in a way that dismisses what she's saying even as she calls attention to it.

It is a brave, risky conception that even comes across as grotesque at moments, a feeling underscored by the fact that Ms. McTeer is no doll-size ingenue but a woman of towering height and erotic presence. (She compliantly bends her knees for her long, frequent kisses with Torvald.) She's a fluttery geisha in overdrive, on call to entertain and make merry whenever her husband chooses to appear from his invincible fortress of a study.

What cannot be doubted is that Nora behaves like this out of love for the man she married. It's the same impulse that drove her to commit the criminal act—the forging of her father's signature when she needed to borrow money to take her ailing husband to Italy—that provides the play with its plot. And this production ingeniously melds Nora's apprehension about being exposed by the embittered money lender Nils Krogstad (Peter Gowen) with the encroaching awareness that her love for Torvald, the center of her existence, is built on sand.

There are moments throughout, especially in Nora's scenes with her childhood friend Kristine Linde (Jan Maxwell) and her cynical admirer, Dr. Rank (John Carlisle), when shafts of light break into the doll's house, a sense of how hard and unfair the world can be and of the imbalance in the Helmers' marriage.

The scene when, in conversation with Dr. Rank, Nora realizes that her relationship with her husband is like that she had with her doting father, is remarkable both for how the perception astonishes her and for how she seems to brush it away. So when the play reaches its climax, it feels less like an abrupt turn than the inevitable end of a single, well-paved road.

Mr. Page, best known here for his productions of "Heartbreak House" (with Rex Harrison and Rosemary Harris) and "Inadmissible Evidence" (with Nicol Williamson), reminds you of the virtues of pure naturalism in theater. There's a ripe physicality to the production, an awareness of the comforts of the warmth of home and clothing (deliciously embodied by Deirdre Clancy's set and costumes) and of the literal coldness outside. (This is the first production of "A Doll's House" I've seen in which, when Nora makes her famous final exit, I worried whether she was dressed warmly enough.)

There is a definite sensual heat as well. It's apparent in the coded, tantalizing body language between Nora and Helmer; in the hungry kisses stolen by Kristine and Nils after they declare their love for each other; in Nora's mischievously displaying her silk stockings to the terminally ill Dr. Rank, an act that registers as one of infinite, if misplaced, kindness to a dying man; and, above all, in Ms. McTeer's dancing the tarantella as a giddy, erotic collapse into nervous exhaustion.

It is also hard to imagine a more persuasively balanced ensemble. Mr. Carlisle's flinty, troubled doctor; Ms. Maxwell's sober, pragmatic Kristine (a perfect foil to Ms. McTeer's agitation); Mr. Gowen's all-too-human, self-preserving desperation: these performances remind you that Ibsen did indeed create complete characters who are always waiting to be rediscovered.

As Torvald, the handsome, imposingly centered Mr. Teale couldn't be better. For once, you understand the magnetic hold this husband has over his wife, as well as why he is destined to lose her. His blunt air of authority is so compelling that when it finally shatters, the effect is devastating.

Nora leaves this broken man less in anger than in sorrow, a fitting conclusion to an evening infused not with polemical rage but with a sad compassion for the mess people make of their lives. The "something glorious" that Nora so ravenously craves, a heroic act from her husband that would redeem their marriage, doesn't happen, of course. But thanks to Ms. McTeer and company, something glorious is very definitely occurring at the Belasco.

INTERVIEW WITH JANET McTEER

"I always thought the problem was Torvald," she [McTeer] said, sitting in her dressing room recently in the Belasco Theater on West 44th Street. Often he is played as a pompous older man. "And when he's played like that," she added, "the tension is gone before it's started. From a theatrical point of view, it's a much more interesting concept to start from A and go to Zed, to have a young and vital Torvald, have them in a real marriage."

If Ms. McTeer, who on Sunday night won a Tony Award for best actress in a play, has more than her own performance on her mind, it's because the idea for

From "A Nora Beyond All Pretense," by Peter Marks, *New York Times*, 3 June, 1997.

the production—which also won Tonys for best revival, best director and best featured actor—was hatched by Ms. McTeer herself. And though she says that casting a Welsh actor, Owen Teale, as a particularly virile and domineering Torvald gave the play a rationale and emotional balance that it usually lacks, it is her frenetic, sensual performance that has drawn the most attention. . . . Fierce debates often break out among theatergoers these days over Ms. McTeer's approach to the role, especially her wildly theatrical entrance in Act I, when her Amazonian (she's 6 foot 1) dervish of a Nora, in flowing blond tresses and flouncy skirt, preens, flutters and virtually bounces off the walls of the set designer Deirdre Clancy's evocation of a home in a small Norwegian town, circa 1879. . . .

To the 35-year-old British actress, Nora is not merely Torvald's kitten. She is a caged animal who, in the course of the . . . play, . . . comes to a realization that allows her to wrestle free of the constraints that have been imposed on her, first by her father and then by her husband.

By the play's end, her Nora simply stops play-acting her role, the one assigned by societal convention. The pretense dropped, Ms. McTeer's mannerisms disappear too, as if Nora has stepped out of her neuroses.

It's a remarkable stripping away in what is a meticulously detailed and controlled performance. Ms. McTeer is able to convey the unnaturalness of a flamingo forced to act the hummingbird. "My basic contention is that she has no self-esteem," said the actress, who wears her reddish-brown hair cropped short under Nora's Barbie-dollish wig. "And she is discovering everything about herself in the moment. When she doesn't want to confront something, she flaps her hands to wave it away. It's such a psychological gesture."

"Every character I play is 6 foot 1," she added. "But I play Nora as if she doesn't want to be.". . .

Two years ago, after the actress had played Nora in a radio version for the BBC, she began to wonder if she could recreate it on the stage. The obstacle, she believed, was her height; Torvald constantly refers to Nora in diminutive terms. "I thought I was far too big to do it in real life," Ms. McTeer said, adding that she turned to a friend, the producer Thelma Holt, who encouraged her to take it on anyway. "You always see Nora as a slight, fluffy little thing," said Ms. Holt, who would go on to produce the British version and then presented it in New York with Bill Kenwright. "Here, we had the Valkyrie. She didn't see Nora as a fluffy little thing. She only saw the terror of the woman.". . .

Physical differences aside, Ms. McTeer says she felt a strange kinship with Nora. "It is, in some ways, a play about someone who's never had their own voice, and I had always felt like the odd one out." She grew up in York, in the north of England, in a family with no theatrical experience or aspirations. The closest Ms. McTeer herself had got to the stage, in fact, was the concession stand at a local theater where she sold coffee. Watching a local production of *She Stoops to Conquer,* she decided that "if I don't have a go at this, I'll regret it." So at 17 she traveled to London to audition for the major theater schools. She recalled her first audition: "I read Juliet in four-inch heels. They didn't even look up." But she prepared some other speeches, and apparently communicated an innate talent. Upon completing a monologue at one tryout, the proctor looked astonished: "He said, 'Who helped you with this speech?'" Ms. McTeer recalled. "I said, 'No one.' He said 'Where did you practice?' I said, 'In front of my mirror.'"

She was admitted to three of London's most prestigious schools, chose the Royal Academy, and has been working her way through the classical canon ever since. Asked where she had acquired the nerve to apply in the first place, she shrugged and laughed heartily. "I've always had confidence in my ability as an actor," she said, munching a chocolate chip cookie and sipping tea before an evening performance. "I'm just uncompromising."

Perhaps it takes an actress who might dive into a pool without a glance at the depth of the water to look at a character like Nora in an entirely new way. In this production, she was certainly assisted by her fellow actors, particularly Mr. Teale, whose Torvald is almost as much of a surprise as Nora. The sexual tension between them is almost palpable; if Ms. McTeer's Nora is an Amazon, Mr. Teale's Torvald is a Viking. When he sweeps her into his arms in one of many romantic moments, it's as if he means to smother her with a kiss. "It's a jigsaw; they fit each other," said Mr. Teale, who also won a Tony on Sunday night. "He asks her to play a role, and she plays it."

To some critics and other theatergoers, the play's final 20 minutes between Nora and Torvald, in which Nora explains her decision to leave her husband and children, has never seemed more lucid and wrenching. Ms. McTeer says that audiences may find the scene so powerful because, in her view, it's only in those concluding moments that Nora begins to see what a waste her life has been. It is not, in the actress's view, an angry feminist manifesto, but the announcement of the start of a search. "She doesn't know who she is," Ms. McTeer said, "but she's going to have a try."

AUGUST STRINDBERG

1849–1912

Throughout his life Strindberg suffered from a variety of psychological anxieties and compulsions, and throughout his career he exploited his personal and psychic life in his novels, short stories, poetry, essays, and plays. He was raised in Stockholm, Sweden, the fourth of twelve children and the first born in wedlock. His mother died when he was thirteen, and his father immediately married the housekeeper. Strindberg himself was married three times and divorced three times, and each of his marriages was a tormenting experience both for him and the woman, particularly his first marriage to Siri von Essen, an aspiring actress of little talent who divorced her husband, a baron, in order to marry Strindberg. Before the marriage, Strindberg had worked briefly in various jobs, as a tutor, a telegraph clerk, an actor, and a librarian, but once he became involved with Siri he devoted himself almost exclusively to his writing. They remained married from 1877 to 1891, but long before they were divorced their affection for one another had given way to sexual quarrels, mutual jealousies, and bitter recriminations. During the disintegration of the marriage, Strindberg turned out a series of autobiographical novels, among them *A Fool's Defence* (1886), based on his involvement with Siri and her former husband, as well as a series of powerful naturalistic plays, all dealing with forms of psychological and sexual strife between men and women, including *The Father* (1887), *Miss Julie* (1888), *The Creditors* (1889), and *The Stronger* (1890).

Strindberg married once again in 1893, this time a young Austrian journalist, but their relationship quickly disintegrated into many of the same patterns that had characterized his first marriage. And by 1894 Strindberg himself was beginning to experience a psychological disintegration that was to extend over the next two years, a period during which he suffered from a profound sense of guilt and spiritual torment, as well as from a variety of paranoiac hallucinations, focusing both on supernatural powers and on the doctor to whom he eventually committed himself for treatment. During this period he immersed himself in the mystical works of Emanuel Swedenborg and other religious writers, and turned his hand to painting and experiments in alchemy. By 1897, he had already chronicled his psychological and spiritual crisis in a thinly veiled autobiographical novel, *Inferno,* and by 1898 he had begun another immensely productive period of writing that was to continue until the end of his life. Overall, he produced more than seventy plays and dramatic fragments.

During the period following his psychological inferno, Strindberg turned out a series of twenty-one chronicle plays, many of them in the manner of Shakespeare's, dealing with figures and periods in Swedish history from the thirteenth to the eighteenth century. But the most important plays of his later period reflect the preoccupations that flowed from his spiritual and emotional crisis. The plays are concerned with the exposure of evil, as in *The Dance of Death* (1901), *A Dream Play* (1902), and *The Ghost Sonata* (1907), or with guilt and expiation, as in *Crime and Crime* (1899) and *Easter* (1901), or with spiritual pilgrimage, as in *To Damascus*

(1898–1904) and *The Great Highway* (1909). In these plays, Strindberg turned away from the purely naturalistic methods of his earlier plays, using expressionistic and symbolic techniques to dramatize his troubled vision of human experience. In *A Dream Play,* for example, the world is seen entirely through the experience and perception of the Daughter of Indra, the child of a deity, whose descent to earth and subsequent encounters with various human beings reflect and reproduce, as Strindberg explained in his note on the play, "the disconnected but apparently logical form of a dream." Because it is a dream, "Anything can happen; everything is possible and probable. . . . The characters are split, double and multiply; they evaporate, crystallise, scatter and converge. But a single consciousness holds sway over them all—that of the dreamer." The dreamer, of course, was Strindberg himself, and the disconnected events of the play vividly project his melancholy vision of the human landscape. *The Ghost Sonata* is another expressionistic and symbolic fantasy, this time displaying the macabre spectacle of a demonic household as it is progressively unveiled to the eyes of a young student—clearly Strindberg's alter ego—who ends the play by proclaiming the world to be "this madhouse, this prison, this charnelhouse." In their expressionistic techniques, these later plays prefigure a major aspect of modern and contemporary drama. In their preoccupation with dreams and the disconnected logic of psychic experience, they are arresting parallels to the work of Freud, whose first important study of the unconscious, *The Interpretation of Dreams,* did not appear until 1900.

But even in his naturalistic plays of the eighties, such as *Miss Julie,* Strindberg was advanced for his time, both in his dramatic techniques and in his psychological insight. He took great pains to identify his innovations in a lengthy foreword to *Miss Julie* that he wrote after the play was accepted for publication (see Ideas of Drama). He called attention, for example, to the improvisational miming of Kristin early in the play, to the improvisational miming and dancing of the peasants, and to the improvisational monologue of Kristin mumbling in her sleep. He was aware of the classical precedents for mime, dancing, and monologue in drama, much as he was aware of the Italian Renaissance precedents for improvisational performance, but he also recognized that realistic conventions of his time had excluded these dramatic possibilities from the stage, whereas he considered them not only consistent with but essential to a naturalistic illusion. In the same context, he also called attention to the fact that the play is designed to be staged without intermission, and that the set is to be diagonally arranged, "so that the actors may play full-face and in half-profile when they are sitting opposite one another at the table." He might also have pointed out that the action is set in a kitchen that really functions, for the play begins with Kristin frying a piece of kidney on the stove, and it reaches a climax with Jean beheading Julie's greenfinch on the kitchen chopping block. In all these respects, Strindberg carried naturalistic theater further than any of his contemporaries—extending it to its logical and psychological limits.

In the psychological conception of Jean and Julie, as well as in the unfolding of their relationship, Strindberg also challenged his contemporaries, particularly Emile Zola, the first major proponent of naturalism, who in 1874 had written a manifesto proclaiming that heredity and environment are the sole determinants of human nature and behavior, and that dramatists are, therefore, obliged to reflect these circumstances in their plays. Strindberg, however, was clearly not content to limit himself to so narrow a conception of human behavior as he makes clear in the foreword to *Miss Julie:*

> I see Miss Julie's tragic fate to be the result of many circumstances: the mother's character, the father's mistaken upbringing of the girl, her own weak nature, and the influence of her fiancé on a weak, degenerate mind. Also, more directly, the festive mood of Midsummer Eve, her father's absence, her monthly indisposition, her pre-occupation with animals, the excitement of dancing, the magic of dusk, the strongly aphrodisiac influence of flowers, and finally the chance that drives the couple into a room alone—to which must be added the urgency of the excited man.
>
> My treatment of the theme, moreover, is neither exclusively physiological nor psychological. I have not put the blame wholly on the inheritance from her mother, nor on her physical condition at the time, nor on immorality. I have not even preached a moral sermon; in the absence of a priest I leave this to the cook.
>
> I congratulate myself on this multiplicity of motives as being up-to-date, and if others have done the same thing before me, then I congratulate myself on not being alone in my "paradoxes," as all innovations are called.

Strindberg's comments here and elsewhere in the foreword may well serve as a warning against trying to interpret the play within any kind of simplistic framework. It is an enactment of a class struggle, as Strindberg notes, and as is repeatedly evident in the play from the dialogue and action of Julie, Jean, and Kristin. It is also, in part, an enactment of sexual warfare, as Strindberg and the play make painfully clear. But these two aspects of the conflict are inextricably woven together and complicated further by the subtle aspects of personality that mark both Jean and Julie as individuals rather than social or sexual types. The unfolding of their conflict is thus continually surprising and revealing, and until the very end of the play when Julie walks out of the kitchen with the razor in her hand, the resolution of their conflict is never predictable, though it is thoroughly plausible.

The complexity and the intensity of the struggle between Julie and Jean seemed fully realized in the production by the Royal Dramatic Theater of Sweden, presented at the Brooklyn Academy of Music in 1991. The costuming, for example, vividly displayed the diffference between the two women in Jean's life: Miss Julie in her bright-red low-cut dress and Kristin, severely buttoned up for church, and life, in sober black (Figure 3). Julie's red dress clearly marked her as sexually available, while Jean's removal of his long-sleeved black coat, revealing his rolled-up sleeves, signified the change from "valet" to "lover." The changing relationship between Jean and Julie can also be seen in the bold dramatic blocking and gestures that display the exuberant moment when Jean describes his dream of climbing a high tree, as Julie listens wistfully (Figure 1); the depressed, postcoital scene in which Julie talks about her past (Figure 2); and the moment when Jean attacks Julie's romantic talk about honor and shame (Figure 4). In this stage production, as in his well-known films, Ingmar Bergman directed *Miss Julie* not only to heighten the sexual tensions it embodies but also to explore the questions of power and domination at the heart of those tensions.

MISS JULIE

BY AUGUST STRINDBERG / TRANSLATED BY ELIZABETH SPRIGGE

CHARACTERS

MISS JULIE, *aged 25*
JEAN, *the valet, aged 30*
KRISTIN, *the cook, aged 35*

SCENE

The large kitchen of a Swedish manor house in a country district in the 1880s.

(Midsummer Eve.
The kitchen has three doors, two small ones into JEAN's *and* KRISTIN's *bedrooms, and a large, glass-fronted double one, opening on to a courtyard. This is the only way to the rest of the house.*
Through these glass doors can be seen part of a fountain with a cupid, lilac bushes in flower and the tops of some Lombardy poplars. On one wall are shelves edged with scalloped paper on which are kitchen utensils of copper, iron and tin.
To the left is the corner of a large tiled range and part of its chimney-hood, to the right the end of the servants' dinner table with chairs beside it.
The stove is decorated with birch boughs, the floor strewn with twigs of juniper. On the end of the table is a large Japanese spice jar full of lilac.
There are also an ice-box, a scullery table and a sink.
Above the double door hangs a big old-fashioned bell; near it is a speaking-tube.
A fiddle can be heard from the dance in the barn near-by.
KRISTIN *is standing at the stove, frying something in a pan. She wears a light-colored cotton dress and a big apron.*
JEAN *enters, wearing livery and carrying a pair of large riding-boots with spurs, which he puts in a conspicuous place.)*

JEAN: Miss Julie's crazy again to-night, absolutely crazy.
KRISTIN: Oh, so you're back, are you?
JEAN: When I'd taken the Count to the station, I came back and dropped in at the Barn for a dance. And who did I see there but our young lady leading off with the gamekeeper. But the moment she sets eyes on me, up she rushes and invites me to waltz with her. And how she waltzed—I've never seen anything like it! She's crazy.
KRISTIN: Always has been, but never so bad as this last fortnight since the engagement was broken off.
JEAN: Yes, that was a pretty business, to be sure. He's a decent enough chap, too, even if he isn't rich. Oh, but they're choosy! *(Sits down at the end of the table.)* In any case, it's a bit odd that our young—er—lady would rather stay at home with yokels than go with her father to visit her relations.

KRISTIN: Perhaps she feels a bit awkward, after that bust-up with her fiancé.
JEAN: Maybe. That chap had some guts, though. Do you know the sort of thing that was going on, Kristin? I saw it with my own eyes, though I didn't let on I had.
KRISTIN: You saw them. . . ?
JEAN: Didn't I just! Came across the pair of them one evening in the stable-yard. Miss Julie was doing what she called "training" him. Know what that was? Making him jump over her riding-whip—the way you teach a dog. He did it twice and got a cut each time for his pains, but when it came to the third go, he snatched the whip out of her hand and broke it into smithereens. And then he cleared off.
KRISTIN: What goings on! I never did!
JEAN: Well, that's how it was with that little affair . . . Now, what have you got for me, Kristin? Something tasty?
KRISTIN *(serving from the pan to his plate)*: Well, it's just a little bit of kidney I cut off their joint.
JEAN *(smelling it)*: Fine! That's my special *délice*.° *(Feels the plate.)* But you might have warmed the plate.
KRISTIN: When you choose to be finicky you're worse than the Count himself. *(Pulls his hair affectionately.)*
JEAN *(crossly)*: Stop pulling my hair. You know how sensitive I am.
KRISTIN: There, there! It's only love, you know.

*(*JEAN *eats.* KRISTIN *brings a bottle of beer.)*

JEAN: Beer on Midsummer Eve? No thanks! I've got something better than that. *(From a drawer in the table brings out a bottle of red wine with a yellow seal.)* Yellow seal, see! Now get me a glass. You use a glass with a stem of course when you're drinking it straight.
KRISTIN *(giving him a wine-glass)*: Lord help the woman who gets you for a husband, you old fusser! *(She*

---

délice, delight.

puts the beer in the ice-box and sets a small saucepan on the stove.)

JEAN: Nonsense! You'll be glad enough to get a fellow as smart as me. And I don't think it's done you any harm, people calling me your fiancé. *(Tastes the wine.)* Good. Very good indeed. But not quite warmed enough. *(Warms the glass in his hand.)* We bought this in Dijon. Four francs the liter without the bottle, and duty on top of that. What are you cooking now? It stinks.

KRISTIN: Some bloody muck Miss Julie wants for Diana.

JEAN: You should be more refined in your speech, Kristin. But why should you spend a holiday cooking for that bitch? Is she sick or what?

KRISTIN: Yes, she's sick. She sneaked out with the pug at the lodge and got in the usual mess. And that, you know, Miss Julie won't have.

JEAN: Miss Julie's too high-and-mighty in some respects, and not enough in others, just like her mother before her. The Countess was more at home in the kitchen and cowsheds than anywhere else, but would she ever go driving with only one horse? She went round with her cuffs filthy, but she had to have the coronet on the cufflinks. Our young lady—to come back to her—hasn't any proper respect for herself or her position. I mean she isn't refined. In the Barn just now she dragged the gamekeeper away from Anna and made him dance with her—no waiting to be asked. We wouldn't do a thing like that. But that's what happens when the gentry try to behave like the common people—they become common . . . Still she's a fine girl. Smashing! What shoulders! And what—er—etcetera!

KRISTIN: Oh come off it! I know what Clara says, and she dresses her.

JEAN: Clara? Pooh, you're all jealous! But I've been out riding with her . . . and as for her dancing!

KRISTIN: Listen, Jean. You will dance with me, won't you, as soon as I'm through.

JEAN: Of course I will.

KRISTIN: Promise?

JEAN: Promise? When I say I'll do a thing I do it. Well thanks for the supper. It was a real treat. *(Corks the bottle.)*

(JULIE appears in the doorway, speaking to someone outside.)

JULIE: I'll be back in a moment. Don't wait.

(JEAN slips the bottle into the drawer and rises respectfully. JULIE enters and joins KRISTIN at the stove.)

Well, have you made it? *(KRISTIN signs that JEAN is near them.)*

JEAN *(gallantly)*: Have you ladies got some secret?

JULIE *(flipping his face with her handkerchief)*: You're very inquisitive.

JEAN: What a delicious smell! Violets.

JULIE *(coquettishly)*: Impertinence! Are you an expert of scent too? I must say you know how to dance. Now don't look. Go away. *(The music of a schottische begins.)*

JEAN *(with impudent politeness)*: Is it some witches' brew you're cooking on Midsummer Eve? Something to tell your stars by, so you can see your future?

JULIE *(sharply)*: If you could see that you'd have good eyes. *(to KRISTIN)* Put it in a bottle and cork it tight. Come and dance this schottische with me, Jean.

JEAN *(hesitating)*: I don't want to be rude, but I've promised to dance this one with Kristin.

JULIE: Well, she can have another, can't you, Kristin? You'll lend me Jean, won't you?

KRISTIN *(bottling)*: It's nothing to do with me. When you're so condescending, Miss, it's not his place to say no. Go on, Jean, and thank Miss Julie for the honor.

JEAN: Frankly speaking, Miss, and no offense meant, I wonder if it's wise for you to dance twice running with the same partner, specially as those people are so ready to jump to conclusions.

JULIE *(flaring up)*: What did you say? What sort of conclusions? What do you mean?

JEAN *(meekly)*: As you choose not to understand, Miss Julie, I'll have to speak more plainly. It looks bad to show a preference for one of your retainers when they're all hoping for the same unusual favor.

JULIE: Show a preference! The very idea! I'm surprised at you. I'm doing the people an honor by attending their ball when I'm mistress of the house, but if I'm really going to dance, I mean to have a partner who can lead and doesn't make me look ridiculous.

JEAN: If those are your orders, Miss, I'm at your service.

JULIE *(gently)*: Don't take it as an order. Tonight we're all just people enjoying a party. There's no question of class. So now give me your arm. Don't worry, Kristin, I shan't steal your sweetheart.

(JEAN gives JULIE his arm and leads her out. Left alone, KRISTIN plays her scene in an unhurried, natural way, humming to the tune of the schottische, played on a distant violin. She clears JEAN's place, washes up and puts things away, then takes off her apron, brings out a small mirror from a drawer, props it against the jar of lilac, lights a candle, warms a small pair of tongs and curls her fringe. She goes to the door and listens, then turning back to the table finds MISS JULIE's handkerchief. She smells it, then meditatively smoothes it out and folds it. Enter JEAN.)

JEAN: She really *is* crazy. What a way to dance! With people standing grinning at her too from behind the doors. What's got into her, Kristin?

KRISTIN: Oh, it's just her time coming on. She's always queer then. Are you going to dance with me now?

JEAN: Then you're not wild with me for cutting that one.

KRISTIN: You know I'm not—for a little thing like that. Besides, I know my place.

JEAN (*putting his arm round her waist*): You're a sensible girl, Kristin, and you'll make a very good wife . . .

(*Enter* JULIE, *unpleasantly surprised.*)

JULIE (*with forced gaiety*): You're a fine beau—running away from your partner.

JEAN: Not away, Miss Julie, but as you see back to the one I deserted.

JULIE (*changing her tone*): You really can dance, you know. But why are you wearing your livery on a holiday. Take it off at once.

JEAN: Then I must ask you to go away for a moment, Miss. My black coat's here. (*Indicates it hanging on the door to his room.*)

JULIE: Are you so shy of me—just over changing a coat? Go into your room then—or stay here and I'll turn my back.

JEAN: Excuse me then, Miss. (*He goes to his room and is partly visible as he changes his coat.*)

JULIE: Tell me, Kristin, is Jean your fiancé? You seem very intimate.

KRISTIN: My fiancé? Yes, if you like. We call it that.

JULIE: Call it?

KRISTIN: Well, you've had a fiancé yourself, Miss, and . . .

JULIE: But we really were engaged.

KRISTIN: All the same it didn't come to anything.

(JEAN *returns in his black coat.*)

JULIE: *Très gentil, Monsieur Jean. Très gentil.*°

JEAN: *Vous voulez plaisanter, Madame.*°

JULIE: *Et vous voulez parler français.*° Where did you learn it?

JEAN: In Switzerland, when I was steward at one of the biggest hotels in Lucerne.

JULIE: You look quite the gentleman in that get-up. Charming. (*Sits at the table.*)

JEAN: Oh, you're just flattering me!

JULIE (*annoyed*): Flattering you?

JEAN: I'm too modest to believe you would pay real compliments to a man like me, so I must take it you are exaggerating—that this is what's known as flattery.

JULIE: Where on earth did you learn to make speeches like that? Perhaps you've been to the theater a lot.

JEAN: That's right. And traveled a lot too.

Très . . . gentil, Very nice, Monsieur Jean, very nice. *Vous . . . Madame,* You like to joke, Madame. *Et . . . français,* And you want to speak French.

JULIE: But you come from this neighborhood, don't you?

JEAN: Yes, my father was a laborer on the next estate— the District Attorney's place. I often used to see you, Miss Julie, when you were little, though you never noticed me.

JULIE: Did you really?

JEAN: Yes. One time specially I remember . . . but I can't tell you about that.

JULIE: Oh do! Why not? This is just the time.

JEAN: No, I really can't now. Another time perhaps.

JULIE: Another time means never. What harm in now?

JEAN: No harm, but I'd rather not. (*Points to* KRISTIN, *now fast asleep.*) Look at her.

JULIE: She'll make a charming wife, won't she? I wonder if she snores.

JEAN: No, she doesn't, but she talks in her sleep.

JULIE (*cynically*): How do you know she talks in her sleep?

JEAN (*brazenly*): I've heard her. (*Pause. They look at one another.*)

JULIE: Why don't you sit down?

JEAN: I can't take such a liberty in your presence.

JULIE: Supposing I order you to.

JEAN: I'll obey.

JULIE: Then sit down. No, wait a minute. Will you get me a drink first?

JEAN: I don't know what's in the ice-box. Only beer, I expect.

JULIE: There's no only about it. My taste is so simple I prefer it to wine.

(JEAN *takes a bottle from the ice-box, fetches a glass and plate and serves the beer.*)

JEAN: At your service.

JULIE: Thank you. Won't you have some yourself?

JEAN: I'm not really a beer-drinker, but if it's an order. . . .

JULIE: Order? I should have thought it was ordinary manners to keep your partner company.

JEAN: That's a good way of putting it. (*He opens another bottle and fetches a glass.*)

JULIE: Now drink my health. (*He hesitates.*) I believe the man really is shy.

(JEAN *kneels and raises his glass with mock ceremony.*)

JEAN: To the health of my lady!

JULIE: Bravo! Now kiss my shoe and everything will be perfect. (*He hesitates, then boldly takes hold of her foot and lightly kisses it.*) Splendid. You ought to have been an actor.

JEAN (*rising*): We can't go on like this, Miss Julie. Someone might come in and see us.

JULIE: Why would that matter?

JEAN: For the simple reason that they'd talk. And if you knew the way their tongues were wagging out there just now, you . . .

JULIE: What were they saying? Tell me. Sit down.

JEAN *(sitting)*: No offense meant, Miss, but . . . well, their language wasn't nice, and they were hinting . . . oh, you know quite well what. You're not a child, and if a lady's seen drinking alone at night with a man—and a servant at that—then . . .

JULIE: Then what? Besides, we're not alone. Kristin's here.

JEAN: Yes, asleep.

JULIE: I'll wake her up. *(Rises.)* Kristin, are you asleep? *(KRISTIN mumbles in her sleep.)* Kristin! Goodness, how she sleeps!

KRISTIN *(in her sleep)*: The Count's boots are cleaned —put the coffee on—yes, yes, at once . . . *(Mumbles incoherently.)*

JULIE *(tweaking her nose)*: Wake up, can't you!

JEAN *(sharply)*: Let her sleep.

JULIE: What?

JEAN: When you've been standing at the stove all day you're likely to be tired at night. And sleep should be respected.

JULIE *(changing her tone)*: What a nice idea. It does you credit. Thank you for it. *(Holds out her hand to him.)* Now come out and pick some lilac for me. *(During the following KRISTIN goes sleepily in to her bedroom.)*

JEAN: Out with you, Miss Julie?

JULIE: Yes.

JEAN: It wouldn't do. It really wouldn't.

JULIE: I don't know what you mean. You can't possibly imagine that . . .

JEAN: I don't, but others do.

JULIE: What? That I'm in love with the valet?

JEAN: I'm not a conceited man, but such a thing's been known to happen, and to these rustics nothing's sacred.

JULIE: You, I take it, are an aristocrat.

JEAN: Yes, I am.

JULIE: And I am coming down in the world.

JEAN: Don't come down, Miss Julie. Take my advice. No one will believe you came down of your own accord. They'll all say you fell.

JULIE: I have a higher opinion of our people than you. Come and put it to the test. Come on. *(Gazes into his eyes.)*

JEAN: You're very strange, you know.

JULIE: Perhaps I am, but so are you. For that matter everything is strange. Life, human beings, everything, just scum drifting about on the water until it sinks—down and down. That reminds me of a dream I sometimes have, in which I'm on top of a pillar and can't see any way of getting down. When I look down I'm dizzy; I have to get down but I haven't the courage to jump. I can't stay there and I long to fall, but I don't fall. There's no respite. There can't be any peace at all for me until I'm down, right down on the ground. And if I did get to the ground I'd want to be under the ground . . . Have you ever felt like that?

JEAN: No. In my dream I'm lying under a great tree in a dark wood. I want to get up, up to the top of it, and look out over the bright landscape where the sun is shining and rob that high nest of its golden eggs. And I climb and climb, but the trunk is so thick and smooth and it's so far to the first branch. But I know if I can once reach that first branch I'll go to the top just as if I'm on a ladder. I haven't reached it yet, but I shall get there, even if only in my dreams.

JULIE: Here I am chattering about dreams with you. Come on. Only into the park. *(She takes his arm and they go toward the door.)*

JEAN: We must sleep on nine midsummer flowers tonight; then our dreams will come true, Miss Julie. *(They turn at the door. He has a hand to his eye.)*

JULIE: Have you got something in your eye? Let me see.

JEAN: Oh, it's nothing. Just a speck of dust. It'll be gone in a minute.

JULIE: My sleeve must have rubbed against you. Sit down and let me see to it. *(Takes him by the arm and makes him sit down, bends his head back and tries to get the speck out with the corner of her handkerchief.)* Keep still now, quite still. *(Slaps his hand.)* Do as I tell you. Why, I believe you're trembling, big, strong man though you are! *(Feels his biceps.)* What muscles!

JEAN *(warning)*: Miss Julie!

JULIE: Yes, Monsieur Jean?

JEAN: *Attention. Je ne suis qu'un homme.*°

JULIE: Will you stay still! There now. It's out. Kiss my hand and say thank you.

JEAN *(rising)*: Miss Julie, listen, Kristin's gone to bed now. Will you listen?

JULIE: Kiss my hand first.

JEAN: Very well, but you'll have only yourself to blame.

JULIE: For what?

JEAN: For what! Are you still a child at twenty-five? Don't you know it's dangerous to play with fire?

JULIE: Not for me. I'm insured.

JEAN *(bluntly)*: No, you're not. And even if you are, there's still stuff here to kindle a flame.

JULIE: Meaning yourself?

JEAN: Yes. Not because I'm me, but because I'm a man and young and . . .

JULIE: And good looking? What incredible conceit! A Don Juan perhaps? Or a Joseph? Good Lord, I do believe you are a Joseph!

JEAN: Do you?

JULIE: I'm rather afraid so.

(JEAN goes boldly up and tries to put his arms round her and kiss her. She boxes his ears.)

Attention . . . homme, Careful, I'm only a man.

How dare you!

JEAN: Was that in earnest or a joke?

JULIE: In earnest.

JEAN: Then what went before was in earnest too. You take your games too seriously and that's dangerous. Anyhow I'm tired of playing now and beg leave to return to my work. The Count will want his boots first thing and it's past midnight now.

JULIE: Put those boots down.

JEAN: No. This is my work, which it's my duty to do. But I never undertook to be your playfellow and I never will be. I consider myself too good for that.

JULIE: You're proud.

JEAN: In some ways—not all.

JULIE: Have you ever been in love?

JEAN: We don't put it that way, but I've been gone on quite a few girls. And once I went sick because I couldn't have the one I wanted. Sick, I mean, like those princes in the Arabian Nights who couldn't eat or drink for love.

JULIE: Who was she? *(No answer.)* Who was she?

JEAN: You can't force me to tell you that.

JULIE: If I ask as an equal, ask as a—friend? Who was she?

JEAN: You.

JULIE *(sitting)*: How absurd!

JEAN: Yes, ludicrous if you like. That's the story I wouldn't tell you before, see, but now I will . . . Do you know what the world looks like from below? No, you don't. No more than the hawks and falcons do whose backs one hardly ever sees because they're always soaring up aloft. I lived in a laborer's hovel with seven other children and a pig, out in the gray fields where there isn't a single tree. But from the window I could see the wall round the Count's park with apple-trees above it. That was the Garden of Eden, guarded by many terrible angels with flaming swords. All the same I and the other boys managed to get to the tree of life. Does all this make you despise me?

JULIE: Goodness, all boys steal apples!

JEAN: You say that now, but all the same you do despise me. However, one time I went into the Garden of Eden with my mother to weed the onion beds. Close to the kitchen garden there was a Turkish pavilion hung all over with jasmine and honeysuckle. I hadn't any idea what it was used for, but I'd never seen such a beautiful building. People used to go in and then come out again, and one day the door was left open. I crept up and saw the walls covered with pictures of kings and emperors, and the windows had red curtains with fringes—you know now what the place was, don't you? I . . . *(Breaks off a piece of lilac and holds it for* JULIE *to smell. As he talks, she takes it from him.)* I had never been inside the manor, never seen anything but the church, and this was more beautiful. No matter where my thoughts went, they always came back—to that place. The longing went on growing in me to enjoy it fully, just once. *Enfin,*° I sneaked in, gazed and admired. Then I heard someone coming. There was only one way out for the gentry, but for me there was another and I had no choice but to take it. *(*JULIE *drops the lilac on the table.)* Then I took to my heels, plunged through the raspberry canes, dashed across the strawberry beds and found myself on the rose terrace. There I saw a pink dress and a pair of white stockings—it was you. I crawled into a weed pile and lay there right under it among prickly thistles and damp rank earth. I watched you walking among the roses and said to myself: "If it's true that a thief can get to heaven and be with the angels, it's pretty strange that a laborer's child here on God's earth mayn't come in the park and play with the Count's daughter."

JULIE *(sentimentally)*: Do you think all poor children feel the way you did?

JEAN *(taken aback, then rallying)*: *All* poor children? . . . Yes, of course they do. Of course.

JULIE: It must be terrible to be poor.

JEAN *(with exaggerated distress)*: Oh yes, Miss Julie, yes. A dog may lie on the Countess's sofa, a horse may have his nose stroked by a young lady, but a servant . . . *(Change of tone.)* well, yes, now and then you meet one with guts enough to rise in the world, but how often? Anyhow, do you know what I did? Jumped into the millstream with my clothes on, was pulled out and got a hiding. But the next Sunday, when Father and all the rest went to Granny's, I managed to get left behind. Then I washed with soap and hot water, put my best clothes on and went to church so as to see you. I did see you and went home determined to die. But I wanted to die beautifully and peacefully, without any pain. Then I remembered it was dangerous to sleep under an elder bush. We had a big one in full bloom, so I stripped it and climbed into the oats-bin with the flowers. Have you ever noticed how smooth oats are? Soft to touch as human skin . . . Well, I closed the lid and shut my eyes, fell asleep, and when they woke me I was very ill. But I didn't die, as you see. What I meant by all that I don't know. There was no hope of winning you—you were simply a symbol of the hopelessness of ever getting out of the class I was born in.

Enfin, well.

JULIE: You put things very well, you know. Did you go to school?

JEAN: For a while. But I've read a lot of novels and been to the theater. Besides, I've heard educated folk talking—that's what's taught me most.

JULIE: Do you stand round listening to what we're saying?

JEAN: Yes, of course. And I've heard quite a bit too! On the carriage box or rowing the boat. Once I heard you, Miss Julie, and one of your young lady friends . . .

JULIE: Oh! Whatever did you hear?

JEAN: Well, it wouldn't be nice to repeat it. And I must say I was pretty startled. I couldn't think where you had learnt such words. Perhaps, at bottom, there isn't as much difference between people as one's led to believe.

JULIE: How dare you! We don't behave as you do when we're engaged.

JEAN (looking hard at her): Are you sure? It's no use making out so innocent to me.

JULIE: The man I gave my love to was a scoundrel.

JEAN: That's what you always say—afterward.

JULIE: Always?

JEAN: I think it must be always. I've heard the expression several times in similar circumstances.

JULIE: What circumstances?

JEAN: Like those in question. The last time . . .

JULIE (rising): Stop. I don't want to hear any more.

JEAN: Nor did she—curiously enough. May I go to bed now please?

JULIE (gently): Go to bed on Midsummer Eve?

JEAN: Yes. Dancing with that crowd doesn't really amuse me.

JULIE: Get the key of the boathouse and row me out on the lake. I want to see the sun rise.

JEAN: Would that be wise?

JULIE: You sound as though you're frightened for your reputation.

JEAN: Why not? I don't want to be made a fool of, nor to be sent packing without references when I'm trying to better myself. Besides, I have Kristin to consider.

JULIE: So now it's Kristin.

JEAN: Yes, but it's you I'm thinking about too. Take my advice and go to bed.

JULIE: Am I to take orders from you?

JEAN: Just this once, for your own sake. Please. It's very late and sleepiness goes to one's head and makes one rash. Go to bed. What's more, if my ears don't deceive me, I hear people coming this way. They'll be looking for me, and if they find us here, you're done for.

(The CHORUS approaches, singing. During the following dialogue the song is heard in snatches, and in full when the peasants enter.)

Out of the wood two women came,
Tridiri-ralla, tridiri-ra.
The feet of one were bare and cold,
Tridiri-ralla-la.

The other talked of bags of gold,
Tridiri-ralla, tridiri-ra.
But neither had a sou to her name,
Tridiri-ralla-la.

The bridal wreath I give to you,
Tridiri-ralla, tridiri-ra.
But to another I'll be true,
Tridiri-ralla-la.

JULIE: I know our people and I love them, just as they do me. Let them come. You'll see.

JEAN: No, Miss Julie, they don't love you. They take your food, then spit at it. You must believe me. Listen to them, just listen to what they're singing . . . No, don't listen.

JULIE (listening): What are they singing?

JEAN: They're mocking—you and me.

JULIE: Oh no! How horrible! What cowards!

JEAN: A pack like that's always cowardly. But against such odds there's nothing we can do but run away.

JULIE: Run away? Where to? We can't get out and we can't go into Kristin's room.

JEAN: Into mine then. Necessity knows no rules. And you can trust me. I really am your true and devoted friend.

JULIE: But supposing . . . supposing they were to look for you in there?

JEAN: I'll bolt the door, and if they try to break in I'll shoot. Come on. (Pleading.) Please come.

JULIE (tensely): Do you promise. . . ?

JEAN: I swear!

(JULIE *goes quickly into his room and he excitedly follows her. Led by the fiddler, the peasants enter in festive attire with flowers in their hats. They put a barrel of beer and a keg of spirits, garlanded with leaves, on the table, fetch glasses and begin to carouse. The scene becomes a ballet. They form a ring and dance and sing and mime.* "Out of the wood two women came." *Finally they go out, still singing.* JULIE *comes in alone. She looks at the havoc in the kitchen, wrings her hands, then takes out her powder puff and powders her face.* JEAN *enters in high spirits.*)

JEAN: Now you see! And you heard, didn't you? Do you still think it's possible for us to stay here?

JULIE: No, I don't. But what can we do?

JEAN: Run away. Far away. Take a journey.

JULIE: Journey? But where to?

JEAN: Switzerland. The Italian lakes. Ever been there?

JULIE: No. Is it nice?

JEAN: Ah! Eternal summer, oranges, evergreens . . . ah!

JULIE: But what would we do there?

JEAN: I'll start a hotel. First-class accommodation and first-class customers.

JULIE: Hotel?

JEAN: There's life for you. New faces all the time, new languages—no time for nerves or worries, no need to look for something to do—work rolling up of its own accord. Bells ringing night and day, trains whistling, buses coming and going, and all the time gold pieces rolling on to the counter. There's life for you!

JULIE: For *you*. And I?

JEAN: Mistress of the house, ornament of the firm. With your looks, and your style . . . oh, it's bound to be a success! Terrific! You'll sit like a queen in the office and set your slaves in motion by pressing an electric button. The guests will file past your throne and nervously lay their treasure on your table. You've no idea the way people tremble when they get their bills. I'll salt the bills and you'll sugar them with your sweetest smiles. Ah, let's get away from here! *(Produces a timetable.)* At once, by the next train. We shall be at Malmö at six-thirty, Hamburg eight-forty next morning, Frankfort-Basle the following day, and Como by the St. Gotthard Pass in—let's see—three days. Three days!

JULIE: That's all very well. But Jean, you must give me courage. Tell me you love me. Come and take me in your arms.

JEAN *(reluctantly)*: I'd like to, but I daren't. Not again in this house. I love you—that goes without saying. You can't doubt that, Miss Julie, can you?

JULIE *(shyly, very feminine)*: Miss? Call me Julie. There aren't any barriers between us now. Call me Julie.

JEAN *(uneasily)*: I can't. As long as we're in this house, there *are* barriers between us. There's the past and there's the Count. I've never been so servile to anyone as I am to him. I've only to hear his bell and I shy like a horse. Even now, when I look at his boots, standing there so proud and stiff, I feel my back beginning to bend. *(Kicks the boots.)* It's those old, narrow-minded notions drummed into us as children . . . but they can soon be forgotten. You've only got to get to another country, a republic, and people will bend themselves double before my porter's livery. Yes, double they'll bend themselves, but I shan't. I wasn't born to bend. I've got guts. I've got character, and once I reach that first branch, you'll watch me climb. Today I'm valet, next year I'll be proprietor, in ten years I'll have made a fortune, and then I'll go to Rumania, get myself decorated and I may, I only say *may*, mind you, end up as a Count.

JULIE *(sadly)*: That would be very nice.

JEAN: You see in Rumania one can buy a title, and then you'll be a Countess after all. My Countess.

JULIE: What do I care about all that? I'm putting those things behind me. Tell me you love me, because if you don't . . . if you don't, what am I?

JEAN: I'll tell you a thousand times over—later. But not here. No sentimentality now or everything will be lost. We must consider this thing calmly like reasonable people. *(Takes a cigar, cuts and lights it.)* You sit down there and I'll sit here and we'll talk as if nothing happened.

JULIE: My God, have you no feelings at all?

JEAN: Nobody has more. But I know how to control them.

JULIE: A short time ago you were kissing my shoe. And now . . .

JEAN *(harshly)*: Yes, that was then. Now we have something else to think about.

JULIE: Don't speak to me so brutally.

JEAN: I'm not. Just sensibly. One folly's been committed, don't let's have more. The Count will be back at any moment and we've got to settle our future before that. Now, what do you think of my plans? Do you approve?

JULIE: It seems a very good idea—but just one thing. Such a big undertaking would need a lot of capital. Have you got any?

JEAN *(chewing his cigar)*: I certainly have. I've got my professional skill, my wide experience, and my knowledge of foreign languages. That's capital worth having, it seems to me.

JULIE: But it won't buy even one railway ticket.

JEAN: Quite true. That's why I need a backer to advance some ready cash.

JULIE: How could you get that at a moment's notice?

JEAN: You must get it, if you want to be my partner.

JULIE: I can't. I haven't any money of my own. *(Pause.)*

JEAN: Then the whole thing's off.

JULIE: And. . . ?

JEAN: We go on as we are.

JULIE: Do you think I'm going to stay under this roof as your mistress? With everyone pointing at me. Do you think I can face my father after this? No. Take me away from here, away from this shame, this humiliation. Oh my God, what have I done? My God, my God! *(Weeps.)*

JEAN: So that's the tune now, is it? What have you done? Same as many before you.

JULIE *(hysterically)*: And now you despise me. I'm falling, I'm falling.

JEAN: Fall as far as me and I'll lift you up again.

JULIE: Why was I so terribly attracted to you? The weak to the strong, the falling to the rising? Or was it love? Is that love? Do you know what love is?

JEAN: Do I? You bet I do. Do you think I never had a girl before?

JULIE: The things you say, the things you think!

JEAN: That's what life's taught me, and that's what I am. It's no good getting hysterical or giving yourself airs. We're both in the same boat now. Here, my dear girl, let me give you a glass of something special. (*Opens the drawer, takes out the bottle of wine and fills two used glasses.*)

JULIE: Where did you get that wine?

JEAN: From the cellar.

JULIE: My father's burgundy.

JEAN: Why not, for his son-in-law?

JULIE: And I drink beer.

JEAN: That only shows your taste's not so good as mine.

JULIE: Thief!

JEAN: Are you going to tell on me?

JULIE: Oh God! The accomplice of a petty thief! Was I blind drunk? Have I dreamt this whole night? Midsummer Eve, the night for innocent merry-making.

JEAN: Innocent, eh?

JULIE: Is anyone on earth as wretched as I am now?

JEAN: Why should *you* be? After such a conquest. What about Kristin in there? Don't you think she has any feelings?

JULIE: I did think so, but I don't any longer. No. A menial is a menial . . .

JEAN: And a whore is a whore.

JULIE (*falling to her knees, her hands clasped*): O God in heaven, put an end to my miserable life! Lift me out of this filth in which I'm sinking. Save me! Save me!

JEAN: I must admit I'm sorry for you. When I was in the onion bed and saw you up there among the roses, I . . . yes, I'll tell you now . . . I had the same dirty thoughts as all boys.

JULIE: You, who wanted to die because of me?

JEAN: In the oats-bin? That was just talk.

JULIE: Lies, you mean.

JEAN (*getting sleepy*): More or less. I think I read a story in some paper about a chimney-sweep who shut himself up in a chest full of lilac because he'd been summonsed for not supporting some brat . . .

JULIE: So this is what you're like.

JEAN: I had to think up something. It's always the fancy stuff that catches the women.

JULIE: Beast!

JEAN: *Merde!*

JULIE: Now you have seen the falcon's back.

JEAN: Not exactly its *back*.

JULIE: I was to be the first branch.

JEAN: But the branch was rotten.

JULIE: I was to be a hotel sign.

JEAN: And I the hotel.

JULIE: Sit at your counter, attract your clients and cook their accounts.

JEAN: I'd have done that myself.

JULIE: That any human being can be so steeped in filth!

JEAN: Clean it up then.

JULIE: Menial! Lackey! Stand up when I speak to you.

JEAN: Menial's whore, lackey's harlot, shut your mouth and get out of here! Are you the one to lecture me for being coarse? Nobody of my kind would ever be as coarse as you were tonight. Do you think any servant girl would throw herself at a man that way? Have you ever seen a girl of my class asking for it like that? I haven't. Only animals and prostitutes.

JULIE (*broken*): Go on. Hit me, trample on me—it's all I deserve. I'm rotten. But help me! If there's any way out at all, help me.

JEAN (*more gently*): I'm not denying myself a share in the honor of seducing you, but do you think anybody in my place would have dared look in your direction if you yourself hadn't asked for it? I'm still amazed . . .

JULIE: And proud.

JEAN: Why not? Though I must admit the victory was too easy to make me lose my head.

JULIE: Go on hitting me.

JEAN (*rising*): No. On the contrary I apologize for what I've said. I don't hit a person who's down—least of all a woman. I can't deny there's a certain satisfaction in finding that what dazzled one below was just moonshine, that the falcon's back is gray after all, that there's powder on the lovely cheek, that polished nails can have black tips, that the handkerchief is dirty although it smells of scent. On the other hand it hurts to find that what I was struggling to reach wasn't high and isn't real. It hurts to see you fallen so low you're far lower than your own cook. Hurts like when you see the last flowers of summer lashed to pieces by rain and turned to mud.

JULIE: You're talking as if you're already my superior.

JEAN: I am. I might make you a Countess, but you could never make me a Count, you know.

JULIE: But I am the child of a Count, and you could never be that.

JEAN: True, but I might be the father of Counts if . . .

JULIE: You're a thief. I'm not.

JEAN: There are worse things than being a thief—much lower. Besides, when I'm in a place I regard myself as a member of the family to some extent, as one of the children. You don't call it stealing when children pinch a berry from overladen bushes. (*His passion is roused again.*) Miss Julie, you're a glorious woman, far too good for a man like me. You were carried away by some kind of madness, and now you're trying to cover up your mistake by persuading yourself you're in love with me. You're not, although you may find me physically attractive, which means your love's no better than mine. But I wouldn't be satisfied with being nothing but an animal for you, and I could never make you love me.

JULIE: Are you sure?

JEAN: You think there's a chance? Of my loving you, yes, of course. You're beautiful, refined *(Takes her hand)* educated, and you can be nice when you want to be. The fire you kindle in a man isn't likely to go out. *(Puts his arm round her.)* You're like mulled wine, full of spices, and your kisses . . . *(He tries to pull her to him, but she breaks away.)*

JULIE: Let go of me! You won't win me that way.

JEAN: Not that way, how then? Not by kisses and fine speeches, not by planning the future and saving you from shame? How then?

JULIE: How? How? I don't know. There isn't any way. I loathe you—loathe you as I loathe rats, but I can't escape from you.

JEAN: Escape with me.

JULIE *(pulling herself together)*: Escape? Yes, we must escape. But I'm so tired. Give me a glass of wine. *(He pours it out. She looks at her watch.)* First we must talk. We still have a little time. *(Empties the glass and holds it out for more.)*

JEAN: Don't drink like that. You'll get tipsy.

JULIE: What's that matter?

JEAN: What's it matter? It's vulgar to get drunk. Well, what have you got to say?

JULIE: We've got to run away, but we must talk first—or rather, I must, for so far you've done all the talking. You've told me about your life, now I want to tell you about mine, so that we really know each other before we begin this journey together.

JEAN: Wait. Excuse my saying so, but don't you think you may be sorry afterward if you give away your secrets to me?

JULIE: Aren't you my friend?

JEAN: On the whole. But don't rely on me.

JULIE: You can't mean that. But anyway everyone knows my secrets. Listen. My mother wasn't well-born; she came of quite humble people, and was brought up with all those new ideas of sex-equality and women's rights and so on. She thought marriage was quite wrong. So when my father proposed to her, she said she would never become his *wife* . . . but in the end she did. I came into the world, as far as I can make out, against my mother's will, and I was left to run wild, but I had to do all the things a boy does—to prove women are as good as men. I had to wear boys' clothes; I was taught to handle horses—and I wasn't allowed in the dairy. She made me groom and harness and go out hunting; I even had to try to plough. All the men on the estate were given the women's jobs, and the women the men's, until the whole place went to rack and ruin and we were the laughing-stock of the neighborhood. At last my father seemed to have come to his senses and rebelled. He changed everything and ran the place his own way. My mother got ill—I don't know what was the matter with her, but she used to have strange attacks and hide herself in the attic or the garden. Sometimes she stayed out all night. Then came the great fire which you have heard people talking about. The house and the stables and the barns—the whole place burnt to the ground. In very suspicious circumstances. Because the accident happened the very day the insurance had to be renewed, and my father had sent the new premium, but through some carelessness of the messenger it arrived too late. *(Refills her glass and drinks.)*

JEAN: Don't drink any more.

JULIE: Oh, what does it matter? We were destitute and had to sleep in the carriages. My father didn't know how to get money to rebuild, and then my mother suggested he should borrow from an old friend of hers, a local brick manufacturer. My father got the loan and, to his surprise, without having to pay interest. So the place was rebuilt. *(Drinks.)* Do you know who set fire to it?

JEAN: Your lady mother.

JULIE: Do you know who the brick manufacturer was?

JEAN: Your mother's lover?

JULIE: Do you know whose the money was?

JEAN: Wait . . . no, I don't know that.

JULIE: It was my mother's.

JEAN: In other words the Count's, unless there was a settlement.

JULIE: There wasn't any settlement. My mother had a little money of her own which she didn't want my father to control, so she invested it with her—friend.

JEAN: Who grabbed it.

JULIE: Exactly. He appropriated it. My father came to know all this. He couldn't bring an action, couldn't pay his wife's lover, nor prove it was his wife's money. That was my mother's revenge because he made himself master in his own house. He nearly shot himself then—at least there's a rumor he tried and didn't bring it off. So he went on living, and my mother had to pay dearly for what she'd done. Imagine what those five years were like for me. My natural sympathies were with my father, yet I took my mother's side, because I didn't know the facts. I'd learnt from her to hate and distrust men—you know how she loathed the whole male sex. And I swore to her I'd never become the slave of any man.

JEAN: And so you got engaged to that attorney.

JULIE: So that he should be my slave.

JEAN: But he wouldn't be.

JULIE: Oh yes, he wanted to be, but he didn't have the chance. I got bored with him.

JEAN: Is that what I saw—in the stable-yard?

JULIE: What did you see?

JEAN: What I saw was him breaking off the engagement.

JULIE: That's a lie. It was I who broke it off. Did he say it was him? The cad.

JEAN: He's not a cad. Do you hate men, Miss Julie?

JULIE: Yes . . . most of the time. But when that weakness comes, oh . . . the shame!

JEAN: Then do you hate me?

JULIE: Beyond words. I'd gladly have you killed like an animal.

JEAN: Quick as you'd shoot a mad dog, eh?

JULIE: Yes.

JEAN: But there's nothing here to shoot with—and there isn't a dog. So what do we do now?

JULIE: Go abroad.

JEAN: To make each other miserable for the rest of our lives?

JULIE: No, to enjoy ourselves for a day or two, for a week, for as long as enjoyment lasts, and then—to die . . .

JEAN: Die? How silly! I think it would be far better to start a hotel.

JULIE (without listening): . . . die on the shores of Lake Como, where the sun always shines and at Christmas time there are green trees and glowing oranges.

JEAN: Lake Como's a rainy hole and I didn't see any oranges outside the shops. But it's a good place for tourists. Plenty of villas to be rented by—er—honeymoon couples. Profitable business that. Know why? Because they all sign a lease for six months and all leave after three weeks.

JULIE (naïvely): After three weeks? Why?

JEAN: They quarrel, of course. But the rent has to be paid just the same. And then it's let again. So it goes on and on, for there's plenty of love although it doesn't last long.

JULIE: You don't want to die with me?

JEAN: I don't want to die at all. For one thing I like living and for another I consider suicide's a sin against the Creator who gave us life.

JULIE: You believe in God—you?

JEAN: Yes, of course. And I go to church every Sunday. Look here. I'm tired of all this. I'm going to bed.

JULIE: Indeed! And do you think I'm going to leave things like this? Don't you know what you owe the woman you've ruined?

JEAN (taking out his purse and throwing a silver coin on the table): There you are. I don't want to be in anybody's debt.

JULIE (pretending not to notice the insult): Don't you know what the law is?

JEAN: There's no law unfortunately that punishes a woman for seducing a man.

JULIE: But can you see anything for it but to go abroad, get married and then divorce?

JEAN: What if I refuse this mésalliance?

JULIE: Mésalliance?

JEAN: Yes for me. I'm better bred than you, see! Nobody in my family committed arson.

JULIE: How do you know?

JEAN: Well, you can't prove otherwise, because we haven't any family records outside the Registrar's office. But I've seen your family tree in that book on the drawing-room table. Do you know who the founder of your family was? A miller who let his wife sleep with the King one night during the Danish war. I haven't any ancestors like that. I haven't any ancestors at all, but I might become one.

JULIE: This is what I get for confiding in someone so low, for sacrificing my family honor . . .

JEAN: Dishonor! Well, I told you so. One shouldn't drink because then one talks. And one shouldn't talk.

JULIE: Oh, how ashamed I am, how bitterly ashamed! If at least you loved me!

JEAN: Look here—for the last time—what do you want? Am I to burst into tears? Am I to jump over your riding whip? Shall I kiss you and carry you off to Lake Como for three weeks, after which . . . What am I to do? What do you want? This is getting unbearable, but that's what comes of playing around with women. Miss Julie, I can see how miserable you are; I know you're going through hell, but I don't understand you. We don't have scenes like this; we don't go in for hating each other. We make love for fun in our spare time, but we haven't all day and all night for it like you. I think you must be ill. I'm sure you're ill.

JULIE: Then you must be kind to me. You sound almost human now.

JEAN: Well, be human yourself. You spit at me, then won't let me wipe it off—on you.

JULIE: Help me, help me! Tell me what to do, where to go.

JEAN: Jesus, as if I knew!

JULIE: I've been mad, raving mad, but there must be a way out.

JEAN: Stay here and keep quiet. Nobody knows anything.

JULIE: I can't. People do know. Kristin knows.

JEAN: They don't know and they wouldn't believe such a thing.

JULIE (hesitating): But—it might happen again.

JEAN: That's true.

JULIE: And there might be—consequences.

JEAN (in panic): Consequences! Fool that I am I never thought of that. Yes, there's nothing for it but to go. At once. I can't come with you. That would be a complete give-away. You must go alone—abroad—anywhere.

JULIE: Alone! Where to? I can't.

JEAN: You must. And before the Count gets back. If you stay, we know what will happen. Once you've sinned you feel you might as well go on, as the harm's done. Then you get more and more reckless and in the end you're found out. No. You must go abroad. Then write to the Count and tell him everything, except that it was me. He'll never guess that—and I don't think he'll want to.

JULIE: I'll go if you come with me.

JEAN: Are you crazy, woman? "Miss Julie elopes with valet." Next day it would be in the headlines, and the Count would never live it down.

JULIE: I can't go. I can't stay. I'm so tired, so completely worn out. Give me orders. Set me going. I can't think any more, can't act . . .

JEAN: You see what weaklings you are. Why do you give yourselves airs and turn up your noses as if you're the lords of creation? Very well, I'll give you your orders. Go upstairs and dress. Get money for the journey and come down here again.

JULIE (softly): Come up with me.

JEAN: To your room? Now you've gone crazy again. (Hesitates a moment.) No! Go along at once. (Takes her hand and pulls her to the door.)

JULIE (as she goes): Speak kindly to me, Jean.

JEAN: Orders always sound unkind. Now you know. Now you know.

(Left alone, JEAN sighs with relief, sits down at the table, takes out a note-book and pencil and adds up figures, now and then aloud. Dawn begins to break. KRISTIN enters dressed for church, carrying his white dickey and tie.)

KRISTIN: Lord Jesus, look at the state the place is in! What have you been up to? (Turns out the lamp.)

JEAN: Oh, Miss Julie invited the crowd in. Did you sleep through it? Didn't you hear anything?

KRISTIN: I slept like a log.

JEAN: And dressed for church already.

KRISTIN: Yes, you promised to come to Communion with me today.

JEAN: Why, so I did. And you've got my bib and tucker. I see. Come on then. (Sits. KRISTIN begins to put his things on. Pause. Sleepily.) What's the lesson today?

KRISTIN: It's about the beheading of John the Baptist, I think.

JEAN: That's sure to be horribly long. Hi, you're choking me! Oh Lord, I'm so sleepy, so sleepy!

KRISTIN: Yes, what have you been doing up all night? You look absolutely green.

JEAN: Just sitting here talking with Miss Julie.

KRISTIN: She doesn't know what's proper, that one. (Pause.)

JEAN: I say, Kristin.

KRISTIN: What?

JEAN: It's queer really, isn't it, when you come to think of it? Her.

KRISTIN: What's queer?

JEAN: The whole thing. (Pause.)

KRISTIN (looking at the half-filled glasses on the table): Have you been drinking together too?

JEAN: Yes.

KRISTIN: More shame you. Look me straight in the face.

JEAN: Yes.

KRISTIN: Is it possible? Is it possible?

JEAN (after a moment): Yes, it is.

KRISTIN: Oh! This I would never have believed. How low!

JEAN: You're not jealous of her, surely?

KRISTIN: No, I'm not. If it had been Clara or Sophie I'd have scratched your eyes out. But not of her. I don't know why; that's how it is though. But it's disgusting.

JEAN: You're angry with her then.

KRISTIN: No. With you. It was wicked of you, very very wicked. Poor girl. And, mark my words, I won't stay here any longer now—in a place where one can't respect one's employers.

JEAN: Why should one respect them?

KRISTIN: You should know since you're so smart. But you don't want to stay in the service of people who aren't respectable, do you? I wouldn't demean myself.

JEAN: But it's rather a comfort to find out they're no better than us.

KRISTIN: I don't think so. If they're no better there's nothing for us to live up to. Oh and think of the Count! Think of him. He's been through so much already. No I won't stay in the place any longer. A fellow like you too! If it had been that attorney now or somebody of her own class . . .

JEAN: Why, what's wrong with . . .

KRISTIN: Oh, you're all right in your own way, but when all's said and done there is a difference between one class and another. No, this is something I'll never be able to stomach. That our young lady who was so proud and so down on men you'd never believe she'd let one come near her should go and give herself to one like you. She who wanted to have poor Diana shot for running after the lodge-keeper's pug. No. I must say. . . ! Well, I won't stay here any longer. On the twenty-fourth of October, I quit.

JEAN: And then?

KRISTIN: Well, since you mention it, it's about time you began to look around, if we're ever going to get married.

JEAN: But what am I to look for? I shan't get a place like this when I'm married.

KRISTIN: I know you won't. But you might get a job as porter or caretaker in some public institution. Government rations are small but sure, and there's a pension for the widow and children.

JEAN: That's all very fine, but it's not in my line to start thinking at once about dying for my wife and children. I must say I had rather bigger ideas.

KRISTIN: You and your ideas! You've got obligations too, and you'd better start thinking about them.

JEAN: Don't *you* start pestering me about obligations. I've had enough of that. (*Listens to a sound upstairs.*) Anyway we've got plenty of time to work things out. Go and get ready now and we'll be off to church.

KRISTIN: Who's that walking about upstairs?

JEAN: Don't know—unless it's Clara.

KRISTIN (*going*): You don't think the Count could have come back without our hearing him?

JEAN (*scared*): The Count? No, he can't have. He'd have rung for me.

KRISTIN: God help us! I've never known such goings on. (*Exit.*)

(*The sun has now risen and is shining on the treetops. The light gradually changes until it slants in through the windows.* JEAN *goes to the door and beckons.* JULIE *enters in traveling clothes, carrying a small bird-cage covered with a cloth which she puts on a chair.*)

JULIE: I'm ready.

JEAN: Hush! Kristin's up.

JULIE (*in a very nervous state*): Does she suspect anything?

JEAN: Not a thing. But, my God, what a sight you are!

JULIE: Sight! What do you mean?

JEAN: You're white as a corpse and—pardon me—your face is dirty.

JULIE: Let me wash then. (*Goes to the sink and washes her face and hands.*) There. Give me a towel. Oh! The sun is rising!

JEAN: And that breaks the spell.

JULIE: Yes. The spell of Midsummer Eve . . . But listen, Jean. Come with me. I've got the money.

JEAN (*skeptically*): Enough?

JULIE: Enough to start with. Come with me. I can't travel alone today. It's Midsummer Day, remember. I'd be packed into a suffocating train among crowds of people who'd all stare at me. And it would stop at every station while I yearned for wings. No, I can't do that. I simply can't. There will be memories too; memories of Midsummer Days when I was little. The leafy church—birch and lilac—the gaily spread dinner table, relatives, friends—everything in the park—dancing and music and flowers and fun. Oh, however far you run away—there'll always be memories in the baggage car—and remorse and guilt.

JEAN: I will come with you, but quickly now then, before it's too late. At once.

JULIE: Put on your things. (*Picks up the cage.*)

JEAN: No luggage, mind. That would give us away.

JULIE: No, only what we can take with us in the carriage.

JEAN (*fetching his hat*): What on earth have you got there? What is it?

JULIE: Only my greenfinch. I don't want to leave it behind.

JEAN: Well, I'll be damned! We're to take a bird-cage along, are we? You're crazy. Put that cage down.

JULIE: It's the only thing I'm taking from my home. The only living creature who cares for me since Diana went off like that. Don't be cruel. Let me take it.

JEAN: Put that cage down, I tell you—and don't talk so loud. Kristin will hear.

JULIE: No, I won't leave it in strange hands. I'd rather you killed it.

JEAN: Give the little beast here then and I'll wring its neck.

JULIE: But don't hurt it, don't . . . no, I can't.

JEAN: Give it here, I *can*.

JULIE (*taking the bird out of the cage and kissing it*): Dear little Serena, must you die and leave your mistress?

JEAN: Please don't make a scene. It's *your* life and future we're worrying about. Come on, quick now!

(*He snatches the bird from her, puts it on a board and picks up a chopper.* JULIE *turns away.*)

You should have learnt how to kill chickens instead of target-shooting. Then you wouldn't faint at a drop of blood.

JULIE (*screaming*): Kill me too! Kill me! You who can butcher an innocent creature without a quiver. Oh, how I hate you, how I loathe you! There is blood between us now. I curse the hour I first saw you. I curse the hour I was conceived in my mother's womb.

JEAN: What's the use of cursing. Let's go.

JULIE (*going to the chopping-block as if drawn against her will*): No, I won't go yet. I can't . . . I must look. Listen! There's a carriage. (*Listens without taking her eyes off the board and chopper.*) You don't think I can bear the sight of blood. You think I'm so weak. Oh, how I should like to see your blood and your brains on a chopping-block! I'd like to see the whole of your sex swimming like that in a sea of blood. I think I could drink out of your skull, bathe my feet in your broken breast and eat your heart roasted whole. You think I'm weak. You think I love you, that my womb yearned for your seed and I want to carry your offspring under my heart and nourish it with my blood. You think I want to bear your child and take your name. By the way, what is your name? I've never heard your surname. I don't suppose you've got one. I should be "Mrs. Hovel" or "Madam Dunghill." You dog wearing my collar, you lackey with my crest on your buttons! I share you with my cook; I'm my own servant's rival! Oh! Oh! Oh! . . . You think I'm a coward and will run away. No, now

I'm going to stay—and let the storm break. My father will come back . . . find his desk broken open . . . his money gone. Then he'll ring the bell—twice for the valet—and then he'll send for the police . . . and I shall tell everything. Everything. Oh how wonderful to make an end of it all—a real end! He has a stroke and dies and that's the end of all of us. Just peace and quietness . . . eternal rest. The coat of arms broken on the coffin and the Count's line extinct . . . But the valet's line goes on in an orphanage, wins laurels in the gutter and ends in jail.

JEAN: There speaks the noble blood! Bravo, Miss Julie. But now, don't let the cat out of the bag.

(KRISTIN *enters dressed for church, carrying a prayerbook.* JULIE *rushes to her and flings herself into her arms for protection.*)

JULIE: Help me, Kristin! Protect me from this man!

KRISTIN (*unmoved and cold*): What goings-on for a feast day morning! (*Sees the board.*) And what a filthy mess. What's it all about? Why are you screaming and carrying on so?

JULIE: Kristin, you're a woman and my friend. Beware of that scoundrel!

JEAN (*embarrassed*): While you ladies are talking things over, I'll go and shave. (*Slips into his room.*)

JULIE: You must understand. You must listen to me.

KRISTIN: I certainly don't understand such loose ways. Where are you off to in those traveling clothes? And he had his hat on, didn't he, eh?

JULIE: Listen, Kristin. Listen, I'll tell you everything.

KRISTIN: I don't want to know anything.

JULIE: You must listen.

KRISTIN: What to? Your nonsense with Jean? I don't care a rap about that; it's nothing to do with me. But if you're thinking of getting him to run off with you, we'll soon put a stop to that.

JULIE (*very nervously*): Please try to be calm, Kristin, and listen. I can't stay here, nor can Jean—so we must go abroad.

KRISTIN: Hm, hm!

JULIE (*brightening*): But you see, I've had an idea. Supposing we all three go—abroad—to Switzerland and start a hotel together . . . I've got some money, you see . . . and Jean and I could run the whole thing—and I thought you would take charge of the kitchen. Wouldn't that be splendid? Say yes, do. If you come with us everything will be fine. Oh do say yes! (*Puts her arms round* KRISTIN.)

KRISTIN (*coolly thinking*): Hm, hm.

JULIE (*presto tempo*): You've never traveled, Kristin. You should go abroad and see the world. You've no idea how nice it is traveling by train—new faces all the time and new countries. On our way through Hamburg we'll go to the zoo—you'll love that—and we'll go to the theater and the opera too . . . and when we get to Munich there'll be the museums, dear, and pictures by Rubens and Raphael—the great painters, you know . . . You've heard of Munich, haven't you? Where King Ludwig lived—you know, the king who went mad, . . . We'll see his castles—some of his castles are still just like in fairy-tales . . . and from there it's not far to Switzerland—and the Alps. Think of the Alps, Kristin dear, covered with snow in the middle of summer . . . and there are oranges there and trees that are green the whole year round . . .

(JEAN *is seen in the door of his room, sharpening his razor on a strop which he holds with his teeth and his left hand. He listens to the talk with satisfaction and now and then nods approval.* JULIE *continues,* tempo prestissimo.°)

And then we'll get a hotel . . . and I'll sit at the desk, while Jean receives the guests and goes out marketing and writes letters . . . There's life for you! Trains whistling, buses driving up, bells ringing upstairs and downstairs . . . and I shall make out the bills—and I shall cook them too . . . you've no idea how nervous travelers are when it comes to paying their bills. And you—you'll sit like a queen in the kitchen . . . of course there won't be any standing at the stove for you. You'll always have to be nicely dressed and ready to be seen, and with your looks—no, I'm not flattering you—one fine day you'll catch yourself a husband . . . some rich Englishman, I shouldn't wonder—they're the ones who are easy (*Slowing down.*) to catch . . . and then we'll get rich and build ourselves a villa on Lake Como . . . of course it rains there a little now and then—but (*Dully.*) the sun must shine there too sometimes—even though it seems gloomy—and if not—then we can come home again—come back—(*Pause.*)—here—or somewhere else . . .

KRISTIN: Look here, Miss Julie, do you believe all that yourself?

JULIE (*exhausted*): Do I believe it?

KRISTIN: Yes.

JULIE (*wearily*): I don't know. I don't believe anything any more. (*Sinks down on the bench; her head in her arms on the table.*) Nothing. Nothing at all.

KRISTIN (*turning to* JEAN): So you meant to beat it, did you?

JEAN (*disconcerted, putting the razor on the table*): Beat it? What are you talking about? You've heard Miss Julie's plan, and though she's tired now with being up all night, it's a perfectly sound plan.

KRISTIN: Oh, is it? If you thought I'd work for that . . .

JEAN (*interrupting*): Kindly use decent language in front of your mistress. Do you hear?

KRISTIN: Mistress?

---

tempo prestissimo, with a very rapid pace.

JEAN: Yes.

KRISTIN: Well, well, just listen to that!

JEAN: Yes, it would be a good thing if you did listen and talked less. Miss Julie is your mistress and what's made you lose your respect for her now ought to make you feel the same about yourself.

KRISTIN: I've always had enough self-respect—

JEAN: To despise other people.

KRISTIN: —not to go below my own station. Has the Count's cook ever gone with the groom or the swineherd? Tell me that.

JEAN: No, you were lucky enough to have a high-class chap for your beau.

KRISTIN: High-class all right—selling the oats out of the Count's stable.

JEAN: You're a fine one to talk—taking a commission on the groceries and bribes from the butcher.

KRISTIN: What the devil. . . ?

JEAN: And now you can't feel any respect for your employers. You, you!

KRISTIN: Are you coming to church with me? I should think you need a good sermon after your fine deeds.

JEAN: No, I'm not going to church today. You can go alone and confess your own sins.

KRISTIN: Yes, I'll do that and bring back enough forgiveness to cover yours too. The Saviour suffered and died on the cross for all our sins, and if we go to Him with faith and a penitent heart, He takes all our sins upon Himself.

JEAN: Even grocery thefts?

JULIE: Do you believe that, Kristin?

KRISTIN: That is my living faith, as sure as I stand here. The faith I learnt as a child and have kept ever since, Miss Julie. "But where sin abounded, grace did much more abound."

JULIE: Oh, if I had your faith! Oh, if . . .

KRISTIN: But you see you can't have it without God's special grace, and it's not given to all to have that.

JULIE: Who is it given to then?

KRISTIN: That's the great secret of the workings of grace, Miss Julie. God is no respecter of persons, and with Him the last shall be first . . .

JULIE: Then I suppose He does respect the last.

KRISTIN (continuing): . . . and it is easier for a camel to go through the eye of a needle than for a rich man to enter into the kingdom of God. That's how it is, Miss Julie. Now I'm going—alone, and on my way I shall tell the groom not to let any of the horses out, in case anyone should want to leave before the Count gets back. Good-by. (Exit.)

JEAN: What a devil! And all on account of a greenfinch.

JULIE (wearily): Never mind the greenfinch. Do you see any way out of this, any end to it?

JEAN (pondering): No.

JULIE: If you were in my place, what would you do?

JEAN: In your place? Wait a bit. If I was a woman—a lady of rank who had—fallen. I don't know. Yes, I do know now.

JULIE (picking up the razor and making a gesture): This?

JEAN: Yes. But I wouldn't do it, you know. There's a difference between us.

JULIE: Because you're a man and I'm a woman? What is the difference?

JEAN: The usual difference—between man and woman.

JULIE (holding the razor): I'd like to. But I can't. My father couldn't either, that time he wanted to.

JEAN: No, he didn't want to. He had to be revenged first.

JULIE: And now my mother is revenged again, through me.

JEAN: Didn't you ever love your father, Miss Julie?

JULIE: Deeply, but I must have hated him too—unconsciously. And he let me be brought up to despise my own sex, to be half woman, half man. Whose fault is what's happened? My father's, my mother's, or my own? My own? I haven't anything that's my own. I haven't one single thought that I didn't get from my father, one emotion that didn't come from my mother, and as for this last idea—about all people being equal—I got that from him, my fiancé—that's why I call him a cad. How can it be my fault? Push the responsibility on to Jesus, like Kristin does? No, I'm too proud and—thanks to my father's teaching—too intelligent. As for all that about a rich person not being able to get into heaven, it's just a lie, but Kristin, who has money in the savings-bank, will certainly not get in. Whose fault is it? What does it matter whose fault it is? In any case I must take the blame and bear the consequences.

JEAN: Yes, but . . . (There are two sharp rings on the bell. JULIE jumps to her feet. JEAN changes into his livery.) The Count is back. Supposing Kristin . . . (Goes to the speaking-tube, presses it and listens.)

JULIE: Has he been to his desk yet?

JEAN: This is Jean, sir. (Listens.) Yes, sir. (Listens.) Yes, sir, very good, sir. (Listens.) At once, sir? (Listens.) Very good, sir. In half an hour.

JULIE (in panic): What did he say? My God, what did he say?

JEAN: He ordered his boots and his coffee in half an hour.

JULIE: Then there's half an hour . . . Oh, I'm so tired! I can't do anything. Can't be sorry, can't run away, can't stay, can't live—can't die. Help me. Order me, and I'll obey like a dog. Do me this last service—save my honor, save his name. You know what I ought to do, but haven't the strength to do. Use your strength and order me to do it.

JEAN: I don't know why—I can't now—I don't understand . . . It's just as if this coat made me—I can't give you orders—and now that the Count has spoken to me—I can't quite explain, but . . . well, that devil of a lackey is bending my back again. I believe if the Count came down now and ordered me to cut my throat, I'd do it on the spot.

JULIE: Then pretend you're him and I'm you. You did some fine acting before, when you knelt to me and played the aristocrat. Or . . . Have you ever seen a hypnotist at the theater? *(He nods.)* He says to the person "Take the broom," and he takes it. He says "Sweep," and he sweeps . . .

JEAN: But the person has to be asleep.

JULIE *(as if in a trance)*: I am asleep already . . . the whole room has turned to smoke—and you look like a stove—a stove like a man in black with a tall hat—your eyes are glowing like coals when the fire is low—and your face is a white patch like ashes. *(The sunlight has now reached the floor and lights up* JEAN.*)* How nice and warm it is! *(She holds out her hands as though warming them at a fire.)* And so light—and so peaceful.

JEAN *(putting the razor in her hand)*: Here is the broom. Go now while it's light—out to the barn—and . . . *(Whispers in her ear.)*

JULIE *(waking)*: Thank you. I am going now—to rest.

But just tell me that even the first can receive the gift of grace.

JEAN: The first? No, I can't tell you that. But wait . . . Miss Julie, I've got it! You aren't one of the first any longer. You're one of the last.

JULIE: That's true, I'm one of the very last. I *am* the last. Oh! . . . But now I can't go. Tell me again to go.

JEAN: No, I can't now either. I can't.

JULIE: And the first shall be last.

JEAN: Don't think, don't think. You're taking my strength away too and making me a coward. What's that? I thought I saw the bell move . . . To be so frightened of a bell! Yes, but it's not just a bell. There's somebody behind it—a hand moving it— and something else moving the hand—and if you stop your ears—if you stop your ears—yes, then it rings louder than ever. Rings and rings until you answer—and then it's too late. Then the police come and . . . and . . . *(The bell rings twice loudly.* JEAN *flinches, then straightens himself up.)* It's horrible. But there's no other way to end it . . . Go!

(JULIE walks firmly out through the door.)

CURTAIN

Figure 1. Jean (Peter Stormare) describes his ambitious dream to Julie (Lena Olin) in the Royal Dramatic Theater of Sweden production of *Miss Julie,* directed by Ingmar Bergman, 1991. (Photograph: Bengt Wanselius.)

Figure 2. The Bergman production shows Jean (Peter Stormare) and Julie (Lena Olin), exhausted and depressed after their sexual encounter. (Photograph: Bengt Wanselius.)

Figure 3. In the Bergman production, Jean (Peter Stormare) embraces Kristin (Gerthi Kulle), who is dressed for church. (Photograph: Bengt Wanselius.)

Figure 4. The Bergman production's Jean (Peter Stormare), irritated and frustrated by Julie's talk of honor and shame, attacks the woman he has earlier seduced. (Photograph: Bengt Wanselius.)

Staging of *Miss Julie*

REVIEW OF THE ROYAL DRAMATIC THEATER
OF SWEDEN PRODUCTION AT THE BROOKLYN
ACADEMY OF MUSIC, 1991, BY MEL GUSSOW

It is midsummer night and the light through the windows of the kitchen has an unnatural glow. In the course of Ingmar Bergman's staging of Strindberg's "Miss Julie," that light will go through many subtle changes, counterpointing the emotional turbulence of the characters onstage. Their duel is a class war as well as a fierce battle of the sexes.

Despite all the portent, the play never loses its personal dimension, its sense of wounds mutually inflicted. Strindberg called "Miss Julie" a naturalistic tragedy, a fact that has never been so evident as in Mr. Bergman's stunning production. This is the opening play of the Royal Dramatic Theater of Sweden's all too brief season at the Brooklyn Academy of Music.

As the production flawlessly unfolds on stage at the Majestic Theater, one necessarily thinks of Bergman films like "Persona," in which the director confines disparate characters in domestic disharmony. Though the play remains firmly fixed within that kitchen, there is a feeling of life outside the room. "Miss Julie" is commonly regarded as a small-scale intimate drama. The director enlarges its dramatic vision so that the audience more clearly understands the psychological and societal forces that drive the title character to her destructive acts.

Initially, we see only the inhabitants of the kitchen: Jean, the valet, and Kristin, the cook. Jean (Peter Stormare) exudes fastidiousness. Pouring himself a glass of wine, he pretends to be both servant and master, and, after a sip, he offers himself an approving glance. Except for the accident of his birth, he could be an aristocrat. Later we will see that Miss Julie (Lena Olin) has a vulgarity that would be unacceptable in the servant class. Kristin (Gerthi Kulle) is quietly submissive in the background, demeaning herself to Jean's wishes.

Gunilla Palmstierna-Weiss's pale gray setting is perfect—everything neatly arranged in a pristine, painterly environment. There is as much significant and unobtrusive atmospheric detail in this room as in Mr. Bergman's "Fanny and Alexander."

Suddenly Miss Julie enters, her red dress and her forthright manner a brusque intrusion on the placidity of the room. Miss Olin brings with her a swirl of sensuality and immediately embarks on the seduction of Jean. But which one is the predator? Both could answer the call, as each is, to use the title of a related Strindberg drama, "playing with fire."

Miss Olin is a glamorous figure and she and Mr. Stormare are mutually attracted—with good reason. They are so evenly matched that a newcomer to the play might not be aware which character is the stronger. Although Miss Julie grasps control of her fate, it is Jean who will survive the "spell of this magical night."

Theatergoers can hear the dialogue in English on headsets, although without the translation, one is still aware of the themes—of submission, dishonor and revenge, of the urge but not the will toward flight. Even in moments of silence, the production never loses its highly charged intensity.

Just as the play alternates currents, Miss Olin is mercurial as Miss Julie. She is demanding in her approach to Jean, yet at odd times seems almost unsure of herself, summoning demons she is unable to control. The actress offers a beautifully seductive, virtuosic performance, one that translates in any language.

Mr. Stormare, who played the title role in Mr. Bergman's version of "Hamlet" several seasons ago at the Brooklyn Academy, also reveals the breadth of his artistry. His Jean is cool in his arrogance and childlike about receiving his due, whether it is the admiration of Kristin or a fulfillment of a youthful dream of paradise on earth.

Jean can seem stiff and fussy. Mr. Stormare keeps him aggressively masculine and also locates the self-mocking humor, as in his response to Miss Julie's suggestion that death may be his solution. "Die?" he says, dismissing the notion. "That's stupid. I'd rather start a hotel."

In a role that is often neglected, Miss Kulle offers a proud and watchful portrait of Kristin. She endures indignities, while shrinking from all of Miss Olin's patronizing overtures. Because the actress is herself attractive, she poses more of an alternative to Miss Julie than in many productions.

The director devises an evocative variation on the servants who dance onstage in a mime show. Instead of having them represent a joy of life, they are all self-indulgently drunk, falling over themselves like figures in a Breughel canvas.

The production runs almost two hours rather than the author's suggested 90 minutes. Mr. Bergman has slightly expanded the text by inserting a passage cut by Strindberg. But the primary reason for the length is that the director, with his cinematic eye, takes time for subtext, using the kitchen as an active presence and dramatizing mood along with character. This is an eloquent performance of a masterwork, in every sense a transcendent evening of theater.

OSCAR WILDE

1854–1900

While still an undergraduate at Oxford University, Oscar Wilde was already notorious for a devotion to style, thanks to his flamboyant clothes and witty repartee. Yet he also had a successful academic career, earning a First—top marks—in Classics and the Newdigate Prize for Poetry. Before he was thirty, Wilde had become so prominent in English society that he served as the model for characters in one novel, two plays, and, most notably, Gilbert and Sullivan's operetta, *Patience* (1881), in which the poet Bunthorne stands out as a satiric embodiment of Wilde's aesthetic credo and style. Although he came from a well-known Dublin family—his father was an eye surgeon who held a royal appointment and his mother a committed Irish nationalist—Wilde inherited little money from his father, and thus needed to earn both money and status by his wits. He succeeded brilliantly, as evidenced by a remunerative lecture tour to the United States; new friends in the theatrical and literary spotlight; a new play written originally in French (*Salomé*, 1893) for Sarah Bernhardt, the greatest actress of her generation; and short stories, a novel, and four more plays, written in just four years. By February 1895, when *The Importance of Being Earnest* opened on Valentine's Day, barely six weeks after the opening of *An Ideal Husband,* Wilde's professional achievement was stunning.

During that same period, however, Wilde's private life had become increasingly more complex and difficult. Though he married Constance Lloyd in 1884 and fathered two sons, he was also increasingly drawn to the company of young men, especially Lord Alfred Douglas, the youngest son of the Marquis of Queensbury, the man who established the international rules for boxing. Queensbury, rightly suspecting that the two men were lovers, objected strenuously to their relationship, and on the opening night of *The Importance of Being Earnest,* showed up at St. James's Theatre carrying a "bouquet" of vegetables, but was prevented from entering. Enraged, Queensbury went the next day to the Albemarle Club and left a card for Wilde with the somewhat cryptic (and misspelled) message: "To Oscar Wilde, posing somdomite." If Wilde had simply ignored this communication—which, after all, did not actually accuse him of homosexual behavior, but of posing as a homosexual—he might have avoided the disgrace that followed. Instead, probably urged on by Lord Alfred's dislike of his father, Wilde sued Queensbury for libel. The exposure of Wilde's homosexual behavior, not simply with Douglas, but with paid male prostitutes, led him to withdraw the libel case, and then to be tried for "indecent behavior." Convicted, he went to jail for two years, and after his release spent the last three years of his life abroad, separated from his family, from the glittering society that had once idolized him, and even, finally, from Lord Alfred Douglas, who agreed not to see Wilde again in exchange for financial support from his mother.

Since homosexual behavior was criminal in England (and remained so until 1967), it is not surprising that Wilde attempted to deny Queensbury's accusations. Yet Wilde surely knew that he was leading a double life, so it is also not surprising that, throughout his writing, he returns—almost obsessively—to characters and situations that dramatize the problematic nature of individual integrity, the stain of the past, and the puritanical judgments that people make so easily. *Lady Windermere's Fan* (1891) and *A Woman of No Importance* (1893) both focus on women who have borne illegitimate children and who are therefore ostracized by society. Lady Windermere, the young and naïve heroine of Wilde's first comedy who admits that she has "something of the Puritan" in her, condemns Mrs. Erlynne, a woman with a "past," only later to find out that Mrs. Erlynne is her mother. Similarly, Mrs. Arbuthnot, the "woman of no importance" who has a son out of wedlock, confesses her past to that son in order to keep him from becoming corrupted by his father; Lord Illingworth, the man who once seduced her and who tries to seduce their son by offering him financial and social security, is finally dismissed by Mrs. Arbuthnot, first directly when she refuses to marry him (the proposal is, after all, twenty years too late) and then, after his exit, when she refers to him as "a man of no importance."

Both of these plays center around women's moral and social predicaments, perhaps because late Victorian society seemed so quick to condemn female sexuality. But in *The Picture of Dorian Gray* (1890), Wilde's only novel, the perils of a double life are hauntingly detailed in the Gothic story of a character who retains his youthful good looks despite an increasingly dissolute life, the ravages of which are mysteriously recorded on a picture of him that grows steadily older and more vicious looking compared to his own mirror image. And in *An Ideal Husband* (1895), the protagonist with a secret past is Sir Robert Chiltern, a man who had, eighteen years earlier, given confidential government information to a financier in return for money that enabled Chiltern to move out of his job as secretary to a cabinet minister and into an increasingly brilliant political career. Chiltern is not the only one with secrets in the play; indeed, his blackmailer, Mrs. Cheveley, turns out to be a thief. Moreover, as Wilde makes clear when Chiltern appeals to his wife not to judge too harshly, idealism as well as deception can be a mistake. Chiltern's cry for forgiveness, "All sins, except a sin against itself, Love should forgive. All lives, save loveless lives, true Love should pardon," resonates with Wilde's own hidden identity.

Though all Wilde's comic plays contain elements of melodrama—the "fallen woman," the long-lost child, the devastating secret that might destroy a marriage, the blackmailer—they are also elegant and witty portrayals of upper-class society, of a world dominated by fashionable appearance, social status, and gossip. Each play features a character who functions both as a savvy commentator on that society, and as a member of it. That character—the wealthy man-about-town—is, at first, the speaker of lines that sound like Wilde himself, emphasizing not morality but style. One can hear the flamboyant wit of Wilde when Lord Darlington says to Lady Windermere, "It is absurd to divide people into good and bad. People are either charming or tedious," or when Lord Illingworth (in *A Woman of No Importance*) epigrammatically describes hunting—"The English country gentleman galloping after a fox—the unspeakable in full pursuit of the uneatable," or when Lord Goring (in *An Ideal Husband*) declares, "I love talking about nothing. It is the only thing I know anything about." Yet each of these characters is eventually moved by the melodramatic plot away from their seemingly detached position into an involvement in the action of the play.

What sets *The Importance of Being Earnest* apart from these other comedies is not the milieu so much as a thorough transformation of the basic situation that gives rise to the mixture of melodrama and flippancy in the earlier comedies. Though Wilde retained the element of secrecy, he transformed it from the concealment of a sexual or moral impropriety to the creation of a hidden but essentially harmless identity, devised merely to escape from societal pressures. And in keeping with his abandonment of a heavy moral burden, Wilde allows almost everyone in the play the power and pleasure of aphoristic wit, including not only the main characters, but also Lane, Algernon's butler; Miss Prism, Cecily's governess; and even the mild-mannered and naïve vicar, Chasuble.

Although the play is justly famed for its dazzling verbal wit, *The Importance of Being Earnest* draws much of its power from its high-handed rewriting of a familiar plot and its equally vivid portrayal of shamelessly egotistical people. As many critics have noted, the story of the child lost almost from birth and finally reunited with his parents is drawn not only from melodrama (and from Wilde's own *Lady Windermere's Fan*) but also from *Oedipus Rex*. Though Sophocles' play builds to the horror of Oedipus' recognition and Wilde's to the comic moment when Jack thinks that Lady Bracknell, mother of his beloved Gwendolen, may also be his own mother, tragedy is skirted and the truth, so carelessly dismissed by Algernon, is finally revealed. And though Wilde's comic characters all sound as stylishly witty as their author, they are nonetheless more than a collection of epigrams. Lady Bracknell, one of the great comic roles for women in Western drama, is both the dogmatic arbitress of societal norms and the target of satirical jabs. Algernon, the dandy-turned-lover, is also a hungry child, gobbling up cucumber sandwiches and muffins at an amazing rate. Even Cecily, growing up on a country estate, is not as unspoiled and naïve as one might think, but coolly and efficiently devastates Gwendolen's assurance in the tea-party scene. If the play looks back to the Restoration and eighteenth-century comedy of manners—one thinks of Sheridan's Mrs. Malaprop (*The Rivals*, 1775) as a linguistically challenged Lady Bracknell—it also looks forward to contemporary plays. Noel Coward foregrounds the sexual attraction/hostility between the central witty couple in *Private Lives* (1930); Joe Orton rewrites the lost child plot with increasingly complicated sexual relationships in *What the Butler Saw* (1969); and Tom Stoppard uses *The Importance of Being Earnest* as his central text in *Travesties* (1974), a play about revolution, both in politics and literature.

One of the recurring questions in producing this stylish play is how much emphasis to put on its wit and social artifice and how much (if any) on the complex personal reality that exists at the heart of the play. Desmond McCarthy, reviewing the famous 1939 production led by John Gielgud as Jack and Edith Evans as Lady Bracknell insisted that in "artificial comedy," as he called Wilde's play, "every gesture and intonation should be self-delighting; never a betrayal of direct feeling." The gestures and body language of Gwendolen and Cecily in 1939, responding to the offer by Jack and Algernon to be christened (see Figure 1) clearly display staged—rather than real—feelings. Edith Evans' performance, from her overbearing demeanor to her amazingly ornate hats (see Figure 2) to her unforgettable vocalization of "A handbag?" has been captured on film (1952) and still remains in the memory of audiences. Indeed, when Peter Hall staged the play at London's National Theatre in 1982, many critics commented that Judi Dench, then 47, was too young for the role (see Figure 3), conveniently forgetting that Edith Evans was just 49 when she first played the part. More crucially, Hall's cast avoided "campy artifice" and worked instead to present "plausible people in a slightly askew world" (see Michael Billington's review following the play, and Figure 4). For some reviewers, the production lacked charm and sparkle, but for others, the production revealed what Billington called "a daisy-chain of serious comment," a paradoxical description mirroring Wilde's own subtitle, "a trivial comedy for serious people." The paradoxes that pervade the play's linguistic surface work not only because they are witty, but because they vividly remind us of the perennial struggle between social appearance and private reality, a struggle that was deeply painful in Wilde's own life, and continues to be compelling for audiences today.

THE IMPORTANCE OF BEING EARNEST

BY OSCAR WILDE

CHARACTERS

JOHN WORTHING, J.P.
ALGERNON MONCRIEFF
REV. CANON CHASUBLE, D.D.
MERRIMAN, *butler*
LANE, *manservant*
LADY BRACKNELL
HON. GWENDOLEN FAIRFAX
CECILY CARDEW
MISS PRISM, *governess*

THE SCENES OF THE PLAY

ACT 1—*Algernon Moncrieff's flat in Half-Moon Street, W.°*
ACT 2—*The Garden at the Manor House, Woolton.*
ACT 3—*Drawing-Room at the Manor House, Woolton.*

ACT 1

(Morning-room in ALGERNON *'s flat in Half-Moon Street. The room is luxuriously and artistically furnished. The sound of a piano is heard in the adjoining room.)*
*(*LANE *is arranging afternoon tea on the table, and after the music has ceased,* ALGERNON *enters.)*

ALGERNON: Did you hear what I was playing, Lane?

LANE: I didn't think it polite to listen, sir.

ALGERNON: I'm sorry for that, for your sake. I don't play accurately—anyone can play accurately—but I play with wonderful expression. As far as the piano is concerned, sentiment is my forte. I keep science for life.

LANE: Yes, sir.

ALGERNON: And, speaking of the science of life, have you got the cucumber sandwiches out for Lady Bracknell?

LANE: Yes, sir. *(Hands them on a salver.)*

ALGERNON: *(Inspects them, takes two, and sits down on the sofa.)* Oh! . . . by the way, Lane, I see from your book that on Thursday night, when Lord Shoreham and Mr Worthing were dining with me, eight bottles of champagne are entered as having been consumed.

LANE: Yes, sir; eight bottles and a pint.

ALGERNON: Why is it that at a bachelor's establishment the servants invariably drink the champagne? I ask merely for information.

LANE: I attribute it to the superior quality of the wine, sir. I have often observed that in married households the champagne is rarely of a first-rate brand.

ALGERNON: Good Heavens! Is marriage so demoralizing as that?

LANE: I believe it *is* a very pleasant state, sir. I have had very little experience of it myself up to the present. I have only been married once. That was in consequence of a misunderstanding between myself and a young person.

ALGERNON: *(Languidly.)* I don't know that I am much interested in your family life, Lane.

LANE: No, sir; it is not a very interesting subject. I never think of it myself.

ALGERNON: Very natural, I am sure. That will do, Lane, thank you.

LANE: Thank you, sir. *(*LANE *goes out.)*

ALGERNON: Lane's views on marriage seem somewhat lax. Really, if the lower orders don't set us a good example, what on earth is the use of them? They seem, as a class, to have absolutely no sense of moral responsibility.

(Enter LANE.*)*

LANE: Mr Ernest Worthing.

(Enter JACK.*)* *(*LANE *goes out.)*

ALGERNON: How are you, my dear Ernest? What brings you up to town?

JACK: Oh, pleasure, pleasure! What else should bring one anywhere? Eating as usual, I see, Algy!

ALGERNON: *(Stiffly.)* I believe it is customary in good society to take some slight refreshment at five o'clock. Where have you been since last Thursday?

JACK: *(Sitting down on the sofa.)* In the country.

ALGERNON: What on earth do you do there?

JACK: *(Pulling off his gloves.)* When one is in town one

Half-Moon Street, W., fashionable street in central London.

617

amuses oneself. When one is in the country one amuses other people. It is excessively boring.

ALGERNON: And who are the people you amuse?

JACK: *(Airily)* Oh, neighbours, neighbours.

ALGERNON: Got nice neighbours in your part of Shropshire?

JACK: Perfectly horrid! Never speak to one of them.

ALGERNON: How immensely you must amuse them! *(Goes over and takes sandwich.)* By the way, Shropshire is your county, is it not?

JACK: Eh? Shropshire? Yes, of course. Hallo! Why all these cups? Why cucumber sandwiches? Why such reckless extravagance in one so young? Who is coming to tea?

ALGERNON: Oh! merely Aunt Augusta and Gwendolen.

JACK: How perfectly delightful!

ALGERNON: Yes, that is all very well; but I am afraid Aunt Augusta won't quite approve of your being here.

JACK: May I ask why?

ALGERNON: My dear fellow, the way you flirt with Gwendolen is perfectly disgraceful. It is almost as bad as the way Gwendolen flirts with you.

JACK: I am in love with Gwendolen. I have come up to town expressly to propose to her.

ALGERNON: I thought you had come up for pleasure? . . . I call that business.

JACK: How utterly unromantic you are!

ALGERNON: I really don't see anything romantic in proposing. It is very romantic to be in love. But there is nothing romantic about a definite proposal. Why, one may be accepted. One usually is, I believe. Then the excitement. If ever I get married, I'll certainly try to forget the fact.

JACK: I have no doubt about that, dear Algy. The Divorce Court was specially invented for people whose memories are so curiously constituted.

ALGERNON: Oh! there is no use speculating on that subject. Divorces are made in Heaven—*(JACK puts out his hand to take a sandwich. ALGERNON at once interferes.)* Please don't touch the cucumber sandwiches. They are ordered specially for Aunt Augusta. *(Takes one and eats it.)*

JACK: Well, you have been eating them all the time.

ALGERNON: That is quite a different matter. She is my aunt. *(Takes plate from below.)* Have some bread and butter. The bread and butter is for Gwendolen. Gwendolen is devoted to bread and butter.

JACK: *(Advancing to table and helping himself.)* And very good bread and butter it is too.

ALGERNON: Well, my dear fellow, you need not eat as if you were going to eat it all. You behave as if you were married to her already. You are not married to her already, and I don't think you ever will be.

JACK: Why on earth do you say that?

ALGERNON: Well, in the first place, girls never marry the men they flirt with. Girls don't think it right.

JACK: Oh, that is nonsense!

ALGERNON: It isn't. It is a great truth. It accounts for the extraordinary number of bachelors that one sees all over the place. In the second place, I don't give my consent.

JACK: Your consent!

ALGERNON: My dear fellow, Gwendolen is my first cousin. And before I allow you to marry her, you will have to clear up the whole question of Cecily. *(Rings bell.)*

JACK: Cecily! What on earth do you mean? What do you mean, Algy, by Cecily? I don't know anyone of the name of Cecily.

(Enter LANE.)

ALGERNON: Bring me that cigarette case Mr Worthing left in the smoking-room the last time he dined here.

LANE: Yes, sir. *(LANE goes out.)*

JACK: Do you mean to say you have had my cigarette case all this time? I wish to goodness you had let me know. I have been writing frantic letters to Scotland Yard about it. I was very nearly offering a large reward.

ALGERNON: Well, I wish you would offer one. I happen to be more than usually hard up.

JACK: There is no good offering a large reward now that the thing is found.

(Enter LANE with the cigarette case on a salver. ALGERNON takes it at once. LANE goes out.)

ALGERNON: I think that is rather mean of you, Ernest, I must say. *(Opens case and examines it.)* However, it makes no matter, for, now that I look at the inscription inside, I find that the thing isn't yours after all.

JACK: Of course it's mine. *(Moving to him.)* You have seen me with it a hundred times, and you have no right whatsoever to read what is written inside. It is a very ungentlemanly thing to read a private cigarette case.

ALGERNON: Oh! it is absurd to have a hard-and-fast rule about what one should read and what one shouldn't. More than half of modern culture depends on what one shouldn't read.

JACK: I am quite aware of the fact, and I don't propose to discuss modern culture. It isn't the sort of thing one should talk of in private. I simply want my cigarette case back.

ALGERNON: Yes; but this isn't your cigarette case. This cigarette case is a present from someone of the name of Cecily, and you said you didn't know anyone of that name.

JACK: Well, if you want to know, Cecily happens to be my aunt.

ALGERNON: Your aunt!

JACK: Yes. Charming old lady she is, too. Lives at Tunbridge Wells.° Just give it back to me, Algy.

ALGERNON: *(Retreating to back of sofa.)* But why does she call herself little Cecily if she is your aunt and lives at Tunbridge Wells? *(Reading.)* 'From little Cecily with her fondest love.'

JACK: *(Moving to sofa and kneeling upon it.)* My dear fellow, what on earth is there in that? Some aunts are tall, some aunts are not tall. That is a matter that surely an aunt may be allowed to decide for herself. You seem to think that every aunt should be exactly like your aunt! That is absurd! For Heaven's sake give me back my cigarette case. *(Follows* ALGERNON *round the room.)*

ALGERNON: Yes. But why does your aunt call you her uncle? 'From little Cecily, with her fondest love to her dear Uncle Jack.' There is no objection, I admit, to an aunt being a small aunt, but why an aunt, no matter what her size may be, should call her own nephew her uncle, I can't quite make out. Besides, your name isn't Jack at all; it is Ernest.

JACK: It isn't Ernest; it's Jack.

ALGERNON: You have always told me it was Ernest. I have introduced you to everyone as Ernest. You answer to the name of Ernest. You look as if your name was Ernest. You are the most earnest looking person I ever saw in my life. It is perfectly absurd your saying that your name isn't Ernest. It's on your cards. Here is one of them. *(Taking it from case)* 'Mr Ernest Worthing, B. 4, The Albany.' I'll keep this as a proof that your name is Ernest if ever you attempt to deny it to me, or to Gwendolen, or to anyone else. *(Puts the card in his pocket.)*

JACK: Well, my name is Ernest in town and Jack in the country, and the cigarette case was given to me in the country.

ALGERNON: Yes, but that does not account for the fact that your small Aunt Cecily, who lives at Tunbridge Wells, calls you her dear uncle. Come, old boy, you had much better have the thing out at once.

JACK: My dear Algy, you talk exactly as if you were a dentist. It is very vulgar to talk like a dentist when one isn't a dentist. It produces a false impression.

ALGERNON: Well, that is exactly what dentists always do. Now, go on! Tell me the whole thing. I may mention that I have always suspected you of being a confirmed and secret Bunburyist; and I am quite sure of it now.

JACK: Bunburyist? What on earth do you mean by a Bunburyist?

ALGERNON: I'll reveal to you the meaning of that incomparable expression as soon as you are kind enough to inform me why you are Ernest in town and Jack in the country.

JACK: Well, produce my cigarette case first.

ALGERNON: Here it is. *(Hands cigarette case.)* Now produce your explanation, and pray make it improbable. *(Sits on sofa.)*

JACK: My dear fellow, there is nothing improbable about my explanation at all. In fact it's perfectly ordinary. Old Mr Thomas Cardew, who adopted me when I was a little boy, made me in his will guardian to his granddaughter, Miss Cecily Cardew. Cecily, who addresses me as her uncle from motives of respect that you could not possibly appreciate, lives at my place in the country under the charge of her admirable governess, Miss Prism.

ALGERNON: Where is that place in the country, by the way?

JACK: That is nothing to you, dear boy. You are not going to be invited. . . . I may tell you candidly that the place is not in Shropshire.

ALGERNON: I suspected that, my dear fellow! I have Bunburyed all over Shropshire on two separate occasions. Now, go on. Why are you Ernest in town and Jack in the country?

JACK: My dear Algy, I don't know whether you will be able to understand my real motives. You are hardly serious enough. When one is placed in the position of guardian, one has to adopt a very high moral tone on all subjects. It's one's duty to do so. And as a high moral tone can hardly be said to conduce very much to either one's health or one's happiness, in order to get up to town I have always pretended to have a younger brother of the name of Ernest, who lives in the Albany, and gets into the most dreadful scrapes. That, my dear Algy, is the whole truth pure and simple.

ALGERNON: The truth is rarely pure and never simple. Modern life would be very tedious if it were either and modern literature a complete impossibility!

JACK: That wouldn't be at all a bad thing.

ALGERNON: Literary criticism is not your forte, my dear fellow. Don't try it. You should leave that to people who haven't been at a University. They do it so well in the daily papers. What you really are is a Bunburyist. I was quite right in saying you were a Bunburyist. You are one of the most advanced Bunburyists I know.

JACK: What on earth do you mean?

ALGERNON: You have invented a very useful younger brother called Ernest, in order that you may be able to come up to town as often as you like. I have invented an invaluable permanent invalid called Bunbury, in order that I may be able to go down into the country whenever I choose.

Tunbridge Wells, fashionable spa town in Kent.

Bunbury is perfectly invaluable. If it wasn't for Bunbury's extraordinary bad health, for instance, I wouldn't be able to dine with you at Willis's tonight, for I have been really engaged to Aunt Augusta for more than a week.

JACK: I haven't asked you to dine with me anywhere tonight.

ALGERNON: I know. You are absurdly careless about sending out invitations. It is very foolish of you. Nothing annoys people so much as not receiving invitations.

JACK: You had much better dine with your Aunt Augusta.

ALGERNON: I haven't the smallest intention of doing anything of the kind. To begin with, I dined there on Monday, and once a week is quite enough to dine with one's own relations. In the second place, whenever I do dine there I am always treated as a member of the family, and sent down with either no woman at all, or two. In the third place, I know perfectly well whom she will place me next to, tonight. She will place me next Mary Farquhar, who always flirts with her own husband across the dinner table. That is not very pleasant. Indeed, it is not even decent . . . and that sort of thing is enormously on the increase. The amount of women in London who flirt with their own husbands is perfectly scandalous. It looks so bad. It is simply washing one's clean linen in public. Besides, now that I know you to be a confirmed Bunburyist, I naturally want to talk to you about Bunburying. I want to tell you the rules.

JACK: I'm not a Bunburyist at all. If Gwendolen accepts me, I am going to kill my brother, indeed I think I'll kill him in any case. Cecily is a little too much interested in him. It is rather a bore. So I am going to get rid of Ernest. And I strongly advise you to do the same with Mr . . . with your invalid friend who has the absurd name.

ALGERNON: Nothing will induce me to part with Bunbury, and if you ever get married, which seems to me extremely problematic, you will be very glad to know Bunbury. A man who marries without knowing Bunbury has a very tedious time of it.

JACK: That is nonsense. If I marry a charming girl like Gwendolen, and she is the only girl I ever saw in my life that I would marry, I certainly won't want to know Bunbury.

ALGERNON: Then your wife will. You don't seem to realize, that in married life three is company and two is none.

JACK: (Sententiously) That, my dear young friend, is the theory that the corrupt French Drama has been propounding for the last fifty years.

ALGERNON: Yes; and that the happy English home has proved in half the time.

JACK: For Heaven's sake, don't try to be cynical. It's perfectly easy to be cynical.

ALGERNON: My dear fellow, it isn't easy to be anything nowadays. There's such a lot of beastly competition about. (The sound of an electric bell is heard.) Ah! that must be Aunt Augusta. Only relatives, or creditors, ever ring in that Wagnerian manner. Now, if I get her out of the way for ten minutes, so that you can have an opportunity for proposing to Gwendolen, may I dine with you tonight at Willis's?

JACK: I suppose so, if you want to.

ALGERNON: Yes, but you must be serious about it. I hate people who are not serious about meals. It is so shallow of them.

(Enter LANE.)

LANE: Lady Bracknell and Miss Fairfax.

(ALGERNON goes forward to meet them. Enter LADY BRACKNELL and GWENDOLEN.)

LADY BRACKNELL: Good afternoon, dear Algernon, I hope you are behaving very well.

ALGERNON: I'm feeling very well, Aunt Augusta.

LADY BRACKNELL: That's not quite the same thing. In fact the two things rarely go together. (Sees JACK and bows to him with icy coldness.)

ALGERNON: (To GWENDOLEN) Dear me, you are smart!

GWENDOLEN: I am always smart! Aren't I, Mr Worthing?

JACK: You're quite perfect, Miss Fairfax.

GWENDOLEN: Oh! I hope I am not that. It would leave no room for developments, and I intend to develop in many directions. (GWENDOLEN and JACK sit down together in the corner.)

LADY BRACKNELL: I'm sorry if we are a little late, Algernon, but I was obliged to call on dear Lady Harbury. I hadn't been there since her poor husband's death. I never saw a woman so altered; she looks quite twenty years younger. And now I'll have a cup of tea, and one of those nice cucumber sandwiches you promised me.

ALGERNON: Certainly, Aunt Augusta. (Goes over to tea-table.)

LADY BRACKNELL: Won't you come and sit here, Gwendolen?

GWENDOLEN: Thanks, Mamma, I'm quite comfortable where I am.

ALGERNON: (Picking up empty plate in horror.) Good heavens! Lane! Why are there no cucumber sandwiches? I ordered them specially.

LANE: (Gravely.) There were no cucumbers in the market this morning, sir. I went down twice.

ALGERNON: No cucumbers!

LANE: No, sir. Not even for ready money.

ALGERNON: That will do, Lane, thank you.

LANE: Thank you, sir.

ALGERNON: I am greatly distressed, Aunt Augusta, about there being no cucumbers, not even for ready money.

LADY BRACKNELL: It really makes no matter, Algernon. I had some crumpets with Lady Harbury, who seems to me to be living entirely for pleasure now.

ALGERNON: I hear her hair has turned quite gold from grief.

LADY BRACKNELL: It certainly has changed its color. From what cause I, of course, cannot say. (ALGERNON crosses and hands tea.) Thank you. I've quite a treat for you tonight, Algernon. I am going to send you down with Mary Farquhar. She is such a nice woman, and so attentive to her husband. It's delightful to watch them.

ALGERNON: I am afraid, Aunt Augusta, I shall have to give up the pleasure of dining with you tonight after all.

LADY BRACKNELL: (Frowning) I hope not, Algernon. It would put my table completely out. Your uncle would have to dine upstairs. Fortunately he is accustomed to that.

ALGERNON: It is a great bore, and, I need hardly say, a terrible disappointment to me, but the fact is I have just had a telegram to say that my poor friend Bunbury is very ill again. (Exchanges glances with JACK.) They seem to think I should be with him.

LADY BRACKNELL: It is very strange. This Mr Bunbury seems to suffer from curiously bad health.

ALGERNON: Yes; poor Bunbury is a dreadful invalid.

LADY BRACKNELL: Well, I must say, Algernon, that I think it is high time that Mr Bunbury made up his mind whether he was going to live or to die. This shilly-shallying with the question is absurd. Nor do I in any way approve of the modern sympathy with invalids. I consider it morbid. Illness of any kind is hardly a thing to be encouraged in others. Health is the primary duty of life. I am always telling that to your poor uncle, but he never seems to take much notice . . . as far as any improvement in his ailments goes. I should be much obliged if you would ask Mr Bunbury, from me, to be kind enough not to have a relapse on Saturday, for I rely on you to arrange my music for me. It is my last reception, and one wants something that will encourage conversation, particularly at the end of the season when everyone has practically said whatever they had to say, which, in most cases, was probably not much.

ALGERNON: I'll speak to Bunbury, Aunt Augusta, if he is still conscious, and I think I can promise you he'll be all right by Saturday. Of course the music is a great difficulty. You see, if one plays good music, people don't listen, and if one plays bad music, people don't talk. But I'll run over the programme I've drawn out, if you will kindly come into the next room for a moment.

LADY BRACKNELL: Thank you, Algernon. It is very thoughtful of you. (Rising, and following ALGERNON.) I'm sure the programme will be delightful, after a few expurgations. French songs I cannot possibly allow. People always seem to think that they are improper, and either look shocked, which is vulgar, or laugh, which is worse. But German sounds a thoroughly respectable language, and indeed, I believe is so. Gwendolen, you will accompany me.

GWENDOLEN: Certainly, Mamma.

(LADY BRACKNELL and ALGERNON go into the music-room. GWENDOLEN remains behind.)

JACK: Charming day it has been, Miss Fairfax.

GWENDOLEN: Pray don't talk to me about the weather, Mr Worthing. Whenever people talk to me about the weather, I always feel quite certain that they mean something else. And that makes me so nervous.

JACK: I do mean something else.

GWENDOLEN: I thought so. In fact, I am never wrong.

JACK: And I would like to be allowed to take advantage of Lady Bracknell's temporary absence. . . .

GWENDOLEN: I would certainly advise you to do so. Mamma has a way of coming back suddenly into a room that I have often had to speak to her about.

JACK: (Nervously.) Miss Fairfax, ever since I met you I have admired you more than any girl . . . I have ever met since . . . I met you.

GWENDOLEN: Yes, I am quite aware of the fact. And I often wish that in public, at any rate, you had been more demonstrative. For me you have always had an irresistible fascination. Even before I met you I was far from indifferent to you. (JACK looks at her in amazement.) We live, as I hope you know, Mr Worthing, in an age of ideals. The fact is constantly mentioned in the more expensive monthly magazines, and has reached the provincial pulpits I am told: and my ideal has always been to love someone of the name of Ernest. There is something in that name that inspires absolute confidence. The moment Algernon first mentioned to me that he had a friend called Ernest, I knew I was destined to love you.

JACK: You really love me, Gwendolen?

GWENDOLEN: Passionately!

JACK: Darling! You don't know how happy you've made me.

GWENDOLEN: My own Ernest!

JACK: But you don't mean to say that you couldn't love me if my name wasn't Ernest?

GWENDOLEN: But your name is Ernest.

JACK: Yes, I know it is. But supposing it was something

else? Do you mean to say you couldn't love me then?

GWENDOLEN: *(Glibly.)* Ah! that is clearly a metaphysical speculation, and like most metaphysical speculations has very little reference at all to the actual facts of real life, as we know them.

JACK: Personally, darling, to speak quite candidly, I don't much care about the name of Ernest . . . I don't think the name suits me at all.

GWENDOLEN: It suits you perfectly. It is a divine name. It has a music of its own. It produces vibrations.

JACK: Well, really, Gwendolen, I must say that I think there are lots of other much nicer names. I think Jack, for instance, a charming name.

GWENDOLEN: Jack? . . . No, there is very little music in the name Jack, if any at all, indeed. It does not thrill. It produces absolutely no vibrations. . . . I have known several Jacks, and they all, without exception, were more than usually plain. Besides, Jack is a notorious domesticity for John! And I pity any woman who is married to a man called John. She would probably never be allowed to know the entrancing pleasure of a single moment's solitude. The only really safe name is Ernest.

JACK: Gwendolen, I must get christened at once—I mean we must get married at once. There is no time to be lost.

GWENDOLEN: Married, Mr Worthing?

JACK: *(Astounded.)* Well . . . surely. You know that I love you, and you led me to believe, Miss Fairfax, that you were not absolutely indifferent to me.

GWENDOLEN: I adore you. But you haven't proposed to me yet. Nothing has been said at all about marriage. The subject has not even been touched on.

JACK: Well . . . may I propose to you now?

GWENDOLEN: I think it would be an admirable opportunity. And to spare you any possible disappointment, Mr Worthing, I think it only fair to tell you quite frankly beforehand that I am fully determined to accept you.

JACK: Gwendolen!

GWENDOLEN: Yes, Mr Worthing, what have you got to say to me?

JACK: You know what I have got to say to you.

GWENDOLEN: Yes, but you don't say it.

JACK: Gwendolen, will you marry me? *(Goes on his knees.)*

GWENDOLEN: Of course I will, darling. How long you have been about it! I am afraid you have had very little experience in how to propose.

JACK: My own one, I have never loved anyone in the world but you.

GWENDOLEN: Yes, but men often propose for practice. I know my brother Gerald does. All my girlfriends tell me so. What wonderfully blue eyes you have, Ernest! They are quite, quite blue. I hope you will always look at me just like that, especially when there are other people present.

(Enter LADY BRACKNELL.)

LADY BRACKNELL: Mr Worthing! Rise, sir, from this semi-recumbent posture. It is most indecorous.

GWENDOLEN: Mamma! *(He tries to rise; she restrains him.)* I must beg you to retire. This is no place for you. Besides, Mr Worthing has not quite finished yet.

LADY BRACKNELL: Finished what, may I ask?

GWENDOLEN: I am engaged to Mr Worthing, Mamma. *(They rise together.)*

LADY BRACKNELL: Pardon me, you are not engaged to anyone. When you do become engaged to someone, I, or your father, should his health permit him, will inform you of the fact. An engagement should come on a young girl as a surprise, pleasant or unpleasant, as the case may be. It is hardly a matter that she could be allowed to arrange for herself. . . . And now I have a few questions to put to you, Mr Worthing. While I am making these inquiries, you, Gwendolen, will wait for me below in the carriage.

GWENDOLEN: *(Reproachfully.)* Mamma!

LADY BRACKNELL: In the carriage, Gwendolen!

(GWENDOLEN goes to the door. She and JACK blow kisses to each other behind LADY BRACKNELL's back. LADY BRACKNELL looks vaguely about as if she could not understand what the noise was. Finally turns round.) Gwendolen, the carriage!

GWENDOLEN: Yes, Mamma. *(Goes out, looking back at JACK.)*

LADY BRACKNELL: *(Sitting down.)* You can take a seat, Mr Worthing. *(Looks in her pocket for note-book and pencil.)*

JACK: Thank you, Lady Bracknell, I prefer standing.

LADY BRACKNELL: *(Pencil and note-book in hand.)* I feel bound to tell you that you are not down on my list of eligible young men, although I have the same list as the dear Duchess of Bolton has. We work together, in fact. However, I am quite ready to enter your name, should your answers be what a really affectionate mother requires. Do you smoke?

JACK: Well, yes, I must admit I smoke.

LADY BRACKNELL: I am glad to hear it. A man should always have an occupation of some kind. There are far too many idle men in London as it is. How old are you?

JACK: Twenty-nine.

LADY BRACKNELL: A very good age to be married at. I have always been of opinion that a man who desires to get married should know either everything or nothing. Which do you know?

JACK: *(After some hesitation.)* I know nothing, Lady Bracknell.

LADY BRACKNELL: I am pleased to hear it. I do not approve of anything that tampers with natural ignorance. Ignorance is like a delicate exotic fruit; touch it and the bloom is gone. The whole theory of modern education is radically unsound. Fortunately in England, at any rate, education produces no effect whatsoever. If it did, it would prove a serious danger to the upper classes, and probably lead to acts of violence in Grosvenor Square.° What is your income?

JACK: Between seven and eight thousand a year.°

LADY BRACKNELL: *(Makes a note in her book.)* In land, or in investments?

JACK: In investments, chiefly.

LADY BRACKNELL: That is satisfactory. What between the duties expected of one during one's lifetime, and the duties exacted from one after one's death, land has ceased to be either a profit or a pleasure. It gives one position, and prevents one from keeping it up. That's all that can be said about land.

JACK: I have a country house with some land, of course, attached to it, about fifteen hundred acres, I believe; but I don't depend on that for my real income. In fact, as far as I can make out, the poachers are the only people who make anything out of it.

LADY BRACKNELL: A country house! How many bedrooms? Well, that point can be cleared up afterwards. You have a town house, I hope? A girl with a simple, unspoiled nature, like Gwendolen, could hardly be expected to reside in the country.

JACK: Well, I own a house in Belgrave Square,° but it is let by the year to Lady Bloxham. Of course, I can get it back whenever I like, at six months' notice.

LADY BRACKNELL: Lady Bloxham? I don't know her.

JACK: Oh, she goes about very little. She is a lady considerably advanced in years.

LADY BRACKNELL: Ah, nowadays that is no guarantee of respectability of character. What number in Belgrave Square?

JACK: 149.

LADY BRACKNELL: *(Shaking her head.)* The unfashionable side. I thought there was something. However, that could easily be altered.

JACK: Do you mean the fashion, or the side?

LADY BRACKNELL: *(Sternly.)* Both, if necessary, I presume. What are your politics?

JACK: Well, I am afraid I really have none. I am a Liberal Unionist.°

LADY BRACKNELL: Oh, they count as Tories. They dine with us. Or come in the evening, at any rate. Now to minor matters. Are your parents living?

JACK: I have lost both my parents.

LADY BRACKNELL: Both? . . . That seems like carelessness. Who was your father? He was evidently a man of some wealth. Was he born in what the Radical papers call the purple of commerce, or did he rise from the ranks of the aristocracy?

JACK: I am afraid I really don't know. The fact is, Lady Bracknell, I said I had lost my parents. It would be nearer the truth to say that my parents seem to have lost me. . . . I don't actually know who I am by birth. I was . . . well, I was found.

LADY BRACKNELL: Found!

JACK: The late Mr Thomas Cardew, an old gentleman of a very charitable and kindly disposition, found me, and gave me the name of Worthing, because he happened to have a first-class ticket for Worthing in his pocket at the time. Worthing is a place in Sussex. It is a seaside resort.

LADY BRACKNELL: Where did the charitable gentleman who had a first-class ticket for this seaside resort find you?

JACK: *(Gravely.)* In a handbag.

LADY BRACKNELL: A handbag?

JACK: *(Very seriously.)* Yes, Lady Bracknell. I was in a handbag—a somewhat large, black leather handbag, with handles to it—an ordinary handbag in fact.

LADY BRACKNELL: In what locality did this Mr James, or Thomas, Cardew come across this ordinary handbag?

JACK: In the cloakroom at Victoria Station. It was given to him in mistake for his own.

LADY BRACKNELL: The cloakroom at Victoria Station?

JACK: Yes. The Brighton line.

LADY BRACKNELL: The line is immaterial. Mr Worthing, I confess I feel somewhat bewildered by what you have just told me. To be born, or at any rate, bred in a handbag, whether it had handles or not, seems to me to display a contempt for the ordinary decencies of family life that reminds one of the worst excesses of the French Revolution. And I presume you know what that unfortunate movement led to? As for the particular locality in which the handbag was found, a cloakroom at a railway station might serve to conceal a social indiscretion—has probably, indeed, been used for that purpose before now—but it could hardly be regarded as an assured basis for a recognized position in good society.

JACK: May I ask you then what you would advise me to do? I need hardly say I would do anything in the world to ensure Gwendolen's happiness.

LADY BRACKNELL: I would strongly advise you, Mr Worthing, to try and acquire some relations as

---

Grosvenor Square, central square in Mayfair, the most expensive residential area in London. **seven and eight thousand a year,** approximately $35,000 to $40,000 in 1895, but worth much more in terms of purchasing power today. **Belgrave Square,** select residential area in London. **Liberal Unionists,** conservative wing of Liberal party, and thus acceptable to Lady Bracknell.

soon as possible, and to make a definite effort to produce at any rate one parent, of either sex, before the season is quite over.

JACK: Well, I don't see how I could possibly manage to do that. I can produce the handbag at any moment. It is in my dressing-room at home. I really think that should satisfy you, Lady Bracknell.

LADY BRACKNELL: Me, sir! What has it to do with me? You can hardly imagine that I and Lord Bracknell would dream of allowing our only daughter—a girl brought up with the utmost care—to marry into a cloakroom, and form an alliance with a parcel? Good morning, Mr Worthing!

(LADY BRACKNELL *sweeps out in majestic indignation.*)

JACK: Good morning! (ALGERNON, *from the other room, strikes up the* Wedding March. JACK *looks perfectly furious, and goes to the door.*) For goodness' sake don't play that ghastly tune, Algy! How idiotic you are!

(*The music stops, and* ALGERNON *enters cheerily.*)

ALGERNON: Didn't it go off all right, old boy? You don't mean to say Gwendolen refused you? I know it is a way she has. She is always refusing people. I think it is most ill-natured of her.

JACK: Oh, Gwendolen is as right as a trivet. As far as she is concerned, we are engaged. Her mother is perfectly unbearable. Never met such a gorgon . . . I don't really know what a gorgon is like, but I am quite sure that Lady Bracknell is one. In any case, she is a monster, without being a myth, which is rather unfair . . . I beg your pardon, Algy, I suppose I shouldn't talk about your own aunt in that way before you.

ALGERNON: My dear boy, I love hearing my relations abused. It is the only thing that makes me put up with them at all. Relations are simply a tedious pack of people who haven't got the remotest knowledge of how to live, nor the smallest instinct about when to die.

JACK: Oh, that is nonsense!

ALGERNON: It isn't!

JACK: Well, I won't argue about the matter. You always want to argue about things.

ALGERNON: That is exactly what things were originally made for.

JACK: Upon my word, if I thought that, I'd shoot myself. . . . (*A pause.*) You don't think there is any chance of Gwendolen becoming like her mother in about a hundred and fifty years, do you, Algy?

ALGERNON: All women become like their mothers. That is their tragedy. No man does. That's his.

JACK: Is that clever?

ALGERNON: It is perfectly phrased! and quite as true as any observation in civilized life should be.

JACK: I am sick to death of cleverness. Everybody is clever nowadays. You can't go anywhere without meeting clever people. The thing has become an absolute public nuisance. I wish to goodness we had a few fools left.

ALGERNON: We have.

JACK: I should extremely like to meet them. What do they talk about?

ALGERNON: The fools! Oh! about the clever people, of course.

JACK: What fools!

ALGERNON: By the way, did you tell Gwendolen the truth about your being Ernest in town, and Jack in the country?

JACK: (*In a very patronizing manner.*) My dear fellow, the truth isn't quite the sort of thing one tells to a nice sweet refined girl. What extraordinary ideas you have about the way to behave to a woman!

ALGERNON: The only way to behave to a woman is to make love to her, if she is pretty, and to someone else if she is plain.

JACK: Oh, that is nonsense.

ALGERNON: What about your brother? What about the profligate Ernest?

JACK: Oh, before the end of the week I shall have got rid of him. I'll say he died in Paris of apoplexy. Lots of people die of apoplexy, quite suddenly, don't they?

ALGERNON: Yes, but it's hereditary, my dear fellow. It's a sort of thing that runs in families. You had much better say a severe chill.

JACK: You are sure a severe chill isn't hereditary, or anything of that kind?

ALGERNON: Of course it isn't!

JACK: Very well, then. My poor brother Ernest is carried off suddenly in Paris, by a severe chill. That gets rid of him.

ALGERNON: But I thought you said that . . . Miss Cardew was a little too much interested in your poor brother Ernest? Won't she feel his loss a good deal?

JACK: Oh, that is all right. Cecily is not a silly romantic girl, I am glad to say. She has got a capital appetite, goes long walks, and pays no attention at all to her lessons.

ALGERNON: I would rather like to see Cecily.

JACK: I will take very good care you never do. She is excessively pretty, and she is only just eighteen.

ALGERNON: Have you told Gwendolen yet that you have an excessively pretty ward who is only just eighteen?

JACK: Oh! one doesn't blurt these things out to people. Cecily and Gwendolen are perfectly certain to be extremely great friends. I'll bet you anything you like that half an hour after they have met, they will be calling each other sister.

ALGERNON: Women only do that when they have

called each other a lot of other things first. Now, my dear boy, if we want to get a good table at Willis's, we really must go and dress. Do you know it is nearly seven?

JACK: *(Irritably)* Oh! it always is nearly seven.

ALGERNON: Well, I'm hungry.

JACK: I never knew you when you weren't. . . .

ALGERNON: What shall we do after dinner? Go to a theater?

JACK Oh, no! I loathe listening.

ALGERNON: Well, let us go to the club?

JACK: Oh, no! I hate talking.

ALGERNON: Well, we might trot round to the Empire° at ten?

JACK: Oh, no! I can't bear looking at things. It is so silly.

ALGERNON: Well, what shall we do?

JACK: Nothing!

ALGERNON: It is awfully hard work doing nothing. However, I don't mind hard work where there is no definite object of any kind.

(Enter LANE.*)*

LANE: Miss Fairfax.

(Enter GWENDOLEN. LANE *goes out.)*

ALGERNON: Gwendolen, upon my word!

GWENDOLEN: Algy, kindly turn your back. I have something very particular to say to Mr Worthing.

ALGERNON: Really, Gwendolen, I don't think I can allow this at all.

GWENDOLEN: Algy, you always adopt a strictly immoral attitude towards life. You are not quite old enough to do that. *(ALGERNON retires to the fireplace.)*

JACK: My own darling!

GWENDOLEN: Ernest, we may never be married. From the expression on Mamma's face I fear we never shall. Few parents nowadays pay any regard to what their children say to them. The old-fashioned respect for the young is fast dying out. Whatever influence I ever had over Mamma, I lost at the age of three. But although she may prevent us from becoming man and wife, and I may marry someone else, and marry often, nothing that she can possibly do can alter my eternal devotion to you.

JACK: Dear Gwendolen!

GWENDOLEN: The story of your romantic origin, as related to me by Mamma, with unpleasing comments, has naturally stirred the deeper fibers of my nature. Your Christian name has an irresistible fascination. The simplicity of your character makes you exquisitely incomprehensible to

me. Your town address at the Albany I have. What is your address in the country?

JACK: The Manor House, Woolton, Hertfordshire.

(ALGERNON, who has been carefully listening, smiles to himself, and writes the address on his shirt-cuff. Then picks up the Railway Guide.)

GWENDOLEN: There is a good postal service, I suppose? It may be necessary to do something desperate. That of course will require serious consideration. I will communicate with you daily.

JACK: My own one!

GWENDOLEN: How long do you remain in town?

JACK: Till Monday.

GWENDOLEN: Good! Algy, you may turn round now.

ALGERNON: Thanks, I've turned round already.

GWENDOLEN: You may also ring the bell.

JACK: You will let me see you to your carriage, my own darling?

GWENDOLEN: Certainly.

JACK: *(To* LANE, *who now enters.)* I will see Miss Fairfax out.

LANE: Yes, sir. *(*JACK *and* GWENDOLEN *go off.)*

*(*LANE *presents several letters on a salver to* ALGERNON. *It is to be surmised that they are bills, as* ALGERNON, *after looking at the envelopes, tears them up.)*

ALGERNON: A glass of sherry, Lane.

LANE: Yes, sir.

ALGERNON: Tomorrow, Lane, I'm going Bunburying.

LANE: Yes, sir.

ALGERNON: I shall probably not be back till Monday. You can put up my dress clothes, my smoking jacket, and all the Bunbury suits. . . .

LANE: Yes, sir. *(Handing sherry.)*

ALGERNON: I hope tomorrow will be a fine day, Lane.

LANE: It never is, sir.

ALGERNON: Lane, you're a perfect pessimist.

LANE: I do my best to give satisfaction, sir.

(Enter JACK. LANE *goes off.)*

JACK: There's a sensible, intellectual girl! The only girl I ever cared for in my life. *(*ALGERNON *is laughing immoderately.)* What on earth are you so amused at?

ALGERNON: Oh, I'm a little anxious about poor Bunbury, that is all.

JACK: If you don't take care, your friend Bunbury will get you into a serious scrape some day.

ALGERNON: I love scrapes. They are the only things that are never serious.

JACK: Oh, that's nonsense, Algy. You never talk anything but nonsense.

ALGERNON: Nobody ever does.

*(*JACK *looks indignantly at him, and leaves the room.* ALGERNON *lights a cigarette, reads his shirt-cuff, and smiles.)*

ACT-DROP.

Empire, variety theater in Leicester Square.

ACT 2

(Garden at the Manor House. A flight of gray stone steps leads up to the house. The garden, an old-fashioned one, full of roses. Time of year, July. Basket chairs,° and a table covered with books, are set under a large yew tree.)

(MISS PRISM discovered seated at the table. CECILY is at the back watering flowers.)

MISS PRISM: *(Calling)* Cecily, Cecily! Surely such a utilitarian occupation as the watering of flowers is rather Moulton's° duty than yours? Especially at a moment when intellectual pleasures await you. Your German grammar is on the table. Pray open it at page fifteen. We will repeat yesterday's lesson.

CECILY: *(Coming over very slowly.)* But I don't like German. It isn't at all a becoming language. I know perfectly well that I look quite plain after my German lesson.

MISS PRISM: Child, you know how anxious your guardian is that you should improve yourself in every way. He laid particular stress on your German, as he was leaving for town yesterday. Indeed, he always lays stress on your German when he is leaving for town.

CECILY: Dear Uncle Jack is so very serious! Sometimes he is so serious that I think he cannot be quite well.

MISS PRISM: *(Drawing herself up.)* Your guardian enjoys the best of health, and his gravity of demeanor is especially to be commended in one so comparatively young as he is. I know no one who has a higher sense of duty and responsibility.

CECILY: I suppose that is why he often looks a little bored when we three are together.

MISS PRISM: Cecily! I am surprised at you. Mr Worthing has many troubles in his life. Idle merriment and triviality would be out of place in his conversation. You must remember his constant anxiety about that unfortunate young man his brother.

CECILY: I wish Uncle Jack would allow that unfortunate young man, his brother, to come down here sometimes. We might have a good influence over him, Miss Prism. I am sure you certainly would. You know German, and Geology, and things of that kind influence a man very much. (CECILY *begins to write in her diary.)*

MISS PRISM: *(Shaking her head.)* I do not think that even I could produce any effect on a character that according to his own brother's admission is irretrievably weak and vacillating. Indeed I am not sure that I would desire to reclaim him. I am not in favor of this modern mania for turning bad people into good people at a moment's notice. As a man sows so let him reap. You must put away your diary, Cecily. I really don't see why you should keep a diary at all.

CECILY: I keep a diary in order to enter the wonderful secrets of my life. If I didn't write them down I should probably forget all about them.

MISS PRISM: Memory, my dear Cecily, is the diary that we all carry about with us.

CECILY: Yes, but it usually chronicles the things that have never happened, and couldn't possibly have happened. I believe that memory is responsible for nearly all the three-volume novels that Mudie° sends us.

MISS PRISM: Do not speak slightingly of the three-volume novel, Cecily. I wrote one myself in earlier days.

CECILY: Did you really, Miss Prism? How wonderfully clever you are! I hope it did not end happily? I don't like novels that end happily. They depress me so much.

MISS PRISM: The good ended happily, and the bad unhappily. That is what fiction means.

CECILY: I suppose so. But it seems very unfair. And was your novel ever published?

MISS PRISM: Alas! no. The manuscript unfortunately was abandoned. I use the word in the sense of lost or mislaid. To your work, child, these speculations are profitless.

CECILY: *(Smiling.)* But I see dear Dr Chasuble coming up through the garden.

MISS PRISM: *(Rising and advancing.)* Dr Chasuble! This is indeed a pleasure.

(Enter CANON CHASUBLE.)

CHASUBLE: And how are we this morning? Miss Prism, you are, I trust, well?

CECILY: Miss Prism has just been complaining of a slight headache. I think it would do her so much good to have a short stroll with you in the Park, Dr Chasuble.

MISS PRISM: Cecily, I have not mentioned anything about a headache.

CECILY: No, dear Miss Prism, I know that, but I felt instinctively that you had a headache. Indeed I was thinking about that, not about my German lesson, when the Rector came in.

CHASUBLE: I hope, Cecily, you are not inattentive.

CECILY: Oh, I am afraid I am.

CHASUBLE: That is strange. Were I fortunate enough to be Miss Prism's pupil, I would hang upon her lips. (MISS PRISM *glares.)* I spoke metaphorically.—My

---

Basket chairs, wickerwork chairs. **Moulton,** the name of a gardener who never appears in the play.

Mudie, Mudie's Library was a lending library, and three-volume novels were among its staple selections.

metaphor was drawn from bees. Ahem! Mr Worthing, I suppose, has not returned from town yet?

MISS PRISM: We do not expect him till Monday afternoon.

CHASUBLE: Ah yes, he usually likes to spend his Sunday in London. He is not one of those whose sole aim is enjoyment, as, by all accounts, that unfortunate young man his brother seems to be. But I must not disturb Egeria° and her pupil any longer.

MISS PRISM: Egeria? My name is Lætitia,° Doctor.

CHASUBLE: (Bowing.) A classical allusion merely, drawn from the pagan authors. I shall see you both no doubt at Evensong?

MISS PRISM: I think, dear Doctor, I will have a stroll with you. I find I have a headache after all, and a walk might do it good.

CHASUBLE: With pleasure, Miss Prism, with pleasure. We might go as far as the schools and back.

MISS PRISM: That would be delightful. Cecily, you will read your Political Economy in my absence. The chapter on the Fall of the Rupee° you may omit. It is somewhat too sensational. Even these metallic problems have their melodramatic side.

(Goes down the garden with DR CHASUBLE.)

CECILY: (Picks up books and throws them back on table.) Horrid Political Economy! Horrid Geography! Horrid, horrid German!

(Enter MERRIMAN with a card on a salver.)

MERRIMAN: Mr Ernest Worthing has just driven over from the station. He has brought his luggage with him.

CECILY: (Takes the card and reads it.) 'Mr Ernest Worthing, B. 4, The Albany, W.' Uncle Jack's brother! Did you tell him Mr Worthing was in town?

MERRIMAN: Yes, Miss. He seemed very much disappointed. I mentioned that you and Miss Prism were in the garden. He said he was anxious to speak to you privately for a moment.

CECILY: Ask Mr Ernest Worthing to come here. I suppose you had better talk to the housekeeper about a room for him.

MERRIMAN: Yes, Miss. (MERRIMAN goes off.)

CECILY: I have never met any really wicked person before. I feel rather frightened. I am so afraid he will look just like everyone else.

(Enter ALGERNON, very gay and debonair.)

He does!

Egeria, nymph thought to have dictated laws to a Roman king; the name connotes chastity. Lætitia, Roman name for happiness. Fall of the Rupee, the Indian currency had been devalued in the 1890s.

ALGERNON: (Raising his hat.) You are my little cousin Cecily, I'm sure.

CECILY: You are under some strange mistake. I am not little. In fact, I believe I am more than usually tall for my age. (ALGERNON is rather taken aback.) But I am your cousin Cecily. You, I see from your card, are Uncle Jack's brother, my cousin Ernest, my wicked cousin Ernest.

ALGERNON: Oh! I am not really wicked at all, cousin Cecily. You mustn't think that I am wicked.

CECILY: If you are not, then you have certainly been deceiving us all in a very inexcusable manner. I hope you have not been leading a double life, pretending to be wicked and being really good all the time. That would be hypocrisy.

ALGERNON: (Looks at her in amazement.) Oh! Of course I have been rather reckless.

CECILY: I am glad to hear it.

ALGERNON: In fact, now you mention the subject, I have been very bad in my own small way.

CECILY: I don't think you should be so proud of that, though I am sure it must have been very pleasant.

ALGERNON: It is much pleasanter being here with you.

CECILY: I can't understand how you are here at all. Uncle Jack won't be back till Monday afternoon.

ALGERNON: That is a great disappointment. I am obliged to go up by the first train on Monday morning. I have a business appointment that I am anxious . . . to miss.

CECILY: Couldn't you miss it anywhere but in London?

ALGERNON: No; the appointment is in London.

CECILY: Well, I know, of course, how important it is not to keep a business engagement, if one wants to retain any sense of the beauty of life, but still I think you had better wait till Uncle Jack arrives. I know he wants to speak to you about your emigrating.

ALGERNON: About my what?

CECILY: Your emigrating. He has gone up to buy your outfit.

ALGERNON: I certainly wouldn't let Jack buy my outfit. He has no taste in neckties at all.

CECILY: I don't think you will require neckties. Uncle Jack is sending you to Australia.

ALGERNON: Australia? I'd sooner die.

CECILY: Well, he said at dinner on Wednesday night, that you would have to choose between this world, the next world, and Australia.

ALGERNON: Oh, well! The accounts I have received of Australia and the next world are not particularly encouraging. This world is good enough for me, cousin Cecily.

CECILY: Yes, but are you good enough for it?

ALGERNON: I'm afraid I'm not that. That is why I want you to reform me. You might make that your mission, if you don't mind, cousin Cecily.

CECILY: I'm afraid I've no time, this afternoon.

ALGERNON: Well, would you mind my reforming myself this afternoon?

CECILY: It is rather quixotic of you. But I think you should try.

ALGERNON: I will. I feel better already.

CECILY: You are looking a little worse.

ALGERNON: That is because I am hungry.

CECILY: How thoughtless of me. I should have remembered that when one is going to lead an entirely new life, one requires regular and wholesome meals. Won't you come in?

ALGERNON: Thank you. Might I have a button-hole first? I never have any appetite unless I have a button-hole first.

CECILY: A Maréchal Niel?° *(Picks up scissors.)*

ALGERNON: No, I'd sooner have a pink rose.

CECILY: Why? *(Cuts a flower.)*

ALGERNON: Because you are like a pink rose, cousin Cecily.

CECILY: I don't think it can be right for you to talk to me like that. Miss Prism never says such things to me.

ALGERNON: Then Miss Prism is a short-sighted old lady. *(CECILY puts the rose in his button-hole.)* You are the prettiest girl I ever saw.

CECILY: Miss Prism says that all good looks are a snare.

ALGERNON: They are a snare that every sensible man would like to be caught in.

CECILY: Oh! I don't think I would care to catch a sensible man. I shouldn't know what to talk to him about.

(They pass into the house. MISS PRISM and DR CHASUBLE return.)

MISS PRISM: You are too much alone, dear Dr Chasuble. You should get married. A misanthrope I can understand—a womanthrope, never!

CHASUBLE: *(With a scholar's shudder.)* Believe me, I do not deserve so neologistic a phrase. The precept as well as the practice of the Primitive Church was distinctly against matrimony.

MISS PRISM: *(Sententiously.)* That is obviously the reason why the Primitive Church has not lasted up to the present day. And you do not seem to realize, dear Doctor, that by persistently remaining single, a man converts himself into a permanent public temptation. Men should be more careful; this very celibacy leads weaker vessels astray.

CHASUBLE: But is a man not equally attractive when married?

MISS PRISM: No married man is ever attractive except to his wife.

CHASUBLE: And often, I've been told, not even to her.

MISS PRISM: That depends on the intellectual sympa-
thies of the woman. Maturity can always be depended on. Ripeness can be trusted. Young women are green. *(DR CHASUBLE starts.)* I spoke horticulturally. My metaphor was drawn from fruits. But where is Cecily?

CHASUBLE: Perhaps she followed us to the schools.

(Enter JACK slowly from the back of the garden. He is dressed in the deepest mourning, with crêpe hatband and black gloves.)

MISS PRISM: Mr Worthing!

CHASUBLE: Mr Worthing?

MISS PRISM: This is indeed a surprise. We did not look for you till Monday afternoon.

JACK: *(Shakes MISS PRISM's hand in a tragic manner.)* I have returned sooner than I expected. Dr Chasuble, I hope you are well?

CHASUBLE: Dear Mr Worthing, I trust this garb of woe does not betoken some terrible calamity?

JACK: My brother.

MISS PRISM: More shameful debts and extravagance?

CHASUBLE: Still leading his life of pleasure?

JACK: *(Shaking his head.)* Dead!

CHASUBLE: Your brother Ernest dead?

JACK: Quite dead.

MISS PRISM: What a lesson for him! I trust he will profit by it.

CHASUBLE: Mr Worthing, I offer you my sincere condolence. You have at least the consolation of knowing that you were always the most generous and forgiving of brothers.

JACK: Poor Ernest! He had many faults, but it is a sad, sad blow.

CHASUBLE: Very sad indeed. Were you with him at the end?

JACK: No. He died abroad; in Paris, in fact. I had a telegram last night from the manager of the Grand Hotel.

CHASUBLE: Was the cause of death mentioned?

JACK: A severe chill, it seems.

MISS PRISM: As a man sows, so shall he reap.

CHASUBLE: *(Raising his hand.)* Charity, dear Miss Prism, charity! None of us are perfect. I myself am peculiarly susceptible to drafts. Will the interment take place here?

JACK: No. He seemed to have expressed a desire to be buried in Paris.

CHASUBLE: In Paris! *(Shakes his head.)* I fear that hardly points to any very serious state of mind at the last. You would no doubt wish me to make some slight allusion to this tragic domestic affliction next Sunday. *(JACK presses his hand convulsively.)* My sermon on the meaning of the manna in the wilderness°

Maréchal Niel, a yellow rose.

manna in the wilderness, white substance miraculously provided to the Israelites as they journeyed to the Holy Land (Exodus, 16).

can be adapted to almost any occasion, joyful, or, as in the present case, distressing. *(All sigh.)* I have preached it at harvest celebrations, christenings, confirmations, on days of humiliation and festal days. The last time I delivered it was in the Cathedral, as a charity sermon on behalf of the Society for the Prevention of Discontent among the Upper Orders. The Bishop, who was present, was much struck by some of the analogies I drew.

JACK: Ah! that reminds me, you mentioned christenings I think, Dr Chasuble? I suppose you know how to christen all right? *(DR CHASUBLE looks astounded.)* I mean, of course, you are continually christening, aren't you?

MISS PRISM: It is, I regret to say, one of the Rector's most constant duties in this parish. I have often spoken to the poorer classes on the subject. But they don't seem to know what thrift is.

CHASUBLE: But is there any particular infant in whom you are interested, Mr Worthing? Your brother was, I believe, unmarried, was he not?

JACK: Oh yes.

MISS PRISM: *(Bitterly.)* People who live entirely for pleasure usually are.

JACK: But it is not for any child, dear Doctor. I am very fond of children. No! the fact is, I would like to be christened myself, this afternoon, if you have nothing better to do.

CHASUBLE: But surely, Mr Worthing, you have been christened already?

JACK: I don't remember anything about it.

CHASUBLE: But have you any grave doubts on the subject?

JACK: I certainly intend to have. Of course I don't know if the thing would bother you in any way, or if you think I am a little too old now.

CHASUBLE: Not at all. The sprinkling, and, indeed, the immersion of adults is a perfectly canonical practice.

JACK: Immersion!

CHASUBLE: You need have no apprehensions. Sprinkling is all that is necessary, or indeed I think advisable. Our weather is so changeable. At what hour would you wish the ceremony performed?

JACK: Oh, I might trot round about five if that would suit you.

CHASUBLE: Perfectly, perfectly! In fact I have two similar ceremonies to perform at that time. A case of twins that occurred recently in one of the outlying cottages on your own estate. Poor Jenkins the carter, a most hardworking man.

JACK: Oh! I don't see much fun in being christened along with other babies. It would be childish. Would half-past five do?

CHASUBLE: Admirably! Admirably! *(Takes out watch.)* And now, dear Mr Worthing, I will not intrude any longer into a house of sorrow. I would merely beg you not to be too much bowed down by grief. What seems to us bitter trials are often blessings in disguise.

MISS PRISM: This seems to me a blessing of an extremely obvious kind.

(Enter CECILY from the house.)

CECILY: Uncle Jack! Oh, I am pleased to see you back. But what horrid clothes you have got on! Do go and change them.

MISS PRISM: Cecily!

CHASUBLE: My child! my child! *(CECILY goes towards JACK; he kisses her brow in a melancholy manner.)*

CECILY: What is the matter, Uncle Jack? Do look happy! You look as if you had toothache, and I have got such a surprise for you. Who do you think is in the dining-room? Your brother!

JACK: Who?

CECILY: Your brother Ernest. He arrived about half an hour ago.

JACK: What nonsense! I haven't got a brother.

CECILY: Oh, don't say that. However badly he may have behaved to you in the past he is still your brother. You couldn't be so heartless as to disown him. I'll tell him to come out. And you will shake hands with him, won't you, Uncle Jack? *(Runs back into the house.)*

CHASUBLE: These are very joyful tidings.

MISS PRISM: After we had all been resigned to his loss, his sudden return seems to me peculiarly distressing.

JACK: My brother is in the dining-room? I don't know what it all means. I think it is perfectly absurd.

(Enter ALGERNON and CECILY hand in hand. They come slowly up to Jack.)

JACK: Good heavens! *(Motions ALGERNON away.)*

ALGERNON: Brother John, I have come down from town to tell you that I am very sorry for all the trouble I have given you, and that I intend to lead a better life in the future. *(JACK glares at him and does not take his hand.)*

CECILY: Uncle Jack, you are not going to refuse your own brother's hand?

JACK: Nothing will induce me to take his hand. I think his coming down here disgraceful. He knows perfectly well why.

CECILY: Uncle Jack, do be nice. There is some good in everyone. Ernest has just been telling me about his poor invalid friend Mr Bunbury whom he goes to visit so often. And surely there must be much good in one who is kind to an invalid, and leaves the pleasures of London to sit by a bed of pain.

JACK Oh! he has been talking about Bunbury has he?

CECILY: Yes, he has told me all about poor Mr Bunbury, and his terrible state of health.

JACK: Bunbury! Well, I won't have him talk to you about Bunbury or about anything else. It is enough to drive one perfectly frantic.

ALGERNON: Of course I admit that the faults were all on my side. But I must say that I think that Brother John's coldness to me is peculiarly painful. I expected a more enthusiastic welcome, especially considering it is the first time I have come here.

CECILY: Uncle Jack, if you don't shake hands with Ernest, I will never forgive you.

JACK: Never forgive me?

CECILY: Never, never, never!

JACK: Well, this is the last time I shall ever do it. *(Shakes hands with* ALGERNON *and glares.)*

CHASUBLE: It's pleasant, is it not, to see so perfect a reconciliation? I think we might leave the two brothers together.

MISS PRISM: Cecily, you will come with us.

CECILY: Certainly, Miss Prism. My little task of reconciliation is over.

CHASUBLE: You have done a beautiful action today, dear child.

MISS PRISM: We must not be premature in our judgements.

CECILY: I feel very happy. *(They all go off.)*

JACK: You young scoundrel, Algy, you must get out of this place as soon as possible. I don't allow any Bunburying here.

(Enter MERRIMAN.*)*

MERRIMAN: I have put Mr Ernest's things in the room next to yours, sir. I suppose that is all right?

JACK: What?

MERRIMAN: Mr Ernest's luggage, sir. I have unpacked it and put it in the room next to your own.

JACK: His luggage?

MERRIMAN: Yes, sir. Three portmanteaus, a dressing-case, two hat boxes, and a large luncheon-basket.

ALGERNON: I am afraid I can't stay more than a week this time.

JACK: Merriman, order the dog-cart° at once. Mr Ernest has been suddenly called back to town.

MERRIMAN: Yes, sir. *(Goes back into the house.)*

ALGERNON: What a fearful liar you are, Jack. I have not been called back to town at all.

JACK: Yes, you have.

ALGERNON: I haven't heard anyone call me.

JACK: Your duty as a gentleman calls you back.

ALGERNON: My duty as a gentleman has never interfered with my pleasures in the smallest degree.

JACK: I can quite understand that.

ALGERNON: Well, Cecily is a darling.

---

dog-cart, two-wheeled horse-drawn carriage.

JACK: You are not to talk of Miss Cardew like that. I don't like it.

ALGERNON: Well, I don't like your clothes. You look perfectly ridiculous in them. Why on earth don't you go up and change? It is perfectly childish to be in deep mourning for a man who is actually staying for a whole week in your house as a guest. I call it grotesque.

JACK: You are certainly not staying with me for a whole week as a guest or anything else. You have got to leave . . . by the four-five train.

ALGERNON: I certainly won't leave you so long as you are in mourning. It would be most unfriendly. If I were in mourning you would stay with me, I suppose. I should think it very unkind if you didn't.

JACK: Well, will you go if I change my clothes?

ALGERNON: Yes, if you are not too long. I never saw anybody take so long to dress, and with such little result.

JACK: Well, at any rate, that is better than being always overdressed as you are.

ALGERNON: If I am occasionally a little overdressed, I make up for it by being always immensely over-educated.

JACK: Your vanity is ridiculous, your conduct an outrage, and your presence in my garden utterly absurd. However, you have got to catch the four-five, and I hope you will have a pleasant journey back to town. This Bunburying, as you call it, has not been a great success for you.

(Goes into the house.)

ALGERNON: I think it has been a great success. I'm in love with Cecily, and that is everything. *(Enter* CECILY *at the back of the garden. She picks up the can and begins to water the flowers.)* But I must see her before I go, and make arrangements for another Bunbury. Ah, there she is.

CECILY: Oh, I merely came back to water the roses. I thought you were with Uncle Jack.

ALGERNON: He's gone to order the dog-cart for me.

CECILY: Oh, is he going to take you for a nice drive?

ALGERNON: He's going to send me away.

CECILY: Then have we got to part?

ALGERNON: I am afraid so. It's a very painful parting.

CECILY: It is always painful to part from people whom one has known for a very brief space of time. The absence of old friends one can endure with equanimity. But even a momentary separation from anyone to whom one has just been introduced is almost unbearable.

ALGERNON: Thank you.

(Enter MERRIMAN.*)*

MERRIMAN: The dog-cart is at the door, sir. (ALGERNON *looks appealingly at* CECILY.)

CECILY: It can wait, Merriman . . . for . . . five minutes.

MERRIMAN: Yes, miss. (*Exit* MERRIMAN.)

ALGERNON: I hope, Cecily, I shall not offend you if I state quite frankly and openly that you seem to me to be in every way the visible personification of absolute perfection.

CECILY: I think your frankness does you great credit, Ernest. If you will allow me I will copy your remarks into my diary. (*Goes over to table and begins writing in diary.*)

ALGERNON: Do you really keep a diary? I'd give anything to look at it. May I?

CECILY: Oh no. (*Puts her hand over it.*) You see, it is simply a very young girl's record of her own thoughts and impressions, and consequently meant for publication. When it appears in volume form I hope you will order a copy. But pray, Ernest, don't stop. I delight in taking down from dictation. I have reached 'absolute perfection.' You can go on. I am quite ready for more.

ALGERNON: (*Somewhat taken aback.*) Ahem! Ahem!

CECILY: Oh, don't cough, Ernest. When one is dictating one should speak fluently and not cough. Besides, I don't know how to spell a cough. (*Writes as* ALGERNON *speaks.*)

ALGERNON: (*Speaking very rapidly.*) Cecily, ever since I first looked upon your wonderful and incomparable beauty, I have dared to love you wildly, passionately, devotedly, hopelessly.

CECILY: I don't think that you should tell me that you love me wildly, passionately, devotedly, hopelessly. Hopelessly doesn't seem to make much sense, does it?

ALGERNON: Cecily!

(*Enter* MERRIMAN.)

MERRIMAN: The dog-cart is waiting, sir.

ALGERNON: Tell it to come round next week, at the same hour.

MERRIMAN: (*Looks at* CECILY, *who makes no sign.*) Yes, sir.

(MERRIMAN *retires.*)

CECILY: Uncle Jack would be very much annoyed if he knew you were staying on till next week, at the same hour.

ALGERNON: Oh, I don't care about Jack. I don't care for anybody in the whole world but you. I love you, Cecily. You will marry me, won't you?

CECILY: You silly boy! Of course. Why, we have been engaged for the last three months.

ALGERNON: For the last three months?

CECILY: Yes, it will be exactly three months on Thursday.

ALGERNON: But how did we become engaged?

CECILY: Well, ever since dear Uncle Jack first confessed to us that he had a younger brother who was very wicked and bad, you of course have formed the chief topic of conversation between myself and Miss Prism. And of course a man who is much talked about is always very attractive. One feels there must be something in him after all. I daresay it was foolish of me, but I fell in love with you, Ernest.

ALGERNON: Darling! And when was the engagement actually settled?

CECILY: On the 14th of February last. Worn out by your entire ignorance of my existence, I determined to end the matter one way or the other, and after a long struggle with myself I accepted you under this dear old tree here. The next day I bought this little ring in your name, and this is the little bangle with the true lovers' knot I promised you always to wear.

ALGERNON: Did I give you this? It's very pretty, isn't it?

CECILY: Yes, you've wonderfully good taste, Ernest. It's the excuse I've always given for your leading such a bad life. And this is the box in which I keep all your dear letters. (*Kneels at table, opens box, and produces letters tied up with blue ribbon.*)

ALGERNON: My letters! But my own sweet Cecily, I have never written you any letters.

CECILY: You need hardly remind me of that, Ernest. I remember only too well that I was forced to write your letters for you. I always wrote three times a week, and sometimes oftener.

ALGERNON: Oh, do let me read them, Cecily?

CECILY: Oh, I couldn't possibly. They would make you far too conceited. (*Replaces box.*) The three you wrote me after I had broken off the engagement are so beautiful, and so badly spelled, that even now I can hardly read them without crying a little.

ALGERNON: But was our engagement ever broken off?

CECILY: Of course it was. On the 22nd of last March. You can see the entry if you like. (*Shows diary.*) 'Today I broke off my engagement with Ernest. I feel it is better to do so. The weather still continues charming.'

ALGERNON: But why on earth did you break it off? What had I done? I had done nothing at all. Cecily, I am very much hurt indeed to hear you broke it off. Particularly when the weather was so charming.

CECILY: It would hardly have been a really serious engagement if it hadn't been broken off at least once. But I forgave you before the week was out.

ALGERNON: (*Crossing to her, and kneeling.*) What a perfect angel you are, Cecily.

CECILY: You dear romantic boy. (*He kisses her, she puts her fingers through his hair.*) I hope your hair curls naturally, does it?

ALGERNON: Yes, darling, with a little help from others.

CECILY: I am so glad.

ALGERNON: You'll never break off our engagement again, Cecily?

CECILY: I don't think I could break it off now that I

have actually met you. Besides, of course, there is the question of your name.

ALGERNON: Yes, of course. (*Nervously.*)

CECILY: You must not laugh at me, darling, but it had always been a girlish dream of mine to love someone whose name was Ernest. (ALGERNON *rises,* CECILY *also.*) There is something in that name that seems to inspire absolute confidence. I pity any poor married woman whose husband is not called Ernest.

ALGERNON: But, my dear child, do you mean to say you could not love me if I had some other name?

CECILY: But what name?

ALGERNON: Oh, any name you like—Algernon—for instance. . . .

CECILY: But I don't like the name of Algernon.

ALGERNON: Well, my own dear, sweet, loving little darling, I really can't see why you should object to the name of Algernon. It is not at all a bad name. In fact, it is rather an aristocratic name. Half of the chaps who get into the Bankruptcy Court are called Algernon. But seriously, Cecily . . . (*Moving to her*) . . . if my name was Algy, couldn't you love me?

CECILY: (*Rising.*) I might respect you, Ernest, I might admire your character, but I fear that I should not be able to give you my undivided attention.

ALGERNON: Ahem! Cecily! (*Picking up hat.*) Your Rector here is, I suppose, thoroughly experienced in the practice of all the rites and ceremonials of the Church?

CECILY: Oh, yes. Dr Chasuble is a most learned man. He has never written a single book, so you can imagine how much he knows.

ALGERNON: I must see him at once on a most important christening—I mean on most important business.

CECILY: Oh!

ALGERNON: I shan't be away more than half an hour.

CECILY: Considering that we have been engaged since February the 14th, and that I only met you today for the first time, I think it is rather hard that you should leave me for so long a period as half an hour. Couldn't you make it twenty minutes?

ALGERNON: I'll be back in no time.

(*Kisses her and rushes down the garden.*)

CECILY: What an impetuous boy he is! I like his hair so much. I must enter his proposal in my diary.

(*Enter* MERRIMAN.)

MERRIMAN: A Miss Fairfax has just called to see Mr Worthing. On very important business Miss Fairfax states.

CECILY: Isn't Mr Worthing in his library?

MERRIMAN: Mr Worthing went over in the direction of the Rectory some time ago.

CECILY: Pray ask the lady to come out here; Mr Worthing is sure to be back soon. And you can bring tea.

MERRIMAN: Yes, Miss. (*Goes out.*)

CECILY: Miss Fairfax! I suppose one of the many good elderly women who are associated with Uncle Jack in some of his philanthropic work in London. I don't quite like women who are interested in philanthropic work. I think it is so forward of them.

(*Enter* MERRIMAN.)

MERRIMAN: Miss Fairfax.

(*Enter* GWENDOLEN.) (*Exit* MERRIMAN.)

CECILY: (*Advancing to meet her.*) Pray let me introduce myself to you. My name is Cecily Cardew.

GWENDOLEN: Cecily Cardew? (*Moving to her and shaking hands.*) What a very sweet name! Something tells me that we are going to be great friends. I like you already more than I can say. My first impressions of people are never wrong.

CECILY: How nice of you to like me so much after we have known each other such a comparatively short time. Pray sit down.

GWENDOLEN: (*Still standing up*) I may call you Cecily, may I not?

CECILY: With pleasure!

GWENDOLEN: And you will always call me Gwendolen, won't you?

CECILY: If you wish.

GWENDOLEN: Then that is all quite settled, is it not?

CECILY: I hope so. (*A pause. They both sit down together.*)

GWENDOLEN: Perhaps this might be a favorable opportunity for my mentioning who I am. My father is Lord Bracknell. You have never heard of Papa, I suppose?

CECILY: I don't think so.

GWENDOLEN: Outside the family circle, Papa, I am glad to say, is entirely unknown. I think that is quite as it should be. The home seems to me to be the proper sphere for the man. And certainly once a man begins to neglect his domestic duties he becomes painfully effeminate, does he not? And I don't like that. It makes men so very attractive. Cecily, Mamma, whose views on education are remarkably strict, has brought me up to be extremely short-sighted; it is part of her system; so do you mind my looking at you through my glasses?

CECILY: Oh! not at all, Gwendolen. I am very fond of being looked at.

GWENDOLEN: (*After examining* CECILY *carefully through a lorgnette.*) You are here on a short visit I suppose?

CECILY: Oh no! I live here.

GWENDOLEN: (*Severely.*) Really? Your mother, no doubt, or some female relative of advanced years, resides here also?

CECILY: Oh no! I have no mother, nor, in fact, any relations.

GWENDOLEN: Indeed?

CECILY: My dear guardian, with the assistance of Miss Prism, has the arduous task of looking after me.

GWENDOLEN: Your guardian?

CECILY: Yes, I am Mr Worthing's ward.

GWENDOLEN: Oh! It is strange he never mentioned to me that he had a ward. How secretive of him! He grows more interesting hourly. I am not sure, however, that the news inspires me with feelings of unmixed delight. *(Rising and going to her.)* I am very fond of you, Cecily; I have liked you ever since I met you! But I am bound to state that now that I know that you are Mr Worthing's ward, I cannot help expressing a wish you were—well just a little older than you seem to be—and not quite so very alluring in appearance. In fact, if I may speak candidly—

CECILY: Pray do! I think that whenever one has anything unpleasant to say, one should always be quite candid.

GWENDOLEN: Well, to speak with perfect candor, Cecily, I wish that you were fully forty-two, and more than usually plain for your age. Ernest has a strong upright nature. He is the very soul of truth and honor. Disloyalty would be as impossible to him as deception. But even men of the noblest possible moral character are extremely susceptible to the influence of the physical charms of others. Modern, no less than ancient history, supplies us with many most painful examples of what I refer to. If it were not so, indeed, history would be quite unreadable.

CECILY: I beg your pardon, Gwendolen, did you say Ernest?

GWENDOLEN: Yes.

CECILY: Oh, but it is not Mr Ernest Worthing who is my guardian. It is his brother—his elder brother.

GWENDOLEN: *(Sitting down again.)* Ernest never mentioned to me that he had a brother.

CECILY: I am sorry to say they have not been on good terms for a long time.

GWENDOLEN: Ah! that accounts for it. And now that I think of it I have never heard any man mention his brother. The subject seems distasteful to most men. Cecily, you have lifted a load from my mind. I was growing almost anxious. It would have been terrible if any cloud had come across a friendship like ours, would it not? Of course you are quite, quite sure that it is not Mr Ernest Worthing who is your guardian?

CECILY: Quite sure. *(A pause.)* In fact, I am going to be his.

GWENDOLEN: *(Enquiringly.)* I beg your pardon?

CECILY: *(Rather shy and confidingly.)* Dearest Gwendolen, there is no reason why I should make a secret of it to you. Our little county newspaper is sure to chronicle the fact next week. Mr Ernest Worthing and I are engaged to be married.

GWENDOLEN: *(Quite politely, rising.)* My darling Cecily, I think there must be some slight error. Mr Ernest Worthing is engaged to me. The announcement will appear in the *Morning Post* on Saturday at the latest.

CECILY: *(Very politely, rising)* I am afraid you must be under some misconception. Ernest proposed to me exactly ten minutes ago. *(Shows diary.)*

GWENDOLEN: *(Examines diary through her lorgnette carefully.)* It is certainly very curious, for he asked me to be his wife yesterday afternoon at 5:30. If you would care to verify the incident, pray do so. *(Produces diary of her own.)* I never travel without my diary. One should always have something sensational to read in the train. I am so sorry, dear Cecily, if it is any disappointment to you, but I am afraid *I* have the prior claim.

CECILY: It would distress me more than I can tell you, dear Gwendolen, if it caused you any mental or physical anguish, but I feel bound to point out that since Ernest proposed to you he clearly has changed his mind.

GWENDOLEN: *(Meditatively.)* If the poor fellow has been entrapped into any foolish promise I shall consider it my duty to rescue him at once, and with a firm hand.

CECILY: *(Thoughtfully and sadly.)* Whatever unfortunate entanglement my dear boy may have got into, I will never reproach him with it after we are married.

GWENDOLEN: Do you allude to me, Miss Cardew, as an entanglement? You are presumptuous. On an occasion of this kind it becomes more than a moral duty to speak one's mind. It becomes a pleasure.

CECILY: Do you suggest, Miss Fairfax, that I entrapped Ernest into an engagement? How dare you? This is no time for wearing the shallow mask of manners. When I see a spade I call it a spade.

GWENDOLEN: *(Satirically.)* I am glad to say that I have never seen a spade. It is obvious that our social spheres have been widely different.

(Enter MERRIMAN, *followed by the footman. He carries a salver, table cloth, and plate stand.* CECILY *is about to retort. The presence of the servants exercises a restraining influence, under which both girls chafe.)*

MERRIMAN: Shall I lay tea here as usual, miss?

CECILY: *(Sternly, in a calm voice.)* Yes, as usual. *(*MERRIMAN *begins to clear table and lay cloth. A long pause.* CECILY *and* GWENDOLEN *glare at each other.)*

GWENDOLEN: Are there many interesting walks in the vicinity, Miss Cardew?

CECILY: Oh! Yes! a great many. From the top of one of the hills quite close one can see five counties.

GWENDOLEN: Five counties! I don't think I should like that. I hate crowds.

CECILY: (Sweetly.) I suppose that is why you live in town? (GWENDOLEN bites her lip, and beats her foot nervously with her parasol.)

GWENDOLEN: (Looking round.) Quite a well-kept garden this is, Miss Cardew.

CECILY: So glad you like it, Miss Fairfax.

GWENDOLEN: I had no idea there were any flowers in the country.

CECILY: Oh, flowers are as common here, Miss Fairfax, as people are in London.

GWENDOLEN: Personally I cannot understand how anybody manages to exist in the country, if anybody who is anybody does. The country always bores me to death.

CECILY: Ah! This is what the newspapers call agricultural depression, is it not? I believe the aristocracy are suffering very much from it just at present. It is almost an epidemic amongst them, I have been told. May I offer you some tea, Miss Fairfax?

GWENDOLEN: (With elaborate politeness.) Thank you. (Aside.) Detestable girl! But I require tea!

CECILY: (Sweetly.) Sugar?

GWENDOLEN: (Superciliously.) No, thank you. Sugar is not fashionable any more. (CECILY looks angrily at her, takes up the tongs, and puts four lumps of sugar into the cup.)

CECILY: (Severely.) Cake or bread and butter?

GWENDOLEN: (In a bored manner.) Bread and butter, please. Cake is rarely seen at the best houses nowadays.

CECILY: (Cuts a very large slice of cake, and puts it on the tray.) Hand that to Miss Fairfax. (MERRIMAN does so, and goes out with footman. GWENDOLEN drinks the tea and makes a grimace. Puts down cup at once, reaches out her hand to the bread and butter, looks at it, and finds it is cake. Rises in indignation.)

GWENDOLEN: You have filled my tea with lumps of sugar, and though I asked most distinctly for bread and butter, you have given me cake. I am known for the gentleness of my disposition, and the extraordinary sweetness of my nature, but I warn you, Miss Cardew, you may go too far.

CECILY: (Rising.) To save my poor, innocent, trusting boy from the machinations of any other girl there are no lengths to which I would not go.

GWENDOLEN: From the moment I saw you I distrusted you. I felt that you were false and deceitful. I am never deceived in such matters. My first impressions of people are invariably right.

CECILY: It seems to me, Miss Fairfax, that I am trespassing on your valuable time. No doubt you have many other calls of a similar character to make in the neighborhood.

(Enter JACK.)

GWENDOLEN: (Catching sight of him.) Ernest! My own Ernest!

JACK: Gwendolen! Darling! (Offers to kiss her.)

GWENDOLEN: (Drawing back.) A moment! May I ask if you are engaged to be married to this young lady? (Points to CECILY.)

JACK: (Laughing.) To dear little Cecily! Of course not! What could have put such an idea into your pretty little head?

GWENDOLEN: Thank you. You may! (Offers her cheek.)

CECILY: (Very sweetly.) I knew there must be some misunderstanding, Miss Fairfax. The gentleman whose arm is at present round your waist is my dear guardian, Mr John Worthing.

GWENDOLEN: I beg your pardon?

CECILY: This is Uncle Jack.

GWENDOLEN: (Receding.) Jack! Oh!

(Enter ALGERNON.)

CECILY: Here is Ernest.

ALGERNON: (Goes straight over to CECILY without noticing anyone else.) My own love! (Offers to kiss her.)

CECILY: (Drawing back.) A moment, Ernest! May I ask you—are you engaged to be married to this young lady?

ALGERNON: (Looking round.) To what young lady? Good heavens! Gwendolen!

CECILY: Yes! to good heavens, Gwendolen, I mean to Gwendolen.

ALGERNON: (Laughing.) Of course not! What could have put such an idea into your pretty little head?

CECILY: Thank you. (Presenting her cheek to be kissed.) You may. (ALGERNON kisses her.)

GWENDOLEN: I felt there was some slight error, Miss Cardew. The gentleman who is now embracing you is my cousin, Mr Algernon Moncrieff.

CECILY: (Breaking away from ALGERNON) Algernon Moncrieff! Oh! (The two girls move towards each other and put their arms round each other's waists as if for protection.)

CECILY: Are you called Algernon?

ALGERNON: I cannot deny it.

CECILY: Oh!

GWENDOLEN: Is your name really John?

JACK: (Standing rather proudly.) I could deny it if I liked. I could deny anything if I liked. But my name certainly is John. It has been John for years.

CECILY: (To GWENDOLEN.) A gross deception has been practiced on both of us.

GWENDOLEN: My poor wounded Cecily!

CECILY: My sweet wronged Gwendolen!

GWENDOLEN: (Slowly and seriously.) You will call me sister, will you not? (They embrace. JACK and ALGERNON groan and walk up and down.)

CECILY: (Rather brightly.) There is just one question I would like to be allowed to ask my guardian.

GWENDOLEN: An admirable idea! Mr Worthing, there

is just one question I would like to be permitted to put to you. Where is your brother Ernest? We are both engaged to be married to your brother Ernest, so it is a matter of some importance to us to know where your brother Ernest is at present.

JACK: *(Slowly and hesitatingly.)* Gwendolen—Cecily—it is very painful for me to be forced to speak the truth. It is the first time in my life that I have ever been reduced to such a painful position, and I am really quite inexperienced in doing anything of the kind. However I will tell you quite frankly that I have no brother Ernest. I have no brother at all. I never had a brother in my life, and I certainly have not the smallest intention of ever having one in the future.

CECILY: *(Surprised.)* No brother at all?

JACK: *(Cheerily.)* None!

GWENDOLEN: *(Severely.)* Had you never a brother of any kind?

JACK: *(Pleasantly.)* Never. Not even of any kind.

GWENDOLEN: I am afraid it is quite clear, Cecily, that neither of us is engaged to be married to anyone.

CECILY: It is not a very pleasant position for a young girl suddenly to find herself in. Is it?

GWENDOLEN: Let us go into the house. They will hardly venture to come after us there.

CECILY: No, men are so cowardly, aren't they?

(They retire into the house with scornful looks.)

JACK: This ghastly state of things is what you call Bun-burying, I suppose?

ALGERNON: Yes, and a perfectly wonderful Bunbury it is. The most wonderful Bunbury I have ever had in my life.

JACK: Well, you've no right whatsoever to Bunbury here.

ALGERNON: That is absurd. One has a right to Bun-bury anywhere one chooses. Every serious Bun-buryist knows that.

JACK: Serious Bunburyist! Good heavens!

ALGERNON: Well, one must be serious about some-thing, if one wants to have any amusement in life. I happen to be serious about Bunburying. What on earth you are serious about I haven't got the remotest idea. About everything, I should fancy. You have such an absolutely trivial nature.

JACK: Well, the only small satisfaction I have in the whole of this wretched business is that your friend Bunbury is quite exploded. You won't be able to run down to the country quite so often as you used to do, dear Algy. And a very good thing too.

ALGERNON: Your brother is a little off color, isn't he, dear Jack? You won't be able to disappear to Lon-don quite so frequently as your wicked custom was. And not a bad thing either.

JACK: As for your conduct towards Miss Cardew, I must say that your taking in a sweet, simple, inno-cent girl like that is quite inexcusable. To say nothing of the fact that she is my ward.

ALGERNON: I can see no possible defense at all for your deceiving a brilliant, clever, thoroughly ex-perienced young lady like Miss Fairfax. To say nothing of the fact that she is my cousin.

JACK: I wanted to be engaged to Gwendolen, that is all. I love her.

ALGERNON: Well, I simply wanted to be engaged to Cecily. I adore her.

JACK: There is certainly no chance of your marrying Miss Cardew.

ALGERNON: I don't think there is much likelihood, Jack, of you and Miss Fairfax being united.

JACK: Well, that is no business of yours.

ALGERNON: If it was my business, I wouldn't talk about it. *(Begins to eat muffins.)* It is very vulgar to talk about one's business. Only people like stockbro-kers do that, and then merely at dinner parties.

JACK: How you can sit there, calmly eating muffins when we are in this horrible trouble, I can't make out. You seem to me to be perfectly heartless.

ALGERNON: Well, I can't eat muffins in an agitated manner. The butter would probably get on my cuffs. One should always eat muffins quite calmly. It is the only way to eat them.

JACK: I say it's perfectly heartless your eating muffins at all, under the circumstances.

ALGERNON: When I am in trouble, eating is the only thing that consoles me. Indeed, when I am in really great trouble, as anyone who knows me inti-mately will tell you, I refuse everything except food and drink. At the present moment I am eat-ing muffins because I am unhappy. Besides, I am particularly fond of muffins. *(Rising.)*

JACK: *(Rising.)* Well, that is no reason why you should eat them all in that greedy way. *(Takes muffins from ALGERNON.)*

ALGERNON: *(Offering tea-cake.)* I wish you would have tea-cake instead. I don't like tea-cake.

JACK: Good heavens! I suppose a man may eat his own muffins in his own garden.

ALGERNON: But you have just said it was perfectly heartless to eat muffins.

JACK: I said it was perfectly heartless of you, under the circumstances. That is a very different thing.

ALGERNON: That may be. But the muffins are the same. *(He seizes the muffin-dish from JACK.)*

JACK: Algy, I wish to goodness you would go.

ALGERNON: You can't possibly ask me to go without having some dinner. It's absurd. I never go with-out my dinner. No one ever does, except vegetari-ans and people like that. Besides I have just made arrangements with Dr Chasuble to be christened at a quarter to six under the name of Ernest.

JACK: My dear fellow, the sooner you give up that nonsense the better. I made arrangements this morning with Dr Chasuble to be christened myself at 5:30, and I naturally will take the name of Ernest. Gwendolen would wish it. We can't both be christened Ernest. It's absurd. Besides, I have a perfect right to be christened if I like. There is no evidence at all that I ever have been christened by anybody. I should think it extremely probable I never was, and so does Dr Chasuble. It is entirely different in your case. You have been christened already.

ALGERNON: Yes, but I have not been christened for years.

JACK: Yes, but you have been christened. That is the important thing.

ALGERNON: Quite so. So I know my constitution can stand it. If you are not quite sure about your ever having been christened, I must say I think it rather dangerous your venturing on it now. It might make you very unwell. You can hardly have forgotten that someone very closely connected with you was very nearly carried off this week in Paris by a severe chill.

JACK: Yes, but you said yourself that a severe chill was not hereditary.

ALGERNON: It usen't to be, I know—but I daresay it is now. Science is always making wonderful improvements in things.

JACK: *(Picking up the muffin-dish.)* Oh, that is nonsense; you are always talking nonsense.

ALGERNON: Jack, you are at the muffins again! I wish you wouldn't. There are only two left. *(Takes them.)* I told you I was particularly fond of muffins.

JACK: But I hate tea-cake.

ALGERNON: Why on earth then do you allow tea-cake to be served up for your guests? What ideas you have of hospitality!

JACK: Algernon! I have already told you to go. I don't want you here. Why don't you go!

ALGERNON: I haven't quite finished my tea yet! and there is still one muffin left. *(JACK groans, and sinks into a chair, ALGERNON still continues eating.)*
ACT-DROP.

ACT 3

(Morning room at the Manor House.)
(GWENDOLEN and CECILY are at the window, looking out into the garden.)

GWENDOLEN: The fact that they did not follow us at once into the house, as anyone else would have done, seems to me to show that they have some sense of shame left.

CECILY: They have been eating muffins. That looks like repentance.

GWENDOLEN: *(After a pause.)* They don't seem to notice us at all. Couldn't you cough?

CECILY: But I haven't got a cough.

GWENDOLEN: They're looking at us. What effrontery!

CECILY: They're approaching. That's very forward of them.

GWENDOLEN: Let us preserve a dignified silence.

CECILY: Certainly. It's the only thing to do now.

(Enter JACK followed by ALGERNON. They whistle some dreadful popular air from a British opera.)

GWENDOLEN: This dignified silence seems to produce an unpleasant effect.

CECILY: A most distasteful one.

GWENDOLEN: But we will not be the first to speak.

CECILY: Certainly not.

GWENDOLEN: Mr Worthing, I have something very particular to ask you. Much depends on your reply.

CECILY: Gwendolen, your common sense is invaluable. Mr Moncrieff, kindly answer me the following question. Why did you pretend to be my guardian's brother?

ALGERNON: In order that I might have an opportunity of meeting you.

CECILY: *(To GWENDOLEN.)* That certainly seems a satisfactory explanation, does it not?

GWENDOLEN: Yes, dear, if you can believe him.

CECILY: I don't. But that does not affect the wonderful beauty of his answer.

GWENDOLEN: True. In matters of grave importance, style, not sincerity is the vital thing. Mr Worthing, what explanation can you offer to me for pretending to have a brother? Was it in order that you might have an opportunity of coming up to town to see me as often as possible?

JACK: Can you doubt it, Miss Fairfax?

GWENDOLEN: I have the gravest doubts upon the subject. But I intend to crush them. This is not the moment for German skepticism. *(Moving to CECILY.)* Their explanations appear to be quite satisfactory, especially Mr Worthing's. That seems to me to have the stamp of truth upon it.

CECILY: I am more than content with what Mr Moncrieff said. His voice alone inspires one with absolute credulity.

GWENDOLEN: Then you think we should forgive them?

CECILY: Yes. I mean no.

GWENDOLEN: True! I had forgotten. There are principles at stake that one cannot surrender. Which of us should tell them? The task is not a pleasant one.

CECILY: Could we not both speak at the same time?

GWENDOLEN: An excellent idea! I nearly always speak at the same time as other people. Will you take the time from me?

CECILY: Certainly. *(GWENDOLYN beats time with uplifted finger.)*

GWENDOLEN AND CECILY: *(Speaking together.)* Your Christian names are still an insuperable barrier. That is all!

JACK AND ALGERNON: *(Speaking together.)* Our Christian names! Is that all? But we are going to be christened this afternoon.

GWENDOLEN: *(To* JACK.*)* For my sake you are prepared to do this terrible thing?

JACK: I am.

CECILY: *(To* ALGERNON.*)* To please me you are ready to face this fearful ordeal?

ALGERNON: I am!

GWENDOLEN: How absurd to talk of the equality of the sexes! Where questions of self-sacrifice are concerned, men are infinitely beyond us.

JACK: We are! *(Clasps hands with* ALGERNON.*)*

CECILY: They have moments of physical courage of which we women know absolutely nothing.

GWENDOLEN: *(To* JACK.*)* Darling!

ALGERNON: *(To* CECILY.*)* Darling! *(They fall into each other's arms.)*

(Enter MERRIMAN. *When he enters he coughs loudly, seeing the situation.)*

MERRIMAN: Ahem! Ahem! Lady Bracknell!

JACK: Good heavens!

(Enter LADY BRACKNELL. *The couples separate, in alarm. Exit* MERRIMAN.*)*

LADY BRACKNELL: Gwendolen! What does this mean?

GWENDOLEN: Merely that I am engaged to be married to Mr Worthing, Mamma.

LADY BRACKNELL: Come here. Sit down. Sit down immediately. Hesitation of any kind is a sign of mental decay in the young, of physical weakness in the old. *(Turns to* JACK.*)* Apprised, sir, of my daughter's sudden flight by her trusty maid, whose confidence I purchased by means of a small coin, I followed her at once by a luggage train. Her unhappy father is, I am glad to say, under the impression that she is attending a more than usually lengthy lecture by the University Extension Scheme on the influence of a permanent income on thought. I do not propose to undeceive him. Indeed I have never undeceived him on any question. I would consider it wrong. But of course, you will clearly understand that all communication between yourself and my daughter must cease immediately from this moment. On this point, as indeed on all points, I am firm.

JACK: I am engaged to be married to Gwendolen, Lady Bracknell!

LADY BRACKNELL: You are nothing of the kind, sir. And now, as regards Algernon! . . . Algernon!

ALGERNON: Yes, Aunt Augusta.

LADY BRACKNELL: May I ask if it is in this house that your invalid friend Mr Bunbury resides?

ALGERNON: *(Stammering.)* Oh! No! Bunbury doesn't live here. Bunbury is somewhere else at present. In fact, Bunbury is dead.

LADY BRACKNELL: Dead! When did Mr Bunbury die? His death must have been extremely sudden.

ALGERNON: *(Airily.)* Oh! I killed Bunbury this afternoon. I mean poor Bunbury died this afternoon.

LADY BRACKNELL: What did he die of?

ALGERNON: Bunbury? Oh, he was quite exploded.

LADY BRACKNELL: Exploded! Was he the victim of a revolutionary outrage? I was not aware that Mr Bunbury was interested in social legislation. If so, he is well punished for his morbidity.

ALGERNON: My dear Aunt Augusta, I mean he was found out! The doctors found out that Bunbury could not live, that is what I mean—so Bunbury died.

LADY BRACKNELL: He seems to have had great confidence in the opinion of his physicians. I am glad, however, that he made up his mind at the last to some definite course of action, and acted under proper medical advice. And now that we have finally got rid of this Mr Bunbury, may I ask, Mr Worthing, who is that young person whose hand my nephew Algernon is now holding in what seems to me a peculiarly unnecessary manner?

JACK: That lady is Miss Cecily Cardew, my ward. *(*LADY BRACKNELL *bows coldly to* CECILY.*)*

ALGERNON: I am engaged to be married to Cecily, Aunt Augusta.

LADY BRACKNELL: I beg your pardon?

CECILY: Mr Moncrieff and I are engaged to be married, Lady Bracknell.

LADY BRACKNELL: *(With a shiver, crossing to the sofa and sitting down.)* I do not know whether there is anything peculiarly exciting in the air of this particular part of Hertfordshire, but the number of engagements that go on seems to me considerably above the proper average that statistics have laid down for our guidance. I think some preliminary enquiry on my part would not be out of place. Mr Worthing, is Miss Cardew at all connected with any of the larger railway stations in London? I merely desire information. Until yesterday I had no idea that there were any families or persons whose origin was a Terminus. *(*JACK *looks perfectly furious, but restrains himself.)*

JACK: *(In a clear, cold voice.)* Miss Cardew is the granddaughter of the late Mr Thomas Cardew of 149, Belgrave Square, SW; Gervase Park, Dorking, Surrey; and the Sporran, Fifeshire, NB.

LADY BRACKNELL: That sounds not unsatisfactory. Three addresses always inspire confidence, even in tradesmen. But what proof have I of their authenticity?

JACK: I have carefully preserved the Court Guides of the period. They are open to your inspection, Lady Bracknell.

LADY BRACKNELL: *(Grimly.)* I have known strange errors in that publication.

JACK: Miss Cardew's family solicitors are Messrs. Markby, Markby, and Markby.

LADY BRACKNELL: Markby, Markby, and Markby? A firm of the very highest position in their profession. Indeed I am told that one of the Mr Markbys is occasionally to be seen at dinner parties. So far I am satisfied.

JACK: *(Very irritably.)* How extremely kind of you, Lady Bracknell! I have also in my possession, you will be pleased to hear, certificates of Miss Cardew's birth, baptism, whooping cough, registration, vaccination, confirmation, and the measles; both the German and the English variety.

LADY BRACKNELL: Ah! A life crowded with incident, I see; though perhaps somewhat too exciting for a young girl. I am not myself in favor of premature experiences. *(Rises, looks at her watch.)* Gwendolen! the time approaches for our departure. We have not a moment to lose. As a matter of form, Mr Worthing, I had better ask you if Miss Cardew has any little fortune?

JACK: Oh! about a hundred and thirty thousand pounds in the Funds.° That is all. Good-bye, Lady Bracknell. So pleased to have seen you.

LADY BRACKNELL: *(Sitting down again.)* A moment, Mr Worthing. A hundred and thirty thousand pounds! And in the Funds! Miss Cardew seems to me a most attractive young lady, now that I look at her. Few girls of the present day have any really solid qualities, any of the qualities that last, and improve with time. We live, I regret to say, in an age of surfaces. *(To CECILY.)* Come over here, dear. *(CECILY goes across.)* Pretty child! your dress is sadly simple, and your hair seems almost as nature might have left it. But we can soon alter all that. A thoroughly experienced French maid produces a really marvelous result in a very brief space of time. I remember recommending one to young Lady Lancing, and after three months her own husband did not know her.

JACK: *(Aside.)* And after six months nobody knew her.

LADY BRACKNELL: *(Glares at JACK for a few moments. Then bends, with a practiced smile, to CECILY.)* Kindly turn round, sweet child. *(CECILY turns completely round.)* No, the side view is what I want. *(CECILY presents her profile.)* Yes, quite as I expected. There are distinct social possibilities in your profile. The two weak points in our age are its want of principle and its want of profile. The chin a little higher, dear. Style largely depends on the way the chin is worn. They are worn very high, just at present. Algernon!

ALGERNON: Yes, Aunt Augusta!

LADY BRACKNELL: There are distinct social possibilities in Miss Cardew's profile.

ALGERNON: Cecily is the sweetest, dearest, prettiest girl in the whole world. And I don't care twopence about social possibilities.

LADY BRACKNELL: Never speak disrespectfully of Society, Algernon. Only people who can't get into it do that. *(To CECILY.)* Dear child, of course you know that Algernon has nothing but his debts to depend upon. But I do not approve of mercenary marriages. When I married Lord Bracknell I had no fortune of any kind. But I never dreamed for a moment of allowing that to stand in my way. Well, I suppose I must give my consent.

ALGERNON: Thank you, Aunt Augusta.

LADY BRACKNELL: Cecily, you may kiss me!

CECILY: *(Kisses her.)* Thank you, Lady Bracknell.

LADY BRACKNELL: You may also address me as Aunt Augusta for the future.

CECILY: Thank you, Aunt Augusta.

LADY BRACKNELL: The marriage, I think, had better take place quite soon.

ALGERNON: Thank you, Aunt Augusta.

CECILY: Thank you, Aunt Augusta.

LADY BRACKNELL: To speak frankly, I am not in favor of long engagements. They give people the opportunity of finding out each other's character before marriage, which I think is never advisable.

JACK: I beg your pardon for interrupting you, Lady Bracknell, but this engagement is quite out of the question. I am Miss Cardew's guardian, and she cannot marry without my consent until she comes of age. That consent I absolutely decline to give.

LADY BRACKNELL: Upon what grounds may I ask? Algernon is an extremely, I may almost say an ostentatiously, eligible young man. He has nothing, but he looks everything. What more can one desire?

JACK: It pains me very much to have to speak frankly to you, Lady Bracknell, about your nephew, but the fact is that I do not approve at all of his moral character. I suspect him of being untruthful. *(ALGERNON and CECILY look at him in indignant amazement.)*

LADY BRACKNELL: Untruthful! My nephew Algernon? Impossible! He is an Oxonian.°

JACK: I fear there can be no possible doubt about the matter. This afternoon, during my temporary absence in London on an important question of romance, he obtained admission to my house by means of the false pretense of being my brother.

---

a hundred and thirty thousand pounds in the Funds, approximately $650,000 invested in government bonds, a safe form of investment.

Oxonian, a graduate of the University of Oxford.

Under an assumed name he drank, I've just been informed by my butler, an entire pint bottle of my Perrier-Jouet, Brut,° '89; a wine I was specially reserving for myself. Continuing his disgraceful deception, he succeeded in the course of the afternoon in alienating the affections of my only ward. He subsequently stayed to tea, and devoured every single muffin. And what makes his conduct all the more heartless is, that he was perfectly well aware from the first that I have no brother, that I never had a brother, and that I don't intend to have a brother, not even of any kind. I distinctly told him so myself yesterday afternoon.

LADY BRACKNELL: Ahem! Mr Worthing, after careful consideration I have decided entirely to overlook my nephew's conduct to you.

JACK: That is very generous of you, Lady Bracknell. My own decision, however, is unalterable. I decline to give my consent.

LADY BRACKNELL: (*To* CECILY.) Come here, sweet child. (CECILY *goes over.*) How old are you, dear?

CECILY: Well, I am really only eighteen, but I always admit to twenty when I go to evening parties.

LADY BRACKNELL: You are perfectly right in making some slight alteration. Indeed, no woman should ever be quite accurate about her age. It looks so calculating. . . . (*In a meditative manner.*) Eighteen, but admitting to twenty at evening parties. Well, it will not be very long before you are of age and free from the restraints of tutelage. So I don't think your guardian's consent is, after all, a matter of any importance.

JACK: Pray excuse me, Lady Bracknell, for interrupting you again, but it is only fair to tell you that according to the terms of her grandfather's will Miss Cardew does not come legally of age till she is thirty-five.

LADY BRACKNELL: That does not seem to me to be a grave objection. Thirty-five is a very attractive age. London society is full of women of the very highest birth who have, of their own free choice, remained thirty-five for years. Lady Dumbleton is an instance in point. To my own knowledge she has been thirty-five ever since she arrived at the age of forty, which was many years ago now. I see no reason why our dear Cecily should not be even still more attractive at the age you mention than she is at present. There will be a large accumulation of property.

CECILY: Algy, could you wait for me till I was thirty-five?

ALGERNON: Of course I could, Cecily. You know I could.

CECILY: Yes, I felt it instinctively, but I couldn't wait all that time. I hate waiting even five minutes for anybody. It always makes me rather cross. I am not punctual myself, I know, but I do like punctuality in others, and waiting, even to be married, is quite out of the question.

ALGERNON: Then what is to be done, Cecily?

CECILY: I don't know, Mr Moncrieff.

LADY BRACKNELL: My dear Mr Worthing, as Miss Cardew states positively that she cannot wait till she is thirty-five—a remark which I am bound to say seems to me to show a somewhat impatient nature—I would beg of you to reconsider your decision.

JACK: But my dear Lady Bracknell, the matter is entirely in your own hands. The moment you consent to my marriage with Gwendolen, I will most gladly allow your nephew to form an alliance with my ward.

LADY BRACKNELL: (*Rising and drawing herself up.*) You must be quite aware that what you propose is out of the question.

JACK: Then a passionate celibacy is all that any of us can look forward to.

LADY BRACKNELL: That is not the destiny I propose for Gwendolen. Algernon, of course, can choose for himself. (*Pulls out her watch.*) Come, dear; (GWENDOLEN *rises*) we have already missed five, if not six, trains. To miss any more might expose us to comment on the platform.

(*Enter* DR CHASUBLE.)

CHASUBLE: Everything is quite ready for the christenings.

LADY BRACKNELL: The christenings, sir! Is not that somewhat premature?

CHASUBLE: (*Looking rather puzzled, and pointing to* JACK *and* ALGERNON.) Both these gentlemen have expressed a desire for immediate baptism.

LADY BRACKNELL: At their age? The idea is grotesque and irreligious! Algernon, I forbid you to be baptized. I will not hear of such excesses. Lord Bracknell would be highly displeased if he learned that that was the way in which you wasted your time and money.

CHASUBLE: Am I to understand then that there are to be no christenings at all this afternoon?

JACK: I don't think that, as things are now, it would be of much practical value to either of us, Dr Chasuble.

CHASUBLE: I am grieved to hear such sentiments from you, Mr Worthing. They savor of the heretical views of the Anabaptists, views that I have completely refuted in four of my unpublished sermons. However, as your present mood seems to be one peculiarly secular, I will return to the church at once. Indeed, I have just been informed

---

Perrier-Jouet, Brut, champagne.

by the pew-opener° that for the last hour and a half Miss Prism has been waiting for me in the vestry.

LADY BRACKNELL: (*Starting.*) Miss Prism! Did I hear you mention a Miss Prism?

CHASUBLE: Yes, Lady Bracknell. I am on my way to join her.

LADY BRACKNELL: Pray allow me to detain you for a moment. This matter may prove to be one of vital importance to Lord Bracknell and myself. Is this Miss Prism a female of repellent aspect, remotely connected with education?

CHASUBLE: (*Somewhat indignantly.*) She is the most cultivated of ladies, and the very picture of respectability.

LADY BRACKNELL: It is obviously the same person. May I ask what position she holds in your household?

CHASUBLE: (*Severely.*) I am a celibate, madam.

JACK: (*Interposing.*) Miss Prism, Lady Bracknell, has been for the last three years Miss Cardew's esteemed governess and valued companion.

LADY BRACKNELL: In spite of what I hear of her, I must see her at once. Let her be sent for.

CHASUBLE: (*Looking off.*) She approaches; she is nigh.

(*Enter* MISS PRISM *hurriedly.*)

MISS PRISM: I was told you expected me in the vestry, dear Canon. I have been waiting for you there for an hour and three-quarters. (*Catches sight of* LADY BRACKNELL *who has fixed her with a stony glare.* MISS PRISM *grows pale and quails. She looks anxiously round as if desirous to escape.*)

LADY BRACKNELL: (*In a severe, judicial voice.*) Prism! (MISS PRISM *bows her head in shame.*) Come here, Prism! (MISS PRISM *approaches in a humble manner.*) Prism! Where is that baby? (*General consternation. The* CANON *starts back in horror.* ALGERNON *and* JACK *pretend to be anxious to shield* CECILY *and* GWENDOLEN *from hearing the details of a terrible public scandal.*) Twenty-eight years ago, Prism, you left Lord Bracknell's house, Number 104, Upper Grosvenor Street, in charge of a perambulator that contained a baby, of the male sex. You never returned. A few weeks later, through the elaborate investigations of the Metropolitan police, the perambulator was discovered at midnight, standing by itself in a remote corner of Bayswater. It contained the manuscript of a three-volume novel of more than usually revolting sentimentality. (MISS PRISM *starts in involuntary indignation.*) But the baby was not there! (*Everyone looks at* MISS PRISM.) Prism! Where is that baby? (*A pause.*)

MISS PRISM: Lady Bracknell, I admit with shame that I do not know. I only wish I did. The plain facts of

the case are these. On the morning of the day you mention, a day that is forever branded on my memory, I prepared as usual to take the baby out in its perambulator. I had also with me a somewhat old, but capacious handbag in which I had intended to place the manuscript of a work of fiction that I had written during my few unoccupied hours. In a moment of mental abstraction, for which I never can forgive myself, I deposited the manuscript in the bassinette,° and placed the baby in the handbag.

JACK: (*Who has been listening attentively.*) But where did you deposit the handbag?

MISS PRISM: Do not ask me, Mr Worthing.

JACK: Miss Prism, this is a matter of no small importance to me. I insist on knowing where you deposited the handbag that contained that infant.

MISS PRISM: I left it in the cloakroom of one of the larger railway stations in London.

JACK: What railway station?

MISS PRISM: (*Quite crushed.*) Victoria. The Brighton line. (*Sinks into a chair.*)

JACK: I must retire to my room for a moment. Gwendolen, wait here for me.

GWENDOLEN: If you are not too long, I will wait here for you all my life. (*Exit* JACK *in great excitement.*)

CHASUBLE: What do you think this means, Lady Bracknell?

LADY BRACKNELL: I dare not even suspect, Dr Chasuble. I need hardly tell you that in families of high position strange coincidences are not supposed to occur. They are hardly considered the thing. (*Noises heard overhead as if someone was throwing trunks about. Everyone looks up.*)

CECILY: Uncle Jack seems strangely agitated.

CHASUBLE: Your guardian has a very emotional nature.

LADY BRACKNELL: This noise is extremely unpleasant. It sounds as if he was having an argument. I dislike arguments of any kind. They are always vulgar, and often convincing.

CHASUBLE: (*Looking up.*) It has stopped now. (*The noise is redoubled.*)

LADY BRACKNELL: I wish he would arrive at some conclusion.

GWENDOLEN: This suspense is terrible. I hope it will last.

(*Enter* JACK *with a handbag of black leather in his hand.*)

JACK: (*Rushing over to* MISS PRISM.) Is this the handbag, Miss Prism? Examine it carefully before you speak. The happiness of more than one life depends on your answer.

MISS PRISM: (*Calmly.*) It seems to be mine. Yes, here is the injury it received through the upsetting of a Gower Street omnibus in younger and happier

---

pew-opener, person employed in church to open the private pews of eminent persons.

bassinette, hooded baby carriage.

days. Here is the stain on the lining caused by the explosion of a temperance beverage, an incident that occurred at Leamington. And here, on the lock, are my initials. I had forgotten that in an extravagant mood I had had them placed there. The bag is undoubtedly mine. I am delighted to have it so unexpectedly restored to me. It has been a great inconvenience being without it all these years.

JACK: *(In a pathetic voice.)* Miss Prism, more is restored to you than this handbag. I was the baby you placed in it.

MISS PRISM: *(Amazed.)* You?

JACK: *(Embracing her.)* Yes . . . mother!

MISS PRISM: *(Recoiling in indignant astonishment.)* Mr Worthing! I am unmarried!

JACK: Unmarried! I do not deny that is a serious blow. But after all, who has the right to cast a stone against one who has suffered? Cannot repentance wipe out an act of folly? Why should there be one law for men, and another for women? Mother, I forgive you. *(Tries to embrace her again.)*

MISS PRISM: *(Still more indignant.)* Mr Worthing, there is some error. *(Pointing to* LADY BRACKNELL.*)* There is the lady who can tell you who you really are.

JACK: *(After a pause.)* Lady Bracknell, I hate to seem inquisitive, but would you kindly inform me who I am?

LADY BRACKNELL: I am afraid that the news I have to give you will not altogether please you. You are the son of my poor sister, Mrs Moncrieff, and consequently Algernon's elder brother.

JACK: Algy's elder brother! Then I have a brother after all. I knew I had a brother! I always said I had a brother! Cecily,—how could you have ever doubted that I had a brother. *(Seizes hold of* ALGERNON.*)* Dr Chasuble, my unfortunate brother. Miss Prism, my unfortunate brother. Gwendolen, my unfortunate brother. Algy, you young scoundrel, you will have to treat me with more respect in the future. You have never behaved to me like a brother in all your life.

ALGERNON: Well, not till today, old boy, I admit. I did my best, however, though I was out of practice. *(Shakes hands.)*

GWENDOLEN: *(to* JACK.*)* My own! But what own are you? What is your Christian name, now that you have become someone else?

JACK: Good heavens! . . . I had quite forgotten that point. Your decision on the subject of my name is irrevocable, I suppose?

GWENDOLEN: I never change, except in my affections.

CECILY: What a noble nature you have, Gwendolen!

JACK: Then the question had better be cleared up at once. Aunt Augusta, a moment. At the time when Miss Prism left me in the handbag, had I been christened already?

LADY BRACKNELL: Every luxury that money could buy, including christening, had been lavished on you by your fond and doting parents.

JACK: Then I was christened! That is settled. Now, what name was I given? Let me know the worst.

LADY BRACKNELL: Being the eldest son you were naturally christened after your father.

JACK: *(Irritably.)* Yes, but what was my father's Christian name?

LADY BRACKNELL: *(Meditatively.)* I cannot at the present moment recall what the General's Christian name was. But I have no doubt he had one. He was eccentric, I admit. But only in later years. And that was the result of the Indian climate, and marriage, and indigestion, and other things of that kind.

JACK: Algy! Can't you recollect what our father's Christian name was?

ALGERNON: My dear boy, we were never even on speaking terms. He died before I was a year old.

JACK: His name would appear in the Army Lists of the period, I suppose, Aunt Augusta?

LADY BRACKNELL: The General was essentially a man of peace, except in his domestic life. But I have no doubt his name would appear in any military directory.

JACK: The Army Lists of the last forty years are here. These delightful records should have been my constant study. *(Rushes to bookcase and tears the books out.)* M. Generals . . . Mallam, Maxbohm, Magley, what ghastly names they have—Markby, Migsby, Mobbs, Moncrieff! Lieutenant 1840, Captain, Lieutenant-Colonel, Colonel, General 1869, Christian names, Ernest John. *(Puts book very quietly down and speaks quite calmly.)* I always told you, Gwendolen, my name was Ernest, didn't I? Well, it is Ernest after all. I mean it naturally is Ernest.

LADY BRACKNELL: Yes, I remember now that the General was called Ernest. I knew I had some particular reason for disliking the name.

GWENDOLEN: Ernest! My own Ernest! I felt from the first that you could have no other name!

JACK: Gwendolen, it is a terrible thing for a man to find out suddenly that all his life he has been speaking nothing but the truth. Can you forgive me?

GWENDOLEN: I can. For I feel that you are sure to change.

JACK: My own one!

CHASUBLE: *(to* MISS PRISM.*)* Lætitia! *(Embraces her.)*

MISS PRISM: *(Enthusiastically.)* Frederick! At last!

ALGERNON: Cecily! *(Embraces her.)* At last!

JACK: Gwendolen! *(Embraces her.)* At last!

LADY BRACKNELL: My nephew, you seem to be displaying signs of triviality.

JACK: On the contrary, Aunt Augusta, I've now realized for the first time in my life the vital Importance of Being Earnest.

CURTAIN.

Figure 1. Flanked by Jack (John Gielgud, *left*) and Algernon (Jack Hawkins, *right*), Gwendolen (Gwen Ffrangçon-Davies) and Cecily (Peggy Ashcroft) are horrified to discover that neither man is really named Ernest. The 1939 production of *The Importance of Being Earnest* at the Globe Theatre, London, was directed by John Gielgud. (Photograph: Angus McBean, Harvard Theatre Collection.)

Figure 2. "Rise, sir, from this semi-recumbent posture," demands Lady Bracknell (Edith Evans) as she surprises Jack (John Gielgud) proposing to Gwendolen (Gwen Ffrangçon-Davies) in the 1939 production. (Photograph: Angus McBean, Harvard Theatre Collection.)

Figure 3. Lady Bracknell, notebook in hand (Judi Dench) quizzes Jack (Martin Jarvis) about his suitability as Gwendolen's future husband in the 1982 National Theatre production directed by Peter Hall. (Photograph: Zoe Dominic.)

Figure 4. The stylized set for the second act of the 1982 National Theatre production, with its reflecting surface, potted plants, and silhouetted village, is the background for the confrontations of Jack and Gwendolen (Martin Jarvis and Zoe Wanamaker, *to left*) and Algernon and Cecily (Nigel Havers and Elizabeth Garvie, *right*). (Photograph: Zoe Dominic.)

Staging of *The Importance of Being Earnest*

REVIEW OF THE NATIONAL
THEATRE PRODUCTION, 1982,
BY MICHAEL BILLINGTON

All too often productions of The Importance of Being Earnest are swathed in campy artifice. But Peter Hall's fine new version at the Lyttelton not only strips the play of the usual fussy accretions but hits the perfect balance between realism and style. The people themselves are motivated by recognisable passions like lust and greed; yet the world they inhabit, half-way between W. S. Gilbert and Alice in Wonderland, exists at a slight tangent to normality.

You recognise from the start that you are in safe hands. Martin Jarvis's Jack Worthing, with his wing-collar, cruel specs and severe swept-back hair, has the dry formality of Redgrave's Crocker-Harris in The Browning Version. Not only does this establish an obvious physical contrast with Nigel Havers's floppy-cravatted, curly-haired, insouciant Algernon. It also pinpoints one of the play's main themes: the Victorian double-standard ("Ernest in town and Jack in the country") that enabled respectable pillars of society to have a secret, camouflaged life.

But the great merit of the production is that, instead of a lot of elegant people saying witty things, it offers genuine emotional reality. And nowhere is this better seen than in Judi Dench's superb Lady Bracknell. It would be an exaggeration to say that she is more Zola than gorgon but she does present us with a woman prey to quicksilver feelings. Thus she starts the famous interview with Mr Worthing with a voracious, note-taking delight in his financial prospects: even the news that he inhabits the unfashionable side of Belgrave Square elicits nothing more than a mercurial giggle.

Warming to her task, she invites him to sit alongside her on the sofa. But the shattering news of his origins is greeted not with a sub-Evans swoop but with a very slow, incredulous removal of her glasses and a sotto voce rendering of "A handbag?" in thunderstruck disbelief. Ostentatiously tearing up her notes, she conducts the rest of the interrogation with the hurried politeness of someone anxious to catch a train. I cite this as only one example of a totally re-thought performance that takes us on a conducted tour of the character: the whaleboned snobbery, the hunger for loot, the contempt for her husband (always referred to in a voice-dropping aside as if he were a leper), the ill-concealed delight in her own bon mots. Ms Dench gives us a woman rather than an exercise in style.

But this is only one example of the production's ability to present us with plausible people in a slightly askew world. Anna Massey's Miss Prism, for example, is no caricature-spinster but a perky lady of considerable literary vanity (she visibly reels at the description of her three-volume novel as of "more than usually revolting sentimentality") and limited imagination: she is more excited at the recovery of her voluminous handbag which she inspects like Arthur Negus than at its sensational implications. And Paul Rogers's Canon Chasuble is funny precisely because he is a Hertfordshire Holofernes, vastly proud of his scholarship, and not because clerics are automatically hilarious.

What Hall's production also brings out is the bedrock of love and lust that underpins all the famous Wildean epigrams. This is an unequivocally hetero production (I suspect there was nothing the least effete about the original version) in which Zoe Wanamaker's Gwendolen is no Dresden doll but a raunchy lady who, when asked by Mr Worthing if she loves him, replies, "Passionately," in a voice of throaty sexiness. And Elizabeth Garvie's Cecily, though looking like a bonneted Lewis Carroll Alice, is as determined as the Mounties to get her man.

The passions are real. But the problem with the play is that it does have a strange topsy-turvy, Gilbertian quality. And John Bury's designs hint at this in their faint stylisation. The second-act garden, for instance, has a glassy, reflecting surface, sporadic rose-tree (again a hint of Alice?) and a silhouetted village background. Visually, the production makes the point that Wilde transports us into a timeless, Victorian fairy-land. But, textually, it never lets us forget that Wilde also offers us a daisy-chain of serious comment on death, marriage, morals, the class-system, the decline of aristocracy. Eric Bently once said that the play "intermittently shows the English upper class in a harsh, bizarre light." And the achievement of this production is that it reflects the play's historic importance without itself ever becoming earnest.

JOHN MILLINGTON SYNGE

1871–1909

Although John Millington (J. M.) Synge lived only long enough to write six plays, all of them during the last several years of his life, these six plays about Irish folk experience are so powerful and evocative that they have established him as the first great playwright of the modern Irish theater. Such a notable achievement could hardly have been predicted from either his childhood or his educational experience, for he was born and reared in Dublin in a repressive Calvinistic household and educated at Trinity College, Dublin, where he studied natural science, music, as well as the Gaelic and Hebrew languages. His theatrical career could not even have been anticipated from his early adulthood, for after graduating from Trinity College in 1892, he left Ireland to travel in Germany, Italy, and France, and then settled down in Paris to study at the Sorbonne. While in Paris, he devoted himself to learning French and Italian, as well as to writing poems and reviews. But in 1896, Synge had a prophetic encounter with the great Irish poet William Butler Yeats, who gave him the following advice:

> Give up Paris, you will never create anything by reading Racine, and Arthur Symons will always be a better critic of French literature. Go to the Aran Islands. Live there as if you were one of the people themselves; express a life that has never found expression.

By 1898, Synge had finally given up on his desire to make a literary career in Paris, and he acted on Yeats's advice. From 1898 to 1902, he spent every summer in the Aran Islands, off the western coast of Ireland, immersing himself in the experience of peasant life and keeping a record of impressions that he subsequently drew on in the plays he wrote between 1902 and 1909. Life on those barren islands was clearly a harsh, almost primitive, struggle for existence, as Synge made evident in the published version of his journal, *The Aran Islands* (1904). But the dignity and joy with which those peasants endured hardship clearly stimulated Synge's imagination, as did the richness and wildness of their colloquial language, which he sought to reflect in all his plays.

Synge was also stimulated by a new theatrical movement that developed in Dublin between 1899 and 1902, when Yeats, with the support of his wealthy literary friend Lady Augusta Gregory and the collaboration of other Irish writers, was in the process of launching the Irish Literary Theatre, a repertory group dedicated to developing a native Irish drama that would "bring upon the stage the deeper thoughts and emotions of Ireland." This group, which is now known as the Abbey Theatre for the playhouse that was donated to it in 1904, deliberately aimed to set itself apart from the naturalistic drama of Ibsen and Strindberg that was then thriving on the Continent, seeking instead to echo the richly poetic language of Irish experience. These artistic goals clearly appealed to Synge, for as he indicated in his preface to *The Playboy of the Western World,* he too regarded Ibsen as "dealing with the reality of life in joyless and pallid words," and he too believed that the language of Irish drama should reflect "a popular imagination that is fiery and magnificent, and tender." Synge readily accepted Yeats's invitation to join the new group, and from 1902 on he wrote and directed for the Abbey Theatre.

Synge's six plays reflect his conviction that "on the stage one must have reality, and one must have joy," although not necessarily at the same time. Thus, in his first play, *Riders to the Sea* (written in 1902, but not produced until 1904), Synge used his evocative language to dramatize the nobility of a brave old peasant woman as she endures the loss of her last son to the sea after already having lost her husband and her other five sons to it—a loss that she finally transcends through the ironic reflection that "They're all gone now, and there isn't anything more the sea can do to me." So powerful is Synge's portrayal of the unrelenting world that it has inspired writers from other cultures to rewrite the play, most notably Derek Walcott, whose 1954 play *The Sea at Dauphin* resets Synge's play in a Caribbean context focusing on the fishermen rather than the women they leave behind. Synge's first full-length play, *The Well of the Saints* (1905), is less indebted to the reality of the Aran Islands than to Irish folklore. In this seriocomic three-act play, Synge depicts the vanities and escapism of an old blind couple who miraculously have their sight temporarily restored by a saint, only to discover their physical ugliness. When the saint offers to perpetuate their sight, they choose instead to return to the illusions of their blindness that the husband sustains through the flights of his poetic imagination.

Synge's persistent concern with the mythic power of the Irish imagination reached its most thoroughgoing and boisterous expression in his next work, *The Playboy of the Western World* (1907). From the moment that Christy Mahon staggers into Michael James's pub and proceeds to tell his bloody tale of having murdered his tyrannical father, he transforms the lives of the desolate villagers, who in turn transform him into their hero. Imagination works powerfully on the lives of everyone in the play, especially the barmaid Pegeen, who falls in love with Christy. But when Christy's father unexpectedly enters the pub, Christy's heroic stature in the eyes of the villagers is suddenly shattered, and the play subsequently turns into an archetypal struggle for survival between father and son. In this sense, it may be seen as a variation on the theme of patricide embodied in *Oedipus Rex.* The variation is arresting, because it initially dramatizes the villagers' tacit approval of patricide in their celebration of Christy's supposed murder, but in the end it exposes their horror of the act when they are faced with the possibility that it might occur in their presence. As Pegeen proclaims, "There's a great gap between a gallous [splendid] story and a dirty deed." It is as if Christy has forced the villagers to recognize within themselves the imaginative appeal of violating so powerful a taboo, a violation that he is at least willing to make and that his father is even willing to accept. Despite all its boisterous and farcical activity, *The Playboy of the Western World* plays seriously with the themes of imagination and reality.

Synge's achievement in this play was at first overshadowed by the furious response it evoked from its very first audience. When Christy claims near the end of the play that he only loves Pegeen and would reject "a drift of chosen females, standing in their shifts itself," the Dublin audience, already outraged by Synge's apparent portrayal of Irishmen as a foul-mouthed group of country bumpkins delighting in violence, erupted in vocal protest at Christy's allusion to underwear-clad women. Police were needed for several more performances, and irate letters appeared in newspapers. Though the *Playboy* "riots" may now seem strange given the graphic violence and sexuality of contemporary popular culture, those riots actually reflect the power of theater within that Irish culture. Moreover, the anger of the audience suggests how successful Synge was in creating a realistic world on stage, a world whose values seemed to challenge those of the audience.

In fact, Synge's first-produced play, *In the Shadow of the Glen* (1903), created a similar stir. Prominent Irish nationalists, including Maud Gonne, walked out of the first performance and a review in the *Irish Times* found the play "exceedingly distasteful." Letters to another newspaper, the *United Irishman,* from both W. B. Yeats and his father, the noted painter J. B. Yeats, kept the controversy alive, with both father and son defending Synge's play and its honest portrayal of "our Irish institution, the loveless marriage." W. B. Yeats argued for Synge's play in an even broader context, claiming that Irish writers must be free to write on any subject, even if audiences were indifferent or hostile.

The power of Synge's short play derives not only from its central situation—the marital incompatibility between a jealous old man and a sensitive young woman—but from the language he used to portray them. Later Synge would assert that "In a good play every speech should be as fully flavored as a nut or apple, and such speeches cannot be written by anyone who works among people who have shut their lips on poetry." Everyone in the play speaks that "fully flavored" language, language that Synge created for characters he had heard about when visiting the Aran Islands. Indeed, reading Synge's account of the story (see excerpt following the play) and then reading the play makes clear how thoroughly he transformed a compelling anecdote into a play that is both serious and comic, poetic and harsh. And although Synge would later condemn Ibsen's language, he nonetheless named his central character Nora, and, like Ibsen in *A Doll's House,* imagined her escaping from her repressive marriage.

Riders to the Sea and *In the Shadow of the Glen* are in some ways complementary plays, one dealing somberly with fate and human acceptance, the other portraying an ironic world of compromise and change. When the Royal Shakespeare Company presented an evening of three Irish plays in 1998, Synge's one-acts and Yeats's last play, *Purgatory,* the collective title *Shadows* reminded the audience of the centrality of death to each play, and, as the director John Crowley put it, "the refusal of the dead to leave the living alone." While reviewers differed in their response to the combination of plays, they all paid tribute to Yeats and, particularly, Synge as the sources of contemporary Irish drama (see Alastair Macaulay's review following the play). The contradictory moods of *In the Shadow of the Glen* emerge from moments such as the husband threatening his younger rival, Michael Dara, a threat made less violent by the nightgown the supposed dead man is wearing (see Figure 1), or the sadness evident in Nora's eyes as she speaks of her lonely life (see Figure 2), or from the play's closing moments when the rejected husband and the rejected suitor drink together. Those last lines may reveal ironic pragmatism or genuine reconciliation, just as Nora's departure can reflect naïve optimism or determined individuality or even wistful compromise. Synge's writing about Irish folk and folklore came from his observation and listening, but also from his perceptive understanding of the complex and often ambiguous nature of human relationships.

IN THE SHADOW OF THE GLEN

BY J. M. SYNGE

CHARACTERS

DAN BURKE, *farmer and herd*
NORA BURKE, *his wife*
MICHAEL DARA, *a young herd*
A TRAMP

SCENE

The last cottage at the head of a long glen in County Wicklow.°
(Cottage kitchen; turf fire on the right; a bed near it against the wall, with a body lying on it covered with a sheet. A door is at the other end of the room, with a low table near it, and stools, or wooden chairs. There are a couple of glasses on the table, and a bottle of whisky, as if for a wake,° with two cups, a tea-pot, and a home-made cake. There is another small door near the bed. NORA BURKE *is moving about the room, settling a few things, and lighting candles on the table, looking now and then at the bed with an uneasy look. Someone knocks softly at the door. She takes up a stocking with money from the table and puts it in her pocket. Then she opens the door.)*

TRAMP *(outside)*: Good evening to you, lady of the house.

NORA: Good evening kindly, stranger; it's a wild night, God help you, to be out in the rain falling.

TRAMP: It is, surely, and I walking to Brittas from the Aughrim fair.°

NORA: Is it walking on your feet, stranger?

TRAMP: On my two feet, lady of the house, and when I saw the light below I thought may be if you'd a sup of new milk and a quiet, decent corner where a man could sleep . . . *(He looks in past her and sees the dead man.)* The Lord have mercy on us all!

NORA: It doesn't matter anyway, stranger; come in out of the rain.

TRAMP *(coming in slowly and going towards the bed)*: Is it departed he is?

NORA: It is, stranger. He's after dying on me, God forgive him, and there I am now with a hundred sheep beyond on the hills, and no turf drawn for the winter.°

TRAMP *(looking closely at the dead man)*: It's a queer look is on him for a man that's dead.

NORA *(half humorously)*: He was always queer, stranger; and I suppose them that's queer and they living men will be queer bodies after.

TRAMP: Isn't it a great wonder you're letting him lie there, and he not tidied, or laid out itself?

NORA *(coming to the bed)*: I was afeard, stranger, for he put a black curse on me this morning if I'd touch his body the time he'd die sudden, or let any one touch it except his sister only, and it's ten miles away she lives, in the big glen over the hill.

TRAMP *(looking at her and nodding slowly)*: It's a queer story he wouldn't let his own wife touch him, and he dying quiet in his bed.

NORA: He was an old man, and an odd man, stranger, and it's always up on the hills he was, thinking thoughts in the dark mist. . . . *(She pulls back a bit of the sheet.)* Lay your hand on him now, and tell me if it's cold he is surely.

TRAMP: Is it getting the curse on me you'd be, woman of the house? I wouldn't lay my hand on him for the Lough Nahanagan° and it filled with gold.

NORA *(looking uneasily at the body)*: Maybe cold would be no sign of death with the like of him, for he was always cold, every day since I knew him . . . and every night, stranger . . . *(she covers up his face and comes away from the bed)*; but I'm thinking it's dead he is surely, for he's complaining a while back of a pain in his heart, and this morning, the time he was going off to Brittas for three days or four, he was taken with a sharp turn. Then he went into his bed, and he was saying it was destroyed he was, the time the shadow was going

---

County Wicklow, county south of Dublin, where Synge spent much of his boyhood. Though Synge heard the story when he was visiting the Aran Islands off the west coast of Ireland, he set the play near the east coast, in territory he knew even better. *wake,* ritual ceremony in honor of the dead, including drinks and food, and the offering of a new pipe to each visitor. *Brittas from the Aughrim fair,* the tramp has been walking either across the whole of Ireland (Aughrim in County Galway) or just twenty miles (Aughrim in County Wicklow). *no turf drawn for the winter,* slabs of peat collected to use for fuel.

Lough Nahanagan, local lake with the reputation of being inhabited by a sea monster.

651

up through the glen, and when the sun set on the bog beyond he made a great lep, and let a great cry out of him, and stiffened himself out the like of a dead sheep.

TRAMP (*crosses himself*): God rest his soul.

NORA (*pouring him out a glass of whisky*): Maybe that would do you better than the milk of the sweetest cow in County Wicklow.

TRAMP: The Almighty God reward you and may it be to your good health. (*He drinks.*)

NORA (*giving him a pipe and tobacco*): I've no pipes saving his own, stranger, but they're sweet pipes to smoke.

TRAMP: Thank you kindly, lady of the house.

NORA: Sit down now, stranger, and be taking your rest.

TRAMP (*filling a pipe and looking about the room*): I've walked a great way through the world, lady of the house, and seen great wonders, but I never seen a wake till this day with fine spirits, and good tobacco, and the best of pipes, and no one to taste them but a woman only.

NORA: Didn't you hear me say it was only after dying on me he was when the sun went down, and how would I go out into the glen and tell the neighbours, and I a lone woman with no house near me?

TRAMP (*drinking*): There's no offence, lady of the house?

NORA: No offence in life, stranger. How would the like of you, passing in the dark night, know the lonesome way I was with no house near me at all?

TRAMP (*sitting down*): I knew rightly. (*He lights his pipe, so that there is a sharp light beneath his haggard face.*) And I was thinking, and I coming in through the door, that it's many a lone woman would be afeard of the like of me in the dark night, in a place wouldn't be as lonesome as this place, where there aren't two living souls would see the little light you have shining from the glass.

NORA (*slowly*): I'm thinking many would be afeard, but I never knew what way I'd be afeard of beggar or bishop or any man of you at all.... (*She looks towards the window and lowers her voice.*) It's other things than the like of you, stranger, would make a person afeard.

TRAMP (*looking round with a half shudder*): It is surely, God help us all!

NORA (*looking at him for a moment with curiosity*): You're saying that, stranger, as if you were easy afeard.

TRAMP (*speaking mournfully*): Is it myself, lady of the house, that does be walking round in the long nights, and crossing the hills when the fog is on them, the time a little stick would seem as big as your arm, and a rabbit as big as a bay horse, and a stack of turf as big as a towering church in the city of Dublin? If myself was easy afeard, I'm telling you, it's long ago I'd have been locked into the Richmond Asylum,° or maybe have run up into the back hills with nothing on me but an old shirt, and been eaten by the crows the like of Patch Darcy—the Lord have mercy on him—in the year that's gone.

NORA (*with interest*): You knew Darcy?

TRAMP: Wasn't I the last one heard his living voice in the whole world?

NORA: There were great stories of what was heard at that time, but would any one believe the things they do be saying in the glen?

TRAMP: It was no lie, lady of the house. . . . I was passing below on a dark night the like of this night, and the sheep were lying under the ditch and every one of them coughing and choking like an old man, with the great rain and the fog. Then I heard a thing talking—queer talk, you wouldn't believe it at all, and you out of your dreams—and "Merciful God," says I, "if I begin hearing the like of that voice out of the thick mist, I'm destroyed surely." Then I run and I run till I was below in Rathvanna.° I got drunk that night, I got drunk in the morning, and drunk the day after—I was coming from the races beyond—and the third day they found Darcy. . . . Then I knew it was himself I was after hearing, and I wasn't afeard any more.

NORA (*speaking sorrowfully and slowly*): God spare Darcy; he'd always look in here and he passing up or passing down, and it's very lonesome I was after him a long while (*she looks over at the bed and lowers her voice, speaking very slowly*), and then I got happy again—if it's ever happy we are, stranger—for I got used to being lonesome. (*A short pause; then she stands up.*) Was there any one on the last bit of the road, stranger, and you coming from Aughrim?

TRAMP: There was a young man with a drift° of mountain ewes, and he running after them this way and that.

NORA (*with a half smile*): Far down, stranger?

TRAMP: A piece only.

(NORA *fills the kettle and puts it on the fire.*)

NORA: Maybe, if you're not easy afeard, you'd stay here a short while alone with himself.

TRAMP: I would surely. A man that's dead can do no hurt.

NORA (*speaking with a sort of constraint*): I'm going a little back to the west, stranger, for himself would go there one night and another and whistle at that place, and then the young man you're after seeing—a kind of a farmer has come up from the

---

Richmond Asylum, Dublin hospital, originally a prison. *Rathvanna,* possibly a combination of Wicklow villages Rathdrum and Aughavanna. *drift,* small flock.

sea to live in a cottage beyond—would walk round to see if there was a thing we'd have to be done, and I'm wanting him this night, the way he can go down into the glen when the sun goes up and tell the people that himself is dead.

TRAMP (*looking at the body in the sheet*): It's myself will go for him, lady of the house, and let you not be destroying yourself with the great rain.

NORA: You wouldn't find your way, stranger, for there's a small path only, and it running up between two sluigs° where an ass and cart would be drowned. (*She puts a shawl over her head*). Let you be making yourself easy, and saying a prayer for his soul, and it's not long I'll be coming again.

TRAMP (*moving uneasily*): Maybe if you'd a piece of a grey thread and a sharp needle—there's great safety in a needle,° lady of the house—I'd be putting a little stitch here and there in my old coat, the time I'll be praying for his soul, and it going up naked to the saints of God.

NORA (*takes a needle and thread from the front of her dress and gives it to him*): There's the needle, stranger, and I'm thinking you won't be lonesome, and you used to the back hills, for isn't a dead man itself more company than to be sitting alone, and hearing the winds crying, and you not knowing on what thing your mind would stay?

TRAMP (*slowly*): It's true, surely, and the Lord have mercy on us all!

(NORA *goes out. The tramp begins stitching one of the tags in his coat, saying the "De Profundis"° under his breath. In an instant the sheet is drawn lowly down, and* DAN BURKE *looks out. The tramp moves uneasily, then looks up, and springs to his feet with a movement of terror.*)

DAN (*with a hoarse voice*): Don't be afeard, stranger; a man that's dead can do no hurt.

TRAMP (*trembling*): I meant no harm, your honour; and won't you leave me easy to be saying a little prayer for your soul?

(*A long whistle is heard outside.*)

DAN (*sitting up in his bed and speaking fiercely*): Ah, the devil mend her. . . . Do you hear that, stranger? Did ever you hear another woman could whistle the like of that with two fingers in her mouth? (*He looks at the table hurriedly.*) I'm destroyed with the drouth,° and let you bring me a drop quickly before herself will come back.

TRAMP (*doubtfully*): Is it not dead you are?

DAN: How would I be dead, and I as dry as a baked bone, stranger?

TRAMP (*pouring out the whisky*): What will herself say if she smells the stuff on you, for I'm thinking it's not for nothing you're letting on° to be dead?

DAN: It is not, stranger; but she won't be coming near me at all, and it's not long now I'll be letting on, for I've a cramp in my back, and my hip's asleep on me, and there's been the devil's own fly itching my nose. It's near dead I was wanting to sneeze, and you blathering about the rain, and Darcy (*bitterly*)—the devil choke him—and the towering church. (*Crying out impatiently.*) Give me that whisky. Would you have herself come back before I taste a drop at all?

(TRAMP *gives him the glass.*)

(*After drinking.*) Go over now to that cupboard, and bring me a black stick you'll see in the west corner by the wall.

TRAMP (*taking a stick from the cupboard*): Is it that, your honour?

DAN: It is, stranger; it's a long time I'm keeping that stick, for I've a bad wife in the house.

TRAMP (*with a queer look*): Is it herself, master of the house, and she a grand woman to talk?

DAN: It's herself, surely, it's a bad wife she is—a bad wife for an old man, and I'm getting old, God help me, though I've an arm to me still. (*He takes the stick in his hand.*) Let you wait now a short while, and it's a great sight you'll see in this room in two hours or three. (*He stops to listen.*) Is that somebody above?

TRAMP (*listening*): There's a voice speaking on the path.

DAN: Put that stick here in the bed and smooth the sheet the way it was lying. (*He covers himself up hastily.*) Be falling to sleep now, and don't let on you know anything, or I'll be having your life. I wouldn't have told you at all but it's destroyed with the drouth I was.

TRAMP (*covering his head*): Have no fear, master of the house. What is it I know of the like of you that I'd be saying a word or putting out my hand to stay you at all? (*He goes back to the fire, sits down on a stool with his back to the bed, and goes on stitching his coat.*)

DAN (*under the sheet, querulously*): Stranger!

TRAMP (*quickly*): Whisht! whisht! Be quiet, I'm telling you; they're coming now at the door.

(NORA *comes in with* MICHAEL DARA, *a tall, innocent young man, behind her.*)

NORA: I wasn't long at all, stranger, for I met himself on the path.

TRAMP: You were middling long, lady of the house.

---

sluigs, mires or morasses, as contrasted with a walkable bog. *great safety in a needle,* refers to the folk belief that a sharp needle protected a person against the fairies. *De Profundis,* Psalm 130, another protection against the supernatural. *drouth,* thirst, dryness.

letting on, pretending.

NORA: There was no sign from himself?

TRAMP: No sign at all, lady of the house.

NORA (to MICHAEL): Go over now and pull down the sheet, and look on himself, Michael Dara, and you'll see it's the truth I'm telling you.

MICHAEL: I will not, Nora; I do be afeard of the dead.

(He sits down on a stool next the table, facing the TRAMP. NORA *puts the kettle on a lower hook of the pot-hooks, and piles turf under it.)*

NORA (turning to TRAMP): Will you drink a sup of tea with myself and the young man, stranger, or *(speaking more persuasively)* will you go into the little room and stretch yourself a short while on the bed? I'm thinking it's destroyed you are walking the length of that way in the great rain.

TRAMP: Is it go away and leave you, and you having a wake, lady of the house? I will not, surely. *(He takes a drink from his glass, which he has beside him.)* And it's none of your tea I'm asking either.

(He goes on stitching. NORA *makes the tea.)*

MICHAEL (after looking at the TRAMP rather scornfully for a moment): That's a poor coat you have, God help you, and I'm thinking it's a poor tailor you are with it.

TRAMP: If it's a poor tailor I am, I'm thinking it's a poor herd does be running backward and forward after a little handful of ewes, the way I seen yourself running this day, young fellow, and you coming from the fair.

*(*NORA *comes back to the table.)*

NORA (to MICHAEL, in a low voice): Let you not mind him at all, Michael Dara; he has a drop taken, and it's soon he'll be falling asleep.

MICHAEL: It's no lie he's telling; I was destroyed, surely. They were that wilful they were running off into one man's bit of oats, and another man's bit of hay, and tumbling into the red bog till it's more like a pack of old goats than sheep they were. . . . Mountain ewes is a queer breed, Nora Burke, and I not used to them at all.

NORA (settling the tea-things): There's no one can drive a mountain ewe but the men do be reared in the Glenmalure, I've heard them say, and above by Rathvanna, and the Glen Imaal°—men the like of Patch Darcy, God spare his soul, who would walk through five hundred sheep and miss one of them, and he not reckoning them at all.

MICHAEL (uneasily): Is it the man went queer in his head the year that's gone?

NORA: It is, surely.

TRAMP (plaintively): That was a great man, young fel-low—a great man, I'm telling you. There was never a lamb from his own ewes he wouldn't know before it was marked, and he'd run from this to the city of Dublin and never catch for his breath.

NORA (turning round quickly): He was a great man surely, stranger; and isn't it a grand thing when you hear a living man saying a good word of a dead man, and he mad dying?

TRAMP: It's the truth I'm saying, God spare his soul.

(He puts the needle under the collar of his coat, and settles himself to sleep in the chimney corner. NORA *sits down at the table:* NORA *and* MICHAEL*'s backs are turned to the bed.)*

MICHAEL (looking at her with a queer look): I heard tell this day, Nora Burke, that it was on the path below Patch Darcy would be passing up and passing down, and I heard them say he'd never pass it night or morning without speaking with yourself.

NORA (in a low voice): It was no lie you heard, Michael Dara.

MICHAEL: I'm thinking it's a power of men you're after knowing if it's in a lonesome place you live itself.

NORA (giving him his tea): It's in a lonesome place you do have to be talking with someone, and looking for someone, in the evening of the day, and if it's a power of men I'm after knowing they were fine men, for I was a hard child to please, and a hard girl to please *(she looks at him a little sternly)*, and it's a hard woman I am to please this day, Michael Dara, and it's no lie I'm telling you.

MICHAEL (looking over to see that the TRAMP is asleep, and then pointing to the dead man): Was it a hard woman to please you were when you took himself for your man?

NORA: What way would I live, and I an old woman, if I didn't marry a man with a bit of a farm, and cows on it, and sheep on the back hills?

MICHAEL (considering): That's true, Nora, and maybe it's no fool you were, for there's good grazing on it, if it is a lonesome place, and I'm thinking it's a good sum he's left behind.

NORA (taking the stocking with the money from her pocket, and putting it on the table): I do be thinking in the long nights it was a big fool I was that time, Michael Dara; for what good is a bit of a farm with cows on it, and sheep on the back hills, when you do be sitting looking out from a door the like of that door, and seeing nothing but the mists rolling down the bog, and the mists again and they rolling up the bog, and hearing nothing but the wind crying out in the bits of broken trees were left from the great storm, and the streams roaring with the rain.

MICHAEL (looking at her uneasily): What is it ails you this

Glenmalure . . . Glen Imaal, valleys in Wicklow.

night, Nora Burke? I've heard tell it's the like of that talk you do hear from men, and they after being a great while on the back hills.°

NORA (*putting out the money on the table*): It's a bad night, and a wild night, Michael Dara, and isn't it a great while I am at the foot of the back hills, sitting up here boiling food for himself, and food for the brood sow, and baking a cake when the night falls? (*She puts up the money listlessly in little piles on the table.*) Isn't it a long while I am sitting here in the winter and the summer, and the fine spring, with the young growing behind me and the old passing, saying to myself one time to look on Mary Brien, who wasn't that height (*holding out her hand*) and I a fine girl growing up, and there she is now with two children, and another coming on her in three months or four. (*She pauses.*)

MICHAEL (*moving over three of the piles*): That's three pounds we have now, Nora Burke.

NORA (*continuing in the same voice*): And saying to myself another time, to look on Peggy Cavanagh, who had the lightest hand at milking a cow that wouldn't be easy, or turning a cake, and there she is now walking round on the roads, or sitting in a dirty old house, with no teeth in her mouth, and no sense, and no more hair than you'd see on a bit of hill and they after burning the furze from it.

MICHAEL: That's five pounds and ten notes, a good sum, surely! . . . It's not that way you'll be talking when you marry a young man, Nora Burke, and they were saying in the fair my lambs were the best lambs, and I got a grand price, for I'm no fool now at making a bargain when my lambs are good.

NORA: What was it you got?

MICHAEL: Twenty pounds for the lot, Nora Burke. . . . We'd do right to wait now till himself will be quiet awhile in the Seven Churches,° and then you'll marry me in the chapel of Rathvanna, and I'll bring the sheep up on the bit of a hill you have on the back mountain, and we won't have anything we'd be afeard to let our minds on when the mist is down.

NORA (*pouring him out some whisky*): Why would I marry you, Mike Dara? You'll be getting old and I'll be getting old, and in a little while, I'm telling you, you'll be sitting up in your bed—the way himself was sitting—with a shake in your face, and your teeth falling, and the white hair sticking out round you like an old bush where sheep do be leaping a gap.

(DAN BURKE *sits up noiselessly from under the sheet, with his hand to his face. His white hair is sticking out round his head.* NORA *goes on slowly without hearing him.*)

It's a pitiful thing to be getting old, but it's a queer thing surely. It's a queer thing to see an old man sitting up there in his bed with no teeth in him, and a rough word in his mouth, and his chin the way it would take the bark from the edge of an oak board you'd have building a door. . . . God forgive me, Michael Dara, we'll all be getting old, but it's a queer thing surely.

MICHAEL: It's too lonesome you are from living a long time with an old man, Nora, and you're talking again like a herd that would be coming down from the thick mist (*he puts his arm round her*), but it's a fine life you'll have now with a young man— a fine life, surely. . . .

(DAN *sneezes violently.* MICHAEL *tries to get to the door, but before he can do so* DAN *jumps out of the bed in queer white clothes, with the stick in his hand, and goes over and puts his back against it.*)

Son of God deliver us! (*Crosses himself, and goes backward across the room.*)

DAN (*holding up his hand at him*): Now you'll not marry her the time I'm rotting below in the Seven Churches, and you'll see the thing I'll give you will follow you on the back mountains when the wind is high.

MICHAEL (*to* NORA): Get me out of it, Nora, for the love of God. He always did what you bid him, and I'm thinking he would do it now.

NORA (*looking at the* TRAMP): Is it dead he is or living?

DAN (*turning towards her*): It's little you care if it's dead or living I am; but there'll be an end now of your fine times, and all the talk you have of young men and old men, and of the mist coming up or going down. (*He opens the door.*) You'll walk out now from that door, Nora Burke; and it's not to-morrow, or the next day, or any day of your life, that you'll put in your foot through it again.

TRAMP (*standing up*): It's a hard thing you're saying for an old man, master of the house; and what would the like of her do if you put her out on the roads?

DAN: Let her walk round the like of Peggy Cavanagh below, and be begging money at the cross-roads, or selling songs to the men. (*To* NORA.) Walk out now, Nora Burke, and it's soon you'll be getting old with that life, I'm telling you; it's soon your teeth'll be falling and your head'll be the like of a bush where sheep do be leaping a gap.

(*He pauses;* NORA *looks round at* MICHAEL.)

MICHAEL (*timidly*): There's a fine Union° below in Rathdrum.

DAN: The like of her would never go there. . . . It's

---

black hills, remote areas, only fit for mountain sheep.
Seven Churches, in Glendalough, a former religious center.

Union, workhouse (where the homeless might stay).

lonesome roads she'll be going and hiding herself away till the end will come, and they find her stretched like a dead sheep with the frost on her, or the big spiders maybe, and they putting their webs on her, in the butt of a ditch.

NORA (angrily): What way will yourself be that day, Daniel Burke? What way will you be that day and you lying down a long while in your grave? For it's bad you are living, and it's bad you'll be when you're dead. (She looks at him a moment fiercely, then half turns away and speaks plaintively again.) Yet, if it is itself, Daniel Burke, who can help it at all, and let you be getting up into your bed, and not be taking your death with the wind blowing on you, and the rain with it, and you half in your skin.

DAN: It's proud and happy you'd be if I was getting my death the day I was shut of yourself. (Pointing to the door.) Let you walk out through that door, I'm telling you, and let you not be passing this way if it's hungry you are, or wanting a bed.

TRAMP (pointing to MICHAEL): Maybe himself would take her.

NORA: What would he do with me now?

TRAMP: Give you the half of a dry bed, and good food in your mouth.

DAN: Is it a fool you think him, stranger, or is it a fool you were born yourself? Let her walk out of that door, and let you go along with her, stranger—if it's raining itself—for it's too much talk you have surely.

TRAMP (going over to NORA): We'll be going now, lady of the house; the rain is falling, but the air is kind, and maybe it'll be a grand morning, by the grace of God.

NORA: What good is a grand morning when I'm destroyed surely, and I going out to get my death walking the roads?

TRAMP: You'll not be getting your death with myself, lady of the house, and I knowing all the ways a man can put food in his mouth. . . . We'll be going now, I'm telling you, and the time you'll be feeling the cold, and the frost, and the great rain, and the sun again, and the south wind blowing in the glens, you'll not be sitting up on a wet ditch, the way you're after sitting in this place, making yourself old with looking on each day, and it passing you by. You'll be saying one time: "It's a grand evening, by the grace of God," and another time, "It's a wild night, God help us; but it'll pass, surely." You'll be saying . . .

DAN (goes over to them, crying out impatiently): Go out of that door, I'm telling you, and do your blathering below in the glen.

(NORA gathers a few things into her shawl.)

TRAMP (at the door): Come along with me now, lady of the house, and it's not my blather you'll be hearing only, but you'll be hearing the herons crying out over the black lakes, and you'll be hearing the grouse and the owls with them, and the larks and the big thrushes when the days are warm; and it's not from the like of them you'll be hearing a tale of getting old like Peggy Cavanagh, and losing the hair off you, and the light of your eyes, but it's fine songs you'll be hearing when the sun goes up, and there'll be no old fellow wheezing, the like of a sick sheep, close to your ear.

NORA: I'm thinking it's myself will be wheezing that time with lying down under the heavens when the night is cold; but you've a fine bit of talk, stranger, and it's with yourself I'll go. (She goes towards the door, then turns to DAN.) You think it's a grand thing you're after doing with your letting on to be dead, but what is it at all? What way would a woman live in a lonesome place the like of this place, and she not making a talk with the men passing? And what way will yourself live from this day, with none to care you? What is it you'll have now but a black life, Daniel Burke; and it's not long, I'm telling you, till you'll be lying again under that sheet, and you dead surely.

(She goes out with the TRAMP. MICHAEL is slinking after them, but DAN stops him.)

DAN: Sit down now and take a little taste of the stuff, Michael Dara. There's a great drouth on me, and the night is young.

MICHAEL (coming back to the table): And it's very dry I am, surely, with the fear of death you put on me, and I after driving mountain ewes since the turn of the day.

DAN (throwing away his stick): I was thinking to strike you, Michael Dara; but you're a quiet man, God help you, and I don't mind you at all. (He pours out two glasses of whisky, and gives one to MICHAEL.) Your good health, Michael Dara.

MICHAEL: God reward you, Daniel Burke, and may you have a long life and a quiet life, and good health with it.

(They drink.)

CURTAIN

Figure 1. Dan Burke (Lalor Roddy) brandishes his blackthorn stick as he threatens Michael Dara in the 1998 Royal Shakespeare Company production of *In the Shadow of the Glen*, directed by John Crowley. (Photograph: Malcolm Davies, Shakespeare Centre Library, Stratford-upon-Avon.)

Figure 2. Nora (Mairead McKinley) reflects both sadness and defiance in the 1998 production. (Photograph: Malcolm Davies, Shakespeare Centre Library, Stratford-upon-Avon.)

Staging of *In the Shadow of the Glen*

REVIEW OF THE ROYAL SHAKESPEARE
COMPANY PRODUCTION, 1998,
BY ALASTAIR MACAULAY

Now that the Irish play has become an exceptionally lively genre of British theatre, it is good to go back to some of the plays by J.M. Synge and W.B. Yeats that helped, beautifully, to define the genre. To, in particular, the seldom-performed half-hour plays.

In *Shadows,* a new programme at The Other Place, the Royal Shakespeare Company is now giving a "trinity" of such plays: Synge's *Riders to the Sea* and *The Shadow of the Glen* (both 1903) and Yeats's *Purgatory* (1939). The plays are given in quick succession, the six actors of the first play also returning for the other two; and so, since the plays share common themes (small rural households, the recent dead), they add up here to create a folk idea of Ireland, an Ireland where the particular events of each play are in fact general events, events that have occurred in more neighbourhoods than one, events that have indeed shaped the Irish idea of what Ireland is. There is a grim resignation in each play to the cruelty of fate and death. And deeper than events, these plays catch language, a folk style of Irish speech that is richly poetic.

In *Riders to the Sea,* a mother and her two daughters discover that one, no, two of her sons are dead in the sea. In *The Shadow of the Glen,* a wife who has assumed that her grim old husband is dead and receives the courtship of two younger men is thrown out of house by her husband when he leaps from his bed. In *Purgatory,* a man, after telling his son how he killed his father, now kills his son too. John Crowley directs this trinity with perfect economy, using again where appropriate the few pieces of furniture from one play in the next, suggesting the large blank rural quiet that encompasses the milieu of each play.

Lalor Roddy and Owen Sharp, who play small roles in *Riders,* are the old husband and the unsuccessful suitor in *The Shadow,* and then the parricide and his filial victim in *Purgatory;* Mairead McKinley and Stephen Kennedy are likewise involved in all three, even if only as silent presences in the last; and the brief scene-changes between the plays involve all six actors with music, as if showing a glimpse or hint of an Irish wake.

All the performances are very fine. My only cavil is that the actors do not give quite enough weight to some of the early threads of plot in *Riders to the Sea;* and yet it is this play that leaves the deepest and most beautiful impression. Stella McCusker plays Maurya, the mother who has learnt from the loss of so many of her menfolk to be so emotionally guarded that she neglects to give a parting blessing to her last remaining son, and who all too soon finds herself mourning him too. She responds with elegiac resignation. "They're all gone now, and there isn't anything more the sea can do to me . . . They're all together this time, and the end is come . . . No man at all can be living for ever, and we must be satisfied." McCusker's gaunt stillness and soft sorrow are superb.

The seeds of Beckett and even of wee Martin McDonagh are to be discerned in these plays. But the beauty of *Shadows* lies not in its historical importance to subsequent drama. The beauty lies in lines like: "It's the life of a young man to be going on the sea, and who would listen to an old woman with one thing and she saying it over?" *(Riders);* and "He was an old man, and an odd man, stranger, and it's always up on the hills he was, thinking thoughts in the dark mist" *(The Shadow);* and "I killed that lad because had he grown up/ He would have struck a woman's fancy,/ Begot, and passed pollution on," *(Purgatory).*

I find the prose of Synge's plays yet more wonderful than the poetry of Yeats's: it loops the patterns of Irish talk back to the King James Bible and to Homer. But these plays of folk experience are also plays that catch the ironic mood of the modern era. Both Synge and Yeats, in putting Ireland on the map of world drama, also helped to define the thought of the 20th century.

J. M. SYNGE ON THE SOURCE
OF THE PLAY, 1904

. . . Pat told me a story of an unfaithful wife, which I will give further down, and then broke into a moral dispute with the visitor, which caused immense delight to some young men who had come down to listen to the story. Unfortunately it was carried on so rapidly in Gaelic that I lost most of the points.

This old man talks usually in a mournful tone about his ill-health, and his death, which he feels to be approaching, yet he has occasional touches of humour that remind me of old Mourteen on the north island. To-day a grotesque twopenny doll was lying on the floor near the old woman. He picked it up and examined it as if comparing it with her. Then he held it up: 'Is it you is after bringing that thing into the world,' he said, 'woman of the house?'

Here is the story:—

One day I was travelling on foot from Galway to Dublin, and the darkness came on me and I ten miles from the town I was wanting to pass the night in. Then a hard rain began to fall and I was tired walking, so when I saw a sort of a house with no roof on it up against the road, I got in the way the walls would give me shelter.

As I was looking round I saw a light in some trees two perches off, and thinking any sort of a house would be better than where I was, I got over a wall and went up to the house to look in at the window.

I saw a dead man laid on a table, and candles lighted, and a woman watching him. I was frightened when I saw him, but it was raining hard, and I said to myself, if he was dead he couldn't hurt me. Then I knocked on the door and the woman came and opened it.

'Good evening, ma'am,' says I.

In the author's foreword to *The Aran Islands,* Synge claims: "I have given a direct account of my life on the islands, and of what I met with among them, inventing nothing, and changing nothing that is essential. As far as possible, however, I have disguised the identity of the people I speak of, by making changes in their names, and in the letters I quote, and by altering some local and family relationships." The story told by an old man, Pat Dirane, became the basis for Synge's play, *In the Shadow of the Glen.*

'Good evening kindly, stranger,' says she. 'Come in out of the rain.'

Then she took me in and told me her husband was after dying on her, and she was watching him that night.

'But it's thirsty you'll be, stranger,' says she. 'Come into the parlour.'

Then she took me into the parlour—and it was a fine clean house—and she put a cup, with a saucer under it, on the table before me with fine sugar and bread.

When I'd had a cup of tea I went back into the kitchen where the dead man was lying, and she gave me a fine new pipe off the table with a drop of spirits.

'Stranger,' says she, 'would you be afeard to be alone with himself?'

'Not a bit in the world, ma'am,' says I; 'he that's dead can do no hurt.'

Then she said she wanted to go over and tell the neighbours the way her husband was after dying on her, and she went out and locked the door behind her.

I smoked one pipe, and I leaned out and took another off the table. I was smoking it with my hand on the back of my chair—the way you are yourself this minute, God bless you—and I looking on the dead man, when he opened his eyes as wide as myself and looked at me.

'Don't be afraid, stranger,' said the dead man; 'I'm not dead at all in the world. Come here and help me up and I'll tell you all about it.'

Well, I went up and took the sheet off of him, and I saw that he had a fine clean shirt on his body, and fine flannel drawers.

He sat up then, and says he—

'I've got a bad wife, stranger, and I let on to be dead the way I'd catch her goings on.'

Then he got two fine sticks he had to keep down his wife, and he put them at each side of his body, and he laid himself out again as if he was dead.

In half an hour his wife came back and a young man along with her. Well, she gave him his tea, and she told him he was tired, and he would do right to go and lie down in the bedroom.

The young man went in and the woman sat down to watch by the dead man. A while after she got up and 'Stranger,' says she, 'I'm going in to get the candle out of the room; I'm thinking the young man will be asleep by this time.' She went into the bedroom, but the divil a bit of her came back.

Then the dead man got up, and he took one stick, and he gave the other to myself. We went in and saw them lying together with her head on his arm.

The dead man hit him a blow with the stick so that the blood out of him leapt up and hit the gallery.

That is my story.

In stories of this kind he always speaks in the first person, with minute details to show that he was actually present at the scenes that are described.

At the beginning of this story he gave me a long account of what had made him be on his way to Dublin on that occasion, and told me about all the rich people he was going to see in the finest streets of the city.

ANTON CHEKHOV

1860–1904

Anton Chekhov was born in Taganrog, a Crimean resort not far from Yalta, where he wrote his last play, *The Cherry Orchard,* when he was dying of tuberculosis. Although his grandfather had been a serf who amassed enough money to buy not only his freedom but also an estate, his father, plagued by the debts of an unsuccessful grocery, was forced to leave Taganrog and move the family to Moscow. Chekhov himself remained in Taganrog to finish his schooling, but his years there could hardly have been pleasant ones, for his poverty compelled him to earn money by doing homework for his fellow students, and Taganrog itself, like most seaside resorts of that era, was filled with the sick and aged. So it is not surprising that the resorts that appear repeatedly in Chekhov's works, such as the "villas" that Lopakhin proposes to build along the river bank, are always associated with tedium and futility. By 1880, Chekhov, too, had left Taganrog and moved to Moscow, where he entered medical school and started to write short stories to help support himself and his family. He became a physician and practiced medicine for a time, yet he gradually came to spend more and more effort on his writing, and less and less on medicine. By 1888, he was practicing only during epidemics, when there was a shortage of doctors, but was writing so much that he had already published 300 stories. During the 1880s, Chekhov had also started writing for the stage—first one-act plays, which he began doing in 1884, the year of his graduation from medical school, then full-length works, the earliest of which appeared in 1887. Most of his one-act plays are farcical studies of middle-class aspirations to sophisticated society, such as *The Boor* and *The Marriage Proposal,* which were well received and still continue to be performed. His early full-length works—such as *Ivanov* (1887) and *The Wood Demon* (1889), an early version of *Uncle Vanya*—were bitter failures, so much so that he did not write another serious full-length play until *The Seagull* (1896), which was first produced in St. Petersburg.

The Seagull, a psychologically realistic play, which bears witness to the drama of human loneliness and frustration, failed dismally in its opening production, for it was a radical departure from Russian theatrical tastes of the time. Chekhov's audience was unaccustomed to his low-key realism, to his subtle revelations of character, to his apparently plotless drama of Russian life, for this kind of drama was completely at odds with the melodramatic thrillers then being imported from Paris. The Russian actors were also unprepared for it, since they had never tried, nor seen, any style of performance other than the bombastic acting of the period that had been popularized by the English actor Edmund Kean. And the management of the theater where the play was produced did not give the actors much of a chance to develop an appropriately low-key style, allowing them only nine days for rehearsals. *The Seagull* was literally laughed off the stage in St. Petersburg. Although Chekhov vowed never to write another play, he did permit *The Seagull* to be printed in a literary magazine, where it caught the interest of two wealthy young men, Konstantin Stanislavsky and Vladimir Nemirovich-Danchenko, whose theatrical ambitions brought them together in 1898 to form the Moscow Art Theatre. This group was based on the new principles of ensemble acting then being attempted throughout Europe, where acting companies were following the model established by the German troupe of the Duke of Saxe-Meinegen. But Stanislavsky and Nemirovich-Danchenko were not content simply to develop an ensemble. They aimed to develop an acting company with a distinctively new style of performance, a style that was understated rather than overstated, realistic instead of melodramatic (see Ideas of Drama). That style was perfectly attuned to the psychological nuances of *The Seagull*, and thus they chose to conclude their first season with a revival of the play. That revival turned out to be the making of both Chekhov and the Moscow Art Theatre, for though the rest of their season had been a series of failures, *The Seagull* was met with thunderous applause by the audience.

Chekhov's plays do not actually try to elicit dynamic roars of approval. Indeed, they are all wry, sometimes weary, sometimes satirical displays of futility in human behavior—of the inability to act decisively, even when such action would seem to be easily within the range of human capacity. In *Uncle Vanya* (1899), for example, the central character learns that the professor for whom he has slaved without reward is not the personification of wisdom, as he had thought, but is instead a mediocre academic windbag. Consequently, he is moved to shoot the professor at point-blank range, but misses him. And he is seen at the end of the play repressing his knowledge of his own wasted life, unlearning what he has learned by a titanic effort in futility. Chekhov's next play, *The Three Sisters* (1901), is a study of shared futility, enacted by the title characters who, though left with an ample inheritance, never fulfill any of their personal hopes, professional ambitions, or mundane desires—not even the simple desire that moves them throughout the play: to go to Moscow. *The Three Sisters* was followed three years later by the production of *The Cherry Orchard* in January 1904, six months before Chekhov died of tuberculosis.

The Cherry Orchard may be seen as a full-scale version of cultural futility—the inability of an old aristocratic social order to preserve itself, and the inability of a new bourgeois order to find meaning in anything beyond the acquisition of money and land. Everyone in the play owns, wants to own, or wants to maintain ownership of someone or something, and the play witnesses everyone gaining or losing the things they wish to own. Whether the audience is to laugh at this spectacle, to weep, or simply to be bemused is a difficult question. Chekhov called the play a comedy, and he apparently intended it to be comic, judging from correspondence with Stanislavsky and Nemirovich-Danchenko. Yet Stanislavsky's letters just as clearly show that he did not consider it a comedy at all—that he viewed it as a tragic expression of Russian life:

> It is not a comedy, not a farce, as you wrote—it is a tragedy no matter if you do indicate a way out into a better world in the last act . . . when I read it for the second time . . . I wept like a woman, I tried to control myself, but could not. I can hear you say: "But please, this is a farce . . ." No, for the ordinary person this is a tragedy.

Stanislavsky's decision to produce the play as a tragedy moved Chekhov to complain that he was turning it into a piece of sniveling sentimentality. Stanislavsky did modify his interpretation somewhat during the next thirty years that he produced it, but he never came around to seeing the characters as laughable.

The conflict between Chekhov and Stanislavsky is, of course, irreconcilable because *The Cherry Orchard* repeatedly hovers between the comic and the tragic. John Gross of the *Sunday Telegraph,* writing about the 1995 production by the Royal Shakespeare Company, even wondered "why people go on arguing about whether his [Chekhov's] vision of life was tragic or comic, when it was so unmistakably both." Review after review noted how that production juxtaposed moments of comedy with moments of pain, often involving the same character. David Troughton's Lopakhin, for example, returned from buying the cherry orchard and bragged about it with drunken cheerfulness. But as he spoke of owning the estate where his grandfather had been a slave, his long-repressed anger became frighteningly visible to the audience, both offstage and on (see Figure 1). Though Penelope Wilton's Mrs. Ranevsky listened to Lopakhin with frozen horror, she was, in Wilton's eyes, "not a snob" but rather a person who, at other moments, both admired Lopakhin and hoped to get money from him. Indeed, as Wilton describes her (see commentary following the text), Mrs. Ranevsky's complexities clearly unfold: selfish, a loving mother, grief-stricken, ruled by her heart. As Wilton also noted, Mrs. Ranevsky has a relationship with almost every character in the play, and the production's staging made clear her centrality (see Figure 2) except for the moment when Lopakhin takes over and she is both physically and metaphorically relegated to the background. All of the play's complicated relationships seemed clearer on the almost-bare wooden stage of the Swan Theatre, a stage furnished with only a few pieces of furniture, until the last act. Then, as Mrs. Ranevsky prepared to leave the house, servants brought in piles of trunks and suitcases, creating not just a sense of how extravagantly the family had lived—and would continue to live—but also a metaphoric wall to separate Lopakhin and Varya (Figure 3). And when servants then removed all of those suitcases, the stage felt emptier than before, a fitting emblem of the loneliness and sadness that this play can evoke. The play's—and the production's—final image is of Firs, the old servant who insists on past tradition (see his formal attire in Figure 2), but who is forgotten by the family and left to die alone (see Figure 4). The cherry orchard so often mentioned in the text but never seen in this production remains, for the audience as well as for the characters, a vision of a happier past that no one can reclaim.

THE CHERRY ORCHARD

BY ANTON CHEKHOV / TRANSLATED BY DAVID MAGARSHACK

CHARACTERS

LYUBOV (LYUBA) ANDREYEVNA RANEVSKY, *a landowner*
ANYA, *her daughter, aged seventeen*
VARYA, *her adopted daughter, aged twenty-four*
LEONID ANDREYEVICH GAYEV, *Mrs. Ranevsky's brother*
YERMOLAY ALEXEYEVICH LOPAKHIN, *a businessman*
PETER (PYOTR) SERGEYEVICH TROFIMOV, *a student*
BORIS BORISOVICH SIMEONOV-PISHCHIK, *a landowner*
CHARLOTTE IVANOVNA, *a governess*
SIMON PANTELEYEVICH YEPIKHODOV, *a clerk*

DUNYASHA, *a maid*
FIRS, *a manservant, aged eighty-seven*
YASHA, *a young manservant*
A HIKER
A STATIONMASTER
A POST OFFICE CLERK
GUESTS *and* SERVANTS

SCENE

The action takes place on MRS. RANEVSKY'S *estate.*

ACT 1

(A room which is still known as the nursery. One of the doors leads to ANYA'S *room. Daybreak; the sun will be rising soon. It is May. The cherry trees are in blossom, but it is cold in the orchard. Morning frost. The windows of the room are shut. Enter* DUNYASHA, *carrying a candle, and* LOPAKHIN *with a book in his hand.)*

LOPAKHIN: The train's arrived, thank goodness. What's the time?

DUNYASHA: Nearly two o'clock, sir. *(Blows out the candle.)* It's light already.

LOPAKHIN: How late was the train? Two hours at least. *(Yawns and stretches.)* What a damn fool I am! Came here specially to meet them at the station and fell asleep.... Sat down in a chair and dropped off. What a nuisance! Why didn't you wake me?

DUNYASHA: I thought you'd gone, sir. *(Listens.)* I think they're coming.

LOPAKHIN *(listening)*: No.... I should have been there to help them with the luggage and so on. *(Pause.)* Mrs. Ranevsky's been abroad for five years. I wonder what she's like now.... She's such a nice person. Simple, easy-going. I remember when I was a lad of fifteen, my late father—he used to keep a shop in the village—punched me in the face and made my nose bleed. We'd gone into the yard to fetch something, and he was drunk. Mrs. Ranevsky—I remember it as if it happened yesterday, she was such a young girl then and so slim—took me to the washstand in this very room, the nursery. "Don't cry, little peasant," she said, "it won't matter by the time you're wed." *(Pause.)* Little peasant ... It's quite true my father was a peasant, but here I am wearing a white waistcoat and brown shoes. A dirty peasant in a fashionable shop.... Except, of course, that I'm a rich man now, rolling in money. But, come to

think of it, I'm a plain peasant still.... *(Turns the pages of his book.)* Been reading this book and haven't understood a word. Fell asleep reading it.

(Pause.)

DUNYASHA: The dogs have been awake all night; they know their masters are coming.

LOPAKHIN: What's the matter, Dunyasha? Why are you in such a state?

DUNYASHA: My hands are shaking. I think I'm going to faint.

LOPAKHIN: A little too refined, aren't you, Dunyasha? Quite the young lady. Dress, hair. It won't do, you know. Remember your place!

(Enter YEPIKHODOV *with a bunch of flowers; he wears a jacket and brightly polished high-boots which squeak loudly; on coming in, he drops the flowers.)*

YEPIKHODOV *(picking up the flowers)*: The gardener sent these. Said to put them in the dining room. *(Hands the flowers to* DUNYASHA.)

LOPAKHIN: Bring me some kvass while you're about it.

DUNYASHA: Yes, sir. *(Goes out.)*

YEPIKHODOV: Thirty degrees, morning frost, and the cherry trees in full bloom. Can't say I think much of our climate, sir. *(Sighs.)* Our climate isn't particularly accommodating, is it, sir? Not when you want it to be, anyway. And another thing. The other day I bought myself this pair of boots, and believe me, sir, they squeak so terribly that it's more than a man can endure. Do you happen to know of something I could grease them with?

LOPAKHIN: Go away. You make me tired.

YEPIKHODOV: Every day, sir, I'm overtaken by some calamity. Not that I mind. I'm used to it. I just smile. *(*DUNYASHA *comes in and hands* LOPAKHIN *the kvass.)* I'll be off. *(Bumps into a chair and knocks it over.)* There you are, sir. *(Triumphantly.)* You see, sir, pardon the expression, this sort of circumstance . . . I mean to say . . . Remarkable! Quite remarkable! *(Goes out.)*

DUNYASHA: I simply must tell you, sir: Yepikhodov has proposed to me.

LOPAKHIN: Oh?

DUNYASHA: I really don't know what to do, sir. He's ever such a quiet fellow, except that sometimes he starts talking and you can't understand a word he says. It sounds all right and it's ever so moving, only you can't make head or tail of it. I like him a little, I think. I'm not sure though. He's madly in love with me. He's such an unlucky fellow, sir. Every day something happens to him. Everyone teases him about it. They've nicknamed him Twenty-two Calamities.

LOPAKHIN *(listens)*: I think I can hear them coming.

DUNYASHA: They're coming! Goodness, I don't know what's the matter with me. I've gone cold all over.

LOPAKHIN: Yes, they are coming all right. Let's go and meet them. Will she recognize me? We haven't seen each other for five years.

DUNYASHA *(agitated)*: I'm going to faint. Oh dear, I'm going to faint!

(Two carriages can be heard driving up to the house. LOPAKHIN and DUNYASHA go out quickly. The stage is empty. People can be heard making a noise in the adjoining rooms. FIRS, *who has been to meet* MRS. RANEVSKY *at the station, walks across the stage hurriedly, leaning on a stick. He wears an old-fashioned livery coat and a top hat; he keeps muttering to himself, but it is impossible to make out a single word. The noise offstage becomes louder. A voice is heard: "Let's go through here."* MRS. RANEVSKY, ANYA, *and* CHARLOTTE, *with a lap dog on a little chain, all wearing traveling clothes,* VARYA, *wearing an overcoat and a head scarf,* GAYEV, SIMEONOV-PISHCHIK, LOPAKHIN, DUNYASHA, *carrying a bundle and an umbrella, and other* SERVANTS *with luggage walk across the stage.)*

ANYA: Let's go through here. Remember this room, Mother?

MRS. RANEVSKY *(joyfully, through tears)*: The nursery!

VARYA: It's so cold. My hands are quite numb. *(to* MRS. RANEVSKY*)* Your rooms, the white one and the mauve one, are just as you left them, Mother dear.

MRS. RANEVSKY: The nursery! My dear, my beautiful room! I used to sleep here when I was a little girl. *(Cries.)* I feel like a little girl again now. *(Kisses her brother and* VARYA, *and then her brother again.)* Varya is the same as ever. Looks like a nun. And I also recognized Dunyasha. *(Kisses* DUNYASHA.*)*

GAYEV: The train was two hours late. How do you like that? What a way to run a railway!

CHARLOTTE *(to* PISHCHIK*)*: My dog also eats nuts.

PISHCHIK *(surprised)*: Good Lord!

(All, except ANYA *and* DUNYASHA, *go out.)*

DUNYASHA: We thought you'd never come. *(Helps* ANYA *off with her coat and hat.)*

ANYA: I haven't slept for four nights on our journey. Now I'm chilled right through.

DUNYASHA: You left before Easter. It was snowing and freezing then. It's different now, isn't it? Darling Anya! *(Laughs and kisses her.)* I've missed you so much, my darling, my precious! Oh, I must tell you at once! I can't keep it to myself a minute longer. . . .

ANYA *(apathetically)*: What is it this time?

DUNYASHA: Our clerk, Yepikhodov, proposed to me after Easter.

ANYA: Always the same. *(Tidying her hair.)* I've lost all my hairpins. *(She is so tired, she can hardly stand.)*

DUNYASHA: I don't know what to think. He loves me so much, so much!

ANYA *(tenderly, looking through the door into her room)*: My own room, my own windows, just as if I'd never been away! I'm home again! As soon as I get up in the morning, I'll run out into the orchard. . . . Oh, if only I could sleep. I didn't sleep all the way back, I was so worried.

DUNYASHA: Mr. Trofimov arrived the day before yesterday.

ANYA *(joyfully)*: Peter!

DUNYASHA: He's asleep in the bathhouse. He's been living there. Afraid of being a nuisance, he says. *(Glancing at her watch.)* I really ought to wake him, except that Miss Varya told me not to. "Don't you dare wake him!" she said.

*(*VARYA *comes in with a bunch of keys at her waist.)*

VARYA: Dunyasha, coffee quick! Mother's asking for some.

DUNYASHA: I won't be a minute! *(Goes out.)*

VARYA: Well, thank goodness you're all back. You're home again, my darling. *(Caressing her.)* My darling is home again! My sweet child is home again.

ANYA: I've had such an awful time!

VARYA: I can imagine it.

ANYA: I left before Easter. It was terribly cold then. All the way Charlotte kept talking and doing her conjuring tricks. Why did you force Charlotte on me?

VARYA: But you couldn't have gone alone, darling, could you? You're only seventeen!

ANYA: In Paris it was also cold and snowing. My French is awful. I found Mother living on the fourth floor. When I got there, she had some French visitors, a few ladies and an old Catholic priest with a book. The place was full of tobacco smoke and terribly uncomfortable. Suddenly I felt sorry for Mother, so sorry that I took her head in my arms, held it tightly, and couldn't let go. Afterwards Mother was very sweet to me. She was crying all the time.

VARYA *(through tears)*: Don't go on, Anya. Please don't.

ANYA: She'd already sold her villa near Mentone. She had nothing left. Nothing! I hadn't any money, either. There was hardly enough for the journey. Mother just won't understand! We had dinner at the station and she would order the most expensive things and tip the waiters a ruble each. Charlotte was just the same. Yasha, too, demanded to be given the same kind of food. It was simply awful! You see, Yasha is Mother's manservant. We've brought him back with us.

VARYA: Yes, I've seen the scoundrel.

ANYA: Well, what's been happening? Have you paid the interest on the mortgage?

VARYA: Heavens, no!

ANYA: Dear, oh dear . . .

VARYA: The estate will be up for sale in August.

ANYA: Oh dear!

LOPAKHIN (*puts his head through the door and bleats*): Bah-h-h! (*Goes out.*)

VARYA (*through tears*): Oh, I'd like to hit him! (*Shakes her fist.*)

ANYA (*gently embracing* VARYA): Varya, has he proposed to you? (VARYA *shakes her head.*) But he loves you. Why don't you two come to an understanding? What are you waiting for?

VARYA: I don't think anything will come of it. He's so busy. He can't be bothered with me. Why, he doesn't even notice me. I wish I'd never known him. I can't stand the sight of him. Everyone's talking about our wedding, everyone's congratulating me, while there's really nothing in it. It's all so unreal. Like a dream. (*In a different tone of voice.*) You've got a new brooch. Like a bee, isn't it?

ANYA (*sadly*): Yes, Mother bought it. (*Goes to her room, talking quite happily, like a child.*) You know, I went up in a balloon in Paris!

VARYA: My darling's home again! My dearest one's home again! (DUNYASHA *has come back with a coffeepot and is making coffee;* VARYA *is standing at the door of* ANYA's *room.*) All day long, darling, I'm busy about the house, and all the time I'm dreaming, dreaming. If only we could find a rich husband for you! My mind would be at rest then. I'd go into a convent and later on a pilgrimage to Kiev . . . to Moscow. Just keep going from one holy place to another. On and on. . . . Wonderful!

ANYA: The birds are singing in the orchard. What's the time?

VARYA: It's past two. It's time you were asleep, darling. (*Goes into* ANYA's *room.*) Wonderful!

(*Enter* YASHA *with a traveling rug and a small bag.*)

YASHA (*crossing the stage, in an affected genteel voice*): May I be permitted to go through here?

DUNYASHA: I can hardly recognize you, Yasha. You've changed so much abroad.

YASHA: Hmmm . . . And who are you, may I ask?

DUNYASHA: When you left, I was no bigger than this. (*Shows her height from the floor with her hand.*) I'm Dunyasha, Fyodor Kozoedov's daughter. Don't you remember me?

YASHA: Mmmm . . . Juicy little cucumber! (*Looks round, then puts his arms around her; she utters a little scream and drops a saucer.* YASHA *goes out hurriedly.*)

VARYA (*in the doorway, crossly*): What's going on there?

DUNYASHA (*in tears*): I've broken a saucer.

VARYA: That's lucky.

ANYA (*coming out of her room*): Mother must be told Peter's here.

VARYA: I gave orders not to wake him.

ANYA (*pensively*): Father died six years ago. A month after that our brother, Grisha, was drowned in the river. Such a pretty little boy. He was only seven. Mother took it badly. She went away, went away never to come back. (*Shudders.*) Peter Trofimov was Grisha's tutor. He might remind her . . .

(FIRS *comes in, wearing a jacket and a white waistcoat.*)

FIRS (*walks up to the coffeepot anxiously*): Madam will have her coffee here. (*Puts on white gloves.*) Is the coffee ready? (*Sternly, to* DUNYASHA.) You there! Where's the cream?

DUNYASHA: Oh dear! (*Goes out quickly.*)

FIRS (*fussing round the coffeepot*): The nincompoop! (*Muttering to himself.*) She's come from Paris. . . . Master used to go to Paris. . . . Aye, by coach. . . . (*Laughs.*)

VARYA: What are you talking about, Firs?

FIRS: Sorry, what did you say? (*Joyfully.*) Madam is home again! Home at last! I can die happy now. (*Weeps with joy.*)

(*Enter* MRS. RANEVSKY, GAYEV, [LOPAKHIN], *and* SIMEONOV-PISHCHIK, *the last one wearing a Russian long-waisted coat of expensive cloth and wide trousers. As he enters,* GAYEV *moves his arms and body as if he were playing billiards.*)

MRS. RANEVSKY: How does it go now? Let me think. Pot the red in the corner. Double into the middle pocket.

GAYEV: And straight into the corner! A long time ago, Lyuba, you and I slept in this room. Now I'm fifty-one. . . . Funny, isn't it!

LOPAKHIN: Aye, time flies.

GAYEV: I beg your pardon?

LOPAKHIN: "Time flies," I said.

GAYEV: The place reeks of patchouli.

ANYA: I'm off to bed. Good night, Mother. (*Kisses her mother.*)

MRS. RANEVSKY: My sweet little darling! (*Kisses her hands.*) You're glad to be home, aren't you? I still can't believe it.

ANYA: Good night, Uncle.

GAYEV (*kissing her face and hands*): God bless you. You're

so like your mother! *(to his sister)* You were just like her at that age, Lyuba.

(ANYA shakes hands with LOPAKHIN and PISHCHIK. Goes out and shuts the door behind her.)

MRS. RANEVSKY: She's terribly tired.

PISHCHIK: It was a long journey.

VARYA *(to LOPAKHIN and PISHCHIK)*: Well, gentlemen, it's past two o'clock. You mustn't outstay your welcome, must you?

MRS. RANEVSKY *(laughs)*: You're just the same, Varya. *(Draws VARYA to her and kisses her.)* Let me have my coffee first and then we'll all go. *(FIRS puts a little cushion under her feet.)* Thank you, Firs dear. I've got used to having coffee. I drink it day and night. Thank you, Firs, thank you, my dear old man. *(Kisses FIRS.)*

VARYA: I'd better make sure they've brought all the things in. *(Goes out.)*

MRS. RANEVSKY: Is it really me sitting here? *(Laughs.)* I feel like jumping about, waving my arms. *(Covers her face with her hands.)* And what if it's all a dream? God knows, I love my country. I love it dearly. I couldn't look out of the train for crying. *(Through tears.)* But, I suppose I'd better have my coffee. Thank you, Firs, thank you, dear old man. I'm so glad you're still alive.

FIRS: The day before yesterday . . .

GAYEV: He's a little deaf.

LOPAKHIN: At five o'clock I've got to leave for Kharkov. What a nuisance! I wish I could have had a good look at you, a good talk with you. You're still as magnificent as ever. . . .

PISHCHIK *(breathing heavily)*: Lovelier, I'd say. Dressed in the latest Paris fashion. If only I were twenty years younger—ho-ho-ho!

LOPAKHIN: This brother of yours says that I'm an ignorant oaf, a tightfisted peasant, but I don't mind. Let him talk. All I want is that you should believe in me as you used to, that you should look at me as you used to with those wonderful eyes of yours. Merciful heavens! My father was a serf of your father and your grandfather, but you, you alone, did so much for me in the past that I forgot everything, and I love you just as if you were my own flesh and blood, more than my own flesh and blood.

MRS. RANEVSKY: I can't sit still, I can't. . . . *(Jumps up and walks about the room in great agitation.)* This happiness is more than I can bear. Laugh at me if you like. I'm making such a fool of myself. Oh, my darling little bookcase . . . *(Kisses the bookcase.)* My sweet little table . . .

GAYEV: You know, of course, that Nanny died here while you were away.

MRS. RANEVSKY *(sits down and drinks her coffee)*: Yes, God rest her soul. They wrote to tell me about it.

GAYEV: Anastasy, too, is dead. Boss-eyed Peter left me for another job. He's with the Police Superintendent in town now. *(Takes a box of fruit drops out of his pocket and sucks one.)*

PISHCHIK: My daughter Dashenka—er—wishes to be remembered to you.

LOPAKHIN: I'd like to say something very nice and cheerful to you. *(Glances at his watch.)* I shall have to be going in a moment and there isn't much time to talk. As you know, your cherry orchard's being sold to pay your debts. The auction is on the twenty-second of August. But there's no need to worry, my dear. You can sleep soundly. There's a way out. Here's my plan. Listen carefully, please. Your estate is only about twelve miles from town, and the railway is not very far away. Now, all you have to do is break up your cherry orchard and the land along the river into building plots and lease them out for country cottages. You'll then have an income of at least twenty-five thousand a year.

GAYEV: I'm sorry, but what utter nonsense!

MRS. RANEVSKY: I don't quite follow you, Lopakhin.

LOPAKHIN: You'll be able to charge your tenants at least twenty-five rubles a year for a plot of about three acres. I bet you anything that if you advertise now, there won't be a single plot left by the autumn. They will all be snapped up. In fact, I congratulate you. You are saved. The site is magnificent and the river is deep enough for bathing. Of course, the place will have to be cleared, tidied up. . . . I mean, all the old buildings will have to be pulled down, including, I'm sorry to say, this house, but it isn't any use to anybody any more, is it? The old cherry orchard will have to be cut down.

MRS. RANEVSKY: Cut down? My dear man, I'm very sorry but I don't think you know what you're talking about. If there's anything of interest, anything quite remarkable, in fact, in the whole county, it's our cherry orchard.

LOPAKHIN: The only remarkable thing about this orchard is that it's very large. It only produces a crop every other year, and even then you don't know what to do with the cherries. Nobody wants to buy them.

GAYEV: Why, you'll find our orchard mentioned in the encyclopedia.

LOPAKHIN *(glancing at his watch)*: If we can't think of anything and if we can't come to any decision, it won't be only your cherry orchard but your whole estate that will be sold at auction on the twenty-second of August. Make up your mind. I tell you, there is no other way. Take my word for it. There isn't.

FIRS: In the old days, forty or fifty years ago, the cherries used to be dried, preserved, made into jam, and sometimes—

GAYEV: Do shut up, Firs.

FIRS: —and sometimes cartloads of dried cherries were sent to Moscow and Kharkov. Fetched a lot of money, they did. Soft and juicy, those cherries were. Sweet and such a lovely smell . . . They knew the recipe then. . . .

MRS. RANEVSKY: And where's the recipe now?

FIRS: Forgotten. No one remembers it.

PISHCHIK (to MRS. RANEVSKY): What was it like in Paris? Eh? Eat any frogs?

MRS. RANEVSKY: I ate crocodiles.

PISHCHIK: Good Lord!

LOPAKHIN: Till recently there were only the gentry and the peasants in the country. Now we have holiday-makers. All our towns, even the smallest, are surrounded by country cottages. I shouldn't be surprised if in twenty years the holiday-maker multiplies enormously. All your holiday-maker does now is drink tea on the veranda, but it's quite in the cards that if he becomes the owner of three acres of land, he'll do a bit of farming on the side, and then your cherry orchard will become a happy, prosperous, thriving place.

GAYEV (indignantly): What nonsense!

(Enter VARYA and YASHA.)

VARYA: I've got two telegrams in here for you, Mother dear. (Picks out a key and unlocks the old-fashioned bookcase with a jingling noise.) Here they are.

MRS. RANEVSKY: They're from Paris. (Tears the telegrams up without reading them.) I've finished with Paris.

GAYEV: Do you know how old this bookcase is, Lyuba? Last week I pulled out the bottom drawer and saw some figures burned into it. This bookcase was made exactly a hundred years ago. What do you think of that? Eh? We ought really to celebrate its centenary. An inanimate object, but say what you like, it's a bookcase after all.

PISHCHIK (amazed): A hundred years! Good Lord!

GAYEV: Yes, indeed. It's quite something. (Feeling round the bookcase with his hands.) Dear, highly esteemed bookcase, I salute you. For over a hundred years you have devoted yourself to the glorious ideals of goodness and justice. Throughout the hundred years your silent appeal to fruitful work has never faltered. It sustained (through tears) in several generations of our family, their courage and faith in a better future and fostered in us the ideals of goodness and social consciousness.

(Pause.)

LOPAKHIN: Aye. . . .

MRS. RANEVSKY: You haven't changed a bit, have you, darling Leonid?

GAYEV (slightly embarrassed): Off the right into a corner! Pot into the middle pocket!

LOPAKHIN (glancing at his watch): Well, afraid it's time I was off.

YASHA (handing MRS. RANEVSKY her medicine): Your pills, ma'am.

PISHCHIK: Never take any medicines, dear lady. I don't suppose they'll do you much harm, but they won't do you any good either. Here, let me have 'em, my dear lady. (Takes the box of pills from her, pours the pills into the palm of his hand, blows on them, puts them all into his mouth, and washes them down with kvass.) There!

MRS. RANEVSKY (alarmed): You're mad!

PISHCHIK: Swallowed the lot.

LOPAKHIN: The glutton!

(All laugh.)

FIRS: He was here at Easter, the gentleman was. Ate half a bucketful of pickled cucumbers, he did. . . . (Mutters.)

MRS. RANEVSKY: What is he saying?

VARYA: He's been muttering like that for the last three years. We've got used to it.

YASHA: Old age!

(CHARLOTTE, in a white dress, very thin and tightly laced, a lorgnette dangling from her belt, crosses the stage.)

LOPAKHIN: I'm sorry, Miss Charlotte, I haven't had the chance of saying how-do-you-do to you. (Tries to kiss her hand.)

CHARLOTTE (snatching her hand away): If I let you kiss my hand, you'll want to kiss my elbow, then my shoulder . . .

LOPAKHIN: It's not my lucky day. (They all laugh.) My dear Charlotte, show us a trick, please.

MRS. RANEVSKY: Yes, do show us a trick, Charlotte.

CHARLOTTE: I won't. I'm off to bed. (Goes out.)

LOPAKHIN: We'll meet again in three weeks. (Kisses MRS. RANEVSKY's hand.) Good-bye for now. I must go. (to GAYEV) So long. (Embraces PISHCHIK.) So long. (Shakes hands with VARYA and then with FIRS and YASHA.) I wish I didn't have to go. (to MRS. RANEVSKY) Let me know if you make up your mind about the country cottages. If you decide to go ahead, I'll get you a loan of fifty thousand or more. Think it over seriously.

VARYA (angrily): For goodness' sake, go!

LOPAKHIN: I'm going, I'm going. . . . (Goes out.)

GAYEV: The oaf! However, I'm sorry. Varya's going to marry him, isn't she? He's Varya's intended.

VARYA: Don't say things you'll be sorry for, Uncle.

MRS. RANEVSKY: But why not, Varya? I should be only too glad. He's a good man.

PISHCHIK: A most admirable fellow, to tell the truth. My Dashenka—er—also says that—er—says all sorts of things. (Drops off and snores, but wakes up immediately.) By the way, my dear lady, you will lend me two hundred and forty rubles, won't you? Must pay the interest on the mortgage tomorrow.

VARYA (terrified): We have no money; we haven't!

MRS. RANEVSKY: We really haven't any, you know.

PISHCHIK: Have a good look around—you're sure to find it. (Laughs.) I never lose hope. Sometimes I think it's all over with me, I'm done for, then— hey presto—they build a railway over my land and pay me for it. Something's bound to turn up, if not today, then tomorrow. I'm certain of it. Dashenka might win two hundred thousand. She's got a ticket in the lottery, you know.

MRS. RANEVSKY: Well, I've finished my coffee. Now to bed.

FIRS (brushing GAYEV's clothes admonishingly): Put the wrong trousers on again, sir. What am I to do with you?

VARYA (in a low voice): Anya's asleep. (Opens a window quietly.) The sun has risen. It's no longer cold. Look, Mother dear. What lovely trees! Heavens, what wonderful air! The starlings are singing.

GAYEV (opens another window): The orchard's all white. Lyuba, you haven't forgotten, have you? The long avenue there—it runs on and on, straight as an arrow. It gleams on moonlit nights. Remember? You haven't forgotten, have you?

MRS. RANEVSKY (looking through the window at the orchard): Oh, my childhood, oh, my innocence! I slept in this nursery. I used to look out at the orchard from here. Every morning happiness used to wake with me. The orchard was just the same in those days. Nothing has changed. (Laughs happily.) White, all white! Oh, my orchard! After the dark, rainy autumn and the cold winter, you're young again, full of happiness; the heavenly angels haven't forsaken you. If only this heavy load could be lifted from my heart; if only I could forget my past!

GAYEV: Well, and now they're going to sell the orchard to pay our debts. Funny, isn't it?

MRS. RANEVSKY: Look! Mother's walking in the orchard in . . . a white dress! (Laughs happily.) It is Mother!

GAYEV: Where?

VARYA: Really, Mother dear, what are you saying?

MRS. RANEVSKY: There's no one there. I just imagined it. Over there, on the right, near the turning to the summer house, a little white tree's leaning over. It looks like a woman. (Enter TROFIMOV. He is dressed in a shabby student's uniform and wears glasses.) What an amazing orchard! Masses of white blossom. A blue sky . . .

TROFIMOV: I say, Mrs. Ranevsky . . . (She looks round at him.) I've just come to say hello. I'll go at once. (Kisses her hand warmly.) I was told to wait till morning, but I—I couldn't, I couldn't.

(MRS. RANEVSKY gazes at him in bewilderment.)

VARYA (through tears): This is Peter Trofimov.

TROFIMOV: Peter Trofimov. Your son Grisha's old tutor. I haven't changed so much, have I?

(MRS. RANEVSKY embraces him and weeps quietly.)

GAYEV (embarrassed): There, there, Lyuba.

VARYA (cries): I did tell you to wait till tomorrow, didn't I, Peter?

MRS. RANEVSKY: Grisha, my . . . little boy. Grisha . . . my son.

VARYA: It can't be helped, Mother. It was God's will.

TROFIMOV (gently, through tears): Now, now . . .

MRS. RANEVSKY (weeping quietly): My little boy died, drowned. Why? Why, my friend? (More quietly.) Anya's asleep in there and here I am shouting, making a noise. . . . Well, Peter? You're not as good-looking as you were, are you? Why not? Why have you aged so much?

TROFIMOV: A peasant woman in a railway carriage called me "a moth-eaten gentleman."

MRS. RANEVSKY: You were only a boy then. A charming young student. Now you're growing thin on top, you wear glasses. . . . You're not still a student, are you? (Walks toward the door.)

TROFIMOV: I expect I shall be an eternal student.

MRS. RANEVSKY (kisses her brother and then VARYA): Well, go to bed now. You, Leonid, have aged too.

PISHCHIK (following her): So, we're off to bed now, are we? Oh dear, my gout! I think I'd better stay the night here. Now, what about letting me have the—er—two hundred and forty rubles tomorrow morning, dear lady? Early tomorrow morning. . . .

GAYEV: He does keep on, doesn't he?

PISHCHIK: Two hundred and forty rubles—to pay the interest on the mortgage.

MRS. RANEVSKY: But I haven't any money, my dear man.

PISHCHIK: I'll pay you back, dear lady. Such a trifling sum.

MRS. RANEVSKY: Oh, all right. Leonid will let you have it. Let him have it, Leonid.

GAYEV: Let him have it? The hell I will.

MRS. RANEVSKY: What else can we do? Let him have it, please. He needs it. He'll pay it back.

(MRS. RANEVSKY, TROFIMOV, PISHCHIK, and FIRS go out. GAYEV, VARYA, and YASHA remain.)

GAYEV: My sister hasn't got out of the habit of throwing money about. (to YASHA) Out of my way, fellow. You reek of the hen house.

YASHA (grins): And you, sir, are the same as ever.

GAYEV: I beg your pardon? (to VARYA) What did he say?

VARYA (to YASHA): Your mother's come from the

village. She's been sitting in the servants' quarters since yesterday. She wants to see you.

YASHA: Oh, bother her!

VARYA: You shameless bounder!

YASHA: I don't care. She could have come tomorrow, couldn't she? *(Goes out.)*

VARYA: Dear Mother is just the same as ever. Hasn't changed a bit. If you let her, she'd give away everything.

GAYEV: I suppose so. *(Pause.)* When a lot of remedies are suggested for an illness, it means that the illness is incurable. I've been thinking, racking my brains; I've got all sorts of remedies, lots of them, which, of course, means that I haven't got one. It would be marvelous if somebody left us some money. It would be marvelous if we found a very rich husband for Anya. It would be marvelous if one of us went to Yaroslavl to try our luck with our great-aunt, the Countess. She's very rich, you know. Very rich.

VARYA *(crying)*: If only God would help us.

GAYEV: Don't howl! Our aunt is very rich, but she doesn't like us. First, because my sister married a lawyer and not a nobleman.... *(ANYA appears in the doorway.)* She did not marry a nobleman, and she has not been leading an exactly blameless life, has she? She's a good, kind, nice person. I love her very much. But, however much you try to make allowances for her, you have to admit that she is an immoral woman. You can sense it in every movement she makes.

VARYA *(in a whisper)*: Anya's standing in the doorway.

GAYEV: I beg your pardon? *(Pause.)* Funny thing, there's something in my right eye. Can't see properly. On Thursday, too, in the district court . . .

(ANYA comes in.)

VARYA: Why aren't you asleep, Anya?

ANYA: I can't sleep, I can't.

GAYEV: My little darling! *(Kisses ANYA's face and hands.)* My dear child! *(Through tears.)* You're not my niece, you're my angel. You're everything to me. Believe me. Do believe me.

ANYA: I believe you, Uncle. Everyone loves you, everyone respects you, but, dear Uncle, you shouldn't talk so much. What were you saying just now about Mother, about your own sister? What did you say it for?

GAYEV: Well, yes, yes. *(He takes her hand and covers his face with it.)* You're quite right. It was dreadful. Dear God, dear God, help me! That speech I made to the bookcase today—it was so silly. The moment I finished it, I realized how silly it was.

VARYA: It's quite true, Uncle dear. You oughtn't to talk so much. Just don't talk, that's all.

ANYA: If you stopped talking, you'd feel much happier yourself.

GAYEV: Not another word. *(Kisses ANYA's and VARYA's hands.)* Not another word. Now to business. Last Thursday I was at the county court, and, well—er—I met a lot of people there, and we started talking about this and that, and—er—it would seem that we might manage to raise some money on a promissory note and pay the interest to the bank.

VARYA: Oh, if only God would help us!

GAYEV: I shall be there again on Tuesday, and I'll have another talk. *(to VARYA)* For goodness' sake, don't howl! *(to ANYA)* Your mother will have a talk with Lopakhin. I'm sure he won't refuse her. After you've had your rest, you'll go to Yaroslavl to see your great-aunt, the Countess. That's how we shall tackle the problem from three different sides, and I'm sure we'll get it settled. The interest we shall pay. Of that I'm quite sure. *(Puts a fruit drop in his mouth.)* I give you my word of honor, I swear by anything you like, the estate will not be sold! *(Excitedly.)* Why, I'll stake my life on it! Here's my hand; call me a rotten scoundrel if I allow the auction to take place. I stake my life on it!

ANYA *(has regained her composure; she looks happy)*: You're so good, Uncle dear! So clever! *(Embraces him.)* I'm no longer worried now. Not a bit worried. I'm happy.

(Enter FIRS.)

FIRS *(reproachfully)*: Have you no fear of God, sir? When are you going to bed?

GAYEV: Presently, presently. Go away, Firs. Never mind, I'll undress this time. Well, children, bye-bye now. More about it tomorrow. Now you must go to bed. *(Kisses ANYA and VARYA.)* I'm a man of the eighties. People don't think much of that time, but let me tell you, I've suffered a great deal for my convictions during my life. It's not for nothing that the peasants love me. You have to know your peasant, you have to know how to—

ANYA: There you go again, Uncle.

VARYA: Please, Uncle dear, don't talk so much.

FIRS *(angrily)*: Sir!

GAYEV: I'm coming, I'm coming. You two go to bed. Off two cushions into the middle. Pot the white!

(GAYEV goes out, FIRS shuffling off after him.)

ANYA: I'm not worried any longer now. I don't feel like going to Yaroslavl. I don't like my great-aunt, but I'm no longer worried. I ought to thank Uncle for that. *(Sits down.)*

VARYA: I ought to go to bed, and I shall be going in a moment, I must tell you first that something unpleasant happened here while you were away. You know, of course, that only a few old servants live in the old servants' quarters: Yefimushka,

Polia, Evstigney, and, well, also Karp. They had been letting some tramps sleep there, but I didn't say anything about it. Then I heard that they were telling everybody that I'd given orders for them to be fed on nothing but dried peas. I'm supposed to be a miser, you see. It was all that Evstigney's doing. Well, I said to myself, if that's how it is, you just wait! So I sent for Evstigney. *(Yawns.)* He comes. "What do you mean," I said, "Evstigney, you silly old fool?" *(Looks at* ANYA*)* Darling! *(Pause.)* Asleep . . . *(Takes* ANYA *by the arm.)* Come to bed, dear. . . . Come on! *(Leads her by the arm.)* My darling's fallen asleep. Come along. *(They go out. A shepherd's pipe is heard playing from far away on the other side of the orchard.* TROFIMOV *walks across the stage and, catching sight of* VARYA *and* ANYA, *stops.)* Shh! She's asleep, asleep. Come along, my sweet.

ANYA *(softly, half asleep)*: I'm so tired. . . . I keep hearing harness bells. Uncle . . . dear . . . Mother and Uncle . . .

VARYA: Come on, my sweet, come on. . . .

(They go into ANYA's *room.)*

TROFIMOV *(deeply moved)*: My sun! My spring!

CURTAIN

ACT 2

(Open country. A small tumbledown wayside chapel. Near it, a well, some large stones, which look like old gravestones, and an old bench. A road can be seen leading to GAYEV's *estate. On one side, a row of tall dark poplars; it is there that the cherry orchard begins. In the distance, some telegraph poles, and far, far away on the horizon, the outlines of a large town that is visible only in very fine, clear weather. The sun is about to set.* CHARLOTTE, YASHA, *and* DUNYASHA *are sitting on the bench;* YEPIKHODOV *is standing nearby and is playing a guitar; they all sit sunk in thought.* CHARLOTTE *wears a man's old peaked hat; she has taken a shotgun from her shoulder and is adjusting the buckle on the strap.)*

CHARLOTTE *(pensively)*: I haven't a proper passport, I don't know how old I am, and I can't help thinking that I'm still a young girl. When I was a little girl, my father and mother used to travel the fairs and give performances—very good ones. I used to do the *salto mortale* and all sorts of other tricks. When Father and Mother died, a German lady adopted me and began educating me. Very well. I grew up and became a governess, but where I came from and who I am, I do not know. Who my parents were, I do not know either. They may not even have been married. I don't know. *(Takes a cucumber out of her pocket and starts eating it.)* I don't know anything. *(Pause.)* I'm longing to talk to someone, but there is no one to talk to. I haven't anyone. . . .

YEPIKHODOV *(plays his guitar and sings)*: "What care I for the world and its bustle? What care I for my friends and my foes?". . . Nice to play a mandolin.

DUNYASHA: It's a guitar, not a mandolin. *(She looks at herself in a hand mirror and powders her face.)*

YEPIKHODOV: To a madman in love, it's a mandolin. *(Sings softly.)* "If only my heart was warmed by the fire of love requited."

*(*YASHA *joins in.)*

CHARLOTTE: How terribly these people sing! Ugh! Like hyenas.

DUNYASHA *(to* YASHA*)*: All the same, you're ever so lucky to have been abroad.

YASHA: Why, of course. Can't help agreeing with you there. *(Yawns, then lights a cigar.)*

YEPIKHODOV: Stands to reason. Abroad, everything's in excellent complexion. Been like that for ages.

YASHA: Naturally.

YEPIKHODOV: I'm a man of some education, I read all sorts of remarkable books, but what I simply can't understand is where it's all leading to. I mean, what do I really want—to live or to shoot myself? In any case, I always carry a revolver. Here it is. *(Shows them his revolver.)*

CHARLOTTE: That's done. Now I can go. *(Puts the shotgun over her shoulder.)* You're a very clever man, Yepikhodov. You frighten me to death. Women must be madly in love with you. Brrr! *(Walking away.)* These clever people are all so stupid. I've no one to talk to. Always alone, alone, I've no one, and who I am and what I am for is a mystery. *(Walks off slowly.)*

YEPIKHODOV: Strictly speaking, and apart from all other considerations, what I ought to say about myself, among other things, is that Fate treats me without mercy, like a storm a small boat. Even supposing I'm mistaken, why in that case should I wake up this morning and suddenly find a spider of quite enormous dimensions on my chest? As big as that. *(Uses both hands to show the spider's size.)* Or again, I pick up a jug of kvass and there's something quite outrageously indecent in it, like a cockroach. *(Pause.)* Have you ever read Buckle's *History of Civilization?* *(Pause.)* May I have a word or two with you, Dunyasha?

DUNYASHA: Oh, all right. What is it?

YEPIKHODOV: I'd be very much obliged if you'd let me speak to you in private. *(Sighs.)*

DUNYASHA *(embarrassed)*: All right, only first bring me my cape, please. It's hanging near the wardrobe. It's so damp here.

YEPIKHODOV: Very well, I'll fetch it. . . . Now I know what to do with my revolver. *(Picks up his guitar and goes out strumming it.)*

YASHA: Twenty-two Calamities! A stupid fellow, between you and me. (*Yawns.*)

DUNYASHA: I hope to goodness he won't shoot himself. (*Pause.*) I'm ever so nervous. I can't help being worried all the time. I was taken into service when I was a little girl, and now I can't live like a peasant any more. See my hands? They're ever so white, as white as a young lady's. I've become so nervous, so sensitive, so like a lady. I'm afraid of everything. I'm simply terrified. So if you deceived me, Yasha, I don't know what would happen to my nerves.

YASHA (*kisses her*): Little cucumber! Mind you, I expect every girl to be respectable. What I dislike most is for a girl to misbehave herself.

DUNYASHA: I've fallen passionately in love with you, Yasha. You're so educated. You can talk about anything.

(*Pause.*)

YASHA (*yawning*): You see, in my opinion, if a girl is in love with somebody, it means she's immoral. (*Pause.*) It is so pleasant to smoke a cigar in the open air. (*Listens.*) Someone's coming. It's them.... (DUNYASHA *embraces him impulsively.*) Please go home and look as if you've been down to the river for a swim. Take that path or they'll think I had arranged to meet you here. Can't stand that sort of thing.

DUNYASHA (*coughing quietly*): Your cigar has given me an awful headache. (*Goes out.*)

(YASHA *remains sitting near the chapel. Enter* MRS. RANEVSKY, GAYEV, *and* LOPAKHIN.)

LOPAKHIN: You must make up your minds once and for all. There's not much time left. After all, it's quite a simple matter. Do you agree to lease your land for country cottages or don't you? Answer me in one word: yes or no. Just one word.

MRS. RANEVSKY: Who's been smoking such horrible cigars here? (*Sits down.*)

GAYEV: Now that they've built the railway, things are much more convenient. (*Sits down.*) We've been to town for lunch—pot the red in the middle! I really should have gone in to have a game first.

MRS. RANEVSKY: There's plenty of time.

LOPAKHIN: Just one word. (*Imploringly.*) Please give me your answer!

GAYEV (*yawns*): I beg your pardon?

MRS. RANEVSKY (*looking in her purse*): Yesterday I had a lot of money, but I've hardly any left today. My poor Varya! Tries to economize by feeding everybody on milk soup and the old servants in the kitchen on peas, and I'm just throwing money about stupidly. (*Drops her purse, scattering some gold coins.*) Goodness gracious, all over the place! (*She looks annoyed.*)

YASHA: Allow me to pick 'em up, madam. It won't take a minute. (*Starts picking up the coins.*)

MRS. RANEVSKY: Thank you, Yasha. Why on earth did I go out to lunch? That disgusting restaurant of yours with its stupid band, and those tablecloths smelling of soap. Why did you have to drink so much, Leonid? Or eat so much? Or talk so much? You did talk a lot again in the restaurant today and all to no purpose. About the seventies and the decadents ... And who to? Talking about the decadents to waiters!

LOPAKHIN: Aye....

GAYEV (*waving his arm*): I'm incorrigible, that's clear. (*Irritably to* YASHA.) What are you hanging around here for?

YASHA (*laughs*): I can't hear your voice without laughing, sir.

GAYEV (*to his sister*): Either he or I.

MRS. RANEVSKY: Go away, Yasha. Run along.

YASHA (*returning the purse to* MRS. RANEVSKY): At once, madam. (*Is hardly able to suppress his laughter.*) This very minute. (*Goes out.*)

LOPAKHIN: The rich merchant Deriganov is thinking of buying your estate. I'm told he's coming to the auction himself.

MRS. RANEVSKY: Where did you hear that?

LOPAKHIN: That's what they're saying in town.

GAYEV: Our Yaroslavl great-aunt has promised to send us money, but when and how much we do not know.

LOPAKHIN: How much will she send? A hundred thousand? Two hundred?

MRS. RANEVSKY: Well, I hardly think so. Ten or fifteen thousand at most. We must be thankful for that.

LOPAKHIN: I'm sorry, but such improvident people as you, such peculiar, unbusinesslike people, I've never met in my life! You're told in plain language that your estate's going to be sold, and you don't seem to understand.

MRS. RANEVSKY: But what are we to do? Tell us, please.

LOPAKHIN: I tell you every day. Every day I go on repeating the same thing over and over again. You must let out the cherry orchard and the land for country cottages, and you must do it now, as quickly as possible. The auction is on top of you! Try to understand! The moment you decide to let your land, you'll be able to raise as much money as you like, and you'll be saved.

MRS. RANEVSKY: Country cottages, holiday-makers—I'm sorry, but it's so vulgar.

GAYEV: I'm of your opinion entirely.

LOPAKHIN: I shall burst into tears or scream or have a fit. I can't stand it. You've worn me out! (*to* GAYEV) You're a silly old woman!

GAYEV: I beg your pardon?

LOPAKHIN: A silly old woman! (*He gets up to go.*)

MRS. RANEVSKY (*in dismay*): No, don't go. Please stay. I beg you. Perhaps we'll think of something.

LOPAKHIN: What is there to think of?

MRS. RANEVSKY: Please don't go. I beg you. Somehow I feel so much more cheerful with you here. (*Pause.*) I keep expecting something to happen, as though the house was going to collapse on top of us.

GAYEV (*deep in thought*): Cannon off the cushion. Pot into the middle pocket. . . .

MRS. RANEVSKY: I'm afraid we've sinned too much—

LOPAKHIN: You sinned!

GAYEV (*putting a fruit drop into his mouth*): They say I squandered my entire fortune on fruit drops. (*Laughs.*)

MRS. RANEVSKY: Oh, my sins! . . . I've always thrown money about aimlessly, like a madwoman. Why, I even married a man who did nothing but pile up debts. My husband died of champagne. He drank like a fish. Then, worse luck, I fell in love with someone, had an affair with him, and it was just at that time—it was my first punishment, a blow that nearly killed me—that my boy was drowned in the river here. I went abroad, never to come back, never to see that river again. I shut my eyes and ran, beside myself, and *he* followed me—pitilessly, brutally. I bought a villa near Mentone because *he* had fallen ill. For the next three years I knew no rest, nursing him day and night. He wore me out. Everything inside me went dead. Then, last year, I had to sell the villa to pay my debts. I left for Paris, where he robbed me, deserted me, and went to live with another woman. I tried to poison myself. Oh, it was all so stupid, so shaming. . . . It was then that I suddenly felt an urge to go back to Russia, to my homeland, to my daughter. (*Dries her eyes.*) Lord, O Lord, be merciful! Forgive me my sins! Don't punish me any more! (*Takes a telegram from her pocket.*) I received this telegram from Paris today. He asks me to forgive him. He implores me to go back. (*Tears up the telegram.*) What's that? Music? (*Listens intently.*)

GAYEV: That's our famous Jewish band. Remember? Four fiddles, a flute, and a double bass.

MRS. RANEVSKY: Does it still exist? We ought to arrange a party and have them over to the house.

LOPAKHIN (*listening*): I don't hear anything. (*Sings quietly.*) "And the Germans, if you pay 'em, will turn a Russian into a Frenchman." (*Laughs.*) I saw an excellent play at the theatre last night. It was very amusing.

MRS. RANEVSKY: I don't suppose it was amusing at all. You shouldn't be watching plays, but should be watching yourselves more often. What dull lives you live. What nonsense you talk.

LOPAKHIN: Perfectly true. Let's admit quite frankly that the life we lead is utterly stupid. (*Pause.*) My father was a peasant, an idiot. He understood nothing. He taught me nothing. He just beat me when he was drunk and always with a stick. As a matter of fact, I'm just as big a blockhead and an idiot myself. I never learnt anything, and my handwriting is so abominable that I'm ashamed to let people see it.

MRS. RANEVSKY: You ought to get married, my friend.

LOPAKHIN: Yes. That's true.

MRS. RANEVSKY: Married to our Varya. She's a nice girl.

LOPAKHIN: Aye. . . .

MRS. RANEVSKY: Her father was a peasant too. She's a hard-working girl, and she loves you. That's the important thing. Why, you've been fond of her for a long time yourself.

LOPAKHIN: Very well. I've no objection. She's a good girl.

(*Pause.*)

GAYEV: I've been offered a job in a bank. Six thousand a year. Have you heard, Lyuba?

MRS. RANEVSKY: You in a bank! You'd better stay where you are.

(FIRS *comes in carrying an overcoat.*)

FIRS (*to* GAYEV): Please put it on, sir. It's damp out here.

GAYEV (*putting on the overcoat*): You're a damned nuisance, my dear fellow.

FIRS: Come along, sir. Don't be difficult. . . . This morning, too, you went off without saying a word. (*Looks him over.*)

MRS. RANEVSKY: How you've aged, Firs!

FIRS: What's that, ma'am?

LOPAKHIN: Your mistress says you've aged a lot.

FIRS: I've been alive a long time. They were trying to marry me off before your dad was born. . . . (*Laughs.*) When freedom came, I was already chief valet. I refused to accept freedom and stayed on with my master. (*Pause.*) I well remember how glad everyone was, but what they were glad about, they did not know themselves.

LOPAKHIN: It wasn't such a bad life before, was it? At least, they flogged you.

FIRS (*not hearing him*): I should say so. The peasants stuck to their masters and the masters to their peasants. Now everybody does what he likes. You can't understand nothing.

GAYEV: Shut up, Firs. I have to go to town tomorrow. I've been promised an introduction to a general who might lend us some money on a promissory note.

LOPAKHIN: Nothing will come of it. You won't pay the interest, either. You may be sure of that.

MRS. RANEVSKY: Oh, he's just imagining things. There aren't any generals.

(Enter TROFIMOV, ANYA, *and* VARYA.*)*

GAYEV: Here they are at last.

ANYA: There's Mother.

MRS. RANEVSKY *(affectionately)*: Come here, come here, my dears. *(Embracing* ANYA *and* VARYA.*)* If you only knew how much I love you both. Sit down beside me. That's right.

(All sit down.)

LOPAKHIN: Our eternal student is always walking about with the young ladies.

TROFIMOV: Mind your own business.

LOPAKHIN: He's nearly fifty and he's still a student.

TROFIMOV: Do drop your idiotic jokes.

LOPAKHIN: Why are you so angry, you funny fellow?

TROFIMOV: Well, stop pestering me.

LOPAKHIN *(laughs)*: Tell me, what do you think of me?

TROFIMOV: Simply this: You're a rich man and you'll soon be a millionaire. Now, just as a beast of prey devours everything in its path and so helps to preserve the balance of nature, so you, too, perform a similar function.

(They all laugh.)

VARYA: You'd better tell us about the planets, Peter.

MRS. RANEVSKY: No, let's carry on with what we were talking about yesterday.

TROFIMOV: What was that?

GAYEV: Pride.

TROFIMOV: We talked a lot yesterday, but we didn't arrive at any conclusion. As you see it, there's something mystical about the proud man. You may be right for all I know. But try to look at it simply, without being too clever. What sort of pride is it, is there any sense in it, if, physiologically, man is far from perfect? If, in fact, he is, in the vast majority of cases, coarse, stupid, and profoundly unhappy? It's time we stopped admiring ourselves. All we must do is—work!

GAYEV: We're going to die all the same.

TROFIMOV: Who knows? And what do you mean by "we're going to die"? A man may possess a hundred senses. When he dies, he loses only the five we know. The other ninety-five live on.

MRS. RANEVSKY: How clever you are, Peter!

LOPAKHIN *(ironically)*: Oh, frightfully!

TROFIMOV: Mankind marches on, perfecting its powers. Everything that is incomprehensible to us now, will one day become familiar and comprehensible. All we have to do is to work and do our best to assist those who are looking for truth. Here in Russia only a few people are working so far. The vast majority of the educated people I know, do nothing. They aren't looking for anything. They are quite incapable of doing any work. They call themselves intellectuals, but speak to their servants as inferiors and treat the peasants like animals. They're not particularly keen on their studies, they don't do any serious reading, they are bone idle, they merely talk about science, and they understand very little about art. They are all so solemn, they look so very grave, they talk only of important matters, they philosophize. Yet anyone can see that our workers are abominably fed, sleep on bare boards, thirty and forty to a room—bedbugs everywhere, stench, damp, moral turpitude. It's therefore obvious that all our fine phrases are merely a way of deluding ourselves and others. Tell me, where are all those children's crèches people are talking so much about? Where are the reading rooms? You find them only in novels. Actually, we haven't any. All we have is dirt, vulgarity, brutality. I dislike and I'm frightened of all these solemn countenances, just as I'm frightened of all serious conversations. Why not shut up for once?

LOPAKHIN: Well, I get up at five o'clock in the morning. I work from morning till night, and I've always lots of money on me—mine and other people's—and I can see what the people around me are like. One has only to start doing something to realize how few honest, decent people there are about. Sometimes when I lie awake, I keep thinking: Lord, you've given us vast forests, boundless plains, immense horizons, and living here, we ourselves ought really to be giants—

MRS. RANEVSKY: You want giants, do you? They're all right only in fairy tales. Elsewhere they frighten me. (YEPIKHODOV *crosses the stage in the background, playing his guitar. Pensively.)* There goes Yepikhodov.

ANYA *(pensively)*: There goes Yepikhodov.

GAYEV: The sun's set, ladies and gentlemen.

TROFIMOV: Yes.

GAYEV *(softly, as though declaiming)*: Oh, nature, glorious nature! Glowing with eternal radiance, beautiful and indifferent, you, whom we call Mother, uniting in yourself both life and death, you—lifegiver and destroyer . . .

VARYA *(imploringly)*: Darling Uncle!

ANYA: Uncle, again!

TROFIMOV: You'd far better pot the red in the middle.

GAYEV: Not another word! Not another word!

(They all sit deep in thought. Everything is still. The silence is broken only by the subdued muttering of FIRS. *Suddenly a distant sound is heard. It seems to come from the sky, the sound of a breaking string, slowly dying away, melancholy.)*

MRS. RANEVSKY: What's that?

LOPAKHIN: I don't know. I expect a bucket must have broken somewhere far away in a coal mine, but somewhere a very long distance away.

GAYEV: Perhaps it was a bird, a heron or something.

TROFIMOV: Or an eagle-owl.

MRS. RANEVSKY (*shudders*): It makes me feel dreadful for some reason.

(*Pause.*)

FIRS: Same thing happened before the misfortune: the owl hooted and the samovar kept hissing.

GAYEV: Before what misfortune?

FIRS: Before they gave us our freedom.

(*Pause.*)

MRS. RANEVSKY: Come, let's go in, my friends. It's getting dark. (*to* ANYA) There are tears in your eyes. What's the matter, darling. (*Embraces her.*)

ANYA: It's nothing, Mother. Nothing.

TROFIMOV: Someone's coming.

(*A* HIKER *appears. He wears a shabby white peaked cap and an overcoat; he is slightly drunk.*)

HIKER: Excuse me, is this the way to the station?

GAYEV: Yes, follow that road.

HIKER: I'm greatly obliged to you sir. (*Coughs.*) Glorious weather . . . (*Declaiming.*) Brother, my suffering brother, come to the Volga, you whose groans . . . (*to* VARYA) Mademoiselle, won't you give thirty kopecks to a starving Russian citizen?

(VARYA, *frightened, utters a little scream.*)

LOPAKHIN (*angrily*): There's a limit to the most disgraceful behavior.

MRS. RANEVSKY (*at a loss*): Here, take this. (*Looks for some money in her purse.*) No silver. Never mind, have this gold one.

HIKER: Profoundly grateful to you, ma'am. (*Goes out.*)

(*Laughter.*)

VARYA (*frightened*): I'm going away. I'm going away. Good heavens, Mother dear, there's no food for the servants in the house, and you gave him a gold sovereign!

MRS. RANEVSKY: What's to be done with a fool like me? I'll give you all I have when we get home. You'll lend me some more money, Lopakhin, won't you?

LOPAKHIN: With pleasure.

MRS. RANEVSKY: Let's go in. It's time. By the way, Varya, we've found you a husband here. Congratulations.

VARYA (*through tears*): This isn't a joking matter, Mother.

LOPAKHIN: Okhmelia, go to a nunnery!

GAYEV: Look at my hands. They're shaking. It's a long time since I had a game of billiards.

LOPAKHIN: Okhmelia, O nymph, remember me in your prayers!

MRS. RANEVSKY: Come along, come along, it's almost supper time.

VARYA: That man frightened me. My heart's still pounding.

LOPAKHIN: Let me remind you, ladies and gentlemen: The cherry orchard is up for sale on the twenty-second of August. Think about it! Think!

(*They all go out except* TROFIMOV *and* ANYA.)

ANYA (*laughing*): I'm so glad the hiker frightened Varya. Now we are alone.

TROFIMOV: Varya's afraid we might fall in love. That's why she follows us around for days on end. With her narrow mind she cannot grasp that we are above love. The whole aim and meaning of our life is to bypass everything that is petty and illusory, that prevents us from being free and happy. Forward! Let us march on irresistibly toward the bright star shining there in the distance! Forward! Don't lag behind, friends!

ANYA (*clapping her hands excitedly*): You talk so splendidly! (*Pause.*) It's so heavenly here today!

TROFIMOV: Yes, the weather is wonderful.

ANYA: What have you done to me, Peter? Why am I no longer as fond of the cherry orchard as before? I loved it so dearly. I used to think there was no lovelier place on earth than our orchard.

TROFIMOV: The whole of Russia is our orchard. The earth is great and beautiful. There are lots of lovely places on it. (*Pause.*) Think, Anya: your grandfather, your great-grandfather, and all your ancestors owned serfs. They owned living souls. Can't you see human beings looking at you from every cherry tree in your orchard, from every leaf and every tree trunk? Don't you hear their voices? To own living souls—that's what has changed you all so much, you who are living now and those who lived before you. That's why your mother, you yourself, and your uncle no longer realize that you are living on borrowed capital, at other people's expense, at the expense of those whom you don't admit farther than your entrance hall. We are at least two hundred years behind the times. We haven't got anything at all. We have no definite attitude toward our past. We just philosophize, complain of depression, or drink vodka. Isn't it abundantly clear that before we start living in the present, we must atone for our past, make an end of it? And atone for it we can only by suffering, by extraordinary, unceasing labor. Understand that, Anya.

ANYA: The house we live in hasn't really been ours for a long time. I'm going to leave it. I give you my word.

TROFIMOV: If you have the keys of the house, throw them into the well and go away. Be free as the wind.

ANYA (*rapturously*): How well you said it!

TROFIMOV: Believe me, Anya, believe me! I'm not yet

thirty, I'm young, I'm still a student, but I've been through hell more than once. I'm driven from pillar to post. In winter I'm half-starved, I'm ill, worried, poor as a beggar. You can't imagine the terrible places I've been to! And yet, always, every moment of the day and night, my heart was full of ineffable visions of the future. I feel, I'm quite sure, that happiness is coming, Anya. I can see it coming already.

ANYA (*pensively*): The moon is rising.

(YEPIKHODOV *can be heard playing the same sad tune as before on his guitar. The moon rises. Somewhere near the poplars* VARYA *is looking for* ANYA *and calling, "Anya, where are you?"*)

TROFIMOV: Yes, the moon is rising. (*Pause.*) There it is—happiness! It's coming nearer and nearer. Already I can hear its footsteps, and if we never see it, if we never know it, what does that matter? Others will see it.

VARYA (*offstage*): Anya, where are you?

TROFIMOV: That Varya again! (*Angrily.*) Disgusting!

ANYA: Never mind, let's go to the river. It's lovely there.

TROFIMOV: Yes, let's.

(*They go out.*)

VARYA (*offstage*): Anya! Anya!

CURTAIN

ACT 3

(*The drawing room, separated by an archway from the ballroom. A candelabra is alight. The Jewish band can be heard playing in the entrance hall. It is the same band that is mentioned in Act Two. Evening. In the ballroom people are dancing the Grande Ronde.* SIMEONOV-PISHCHIK'*s voice can be heard crying out, "Promenade à une paire!" They all come out into the drawing room:* PISHCHIK *and* CHARLOTTE *the first couple,* TROFIMOV *and* MRS. RANEVSKY *the second,* ANYA *and a* POST OFFICE CLERK *the third,* VARYA *and the* STATIONMASTER *the fourth, and so on.* VARYA *is quietly crying and dries her eyes as she dances. The last couple consists of* DUNYASHA *and a partner. They walk across the drawing room.* PISHCHIK *shouts, "Grande Ronde balancez!" and "Les cavaliers à genoux et remerciez vos dames!"*)

(FIRS, *wearing a tailcoat, brings in soda water on a tray.* PISHCHIK *and* TROFIMOV *come into the drawing room.*)

PISHCHIK: I've got high blood-pressure. I've had two strokes already, and I find dancing hard work. But, as the saying goes, if you're one of a pack, wag your tail, whether you bark or not. As a matter of fact, I'm as strong as a horse. My father, may he rest in peace, liked his little joke, and speaking about our family pedigree, he used to say that the ancient Simeonov-Pishchiks came from the horse that Caligula had made a senator. (*Sits down.*) But you see, the trouble is that I have no money. A hungry dog believes only in meat. (*Snores, but wakes up again at once.*) I'm just the same. All I can think of is money.

TROFIMOV: There really is something horsy about you.

PISHCHIK: Well, a horse is a good beast. You can sell a horse.

(*From an adjoining room comes the sound of people playing billiards.* VARYA *appears in the ballroom under the archway.*)

TROFIMOV (*teasing her*): Mrs. Lopakhin! Mrs. Lopakhin!

VARYA (*angrily*): Moth-eaten gentleman!

TROFIMOV: Well, I am a moth-eaten gentleman and proud of it.

VARYA (*brooding bitterly*): We've hired a band, but how we are going to pay for it, I don't know. (*Goes out.*)

TROFIMOV (*to* PISHCHIK): If the energy you have wasted throughout your life looking for money to pay the interest on your debts had been spent on something else, you'd most probably have succeeded in turning the world upside down.

PISHCHIK: Nietzsche, the famous philosopher—a great man, a man of great intellect—says in his works that there's nothing wrong about forging bank notes.

TROFIMOV: Have you read Nietzsche?

PISHCHIK: Well, actually, Dashenka told me about it. I don't mind telling you, though, that in my present position I might even forge bank notes. The day after tomorrow I've got to pay three hundred and ten rubles. I've already got one hundred and thirty. (*Feels his pockets in alarm.*) My money's gone, I've lost my money! (*Through tears.*) Where is it? (*Happily.*) Ah, here it is, in the lining. Lord the shock brought me out in a cold sweat!

(*Enter* MRS. RANEVSKY *and* CHARLOTTE.)

MRS. RANEVSKY (*hums a popular Georgian dance tune*): Why is Leonid so late? What's he doing in town? (*to* DUNYASHA) Offer the band tea, please.

TROFIMOV: I don't suppose the auction has taken place.

MRS. RANEVSKY: What a time to have a band! What a time to give a party! Oh, well, never mind. (*Sits down and hums quietly.*)

CHARLOTTE (*hands* PISHCHIK *a pack of cards*): Here's a pack of cards. Think of a card.

PISHCHIK: All right.

CHARLOTTE: Now shuffle the pack. That's right. Now give it to me. Now, then, my dear Mr. Pishchik, *eins, zwei, drei!* Look in your breast pocket. Is it there?

PISHCHIK (*takes the card out of his breast pocket*): The eight of spades! Absolutely right! (*Surprised.*) Good Lord!

CHARLOTTE (*holding a pack of cards on the palm of her hand, to* TROFIMOV): Tell me, quick, what's the top card?

TROFIMOV: Well, let's say the queen of spades.

CHARLOTTE: Here it is. (*to* PISHCHIK): What's the top card now?

PISHCHIK: The ace of hearts.

CHARLOTTE: Here you are! (*Claps her hands and the pack of cards disappears.*) What lovely weather we're having today. (*A mysterious female voice, which seems to come from under the floor, answers: "Oh yes, glorious weather, madam!"*) You're my ideal, you're so nice! (*The voice: "I like you very much too, madam."*)

STATIONMASTER (*clapping his hands*): Bravo, Madam Ventriloquist!

PISHCHIK (*looking surprised*): Good Lord! Enchanting, Miss Charlotte, I'm simply in love with you.

CHARLOTTE: In love! Are you sure you can love? *Guter Mensch, aber schlechter Musikant.* [A good man, but a poor musician.]

TROFIMOV (*claps* PISHCHIK *on the shoulder*): Good old horse!

CHARLOTTE: Attention, please. One more trick. (*She takes a rug from a chair.*) Here's a very good rug. I'd like to sell it. (*Shaking it.*) Who wants to buy it?

PISHCHIK (*surprised*): Good Lord!

CHARLOTTE: *Eins, zwei, drei!* (*Quickly snatching up the rug, which she had let fall, she reveals* ANYA *standing behind it.* ANYA *curtseys, runs to her mother, embraces her, and runs back to the ballroom, amid general enthusiasm.*)

MRS. RANEVSKY (*applauding*): Bravo, bravo!

CHARLOTTE: Now, once more. *Eins, zwei, drei!* (*Lifts the rug; behind it stands* VARYA, *who bows.*)

PISHCHIK (*surprised*): Good Lord!

CHARLOTTE: The end! (*Throws the rug over* PISHCHIK, *curtseys, and runs off to the ballroom.*)

PISHCHIK (*running after her*): The hussy! What a woman, eh? What a woman! (*Goes out.*)

MRS. RANEVSKY: Still no Leonid. I can't understand what he can be doing in town all this time. It must be over now. Either the estate has been sold or the auction didn't take place. Why keep us in suspense so long?

VARYA (*trying to comfort her*): I'm certain Uncle must have bought it.

TROFIMOV (*sarcastically*): Oh, to be sure!

VARYA: Our great-aunt sent him power of attorney to buy the estate in her name and transfer the mortgage to her. She's done it for Anya's sake. God will help us and Uncle will buy it. I'm sure of it.

MRS. RANEVSKY: Your great-aunt sent fifteen thousand to buy the estate in her name. She doesn't trust us—but the money wouldn't even pay the interest. (*She covers her face with her hands.*) My whole future is being decided today, my future. . . .

TROFIMOV (*teasing* VARYA): Mrs. Lopakhin!

VARYA (*crossly*): Eternal student! Expelled twice from the university, weren't you?

MRS. RANEVSKY: Why are you so cross, Varya? He's teasing you about Lopakhin. Well, what of it? Marry Lopakhin if you want to. He is a nice, interesting man. If you don't want to, don't marry him. Nobody's forcing you, darling.

VARYA: I regard such a step seriously, Mother dear. I don't mind being frank about it: He is a nice man, and I like him.

MRS. RANEVSKY: Well, marry him. What are you waiting for? That's what I can't understand.

VARYA: But, Mother dear, I can't very well propose to him myself, can I? Everyone's been talking to me about him for the last two years. Everyone! But he either says nothing or makes jokes. I quite understand. He's making money. He has his business to think of, and he hasn't time for me. If I had any money, just a little, a hundred rubles, I'd give up everything and go right away as far as possible. I'd have gone into a convent.

TROFIMOV: Wonderful!

VARYA (*to* TROFIMOV): A student ought to be intelligent! (*In a gentle voice, through tears.*) How plain you've grown, Peter! How you've aged! (*to* MRS. RANEVSKY, *no longer crying*) I can't live without having something to do, Mother! I must be doing something all the time.

(*Enter* YASHA.)

YASHA (*hardly able to restrain his laughter*): Yepikhodov's broken a billiard cue! (*Goes out.*)

VARYA: What's Yepikhodov doing here? Who gave him permission to play billiards? Can't understand these people! (*Goes out.*)

MRS. RANEVSKY: Don't tease her, Peter. Don't you see she is unhappy enough already?

TROFIMOV: She's a bit too conscientious. Pokes her nose into other people's affairs. Wouldn't leave me and Anya alone all summer. Afraid we might have an affair. What business is it of hers? Besides, the idea never entered my head. Such vulgarity is beneath me. We are above love.

MRS. RANEVSKY: So, I suppose I must be beneath love. (*In great agitation.*) Why isn't Leonid back? All I want to know is: Has the estate been sold or not? Such a calamity seems so incredible to me that I don't know what to think. I'm completely at a loss. I feel like screaming, like doing something silly. Help me, Peter. Say something. For God's sake, say something!

TROFIMOV: What does it matter whether the estate's been sold today or not? The estate's been finished and done with long ago. There's no turning back. The road to it is closed. Stop worrying, my dear. You mustn't deceive yourself. Look the truth straight in the face for once in your life.

MRS. RANEVSKY: What truth? You can see where truth is and where it isn't, but I seem to have gone blind. I see nothing. You boldly solve all important problems, but tell me, dear boy, isn't it because you're young, isn't it because you haven't had the time to live through the consequences of any of your problems? You look ahead boldly, but isn't it because you neither see nor expect anything terrible to happen to you, because life is still hidden from your young eyes? You're bolder, more honest, you see much deeper than any of us, but think carefully, try to understand our position, be generous even a little, spare me. I was born here, you know. My father and mother lived here, and my grandfather also. I love this house. Life has no meaning for me without the cherry orchard, and if it has to be sold, then let me be sold with it. (*Embraces* TROFIMOV *and kisses him on the forehead.*) Don't you see, my son was drowned here. (*Weeps.*) Have pity on me, my good, kind friend.

TROFIMOV: You know I sympathize with you with all my heart.

MRS. RANEVSKY: You should have put it differently. (*Takes out her handkerchief. A telegram falls on the floor.*) My heart is so heavy today. You can't imagine how heavy. I can't bear this noise. The slightest sound makes me shudder. I'm trembling all over. I'm afraid to go to my room. I'm terrified to be alone. . . . Don't condemn me, Peter. I love you as my own son. I'd gladly let Anya marry you, I swear I would. Only, my dear boy, you must study, you must finish your course at the university. You never do anything. You just drift from one place to another. That's what's so strange. Isn't that so? Isn't it? And you should do something about your beard. Make it grow, somehow. (*Laughs.*) You are funny!

TROFIMOV (*picking up the telegram*): I have no wish to be handsome.

MRS. RANEVSKY: That telegram's from Paris. I get one every day. Yesterday and today. That wild man is ill again, in trouble again. He asks me to forgive him. He begs me to come back to him, and I really think I ought to be going back to Paris to be near him for a bit. You're looking very stern, Peter. But what's to be done, my dear boy? What am I to do? He's ill. He's lonely. He's unhappy. Who'll look after him there? Who'll stop him from doing something silly? Who'll give him his medicine at the right time? And, why hide it? Why be silent about it? I love him. That's obvious. I love him. I love him. He's a millstone round my neck and he's dragging me down to the bottom with him, but I love the millstone, and I can't live without it. (*Presses* TROFIMOV*'s hand.*) Don't think badly of me, Peter. Don't say anything. Don't speak.

TROFIMOV (*through tears*): For God's sake—forgive my being so frank, but he left you penniless!

MRS. RANEVSKY: No, no, no! You mustn't say that. (*Puts her hands over her ears.*)

TROFIMOV: Why, he's a scoundrel, and you're the only one who doesn't seem to know it. He's a petty scoundrel, a nonentity.

MRS. RANEVSKY (*angry but restraining herself*): You're twenty-six or twenty-seven, but you're still a schoolboy—a sixth-grade schoolboy!

TROFIMOV: What does that matter?

MRS. RANEVSKY: You ought to be a man. A person of your age ought to understand people who are in love. You ought to be in love yourself. You ought to fall in love. (*Angrily.*) Yes! Yes! And you're not so pure either. You're just a prude, a ridiculous crank, a freak!

TROFIMOV (*horrified*): What is she saying?

MRS. RANEVSKY: "I'm above love!" You're not above love, you're simply what Firs calls a nincompoop. Not have a mistress at your age!

TROFIMOV (*horrified*): This is terrible! What is she saying? (*Walks quickly into the ballroom, clutching his head.*) It's dreadful! I can't! I'll go away! (*Goes out but immediately comes back.*) All is at an end between us! (*Goes out into the hall.*)

MRS. RANEVSKY (*shouting after him*): Peter, wait! You funny boy, I was only joking. Peter!

(*Someone can be heard running rapidly up the stairs and then suddenly falling downstairs with a crash.* ANYA *and* VARYA *scream, followed immediately by laughter.*)

MRS. RANEVSKY: What's happened?

ANYA (*laughing, runs in*): Peter's fallen down the stairs! (*Runs out.*)

MRS. RANEVSKY: What an eccentric! (*The* STATIONMASTER *stands in the middle of the ballroom and recites* "The Fallen Woman" *by Alexey Tolstoy. The others listen. But he has hardly time to recite a few lines when the sound of a waltz comes from the entrance hall, and the recitation breaks off. Everyone dances.* TROFIMOV, ANYA, VARYA, *and* MRS. RANEVSKY *enter from the hall.*) Well, Peter dear, you pure soul, I'm sorry. . . . Come, let's dance. (*Dances with* TROFIMOV.)

(ANYA *and* VARYA *dance together.* FIRS *comes in and stands his walking stick near the side door.* YASHA *has also come in from the drawing room and is watching the dancing.*)

YASHA: Well, Grandpa!

FIRS: I'm not feeling too well. We used to have generals, barons, and admirals at our dances before, but now we send for the post office clerk and the stationmaster. Even they are not too keen to come. Afraid I'm getting weak. The old master, the mistress's grandfather that is, used to give us powdered sealing wax for medicine. It was his prescription for all illnesses. I've been taking sealing wax every day for the last twenty years or more. That's perhaps why I'm still alive.

YASHA: You make me sick, Grandpa. *(Yawns).* I wish you was dead.

FIRS: Ugh, you nincompoop! *(Mutters.)*

(TROFIMOV and MRS. RANEVSKY dance in the ballroom and then in the drawing room.)

MRS. RANEVSKY: *Merci.* I think I'll sit down a bit. *(Sits down.)* I'm tired.

(Enter ANYA.)

ANYA *(agitated)*: A man in the kitchen said just now that the cherry orchard has been sold today.

MRS. RANEVSKY: Sold? Who to?

ANYA: He didn't say. He's gone away now.

(ANYA dances with TROFIMOV; both go off to the ballroom.)

YASHA: Some old man gossiping, madam. A stranger.

FIRS: Master Leonid isn't here yet. Hasn't returned. Wearing his light autumn overcoat. He might catch cold. Oh, these youngsters!

MRS. RANEVSKY: I shall die! Yasha, go and find out who bought it.

YASHA: But he's gone, the old man has. *(Laughs.)*

MRS. RANEVSKY *(a little annoyed)*: Well, what are you laughing at? What are you so pleased about?

YASHA: Yepikhodov's a real scream. Such a fool. Twenty-two Calamities!

MRS. RANEVSKY: Firs, where will you go if the estate's sold?

FIRS: I'll go wherever you tell me, ma'am.

MRS. RANEVSKY: You look awful! Are you ill? You'd better go to bed.

FIRS: Me to bed, ma'am? *(Ironically.)* If I goes to bed, who's going to do the waiting? Who's going to look after everything? I'm the only one in the whole house.

YASHA *(to MRS. RANEVSKY)*: I'd like to ask you a favor, madam. If you go back to Paris, will you take me with you? It's quite impossible for me to stay here. *(Looking round, in an undertone.)* You know perfectly well yourself what an uncivilized country this is—the common people are so immoral— and besides, it's so boring here, the food in the kitchen is disgusting, and on top of it, there's that old Firs wandering about, muttering all sorts of inappropriate words. Take me with you, madam, please!

(Enter PISHCHIK.)

PISHCHIK: May I have the pleasure of a little dance, fair lady? *(MRS. RANEVSKY goes with him.)* I'll have one hundred and eighty rubles off you all the same, my dear, charming lady. . . . I will, indeed. *(They dance.)* One hundred and eighty rubles. . . .

(They go into the ballroom.)

YASHA *(singing softly)*: "Could you but feel the agitated beating of my heart."

(In the ballroom a woman in a gray top hat and check trousers can be seen jumping about and waving her arms. Shouts of "Bravo, Charlotte! Bravo!")

DUNYASHA *(stops to powder her face)*: Miss Anya told me to join the dancers because there are lots of gentlemen and very few ladies. But dancing makes me dizzy and my heart begins beating so fast. I say, Firs, the post office clerk said something to me just now that quite took my breath away.

(The music becomes quieter.)

FIRS: What did he say to you?

DUNYASHA: "You're like a flower," he said.

YASHA *(yawning)*: What ignorance! *(Goes out.)*

DUNYASHA: Like a flower! I'm ever so delicate, and I love people saying nice things to me!

FIRS: You'll come to a bad end, my girl. Mark my words.

(Enter YEPIKHODOV.)

YEPIKHODOV: You seem to avoid me, Dunyasha. Just as if I was some insect. *(Sighs.)* Oh, life!

DUNYASHA: What do you want?

YEPIKHODOV: No doubt you may be right. *(Sighs.)* But, of course, if one looks at things from a certain point of view, then, if I may say so and if you'll forgive my frankness, you have reduced me absolutely to a state of mind. I know what Fate has in store for me. Every day some calamity overtakes me, but I got used to it so long ago that I just look at my Fate and smile. You gave me your word, and though I—

DUNYASHA: Let's talk about it some other time. Leave me alone now. Now, I am dreaming. *(Plays with her fan.)*

YEPIKHODOV: Every day some calamity overtakes me, and I—let me say it quite frankly—why, I just smile, laugh even.

(Enter VARYA from the ballroom.)

VARYA: Are you still here, Simon! What an ill-mannered fellow you are, to be sure! *(to DUNYASHA)* Be off with you, Dunyasha. *(to YEPIKHODOV)* First you go and play billiards and break a cue, and now you wander about the drawing room as if you were a guest.

YEPIKHODOV: It's not your place to reprimand me, if you don't mind my saying so.

VARYA: I'm not reprimanding you. I'm telling you. All you do is drift about from one place to another without ever doing a stroke of work. We're employing an office clerk, but goodness knows why.

YEPIKHODOV *(offended)*: Whether I work or drift about,

whether I eat or play billiards, is something which only people older than you, people who know what they're talking about, should decide.

VARYA: How dare you talk to me like that? *(Flaring up.)* How dare you? I don't know what I'm talking about, don't I? Get out of here! This instant!

YEPIKHODOV *(cowed)*: Express yourself with more delicacy, please.

VARYA *(beside herself)*: Get out of here this minute! Out! *(He goes toward the door, and she follows him.)* Twenty-two Calamities! Don't let me see you here again! Never set foot here again! *(YEPIKHODOV goes out. He can be heard saying behind the door: "I'll lodge a complaint.")* Oh, so you're coming back, are you? *(Picks up the stick which FIRS has left near the door.)* Come on, come on, I'll show you! Coming are you? Well, take that! *(Swings the stick as LOPAKHIN comes in.)*

LOPAKHIN: Thank you very much!

VARYA *(angrily and derisively)*: I'm so sorry!

LOPAKHIN: It's quite all right. Greatly obliged to you for the kind reception.

VARYA: Don't mention it. *(Walks away, then looks round and inquires gently.)* I didn't hurt you, did I?

LOPAKHIN: Oh no, not at all. There's going to be an enormous bump on my head for all that.

(Voices in the ballroom: "Lopakhin's arrived. Lopakhin!")

PISHCHIK: Haven't heard from you or seen you for ages, my dear fellow! *(Embraces LOPAKHIN.)* Do I detect a smell of brandy, dear boy? We're doing very well here, too.

(Enter MRS. RANEVSKY.)

MRS. RANEVSKY: Is it you, Lopakhin? Why have you been so long? Where's Leonid?

LOPAKHIN: He came back with me. He'll be here in a moment.

MRS. RANEVSKY *(agitated)*: Well, what happened? Did the auction take place? Speak, for heaven's sake!

LOPAKHIN *(embarrassed, fearing to betray his joy)*: The auction was over by four o'clock. We missed our train and had to wait till half past nine. *(With a deep sigh.)* Oh dear, I'm afraid I feel a little dizzy.

(Enter GAYEV. He carries some parcels in his right hand and wipes away his tears with his left.)

MRS. RANEVSKY: What's the matter, Leonid? Well! *(Impatiently, with tears.)* Quick, tell me for heaven's sake!

GAYEV *(doesn't answer, only waves his hands resignedly; to FIRS, weeping)*: Here, take these—anchovies, Kerch herrings . . . I've had nothing to eat all day. I've had a terrible time. *(The door of the billiard room is open; the click of billiard balls can be heard and YASHA's voice: "Seven and eighteen!" GAYEV's expression changes. He is no longer crying.)* I'm awfully tired. Come and help me change, Firs.

(GAYEV goes off through the ballroom to his own room, followed by FIRS.)

PISHCHIK: Well, what happened at the auction? Come, tell us!

MRS. RANEVSKY: Has the cherry orchard been sold?

LOPAKHIN: It has.

MRS. RANEVSKY: Who bought it?

LOPAKHIN: I bought it. *(Pause.* MRS. RANEVSKY *is crushed; she would have collapsed on the floor if she had not been standing near an armchair.* VARYA *takes the keys from her belt, throws them on the floor in the center of the drawing room, and goes out.)* I bought it! One moment, please, ladies and gentlemen. I feel dazed. I can't talk. . . . *(Laughs.)* Deriganov was already there when we got to the auction. Gayev had only fifteen thousand, and Deriganov began his bidding at once with thirty thousand over and above the mortgage. I realized the position at once and took up his challenge. I bid forty. He bid forty-five. He kept raising his bid by five thousand and I by adding another ten thousand. Well, it was soon over. I bid ninety thousand on top of the arrears, and the cherry orchard was knocked down to me. Now the cherry orchard is mine! Mine! *(Laughs loudly.)* Merciful heavens, the cherry orchard's mine! Come on, tell me, tell me I'm drunk. Tell me I'm out of my mind. Tell me I'm imagining it all. *(Stamps his feet.)* Don't laugh at me! If my father and my grandfather were to rise from their graves and see what's happened, see how their Yermolay, their beaten and half-literate Yermolay, Yermolay who used to run around barefoot in winter, see how that same Yermolay bought this estate, the most beautiful estate in the world! I've bought the estate where my father and grandfather were slaves, where they weren't even allowed inside the kitchen. I must be dreaming. I must be imagining it all. It can't be true. It's all a figment of your imagination, shrouded in mystery. *(Picks up the keys, smiling affectionately.)* She's thrown down the keys. Wants to show she's no longer the mistress here. *(Jingles the keys.)* Oh well, never mind. *(The band is heard tuning up.)* Hey you, musicians, play something! I want to hear you. Come, all of you! Come and watch Yermolay Lopakhin take an axe to the cherry orchard. Watch the trees come crashing down. We'll cover the place with country cottages, and our grandchildren and great-grandchildren will see a new life springing up here. Strike up the music! *(The band plays.* MRS. RANEVSKY *has sunk into a chair and is weeping bitterly. Reproachfully.)* Why did you not listen to me? You poor dear, you will never get it back now. *(With tears.)* Oh, if only all this could be over soon, if only our unhappy, disjointed life could somehow be changed soon.

PISHCHIK (*takes his arm, in an undertone*): She's crying. Let's go into the ballroom. Let's leave her alone. Come on. (*Takes his arm and leads him away to the ballroom.*)

LOPAKHIN: What's the matter? You there in the band, play up, play up! Let's hear you properly. Let's have everything as I want it now. (*Ironically.*) Here comes the new landowner, the owner of the cherry orchard! (*Knocks against a small table accidentally and nearly knocks over the candelabra.*) I can pay for everything!

(LOPAKHIN *goes out with* PISHCHIK. *There is no one left in the ballroom except* MRS. RANEVSKY, *who remains sitting in a chair, hunched up and crying bitterly. The band plays quietly.* ANYA *and* TROFIMOV *come in quickly.* ANYA *goes up to her mother and kneels in front of her.* TROFIMOV *remains standing by the entrance to the ballroom.*)

ANYA: Mother, Mother, why are you crying? My dear, good, kind Mother, my darling Mother, I love you; God bless you, Mother. The cherry orchard is sold. It's gone. That's true, quite true, but don't cry, Mother. You still have your life ahead of you, and you've still got your kind and pure heart. . . . Come with me, darling. Come. Let's go away from here. We shall plant a new orchard, an orchard more splendid than this one. You will see it, you will understand, and joy, deep, serene joy, will steal into your heart, sink into it like the sun in the evening, and you will smile, Mother! Come, darling! Come!

CURTAIN

ACT 4

(*The scene is the same as in the first act. There are no curtains at the windows or pictures on the walls. Only a few pieces of furniture are left. They have been stacked in one corner as if for sale. There is a feeling of emptiness. Near the front door and at the back of the stage, suitcases, traveling bags, etc., are piled up. The door on the left is open and the voices of* VARYA *and* ANYA *can be heard.* LOPAKHIN *stands waiting.* YASHA *is holding a tray with glasses of champagne. In the entrance hall* YEPIKHODOV *is tying up a box. There is a constant murmur of voices offstage, the voices of peasants who have come to say good-bye.* GAYEV's *voice is heard: "Thank you, my dear people, thank you."*)

YASHA: The peasants have come to say good-bye. In my opinion, sir, the peasants are decent enough fellows, but they don't understand a lot.

(*The murmur of voices dies away.* MRS. RANEVSKY *and* GAYEV *come in through the entrance hall; she is not crying, but she is pale. Her face is quivering. She cannot speak.*)

GAYEV: You gave them your purse, Lyuba. You shouldn't. You really shouldn't!

MRS. RANEVSKY: I—I couldn't help it. I just couldn't help it.

(*Both go out.*)

LOPAKHIN (*calling through the door after them*): Please take a glass of champagne. I beg you. One glass each before we leave. I forgot to bring any from town, and I could find only one bottle at the station. Please! (*Pause.*) Why, don't you want any? (*Walks away from the door.*) If I'd known, I wouldn't have bought it. Oh well, I don't think I'll have any, either. (YASHA *puts the tray down carefully on a chair.*) You'd better have some, Yasha.

YASHA: Thank you, sir. To those who're going away! And here's to you, sir, who's staying behind! (*Drinks.*) This isn't real champagne. Take it from me, sir.

LOPAKHIN: Paid eight rubles a bottle. (*Pause.*) Damn cold here.

YASHA: The stoves haven't been lit today. We're leaving, anyway. (*Laughs.*)

LOPAKHIN: What's so funny?

YASHA: Oh, nothing. Just feeling happy.

LOPAKHIN: It's October, but it might just as well be summer: it's so sunny and calm. Good building weather. (*Glances at his watch and calls through the door.*) I say, don't forget the train leaves in forty-seven minutes. In twenty minutes we must start for the station. Hurry up!

(TROFIMOV *comes in from outside, wearing an overcoat.*)

TROFIMOV: I think it's about time we were leaving. The carriages are at the door. Where the blazes could my galoshes have got to? Disappeared without a trace. (*Through the door.*) Anya, I can't find my galoshes! Can't find them!

LOPAKHIN: I've got to go to Kharkov. I'll leave with you on the same train. I'm spending the winter in Kharkov. I've been hanging about here too long. I'm worn out with having nothing to do. I can't live without work. Don't know what to do with my hands. They just flop about as if they belonged to someone else.

TROFIMOV: Well, we'll soon be gone and then you can resume your useful labors.

LOPAKHIN: Come on, have a glass of champagne.

TROFIMOV: No, thank you.

LOPAKHIN: So you're off to Moscow, are you?

TROFIMOV: Yes. I'll see them off to town, and I'm off to Moscow tomorrow.

LOPAKHIN: I see. I suppose the professors have stopped lecturing while you've been away. They're all waiting for you to come back.

TROFIMOV: Mind your own business.

LOPAKHIN: How many years have you been studying at the university?

TROFIMOV: Why don't you think of something new for a change? This is rather old, don't you think?— and stale. *(Looking for his galoshes.)* I don't suppose we shall ever meet again, so let me give you a word of advice as a farewell gift: Don't wave your arms about. Get rid of the habit of throwing your arms about. And another thing: To build country cottages in the hope that in the fullness of time vacationers will become landowners is the same as waving your arms about. Still, I like you in spite of everything. You've got fine sensitive fingers, like an artist's, and you have a fine sensitive soul.

LOPAKHIN *(embraces him)*: My dear fellow, thanks for everything. Won't you let me lend you some money for your journey? You may need it.

TROFIMOV: Need it? Whatever for?

LOPAKHIN: But you haven't any, have you?

TROFIMOV: Oh, but I have. I've just got some money for a translation. Got it here in my pocket. *(Anxiously.)* Where could those galoshes of mine have got to?

VARYA *(from another room)*: Oh, take your filthy things! *(Throws a pair of galoshes onto the stage.)*

TROFIMOV: Why are you so cross, Varya? Good heavens, these are not my galoshes!

LOPAKHIN: I had about three thousand acres of poppy sown last spring. Made a clear profit of forty thousand. When my poppies were in bloom, what a beautiful sight they were! Well, so you see, I made forty thousand and I'd be glad to lend you some of it because I can afford to. So why be so high and mighty? I'm a peasant. . . . I'm offering it to you without ceremony.

TROFIMOV: Your father was a peasant, my father was a pharmacist, all of which proves exactly nothing. *(LOPAKHIN takes out his wallet.)* Put it back! Put it back! If you offered me two hundred thousand, I wouldn't accept it. I'm a free man. Everything you prize so highly, everything that means so much to all of you, rich or poor, has no more power over me than a bit of fluff blown about in the air. I can manage without you. I can pass you by. I'm strong and proud. Mankind is marching toward a higher truth, toward the greatest happiness possible on earth, and I'm in the front ranks!

LOPAKHIN: Will you get there?

TROFIMOV: I will. *(Pause.)* I will get there or show others the way to get there.

(The sound of an axe striking a tree can be heard in the distance.)

LOPAKHIN: Well, good-bye, my dear fellow. Time to go. You and I are trying to impress one another, but life goes on regardless. When I work hard for hours on end, I can think more clearly, and then I can't help feeling that I, too, know what I live for. Have you any idea how many people in Russia exist goodness only knows why? However, no matter. It isn't they who make the world go round. I'm told Gayev has taken a job at the bank at six thousand a year. He'll never stick to it. Too damn lazy.

ANYA *(in the doorway)*: Mother asks you not to begin cutting the orchard down till she's gone.

TROFIMOV: Really, haven't you any tact at all? *(Goes out through the hall.)*

LOPAKHIN: Sorry, I'll see to it at once, at once! The damned idiots! *(Goes out after TROFIMOV.)*

ANYA: Has Firs been taken to the hospital?

YASHA: I told them to this morning. They must have taken him, I should think.

ANYA *(to YEPIKHODOV, who is crossing the ballroom)*: Please find out if Firs has been taken to the hospital.

YASHA *(offended)*: I told Yegor this morning. I haven't got to tell him a dozen times, have I?

YEPIKHODOV: Old man Firs, if you want my final opinion, is beyond repair, and it's high time he was gathered to his fathers. So far as I'm concerned, I can only envy him. *(Puts a suitcase on a hatbox and squashes it.)* There, you see! I knew it. *(Goes out.)*

YASHA *(sneeringly)*: Twenty-two Calamities!

VARYA *(from behind the door)*: Has Firs been taken to the hospital?

ANYA: He has.

VARYA: Why didn't they take the letter for the doctor?

ANYA: We'd better send it on after him. *(Goes out.)*

VARYA *(from the next room)*: Where's Yasha? Tell him his mother's here. She wants to say good-bye to him.

YASHA *(waves his hand impatiently)*: Oh, that's too much!

(All this time DUNYASHA has been busy with the luggage. Now that YASHA is alone, she goes up to him.)

DUNYASHA: You haven't even looked at me once, Yasha. You're going away, leaving me behind. *(Bursts out crying and throws her arms around his neck.)*

YASHA: Must you cry? *(Drinks champagne.)* I'll be back in Paris in a week. Tomorrow we catch the express and off we go! That's the last you'll see of us. I can hardly believe it, somehow. *Vive la France!* I hate it here. It doesn't suit me at all. It's not the kind of life I like. I'm afraid it can't be helped. I've had enough of all this ignorance. More than enough. *(Drinks champagne.)* So what's the use of crying? Behave yourself and you won't end up crying.

DUNYASHA *(powdering her face, looking in a hand mirror)*: Write to me from Paris, please. I did love you, Yasha, after all. I loved you so much. I'm such an affectionate creature, Yasha.

YASHA: They're coming here. (*Busies himself around the suitcases, humming quietly.*)

(*Enter* MRS. RANEVSKY, GAYEV, ANYA, *and* CHARLOTTE.)

GAYEV: We ought to be going. There isn't much time left. (*Looking at* YASHA.) Who's smelling of pickled herrings here?

MRS. RANEVSKY: In another ten minutes we ought to be getting into the carriages. (*Looks round the room.*) Good-bye, dear house, good-bye, old grandfather house! Winter will pass, spring will come, and you won't be here any more. They'll have pulled you down. The things these walls have seen! (*Kisses her daughter affectionately.*) My precious one, you look radiant. Your eyes are sparkling like diamonds. Happy? Very happy?

ANYA: Oh yes, very! A new life is beginning, Mother!

GAYEV (*gaily*): It is, indeed. Everything's all right now. We were all so worried and upset before the cherry orchard was sold, but now, when everything has been finally and irrevocably settled, we have all calmed down and even cheered up. I'm a bank official now, a financier. Pot the red in the middle. As for you, Lyuba, say what you like, but you too are looking a lot better. There's no doubt about it.

MRS. RANEVSKY: Yes, my nerves are better, that's true. (*Someone helps her on with her hat and coat.*) I sleep well. Take my things out, Yasha. It's time. (*to* ANYA) We'll soon be seeing each other again, darling. I'm going to Paris. I'll live there on the money your great-aunt sent from Yaroslavl to buy the estate—three cheers for Auntie!—but the money won't last long, I'm afraid.

ANYA: You'll come home soon, Mother, very soon. I'm going to study, pass my school exams, and then I'll work and help you. We shall read all sorts of books together, won't we, Mother? (*Kisses her mother's hands.*) We shall read during the autumn evenings. We'll read lots and lots of books, and a new, wonderful world will open up to us. (*Dreamily.*) Oh, do come back, Mother!

MRS. RANEVSKY: I'll come back, my precious. (*Embraces her daughter.*)

(*Enter* LOPAKHIN. CHARLOTTE *quietly hums a tune.*)

GAYEV: Happy Charlotte! She's singing!

CHARLOTTE (*picks up a bundle that looks like a baby in swaddling clothes*): My darling baby, go to sleep, my baby. (*A sound of a baby crying is heard.*) Hush, my sweet, my darling boy. (*The cry is heard again.*) Poor little darling, I'm so sorry for you! (*Throws the bundle down.*) So you will find me another job, won't you? I can't go on like this.

LOPAKHIN: We'll find you one, don't you worry.

GAYEV: Everybody's leaving us. Varya's going away. All of a sudden, we're no longer wanted.

CHARLOTTE: I haven't anywhere to live in town. I must go away. (*Sings quietly.*) It's all the same to me. . . .

(*Enter* PISHCHIK.)

LOPAKHIN: The nine days' wonder!

PISHCHIK (*out of breath*): Oh dear, let me get my breath back! I'm all in. Dear friends . . . a drink of water, please.

GAYEV: Came to borrow some money, I'll be bound. Not from me this time. Better make myself scarce. (*Goes out.*)

PISHCHIK: Haven't seen you for ages, dearest lady. (*to* LOPAKHIN) You here too? Glad to see you . . . man of immense intellect. . . . Here, that's for you, take it. (*Gives* LOPAKHIN *money.*) Four hundred rubles. That leaves eight hundred and forty I still owe you.

LOPAKHIN (*puzzled, shrugging his shoulders*): I must be dreaming. Where did you get it?

PISHCHIK: One moment . . . Terribly hot . . . Most extraordinary thing happened. Some Englishmen came to see me. They found some kind of white clay on my land. (*to* MRS. RANEVSKY) Here's four hundred for you too, beautiful ravishing lady. (*Gives her the money.*) The rest later. (*Drinks some water.*) Young fellow in the train just now was telling me that some—er—great philosopher advises people to jump off roofs. "Jump!" he says, and that'll solve all your problems. (*With surprise.*) Good Lord! More water, please.

LOPAKHIN: Who were these Englishmen?

PISHCHIK: I let them a plot of land with the clay on a twenty-four years' lease. And now you must excuse me, my friends. I'm in a hurry. Must be rushing off somewhere else. To Znoykov's, to Kardamonov's . . . Owe them all money. (*Drinks.*) Good-bye. I'll look in on Thursday.

MRS. RANEVSKY: We're just leaving for town. I'm going abroad tomorrow.

PISHCHIK: What? (*In a worried voice.*) Why are you going to town? Oh! I see! The furniture, the suitcases . . . Well, no matter. (*Through tears.*) No matter. Men of immense intellect, these Englishmen. . . . No matter. . . . No matter. I wish you all the best. May God help you. . . . No matter. Everything in this world comes to an end. (*Kisses* MRS. RANEVSKY*'s hand.*) When you hear that my end has come, remember the—er—old horse and say: Once there lived a man called Simeonov-Pishchik; may he rest in peace. Remarkable weather we've been having. . . . Yes. (*Goes out in great embarrassment, but immediately comes back and says, standing in the doorway.*) My Dashenka sends her regards. (*Goes out.*)

MRS. RANEVSKY: Well, we can go now. I'm leaving with two worries on my mind. One concerns Firs. He's ill. *(With a glance at her watch.)* We still have about five minutes.

ANYA: Firs has been taken to the hospital, Mother. Yasha sent him off this morning.

MRS. RANEVSKY: My other worry concerns Varya. She's used to getting up early and working. Now that she has nothing to do, she's like a fish out of water. She's grown thin and pale, and she's always crying, poor thing. *(Pause.)* You must have noticed it, Lopakhin. As you very well know, I'd always hoped to see her married to you. Indeed, everything seemed to indicate that you two would get married. *(She whispers to* ANYA, *who nods to* CHARLOTTE, *and they both go out.)* She loves you, you like her, and I simply don't know why you two always seem to avoid each other. I don't understand it.

LOPAKHIN: To tell you the truth, neither do I. The whole thing's odd somehow. If there's still time, I'm ready even now. . . . Let's settle it at once and get it over. I don't feel I'll ever propose to her without you here.

MRS. RANEVSKY: Excellent! Why, it shouldn't take more than a minute. I'll call her at once.

LOPAKHIN: And there's champagne here too. Appropriate to the occasion. *(Looks at the glasses.)* They're empty. Someone must have drunk it. *(*YASHA *coughs.)* Lapped it up, I call it.

MRS. RANEVSKY *(excitedly)*: Fine! We'll go out. Yasha, *allez!* I'll call her. *(Through the door.)* Varya, leave what you're doing and come here for a moment. Come on.

*(*MRS. RANEVSKY *goes out with* YASHA.*)*

LOPAKHIN *(glancing at his watch)*: Aye. . . .

(Pause. Behind the door suppressed laughter and whispering can be heard. Enter VARYA.*)*

VARYA *(spends a long time examining the luggage)*: Funny, can't find it.

LOPAKHIN: What are you looking for?

VARYA: Packed it myself, and can't remember.

(Pause.)

LOPAKHIN: Where are you going now, Varya?

VARYA: Me? To the Ragulins'. I've agreed to look after their house—to be their housekeeper, I suppose.

LOPAKHIN: In Yashnevo, isn't it? About fifty miles from here. *(Pause.)* Aye. . . . So life's come to an end in this house.

VARYA *(examining the luggage)*: Where can it be? Must have put it in the trunk. Yes, life's come to an end in this house. It will never come back.

LOPAKHIN: I'm off to Kharkov by the same train. Lots to see to there. I'm leaving Yepikhodov here to keep an eye on things. I've given him the job.

VARYA: Have you?

LOPAKHIN: This time last year it was already snowing, you remember. Now it's calm and sunny. A bit cold, though. Three degrees of frost.

VARYA: I haven't looked. *(Pause.)* Anyway, our thermometer's broken.

(Pause. A voice from outside, through the door: "Mr. Lopakhin!")

LOPAKHIN *(as though he had long been expecting this call)*: Coming! *(Goes out quickly.)*

*(*VARYA *sits down on the floor, lays her head on a bundle of clothes, and sobs quietly. The door opens and* MRS. RANEVSKY *comes in cautiously.)*

MRS. RANEVSKY: Well? *(Pause.)* We must go.

VARYA *(no longer crying, dries her eyes)*: Yes, it's time, Mother dear. I'd like to get to the Ragulins' today, I only hope we don't miss the train.

MRS. RANEVSKY *(calling through the door)*: Anya, put your things on.

(Enter ANYA, *followed by* GAYEV *and* CHARLOTTE. GAYEV *wears a warm overcoat with a hood.* SERVANTS *and* COACHMEN *come in.* YEPIKHODOV *is busy with the luggage.)*

MRS. RANEVSKY: Now we can be on our way.

ANYA *(joyfully)*: On our way. Oh, yes!

GAYEV: My friends, my dear, dear friends, leaving this house for good, how can I remain silent, how can I, before parting from you, refrain from expressing the feelings which now pervade my whole being—

ANYA *(imploringly)*: Uncle!

VARYA: Uncle dear, please don't.

GAYEV *(dejectedly)*: Double the red into the middle. . . . Not another word!

(Enter TROFIMOV, *followed by* LOPAKHIN.*)*

TROFIMOV: Well, ladies and gentlemen, it's time to go.

LOPAKHIN: Yepikhodov, my coat!

MRS. RANEVSKY: Let me sit down a minute. I feel as though I've never seen the walls and ceilings of this house before. I look at them now with such eagerness, with such tender emotion. . . .

GAYEV: I remember when I was six years old sitting on this window sill on Trinity Sunday and watching Father going to church.

MRS. RANEVSKY: Have all the things been taken out?

LOPAKHIN: I think so. *(To* YEPIKHODOV *as he puts on his coat.)* Mind, everything's all right here, Yepikhodov.

YEPIKHODOV *(in a hoarse voice)*: Don't you worry, sir.

LOPAKHIN: What's the matter with your voice?

YEPIKHODOV: I've just had a drink of water and I must have swallowed something.

YASHA *(contemptuously)*: What ignorance!

MRS. RANEVSKY: There won't be a soul left in this place when we've gone.

LOPAKHIN: Not till next spring.

(VARYA *pulls an umbrella out of a bundle of clothes with such force that it looks as if she were going to hit someone with it;* LOPAKHIN *pretends to be frightened.*)

VARYA: Good heavens, you didn't really think that—

TROFIMOV: Come on, let's get into the carriages! It's time. The train will be in soon.

VARYA: There are your galoshes, Peter. By that suitcase. (*Tearfully.*) Oh, how dirty they are, how old. . . .

TROFIMOV (*putting on his galoshes*): Come along, ladies and gentlemen.

(*Pause.*)

GAYEV (*greatly put out, afraid of bursting into tears*): Train . . . station . . . in off into the middle pocket . . . double the white into the corner.

MRS. RANEVSKY: Come along!

LOPAKHIN: Is everyone here? No one left behind? (*Locks the side door on the left.*) There are some things in there. I'd better keep it locked. Come on!

ANYA: Good-bye, old house! Good-bye, old life!

TROFIMOV: Welcome new life!

(TROFIMOV *goes out with* ANYA. VARYA *casts a last look round the room and goes out unhurriedly.* YASHA *and* CHARLOTTE, *carrying her lap dog, go out.*)

LOPAKHIN: So, it's till next spring. Come along, ladies and gentlemen. Till we meet again. (*Goes out.*)

(MRS. RANEVSKY *and* GAYEV *are left alone. They seem to have been waiting for this moment. They fling their arms around each other, sobbing quietly, restraining themselves, as though afraid of being overheard.*)

GAYEV (*in despair*): My sister! My sister!

MRS. RANEVSKY: Oh, my dear, my sweet, my beautiful orchard! My life, my youth, my happiness, good-bye! . . .

ANYA (*offstage, happily, appealingly*): Mo-ther!

TROFIMOV (*offstage, happily, excited*): Where are you?

MRS. RANEVSKY: One last look at the walls and the windows. Mother loved to walk in this room.

GAYEV: My sister, my sister!

ANYA (*offstage*): Mo-ther!

TROFIMOV (*offstage*): Where are you?

MRS. RANEVSKY: We're coming.

(*They go out. The stage is empty. The sound of all the doors being locked is heard, then of carriages driving off. It grows quiet. The silence is broken by the muffled noise of an axe striking a tree, sounding forlorn and sad. Footsteps can be heard.* FIRS *appears from the door on the right. He is dressed, as always, in a jacket and white waistcoat. He is wearing slippers. He looks ill.*)

FIRS (*walks up to the door and tries the handle*): Locked! They've gone. (*Sits down on the sofa.*) Forgot all about me. Never mind. Let me sit down here for a bit. Forgotten to put on his fur coat, the young master has. Sure of it. Gone off in his light overcoat. (*Sighs anxiously.*) I should have seen to it. . . . Oh, these youngsters! (*Mutters something which cannot be understood.*) My life's gone just as if I'd never lived. . . . (*Lies down.*) I'll lie down a bit. No strength left. Nothing's left. Nothing. Ugh, you— nincompoop! (*Lies motionless.*)

(*A distant sound is heard, which seems to come from the sky, the sound of a breaking string, slowly dying away, melancholy. It is followed by silence, broken only by the sound of an axe striking a tree far away in the orchard.*)

CURTAIN

Figure 1. "Don't laugh at me!" yells Lopakhin (David Troughton) as he brags about buying the cherry orchard and the estate. Behind him, watching in stunned disbelief are Pishchik (James Hayes, *left*), Mrs. Ranevsky (Penelope Wilton, *seated*), and, in the background, Yepikhodov (John Douglass), the Stationmaster (Gary Taylor), Servant (Lisé Stevenson), and Yasha (Mark Lockyer). The 1995 Royal Shakespeare Company production of *The Cherry Orchard* was directed by Adrian Noble. (Photograph: Malcolm Davies, Shakespeare Centre Library.)

Figure 2. The strange and distant sound, described by Chekhov as "a breaking string," startles the listeners in Act 2 of *The Cherry Orchard* in the 1995 Royal Shakespeare Company production. Firs (Peter Copley, *left*) and Trofimov (Sean Murray, *right*) frame the central group: Mrs. Ranevsky (Penelope Wilton, *center*), Varya (Kate Duchêne, *seated left*), Anya (Lucy Whybrow, *seated right*), Gayev (Alec McCowen, *standing behind bench*), and Lopakhin (David Troughton, on *floor*). (Photograph: Malcolm Davies, Shakespeare Centre Library.)

Figure 3. In the Royal Shakespeare Company production, Varya (Kate Duchêne) pretends to search for something in one of the many suitcases piled up before Mrs. Ranevsky's departure while actually waiting for Lopakhin (David Troughton) to propose marriage. (Photograph: Malcolm Davies, Shakespeare Centre Library.)

Figure 4. In the last minutes of the Royal Shakespeare Company production, the aged Firs (Peter Copley) is left alone on an empty stage, in an empty house. (Photograph: Malcolm Davies, Shakespeare Centre Library.)

Staging of *The Cherry Orchard*

PENELOPE WILTON ON PLAYING
MADAME RANEVSKAYA

Madame Ranevskaya's° journey is very complicated. Her name, Luba,° means light, and I don't think Chekhov chose that by mistake. She is light. When she comes into a room, people like to be with her. She makes things happen. When she's not there, nothing happens, it's dead. I think she is a selfish woman, but she's not selfish insofar as she's cruelly selfish, she's selfish because she's a survivor. She adores her children, but the most important person in the play, to her, is her lover in Paris, whom she's obsessed by. And I think that's a very sexual relationship, so those telegrams that keep coming, churn her up. She's left because he's behaved appallingly; he's left her for another woman, gone through all her money, she's got nothing left, and she comes home. But she does come from a period of time where people of her class were hopeless. She's never had to do a thing in her life, there's been an enormous estate, they've gone through the money, she and her brother. She married the wrong person; she's ruled by her heart; she didn't marry an aristocrat as she was supposed to, in the world she comes from. She married for love; he turned out to be a drunk, then she fell in love with someone else, and she went away, and he followed her. She went away because her son died, he was drowned; she has had enormous tragedy in her life. A son drowning at 7 is the most terrible thing. She lives for the moment, she lives life to the full.

I think that the character of Madame Ranevskaya, the Russians knew about. As with *War and Peace,* there's this aristocratic woman who follows her heart, and they're always looked on by the society from which they come as being terrible, but actually they're rather impulsive, very warm people, who love life. If life is terrible, let's throw a party. The sort of people that people like to read about in *Hello* magazine; people live vicariously through them; they see them, and they think, 'Oh, isn't it terrible, she's had this child when she wasn't married, or she's gone off with her lover'. I think he's written her very, very clearly. And she's a mother, a very loving mother. If things had been better in Paris, I think she'd have sent for Anya. But if you're going around Europe with a lover that's behaving appallingly, you can't manage to have a ten-year-old child with you. Her little boy had died, and I think she was grief-stricken and wanted to get out.

I'm afraid of what happens to her, after the play is over. I mean, she is entirely selfish, and she takes the money that the great-aunt sent from Yaroslava, which was about 15,000 roubles, and goes to Paris, and I think she'll stay somewhere and her lover will come back to her, and as soon as the money goes, he'll push off again. This is me, the actress speaking. Madame Ranevskaya doesn't look about tomorrow, or next week, she wants to get back to him more than anything. But I think, as the actress, what will happen to her is that he will go through the money and leave her again, and she'll end up in one of those cosmopolitan cafés telling people that she once had a big estate in Russia, and people will say 'Ah,' and she'll have a bed-sitting room, and go to the Russian Orthodox church, and be known as an eccentric.

I think one has to understand the relationship that Russian aristocracy had with servants. It's not like an English relationship. We had servants, but it was based on class in a way that I don't think was the same in Russia. The English class system is much more snobbish— you don't talk to servants. I don't think that was entirely the case in Russia, it was much more a family thing, much more patriarchal, you looked after everybody. I think the relationship with Lopakhin, for example, is one partly of necessity and partly because she's not a snob. She's had a much more worldly view of life, and she likes people. I don't think it's a complicated relationship. She admires him, and also he's a source of money! And he might marry Varya. When we were rehearsing this play, it was interesting to work out who you actually spoke to in the play, and who you didn't. I never once address Charlotte, or mention her name. I never once mention Epihodov's name, but I think I speak to everybody else. If you put into a room all those actors, and say 'Go and stand next to whom you stand by,' they all talk to me, except for Epihodov and Charlotte. It's interesting; she has a relationship with nearly everybody.

Another thing about Ranevskaya is her grief over the loss of her little boy. I don't think you get over grief. You think about it less, but when you're met with it again, I don't think you ever quite manage it. That's been my experience. My mother died very sadly of cancer, very badly, and I don't ever get over that. If I allowed myself to think about it, it would upset me as

---

Ranevskaya, Russian feminine form of Ranevsky, retained in some translations of this play.   *Luba*, actually Lyuba, is the nickname for Lyubov, which means *love*.

much now as it ever did. As time passes you think about it less. My sister gave me a photograph—of my mother and my father, who are both dead now—just the other day, of them laughing, and I immediately burst into tears, because it's just so: 'They're not there.' And that's the same thing in *The Cherry Orchard,* Trofimov catches her at a very, very vulnerable moment. She's very tired, it's two o'clock in the morning; seeing everybody again, she hasn't seen anyone for five years, and then this person from the past walks in—that's where Chekhov is brilliant, to bring him in at that moment—and I think it's too much. 'Why was he drowned, why? Why was it my son?' That's the question people always ask when something terrible happens. It's a mixture of enormous sadness and anger. I think that bond with Trofimov is based on the fact that he was my son's tutor, he was the nearest thing to my little boy. I can only remember thinking 'What would I feel if I were suddenly reminded of my little boy's death?' You don't see a person from your past for a long time, and then suddenly, there is the person who was as close to your little boy as you were, and she nearly collapses. It's a movement that came about in rehearsal, and that's what we'd decided to do. It doesn't change. Sometimes it's better than other times, because it's not easy to act that sort of thing every night. I just try and get better. You're never, and this is not being falsely modest, you're never really pleased. I mean there are a few times when you're really delighted. As you get older, you essentially try to do less, and it goes deeper, and it becomes more fermented. That's what you try to do.

BERNARD SHAW

1856–1950

Shaw did not write his first play until he was thirty-six, but by the time of his death he had written forty-seven full-length plays as well as a number of playlets and thus had become one of the most prolific dramatists in the history of the English theater. He was born and raised in Dublin in the midst of an unhappy marriage, his father an unsuccessful merchant who turned to drink, his mother a talented singer who scorned the domestic chores of tending a household. By the time he was fifteen, he had dropped out of school, where according to his own account he learned only that schools are a form of imprisonment; by the time he was twenty he had abandoned an office job in Dublin and gone to live in London with his mother, who was a professional teacher of music. Shaw had vowed never to do another "honest day's work" but to make his way in the world as a writer, and from 1876 to 1885 he leaned on his mother for financial support while he turned out five novels, none of which he was able to get published.

Although the early 1880s were a period of literary frustration for Shaw, they proved to be a time in which he made intellectual discoveries that were to influence most of his thinking and writing. In 1882 he first heard about Karl Marx and subsequently became a lifelong convert to socialism, confessing later that "the importance of the economic basis of society dawned on me" and that "Marx made a man of me." Then in 1884, having studied *Das Kapital* in a Marxist reading circle, he joined the Fabians, a socialist group that, though influenced by Marx, regarded the state not as a class structure to be overthrown but as a social mechanism to be gradually altered and used for the promotion of public welfare. To achieve this goal, Shaw and his Fabian colleagues publicized their positions on every economic, political, and social issue of the day—from local government reform to reform of the poor laws, from trade unionism to women's rights—making their views known in leaflets, newspapers, pamphlets, and books, in lecture halls and on street corners. By the late 1880s Shaw was also writing art criticism, book reviews, and music criticism for several London newspapers. And in 1891, he also made his views known on the state of drama by publishing *The Quintessence of Ibsenism,* a fiery little book in which he sought to awaken English theatergoers to the social consciousness embodied in Ibsen's plays (see Ideas of Drama).

Having sharpened his prose on so wide a variety of cultural and social issues, Shaw himself was uniquely prepared to become the English counterpart of Ibsen, and in 1892 he launched his theatrical career with *Widowers' Houses,* a dramatic attack on the evils of slum landlordism, which he showed to be an emblem of the capitalist system. But even in this first play, as in nearly all of the others he was to write, Shaw's dramatic technique was vastly different from that of Ibsen. Whereas Ibsen had probed the inner lives and problems of his characters in plays suffused with a Scandinavian air of gloom, Shaw turned his characters into witty spokespersons for his social and political views. Shaw's experience in politics and critical reviewing had clearly taught him that comic wit is often the most powerful means of awakening an audience and winning its support.

In the years that followed his first play, Shaw used his comic techniques to expose and satirize an astonishing array of follies or evils in economics, politics, society, theology, morality, and science. In *Mrs. Warren's Profession* (1893), a play about prostitution, he showed that "rich men without conviction are more dangerous in modern society than poor women without chastity." In *Arms and the Man* (1894), he mocked romantic notions about love and war by making his hero a blunt realist who throws away his cartridges and replaces them with chocolates because he knows enough to realize that cartridges will be useless during a cavalry charge but chocolates will be invaluable after the charge is over. In *Candida* (1895), he challenged conventional ideas of marriage by creating as his heroine a very superior woman whose strength is revealed to lie in the way she conceals her strength. In *Caesar and Cleopatra* (1899), he mocked Shakespeare's view of Roman history, as it had been presented in *Julius Caesar* and *Antony and Cleopatra,* by turning Cleopatra into a naive and fearful sixteen-year-old, who is schooled in political wisdom by the hero of the play, Caesar. For Shaw, Caesar was a "naturally great" man precisely because he was free from conventional moral beliefs as well as charmingly self-aware of his limitations.

Though Shaw saw clearly how human beings are often imprisoned by conventional morality, he could imagine the possibility of human beings and social institutions liberating themselves as well. In *Major Barbara* (1905), he created one of his most compelling embodiments of the "life force," Andrew Undershaft, who overturns sentimental moralizing about poverty by providing well-paying jobs rather than Salvation Army handouts; the munitions maker is thus both the merchant of destruction and the creator of meaningful labor. And yet when the weapons of Undershaft came to dominate Europe during World War I, Shaw was quick to dramatize the destructive social and political bankruptcy of his generation. For example, in *Heartbreak House* (1919, though he began writing it in 1913), Shaw portrayed his withering vision of "cultured, leisured Europe before the war" by showing it to be incapable of shaking off its laziness and shallowness. Later, *Saint Joan* (1923) dramatized the tragic conflict between political institutions and genius, ending with a scene in which the martyred Joan returns as a dream-vision twenty-five years after she has been burnt. But when she offers to return as a living woman, everyone shrinks from the prospect in dismay.

Shaw expressed his views not only in his plays but also in prefaces and notes that he wrote for the published versions of the plays. By means of these commentaries, which were often as long as the plays themselves, Shaw used his incisive prose style to explicate his characters, plots, and themes as well as to gain a wider audience for his ideas than was possible in the theater. *Man and Superman* (1903), for example, which brilliantly dramatizes Shaw's ideas of the "life force" and "creative evolution," was published with a lengthy essay on modern society and the need for the superman, and with a tract called "The Revolutionists Handbook and Pocket Companion," which had been mentioned in the first act of the play.

For *Pygmalion* (1913), Shaw provided not only a preface but, more strikingly, an afterword, reprinted here following the play, in which he went on to explain what happened to his characters after the play. Shaw's insistence in the afterword that

Henry Higgins, the phonetics teacher, and Eliza Doolittle, the Cockney flower girl whose speech—and life—he transforms, *would not* get married constitutes an extraordinary attempt to control the audience's experience and understanding of the play as fully as possible. That Shaw ever attempted to exert such total control over his audience seems particularly ironic given the fact that both the play itself and the myth on which it is based are concerned with the problems that arise when one human being tries to exert such control over another. Within the play, Shaw explores the theme of control by turning the story of the mythical Greek sculptor Pygmalion, who created a beautiful statue and then saw it come to life, into the story of Higgins, who transforms a "draggletailed guttersnipe" into "a duchess." He corrects her accent, teaches her proper grammar, dresses her in beautiful clothes, and then watches with pride as the once dirty-faced flower girl moves successfully into "polite society."

But Shaw shows us that the reshaping of Eliza raises serious questions about any attempt to control or shape the lives of other people, especially those over whom one has some power, whether the power comes from class status or money or gender. Even before Higgins starts to teach Eliza, his housekeeper Mrs. Pearce asks, "And what is to become of her when youve finished your teaching?" Higgins's reply is flippant: "Whats to become of her if I leave her in the gutter?" Though Colonel Pickering, Higgins's friend, addresses Eliza politely as "Miss Doolittle," he is astonished to find out that Eliza has run away after her success at the ball and asks naïvely, "What did we do to her?" From Eliza's point of view, what they have done, rather than make a princess out of Cinderella, is destroy her life as a flower girl without offering her any new possibilities. Yet in the process of railing against her predicament, Eliza discovers that she has become independent, that she can teach others what Higgins has taught her. The real transformation, as Higgins realizes, is not in her speech but in her soul: "I said I'd make a woman of you; and I have."

Having made a woman of Eliza, Higgins comes tantalizingly close to finding himself in the situation of his mythic counterpart Pygmalion, who fell in love with the statue he had created. Thus Shaw examines the theme of control by dramatizing its effect not only on Eliza but also on Higgins—on the controller as well as on the one controlled. In flirting constantly with the possibility of a romantic relationship between Higgins and Eliza, Shaw ultimately invites his audience to ponder the fascinating—and disturbing—question of whether a seemingly amoral and heartless creator can be redeemed or transformed by his creation. Though Shaw left the question open in the play itself and answered it negatively in the afterword, the film of *Pygmalion,* for which Shaw wrote the screenplay and received an Academy Award, ends with a scene that implies a distinctly different answer from his afterword. Specifically, as Higgins is shown sitting alone in his study, listening to the recording he made when Eliza first appeared there, Eliza herself returns, her own voice replacing the mechanical one. Shaw probably did not write this scene, though he seems to have given it tacit approval, but it is the same scene that also comes at the end of *My Fair Lady* (1956), the highly successful musical based on *Pygmalion.*

Yet, as Ronald Bryden's review of the 1974 London production of *Pygmalion* makes clear, Shaw's insistence that Eliza does not marry Higgins is also stageworthy and even more relevant to contemporary audiences. Though Higgins may have power because of his education and because he is a man, he is finally unwilling to change and to grow or, in Alec McCowen's portrayal, to grow up. By contrast, Diana Rigg's Eliza, beginning as a messy figure with tattered gloves and wildly feathered hat (see Figure 1) can change, as she is first transformed into an elegantly gowned woman who fascinates polite society (see Figure 3). But the real transformation is internal. Rigg's Eliza ends as a poised figure even with Higgins's hand on her throat (see Figure 2). Indeed, the look on her face makes clear that, while she may be attracted to Higgins, she can also resist both the visible threat and the implied caress. Yet the fact that Shaw had to argue so long for that resistance indicates the enduring power of the desire for romance, a desire *Pygmalion* continues to evoke and to question.

PYGMALION

BY BERNARD SHAW

CHARACTERS

CLARA EYNSFORD HILL, *daughter of*
MRS EYNSFORD HILL, *a lady*
FREDDY EYNSFORD HILL, *the lady's son*
ELIZA DOOLITTLE, *a flower girl*
COLONEL PICKERING, *British officer, amateur phonetician*
PROFESSOR HENRY HIGGINS, *a phonetician*

MRS PEARCE, *Professor Higgins's housekeeper*
ALFRED DOOLITTLE, *Eliza's father, a dust (garbage) man*
MRS HIGGINS, *Professor Higgins's mother*

SCENE

The present

PREFACE TO PYGMALION
A Professor of Phonetics

As will be seen later on, Pygmalion needs, not a preface, but a sequel, which I have supplied in its due place.

The English have no respect for their language, and will not teach their children to speak it. They spell it so abominably that no man can teach himself what it sounds like. It is impossible for an Englishman to open his mouth without making some other Englishman hate or despise him. German and Spanish are accessible to foreigners: English is not accessible even to Englishmen. The reformer England needs today is an energetic phonetic enthusiast: that is why I have made such a one the hero of a popular play. There have been heroes of that kind crying in the wilderness for many years past. When I became interested in the subject towards the end of the eighteen-seventies, the illustrious Alexander Melville Bell, the inventor of Visible Speech, had emigrated to Canada, where his son invented the telephone; but Alexander J. Ellis was still a London patriarch, with an impressive head always covered by a velvet skull cap, for which he would apologize to public meetings in a very courtly manner. He and Tito Pagliardini, another phonetic veteran, were men whom it was impossible to dislike. Henry Sweet, then a young man, lacked their sweetness of character: he was about as conciliatory to conventional mortals as Ibsen or Samuel Butler. His great ability as a phonetician (he was, I think, the best of them all at his job) would have entitled him to high official recognition, and perhaps enabled him to popularize his subject, but for his Satanic contempt for all academic dignitaries and persons in general who thought more of Greek than of phonetics. Once, in the days when the Imperial Institute rose in South Kensington, and Joseph Chamberlain was booming the Empire, I induced the editor of a leading monthly review to commission an article from Sweet on the imperial importance of his subject. When it arrived, it contained nothing but a savagely derisive attack on a professor of language and literature whose chair Sweet regarded as proper to a phonetic expert only. The article, being libellous, had to be returned as impossible; and I had to renounce my dream of dragging its author into the limelight. When I met him afterwards, for the first time for many years, I found to my astonishment that he, who had been a quite tolerably presentable young man, had actually managed by sheer scorn to alter his personal appearance until he had become a sort of walking repudiation of Oxford and all its traditions. It must have been largely in his own despite that he was squeezed into something called a Readership of phonetics there. The future of phonetics rests probably with his pupils, who all swore by him; but nothing could bring the man himself into any sort of compliance with the university to which he nevertheless clung by divine right in an intensely Oxonian way. I daresay his papers, if he has left any, include some satires that may be published without too destructive results fifty years hence. He was, I believe, not in the least an ill-natured man: very much the opposite, I should say; but he would not suffer fools gladly.

Those who knew him will recognize in my third act the allusion to the patent shorthand in which he used to write postcards, and which may be acquired from a four and sixpenny manual published by the Clarendon Press. The postcards which Mrs Higgins describes are such as I have received from Sweet. I would decipher a sound which a cockney would represent by *zerr,* and a Frenchman by *seu,* and then write demanding with some heat what on earth it meant. Sweet, with boundless contempt for my stupidity, would reply that it not only meant but obviously was the word Result, as no other word containing that sound, and capable of making sense with the context, existed in any language spoken on earth. That less expert mortals should require fuller indications was beyond Sweet's patience. Therefore, though the whole point of his

Current Shorthand is that it can express every sound in the language perfectly, vowels as well as consonants, and that your hand has to make no stroke except the easy and current ones with which you write m, n, and u, l, p, and q, scribbling them at whatever angle comes easiest to you, his unfortunate determination to make this remarkable and quite legible script serve also as a shorthand reduced it in his own practice to the most inscrutable of cryptograms. His true objective was the provision of a full, accurate, legible script for our noble but ill-dressed language; but he was led past that by his contempt for the popular Pitman system of shorthand, which he called the Pitfall system. The triumph of Pitman was a triumph of business organization: there was a weekly paper to persuade you to learn Pitman: there were cheap textbooks and exercise books and transcripts of speeches for you to copy, and schools where experienced teachers coached you up to the necessary proficiency. Sweet could not organize his market in that fashion. He might as well have been the Sybil who tore up the leaves of prophecy that nobody would attend to. The four and sixpenny manual, mostly in his lithographed handwriting, that was never vulgarly advertized, may perhaps some day be taken up by a syndicate and pushed upon the public as The Times pushed the Encyclopædia Britannica; but until then it will certainly not prevail against Pitman. I have bought three copies of it during my lifetime; and I am informed by the publishers that its cloistered existence is still a steady and healthy one. I actually learned the system two several times; and yet the shorthand in which I am writing these lines is Pitman's. And the reason is, that my secretary cannot transcribe Sweet, having been perforce taught in the schools of Pitman. Therefore, Sweet railed at Pitman as vainly as Thersites railed at Ajax: his raillery, however it may have eased his soul, gave no popular vogue to Current Shorthand.

Pygmalion Higgins is not a portrait of Sweet, to whom the adventure of Eliza Doolittle would have been impossible; still, as will be seen, there are touches of Sweet in the play. With Higgins's physique and temperament Sweet might have set the Thames on fire. As it was, he impressed himself professionally on Europe to an extent that made his comparative personal obscurity, and the failure of Oxford to do justice to his eminence, a puzzle to foreign specialists in his subject. I do not blame Oxford, because I think Oxford is quite right in demanding a certain social amenity from its nurslings (heaven knows it is not exorbitant in its requirements!); for although I well know how hard it is for a man of genius with a seriously underrated subject to maintain serene and kindly relations with the men who underrate it, and who keep all the best places for less important subjects which they profess without originality and sometimes without much capacity for them, still, if he overwhelms

them with wrath and disdain, he cannot expect them to heap honors on him.

Of the later generations of phoneticians I know little. Among them towers the Poet Laureate, to whom perhaps Higgins may owe his Miltonic sympathies, though here again I must disclaim all portraiture. But if the play makes the public aware that there are such people as phoneticians, and that they are among the most important people in England at present, it will serve its turn.

I wish to boast that Pygmalion has been an extremely successful play all over Europe and North America as well as at home. It is so intensely and deliberately didactic, and its subject is esteemed so dry, that I delight in throwing it at the heads of the wiseacres who repeat the parrot cry that art should never be didactic. It goes to prove my contention that art should never be anything else.

Finally, and for the encouragement of people troubled with accents that cut them off from all high employment, I may add that the change wrought by Professor Higgins in the flower-girl is neither impossible nor uncommon. The modern concierge's daughter who fulfills her ambition by playing the Queen of Spain in Ruy Blas at the Théâtre Français is only one of many thousands of men and women who have sloughed off their native dialects and acquired a new tongue. But the thing has to be done scientifically, or the last state of the aspirant may be worse than the first. An honest and natural slum dialect is more tolerable than the attempt of a phonetically untaught person to imitate the vulgar dialect of the golf club; and I am sorry to say that in spite of the efforts of our Royal Academy of Dramatic Art, there is still too much sham golfing English on our stage, and too little of the noble English of Forbes Robertson.

ACT 1

(Covent Garden at 11.15 p.m. Torrents of heavy summer rain. Cab whistles blowing frantically in all directions. Pedestrians running for shelter into the market and under the portico of St Paul's Church, where there are already several people, among them a lady and her daughter in evening dress. They are all peering out gloomily at the rain, except one man with his back turned to the rest, who seems wholly preoccupied with a notebook in which he is writing busily.

The church clock strikes the first quarter.)

THE DAUGHTER *(in the space between the central pillars, close to the one on her left)*: I'm getting chilled to the bone. What can Freddy be doing all this time? He's been gone twenty minutes.

THE MOTHER *(on her daughter's right)*: Not so long. But he ought to have got us a cab by this.

A BYSTANDER *(on the lady's right)*: He wont get no cab

not until half-past eleven, missus, when they come back after dropping their theatre fares.

THE MOTHER: But we must have a cab. We cant stand here until half-past eleven. It's too bad.

THE BYSTANDER: Well, it aint my fault, missus.

THE DAUGHTER: If Freddy had a bit of gumption, he would have got one at the theatre door.

THE MOTHER: What could he have done, poor boy?

THE DAUGHTER: Other people got cabs. Why couldnt he?

(FREDDY *rushes in out of the rain from the Southampton Street side, and comes between them closing a dripping umbrella. He is a young man of twenty, in evening dress, very wet round the ankles.*)

THE DAUGHTER: Well, havnt you got a cab?

FREDDY: Theres not one to be had for love or money.

THE MOTHER: Oh, Freddy, there must be one. You cant have tried.

THE DAUGHTER: It's too tiresome. Do you expect us to go and get one ourselves?

FREDDY: I tell you theyre all engaged. The rain was so sudden: nobody was prepared; and everybody had to take a cab. Ive been to Charing Cross one way and nearly to Ludgate Circus the other; and they were all engaged.

THE MOTHER: Did you try Trafalgar Square?

FREDDY: There wasnt one at Trafalgar Square.

THE DAUGHTER: Did you try?

FREDDY: I tried as far as Charing Cross station. Did you expect me to walk to Hammersmith?

THE DAUGHTER: You havnt tried at all.

THE MOTHER: You really are very helpless, Freddy. Go again; and dont come back until you have found a cab.

FREDDY: I shall simply get soaked for nothing.

THE DAUGHTER: And what about us? Are we to stay here all night in this draught, with next to nothing on? You selfish pig—

FREDDY: Oh, very well: I'll go, I'll go. (*He opens his umbrella and dashes off Strandwards, but comes into collision with a flower girl, who is hurrying in for shelter, knocking her basket out of her hands. A blinding flash of lightning, followed instantly by a rattling peal of thunder, orchestrates the incident.*)

THE FLOWER GIRL: Nah then, Freddy: look wh'y' gowin, deah.

FREDDY: Sorry (*he rushes off*).

THE FLOWER GIRL (*picking up her scattered flowers and replacing them in the basket*): Theres menners f' yer! Te-oo banches o voylets trod into the mad. (*She sits down on the plinth of the column, sorting her flowers, on the lady's right. She is not at all an attractive person. She is perhaps eighteen, perhaps twenty, hardly older. She wears a little sailor hat of black straw that has long been exposed to the dust and soot of London and has seldom if ever been brushed. Her hair needs washing rather*

badly: its mousy color can hardly be natural. She wears a shoddy black coat that reaches nearly to her knees and is shaped to her waist. She has a brown skirt with a coarse apron. Her boots are much the worse for wear. She is no doubt as clean as she can afford to be; but compared to the ladies she is very dirty. Her features are no worse than theirs; but their condition leaves something to be desired; and she needs the services of a dentist.)

THE MOTHER: How do you know that my son's name is Freddy, pray?

THE FLOWER GIRL: Ow, eez ye-ooa san, is e? Wal, fewd dan y' de-ooty bawmz a mather should, eed now bettern to spawl a pore gel's flahrzn than ran awy athaht pyin. Will ye-oo py me f'them? (*Here, with apologies, this desperate attempt to present her dialect without a phonetic alphabet must be abandoned as unintelligible outside London.*)

THE DAUGHTER: Do nothing of the sort, mother. The idea!

THE MOTHER: Please allow me, Clara. Have you any pennies?

THE DAUGHTER: No. I've nothing smaller than sixpence.

THE FLOWER GIRL (*hopefully*): I can give you change for a tanner, kind lady.

THE MOTHER (*to CLARA*): Give it to me. (CLARA *parts reluctantly.*) Now (*to the girl*) this is for your flowers.

THE FLOWER GIRL: Thank you kindly, lady.

THE DAUGHTER: Make her give you the change. These things are only a penny a bunch.

THE MOTHER: Do hold your tongue, Clara. (*To the girl*) You can keep the change.

THE FLOWER GIRL: Oh, thank you, lady.

THE MOTHER: Now tell me how you know that young gentleman's name.

THE FLOWER GIRL: I didnt.

THE MOTHER: I heard you call him by it. Dont try to deceive me.

THE FLOWER GIRL (*protesting*): Who's trying to deceive you? I called him Freddy or Charlie same as you might yourself if you was talking to a stranger and wished to be pleasant. (*She sits down beside her basket.*)

THE DAUGHTER: Sixpence thrown away! Really, mamma, you might have spared Freddy that. (*She retreats in disgust behind the pillar.*)

(*An elderly gentleman of the amiable military type rushes into the shelter, and closes a dripping umbrella. He is in the same plight as* FREDDY, *very wet about the ankles. He is in evening dress, with a light overcoat. He takes the place left vacant by the daughter's retirement.*)

THE GENTLEMAN: Phew!

THE MOTHER (*to the gentleman*): Oh, sir, is there any sign of its stopping?

THE GENTLEMAN: I'm afraid not. It started worse than ever about two minutes ago (*he goes to the plinth beside the flower girl; puts up his foot on it; and stoops to turn down his trouser ends.)*

THE MOTHER: Oh dear! *(She retires sadly and joins her daughter.)*

THE FLOWER GIRL *(taking advantage of the military gentleman's proximity to establish friendly relations with him)*: If it's worse, it's a sign it's nearly over. So cheer up, Captain; and buy a flower off a poor girl.

THE GENTLEMAN: I m sorry. I havnt any change.

THE FLOWER GIRL: I can give you change, Captain.

THE GENTLEMAN: For a sovereign? Ive nothing less.

THE FLOWER GIRL: Garn! Oh do buy a flower off me, Captain. I can change half-a-crown. Take this for tuppence.

THE GENTLEMAN: Now dont be troublesome: theres a good girl. *(Trying his pockets)* I really havnt any change—Stop: heres three hapence, if thats any use to you *(he retreats to the other pillar).*

THE FLOWER GIRL *(disappointed, but thinking three half-pence better than nothing)*: Thank you, sir.

THE BYSTANDER *(to the girl)*: You be careful: give him a flower for it. Theres a bloke here behind taking down every blessed word youre saying. *(All turn to the man who is taking notes.)*

THE FLOWER GIRL *(springing up terrified)*: I aint done nothing wrong by speaking to the gentleman. Ive a right to sell flowers if I keep off the kerb. *(Hysterically)* I'm a respectable girl: so help me, I never spoke to him except to ask him to buy a flower off me. *(General hubbub, mostly sympathetic to the flower girl, but deprecating her excessive sensibility. Cries of* Dont start hollerin. Who's hurting you? Nobody's going to touch you. Whats the good of fussing? Steady on. Easy easy, etc., *come from the elderly staid spectators, who pat her comfortingly. Less patient ones bid her shut her head, or ask her roughly what is wrong with her. A remoter group, not knowing what the matter is, crowd in and increase the noise with question and answer:* Whats the row? Whatshe do? Where is he? A tec taking her down. What! him? Yes: him over there: Took money off the gentleman, etc. *The flower girl, distraught and mobbed, breaks through them to the gentleman, crying wildly)* Oh, sir, dont let him charge me. You dunno what it means to me. Theyll take away my character and drive me on the streets for speaking to gentlemen. They—

THE NOTE TAKER *(coming forward on her right, the rest crowding after him)*: There, there, there, there! who's hurting you, you silly girl? What do you take me for?

THE BYSTANDER: It's all right: he's a gentleman: look at his boots. *(Explaining to the note taker)* She thought you was a copper's nark, sir.

THE NOTE TAKER *(with quick interest)*: Whats a copper's nark?

THE BYSTANDER *(inapt at definition)*: It's a—well, it's a copper's nark, as you might say. What else would you call it? A sort of informer.

THE FLOWER GIRL *(still hysterical)*: I take my Bible oath I never said a word—

THE NOTE TAKER *(overbearing but good-humored)*: Oh, shut up, shut up. Do I look like a policeman?

THE FLOWER GIRL *(far from reassured)*: Then what did you take down my words for? How do I know whether you took me down right? You just shew me what youve wrote about me. *(The note taker opens his book and holds it steadily under her nose, though the pressure of the mob trying to read it over his shoulders would upset a weaker man.)* Whats that? That aint proper writing. I cant read that.

THE NOTE TAKER: I can. *(Reads, reproducing her pronunciation exactly)* "Cheer ap, Keptin; n' baw ya flahr orf a pore gel."

THE FLOWER GIRL *(much distressed)*: It's because I called him Captain. I meant no harm. *(To the gentleman)* Oh, sir, dont let him lay a charge agen me for a word like that. You—

THE GENTLEMAN: Charge! I make no charge. *(To the note taker)* Really, sir, if you are a detective, you need not begin protecting me against molestation by young women until I ask you. Anybody could see that the girl meant no harm.

THE BYSTANDERS GENERALLY *(demonstrating against police espionage)*: Course they could. What business is it of yours? You mind your own affairs. He wants promotion, he does. Taking down people's words! Girl never said a word to him. What harm if she did? Nice thing a girl cant shelter from the rain without being insulted, etc., etc., etc. *(She is conducted by the more sympathetic demonstrators back to her plinth, where she resumes her seat and struggles with her emotion.)*

THE BYSTANDER: He aint a tec. He's a blooming busybody: thats what he is. I tell you, look at his boots.

THE NOTE TAKER *(turning on him genially)*: And how are all your people down at Selsey?

THE BYSTANDER *(suspiciously)*: Who told you my people come from Selsey?

THE NOTE TAKER: Never you mind. They did. *(To the girl)* How do you come to be up so far east? You were born in Lisson Grove.

THE FLOWER GIRL *(appalled)*: Oh, what harm is there in my leaving Lisson Grove? It wasnt fit for a pig to live in; and I had to pay four-and-six a week. *(In tears)* Oh, boo—hoo—oo—

THE NOTE TAKER: Live where you like; but stop that noise.

THE GENTLEMAN *(to the girl)*: Come, come! he cant touch you: you have a right to live where you please.

A SARCASTIC BYSTANDER *(thrusting himself between the note taker and the gentleman)*: Park Lane, for instance. I'd like to go into the Housing Question with you, I would.

THE FLOWER GIRL (*subsiding into a brooding melancholy over her basket, and talking very low-spiritedly to herself*): I'm a good girl, I am.

THE SARCASTIC BYSTANDER (*not attending to her*): Do you know where *I* come from?

THE NOTE TAKER (*promptly*): Hoxton.

(*Titterings. Popular interest in the note taker's performance increases.*)

THE SARCASTIC ONE (*amazed*): Well, who said I didnt? Bly me! You know everything, you do.

THE FLOWER GIRL (*still nursing her sense of injury*): Aint no call to meddle with me, he aint.

THE BYSTANDER (*to her*): Of course he aint. Dont you stand it from him. (*To the note taker*) See here: what call have you to know about people what never offered to meddle with you? Wheres your warrant?

SEVERAL BYSTANDERS (*encouraged by this seeming point of law*): Yes: wheres your warrant?

THE FLOWER GIRL: Let him say what he likes. I dont want to have no truck with him.

THE BYSTANDER: You take us for dirt under your feet, dont you? Catch you taking liberties with a gentleman!

THE SARCASTIC BYSTANDER: Yes: tell him where he come from if you want to go fortune-telling.

THE NOTE TAKER: Cheltenham, Harrow, Cambridge, and India.

THE GENTLEMAN: Quite right. (*Great laughter. Reaction in the note taker's favor. Exclamations of* He knows all about it. Told him proper. Hear him tell the toff where he come from? *etc.*) May I ask, sir, do you do this for your living at a music hall?

THE NOTE TAKER: Ive thought of that. Perhaps I shall some day.

(*The rain has stopped; and the persons on the outside of the crowd begin to drop off.*)

THE FLOWER GIRL (*resenting the reaction*): He's no gentleman, he aint, to interfere with a poor girl.

THE DAUGHTER (*out of patience, pushing her way rudely to the front and displacing the gentleman, who politely retires to the other side of the pillar*): What on earth is Freddy doing? I shall get pneumonia if I stay in this draught any longer.

THE NOTE TAKER (*to himself, hastily making a note of her pronunciation of "monia"*): Earlscourt.

THE DAUGHTER (*violently*): Will you please keep your impertinent remarks to yourself.

THE NOTE TAKER: Did I say that out loud? I didnt mean to. I beg your pardon. Your mother's Epsom, unmistakably.

THE MOTHER (*advancing between her daughter and the note taker*): How very curious! I was brought up in Largelady Park, near Epsom.

THE NOTE TAKER (*uproariously amused*): Ha! ha! What a devil of a name! Excuse me. (*To the daughter*) You want a cab, do you?

THE DAUGHTER: Dont dare speak to me.

THE MOTHER: Oh please, please, Clara. (*Her daughter repudiates her with an angry shrug and retires haughtily.*) We should be so grateful to you, sir, if you found us a cab. (*The note taker produces a whistle.*) Oh, thank you. (*She joins her daughter.*)

(*The note taker blows a piercing blast.*)

THE SARCASTIC BYSTANDER: There! I knowed he was a plain-clothes copper.

THE BYSTANDER: That aint a police whistle: thats a sporting whistle.

THE FLOWER GIRL (*still preoccupied with her wounded feelings*): He's no right to take away my character. My character is the same as any lady's.

THE NOTE TAKER: I dont know whether youve noticed it; but the rain stopped about two minutes ago.

THE BYSTANDER: So it has. Why didnt you say so before? and us losing our time listening to your silliness! (*He walks off towards the Strand.*)

THE SARCASTIC BYSTANDER: I can tell where you come from. You come from Anwell. Go back there.

THE NOTE TAKER (*helpfully*): Hanwell.

THE SARCASTIC BYSTANDER (*affecting great distinction of speech*): Thenk you, teacher. Haw haw! So long (*he touches his hat with mock respect and strolls off*).

THE FLOWER GIRL: Frightening people like that! How would he like it himself?

THE MOTHER: It's quite fine now, Clara. We can walk to a motor bus. Come. (*She gathers her skirts above her ankles and hurries off towards the Strand.*)

THE DAUGHTER: But the cab—(*her mother is out of hearing*). Oh, how tiresome! (*She follows angrily.*)

(*All the rest have gone except the note taker, the gentleman, and the flower girl, who sits arranging her basket and still pitying herself in murmurs.*)

THE FLOWER GIRL: Poor girl! Hard enough for her to live without being worrited and chivied.

THE GENTLEMAN (*returning to his former place on the note taker's left*): How do you do it, if I may ask?

THE NOTE TAKER: Simply phonetics. The science of speech. Thats my profession: also my hobby. Happy is the man who can make a living by his hobby! You can spot an Irishman or a Yorkshireman by his brogue. *I* can place any man within six miles. I can place him within two miles in London. Sometimes within two streets.

THE FLOWER GIRL: Ought to be ashamed of himself, unmanly coward!

THE GENTLEMAN: But is there a living in that?

THE NOTE TAKER: Oh yes. Quite a fat one. This is an age of upstarts. Men begin in Kentish Town with £80 a year, and end in Park Lane with a hundred thousand. They want to drop Kentish Town; but they give themselves away every time they open their mouths. Now I can teach them—

THE FLOWER GIRL: Let him mind his own business and leave a poor girl—

THE NOTE TAKER (*explosively*): Woman: cease this detestable boohooing instantly; or else seek the shelter of some other place of worship.

THE FLOWER GIRL (*with feeble defiance*): Ive a right to be here if I like, same as you.

THE NOTE TAKER: A woman who utters such depressing and disgusting sounds has no right to be anywhere—no right to live. Remember that you are a human being with a soul and the divine gift of articulate speech: that your native language is the language of Shakespeare and Milton and The Bible: and dont sit there crooning like a bilious pigeon.

THE FLOWER GIRL (*quite overwhelmed, looking up at him in mingled wonder and deprecation without daring to raise her head*): Ah-ah-ah-ow-ow-ow-oo!

THE NOTE TAKER (*whipping out his book*): Heavens! what a sound! (*He writes; then holds out the book and reads, reproducing her vowels exactly*) Ah-ah-ah-ow-ow-ow-oo!

THE FLOWER GIRL (*tickled by the performance, and laughing in spite of herself*): Garn!

THE NOTE TAKER: You see this creature with her kerbstone English: the English that will keep her in the gutter to the end of her days. Well, sir, in three months I could pass that girl off as a duchess at an ambassador's garden party. I could even get her a place as lady's maid or shop assistant, which requires better English. Thats the sort of thing I do for commercial millionaires. And on the profits of it I do genuine scientific work in phonetics, and a little as a poet on Miltonic lines.

THE GENTLEMAN: I am myself a student of Indian dialects; and—

THE NOTE TAKER (*eagerly*): Are you? Do you know Colonel Pickering, the author of Spoken Sanscrit?

THE GENTLEMAN: I am Colonel Pickering. Who are you?

THE NOTE TAKER: Henry Higgins, author of Higgins's Universal Alphabet.

PICKERING (*with enthusiasm*): I came from India to meet you.

HIGGINS: I was going to India to meet you.

PICKERING: Where do you live?

HIGGINS: 27A Wimpole Street. Come and see me tomorrow.

PICKERING: I'm at the Carlton. Come with me now and lets have a jaw over some supper.

HIGGINS: Right you are.

THE FLOWER GIRL (*to* PICKERING, *as he passes her*): Buy a flower, kind gentleman. I'm short for my lodging.

PICKERING: I really havnt any change. I'm sorry (*he goes away*).

HIGGINS (*shocked at the girl's mendacity*): Liar. You said you could change half-a-crown.

THE FLOWER GIRL (*rising in desperation*): You ought to be stuffed with nails, you ought. (*Flinging the basket at his feet*) Take the whole blooming basket for sixpence.

(*The church clock strikes the second quarter.*)

HIGGINS (*hearing in it the voice of God, rebuking him for his Pharisaic want of charity to the poor girl*): A reminder. (*He raises his hat solemnly; then throws a handful of money into the basket and follows* PICKERING.)

THE FLOWER GIRL (*picking up a half-crown*): Ah-ow-ooh! (*Picking up a couple of florins*) Aaah-ow-ooh! (*Picking up several coins*) Aaaaaah-ow-ooh! (*Picking up a half-sovereign*) Aaaaaaaaaaaah-ow-ooh!!!

FREDDY (*springing out of a taxicab*): Got one at last. Hallo! (*To the girl*) Where are the two ladies that were here?

THE FLOWER GIRL: They walked to the bus when the rain stopped.

FREDDY: And left me with a cab on my hands! Damnation!

THE FLOWER GIRL (*with grandeur*): Never mind, young man. *I'm* going home in a taxi. (*She sails off to the cab. The driver puts his hand behind him and holds the door firmly shut against her. Quite understanding his mistrust, she shews him her handful of money.*) Eightpence aint no object to me, Charlie. (*He grins and opens the door.*) Angel Court, Drury Lane, round the corner of Micklejohn's oil shop. Lets see how fast you can make her hop it. (*She gets in and pulls the door to with a slam as the taxicab starts.*)

FREDDY: Well, I'm dashed!

ACT 2

(*Next day at 11 a.m.* HIGGINS'*s laboratory in Wimpole Street. It is a room on the first floor, looking on the street, and was meant for the drawing room. The double doors are in the middle of the back wall; and persons entering find in the corner to their right two tall file cabinets at right angles to one another against the walls. In this corner stands a flat writing-table, on which are a phonograph, a laryngoscope, a row of tiny organ pipes with bellows, a set of lamp chimneys for singing flames with burners attached to a gas plug in the wall by an india-rubber tube, several tuning-forks of different sizes, a life-size image of half a human head, shewing in section the vocal organs, and a box containing a supply of wax cylinders for the phonograph.*

Further down the room, on the same side, is a fireplace, with a comfortable leather-covered easy-chair at the side of the hearth nearest the door, and a coal-scuttle. There is a clock on the mantelpiece. Between the fireplace and the phonograph table is a stand for newspapers.

On the other side of the central door, to the left of the vis-

itor, is a cabinet of shallow drawers. On it is a telephone and the telephone directory. The corner beyond, and most of the side wall, is occupied by a grand piano, with the keyboard at the end furthest from the door, and a bench for the player extending the full length of the keyboard. On the piano is a dessert dish heaped with fruit and sweets, mostly chocolates.

The middle of the room is clear. Besides the easy-chair, the piano bench, and two chairs at the phonograph table, there is one stray chair. It stands near the fireplace. On the walls, engravings: mostly Piranesis and mezzotint portraits. No paintings.

PICKERING is seated at the table, putting down some cards and a tuning-fork which he has been using. HIGGINS is standing up near him, closing two or three file drawers which are hanging out. He appears in the morning light as a robust, vital, appetizing sort of man of forty or thereabouts, dressed in a professional-looking black frock-coat with a white linen collar and black silk tie. He is of the energetic, scientific type, heartily, even violently interested in everything that can be studied as a scientific subject, and careless about himself and other people, including their feelings. He is, in fact, but for his years and size, rather like a very impetuous baby "taking notice" eagerly and loudly, and requiring almost as much watching to keep him out of unintended mischief. His manner varies from genial bullying when he is in a good humor to stormy petulance when anything goes wrong; but he is so entirely frank and void of malice that he remains likeable even in his least reasonable moments.)

HIGGINS (*as he shuts the last drawer*): Well, I think thats the whole show.

PICKERING: It's really amazing. I havnt taken half of it in, you know.

HIGGINS: Would you like to go over any of it again?

PICKERING (*rising and coming to the fireplace, where he plants himself with his back to the fire*): No, thank you; not now. I'm quite done up for this morning.

HIGGINS (*following him, and standing beside him on his left*): Tired of listening to sounds?

PICKERING: Yes. It's a fearful strain. I rather fancied myself because I can pronounce twenty-four distinct vowel sounds; but your hundred and thirty beat me. I cant hear a bit of difference between most of them.

HIGGINS (*chuckling, and going over to the piano to eat sweets*): Oh, that comes with practice. You hear no difference at first; but you keep on listening, and presently you find theyre all as different as A from B. (MRS PEARCE *looks in: she is* HIGGINS's *housekeeper.*) Whats the matter?

MRS PEARCE (*hesitating, evidently perplexed*): A young woman wants to see you sir.

HIGGINS: A young woman! What does she want?

MRS PEARCE: Well, sir, she says youll be glad to see her when you know what she's come about. She's

quite a common girl, sir. Very common indeed. I should have sent her away, only I thought perhaps you wanted her to talk into your machines. I hope Ive not done wrong; but really you see such queer people sometimes—youll excuse me, I'm sure, sir—

HIGGINS: Oh, thats all right, Mrs Pearce. Has she an interesting accent?

MRS PEARCE: Oh, something dreadful, sir, really. I dont know how you can take an interest in it.

HIGGINS (*to* PICKERING): Lets have her up. Shew her up, Mrs Pearce (*he rushes across to his working table and picks out a cylinder to use on the phonograph*).

MRS PEARCE (*only half resigned to it*): Very well, sir. It's for you to say. (*She goes downstairs.*)

HIGGINS: This is rather a bit of luck. I'll shew you how I make records. We'll set her talking; and I'll take it down first in Bell's visible Speech; then in broad Romic; and then we'll get her on the phonograph so that you can turn her on as often as you like with the written transcript before you.

MRS PEARCE (*returning*): This is the young woman, sir.

(*The flower girl enters in state. She has a hat with three ostrich feathers, orange, sky-blue, and red. She has a nearly clean apron, and the shoddy coat has been tidied a little. The pathos of this deplorable figure, with its innocent vanity and consequential air, touches* PICKERING, *who has already straightened himself in the presence of* MRS PEARCE. *But as to* HIGGINS, *the only distinction he makes between men and women is that when he is neither bullying nor exclaiming to the heavens against some feather-weight cross, he coaxes women as a child coaxes its nurse when it wants to get anything out of her.*)

HIGGINS (*brusquely, recognizing her with unconcealed disappointment, and at once, babylike, making an intolerable grievance of it*): Why, this is the girl I jotted down last night. She's no use: Ive got all the records I want of the Lisson Grove lingo; and I'm not going to waste another cylinder on it. (*To the girl*) Be off with you: I dont want you.

THE FLOWER GIRL: Dont you be so saucy. You aint heard what I come for yet. (*To* MRS PEARCE, *who is waiting at the door for further instructions*) Did you tell him I come in a taxi?

MRS PEARCE: Nonsense, girl! what do you think a gentleman like Mr Higgins cares what you came in?

THE FLOWER GIRL: Oh, we are proud! He aint above giving lessons, not him: I heard him say so. Well, I aint come here to ask for any compliment; and if my money's not good enough I can go elsewhere.

HIGGINS: Good enough for what?

THE FLOWER GIRL: Good enough for ye-oo. Now you know, dont you? I'm come to have lessons, I am. And to pay for em too: make no mistake.

HIGGINS (*stupent*): Well!!! (*Recovering his breath with a gasp*) What do you expect me to say to you?

THE FLOWER GIRL: Well, if you was a gentleman, you might ask me to sit down, I think. Dont I tell you I'm bringing you business?

HIGGINS: Pickering: shall we ask this baggage to sit down, or shall we throw her out of the window?

THE FLOWER GIRL (*running away in terror to the piano, where she turns at bay*): Ah-ah-oh-ow-ow-ow-oo! (*Wounded and whimpering*) I wont be called a baggage when Ive offered to pay like any lady.

(*Motionless, the two men stare at her from the other side of the room, amazed.*)

PICKERING (*gently*): What is it you want, my girl?

THE FLOWER GIRL: I want to be a lady in a flower shop stead of selling at the corner of Tottenham Court Road. But they wont take me unless I can talk more genteel. He said he could teach me. Well, here I am ready to pay him—not asking any favor—and he treats me as if I was dirt.

MRS PEARCE: How can you be such a foolish ignorant girl as to think you could afford to pay Mr Higgins?

THE FLOWER GIRL: Why shouldnt I? I know what lessons cost as well as you do; and I'm ready to pay.

HIGGINS: How much?

THE FLOWER GIRL (*coming back to him, triumphant*): Now youre talking! I thought youd come off it when you saw a chance of getting back a bit of what you chucked at me last night. (*Confidently*) Youd had a drop in, hadnt you?

HIGGINS (*peremptorily*): Sit down.

THE FLOWER GIRL: Oh, if youre going to make a compliment of it—

HIGGINS (*thundering at her*): Sit down.

MRS PEARCE (*severely*): Sit down, girl. Do as youre told.

(*She places the stray chair near the hearthrug between HIGGINS and PICKERING, and stands behind it waiting for the girl to sit down.*)

THE FLOWER GIRL: Ah-ah-ah-ow-ow-oo! (*She stands, half rebellious, half bewildered.*)

PICKERING (*very courteous*): Wont you sit down?

THE FLOWER GIRL (*coyly*): Dont mind if I do. (*She sits down. PICKERING returns to the hearthrug.*)

HIGGINS: Whats your name?

THE FLOWER GIRL: Liza Doolittle.

HIGGINS (*declaiming gravely*):
Eliza, Elizabeth, Betsy, and Bess,
They went to the woods to get a bird's nes':

PICKERING: They found a nest with four eggs in it:

HIGGINS: They took one apiece, and left three in it.

(*They laugh heartily at their own wit.*)

LIZA: Oh, dont be silly.

MRS PEARCE: You mustnt speak to the gentleman like that.

LIZA: Well, why wont he speak sensible to me?

HIGGINS: Come back to business. How much do you propose to pay me for the lessons?

LIZA: Oh, I know whats right. A lady friend of mine gets French lessons for eighteenpence an hour from a real French gentleman. Well, you wouldnt have the face to ask me the same for teaching me my own language as you would for French; so I wont give more than a shilling. Take it or leave it.

HIGGINS (*walking up and down the room, rattling his keys and his cash in his pockets*): You know, Pickering, if you consider a shilling, not as a simple shilling, but as a percentage of this girl's income, it works out as fully equivalent to sixty or seventy guineas from a millionaire.

PICKERING: How so?

HIGGINS: Figure it out. A millionaire has about £150 a day. She earns about half-a-crown.

LIZA (*haughtily*): Who told you I only—

HIGGINS (*continuing*): She offers me two-fifths of her day's income for a lesson. Two-fifths of a millionaire's income for a day would be somewhere about £60. It's handsome. By George, it's enormous! it's the biggest offer I ever had.

LIZA (*rising, terrified*): Sixty pounds! What are you talking about? I never offered you sixty pounds. Where would I get—

HIGGINS: Hold your tongue.

LIZA (*weeping*): But I aint got sixty pounds. Oh—

MRS PEARCE: Dont cry, you silly girl. Sit down. Nobody is going to touch your money.

HIGGINS: Somebody is going to touch you, with a broomstick, if you dont stop snivelling. Sit down.

LIZA (*obeying slowly*): Ah-ah-ah-ow-oo-o! One would think you was my father.

HIGGINS: If I decide to teach you, I'll be worse than two fathers to you. Here (*he offers her his silk handkerchief*)!

LIZA: Whats this for?

HIGGINS: To wipe your eyes. To wipe any part of your face that feels moist. Remember: thats your handkerchief; and thats your sleeve. Dont mistake the one for the other if you wish to become a lady in a shop.

(*LIZA, utterly bewildered, stares helplessly at him.*)

MRS PEARCE: It's no use talking to her like that, Mr Higgins: she doesnt understand you. Besides, youre quite wrong: she doesnt do it that way at all (*she takes the handkerchief*).

LIZA (*snatching it*): Here! You give me that handkerchief. He give it to me, not to you.

PICKERING (*laughing*): He did. I think it must be regarded as her property, Mrs Pearce.

MRS PEARCE (*resigning herself*): Serve you right, Mr Higgins.

PICKERING: Higgins: I'm interested. What about the

ambassador's garden party? I'll say youre the greatest teacher alive if you make that good. I'll bet you all the expenses of the experiment you cant do it. And I'll pay for the lessons.

LIZA: Oh, you are real good. Thank you, Captain.

HIGGINS (*tempted, looking at her*): It's almost irresistible. She's so deliciously low—so horribly dirty—

LIZA (*protesting extremely*): Ah-ah-ah-ah-ow-ow-oo-oo!!! I aint dirty: I washed my face and hands afore I come, I did.

PICKERING: Youre certainly not going to turn her head with flattery, Higgins.

MRS PEARCE (*uneasy*): Oh, dont say that, sir: theres more ways than one of turning a girl's head; and nobody can do it better than Mr Higgins, though he may not always mean it. I do hope, sir, you wont encourage him to do anything foolish.

HIGGINS (*becoming excited as the idea grows on him*): What is life but a series of inspired follies? The difficulty is to find them to do. Never lose a chance: it doesnt come every day. I shall make a duchess of this draggletailed guttersnipe.

LIZA (*strongly deprecating this view of her*): Ah-ah-ah-ow-ow-oo!

HIGGINS (*carried away*): Yes: in six months—in three if she has a good ear and a quick tongue—I'll take her anywhere and pass her off as anything. We'll start today: now! this moment! Take her away and clean her, Mrs Pearce. Monkey Brand, if it wont come off any other way. Is there a good fire in the kitchen?

MRS PEARCE (*protesting*): Yes; but—

HIGGINS (*storming on*): Take all her clothes off and burn them. Ring up Whiteley or somebody for new ones. Wrap her up in brown paper til they come.

LIZA: Youre no gentleman, youre not, to talk of such things. I'm a good girl, I am; and I know what the like of you are, I do.

HIGGINS: We want none of your Lisson Grove prudery here, young woman. Youve got to learn to behave like a duchess. Take her away, Mrs Pearce. If she gives you any trouble, wallop her.

LIZA (*springing up and running between* PICKERING *and* MRS PEARCE *for protection*): No! I'll call the police, I will.

MRS PEARCE: But Ive no place to put her.

HIGGINS: Put her in the dustbin.

LIZA: Ah-ah-ah-ow-ow-oo!

PICKERING: Oh come, Higgins! be reasonable.

MRS PEARCE (*resolutely*): You must be reasonable, Mr Higgins: really you must. You cant walk over everybody like this.

(HIGGINS, *thus scolded, subsides. The hurricane is succeeded by a zephyr of amiable surprise.*)

HIGGINS (*with professional exquisiteness of modulation*): I

walk over everybody! My dear Mrs Pearce, my dear Pickering, I never had the slightest intention of walking over anyone. All I propose is that we should be kind to this poor girl. We must help her to prepare and fit herself for her new station in life. If I did not express myself clearly it was because I did not wish to hurt her delicacy, or yours.

(LIZA, *reassured, steals back to her chair.*)

MRS PEARCE (*to* PICKERING): Well, did you ever hear anything like that, sir?

PICKERING (*laughing heartily*): Never, Mrs Pearce: never.

HIGGINS (*patiently*): Whats the matter?

MRS PEARCE: Well, the matter is, sir, that you cant take a girl up like that as if you were picking up a pebble on the beach.

HIGGINS: Why not?

MRS PEARCE: Why not! But you dont know anything about her. What about her parents? She may be married.

LIZA: Garn!

HIGGINS: There! As the girl very properly says, Garn! Married indeed! Dont you know that a woman of that class looks a worn out drudge of fifty a year after she's married?

LIZA: Whood marry me?

HIGGINS (*suddenly resorting to the most thrillingly beautiful low tones in his best elocutionary style*): By George, Eliza, the streets will be strewn with the bodies of men shooting themselves for your sake before Ive done with you.

MRS PEARCE: Nonsense sir. You mustnt talk like that to her.

LIZA (*rising and squaring herself determinedly*): I'm going away. He's off his chump, he is. I dont want no balmies teaching me.

HIGGINS (*wounded in his tenderest point by her insensibility to his elocution*): Oh, indeed! I'm mad, am I? Very well, Mrs Pearce: you neednt order the new clothes for her. Throw her out.

LIZA (*whimpering*): Nah-ow. You got no right to touch me.

MRS PEARCE: You see now what comes of being saucy. (*Indicating the door*) This way, please.

LIZA (*almost in tears*): I didnt want no clothes. I wouldnt have taken them (*she throws away the handkerchief*). I can buy my own clothes.

HIGGINS (*deftly retrieving the handkerchief and intercepting her on her reluctant way to the door*): Youre an ungrateful wicked girl. This is my return for offering to take you out of the gutter and dress you beautifully and make a lady of you.

MRS PEARCE: Stop, Mr Higgins. I wont allow it. It's you that are wicked. Go home to your parents, girl; and tell them to take better care of you.

LIZA: I aint got no parents. They told me I was big enough to earn my own living and turned me out.

MRS PEARCE: Wheres your mother?

LIZA: I aint got no mother. Her that turned me out was my sixth stepmother. But I done without them. And I'm a good girl, I am.

HIGGINS: Very well, then, what on earth is all this fuss about? The girl doesnt belong to anybody—is no use to anybody but me. (*He goes to* MRS PEARCE *and begins coaxing.*) You can adopt her, Mrs Pearce: I'm sure a daughter would be a great amusement to you. Now dont make any more fuss. Take her downstairs; and—

MRS PEARCE: But whats to become of her? Is she to be paid anything? Do be sensible, sir.

HIGGINS: Oh, pay her whatever is necessary: put it down in the housekeeping book. (*Impatiently*) What on earth will she want with money? She'll have her food and her clothes. She'll only drink if you give her money.

LIZA (*turning on him*): Oh you are a brute. It's a lie: nobody ever saw the sign of liquor on me. (*She goes back to her chair and plants herself there defiantly.*)

PICKERING (*in good-humored remonstrance*): Does it occur to you, Higgins, that the girl has some feelings?

HIGGINS (*looking critically at her*): Oh no, I dont think so. Not any feelings that we need bother about. (*Cheerily*) Have you, Eliza?

LIZA: I got my feelings same as anyone else.

HIGGINS (*to* PICKERING, *reflectively*): You see the difficulty?

PICKERING: Eh? What difficulty?

HIGGINS: To get her to talk grammar. The mere pronunciation is easy enough.

LIZA: I dont want to talk grammar. I want to talk like a lady.

MRS PEARCE: Will you please keep to the point, Mr Higgins? I want to know on what terms the girl is to be here. Is she to have any wages? And what is to become of her when youve finished your teaching? You must look ahead a little.

HIGGINS (*impatiently*): Whats to become of her if I leave her in the gutter? Tell me that, Mrs Pearce.

MRS PEARCE: Thats her own business, not yours, Mr Higgins.

HIGGINS: Well, when Ive done with her, we can throw her back into the gutter; and then it will be her own business again; so thats all right.

LIZA: Oh, youve no feeling heart in you: you dont care for nothing but yourself (*she rises and takes the floor resolutely*). Here! Ive had enough of this. I'm going (*making for the door*). You ought to be ashamed of yourself, you ought.

HIGGINS (*snatching a chocolate cream from the piano, his eyes suddenly beginning to twinkle with mischief*): Have some chocolates, Eliza.

LIZA (*halting, tempted*): How do I know what might be in them? Ive heard of girls being drugged by the like of you.

(HIGGINS *whips out his penknife; cuts a chocolate in two; puts one half into his mouth and bolts it; and offers her the other half.*)

HIGGINS: Pledge of good faith, Eliza. I eat one half: you eat the other. (LIZA *opens her mouth to retort: he pops the half chocolate into it.*) You shall have boxes of them, barrels of them, every day. You shall live on them. Eh?

LIZA (*who has disposed of the chocolate after being nearly choked by it*): I wouldnt have ate it, only I'm too ladylike to take it out of my mouth.

HIGGINS: Listen, Eliza. I think you said you came in a taxi.

LIZA: Well, what if I did? Ive as good a right to take a taxi as anyone else.

HIGGINS: You have, Eliza; and in future you shall have as many taxis as you want. You shall go up and down and round the town in a taxi every day. Think of that, Eliza.

MRS PEARCE: Mr Higgins: youre tempting the girl. It's not right. She should think of the future.

HIGGINS: At her age! Nonsense! Time enough to think of the future when you havnt any future to think of. No, Eliza: do as this lady does: think of other people's futures; but never think of your own. Think of chocolates, and taxis, and gold, and diamonds.

LIZA: No: I dont want no gold and no diamonds. I'm a good girl, I am. (*She sits down again, with an attempt at dignity.*)

HIGGINS: You shall remain so, Eliza, under the care of Mrs Pearce. And you shall marry an officer in the Guards, with a beautiful moustache: the son of a marquis, who will disinherit him for marrying you, but will relent when he sees your beauty and goodness—

PICKERING: Excuse me, Higgins; but I really must interfere. Mrs Pearce is quite right. If this girl is to put herself in your hands for six months for an experiment in teaching, she must understand thoroughly what she's doing.

HIGGINS: How can she? She's incapable of understanding anything. Besides, do any of us understand what we are doing? If we did, would we ever do it?

PICKERING: Very clever, Higgins; but not sound sense. (*To* ELIZA) Miss Doolittle—

LIZA (*overwhelmed*): Ah-ah-ow-oo!

HIGGINS: There! Thats all youll get out of Eliza. Ah-ah-ow-oo! No use explaining. As a military man you ought to know that. Give her her orders: thats what she wants. Eliza: you are to live here for the next six months, learning how to speak beautifully, like a lady in a florist's shop. If youre good and do whatever youre told, you shall sleep in a proper bedroom, and have lots to eat, and money to buy chocolates and take rides in taxis. If youre naughty and idle you will sleep in the back kitchen among the black beetles, and be walloped by Mrs Pearce with a broomstick. At the end of six months you shall go to Buckingham Palace in a carriage, beautifully dressed. If the King finds out youre not a lady, you will be taken by the police to the Tower of London, where your head will be cut off as a warning to other presumptuous flower girls. If you are not found out, you shall have a present of seven-and-sixpence to start life with as a lady in a shop. If you refuse this offer you will be a most ungrateful and wicked girl; and the angels will weep for you. *(To* PICKERING*)* Now are you satisfied, Pickering? *(To* MRS PEARCE*)* Can I put it more plainly and fairly, Mrs Pearce?

MRS PEARCE *(patiently)*: I think youd better let me speak to the girl properly in private. I dont know that I can take charge of her or consent to the arrangement at all. Of course I know you dont mean her any harm; but when you get what you call interested in people's accents, you never think or care what may happen to them or you. Come with me, Eliza.

HIGGINS: Thats all right. Thank you, Mrs Pearce. Bundle her off to the bathroom.

LIZA *(rising reluctantly and suspiciously)*: Youre a great bully, you are. I wont stay here if I dont like. I wont let nobody wallop me. I never asked to go to Bucknam Palace, I didnt. I was never in trouble with the police, not me. I'm a good girl—

MRS PEARCE: Dont answer back, girl. You dont understand the gentleman. Come with me. *(She leads the way to the door, and holds it open for* ELIZA*.)*

LIZA *(as she goes out)*: Well, what I say is right. I wont go near the King, not if I'm going to have my head cut off. If I'd known what I was letting myself in for, I wouldnt have come here. I always been a good girl; and I never offered to say a word to him; and I dont owe him nothing; and I dont care; and I wont be put upon; and I have my feelings the same as anyone else—

(MRS PEARCE shuts the door; and ELIZA's plaints are no longer audible. PICKERING *comes from the hearth to the chair and sits astride it with his arms on the back.)*

PICKERING: Excuse the straight question, Higgins. Are you a man of good character where women are concerned?

HIGGINS *(moodily)*: Have you ever met a man of good character where women are concerned?

PICKERING: Yes: very frequently.

HIGGINS *(dogmatically, lifting himself on his hands to the level of the piano, and sitting on it with a bounce)*: Well, I havnt. I find that the moment I let a woman make friends with me, she becomes jealous, exacting, suspicious, and a damned nui-

sance. I find that the moment I let myself make friends with a woman, I become selfish and tyrannical. Women upset everything. When you let them into your life, you find that the woman is driving at one thing and youre driving at another.

PICKERING: At what, for example?

HIGGINS *(coming off the piano restlessly)*: Oh, Lord knows! I suppose the woman wants to live her own life; and the man wants to live his; and each tries to drag the other on to the wrong track. One wants to go north and the other south; and the result is that both have to go east, though they both hate the east wind. *(He sits down on the bench at the keyboard.)* So here I am, a confirmed old bachelor, and likely to remain so.

PICKERING *(rising and standing over him gravely)*: Come, Higgins! You know what I mean. If I'm to be in this business I shall feel responsible for that girl. I hope it's understood that no advantage is to be taken of her position.

HIGGINS: What! That thing! Sacred, I assure you. *(Rising to explain)* You see, she'll be a pupil; and teaching would be impossible unless pupils were sacred. Ive taught scores of American millionairesses how to speak English: the best looking women in the world. I'm seasoned. They might as well be blocks of wood. *I* might as well be a block of wood. It's—

(MRS PEARCE opens the door. She has ELIZA's hat in her hand. PICKERING *retires to the easy-chair at the hearth and sits down.)*

HIGGINS *(eagerly)*: Well, Mrs Pearce: is it all right?

MRS PEARCE *(at the door)*: I just wish to trouble you with a word, if I may, Mr Higgins.

HIGGINS: Yes, certainly. Come in. *(She comes forward.)* Dont burn that, Mrs Pearce. I'll keep it as a curiosity. *(He takes the hat.)*

MRS PEARCE: Handle it carefully, sir, please. I had to promise her not to burn it; but I had better put it in the oven for a while.

HIGGINS *(putting it down hastily on the piano)*: Oh! thank you. Well, what have you to say to me?

PICKERING: Am I in the way?

MRS PEARCE: Not at all, sir. Mr Higgins: will you please be very particular what you say before the girl?

HIGGINS *(sternly)*: Of course. I'm always particular about what I say. Why do you say this to me?

MRS PEARCE *(unmoved)*: No, sir: youre not at all particular when youve mislaid anything or when you get a little impatient. Now it doesnt matter before me: I'm used to it. But you really must not swear before the girl.

HIGGINS *(indignantly)*: *I* swear! *(Most emphatically)* I never swear. I detest the habit. What the devil do you mean?

MRS PEARCE *(stolidly)*: Thats what I mean, sir. You

swear a great deal too much. I dont mind your damning and blasting, and what the devil and where the devil and who the devil—

HIGGINS: Mrs Pearce: this language from your lips! Really!

MRS PEARCE (*not to be put off*): —but there is a certain word I must ask you not to use. The girl has just used it herself because the bath was too hot. It begins with the same letter as bath. She knows no better: she learnt it at her mother's knee. But she must not hear it from your lips.

HIGGINS (*loftily*): I cannot charge myself with having ever uttered it, Mrs Pearce. (*She looks at him steadfastly. He adds, hiding an uneasy conscience with a judicial air*) Except perhaps in a moment of extreme and justifiable excitement.

MRS PEARCE: Only this morning, sir, you applied it to your boots, to the butter, and to the brown bread.

HIGGINS: Oh, that! Mere alliteration, Mrs Pearce, natural to a poet.

MRS PEARCE: Well, sir, whatever you choose to call it, I beg you not to let the girl hear you repeat it.

HIGGINS: Oh, very well, very well. Is that all?

MRS PEARCE: No, sir. We shall have to be very particular with this girl as to personal cleanliness.

HIGGINS: Certainly. Quite right. Most important.

MRS PEARCE: I mean not to be slovenly about her dress or untidy in leaving things about.

HIGGINS (*going to her solemnly*): Just so. I intended to call your attention to that. (*He passes on to* PICKERING, *who is enjoying the conversation immensely.*) It is these little things that matter, Pickering. Take care of the pence and the pounds will take care of themselves is as true of personal habits as of money. (*He comes to anchor on the hearthrug, with the air of a man in an unassailable position.*)

MRS PEARCE: Yes, sir. Then might I ask you not to come down to breakfast in your dressing-gown, or at any rate not to use it as a napkin to the extent you do, sir. And if you would be so good as not to eat everything off the same plate, and to remember not to put the porridge saucepan out of your hand on the clean tablecloth, it would be a better example to the girl. You know you nearly choked yourself with a fishbone in the jam only last week.

HIGGINS (*routed from the hearthrug and drifting back to the piano*): I may do these things sometimes in absence of mind; but surely I dont do them habitually. (*Angrily*) By the way: my dressing-gown smells most damnably of benzine.

MRS PEARCE: No doubt it does, Mr Higgins. But if you will wipe your fingers—

HIGGINS (*yelling*): Oh very well, very well: I'll wipe them in my hair in future.

MRS PEARCE: I hope youre not offended, Mr Higgins.

HIGGINS (*shocked at finding himself thought capable of an unamiable sentiment*): Not at all, not at all. Youre quite right, Mrs Pearce: I shall be particularly careful before the girl. Is that all?

MRS PEARCE: No, sir. Might she use some of those Japanese dresses you brought from abroad? I really cant put her back into her old things.

HIGGINS: Certainly. Anything you like. Is that all?

MRS PEARCE: Thank you, sir. Thats all. (*She goes out.*)

HIGGINS: You know, Pickering, that woman has the most extraordinary ideas about me. Here I am, a shy, diffident sort of man. Ive never been able to feel really grown-up and tremendous, like other chaps. And yet she's firmly persuaded that I'm an arbitrary overbearing bossing kind of person. I cant account for it.

(MRS PEARCE *returns.*)

MRS PEARCE: If you please, sir, the trouble's beginning already. Theres a dustman downstairs, Alfred Doolittle, wants to see you. He says you have his daughter here.

PICKERING (*rising*): Phew! I say! (*He retreats to the hearthrug.*)

HIGGINS (*promptly*): Send the blackguard up.

MRS PEARCE: Oh, very well, sir. (*She goes out.*)

PICKERING: He may not be a blackguard, Higgins.

HIGGINS: Nonsense. Of course he's a blackguard.

PICKERING: Whether he is or not, I'm afraid we shall have some trouble with him.

HIGGINS (*confidently*): Oh no: I think not. If theres any trouble he shall have it with me, not I with him. And we are sure to get something interesting out of him.

PICKERING: About the girl?

HIGGINS: No. I mean his dialect.

PICKERING: Oh!

MRS PEARCE (*at the door*): Doolittle, sir. (*She admits* DOOLITTLE *and retires.*)

(ALFRED DOOLITTLE *is an elderly but vigorous dustman, clad in the costume of his profession, including a hat with a back brim covering his neck and shoulders. He has well marked and rather interesting features, and seems equally free from fear and conscience. He has a remarkably expressive voice, the result of a habit of giving vent to his feelings without reserve. His present pose is that of wounded honor and stern resolution.*)

DOOLITTLE (*at the door, uncertain which of the two gentlemen is his man*): Professor Higgins?

HIGGINS: Here. Good morning. Sit down.

DOOLITTLE: Morning, Governor. (*He sits down magisterially.*) I come about a very serious matter, Governor.

HIGGINS (*to* PICKERING): Brought up in Hounslow. Mother Welsh, I should think. (DOOLITTLE *opens his mouth, amazed.* HIGGINS *continues*) What do you want, Doolittle?

DOOLITTLE *(menacingly)*: I want my daughter: thats what I want. See?

HIGGINS: Of course you do. Youre her father, arnt you? You dont suppose anyone else wants her, do you? I'm glad to see you have some spark of family feeling left. She's upstairs. Take her away at once.

DOOLITTLE *(rising, fearfully taken aback)*: What!

HIGGINS: Take her away. Do you suppose I'm going to keep your daughter for you?

DOOLITTLE *(remonstrating)*: Now, now, look here, Governor. Is this reasonable? Is it fairity to take advantage of a man like this? The girl belongs to me. You got her. Where do I come in? *(He sits down again.)*

HIGGINS: Your daughter had the audacity to come to my house and ask me to teach her how to speak properly so that she could get a place in a flower-shop. This gentleman and my housekeeper have been here all the time. *(Bullying him)* How dare you come here and attempt to blackmail me? You sent her here on purpose.

DOOLITTLE *(protesting)*: No, Governor.

HIGGINS: You must have. How else could you possibly know that she is here?

DOOLITTLE: Dont take a man up like that, Governor.

HIGGINS: The police shall take you up. This is a plant—a plot to extort money by threats. I shall telephone for the police. *(He goes resolutely to the telephone and opens the directory.)*

DOOLITTLE: Have I asked you for a brass farthing? I leave it to the gentleman here: have I said a word about money?

HIGGINS *(throwing the book aside and marching down on* DOOLITTLE *with a poser)*: What else did you come for?

DOOLITTLE *(sweetly)*: Well, what would a man come for? Be human, Governor.

HIGGINS *(disarmed)*: Alfred: did you put her up to it?

DOOLITTLE: So help me, Governor, I never did. I take my Bible oath I aint seen the girl these two months past.

HIGGINS: Then how did you know she was here?

DOOLITTLE *("most musical, most melancholy")*: I'll tell you, Governor, if youll only let me get a word in. I'm willing to tell you. I'm wanting to tell you. I'm waiting to tell you.

HIGGINS: Pickering: this chap has a certain natural gift of rhetoric. Observe the rhythm of his native woodnotes wild. "I'm willing to tell you: I'm wanting to tell you: I'm waiting to tell you." Sentimental rhetoric! thats the Welsh strain in him. It also accounts for his mendacity and dishonesty.

PICKERING: Oh, please, Higgins: I'm west country myself. *(To* DOOLITTLE*)* How did you know the girl was here if you didnt send her?

DOOLITTLE: It was like this, Governor. The girl took a boy in the taxi to give him a jaunt. Son of her landlady, he is. He hung about on the chance of her giving him another ride home. Well, she sent him back for her luggage when she heard you was willing for her to stop here. I met the boy at the corner of Long Acre and Endell Street.

HIGGINS: Public house. Yes?

DOOLITTLE: The poor man's club, Governor: why shouldnt I?

PICKERING: Do let him tell his story, Higgins.

DOOLITTLE: He told me what was up. And I ask you, what was my feelings and my duty as a father? I says to the boy, "You bring me the luggage," I says—

PICKERING: Why didnt you go for it yourself?

DOOLITTLE: Landlady wouldnt have trusted me with it, Governor. She's that kind of woman: you know. I had to give the boy a penny afore he trusted me with it, the little swine. I brought it to her just to oblige you like, and make myself agreeable. Thats all.

HIGGINS: How much luggage?

DOOLITTLE: Musical instrument, Governor. A few pictures, a trifle of jewelry, and a bird-cage. She said she didnt want no clothes. What was I to think from that, Governor? I ask you as a parent what was I to think?

HIGGINS: So you came to rescue her from worse than death, eh?

DOOLITTLE *(appreciatively: relieved at being so well understood)*: Just so, Governor. Thats right.

PICKERING: But why did you bring her luggage if you intended to take her away?

DOOLITTLE: Have I said a word about taking her away? Have I now?

HIGGINS *(determinedly)*: Youre going to take her away, double quick. *(He crosses to the hearth and rings the bell.)*

DOOLITTLE *(rising)*: No, Governor. Dont say that. I'm not the man to stand in my girl's light. Heres a career opening for her, as you might say; and—

*(*MRS PEARCE *opens the door and awaits orders.)*

HIGGINS: Mrs Pearce: this is Eliza's father. He has come to take her away. Give her to him. *(He goes back to the piano, with an air of washing his hands of the whole affair.)*

DOOLITTLE: No. This is a misunderstanding. Listen here—

MRS PEARCE: He cant take her away, Mr Higgins: how can he? You told me to burn her clothes.

DOOLITTLE: Thats right. I cant carry the girl through the streets like a blooming monkey, can I? I put it to you.

HIGGINS: You have put it to me that you want your daughter. Take your daughter. If she has no clothes go out and buy her some.

DOOLITTLE (*desperate*): Wheres the clothes she come in? Did I burn them or did your missus here?

MRS PEARCE: I am the housekeeper, if you please. I have sent for some clothes for your girl. When they come you can take her away. You can wait in the kitchen. This way, please.

(DOOLITTLE, *much troubled, accompanies her to the door; then hesitates; finally turns confidentially to* HIGGINS.)

DOOLITTLE: Listen here, Governor. You and me is men of the world, aint we?

HIGGINS: Oh! Men of the world, are we? Youd better go, Mrs Pearce.

MRS PEARCE: I think so, indeed, sir. (*She goes, with dignity.*)

PICKERING: The floor is yours, Mr Doolittle.

DOOLITTLE (*to* PICKERING): I thank you, Governor. (*To* HIGGINS, *who takes refuge on the piano bench, a little overwhelmed by the proximity of his visitor; for* DOOLITTLE *has a professional flavor of dust about him.*) Well, the truth is, Ive taken a sort of fancy to you, Governor; and if you want the girl, I'm not so set on having her back home again but what I might be open to an arrangement. Regarded in the light of a young woman, she's a fine handsome girl. As a daughter she's not worth her keep; and so I tell you straight. All I ask is my rights as a father; and youre the last man alive to expect me to let her go for nothing; for I can see youre one of the straight sort, Governor. Well, whats a five-pound note to you? And whats Eliza to me? (*He returns to his chair and sits down judicially.*)

PICKERING: I think you ought to know, Doolittle, that Mr Higgins's intentions are entirely honorable.

DOOLITTLE: Course they are, Governor. If I thought they wasnt, I'd ask fifty.

HIGGINS (*revolted*): Do you mean to say, you callous rascal, that you would sell your daughter for £50?

DOOLITTLE: Not in a general way I wouldnt; but to oblige a gentleman like you I'd do a good deal, I do assure you.

PICKERING: Have you no morals, man?

DOOLITTLE (*unabashed*): Cant afford them, Governor. Neither could you if you was as poor as me. Not that I mean any harm, you know. But if Liza is going to have a bit out of this, why not me too?

HIGGINS (*troubled*): I dont know what to do, Pickering. There can be no question that as a matter of morals it's a positive crime to give this chap a farthing. And yet I feel a sort of rough justice in his claim.

DOOLITTLE: Thats it, Governor. Thats all I say. A father's heart, as it were.

PICKERING: Well, I know the feeling; but really it seems hardly right—

DOOLITTLE: Dont say that, Governor. Dont look at it that way. What am I, Governors both? I ask you, what am I? I'm one of the undeserving poor: thats what I am. Think of what that means to a man. It means that he's up agen middle class morality all the time. If theres anything going, and I put in for a bit of it, it's always the same story. "Youre undeserving; so you cant have it." But my needs is as great as the most deserving widow's that ever got money out of six different charities in one week for the death of the same husband. I dont need less than a deserving man: I need more. I dont eat less hearty than him; and I drink a lot more. I want a bit of amusement, cause I'm a thinking man. I want cheerfulness and a song and a band when I feel low. Well, they charge me just the same for everything as they charge the deserving. What is middle class morality? Just an excuse for never giving me anything. Therefore, I ask you, as two gentlemen, not to play that game on me. I'm playing straight with you. I aint pretending to be deserving. I'm undeserving; and I mean to go on being undeserving. I like it; and thats the truth. Will you take advantage of a man's nature to do him out of the price of his own daughter what he's brought up and fed and clothed by the sweat of his brow until she's growed big enough to be interesting to you two gentlemen? Is five pounds reasonable? I put it to you; and I leave it to you.

HIGGINS (*rising, and going over to* PICKERING): Pickering: if we were to take this man in hand for three months, he could choose between a seat in the Cabinet and a popular pulpit in Wales.

PICKERING: What do you say to that, Doolittle?

DOOLITTLE: Not me, Governor, thank you kindly. Ive heard all the preachers and all the prime ministers—for I'm a thinking man and game for politics or religion or social reform same as all the other amusements—and I tell you it's a dog's life any way you look at it. Undeserving poverty is my line. Taking one station in society with another, it's—it's—well, it's the only one that has any ginger in it, to my taste.

HIGGINS: I suppose we must give him a fiver.

PICKERING: He'll make a bad use of it, I'm afraid.

DOOLITTLE: Not me, Governor, so help me I wont. Dont you be afraid that I'll save it and spare it and live idle on it. There wont be a penny of it left by Monday: I'll have to go to work same as if I'd never had it. It wont pauperize me, you bet. Just one good spree for myself and the missus, giving pleasure to ourselves and employment to others, and satisfaction to you to think it's not been throwed away. You couldnt spend it better.

HIGGINS (*taking out his pocket book and coming between* DOOLITTLE *and the piano*): This is irresistible. Lets give him ten. (*He offers two notes to the dustman.*)

DOOLITTLE: No, Governor. She wouldnt have the heart to spend ten; and perhaps I shouldnt neither. Ten pounds is a lot of money: it makes a man feel prudent like; and then goodbye to happiness. You give me what I ask you, Governor: not a penny more, and not a penny less.

PICKERING: Why dont you marry that missus of yours? I rather draw the line at encouraging that sort of immorality.

DOOLITTLE: Tell her so, Governor: tell her so. *I*'m willing. It's me that suffers by it. Ive no hold on her. I got to be agreeable to her. I got to give her presents. I got to buy her clothes something sinful. I'm a slave to that woman, Governor, just because I'm not her lawful husband. And she knows it too. Catch her marrying me! Take my advice, Governor: marry Eliza while she's young and dont know no better. If you dont youll be sorry for it after. If you do, she'll be sorry for it after; but better her than you, because youre a man, and she's only a woman and dont know how to be happy anyhow.

HIGGINS: Pickering: if we listen to this man another minute, we shall have no convictions left. *(To* DOOLITTLE*)* Five pounds I think you said.

DOOLITTLE: Thank you kindly, Governor.

HIGGINS: Youre sure you wont take ten?

DOOLITTLE: Not now. Another time, Governor.

HIGGINS *(handing him a five-pound note)*: Here you are.

DOOLITTLE: Thank you, Governor. Good morning.
(He hurries to the door, anxious to get away with his booty. When he opens it he is confronted with a dainty and exquisitely clean young Japanese lady in a simple blue cotton kimono printed cunningly with small white jasmine blossoms. MRS PEARCE *is with her. He gets out of her way deferentially and apologizes.)* Beg pardon, miss.

THE JAPANESE LADY: Garn! Dont you know your own daughter?

DOOLITTLE:	*(exclaiming*	Bly me! it's Eliza!
HIGGINS:	*simultaneously)*	Whats that! This!
PICKERING:		By Jove!

LIZA: Dont I look silly?

HIGGINS: Silly?

MRS. PEARCE *(at the door)*: Now, Mr Higgins, please dont say anything to make the girl conceited about herself.

HIGGINS *(conscientiously)*: Oh! Quite right, Mrs Pearce. *(To* ELIZA*)* Yes: damned silly.

MRS PEARCE: Please, sir.

HIGGINS *(correcting himself)*: I mean extremely silly.

LIZA: I should look all right with my hat on. *(She takes up her hat; puts it on; and walks across the room to the fireplace with a fashionable air.)*

HIGGINS: A new fashion, by George! And it ought to look horrible!

DOOLITTLE *(with fatherly pride)*: Well, I never thought she'd clean up as good looking as that, Governor. She's a credit to me, aint she?

LIZA: I tell you, it's easy to clean up here. Hot and

cold water on tap, just as much as you like, there is. Woolly towels, there is; and a towel horse so hot, it burns your fingers. Soft brushes to scrub yourself, and a wooden bowl of soap smelling like primroses. Now I know why ladies is so clean. Washing's a treat for them. Wish they saw what it is for the like of me!

HIGGINS: I'm glad the bathroom met with your approval.

LIZA: It didnt: not all of it; and I dont care who hears me say it. Mrs Pearce knows.

HIGGINS: What was wrong, Mrs Pearce?

MRS PEARCE *(blandly)*: Oh, nothing sir. It doesnt matter.

LIZA: I had a good mind to break it. I didnt know which way to look. But I hung a towel over it, I did.

HIGGINS: Over what?

MRS PEARCE: Over the looking-glass, sir.

HIGGINS: Doolittle: you have brought your daughter up too strictly.

DOOLITTLE: Me! I never brought her up at all, except to give her a lick of a strap now and again. Dont put it on me, Governor. She aint accustomed to it, you see: thats all. But she'll soon pick up your free-and-easy ways.

LIZA: I'm a good girl, I am; and I won't pick up no free-and-easy ways.

HIGGINS: Eliza: if you say again that youre a good girl, your father shall take you home.

LIZA: Not him. You dont know my father. All he come here for was to touch you for some money to get drunk on.

DOOLITTLE: Well, what else would I want money for? To put into the plate in church, I suppose. *(She puts out her tongue at him. He is so incensed by this that* PICKERING *presently finds it necessary to step between them.)* Dont you give me none of your lip; and dont let me hear you giving this gentleman any of it neither, or youll hear from me about it. See?

HIGGINS: Have you any further advice to give her before you go, Doolittle? Your blessing, for instance.

DOOLITTLE: No, Governor: I aint such a mug as to put up my children to all I know myself. Hard enough to hold them in without that. If you want Eliza's mind improved, Governor, you do it yourself with a strap. So long, gentlemen. *(He turns to go.)*

HIGGINS *(impressively)*: Stop. Youll come regularly to see your daughter. It's your duty, you know. My brother is a clergyman; and he could help you in your talks with her.

DOOLITTLE *(evasively)*: Certainly. I'll come, Governor. Not just this week, because I have a job at a distance. But later on you may depend on me. Afternoon, Gentlemen. Afternoon, maam. *(He takes off his hat to* MRS PEARCE, *who disdains the salutation and goes out. He winks at* HIGGINS, *thinking him probably a fellow sufferer from* MRS PEARCE's *difficult disposition, and follows her.*)

LIZA: Dont you believe the old liar. He'd as soon you set a bull-dog on him as a clergyman. You wont see him again in a hurry.

HIGGINS: I dont want to, Eliza. Do you?

LIZA: Not me. I dont want never to see him again, I dont. He's a disgrace to me, he is, collecting dust, instead of working at his trade.

PICKERING: What is his trade, Eliza?

LIZA: Taking money out of other people's pockets into his own. His proper trade's a navvy; and he works at it sometimes too—for exercise—and earns good money at it. Aint you going to call me Miss Doolittle any more?

PICKERING: I beg your pardon, Miss Doolittle. It was a slip of the tongue.

LIZA: Oh, I dont mind; only it sounded so genteel. I should just like to take a taxi to the corner of Tottenham Court Road and get out there and tell it to wait for me, just to put the girls in their place a bit. I wouldnt speak to them, you know.

PICKERING: Better wait til we get you something really fashionable.

HIGGINS: Besides, you shouldnt cut your old friends now that you have risen in the world. Thats what we call snobbery.

LIZA: You dont call the like of them my friends now, I should hope. Theyve took it out of me often enough with their ridicule when they had the chance; and now I mean to get a bit of my own back. But if I'm to have fashionable clothes, I'll wait. I should like to have some. Mrs Pearce says youre going to give me some to wear in bed at night different to what I wear in the daytime; but it do seem a waste of money when you could get something to shew. Besides, I never could fancy changing into cold things on a winter night.

MRS PEARCE (coming back): Now, Eliza. The new things have come for you to try on.

LIZA: Ah-ow-oo-ooh! (She rushes out.)

MRS PEARCE (following her): Oh, dont rush about like that, girl. (She shuts the door behind her.)

HIGGINS: Pickering: we have taken on a stiff job.

PICKERING (with conviction): Higgins: we have.

ACT 3

(*It is* MRS HIGGINS's *at-home day. Nobody has yet arrived. Her drawing room, in a flat on Chelsea Embankment, has three windows looking on the river; and the ceiling is not so lofty as it would be in an older house of the same pretension. The windows are open, giving access to a balcony with flowers in pots. If you stand with your face to the windows, you have the fireplace on your left and the door in the right-hand wall close to the corner nearest the windows.*

MRS HIGGINS *was brought up on Morris and Burne Jones; and her room, which is very unlike her son's room in Wimpole Street, is not crowded with furniture and little tables and nicknacks. In the middle of the room there is a big ottoman; and this, with the carpet, the Morris wallpapers, and the Morris chintz window curtains and brocade covers of the ottoman and its cushions, supply all the ornament, and are much too handsome to be hidden by odds and ends of useless things. A few good oil-paintings from the exhibitions in the Grosvenor Gallery thirty years ago (the Burne Jones, not the Whistler side of them) are on the walls. The only landscape is a Cecil Lawson on the scale of a Rubens. There is a portrait of* MRS HIGGINS *as she was when she defied fashion in her youth in one of the beautiful Rossettian costumes which, when caricatured by people who did not understand, led to the absurdities of popular estheticism in the eighteen-seventies.*

In the corner diagonally opposite the door MRS HIGGINS, *now over sixty and long past taking the trouble to dress out of the fashion, sits writing at an elegantly simple writing-table with a bell button within reach of her hand. There is a Chippendale chair further back in the room between her and the window nearest her side. At the other side of the room, further forward, is an Elizabethan chair roughly carved in the taste of Inigo Jones. On the same side a piano in a decorated case. The corner between the fireplace and the window is occupied by a divan cushioned in Morris chintz.*

It is between four and five in the afternoon.

The door is opened violently; and HIGGINS *enters with his hat on.*)

MRS HIGGINS (dismayed): Henry (scolding him)! What are you doing here to-day? It is my at-home day: you promised not to come. (As he bends to kiss her, she takes his hat off, and presents it to him.)

HIGGINS: Oh bother! (He throws the hat down on the table.)

MRS HIGGINS: Go home at once.

HIGGINS (kissing her): I know, mother. I came on purpose.

MRS HIGGINS: But you mustnt. I'm serious, Henry. You offend all my friends: they stop coming whenever they meet you.

HIGGINS: Nonsense! I know I have no small talk; but people dont mind. (He sits on the settee.)

MRS HIGGINS: Oh! dont they? Small talk indeed! What about your large talk? Really, dear, you mustnt stay.

HIGGINS: I must. Ive a job for you. A phonetic job.

MRS HIGGINS: No use, dear. I'm sorry; but I cant get round your vowels; and though I like to get pretty postcards in your patent shorthand, I always have to read the copies in ordinary writing you so thoughtfully send me.

HIGGINS: Well, this isnt a phonetic job.

MRS HIGGINS: You said it was.

HIGGINS: Not your part of it. Ive picked up a girl.

MRS HIGGINS: Does that mean that some girl has picked you up?

HIGGINS: Not at all. I dont mean a love affair.

MRS HIGGINS: What a pity!

HIGGINS: Why?

MRS HIGGINS: Well, you never fall in love with anyone under forty-five. When will you discover that there are some rather nice-looking young women about?

HIGGINS: Oh, I cant be bothered with young women. My idea of a lovable woman is something as like you as possible. I shall never get into the way of seriously liking young women: some habits lie too deep to be changed. (*Rising abruptly and walking about, jingling his money and his keys in his trouser pockets*) Besides, theyre all idiots.

MRS HIGGINS: Do you know what you would do if you really loved me, Henry?

HIGGINS: Oh bother! What? Marry, I suppose?

MRS HIGGINS: No. Stop fidgeting and take your hands out of your pockets. (*With a gesture of despair, he obeys and sits down again.*) Thats a good boy. Now tell me about the girl.

HIGGINS: She's coming to see you.

MRS HIGGINS: I dont remember asking her.

HIGGINS: You didnt. *I* asked her. If youd known her you wouldnt have asked her.

MRS HIGGINS: Indeed! Why?

HIGGINS: Well, it's like this. She's a common flower girl. I picked her off the kerbstone.

MRS HIGGINS: And invited her to my at-home!

HIGGINS (*rising and coming to her to coax her*): Oh, thatll be all right. Ive taught her to speak properly; and she has strict orders as to her behavior. She's to keep to two subjects: the weather and everybody's health—Fine day and How do you do, you know—and not to let herself go on things in general. That will be safe.

MRS HIGGINS: Safe! To talk about our health! about our insides! perhaps about our outsides! How could you be so silly, Henry?

HIGGINS (*impatiently*): Well, she must talk about something. (*He controls himself and sits down again.*) Oh, she'll be all right: dont you fuss. Pickering is in it with me. Ive a sort of bet on that I'll pass her off as a duchess in six months. I started on her some months ago; and she's getting on like a house on fire. I shall win my bet. She has a quick ear; and she's been easier to teach than my middle-class pupils because she's had to learn a complete new language. She talks English almost as you talk French.

MRS HIGGINS: Thats satisfactory, at all events.

HIGGINS: Well, it is and it isnt.

MRS HIGGINS: What does that mean?

HIGGINS: You see, Ive got her pronunciation all right; but you have to consider not only how a girl pronounces, but what she pronounces; and thats where—

(*They are interrupted by the parlor-maid, announcing guests.*)

THE PARLOR-MAID: Mrs and Miss Eynsford Hill. (*She withdraws.*)

HIGGINS: Oh Lord! (*He rises; snatches his hat from the table; and makes for the door; but before he reaches it his mother introduces him.*)

(MRS *and* MISS EYNSFORD HILL *are the mother and daughter who sheltered from the rain in Covent Garden. The mother is well bred, quiet, and has the habitual anxiety of straitened means. The daughter has acquired a gay air of being very much at home in society: the bravado of genteel poverty.*)

MRS EYNSFORD HILL (*to* MRS HIGGINS): How do you do? (*They shake hands.*)

MISS EYNSFORD HILL: How d'you do? (*She shakes.*)

MRS HIGGINS (*introducing*): My son Henry.

MRS EYNSFORD HILL: Your celebrated son! I have so longed to meet you, Professor Higgins.

HIGGINS (*glumly, making no movement in her direction*): Delighted. (*He backs against the piano and bows brusquely.*)

MISS EYNSFORD HILL (*going to him with confident familiarity*): How do you do?

HIGGINS (*staring at her*): Ive seen you before somewhere. I havnt the ghost of a notion where; but Ive heard your voice. (*Drearily*) It doesnt matter. Youd better sit down.

MRS HIGGINS: I'm sorry to say that my celebrated son has no manners. You mustnt mind him.

MISS EYNSFORD HILL (*gaily*): I dont. (*She sits in the Elizabethan chair.*)

MRS EYNSFORD HILL (*a little bewildered*): Not at all. (*She sits on the ottoman between her daughter and* MRS HIGGINS, *who has turned her chair away from the writing table.*)

HIGGINS: Oh, have I been rude? I didnt mean to be.

(*He goes to the central window, through which, with his back to the company, he contemplates the river and the flowers in Battersea Park on the opposite bank as if they were a frozen desert.*
The parlor-maid returns, ushering in PICKERING.)

THE PARLOR-MAID: Colonel Pickering. (*She withdraws.*)

PICKERING: How do you do, Mrs Higgins?

MRS HIGGINS: So glad youve come. Do you know Mrs Eynsford Hill—Miss Eynsford Hill? (*Exchange of bows. The* COLONEL *brings the Chippendale chair a little forward between* MRS HILL *and* MRS HIGGINS, *and sits down.*)

PICKERING: Has Henry told you what weve come for?

HIGGINS (*over his shoulder*): We were interrupted: damn it!

MRS HIGGINS: Oh Henry, Henry, really!

MRS EYNSFORD HILL (*half rising*): Are we in the way?

MRS HIGGINS (*rising and making her sit down again*): No, no. You couldnt have come more fortunately: we want you to meet a friend of ours.

HIGGINS (*turning hopefully*): Yes, by George! We want two or three people. Youll do as well as anybody else.

(*The parlor-maid returns, ushering* FREDDY.)

THE PARLOR-MAID: Mr Eynsford Hill.

HIGGINS (*almost audibly, past endurance*): God of Heaven! another of them.

FREDDY (*shaking hands with* MRS HIGGINS): Ahdedo?

MRS HIGGINS: Very good of you to come. (*Introducing*) Colonel Pickering.

FREDDY (*bowing*): Ahdedo?

MRS HIGGINS: I dont think you know my son, Professor Higgins.

FREDDY (*going to* HIGGINS): Ahdedo?

HIGGINS (*looking at him much as if he were a pickpocket*): I'll take my oath Ive met you before somewhere. Where was it?

FREDDY: I dont think so.

HIGGINS (*resignedly*): It dont matter, anyhow. Sit down.

(*He shakes* FREDDY's *hand, and almost slings him on to the ottoman with his face to the windows; then comes round to the other side of it.*)

HIGGINS: Well, here we are, anyhow! (*He sits down on the ottoman next* MRS EYNSFORD HILL, *on her left.*) And now, what the devil are we going to talk about until Eliza comes?

MRS HIGGINS: Henry: you are the life and soul of the Royal Society's soirées; but really youre rather trying on more commonplace occasions.

HIGGINS: Am I? Very sorry. (*Beaming suddenly*) I suppose I am, you know. (*Uproariously*) Ha, ha!

MISS EYNSFORD HILL (*who considers* HIGGINS *quite eligible matrimonially*): I sympathize. *I* havnt any small talk. If people would only be frank and say what they really think!

HIGGINS (*relapsing into gloom*): Lord forbid!

MRS EYNSFORD HILL (*taking up her daughter's cue*): But why?

HIGGINS: What they think they ought to think is bad enough, Lord knows; but what they really think would break up the whole show. Do you suppose it would be really agreeable if I were to come out now with what *I* really think?

MISS EYNSFORD HILL (*gaily*): Is it so very cynical?

HIGGINS: Cynical! Who the dickens said it was cynical? I mean it wouldnt be decent.

MRS EYNSFORD HILL (*seriously*): Oh! I'm sure you dont mean that, Mr Higgins.

HIGGINS: You see, we're all savages, more or less. We're supposed to be civilized and cultured—to know all about poetry and philosophy and art and science, and so on; but how many of us know even the meanings of these names? (*To* MISS HILL) What do you know of poetry? (*To* MRS HILL) What do you know of science? (*Indicating* FREDDY) What does he know of art or science or anything else? What the devil do you imagine I know of philosophy?

MRS HIGGINS (*warningly*): Or of manners, Henry?

THE PARLOR-MAID (*opening the door*): Miss Doolittle. (*She withdraws.*)

HIGGINS (*rising hastily and running to* MRS HIGGINS): Here she is, mother. (*He stands on tiptoe and makes signs over his mother's head to* ELIZA *to indicate to her which lady is her hostess*).

(ELIZA, *who is exquisitely dressed, produces an impression of such remarkable distinction and beauty as she enters that they all rise, quite fluttered. Guided by* HIGGINS's *signals, she comes to* MRS HIGGINS *with studied grace.*)

LIZA (*speaking with pedantic correctness of pronunciation and great beauty of tone*): How do you do, Mrs Higgins? (*She gasps slightly in making sure of the H in* HIGGINS, *but is quite successful.*) Mr Higgins told me I might come.

MRS HIGGINS (*cordially*): Quite right: I'm very glad indeed to see you.

PICKERING: How do you do, Miss Doolittle?

LIZA (*shaking hands with him*): Colonel Pickering, is it not?

MRS EYNSFORD HILL: I feel sure we have met before, Miss Doolittle. I remember your eyes.

LIZA: How do you do? (*She sits down on the ottoman gracefully in the place just left vacant by* HIGGINS.)

MRS EYNSFORD HILL (*introducing*): My daughter Clara.

LIZA: How do you do?

CLARA (*impulsively*): How do you do? (*She sits down on the ottoman beside* ELIZA, *devouring her with her eyes.*)

FREDDY (*coming to their side of the ottoman*): Ive certainly had the pleasure.

MRS EYNSFORD HILL (*introducing*): My son Freddy.

LIZA: How do you do?

(FREDDY *bows and sits down in the Elizabethan chair, infatuated.*)

HIGGINS (*suddenly*): By George, yes: it all comes back to me! (*They stare at him.*) Covent Garden! (*Lamentably*) What a damned thing!

MRS HIGGINS: Henry, please! (*He is about to sit on the edge of the table*) Dont sit on my writing-table: youll break it.

HIGGINS (*sulkily*): Sorry.

(*He goes to the divan, stumbling into the fender and over the fire-irons on his way; extricating himself with muttered imprecations; and finishing his disastrous journey by throwing himself so impatiently on the divan that he almost breaks it.* MRS HIGGINS *looks at him, but controls herself and says nothing.*

A long and painful pause ensues.)

MRS HIGGINS *(at last, conversationally)*: Will it rain, do you think?

LIZA: The shallow depression in the west of these islands is likely to move slowly in an easterly direction. There are no indications of any great change in the barometrical situation.

FREDDY: Ha! ha! how awfully funny!

LIZA: What is wrong with that, young man? I bet I got it right.

FREDDY: Killing!

MRS EYNSFORD HILL: I'm sure I hope it wont turn cold. Theres so much influenza about. It runs right through our whole family regularly every spring.

LIZA *(darkly)*: My aunt died of influenza: so they said.

MRS EYNSFORD HILL *(clicks her tongue sympathetically)*: !!!

LIZA *(in the same tragic tone)*: But it's my belief they done the old woman in.

MRS HIGGINS *(puzzled)*: Done her in?

LIZA: Y-e-e-e-es, Lord love you! Why should she die of influenza? She come through diphtheria right enough the year before. I saw her with my own eyes. Fairly blue with it, she was. They all thought she was dead; but my father he kept ladling gin down her throat til she came to so sudden that she bit the bowl off the spoon.

MRS EYNSFORD HILL *(startled)*: Dear me!

LIZA *(piling up the indictment)*: What call would a woman with that strength in her have to die of influenza? What become of her new straw hat that should have come to me? Somebody pinched it; and what I say is, them as pinched it done her in.

MRS EYNSFORD HILL: What does doing her in mean?

HIGGINS *(hastily)*: Oh, thats the new small talk. To do a person in means to kill them.

MRS EYNSFORD HILL *(to ELIZA, horrified)*: You surely dont believe that your aunt was killed?

LIZA: Do I not! Them she lived with would have killed her for a hat-pin, let alone a hat.

MRS EYNSFORD HILL: But it cant have been right for your father to pour spirits down her throat like that. It might have killed her.

LIZA: Not her. Gin was mother's milk to her. Besides, he'd poured so much down his own throat that he knew the good of it.

MRS EYNSFORD HILL: Do you mean that he drank?

LIZA: Drank! My word! Something chronic.

MRS EYNSFORD HILL: How dreadful for you!

LIZA: Not a bit. It never did him no harm what I could see. But then he did not keep it up regular. *(Cheerfully)* On the burst, as you might say, from time to

time. And always more agreeable when he had a drop in. When he was out of work, my mother used to give him fourpence and tell him to go out and not come back until he'd drunk himself cheerful and loving-like. Theres lots of women has to make their husbands drunk to make them fit to live with. *(Now quite at her ease)* You see, it's like this. If a man has a bit of a conscience, it always takes him when he's sober; and then it makes him low-spirited. A drop of booze just takes that off and makes him happy. *(To FREDDY, who is in convulsions of suppressed laughter)* Here! what are you sniggering at?

FREDDY: The new small talk. You do it so awfully well.

LIZA: If I was doing it proper, what was you laughing at? *(To HIGGINS)* Have I said anything I oughtnt?

MRS HIGGINS *(interposing)*: Not at all, Miss Doolittle.

LIZA: Well, thats a mercy, anyhow. *(Expansively)* What I always say is—

HIGGINS *(rising and looking at his watch)*: Ahem!

LIZA *(looking round at him; taking the hint; and rising)*: Well: I must go. *(They all rise.* FREDDY *goes to the door.)* So pleased to have met you. Goodbye. *(She shakes hands with* MRS HIGGINS.*)*

MRS HIGGINS: Goodbye.

LIZA: Goodbye, Colonel Pickering.

PICKERING: Goodbye, Miss Doolittle. *(They shake hands.)*

LIZA *(nodding to the others)*: Goodbye, all.

FREDDY *(opening the door for her)*: Are you walking across the Park, Miss Doolittle? If so—

LIZA: Walk! Not bloody likely. *(Sensation.)* I am going in a taxi. *(She goes out.)*

*(*PICKERING *gasps and sits down.* FREDDY *goes out on the balcony to catch another glimpse of* ELIZA.*)*

MRS EYNSFORD HILL *(suffering from shock)*: Well, I really cant get used to the new ways.

CLARA *(throwing herself discontentedly into the Elizabethan chair)*: Oh, it's all right, mamma, quite right. People will think we never go anywhere or see anybody if you are so old-fashioned.

MRS EYNSFORD HILL: I daresay I am very old-fashioned; but I do hope you wont begin using that expression, Clara. I have got accustomed to hear you talking about men as rotters, and calling everything filthy and beastly; though I do think it horrible and unladylike. But this last is really too much. Dont you think so, Colonel Pickering?

PICKERING: Dont ask me. Ive been away in India for several years; and manners have changed so much that I sometimes dont know whether I'm at a respectable dinner-table or in a ship's forecastle.

CLARA: It's all a matter of habit. Theres no right or wrong in it. Nobody means anything by it. And it's so quaint, and gives such a smart emphasis to things that are not in themselves very witty. I find the new small talk delightful and quite innocent.

MRS EYNSFORD HILL (*rising*): Well, after that, I think it's time for us to go.

(PICKERING *and* HIGGINS *rise.*)

CLARA (*rising*): Oh yes: we have three at-homes to go to still. Goodbye, Mrs Higgins. Goodbye, Colonel Pickering. Goodbye, Professor Higgins.

HIGGINS (*coming grimly at her from the divan, and accompanying her to the door*): Goodbye. Be sure you try on that small talk at the three at-homes. Dont be nervous about it. Pitch it in strong.

CLARA (*all smiles*): I will. Goodbye. Such nonsense, all this early Victorian prudery!

HIGGINS (*tempting her*): Such damned nonsense!

CLARA: Such bloody nonsense!

MRS EYNSFORD HILL (*convulsively*): Clara!

CLARA: Ha! ha! (*She goes out radiant, conscious of being thoroughly up to date, and is heard descending the stairs in a stream of silvery laughter.*)

FREDDY (*to the heavens at large*): Well, I ask you—(*He gives it up, and comes to* MRS HIGGINS.) Goodbye.

MRS HIGGINS (*shaking hands*): Goodbye. Would you like to meet Miss Doolittle again?

FREDDY (*eagerly*): Yes, I should, most awfully.

MRS HIGGINS: Well, you know my days.

FREDDY: Yes. Thanks awfully. Goodbye. (*He goes out.*)

MRS EYNSFORD HILL: Goodbye, Mr Higgins.

HIGGINS: Goodbye. Goodbye.

MRS EYNSFORD HILL (*to* PICKERING): It's no use. I shall never be able to bring myself to use that word.

PICKERING: Dont. It's not compulsory, you know. Youll get on quite well without it.

MRS EYNSFORD HILL: Only, Clara is so down on me if I am not positively reeking with the latest slang. Goodbye.

PICKERING: Goodbye. (*They shake hands.*)

MRS EYNSFORD HILL (*to* MRS HIGGINS): You mustnt mind Clara. (PICKERING, *catching from her lowered tone that this is not meant for him to hear, discreetly joins* HIGGINS *at the window.*) We're so poor! and she gets so few parties, poor child! She doesnt quite know. (MRS HIGGINS, *seeing that her eyes are moist, takes her hand sympathetically and goes with her to the door.*) But the boy is nice. Dont you think so?

MRS HIGGINS: Oh, quite nice. I shall always be delighted to see him.

MRS EYNSFORD HILL: Thank you, dear. Goodbye. (*She goes out.*)

HIGGINS (*eagerly*): Well? Is Eliza presentable? (*He swoops on his mother and drags her to the ottoman, where she sits down in* ELIZA's *place with her son on her left.*)

(PICKERING *returns to his chair on her right.*)

MRS HIGGINS: You silly boy, of course she's not presentable. She's a triumph of your art and of her dressmaker's; but if you suppose for a moment that she doesnt give herself away in every sentence she utters, you must be perfectly cracked about her.

PICKERING: But dont you think something might be done? I mean something to eliminate the sanguinary element from her conversation.

MRS HIGGINS: Not as long as she is in Henry's hands.

HIGGINS (*aggrieved*): Do you mean that my language is improper?

MRS HIGGINS: No, dearest: it would be quite proper—say on a canal barge; but it would not be proper for her at a garden party.

HIGGINS (*deeply injured*): Well I must say—

PICKERING (*interrupting him*): Come, Higgins: you must learn to know yourself. I havnt heard such language as yours since we used to review the volunteers in Hyde Park twenty years ago.

HIGGINS (*sulkily*): Oh, well, if you say so, I suppose I dont always talk like a bishop.

MRS HIGGINS (*quieting* HENRY *with a touch*): Colonel Pickering: will you tell me what is the exact state of things in Wimpole Street?

PICKERING (*cheerfully: as if this completely changed the subject*): Well, I have come to live there with Henry. We work together at my Indian Dialects; and we think it more convenient—

MRS HIGGINS: Quite so. I know all about that: it's an excellent arrangement. But where does this girl live?

HIGGINS: With us, of course. Where should she live?

MRS HIGGINS: But on what terms? Is she a servant? If not, what is she?

PICKERING (*slowly*): I think I know what you mean, Mrs Higgins.

HIGGINS: Well, dash me if *I* do! Ive had to work at the girl every day for months to get her to her present pitch. Besides, she's useful. She knows where my things are, and remembers my appointments and so forth.

MRS HIGGINS: How does your housekeeper get on with her?

HIGGINS: Mrs Pearce? Oh, she's jolly glad to get so much taken off her hands; for before Eliza came, she used to have to find things and remind me of my appointments. But she's got some silly bee in her bonnet about Eliza. She keeps saying "You dont think sir": doesnt she, Pick?

PICKERING: Yes: thats the formula. "You dont think, sir." Thats the end of every conversation about Eliza.

HIGGINS: As if I ever stop thinking about the girl and her confounded vowels and consonants. I'm worn out, thinking about her, and watching her lips and her teeth and her tongue, not to mention her soul, which is the quaintest of the lot.

MRS HIGGINS: You certainly are a pretty pair of babies, playing with your live doll.

HIGGINS: Playing! The hardest job I ever tackled: make no mistake about that, mother. But you have no idea how frightfully interesting it is to take a human being and change her into a quite different human being by creating a new speech for her. It's filling up the deepest gulf that separates class from class and soul from soul.

PICKERING (*drawing his chair closer to* MRS HIGGINS *and bending over to her eagerly*): Yes: it's enormously interesting. I assure you, Mrs Higgins, we take Eliza very seriously. Every week—every day almost—there is some new change. (*Closer again*) We keep records of every stage—dozens of gramophone disks and photographs—

HIGGINS (*assailing her at the other ear*): Yes, by George: it's the most absorbing experiment I ever tackled. She regularly fills our lives up: doesnt she, Pick?

PICKERING: We're always talking Eliza.

HIGGINS: Teaching Eliza.

PICKERING: Dressing Eliza.

MRS HIGGINS: What!

HIGGINS: Inventing new Elizas.

HIGGINS:	(*speaking together*)	You know, she has the most extraordinary quickness of ear:
PICKERING:		I assure you, my dear Mrs Higgins, that girl
HIGGINS:		just like a parrot. I've tried her with every
PICKERING:		is a genius. She can play the piano quite beautifully.
HIGGINS:		possible sort of sound that a human being can make—
PICKERING:		We have taken her to classical concerts and to music
HIGGINS:		Continental dialects, African dialects, Hottentot
PICKERING:		halls; and it's all the same to her: she plays everything
HIGGINS:		clicks, things it took me years to get hold of; and
PICKERING:		she hears right off when she comes home, whether it's
HIGGINS:		she picks them up like a shot, right away, as if she had
PICKERING:		Beethoven and Brahms or Lehar and Lionel Monckton;
HIGGINS:		been at it all her life.
PICKERING:		though six months ago, she'd never as much as touched a piano—

MRS HIGGINS (*putting her fingers in her ears, as they are by this time shouting one another down with an intolerable noise*): Sh-sh-sh—sh! (*They stop.*)

PICKERING: I beg your pardon. (*He draws his chair back apologetically.*)

HIGGINS: Sorry. When Pickering starts shouting nobody can get a word in edgeways.

MRS HIGGINS: Be quiet, Henry. Colonel Pickering: dont you realize that when Eliza walked into Wimpole Street, something walked in with her?

PICKERING: Her father did. But Henry soon got rid of him.

MRS HIGGINS: It would have been more to the point if her mother had. But as her mother didnt something else did.

PICKERING: But what?

MRS HIGGINS (*unconsciously dating herself by the word*): A problem.

PICKERING: Oh, I see. The problem of how to pass her off as a lady.

HIGGINS: I'll solve that problem. Ive half solved it already.

MRS HIGGINS: No, you two infinitely stupid male creatures: the problem of what is to be done with her afterwards.

HIGGINS: I dont see anything in that. She can go her own way, with all the advantages I have given her.

MRS HIGGINS: The advantages of that poor woman who was here just now! The manners and habits that disqualify a fine lady from earning her own living without giving her a fine lady's income! Is that what you mean?

PICKERING (*indulgently, being rather bored*): Oh, that will be all right, Mrs Higgins. (*He rises to go.*)

HIGGINS (*rising also*): We'll find her some light employment.

PICKERING: She's happy enough. Dont you worry about her. Goodbye. (*He shakes hands as if he were consoling a frightened child, and makes for the door.*)

HIGGINS: Anyhow, theres no good bothering now. The thing's done. Goodbye, mother. (*He kisses her, and follows* PICKERING.)

PICKERING (*turning for a final consolation*): There are plenty of openings. We'll do whats right. Goodbye.

HIGGINS (*to* PICKERING *as they go out together*): Let's take her to the Shakespear exhibition at Earls Court.

PICKERING: Yes: lets. Her remarks will be delicious.

HIGGINS: She'll mimic all the people for us when we get home.

PICKERING: Ripping. (*Both are heard laughing as they go downstairs.*)

MRS HIGGINS (*rises with an impatient bounce, and returns to her work at the writing-table. She sweeps a litter of disarranged papers out of her way; snatches a sheet of paper from her stationery case; and tries resolutely to write. At the third line she gives it up; flings down her pen; grips the table angrily and exclaims*): Oh, men! men!! men!!!

ACT 4

(The Wimpole Street laboratory. Midnight. Nobody in the room. The clock on the mantelpiece strikes twelve. The fire is not alight: it is a summer night.

Presently HIGGINS *and* PICKERING *are heard on the stairs.)*

HIGGINS *(calling down to* PICKERING*)*: I say, Pick: lock up, will you? I shant be going out again.

PICKERING: Right. Can Mrs Pearce go to bed? We dont want anything more, do we?

HIGGINS: Lord, no!

*(*ELIZA *opens the door and is seen on the lighted landing in opera cloak, brilliant evening dress, and diamonds, with fan, flowers, and all accessories. She comes to the hearth, and switches on the electric lights there. She is tired: her pallor contrasts strongly with her dark eyes and hair; and her expression is almost tragic. She takes off her cloak; puts her fan and flowers on the piano; and sits down on the bench, brooding and silent.* HIGGINS, *in evening dress, with overcoat and hat, comes in, carrying a smoking jacket which he has picked up downstairs. He takes off the hat and overcoat; throws them carelessly on the newspaper stand; disposes of his coat in the same way; puts on the smoking jacket; and throws himself wearily into the easy-chair at the hearth.* PICKERING, *similarly attired, comes in. He also takes off his hat and overcoat, and is about to throw them on* HIGGINS's *when he hesitates.)*

PICKERING: I say: Mrs Pearce will row if we leave these things lying about in the drawing room.

HIGGINS: Oh, chuck them over the bannisters into the hall. She'll find them there in the morning and put them away all right. She'll think we were drunk.

PICKERING: We are, slightly. Are there any letters?

HIGGINS: I didnt look. *(*PICKERING *takes the overcoats and hats and goes downstairs.* HIGGINS *begins half singing half yawning an air from La Fanciulla del Golden West. Suddenly he stops and exclaims)* I wonder where the devil my slippers are!

*(*ELIZA *looks at him darkly; then rises suddenly and leaves the room.*

HIGGINS *yawns again, and resumes his song.*

PICKERING *returns, with the contents of the letter-box in his hand.)*

PICKERING: Only circulars, and this coroneted billet-doux for you. *(He throws the circulars into the fender, and posts himself on the hearthrug, with his back to the grate.)*

HIGGINS *(glancing at the billet-doux)*: Money-lender. *(He throws the letter after the circulars.)*

*(*ELIZA *returns with a pair of large down-at-heel slippers. She places them on the carpet before* HIGGINS, *and sits as before without a word.)*

HIGGINS *(yawning again)*: Oh Lord! What an evening! What a crew! What a silly tomfoolery! *(He raises his shoe to unlace it, and catches sight of the slippers. He stops unlacing and looks at them as if they had appeared there of their own accord.)* Oh! theyre there, are they?

PICKERING *(stretching himself)*: Well, I feel a bit tired. It's been a long day. The garden party, a dinner party, and the opera! Rather too much of a good thing. But youve won your bet, Higgins. Eliza did the trick, and something to spare, eh?

HIGGINS *(fervently)*: Thank God it's over!

*(*ELIZA *flinches violently; but they take no notice of her; and she recovers herself and sits stonily as before.)*

PICKERING: Were you nervous at the garden party? *I* was. Eliza didnt seem a bit nervous.

HIGGINS: Oh, she wasnt nervous. I knew she'd be all right. No: it's the strain of putting the job through all these months that has told on me. It was interesting enough at first, while we were at the phonetics; but after that I got deadly sick of it. If I hadnt backed myself to do it I should have chucked the whole thing up two months ago. It was a silly notion: the whole thing has been a bore.

PICKERING: Oh come! the garden party was frightfully exciting. My heart began beating like anything.

HIGGINS: Yes, for the first three minutes. But when I saw we were going to win hands down, I felt like a bear in a cage, hanging about doing nothing. The dinner was worse: sitting gorging there for over an hour, with nobody but a damned fool of a fashionable woman to talk to! I tell you, Pickering, never again for me. No more artificial duchesses. The whole thing has been simple purgatory.

PICKERING: Youve never been broken in properly to the social routine. *(Strolling over to the piano)* I rather enjoy dipping into it occasionally myself: it makes me feel young again. Anyhow, it was a great success: an immense success. I was quite frightened once or twice because Eliza was doing it so well. You see, lots of the real people cant do it at all: theyre such fools that they think style comes by nature to people in their position; and so they never learn. Theres always something professional about doing a thing superlatively well.

HIGGINS: Yes: thats what drives me mad: the silly people dont know their own silly business. *(Rising)* However, it's over and done with; and now I can go to bed at last without dreading tomorrow.

*(*ELIZA's *beauty becomes murderous.)*

PICKERING: I think I shall turn in too. Still, it's been a great occasion: a triumph for you. Goodnight. *(He goes.)*

HIGGINS *(following him)*: Goodnight. *(Over his shoulder, at the door)* Put out the lights, Eliza; and tell Mrs

Pearce not to make coffee for me in the morning: I'll take tea. (*He goes out.*)

(ELIZA *tries to control herself and feel indifferent as she rises and walks across to the hearth to switch off the lights. By the time she gets there she is on the point of screaming. She sits down in* HIGGINS's *chair and holds on hard to the arms. Finally she gives way and flings herself furiously on the floor, raging.*)

HIGGINS (*in despairing wrath outside*): What the devil have I done with my slippers? (*He appears at the door.*)

LIZA (*snatching up the slippers, and hurling them at him one after the other with all her force*): There are your slippers. And there. Take your slippers; and may you never have a day's luck with them!

HIGGINS (*astounded*): What on earth—! (*He comes to her.*) Whats the matter? Get up. (*He pulls her up.*) Anything wrong?

LIZA (*breathless*): Nothing wrong—with you. Ive won your bet for you, havnt I? Thats enough for you. *I* dont matter, I suppose.

HIGGINS: You won my bet! You! Presumptuous insect! *I* won it. What did you throw those slippers at me for?

LIZA: Because I wanted to smash your face. I'd like to kill you, you selfish brute. Why didnt you leave me where you picked me out of—in the gutter? You thank God it's all over, and that now you can throw me back again there, do you? (*She crisps her fingers frantically.*)

HIGGINS (*looking at her in cool wonder*): The creature is nervous, after all.

LIZA (*gives a suffocated scream of fury, and instinctively darts her nails at his face*): !!

HIGGINS (*catching her wrists*): Ah! would you? Claws in, you cat. How dare you shew your temper to me? Sit down and be quiet. (*He throws her roughly into the easy-chair.*)

LIZA (*crushed by superior strength and weight*): Whats to become of me? Whats to become of me?

HIGGINS: How the devil do I know whats to become of you? What does it matter what becomes of you?

LIZA: You dont care. I know you dont care. You wouldnt care if I was dead. I'm nothing to you—not so much as them slippers.

HIGGINS (*thundering*): Those slippers.

LIZA (*with bitter submission*): Those slippers. I didnt think it made any difference now.

(*A pause.* ELIZA *hopeless and crushed.* HIGGINS *a little uneasy.*)

HIGGINS (*in his loftiest manner*): Why have you begun going on like this? May I ask whether you complain of your treatment here?

LIZA: No.

HIGGINS: Has anybody behaved badly to you? Colonel Pickering? Mrs Pearce? Any of the servants?

LIZA: No.

HIGGINS: I presume you dont pretend that *I* have treated you badly?

LIZA: No.

HIGGINS: I am glad to hear it. (*He moderates his tone.*) Perhaps youre tired after the strain of the day. Will you have a glass of champagne? (*He moves towards the door.*)

LIZA: No. (*Recollecting her manners*) Thank you.

HIGGINS (*good-humored again*): This has been coming on you for some days. I suppose it was natural for you to be anxious about the garden party. But thats all over now. (*He pats her kindly on the shoulder. She writhes.*) Theres nothing more to worry about.

LIZA: No. Nothing more for you to worry about. (*She suddenly rises and gets away from him by going to the piano bench, where she sits and hides her face.*) Oh God! I wish I was dead.

HIGGINS (*staring after her in sincere surprise*): Why? In heaven's name, why? (*Reasonably, going to her*) Listen to me, Eliza. All this irritation is purely subjective.

LIZA: I dont understand. I'm too ignorant.

HIGGINS: It's only imagination. Low spirits and nothing else. Nobody's hurting you. Nothing's wrong. You go to bed like a good girl and sleep it off. Have a little cry and say your prayers: that will make you comfortable.

LIZA: I heard your prayers. "Thank God it's all over!"

HIGGINS (*impatiently*): Well, dont you thank God it's all over? Now you are free and can do what you like.

LIZA (*pulling herself together in desperation*): What am I fit for? What have you left me fit for? Where am I to go? What am I to do? Whats to become of me?

HIGGINS (*enlightened, but not at all impressed*): Oh thats whats worrying you, is it? (*He thrusts his hands into his pockets, and walks about in his usual manner, rattling the contents of his pockets, as if condescending to a trivial subject out of pure kindness.*) I shouldnt bother about it if I were you. I should imagine you wont have much difficulty in settling yourself somewhere or other, though I hadnt quite realized that you were going away. (*She looks quickly at him: he does not look at her, but examines the dessert stand on the piano and decides that he will eat an apple.*) You might marry, you know. (*He bites a large piece out of the apple and munches it noisily.*) You see, Eliza, all men are not confirmed old bachelors like me and the Colonel. Most men are the marrying sort (poor devils!); and youre not bad-looking: it's quite a pleasure to look at you sometimes—not now, of course, because youre crying and looking as ugly as the very devil; but when youre all right and quite yourself, youre what I should call attractive. That is, to the people in the marrying line, you understand. You go to bed and have a good nice rest; and then get up and look at yourself in the glass; and you wont feel so cheap.

(ELIZA *again looks at him, speechless, and does not stir. The look is quite lost on him: he eats his apple with a dreamy expression of happiness, as it is quite a good one.*)

HIGGINS (*a genial afterthought occurring to him*): I daresay my mother could find some chap or other who would do very well.

LIZA: We were above that at the corner of Tottenham Court Road.

HIGGINS (*waking up*): What do you mean?

LIZA: I sold flowers. I didnt sell myself. Now youve made a lady of me I'm not fit to sell anything else. I wish youd left me where you found me.

HIGGINS (*slinging the core of the apple decisively into the grate*): Tosh, Eliza. Dont you insult human relations by dragging all this cant about buying and selling into it. You neednt marry the fellow if you dont like him.

LIZA: What else am I to do?

HIGGINS: Oh, lots of things. What about your old idea of a florist's shop? Pickering could set you up in one: he's lots of money. (*Chuckling*) He'll have to pay for all those togs you have been wearing today; and that, with the hire of the jewellery, will make a big hole in two hundred pounds. Why, six months ago you would have thought it the millennium to have a flower shop of your own. Come! youll be all right. I must clear off to bed: I'm devilish sleepy. By the way, I came down for something: I forget what it was.

LIZA: Your slippers.

HIGGINS: Oh yes, of course. You shied them at me. (*He picks them up, and is going out when she rises and speaks to him.*)

LIZA: Before you go, sir—

HIGGINS (*dropping the slippers in his surprise at her calling him Sir*): Eh?

LIZA: Do my clothes belong to me or to Colonel Pickering?

HIGGINS (*coming back into the room as if her question were the very climax of unreason*): What the devil use would they be to Pickering?

LIZA: He might want them for the next girl you pick up to experiment on.

HIGGINS (*shocked and hurt*): Is that the way you feel towards us?

LIZA: I dont want to hear anything more about that. All I want to know is whether anything belongs to me. My own clothes were burnt.

HIGGINS: But what does it matter? Why need you start bothering about that in the middle of the night?

LIZA: I want to know what I may take away with me. I dont want to be accused of stealing.

HIGGINS (*now deeply wounded*): Stealing! You shouldnt have said that, Eliza. That shews a want of feeling.

LIZA: I'm sorry. I'm only a common ignorant girl; and in my station I have to be careful. There cant be any feelings between the like of you and the like of me. Please will you tell me what belongs to me and what doesnt?

HIGGINS (*very sulky*): You may take the whole damned houseful if you like. Except the jewels. Theyre hired. Will that satisfy you? (*He turns on his heel and is about to go in extreme dudgeon.*)

LIZA (*drinking in his emotion like nectar, and nagging him to provoke a further supply*): Stop, please. (*She takes off her jewels.*) Will you take these to your room and keep them safe? I dont want to run the risk of their being missing.

HIGGINS (*furious*): Hand them over. (*She puts them into his hands.*) If these belonged to me instead of to the jeweller, I'd ram them down your ungrateful throat. (*He perfunctorily thrusts them into his pockets, unconsciously decorating himself with the protruding ends of the chains.*)

LIZA (*taking a ring off*): This ring isnt the jeweller's: it's the one you bought me in Brighton. I dont want it now. (HIGGINS *dashes the ring violently into the fireplace, and turns on her so threateningly that she crouches over the piano with her hands over her face, and exclaims*) Dont you hit me.

HIGGINS: Hit you! You infamous creature, how dare you accuse me of such a thing? It is you who have hit me. You have wounded me to the heart.

LIZA (*thrilling with hidden joy*): I'm glad. Ive got a little of my own back, anyhow.

HIGGINS (*with dignity, in his finest professional style*): You have caused me to lose my temper: a thing that has hardly ever happened to me before. I prefer to say nothing more tonight. I am going to bed.

LIZA (*pertly*): Youd better leave a note for Mrs Pearce about the coffee; for she wont be told by me.

HIGGINS (*formally*): Damn Mrs Pearce; and damn the coffee; and damn you; and damn my own folly in having lavished hard-earned knowledge and the treasure of my regard and intimacy on a heartless guttersnipe. (*He goes out with impressive decorum, and spoils it by slamming the door savagely.*)

(ELIZA *smiles for the first time; expresses her feelings by a wild pantomime in which an imitation of* HIGGINS's *exit is confused with her own triumph; and finally goes down on her knees on the hearthrug to look for the ring.*)

ACT 5

(MRS HIGGINS's *drawing room. She is at her writing-table as before. The parlor-maid comes in.*)

THE PARLOR-MAID (*at the door*): Mr Henry, maam, is downstairs with Colonel Pickering.

MRS HIGGINS: Well, shew them up.

THE PARLOR-MAID: Theyre using the telephone, maam. Telephoning to the police, I think.

MRS HIGGINS: What!

THE PARLOR-MAID *(coming further in and lowering her voice)*: Mr Henry is in a state, maam. I thought I'd better tell you.

MRS HIGGINS: If you had told me that Mr Henry was not in a state it would have been more surprising. Tell them to come up when theyve finished with the police. I suppose he's lost something.

THE PARLOR-MAID: Yes, maam *(going).*

MRS HIGGINS: Go upstairs and tell Miss Doolittle that Mr Henry and the Colonel are here. Ask her not to come down til I send for her.

THE PARLOR-MAID: Yes, maam.

(HIGGINS bursts in. He is, as the parlor-maid has said, in a state.)

HIGGINS: Look here, mother: heres a confounded thing!

MRS HIGGINS: Yes, dear. Good morning. *(He checks his impatience and kisses her, whilst the parlor-maid goes out.)* What is it?

HIGGINS: Eliza's bolted.

MRS HIGGINS *(calmly continuing her writing)*: You must have frightened her.

HIGGINS: Frightened her! nonsense! She was left last night, as usual, to turn out the lights and all that; and instead of going to bed she changed her clothes and went right off: her bed wasnt slept in. She came in a cab for her things before seven this morning; and that fool Mrs Pearce let her have them without telling me a word about it. What am I to do?

MRS HIGGINS: Do without, I'm afraid, Henry. The girl has a perfect right to leave if she chooses.

HIGGINS *(wandering distractedly across the room)*: But I cant find anything. I dont know what appointments Ive got. I'm—(PICKERING comes in. MRS HIGGINS puts down her pen and turns away from the writing-table.)

PICKERING *(shaking hands)*: Good morning, Mrs Higgins. Has Henry told you? *(He sits down on the ottoman.)*

HIGGINS: What does that ass of an inspector say? Have you offered a reward?

MRS HIGGINS *(rising in indignant amazement)*: You dont mean to say you have set the police after Eliza.

HIGGINS: Of course. What are the police for? What else could we do? *(He sits in the Elizabethan chair.)*

PICKERING: The inspector made a lot of difficulties. I really think he suspected us of some improper purpose.

MRS HIGGINS: Well, of course he did. What right have you to go to the police and give the girl's name as if she were a thief, or a lost umbrella, or something? Really! *(She sits down again, deeply vexed.)*

HIGGINS: But we want to find her.

PICKERING: We cant let her go like this, you know, Mrs Higgins. What were we to do?

MRS HIGGINS: You have no more sense, either of you, than two children. Why—

(The parlor-maid comes in and breaks off the conversation.)

THE PARLOR-MAID: Mr Henry: a gentleman wants to see you very particular. He's been sent on from Wimpole Street.

HIGGINS: Oh, bother! I cant see anyone now. Who is it?

THE PARLOR-MAID: A Mr Doolittle, sir.

PICKERING: Doolittle! Do you mean the dustman?

THE PARLOR-MAID: Dustman! Oh no, sir: a gentleman.

HIGGINS *(springing up excitedly)*: By George, Pick, it's some relative of hers that she's gone to. Somebody we know nothing about. *(To the parlor-maid)* Send him up, quick.

THE PARLOR-MAID: Yes, sir. *(She goes.)*

HIGGINS *(eagerly, going to his mother)*: Genteel relatives! now we shall hear something. *(He sits down in the Chippendale chair.)*

MRS HIGGINS: Do you know any of her people?

PICKERING: Only her father: the fellow we told you about.

THE PARLOR-MAID *(announcing)*: Mr Doolittle. *(She withdraws.)*

(DOOLITTLE enters. He is brilliantly dressed in a new fashionable frock-coat, with white waistcoat and grey trousers. A flower in his buttonhole, a dazzling silk hat, and patent leather shoes complete the effect. He is too concerned with the business he has come on to notice MRS HIGGINS. He walks straight to HIGGINS, and accosts him with vehement reproach.)

DOOLITTLE *(indicating his own person)*: See here! Do you see this? You done this.

HIGGINS: Done what, man?

DOOLITTLE: This, I tell you. Look at it. Look at this hat. Look at this coat.

PICKERING: Has Eliza been buying you clothes?

DOOLITTLE: Eliza! not she. Not half. Why would she buy me clothes?

MRS HIGGINS: Good morning, Mr Doolittle. Wont you sit down?

DOOLITTLE *(taken aback as he becomes conscious that he has forgotten his hostess)*: Asking your pardon, maam. *(He approaches her and shakes her proffered hand.)* Thank you. *(He sits down on the ottoman, on PICKERING's right.)* I am that full of what has happened to me that I cant think of anything else.

HIGGINS: What the dickens has happened to you?

DOOLITTLE: I shouldnt mind if it had only happened to me: anything might happen to anybody and nobody to blame but Providence, as you might say. But this is something that you done to me: yes, you, Henry Higgins.

HIGGINS: Have you found Eliza? Thats the point.

DOOLITTLE: Have you lost her?

HIGGINS: Yes.

DOOLITTLE: You have all the luck, you have. I aint found her; but she'll find me quick enough now after what you done to me.

MRS HIGGINS: But what has my son done to you, Mr Doolittle?

DOOLITTLE: Done to me! Ruined me. Destroyed my happiness. Tied me up and delivered me into the hands of middle class morality.

HIGGINS (rising intolerantly and standing over DOOLITTLE): Youre raving. Youre drunk. Youre mad. I gave you five pounds. After that I had two conversations with you, at half-a-crown an hour. Ive never seen you since.

DOOLITTLE: Oh! Drunk! am I? Mad! am I? Tell me this. Did you or did you not write a letter to an old blighter in America that was giving five millions to found Moral Reform Societies all over the world, and that wanted you to invent a universal language for him?

HIGGINS: What! Ezra D. Wannafeller! He's dead. (He sits down again carelessly.)

DOOLITTLE: Yes: he's dead; and I'm done for. Now did you or did you not write a letter to him to say that the most original moralist at present in England, to the best of your knowledge, was Alfred Doolittle, a common dustman.

HIGGINS: Oh, after your last visit I remember making some silly joke of the kind.

DOOLITTLE: Ah! you may well call it a silly joke. It put the lid on me right enough. Just give him the chance he wanted to shew that Americans is not like us: that they recognize and respect merit in every class of life, however humble. Them words is in his blooming will, in which, Henry Higgins, thanks to your silly joking, he leaves me a share in his Predigested Cheese Trust worth three thousand a year on condition that I lecture for his Wannafeller Moral Reform World League as often as they ask me up to six times a year.

HIGGINS: The devil he does! Whew! (Brightening suddenly) What a lark!

PICKERING: A safe thing for you, Doolittle. They wont ask you twice.

DOOLITTLE: It aint the lecturing I mind. I'll lecture them blue in the face, I will, and not turn a hair. It's making a gentleman of me that I object to. Who asked him to make a gentleman of me? I was happy. I was free. I touched pretty nigh everybody for money when I wanted it, same as I touched you, Henry Higgins. Now I am worrited; tied neck and heels; and everybody touches me for money.

It's a fine thing for you, says my solicitor. Is it? says I. You mean it's a good thing for you, I says. When I was a poor man and had a solicitor once when they found a pram in the dust cart, he got me off, and got shut of me and got me shut of him as quick as he could. Same with the doctors: used to shove me out of the hospital before I could hardly stand on my legs, and nothing to pay. Now they finds out that I'm not a healthy man and cant live unless they looks after me twice a day. In the house I'm not let do a hand's turn for myself: somebody else must do it and touch me for it. A year ago I hadnt a relative in the world except two or three that wouldnt speak to me. Now Ive fifty, and not a decent week's wages among the lot of them. I have to live for others and not for myself: thats middle class morality. You talk of losing Eliza. Dont you be anxious: I bet she's on my doorstep by this: she that could support herself easy by selling flowers if I wasnt respectable. And the next one to touch me will be you, Henry Higgins. I'll have to learn to speak middle class language from you, instead of speaking proper English. Thats where youll come in; and I daresay thats what you done it for.

MRS HIGGINS: But, my dear Mr Doolittle, you need not suffer all this if you are really in earnest. Nobody can force you to accept this bequest. You can repudiate it. Isnt that so, Colonel Pickering?

PICKERING: I believe so.

DOOLITTLE (softening his manner in deference to her sex): Thats the tragedy of it, maam. It's easy to say chuck it; but I havnt the nerve. Which of us has? We're all intimidated. Intimidated, maam: thats what we are. What is there for me if I chuck it but the workhouse in my old age? I have to dye my hair already to keep my job as a dustman. If I was one of the deserving poor, and had put by a bit, I could chuck it; but then why should I, acause the deserving poor might as well be millionaires for all the happiness they ever has. They dont know what happiness is. But I, as one of the undeserving poor, have nothing between me and the pauper's uniform but this here blasted three thousand a year that shoves me into the middle class. (Excuse the expression, maam: youd use it yourself if you had my provocation.) Theyve got you every way you turn: it's a choice between the Skilly of the workhouse and the Char Bydis of the middle class; and I havnt the nerve for the workhouse. Intimidated: thats what I am. Broke. Bought up. Happier men than me will call for my dust, and touch me for their tip; and I'll look on helpless, and envy them. And thats what your son has brought me to. (He is overcome by emotion.)

MRS HIGGINS: Well, I'm very glad youre not going to do anything foolish, Mr Doolittle. For this solves the problem of Eliza's future. You can provide for her now.

DOOLITTLE (*with melancholy resignation*): Yes, maam: I'm expected to provide for everyone now, out of three thousand a year.

HIGGINS (*jumping up*): Nonsense! he cant provide for her. He shant provide for her. She doesnt belong to him. I paid him five pounds for her. Doolittle: either youre an honest man or a rogue.

DOOLITTLE (*tolerantly*): A little of both, Henry, like the rest of us: a little of both.

HIGGINS: Well, you took that money for the girl; and you have no right to take her as well.

MRS HIGGINS: Henry: dont be absurd. If you want to know where Eliza is, she is upstairs.

HIGGINS (*amazed*): Upstairs!!! Then I shall jolly soon fetch her downstairs. (*He makes resolutely for the door.*)

MRS HIGGINS (*rising and following him*): Be quiet, Henry. Sit down.

HIGGINS: I—

MRS HIGGINS: Sit down, dear; and listen to me.

HIGGINS: Oh very well, very well, very well. (*He throws himself ungraciously on the ottoman, with his face towards the windows.*) But I think you might have told us this half an hour ago.

MRS HIGGINS: Eliza came to me this morning. She passed the night partly walking about in a rage, partly trying to throw herself into the river and being afraid to, and partly in the Carlton Hotel. She told me of the brutal way you two treated her.

HIGGINS (*bounding up again*): What!

PICKERING (*rising also*): My dear Mrs Higgins, she's been telling you stories. We didnt treat her brutally. We hardly said a word to her; and we parted on particularly good terms. (*Turning on* HIGGINS.) Higgins: did you bully her after I went to bed?

HIGGINS: Just the other way about. She threw my slippers in my face. She behaved in the most outrageous way. I never gave her the slightest provocation. The slippers came bang into my face the moment I entered the room—before I had uttered a word. And used perfectly awful language.

PICKERING (*astonished*): But why? What did we do to her?

MRS HIGGINS: I think I know pretty well what you did. The girl is naturally rather affectionate, I think. Isnt she, Mr Doolittle?

DOOLITTLE: Very tender-hearted, maam. Takes after me.

MRS HIGGINS: Just so. She had become attached to you both. She worked very hard for you, Henry! I dont think you quite realize what anything in the nature of brain work means to a girl like that. Well, it seems that when the great day of trial came, and she did this wonderful thing for you without making a single mistake, you two sat there and never said a word to her, but talked together of how glad you were that it was all over and how you had been bored with the whole thing. And then you were surprised because she threw your slippers at you! *I* should have thrown the fire-irons at you.

HIGGINS: We said nothing except that we were tired and wanted to go to bed. Did we, Pick?

PICKERING (*shrugging his shoulders*): That was all.

MRS HIGGINS (*ironically*): Quite sure?

PICKERING: Absolutely. Really, that was all.

MRS HIGGINS: You didnt thank her, or pet her, or admire her, or tell her how splendid she'd been.

HIGGINS (*impatiently*): But she knew all about that. We didnt make speeches to her, if thats what you mean.

PICKERING (*conscience stricken*): Perhaps we were a little inconsiderate. Is she very angry?

MRS HIGGINS (*returning to her place at the writing-table*): Well, I'm afraid she wont go back to Wimpole Street, especially now that Mr Doolittle is able to keep up the position you have thrust on her; but she says she is quite willing to meet you on friendly terms and to let bygones be bygones.

HIGGINS (*furious*): Is she, by George? Ho!

MRS HIGGINS: If you promise to behave yourself, Henry, I'll ask her to come down. If not, go home; for you have taken up quite enough of my time.

HIGGINS: Oh, all right. Very well. Pick: you behave yourself. Let us put on our best Sunday manners for this creature that we picked out of the mud. (*He flings himself sulkily into the Elizabethan chair.*)

DOOLITTLE (*remonstrating*): Now, now, Henry Higgins! have some consideration for my feelings as a middle class man.

MRS HIGGINS: Remember your promise, Henry. (*She presses the bell-button on the writing-table.*) Mr Doolittle: will you be so good as to step out on the balcony for a moment. I dont want Eliza to have the shock of your news until she has made it up with these two gentlemen. Would you mind?

DOOLITTLE: As you wish, lady. Anything to help Henry to keep her off my hands. (*He disappears through the window.*)

(*The parlor-maid answers the bell.* PICKERING *sits down in* DOOLITTLE's *place.*)

MRS HIGGINS: Ask Miss Doolittle to come down, please.

THE PARLOR-MAID: Yes, maam. (*She goes out.*)

MRS HIGGINS: Now, Henry: be good.

HIGGINS: I am behaving myself perfectly.

PICKERING: He is doing his best, Mrs Higgins.

(*A pause.* HIGGINS *throws back his head; stretches out his legs; and begins to whistle.*)

MRS HIGGINS: Henry, dearest, you dont look at all nice in that attitude.

HIGGINS (*pulling himself together*): I was not trying to look nice, mother.

MRS HIGGINS: It doesnt matter, dear. I only wanted to make you speak.

HIGGINS: Why?

MRS HIGGINS: Because you cant speak and whistle at the same time.

(HIGGINS *groans. Another very trying pause.*)

HIGGINS (*springing up, out of patience*): Where the devil is that girl? Are we to wait here all day?

(ELIZA *enters, sunny, self-possessed, and giving a staggeringly convincing exhibition of ease of manner. She carries a little work-basket, and is very much at home.* PICKERING *is too much taken aback to rise.*)

LIZA: How do you do, Professor Higgins? Are you quite well?

HIGGINS (*choking*): Am I—(*He can say no more.*)

LIZA: But of course you are: you are never ill. So glad to see you again, Colonel Pickering. (*He rises hastily; and they shake hands.*) Quite chilly this morning, isnt it? (*She sits down on his left. He sits beside her.*)

HIGGINS: Dont you dare try this game on me. I taught it to you; and it doesnt take me in. Get up and come home; and dont be a fool.

(ELIZA *takes a piece of needlework from her basket, and begins to stitch at it, without taking the least notice of this outburst.*)

MRS HIGGINS: Very nicely put, indeed, Henry. No woman could resist such an invitation.

HIGGINS: You let her alone, mother. Let her speak for herself. You will jolly soon see whether she has an idea that I havnt put into her head or a word that I havnt put into her mouth. I tell you I have created this thing out of the squashed cabbage leaves of Covent Garden; and now she pretends to play the fine lady with me.

MRS HIGGINS (*placidly*): Yes, dear; but youll sit down, wont you?

(HIGGINS *sits down again, savagely.*)

LIZA (*to* PICKERING, *taking no apparent notice of* HIGGINS, *and working away deftly*): Will you drop me altogether now that the experiment is over, Colonel Pickering?

PICKERING: Oh dont. You mustnt think of it as an experiment. It shocks me, somehow.

LIZA: Oh, I'm only a squashed cabbage leaf—

PICKERING (*impulsively*): No.

LIZA (*continuing quietly*): —but I owe so much to you that I should be very unhappy if you forgot me.

PICKERING: It's very kind of you to say so, Miss Doolittle.

LIZA: It's not because you paid for my dresses. I know you are generous to everybody with money. But it was from you that I learnt really nice manners; and that is what makes one a lady, isnt it? You see it was so very difficult for me with the example of Professor Higgins always before me. I was brought up to be just like him, unable to control myself, and using bad language on the slightest provocation. And I should never have known that ladies and gentlemen didnt behave like that if you hadnt been there.

HIGGINS: Well!!

PICKERING: Oh, thats only his way, you know. He doesnt mean it.

LIZA: Oh, *I* didnt mean it either, when I was a flower girl. It was only my way. But you see I did it; and thats what makes the difference after all.

PICKERING: No doubt. Still, he taught you to speak; and I couldnt have done that, you know.

LIZA (*trivially*): Of course: that is his profession.

HIGGINS: Damnation!

LIZA (*continuing*): It was just like learning to dance in the fashionable way: there was nothing more than that in it. But do you know what began my real education?

PICKERING: What?

LIZA (*stopping her work for a moment*): Your calling me Miss Doolittle that day when I first came to Wimpole Street. That was the beginning of self-respect for me. (*She resumes her stitching.*) And there were a hundred little things you never noticed, because they came naturally to you. Things about standing up and taking off your hat and opening doors—

PICKERING: Oh, that was nothing.

LIZA: Yes: things that shewed you thought and felt about me as if I were something better than a scullery-maid; though of course I know you would have been just the same to a scullery-maid if she had been let into the drawing room. You never took off your boots in the dining room when I was there.

PICKERING: You mustnt mind that. Higgins takes off his boots all over the place.

LIZA: I know. I am not blaming him. It is his way, isnt it? But it made such a difference to me that you didnt do it. You see, really and truly, apart from the things anyone can pick up (the dressing and the proper way of speaking, and so on), the difference between a lady and a flower girl is not how she behaves, but how she's treated. I shall always be a flower girl to Professor Higgins, because he always treats me as a flower girl, and always will; but I know I can be a lady to you, because you always treat me as a lady, and always will.

MRS HIGGINS: Please dont grind your teeth, Henry.

PICKERING: Well, this is really very nice of you, Miss Doolittle.

LIZA: I should like you to call me Eliza, now, if you would.

PICKERING: Thank you. Eliza, of course.

LIZA: And I should like Professor Higgins to call me Miss Doolittle.

HIGGINS: I'll see you damned first.

MRS HIGGINS: Henry! Henry!

PICKERING (*laughing*): Why dont you slang back at him? Dont stand it. It would do him a lot of good.

LIZA: I cant. I could have done it once; but now I cant go back to it. Last night, when I was wandering about, a girl spoke to me; and I tried to get back into the old way with her; but it was no use. You told me, you know, that when a child is brought to a foreign country, it picks up the language in a few weeks, and forgets its own. Well, I am a child in your country. I have forgotten my own language, and can speak nothing but yours. Thats the real break-off with the corner of Tottenham Court Road. Leaving Wimpole Street finishes it.

PICKERING (*much alarmed*): Oh! but youre coming back to Wimpole Street, arnt you? Youll forgive Higgins?

HIGGINS (*rising*): Forgive! Will she, by George! Let her go. Let her find out how she can get on without us. She will relapse into the gutter in three weeks without me at her elbow.

(DOOLITTLE *appears at the center window. With a look of dignified reproach at* HIGGINS, *he comes slowly and silently to his daughter, who, with her back to the window, is unconscious of his approach.*)

PICKERING: He's incorrigible, Eliza. You wont relapse, will you?

LIZA: No: not now. Never again. I have learnt my lesson. I dont believe I could utter one of the old sounds if I tried. (DOOLITTLE *touches her on her left shoulder. She drops her work, losing her self-possession utterly at the spectacle of her father's splendor*) A-a-a-a-ah-ow-ooh!

HIGGINS (*with a crow of triumph*): Aha! Just so. A-a-a-ahowooh! A-a-a-ahowooh! A-a-a-ahowooh! Victory! Victory! (*He throws himself on the divan, folding his arms, and spraddling arrogantly.*)

DOOLITTLE: Can you blame the girl? Dont look at me like that, Eliza. It aint my fault. Ive come into some money.

LIZA: You must have touched a millionaire this time, dad.

DOOLITTLE: I have. But I'm dressed something special today. I'm going to St George's, Hanover Square. Your stepmother is going to marry me.

LIZA (*angrily*): Youre going to let yourself down to marry that low common woman!

PICKERING (*quietly*): He ought to, Eliza. (*To* DOOLITTLE) Why has she changed her mind?

DOOLITTLE (*sadly*): Intimidated, Governor. Intimidated. Middle class morality claims its victim. Wont you put on your hat, Liza, and come and see me turned off?

LIZA: If the Colonel says I must, I—I'll (*almost sobbing*) I'll demean myself. And get insulted for my pains, like enough.

DOOLITTLE: Dont be afraid: she never comes to words with anyone now, poor woman! respectability has broke all the spirit out of her.

PICKERING (*squeezing* ELIZA's *elbow gently*): Be kind to them, Eliza. Make the best of it.

LIZA (*forcing a little smile for him through her vexation*): Oh well, just to shew theres no ill feeling. I'll be back in a moment. (*She goes out.*)

DOOLITTLE (*sitting down beside* PICKERING): I feel uncommon nervous about the ceremony, Colonel. I wish youd come and see me through it.

PICKERING: But youve been through it before, man. You were married to Eliza's mother.

DOOLITTLE: Who told you that, Colonel?

PICKERING: Well, nobody told me. But I concluded—naturally—

DOOLITTLE: No: that aint the natural way, Colonel: it's only the middle class way. My way was always the undeserving way. But dont say nothing to Eliza. She dont know: I always had a delicacy about telling her.

PICKERING: Quite right. We'll leave it so, if you dont mind.

DOOLITTLE: And youll come to the church, Colonel, and put me through straight?

PICKERING: With pleasure. As far as a bachelor can.

MRS HIGGINS: May I come, Mr Doolittle? I should be very sorry to miss your wedding.

DOOLITTLE: I should indeed be honored by your condescension, maam; and my poor old woman would take it as a tremenjous compliment. She's been very low, thinking of the happy days that are no more.

MRS HIGGINS (*rising*): I'll order the carriage and get ready. (*The men rise, except* HIGGINS.) I shant be more than fifteen minutes. (*As she goes to the door* ELIZA *comes in, hatted and buttoning her gloves.*) I'm going to the church to see your father married, Eliza. You had better come in the brougham with me. Colonel Pickering can go on with the bridegroom.

(MRS HIGGINS *goes out.* ELIZA *comes to the middle of the room between the center window and the ottoman.* PICKERING *joins her.*)

DOOLITTLE: Bridegroom! What a word! It makes a man realize his position, somehow. (*He takes up his hat and goes towards the door.*)

PICKERING: Before I go, Eliza, do forgive him and come back to us.

LIZA: I dont think papa would allow me. Would you, dad?

DOOLITTLE (sad but magnanimous): They played you off very cunning, Eliza, them two sportsmen. If it had been only one of them, you could have nailed him. But you see, there was two; and one of them chaperoned the other, as you might say. (To PICKERING) It was artful of you, Colonel; but I bear no malice: I should have done the same myself. I been the victim of one woman after another all my life; and I dont grudge you two getting the better of Eliza. I shant interfere. It's time for us to go, Colonel. So long, Henry. See you in St George's, Eliza. (He goes out.)

PICKERING (coaxing): Do stay with us, Eliza. (He follows Doolittle.)

(ELIZA goes out on the balcony to avoid being alone with HIGGINS. He rises and joins her there. She immediately comes back into the room and makes for the door; but he goes along the balcony quickly and gets his back to the door before she reaches it.)

HIGGINS: Well, Eliza, youve had a bit of your own back, as you call it. Have you had enough? and are you going to be reasonable? Or do you want any more?

LIZA: You want me back only to pick up your slippers and put up with your tempers and fetch and carry for you.

HIGGINS: I havnt said I wanted you back at all.

LIZA: Oh, indeed. Then what are we talking about?

HIGGINS: About you, not about me. If you come back I shall treat you just as I have always treated you. I cant change my nature; and I dont intend to change my manners. My manners are exactly the same as Colonel Pickering's.

LIZA: Thats not true. He treats a flower girl as if she was a duchess.

HIGGINS: And I treat a duchess as if she was a flower girl.

LIZA: I see. (She turns away composedly, and sits on the ottoman, facing the window.) The same to everybody.

HIGGINS: Just so.

LIZA: Like father.

HIGGINS (grinning, a little taken down): Without accepting the comparison at all points, Eliza, it's quite true that your father is not a snob, and that he will be quite at home in any station of life to which his eccentric destiny may call him. (Seriously) The great secret, Eliza, is not having bad manners or good manners or any other particular sort of manners, but having the same manner for all human souls: in short, behaving as if you were in Heaven, where there are no third-class carriages, and one soul is as good as another.

LIZA: Amen. You are a born preacher.

HIGGINS (irritated): The question is not whether I treat you rudely, but whether you ever heard me treat anyone else better.

LIZA (with sudden sincerity): I dont care how you treat me. I dont mind your swearing at me. I dont mind a black eye: Ive had one before this. But (standing up and facing him) I wont be passed over.

HIGGINS: Then get out of my way; for I wont stop for you. You talk about me as if I were a motor bus.

LIZA: So you are a motor bus: all bounce and go, and no consideration for anyone. But I can do without you: dont think I cant.

HIGGINS: I know you can. I told you you could.

LIZA (wounded, getting away from him to the other side of the ottoman with her face to the hearth): I know you did, you brute. You wanted to get rid of me.

HIGGINS: Liar.

LIZA: Thank you. (She sits down with dignity.)

HIGGINS: You never asked yourself, I suppose, whether I could do without you.

LIZA (earnestly): Dont you try to get round me. Youll have to do without me.

HIGGINS (arrogant): I can do without anybody. I have my own soul: my own spark of divine fire. But (with sudden humility) I shall miss you, Eliza. (He sits down near her on the ottoman.) I have learnt something from your idiotic notions: I confess that humbly and gratefully. And I have grown accustomed to your voice and appearance. I like them, rather.

LIZA: Well, you have both of them on your gramophone and in your book of photographs. When you feel lonely without me, you can turn the machine on. It's got no feelings to hurt.

HIGGINS: I cant turn your soul on. Leave me those feelings; and you can take away the voice and the face. They are not you.

LIZA: Oh, you are a devil. You can twist the heart in a girl as easy as some could twist her arms to hurt her. Mrs Pearce warned me. Time and again she has wanted to leave you; and you always got round her at the last minute. And you dont care a bit for her. And you dont care a bit for me.

HIGGINS: I care for life, for humanity; and you are a part of it that has come my way and been built into my house. What more can you or anyone ask?

LIZA: I wont care for anybody that doesnt care for me.

HIGGINS: Commercial principles, Eliza. Like (reproducing her Covent Garden pronunciation with professional exactness) s'yollin voylets (selling violets), isnt it?

LIZA: Dont sneer at me. It's mean to sneer at me.

HIGGINS: I have never sneered in my life. Sneering doesnt become either the human face or the human soul. I am expressing my righteous contempt for Commercialism. I dont and wont trade in affection. You call me a brute because you couldnt buy a claim on me by fetching my slippers and finding my spectacles. You were a fool: I think a woman fetching a man's slippers is a disgusting sight: did I ever fetch your slippers? I think a good deal more of you for throwing them in my face. No use slaving for me and then saying you want to be cared for: who cares for a slave? If you come back, come back for the sake of good fellowship; for youll get nothing else. Youve had a thousand times as much out of me as I have out of you; and if you dare to set up your little dog's tricks of fetching and carrying slippers against my creation of a Duchess Eliza, I'll slam the door in your silly face.

LIZA: What did you do it for if you didnt care for me?

HIGGINS (heartily): Why, because it was my job.

LIZA: You never thought of the trouble it would make for me.

HIGGINS: Would the world ever have been made if its maker had been afraid of making trouble? Making life means making trouble. Theres only one way of escaping trouble; and thats killing things. Cowards, you notice, are always shrieking to have troublesome people killed.

LIZA: I'm no preacher: I dont notice things like that. I notice that you dont notice me.

HIGGINS (jumping up and walking about intolerantly): Eliza: youre an idiot. I waste the treasures of my Miltonic mind by spreading them before you. Once for all, understand that I go my way and do my work without caring twopence what happens to either of us. I am not intimidated, like your father and your stepmother. So you can come back or go to the devil: which you please.

LIZA: What am I to come back for?

HIGGINS (bounding up on his knees on the ottoman and leaning over it to her): For the fun of it. Thats why I took you on.

LIZA (with averted face): And you may throw me out tomorrow if I dont do everything you want me to?

HIGGINS: Yes; and you may walk out tomorrow if I dont do everything you want me to.

LIZA: And live with my stepmother?

HIGGINS: Yes, or sell flowers.

LIZA: Oh! if I only could go back to my flower basket! I should be independent of both you and father and all the world! Why did you take my independence from me? Why did I give it up? I'm a slave now, for all my fine clothes.

HIGGINS: Not a bit. I'll adopt you as my daughter and settle money on you if you like. Or would you rather marry Pickering?

LIZA (looking fiercely round at him): I wouldnt marry you if you asked me; and youre nearer my age than what he is.

HIGGINS (gently): Than he is: not "than what he is."

LIZA (losing her temper and rising): I'll talk as I like. Youre not my teacher now.

HIGGINS (reflectively): I dont suppose Pickering would, though. He's as confirmed an old bachelor as I am.

LIZA: Thats not what I want; and dont you think it. Ive always had chaps enough wanting me that way. Freddy Hill writes to me twice and three times a day, sheets and sheets.

HIGGINS (disagreeably surprised): Damn his impudence! (He recoils and finds himself sitting on his heels.)

LIZA: He has a right to if he likes, poor lad. And he does love me.

HIGGINS (getting off the ottoman): You have no right to encourage him.

LIZA: Every girl has a right to be loved.

HIGGINS: What! By fools like that?

LIZA: Freddy's not a fool. And if he's weak and poor and wants me, may be he'd make me happier than my betters that bully me and dont want me.

HIGGINS: Can he make anything of you? Thats the point.

LIZA: Perhaps I could make something of him. But I never thought of us making anything of one another; and you never think of anything else. I only want to be natural.

HIGGINS: In short, you want me to be as infatuated about you as Freddy? Is that it?

LIZA: No I dont. Thats not the sort of feeling I want from you. And dont you be too sure of yourself or of me. I could have been a bad girl if I'd liked. Ive seen more of some things than you, for all your learning. Girls like me can drag gentlemen down to make love to them easy enough. And they wish each other dead the next minute.

HIGGINS: Of course they do. Then what in thunder are we quarrelling about?

LIZA (much troubled): I want a little kindness. I know I'm a common ignorant girl, and you a book-learned gentleman; but I'm not dirt under your feet. What I done (correcting herself) what I did was not for the dresses and the taxis: I did it because we were pleasant together and I come—came—to care for you; not to want you to make love to me, and not forgetting the difference between us, but more friendly like.

HIGGINS: Well, of course. Thats just how I feel. And how Pickering feels. Eliza: youre a fool.

LIZA: Thats not a proper answer to give me (she sinks on the chair at the writing-table in tears).

HIGGINS: It's all youll get until you stop being a common idiot. If youre going to be a lady, youll have to give up feeling neglected if the men you know dont spend half their time snivelling over you and the other half giving you black eyes. If you cant stand the coldness of my sort of life, and the strain of it, go back to the gutter. Work til you are more a brute than a human being; and then cuddle and squabble and drink til you fall asleep. Oh, it's a fine life, the life of the gutter. It's real: it's warm: it's violent: you can feel it through the thickest skin: you can taste it and smell it without any training or any work. Not like Science and Literature and Classical Music and Philosophy and Art. You find me cold, unfeeling, selfish, dont you? Very well: be off with you to the sort of people you like. Marry some sentimental hog or other with lots of money, and a thick pair of lips to kiss you with and a thick pair of boots to kick you with. If you cant appreciate what youve got, youd better get what you can appreciate.

LIZA (desperate): Oh, you are a cruel tyrant. I cant talk to you: you turn everything against me: I'm always in the wrong. But you know very well all the time that youre nothing but a bully. You know I cant go back to the gutter, as you call it, and that I have no real friends in the world but you and the Colonel. You know well I couldnt bear to live with a low common man after you two; and it's wicked and cruel of you to insult me by pretending I could. You think I must go back to Wimpole Street because I have nowhere else to go but father's. But dont you be too sure that you have me under your feet to be trampled on and talked down. I'll marry Freddy, I will, as soon as he's able to support me.

HIGGINS (sitting down beside her): Rubbish! you shall marry an ambassador. You shall marry the Governor-General of India or the Lord-Lieutenant of Ireland, or somebody who wants a deputy-queen. I'm not going to have my masterpiece thrown away on Freddy.

LIZA: You think I like you to say that. But I havnt forgot what you said a minute ago; and I wont be coaxed round as if I was a baby or a puppy. If I cant have kindness, I'll have independence.

HIGGINS: Independence? Thats middle class blasphemy. We are all dependent on one another, every soul of us on earth.

LIZA (rising determinedly): I'll let you see whether I'm dependent on you. If you can preach, I can teach. I'll go and be a teacher.

HIGGINS: Whatll you teach, in heaven's name?

LIZA: What you taught me. I'll teach phonetics.

HIGGINS: Ha! ha! ha!

LIZA: I'll offer myself as an assistant to Professor Nepean.

HIGGINS (rising in a fury): What! That impostor! that humbug! that toadying ignoramus! Teach him my methods! my discoveries! You take one step in his direction and I'll wring your neck. (He lays hands on her.) Do you hear?

LIZA (defiantly non-resistant): Wring away. What do I care? I knew youd strike me some day. (He lets her go, stamping with rage at having forgotten himself, and recoils so hastily that he stumbles back into his seat on the ottoman.) Aha! Now I know how to deal with you. What a fool I was not to think of it before! You cant take away the knowledge you gave me. You said I had a finer ear than you. And I can be civil and kind to people, which is more than you can. Aha! Thats done you, Henry Higgins, it has. Now I dont care that (snapping her fingers) for your bullying and your big talk. I'll advertize it in the papers that your duchess is only a flower girl that you taught, and that she'll teach anybody to be a duchess just the same in six months for a thousand guineas. Oh, when I think of myself crawling under your feet and being trampled on and called names, when all the time I had only to lift up my finger to be as good as you, I could just kick myself.

HIGGINS (wondering at her): You damned impudent slut, you! But it's better than snivelling; better than fetching slippers and finding spectacles, isnt it? (Rising) By George, Eliza, I said I'd make a woman of you; and I have. I like you like this.

LIZA: Yes: you turn round and make up to me now that I'm not afraid of you, and can do without you.

HIGGINS: Of course I do, you little fool. Five minutes ago you were like a millstone round my neck. Now youre a tower of strength: a consort battleship. You and I and Pickering will be three old bachelors together instead of only two men and a silly girl.

(MRS HIGGINS returns, dressed for the wedding. ELIZA instantly becomes cool and elegant.)

MRS HIGGINS: The carriage is waiting, Eliza. Are you ready?

LIZA: Quite. Is the Professor coming?

MRS HIGGINS: Certainly not. He cant behave himself in church. He makes remarks out loud all the time on the clergyman's pronunciation.

LIZA: Then I shall not see you again, Professor. Goodbye. (She goes to the door.)

MRS HIGGINS (coming to HIGGINS): Goodbye, dear.

HIGGINS: Goodbye, mother. (He is about to kiss her, when he recollects something.) Oh, by the way, Eliza, order a ham and a Stilton cheese, will you? And buy me a pair of reindeer gloves, number eights, and a tie to match that new suit of mine, at Eale & Binman's. You can choose the color. (His cheerful, careless, vigorous voice shows that he is incorrigible.)

LIZA (disdainfully): Buy them yourself. (She sweeps out.)

MRS HIGGINS: I'm afraid youve spoiled that girl, Henry. But never mind, dear: I'll buy you the tie and gloves.

HIGGINS *(sunnily)*: Oh, dont bother. She'll buy em all right enough. Goodbye.

(They kiss. MRS HIGGINS *runs out.* HIGGINS *left alone, rattles his cash in his pocket; chuckles; and disports himself in a highly self-satisfied manner.)*

*   *   *

The rest of the story need not be shewn in action, and indeed, would hardly need telling if our imaginations were not so enfeebled by their lazy dependence on the ready-mades and reach-me-downs of the rag-shop in which Romance keeps its stock of "happy endings" to misfit all stories. Now, the history of Eliza Doolittle, though called a romance because the transfiguration it records seems exceedingly improbable, is common enough. Such transfigurations have been achieved by hundreds of resolutely ambitious young women since Nell Gwynne set them the example by playing queens and fascinating kings in the theatre in which she began by selling oranges. Nevertheless, people in all directions have assumed, for no other reason than that she became the heroine of a romance, that she must have married the hero of it. This is unbearable, not only because her little drama, if acted on such a thoughtless assumption, must be spoiled, but because the true sequel is patent to anyone with a sense of human nature in general, and of feminist instinct in particular.

Eliza, in telling Higgins she would not marry him if he asked her, was not coquetting: she was announcing a well-considered decision. When a bachelor interests, and dominates, and teaches, and becomes important to a spinster, as Higgins with Eliza, she always, if she has character enough to be capable of it, considers very seriously indeed whether she will play for becoming that bachelor's wife, especially if he is so little interested in marriage that a determined and devoted woman might capture him if she set herself resolutely to do it. Her decision will depend a good deal on whether she is really free to choose; and that, again, will depend on her age and income. If she is at the end of her youth, and has no security for her livelihood, she will marry him because she must marry anybody who will provide for her. But at Eliza's age a good-looking girl does not feel that pressure: she feels free to pick and choose. She is therefore guided by her instinct in the matter. Eliza's instinct tells her not to marry Higgins. It does not tell her to give him up. It is not in the slightest doubt as to his remaining one of the strongest personal interests in her life. It would be very sorely strained if there was another woman likely to supplant her with him. But as she feels sure of him on that last point, she has no doubt at all as to her course, and would not have any, even if the difference of twenty years in age, which seems so great to youth, did not exist between them.

As our own instincts are not appealed to by her con-clusion, let us see whether we cannot discover some reason in it. When Higgins excused his indifference to young women on the ground that they had an irresistible rival in his mother, he gave the clue to his inveterate old-bachelordom. The case is uncommon only to the extent that remarkable mothers are uncommon. If an imaginative boy has a sufficiently rich mother who has intelligence, personal grace, dignity of character without harshness, and a cultivated sense of the best art of her time to enable her to make her house beautiful, she sets a standard for him against which very few women can struggle, besides effecting for him a disengagement of his affections, his sense of beauty, and his idealism from his specifically sexual impulses. This makes him a standing puzzle to the huge number of uncultivated people who have been brought up in tasteless homes by commonplace or disagreeable parents, and to whom, consequently, literature, painting, sculpture, music, and affectionate personal relations come as modes of sex if they come at all. The word passion means nothing else to them; and that Higgins could have a passion for phonetics and idealize his mother instead of Eliza, would seem to them absurd and unnatural. Nevertheless, when we look round and see that hardly anyone is too ugly or disagreeable to find a wife or a husband if he or she wants one, whilst many old maids and bachelors are above the average in quality and culture, we cannot help suspecting that the disentanglement of sex from the associations with which it is so commonly confused, a disentanglement which persons of genius achieve by sheer intellectual analysis, is sometimes produced or aided by parental fascination.

Now, though Eliza was incapable of thus explaining to herself Higgins's formidable powers of resistance to the charm that prostrated Freddy at the first glance, she was instinctively aware that she could never obtain a complete grip of him, or come between him and his mother (the first necessity of the married woman). To put it shortly, she knew that for some mysterious reason he had not the makings of a married man in him, according to her conception of a husband as one to whom she would be his nearest and fondest and warmest interest. Even had there been no mother-rival, she would still have refused to accept an interest in herself that was secondary to philosophic interests. Had Mrs Higgins died, there would still have been Milton and the Universal Alphabet. Landor's remark that to those who have the greatest power of loving, love is a secondary affair, would not have recommended Landor to Eliza. Put that along with her resentment of Higgins's domineering superiority, and her mistrust of his coaxing cleverness in getting round her and evading her wrath when he had gone too far with his impetuous bullying, and you will see that Eliza's instinct had good grounds for warning her not to marry her Pygmalion.

And now, whom did Eliza marry? For if Higgins was a predestinate old bachelor, she was most certainly not a predestinate old maid. Well, that can be told very shortly to those who have not guessed it from the indications she has herself given them.

Almost immediately after Eliza is stung into proclaiming her considered determination not to marry Higgins, she mentions the fact that young Mr Frederick Eynsford Hill is pouring out his love for her daily through the post. Now Freddy is young, practically twenty years younger than Higgins: he is a gentleman (or, as Eliza would qualify him, a toff), and speaks like one; he is nicely dressed, is treated by the Colonel as an equal, loves her unaffectedly, and is not her master, nor ever likely to dominate her in spite of his advantage of social standing. Eliza has no use for the foolish romantic tradition that all women love to be mastered, if not actually bullied and beaten. "When you go to women," says Nietzsche, "take your whip with you." Sensible despots have never confined that precaution to women: they have taken their whips with them when they have dealt with men, and been slavishly idealized by the men over whom they have flourished the whip much more than by women. No doubt there are slavish women as well as slavish men: and women, like men, admire those that are stronger than themselves. But to admire a strong person and to live under that strong person's thumb are two different things. The weak may not be admired and hero-worshipped; but they are by no means disliked or shunned; and they never seem to have the least difficulty in marrying people who are too good for them. They may fail in emergencies; but life is not one long emergency: it is mostly a string of situations for which no exceptional strength is needed, and with which even rather weak people can cope if they have a stronger partner to help them out. Accordingly, it is a truth everywhere in evidence that strong people, masculine or feminine, not only do not marry stronger people, but do not shew any preference for them in selecting their friends. When a lion meets another with a louder roar "the first lion thinks the last a bore." The man or woman who feels strong enough for two, seeks for every other quality in a partner than strength.

The converse is also true. Weak people want to marry strong people who do not frighten them too much; and this often leads them to make the mistake we describe metaphorically as "biting off more than they can chew." They want too much for too little; and when the bargain is unreasonable beyond all bearing, the union becomes impossible: it ends in the weaker party being either discarded or borne as a cross, which is worse. People who are not only weak, but silly or obtuse as well, are often in these difficulties.

This being the state of human affairs, what is Eliza fairly sure to do when she is placed between Freddy and Higgins? Will she look forward to a lifetime of fetching Higgins's slippers or to a lifetime of Freddy fetching hers? There can be no doubt about the answer. Unless Freddy is biologically repulsive to her, and Higgins biologically attractive to a degree that overwhelms all her other instincts, she will, if she marries either of them, marry Freddy.

And that is just what Eliza did.

Complications ensued; but they were economic, not romantic. Freddy had no money and no occupation. His mother's jointure, a last relic of the opulence of Largelady Park, had enabled her to struggle along in Earlscourt with an air of gentility, but not to procure any serious secondary education for her children, much less give the boy a profession. A clerkship at thirty shillings a week was beneath Freddy's dignity, and extremely distasteful to him besides. His prospects consisted of a hope that if he kept up appearances somebody would do something for him. The something appeared vaguely to his imagination as a private secretaryship or a sinecure of some sort. To his mother it perhaps appeared as a marriage to some lady of means who could not resist her boy's niceness. Fancy her feelings when he married a flower girl who had become déclassée under extraordinary circumstances which were now notorious!

It is true that Eliza's situation did not seem wholly ineligible. Her father, though formerly a dustman, and now fantastically disclassed, had become extremely popular in the smartest society by a social talent which triumphed over every prejudice and every disadvantage. Rejected by the middle class, which he loathed, he had shot up at once into the highest circles by his wit, his dustmanship (which he carried like a banner), and his Nietzschean transcendence of good and evil. At intimate ducal dinners he sat on the right hand of the Duchess; and in country houses he smoked in the pantry and was made much of by the butler when he was not feeding in the dining room and being consulted by cabinet ministers. But he found it almost as hard to do all this on four thousand a year as Mrs Eynsford Hill to live in Earlscourt on an income so pitiably smaller that I have not the heart to disclose its exact figure. He absolutely refused to add the last straw to his burden by contributing to Eliza's support.

Thus Freddy and Eliza, now Mr and Mrs Eynsford Hill, would have spent a penniless honeymoon but for a wedding present of £500 from the Colonel to Eliza. It lasted a long time because Freddy did not know how to spend money, never having had any to spend, and Eliza, socially trained by a pair of old bachelors, wore her clothes as long as they held together and looked pretty, without the least regard to their being many months out of fashion. Still, £500 will not last two young people for ever; and they both knew, and Eliza felt as well, that they must shift for themselves in the end. She could quarter herself on Wimpole Street because it had come to be her home; but she was quite aware that she ought not to quarter Freddy there, and that it would not be good for his character if she did.

Not that the Wimpole Street bachelors objected. When she consulted them, Higgins declined to be bothered about her housing problem when that solution was so simple. Eliza's desire to have Freddy in the house with her seemed of no more importance than if she had wanted an extra piece of bedroom furniture. Pleas as to Freddy's character, and the moral obligation on him to earn his own living, were lost on Higgins. He denied that Freddy had any character, and declared that if he tried to do any useful work some competent person would have the trouble of undoing it: a procedure involving a net loss to the community, and great unhappiness to Freddy himself, who was obviously intended by Nature for such light work as amusing Eliza, which, Higgins declared, was a much more useful and honorable occupation than working in the city. When Eliza referred again to her project of teaching phonetics, Higgins abated not a jot of his violent opposition to it. He said she was not within ten years of being qualified to meddle with his pet subject; and as it was evident that the Colonel agreed with him, she felt she could not go against them in this grave matter, and that she had no right, without Higgins's consent, to exploit the knowledge he had given her; for his knowledge seemed to her as much his private property as his watch: Eliza was no communist. Besides, she was superstitiously devoted to them both, more entirely and frankly after her marriage than before it.

It was the Colonel who finally solved the problem, which had cost him much perplexed cogitation. He one day asked Eliza, rather shyly, whether she had quite given up her notion of keeping a flower shop. She replied that she had thought of it, but had put it out of her head, because the Colonel had said, that day at Mrs Higgins's, that it would never do. The Colonel confessed that when he said that, he had not quite recovered from the dazzling impression of the day before. They broke the matter to Higgins that evening. The sole comment vouchsafed by him very nearly led to a quarrel with Eliza. It was to the effect that she would have in Freddy an ideal errand boy.

Freddy himself was next sounded on the subject. He said he had been thinking of a shop himself; though it had presented itself to his pennilessness as a small place in which Eliza should sell tobacco at one counter whilst he sold newspapers at the opposite one. But he agreed that it would be extraordinarily jolly to go early every morning with Eliza to Covent Garden and buy flowers on the scene of their first meeting: a sentiment which earned him many kisses from his wife. He added that he had always been afraid to propose anything of the sort, because Clara would make an awful row about a step that must damage her matrimonial chances, and his mother could not be expected to like it after clinging for so many years to that step of the social ladder on which retail trade is impossible.

This difficulty was removed by an event highly unexpected by Freddy's mother. Clara, in the course of her incursions into those artistic circles which were the highest within her reach, discovered that her conversational qualifications were expected to include a grounding in the novels of Mr H. G. Wells. She borrowed them in various directions so energetically that she swallowed them all within two months. The result was a conversion of a kind quite common today. A modern Acts of the Apostles would fill fifty whole Bibles if anyone were capable of writing it.

Poor Clara, who appeared to Higgins and his mother as a disagreeable and ridiculous person, and to her own mother as in some inexplicable way a social failure, had never seen herself in either light; for though so some extent ridiculed and mimicked in West Kensington like everybody else there, she was accepted as a rational and normal—or shall we say inevitable?—sort of human being. At worst they called her The Pusher; but to them no more than to herself had it ever occurred that she was pushing the air, and pushing it in a wrong direction. Still, she was not happy. She was growing desperate. Her one asset, the fact that her mother was what the Epsom greengrocer called a carriage lady, had no exchange value, apparently. It had prevented her from getting educated, because the only education she could have afforded was education with the Earlscourt greengrocer's daughter. It had led her to seek the society of her mother's class; and that class simply would not have her, because she was much poorer than the greengrocer, and, far from being able to afford a maid, could not afford even a housemaid, and had to scrape along at home with an illiberally treated general servant. Under such circumstances nothing could give her an air of being a genuine product of Largelady Park. And yet its tradition made her regard a marriage with anyone within her reach as an unbearable humiliation. Commercial people and professional people in a small way were odious to her. She ran after painters and novelists; but she did not charm them; and her bold attempts to pick up and practice artistic and literary talk irritated them. She was, in short, an utter failure, an ignorant, incompetent, pretentious, unwelcome, penniless, useless little snob; and though she did not admit these disqualifications (for nobody ever faces unpleasant truths of this kind until the possibility of a way out dawns on them) she felt their effects too keenly to be satisfied with her position.

Clara had a startling eyeopener when, on being suddenly wakened to enthusiasm by a girl of her own age who dazzled her and produced in her a gushing desire to take her for a model, and gain her friendship, she discovered that this exquisite apparition had graduated from the gutter in a few months time. It shook her so violently, that when Mr H. G. Wells lifted her on the point of his puissant pen, and placed her at the angle of view from which the life she was leading and the society to which she clung appeared in its true relation to real human needs and worthy social structure, he effected a conversion and a conviction of sin comparable to the most sensational feats of General Booth or Gypsy Smith. Clara's snobbery went bang. Life suddenly began to move with her. Without knowing how or why, she began to make friends and enemies. Some of the acquaintances to whom she had been a tedious or indifferent or ridiculous affliction, dropped her: others became cordial. To her amazement she found that some "quite nice" people were saturated with Wells, and that this accessibility to ideas was the secret of their niceness. People she had thought deeply religious, and had tried to conciliate on that track with disastrous results, suddenly took an interest in her, and revealed a hostility to conventional religion which she had never conceived possible except among the most desperate characters. They made her read Galsworthy; and Galsworthy exposed the vanity of Largelady Park and finished her. It exasperated her to think that the dungeon in which she had languished for so many unhappy years had been unlocked all the time, and that the impulses she had so carefully struggled with and stifled for the sake of keeping well with society, were precisely those by which alone she could have come into any sort of sincere human contact. In the radiance of these discoveries, and the tumult of their reaction, she made a fool of herself as freely and conspicuously as when she so rashly adopted Eliza's expletive in Mrs Higgins's drawing room; for the new-born Wellsian had to find her bearings almost as ridiculously as a baby; but nobody hates a baby for its ineptitudes, or thinks the worse of it for trying to eat the matches; and Clara lost no friends by her follies. They laughed at her to her face this time; and she had to defend herself and fight it out as best she could.

When Freddy paid a visit to Earlscourt (which he never did when he could possibly help it) to make the desolating announcement that he and his Eliza were thinking of blackening the Largelady scutcheon by opening a shop, he found the little household already convulsed by a prior announcement from Clara that she also was going to work in an old furniture shop in Dover Street, which had been started by a fellow Wellsian. This appointment Clara owed, after all, to her old social accomplishment of Push. She had made up her mind that, cost what it might, she would see Mr Wells in the flesh; and she had achieved her end at a garden party. She had better luck than so rash an enterprise deserved. Mr Wells came up to her expectations. Age had not withered him, nor could custom stale his infinite variety in half an hour. His pleasant

neatness and compactness, his small hands and feet, his teeming ready brain, his unaffected accessibility, and a certain fine apprehensiveness which stamped him as susceptible from his topmost hair to his tipmost toe, proved irresistible. Clara talked of nothing else for weeks and weeks afterwards. And as she happened to talk to the lady of the furniture shop, and that lady also desired above all things to know Mr Wells and sell pretty things to him, she offered Clara a job on the chance of achieving that end through her.

And so it came about that Eliza's luck held, and the expected opposition to the flower shop melted away. The shop is in the arcade of a railway station not very far from the Victoria and Albert Museum; and if you live in that neighborhood you may go there any day and buy a buttonhole from Eliza.

Now here is a last opportunity for romance. Would you not like to be assured that the shop was an immense success, thanks to Eliza's charms and her early business experience in Covent Garden? Alas! the truth is the truth: the shop did not pay for a long time, simply because Eliza and her Freddy did not know how to keep it. True, Eliza had not to begin at the very beginning: she knew the names and prices of the cheaper flowers; and her elation was unbounded when she found that Freddy, like all youths educated at cheap, pretentious, and thoroughly inefficient schools, knew a little Latin. It was very little, but enough to make him appear to her a Porson or Bentley, and to put him at his ease with botanical nomenclature. Unfortunately he knew nothing else; and Eliza, though she could count money up to eighteen shillings or so, and had acquired a certain familiarity with the language of Milton from her struggles to qualify herself for winning Higgins's bet, could not write out a bill without utterly disgracing the establishment. Freddy's power of stating in Latin that Balbus built a wall and that Gaul was divided into three parts did not carry with it the slightest knowledge of accounts or business: Colonel Pickering had to explain to him what a cheque book and a bank account meant. And the pair were by no means easily teachable. Freddy backed up Eliza in her obstinate refusal to believe that they could save money by engaging a bookkeeper with some knowledge of the business. How, they argued, could you possibly save money by going to extra expense when you already could not make both ends meet? But the Colonel, after making the ends meet over and over again, at last gently insisted; and Eliza, humbled to the dust by having to beg from him so often, and stung by the uproarious derision of Higgins, to whom the notion of Freddy succeeding at anything was a joke that never palled, grasped the fact that business, like phonetics, has to be learned.

On the piteous spectacle of the pair spending their evenings in shorthand schools and polytechnic classes, learning bookkeeping and typewriting with incipient junior clerks, male and female, from the elementary schools, let me not dwell. There were even classes at the London School of Economics, and a humble personal appeal to the director of that institution to recommend a course bearing on the flower business. He, being a humorist, explained to them the method of the celebrated Dickensian essay on Chinese Metaphysics by the gentleman who read an article on China and an article on Metaphysics and combined the information. He suggested that they should combine the London School with Kew Gardens. Eliza, to whom the procedure of the Dickensian gentleman seemed perfectly correct (as in fact it was) and not in the least funny (which was her only ignorance), took his advice with entire gravity. But the effort that cost her the deepest humiliation was a request to Higgins, whose pet artistic fancy, next to Milton's verse, was calligraphy, and who himself wrote a most beautiful Italian hand, that he would teach her to write. He declared that she was congenitally incapable of forming a single letter worthy of the least of Milton's words; but she persisted; and again he suddenly threw himself into the task of teaching her with a combination of stormy intensity, concentrated patience, and occasional bursts of interesting disquisition on the beauty and nobility, the august mission and destiny, of human handwriting. Eliza ended by acquiring an extremely uncommercial script which was a positive extension of her personal beauty, and spending three times as much on stationery as anyone else because certain qualities and shapes of paper became indispensable to her. She could not even address an envelope in the usual way because it made the margins all wrong.

Their commercial schooldays were a period of disgrace and despair for the young couple. They seemed to be learning nothing about flower shops. At last they gave it up as hopeless, and shook the dust of the shorthand schools, and the polytechnics, and the London School of Economics from their feet for ever. Besides, the business was in some mysterious way beginning to take care of itself. They had somehow forgotten their objections to employing other people. They came to the conclusion that their own way was the best, and that they had really a remarkable talent for business. The Colonel, who had been compelled for some years to keep a sufficient sum on current account at his bankers to make up their deficits, found that the provision was unnecessary: the young people were prospering. It is true that there was not quite fair play between them and their competitors in trade. Their week-ends in the country cost them nothing, and

saved them the price of their Sunday dinners; for the motor car was the Colonel's; and he and Higgins paid the hotel bills. Mr F. Hill, florist and greengrocer (they soon discovered that there was money in asparagus; and asparagus led to other vegetables), had an air which stamped the business as classy; and in private life he was still Frederick Eynsford Hill, Esquire. Not that there was any swank about him: nobody but Eliza knew that he had been christened Frederick Challoner. Eliza herself swanked like anything.

That is all. That is how it has turned out. It is astonishing how much Eliza still manages to meddle in the housekeeping at Wimpole Street in spite of the shop and her own family. And it is notable that though she never nags her husband, and frankly loves the Colonel as if she were his favorite daughter, she has never got out of the habit of nagging Higgins that was established on the fatal night when she won his bet for him. She snaps his head off on the faintest provocation, or on none. He no longer dares to tease her by assuming an abysmal inferiority of Freddy's mind to his own. He storms and bullies and derides: but she stands up to him so ruthlessly that the Colonel has to ask her from time to time to be kinder to Higgins; and it is the only request of his that brings a mulish expression into her face. Nothing but some emergency or calamity great enough to break down all likes and dislikes, and throw them both back on their common humanity—and may they be spared any such trial!—will ever alter this. She knows that Higgins does not need her, just as her father did not need her. The very scrupulousness with which he told her that day that he had become used to having her there, and dependent on her for all sorts of little services, and that he should miss her if she went away (it would never have occurred to Freddy or the Colonel to say anything of the sort) deepens her inner certainty that she is "no more to him than them slippers"; yet she has a sense, too, that his indifference is deeper than the infatuation of commoner souls. She is immensely interested in him. She has even secret mischievous moments in which she wishes she could get him alone, on a desert island, away from all ties and with nobody else in the world to consider, and just drag him off his pedestal and see him making love like any common man. We all have private imaginations of that sort. But when it comes to business, to the life that she really leads as distinguished from the life of dreams and fancies, she likes Freddy and she likes the Colonel; and she does not like Higgins and Mr Doolittle. Galatea never does quite like Pygmalion: his relation to her is too godlike to be altogether agreeable.

Figure 1. A shabbily dressed and hesitant Eliza (Diana Rigg) listens to Higgins (Alec McCowen) explaining his plan to teach her how to speak properly. The 1974 London production of *Pygmalion* was directed by John Dexter. (Photograph: Zoë Dominic, London.)

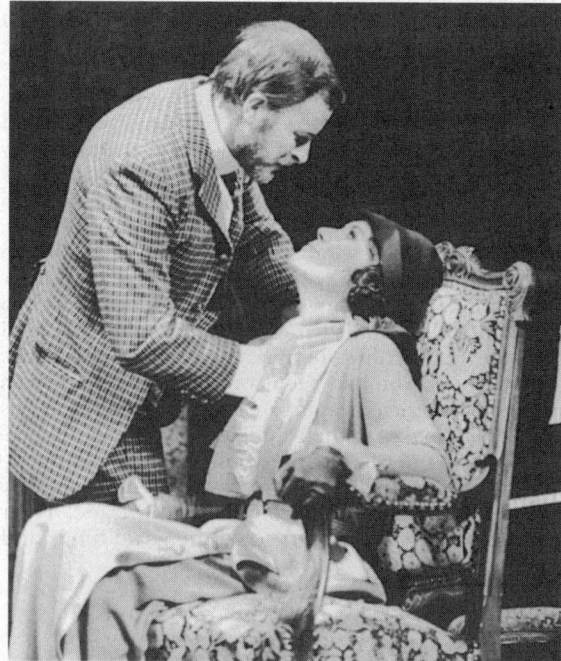

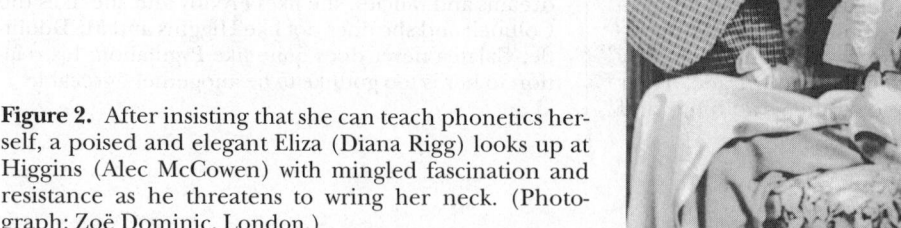

Figure 2. After insisting that she can teach phonetics herself, a poised and elegant Eliza (Diana Rigg) looks up at Higgins (Alec McCowen) with mingled fascination and resistance as he threatens to wring her neck. (Photograph: Zoë Dominic, London.)

Figure 3. Beautifully outfitted, Eliza (Diana Rigg, *center*) tries out her new pronunciation and vocabulary at Mrs. Higgins's tea party. Listening to her are, *left to right,* Mrs. Higgins (Ellen Pollock), Colonel Pickering (Jack May), Mrs. Eynsford Hill (Margaret Ward), Clara Eynsford Hill (Sarah Atkinson), Higgins (Alec McCowen), and Freddy Eynsford Hill (Anthony Naylor). The richly detailed set and costumes were designed by Jocelyn Herbert and Andrew Sanders. (Photograph: Zoë Dominic, London.)

Staging of *Pygmalion*

**REVIEW OF THE LONDON PRODUCTION, 1974,
BY RONALD BRYDEN**

As a rule, Norfolk has no flatness to match the second night of a show acclaimed to be a hit by the morning papers singing together. The nervous chemistry which triggered ovations is spent. The exhausted cast, carousing all night, have already passed from excitement to boredom at the certainty of a long run. The audience, serious playgoers in real clothes as opposed to the first night's fancy dress rout of backers' friends, sit baffled, wondering what the shouting was about. The revival of *Pygmalion* at the Old New, as I shall always think of the Albery Theatre, was the exception. Clearly the cast found it impossible to believe a success, in these days, wholly earned and deserved. Even at the second performance [they] were still beavering away earning it all over again.

Presumably they needed reassurance that one could market *My Fair Lady* without the songs and sentiment. Joy to the world, they were wrong. The man deserving their success most is Eddie Kulukundis, first impresario to recognise that beneath the mountain of royalties from Lerner and Loewe's extravaganza lay the 20th century classic ripest for rediscovery. Alongside the familiar pleasure of the real Eliza Doolittle's revelation within the bedraggled Covent Garden guttersnipe runs, in this production, the pleasure of the revelation of the play Shaw really wrote, crisp and twice as pertinent as the day he wrote it.

Did you think the day gone by when a comedy about a Cockney learning to talk Knightsbridge posh had anything to say to our cultural revolution, with its thousand local accents blooming together in the halls of Reith? You were thinking of the wrong play: not Shaw's but Alan Lerner's. Shaw's Professor Higgins is a modern phoneticist, with no preference between the accents by which England's classes proclaim themselves—"good English" to him is simply clear English, attainable only by foreigners, and he's as scathing about Mayfair's drawl as about Eliza's tortured vowels. The high point of the Shaw version isn't Cinderella going to the ball, but Cinderella shying the slipper in the prince's face and asking what made him think any girl in her right mind could want a life as useless as a princess's?

For, of course, there never was a ball scene in Shaw's *Pygmalion*. He pretended he left it out because it would cost too much even for Beerbohm Tree's Edwardian palace of spectacle, Her Majesty's. In fact, he knew perfectly well it could only obscure his real story line, as it has so fatally for the two generations brought up on Anthony Asquith's pre-war film and Lerner and Loewe's coster fantasia. One of the keenest pleasures of John Dexter's production is the beautifully ruthless cut from Mrs. Higgins' third-act question, "What's to become of her afterwards?" to afterwards itself—Eliza slumped despairingly in her diamonds on the same stool where she timidly perched on her arrival in Higgins' laboratory, fit for nothing but evenings as pointless and boring as the one she's just spent.

Indeed, the play has so many modern resonances you wonder whether Shaw wasn't in fact the last of the prophets. Acquired in a fit of absent-mindedness, Eliza in her helpless gentrification could stand for any former British colony left to its own devices with the crippling legacy of a one-crop economy, an education system geared to Oxbridge entry and class structure based on shades of Nordic pallor. Until Soyinka, one of the Naipauls or their equal replaces it, *Pygmalion* is the best play on post-imperialism we have. It's also the best answer yet to Germaine Greer and sisters. When Eliza sniffles about what she's been "made into" by her masters in speech, Higgins roars at her to forget how men treat her and stand on her own feet—she won't be independent until she stops whining for men to recognise her independence, and takes it.

So that, for the first time since Beerbohm Tree bowdlerised the final curtain by tossing flowers to the departing Mrs. Patrick Campbell, the happy ending is the one Shaw wrote. Eliza takes her independence and goes out slamming the door, to turn Freddie Eynsford Hill into the same sort of full-grown human being Higgins has goaded her to become. Any other conclusion would be as bathetic as Mrs. Gandhi pleading for India's reannexation by the United Kingdom or Mrs. Pankhurst telling Lloyd George she didn't really want votes for women, thank you, she'd only done it because she secretly enjoyed forcible feeding.

The impossibility of Higgins and Eliza finally falling into each other's arms is underlined here by the presence of Alec McCowen and Diana Rigg in the roles. They make the characters fundamentally incompatible by being the same kind of actors. The strongest weapon of both is precision, verging on overcalculatedness. One can imagine their two minds meeting in the phonetic lessons, revelling in precise discrimination of sounds and precise imitation of them. Once their precision turns to any larger relationship between the pedant and his Galatea, it's clear the negotiations can never succeed. Precisely as Millamant and Mirabell hammer out the terms of their marriage contract in *The Way of the World*, this Eliza and Higgins haggle over the fine print of a possible merger and recognise that it will not work.

Neither is perfectly cast. The second level of Shaw's joke was that his "companion dreadnoughts" should be played by two sacred monsters of theatrical egotism like Tree and Mrs. Pat. He was fortunate that George Alexander's refusal of the play gave Higgins to Tree, the ultimate actor-manager. Higgins could become a parody of Tree's Svengali, a power-mad scientist into whose clutches the flower-girl falls, only to destroy him with the greater monstrosity of her Cockney sanity. (The nearest modern approach to Tree's Higgins would surely be Donald Sinden's; may it be soon.) McCowen can't play that. Instead he mines the role for the nuggets of psychology with which Shaw underpinned Tree's flamboyance: Higgins' admission that he never feels completely grown-up among other men; his dependence on his mother; his defensive barricading of himself behind the minutiae of a science concerned with self-presentation.

McCowen's precision can flower here—watch the marvellous, three-second movement with which he drops Eliza's hat when his housekeeper warns him of lice, shakes his fingers fastidiously, tells himself not to be ridiculous and hides the gesture by plunging his hands under his arms in a habitual Napoleonic stance of self-sufficiency. Instead of virtuoso floods of actor-managerish charm and temperament, he gives the subtext: the insecurity which makes Higgins all bark, botanical and canine. It's a colder reading than usual, but not without emotion. Implicit in his teaching of Eliza is his recognition of a being in the same need to learn self-presentation as himself. When she walks out at the end, his shoulders sag in recognition that he has created in her a strength beyond his own.

Against the odds, he earns success in the role. So in another way does Diana Rigg. The germ of Shaw's comedy was his detection beneath Mrs. Pat's *grande dame* languors of a coarse, quarrelsome strain of Cockney vulgarity. That layer of the part is beyond Miss Rigg, so she cleverly builds her performance from its other pole. Her Cockney is not raucous but muffled: she makes its uncertainty Eliza's. The girl who walks into Higgins' parlour is only a fraction of herself. She mumbles, talks to herself, uses her limbs awkwardly. In the tea-party scene, she is a doll coming to life, Coppélia spinning out of control as selfhood floods into her wooden gestures.

Her brand of preciseness comes into its own here: I've never seen it played better. In the final acts, intelligence can take over. Eliza is herself, contained, exact and beautiful. The self-pity is played as a duty to herself, part of her negotiations with Higgins, but it's clear she would rather know where she stands than risk ambiguity staying with him. The incompleteness of characterisation is turned into the character: the full Eliza is only there at the end of the play. You can fault individual early bits, but you can't fault the whole conception, its acuteness or skill.

The leads justify casting against the grain by evolving during their performances. Bob Hoskins' Doolittle is all there from the moment he takes the stage, a philosophical walrus who puts a curve on his rhetoric rather as sealions curve their torsos to catch a fish. Ellen Pollock's Mrs. Higgins shapes itself beautifully against the two leads: you can see her demonstrating to Eliza the meaning of graceful movement, while relishing with a private vanity her son's admiration of it. So does Hilda Fenemore's Mrs. Pearce: it's clear that the housekeeper has found Higgins' weakness and exploits it, whereas once she finds Eliza's strength she stands back and washes her hands of her. The dove-tailing of these performances I suppose is John Dexter's special triumph: it's the tightest-woven stage household we've seen since his *Woman Killed with Kindness.* Jocelyn Herbert's and Andrew Sanders' sets are probably the best summary of the production: a shade diagrammatic, drawn rather than embodied, they earn success by sheer accuracy of line. It's a better kind of success, I'd say, than many more full-blown.

LUIGI PIRANDELLO

1867–1936

Pirandello, whose life was in many respects as problematic as the existence of the characters in his plays, playfully acknowledged its confusion by declaring himself to be "the son of Chaos." His father was the owner of a lucrative sulfur mine, and Pirandello was born on his father's country estate in a southern Sicilian locale whose name was derived from the Greek word "chaos." Although his father had intended him to have a career in business, Pirandello was already writing poetry by the time he was sixteen. When he was eighteen, having failed in a brief business venture, his father sent him off to the University of Rome. Pirandello subsequently attended the University of Bonn, where in 1891 he earned a doctorate in philology, but instead of pursuing a career in teaching and research he returned to Rome and immersed himself in writing poetry and fiction. By 1894, he had already published two volumes of poetry and a collection of short stories. Also in 1894, he was married off in an arrangement negotiated by his father and another sulfur-mine owner who wanted to unite their business interests. For its first ten years, the marriage was evidently a happy one, supported by the substantial wealth of both sets of parents, but in 1904 both sulfur mines were destroyed by a flood. The news of this disaster was so shocking to Pirandello's wife that she fainted on hearing it, was subsequently completely paralyzed for six months, and then gradually went insane. Pirandello was forced to take a position teaching literature at a girls' school, an arrangement that provoked his wife to have hysterical fits of jealousy. Her derangement repeatedly caused her to become physically violent, yet Pirandello persisted in taking care of her himself for fifteen years, until in 1919 his friends finally convinced him to have her committed to a mental institution.

Pirandello continued to write during all the years of living through his wife's insanity and through the insanity of World War I, which divided his allegiances between Germany, a country he admired for its learning and scholarship, and Italy, his own country, which entered the conflict in 1916 on the side of the English and French. By 1916, he had published several volumes of short stories, several novels, several collections of poetry, and three one-act plays, and in virtually all these works he expressed a relativistic view of existence that he appears to have been driven to by the chaotic nature of his own personal experience. In his most well-known novel, *The Late Mattia Pascal* (1905), for example, he told the story of a man who discovers that because he left some belongings on a bridge, everyone thinks he has committed suicide. Having made this discovery, the man decides to capitalize on the misunderstanding by trying to start a new life, free of the deceptions and role-playing that had characterized his old one. But he at once realizes that he must take a new role in order to prevent his earlier identity from being discovered, and thus gradually recognizes that his personality is not his own creation but an appearance forced on him by what is expected in his own society.

The predicament of Mattia Pascal epitomizes Pirandello's persistent concern regarding the inescapable compulsion of human beings to play roles, to assume so many guises, in fact, that they can never be certain even of their own personal character, much less that of anyone else they encounter in the world. Pirandello explicitly defined his concern with these problems in 1920, shortly before the appearance of *Six Characters in Search of an Author* (1922):

> I think that life is a very sad piece of buffoonery: because we have in ourselves, without being able to know why, wherefore or whence, the need to deceive ourselves constantly by creating a reality (one for each and never the same for all), which from time to time is discovered to be vain and illusory.

The vanity and the illusoriness of this "buffoonery" provided Pirandello with the grounds for all of his writing:

> My art is full of bitter compassion for all those who deceive themselves; but this compassion cannot fail to be followed by the ferocious derision of destiny which condemns man to deception.

His "bitter compassion," fed by the irrationality of the war, evidently moved him to turn to playwriting, for between 1916 and 1921 in a fury of productivity he produced a total of fifteen plays.

Pirandello dramatized his relativistic vision most explicitly in a play appropriately titled *Right You Are, If You Think You Are* (1917), which depicts the futile attempts of an Italian community to unravel the truth about a husband, his wife, and his mother-in-law who have come to live in their city. The mother-in-law tells one story about their situation, which is subsequently contradicted by that of the husband, who appears to demonstrate that his mother-in-law is insane, but his version of their situation is, in turn, discredited by another story from his mother-in-law that appears to prove that he is a madman, and the action of the play repeatedly complicates the problem of determining the truth about the family without ever resolving it. As the wife (who appears only at the end of the play) says, "I am the one that each of you thinks I am." Truth is thus presented to be as unstable, as variable, as the differing perceptions of every member in the community. The maddening implications of this vision were dramatized by Pirandello in *Enrico IV* (1922), a play that portrays the schizophrenic experience of a man who recovers from a long psychotic delusion about himself only to perpetuate his madness as a deliberate pose. But at the end of the play, his deliberate choice turns into an eternal necessity, when he kills a man who has accused him of being sane and finds that in order to escape a charge of murder he must retreat forever into the role of being a madman.

By the end of his life, Pirandello had dramatized his haunting view of existence in nearly forty plays, but none of them achieved the enduring fame of *Six Characters in Search of an Author*. Its unique dramatic power is in large part the result of Pirandello's reclaiming of a traditional dramatic form—the play within the play—and a traditional dramatic metaphor for the vanity of existence—"Life's but . . . a poor player that struts and frets his hour upon the stage and then is heard no more." Pirandello has used these traditional elements to present his relativistic vision in its most disturbingly complicated form. From the moment the six characters appear on stage seeking an author to tell their story and a producer to dramatize their experience, Pirandello gradually unfolds the dizzying ramifications of his relativistic view: in the Father's repeated explanations of it that the Producer repeatedly denies, even in the face of the hopeless confusion unfolding before him; in the repeated attempts of the Stepdaughter to have the story played from her perspective that the Father repeatedly claims to be a distortion of his true character; in the almost inarticulate desire of the Mother to have her older son express the affection and forgiveness that she feels is warranted from her point of view; in the Son's attempt to proclaim his lack of complicity in the gruesome tragedy, despite being one of the villains of the piece; and, of course, in the inability of any of the characters or actors to understand each other at all. The play moves inexorably to its final frenzy of yelling, one side shouting "Reality!" the other "Make-believe!" And Pirandello's symbolic comment on this confusion is to plunge the theater into darkness, so that even the Producer, so staunchly sure of the truth, cannot see where he is going. Although the play is clearly an enactment of Pirandello's relativistic philosophy, it may also be seen as dramatizing the problematic relationship between art and life, between performance and existence. The characters' search for an author may also be viewed as a compelling psychological study of the anxiety—even the schizophrenia—that results from the felt absence of a stable authority figure. Even the Father, the traditional image of authority, is seeking a reliable source of authority, but the only authority figure in the play, the Producer, is equally unreliable.

When *Six Characters* was first produced in Rome in 1922, the audience turned into a madhouse of excitement at the end of the play. When it was produced in Paris in 1923, it stunned the French theatrical world and led to a torrent of dramatic imitations. Since then, the phrase "appearance and reality" has become such a cliché that contemporary audiences may well wonder what all the fuss was about. Successful contemporary productions have highlighted the conflict between the "real" actors who are rehearsing a play and the "imaginary" characters who suddenly appear and demand to have their story staged. Thus, the American Repertory Theatre in Cambridge has staged the play repeatedly since 1984, and in each production the actors are rehearsing a play actually in the A.R.T. repertory (by Molière in 1984 and 1988, by Carlo Gozzi in 1996), and are identified by their actual names. Taking a distinctly different approach, the 2001 Young Vic production had its actors rehearse another Pirandello play, as called for in the original version of the play, but added a slide-lecture about Pirandello's life—the characters bursting through the screen when they interrupted the rehearsal. That surprising entrance is emblematic of the conflict that the characters constantly experience during the play as they try to make the director and the actors understand their story. One has only to look at the incongruity of the Stepdaughter's schoolgirl hat on the suavely coiffed Leading Lady (see Figure 1) to see how little the actors resemble the characters they are asked to play. While the characters appear always in black, the actors wear much lighter colors (see Figure 2). And their total misunderstanding of the characters' story is evident when the Producer, rebuked by Madame Pace for laughing at her broken English, then decides that a "little comic relief" is just what is needed to heighten the central dramatic encounter of the Father and Stepdaughter in a brothel (see Figure 3). John Peter's review of the production, reprinted following the play, suggests that "*Six Characters* is a tragedy with laughter," and that even the guilty figure of the father is somehow laughable when he wishes to have an actor play his part. Laughable, and even melodramatic, though the characters may sometimes be, Pirandello uses their strange plight to raise disturbing and perhaps unanswerable questions about the nature of theatrical representation and the limits of life on stage—questions of compelling importance not only for the characters in the play but also for the audience watching them.

SIX CHARACTERS IN SEARCH OF AN AUTHOR

BY LUIGI PIRANDELLO / TRANSLATED BY FREDERICK MAY

CHARACTERS OF THE PLAY IN THE MAKING

THE FATHER
THE MOTHER
THE STEPDAUGHTER
THE SON
THE BOY *(nonspeaking)*
THE LITTLE GIRL *(nonspeaking)*
MADAME PACE *(who is called into being)*

THE ACTORS IN THE COMPANY

THE PRODUCER *(Director)*
THE LEADING LADY
THE LEADING MAN
THE SECOND FEMALE LEAD *(referred to as* THE SECOND
    ACTRESS *in the text)*
THE INGENUE
THE JUVENILE LEAD
OTHER ACTORS AND ACTRESSES

THE STAGE MANAGER
THE PROMPTER
THE PROPERTY MAN
THE FOREMAN OF THE STAGE CREW
THE PRODUCER'S SECRETARY
THE COMMISSIONAIRE
STAGEHANDS AND OTHER THEATRE PERSONNEL

SCENE

Daytime: The Stage of a Theatre

N.B. The play has neither acts nor scenes. Its performance will be interrupted twice: once—though the curtain will not be lowered—when the PRODUCER *and the principal* CHARACTERS *go away to write the script and the* ACTORS *leave the stage, and a second time when the Man on the Curtain lets it fall by mistake.*

ACT 1

(When the audience enters the auditorium the curtain is up and the stage is just as it would be during the daytime. There is no set and there are no wings; it is empty and in almost total darkness. This is in order that right from the very beginning the audience shall receive the impression of being present, not at a performance of a carefully rehearsed play, but at a performance of a play that suddenly happens.

Two small flights of steps, one right and one left, give access to the stage from the auditorium.

On the stage itself, the prompter's dome has been removed, and is standing just to one side of the prompt box.

Downstage, on the other side, a small table and an armchair with its back turned to the audience have been set for the PRODUCER.

Two more small tables, one rather larger than the other, together with several chairs, have been set downstage so that they are ready if needed for the rehearsal. There are other chairs scattered about to the left and to the right for the actors, and, in the background, to one side and almost hidden, there is a pianoforte.

When the house lights go down the FOREMAN *comes on to the stage through the back door. He is dressed in blue dungarees and carries his tools in a bag slung at his belt. From a corner at the back of the stage he takes one or two slats of wood, brings them down front, kneels down and starts nailing them together. At the sound of his hammer the* STAGE MANAGER *rushes in from the direction of the dressing-rooms.)*

STAGE MANAGER: Hey! What are you doing?

FOREMAN: What am I doing? Hammering . . . nails.

STAGE MANAGER: At this time of day? *(He looks at his watch.)* It's gone half-past ten! The Producer'll be here any minute now and he'll want to get on with his rehearsal.

FOREMAN: And let me tell *you* something . . . I've got to have time to do *my* work, too.

STAGE MANAGER: You'll get it, you'll get it. . . . But you can't do that *now.*

FOREMAN: When can I do it then?

STAGE MANAGER: After the rehearsal. Now, come on. . . . Clear up all this mess, and let me get on with setting the second act of *The Game As He Played It.*

(The FOREMAN *gathers his pieces of wood together, muttering and grumbling all the while, and goes off. Meanwhile, the* ACTORS OF THE COMPANY *have begun to come on to the stage through the door back. First one comes in, then another, then two together . . . just as they please. There are nine or ten of them in all—as many as you would suppose you would need for the rehearsal of Pirandello's play,* The Game As He Played It, *which has been called for today.*

As they come in they greet one another and the STAGE MANAGER *with a cheery 'Good morning.' Some of them go off to their dressing-rooms; others, and among them the* PROMPTER, *who is carrying the prompt copy rolled up under his arm, remain on the stage, waiting for the* PRODUCER *to come and start the rehearsal. While they are waiting—some of them standing, some seated about in small groups—they exchange a few words among themselves. One lights a cigarette, another complains about the part that he's been given and a third reads out an item of news from a theatrical journal for the benefit of the other actors. It would be best if all the* ACTORS *and* ACTRESSES *could be dressed in rather bright and gay clothes. This first improvised scene should be played very naturally and with great vivacity. After a while, one of the comedy men can sit down at the piano and start playing a dance-tune. The younger* ACTORS *and* ACTRESSES *start dancing.)*

STAGE MANAGER *(clapping his hands to restore order)*: Come on, now, come on! That's enough of that! Here's the producer!

(The music and dancing come to a sudden stop. The ACTORS *turn and look out into the auditorium and see the* PRODUCER, *who is coming in through the door. He comes up the gangway between the stalls, bowler hat on head, stick under arm, and a large cigar in his mouth, to the accompaniment of a chorus of 'Good mornings' from the* ACTORS *and climbs up one of the flights of steps on to the stage. His* SECRETARY *offers him his post—a newspaper or so, a script.)*

PRODUCER: Any letters?

SECRETARY: None at all. This is all the post there is.

PRODUCER *(handing him back the script)*: Put it in my office. *(Then, looking around and turning to the* STAGE MANAGER.*)* Oh, you can't see a thing here! Ask them to give us a spot of light, please.

STAGE MANAGER: Right you are!

(He goes off to give the order and a short while after the whole of the right side of the stage, where the ACTORS *are standing, is lit up by a bright white light. In the meantime the* PROMPTER *has taken his place in his box, switched on his light and spread his script out in front of him.)*

PRODUCER *(clapping his hands)*: Come on, let's get started! *(to the* STAGE MANAGER*)* Anyone missing?

STAGE MANAGER: The Leading Lady.

PRODUCER: As usual! *(Looks at his watch.)* We're ten minutes late already. Make a note, will you, please, to remind me to give her a good talking-to about being so late! It might teach her to get to rehearsals on time in the future.

(He has scarcely finished his rebuke when the voice of the LEADING LADY *is heard at the back of the auditorium.)*

LEADING LADY: No, please don't! Here I am! Here I am! *(She is dressed completely in white, with a large and rather dashing and provocative hat, and is carry-ing a dainty little lap-dog. She runs down the aisle and hastily climbs up the steps on to the stage.)*

PRODUCER: You've set your heart on always keeping us waiting, haven't you?

LEADING LADY: Forgive me! I hunted everywhere for a taxi so that I should get here on time! But you haven't started yet, anyway. And I don't come on immediately. *(Then, calling the* STAGE MANAGER *by name, she gives him the lap-dog.)* Please put him in my dressing-room . . . and mind you shut the door!

PRODUCER *(grumblingly)*: And she has to bring a dog along too! As if there weren't enough dogs around here! *(He claps his hands again and turns to the* PROMPTER.*)* Come on now, let's get on with Act II of *The Game As He Played It*. *(He sits down in the armchair.)* Now, ladies and gentlemen, who's on?

(The ACTORS *and* ACTRESSES *clear away from the front of the stage and go and sit to one side, except for the three who start the scene, and the* LEADING LADY. *She has paid no attention to the* PRODUCER's *question and has seated herself at one of the little tables.)*

PRODUCER *(to the* LEADING LADY*)*: Ah! So you're in this scene, are you?

LEADING LADY: Me? Oh, no!

PRODUCER *(annoyed)*: Then for God's sake get off!

(And the LEADING LADY *gets up and goes and sits with the others.)*

PRODUCER *(to the* PROMPTER*)*: Now, let's get started!

PROMPTER *(reading from his script)*: "The house of Leone Gala. A strange room, half dining-room, half study."

PRODUCER *(turning to the* STAGE MANAGER*)*: We'll use the red set.

STAGE MANAGER *(making a note on a sheet of paper)*: The red set. Right!

PROMPTER *(continuing to read from his script)*: "A table laid for a meal and a desk with books and papers. Bookshelves with books on them. Glass-fronted cupboards containing valuable china. A door back leading into Leone's bedroom. A side door left, leading into the kitchen. The main entrance is right."

PRODUCER *(getting up and pointing)*: Right! Now listen carefully—over there, the main entrance. And over here, the kitchen. *(Turning to the* ACTOR *who is to play the part of Socrates.)* You'll make your entrances and exits this side. *(to the* STAGE MANAGER*)* We'll have that green-baize door at the back there . . . and some curtains. *(He goes and sits down again.)*

STAGE MANAGER *(making a note)*: Right you are!

PROMPTER *(reading)*: "Scene I. Leone Gala, Guido Venanzi, Filippo, who is called Socrates." *(to the* PRODUCER*)* Do I have to read the stage directions as well?

PRODUCER: Yes, yes, of course! I've told you that a hundred times!

PROMPTER *(reading)*: "When the curtain rises, Leone Gala, wearing a cook's hat and apron, is busy beating an egg in a basin, with a wooden spoon. Filippo, also dressed as a cook, is beating another egg. Guido Venanzi is sitting listening to them."

LEADING MAN *(to the* PRODUCER*)*: Excuse me, but do I really have to wear a cook's hat?

PRODUCER *(irritated by this observation)*: So it seems! That's certainly what's written there! *(He points to the script.)*

LEADING MAN: Forgive me for saying so, but it's ridiculous.

PRODUCER *(bounding to feet in fury)*: Ridiculous! Ridiculous! What do you expect me to do if the French haven't got any more good comedies to send us, and we're reduced to putting on plays by Pirandello? And if you can understand *his* plays . . . you're a better man than I am! He deliberately goes out of his way to annoy people, so that by the time the play's through everybody's fed up . . . actors, critics, audience, everybody! *(The* ACTORS *laugh. Then getting up and going over to the* LEADING MAN, *the* PRODUCER *cries.)* Yes, my dear fellow, a cook's hat! And you beat eggs! And do you think that, having these eggs to beat, you then have nothing more on your hands? Oh, no, not a bit of it. . . . You have to represent the shell of the eggs that you're beating! *(The* ACTORS *start laughing again and begin to make ironical comments among themselves.)* Shut up! And listen when I'm explaining things! *(Turning again to the* LEADING MAN*.)* Yes, my dear fellow, the shell . . . or, as you might say, the empty form of reason, without that content of instinct which is blind! You are reason and your wife is instinct, in a game where you play the parts which have been given you. And all the time you're playing your part, you are the self-willed puppet of yourself. Understand?

LEADING MAN *(spreading out his hands)*: Me? No!

PRODUCER *(returning to his seat)*: Neither do I! However, let's get on with it! It's going to be a wonderful flop, anyway! *(In a confidential tone.)* I suggest you turn to the audience a bit more . . . about three-quarters face. Otherwise, what with the abstruseness of the dialogue, and the audience's not being able to hear you, the whole thing'll go to hell. *(Clapping his hands again.)* Now, come along! *Come along!* Let's get started!

PROMPTER: Excuse me, sir, do you mind if I put the top back on my box? There's a bit of a draught.

PRODUCER: Of course! Go ahead! Go ahead!

(Meanwhile the COMMISSIONAIRE *has entered the auditorium. He is wearing a braided cap and, having covered the length of the aisle, he comes up to the edge of the stage to announce the arrival of the* SIX CHARACTERS *to the* PRODUCER. *They have followed the* COMMISSIONAIRE *into the auditorium and have walked behind him as he has come up to the stage. They look about them, a little perplexed and a little dismayed.*

In any production of this play it is imperative that the producer should use every means possible to avoid any confusion between the SIX CHARACTERS *and the* ACTORS. *The placing of the two groups, as they will be indicated in the stage-directions once the* CHARACTERS *are on the stage, will no doubt help. So, too, will their being lit in different colors. But the most effective and most suitable method of distinguishing them that suggests itself, is the use of special masks for the* CHARACTERS, *masks specially made from some material which will not grow limp with perspiration and will at the same time be light enough to be worn by the actors playing these parts. They should be cut so as to leave the eyes, the nose and the mouth free. In this way the deep significance of the play can be brought out. The* CHARACTERS *should not, in fact, appear as phantasms, but as created realities, unchangeable creations of the imagination and, therefore, more real and more consistent than the ever-changing naturalness of the* ACTORS.

The masks will assist in giving the impression of figures constructed by art, each one fixed immutably in the expression of that sentiment which is fundamental to it. That is to say in REMORSE *for the* FATHER, REVENGE *for the* STEPDAUGHTER, CONTEMPT *for the* SON *and* SORROW *for the* MOTHER. *Her mask should have wax tears fixed in the corners of the eyes and coursing down the cheeks, just like those which are carved and painted in the representations of the Mater Dolorosa that are to be seen in churches.*

Her dress, too, should be of a special material and cut. It should be severely plain, its folds stiff, giving in fact the appearance of having been carved, and not of being made of any material that you can just go out and buy or have cut-out and made up into a dress by any ordinary dressmaker.

The FATHER *is a man of about fifty. He is not bald but his reddish hair is thin at the temples. His moustache is thick and coils over his still rather youthful-looking mouth, which all too often falls open in a purposeless, uncertain smile. His complexion is pale and this is especially noticeable when one has occasion to look at his forehead, which is particularly broad. His blue, oval-shaped eyes are very clear and piercing. He is wearing a dark jacket and light-coloured trousers. At times his manner is all sweetness and light, at others it is hard and harsh.*

The MOTHER *appears as a woman crushed and terrified by an intolerable weight of shame and abasement. She is dressed in a modest black and wears a thick crepe widow's veil. When she lifts her veil she reveals a wax-like face; it is not, however at all sickly looking. She keeps her eyes downcast all the time. The* STEPDAUGHTER, *who is eighteen, is defiant, bold, arrogant—almost shamelessly so. She is very beautiful. She, too, is dressed in mourning but carries it with a decided air of showy elegance. She shows contempt for the very timid, dejected, half-frightened manner of her younger brother, a rather grubby and unprepossessing* BOY *of fourteen, who is also dressed in black. On the other hand she displays a very lively tenderness for her small sister, a* LITTLE GIRL *of about four, who is wearing a white frock with a black silk sash round her waist.*

The SON *is a tall young man of twenty-two. He is wearing a mauve-coloured overcoat and has a long green scarf twisted round his neck. He appears as if he has stiffened into an attitude of contempt for the* FATHER *and of supercilious indifference toward the* MOTHER.*)*

COMMISSIONAIRE *(cap in hand)*: Excuse me, sir.

PRODUCER *(snapping at him rudely)*: Now what's the matter?

COMMISSIONAIRE: There are some people here, sir, asking for you.

(The PRODUCER *and the* ACTORS *turn in astonishment and look out into the auditorium.)*

PRODUCER *(furiously)*: But I've got a rehearsal on at the moment! And you know quite well that no one's allowed in here while a rehearsal's going on. *(Then addressing the* CHARACTERS.*)* Who are you? What do you want?

FATHER *(he steps forward, followed by the others, and comes to the foot of one of the flights of steps)*: We are here in search of an author.

PRODUCER *(caught between anger and utter astonishment)*: In search of an author? Which author?

FATHER: Any author, sir.

PRODUCER: But there's no author here. . . . We're rehearsing a new play.

STEPDAUGHTER *(vivaciously, as she rushes up the steps)*: So much the better! Then so much the better, sir! We can be your new play.

ONE OF THE ACTORS *(amidst the lively comments and laughter of the others)*: Oh, just listen to her! *Listen* to her!

FATHER *(following the* STEPDAUGHTER *on to the stage)*: Yes, but if there isn't any author. . . . *(to the* PRODUCER*)* Unless you'd like to be the author. . . .

(Holding the LITTLE GIRL *by the hand, the* MOTHER, *followed by the* BOY, *climbs up the first steps leading to the stage and stands there expectantly. The* SON *remains morosely below.)*

PRODUCER: Are you people trying to be funny?

FATHER: No. . . . How can you suggest such a thing? On the contrary, we are bringing you a terrible and grievous drama.

STEPDAUGHTER: And we might make your fortune for you.

PRODUCER: Perhaps you'll do me the kindness of getting out of this theatre! We've got no time to waste on lunatics!

FATHER *(he is wounded by this, but replies in a gentle tone)*: Oh . . . But you know very well, don't you, that life is full of things that are infinitely absurd, things that, for all their impudent absurdity, have no need to masquerade as truth, because they are true.

PRODUCER: What the devil are you talking about?

FATHER: What I'm saying is that reversing the usual order of things, forcing oneself to a contrary way of action, may well be construed as madness. As, for instance, when we create things which have all the appearance of reality in order that they shall look like the realities themselves. But allow me to observe that if this indeed be madness, it is, nonetheless, the sole *raison d'être* of your profession.

(The ACTORS *stir indignantly at this.)*

PRODUCER *(getting up and looking him up and down)*: Oh, yes? do you think ours is a profession of lunatics, do you?

FATHER: Yes, making what isn't true *seem* true . . . without having to . . . for fun. . . . Isn't it your function to give life on the stage to imaginary characters?

PRODUCER *(immediately, making himself spokesman for the growing anger of his actors)*: I should like you to know, my dear sir, that the actor's profession is a most noble one, and although nowadays, with things in the state they are, our playwrights give us stupid comedies to act, and puppets to represent instead of men, I'd have you know that it is our boast that we have given life, here on these very boards, to immortal works!

(The ACTORS *satisfiedly murmur their approval and applaud the* PRODUCER.*)*

FATHER *(breaking in and following hard on his argument)*: There you are! Oh, that's it exactly! To living beings . . . to beings who are more alive than those who breathe and wear clothes! Less real, perhaps, but truer! We're in complete agreement!

(The ACTORS *look at each other in utter astonishment.)*

PRODUCER: But . . . What on earth! . . . But you said just now . . .

FATHER: No, I said that because of your . . . because you shouted at us that you had no time to waste on lunatics . . . while nobody can know better than you that nature makes use of the instrument of human fantasy to pursue her work of creation on a higher level.

PRODUCER: True enough! True enough! But where does all this get us?

FATHER: Nowhere. I only wish to show you that one is born into life in so many ways, in so many forms. . . . As a tree, or as a stone; as water or as a butterfly. . . . Or as a woman. And that one can be born a character.

PRODUCER (*ironically, feigning amazement*): And you to- gether with these other people, were born a char- acter?

FATHER: Exactly. And alive, as you see. (*The* PRODUCER *and the* ACTORS *burst out laughing as if at some huge joke.*) (*Hurt.*) I'm sorry that you laugh like that because, I repeat, we carry within ourselves a terrible and grievous drama, as you can deduce for yourselves from this woman veiled in black.

(*And so saying, he holds out his hand to the* MOTHER *and helps her up the last few steps and, continuing to hold her hand, leads her with a certain tragic solemnity to the other side of the stage, which immediately lights up with a fantastic kind of light. The* LITTLE GIRL *and the* BOY *follow their* MOTHER. *Next the* SON *comes up and goes and stands to one side, in the background. Then the* STEP- DAUGHTER *follows him on to the stage; she stands down- stage, leaning against the proscenium arch. The* ACTORS *are at first completely taken aback and then, caught in admiration at this development, they burst into applause— just as if they had had a show put on for their benefit.*)

PRODUCER (*at first utterly astonished and then indignant*): Shut up! what the. . . ! (*Then turning to the* CHAR- ACTERS.) And you get out of here! Clear out of here! (*to the* STAGE MANAGER) For God's sake, clear them out!

STAGE MANAGER (*coming forward, but then stopping as if held back by some strange dismay*): Go away! Go away!

FATHER (*to the* PRODUCER): No, no! Listen. . . . We. . . .

PRODUCER (*shouting*): I tell you, we've got work to do!

LEADING MAN: You can't go about playing practical jokes like this. . . .

FATHER (*resolutely coming forward*): I wonder at your incredulity. Is it perhaps that you're not accus- tomed to seeing the characters created by an author leaping to life up here on the stage, when they come face to face with each other? Or is it, perhaps, that there's no script there (*He points to the prompt box.*) that contains us?

STEPDAUGHTER (*smiling, she steps toward the* PRODUCER; *then, in a wheedling voice*): Believe me, sir, we really are six characters . . . and very, very interest- ing! But we've been cut adrift.

FATHER (*brushing her aside*): Yes, that's it, we've been cut adrift. (*And then immediately to the* PRODUCER.) In the sense, you understand, that the author who created us as living beings, either couldn't or wouldn't put us materially into the world of art. And it was truly a crime . . . because he who has the good fortune to be born a living character may snap his fingers at Death even. He will never die! Man . . . The writer . . . The instrument of creation . . . Will die. . . . But what is created by him will never die. And in order to live eternally he has not the slightest need of extraordinary

gifts or of accomplishing prodigies. Who was San- cho Panza? Who was Don Abbondio? And yet they live eternally because—living seeds—they had the good fortune to find a fruitful womb—a fantasy which knew how to raise and nourish them, and to make them live through all eternity.

PRODUCER: All this is very, very fine indeed. . . . But what do you want here?

FATHER: We wish to live, sir!

PRODUCER (*ironically*): Through all eternity?

FATHER: No sir; just a moment . . . in you.

AN ACTOR: Listen to him! . . . listen to him!

LEADING LADY: They want to live in us!

JUVENILE LEAD (*pointing to the* STEPDAUGHTER): I've no objection . . . so long as I get her.

FATHER: Listen! Listen! The play is in the making. (*to the* PRODUCER) But if you and your actors are will- ing, we can settle it all between us without further delay.

PRODUCER (*annoyed*): But what do you want to settle? We don't go in for that sort of concoction here! We put on comedies and dramas here.

FATHER: Exactly! That's the very reason why we came to you.

PRODUCER: And where's the script?

FATHER: It is in us, sir. (*The* ACTORS *laugh.*) The drama is in us. We are the drama and we are impatient to act it—so fiercely does our inner passion urge us on.

STEPDAUGHTER (*scornful, treacherous, alluring, with delib- erate shamelessness*): My passion. . . . If you only knew! My passion . . . for him! (*She points to the* FATHER *and makes as if to embrace him, but then bursts into strident laughter.*)

FATHER (*at once, angrily*): You keep out of this for the moment! And please don't laugh like that!

STEPDAUGHTER: Oh . . . mayn't I? Then perhaps you'll allow me, ladies and gentlemen. . . . Although it's scarcely two months since my father died . . . just you watch how I can dance and sing! (*Mischie- vously she starts to sing Dave Stamper's "Prends garde à Tchou-Tchin-Tchou" in the fox-trot or slow one-step version by François Salabert. She sings the first verse, accompanying it with a dance.*)

Les chinois sont un peuple malin,
De Shangai à Pékin,
Ils ont mis des écriteaux partout:
Prenez garde à Tchou-Tchin-Tchou!

(*While she is singing and dancing, the* ACTORS, *and espe- cially the younger ones, as if attracted by some strange fas- cination, move toward her and half raise their hands as though to catch hold of her. She runs away, and when the* ACTORS *burst into applause, and the* PRODUCER *rebukes her, she stands where she is, quietly, abstractedly, and as if her thoughts were far away.*)

ACTORS *and* ACTRESSES (*laughing and clapping*): Well done! Jolly good!

PRODUCER (*irately*): Shut up! What do you think this is . . . a cabaret? (*Then taking the* FATHER *a little to one side, he says with a certain amount of consternation.*) Tell me something. . . . Is she mad?

FATHER: What do you mean, mad? It's worse than that!

STEPDAUGHTER (*immediately rushing up to the* PRODUCER): Worse! Worse! Oh it's something very much worse than that! Listen! Let's put this drama on at once . . . Please! Then you'll see that at a certain moment I . . . when this little darling here. . . . (*Takes the* LITTLE GIRL *by the hand and brings her over to the* PRODUCER.) . . . Isn't she a dear? (*Takes her in her arms and kisses her.*) You little darling! . . . You dear little darling! (*Puts her down again, adding in a moved tone, almost without wishing to.*) Well, when God suddenly takes this child away from her poor mother, and that little imbecile there (*Roughly grabbing hold of the* BOY *by the sleeve and thrusting him forward.*) does the stupidest of all stupid things, like the idiot he is (*Pushing him back toward the* MOTHER.) . . . Then you will see me run away. Yes, I shall run away! And, oh, how I'm longing for that moment to come! Because after all the very intimate things that have happened between him and me (*With a horrible wink in the direction of the* FATHER.) I can't remain any longer with these people . . . having to witness my mother's anguish because of that queer fish there (*Pointing to the* SON.) Look at him! Look at him! See how indifferent, how frigid he is . . . because he's the legitimate son . . . *he* is! He despises me, he despises him (*Pointing to the* BOY.), he despises that dear little creature. . . . Because we're bastards! Do you understand? . . . Because we're *bastards!* (*She goes up to the* MOTHER *and embraces her.*) And he doesn't want to recognize this poor woman as his mother. . . . This poor woman . . . who is the mother of us all! He looks down at her as if she were only the mother of us three bastards! The wretch! (*She says all this very quickly and very excitedly. She raises her voice at the word "bastards" and the final "wretch" is delivered in a low voice and almost spat out.*)

MOTHER (*to the* PRODUCER, *an infinity of anguish in her voice*): Please, in the name of these two little children . . . I beg you. . . . (*She grows faint and sways on her feet.*) Oh, my God! (*Consternation and bewilderment among the* ACTORS.)

FATHER (*rushing over to support her, accompanied by most of the* ACTORS): Quick . . . a chair. . . . A chair for this poor widow!

ACTORS (*rushing over*): Has she fainted? Has she fainted?

PRODUCER: Quick, get a chair . . . get a chair!

(*One of the* ACTORS *brings a chair, the others stand around, anxious to help in any way they can. The* MOTHER *sits on the chair; she attempts to prevent the* FATHER *from lifting the veil which hides her face.*)

FATHER: Look at her. . . . Look at her. . . .

MOTHER: No, no! My God! Stop it, please!

FATHER: Let them see you. (*He lifts her veil.*)

MOTHER (*rising and covering her face with her hands in desperation*): I beg you, sir, . . . Don't let this man carry out his plan! You must prevent him. . . . It's horrible!

PRODUCER (*utterly dumbfounded*): I don't get this at all. . . . I haven't got the slightest idea what you're talking about. (*to the* FATHER) Is this lady your wife?

FATHER (*immediately*): Yes, sir, my wife.

PRODUCER: Then how does it come about that she's a widow if you're still alive?

(*The* ACTORS *find relief for their bewilderment and astonishment in a noisy burst of laughter.*)

FATHER (*wounded, speaking with sharp resentment*): Don't laugh! Don't laugh like that, for pity's sake! It is in this fact that her drama lies. She had another man. Another man who ought to be here.

MOTHER (*with a cry*): No! No!

STEPDAUGHTER: He's got the good luck to be dead. . . . He died two months ago, as I just told you. We're still wearing mourning for him, as you can see.

FATHER: But it's not because he's dead that he's not here. No, he's not here because . . . Look at her! Look at her, please, and you'll understand immediately! Her drama does not lie in the love of two men for whom she, being incapable of love, could feel nothing. . . . Unless, perhaps, it be a little gratitude . . . to him, not to me. She is not a woman. . . . She is a mother. And her drama. . . . And how powerful it is! How powerful it is! . . . Her drama lies entirely, in fact, in these four children . . . The children of the two men that she had.

MOTHER: Did you say that I had them? Do you dare to say that I *had* these two men . . . to suggest that I wanted them? (*to the* PRODUCER) It was his doing. He gave him to me! He forced him on me! He forced me. . . . He forced me to go away with that other man!

STEPDAUGHTER (*at once, indignantly*): It's not true!

MOTHER (*startled*): Not true?

STEPDAUGHTER: It's not true! It's not true, I say.

MOTHER: And what can you possibly know about it?

STEPDAUGHTER: It's not true! (*to the* PRODUCER) Don't believe her! Do you know why she said that? Because of him. (*Pointing to the* SON.) That's why she said it! Because she tortures herself, wears herself out with anguish, because of the indifference of that son of hers. She wants him to believe that if she abandoned him when he was two years old it was because he *(Pointing to the* FATHER.*)* forced her to do it.

MOTHER *(forcefully)*: He forced me to do it! He forced me, as God is my witness! *(to the* PRODUCER*)* Ask him *(Pointing to her* HUSBAND.*)* if it's not true! Make him tell my son! She *(Pointing to her* DAUGHTER.*)* knows nothing at all about the matter.

STEPDAUGHTER: I know that while my father lived you were always happy.... You had a peaceful and contented life together. Deny it if you can!

MOTHER: I don't deny it! No....

STEPDAUGHTER: He was always most loving, always kindness itself towards you. *(to the* BOY, *angrily)* Isn't it true? Go on.... Say it's true! Why don't you speak, you stupid little idiot?

MOTHER: Leave the poor boy alone! Why do you want to make me appear an ungrateful woman? I don't want to say anything against your father.... I only said that it wasn't my fault, and that it wasn't just to satisfy my own desires that I left his house and abandoned my son.

FATHER: What she says is true. It was my doing.

(There is a pause.)

LEADING MAN *(to the other* ACTORS*)*: My God! What a show!

LEADING LADY: And we're the audience this time!

JUVENILE LEAD: For once in a while.

PRODUCER *(who is beginning to show a lively interest)*: Let's listen to this! Let's hear what they've got to say! *(And saying this he goes down the steps into the auditorium and stands in front of the stage, as if to get an impression of the scene from the audience's point of view.)*

SON *(without moving from where he is, speaking coldly, softly, ironically)*: Yes! Listen to the chunk of philosophy you're going to get now. He will tell you all about the Demon of Experiment.

FATHER: You're a cynical idiot, as I've told you a hundred times. *(Down to the* PRODUCER.*)* He mocks me because of this expression that I've discovered in my own defence.

SON *(contemptuously)*: Words! Words!

FATHER: Yes! Words! Words! They can always bring consolation to us.... To every one of us.... When we're confronted by something for which there's no explanation.... When we're face to face with an evil that consumes us.... The consolation of finding a word that tells us nothing, but that brings us peace.

STEPDAUGHTER: And dulls our sense of remorse, too. Yes! That above all!

FATHER: Dulls our sense of remorse? No, that's not true. It wasn't with words alone that I quietened remorse within me.

STEPDAUGHTER: No, you did it with a little money as well. Yes! Oh, yes! with a little money as well! With

the hundred lire that he was going to offer me ... as payment, ladies and gentlemen!

(A movement of horror on the part of the ACTORS.*)*

SON *(contemptuously to his* STEPSISTER*)*: That was vile!

STEPDAUGHTER: Vile? There they were, in a pale blue envelope, on the little mahogany table in the room behind Madame Pace's shop. Madame Pace.... One of those *Madames* who pretend to sell *Robes et Manteaux* so that they can attract us poor girls from decent families into their workrooms.

SON: And she's bought the right to tyrannise over the whole lot of us with those hundred lire that he was going to pay her.... But by good fortune.... And let me emphasise this.... He had no reason to pay her anything.

STEPDAUGHTER: Yes, but it was a very near thing! Oh, yes, it was, you know! *(She bursts out laughing.)*

MOTHER *(rising to protest)*: For shame! For shame!

STEPDAUGHTER *(immediately)*: Shame? No! This is my revenge! I'm trembling with desire.... Simply trembling with desire to live that scene! That room.... Over there the divan, the long mirror and a screen.... And in front of the window that little mahogany table.... And the pale blue envelope with the hundred lire inside. Yes, I can see it quite clearly! I'd only have to stretch out my hand and I could pick it up! But you gentlemen really ought to turn your backs now, because I'm almost naked. I no longer blush, because he's the one who does the blushing now. *(Pointing to* FATHER.*)* But, let me tell you, he was very pale then.... Very pale indeed! *(to the* PRODUCER*)* You can believe *me!*

PRODUCER: I haven't the vaguest idea what you're talking about!

FATHER: I can well believe it! When you get things hurled at you like that. Put your foot down.... And let me speak before you believe all these horrible slanders she's so viciously heaping upon me.... Without letting me get a word of explanation in.

STEPDAUGHTER: Ah, but this isn't the place for your long-winded fairy-stories, you know!

FATHER: But I'm not going to.... I want to explain things to him!

STEPDAUGHTER: Oh yes ... I bet you do! You'll explain everything so that it suits you, won't you?

(At this point the PRODUCER *comes back on stage to restore order.)*

FATHER: But can't you see that here we have the cause of all the trouble! In the use of words! Each one of us has a whole world of things inside him.... And each one of us has his own particular world. How can we understand each other if into the words which I speak I put the sense and the value of things as I understand them within myself. . . . While at the same time whoever is listening to them inevitably assumes them to have the sense and value that they have for him. . . . The sense and value that they have in the world that he has within him? We think we understand one another. . . . But we never really do understand! Look at this situation, for example! All my pity, all the pity that I feel for this woman (*Pointing to the* MOTHER.) she sees as the most ferocious cruelty.

MOTHER: But you turned me out of the house!

FATHER: There! Do you hear? I turned her out! She really believed that I was turning her out!

MOTHER: You know how to talk . . . I don't. . . . But believe me (*Turning to the* PRODUCER.) after he had married me. . . . Goodness knows why! For I was a poor, humble woman. . . .

FATHER: But it was just because of that. . . . It was your humility that I loved in you. I married you for your humility, believing . . . (*He breaks off, for she is making gestures of contradiction. Then, seeing how utterly impossible it is to make her understand him, he opens his arms wide in a gesture of despair and turns to the* PRODUCER.) No! . . . You see? She says no! It's terrifying, believe me! It's really terrifying, this deafness (*He taps his forehead.*). . . . This mental deafness of hers! Affection. . . . Yes! . . . For her children! But deaf . . . Mentally deaf. . . . Deaf to the point of desperation.

STEPDAUGHTER: True enough! But now you make him tell us what good all his cleverness has ever done us.

FATHER: If we could only foresee all the ill that can result from the good that we believe we are doing.

(*Meanwhile the* LEADING LADY, *with ever-increasing fury, has been watching the* LEADING MAN, *who is busy carrying on a flirtation with the* STEPDAUGHTER. *Unable to stand it any longer she now steps forward and says to the* PRODUCER.)

LEADING LADY: Excuse me, but are you going on with the rehearsal?

PRODUCER: Why, of course! Of course! But just at the moment I want to hear what these people have to say!

JUVENILE LEAD: This is really something quite new!

INGENUE: It's most interesting!

LEADING LADY: For those that are interested! (*And she looks meaningly in the direction of the* LEADING MAN.)

PRODUCER (*to the* FATHER): But you'll have to explain everything clearly. (*He goes and sits down.*)

FATHER: Yes. . . . Well. . . . You see . . . I had a poor man working under me. . . . He was my secretary, and devoted to me. . . . Who understood her in every way . . . In everything (*Pointing to the* MOTHER.) Oh, there wasn't the slightest suspicion of anything

wrong. He was a good man. A humble man. . . . Just like her. . . . They were incapable . . . both of them . . . not only of doing evil . . . but even of thinking it!

STEPDAUGHTER: So, instead, he thought about it for them! And then got on with it.

FATHER: It's not true! I thought that what I should be doing would be for their good. . . . And for mine, too . . . I confess it! Yes, things had come to such a pass that I couldn't say a single word to either of them without their immediately exchanging an understanding look. . . . Without the one's immediately trying to catch the other's eye. . . . For advice as to how to take what I had said. . . . So that I shouldn't get into a bad temper. As you'll readily appreciate it was enough to keep me in a state of continual fury. . . . Of intolerable exasperation!

PRODUCER: But. . . . Forgive my asking. . . . Why didn't you give this secretary of yours the sack?

FATHER: That's exactly what I did do, as a matter of fact. But then I had to watch that poor woman wandering forlornly about the house like some poor lost creature . . . Like one of those stray animals you take in out of charity.

MOTHER: But . . .

FATHER (*immediately turning on her, as if to forestall what she is about to say*): Your son! You were going to tell him about your son, weren't you?

MOTHER: But first of all he tore my son away from me!

FATHER: Not out of any desire to be cruel though! I took him away so that, by living in the country, in contact with Nature, he might grow up strong and healthy.

STEPDAUGHTER (*pointing to him, ironically*): And just look at him!

FATHER (*immediately*): And is it my fault, too, that he's grown up the way he has? I sent him to a wet-nurse in the country . . . a peasant's wife . . . because my wife didn't seem strong enough to me. . . . Although she came of a humble family, and it was for that reason that I'd married her! Just a whim maybe. . . . But then . . . what was I to do? I've always had this cursed longing for a certain solid moral healthiness.

(*At this the* STEPDAUGHTER *breaks out afresh into noisy laughter.*)

Make her stop that noise! I can't stand it!

PRODUCER: Be quiet! Let me hear what he has to say, for God's sake!

(*At the* PRODUCER's *rebuke she immediately returns to her former attitude. . . . Absorbed and distant, a half-smile on her lips. The* PRODUCER *comes down off the stage again to see how it looks from the auditorium.*)

FATHER: I could no longer stand the sight of that

woman near me *(Pointing to the* MOTHER.*)* Not so much because of the irritation she caused me . . . the nausea . . . the very real nausea with which she inspired me. . . . But rather because of the pain . . . the pain and the anguish that I was suffering on her account.

MOTHER: And he sent me away!

FATHER: Well provided with everything. . . . To that other man. . . . So that she might be free of me.

MOTHER: And so that he might be free as well!

FATHER: Yes, I admit it. And a great deal of harm came as a result of it. . . . But I meant well. . . . And I did it more for her sake than for my own. I swear it! *(He folds his arms. Then immediately turning to the* MOTHER.*)* Did I ever lose sight of you? Tell me, did I ever lose sight of you until that fellow took you away suddenly to some other town . . . all unknown to me. . . . Just because he'd got some queer notion into his head about the interest I was showing in you. . . . An interest which was pure, I assure you, sir. . . . Without the slightest suspicion of any ulterior motive about it! I watched the new little family that grew up around her with incredible tenderness. She can testify to that. *(He points to the* STEPDAUGHTER.*)*

STEPDAUGHTER: Oh, I most certainly can! I was such a sweet little girl. . . . Such a sweet little girl, you see. . . . With plaits down to my shoulders . . . and my knickers a little bit longer than my frock. I used to see him standing there by the door of the school as I came out. He came to see how I was growing up. . . .

FATHER: Oh, this is vile! Treacherous! Infamous!

STEPDAUGHTER: Oh, no! What makes you say it's infamous?

FATHER: It's infamous! Infamous! *(Then turning excitedly to the* PRODUCER *he goes on in an explanatory tone.)* After she'd gone away *(Pointing to the* MOTHER*)*, my house suddenly seemed empty. She had been a burden on my spirit, but she had filled my house with her presence! Left alone I wandered through the rooms like some lost soul. This boy here *(Pointing to the* SON*)*, having been brought up away from home. . . . I don't know . . . But . . . but when he returned home he no longer seemed to be my son. With no mother to link him to me, he grew up entirely on his own. . . . A creature apart . . . absorbed in himself . . . with no tie of intellect or affection to bind him to me. And then. . . . And, strange as it may seem, it's the simple truth . . . I became curious about her little family. . . . Gradually I was attracted to this family which had come into being as a result of what I had done. And the thought of it began to fill the emptiness that I felt all around me. I felt a real need . . . a very real need . . . to believe that she was happy, at peace, absorbed in the simple every-day duties of life. I wanted to look on her as being fortunate because she was far removed from the complicated torments of my spirit. And so, to have some proof of this, I used to go and watch that little girl come out of school.

STEPDAUGHTER: I should just say he did! He used to follow me along the street. He would smile at me and when I reached home he'd wave to me . . . like this. I would look at him rather provocatively, opening my eyes wide. I didn't know who he might be. I told my mother about him and she knew at once who it must be. *(The* MOTHER *nods agreement.)* At first she didn't want to let me go to school again. . . . And she kept me away for several days. And when I did go back, I saw him waiting for me at the door again . . . looking ridiculous . . . with a brown paper bag in his hand. He came up to me and patted me. . . . And then he took a lovely large straw hat out of the bag . . . with lots of lovely roses on it . . . And all for me.

PRODUCER: This is a bit off the point, you know.

SON *(contemptuously)*: Yes. . . . Literature! Literature!

FATHER: Literature indeed! This is life! Passion!

PRODUCER: It may be. But you certainly can't act this sort of stuff!

FATHER: I agree with you. Because all this is only leading up to the main action. I'm not suggesting that this part should be acted. And as a matter of fact, as you can quite well see, she *(Pointing to the* STEPDAUGHTER.*)* is no longer that little girl with plaits down to her shoulders. . . .

STEPDAUGHTER: . . . and her knickers a little bit longer than her frock!

FATHER: It is now that the drama comes! Something new, something complex. . . .

STEPDAUGHTER *(coming forward, her voice gloomy, fierce)*: As soon as my father died. . . .

FATHER *(at once, not giving her a chance to continue)*: . . . they fell into the most wretched poverty! They came back here. . . . And because of her stupidity *(Pointing to the* MOTHER.*)* I didn't know a thing about it. It's true enough that she can hardly write her own name. . . . But she might have got her daughter or that boy to write and tell me that they were in need!

MOTHER: Now tell me, sir, how was I to know that this was how he'd feel?

FATHER: That's exactly where you went wrong, in never having got to know how I felt about something.

MOTHER: After so many years away from him. . . . And after all that had happened. . . .

FATHER: And is it my fault that that fellow took you away from here as he did? *(Turning to the* PRODUCER.*)* I tell you, they disappeared overnight. . . . He'd found some sort of a job away from here . . .

I couldn't trace them at all. . . . So, of necessity, my interest in them dwindled. And this was how it was for quite a number of years. The drama broke out, unforeseen, and violent in its intensity, when they returned. . . . When I was impelled by the demands of my miserable flesh, which is still alive with desire. . . . Oh, the wretchedness, the unutterable wretchedness of the man who's alone and who detests the vileness of casual affairs! When he's not old enough to do without a woman, and not really young enough to be able to go and look for one without feeling a sense of shame. Wretchedness, did I say? It's horrible! It's horrible! Because no woman is any longer capable of giving him love. And when he realises this, he ought to do without. . . . Yes, yes, I know! . . . Each one of us, when he appears before his fellow men, is clothed with a certain dignity. But deep down inside himself he knows what unconfessable things go on in the secrecy of his own heart. We give way . . . we give way to temptation. . . . Only to rise up again immediately, filled with a great eagerness to reestablish our dignity in all its solid entirety. . . . Just as if it were a tombstone on some grave in which we had buried, in which we had hidden from our eyes, every sign, and the very memory itself of our shame. And everyone is just like that! Only there are some of us who lack the courage to talk about certain things.

STEPDAUGHTER: They've got the courage to do them, though. . . . All of them!

FATHER: Yes, all of them! But only in secret! And that's why it needs so much more courage to talk about them! A man's only got to mention these things, and the words have hardly left his lips before he's been labelled a cynic. And all the time it's not true. He's just like everybody else. . . . In fact he's better than they are, because he's not afraid to reveal with the light of his intelligence that red blush of shame which is inherent in human bestiality. . . . That shame to which bestial man closes his eyes, in order not to see it. And woman. . . . Yes, woman. . . . What kind of a being is she? She looks at you, tantalisingly, invitingly. You take her in your arms. And no sooner is she clasped firmly in your arms than she shuts her eyes. It is the sign of her mission, the sign by which she says to man, "Blind yourself, for I am blind."

STEPDAUGHTER: And what about when she no longer shuts her eyes? When she no longer feels the need to hide her blushing shame from herself by closing her eyes? When she sees instead . . . dry-eyed and dispassionate . . . the blushing shame of man, who has blinded himself without love? Oh, what disgust, what unutterable disgust, does she feel then for all these intellectual complications, for all this philosophy which reveals the beast in man and then tries to save him, tries to excuse him . . . I just can't stand here and listen to him! Because when a man is obliged to 'simplify' life bestially like that—when he throws overboard every vestige of 'humanity', every chaste desire, every pure feeling. . . . All sense of idealism, of duty, or modesty and of shame. . . . Then nothing is more contemptible, infuriating and revoltingly nauseating than their maudlin remorse. . . . Those crocodile tears!

PRODUCER: Now let's get back to the point! Let's get to the point! This is just a lot of beating about the bush!

FATHER: Very well. But a fact is like a sack. . . . When it's empty it won't stand up. And in order to make it stand up you must first of all pour into it all the reasons and all the feelings which have caused it to exist. I couldn't possibly be expected to know that when that man died and they returned here in such utter poverty, she (*Pointing to the* MOTHER.) would go out to work as a dress-maker in order to support the children. . . . Nor that, of all people, she'd gone to work for that . . . for Madame Pace.

STEPDAUGHTER: Who's a high-class dress-maker, if you ladies and gentlemen would really like to know. On the surface she does work for only the best sort of people. But she arranges things so that these fine ladies act as a screen . . . without prejudice to the others . . . who are only so-so.

MOTHER: Believe me, it never entered my head for one moment that that old hag gave me work because she had her eye on my daughter. . . .

STEPDAUGHTER: Poor Mummy! Do you know what that woman used to do when I took her back the work that my mother had done? She would point out to me how the material had been ruined by giving it to my mother to sew. . . . Oh, she'd grumble about this! And she'd grumble about that! And so, you understand, I had to pay for it. . . . And all the time this poor creature thought she was sacrificing herself for me and for those two children, as she sat up all night sewing away at work for Madame Pace. (*Gestures and exclamations of indignation from the* ACTORS.)

PRODUCER (*immediately*): And it was there, one day, that you met . . .

STEPDAUGHTER (*pointing to the* FATHER): . . . him! Yes, him! An old client! Now there's a scene for you to put on! Absolutely superb!

FATHER: With her . . . the Mother . . . arriving. . . .

STEPDAUGHTER (*immediately, treacherously*): . . . almost in time!

FATHER (*a cry*): No! In time! In time! Fortunately I recognized her in time! And I took them all back home with me! Now you can imagine what the situation is like for both of us. She, just as you see her. . . . And I no longer able to look her in the face.

STEPDAUGHTER: It's utterly ridiculous! How can I possibly be expected, after all that, to be a modest young miss . . . well-bred and virtuous . . . in accordance with his confounded aspirations for a "solid moral healthiness"?

FATHER: My drama lies entirely in this one thing. . . . In my being conscious that each one of us believes himself to be a single person. But it's not true. . . . Each one of us is many persons. . . . Many persons . . . according to all the possibilities of being that there are within us. . . . With some people we are one person. . . . With others we are somebody quite different. . . . And all the time we are under the illusion of always being one and the same person for everybody. . . . We believe that we are always this one person in whatever it is we may be doing. But it's not true! It's not true! And we see this very clearly when by some tragic chance we are, as it were, caught up whilst in the middle of doing something and find ourselves suspended in midair. And then we perceive that all of us was not in what we were doing, and that it would, therefore, be an atrocious injustice to us to judge us by that action alone . . . to keep us suspended like that. . . . To keep us in a pillory . . . throughout all existence . . . as if our whole life were completely summed up in that one deed. Now do you understand the treachery of this girl? She surprised me somewhere where I shouldn't have been . . . and doing something that I shouldn't have been doing with her. . . . She surprised an aspect of me that should never have existed for her. And now she is trying to attach to me a reality such as I could never have expected I should have to assume for her. . . . The reality that lies in one fleeting, shameful moment of my life. And this, this above all, is what I feel most strongly about. And as you can see, the drama acquires a tremendous value from this concept. Then there's the position of the others. . . . His . . . (Pointing to the SON.)

SON (shrugging his shoulders scornfully): Leave me alone! I've got nothing to do with all this!

FATHER: What do you mean . . . you've got nothing to do with all this?

SON: I've got nothing to do with it. . . . And I don't want to have anything to do with it, because, as you quite well know, I wasn't meant to be mixed up in all this with the rest of you!

STEPDAUGHTER: Common, that's what we are! And he's a fine gentleman! But, as you may have noticed, every now and again I fix him with a contemptuous look, and he lowers his eyes. . . . Because he knows the harm he's done me!

SON (scarcely looking at her): I?

STEPDAUGHTER: Yes, you! You! It's all your fault that I became a prostitute! (A movement of horror from the ACTORS.) Did you or did you not deny us, by the attitude you adopted—I won't say the intimacy of your home—but even that mere hospitality which makes guests feel at their ease? We were invaders who had come to disturb the kingdom of your legitimacy. I should just like you (This to the PRODUCER.) to be present at certain little scenes that took place between him and me. He says that I tyrannised over everybody. . . . But it was just because of the way that he behaved that I took advantage of the thing that he calls 'vile.' . . . Why I exploited the reason for my coming into his house with my mother . . . Who is his mother as well! And I went into that house as mistress of it!

SON (slowly coming forward): It's all very easy for them. . . . It's fine sport. . . . All of them ganging up against me. But just imagine the position of a son whose fate it is one fine day, while he's sitting quietly at home, to see arriving an impudent and brazen young woman who asks for his father— and heaven knows what her business is with him! Later he sees her come back, as brazen as ever, bringing that little girl with her. And finally he sees her treating her father—without knowing in the least why—in a very equivocal and very much to-the-point manner . . . asking him for money, in a tone of voice which leads you to suppose that he must give it to her. . . . Must give it to her, because he has every obligation to do so. . . .

FATHER: As indeed I have! It's an obligation I owe your mother!

SON: How should I know that? When I had never seen or even heard of her? Then one day I see her arrive with her (Pointing to the STEPDAUGHTER.) together with that boy and the little girl. And they say to me, "This is your mother, too, you know." Little by little I begin to understand. . . . Largely as a result of the way she goes on (Pointing to the STEPDAUGHTER again.) . . . . Why is it that they've come to live with us. . . . So suddenly . . . So unexpectedly. . . . What I feel, what I experience, I neither wish, nor am able, to express. I wouldn't even wish to confess it to myself. No action, therefore, can be hoped for from me in this affair. Believe me, I am a dramatically unrealised character . . . and I do not feel the least bit at ease in their company. So please leave me out of it!

FATHER: What! But it's just because you're like that. . . .

SON (in violent exasperation): And what do you know about it? How do you know what I'm like? When have you ever bothered yourself about me?

FATHER: I admit it! I admit it! But isn't that a dramatic situation in itself? This aloofness of yours, which is so cruel to me and to your mother. . . . Your mother who returns home and sees you almost for the first time . . . You're so grown up that she doesn't recognise you, but she knows that you're her son. (*Pointing to the* MOTHER *and addressing the* PRODUCER.) There, look! She's crying!

STEPDAUGHTER (*angrily, stamping her foot*): Like the fool she is!

FATHER (*pointing to the* STEPDAUGHTER): She can't stand him! (*Then returning to the subject of the* SON.) He says he's got nothing to do with all this, when, as a matter of fact, almost the whole action hinges on him. Look at that little boy. . . . See how he clings to his mother all the time, frightened and humiliated. . . . And it's *his* fault that he's like that! Perhaps his position is the most painful of all. . . . More than any of them he feels himself to be an outsider. And so the poor little chap feels mortified, humiliated at being taken into my home . . . out of charity, as it were. (*Confidentially.*) He's just like his father. Humble. . . . Doesn't say a word. . . .

PRODUCER: I don't think it's a good idea to have him in. You've no idea what a nuisance boys are on the stage.

FATHER: Oh, . . . but he won't be a nuisance for long . . . He disappears almost immediately. And the little girl, too. . . . In fact, she's the first to go.

PRODUCER: This is excellent! I assure you I find this all very interesting. . . . Very interesting indeed! I can see we've got the makings of a pretty good play here.

STEPDAUGHTER (*trying to butt in*): When you've got a character like me!

FATHER (*pushing her to one side in his anxiety to hear what decision the* PRODUCER *has come to*): You be quiet!

PRODUCER (*continuing, heedless of the interruption*): And it's certainly something new. . . . Ye-es! . . .

FATHER: Absolutely brand new!

PRODUCER: You had a nerve, though. I must say. . . . Coming here and chucking the idea at me like that. . . .

FATHER: Well, you understand, born as we are for the stage. . . .

PRODUCER: Are you amateur actors?

FATHER: No . . . I say that we're born for the stage because . . .

PRODUCER: Oh, don't try and con me with that one! You're an old hand at this game.

FATHER: No. I only act as much as anyone acts the part that he sets himself to perform, or the part that he is given in life. And in me it is passion itself, as you can see, that always becomes a little theatrical of its own accord . . . as it does in everyone . . . once it becomes exalted.

PRODUCER: Oh well, that as may be! That as may be! . . . But you do understand, without an author . . . I could give you the address of somebody who'd . . .

FATHER: No! . . . Look here. . . . You be the author!

PRODUCER: Me? What the devil are you talking about?

FATHER: Yes, you! You! Why not?

PRODUCER: Because I've never written anything in my life! That's why not!

FATHER: Then why not try your hand at it now? There's nothing to it. Everybody's doing it! And your job's made all the easier for you because we are here, all of us, alive before you. . . .

PRODUCER: That's not enough!

FATHER: Not enough? When you see us live our drama . . .

PRODUCER: Yes! Yes! But we'll still need somebody to write the play.

FATHER: No. . . . Someone to take it down possibly, while we act it out, scene by scene. It'll be quite sufficient if we make a rough sketch of it first and then have a run through.

PRODUCER (*climbing back on to the stage, tempted by this*): H'm! . . . You almost succeed in tempting me. . . . H'm! It would be rather fun! We could certainly have a shot at it.

FATHER: Of course! Oh, you'll see what wonderful scenes'll emerge! I can tell you what they are here and now.

PRODUCER: You tempt me. . . . You tempt me. . . . Let's have a go at it! . . . Come with me into my office. (*Turning to the* ACTORS.) You can have a few minutes' break. . . . But don't go too far away. I want you all back again in about a quarter of an hour or twenty minutes. (*To the* FATHER.) Well, let's see what we can make of it! We might get something really extraordinary out of it. . . .

FATHER: There's no *might* about it! They'd better come along too, don't you think? (*Pointing to the other* CHARACTERS.)

PRODUCER: Yes, bring 'em along! Bring 'em along! (*Starts going off and then turns back to the* ACTORS.) Now remember, don't be late back! You've got a quarter of an hour!

(*The* PRODUCER *and the* SIX CHARACTERS *cross the stage and disappear. The* ACTORS *remain looking at one another in astonishment.*)

LEADING MAN: Is he serious? What's he going to do?

JUVENILE LEAD: This is utter madness!

A THIRD ACTOR: Does he expect us to knock up a play in five minutes?

JUVENILE LEAD: Yes . . . like the actors in the old Commedia dell'Arte.

LEADING LADY: Well, if he thinks that I'm going to have anything to do with fun and games of that sort. . . .

INGENUE: And you certainly won't catch me joining in!

A FOURTH ACTOR: I should like to know who those people are. (*He is alluding to the* CHARACTERS.)

THIRD ACTOR: Who do you think they're likely to be? They're probably escaped lunatics. . . . Or crooks!

JUVENILE LEAD: And does he really take what they say seriously?

INGENUE: Vanity! That's what it is. . . . The vanity of appearing as an author!

LEADING MAN: It's absolutely unheard of! If the stage has come to this. . . .

A FIFTH ACTOR: I'm rather enjoying it!

THIRD ACTOR: Oh, well! After all, we shall have the pleasure of seeing what comes of it all!

(And talking among themselves in this way the ACTORS *leave the stage. Some go out through the door back, some go in the direction of the dressing-rooms. The curtain remains up.)*

(The performance is suspended for twenty minutes.)

ACT 2

(The call-bells ring, warning the audience that the performance is about to be resumed. The ACTORS, *the* STAGE MANAGER, *the* FOREMAN *of the stage crew, the* PROMPTER *and the* PROPERTY MAN *reassemble on stage. Some come from the dressing-rooms, some through the door back, some even from the auditorium. The* PRODUCER *enters from his office accompanied by the* SIX CHARACTERS. *The houselights are extinguished and the stage lighting is as before.)*

PRODUCER: Now come on, ladies and gentlemen! Are we all here? Let me have your attention please! Now let's make a start! *(Then calls the* FOREMAN.*)*

FOREMAN: Yes, sir?

PRODUCER: Set the stage for the parlour scene. A couple of flats and a door will do. As quickly as you can!

(The FOREMAN *runs off at once to carry out this order and is setting the stage as directed whilst the* PRODUCER *is making his arrangements with the* STAGE MANAGER, *the* PROPERTY MAN, *the* PROMPTER *and the* ACTORS. *The flats he has set up are painted in pink and gold stripes.)*

PRODUCER *(to* PROPERTY MAN*)*: Just have a look, please, and see if we've got some sort of sofa or divan in the props room.

PROPERTY MAN: There's the green one, sir.

STEPDAUGHTER: No, no, green won't do! It was yellow . . . yellow flowered plush. . . . A huge thing . . . and most comfortable.

PROPERTY MAN: Well, we haven't got anything like that.

PRODUCER: It doesn't matter! Give me what there is!

STEPDAUGHTER: What do you mean, it doesn't matter? Madame Pace's famous sofa!

PRODUCER: We only want it for this run-through. Please don't interfere. *(to the* STAGE MANAGER*)* Oh, and see if we've got a shop-window . . . something rather long and narrowish is what we want.

STEPDAUGHTER: And a little table . . . the little mahogany table for the pale blue envelope!

STAGE MANAGER *(to* PRODUCER*)*: There's that little one. . . . You know, the gold-painted one.

PRODUCER: That'll do fine! Shove it on!

FATHER: You need a long mirror.

STEPDAUGHTER: And the screen! I must have a screen, please. . . . Else how can I manage?

STAGE MANAGER: Don't you worry, Miss! We've got masses of them!

PRODUCER *(to the* STEPDAUGHTER*)*: And some clothes-hangers and so on, h'm?

STEPDAUGHTER: Oh, yes, lots!

PRODUCER *(to the* STAGE MANAGER*)*: See how many we've got and get somebody to bring them up.

STAGE MANAGER: Right you are, sir, I'll see to it!

(The STAGE MANAGER *goes off about his business and while the* PRODUCER *is talking to the* PROMPTER *and later to the* CHARACTERS *and* ACTORS, *he gets the stage hands to bring up the furniture and properties and proceeds to arrange them in what he thinks is the best sort of order.)*

PRODUCER *(to the* PROMPTER*)*: Now if you'll get into position while they're setting the stage. . . . Look, here's an outline of the thing. . . . Act I . . . Act II . . . *(he holds out some sheets of paper to him).* But you'll really have to excel yourself this time.

PROMPTER: You mean, take it down in shorthand?

PRODUCER *(pleasantly surprised)*: Oh, good man! Can you do shorthand?

PROMPTER: I mayn't know much about prompting, but shorthand. . . .

PRODUCER: Better and better. *(Turning to a* STAGEHAND.*)* Go and get some paper out of my room. . . . A large wadge.° . . . As much as you can find!

(The STAGEHAND *hurries off and returns shortly with a thick wad of paper which he gives to the* PROMPTER.*)*

PRODUCER *(to the* PROMPTER*)*: Follow the scenes closely as we play them and try to fix the lines . . . or at least the most important ones. *(Then, turning to the* ACTORS.*)* Right, ladies and gentlemen, clear the stage, please! No, come over this side *(He waves them over to his left.)* . . . and pay careful attention to what goes on.

LEADING LADY: Excuse me, but we . . .

PRODUCER *(forestalling what she is going to say)*: There won't be any improvising to do, don't you worry!

LEADING MAN: What do we have to do, then?

PRODUCER: Nothing. For the moment all you've got to do is to stay over there and watch what happens. You'll get your parts later. Just now we're

---

wadge, bundle.

going to have a rehearsal . . . or as much of one as we can in the circumstances! And they'll be doing the rehearsing. *(He points to the* CHARACTERS.*)*

FATHER *(in consternation, as if he had tumbled from the clouds into the midst of all the confusion on stage)*: We are? But, excuse me, in what way will it be a rehearsal?

PRODUCER: Well . . . a rehearsal . . . a rehearsal for their benefit. *(He points to the* ACTORS.*)*

FATHER: But if we're the characters . . .

PRODUCER: Just so, "the characters." But it's not characters that act here. It's actors who do the acting here. The characters remain there, in the script. *(He points to the prompt-box.)* . . . When there is a script!

FATHER: Precisely! And since there is no script and you have the good fortune to have the characters here alive before your very eyes. . . .

PRODUCER: Oh, this is wonderful! Do you want to do everything on your own? Act . . . present yourselves to the public!

FATHER: Yes, just as we are.

PRODUCER: And let me tell you you'd make a wonderful sight!

LEADING MAN: And what use should we be then?

PRODUCER: You're not going to pretend that you can act, are you? Why, it's enough to make a cat laugh. . . . *(And as a matter of fact, the* ACTORS *burst out laughing.)* There you are, you see, they're laughing at the idea! *(Then, remembering.)* But, to the point! I must tell you what your parts are. That's not so very difficult. They pretty well cast themselves. *(to the* SECOND ACTRESS*)* You, the MOTHER. *(to the* FATHER*)* We'll have to find a name for her.

FATHER: Amalia.

PRODUCER: But that's your wife's name. We can hardly call her by her real name.

FATHER: And why not, when that's her name? But, perhaps, it is has to be that lady . . . *(A slight gesture to indicate the* SECOND ACTRESS.*)* I see *her (Pointing to the* MOTHER.*)* as Amalia. But do as you like. . . . *(His confusion grows.)* I don't know what to say to you. . . . I'm already beginning. . . . I don't know how to express it . . . to hear my own words ringing false . . . as if they had another sound from the one I had meant to give them. . . .

PRODUCER: Now don't you worry about that! Don't you worry about it at all! We'll think about how to get the right tone of voice. And as for the name. . . . If you want it to be Amalia, Amalia it shall be. Or we'll find some other name. Just for the present we'll refer to the characters in this way. *(to the* JUVENILE LEAD*)* You, the Son . . . *(to the* LEADING LADY*)* And you'll play the Stepdaughter, of course. . . .

STEPDAUGHTER *(excitedly)*: What! What did you say? That woman there. . . . Me! *(She bursts out laughing.)*

PRODUCER *(angrily)*: And what's making you laugh?

LEADING LADY *(indignantly)*: Nobody has ever dared to laugh at me before! Either you treat me with respect or I'm walking out!

STEPDAUGHTER: Oh, no, forgive me! I wasn't laughing at you.

PRODUCER *(to* STEPDAUGHTER*)*: You should feel yourself honoured to be played by . . .

LEADING LADY *(immediately, disdainfully)*: . . . "that woman there."

STEPDAUGHTER: But my remark wasn't meant as a criticism of you . . . I was thinking about myself. . . . Because I can't see myself in you at all. I don't know how to . . . you're not a bit like me!

FATHER: Yes, that's the point I wanted to make! Look . . . all that we express. . . .

PRODUCER: What do you mean . . . *all that you express?* Do you think that this whatever-it-is that you express is something you've got inside you? Not a bit of it.

FATHER: Why . . . aren't even the things we express our own?

PRODUCER: Of course they aren't! The things that you express become material here for the actors, who give it body and form, voice and gesture. And, let me tell you, my actors have given expression to much loftier material than this. This stuff of yours is so trivial that, believe me, if it comes off on the stage, the credit will all be due to my actors.

FATHER: I don't dare to contradict you! But please believe me when I tell you that we . . . who have these bodies . . . these features. . . . Who are as you see us now . . . We are suffering horribly. . . .

PRODUCER *(cutting in impatiently)*: . . . But the makeup will remedy all that. . . . At least as far as your faces are concerned!

FATHER: Perhaps. . . . But what about our voices? . . . What about our gestures? . . .

PRODUCER: Now, look here! You, as yourself, just cannot exist here! Here there's an actor who'll play you. And let that be an end to all this argument!

FATHER: I understand. . . . And now I think I see why our author didn't wish to put us on the stage after all. . . . He saw us as we are. . . . Alive. . . . He saw us as living beings. . . . I don't want to offend your actors. . . . Heaven forbid that I should! . . . But I think that seeing myself acted now . . . by I don't know whom . . .

LEADING MAN *(rising with some dignity and coming over, followed by a laughing group of young actresses)*: By me, if you have no objection.

FATHER *(humbly, mellifluously)*: I am deeply honoured, sir. *(He bows.)* But. . . . Well. . . . I think that however much of his art this gentleman puts into absorbing me into himself. . . . However much he wills it. . . . *(He becomes confused.)*

LEADING MAN: Go on! Go on! *(The actresses laugh.)*

FATHER: Well, I should say that the performance he'll give. . . . Even if he makes himself up to look as much like me as he can. . . . I should say that with his figure . . . *(All the ACTORS laugh.)* . . . it will be difficult for it to be a performance of me . . . of me as I really am. It will rather be . . . leaving aside the question of his appearance. . . . It will be how he interprets what I am . . . how he sees me. . . . If he sees me as anything at all. . . . And not as I, deep down within myself, feel myself to be. And it certainly seems to me that whoever is called upon to criticise us will have to take this into account.

PRODUCER: So you're already thinking about what the critics will say, are you? And here I am, still trying to get the play straight! The critics can say what they like. We'd be much better occupied in thinking about getting the play on. . . . If we can. *(Stepping out of the group and looking around him.)* Now, come on, let's make a start! Is everything ready? *(to the ACTORS and CHARACTERS)* Come on, don't clutter up the place! Let me see how it looks! *(He comes down from the stage.)* And now, don't let's lose any more time! *(to the STEPDAUGHTER)* Do you think the set looks all right?

STEPDAUGHTER: To be perfectly honest, I just don't recognise it at all!

PRODUCER: Good Lord, you surely didn't hope that we were going to reconstruct that room behind Madame Pace's shop here on the stage, did you? *(to the FATHER)* You did tell me it had flowered wallpaper, didn't you?

FATHER: Yes, white.

PRODUCER: Well, it's not white—and it's got stripes on it—but it'll have to do! As for the furniture, I think we've more or less got everything we need. Bring that little table down here a bit! *(The STAGE-HANDS do so. Then he says to the PROPERTY MAN.)* Now, will you go and get an envelope. . . . A pale blue one if you can. . . . And give it to that gentleman. *(He points to the FATHER.)*

PROPERTY MAN: The kind you put letters in?

PRODUCER *and* FATHER: Yes, the kind you put letters in!

PROPERTY MAN: Yes, sir! At once, sir! *(Exit.)*

PRODUCER: Now, come on! First scene—the young lady. *(The LEADING LADY comes forward.)* No! No! Wait a moment! I said the young lady! *(Pointing to the STEPDAUGHTER.)* You stay there and watch. . . .

STEPDAUGHTER *(immediately adding)*: . . . how I make it live!

LEADING LADY *(resentfully)*: I'll know how to make it live, don't you worry, once I get started!

PRODUCER *(with his hands to his head)*: Ladies and gentlemen, don't let's have any arguing! Please! Right! Now . . . The first scene is between the young lady and Madame Pace. Oh! *(He looks around rather helplessly and then comes back on stage.)* What about this Madame Pace?

FATHER: She's not with us, sir.

PRODUCER: And what do we do about her?

FATHER: But she's alive! She's alive too!

PRODUCER: Yes, yes! But where is she?

FATHER: If you'll just allow me to have a word with your people. . . . *(Turning to the ACTRESSES.)* I wonder if you ladies would do me the kindness of lending me your hats for a moment.

THE ACTRESSES *(a chorus . . . half-laughing, half-surprised)*: What?
Our hats?
What did he say?
Why?
Listen to the man!

PRODUCER: What are you going to do with the women's hats?

(The ACTORS laugh.)

FATHER: Oh, nothing . . . I just want to put them on these pegs for a moment. And perhaps one of you ladies would be so kind as to take off your coat, too.

THE ACTORS *(laughter and surprise in their voices)*: Their coats as well? And after that? The man must be mad!

ONE OR TWO OF THE ACTRESSES *(surprise and laughter in their voices)*: But why?
Only our coats?

FATHER: So that I can hang them here. . . . Just for a moment or so. . . . Please do me this favour. Will you?

THE ACTRESSES *(they take off their hats. One or two take off their coats as well, all laughing the while. They go over and hang the coats here and there on the pegs and hangers)*:
And why not?
Here you are!
This really is funny!
Do we have to put them on show?

FATHER: Precisely. . . . You have to put them on show . . . Like this!

PRODUCER: Is one allowed to know what you're up to?

FATHER: Why yes. If we set the stage better, who knows whether she may not be attracted by the objects of her trade and perhaps appear among us. . . . *(He invites them to look toward the door at the back of the stage.)* Look! Look!

(The door opens and MADAME PACE comes in and takes a few steps forward. She is an enormously fat old harridan

of a woman, wearing a pompous carrot-coloured tow wig with a red rose stuck into one side of it, in the Spanish manner. She is heavily made up and dressed with clumsy elegance in a stylish red silk dress. In one hand she carries an ostrich feather fan; the other hand is raised and a lighted cigarette is poised between two fingers. Immediately they see this apparition, the ACTORS *and the* PRODUCER *bound off the stage with howls of fear, hurling themselves down the steps into the auditorium and making as if to dash up the aisle. The* STEPDAUGHTER, *however, rushes humbly up to* MADAME PACE, *as if greeting her mistress.)*

STEPDAUGHTER *(rushing up to her)*: Here she is! Here she is!

FATHER *(beaming)*: It's Madame Pace! What did I tell you? Here she is!

PRODUCER *(his first surprise overcome, he is now indignant)*: What sort of a game do you call this?

LEADING MAN:
JUVENILE LEAD: } *almost at the same moment and all speaking at once.* { Hang it all, what's going on?
INGENUE: Where did *she* spring from?
LEADING LADY: They were keeping her in reserve!
So it's back to the music hall and conjuring tricks, is it?

FATHER *(dominating the protesting voices)*: One moment, please! Why should you wish to destroy this prodigy of reality, which was born, which was evoked, attracted and formed by this scene itself? . . . A reality which has more right to live here than you have. . . . Because it is so very much more alive than you are. . . . Why do you want to spoil it all, just because of some niggling, vulgar convention of truth? . . . Which of you actresses will be playing the part of Madame Pace? Well, *that* woman is Madame Pace! Grant me at least that the actress who plays her will be less true than she is. . . . For *she* is Madame Pace in person! Look! My daughter recognised her and went up to her at once. Now, watch the scene! Just watch it! *(Hesitantly the* PRODUCER *and the* ACTORS *climb back on to the stage. But while the* ACTORS *have been protesting and the* FATHER *has been replying to them, the scene between the* STEPDAUGHTER *and* MADAME PACE *has begun. It is carried on in an undertone, very quietly—naturally in fact—in a manner that would be quite impossible on the stage. When the* ACTORS *obey the* FATHER'S *demand that they shall watch what is happening, they see that* MADAME PACE *has already put her hand under the* STEPDAUGHTER'S *chin to raise her head and is talking to her. Hearing her speak in a completely unintelligible manner they are held for a moment. But almost immediately their attention flags.)*

PRODUCER: Well?

LEADING MAN: But what's she saying?

LEADING LADY: We can't hear a thing!

JUVENILE LEAD: Speak up! Louder!

STEPDAUGHTER *(she leaves* MADAME PACE *and comes down to the group of* ACTORS. MADAME PACE *smiles— a priceless smile)*: Did you say, 'Louder?' What do you mean, 'Louder?' What we're talking about is scarcely the sort of thing to be shouted from the roof-tops. I was able to yell it out just now so that I could shame *him (Pointing to the* FATHER.*)* . . . So that I could have my revenge! But it's quite another matter for Madame Pace. . . . It would mean prison for her.

PRODUCER: Indeed? So that's how it is, is it? But let me tell you something, my dear young lady. . . . Here in the theatre you've got to make yourself heard! The way you're doing this bit at the moment even those of us who're on stage can't hear you! Just imagine what it'll be like with an audience out front. This scene's got to be got over. And anyway there's nothing to prevent you from speaking up when you're on together. . . . We shan't be here to listen to you. . . . We're only here now because it's a rehearsal. Pretend you're alone in the room behind the shop, where nobody can hear you.

(The STEPDAUGHTER *elegantly, charmingly—and with a mischievous smile—wags her finger two or three times in disagreement.)*

PRODUCER: What do you mean, 'No?'

STEPDAUGHTER *(in a mysterious whisper)*: There's someone who'll hear us if she *(Pointing to* MADAME PACE.*)* speaks up.

PRODUCER *(in utter consternation)*: Do you mean to say that there's somebody else who's going to burst in on us? *(The* ACTORS *make as if to dive off the stage again.)*

FATHER: No! No! They're alluding to me. I have to be there, waiting behind the door. . . . And Madame Pace knows it. So, if you'll excuse me, I'll go. . . . So that I'm all ready to make my entrance. *(He starts off toward the back of the stage.)*

PRODUCER *(stopping him)*: No! No! Wait a moment! When you're here you have to respect the conventions of the theatre! Before you get ready to go on to that bit. . . .

STEPDAUGHTER: No! Let's get on with it at once! At once! I'm dying with desire, I tell you . . . to live this scene. . . . To live it! If he wants to get on with it right away, I'm more than ready!

PRODUCER *(shouting)*: But first of all, the scene between you and her *(Pointing to* MADAME PACE.*)* has got to be over! Do you understand?

STEPDAUGHTER: Oh, my God! She's just been telling me what you already know. . . . That once again my mother's work has been badly done. . . . That the dress is spoilt . . . And that I must be patient if she is to go on helping us in our misfortune.

MADAME PACE (*stepping forward, a grand air of importance about her*): But, yes, señor, porque I not want to make profit . . . to take advantage. . . .

PRODUCER (*more than a touch of terror in his voice*): What? Does she speak like that?

(*The* ACTORS *burst into noisy laughter.*)

STEPDAUGHTER (*laughing too*): Yes, she speaks like that, half in English, half in Spanish. . . . It's most comical.

MADAME PACE: Ah, no, it does not to me seem good manners that you laugh of me when I . . . force myself to . . . hablar, as I can, English, señor!

PRODUCER: Indeed, no! It's very wrong of us! You speak like that! Yes, speak like that, Madame! It'll bring the house down! We couldn't ask for anything better. It'll bring a little comic relief into the crudity of the situation. Yes, you talk like that! It's absolutely wonderful!

STEPDAUGHTER: Wonderful! And why not? When you hear a certain sort of suggestion made to you in a lingo like that. . . . There's not much doubt about what your answer's going to be. . . . Because it almost seems like a joke. You feel inclined to laugh when you hear there's an 'old señor', who wants to 'amuse himself with me'. An 'old señor', eh, Madame?

MADAME PACE: Not so very old. . . . Not quite so young, yes? And if he does not please to you. . . . Well, he has . . . *prudencia.*

MOTHER (*absorbed as they are in the scene, the* ACTORS *have been paying no attention to her. Now, to their amazement and consternation, she leaps up and attacks* MADAME PACE. *At her cry they jump, then hasten smilingly to restrain her, for she, meanwhile, has snatched off* MADAME PACE'*s wig and has thrown it to the ground*): You old devil! You old witch! You murderess! Oh, my daughter!

STEPDAUGHTER (*rushing over to restrain her* MOTHER): No, Mummy, no! Please!

FATHER (*rushing over at the same time*): Calm yourself, my dear! Just be calm! Now . . . come and sit down again!

MOTHER: Take that woman out of my sight, then!

(*In the general excitement the* PRODUCER, *too, has rushed over and the* STEPDAUGHTER *now turns to him.*)

STEPDAUGHTER: It's impossible for my mother to remain here!

FATHER (*to the* PRODUCER): They can't be here together. That's why, when we first came, that woman wasn't with us. If they're on at the same time the whole thing is inevitably given away in advance.

PRODUCER: It doesn't matter! It doesn't matter a bit!

This is only a first run-through. . . . Just to give us a rough idea how it goes. Everything'll come in useful . . . I can sort out the bits and pieces later. . . . I'll make something out of it, even if it is all jumbled up. (*Turning to the* MOTHER *and leading her back to her chair.*) Now, please be calm, and sit down here, nice and quietly.

(*Meanwhile the* STEPDAUGHTER *has gone down centre stage again. She turns to* MADAME PACE.)

STEPDAUGHTER: Go on, Madame, go on!

MADAME PACE (*offended*): Ah, no thank you! Here I do not do nothing more with your mother present!

STEPDAUGHTER: Now, come on! Show in the 'old señor' who wants to 'amuse himself with me'. (*Turning imperiously on the rest.*) Yes, this scene has got to be played. So let's get on with it! (*to* MADAME PACE) You can go!

MADAME PACE: Ah, I am going . . . I am going. . . . Most assuredly I am going! (*Exit furiously, ramming her wig back on and glowering at the* ACTORS, *who mockingly applaud her.*)

STEPDAUGHTER (*to the* FATHER): And now you make your entrance! There's no need for you to go out and come in again! Come over here! Pretend that you've already entered! Now, I'm standing here modestly, my eyes on the ground. Come on! Speak up! Say, 'Good afternoon, Miss,' in that special tone of voice . . . you know. . . . Like somebody who's just come in from the street.

PRODUCER (*by this time he is down off the stage*): Listen to her! Are you running this rehearsal, or am I? (*To the* FATHER, *who is looking perplexed and undecided*) Go on, do as she tells you! Go to the back of the stage. . . . Don't exit! . . . And then come forward again.

(*The* FATHER *does as he is told. He is troubled and very pale. But as he approaches from the back of the stage he smiles, already absorbed in the reality of his created life. He smiles as if the drama which is about to break upon him is as yet unknown to him. The* ACTORS *become intent on the scene which is beginning.*)

PRODUCER (*whispering quickly to the* PROMPTER, *who has taken up his position*): Get ready to write now!

THE SCENE

FATHER (*coming forward, a new note in his voice*): Good afternoon, Miss.

STEPDAUGHTER (*her head bowed, speaking with restrained disgust*): Good afternoon!

FATHER (*studying her a little, looking up into her face from under the brim of her hat* [*which almost hides it*], *and perceiving that she is very young, exclaims, almost to himself, a little out of complacency, a little, too, from the fear of compromising himself in a risky adventure*):

H'm! But. . . . M'm. . . . This won't be the first time, will it? The first time that you've been here?

STEPDAUGHTER *(as before)*: No, sir.

FATHER: You've been in here before? *(And since the* STEPDAUGHTER *nods in affirmation.)* More than once? *(He waits a little while for her reply, resumes his study of her, again looking up into her face from under the brim of her hat, smiles and then says.)* Then . . . well . . . it shouldn't any longer be so. . . . May I take off your hat?

STEPDAUGHTER *(immediately forestalling him, unable to restrain her disgust)*: No, sir, I'll take it off myself! *(Convulsed, she hurriedly takes it off.)*

(The MOTHER *is on tenterhooks throughout. The* TWO CHILDREN *cling to their* MOTHER *and they, she and the* SON *form a group on the side opposite the* ACTORS, *watching the scene. The* MOTHER *follows the words and the actions of the* STEPDAUGHTER *and the* FATHER *with varying expressions of sorrow, of indignation, of anxiety and of horror; from time to time she hides her face in her hands and sobs.)*

MOTHER: Oh, my God! My God!

FATHER *(he remains for a moment as if turned to stone by this sob. Then he resumes in the same tone of voice as before)*: Here, let me take it. I'll hang it up for you. *(He takes the hat from her hands.)* But such a charming, such a dear little head really ought to have a much smarter hat than this! Would you like to come and help me choose one from among these hats of Madame's? Will you?

INGENUE *(breaking in)*: Oh, I say! Those are *our* hats!

PRODUCER *(at once, furiously)*: For God's sake, shut up! Don't try to be funny! We're doing our best to rehearse this scene, in case you weren't aware of the fact! *(Turning to* STEPDAUGHTER.*)* Go on from where you left off, please.

STEPDAUGHTER *(continuing)*: No thank you, sir.

FATHER: Come now, don't say no. Do say you'll accept it. . . . Just to please me. I shall be most upset if you won't. . . . Look, here are some rather nice ones. And then it would please Madame. She puts them out on show on purpose, you know.

STEPDAUGHTER: No . . . listen! I couldn't wear it.

FATHER: You're thinking perhaps about what they'll say when you come home wearing a new hat? Well now, shall I tell you what to do? Shall I tell you what to say when you get home?

STEPDAUGHTER *(quickly—she is at the end of her tether)*: No, it's not that! I couldn't wear it because I'm . . . As you see. . . . You should have noticed already . . . *(indicating her black dress.)*

FATHER: That you're in mourning! Of course. . . . Oh, forgive me! Of course! Oh, I beg your pardon! Believe me. . . . I'm most profoundly sorry. . . .

STEPDAUGHTER *(summoning all her strength and forcing herself to conquer her contempt, her indignation and her nausea)*: Stop! Please don't say any more! I really ought to be thanking you. There's no need for you to feel so very sorry or upset! Please don't give another thought to what I said! I, too, you understand. . . . *(Tries hard to smile and adds.)* I really must forget that I'm dressed like this!

PRODUCER *(interrupting them; he climbs back on the stage and turns to the* PROMPTER*)*: Hold it! Stop a minute! Don't write that down. Leave out that last bit. *(Turning to the* FATHER *and the* STEPDAUGHTER.*)* It's going very well! Very well indeed! *(Then to the* FATHER.*)* And then you go on as we arranged. *(to the* ACTORS*)* Rather delightful, that bit where he offers her the hat, don't you think?

STEPDAUGHTER: Ah, but the best bit's coming now! Why aren't we going on?

PRODUCER: Now be patient, please! Just for a little while! *(Turning to the* ACTORS.*)* Of course it'll have to be treated rather lightly. . . .

LEADING MAN: . . . M'm . . . and put over slickly. . . .

LEADING LADY: Of course! There's nothing difficult about it at all. *(to the* LEADING MAN*)* Shall we try it now?

LEADING MAN: As far as I'm . . . I'll go and get ready for my entrance. *(Exits to take up his position outside the door back.)*

PRODUCER *(to the* LEADING LADY*)*: Now look. . . . The scene between you and Madame Pace is finished. I'll get down to writing it up properly afterwards. You're standing. . . . Where are you going?

LEADING LADY: Just a moment! I want to put my hat back on. . . . *(Goes over, takes her hat down and puts it on.)*

PRODUCER: Good! Now you stand here. With your head bowed down a bit.

STEPDAUGHTER *(amused)*: But she's not dressed in black!

LEADING LADY: I *shall* be dressed in black. . . . And much more becomingly than you are!

PRODUCER *(to the* STEPDAUGHTER*)*: Shut up . . . please! And watch! You'll learn something. *(Claps his hands.)* Now come on! Let's get going! Entrance! *(He goes down from the stage again to see how it looks from out front. The door back opens and the* LEADING MAN *steps forward. He has the lively, raffish, self-possessed air of an elderly gallant. The playing of this scene by the* ACTORS *will appear from the very first words as something completely different from what was played before, without its having, even in the slightest degree, the air of a parody. It should appear rather as if the scene has been touched up. Quite naturally the* FATHER *and the* STEPDAUGHTER, *not being able to recognise themselves at all in the* LEADING LADY *and* LEADING MAN, *yet hearing them deliver the very words they used, react in a variety of ways, now with a gesture, now with a smile, with open protest even, to the impres-*

sion they receive. They are surprised, lost in wonder, in suffering . . . as we shall see. The PROMPTER's *voice is clearly heard throughout the scene.)*

LEADING MAN: Good afternoon, Miss!

FATHER *(immediately, unable to restrain himself)*: No! No! *(And the* STEPDAUGHTER, *seeing the* LEADING MAN *enter in this way, bursts out laughing.)*

PRODUCER *(infuriated)*: Shut up! And once and for all . . . Stop that laughing! We shan't get anywhere if we go on like this!

STEPDAUGHTER *(moving away from the proscenium)*: Forgive me . . . but I couldn't help laughing! This lady *(Pointing to the* LEADING LADY.) stands just where you put her, without budging an inch . . . But if she's meant to be me. . . . I can assure you that if I heard anybody saying 'Good afternoon' to me in that way and in that tone of voice I'd burst out laughing. . . . So I had to, you see.

FATHER *(coming forward a little, too)*: Yes, that's it exactly. . . . His manner. . . . The tone of voice. . . .

PRODUCER: To hell with your manner and your tone of voice! Just stand to one side, if you don't mind, and let me get a look at this rehearsal.

LEADING MAN *(coming forward)*: Now if I've got to play an old fellow who's coming into a house of rather doubtful character. . . .

PRODUCER: Oh, don't take any notice of him! Now, *please!* Start again, please! It was going very nicely. *(There is a pause—he is clearly waiting for the* LEADING MAN *to begin again.)* Well?

LEADING MAN: Good afternoon, Miss.

LEADING LADY: Good afternoon!

LEADING MAN *(repeating the* FATHER's *move—that is, looking up into the* LEADING LADY's *face from under the brim of her hat; but then expressing very clearly first his satisfaction and then his fear)*: M'm . . . this won't be the first time, I hope. . . .

FATHER *(unable to resist the temptation to correct him)*: Not 'hope'—'will it?', 'will it?'

PRODUCER: You say 'will it?' . . . It's a question.

LEADING MAN *(pointing to the* PROMPTER): I'm sure he said, 'hope.'

PRODUCER: Well, it's all one! 'Hope' or whatever it was! Go on, please! Go on. . . . Oh, there was one thing . . . I think perhaps it ought not to be quite so heavy. . . . Hold on, I'll show you what I mean. Watch me. . . . *(Comes back on to the stage. Then, making his entrance, he proceeds to play the part.)* Good afternoon, Miss.

LEADING LADY: Good afternoon. . . .

PRODUCER: M'm. . . . *(Turning to the* LEADING MAN *to impress on him the way he has looked up at the* LEADING LADY *from under the brim of her hat.)* Surprise, fear and satisfaction. *(Then turning back to the* LEADING LADY.) It won't be the first time, will it, that you've been here? *(Turning again to the* LEADING MAN *enquiringly.)* Is that clear? *(to the* LEADING

LADY*)* And then you say, 'No, sir.' *(to the* LEADING MAN*)* There you are. . . . It wants to be a little more . . . what shall I say? . . . A little more *flexible.* A little more *souple!* *(He goes down from the stage again.)*

LEADING LADY: No, sir. . . .

LEADING MAN: You've been here before? More than once?

PRODUCER: Wait a minute! You must let her *(pointing to the* LEADING LADY.) get her nod in first. You've been here before? *(The* LEADING LADY *lifts her head a little, closing her eyes painfully as if in disgust and then when the* PRODUCER *says* DOWN, *nods twice.)*

STEPDAUGHTER *(unable to restrain herself)*: Oh, my God! *(And immediately she puts her hand over her mouth to stifle her laughter.)*

PRODUCER *(turning)*: What's the matter?

STEPDAUGHTER *(immediately)*: Nothing! Nothing!

PRODUCER *(to the* LEADING MAN): It's your cue. . . . Carry straight on.

LEADING MAN: More than once? Well then . . . Come along . . . May I take off your hat? *(The* LEADING MAN *says this last line in such a tone of voice and accompanies it with such a gesture that the* STEPDAUGHTER, *who has remained with her hands over her mouth, can no longer restrain herself. She tries desperately to prevent herself from laughing but a noisy burst of laughter comes irresistibly through her fingers.)*

LEADING LADY *(turning indignantly)*: I'm not going to stand here and be made a fool of by that woman!

LEADING MAN: And neither am I. Let's pack the whole thing in.

PRODUCER *(shouting at the* STEPDAUGHTER): Once and for all, will you shut up!

STEPDAUGHTER: Yes. . . . Forgive me, please! . . . Forgive me!

PRODUCER: The trouble with you is that you've got no manners! You go too far!

FATHER *(trying to intervene)*: Yes, sir, you're quite right! Quite right! But you must forgive her. . . .

PRODUCER *(climbing back on to the stage)*: What do you want me to forgive? It's absolutely disgusting the way she's behaving!

FATHER: Yes. . . . But . . . Oh, believe me . . . Believe me, it has such a strange effect. . . .

PRODUCER: Strange! How do you mean, 'Strange'? What's so strange about it?

FATHER: You see, sir, I admire . . . I admire your actors . . . That gentleman there *(Pointing to the* LEADING MAN.) and that lady *(Pointing to the* LEADING LADY.) . . . But . . . Well . . . The truth is . . . They're certainly not us!

PRODUCER: I should hope not! How do you expect them to be you if they're actors?

FATHER: Just so, actors. And they play our parts well, both of them. But when they act . . . To us they seem to be doing something quite different. They want to be the same . . . And all the time they just aren't.

PRODUCER: But how aren't they the same? What are they then?

FATHER: Something that becomes theirs . . . And no longer ours.

PRODUCER: But that's inevitable! I've told you that already.

FATHER: Yes. I understand . . . I understand that. . . .

PRODUCER: Well then, let's hear no more on the subject! *(Turning to the* ACTORS.) We'll run through it later by ourselves in the usual way. I've always had a strong aversion to holding rehearsals with the author present. He's never satisfied! *(Turning to the* FATHER *and the* STEPDAUGHTER.) Now, come on, Let's get on with it! And let's see if we can have no more laughing! *(to the* STEPDAUGHTER.)

STEPDAUGHTER: Oh, I shan't laugh any more! I promise you! My big bit's coming now. . . . Just you wait and see!

PRODUCER: Well, then. . . . When you say, 'Please don't give another thought to what I said! I, too, you understand. . . .' *(Turning to the* FATHER.) You come in at once with, 'I understand! I understand! and immediately ask . . .

STEPDAUGHTER *(interrupting him)*: What? What does he ask?

PRODUCER: . . . why you're in mourning.

STEPDAUGHTER: Oh, no! That's not it at all! Listen! When I told him that I mustn't think about my being in mourning, do you know what his answer was? 'Well, then, let's take this little frock off at once, shall we!'

PRODUCER: That would be wonderful! Wonderful! That *would* bring the house down!

STEPDAUGHTER: But it's the truth!

PRODUCER: But what's the truth got to do with it? Acting's what we're here for! Truth's all very fine. . . . But only up to a point.

STEPDAUGHTER: And what do you want then?

PRODUCER: You'll see! You'll see. Leave everything to me.

STEPDAUGHTER: No, I won't! What you'd like to do, no doubt, is to concoct a romantic, sentimental little affair out of my disgust, out of all the reasons, each more cruel, each viler than the other, why I am this sort of woman, why I am what I am! An affair with him! He asks me why I'm in mourning and I reply with tears in my eyes that my father died only two months ago. No! No! He must say what he said then, 'Well, then, let's take this little frock off at once, shall we? And I . . . my heart still grieving for my father's death. . . . I went behind there. . . . Do you understand? . . . There, behind that screen! And then, my fingers trembling with shame and disgust, I took off my frock, undid my brassiere. . . .

PRODUCER *(running his hands through his hair)*: For God's sake! What on earth are you saying, girl?

STEPDAUGHTER *(crying out excitedly)*: The truth! The truth!

PRODUCER: Yes, it probably is the truth! I'm not denying it! And I understand . . . I fully appreciate all your horror! But you must realise that we simply can't put this kind of thing on the stage.

STEPDAUGHTER: Oh, you can't, can't you? If that's how things are, thanks very much! I'm going!

PRODUCER: No! No! Look here! . . .

STEPDAUGHTER: I'm going! I'm not stopping here! You worked it all out together, didn't you? . . . The pair of you. . . . You and him. . . . When you were in there. . . . You worked out what was going to be possible on the stage. Oh, thanks very much! I understand! He wants to jump to the bit where he presents his spiritual torments! *(This is said harshly.)* But I want to present my own drama! Mine! Mine!

PRODUCER *(his shoulders shaking with annoyance)*: Ah! There we have it! *Your* drama! Look here . . . you'll have to forgive me for telling you this . . . but there isn't only your part to be considered! Each of the others has his drama, too. *(He points to the* FATHER.) He has his and your Mother has hers. You can't have one character coming along like this, becoming too prominent, invading the stage in and out of season and overshadowing all the rest. All the characters must be contained within one harmonious picture, and presenting only what it is proper to present. I'm very well aware that everyone carries a complete life within himself and that he wants to put it before the whole world. But it's here that we run into difficulties: how are we to bring out only just so much as is absolutely necessary? . . . And at the same time, of course, to take into account all the other characters. . . . And yet in that small fragment we have to be able to hint at all the rest of the secret life of that character. Ah, it would be all very pleasant if each character could have a nice little monologue. . . . Or without making any bones about it, give a lecture, in which he could tell his audience what's bubbling and boiling away inside him. *(His tone is good-humoured, conciliatory.)* You must restrain yourself. And believe me, it's in your own interest, too. Because all this fury . . . this exasperation and this disgust . . . They make a bad impression. Especially when . . . And pardon me for mentioning this. . . . You yourself have confessed that you'd had other men there at Madame Pace's before him. . . . And more than once!

STEPDAUGHTER *(bowing her head. She pauses a moment in recollection and then, a deeper note in her voice)*: That is true! But you must remember that those other men mean *him* for me, just as much as he himself does!

PRODUCER (*uncomprehending*): What? The other men mean *him*? What do you mean?

STEPDAUGHTER: Isn't it true that in the case of someone who's gone wrong, the person who was responsible for the first fault is responsible for all the faults which follow? And in my case, he is responsible.... Has been ever since before I was born. Look at him, and see if it isn't true!

PRODUCER: Very well, then! And does this terrible weight of remorse that is resting on his spirit seem so slight a thing to you? Give him the chance of acting it!

STEPDAUGHTER: How? How can he act all his 'noble' remorse, all his 'moral' torments, if you want to spare him all the horror of one day finding in his arms.... After he had asked her to take off her frock ... her grief still undulled by time.... The horror of finding in his arms that child.... A woman now, and a fallen woman already.... That child whom he used to go and watch as she came out of school? (*She says these last words in a voice trembling with emotion. The* MOTHER, *hearing her talk like this, is overcome by distress which expresses itself at first in stifled sobs. Finally she breaks out into a fit of bitter crying. Everyone is deeply moved. There is a long pause.*)

STEPDAUGHTER (*gravely and resolutely, as soon as the* MOTHER *shows signs of becoming a little quieter*): At the moment we are here, unknown as yet by the public. Tomorrow you will present us as you wish.... Making up your play in your own way. But would you really like to see our drama? To see it flash into life as it did in reality?

PRODUCER: Why, of course! I couldn't ask for anything better, so that from now on I can use as much as possible of it.

STEPDAUGHTER: Well, then, ask my Mother to leave us.

MOTHER (*rising, her quiet weeping changed to a sharp cry*): No! No! Don't you allow them to do it! Don't allow them to do it!

PRODUCER: But it's only so that I can see how it goes.

MOTHER: I can't bear it! I can't bear it!

PRODUCER: But since it's already happened, I don't understand!

MOTHER: No, it's happening now! It happens all the time! My torment is no pretence, sir. I am alive and I am present always.... At every moment of my torment ... A torment which is for ever renewing itself. Always alive and always present. But those two children there ... Have you heard them say a single word? They can no longer speak! They cling to me still.... In order to keep my torment living and present! But for themselves they no longer exist! They no longer exist! And she (*Pointing to the* STEPDAUGHTER.) ... She

has run away.... Run away from me and is lost.... Lost! ... And if I see her here before me it is for this reason and for this reason alone.... To renew at all times.... Forever.... To bring before me again, present and living, the anguish that I have suffered on her account too.

FATHER (*solemnly*): The eternal moment, as I told you, sir. She (*He points to the* STEPDAUGHTER.) ... She is here in order to fix me.... To hold me suspended throughout all eternity.... In the pillory of that one fleeting shameful moment in my life. She cannot renounce her role ... And you, sir, cannot really spare me my agony.

PRODUCER: Quite so, but I didn't say that I wouldn't present it. As a matter of fact it'll form the basis of the first act.... Up to the point where she surprises you. (*Pointing to the* MOTHER.)

FATHER: That is right. Because it is my sentence. All our passion.... All our suffering.... Which must culminate in *her* cry. (*Pointing to the* MOTHER.)

STEPDAUGHTER: I can still hear it ringing in my ears! That cry sent me mad! You can play me just as you like ... It doesn't matter. Dressed, if you like, provided that I can have my arms bare at least.... Just my arms bare.... Because, you see, standing there.... (*She goes up to the* FATHER *and rests her head on his chest.*) With my head resting on his chest like this ... and with my arms round his neck ... I could see a vein throbbing away in my arm. And then ... Just as if that pulsing vein alone gave me a sense of horror ... I shut my eyes tight and buried my head in his chest. (*Turning towards the* MOTHER.) Scream, Mummy! Scream! (*She buries her head in the* FATHER's *chest and, raising her shoulders as if in order not to hear the cry, adds in a voice stifled with torment.*) Scream, as you screamed then!

MOTHER (*rushing upon them to separate them*): No! No! She's my daughter! (*And having torn her daughter away.*) You brute! You brute! She's my daughter! Can't you see that she's my daughter?

PRODUCER (*retreating at the cry right up to the footlights, amid the general dismay of the* ACTORS): Excellent! Excellent! And then ... Curtain! Curtain!

FATHER (*rushing over to him convulsively*): Yes, because that's how it really happened!

PRODUCER (*quite convinced, admiration in his voice*): Oh, yes, we must have the curtain there.... That cry and then ... Curtain! Curtain!

(*At the repeated shouts of the* PRODUCER *the* STAGEHAND *on the curtain lets it down, leaving the* PRODUCER *and the* FATHER *between it and the footlights.*)

PRODUCER (*looking up, his arms raised*): Oh, the damned fool! I say, 'Curtain' ... Meaning that I want the act to end there.... And he really does go and bring the curtain down. (*to the* FATHER, *lifting up a corner of the curtain.*) Oh, yes! That's absolutely wonderful! Very good indeed! That'll get them! There's no *if* or *but* about it. . . . That line and then . . . *Curtain!* We've got something in that first act . . . or I'm a Dutchman! (*Disappears through the curtain with the* FATHER.)

ACT 3

(*When the curtain goes up again the audience sees that the* STAGEHANDS *have dismantled the previous set and put on in its place a small garden fountain. On one side of the stage the* ACTORS *are sitting in a row, and on the other side, the* CHARACTERS. *The* PRODUCER *is standing in a meditative attitude in the middle of the stage with his hand clenched over his mouth. There is a brief pause.*)

PRODUCER (*with a shrug of his shoulders*): Oh, well! . . . Let's get on with Act II! Now if you'll only leave it all to me, as we agreed, everything'll sort itself out.

STEPDAUGHTER: This is where we make our entry into his house . . . (*Pointing to the* FATHER.) In spite of him! (*Pointing to the* SON.)

PRODUCER (*out of patience*): Yes, yes! But leave it to me, I tell you!

STEPDAUGHTER: Well. . . . So long as it's made quite clear that it was against his wishes.

MOTHER (*from the corner, shaking her head*): For all the good that's come of it. . . .

STEPDAUGHTER (*turning to her quickly*): That doesn't matter! The more harm that it's done us, the more remorse for him!

PRODUCER (*impatiently*): I understand all that! I'll take it all into account! don't you worry about it!

MOTHER (*a supplicant note in her voice*): But I do beg you sir . . . To set my conscience at rest. . . . To make it quite plain that I tried in every way I could to . . .

STEPDAUGHTER (*interrupting contemptuously and continuing her* MOTHER's *speech*): . . . to pacify me, to persuade me not to get my own back. . . . (*to the* PRODUCER) Go on . . . do what she asks you! Give her that satisfaction. . . . Because she's quite right, you know! I'm enjoying myself no end, because . . . Well, just look . . . The meeker she is, the more she tries to wriggle her way into his heart, the more he holds himself aloof, the more distant he becomes. I can't think why she bothers!

PRODUCER: Are we going to get started on the second act or are we not?

STEPDAUGHTER: I won't say another word! But, you know, it won't be possible to play it all in the garden, as you suggested.

PRODUCER: Why not?

STEPDAUGHTER: Because he (*Pointing to the* SON *again.*) shuts himself up in his room all the time. . . . Holding himself aloof. . . . And, what's more, there's all the boy's part. . . . Poor bewildered little devil. . . . As I told you, all that takes place indoors.

PRODUCER: I know all about that! On the other hand you do understand that we can hardly stick up notices telling the audience what the scene is. . . . Or change the set three or four times in one act.

LEADING MAN: They used to in the good old days.

PRODUCER: Oh, yes. . . . When the intelligence of the audience was about up to the level of that little girl's there. . . .

LEADING LADY: And it does make it easier to get the sense of illusion.

FATHER (*immediately, rising*): Illusion, did you say? For Heaven's sake, please don't use the word illusion! Please don't use that word. . . . It's a particularly cruel one for us!

PRODUCER (*astounded*): And why's that?

FATHER: It's cruel! Cruel! You should have known that!

PRODUCER: What ought we to say then? We were referring to the illusion that we have to create on this stage . . . for the audience. . . .

LEADING MAN: . . . with our acting. . . .

PRODUCER: . . . the illusion of a reality!

FATHER: I understand, sir. But you . . . Perhaps you can't understand us. Forgive me! Because . . . you see . . . for you and for your actors, all this is only . . . and quite rightly so. . . . All this is only a game.

LEADING LADY (*indignantly interrupting him*): What do you mean, a game? We're not children! We're serious actors!

FATHER: I don't deny it! And in fact, in using the term, I was referring to your art which must, as this gentleman has said, create a perfect illusion of reality.

PRODUCER: Precisely!

FATHER: Now just consider the fact that we (*Pointing quickly to himself and to the other* FIVE CHARACTERS.) as ourselves, have no other reality outside this illusion!

PRODUCER (*in utter astonishment, looking round at his actors who show the same bewildered amazement*): And what does all that mean?

FATHER (*the ghost of a smile on his face. There is a brief pause while he looks at them all*): As I said. . . . What other reality should we have? What for you is an illusion that you have to create, for us, on the other hand, is our sole reality. The only reality we know. (*There he takes a step or two toward the* PRODUCER *and adds.*) But it's not only true in our case, you know. Just think it over. (*He looks into his eyes.*) Can you tell me who you are? (*And he stands there pointing his index finger at him.*)

PRODUCER (*disturbed, a half-smile on his lips*): What? Who am I? I'm myself!

FATHER: And suppose I were to tell you that that

wasn't true? Suppose I told you that you were me? . . .

PRODUCER: I should say that you were mad! (*The* ACTORS *laugh.*)

FATHER: You're quite right to laugh, because here everything's a game. (*to the* PRODUCER) And you can object, therefore, that it's only in fun that that gentleman (*Pointing to the* LEADING MAN.) who is *himself* must be *me* who, on the contrary, am myself. . . . That is, *the person you see here.* There, you see. I've caught you in a trap! (*The* ACTORS *laugh again.*)

PRODUCER (*annoyed*): But you said all this not ten minutes ago! Do we have to go over all that again?

FATHER: No. As a matter of fact that wasn't what I intended. I should like to invite you to abandon this game . . . (*Looking at the* LEADING LADY *as if to forestall what she will say.*) Your art! Your art! . . . The game that it is customary for you and your actors to play here in this theatre. And once again I ask you in all seriousness. . . . Who are you?

PRODUCER (*turning to the* ACTORS *in utter amazement, an amazement not unmixed with irritation*): What a cheek the fellow has! A man who calls himself a character comes here and asks me who I am!

FATHER (*with dignity, but in no way haughtily*): A character, sir, may always ask a man who he is. Because a character has a life which is truly his, marked with his own special characteristics. . . . And as a result he is always somebody! Whilst a man . . . . And I'm not speaking of you personally at the moment. . . . Man in general . . . Can quite well be nobody.

PRODUCER: That is as may be! But you're asking *me* these questions. Me, do you understand? The Producer! The boss!

FATHER (*softly, with gentle humility*): But only in order to know if you, you as you really are now, are seeing yourself as, for instance, after all the time that has gone by, you see yourself as you were at some point in the past. . . . With all the illusions that you had then . . . with everything . . . all the things you had deep down inside you . . . everything that made up your external world . . . everything as it appeared to you then . . . and as it *was*, as it was in reality for you then! Well . . . thinking back on those illusions which you no longer have . . . on all those things that no longer *seem* to be what they *were* once upon a time . . . don't you feel that . . . I won't say these boards. . . . No! . . . That the very earth itself is slipping away from under your feet, when you reflect that in the same way this *you* that you now feel yourself to be . . . all your reality as it is today . . . is destined to seem an illusion tomorrow?

PRODUCER (*not having understood much of all this, and somewhat taken aback by this argument*): Well? And where does all this get us, anyway?

FATHER: Nowhere. I only want to make you see that if we (*Again pointing to himself and to the other* CHARACTERS.) have no reality outside the world of illusion, it would be as well if you mistrusted your own reality. . . . The reality that you breathe and touch today . . . Because like the reality of yesterday, it is fated to reveal itself as a mere illusion tomorrow.

PRODUCER (*deciding to make fun of him*): Oh, excellent! And so you'd say that you and this play of yours that you've been putting on for my benefit are more real than I am?

FATHER (*with the utmost seriousness*): Oh, without a doubt.

PRODUCER: Really?

FATHER: I thought that you'd understood that right from the very beginning.

PRODUCER: More real than I am?

FATHER: If your reality can change from one day to the next. . . .

PRODUCER: But everybody knows that it can change like that! It's always changing. . . . Just like everybody else's.

FATHER (*with a cry*): No, ours doesn't change! You see. . . . That's the difference between us! Our reality doesn't change. . . . It can't change. . . . It can never be in any way different from what it is. . . . Because it is already fixed. . . . Just as it is. . . . For ever! For ever it is *this* reality. . . . It's terrible! . . . This immutable reality. . . . It should make you shudder to come near us!

PRODUCER (*quickly, suddenly struck by an idea. He moves over and stands squarely in front of him*): I should like to know, however, when anyone ever saw a character step out of his part and begin a long dissertation on it like the one you've just been making. . . . Expounding it. . . . Explaining it. . . . Can you tell me? . . . I've never seen it happen before!

FATHER: You have never seen it happen before because authors usually hide the details of their work of creation. Once the characters are alive. . . . Once they are standing truly alive before their author. . . . He does nothing but follow the words and gestures that they suggest to him. . . . And he must want them to be what they themselves want to be. For woe betide him if he doesn't do what they wish him to do! When a character is born he immediately acquires such an independence . . . Even of his own author. . . . That everyone can imagine him in a whole host of situations in which his author never thought of placing him. . . . They can even imagine his acquiring, sometimes, a significance that the author never dreamt of giving him.

PRODUCER: Yes. . . . I know all that!

FATHER: Well, then, why are you so astonished at see-ing us? Just imagine what a misfortune it is for a character to be born alive.... Created by the imagination of an author who afterwards sought to deny him life.... Now tell me whether a char-acter who has been left unrealised in this way.... Living, yet without a life.... Whether this charac-ter hasn't the right to do what we are doing now.... Here and now.... For your benefit? ... After we had spent ... Oh, such ages, believe me! ... Doing it for his benefit ... Trying to per-suade him, trying to urge him to realise us.... First of all I would present myself to him.... Then she would ... *(Pointing to the* STEPDAUGH-TER.*)* ... And then her poor Mother....

STEPDAUGHTER *(coming forward as if in a trance)*: Yes, what he says is true.... I would go and tempt him.... There, in his gloomy study.... Just at twilight.... He would be sitting there, sunk in an armchair.... Not bothering to stir himself and switch on the light.... Content to let the room get darker and darker.... Until the whole room was filled with a darkness that was alive with our presence.... We were there to tempt him.... *(And then, as if she saw herself as still in that study and irritated by the presence of all those actors.)* Oh, go away.... All of you! Leave us alone! Mummy ... and her son.... I and the little girl.... The boy by himself.... Always by himself.... Then he and I together. *(A faint gesture in the direction of the* FATHER.*)* And then.... By myself.... By myself ... alone in that darkness. *(A sudden turn round as if she wished to seize and fix the vision that she has of herself, the living vision of herself that she sees shining in the darkness.)* Yes, my life! Ah, what scenes, what wonderful scenes we suggested to him! And I ... I tempted him more than any of them....

FATHER: Indeed you did! And it may well be that it's all your fault that he wouldn't give us the life we asked for.... You were too persistent.... Too impudent.... You exaggerated too much....

STEPDAUGHTER: What? When it was he who wanted me to be what I am? *(She goes up to the* PRODUCER *and says confidentially.)* I think it's much more likely that he refused because he felt depressed ... or because of his contempt for the theatre.... Or at least, for the present-day the-atre with all its pandering to the box-office....

PRODUCER: Let's get on! Let's get on, for God's sake! Let's have some action!

STEPDAUGHTER: It looks to me as if we've got too much action for you already.... Just staging our entry into his house. *(Pointing to the* FATHER.*)* You yourself said that you couldn't stick up notices or be changing the set every five minutes.

PRODUCER: And neither can we! Of course we can't!

What we've got to do is to combine and group all the action into one continuous well-knit scene.... Not the sort of thing that you want.... With, first of all, your younger brother coming home from school and wandering about the house like some lost soul.... Hiding behind doors and brooding on a plan that ... What did you say it does to him?

STEPDAUGHTER: Dries him up.... Shrivels him up completely.

PRODUCER: M'm! Well, as you said.... And all the time you can see it more and more clearly in his eyes.... Wasn't that what you said?

STEPDAUGHTER: Yes.... just look at him! *(Pointing to where he is standing by his* MOTHER.*)*

PRODUCER: And then, at the same time, you want the child to be playing in the garden, blissfully unaware of everything. The boy in the house, the little girl in the garden.... I ask you!

STEPDAUGHTER: Yes ... happily playing in the sun! That is the only pleasure that I have.... Her hap-piness.... All the joy that she gets from playing in the garden.... After the wretchedness and the squalor of that horrible room where we all four slept together.... And she had to sleep with me.... Just think of it.... My vile contaminated body next to hers! ... With her holding me tight in her loving, innocent, little arms! She only had to get a glimpse of me in the garden and she'd run up to me and take me by the hand. She wasn't interested in the big flowers ... she'd run about looking for the ... 'weeny' ones.... So that she could point them out to me.... And she'd be so happy.... So excited.... *(As she says this she is torn by the memory of it all and gives a long, despairing cry, dropping her head on to her hands which are lying loosely on the little table in front of her. At the sight of her emotion everyone is deeply moved. The* PRODUCER *goes up to her almost paternally and says comfortingly.)*

PRODUCER: We'll have the garden in ... don't you worry.... We'll have the garden scene in.... Just you wait and see.... You'll be quite satisfied with how I arrange it.... We'll play everything in the garden. *(Calling a* STAGEHAND.*)* Hey *(his name)*! Let me have something in the shape of a tree or two.... A couple of not-too-large cypresses in front of this fountain! *(Two small cypresses descend from the flies. The* FOREMAN *dashes up and fixes them with struts and nails.)*

PRODUCER *(to the* STEPDAUGHTER*)*: That'll do.... For the moment anyway.... It'll give us a rough idea. *(Calls to the* STAGEHAND *again.)* Oh *(his name)*, let me have something for a sky, will you?

STAGEHAND *(up aloft)*: Eh?

PRODUCER: Something for a sky! A flat to go behind the fountain! *(And a white backcloth descends from the flies.)*

PRODUCER: Not white! I said I wanted a sky! Oh, well, it doesn't matter. . . . Leave it! Leave it! . . . I'll fix it myself. . . . *(Calls.)* Hey! . . . You there on the lights! . . . Everything off. . . . And let me have the moonlight blues on! . . . Blues in the batten! . . . A couple of blue spots on the backcloth! . . . Yes, that's it! That's just right!

(There is now a mysterious moonlit effect about the scene, and the ACTORS *are prompted to move about and to speak as they would if they were indeed walking in a moonlit garden.)*

PRODUCER *(to the* STEPDAUGHTER*)*: There, do you see? Now the Boy, instead of hiding behind doors inside the house, can move about the garden and hide behind these trees. But, you know, it'll be rather difficult to find a little girl to play that scene with you. . . . The one where she shows you the flowers. *(Turning to the* BOY*.)* Now come down here a bit! Let's see how it works out! *(Then, since the* BOY *doesn't move.)* Come on! Come on! *(He drags him forward and tries to make him hold his head up. But after every attempt down it falls again.)* Good God, here's a fine how d'ye do. . . . There's something queer about this boy. . . . What's the matter with him? . . . My God, he'll have to say *something.* . . . *(He goes up to him, puts a hand on his shoulder and places him behind one of the trees.)* Now. . . . Forward a little! . . . Let me see you! . . . M'm! . . . Now hide yourself. . . . That's it! Now try popping your head out a bit. . . . Take a look round. . . . *(He goes to one side to study the effect and the* BOY *does what he has been told to do. The* ACTORS *look on, deeply affected and quite dismayed.)* That's excellent! . . . Yes, excellent! *(Turning again to the* STEPDAUGHTER*.)* Suppose the little girl were to catch sight of him there as he was looking out, and run over to him. . . . Wouldn't that drag a word or two out of him?

STEPDAUGHTER *(rising)*: It's no use your hoping that he'll speak. . . . At least not so long as *he's* here. *(Pointing to the* SON*.)* If you want him to speak, you'll have to send *him* away first.

SON *(going resolutely toward the steps down into the auditorium)*: Willingly! I'm only too happy to oblige. Nothing could possibly suit me better!

PRODUCER *(immediately catching hold of him)*: Hey! Oh no you don't! Where are you going? You hang on a minute!

(The MOTHER *rises in dismay, filled with anguish at the thought that he really is going away. She instinctively raises her arms to prevent him from going, without, however, moving from where she is standing.)*

SON *(he has reached the footlights)*: I tell you . . . There's absolutely nothing for me to do here! Let me go, please! Let me go! (This to the PRODUCER.)

PRODUCER: What do you mean . . . There's nothing for you to do?

STEPDAUGHTER *(placidly, ironically)*: Don't bother to hold him back! He won't go away!

FATHER: He has to play that terrible scene with his Mother in the garden.

SON *(immediately, fiercely, resolutely)*: I'm not playing anything! I've said that all along! *(To the* PRODUCER*)* Let me go!

STEPDAUGHTER *(running over, then addressing the* PRODUCER*)* Do you mind? *(She gets him to lower the hand with which he has been restraining the* SON*.)* Let him go! *(Then turning to the* SON, *as soon as the* PRODUCER *has dropped his arm.)* Well, go on. . . . Leave us!

(The SON *stands where he is, still straining in the direction of the steps, but, as if held back by some mysterious force, he cannot go down them. Then, amidst the utter dismay and anxious bewilderment of the* ACTORS, *he wanders slowly along the length of the footlights in the direction of the other flight of steps. Once there, he again finds himself unable to descend, much as he would wish to. The* STEPDAUGHTER *has watched his progress intently, her eyes challenging, defiant. Now she bursts out laughing.)*

STEPDAUGHTER: He can't, you see! He can't leave us! He must remain here. . . . He has no choice but to remain with us! He's chained to us. . . . Irrevocably! But if I . . . Who really do run away when what is inevitable happens. . . . And I run away because of my hatred for him. . . . I run away just because I can no longer bear the sight of him. . . . Well, if I can still stay here. . . . If I can still put up with his company and with having to have him here before my eyes. . . . Do you think it's likely that he can run away? Why, he was to stay here with that precious father of his. . . . With his mother. . . . Because now she has no other children but him. . . . *(Turning to her* MOTHER.*)* Come on, Mummy! Come on. . . . *(Turning to the* PRODUCER *and pointing to the* MOTHER.*)* There. . . . you see. . . . She'd got up to prevent him from going. . . . *(to her* MOTHER, *as if willing her actions by some magic power)* Come on! Come on! *(Then to the* PRODUCER.*)* You can imagine just how reluctant she is to give this proof of her affection in front of your actors. But so great is her desire to be with him that . . . There! . . . You see? . . . She's willing to live out again her scene with him! *(And as a matter of fact the* MOTHER *has gone up to her* SON, *and scarcely has the* STEPDAUGHTER *finished speaking before she makes a gesture to indicate her agreement.)*

SON *(immediately)*: No! No! You're not going to drag me into this! If I can't get away, I shall stay here! But I repeat that I'm not going to do any acting at all!

FATHER (*trembling with excitement, to the* PRODUCER):
You can force him to act!

SON: Nobody can force me!

FATHER: I can and I will!

STEPDAUGHTER: Wait! Wait! First of all the little girl has to go to the fountain.... (*Goes over to the* LITTLE GIRL. *She drops on to her knees in front of her and takes her face in her hands.*) Poor little darling.... You're looking so bewildered.... With those beautiful eyes.... You must be wondering just where you are. We're on a stage, dear! What's a stage? Well ... It's a place where you play at being serious. They put on plays here. And now we're putting a play on. Really and truly! Even you.... (*Embracing her, clasping her to her breast and rocking her for a moment or so*) Oh, you little darling.... My dear little darling, what a terrible play for you.... What a horrible end they've thought out for you! The garden, the fountain.... Yes, it's a make-believe fountain ... The pity is, darling, that everything's make-believe here ... But perhaps you like a make-believe fountain better than a real one.... So that you can play in it.... M'm? No.... It'll be a game for the others.... Not for you unfortunately ... Because you're real.... And you really play by a real fountain.... A lovely big green one, with masses of bamboo palms casting shadows.... Looking at your reflection in the water.... And lots and lots of little baby ducklings swimming about in it, breaking the shadow into a thousand little ripples. You try to take hold of one of the ducklings.... (*With a shriek which fills everybody with dismay.*) No, Rosetta, no! Your Mummy's not looking after you.... And all because of that swine there.... Her son! I feel as if all the devils in hell were loose inside me.... And he ... (*Leaves the* LITTLE GIRL *and turns with her usual scorn to the* BOY.) What are you doing ... drooping there like that? ... Always the little beggar-boy! It'll be your fault too if that baby drowns.... Because of the way you go on.... As if I didn't pay for everybody when I got you into this house. (*Seizing his arm to make him take his hand out of his pocket.*) What have you got there? What are you trying to hide? Out with it! Take that hand out of your pocket. (*She snatches his hand out of his pocket and to everybody's horror reveals that it is clenched round a revolver. She looks at him for a little while, as if satisfied. Then she says somberly.*) M'm! Where did you get that gun from? ... And how did you manage to lay your hands on it? (*And since the* BOY, *in his utter dismay—his eyes are staring and vacant—does not reply.*) You idiot! If I'd been you I shouldn't have killed myself.... I'd have killed one of *them*.... Or the pair of them! Father and son together! (*She hides them behind the*

cypress tree where he was lurking before. Then she takes the LITTLE GIRL *by the hand and leads her towards the fountain. She puts her into the basin of the fountain, and makes her lie down so that she is completely hidden. Finally she goes down on her knees and buries her head in her hands on the rim of the basin of the fountain.*)

PRODUCER: That's it! Good! (*Turning to the* SON.) And at the same time....

SON (*angrily*): What do you mean ... 'And at the same time'? Oh, no! ... Nothing of the sort! There never was any scene between her and me! (*Pointing to the* MOTHER.) You make her tell you what really happened! (*Meanwhile the* SECOND ACTRESS *and the* JUVENILE LEAD *have detached themselves from the group of* ACTORS *and are standing gazing intently at the* MOTHER *and the* SON *so that later they can act these parts.*)

MOTHER: Yes, it's true, sir! I'd gone to his room at the time.

SON: There! Did you hear? To my room! Not into the garden!

PRODUCER: That doesn't matter at all! As I said we'll have to run all the action together into one composite scene!

SON (*becoming aware that the* JUVENILE LEAD *is studying him*): What do you want?

JUVENILE LEAD: Nothing! I was just looking at you.

SON (*turning to the* SECOND ACTRESS): Oh! ... And *you're* here too, are you? All ready to play *her* part, I suppose? (*Pointing to the* MOTHER.)

PRODUCER: That's the idea! And if you want my opinion you ought to be damned grateful for all the attention they're paying you.

SON: Indeed? Thank you! But hasn't it dawned on you yet that you aren't going to be able to stage this play? Not even the tiniest vestige of us is to be found in you.... And all the time your actors are studying us from the outside. Do you think it's possible for us to live confronted by a mirror which, not merely content with freezing us in that particular picture which is the fixing of our expression, has to throw an image back at us which we can no longer recognise? ... Our own features, yes.... But twisted into a horrible grimace.

FATHER: He's quite right! He's quite right, you know!

PRODUCER (*to the* JUVENILE LEAD *and* SECOND ACTRESS): Right you are! Get back with the others!

SON: It's no use your bothering! I'm not having anything to do with this!

PRODUCER: You be quiet for the moment, and let me listen to what your mother has to say. (*to the* MOTHER) You were saying? ... You'd gone to his room? ...

MOTHER: Yes, I'd gone to his room.... I couldn't bear the strain any longer! I wanted to pour out my heart to him.... I wanted to tell him of all the anguish that was tormenting me. . . . But as soon as he saw me come in . . .

SON: There was no scene between us! I rushed out of the room. . . . I didn't want to get involved in any scenes! Because I never have been involved in any! Do you understand?

MOTHER: Yes! That *is* what happened! That is what happened.

PRODUCER: But for the purposes of this play we've simply *got* to have a scene between you and him! Why . . . it's absolutely *essential!*

MOTHER: I'm quite ready to take part in one! Oh, if you could only find some way to give me an opportunity of speaking to him . . . if only for a moment. . . . So that I can pour out my heart to him!

FATHER (*going up to the* SON, *in a great rage*): You'll do what she asks, do you understand? You'll do what your Mother asks!

SON (*more stubbornly than ever*): I'm doing nothing!

FATHER (*taking hold of him by the lapels of his coat and shaking him*): My God, you'll do what I tell you! Or else . . . Can't you hear how she's pleading with you? Haven't you a spark of feeling in you for your Mother?

SON (*grappling with the* FATHER): No, I haven't! For God's sake, let's have done with all this. . . . Once and for all, let's have done with it!

(*General agitation. The* MOTHER *is terrified and tries to get between them in order to separate them.*)

MOTHER: Please! Please!

FATHER (*without relinquishing his hold*): You must obey me! You *must!*

SON (*struggling with him and finally hurling him to the ground. He falls near the steps amidst general horror*): What's come over you? Why are you in this terrible state of frenzy? Haven't you any sense of decency? . . . Going about parading your shame. . . . And ours, too. I'm having nothing to do with this affair! Nothing, do you hear? And by making this stand I am interpreting the wishes of our author, who didn't wish to put us on the stage!

PRODUCER: Oh, God! You come along here and . . .

SON (*pointing to the* FATHER): *He* did! I didn't.

PRODUCER: Aren't you here now?

SON: It was he who wanted to come. . . . And he dragged us all along with him. Then the pair of them went in there with you and agreed on what was to go into the play. But he didn't only stick to what really did occur. . . . No, as if that wasn't enough for any man, he had to put in things that never even happened.

PRODUCER: Well, then, you tell me what really happened! You can at least do that! You rushed out of your room without saying a word?

SON (*he hesitates for a moment*): Without saying a word! I didn't want to get involved in a scene!

PRODUCER (*pressing him*): And then? What did you do then?

SON (*everybody's attention is on him; amidst the anguished silence he takes a step or two across the front of the stage*): Nothing. . . . As I was crossing the garden . . . (*He breaks off and becomes gloomy and absorbed.*)

PRODUCER (*urging him to speak, very much moved by this extraordinary reserve*): Well? As you were crossing the garden?

SON (*in exasperation, shielding his face with his arm*): Why do you want to force me to tell you? It's horrible!

(*The* MOTHER *is trembling all over and stifled sobs come from her as she looks toward the fountain.*)

PRODUCER (*slowly, quietly . . . he has seen where the* MOTHER *is looking and he now turns to the* SON *with growing apprehension*): The little girl?

SON (*staring straight in front of him, out into the auditorium*): There . . . In the fountain. . . .

FATHER (*from where he is on the floor, pointing with tender pity to the* MOTHER): She was following him. . . .

PRODUCER (*anxiously to the* SON): And what did you do?

SON (*slowly, continuing to stare in front of him*): I rushed up to the fountain. . . . I was about to dive in and fish her out. . . . Then all of a sudden I pulled up short. . . . Behind that tree I saw something that made my blood run cold. . . . The boy. . . . The boy was standing there. . . . Stock still. . . . With madness in his eyes. . . . Staring like some insane creature at his little sister, who was lying drowned in the fountain! (*The* STEPDAUGHTER, *who has all this while been bent over the fountain in order to hide the* LITTLE GIRL, *is sobbing desperately—her sobs coming like an echo from the background. There is a pause.*) I moved towards him. . . . And then . . . (*And from behind the trees where the* BOY *is hidden a revolver shot rings out.*)

MOTHER (*with a heartrending cry she rushes behind the trees accompanied by the* SON *and all the* ACTORS. *There is general confusion*): Oh, my son! My son! (*And then amidst the general hubbub and shouting.*) Help! Oh, help!

PRODUCER (*amidst all the shouting, he tries to clear a space while the* BOY *is carried off behind the skycloth*): Is he wounded? Is he badly hurt?

(*By now everybody, except for the* PRODUCER *and the* FATHER, *who is still on the ground by the steps, has disappeared behind the skycloth. They can be heard muttering and exclaiming in great consternation. Then first from one side, then from the other, the* ACTORS *re-enter.*)

LEADING LADY (*re-entering right, very much moved*): He's dead, poor boy! He's dead! Oh what a terrible thing to happen!

LEADING MAN (*re-entering left, laughing*): What do you mean, dead? It's all make-believe! It's all just a pretence! Don't get taken in by it!

OTHER ACTORS (*entering from the right*): Make-believe? Pretence? Reality! Reality! He's dead!

OTHERS (*from the left*): No! Make-believe! It's all a pretence!

FATHER (*rising and crying out to them*): What do you mean, pretence? Reality, ladies and gentlemen, reality! Reality! (*And desperation in his face, he too disappears behind the backcloth.*)

PRODUCER (*at the end of his tether*): Pretence! Reality! Go to hell, the whole lot of you! Lights! Lights! Lights!

(*The stage and the auditorium are suddenly flooded with very bright light. The PRODUCER breathes again as if freed from a tremendous burden. They all stand there looking into one another's eyes, in an agony of suspense and dismay.*)

PRODUCER: My God! Nothing like this has ever happened to me before! I've lost a whole day on their account! (*He looks at his watch.*) You can go home now. . . . All of you! There's nothing we can do now! It's too late to start rehearsing again! I'll see you all this evening. (*And as soon as the ACTORS have said 'Goodbye!' and gone he calls out to the ELECTRICIAN.*) Hey (*his name*) Everything off! (*He has hardly got the words out before the theatre is plunged for a moment into utter darkness.*) Hell! You might at least leave me one light on, so that I can see where I'm going!

(*And immediately behind the backcloth, a green flood lights up. It projects the silhouettes of the CHARACTERS [minus the BOY and the LITTLE GIRL], clear-cut and huge, on to the backcloth. The PRODUCER is terrified and leaps off the stage. As he does so the green flood is switched off—rather as if its having come on in the first instance had been due to the ELECTRICIAN's having pulled the wrong switch—and the stage is again lit in blue. Slowly the CHARACTERS come in and advance to the front of the stage. The SON comes in first, from the right, followed by the MOTHER, who has her arms outstretched toward him. Then the FATHER comes in from the left. They stop halfway down the stage and stand there like people in a trance. Last of all the STEPDAUGHTER comes in from the left and runs toward the steps which lead down into the auditorium. With her foot on the top step she stops for a moment to look at the other three and bursts into strident laughter. Then she hurls herself down the steps and runs up the aisle. She stops at the back of the auditorium and turns to look at the three figures standing on the stage. She bursts out laughing again. And when she has disappeared from the auditorium you can still hear her terrible laughter coming from the foyer beyond. A short pause and then, CURTAIN.*)

Figure 1. The Director (Darrell D'Silva) listens to the sophisticated Leading Actress (Liza Sadovy) "acting" as the Stepdaughter in the Young Vic 2001 production of *Six Characters Looking for an Author,* directed by Richard Jones, London. The translator, David Harrower, provided the new title. (Photograph: Donald Cooper.)

Figure 2. The Father (Stephen Boxer, *left*) and the Stepdaughter (Leah Muller, *in black dress*) confront the Director (Darrell D'Silva, *seated*) in the Young Vic production. Other members of the acting company look on, including, from left to right, the Director's Assistant (Catherine Malone), the Leading Actor (Dale Rapley), the Young Actor (David Fairweather), and the Young Actress (Elizabeth Hopley). (Photograph: Donald Cooper.)

Figure 3. Stunned by Madame Pace's accent, the Director (Darrell D'Silva) interrupts the scene between the Stepdaughter (Leah Muller) and Madame Pace (Michelle Wade) in the Young Vic production. (Photograph: Donald Cooper.)

Staging of *Six Characters in Search of an Author*

REVIEW OF THE YOUNG VIC PRODUCTION, 2001, BY JOHN PETER

I used to think of it as a once-in-a-lifetime play: it has a central *coup de théâtre* that is a surprise, and you are unlikely to forget it. No surprise, no argument. No argument, no play. It has taken Richard Jones's new production of Luigi Pirandello's *Six Characters Looking for an Author** (Young Vic) to make me see that there is more life in this fabulous beast than I had thought.

Rereading the play would not have been enough in itself—and this has its own irony. Pirandello is writing, among other things, about the inability of the theatre to show life as it is; and it has taken a live performance, theatre at its swaggering best, to make the play rise above its own theatricality.

The scene is a rehearsal room. The Young Vic has turned itself into a proscenium-arch theatre for the occasion, and the way the curtain is used mocks the proceedings with sly elegance. Giles Cadle's wide, shallow set is dominated by the word TEATRO on the wall, with an arrow pointing to the right. You get the message: this is life, the theatre is offstage. A young woman is getting the place ready, clearly for the imminent arrival of somebody who wants things just right. She is the Director's Assistant (Catherine Malone).

Enter the Director (Darrell D'Silva). He is a spoilt, preening martinet whose life relies on a series of theatrical attitudes: he is playing the character he thinks directors are expected to have. Be superior, demanding, temperamental, ruthless. Be avuncular or warmhearted if absolutely necessary. Don't let your actors find their own way of playing their roles; show them how, and don't let them protest. Reach your hand out for your coffee without even looking up, like a new Labour spin doctor who expects to be silently serviced. D'Silva has been growing in stature and technical expertise since I first saw him in Stratford; here he creates a narcissistic monster whom you watch with amused dislike, but who also knows more about his trade than you would like to admit.

Now the company arrive, including the Leading Actor (Dale Rapley), a smug, handsome hunk who knows he is irresistible to anything in skirts. The Leading Actress (Liza Sadovy) is late, naturally, making a

grand entrance, apologising ostentatiously, and presenting a well-rehearsed picture of a purring lioness who has to be lusted after but never approached.

It is at this point that you understand what Jones has done. He has opened the darkened windows on the play and let in the light and the bracing wind of comedy. *Six Characters* is a tragedy with laughter as well as the other thing. It is the best dramatisation of the theatrical experience—its almost primitive simplicity but also its sophistication, its gift for causing moral discomfort, and its dangerous charm—since *A Midsummer Night's Dream*, with its deceptively funny subplot of the Rude Mechanicals.

Like Shakespeare, Pirandello sees things from both sides. It was the existential philosophers—Merleau-Ponty, Sartre et al.—who first described the great need, and the fatal trap, of human beings to be seen to be perceived, and how this need influences their behaviour. You become what you want people to see. The theatre, of course, has known this for ever. Actors are people for whom being seen is a vocation and a passion.

Now enter a group of people in black. This is the pivotal *coup de théâtre* of the play. This is a family of six people, adults and children. Something terrible has happened to them, and they are offering the story as material for a play. The story is pure melodrama, and it makes the Director incredulous. At this point, Pirandello's play, too, teeters at the edge of improbability. This is quite deliberate. You realise that there's something laughable, as well as fascinating, about the professional pretence called theatre. Yet for the family in black, being represented in a play holds out the possibility of justification, a sense of permanence and a hope that, through it, people will understand what happened to them. It is a more complex version of Renaissance princes and merchants wanting to be painted, preferably in attitudes of prayer, in the pictures they commissioned.

The family is led by the Father (Stephen Boxer) and the Mother (Yolanda Vasquez). The Stepdaughter (Leah Muller) is the centre of attention. What happened to her in the shop owned by Madame Pace (Michelle Wade)? Boxer gives one of his subtlest and most harrowing performances: both aggressor and victim, both sinned against and sinning, he has the air of anger and guilt beyond healing. At the same time,

---

*The Young Vic production featured a new translation by David Harrower, with this slightly revised title.

there is something painfully and pitifully laughable about him and his anxiety to be played by an actor, as if that might justify his existence and make it bearable.

But will the actors be able to play the family? Here is the crux of the play. What is real in life may not look real in the theatre. The six characters want their lives to be imitated, but the theatre can only represent. The theatre is controlled, shaped by our old friends beginning, middle and end; life is shapeless, unpredictable, open-ended. People think their life is theatrical; actors are obsessed with how lifelike acting is. Each aspires to the condition of the other. The theatre feeds off life, but keeps it at arm's length; but once the actor is onstage, life becomes something outside, potentially dangerous and disruptive. The theatre is busy holding a mirror up to nature, but nature sticks out its tongue at it.

Pirandello's play is a lesson in how to bear unreality. The better the play and its production, the less you believe that it is like life, and yet you apprehend in it an absurd, elusive, insistent reality. We like our art to be affirmative because that is comforting; Pirandello, showman and cynic, knows that you only achieve anything like adulthood if you can accept the unreliability of everything. In the second act, set in the "theatre", the set is dominated by the word USCITA: exit. There is a world outside; make of it what you will. Escape from the theatre into life, or from life into the theatre, and the best of luck. That is what this shockingly brilliant play, and Jones's brilliant production, are about.

EUGENE O'NEILL

1888–1953

Before his death of a rare degenerative disease that made it almost impossible for him to write during the last several years of his life, O'Neill produced more than fifty plays whose theatrical range and vision have firmly established him as the greatest playwright in the history of American drama. From the very beginning of his life the theater was an inextricable part of his experience, for he was the son of one of America's most famous matinee idols, the romantic actor James O'Neill, who achieved theatrical fame as the star of *The Count of Monte Cristo* and continued to tour in the play until he was well into his sixties. O'Neill was born in a hotel in the theater district of New York, and during his early childhood he traveled with his father on theatrical tours that took him throughout the United States. The chaotic life of his father's career and the morphine addiction that his mother developed after taking the drug to alleviate the pain of O'Neill's birth were also an indelible part of his experience, which he reflected in a number of late autobiographical plays that constitute the greatest achievement of his career, among them *Long Day's Journey into Night* (1940) and *A Moon for the Misbegotten* (1943). In these and other late plays, O'Neill confronted the most painful aspects of his family's and his own personal experience—his father's extramarital affairs, his mother's morphine addiction, his brother's inability to hold a job, his father's alcoholism, his brother's alcoholism, his own alcoholism that drove him to attempt suicide at a Bowery bar in 1912, and the endless cycle of bitter accusation and shamefaced apology that consumed the family throughout his life, leaving him obsessively torn between love and hatred for all its members. But the writing of these plays was more than a psychological milestone of honestly confronting his own past, for they also represent the artistic climax to his many years of searching for an appropriate dramatic form in which to convey his vision of modern experience.

O'Neill turned to playwriting in 1912, after a hectic period of several years, during which he got secretly married to a young woman, whom he promptly left to go prospecting for gold in Honduras, returned after a year to join his father as an actor and assistant stage manager on tour, went to sea again for a brief period, returned and took a job as a reporter on a small-town newspaper in Connecticut, and then came down with tuberculosis, brought on no doubt by his dissolute life, which forced him to be hospitalized for an extended period of time. During 1912, he became an avid reader of drama and decided to make his career as a dramatist. He began writing plays in 1913, enrolled in a playwriting course at Harvard during 1914, and moved to Greenwich Village in 1915, where he joined up with a group of avant-garde writers who had formed a repertory company that came to be known as the Provincetown Players, after the Massachusetts village where the writers spent the summer. The company, started by Susan Glaspell (author of *Trifles*), her husband, and their friends, would become one of the most influential groups in American theater, largely because of the plays that O'Neill produced for it during his early career.

O'Neill first wrote a series of one-act plays based on his earlier experiences at sea—strictly realistic plays in which he dramatized the illusions and preoccupations of men adrift in the world. By the early 1920s, he turned to full-length plays, still drawing on his attachment to the sea but conveying a complex vision of tragic fate and frustration, as in the Pulitzer Prize-winning *Beyond the Horizon* (1920) and *Anna Christie* (1921). He then began to experiment with expressionist techniques (see p. 526) in *The Emperor Jones* (1920), a one-act psychodrama about a negro "emperor" who flees a palace revolution and succumbs to his own fantasies and "the Little Formless Fears." The most striking innovation in this play was O'Neill's use of a drumbeat that began at pulse rate and gradually accelerated as Jones came closer and closer to death, ceasing only when he died. In *The Hairy Ape* (1922), O'Neill went even further with expressionist techniques by using contrasting symbolic settings (a furnace room versus fashionable Fifth Avenue) as well as choral speeches and socially emblematic characters to dramatize the destruction of a young stoker named Yank, who is unable to move outside of his class.

By the mid-1920s, O'Neill's fascination with Freudian psychology had already become evident in *Desire under the Elms* (1924), a play dramatizing the tragic sexual attraction between a young man and his young stepmother. The Freudian notion that human beings are torn between their social/familial roles and their conflicting inner drives found striking expression in *The Great God Brown* (1926) where, borrowing from Greek drama, O'Neill had his actors wear masks to reflect their assumed personalities. Obsessed with finding stage techniques to reveal the inner thoughts of characters, O'Neill moved from masks to monologues in the nine-act play *Strange Interlude* (1928), where the characters frequently interrupt their dialogue with each other and speak directly to the audience. And in *Days without End* (1934), he carried his expressionistic rendering of Freudian themes to the logical extreme by having two actors play the conflicting sides of the main character.

Yet even during this period when he was exploring the psychopathology of the human mind through a series of unusual dramatic techniques, O'Neill's subject was, repeatedly, the dysfunctional family, a family where love and hate are strongly intertwined, a family strikingly similar to his own, with his egocentric father, his alcoholic brother, and his morphine-addicted mother. *All God's Chillun Got Wings* (1924) seemed to portray the interracial marriage of Jim and Ella, but those characters are modeled on his parents, James and Ella. In *Ah, Wilderness* (1933), O'Neill wrote his only comedy, a nostalgic play in a realistic style, transforming the family's alcoholism into comic moments. When O'Neill was finally able, in his words, "to face my dead at last," he wrote more directly of himself and his family. *The Iceman Cometh* (1939), set in a New York saloon very much like the one where O'Neill had lived and had tried to kill himself, dramatized at length O'Neill's painful awareness of human frailty and self-deception. In *Long Day's Journey into Night* and *A Moon for the Misbegotten*, he renamed his family (Ireland's County Tyrone was the historic home of the O'Neill clan) but otherwise drew many of the details from his own experience, creating plays both unsparing in their condemnation and overwhelming in their love for "the four haunted Tyrones."

The bridge between his late autobiographical plays, with their brutal honesty about family love-hate conflicts, and the earlier plays, where the conflicts were often overpowered by elaborate stylistic devices such as masks and interior monologues, can be found in O'Neill's 1931 trilogy, *Mourning Becomes Electra*. Working from the *Oresteia* of Aeschylus, O'Neill dramatized the tragic fate of a family across several generations—a fate determined not by pride and ambition, as in the Greek drama, but by sexual instincts, psychic guilt, suicide, and remorse. The idea of creating a "modern psychological drama using one of the old legend plots of Greek tragedy" occurred to O'Neill in 1926. During a five-year period, he kept refining his original idea, as evidenced by his working notes in which he considered three distinctly different American settings (the Revolutionary period, the First World War, and the Civil War) before deciding on the Civil War because it was a period "not too distant for audience to associate itself with, yet possessing costume, etc.—possessing sufficient mask of time and space, so that audience will unconsciously grasp at once, it is primarily drama of hidden life forces—fate—behind lives of characters." Thus, within the context of that historical setting, O'Neill created a vividly naturalistic work whose frank psychological exposure of a family torn apart by incestuous attachments and jealous conflicts remains as compelling, disturbing, and relevant today as it was when it first appeared.

As he began drafting the play, O'Neill realized that he had too much material for a single play, so, in keeping with the Greek dramas that inspired him, he planned a trilogy, first writing a scenario for each play *(Homecoming, The Hunted, The Haunted),* and then a series of drafts. He gave his characters names that would reflect their nineteenth-century New England background and at the same time echo their Greek counterparts. So Agamemnon became Ezra Mannon; Clytemnestra became Christine; Aegisthus became Adam Brant; Orestes easily turned into Orin; and Electra, the invention of Aeschylus, became Lavinia. O'Neill's notes also reveal how carefully he shaped his trilogy—planning, for example, the pattern of alternating exterior and interior scenes, or using the sea chanty "Shenandoah" as "a sort of theme song." But he struggled to find the appropriate style for the play, writing it first as "straight realism," then again in a version with half-masks for the characters and self-revealing monologues (as in *Strange Interlude*), and finally in a version that cut the asides and the masks for the characters. He did, however, keep the mask "concept" with his repeated stage direction about the mask-like quality of the character's face in repose. And, like Aeschylus, he created three separate plays, each capable of being understood separately, but each gaining power when seen with the others. The first play, *Homecoming,* corresponding to *Agamemnon,* is printed here.

When O'Neill's trilogy was first staged in New York—in a production lasting six hours, plus a dinner intermission—Brooks Atkinson of the *New York Times* pronounced it "Mr. O'Neill's masterpiece and also one of the supreme achievements of the modern theatre." Since then, the three plays have always been produced together, although any theater company choosing to stage the trilogy must solve a variety of problems—from the length of the three plays, to the casting of actors able to suggest both the grandeur and the vulnerability of O'Neill's characters, to the creation of sets that include indoor rooms, the outdoor façade of the house, and even a ship (for the second play, *The Hunted*). While the designers of the 1997 production at Washington, D.C.'s, Shakespeare Theatre—Ming Cho Lee (set) and Jane Greenwood (costumes)—had different responses to O'Neill's highly detailed stage directions (see interview reprinted following the text), both were fascinated by the challenges of the play. Jane Greenwood's design for Lavinia's black dress (see Figure 1) cleverly incorporates O'Neill's direction about Lavinia's military bearing into the black velvet military trim on the dress; in contrast, Christine's lavish green dress (see Figure 1) represents her sensual aspect. The casting and makeup of the actors playing Ezra Mannon and Adam Brant, Christine's husband and lover, respectively, emphasize, as did O'Neill, their remarkable similarity (see Figures 1 and 2). The Mannon house (see Figure 3) was dominated outdoors by "the impossibly tall doors of set designer Ming Cho Lee's soaring, revolving white box of a house" (Nelson Pressley, writing in the *Washington Times*) and indoors by the portrait of Ezra Mannon as a judge (see Figure 4). The huge doors dwarf the characters seated on benches, while the portrait looms over Lavinia and implicitly reproaches Christine. The stage picture becomes a visual expression of the contradictions O'Neill set himself to explore: a family bound together by love and hate, in a world where homecoming means death.

HOMECOMING
Part One of the Trilogy: Mourning Becomes Electra

BY EUGENE O'NEILL

CHARACTERS

BRIGADIER-GENERAL EZRA MANNON
CHRISTINE, *his wife*
LAVINIA, *their daughter*
CAPTAIN ADAM BRANT, *of the clipper "Flying Trades"*
CAPTAIN PETER NILES, *U.S. Artillery*
HAZEL NILES, *his sister*
SETH BECKWITH
AMOS AMES
LOUISA, *his wife*
MINNIE, *her cousin*

SCENES

ACT 1—*Exterior of the* MANNON *house in New England—April, 1865.*
ACT 2—EZRA MANNON's *study in the house—no time has elapsed.*
ACT 3—*The same as Act 1—exterior of the house—a night a week later.*
ACT 4—*A bedroom in the house—later the same night.*

ACT 1

(Exterior of the MANNON *house on a late afternoon in April, 1865. At front is the driveway which leads up to the house from the two entrances on the street. Behind the driveway the white Grecian temple portico with its six tall columns extends across the stage. A big pine tree is on the lawn at the edge of the drive before the right corner of the house. Its trunk is a black column in striking contrast to the white columns of the portico. By the edge of the drive, left front, is a thick clump of lilacs and syringas. A bench is placed on the lawn at front of this shrubbery which partly screens anyone sitting on it from the front of the house.*

It is shortly before sunset and the soft light of the declining sun shines directly on the front of the house, shimmering in a luminous mist on the white portico and the gray stone wall behind, intensifying the whiteness of the columns, the somber grayness of the wall, the green of the open shutters, the green of the lawn and shrubbery, the black and green of the pine tree. The white columns cast black bars of shadow on the gray wall behind them. The windows of the lower floor reflect the sun's rays in a resentful glare. The temple portico is like an incongruous white mask fixed on the house to hide its somber gray ugliness.

In the distance, from the town, a band is heard playing "John Brown's Body." Borne on the light puffs of wind this music is at times quite loud, then sinks into faintness as the wind dies.

From the left rear, a man's voice is heard singing the chanty "Shenandoah"—a song that more than any other holds in it the brooding rhythm of the sea. The voice grows quickly nearer. It is thin and aged, the wraith of what must once have been a good baritone.)

Oh, Shenandoah, I long to hear you
A-way, my rolling river
Oh, Shenandoah, I can't get near you
Way-ay, I'm bound away
Across the wide Missouri.

(The singer, SETH BECKWITH, *finishes the last line as he enters from around the corner of the house. Closely following him are* AMOS AMES, *his wife,* LOUISA, *and her cousin* MINNIE.

SETH BECKWITH, *the* MANNONS' *gardener and man of all work, is an old man of seventy-five with white hair and beard, tall, raw-boned and stoop-shouldered, his joints stiffened by rheumatism, but still sound and hale. He has a gaunt face that in repose gives one the strange impression of a life-like mask. It is set in a grim expression, but his small, sharp eyes still peer at life with a shrewd prying avidity and his loose mouth has a strong suggestion of ribald humor. He wears his earth-stained working clothes.*

AMOS AMES, *carpenter by trade but now taking a holiday and dressed in his Sunday best, as are his wife and her cousin, is a fat man in his fifties. In character he is the townsfolk type of garrulous gossip-monger who is at the same time devoid of evil intent, scandal being for him merely the subject most popular with his audience.*

His wife, LOUISA, *is taller and stouter than he and about the same age. Of a similar scandal-bearing type, her tongue is sharpened by malice.*

Her cousin, MINNIE, *is a plump little woman of forty, of the meek, eager-listener type, with a small round face, round stupid eyes, and a round mouth pursed out to drink in gossip.*

These last three are types of townsfolk rather than

779

individuals, a chorus representing the town come to look and listen and spy on the rich and exclusive MANNONS.

Led by SETH, *they come forward as far as the lilac clump and stand staring at the house.* SETH, *in a mood of aged playfulness, is trying to make an impression on* MINNIE. *His singing has been for her benefit. He nudges her with his elbow, grinning.*)

SETH: How's that fur singin' fur an old feller? I used to be noted fur my chanties. (*Seeing she is paying no attention to him but is staring with open-mouthed awe at the house, he turns to* AMES—*jubilantly*) By jingo, Amos, if that news is true, there won't be a sober man in town tonight! It's our patriotic duty to celebrate!

AMES (*with a grin*): We'd ought to, that's sartin!

LOUISA: You ain't goin' to git Amos drunk tonight, surrender or no surrender! An old reprobate, that's what you be!

SETH (*pleased*): Old nothin'! On'y seventy-five! My old man lived to be ninety! Licker can't kill the Beckwiths! (*He and* AMES *laugh.* LOUISA *smiles in spite of herself.* MINNIE *is oblivious, still staring at the house.*)

MINNIE: My sakes! What a purty house!

SETH: Wal, I promised Amos I'd help show ye the sights when you came to visit him. 'Taint everyone can git to see the Mannon place close to. They're strict about trespassin'.

MINNIE: My! They must be rich! How'd they make their money?

SETH: Ezra's made a pile, and before him, his father, Abe Mannon, he inherited some and made a pile more in shippin'. Started one of the fust Western Ocean packet lines.

MINNIE: Ezra's the General, ain't he?

SETH (*proudly*): Ayeh. The best fighter in the hull of Grant's army!

MINNIE: What kind is he?

SETH (*boastfully expanding*): He's able, Ezra is! Folks think he's cold-blooded and uppish, 'cause he's never got much to say to 'em. But that's only the Mannons' way. They've been top dog around here for near on two hundred years and don't let folks fergit it.

MINNIE: How'd he come to jine the army if he's so rich?

SETH: Oh, he'd been a soldier afore this war. His paw made him go to West P'int. He went to the Mexican war and come out a major. Abe died that same year and Ezra give up the army and took holt of the shippin' business here. But he didn't stop there. He learned law on the side and got made a judge. Went in fur politics and got 'lected mayor. He was mayor when this war broke out but he resigned to once and jined the army again. And now he's riz to be General. Oh, he's able, Ezra is!

AMES: Ayeh. This town's real proud of Ezra.

LOUISA: Which is more'n you kin say fur his wife. Folks all hates her! She ain't the Mannon kind. French and Dutch descended, she is. Furrin lookin' and queer. Her father's a doctor in New York, but he can't be much of a one 'cause she didn't bring no money when Ezra married her.

SETH (*his face growing grim—sharply*): Never mind her. We ain't talkin' 'bout her. (*then abruptly changing the subject*) Wal, I've got to see Vinnie. I'm goin' round by the kitchen. You wait here. And if Ezra's wife starts to run you off fur trespassin', you tell her I got permission from Vinnie to show you round. (*He goes off around the corner of the house, left. The three stare about them gawkily, awed and uncomfortable. They talk in low voices.*)

LOUISA: Seth is so proud of his durned old Mannons! I couldn't help givin' him a dig about Ezra's wife.

AMES: Wal, don't matter much. He's allus hated her.

LOUISA: Ssshh! Someone's comin' out. Let's get back here! (*They crowd to the rear of the bench by the lilac clump and peer through the leaves as the front door is opened and* CHRISTINE MANNON *comes out to the edge of the portico at the top of the steps.* LOUISA *prods her cousin and whispers excitedly*) That's her! (CHRISTINE MANNON *is a tall striking-looking woman of forty but she appears younger. She has a fine, voluptuous figure and she moves with a flowing animal grace. She wears a green satin dress, smartly cut and expensive, which brings out the peculiar color of her thick curly hair, partly a copper brown, partly a bronze gold, each shade distinct and yet blending with the other. Her face is unusual, handsome rather than beautiful. One is struck at once by the strange impression it gives in repose of being not living flesh but a wonderfully life-like pale mask, in which only the deep-set eyes, of a dark violet blue, are alive. Her black eyebrows meet in a pronounced straight line above her strong nose. Her chin is heavy, her mouth large and sensual, the lower lip full, the upper a thin bow, shadowed by a line of hair. She stands and listens defensively, as if the music held some meaning that threatened her. But at once she shrugs her shoulders with disdain and comes down the steps and walks off toward the flower garden, passing behind the lilac clump without having noticed* AMES *and the women.*)

MINNIE (*in an awed whisper*): My! She's awful handsome, ain't she?

LOUISA: Too furrin lookin' fur my taste.

MINNIE: Ayeh. There's somethin' queer lookin' about her face.

AMES: Secret lookin'—'s if it was a mask she'd put on. That's the Mannon look. They all has it. They grow it on their wives. Seth's growed it on too, didn't you notice—from bein' with 'em all his life. They don't want folks to guess their secrets.

MINNIE (*breathlessly eager*): Secrets?

LOUISA: The Mannons got skeletons in their closets same as others! Worse ones. *(lowering her voice almost to a whisper—to her husband)* Tell Minnie about old Abe Mannon's brother David marryin' that French Canuck nurse girl he'd got into trouble.

AMES: Ssshh! Shet up, can't you? Here's Seth comin'. *(But he whispers quickly to MINNIE)* That happened way back when I was a youngster. I'll tell you later. *(SETH has appeared from around the left corner of the house and now joins them.)*

SETH: That durned nigger cook is allus askin' me to fetch wood fur her! You'd think I was her slave! That's what we get fur freein' 'em! *(then briskly)* Wal, come along, folks. I'll show you the peach orchard and then we'll go to my greenhouse. I couldn't find Vinnie. *(They are about to start when the front door of the house is opened and LAVINIA comes out to the top of the steps where her mother had stood. She is twenty-three but looks considerably older. Tall like her mother, her body is thin, flat-breasted and angular, and its unattractiveness is accentuated by her plain black dress. Her movements are stiff and she carries herself with a wooden, square-shouldered, military bearing. She has a flat dry voice and a habit of snapping out her words like an officer giving orders. But in spite of these dissimilarities, one is immediately struck by her facial resemblance to her mother. She has the same peculiar shade of copper-gold hair, the same pallor and dark violet-blue eyes, the black eyebrows meeting in a straight line above her nose, the same sensual mouth, the same heavy jaw. Above all, one is struck by the same strange, life-like mask impression her face gives in repose. But it is evident LAVINIA does all in her power to emphasize the dissimilarity rather than the resemblance to her parent. She wears her hair pulled tightly back, as if to conceal its natural curliness, and there is not a touch of feminine allurement to her severely plain get-up. Her head is the same size as her mother's, but on her thin body it looks too large and heavy.)*

SETH *(seeing her)*: There she be now. *(He starts for the steps—then sees she has not noticed their presence, and stops and stands waiting, struck by something in her manner. She is looking off right, watching her mother as she strolls through the garden to the greenhouse. Her eyes are bleak and hard with an intense, bitter enmity. Then her mother evidently disappears in the greenhouse, for LAVINIA turns her head, still oblivious to SETH and his friends, and looks off left, her attention caught by the band, the music of which, borne on a freshening breeze, has suddenly become louder. It is still playing "John Brown's Body." LAVINIA listens, as her mother had a moment before, but her reaction is the direct opposite to what her mother's had been. Her eyes light up with a grim satisfaction, and an expression of strange vindictive triumph comes into her face.)*

LOUISA *(in a quick whisper to MINNIE)*: That's Lavinia!

MINNIE: She looks like her mother in face—queer lookin'—but she ain't purty like her.

SETH: You git along to the orchard, folks. I'll jine you there. *(They walk back around the left of the house and disappear. He goes to LAVINIA eagerly.)* Say, I got fine news fur you, Vinnie. The telegraph feller says Lee is a goner sure this time! They're only waitin' now fur the news to be made official. You can count on your paw comin' home!

LAVINIA *(grimly)*: I hope so. It's time.

SETH *(with a keen glance at her—slowly)*: Ayeh.

LAVINIA *(turning on him sharply)*: What do you mean, Seth?

SETH *(avoiding her eyes—evasively)*: Nothin'—'cept what you mean. *(LAVINIA stares at him. He avoids her eyes—then heavily casual)* Where was you gallivantin' night afore last and all yesterday?

LAVINIA *(starts)*: Over to Hazel and Peter's house.

SETH: Ayeh. There's where Hannah said you'd told her you was goin'. That's funny now—'cause I seen Peter upstreet yesterday and he asked me where you was keepin' yourself.

LAVINIA *(again starts—then slowly as if admitting a secret understanding between them)*: I went to New York, Seth.

SETH: Ayeh. That's where I thought you'd gone, mebbe. *(then with deep sympathy)* It's durned hard on you, Vinnie. It's a durned shame.

LAVINIA *(stiffening—curtly)*: I don't know what you're talking about.

SETH *(nods comprehendingly)*: All right, Vinnie. Just as you say. *(He pauses—then after hesitating frowningly for a moment, blurts out)* There's somethin' been on my mind lately I want to warn you about. It's got to do with what's worryin' you—that is, if there's anythin' in it.

LAVINIA *(stiffly)*: There's nothing worrying me. *(then sharply)* Warn me? About what?

SETH: Mebbe it's nothin'—and then again mebbe I'm right, and if I'm right, then you'd ought t'be warned. It's to do with that Captain Brant.

LAVINIA *(starts again but keeps her tone cold and collected)*: What about him?

SETH: Somethin' I calc'late no one'd notice 'specially 'ceptin' me, because— *(then hastily as he sees someone coming up the drive)* Here's Peter and Hazel comin'. I'll tell you later, Vinnie. I ain't got time now anyways. Those folks are waitin' for me.

LAVINIA: I'll be sitting here. You come back afterwards. *(then her cold disciplined mask breaking for a moment—tensely)* Oh, why do Peter and Hazel have to come now? I don't want to see anyone! *(She starts as if to go into the house.)*

SETH: You run in. I'll git rid of 'em fur you.

LAVINIA *(recovering herself—curtly)*: No. I'll see them. *(SETH goes back around the corner of the house, left. A moment later HAZEL and PETER NILES enter along the drive from left, front.* HAZEL *is a pretty, healthy girl of nineteen, with dark hair and eyes. Her features are small but clearly modelled. She has a strong chin and a capable, smiling mouth. One gets a sure impression of her character at a glance—frank, innocent, amiable and good—not in a negative but in a positive, self-possessed way. Her brother,* PETER, *is very like her in character—straightforward, guileless and good-natured. He is a heavily built young fellow of twenty-two, awkward in movement and hesitating in speech. His face is broad, plain, with a snubby nose, curly brown hair, fine gray eyes and a big mouth. He wears the uniform of an artillery captain in the Union Army.)*

LAVINIA *(with forced cordiality)*: Good afternoon. How are you? *(She and* HAZEL *kiss and she shakes hands with* PETER.*)*

HAZEL: Oh, we're all right. But how are you, Vinnie, that's the question? Seems as if we hadn't seen you in ages! You haven't been sick, I hope!

LAVINIA: Well—if you call a pesky cold sick.

PETER: Gosh, that's too bad! All over it now?

LAVINIA: Yes—almost. Do sit down, won't you? *(*HAZEL *sits at left of bench,* LAVINIA *beside her in the middle.* PETER *sits gingerly on the right edge so that there is an open space between him and* LAVINIA.*)*

HAZEL: Peter can stay a while if you want him to, but I just dropped in for a second to find out if you'd had any more news from Orin.

LAVINIA: Not since the letter I showed you.

HAZEL: But that was ages ago! And I haven't had a letter in months. I guess he must have met another girl some place and given me the go by. *(She forces a smile but her tone is really hurt.)*

PETER: Orin not writing doesn't mean anything. He never was much of a hand for letters.

HAZEL: I know that, but—you don't think he's been wounded, do you, Vinnie?

LAVINIA: Of course not. Father would have let us know.

PETER: Sure he would. Don't be foolish, Hazel! *(then after a little pause)* Orin ought to be home before long now. You've heard the good news, of course, Vinnie?

HAZEL: Peter won't have to go back. Isn't that fine?

PETER: My wound is healed and I've got orders to leave tomorrow but they'll be cancelled, I guess. *(grinning)* I won't pretend I'm the sort of hero that wants to go back, either! I've had enough!

HAZEL *(impulsively)*: Oh, it will be so good to see Orin again. *(then embarrassed, forces a self-conscious laugh and gets up and kisses* LAVINIA*)* Well, I must run. I've got to meet Emily. Good-bye, Vinnie. Do take care of yourself and come to see us soon. *(with a teasing glance at her brother)* And be kind to Peter. He's nice—when he's asleep. And he has something he's just dying to ask you!

PETER *(horribly embarrassed)*: Darn you! *(*HAZEL *laughs*

and goes off down the drive, left front. PETER *fidgets, his eyes on the ground.* LAVINIA *watches him. Since* HAZEL*'s teasing statement, she has visibly withdrawn into herself and is on the defensive. Finally* PETER *looks up and blurts out awkwardly)* Hazel feels bad about Orin not writing. Do you think he really—loves her?

LAVINIA *(stiffening—brusquely)*: I don't know anything about love! I don't want to know anything! *(intensely)* I hate love!

PETER *(crushed by this but trying bravely to joke)*: Gosh, then, if that's the mood you're in, I guess I better not ask—something I'd made up my mind to ask you today.

LAVINIA: It's what you asked me a year ago when you were home on leave, isn't it?

PETER: And you said wait till the war was over. Well, it's over now.

LAVINIA *(slowly)*: I can't marry anyone, Peter. I've got to stay home. Father needs me.

PETER: He's got your mother.

LAVINIA *(sharply)*: He needs me more! *(A pause. Then she turns pityingly and puts her hand on his shoulder.)* I'm sorry, Peter.

PETER *(gruffly)*: Oh, that's all right.

LAVINIA: I know it's what girls always say in books, but I do love you as a brother, Peter. I wouldn't lose you as a brother for anything. We've been like that ever since we were little and started playing together—you and Orin and Hazel and I. So please don't let this come between us.

PETER: 'Course it won't. What do you think I am? *(doggedly)* Besides, I'm not giving up hope but what you'll change your mind in time. That is, unless it's because you love someone else—

LAVINIA *(snatching her hand back)*: Don't be stupid, Peter!

PETER: But how about this mysterious clipper captain that's been calling?

LAVINIA *(angrily)*: Do you think I care anything about that—that—!

PETER: Don't get mad. I only meant, folks say he's courting you.

LAVINIA: Folks say more than their prayers!

PETER: Then you don't—care for him?

LAVINIA *(intensely)*: I hate the sight of him!

PETER: Gosh! I'm glad to hear you say that, Vinnie. I was afraid—I imagined girls all liked him. He's such a darned romantic-looking cuss. Looks more like a gambler or a poet than a ship captain. I got a look as he was coming out of your gate—I guess it was the last time he was here. Funny, too. He reminded me of someone. But I couldn't place who it was.

LAVINIA *(startled, glances at him uneasily)*: No one around here, that's sure. He comes from out West. Grandfather Hamel happened to meet him in New York and took a fancy to him, and Mother met him at Grandfather's house.

PETER: Who is he, anyway, Vinnie?

LAVINIA: I don't know much about him in spite of what you think. Oh, he did tell me the story of his life to make himself out romantic, but I didn't pay much attention. He went to sea when he was young and was in California for the Gold Rush. He's sailed all over the world—he lived on a South Sea island once, so he says.

PETER (grumpily): He seems to have had plenty of romantic experience, if you can believe him!

LAVINIA (bitterly): That's his trade—being romantic! (then agitatedly) But I don't want to talk any more about him. (She gets up and walks toward right to conceal her agitation, keeping her back turned to PETER.)

PETER (with a grin): Well, I don't either. I can think of more interesting subjects. (CHRISTINE MANNON appears from left, between the clump of lilacs and the house. She is carrying a big bunch of flowers. LAVINIA senses her presence and whirls around. For a moment, mother and daughter stare into each other's eyes. In their whole tense attitudes is clearly revealed the bitter antagonism between them. But CHRISTINE quickly recovers herself and her air resumes its disdainful aloofness.)

CHRISTINE: Ah, here you are at last! (Then she sees PETER, who is visibly embarrassed by her presence.) Why, good afternoon, Peter, I didn't see you at first.

PETER: Good afternoon, Mrs. Mannon. I was just passing and dropped in for a second. I guess I better run along now, Vinnie.

LAVINIA (with an obvious eagerness to get him off—quickly): All right. Good-bye, Peter.

PETER: Good-bye. Good-bye, Mrs. Mannon.

CHRISTINE: Good-bye, Peter. (He disappears from the drive, left. CHRISTINE comes forward.) I must say you treat your one devoted swain pretty rudely. (LAVINIA doesn't reply. CHRISTINE goes on coolly.) I was wondering when I was going to see you. When I returned from New York last night you seemed to have gone to bed.

LAVINIA: I had gone to bed.

CHRISTINE: You usually read long after that. I tried your door—but you had locked yourself in. When you kept yourself locked in all day I was sure you were intentionally avoiding me. But Annie said you had a headache. (While she has been speaking she has come toward LAVINIA until she is now within arm's reach of her. The facial resemblance, as they stand there, is extraordinary. CHRISTINE stares at her coolly, but one senses an uneasy wariness beneath her pose.) Did you have a headache?

LAVINIA: No. I wanted to be alone—to think over things.

CHRISTINE: What things, if I may ask? (Then, as if she were afraid of an answer to this question, she abruptly changes the subject.) Who are those people I saw wandering about the grounds?

LAVINIA: Some friends of Seth's.

CHRISTINE: Because they know that lazy old sot, does it give them the privilege of trespassing?

LAVINIA: I gave Seth permission to show them around.

CHRISTINE: And since when have you the right without consulting me?

LAVINIA: I couldn't very well consult you when Seth asked me. You had gone to New York—(she pauses a second—then adds slowly, staring fixedly at her mother) to see Grandfather. Is he feeling any better? He seems to have been sick so much this past year.

CHRISTINE (casually, avoiding her eyes): Yes. He's much better now. He'll soon be going the rounds to his patients again, he hopes. (as if anxious to change the subject, looking at the flowers she carries) I've been to the greenhouse to pick these. I felt our tomb needed a little brightening. (She nods scornfully toward the house.) Each time I come back after being away it appears more like a sepulchre! The "whited" one of the Bible—pagan temple front stuck like a mask on Puritan gray ugliness! It was just like old Abe Mannon to build such a monstrosity—as a temple for his hatred. (then with a little mocking laugh) Forgive me, Vinnie. I forgot you liked it. And you ought to. It suits your temperament. (LAVINIA stares at her but remains silent. CHRISTINE glances at her flowers again and turns toward the house.) I must put these in water. (She moves a few steps toward the house—then turns again—with a studied casualness) By the way, before I forget, I happened to run into Captain Brant on the street in New York. He said he was coming up here today to take over his ship and asked me if he might drop in to see you. I told him he could—and stay to supper with us. (without looking at LAVINIA, who is staring at her with a face grown grim and hard) Doesn't that please you, Vinnie? Or do you remain true to your one and only beau, Peter?

LAVINIA: Is that why you picked the flowers—because he is coming? (Her mother does not answer. She goes on with a threatening undercurrent in her voice.) You have heard the news, I suppose? It means Father will be home soon!

CHRISTINE (without looking at her—coolly): We've had so many rumors lately. This report hasn't been confirmed yet, has it? I haven't heard the fort firing a salute.

LAVINIA: You will before long!

CHRISTINE: I'm sure I hope so as much as you.

LAVINIA: You can say that!

CHRISTINE (*concealing her alarm—coldly*): What do you mean? You will kindly not take that tone with me, please! (*cuttingly*) If you are determined to quarrel, let us go into the house. We might be overheard out here. (*She turns and sees* SETH *who has just come to the corner of the house, left, and is standing there watching them.*) See. There is your old crony doing his best to listen now! (*moving to the steps*) I am going in and rest a while. (*She walks up the steps.*)

LAVINIA (*harshly*): I've got to have a talk with you, Mother—before long!

CHRISTINE (*turning defiantly*): Whenever you wish. Tonight after the Captain leaves you, if you like. But what is it you want to talk about?

LAVINIA: You'll know soon enough!

CHRISTINE (*staring at her with a questioning dread—forcing a scornful smile*): You always make such a mystery of things, Vinnie. (*She goes into the house and closes the door behind her.* SETH *comes forward from where he had withdrawn around the corner of the house.* LAVINIA *makes a motion for him to follow her, and goes and sits on the bench at left. A pause. She stares straight ahead, her face frozen, her eyes hard. He regards her understandingly.*)

LAVINIA (*abruptly*): Well? What is it about Captain Brant you want to warn me against? (*then as if she felt she must defend her question from some suspicion that she knows is in his mind*) I want to know all I can about him because—he seems to be calling to court me.

SETH (*managing to convey his entire disbelief of this statement in one word*): Ayeh.

LAVINIA (*sharply*): You say that as if you didn't believe me.

SETH: I believe anything you tell me to believe. I ain't been with the Mannons for sixty years without learning that. (*A pause. Then he asks slowly*) Ain't you noticed this Brant reminds you of someone in looks?

LAVINIA (*struck by this*): Yes. I have—ever since I first saw him—but I've never been able to place who—Who do you mean?

SETH: Your Paw, ain't it, Vinnie?

LAVINIA (*startled—agitatedly*): Father? No! It can't be! (*then as if the conviction were forcing itself on her in spite of herself*) Yes! He does—something about his face—that must be why I've had the strange feeling I've known him before—why I've felt—(*then tensely as if she were about to break down*) Oh! I won't believe it! You must be mistaken, Seth! That would be too—!

SETH: He ain't only like your Paw. He's like Orin, too—and all the Mannons I've known.

LAVINIA (*frightenedly*): But why—why should he—?

SETH: More speshully he calls to my mind your Grandpaw's brother, David. How much do you know about David Mannon, Vinnie? I know his name's never been allowed to be spoke among Mannons since the day he left—but you've likely heard gossip, ain't you—even if it all happened before you was born.

LAVINIA: I've heard that he loved the Canuck nurse girl who was taking care of Father's little sister who died, and had to marry her because she was going to have a baby; and that Grandfather put them both out of the house and then afterwards tore it down and built this one because he wouldn't live where his brother had disgraced the family. But what has that old scandal got to do with—

SETH: Wait. Right after they was throwed out they married and went away. There was talk they'd gone out West, but no one knew nothin' about 'em afterwards—'ceptin' your Grandpaw let out to me one time she'd had the baby—a boy. He was cussin' it. (*then impressively*) It's about her baby I've been thinkin', Vinnie.

LAVINIA (*a look of appalled comprehension growing on her face*): Oh!

SETH: How old is that Brant, Vinnie?

LAVINIA: Thirty-six, I think.

SETH: Ayeh! That'd make it right. And here's another funny thing—his name. Brant's sort of queer fur a name. I ain't never heard tell of it before. Sounds made up to me—like short fur somethin' else. Remember what that Canuck girl's name was, do you, Vinnie? Marie Brantôme! See what I'm drivin' at?

LAVINIA (*agitatedly, fighting against a growing conviction*): But—don't be stupid, Seth—his name would be Mannon and he'd be only too proud of it.

SETH: He'd have good reason not to use the name of Mannon when he came callin' here, wouldn't he? If your Paw ever guessed—!

LAVINIA (*breaking out violently*): No! It can't be! God wouldn't let it! It would be too horrible—on top of—! I won't even think of it, do you hear? Why did you have to tell me?

SETH (*calmingly*): There now! Don't take on, Vinnie. No need gettin' riled at me. (*He waits—then goes on insistently.*) All I'm drivin' at is that it's durned funny—his looks and the name—and you'd ought fur your paw's sake to make sartin.

LAVINIA: How can I make certain?

SETH: Catch him off guard sometime and put it up to him strong—as if you knowed it—and see if mebbe he don't give himself away. (*He starts to go—looks down the drive at left.*) Looks like him comin' up the drive now, Vinnie. There's somethin' about his walk calls back David Mannon, too. If I didn't know it was him I'd think it was David's ghost comin' home. (*He turns away abruptly.*) Wal, calc'late I better git back to work.

(He walks around the left corner of the house. A pause. Then CAPTAIN ADAM BRANT *enters from the drive, left, front. He starts on seeing* LAVINIA *but immediately puts on his most polite, winning air. One is struck at a glance by the peculiar quality his face in repose has of being a life-like mask rather than living flesh. He has a broad, low forehead, framed by coal-black straight hair which he wears noticeably long, pushed back carelessly from his forehead as a poet's might be. He has a big aquiline nose, bushy eyebrows, swarthy complexion, hazel eyes. His wide mouth is sensual and moody—a mouth that can be strong and weak by turns. He wears a mustache, but his heavy cleft chin is clean-shaven. In figure he is tall, broad-shouldered and powerful. He gives the impression of being always on the offensive or defensive, always fighting life. He is dressed with an almost foppish extravagance, with touches of studied carelessness, as if a romantic Byronic appearance were the ideal in mind. There is little of the obvious ship captain about him, except his big, strong hands and his deep voice.)*

BRANT *(bowing with an exaggerated politeness)*: Good afternoon. *(coming and taking her hand which she forces herself to hold out to him)* Hope you don't mind my walking in on you without ceremony. Your mother told me—

LAVINIA: I know. She had to go out for a while and she said I was to keep you company until she returned.

BRANT *(gallantly)*: Well, I'm in good luck, then. I hope she doesn't hurry back to stand watch over us. I haven't had a chance to be alone with you since— that night we went walking in the moonlight, do you remember? *(He has kept her hand and he drops his voice to a low, lover-like tone.* LAVINIA *cannot repress a start, agitatedly snatching her hand from his and turning away from him.)*

LAVINIA *(regaining command of herself—slowly)*: What do you think of the news of Lee surrendering, Captain? We expect my father home very soon now. *(At something in her tone he stares at her suspiciously, but she is looking straight before her.)* Why don't you sit down?

BRANT: Thank you. *(He sits on the bench at her right. He has become wary now, feeling something strange in her attitude but not able to make her out—casually)* Yes, you must be very happy at the prospect of seeing your father again. Your mother has told me how close you've always been to him.

LAVINIA: Did she? *(then with intensity)* I love Father better than anyone in the world. There is nothing I wouldn't do—to protect him from hurt!

BRANT *(watching her carefully—keeping his casual tone)*: You care more for him than for your mother?

LAVINIA: Yes.

BRANT: Well, I suppose that's the usual way of it. A daughter feels closer to her father and a son to his mother. But I should think you ought to be a born exception to that rule.

LAVINIA: Why?

BRANT: You're so like your mother in some ways. Your face is the dead image of hers. And look at your hair. You won't meet hair like yours and hers again in a month of Sundays. I only know of one other woman who had it. You'll think it strange when I tell you. It was my mother.

LAVINIA *(with a start)*: Ah!

BRANT *(dropping his voice to a reverent, hushed tone)*: Yes, she had beautiful hair like your mother's, that hung down to her knees, and big, deep, sad eyes that were blue as the Caribbean sea!

LAVINIA *(harshly)*: What do looks amount to? I'm not a bit like her! Everybody knows I take after Father!

BRANT *(brought back with a shock, astonished at her tone)*: But—you're not angry at me for saying that, are you? *(then filled with uneasiness and resolving he must establish himself on an intimate footing with her again—with engaging bluntness)* You're puzzling today, Miss Lavinia. You'll excuse me if I come out with it bluntly. I've lived most of my life at sea and in camps and I'm used to straight speaking. What are you holding against me? If I've done anything to offend you, I swear it wasn't meant. *(She is silent, staring before her with hard eyes, rigidly upright. He appraises her with a calculating look, then goes on.)* I wouldn't have bad feeling come between us for the world. I may only be flattering myself, but I thought you liked me. Have you forgotten that night walking along the shore?

LAVINIA *(in a cold, hard voice)*: I haven't forgotten. Did Mother tell you you could kiss me?

BRANT: What—what do you mean? *(But he at once attributes the question to her naïveté—laughingly)* Oh! I see! But, come now, Lavinia, you can't mean, can you, I should have asked her permission?

LAVINIA: Shouldn't you?

BRANT *(again uneasy—trying to joke it off)*: Well, I wasn't brought up that strictly and, should or shouldn't, at any rate, I didn't—and it wasn't the less sweet for that! *(Then at something in her face he hurriedly goes off on another tack.)* I'm afraid I gabbed too much that night. Maybe I bored you with my talk of clipper ships and my love for them?

LAVINIA *(dryly)*: "Tall, white clippers," you called them. You said they were like beautiful, pale women to you. You said you loved them more than you'd ever loved a woman. Is that true, Captain?

BRANT *(with forced gallantry)*: Aye. But I meant, before I met you. *(then thinking he has at last hit on the cause of her changed attitude toward him—with a laugh)* So that's what you're holding against me, is it? Well, I might have guessed. Women are jealous of ships. They always suspect the sea. They know they're three of a kind when it comes to a man!

(He laughs again but less certainly this time, as he regards her grim, set expression.) Yes, I might have seen you didn't appear much taken by my sea gamming that night. I suppose clippers are too old a story to the daughter of a ship builder. But unless I'm much mistaken, you were interested when I told you of the islands in the South Seas where I was shipwrecked my first voyage at sea.

LAVINIA *(in a dry, brittle tone)*: I remember your admiration for the naked native women. You said they had found the secret of happiness because they had never heard that love can be a sin.

BRANT *(surprised—sizing her up puzzledly)*: So you remember that, do you? *(then romantically)* Aye! And they live in as near the Garden of Paradise before sin was discovered as you'll find on this earth! Unless you've seen it, you can't picture the green beauty of their land set in the blue of the sea! The clouds like down on the mountain tops, the sun drowsing in your blood, and always the surf on the barrier reef singing a croon in your ears like a lullaby! The Blessed Isles, I'd call them! You can forget there all men's dirty dreams of greed and power!

LAVINIA: And their dirty dreams—of love?

BRANT *(startled again—staring at her uneasily)*: Why do you say that? What do you mean, Lavinia?

LAVINIA: Nothing. I was only thinking—of your Blessed Isles.

BRANT *(uncertainly)*: Oh! But you said— *(Then with a confused, stupid persistence he comes closer to her, dropping his voice again to his love-making tone.)* Whenever I remember those islands now, I will always think of you, as you walked beside me that night with your hair blowing in the sea wind and the moonlight in your eyes! *(He tries to take her hand, but at his touch she pulls away and springs to her feet.)*

LAVINIA *(with cold fury)*: Don't you touch me! Don't you dare—! You liar! You—! *(Then as he starts back in confusion, she seizes this opportunity to follow* SETH*'s advice—staring at him with deliberately insulting scorn)* But I suppose it would be foolish to expect anything but cheap romantic lies from the son of a low Canuck nurse girl!

BRANT *(stunned)*: What's that? *(then rage at the insult to his mother overcoming all prudence—springs to his feet threateningly)* Belay, damn you!—or I'll forget you're a woman—no Mannon can insult her while I—

LAVINIA *(appalled now she knows the truth)*: So—it is true— You are her son! Oh!

BRANT *(fighting to control himself—with harsh defiance)*: And what if I am? I'm proud to be! My only shame is my dirty Mannon blood! So that's why you couldn't stand my touching you just now, is it? You're too good for the son of a servant, eh? By God, you were glad enough before—!

LAVINIA *(fiercely)*: It's not true! I was only leading you on to find out things!

BRANT: Oh, no! It's only since you suspected who I was! I suppose your father has stuffed you with his lies about my mother! But, by God, you'll hear the truth of it, now you know who I am— And you'll see if you or any Mannon has the right to look down on her!

LAVINIA: I don't want to hear— *(She starts to go toward the house.)*

BRANT *(grabbing her by the arm—tauntingly)*: You're a coward, are you, like all Mannons, when it comes to facing the truth about themselves? *(She turns on him defiantly. He drops her arm and goes on harshly.)* I'll bet he never told you your grandfather, Abe Mannon, as well as his brother, loved my mother!

LAVINIA: It's a lie!

BRANT: It's the truth. It was his jealous revenge made him disown my father and cheat him out of his share of the business they'd inherited!

LAVINIA: He didn't cheat him! He bought him out!

BRANT: Forced him to sell for one-tenth its worth, you mean! He knew my father and mother were starving! But the money didn't last my father long! He'd taken to drink. He was a coward—like all Mannons—once he felt the world looked down on him. He skulked and avoided people. He grew ashamed of my mother—and me. He sank down and down and my mother worked and supported him. I can remember when men from the corner saloon would drag him home and he'd fall in the door, a sodden carcass. One night when I was seven he came home crazy drunk and hit my mother in the face. It was the first time he'd ever struck her. It made me blind mad. I hit at him with the poker and cut his head. My mother pulled me back and gave me a hiding. Then she cried over him. She'd never stopped loving him.

LAVINIA: Why do you tell me this? I told you once I don't want to hear—

BRANT *(grimly)*: You'll see the point of it damned soon! *(unheeding—as if the scene were still before his eyes)* For days after, he sat and stared at nothing. One time when we were alone he asked me to forgive him hitting her. But I hated him and I wouldn't forgive him. Then one night he went out and he didn't come back. The next morning they found him hanging in a barn!

LAVINIA *(with a shudder)*: Oh!

BRANT *(savagely)*: The only decent thing he ever did!

LAVINIA: You're lying! No Mannon would ever—

BRANT: Oh, wouldn't they? They are all fine, honorable gentlemen, you think! Then listen a bit and you'll hear something about another of them! *(then going on bitterly with his story)* My mother sewed for a living and sent me to school. She was very strict with me. She blamed me for his killing himself. But she was bound she'd make a gentleman of me—like he was!—if it took her last cent and her last strap! *(with a grim smile)* She didn't succeed, as you notice! At seventeen I ran away to sea—and forgot I had a mother, except I took part of her name—Brant was short and easy on ships—and I wouldn't wear the name of Mannon. I forgot her until two years ago when I came back from the East. Oh, I'd written to her now and then and sent her money when I happened to have any. But I'd forgotten her just the same—and when I got to New York I found her dying—of sickness and starvation! And I found out that when she'd been laid up, not able to work, not knowing where to reach me, she'd sunk her last shred of pride and written to your father asking for a loan. He never answered her. And I came too late. She died in my arms. *(with vindictive passion)* He could have saved her—and he deliberately let her die! He's as guilty of murder as anyone he ever sent to the rope when he was a judge!

LAVINIA *(springing to her feet—furiously)*: You dare say that about Father! If he were here—

BRANT: I wish to God he was! I'd tell him what I tell you now—that I swore on my mother's body I'd revenge her death on him.

LAVINIA *(with cold deadly intensity)*: And I suppose you boast that now you've done so, don't you?—in the vilest, most cowardly way—like the son of a servant you are!

BRANT *(again thrown off guard—furiously)*: Belay, I told you, with that kind of talk!

LAVINIA: She is only your means of revenge on Father, is that it?

BRANT *(stunned—stammers in guilty confusion)*: What?—She?—Who?—I don't know what you're talking about!

LAVINIA: Then you soon will know! And so will she! I've found out all I wanted to from you. I'm going in to talk to her now. You wait here until I call you!

BRANT *(furious at her tone)*: No! Be damned if you can order me about as if I was your servant!

LAVINIA *(icily)*: If you have any consideration for her, you'll do as I say and not force me to write my father. *(She turns her back on him and walks to the steps woodenly erect and square-shouldered.)*

BRANT *(desperately now—with a grotesque catching at his lover's manner)*: I don't know what you mean, Lavinia. I swear before God it is only you I— *(She turns at the top of the steps at this and stares at him with such a passion of hatred that he is silenced. Her lips move as if she were going to speak, but she fights back the words, turns stiffly and goes into the house and closes the door behind her.)*

CURTAIN

ACT 2

*(In the house—*EZRA MANNON*'s study. No time has elapsed.*

The study is a large room with a stiff, austere atmosphere. The furniture is old colonial. The walls are plain plastered surfaces tinted a dull gray with a flat white trim. At rear, right, is a door leading to the hall. On the right wall is a painting of George Washington in a gilt frame, flanked by smaller portraits of Alexander Hamilton and John Marshall. At rear, center, is an open fireplace. At left of fireplace, a bookcase filled with law books. Above the fireplace, in a plain frame, is a large portrait of EZRA MANNON *himself, painted ten years previously. One is at once struck by the startling likeness between him and* ADAM BRANT. *He is a tall man in his early forties, with a spare, wiry frame, seated stiffly in an armchair, his hands on the arms, wearing his black judge's robe. His face is handsome in a stern, aloof fashion. It is cold and emotionless and has the same strange semblance of a life-like mask that we have already seen in the faces of his wife and daughter and* BRANT.

On the left are two windows. Between them a desk. A large table with an armchair on either side, right and left, stands at left center, front. At right center is another chair. There are hooked rugs on the floor.

Outside the sun is beginning to set and its glow fills the room with a golden mist. As the action progresses this becomes brighter, then turns to crimson, which darkens to somberness at the end.

LAVINIA *is discovered standing by the table. She is fighting to control herself, but her face is torn by a look of stricken anguish. She turns slowly to her father's portrait and for a moment stares at it fixedly. Then she goes to it and puts her hand over one of his hands with a loving, protecting gesture.)*

LAVINIA: Poor Father! *(She hears a noise in the hall and moves hastily away. The door from the hall is opened and* CHRISTINE *enters. She is uneasy underneath, but affects a scornful indignation.)*

CHRISTINE: Really, this unconfirmed report must have turned your head—otherwise I'd find it difficult to understand your sending Annie to disturb me when you knew I was resting.

LAVINIA: I told you I had to talk to you.

CHRISTINE *(looking around the room with aversion)*: But why in this musty room, of all places?

LAVINIA *(indicating the portrait—quietly)*: Because it's Father's room.

CHRISTINE *(starts, looks at the portrait and quickly drops her eyes.* LAVINIA *goes to the door and closes it.* CHRISTINE *says with forced scorn)*: More mystery?

LAVINIA: You better sit down. *(*CHRISTINE *sits in the chair at rear center.* LAVINIA *goes back to her father's chair at left of table.)*

CHRISTINE: Well—if you're quite ready, perhaps you will explain.

LAVINIA: I suppose Annie told you I'd been to visit Hazel and Peter while you were away.

CHRISTINE: Yes. I thought it peculiar. You never visit anyone overnight. Why did you suddenly take that notion?

LAVINIA: I didn't.

CHRISTINE: You didn't visit them?

LAVINIA: No.

CHRISTINE: Then where did you go?

LAVINIA *(accusingly)*: To New York! *(CHRISTINE starts. LAVINIA hurries on a bit incoherently.)* I've suspected something—lately—the excuse you've made for all your trips there the past year, that Grandfather was sick— *(as CHRISTINE is about to protest indignantly)* Oh! I know he has been—and you've stayed at his house—but I've suspected lately that wasn't the real reason—and now I can prove it isn't! Because I waited outside Grandfather's house and followed you. I saw you meet Brant!

CHRISTINE *(alarmed but concealing it—coolly)*: Well, what if you did? I told you myself I ran into him by accident—

LAVINIA: You went to his room!

CHRISTINE *(shaken)*: He asked me to meet a friend of his—a lady. It was her house we went to.

LAVINIA: I asked the woman in the basement. He had hired the room under another name, but she recognized his description. And yours too. She said you had come there often in the past year.

CHRISTINE *(desperately)*: It was the first time I had ever been there. He insisted on my going. He said he had to talk to me about you. He wanted my help to approach your father—

LAVINIA *(furiously)*: How can you lie like that? How can you be so vile as to try to use me to hide your adultery?

CHRISTINE *(springing up—with weak indignation)*: Vinnie!

LAVINIA: Your adultery, I said!

CHRISTINE: No!

LAVINIA: Stop lying, I tell you! I went upstairs! I heard you telling him— "I love you, Adam"—and kissing him! *(with a cold bitter fury)* You vile—! You're shameless and evil! Even if you are my mother, I say it! *(CHRISTINE stares at her, overwhelmed by this onslaught, her poise shattered for the moment. She tries to keep her voice indifferent but it trembles a little.)*

CHRISTINE: I—I knew you hated me, Vinnie—but not as bitterly as that! *(then with a return of her defiant coolness)* Very well! I love Adam Brant. What are you going to do?

LAVINIA: How you say that—without any shame! You don't give one thought to Father—who is so good—who trusts you! Oh, how could you do this to Father? How could you?

CHRISTINE *(with strident intensity)*: You would understand if you were the wife of a man you hated!

LAVINIA *(horrified—with a glance at the portrait)*: Don't! Don't say that—before him! I won't listen!

CHRISTINE *(grabbing her by the arm)*: You will listen! I'm talking to you as a woman now, not as mother to daughter! That relationship has no meaning between us! You've called me vile and shameless! Well, I want you to know that's what I've felt about myself for over twenty years, giving my body to a man I—

LAVINIA *(trying to break away from her, half putting her hands up to her ears)*: Stop telling me such things! Let me go! *(She breaks away, shrinking from her mother with a look of sick repulsion. A pause. She stammers)* You—then you've always hated Father?

CHRISTINE *(bitterly)*: No. I loved him once—before I married him—incredible as that seems now! He was handsome in his lieutenant's uniform! He was silent and mysterious and romantic! But marriage soon turned his romance into—disgust!

LAVINIA *(wincing again—stammers harshly)*: So I was born of your disgust! I've always guessed that, Mother—ever since I was little—when I used to come to you—with love—but you would always push me away! I've felt it ever since I can remember—your disgust! *(then with a flare-up of bitter hatred)* Oh, I hate you! It's only right I should hate you!

CHRISTINE *(shaken—defensively)*: I tried to love you. I told myself it wasn't human not to love my own child, born of my body. But I never could make myself feel you were born of any body but his! You were always my wedding night to me—and my honeymoon!

LAVINIA: Stop saying that! How can you be so—! *(then suddenly—with a strange jealous bitterness)* You've loved Orin! Why didn't you hate him, too?

CHRISTINE: Because by then I had forced myself to become resigned in order to live! And most of the time I was carrying him, your father was with the army in Mexico. I had forgotten him. And when Orin was born he seemed my child, only mine, and I loved him for that! *(bitterly)* I loved him until he let you and your father nag him into the war, in spite of my begging him not to leave me alone. *(staring at LAVINIA with hatred)* I know his leaving me was your doing principally, Vinnie!

LAVINIA *(sternly)*: It was his duty as a Mannon to go! He'd have been sorry the rest of his life if he hadn't! I love him better than you! I was thinking of him!

CHRISTINE: Well, I hope you realize I never would have fallen in love with Adam if I'd had Orin with me. When he had gone there was nothing left—but hate and a desire to be revenged—and a longing for love! And it was then I met Adam. I saw he loved me—

LAVINIA *(with taunting scorn)*: He doesn't love you!

You're only his revenge on Father! Do you know who he really is? He's the son of that low nurse girl Grandfather put out of our house!

CHRISTINE (*concealing a start—coolly*): So you've found that out? Were you hoping it would be a crushing surprise to me? I've known it all along. He told me when he said he loved me.

LAVINIA: Oh! And I suppose knowing who he was gave you all the more satisfaction—to add that disgrace!

CHRISTINE (*cuttingly*): Will you kindly come to the point and tell me what you intend doing? I suppose you'll hardly let your father get in the door before you tell him!

LAVINIA (*suddenly becoming rigid and cold again—slowly*): No. Not unless you force me to. (*then as she sees her mother's astonishment—grimly*) I don't wonder you're surprised! You know you deserve the worst punishment you could get. And Father would disown you publicly, no matter how much the scandal cost him!

CHRISTINE: I realize that. I know him even better than you do!

LAVINIA: And I'd like to see you punished for your wickedness! So please understand this isn't for your sake. It's for Father's. He hasn't been well lately. I'm not going to have him hurt! It's my first duty to protect him from you!

CHRISTINE: I know better than to expect any generosity on my account.

LAVINIA: I won't tell him, provided you give up Brant and never see him again—and promise to be a dutiful wife to Father and make up for the wrong you've done him!

CHRISTINE (*stares at her daughter—a pause—then she laughs dryly*): What a fraud you are, with your talk of your father and your duty! Oh, I'm not denying you want to save his pride—and I know how anxious you are to keep the family from more scandal! But all the same, that's not your real reason for sparing me!

LAVINIA (*confused—guiltily*): It is!

CHRISTINE: You wanted Adam Brant yourself!

LAVINIA: That's a lie!

CHRISTINE: And now you know you can't have him, you're determined that at least you'll take him from me!

LAVINIA: No!

CHRISTINE: But if you told your father, I'd have to go away with Adam. He'd be mine still. You can't bear that thought, even at the price of my disgrace, can you?

LAVINIA: It's your evil mind!

CHRISTINE: I know you, Vinnie! I've watched you ever since you were little, trying to do exactly what you're doing now! You've tried to become the wife of your father and the mother of Orin! You've always schemed to steal my place!

LAVINIA (*wildly*): No! It's you who have stolen all love from me since the time I was born! (*then her manner becoming threatening*) But I don't want to listen to any more of your lies and excuses! I want to know right now whether you're going to do what I told you or not!

CHRISTINE: Suppose I refuse! Suppose I go off openly with Adam! Where will you and your father and the family name be after that scandal? And what if I were disgraced myself? I'd have the man I love, at least!

LAVINIA (*grimly*): Not for long! Father would use all his influence and get Brant blacklisted so he'd lose his command and never get another! You know how much the "Flying Trades" means to him. And Father would never divorce you. You could never marry. You'd be an anchor around his neck. Don't forget you're five years older than he is! He'll still be in his prime when you're an old woman with all your looks gone! He'd grow to hate the sight of you!

CHRISTINE (*stung beyond bearing—makes a threatening move as if to strike her daughter's face*): You devil! You mean little—! (*But* LAVINIA *stares back coldly into her eyes and she controls herself and drops her hand.*)

LAVINIA: I wouldn't call names if I were you! There is one you deserve!

CHRISTINE (*turning away—her voice still trembling*): I'm a fool to let you make me lose my temper—over your jealous spite! (*A pause.* LAVINIA *stares at her.* CHRISTINE *seems considering something. A sinister expression comes to her face. Then she turns back to* LAVINIA—*coldly*) But you wanted my answer, didn't you? Well, I agree to do as you said. I promise you I'll never see Adam again after he calls this evening. Are you satisfied?

LAVINIA (*stares at her with cold suspicion*): You seem to take giving him up pretty easily!

CHRISTINE (*hastily*): Do you think I'll ever give you the satisfaction of seeing me grieve? Oh, no, Vinnie! You'll never have a chance to gloat!

LAVINIA (*still suspiciously—with a touch of scorn*): If I loved anyone—!

CHRISTINE (*tauntingly*): If? I think you do love him—as much as you can love! (*with a sudden flurry of jealousy*) You little fool! Don't you know I made him flirt with you, so you wouldn't be suspicious?

LAVINIA (*gives a little shudder—then fiercely*): He didn't fool me! I saw what a liar he was! I just led him on—to find out things! I always hated him! (CHRISTINE *smiles mockingly and turns away, as if to go out of the room.* LAVINIA*'s manner becomes threatening again.*) Wait! I don't trust you! I know you're thinking already how you can fool me and break the promise you've just made! But you better not try it! I'll be watching you every minute! And I won't be the only one! I wrote to Father and Orin as soon as I got back from New York!

CHRISTINE (*startled*): About Adam?

LAVINIA: Only enough so they'd be suspicious and watch you too. I said a Captain Brant had been calling and folks had begun to gossip.

CHRISTINE: Ah! I see what it's going to mean—that you'll always have this to hold over me and I'll be under your thumb for the rest of my life! (*She cannot restrain her rage—threateningly*) Take care, Vinnie! You'll be responsible if—! (*She checks herself abruptly.*)

LAVINIA (*suspiciously*): If what?

CHRISTINE (*quickly*): Nothing. I only meant if I went off with Adam. But of course you know I won't do that. You know there's nothing I can do now—but obey your orders!

LAVINIA (*continues to stare at her suspiciously—grimly*): You ought to see it's your duty to Father, not my orders—if you had any honor or decency! (*then brusquely*) Brant is waiting outside. You can tell him what you've got to do—and tell him if he ever dares come here again—! (*forcing back her anger*) And see that you get rid of him right now! I'm going upstreet to get the latest news. I won't be gone more than a half-hour and I want him out of the house by the time I get back, do you hear? If he isn't, I'll write Father again. I won't even wait for him to come home! (*She turns her back on her mother and marches out the door, square-shouldered and stiff, without a backward glance.* CHRISTINE *looks after her, waiting until she hears the side door of the house close after her. Then she turns and stands in tense calculating thought. Her face has become like a sinister evil mask. Finally, as if making up her mind irrevocably, she comes to the table, tears off a slip of paper and writes two words on it. She tucks this paper in the sleeve of her dress and goes to the open window and calls*)

CHRISTINE: Adam! (*She moves toward the door to wait for him. Her eyes are caught by the eyes of her husband in the portrait over the fireplace. She stares at him with hatred and addresses him vindictively, half under her breath.*) You can thank Vinnie, Ezra! (*She goes to the door and reaches it just as* BRANT *appears from the hall. She takes his hand and draws him into the room, closing the door behind him. One is immediately struck by the resemblance between his face and that of the portrait of* EZRA MANNON.)

BRANT (*glancing uneasily at her, as they come to the center of the room*): She knows—?

CHRISTINE: Yes. She followed me to New York. And she's found out who you are too, Adam.

BRANT (*with a grim smile*): I know. She got that out of me—the proof of it, at any rate. Before I knew what was up I'd given myself away.

CHRISTINE: She must have noticed your resemblance to Orin. I was afraid that might start her thinking.

BRANT (*sees the portrait for the first time. Instantly his body shifts to a fighting tenseness. It is as if he were going to spring at the figure in the painting. He says slowly*): That, I take it, is General Mannon?

CHRISTINE: Judge Mannon then. Don't forget he used to be a judge. He won't forget it.

BRANT (*his eyes still fixed on the portrait—comes and sits in* MANNON's *chair on the left of table. Unconsciously he takes the same attitude as* MANNON, *sitting erect, his hands on the arms of the chair—slowly*): Does Orin by any chance resemble his father?

CHRISTINE (*stares at him—agitatedly*): No! Of course not! What put such a stupid idea in your head?

BRANT: It would be damned queer if you fell in love with me because I recalled Ezra Mannon to you!

CHRISTINE (*going to him and putting an arm around his shoulder*): No, no, I tell you! It was Orin you made me think of! It was Orin!

BRANT: I remember that night we were introduced and I heard the name Mrs. Ezra Mannon! By God, how I hated you then for being his! I thought, by God, I'll take her from him and that'll be part of my revenge! And out of that hatred my love came! It's damned queer, isn't it?

CHRISTINE (*hugging him to her*): Are you going to let him take me from you now, Adam?

BRANT (*passionately*): You ask that!

CHRISTINE: You swear you won't—no matter what you must do?

BRANT: By God, I swear it!

CHRISTINE (*kisses him*): Remember that oath! (*She glances at the portrait—then turns back to* BRANT *with a little shiver—nervously*) What made you sit there? It's his chair. I've so often seen him sitting there— (*forcing a little laugh*) Your silly talk about resemblances— Don't sit there. Come. Bring that chair over here. (*She moves to the chair at right center. He brings the chair at right of table close to hers.*)

BRANT: We've got to decide what we must do. The time for skulking and lying is over—and by God I'm glad of it! It's a coward's game I have no stomach for! (*He has placed the chair beside hers. She is staring at the portrait.*) Why don't you sit down, Christine?

CHRISTINE (*slowly*): I was thinking—perhaps we had better go to the sitting-room. (*then defiantly*) No! I've been afraid of you long enough, Ezra! (*She sits down.*)

BRANT: I felt there was something wrong the moment I saw her. I tried my damndest to put her off the course by giving her some soft-soap—as you'd told me to do to blind her. (*frowning*) That was a mistake, Christine. It made her pay too much attention to me—and opened her eyes!

CHRISTINE: Oh, I know I've made one blunder after

another. It's as if love drove me on to do everything I shouldn't. I never should have brought you to this house. Seeing you in New York should have been enough for me. But I loved you too much. I wanted you every possible moment we could steal! And I simply couldn't believe that he ever would come home. I prayed that he should be killed in the war so intensely that I finally believed it would surely happen! *(with savage intensity)* Oh, if he were only dead!

BRANT: That chance is finished now.

CHRISTINE *(slowly—without looking at him)*: Yes—in that way.

BRANT *(stares at her)*: What do you mean? *(She remains silent. He changes the subject uneasily.)* There's only one thing to do! When he comes home I'll wait for him and not give Vinnie the satisfaction of telling him. I'll tell him myself. *(vindictively)* By God! I'd give my soul to see his face when he knows you love Marie Brantôme's son! And then I'll take you away openly and laugh at him! And if he tries to stop me—! *(He stops and glances with savage hatred at the portrait.)*

CHRISTINE: What would you do then?

BRANT: If ever I laid hands on him, I'd kill him!

CHRISTINE: And then? You would be hanged for murder! And where would I be? There would be nothing left for me but to kill myself!

BRANT: If I could catch him alone, where no one would interfere, and let the best man come out alive—as I've often seen it done in the West!

CHRISTINE: This isn't the West.

BRANT: I could insult him on the street before everyone and make him fight me! I could let him shoot first and then kill him in self-defense.

CHRISTINE *(scornfully)*: Do you imagine you could force him to fight a duel with you? Don't you know duelling is illegal? Oh, no! He'd simply feel bound to do his duty as a former judge and have you arrested! *(She adds calculatingly, seeing he is boiling inside)* It would be a poor revenge for your mother's death to let him make you a laughing stock!

BRANT: But when I take you off, the laugh will be on him! You can come on the "Flying Trades."

CHRISTINE *(calculatingly reproachful)*: I don't think you'd propose that, Adam, if you stopped thinking of your revenge for a moment and thought of me! Don't you realize he would never divorce me, out of spite? What would I be in the world's eyes? My life would be ruined and I would ruin yours! You'd grow to hate me!

BRANT *(passionately)*: Don't talk like that! It's a lie and you know it!

CHRISTINE *(with bitter yearning)*: If I could only believe that, Adam! But I'll grow old so soon! And I'm afraid of time! *(then abruptly changing tone)* As for

my sailing on your ship, you'll find you won't have a ship! He'll see to it you lose this command and get you blacklisted so you'll have no chance of getting another.

BRANT *(angrily)*: Aye! He can do that if he sets about it. There are twice as many skippers as ships these days.

CHRISTINE *(calculatingly—without looking at him)*: If he had only been killed, we could be married now and I would bring you my share of the Mannon estate. That would only be justice. It's yours by right. It's what his father stole from yours.

BRANT: That's true enough, damn him!

CHRISTINE: You wouldn't have to worry about commands or owners' favors then. You could buy your own ship and be your own master!

BRANT *(yearningly)*: That's always been my dream—some day to own my own clipper! And Clark and Dawson would be willing to sell the "Flying Trades." *(then forgetting everything in his enthusiasm)* You've seen her, Christine. She's as beautiful a ship as you're a woman. Aye, the two of you are like sisters. If she was mine, I'd take you on a honeymoon then! To China—and on the voyage back, we'd stop at the South Pacific Islands I've told you about. By God, there's the right place for love and a honeymoon!

CHRISTINE *(slowly)*: Yes—but Ezra is alive!

BRANT *(brought back to earth—gloomily)*: I know it's only a dream.

CHRISTINE *(turning to stare at him—slowly)*: You can have your dream—and I can have mine. There is a way. *(then turning away again)* You remember my telling you he had written complaining of pains about his heart?

BRANT: You're surely not hoping—

CHRISTINE: No. He said it was nothing serious. But I've let it be known that he has heart trouble. I went to see our old family doctor and told him about Ezra's letter. I pretended to be dreadfully worried, until I got him worried too. He's the town's worst old gossip. I'm sure everyone knows about Ezra's weak heart by this time.

BRANT: What are you driving at, Christine?

CHRISTINE: Something I've been thinking of ever since I realized he might soon come home. And now that Vinnie—but even if we didn't have to consider her, it'd be the only way! I couldn't fool him long. He's a strange, hidden man. His silence always creeps into my thoughts. Even if he never spoke, I would feel what was in his mind and some night, lying beside him, it would drive me mad and I'd have to kill his silence by screaming out the truth! *(She has been staring before her—now she suddenly turns on BRANT—slowly)* If he died suddenly now, no one would think it was anything but heart failure. I've been reading a book in

Father's medical library. I saw it there one day a few weeks ago—it was as if some fate in me forced me to see it! *(She reaches in the sleeve of her dress and takes out the slip of paper she had written on.)* I've written something here. I want you to get it for me. *(His fingers close on it mechanically. He stares at it with a strange stupid dread. She hurries on so as not to give him time for reflection.)* The work on the "Flying Trades" is all finished, isn't it? You sail to Boston tomorrow, to wait for cargo?

BRANT *(dully)*: Aye.

CHRISTINE: Get this at some druggist's down by the waterfront the minute you reach there. You can make up some story about a sick dog on your ship. As soon as you get it, mail it to me here. I'll be on the lookout, so Vinnie will never know it came. Then you must wait on the "Flying Trades" until you hear from me or I come to you—afterward!

BRANT *(dully)*: But how can you do it—so no one will suspect?

CHRISTINE: He's taking medicine. I'll give him his medicine. Oh, I've planned it carefully.

BRANT: But—if he dies suddenly, won't Vinnie—

CHRISTINE: There'll be no reason for her to suspect. She's worried already about his heart. Besides, she may hate me, but she would never think—

BRANT: Orin will be coming home, too.

CHRISTINE: Orin will believe anything I want him to. As for the people here, they'd never dream of such a thing in the Mannon house! And the sooner I do it, the less suspicion there'll be! They will think the excitement of coming home and the reaction were too much for his weak heart! Doctor Blake will think so. I'll see that's what he thinks.

BRANT *(harshly)*: Poison! It's a coward's trick!

CHRISTINE *(with fierce scorn now, seeing the necessity of goading him)*: Do you think you would be braver to give me up to him and let him take away your ship?

BRANT: No!

CHRISTINE: Didn't you say you wanted to kill him?

BRANT: Aye! But I'd give him his chance!

CHRISTINE: Did he give your mother her chance?

BRANT *(aroused)*: No, damn him!

CHRISTINE: Then what makes you suddenly so scrupulous about his death? *(with a sneer)* It must be the Mannon in you coming out! Are you going to prove, the first time your love is put to a real test, that you're a weak coward like your father?

BRANT: Christine! If it was any man said that to me—!

CHRISTINE *(passionately)*: Have you thought of this side of his homecoming—that he's coming back to my bed? If you love me as much as you claim, I should think that would rid you of any scruples! If it was a question of some woman taking you from me, I wouldn't have qualms about which was or wasn't the way to kill her! *(more tauntingly)* But perhaps your love has been only a lie you told me—to take the sneaking revenge on him of being a backstairs lover! Perhaps—

BRANT *(stung, grabbing her by the shoulders—fiercely)*: Stop it! I'll do anything you want! You know it! *(then with a change to somber grimness—putting the paper in his pocket)* And you're right. I'm a damn fool to have any feeling about how Ezra Mannon dies!

CHRISTINE *(A look of exultant satisfaction comes to her face as she sees he is definitely won over now. She throws her arms around him and kisses him passionately.)*: Ah! Now you're the man I love again, not a hypocritical Mannon! Promise me, no more cowardly romantic scruples! Promise me!

BRANT: I promise. *(The boom of a cannon sounds from the fort that guards the harbor. He and CHRISTINE start frightenedly and stand staring at each other. Another boom comes, reverberating, rattling the windows. CHRISTINE recovers herself.)*

CHRISTINE: You hear? That's the salute to his homecoming! *(She kisses him—with fierce insistence)* Remember your mother's death! Remember your dream of your own ship! Above all, remember you'll have me!—all your own—your wife! *(then urgently)* And now you must go! She'll be coming back—and you're not good at hiding your thoughts. *(urging him toward the door)* Hurry! I don't want you to meet her! *(The cannon at the fort keep booming at regular intervals until the end of the scene. BRANT goes out in the hall and a moment later the front door is heard closing after him. CHRISTINE hurries from the door to the window and watches him from behind the curtains as he goes down the drive. She is in a state of tense, exultant excitement. Then, as if an idea had suddenly come to her, she speaks to his retreating figure with a strange sinister air of elation.)* You'll never dare leave me now, Adam—for your ships or your sea or your naked Island girls—when I grow old and ugly! *(She turns back from the window. Her eyes are caught by the eyes of her husband in the portrait and for a moment she stares back into them, as if fascinated. Then she jerks her glance away and, with a little shudder she cannot repress, turns and walks quickly from the room and closes the door behind her.)*

CURTAIN

ACT 3

(The same as Act 1, Scene One—exterior of the MANNON house. It is around nine o'clock of a night a week later. The light of a half moon falls on the house, giving it an unreal, detached, eerie quality. The pure white temple front seems more than ever like an incongruous mask fixed on the somber, stone house. All the shutters are closed. The

*white columns of the portico cast black bars of shadow on
the gray wall behind them. The trunk of the pine at right is
an ebony pillar, its branches a mass of shade.*

LAVINIA *is sitting on the top of the steps to the portico.
She is dressed, as before, severely in black. Her thin figure,
seated stiffly upright, arms against her sides, the legs close
together, the shoulders square, the head upright, is like that
of an Egyptian statue. She is staring straight before her.
The sound of* SETH's *thin, aged baritone mournfully
singing the chanty "Shenandoah" is heard from down the
drive, off right front. He is approaching the house and the
song draws quickly nearer.)*

> *Oh, Shenandoah, I long to hear you
> A-way, my rolling river.
> Oh, Shenandoah, I can't get near you
> Way-ay, I'm bound away
> Across the wide Missouri.*
>
> *Oh, Shenandoah, I love your daughter
> A-way, my rolling river.*

*(He enters right front. He is a bit drunk but holding his
liquor well. He walks up by the lilacs starting the next line
"Oh, Shenandoah"—then suddenly sees* LAVINIA *on the
steps and stops abruptly, a bit sheepish.)*

LAVINIA *(disapprovingly)*: This is the second time this
week I've caught you coming home like this.

SETH *(unabashed, approaches the steps—with a grin)*: I'm
aimin' to do my patriotic duty, Vinnie. The first
time was celebratin' Lee's surrender and this time
is drownin' my sorrow for the President gittin'
shot! And the third'll be when your Paw gits home!

LAVINIA: Father might arrive tonight.

SETH: Gosh, Vinnie, I never calc'lated he could git
here so soon!

LAVINIA: Evidently you didn't. He'd give you fits if he
caught you drunk. Oh, I don't believe he'll come,
but it's possible he might.

SETH *(is evidently trying to pull himself together. He suddenly leans over toward her and, lowering his voice,
asks soberly)*: Did you find out anything about that
Brant?

LAVINIA *(sharply)*: Yes. There's no connection. It was
just a silly idea of yours.

SETH *(stares at her—then understandingly)*: Wal, if you
want it left that way, I'll leave it that way. *(A pause.
He continues to stand looking at her, while she stares in
front of her.)*

LAVINIA *(in a low voice)*: What was that Marie Brantôme like, Seth?

SETH: Marie? She was always laughin' and singin'—
frisky and full of life—with something free and
wild about her like an animile. Purty she was, too!
(then he adds) Hair just the color of your Maw's
and yourn she had.

LAVINIA: I know.

SETH: Oh, everyone took to Marie—couldn't help it.
Even your Paw. He was only a boy then, but he was
crazy about her, too, like a youngster would be.
His mother was stern with him, while Marie, she
made a fuss over him and petted him.

LAVINIA: Father, too!

SETH: Ayeh—but he hated her worse than anyone
when it got found out she was his Uncle David's
fancy woman.

LAVINIA: *(in a low voice, as if to herself, staring at the
house)* It's all so strange! It frightens me! *(She
checks herself abruptly—turns to* SETH, *curtly)* I don't
believe that about Father. You've had too much
whiskey. Go to bed and sleep it off. *(She walks up
the steps again.)*

SETH *(gazes at her with understanding)*: Ayeh. *(then
warningly, making a surreptitious signal as he sees the
front door opening behind her)* Ssstt! (CHRISTINE
*appears outlined in the light from the hall. She is
dressed in a gown of green velvet that sets off her hair.
The light behind her glows along the edges of the dress
and in the color of her hair. She closes the door and
comes into the moonlight at the edge of the steps, standing above and a little to the right of* LAVINIA. *The
moonlight, falling full on them, accentuates strangely
the resemblance between their faces and at the same time
the hostile dissimilarity in body and dress.* LAVINIA *does
not turn or give any sign of knowing her mother is
behind her. There is a second's uncomfortable silence.*
SETH *moves off left.)* Wal, I'll trot along! *(He disappears around the corner of the house. There is a pause.
Then* CHRISTINE *speaks in a dry mocking tone.)*

CHRISTINE: What are you moongazing at? Puritan
maidens shouldn't peer too inquisitively into
Spring! Isn't beauty an abomination and love a
vile thing? *(She laughs with bitter mockery—then
tauntingly)* Why don't you marry Peter? You don't
want to be left an old maid, do you?

LAVINIA *(quietly)*: You needn't hope to get rid of me
that way. I'm not marrying anyone. I've got my
duty to Father.

CHRISTINE: Duty! How often I've heard that word in
this house! Well, you can't say I didn't do mine all
these years. But there comes an end.

LAVINIA *(grimly)*: And there comes another end—and
you must do your duty again!

CHRISTINE *(starts as if to retort defiantly—then says calmly)*:
Yes, I realize that.

LAVINIA *(after a pause—suspiciously)*: What's going on
at the bottom of your mind? I know you're plotting something!

CHRISTINE *(controlling a start)*: Don't be stupid, please!

LAVINIA: Are you planning how you can see Adam
again? You better not!

CHRISTINE *(calmly)*: I'm not so foolish. I said good-bye
once. Do you think I want to make it harder for
myself?

LAVINIA: Has it been hard for you? I'd never guess it—and I've been watching you.

CHRISTINE: I warned you you would have no chance to gloat! *(after a pause)* When do you expect your father home? You want me to play my part well when he comes, don't you?—for his sake. I'd like to be forewarned.

LAVINIA: His letter said he wouldn't wait until his brigade was disbanded but would try to get leave at once. He might arrive tonight—or tomorrow—or the next day. I don't know.

CHRISTINE: You think he might come tonight? *(then with a mocking smile)* So he's the beau you're waiting for in the spring moonlight! *(then after a pause)* But the night train got in long ago.

LAVINIA *(glances down the drive, left front—then starts to her feet excitedly)*: Here's someone! (CHRISTINE *slowly rises. There is the sound of footsteps. A moment later* EZRA MANNON *enters from left, front. He stops short in the shadow for a second and stands, erect and stiff, as if at attention, staring at his house, his wife and daughter. He is a tall, spare, big-boned man of fifty, dressed in the uniform of a Brigadier-General. One is immediately struck by the mask-like look of his face in repose, more pronounced in him than in the others. He is exactly like the portrait in his study, which we have seen in Act 2, except that his face is more lined and lean and the hair and beard are grizzled. His movements are exact and wooden and he has a mannerism of standing and sitting in stiff, posed attitudes that suggest the statues of military heroes. When he speaks, his deep voice has a hollow repressed quality, as if he were continually withholding emotion from it. His air is brusque and authoritative.)*

LAVINIA *(seeing the man's figure stop in the shadow—calls excitedly)*: Who's that?

MANNON *(stepping forward into the moonlight)*: It's I.

LAVINIA *(with a cry of joy)*: Father! *(She runs to him and throws her arms around him and kisses him.)* Oh, Father! *(She bursts into tears and hides her face against his shoulder.)*

MANNON *(embarrassed—patting her head—gruffly)*: Come! I thought I'd taught you never to cry.

LAVINIA *(obediently forcing back her tears)*: I'm sorry, Father—but I'm so happy!

MANNON *(awkwardly moved)*: Tears are queer tokens of happiness! But I appreciate your—your feeling.

CHRISTINE *(has slowly descended the steps, her eyes fixed on him—tensely)*: Is it really you, Ezra? We had just given up hope of your coming tonight.

MANNON *(going stiffly to meet her)*: Train was late. The railroad is jammed up. Everybody has got leave. *(He meets her at the foot of the steps and kisses her with a chill dignity—formally)* I am glad to see you, Christine. You are looking well. *(He steps back and stares at her—then in a voice that betrays a deep undercurrent of suppressed feeling)* You have changed,

somehow. You are prettier than ever—But you always were pretty.

CHRISTINE *(forcing a light tone)*: Compliments from one's husband! How gallant you've become, Ezra! *(then solicitously)* You must be terribly tired. Wouldn't you like to sit here on the steps for a while? The moonlight is so beautiful.

LAVINIA *(who has been hovering about jealously, now manages to worm herself between them—sharply)*: No. It's too damp out here. And Father must be hungry. *(taking his arm)* Come inside with me and I'll get you something to eat. You poor dear! You must be starved.

MANNON *(really revelling in his daughter's coddling but embarrassed before his wife—pulling his arm back—brusquely)*: No, thanks! I would rather rest here for a spell. Sit down, Vinnie. (CHRISTINE *sits on the top step at center; he sits on the middle step at right;* LAVINIA *on the lowest step at left. While they are doing this he keeps on talking in his abrupt sentences, as if he were trying to cover up some hidden uneasiness.)* I've got leave for a few days. Then I must go back and disband my brigade. Peace ought to be signed soon. The President's assassination is a frightful calamity. But it can't change the course of events.

LAVINIA: Poor man! It's dreadful he should die just at his moment of victory.

MANNON: Yes! *(then after a pause—somberly)* All victory ends in the defeat of death. That's sure. But does defeat end in the victory of death? That's what I wonder! *(They both stare at him,* LAVINIA *in surprise,* CHRISTINE *in uneasy wonder. A pause.)*

CHRISTINE: Where is Orin? Couldn't you get leave for him too?

MANNON *(hesitates—then brusquely)*: I've been keeping it from you. Orin was wounded.

LAVINIA: Wounded! You don't mean—badly hurt?

CHRISTINE *(half starting to her feet impulsively—with more of angry bitterness than grief)*: I knew it! I knew when you forced him into your horrible war—! *(then sinking back—tensely)* You needn't trouble to break the news gradually, Ezra. Orin is dead, isn't he?

LAVINIA: Don't say that! It isn't true, is it, Father?

MANNON *(curtly—a trace of jealousy in his tone)*: Of course it isn't! If your mother would permit me to finish instead of jumping at conclusions about her baby—! *(with a grim, proud satisfaction)* He's no baby now. I've made a man of him. He did one of the bravest things I've seen in the war. He was wounded in the head—a close shave but it turned out only a scratch. But he got brain fever from the shock. He's all right now. He was in a rundown condition, they say at the hospital. I never guessed it. Nerves. I wouldn't notice nerves. He's always been restless. *(half turning to* CHRISTINE*)* He gets that from you.

CHRISTINE: When will he be well enough to come home?

MANNON: Soon. The doctor advised a few more days' rest. He's still weak. He was out of his head for a long time. Acted as if he were a little boy again. Seemed to think you were with him. That is, he kept talking to "Mother."

CHRISTINE (*with a tense intake of breath*): Ah!

LAVINIA (*pityingly—with a tinge of scorn in her voice*): Poor Orin!

MANNON: I don't want you to baby him when he comes home, Christine. It would be bad for him to get tied to your apron strings again.

CHRISTINE: You needn't worry. That passed—when he left me. (*Another pause. Then* LAVINIA *speaks.*)

LAVINIA: How is the trouble with your heart, Father? I've been so afraid you might be making it out less serious than it really was to keep us from worrying.

MANNON (*gruffly*): If it was serious, I'd tell you, so you'd be prepared. If you'd seen as much of death as I have in the past four years, you wouldn't be afraid of it. (*suddenly jumping to his feet—brusquely*) Let's change the subject! I've had my fill of death. What I want now is to forget it. (*He turns and paces up and down to the right of steps.* LAVINIA *watches him worriedly.*) All I know is the pain is like a knife. It puts me out of commission while it lasts. The doctor gave me orders to avoid worry or any over-exertion or excitement.

CHRISTINE (*staring at him*): You don't look well. But probably that's because you're so tired. You must go to bed soon, Ezra.

MANNON (*comes to a stop in his pacing directly before her and looks into her eyes—a pause—then he says in a voice that he tries to make ordinary*): Yes, I want to—soon.

LAVINIA (*who has been watching him jealously—suddenly pulling him by the arm—with a childish volubility*): No! Not yet! Please, Father! You've only just come! We've hardly talked at all! (*defiantly to her mother*) How can you tell him he looks tired? He looks as well as I've ever seen him. (*then to her father, with a vindictive look at* CHRISTINE) We've so much to tell you. All about Captain Brant. (*If she had expected her mother to flinch at this, she is disappointed.* CHRISTINE *is prepared and remains unmoved beneath the searching, suspicious glance* MANNON *now directs at her.*)

MANNON: Vinnie wrote me you'd had company. I never heard of him. What business had he here?

CHRISTINE (*with an easy smile*): You had better ask Vinnie! He's her latest beau! She even went walking in the moonlight with him!

LAVINIA (*with a gasp at being defied so brazenly*): Oh!

MANNON (*now jealous and suspicious of his daughter*): I notice you didn't mention that in your letter, young lady!

LAVINIA: I only went walking once with him—and that was before— (*She checks herself abruptly.*)

MANNON: Before what?

LAVINIA: Before I knew he's the kind who chases after every woman he sees.

MANNON (*angrily to* CHRISTINE): A fine guest to receive in my absence!

LAVINIA: I believe he even thought Mother was flirting with him. That's why I felt it my duty to write you. You know how folks in town gossip, Father. I thought you ought to warn Mother she was foolish to allow him to come here.

MANNON: Foolish! It was downright—!

CHRISTINE (*coldly*): I would prefer not to discuss this until we are alone, Ezra—if you don't mind! And I think Vinnie is extremely inconsiderate the moment you're home—to annoy you with such ridiculous nonsense! (*She turns to* LAVINIA.) I think you've done enough mischief. Will you kindly leave us?

LAVINIA: No.

MANNON (*sharply*): Stop your squabbling, both of you! I hoped you had grown out of that nonsense! I won't have it in my house!

LAVINIA (*obediently*): Yes, Father.

MANNON: It must be your bedtime, Vinnie.

LAVINIA: Yes, Father. (*She comes and kisses him—excitedly*) Oh, I'm so happy you're here! Don't let Mother make you believe I— You're the only man I'll ever love! I'm going to stay with you!

MANNON (*patting her hair—with gruff tenderness*): I hope so. I want you to remain my little girl—for a while longer, at least. (*then suddenly catching* CHRISTINE's *scornful glance—pushes* LAVINIA *away—brusquely*) March now!

LAVINIA: Yes, Father. (*She goes up the steps past her mother without a look. Behind her mother, in the portico, she stops and turns.*) Don't let anything worry you, Father. I'll always take care of you. (*She goes in.* MANNON *looks at his wife who stares before her. He clears his throat as if about to say something—then starts pacing self-consciously up and down at the right of steps.*)

CHRISTINE (*forcing a gentle tone*): Sit down, Ezra. You will only make yourself more tired, keeping on your feet. (*He sits awkwardly two steps below her, on her left, turned sideways to face her. She asks with disarming simplicity*) Now please tell me just what it is you suspect me of?

MANNON (*taken aback*): What makes you think I suspect you?

CHRISTINE: Everything! I've felt your distrust from the moment you came. Your eyes have been probing me, as if you were a judge again and I were the prisoner.

MANNON (*guiltily*): I—?

CHRISTINE: And all on account of a stupid letter

Vinnie had no business to write. It seems to me a late day, when I am an old woman with grown-up children, to accuse me of flirting with a stupid ship captain!

MANNON (*impressed and relieved—placatingly*): There's no question of accusing you of that. I only think you've been foolish to give the gossips a chance to be malicious.

CHRISTINE: Are you sure that's all you have in your heart against me?

MANNON: Yes! Of course! What else? (*patting her hand embarrassedly*) We'll say no more about it. (*Then he adds gruffly*) But I'd like you to explain how this Brant happened—

CHRISTINE: I'm only too glad to! I met him at Father's. Father has taken a fancy to him for some reason. So when he called here I couldn't be rude, could I? I hinted that his visits weren't welcome, but men of his type don't understand hints. But he's only been here four times in all, I think. And as for there having been gossip, that's nonsense! The only talk has been that he came to court Vinnie! You can ask anyone in town.

MANNON: Damn his impudence! It was your duty to tell him flatly he wasn't wanted!

CHRISTINE (*forcing a contrite air*): Well, I must confess I didn't mind his coming as much as I might have—for one reason. He always brought me news of Father. Father's been sick for the past year, as I wrote you. (*then with a twitch of the lips, as if she were restraining a derisive smile*) You can't realize what a strain I've been under—worrying about Father and Orin and—you.

MANNON (*deeply moved, turns to her and takes her hand in both of his—awkwardly*): Christine—I deeply regret—having been unjust. (*He kisses her hand impulsively—then embarrassed by this show of emotion, adds in a gruff, joking tone*) Afraid old Johnny Reb would pick me off, were you?

CHRISTINE (*controlling a wild impulse to burst into derisive laughter*): Do you need to ask that? (*A pause. He stares at her, fascinated and stirred.*)

MANNON (*finally blurts out*): I've dreamed of coming home to you, Christine! (*leans toward her, his voice trembling with desire and a feeling of strangeness and awe—touching her hair with an awkward caress*) You're beautiful! You look more beautiful than ever—and strange to me. I don't know you. You're younger. I feel like an old man beside you. Only your hair is the same—your strange beautiful hair I always—

CHRISTINE (*with a start of repulsion, shrinking from his hand*): Don't! (*then as he turns away, hurt and resentful at this rebuff—hastily*) I'm sorry, Ezra. I didn't mean—I—I'm nervous tonight. (MANNON *paces to the right and stands looking at the trees.* CHRISTINE *stares at his back with hatred. She sighs*

with affected weariness and leans back and closes her eyes.)

CHRISTINE: I'm tired, Ezra.

MANNON (*blurts out*): I shouldn't have bothered you with that foolishness about Brant tonight. (*He forces a strained smile.*) But I was jealous a mite, to tell you the truth. (*He forces himself to turn and, seeing her eyes are shut, suddenly comes and leans over her awkwardly, as if to kiss her, then is stopped by some strangeness he feels about her still face.*)

CHRISTINE (*feeling his desire and instinctively shrinking—without opening her eyes*): Why do you look at me like that?

MANNON (*turns away guiltily*): Like what? (*uneasily*) How do you know? Your eyes are shut. (*Then, as if some burden of depression were on him that he had to throw off, he blurts out hastily*) I can't get used to home yet. It's so lonely. I've got used to the feel of camps with thousands of men around me at night—a sense of protection, maybe! (*suddenly uneasy again*) Don't keep your eyes shut like that! Don't be so still! (*then, as she opens her eyes—with an explosive appeal*) God, I want to talk to you, Christine! I've got to explain some things—inside me—to my wife—try to, anyway! (*He sits down beside her.*) Shut your eyes again! I can talk better. It has always been hard for me to talk—about feelings. I never could when you looked at me. Your eyes were always so—so full of silence! That is, since we've been married. Not before, when I was courting you. They used to speak then. They made me talk—because they answered.

CHRISTINE (*her eyes closed—tensely*): Don't talk, Ezra.

MANNON (*as if he had determined, once started, to go on doggedly without heeding any interruption*): It was seeing death all the time in this war got me to thinking these things. Death was so common, it didn't mean anything. That freed me to think of life. Queer, isn't it? Death made me think of life. Before that life had only made me think of death!

CHRISTINE (*without opening her eyes*): Why are you talking of death?

MANNON: That's always been the Mannons' way of thinking. They went to the white meeting-house on Sabbaths and meditated on death. Life was a dying. Being born was starting to die. Death was being born. (*shaking his head with a dogged bewilderment*) How in hell people ever got such notions! That white meeting-house. It stuck in my mind—clean-scrubbed and whitewashed—a temple of death! But in this war I've seen too many white walls splattered with blood that counted no more than dirty water. I've seen dead men scattered about, no more important than rubbish to be got rid of. That made the white meeting-house seem meaningless—making so much solemn fuss over death!

CHRISTINE (*opens her eyes and stares at him with a strange terror*): What has this talk of death to do with me?

MANNON (*avoiding her glance—insistently*): Shut your eyes again. Listen and you'll know. (*She shuts her eyes. He plods on with a note of desperation in his voice.*) I thought about my life—lying awake nights—and about your life. In the middle of battle I'd think maybe in a minute I'll be dead. But my life as just me ending, that didn't appear worth a thought one way or another. But listen, me as your husband being killed that seemed queer and wrong—like something dying that had never lived. Then all the years we've been man and wife would rise up in my mind and I would try to look at them. But nothing was clear except that there'd always been some barrier between us—a wall hiding us from each other! I would try to make up my mind exactly what that wall was but I never could discover. (*with a clumsy appealing gesture*) Do you know?

CHRISTINE (*tensely*): I don't know what you're talking about.

MANNON: But you've known it was there! Don't lie, Christine! (*He looks at her still face and closed eyes, imploring her to reassure him—then blunders on doggedly*) Maybe you've always known you didn't love me. I call to mind the Mexican War. I could see you wanted me to go. I had a feeling you'd grown to hate me. Did you? (*She doesn't answer.*) That was why I went. I was hoping I might get killed. Maybe you were hoping that too. Were you?

CHRISTINE (*stammers*): No, no, I—What makes you say such things?

MANNON: When I came back you had turned to your new baby, Orin. I was hardly alive for you any more. I saw that. I tried not to hate Orin. I turned to Vinnie, but a daughter's not a wife. Then I made up my mind I'd do my work in the world and leave you alone in your life and not care. That's why the shipping wasn't enough—why I became a judge and a mayor and such vain truck, and why folks in town look on me as so able! Ha! Able for what? Not for what I wanted most in life! Not for your love! No! Able only to keep my mind from thinking of what I'd lost! (*He stares at her—then asks pleadingly*) For you did love me before we were married. You won't deny that, will you?

CHRISTINE (*desperately*): I don't deny anything!

MANNON (*drawing himself up with a stern pride and dignity and surrendering himself like a commander against hopeless odds*): All right, then. I came home to surrender to you—what's inside me. I love you. I loved you then, and all the years between, and I love you now.

CHRISTINE (*distractedly*): Ezra! Please!

MANNON: I want that said! Maybe you have forgotten it. I wouldn't blame you. I guess I haven't said it or showed it much—ever. Something queer in me keeps me mum about the things I'd like most to say—keeps me hiding the things I'd like to show. Something keeps me sitting numb in my own heart—like a statue of a dead man in a town square. (*Suddenly he reaches over and takes her hand.*) I want to find what that wall is marriage put between us! You've got to help me smash it down! We have twenty good years still before us! I've been thinking of what we could do to get back to each other. I've a notion if we'd leave the children and go off on a voyage together—to the other side of the world—find some island where we could be alone a while. You'll find I have changed, Christine. I'm sick of death! I want life! Maybe you could love me now! (*in a note of final desperate pleading*) I've got to make you love me!

CHRISTINE (*pulls her hand away from him and springs to her feet wildly*): For God's sake, stop talking. I don't know what you're saying. Leave me alone! What must be, must be! You make me weak! (*then abruptly*) It's getting late.

MANNON (*terribly wounded, withdrawn into his stiff soldier armor—takes out his watch mechanically*): Yes—six past eleven. Time to turn in. (*He ascends two steps, his face toward the door. He says bitterly*) You tell me to stop talking! By God, that's funny!

CHRISTINE (*collected now and calculating—takes hold of his arm, seductively*): I meant—what is the good of words? There is no wall between us. I love you.

MANNON (*grabs her by the shoulders and stares into her face*): Christine! I'd give my soul to believe that—but—I'm afraid! (*She kisses him. He presses her fiercely in his arms—passionately*) Christine! (*The door behind him is opened and* LAVINIA *appears at the edge of the portico behind and above him. She wears slippers over her bare feet and has a dark dressing-gown over her night dress. She shrinks back from their embrace with aversion. They separate, startled.*)

MANNON (*embarrassed—irritably*): Thought you'd gone to bed, young lady!

LAVINIA (*woodenly*): I didn't feel sleepy. I thought I'd walk a little. It's such a fine night.

CHRISTINE: We are just going to bed. Your father is tired. (*She moves up, past her daughter, taking* MANNON*'s hand, leading him after her to the door.*)

MANNON: No time for a walk, if you ask me. See you turn in soon.

LAVINIA: Yes, Father.

MANNON: Good night. (*The door closes behind them.* LAVINIA *stands staring before her—then walks stiffly down the steps and stands again. Light appears between the chinks of the shutters in the bedroom on the second floor to the left. She looks up.*)

LAVINIA (*in an anguish of jealous hatred*): I hate you! You steal even Father's love from me again! You stole all love from me when I was born! *(then almost with a sob, hiding her face in her hands)* Oh, Mother! Why have you done this to me? What harm had I done you? *(then looking up at the window again—with passionate disgust)* Father, how can you love that shameless harlot? *(then frenziedly)* I can't bear it! I won't! It's my duty to tell him about her! I will! *(She calls desperately)* Father! Father! *(The shutter of the bedroom is pushed open and* MANNON *leans out.)*

MANNON *(sharply)*: What is it? Don't shout like that!

LAVINIA *(stammers lamely)*: I—I remembered I forgot to say good night, Father.

MANNON *(exasperated)*: Good heavens! What— *(then gently)* Oh—all right—good night, Vinnie. Get to bed soon, like a good girl.

LAVINIA: Yes, Father. Good night. *(He goes back in the bedroom and pulls the shutter closed. She stands staring fascinatedly up at the window, wringing her hands in a pitiful desperation.)*

CURTAIN

ACT 4

(EZRA MANNON's bedroom. A big four-poster bed is at rear, center, the foot front, the head against the rear wall. A small stand, with a candle on it, is by the head of the bed on the left. To the left of the stand is a door leading into CHRISTINE's room. The door is open. In the left wall are two windows. At left, front, is a table with a lamp on it and a chair beside it. In the right wall, front, is a door leading to the hall. Further back, against the wall, is a bureau.

None of these details can be discerned at first because the room is in darkness, except for what moonlight filters feebly through the shutters. It is around dawn of the following morning.

CHRISTINE's form can be made out, a pale ghost in the darkness, as she slips slowly and stealthily from the bed. She tiptoes to the table, left front, and picks up a light-colored dressing-gown that is flung over the chair and puts it on. She stands listening for some sound from the bed. A pause. Then MANNON's voice comes suddenly from the bed, dull and lifeless.)

MANNON: Christine.

CHRISTINE *(starts violently—in a strained voice)*: Yes.

MANNON: Must be near daybreak, isn't it?

CHRISTINE: Yes. It is beginning to get gray.

MANNON: What made you jump when I spoke? Is my voice so strange to you?

CHRISTINE: I thought you were asleep.

MANNON: I haven't been able to sleep. I've been lying here thinking. What makes you so uneasy?

CHRISTINE: I haven't been able to sleep either.

MANNON: You slunk out of bed so quietly.

CHRISTINE: I didn't want to wake you.

MANNON *(bitterly)*: Couldn't you bear it—lying close to me?

CHRISTINE: I didn't want to disturb you by tossing around.

MANNON: We'd better light the light and talk a while.

CHRISTINE *(with dread)*: I don't want to talk! I prefer the dark.

MANNON: I want to see you. *(He takes matches from the stand by the bed and lights the candle on it.* CHRISTINE *hastily sits down in the chair by the table, pushing it so she sits facing left, front, with her face turned three-quarters away from him. He pushes his back up against the head of the bed in a half-sitting position. His face, with the flickering candle light on its side, has a grim, bitter expression.)* You like the dark where you can't see your old man of a husband, is that it?

CHRISTINE: I wish you wouldn't talk like that, Ezra. If you are going to say stupid things, I'll go in my own room. *(She gets to her feet but keeps her face turned away from him.)*

MANNON: Wait! *(then a note of pleading in his voice)* Don't go. I don't want to be alone. *(She sits again in the same position as before. He goes on humbly.)* I didn't mean to say those things. I guess there's bitterness inside me—my own cussedness, maybe—and sometimes it gets out before I can stop it.

CHRISTINE: You have always been bitter.

MANNON: Before we married?

CHRISTINE: I don't remember.

MANNON: You don't want to remember you ever loved me!

CHRISTINE *(tensely)*: I don't want to talk of the past! *(abruptly changing the subject)* Did you hear Vinnie the first part of the night? She was pacing up and down before the house like a sentry guarding you. She didn't go to bed until two. I heard the clock strike.

MANNON: There is one who loves me, at least! *(then after a pause)* I feel strange, Christine.

CHRISTINE: You mean—your heart? You don't think you are going to be—taken ill, do you?

MANNON *(harshly)*: No! *(a pause—then accusingly)* Is that what you're waiting for? Is that why you were so willing to give yourself tonight? Were you hoping—?

CHRISTINE *(springing up)*: Ezra! Stop talking like that! I can't stand it! *(She moves as if to go into her own room.)*

MANNON: Wait! I'm sorry I said that. *(Then, as she sits down again, he goes on gloomily.)* It isn't my heart. It's something uneasy troubling my mind—as if something in me was listening, watching, waiting for something to happen.

CHRISTINE: Waiting for what to happen?

MANNON: I don't know. *(A pause—then he goes on somberly.)* This house is not my house. This is not my room nor my bed. They are empty—waiting for someone to move in! And you are not my wife! You are waiting for something!

CHRISTINE (*beginning to snap under the strain—jumps to her feet again*): What would I be waiting for?

MANNON: For death—to set you free!

CHRISTINE: Leave me alone! Stop nagging at me with your crazy suspicions! (*then anger and hatred come into her voice*) Not your wife! You acted as if I were your wife—your property—not so long ago!

MANNON (*with bitter scorn*): Your body? What are bodies to me? I've seen too many rotting in the sun to make grass greener! Ashes to ashes, dirt to dirt! Is that your notion of love? Do you think I married a body? (*then, as if all the bitterness and hurt in him had suddenly burst its dam*) You were lying to me tonight as you've always lied! You were only pretending love! You let me take you as if you were a nigger slave I'd bought at auction! You made me appear a lustful beast in my own eyes!—as you've always done since our first marriage night! I would feel cleaner now if I had gone to a brothel! I would feel more honor between myself and life!

CHRISTINE (*in a stifled voice*): Look out, Ezra! I won't stand—

MANNON (*with a harsh laugh*): And I had hoped my homecoming would mark a new beginning—new love between us! I told you my secret feelings. I tore my insides out for you—thinking you'd understand! By God, I'm an old fool!

CHRISTINE (*her voice grown strident*): Did you think you could make me weak—make me forget all the years? Oh no, Ezra! It's too late! (*Then her voice changes, as if she had suddenly resolved on a course of action, and becomes deliberately taunting.*) You want the truth? You've guessed it! You've used me, you've given me children, but I've never once been yours! I never could be! And whose fault is it? I loved you when I married you! I wanted to give myself! But you made me so I couldn't give! You filled me with disgust!

MANNON (*furiously*): You say that to me! (*then trying to calm himself—stammers*) No! Be quiet! We mustn't fight! I mustn't lose my temper! It will bring on—!

CHRISTINE (*goading him with calculating cruelty*): Oh, no! You needn't adopt that pitiful tone! You wanted the truth and you're going to hear it now!

MANNON (*frightened—almost pleading*): Be quiet, Christine!

CHRISTINE: I've lied about everything! I lied about Captain Brant! He is Marie Brantôme's son! And it was I he came to see, not Vinnie! I made him come!

MANNON (*seized with fury*): You dared—! You—! The son of that—!

CHRISTINE: Yes, I dared! And all my trips to New York weren't to visit Father but to be with Adam! He's gentle and tender, he's everything you've never been. He's what I've longed for all these years with you—a lover! I love him! So now you know the truth!

MANNON (*in a frenzy—struggling to get out of bed*): You—you whore—I'll kill you! (*Suddenly he falls back, groaning, doubled up on his left side, with intense pain.*)

CHRISTINE (*with savage satisfaction*): Ah! (*She hurries through the doorway into her room and immediately returns with a small box in her hand. He is facing away from her door, and, even if the intense pain left him any perception, he could not notice her departure and return, she moves so silently.*)

MANNON (*gaspingly*): Quick—medicine!

CHRISTINE (*turned away from him, takes a pellet from the box, asking tensely as she does so*): Where is your medicine?

MANNON: On the stand! Hurry!

CHRISTINE: Wait. I have it now. (*She pretends to take something from the stand by the head of the bed—then holds out the pellet and a glass of water which is on the stand.*) Here. (*He turns to her, groaning and opens his mouth. She puts the pellet on his tongue and presses the glass of water to his lips.*) Now drink.

MANNON (*takes a swallow of water—then suddenly a wild look of terror comes over his face. He gasps*): That's not—my medicine! (*She shrinks back to the table, the hand with the box held out behind her, as if seeking a hiding place. Her fingers release the box on the table top and she brings her hand in front of her as if instinctively impelled to prove to him she has nothing. His eyes are fixed on her in a terrible accusing glare. He tries to call for help but his voice fades to a wheezy whisper.*) Help! Vinnie! (*He falls back in a coma, breathing stertorously.* CHRISTINE *stares at him fascinatedly—then starts with terror as she hears a noise from the hall and frantically snatches up the box from the table and holds it behind her back, turning to face the door as it opens and* LAVINIA *appears in the doorway. She is dressed as at the end of Act 3, in nightgown, wrapper, and slippers. She stands, dazed and frightened and hesitating, as if she had just awakened.*)

LAVINIA: I had a horrible dream—I thought I heard Father calling me—it woke me up—

CHRISTINE (*trembling with guilty terror—stammers*): He just had—an attack.

LAVINIA (*hurries to the bed*): Father! (*She puts her arms around him.*) He's fainted!

CHRISTINE: No. He's all right now. Let him sleep. (*At this moment* MANNON, *with a last dying effort, straightens up in a sitting position in* LAVINIA's *arms, his eyes glaring at his wife and manages to raise his arm and point an accusing finger at her.*)

MANNON (*gasps*): She's guilty—not medicine! (*He falls back limply.*)

LAVINIA: Father! *(Frightenedly she feels for his pulse, puts her ear against his chest to listen for a heartbeat.)*

CHRISTINE: Let him alone. He's asleep.

LAVINIA: He's dead!

CHRISTINE *(repeats mechanically)*: Dead? *(then in a strange flat tone)* I hope—he rests in peace.

LAVINIA *(turning on her with hatred)*: Don't you dare pretend—! You wanted him to die! You— *(She stops and stares at her mother with a horrified suspicion—then harshly accusing)* Why did he point at you like that? Why did he say you were guilty? Answer me!

CHRISTINE *(stammers)*: I told him—Adam was my lover.

LAVINIA *(aghast)*: You told him that—when you knew his heart—! Oh! You did it on purpose! You murdered him!

CHRISTINE: No—it was your fault—you made him suspicious—he kept talking of love and death—he forced me to tell him! *(Her voice becomes thick, as if she were drowsy and fighting off sleep. Her eyes half close.)*

LAVINIA *(grabbing her by the shoulders—fiercely)*: Listen! Look at me! He said "not medicine"! What did he mean?

CHRISTINE *(keeping the hand with the poison pressed against her back)*: I—I don't know.

LAVINIA: You do know! What was it? Tell me!

CHRISTINE *(with a last effort of will manages to draw herself up and speak with a simulation of outraged feeling)*: Are you accusing your mother of—

LAVINIA: Yes! I—! *(then distractedly)* No—you can't be that evil!

CHRISTINE *(her strength gone—swaying weakly)*: I don't know what—you're talking about. *(She edges away from LAVINIA toward her bedroom door, the hand with the poison stretched out behind her—weakly)* I—feel faint. I must go—and lie down. I— *(She turns as if to run into the room, takes a tottering step—then her knees suddenly buckle under her and she falls in a dead faint at the foot of the bed. As her hand strikes the floor the fingers relax and the box slips out onto one of the hooked rugs.)*

LAVINIA *(does not notice this. Startled by CHRISTINE's collapse, she automatically bends on one knee beside her and hastily feels for her pulse. Then satisfied she has only fainted, her anguished hatred immediately returns and she speaks with strident denunciation.)*: You murdered him just the same—by telling him! I suppose you think you'll be free to marry Adam now! But you won't! Not while I'm alive! I'll make you pay for your crime! I'll find a way to punish you! *(She is starting to her feet when her eyes fall on the little box on the rug. Immediately she snatches it up and stares at it, the look of suspicion changing to a dreadful, horrified certainty. Then with a shuddering cry she shrinks back along the side of the bed, the box clutched in her hand, and sinks on her knees by the head of the bed, and flings her arms around the dead man. With anguished beseeching)* Father! Don't leave me alone! Come back to me! Tell me what to do!

CURTAIN

Figure 1. Lavinia (Kelly McGillis) warmly and possessively greets her father, Ezra Mannon (Ted van Griethuysen), just returned from the Civil War, while her mother, Christine (Franchelle Stewart Dorn), looks on in cold disapproval. The Shakespeare Theatre production of *Mourning Becomes Electra* was directed by Michael Kahn, Washington, D.C., 1997. (Photograph: © Carol Rosegg.)

Figure 2. Christine (Franchelle Stewart Dorn) and her lover, Adam Brant (Brett Porter), dream of their new life together in the Shakespeare Theatre production of *Mourning Becomes Electra*. (Photograph: © Carol Rosegg.)

Figure 3. Lavinia (Kelly McGillis) and Adam Brant (Brett Porter), sitting on benches outside the Mannon house, begin their first-act conversation in formal politeness in the Shakespeare Theatre production of *Mourning Becomes Electra*. (Photograph: © Carol Rosegg.)

Figure 4. Lavinia (Kelly McGillis, *left*) confronts Christine (Franchelle Stewart Dorn, *right*) about Christine's affair with Adam Brant. The larger-than-life portrait of Lavinia's father and Christine's husband, Judge Mannon, dominates the set in the Shakespeare Theatre production of *Mourning Becomes Electra*. (Photograph: © Carol Rosegg.)

Staging of *Homecoming*

When set designer Ming Cho Lee and costume designer Jane Greenwood bring their unique artistic expertise to *Mourning Becomes Electra,* they bring with them the wisdom of their years as friends and collaborators. Interviewed by phone in the midst of their hectic, international careers, they offered complementary insights into this difficult work.

While Shakespeare and his contemporaries offer little if any guidance regarding a production's physical elements, O'Neill is very specific about his vision. Stage directions include lengthy descriptions of sets and costumes that might be seen as threats to the imagination of a designer.

Greenwood doesn't see it that way. "I was just talking to Alfred Uhry about this exact thing," she said, referring to the author of *Driving Miss Daisy* and *Last Night of Ballyhoo,* currently on Broadway. "In his new play, which I'm working on, he was very specific about a blue velvet dress and he asked me, 'Jane, does that drive you crazy when I write something like that?' And I told him, 'No! I love it!' I do. I think it's wonderful for a playwright to say something like that if he feels strongly about it. That's one of the reasons I love O'Neill, because he's so clear."

Lee agreed, with reservations. "I tell everyone that you really should respect the playwright's vision because if you're doing designs for Ibsen or Shaw, who do such specific research, or O'Neill, you should trust that the playwright knows what he or she is doing. On the other hand when you have a script like *Mourning Becomes Electra,* where the description of the characters and how they stand and how they speak is so specific, it can be rather limiting. The first time I read through the play, I read every word. When I went through it a second time I deliberately blocked out all the italics. I just read the dialogue. That freed me up a bit."

Among O'Neill's specifications is a frequent reference to green, first for Christine's gowns and later for those of her daughter Lavinia. The ambiguity about shade and tone, however, left plenty for Greenwood to work with. "It was a very fashionable color in the Victorian period," she explained, "and we would use a Victorian shade of green if we were doing a period piece. Ming has chosen an abstract design so I expect our greens will be more heightened." Greenwood was quick to add that playwrights often use color as a key to character, and sometimes as a symbolic reference. "For me, use of the color green tells us many different things about Christine," she said. "It tells us that she's vain; that she knows that it complements the golden red in her hair. For Christine, a green dress has an emotional context. It tells us that she's envious, even a little vicious."

As for the men, Greenwood commented, "A uniform is a uniform. We've all seen Ken Burns's Civil War series. We know what those men looked like. And for the civilian clothes, there are hundreds of wonderful photographs to go by."

In designing the set, Lee was faced not only with the demands of the text but with the limitations of the Shakespeare Theatre stage. "There is specific business written into the text that dictates design elements," he explained. "There's action on the porch while the father is upstairs. Lavinia is on the stairs calling up and he shuts the window." The need for a second story presented difficulties in a theatre where fly space is extremely limited. "The idea of having that second floor and having to get rid of it to get into the bedroom for the next scene was very perplexing. It also just didn't feel right," Lee said. "So I said to hell with it."

The designer went through a series of intriguing ideas before settling on a final concept. He started with a square room filled with grass. "We would just put the furniture on the grass," he explained. "It's a postmodern cliché, breaking the mold, combining the interior and exterior. It didn't work too badly, but I couldn't decide how to move from one scene to another. Then I thought that a turntable was what I needed but that didn't quite work out either. So I thought of putting one room inside another bigger room. Finally I had an image of both women climbing a long, long staircase so I thought, we'll need a long staircase to a second floor. So I ended up with a second floor after all. The hardest part, of course, will be the boat." The Lee/Greenwood collaboration has been formed over years of working together and through shared teaching duties at Yale University. Asked about their collaborative process, Greenwood answered with a laugh. "We take the train from New York to Yale once a week so we know that every Wednesday we've got two hours together. We don't just talk about our work; we talk about many things." "I don't believe in too much talk," Lee added. "Too much talk about visual things tends to be not only boring but can really lead you in the wrong direction. If everyone is reading the same play and if they're good, something will come together."

FEDERICO GARCIA LORCA

1898-1936

Before he was executed by the Fascists at the beginning of the Spanish civil war, Lorca had written twelve plays. But his last three works—tragedies of rural life—are such powerful evocations of an archetypal conflict between passionate human instincts and traditional codes of conduct that they alone have been sufficient to establish his reputation as the most culturally conscious and theatrically intense dramatist to emerge in Spain during the twentieth century. He was born near the city of Granada, in southern Spain, a region deeply influenced by the Andalusian and Gypsy folk traditions of balladry and dance—traditions that left their mark on both his poetry and plays. He was also influenced by his wealthy father and his cultivated mother, who evidently encouraged him to develop his widely varied artistic talents, for he was not only a poet and playwright but also an accomplished pianist and painter. By the time he was eight, he was already improvising plays in the courtyard of his parents' home, and before he entered the University of Granada at the age of sixteen he was writing ballads, poems, and prose descriptions of the Spanish landscape that he subsequently included in published collections of his works. When he entered the university, he planned to study for a career in law, but he quickly changed his mind and moved on to studies in philosophy and literature, which he continued at the University of Madrid. When he moved to Madrid in 1919, he had already published *Impressions and Landscapes* (1918), an evocative series of impressions based on his travels throughout Spain, and he had in hand a manuscript of poems that he shared with his fellow students in public readings. Lorca, in fact, was an inveterate performer, and throughout his life he evidently took much greater pleasure in reading his works or seeing them produced than in rushing them into print. He usually published his work well after it had been written, and much of it remained unpublished even at the time of his death.

Lorca's playwriting career began in earnest during the 1920s, a period when he experimented in a variety of forms and turned out a number of works, including a parable play about a cockroach who becomes entranced by the enchanting world of a butterfly; a comedy based on the traditional Spanish puppet character Don Cristobal; a series of farces based on the films of Buster Keaton; a surrealist work involving a young man, his fiancée, a mannequin, a dead child, and a cat; a verse play about Mariana Pineda, a nineteenth-century figure who died in the liberation of Madrid; and a tragic farce about an old bachelor who falls in love with a naïve and sensual young girl. These works, together with his numerous public readings and his publication of two collections of poems and a collection of ballads, had turned Lorca into a widely celebrated Spanish writer by the end of the 1920s. In 1929, he left Spain temporarily to visit Paris and London before traveling to America, where he spent a year at Columbia University, but he evidently did not find

New York a congenial place, and by 1930 he had left to visit Cuba, Argentina, and other Latin American countries before returning permanently to Spain.

His travel abroad had also apparently turned him away from all the cosmopolitan movements in drama that were then astir in the major theatrical centers, for when he returned to Spain in 1931, he organized a government-sponsored theatrical troupe and began touring the provinces, producing the Spanish classics of the seventeenth century wherever he could find an audience in small Spanish towns and villages. His sustained immersion in the folk life of the Spanish provinces must have led him to develop the subjects that resulted in the major works of his career—his three tragedies of rural experience—which he wrote during his last five years. In each of these, he focused on the predicament of characters who are torn between their allegiance to traditional Spanish codes of honor and religious belief, on the one hand, and their passionate human desires, on the other. And, in each case, he dramatized the tragic frustration of natural human impulses that he evidently perceived as the inescapable outcome of being forced to submit to rigid and anachronistic codes of behavior. Lorca's emphasis on such frustration may also reflect a covert attack on a variety of repressive forces in his own life: the dogmatic power of the Catholic Church, the political conservatism of the governing Fascists who would execute Lorca in 1936, and the hostility of a predominantly heterosexual society that degraded and ostracized homosexuals like himself.

In the earliest of the tragedies, *Blood Wedding* (1933), a work heavily interspersed with lyric scenes, Lorca dramatized the primal power of the blood in the person of a young woman "burning with desire," who finds herself betrothed and married to a man whom she regards as "a little bit of water." Immediately after the marriage ceremony she runs off with another man, the husband of her cousin, a man whose family had killed the father and brother of her own husband in a blood feud, but a man whom she had always loved because he was for her "a dark river, choked with brush, that brought near me the undertone of its rushes and its whispered song." The two lovers thus violate all the codes of belief and honor in their community and escape into the forest, where they are pursued by the newly married groom, which results in a doubly fatal encounter between the groom and his rival. The bride is thus left "without a single man ever having seen himself in the whiteness of my breasts," a condition that is at once the measure of her conventional purity and her intense frustration. And the mother of the groom, in a final chorus, is seen lamenting the death of her last son at the hands of the same family that had previously killed her husband and her other son. The conflict between traditional codes and human desires is, therefore, presented as bringing profound suffering to all the central characters, old and young, conventional and rebellious alike. In his second tragedy of rural experience, *Yerma* (1934), Lorca examined the plight of a married woman whose frustrated maternal desire ultimately drives her to the act of killing her impotent and unsympathetic husband—an act that in turn moves her to cry out, "I'm going to rest without ever waking to see whether my blood has announced the coming of new blood. My body barren forever."

Like his other mature plays, *The House of Bernarda Alba,* finished a few months before Lorca's death in 1936 but not produced until 1945, is dramatically preoccupied with the frustration of natural human desire. And like these other plays, it dramatizes this problem by focusing on the experience of women, exploring the sentiment voiced by Amelia, "To be born a woman's the worst possible punishment." Indeed, in this play there are no men on stage at all, though every speech resounds either with the memory of Bernarda's recently dead husband or with the yearning of all her daughters for the virile figure of Pepe el Romano. (So vividly does Lorca evoke that offstage male world that half a century later Cuban-born playwright Eduardo Machado would write *Crocodile Eyes* (1999), focusing on Pepe and his male friends.) The world of the play, as indicated by its title, is dominated by Bernarda, whose tyrannical honor and pride and piety and repressiveness are epitomized by the starkly white color of her house, by the black colors of mourning she enforces upon her daughters, and by her big stick that thumps over and over again on the stage. The play repeatedly emphasizes repression: Bernarda's announcement of eight years of mourning, Maria Josefa gagged so that she won't shout, the stallion locked in the stall. Even when La Poncia, the earthy maid who is willing to confront Bernarda directly, imagines revenge, she invokes the prevailing sense of a household that is really a prison: "Then I'll lock myself up in a room with her and spit in her face—a whole year."

Staging a play whose characters almost always seem at emotional breaking points is not easy, but Nuria Espert, a well-known Spanish actress and director, succeeded in her 1986 production (first staged at the Lyric, Hammersmith, then transferred to the West End). As Michael Billington points out in his review, and as a number of other critics noted, the set itself was crucial, its white stone walls and barred windows harshly looming over the black-clad actresses (see Figure 1). Espert's three older actresses, differing noticeably in physical stature, emphasize the conflict between contrasting views of womanhood. Patricia Hayes as Maria Josefa appears always in white (see Figure 3), symbolizing both the bride she wishes to become and the innocence of the lamb she carries in the last act, an innocence her daughter Bernarda has imprisoned and thus distorted into madness. Glenda Jackson's thin angular features and her ramrod-straight posture (see Figure 3) aptly reflect Bernarda's condemnation of everyone beneath her in social standing or in moral outlook. Joan Plowright's rounder features and full curls (see Figure 2) suggest that La Poncia is a woman able to remember her husband with delight, a woman able to understand the sexual longings of Martirio and Adela, longings that Bernarda can only try to repress. Given the irrepressibility of such desires, it's not surprising that Bernarda at the end turns into a screaming banshee, driving off Pepe el Romano (see Figure 4) and thus driving Adela to suicide. She may command her house, but it is a house dominated by death.

THE HOUSE OF BERNARDA ALBA
A Drama about Women in the Villages of Spain

BY FEDERICO GARCIA LORCA / TRANSLATED BY JAMES GRAHAM-LUJÁN AND RICHARD L. O'CONNELL

CHARACTERS

BERNARDA *(age 60)*
MARIA JOSEFA, *Bernarda's mother (age 80)*
ANGUSTIAS, *Bernarda's daughter (age 39)*
MAGDALENA, *Bernarda's daughter (age 30)*
AMELIA, *Bernarda's daughter (age 27)*
MARTIRIO, *Bernarda's daughter (age 24)*
ADELA, *Bernarda's daughter (age 20)*

A MAID *(age 50)*
LA PONCIA, *a maid (age 60)*
PRUDENCIA *(age 50)*
WOMEN IN MOURNING
BEGGAR WOMAN

The writer states that these Three Acts are intended as a photographic document.

ACT 1

(A very white room in BERNARDA ALBA's *house. The walls are white. There are arched doorways with jute curtains tied back with tassels and ruffles. Wicker chairs. On the walls, pictures of unlikely landscapes full of nymphs or legendary kings.*

It is summer. A great brooding silence fills the stage. It is empty when the curtain rises. Bells can be heard tolling outside.)

MAIDSERVANT *(entering)*: The tolling of those bells hits me right between the eyes.

PONCIA *(she enters, eating bread and sausage)*: More than two hours of mumbo jumbo. Priests are here from all the towns. The church looks beautiful. At the first responsory for the dead, Magdalena fainted.

SERVANT: She's the one who's left most alone.

PONCIA: She's the only one who loved her father. Ay! Thank God we're alone for a little. I came over to eat.

SERVANT: If Bernarda sees you. . . !

PONCIA: She's not eating today so she'd just as soon we'd all die of hunger! Domineering old tyrant! But she'll be fooled! I opened the sausage crock.

SERVANT *(with an anxious sadness)*: Couldn't you give me some for my little girl, Poncia?

PONCIA: Go ahead! And take a fistful of peas too. She won't know the difference today.

VOICE *(within)*: Bernarda!

PONCIA: There's the grandmother! Isn't she locked up tight?

SERVANT: Two turns of the key.

PONCIA: You'd better put the cross-bar up too. She's got the fingers of a lock-picker!

VOICE *(within)*: Bernarda!

PONCIA *(shouting)*: She's coming! *(to the* SERVANT*)* Clean everything up good. If Bernarda doesn't find things shining, she'll pull out the few hairs I have left.

SERVANT: What a woman!

PONCIA: Tyrant over everyone around her. She's perfectly capable of sitting on your heart and watching you die for a whole year without turning off that cold little smile she wears on her wicked face. Scrub, scrub those dishes!

SERVANT: I've got blood on my hands from so much polishing of everything.

PONCIA: She's the cleanest, she's the decentest, she's the highest everything! A good rest her poor husband's earned!

(The bells stop.)

SERVANT: Did all the relatives come?

PONCIA: Just hers. His people hate her. They came to see him dead and make the sign of the cross over him; that's all.

SERVANT: Are there enough chairs?

PONCIA: More than enough. Let them sit on the floor. When Bernarda's father died people stopped coming under this roof. She doesn't want them to see her in her "domain." Curse her!

SERVANT: She's been good to you.

PONCIA: Thirty years washing her sheets. Thirty years eating her leftovers. Nights of watching when she had a cough. Whole days peeking through a crack in the shutters to spy on the neighbors and carry her the tale. Life without secrets one from the other. But in spite of that—curse her!

May the "pain of the piercing nail" strike her in the eyes.

SERVANT: Poncia!

PONCIA: But I'm a good watchdog! I bark when I'm told and bite beggars' heels when she sics me on 'em. My sons work in her fields—both of them already married, but one of these days I'll have enough.

SERVANT: And then. . . ?

PONCIA: Then I'll lock myself up in a room with her and spit in her face—a whole year. "Bernarda, here's for this, that and the other!" Till I leave her—just like a lizard the boys have squashed. For that's what she is—she and her whole family! Not that I envy her her life. Five girls are left her, five ugly daughters—not counting Angustias the eldest, by her first husband, who has money—the rest of them, plenty of eyelets to embroider, plenty of linen petticoats, but bread and grapes when it comes to inheritance.

SERVANT: Well, *I'd* like to have what they've got!

PONCIA: All we have is our hands and a hole in God's earth.

SERVANT: And that's the only earth they'll ever leave to us—to us who have nothing!

PONCIA (*at the cupboard*): This glass has some specks.

SERVANT: Neither soap nor rag will take them off.

(*The bells toll.*)

PONCIA: The last prayer! I'm going over and listen. I certainly like the way our priest sings. In the Pater Noster his voice went up, and up—like a pitcher filling with water little by little. Of course, at the end his voice cracked, but it's glorious to hear it. No, there never was anybody like the old Sacristan—Tronchapinos. At my mother's Mass, may she rest in peace, he sang. The walls shook—and when he said "Amen," it was as if a wolf had come into the church.

(*Imitating him.*)

A-a-a-a-men!

(*She starts coughing.*)

SERVANT: Watch out—you'll strain your windpipe!

PONCIA: I'd rather strain something else!

(*Goes out laughing.*)
(*The* SERVANT *scrubs. The bells toll.*)

SERVANT (*imitating the bells*): Dong, dong, dong. Dong, dong, dong. May God forgive him!

BEGGAR WOMAN (*at the door, with a little girl*): Blesséd be God!

SERVANT: Dong, dong, dong. I hope he waits many years for us! Dong, dong, dong.

BEGGAR (*loudly, a little annoyed*): Blesséd be God!

SERVANT (*annoyed*): Forever and ever!

BEGGAR: I came for the scraps.

(*The bells stop tolling.*)

SERVANT: You can go right out the way you came in. Today's scraps are for me.

BEGGAR: But you have somebody to take care of you— and my little girl and I are all alone!

SERVANT: Dogs are alone too, and they live.

BEGGAR: They always give them to me.

SERVANT: Get out of here! Who let you in anyway? You've already tracked up the place.

(*The* BEGGAR WOMAN *and* LITTLE GIRL *leave. The* SERVANT *goes on scrubbing.*)

Floors finished with oil, cupboards, pedestals, iron beds—but us servants, we can suffer in silence—and live in mud huts with a plate and a spoon. I hope someday not a one will be left to tell it.

(*The bells sound again.*)

Yes, yes—ring away. Let them put you in a coffin with gold inlay and brocade to carry it on—you're no less dead I'll be, so take what's coming to you, Antonio María Benavides—stiff in your broadcloth suit and your high boots—take what's coming to you! You'll never again lift my skirts behind the corral door!

(*From the rear door, two by two, women in mourning with large shawls and black skirts and fans, begin to enter. They come in slowly until the stage is full.*)

SERVANT (*breaking into a wail*): Oh, Antonio María Benavides, now you'll never see these walls, nor break bread in this house again! I'm the one who loved you most of all your servants.

(*Pulling her hair.*)

Must I live on after you've gone? Must I go on living?

(*The two hundred women finish coming in, and* BERNARDA *and her five daughters enter.* BERNARDA *leans on a cane.*)

BERNARDA (*to the* SERVANT): Silence!

SERVANT (*weeping*): Bernarda!

BERNARDA: Less shrieking and more work. You should have had all this cleaner for the wake. Get out. This isn't your place.

(*The* SERVANT *goes off crying.*)

The poor are like animals—they seem to be made of different stuff.

FIRST WOMAN: The poor feel their sorrows too.

BERNARDA: But they forget them in front of a plateful of peas.

FIRST GIRL (*timidly*): Eating is necessary for living.

BERNARDA: At your age one doesn't talk in front of older people.

WOMAN: Be quiet, child.

BERNARDA: I've never taken lessons from anyone. Sit down.

(They sit down. Pause. Loudly.)

Magdalena, don't cry. If you want to cry, get under your bed. Do you hear me?

SECOND WOMAN *(to BERNARDA)*: Have you started to work the fields?

BERNARDA: Yesterday.

THIRD WOMAN: The sun comes down like lead.

FIRST WOMAN: I haven't known heat like this for years.

(Pause. They all fan themselves.)

BERNARDA: Is the lemonade ready?

PONCIA: Yes, Bernarda.

(She brings in a large tray full of little white jars which she distributes.)

BERNARDA: Give the men some.

PONCIA: They're already drinking in the patio.

BERNARDA: Let them get out the way they came in. I don't want them walking through here.

A GIRL *(to ANGUSTIAS)*: Pepe el Romano was with the men during the service.

ANGUSTIAS: There he was.

BERNARDA: His mother was there. She saw his mother. Neither she nor I saw Pepe . . .

GIRL: I thought . . .

BERNARDA: The one who *was* there was Darajalí, the widower. Very close to your Aunt. We all of us saw him.

SECOND WOMAN *(aside, in a low voice)*: Wicked, worse than wicked woman!

THIRD WOMAN: A tongue like a knife!

BERNARDA: Women in church shouldn't look at any man but the priest—and him only because he wears skirts. To turn your head is to be looking for the warmth of corduroy.

FIRST WOMAN: Sanctimonious old snake!

PONCIA *(between her teeth)*: Itching for a man's warmth.

BERNARDA *(beating with her cane on the floor)*: Bléssed be God!

ALL *(crossing themselves)*: Forever blesséd and praised.

BERNARDA: Rest in peace with holy company at your head.

ALL: Rest in peace!

BERNARDA: With the Angel Saint Michael, and his sword of justice.

ALL: Rest in peace!

BERNARDA: With the key that opens, and the hand that locks.

ALL: Rest in peace!

BERNARDA: With the most blesséd, and the little lights of the field.

ALL: Rest in peace!

BERNARDA: With our holy charity, and all souls on land and sea.

ALL: Rest in peace!

BERNARDA: Grant rest to your servant, Antonio María Benavides, and give him the crown of your blesséd glory.

ALL: Amen.

BERNARDA *(she rises and chants)*: *Requiem aeternam donat eis domine.*

ALL *(standing and chanting in the Gregorian fashion)*: *Et lux perpetua luce ab eis.*

(They cross themselves.)

FIRST WOMAN: May you have health to pray for his soul. *(They start filing out.)*

THIRD WOMAN: You won't lack loaves of hot bread.

SECOND WOMAN: Nor a roof for your daughters.

(They are all filing in front of BERNARDA and going out. ANGUSTIAS leaves by the door to the patio.)

FOURTH WOMAN: May you go on enjoying your wedding wheat.

PONCIA *(she enters, carrying a money bag)*: From the men—this bag of money for Masses.

BERNARDA: Thank them—and let them have a glass of brandy.

GIRL *(to MAGDALENA)*: Magdalena . . .

BERNARDA *(to MAGDALENA, who is starting to cry)*: Sh-h-h-h!

(She beats with her cane on the floor.)
(All the women have gone out.)

BERNARDA *(to the women who have just left)*: Go back to your houses and criticize everything you've seen! I hope it'll be many years before you pass under the archway of my door again.

PONCIA: You've nothing to complain about. The whole town came.

BERNARDA: Yes, to fill my house with the sweat from their wraps and the poison of their tongues.

AMELIA: Mother, don't talk like that.

BERNARDA: What other way is there to talk about this curséd village with no river—this village full of wells where you drink water always fearful it's been poisoned?

PONCIA: Look what they've done to the floor!

BERNARDA: As though a herd of goats had passed through.

(PONCIA cleans the floor.)

Adela, give me a fan.

ADELA: Take this one.

(She gives her a round fan with green and red flowers.)

BERNARDA *(throwing the fan on the floor)*: Is that the fan to give to a widow? Give me a black one and learn to respect your father's memory.

MARTIRIO: Take mine.

BERNARDA: And you?

MARTIRIO: I'm not hot.

BERNARDA: Well, look for another, because you'll need it. For the eight years of mourning, not a breath of air will get in this house from the street. We'll act as if we'd sealed up doors and windows with bricks. That's what happened in my father's house—and in my grandfather's house. Meantime, you can all start embroidering your hope-chest linens. I have twenty bolts of linen in the chest from which to cut sheets and coverlets. Magdalena can embroider them.

MAGDALENA: It's all the same to me.

ADELA (sourly): If you don't want to embroider them—they can go without. That way yours will look better.

MAGDALENA: Neither mine nor yours. I know I'm not going to marry. I'd rather carry sacks to the mill. Anything except sit here day after day in this dark room.

BERNARDA: That's what a woman is for.

MAGDALENA: Cursed be all women.

BERNARDA: In this house you'll do what I order. You can't run with the story to your father any more. Needle and thread for women. Whiplash and mules for men. That's the way it has to be for people who have certain obligations.

(ADELA goes out.)

VOICE: Bernarda! Let me out!

BERNARDA (calling): Let her out now!

(The FIRST SERVANT enters.)

FIRST SERVANT: I had a hard time holding her. In spite of her eighty years, your mother's strong as an oak.

BERNARDA: It runs in the family. My grandfather was the same way.

SERVANT: Several times during the wake I had to cover her mouth with an empty sack because she wanted to shout out to you to give her dishwater to drink at least, and some dogmeat, which is what she says you feed her.

MARTIRIO: She's mean!

BERNARDA (to SERVANT): Let her get some fresh air in the patio.

SERVANT: She took her rings and the amethyst earrings out of the box, put them on, and told me she wants to get married.

(The daughters laugh.)

BERNARDA: Go with her and be careful she doesn't get near the well.

SERVANT: You don't need to be afraid she'll jump in.

BERNARDA: It's not that—but the neighbors can see her there from their windows.

(The SERVANT leaves.)

MARTIRIO: We'll go change our clothes.

BERNARDA: Yes, but don't take the kerchiefs from your heads.

(ADELA enters.)

And Angustias?

ADELA (meaningfully): I saw her looking out through the cracks of the back door. The men had just gone.

BERNARDA: And you, what were you doing at the door?

ADELA: I went there to see if the hens had laid.

BERNARDA: But the men had already gone!

ADELA (meaningfully): A group of them were still standing outside.

BERNARDA (furiously): Angustias! Angustias!

ANGUSTIAS (entering): Did you want something?

BERNARDA: For what—and at whom—were you looking?

ANGUSTIAS: Nobody.

BERNARDA: Is it decent for a woman of your class to be running after a man the day of her father's funeral? Answer me! Whom were you looking at?

(Pause.)

ANGUSTIAS: I . . .

BERNARDA: Yes, you!

ANGUSTIAS: Nobody.

BERNARDA: Soft! Honeytongue!

(She strikes her.)

PONCIA (running to her): Bernarda, calm down!

(She holds her. ANGUSTIAS weeps.)

BERNARDA: Get out of here, all of you!

(They all go out.)

PONCIA: She did it not realizing what she was doing—although it's bad, of course. It really disgusted me to see her sneak along to the patio. Then she stood at the window listening to the men's talk, which, as usual, was not the sort one should listen to.

BERNARDA: That's what they come to funerals for. (With curiosity.) What were they talking about?

PONCIA: They were talking about Paca la Roseta. Last night they tied her husband up in a stall, stuck her on a horse behind the saddle, and carried her away to the depths of the olive grove.

BERNARDA: And what did she do?

PONCIA: She? She was just as happy—they say her breasts were exposed and Maximiliano held on to her as if he were playing a guitar. Terrible!

BERNARDA: And what happened?

PONCIA: What had to happen. They came back almost at daybreak. Paca la Roseta with her hair loose and a wreath of flowers on her head.

BERNARDA: She's the only bad woman we have in the village.

PONCIA: Because she's not from here. She's from far away. And those who went with her are the sons of outsiders too. The men from here aren't up to a thing like that.

BERNARDA: No, but they like to see it, and talk about it, and suck their fingers over it.

PONCIA: They were saying a lot more things.

BERNARDA (*looking from side to side with a certain fear*): What things?

PONCIA: I'm ashamed to talk about them.

BERNARDA: And my daughter heard them?

PONCIA: Of course!

BERNARDA: That one takes after her Aunts: white and mealy-mouthed and casting sheep's eyes at any little barber's compliment. Oh, what one has to go through and put up with so people will be decent and not too wild!

PONCIA: It's just that your daughters are of an age when they ought to have husbands. Mighty little trouble they give you. Angustias must be much more than thirty now.

BERNARDA: Exactly thirty-nine.

PONCIA: Imagine. And she's never had a beau . . .

BERNARDA (*furiously*): None of them has ever had a beau and they've never needed one! They get along very well.

PONCIA: I didn't mean to offend you.

BERNARDA: For a hundred miles around there's no one good enough to come near them. The men in this town are not of their class. Do you want me to turn them over to the first shepherd?

PONCIA: You should have moved to another town.

BERNARDA: That's it. To sell them!

PONCIA: No, Bernarda, to change. . . . Of course, any place else, they'd be the poor ones.

BERNARDA: Hold your tormenting tongue!

PONCIA: One can't even talk to you. Do we, or do we not share secrets?

BERNARDA: We do not. You're a servant and I pay you. Nothing more.

PONCIA: But . . .

SERVANT (*entering*): Don Arturo's here. He's come to see about dividing the inheritance.

BERNARDA: Let's go. (*to the* SERVANT) You start white-washing the patio. (*to* LA PONCIA) And you start putting all the dead man's clothes away in the chest.

PONCIA: We could give away some of the things.

BERNARDA: Nothing—not a button even! Not even the cloth we covered his face with.

(*She goes out slowly, leaning on her cane. At the door she turns to look at the two servants. They go out. She leaves.*)
(AMELIA *and* MARTIRIO *enter.*)

AMELIA: Did you take the medicine?

MARTIRIO: For all the good it'll do me.

AMELIA: But you took it?

MARTIRIO: I do things without any faith, but like clockwork.

AMELIA: Since the new doctor came you look livelier.

MARTIRIO: I feel the same.

AMELIA: Did you notice? Adelaida wasn't at the funeral.

MARTIRIO: I know. Her sweetheart doesn't let her go out even to the front doorstep. Before, she was gay. Now, not even powder on her face.

AMELIA: These days a girl doesn't know whether to have a beau or not.

MARTIRIO: It's all the same.

AMELIA: The whole trouble is all these wagging tongues that won't let us live. Adelaida has probably had a bad time.

MARTIRIO: She's afraid of our mother. Mother is the only one who knows the story of Adelaida's father and where he got his lands. Every time she comes here, Mother twists the knife in the wound. Her father killed his first wife's husband in Cuba so he could marry her himself. Then he left her there and went off with another woman who already had one daughter, and then he took up with this other girl, Adelaida's mother, and married her after his second wife died insane.

AMELIA: But why isn't a man like that put in jail?

MARTIRIO: Because men help each other cover up things like that and no one's able to tell on them.

AMELIA: But Adelaida's not to blame for any of that.

MARTIRIO: No. But history repeats itself. I can see that everything is a terrible repetition. And she'll have the same fate as her mother and grandmother—both of them wife to the man who fathered her.

AMELIA: What an awful thing!

MARTIRIO: It's better never to look at a man. I've been afraid of them since I was a little girl. I'd see them in the yard, yoking the oxen and lifting grain sacks, shouting and stamping, and I was always afraid to grow up for fear one of them would suddenly take me in his arms. God has made me weak and ugly and has definitely put such things away from me.

AMELIA: Don't say that! Enrique Humanas was after you and he liked you.

MARTIRIO: That was just people's ideas! One time I stood in my nightgown at the window until day-break because he let me know through his shepherd's little girl that he was going to come, and he didn't. It was all just talk. Then he married someone else who had more money than I.

AMELIA: And ugly as the devil.

MARTIRIO: What do men care about ugliness? All they care about is lands, yokes of oxen, and a submissive bitch who'll feed them.

AMELIA: Ay!

(MAGDALENA enters.)

MAGDALENA: What are you doing?

MARTIRIO: Just here.

AMELIA: And you?

MAGDALENA: I've been going through all the rooms. Just to walk a little, and look at Grandmother's needlepoint pictures—the little woolen dog, and the black man wrestling with the lion—which we liked so much when we were children. Those were happier times. A wedding lasted ten days and evil tongues weren't in style. Today people are more refined. Brides wear white veils, just as in the cities, and we drink bottled wine, but we rot inside because of what people might say.

MARTIRIO: Lord knows what went on then!

AMELIA *(to MAGDALENA)*: One of your shoelaces has come untied.

MAGDALENA: What of it?

AMELIA: You'll step on it and fall.

MAGDALENA: One less!

MARTIRIO: And Adela?

MAGDALENA: Ah! She put on the green dress she made to wear for her birthday, went out to the yard, and began shouting: "Chickens! Chickens, look at me!" I had to laugh.

AMELIA: If Mother had only seen her!

MAGDALENA: Poor little thing! She's the youngest one of us and still has her illusions. I'd give something to see her happy.

(Pause. ANGUSTIAS crosses the stage, carrying some towels.)

ANGUSTIAS: What time is it?

MAGDALENA: It must be twelve.

ANGUSTIAS: So late?

AMELIA: It's about to strike.

(ANGUSTIAS goes out.)

MAGDALENA *(meaningfully)*: Do you know what?

(Pointing after ANGUSTIAS.)

AMELIA: No.

MAGDALENA: Come on!

MARTIRIO: I don't know what you're talking about!

MAGDALENA: Both of you know it better than I do, always with your heads together, like two little sheep, but not letting anybody else in on it. I mean about Pepe el Romano!

MARTIRIO: Ah!

MAGDALENA *(mocking her)*: Ah! The whole town's talking about it. Pepe el Romano is coming to marry Angustias. Last night he was walking around the house and I think he's going to send a declaration soon.

MARTIRIO: I'm glad. He's a good man.

AMELIA: Me too. Angustias is well off.

MAGDALENA: Neither one of you is glad.

MARTIRIO: Magdalena! What do you mean?

MAGDALENA: If he were coming because of Angustias' looks, for Angustias as a woman, I'd be glad too, but he's coming for her money. Even though Angustias is our sister, we're her family here and we know she's old and sickly, and always has been the least attractive one of us! Because if she looked like a dressed-up stick at twenty, what can she look like now, now that she's forty?

MARTIRIO: Don't talk like that. Luck comes to the one who least expects it.

AMELIA: But Magdalena's right after all! Angustias has all her father's money; she's the only rich one in the house and that's why, now that Father's dead and the money will be divided, they're coming for her.

MAGDALENA: Pepe el Romano is twenty-five years old and the best looking man around here. The natural thing would be for him to be after you, Amelia, or our Adela, who's twenty—not looking for the least likely one in this house, a woman who, like her father, talks through her nose.

MARTIRIO: Maybe he likes that!

MAGDALENA: I've never been able to bear your hypocrisy.

MARTIRIO: Heavens!

(ADELA enters.)

MAGDALENA: Did the chickens see you?

ADELA: What did you want me to do?

AMELIA: If Mother sees you, she'll drag you by your hair!

ADELA: I had a lot of illusions about this dress. I'd planned to put it on the day we were going to eat watermelons at the well. There wouldn't have been another like it.

MARTIRIO: It's a lovely dress.

ADELA: And one that looks very good on me. It's the best thing Magdalena's ever cut.

MAGDALENA: And the chickens, what did they say to you?

ADELA: They presented me with a few fleas that riddled my legs.

(They laugh.)

MARTIRIO: What you can do is dye it black.

MAGDALENA: The best thing you can do is give it to Angustias for her wedding with Pepe el Romano.

ADELA *(with hidden emotion)*: But Pepe el Romano . . .

AMELIA: Haven't you heard about it?

ADELA: No.

MAGDALENA: Well, now you know!

ADELA: But it can't be!

MAGDALENA: Money can do anything.

ADELA: Is that why she went out after the funeral and stood looking through the door?

(Pause.)

And that man would . . .

MAGDALENA: Would do anything.

(Pause.)

MARTIRIO: What are you thinking, Adela?

ADELA: I'm thinking that this mourning has caught me at the worst moment of my life for me to bear it.

MAGDALENA: You'll get used to it.

ADELA *(bursting out, crying with rage)*: I will not get used to it! I can't be locked up. I don't want my skin to look like yours. I don't want my skin's whiteness lost in these rooms. Tomorrow I'm going to put on my green dress and go walking in the streets. I want to go out!

(The FIRST SERVANT enters.)

MAGDALENA *(in a tone of authority)*: Adela!

SERVANT: The poor thing! How she misses her father. . . .

(She goes out.)

MARTIRIO: Hush!

AMELIA: What happens to one will happen to all of us.

(ADELA grows calm.)

MAGDALENA: The servant almost heard you.

SERVANT *(entering)*: Pepe el Romano is coming along at the end of the street.

(AMELIA, MARTIRIO and MAGDALENA run hurriedly.)

MAGDALENA: Let's go see him!

(They leave rapidly.)

SERVANT *(to ADELA)*: Aren't you going?

ADELA: It's nothing to me.

SERVANT: Since he has to turn the corner, you'll see him better from the window of your room.

(The SERVANT goes out. ADELA is left on the stage, standing doubtfully; after a moment, she also leaves rapidly, going toward her room. BERNARDA and LA PONCIA come in.)

BERNARDA: Damned portions and shares.

PONCIA: What a lot of money is left to Angustias!

BERNARDA: Yes.

PONCIA: And for the others, considerably less.

BERNARDA: You've told me that three times now, when you know I don't want it mentioned! Considerably less; a lot less! Don't remind me any more.

(ANGUSTIAS comes in, her face heavily made up.)

Angustias!

ANGUSTIAS: Mother.

BERNARDA: Have you dared to powder your face? Have you dared to wash your face on the day of your father's death?

ANGUSTIAS: He wasn't my father. Mine died a long time ago. Have you forgotten that already?

BERNARDA: You owe more to this man, father of your sisters, than to your own. Thanks to him, your fortune is intact.

ANGUSTIAS: We'll have to see about that first!

BERNARDA: Even out of decency! Out of respect!

ANGUSTIAS: Let me go out, mother!

BERNARDA: Let you go out? After I've taken that powder off your face, I will. Spineless! Painted hussy! Just like your aunts!

(She removes the powder violently with her handkerchief.)

Now get out!

PONCIA: Bernarda, don't be so hateful!

BERNARDA: Even though my mother is crazy, I still have my five senses and I know what I'm doing.

(They all enter.)

MAGDALENA: What's going on here?

BERNARDA: Nothing's "going on here"!

MAGDALENA *(to ANGUSTIAS)*: If you're fighting over the inheritance, you're the richest one and can hang on to it all.

ANGUSTIAS: Keep your tongue in your pocketbook!

BERNARDA *(beating on the floor)*: Don't fool yourselves into thinking you'll sway me. Until I go out of this house feet first I'll give the orders for myself and for you!

(Voices are heard and MARIA JOSEFA, BERNARDA's mother, enters. She is very old and has decked out her head and breast with flowers.)

MARIA JOSEFA: Bernarda, where is my mantilla? Nothing, nothing of what I own will be for any of you. Not my rings nor my black moiré dress. Because not a one of you is going to marry—not a one. Bernarda, give me my necklace of pearls.

BERNARDA *(to the SERVANT)*: Why did you let her in here?

SERVANT *(trembling)*: She got away from me!

MARIA JOSEFA: I ran away because I want to marry—I want to get married to a beautiful manly man from the shore of the sea. Because here the men run from women.

BERNARDA: Hush, hush, Mother!

MARIA JOSEFA: No, no—I won't hush. I don't want to see these single women, longing for marriage, turning their hearts to dust; and I want to go to my home town. Bernarda, I want a man to get married to and be happy with!

BERNARDA: Lock her up!

MARIA JOSEFA: Let me go out, Bernarda!

(The SERVANT seizes MARIA JOSEFA.)

BERNARDA: Help her, all of you!

(They all grab the old woman.)

MARIA JOSEFA: I want to get away from here! Bernarda! To get married by the shore of the sea—by the shore of the sea!

(Quick, curtain.)

ACT 2

(A white room in BERNARDA'*s house. The doors on the left lead to the bedrooms.* BERNARDA'*s* DAUGHTERS *are seated on low chairs, sewing.* MAGDALENA *is embroidering.* LA PONCIA *is with them.)*

ANGUSTIAS: I've cut the third sheet.

MARTIRIO: That one goes to Amelia.

MAGDALENA: Angustias, shall I put Pepe's initials here too?

ANGUSTIAS *(dryly)*: No.

MAGDALENA *(calling, from off stage to* ADELA*)*: Adela, aren't you coming?

AMELIA: She's probably stretched out on the bed.

PONCIA: Something's wrong with that one. I find her restless, trembling, frightened—as if a lizard were between her breasts.

MARTIRIO: There's nothing, more or less, wrong with her than there is with all of us.

MAGDALENA: All of us except Angustias.

ANGUSTIAS: I feel fine, and anybody who doesn't like it can pop.

MAGDALENA: We all have to admit the nicest things about you are your figure and your tact.

ANGUSTIAS: Fortunately, I'll soon be out of this hell.

MAGDALENA: Maybe you won't get out!

MARTIRIO: Stop this talk!

ANGUSTIAS: Besides, a good dowry is better than dark eyes in one's face!

MAGDALENA: All you say just goes in one ear and out the other.

AMELIA *(to* LA PONCIA*)*: Open the patio door and see if we can get a bit of a breeze.

*(*LA PONCIA *opens the door.)*

MARTIRIO: Last night I couldn't sleep because of the heat.

AMELIA: Neither could I.

MAGDALENA: I got up for a bit of air. There was a black storm cloud and a few drops even fell.

PONCIA: It was one in the morning and the earth seemed to give off fire. I got up too. Angustias was still at the window with Pepe.

MAGDALENA *(with irony)*: That late? What time did he leave?

ANGUSTIAS: Why do you ask, if you saw him?

AMELIA: He must have left about one-thirty.

ANGUSTIAS: Yes. How did you know?

AMELIA: I heard him cough and heard his mare's hoofbeats.

PONCIA: But I heard him leave around four.

ANGUSTIAS: It must have been someone else!

PONCIA: No, I'm sure of it!

AMELIA: That's what it seemed to me, too.

MAGDALENA: That's very strange!

(Pause.)

PONCIA: Listen, Angustias, what did he say to you the first time he came by your window?

ANGUSTIAS: Nothing. What should he say? Just talked.

MARTIRIO: It's certainly strange that two people who never knew each other should suddenly meet at a window and be engaged.

ANGUSTIAS: Well, I didn't mind.

AMELIA: I'd have felt very strange about it.

ANGUSTIAS: No, because when a man comes to a window he knows, from all the busybodies who come and go and fetch and carry, that he's going to be told "yes."

MARTIRIO: All right, but he'd have to ask you.

ANGUSTIAS: Of course!

AMELIA *(inquisitively)*: And how did he ask you?

ANGUSTIAS: Why, no way:—"You know I'm after you. I need a good, well brought up woman, and that's you—if it's agreeable."

AMELIA: These things embarrass me!

ANGUSTIAS: They embarrass me too, but one has to go through it!

PONCIA: And did he say anything more?

ANGUSTIAS: Yes, he did all the talking.

MARTIRIO: And you?

ANGUSTIAS: I couldn't have said a word. My heart was almost coming out of my mouth. It was the first time I'd ever been alone at night with a man.

MAGDALENA: And such a handsome man.

ANGUSTIAS: He's not bad looking!

PONCIA: Those things happen among people who have an idea how to do things, who talk and say and move their hand. The first time my husband, Evaristo the Short-tailed, came to my window . . . Ha! Ha! Ha!

AMELIA: What happened?

PONCIA: It was very dark. I saw him coming along and as he went by he said, "Good evening." "Good evening," I said. Then we were both silent for more than half an hour. The sweat poured down my body. Then Evaristo got nearer and nearer as if he wanted to squeeze in through the bars and said in a very low voice—"Come here and let me feel you!"

(They all laugh. AMELIA *gets up, runs, and looks through the door.)*

AMELIA: Ay, I thought mother was coming!

MAGDALENA: What she'd have done to us!

(They go on laughing.)

AMELIA: Sh-h-h! She'll hear us.

PONCIA: Then he acted very decently. Instead of getting some other idea, he went to raising birds, until he died. You aren't married but it's good for you to know, anyway, that two weeks after the wedding a man gives up the bed for the table, then the table for the tavern, and the woman who doesn't like it can just rot, weeping in a corner.

AMELIA: You liked it.

PONCIA: I learned how to handle him!

MARTIRIO: Is it true that you sometimes hit him?

PONCIA: Yes, and once I almost poked out one of his eyes!

MAGDALENA: All women ought to be like that!

PONCIA: I'm one of your mother's school. One time I don't know what he said to me, and then I killed all his birds—with the pestle!

(They laugh.)

MAGDALENA: Adela, child! Don't miss this.

AMELIA: Adela!

(Pause.)

MAGDALENA: I'll go see!

(She goes out.)

PONCIA: That child is sick!

MARTIRIO: Of course. She hardly sleeps!

PONCIA: What *does* she do, then?

MARTIRIO: How do I know what she does?

PONCIA: You probably know better than we do, since you sleep with just a wall between you.

ANGUSTIAS: Envy gnaws on people.

AMELIA: Don't exaggerate.

ANGUSTIAS: I can tell it in her eyes. She's getting the look of a crazy woman.

MARTIRIO: Don't talk about crazy women. This is one place you're not allowed to say that word.

(MAGDALENA and ADELA enter.)

MAGDALENA: Didn't you say she was asleep?

ADELA: My body aches.

MARTIRIO *(with a hidden meaning)*: Didn't you sleep well last night?

ADELA: Yes.

MARTIRIO: Then?

ADELA *(loudly)*: Leave me alone. Awake or asleep, it's no affair of yours. I'll do whatever I want to with my body.

MARTIRIO: I was just concerned about you!

ADELA: Concerned?—curious! Weren't you sewing? Well, continue! I wish I were invisible so I could pass through a room without being asked where I was going!

SERVANT *(entering)*: Bernarda is calling you. The man with the laces is here.

(All but ADELA and LA PONCIA go out, and as MARTIRIO leaves, she looks fixedly at ADELA.)

ADELA: Don't look at me like that! If you want, I'll give you my eyes, for they're younger, and my back to improve that hump you have, but look the other way when I go by.

PONCIA: Adela, she's your sister, and the one who most loves you besides!

ADELA: She follows me everywhere. Sometimes she looks in my room to see if I'm sleeping. She won't let me breathe, and always, "Too bad about that face!" "Too bad about that body! It's going to waste!" But I won't let that happen. My body will be for whomever I choose.

PONCIA *(insinuatingly, in a low voice)*: For Pepe el Romano, no?

ADELA *(frightened)*: What do you mean?

PONCIA: What I said, Adela!

ADELA: Shut up!

PONCIA *(loudly)*: Don't you think I've noticed?

ADELA: Lower your voice!

PONCIA: Then forget what you're thinking about!

ADELA: What do you know?

PONCIA: We old ones can see through walls. Where do you go when you get up at night?

ADELA: I wish you were blind!

PONCIA: But my head and hands are full of eyes, where something like this is concerned. I couldn't possibly guess your intentions. Why did you sit almost naked at your window, and with the light on and the window open, when Pepe passed by the second night he came to talk with your sister?

ADELA: That's not true!

PONCIA: Don't be a child! Leave your sister alone. And if you like Pepe el Romano, keep it to yourself.

(ADELA weeps.)

Besides, who says you can't marry him? Your sister Angustias is sickly. She'll die with her first child. Narrow waisted, old—and out of my experience I can tell you she'll die. Then Pepe will do what all widowers do in these parts: he'll marry the youngest and most beautiful, and that's you. Live on that hope, forget him, anything; but don't go against God's law.

ADELA: Hush!

PONCIA: I won't hush!

ADELA: Mind your own business. Snooper, traitor!

PONCIA: I'm going to stick to you like a shadow!

ADELA: Instead of cleaning the house and then going to bed and praying for the dead, you root around like an old sow about goings on between men and women—so you can drool over them.

PONCIA: I keep watch; so people won't spit when they pass our door.

ADELA: What a tremendous affection you've suddenly conceived for my sister.

PONCIA: I don't have any affection for any of you. I want to live in a decent house. I don't want to be dirtied in my old age!

ADELA: Save your advice. It's already too late. For I'd leap not over you, just a servant, but over my mother to put out this fire I feel in my legs and my mouth. What can you possibly say about me? That I lock myself in my room and will not open the door? That I don't sleep? I'm smarter than you! See if you can catch the hare with your hands.

PONCIA: Don't defy me, Adela, don't defy me! Because I can shout, light lamps, and make bells ring.

ADELA: Bring four thousand yellow flares and set them about the walls of the yard. No one can stop what has to happen.

PONCIA: You like him that much?

ADELA: That much! Looking in his eyes I seem to drink his blood in slowly.

PONCIA: I won't listen to you.

ADELA: Well, you'll have to. I've been afraid of you. But now I'm stronger than you!

(ANGUSTIAS enters.)

ANGUSTIAS: Always arguing!

PONCIA: Certainly. She insists that in all this heat I have to go bring her I don't know what from the store.

ANGUSTIAS: Did you buy me the bottle of perfume?

PONCIA: The most expensive one. And the face powder. I put them on the table in your room.

(ANGUSTIAS goes out.)

ADELA: And be quiet!

PONCIA: We'll see!

(MARTIRIO and AMELIA enter.)

MARTIRIO *(to ADELA)*: Did you see the laces?

AMELIA: Angustias', for her wedding sheets, are beautiful.

ADELA *(to MARTIRIO, who is carrying some lace)*: And these?

MARTIRIO: They're for me. For a nightgown.

ADELA *(with sarcasm)*: One needs a sense of humor around here!

MARTIRIO *(meaningfully)*: But only for me to look at. I don't have to exhibit myself before anybody.

PONCIA: No one ever sees us in our nightgowns.

MARTIRIO *(meaningfully, looking at ADELA)*: Sometimes they don't! But I love nice underwear. If I were rich, I'd have it made of Holland Cloth. It's one of the few tastes I've left.

PONCIA: These laces are beautiful for babies' caps and christening gowns. I could never afford them for my own. Now let's see if Angustias will use them for hers. Once she starts having children, they'll keep her running night and day.

MAGDALENA: I don't intend to sew a stitch on them.

AMELIA: And much less bring up some stranger's children. Look how our neighbors across the road are—making sacrifices for four brats.

PONCIA: They're better off than you. There at least they laugh and you can hear them fight.

MARTIRIO: Well, you go work for them, then.

PONCIA: No, fate has sent me to this nunnery!

(Tiny bells are heard distantly as though through several thicknesses of wall.)

MAGDALENA: It's the men going back to work.

PONCIA: It was three o'clock a minute ago.

MARTIRIO: With this sun!

ADELA *(sitting down)*: Ay! If only we could go out in the fields too!

MAGDALENA *(sitting down)*: Each class does what it has to!

MARTIRIO *(sitting down)*: That's it!

AMELIA *(sitting down)*: Ay!

PONCIA: There's no happiness like that in the fields right at this time of year. Yesterday morning the reapers arrived. Forty or fifty handsome young men.

MAGDALENA: Where are they from this year?

PONCIA: From far, far away. They came from the mountains! Happy! Like weathered trees! Shouting and throwing stones! Last night a woman who dresses in sequins and dances, with an accordion, arrived, and fifteen of them made a deal with her to take her to the olive grove. I saw them from far away. The one who talked with her was a boy with green eyes—tight knit as a sheaf of wheat.

AMELIA: Really?

ADELA: Are you sure?

PONCIA: Years ago another one of those women came here, and I myself gave my eldest son some money so he could go. Men need things like that.

ADELA: Everything's forgiven *them*.

AMELIA: To be born a woman's the worst possible punishment.

MAGDALENA: Even our eyes aren't our own.

(A distant song is heard, coming nearer.)

PONCIA: There they are. They have a beautiful song.

AMELIA: They're going out to reap now.

CHORUS:

> *The reapers have set out*
> *Looking for ripe wheat;*
> *They'll carry off the hearts*
> *Of any girls they meet.*

(Tambourines and carrañacas are heard. Pause. They all listen in the silence cut by the sun.)

AMELIA: And they don't mind the sun!

MARTIRIO: They reap through flames.

ADELA: How I'd like to be a reaper so I could come and go as I pleased. Then we could forget what's eating us all.

MARTIRIO: What do you have to forget?

ADELA: Each one of us has something.

MARTIRIO (intensely): Each one!

PONCIA: Quiet! Quiet!

CHORUS (very distantly):

Throw wide your doors and windows,
You girls who live in the town
The reaper asks you for roses
With which to deck his crown.

PONCIA: What a song!

MARTIRIO (with nostalgia):

Throw wide your doors and windows,
You girls who live in the town.

ADELA (passionately):

The reaper asks you for roses
With which to deck his crown.

(The song grows more distant.)

PONCIA: Now they're turning the corner.

ADELA: Let's watch them from the window of my room.

PONCIA: Be careful not to open the shutters too much because they're likely to give them a push to see who's looking.

(The three leave. MARTIRIO is left sitting on the low chair with her head between her hands.)

AMELIA (drawing near her): What's wrong with you?

MARTIRIO: The heat makes me feel ill.

AMELIA: And it's no more than that?

MARTIRIO: I was wishing it were November, the rainy days, the frost—anything except this unending summertime.

AMELIA: It'll pass and come again.

MARTIRIO: Naturally.

(Pause.)

What time did you go to sleep last night?

AMELIA: I don't know. I sleep like a log. Why?

MARTIRIO: Nothing. Only I thought I heard someone in the yard.

AMELIA: Yes?

MARTIRIO: Very late.

AMELIA: And weren't you afraid?

MARTIRIO: No. I've heard it other nights.

AMELIA: We'd better watch out! Couldn't it have been the shepherds?

MARTIRIO: The shepherds come at six.

AMELIA: Maybe a young, unbroken mule?

MARTIRIO (to herself, with double meaning): That's it! That's it. An unbroken little mule.

AMELIA: We'll have to set a watch.

MARTIRIO: No. No. Don't say anything. It may be I've just imagined it.

AMELIA: Maybe.

(Pause. AMELIA starts to go.)

MARTIRIO: Amelia!

AMELIA (at the door): What?

(Pause.)

MARTIRIO: Nothing.

(Pause.)

AMELIA: Why did you call me?

(Pause.)

MARTIRIO: It just came out. I didn't mean to.

(Pause.)

AMELIA: Lie down for a little.

ANGUSTIAS (she bursts in furiously, in a manner that makes a great contrast with previous silence): Where's that picture of Pepe I had under my pillow? Which one of you has it?

MARTIRIO: No one.

AMELIA: You'd think he was a silver St. Bartholomew.

ANGUSTIAS: Where's the picture?

(PONCIA, MAGDALENA and ADELA enter.)

ADELA: What picture?

ANGUSTIAS: One of you has hidden it from me.

MAGDALENA: Do you have the effrontery to say that?

ANGUSTIAS: I had it in my room, and now it isn't there.

MARTIRIO: But couldn't it have jumped out into the yard at midnight? Pepe likes to walk around in the moonlight.

ANGUSTIAS: Don't joke with me! When he comes I'll tell him.

PONCIA: Don't do that! Because it'll turn up.

(Looking at ADELA.)

ANGUSTIAS: I'd like to know which one of you has it.

ADELA (looking at MARTIRIO): Somebody has it! But not me!

MARTIRIO (with meaning): Of course not you!

BERNARDA (entering with her cane): What scandal is this in my house in the heat's heavy silence? The neighbors must have their ears glued to the walls.

ANGUSTIAS: They've stolen my sweetheart's picture!

BERNARDA (fiercely): Who? Who?

ANGUSTIAS: They have!

BERNARDA: Which one of you?

(Silence.)

Answer me!

(Silence.) (To LA PONCIA.*)*

Search their rooms! Look in their beds. This comes of not tying you up with shorter leashes. But I'll teach you now! *(to* ANGUSTIAS*)* Are you sure?

ANGUSTIAS: Yes.

BERNARDA: Did you look everywhere?

ANGUSTIAS: Yes, Mother.

(They all stand in an embarrassed silence.)

BERNARDA: At the end of my life—to make me drink the bitterest poison a mother knows. *(to* PONCIA*)* Did you find it?

PONCIA: Here it is.

BERNARDA: Where did you find it?

PONCIA: It was . . .

BERNARDA: Say it! Don't be afraid.

PONCIA *(wonderingly)*: Between the sheets in Martirio's bed.

BERNARDA *(to* MARTIRIO*)*: Is that true?

MARTIRIO: It's true.

BERNARDA *(advancing on her, beating her with her cane)*: You'll come to a bad end yet, you hypocrite! Trouble maker!

MARTIRIO *(fiercely)*: Don't hit me, Mother!

BERNARDA: All I want to!

MARTIRIO: If I let you! You hear me? Get back!

PONCIA: Don't be disrespectful to your mother!

ANGUSTIAS *(holding* BERNARDA*)*: Let her go, please!

BERNARDA: Not even tears in your eyes.

MARTIRIO: I'm not going to cry just to please you.

BERNARDA: Why did you take the picture?

MARTIRIO: Can't I play a joke on my sister? What else would I want it for?

ADELA *(leaping forward, full of jealousy)*: It wasn't a joke! You never liked to play jokes. It was something else bursting in her breast—trying to come out. Admit it openly now.

MARTIRIO: Hush, and don't make me speak; for if I should speak the walls would close together one against the other with shame.

ADELA: An evil tongue never stops inventing lies.

BERNARDA: Adela!

MAGDALENA: You're crazy.

AMELIA: And you stone us all with your evil suspicions.

MARTIRIO: But some others do things more wicked!

ADELA: Until all at once they stand forth stark naked and the river carries them along.

BERNARDA: Spiteful!

ANGUSTIAS: It's not my fault Pepe el Romano chose me!

ADELA: For your money.

ANGUSTIAS: Mother!

BERNARDA: Silence!

MARTIRIO: For your fields and your orchards.

MAGDALENA: That's only fair.

BERNARDA: Silence, I say! I saw the storm coming but I didn't think it'd burst so soon. Oh, what an avalanche of hate you've thrown on my heart! But I'm not old yet—I have five chains for you, and this house my father built, so not even the weeds will know of my desolation. Out of here!

(They go out. BERNARDA *sits down desolately.* LA PONCIA *is standing close to the wall.* BERNARDA *recovers herself, and beats on the floor.)*

I'll have to let them feel the weight of my hand! Bernarda, remember your duty!

PONCIA: May I speak?

BERNARDA: Speak. I'm sorry you heard. A stranger is always out of place in a family.

PONCIA: What I've seen, I've seen.

BERNARDA: Angustias must get married right away.

PONCIA: Certainly. We'll have to get her away from here.

BERNARDA: Not her, him!

PONCIA: Of course. He's the one to get away from here. You've thought it all out.

BERNARDA: I'm not thinking. These are things that shouldn't and can't be thought out. I give orders.

PONCIA: And you think he'll be satisfied to go away?

BERNARDA *(rising)*: What are you imagining now?

PONCIA: He will, of course, marry Angustias.

BERNARDA: Speak up! I know you well enough to see that your knife's out for me.

PONCIA: I never knew a warning could be called murder.

BERNARDA: Have you some "warning" for me?

PONCIA: I'm not making any accusations, Bernarda. I'm only telling you to open your eyes and you'll see.

BERNARDA: See what?

PONCIA: You've always been smart, Bernarda. You've seen other people's sins a hundred miles away. Many times I've thought you could read minds. But, your children are your children, and now you're blind.

BERNARDA: Are you talking about Martirio?

PONCIA: Well, yes—about Martirio . . .

(With curiosity.)

I wonder why she hid the picture?

BERNARDA *(shielding her daughter)*: After all, she says it was a joke. What else could it be?

PONCIA *(scornfully)*: Do you believe that?

BERNARDA *(sternly)*: I don't merely believe it. It's so!

PONCIA: Enough of this. We're talking about your family. But if we were talking about your neighbor across the way, what would it be?

BERNARDA: Now you're beginning to pull the point of the knife out.

PONCIA (*always cruelly*): No, Bernarda. Something very grave is happening here. I don't want to put the blame on your shoulders, but you've never given your daughters any freedom. Martirio is lovesick. I don't care what you say. Why didn't you let her marry Enrique Humanas? Why, on the very day he was coming to her window did you send him a message not to come?

BERNARDA (*loudly*): I'd do it a thousand times over! My blood won't mingle with the Humanas' while I live! His father was a shepherd.

PONCIA: And you see now what's happening to you with these airs!

BERNARDA: I have them because I can afford to. And you don't have them because you know where you came from!

PONCIA (*with hate*): Don't remind me! I'm old now. I've always been grateful for your protection.

BERNARDA (*emboldened*): You don't seem so!

PONCIA (*with hate, behind softness*): Martirio will forget this.

BERNARDA: And if she doesn't—the worse for her. I don't believe this is that "very grave thing" that's happening here. Nothing's happening here. It's just that you wish it would! And if it should happen one day, you can be sure it won't go beyond these walls.

PONCIA: I'm not so sure of that! There are people in town who can also read hidden thoughts, from afar.

BERNARDA: How you'd like to see me and my daughters on our way to a whorehouse!

PONCIA: No one knows her own destiny!

BERNARDA: I know my destiny! And my daughters'! The whorehouse was for a certain woman, already dead. . . .

PONCIA (*fiercely*): Bernarda, respect the memory of my mother!

BERNARDA: Then don't plague me with your evil thoughts!

(*Pause.*)

PONCIA: I'd better stay out of everything.

BERNARDA: That's what you ought to do. Work and keep your mouth shut. The duty of all who work for a living.

PONCIA: But we can't do that. Don't you think it'd be better for Pepe to marry Martirio or . . . yes! . . . Adela?

BERNARDA: No, I *don't* think so.

PONCIA (*with meaning*): Adela! She's Romano's real sweetheart!

BERNARDA: Things are never the way we want them!

PONCIA: But it's hard work to turn them from their destined course. For Pepe to be with Angustias seems wrong to me—and to other people—and even to the wind. Who knows if they'll get what they want?

BERNARDA: There you go again! Sneaking up on me—giving me bad dreams. But I won't listen to you, because if all you say should come to pass—I'd scratch your face.

PONCIA: Frighten someone else with that.

BERNARDA: Fortunately, my daughters respect me and have never gone against my will!

PONCIA: That's right! But, as soon as they break loose they'll fly to the rooftops!

BERNARDA: And I'll bring them down with stones!

PONCIA: Oh, yes! You were always the bravest one!

BERNARDA: I've always enjoyed a good fight!

PONCIA: But aren't people strange. You should see Angustias' enthusiasm for her lover, at her age! And he seems very smitten too. Yesterday my oldest son told me that when he passed by with the oxen at four-thirty in the morning they were still talking.

BERNARDA: At four-thirty?

ANGUSTIAS (*entering*): That's a lie!

PONCIA: That's what he told me.

BERNARDA (*to* ANGUSTIAS): Speak up!

ANGUSTIAS: For more than a week Pepe has been leaving at one. May God strike me dead if I'm lying.

MARTIRIO (*entering*): I heard him leave at four too.

BERNARDA: But did you see him with your eyes?

MARTIRIO: I didn't want to look out. Don't you talk now through the side window?

ANGUSTIAS: We talk through my bedroom window.

(ADELA *appears at the door.*)

MARTIRIO: Then . . .

BERNARDA: What's going on here?

PONCIA: If you're not careful, you'll find out! At least Pepe was at *one* of your windows—and at four in the morning too!

BERNARDA: Are you sure of that?

PONCIA: You can't be sure of anything in this life!

ADELA: Mother, don't listen to someone who wants us to lose everything we have.

BERNARDA: I know how to take care of myself! If the townspeople want to come bearing false witness against me, they'll run into a stone wall! Don't any of you talk about this! Sometimes other people try to stir up a wave of filth to drown us.

MARTIRIO: I don't like to lie.

PONCIA: So there must be something.

BERNARDA: There won't be anything. I was born to have my eyes always open. Now I'll watch without closing them 'til I die.

ANGUSTIAS: I have the right to know.

BERNARDA: You don't have any right except to obey. No one's going to fetch and carry for me. (*to* LA PONCIA) And don't meddle in our affairs. No one will take a step without my knowing it.

SERVANT (*entering*): There's a big crowd at the top of the street, and all the neighbors are at their doors!

BERNARDA (*to* PONCIA): Run see what's happening!

(*The* GIRLS *are about to run out.*)

Where are you going? I always knew you for window-watching women and breakers of your mourning. All of you, to the patio!

(*They go out.* BERNARDA *leaves. Distant shouts are heard.*)

(MARTIRIO *and* ADELA *enter and listen, not daring to step farther than the front door.*)

MARTIRIO: You can be thankful I didn't happen to open my mouth.

ADELA: I would have spoken too.

MARTIRIO: And what were you going to say? Wanting isn't doing!

ADELA: I do what I can and what happens to suit me. You've wanted to, but haven't been able.

MARTIRIO: You won't go on very long.

ADELA: I'll have everything!

MARTIRIO: I'll tear you out of his arms!

ADELA (*pleadingly*): Martirio, let me be!

MARTIRIO: None of us will have him!

ADELA: He wants me for his house!

MARTIRIO: I saw how he embraced you!

ADELA: I didn't want him to. It's as if I were dragged by a rope.

MARTIRIO: I'll see you dead first!

(MAGDALENA *and* ANGUSTIAS *look in. The tumult is increasing. A* SERVANT *enters with* BERNARDA. PONCIA *also enters from another door.*)

PONCIA: Bernarda!

BERNARDA: What's happening?

PONCIA: Librada's daughter, the unmarried one, had a child and no one knows whose it is!

ADELA: A child?

PONCIA: And to hide her shame she killed it and hid it under the rocks, but the dogs, with more heart than most Christians, dug it out and, as though directed by the hand of God, left it at her door. Now they want to kill her. They're dragging her through the streets—and down the paths and across the olive groves the men are coming, shouting so the fields shake.

BERNARDA: Yes, let them all come with olive whips and hoe handles—let them all come and kill her!

ADELA: No, not to kill her!

MARTIRIO: Yes—and let us go out too!

BERNARDA: And let whoever loses her decency pay for it!

(*Outside a woman's shriek and a great clamor is heard.*)

ADELA: Let her escape! Don't you go out!

MARTIRIO (*looking at* ADELA): Let her pay what she owes!

BERNARDA (*at the archway*): Finish her before the guards come! Hot coals in the place where she sinned!

ADELA (*holding her belly*): No! No!

BERNARDA: Kill her! Kill her!

(*Curtain.*)

ACT 3

(*Four white walls, lightly washed in blue, of the interior patio of* BERNARDA ALBA*'s house. The doorways, illumined by the lights inside the rooms, give a tenuous glow to the stage. At the center there is a table with a shaded oil lamp about which* BERNARDA *and her* DAUGHTERS *are eating.* LA PONCIA *serves them.* PRUDENCIA *sits apart. When the curtain rises, there is a great silence interrupted only by the noise of plates and silverware.*)

PRUDENCIA: I'm going. I've made you a long visit.

(*She rises.*)

BERNARDA: But wait, Prudencia. We never see one another.

PRUDENCIA: Have they sounded the last call to rosary?

PONCIA: Not yet.

(PRUDENCIA *sits down again.*)

BERNARDA: And your husband, how's he getting on?

PRUDENCIA: The same.

BERNARDA: We never see him either.

PRUDENCIA: You know how he is. Since he quarrelled with his brothers over the inheritance, he hasn't used the front door. He takes a ladder and climbs over the back wall.

BERNARDA: He's a real man! And your daughter?

PRUDENCIA: He's never forgiven her.

BERNARDA: He's right.

PRUDENCIA: I don't know what he told you. I suffer because of it.

BERNARDA: A daughter who's disobedient stops being a daughter and becomes an enemy.

PRUDENCIA: I let water run. The only consolation I've left is to take refuge in the church, but, since I'm losing my sight, I'll have to stop coming so the children won't make fun of me.

(*A heavy blow is heard against the walls.*)

What's that?

BERNARDA: The stallion. He's locked in the stall and he kicks against the wall of the house.

(*Shouting.*)

Tether him and take him out in the yard!

(*In a lower voice.*)

He must be too hot.

PRUDENCIA: Are you going to put the new mares to him?

BERNARDA: At daybreak.

PRUDENCIA: You've known how to increase your stock.

BERNARDA: By dint of money and struggling.

PONCIA (interrupting): And she has the best herd in these parts. It's a shame that prices are low.

BERNARDA: Do you want a little cheese and honey?

PRUDENCIA: I have no appetite.

(The blow is heard again.)

PONCIA: My God!

PRUDENCIA: It quivered in my chest.

BERNARDA (rising, furiously): Do I have to say things twice? Let him out to roll on the straw.

(Pause. Then, as though speaking to the stableman.)

Well then, lock the mares in the corral, but let him run free or he may kick down the walls.

(She returns to the table and sits again.)

Ay, what a life!

PRUDENCIA: You have to fight like a man.

BERNARDA: That's it.

(ADELA gets up from the table.)

Where are you going?

ADELA: For a drink of water.

BERNARDA (raising her voice): Bring a pitcher of cool water. (to ADELA) You can sit down. (ADELA sits down.)

PRUDENCIA: And Angustias, when will she get married?

BERNARDA: They're coming to ask for her within three days.

PRUDENCIA: You must be happy.

ANGUSTIAS: Naturally!

AMELIA (to MAGDALENA): You've spilled the salt!

MAGDALENA: You can't possibly have worse luck than you're having.

AMELIA: It always brings bad luck.

BERNARDA: That's enough!

PRUDENCIA (to ANGUSTIAS): Has he given you the ring yet?

ANGUSTIAS: Look at it.

(She holds it out.)

PRUDENCIA: It's beautiful. Three pearls. In my day, pearls signified tears.

ANGUSTIAS: But things have changed now.

ADELA: I don't think so. Things go on meaning the same. Engagement rings should be diamonds.

PONCIA: The most appropriate.

BERNARDA: With pearls or without them, things are as one proposes.

MARTIRIO: Or as God disposes.

PRUDENCIA: I've been told your furniture is beautiful.

BERNARDA: It cost sixteen thousand *reales*.

PONCIA (interrupting): The best is the wardrobe with the mirror.

PRUDENCIA: I never saw a piece like that.

BERNARDA: We had chests.

PRUDENCIA: The important thing is that everything be for the best.

ADELA: And that you never know.

BERNARDA: There's no reason why it shouldn't be.

(Bells are heard very distantly.)

PRUDENCIA: The last call. (to ANGUSTIAS) I'll be coming back to have you show me your clothes.

ANGUSTIAS: Whenever you like.

PRUDENCIA: Good evening—God bless you!

BERNARDA: Good-bye, Prudencia.

ALL FIVE DAUGHTERS (at the same time): God go with you!

(Pause. PRUDENCIA goes out.)

BERNARDA: Well, we've eaten.

(They rise.)

ADELA: I'm going to walk as far as the gate to stretch my legs and get a bit of fresh air.

(MAGDALENA sits down in a low chair and leans against the wall.)

AMELIA: I'll go with you.

MARTIRIO: I too.

ADELA (with contained hate): I'm not going to get lost!

AMELIA: One needs company at night.

(They go out. BERNARDA sits down. ANGUSTIAS is clearing the table.)

BERNARDA: I've told you once already! I want you to talk to your sister Martirio. What happened about the picture was a joke and you must forget it.

ANGUSTIAS: You know she doesn't like me.

BERNARDA: Each one knows what she thinks inside. I don't pry into anyone's heart, but I want to put up a good front and have family harmony. You understand?

ANGUSTIAS: Yes.

BERNARDA: Then that's settled.

MAGDALENA (she is almost asleep): Besides, you'll be gone in no time.

(She falls asleep.)

ANGUSTIAS: Not soon enough for me.

BERNARDA: What time did you stop talking last night?

ANGUSTIAS: Twelve-thirty.

BERNARDA: What does Pepe talk about?

ANGUSTIAS: I find him absent-minded. He always talks to me as though he were thinking of something else. If I ask him what's the matter, he answers— "We men have our worries."

BERNARDA: You shouldn't ask him. And when you're married, even less. Speak if he speaks, and look at him when he looks at you. That way you'll get along.

ANGUSTIAS: But, Mother, I think he's hiding things from me.

BERNARDA: Don't try to find out. Don't ask him, and above all, never let him see you cry.

ANGUSTIAS: I should be happy, but I'm not.

BERNARDA: It's all the same.

ANGUSTIAS: Many nights I watch Pepe very closely through the window bars and he seems to fade away—as though he were hidden in a cloud of dust like those raised by the flocks.

BERNARDA: That's just because you're not strong.

ANGUSTIAS: I hope so!

BERNARDA: Is he coming tonight?

ANGUSTIAS: No, he went into town with his mother.

BERNARDA: Good, we'll get to bed early. Magdalena!

ANGUSTIAS: She's asleep.

(ADELA, MARTIRIO and AMELIA enter.)

AMELIA: What a dark night!

ADELA: You can't see two steps in front of you.

MARTIRIO: A good night for robbers, for anyone who needs to hide.

ADELA: The stallion was in the middle of the corral. White. Twice as large. Filling all the darkness.

AMELIA: It's true. It was frightening. Like a ghost.

ADELA: The sky has stars as big as fists.

MARTIRIO: This one stared at them till she almost cracked her neck.

ADELA: Don't you like them up there?

MARTIRIO: What goes on over the roof doesn't mean a thing to me. I have my hands full with what happens under it.

ADELA: Well, that's the way it goes with you!

BERNARDA: And it goes the same for you as for her.

ANGUSTIAS: Good night.

ADELA: Are you going to bed now?

ANGUSTIAS: Yes, Pepe isn't coming tonight.

(She goes out.)

ADELA: Mother, why, when a star falls or lightning flashes, does one say:
Holy Barbara, blessed on high
May your name be in the sky
With holy water written high?

BERNARDA: The old people know many things we've forgotten.

AMELIA: I close my eyes so I won't see them.

ADELA: Not I. I like to see what's quiet and been quiet for years on end, running with fire.

MARTIRIO: But all that has nothing to do with us.

BERNARDA: And it's better not to think about it.

ADELA: What a beautiful night! I'd like to stay up till very late and enjoy the breeze from the fields.

BERNARDA: But we have to go to bed. Magdalena!

AMELIA: She's just dropped off.

BERNARDA: Magdalena!

MAGDALENA *(annoyed)*: Leave me alone!

BERNARDA: To bed!

MAGDALENA *(rising, in a bad humor)*: You don't give anyone a moment's peace!

(She goes off grumbling.)

AMELIA: Good night!

(She goes out.)

BERNARDA: You two get along, too.

MARTIRIO: How is it Angustias' sweetheart isn't coming tonight?

BERNARDA: He went on a trip.

MARTIRIO *(looking at* ADELA*)*: Ah!

ADELA: I'll see you in the morning!

(She goes out. MARTIRIO *drinks some water and goes out slowly, looking at the door to the yard.* LA PONCIA *enters.)*

PONCIA: Are you still here?

BERNARDA: Enjoying this quiet and not seeing anywhere the "very grave thing" that's happening here—according to you.

PONCIA: Bernarda, let's not go any further with this.

BERNARDA: In this house there's no question of a yes or a no. My watchfulness can take care of anything.

PONCIA: Nothing's happening outside. That's true, all right. Your daughters act and are as though stuck in a cupboard. But neither you nor anyone else can keep watch inside a person's heart.

BERNARDA: My daughters breathe calmly enough.

PONCIA: That's your business, since you're their mother. I have enough to do just with serving you.

BERNARDA: Yes, you've turned quiet now.

PONCIA: I keep my place—that's all.

BERNARDA: The trouble is you've nothing to talk about. If there were grass in this house, you'd make it your business to put the neighbors' sheep to pasture here.

PONCIA: I hide more than you think.

BERNARDA: Do your sons still see Pepe at four in the morning? Are they still repeating this house's evil litany?

PONCIA: They say nothing.

BERNARDA: Because they can't. Because there's nothing for them to sink their teeth in. And all because my eyes keep constant watch!

PONCIA: Bernarda, I don't want to talk about this because I'm afraid of what you'll do. But don't you feel so safe.

BERNARDA: Very safe!

PONCIA: Who knows, lightning might strike suddenly. Who knows but what all of a sudden, in a rush of blood, your heart might stop.

BERNARDA: Nothing will happen here. I'm on guard now against all your suspicions.

PONCIA: All the better for you.

BERNARDA: Certainly, all the better!

SERVANT (*entering*): I've just finished with the dishes. Is there anything else, Bernarda?

BERNARDA (*rising*): Nothing. I'm going to get some rest.

PONCIA: What time do you want me to call you?

BERNARDA: No time. Tonight I intend to sleep well.

(*She goes out.*)

PONCIA: When you're powerless against the sea, it's easier to turn your back on it and not look at it.

SERVANT: She's so proud! She herself pulls the blindfold over her eyes.

PONCIA: I can do nothing. I tried to head things off, but now they frighten me too much. You feel this silence?—in each room there's a thunderstorm—and the day it breaks, it'll sweep all of us along with it. But I've said what I had to say.

SERVANT: Bernarda thinks nothing can stand against her, yet she doesn't know the strength a man has among women alone.

PONCIA: It's not all the fault of Pepe el Romano. It's true last year he was running after Adela; and she was crazy about him—but she ought to keep her place and not lead him on. A man's a man.

SERVANT: And some there are who believe he didn't have to talk many times with Adela.

PONCIA: That's true.

(*In a low voice.*)

And some other things.

SERVANT: I don't know what's going to happen here.

PONCIA: How I'd like to sail across the sea and leave this house, this battleground, behind!

SERVANT: Bernarda's hurrying the wedding and it's possible nothing will happen.

PONCIA: Things have gone much too far already. Adela is set no matter what comes, and the rest of them watch without rest.

SERVANT: Martirio too . . . ?

PONCIA: That one's the worst. She's a pool of poison. She sees El Romano is not for her, and she'd sink the world if it were in her hand to do so.

SERVANT: How bad they all are!

PONCIA: They're women without men, that's all. And in such matters even blood is forgotten. Sh-h-h-h!

(*She listens.*)

SERVANT: What's the matter?

PONCIA (*she rises*): The dogs are barking.

SERVANT: Someone must have passed by the back door.

(ADELA *enters wearing a white petticoat and corselet.*)

PONCIA: Aren't you in bed yet?

ADELA: I want a drink of water.

(*She drinks from a glass on the table.*)

PONCIA: I imagined you were asleep.

ADELA: I got thirsty and woke up. Aren't you two going to get some rest?

SERVANT: Soon now.

(ADELA *goes out.*)

PONCIA: Let's go.

SERVANT: We've certainly earned some sleep. Bernarda doesn't let me rest the whole day.

PONCIA: Take the light.

SERVANT: The dogs are going mad.

PONCIA: They're not going to let us sleep.

(*They go out. The stage is left almost dark.* MARIA JOSEFA *enters with a lamb in her arms.*)

MARIA JOSEFA (*singing*):

> Little lamb, child of mine,
> Let's go to the shore of the sea,
> The tiny ant will be at his doorway,
> I'll nurse you and give you your bread.
> Bernarda, old leopard-face,
> And Magdalena, hyena-face,
> Little lamb . . .
> Rock, rock-a-bye,
> Let's go to the palms at Bethlehem's gate.

(*She laughs.*)

> Neither you nor I would want to sleep
> The door will open by itself
> And on the beach we'll go and hide
> In a little coral cabin.
> Bernarda, old leopard-face,
> And Magdalena, hyena-face,
> Little lamb . . .
> Rock, rock-a-bye,
> Let's go to the palms at Bethlehem's gate.

(*She goes off singing.*)

(ADELA *enters. She looks about cautiously and disappears out the door leading to the corral.* MARTIRIO *enters by another door and stands in anguished watchfulness near the center of the stage. She also is in petticoats. She covers herself with a small black scarf.* MARIA JOSEFA *crosses before her.*)

MARTIRIO: Grandmother, where are you going?

MARIA JOSEFA: You are going to open the door for me? Who are you?

MARTIRIO: How did you get out here?

MARIA JOSEFA: I escaped. You, who are you?

MARTIRIO: Go back to bed.

MARIA JOSEFA: You're Martirio. Now I see you. Martirio, face of a martyr. And when are you going to have a baby? I've had this one.

MARTIRIO: Where did you get that lamb?

MARIA JOSEFA: I know it's a lamb. But can't a lamb be a baby? It's better to have a lamb than not to have anything. Old Bernarda, leopard-face, and Magdalena, hyena-face!

MARTIRIO: Don't shout.

MARIA JOSEFA: It's true. Everything's very dark. Just because I have white hair you think I can't have babies, but I can—babies and babies and babies. This baby will have white hair, and I'd have *this* baby, and another, and this *one* other; and with all of us with snow white hair we'll be like the waves— one, then another, and another. Then we'll all sit down and all of us will have white heads, and we'll be seafoam. Why isn't there any seafoam here? Nothing but mourning shrouds here.

MARTIRIO: Hush, hush.

MARIA JOSEFA: When my neighbor had a baby, I'd carry her some chocolate and later she'd bring me some, and so on—always and always and always. You'll have white hair, but your neighbors won't come. Now I have to go away, but I'm afraid the dogs will bite me. Won't you come with me as far as the fields? I don't like fields. I like houses, but open houses, and the neighbor women asleep in their beds with their little tiny tots, and the men outside sitting in their chairs. Pepe el Romano is a giant. All of you love him. But he's going to devour you because you're grains of wheat. No, not grains of wheat. Frogs with no tongues!

MARTIRIO (*angrily*): Come, off to bed with you.

(*She pushes her.*)

MARIA JOSEFA: Yes, but then you'll open the door for me, won't you?

MARTIRIO: Of course.

MARIA JOSEFA (*weeping*):

> Little lamb, child of mine,
> Let's go to the shore of the sea,
> The tiny ant will be at his doorway,
> I'll nurse you and give you your bread.

(MARTIRIO *locks the door through which* MARIA JOSEFA *came out and goes to the yard door. There she hesitates, but goes two steps farther.*)

MARTIRIO (*in a low voice*): Adela! (*Pause. She advances to the door. Then, calling.*) Adela!

(ADELA *enters. Her hair is disarranged.*)

ADELA: And what are you looking for me for?

MARTIRIO: Keep away from him.

ADELA: Who are you to tell me that?

MARTIRIO: That's no place for a decent woman.

ADELA: How you wish *you'd* been there!

MARTIRIO (*shouting*): This is the moment for me to speak. This can't go on.

ADELA: This is just the beginning. I've had strength enough to push myself forward—the spirit and looks you lack. I've seen death under this roof,

and gone out to look for what was mine, what belonged to me.

MARTIRIO: That soulless man came for another woman. You pushed yourself in front of him.

ADELA: He came for the money, but his eyes were always on me.

MARTIRIO: I won't allow you to snatch him away. He'll marry Angustias.

ADELA: You know better than I he doesn't love her.

MARTIRIO: I know.

ADELA: You know because you've seen—he loves me, me!

MARTIRIO (*desperately*): Yes.

ADELA (*close before her*): He loves me, *me!* He loves me, *me!*

MARTIRIO: Stick me with a knife if you like, but don't tell me that again.

ADELA: That's why you're trying to fix it so I won't go away with him. It makes no difference to you if he puts his arms around a woman he doesn't love. Nor does it to me. He could be a hundred years with Angustias, but for him to have his arms around me seems terrible to you—because you too love him! You love him!

MARTIRIO (*dramatically*): Yes! Let me say it without hiding my head. Yes! my breast's bitter, bursting like a pomegranate. I love him!

ADELA (*impulsively, hugging her*): Martirio, Martirio, I'm not to blame!

MARTIRIO: Don't put your arms around me! Don't try to smooth it over. My blood's no longer yours, and even though I try to think of you as a sister, I see you as just another woman.

(*She pushes her away.*)

ADELA: There's no way out here. Whoever has to drown—let her drown. Pepe is mine. He'll carry me to the rushes along the river bank. . . .

MARTIRIO: He won't!

ADELA: I can't stand this horrible house after the taste of his mouth. I'll be what he wants me to be. Everybody in the village against me, burning me with their fiery fingers; pursued by those who claim they're decent, and I'll wear, before them all, the crown of thorns that belongs to the mistress of a married man.

MARTIRIO: Hush!

ADELA: Yes, yes. (*In a low voice.*) Let's go to bed. Let's let him marry Angustias. I don't care any more, but I'll go off alone to a little house where he'll come to see me whenever he wants, whenever he feels like it.

MARTIRIO: That'll never happen! Not while I have a drop of blood left in my body.

ADELA: Not just weak you, but a wild horse I could force to his knees with just the strength of my little finger.

MARTIRIO: Don't raise that voice of yours to me. It irritates me. I have a heart full of a force so evil that, without my wanting to be, I'm drowned by it.

ADELA: You show us the way to love our sisters. God must have meant to leave me alone in the midst of darkness because I can see you as I've never seen you before.

(A whistle is heard and ADELA *runs toward the door, but* MARTIRIO *gets in front of her.)*

MARTIRIO: Where are you going?

ADELA: Get away from that door!

MARTIRIO: Get by me if you can!

ADELA: Get away!

(They struggle.)

MARTIRIO *(shouts)*: Mother! Mother!

ADELA: Let me go!

*(*BERNARDA *enters. She wears petticoats and a black shawl.)*

BERNARDA: Quiet! Quiet! How poor I am without even a man to help me!

MARTIRIO *(pointing to* ADELA*)*: She was with him. Look at those skirts covered with straw!

BERNARDA *(going furiously toward* ADELA*)*: That's the bed of a bad woman!

ADELA *(facing her)*: There'll be an end to prison voices here! *(*ADELA *snatches away her mother's cane and breaks it in two.)* This is what I do with the tyrant's cane. Not another step. No one but Pepe commands me!

*(*MAGDALENA *enters.)*

MAGDALENA: Adela!

*(*LA PONCIA *and* ANGUSTIAS *enter.)*

ADELA: I'm his. *(to* ANGUSTIAS*)* Know that—and go out in the yard and tell him. He'll be master in this house.

ANGUSTIAS: My God!

BERNARDA: The gun! Where's the gun?

(She rushes out. LA PONCIA *runs ahead of her.* AMELIA *enters and looks on frightened, leaning her head against the wall. Behind her comes* MARTIRIO.*)*

ADELA: No one can hold me back!

(She tries to go out.)

ANGUSTIAS *(holding her)*: You're not getting out of here with your body's triumph! Thief! Disgrace of this house!

MAGDALENA: Let her go where we'll never see her again!

(A shot is heard.)

BERNARDA *(entering)*: Just try looking for him now!

MARTIRIO *(entering)*: That does away with Pepe el Romano.

ADELA: Pepe! My God! Pepe!

(She runs out.)

PONCIA: Did you kill him?

MARTIRIO: No. He raced away on his mare!

BERNARDA: It was my fault. A woman can't aim.

MAGDALENA: Then, why did you say. . . ?

MARTIRIO: For her! I'd like to pour a river of blood over her head!

PONCIA: Curse you!

MAGDALENA: Devil!

BERNARDA: Although it's better this way!

(A thud is heard.)

Adela! Adela!

PONCIA *(at her door)*: Open this door!

BERNARDA: Open! Don't think the walls will hide your shame!

SERVANT *(entering)*: All the neighbors are up!

BERNARDA *(in a low voice, but like a roar)*: Open! Or I'll knock the door down!

(Pause. Everything is silent.)

Adela!

(She walks away from the door.)

A hammer!

*(*LA PONCIA *throws herself against the door. It opens and she goes in. As she enters, she screams and backs out.)*

What is it?

PONCIA *(she puts her hands to her throat)*: May we never die like that!

(The SISTERS *fall back. The* SERVANT *crosses herself.* BERNARDA *screams and goes forward.)*

Don't go in!

BERNARDA: No, not I! Pepe, you're running now, alive in the darkness, under the trees, but another day you'll fall. Cut her down! My daughter died a virgin. Take her to another room and dress her as though she were a virgin. No one will say anything about this! She died a virgin. Tell them, so that at dawn, the bells will ring twice.

MARTIRIO: A thousand times happy she, who had him.

BERNARDA: And I want no weeping. Death must be looked at face to face. Silence!

(To one daughter.)

Be still, I said!

(To another daughter.)

Tears when you're alone! We'll drown ourselves in a sea of mourning. She, the youngest daughter of Bernarda Alba, died a virgin. Did you hear me? Silence, silence, I said. Silence!

CURTAIN

Figure 1. The entire household of Bernarda Alba and the neighbor women join in mourning for Bernarda's late husband in Nuria Espert's 1986 production at the Lyric, Hammersmith. (Photograph: © Donald Cooper/Photostage.)

Figure 2. Poncia (Joan Plowright, *arms outstretched*) tells Angustias (Julie Legrand, *left*), Magdalena (Christine Edmonds), Amelia (Chloe Salaman), and Martirio (Deborah Findlay) about her courtship in Nuria Espert's 1986 production. (Photograph: © Donald Cooper/Photostage.)

Figure 3. Maria Josefa (Patricia Hayes, *center*) insists that she wants to marry; Bernarda (Glenda Jackson) stares at her in anger, and Poncia (Joan Plowright) tries to restrain her in Nuria Espert's 1986 production. (Photograph: © Donald Cooper/Photostage.)

Figure 4. "Just try looking for him now!" screams Bernarda Alba (Glenda Jackson, *center, with rifle*) after firing at Pepe el Romano; Adela (Amanda Root, *standing front right*) is about to rush out, distraught, to her death in Nuria Espert's 1986 production (as seen at the Globe Theatre in 1987). (Photograph: © Donald Cooper/Photostage.)

Staging of *The House of Bernarda Alba*

REVIEW OF THE LYRIC, HAMMERSMITH PRODUCTION, 1986, BY MICHAEL BILLINGTON

The British theatre suddenly seems to be shedding its insularity. Peter James's internationalist policy at the Lyric, Hammersmith, brings us a moving, austerely impressive production of Lorca's 50-year-old *The House of Bernarda Alba,* directed by Nuria Espert, that proves several things: that British actresses can play Spanish tragedy, that Lorca is translatable (at least by Robert David Macdonald), and that a suburban theatre can yield a production that would not disgrace—indeed would enhance—the stages of our national companies.

The set has a lot to do with it. Ezio Frigerio (Strehler's designer) has taken the title literally and made the house one of the stars of the evening. Lorca's play is about the passion and frustration of the five, immured daughters of the widowed, tyrannical Bernarda Alba: and Frigerio has surrounded them by towering, white, age-pocked Granada walls inset with tiny, barred windows and culminating in a grating, flagstone floor.

The impression, simultaneously, is of a prison courtyard, a nunnery and an asylum; and, even if the sense of Andalusian heat is not very strong, the claustrophobia is heightened by the lowering space and by Franca Squarciatino's black costumes giving the women the look of bottled insects.

The difficulty lies in creating, for an English audience, a world dominated by honour, tradition, toil and sexual restraint from which there is only one escape: an arranged marriage has been fixed between the eldest daughter, Angustias, and the unseen Pepe el Romano who, it tragically transpires, is the lover of her youngest sister, Adela.

The power of Lorca's play lies in its portrait of a specific family. But even in the canopied courtyard, while outside the men go off to harvest, they are enclosed by the house, history, sexual custom and an overpowering sense of fate. "I should be happy but I'm not," says Angustias. "It's all the same either way," her mother replies, sealing their collective doom.

Nuria Espert breaks through Anglo-Saxon optimism to create this sense of entrapment and she does this by assembling a crack company in which no one is allowed to give a selfish-star-performance. Gillian Hanna's Maid, dutifully scrubbing stone floors and driven mad by the noise of the funeral bells, is as vital to the atmosphere as Glenda Jackson's tyrannical matriarch who rules over her brood like a female leopard (she even brandishes a claw at a recalcitrant daughter) and who howls with sadistic relish as an errant village woman is dragged through the streets.

At first hard to distinguish, her five daughters gradually take on individual life: Deborah Findlay's Martirio, caressing a black-stockinged ankle as she talks of the men yoking bullocks in the yard, implies a sensuality balefully repressed, while Amanda Root's Adela in her green dress embodies a dream of freedom.

But the vital tonal contrast is supplied by Joan Plowright in a marvellous performance as the servant Poncia: she is earthy, robust, sensual but the way she smoothes the nap of the folded linen evokes a lifetime of drudgery and suggests she is as much part of a doomed, mechanistic universe as the sisters. Patricia Hayes, stark-naked in a white shift, also gives a highly courageous performance as the mad, locked-in grandmother symbolising the fate awaiting Bernarda's daughters.

A needless interval dissipates the tension. But otherwise this is a vivid realisation of Lorca's play that conveys much of its meaning through a series of resonant images: of the sisters breaking into dreamy, private dances as the men go off to reap and of the family dining in a corner of the courtyard in a state of imprisoned festivity. Nuria Espert has put before us an enclosed world: at the same time, she has opened up the possibility of Lorca on the British stage.

BERTOLT BRECHT

1898–1956

The social and political upheavals of the twentieth century profoundly influenced Brecht's life and his plays. World War I put an end to his medical studies in Munich and marked the beginning of his intense political consciousness, which he expressed in "The Legend of the Dead Soldier" (1918), a poem the Nazis were later to cite as evidence for denying him German citizenship. Shortly after the war, in 1919, he took part in an unsuccessful revolution in his native Bavaria, a bitter experience that provided the basis for his first successful play, *Drums in the Night* (1922). By 1922, Brecht had also become dramaturg (a resident playwright and adapter) at the Munich Kammerspiele, a theater for which he wrote *In the Jungle of the Cities* (1923). There, too, he directed *Edward II* (1924), his revision of Marlowe's history play, in a striking production that featured a battle scene with the faces of the soldiers painted stark white.

But it was in Berlin, where Brecht moved to in 1924, that he was to become widely known—and where he was to develop his revolutionary concept of "epic theater": a form of drama and dramatic production intended to provoke spectators into a heightened social and political awareness, rather than involve them emotionally in a realistic or naturalistic situation (see "Theatre for Pleasure, or Theatre for Instruction," in Ideas of Drama). To prevent spectators from empathizing with his characters, Brecht advocated an "alienation effect" both in acting and playwriting. Brecht's approach to acting directly countered the method of Stanislavsky. Brecht asked actors to distance themselves from the inner life of a role and not immerse themselves in it, to deliver lines in a mocking or dispassionate tone instead of an emotionally convincing voice, and in general to act a part in a manner that conveyed the awareness of being a performer rather than the involvement of being a character. To jerk spectators into a heightened social and political consciousness, Brecht abandoned the carefully elaborated plots of realistic drama in favor of an episodic structure he learned from reading and viewing the expressionistic political plays of his German contemporaries. Brecht created this jerky, episodic effect by using short scenes in rapidly changing locales, with frequent shifts from prose to verse to song. And to further awaken the audience to his political message, Brecht incorporated a variety of nonrealistic staging devices used by the radical German producer Erwin Piscator—posters, slide projections, motion pictures, stylized sets, and garish lighting effects.

Brecht synthesized all these elements for the first time in *Man Is Man* (1926), a fiercely anticolonial, antiwar play, which is set in India during the British imperial rule and depicts the transformation of a poor dock worker into a soldier and military hero—a transformation that also changes him from a human being into a monster of nature. Two years later, Brecht produced his most popular and successful piece of epic theater, *The Threepenny Opera* (1928), a biting attack on capitalistic society, a society in which "money rules the world" and in which "Mankind can keep alive thanks to its brilliance in keeping its humanity repressed." To this political satire, Brecht adds romantic satire, mocking Polly Peachum's naïve attachment to the lusty Macheath. The fame and money Brecht gained from this work, the popularity of which derived not just from Brecht's clever reworking of John Gay's *The Beggar's Opera* (1728) but from Kurt Weill's pungent score, gave Brecht the freedom to create a wide variety of theatrical works: his dogmatically Marxist plays, which he called "Lehrstücke" (literally, learning pieces), including *The Measures Taken* (1930) and *The Exception and the Rule* (1930); his less dogmatic but still socialist plays, such as *The Mother* (1932) and *St. Joan of the Stockyards* (1932); and his other musical collaborations with Weill, *Happy End* (1929), *The Rise and Fall of the City of Mahagonny* (1929), and *The Seven Deadly Sins* (1933). The overtly didactic message in all these plays was, in essence, a challenge to the audience to change an existing social order that Brecht perceived as enslaving human beings through bureaucracy, war, and capitalism.

In 1933, political upheaval once again altered the course of Brecht's life, for when Hitler came to power Brecht was compelled to flee Nazi Germany—the communist politics of his plays had led to the danger of his being tried for high treason. He stayed briefly in Switzerland, then made his home in Denmark until 1939, when an impending Nazi invasion of that country forced him to move his family and his acting company to Sweden. But in 1940, the fear that Sweden would be invaded drove Brecht and his entourage to Finland. In 1941, he obtained a visa to the United States and settled in Santa Monica, California, where he lived until 1947, when his communist allegiances brought him under investigation by the House Committee on Un-American Activities, and he was forced to return to Germany. He spent his remaining years in East Berlin, where he devoted himself primarily to producing his already written plays and to turning his acting company, the Berliner Ensemble, into one of the most distinguished theatrical groups in the world.

During his exile from Germany, Brecht composed his most powerful plays—among them *Mother Courage and Her Children* (1939), *The Good Woman of Setzuan* (1943), *The Caucasian Chalk Circle* (1945), and *Galileo,* which he wrote and rewrote between 1938 and 1954. In all of these plays, the overt, even strident didacticism of his earlier Marxist plays gives way to a broader socialist message. Oppression is still the enemy, but in these plays it is seen as residing not only in social institutions but in the acts of individual human beings. And it is in these plays, too, that the split between Brecht's theories of epic theater and his actual practice become most noticeable, for the plays seem to invite an audience to become passionately involved in the problems of their central characters. Although Brecht's notes on Mother Courage repeatedly emphasize the distasteful qualities he had hoped to reveal in her—her pettiness, her moral deformity, her incurable political ignorance—audiences invariably become engaged by her tenacity and indomitability. The female protagonist of *The Good Woman of Setzuan* must adopt a male disguise and ruthless behavior in order to enjoy the good fortune that suddenly befalls her, but although Brecht offers no solution to her dilemma (how can one be good and still survive in a grasping, materialistic world?), the strength of Shen Te's idealism still engages the audience's sympathies. And although Brecht's notes to *Galileo* indicate that he meant to portray the famous scientist as having betrayed his calling, the play itself invites a more spacious and sympathetic view of the man.

Brecht's three versions of the play show his continuing fascination with the character of Galileo as well as his perception that Galileo's recantation of his scientific discoveries could be interpreted in a variety of ways. In the first version, written in 1938 and titled *The Earth Moves,* Galileo's revolutionary experiments and discoveries are depicted as profoundly disturbing to the religious authorities because they replace a geocentric view of planetary relationships with a heliocentric one and thereby remove human beings from the center of God's universe—a decentering that challenges the centrality of the Catholic Church itself. But after 1945, when American war planes dropped atomic bombs on Hiroshima and Nagasaki, Brecht, aided by Charles Laughton, rewrote the play in English to mock not only the institutions of the church but also Galileo himself as a kind of self-serving intellectual who would do anything, even recant his own scientific work, to save his skin. In this version, the play turns into a condemnation of the scientist as a man who might have changed human understanding but who failed to do so and in that failure indirectly contributed to something as horrific as the dropping of the bomb. The play's final version, in German again, is the longest, containing Brecht's bitterest attack on Galileo's failure to resist the Inquisition.

The balance and clarity of the "Laughton version" reflect the unusual working conditions that created the text. Meeting every morning in Laughton's large house overlooking the Pacific Ocean, the famous actor who spoke no German and the famous playwright whose English was limited communicated through their common language—theatrical gesture. Brecht reports that he would act out a piece of dialogue in "bad English or even in German," Laughton would act it back in "proper English," and finally Brecht would consent to a line, which Laughton would then write down.

Photographs from the 1947 New York production show Laughton's ability to convey different facets of Galileo's personality: his wary suspicion of the Inquisitor (Figure 1), his comfortably relaxed enjoyment of his friends (Figure 2), and his intense concentration (Figure 3). In that final photograph, one sees too the pain of the "stony and scientifically accurate self-knowledge" that Irwin Shaw found so memorable. Galileo's chilling view of himself as a man who betrayed his profession seemed for Irwin Shaw "the very core of truth." Yet the play follows Galileo's long speech of self-recrimination with Andrea's view that Galileo's recantation was strategic, something that enabled him to live and continue his writing. Who, then, has the last word? In the play's final scene, Andrea smuggles Galileo's manuscript out of Italy, trying to explain the truth to a young boy just as Galileo had explained it to him. And though the almost-blind Galileo can no longer see the sky, it is nonetheless bright.

GALILEO

BY BERTOLT BRECHT / TRANSLATED BY CHARLES LAUGHTON

It is my opinion that the earth is very noble and admirable by reason of so many and so different alterations and generations which are incessantly made therein.

—GALILEO GALILEI

CHARACTERS

GALILEO GALILEI
ANDREA SARTI, *two actors: boy and man*
MRS. SARTI
LUDOVICO MARSILI
PRIULI, *the curator*
SAGREDO, GALILEO'S *friend*
VIRGINIA GALILEI
TWO SENATORS
MATTI, *an iron founder*
PHILOSOPHER, *later,* RECTOR OF THE UNIVERSITY
ELDERLY LADY
YOUNG LADY
FEDERZONI, *assistant to* GALILEO
MATHEMATICIAN
LORD CHAMBERLAIN
FAT PRELATE
TWO SCHOLARS
TWO MONKS
INFURIATED MONK
OLD CARDINAL
ATTENDANT MONK
CHRISTOPHER CLAVIUS

LITTLE MONK
TWO SECRETARIES
CARDINAL BELLARMIN
CARDINAL BARBERINI
CARDINAL INQUISITOR
YOUNG GIRL
HER FRIEND
GIUSEPPE
STREET SINGER
HIS WIFE
REVELLER
A LOUD VOICE
INFORMER
TOWN CRIER
OFFICIAL
PEASANT
CUSTOMS OFFICER
BOY
SENATORS, OFFICIALS, PROFESSORS, LADIES, GUESTS, CHILDREN

There are two wordless roles: The Doge in scene 2 and Prince Cosmo de Medici in scene 4. The ballad of scene 9 is filled out by a pantomime: among the individuals in the pantomimic crowd are three extras (including the "King of Hungary"), Cobbler's Boy, Three Children, Peasant Woman, Monk, Rich Couple, Dwarf, Beggar, and Girl.

SCENE 1

In the year sixteen hundred and nine
Science's light began to shine.
At Padua City, in a modest house
Galileo Galilei set out to prove
The sun is still, the earth is on the move.

(GALILEO's *scantily furnished study. Morning.* GALILEO *is washing himself. A barefooted boy,* ANDREA, *son of his housekeeper,* MRS. SARTI, *enters with a big astronomical model.*)

GALILEO: Where did you get that thing?
ANDREA: The coachman brought it.
GALILEO: Who sent it?
ANDREA: It said "From the Court of Naples" on the box.
GALILEO: I don't want their stupid presents. Illuminated manuscripts, a statue of Hercules the size of an elephant—they never send money.
ANDREA: But isn't this an astronomical instrument, Mr. Galilei?
GALILEO: This is an antique too. An expensive toy.
ANDREA: What's it for?

GALILEO: It's a map of the sky according to the wise men of ancient Greece. Bosh! We'll try and sell it to the university. They still teach it there.
ANDREA: How does it work, Mr. Galilei?
GALILEO: It's complicated.
ANDREA: I think I could understand it.
GALILEO (*interested*): Maybe. Let's begin at the beginning. Description!
ANDREA: There are metal rings, a lot of them.
GALILEO: How many?
ANDREA: Eight.
GALILEO: Correct. And?
ANDREA: There are words painted on the bands.
GALILEO: What words?
ANDREA: The names of stars.
GALILEO: Such as?
ANDREA: Here is a band with the sun on it and on the inside band is the moon.
GALILEO: Those metal bands represent crystal globes, eight of them.
ANDREA: Crystal?
GALILEO: Like huge soap bubbles one inside the other and the stars are supposed to be tacked on to

them. Spin the band with the sun on it. (ANDREA *does.*) You see the fixed ball in the middle?

ANDREA: Yes.

GALILEO: That's the earth. For two thousand years man has chosen to believe that the sun and all the host of stars revolve about him. Well. The Pope, the Cardinals, the princes, the scholars, captains, merchants, housewives, have pictured themselves squatting in the middle of an affair like that.

ANDREA: Locked up inside?

GALILEO (*triumphant*): Ah!

ANDREA: It's like a cage.

GALILEO: So you sensed that. (*Against the model.*) I like to think the ships began it.

ANDREA: Why?

GALILEO: They used to hug the coasts and then all of a sudden they left the coasts and spread over the oceans. A new age was coming. I was on to it years ago. I was a young man, in Siena. There was a group of masons arguing. They had to raise a block of granite. It was hot. To help matters, one of them wanted to try a new arrangement of ropes. After five minutes' discussion, out went a method which had been employed for a thousand years. The millennium of faith is ended, said I, this is the millennium of doubt. And we are pulling out of that contraption. The sayings of the wise men won't wash anymore. Everybody, at last, is getting nosy. I predict that in our time astronomy will become the gossip of the marketplace and the sons of fishwives will pack the schools.

ANDREA: You're off again, Mr. Galilei. Give me the towel. (*He wipes some soap from* GALILEO's *back.*)

GALILEO: By that time, with any luck, they will be learning that the earth rolls around the sun, and that their mothers, the captains, the scholars, the princes, and the Pope are rolling with it.

ANDREA: That turning-round-business is no good. I can see with my own eyes that the sun comes up in one place in the morning and goes down in a different place in the evening. It doesn't stand still, I can see it move.

GALILEO: You see nothing, all you do is gawk. Gawking is not seeing. (*He puts the iron washstand in the middle of the room.*) Now: that's the sun. Sit down. (ANDREA *sits on a chair.* GALILEO *stands behind him.*) Where is the sun, on your right or on your left?

ANDREA: Left.

GALILEO: And how will it get to the right?

ANDREA: By your putting it there, of course.

GALILEO: Of course? (*He picks* ANDREA *up, chair and all, and carries him round to the other side of the washstand.*) Now where is the sun?

ANDREA: On the right.

GALILEO: And did it move?

ANDREA: I did.

GALILEO: Wrong. Stupid! The chair moved.

ANDREA: But I was on it.

GALILEO: Of course. The chair is the earth, and you're sitting on it.

(MRS. SARTI, *who has come in with a glass of milk and a roll, has been watching.*)

MRS. SARTI: What are you doing with my son, Mr. Galilei?

ANDREA: Now, mother, you don't understand.

MRS. SARTI: You understand, don't you? Last night he tried to tell me that the earth goes round the sun. You'll soon have him saying that two times two is five.

GALILEO (*eating his breakfast*): Apparently we are on the threshold of a new era, Mrs. Sarti.

MRS. SARTI: Well, I hope we can pay the milkman in this new era. A young gentleman is here to take private lessons and he is well-dressed and don't you frighten him away like you did the others. Wasting your time with Andrea! (*To* ANDREA.) How many times have I told you not to wheedle free lessons out of Mr. Galilei? (MRS. SARTI *goes.*)

GALILEO: So you thought enough of the turning-round-business to tell your mother about it.

ANDREA: Just to surprise her.

GALILEO: Andrea, I wouldn't talk about our ideas outside.

ANDREA: Why not?

GALILEO: Certain of the authorities won't like it.

ANDREA: Why not, if it's the truth?

GALILEO (*laughs*): Because we are like the worms who are little and have dim eyes and can hardly see the stars at all, and the new astronomy is a framework of guesses or very little more—yet.

(MRS. SARTI *shows in* LUDOVICO MARSILI, *a presentable young man.*)

GALILEO: This house is like a marketplace. (*Pointing to the model.*) Move that out of the way! Put it down there!

(LUDOVICO *does.*)

LUDOVICO: Good morning, sir. My name is Ludovico Marsili.

GALILEO (*reading a letter of recommendation he has brought*): You came by way of Holland and your family lives in the Campagna? Private lessons, thirty scudi a month.

LUDOVICO: That's all right, of course, sir.

GALILEO: What is your subject?

LUDOVICO: Horses.

GALILEO: Aha.

LUDOVICO: I don't understand science, sir.

GALILEO: Aha.

LUDOVICO: They showed me an instrument like that in Amsterdam. You'll pardon me, sir, but it didn't make sense to me at all.

GALILEO: It's out of date now.

(ANDREA *goes*.)

LUDOVICO: You'll have to be patient with me, sir. Nothing in science makes sense to me.

GALILEO: Aha.

LUDOVICO: I saw a brand new instrument° in Amsterdam. A tube affair. "See things five times as large as life!" It had two lenses, one at each end, one lens bulged and the other was like that. (*Gesture*.) Any normal person would think that different lenses cancel each other out. They didn't! I just stood and looked a fool.

GALILEO: I don't quite follow you. What does one see enlarged?

LUDOVICO: Church steeples, pigeons, boats. Anything at a distance.

GALILEO: Did you yourself—see things enlarged?

LUDOVICO: Yes, sir.

GALILEO: And the tube had two lenses? Was it like this? (*He has been making a sketch*.)

(LUDOVICO *nods*.)

GALILEO: A recent invention?

LUDOVICO: It must be. They only started peddling it on the streets a few days before I left Holland.

GALILEO (*starts to scribble calculations on the sketch; almost friendly*): Why do you bother your head with science? Why don't you just breed horses?

(*Enter* MRS. SARTI. GALILEO *doesn't see her. She listens to the following*.)

LUDOVICO: My mother is set on the idea that science is necessary nowadays for conversation.

GALILEO: Aha. You'll find Latin or philosophy easier. (MRS. SARTI *catches his eye*.) I'll see you on Tuesday afternoon.

LUDOVICO: I shall look forward to it, sir.

GALILEO: Good morning. (*He goes to the window and shouts into the street*.) Andrea! Hey, Redhead, Redhead!

MRS. SARTI: The curator of the museum is here to see you.

GALILEO: Don't look at me like that. I took him, didn't I?

---

brand new instrument, The telescope was thought erroneously to have been invented by Hans Lippershey, who made and sold telescopes in Middelburg, Netherlands, in 1608. When he applied for a patent, he was refused on the grounds that the idea was widespread. Telescopes were available for sale in Paris in 1609, then Germany, Italy, and London in the same year. Galileo reinvented the instrument by calculating the mathematical relationship of the focal lengths of lenses. His versions were on the order of ten times more powerful than those available, and they also permitted the viewer to see things right side up, which Lippershey's did not.

MRS. SARTI: I caught your eye in time.

GALILEO: Show the curator in.

(*She goes. He scribbles something on a new sheet of paper. The* CURATOR *comes in*.)

CURATOR: Good morning, Mr. Galilei.

GALILEO: Lend me a scudo. (*He takes it and goes to the window, wrapping the coin in the paper on which he has been scribbling*.) Redhead, run to the spectacle-maker and bring me two lenses; here are the measurements. (*He throws the paper out of the window. During the following scene* GALILEO *studies his sketch of the lenses*.)

CURATOR: Mr. Galilei, I have come to return your petition for an honorarium. Unfortunately I am unable to recommend your request.

GALILEO: My good sir, how can I make ends meet on five hundred scudi?

CURATOR: What about your private students?

GALILEO: If I spend all my time with students, when am I to study? My particular science is on the threshold of important discoveries. (*He throws a manuscript on the table*.) Here are my findings on the laws of falling bodies. That should be worth two hundred scudi.

CURATOR: I am sure that any paper of yours is of infinite worth, Mr. Galilei. . . .

GALILEO: I was limiting it to two hundred scudi.

CURATOR (*cool*): Mr. Galilei, if you want money and leisure, go to Florence. I have no doubt Prince Cosmo de Medici will be glad to subsidize you, but eventually you will be forbidden to think—in the name of the Inquisition. (GALILEO *says nothing*.) Now let us not make a mountain out of a molehill. You are happy here in the Republic of Venice but you need money. Well, that's human, Mr. Galilei, may I suggest a simple solution? You remember that chart you made for the army to extract cube roots without any knowledge of mathematics? Now that was practical!

GALILEO: Bosh!

CURATOR: Don't say bosh about something that astounded the Chamber of Commerce. Our city elders are businessmen. Why don't you invent something useful that will bring them a little profit?

GALILEO (*playing with the sketch of the lenses; suddenly*): I see. Mr. Priuli, I may have something for you.

CURATOR: You don't say so.

GALILEO: It's not quite there yet, but . . .

CURATOR: You've never let me down yet, Galilei.

GALILEO: You are always an inspiration to me, Priuli.

CURATOR: You are a great man: a discontented man, but I've always said you are a great man.

GALILEO (*tartly*): My discontent, Priuli, is for the most part with myself. I am forty-six years of age and have achieved nothing which satisfies me.

CURATOR: I won't disturb you any further.

GALILEO: Thank you. Good morning.

CURATOR: Good morning. And thank you.

(He goes. GALILEO *sighs.* ANDREA *returns, bringing lenses.)*

ANDREA: One scudo was not enough. I had to leave my cap with him before he'd let me take them away.

GALILEO: We'll get it back someday. Give them to me. *(He takes the lenses over to the window, holding them in the relation they would have in a telescope.)*

ANDREA: What are those for?

GALILEO: Something for the senate. With any luck, they will rake in two hundred scudi. Take a look!

ANDREA: My, things look close! I can read the copper letters on the bell in the Campanile. And the washerwomen by the river, I can see their washboards!

GALILEO: Get out of the way. *(Looking through the lenses himself.)* Aha!

SCENE 2

No one's virtue is complete:
Great Galileo liked to eat.
You will not resent, we hope,
The truth about his telescope.

(The great arsenal of Venice, overlooking the harbor full of ships. SENATORS *and* OFFICIALS *on one side,* GALILEO, *his daughter* VIRGINIA, *and his friend* SAGREDO *on the other side. They are dressed in formal, festive clothes.* VIRGINIA *is fourteen and charming. She carries a velvet cushion on which lies a brand new telescope. Behind* GALILEO *are some* ARTISANS *from the arsenal. There are onlookers,* LUDOVICO *amongst them.)*

CURATOR *(announcing)*: Senators, Artisans of the Great Arsenal of Venice; Mr. Galileo Galilei, professor of mathematics at your University of Padua.

*(*GALILEO *steps forward and starts to speak.)*

GALILEO: Members of the High Senate! Gentlemen: I have great pleasure, as director of this institute, in presenting for your approval and acceptance an entirely new instrument originating from this our great arsenal of the Republic of Venice. As professor of mathematics at your University of Padua, your obedient servant has always counted it his privilege to offer you such discoveries and inventions as might prove lucrative to the manufacturers and merchants of our Venetian Republic. Thus, in all humility, I tender you this, my optical tube, or telescope, constructed, I assure you, on the most scientific and Christian principles, the product of seventeen years patient research at your University of Padua.

*(*GALILEO *steps back. The* SENATORS *applaud.)*

SAGREDO *(aside to* GALILEO*)*: Now you will be able to pay your bills.

GALILEO: Yes. It will make money for them. But you realize that it is more than a money-making gadget?—I turned it on the moon last night . . .

CURATOR *(in his best chamber-of-commerce manner)*: Gentlemen: Our Republic is to be congratulated not only because this new acquisition will be one more feather in the cap of Venetian culture . . . *(polite applause)* . . . not only because our own Mr. Galilei has generously handed this fresh product of his teeming brain entirely over to you, allowing you to manufacture as many of these highly salable articles as you please. . . . *(Considerable applause.)* But Gentlemen of the Senate, has it occurred to you that—with the help of this remarkable new instrument—the battle fleet of the enemy will be visible to us a full two hours before we are visible to him? *(Tremendous applause.)*

GALILEO *(aside to* SAGREDO*)*: We have been held up three generations for lack of a thing like this. I want to go home.

SAGREDO: What about the moon?

GALILEO: Well, for one thing, it doesn't give off its own light.

CURATOR *(continuing his oration)*: And now, Your Excellency, and Members of the Senate, Mr. Galilei entreats you to accept the instrument from the hands of his charming daughter Virginia.

(Polite applause. He beckons to VIRGINIA *who steps forward and presents the telescope to the* DOGE.*)*

CURATOR *(during this)*: Mr. Galilei gives his invention entirely into your hands, Gentlemen, enjoining you to construct as many of these instruments as you may please.

(More applause. The SENATORS *gather round the telescope, examining it, and looking through it.)*

GALILEO *(aside to* SAGREDO*)*: Do you know what the Milky Way is made of?

SAGREDO: No.

GALILEO: I do.

CURATOR *(interrupting)*: Congratulations, Mr. Galilei. Your extra five hundred scudi a year are safe.

GALILEO: Pardon? What? Of course, the five hundred scudi! Yes!

(A prosperous man is standing beside the CURATOR.*)*

CURATOR: Mr. Galilei, Mr. Matti of Florence.

MATTI: You're opening new fields, Mr. Galilei. We could do with you at Florence.

CURATOR: Now, Mr. Matti, leave something to us poor Venetians.

MATTI: It is a pity that a great republic has to seek an excuse to pay its great men their right and proper dues.

CURATOR: Even a great man has to have an incentive. *(He joins the* SENATORS *at the telescope.)*

MATTI: I am an iron founder.

GALILEO: Iron founder!

MATTI: With factories at Pisa and Florence. I wanted to talk to you about a machine you designed for a friend of mine in Padua.

GALILEO: I'll put you on to someone to copy it for you, I am not going to have the time.—How are things in Florence?

(They wander away.)

FIRST SENATOR *(peering)*: Extraordinary! They're having their lunch on that frigate. Lobsters! I'm hungry!

(Laughter.)

SECOND SENATOR: Oh, good heavens, look at her! I must tell my wife to stop bathing on the roof. When can I buy one of these things?

(Laughter. VIRGINIA *has spotted* LUDOVICO *among the onlookers and drags him to* GALILEO.)

VIRGINIA *(to* LUDOVICO*)*: Did I do it nicely?

LUDOVICO: I thought so.

VIRGINIA: Here's Ludovico to congratulate you, father.

LUDOVICO *(embarrassed)*: Congratulations, sir.

GALILEO: I improved it.

LUDOVICO: Yes, sir. I am beginning to understand science.

*(GALILEO *is surrounded.)*

VIRGINIA: Isn't father a great man?

LUDOVICO: Yes.

VIRGINIA: Isn't that new thing father made pretty?

LUDOVICO: Yes, a pretty red. Where I saw it first it was covered in green.

VIRGINIA: What was?

LUDOVICO: Never mind. *(A short pause.)* Have you ever been to Holland?

(They go. All Venice is congratulating GALILEO, *who wants to go home.)*

SCENE 3

January ten, sixteen ten;
Galileo Galilei abolishes heaven.

(GALILEO's study at Padua. It is night. GALILEO *and* SAGREDO *at a telescope.)*

SAGREDO *(softly)*: The edge of the crescent is jagged. All along the dark part, near the shiny crescent, bright particles of light keep coming up, one after the other and growing larger and merging with the bright crescent.

GALILEO: How do you explain those spots of light?

SAGREDO: It can't be true . . .

GALILEO: It *is* true: they are high mountains.

SAGREDO: On a star?

GALILEO: Yes. The shining particles are mountain peaks catching the first rays of the rising sun while the slopes of the mountains are still dark, and what you see is the sunlight moving down from the peaks into the valleys.

SAGREDO: But this gives the lie to all the astronomy that's been taught for the last two thousand years.

GALILEO: Yes. What you are seeing now has been seen by no other man beside myself.

SAGREDO: But the moon can't be an earth with mountains and valleys like our own any more than the earth can be a star.

GALILEO: The moon *is* an earth with mountains and valleys—and the earth *is* a star. As the moon appears to us, so we appear to the moon. From the moon, the earth looks something like a crescent, sometimes like a half-globe, sometimes a full globe, and sometimes it is not visible at all.

SAGREDO: Galileo, this is frightening.

(An urgent knocking on the door.)

GALILEO: I've discovered something else, something even more astonishing.

(More knocking. GALILEO *opens the door and the* CURATOR *comes in.)*

CURATOR: There it is—your "miraculous optical tube." Do you know that this invention he so picturesquely termed "the fruit of seventeen years research" will be on sale tomorrow for two scudi apiece at every street corner in Venice? A shipload of them has just arrived from Holland.

SAGREDO: Oh, dear!

*(GALILEO *turn his back and adjusts the telescope.)*

CURATOR: When I think of the poor gentlemen of the senate who believed they were getting an invention they could monopolize for their own profit. . . . Why, when they took their first look through the glass, it was only by the merest chance that they didn't see a peddler, seven times enlarged, selling tubes exactly like it at the corner of the street.

SAGREDO: Mr. Priuli, with the help of this instrument, Mr. Galilei has made discoveries that will revolutionize our concept of the universe.

CURATOR: Mr. Galilei provided the city with a first rate water pump and the irrigation works he designed function splendidly. How was I to expect this?

GALILEO *(still at the telescope)*: Not so fast, Priuli. I may be on the track of a very large gadget. Certain of the stars appear to have regular movements. If there were a clock in the sky, it could be seen from anywhere. That might be useful for your shipowners.

CURATOR: I won't listen to you. I listened to you before, and as a reward for my friendship you have made me the laughingstock of the town. You can laugh—you got your money. But let me tell you this: you've destroyed my faith in a lot of things, Mr. Galilei. I'm disgusted with the world. That's all I have to say. (He storms out.)

GALILEO (embarrassed): Businessmen bore me, they suffer so. Did you see the frightened look in his eyes when he caught sight of a world not created solely for the purpose of doing business?

SAGREDO: Did you know that telescopes had been made in Holland?

GALILEO: I'd heard about it. But the one I made for the Senators was twice as good as any Dutchman's. Besides, I needed the money. How can I work, with the tax collector on the doorstep? And my poor daughter will never acquire a husband unless she has a dowry, she's not too bright. And I like to buy books—all kinds of books. Why not? And what about my appetite? I don't think well unless I eat well. Can I help it if I get my best ideas over a good meal and a bottle of wine? They don't pay me as much as they pay the butcher's boy. If only I could have five years to do nothing but research! Come on. I am going to show you something else.

SAGREDO: I don't know that I want to look again.

GALILEO: This is one of the brighter nebulae of the Milky Way. What do you see?

SAGREDO: But it's made up of stars—countless stars.

GALILEO: Countless worlds.

SAGREDO (hesitating): What about the theory that the earth revolves round the sun? Have you run across anything about that?

GALILEO: No. But I noticed something on Tuesday that might prove a step towards even that. Where's Jupiter? There are four lesser stars near Jupiter. I happened on them on Monday but didn't take any particular note of their position. On Tuesday I looked again. I could have sworn they had moved. They have changed again. Tell me what you see.

SAGREDO: I only see three.

GALILEO: Where's the fourth? Let's get the charts and settle down to work.

(They work and the lights dim. The lights go up again. It is near dawn.)

GALILEO: The only place the fourth can be is round at the back of the larger star where we cannot see it. This means there are small stars revolving around a big star. Where are the crystal shells now that the stars are supposed to be fixed to?

SAGREDO: Jupiter can't be attached to anything: there are other stars revolving round it.

GALILEO: There is no support in the heavens. (SAGREDO laughs awkwardly.) Don't stand there looking at me as if it weren't true.

SAGREDO: I suppose it is true. I'm afraid.

GALILEO: Why?

SAGREDO: What do you think is going to happen to you for saying that there is another sun around which other earths revolve? And that there are only stars and no difference between earth and heaven? Where is God then?

GALILEO: What do you mean?

SAGREDO: God? Where is God?

GALILEO (angrily): Not there! Any more than he'd be here—if creatures from the moon came down to look for him!

SAGREDO: Then where is He?

GALILEO: I'm not a theologian: I'm a mathematician.

SAGREDO: You are a human being! (Almost shouting.) Where is God in your system of the universe?

GALILEO: Within ourselves. Or—nowhere.

SAGREDO: Ten years ago a man was burned at the stake for saying that.

GALILEO: Giordano Bruno° was an idiot: he spoke too soon. He would never have been condemned if he could have backed up what he said with proof.

SAGREDO (incredulously): Do you really believe proof will make any difference?

GALILEO: I believe in the human race. The only people that can't be reasoned with are the dead. Human beings are intelligent.

SAGREDO: Intelligent—or merely shrewd?

GALILEO: I know they call a donkey a horse when they want to sell it, and a horse a donkey when they want to buy it. But is that the whole story? Aren't they susceptible to truth as well? (He fishes a small pebble out of his pocket.) If anybody were to drop a stone . . . (drops the pebble) . . . and tell them that it didn't fall, do you think they would keep quiet? The evidence of your own eyes is a very seductive thing. Sooner or later everybody must succumb to it.

SAGREDO: Galileo, I am helpless when you talk.

(A church bell has been ringing for some time, calling people to Mass. Enter VIRGINIA, muffled up for Mass, carrying a candle, protected from the wind by a globe.)

Giordano Bruno, Bruno (1548–1600), one of the most distinguished Italian Renaissance thinkers, lectured in England, France, Germany, and other countries in Europe before being imprisoned for heresy by the Inquisition. After a period of confinement and a lengthy trial, he was burned at the stake. He believed, like Galileo, in the Copernican view of astronomy, which asserted that the earth rotated around the sun.

VIRGINIA: Oh, father, you promised to go to bed to-night, and it's five o'clock again.
GALILEO: Why are you up at this hour?
VIRGINIA: I'm going to Mass with Mrs. Sarti. Ludovico is going too. How was the night, father?
GALILEO: Bright.
VIRGINIA: What did you find through the tube?
GALILEO: Only some little specks by the side of a star. I must draw attention to them somehow. I think I'll name them after the Prince of Florence. Why not call them the Medicean planets? By the way, we may move to Florence. I've written to His Highness, asking if he can use me as Court Mathematician.
VIRGINIA: Oh, father, we'll be at the court!
SAGREDO (amazed): Galileo!
GALILEO: My dear Sagredo, I must have leisure. My only worry is that His Highness after all may not take me. I'm not accustomed to writing formal letters to great personages. Here, do you think this is the right sort of thing?
SAGREDO (reads and quotes): "Whose sole desire is to reside in Your Highness' presence—the rising sun of our great age." Cosmo de Medici is a boy of nine.
GALILEO: The only way a man like me can land a good job is by crawling on his stomach. Your father, my dear, is going to take his share of the pleasures of life in exchange for all his hard work, and about time too. I have no patience, Sagredo, with a man who doesn't use his brains to fill his belly. Run along to Mass now.

(VIRGINIA goes.)

SAGREDO: Galileo, do not go to Florence.
GALILEO: Why not?
SAGREDO: The monks are in power there.
GALILEO: Going to Mass is a small price to pay for a full belly. And there are many famous scholars at the court of Florence.
SAGREDO: Court monkeys.
GALILEO: I shall enjoy taking them by the scruff of the neck and making them look through the telescope.
SAGREDO: Galileo, you are traveling the road to disaster. You are suspicious and skeptical in science, but in politics you are as naive as your daughter! How can people in power leave a man at large who tells the truth, even if it be the truth about the distant stars? Can you see the Pope scribbling a note in his diary: "10th of January, 1610, Heaven abolished"? A moment ago, when you were at the telescope, I saw you tied to the stake, and when you said you believed in proof, I smelt burning flesh!
GALILEO: I am going to Florence.

(Before the next scene a curtain with the following legend on it is lowered:

By setting the name of Medici in the sky, I am bestowing immortality upon the stars. I commend myself to you as your most faithful and devoted servant, whose sole desire is to reside in Your Highness' presence, the rising sun of our great age.

—GALILEO GALILEI)

SCENE 4

(GALILEO's house at Florence. Well-appointed. GALILEO is demonstrating his telescope to PRINCE COSMO DE MEDICI, a boy of nine, accompanied by his LORD CHAMBERLAIN, LADIES AND GENTLEMEN OF THE COURT, and an assortment of university PROFESSORS. With GALILEO are ANDREA and FEDERZONI, the new assistant (an old man). MRS. SARTI stands by. Before the scene opens the voice of the PHILOSOPHER can be heard.)

VOICE OF THE PHILOSOPHER: Quaedam miracula universi. Orbes mystice canorae, arcus crystallini, circulatio corporum coelestium. Cyclorum epicyclorumque intoxicatio, integritas tabulae chordarum et architectura elata globorum coelestium.
GALILEO: Shall we speak in everyday language? My colleague Mr. Federzoni does not understand Latin.
PHILOSOPHER: Is it necessary that he should?
GALILEO: Yes.
PHILOSOPHER: Forgive me. I thought he was your mechanic.
ANDREA: Mr. Federzoni is a mechanic and a scholar.
PHILOSOPHER: Thank you, young man. If Mr. Federzoni insists . . .
GALILEO: I insist.
PHILOSOPHER: It will not be as clear, but it's your house. Your Highness . . . (The PRINCE is ineffectually trying to establish contact with ANDREA.) I was about to recall to Mr. Galilei some of the wonders of the universe as they are set down for us in the Divine Classics. (The LADIES "ah.") Remind him of the "mystically musical spheres, the crystal arches, the circulation of the heavenly bodies—"
ELDERLY LADY: Perfect poise!
PHILOSOPHER: "—the intoxication of the cycles and epicycles, the integrity of the tables of chords and the enraptured architecture of the celestial globes."
ELDERLY LADY: What diction!
PHILOSOPHER: May I pose the question: Why should we go out of our way to look for things that can only strike a discord in this ineffable harmony?

(The LADIES applaud.)

FEDERZONI: Take a look through here—you'll be interested.
ANDREA: Sit down here, please.

(The PROFESSORS laugh.)

MATHEMATICIAN: Mr. Galilei, nobody doubts that your brain child—or is it your adopted brain child?—is brilliantly contrived.

GALILEO: Your Highness, one can see the four stars as large as life, you know.

(The PRINCE *looks to the* ELDERLY LADY *for guidance.)*

MATHEMATICIAN: Ah. But has it occurred to you that an eyeglass through which one sees such phenomena might not be a too reliable eyeglass?

GALILEO: How is that?

MATHEMATICIAN: If one could be sure you would keep your temper, Mr. Galilei, I could suggest that what one sees in the eyeglass and what is in the heavens are two entirely different things.

GALILEO *(quietly)*: You are suggesting fraud?

MATHEMATICIAN: No! How could I, in the presence of His Highness?

ELDERLY LADY: The gentlemen are just wondering if Your Highness' stars are really, really there!

(Pause.)

YOUNG LADY *(trying to be helpful)*: Can one see the claws on the Great Bear?

GALILEO: And everything on Taurus the Bull.

FEDERZONI: Are you going to look through it or not?

MATHEMATICIAN: With the greatest of pleasure.

(Pause. Nobody goes near the telescope. All of a sudden the boy ANDREA *turns and marches pale and erect past them through the whole length of the room. The* GUESTS *follow with their eyes.)*

MRS. SARTI *(as he passes her)*: What is the matter with you?

ANDREA *(shocked)*: They are wicked.

PHILOSOPHER: Your Highness, it is a delicate matter and I had no intention of bringing it up, but Mr. Galilei was about to demonstrate the impossible. His new stars would have broken the outer crystal sphere—which we know of on the authority of Aristotle. I am sorry.

MATHEMATICIAN: The last word.

FEDERZONI: He had no telescope.

MATHEMATICIAN: Quite.

GALILEO *(keeping his temper)*: "Truth is the daughter of Time, not of Authority." Gentlemen, the sum of our knowledge is pitiful. It has been my singular good fortune to find a new instrument which brings a small patch of the universe a little bit closer. It is at your disposal.

PHILOSOPHER: Where is all this leading?

GALILEO: Are we, as scholars, concerned with where the truth might lead us?

PHILOSOPHER: Mr. Galilei, the truth might lead us anywhere!

GALILEO: I can only beg you to look through my eyeglass.

MATHEMATICIAN *(wild)*: If I understand Mr. Galilei correctly, he is asking us to discard the teachings of two thousand years.

GALILEO: For two thousand years we have been looking at the sky and didn't see the four moons of Jupiter, and there they were all the time. Why defend shaken teachings? You should be doing the shaking. *(The* PRINCE *is sleepy.)* Your Highness! My work in the Great Arsenal of Venice brought me in daily contact with sailors, carpenters, and so on. These men are unread. They depend on the evidence of their senses. But they taught me many new ways of doing things. The question is whether these gentlemen here want to be found out as fools by men who might not have had the advantages of a classical education but who are not afraid to use their eyes. I tell you that our dockyards are stirring with that same high curiosity which was the true glory of Ancient Greece.

(Pause.)

PHILOSOPHER: I have no doubt Mr. Galilei's theories will arouse the enthusiasm of the dockyards.

CHAMBERLAIN: Your Highness, I find to my amazement that this highly informative discussion has exceeded the time we had allowed for it. May I remind Your Highness that the State Ball begins in three-quarters of an hour?

(The COURT *bows low.)*

ELDERLY LADY: We would really have liked to look through your eyeglass, Mr. Galilei, wouldn't we, Your Highness?

(The PRINCE *bows politely and is led to the door.* GALILEO *follows the* PRINCE, CHAMBERLAIN, *and* LADIES *towards the exit. The* PROFESSORS *remain at the telescope.)*

GALILEO *(almost servile)*: All anybody has to do is look through the telescope, Your Highness.

*(MRS. SARTI *takes a plate with candies to the* PRINCE *as he is walking out.)*

MRS. SARTI: A piece of homemade candy, Your Highness?

ELDERLY LADY: Not now. Thank you. It is too soon before His Highness' supper.

PHILOSOPHER: Wouldn't I like to take that thing to pieces.

MATHEMATICIAN: Ingenious contraption. It must be quite difficult to keep clean. *(He rubs the lens with his handkerchief and looks at the handkerchief.)*

FEDERZONI: We did not paint the Medicean stars on the lens.

ELDERLY LADY *(to the* PRINCE, *who has whispered something to her)*: No, no, no, there is nothing the matter with your stars!

CHAMBERLAIN (*across the stage to* GALILEO): His Highness will of course seek the opinion of the greatest living authority: Christopher Clavius, Chief Astronomer to the Papal College in Rome.

SCENE 5

> *Things take indeed a wondrous turn*
> *When learned men do stoop to learn*
> *Clavius, we are pleased to say,*
> *Upheld Galileo Galilei.*

(*A burst of laughter is heard and the curtains reveal a hall in the Collegium Romanum.* HIGH CHURCHMEN, MONKS, *and* SCHOLARS *standing about talking and laughing.* GALILEO *by himself in a corner.*)

FAT PRELATE (*shaking with laughter*): Hopeless! Hopeless! Hopeless! Will you tell me something people won't believe?

A SCHOLAR: Yes, that you don't love your stomach!

FAT PRELATE: They'd believe that. They only do not believe what's good for them. They doubt the devil, but fill them up with some fiddle-de-dee about the earth rolling like a marble in the gutter and they swallow it hook, line, and sinker. Sancta simplicitas!

(*He laughs until the tears run down his cheeks. The others laugh with him. A group has formed whose members boisterously begin to pretend they are standing on a rolling globe.*)

A MONK: It's rolling fast, I'm dizzy. May I hold on to you, Professor? (*He sways dizzily and clings to one of the* SCHOLARS *for support.*)

THE SCHOLAR: Old Mother Earth's been at the bottle again. Whoa!

MONK: Hey! Hey! We're slipping off! Help!

SECOND SCHOLAR: Look! There's Venus! Hold me, lads. Whee!

SECOND MONK: Don't, don't hurl us off on to the moon. There are nasty sharp mountain peaks on the moon, brethren!

VARIOUSLY: Hold tight! Hold tight! Don't look down! Hold tight! It'll make you giddy!

FAT PRELATE: And we cannot have giddy people in Holy Rome.

(*They rock with laughter. An* INFURIATED MONK *comes out from a large door at the rear holding a Bible in his hand and pointing out a page with his finger.*)

INFURIATED MONK: What does the Bible say—"Sun, stand thou still on Gideon and thou, moon, in the valley of Ajalon." Can the sun come to a standstill if it doesn't ever move? Does the Bible lie?

FAT PRELATE: How did Christopher Clavius, the greatest astronomer we have, get mixed up in an investigation of this kind?

INFURIATED MONK: He's in there with his eye glued to that diabolical instrument.

FAT PRELATE (*to* GALILEO, *who has been playing with his pebble and has dropped it*): Mr. Galilei, something dropped down.

GALILEO: Monsignor, are you sure it didn't drop up?

INFURIATED MONK: As astronomers we are aware that there are phenomena which are beyond us, but man can't expect to understand everything!

(*Enter a very* OLD CARDINAL *leaning on a* MONK *for support. Others move aside.*)

OLD CARDINAL: Aren't they out yet? Can't they reach a decision on that paltry matter? Christopher Clavius ought to know his astronomy after all these years. I am informed that Mr. Galilei transfers mankind from the center of the universe to somewhere on the outskirts. Mr. Galilei is therefore an enemy of mankind and must be dealt with as such. Is it conceivable that God would trust this most precious fruit of His labor to a minor frolicking star? Would He have sent His Son to such a place? How can there be people with such twisted minds that they believe what they're told by the slave of a multiplication table?

FAT PRELATE (*quietly to* CARDINAL): The gentleman is over there.

OLD CARDINAL: So you are the man. You know my eyes are not what they were, but I can see you bear a striking resemblance to the man we burned. What was his name?

MONK: Your Eminence must avoid excitement the doctor said . . .

OLD CARDINAL (*disregarding him*): So you have degraded the earth despite the fact that you live by her and receive everything from her. I won't have it! I won't have it! I won't be a nobody on an inconsequential star briefly twirling hither and thither. I tread the earth, and the earth is firm beneath my feet, and there is no motion to the earth, and the earth is the center of all things, and I am the center of the earth, and the eye of the Creator is upon me. About me revolve, affixed to their crystal shells, the lesser lights of the stars and the great light of the sun, created to give light upon me that God might see me—Man, God's greatest effort, the center of creation. "In the image of God created He him." Immortal . . . (*His strength fails him and he catches for the* MONK *for support.*)

MONK: You mustn't overtax your strength, Your Eminence.

(*At this moment the door at the rear opens and* CHRISTOPHER CLAVIUS *enters followed by his* ASTRONOMERS. *He strides hastily across the hall, looking neither to right nor left. As he goes by we hear him say—*)

CLAVIUS: He is right.

(Deadly silence. All turn to GALILEO.*)*

OLD CARDINAL: What is it? Have they reached a decision?

(No one speaks.)

MONK: It is time that Your Eminence went home.

(The hall is emptying fast. One LITTLE MONK *who had entered with* CLAVIUS *speaks to* GALILEO.*)*

LITTLE MONK: Mr. Galilei, I heard Father Clavius say: "Now it's for the theologians to set the heavens right again." You have won.

(Before the next scene a curtain with the following legend on it is lowered:

. . . As these new astronomical charts enable us to determine longitudes at sea and so make it possible to reach the new continents by the shortest routes, we would beseech Your Excellency to aid us in reaching Mr. Galilei, mathematician to the Court of Florence, who is now in Rome . . .

———From a letter written by a member of the Genoa Chamber of Commerce and Navigation to the Papal Legation)

SCENE 6

When Galileo was in Rome
A Cardinal asked him to his home
He wined and dined him as his guest
And only made one small request.

*(*CARDINAL BELLARMIN*'s house in Rome. Music is heard and the chatter of many guests. Two* SECRETARIES *are at the rear of the stage at a desk.* GALILEO, *his daughter* VIRGINIA, *now twenty-one and* LUDOVICO MARSILI, *who has become her fiancé, are just arriving. A few* GUESTS, *standing near the entrance with masks in their hands, nudge each other and are suddenly silent.* GALILEO *looks at them. They applaud him politely and bow.)*

VIRGINIA: O father! I'm so happy. I won't dance with anyone but you, Ludovico.

GALILEO *(to a* SECRETARY*)*: I was to wait here for His Eminence.

FIRST SECRETARY: His Eminence will be with you in a few minutes.

VIRGINIA: Do I look proper?

LUDOVICO: You are showing some lace.

*(*GALILEO *puts his arms around their shoulders.)*

GALILEO *(quoting mischievously)*: Fret not, daughter, if perchance
You attract a wanton glance.
The eyes that catch a trembling lace

Will guess the heartbeat's quickened pace.
Lovely woman still may be
Careless with felicity.

VIRGINIA *(to* GALILEO*)*: Feel my heart.

GALILEO *(to* LUDOVICO*)*: It's thumping.

VIRGINIA: I hope I always say the right thing.

LUDOVICO: She's afraid she's going to let us down.

VIRGINIA: Oh, I want to look beautiful.

GALILEO: You'd better. If you don't they'll start saying all over again that the earth doesn't turn.

LUDOVICO *(laughing)*: It *doesn't* turn, sir.

*(*GALILEO *laughs.)*

GALILEO: Go and enjoy yourselves. *(He speaks to one of the* SECRETARIES.*)* A large fête?

FIRST SECRETARY: Two hundred and fifty guests, Mr. Galilei. We have represented here this evening most of the great families of Italy, the Orsinis, the Villanis, the Nuccolis, the Soldanieris, the Canes, the Lecchis, the Estensis, the Colombinis, the . . .

*(*VIRGINIA *comes running back.)*

VIRGINIA: Oh father, I didn't tell you: you're famous.

GALILEO: Why?

VIRGINIA: The hairdresser in the Via Vittorio kept four other ladies waiting and took me first. *(Exit.)*

GALILEO *(at the stairway, leaning over the well)*: Rome!

(Enter CARDINAL BELLARMIN, *wearing the mask of a lamb, and* CARDINAL BARBERINI, *wearing the mask of a dove.)*

SECRETARIES: Their Eminences, Cardinals Bellarmin and Barberini.

(The CARDINALS *lower their masks.)*

GALILEO *(to* BELLARMIN*)*: Your Eminence.

BELLARMIN: Mr. Galilei, Cardinal Barberini.

GALILEO: Your Eminence.

BARBERINI: So you are the father of that lovely child!

BELLARMIN: Who is inordinately proud of being her father's daughter.

(They laugh.)

BARBERINI *(points his finger at* GALILEO*)*: "The sun riseth and setteth and returneth to its place," saith the Bible. What saith Galilei?

GALILEO: Appearances are notoriously deceptive, Your Eminence. Once when I was so high, I was standing on a ship that was pulling away from the shore and I shouted, "The shore is moving!" I know now that it was the ship which was moving.

BARBERINI *(laughs)*: You can't catch that man. I tell you, Bellarmin, his moons around Jupiter are hard nuts to crack. Unfortunately for me I happened to glance at a few papers on astronomy once. It is harder to get rid of than the itch.

BELLARMIN: Let's move with the times. If it makes

navigation easier for sailors to use new charts based on a new hypothesis let them have them. We only have to scotch doctrines that contradict Holy Writ.

(He leans over the balustrade of the well and acknowledges various GUESTS.*)*

BARBERINI: But Bellarmin, you haven't caught on to this fellow. The scriptures don't satisfy him. Copernicus does.

GALILEO: Copernicus? "He that withholdeth corn the people shall curse him." Book of Proverbs.

BARBERINI: "A prudent man concealeth knowledge." Also Book of Proverbs.

GALILEO: "Where no oxen are, the stable is clean, but much increase is by the strength of the ox."

BARBERINI: "He that ruleth his spirit is better than he that taketh a city."

GALILEO: "But a broken spirit drieth up the bones." *(Pause.)* "Doth not wisdom cry?"

BARBERINI: "Can one walk on hot coals and his feet not be scorched?"—Welcome to Rome, Friend Galileo. You recall the legend of our city's origin? Two small boys found sustenance and refuge with a she-wolf and from that day we have paid the price for the she-wolf's milk. But the place is not bad. We have everything for your pleasure—from a scholarly dispute with Bellarmin to ladies of high degree. Look at that woman flaunting herself. No? He wants a weighty discussion! All right! *(To* GALILEO.*)* You people speak in terms of circles and ellipses and regular velocities—simple movements that the human mind can grasp—very convenient—but suppose Almighty God had taken it into his head to make the stars move like that . . . *(he describes an irregular motion with his finger through the air)* . . . then where would you be?

GALILEO: My good man—the Almighty would have endowed us with brains like that . . . *(repeats the movement)* . . . so that we could grasp the movements . . . *(repeats the movement)* . . . like that. I believe in the brain.

BARBERINI: I consider the brain inadequate. He doesn't answer. He is too polite to tell me he considers *my* brain inadequate. What is one to do with him? Butter wouldn't melt in his mouth. All he wants to do is to prove that God made a few boners in astronomy. God didn't study his astronomy hard enough before he composed Holy Writ. *(To the* SECRETARIES.*)* Don't take anything down. This is a scientific discussion among friends.

BELLARMIN: *(to* GALILEO*)*: Does it not appear more probable—even to you—that the Creator knows more about his work than the created?

GALILEO: In his blindness man is liable to misread not only the sky but also the Bible.

BELLARMIN: The interpretation of the Bible is a matter for the ministers of God. *(*GALILEO *remains silent.)* At last you are quiet. *(He gestures to the* SECRETARIES. *They start writing.)* Tonight the Holy Office has decided that the theory according to which the earth goes around the sun is foolish, absurd, and a heresy. I am charged, Mr. Galilei, with cautioning you to abandon these teachings. *(To the* FIRST SECRETARY.*)* Would you repeat that?

FIRST SECRETARY *(reading)*: "His Eminence, Cardinal Bellarmin, to the aforesaid Galilei: The Holy Office has resolved that the theory according to which the earth goes around the sun is foolish, absurd, and a heresy. I am charged, Mr. Galilei, with cautioning you to abandon these teachings."

GALILEO *(rocking on his base)*: But the facts!

BARBERINI *(consoling)*: Your findings have been ratified by the Papal Observatory, Galilei. That should be most flattering to you . . .

BELLARMIN *(cutting in)*: The Holy Office formulated the decree without going into details.

GALILEO *(to* BARBERINI*)*: Do you realize, the future of all scientific research is . . .

BELLARMIN *(cutting in)*: Completely assured, Mr. Galilei. It is not given to man to know the truth: it is granted to him to seek after the truth. Science is the legitimate and beloved daughter of the Church. She must have confidence in the Church.

GALILEO *(infuriated)*: I would not try confidence by whistling her too often.

BARBERINI *(quickly)*: Be careful what you're doing—you'll be throwing out the baby with the bath water, friend Galilei. *(Serious.)* We need you more than you need us.

BELLARMIN: Well, it is time we introduced our distinguished friend to our guests. The whole country talks of him!

BARBERINI: Let us replace our masks, Bellarmin. Poor Galilei hasn't got one.

(He laughs. They take GALILEO *out.)*

FIRST SECRETARY: Did you get his last sentence?

SECOND SECRETARY: Yes. Do you have what he said about believing in the brain?

(Another cardinal—the INQUISITOR—*enters.)*

INQUISITOR: Did the conference take place?

(The FIRST SECRETARY *hands him the papers and the* INQUISITOR *dismisses the* SECRETARIES. *They go. The* INQUISITOR *sits down and starts to read the transcription. Two or three* YOUNG LADIES *skitter across the stage; they see the* INQUISITOR *and curtsy as they go.)*

YOUNG GIRL: Who was that?

HER FRIEND: The Cardinal Inquisitor.

(They giggle and go. Enter VIRGINIA. *She curtsies as she goes. The* INQUISITOR *stops her.)*

INQUISITOR: Good evening, my child. Beautiful night.

May I congratulate you on your betrothal? Your young man comes from a fine family. Are you staying with us here in Rome?

VIRGINIA: Not now, Your Eminence. I must go home to prepare for the wedding.

INQUISITOR: Ah. You are accompanying your father to Florence. That should please him. Science must be cold comfort in a home. Your youth and warmth will keep him down to earth. It is easy to get lost up there. (*He gestures to the sky.*)

VIRGINIA: He doesn't talk to me about the stars, Your Eminence.

INQUISITOR: No. (*He laughs.*) They don't eat fish in the fisherman's house. I can tell you something about astronomy. My child, it seems that God has blessed our modern astronomers with imaginations. It is quite alarming! Do you know that the earth—which we old fogies supposed to be so large—has shrunk to something no bigger than a walnut, and the new universe has grown so vast that prelates—and even cardinals—look like ants. Why, God Almighty might lose sight of a Pope! I wonder if I know your Father Confessor.

VIRGINIA: Father Christopherus, from Saint Ursula's at Florence, Your Eminence.

INQUISITOR: My dear child, your father will need you. Not so much now perhaps, but one of these days. You are pure, and there is strength in purity. Greatness is sometimes, indeed often, too heavy a burden for those to whom God has granted it. What man is so great that he has no place in a prayer? But I am keeping you, my dear. Your fiancé will be jealous of me, and I am afraid your father will never forgive me for holding forth on astronomy. Go to your dancing and remember me to Father Christopherus.

(VIRGINIA *kisses his ring and runs off. The* INQUISITOR *resumes his reading.*)

SCENE 7

Galileo, feeling grim,
A young monk came to visit him.
The monk was born of common folk.
It was of science that they spoke.

(*Garden of Florentine Ambassador in Rome. Distant hum of a great city.* GALILEO *and the* LITTLE MONK *of scene 5 are talking.*)

GALILEO: Let's hear it. That robe you're wearing gives you the right to say whatever you want to say. Let's hear it.

LITTLE MONK: I have studied physics, Mr. Galilei.

GALILEO: That might help us if it enabled you to admit that two and two are four.

LITTLE MONK: Mr. Galilei, I have spent four sleepless nights trying to reconcile the decree that I have read with the moons of Jupiter that I have seen. This morning I decided to come to see you after I had said Mass.

GALILEO: To tell me that Jupiter has no moons?

LITTLE MONK: No, I found out that I think the decree a wise decree. It has shocked me into realizing that free research has its dangers. I have had to decide to give up astronomy. However, I felt the impulse to confide in you some of the motives which have impelled even a passionate physicist to abandon his work.

GALILEO: Your motives are familiar to me.

LITTLE MONK: You mean, of course, the special powers invested in certain commissions of the Holy Office? But there is something else. I would like to talk to you about my family. I do not come from the great city. My parents are peasants in the Campagna, who know about the cultivation of the olive tree, and not much about anything else. Too often these days when I am trying to concentrate on tracking down the moons of Jupiter, I see my parents. I see them sitting by the fire with my sister, eating their curded cheese. I see the beams of the ceiling above them, which the smoke of centuries has blackened, and I can see the veins stand out on their toil-worn hands, and the little spoons in their hands. They scrape a living, and underlying their poverty there is a sort of order. There are routines. The routine of scrubbing the floors, the routine of the seasons in the olive orchard, the routine of paying taxes. The troubles that come to them are recurrent troubles. My father did not get his poor bent back all at once, but little by little, year by year, in the olive orchard; just as year after year, with unfailing regularity, childbirth has made my mother more and more sexless. They draw the strength they need to sweat with their loaded baskets up the stony paths, to bear children, even to eat, from the sight of the trees greening each year anew, from the reproachful face of the soil, which is never satisfied, and from the little church and Bible texts they hear there on Sunday. They have been told that God relies upon them and that the pageant of the world has been written around them that they may be tested in the important or unimportant parts handed out to them. How could they take it, were I to tell them that they are on a lump of stone ceaselessly spinning in empty space, circling around a second-rate star? What, then, would be the use of their patience, their acceptance of misery? What comfort, then, the Holy Scriptures, which have mercifully explained their crucifixion? The Holy Scriptures would then be proved full of mistakes. No, I see them begin to look frightened. I see them slowly put their spoons down on the table. They would feel cheated. "There is no eye watching over us, after all," they would say. "We have to start out on our own, at our time of life. Nobody has planned a part for us beyond this wretched one on a worthless star. There is no meaning in our misery. Hunger is just not having eaten. It is no test of strength. Effort is just stooping and carrying. It is not a virtue." Can you understand that I read into the decree of the Holy Office a noble motherly pity and a great goodness of the soul?

GALILEO *(embarrassed)*: Hm, well at least you have found out that it is not a question of the satellites of Jupiter, but of the peasants of the Campagna! And don't try to break me down by the halo of beauty that radiates from old age. How does a pearl develop in an oyster? A jagged grain of sand makes its way into the oyster's shell and makes its life unbearable. The oyster exudes slime to cover the grain of sand and the slime eventually hardens into a pearl. The oyster nearly dies in the process. To hell with the pearl, give me the healthy oyster! And virtues are not exclusive to misery. If your parents were prosperous and happy, they might develop the virtues of happiness and prosperity. Today the virtues of exhaustion are caused by the exhausted land. For that my new water pumps could work more wonders than their ridiculous superhuman efforts. Be fruitful and multiply: for war will cut down the population, and our fields are barren! *(A pause.)* Shall I lie to your people?

LITTLE MONK: We must be silent from the highest of motives: the inward peace of less fortunate souls.

GALILEO: My dear man, as a bonus for not meddling with your parents' peace, the authorities are tendering me, on a silver platter, persecution-free, my share of the fat sweated from your parents, who, as you know, were made in God's image. Should I condone this decree, my motives might not be disinterested: easy life, no persecution, and so on.

LITTLE MONK: Mr. Galilei, I am a priest.

GALILEO: You are also a physicist. How can new machinery be evolved to domesticate the river water if we physicists are forbidden to study, discuss, and pool our findings about the greatest machinery of all, the machinery of the heavenly bodies? Can I reconcile my findings on the paths of falling bodies with the current belief in the tracks of witches on broom sticks? *(A pause.)* I am sorry—I shouldn't have said that.

LITTLE MONK: You don't think that the truth, if it is the truth, would make its way without us?

GALILEO: No! No! No! As much of the truth gets through as we push through. You talk about the Campagna peasants as if they were the moss on their huts. Naturally, if they don't get a move on

and learn to think for themselves, the most efficient of irrigation systems cannot help them. I can see their divine patience, but where is their divine fury?

LITTLE MONK *(helpless)*: They are old!

(GALILEO stands for a moment, beaten; he cannot meet the LITTLE MONK's eyes. He takes a manuscript from the table and throws it violently on the ground.)

LITTLE MONK: What is that?

GALILEO: Here is writ what draws the ocean when it ebbs and flows. Let it lie there. Thou shalt not read. *(LITTLE MONK has picked up the manuscript.)* Already! An apple of the tree of knowledge, he can't wait, he wolfs it down. He will rot in hell for all eternity. Look at him, where are his manners?—Sometimes I think I would let them imprison me in a place a thousand feet beneath the earth where no light could reach me, if in exchange I could find out what stuff that is: "Light." The bad thing is that, when I find something, I have to boast about it like a lover or a drunkard or a traitor. That is a hopeless vice and leads to the abyss. I wonder how long I shall be content to discuss it with my dog!

LITTLE MONK *(immersed in the manuscript)*: I don't understand this sentence.

GALILEO: I'll explain it to you, I'll explain it to you.

(They are sitting on the floor.)

SCENE 8

Eight long years with tongue in cheek
Of what he knew he did not speak.
Then temptation grew too great
And Galileo challenged fate.

(GALILEO's house in Florence again. GALILEO is supervising his ASSISTANTS—ANDREA, FEDERZONI, and the LITTLE MONK—who are about to prepare an experiment. MRS. SARTI and VIRGINIA are at a long table sewing bridal linen. There is a new telescope, larger than the old one. At the moment it is covered with a cloth.)

ANDREA *(looking up a schedule)*: Thursday. Afternoon. Floating bodies again. Ice, bowl of water, scales, and it says here an iron needle. Aristotle.

VIRGINIA: Ludovico likes to entertain. We must take care to be neat. His mother notices every stitch. She doesn't approve of father's books.

MRS. SARTI: That's all a thing of the past. He hasn't published a book for years.

VIRGINIA: That's true. Oh Sarti, it's fun sewing a trousseau.

MRS. SARTI: Virginia, I want to talk to you. You are very young, and you have no mother, and your father is putting those pieces of ice in water, and marriage is too serious a business to go into blind. Now you should go to see a real astronomer from the university and have him cast your horoscope so you know where you stand. (VIRGINIA *giggles.*) What's the matter?

VIRGINIA: I've been already.

MRS. SARTI: Tell Sarti.

VIRGINIA: I have to be careful for three months now because the sun is in Capricorn, but after that I get a favorable ascendant, and I can undertake a journey if I am careful of Uranus, as I'm a Scorpion.

MRS. SARTI: What about Ludovico?

VIRGINIA: He's a Leo, the astronomer said. Leos are sensual. (*Giggles.*)

(*There is a knock at the door, it opens. Enter the* RECTOR OF THE UNIVERSITY, *the philosopher of scene 4, bringing a book.*)

RECTOR (*to* VIRGINIA): This is about the burning issue of the moment. He may want to glance over it. My faculty would appreciate his comments. No, don't disturb him now, my dear. Every minute one takes of your father's time is stolen from Italy. (*He goes.*)

VIRGINIA: Federzoni! The rector of the university brought this.

(FEDERZONI *takes it.*)

GALILEO: What's it about?

FEDERZONI (*spelling*): DE MACULIS IN SOLE.

ANDREA: Oh, it's on the sun spots!

(ANDREA *comes to one side, and the* LITTLE MONK *the other, to look at the book.*)

ANDREA: A new one!

(FEDERZONI *resentfully puts the book into their hands and continues with the preparation of the experiment.*)

ANDREA: Listen to this dedication. (*Quotes.*) "To the greatest living authority on physics, Galileo Galilei."—I read Fabricius' paper the other day. Fabricius says the spots are clusters of planets between us and the sun.

LITTLE MONK: Doubtful.

GALILEO (*noncommittal*): Yes?

ANDREA: Paris and Prague hold that they are vapors from the sun. Federzoni doubts that.

FEDERZONI: Me? You leave me out. I said "hm," that was all. And don't discuss new things before me. I can't read the material, it's in Latin. (*He drops the scales and stands trembling with fury.*) Tell me, can I doubt anything?

(GALILEO *walks over and picks up the scales silently. Pause.*)

LITTLE MONK: There is happiness in doubting, I wonder why.

ANDREA: Aren't we going to take this up?

GALILEO: At the moment we are investigating floating bodies.

ANDREA: Mother has baskets full of letters from all over Europe asking his opinion.

FEDERZONI: The question is whether you can afford to remain silent.

GALILEO: I cannot afford to be smoked on a wood fire like a ham.

ANDREA (*surprised*): Ah. You think the sun spots may have something to do with that again? (GALILEO *does not answer.*) Well, we stick to fiddling about with bits of ice in water. That can't hurt you.

GALILEO: Correct.—Our thesis!

ANDREA: All things that are lighter than water float, and all things that are heavier sink.

GALILEO: Aristotle says—

LITTLE MONK (*reading out of a book, translating*): "A broad and flat disk of ice, although heavier than water, still floats, because it is unable to divide the water."

GALILEO: Well. Now I push the ice below the surface. I take away the pressure of my hands. What happens?

(*Pause.*)

LITTLE MONK: It rises to the surface.

GALILEO: Correct. It seems to be able to divide the water as it's coming up, doesn't it?

LITTLE MONK: Could it be lighter than water after all?

GALILEO: Aha!

ANDREA: Then all things that are lighter than water float, and all things that are heavier sink. Q.e.d.°

GALILEO: Not at all. Hand me that iron needle. Heavier than water? (*They all nod.*) A piece of paper. (*He places the needle on a piece of paper and floats it on the surface of the water. Pause.*) Do not be hasty with your conclusion. (*Pause.*) What happens?

FEDERZONI: The paper has sunk, the needle is floating.

VIRGINIA: What's the matter?

MRS. SARTI: Every time I hear them laugh it sends shivers down my spine.

(*There is a knocking at the outer door.*)

MRS. SARTI: Who's that at the door?

(*Enter* LUDOVICO. VIRGINIA *runs to him. They embrace.* LUDOVICO *is followed by a* SERVANT *with baggage.*)

Q.e.d., In Latin, *quod erat demonstrandum,* "which was to be demonstrated," is the usual ending on a logical examination using Aristotelian logic. The point is that it is not demonstrated; the following experiment with the needle and the paper demonstrates the power of surface tension, which contradicts Andrea's earlier statement. Experimentation in other words, is the final arbiter of what is true, not rules such as Andrea establishes.

MRS. SARTI: Well!

VIRGINIA: Oh! Why didn't you write that you were coming?

LUDOVICO: I decided on the spur of the moment. I was over inspecting our vineyards at Bucciole. I couldn't keep away.

GALILEO: Who's that?

LITTLE MONK: Miss Virginia's intended. What's the matter with your eyes?

GALILEO (blinking): Oh yes, it's Ludovico, so it is. Well! Sarti, get a jug of that Sicilian wine, the old kind. We celebrate.

(Everybody sits down. MRS. SARTI has left, followed by LUDOVICO's SERVANT.)

GALILEO: Well, Ludovico, old man. How are the horses?

LUDOVICO: The horses are fine.

GALILEO: Fine.

LUDOVICO: But those vineyards need a firm hand. (To VIRGINIA.) You look pale. Country life will suit you. Mother's planning on September.

VIRGINIA: I suppose I oughtn't, but stay here, I've got something to show you.

LUDOVICO: What?

VIRGINIA: Never mind. I won't be ten minutes. (She runs out.)

LUDOVICO: How's life these days, sir?

GALILEO: Dull.—How was the journey?

LUDOVICO: Dull.—Before I forget, mother sends her congratulations on your admirable tact over the latest rumblings of science.

GALILEO: Thank her from me.

LUDOVICO: Christopher Clavius had all Rome on its ears. He said he was afraid that the turning-around-business might crop up again on account of these spots on the sun.

ANDREA: Clavius is on the same track! (To LUDOVICO.) My mother's baskets are full of letters from all over Europe asking Mr. Galilei's opinion.

GALILEO: I am engaged in investigating the habits of floating bodies. Any harm in that?

(MRS. SARTI reenters, followed by the SERVANT. They bring wine and glasses on a tray.)

GALILEO (hands out the wine): What news from the Holy City, apart from the prospect of my sins?

LUDOVICO: The Holy Father is on his death bed. Hadn't you heard?

LITTLE MONK: My goodness! What about the succession?

LUDOVICO: All the talk is of Barberini.

GALILEO: Barberini?

ANDREA: Mr. Galilei knows Barberini.

LITTLE MONK: Cardinal Barberini is a mathematician.

FEDERZONI: A scientist in the chair of Peter!

(Pause.)

GALILEO (cheering up enormously): This means change. We might live to see the day, Federzoni, when we don't have to whisper that two and two are four. (To LUDOVICO.) I like this wine. Don't you, Ludovico?

LUDOVICO: I like it.

GALILEO: I know the hill where it is grown. The slope is steep and stony, the grape almost blue. I am fond of this wine.

LUDOVICO: Yes, sir.

GALILEO: There are shadows in this wine. It is almost sweet but just stops short.—Andrea, clear that stuff away, ice, bowl and needle.—I cherish the consolations of the flesh. I have no patience with cowards who call them weaknesses. I say there is a certain achievement in enjoying things.

(The PUPILS get up and go to the experiment table.)

LITTLE MONK: What are we to do?

FEDERZONI: He is starting on the sun.

(They begin with clearing up.)

ANDREA (singing in a low voice): The Bible proves the earth stands still,
The Pope, he swears with tears:
The earth stands still. To prove it so
He takes it by the ears.

LUDOVICO: What's the excitement?

MRS. SARTI: You're not going to start those hellish goings-on again, Mr. Galilei?

ANDREA: And gentlefolk, they say so too.
Each learned doctor proves,
(If you grease his palm): The earth stands still.
And yet—and yet it moves.

GALILEO: Barberini is in the ascendant, so your mother is uneasy, and you're sent to investigate me. Correct me if I am wrong, Ludovico. Clavius is right: These spots on the sun interest me.

ANDREA: We might find out that the sun also revolves. How would you like that, Ludovico?

GALILEO: Do you like my wine, Ludovico?

LUDOVICO: I told you I did, sir.

GALILEO: You really like it?

LUDOVICO: I like it.

GALILEO: Tell me, Ludovico, would you consider going so far as to accept a man's wine or his daughter without insisting that he drop his profession? I have no wish to intrude, but have the moons of Jupiter affected Virginia's bottom?

MRS. SARTI: That isn't funny, it's just vulgar. I am going for Virginia.

LUDOVICO (keeps her back): Marriages in families such as mine are not arranged on a basis of sexual attraction alone.

GALILEO: Did they keep you back from marrying my daughter for eight years because I was on probation?

LUDOVICO: My future wife must take her place in the family pew.

GALILEO: You mean, if the daughter of a bad man sat in your family pew, your peasants might stop paying the rent?

LUDOVICO: In a sort of way.

GALILEO: When I was your age, the only person I allowed to rap me on the knuckles was my girl.

LUDOVICO: My mother was assured that you had undertaken not to get mixed up in this turning-around-business again, sir.

GALILEO: We had a conservative Pope then.

MRS. SARTI: Had! His Holiness is not dead yet!

GALILEO (with relish): Pretty nearly.

MRS. SARTI: That man will weigh a chip of ice fifty times, but when it comes to something that's convenient, he believes it blindly. "Is His Holiness dead?"—"Pretty nearly!"

LUDOVICO: You will find, sir, if His Holiness passes away, the new Pope, whoever he turns out to be, will respect the convictions held by the solid families of the country.

GALILEO (to ANDREA): That remains to be seen.—Andrea, get out the screen. We'll throw the image of the sun on our screen to save our eyes.

LITTLE MONK: I thought you'd been working at it. Do you know when I guessed it? When you didn't recognize Mr. Marsili.

MRS. SARTI: If my son has to go to hell for sticking to you, that's my affair, but you have no right to trample on your daughter's happiness.

LUDOVICO (to his SERVANT): Giuseppe, take my baggage back to the coach, will you?

MRS. SARTI: This will kill her. (She runs out, still clutching the jug.)

LUDOVICO (politely): Mr. Galilei, if we Marsilis were to countenance teachings frowned on by the church, it would unsettle our peasants. Bear in mind: these poor people in their brute state get everything upside down. They are nothing but animals. They will never comprehend the finer points of astronomy. Why, two months ago a rumor went around, an apple had been found on a pear tree, and they left their work in the fields to discuss it.

GALILEO (interested): Did they?

LUDOVICO: I have seen the day when my poor mother has had to have a dog whipped before their eyes to remind them to keep their place. Oh, you may have seen the waving corn from the window of your comfortable coach. You have, no doubt, nibbled our olives, and absentmindedly eaten our cheese, but you can have no idea how much responsibility that sort of thing entails.

GALILEO: Young man, I do not eat my cheese absentmindedly. (To ANDREA.) Are we ready?

ANDREA: Yes, sir.

GALILEO (leaves LUDOVICO and adjusts the mirror): You would not confine your whippings to dogs to remind your peasants to keep their places, would you, Marsili?

LUDOVICO (after a pause): Mr. Galilei, you have a wonderful brain, it's a pity.

LITTLE MONK (astonished): He threatened you.

GALILEO: Yes. And he threatened you too. We might unsettle his peasants. Your sister, Fulganzio, who works the lever of the olive press, might laugh out loud if she heard the sun is not a gilded coat of arms but a lever too. The earth turns because the sun turns it.

ANDREA: That could interest his steward too and even his money lender—and the seaport towns . . .

FEDERZONI: None of them speak Latin.

GALILEO: I might write in plain language. The work we do is exacting. Who would go through the strain for less than the population at large!

LUDOVICO: I see you have made your decision. It was inevitable. You will always be a slave of your passions. Excuse me to Virginia, I think it's as well I don't see her now.

GALILEO: The dowry is at your disposal at any time.

LUDOVICO: Good afternoon. (He goes, followed by the SERVANT.)

ANDREA: Exit Ludovico. To hell with all Marsilis, Villanis, Orsinis, Canes, Nuccolis, Soldanieris . . .

FEDERZONI: . . . who ordered the earth stand still because their castles might be shaken loose if it revolves . . .

LITTLE MONK: . . . and who only kiss the Pope's feet as long as he uses them to trample on the people. God made the physical world, God made the human brain. God will allow physics.

ANDREA: They will try to stop us.

GALILEO: Thus we enter the observation of these spots on the sun in which we are interested, at our own risk, not counting on protection from a problematical new Pope . . .

ANDREA: . . . but with great likelihood of dispelling Fabricius' vapors, and the shadows of Paris and Prague, and of establishing the rotation of the sun . . .

GALILEO: . . . and with *some* likelihood of establishing the rotation of the sun. My intention is not to prove that I was right but to find out *whether* I was right. "Abandon hope all ye who enter—an observation." Before assuming these phenomena are spots, which would suit us, let us first set about proving that they are not—fried fish. We crawl by inches. What we find today we will wipe from the blackboard tomorrow and reject it—unless it shows up again the day after tomorrow. And if we find anything which would suit us, that thing we will eye with particular distrust. In fact, we will approach this observing of the sun with the implacable determination to prove that the earth stands still and only if hopelessly defeated in this pious undertaking can we allow ourselves to wonder if we may not have been right all the time: the earth revolves. Take the cloth off the telescope and turn it on the sun.

(Quietly they start work. When the coruscating image of the sun is focused on the screen, VIRGINIA *enters hurriedly, her wedding dress on, her hair disheveled,* MRS. SARTI *with her, carrying her wedding veil. The two women realize what has happened.* VIRGINIA *faints.* ANDREA, LITTLE MONK, *and* GALILEO *rush to her.* FEDERZONI *continues working.)*

SCENE 9

On April Fool's Day, thirty two,
Of science there was much ado.
People had learned from Galilei:
They used his teaching in their way.

(Around the corner from the marketplace a STREET SINGER *and his* WIFE, *who is costumed to represent the earth in a skeleton globe made of thin bands of brass, are holding the attention of a sprinkling of representative citizens, some in masquerade who were on their way to see the carnival procession. From the marketplace the noise of an impatient crowd.)*

BALLAD SINGER *(accompanied by his* WIFE *on the guitar)*:
When the Almighty made the universe
He made the earth and then he made the sun.
Then round the earth he bade the sun to turn—
That's in the Bible, Genesis, Chapter One.
And from that time all beings here below
Were in obedient circles meant to go:

Around the Pope the cardinals
Around the cardinals the bishops
Around the bishops the secretaries
Around the secretaries the aldermen
Around the aldermen the craftsmen
Around the craftsmen the servants
Around the servants the dogs, the chickens, and
the beggars.

(A conspicuous REVELLER—*henceforth called the* SPINNER—*has slowly caught on and is exhibiting his idea of spinning around. He does not lose dignity, he faints with mock grace.)*

BALLAD SINGER: Up stood the learned Galileo
Glanced briefly at the sun
And said: "Almighty God was wrong
In Genesis, Chapter One!"

Now that was rash, my friends, it is no matter
small
For heresy will spread today like foul diseases.

Change Holy Writ, forsooth? What will be left at all?
Why: each of us would say and do just what he pleases!

(Three wretched EXTRAS, *employed by the chamber of commerce, enter. Two of them, in ragged costumes, moodily bear a litter with a mock throne. The third sits on the throne. He wears sacking, a false beard, a prop crown, he carries a prop orb and sceptre, and around his chest the inscription* "THE KING OF HUNGARY." *The litter has a card with* "No. 4" *written on it. The litter bearers dump him down and listen to the* BALLAD SINGER.)*

BALLAD SINGER: Good people, what will come to pass
If Galileo's teachings spread?
No altar boy will serve the Mass
No servant girl will make the bed.
Now that is grave, my friends, it is no matter
small:
For independent spirit spreads like foul diseases!
(Yet life is sweet and man is weak and after all—
How nice it is, for a little change, to do just as
one pleases!)

(The BALLAD SINGER *takes over the guitar. His* WIFE *dances around him, illustrating the motion of the earth. A* COBBLER'S BOY *with a pair of resplendent lacquered boots hung over his shoulder has been jumping up and down in mock excitement. There are three more* CHILDREN, *dressed as grownups among the* SPECTATORS, *two together and a single one with mother. The* COBBLER'S BOY *takes the three* CHILDREN *in hand, forms a chain, and leads it, moving to the music, in and out among the* SPECTATORS, *"whipping" the chain so that the last child bumps into people. On the way past a* PEASANT WOMAN, *he steals an egg from her basket. She gestures to him to return it. As he passes her again he quietly breaks the egg over her head. The* KING OF HUNGARY *ceremoniously hands his orb to one of his bearers, marches down with mock dignity, and chastises the* COBBLER'S BOY. *The parents remove the three* CHILDREN. *The unseemliness subsides.)*

BALLAD SINGER: The carpenters take wood and build
Their houses—not the church's pews.
And members of the cobblers' guild
Now boldly walk the streets—in shoes.
The tenant kicks the noble lord
Quite off the land he owned—like that!
The milk his wife once gave the priest
Now makes *(at last!)* her children fat.

Ts, ts, ts, ts, my friends, this is no matter small
For independent spirit spreads like foul diseases
People must keep their place, some down and
some on top!
(Though it is nice, for a little change, to do just as
one pleases!)

(*The* COBBLER'S BOY *has put on the lacquered boots he was carrying. He struts off. The* BALLAD SINGER *takes over the guitar again. His* WIFE *dances around him in increased tempo. A* MONK *has been standing near a* RICH COUPLE, *who are in subdued costly clothes, without masks: shocked at the song, he now leaves. A* DWARF *in the costume of an astronomer turns his telescope on the departing* MONK, *thus drawing attention to the* RICH COUPLE. *In imitation of the* COBBLER'S BOY, *the* SPINNER *forms a chain of grownups. They move to the music, in and out, and between the* RICH COUPLE. *The* SPINNER *changes the* GENTLEMAN's *bonnet for the ragged hat of a* BEGGAR. *The* GENTLEMAN *decides to take this in good part, and a* GIRL *is emboldened to take his dagger. The* GENTLEMAN *is miffed, throws the* BEGGAR's *hat back. The* BEGGAR *discards the* GENTLEMAN's *bonnet and drops it on the ground. The* KING OF HUNGARY *has walked from his throne, taken an egg from the* PEASANT WOMAN, *and paid for it. He now ceremoniously breaks it over the* GENTLEMAN's *head as he is bending down to pick up his bonnet. The* GENTLEMAN *conducts the* LADY *away from the scene. The* KING OF HUNGARY, *about to resume his throne, finds one of the* CHILDREN *sitting on it. The* GENTLEMAN *returns to retrieve his dagger. Merriment. The* BALLAD SINGER *wanders off. This is part of his routine. His* WIFE *sings to the* SPINNER.)

WIFE: Now speaking for myself I feel
    That I could also do with a change.
    You know, for me . . . (*Turning to a reveller*)
        . . . *you* have appeal
    Maybe tonight we could arrange . . .

(*The* DWARF-ASTRONOMER *has been amusing the people by focusing his telescope on her legs. The* BALLAD SINGER *has returned.*)

BALLAD SINGER: No, no, no, no, no, stop, Galileo,
        stop!
    For independent spirit spreads like foul diseases
    People must keep their place, some down and
        some on top!
    (Though it is nice, for a little change, to do just
        as one pleases!)

(*The* SPECTATORS *stand embarrassed. A* GIRL *laughs loudly.*)

BALLAD SINGER AND HIS WIFE: Good people who
        have trouble here below
    In serving cruel lords and gentle Jesus
    Who bids you turn the other cheek just so . . .
        (*With mimicry.*)
    While they prepare to strike the second blow:
    Obedience will never cure your woe
    So each of you wake up and do just as he
        pleases!

(*The* BALLAD SINGER *and his* WIFE *hurriedly start to try to sell pamphlets to the* SPECTATORS.)

BALLAD SINGER: Read all about the earth going round the sun, two centesimi only. As proved by the great Galileo. Two centesimi only. Written by a local scholar. Understandable to one and all. Buy one for your friends, your children and your aunty Rosa, two centesimi only. Abbreviated but complete. Fully illustrated with pictures of the planets, including Venus, two centesimi only.

(*During the speech of the* BALLAD SINGER *we hear the carnival procession approaching followed by laughter. A* REVELLER *rushes in.*)

REVELLER: The procession!

(*The litter bearers speedily joggle out the* KING OF HUNGARY. *The* SPECTATORS *turn and look at the first float of the procession, which now makes its appearance. It bears a gigantic figure of* GALILEO, *holding in one hand an open Bible with the pages crossed out. The other hand points to the Bible, and the head mechanically turns from side to side as if to say "No! No!")*

A LOUD VOICE: Galileo, the Bible killer!

(*The laughter from the marketplace becomes uproarious. The* MONK *comes flying from the marketplace followed by delighted* CHILDREN.)

SCENE 10

> The depths are hot, the heights are chill
> The streets are loud, the court is still.

(*Antechamber and staircase in the Medicean palace in Florence.* GALILEO, *with a book under his arm, waits with his* DAUGHTER *to be admitted to the presence of the* PRINCE.)

VIRGINIA: They are a long time.
GALILEO: Yes.
VIRGINIA: Who is that funny-looking man? (*She indicates the* INFORMER *who has entered casually and seated himself in the background, taking no apparent notice of* GALILEO.)
GALILEO: I don't know.
VIRGINIA: It's not the first time I have seen him around. He gives me the creeps.
GALILEO: Nonsense. We're in Florence, not among robbers in the mountains of Corsica.
VIRGINIA: Here comes the Rector.

(*The* RECTOR *comes down the stairs.*)

GALILEO: Gaffone is a bore. He attaches himself to you.

(*The* RECTOR *passes, scarcely nodding.*)

GALILEO: My eyes are bad today. Did he acknowledge us?
VIRGINIA: Barely. (*Pause.*) What's in your book? Will they say it's heretical?

GALILEO: You hang around church too much. And getting up at dawn and scurrying to Mass is ruining your skin. You pray for me, don't you?

(A MAN *comes down the stairs.)*

VIRGINIA: Here's Mr. Matti. You designed a machine for his iron foundries.

MATTI: How were the squabs, Mr. Galilei? *(Low.)* My brother and I had a good laugh the other day. He picked up a racy pamphlet against the Bible somewhere. It quoted you.

GALILEO: The squabs, Matti, were wonderful, thank you again. Pamphlets I know nothing about. The Bible and Homer are my favorite reading.

MATTI: No necessity to be cautious with me, Mr. Galilei. I am on your side. I am not a man who knows about the motions of the stars, but you have championed the freedom to teach new things. Take that mechanical cultivator they have in Germany which you described to me. I can tell you, it will never be used in this country. The same circles that are hampering you now will forbid the physicians at Bologna to cut up corpses for research. Do you know, they have such things as money markets in Amsterdam and in London? Schools for business, too. Regular papers with news. Here we are not even free to make money. I have a stake in your career. They are against iron foundries because they say the gathering of so many workers in one place fosters immorality! If they ever try anything, Mr. Galilei, remember you have friends in all walks of life including an iron founder. Good luck to you. *(He goes.)*

GALILEO: Good man, but need he be so affectionate in public? His voice carries. They will always claim me as their spiritual leader particularly in places where it doesn't help me at all. I have written a book about the mechanics of the firmament, that is all. What they do or don't do with it is not my concern.

VIRGINIA *(loud)*: If people only knew how you disagreed with those goings-on all over the country last All Fools' day.

GALILEO: Yes. Offer honey to a bear, and lose your arm if the beast is hungry.

VIRGINIA *(low)*: Did the Prince ask you to come here today?

GALILEO: I sent word I was coming. He will want the book, he has paid for it. My health hasn't been any too good lately. I may accept Sagredo's invitation to stay with him in Padua for a few weeks.

VIRGINIA: You couldn't manage without your books.

GALILEO: Sagredo has an excellent library.

VIRGINIA: We haven't had this month's salary yet—

GALILEO: Yes. *(The* CARDINAL INQUISITOR *passes down the staircase. He bows deeply in answer to* GALILEO's *bow.)* What is he doing in Florence? If they try to do anything to me, the new Pope will meet them with an iron NO. And the Prince is my pupil, he would never have me extradited.

VIRGINIA: Psst. The Lord Chamberlain.

(The LORD CHAMBERLAIN *comes down the stairs.)*

LORD CHAMBERLAIN: His Highness had hoped to find time for you, Mr. Galilei. Unfortunately, he has to leave immediately to judge the parade at the Riding Academy. On what business did you wish to see His Highness?

GALILEO: I wanted to present my book to His Highness.

LORD CHAMBERLAIN: How are your eyes today?

GALILEO: So, so. With His Highness' permission, I am dedicating the book . . .

LORD CHAMBERLAIN: Your eyes are a matter of great concern to His Highness. Could it be that you have been looking too long and too often through your marvelous tube? *(He leaves without accepting the book.)*

VIRGINIA *(greatly agitated)*: Father, I am afraid.

GALILEO: He didn't take the book, did he? *(Low and resolute.)* Keep a straight face. We are not going home, but to the house of the lens-grinder. There is a coach and horses in his backyard. Keep your eyes to the front, don't look back at that man.

(They start. The LORD CHAMBERLAIN *comes back.)*

LORD CHAMBERLAIN: Oh, Mr. Galilei! His Highness has just charged me to inform you that the Florentine Court is no longer in a position to oppose the request of the Holy Inquisition to interrogate you in Rome.

SCENE 11

The Pope

(A chamber in the Vatican. The POPE, URBAN VIII—*formerly* CARDINAL BARBERINI—*is giving audience to the* CARDINAL INQUISITOR. *The trampling and shuffling of many feet is heard throughout the scene from the adjoining corridors. During the scene the* POPE *is being robed for the conclave he is about to attend: at the beginning of the scene he is plainly* BARBERINI, *but as the scene proceeds he is more and more obscured by grandiose vestments.)*

POPE: No! No! No!

INQUISITOR *(referring to the owners of the shuffling feet)*: Doctors of all chairs from the universities, representatives of the special orders of the church, representatives of the clergy as a whole who have come believing with childlike faith in the word of God as set forth in the Scriptures, who have come to hear Your Holiness confirm their faith: and Your Holiness is really going to tell them that the Bible can no longer be regarded as the alphabet of truth?

POPE: I will not set myself up against the multiplication table. No!

INQUISITOR: Ah, that is what these people say, that it is the multiplication table. Their cry is, "The figures compel us," but where do these figures come from? Plainly they come from doubt. These men doubt everything. Can society stand on doubt and not on faith? "Thou are my master, but I doubt whether it is for the best." "This is my neighbor's house and my neighbor's wife, but why shouldn't they belong to me?" After the plague, after the new war, after the unparalleled disaster of the Reformation, your dwindling flock look to their shepherd, and now the mathematicians turn their tubes on the sky and announce to the world that you have not the best advice about the heavens either—up to now your only uncontested sphere of influence. This Galilei started meddling in machines at an early age. Now that men in ships are venturing on the great oceans—I am not against that of course—they are putting their faith in a brass bowl they call a compass and not in Almighty God.

POPE: This man is the greatest physicist of our time. He is the light of Italy, and not just any muddlehead.

INQUISITOR: Would we have had to arrest him otherwise? This bad man knows what he is doing, not writing his books in Latin, but in the jargon of the marketplace.

POPE (occupied with the shuffling feet): That was not in the best of taste. (A pause.) These shuffling feet are making me nervous.

INQUISITOR: May they be more telling than my words, Your Holiness. Shall all these go from you with doubt in their hearts?

POPE: This man has friends. What about Versailles?° What about the Viennese court? They will call Holy Church a cesspool for defunct ideas. Keep your hands off him.

INQUISITOR: In practice it will never get far. He is a man of the flesh. He would soften at once.

POPE: He has more enjoyment in him than any man I ever saw. He loves eating and drinking and thinking. To excess. He indulges in thinking bouts! He cannot say no to an old wine or a new thought. (Furious.) I do not want a condemnation of physical facts. I do not want to hear battle cries: Church, church, church! Reason, reason, reason! (Pause.) These shuffling feet are intolerable. Has the whole world come to my door?

INQUISITOR: Not the whole world, Your Holiness. A select gathering of the faithful.

Versailles, The Pope refers to Versailles as the center of the French court, even though Louis XIV's massive palace would not be built until the 1660s.

(Pause.)

POPE (exhausted): It is clearly understood: he is not to be tortured. (Pause.) At the very most, he may be shown the instruments.

INQUISITOR: That will be adequate, Your Holiness. Mr. Galilei understands machinery.

(The eyes of BARBERINI look helplessly at the CARDINAL INQUISITOR from under the completely assembled panoply of POPE URBAN VIII.)

SCENE 12

June twenty-second, sixteen thirty-three,
A momentous date for you and me.
Of all the days that was the one
An age of reason could have begun.

(Again the garden of the Florentine Ambassador at Rome, where GALILEO's assistants wait the news of the trial. The LITTLE MONK and FEDERZONI are attempting to concentrate on a game of chess. VIRGINIA kneels in a corner, praying and counting her beads.)

LITTLE MONK: The Pope didn't even grant him an audience.

FEDERZONI: No more scientific discussions.

ANDREA: The "Discorsi" will never be finished. The sum of his findings. They will kill him.

FEDERZONI (stealing a glance at him): Do you really think so?

ANDREA: He will never recant.

(Silence.)

LITTLE MONK: You know when you lie awake at night how your mind fastens on to something irrelevant. Last night I kept thinking: if only they would let him take his little stone in with him, the appeal-to-reason-pebble that he always carries in his pocket.

FEDERZONI: In the room *they'll* take him to, he won't have a pocket.

ANDREA: But he will not recant.

LITTLE MONK: How can they beat the truth out of a man who gave his sight in order to see?

FEDERZONI: Maybe they can't.

(Silence.)

ANDREA (speaking about VIRGINIA): She is praying that he will recant.

FEDERZONI: Leave her alone. She doesn't know whether she's on her head or on her heels since they got hold of her. They brought her Father Confessor from Florence.

(The INFORMER of scene 10 enters.)

INFORMER: Mr. Galilei will be here soon. He may need a bed.

FEDERZONI: Have they let him out?

INFORMER: Mr. Galilei is expected to recant at five o'clock. The big bell of Saint Marcus will be rung and the complete text of his recantation publicly announced.

ANDREA: I don't believe it.

INFORMER: Mr. Galilei will be brought to the garden gate at the back of the house, to avoid the crowds collecting in the streets. (He goes.)

(Silence.)

ANDREA: The moon is an earth because the light of the moon is not her own. Jupiter is a fixed star, and four moons turn around Jupiter, therefore we are not shut in by crystal shells. The sun is the pivot of our world, therefore the earth is not the center. The earth moves, spinning about the sun. And he showed us. You can't make a man unsee what he has seen.

(Silence.)

FEDERZONI: Five o'clock in one minute.

(VIRGINIA prays louder.)

ANDREA: Listen all of you, they are murdering the truth.

(He stops up his ears with his fingers. The two other pupils do the same. FEDERZONI goes over to the LITTLE MONK, and all of them stand absolutely still in cramped positions. Nothing happens. No bell sounds. After a silence, filled with the murmur of VIRGINIA's prayers, FEDERZONI runs to the wall to look at the clock. He turns around, his expression changed. He shakes his head. They drop their hands.)

FEDERZONI: No. No bell. It is three minutes after.

LITTLE MONK: He hasn't.

ANDREA: He held true. It is all right, it is all right.

LITTLE MONK: He did not recant.

FEDERZONI: No.

(They embrace each other, they are delirious with joy.)

ANDREA: So force cannot accomplish everything. What has been seen can't be unseen. Man is constant in the face of death.

FEDERZONI: June 22, 1633: dawn of the age of reason. I wouldn't have wanted to go on living if he had recanted.

LITTLE MONK: I didn't say anything, but I was in agony. Oh, ye of little faith!

ANDREA: I was sure.

FEDERZONI: It would have turned our morning to night.

ANDREA: It would have been as if the mountain had turned to water.

LITTLE MONK (kneeling down, crying): Oh God, I thank Thee.

ANDREA: Beaten humanity can lift its head. A man has stood up and said "no."

(At this moment the bell of Saint Marcus begins to toll. They stand like statues. VIRGINIA stands up.)

VIRGINIA: The bell of Saint Marcus. He is not damned.

(From the street one hears the TOWN CRIER reading GALILEO's recantation.)

TOWN CRIER: I, Galileo Galilei, Teacher of Mathematics and Physics, do hereby publicly renounce my teaching that the earth moves. I foreswear this teaching with a sincere heart and unfeigned faith and detest and curse this and all other errors and heresies repugnant to the Holy Scriptures.

(The lights dim; when they come up again the bell of Saint Marcus is petering out. VIRGINIA has gone but the SCHOLARS are still there waiting.)

ANDREA (loud): The mountain did turn to water.

(GALILEO has entered quietly and unnoticed. He is changed, almost unrecognizable. He has heard ANDREA. He waits some seconds by the door for somebody to greet him. Nobody does. They retreat from him. He goes slowly and, because of his bad sight, uncertainly, to the front of the stage where he finds a chair, and sits down.)

ANDREA: I can't look at him. Tell him to go away.

FEDERZONI: Steady.

ANDREA (hysterically): He saved his big gut.

FEDERZONI: Get him a glass of water.

(The LITTLE MONK fetches a glass of water for ANDREA. Nobody acknowledges the presence of GALILEO, who sits silently on his chair listening to the voice of the TOWN CRIER, now in another street.)

ANDREA: I can walk. Just help me a bit.

(They help him to the door.)

ANDREA (in the door): "Unhappy is the land that breeds no hero."

GALILEO: No, Andrea: "Unhappy is the land that needs a hero."

(Before the next scene a curtain with the following legend on it is lowered:

   You can plainly see that if a horse were to fall from a height of three or four feet, it could break its bones, whereas a dog would not suffer injury. The same applies to a cat from a height of as much as eight or ten feet, to a grasshopper from the top of a tower, and to an ant falling down from the moon. Nature could not allow a horse to become as big as twenty horses nor a giant as big as ten men, unless she were to change the proportions of all its members, particularly the bones. Thus the common assumption that great and small structures are equally tough is obviously wrong.

                                        —From the Discorsi)

SCENE 13

1633–1642.
Galileo Galilei remains a prisoner
of the Inquisition until his death.

(A country house near Florence. A large room simply fur-
nished. There is a huge table, a leather chair, a globe of the
world on a stand, and a narrow bed. A portion of the
adjoining anteroom is visible, and the front door which
opens into it.)

(An OFFICIAL OF THE INQUISITION *sits on guard in*
the anteroom.)

(In the large room, GALILEO *is quietly experimenting*
with a bent wooden rail and a small ball of wood. He is
still vigorous but almost blind.)

(After a while there is a knocking at the outside door. The
OFFICIAL *opens it to a* PEASANT *who brings a plucked*
goose. VIRGINIA *comes from the kitchen. She is past forty.)*

PEASANT *(handing the goose to* VIRGINIA*):* I was told to
deliver this here.

VIRGINIA: I didn't order a goose.

PEASANT: I was told to say it's from someone who was
passing through.

*(*VIRGINIA *takes the goose, surprised. The* OFFICIAL *takes*
it from her and examines it suspiciously. Then, reassured,
he hands it back to her. The PEASANT *goes.* VIRGINIA
brings the goose in to GALILEO*.)*

VIRGINIA: Somebody who was passing through sent
you something.

GALILEO: What is it?

VIRGINIA: Can't you see it?

GALILEO: No. *(He walks over.)* A goose. Any name?

VIRGINIA: No.

GALILEO *(weighing the goose)*: Solid.

VIRGINIA *(cautiously)*: Will you eat the liver, if I have it
cooked with a little apple?

GALILEO: I had my dinner. Are you under orders to
finish me off with food?

VIRGINIA: It's not rich. And what is wrong with your
eyes again? You should be able to see it.

GALILEO: You were standing in the light.

VIRGINIA: I was not.—You haven't been writing again?

GALILEO *(sneering)*: What do you think?

*(*VIRGINIA *takes the goose out into the anteroom and*
speaks to the OFFICIAL*.)*

VIRGINIA: You had better ask Monsignor Carpula to
send the doctor. Father couldn't see this goose
across the room.—Don't look at me like that. He
has not been writing. He dictates everything to
me, as you know.

OFFICIAL: Yes?

VIRGINIA: He abides by the rules. My father's repentance is sincere. I keep an eye on him. *(She hands*

him the goose.) Tell the cook to fry the liver with an
apple and an onion. *(She goes back into the large*
room.) And you have no business to be doing that
with those eyes of yours, father.

GALILEO: You may read me some Horace.

VIRGINIA: We should go on with your weekly letter to
the Archbishop. Monsignor Carpula to whom we
owe so much was all smiles the other day because
the Archbishop had expressed his pleasure at
your collaboration.

GALILEO: Where were we?

VIRGINIA *(sits down to take his dictation)*: Paragraph
four.

GALILEO: Read what you have.

VIRGINIA: "The position of the church in the matter
of the unrest at Genoa. I agree with Cardinal Spoletti in the matter of the unrest among the Venetian ropemakers . . ."

GALILEO: Yes. *(Dictates.)* I agree with Cardinal Spoletti
in the matter of the unrest among the Venetian
ropemakers: it is better to distribute good nourishing food in the name of charity than to pay
them more for their bellropes. It being surely better to strengthen their faith than to encourage
their acquisitiveness. St. Paul says: Charity never
faileth.—How is that?

VIRGINIA: It's beautiful, father.

GALILEO: It couldn't be taken as irony?

VIRGINIA: No. The Archbishop will like it. It's so practical.

GALILEO: I trust your judgment. Read it over slowly.

VIRGINIA: "The position of the Church in the matter
of the unrest . . ."

(There is a knocking at the outside door. VIRGINIA *goes into*
the anteroom. The OFFICIAL *opens the door. It is* ANDREA*.)*

ANDREA: Good evening. I am sorry to call so late, I'm
on my way to Holland. I was asked to look him up.
Can I go in?

VIRGINIA: I don't know whether he will see you. You
never came.

ANDREA: Ask him.

*(*GALILEO *recognizes the voice. He sits motionless.* VIR-
GINIA *comes in to* GALILEO*.)*

GALILEO: Is that Andrea?

VIRGINIA: Yes. *(Pause.)* I will send him away.

GALILEO: Show him in.

*(*VIRGINIA *shows* ANDREA *in.* VIRGINIA *sits,* ANDREA *re-*
mains standing.)

ANDREA *(cool)*: Have you been keeping well, Mr. Galilei?

GALILEO: Sit down. What are you doing these days?
What are you working on? I heard it was something about hydraulics in Milan.

ANDREA: As he knew I was passing through, Fabricius of Amsterdam asked me to visit you and inquire about your health.

(Pause.)

GALILEO: I am very well.

ANDREA *(formally)*: I am glad I can report you are in good health.

GALILEO: Fabricius will be glad to hear it. And you might inform him that, on account of the depth of my repentance, I live in comparative comfort.

ANDREA: Yes, we understand that the church is more than pleased with you. Your complete acceptance has had its effect. Not one paper expounding a new thesis has made its appearance in Italy since your submission.

(Pause.)

GALILEO: Unfortunately there are countries not under the wing of the church. Would you not say the erroneous condemned theories are still taught—there?

ANDREA *(relentless)*: Things are almost at a standstill.

GALILEO: Are they? *(Pause.)* Nothing from Descartes in Paris?

ANDREA: Yes. On receiving the news of your recantation, he shelved his treatise on the nature of light.

GALILEO: I sometimes worry about my assistants whom I led into error. Have they benefited by my example?

ANDREA: In order to work I have to go to Holland.

GALILEO: Yes.

ANDREA: Federzoni is grinding lenses again, back in some shop.

GALILEO: He can't read the books.

ANDREA: Fulganzio, our little monk, has abandoned research and is resting in peace in the church.

GALILEO: So. *(Pause.)* My superiors are looking forward to my spiritual recovery. I am progressing as well as can be expected.

VIRGINIA: You are doing well, father.

GALILEO: Virginia, leave the room.

(VIRGINIA rises uncertainly and goes out.)

VIRGINIA *(to the OFFICIAL)*: He was his pupil, so now he is his enemy.—Help me in the kitchen.

(She leaves the anteroom with the OFFICIAL.)

ANDREA: May I go now, sir?

GALILEO: I do not know why you came, Sarti. To unsettle me? I have to be prudent.

ANDREA: I'll be on my way.

GALILEO: As it is, I have relapses. I completed the "Discorsi."

ANDREA: You completed what?

GALILEO: My "Discorsi."

ANDREA: How?

GALILEO: I am allowed pen and paper. My superiors are intelligent men. They know the habits of a lifetime cannot be broken abruptly. But they protect me from any unpleasant consequences: they lock my pages away as I dictate them. And I should know better than to risk my comfort. I wrote the "Discorsi" out again during the night. The manuscript is in the globe. My vanity has up to now prevented me from destroying it. If you consider taking it, you will shoulder the entire risk. You will say it was pirated from the original in the hands of the Holy Office.

(ANDREA, as in a trance, has gone to the globe. He lifts the upper half and gets the book. He turns the pages as if wanting to devour them. In the background the opening sentences of the Discorsi *appear:*

MY PURPOSE IS TO SET FORTH A VERY NEW SCIENCE DEALING WITH A VERY ANCIENT SUBJECT—MOTION. . . . AND I HAVE DISCOVERED BY EXPERIMENT SOME PROPERTIES OF IT WHICH ARE WORTH KNOWING. . . .)

GALILEO: I had to employ my time somehow.

(The text disappears.)

ANDREA: Two new sciences! This will be the foundation stone of a new physics.

GALILEO: Yes. Put it under your coat.

ANDREA: And we thought you had deserted. *(In a low voice.)* Mr. Galilei, how can I begin to express my shame. Mine has been the loudest voice against you.

GALILEO: That would seem to have been proper. I taught you science and I decried the truth.

ANDREA: Did you? I think not. Everything is changed!

GALILEO: What is changed?

ANDREA: You shielded the truth from the oppressor. Now I see! In your dealings with the Inquisition you used the same superb common sense you brought to physics.

GALILEO: Oh!

ANDREA: We lost our heads. With the crowd at the street corners we said: "He will die, he will never surrender!" You came back: "I surrendered but I am alive." We cried: "Your hands are stained!" You say: "Better stained than empty."

GALILEO: "Better stained than empty."—It sounds realistic. Sounds like me.

ANDREA: And I of all people should have known. I was twelve when you sold another man's telescope to the Venetian Senate, and saw you put it to immortal use. Your friends were baffled when you bowed to the Prince of Florence: Science gained a wider audience. You always laughed at heroics. "People who suffer bore me," you said. "Misfortunes are due mainly to miscalculations." And: "If there are obstacles, the shortest line between two points may be the crooked line."

GALILEO: It makes a picture.

ANDREA: And when you stooped to recant in 1633, I should have understood that you were again about your business.

GALILEO: My business being?

ANDREA: Science. The study of the properties of motion, mother of the machines which will themselves change the ugly face of the earth.

GALILEO: Aha!

ANDREA: You gained time to write a book that only you could write. Had you burned at the stake in a blaze of glory they would have won.

GALILEO: They have won. And there is no such thing as a scientific work that only one man can write.

ANDREA: Then why did you recant, tell me that!

GALILEO: I recanted because I was afraid of physical pain.

ANDREA: No!

GALILEO: They showed me the instruments.

ANDREA: It was not a plan?

GALILEO: It was not.

(Pause.)

ANDREA: But you have contributed. Science has only one commandment: contribution. And you have contributed more than any man for a hundred years.

GALILEO: Have I? Then welcome to my gutter, dear colleague in science and brother in treason: I sold out, you are a buyer. The first sight of the book! His mouth watered and his scoldings were drowned. Blessed be our bargaining, whitewashing, death-fearing community!

ANDREA: The fear of death is human.

GALILEO: Even the church will teach you that to be weak is not human. It is just evil.

ANDREA: The church, yes! But science is not concerned with our weaknesses.

GALILEO: No? My dear Sarti, in spite of my present convictions, I may be able to give you a few pointers as to the concerns of your chosen profession.

(Enter VIRGINIA *with a platter.)*

In my spare time, I happen to have gone over this case. I have spare time.—Even a man who sells wool, however good he is at buying wool cheap and selling it dear, must be concerned with the standing of the wool trade. The practice of science would seem to call for valor. She trades in knowledge, which is the product of doubt. And this new art of doubt has enchanted the public. The plight of the multitude is old as the rocks, and is believed to be basic as the rocks. But now they have learned to doubt. They snatched the telescopes out of our hands and had them trained on their tormentors: prince, official, public moralist. The mechanism of the heavens was clearer, the mechanism of their courts was still murky. The battle to measure the heavens is won by doubt; by credulity the Roman housewife's battle for milk will always be lost. Word is passed down that this is of no concern to the scientist who is told he will only release such of his findings as do not disturb the peace, that is, the peace of mind of the well-to-do. Threats and bribes fill the air. Can the scientist hold out on the numbers?—For what reason do you labor? I take it the intent of science is to ease human existence. If you give way to coercion, science can be crippled, and your new machines may simply suggest new drudgeries. Should you then, in time, discover all there is to be discovered, your progress must then become a progress away from the bulk of humanity. The gulf might even grow so wide that the sound of your cheering at some new achievement would be echoed by a universal howl of horror.—As a scientist I had an almost unique opportunity. In my day astronomy emerged into the marketplace. At that particular time, had one man put up a fight, it could have had wide repercussions. I have come to believe that I was never in real danger; for some years I was as strong as the authorities, and I surrendered my knowledge to the powers that be, to use it, no, not *use* it, *abuse* it, as it suits their ends. I have betrayed my profession. Any man who does what I have done must not be tolerated in the ranks of science.

*(*VIRGINIA, *who has stood motionless, puts the platter on the table.)*

VIRGINIA: You are accepted in the ranks of the faithful, father.

GALILEO *(sees her)*: Correct. *(He goes over to the table.)* I have to eat now.

VIRGINIA: We lock up at eight.

ANDREA: I am glad I came. *(He extends his hand.* GALILEO *ignores it and goes over to his meal.)*

GALILEO *(examining the plate; to* ANDREA*)*: Somebody who knows me sent me a goose. I still enjoy eating.

ANDREA: And your opinion is now that the "new age" was an illusion?

GALILEO: Well.—This age of ours turned out to be a whore, spattered with blood. Maybe, new ages look like blood-spattered whores. Take care of yourself.

ANDREA: Yes. *(Unable to go.)* With reference to your evaluation of the author in question—I do not know the answer. But I cannot think that your savage analysis is the last word.

GALILEO: Thank you, sir.

(OFFICIAL *knocks at the door.*)

VIRGINIA (*showing* ANDREA *out*): I don't like visitors from the past, they excite him.

(*She lets him out. The* OFFICIAL *closes the iron door.* VIRGINIA *returns.*)

GALILEO (*eating*): Did you try and think who sent the goose?

VIRGINIA: Not Andrea.

GALILEO: Maybe not. I gave Redhead his first lesson; when he held out his hand, I had to remind myself he is teaching now.—How is the sky tonight?

VIRGINIA (*at the window*): Bright.

(GALILEO *continues eating.*)

SCENE 14

The great book o'er the border went
And, good folk, that was the end.
But we hope you'll keep in mind
You and I were left behind.

(*Before a little Italian customs house early in the morning.* ANDREA *sits upon one of his traveling trunks at the barrier and reads* GALILEO's *book. The window of a small house is still lit, and a big grotesque shadow, like an old witch and her cauldron, falls upon the house wall beyond. Barefoot* CHILDREN *in rags see it and point to the little house.*)

CHILDREN (*singing*): One, two, three, four, five, six,
Old Marina is a witch.
At night, on a broomstick she sits
And on the church steeple she spits.

CUSTOMS OFFICER (*to* ANDREA) Why are you making this journey?

ANDREA: I am a scholar.

CUSTOMS OFFICER (*to his* CLERK): Put down under "reason for leaving the country": Scholar. (*He points to the baggage.*) Books! Anything dangerous in these books?

ANDREA: What is dangerous?

CUSTOMS OFFICER: Religion. Politics.

ANDREA: These are nothing but mathematical formulas.

CUSTOMS OFFICER: What's that?

ANDREA: Figures.

CUSTOMS OFFICER: Oh, figures. No harm in figures. Just wait a minute, sir, we will soon have your papers stamped. (*He exits with* CLERK.)

(*Meanwhile, a little council of war among the* CHILDREN *has taken place.* ANDREA *quietly watches. One of the* BOYS, *pushed forward by the others, creeps up to the little house from which the shadow comes and takes the jug of milk on the doorstep.*)

ANDREA (*quietly*): What are you doing with that milk?

BOY (*stopping in mid-movement*): She is a witch.

(*The other* CHILDREN *run away behind the customs house. One of them shouts, "Run, Paolo!"*)

ANDREA: Hmm!—And because she is a witch she mustn't have milk. Is that the idea?

BOY: Yes.

ANDREA: And how do you know she is a witch?

BOY (*points to shadow on house wall*): Look!

ANDREA: Oh! I see.

BOY: And she rides on a broomstick at night—and she bewitches the coachman's horses. My cousin Luigi looked through the hole in the stable roof, that the snowstorm made, and heard the horses coughing something terrible.

ANDREA: Oh!—How big was the hole in the stable roof?

BOY: Luigi didn't tell. Why?

ANDREA: I was asking because maybe the horses got sick because it was cold in the stable. You had better ask Luigi how big that hole is.

BOY: You are not going to say Old Marina isn't a witch, because you can't.

ANDREA: No, I can't say she isn't a witch. I haven't looked into it. A man can't know about a thing he hasn't looked into, or can he?

BOY: No!—But THAT! (*He points to the shadow.*) She is stirring hell-broth.

ANDREA: Let's see. Do you want to take a look? I can lift you up.

BOY: You lift me to the window, mister! (*He takes a slingshot out of his pocket.*) I can really bash her from there.

ANDREA: Hadn't we better make sure she is a witch before we shoot? I'll hold that.

(*The* BOY *puts the milk jug down and follows him reluctantly to the window.* ANDREA *lifts the boy up so that he can look in.*)

ANDREA: What do you see?

BOY (*slowly*): Just an old girl cooking porridge.

ANDREA: Oh! Nothing to it then. Now look at her shadow, Paolo.

(*The* BOY *looks over his shoulder and back and compares the reality and the shadow.*)

BOY: The big thing is a soup ladle.

ANDREA: Ah! A ladle! You see, I would have taken it for a broomstick, but I haven't looked into the matter as you have, Paolo. Here is your sling.

CUSTOMS OFFICER (*returning with the* CLERK *and handing* ANDREA *his papers*): All present and correct. Good luck, sir.

(ANDREA *goes, reading* GALILEO's *book. The* CLERK *starts to bring his baggage after him. The barrier rises.* ANDREA *passes through, still reading the book. The* BOY *kicks over the milk jug.*)

BOY (*shouting after* ANDREA): She *is* a witch! She *is* a witch!

ANDREA: You saw with your own eyes: think it over!

(*The* BOY *joins the others. They sing.*)

One, two, three, four, five, six,
Old Marina is a witch.
At night, on a broomstick she sits
And on the church steeple she spits.

(*The* CUSTOMS OFFICERS *laugh.* ANDREA *goes.*)

Figure 1. Galileo (Charles Laughton) glances warily at the Inquisitor (John Carradine) while Virginia (Joan McCracken) curtsies demurely in the 1947 New York production of *Galileo,* directed by Joseph Losey. (Photograph: Billy Rose Theatre Collection. The New York Public Library for the Performing Arts. Astor, Lenox, and Tilden Foundations.)

Figure 2. A relaxed Galileo (Charles Laughton) chats with his co-workers and Ludovico while Mrs. Sarti (Hester Sondergard) looks on disapprovingly. Around the table are Ludovico (Philip Swander), Andrea (Nehemiah Persoff), and the Little Monk (Donald Symington), while Federzoni (Dwight Marfield) stands in the background. (Photograph: Billy Rose Theatre Collection. The New York Public Library for the Performing Arts. Astor, Lenox, and Tilden Foundations.)

Figure 3. Almost blind, the imprisoned Galileo (Charles Laughton) "is quietly experimenting with a bent wooden rail and a small ball of wood" in the final scene of the 1947 New York production. (Photograph: Billy Rose Theatre Collection. The New York Public Library for the Performing Arts. Astor, Lenox, and Tilden Foundations.)

Staging of *Galileo*

REVIEW OF THE NEW YORK PRODUCTION, 1947, BY IRWIN SHAW

There has been considerable discussion, some of it quite acrimonious, about the propriety of having an institution called the Experimental Theatre put on a work in which an actor of Charles Laughton's standing plays the leading part. The argument has leaked over to include the Experimental Theatre's next production, "Skipper Next to God," with John Garfield. According to the critics of the enterprise, it would seem that nothing a well-known actor can do on a stage can properly be considered an experiment. This, of course, is nonsense, and the sponsors of the project are to be congratulated for fulfilling handsomely, in Bertolt Brecht's "Galileo," the promise of the organization's title.

The play is noble in theme, relentlessly unconventional in execution, and it permits Laughton to escape, if only for six performances, the absurd, minor warblings which have recently been his lot in Hollywood. Equipped with an abstract set, a fluttering gauze curtain that is drawn at the end of each scene by a small boy with a pole, projections of Renaissance drawings and paintings, and intermittent choruses with music by Hanns Eisler, sung by three choirboys, it could hardly be called a standard Broadway performance.

Aside from its technical innovations, the story of Galileo's martyrdom by Authority is bitterly apposite for today's audiences. The heresy hunters are almost as busy today in Washington as they ever were in Florence, and recantations fill the air in a medieval blizzard of fear. *Time, Life* and Hearst have replaced the rack, and the Representative from New Jersey has donned the Inquisitor's dark satin. The sobbing "I was wrong" of the matinee idol is now to be heard, instead of the "I have sinned" of the old astronomer, but the pattern, as Brecht bleakly points out, is the same. Truth dies with conformity, this year or last.

Cool demands. Brecht's method of saying these things, in accordance with his theories of the "Epic" theater, is abstract, cold and didactic. He assumes the air of the passionless teacher lecturing to students who are not so bright as they should be. He disdains all emotionalism; scornfully, he refuses to amuse us with the usual dramatist's tricks. His characters are symbols, not people; his action the functioning of huge forces, not the clash of human beings. The final effect is interesting, but aggravating. We get the unpleasant feeling that Brecht regards the human race, or at least that part of it which goes to the theater, as animals equipped with only the most rudimentary ability to reason. His Olympian condescension is bound to annoy us, even when we agree with him most heartily.

Joseph Losey's staging meets, I suppose, with Brecht's cool demands, but it is only in three magnificently searching and eloquent scenes in the second half that the play comes really alive. One is in a garden, in which a young monk tells Galileo the reasons of conscience for which he is giving up the study of physics; another is in the Pope's robing room, in which the humanitarian prelate is forced by the logic of his position to agree to the limited torture of the scientist; and the third is the last scene of the play, in which Galileo explores the most profound and complex depths of compromise, cowardice and treachery.

It is in this scene, seated quietly on the almost empty stage, that Laughton gives us one of the most memorable moments of the recent theater. With a stony and scientifically accurate self-knowledge, he appraises himself and the world. Tragically clear, half-victor half-victim, the old giant delivers himself of a monumental monologue, and for a time, on the stage of the Maxine Elliot, we seem to be at the very core of truth.

It is devoutly to be hoped that the commercial theater will rise to the challenge of "Galileo" and put it on the boards where all may see it.

ARTHUR MILLER

1915–

> In all my plays and books I try to take settings and dramatic situations from life which involve real questions of right and wrong. Then I set out, rather implacably and in the most realistic situations I can find, the moral dilemma and try to point a real, though hard, path out. I don't see how you can write anything decent without using the question of right and wrong as the basis.

That uncompromising statement from Arthur Miller, one of America's most significant contemporary dramatists, focuses directly on the lifelong concern with the intersection of social and moral responsibility that he has repeatedly dramatized in a career lasting over fifty years. Miller's achievements—and especially his ability to question the American dream of "success"—are even more noteworthy, given the financial difficulties of his younger life. Born in Harlem at a time when his father was still struggling to establish a successful clothing manufacturing business, he was raised in a suburb of Brooklyn after his father's business had become well established. But the depression of 1929 nearly ruined his father, so Miller had to work in an automobile warehouse to save up enough money for college at the University of Michigan. After a series of jobs during college, he then worked briefly for a federal government playwriting project and, during the war, wrote radio plays and other pieces to help support civilian morale at home. Before the end of the war, he had also completed his first full-length play to be produced on Broadway, *The Man Who Had All the Luck* (1944), and though it closed after only four performances, it clearly anticipated the concern with moral responsibility and guilt that has been central to virtually all of Miller's work for the theater.

Those issues recur, in various forms, in many of his major plays. *All My Sons* (1947), which won the New York Drama Critics Circle award for the best play of the season, portrays the crisis of Joe Keller, a small armaments manufacturer, whose son discovers that Joe sold defective airplane parts to the army. Joe's claim that he wanted to preserve the business and support his family finally gives way to an acknowledgment of his moral responsibility to the world beyond the limits of his own family. *The Crucible* (1953) deals with two widely separated historical events; by dramatizing a story set during the seventeenth-century Salem witch trials, Miller challenged the politically repressive hearings of the 1950s House Un-American Activities Committee. His protagonist, John Proctor, finally must confront the kind of dilemma that Miller himself faced when he, like many other artists, was asked to testify about his political beliefs—and those of his friends. Proctor confesses his own failings, but when asked to implicate others, he refuses to do so. Another dramatization of betrayal appears in *A View from the Bridge* (1956), where Eddie Carbone's unacknowledged sexual jealousy leads him to reveal the presence of illegal immigrants, even though they are his own relations. And in *Incident at Vichy* (1964) Miller focused on a group of detainees waiting to be interrogated by Nazi officials in occupied France, thus setting the problems of individual conscience and compromise against the background of the Holocaust.

Miller's long career has continued with new plays, *The Ride Down Mt. Morgan* (1991), *Broken Glass* (1994), and *Resurrection Blues* (2002); a film, *Focus* (2001), based on his 1945 novel of the same name; and numerous revivals of his earlier plays. And of those plays, none is more honored and produced than *Death of a Salesman* (1949), Miller's consummate dramatization of the most disturbing aspects in the modern American version of "success." Miller chose for his protagonist an archetypal figure in American culture—the traveling salesman—and he endowed that figure with all the conventional American aspirations, including not only the desire to succeed by being "well liked" but also the desire to be respected by one's friends, to be loved and admired by one's family, to contribute to the success of one's children, to pay one's bills on time, and to own one's own home. Then, in order to explore the failure of such middle-class values, Miller made the strategic decision of focusing on the archetypal salesman at the vulnerable moment in his life, when he is "tired to death by his age and by the disappointment of all his hopes." That, in essence, is the formula for the play, but the play itself goes far beyond the formula, largely because Miller does not confine himself to making an indictment of American cultural values.

Admittedly, the play can be read as an exposure of the cruelty, the cynicism, the stupidity, and the immorality that result from a blind commitment to American materialistic values, for those qualities are repeatedly displayed in Willy's behavior toward his wife, his sons, his friends, his boss, and—above all—in the symbolic spectacle of Willy's brother Ben preaching the law of the jungle to Biff: "Never fight fair with a stranger, boy. You'll never get out of the jungle that way." The play can also be read as a tragedy of the common man—a view of the work that Miller sought to define in an essay he published along with the play, "Tragedy and the Common Man" (reprinted in Ideas of Drama). In that essay, Miller sought to challenge the traditional notion of the "well placed" or "exalted" tragic figure, arguing instead for a redefinition of tragedy applicable to the "lowly": "the underlying fear of being displaced, the disaster inherent in being torn away from our chosen image of what and who we are in the world."

But the power of the play, at last, derives less from its socially conscious tragic vision than from the way Miller dramatizes that vision by concentrating on Willy's mental and emotional experiences during the moment of his tragic crisis. Willy would not, after all, be such a compelling figure if he were merely a common social type. He is, in fact, highly particularized through the detailed exposure of his tortured consciousness—through the expressionistic presentation of his mental processes as he repeatedly shifts back and forth between past and present experience, mingling memory with immediate reality with hallucination. When he is shown, for example, in the first act, on the verge of embracing his wife, Linda, only to find himself engulfed by the memory of his adulterous escapade with another woman, Willy is poignantly revealed as a particular human being overwhelmed by guilt and by the painful isolation that it creates between him and his family. His sense of isolation increases throughout the play as he is incessantly bombarded by both painful memories from the past and disappointments in the present. Yet he does not simply acquiesce to the relentless flow of events in his world and in his mind, but seeks to resist them, indeed to alter them with all the force of his being. His final act—his suicide—is in part an act of resistance, but even more an act of love for his family. He thus escapes from the enslavement of being a salesman and becomes a person bound by authentic human attachments, free at last "to do the right thing."

In the years immediately following its first appearance, *Death of a Salesman* was interpreted in the United States and throughout the world as being primarily a statement about American culture. But its persistent appeal to audiences suggests that it speaks to even larger concerns—to the dismay that all human beings experience when they find themselves profoundly dissatisfied with the trajectory of their lives—unable to accept what they have done to others, what others have done to them, and what they have become as a consequence. So universal is the play's appeal that Miller was asked to direct its first Chinese production at the Beijing People's Art Theatre in 1983. Though the capitalist, market-driven culture of Miller's play might seem incomprehensible in communist China, the production was tremendously successful because Chinese actors and audiences were able to understand the characters as human beings, not just as emblems of American culture.

More recently, the fiftieth anniversary of the play's premiere called forth numerous articles about Miller and his play. One of the most fascinating of those pieces is John Lahr's "Making Willy Loman" (reprinted after the play), for it offers a series of illuminating details from Miller's notebook about the play. In those notes, as Lahr explains, Miller reveals a series of sources for the play, some deeply personal, even idiosyncratic, such as the revelation that Willy Loman's last name comes from a scene in a 1933 film. They also show the playwright's growing sense that he needed to find a new dramatic language and form—one that could evoke past and present simultaneously. Jo Mielziner's set for the first production (see Figure 1), a backdrop of tall buildings surrounding the house, vividly suggested a modern world closing in on Willy's older center of security, his home, and it allowed the action to flow easily and naturally from one place to another without set changes. On February 10, 1999, exactly fifty years after the premiere, a highly praised new production of the play from Chicago's Goodman Theatre opened in New York. That production made clear that the play is also "a love story," as Elia Kazan, its first director, had said to Miller. That love story is manifest not only in the intimacy and pain of the relationship between Willy and his wife, Linda (see Figure 2), but also in the abiding love of Willy for his two sons, especially Biff, the older one (see Figure 3). Brian Dennehy's Willy was one in a long series of distinguished realizations of that role—from Lee J. Cobb (who created the role) to George C. Scott (1975) to Dustin Hoffman (1984). But no matter who plays the role, the play itself evokes powerful—and sometimes audible—emotional responses from its audiences. Benedict Nightingale began his review of the 1984 production by asking, "What was that strange sniffling sound?" while Ben Brantley concluded his review of the 1999 New York production, "I could hear people around me not just sniffling but sobbing." The first production left people—in Arthur Miller's words— silent, "sitting there with handkerchiefs over their faces." Willy's story, in its striving for success and its confrontation with failure, continues to speak to the human condition throughout the world.

DEATH OF A SALESMAN

BY ARTHUR MILLER

CHARACTERS

WILLY LOMAN
LINDA
BIFF
HAPPY
BERNARD
THE WOMAN
CHARLEY
UNCLE BEN
HOWARD WAGNER

JENNY
STANLEY
MISS FORSYTHE
LETTA

SCENE

The action takes place in WILLY LOMAN'*s house and yard and in various places he visits in the New York and Boston of today.*

ACT 1

(A melody is heard, played upon a flute. It is small and fine, telling of grass and trees and the horizon. The curtain rises.

Before us is the Salesman's house. We are aware of towering, angular shapes behind it, surrounding it on all sides. Only the blue light of the sky falls upon the house and forestage; the surrounding area shows an angry glow of orange. As more light appears, we see a solid vault of apartment houses around the small, fragile-seeming home. An air of the dream clings to the place, a dream rising out of reality. The kitchen at center seems actual enough, for there is a kitchen table with three chairs, and a refrigerator. But no other fixtures are seen. At the back of the kitchen there is a draped entrance, which leads to the living-room. To the right of the kitchen, on a level raised two feet, is a bedroom furnished only with a brass bedstead and a straight chair. On a shelf over the bed a silver athletic trophy stands. A window opens onto the apartment house at the side.

Behind the kitchen, on a level raised six and a half feet, is the boys' bedroom, at present barely visible. Two beds are dimly seen, and at the back of the room a dormer window. [This bedroom is above the unseen living-room.] At the left a stairway curves up to it from the kitchen.

The entire setting is wholly or, in some places, partially transparent. The roof-line of the house is one-dimensional; under and over it we see the apartment buildings. Before the house lies an apron, curving beyond the forestage into the orchestra. This forward area serves as the back yard as well as the locale of all WILLY'*s imaginings and of his city scenes. Whenever the action is in the present the actors observe the imaginary wall-lines, entering the house only through its door at the left. But in the scenes of the past these boundaries are broken, and characters enter or leave a room by stepping "through" a wall onto the forestage.*

From the right, WILLY LOMAN, *the Salesman, enters, carrying two large sample cases. The flute plays on. He* hears but is not aware of it. He is past sixty years of age, dressed quietly. Even as he crosses the stage to the doorway of the house, his exhaustion is apparent. He unlocks the door, comes into the kitchen, and thankfully lets his burden down, feeling the soreness of his palms. A word-sigh escapes his lips—it might be "Oh, boy, oh, boy." He closes the door, then carries his cases out into the living-room, through the draped kitchen doorway.*

LINDA, *his wife, has stirred in her bed at the right. She gets out and puts on a robe, listening. Most often jovial, she has developed an iron repression of her exceptions to* WILLY'*s behavior—she more than loves him, she admires him, as though his mercurial nature, his temper, his massive dreams and little cruelties, served her only as sharp reminders of the turbulent longings within him, longings which she shares but lacks the temperament to utter and follow to their end.)*

LINDA *(hearing* WILLY *outside the bedroom, calls with some trepidation):* Willy!

WILLY: It's all right. I came back.

LINDA: Why? What happened? *(Slight pause.)* Did something happen, Willy?

WILLY: No, nothing happened.

LINDA: You didn't smash the car, did you?

WILLY *(with casual irritation):* I said nothing happened. Didn't you hear me?

LINDA: Don't you feel well?

WILLY: I'm tired to the death. *(The flute has faded away. He sits on the bed beside her, a little numb.)* I couldn't make it. I just couldn't make it, Linda.

LINDA *(very carefully, delicately):* Where were you all day? You look terrible.

WILLY: I got as far as a little above Yonkers. I stopped for a cup of coffee. Maybe it was the coffee.

LINDA: What?

WILLY *(after a pause):* I suddenly couldn't drive any more. The car kept going off onto the shoulder, y'know?

LINDA (*helpfully*): Oh. Maybe it was the steering again. I don't think Angelo knows the Studebaker.

WILLY: No, it's me, it's me. Suddenly I realize I'm goin' sixty miles an hour and I don't remember the last five minutes. I'm—I can't seem to—keep my mind to it.

LINDA: Maybe it's your glasses. You never went for your new glasses.

WILLY: No, I see everything. I came back ten miles an hour. It took me nearly four hours from Yonkers.

LINDA (*resigned*): Well, you'll just have to take a rest, Willy, you can't continue this way.

WILLY: I just got back from Florida.

LINDA: But you didn't rest your mind. Your mind is overactive, and the mind is what counts, dear.

WILLY: I'll start out in the morning. Maybe I'll feel better in the morning. (*She is taking off his shoes.*) These goddam arch supports are killing me.

LINDA: Take an aspirin. Should I get you an aspirin? It'll soothe you.

WILLY (*with wonder*): I was driving along, you understand? And I was fine. I was even observing the scenery. You can imagine, me looking at scenery, on the road every week of my life. But it's so beautiful up there, Linda, the trees are so thick, and the sun is warm. I opened the windshield and just let the warm air bathe over me. And then all of a sudden I'm goin' off the road! I'm tellin' ya, I absolutely forgot I was driving. If I'd've gone the other way, over the white line I might've killed somebody. So I went on again—and five minutes later I'm dreamin' again, and I nearly—(*He presses two fingers against his eyes.*) I have such thoughts, I have such strange thoughts.

LINDA: Willy, dear. Talk to them again. There's no reason why you can't work in New York.

WILLY: They don't need me in New York. I'm the New England man. I'm vital in New England.

LINDA: But you're sixty years old. They can't expect you to keep traveling every week.

WILLY: I'll have to send a wire to Portland. I'm supposed to see Brown and Morrison tomorrow morning at ten o'clock to show the line. Goddammit, I could sell them! (*He starts putting on his jacket.*)

LINDA (*taking the jacket from him*): Why don't you go down to the place tomorrow and tell Howard you've simply got to work in New York? You're too accommodating, dear.

WILLY: If old man Wagner was alive I'd a been in charge of New York now! That man was a prince, he was a masterful man. But that boy of his, that Howard, he don't appreciate. When I was north the first time, the Wagner Company didn't know where New England was!

LINDA: Why don't you tell those things to Howard, dear?

WILLY (*encouraged*): I will, I definitely will. Is there any cheese?

LINDA: I'll make you a sandwich.

WILLY: No, go to sleep. I'll take some milk. I'll be up right away. The boys in?

LINDA: They're sleeping. Happy took Biff on a date tonight.

WILLY (*interested*): That so?

LINDA: It was so nice to see them shaving together, one behind the other, in the bathroom. And going out together. You notice? The whole house smells of shaving lotion.

WILLY: Figure it out. Work a lifetime to pay off a house. You finally own it, and there's nobody to live in it.

LINDA: Well, dear, life is a casting off. It's always that way.

WILLY: No, no, some people—some people accomplish something. Did Biff say anything after I went this morning?

LINDA: You shouldn't have criticized him, Willy, especially after he just got off the train. You mustn't lose your temper with him.

WILLY: When the hell did I lose my temper? I simply asked him if he was making any money. Is that a criticism?

LINDA: But, dear, how could he make any money?

WILLY (*worried and angered*): There's such an undercurrent in him. He became a moody man. Did he apologize when I left this morning?

LINDA: He was crestfallen, Willy. You know how he admires you. I think if he finds himself, then you'll both be happier and not fight any more.

WILLY: How can he find himself on a farm? Is that a life? A farmhand? In the beginning, when he was young, I thought, well, a young man, it's good for him to tramp around, take a lot of different jobs. But it's more than ten years now and he has yet to make thirty-five dollars a week!

LINDA: He's finding himself, Willy.

WILLY: Not finding yourself at the age of thirty-four is a disgrace!

LINDA: Shh!

WILLY: The trouble is he's lazy, goddammit!

LINDA: Willy, please!

WILLY: Biff is a lazy bum.

LINDA: They're sleeping. Get something to eat. Go on down.

WILLY: Why did he come home? I would like to know what brought him home.

LINDA: I don't know. I think he's still lost, Willy. I think he's very lost.

WILLY: Biff Loman is lost. In the greatest country in the world a young man with such—personal attractiveness, gets lost. And such a hard worker. There's one thing about Biff—he's not lazy.

LINDA: Never.

WILLY (*with pity and resolve*): I'll see him in the morning; I'll have a nice talk with him. I'll get him a job selling. He could be big in no time. My God! Remember how they used to follow him around in high school? When he smiled at one of them their faces lit up. When he walked down the street . . . (*He loses himself in reminiscences.*)

LINDA (*trying to bring him out of it*): Willy, dear, I got a new kind of American-type cheese today. It's whipped.

WILLY: Why do you get American when I like Swiss?

LINDA: I just thought you'd like a change—

WILLY: I don't want a change! I want Swiss cheese. Why am I always being contradicted?

LINDA (*with a covering laugh*): I thought it would be a surprise.

WILLY: Why don't you open a window in here, for God's sake?

LINDA (*with infinite patience*): They're all open, dear.

WILLY: The way they boxed us in here. Bricks and windows, windows and bricks.

LINDA: We should've bought the land next door.

WILLY: The street is lined with cars. There's not a breath of fresh air in the neighborhood. The grass don't grow any more, you can't raise a carrot in the back yard. They should've had a law against apartment houses. Remember those two beautiful elm trees out there? When I and Biff hung the swing between them?

LINDA: Yeah, like being a million miles from the city.

WILLY: They should've arrested the builder for cutting those down. They massacred the neighborhood. (*Lost.*) More and more I think of those days, Linda. This time of year it was lilac and wisteria. And then the peonies would come out, and the daffodils. What fragrance in this room!

LINDA: Well, after all, people had to move somewhere.

WILLY: No, there's more people now.

LINDA: I don't think there's more people. I think—

WILLY: There's more people! That's what's ruining this country! Population is getting out of control. The competition is maddening! Smell the stink from that apartment house! And another one on the other side . . . How can they whip cheese?

(*On* WILLY'*s last line,* BIFF *and* HAPPY *raise themselves up in their beds, listening.*)

LINDA: Go down, try it. And be quiet.

WILLY (*turning to* LINDA, *guiltily*): You're not worried about me, are you, sweetheart?

BIFF: What's the matter?

HAPPY: Listen!

LINDA: You've got too much on the ball to worry about.

WILLY: You're my foundation and my support, Linda.

LINDA: Just try to relax, dear. You make mountains out of molehills.

WILLY: I won't fight him any more. If he wants to go back to Texas, let him go.

LINDA: He'll find his way.

WILLY: Sure. Certain men just don't get started till later in life. Like Thomas Edison, I think. Or B. F. Goodrich. One of them was deaf. (*He starts for the bedroom doorway.*) I'll put my money on Biff.

LINDA: And Willy—if it's warm Sunday we'll drive in the country. And we'll open the windshield, and take lunch.

WILLY: No, the windshields don't open on the new cars.

LINDA: But you opened it today.

WILLY: Me? I didn't. (*He stops.*) Now isn't that peculiar! Isn't that a remarkable—(*He breaks off in amazement and fright as the flute is heard distantly.*)

LINDA: What, darling?

WILLY: That is the most remarkable thing.

LINDA: What, dear?

WILLY: I was thinking of the Chevvy. (*Slight pause.*) Nineteen twenty-eight . . . when I had that red Chevvy—(*Breaks off.*) That funny? I coulda sworn I was driving that Chevvy today.

LINDA: Well, that's nothing. Something must've reminded you.

WILLY: Remarkable. Ts. Remember those days? The way Biff used to simonize that car? The dealer refused to believe there was eighty thousand miles on it. (*He shakes his head.*) Heh! (*to* LINDA) Close your eyes, I'll be right up. (*He walks out of the bedroom.*)

HAPPY (*to* BIFF): Jesus, maybe he smashed up the car again!

LINDA (*calling after* WILLY): Be careful on the stairs, dear! The cheese is on the middle shelf! (*She turns, goes over to the bed, takes his jacket, and goes out of the bedroom.*)

(*Light has risen on the boys' room. Unseen,* WILLY *is heard talking to himself, "Eighty thousand miles," and a little laugh.* BIFF *gets out of bed, comes downstage a bit, and stands attentively.* BIFF *is two years older than his brother* HAPPY, *well built, but in these days bears a worn air and seems less self-assured. He has succeeded less, and his dreams are stronger and less acceptable than* HAPPY'*s.* HAPPY *is tall, powerfully made. Sexuality is like a visible color on him, or a scent that many women have discovered. He, like his brother, is lost, but in a different way, for he has never allowed himself to turn his face toward defeat and is thus more confused and hard-skinned, although seemingly more content.*)

HAPPY (*getting out of bed*): He's going to get his license taken away if he keeps that up. I'm getting nervous about him, y'know, Biff?

BIFF: His eyes are going.

HAPPY: No, I've driven with him. He sees all right. He just doesn't keep his mind on it. I drove into the city with him last week. He stops at a green light and then it turns red and he goes. *(He laughs.)*

BIFF: Maybe he's color-blind.

HAPPY: Pop? Why he's got the finest eye for color in the business. You know that.

BIFF *(sitting down on his bed)*: I'm going to sleep.

HAPPY: You're not still sour on Dad, are you, Biff?

BIFF: He's all right, I guess.

WILLY *(underneath them, in the living-room)*: Yes, sir, eighty thousand miles—eighty-two thousand!

BIFF: You smoking?

HAPPY *(holding out a pack of cigarettes)*: Want one?

BIFF *(taking a cigarette)*: I can never sleep when I smell it.

WILLY: What a simonizing job, heh!

HAPPY *(with deep sentiment)*: Funny, Biff, y'know? Us sleeping in here again? The old beds. *(He pats his bed affectionately.)* All the talk that went across those two beds, huh? Our whole lives.

BIFF: Yeah. Lotta dreams and plans.

HAPPY *(with a deep and masculine laugh)*: About five hundred women would like to know what was said in this room.

(They share a soft laugh.)

BIFF: Remember that big Betsy something—what the hell was her name—over on Bushwick Avenue?

HAPPY *(combing his hair)*: With the collie dog!

BIFF: That's the one. I got you in there, remember?

HAPPY: Yeah, that was my first time—I think. Boy, there was a pig! *(They laugh, almost crudely.)* You taught me everything I know about women. Don't forget that.

BIFF: I bet you forgot how bashful you used to be. Especially with girls.

HAPPY: Oh, I still am, Biff.

BIFF: Oh, go on.

HAPPY: I just control it, that's all. I think I got less bashful and you got more so. What happened, Biff? Where's the old humor, the old confidence? *(He shakes* BIFF*'s knee.* BIFF *gets up and moves restlessly about the room.)* What's the matter?

BIFF: Why does Dad mock me all the time?

HAPPY: He's not mocking you, he—

BIFF: Everything I say there's a twist of mockery on his face. I can't get near him.

HAPPY: He just wants you to make good, that's all. I wanted to talk to you about Dad for a long time, Biff. Something's—happening to him. He—talks to himself.

BIFF: I noticed that this morning. But he always mumbled.

HAPPY: But not so noticeable. It got so embarrassing I sent him to Florida. And you know something? Most of the time he's talking to you.

BIFF: What's he say about me?

HAPPY: I can't make it out.

BIFF: What's he say about me?

HAPPY: I think the fact that you're not settled, that you're still kind of up in the air . . .

BIFF: There's one or two other things depressing him, Happy.

HAPPY: What do you mean?

BIFF: Never mind. Just don't lay it all to me.

HAPPY: But I think if you just got started—I mean—is there any future for you out there?

BIFF: I tell ya, Hap, I don't know what the future is. I don't know—what I'm supposed to want.

HAPPY: What do you mean?

BIFF: Well, I spent six or seven years after high school trying to work myself up. Shipping clerk, salesman, business of one kind or another. And it's a measly manner of existence. To get on that subway on the hot mornings in summer. To devote your whole life to keeping stock, or making phone calls, or selling or buying. To suffer fifty weeks of the year for the sake of a two-week vacation, when all you really desire is to be outdoors, with your shirt off. And always to have to get ahead of the next fella. And still—that's how you build a future.

HAPPY: Well, you really enjoy it on a farm? Are you content out there?

BIFF *(with rising agitation)*: Hap, I've had twenty or thirty different kinds of jobs since I left home before the war, and it always turns out the same. I just realized it lately. In Nebraska when I herded cattle, and the Dakotas, and Arizona, and now in Texas. It's why I came home now, I guess, because I realized it. This farm I work on, it's spring there now, see? And they've got about fifteen new colts. There's nothing more inspiring or—beautiful than the sight of a mare and a new colt. And it's cool there now, see? Texas is cool now, and it's spring. And whenever spring comes to where I am, I suddenly get the feeling, my God, I'm not gettin' anywhere! What the hell am I doing, playing around with horses, twenty-eight dollars a week! I'm thirty-four years old, I oughta be makin' my future. That's when I come running home. And now, I get here, and I don't know what to do with myself. *(After a pause.)* I've always made a point of not wasting my life, and everytime I come back here I know that all I've done is to waste my life.

HAPPY: You're a poet, you know that, Biff? You're a—you're an idealist!

BIFF: No, I'm mixed up very bad. Maybe I oughta get married. Maybe I oughta get stuck into something. Maybe that's my trouble. I'm like a boy. I'm not married, I'm not in business, I just—I'm like a boy. Are you content, Hap? You're a success, aren't you? Are you content?

HAPPY: Hell, no!

BIFF: Why? You're making money, aren't you?

HAPPY (*moving about with energy, expressiveness*): All I can do now is wait for the merchandise manager to die. And suppose I get to be merchandise manager? He's a good friend of mine, and he just built a terrific estate on Long Island. And he lived there about two months and sold it, and now he's building another one. He can't enjoy it once it's finished. And I know that's just what I would do. I don't know what the hell I'm workin' for. Sometimes I sit in my apartment—all alone. And I think of the rent I'm paying. And it's crazy. But then, it's what I always wanted. My own apartment, a car, and plenty of women. And still, goddammit, I'm lonely.

BIFF (*with enthusiasm*): Listen, why don't you come out West with me?

HAPPY: You and I, heh?

BIFF: Sure, maybe we could buy a ranch. Raise cattle, use our muscles. Men built like we are should be working out in the open.

HAPPY (*avidly*): The Loman Brothers, heh?

BIFF (*with vast affection*): Sure, we'd be known all over the counties!

HAPPY (*enthralled*): That's what I dream about, Biff. Sometimes I want to just rip my clothes off in the middle of the store and outbox that goddam merchandise manager. I mean I can outbox, outrun, and outlift anybody in that store, and I have to take orders from those common, petty sons-of-bitches till I can't stand it any more.

BIFF: I'm tellin' you, kid, if you were with me I'd be happy out there.

HAPPY (*enthused*): See, Biff, everybody around me is so false that I'm constantly lowering my ideals . . .

BIFF: Baby, together we'd stand up for one another, we'd have someone to trust.

HAPPY: If I were around you—

BIFF: Hap, the trouble is we weren't brought up to grub for money. I don't know how to do it.

HAPPY: Neither can I!

BIFF: Then let's go!

HAPPY: The only thing is—what can you make out there?

BIFF: But look at your friend. Builds an estate and then hasn't the peace of mind to live in it.

HAPPY: Yeah, but when he walks into the store the waves part in front of him. That's fifty-two thousand dollars a year coming through the revolving door, and I got more in my pinky finger than he's got in his head.

BIFF: Yeah, but you just said—

HAPPY: I gotta show some of those pompous, self-important executives over there that Hap Loman can make the grade. I want to walk into the store the way he walks in. Then I'll go with you, Biff.

We'll be together yet, I swear. But take those two we had tonight. Now weren't they gorgeous creatures?

BIFF: Yeah, yeah, most gorgeous I've had in years.

HAPPY: I get that any time I want, Biff. Whenever I feel disgusted. The only trouble is, it gets like bowling or something. I just keep knockin' them over and it doesn't mean anything. You still run around a lot?

BIFF: Naa. I'd like to find a girl—steady, somebody with substance.

HAPPY: That's what I long for.

BIFF: Go on! You'd never come home.

HAPPY: I would! Somebody with character, with resistance! Like Mom, y'know? You're gonna call me a bastard when I tell you this. That girl Charlotte I was with tonight is engaged to be married in five weeks. (*He tries on his new hat.*)

BIFF: No kiddin'!

HAPPY: Sure, the guy's in line for the vice-presidency of the store. I don't know what gets into me, maybe I just have an overdeveloped sense of competition or something, but I went and ruined her, and furthermore I can't get rid of her. And he's the third executive I've done that to. Isn't that a crummy characteristic? And to top it all, I go to their weddings! (*Indignantly, but laughing.*) Like I'm not supposed to take bribes. Manufacturers offer me a hundred-dollar bill now and then to throw an order their way. You know how honest I am, but it's like this girl, see. I hate myself for it. Because I don't want the girl, and, still, I take it and—I love it!

BIFF: Let's go to sleep.

HAPPY: I guess we didn't settle anything, heh?

BIFF: I just got one idea that I think I'm going to try.

HAPPY: What's that?

BIFF: Remember Bill Oliver?

HAPPY: Sure, Oliver is very big now. You want to work for him again?

BIFF: No, but when I quit he said something to me. He put his arm on my shoulder, and he said, "Biff, if you ever need anything, come to me."

HAPPY: I remember that. That sounds good.

BIFF: I think I'll go to see him. If I could get ten thousand or even seven or eight thousand dollars I could buy a beautiful ranch.

HAPPY: I bet he'd back you. 'Cause he thought highly of you, Biff. I mean, they all do. You're well liked, Biff. That's why I say to come back here, and we both have the apartment. And I'm tellin' you, Biff, any babe you want . . .

BIFF: No, with a ranch I could do the work I like and still be something. I just wonder though. I wonder if Oliver still thinks I stole that carton of basketballs.

HAPPY: Oh, he probably forgot that long ago. It's almost ten years. You're too sensitive. Anyway, he didn't really fire you.

BIFF: Well, I think he was going to. I think that's why I quit. I was never sure whether he knew or not. I know he thought the world of me, though. I was the only one he'd let lock up the place.

WILLY (*below*): You gonna wash the engine, Biff?

HAPPY: Shh!

(BIFF *looks at* HAPPY, *who is gazing down, listening.* WILLY *is mumbling in the parlor.*)

HAPPY: You hear that?

(*They listen.* WILLY *laughs warmly.*)

BIFF (*growing angry*): Doesn't he know Mom can hear that?

WILLY: Don't get your sweater dirty, Biff!

(*A look of pain crosses* BIFF'*s face.*)

HAPPY: Isn't that terrible? Don't leave again, will you? You'll find a job here. You gotta stick around. I don't know what to do about him, it's getting embarrassing.

WILLY: What a simonizing job!

BIFF: Mom's hearing that!

WILLY: No kiddin', Biff, you got a date? Wonderful!

HAPPY: Go on to sleep. But talk to him in the morning, will you?

BIFF (*reluctantly getting into bed*): With her in the house. Brother!

HAPPY (*getting into bed*): I wish you'd have a good talk with him.

(*The light on their room begins to fade.*)

BIFF (*to himself in bed*): That selfish, stupid . . .

HAPPY: Sh . . . Sleep, Biff.

(*Their light is out. Well before they have finished speaking,* WILLY'*s form is dimly seen below in the darkened kitchen. He opens the refrigerator, searches in there, and takes out a bottle of milk. The apartment houses are fading out, and the entire house and surroundings become covered with leaves. Music insinuates itself as the leaves appear.*)

WILLY: Just wanna be careful with those girls, Biff, that's all. Don't make any promises. No promises of any kind. Because a girl, y'know, they always believe what you tell 'em, and you're very young, Biff, you're too young to be talking seriously to girls.

(*Light rises on the kitchen.* WILLY, *talking, shuts the refrigerator door and comes downstage to the kitchen table. He pours milk into a glass. He is totally immersed in himself, smiling faintly.*)

WILLY: Too young entirely, Biff. You want to watch your schooling first. Then when you're all set, there'll be plenty of girls for a boy like you. (*He smiles broadly at a kitchen chair.*) That so? The girls pay for you? (*He laughs.*) Boy, you must really be makin' a hit.

(WILLY *is gradually addressing—physically—a point off-stage, speaking through the wall of the kitchen, and his voice has been rising in volume to that of a normal conversation.*)

WILLY: I been wondering why you polish the car so careful. Ha! Don't leave the hubcaps, boys. Get the chamois to the hubcaps. Happy, use newspaper on the windows, it's the easiest thing. Show him how to do it, Biff! You see, Happy? Pad it up, use it like a pad. That's it, that's it, good work. You're doin' all right, Hap. (*He pauses, then nods in approbation for a few seconds, then looks upward.*) Biff, first thing we gotta do when we get time is clip that big branch over the house. Afraid it's gonna fall in a storm and hit the roof. Tell you what. We get a rope and sling her around, and then we climb up there with a couple of saws and take her down. Soon as you finish the car, boys, I wanna see ya. I got a surprise for you, boys.

BIFF (*offstage*): Whatta ya got, Dad?

WILLY: No, you finish first. Never leave a job till you're finished—remember that. (*Looking toward the "big trees."*) Biff, up in Albany I saw a beautiful hammock. I think I'll buy it next trip, and we'll hang it right between those two elms. Wouldn't that be something? Just swingin' there under those branches. Boy, that would be . . .

(YOUNG BIFF *and* YOUNG HAPPY *appear from the direction* WILLY *was addressing.* HAPPY *carries rags and a pail of water.* BIFF, *wearing a sweater with a block "S," carries a football.*)

BIFF (*pointing in the direction of the car offstage*): How's that, Pop, professional?

WILLY: Terrific. Terrific job, boys. Good work, Biff.

HAPPY: Where's the surprise, Pop?

WILLY: In the back seat of the car.

HAPPY: Boy! (*He runs off.*)

BIFF: What is it, Dad? Tell me, what'd you buy?

WILLY (*laughing, cuffs him*): Never mind, something I want you to have.

BIFF (*turns and starts off*): What is it, Hap?

HAPPY (*offstage*): It's a punching bag!

BIFF: Oh, Pop!

WILLY: It's got Gene Tunney's signature on it!

(HAPPY *runs onstage with a punching bag.*)

BIFF: Gee, how'd you know we wanted a punching bag?

WILLY: Well, it's the finest thing for the timing.

HAPPY (*lies down on his back and pedals with his feet*): I'm losing weight, you notice, Pop?

WILLY (*to* HAPPY): Jumping rope is good too.

BIFF: Did you see the new football I got?

WILLY (*examining the ball*): Where'd you get a new ball?

BIFF: The coach told me to practice my passing.

WILLY: That so? And he gave you the ball, heh?

BIFF: Well, I borrowed it from the locker room. (*He laughs confidentially.*)

WILLY (*laughing with him at the theft*): I want you to return that.

HAPPY: I told you he wouldn't like it!

BIFF (*angrily*): Well, I'm bringing it back!

WILLY (*stopping the incipient argument, to* HAPPY): Sure, he's gotta practice with a regulation ball, doesn't he? (*to* BIFF) Coach'll probably congratulate you on your initiative!

BIFF: Oh, he keeps congratulating my initiative all the time, Pop.

WILLY: That's because he likes you. If somebody else took that ball there'd be an uproar. So what's the report, boys, what's the report?

BIFF: Where'd you go this time, Dad? Gee we were lonesome for you.

WILLY (*pleased, puts an arm around each boy and they come down to the apron*): Lonesome, heh?

BIFF: Missed you every minute.

WILLY: Don't say? Tell you a secret, boys. Don't breathe it to a soul. Someday I'll have my own business, and I'll never have to leave home any more.

HAPPY: Like Uncle Charley, heh?

WILLY: Bigger than Uncle Charley! Because Charley is not—liked. He's liked, but he's not—well liked.

BIFF: Where'd you go this time, Dad?

WILLY: Well, I got on the road, and I went north to Providence. Met the Mayor.

BIFF: The Mayor of Providence!

WILLY: He was sitting in the hotel lobby.

BIFF: What'd he say?

WILLY: He said, "Morning!" and I said, "You got a fine city here, Mayor." And then he had coffee with me. And then I went to Waterbury. Waterbury is a fine city. Big clock city, the famous Waterbury clock. Sold a nice bill there. And then Boston—Boston is the cradle of the Revolution. A fine city. And a couple of other towns in Mass., and on to Portland and Bangor and straight home!

BIFF: Gee, I'd love to go with you sometime, Dad.

WILLY: Soon as summer comes.

HAPPY: Promise?

WILLY: You and Hap and I, and I'll show you all the towns. America is full of beautiful towns and fine, upstanding people. And they know me, boys, they know me up and down New England. The finest people. And when I bring you fellas up, there'll be an open sesame for all of us, 'cause one thing, boys: I have friends. I can park my car in any street in New England, and the cops protect it like their own. This summer, heh?

BIFF *and* HAPPY (*together*): Yeah! You bet!

WILLY: We'll take our bathing suits.

HAPPY: We'll carry your bags, Pop!

WILLY: Oh, won't that be something! Me comin' into the Boston stores with you boys carryin' my bags. What a sensation!

(BIFF *is prancing around, practicing passing the ball.*)

WILLY: You nervous, Biff, about the game?

BIFF: Not if you're gonna be there.

WILLY: What do they say about you in school, now that they made you captain?

HAPPY: There's a crowd of girls behind him everytime the classes change.

BIFF (*taking* WILLY'*s hand*): This Saturday, Pop, this Saturday—just for you, I'm going to break through for a touchdown.

HAPPY: You're supposed to pass.

BIFF: I'm takin' one play for Pop. You watch me, Pop, and when I take off my helmet, that means I'm breakin' out. Then you watch me crash through that line!

WILLY (*kisses* BIFF): Oh, wait'll I tell this in Boston!

(BERNARD *enters in knickers. He is younger than* BIFF, *earnest and loyal, a worried boy.*)

BERNARD: Biff, where are you? You're supposed to study with me today.

WILLY: Hey, looka Bernard. What're you lookin' so anemic about, Bernard?

BERNARD: He's gotta study, Uncle Willy. He's got Regents next week.

HAPPY (*tauntingly, spinning* BERNARD *around*): Let's box, Bernard!

BERNARD: Biff! (*He gets away from* HAPPY.) Listen, Biff, I heard Mr. Birnbaum say that if you don't start studyin' math he's gonna flunk you, and you won't graduate. I heard him!

WILLY: You better study with him, Biff. Go ahead now.

BERNARD: I heard him!

BIFF: Oh, Pop, you didn't see my sneakers! (*He holds up a foot for* WILLY *to look at.*)

WILLY: Hey, that's a beautiful job of printing!

BERNARD (*wiping his glasses*): Just because he printed University of Virginia on his sneakers doesn't mean they've got to graduate him, Uncle Willy!

WILLY (*angrily*): What're you talking about? With scholarships to three universities they're gonna flunk him?

BERNARD: But I heard Mr. Birnbaum say—

WILLY: Don't be a pest, Bernard! (*to his boys*) What an anemic!

BERNARD: Okay, I'm waiting for you in my house, Biff.

(BERNARD *goes off. The* LOMANS *laugh.*)

WILLY: Bernard is not well liked, is he?

BIFF: He's liked, but he's not well liked.

HAPPY: That's right, Pop.

WILLY: That's just what I mean. Bernard can get the best marks in school, y'understand, but when he gets out in the business world, y'understand, you are going to be five times ahead of him. That's why I thank Almighty God you're both built like Adonises. Because the man who makes an appearance in the business world, the man who creates personal interest, is the man who gets ahead. Be liked and you will never want. You take me, for instance. I never have to wait in line to see a buyer. "Willy Loman is here!" That's all they have to know, and I go right through.

BIFF: Did you knock them dead, Pop?

WILLY: Knocked 'em cold in Providence, slaughtered 'em in Boston.

HAPPY (on his back, pedaling again): I'm losing weight, you notice, Pop?

(LINDA enters, as of old, a ribbon in her hair, carrying a basket of washing.)

LINDA (with youthful energy): Hello, dear!

WILLY: Sweetheart!

LINDA: How'd the Chevvy run?

WILLY: Chevrolet, Linda, is the greatest car ever built. (to the boys) Since when do you let your mother carry wash up the stairs?

BIFF: Grab hold there, boy!

HAPPY: Where to, Mom?

LINDA: Hang them up on the line. And you better go down to your friends, Biff. The cellar is full of boys. They don't know what to do with themselves.

BIFF: Ah, when Pop comes home they can wait!

WILLY (laughs appreciatively): You better go down and tell them what to do, Biff.

BIFF: I think I'll have them sweep out the furnace room.

WILLY: Good work, Biff.

BIFF (goes through wall-line of kitchen to doorway at back and calls down): Fellas! Everybody sweep out the furnace room! I'll be right down!

VOICES: All right! Okay, Biff.

BIFF: George and Sam and Frank, come out back! We're hangin' up the wash! Come on, Hap, on the double! (He and HAPPY carry out the basket.)

LINDA: The way they obey him!

WILLY: Well, that's training, the training. I'm tellin' you, I was sellin' thousands and thousands, but I had to come home.

LINDA: Oh, the whole block'll be at that game. Did you sell anything?

WILLY: I did five hundred gross in Providence and seven hundred gross in Boston.

LINDA: No! Wait a minute, I've got a pencil. (She pulls pencil and paper out of her apron pocket.) That makes your commission . . . Two hundred—my God! Two hundred and twelve dollars!

WILLY: Well, I didn't figure it yet, but . . .

LINDA: How much did you do?

WILLY: Well, I—I did—about a hundred and eighty gross in Providence. Well, no—it came to— roughly two hundred gross on the whole trip.

LINDA (without hesitation): Two hundred gross. That's . . . (She figures.)

WILLY: The trouble was that three of the stores were half closed for inventory in Boston. Otherwise I woulda broke records.

LINDA: Well, it makes seventy dollars and some pennies. That's very good.

WILLY: What do we owe?

LINDA: Well, on the first there's sixteen dollars on the refrigerator—

WILLY: Why sixteen?

LINDA: Well, the fan belt broke, so it was a dollar eighty.

WILLY: But it's brand new.

LINDA: Well, the man said that's the way it is. Till they work themselves in, y'know.

(They move through the wall-line into the kitchen.)

WILLY: I hope we didn't get stuck on that machine.

LINDA: They got the biggest ads of any of them!

WILLY: I know, it's a fine machine. What else?

LINDA: Well, there's nine-sixty for the washing machine. And for the vacuum cleaner there's three and a half due on the fifteenth. Then the roof, you got twenty-one dollars remaining.

WILLY: It don't leak, does it?

LINDA: No, they did a wonderful job. Then you owe Frank for the carburetor.

WILLY: I'm not going to pay that man! That goddam Chevrolet, they ought to prohibit the manufacture of that car!

LINDA: Well, you owe him three and a half. And odds and ends, comes to around a hundred and twenty dollars by the fifteenth.

WILLY: A hundred and twenty dollars! My God, if business don't pick up I don't know what I'm gonna do!

LINDA: Well, next week you'll do better.

WILLY: Oh, I'll knock 'em dead next week. I'll go to Hartford. I'm very well liked in Hartford. You know, the trouble is, Linda, people don't seem to take to me.

(They move onto the forestage.)

LINDA: Oh, don't be foolish.

WILLY: I know it when I walk in. They seem to laugh at me.

LINDA: Why? Why would they laugh at you? Don't talk that way, Willy.

(WILLY *moves to the edge of the stage.* LINDA *goes into the kitchen and starts to darn stockings.*)

WILLY: I don't know the reason for it, but they just pass me by. I'm not noticed.

LINDA: But you're doing wonderful, dear. You're making seventy to a hundred dollars a week.

WILLY: But I gotta be at it ten, twelve hours a day. Other men—I don't know—they do it easier. I don't know why—I can't stop myself—I talk too much. A man oughta come in with a few words. One thing about Charley. He's a man of few words, and they respect him.

LINDA: You don't talk too much, you're just lively.

WILLY (*smiling*): Well, I figure, what the hell, life is short, a couple of jokes. (*to himself*) I joke too much! (*The smile goes.*)

LINDA: Why? You're—

WILLY: I'm fat. I'm very—foolish to look at, Linda. I didn't tell you, but Christmas time I happened to be calling on F. H. Stewarts, and a salesman I know, as I was going in to see the buyer I heard him say something about—walrus. And I—I cracked him right across the face. I won't take that. I simply will not take that. But they do laugh at me. I know that.

LINDA: Darling . . .

WILLY: I gotta overcome it. I know I gotta overcome it. I'm not dressing to advantage, maybe.

LINDA: Willy, darling, you're the handsomest man in the world—

WILLY: Oh, no, Linda.

LINDA: To me you are. (*Slight pause.*) The handsomest.

(*From the darkness is heard the laughter of a woman.* WILLY *doesn't turn to it, but it continues through* LINDA's *lines.*)

LINDA: And the boys, Willy. Few men are idolized by their children the way you are.

(*Music is heard as behind a scrim, to the left of the house,* THE WOMAN, *dimly seen, is dressing.*)

WILLY (*with great feeling*): You're the best there is, Linda, you're a pal, you know that? On the road—on the road I want to grab you sometimes and just kiss the life outa you.

(*The laughter is loud now, and he moves into a brightening area at the left, where* THE WOMAN *has come from behind the scrim and is standing, putting on her hat, looking into a "mirror" and laughing.*)

WILLY: 'Cause I get so lonely—especially when business is bad and there's nobody to talk to. I get the feeling that I'll never sell anything again, that I won't make a living for you, or a business, a business for the boys. (*He talks through* THE WOMAN's *subsiding laughter;* THE WOMAN *primps at the "mirror."*) There's so much I want to make for—

THE WOMAN: Me? You didn't make me, Willy. I picked you.

WILLY (*pleased*): You picked me?

THE WOMAN (*who is quite proper-looking,* WILLY's *age*): I did. I've been sitting at that desk watching all the salesmen go by, day in, day out. But you've got such a sense of humor, and we do have such a good time together, don't we?

WILLY: Sure, sure. (*He takes her in his arms.*) Why do you have to go now?

THE WOMAN: It's two o'clock . . .

WILLY: No, come on in! (*He pulls her.*)

THE WOMAN: . . . my sisters'll be scandalized. When'll you be back?

WILLY: Oh, two weeks about. Will you come up again?

THE WOMAN: Sure thing. You do make me laugh. It's good for me. (*She squeezes his arm, kisses him.*) And I think you're a wonderful man.

WILLY: You picked me, heh?

THE WOMAN: Sure. Because you're so sweet. And such a kidder.

WILLY: Well, I'll see you next time I'm in Boston.

THE WOMAN: I'll put you right through to the buyers.

WILLY (*slapping her bottom*): Right, well, bottoms up!

THE WOMAN (*slaps him gently and laughs*): You just kill me, Willy. (*He suddenly grabs her and kisses her roughly.*) You kill me. And thanks for the stockings. I love a lot of stockings. Well, good night.

WILLY: Good night. And keep your pores open!

THE WOMAN: Oh, Willy!

(THE WOMAN *bursts out laughing, and* LINDA's *laughter blends in.* THE WOMAN *disappears into the dark. Now the area at the kitchen table brightens.* LINDA *is sitting where she was at the kitchen table, but now is mending a pair of her silk stockings.*)

LINDA: You are, Willy. The handsomest man. You've got no reason to feel that—

WILLY (*coming out of* THE WOMAN's *dimming area and going over to* LINDA): I'll make it all up to you, Linda, I'll—

LINDA: There's nothing to make up, dear. You're doing fine, better than—

WILLY (*noticing her mending*): What's that?

LINDA: Just mending my stockings. They're so expensive—

WILLY (*angrily, taking them from her*): I won't have you mending stockings in this house! Now throw them out!

(LINDA *puts the stockings in her pocket.*)

BERNARD (*entering on the run*): Where is he? If he doesn't study!

WILLY (*moving to the forestage, with great agitation*): You'll give him the answers!

BERNARD: I do, but I can't on a Regents! That's a state exam! They're liable to arrest me!

WILLY: Where is he? I'll whip him, I'll whip him!

LINDA: And he'd better give back that football, Willy, it's not nice.

WILLY: Biff! Where is he? Why is he taking everything?

LINDA: He's too rough with the girls, Willy. All the mothers are afraid of him!

WILLY: I'll whip him!

BERNARD: He's driving the car without a license!

(THE WOMAN's *laugh is heard.*)

WILLY: Shut up!

LINDA: All the mothers—

WILLY: Shut up!

BERNARD (*backing quietly away and out*): Mr. Birnbaum says he's stuck up.

WILLY: Get outa here!

BERNARD: If he doesn't buckle down he'll flunk math! (*He goes off.*)

LINDA: He's right, Willy, you've gotta—

WILLY (*exploding at her*): There's nothing the matter with him! You want him to be a worm like Bernard? He's got spirit, personality . . .

(*As he speaks,* LINDA, *almost in tears, exits into the living-room.* WILLY *is alone in the kitchen, wilting and staring. The leaves are gone. It is night again, and the apartment houses look down from behind.*)

WILLY: Loaded with it. Loaded! What is he stealing? He's giving it back, isn't he? Why is he stealing? What did I tell him? I never in my life told him anything but decent things.

(HAPPY *in pajamas has come down the stairs;* WILLY *suddenly becomes aware of* HAPPY's *presence.*)

HAPPY: Let's go now, come on.

WILLY (*sitting down at the kitchen table*): Huh! Why did she have to wax the floors herself? Everytime she waxes the floors she keels over. She knows that!

HAPPY: Shh! Take it easy. What brought you back tonight?

WILLY: I got an awful scare. Nearly hit a kid in Yonkers. God! Why didn't I go to Alaska with my brother Ben that time! Ben! That man was a genius, that man was success incarnate! What a mistake! He begged me to go.

HAPPY: Well, there's no use in—

WILLY: You guys! There was a man started with the clothes on his back and ended up with diamond mines!

HAPPY: Boy, someday I'd like to know how he did it.

WILLY: What's the mystery? The man knew what he wanted and went out and got it! Walked into a jungle, and comes out, the age of twenty-one, and he's rich! The world is an oyster, but you don't crack it open on a mattress!

HAPPY: Pop, I told you I'm gonna retire you for life.

WILLY: You'll retire me for life on seventy goddam dollars a week? And your women and your car and your apartment, and you'll retire me for life! Christ's sake, I couldn't get past Yonkers today! Where are you guys, where are you? The woods are burning! I can't drive a car!

(CHARLEY *has appeared in the doorway. He is a large man, slow of speech, laconic, immovable. In all he says, despite what he says, there is pity, and, now, trepidation. He has a robe over pajamas, slippers on his feet. He enters the kitchen.*)

CHARLEY: Everything all right?

HAPPY: Yeah, Charley, everything's . . .

WILLY: What's the matter?

CHARLEY: I heard some noise. I thought something happened. Can't we do something about the walls? You sneeze in here, and in my house hats blow off.

HAPPY: Let's go to bed, Dad, Come on.

(CHARLEY *signals to* HAPPY *to go.*)

WILLY: You go ahead, I'm not tired at the moment.

HAPPY (*to* WILLY): Take it easy, huh? (*He exits.*)

WILLY: What're you doin' up?

CHARLEY (*sitting down at the kitchen table opposite* WILLY): Couldn't sleep good. I had a heartburn.

WILLY: Well, you don't know how to eat.

CHARLEY: I eat with my mouth.

WILLY: No, you're ignorant. You gotta know about vitamins and things like that.

CHARLEY: Come on, let's shoot. Tire you out a little.

WILLY (*hesitantly*): All right. You got cards?

CHARLEY (*taking a deck from his pocket*): Yeah, I got them. Someplace. What is it with those vitamins?

WILLY (*dealing*): They build up your bones. Chemistry.

CHARLEY: Yeah, but there's no bones in a heartburn.

WILLY: What are you talkin' about? Do you know the first thing about it?

CHARLEY: Don't get insulted.

WILLY: Don't talk about something you don't know anything about.

(*They are playing. Pause.*)

CHARLEY: What're you doin' home?

WILLY: A little trouble with the car.

CHARLEY: Oh. (*Pause.*) I'd like to take a trip to California.

WILLY: Don't say.

CHARLEY: You want a job?

WILLY: I got a job, I told you that. (*After a slight pause.*) What the hell are you offering me a job for?

CHARLEY: Don't get insulted.

WILLY: Don't insult me.

CHARLEY: I don't see no sense in it. You don't have to go on this way.

WILLY: I got a good job. *(Slight pause.)* What do you keep comin' in here for?

CHARLEY: You want me to go?

WILLY *(after a pause, withering)*: I can't understand it. He's going back to Texas again. What the hell is that?

CHARLEY: Let him go.

WILLY: I got nothin' to give him, Charley, I'm clean, I'm clean.

CHARLEY: He won't starve. None a them starve. Forget about him.

WILLY: Then what have I got to remember?

CHARLEY: You take it too hard. To hell with it. When a deposit bottle is broken you don't get your nickel back.

WILLY: That's easy enough for you to say.

CHARLEY: That ain't easy for me to say.

WILLY: Did you see the ceiling I put up in the living-room?

CHARLEY: Yeah, that's a piece of work. To put up a ceiling is a mystery to me. How do you do it?

WILLY: What's the difference?

CHARLEY: Well, talk about it.

WILLY: You gonna put up a ceiling?

CHARLEY: How could I put up a ceiling?

WILLY: Then what the hell are you bothering me for?

CHARLEY: You're insulted again.

WILLY: A man who can't handle tools is not a man. You're disgusting.

CHARLEY: Don't call me disgusting, Willy.

(UNCLE BEN, carrying a valise and an umbrella, enters the forestage from around the right corner of the house. He is a stolid man, in his sixties, with a mustache and an authoritative air. He is utterly certain of his destiny, and there is an aura of far places about him. He enters exactly as WILLY speaks.)

WILLY: I'm getting awfully tired, Ben.

(BEN's music is heard. BEN looks around at everything.)

CHARLEY: Good, keep playing; you'll sleep better. Did you call me Ben?

(BEN looks at his watch.)

WILLY: That's funny. For a second there you reminded me of my brother Ben.

BEN: I only have a few minutes. *(He strolls, inspecting the place. WILLY and CHARLEY continue playing.)*

CHARLEY: You never heard from him again, heh? Since that time?

WILLY: Didn't Linda tell you? Couple of weeks ago we got a letter from his wife in Africa. He died.

CHARLEY: That so.

BEN *(chuckling)*: So this is Brooklyn, eh?

CHARLEY: Maybe you're in for some of his money.

WILLY: Naa, he had seven sons. There's just one opportunity I had with that man . . .

BEN: I must make a train, William. There are several properties I'm looking at in Alaska.

WILLY: Sure, sure! If I'd gone with him to Alaska that time, everything would've been totally different.

CHARLEY: Go on, you'd froze to death up there.

WILLY: What're you talking about?

BEN: Opportunity is tremendous in Alaska, William. Surprised you're not up there.

WILLY: Sure, tremendous.

CHARLEY: Heh?

WILLY: There was the only man I ever met who knew the answers.

CHARLEY: Who?

BEN: How are you all?

WILLY *(taking a pot, smiling)*: Fine, fine.

CHARLEY: Pretty sharp tonight.

BEN: Is Mother living with you?

WILLY: No, she died a long time ago.

CHARLEY: Who?

BEN: That's too bad. Fine specimen of a lady, Mother.

WILLY *(to CHARLEY)*: Heh?

BEN: I'd hoped to see the old girl.

CHARLEY: Who died?

BEN: Heard anything from Father, have you?

WILLY *(unnerved)*: What do you mean, who died?

CHARLEY *(taking a pot)*: What're you talkin' about?

BEN *(looking at his watch)*: William, it's half-past eight!

WILLY *(as though to dispel his confusion he angrily stops CHARLEY's hand)*: That's my build!

CHARLEY: I put the ace—

WILLY: If you don't know how to play the game I'm not gonna throw my money away on you!

CHARLEY *(rising)*: It was my ace, for God's sake!

WILLY: I'm through, I'm through!

BEN: When did Mother die?

WILLY: Long ago. Since the beginning you never knew how to play cards.

CHARLEY *(picks up the cards and goes to the door)*: All right! Next time I'll bring a deck with five aces.

WILLY: I don't play that kind of game!

CHARLEY *(turning to him)*: You ought to be ashamed of yourself!

WILLY: Yeah?

CHARLEY: Yeah! *(He goes out.)*

WILLY *(slamming the door after him)*: Ignoramus!

BEN *(as WILLY comes toward him through the wall-line of the kitchen)*: So you're William.

WILLY *(shaking BEN's hand)*: Ben! I've been waiting for you so long! What's the answer? How did you do it?

BEN: Oh, there's a story in that.

(LINDA enters the forestage, as of old, carrying the wash basket.)

LINDA: Is this Ben?

BEN *(gallantly)*: How do you do, my dear.

LINDA: Where've you been all these years? Willy's always wondered why you—

WILLY (*pulling* BEN *away from her impatiently*): Where is Dad? Didn't you follow him? How did you get started?

BEN: Well, I don't know how much you remember.

WILLY: Well, I was just a baby, of course, only three or four years old—

BEN: Three years and eleven months.

WILLY: What a memory, Ben!

BEN: I have many enterprises, William, and I have never kept books.

WILLY: I remember I was sitting under the wagon in— was it Nebraska?

BEN: It was South Dakota, and I gave you a bunch of wild flowers.

WILLY: I remember you walking away down some open road.

BEN (*laughing*): I was going to find Father in Alaska.

WILLY: Where is he?

BEN: At that age I had a very faulty view of geography, William. I discovered after a few days that I was heading due south, so instead of Alaska, I ended up in Africa.

LINDA: Africa!

WILLY: The Gold Coast!

BEN: Principally diamond mines.

LINDA: Diamond mines!

BEN: Yes, my dear. But I've only a few minutes—

WILLY: No! Boys! Boys! (YOUNG BIFF *and* HAPPY *appear.*) Listen to this. This is your Uncle Ben, a great man! Tell my boys, Ben!

BEN: Why, boys, when I was seventeen I walked into the jungle, and when I was twenty-one I walked out. (*He laughs.*) And by God I was rich.

WILLY (*to the boys*): You see what I been talking about? The greatest things can happen!

BEN (*glancing at his watch*): I have an appointment in Ketchikan Tuesday week.

WILLY: No, Ben! Please tell about Dad. I want my boys to hear. I want them to know the kind of stock they spring from. All I remember is a man with a big beard, and I was in Mamma's lap, sitting around a fire, and some kind of high music.

BEN: His flute. He played the flute.

WILLY: Sure, the flute, that's right!

(*New music is heard, a high, rollicking tune.*)

BEN: Father was a very great and a very wild-hearted man. We would start in Boston, and he'd toss the whole family into the wagon, and then he'd drive the team right across the country; through Ohio, and Indiana, Michigan, Illinois, and all the Western states. And we'd stop in the towns and sell the flutes that he'd made on the way. Great inventor, Father. With one gadget he made more in a week than a man like you could make in a lifetime.

WILLY: That's just the way I'm bringing them up, Ben—rugged, well liked, all-around.

BEN: Yeah? (*to* BIFF) Hit that, boy—hard as you can. (*He pounds his stomach.*)

BIFF: Oh, no, sir!

BEN (*taking boxing stance*): Come on, get to me! (*He laughs.*)

WILLY: Go to it, Biff! Go ahead, show him!

BIFF: Okay! (*He cocks his fists and starts in.*)

LINDA (*to* WILLY): Why must he fight, dear?

BEN (*sparring with* BIFF): Good boy! Good boy!

WILLY: How's that, Ben, heh?

HAPPY: Give him the left, Biff!

LINDA: Why are you fighting?

BEN: Good boy! (*Suddenly comes in, trips* BIFF, *and stands over him, the point of his umbrella poised over* BIFF*'s eye.*)

LINDA: Look out, Biff!

BIFF: Gee!

BEN (*patting* BIFF*'s knee*): Never fight fair with a stranger, boy. You'll never get out of the jungle that way. (*Taking* LINDA*'s hand and bowing.*) It was an honor and a pleasure to meet you, Linda.

LINDA (*withdrawing her hand coldly, frightened*): Have a nice—trip.

BEN (*to* WILLY): And good luck with your—what do you do?

WILLY: Selling.

BEN: Yes. Well . . . (*He raises his hand in farewell to all.*)

WILLY: No, Ben, I don't want you to think . . . (*He takes* BEN*'s arm to show him.*) It's Brooklyn, I know, but we hunt too.

BEN: Really, now.

WILLY: Oh, sure, there's snakes and rabbits and— that's why I moved out here. Why, Biff can fell any one of these trees in no time! Boys! Go right over to where they're building the apartment house and get some sand. We're gonna rebuild the entire front stoop right now! Watch this, Ben!

BIFF: Yes, sir! On the double, Hap!

HAPPY (*as he and* BIFF *run off*): I lost weight, Pop, you notice?

(CHARLEY *enters in knickers, even before the boys are gone.*)

CHARLEY: Listen, if they steal any more from that building the watchman'll put the cops on them!

LINDA (*to* WILLY): Don't let Biff . . .

(BEN *laughs lustily.*)

WILLY: You shoulda seen the lumber they brought home last week. At least a dozen six-by-tens worth all kinds a money.

CHARLEY: Listen, if that watchman—

WILLY: I gave them hell, understand. But I got a couple of fearless characters there.

CHARLEY: Willy, the jails are full of fearless characters.

BEN (*clapping* WILLY *on the back, with a laugh at* CHARLEY): And the stock exchange, friend!

WILLY (*joining in* BEN'*s laughter*): Where are the rest of your pants?

CHARLEY: My wife bought them.

WILLY: Now all you need is a golf club and you can go upstairs and go to sleep. (*to* BEN) Great athlete! Between him and his son Bernard they can't hammer a nail!

BERNARD (*rushing in*): The watchman's chasing Biff!

WILLY (*angrily*): Shut up! He's not stealing anything!

LINDA (*alarmed, hurrying off left*): Where is he? Biff, dear! (*She exits.*)

WILLY (*moving toward the left, away from* BEN): There's nothing wrong. What's the matter with you?

BEN: Nervy boy. Good!

WILLY (*laughing*): Oh, nerves of iron, that Biff!

CHARLEY: Don't know what it is. My New England man comes back and he's bleedin', they murdered him up there.

WILLY: It's contacts, Charley, I got important contacts!

CHARLEY (*sarcastically*): Glad to hear it, Willy. Come in later, we'll shoot a little casino. I'll take some of your Portland money. (*He laughs at* WILLY *and exits.*)

WILLY (*turning to* BEN): Business is bad, it's murderous. But not for me, of course.

BEN: I'll stop by on my way back to Africa.

WILLY (*longingly*): Can't you stay a few days? You're just what I need, Ben, because I—I have a fine position here, but I—well, Dad left when I was such a baby and I never had a chance to talk to him and I still feel—kind of temporary about myself.

BEN: I'll be late for my train.

(*They are at opposite ends of the stage.*)

WILLY: Ben, my boys—can't we talk? They'd go into the jaws of hell for me, see, but I—

BEN: William, you're being first-rate with your boys. Outstanding, manly chaps!

WILLY (*hanging on to his words*): Oh, Ben, that's good to hear! Because sometimes I'm afraid that I'm not teaching them the right kind of—Ben, how should I teach them?

BEN (*giving great weight to each word, and with a certain vicious audacity*): William, when I walked into the jungle, I was seventeen. When I walked out I was twenty-one. And, by God, I was rich! (*He goes off into darkness around the right corner of the house.*)

WILLY: . . . was rich! That's just the spirit I want to imbue them with! To walk into a jungle! I was right! I was right! I was right!

(BEN *is gone, but* WILLY *is still speaking to him as* LINDA, *in nightgown and robe, enters the kitchen, glances around for* WILLY, *then goes to the door of the house, looks out and sees him. Comes down to his left. He looks at her.*)

LINDA: Willy, dear? Willy?

WILLY: I was right!

LINDA: Did you have some cheese? (*He can't answer.*) It's very late, darling. Come to bed, heh?

WILLY (*looking straight up*): Gotta break your neck to see a star in this yard.

LINDA: You coming in?

WILLY: Whatever happened to that diamond watch fob? Remember? When Ben came from Africa that time? Didn't he give me a watch fob with a diamond in it?

LINDA: You pawned it, dear. Twelve, thirteen years ago. For Biff's radio correspondence course.

WILLY: Gee, that was a beautiful thing. I'll take a walk.

LINDA: But you're in your slippers.

WILLY (*starting to go around the house at the left*): I was right! I was! (*Half to* LINDA, *as he goes, shaking his head.*) What a man! There was a man worth talking to. I was right!

LINDA (*calling after* WILLY): But in your slippers, Willy!

(WILLY *is almost gone when* BIFF, *in his pajamas, comes down the stairs and enters the kitchen.*)

BIFF: What is he doing out there?

LINDA: Sh!

BIFF: God Almighty, Mom, how long has he been doing this?

LINDA: Don't, he'll hear you.

BIFF: What the hell is the matter with him?

LINDA: It'll pass by morning.

BIFF: Shouldn't we do anything?

LINDA: Oh, my dear, you should do a lot of things, but there's nothing to do, so go to sleep.

(HAPPY *comes down the stairs and sits on the steps.*)

HAPPY: I never heard him so loud, Mom.

LINDA: Well, come around more often; you'll hear him. (*She sits down at the table and mends the lining of* WILLY'*s jacket.*)

BIFF: Why didn't you ever write me about this, Mom?

LINDA: How would I write to you? For over three months you had no address.

BIFF: I was on the move. But you know I thought of you all the time. You know that, don't you, pal?

LINDA: I know, dear, I know. But he likes to have a letter. Just to know that there's still a possibility for better things.

BIFF: He's not like this all the time, is he?

LINDA: It's when you come home he's always the worst.

BIFF: When I come home?

LINDA: When you write you're coming, he's all smiles, and talks about the future, and—he's just wonderful. And then the closer you seem to come, the more shaky he gets, and then, by the time you get here, he's arguing, and he seems angry at you. I think it's just that maybe he can't bring himself to—to open up to you. Why are you so hateful to each other? Why is that?

BIFF (evasively): I'm not hateful, Mom.

LINDA: But you no sooner come in the door than you're fighting!

BIFF: I don't know why. I mean to change. I'm tryin', Mom, you understand?

LINDA: Are you home to stay now?

BIFF: I don't know. I want to look around, see what's doin'.

LINDA: Biff, you can't look around all your life, can you?

BIFF: I just can't take hold, Mom. I can't take hold of some kind of a life.

LINDA: Biff, a man is not a bird, to come and go with the springtime.

BIFF: Your hair . . . (He touches her hair.) Your hair got so gray.

LINDA: Oh, it's been gray since you were in high school. I just stopped dyeing it, that's all.

BIFF: Dye it again, will ya? I don't want my pal looking old. (He smiles.)

LINDA: You're such a boy! You think you can go away for a year and . . . You've got to get it into your head now that one day you'll knock on this door and there'll be strange people here—

BIFF: What are you talking about? You're not even sixty, Mom.

LINDA: But what about your father?

BIFF (lamely): Well, I meant him too.

HAPPY: He admires Pop.

LINDA: Biff, dear, if you don't have any feeling for him, then you can't have any feeling for me.

BIFF: Sure I can, Mom.

LINDA: No. You can't just come to see me, because I love him. (With a threat, but only a threat, of tears.) He's the dearest man in the world to me, and I won't have anyone making him feel unwanted and low and blue. You've got to make up your mind now, darling, there's no leeway any more. Either he's your father and you pay him that respect, or else you're not to come here. I know he's not easy to get along with—nobody knows that better than me—but . . .

WILLY (from the left, with a laugh): Hey, hey, Biffo!

BIFF (starting to go out after WILLY): What the hell is the matter with him? (HAPPY stops him.)

LINDA: Don't—don't go near him!

BIFF: Stop making excuses for him! He always, always wiped the floor with you. Never had an ounce of respect for you.

HAPPY: He's always had respect for—

BIFF: What the hell do you know about it?

HAPPY (surlily): Just don't call him crazy!

BIFF: He's got no character—Charley wouldn't do this. Not in his own house—spewing out that vomit from his mind.

HAPPY: Charley never had to cope with what he's got to.

BIFF: People are worse off than Willy Loman. Believe me, I've seen them!

LINDA: Then make Charley your father, Biff. You can't do that, can you? I don't say he's a great man. Willy Loman never made a lot of money. His name was never in the paper. He's not the finest character that ever lived. But he's a human being, and a terrible thing is happening to him. So attention must be paid. He's not to be allowed to fall into his grave like an old dog. Attention, attention must be finally paid to such a person. You called him crazy—

BIFF: I didn't mean—

LINDA: No, a lot of people think he's lost his—balance. But you don't have to be very smart to know what his trouble is. The man is exhausted.

HAPPY: Sure!

LINDA: A small man can be just as exhausted as a great man. He works for a company thirty-six years this March, opens up unheard-of territories to their trademark, and now in his old age they take his salary away.

HAPPY (indignantly): I didn't know that, Mom.

LINDA: You never asked, my dear! Now that you get your spending money someplace else you don't trouble your mind with him.

HAPPY: But I gave you money last—

LINDA: Christmas time, fifty dollars! To fix the hot water it cost ninety-seven fifty! For five weeks he's been on straight commission, like a beginner, an unknown!

BIFF: Those ungrateful bastards!

LINDA: Are they any worse than his sons? When he brought them business, when he was young, they were glad to see him. But now his old friends, the old buyers that loved him so and always found some order to hand him in a pinch—they're all dead, retired. He used to be able to make six, seven calls a day in Boston. Now he takes his valises out of the car and puts them back and takes them out again and he's exhausted. Instead of walking he talks now. He drives seven hundred miles, and when he gets there no one knows him any more, no one welcomes him. And what goes through a man's mind, driving seven hundred miles home without having earned a cent? Why shouldn't he talk to himself? Why? When he has to go to Charley and borrow fifty dollars a week and pretend to me that it's his pay? How long can that go on? How long? You see what I'm sitting here and waiting for? And you tell me he has no character? The man who never worked a day but for your benefit? When does he get the medal for that? Is this his reward—to turn around at the age of sixty-three and find his sons, who he loved better than his life, one a philandering bum—

HAPPY: Mom!

LINDA: That's all you are, my baby! (*to* BIFF) And you! What happened to the love you had for him? You were such pals! How you used to talk to him on the phone every night! How lonely he was till he could come home to you!

BIFF: All right, Mom. I'll live here in my room, and I'll get a job. I'll keep away from him, that's all.

LINDA: No, Biff. You can't stay here and fight all the time.

BIFF: He threw me out of this house, remember that.

LINDA: Why did he do that? I never knew why.

BIFF: Because I know he's a fake and he doesn't like anybody around who knows!

LINDA: Why a fake? In what way? What do you mean?

BIFF: Just don't lay it all at my feet. It's between me and him—that's all I have to say. I'll chip in from now on. He'll settle for half my pay check. He'll be all right. I'm going to bed. (*He starts for the stairs.*)

LINDA: He won't be all right.

BIFF (*turning on the stairs, furiously*): I hate this city and I'll stay here. Now what do you want?

LINDA: He's dying, Biff.

(HAPPY *turns quickly to her, shocked.*)

BIFF (*after a pause*): Why is he dying?

LINDA: He's been trying to kill himself.

BIFF (*with great horror*): How?

LINDA: I live from day to day.

BIFF: What're you talking about?

LINDA: Remember I wrote you that he smashed up the car again? In February?

BIFF: Well?

LINDA: The insurance inspector came. He said that they have evidence. That all these accidents in the last year—weren't—weren't—accidents.

HAPPY: How can they tell that? That's a lie.

LINDA: It seems there's a woman . . . (*She takes a breath as . . .*)

BIFF (*sharply but contained*): What woman?

LINDA (*simultaneously*): . . . and this woman . . .

LINDA: What?

BIFF: Nothing. Go ahead.

LINDA: What did you say?

BIFF: Nothing. I just said what woman?

HAPPY: What about her?

LINDA: Well, it seems she was walking down the road and saw his car. She says that he wasn't driving fast at all, and that he didn't skid. She says he came to that little bridge, and then deliberately smashed into the railing, and it was only the shallowness of the water that saved him.

BIFF: Oh, no, he probably just fell asleep again.

LINDA: I don't think he fell asleep.

BIFF: Why not?

LINDA: Last month . . . (*With great difficulty.*) Oh, boys, it's so hard to say a thing like this! He's just a big stupid man to you, but I tell you there's more good in him than in many other people. (*She chokes, wipes her eyes.*) I was looking for a fuse. The lights blew out, and I went down the cellar. And behind the fuse box—it happened to fall out—was a length of rubber pipe—just short.

HAPPY: No kidding?

LINDA: There's a little attachment on the end of it. I knew right away. And sure enough, on the bottom of the water heater there's a new little nipple on the gas pipe.

HAPPY (*angrily*): That—jerk.

BIFF: Did you have it taken off?

LINDA: I'm—I'm ashamed to. How can I mention it to him? Every day I go down and take away that little rubber pipe. But, when he comes home, I put it back where it was. How can I insult him that way? I don't know what to do. I live from day to day, boys. I tell you, I know every thought in his mind. It sounds so old-fashioned and silly, but I tell you he put his whole life into you and you've turned your backs on him. (*She is bent over in the chair, weeping, her face in her hands.*) Biff, I swear to God! Biff, his life is in your hands!

HAPPY (*to* BIFF): How do you like that damned fool!

BIFF (*kissing her*): All right, pal, all right. It's all settled now. I've been remiss. I know that, Mom. But now I'll stay, and I swear to you, I'll apply myself. (*Kneeling in front of her, in a fever of self-reproach*) It's just—you see, Mom, I don't fit in business. Not that I won't try. I'll try, and I'll make good.

HAPPY: Sure you will. The trouble with you in business was you never tried to please people.

BIFF: I know, I—

HAPPY: Like when you worked for Harrison's. Bob Harrison said you were tops, and then you go and do some damn fool thing like whistling whole songs in the elevator like a comedian.

BIFF (*against* HAPPY): So what? I like to whistle sometimes.

HAPPY: You don't raise a guy to a responsible job who whistles in the elevator!

LINDA: Well, don't argue about it now.

HAPPY: Like when you'd go off and swim in the middle of the day instead of taking the line around.

BIFF (*his resentment rising*): Well, don't you run off?

You take off sometimes, don't you? On a nice summer day?

HAPPY: Yeah, but I cover myself!

LINDA: Boys!

HAPPY: If I'm going to take a fade the boss can call any number where I'm supposed to be and they'll swear to him that I just left. I'll tell you something that I hate to say, Biff, but in the business world some of them think you're crazy.

BIFF (angered): Screw the business world!

HAPPY: All right, screw it! Great, but cover yourself!

LINDA: Hap, Hap!

BIFF: I don't care what they think! They've laughed at Dad for years, and you know why? Because we don't belong in this nuthouse of a city! We should be mixing cement on some open plain, or—or carpenters. A carpenter is allowed to whistle!

(WILLY walks in from the entrance of the house, at left.)

WILLY: Even your grandfather was better than a carpenter. (Pause. They watch him.) You never grew up. Bernard does not whistle in the elevator, I assure you.

BIFF (as though to laugh WILLY out of it): Yeah, but you do, Pop.

WILLY: I never in my life whistled in an elevator! And who in the business world thinks I'm crazy!

BIFF: I didn't mean it like that, Pop. Now don't make a whole thing out of it, will ya?

WILLY: Go back to the West! Be a carpenter, a cowboy, enjoy yourself!

LINDA: Willy, he was just saying—

WILLY: I heard what he said!

HAPPY (trying to quiet WILLY): Hey, Pop, come on now . . .

WILLY (continuing over HAPPY's line): They laugh at me, heh? Go to Filene's, go to the Hub, go to Slattery's, Boston. Call out the name Willy Loman and see what happens! Big shot!

BIFF: All right, Pop.

WILLY: Big!

BIFF: All right!

WILLY: Why do you always insult me?

BIFF: I didn't say a word. (to LINDA) Did I say a word?

LINDA: He didn't say anything, Willy.

WILLY (going to the doorway of the living-room): All right, good night, good night.

LINDA: Willy, dear, he just decided . . .

WILLY (to BIFF): If you get tired hanging around tomorrow, paint the ceiling I put up in the living-room.

BIFF: I'm leaving early tomorrow.

HAPPY: He's going to see Bill Oliver, Pop.

WILLY (interestedly): Oliver? For what?

BIFF (with reserve, but trying, trying): He always said he'd stake me. I'd like to go into business, say maybe I can take him up on it.

LINDA: Isn't that wonderful?

WILLY: Don't interrupt. What's wonderful about it? There's fifty men in the City of New York who'd stake him. (to BIFF) Sporting goods?

BIFF: I guess so. I know something about it and—

WILLY: He knows something about it! You know sporting goods better than Spalding, for God's sake! How much is he giving you?

BIFF: I don't know, I didn't even see him yet, but—

WILLY: Then what're you talkin' about?

BIFF (getting angry): Well, all I said was I'm gonna see him, that's all!

WILLY (turning away): Ah, you're counting your chickens again.

BIFF (starting left for the stairs): Oh, Jesus, I'm going to sleep!

WILLY (calling after him): Don't curse in this house!

BIFF (turning): Since when did you get so clean?

HAPPY (trying to stop them): What a . . .

WILLY: Don't use that language to me! I won't have it!

HAPPY (grabbing BIFF, shouts): Wait a minute! I got an idea. I got a feasible idea. Come here, Biff, let's talk this over now, let's talk some sense here. When I was down in Florida last time, I thought of a great idea to sell sporting goods. It just came back to me. You and I, Biff—we have a line, the Loman Line. We train a couple of weeks, and put on a couple of exhibitions, see?

WILLY: That's an idea!

HAPPY: Wait! We form two basketball teams, see? Two water-polo teams. We play each other. It's a million dollars' worth of publicity. Two brothers, see? The Loman Brothers. Displays in the Royal Palms—all the hotels. And banners over the ring and the basketball court; "Loman Brothers." Baby, we could sell sporting goods!

WILLY: This is a one-million-dollar idea!

LINDA: Marvelous!

BIFF: I'm in great shape as far as that's concerned.

HAPPY: And the beauty of it is, Biff, it wouldn't be like a business. We'd be out playin' ball again . . .

BIFF (enthused): Yeah, that's . . .

WILLY: Million-dollar . . .

HAPPY: And you wouldn't get fed up with it, Biff. It'd be the family again. There'd be the old honor, and comradeship, and if you wanted to go off for a swim or somethin'—well, you'd do it! Without some smart cooky gettin' up ahead of you!

WILLY: Lick the world! You guys together could absolutely lick the civilized world.

BIFF: I'll see Oliver tomorrow. Hap, if we could work that out . . .

LINDA: Maybe things are beginning to—

WILLY (wildly enthused, to LINDA): Stop interrupting! (To BIFF) But don't wear sport jacket and slacks when you see Oliver.

BIFF: No, I'll—

WILLY: A business suit, and talk as little as possible, and don't crack any jokes.

BIFF: He did like me. Always liked me.

LINDA: He loved you!

WILLY (*to* LINDA): Will you stop! (*to* BIFF) Walk in very serious. You are not applying for a boy's job. Money is to pass. Be quiet, fine, and serious. Everybody likes a kidder, but nobody lends him money.

HAPPY: I'll try to get some myself, Biff. I'm sure I can.

WILLY: I see great things for you kids. I think your troubles are over. But remember, start big and you'll end big. Ask for fifteen. How much you gonna ask for?

BIFF: Gee, I don't know—

WILLY: And don't say "Gee." "Gee" is a boy's word. A man walking in for fifteen thousand dollars does not say "Gee!"

BIFF: Ten, I think would be top though.

WILLY: Don't be so modest. You always started too low. Walk in with a big laugh. Don't look worried. Start off with a couple of your good stories to lighten things up. It's not what you say, it's how you say it—because personality always wins the day.

LINDA: Oliver always thought the highest of him—

WILLY: Will you let me talk?

BIFF: Don't yell at her, Pop, will ya?

WILLY (*angrily*): I was talking, wasn't I?

BIFF: I don't like you yelling at her all the time, and I'm tellin' you, that's all.

WILLY: What're you, takin' over this house?

LINDA: Willy—

WILLY (*turning on her*): Don't take his side all the time, goddammit!

BIFF (*furiously*): Stop yelling at her!

WILLY (*suddenly pulling on his cheek, beaten down, guilt ridden*): Give my best to Bill Oliver—he may remember me. (*He exits through the living-room doorway.*)

LINDA (*her voice subdued*): What'd you have to start that for? (BIFF *turns away.*) You see how sweet he was as soon as you talked hopefully? (*She goes over to* BIFF.) Come up and say good night to him. Don't let him go to bed that way.

HAPPY: Come on, Biff, let's buck him up.

LINDA: Please, dear. Just say good night. It takes so little to make him happy. Come. (*She goes through the living-room doorway, calling upstairs from within the living-room.*) Your pajamas are hanging in the bathroom, Willy!

HAPPY (*looking toward where* LINDA *went out*): What a woman! They broke the mold when they made her. You know that, Biff?

BIFF: He's off salary. My God, working on commission!

HAPPY: Well, let's face it: he's no hot-shot selling man. Except that sometimes, you have to admit, he's a sweet personality.

BIFF (*deciding*): Lend me ten bucks, will ya? I want to buy some new ties.

HAPPY: I'll take you to a place I know. Beautiful stuff. Wear one of my striped shirts tomorrow.

BIFF: She got gray. Mom got awful old. Gee, I'm gonna go in to Oliver tomorrow and knock him for a—

HAPPY: Come on up. Tell that to Dad. Let's give him a whirl. Come on.

BIFF (*steamed up*): You know, with ten thousand bucks, boy!

HAPPY (*as they go into the living-room*): That's the talk, Biff, that's the first time I've heard the old confidence out of you! (*From within the living-room, fading off.*) You're gonna live with me, kid, and any babe you want just say the word . . . (*The last lines are hardly heard. They are mounting the stairs to their parents' bedroom.*)

LINDA (*entering her bedroom and addressing* WILLY, *who is in the bathroom. She is straightening the bed for him*): Can you do anything about the shower? It drips.

WILLY (*from the bathroom*): All of a sudden everything falls to pieces! Goddam plumbing, oughta be sued, those people. I hardly finished putting it in and the thing . . . (*His words rumble off.*)

LINDA: I'm just wondering if Oliver will remember him. You think he might?

WILLY (*coming out of the bathroom in his pajamas*): Remember him? What's the matter with you, you crazy? If he'd've stayed with Oliver he'd be on top by now! Wait'll Oliver gets a look at him. You don't know the average caliber any more. The average young man today—(*He is getting into bed.*)—is got a caliber of zero. Greatest thing in the world for him was to bum around.

(BIFF *and* HAPPY *enter the bedroom. Slight pause.*)

WILLY (*stops short, looking at* BIFF): Glad to hear it, boy.

HAPPY: He wanted to say good night to you, sport.

WILLY (*to* BIFF): Yeah. Knock him dead, boy. What'd you want to tell me?

BIFF: Just take it easy, Pop. Good night. (*He turns to go.*)

WILLY (*unable to resist*): And if anything falls off the desk while you're talking to him—like a package or something—don't you pick it up. They have office boys for that.

LINDA: I'll make a big breakfast—

WILLY: Will you let me finish? (*to* BIFF) Tell him you were in the business in the West. Not farm work.

BIFF: All right, Dad.

LINDA: I think everything—

WILLY (*going right through her speech*): And don't undersell yourself. No less than fifteen thousand dollars.

BIFF (*unable to bear him*): Okay. Good night, Mom. (*He starts moving.*)

WILLY: Because you got a greatness in you, Biff, remember that. You got all kinds a greatness . . . (*He lies back, exhausted.* BIFF *walks out.*)

LINDA (*calling after* BIFF): Sleep well, darling!

HAPPY: I'm gonna get married, Mom. I wanted to tell you.

LINDA: Go to sleep, dear.

HAPPY (*going*): I just wanted to tell you.

WILLY: Keep up the good work. (HAPPY *exits.*) God . . . remember that Ebbets Field game? The championship of the city?

LINDA: Just rest. Should I sing to you?

WILLY: Yeah. Sing to me. (LINDA *hums a soft lullaby.*) When that team came out—he was the tallest, remember?

LINDA: Oh, yes. And in gold.

(BIFF *enters the darkened kitchen, takes a cigarette and leaves the house. He comes downstage into a golden pool of light. He smokes, staring at the night.*)

WILLY: Like a young god. Hercules—something like that. And the sun, the sun all around him. Remember how he waved to me? Right up from the field, with the representatives of three colleges standing by? And the buyers I brought, and the cheers when he came out—Loman, Loman, Loman! God Almighty, he'll be great yet. A star like that, magnificent, can never really fade away!

(*The light on* WILLY *is fading. The gas heater begins to glow through the kitchen wall, near the stairs, a blue flame beneath red coils.*)

LINDA (*timidly*): Willy dear, what has he got against you?

WILLY: I'm so tired. Don't talk any more.

(BIFF *slowly returns to the kitchen. He stops, stares toward the heater.*)

LINDA: Will you ask Howard to let you work in New York?

WILLY: First thing in the morning. Everything'll be all right.

(BIFF *reaches behind the heater and draws out a length of rubber tubing. He is horrified and turns his head toward* WILLY*'s room, still dimly lit, from which the strains of* LINDA*'s desperate but monotonous humming rise.*)

WILLY (*staring through the window into the moonlight*): Gee, look at the moon moving between the buildings!

(BIFF *wraps the tubing around his hand and quickly goes up the stairs.*)

ACT 2

(*Music is heard, gay and bright. The curtain rises as the music fades away.* WILLY, *in shirt sleeves, is sitting at the kitchen table, sipping coffee, his hat in his lap.* LINDA *is filling his cup when she can.*)

WILLY: Wonderful coffee. Meal in itself.

LINDA: Can I make you some eggs?

WILLY: No. Take a breath.

LINDA: You look so rested, dear.

WILLY: I slept like a dead one. First time in months. Imagine, sleeping till ten on a Tuesday morning. Boys left nice and early, heh?

LINDA: They were out of here by eight o'clock.

WILLY: Good work!

LINDA: It was so thrilling to see them leaving together. I can't get over the shaving lotion in this house!

WILLY (*smiling*): Mmm—

LINDA: Biff was very changed this morning. His whole attitude seemed to be hopeful. He couldn't wait to get downtown to see Oliver.

WILLY: He's heading for a change. There's no question, there simply are certain men that take longer to get—solidified. How did he dress?

LINDA: His blue suit. He's so handsome in that suit. He could be a—anything in that suit!

(WILLY *gets up from the table.* LINDA *holds his jacket for him.*)

WILLY: There's no question, no question at all. Gee, on the way home tonight I'd like to buy some seeds.

LINDA (*laughing*): That'd be wonderful. But not enough sun gets back there. Nothing'll grow any more.

WILLY: You wait, kid, before it's all over we're gonna get a little place out in the country, and I'll raise some vegetables, a couple of chickens . . .

LINDA: You'll do it yet, dear.

(WILLY *walks out of his jacket.* LINDA *follows him.*)

WILLY: And they'll get married, and come for a weekend. I'd build a little guest house. 'Cause I got so many fine tools, all I'd need would be a little lumber and some peace of mind.

LINDA (*joyfully*): I sewed the lining . . .

WILLY: I could build two guest houses, so they'd both come. Did he decide how much he's going to ask Oliver for?

LINDA (*getting him into the jacket*): He didn't mention it, but I imagine ten or fifteen thousand. You going to talk to Howard today?

WILLY: Yeah, I'll put it to him straight and simple. He'll just have to take me off the road.

LINDA: And Willy, don't forget to ask for a little advance,

because we've got the insurance premium. It's the grace period now.

WILLY: That's a hundred . . . ?

LINDA: A hundred and eight, sixty-eight. Because we're a little short again.

WILLY: Why are we short?

LINDA: Well, you had the motor job on the car . . .

WILLY: That goddam Studebaker!

LINDA: And you got one more payment on the refrigerator . . .

WILLY: But it just broke again!

LINDA: Well, it's old, dear.

WILLY: I told you we should've bought a well-advertised machine. Charley bought a General Electric and it's twenty years old and it's still good, that son-of-a-bitch.

LINDA: But, Willy—

WILLY: Whoever heard of a Hastings refrigerator? Once in my life I would like to own something outright before it's broken! I'm always in a race with the junkyard! I just finished paying for the car and it's on its last legs. The refrigerator consumes belts like a goddam maniac. They time those things. They time them so when you finally paid for them, they're used up.

LINDA (buttoning up his jacket as he unbuttons it): All told, about two hundred dollars would carry us, dear. But that includes the last payment on the mortgage. After this payment, Willy, the house belongs to us.

WILLY: It's twenty-five years!

LINDA: Biff was nine years old when we bought it.

WILLY: Well, that's a great thing. To weather a twenty-five year mortgage is—

LINDA: It's an accomplishment.

WILLY: All the cement, the lumber, the reconstruction I put in this house! There ain't a crack to be found in it any more.

LINDA: Well, it served its purpose.

WILLY: What purpose? Some stranger'll come along, move in, and that's that. If only Biff would take this house, and raise a family . . . (He starts to go.) Good-by, I'm late.

LINDA (suddenly remembering): Oh, I forgot! You're supposed to meet them for dinner.

WILLY: Me?

LINDA: At Frank's Chop House on Forty-eighth near Sixth Avenue.

WILLY: Is that so! How about you?

LINDA: No, just the three of you. They're gonna blow you to a big meal!

WILLY: Don't say! Who thought of that?

LINDA: Biff came to me this morning, Willy, and he said, "Tell Dad, we want to blow him to a big meal." Be there six o'clock. You and your two boys are going to have dinner.

WILLY: Gee whiz! That's really somethin'. I'm gonna knock Howard for a loop, kid. I'll get an advance, and I'll come home with a New York job. Goddammit, now I'm gonna do it!

LINDA: Oh, that's the spirit, Willy!

WILLY: I will never get behind a wheel the rest of my life!

LINDA: It's changing, Willy, I can feel it changing!

WILLY: Beyond a question. G'by, I'm late. (He starts to go again.)

LINDA (calling after him as she runs to the kitchen table for a handkerchief): You got your glasses?

WILLY (feels for them, then comes back in): Yeah, yeah, got my glasses.

LINDA (giving him the handkerchief): And a handkerchief.

WILLY: Yeah, handkerchief.

LINDA: And your saccharine?

WILLY: Yeah, my saccharine.

LINDA: Be careful on the subway stairs.

(She kisses him, and a silk stocking is seen hanging from her hand. WILLY notices it.)

WILLY: Will you stop mending stockings? At least while I'm in the house. It gets me nervous. I can't tell you. Please.

(LINDA hides the stocking in her hand as she follows WILLY across the forestage in front of the house.)

LINDA: Remember, Frank's Chop House.

WILLY (passing the apron): Maybe beets would grow out there.

LINDA (laughing): But you tried so many times.

WILLY: Yeah. Well, don't work hard today. (He disappears around the right corner of the house.)

LINDA: Be careful!

(As WILLY vanishes, LINDA waves to him. Suddenly the phone rings. She runs across the stage and into the kitchen and lifts it.)

LINDA: Hello? Oh, Biff! I'm so glad you called, I just . . . Yes, sure, I just told him. Yes, he'll be there for dinner at six o'clock, I didn't forget. Listen, I was just dying to tell you. You know that little rubber pipe I told you about? That he connected to the gas heater? I finally decided to go down the cellar this morning and take it away and destroy it. But it's gone! Imagine! He took it away himself, it isn't there! (She listens.) When? Oh, then you took it. Oh—nothing, it's just that I'd hoped he'd taken it away himself. Oh, I'm not worried, darling, because this morning he left in such high spirits, it was like the old days! I'm not afraid any more. Did Mr. Oliver see you? . . . Well, you wait there then. And make a nice impression on him, darling. Just don't perspire too much before you see him. And have a nice time with Dad. He may have big news too! . . . That's right, a New York job. And be sweet to him tonight, dear. Be loving to him. Because he's only a little boat looking for a harbor. *(She is trembling with sorrow and joy.)* Oh, that's wonderful, Biff, you'll save his life. Thanks, darling. Just put your arm around him when he comes into the restaurant. Give him a smile. That's the boy . . . Good-by, dear. . . . You got your comb? . . . That's fine. Good-by, Biff dear.

(In the middle of her speech, HOWARD WAGNER, *thirty-six, wheels in a small typewriter table on which is a wire-recording machine and proceeds to plug it in. This is on the left forestage. Light slowly fades on* LINDA *as it rises on* HOWARD. HOWARD *is intent on threading the machine and only glances over his shoulder as* WILLY *appears.)*

WILLY: Pst! Pst!

HOWARD: Hello, Willy, come in.

WILLY: Like to have a little talk with you, Howard.

HOWARD: Sorry to keep you waiting. I'll be with you in a minute.

WILLY: What's that, Howard?

HOWARD: Didn't you ever see one of these? Wire recorder.

WILLY: Oh. Can we talk a minute?

HOWARD: Records things. Just got delivery yesterday. Been driving me crazy, the most terrific machine I ever saw in my life. I was up all night with it.

WILLY: What do you do with it?

HOWARD: I bought it for dictation, but you can do anything with it. Listen to this. I had it home last night. Listen to what I picked up. The first one is my daughter. Get this. *(He flicks the switch and "Roll out the Barrel" is heard being whistled.)* Listen to that kid whistle.

WILLY: That is lifelike, isn't it?

HOWARD: Seven years old. Get that tone.

WILLY: Ts, ts. Like to ask a little favor if you . . .

(The whistling breaks off, and the voice of HOWARD's *daughter is heard.)*

HIS DAUGHTER: "Now you, Daddy."

HOWARD: She's crazy for me! *(Again the same song is whistled.)* That's me! Ha! *(He winks.)*

WILLY: You're very good!

(The whistling breaks off again. The machine runs silent for a moment.)

HOWARD: Sh! Get this now, this is my son.

HIS SON: "The capital of Alabama is Montgomery; the capital of Arizona is Phoenix; the capital of Arkansas is Little Rock; the capital of California is Sacramento . . ." *(and on, and on.)*

HOWARD *(holding up five fingers)*: Five years old, Willy!

WILLY: He'll make an announcer some day!

HIS SON *(continuing)*: "The capital . . ."

HOWARD: Get that—alphabetical order! *(The machine*

breaks off suddenly.) Wait a minute. The maid kicked the plug out.

WILLY: It certainly is a—

HOWARD: Sh, for God's sake!

HIS SON: "It's nine o'clock, Bulova watch time. So I have to go to sleep."

WILLY: That really is—

HOWARD: Wait a minute! The next is my wife.

(They wait.)

HOWARD'S VOICE: "Go on, say something." *(Pause.)* "Well, you gonna talk?"

HIS WIFE: "I can't think of anything."

HOWARD'S VOICE: "Well, talk—it's turning."

HIS WIFE *(shyly, beaten)*: "Hello." *(Silence.)* "Oh, Howard, I can't talk into this . . ."

HOWARD *(snapping the machine off)*: That was my wife.

WILLY: This is a wonderful machine. Can we—

HOWARD: I tell you, Willy, I'm gonna take my camera, and my bandsaw, and all my hobbies, and out they go. This is the most fascinating relaxation I ever found.

WILLY: I think I'll get one myself.

HOWARD: Sure, they're only a hundred and a half. You can't do without it. Supposing you wanna hear Jack Benny, see? But you can't be at home at that hour. So you tell the maid to turn the radio on when Jack Benny comes on, and this automatically goes on with the radio . . .

WILLY: And when you come home you . . .

HOWARD: You can come home twelve o'clock, one o'clock, any time you like, and you get yourself a Coke and sit yourself down, throw the switch, and there's Jack Benny's program in the middle of the night!

WILLY: I'm definitely going to get one. Because lots of time I'm on the road, and I think to myself, what I must be missing on the radio!

HOWARD: Don't you have a radio in the car?

WILLY: Well, yeah, but who ever thinks of turning it on?

HOWARD: Say, aren't you supposed to be in Boston?

WILLY: That's what I want to talk to you about, Howard. You got a minute? *(He draws a chair in from the wing.)*

HOWARD: What happened? What're you doing here?

WILLY: Well . . .

HOWARD: You didn't crack up again, did you?

WILLY: Oh, no. No . . .

HOWARD: Geez, you had me worried there for a minute. What's the trouble?

WILLY: Well, tell you the truth, Howard. I've come to the decision that I'd rather not travel any more.

HOWARD: Not travel! Well, what'll you do?

WILLY: Remember, Christmas time, when you had the party here? You said you'd try to think of some spot for me here in town.

HOWARD: With us?

WILLY: Well, sure.

HOWARD: Oh, yeah, yeah, I remember. Well, I couldn't think of anything for you, Willy.

WILLY: I tell ya, Howard. The kids are all grown up, y'know. I don't need much any more. If I could take home—well, sixty-five dollars a week, I could swing it.

HOWARD: Yeah, but Willy, see I—

WILLY: I tell ya why, Howard. Speaking frankly and between the two of us, y'know—I'm just a little tired.

HOWARD: Oh, I could understand that, Willy. But you're a road man, Willy, and we do a road business. We've only got a half-dozen salesmen on the floor here.

WILLY: God knows, Howard, I never asked a favor of any man. But I was with the firm when your father used to carry you in here in his arms.

HOWARD: I know that, Willy, but—

WILLY: Your father came to me the day you were born and asked me what I thought of the name of Howard, may he rest in peace.

HOWARD: I appreciate that, Willy, but there just is no spot here for you. If I had a spot I'd slam you right in, but I just don't have a single solitary spot.

(He looks for his lighter. WILLY has picked it up and gives it to him. Pause.)

WILLY (with increasing anger): Howard, all I need to set my table is fifty dollars a week.

HOWARD: But where am I going to put you, kid?

WILLY: Look, it isn't a question of whether I can sell merchandise, is it?

HOWARD: No, but it's a business, kid, and everybody's gotta pull his own weight.

WILLY (desperately): Just let me tell you a story, Howard—

HOWARD: 'Cause you gotta admit, business is business.

WILLY (angrily): Business is definitely business, but just listen for a minute. You don't understand this. When I was a boy—eighteen, nineteen—I was already on the road. And there was a question in my mind as to whether selling had a future for me. Because in those days I had a yearning to go to Alaska. See, there were three gold strikes in one month in Alaska, and I felt like going out. Just for the ride, you might say.

HOWARD (barely interested): Don't say.

WILLY: Oh, yeah, my father lived many years in Alaska. He was an adventurous man. We've got quite a little streak of self-reliance in our family. I thought I'd go out with my older brother and try to locate him, and maybe settle in the North with the old man. And I was almost decided to go, when I met a salesman in the Parker House. His name was Dave Singleman. And he was eighty-four years old, and he'd drummed merchandise in thirty-one states. And old Dave, he'd go up to his room, y'understand, put on his green velvet slippers—I'll never forget—and pick up his phone and call the buyers, and without ever leaving his room, at the age of eighty-four, he made his living. And when I saw that, I realized that selling was the greatest career a man could want. 'Cause what could be more satisfying than to be able to go, at the age of eighty-four, into twenty or thirty different cities, and pick up a phone, and be remembered and loved and helped by so many different people? Do you know? when he died—and by the way he died the death of a salesman, in his green velvet slippers in the smoker of the New York, New Haven and Hartford, going into Boston—when he died, hundreds of salesmen and buyers were at his funeral. Things were sad on a lotta trains for months after that. (He stands up. HOWARD has not looked at him.) In those days there was personality in it, Howard. There was respect, and comradeship, and gratitude in it. Today, it's all cut and dried, and there's no chance for bringing friendship to bear—or personality. You see what I mean? They don't know me any more.

HOWARD (moving away, to the right): That's just the thing, Willy.

WILLY: If I had forty dollars a week—that's all I'd need. Forty dollars, Howard.

HOWARD: Kid, I can't take blood from a stone, I—

WILLY (desperation is on him now): Howard, the year Al Smith was nominated, your father came to me and—

HOWARD (starting to go off): I've got to see some people, kid.

WILLY (stopping him): I'm talking about your father! There were promises made across this desk! You mustn't tell me you've got people to see—I put thirty-four years into this firm, Howard, and now I can't pay my insurance! You can't eat the orange and throw the peel away—a man is not a piece of fruit! (After a pause.) Now pay attention. Your father—in 1928 I had a big year. I averaged a hundred and seventy dollars a week in commissions.

HOWARD (impatiently): Now, Willy, you never averaged—

WILLY (banging his hand on the desk): I averaged a hundred and seventy dollars a week in the year of 1928! And your father came to me—or rather, I was in the office here—it was right over this desk—and he put his hand on my shoulder—

HOWARD (getting up): You'll have to excuse me, Willy, I

gotta see some people. Pull yourself together. *(Going out.)* I'll be back in a little while.

(On HOWARD's *exit, the light of his chair grows very bright and strange.)*

WILLY: Pull myself together! What the hell did I say to him? My God, I was yelling at him! How could I! *(*WILLY *breaks off, staring at the light, which occupies the chair, animating it. He approaches this chair, standing across the desk from it.)* Frank, Frank, don't you remember what you told me that time? How you put your hand on my shoulder, and Frank . . . *(He leans on the desk and as he speaks the dead man's name he accidentally switches on the recorder, and instantly)*

HOWARD'S SON: " . . . of New York is Albany. The capital of Ohio is Cincinnati, the capital of Rhode Island is . . ." *(The recitation continues.)*

WILLY *(leaping away with fright, shouting)*: Ha! Howard! Howard! Howard!

HOWARD *(rushing in)*: What happened?

WILLY *(pointing at the machine, which continues nasally, childishly, with the capital cities)*: Shut it off! Shut it off!

HOWARD *(pulling the plug out)*: Look, Willy . . .

WILLY *(pressing his hands to his eyes)*: I gotta get myself some coffee. I'll get some coffee . . .

*(*WILLY *starts to walk out.* HOWARD *stops him.)*

HOWARD *(rolling up the cord)*: Willy, Look . . .

WILLY: I'll go to Boston.

HOWARD: Willy, you can't go to Boston for us.

WILLY: Why can't I go?

HOWARD: I don't want you to represent us. I've been meaning to tell you for a long time now.

WILLY: Howard, are you firing me?

HOWARD: I think you need a good long rest, Willy.

WILLY: Howard—

HOWARD: And when you feel better, come back, and we'll see if we can work something out.

WILLY: But I gotta earn money, Howard. I'm in no position to—

HOWARD: Where are your sons? Why don't your sons give you a hand?

WILLY: They're working on a very big deal.

HOWARD: This is no time for false pride, Willy. You go to your sons and you tell them that you're tired. You've got two great boys, haven't you?

WILLY: Oh, no question, no question, but in the meantime . . .

HOWARD: Then that's that, heh?

WILLY: All right, I'll go to Boston tomorrow.

HOWARD: No, no.

WILLY: I can't throw myself on my sons. I'm not a cripple!

HOWARD: Look, kid, I'm busy this morning.

WILLY *(grasping* HOWARD's *arm)*: Howard, you've got to let me go to Boston!

HOWARD *(hard, keeping himself under control)*: I've got a line of people to see this morning. Sit down, take five minutes, and pull yourself together, and then go home, will ya? I need the office, Willy. *(He starts to go; turns, remembering the recorder, starts to push off the table holding the recorder.)* Oh, yeah. Whenever you can this week, stop by and drop off the samples. You'll feel better, Willy, and then come back and we'll talk. Pull yourself together, kid, there's people outside.

*(*HOWARD *exits, pushing the table off left.* WILLY *stares into space, exhausted. Now the music is heard—*BEN's *music—first distantly, then closer, closer. As* WILLY *speaks,* BEN *enters from the right. He carries valise and umbrella.)*

WILLY: Oh, Ben, how did you do it? What is the answer? Did you wind up the Alaska deal already?

BEN: Doesn't take much time if you know what you're doing. Just a short business trip. Boarding ship in an hour. Wanted to say good-by.

WILLY: Ben, I've got to talk to you.

BEN *(glancing at his watch)*: Haven't the time, William.

WILLY *(crossing the apron to* BEN*)*: Ben, nothing's working out. I don't know what to do.

BEN: Now look here, William. I've bought timberland in Alaska and I need a man to look after things for me.

WILLY: God, timberland! Me and my boys in those grand outdoors!

BEN: You've a new continent at your doorstep, William. Get out of these cities, they're full of talk and time payments and courts of law. Screw on your fists and you can fight for a fortune up there.

WILLY: Yes, yes! Linda, Linda!

*(*LINDA *enters as of old, with the wash.)*

LINDA: Oh, you're back?

BEN: I haven't much time.

WILLY: No, wait! Linda, he's got a proposition for me in Alaska.

LINDA: But you've got—*(to* BEN*)* He's got a beautiful job here.

WILLY: But in Alaska, kid, I could—

LINDA: You're doing well enough, Willy!

BEN *(to* LINDA*)*: Enough for what, my dear?

LINDA *(frightened of* BEN *and angry at him)*: Don't say those things to him! Enough to be happy right here, right now. *(to* WILLY, *while* BEN *laughs)* Why must everybody conquer the world? You're well liked, and the boys love you, and someday—*(to* BEN*)*—why, old man Wagner told him just the other day that if he keeps it up he'll be a member of the firm, didn't he, Willy?

WILLY: Sure, sure. I am building something with this firm, Ben, and if a man is building something he must be on the right track, mustn't he?

BEN: What are you building? Lay your hand on it. Where is it?

WILLY *(hesitantly)*: That's true, Linda, there's nothing.

LINDA: Why? *(to BEN)* There's a man eighty-four years old—

WILLY: That's right, Ben, that's right. When I look at that man I say, what is there to worry about?

BEN: Bah!

WILLY: It's true, Ben. All he has to do is go into any city, pick up the phone, and he's making his living and you know why?

BEN *(picking up his valise)*: I've got to go.

WILLY *(holding BEN back)*: Look at this boy!

(BIFF, in his high school sweater, enters carrying suitcase. HAPPY carries BIFF's shoulder guards, gold helmet, and football pants.)

WILLY: Without a penny to his name, three great universities are begging for him, and from there the sky's the limit, because it's not what you do, Ben. It's who you know and the smile on your face! It's contacts, Ben, contacts! The whole wealth of Alaska passes over the lunch table at the Commodore Hotel, and that's the wonder, the wonder of this century, that a man can end with diamonds here on the basis of being liked! *(He turns to BIFF.)* And that's why when you get out on that field today it's important. Because thousands of people will be rooting for you and loving you. *(to BEN, who has again begun to leave)* And Ben! when he walks into a business office his name will sound out like a bell and all the doors will open to him! I've seen it, Ben, I've seen it a thousand times! You can't feel it with your hand like timber, but it's there!

BEN: Good-by, William.

WILLY: Ben, am I right? Don't you think I'm right? I value your advice.

BEN: There's a new continent at your doorstep, William. You could walk out rich. Rich! *(He is gone.)*

WILLY: We'll do it here, Ben! You hear me? We're gonna do it here!

(YOUNG BERNARD rushes in. The gay music of the Boys is heard.)

BERNARD: Oh, gee, I was afraid you left already!

WILLY: Why? What time is it?

BERNARD: It's half-past one!

WILLY: Well, come on, everybody! Ebbets Field next stop! Where's the pennants? *(He rushes through the wall-line of the kitchen and out into the living-room.)*

LINDA *(to BIFF)*: Did you pack fresh underwear?

BIFF *(who has been limbering up)*: I want to go!

BERNARD: Biff, I'm carrying your helmet, ain't I?

HAPPY: No, I'm carrying the helmet.

BERNARD: Oh, Biff, you promised me.

HAPPY: I'm carrying the helmet.

BERNARD: How am I going to get in the locker room?

LINDA: Let him carry the shoulder guards. *(She puts her coat and hat on in the kitchen.)*

BERNARD: Can I, Biff? 'Cause I told everybody I'm going to be in the locker room.

HAPPY: In Ebbets Field it's the clubhouse.

BERNARD: I meant the clubhouse, Biff!

HAPPY: Biff!

BIFF *(grandly, after a slight pause)*: Let him carry the shoulder guards.

HAPPY *(as he gives BERNARD the shoulder guards)*: Stay close to us now.

(WILLY rushes in with the pennants.)

WILLY *(handing them out)*: Everybody wave when Biff comes out on the field. *(HAPPY and BERNARD run off.)* You set now, boy?

(The music has died away.)

BIFF: Ready to go, Pop. Every muscle is ready.

WILLY *(at the edge of the apron)*: You realize what this means?

BIFF: That's right, Pop.

WILLY *(feeling BIFF's muscles)*: You're comin' home this afternoon captain of the All-Scholastic Championship Team of the City of New York.

BIFF: I got it, Pop. And remember, pal, when I take off my helmet, that touchdown is for you.

WILLY: Let's go! *(He is starting out, with his arm around BIFF, when CHARLEY enters, as of old, in knickers.)* I got no room for you, Charley.

CHARLEY: Room? For what?

WILLY: In the car.

CHARLEY: You goin' for a ride? I wanted to shoot some casino.

WILLY *(furiously)*: Casino! *(Incredulously.)* Don't you realize what today is?

LINDA: Oh, he knows, Willy. He's just kidding you.

WILLY: That's nothing to kid about!

CHARLEY: No, Linda, what's goin' on?

LINDA: He's playing in Ebbets Field.

CHARLEY: Baseball in this weather?

WILLY: Don't talk to him. Come on, come on! *(He is pushing them out.)*

CHARLEY: Wait a minute, didn't you hear the news?

WILLY: What?

CHARLEY: Don't you listen to the radio? Ebbets Field just blew up.

WILLY: You go to hell! *(CHARLEY laughs. Pushing them out.)* Come on, come on! We're late.

CHARLEY *(as they go)*: Knock a homer, Biff, knock a homer!

WILLY *(the last to leave, turning to CHARLEY)*: I don't

think that was funny, Charley. This is the greatest day of his life.

CHARLEY: Willy, when are you going to grow up?

WILLY: Yeah, heh? When this game is over, Charley, you'll be laughing out of the other side of your face. They'll be calling him another Red Grange. Twenty-five thousand a year.

CHARLEY (kidding): Is that so?

WILLY: Yeah, that's so.

CHARLEY: Well, then, I'm sorry, Willy. But tell me something.

WILLY: What?

CHARLEY: Who is Red Grange?

WILLY: Put up your hands. Goddam you, put up your hands!

(CHARLEY, chuckling, shakes his head and walks away, around the left corner of the stage. WILLY follows him. The music rises to a mocking frenzy.)

WILLY: Who the hell do you think you are, better than everybody else? You don't know everything, you big, ignorant, stupid . . . Put up your hands!

(Light rises, on the right side of the forestage, on a small table in the reception room of CHARLEY's office. Traffic sounds are heard. BERNARD, now mature, sits whistling to himself. A pair of tennis rackets and an overnight bag are on the floor beside him.)

WILLY (offstage): What are you walking away for? Don't walk away! If you're going to say something say it to my face! I know you laugh at me behind my back. You'll laugh out of the other side of your goddam face after this game. Touchdown! Touchdown! Eighty thousand people! Touchdown! Right between the goal posts.

(BERNARD is a quiet, earnest, but self-assured young man. WILLY's voice is coming from right upstage now. BERNARD lowers his feet off the table and listens. JENNY, his father's secretary, enters.)

JENNY (distressed): Say, Bernard, will you go out in the hall?

BERNARD: What is that noise? Who is it?

JENNY: Mr. Loman. He just got off the elevator.

BERNARD (getting up): Who's he arguing with?

JENNY: Nobody. There's nobody with him. I can't deal with him any more, and your father gets all upset everytime he comes. I've got a lot of typing to do, and your father's waiting to sign it. Will you see him?

WILLY (entering): Touchdown! Touch—(He sees JENNY.) Jenny, Jenny, good to see you. How're ya? Workin'? Or still honest?

JENNY: Fine. How've you been feeling?

WILLY: Not much any more, Jenny. Ha, ha! (He is surprised to see the rackets.)

BERNARD: Hello, Uncle Willy.

WILLY (almost shocked): Bernard! Well, look who's here! (He comes quickly, guiltily, to BERNARD and warmly shakes his hand.)

BERNARD: How are you? Good to see you.

WILLY: What are you doing here?

BERNARD: Oh, just stopped by to see Pop. Get off my feet till my train leaves. I'm going to Washington in a few minutes.

WILLY: Is he in?

BERNARD: Yes, he's in his office with the accountant. Sit down.

WILLY (sitting down): What're you going to do in Washington?

BERNARD: Oh, just a case I've got there, Willy.

WILLY: That so? (Indicating the rackets.) You going to play tennis there?

BERNARD: I'm staying with a friend who's got a court.

WILLY: Don't say. His own tennis court. Must be fine people, I bet.

BERNARD: They are, very nice. Dad tells me Biff's in town.

WILLY (with a big smile): Yeah, Biff's in. Working on a very big deal, Bernard.

BERNARD: What's Biff doing?

WILLY: Well, he's been doing very big things in the West. But he decided to establish himself here. Very big. We're having dinner. Did I hear your wife had a boy?

BERNARD: That's right. Our second.

WILLY: Two boys! What do you know!

BERNARD: What kind of a deal has Biff got?

WILLY: Well, Bill Oliver—very big sporting-goods man—he wants Biff very badly. Called him in from the West. Long distance, carte blanche, special deliveries. Your friends have their own private tennis court?

BERNARD: You still with the old firm, Willy?

WILLY (after a pause): I'm—I'm overjoyed to see how you made the grade, Bernard, overjoyed. It's an encouraging thing to see a young man really—really—Looks very good for Biff—very—(He breaks off, then.) Bernard—(He is so full of emotion, he breaks off again.)

BERNARD: What is it, Willy?

WILLY (small and alone): What—what's the secret?

BERNARD: What secret?

WILLY: How—how did you? Why didn't he ever catch on?

BERNARD: I wouldn't know that, Willy.

WILLY (confidentially, desperately): You were his friend, his boyhood friend. There's something I don't understand about it. His life ended after that Ebbets Field game. From the age of seventeen nothing good ever happened to him.

BERNARD: He never trained himself for anything.

WILLY: But he did, he did. After high school he took so many correspondence courses. Radio mechanics;

television; God knows what, and never made the slightest mark.

BERNARD (*taking off his glasses*): Willy, do you want to talk candidly?

WILLY (*rising, faces* BERNARD): I regard you as a very brilliant man, Bernard. I value your advice.

BERNARD: Oh, the hell with the advice, Willy. I couldn't advise you. There's just one thing I've always wanted to ask you. When he was supposed to graduate, and the math teacher flunked him—

WILLY: Oh, that son-of-a-bitch ruined his life.

BERNARD: Yeah, but, Willy, all he had to do was go to summer school and make up that subject.

WILLY: That's right, that's right.

BERNARD: Did you tell him not to go to summer school?

WILLY: Me? I begged him to go. I ordered him to go!

BERNARD: Then why wouldn't he go?

WILLY: Why? Why! Bernard, that question has been trailing me like a ghost for the last fifteen years. He flunked the subject, and laid down and died like a hammer hit him!

BERNARD: Take it easy, kid.

WILLY: Let me talk to you—I got nobody to talk to. Bernard, Bernard, was it my fault? Y'see? It keeps going around in my mind, maybe I did something to him. I got nothing to give him.

BERNARD: Don't take it so hard.

WILLY: Why did he lay down? What is the story there? You were his friend!

BERNARD: Willy, I remember, it was June, and our grades came out. And he'd flunked math.

WILLY: That son-of-a-bitch!

BERNARD: No, it wasn't right then. Biff just got very angry, I remember, and he was ready to enroll in summer school.

WILLY (*surprised*): He was?

BERNARD: He wasn't beaten by it at all. But then, Willy, he disappeared from the block for almost a month. And I got the idea that he'd gone up to New England to see you. Did he have a talk with you then?

(WILLY *stares in silence.*)

BERNARD: Willy?

WILLY (*with a strong edge of resentment in his voice*): Yeah, he came to Boston. What about it?

BERNARD: Well, just that when he came back—I'll never forget this, it always mystifies me. Because I'd thought so well of Biff, even though he'd always taken advantage of me. I loved him, Willy, y'know? And he came back after that month and took his sneakers—remember those sneakers with "University of Virginia" printed on them? He was so proud of those, wore them every day. And he took them down in the cellar, and burned them up in the furnace. We had a fist fight. It lasted at least half an hour. Just the two of us, punching each other down the cellar, and crying right through it. I've often thought of how strange it was that I knew he'd given up his life. What happened in Boston, Willy?

(WILLY *looks at him as at an intruder.*)

BERNARD: I just bring it up because you asked me.

WILLY (*angrily*): Nothing. What do you mean, "What happened?" What's that got to do with anything?

BERNARD: Well, don't get sore.

WILLY: What are you trying to do, blame it on me? If a boy lays down is that my fault?

BERNARD: Now, Willy, don't get—

WILLY: Well, don't—don't talk to me that way! What does that mean, "What happened?"

(CHARLEY *enters. He is in his vest, and he carries a bottle of bourbon.*)

CHARLEY: Hey, you're going to miss that train. (*He waves the bottle.*)

BERNARD: Yeah, I'm going. (*He takes the bottle.*) Thanks, Pop. (*He picks up his rackets and bag.*) Good-by, Willy, and don't worry about it. You know, "If at first you don't succeed . . ."

WILLY: Yes, I believe in that.

BERNARD: But sometimes, Willy, it's better for a man just to walk away.

WILLY: Walk away?

BERNARD: That's right.

WILLY: But if you can't walk away?

BERNARD (*after a slight pause*): I guess that's when it's tough. (*Extending his hand.*) Good-by, Willy.

WILLY (*shaking* BERNARD's *hand*): Good-by, boy.

CHARLEY (*an arm on* BERNARD's *shoulder*): How do you like this kid? Gonna argue a case in front of the Supreme Court.

BERNARD (*protesting*): Pop!

WILLY (*genuinely shocked, pained, and happy*): No! The Supreme Court!

BERNARD: I gotta run. 'By, Dad!

CHARLEY: Knock 'em dead, Bernard!

(BERNARD *goes off.*)

WILLY (*as* CHARLEY *takes out his wallet*): The Supreme Court! And he didn't even mention it!

CHARLEY (*counting out money on the desk*): He don't have to—he's gonna do it.

WILLY: And you never told him what to do, did you? You never took any interest in him.

CHARLEY: My salvation is that I never took any interest in anything. There's some money—fifty dollars. I got an accountant inside.

WILLY: Charley, look . . . (*With difficulty.*) I got my insurance to pay. If you can manage it—I need a hundred and ten dollars.

(CHARLEY *doesn't reply for a moment; merely stops moving.*)

WILLY: I'd draw it from my bank but Linda would know, and I . . .

CHARLEY: Sit down, Willy.

WILLY (moving toward the chair): I'm keeping an account of everything, remember. I'll pay every penny back. (He sits.)

CHARLEY: Now listen to me, Willy.

WILLY: I want you to know I appreciate . . .

CHARLEY (sitting down on the table): Willy, what're you doin'? What the hell is goin' on in your head?

WILLY: Why? I'm simply . . .

CHARLEY: I offered you a job. You can make fifty dollars a week. And I won't send you on the road.

WILLY: I've got a job.

CHARLEY: Without pay? What kind of a job is a job without pay? (He rises.) Now, look, kid, enough is enough. I'm no genius but I know when I'm being insulted.

WILLY: Insulted!

CHARLEY: Why don't you want to work for me?

WILLY: What's the matter with you? I've got a job.

CHARLEY: Then what're you walkin' in here every week for?

WILLY (getting up): Well, if you don't want me to walk in here—

CHARLEY: I am offering you a job.

WILLY: I don't want your goddam job!

CHARLEY: When the hell are you going to grow up?

WILLY (furiously): You big ignoramus, if you say that to me again I'll rap you one! I don't care how big you are! (He's ready to fight.)

(Pause.)

CHARLEY (kindly, going to him): How much do you need, Willy?

WILLY: Charley, I'm strapped, I'm strapped. I don't know what to do. I was just fired.

CHARLEY: Howard fired you?

WILLY: That snotnose. Imagine that? I named him. I named him Howard.

CHARLEY: Willy, when're you gonna realize that them things don't mean anything? You named him Howard, but you can't sell that. The only thing you got in this world is what you can sell. And the funny thing is that you're a salesman, and you don't know that.

WILLY: I've always tried to think otherwise, I guess. I always felt that if a man was impressive, and well liked, that nothing—

CHARLEY: Why must everybody like you? Who liked J. P. Morgan? Was he impressive? In a Turkish bath he'd look like a butcher. But with his pockets on he was very well liked. Now listen, Willy, I know you don't like me, and nobody can say I'm in love with you, but I'll give you a job because—just for the hell of it, put it that way. Now what do you say?

WILLY: I—I just can't work for you, Charley.

CHARLEY: What're you, jealous of me?

WILLY: I can't work for you, that's all, don't ask me why.

CHARLEY (angered, takes out more bills): You been jealous of me all your life, you damned fool! Here, pay your insurance. (He puts the money in WILLY's hand.)

WILLY: I'm keeping strict accounts.

CHARLEY: I've got some work to do. Take care of yourself. And pay your insurance.

WILLY (moving to the right): Funny, y'know? After all the highways, and the trains, and the appointments, and the years, you end up worth more dead than alive.

CHARLEY: Willy, nobody's worth nothin' dead. (After a slight pause.) Did you hear what I said?

(WILLY stands still, dreaming.)

CHARLEY: Willy!

WILLY: Apologize to Bernard for me when you see him. I didn't mean to argue with him. He's a fine boy. They're all fine boys, and they'll end up big—all of them. Someday they'll all play tennis together. Wish me luck, Charley. He saw Bill Oliver today.

CHARLEY: Good luck.

WILLY (on the verge of tears): Charley, you're the only friend I got. Isn't that a remarkable thing? (He goes out.)

CHARLEY: Jesus!

(CHARLEY stares after him a moment and follows. All light blacks out. Suddenly raucous music is heard, and a red glow rises behind the screen at right. STANLEY, a young waiter, appears, carrying a table, followed by HAPPY, who is carrying two chairs.)

STANLEY (putting the table down): That's all right, Mr. Loman, I can handle it myself. (He turns and takes the chairs from HAPPY and places them at the table.)

HAPPY (glancing around): Oh, this is better.

STANLEY: Sure, in the front there you're in the middle of all kinds a noise. Whenever you got a party, Mr. Loman, you just tell me and I'll put you back here. Y'know, there's a lotta people they don't like it private, because when they go out they like to see a lotta action around them because they're sick and tired to stay in the house by theirself. But I know you, you ain't from Hackensack. You know what I mean?

HAPPY (sitting down): So how's it coming, Stanley?

STANLEY: Ah, it's a dog's life. I only wish during the war they'd a took me in the Army. I coulda been dead by now.

HAPPY: My brother's back, Stanley.

STANLEY: Oh, he come back, heh? From the Far West.

HAPPY: Yeah, big cattle man, my brother, so treat him right. And my father's coming too.

STANLEY: Oh, your father too!

HAPPY: You got a couple of nice lobsters?

STANLEY: Hundred per cent, big.

HAPPY: I want them with the claws.

STANLEY: Don't worry, I don't give you no mice. (HAPPY *laughs.*) How about some wine? It'll put a head on the meal.

HAPPY: No. You remember, Stanley, that recipe I brought you from overseas? With the champagne in it?

STANLEY: Oh, yeah, sure. I still got it tacked up yet in the kitchen. But that'll have to cost a buck apiece anyways.

HAPPY: That's all right.

STANLEY: What'd you, hit a number or somethin'?

HAPPY: No, it's a little celebration. My brother is—I think he pulled off a big deal today. I think we're going into business together.

STANLEY: Great! That's the best for you. Because a family business, you know what I mean?—that's the best.

HAPPY: That's what I think.

STANLEY: 'Cause what's the difference? Somebody steals? It's in the family. Know what I mean? (*Sotto voce.*) Like this bartender here. The boss is goin' crazy what kinda leak he's got in the cash register. You put it in but it don't come out.

HAPPY (*raising his head*): Sh!

STANLEY: What?

HAPPY: You notice I wasn't lookin' right or left, was I?

STANLEY: No.

HAPPY: And my eyes are closed.

STANLEY: So what's the—?

HAPPY: Strudel's comin'.

STANLEY (*catching on, looks around*): Ah, no, there's no—

(*He breaks off as a furred, lavishly dressed girl enters and sits at the next table. Both follow her with their eyes.*)

STANLEY: Geez, how d'ya know?

HAPPY: I got radar or something. (*Staring directly at her profile.*) Oooooooo . . . Stanley.

STANLEY: I think that's for you, Mr. Loman.

HAPPY: Look at that mouth. Oh, God. And the binoculars.

STANLEY: Geez, you got a life, Mr. Loman.

HAPPY: Wait on her.

STANLEY (*going to the girl's table*): Would you like a menu, ma'am?

GIRL: I'm expecting someone, but I'd like a—

HAPPY: Why don't you bring her—excuse me, miss, do you mind? I sell champagne, and I'd like you to try my brand. Bring her a champagne, Stanley.

GIRL: That's awfully nice of you.

HAPPY: Don't mention it. It's all company money. (*He laughs.*)

GIRL: That's a charming product to be selling, isn't it?

HAPPY: Oh, gets to be like everything else. Selling is selling, y'know.

GIRL: I suppose.

HAPPY: You don't happen to sell, do you?

GIRL: No, I don't sell.

HAPPY: Would you object to a compliment from a stranger? You ought to be on a magazine cover.

GIRL (*looking at him a little archly*): I have been.

(STANLEY *comes in with a glass of champagne.*)

HAPPY: What'd I say before, Stanley? You see? She's a cover girl.

STANLEY: Oh, I could see, I could see.

HAPPY (*to the* GIRL): What magazine?

GIRL: Oh, a lot of them. (*She takes the drink.*) Thank you.

HAPPY: You know what they say in France, don't you? "Champagne is the drink of the complexion"— Hya, Biff!

(BIFF *has entered and sits with* HAPPY.)

BIFF: Hello, kid. Sorry I'm late.

HAPPY: I just got here. Uh, Miss—?

GIRL: Forsythe.

HAPPY: Miss Forsythe, this is my brother.

BIFF: Is Dad here?

HAPPY: His name is Biff. You might've heard of him. Great football player.

GIRL: Really? What team?

HAPPY: Are you familiar with football?

GIRL: No, I'm afraid I'm not.

HAPPY: Biff is quarterback with the New York Giants.

GIRL: Well, that is nice, isn't it? (*She drinks.*)

HAPPY: Good health.

GIRL: I'm happy to meet you.

HAPPY: That's my name. Hap. It's really Harold, but at West Point they called me Happy.

GIRL (*now really impressed*): Oh, I see. How do you do? (*She turns her profile.*)

BIFF: Isn't Dad coming?

HAPPY: You want her?

BIFF: Oh, I could never make that.

HAPPY: I remember the time that idea would never come into your head. Where's the old confidence, Biff?

BIFF: I just saw Oliver—

HAPPY: Wait a minute. I've got to see that old confidence again. Do you want her? She's on call.

BIFF: Oh, no. (*He turns to look at the* GIRL.)

HAPPY: I'm telling you. Watch this. (*Turning to the* GIRL.) Honey? (*She turns to him.*) Are you busy?

GIRL: Well, I am . . . but I could make a phone call.

HAPPY: Do that, will you, honey? And see if you can get a friend. We'll be here for a while. Biff is one of the greatest football players in the country.

GIRL (*standing up*): Well, I'm certainly happy to meet you.

HAPPY: Come back soon.

GIRL: I'll try.

HAPPY: Don't try, honey, try hard.

(*The* GIRL *exits.* STANLEY *follows, shaking his head in bewildered admiration.*)

HAPPY: Isn't that a shame now? A beautiful girl like that? That's why I can't get married. There's not a good woman in a thousand. New York is loaded with them, kid!

BIFF: Hap, look—

HAPPY: I told you she was on call!

BIFF (*strangely unnerved*): Cut it out, will ya? I want to say something to you.

HAPPY: Did you see Oliver?

BIFF: I saw him all right. Now look, I want to tell Dad a couple of things and I want you to help me.

HAPPY: What? Is he going to back you?

BIFF: Are you crazy? You're out of your goddam head, you know that?

HAPPY: Why? What happened?

BIFF (*breathlessly*): I did a terrible thing today, Hap. It's been the strangest day I ever went through. I'm all numb, I swear.

HAPPY: You mean he wouldn't see you?

BIFF: Well, I waited six hours for him, see? All day. Kept sending my name in. Even tried to date his secretary so she'd get me to him, but no soap.

HAPPY: Because you're not showin' the old confidence, Biff. He remembered you, didn't he?

BIFF (*stopping* HAPPY *with a gesture*): Finally, about five o'clock, he comes out. Didn't remember who I was or anything. I felt like such an idiot, Hap.

HAPPY: Did you tell him my Florida idea?

BIFF: He walked away. I saw him for one minute. I got so mad I could've torn the walls down! How the hell did I ever get the idea I was a salesman there? I even believed myself that I'd been a salesman for him! And then he gave me one look and—I realized what a ridiculous lie my whole life has been! We've been talking in a dream for fifteen years. I was a shipping clerk.

HAPPY: What'd you do?

BIFF (*with great tension and wonder*): Well, he left, see. And the secretary went out. I was all alone in the waiting-room. I don't know what came over me, Hap. The next thing I know I'm in his office—paneled walls, everything. I can't explain it. I—Hap, I took his fountain pen.

HAPPY: Geez, did he catch you?

BIFF: I ran out. I ran down all eleven flights. I ran and ran and ran.

HAPPY: That was an awful dumb—what'd you do that for?

BIFF (*agonized*): I don't know, I just—wanted to take something, I don't know. You gotta help me, Hap, I'm gonna tell Pop.

HAPPY: You crazy? What for?

BIFF: Hap, he's got to understand that I'm not the man somebody lends that kind of money to. He thinks I've been spiting him all these years and it's eating him up.

HAPPY: That's just it. You tell him something nice.

BIFF: I can't.

HAPPY: Say you got a lunch date with Oliver tomorrow.

BIFF: So what do I do tomorrow?

HAPPY: You leave the house tomorrow and come back at night and say Oliver is thinking it over. And he thinks it over for a couple of weeks, and gradually it fades away and nobody's the worse.

BIFF: But it'll go on forever!

HAPPY: Dad is never so happy as when he's looking forward to something!

(WILLY *enters.*)

HAPPY: Hello, scout!

WILLY: Gee, I haven't been here in years!

(STANLEY *has followed* WILLY *in and sets a chair for him.* STANLEY *starts off but* HAPPY *stops him.*)

HAPPY: Stanley!

(STANLEY *stands by, waiting for an order.*)

BIFF (*going to* WILLY *with guilt, as to an invalid*): Sit down, Pop. You want a drink?

WILLY: Sure, I don't mind.

BIFF: Let's get a load on.

WILLY: You look worried.

BIFF: N-no. (*to* STANLEY) Scotch all around. Make it doubles.

STANLEY: Doubles, right. (*He goes.*)

WILLY: You had a couple already, didn't you?

BIFF: Just a couple, yeah.

WILLY: Well, what happened, boy? (*Nodding affirmatively, with a smile.*) Everything go all right?

BIFF (*takes a breath, then reaches out and grasps* WILLY*'s hand*): Pal . . . (*He is smiling bravely, and* WILLY *is smiling too.*) I had an experience today.

HAPPY: Terrific, Pop.

WILLY: That so? What happened?

BIFF (*high, slightly alcoholic, above the earth*): I'm going to tell you everything from first to last. It's been a strange day. (*Silence. He looks around, composes himself as best he can, but his breath keeps breaking the rhythm of his voice.*) I had to wait quite a while for him, and—

WILLY: Oliver?

BIFF: Yeah, Oliver. All day, as a matter of cold fact. And a lot of—instances—facts, Pop, facts about my life came back to me. Who was it, Pop? Who ever said I was a salesman with Oliver?

WILLY: Well, you were.

BIFF: No, Dad, I was a shipping clerk.

WILLY: But you were practically—

BIFF (*with determination*): Dad, I don't know who said it first, but I was never a salesman for Bill Oliver.

WILLY: What're you talking about?

BIFF: Let's hold on to the facts tonight, Pop. We're not going to get anywhere bullin' around. I was a shipping clerk.

WILLY (*angrily*): All right, now listen to me—

BIFF: Why don't you let me finish?

WILLY: I'm not interested in stories about the past or any crap of that kind because the woods are burning, boys, you understand? There's a big blaze going on all around. I was fired today.

BIFF (*shocked*): How could you be?

WILLY: I was fired, and I'm looking for a little good news to tell your mother, because the woman has waited and the woman has suffered. The gist of it is that I haven't got a story left in my head, Biff. So don't give me a lecture about facts and aspects. I am not interested. Now what've you got to say to me?

(STANLEY *enters with three drinks. They wait until he leaves.*)

WILLY: Did you see Oliver?

BIFF: Jesus, Dad!

WILLY: You mean you didn't go up there?

HAPPY: Sure he went up there.

BIFF: I did. I—saw him. How could they fire you?

WILLY (*on the edge of his chair*): What kind of a welcome did he give you?

BIFF: He won't even let you work on commission?

WILLY: I'm out! (*Driving.*) So tell me, he gave you a warm welcome?

HAPPY: Sure, Pop, sure!

BIFF (*driven*): Well, it was kind of—

WILLY: I was wondering if he'd remember you. (*to* HAPPY.) Imagine, man doesn't see him for ten, twelve years, and gives him that kind of a welcome!

HAPPY: Damn right!

BIFF (*trying to return to the offensive*): Pop, look—

WILLY: You know why he remembered you, don't you? Because you impressed him in those days.

BIFF: Let's talk quietly and get this down to the facts, huh?

WILLY (*as though* BIFF *had been interrupting*): Well, what happened? It's great news, Biff. Did he take you into his office or'd you talk in the waiting-room?

BIFF: Well, he came in, see, and—

WILLY (*with a big smile*): What'd he say? Betcha he threw his arm around you.

BIFF: Well, he kinda—

WILLY: He's a fine man. (*to* HAPPY.) Very hard man to see, y'know.

HAPPY (*agreeing*): Oh, I know.

WILLY (*to* BIFF): Is that where you had the drinks?

BIFF: Yeah, he gave me a couple of—no, no!

HAPPY (*cutting in*): He told him my Florida idea.

WILLY: Don't interrupt. (*to* BIFF) How'd he react to the Florida idea?

BIFF: Dad, will you give me a minute to explain?

WILLY: I've been waiting for you to explain since I sat down here! What happened? He took you into his office and what?

BIFF: Well—I talked. And—and he listened, see.

WILLY: Famous for the way he listens, y'know. What was his answer?

BIFF: His answer was—(*He breaks off, suddenly angry.*) Dad, you're not letting me tell you what I want to tell you!

WILLY (*accusing, angered*): You didn't see him, did you?

BIFF: I did see him!

WILLY: What'd you insult him or something? You insulted him, didn't you?

BIFF: Listen, will you let me out of it, will you just let me out of it!

HAPPY: What the hell!

WILLY: Tell me what happened!

BIFF (*to* HAPPY): I can't talk to him!

(*A single trumpet note jars the ear. The light of green leaves stains the house, which holds the air of night and a dream.* YOUNG BERNARD *enters and knocks on the door of the house.*)

YOUNG BERNARD (*frantically*): Mrs. Loman, Mrs. Loman!

HAPPY: Tell him what happened!

BIFF (*to* HAPPY): Shut up and leave me alone!

WILLY: No, no! You had to go and flunk math!

BIFF: What math? What're you talking about?

YOUNG BERNARD: Mrs. Loman, Mrs. Loman!

(LINDA *appears in the house, as of old.*)

WILLY (*wildly*): Math, math, math!

BIFF: Take it easy, Pop!

YOUNG BERNARD: Mrs. Loman!

WILLY (*furiously*): If you hadn't flunked you'd've been set by now!

BIFF: Now, look, I'm gonna tell you what happened, and you're going to listen to me.

YOUNG BERNARD: Mrs. Loman!

BIFF: I waited six hours—

HAPPY: What the hell are you saying?

BIFF: I kept sending in my name but he wouldn't see me. So finally he . . . (*He continues unheard as light fades low on the restaurant.*)

YOUNG BERNARD: Biff flunked math!

LINDA: No!

YOUNG BERNARD: Birnbaum flunked him! They won't graduate him!

LINDA: But they have to. He's gotta go to the university. Where is he? Biff! Biff!

YOUNG BERNARD: No, he left. He went to Grand Central.

LINDA: Grand—You mean he went to Boston!

YOUNG BERNARD: Is Uncle Willy in Boston?

LINDA: Oh, maybe Willy can talk to the teacher. Oh, the poor, poor boy!

(Light on house area snaps out.)

BIFF *(at the table, now audible, holding up a gold fountain pen)*: . . . so I'm washed up with Oliver, you understand? Are you listening to me?

WILLY *(at a loss)*: Yeah, sure. If you hadn't flunked—

BIFF: Flunked what? What're you talking about?

WILLY: Don't blame everything on me! I didn't flunk math—you did! What pen?

HAPPY: That was awful dumb, Biff, a pen like that is worth—

WILLY *(seeing the pen for the first time)*: You took Oliver's pen?

BIFF *(weakening)*: Dad, I just explained it to you.

WILLY: You stole Bill Oliver's fountain pen!

BIFF: I didn't exactly steal it! That's just what I've been explaining to you!

HAPPY: He had it in his hand and just then Oliver walked in, so he got nervous and stuck it in his pocket!

WILLY: My God, Biff!

BIFF: I never intended to do it, Dad!

OPERATOR'S VOICE: Standish Arms, good evening!

WILLY *(shouting)*: I'm not in my room!

BIFF *(frightened)*: Dad, what's the matter? *(He and* HAPPY *stand up.)*

OPERATOR: Ringing Mr. Loman for you!

WILLY: I'm not there, stop it!

BIFF *(horrified, gets down on one knee before* WILLY*)*: Dad, I'll make good, I'll make good. *(*WILLY *tries to get to his feet.* BIFF *holds him down.)* Sit down now.

WILLY: No, you're no good, you're no good for anything.

BIFF: I am, Dad, I'll find something else, you understand? Now don't worry about anything. *(He holds up* WILLY*'s face.)* Talk to me, Dad.

OPERATOR: Mr. Loman does not answer. Shall I page him.

WILLY *(attempting to stand, as though to rush and silence the* OPERATOR*)*: No, no, no!

HAPPY: He'll strike something, Pop.

WILLY: No, no . . .

BIFF *(desperately, standing over* WILLY*)*: Pop, listen! Listen to me! I'm telling you something good. Oliver talked to his partner about the Florida idea. You listening? He—he talked to his partner, and he came to me . . . I'm going to be all right, you hear? Dad, listen to me, he said it was just a question of the amount!

WILLY: Then you . . . got it?

HAPPY: He's gonna be terrific, Pop!

WILLY *(trying to stand)*: Then you got it, haven't you? You got it! You got it!

BIFF *(agonized, holds* WILLY *down)*: No, no. Look, Pop. I'm supposed to have lunch with them tomorrow. I'm just telling you this so you'll know that I can still make an impression, Pop. And I'll make good somewhere, but I can't go tomorrow, see?

WILLY: Why not? You simply—

BIFF: But the pen, Pop!

WILLY: You give it to him and tell him it was an oversight!

HAPPY: Sure, have lunch tomorrow!

BIFF: I can't say that—

WILLY: You were doing a crossword puzzle and accidentally used his pen!

BIFF: Listen, kid, I took those balls years ago, now I walk in with his fountain pen? That clinches it, don't you see? I can't face him like that! I'll try elsewhere.

PAGE'S VOICE: Paging Mr. Loman!

WILLY: Don't you want to be anything?

BIFF: Pop, how can I go back?

WILLY: You don't want to be anything, is that what's behind it?

BIFF *(now angry at* WILLY *for not crediting his sympathy)*: Don't take it that way! You think it was easy walking into that office after what I'd done to him? A team of horses couldn't have dragged me back to Bill Oliver!

WILLY: Then why'd you go?

BIFF: Why did I go? Why did I go! Look at you! Look at what's become of you!

(Off left, THE WOMAN *laughs.)*

WILLY: Biff, you're going to go to that lunch tomorrow, or—

BIFF: I can't go. I've got no appointment!

HAPPY: Biff, for. . . !

WILLY: Are you spiting me?

BIFF: Don't take it that way! Goddammit!

WILLY *(strikes* BIFF *and falters away from the table)*: You rotten little louse! Are you spiting me?

THE WOMAN: Someone's at the door, Willy!

BIFF: I'm no good, can't you see what I am?

HAPPY *(separating them)*: Hey, you're in a restaurant! Now cut it out, both of you! *(The* GIRLS *enter.)* Hello, girls, sit down.

*(*THE WOMAN *laughs, off left.)*

MISS FORSYTHE: I guess we might as well. This is Letta.

THE WOMAN: Willy, are you going to wake up?

BIFF *(ignoring* WILLY*)*: How're ya, miss, sit down. What do you drink?

MISS FORSYTHE: Letta might not be able to stay long.

LETTA: I gotta get up very early tomorrow. I got jury duty. I'm so excited! Were you fellows ever on a jury?

BIFF: No, but I been in front of them! *(The* GIRLS *laugh.)* This is my father.

LETTA: Isn't he cute? Sit down with us, Pop.

HAPPY: Sit him down, Biff!

BIFF (*going to him*): Come on, slugger, drink us under the table. To hell with it! Come on, sit down, pal.

(*On* BIFF's *last insistence,* WILLY *is about to sit.*)

THE WOMAN (*now urgently*): Willy, are you going to answer the door!

(THE WOMAN's *call pulls* WILLY *back. He starts right, befuddled.*)

BIFF: Hey, where are you going?

WILLY: Open the door.

BIFF: The door?

WILLY: The washroom . . . the door . . . where's the door?

BIFF (*leading* WILLY *to the left*): Just go straight down.

(WILLY *moves left.*)

THE WOMAN: Willy, Willy, are you going to get up, get up, get up, get up?

(WILLY *exits left.*)

LETTA: I think it's sweet you bring your daddy along.

MISS FORSYTHE: Oh, he isn't really your father!

BIFF (*at left, turning to her resentfully*): Miss Forsythe, you've just seen a prince walk by. A fine, troubled prince. A hard-working, unappreciated prince. A pal, you understand? A good companion. Always for his boys.

LETTA: That's so sweet.

HAPPY: Well, girls, what's the program? We're wasting time. Come on, Biff. Gather round. Where would you like to go?

BIFF: Why don't you do something for him?

HAPPY: Me!

BIFF: Don't you give a damn for him, Hap?

HAPPY: What're you talking about? I'm the one who—

BIFF: I sense it, you don't give a good goddam about him. (*He takes the rolled-up hose from his pocket and puts it on the table in front of* HAPPY.) Look what I found in the cellar, for Christ's sake. How can you bear to let it go on?

HAPPY: Me? Who goes away? Who runs off and—

BIFF: Yeah, but he doesn't mean anything to you. You could help him—I can't! Don't you understand what I'm talking about? He's going to kill himself, don't you know that?

HAPPY: Don't I know it! Me!

BIFF: Hap, help him! Jesus . . . help him . . . Help me, help me, I can't bear to look at his face! (*Ready to weep, he hurries out, up right.*)

HAPPY (*starting after him*): Where are you going?

MISS FORSYTHE: What's he so mad about?

HAPPY: Come on, girls, we'll catch up with him.

MISS FORSYTHE (*as* HAPPY *pushes her out*): Say, I don't like that temper of his!

HAPPY: He's just a little overstrung, he'll be all right!

WILLY (*off left, as* THE WOMAN *laughs*): Don't answer! Don't answer!

LETTA: Don't you want to tell your father—

HAPPY: No, that's not my father. He's just a guy. Come on, we'll catch Biff, and, honey, we're going to paint this town! Stanley, where's the check! Hey, Stanley!

(*They exit.* STANLEY *looks toward left.*)

STANLEY (*calling to* HAPPY *indignantly*): Mr. Loman! Mr. Loman!

(STANLEY *picks up a chair and follows them off. Knocking is heard off left.* THE WOMAN *enters, laughing.* WILLY *follows her. She is in a black slip, he is buttoning his shirt. Raw, sensuous music accompanies their speech.*)

WILLY: Will you stop laughing? Will you stop?

THE WOMAN: Aren't you going to answer the door? He'll wake the whole hotel.

WILLY: I'm not expecting anybody.

THE WOMAN: Whyn't you have another drink, honey, and stop being so damn self-centered?

WILLY: I'm so lonely.

THE WOMAN: You know you ruined me, Willy? From now on, whenever you come to the office, I'll see that you go right through to the buyers. No waiting at my desk any more, Willy. You ruined me.

WILLY: That's nice of you to say that.

THE WOMAN: Gee, you are self-centered! Why so sad? You are the saddest, self-centeredest soul I ever did see-saw. (*She laughs. He kisses her.*) Come on inside, drummer boy. It's silly to be dressing in the middle of the night. (*As knocking is heard.*) Aren't you going to answer the door?

WILLY: They're knocking on the wrong door.

THE WOMAN: But I felt the knocking. And he heard us talking in here. Maybe the hotel's on fire!

WILLY (*his terror rising*): It's a mistake.

THE WOMAN: Then tell him to go away!

WILLY: There's nobody there.

THE WOMAN: It's getting on my nerves, Willy. There's somebody standing out there and it's getting on my nerves!

WILLY (*pushing her away from him*): All right, stay in the bathroom here, and don't come out. I think there's a law in Massachusetts about it, so don't come out. It may be that new room clerk. He looked very mean. So don't come out. It's a mistake, there's no fire.

(*The knocking is heard again. He takes a few steps away from her, and she vanishes into the wing. The light follows him, and now he is facing* YOUNG BIFF, *who carries a suitcase.* BIFF *steps toward him. The music is gone.*)

BIFF: Why didn't you answer?

WILLY: Biff! What are you doing in Boston?

BIFF: Why didn't you answer? I've been knocking for five minutes, I called you on the phone—

WILLY: I just heard you. I was in the bathroom and had the door shut. Did anything happen home?

BIFF: Dad—I let you down.

WILLY: What do you mean?

BIFF: Dad . . .

WILLY: Biffo, what's this about? *(Putting his arm around* BIFF.*)* Come on, let's go downstairs and get you a malted.

BIFF: Dad, I flunked math.

WILLY: Not for the term?

BIFF: The term. I haven't got enough credits to graduate.

WILLY: You mean to say Bernard wouldn't give you the answers?

BIFF: He did, he tried, but I only got a sixty-one.

WILLY: And they wouldn't give you four points?

BIFF: Birnbaum refused absolutely. I begged him, Pop, but he won't give me those points. You gotta talk to him before they close the school. Because if he saw the kind of man you are, and you just talked to him in your way, I'm sure he'd come through for me. The class came right before practice, see, and I didn't go enough. Would you talk to him? He'd like you, Pop. You know the way you could talk.

WILLY: You're on. We'll drive right back.

BIFF: Oh, Dad, good work! I'm sure he'll change it for you!

WILLY: Go downstairs and tell the clerk I'm checkin' out. Go right down.

BIFF: Yes, sir! See, the reason he hates me, Pop—one day he was late for class so I got up at the blackboard and imitated him. I crossed my eyes and talked with a lithp.

WILLY *(laughing)*: You did? The kids like it?

BIFF: They nearly died laughing!

WILLY: Yeah? What'd you do?

BIFF: The thquare root of thixthy twee is . . . *(*WILLY *bursts out laughing;* BIFF *joins him.)* And in the middle of it he walked in!

*(*WILLY *laughs and* THE WOMAN *joins in offstage.)*

WILLY *(without hesitation)*: Hurry downstairs and—

BIFF: Somebody in there?

WILLY: No, that was next door.

*(*THE WOMAN *laughs offstage.)*

BIFF: Somebody got in your bathroom!

WILLY: No, it's the next room, there's a party—

THE WOMAN *(enters, laughing. She lisps this)*: Can I come in? There's something in the bathtub, Willy, and it's moving!

*(*WILLY *looks at* BIFF, *who is staring open-mouthed and horrified at* THE WOMAN.*)*

WILLY: Ah—you better go back to your room. They must be finished painting by now. They're painting her room so I let her take a shower here. Go back, go back . . . *(He pushes her.)*

THE WOMAN *(resisting)*: But I've got to get dressed Willy, I can't—

WILLY: Get out of here! Go back, go back . . . *(Suddenly striving for the ordinary.)* This is Miss Francis, Biff, she's a buyer. They're painting her room. Go back, Miss Francis, go back . . .

THE WOMAN: But my clothes, I can't go out naked in the hall!

WILLY *(pushing her offstage)*: Get outa here! Go back, go back!

*(*BIFF *slowly sits down on his suitcase as the argument continues offstage.)*

THE WOMAN: Where's my stockings? You promised me stockings, Willy!

WILLY: I have no stockings here!

THE WOMAN: You had two boxes of size nine sheers for me, and I want them!

WILLY: Here, for God's sake, will you get outa here!

THE WOMAN *(enters holding a box of stockings)*: I just hope there's nobody in the hall. That's all I hope. *(to* BIFF*)* Are you football or baseball?

BIFF: Football.

THE WOMAN *(angry, humiliated)*: That's me too. G'night. *(She snatches her clothes from* WILLY, *and walks out.)*

WILLY *(after a pause)*: Well, better get going. I want to get to the school first thing in the morning. Get my suits out of the closet. I'll get my valise. *(*BIFF *doesn't move.)* What's the matter? *(*BIFF *remains motionless, tears falling.)* She's a buyer. Buys for J. H. Simmons. She lives down the hall—they're painting. You don't imagine—*(He breaks off. After a pause.)* Now listen, pal, she's just a buyer. She sees merchandise in her room and they have to keep it looking just so . . . *(Pause. Assuming command.)* All right, get my suits. *(*BIFF *doesn't move.)* Now stop crying and do as I say. I gave you an order. Biff, I gave you an order! Is that what you do when I give you an order? How dare you cry! *(Putting his arm around* BIFF.*)* Now look, Biff, when you grow up you'll understand about these things. You mustn't—you mustn't overemphasize a thing like this. I'll see Birnbaum first thing in the morning.

BIFF: Never mind.

WILLY *(getting down beside* BIFF*)*: Never mind! He's going to give you those points. I'll see to it.

BIFF: He wouldn't listen to you.

WILLY: He certainly will listen to me. You need those points for the U. of Virginia.

BIFF: I'm not going there.

WILLY: Heh? If I can't get him to change that mark you'll make it up in summer school. You've got all summer to—

BIFF (*his weeping breaking from him*): Dad . . .

WILLY (*infected by it*): Oh, my boy . . .

BIFF: Dad . . .

WILLY: She's nothing to me, Biff. I was lonely, I was terribly lonely.

BIFF: You—you gave her Mama's stockings! (*His tears break through and he rises to go.*)

WILLY (*grabbing for* BIFF): I gave you an order!

BIFF: Don't touch me, you—liar!

WILLY: Apologize for that!

BIFF: You fake! You phony little fake! You fake! (*Overcome, he turns quickly and weeping fully goes out with his suitcase.* WILLY *is left on the floor on his knees.*)

WILLY: I gave you an order! Biff, come back here or I'll beat you! Come back here! I'll whip you!

(STANLEY *comes quickly in from the right and stands in front of* WILLY.)

WILLY (*shouts at* STANLEY): I gave you an order . . .

STANLEY: Hey, let's pick it up, pick it up, Mr. Loman. (*He helps* WILLY *to his feet.*) Your boys left with the chippies. They said they'll see you home.

(*A second waiter watches some distance away.*)

WILLY: But we were supposed to have dinner together.

(*Music is heard,* WILLY's *theme.*)

STANLEY: Can you make it?

WILLY: I'll—sure, I can make it. (*Suddenly concerned about his clothes.*) Do I—I look all right?

STANLEY: Sure, you look all right. (*He flicks a speck off* WILLY's *lapel.*)

WILLY: Here—here's a dollar.

STANLEY: Oh, your son paid me. It's all right.

WILLY (*putting it in* STANLEY's *hand*): No, take it. You're a good boy.

STANLEY: Oh, no, you don't have to . . .

WILLY: Here—here's some more, I don't need it any more. (*After a slight pause.*) Tell me—is there a seed store in the neighborhood?

STANLEY: Seeds? You mean like to plant?

(*As* WILLY *turns,* STANLEY *slips the money back into his jacket pocket.*)

WILLY: Yes. Carrots, peas . . .

STANLEY: Well, there's hardware stores on Sixth Avenue, but it may be too late now.

WILLY (*anxiously*): Oh, I'd better hurry. I've got to get some seeds. (*He starts off to the right.*) I've got to get some seeds, right away. Nothing's planted. I don't have a thing in the ground.

(WILLY *hurries out as the light goes down.* STANLEY *moves over to the right after him, watches him off. The other waiter has been staring at* WILLY.)

STANLEY (*to the waiter*): Well, whatta you looking at?

(*The waiter picks up the chairs and moves off right. Stanley takes the table and follows him. The light fades on this area. There is a long pause, the sound of the flute coming over. The light gradually rises on the kitchen, which is empty.* HAPPY *appears at the door of the house, followed by* BIFF. HAPPY *is carrying a large bunch of long-stemmed roses. He enters the kitchen, looks around for* LINDA. *Not seeing her, he turns to* BIFF, *who is just outside the house door, and makes a gesture with his hands, indicating "Not here, I guess." He looks into the living-room and freezes. Inside,* LINDA, *unseen, is seated,* WILLY's *coat on her lap. She rises ominously and quietly and moves toward* HAPPY, *who backs up into the kitchen, afraid.*)

HAPPY: Hey, what're you doing up? (LINDA *says nothing but moves toward him implacably.*) Where's Pop? (*He keeps backing to the right, and now* LINDA *is in full view in the doorway to the living-room.*) Is he sleeping?

LINDA: Where were you?

HAPPY (*trying to laugh it off*): We met two girls, Mom, very fine types. Here, we brought you some flowers. (*Offering them to her.*) Put them in your room, Ma.

(*She knocks them to the floor at* BIFF's *feet. He has now come inside and closed the door behind him. She stares at* BIFF, *silent.*)

HAPPY: Now, what'd you do that for? Mom, I want you to have some flowers—

LINDA (*cutting* HAPPY *off, violently to* BIFF): Don't you care whether he lives or dies?

HAPPY (*going to the stairs*): Come upstairs, Biff.

BIFF (*with a flare of disgust, to* HAPPY): Go away from me! (*to* LINDA) What do you mean, lives or dies? Nobody's dying around here, pal.

LINDA: Get out of my sight! Get out of here!

BIFF: I wanna see the boss.

LINDA: You're not going near him!

BIFF: Where is he? (*He moves into the living-room and* LINDA *follows.*)

LINDA (*shouting after* BIFF): You invite him for dinner. He looks forward to it all day—(BIFF *appears in his parents' bedroom, looks around, and exits.*)—and then you desert him there. There's no stranger you'd do that to!

HAPPY: Why? He had a swell time with us. Listen, When I—(LINDA *comes back into the kitchen.*)—desert him I hope I don't outlive the day!

LINDA: Get out of here!

HAPPY: Now look, Mom . . .

LINDA: Did you have to go to women tonight? You and your lousy rotten whores!

(BIFF *re-enters the kitchen.*)

HAPPY: Mom, all we did was follow Biff around trying to cheer him up! (*To* BIFF) Boy, what a night you gave me!

LINDA: Get out of here, both of you, and don't come back! I don't want you tormenting him any more. Go on now, get your things together! *(to* BIFF*)* You can sleep in his apartment. *(She starts to pick up the flowers and stops herself.)* Pick up this stuff, I'm not your maid any more. Pick it up, you bum, you!

*(*HAPPY *turns his back to her in refusal.* BIFF *slowly moves over and gets down on his knees, picking up the flowers.)*

LINDA: You're a pair of animals! No one, not another living soul would have had the cruelty to walk out on that man in a restaurant!

BIFF *(not looking at her)*: Is that what he said?

LINDA: He didn't have to say anything. He was so humiliated he nearly limped when he came in.

HAPPY: But, Mom, he had a great time with us—

BIFF *(cutting him off violently)*: Shut up!

(Without another word, HAPPY *goes upstairs.)*

LINDA: You! You didn't even go in to see if he was all right!

BIFF *(still on the floor in front of* LINDA, *the flowers in his hand; with self-loathing)*: No. Didn't. Didn't do a damned thing. How do you like that, heh? Left him babbling in a toilet.

LINDA: You louse. You . . .

BIFF: Now you hit it on the nose! *(He gets up, throws the flowers in the wastebasket).* The scum of the earth, and you're looking at him!

LINDA: Get out of here!

BIFF: I gotta talk to the boss, Mom. Where is he?

LINDA: You're not going near him. Get out of this house!

BIFF *(with absolute assurance, determination)*: No. We're gonna have an abrupt conversation, him and me.

LINDA: You're not talking to him!

(Hammering is heard from outside the house, off right. BIFF *turns toward the noise.)*

LINDA *(suddenly pleading)*: Will you please leave him alone?

BIFF: What's he doing out there?

LINDA: He's planting the garden!

BIFF *(quietly)*: Now? Oh, my God!

*(*BIFF *moves outside,* LINDA *following. The light dies down on them and comes up on the center of the apron as* WILLY *walks into it. He is carrying a flashlight, a hoe, and a handful of seed packets. He raps the top of the hoe sharply to fix it firmly, and then moves to the left, measuring off the distance with his foot. He holds the flashlight to look at the seed packets, reading off the instructions. He is in the blue of night.)*

WILLY: Carrots . . . quarter-inch apart. Rows . . . one-foot rows. *(He measures it off.)* One foot. *(He puts down a package and measures off.)* Beets. *(He puts down another package and measures again.)* Lettuce.

(He reads the package, puts it down.) One foot—*(He breaks off as* BEN *appears at the right and moves slowly down to him.)* What a proposition, ts, ts. Terrific, terrific. 'Cause she's suffered, Ben, the woman has suffered. You understand me? A man can't go out the way he came in, Ben, a man has got to add up to something. You can't, you can't—*(*BEN *moves toward him as though to interrupt.)* You gotta consider, now. Don't answer so quick. Remember, it's a guaranteed twenty-thousand-dollar proposition. Now look, Ben, I want you to go through the ins and outs of this thing with me. I've got nobody to talk to, Ben, and the woman has suffered, you hear me?

BEN *(standing still, considering)*: What's the proposition?

WILLY: It's twenty thousand dollars on the barrelhead. Guaranteed, gilt-edged, you understand?

BEN: You don't want to make a fool of yourself. They might not honor the policy.

WILLY: How can they dare refuse? Didn't I work like a coolie to meet every premium on the nose? And now they don't pay off? Impossible!

BEN: It's called a cowardly thing, William.

WILLY: Why? Does it take more guts to stand here the rest of my life ringing up a zero?

BEN *(yielding)*: That's a point, William. *(He moves, thinking, turns.)* And twenty thousand—that *is* something one can feel with the hand, it is there.

WILLY *(now assured, with rising power)*: Oh, Ben, that's the whole beauty of it! I see it like a diamond, shining in the dark, hard and rough, that I can pick up and touch in my hand. Not like—like an appointment! This would not be another damned-fool appointment, Ben, and it changes all the aspects. Because he thinks I'm nothing, see, and so he spites me. But the funeral—*(Straightening up.)* Ben, that funeral will be massive! They'll come from Maine, Massachusetts, Vermont, New Hampshire! All the old-timers with the strange license plates—that boy will be thunder-struck, Ben, because he never realized—I am known! Rhode Island, New York, New Jersey—I am known, Ben, and he'll see it with his eyes once and for all. He'll see what I am, Ben! He's in for a shock, that boy!

BEN *(coming down to the edge of the garden)*: He'll call you a coward.

WILLY *(suddenly fearful)*: No, that would be terrible.

BEN: Yes. And a damned fool.

WILLY: No, no, he mustn't, I won't have that! *(He is broken and desperate.)*

BEN: He'll hate you, William.

(The gay music of the BOYS *is heard.)*

WILLY: Oh, Ben, how do we get back to all the great times? Used to be so full of light, and comradeship, the sleigh-riding in winter, and the ruddiness on his cheeks. And always some kind of good news coming up, always something nice coming up ahead. And never even let me carry the valises in the house, and simonizing, simonizing that little red car! Why, why can't I give him something and not have him hate me?

BEN: Let me think about it. (*He glances at his watch.*) I still have a little time. Remarkable proposition, but you've got to be sure you're not making a fool of yourself.

(BEN *drifts off upstage and goes out of sight.* BIFF *comes down from the left.*)

WILLY (*suddenly conscious of* BIFF, *turns and looks up at him, then begins picking up the packages of seeds in confusion*): Where the hell is that seed? (*Indignantly*) You can't see nothing out here! They boxed in the whole goddam neighborhood!

BIFF: There are people all around here. Don't you realize that?

WILLY: I'm busy. Don't bother me.

BIFF (*taking the hoe from* WILLY): I'm saying good-by to you, Pop. (WILLY *looks at him, silent, unable to move.*) I'm not coming back any more.

WILLY: You're not going to see Oliver tomorrow?

BIFF: I've got no appointment, Dad.

WILLY: He put his arm around you, and you've got no appointment?

BIFF: Pop, get this now, will you? Everytime I've left it's been a fight that sent me out of here. Today I realized something about myself and I tried to explain it to you and I—I think I'm just not smart enough to make any sense out of it for you. To hell with whose fault it is or anything like that. (*He takes* WILLY's *arm.*) Let's just wrap it up, heh? Come on in, we'll tell Mom. (*He gently tries to pull* WILLY *to left.*)

WILLY (*frozen, immobile, with guilt in his voice*): No, I don't want to see her.

BIFF: Come on! (*He pulls again, and* WILLY *tries to pull away.*)

WILLY (*highly nervous*): No, no, I don't want to face her.

BIFF (*tries to look into* WILLY's *face, as if to find the answer there*): Why don't you want to see her?

WILLY (*more harshly now*): Don't bother me, will you?

BIFF: What do you mean, you don't want to see her? You don't want them calling you yellow, do you? This isn't your fault; it's me, I'm a bum. Now come inside! (WILLY *strains to get away.*) Did you hear what I said to you?

(WILLY *pulls away and quickly goes by himself into the house.* BIFF *follows.*)

LINDA (*to* WILLY): Did you plant, dear?

BIFF (*at the door, to* LINDA): All right, we had it out. I'm going and I'm not writing any more.

LINDA (*going to* WILLY *in the kitchen*): I think that's the best way, dear. 'Cause there's no use drawing it out, you'll just never get along.

(WILLY *doesn't respond.*)

BIFF: People ask where I am and what I'm doing, you don't know, and you don't care. That way it'll be off your mind and you can start brightening up again. All right? That clears it, doesn't it? (WILLY *is silent, and* BIFF *goes to him.*) You gonna wish me luck, scout? (*He extends his hand.*) What do you say?

LINDA: Shake his hand, Willy.

WILLY (*turning to her, seething with hurt*): There's no necessity to mention the pen at all, y'know.

BIFF (*gently*): I've got no appointment, Dad.

WILLY (*erupting fiercely*): He put his arm around . . . ?

BIFF: Dad, you're never going to see what I am, so what's the use of arguing? If I strike oil I'll send you a check. Meantime forget I'm alive.

WILLY (*to* LINDA): Spite, see?

BIFF: Shake hands, Dad.

WILLY: Not my hand.

BIFF: I was hoping not to go this way.

WILLY: Well, this is the way you're going. Good-by.

(BIFF *looks at him a moment, then turns sharply and goes to the stairs.*)

WILLY (*stops him with*): May you rot in hell if you leave this house!

BIFF (*turning*): Exactly what is it that you want from me?

WILLY: I want you to know, on the train, in the mountains, in the valleys, wherever you go, that you cut down your life for spite!

BIFF: No, no.

WILLY: Spite, spite, is the word of your undoing! And when you're down and out, remember what did it. When you're rotting somewhere beside the railroad tracks, remember, and don't you dare blame it on me!

BIFF: I'm not blaming it on you!

WILLY: I won't take the rap for this, you hear?

(HAPPY *comes down the stairs and stands on the bottom step, watching.*)

BIFF: That's just what I'm telling you!

WILLY (*sinking into a chair at the table, with full accusation*): You're trying to put a knife in me—don't think I don't know what you're doing!

BIFF: All right, phony! Then let's lay it on the line. (*He whips the rubber tube out of his pocket and puts it on the table.*)

HAPPY: You crazy—

LINDA: Biff! *(She moves to grab the hose, but* BIFF *holds it down with his hand.)*

BIFF: Leave it there! Don't move it!

WILLY *(not looking at it)*: What is that?

BIFF: You know goddam well what that is.

WILLY *(caged, wanting to escape)*: I never saw that.

BIFF: You saw it. The mice didn't bring it into the cellar! What is this supposed to do, make a hero out of you? This supposed to make me sorry for you?

WILLY: Never heard of it.

BIFF: There'll be no pity for you, you hear it? No pity!

WILLY *(to* LINDA*)*: You hear the spite!

BIFF: No, you're going to hear the truth—what you are and what I am!

LINDA: Stop it!

WILLY: Spite!

HAPPY *(coming down toward* BIFF*)*: You cut it now!

BIFF *(to* HAPPY*)*: The man don't know who we are! The man is gonna know! *(to* WILLY*)* We never told the truth for ten minutes in this house!

HAPPY: We always told the truth!

BIFF *(turning on him)*: You big blow, are you the assistant buyer? You're one of the two assistants to the assistant, aren't you?

HAPPY: Well, I'm practically—

BIFF: You're practically full of it! We all are! And I'm through with it. *(to* WILLY*)* Now hear this, Willy, this is me.

WILLY: I know you!

BIFF: You know why I had no address for three months? I stole a suit in Kansas City and I was in jail. *(to* LINDA, *who is sobbing)* Stop crying. I'm through with it.

*(*LINDA *turns away from them, her hands covering her face.)*

WILLY: I suppose that's my fault!

BIFF: I stole myself out of every good job since high school!

WILLY: And whose fault is that?

BIFF: And I never got anywhere because you blew me so full of hot air I could never stand taking orders from anybody! That's whose fault it is!

WILLY: I hear that!

LINDA: Don't, Biff!

BIFF: It's goddam time you heard that! I had to be boss big shot in two weeks, and I'm through with it!

WILLY: Then hang yourself! For spite, hang yourself!

BIFF: No! Nobody's hanging himself, Willy! I ran down eleven flights with a pen in my hand today. And suddenly I stopped, you hear me? And in the middle of that office building, do you hear this? I stopped in the middle of that building and I saw—the sky. I saw the things that I love in this world. The work and the food and time to sit and smoke. And I looked at the pen and said to myself, what the hell am I grabbing this for? Why am I trying to become what I don't want to be? What am I doing in an office, making a contemptuous, begging fool of myself, when all I want is out there, waiting for me the minute I say I know who I am! Why can't I say that, Willy? *(He tries to make* WILLY *face him, but* WILLY *pulls away and moves to the left.)*

WILLY *(with hatred, threateningly)*: The door of your life is wide open!

BIFF: Pop! I'm a dime a dozen, and so are you!

WILLY *(turning on him now in an uncontrolled outburst)*: I am not a dime a dozen! I am Willy Loman and you are Biff Loman!

*(*BIFF *starts for* WILLY, *but is blocked by* HAPPY. *In his fury,* BIFF *seems on the verge of attacking his father.)*

BIFF: I am not a leader of men, Willy, and neither are you. You were never anything but a hard-working drummer who landed in the ash can like all the rest of them! I'm one dollar an hour, Willy! I tried seven states and couldn't raise it. A buck an hour! Do you gather my meaning? I'm not bringing home any prizes any more, and you're going to stop waiting for me to bring them home!

WILLY *(directly to* BIFF*)*: You vengeful, spiteful mutt!

*(*BIFF *breaks from* HAPPY. WILLY, *in fright, starts up the stairs.* BIFF *grabs him.)*

BIFF *(at the peak of his fury)*: Pop, I'm nothing! I'm nothing, Pop. Can't you understand that? There's no spite in it any more. I'm just what I am, that's all.

*(*BIFF*'s fury has spent itself, and he breaks down, sobbing, holding on to* WILLY, *who dumbly fumbles for* BIFF*'s face.)*

WILLY *(astonished)*: What're you doing? What're you doing? *(to* LINDA*)* Why is he crying?

BIFF *(crying, broken)*: Will you let me go, for Christ's sake? Will you take that phony dream and burn it before something happens? *(Struggling to contain himself, he pulls away and moves to the stairs.)* I'll go in the morning. Put him—put him to bed. *(Exhausted,* BIFF *moves up the stairs to his room.)*

WILLY *(after a long pause, astonished, elevated)*: Isn't that—isn't that remarkable? Biff—he likes me!

LINDA: He loves you, Willy!

HAPPY *(deeply moved)*: Always did, Pop.

WILLY: Oh, Biff! *(Staring wildly.)* He cried! Cried to me. *(He is choking with his love, and now cries out his promise.)* That boy—that boy is going to be magnificent!

*(*BEN *appears in the light just outside the kitchen.)*

BEN: Yes, outstanding, with twenty thousand behind him.

LINDA *(sensing the racing of his mind, fearfully, carefully)*: Now come to bed, Willy. It's all settled now.

WILLY (*finding it difficult not to rush out of the house*): Yes, we'll sleep. Come on. Go to sleep, Hap.

BEN: And it does take a great kind of a man to crack the jungle.

(*In accents of dread,* BEN's *idyllic music starts up.*)

HAPPY (*his arm around* LINDA): I'm getting married, Pop, don't forget it. I'm changing everything. I'm gonna run that department before the year is up. You'll see, Mom. (*He kisses her.*)

BEN: The jungle is dark but full of diamonds, Willy.

(WILLY *turns, moves, listening to* BEN.)

LINDA: Be good. You're both good boys, just act that way, that's all.

HAPPY: 'Night, Pop. (*He goes upstairs.*)

LINDA (*to* WILLY): Come, dear.

BEN (*with greater force*): One must go in to fetch a diamond out.

WILLY (*to* LINDA, *as he moves slowly along the edge of the kitchen, toward the door*): I just want to get settled down, Linda. Let me sit alone for a little.

LINDA (*almost uttering her fear*): I want you upstairs.

WILLY (*taking her in his arms*): In a few minutes, Linda. I couldn't sleep right now. Go on, you look awful tired. (*He kisses her.*)

BEN: Not like an appointment at all. A diamond is rough and hard to the touch.

WILLY: Go on now. I'll be right up.

LINDA: I think this is the only way, Willy.

WILLY: Sure, it's the best thing.

BEN: Best thing!

WILLY: The only way. Everything is gonna be—go on, kid, go to bed. You look so tired.

LINDA: Come right up.

WILLY: Two minutes.

(LINDA *goes into the living-room, then reappears in her bedroom.* WILLY *moves just outside the kitchen door.*)

WILLY: Loves me. (*Wonderingly.*) Always loved me. Isn't that a remarkable thing? Ben, he'll worship me for it!

BEN (*with promise*): It's dark there, but full of diamonds.

WILLY: Can you imagine that magnificence with twenty thousand dollars in his pocket?

LINDA (*calling from her room*): Willy! Come up!

WILLY (*calling into the kitchen*): Yes! Yes. Coming! It's very smart, you realize that, don't you sweetheart? Even Ben sees it. I gotta go, baby. 'By! 'By! (*Going over to* BEN, *almost dancing*) Imagine? When the mail comes he'll be ahead of Bernard again!

BEN: A perfect proposition all around.

WILLY: Did you see how he cried to me? Oh, if I could kiss him, Ben!

BEN: Time, William, time!

WILLY: Oh, Ben, I always knew one way or another we were gonna make it, Biff and I!

BEN (*looking at his watch*): The boat. We'll be late. (*He moves slowly off into the darkness.*)

WILLY (*elegiacally, turning to the house*): Now when you kick off, boy, I want a seventy-yard boot, and get right down the field under the ball, and when you hit, hit low and hit hard, because it's important, boy. (*He swings around and faces the audience.*) There's all kinds of important people in the stands, and the first thing you know . . . (*Suddenly realizing he is alone.*) Ben! Ben, where do I . . . ? (*He makes a sudden movement of search.*) Ben, how do I . . . ?

LINDA (*calling*): Willy, you coming up?

WILLY (*uttering a gasp of fear, whirling about as if to quiet her*): Sh! (*He turns around as if to find his way; sounds, faces, voices, seem to be swarming in upon him and he flicks at them, crying.*) Sh! Sh! (*Suddenly music, faint and high, stops him. It rises in intensity, almost to an unbearable scream. He goes up and down on his toes, and rushes off around the house.*) Shhh!

LINDA: Willy?

(*There is no answer.* LINDA *waits.* BIFF *gets up off his bed. He is still in his clothes.* HAPPY *sits up.* BIFF *stands listening.*)

LINDA (*with real fear*): Willy, answer me! Willy!

(*There is the sound of a car starting and moving away at full speed.*)

LINDA: No!

BIFF (*rushing down the stairs*): Pop!

(*As the car speeds off, the music crashes down in a frenzy of sound, which becomes the soft pulsation of a single cello string.* BIFF *slowly returns to his bedroom. He and* HAPPY *gravely don their jackets.* LINDA *slowly walks out of her room. The music has developed into a dead march. The leaves of day are appearing over everything.* CHARLEY *and* BERNARD, *somberly dressed, appear and knock on the kitchen door.* BIFF *and* HAPPY *slowly descend the stairs to the kitchen as* CHARLEY *and* BERNARD *enter. All stop a moment when* LINDA, *in clothes of mourning, bearing a little bunch of roses, comes through the draped doorway into the kitchen. She goes to* CHARLEY *and takes his arm. Now all move toward the audience, through the wall-line of the kitchen. At the limit of the apron,* LINDA *lays down the flowers, kneels, and sits back on her heels. All stare down at the grave.*)

REQUIEM

CHARLEY: It's getting dark, Linda.

(LINDA *doesn't react. She stares at the grave.*)

BIFF: How about it, Mom? Better get some rest, heh? They'll be closing the gate soon.

(LINDA *makes no move. Pause.*)

HAPPY *(deeply angered)*: He had no right to do that. There was no necessity for it. We would've helped him.

CHARLEY *(grunting)*: Hmmm.

BIFF: Come along, Mom.

LINDA: Why didn't anybody come?

CHARLEY: It was a very nice funeral.

LINDA: But where are all the people he knew? Maybe they blame him.

CHARLEY: Naa. It's a rough world, Linda. They wouldn't blame him.

LINDA: I can't understand it. At this time especially. First time in thirty-five years we were just about free and clear. He only needed a little salary. He was even finished with the dentist.

CHARLEY: No man only needs a little salary.

LINDA: I can't understand it.

BIFF: There were a lot of nice days. When he'd come home from a trip; or on Sundays, making the stoop; finishing the cellar; putting on the new porch; when he built the extra bathroom; and put up the garage. You know something, Charley, there's more of him in that front stoop than in all the sales he ever made.

CHARLEY: Yeah. He was a happy man with a batch of cement.

LINDA: He was so wonderful with his hands.

BIFF: He had the wrong dreams. All, all, wrong.

HAPPY *(almost ready to fight BIFF)*: Don't say that!

BIFF: He never knew who he was.

CHARLEY *(stopping HAPPY's movement and reply. To BIFF)*: Nobody dast blame this man. You don't understand: Willy was a salesman. And for a salesman, there is no rock bottom to the life. He don't put a bolt to a nut, he don't tell you the law or give you medicine. He's a man way out there in the blue, riding on a smile and a shoeshine. And when they start not smiling back—that's an earthquake. And then you get yourself a couple of spots on your hat, and you're finished. Nobody dast blame this man. A salesman is got to dream, boy. It comes with the territory.

BIFF: Charley, the man didn't know who he was.

HAPPY *(infuriated)*: Don't say that!

BIFF: Why don't you come with me, Happy?

HAPPY: I'm not licked that easily. I'm staying right in this city and I'm gonna beat this racket! *(He looks at BIFF, his chin set.)* The Loman Brothers!

BIFF: I know who I am, kid.

HAPPY: All right, boy. I'm gonna show you and everybody else that Willy Loman did not die in vain. He had a good dream. It's the only dream you can have—to come out number-one man. He fought it out here, and this is where I'm gonna win it for him.

BIFF *(with a hopeless glance at HAPPY, bends toward his mother)*: Let's go, Mom.

LINDA: I'll be with you in a minute. Go on, Charley. *(He hesitates.)* I want to, just for a minute. I never had a chance to say good-by.

(CHARLEY moves away, followed by HAPPY. BIFF remains a slight distance up and left of LINDA. She sits there, summoning herself. The flute begins, not far away, playing behind her speech.)

LINDA: Forgive me, dear, I can't cry. I don't know what it is, but I can't cry. I don't understand it. Why did you ever do that? Help me, Willy, I can't cry. It seems to me that you're just on another trip. I keep expecting you. Willy, dear, I can't cry. Why did you do it? I search and search and I search, and I can't understand it, Willy. I made the last payment on the house today. Today, dear. And there'll be nobody home. *(A sob rises in her throat.)* We're free and clear. *(Sobbing more fully, released.)* We're free. *(BIFF comes slowly toward her.)* We're free . . . We're free . . .

(BIFF lifts her to her feet and moves out up right with her in his arms. LINDA sobs quietly. BERNARD and CHARLEY come together and follow them, followed by HAPPY. Only the music of the flute is left on the darkening stage as over the house the hard towers of the apartment buildings rise into sharp focus, and

THE CURTAIN FALLS.)

Figure 1. Jo Mielziner's set for the first production of *Death of a Salesman,* Morosco Theatre, New York, 1949. (Photograph: Billy Rose Theatre Collection. The New York Public Library of the Performing Arts. Astor, Lenox, and Tilden Foundations.)

Figure 2. Linda (Elizabeth Franz) comforts Willy (Brian Dennehy) in the Goodman Theatre's 1998 production of *Death of a Salesman,* directed by Robert Falls. (Photograph: Eric Y. Exit/The Goodman Theatre.)

Figure 3. "Someday I'll have my own business," Willy (Brian Dennehy, *center*) promises his sons, here seen in the Goodman Theatre production as their younger selves, with Biff (Kevin Anderson, *left*) in his letterman's sweater and Happy (Ted Koch, *right*) looking anxiously at his father for his approval. (Photograph: Eric Y. Exit/The Goodman Theatre.)

Staging of *Death of a Salesman*

MAKING WILLY LOMAN: A LOOK AT MILLER'S NOTEBOOK, 1999, BY JOHN LAHR

On a crisp April weekend in 1948, Arthur Miller, then only thirty-three and enjoying the first flush of fame after the Broadway success the previous year of "All My Sons," waved goodbye to his first wife, Mary, and their two young kids, in Brooklyn, and set off for Roxbury, Connecticut, where he intended to build a cabin on a hillock just behind a Colonial house he had recently purchased for the family, which stood at the aptly named crossroads of Tophet (another name for Hell) and Gold Mine. "It was a purely instinctive act," Miller, who long ago traded up from that first forty-four-acre property to a four-hundred-acre spread on Painter Hill, a few miles down the road, told me recently. "I had never built a building in my life."

Miller had a play in mind, too; his impulse for the cabin was "to sit in the middle of it, and shut the door, and let things happen." All Miller knew about his new play was that it would be centered on a travelling salesman who would die at the end and that two of the lines were "Willy?" "It's all right. I came back"—words that to Miller spoke "the whole disaster in a nutshell." He says, "I mean, imagine a salesman who can't get past Yonkers. It's the end of the world. It's like an actor saying 'It's all right. I can't speak.'" As he worked away on his cabin, he repeated the play's two lines like a kind of mantra. "I kept saying, 'As soon as I get the roof on and the windows in, I'm gonna start this thing,'" he recalls. "And indeed I started on a morning in spring. Everything was starting to bud. Beautiful weather."

Miller had fashioned a desk out of an old door. As he sat down to it his tools and nails were still stashed in a corner of the studio, which was as yet unpainted and smelled of raw wood. "I started in the morning, went through the day, then had dinner, and then I went back there and worked till—I don't know—one or two o'clock in the morning," he says. "It sort of unveiled itself. I was the stenographer. I could hear them. I could hear them, literally." When Miller finally lay down to sleep that first night, he realized he'd been crying. "My eyes still burned and my throat was sore from talking it all out and shouting and laughing," he later wrote in his autobiography, "Timebends." In one day, he had produced, almost intact, the first act of "Death of a Salesman," which has since sold about eleven million copies, making it probably the most successful modern play ever published. The show, which is being put on somewhere in the world almost every day of the year, celebrates its fiftieth anniversary next month with a Broadway revival from Chicago's Goodman Theatre, directed by Robert Falls and starring Brian Dennehy as the fanatical and frazzled drummer Willy Loman.

"He didn't write 'Death of a Salesman'; he *released* it," the play's original director, Elia Kazan, said in his autobiography, "A Life." "It was there inside him, stored up waiting to be turned loose." To Miller, there was a "dream's quality in my memory of the writing and the day or two that followed its completion." In his notebook for "Death of a Salesman"—a sixty-six-page document chronicling the play's creation, which is kept with his papers at the University of Texas at Austin—he wrote, "He who understands everything about his subject cannot write it. I write as much to discover as to explain." After that first day of inspiration, it took Miller six weeks to call forth the second act and to make Willy remember enough "so he would kill himself." The form of the play—where past and present coalesce in a lyrical dramatic arc—was one that Miller felt he'd been "searching for since the beginning of my writing life." "Death of a Salesman" seems to spill out of Willy's panic-stricken, protean imagination, and not out of a playwright's detached viewpoint. "The play is written from the sidewalk instead of from a skyscraper," Miller says of its first-person urgency. But, ironically, it was from the deck of a skyscraper that Miller contemplated beginning his drama, in a kind of Shakespearean foreshadowing of Willy's suicidal delirium. The notebook's first entry reads:

> Scene 1—Atop Empire State. 2 guards. "Who will die today? It's that kind of day . . . fog, and poor visibility. They like to jump into a cloud. Who will it be today?"

As Miller navigated his way through the rush of characters and plot ideas, the notebook acted as ballast. "In every scene remember his size, ugliness," Miller reminds himself about Loman on its second page. "Remember his own attitude. Remember *pity*." He analyzes his characters' motives. "Willy wants his sons to destroy his failure," he writes, and on a later page, "Willy resents Linda's unbroken, patient forgiveness (knowing there must be great hidden hatred for him in her heart)." In Miller's notebook, characters emerge sound and fully formed. For instance, of Willy's idealized elder son, Biff, who is a lost soul fallen from his high-school glory and full of hate for his father, he writes, "Biff is travelled, oppressed by guilt of failure, of not making money although a kind of indolence pleases him: an easygoing way of life. . . . Truthfully, Biff is not really bright enough to make a businessman. *Wants everything too fast.*" Miller also talks to himself about the emotional stakes and the trajectory of scenes:

> Have it happen that Willy's life is in Biff's hands—aside from Biff succeeding. There is Willy's guilt to Biff re: The Woman. But is that retrievable? There is Biff's disdain for Willy's character, his false aims, his pretense and these Biff cannot finally give up or alter. Discover the link between Biff's work views and his anti-work feelings.

Although the notebook begins with a series of choppy asides and outlines, it soon becomes an expansive, exact handwritten log of Miller's contact with his inner voices. For instance, it reveals the development of Charley, Loman's benevolent next-door neighbor, whose laconic evenhandedness was, in Miller's eyes, partly a projection of his own father. Charley speaks poignantly to Biff at Willy's graveside ("Nobody dast blame this man"); what appears in the last scene as a taut and memorable nine-line speech, a kind of eulogy, was mined from words (here indicated in italics) that were part of a much longer improvisation in the notebook:

> A salesman doesn't build anything, *he don't put a bolt to a nut* or a seed in the ground. A man who doesn't build anything must be liked. He must be cheerful on bad days. Even calamities mustn't break through. Cause one thing, he has got to be liked. *He don't tell you the law or give you medicine.* So there's no rock bottom to your life. All you know is that on good days or bad, you gotta come in cheerful. No calamity must be permitted to break through, Cause one thing, always, you're a man who's gotta be believed. You're way out there *riding on a smile and a shoeshine. And when they start not smilin' back,* the sky falls in. *And then you get a couple of spots on your hat, and you're finished. Cause there's no rock bottom to your life.*

Here, as in all his notes for the play, Miller's passion and his flow are apparent in the surprising absence of cross-outs; the pages exude a startling alertness. He is listening not just to the voices of his characters but to the charmed country silence around him, which seems to define his creative state of grace:

> Roxbury—At night the insects softly thumping the screens like a blind man pushing with his fingers in the dark. . . . The crickets, frogs, whippoorwills altogether, a scream from the breast of the earth when everyone is gone. The evening sky, faded gray, like the sea pressing up against the windows, or an opaque gray screen. (Through which someone is looking in at me?)

On a bright-blue December afternoon last year, Miller, now eighty-three, returned to the cabin with his third wife, the photographer Inge Morath. Although she has lived with Miller for more than three decades, only one mile away from the "Salesman" studio, she had never seen the place. "The main house was occupied by people I didn't know. They were sort of engineer people. Very antipathetic," Miller said, swinging his red Volkswagen into the driveway of the new, friendly writer-owners. In a tan windbreaker and a baseball cap, he looked as rough-hewn and handy as any local farmer. (The diningroom tables and chairs in his current, cluttered 1782 farmhouse are Miller's handiwork, produced in his carpentry workshop.) After a cursory inspection of his old home, Miller, who is six feet three and stoops a little now, set off toward the cabin, up a steep hump that sits a few hundred paces from the back of the house. "In those days, I didn't think this hill was quite as steep," he said.

The cabin, a white clapboard construction in somewhat urgent need of a new coat of paint, stood just over the top of the rise, facing west, toward a thicket of birch trees and a field. "Oh, it will last as long as it's painted," Miller said, inspecting what he had wrought. "See, if a building has a sound roof, that's it, you'll keep it."

"I didn't know it was so tiny," Morath said. She snapped off a few photos, then waved her husband into the foreground for a picture before we all crowded into what proved to be a single high-ceilinged room. Except for a newly installed fluorescent light and some red linoleum that had been fitted over the floorboards, what Miller saw was what he'd built. He stepped outside to see if the cabin had been wired for electricity. (It had.) He inspected the three cinder blocks on which it was securely perched against the side of the hill. "I did the concrete," he recalled. Leaving, he turned to take a last look. "I learned a lot doing it," he said. "The big problem was getting the rafters of the roof up there alone. I finally built it on the ground and then swung them up." He added, "It's a bit like playwriting, you know. You get to a certain point, you gotta squeeze your way out of it."

Where does the alchemy of a great play begin? The seeds of "Death of a Salesman" were planted decades before Miller stepped into his cabin. "Selling was in the air through my boyhood," says Miller, whose father, Isidore, was the salesman-turned-owner of the Miltex Coat and Suit Company, which was a thriving enough business to provide the family with a spacious apartment on 110th Street in Harlem, a country bungalow, and a limousine and driver. "The whole idea of selling successfully was very important." Just as Miller was entering his teens, however, his father's business was wiped out by the Depression. Isidore's response was silence and sleep ("My father had trouble staying awake"); his son's response was anger. "I had never raised my voice against my father, nor did he against me, then or ever," wrote Miller, who had to postpone going to college for two years—until 1934—because "nobody was in possession of the fare." "As I knew perfectly well, it was not he who angered me, only his failure to cope with his fortune's collapse," Miller went on in his autobiography. "Thus I had two fathers, the real one and the metaphoric, and the latter I resented because he did not know how to win out over the general collapse.

"Death of a Salesman" is a lightning rod both for a father's bewilderment ("What's the secret?" Willy asks various characters) and for a son's fury at parental powerlessness ("You fake! You phoney little fake!" Biff tells Willy when they finally square off, in Act II). After the play's success, Miller's mother, Augusta, found an early manuscript called "In Memoriam," a forgotten autobiographical fragment that Miller had written when he was about seventeen. The piece, which was published in these pages in 1995, is about a Miltex salesman called Schoenzeit, who had once asked Miller for subway fare when Miller was helping him carry samples to an uptown buyer. The real Schoenzeit killed himself the next day by throwing himself in front of the El train; the character's "dejected soul"—a case of exhaustion masquerading as gaiety—is the first sighting of what would become Willy Loman. "His emotions were displayed at the wrong times always, and he knew when to laugh," Miller wrote. In 1952, Miller, rummaging through his papers, found a 1937 notebook in which he had made embryonic sketches of Willy, Biff, and Willy's second son, Happy. "It was the same family," he says of the twenty pages of realistic dialogue. "But I was unable in that straightforward, realistic form to contain what I thought of as the man's poetry—that is, the zigzag shots of his mind." He adds, "I just blotted it out."

Every masterpiece is a story of accident and accomplishment. Of all the historical and personal forces that fed the making of "Death of a Salesman," none was more important than a moment in 1947 when Miller's uncle Manny Newman accosted him in the lobby of the Colonial Theatre in Boston after a matinée of "All My Sons." "People regarded him as a kind of strange, completely untruthful personality," Miller says of Newman, a salesman and a notorious fabulist, who within the year would commit suicide. "I thought of him as a kind of wonderful inventor. There was something in him which was terribly moving, because his suffering was right on his skin, you see. He was the ultimate climber up the ladder who was constantly being stepped on by those climbing past him. My empathy for him was immense. I mean, how could he possibly have succeeded? There was no way." According to Miller, Newman was "cute and ugly, a bantam with a lisp. Very charming." He and his family, including two sons, Abby and Buddy, lived modestly in Brooklyn. "It was a house without irony, trembling with resolutions and shouts of victories that had not

yet taken place but surely would tomorrow," Miller recalled in "Timebends." Newman was fiercely, wackily competitive; even when Miller was a child, in the few hours he spent in Newman's presence his uncle drew him into some kind of imaginary contest "which never stopped in his mind." Miller, who was somewhat ungainly as a boy, was often compared unfavorably with his cousins, and whenever he visited them, he said, "I always had to expect some kind of insinuation of my entire life's probable failure."

When Newman approached Miller after that matinée, he had not seen his nephew for more than a decade. He had tears in his eyes, but, instead of complimenting the playwright, he told Miller, "Buddy is doing very well." Miller says now, "He had simply picked up the conversation from fifteen years before. That element of competitiveness—his son competing with me—was so alive in his head that there was no gate to keep it from his mouth. He was living in two places at the same time." Miller continues, "So everything is in the present. For him to say 'Buddy is doing very well'—there are no boundaries. It's all now. It's all now. And that to me was wonderful."

At the time, Miller was absorbed in the tryout of "All My Sons" and had "not the slightest interest in writing about a salesman." Until "All My Sons," Miller's plays had not been naturalistic in style; he had "resolved to write a play that could be put on," and had "put two years into 'All My Sons' to be sure that I believed every page of it." But Miller found naturalism, with its chronological exposition, "not sensuous enough" as a style; he began to imagine a kind of play where, as in Greek drama, issues were confronted head on, and where the transitions between scenes were pointed rather than disguised. The success of "All My Sons" emboldened him. "I could now move into unknown territory," Miller says. "And that unknown territory was basically that we're thinking on several planes at the same time. I wanted to find a way to try to make everything happen at once." In his introduction to the fiftieth-anniversary edition of "Death of a Salesman," Miller writes, "The play had to move forward not by following a narrow discreet line, but as a phalanx." He continues, "There was no model I could adapt for this play, no past history for the kind of work I felt it could become." The notebook for the play shows Miller formulating a philosophy for the kind of Cubist stage pictures that would become his new style:

> Life is formless—its interconnections are cancelled by lapses of time, by events occurring in separate places, by the hiatus of memory. We live in the world made by man and the past. Art suggests or makes the interconnection palpable. Form is the tension of these interconnections: man with man, man with the past and present environment. The drama at its best is a mass experience of this tension.

At first, the Manny Newman encounter inspired in Miller only the intimation of a new, slashing sense of dramatic form. The play's structure is embedded in the structure of Loman's turbulent mind, which, Miller says, destroys the boundaries between then and now. As a result, "there are no flashbacks, strictly speaking, in 'Death of a Salesman,'" he says. "It's always moving forward." In this way, Miller jettisoned what he calls "the daylight continuity" of naturalism for the more fluid dark logic of dreams. "In a dream you don't have transitional material," Miller says. "The dream starts where it starts to mean something." He continues, "I wanted to start every scene at the last possible instant, no matter where that instant happened to be." He picked up a copy of his play and read me its first beats: "'Willy?' 'It's all right. I came back.' 'Why? What happened? Did something happen, Willy?' 'No, nothing happened.'" He added, "We're into the thing in three lines." His new structure jump-started both the scenes and the stage language, whose intensity Miller called "emergency speech"—an "unashamedly open" idiom that replaced "the crabbed dramatic hints and pretexts of the natural." Willy dies without a secret; the play's structure, with its crosscutting between heightened moments, encouraged the idea of revelation. The audience response that Miller wanted to incite, he said, "was not 'What happens next and why?' so much as 'Oh, God, of course.'"

When, early in 1948, Miller visited his cousin Abby Newman to talk about the blighted life of his late father, Miller himself had just such an epiphany. Newman told Miller, "He wanted a business for us. So we could all work together. A business for the boys." Miller, who repeated Newman's words in the play, wrote in his autobiography, "This conventional, mundane wish was a shot of electricity that switched all the random iron filings in my mind in one direction. A hopelessly distracted Manny was transformed into a man with a purpose: he had been trying to make a gift that would crown all those striving years; all those lies he told, all his imaginings and crazy exaggerations, even the almost military discipline he had laid on his boys, were in this instant given form and point. I suddenly understood him with my very blood."

Willy Loman is a salesman, but we're never told what product he lugs around in his two large sample cases. Once, a theatregoer buttonholed Miller and put the question to him: "What's he selling? You never say what he's selling." Miller quipped, "Well, himself. That's who's in the valise." Miller adds, "You sell yourself. You sell the goods. You become the commodity." Willy's house echoes with exhortations to his two floundering sons about the presentation of self ("The man who creates personal interest is the man who gets ahead. Be liked and you will never want") and the imperialism of self ("Lick the world. You guys together could absolutely lick the civilized world"). In his note-

book Miller writes, "Willy longs to take off, be great," and "Willy wants his boys prepared for any life. 'Nobody will laugh at them—take advantage. They'll be big men.' It's the big men who command respect." In Willy's frenzied and exhausted attempt to claim himself, Miller had stumbled onto a metaphor for a postwar society's eagerness to pursue its self-interest after years of postponed life. In Willy's desperate appetite for success and in the brutal dicta offered by his rich brother Ben ("Never fight fair with a stranger, boy. You'll never get out of the jungle that way") "Death of a Salesman" caught the spirit of self-aggrandizement being fed by what Miller calls "the biggest boom in the history of the world." Americans had struggled through the Depression, then fought a world war to keep the nation's democratic dream alive; that dream was, broadly speaking, a dream of self-realization. America, with its ideal of freedom, challenged its citizens to see how far they could go in a lifetime—"to end up big," as Willy says. (In the play, Ben, whom Willy looks to for answers—the notebook points to him as "the visible evidence of what the boys can do and be. Superior family"—is literally the predatory imperialist who at seventeen walked into the African jungle and emerged four years later as a millionaire.) Miller was not the first to dramatize the barbarity of American individualism; but, in a shift that signalled the changing cultural mood, he was the first to stage this spiritual battle of attrition as a journey to the interior of the American psyche. "In a certain sense, Willy is all the voices," Miller said later. In fact, "The Inside of His Head" was Miller's first title for the play; he also briefly toyed with the idea of having the proscenium designed in the shape of a head and having the action take place inside it.

In the economic upheavals of the thirties, social realism reflected the country's mood; plays held a mirror up to the external world, not an internal one. But in the postwar boom Tennessee Williams's "The Glass Menagerie" (1945) and "A Streetcar Named Desire" (1947), written in what Williams called his "personal lyricism," suddenly found an audience and struck a deep new chord in American life. The plays were subjective, poetic, symbolic; they made a myth of the self, not of social remedies. Indeed, the name "Willy Loman" was not intended by Miller as a sort of socioeconomic indicator ("low man"). Miller took it from a chilling moment in Fritz Lang's film "The Testament of Dr. Mabuse" (1933) when, after a long and terrifying stakeout, a disgraced detective who thinks he can redeem himself by exposing a gang of forgers is pursued and duped by them. The chase ends with the detective on the phone to his former boss ("Lohmann? Help me, for God's sake! Lohmann!"); when we see him next, he is in an asylum, gowned and frightened and shouting into an invisible phone ("Lohmann? Lohmann? Lohmann?"). "What the name really meant to me was a terrified man calling into the void for help that will never come," Miller said.

Willy Loman's particular terror goes to the core of American individualism, in which the reputable self and the issue of wealth are hopelessly tangled. "A man can't go out the way he came in," Willy says to Ben. "A man has got to add up to something." Willy, who, at sixty, has no job, no money, no loyalty from his boys, is sensationally lacking in assets and in their social corollary—a sense of blessing. "He envies those who are blessed; he feels unblessed, but he's striving for it," Miller says. Although Willy's wife, Linda, famously says of him that "attention must be paid," he feels invisible to the world. "I'm not noticed," he says. Later, Linda confides to the boys, "For five weeks he's been on straight commission, like a beginner, an unknown!" As Miller puts it now, "The whole idea of people failing with us is that they can no longer be loved. You haven't created a persona which people will pay for, see, experience, or come close to. It's almost like death. You have a deathly touch. People who succeed are loved because they exude some magical formula for fending off destruction, fending off death." He continues, "It's the most brutal way of looking at life that one can imagine, because it discards anyone who does not measure up. It wants to destroy them. It's been going on since the Puritan times. You are beyond the blessing of God. You're beyond the reach of God. That God rewards those who deserve it. It's a moral condemnation that goes on. You don't want to be near this failure."

"Death of a Salesman" was the first play to dramatize this punishing—and particularly American—interplay of panic and achievement. Before "Salesman," Eugene O'Neill's "The Iceman Cometh" (1946) raised the issue in the eerie calm of Harry Hope's bar, whose sodden habitués have retreated from competitiveness into a perverse contentment; as one of the characters says, "No one here has to worry about where they're going next, because there is no farther they can go." But in Willy Loman, Miller was able to bring both the desperation and the aspiration of American life together in one character.

Willy is afflicted by the notion of winning—what Brecht called "the black addiction of the brain." He cheats at cards; he encourages his boys to seek every advantage. Victory haunts him and his feckless sons. In a scene from the notebook, Biff and Happy tell Willy of their plan to go into business. "Step on it, boys, there ain't a minute to lose," Willy tells them, but their souls are strangled by their father's heroic dreams, which hang over them like some sort of spiritual kudzu. In another notebook entry, Biff rounds fiercely on Willy: "I don't care if you live or die. You think I'm mad at you because of the Woman, don't you? I am, but I'm madder because you botched up my life, because I can't tear you out of my heart, because I keep trying to make good, be something for you, to succeed for you."

In dramatizing the fantasy of competition, Miller's play was the first to dissect cultural envy in action—that process of invidious comparison which drives society forward but also drives it crazy. "You lose your life to it!" Miller says of the envy that feeds Willy's restlessness. "It's the ultimate outer-directional emotion. In other words, I am doing this not because it's flowing from me but because it's flowing against him." He goes on, "You're living in a mirror. It's a life of reflections. Emptiness. Emptiness. Emptiness. Hard to go to sleep at night. And hard to wake up." In his mind, Willy is competing with his brother Ben; with Dave Singleman, a successful old salesman who could make a living "without ever leaving his room" and who died a placid, accomplished death on a train to Boston; with his neighbor Charley, who owns his own business; and with Charley's successful lawyer son, Bernard. "Where's Willy in all this?" Miller asks. "He's competed himself to death. He's not existing anymore, or hardly."

In his notebook Miller wrote, "It is the combination of guilt (of failure), hate, and love—all in conflict that he resolves by 'accomplishing' a 20,000 dollar death." In death, Willy is worth more than in life. His suicide is the ultimate expression of his confusion of success with love and also of his belief in winning at all costs. As a father, he overlooked Biff's small childhood acts of larceny—taking sand from a building site, stealing basketballs, getting the answers for tests from the nerdy, studious Bernard—and Biff has continued his habit into adulthood, out of a combination of envy and revenge. A notebook citation reads, "It is necessary to (1) reveal to Willy that Biff stole to queer himself, and did it to hurt Willy," and "(2) And that he did it because of the Woman and all the disillusionment it implied." In the final version of the play, Biff, admitting in passing that he spent three months in a Kansas City jail for lifting a suit, tells Willy, "I stole myself out of every good job since high school!" At first, Miller saw the twenty thousand dollars of insurance money as cash to put Biff on the straight and narrow. "My boy's a thief—with 20,000 he'd stop it,'" he wrote in the notebook. Instead, Willy's suicide—the final show of force and fraud, in keeping with his demented competitive fantasies—is pitched on a more grandiose and perverse note. In an early draft of the terrific penultimate scene, where Biff exposes Willy and calls it quits with him and his dream, there is this exchange:

BIFF (to him): What the hell do you want from me? What do you want from me?
WILLY: —Greatness—
BIFF: No—

In Miller's final draft, Willy, who will not accept his son's confession of thievery, takes Biff's greatness as a given as he visualizes his own suicide. "Can you imagine that magnificence with twenty thousand dollars in his pocket?" he says to Ben. He adds, "Imagine? When the mail comes he'll be ahead of Bernard again." When he goes to his death, Willy, in his mind, is on a football field with Biff, and full of vindictive triumph ("When you hit, hit low and hit hard, because it's important, boy"). "He dies sending his son through the goalposts," Miller says. "He dies moving." Miller pauses. "I think now that Kazan had it right from the beginning. He said, 'It's a love story.'"

On the last page of his notebook, Miller scribbled a short speech to give to the original cast after its members had read the play in galleys: "I want you all to know now that the cannons are quiet that this production has been the most gratifying I have known. I believe you are the finest ever gathered for any play and I am exceedingly proud and gratified not only for myself but for the American theatre." (The original cast included Lee J. Cobb as Willy, with Mildred Dunnock, Arthur Kennedy, and Cameron Mitchell.) In its passage to greatness, "Death of a Salesman" was enhanced enormously by the poetic set design of Jo Mielziner, who created a series of platforms, with Willy's house as a haunting omnipresent background. However, as Elia Kazan pointed out in his autobiography, "The stage direction in the original manuscript that Art gave me to read directly after he'd finished it does not mention a home as a scenic element. It reads, 'A pinpoint travelling spot lights a small area on stage left. The Salesman is revealed. He takes out his keys and opens an invisible door.'" Kazan continues, "It was a play waiting for a directorial solution." It got it. "Death of a Salesman" also got its share of bad suggestions. Kazan's then wife, Molly Day Thacher, who was a playreader for the Group Theatre and had some influence over Kazan, tried to get Miller, as he remembers it, "to cut out Uncle Ben, all the memory scenes, and simply make it a realistic little narrative." And the coproducer, Kermit Bloomgarden, nervous of a play with "Death" in its title, took a poll among theatregoers which asked, "Would you go to see a play called 'Death of a Salesman'?" Nobody would. "They had a list of about fif-

teen titles," Miller says. "One was 'Free and Clear.' I'll never forget that."

In the intervening half century, the surface of American life has changed, but its mad competitiveness hasn't. "I'm not aware of any change in the way people look at this play," Miller says, but he admits that Willy's complaints about loyalty from the head office ring strange to contemporary ears. "Workers now—not just workers but management—know that nobody will have much pity for them." Last year, in a poll taken by the Royal National Theatre of eight hundred English theatre professionals, Miller was voted the greatest contemporary playwright; but in America, where in some quarters he's seen as a kind of Jeremiah, Miller is not accorded quite the same honor. He ascribes his decline in popularity to the erosion of the "unified audience" that came with the rise of the avant-garde in the early sixties. "The only theatre available to a playwright in the late forties was Broadway," Miller writes in the fiftieth-anniversary edition of "Salesman." "That theatre had one single audience . . . catering to very different levels of age, culture, education, and intellectual sophistication." He continues, "One result of this mix was the ideal, if not frequent fulfillment, of a kind of play that would be complete rather than fragmentary, an emotional rather than an intellectual experience, a play basically of heart with its ulterior moral gesture integrated with action rather than rhetoric. In fact, it was a Shakespearean ideal, a theatre for anyone with an understanding of English and perhaps some common sense."

But there was nothing Shakespearean in the response to "that damned disturbing play," as Kazan called it, on the night of its début, February 10, 1949, in Philadelphia. "The curtain came down and nothing happened," Miller says. "People sat there a good two or three minutes, then somebody stood up with his coat. Several men—I didn't see women doing this—were helpless. They were sitting there with handkerchiefs over their faces. It was like a funeral." He continues, "I didn't know whether the show was dead or alive. The cast was back there wondering what had happened. Nobody'd pulled the curtain up. Finally, someone thought to applaud, and then the house came apart."

TENNESSEE WILLIAMS

1911–1983

Despite his first name, a nickname he adopted during his college days, Williams was born in Mississippi and lived there until 1918, when his father, a traveling salesman, was promoted to an office in St. Louis. That move to the Midwest, according to Williams, was a "tragic" experience. He was mocked for his southern accent, he was pained by the heightened awareness of being poor, and thus he never adjusted to life in St. Louis. Looking back on his childhood there, Williams once described it as "the beginning of the social consciousness which I think has marked most of my writing." Williams lived in St. Louis until his mid-twenties, and those years with his family—with his tyrannical father, his overprotective mother, and his mentally withdrawn sister—evidently gave rise to the acute psychological awareness that has also marked virtually all of his writing. Those years with his family in St. Louis certainly must have given rise to his abiding concern with the painful experience of the outsider: the artist, the dreamer, the physically crippled, the mentally disturbed, and the sexually driven. As a child, he had been afflicted by diptheria, which for many years left him with paralyzed legs and weakened kidneys. As a teenager, he suffered the taunts of his father who repeatedly called him "Miss Nancy" because of his literary inclinations and his effeminacy. In his mid-twenties, he worked himself into a nervous and physical breakdown, selling shoes during the day at his father's insistence and writing plays late into the night to escape his miserable existence. During this time he also witnessed the permanent mental breakdown of his introverted sister, with whom he had been close throughout his years in Mississippi and St. Louis.

These painful experiences of his childhood and youth clearly provided Williams with material for his first major stage success, *The Glass Menagerie* (1944), "a memory play" whose protagonist-narrator, Tom Wingfield, is clearly modeled on Williams himself, much as Laura Wingfield is modeled on Williams's sister Rose. Tom, for example, is portrayed as a poet and dreamer, yearning for escape from the suffocating world of business, while Laura is depicted as a pathologically shy young woman who lives in a private world of glass animals and old phonograph records. Indeed, it might well be said that Williams reflected the personality and dispositions of his father, his mother, his sister, and himself in virtually all his work. His father's personality is echoed in the cynically practical and coarsely domineering men who often figure prominently in his plays, such as Stanley Kowalski in *A Streetcar Named Desire* (1947) or Big Daddy in *Cat on a Hot Tin Roof* (1955). His mother is echoed in the long-suffering women who patiently endure the afflictions of being married to these domineering characters, such as Stella Kowalski or Big Mama. His sister is echoed in psychologically fragile women who have retreated from life, such as Blanche, a faded southern "gentlewoman" who clings desperately to the memory of her lost plantation in *A Streetcar Named Desire*, or Alma, the virginal spinster in *Summer and Smoke* (1948), or Hannah Jelkes, the "ethereal, almost ghostly" figure in *The Night of the Iguana* (1961). And Williams's homosexual self, a self he did not acknowledge publicly for many years, is echoed in the relationship between Brick and Skipper in *Cat on a Hot Tin Roof.* Indeed, Williams echoed himself in all his artists and poets and dreamers—men and women characters alike—who suffer from the brutality of the coarsely practical worlds they inhabit.

But Williams by no means limited himself to characters modeled on his own family, as is evident simply from all the lusty and vigorous women who figure in his plays, such as Serafina in *The Rose Tattoo* (1950), Maxine Faulk in *The Night of the Iguana,* or Maggie in *Cat on a Hot Tin Roof.* Indeed, it would be mistaken to regard Williams as a strictly autobiographical dramatist, for he repeatedly transformed his personal experience so that his characters and their experiences point to timeless human concerns. The plays explore related themes: the experience of the outsider in modern society, human loneliness, the inabiltiy of human beings to communicate with one another, and the irrepressible need to create illusions through which to escape the loneliness and painfulness of existence.

In dramatizing these aspects of experience, Williams was never content to settle for a strictly realistic method of presentation. In his "Production Notes" to *The Glass Menagerie,* for example, he attacked "the straight realistic play with its genuine frigidaire and authentic ice-cubes" by comparing it to a mere "photographic likeness," which he considered inadequate to convey the truth of human experience. To bring the audience closer to the truth, Williams argued in favor of "expressionism and all other unconventional techniques in drama." In *The Glass Menagerie* he relied heavily on suggestive music, lighting, and pantomime to evoke the memories of Tom Wingfield. His notes to the play reveal that he intended even to convey comments on Tom's staged memories through the device of projecting images or phrases on a screen—a device from the epic theater of Brecht. Although Williams agreed to omitting the screen device in the original production of the play, he has persisted in using other techniques of expressionistic theater to evoke the mood and quality of his characters' experience. In his "Notes for the Designer" at the beginning of *Cat on a Hot Tin Roof,* Williams clearly blends realistic and expressionistic approaches by describing the stage furniture in meticulous detail and then concluding with the direction that "the walls below the ceiling should dissolve mysteriously into air." He even turns the furniture into a form of symbolic statement by noting that Brick's "*huge* console combination of radio-phonograph (hi-fi with three speakers) TV set *and* liquor cabinet . . . is a very complete and compact little shrine to virtually all the comforts and illusions behind which we hide from such things as the characters in the play are faced with."

The entire set for *Cat on a Hot Tin Roof*—the bedroom of Brick and Maggie—is a richly symbolic location, for the "big double bed" that it contains tangibly reflects the frustrating relationship of Maggie and Brick, and the bedroom as a whole evokes the problematic relationship of Skipper and Brick through the memories it contains of its original owners, "a pair of old bachelors who shared this room all their lives together." In fact, the image of the bedroom and all that it begets—or fails to beget—is a central concern for everyone in the play, for Big Daddy and Big Mama, for Gooper and Mae alike. It is thus highly appropriate that all the struggles within the family take place within this haunting room.

Despite its frankly suggestive set, when the play opened, the critic Walter Kerr called it "a beautifully written, perfectly directed, stunningly acted play of evasion: evasion on the part of its principal character, evasion perhaps on the part of its playwright." He was referring, of course, to the play's persistent concern with the relationship of Brick and Skipper, the exact nature of which is never clearly established. Williams knew that the relationship would raise questions as to whether or not it was homosexual, and thus he took the unusual step of inserting an interpretative comment into the middle of the play:

> The thing they're discussing, timidly and painfully on the side of BIG DADDY, fiercely, violently on BRICK's side, is the inadmissible thing that SKIPPER died to disavow between them. The fact that if it existed it had to be disavowed to "keep face" in the world they lived in, may be at the heart of the "mendacity" that BRICK drinks to kill his disgust with. It may be the root of his collapse. Or maybe it is only a single manifestation of it, not even the most important. The bird that I hope to catch in the net of this play is not the solution of one man's psychological problem.

In making such remarks, Williams, still putting the matter into the conditional, raises the idea that the problem is not what kind of relationship Brick and Skipper had but their need, created by "the world they lived in," to "keep face." The more important issue, both for Brick and for Williams, is "mendacity." Everyone in the play is guilty of mendacity—of lying and deceiving—and also of betraying and manipulating. And the lies persist only because Big Daddy and Big Mama want to believe them, a condition that suggests the root of public lying is the act of lying to oneself. Williams's concern with the willful perpetuation of illusions is reflected also in the structure of the play, for the first act centers on Maggie trying to get Brick to look at her, while the second act reaches its climax with Big Daddy forcing Brick to look at himself, and the third act derives its power from Brick's final refusal to let Maggie sustain any illusions about him.

Because all the characters in the play are so determinedly bent on their ways yet so undone by the ways they have chosen for themselves, they require very complex performances from actors and actresses—performances that convey both their willfulness and their vulnerability. These qualities were evidently achieved by the American Shakespeare Theater when it revived the play in 1974, as can be seen from a review of that production and from a section of Elizabeth Ashley's autobiography, both reprinted following the text. Photographs from that production convey the sensuality and the helplessness Elizabeth Ashley brought to the role of Maggie (see Figure 1), much as they reveal the obstinacy and the air of defeat Keir Dullea gave to the role of Brick (see Figure 1). They also show the blustery power of Fred Gwynne in the role of Big Daddy (see Figures 2 and 3). Although weakened by disease, that power is still seen in the play as being great enough to hobble virtually everyone in his world.

CAT ON A HOT TIN ROOF

BY TENNESSEE WILLIAMS

CHARACTERS

MARGARET
BRICK
MAE, *sometimes called* SISTER WOMAN
BIG MAMA
DIXIE, *a little girl*
BIG DADDY
REVEREND TOOKER
GOOPER, *sometimes called* BROTHER MAN
DOCTOR BAUGH, *pronounced "Baw"*
LACEY, *a Negro servant*
SOOKEY, *another*
CHILDREN

NOTES FOR THE DESIGNER

The set is the bed-sitting room of a plantation home in the Mississippi Delta. It is along an upstairs gallery which probably runs around the entire house; it has two pairs of very wide doors opening onto the gallery, showing white balustrades against a fair summer sky that fades into dusk and night during the course of the play, which occupies precisely the time of its performance, excepting, of course, the fifteen minutes of intermission.

Perhaps the style of the room is not what you would expect in the home of the Delta's biggest cotton-planter. It is Victorian with a touch of the Far East. It hasn't changed much since it was occupied by the original owners of the place, Jack Straw and Peter Ochello, a pair of old bachelors who shared this room all their lives together. In other words, the room must evoke some ghosts; it is gently and poetically haunted by a relationship that must have involved a tenderness which was uncommon. This may be irrelevant or unnecessary, but I once saw a reproduction of a faded photograph of the verandah of Robert Louis Stevenson's home on that Samoan Island where he spent his last years, and there was a quality of tender light on weathered wood, such as porch furniture made of bamboo and wicker, exposed to tropical suns and tropical rains, which came to mind when I thought about the set for this play, bringing also to mind the grace and comfort of light, the reassurance it gives, on a late and fair afternoon in summer, the way that no matter what, even dread of death, is gently touched and soothed by it. For the set is the background for a play that deals with human extremities of emotion, and it needs that softness behind it.

The bathroom door, showing only pale-blue tile and silver towel racks, is in one side wall; the hall door in the opposite wall. Two articles of furniture need mention: a big double bed which staging should make a functional part of the set as often as suitable, the surface of which should be slightly raked to make figures on it seen more easily; and against the wall space between the two huge double doors upstage: a monumental monstrosity peculiar to our times, a huge console combination of radio-phonograph (hi-fi with three speakers) TV set and liquor cabinet, bearing and containing many glasses and bottles, all in one piece, which is a combination of muted silver tones, and the opalescent tones of reflecting glass, a chromatic link, this thing, between the sepia (tawny gold) tones of the interior and the cool (white and blue) tones of the gallery and sky. This piece of furniture (?!), this monument, is a very complete and compact little shrine to virtually all the comforts and illusions behind which we hide from such things as the characters in the play are faced with.

The set should be far less realistic than I have so far implied in this description of it. I think the walls below the ceiling should dissolve mysteriously into air; the set should be roofed by the sky; stars and moon suggested by traces of milky pallor, as if they were observed through a telescope lens out of focus.

Anything else I can think of? Oh, yes, fanlights (transoms shaped like an open glass fan) above all the doors in the set, with panes of blue and amber, and above all, the designer should take as many pains to give the actors room to move about freely (to show their restlessness, their passion for breaking out) as if it were a set for a ballet.

An evening in summer. The action is continuous, with two intermissions.

Cat on a Hot Tin Roof was rewritten twice by Williams—first, at the request of director Elia Kazan, who requested major changes in the last act for the 1955 Broadway premiere, including the reappearance of Big Daddy, and then for the 1974 production at Stratford, Connecticut. The 1974 version, as critic Clive Barnes indicates in his review, combines elements from the original text (especially the final exchange between Maggie and Brick) and from the text played on Broadway, and is the version reprinted here.

ACT 1

(At the rise of the curtain someone is taking a shower in the bathroom, the door of which is half open. A pretty young woman, with anxious lines in her face, enters the bedroom and crosses to the bathroom door.)

MARGARET *(shouting above roar of water)*: One of those no-neck monsters hit me with a hot buttered biscuit so I have t' change!

*(*MARGARET*'s voice is both rapid and drawling. In her long speeches she has the vocal tricks of a priest delivering a liturgical chant, the lines are almost sung, always continuing a little beyond her breath so she has to gasp for another. Sometimes she intersperses the lines with a little wordless singing, such as "da-da-daaa!")*
(Water turns off and BRICK *calls out to her, but is still unseen. A tone of politely feigned interest, masking indifference, or worse, is characteristic of his speech with* MARGARET.*)*

BRICK: Wha'd you say, Maggie? Water was on s' loud I couldn't hearya. . . .
MARGARET: Well, I!—just remarked that!—one of th' no-neck monsters messed up m' lovely lace dress so I got t'—cha-a-ange. . . . *(She opens and kicks shut drawers of the dresser.)*
BRICK: Why d'ya call Gooper's kiddies no-neck monsters?
MARGARET: Because they've got no necks! Isn't that a good enough reason?
BRICK: Don't they have any necks?
MARGARET: None visible. Their fat little heads are set on their fat little bodies without a bit of connection.
BRICK: That's too bad.
MARGARET: Yes, it's too bad because you can't wring their necks if they've got no necks to wring! Isn't that right, honey? *(She steps out of her dress, stands in a slip of ivory satin and lace.)* Yep, they're no-neck monsters, all no-neck people are monsters . . .

(Children shriek downstairs.)

Hear them? Hear them screaming? I don't know where their voice boxes are located since they don't have necks. I tell you I got so nervous at that table tonight I thought I would throw back my head and utter a scream you could hear across the Arkansas border an' parts of Louisiana an' Tennessee. I said to your charming sister-in-law, Mae, honey, couldn't you feed those precious little things at a separate table with an oilcloth cover? They make such a mess an' the lace cloth looks *so* pretty! She made enormous eyes at me and said, "Ohhh, noooooo! On Big Daddy's birthday? Why, he would never forgive me!" Well, I want you to know, Big Daddy hadn't been at the table two minutes with those five no-neck monsters slobbering and drooling over their food before he threw down his fork an' shouted, "Fo' God's sake, Gooper, why don't you put them pigs at a trough in th' kitchen?"—Well, I swear, I simply could have di-ieed!
  Think of it, Brick, they've got five of them and number six is coming. They've brought the whole bunch down here like animals to display at a county fair. Why, they have those children doin' tricks all the time! "Junior, show Big Daddy how

you do this, show Big Daddy how you do that, say your little piece fo' Big Daddy, Sister. Show your dimples, Sugar. Brother, show Big Daddy how you stand on your head!"—It goes on all the time, along with constant little remarks and innuendos about the fact that you and I have not produced any children, are totally childless and therefore totally useless!—Of course it's comical but it's also disgusting since it's so obvious what they're up to!
BRICK *(without interest)*: What are they up to, Maggie?
MARGARET: Why, you know what they're up to!
BRICK *(appearing)*: No, I don't know what they're up to.

(He stands there in the bathroom doorway drying his hair with a towel and hanging onto the towel rack because one ankle is broken, plastered and bound. He is still slim and firm as a boy. His liquor hasn't started tearing him down outside. He has the additional charm of that cool air of detachment that people have who have given up the struggle. But now and then, when disturbed, something flashes behind it, like lightning in a fair sky, which shows that at some deeper level he is far from peaceful. Perhaps in a stronger light he would show some signs of deliquescence, but the fading, still warm, light from the gallery treats him gently.)

MARGARET: I'll tell you what they're up to, boy of mine!—They're up to cutting you out of your father's estate, and—

(She freezes momentarily before her next remark. Her voice drops as if it were somehow a personally embarrassing admission.)

  —Now we know that Big Daddy's dyin' of—cancer. . . .

(There are voices on the lawn below: long-drawn calls across distance. MARGARET *raises her lovely bare arms and powders her armpits with a light sigh.)*
(She adjusts the angle of a magnifying mirror to straighten an eyelash, then rises fretfully saying.)

  There's so much light in the room it—
BRICK *(softly but sharply)*: Do we?
MARGARET: Do we what?
BRICK: Know Big Daddy's dyin' of cancer?
MARGARET: Got the report today.
BRICK: Oh . . .
MARGARET *(letting down bamboo blinds which cast long, gold-fretted shadows over the room)*: Yep, got th' report just now . . . it didn't surprise me, Baby. . . .

(Her voice has range, and music; sometimes it drops low as a boy's and you have a sudden image of her playing boy's games as a child.)

  I recognized the symptoms soon's we got here last spring, and I'm willin' to bet you that Brother Man and his wife were pretty sure of it, too. That more than likely explains why their usual summer migration to the coolness of the Great Smokies was passed up this summer in favor of—hustlin' down here ev'ry whipstitch with their whole screamin' tribe! And why so many allusions have been made to Rainbow Hill lately. You know what Rainbow Hill is? Place that's famous for treatin' alcoholics an' dope fiends in the movies!

BRICK: I'm not in the movies.

MARGARET: No, and you don't take dope. Otherwise you're a perfect candidate for Rainbow Hill, Baby, and that's where they aim to ship you—over my dead body! Yep, over my dead body they'll ship you there, but nothing would please them better. Then Brother Man could get a-hold of the purse strings and dole out remittances to us, maybe get power of attorney and sign checks for us and cut off our credit wherever, whenever he wanted! Son-of-a-bitch! How'd you like that, Baby?—Well, you've been doin' just about ev'rything in your power to bring it about, you've just been doin' ev'rything you can think of to aid and abet them in this scheme of theirs! Quittin' work, devoting yourself to the occupation of drinkin'!—Breakin' your ankle last night on the high school athletic field: doin' what? Jumpin' hurdles? At two or three in the morning? Just fantastic! Got in the paper. *Clarksdale Register* carried a nice little item about it, human interest story about a well-known former athlete stagin' a one-man track meet on the Glorious Hill High School athletic field last night, but was slightly out of condition and didn't clear the first hurdle! Brother Man Gooper claims he exercised his influence t' keep it from goin' out over AP or UP or every goddam "P."

But, Brick? You still have one big advantage!

(*During the above swift flood of words,* BRICK *has reclined with contrapuntal leisure on the snowy surface of the bed and has rolled over carefully on his side or belly.*)

BRICK (*wryly*): Did you *say* something, Maggie?

MARGARET: Big Daddy dotes on you, honey. And he can't stand Brother Man and Brother Man's wife, that monster of fertility, Mae. Know how I know? By little expressions that flicker over his face when that woman is holding fo'th on one of her choice topics such as—how she refused twilight sleep!—when the twins were delivered! Because she feels motherhood's an experience that a woman ought to experience fully!—in order to fully appreciate the wonder and beauty of it! HAH!—and how she made Brother Man come in an' stand beside her in the delivery room so he would not miss out on the "wonder and beauty" of it either!—producin' those no-neck monsters. . . .

(*A speech of this kind would be antipathetic from almost anybody but* MARGARET; *she makes it oddly funny, because her eyes constantly twinkle and her voice shakes with laughter which is basically indulgent.*)

—Big Daddy shares my attitude toward those two! As for me, well—I give him a laugh now and then and he tolerates me. In fact!—I sometimes suspect that Big Daddy harbors a little unconscious "lech" fo' me. . . .

BRICK: What makes you think that Big Daddy has a lech for you, Maggie?

MARGARET: Way he always drops his eyes down my body when I'm talkin' to him, drops his eyes to my boobs and licks his old chops! Ha ha!

BRICK: That kind of talk is disgusting.

MARGARET: Did anyone ever tell you that you're an ass-aching Puritan, Brick?

I think it's mighty fine that that ole fellow, on the doorstep of death, still takes in my shape with what I think is deserved appreciation!

And you wanta know something else? Big Daddy didn't know how many little Maes and Goopers had been produced! "How many kids have you got?" he asked at the table, just like Brother Man and his wife were new acquaintances to him! Big Mama said he was jokin', but that ole boy wasn't jokin', Lord, no!

And when they infawmed him that they had five already and were turning out number six!—the news seemed to come as a sort of unpleasant surprise . . .

(*Children yell below.*)

Scream, monsters!

(*Turns to* BRICK *with a sudden, gay, charming smile which fades as she notices that he is not looking at her but into fading gold space with a troubled expression.*)
(*It is constant rejection that makes her humor "bitchy."*)

Yes, you should of been at that supper-table, Baby.

(*Whenever she calls him "baby" the word is a soft caress.*)

Y'know, Big Daddy, bless his ole sweet soul, he's the dearest ole thing in the world, but he does hunch over his food as if he preferred not to notice anything else. Well, Mae an' Gooper were side by side at the table, direckly across from Big Daddy, watchin' his face like hawks while they jawed an' jabbered about the cuteness an' brilliance of th' no-neck monsters!

(*She giggles with a hand fluttering at her throat and her breast and her long throat arched.*)
(*She comes downstage and recreates the scene with voice and gesture.*)

And the no-neck monsters were ranged around the table, some in high chairs and some on th'

Books of Knowledge, all in fancy little paper caps in honor of Big Daddy's birthday, and all through dinner, well, I want you to know that Brother Man an' his partner never once, for one moment, stopped exchanging pokes an' pinches an' kicks an' signs an' signals!—Why, they were like a couple of cardsharps fleecing a sucker.—Even Big Mama, bless her ole sweet soul, she isn't th' quickest an' brightest thing in the world, she finally noticed, at last, an' said to Gooper, "Gooper, what are you an' Mae makin' all these signs at each other about?"—I swear t' goodness, I nearly choked on my chicken!

(MARGARET, *back at the dressing table, still doesn't see* BRICK. *He is watching her with a look that is not quite definable—Amused? shocked? contemptuous?—part of those and part of something else.*)

Y'know—your brother Gooper still cherishes the illusion he took a giant step up the social ladder when he married Miss Mae Flynn of the Memphis Flynns.

But I have a piece of Spanish news for Gooper. The Flynns never had a thing in this world but money and they lost that, they were nothing at all but fairly successful climbers. Of course, Mae Flynn came out in Memphis eight years before I made my debut in Nashville, but I had friends at Ward-Belmont who came from Memphis and they used to come to see me and I used to go to see them for Christmas and spring vacations, and so I know who rates an' who doesn't rate in Memphis society. Why, y'know ole Papa Flynn, he barely escaped doing time in the Federal pen for shady manipulations on th' stock market when his chain stores crashed, and as for Mae having been a cotton carnival queen, as they remind us so often, lest we forget, well, that's one honor that I don't envy her for!—Sit on a brass throne on a tacky float an' ride down Main Street, smilin', bowin', and blowin' kisses to all the trash on the street—

(*She picks out a pair of jeweled sandals and rushes to the dressing table.*)

Why, year before last, when Susan McPheeters was singled out fo' that honor, y' know what happened to her? Y'know what happened to poor little Susie McPheeters?
BRICK (*absently*): No. What happened to little Susie McPheeters?
MARGARET: Somebody spit tobacco juice in her face.
BRICK (*dreamily*): Somebody spit tobacco juice in her face?
MARGARET: That's right, some old drunk leaned out of a window in the Hotel Gayoso and yelled, "Hey, Queen, hey, hey, there, Queenie!" Poor Susie looked up and flashed him a radiant smile and he

shot out a squirt of tobacco juice right in poor Susie's face.
BRICK: Well, what d'you know about that.
MARGARET (*gaily*): What do I know about it? I was there, I saw it!
BRICK (*absently*): Must have been kind of funny.
MARGARET: Susie didn't think so. Had hysterics. Screamed like a banshee. They had to stop th' parade an' remove her from her throne an' go on with—

(*She catches sight of him in the mirror, gasps slightly, wheels about to face him. Count ten.*)

—Why are you looking at me like that?
BRICK (*whistling softly, now*): Like what, Maggie?
MARGARET (*intensely, fearfully*): The way y' were lookin' at me just now, befo' I caught your eye in the mirror and you started t' whistle! I don't know how t' describe it but it froze my blood!—I've caught you lookin' at me like that so often lately. What are you thinkin' of when you look at me like that?
BRICK: I wasn't conscious of lookin' at you, Maggie.
MARGARET: Well, I was conscious of it! What were you thinkin'?
BRICK: I don't remember thinking of anything, Maggie.
MARGARET: Don't you think I know that—? Don't you—?—Think I know that—?
BRICK (*coolly*): Know *what,* Maggie?
MARGARET (*struggling for expression*): That I've gone through this—*hideous!—transformation,* become—*hard! Frantic!* (*Then she adds, almost tenderly.*)—*cruel!!*
That's what you've been observing in me lately. How could y' help but observe it? That's all right. I'm not—thin-skinned any more, can't afford t' be thin-skinned any more. (*She is now recovering her power.*) —But Brick? Brick?
BRICK: Did you say something?
MARGARET: I was *goin'* t' say something; that I get—lonely. Very!
BRICK: Ev'rybody gets that . . .
MARGARET: Living with someone you love can be lonelier—than living entirely *alone!*—if the one that y' love doesn't love you. . . .

(*There is a pause.* BRICK *hobbles downstage and asks, without looking at her.*)

BRICK: Would you like to live alone, Maggie?

(*Another pause: then—after she has caught a quick, hurt breath.*)

MARGARET: *No!—God!—I wouldn't!*

(*Another gasping breath. She forcibly controls what must have been an impulse to cry out. We see her deliberately, very forcibly, going all the way back to the world in which you can talk about ordinary matters.*)

Did you have a nice shower?

BRICK: Uh-huh.

MARGARET: Was the water cool?

BRICK: No.

MARGARET: But it made y' feel fresh, huh?

BRICK: Fresher. . . .

MARGARET: I know something would make y' feel *much* fresher!

BRICK: What?

MARGARET: An alcohol rub. Or cologne, a rub with cologne!

BRICK: That's good after a workout but I haven't been workin' out, Maggie.

MARGARET: You've kept in good shape, though.

BRICK (*indifferently*): You think so, Maggie?

MARGARET: I always thought drinkin' men lost their looks, but I was plainly mistaken.

BRICK (*wryly*): Why, thanks, Maggie.

MARGARET: You're the only drinkin' man I know that it never seems t' put fat on.

BRICK: I'm gettin' softer, Maggie.

MARGARET: Well, sooner or later it's bound to soften you up. It was just beginning to soften up Skipper when— (*She stops short.*) I'm sorry. I never could keep my fingers off a sore—I wish you *would* lose your looks. If you did it would make the martyrdom of Saint Maggie a little more bearable. But no such goddam luck. I actually believe you've gotten better looking since you've gone on the bottle. Yeah, a person who didn't know you would think you'd never had a tense nerve in your body or a strained muscle.

(*There are sounds of croquet on the lawn below: the click of mallets, light voices, near and distant.*)

Of course, you always had that detached quality as if you were playing a game without much concern over whether you won or lost, and not that you've lost the game, not lost but just quit playing, you have that rare sort of charm that usually only happens in very old or hopelessly sick people, the charm of the defeated.—You look so cool, so cool, so enviably cool.

REVEREND TOOKER (*off stage right*): Now looka here, boy, lemme show you how to get outa that!

MARGARET: They're playing croquet. The moon has appeared and it's white, just beginning to turn a little bit yellow. . . .

You were a wonderful lover. . . .

Such a wonderful person to go to bed with, and I think mostly because you were really indifferent to it. Isn't that right? Never had any anxiety about it, did it naturally, easily, slowly, with absolute confidence and perfect calm, more like opening a door for a lady or seating her at a table than giving expression to any longing for her. Your indifference made you wonderful at lovemaking— *strange?*—but true. . . .

REVEREND TOOKER: Oh! That's a beauty.

DOCTOR BAUGH: Yeah. I got you boxed.

MARGARET: You know, if I thought you would never, never, *never* make love to me again—I would go downstairs to the kitchen and pick out the longest and sharpest knife I could find and stick it straight into my heart, I swear that I would!

REVEREND TOOKER: Watch out, you're gonna miss it.

DOCTOR BAUGH: You just don't know me, boy!

MARGARET: But one thing I don't have is the charm of the defeated, my hat is still in the ring, and I am determined to win!

(*There is the sound of croquet mallets hitting croquet balls.*)

REVEREND TOOKER: Mmm—You're too slippery for me.

MARGARET: —What is the victory of a cat on a hot tin roof?—I wish I knew. . . .

Just staying on it, I guess, as long as she can. . . .

DOCTOR BAUGH: Jus' like an eel, boy, jus' like an eel!

(*More croquet sounds.*)

MARGARET: Later tonight I'm going to tell you I love you an' maybe by that time you'll be drunk enough to believe me. Yes, they're playing croquet. . . .

Big Daddy is dying of cancer. . . .

What were you thinking of when I caught you looking at me like that? Were you thinking of Skipper?

(BRICK *takes up his crutch, rises.*)

Oh, excuse me, forgive me, but laws of silence don't work! No, laws of silence don't work. . . .

(BRICK *crosses to the bar, takes a quick drink, and rubs his head with a towel.*)

Laws of silence don't work. . . .

When something is festering in your memory or your imagination, laws of silence don't work, it's just like shutting a door and locking it on a house on fire in hope of forgetting that the house is burning. But not facing a fire doesn't put it out. Silence about a thing just magnifies it. It grows and festers in silence, becomes malignant. . . .

(*He drops his crutch.*)

BRICK: Give me my crutch.

(*He has stopped rubbing his hair dry but still stands hanging onto the towel rack in a white towel-cloth robe.*)

MARGARET: Lean on me.

BRICK: No, just give me my crutch.

MARGARET: Lean on my shoulder.

BRICK: *I don't want to lean on your shoulder, I want my crutch!*

(*This is spoken like sudden lightning.*)

Are you going to give me my crutch or do I have to get down on my knees on the floor and—

MARGARET: *Here, here, take it, take it! (She has thrust the crutch at him.)*

BRICK *(hobbling out)*: Thanks . . .

MARGARET: We mustn't scream at each other, the walls in this house have ears. . . .

(He hobbles directly to liquor cabinet to get a new drink.)

—but that's the first time I've heard you raise your voice in a long time, Brick. A crack in the wall?—Of composure?

—I think that's a good sign. . . .

A sign of nerves in a player on the defensive!

(BRICK turns and smiles at her coolly over his fresh drink.)

BRICK: It just hasn't happened yet, Maggie.

MARGARET: What?

BRICK: The click I get in my head when I've had enough of this stuff to make me peaceful. . . .

Will you do me a favor?

MARGARET: Maybe I will. What favor?

BRICK: Just, just keep your voice down!

MARGARET *(in a hoarse whisper)*: I'll do you that favor, I'll speak in a whisper, if not shut up completely, if *you* will do *me* a favor and make that drink your last one till after the party.

BRICK: What party?

MARGARET: Big Daddy's birthday party.

BRICK: Is this Big Daddy's birthday?

MARGARET: You know this is Big Daddy's birthday!

BRICK: No, I don't, I forgot it.

MARGARET: Well, I remembered it for you. . . .

(They are both speaking as breathlessly as a pair of kids after a fight, drawing deep exhausted breaths and looking at each other with faraway eyes, shaking and panting together as if they had broken apart from a violent struggle.)

BRICK: Good for you, Maggie.

MARGARET: You just have to scribble a few lines on this card.

BRICK: You scribble something, Maggie.

MARGARET: It's got to be your handwriting; it's your present, I've given him my present; it's got to be your handwriting!

(The tension between them is building again, the voices becoming shrill once more.)

BRICK: I didn't get him a present.

MARGARET: I got one for you.

BRICK: All right. You write the card, then.

MARGARET: And have him know you didn't remember his birthday?

BRICK: I didn't remember his birthday.

MARGARET: You don't have to prove you didn't!

BRICK: I don't want to fool him about it.

MARGARET: Just write "Love, Brick!" for God's—

BRICK: No.

MARGARET: You've *got* to!

BRICK: I don't have to do anything I don't want to do. You keep forgetting the conditions on which I agreed to stay on living with you.

MARGARET *(out before she knows it)*: I'm not living with you. We occupy the same cage.

BRICK: You've got to remember the conditions agreed on.

SONNY *(off stage)*: Mommy, give it to me. I had it first.

MAE: Hush.

MARGARET: They're impossible conditions!

BRICK: Then why don't you—?

SONNY: I want it, I want it!

MAE: Get away!

MARGARET: HUSH! Who is out there? Is somebody at the door?

(There are footsteps in hall.)

MAE *(outside)*: May I enter a moment?

MARGARET: OH, *you!* Sure. Come in, Mae.

(MAE enters bearing aloft the bow of a young lady's archery set.)

MAE: Brick, is this thing yours?

MARGARET: Why, Sister Woman—that's my Diana Trophy. Won it at the intercollegiate archery contest on the Ole Miss campus.

MAE: It's a mighty dangerous thing to leave exposed round a house full of nawmal rid-blooded children, attracted t'weapons.

MARGARET: "Nawmal rid-blooded children attracted t'weapons" ought t'be taught to keep their hands off things that don't belong to them.

MAE: Maggie, honey, if you had children of your own you'd know how funny that is. Will you please lock this up and put the key out of reach?

MARGARET: Sister Woman, nobody is plotting the destruction of your kiddies. —Brick and I still have our special archers' license. We're goin' deer-huntin' on Moon Lake as soon as the season starts. I love to run with dogs through chilly woods, run, run leap over obstructions— *(She goes into the closet carrying the bow.)*

MAE: How's the injured ankle, Brick?

BRICK: Doesn't hurt. Just itches.

MAE: Oh, my! Brick—Brick, you should've been downstairs after supper! Kiddies put on a show. Polly played the piano, Buster an' Sonny drums, an' then they turned out the lights an' Dixie an' Trixie puhfawmed a toe dance in fairy costume with *spahklus!* Big Daddy just beamed! He just beamed!

MARGARET *(from the closet with a sharp laugh)*: Oh, I bet. It breaks my heart that we missed it! *(She reenters.)* But Mae? Why did y'give dawgs' names to all your kiddies?

MAE: *Dogs'* names?

MARGARET (*sweetly*): Dixie, Trixie, Buster, Sonny, Polly! —Sounds like four dogs and a parrot . . .

MAE: Maggie?

(MARGARET *turns with a smile.*)

Why are you so catty?

MARGARET: Cause I'm a cat! But why can't *you* take a joke, Sister Woman?

MAE: Nothin' pleases me more than a joke that's funny. You know the real names of our kiddies. Buster's real name is Robert. Sonny's real name is Saunders. Trixie's real name is Marlene and Dixie's—

(GOOPER *downstairs calls for her.* "Hey, Mae! Sister Woman, intermission is over!"—*she rushes to door, saying.*)

Intermission is over! See ya later!

MARGARET: I wonder what Dixie's real name is?

BRICK: Maggie, being catty doesn't help things any . . .

MARGARET: I know! *WHY!*—Am I so catty?—Cause I'm consumed with envy an' eaten up with longing?—Brick, I'm going to lay out your beautiful Shantung silk suit from Rome and one of your monogrammed silk shirts. I'll put your cuff links in it, those lovely star sapphires I get you to wear so rarely. . . .

BRICK: I can't get trousers on over this plaster cast.

MARGARET: Yes, you can, I'll help you.

BRICK: I'm not going to get dressed, Maggie.

MARGARET: Will you just put on a pair of white silk pajamas?

BRICK: Yes, I'll do that, Maggie.

MARGARET: *Thank* you, thank you so *much!*

BRICK: Don't mention it.

MARGARET: *Oh, Brick!* How long does it have t' go on? This punishment? Haven't I done time enough, haven't I served my term, can't I apply for a—pardon?

BRICK: Maggie, you're spoiling my liquor. Lately your voice always sounds like you'd been running upstairs to warn somebody that the house was on fire!

MARGARET: Well, no wonder, no wonder. Y'know what I feel like, Brick?
  I feel all the time like a cat on a hot tin roof!

BRICK: Then jump off the roof, jump off it, cats can jump off roofs and land on their four feet uninjured!

MARGARET: Oh, yes!

BRICK: Do it!—fo' God's sake, do it . . .

MARGARET: Do what?

BRICK: Take a lover!

MARGARET: I can't see a man but you! Even with my eyes closed, I just see you! Why don't you get ugly, Brick, why don't you please get fat or ugly or something so I could stand it? (*She rushes to hall door, opens it, listens.*) The concert is still going on!

Bravo, no-necks, bravo! (*She slams and locks door fiercely.*)

BRICK: What did you lock the door for?

MARGARET: To give us a little privacy for a while.

BRICK: You know better, Maggie.

MARGARET: No, I don't know better. . . .

(*She rushes to gallery doors, draws the rose-silk drapes across them.*)

BRICK: Don't make a fool of yourself.

MARGARET: I don't mind makin' a fool of myself over you!

BRICK: I mind, Maggie. I feel embarrassed for you.

MARGARET: Feel embarrassed! But don't continue my torture. I can't live on and on under these circumstances.

BRICK: You agreed to—

MARGARET: I know but—

BRICK: —Accept that condition!

MARGARET: *I CAN'T! I CAN'T! I CAN'T!* (*She seizes his shoulder.*)

BRICK: Let go!

(*He breaks away from her and seizes the small boudoir chair and raises it like a lion-tamer facing a big circus cat.*)
(*Count five. She stares at him with her fist pressed to her mouth, then bursts into shrill, almost hysterical laughter. He remains grave for a moment, then grins and puts the chair down.*)
(BIG MAMA *calls through closed door.*)

BIG MAMA: Son? Son? Son?

BRICK: What is it, Big Mama?

BIG MAMA (*outside*): Oh, son! We got the most wonderful news about Big Daddy. I just had t' run up an' tell you right this— (*She rattles the knob.*) —What's this door doin', locked, faw? You all think there's robbers in the house?

MARGARET: Big Mama, Brick is dressin', he's not dressed yet.

BIG MAMA: That's all right, it won't be the first time I've seen Brick not dressed. Come on, open this door!

(MARGARET, *with a grimace, goes to unlock and open the hall door, as* BRICK *hobbles rapidly to the bathroom and kicks the door shut.* BIG MAMA *has disappeared from the hall.*)

MARGARET: Big Mama?

(BIG MAMA *appears through the opposite gallery doors behind* MARGARET, *huffing and puffing like an old bulldog. She is a short, stout woman; her sixty years and 170 pounds have left her somewhat breathless most of the time; she's always tensed like a boxer, or rather, a Japanese wrestler. Her "family" was maybe a little superior to* BIG

DADDY's *but not much. She wears a black or silver lace dress and at least half a million in flashy gems. She is very sincere.*)

BIG MAMA (*loudly, startling* MARGARET): Here—I come through Gooper's and Mae's gall'ry door. Where's Brick? *Brick*—Hurry on out of there, son, I just have a second and want to give you the news about Big Daddy.—I hate locked doors in a house. . . .

MARGARET (*with affected lightness*): I've noticed you do, Big Mama, but people have got to have *some* moments of privacy, don't they?

BIG MAMA: No, ma'am, not in *my* house. (*Without pause.*) Whacha took off you' dress faw? I thought that little lace dress was so sweet on yuh, honey.

MARGARET: I thought it looked sweet on me, too, but one of m' cute little table-partners used it for a napkin so—!

BIG MAMA (*picking up stockings on floor*): What?

MARGARET: You know, Big Mama, Mae and Gooper's so touchy about those children—thanks, Big Mama . . .

(BIG MAMA *has thrust the picked-up stockings in* MARGARET's *hand with a grunt.*)

—that you just don't dare to suggest there's any room for improvement in their—

BIG MAMA: Brick, hurry out!—Shoot, Maggie, you just don't like children.

MARGARET: I do SO like children! Adore them!—well brought up!

BIG MAMA (*gentle—loving*): Well, why don't you have some and bring them up well, then, instead of all the time pickin' on Gooper's an' Mae's?

GOOPER (*shouting up the stairs*): Hey, hey, Big Mama, Betsy an' Hugh got to go, waitin' t' tell yuh g'by!

BIG MAMA: Tell 'em to hold their hawses, I'll be right down in a jiffy!

GOOPER: Yes ma'am!

(*She turns to the bathroom door and calls out.*)

BIG MAMA: Son? Can you hear me in there?

(*There is a muffled answer.*)

We just got the full report from the laboratory at the Ochsner Clinic, completely negative, son, ev'rything negative, right on down the line! Nothin' a-tall's wrong with him but some little functional thing called a spastic colon. Can you hear me, son?

MARGARET: He can hear you, Big Mama.

BIG MAMA: Then why don't he say something? God Almighty, a piece of news like that should make him shout. It made *me* shout, I can tell you. I shouted and sobbed and fell right down on my knees!—Look! (*She pulls up her skirt.*) See the

bruises where I hit my kneecaps? Took both doctors to haul me back on my feet!

(*She laughs—she always laughs like hell at herself.*)

Big Daddy was furious with me! But ain't that wonderful news?

(*Facing bathroom again, she continues.*)

After all the anxiety we been through to git a report like that on Big Daddy's birthday? Big Daddy tried to hide how much of a load that news took off his mind, but didn't fool *me*. He was mighty close to crying about it *himself*!

(*Goodbyes are shouted downstairs, and she rushes to door.*)

GOOPER: Big Mama!

BIG MAMA: *Hold those people down there, don't let them go!*—Now, git dressed, we're comin' up to this room fo' Big Daddy's birthday party because of your ankle.—How's his ankle, Maggie?

MARGARET: Well, he broke it, Big Mama.

BIG MAMA: I know he broke it.

(*A phone is ringing in hall. A Negro voice answers: "Mistuh Polly's res'dence."*)

I mean does it hurt him much still.

MARGARET: I'm afraid I can't give you that information, Big Mama. You'll have to ask Brick if it hurts much still or not.

SOOKEY (*in the hall*): It's Memphis, Mizz Polly, it's Miss Sally in Memphis.

BIG MAMA: Awright, Sookey.

(BIG MAMA *rushes into the hall and is heard shouting on the phone.*)

Hello, Miss Sally. How are you, Miss Sally?—Yes, well, I was just gonna call you about it. *Shoot!*

MARGARET: Brick, don't!

(BIG MAMA *raises her voice to a bellow.*)

BIG MAMA: *Miss Sally? Don't ever call me from the Gayoso Lobby, too much talk goes on in that hotel lobby, no wonder you can't hear me!* Now listen, Miss Sally. They's nothin' serious wrong with Big Daddy. We got the report just now, they's nothin' wrong but a thing called a—spastic! SPASTIC!—colon . . . (*She appears at the hall door and calls to* MARGARET.) —Maggie, come out here and talk to that fool on the phone. I'm shouted breathless!

MARGARET (*goes out and is heard sweetly at phone*): Miss Sally? This is Brick's wife, Maggie. So nice to hear your voice. Can you hear *mine*? Well, *good*!—Big Mama just wanted you to know that they've got the report from the Ochsner Clinic and what Big Daddy has is a spastic colon. Yes. Spastic colon,

Miss Sally. That's right, spastic colon. *G'bye, Miss Sally, hope I'll see you real soon!*

(Hangs up a little before MISS SALLY *was probably ready to terminate the talk. She returns through the hall door.)*

She heard me perfectly. I've discovered with deaf people the thing to do is not shout at them but just enunciate clearly. My rich old Aunt Cornelia was deaf as the dead but I could make her hear me just by sayin' each word slowly, distinctly, close to her ear. I read her the *Commercial Appeal* ev'ry night, read her the classified ads in it, even, she never missed a word of it. But was she a mean ole thing! Know what I got when she died? Her unexpired subscriptions to five magazines and the Book-of-the-Month Club and a LIBRARY full of ev'ry dull book ever written! All else went to her hellcat of a sister . . . meaner than she was, even!

*(*BIG MAMA *has been straightening things up in the room during this speech.)*

BIG MAMA *(closing closet door on discarded clothes)*: Miss Sally sure is a case! Big Daddy says she's always got her hand out fo' something. He's not mistaken. That poor ole thing always has her hand out fo' somethin'. I don't think Big Daddy gives her as much as he should.

GOOPER: Big Mama! Come on now! Betsy and Hugh can't wait no longer!

BIG MAMA *(shouting)*: I'm comin'!

(She starts out. At the hall door, turns and jerks a forefinger, first toward the bathroom door, then toward the liquor cabinet, meaning: "Has BRICK *been drinking?"* MARGARET *pretends not to understand, cocks her head and raises her brows as if the pantomimic performance was completely mystifying to her.)*

*(*BIG MAMA *rushes back to* MARGARET.*)*

Shoot! Stop playin' so dumb!—I mean has he been drinkin' that stuff much yet?

MARGARET *(with a little laugh)*: Oh! I think he had a highball after supper.

BIG MAMA: Don't laugh about it!—some single men stop drinkin' when they git married and others start! Brick never touched liquor before he—!

MARGARET *(crying out)*: *THAT'S NOT FAIR!*

BIG MAMA: Fair or not fair I want to ask you a question, one question: D'you make Brick happy in bed?

MARGARET: Why don't you ask if he makes *me* happy in bed?

BIG MAMA: Because I know that—

MARGARET: *It works both ways!*

BIG MAMA: Something's not right! You're childless and my son drinks!

GOOPER: Come on, Big Mama!

*(*GOOPER *has called her downstairs and she has rushed to the door on the line above. She turns at the door and points at the bed.)*

—When a marriage goes on the rocks, the rocks are *there*, right *there!*

MARGARET: *That's—*

*(*BIG MAMA *has swept out of the room and slammed the door.)*

—not—*fair* . . .

*(*MARGARET *is alone, completely alone, and she feels it. She draws in, hunches her shoulders, raises her arms with fists clenched, shuts her eyes tight as a child about to be stabbed with a vaccination needle. When she opens her eyes again, what she sees is the long oval mirror and she rushes straight to it, stares into it with a grimace and says: "Who are you?"—Then she crouches a little and answers herself in a different voice which is high, thin, mocking: "I am Maggie the Cat!"—Straightens quickly as bathroom door opens a little and* BRICK *calls out to her.)*

BRICK: Has Big Mama gone?

MARGARET: She's gone.

(He opens the bathroom door and hobbles out, with his liquor glass now empty, straight to the liquor cabinet. He is whistling softly. MARGARET's *head pivots on her long, slender throat to watch him.)*

(She raises a hand uncertainly to the base of her throat, as if it was difficult for her to swallow, before she speaks.)

You know, our sex life didn't just peter out in the usual way, it was cut off short, long before the natural time for it to, and it's going to revive again, just as sudden as that. I'm confident of it. That's what I'm keeping myself attractive for. For the time when you'll see me again like other men see me. Yes, like other men see me. They still see me, Brick, and they like what they see. Uh-huh. Some of them would give their—

Look, Brick!

(She stands before the long oval mirror, touches her breast and then her hips with her two hands.)

How high my body stays on me!—Nothing has fallen on me—not a fraction. . . .

(Her voice is soft and trembling: a pleading child's. At this moment as he turns to glance at her—a look which is like a player passing a ball to another player, third down and goal to go—she has to capture the audience in a grip so tight that she can hold it till the first intermission without any lapse of attention.)

Other men still want me. My face looks strained, sometimes, but I've kept my figure as well as you've kept yours, and men admire it. I still turn heads on the street. Why, last week in Memphis everywhere that I went men's eyes burned holes in my clothes, at the country club and in restaurants and department stores, there wasn't a man I met or walked by that didn't just eat me up with his eyes and turn around when I passed him and look back at me. Why, at Alice's party for her New York cousins, the best-lookin' man in the crowd—followed me upstairs and tried to force his way in the powder room with me, followed me to the door and tried to force his way in!

BRICK: Why didn't you let him, Maggie?

MARGARET: Because I'm not that common, for one thing. Not that I wasn't almost tempted to. You like to know who it was? It was Sonny Boy Maxwell, that's who!

BRICK: Oh, yeah, Sonny Boy Maxwell, he was a good end-runner but had a little injury to his back and had to quit.

MARGARET: He has no injury now and has no wife and still has a lech for me!

BRICK: I see no reason to lock him out of a powder room in that case.

MARGARET: And have someone catch me at it? I'm not that stupid. Oh, I might sometime cheat on you with someone, since you're so insultingly eager to have me do it!—But if I do, you can be damned sure it will be in a place and a time where no one but me and the man could possibly know. Because I'm not going to give you any excuse to divorce me for being unfaithful or anything else. . . .

BRICK: Maggie, I wouldn't divorce you for being unfaithful or anything else. Don't you know that? Hell. I'd be relieved to know that you'd found yourself a lover.

MARGARET: Well, I'm taking no chances. No, I'd rather stay on this hot tin roof.

BRICK: A hot tin roof's 'n uncomfo'table place t' stay on. . . . (He starts to whistle softly.)

MARGARET (through his whistle): Yeah, but I can stay on it just as long as I have to.

BRICK: You could leave me, Maggie.

(He resumes whistle. She wheels about to glare at him.)

MARGARET: Don't want to and will not! Besides if I did, you don't have a cent to pay for it but what you get from Big Daddy and he's dying of cancer!

(For the first time a realization of BIG DADDY's doom seems to penetrate to BRICK's consciousness, visibly, and he looks at MARGARET.)

BRICK: Big Mama just said he wasn't, that the report was okay.

MARGARET: That's what she thinks because she got the same story that they gave Big Daddy. And was just as taken in by it as he was, poor ole things. . . . But tonight they're going to tell her the truth

about it. When Big Daddy goes to bed, they're going to tell her that he is dying of cancer. (She slams the dresser drawer.)—It's malignant and it's terminal.

BRICK: Does Big Daddy know it?

MARGARET: Hell, do they ever know it? Nobody says, "You're dying." You have to fool them. They have to fool themselves.

BRICK: Why?

MARGARET: Why? Because human beings dream of life everlasting, that's the reason! But most of them want it on earth and not in heaven.

(He gives a short, hard laugh at her touch of humor.)

Well. . . . (She touches up her mascara.) That's how it is, anyhow. . . . (She looks about.) Where did I put down my cigarette? Don't want to burn up the home-place, at least not with Mae and Gooper and their five monsters in it!

(She has found it and sucks at it greedily. Blows out smoke and continues.)

So this is Big Daddy's last birthday. And Mae and Gooper, they know it, oh, they know it, all right. They got the first information from the Ochsner Clinic. That's why they rushed down here with their no-neck monsters. Because. Do you know something? Big Daddy's made no will? Big Daddy's never made out any will in his life, and so this campaign's afoot to impress him, forcibly as possible, with the fact that you drink and I've borne no children!

(He continues to stare at her a moment, then mutters something sharp but not audible and hobbles rather rapidly out onto the long gallery in the fading, much faded, gold light.)

MARGARET (continuing her liturgical chant): Y'know, I'm fond of Big Daddy, I am genuinely fond of that old man, I really am, you know. . . .

BRICK (faintly, vaguely): Yes, I know you are. . . .

MARGARET: I've always sort of admired him in spite of his coarseness, his four-letter words and so forth. Because Big Daddy is what he is, and he makes no bones about it. He hasn't turned gentleman farmer, he's still a Mississippi redneck, as much of a redneck as he must have been when he was just overseer here on the old Jack Straw and Peter Ochello place. But he got hold of it an' built it into th' biggest an' finest plantation in the Delta.—I've always liked Big Daddy. . . .

(She crosses to the proscenium.)

Well, this is Big Daddy's last birthday. I'm sorry about it. But I'm facing the facts. It takes money to take care of a drinker and that's the office that I've been elected to lately.

BRICK: You don't have to take care of me.

MARGARET: Yes, I do. Two people in the same boat have got to take care of each other. At least you want money to buy more Echo Spring when this supply is exhausted, or will you be satisfied with a ten-cent beer?

Mae an' Gooper are plannin' to freeze us out of Big Daddy's estate because you drink and I'm childless. But we can defeat that plan. We're *going* to defeat that plan!

Brick, y'know, I've been so God damn disgustingly poor all my life!—That's the *truth*, Brick!

BRICK: I'm not sayin' it isn't.

MARGARET: Always had to suck up to people I couldn't stand because they had money and I was poor as Job's turkey. You don't know what that's like. Well, I'll tell you, it's like you would feel a thousand miles away from Echo Spring!—And had to get back to it on that broken ankle . . . without a crutch!

That's how it feels to be as poor as Job's turkey and have to suck up to relatives that you hated because they had money and all you had was a bunch of hand-me-down clothes and a few old moldy three-per-cent government bonds. My daddy loved his liquor, he fell in love with his liquor the way you've fallen in love with Echo Spring!—And my poor Mama, having to maintain some semblance of social position, to keep appearances up, on an income of one hundred and fifty dollars a month on those old government bonds!

When I came out, the year that I made my debut, I had just two evening dresses! One Mother made me from a pattern in *Vogue*, the other a hand-me-down from a snotty rich cousin I hated!

—The dress that I married you in was my grandmother's weddin' gown. . . .

So that's why I'm like a cat on a hot tin roof!

(BRICK is still on the gallery. Someone below calls up to him in a warm Negro voice, "Hiya, Mistuh Brick, how yuh feelin'?" BRICK raises his liquor glass as if that answered the question.)

MARGARET: You can be young without money, but you can't be old without it. You've got to be old *with* money because to be old without it is just too awful, you've got to be one or the other, either *young* or *with money*, you can't be old and *without* it.—That's the *truth*, Brick. . . .

(BRICK whistles softly, vaguely.)

Well, now I'm dressed, I'm all dressed, there's nothing else for me to do. *(Forlornly, almost fearfully.)* I'm dressed, all dressed, nothing else for me to do. . . .

(She moves about restlessly, aimlessly, and speaks, as if to herself.)

What am I—? Oh!—my bracelets. . . .

(She starts working a collection of bracelets over her hands onto her wrists, about six on each, as she talks.)

I've thought a whole lot about it and now I know when I made my mistake. Yes, I made my mistake when I told you the truth about that thing with Skipper. Never should have confessed it, a fatal error, tellin' you about that thing with Skipper.

BRICK: Maggie, shut up about Skipper. I mean it, Maggie; you got to shut up about Skipper.

MARGARET: You ought to understand that Skipper and I—

BRICK: You don't think I'm serious, Maggie? You're fooled by the fact that I am saying this quiet? Look, Maggie. What you're doing is a dangerous thing to do. You're—you're—you're—foolin' with something that—nobody ought to fool with.

MARGARET: This time I'm going to finish what I have to say to you. Skipper and I made love, if love you could call it, because it made both of us feel a little bit closer to you. You see, you son of a bitch, you asked too much of people, of me, of him, of all the unlucky poor damned sons of bitches that happen to love you, and there was a whole pack of them, yes, there was a pack of them besides me and Skipper, you asked too goddam much of people that loved you, you—superior creature!— you godlike being!—And so we made love to each other to dream it was you, both of us! Yes, yes, yes! Truth, truth! What's so awful about it? I like it, I think the truth is—yeah! I shouldn't have told you. . . .

BRICK *(holding his head unnaturally still and uptilted a bit)*: It was Skipper that told me about it. Not you, Maggie.

MARGARET: I told you!

BRICK: After he told me!

MARGARET: What does it matter who—?

DIXIE: I got your mallet, I got your mallet.

TRIXIE: Give it to me, give it to me, it's mine.

(BRICK turns suddenly out upon the gallery and calls.)

BRICK: Little girl! Hey, little girl!

LITTLE GIRL *(at a distance)*: What, Uncle Brick?

BRICK: Tell the folks to come up!—Bring everybody upstairs!

TRIXIE: It's mine, it's mine.

MARGARET: I can't stop myself! I'd go on telling you this in front of them all, if I had to!

BRICK: Little girl, Go on, go on, will you? Do what I told you, call them!

DIXIE: Okay.

MARGARET: Because it's got to be told and you, you!—you never let me!

(She sobs, then controls herself, and continues almost calmly.)

It was one of those beautiful, ideal things, they tell about in the Greek legends, it couldn't be anything else, you being you, and that's what made it so sad, and that's what made it so awful, because it was love that never could be carried through to anything satisfying or even talked about plainly.

BRICK: Maggie, you gotta stop this.

MARGARET: Brick, I tell you, you got to believe me, Brick, I *do* understand all about it! I—I think it was—*noble!* Can't you tell I'm sincere when I say I respect it? My only point, the only point that I'm making, is life has got to be allowed to continue even after the *dream* of life is—all—over. . . .

(BRICK is without his crutch. Leaning on furniture, he crosses to pick it up as she continues as if possessed by a will outside herself.)

Why I remember when we double-dated at college, Gladys Fitzgerald and I and you and Skipper, it was more like a date between you and Skipper. Gladys and I were just sort of tagging along as if it was necessary to chaperone you!—to make a good public impression—

BRICK *(turns to face her, half lifting his crutch)*: Maggie, you want me to hit you with this crutch? Don't you know I could kill you with this crutch?

MARGARET: Good, Lord, man, d' you think I'd care if you did?

BRICK: One man has one great good true thing in his life. One great good thing which is true!—I had friendship with Skipper.—You are naming it dirty!

MARGARET: I'm not naming it dirty! I am naming it clean.

BRICK: Not love with you, Maggie, but friendship with Skipper was that one great true thing, and you are naming it dirty!

MARGARET: Then you haven't been listenin', not understood what I'm saying! I'm naming it so damn clean that it killed poor Skipper!—You two had something that had to be kept on ice, yes, incorruptible, yes!—and death was the only icebox where you could keep it. . . .

BRICK: I married you, Maggie. Why would I marry you, Maggie, if I was—?

MARGARET: Brick, let me finish!—I know, believe me I know, that it was only Skipper that harbored even any *unconscious* desire for anything not perfectly pure between you two!—Now let me skip a little. You married me early that summer we graduated out of Ole Miss, and we were happy, weren't we, we were blissful, yes, hit heaven together ev'ry time that we loved! But that fall you an' Skipper turned down wonderful offers of jobs in order to keep on bein' football heroes—pro-football heroes. You organized the Dixie Stars that fall, so you could keep on bein' teammates forever! But somethin' was not right with it!—*Me included!*—between you. Skipper began hittin' the bottle . . . you got a spinal injury—couldn't play the Thanks-givin' game in Chicago, watched it on TV from a traction bed in Toledo. I joined Skipper. The Dixie Stars lost because poor Skipper was drunk. We drank together that night all night in the bar of the Blackstone and when cold day was comin' up over the Lake an' we were comin' out drunk to take a dizzy look at it, I said, "SKIPPER! STOP LOVIN' MY HUSBAND OR TELL HIM HE'S GOT TO LET YOU ADMIT IT TO HIM!"—one way or another!

HE SLAPPED ME HARD ON THE MOUTH!—then turned and ran without stopping once, I am sure, all the way back into his room at the Blackstone. . . .

—When I came to his room that night, with a little scratch like a shy little mouse at his door, he made that pitiful, ineffectual little attempt to prove that what I had said wasn't true. . . .

(BRICK strikes at her with crutch, a blow that shatters the gemlike lamp on the table.)

—In this way, I destroyed him, by telling him truth that he and his world which he was born and raised in, yours and his world, had told him could not be told?

From then on Skipper was nothing at all but a receptacle for liquor and drugs. . . .

—*Who shot cock robin? I with my*— *(She throws back her head with tight shut eyes.)* —*merciful arrow!*

(BRICK strikes at her; misses.)

Missed me!—Sorry,—I'm not tryin' to whitewash my behavior, Christ, no! Brick, I'm not good. I don't know why people have to pretend to be good, nobody's good. The rich or the well-to-do can afford to respect moral patterns, conventional moral patterns, but I could never afford to, yeah, but—I'm honest! Give me credit for just that, will you *please?*—Born poor, raised poor, expect to die poor unless I manage to get us something out of what Big Daddy leaves when he dies of cancer! But Brick?!—*Skipper is dead! I'm alive!* Maggie the cat is—

(BRICK hops awkwardly forward and strikes at her again with his crutch.)

—alive! I am alive, alive! I am . . .

(He hurls the crutch at her, across the bed she took refuge behind, and pitches forward on the floor as she completes her speech.)

—alive!

(A little girl, DIXIE, *bursts into the room, wearing an Indian war bonnet and firing a cap pistol at* MARGARET *and shouting: "Bang, bang, bang!")*

(Laughter downstairs floats through the open hall door. MARGARET *had crouched gasping to bed at child's entrance. She now rises and says with cool fury.)*

Little girl, your mother or someone should teach you—*(gasping)*—to knock at a door before you come into a room. Otherwise people might think that you—lack—good breeding. . . .

DIXIE: Yanh, yanh, yanh, what is Uncle Brick doin' on th' floor?

BRICK: I tried to kill your Aunt Maggie, but I failed— and I fell. Little girl, give me my crutch so I can get up off th' floor.

MARGARET: Yes, give your uncle his crutch, he's a cripple, honey, he broke his ankle last night jumping hurdles on the high school athletic field!

DIXIE: What were you jumping hurdles for, Uncle Brick?

BRICK: Because I used to jump them, and people like to do what they used to do, even after they've stopped being able to do it. . . .

MARGARET: That's right, that's your answer, now go away, little girl.

(DIXIE fires cap pistol at MARGARET *three times.)*

Stop, you stop that, monster! You little no-neck monster! *(She seizes the cap pistol and hurls it through gallery door.)*

DIXIE *(with a precocious instinct for the cruelest thing)*: You're *jealous!*—You're just jealous because you can't have babies!

(She sticks out her tongue at MARGARET *as she sashays past her with her stomach stuck out, to the gallery.* MARGARET *slams the gallery doors and leans panting against them. There is a pause.* BRICK *has replaced his spilt drink and sits, faraway, on the great four-poster bed.)*

MARGARET: You see?—they gloat over us being childless, even in front of their five little no-neck monsters!

(Pause. Voices approach on the stairs.)

Brick?—I've been to a doctor in Memphis, a—a gynecologist. . . .

I've been completely examined, and there is no reason why we can't have a child whenever we want one. And this is my time by the calendar to conceive. Are you listening to me? Are you? Are you LISTENING TO ME!

BRICK: Yes. I hear you, Maggie. *(His attention returns to her inflamed face.)* —But how in hell on earth do you imagine—that you're going to have a child by a man that can't stand you?

MARGARET: That's a problem that I will have to work out. *(She wheels about to face the hall door.)*

MAE *(off stage left)*: Come on, Big Daddy. We're all goin' up to Brick's room.

(From off stage left, voices: REVEREND TOOKER, DOCTOR BAUGH, MAE.)*

MARGARET: *Here they come!*

(The lights dim.)

ACT 2

(There is no lapse of time. MARGARET *and* BRICK *are in the same positions they held at the end of Act 1.)*

MARGARET *(at door)*: *Here they come!*

(BIG DADDY appears first, a tall man with a fierce, anxious look, moving carefully not to betray his weakness even, or especially, to himself.)

GOOPER: I read in the *Register* that you're getting a new memorial window.

(Some of the people are approaching through the hall, others along the gallery: voices from both directions. GOOPER *and* REVEREND TOOKER *become visible outside gallery doors, and their voices come in clearly.)*

(They pause outside as GOOPER *lights a cigar.)*

REVEREND TOOKER *(vivaciously)*: Oh, but St. Paul's in Grenada has three memorial windows, and the latest one is a Tiffany stained-glass window that cost twenty-five hundred dollars, a picture of Christ the Good Shepherd with a Lamb in His arms.

MARGARET: Big Daddy.

BIG DADDY: Well, Brick.

BRICK: Hello Big Daddy.—Congratulations!

BIG DADDY: —Crap. . . .

GOOPER: Who give that window, Preach?

REVEREND TOOKER: Clyde Fletcher's widow. Also presented St. Paul's with a baptismal font.

GOOPER: Y'know what somebody ought t' give your church is a *coolin'* system, Preach.

MAE *(almost religiously)*: Let's see now, they've had their *tyyy*-phoid shots, and their tetanus shots, their diptheria shots and their hepatitis shots and their polio shots, they got *those* shots every month from May through September, and— Gooper? Hey! Gooper!—What all have the kiddies been shot faw?

REVEREND TOOKER: Yes, siree, Bob! And y'know what Gus Hamma's family gave in his memory to the church at Two Rivers? A complete new stone parish-house with a basketball court in the basement and a—

BIG DADDY *(uttering a loud barking laugh which is far from truly mirthful*): Hey, Preach! What's all this talk about memorials, Preach? Y' think somebody's about t' kick off around here? 'S that it?

(*Startled by this interjection,* REVEREND TOOKER *decides to laugh at the question almost as loud as he can.*)
(*How he would answer the question we'll never know, as he's spared that embarrassment by the voice of* GOOPER's *wife,* MAE, *rising high and clear as she appears with* "DOC" BAUGH, *the family doctor, through the hall door.*)

MARGARET (*overlapping a bit*): Turn on the hi-fi, Brick! Let's have some music t' start th' party with!

BRICK: You turn it on, Maggie.

(*The talk becomes so general that the room sounds like a great aviary of chattering birds. Only* BRICK *remains unengaged, leaning upon the liquor cabinet with his far-away smile, an ice cube in a paper napkin with which he now and then rubs his forehead. He doesn't respond to* MARGARET's *command. She bounds forward and stoops over the instrument panel of the console.*)

GOOPER: We gave 'em that thing for a third anniversary present, got three speakers in it.

(*The room is suddenly blasted by the climax of a Wagnerian opera or a Beethoven symphony.*)

BIG DADDY: *Turn that damn thing off!*

(*Almost instant silence, almost instantly broken by the shouting charge of* BIG MAMA, *entering through the hall door like a charging rhino.*)

BIG MAMA: *Wha's my Brick, wha's mah precious baby!!*

BIG DADDY: Sorry! Turn it back on!

(*Everyone laughs very loud.* BIG DADDY *is famous for his jokes at* BIG MAMA's *expense, and nobody laughs louder at these jokes than* BIG MAMA *herself, though sometimes they're pretty cruel and* BIG MAMA *has to pick up or fuss with something to cover the hurt that the loud laugh doesn't quite cover.*)
(*On this occasion, a happy occasion because the dread in her heart has also been lifted by the false report on* BIG DADDY's *condition, she giggles, grotesquely, coyly, in* BIG DADDY's *direction and bears down upon* BRICK, *all very quick and alive.*)

BIG MAMA: Here he is, here's my precious baby! What's that you've got in your hand? You put that liquor down, son, your hand was made fo' holdin' somethin' better than that!

GOOPER: Look at Brick put it down!

(BRICK *has obeyed* BIG MAMA *by draining the glass and handing it to her. Again everyone laughs, some high, some low.*)

BIG MAMA: Oh, you bad boy, you, you're my bad little boy. Give Big Mama a kiss, you bad boy, you!— Look at him shy away, will you? Brick never liked

bein' kissed or made a fuss over, I guess because he's always had too much of it!
  Son, you turn that thing off!

(BRICK *has switched on the TV set.*)

I can't stand TV, radio was bad enough but TV has gone it one better, I mean—(*plops wheezing in chair*)—one worse, ha ha! Now what'm I sittin' down here faw? I want t' sit next to my sweetheart on the sofa, hold hands with him and love him up a little!

(BIG MAMA *has on a black and white figured chiffon. The large irregular patterns, like the markings of some massive animal, the luster of her great diamonds and many pearls, the brilliants set in the silver frames of her glasses, her riotous voice, booming laugh, have dominated the room since she entered.* BIG DADDY *has been regarding her with a steady grimace of chronic annoyance.*)

BIG MAMA (*still louder*): Preacher, Preacher, hey, Preach! Give me you' hand an' help me up from this chair!

REVEREND TOOKER: None of your tricks, Big Mama!

BIG MAMA: What tricks? You give me you' hand so I can get up an'—

(REVEREND TOOKER *extends her his hand. She grabs it and pulls him into her lap with a shrill laugh that spans an octave in two notes.*)

Ever seen a preacher in a fat lady's lap? Hey, hey, folks! Ever seen a preacher in a fat lady's lap?

(BIG MAMA *is notorious throughout the Delta for this sort of inelegant horseplay.* MARGARET *looks on with indulgent humor, sipping Dubonnet "on the rocks" and watching* BRICK, *but* MAE *and* GOOPER *exchange signs of humorless anxiety over these antics, the sort of behavior which* MAE *thinks may account for their failure to quite get in with the smartest young married set in Memphis, despite all. One of the Negroes,* LACY *or* SOOKEY, *peeks in, cackling. They are waiting for a sign to bring in the cake and champagne. But* BIG DADDY's *not amused. He doesn't understand why, in spite of the infinite mental relief he's received from the doctor's report, he still has these same old fox teeth in his guts. "This spastic condition is something else," he says to himself, but aloud he roars at* BIG MAMA.)

BIG DADDY: *BIG MAMA, WILL YOU QUIT HORSIN'?*— You're too old an' too fat fo' that sort of crazy kid stuff an' besides a woman with your blood pressure—she had two hundred last spring!—is riskin' a stroke when you mess around like that. . . .

(MAE *blows on a pitch pipe.*)

BIG MAMA: *Here comes Big Daddy's birthday!*

(*Negroes in white jackets enter with an enormous birthday cake ablaze with candles and carrying buckets of champagne with satin ribbons about the bottle necks.* MAE *and* GOOPER *strike up song, and everybody, including the* NEGROES *and* CHILDREN, *joins in. Only* BRICK *remains aloof.*)

EVERYONE:
> Happy birthday to you.
> Happy birthday to you.
> Happy birthday, Big Daddy—

(*Some sing: "Dear, Big Daddy!"*)

> Happy birthday to you.

(*Some sing: "How old are you?"*)
(MAE *has come down center and is organizing her children like a chorus. She gives them a barely audible: "One, two, three!" and they are off in the new tune.*)

CHILDREN:
> Skinamarinka—dinka—dink
> Skinamarinka—do
> We love you.
> Skinamarinka—dinka—dink
> Skinamarinka—do.

(*All together, they turn to* BIG DADDY.)

> Big Daddy, you!

(*They turn back front, like a musical comedy chorus.*)

> We love you in the morning;
> We love you in the night.
> We love you when we're with you,
> And we love you out of sight.
> Skinamarinka—dinka—dink
> Skinamarinka—do.

(MAE *turns to* BIG MAMA.)

> Big Mama, too!

(BIG MAMA *bursts into tears. The* NEGROES *leave.*)

BIG DADDY: Now Ida, what the hell is the matter with you?
MAE: She's just so happy.
BIG MAMA: I'm just so happy, Big Daddy, I have to cry or something.

(*Sudden and loud in the hush.*)

> Brick, do you know the wonderful news that Doc Baugh got from the clinic about Big Daddy? Big Daddy's one hundred per cent!
MARGARET: Isn't that wonderful?
BIG MAMA: He's just one hundred per cent. Passed the examination with flying colors. Now that we know there's nothing wrong with Big Daddy but a spastic colon, I can tell you something. I was worried sick, half out of my mind, for fear Big Daddy might have a thing like—

(MARGARET *cuts through this speech, jumping up and exclaiming shrilly.*)

MARGARET: Brick, honey, aren't you going to give Big Daddy his birthday present?

(*Passing by him, she snatches his liquor glass from him.*)
(*She picks up a fancily wrapped package.*)

> Here it is, Big Daddy, this is from Brick!
BIG MAMA: This is the biggest birthday Big Daddy's ever had, a hundred presents and bushels of telegrams from—
MAE (*at same time*): What is it, Brick?
GOOPER: I bet 500 to 50 that Brick don't *know* what it is.
BIG MAMA: The fun of presents is not knowing what they are till you open the package. Open your present, Big Daddy.
BIG DADDY: Open it you'self. I want to ask Brick somethin'! Come here, Brick.
MARGARET: Big Daddy's callin' you, Brick. (*She is opening the package.*)
BRICK: Tell Big Daddy I'm crippled.
BIG DADDY: I see you're crippled. I want to know how you got crippled.
MARGARET (*making diversionary tactics*): Oh, look, oh, look, why, it's a cashmere robe! (*She holds the robe up for all to see.*)
MAE: You sound surprised, Maggie.
MARGARET: I never saw one before.
MAE: That's funny.—*Hah!*
MARGARET (*turning on her fiercely, with a brilliant smile*): Why is it funny? All my family ever had was family—and luxuries such as cashmere robes still surprise me!
BIG DADDY (*ominously*): Quiet!
MAE (*heedless in her fury*): I don't see how you could be so surprised when you bought it yourself at Loewenstein's in Memphis last Saturday. You know how I know?
BIG DADDY: I said, Quiet!
MAE: —I know because the salesgirl that sold it to you waited on me and said, Oh, Mrs. Pollitt, your sister-in-law just bought a cashmere robe for your husband's father!
MARGARET: Sister Woman! Your talents are wasted as a housewife and mother, you really ought to be with the FBI or—
BIG DADDY: QUIET!

(REVEREND TOOKER's *reflexes are slower than the others'. He finishes a sentence after the bellow.*)

REVEREND TOOKER (*to* DOC BAUGH): —the Stork and the Reaper are running neck and neck!

(*He starts to laugh gaily when he notices the silence and* BIG DADDY's *glare. His laugh dies falsely.*)

BIG DADDY: Preacher, I hope I'm not butting in on more talk about memorial stained-glass windows, am I, Preacher?

(REVEREND TOOKER *laughs feebly, then coughs dryly in the embarrassed silence.*)

Preacher?

BIG MAMA: Now, Big Daddy, don't you pick on Preacher!

BIG DADDY (*raising his voice*): You ever hear that expression all hawk and no spit? You bring that expression to mind with that little dry cough of yours, all hawk an' no spit. . . .

(*The pause is broken only by a short startled laugh from* MARGARET, *the only one there who is conscious of and amused by the grotesque.*)

MAE (*raising her arms and jangling her bracelets*): I wonder if the mosquitoes are active tonight?

BIG DADDY: What's that, Little Mama? Did you make some remark?

MAE: Yes, I said I wondered if the mosquitoes would eat us alive if we went out on the gallery for a while.

BIG DADDY: Well, if they do, I'll have your bones pulverized for fertilizer!

BIG MAMA (*quickly*): Last week we had an airplane spraying the place and I think it done some good, at least I haven't had a—

BIG DADDY (*cutting her speech*): Brick, they tell me, if what they tell me is true, that you done some jumping last night on the high school athletic field?

BIG MAMA: Brick, Big Daddy is talking to you, son.

BRICK (*smiling vaguely over his drink*): What was that, Big Daddy?

BIG DADDY: They said you done some jumping on the high school track field last night.

BRICK: That's what they told me, too.

BIG DADDY: Was it jumping or humping that you were doing out there? What were you doing out there at three A.M., layin' a woman on that cinder track?

BIG MAMA: Big Daddy, you are off the sick-list, now, and I'm not going to excuse you for talkin' so—

BIG DADDY: Quiet!

BIG MAMA: —*nasty* in front of Preacher and—

BIG DADDY: *QUIET!*—I ast you, Brick, if you was cuttin' you'self a piece o' poon-tang last night on that cinder track? I thought maybe you were chasin' poon-tang on that track an' tripped over something in the heat of the chase—'sthat it?

(GOOPER *laughs, loud and false, others nervously following suit.* BIG MAMA *stamps her foot, and purses her lips, crossing to* MAE *and whispering something to her as* BRICK *meets his father's hard, intent, grinning stare with a slow, vague smile that he offers all situations from behind the screen of his liquor.*)

BRICK: No, sir, I don't think so. . . .

MAE (*at the same time, sweetly*): Reverend Tooker, let's you and I take a stroll on the widow's walk.

(*She and the preacher go out on the gallery as* BIG DADDY *says.*)

BIG DADDY: Then what the hell were you doing out there at three o'clock in the morning?

BRICK: Jumping the hurdles, Big Daddy, runnin' and jumpin' the hurdles, but those high hurdles have gotten too high for me, now.

BIG DADDY: Cause you was drunk?

BRICK (*his vague smile fading a little*): Sober I wouldn't have tried to jump the *low* ones. . . .

BIG MAMA (*quickly*): Big Daddy, blow out the candles on your birthday cake!

MARGARET (*at the same time*): I want to propose a toast to Big Daddy Pollitt on his sixty-fifth birthday, the biggest cotton planter in—

BIG DADDY (*bellowing with fury and disgust*): *I told you to stop it, now stop it, quit this—!*

BIG MAMA (*coming in front of* BIG DADDY *with the cake*): Big Daddy, I will not allow you to talk that way, not even on your birthday, I—

BIG DADDY: I'll talk like I want to on my birthday, Ida, or any other goddam day of the year and anybody here that don't like it knows what they can do!

BIG MAMA: You don't mean that!

BIG DADDY: What makes you think I don't mean it?

(*Meanwhile various discreet signals have been exchanged and* GOOPER *has also gone out on the gallery.*)

BIG MAMA: I just know you don't mean it.

BIG DADDY: You don't know a goddam thing and you never did!

BIG MAMA: Big Daddy, you don't mean that.

BIG DADDY: Oh, yes, I do, oh, yes, I do, I mean it! I put up with a whole lot of crap around here because I thought I was dying. And you thought I was dying and you started taking over, well, you can stop taking over now, Ida, because I'm not gonna die, you can just stop now this business of taking over because you're not taking over because I'm not dying, I went through the laboratory and the goddam exploratory operation and there's nothing wrong with me but a spastic colon. And I'm not dying of cancer which you thought I was dying of. Ain't that so? Didn't you think that I was dying of cancer, Ida?

(*Almost everybody is out on the gallery but the two old people glaring at each other across the blazing cake.*)

(BIG MAMA's *chest heaves and she presses a fat fist to her mouth.*)
(BIG DADDY *continues, hoarsely.*)

Ain't that so, Ida? Didn't you have an idea I was dying of cancer and now you could take control of this place and everything on it? I got that impression, I seemed to get that impression. Your loud voice everywhere, your fat old body butting in here and there!

BIG MAMA: Hush! The Preacher!

BIG DADDY: Fuck the goddam preacher!

(BIG MAMA *gasps loudly and sits down on the sofa which is almost too small for her.*)

Did you hear what I said? I said fuck the goddam preacher!

(*Somebody closes the gallery doors from outside just as there is a burst of fireworks and excited cries from the children.*)

BIG MAMA: I never seen you act like this before and I can't think what's got in you!

BIG DADDY: I went through all that laboratory and operation and all just so I would know if you or me was boss here! Well, now it turns out that I am and you ain't—and that's my birthday present— and my cake and champagne!—because for three years now you been gradually taking over. Bossing. Talking. Sashaying your fat old body around the place I made! I made this place! I was overseer on it! I was the overseer on the old Straw and Ochello plantation. I quit school at ten! I quit school at ten years old and went to work like a nigger in the fields. And I rose to be overseer of the Straw and Ochello plantation. And old Straw died and I was Ochello's partner and the place got bigger and bigger and bigger and bigger and bigger! I did all that myself with no goddam help from you, and now you think you're just about to take over. Well, I am just about to tell you that you are not just about to take over, you are not just about to take over a God damn thing. Is that clear to you, Ida? Is that very plain to you, now? Is that understood completely? I been through the laboratory from A to Z. I've had the goddam exploratory operation, and nothing is wrong with me but a spastic colon—made spastic, I guess, by *disgust!* By all the goddam lies and liars that I have had to put up with, and all the goddam hypocrisy that I lived with all these forty years that we been livin' together!

Hey! Ida!! Blow out the candles on the birthday cake! Purse up your lips and draw a deep breath and blow out the goddam candles on the cake!

BIG MAMA: Oh, Big Daddy, oh, oh, oh, Big Daddy!

BIG DADDY: What's the matter with you?

BIG MAMA: *In all these years you never believed that I loved you??*

BIG DADDY: Huh?

BIG MAMA: *And I did. I did so much. I did love you!—* I even loved your hate and your hardness, Big Daddy! (*She sobs and rushes awkwardly out onto the gallery.*)

BIG DADDY (*to himself*): Wouldn't it be funny if that was true. . . .

(*A pause is followed by a burst of light in the sky from the fireworks.*)

BRICK! HEY, BRICK!

(*He stands over his blazing birthday cake.*)
(*After some moments,* BRICK *hobbles in on his crutch, holding his glass.* MARGARET *follows him with a bright, anxious smile.*)

I didn't call you, Maggie. I called Brick.

MARGARET: I'm just delivering him to you.

(*She kisses* BRICK *on the mouth which he immediately wipes with the back of his hand. She flies girlishly back out.* BRICK *and his father are alone.*)

BIG DADDY: Why did you do that?

BRICK: Do what, Big Daddy?

BIG DADDY: Wipe her kiss off your mouth like she'd spit on you.

BRICK: I don't know. I wasn't conscious of it.

BIG DADDY: That woman of yours has a better shape on her than Gooper's but somehow or other they got the same look about them.

BRICK: What sort of look is that, Big Daddy?

BIG DADDY: I don't know how to describe it but it's the same look.

BRICK: They don't look peaceful, do they?

BIG DADDY: No, they sure in hell don't.

BRICK: They look nervous as cats?

BIG DADDY: That's right, they look nervous as cats.

BRICK: Nervous as a couple of cats on a hot tin roof?

BIG DADDY: That's right, boy, they look like a couple of cats on a hot tin roof. It's funny that you and Gooper being so different would pick out the same type of woman.

BRICK: Both of us married into society, Big Daddy.

BIG DADDY: Crap . . . I wonder what gives them both that look?

BRICK: Well. They're sittin' in the middle of a big piece of land, Big Daddy, twenty-eight thousand acres is a pretty big piece of land and so they're squaring off on it, each determined to knock off a bigger piece of it than the other whenever you let it go.

BIG DADDY: I got a surprise for those women. I'm not gonna let it go for a long time yet if that's what they're waiting for.

BRICK: That's right, Big Daddy. You just sit tight and let them scratch each other's eyes out. . . .

BIG DADDY: You bet your life I'm going to sit tight on

it and let those sons of bitches scratch their eyes out, ha ha ha. . . .

But Gooper's wife's a good breeder, you got to admit she's fertile. Hell, at supper tonight she had them all at the table and they had to put a couple of extra leafs in the table to make room for them, she's got five head of them, now, and another one's comin'.

BRICK: Yep, number six is comin'. . . .

BIG DADDY: Six hell, she'll probably drop a litter next time. Brick, you know, I swear to God, I don't know the way it happens.

BRICK: The way what happens, Big Daddy?

BIG DADDY: You git you a piece of land, by hook or crook, an' things start growin' on it, things accumulate on it, and the first thing you know it's completely out of hand, completely out of hand!

BRICK: Well, they say nature hates a vacuum, Big Daddy.

BIG DADDY: That's what they say, but sometimes I think that a vacuum is a hell of a lot better than some of the stuff that nature replaces it with.

Is someone out there by that door?

GOOPER: Hey Mae.

BRICK: Yep.

BIG DADDY: Who? *(He has lowered his voice.)*

BRICK: Someone int'rested in what we say to each other.

BIG DADDY: Gooper?—*GOOPER!*

(After a discreet pause, MAE *appears in the gallery door.)*

MAE: Did you call Gooper, Big Daddy?

BIG DADDY: Aw, it was you.

MAE: Do you want Gooper, Big Daddy?

BIG DADDY: No, and I don't want you. I want some privacy here, while I'm having a confidential talk with my son Brick. Now it's too hot in here to close them doors, but if I have to close those fuckin' doors in order to have a private talk with my son Brick, just let me know and I'll close 'em. Because I hate eavesdroppers, I don't like any kind of sneakin' an' spyin'.

MAE: Why, Big Daddy—

BIG DADDY: You stood on the wrong side of the moon, it threw your shadow!

MAE: I was just—

BIG DADDY: You was just nothing but *spyin'* an' you *know* it!

MAE *(begins to sniff and sob)*: Oh, Big Daddy, you're so unkind for some reason to those that really love you!

BIG DADDY: Shut up, shut up, shut up! I'm going to move you and Gooper out of that room next to this! It's none of your goddam business what goes on in here at night between Brick an' Maggie. You listen at night like a couple of rutten peek-hole spies and go and give a report on what you

hear to Big Mama an' she comes to me and says they say such and such and so and so about what they heard goin' on between Brick an' Maggie, and Jesus, it makes me sick. I'm goin' to move you an' Gooper out of that room, I can't stand sneakin' an' spyin', it makes me puke. . . .

*(*MAE *throws back her head and rolls her eyes heavenward and extends her arms as if invoking God's pity for this unjust martyrdom; then she presses a handkerchief to her nose and flies from the room with a loud swish of skirts.)*

BRICK *(now at the liquor cabinet)*: They listen, do they?

BIG DADDY: Yeah. They listen and give reports to Big Mama on what goes on in here between you and Maggie. They say that— *(He stops as if embarrassed.)* —You won't sleep with her, that you sleep on the sofa. Is that true or not true? If you don't like Maggie, get rid of Maggie!—What are you doin' there now?

BRICK: Fresh'nin up my drink.

BIG DADDY: Son, you know you got a real liquor problem?

BRICK: Yes, sir, yes, I know.

BIG DADDY: Is that why you quit sports-announcing, because of this liquor problem?

BRICK: Yes, sir, yes, sir, I guess so.

(He smiles vaguely and amiably at his father across his replenished drink.)

BIG DADDY: Son, don't guess about it, it's too important.

BRICK *(vaguely)*: Yes, sir.

BIG DADDY: And listen to me, don't look at the damn chandelier. . . .

(Pause. BIG DADDY'S *voice is husky.)*

—Somethin' else we picked up at th' big fire sale in Europe.

(Another pause.)

Life is important. There's nothing else to hold onto. A man that drinks is throwing his life away. Don't do it, hold onto your life. There's nothing else to hold onto. . . .

Sit down over here so we don't have to raise our voices, the walls have ears in this place.

BRICK *(hobbling over to sit on the sofa beside him)*: All right, Big Daddy.

BIG DADDY: Quit!—how'd that come about? Some disappointment?

BRICK: I don't know. Do you?

BIG DADDY: I'm askin' you, God damn it! How in hell would I know if you don't?

BRICK: I just got out there and found that I had a mouth full of cotton. I was always two or three beats behind what was goin' on on the field and so I—

BIG DADDY: Quit!

BRICK (*amiably*): Yes, quit.

BIG DADDY: Son?

BRICK: Huh?

BIG DADDY (*inhales loudly and deeply from his cigar; then bends suddenly a little forward, exhaling loudly and raising a hand to his forehead*): Whew!—ha ha!—I took in too much smoke, it made me a little light-headed. . . .

(*The mantel clock chimes.*)

Why is it so damn hard for people to talk?

BRICK: Yeah. . . .

(*The clock goes on sweetly chiming till it has completed the stroke of ten.*)

—Nice peaceful-soundin' clock, I like to hear it all night. . . .

(*He slides low and comfortable on the sofa;* BIG DADDY *sits straight and rigid with some unspoken anxiety. All his gestures are tense and jerky as he talks. He wheezes and pants and sniffs through his nervous speech, glancing quickly, shyly, from time to time, at his son.*)

BIG DADDY: We got that clock the summer we wint to Europe, me an' Big Mama on that damn Cook's Tour, never had such an awful time in my life. I'm tellin' you, son, those gooks over there, they gouge your eyeballs out in their grand hotels. And Big Mama bought more stuff than you could haul in a couple of boxcars, that's no crap. Everywhere she wint on this whirlwind tour, she bought, bought, bought. Why, half that stuff she bought is still crated up in the cellar, under water last spring! (*He laughs.*)

That Europe is nothin' on earth but a great big auction, that's all it is, that bunch of old worn-out places, it's just a big firesale, the whole fuckin' thing, an' Big Mama wint wild in it, why, you couldn't hold that woman with a mule's harness! Bought, bought, bought!—lucky I'm a rich man, yes siree, Bob, an' half that stuff is mildewin' in th' basement. It's lucky I'm a rich man, it sure is lucky, well, I'm a rich man, Brick, yep, I'm a mighty rich man. (*His eyes light up for a moment.*)

Y'know how much I'm worth? Guess, Brick! Guess how much I'm worth!

(BRICK *smiles vaguely over his drink.*)

Close on ten million in cash an' blue-chip stocks, outside, mind you, of twenty-eight thousand acres of the richest land this side of the valley Nile!

But a man can't buy his life with it, he can't buy back his life with it when his life has been spent, that's one thing not offered in the Europe firesale or in the American markets or any markets on earth, a man can't buy his life with it, he can't buy back his life when his life is finished.

That's a sobering thought, a very sobering thought, and that's a thought that I was turning over in my head, over and over and over—until today. . . .

I'm wiser and sadder, Brick, for this experience which I just gone through. They's one thing else that I remember in Europe.

BRICK: What is that, Big Daddy?

BIG DADDY: The hills around Barcelona in the country of Spain and the children running over those bare hills in their bare skins beggin' like starvin' dogs with howls and screeches, and how fat the priests are on the streets of Barcelona, so many of them and so fat and so pleasant, ha ha!—Y'know I could feed that country? I got money enough to feed that goddam country, but the human animal is a selfish beast and I don't reckon the money I passed out there to those howling children in the hills around Barcelona would more than upholster the chairs in this room, I mean pay to put a new cover on this chair!

Hell, I threw them money like you'd scatter feed corn for chickens, I threw money at them just to get rid of them long enough to climb back into th' car and—drive away. . . .

And then in Morocco, them Arabs, why, I remember one day in Marrakech, that old walled Arab city, I set on a broken-down wall to have a cigar, it was fearful hot there and this Arab woman stood in the road and looked at me till I was embarrassed, she stood stock still in the dusty hot road and looked at me till I was embarrassed. But listen to this. She had a naked child with her, a little naked girl with her, barely able to toddle, and after a while she set this child on the ground and give her a push and whispered something to her.

This child come toward me, barely able t' walk, come toddling up to me and—

Jesus, it makes you sick t' remember a thing like this!

It stuck out its hand and tried to unbutton my trousers!

That child was not yet five! Can you believe me? Or do you think that I am making this up? I wint back to the hotel and said to Big Mama, Git packed! We're clearing out of this country. . . .

BRICK: Big Daddy, you're on a talkin' jag tonight.

BIG DADDY (*ignoring this remark*): Yes, sir, that's how it is, the human animal is a beast that dies but the fact that he's dying don't give him pity for others, no, sir, it—

—Did you say something?

BRICK: Yes.

BIG DADDY: What?

BRICK: Hand me over that crutch so I can get up.

BIG DADDY: Where you goin'?

BRICK: I'm takin' a little short trip to Echo Spring.

BIG DADDY: To where?

BRICK: Liquor cabinet. . . .

BIG DADDY: Yes, sir, boy— (*He hands* BRICK *the crutch*) —the human animal is a beast that dies and if he's got money he buys and buys and buys and I think the reason he buys everything he can buy is that in the back of his mind he has the crazy hope that one of his purchases will be life everlasting!—Which it never can be. . . . The human animal is a beast that—

BRICK (*at the liquor cabinet*): Big Daddy, you sure are shootin' th' breeze here tonight.

(*There is a pause and voices are heard outside.*)

BIG DADDY: I been quiet here lately, spoke not a word, just sat and stared into space. I had something heavy weighing on my mind but tonight that load was took off me. That's why I'm talking.—The sky looks diff'rent to me. . . .

BRICK: You know what I like to hear most?

BIG DADDY: What?

BRICK: Solid quiet. Perfect unbroken quiet.

BIG DADDY: Why?

BRICK: Because it's more peaceful.

BIG DADDY: Man, you'll hear a lot of that in the grave. (*He chuckles agreeably.*)

BRICK: Are you through talkin' to me?

BIG DADDY: Why are you so anxious to shut me up?

BRICK: Well, sir, ever so often you say to me, Brick, I want to have a talk with you, but when we talk, it never materializes. Nothing is said. You sit in a chair and gas about this and that and I look like I listen. I try to look like I listen, but I don't listen, not much. Communication is—awful hard between people an'—somehow between you and me, it just don't—happen.

BIG DADDY: Have you ever been scared? I mean have you ever felt downright terror of something? (*He gets up.*) Just one moment. (*He looks off as if he were going to tell an important secret.*)
　　Brick?

BRICK: What?

BIG DADDY: Son, I thought I had it!

BRICK: Had what? Had what, Big Daddy?

BIG DADDY: Cancer!

BRICK: Oh . . .

BIG DADDY: I thought the old man made out of bones had laid his cold and heavy hand on my shoulder!

BRICK: Well, Big Daddy, you kept a tight mouth about it.

BIG DADDY: A pig squeals. A man keeps a tight mouth about it, in spite of a man not having a pig's advantage.

BRICK: What advantage is that?

BIG DADDY: Ignorance—of mortality—is a comfort. A man don't have that comfort, he's the only living thing that conceives of death, that knows what it is. The others go without knowing which is the way that anything living should go, go without knowing, without any knowledge of it, and yet a pig squeals, but a man sometimes, he can keep a tight mouth about it. Sometimes he—

(*There is a deep smoldering ferocity in the old man.*)

—can keep a tight mouth about it. I wonder if—

BRICK: What, Big Daddy?

BIG DADDY: A whiskey highball would injure this spastic condition?

BRICK: No, sir, it might do it good.

BIG DADDY (*grins suddenly, wolfishly*): Jesus, I can't tell you! The sky is open! Christ, it's open again! It's open boy, it's open!

(BRICK *looks down at his drink.*)

BRICK: You feel better, Big Daddy?

BIG DADDY: Better? Hell! I can breathe!—All of my life I been like a doubled up fist. . . . (*He pours a drink.*) —Poundin', smashin', drivin'!—now I'm going to loosen these doubled-up hands and touch things *easy* with them. . . .

(*He spreads his hands as if caressing the air.*)

You know what I'm contemplating?

BRICK (*vaguely*): No, sir. What are you contemplating?

BIG DADDY: Ha ha!—*Pleasure!*—pleasure with *women!*

(BRICK'*s smile fades a little but lingers.*)

—Yes, boy. I'll tell you something that you might not guess. I still have desire for women and this is my sixty-fifth birthday.

BRICK: I think that's mighty remarkable, Big Daddy.

BIG DADDY: Remarkable?

BRICK: *Admirable*, Big Daddy.

BIG DADDY: You're damn right it is, remarkable and admirable both. I realize now that I never had me enough. I let many chances slip by because of scruples about it, scruples, convention—crap. . . . All that stuff is bull, bull, bull!—It took the shadow of death to make me see it. Now that shadow's lifted, I'm going to cut loose and have, what is it they call it, have me a—ball!

BRICK: A ball, huh?

BIG DADDY: That's right, a ball, a ball! Hell!—I slept with Big Mama till, let's see, five years ago, till I was sixty and she was fifty-eight, and never even liked her, never did!

(The phone has been ringing down the hall. BIG MAMA *enters, exclaiming.)*

BIG MAMA: Don't you men hear that phone ring? I heard it way out on the gall'ry.

BIG DADDY: There's five rooms off this front gall'ry that you could go through. Why do you go through this one?

*(*BIG MAMA *makes a playful face as she bustles out the hall door.)*

Hunh!—Why, when Big Mama goes out of a room, I can't remember what that woman looks like—

BIG MAMA: Hello.

BIG DADDY: But when Big Mama comes back into the room, boy, then I see what she looks like, and I wish I didn't.

(Bends over laughing at this joke till it hurts his guts and he straightens with a grimace. The laugh subsides to a chuckle as he puts the liquor glass a little distrustfully down the table.)

BIG MAMA: Hello, Miss Sally.

*(*BRICK *has risen and hobbled to the gallery doors.)*

BIG DADDY: Hey! Where you goin'?

BRICK: Out for a breather.

BIG DADDY: Not yet you ain't. Stay here till this talk is finished, young fellow.

BRICK: I thought it was finished, Big Daddy.

BIG DADDY: It ain't even begun.

BRICK: My mistake. Excuse me. I just wanted to feel that river breeze.

BIG DADDY: Set back in that chair.

*(*BIG MAMA*'s voice rises, carrying down the hall.)*

BIG MAMA: Miss Sally, you're a case! You're a caution, Miss Sally.

BIG DADDY: Jesus, she's talking to my old maid sister again.

BIG MAMA: Why didn't you give me a chance to explain it to you?

BIG DADDY: Brick, this stuff burns me.

BIG MAMA: Well, goodbye, now, Miss Sally. You come down real soon. Big Daddy's dying to see you.

BIG DADDY: Crap!

BIG MAMA: Yaiss, goodbye, Miss Sally. . . .

(She hangs up and bellows with mirth. BIG DADDY *groans and covers his ears as she approaches.)*
(Bursting in)

Big Daddy, that was Miss Sally callin' from Memphis again! You know what she done, Big Daddy? She called her doctor in Memphis to git him to tell her what that spastic thing is! Ha-*HAAAA!*—And called back to tell me how relieved she was that—Hey! Let me in!

*(*BIG DADDY *has been holding the door half closed against her.)*

BIG DADDY: Naw I ain't. I told you not to come and go through this room. You just back out and go through those five other rooms.

BIG MAMA: Big Daddy? Big Daddy? Oh, Big Daddy!—You didn't mean those things you said to me, did you?

(He shuts door firmly against her but she still calls.)

Sweetheart? Sweetheart? Big Daddy? You didn't mean those awful things you said to me?—I know you didn't. I know you didn't mean those things in your heart. . . .

(The childlike voice fades with a sob and her heavy footsteps retreat down the hall. BRICK *has risen once more on his crutches and starts for the gallery again.)*

BIG DADDY: All I ask of that woman is that she leave me alone. But she can't admit to herself that she makes me sick. That comes of having slept with her too many years. Should of quit much sooner but that old woman she never got enough of it—and I was good in bed . . . I never should of wasted so much of it on her. . . . They say you got just so many and each one is numbered. Well, I got a few left in me, a few, and I'm going to pick me a good one to spend 'em on! I'm going to pick me a choice one, I don't care how much she costs, I'll smother her in—minks! Ha ha! I'll strip her naked and smother her in minks and choke her with diamonds! Ha ha! I'll strip her naked and choke her with diamonds and smother her with minks and hump her from hell to breakfast. *Ha aha ha ha ha!*

MAE *(gaily at door)*: Who's that laughin' in there?

GOOPER: Is Big Daddy laughin' in there?

BIG DADDY: Crap!—them two—*drips.* . . .

(He goes over and touches BRICK'S *shoulder.)*

Yes, son. Brick, boy.—I'm *happy!* I'm happy, son, I'm happy!

(He chokes a little and bites his under lip, pressing his head quickly, shyly against his son's head and then, coughing with embarrassment, goes uncertainly back to the table where he set down the glass. He drinks and makes a grimace as it burns his guts. BRICK *sighs and rises with effort.)*

What makes you so restless? Have you got ants in your britches?

BRICK: Yes, sir . . .

BIG DADDY: Why?

BRICK: —Something—hasn't happened. . . .

BIG DADDY: Yeah? What is that!

BRICK *(sadly)*: —the click. . . .

BIG DADDY: Did you say click?

BRICK: Yes, click.

BIG DADDY: What click?

BRICK: A click that I get in my head that makes me peaceful.

BIG DADDY: I sure in hell don't know what you're talking about, but it disturbs me.

BRICK: It's just a mechanical thing.

BIG DADDY: What is a mechanical thing?

BRICK: This click that I get in my head that makes me peaceful. I got to drink till I get it. It's just a mechanical thing, something like a—like a—like a—

BIG DADDY: Like a—

BRICK: Switch clicking off in my head, turning the hot light off and the cool night on and— (*He looks up, smiling sadly.*) —all of a sudden there's—peace!

BIG DADDY (*whistles long and soft with astonishment; he goes back to* BRICK *and clasps his son's two shoulders*) Jesus! I didn't know it had gotten that bad with you. Why, boy, you're—*alcoholic!*

BRICK: That's the truth, Big Daddy. I'm alcoholic.

BIG DADDY: This shows how I—let things go!

BRICK: I have to hear that little click in my head that makes me peaceful. Usually I hear it sooner than this, sometimes as early as—noon, but—

—Today it's—dilatory. . . .

—I just haven't got the right level of alcohol in my bloodstream yet!

(*This last statement is made with energy as he freshens his drink.*)

BIG DADDY: Uh—huh. Expecting death made me blind. I didn't have no idea that a son of mine was turning into a drunkard under my nose.

BRICK (*gently*): Well, now you do, Big Daddy, the news has penetrated. . . .

BIG DADDY: Uh-huh, yes, now I do. The news has penetrated.

BRICK: And so if you'll excuse me—

BIG DADDY: No, I won't excuse you.

BRICK: —I'd better sit by myself till I hear that click in my head, it's just a mechanical thing but it don't happen except when I'm alone or talking to no one. . . .

BIG DADDY: You got a long, long time to sit still, boy, and talk to no one, but now you're talkin' to me. At least I'm talking to you. And you set there and listen until I tell you the conversation is over!

BRICK: But this talk is like all the others we've ever had together in our lives! It's nowhere, nowhere!—it's—it's *painful*, Big Daddy. . . .

BIG DADDY: All right, then let it be painful, but don't you move from that chair!—I'm going to remove that crutch. . . . (*He seizes the crutch and tosses it across room.*)

BRICK: I can hop on one foot, and if I fall, I can crawl!

BIG DADDY: If you ain't careful you're gonna crawl off this plantation and then, by Jesus, you'll have to hustle your drinks along Skid Row!

BRICK: That'll come, Big Daddy.

BIG DADDY: Naw, it won't. You're my son and I'm going to straighten you out; now that *I'm* straightened out, I'm going to straighten out you!

BRICK: Yeah?

BIG DADDY: Today the report come in from Ochsner Clinic. Y'know what they told me? (*His face glows with triumph.*) The only thing that they could detect with all the instruments of science in that great hospital is a little spastic condition of the colon! And nerves torn to pieces by all that worry about it.

(*A little girl bursts into room with a sparkler clutched in each fist, hops and shrieks like a monkey gone mad and rushes back out again as* BIG DADDY *strikes at her.*)
(*Silence. The two men stare at each other. A woman laughs gaily outside.*)

I want you to know I breathed a sigh of relief almost as powerful as the Vicksburg tornado!

(*There is laughter outside, running footsteps, the soft, plushy sound and light of exploding rockets.*)
(*BRICK stares at him soberly for a long moment; then makes a sort of startled sound in his nostrils and springs up on one foot and hops across the room to grab his crutch, swinging on the furniture for support. He gets the crutch and flees as if in horror for the gallery. His father seizes him by the sleeve of his white silk pajamas.*)

Stay here, you son of a bitch!—till I say go!

BRICK: I can't.

BIG DADDY: You sure in hell will, God damn it.

BRICK: No, I can't. We talk, you talk, in—circles! We get no where, no where! It's always the same, you say you want to talk to me and don't have a fuckin' thing to say to me!

BIG DADDY: Nothin' to say when I'm tellin' you I'm going to live when I thought I was dying?!

BRICK: Oh—*that*—Is that what you have to say to me?

BIG DADDY: Why, you son of a bitch! Ain't that, ain't that—*important*?!

BRICK: Well, you said that, that's said, and now I—

BIG DADDY: Now you set back down.

BRICK: You're all balled up, you—

BIG DADDY: I ain't balled up!

BRICK: You are, you're all balled up!

BIG DADDY: Don't tell me what I am, you drunken whelp! I'm going to tear this coat sleeve off you if you don't set down!

BRICK: Big Daddy—

BIG DADDY: Do what I tell you! I'm the boss here, now! I want you to know I'm back in the driver's seat now!

(*BIG MAMA rushes in, clutching her great heaving bosom.*)

BIG MAMA: Big Daddy!

BIG DADDY: What in hell do you want in here, Big Mama?

BIG MAMA: Oh, Big Daddy! Why are you shouting like that? I just cain't *stainnnnnnnd*—it. . . .

BIG DADDY (*raising the back of his hand above his head*): GIT!—outa here.

(*She rushes back out, sobbing.*)

BRICK (*softly, sadly*): *Christ*. . . .

BIG DADDY (*fiercely*): Yeah! Christ!—is right . . .

(BRICK *breaks loose and hobbles toward the gallery.*)
(BIG DADDY *jerks his crutch from under* BRICK *so he steps with the injured ankle. He utters a hissing cry of anguish, clutches a chair and pulls it over on top of him on the floor.*)

Son of a—tub of—hog fat. . . .

BRICK: Big Daddy! Give me my crutch.

(BIG DADDY *throws the crutch out of reach.*)

Give me that crutch, Big Daddy.

BIG DADDY: Why do you drink?

BRICK: Don't know, give me my crutch!

BIG DADDY: You better think why you drink or give up drinking!

BRICK: Will you please give me my crutch so I can get up off this floor?

BIG DADDY: First you answer my question. Why do you drink? Why are you throwing your life away, boy, like somethin' disgusting you picked up on the street?

BRICK (*getting onto his knees*): Big Daddy, I'm in pain, I stepped on that foot.

BIG DADDY: Good! I'm glad you're not too numb with the liquor in you to feel some pain!

BRICK: You—spilled my—drink . . .

BIG DADDY: I'll make a bargain with you. You tell me why you drink and I'll hand you one. I'll pour the liquor myself and hand it to you.

BRICK: Why do I drink?

BIG DADDY: Yea! Why?

BRICK: Give me a drink and I'll tell you.

BIG DADDY: Tell me first!

BRICK: I'll tell you in one word.

BIG DADDY: What word?

BRICK: DISGUST!

(*The clock chimes softly, sweetly.* BIG DADDY *gives it a short, outraged glance.*)

Now how about that drink?

BIG DADDY: What are you disgusted with? You got to tell me that, first. Otherwise being disgusted don't make no sense!

BRICK: Give me my crutch.

BIG DADDY: You heard me, you got to tell me what I asked you first.

BRICK: I told you, I said to kill my disgust!

BIG DADDY: DISGUST WITH WHAT!

BRICK: You strike a hard bargain.

BIG DADDY: What are you disgusted with?—an' I'll pass you the liquor.

BRICK: I can hop on one foot, and if I fall, I can crawl.

BIG DADDY: You want liquor that bad?

BRICK (*dragging himself up, clinging to bedstead*): Yeah, I want it that bad.

BIG DADDY: If I give you a drink, will you tell me what it is you're disgusted with, Brick?

BRICK: Yes, sir, I will try to.

(*The old man pours him a drink and solemnly passes it to him.*)
(*There is a silence as* BRICK *drinks.*)

Have you ever heard the word "mendacity"?

BIG DADDY: Sure. Mendacity is one of them five dollar words that cheap politicians throw back and forth at each other.

BRICK: You know what it means?

BIG DADDY: Don't it mean lying and liars?

BRICK: Yes, sir, lying and liars.

BIG DADDY: Has someone been lying to you?

CHILDREN (*chanting in chorus offstage*):
We want Big Dad-dee!
We want Big Dad-dee

(GOOPER *appears in the gallery door.*)

GOOPER: Big Daddy, the kiddies are shouting for you out there.

BIG DADDY (*fiercely*): Keep out, Gooper!

GOOPER: 'Scuse *me*!

(BIG DADDY *slams the doors after* GOOPER.)

BIG DADDY: Who's been lying to you, has Margaret been lying to you, has your wife been lying to you about something, Brick?

BRICK: Not her. That wouldn't matter.

BIG DADDY: Then who's been lying to you, and what about?

BRICK: No one single person and no one lie. . . .

BIG DADDY: Then what, what then, for Christ's sake?

BRICK: The whole, the whole—thing. . . .

BIG DADDY: Why are you rubbing your head? You got a headache?

BRICK: No, I'm tryin to—

BIG DADDY: —Concentrate, but you can't because your brain's all soaked with liquor, is that the trouble? Wet brain! (*He snatches the glass from* BRICK's *hand.*) What do you know about this mendacity thing? Hell! I could write a book on it! Don't you know that? I could write a book on it and still not cover the subject. Well, I could, I could write a goddam book on it and still not cover the subject anywhere near enough!!—Think of all the lies I got to put up with!—Pretenses! Ain't that mendacity? Having to pretend stuff you don't think or feel or have any idea of? Having for instance to act like I care for Big Mama!—I haven't been able to stand the sight, sound, or smell of that woman for forty years now!—even when I *laid* her!—regular as a piston. . . .

Pretend to love that son of a bitch of a Gooper and his wife Mae and those five same screechers out there like parrots in a jungle? Jesus! Can't stand to look at 'em!

Church!—it bores the bejesus out of me but I go!—I go an' sit there and listen to the fool preacher!

Clubs!—Elks! Masons! Rotary!—*crap!*

(A spasm of pain makes him clutch his belly. He sinks into a chair and his voice is softer and hoarser.)

You I *do* like for some reason, did always have some kind of real feeling for—affection—respect—yes, always. . . .

You and being a success as a planter is all I ever had any devotion to in my whole life!—and that's the truth. . . .

I don't know why, but it is!

I've lived with mendacity!—Why can't *you* live with it? Hell, you *got* to live with it, there's nothing *else* to *live* with except mendacity, is there?

BRICK: Yes, sir. Yes, sir there is something else that you can live with!

BIG DADDY: What?

BRICK *(lifting his glass)*: This!—Liquor. . . .

BIG DADDY: That's not living, that's dodging away from life.

BRICK: I want to dodge away from it.

BIG DADDY: Then why don't you kill yourself, man?

BRICK: I like to drink. . . .

BIG DADDY: Oh, God, I can't talk to you. . . .

BRICK: I'm sorry, Big Daddy.

BIG DADDY: Not as sorry as I am. I'll tell you something. A little while back when I thought my number was up—

(This speech should have torrential pace and fury.)

—before I found out it was just this—spastic—colon. I thought about you. Should I or should I not, if the jig was up, give you this place when I go—since I hate Gooper an' Mae an' know that they hate me, and since all five same monkeys are little Maes an' Goopers.—And I thought, No!—Then I thought, Yes!—I couldn't make up my mind. I hate Gooper and his five same monkeys and that bitch Mae! Why should I turn over twenty-eight thousand acres of the richest land this side of the valley Nile to not my kind?—But why in hell, on the other hand, Brick—should I subsidize a goddam fool on the bottle?—Liked or not liked, well, maybe even—*loved!*—Why should

I do that?—Subsidize worthless behavior? Rot? Corruption?

BRICK *(smiling)*: I understand.

BIG DADDY: Well, if you do, you're smarter than I am. God damn it, because I don't understand. And this I will tell you frankly. I didn't make up my mind at all on that question and still to this day I ain't made out no will!—Well, now I don't *have* to. The pressure is gone. I can just wait and see if you pull yourself together or if you don't.

BRICK: That's right, Big Daddy.

BIG DADDY: You sound like you thought I was kidding.

BRICK *(rising)*: No, sir, I know you're not kidding.

BIG DADDY: But you don't care—?

BRICK *(hobbling toward the gallery door)*: No, sir, I don't care. . . .

(He stands in the gallery doorway as the night sky turns pink and green and gold with successive flashes of light.)

BIG DADDY: *WAIT!*—Brick. . . .

(His voice drops. Suddenly there is something shy, tender, in his restraining gesture.)

Don't let's—leave it like this, like them other talks we've had, we've always—talked around things, we've—just talked around things for some fuckin' reason. I don't know what, it's always like something was left not spoken, something avoided because neither of us was honest enough with the—other. . . .

BRICK: I never lied to you, Big Daddy.

BIG DADDY: Did I ever to *you?*

BRICK: No, sir. . . .

BIG DADDY: Then there is at least two people that never lied to each other.

BRICK: But we've never *talked* to each other.

BIG DADDY: We can *now.*

BRICK: Big Daddy, there don't seem to be anything much to say.

BIG DADDY: You say that you drink to kill your disgust with lying.

BRICK: You said to give you a reason.

BIG DADDY: Is liquor the only thing that'll kill this disgust?

BRICK: Now. Yes.

BIG DADDY: But not once, huh?

BRICK: Not when I was still young an' believing. A drinking man's someone who wants to forget he isn't still young an' believing.

BIG DADDY: Believing what?

BRICK: Believing. . . .

BIG DADDY: Believing *what?*

BRICK *(stubbornly evasive)*: Believing. . . .

BIG DADDY: I don't know what the hell you mean by believing and I don't think you know what you mean by believing, but if you still got sports in your blood, go back to sports announcing and—

BRICK: Sit in a glass box watching games I can't play? Describing what I can't do while players do it? Sweating out their disgust and confusion in contests I'm not fit for? Drinkin' a coke, half bourbon, so I can stand it? That's no goddam good any more, no help—time just outran me, Big Daddy—got there first . . .

BIG DADDY: I think you're passing the buck.

BRICK: You know many drinkin' men?

BIG DADDY (with a slight, charming smile): I have known a fair number of that species.

BRICK: Could any of them tell you why he drank?

BIG DADDY: Yep, you're passin' the buck to things like time and disgust with "mendacity" and—crap!—if you got to use that kind of language about a thing, it's ninety-proof bull, and I'm not buying any.

BRICK: I had to give you a reason to get a drink!

BIG DADDY: You started drinkin' when your friend Skipper died.

(Silence for five beats. Then BRICK makes a startled movement, reaching for his crutch.)

BRICK: What are you suggesting?

BIG DADDY: I'm suggesting nothing.

(The shuffle and clop of BRICK's rapid hobble away from his father's steady, grave attention.)

—But Gooper an' Mae suggested that there was something not right exactly in your—

BRICK (stopping short downstage as if backed to a wall): "Not right"?

BIG DADDY: Not, well, exactly normal in your friendship with—

BRICK: They suggested that, too? I thought that was Maggie's suggestion.

(BRICK's detachment is at last broken through. His heart is accelerated; his forehead sweat-beaded; his breath becomes more rapid and his voice hoarse. The thing they're discussing, timidly and painfully on the side of BIG DADDY, fiercely, violently on BRICK's side, is the inadmissible thing that SKIPPER died to disavow between them. The fact that if it existed it had to be disavowed to "keep face" in the world they lived in, may be at the heart of the "mendacity" that BRICK drinks to kill his disgust with. It may be the root of his collapse. Or maybe it is only a single manifestation of it, not even the most important. The bird that I hope to catch in the net of this play is not the solution of one man's psychological problem. I'm trying to catch the true quality of experience in a group of people, that cloudy, flickering, evanescent—fiercely charged!—interplay of live human beings in the thundercloud of a common crisis. Some mystery should be left in the revelation of characters in a play, just as a great deal of mystery is always left in the revelation of character in life, even in one's own character to himself. This does not absolve the playwright of his duty to observe and probe as clearly and deeply as he legitimately can: but it should steer him away from "pat" conclusions, facile definitions which make a play just a play, not a snare for the truth of human experience.)

(The following scene should be played with great concentration, with most of the power leashed but palpable in what is left unspoken.)

Who else's suggestion is it, is it yours? How many others thought that Skipper and I were—

BIG DADDY (gently): Now, hold on, hold on a minute, son.—I knocked around in my time.

BRICK: What's that got to do with—

BIG DADDY: I said "Hold on!"—I bummed, I bummed this country till I was—

BRICK: Whose suggestion, who else's suggestion is it?

BIG DADDY: Slept in hobo jungles and railroad Y's and flophouses in all cities before I—

BRICK: Oh, you think so, too, you call me your son and a queer. Oh! Maybe that's why you put Maggie and me in this room that was Jack Straw's and Peter Ochello's, in which that pair of old sisters slept in a double bed where both of 'em died!

BIG DADDY: Now just don't go throwing rocks at—

(Suddenly REVEREND TOOKER appears in the gallery doors, his head slightly, playfully, fatuously cocked, with a practised clergyman's smile, sincere as a bird call blown on a hunter's whistle, the living embodiment of the pious, conventional lie.)

(BIG DADDY gasps a little at this perfectly timed, but incongruous, apparition.)

—What're you lookin' for, Preacher?

REVEREND TOOKER: The gentleman's lavatory, ha ha!—heh, heh . . .

BIG DADDY (with strained courtesy): —Go back out and walk down to the other end of the gallery, Reverend Tooker, and use the bathroom connected with my bedroom, and if you can't find it, ask them where it is!

REVEREND TOOKER: Ah, thanks. (He goes out with a deprecatory chuckle.)

BIG DADDY: It's hard to talk in this place . . .

BRICK: Son of a—!

BIG DADDY (leaving a lot unspoken): —I seen all things and understood a lot of them, till 1910. Christ, the year that—I had worn my shoes through, hocked my—I hopped off a yellow dog freight car half a mile down the road, slept in a wagon of cotton outside the gin—Jack Straw an' Peter Ochello took me in. Hired me to manage this place which grew into this one.—When Jack Straw died—why, old Peter Ochello quit eatin' like a dog does when its master's dead, and died, too!

BRICK: Christ!

BIG DADDY: I'm just saying I understand such—

BRICK (violently): Skipper is dead. I have not quit eating!

BIG DADDY: No, but you started drinking.

(BRICK *wheels on his crutch and hurls his glass across the room shouting.*)

BRICK: YOU THINK SO, TOO?

(*Footsteps run on the gallery. There are women's calls.*)
(BIG DADDY *goes toward the door.*)
(BRICK *is transformed, as if a quiet mountain blew suddenly up in volcanic flame.*)

BRICK: You think so, too? You think so, too? You think me an' Skipper did, did, did!—*sodomy!*—together?
BIG DADDY: Hold—!
BRICK: That what you—
BIG DADDY: —ON—a minute!
BRICK: You think we did dirty things between us, Skipper an'—
BIG DADDY: Why are you shouting like that? Why are you—
BRICK: —Me, is that what you think of Skipper, is that—
BIG DADDY: —so excited? I don't think nothing. I don't know nothing. I'm simply telling you what—
BRICK: You think that Skipper and me were a pair of dirty old men?
BIG DADDY: Now that's—
BRICK: Straw? Ochello? A couple of—
BIG DADDY: Now just—
BRICK: —fucking sissies? Queers? Is that what you—
BIG DADDY: Shhh.
BRICK: —think?

(*He loses his balance and pitches to his knees without noticing the pain. He grabs the bed and drags himself up.*)

BIG DADDY: Jesus!—Whew. . . . Grab my hand!
BRICK: Naw, I don't want your hand. . . .
BIG DADDY: Well, I want yours. Git up!

(*He draws him up, keeps an arm about him with concern and affection.*)

You broken out in a sweat! You're panting like you'd run a race with—
BRICK (*freeing himself from his father's hold*): Big Daddy, you shock me, Big Daddy, you, you—*shock* me! Talkin' so— (*He turns away from his father.*) —casually!—about a—thing like that . . .
    —Don't you know how people *feel* about things like that? How, how *disgusted* they are by things like that? Why, at Ole Miss when it was discovered a pledge to our fraternity, Skipper's and mine, did a, *attempted* to do a, unnatural thing with—
    We not only dropped him like a hot rock!—We told him to git off the campus, and he did, he got!—All the way to— (*He halts, breathless.*)
BIG DADDY: —Where?
BRICK: —North Africa, last I heard!

BIG DADDY: Well, I have come back from further away than that, I have just now returned from the other side of the moon, death's country, son, and I'm not easy to shock by anything here. (*He comes downstage and faces out.*) Always, anyhow, lived with too much space around me to be infected by ideas of other people. One thing you can grow on a big place more important than cotton!—is *tolerance!*—I grown it. (*He returns toward* BRICK.)
BRICK: Why can't exceptional friendship, *real, real, deep, deep friendship!* between two men be respected as something clean and decent without being thought of as—
BIG DADDY: It can, it is, for God's sake.
BRICK: —*Fairies.* . . .

(*In his utterance of this word, we gauge the wide and profound reach of the conventional mores he got from the world that crowned him with early laurel.*)

BIG DADDY: I told Mae an' Gooper—
BRICK: Frig Mae and Gooper, frig all dirty lies and liars!—Skipper and me had a clean, true thing between us!—had a clean friendship, practically all our lives, till Maggie got the idea you're talking about. Normal? No!—it was too rare to be normal, any true thing between two people is too rare to be normal. Oh, once in a while he put his hand on my shoulder or I'd put mine on his, oh, maybe even, when we were touring the country in pro-football an' shared hotel-rooms we'd reach across the space between the two beds and shake hands to say goodnight, yeah, one or two times we—
BIG DADDY: Brick, nobody thinks that's not normal!
BRICK: Well, they're mistaken, it was! It was a pure an' true thing an' that's not normal.
MAE (*off stage*): Big Daddy, they're startin' the fireworks.

(*They both stare straight at each other for a long moment. The tension breaks and both turn away as if tired.*)

BIG DADDY: Yeah, it's—hard t'—talk. . . .
BRICK: All right, then, let's—let it go. . . .
BIG DADDY: Why did Skipper crack up? Why have you?

(BRICK *looks back at his father again. He has already decided, without knowing that he has made this decision, that he is going to tell his father that he is dying of cancer. Only this could even the score between them: one inadmissible thing in return for another.*)

BRICK (*ominously*): All right. You're asking for it, Big Daddy. We're finally going to have that real true talk you wanted. It's too late to stop it, now, we got to carry it through and cover every subject.

(*He hobbles back to the liquor cabinet.*)

Uh-huh.

(He opens the ice bucket and picks up the silver tongs with slow admiration of their frosty brightness.)

Maggie declares that Skipper and I went into pro-football after we left "Ole Miss" because we were scared to grow up . . .

(He moves downstage with the shuffle and clop of a cripple on a crutch. As MARGARET *did when her speech became "recitative," he looks out into the house, commanding its attention by his direct, concentrated gaze—a broken, "tragically elegant" figure telling simply as much as he knows of "the Truth.")*

—Wanted to—keep on tossing—those long, long!—high, high!—passes that—couldn't be intercepted except by time, the aerial attack that made us famous! And so we did, we did, we kept it up for one season, that aerial attack, we held it high!—Yeah, but—

—that summer, Maggie, she laid the law down to me, said, Now or never, and so I married Maggie. . . .

BIG DADDY: How was Maggie in bed?

BRICK *(wryly)*: Great! the greatest!

*(*BIG DADDY *nods as if he thought so.)*

She went on the road that fall with the Dixie Stars. Oh, she made a great show of being the world's best sport. She wore a—wore a—tall bearskin cap! A shako, they call it, a dyed mole-skin coat, a moleskin coat dyed red!—Cut up crazy! Rented hotel ballrooms for victory celebrations, wouldn't cancel them when it—turned out—defeat. . . .

MAGGIE THE CAT! Ha ha!

*(*BIG DADDY *nods.)*

—But Skipper, he had some fever which came back on him which doctors couldn't explain and I got that injury—turned out to be just a shadow on the X-ray plate—and a touch of bursitis. . . .

I lay in a hospital bed, watched our games on TV, saw Maggie on the bench next to Skipper when he was hauled out of a game for stumbles, fumbles!—Burned me up the way she hung on his arm!—Y'know, I think that Maggie had always felt sort of left out because she and me never got any closer together than two people just get in bed, which is not much closer than two cats on a—fence humping. . . .

So! She took this time to work on poor dumb Skipper. He was a less than average student at Ole Miss, you know that, don't you?!—Poured in his mind the dirty, false idea that what we were, him and me, was a frustrated case of that ole pair of sisters that lived in this room, Jack Straw and

Peter Ochello!—He, poor Skipper, went to bed with Maggie to prove it wasn't true, and when it didn't work out, he thought it *was* true!—Skipper broke in two like a rotten stick—nobody ever turned so fast to a lush—or died of it so quick. . . .

—Now are you satisfied?

*(*BIG DADDY *has listened to this story, dividing the grain from the chaff. Now he looks at his son.)*

BIG DADDY: Are *you* satisfied?

BRICK: With what?

BIG DADDY: That half-ass story!

BRICK: What's half-ass about it?

BIG DADDY: Something's left out of that story. What did you leave out?

(The phone has started ringing in the hall.)

GOOPER *(off stage)*: Hello.

(As if it reminded him of something BRICK *glances suddenly toward the sound and says.)*

BRICK: Yes!—I left out a long-distance call which I had from Skipper—

GOOPER: Speaking, go ahead.

BRICK: —In which he made a drunken confession to me and on which I hung up!

GOOPER: No.

BRICK: Last time we spoke to each other in our lives . . .

GOOPER: No, sir.

BIG DADDY: You musta said something to him before you hung up.

BRICK: What could I say to him?

BIG DADDY: Anything. Something.

BRICK: Nothing.

BIG DADDY: Just hung up?

BRICK: Just hung up.

BIG DADDY: Uh-huh. Anyhow now!—we have tracked down the lie with which you're disgusted and which you are drinking to kill your disgust with, Brick. You been passing the buck. This disgust with mendacity is disgust with yourself.

You!—dug the grave of your friend and kicked him in it!—before you'd face truth with him!

BRICK: *His* truth, not *mine!*

BIG DADDY: His truth, okay! But you wouldn't face it with him!

BRICK: Who *can* face truth? Can *you?*

BIG DADDY: Now don't start passin' the rotten buck again, boy!

BRICK: *How about these birthday congratulations, these many, many happy returns of the day, when ev'rybody knows there won't be any except you!*

*(*GOOPER, *who has answered the hall phone, lets out a high, shrill laugh; the voice becomes audible saying: "No, no, you got it all wrong! Upside down. Are you crazy?")* *(*BRICK *suddenly catches his breath as he realizes that he has made a*

shocking disclosure. He hobbles a few paces, then freezes, and without looking at his father's shocked face, says.)

Let's, let's—go out, now, and—watch the fireworks. Come on, Big Daddy.

(BIG DADDY moves suddenly forward and grabs hold of the boy's crutch like it was a weapon for which they were fighting for possession.)

BIG DADDY: Oh, no, no! No one's going out! What did you start to say?

BRICK: I don't remember.

BIG DADDY: "Many happy returns when they know there won't be any"?

BRICK: Aw, hell, Big Daddy, forget it. Come on out on the gallery and look at the fireworks they're shooting off for your birthday. . . .

BIG DADDY: First you finish that remark you were makin' before you cut off. "Many happy returns when they know there won't be any"?—Ain't that what you just said?

BRICK: Look, now. I can get around without that crutch if I have to but it would be a lot easier on the furniture an' glassware if I didn' have to go swinging along like Tarzan of th'—

BIG DADDY: FINISH! WHAT YOU WAS SAYIN'!

(An eerie green glow shows in sky behind him.)

BRICK *(sucking the ice in his glass, speech becoming thick)*: Leave th' place to Gooper and Mae an' their five little same little monkeys. All I want is—

BIG DADDY: "LEAVE TH' PLACE," did you say?

BRICK *(vaguely)*: All twenty-eight thousand acres of the richest land this side of the valley Nile.

BIG DADDY: Who said I was "leaving the place" to Gooper or anybody? This is my sixty-fifth birthday! I got fifteen years or twenty years left in me! I'll outlive *you!* I'll bury you an' have to pay for your coffin!

BRICK: Sure. Many happy returns. Now let's go watch the fireworks, come on, let's—

BIG DADDY: Lying, have they been lying? About the report from th'—clinic? Did they, did they—find something—*Cancer.* Maybe?

BRICK: Mendacity is a system that we live in. Liquor is one way out an' death's the other. . . .

(He takes the crutch from BIG DADDY's loose grip and swings out on the gallery leaving the doors open.)
(A song, "Pick a Bale of Cotton," is heard.)

MAE *(appearing in door)*: Oh, Big Daddy, the field hands are singin' fo' you!

BRICK: I'm sorry, Big Daddy. My head don't work any more and it's hard for me to understand how anybody could care if he lived or died or was dying or cared about anything but whether or not there was liquor left in the bottle and so I said what I

said without thinking. In some ways I'm no better than the others, in some ways worse because I'm less alive. Maybe it's being alive that makes them lie, and being almost *not* alive makes me sort of accidentally truthful—I don't know but—anyway—we've been friends . . .

—And being friends is telling each other the truth. . . .

(There is a pause.)

You told *me!* I told *you!*

BIG DADDY *(slowly and passionately)*: CHRIST—DAMN—

GOOPER *(off stage)*: Let her go!

(Fireworks off stage right.)

BIG DADDY: —ALL—LYING SONS OF—LYING BITCHES!

(He straightens at last and crosses to the inside door. At the door he turns and looks back as if he had some desperate question he couldn't put into words. Then he nods reflectively and says in a hoarse voice.)

Yes, all liars, all liars, all lying dying liars!

(This is said slowly, slowly, with a fierce revulsion. He goes on out.)

—Lying! Dying! Liars!

(BRICK remains motionless as the lights dim out and the curtain falls.)

ACT 3

(There is no lapse of time. BIG DADDY is seen leaving as at the end of Act 2.)

BIG DADDY: ALL LYIN'—DYIN'!—LIARS!—LIARS!—LIARS!

(MARGARET enters.)

MARGARET: Brick, what in the name of God was goin' on in this room?

(DIXIE and TRIXIE enter through the doors and circle around MARGARET shouting. MAE enters from the lower gallery window.)

MAE: Dixie, Trixie, you quit that!

(GOOPER enters through the doors.)

Gooper, will y' please get these kiddies to bed right now!

GOOPER: Mae, you seen Big Mama?

MAE: Not yet.

(GOOPER and kids exit through the doors. REVEREND TOOKER enters through the windows.)

REVEREND TOOKER: Those kiddies are so full of vitality. I think I'll have to be starting back to town.

MAE: Not yet, Preacher. You know we regard you as a member of this family, one of our closest an' dearest, so you just got t' be with us when Doc Baugh gives Big Mama th' actual truth about th' report from the clinic.

MARGARET: Where do you think you're going?

BRICK: Out for some air.

MARGARET: Why'd Big Daddy shout "Liars"?

MAE: Has Big Daddy gone to bed, Brick?

GOOPER (entering): Now where is that old lady?

REVEREND TOOKER: I'll look for her. (He exits to the gallery.)

MAE: Cain'tcha find her, Gooper?

GOOPER: She's avoidin' this talk.

MAE: I think she senses somethin'.

MARGARET (going out to the gallery to BRICK): Brick, they're goin' to tell Big Mama the truth about Big Daddy and she's goin' to need you.

DOCTOR BAUGH: This is going to be painful.

MAE: Painful things cain't always be avoided.

REVEREND TOOKER: I see Big Mama.

GOOPER: Hey, Big Mama, come here.

MAE: Hush, Gooper, don't holler.

BIG MAMA (entering): Too much smell of burnt fireworks makes me feel a little bit sick at my stomach.—Where is Big Daddy?

MAE: That's what I want to know, where has Big Daddy gone?

BIG MAMA: He must have turned in, I reckon he went to baid . . .

GOOPER: Well, then, now we can talk.

BIG MAMA: What is this talk, what talk?

(MARGARET appears on the gallery, talking to DOCTOR BAUGH.)

MARGARET (musically): My family freed their slaves ten years before abolition. My great-great-grandfather gave his slaves their freedom five years before the War between the States started!

MAE: Oh, for God's sake! Maggie's climbed back up in her family tree!

MARGARET (sweetly): What, Mae?

(The pace must be very quick: great Southern animation.)

BIG MAMA (addressing them all): I think Big Daddy was just worn out. He loves his family, he loves to have them around him, but it's a strain on his nerves. He wasn't himself tonight, Big Daddy wasn't himself, I could tell he was all worked up.

REVEREND TOOKER: I think he's remarkable.

BIG MAMA: Yaisss! Just remarkable. Did you all notice the food he ate at that table? Did you all notice the supper he put away? Why he ate like a hawss!

GOOPER: I hope he doesn't regret it.

BIG MAMA: What? Why that man—ate a huge piece of cawn bread with molasses on it! Helped himself twice to hoppin' John.

MARGARET: Big Daddy loves hoppin' John.—We had a real country dinner.

BIG MAMA (overlapping MARGARET): Yaiss, he simply adores it! an' candied yams? Son? That man put away enough food at that table to stuff a field hand!

GOOPER (with grim relish): I hope he don't have to pay for it later on . . .

BIG MAMA (fiercely): What's that, Gooper?

MAE: Gooper says he hopes Big Daddy doesn't suffer tonight.

BIG MAMA: Oh, shoot, Gooper says, Gooper says! Why should Big Daddy suffer for satisfying a normal appetite? There's nothin' wrong with that man but nerves, he's sound as a dollar! And now he knows he is an' that's why he ate such a supper. He had a big load off his mind, knowin' he wasn't doomed t'—what he thought he was doomed to . . .

MARGARET (sadly and sweetly): Bless his old sweet soul . . .

BIG MAMA (vaguely): Yais, bless his heart, where's Brick?

MAE: Outside.

GOOPER: —Drinkin' . . .

BIG MAMA: I know he's drinkin'. Cain't I see he's drinkin' without you continually tellin' me that boy's drinkin'?

MARGARET: Good for you, Big Mama! (She applauds.)

BIG MAMA: Other people drink and have drunk an' will drink, as long as they make that stuff an' put it in bottles.

MARGARET: That's the truth. I never trusted a man that didn't drink.

BIG MAMA: Brick? Brick!

MARGARET: He's still on the gall'ry. I'll go bring him in so we can talk.

BIG MAMA (worriedly): I don't know what this mysterious family conference is about.

(Awkward silence. BIG MAMA looks from face to face, then belches slightly and mutters, "Excuse me . . ." She opens an ornamental fan suspended about her throat. A black lace fan to go with her black lace gown, and fans her wilting corsage, sniffing nervously and looking from face to face in the uncomfortable silence as MARGARET calls "Brick?" and BRICK sings to the moon on the gallery.)

MARGARET: Brick, they're gonna tell Big Mama the truth an' she's gonna need you.

BIG MAMA: I don't know what's wrong here, you all have such long faces! Open that door on the hall and let some air circulate through here, will you please, Gooper?

MAE: I think we'd better leave that door closed, Big Mama, till after the talk.

MARGARET: Brick!

BIG MAMA: Reveren' Tooker, will you please open that door?

REVEREND TOOKER: I sure will, Big Mama.

MAE: I just didn't think we ought t' take any chance of Big Daddy hearin' a word of this discussion.

BIG MAMA: *I swan!* Nothing's going to be said in Big Daddy's house that he cain't hear if he want to!

GOOPER: Well, Big Mama, it's—

(MAE *gives him a quick, hard poke to shut him up. He glares at her fiercely as she circles before him like a burlesque ballerina, raising her skinny bare arms over her head, jangling her bracelets, exclaiming.*)

MAE: *A breeze! A breeze!*

REVEREND TOOKER: I think this house is the coolest house in the Delta.—Did you all know that Halsey Bank's widow put air-conditioning units in the church and rectory at Friar's Point in memory of Halsey?

(*General conversation has resumed; everybody is chatting so that the stage sounds like a bird cage.*)

GOOPER: Too bad nobody cools your church off for you. I bet you sweat in that pulpit these hot Sundays, Reverend Tooker.

REVEREND TOOKER: Yes, my vestments are drenched. Last Sunday the gold in my chasuble faded into the purple.

GOOPER: Reveren', you musta been preachin' hell's fire last Sunday.

MAE (*at the same time to* DOCTOR BAUGH): You reckon those vitamin B12 injections are what they're cracked up t' be, Doc Baugh?

DOCTOR BAUGH: Well if you want to be stuck with something I guess they're as good to be stuck with as anything else.

BIG MAMA (*at the gallery door*): *Maggie, Maggie, aren't you comin' with Brick?*

MAE (*suddenly and loudly, creating a silence*): *I have a strange feeling, I have a peculiar feeling!*

BIG MAMA (*turning from the gallery*): What feeling?

MAE: That Brick said somethin' he shouldn't of said t' Big Daddy.

BIG MAMA: Now what on earth could Brick of said t' Big Daddy that he shouldn't say?

GOOPER: Big Mama, there's somethin'—

MAE: NOW, WAIT!

(*She rushes up to* BIG MAMA *and gives her a quick hug and kiss.* BIG MAMA *pushes her impatiently off.*)

DOCTOR BAUGH: In my day they had what they call the Keeley cure for heavy drinkers.

BIG MAMA: Shoot!

DOCTOR BAUGH: But now I understand they just take some kind of tablets.

GOOPER: They call them "Annie Bust" tablets.

BIG MAMA: *Brick* don't need to take *nothin'.*

(BRICK *and* MARGARET *appear in gallery doors.* BIG MAMA *unaware of his presence behind her.*)

That boy is just broken up over Skipper's death. You know how poor Skipper died. They gave him a big, big dose of that sodium amytal stuff at his home and then they called the ambulance and give him another big, big dose of it at the hospital and that and all of the alcohol in his system fo' months an' months just proved too much for his heart . . . I'm scared of needles! I'm more scared of a needle than the knife . . . I think more people have been needled out of this world than—(*She stops short and wheels about.*)

Oh—here's Brick! My precious baby—

(*She turns upon* BRICK *with short, fat arms extended, at the same time uttering a loud, short sob, which is both comic and touching.* BRICK *smiles and bows slightly, making a burlesque gesture of gallantry for* MARGARET *to pass before him into the room. Then he hobbles on his crutch directly to the liquor cabinet and there is absolute silence, with everybody looking at* BRICK *as everybody has always looked at* BRICK *when he spoke or moved or appeared. One by one he drops ice cubes in his glass, then suddenly, but not quickly, looks back over his shoulder with a wry, charming smile, and says.*)

BRICK: I'm sorry! Anyone else?

BIG MAMA (*sadly*): No, son, I *wish* you wouldn't!

BRICK: I wish I didn't have to, Big Mama, but I'm still waiting for that click in my head which makes it all smooth out!

BIG MAMA: Ow, Brick, you—BREAK MY HEART!

MARGARET (*at same time*): *Brick, go sit with Big Mama!*

BIG MAMA: I just cain't staiiiiiiii-nnnnnnnd-it . . . (*She sobs.*)

MAE: Now that we're all assembled—

GOOPER: We kin talk . . .

BIG MAMA: Breaks my heart . . .

MARGARET: Sit with Big Mama, Brick, and hold her hand.

(BIG MAMA *sniffs very loudly three times, almost like three drumbeats in the pocket of silence.*)

BRICK: You do that, Maggie. I'm a restless cripple. I got to stay on my crutch.

(BRICK *hobbles to the gallery door; leans there as if waiting.*)

(MAE *sits beside* BIG MAMA, *while* GOOPER *moves in front and sits on the end of the couch, facing her.* REVEREND TOOKER *moves nervously into the space between them; on the other side,* DOCTOR BAUGH *stands looking at nothing in particular and lights a cigar.* MARGARET *turns away.*)

BIG MAMA: Why're you all *surroundin'* me—like this? Why're you all starin' at me like this an' makin' signs at each other?

(REVEREND TOOKER *steps back startled.*)

MAE: Calm yourself, Big Mama.

BIG MAMA: Calm you'self, *you'self,* Sister Woman. How could I calm myself with everyone starin' at me as if big drops of blood had broken out on m'face? What's this all about, annh! What?

(GOOPER *coughs and takes a center position.*)

GOOPER: Now, Doc Baugh.

MAE: Doc Baugh?

GOOPER: Big Mama wants to know the complete truth about the report we got from the Ochsner Clinic.

MAE (*eagerly*): —on Big Daddy's condition!

GOOPER: Yais, on Big Daddy's condition, we got to face it.

DOCTOR BAUGH: Well . . .

BIG MAMA (*terrified, rising*): Is there? Something? Something that I? Don't—know?

(*In these few words, this startled, very soft question,* BIG MAMA *reviews the history of her forty-five years with* BIG DADDY, *her great almost embarrassingly true-hearted and simple-minded devotion to* BIG DADDY, *who must have had something* BRICK *has, who made himself loved so much by the "simple expedient" of not loving enough to disturb his charming detachment, also once coupled, like* BRICK, *with virile beauty.*)

(BIG MAMA *has a dignity at this moment; she almost stops being fat.*)

DOCTOR BAUGH (*after a pause, uncomfortably*): Yes?—Well—

BIG MAMA: I!!!—want to—knowwwwww . . .

(*Immediately she thrusts her fist to her mouth as if to deny that statement. Then for some curious reason, she snatches the withered corsage from her breast and hurls it on the floor and steps on it with her short, fat feet.*)

Somebody must be lyin'!—I want to know!

MAE: Sit down, Big Mama, sit down on this sofa.

MARGARET: Brick, go sit with Big Mama.

BIG MAMA: *What is it, what is it?*

DOCTOR BAUGH: I never have seen a more thorough examination than Big Daddy Pollitt was given in all my experience with the Ochsner Clinic.

GOOPER: It's one of the best in the country.

MAE: It's THE best in the country—bar *none!*

(*For some reason she gives* GOOPER *a violent poke as she goes past him. He slaps at her hand without removing his eyes from his mother's face.*)

DOCTOR BAUGH: Of course they were ninety-nine and nine-tenths per cent sure before they even started.

BIG MAMA: Sure of what, sure of what, sure of—*what?* —*what?*

(*She catches her breath in a startled sob.* MAE *kisses her quickly. She thrusts* MAE *fiercely away from her, staring at the* DOCTOR.)

MAE: Mommy, be a brave girl!

BRICK (*in the doorway, softly*): "By the light, by the light, Of the sil-ve-ry mo-oo-n . . ."

GOOPER: Shut up!—Brick.

BRICK: Sorry . . .(*He wanders out on the gallery.*)

DOCTOR BAUGH: But, now, you see, Big Mama, they cut a piece off this growth, a specimen of the tissue and—

BIG MAMA: Growth? You told Big Daddy—

DOCTOR BAUGH: Now wait.

BIG MAMA (*fiercely*): You told me and Big Daddy there wasn't a thing wrong with him but—

MAE: Big Mama, they always—

GOOPER: Let Doc Baugh talk, will yuh?

BIG MAMA: —little spastic condition of—(*Her breath gives out in a sob.*)

DOCTOR BAUGH: Yes, that's what we told Big Daddy. But we had this bit of tissue run through the laboratory and I'm sorry to say the test was positive on it. It's—well—malignant . . .

(*Pause.*)

BIG MAMA: Cancer?! Cancer?!

(DOCTOR BAUGH *nods gravely.* BIG MAMA *gives a long gasping cry.*)

MAE AND GOOPER: Now, now, now. Big Mama, you had to know . . .

BIG MAMA: WHY DIDN'T THEY CUT IT OUT OF HIM? HANH? HANH?

DOCTOR BAUGH: Involved too much, Big Mama, too many organs affected.

MAE: Big Mama, the liver's affected and so's the kidneys, both! It's gone way past what they call a—

GOOPER: A surgical risk.

MAE: —Uh-huh . . .

(BIG MAMA *draws a breath like a dying gasp.*)

REVEREND TOOKER: Tch, tch, tch, tch, tch!

DOCTOR BAUGH: Yes, it's gone past the knife.

MAE: *That's why he's turned yellow, Mommy!*

BIG MAMA: *Git away from me, git away from me, Mae!* (*She rises abruptly.*) *I want Brick! Where's Brick? Where is my only son?*

MAE: Mama! Did she say "*only* son"?

GOOPER: What does that make *me?*

MAE: A sober responsible man with five precious children!—*Six!*

BIG MAMA: I want Brick to tell me! Brick! Brick!

MARGARET (*rising from her reflections in a corner*): Brick was so upset he went back out.

BIG MAMA: *Brick!*

MARGARET: Mama, let *me* tell you!

BIG MAMA: No, no, leave me alone, you're not my blood!

GOOPER: *Mama, I'm your son!* Listen to *me!*

MAE: Gooper's your son, he's your first-born!

BIG MAMA: Gooper never liked Daddy.

MAE (as if terribly shocked): *That's not TRUE!*

(There is a pause. The minister coughs and rises.)

REVEREND TOOKER (to MAE): I think I'd better slip away at this point. *(Discreetly.)* Good night, good night, everybody, and God bless you all . . . on this place . . .

(He slips out.)

(MAE coughs and points at BIG MAMA.*)*

DOCTOR BAUGH: Well, Big Mama . . . *(He sighs.)*

BIG MAMA: It's all a mistake, I know it's just a bad dream.

DOCTOR BAUGH: We're gonna keep Big Daddy as comfortable as we can.

BIG MAMA: Yes, it's just a bad dream, that's all it is, it's just an awful dream.

GOOPER: In my opinion Big Daddy is having some pain but won't admit that he has it.

BIG MAMA: Just a dream, a bad dream.

DOCTOR BAUGH: That's what lots of them do, they think if they don't admit they're having the pain they can sort of escape the fact of it.

GOOPER (with relish): Yes, they get sly about it, they get real sly about it.

MAE: Gooper and I think—

GOOPER: Shut up, Mae! Big Mama, I think—Big Daddy ought to be started on morphine.

BIG MAMA: Nobody's going to give Big Daddy morphine.

DOCTOR BAUGH: Now, Big Mama, when that pain strikes it's going to strike mighty hard and Big Daddy's going to need the needle to bear it.

BIG MAMA: I tell you, nobody's going to give him morphine.

MAE: Big Mama, you don't want to see Big Daddy suffer, you know you—

*(*GOOPER, *standing beside her, gives her a savage poke.)*

DOCTOR BAUGH (placing a package on the table): I'm leaving this stuff here, so if there's a sudden attack you all won't have to send out for it.

MAE: I know how to give a hypo.

BIG MAMA: Nobody's gonna give Big Daddy morphine.

GOOPER: Mae took a course in nursing during the war.

MARGARET: Somehow I don't think Big Daddy would want Mae to give him a hypo.

MAE: You think he'd want *you* to do it?

DOCTOR BAUGH: Well . . .

*(*DOCTOR BAUGH *rises.)*

GOOPER: Doctor Baugh is goin'.

DOCTOR BAUGH: Yes, I got to be goin'. Well, keep your chin up, Big Mama.

GOOPER (with jocularity): She's gonna keep *both* chins up, aren't you, Big Mama?

*(*BIG MAMA *sobs.)*

Now stop that, Big Mama.

GOOPER (at the door with DOCTOR BAUGH): Well, Doc, we sure do appreciate all you done. I'm telling you, we're surely obligated to you for—

*(*DOCTOR BAUGH *has gone out without a glance at him.)*

—I guess that doctor has got a lot on his mind but it wouldn't hurt him to act a little more human . . .

*(*BIG MAMA *sobs.)*

Now be a brave girl, Mommy.

BIG MAMA: It's not true, I know that it's just not true!

GOOPER: Mama, those tests are infallible!

BIG MAMA: Why are you so determined to see your father daid?

MAE: Big Mama!

MARGARET (gently): I know what Big Mama means.

MAE (fiercely): Oh, do you?

MARGARET (quietly and very sadly): Yes, I think I do.

MAE: For a newcomer in the family you sure do show a lot of understanding.

MARGARET: Understanding is needed on this place.

MAE: I guess you must have needed a lot of it in your family, Maggie, with your father's liquor problem and now you've got Brick with his!

MARGARET: Brick does not have a liquor problem at all. Brick is devoted to Big Daddy. This thing is a terrible strain on him.

BIG MAMA: Brick is Big Daddy's boy, but he drinks too much and it worries me and Big Daddy, and, Margaret, you've got to cooperate with us, you've got to cooperate with Big Daddy and me in getting Brick straightened out. Because it will break Big Daddy's heart if Brick don't pull himself together and take hold of things.

MAE: Take hold of *what* things, Big Mama?

BIG MAMA: The place.

(There is a quick violent look between MAE *and* GOOPER.*)*

GOOPER: Big Mama, you've had a shock.

MAE: Yais, we've all had a shock, but . . .

GOOPER: Let's be realistic—

MAE: Big Daddy would never, would *never,* be foolish enough to—

GOOPER: —put this place in irresponsible hands!

BIG MAMA: Big Daddy ain't going to leave the place in anybody's hands; Big Daddy is *not* going to die. I want you to get that in your heads, all of you!

MAE: Mommy, Mommy, Big Mama, we're just as hopeful an' optimistic as you are about Big Daddy's prospects, we have faith in *prayer*—but nevertheless there are certain matters that have to be discussed an' dealt with, because otherwise—

GOOPER: Eventualities have to be considered and now's the time . . . Mae, will you please get my brief case out of our room?

MAE: Yes, honey. (*She rises and goes out through the hall door.*)

GOOPER (*standing over* BIG MAMA): Now, Big Mom. What you said just now was not at all true and you know it. I've always loved Big Daddy in my own quiet way. I never made a show of it, and I know that Big Daddy has always been fond of me in a quiet way, too, and he never made a show of it neither.

(MAE *returns with* GOOPER*'s brief case.*)

MAE: Here's your brief case, Gooper, honey.

GOOPER (*handing the brief case back to her*): Thank you . . . Of cou'se, my relationship with Big Daddy is different from Brick's.

MAE: You're eight years older'n Brick an' always had t' carry a bigger load of th' responsibilities than Brick ever had t' carry. He never carried a thing in his life but a football or a highball.

GOOPER: Mae, will y' let me talk, please?

MAE: Yes, honey.

GOOPER: Now, a twenty-eight-thousand-acre plantation's a mighty big thing t' run.

MAE: Almost singlehanded.

(MARGARET *has gone onto the gallery and can be heard calling softly to* BRICK.)

BIG MAMA: You never had to run this place! What are you talking about? As if Big Daddy was dead and in his grave, you had to run it? Why, you just helped him out with a few business details and had your law practice at the same time in Memphis!

MAE: Oh, Mommy, Mommy, Big Mommy! Let's be fair!

MARGARET: Brick!

MAE: Why, Gooper has given himself body and soul to keeping this place up for the past five years since Big Daddy's health started failing.

MARGARET: Brick!

MAE: Gooper won't say it, Gooper never thought of it as a duty, he just did it. And what did Brick do? Brick kept living in his past glory at college! Still a football player at twenty-seven!

MARGARET (*returning alone*): Who are you talking about now? Brick? A football player? He isn't a football player and you know it. Brick is a sports announcer on TV and one of the best-known ones in the country!

MAE: I'm talking about what he was.

MARGARET: Well, I wish you would just stop talking about my husband.

GOOPER: I've got a right to discuss my brother with other members of MY OWN family, which don't

include *you*. Why don't you go out there and drink with Brick?

MARGARET: I've never seen such malice toward a brother.

GOOPER: How about his for me? Why, he can't stand to be in the same room with me!

MARGARET: This is a deliberate campaign of vilification for the most disgusting and sordid reason on earth, and I know what it is! It's *avarice, greed, greed!*

BIG MAMA: *Oh, I'll scream! I will scream in a moment unless this stops!*

(GOOPER *has stalked up to* MARGARET *with clenched fists at his sides as if he would strike her.* MAE *distorts her face again into a hideous grimace behind* MARGARET'S *back.*)

BIG MAMA (*sobs*): Margaret. Child. Come here. Sit next to Big Mama.

MARGARET: Precious Mommy. I'm sorry, I'm, sorry, I—!

(*She bends her long graceful neck to press her forehead to* BIG MAMA's *bulging shoulder under its black chiffon.*)

MAE: How beautiful, how touching, this display of devotion! Do you know why she's childless? She's childless because that big beautiful athlete husband of hers won't go to bed with her!

GOOPER: You jest won't let me do this in a nice way, will yah? Aw right—I don't give a goddam if Big Daddy likes me or don't like me or did or never did or will or will never! I'm just appealing to a sense of common decency and fair play. I'll tell you the truth. I've resented Big Daddy's partiality to Brick ever since Brick was born, and the way I've been treated like I was just barely good enough to spit on and sometimes not even good enough for that. Big Daddy is dying of cancer, and it's spread all through him and it's attacked all his vital organs including the kidneys and right now he is sinking into uremia, and you all know what uremia is, it's poisoning of the whole system due to the failure of the body to eliminate its poisons.

MARGARET (*to herself, downstage, hissingly*): Poisons, poisons! Venomous thoughts and words! In hearts and minds!—That's poisons!

GOOPER (*overlapping her*): I am asking for a square deal, and by God, I expect to get one. But if I don't get one, if there's any peculiar shenanigans going on around here behind my back, well, I'm not a corporation lawyer for nothing, I know how to protect my own interests.

(BRICK *enters from the gallery with a tranquil, blurred smile, carrying an empty glass with him.*)

BRICK: Storm coming up.

GOOPER: Oh! A late arrival!

MAE: Behold the conquering hero comes!

GOOPER: The fabulous Brick Pollitt! Remember him?
—Who could forget him!

MAE: He looks like he's been injured in a game!

GOOPER: Yep, I'm afraid you'll have to warm the
bench at the Sugar Bowl this year, Brick!

(MAE *laughs shrilly.*)

Or was it the Rose Bowl that he made that famous
run in?—

(*Thunder.*)

MAE: The punch bowl, honey. It was in the punch
bowl, the cut-glass punch bowl!

GOOPER: Oh, that's right, I'm getting the bowls mixed
up!

MARGARET: Why don't you stop venting your malice
and envy on a sick boy?

BIG MAMA: *Now you two hush, I mean it, hush, all of you,
hush!*

DAISY, SOOKEY: Storm! Storm comin'! Storm! Storm!

LACEY: Brightie, close them shutters.

GOOPER: Lacey, put the top up on my Cadillac, will
yuh?

LACEY: Yes, suh, Mistah Pollitt!

GOOPER (*at the same time*): Big Mama, you know it's
necessary for me t' go back to Memphis in th'
mornin' t' represent the Parker estate in a lawsuit.

(MAE *sits on the bed and arranges papers she has taken
from the brief case.*)

BIG MAMA: Is it, Gooper?

MAE: Yaiss.

GOOPER: That's why I'm forced to—to bring up a
problem that—

MAE: Somethin' that's too important t' be put off!

GOOPER: If Brick was sober, he ought to be in on this.

MARGARET: Brick is present; we're present.

GOOPER: Well, good. I will now give you this outline
my partner, Tom Bullitt, an' me have drawn up—
a sort of dummy—trusteeship.

MARGARET: Oh, that's it! You'll be in charge an' dole
out remittances, will you?

GOOPER: This we did as soon as we got the report on
Big Daddy from th' Ochsner Laboratories. We
did this thing, I mean we drew up this dummy
outline with the advice and assistance of the
Chairman of the Boa'd of Directors of th' Southern Plantahs Bank and Trust Company in Memphis, C. C. Bellowes, a man who handles estates
for all th' prominent fam'lies in West Tennessee
and th' Delta.

BIG MAMA: Gooper?

GOOPER (*crouching in front of* BIG MAMA): Now this is
not—not final, or anything like it. This is just a
preliminary outline. But it does provide a basis—
a design—a—possible, feasible—*plan!*

MARGARET: Yes, I'll bet it's a plan.

(*Thunder.*)

MAE: It's a plan to protect the biggest estate in the
Delta from irresponsibility an'—

BIG MAMA: Now you listen to me, all of you, you listen
here? They's not goin' to be any more catty talk in
my house! And Gooper, you put that away before
I grab it out of your hand and tear it right up! I
don't know what the hell's in it, and I don't want
to know what the hell's in it. I'm talkin' in Big
Daddy's language now; I'm his *wife* not his *widow*,
I'm still his *wife!* And I'm talkin' to you in his language an'—

GOOPER: Big Mama, what I have here is—

MAE (*at the same time*): Gooper explained that it's just a
plan . . .

BIG MAMA: I don't care what you got there. Just put it
back where it came from, an' don't let me see it
again, not even the outside of the envelope of it!
Is that understood? Basis! Plan! Preliminary!
Design! I say—what is it Big Daddy always says
when he's disgusted?

BRICK (*from the bar*): Big Daddy says "crap" when he's
disgusted.

BIG MAMA (*rising*): That's right!—CRAP! I say CRAP
too, like Big Daddy!

(*Thunder.*)

MAE: Coarse language doesn't seem called for in this—

GOOPER: Somethin' in me is *deeply outraged* by hearin'
you talk like this.

BIG MAMA: *Nobody's goin' to take nothin'!*—till Big Daddy
lets go of it—maybe, just possibly, not—not even
then! No, not even then!

(*Thunder.*)

MAE: Sookey, hurry up an' git that po'ch furniture
covahed; want th' paint to come off?

GOOPER: Lacey, put mah car away!

LACEY: Caint, Mistah Pollitt, you got the keys!

GOOPER: Naw, you got 'em, man. Where th' keys to th'
car, honey?

MAE: You got 'em in your pocket!

BRICK: "You can always hear me singin' this song,
Show me the way to go home."

(*Thunder distantly.*)

BIG MAMA: Brick! Come here, Brick, I need you. Tonight Brick looks like he used to look when he
was a little boy, just like he did when he played
wild games and used to come home when I
hollered myself hoarse for him, all sweaty and
pink cheeked and sleepy, with his—red curls shining . . .

(BRICK *draws aside as he does from all physical contact
and continues the song in a whisper, opening the ice*

bucket and dropping in the ice cubes one by one as if he were mixing some important chemical formula.)
(Distant thunder.)

Time goes by so fast. Nothin' can outrun it. Death commences too early—almost before you're half acquainted with life—you meet the other . . . Oh, you know we just got to love each other an' stay together, all of us, just as close as we can, especially now that such a *black* thing has come and moved into this place without invitation.

(Awkwardly embracing BRICK, *she presses her head to his shoulder.)*
(A dog howls off stage.)

Oh, Brick, son of Big Daddy, Big Daddy does so love you. Y'know what would be his fondest dream come true? If before he passed on, if Big Daddy has to pass on . . .

(A dog howls.)

. . . you give him a child of yours, a grandson as much like his son as his son is like Big Daddy . . .
MARGARET: I know that's Big Daddy's dream.
BIG MAMA: That's his dream.
MAE: Such a pity that Maggie and Brick can't oblige.
BIG DADDY *(off down stage right on the gallery)*: Looks like the wind was takin' liberties with this place.
SERVANT *(off stage)*: Yes, sir, Mr. Pollitt.
MARGARET *(crossing to the right door)*: Big Daddy's on the gall'ry.

(BIG MAMA has turned toward the hall door at the sound of BIG DADDY's voice on the gallery.)

BIG MAMA: I can't stay here. He'll see somethin' in my eyes.

(BIG DADDY enters the room from up stage right.)

BIG DADDY: Can I come in?

(He puts his cigar in an ash tray.)

MARGARET: Did the storm wake you up, Big Daddy?
BIG DADDY: Which stawm are you talkin' about—th' one outside or th' hullaballoo in here?

(GOOPER squeezes past BIG DADDY.)

GOOPER: 'Scuse me.

(MAE tries to squeeze past BIG DADDY to join GOOPER, but BIG DADDY puts his arm firmly around her.)

BIG DADDY: I heard some mighty loud talk. Sounded like somethin' important was bein' discussed. What was the powwow about?
MAE *(flustered)*: Why—nothin', Big Daddy . . .
BIG DADDY *(crossing to extreme left center, taking MAE with him)*: What is that pregnant-lookin' envelope you're puttin' back in your brief case, Gooper?

GOOPER *(at the foot of the bed, caught, as he stuffs papers into envelope)*: That? Nothin', suh—nothin' much of anythin' at all . . .
BIG DADDY: Nothin'? It looks like a whole lot of nothin'!

(He turns up stage to the group.)

You all know th' story about th' young married couple—
GOOPER: Yes, sir!
BIG DADDY: Hello, Brick—
BRICK: Hello, Big Daddy.

(The group is arranged in a semicircle above BIG DADDY, MARGARET at the extreme right, then MAE and GOOPER, then BIG MAMA, with BRICK at the left.)

BIG DADDY: Young married couple took Junior out to th' zoo one Sunday, inspected all of God's creatures in their cages, with satisfaction.
GOOPER: Satisfaction.
BIG DADDY *(crossing to up stage center, facing front)*: This afternoon was a warm afternoon in spring an' that ole elephant had somethin' else on his mind which was bigger'n peanuts. You know this story, Brick?

(GOOPER nods.)

BRICK: No, sir, I don't know it.
BIG DADDY: Y'see, in th' cage adjoinin' they was a young female elephant in heat!
BIG MAMA *(at BIG DADDY's shoulder)*: Oh, Big Daddy!
BIG DADDY: What's the matter, preacher's gone, ain't he? All right. That female elephant in the next cage was permeatin' the atmosphere about her with a powerful and excitin' odor of female fertility! Huh! Ain't that a nice way to put it, Brick?
BRICK: Yes, sir, nothin' wrong with it!
BIG DADDY: Brick says th's nothin' wrong with it!
BIG MAMA: Oh, Big Daddy!
BIG DADDY *(crossing to down stage center)*: So this ole bull elephant still had a couple of fornications left in him. He reared back his trunk an' got a whiff of that elephant lady next door!—began to paw at the dirt in his cage an' butt his head against the separatin' partition and, first thing y'know, there was a conspicuous change in his *profile*—very *conspicuous!* Ain't I tellin' this story in decent language, Brick?
BRICK: Yes, sir, too fuckin' decent!
BIG DADDY: So, the little boy pointed at it and said, "What's that?" His mama said, "Oh, that's—nothin'!"—His papa said, "She's spoiled!"

(BIG DADDY crosses to BRICK at left.)

You didn't laugh at that story, Brick.

(BIG MAMA crosses to down stage right crying. MARGARET goes to her. MAE and GOOPER hold up stage right center.)

BRICK: No, sir, I didn't laugh at that story.

BIG DADDY: What is the smell in this room? Don't you notice it, Brick? Don't you notice a powerful and obnoxious odor of mendacity in this room?

BRICK: Yes, sir, I think I do, sir.

GOOPER: Mae, Mae . . .

BIG DADDY: There is nothing more powerful. Is there, Brick?

BRICK: No, sir. No, sir there isn't, an' nothin' more obnoxious.

BIG DADDY: Brick agrees with me. The odor of mendacity is a powerful and obnoxious odor an' the stawm hasn't blown it away from this room yet. You notice it, Gooper?

GOOPER: What, sir?

BIG DADDY: How about you, Sister Woman? You notice the unpleasant odor of mendacity in this room?

MAE: Why, Big Daddy, I don't even know what that is.

BIG DADDY: You can smell it. Hell it smells like death!

(BIG MAMA *sobs.* BIG DADDY *looks toward her.*)

What's wrong with that fat woman over there, loaded with diamonds? Hey, what's-you-name, what's the matter with you?

MARGARET (*crossing toward* BIG DADDY): She had a slight dizzy spell, Big Daddy.

BIG DADDY: You better watch that, Big Mama. A stroke is a bad way to go.

MARGARET (*crossing to* BIG DADDY *at center*): Oh, Brick, Big Daddy has on your birthday present to him, Brick, he has on your cashmere robe, the softest material I have ever felt.

BIG DADDY: Yeah, this is my soft birthday, Maggie . . . Not my gold or my silver birthday, but my soft birthday, everything's got to be soft for Big Daddy on this soft birthday.

(MAGGIE *kneels before* BIG DADDY *at center.*)

MARGARET: Big Daddy's got on his Chinese slippers that I gave him, Brick. Big Daddy, I haven't given you my big present yet, but now I will, now's the time for me to present it to you! I have an announcement to make!

MAE: What? What kind of announcement?

GOOPER: A sports announcement, Maggie?

MARGARET: Announcement of life beginning! A child is coming, sired by Brick, and out of Maggie the Cat! I have Brick's child in my body, an' that's my birthday present to Big Daddy on this birthday!

(BIG DADDY *looks at* BRICK *who crosses behind* BIG DADDY *to down stage portal, left.*)

BIG DADDY: Get up, girl, get up off your knees, girl.

(BIG DADDY *helps* MARGARET *to rise. He crosses above her, to her right, bites off the end of a fresh cigar, taken from his bathrobe pocket, as he studies* MARGARET.)

Uh-huh, this girl has life in her body, that's no lie!

BIG MAMA: BIG DADDY'S DREAM COME TRUE!

BRICK: JESUS!

BIG DADDY (*crossing right below wicker stand*): Gooper, I want my lawyer in the mornin'.

BRICK: Where are you goin', Big Daddy?

BIG DADDY: Son, I'm goin' up on the roof, to the belvedere on th' roof to look over my kingdom before I give up my kingdom—twenty-eight thousand acres of th' richest land this side of the valley Nile!

(*He exits through right doors, and down right on the gallery.*)

BIG MAMA (*following*): Sweetheart, sweetheart, sweetheart—can I come with you?

(*She exits down stage right.*)
(MARGARET *is down stage center in the mirror area.* MAE *has joined* GOOPER *and she gives him a fierce poke, making a low hissing sound and a grimace of fury.*)

GOOPER (*pushing her aside.*): Brick, could you possibly spare me one small shot of that liquor?

BRICK: Why, help yourself, Gooper boy.

GOOPER: I will.

MAE (*shrilly*): Of course we know that this is—a lie.

GOOPER: *Be still, Mae.*

MAE: I won't be still! I know she's made this up!

GOOPER: Goddam it, I said shut up!

MARGARET: Gracious! I didn't know that my little announcement was going to provoke such a storm!

MAE: *That* woman isn't *pregnant!*

GOOPER: Who said she was?

MAE: *She* did.

GOOPER: The doctor didn't. Doc Baugh didn't.

MARGARET: I haven't gone to Doc Baugh.

GOOPER: Then who'd you go to, Maggie?

MARGARET: One of the best gynecologists in the South.

GOOPER: Uh huh, uh huh!—I see . . . (*He takes out a pencil and notebook.*)—May we have his name, please?

MARGARET: No, you may not, Mister Prosecuting Attorney!

MAE: He doesn't have any name, he doesn't exist!

MARGARET: Oh, he exists all right, and so does my child, Brick's baby!

MAE: You can't conceive a child by a man that won't sleep with you unless you think you're—

(BRICK *has turned on the phonograph. A scat song cuts* MAE*'s speech.*)

GOOPER: *Turn that off!*

MAE: We know it's a lie because we hear you in here; he won't sleep with you, we hear you! So don't imagine you're going to put a trick over on us, to fool a dying man with a—

(A long drawn cry of agony and rage fills the house. MAR-GARET *turns the phonograph down to a whisper. The cry is repeated.)*

MAE: Did you hear that, Gooper, did you hear that?

GOOPER: Sounds like the pain has struck.

MAE: Go see, Gooper!

GOOPER: Come along and leave these lovebirds together in their nest!

(He goes out first. MAE *follows but turns at the door, contorting her face and hissing at* MARGARET.*)*

MAE: *Liar!*

(She slams the door.)

*(*MARGARET *exhales with relief and moves a little unsteadily to catch hold of* BRICK's *arm.)*

MARGARET: Thank you for—keeping still . . .

BRICK: O.K., Maggie.

MARGARET: It was gallant of you to save my face!

(He now pours down three shots in quick succession and stands waiting, silent. All at once he turns with a smile and says.)

BRICK: *There!*

MARGARET: What?

BRICK: The *click* . . .

(His gratitude seems almost infinite as he hobbles out on the gallery with a drink. We hear his crutch as he swings out of sight. Then, at some distance, he begins singing to himself a peaceful song. MARGARET *holds the big pillow forlornly as if it were her only companion, for a few moments, then throws it on the bed. She rushes to the liquor cabinet, gathers all the bottles in her arms, turns about undecidedly, then runs out of the room with them, leaving the door ajar on the dim yellow hall.* BRICK *is heard hobbling back along the gallery, singing his peaceful song. He comes back in, sees the pillow on the bed, laughs lightly, sadly, picks it up. He has it under his arm as* MARGARET *returns to the room.* MARGARET *softly shuts the door and leans against it, smiling softly at* BRICK.*)*

MARGARET: Brick, I used to think that you were stronger than me and I didn't want to be overpowered by you. But now, since you've taken to liquor—you know what?—I guess it's bad, but now I'm stronger than you and I can love you more truly! Don't move that pillow, I'll move it right back if you do!—Brick?

(She turns out all the lamps but a single rose-silk-shaded one by the bed.)

I really have been to a doctor and I know what to do and—Brick?—this is my time by the calendar to conceive?

BRICK: Yes, I understand, Maggie. But how are you going to conceive a child by a man in love with his liquor?

MARGARET: By locking his liquor up and making him satisfy my desire before I unlock it!

BRICK: Is that what you've done, Maggie?

MARGARET: Look and see. That cabinet's mighty empty compared to before!

BRICK: Well, I'll be a son of a—

(He reaches for his crutch but she beats him to it and rushes out on the gallery, hurls the crutch over the rail and comes back in, panting.)

MARGARET: And so tonight we're going to make the lie true, and when that's done, I'll bring the liquor back here and we'll get drunk together, here, tonight, in this place that death has come into . . . —What do you say?

BRICK: I don't say anything. I guess there's nothing to say.

MARGARET: Oh, you weak people, you weak, beautiful people who give up with such grace. What you want is someone to—

(She turns out the rose-silk lamp.)

—take hold of you.—Gently, gently with love hand your life back to you, like somethin' gold you let go of. I *do* love you, Brick, I *do!*

BRICK *(smiling with charming sadness)*: Wouldn't it be funny if that was true?

Figure 1. Maggie (Elizabeth Ashley) and Brick (Keir Dullea) in the American Shakespeare Theater production of *Cat on a Hot Tin Roof,* directed by Michael Kahn and designed by John Conklin, New York, 1974. (Photograph: Martha Swope/TimePix.)

Figure 2. Mae (Joan Pape, *standing center*), Gooper (Charles Siebert), and their five children perform a musical chorus to celebrate the birthday of Big Daddy (Fred Gwynne), while *(left to right)* Reverend Tooker (Wyman Pendleton), Doctor Baugh (William Larsen), Big Mama (Kate Reid), Sookey (Sarallen), and Lacey look on. This photograph also shows the realistic/expressionistic set with walls that "dissolve mysteriously into air," as Williams specified in his "Notes to the Designer." (Photograph: Martha Swope/TimePix.)

Figure 3. Big Daddy (Fred Gwynne) tells the story of the "ole bull elephant" to Mae (Joan Pape), Big Mama (Kate Reid), and Maggie (Elizabeth Ashley). (Photograph: Martha Swope/TimePix.)

Staging of *Cat on a Hot Tin Roof*

NOTES BY ELIZABETH ASHLEY ON PLAYING
MAGGIE IN THE AMERICAN SHAKESPEARE
THEATER PRODUCTION, 1974

If there was ever a role my whole life summed up into, it was Maggie. I knew her inside and out, down to the marrow of her bones and the stream of her consciousness. She was Southern just like me, and her values and attitudes were all the same ones I grew up with.

She was a delta queen in love with a jock, a woman who knows from her upbringing how to sit down and chit-chat with the old folks in the most high-country-club ladylike way, and then go out to a road house, drink beer and boogie. That was the style where I came from.

She was also someone whose family had good social lines but no money. Her speech in the first act about what it was like to grow up a poor relation and dress in hand-me-downs could have been lifted from my own life.

I also saw something I think a lot of people not from the South had missed, which is that Maggie is wildly funny and funny in a specifically Southern way. Her sense of the ludicrous begins with herself, then extends to everyone and everything else around her. The entire first act is practically a monologue in which she dishes up one funny story after another. I know how to talk that talk. I cut my teeth on it.

The one thing I thought might give me trouble was Maggie's sexuality.

Like a lot of Southern women, her whole identity is based on being beautiful, sexual, and desirable. She has a lot of vanity—which is no bad thing in that part of the country—and when her husband won't go to bed with her it drives her into a frenzy. She becomes like an animal in heat, full of raw hunger and lust. That's the key to her character and the thing that makes the play work. I realized that if I was going to do her justice I would have to get down to the wail and the cry of a low-down dirty blues song. That's what Maggie is, a ballsout lowdown blues song. It moans. . . .

Cat on a Hot Tin Roof is a magnificently built play for the actress doing Maggie. The entire first act is yours. It's practically an hour-long monologue. You're pretty much off for the second act when all the exposition and hard stuff has to get done, and then you come back in for the last act and get to tie it all up with one of the most beautiful speeches ever written in the English language:

"Oh, you weak people, you weak, beautiful people who give up with such grace. What you need is someone to take hold of you—gently, with love, and hand your life back to you, like something gold you let go of."

Does it get any better than that? I don't think so. To be able to say lines like that is a privilege and a trust.

And never was an actress given more of an opportunity to be a star as in that production. As the play opens, Maggie comes into her bedroom, takes off her dress, then sits down on the bed and changes her stockings while she dishes offstage to Brick. Michael Kahn found the largest, whitest bed anyone has ever seen, then placed it smack in the center of the stage and lit it with a bright white spot. No other production ever gave it that kind of prominence.

The first time we rehearsed with the bed he told me, "Okay, Elizabeth, I want you to sit right in the middle of that thing when you do the business with the stockings."

I said, "Jesus, Michael, shouldn't I do it sitting on the side? It's going to be awfully hard to take those stockings off, then put the new ones on and hitch them to my garter belt without being positively lewd."

"Nope, the middle of the bed, however you have to do it. And if you need any further justification, let us not forget that what you're out to do is not change your stockings but to get laid."

I think I milked everything possible out of putting on a pair of stockings. By the time we opened, I probably knew more about putting on stockings than anyone in the world. . . .

As I waited for the house lights to dim [on opening night], I kept telling myself, "The worst thing they can do to you is run you out of town, and you've been run out of town before. The worst thing you can do to yourself is blow it, and you've blown it before. So if you're going to blow it, let's blow it with excess rather than with careful, okay?"

The second I hit the stage all my fear evaporated. . . .

The audience was as up for it as I was. The way the scene starts, Maggie comes blasting through the bedroom door and walks straight down front center stage to a floor-length mirror to look at the stain on her dress. Then playing it right into the mirror, she says the opening lines: "One of those no-neck monsters hit me with a hot buttered biscuit so I have t' change." But when I made my entrance, the applause was so huge that I had to hold my line until they were ready to settle down and listen. You can't just stand there and freeze, so I began turning around and checking my ass in the mirror, pretending to be so hung into it that I did a full circle. And from that moment on I knew I was home free. Maggie was there. She was there with me and in me, more than she'd ever been before.

It was like surfing. The surfer has to know the board and he has to know the water and he has to have the balance and the guts and the balls. He has to have a lot of things, but mainly he has to have the wave. There are dues you have to pay, chops you have to have, and licks you have to know, but if you have all those and you also get the wave and you hit it just right, it's like God hands you a magic bicycle and says, "Okay, kid, you get a free ride. Have fun! That's what it's for!"

But it had to do with more than ego.

I had a mission, and my mission was Tennessee Williams. My mission was to make the people hear the song.

And I was necessary. I was the medium through which the song gets sung.

My mission was to grab those people hard around the heart and say, "Hey, you with your piddling play here and your passable play there, now you listen to *this*! You're telling me that this man is a has-been and can't even get his plays produced? Okay, I'm going to stand in front of you and do nothing but talk for an hour, and I'm going to get you off like you haven't been gotten off since you can't remember when! And you know why? Because it's Tennessee Williams, that's why. And because I know how to do it. So don't bother yourself about whether it's any good or not or whether you like it. Just sit back and have a good time, and don't get in my way."

And they got it. They got it immediately. I could tell from the way they were laughing in the first two minutes.

The way I did Maggie some audiences would laugh in one place and some in another, depending on which aspect of the character they got. That's the joyous thing about playing a character as multi-aspected as Maggie. But that night what cracked them up was Maggie's point of view, which was what I built her from and loved most about her.

And when you have an audience that gets your point of view that quickly, you can't miss unless you start to lie or cheat, which was the very last thing I was going to do with that play.

I couldn't do anything wrong that night. I have never felt so secure before or since, and I know I never will.

When the curtain came down there was a moment of silence like a massive intake of breath, then an explosion of cheers and applause different from anything I'd ever heard before. It was beyond opening-night overreaction and beyond an ego stroke. It was something shared.

It was you and them together breaking through the barrier that separates them as audience from you as performer, them as judges and you as the judged.

All of that was obliterated and ceased to be important in the face of the music, in the face of the song.

REVIEW OF THE AMERICAN SHAKESPEARE THEATER PRODUCTION, 1974, BY CLIVE BARNES

People used to think that Tennessee Williams's plays were about sex and violence. How wrong they were—they are about love and survival. Mr. Williams's "Cat on a Hot Tin Roof" is now 20 years old, and in its first day it was regarded as something of a shocker. Now even though a certain four-letter word has been restored where a euphemism once reigned stupidly supreme, I doubt whether anyone is going to be shocked. . . . But I hope they will be affected. This is a gripping and intensely moving play, a play that can hold its own with anything written in the post-O'Neill American theater.

The Cat is Maggie—a Southern beauty of indefinite lineage. She is married to Brick, a handsome, former football player, now TV sportscaster. The marriage could be perfect, but Brick is an impotent alcoholic who fears that he failed his best friend, apparently a homosexual. Brick's father, Big Daddy, a self-made Southern millionaire, is dying of cancer. He doesn't know it. His wife doesn't know it. But the family, including Brick's brother and sister-in-law, they know it. It is Big Daddy's 65th, and last, birthday.

Michael Kahn's new staging, which opened at the ANTA Theater last night for a limited run, really is new. It originated at the American Shakespeare Theater in Connecticut this summer, and it offers a rewarding new variant on the original play.

As is well known, the Broadway version, directed by Elia Kazan, incorporated in its last act a number of Mr. Kazan's own ideas. Indeed in most printed versions of the play the last act exists in two versions, the so-called "Broadway" version, and the original. In the latter Big Daddy does not appear and Brick, faced with some faint prospect of fatherhood, changes somewhat in his character. Mr. Kahn, presumably with the playwright's permission, seems to have taken the best of both acts—following Mr. Kazan in his inclusion of Big Daddy in the last act (and Kazan was right in his thinking there), and yet following the original in its far more sensitive handling of the final relationship between Brick and Maggie. The result seems to be a definitive version of the play.

Twenty years ago everyone made much of the symbolism in Tennessee Williams, and undoubtedly the symbolism is here. The magnolia scented bedroom that used to belong to the old-maidish bachelors that once owned the plantation, the concept of the bed itself as Maggie's territory, or Brick's possible latent homosexuality symbolized by his hazy impotence—yes, all these are symbols of the sexual warfare that underlies the story. But the story itself, and the compassion Mr. Williams brings to the telling of it, is what really matters.

Mr. Williams has the one vital gift a playwright must possess—he holds the interest. He makes you care by showing you a world. His characters are drawn with rough strokes, for Mr. Williams always demonstrates by exaggeration. He is also a playwright who wants to be very popular (or, rather, very much loved) and this sometimes leads him into cheapness. But he is a master. His plays have a time, a place, a development and ring true.

He is lucky with Mr. Kahn, whose direction seems directly aimed at lowering the play's hot-house temperature, and at making a domestic drama rather than an eternal triangle between a woman, a reluctant man and a bed. As a result Big Daddy becomes rather more important than before.

The imaginative setting by John Conklin, the cleverly evocative costumes by Jane Greenwood and the dappled lighting by Marc B. Weiss, are all splendid, but if Mr. Williams has been fortunate in Mr. Kahn and his collaborators, Mr. Kahn has been equally fortunate in his cast, or at least clever in his casting.

Elizabeth Ashley was much praised for her Maggie in Connecticut, but even then she was sold short. Sensuous, withdrawn, composed and determined, Miss Ashley's Maggie vibrantly combines charm with grit. She can stand outside a conversation like a cobra, or flutter in like a bird. Splendid.

Keir Dullea's ironic, embittered Brick makes her the perfect partner. He has precisely "the charm of the defeated," with his alcoholic eyes staring into the mid-distance of half-forgotten memory, still waiting for the click of oblivion. Both this Brick and this Maggie are oddly vulnerable, which is also the special quality of Fred Gwynne's blustering, hollowed out Big Daddy. These three performances are so right that they detract from the more shallow playing of the rest of the cast, including Kate Reid, slightly too shrill as a miscast Big Mama.

This is a glowing play, memorably staged. It gets Broadway's dramatic season off to a flying start.

CONTEMPORARY THEATER

Most periods in the history of drama are associated with distinctive theatrical structures—the classical Greek with outdoor amphitheaters; the Middle Ages with pageant wagons and platform stages; the Renaissance English with multilevel open-air theaters; the neoclassical with indoor theaters, proscenium stages, and perspective backdrops; the modern with fan-shaped auditoriums and box sets. During the contemporary period, variety is the rule in theatrical structures and staging conventions. The box set and the fan-shaped auditorium of realistic theater (see pages 522 and 524) continue to flourish in many amateur and professional houses. Yet, in addition to this now common pattern, other theatrical arrangements have developed, reflecting a renewed interest in earlier methods of staging. In an attempt to reclaim and combine elements of the classical Greek and Renaissance English theaters, mid-twentieth-century designers created the thrust stage (see Figure 1), in which the audience is seated on rising tiers around three sides of a platform, the fourth side being occupied by a permanent setting that contains multiple acting surfaces. And somewhat earlier in the century, designers reclaimed the medieval style of theater-in-the-round and turned it into the arena stage (see Figure 2), an arrangement placing the audience on all four sides of the actors and using the aisles for entrances and exits. The theatrical freedom of the arena stage has also prompted directors and producers to reclaim another medieval heritage by putting on plays in the street, in public squares, or any other open space that will bring actors and spectators closer to each other than is possible in the traditional theater.

Contemporary set design has been equally flexible, ranging from a total abandonment of settings, set pieces, and props to the use of highly elaborate set designs in a realistic or symbolic style. In part, of course, various styles in set design have been determined by the nature of the theatrical environment. Arena stages and thrust stages clearly do not invite the use of box sets or painted backdrops. But even in a conventional modern theater, where the realism of the box set has been

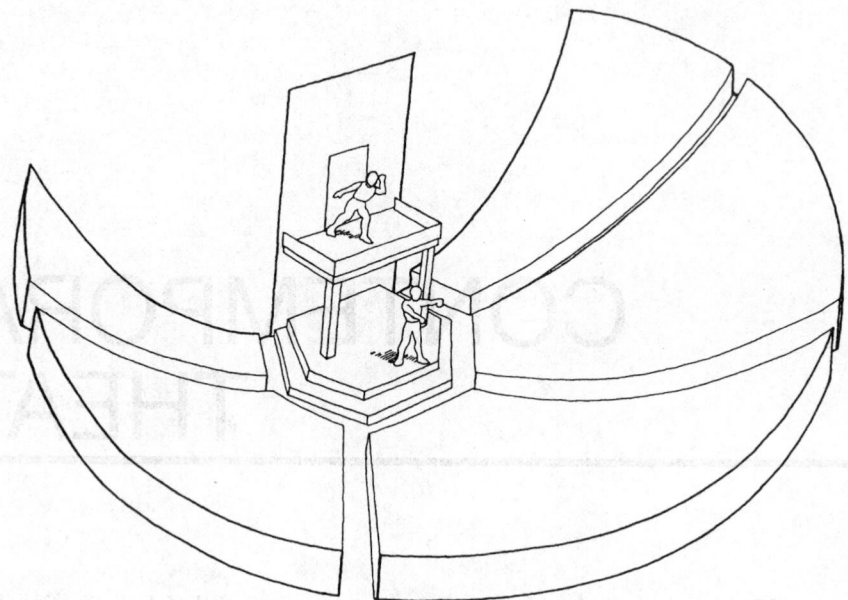

Figure 1. The contemporary thrust stage, showing the multiple acting surfaces adapted from the Renaissance English theater, surrounded on three sides by the rising tiers of seats adapted from the classical Greek theater.

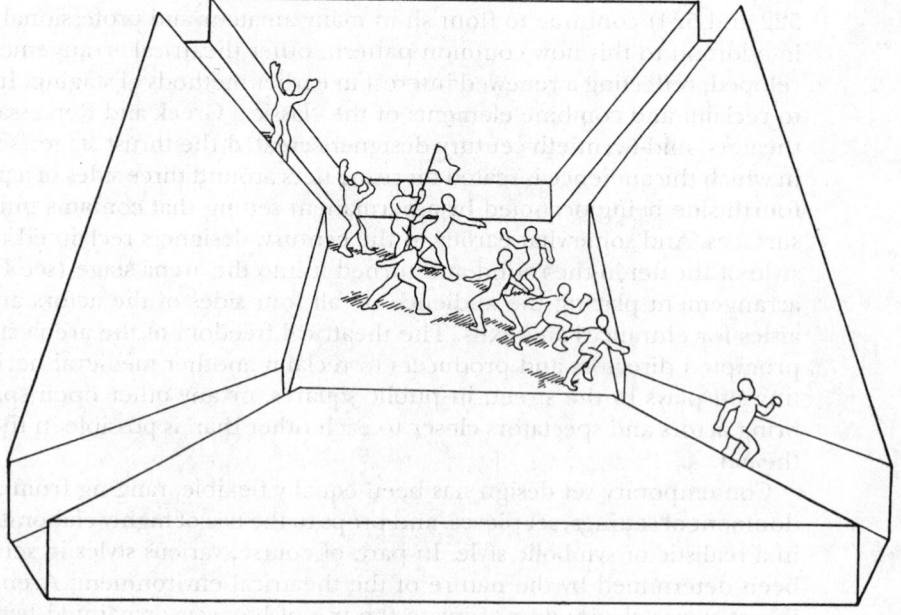

Figure 2. The contemporary arena stage.

readily accessible, designers have taken the liberty of blending and modifying a combination of styles to achieve unique dramatic effects. Harold Pinter sets his short play *Landscape* (1969) in "the kitchen of a country house" and adds the following details: "A long kitchen table. Beth sits in an armchair, which stands away from the table, to its left. Duff sits in a chair at the right corner of the table. The background, of a sink, stove, etc., and a window, is dim. Evening." The kitchen is thus real yet strange; familiar objects (sink, stove, table, chairs) appear, but in a slightly unsettling combination, since Beth is near the table but not at it, separated from Duff who remains at the table. And Pinter's note—"Duff refers normally to Beth, but does not appear to hear her voice. Beth never looks at Duff, and does not appear to hear his voice"—makes the distance implied by the setting even plainer. Pinter thus uses the normal and familiar domesticity of the kitchen to emphasize the disturbing lack of communication between these two people.

The freedom in contemporary theater to choose among a variety of styles has also made it possible for dramatists to reject realistic conventions altogether, as did the playwrights of the most influential movement of the 1950s and 1960s, the theater of the absurd, a movement defined and named by the critic Martin Esslin (see Ideas of Drama). The absurdists—most notably Samuel Beckett, Eugène Ionesco, and Jean Genet—rejected such realistic conventions as psychologically motivated characters and plots, logically consistent dialogue, and familiar styles of presentation, for, as Esslin explained, "The Theatre of the Absurd has renounced arguing about the absurdity of the human condition; it merely presents it in being—that is, in terms of the concrete stage images of the absurdity of existence." Given their acute sense of the malignancy, or meaninglessness, or sterility of existence, the absurdists deliberately favor stage actions and images that will clearly evoke such a view of experience, whether it is the garbage can residents of Beckett's *Endgame* (1957) or the rhinoceros that takes over the world in Ionesco's *Rhinoceros* (1960). The drama that Esslin has labeled absurdist has its roots in avant-garde theater of the late nineteenth and early twentieth century, in such plays as Alfred Jarry's *Ubu Roi* (1896), a scatological and seemingly nonsensical play about a brutal and whimsical ruler, or Guillaume Apollinaire's *The Breasts of Tiresias* (1917), which features a dancing news kiosk and a woman turning into a man when her breasts float away as balloons. Absurdism derives as well from the radical ideas of Antonin Artaud, who in 1938 expounded a "theater of cruelty," which he based on this assumption: "Everything that acts is a cruelty. It is upon this idea of extreme action, pushed beyond all limits, that theatre must be rebuilt." Although absurdist drama, strictly speaking, does not exemplify the theater of cruelty, it does clearly push drama to extreme actions and images.

Not only is absurdist drama a striking instance of the stylistic freedom in contemporary theater but it has also been an influence nurturing even greater experimentation among playwrights, directors, actors, and set designers. After seeing Beckett's *Waiting for Godot* (1952), for example, the dramatist William Saroyan said, "It will make it easier for me and everyone else to write freely in the theatre." Unhampered by expectations about what drama should be, contemporary playwrights have consistently experimented with symbolic and image-centered drama, as indicated by the metaphoric titles of their plays, such as *Endgame, Dutchman, Translations,* and *Angels in America.* The dramatic inventions of the playwrights have, in turn, stimulated designers such as Eiko Ishioka, who created the curving ramp that swirls around the stage in *M. Butterfly.* And the actors themselves, of course, have been forced to develop nonrealistic styles of performance—a challenge that has provoked them to explore the arts of dance, mime, and vaudeville. How, after all, is it possible for an actor to portray "realistically" the process of a man turning into a rhinoceros, or a mute (*Waiting for Godot*) suddenly unleashing a torrent of speech? The need to find new acting styles and to make sense of these plays for an audience has ultimately led to a greatly increased emphasis on the imaginative leadership of the director.

Indeed, contemporary theater, whether it has taken the form of realism, modified realism, or absurdism, has often been determined not only by a playwright's script but also by a director's creative influence upon the script, especially when the director and the playwright work together on a regular basis. Max Stafford-Clark—former artistic director of England's Royal Court Theatre, a nationally subsidized theater devoted to the production of new plays—has worked often and closely with Caryl Churchill. Most of David Mamet's plays were originally directed by Gregory Mosher of Chicago's Goodman Theatre, while August Wilson dedicated *Fences* to "Lloyd Richards, who adds to whatever he touches," publicly acknowledging his debt to the Yale Repertory Theatre director who has directed all of his major works.

Perhaps the most striking example of the creative director in contemporary theater is the Englishman Peter Brook, whose productions of Shakespeare have moved critics to speak of "Brook's *King Lear*" and "Brook's *A Midsummer Night's Dream*," rather than "Shakespeare's." Brook first came to public notice in the early 1940s and 1950s as a "boy genius," directing major productions of Shakespeare in London and Stratford. But his sensational reputation as a revolutionary director did not get established until 1962, when he produced *King Lear* in a style heavily influenced by the starkly expressionistic techniques of Brecht's epic theater. Brook was further influenced by Artaud's theater of cruelty, which led him to argue that cruelty is a necessary "form of self-discipline" for performers; he thus entered into an intense period of physical exercises and improvisations with a group of selected actors, a project culminating in his 1964 production of Peter Weiss's *Marat/Sade,* an elaborate play-within-a-play that features the inmates of a mental asylum staging the events of the French Revolution. Brook's highly disciplined actors kept the stage in a continuous state of theatrical disarray in order to convey the deranged experience of a mental asylum—the actors performing as inmates never stopped moving and drooling and acting out their fantasies. And at the play's conclusion, when the inmates begin attacking the onstage audience who have watched the play, Brook added a final inventive touch: as the audience applauded, the actors lined up and steadily, smirkingly, rhythmically applauded back. Since his work in the 1960s with the Royal Shakespeare Company, Brook has formed his own theater company and established himself in Paris, where he has presented productions as varied as *The Cherry Orchard,* a reworking of Bizet's opera *Carmen,* and a ten-hour adaptation of the great Indian epic *The Mahabharata.*

The revolution in contemporary theater has been carried to its logical extreme by directors who have formed repertory groups committed to a radical alteration of virtually all the traditional conventions of drama. During the late 1960s, for example, the Living Theater of Julian Beck and Judith Malina staged a series of works stressing political activism—an activism they sought to dramatize by deliberately breaking the barrier that has traditionally separated actors from spectators. Members of the Living Theater routinely talked to, touched, and even invited the audience onstage during their performances, and one of their productions, *Paradise Now*, actually climaxed with a "love pile" or "group grope" for both actors and those members of the audience who still remained in the theater. By contrast, Jerzy Grotowski and the Polish Laboratory Theatre deliberately sought to isolate members of the audience, bringing each person in a forty- or fifty-person group into the acting space one by one, sometimes even seating them behind raised walls. Furthermore, by abandoning a permanent stage and choosing to redesign the acting space for each play, by discarding makeup, costumes, props, and music, Grotowski created what has been known as "poor theater" in order to focus on "the personal and scenic technique of the actor as the core of theater art." Other experimental groups of the 1960s and 1970s have applied the rituals of yoga and meditation to theatrical performance, and still others have staged productions in slow motion, creating barely moving visual images in works that run from three to twelve hours in length. Perhaps the most remarkable element in all these experimental groups is not their assault upon theatrical conventions, nor their intense fascination with sound and movement, but their abandonment of scripted plays in favor of improvisation—a phenomenon reminiscent of Artaud's manifesto calling for "No More Masterpieces!"

The 1980s may have brought about a closer working relationship between playwright, director, and actors, especially when one considers the plays of Caryl Churchill, the most notable of which grew out of workshops with actors and directors, or the productions of Ariane Mnouchkine in Paris, whose company of actors and musicians, like that of Peter Brook, has worked with established writers to create scripts for productions such as an eight-hour play about Cambodia and Prince Sihanouk. Great Britain's long tradition of repertory companies has led to these groups either commissioning plays or creating elaborate adaptations, such as a two-part, eight-and-a-half-hour version of Dickens's *Nicholas Nickleby*, which grew out of a collaboration between directors Trevor Nunn and John Caird, playwright David Edgar, and forty-some actors of the Royal Shakespeare Company. In America, several regional theaters have been particularly important in developing new plays and playwrights. The Actors Theatre of Louisville and its artistic director, Jon Jory, have been crucial in the development of Marsha Norman's work, just as the Yale Repertory Theatre and its director, Lloyd Richards, have been central to the career of August Wilson.

While contemporary drama has developed through a series of collaborative theatrical ventures, it also reflects and challenges the most popular art forms of our day—film and television. Because film and television can attract such large audiences, contemporary drama must contend with these popular forms of entertainment. One strategy is to create a strikingly different kind of theatrical experience: contemporary drama is often spare where film is lush, abstract where television is realistic. In Beckett's *Endgame*, people live with only the barest remnants of ordinary life; in Reza's *"Art,"* three different rooms occupy the same stage space, defined simply by three different chairs; in Churchill's *Top Girls*, six of the seven actresses perform at least two different roles, forcing the audience to draw thematic connections as a result of the doubling. But contemporary drama also *uses* the realism associated with film and television. Neil Simon's phenomenally successful career reflects his particular talent for finding humor in details from domestic life and in his characters' inability to cope with such details. The same reliance on realistic detail appears in Marsha Norman's *'night, Mother,* though in this play Jessie's insistence on dealing with the minutiae of everyday life throws into horrifying relief her lack of control over everything else. Much as contemporary drama has drawn on the techniques of film and television, so contemporary dramatists often write for both stage and screen: Harold Pinter, Sam Shepard, and David Mamet are successful film-script writers; Mamet has also written for the television series *Hill Street Blues.* Film and television scripts usually involve many short scenes, perhaps because the medium allows for such fast cutting from one place to another, while realistic stage scripts have often opted for a single set. Yet the blending of the two approaches is also frequent in contemporary drama, as in the many short scenes of *M. Butterfly,* scenes that shift the audience's focus not only from one group of characters to another but from one place to another.

Such "fragmentary" structures are not unique to film or television, as one can see just by looking at the early modern episodic plays of Büchner or of Brecht. And long before them, Elizabethan dramatists often juxtaposed short scenes, frequently contrasting social classes or geographic locales. Indeed, one might argue that what is new in contemporary theater is really an echo of what is old. Just as contemporary theatrical design reflects a variety of staging techniques from the classical, medieval, and Renaissance periods, so the contemporary experimental fascination with sound and movement recalls the religious rituals from which drama first arose. In fact, contemporary drama often alludes to or revises plays, music, and dance from previous eras. Hamm in *Endgame* mimics Shakespearean characters; Derek Walcott combines *Robinson Crusoe* and the traditional English Christmas show, or pantomime, for his exploration of master-servant relationships in *Pantomime;* the South African waiters in *"MASTER HAROLD"* . . . *and the Boys* recreate ballroom dancing through their memories of Fred Astaire and Ginger Rogers; Hwang's *M. Butterfly* rewrites and directly quotes Puccini's opera *Madame Butterfly;* and Mamet's *Oleanna* takes up issues of domination through language and gender in ways that indirectly recall Shaw's *Pygmalion* and Ionesco's *The Lesson.* Thus the history of theater seems to follow a cyclical or echoic pattern, though perhaps it would be more accurate to say, as Peter Brook has, that the theater is not static or unchanging, that "truth in the theater is always on the move." Such movement is inherent in drama, on any stage, at any stage of history, for drama is a living form of art; it draws its life from live actors and a live audience coming together to create the performance.

EUGÈNE IONESCO

1912–1994

When Martin Esslin coined the phrase "the theatre of the absurd," he adopted Albert Camus's idea of the human being as a stranger, "an irremediable exile," caught in the absurd and painful predicament of having neither a past to remember nor a future to hope for. Eugène Ionesco, born in Bucharest, Rumania, to a Rumanian father and a French mother, was in a sense always an exile. When he was very young, his parents took him to France. He lived first in Paris, and then, because he developed anemia, his parents moved him to a farm in the country, a place he would later describe as his lost paradise. In 1925, the family returned to Rumania where, at the age of thirteen, Ionesco learned his native language for the first time. As a young literary critic, he published an attack on three Rumanian writers, only to bring out a second essay a few days later praising the very same authors; then under the title *No!*, he published the two essays together, a first glimpse of the confusing and often contradictory experience that his plays would later dramatize. Ionesco taught French for two years in Bucharest but then returned to France, planning to write a doctoral thesis on contemporary French poetry. Instead he wrote about his childhood, began a novel, and, to support himself, worked in a publishing house. The outbreak of World War II in 1939 compelled him to remain in France, together with his wife and baby daughter.

How then did Ionesco become a playwright? Already fluent in both French and Rumanian, Ionesco decided in 1948 to learn English. Picking up a self-study course in dialogue form, "L'Anglais sans peine" (English without difficulty), he became fascinated by the conversation between the characters: "To my astonishment, Mrs. Smith informed her husband that they had several children, that they lived in the vicinity of London, that their name was Smith, that Mr. Smith was a clerk, that they had a servant, Mary—English, like themselves." As Ionesco copied out the sentences, he found a "tragedy of language" in this conversation so full of clichés as to be meaningless—and thus drafted his "anti-play," *La Cantatrice chauve* (*The Bald Soprano*). The friends to whom he read this play found it not tragic but very funny, so much so that one of them helped to get it produced at a small avant-garde theater. In Ionesco's exuberant adaptation of the English lessons, not only do the Smiths inform each other of facts that they must already know, but their dinner guests, Mr. and Mrs. Martin, begin by addressing each other as strangers but eventually discover that they are married to each other. After building to a crescendo of nonsense words and syllables, the play then begins again, this time with the Martins speaking the lines of the Smiths.

Though *The Bald Soprano* ran for only six weeks in 1950, Ionesco continued to write absurdist plays and to get them produced: *The Lesson* (1951), *The Chairs* (1952), *Amédée, or How to Get Rid of It* (1954), *Jack or the Submission* (1955). Most of these were one-acts, although *Amédée,* which features a corpse that keeps growing and finally floats away into space carrying Amédée with it, is a three-act play, as is *The Killer* (1959). In *The Killer,* whose French title, *Tueur sans gages,* implies that the

967

killer works without payment and thus kills almost randomly, Ionesco presents a world clearly echoing the memories of his idyllic childhood in the French country-side, a "radiant city" where it is always springtime, but a city now deserted because of the mysterious killer. In the last act, the protagonist, Bérenger, tries to appeal to the killer, but hears only chuckling. The ineffectiveness of Bérenger's arguments against such meaningless murder represents Ionesco's most despairing view of humanity. Such helplessness also underlies his next major play, *Rhinoceros* (1960), in which Bérenger, again the protagonist, resists the forces of social/political conformity as represented by the rhinoceros. While *The Killer* shows Bérenger gradually succumbing both to the killer's inexorable chuckling and, in Ionesco's words, to "the vacuity of his own rather commonplace morality," *Rhinoceros* presents at least the possibility that an individual human being might triumph over the thundering menace of mass thinking. Two major productions of *Rhinoceros* in 1960 (the first in Paris, starring the great French actor-manager Jean-Louis Barrault, the second in London, directed by Orson Welles and starring Laurence Olivier) both reflected and contributed to Ionesco's growing public stature.

To many critics, the takeover by the rhinoceroses and the willingness of everyone in the play, except for Bérenger, to change into a rhinoceros was a parable about the success of the Nazi movement. Ionesco had seen the violence of the Nazis when he lived in Rumania, and had felt for himself the difficulty of challenging Fascist doctrine: "When you're twenty years old and you have teachers who offer you scientific or pseudo-scientific theories and explanations, when you have newspapers, when you have a whole atmosphere, doctrines, a whole movement against you, it's really very hard to resist, hard not to let yourself be convinced." And, as the reference to teachers suggests, Ionesco held major doubts about his own life both as a student and then as a teacher.

All of the major themes in Ionesco's plays—the meaningless aspect of language, the human being's tendency to violence, the destructive power of collective thinking—find chilling expression in *The Lesson*. At first, *The Lesson* seems to be a comedy about education, as the young woman coming for a private tutorial with the Professor can hardly remember the capital of France but wishes to qualify for a doctorate in just three weeks. Comically, too, the tutorial begins with arithmetic (the Pupil can't subtract but she can multiply two ten-digit numbers correctly) and then moves to linguistics and comparative philology. Just as Ionesco delights in exposing linguistic clichés in *The Bald Soprano,* so in *The Lesson* the Professor explains how languages differ from one another through "something intangible that one is able to perceive only after very long study, with a great deal of trouble and after the broadest experience." The Professor's discussion of the names of countries, while ridiculous on one level, is also a painful echo of Ionesco's own confusion when he moved from France to Rumania: "At primary school, in France, I'd been taught that French—which was my language—was the most beautiful language in the world, that the French were the bravest people in the world. . . . When I got to Bucharest, my teachers explained that my language was Rumanian, that the most beautiful language in the world was not French but Rumanian. . . ."

By the end of the play, when the Professor attacks the Pupil not only with words but with a knife, Ionesco's perception of the world as one in which "the comic is terrifying, the comic is tragic" becomes frighteningly clear. The donning of an armband with a swastika implies political violence, just as the description of the attack on the Pupil implies not only murder but also rape. The explicit onstage attack, similar to the ending of Baraka's *Dutchman,* dramatizes the struggle for power in terms of sexual relationships. Indeed, more recent plays, such as Robert Athayde's *Miss Margarida's Way* (first American production, 1977) and David Mamet's highly controversial *Oleanna* (1992), have taken the teacher/student relationship and used it, as Ionesco does, as a metaphor for political, social, and sexual domination.

In performance, *The Lesson* has seemed both opaque and accessible, as reflected in reviews of the 1958 New York production. Brooks Atkinson, writing in the *New York Times,* seemed willing to accept *The Chairs* and *The Lesson* as "odd, elliptical fantastifications" and to enjoy a "diverting evening," without feeling bothered by the fact that he couldn't "explain the cosmic significance of M. Ionesco's theme." Walter Kerr, whose review is reprinted following the text, was bothered by the "defiant mindlessness" of both plays, and felt he had followed "a long, tortured, circuitous, pretentious road to a nice, round zero that might be drawn at once." Yet Kerr still responded to the power of the production, with most of his reservations coming afterward when he thought about what he had seen. The theatrical energy of the performance, so strikingly evoked in Kerr's description of Max Adrian and Joan Plowright (see Figure 1), is thus balanced by the "black despair" of the playwright's vision, as the maid comforts the murderous Professor (see Figure 2) and then calmly ushers in the forty-first pupil and the forty-first victim.

THE LESSON
A Comic Drama

BY EUGÈNE IONESCO/TRANSLATED BY DONALD ALLEN

CHARACTERS

THE PROFESSOR, *aged fifty to sixty*
THE YOUNG PUPIL, *aged eighteen*
THE MAID, *aged forty-five to fifty*

SCENE

The office of the old professor, which also serves as a dining room. To the left, a door opens onto the apartment stairs; upstage, to the right, another door opens onto a corridor of the apartment. Upstage, a little left of center, a window, not very large, with plain curtains; on the outside sill of the window are ordinary potted plants. The low buildings with red roofs of a small town can be seen in the distance. The sky is grayish-blue. On the right stands a provincial buffet. The table doubles as a desk, it stands at stage center. There are three chairs around the table, and two more stand on each side of the window. Light-colored wallpaper, some shelves with books.

(When the curtain rises the stage is empty, and it remains so for a few moments. Then we hear the doorbell ring.)

VOICE OF THE MAID *(from the corridor)*: Yes. I'm coming.

(The MAID comes in, after having run down the stairs. She is stout, aged forty-five to fifty, red-faced, and wears a peasant woman's cap. She rushes in, slamming the door to the right behind her, and dries her hands on her apron as she runs towards the door on the left. Meanwhile we hear the doorbell ring again.)

MAID: Just a moment, I'm coming.

(She opens the door. A young PUPIL, aged eighteen, enters. She is wearing a gray student's smock, a small white collar, and carries a student's satchel under her arm.)

MAID: Good morning, miss.
PUPIL: Good morning, madam. Is the Professor at home?
MAID: Have you come for the lesson?
PUPIL: Yes, I have.
MAID: He's expecting you. Sit down for a moment. I'll tell him you're here.
PUPIL: Thank you.

(She seats herself near the table, facing the audience; the hall door is to her left; her back is to the other door, through which the MAID hurriedly exits, calling:)

MAID: Professor, come down please, your pupil is here.
VOICE OF THE PROFESSOR *(rather reedy)*: Thank you. I'm coming . . . in just a moment . . .

(The MAID exits; the PUPIL draws in her legs, holds her satchel on her lap, and waits demurely. She casts a glance or two around the room, at the furniture, at the ceiling too. Then she takes a notebook out of her satchel, leafs through it, and stops to look at a page for a moment as though reviewing a lesson, as though taking a last look at her homework. She seems to be a well-brought-up girl, polite, but lively, gay, dynamic; a fresh smile is on her lips. During the course of the play she progressively loses the lively rhythm of her movement and her carriage, she becomes withdrawn. From gay and smiling she becomes progressively sad and morose; from very lively at the beginning, she becomes more and more fatigued and somnolent. Towards the end of the play her face must clearly express a nervous depression; her way of speaking shows the effects of this, her tongue becomes thick, words come to her memory with difficulty and emerge from her mouth with as much difficulty; she comes to have a manner vaguely paralyzed, the beginning of aphasia.° Firm and determined at the beginning, so much so as to appear to be almost aggressive, she becomes more and more passive, until she is almost a mute and inert object, seemingly inanimate in the PROFESSOR's hands, to such an extent that when he makes his final gesture, she no longer reacts. Insensible, her reflexes deadened, only her eyes in an expressionless face will show inexpressible astonishment and fear. The transition from one manner to the other must of course be made imperceptibly.)

(The PROFESSOR enters. He is a little old man with a little white beard. He wears pince-nez,° a black skull cap, a long black schoolmaster's coat, trousers and shoes of black, detachable white collar, a black tie. Excessively polite, very timid, his voice deadened by his timidity, very proper, very much the teacher. He rubs his hands together constantly; occasionally a lewd gleam comes into his eyes and is quickly repressed.)

(During the course of the play his timidity will disappear progressively, imperceptibly; and the lewd gleams in his eyes will become a steady devouring flame in the end.

---

aphasia, loss of the power of using or understanding words. **pince-nez**, eyeglasses attached to the nose by a spring-clip.

From a manner that is inoffensive at the start, the PRO-
FESSOR *becomes more and more sure of himself, more and
more nervous, aggressive, dominating, until he is able to
do as he pleases with the* PUPIL, *who has become, in his
hands, a pitiful creature. Of course, the voice of the* PRO-
FESSOR *must change too, from thin and reedy, to stronger
and stronger, until at the end it is extremely powerful, ringing, sonorous, while the* PUPIL'*s voice changes from the
very clear and ringing tones that she has at the beginning
of the play until it is almost inaudible. In these first scenes
the* PROFESSOR *might stammer very slightly.*)

PROFESSOR: Good morning, young lady. You . . . I
expect that you . . . that you are the new pupil?

PUPIL (*turns quickly with a lively and self-assured manner;
she gets up, goes toward the* PROFESSOR, *and gives him
her hand*): Yes, Professor. Good morning, Professor. As you see, I'm on time. I didn't want to be
late.

PROFESSOR: That's fine, miss. Thank you, you didn't
really need to hurry. I am very sorry to have kept
you waiting . . . I was just finishing up . . . well . . .
I'm sorry . . . You will excuse me, won't you?

PUPIL: Oh, certainly, Professor. It doesn't matter at
all, Professor.

PROFESSOR: Please excuse me . . . Did you have any
trouble finding the house?

PUPIL: No . . . Not at all. I just asked the way. Everybody knows you around here.

PROFESSOR: For thirty years I've lived in this town.
You've not been here for long? How do you
find it?

PUPIL: It's all right. The town is attractive and even
agreeable, there's a nice park, a boarding school,
a bishop, nice shops and streets . . .

PROFESSOR: That's very true, young lady. And yet, I'd
just as soon live somewhere else. In Paris, or at
least Bordeaux.

PUPIL: Do you like Bordeaux?

PROFESSOR: I don't know. I've never seen it.

PUPIL: But you know Paris?

PROFESSOR: No, I don't know it either, young lady, but
if you'll permit me, can you tell me, Paris is the
capital city of . . . miss?

PUPIL (*searching her memory for a moment, then, happily
guessing*): Paris is the capital city of . . . France?

PROFESSOR: Yes, young lady, bravo, that's very good,
that's perfect. My congratulations. You have your
French geography at your finger tips. You know
your chief cities.

PUPIL: Oh! I don't know them all yet, Professor,
it's not quite that easy, I have trouble learning
them.

PROFESSOR: Oh! it will come . . . you mustn't give
up . . . young lady . . . I beg your pardon . . . have
patience . . . little by little . . . You will see, it will
come in time . . . What a nice day it is today . . . or

rather, not so nice . . . Oh! but then yes it is nice.
In short, it's not too bad a day, that's the main
thing . . . ahem . . . ahem . . . it's not raining and
it's not snowing either.

PUPIL: That would be most unusual, for it's summer
now.

PROFESSOR: Excuse me, miss, I was just going to say
so . . . but as you will learn, one must be ready for
anything.

PUPIL: I guess so, Professor.

PROFESSOR: We can't be sure of anything, young lady,
in this world.

PUPIL: The snow falls in the winter. Winter is one of
the four seasons. The other three are . . . uh . . .
spr . . .

PROFESSOR: Yes?

PUPIL: . . . ing, and then summer . . . and . . . uh . . .

PROFESSOR: It begins like "automobile," miss.

PUPIL: Ah, yes, autumn . . .

PROFESSOR: That's right, miss. That's a good answer,
that's perfect. I am convinced that you will be a
good pupil. You will make real progress. You are
intelligent, you seem to me to be well informed,
and you've a good memory.

PUPIL: I know my seasons, don't I, Professor?

PROFESSOR: Yes, indeed, miss . . . or almost. But it will
come in time. In any case, you're coming along.
Soon you'll know all the seasons, even with your
eyes closed. Just as I do.

PUPIL: It's hard.

PROFESSOR: Oh, no. All it takes is a little effort, a little
good will, miss. You will see. It will come, you may
be sure of that.

PUPIL: Oh, I do hope so, Professor. I have a great
thirst for knowledge. My parents also want me to
get an education. They want me to specialize.
They consider a little general culture, even if it is
solid, is no longer enough, in these times.

PROFESSOR: Your parents, miss, are perfectly right.
You must go on with your studies. Forgive me for
saying so, but it is very necessary. Our contemporary life has become most complex.

PUPIL: And so very complicated too . . . My parents
are fairly rich, I'm lucky. They can help me in my
work, help me in my very advanced studies.

PROFESSOR: And you wish to qualify for . . . ?

PUPIL: Just as soon as possible, for the first doctor's
orals. They're in three weeks' time.

PROFESSOR: You already have your high school
diploma, if you'll pardon the question?

PUPIL: Yes, Professor, I have my science diploma and
my arts diploma, too.

PROFESSOR: Ah, you're very far advanced, even perhaps too advanced for your age. And which doctorate do you wish to qualify for? In the physical
sciences or in moral philosophy?

PUPIL: My parents are very much hoping—if you

think it will be possible in such a short time—they very much hope that I can qualify for the total doctorate.

PROFESSOR: The total doctorate? . . . You have great courage, young lady, I congratulate you sincerely. We will try, miss, to do our best. In any case, you already know quite a bit, and at so young an age too.

PUPIL: Oh, Professor.

PROFESSOR: Then, if you'll permit me, pardon me, please, I do think that we ought to get to work. We have scarcely any time to lose.

PUPIL: Oh, but certainly, Professor, I want to. I beg you to.

PROFESSOR: Then, may I ask you to sit down . . . there . . . Will you permit me, miss, that is if you have no objections, to sit down opposite you?

PUPIL: Oh, of course, Professor, please do.

PROFESSOR: Thank you very much, miss. *(They sit down facing each other at the table, their profiles to the audience.)* There we are. Now have you brought your books and notebooks?

PUPIL *(taking notebooks and books out of her satchel)*: Yes, Professor. Certainly, I have brought all that we'll need.

PROFESSOR: Perfect, miss. This is perfect. Now, if this doesn't bore you . . . shall we begin?

PUPIL: Yes, indeed, Professor, I am at your disposal.

PROFESSOR: At my disposal? *(A gleam comes into his eyes and is quickly extinguished; he begins to make a gesture that he suppresses at once.)* Oh, miss, it is I who am at your disposal. I am only your humble servant.

PUPIL: Oh, Professor . . .

PROFESSOR: If you will . . . now . . . we . . . we . . . I . . . I will begin by making a brief examination of your knowledge, past and present, so that we may chart our future course . . . Good. How is your perception of plurality?

PUPIL: It's rather vague . . . confused.

PROFESSOR: Good. We shall see.

(He rubs his hands together. The MAID *enters, and this appears to irritate the* PROFESSOR. *She goes to the buffet and looks for something, lingering.)*

PROFESSOR: Now, miss, would you like to do a little arithmetic, that is if you want to . . .

PUPIL: Oh, yes, Professor. Certainly, I ask nothing better.

PROFESSOR: It is rather a new science, a modern science, properly speaking, it is more a method than a science . . . And it is also a therapy. *(To the* MAID:) Have you finished, Marie?

MAID: Yes, Professor, I've found the plate. I'm just going . . .

PROFESSOR: Hurry up then. Please go along to the kitchen, if you will.

MAID: Yes, Professor, I'm going. *(She starts to go out.)*

Excuse me, Professor, but take care, I urge you to remain calm.

PROFESSOR: You're being ridiculous, Marie. Now, don't worry.

MAID: That's what you always say.

PROFESSOR: I will not stand for your insinuations. I know perfectly well how to comport myself. I am old enough for that.

MAID: Precisely, Professor. You will do better not to start the young lady on arithmetic. Arithmetic is tiring, exhausting.

PROFESSOR: Not at my age. And anyhow, what business is it of yours? This is my concern. And I know what I'm doing. This is not your department.

MAID: Very well, Professor. But you can't say that I didn't warn you.

PROFESSOR: Marie, I can get along without your advice.

MAID: As you wish, Professor. *(She exits.)*

PROFESSOR: Miss, I hope you'll pardon this absurd interruption . . . Excuse this woman . . . She is always afraid that I'll tire myself. She fusses over my health.

PUPIL: Oh, that's quite all right, Professor. It shows that she's very devoted. She loves you very much. Good servants are rare.

PROFESSOR: She exaggerates. Her fears are stupid. But let's return to our arithmetical knitting.

PUPIL: I'm following you, Professor.

PROFESSOR *(wittily)*: Without leaving your seat!

PUPIL *(appreciating his joke)*: Like you, Professor.

PROFESSOR: Good. Let us arithmetize a little now.

PUPIL: Yes, gladly, Professor.

PROFESSOR: It wouldn't be too tiresome for you to tell me . . .

PUPIL: Not at all, Professor, go on.

PROFESSOR: How much are one and one?

PUPIL: One and one make two.

PROFESSOR *(marveling at the* PUPIL's *knowledge)*: Oh, but that's very good. You appear to me to be well along in your studies. You should easily achieve the total doctorate, miss.

PUPIL: I'm so glad. Especially to have someone like you tell me this.

PROFESSOR: Let's push on: how much are two and one?

PUPIL: Three.

PROFESSOR: Three and one?

PUPIL: Four.

PROFESSOR: Four and one?

PUPIL: Five.

PROFESSOR: Five and one?

PUPIL: Six.

PROFESSOR: Six and one?

PUPIL: Seven.

PROFESSOR: Seven and one?

PUPIL: Eight.

PROFESSOR: Seven and one?

PUPIL: Eight again.

PROFESSOR: Very well answered. Seven and one?

PUPIL: Eight once more.

PROFESSOR: Perfect. Excellent. Seven and one?

PUPIL: Eight again. And sometimes nine.

PROFESSOR: Magnificent. You are magnificent. You are exquisite. I congratulate you warmly, miss. There's scarcely any point in going on. At addition you are a past master. Now, let's look at subtraction. Tell me, if you are not exhausted, how many are four minus three?

PUPIL: Four minus three? . . . Four minus three?

PROFESSOR: Yes. I mean to say: subtract three from four.

PUPIL: That makes . . . seven?

PROFESSOR: I am sorry but I'm obliged to contradict you. Four minus three does not make seven. You are confused: four plus three makes seven, four minus three does not make seven . . . This is not addition anymore, we must subtract now.

PUPIL (trying to understand): Yes . . . yes . . .

PROFESSOR: Four minus three makes . . . How many? . . . How many?

PUPIL: Four?

PROFESSOR: No, miss, that's not it.

PUPIL: Three, then.

PROFESSOR: Not that either, miss . . . Pardon, I'm sorry . . . I ought to say, that's not it . . . excuse me.

PUPIL: Four minus three . . . Four minus three . . . Four minus three? . . . But now doesn't that make ten?

PROFESSOR: Oh, certainly not, miss. It's not a matter of guessing, you've got to think it out. Let's try to deduce it together. Would you like to count?

PUPIL: Yes, Professor. One . . . two . . . uh . . .

PROFESSOR: You know how to count? How far can you count up to?

PUPIL: I can count to . . . infinity.

PROFESSOR: That's not possible, miss.

PUPIL: Well then, let's say to sixteen.

PROFESSOR: That is enough. One must know one's limits. Count then, if you will, please.

PUPIL: One . . . two . . . and after two, comes three . . . then four . . .

PROFESSOR: Stop there, miss. Which number is larger? Three or four?

PUPIL: Uh . . . three or four? Which is the larger? The larger of three or four? In what sense larger?

PROFESSOR: Some numbers are smaller and others are larger. In the large numbers there are more units than in the small . . .

PUPIL: Than in the small numbers?

PROFESSOR: Unless the small ones have smaller units. If they are very small, then there might be more units in the small numbers than in the large . . . if it is a question of other units . . .

PUPIL: In that case, the small numbers can be larger than the large numbers?

PROFESSOR: Let's not go into that. That would take us much too far. You must realize simply that more than numbers are involved here . . . there are also magnitudes, totals, there are groups, there are heaps, heaps of such things as plums, trucks, geese, prune pits, etc. To facilitate our work, let's merely suppose that we have only equal numbers, then the bigger numbers will be those that have the most units.

PUPIL: The one that has the most is the biggest? Ah, I understand, Professor, you are identifying quality with quantity.

PROFESSOR: That is too theoretical, miss, too theoretical. You needn't concern yourself with that. Let us take an example and reason from a definite case. Let's leave the general conclusions for later. We have the number four and the number three, and each has always the same number of units. Which number will be larger, the smaller or the larger?

PUPIL: Excuse me, Professor . . . What do you mean by the larger number? Is it the one that is not so small as the other?

PROFESSOR: That's it, miss, perfect. You have understood me very well.

PUPIL: Then, it is four.

PROFESSOR: What is four—larger or smaller than three?

PUPIL: Smaller . . . no, larger.

PROFESSOR: Excellent answer. How many units are there between three and four? . . . Or between four and three, if you prefer?

PUPIL: There aren't any units, Professor, between three and four. Four comes immediately after three; there is nothing at all between three and four!

PROFESSOR: I haven't made myself very well understood. No doubt, it is my fault. I've not been sufficiently clear.

PUPIL: No, Professor, it's my fault.

PROFESSOR: Look here. Here are three matches. And here is another one, that makes four. Now watch carefully—we have four matches. I take one away, now how many are left?

(We don't see the matches, nor any of the objects that are mentioned. The PROFESSOR gets up from the table, writes on the imaginary blackboard with an imaginary piece of chalk, etc.)

PUPIL: Five. If three and one make four, four and one make five.

PROFESSOR: That's not it. That's not it at all. You always have a tendency to add. But one must be able to subtract too. It's not enough to integrate, you must also disintegrate. That's the way life is. That's philosophy. That's science. That's progress, civilization.

PUPIL: Yes, Professor.

PROFESSOR: Let's return to our matches. I have four of them. You see, there are really four. I take one away, and there remain only . . .

PUPIL: I don't know, Professor.

PROFESSOR: Come now, think. It's not easy, I admit. Nevertheless, you've had enough training to make the intellectual effort required to arrive at an understanding. So?

PUPIL: I can't get it, Professor. I don't know, Professor.

PROFESSOR: Let us take a simpler example. If you had two noses, and I pulled one of them off . . . how many would you have left?

PUPIL: None.

PROFESSOR: What do you mean, none?

PUPIL: Yes, it's because you haven't pulled off any, that's why I have one now. If you had pulled it off, I wouldn't have it anymore.

PROFESSOR: You've not understood my example. Suppose that you have only one ear.

PUPIL: Yes, and then?

PROFESSOR: If I gave you another one, how many would you have then?

PUPIL: Two.

PROFESSOR: Good. And if I gave you still another ear. How many would you have then?

PUPIL: Three ears.

PROFESSOR: Now, I take one away . . . and there remain . . . how many ears?

PUPIL: Two.

PROFESSOR: Good. I take away still another one, how many do you have left?

PUPIL: Two.

PROFESSOR: No. You have two, I take one away, I eat one up, then how many do you have left?

PUPIL: Two.

PROFESSOR: I eat one of them . . . one.

PUPIL: Two.

PROFESSOR: One.

PUPIL: Two.

PROFESSOR: One!

PUPIL: Two!

PROFESSOR: One!!!

PUPIL: Two!!!

PROFESSOR: One!!!

PUPIL: Two!!!

PROFESSOR: One!!!

PUPIL: Two!!!

PROFESSOR: No. No. That's not right. The example is not . . . it's not convincing. Listen to me.

PUPIL: Yes, Professor.

PROFESSOR: You've got . . . you've got . . . you've got . . .

PUPIL: Ten fingers!

PROFESSOR: If you wish. Perfect. Good. You have then ten fingers.

PUPIL: Yes, Professor.

PROFESSOR: How many would you have if you had only five of them?

PUPIL: Ten, Professor.

PROFESSOR: That's not right!

PUPIL: But it is, Professor.

PROFESSOR: I tell you it's not!

PUPIL: You just told me that I had ten . . .

PROFESSOR: I also said, immediately afterwards, that you had five!

PUPIL: I don't have five, I've got ten!

PROFESSOR: Let's try another approach . . . for purposes of subtraction let's limit ourselves to the numbers from one to five . . . Wait now, miss, you'll soon see. I'm going to make you understand.

(The PROFESSOR begins to write on the imaginary blackboard. He moves it closer to the PUPIL, who turns around in order to see it.)

PROFESSOR: Look here, miss . . . (He pretends to draw a stick on the blackboard and the number 1 below the stick; then two sticks and the number 2 below, then three sticks and the number 3 below, then four sticks with the number 4 below.) You see . . .

PUPIL: Yes, Professor.

PROFESSOR: These are sticks, miss, sticks. This is one stick, these are two sticks, and three sticks, then four sticks, then five sticks. One stick, two sticks, three sticks, four and five sticks, these are numbers. When we count the sticks, each stick is a unit, miss . . . What have I just said?

PUPIL: "A unit, miss! What have I just said?"

PROFESSOR: Or a figure! Or a number! One, two, three, four, five, these are the elements of numeration, miss.

PUPIL (hesitant): Yes, Professor. The elements, figures, which are sticks, units and numbers . . .

PROFESSOR: At the same time . . . that's to say, in short—the whole of arithmetic is there.

PUPIL: Yes, Professor. Good, Professor. Thanks, Professor.

PROFESSOR: Now, count, if you will please, using these elements . . . add and subtract . . .

PUPIL (as though trying to impress them on her memory): Sticks are really figures and numbers are units?

PROFESSOR: Hmm . . . so to speak. And then?

PUPIL: One could subtract two units from three units, but can one subtract two twos from three threes? And two figures from four numbers? And three numbers from one unit?

PROFESSOR: No, miss.

PUPIL: Why, Professor?

PROFESSOR: Because, miss.

PUPIL: Because why, Professor? Since one is the same as the other?

PROFESSOR: That's the way it is, miss. It can't be explained. This is only comprehensible through internal mathematical reasoning. Either you have it or you don't.

PUPIL: So much the worse for me.

PROFESSOR: Listen to me, miss, if you don't achieve a profound understanding of these principles, these arithmetical archetypes, you will never be able to perform correctly the functions of a polytechnician. Still less will you be able to teach a course in a polytechnical school . . . or the primary grades. I realize that this is not easy, it is very, very abstract . . . obviously . . . but unless you can comprehend the primary elements, how do you expect to be able to calculate mentally—and this is the least of the things that even an ordinary engineer must be able to do—how much, for example, are three billion seven hundred fifty-five million nine hundred ninety-eight thousand two hundred fifty-one, multiplied by five billion one hundred sixty-two million three hundred and three thousand five hundred and eight?

PUPIL *(very quickly)*: That makes nineteen quintillion three hundred ninety quadrillion two trillion eight hundred forty-four billion two hundred nineteen million one hundred sixty-four thousand five hundred and eight . . .

PROFESSOR *(astonished)*: No. I don't think so. That must make nineteen quintillion three hundred ninety quadrillion two trillion eight hundred forty-four billion two hundred nineteen million one hundred sixty-four thousand five hundred and nine . . .

PUPIL: . . . No . . . five hundred and eight . . .

PROFESSOR *(more and more astonished, calculating mentally)*: Yes . . . you are right . . . the result is indeed . . . *(He mumbles unintelligibly:)* . . . quintillion, quadrillion, trillion, billion, million . . . *(Clearly:)* one hundred sixty-four thousand five hundred and eight . . . *(Stupefied:)* But how did you know that, if you don't know the principles of arithmetical reasoning?

PUPIL: It's easy. Not being able to rely on my reasoning, I've memorized all the products of all possible multiplications.

PROFESSOR: That's pretty good . . . However, permit me to confess to you that that doesn't satisfy me, miss, and I do not congratulate you: in mathematics and in arithmetic especially, the thing that counts—for in arithmetic it is always necessary to count—the thing that counts is, above all, understanding . . . It is by mathematical reasoning, simultaneously inductive and deductive, that you ought to arrive at this result—as well as at any other result. Mathematics is the sworn enemy of memory, which is excellent otherwise, but disastrous, arithmetically speaking! . . . That's why I'm not happy with this . . . this won't do, not at all . . .

PUPIL *(desolated)*: No, Professor.

PROFESSOR: Let's leave it for the moment. Let's go on to another exercise . . .

PUPIL: Yes, Professor.

MAID *(entering)*: Hmm, hmm, Professor . . .

PROFESSOR *(who doesn't hear her)*: It is unfortunate, miss, that you aren't further along in specialized mathematics . . .

MAID *(taking him by the sleeve)*: Professor! Professor!

PROFESSOR: I fear that you will not be able to qualify for the total doctor's orals . . .

PUPIL: Yes, Professor, it's too bad!

PROFESSOR: Unless you . . . *(To the* MAID:*)* Let me be, Marie . . . Look here, why are you bothering me? Go back to the kitchen! To your pots and pans! Go away! Go away! *(To the* PUPIL:*)* We will try to prepare you at least for the partial doctorate . . .

MAID: Professor! . . . Professor! . . . *(She pulls his sleeve.)*

PROFESSOR *(to the* MAID*)*: Now leave me alone! Let me be! What's the meaning of this? . . . *(To the* PUPIL:*)* I must therefore teach you, if you really do insist on attempting the partial doctorate . . .

PUPIL: Yes, Professor.

PROFESSOR: . . . The elements of linguistics and of comparative philology° . . .

MAID: No, Professor, no! . . . You mustn't do that! . . .

PROFESSOR: Marie, you're going too far!

MAID: Professor, especially not philology, philology leads to calamity . . .

PUPIL *(astonished)*: To calamity? *(Smiling, a little stupidly:)* That's hard to believe.

PROFESSOR *(to the* MAID*)*: That's enough now! Get out of here!

MAID: All right, Professor, all right. But you can't say that I didn't warn you! Philology leads to calamity!

PROFESSOR: I'm an adult, Marie!

PUPIL: Yes, Professor.

MAID: As you wish.

(She exits.)

PROFESSOR: Let's continue, miss.

PUPIL: Yes, Professor.

PROFESSOR: I want you to listen now with the greatest possible attention to a lecture I have prepared . . .

PUPIL: Yes, Professor!

PROFESSOR: . . . Thanks to which, in fifteen minutes' time, you will be able to acquire the fundamental principles of the linguistic and comparative philology of the neo-Spanish languages.

PUPIL: Yes, Professor, oh good!

(She claps her hands.)

PROFESSOR *(with authority)*: Quiet! What do you mean by that?

---

philology, study of language.

PUPIL: I'm sorry, Professor.

(Slowly, she replaces her hands on the table.)

PROFESSOR: Quiet! *(He gets up, walks up and down the room, his hands behind his back; from time to time he stops at stage center or near the* PUPIL, *and underlines his words with a gesture of his hand; he orates, but without being too emotional. The* PUPIL *follows him with her eyes, occasionally with some difficulty, for she has to turn her head far around; once or twice, not more, she turns around completely.)* And now, miss, Spanish is truly the mother tongue which gave birth to all the neo-Spanish languages, of which Spanish, Latin, Italian, our own French, Portuguese, Romanian, Sardinian or Sardanapalian, Spanish and neo-Spanish—and also, in certain of its aspects, Turkish which is otherwise very close to Greek, which is only logical, since it is a fact that Turkey is a neighbor of Greece and Greece is even closer to Turkey than you are to me—this is only one more illustration of the very important linguistic law which states that geography and philology are twin sisters . . . You may take notes, miss.

PUPIL *(in a dull voice)*: Yes, Professor!

PROFESSOR: That which distinguishes the neo-Spanish languages from each other and their idioms from the other linguistic groups, such as the group of languages called Austrian and neo-Austrian or Hapsburgian, as well as the Esperanto, Helvetian, Monacan, Swiss, Andorran, Basque, and jai alai° groups, and also the groups of diplomatic and technical languages—that which distinguishes them, I repeat, is their striking resemblance which makes it so hard to distinguish them from each other—I'm speaking of the neo-Spanish languages which one is able to distinguish from each other, however, only thanks to their distinctive characteristics, absolutely indisputable proofs of their extraordinary resemblance, which renders indisputable their common origin, and which, at the same time, differentiates them profoundly—through the continuation of the distinctive traits which I've just cited.

PUPIL: Oooh! Ye-e-e-s-s-s, Professor!

PROFESSOR: But let's not linger over generalities . . .

PUPIL *(regretfully, but won over)*: Oh, Professor . . .

PROFESSOR: This appears to interest you. All the better, all the better.

PUPIL: Oh, yes, Professor . . .

PROFESSOR: Don't worry, miss. We will come back to it later . . . That is if we come back to it at all. Who can say?

---

jai alai, handball-like game.

PUPIL *(enchanted in spite of everything)*: Oh, yes, Professor.

PROFESSOR: Every tongue—you must know this, miss, and remember it *until the hour of your death* . . .

PUPIL: Oh! yes, Professor, until the hour of my death . . . Yes, Professor . . .

PROFESSOR: . . . And this, too, is a fundamental principle, every tongue is at bottom nothing but language, which necessarily implies that it is composed of sounds, or . . .

PUPIL: Phonemes . . .

PROFESSOR: Just what I was going to say. Don't parade your knowledge. You'd do better to listen.

PUPIL: All right, Professor. Yes, Professor.

PROFESSOR: The sounds, miss, must be seized on the wing as they fly so that they'll not fall on deaf ears. As a result, when you set out to articulate, it is recommended, insofar as possible, that you lift up your neck and chin very high, and rise up on the tips of your toes, you see, this way . . .

PUPIL: Yes, Professor.

PROFESSOR: Keep quiet. Remain seated, don't interrupt me . . . And project the sounds very loudly with all the force of your lungs in conjunction with that of your vocal cords. Like this, look: "Butterfly," "Eureka," "Trafalgar," "Papaya." This way, the sounds become filled with a warm air that is lighter than the surrounding air so that they can fly without danger of falling on deaf ears, which are veritable voids, tombs of sonorities. If you utter several sounds at an accelerated speed, they will automatically cling to each other, constituting thus syllables, words, even sentences, that is to say groupings of various importance, purely irrational assemblages of sounds, denuded of all sense, but for that very reason the more capable of maintaining themselves without danger at a high altitude in the air. By themselves, words charged with significance will fall, weighted down by their meaning, and in the end they always collapse, fall . . .

PUPIL: . . . On deaf ears.

PROFESSOR: That's it, but don't interrupt . . . and into the worst confusion . . . Or else burst like balloons. Therefore, miss . . . *(The* PUPIL *suddenly appears to be unwell.)* What's the matter?

PUPIL: I've got a toothache, Professor.

PROFESSOR: That's not important. We're not going to stop for anything so trivial. Let us go on . . .

PUPIL *(appearing to be in more and more pain)*: Yes, Professor.

PROFESSOR: I draw your attention in passing to the consonants that change their nature in combinations. In this case *f* becomes *v*, *d* becomes *t*, *g* becomes *k*, and vice versa, as in these examples that I will cite for you: "That's all right," "hens and chickens," "Welsh rabbit," "lots of nothing," "not at all."*

PUPIL: I've got a toothache.

PROFESSOR: Let's continue.

PUPIL: Yes.

PROFESSOR: To resume: it takes years and years to learn to pronounce. Thanks to science, we can achieve this in a few minutes. In order to project words, sounds and all the rest, you must realize that it is necessary to pitilessly expel air from the lungs, and make it pass delicately, caressingly, over the vocal cords, which, like harps or leaves in the wind, will suddenly shake, agitate, vibrate, vibrate, vibrate or uvulate, or fricate or jostle against each other, or sibilate, sibilate, placing everything in movement, the uvula, the tongue, the palate, the teeth . . .

PUPIL: I have a toothache.

PROFESSOR: . . . And the lips . . . Finally the words come out through the nose, the mouth, the ears, the pores, drawing along with them all the organs that we have named, torn up by the roots, in a powerful, majestic flight, which is none other than what is called, improperly, the voice, whether modulated in singing or transformed into a terrible symphonic storm with a whole procession . . . of garlands of all kinds of flowers, of sonorous artifices: labials, dentals, occlusives, palatals, and others, some caressing, some bitter or violent.

PUPIL: Yes, Professor, I've got a toothache.

PROFESSOR: Let's go on, go on. As for the neo-Spanish languages, they are closely related, so closely to each other, that they can be considered as true second cousins. Moreover, they have the same mother: Spanishe, with a mute *e.* That is why it is so difficult to distinguish them from one another. That is why it is so useful to pronounce carefully, and to avoid errors in pronunciation. Pronunciation itself is worth a whole language. A bad pronunciation can get you into trouble. In this connection, permit me, parenthetically, to share a personal experience with you. *(Slight pause. The* PROFESSOR *goes over his memories for a moment; his features mellow, but he recovers at once.)* I was very young, little more than a child. It was during my military service. I had a friend in the regiment, a vicomte, who suffered from a rather serious defect in his pronunciation: he could not pronounce the letter *f.* Instead of *f,* he said *f.* Thus, instead of "Birds of a feather flock together," he said: "Birds of a feather flock together." He pronounced filly instead of filly, Firmin instead of

Firmin, French bean instead of French bean, go frig yourself instead of go frig yourself, farrago instead of farrago, fee fi fo fum instead of fee fi fo fum, Philip instead of Philip, fictory instead of fictory, February instead of February, March-April instead of March-April, Gerard de Nerval and not as is correct—Gerard de Nerval, Mirabeau instead of Mirabeau, etc., instead of etc., and thus instead of etc., instead of etc., and thus and so forth. However, he managed to conceal his fault so effectively that, thanks to the hats he wore, no one ever noticed it.

PUPIL: Yes, I've got a toothache.

PROFESSOR *(abruptly changing his tone, his voice hardening)*: Let's go on. We'll first consider the points of similarity in order the better to apprehend, later on, that which distinguishes all these languages from each other. The differences can scarcely be recognized by people who are not aware of them. Thus, all the words of all the languages . . .

PUPIL: Uh, yes? . . . I've got a toothache.

PROFESSOR: Let's continue . . . are always the same, just as all the suffixes, all the prefixes, all the terminations, all the roots . . .

PUPIL: Are the roots of words square?

PROFESSOR: Square or cube. That depends.

PUPIL: I've got a toothache.

PROFESSOR: Let's go on. Thus, to give you an example which is little more than an illustration, take the word "front" . . .

PUPIL: How do you want me to take it?

PROFESSOR: However you wish, so long as you take it, but above all do not interrupt.

PUPIL: I've got a toothache.

PROFESSOR: Let's continue . . . I said: Let's continue. Take now the word "front." Have you taken it?

PUPIL: Yes, yes, I've got it. My teeth, my teeth . . .

PROFESSOR: The word "front" is the root of "frontispiece." It is also to be found in "affronted." "Ispiece" is the suffix, and "af" the prefix. They are so called because they do not change. They don't want to.

PUPIL: I've got a toothache.

PROFESSOR: Let's go on. *(Rapidly:)* These prefixes are of Spanish origin. I hope you noticed that, did you?

PUPIL: Oh, how my tooth aches.

PROFESSOR: Let's continue. You've surely also noticed that they've not changed in French. And now, young lady, nothing has succeeded in changing them in Latin either, nor in Italian, nor in Portuguese, nor in Sardanapalian, nor in Sardanapali, nor in Romanian, nor in neo-Spanish, nor in Spanish, nor even in the Oriental: front, frontispiece, affronted, always the same word, invariably with the same root, the same suffix, the same

---

*All to be heavily elided.—Translator's note.

prefix, in all the languages I have named. And it is always the same for all words.

PUPIL: In all languages, these words mean the same thing? I've got a toothache.

PROFESSOR: Absolutely. Moreover, it's more a notion than a word. In any case, you have always the same signification, the same composition, the same sound structure, not only for this word, but for all conceivable words, in all languages. For one single notion is expressed by one and the same word, and its synonyms, in all countries. Forget about your teeth.

PUPIL: I've got a toothache. Yes, yes, yes.

PROFESSOR: Good, let's go on. I tell you, let's go on . . . How would you say, for example, in French: the roses of my grandmother are as yellow as my grandfather who was Asiatic?

PUPIL: My teeth ache, ache, ache.

PROFESSOR: Let's go on, let's go on, go ahead and answer, anyway.

PUPIL: In French?

PROFESSOR: In French.

PUPIL: Uhh . . . I should say in French: the roses of my grandmother are . . . ?

PROFESSOR: As yellow as my grandfather who was Asiatic . . .

PUPIL: Oh well, one would say, in French, I believe, the roses . . . of my . . . how do you say "grandmother" in French?

PROFESSOR: In French? Grandmother.

PUPIL: The roses of my grandmother are as yellow—in French, is it "yellow"?

PROFESSOR: Yes, of course!

PUPIL: Are as yellow as my grandfather when he got angry.

PROFESSOR: No . . . who was A . . .

PUPIL: . . . siatic . . . I've got a toothache.

PROFESSOR: That's it.

PUPIL: I've got a tooth . . .

PROFESSOR: Ache . . . so what . . . let's continue! And now translate the same sentence into Spanish, then into neo-Spanish . . .

PUPIL: In Spanish . . . this would be: the roses of my grandmother are as yellow as my grandfather who was Asiatic.

PROFESSOR: No. That's wrong.

PUPIL: And in neo-Spanish: the roses of my grandmother are as yellow as my grandfather who was Asiatic.

PROFESSOR: That's wrong. That's wrong. That's wrong. You have inverted it, you've confused Spanish with neo-Spanish, and neo-Spanish with Spanish . . . Oh . . . no . . . it's the other way around . . .

PUPIL: I've got a toothache. You're getting mixed up.

PROFESSOR: You're the one who is mixing me up. Pay attention and take notes. I will say the sentence to you in Spanish, then in neo-Spanish, and finally, in Latin. You will repeat after me. Pay attention, for the resemblances are great. In fact, they are identical resemblances. Listen, follow carefully . . .

PUPIL: I've got a tooth . . .

PROFESSOR: . . . Ache.

PUPIL: Let us go on . . . Ah! . . .

PROFESSOR: . . . In Spanish: the roses of my grandmother are as yellow as my grandfather who was Asiatic; in Latin; the roses of my grandmother are as yellow as my grandfather who was Asiatic. Do you detect the differences? Translate this into . . . Romanian.

PUPIL: The . . . how do you say "roses" in Romanian?

PROFESSOR: But "roses," what else?

PUPIL: It's not "roses"? Oh, how my tooth aches!

PROFESSOR: Certainly not, certainly not, since "roses" is a translation in Oriental of the French word "roses," in Spanish "roses," do you get it? In Sardanapali, "roses" . . .

PUPIL: Excuse me, Professor, but . . . Oh, my toothache! . . . I don't get the difference.

PROFESSOR: But it's so simple! So simple! It's a matter of having a certain experience, a technical experience and practice in these diverse languages, which are so diverse in spite of the fact that they present wholly identical characteristics. I'm going to try to give you a key . . .

PUPIL: Toothache . . .

PROFESSOR: That which differentiates these languages, is neither the words, which are absolutely the same, nor the structure of the sentence which is everywhere the same, nor the intonation, which does not offer any differences, nor the rhythm of the language . . . that which differentiates them . . . are you listening?

PUPIL: I've got a toothache.

PROFESSOR: Are you listening to me, young lady? Aah! We're going to lose our temper.

PUPIL: You're bothering me, Professor. I've got a toothache.

PROFESSOR: Son of a cocker spaniel! Listen to me!

PUPIL: Oh well . . . yes . . . yes . . . go on . . .

PROFESSOR: That which distinguishes them from each other, on the one hand, and from their mother, Spanishe with its mute *e*, on the other hand . . . is . . .

PUPIL (*grimacing*): Is what?

PROFESSOR: Is an intangible thing. Something intangible that one is able to perceive only after very long study, with a great deal of trouble and after the broadest experience . . .

PUPIL: Ah?

PROFESSOR: Yes, young lady. I cannot give you any rule. One must have a feeling for it, and well, that's it. But in order to have it, one must study, study, and then study some more.

PUPIL: Toothache.

PROFESSOR: All the same, there are some specific cases where words differ from one language to another . . . but we cannot base our knowledge on these cases, which are, so to speak, exceptional.

PUPIL: Oh, yes? . . . Oh, Professor, I've got a toothache.

PROFESSOR: Don't interrupt! Don't make me lose my temper! I can't answer for what I'll do. I was saying, then . . . Ah, yes, the exceptional cases, the so-called easily distinguished . . . or facilely distinguished . . . or conveniently . . . if you prefer . . . I repeat, if you prefer, for I see that you're not listening to me . . .

PUPIL: I've got a toothache.

PROFESSOR: I say then: in certain expressions in current usage, certain words differ totally from one language to another, so much so that the language employed is, in this case, considerably easier to identify. I'll give you an example: the neo-Spanish expression, famous in Madrid: "My country is the new Spain," becomes in Italian: "My country is . . ."

PUPIL: The new Spain.

PROFESSOR: No! "My country is Italy." Tell me now, by simple deduction, how do you say "Italy" in French?

PUPIL: I've got a toothache.

PROFESSOR: But it's so easy: for the word "Italy," in French we have the word "France," which is an exact translation of it. My country is France. And "France" in Oriental: "Orient!" My country is the Orient. And "Orient" in Portuguese: "Portugal!" The Oriental expression: My country is the Orient is translated then in the same fashion into Portuguese: My country is Portugal! And so on . . .

PUPIL: Oh, no more, no more. My teeth . . .

PROFESSOR: Ache! ache! ache! . . . I'm going to pull them out, I will! One more example. The word "capital"—it takes on, according to the language one speaks, a different meaning. That is to say that when a Spaniard says: "I reside in the capital," the word "capital" does not mean at all the same thing that a Portuguese means when he says: "I reside in the capital." All the more so in the case of a Frenchman, a neo-Spaniard, a Romanian, a Latin, a Sardanapali . . . Whenever you hear it, young lady—young lady, I'm saying this for you! Pooh! Whenever you hear the expression: "I reside in the capital," you will immediately and easily know whether this is Spanish or Spanish, neo-Spanish, French, Oriental, Romanian, or Latin, for it is enough to know which metropolis is referred to by the person who pronounces the sentence . . . at the very moment

he pronounces it . . . But these are almost the only precise examples that I can give you . . .

PUPIL: Oh dear! My teeth . . .

PROFESSOR: Silence! Or I'll bash in your skull!

PUPIL: Just try to! Skulldugger!°

(The PROFESSOR seizes her wrist and twists it.)

PUPIL: Oww!

PROFESSOR: Keep quiet now! Not a word!

PUPIL (whimpering): Toothache . . .

PROFESSOR: One thing that is the most . . . how shall I say it? . . . the most paradoxical . . . yes . . . that's the word . . . the most paradoxical thing, is that a lot of people who are completely illiterate speak these different languages . . . do you understand? What did I just say?

PUPIL: . . . "Speak these different languages! What did I just say?"

PROFESSOR: You were lucky that time! . . . The common people speak a Spanish full of neo-Spanish words that they are entirely unaware of, all the while believing that they are speaking Latin . . . or they speak Latin, full of Oriental words, all the while believing that they're speaking Romanian . . . or Spanish, full of neo-Spanish, all the while believing that they're speaking Sardanapali, or Spanish . . . Do you understand?

PUPIL: Yes! yes! yes! yes! What more do you want . . . ?

PROFESSOR: No insolence, my pet, or you'll be sorry . . . (In a rage:) But the worst of all, young lady, is that certain people, for example, in a Latin that they suppose is Spanish, say: "Both my kidneys are of the same kidney," in addressing themselves to a Frenchman who does not know a word of Spanish, but the latter understands it as if it were his own language. For that matter he thinks it is his own language. And the Frenchman will reply, in French: "Me too, sir, mine are too," and this will be perfectly comprehensible to a Spaniard, who will feel certain that the reply is in pure Spanish and that Spanish is being spoken . . . when, in reality, it was neither Spanish nor French, but Latin in the neo-Spanish dialect . . . Sit still, young lady, don't fidget, stop tapping your feet . . .

PUPIL: I've got a toothache.

PROFESSOR: How do you account for the fact that, in speaking without knowing which language they speak, or even while each of them believes that he is speaking another, the common people understand each other at all?

PUPIL: I wonder.

PROFESSOR: It is simply one of the inexplicable curiosities of the vulgar empiricism of the common people—not to be confused with experience!—a

---

Skulldugger, contemptible person.

paradox, a non-sense, one of the aberrations of human nature, it is purely and simply instinct—to put it in a nutshell . . . That's what is involved here.

PUPIL: Hah! hah!

PROFESSOR: Instead of staring at the flies while I'm going to all this trouble . . . you would do much better to try to be more attentive . . . it is not I who is going to qualify for the partial doctor's orals . . . I passed mine a long time ago . . . and I've won my total doctorate, too . . . and my super-total diploma . . . Don't you realize that what I'm saying is for your own good?

PUPIL: Toothache!

PROFESSOR: Ill-mannered . . . It can't go on like this, it won't do, it won't do, it won't do . . .

PUPIL: I'm . . . listening . . . to you . . .

PROFESSOR: Ahah! In order to learn to distinguish all the different languages, as I've told you, there is nothing better than practice . . . Let's take them up in order. I am going to try to teach you all the translations of the word "knife."

PUPIL: Well, all right . . . if you want . . .

PROFESSOR (calling the MAID): Marie! Marie! She's not there . . . Marie! Marie! . . . Marie, where are you? (He opens the door on the right.) Marie! . . .

(He exits. The PUPIL remains alone several minutes, staring into space, wearing a stupefied expression.)

PROFESSOR (offstage, in a shrill voice): Marie! What are you up to? Why don't you come! When I call you, you must come! (He re-enters, followed by MARIE.) It is I who gives the orders, do you hear? (He points at the PUPIL:) She doesn't understand anything, that girl. She doesn't understand!

MAID: Don't get into such a state, sir, you know where it'll end! You're going to go too far, you're going to go too far.

PROFESSOR: I'll be able to stop in time.

MAID: That's what you always say. I only wish I could see it.

PUPIL: I've got a toothache.

MAID: You see, it's starting, that's the symptom!

PROFESSOR: What symptom? Explain yourself? What do you mean?

PUPIL (in a spiritless voice): Yes, what do you mean? I've got a toothache.

MAID: The final symptom! The chief symptom!

PROFESSOR: Stupid! stupid! stupid! (The MAID starts to exit.) Don't go away like that! I called you to help me find the Spanish, neo-Spanish, Portuguese, French, Oriental, Romanian, Sardanapali, Latin and Spanish knives.

MAID (severely): Don't ask me. (She exits.)

PROFESSOR (makes a gesture as though to protest, then refrains, a little helpless. Suddenly, he remembers): Ah!

(He goes quickly to the drawer where he finds a big knife, invisible or real according to the preference of the director. He seizes it and brandishes it happily.) Here is one, young lady, here is a knife. It's too bad that we only have this one, but we're going to try to make it serve for all the languages, anyway! It will be enough if you will pronounce the word "knife" in all the languages, while looking at the object, very closely, fixedly, and imagining that it is in the language that you are speaking.

PUPIL: I've got a toothache.

PROFESSOR (almost singing, chanting): Now, say "kni," like "kni," "fe," like "fe" . . . And look, look, look at it, watch it . . .

PUPIL: What is this one in? French, Italian or Spanish?

PROFESSOR: That doesn't matter now . . . That's not your concern. Say: "kni."

PUPIL: "Kni."

PROFESSOR: . . . "fe" . . . Look.

(He brandishes the knife under the PUPIL's eyes.)

PUPIL: "fe" . . .

PROFESSOR: Again . . . Look at it.

PUPIL: Oh, no! My God! I've had enough. And besides, I've got a toothache, my feet hurt me, I've got a headache.

PROFESSOR (abruptly): Knife . . . look . . . knife . . . look . . . knife . . . look . . .

PUPIL: You're giving me an earache, too. Oh, your voice! It's so piercing!

PROFESSOR: Say: knife . . . kni . . . fe . . .

PUPIL: No! My ears hurt, I hurt all over . . .

PROFESSOR: I'm going to tear them off, your ears, that's what I'm going to do to you, and then they won't hurt you anymore, my pet.

PUPIL: Oh . . . you're hurting me, oh, you're hurting me . . .

PROFESSOR: Look, come on, quickly, repeat after me: "kni" . . .

PUPIL: Oh, since you insist . . . knife . . . knife . . . (In a lucid moment, ironically:) Is that neo-Spanish . . . ?

PROFESSOR: If you like, yes, it's neo-Spanish, but hurry up . . . we haven't got time . . . And then, what do you mean by that insidious question? What are you up to?

PUPIL (becoming more and more exhausted, weeping, desperate, at the same time both exasperated and in a trance): Ah!

PROFESSOR: Repeat, watch. (He imitates a cuckoo:) Knife, knife . . . knife, knife . . . knife, knife . . . knife, knife . . .

PUPIL: Oh, my head . . . aches . . . (With her hand she caressingly touches the parts of her body as she names them:) . . . My eyes . . .

PROFESSOR (like a cuckoo): Knife, knife . . . knife, knife . . . (They are both standing. The PROFESSOR still brandishes his invisible knife, nearly beside himself, as he *circles around her in a sort of scalp dance, but it is important that this not be exaggerated and that his dance steps be only suggested. The* PUPIL *stands facing the audience, then recoils in the direction of the window, sickly, languid, victimized.)*

PROFESSOR: Repeat, repeat: knife . . . knife . . . knife . . .

PUPIL: I've got a pain . . . my throat, neck . . . oh, my shoulders . . . my breast . . . knife . . .

PROFESSOR: Knife . . . knife . . . knife . . .

PUPIL: My hips . . . knife . . . my thighs . . . kni . . .

PROFESSOR: Pronounce it carefully . . . knife . . . knife . . .

PUPIL: Knife . . . my throat . . .

PROFESSOR: Knife . . . knife . . .

PUPIL: Knife . . . my shoulders . . . my arms, my breast, my hips . . . knife . . . knife . . .

PROFESSOR: That's right . . . Now, you're pronouncing it well . . .

PUPIL: Knife . . . my breast . . . my stomach . . .

PROFESSOR *(changing his voice)*: Pay attention . . . don't break my window . . . the knife kills . . .

PUPIL *(in a weak voice)*: Yes, yes, . . . the knife kills?

PROFESSOR *(striking the* PUPIL *with a very spectacular blow of the knife)*: Aaah! That'll teach you!

*(*PUPIL *also cries "Aah!" then falls, flopping in an immodest position onto a chair which, as though by chance, is near the window. The murderer and his victim shout "Aaah!" at the same moment. After the first blow of the knife, the* PUPIL *flops onto the chair, her legs spread wide and hanging over both sides of the chair. The* PROFESSOR *remains standing in front of her, his back to the audience. After the first blow, he strikes her dead with a second slash of the knife, from bottom to top. After that blow a noticeable convulsion shakes his whole body.)*

PROFESSOR *(winded, mumbling)*: Bitch . . . Oh, that's good, that does me good . . . Ah! Ah! I'm exhausted . . . I can scarcely breathe . . . Aah! *(He breathes with difficulty; he falls—fortunately a chair is there; he mops his brow, mumbles some incomprehensible words; his breathing becomes normal. He gets up, looks at the knife in his hand, looks at the young girl, then as though he were waking up, in a panic:)* What have I done! What's going to happen to me now! What's going to happen! Oh! dear! Oh dear, I'm in trouble! Young lady, young lady, get up! *(He is agitated, still holding onto the invisible knife, which he doesn't know what to do with.)* Come now, young lady, the lesson is over . . . you may go . . . you can pay another time . . . Oh! she is dead . . . dea-ead . . . And by my knife . . . She is dea-ead . . . It's terrible. *(He calls the* MAID:*)* Marie! Marie! My good Marie, come here! Ah! Ah! *(The door on the right opens a little and* MARIE *appears.)* No . . . don't come in . . . I made a mistake . . . I don't need you, Marie . . . I don't need you anymore . . . do you understand? . . .

*(*MAID *enters wearing a stern expression, without saying a word. She sees the corpse.)*

PROFESSOR *(in a voice less and less assured)*: I don't need you, Marie . . .

MAID *(sarcastic)*: Then, you're satisfied with your pupil, she's profited by your lesson?

PROFESSOR *(holding the knife behind his back)*: Yes, the lesson is finished . . . but . . . she . . . she's still there . . . she doesn't want to leave . . .

MAID *(very harshly)*: Is that a fact? . . .

PROFESSOR *(trembling)*: It wasn't I . . . it wasn't I . . . Marie . . . No . . . I assure you . . . it wasn't I, my little Marie . . .

MAID: And who was it? Who was it then? Me?

PROFESSOR: I don't know . . . maybe . . .

MAID: Or the cat?

PROFESSOR: That's possible . . . I don't know . . .

MAID: And today makes it the fortieth time! . . . And every day it's the same thing! Every day! You should be ashamed, at your age . . . and you're going to make yourself sick! You won't have any pupils left. That will serve you right.

PROFESSOR *(irritated)*: It wasn't my fault! She didn't want to learn! She was disobedient! She was a bad pupil! She didn't want to learn!

MAID: Liar! . . .

PROFESSOR *(craftily approaching the* MAID, *holding the knife behind his back)*: It's none of your business! *(He tries to strike her with a great blow of the knife; the* MAID *seizes his wrist in mid-gesture and twists it; the* PROFESSOR *lets the knife fall to the floor)*: . . . I'm sorry!

MAID *(gives him two loud, strong slaps; the* PROFESSOR *falls onto the floor, on his prat; he sobs)*: Little murderer! bastard! You're disgusting! You wanted to do that to me? I'm not one of your pupils, not me! *(She pulls him up by the collar, picks up his skullcap and puts it on his head; he's afraid she'll slap him again and holds his arm up to protect his face, like a child.)* Put the knife back where it belongs, go on! *(The* PROFESSOR *goes and puts it back in the drawer of the buffet, then comes back to her.)* Now didn't I warn you, just a little while ago: arithmetic leads to philology, and philology leads to crime . . .

PROFESSOR: You said "to calamity"!

MAID: It's the same thing.

PROFESSOR: I didn't understand you. I thought that "calamity" was a city and that you meant that philology leads to the city of Calamity . . .

MAID: Liar! Old fox! An intellectual like you is not going to make a mistake in the meanings of words. Don't try to pull the wool over my eyes.

PROFESSOR *(sobbing)*: I didn't kill her on purpose!

MAID: Are you sorry at least?

PROFESSOR: Oh, yes, Marie, I swear it to you!

MAID: I can't help feeling sorry for you! Ah! you're a good boy in spite of everything! I'll try to fix this. But don't start it again . . . It could give you a heart attack . . .

PROFESSOR: Yes, Marie! What are we going to do, now?

MAID: We're going to bury her . . . along with the thirty-nine others . . . that will make forty coffins . . . I'll call the undertakers and my lover, Father Auguste . . . I'll order the wreaths . . .

PROFESSOR: Yes, Marie, thank you very much.

MAID: Well, that's that. And perhaps it won't be necessary to call Auguste, since you yourself are something of a priest at times, if one can believe the gossip.

PROFESSOR: In any case, don't spend too much on the wreaths. She didn't pay for her lesson.

MAID: Don't worry . . . The least you can do is cover her up with her smock, she's not decent that way. And then we'll carry her out . . .

PROFESSOR: Yes, Marie, yes. (*He covers up the body.*) There's a chance that we'll get pinched° . . . with forty coffins . . . Don't you think . . . people will be surprised . . . Suppose they ask us what's inside them?

MAID: Don't worry so much. We'll say that they're empty. And besides, people won't ask questions, they're used to it.

PROFESSOR: Even so . . .

MAID (*she takes out an armband with an insignia, perhaps the Nazi swastika*): Wait, if you're afraid, wear this, then you won't have anything more to be afraid of. (*She puts the armband around his arm.*) . . . That's good politics.

PROFESSOR: Thanks, my little Marie. With this, I won't need to worry . . . You're a good girl, Marie . . . very loyal . . .

MAID: That's enough. Come on, sir. Are you all right?

PROFESSOR: Yes, my little Marie. (*The* MAID *and the* PROFESSOR *take the body of the young girl, one by the shoulders, the other by the legs, and move towards the door on the right.*) Be careful. We don't want to hurt her.

(*They exit. The stage remains empty for several moments. We hear the doorbell ring at the left.*)

VOICE OF THE MAID: Just a moment, I'm coming!

(*She appears as she was at the beginning of the play, and goes towards the door. The doorbell rings again.*)

MAID (*aside*): She's certainly in a hurry, this one! (*Aloud:*) Just a moment! (*She goes to the door on the left, and opens it.*) Good morning, miss! You are the new pupil? You have come for the lesson? The Professor is expecting you. I'll go tell him that you've come. He'll be right down. Come in, miss, come in!

---

pinched, caught, or arrested.

Figure 1. The Professor (Max Adrian) begins to lecture the Pupil (Joan Plowright) on linguistics and comparative philology while the Maid (Paula Bauersmith) looks on with stern disapproval in the 1958 Phoenix Theatre production of *The Lesson*, directed by Tony Richardson. (Photograph: Yale Collection of American Literature. Beinecke Rare Book & Manuscript Library. Yale University.)

Figure 2. After killing the Pupil, the Professor (Max Adrian) clings "like a child" to the comforting Maid (Paula Bauersmith) in the 1958 Phoenix Theatre production. (Photograph: Yale Collection of American Literature. Beinecke Rare Book & Manuscript Library. Yale University.)

Staging of *The Lesson*

REVIEW OF THE PHOENIX THEATRE
PRODUCTION, NEW YORK, 1958,
BY WALTER KERR

I once knew a man who wanted to write a play on the meaninglessness of meaning. I hope he isn't still working on it, for Eugène Ionesco has beaten him to the punch with at least two such treasures, "The Chairs" and "The Lesson," both of which were passionately and perhaps even properly produced at the Phoenix last night.

The first, and far more nerve-wracking, of the pair takes place in what I took to be a lighthouse, beyond which the waters of the sea ripple gently and vacantly. Two toothless and arthritic creatures, played with cackling enthusiasm and considerable skill by Joan Plowright and Eli Wallach, nurse each other's daydreams and blow each other's noses while they wait for a company of invisible friends to assemble so that the old fellow's terribly important "message to mankind" can be delivered by an Orator hired for the occasion.

Before the non-company comes, Mr. Wallach sits on Miss Plowright's lap: she is both his wife and his "mummy." Once the guests are not occupying the several dozens of chairs hurtled onto the stage for them, Miss Plowright explains to her portion of empty air that their only son left them at the age of seven ("the age of discretion"), while Mr. Wallach confides to his vacuum that they have never had any children. When all of the absent guests are assembled, the Orator—looking like Lon Chaney in the role of the Mad Hatter—appears. In a spastic grinding of teeth and tongue, the message is delivered: it is gibberish.

"The Lesson," which affords the extremely adaptable and really talented Miss Plowright an opportunity to wipe off the makeup and appear as a sunny little monster with a toothache, begins with a stoop-shouldered, feverishly intense tutor (Max Adrian, in brilliant form) opening the door to a student who can count to infinity or to 16, whichever is easier. The fact that the child can add but not subtract throws Mr. Adrian into a frenzy ("Integration alone is not enough—disintegration is necessary, too"). The pursuit of mathematics leads the increasingly shaken Adrian to the brink of some secret malaise; as they proceed to the study of words he is toppled over the brink, for "philology is the worst of all." He cuts Miss Plowright's throat, tidies the body away, and opens the door to the next pupil: Miss Plowright. (I wouldn't tell you this if I wasn't pretty certain you'd guess it).

In the course of these two calculated journeys into unreason, some astonishing theatrical effects are spun by director Tony Richardson's ingenious hand: a nightmare cyclone of flapping doors, spinning bodies (only two, it seems like twenty), and whining musical strings; a blur of purple color bleeding downward over the set; a red-and-green electrical storm while confetti uncoils from the heavens. The simple shock value of these violent images is enormous; and the players seem honestly to inherit the wind.

What bothers me about both these exercises, aside from a slight headache that is going away now, is their delicate, insistent assault upon form. I'm not thinking now of the arrogant and fanciful "irregularities" that dot the surface every inch of the way, but of the destiny to which we are being so ruthlessly led: to the defiant mindlessness that is the "answer" in each case. And is, inevitably, "nothing"—intellectual opposites mean the same thing, the only possible message is literally without content: if anything begins over again it is nothing that is beginning again. A philosophy of nihilism is perfectly possible to grasp. But its elaboration into theatrical nonsequiturs becomes a long, tortured, circuitous, pretentious road to a nice, round zero that might be drawn at once. Not the complexity, but the almost juvenile simplicity, of the evening's course is, I think, its undoing.

It is quite as though Lewis Carroll had gone about his work with no playfulness at all, but in black despair, believing hopelessly in every "Off with his head!"

SAMUEL BECKETT

1906–1989

Beckett did not start writing plays until his early forties, but by his mid-fifties he had become internationally recognized as one of the most revolutionary, influential, and philosophically significant dramatists of the contemporary period. Born near Dublin to a wealthy family, he was sent away at the age of fourteen to an Irish boarding school, and from there went on to Trinity College, Dublin, where he proved himself an exceptional student of French and Italian. In 1928, he went to Paris as an exchange teacher and there became acquainted with the most famous Irish author of his day, James Joyce, whose radically new fiction stimulated Beckett to experiment with avant-garde methods of poetry and fiction writing. He returned briefly to Dublin to serve as lecturer in French and to receive his master's degree in 1931 for a study of Marcel Proust, but by the mid-1930s he was on the move again in France and Germany, supporting himself at odd jobs while he continued to write fiction and poetry. Then, in 1937, he settled in Paris, and after World War II broke out and France fell in 1940, he worked for the French resistance movement. Shortly after the end of the war, having taken up permanent residence in Paris, he wrote his first play, *Waiting for Godot*. When it was produced in 1953, it quickly turned into an international sensation.

Waiting for Godot startled audiences and reviewers because it challenged most of their assumptions about the nature of dramatic form. It undercut their ideas of plot with its persistently illogical and purposeless activity; it questioned their ideas of dialogue with its endless contradictions between language and action; it defied their ideas of spectacle with its stage bare except for a tree that is also bare until the second act when it has somehow acquired "four or five leaves." And in all his subsequent plays, Beckett continued to challenge audiences by stripping away more and more of the conventions associated with theater, as if he were seeking to discover how much can be taken away from drama without forsaking the essence of dramatic experience.

In seeking to discover the limits of drama, Beckett progressively stripped away virtually all the elements of theater. Physical action decreased as Beckett's protagonists became less and less mobile. In *Waiting for Godot,* two of the characters are roped to one another, and though everyone can walk they frequently fall down. In *Endgame* (1957), Nagg and Nell are confined to ashbins, Hamm is confined to a wheelchair, and Clov, the only mobile character, hobbles around the stage. In *Happy Days* (1961), Winnie is buried up to her waist in a mound, and by Act 2 the mound has reached her neck. In *Play* (1964), all three characters are immobilized in urns and speak only when a light shines upon them. And in *Not I* (1972), the only visible action is the mouth of a woman speaking. Characters likewise decrease from the five in *Waiting for Godot* to one (and his tape recorder) in *Krapp's Last Tape* (1958). Even language disappears in Beckett's shorter pieces. *Act without Words I* (1957) and *II* (1960) are mime pieces, and *Breath* (1970) lasts for one minute of cries and breaths. Consequently many audiences and reviewers have often been

988 / SAMUEL BECKETT

moved in witnessing Beckett's plays to echo the words of Estragon in *Waiting for Godot*: "Nothing happens, nobody comes, nobody goes, it's awful."

Today, however, *Waiting for Godot* and *Endgame* are recognized as two of the most important plays in contemporary drama, and they have been performed throughout the world to appreciative audiences in Paris and London, on Broadway and off, at San Quentin Prison, and even in community churches. The two couples of *Waiting for Godot*—the tramps Vladimir and Estragon, and the master and his slave, Pozzo and Lucky—have been examined, annotated, and allegorized, yet they still survive. In fact, survival—or existence, to use a more neutral term—is the action of the play. Stranded on a bare stage, in a barren existence, Vladimir and Estragon "wait for Godot," and while they wait they tell stories to each other, they reminisce, they contemplate suicide, they munch carrots and radishes, they pull their boots on and off, and they go through many other routines that Beckett appears to have drawn from the vaudeville world of Charlie Chaplin, Buster Keaton, and the Marx brothers. Estragon sums up their existence when he says, "We always find something, eh Didi, to give us the impression we exist?" Although Godot does not arrive at the end of the first act, nor at the end of the second—though their world grows increasingly hopeless—they sustain themselves through their continued inventiveness. And in contrast to Pozzo and Lucky, who are tied to one another by a rope, Vladimir and Estragon are bound to each other by a friendship that survives repeated separations and quarrels. *Endgame* is a grimmer and tighter play. The two acts of *Godot* have shrunk to a single long act. The two pairs of characters are still present but the emphasis has been drastically changed. The master-slave pair—the blind Hamm and the hobbling Clov—dominate the play, while Nagg and Nell, who are reminiscent of Vladimir and Estragon in their exchanging of memories and food, are confined to ashbins and appear only occasionally. Instead of a road on which the characters might come and go, there is only a room, and the world outside does not appear to contain any sign of life—not even a tree with a few leaves on it.

Endgame has repeatedly tempted critics to define its meaning, in part because it so insistently appears to deny itself significance—Hamm, for example, says "We're not beginning to . . . to . . . mean something?" and Clov replies, "Mean something! You and I, mean something!"—in part because it implicitly alludes to so many interpretive contexts. The chess metaphor of the title is echoed in the physical action of Hamm, the king who can move only in limited ways, and in the "very red faces" of Hamm and Clov contrasted to the "very white faces" of Nagg and Nell. Allusions to Shakespeare abound throughout the play: Hamm's name seems to be a shortened form of Hamlet; he sees himself as a deposed king, like Lear and Richard II; he parodies Richard III's final words when he calls out "My kingdom for a nightman"; and he directly quotes Prospero, "Our revels now are ended," and then throws away his gaff, much as Prospero breaks his magic wand at the end of *The Tempest*. The theatrical metaphor running throughout the play provides another interpretive context. Hamm's first words, for example, are "Me—(*He yawns.*)—to play." Clov looks out at the auditorium and comments, ironically, "I see . . . a multitude . . . in transports . . . of joy." Hamm speaks of the "dialogue," worries that the small boy may provide an "underplot," grumbles when Clov reacts to "an aside," and announces, "I'm warming up for my last soliloquy." Clov starts to leave the stage with the line, "This is what we call making an exit." Thus the stage is, it seems, the only place of life in a world Clov calls "corpsed." And that reference to death is only one of innumerable references to it from the title to the final tableau.

Because *Endgame* is so richly and grimly metaphoric, theater directors have always found it a challenging work to produce. One particular challenge lies in Beckett's insistence on a starkly simple set, an insistence that led him, in 1984, to ask that the American Repertory Theatre production be canceled even before it had opened, because the director had dared to add not only music but a full set suggesting a deserted, perhaps burned-out, subway tunnel, as well as an interracial cast, with Hamm and Nagg played by black actors while Clov and Nell were played by white actors (see Figure 1). Lawyers for the theater company and Beckett's publisher finally reached an out-of-court settlement, and the theater was allowed to stage its production, unchanged, but with a disclaimer from Beckett inserted in the program calling the production "completely unacceptable." In his review of the American Repertory Theatre production, Mel Gussow regards the trash-layered set, which included a derelict train, as an embodiment of Beckett's postnuclear nightmare world, and though recognizing that it differed in detail from Beckett's text, he also considers it true to the spirit of *Endgame*. In 1996, London's Donmar Warehouse mounted a production that was much closer to the letter of Beckett's stage directions. In that production, Clov was not only lame, as the text's mention of his "stiff, staggering walk" implies, but also hunchbacked (see Figure 2). And the set was suitably bleak, with the actual brick walls of the small London theater suggesting some kind of abandoned cellar with Beckett's required windows visible at the back (see Figure 3). As the reviews from Gussow and Taylor make clear, however, the essence of the play lies not in its visual spareness or squalor, but in Beckett's relentless depiction of human beings yoked together, reluctant companions who cannot live with—or without—each other. Both reviews end by citing Nell's paradoxical statement, "Nothing is funnier than unhappiness," a line that sums up Beckett's unforgettably theatrical mixture of comedy and despair.

ENDGAME
A Play in One Act

BY SAMUEL BECKETT

CHARACTERS

NAGG
NELL
HAMM
CLOV

SCENE

Bare interior. Grey light. Left and right back, high up, two small windows, curtains drawn. Front right, a door. Hanging near door, its face to wall, a picture. Front left, touching each other, covered with an old sheet, two ashbins. Center, in an armchair on castors, covered with an old sheet, HAMM. *Motionless by the door, his eyes fixed on* HAMM, CLOV. *Very red face. Brief tableau.*

---

*(*CLOV *goes and stands under window left. Stiff, staggering walk. He looks up at window left. He turns and looks at window right. He goes and stands under window right. He looks up at window right. He turns and looks at window left. He goes out, comes back immediately with a small step-ladder, carries it over and sets it down under window left, gets up on it, draws back curtain. He gets down, takes six steps (for example) towards window right, goes back for ladder, carries it over and sets it down under window right, gets up on it, draws back curtain. He gets down, takes three steps towards window left, goes back for ladder, carries it over and sets it down under window left, gets up on it, looks out of window. Brief laugh. He gets down, goes with ladder towards ashbins, halts, turns, carries back ladder and sets it down under window right, goes to ashbins, removes sheet covering them, folds it over his arm. He raises one lid, stoops and looks into bin. Brief laugh. He closes lid. Same with other bin. He goes to* HAMM, *removes sheet covering him, folds it over his arm. In a dressing-gown, a stiff toque on his head, a large blood-stained handkerchief over his face, a whistle hanging from his neck, a rug over his knees, thick socks on his feet,* HAMM *seems to be asleep.* CLOV *looks him over. Brief laugh. He goes to door, halts, turns towards auditorium.)*

CLOV *(fixed gaze, tonelessly)*: Finished, it's finished, nearly finished, it must be nearly finished.

(Pause.)

Grain upon grain, one by one, and one day, suddenly, there's a heap, a little heap, the impossible heap.

(Pause.)

I can't be punished any more.

(Pause.)

I'll go now to my kitchen, ten feet by ten feet by ten feet, and wait for him to whistle me.

(Pause.)

Nice dimensions, nice proportions, I'll lean on the table, and look at the wall, and wait for him to whistle me.

(He remains a moment motionless, then goes out. He comes back immediately, goes to window right, takes up the ladder and carries it out. Pause. HAMM *stirs. He yawns under the handkerchief. He removes the handkerchief from his face. Very red face. Black glasses.)*

HAMM: Me—*(He yawns.)*—to play.

(He holds the handkerchief spread out before him.)

Old stancher!

(He takes off his glasses, wipes his eyes, his face, the glasses, puts them on again, folds the handkerchief and puts it back neatly in the breast-pocket of his dressing-gown. He clears his throat, joins the tips of his fingers.)

Can there be misery—*(He yawns.)*—loftier than mine? No doubt. Formerly. But now?

(Pause.)

My father?

(Pause.)

My mother?

(Pause.)

My . . . dog?

(Pause.)

Oh I am willing to believe they suffer as much as such creatures can suffer. But does that mean their sufferings equal mine? No doubt.

(Pause.)

No, all is a—*(He yawns.)*—bsolute, *(Proudly.)* the bigger a man is the fuller he is.

(Pause. Gloomily.)

And the emptier.

(He sniffs.)

Clov!

(Pause.)

No, alone.

(Pause.)

What dreams! Those forests!

(Pause.)

Enough, it's time it ended, in the shelter too.

(Pause.)

And yet I hesitate, I hesitate to . . . to end. Yes, there it is, it's time it ended and yet I hesitate to—*(He yawns.)*—to end. *(Yawns.)*

God, I'm tired, I'd be better off in bed.

(He whistles. Enter CLOV *immediately. He halts beside the chair.)*

You pollute the air!

(Pause.)

Get me ready. I'm going to bed.

CLOV: I've just got you up.

HAMM: And what of it?

CLOV: I can't be getting you up and putting you to bed every five minutes, I have things to do.

(Pause.)

HAMM: Did you ever see my eyes?

CLOV: No.

HAMM: Did you never have the curiosity, while I was sleeping, to take off my glasses and look at my eyes?

CLOV: Pulling back the lids?

(Pause.)

No.

HAMM: One of these days I'll show them to you.

(Pause.)

It seems they've gone all white.

(Pause.)

What time is it?

CLOV: The same as usual.

HAMM *(gestures towards window right)*: Have you looked?

CLOV: Yes.

HAMM: Well?

CLOV: Zero.

HAMM: It'd need to rain.

CLOV: It won't rain.

(Pause.)

HAMM: Apart from that, how do you feel?

CLOV: I don't complain.

HAMM: You feel normal?

CLOV *(irritably)*: I tell you I don't complain.

HAMM: I feel a little queer.

(Pause.)

Clov!

CLOV: Yes.

HAMM: Have you not had enough?

CLOV: Yes.

(Pause.)

Of what?

HAMM: Of this . . . this . . . thing.

CLOV: I always had.

(Pause.)

Not you?

HAMM *(gloomily)*: Then there's no reason for it to change.

CLOV: It may end.

(Pause.)

All life long the same questions, the same answers.

HAMM: Get me ready.

*(*CLOV *does not move.)*

Go and get the sheet.

*(*CLOV *does not move.)*

Clov!

CLOV: Yes.

HAMM: I'll give you nothing more to eat.

CLOV: Then we'll die.

HAMM: I'll give you just enough to keep you from dying. You'll be hungry all the time.

CLOV: Then we won't die.

(Pause.)

I'll go and get the sheet.

(He goes toward the door.)

HAMM: No!

*(*CLOV *halts.)*

I'll give you one biscuit per day.

(Pause.)

One and a half.

(Pause.)

Why do you stay with me?

CLOV: Why do you keep me?
HAMM: There's no one else.
CLOV: There's nowhere else.

(Pause.)

HAMM: You're leaving me all the same.
CLOV: I'm trying.
HAMM: You don't love me.
CLOV: No.
HAMM: You loved me once.
CLOV: Once!
HAMM: I've made you suffer too much.

(Pause.)

  Haven't I?
CLOV: It's not that.
HAMM (shocked): I haven't made you suffer too much?
CLOV: Yes!
HAMM (relieved): Ah you gave me a fright!

(Pause. Coldly.)

  Forgive me.

(Pause. Louder.)

  I said, Forgive me.
CLOV: I heard you.

(Pause.)

  Have you bled?
HAMM: Less.

(Pause.)

  Is it not time for my pain-killer?
CLOV: No.

(Pause.)

HAMM: How are your eyes?
CLOV: Bad.
HAMM: How are your legs?
CLOV: Bad.
HAMM: But you can move.
CLOV: Yes.
HAMM (violently): Then move!

(CLOV goes to back wall, leans against it with his forehead and hands.)

  Where are you?
CLOV: Here.
HAMM: Come back!

(CLOV returns to his place beside the chair.)

  Where are you?
CLOV: Here.
HAMM: Why don't you kill me?
CLOV: I don't know the combination of the cupboard.

(Pause.)

HAMM: Go and get two bicycle-wheels.
CLOV: There are no more bicycle-wheels.
HAMM: What have you done with your bicycle?
CLOV: I never had a bicycle.
HAMM: The thing is impossible.
CLOV: When there were still bicycles I wept to have one. I crawled at your feet. You told me to go to hell. Now there are none.
HAMM: And your rounds? When you inspected my paupers. Always on foot?
CLOV: Sometimes on horse.

(The lid of one of the bins lifts and the hands of NAGG appear, gripping the rim. Then his head emerges. Nightcap. Very white face. NAGG yawns, then listens.)

  I'll leave you, I have things to do.
HAMM: In your kitchen?
CLOV: Yes.
HAMM: Outside of here it's death.

(Pause.)

  All right, be off.

(Exit CLOV. Pause.)

  We're getting on.
NAGG: Me pap!
HAMM: Accursed progenitor!
NAGG: Me pap!
HAMM: The old folks at home! No decency left! Guzzle, guzzle, that's all they think of.

(He whistles. Enter CLOV. He halts beside the chair.)

  Well! I thought you were leaving me.
CLOV: Oh not just yet, not just yet.
NAGG: Me pap!
HAMM: Give him his pap.
CLOV: There's no more pap.
HAMM (to NAGG): Do you hear that? There's no more pap. You'll never get any more pap.
NAGG: I want me pap!
HAMM: Give him a biscuit.

(Exit CLOV.)

  Accursed fornicator! How are your stumps?
NAGG: Never mind me stumps.

(Enter CLOV with biscuit.)

CLOV: I'm back again, with the biscuit.

(He gives biscuit to NAGG who fingers it, sniffs it.)

NAGG (plaintively): What is it?
CLOV: Spratt's medium.
NAGG (as before): It's hard! I can't!
HAMM: Bottle him!

(CLOV pushes NAGG back into the bin, closes the lid.)

CLOV (returning to his place beside the chair): If age but knew!

HAMM: Sit on him!

CLOV: I can't sit.

HAMM: True. And I can't stand.

CLOV: So it is.

HAMM: Every man his specialty.

(Pause.)

No phone calls?

(Pause.)

Don't we laugh?

CLOV (after reflection): I don't feel like it.

HAMM (after reflection): Nor I.

(Pause.)

Clov!

CLOV: Yes.

HAMM: Nature has forgotten us.

CLOV: There's no more nature.

HAMM: No more nature! You exaggerate.

CLOV: In the vicinity.

HAMM: But we breathe, we change! We lose our hair, our teeth! Our bloom! Our ideals!

CLOV: Then she hasn't forgotten us.

HAMM: But you say there is none.

CLOV (sadly): No one that ever lived ever thought so crooked as we.

HAMM: We do what we can.

CLOV: We shouldn't.

(Pause.)

HAMM: You're a bit of all right, aren't you?

CLOV: A smithereen.

(Pause.)

HAMM: This is slow work.

(Pause.)

Is it not time for my pain-killer?

CLOV: No.

(Pause.)

I'll leave you, I have things to do.

HAMM: In your kitchen?

CLOV: Yes.

HAMM: What, I'd like to know.

CLOV: I look at the wall.

HAMM: The wall! And what do you see on your wall? Mene, mene? Naked bodies?

CLOV: I see my light dying.

HAMM: Your light dying! Listen to that! Well, it can die just as well here, your light. Take a look at me and then come back and tell me what you think of your light.

(Pause.)

CLOV: You shouldn't speak to me like that.

(Pause.)

HAMM (coldly): Forgive me.

(Pause. Louder.)

I said, Forgive me.

CLOV: I heard you.

(The lid of NAGG's bin lifts. His hands appear, gripping the rim. Then his head emerges. In his mouth the biscuit. He listens.)

HAMM: Did your seeds come up?

CLOV: No.

HAMM: Did you scratch round them to see if they had sprouted?

CLOV: They haven't sprouted.

HAMM: Perhaps it's still too early.

CLOV: If they were going to sprout they would have sprouted.

(Violently.)

They'll never sprout!

(Pause. NAGG takes biscuit in his hand.)

HAMM: This is not much fun.

(Pause.)

But that's always the way at the end of the day, isn't it, Clov?

CLOV: Always.

HAMM: It's the end of the day like any other day, isn't it, Clov?

CLOV: Looks like it.

(Pause.)

HAMM (anguished): What's happening, what's happening?

CLOV: Something is taking its course.

(Pause.)

HAMM: All right, be off.

(He leans back in his chair, remains motionless. CLOV does not move, heaves a great groaning sigh. HAMM sits up.)

I thought I told you to be off.

CLOV: I'm trying.

(He goes to door, halts.)

Ever since I was whelped.

(Exit CLOV.)

HAMM: We're getting on.

(He leans back in his chair, remains motionless. NAGG knocks on the lid of the other bin. Pause. He knocks harder. The lid lifts and the hands of NELL appear, gripping the rim. Then her head emerges. Lace cap. Very white face.)

NELL: What is it, my pet?

(Pause.)

Time for love?

NAGG: Were you asleep?

NELL: Oh no!

NAGG: Kiss me.

NELL: We can't.

NAGG: Try.

(Their heads strain towards each other, fail to meet, fall apart again.)

NELL: Why this farce, day after day?

(Pause.)

NAGG: I've lost me tooth.

NELL: When?

NAGG: I had it yesterday.

NELL *(elegiac)*: Ah yesterday!

(They turn painfully towards each other.)

NAGG: Can you see me?

NELL: Hardly. And you?

NAGG: What?

NELL: Can you see me?

NAGG: Hardly.

NELL: So much the better, so much the better.

NAGG: Don't say that.

(Pause.)

Our sight has failed.

NELL: Yes.

(Pause. They turn away from each other.)

NAGG: Can you hear me?

NELL: Yes. And you?

NAGG: Yes.

(Pause.)

Our hearing hasn't failed.

NELL: Our what?

NAGG: Our hearing.

NELL: No.

(Pause.)

Have you anything else to say to me?

NAGG: Do you remember—

NELL: No.

NAGG: When we crashed on our tandem and lost our shanks.

(They laugh heartily.)

NELL: It was in the Ardennes.

(They laugh less heartily.)

NAGG: On the road to Sedan.

(They laugh still less heartily.)

Are you cold?

NELL: Yes, perished. And you?

NAGG *(pause)*: I'm freezing.

(Pause.)

Do you want to go in?

NELL: Yes.

NAGG: Then go in.

(NELL does not move.)

Why don't you go in?

NELL: I don't know.

(Pause.)

NAGG: Has he changed your sawdust?

NELL: It isn't sawdust.

(Pause. Wearily.)

Can you not be a little accurate, Nagg?

NAGG: Your sand then. It's not important.

NELL: It is important.

(Pause.)

NAGG: It was sawdust once.

NELL: Once!

NAGG: And now it's sand.

(Pause.)

From the shore.

(Pause. Impatiently.)

Now it's sand he fetches from the shore.

NELL: Now it's sand.

NAGG: Has he changed yours?

NELL: No.

NAGG: Nor mine.

(Pause.)

I won't have it!

(Pause. Holding up the biscuit.)

Do you want a bit?

NELL: No.

(Pause.)

Of what?

NAGG: Biscuit. I've kept you half.

(He looks at the biscuit. Proudly.)

Three quarters. For you. Here.

(He proffers the biscuit.)

No?

(Pause.)

Do you not feel well?

HAMM *(wearily)*: Quiet, quiet, you're keeping me awake.

(Pause.)

Talk softer.

(*Pause.*)

If I could sleep I might make love. I'd go into the woods. My eyes would see . . . the sky, the earth. I'd run, run, they wouldn't catch me.

(*Pause.*)

Nature!

(*Pause.*)

There's something dripping in my head.

(*Pause.*)

A heart, a heart in my head.

(*Pause.*)

NAGG (*softly*): Do you hear him? A heart in his head!

(*He chuckles cautiously.*)

NELL: One mustn't laugh at those things, Nagg. Why must you always laugh at them?
NAGG: Not so loud!
NELL (*without lowering her voice*): Nothing is funnier than unhappiness, I grant you that. But—
NAGG (*shocked*): Oh!
NELL: Yes, yes, it's the most comical thing in the world. And we laugh, we laugh, with a will, in the beginning. But it's always the same thing. Yes, it's like the funny story we have heard too often, we still find it funny, but we don't laugh any more.

(*Pause.*)

Have you anything else to say to me?
NAGG: No.
NELL: Are you quite sure?

(*Pause.*)

Then I'll leave you.
NAGG: Do you not want your biscuit?

(*Pause.*)

I'll keep it for you.

(*Pause.*)

I thought you were going to leave me.
NELL: I am going to leave you.
NAGG: Could you give me a scratch before you go?
NELL: No.

(*Pause.*)

Where?
NAGG: In the back.
NELL: No.

(*Pause.*)

Rub yourself against the rim.

NAGG: It's lower down. In the hollow.
NELL: What hollow?
NAGG: The hollow!

(*Pause.*)

Could you not?

(*Pause.*)

Yesterday you scratched me there.
NELL (*elegiac*): Ah yesterday!
NAGG: Could you not?

(*Pause.*)

Would you like me to scratch you?

(*Pause.*)

Are you crying again?
NELL: I was trying.

(*Pause.*)

HAMM: Perhaps it's a little vein.

(*Pause.*)

NAGG: What was that he said?
NELL: Perhaps it's a little vein.
NAGG: What does that mean?

(*Pause.*)

That means nothing.

(*Pause.*)

Will I tell you the story of the tailor?
NELL: No.

(*Pause.*)

What for?
NAGG: To cheer you up.
NELL: It's not funny.
NAGG: It always made you laugh.

(*Pause.*)

The first time I thought you'd die.
NELL: It was on Lake Como.

(*Pause.*)

One April afternoon.

(*Pause.*)

Can you believe it?
NAGG: What?
NELL: That we once went out rowing on Lake Como.

(*Pause.*)

One April afternoon.
NAGG: We had got engaged the day before.
NELL: Engaged!

NAGG: You were in such fits that we capsized. By rights we should have been drowned.

NELL: It was because I felt happy.

NAGG (*indignant*): It was not, it was not, it was my story and nothing else. Happy! Don't you laugh at it still? Every time I tell it. Happy!

NELL: It was deep, deep. And you could see down to the bottom. So white. So clean.

NAGG: Let me tell it again.

(*Raconteur's voice.*)

An Englishman, needing a pair of striped trousers in a hurry for the New Year festivities, goes to his tailor who takes his measurements.

(*Tailor's voice.*)

"That's the lot, come back in four days, I'll have it ready." Good. Four days later.

(*Tailor's voice.*)

"So sorry, come back in a week. I've made a mess of the seat." Good, that's all right, a neat seat can be very ticklish. A week later.

(*Tailor's voice.*)

"Frightfully sorry, come back in ten days, I've made a hash of the crotch." Good, can't be helped, a snug crotch is always a teaser. Ten days later.

(*Tailor's voice.*)

"Dreadfully sorry, come back in a fortnight, I've made a balls of the fly." Good, at a pinch, a smart fly is a stiff proposition.

(*Pause. Normal voice.*)

I never told it worse.

(*Pause. Gloomy.*)

I tell this story worse and worse.

(*Pause. Raconteur's voice.*)

Well, to make it short, the bluebells are blowing and he ballockses the buttonholes.

(*Customer's voice.*)

"God damn you to hell, Sir, no, it's indecent, there are limits! In six days, do you hear me, six days, God made the world. Yes Sir, no less Sir, the WORLD! And you are not bloody well capable of making me a pair of trousers in three months!"

(*Tailor's voice, scandalized.*)

"But my dear Sir, my dear Sir, look—

(*Disdainful gesture, disgustedly.*)

—at the world—

(*Pause.*)

and look—

(*Loving gesture, proudly.*)

—at my TROUSERS!"

(*Pause. He looks at NELL who has remained impassive, her eyes unseeing, breaks into a high forced laugh, cuts it short, pokes his head towards NELL, launches his laugh again.*)

HAMM: Silence!

(*NAGG starts, cuts short his laugh.*)

NELL: You could see down to the bottom.

HAMM (*exasperated*): Have you not finished? Will you never finish?

(*With sudden fury.*)

Will this never finish?

(*NAGG disappears into his bin, closes the lid behind him. NELL does not move. Frenziedly.*)

My kingdom for a nightman!

(*He whistles. Enter CLOV.*)

Clear away this muck! Chuck it in the sea!

(*CLOV goes to bins, halts.*)

NELL: So white.

HAMM: What? What's she blathering about?

(*CLOV stoops, takes NELL's hand, feels her pulse.*)

NELL (*to CLOV*): Desert!

(*CLOV lets go her hand, pushes her back in the bin, closes the lid.*)

CLOV (*returning to his place beside the chair*): She has no pulse.

HAMM: What was she drivelling about?

CLOV: She told me to go away, into the desert.

HAMM: Damn busybody! Is that all?

CLOV: No.

HAMM: What else?

CLOV: I didn't understand.

HAMM: Have you bottled her?

CLOV: Yes.

HAMM: Are they both bottled?

CLOV: Yes.

HAMM: Screw down the lids.

(*CLOV goes towards door.*)

Time enough.

(*CLOV halts.*)

My anger subsides, I'd like to pee.

CLOV (*with alacrity*): I'll go and get the catheter.

(*He goes towards door.*)

HAMM: Time enough.

(CLOV *halts.*)

Give me my pain-killer.

CLOV: It's too soon.

(*Pause.*)

It's too soon on top of your tonic, it wouldn't act.

HAMM: In the morning they brace you up and in the evening they calm you down. Unless it's the other way round.

(*Pause.*)

That old doctor, he's dead naturally?

CLOV: He wasn't old.

HAMM: But he's dead?

CLOV: Naturally.

(*Pause.*)

You ask *me* that?

(*Pause.*)

HAMM: Take me for a little turn.

(CLOV *goes behind the chair and pushes it forward.*)

Not too fast!

(CLOV *pushes chair.*)

Right round the world!

(CLOV *pushes chair.*)

Hug the walls, then back to the center again.

(CLOV *pushes chair.*)

I was right in the center, wasn't I?

CLOV (*pushing*): Yes.

HAMM: We'd need a proper wheel-chair. With big wheels. Bicycle wheels!

(*Pause.*)

Are you hugging?

CLOV (*pushing*): Yes.

HAMM (*groping for wall*): It's a lie! Why do you lie to me?

CLOV (*bearing close to wall*): There! There!

HAMM: Stop!

(CLOV *stops chair close to back wall.* HAMM *lays his hand against the wall.*)

Old wall!

(*Pause.*)

Beyond is the . . . other hell.

(*Pause. Violently.*)

Closer! Closer! Up against!

CLOV: Take away your hand.

(HAMM *withdraws his hand.* CLOV *rams chair against wall.*)

There!

(HAMM *leans towards wall, applies his ear to it.*)

HAMM: Do you hear?

(*He strikes the wall with his knuckles.*)

Do you hear? Hollow bricks!

(*He strikes again.*)

All that's hollow!

(*Pause. He straightens up. Violently.*)

That's enough. Back!

CLOV: We haven't done the round.

HAMM: Back to my place!

(CLOV *pushes chair back to center.*)

Is that my place?

CLOV: Yes, that's your place.

HAMM: Am I right in the center?

CLOV: I'll measure it.

HAMM: More or less! More or less!

CLOV (*moving chair slightly*): There!

HAMM: I'm more or less in the center?

CLOV: I'd say so.

HAMM: You'd say so! Put me right in the center!

CLOV: I'll go and get the tape.

HAMM: Roughly! Roughly!

(CLOV *moves chair slightly.*)

Bang in the center!

CLOV: There!

(*Pause.*)

HAMM: I feel a little too far to the left.

(CLOV *moves chair slightly.*)

Now I feel a little too far to the right.

(CLOV *moves chair slightly.*)

I feel a little too far forward.

(CLOV *moves chair slightly.*)

Now I feel a little too far back.

(CLOV *moves chair slightly.*)

Don't stay there (*i.e., behind the chair*), you give me the shivers.

(CLOV *returns to his place beside the chair.*)

CLOV: If I could kill him I'd die happy.

(*Pause.*)

HAMM: What's the weather like?

CLOV: As usual.

HAMM: Look at the earth.

CLOV: I've looked.

HAMM: With the glass?

CLOV: No need of the glass.

HAMM: Look at it with the glass.

CLOV: I'll go and get the glass.

(Exit CLOV.)

HAMM: No need of the glass!

(Enter CLOV with telescope.)

CLOV: I'm back again, with the glass.

(He goes to window right, looks up at it.)

I need the steps.

HAMM: Why? Have you shrunk?

(Exit CLOV with telescope.)

I don't like that, I don't like that.

(Enter CLOV with ladder, but without telescope.)

CLOV: I'm back again, with the steps.

(He sets down ladder under window right, gets up on it, realizes he has not the telescope, gets down.)

I need the glass.

(He goes towards door.)

HAMM (violently): But you have the glass!

CLOV (halting, violently): No, I haven't the glass!

(Exit CLOV.)

HAMM: This is deadly.

(Enter CLOV with telescope. He goes toward ladder.)

CLOV: Things are livening up.

(He gets up on ladder, raises the telescope, lets it fall.)

I did it on purpose.

(He gets down, picks up the telescope, turns it on auditorium.)

I see . . . a multitude . . . in transports . . . of joy.

(Pause.)

That's what I call a magnifier.

(He lowers the telescope, turns towards HAMM.)

Well? Don't we laugh?

HAMM (after reflection): I don't.

CLOV (after reflection): Nor I.

(He gets up on ladder, turns the telescope on the without.)

Let's see.

(He looks, moving the telescope.)

Zero . . . (He looks.) . . . zero . . . (He looks.) . . . and zero.

HAMM: Nothing stirs. All is—

CLOV: Zer—

HAMM (violently): Wait till you're spoken to!

(Normal voice.)

All is . . . all is . . . all is what?

(Violently.)

All is what?

CLOV: What all is? In a word? Is that what you want to know? Just a moment.

(He turns the telescope on the without, looks, lowers the telescope, turns towards HAMM.)

Corpsed.

(Pause.)

Well? Content?

HAMM: Look at the sea.

CLOV: It's the same.

HAMM: Look at the ocean!

(CLOV gets down, takes a few steps towards window left, goes back for ladder, carries it over and sets it down under window left, gets up on it, turns the telescope on the without, looks at length. He starts, lowers the telescope, examines it, turns it again on the without.)

CLOV: Never seen anything like that!

HAMM (anxiously): What? A sail? A fin? Smoke?

CLOV (looking): The light is sunk.

HAMM (relieved): Pah! We all knew that.

CLOV (looking): There was a bit left.

HAMM: The base.

CLOV (looking): Yes.

HAMM: And now?

CLOV (looking): All gone.

HAMM: No gulls?

CLOV (looking): Gulls!

HAMM: And the horizon? Nothing on the horizon?

CLOV (lowering the telescope, turning toward HAMM, exasperatedly): What in God's name could there be on the horizon?

(Pause.)

HAMM: The waves, how are the waves?

CLOV: The waves?

(He turns the telescope on the waves.)

Lead.

HAMM: And the sun?

CLOV (looking): Zero.

HAMM: But it should be sinking. Look again.

CLOV (looking): Damn the sun.

HAMM: Is it night already then?

CLOV (looking): No.

HAMM: Then what is it?
CLOV (*looking*): Gray.

(*Lowering the telescope, turning towards* HAMM, *louder.*)

Gray!

(*Pause. Still louder.*)

GRRAY!

(*Pause. He gets down, approaches* HAMM *from behind, whispers in his ear.*)

HAMM (*starting*): Gray! Did I hear you say gray?
CLOV: Light black. From pole to pole.
HAMM: You exaggerate.

(*Pause.*)

Don't stay there, you give me the shivers.

(CLOV *returns to his place beside the chair.*)

CLOV: Why this farce, day after day?
HAMM: Routine. One never knows.

(*Pause.*)

Last night I saw inside my breast. There was a big sore.
CLOV: Pah! You saw your heart.
HAMM: No, it was living.

(*Pause. Anguished.*)

Clov!
CLOV: Yes.
HAMM: What's happening?
CLOV: Something is taking its course.

(*Pause.*)

HAMM: Clov!
CLOV (*impatiently*): What is it?
HAMM: We're not beginning to . . . to . . . mean something?
CLOV: Mean something! You and I, mean something!

(*Brief laugh.*)

Ah that's a good one!
HAMM: I wonder.

(*Pause.*)

Imagine if a rational being came back to earth, wouldn't he be liable to get ideas into his head if he observed us long enough.

(*Voice of rational being.*)

Ah, good, now I see what it is, yes, now I understand what they're at!

(CLOV *starts, drops the telescope and begins to scratch his belly with both hands. Normal voice.*)

And without going so far as that, we ourselves . . . (*With emotion.*) . . . we ourselves . . . at certain moments . . . (*Vehemently.*) To think perhaps it won't all have been for nothing!
CLOV (*anguished, scratching himself*): I have a flea!
HAMM: A flea! Are there still fleas?
CLOV: On me, there's one.

(*Scratching.*)

Unless it's a crablouse.
HAMM (*very perturbed*): But humanity might start from there all over again! Catch him, for the love of God!
CLOV: I'll go and get the powder.

(*Exit* CLOV.)

HAMM: A flea! This is awful! What a day!

(*Enter* CLOV *with a sprinkling-tin.*)

CLOV: I'm back again, with the insecticide.
HAMM: Let him have it!

(CLOV *loosens the top of his trousers, pulls it forward and shakes powder into the aperture. He stoops, looks, waits, starts, frenziedly shakes more powder, stoops, looks, waits.*)

CLOV: The bastard!
HAMM: Did you get him?
CLOV: Looks like it.

(*He drops the tin and adjusts his trousers.*)

Unless he's laying doggo.
HAMM: Laying! Lying you mean. Unless he's *lying* doggo.
CLOV: Ah? One says lying? One doesn't say laying?
HAMM: Use your head, can't you. If he was laying we'd be bitched.
CLOV: Ah.

(*Pause.*)

What about that pee?
HAMM: I'm having it.
CLOV: Ah that's the spirit, that's the spirit!

(*Pause.*)

HAMM (*with ardour*): Let's go from here, the two of us! South! You can make a raft and the currents will carry us away, far away, to other . . . mammals!
CLOV: God forbid!
HAMM: Alone, I'll embark alone! Get working on that raft immediately. Tomorrow I'll be gone for ever.
CLOV (*hastening towards door*): I'll start straight away.
HAMM: Wait!

(CLOV *halts.*)

Will there be sharks, do you think?
CLOV: Sharks? I don't know. If there are there will be.

(*He goes towards door.*)

HAMM: Wait!

(CLOV *halts.*)

Is it not yet time for my pain-killer?

CLOV (*violently*): No!

(*He goes towards door.*)

HAMM: Wait!

(CLOV *halts.*)

How are your eyes?

CLOV: Bad.

HAMM: But you can see.

CLOV: All I want.

HAMM: How are your legs?

CLOV: Bad.

HAMM: But you can walk.

CLOV: I come . . . and go.

HAMM: In my house.

(*Pause. With prophetic relish.*)

One day you'll be blind, like me. You'll be sitting there, a speck in the void, in the dark, for ever, like me.

(*Pause.*)

One day you'll say to yourself, I'm tired. I'll sit down, and you'll go and sit down. Then you'll say, I'm hungry, I'll get up and get something to eat. But you won't get up. You'll say, I shouldn't have sat down, but since I have I'll sit on a little longer, then I'll get up and get something to eat. But you won't get up and you won't get anything to eat.

(*Pause.*)

You'll look at the wall a while, then you'll say, I'll close my eyes, perhaps have a little sleep, after that I'll feel better, and you'll close them. And when you open them again there'll be no wall any more.

(*Pause.*)

Infinite emptiness will be all around you, all the resurrected dead of all the ages wouldn't fill it, and there you'll be like a little bit of grit in the middle of the steppe.

(*Pause.*)

Yes, one day you'll know what it is, you'll be like me, except that you won't have anyone with you, because you won't have had pity on anyone and because there won't be anyone left to have pity on.

(*Pause.*)

CLOV: It's not certain.

(*Pause.*)

And there's one thing you forget.

HAMM: Ah?

CLOV: I can't sit down.

HAMM (*impatiently*): Well you'll lie down then, what the hell! Or you'll come to a standstill, simply stop and stand still, the way you are now. One day you'll say, I'm tired. I'll stop. What does the attitude matter?

(*Pause.*)

CLOV: So you all want me to leave you.

HAMM: Naturally.

CLOV: Then I'll leave you.

HAMM: You can't leave us.

CLOV: Then I won't leave you.

(*Pause.*)

HAMM: Why don't you finish us?

(*Pause.*)

I'll tell you the combination of the cupboard if you promise to finish me.

CLOV: I couldn't finish you.

HAMM: Then you won't finish me.

(*Pause.*)

CLOV: I'll leave you, I have things to do.

HAMM: Do you remember when you came here?

CLOV: No. Too small, you told me.

HAMM: Do you remember your father?

CLOV (*wearily*): Same answer.

(*Pause.*)

You've asked me these questions millions of times.

HAMM: I love the old questions.

(*With fervour.*)

Ah the old questions, the old answers, there's nothing like them!

(*Pause.*)

It was I was a father to you.

CLOV: Yes.

(*He looks at* HAMM *fixedly.*)

You were that to me.

HAMM: My house a home for you.

CLOV: Yes.

(*He looks about him.*)

This was that for me.

HAMM (*proudly*): But for me, (*Gesture towards himself.*) no father. But for Hamm, (*Gesture towards surroundings.*) no home.

(*Pause.*)

CLOV: I'll leave you.

HAMM: Did you ever think of one thing?

CLOV: Never.

HAMM: That here we're down in a hole.

(Pause.)

But beyond the hills? Eh? Perhaps it's still green. Eh?

(Pause.)

Flora! Pomona!

(Ecstatically.)

Ceres!

(Pause.)

Perhaps you won't need to go very far.

CLOV: I can't go very far.

(Pause.)

I'll leave you.

HAMM: Is my dog ready?

CLOV: He lacks a leg.

HAMM: Is he silky?

CLOV: He's a kind of Pomeranian.

HAMM: Go and get him.

CLOV: He lacks a leg.

HAMM: Go and get him!

(Exit CLOV.)

We're getting on.

(Enter CLOV holding by one of its three legs a black toy dog.)

CLOV: Your dogs are here.

(He hands the dog to HAMM who feels it, fondles it.)

HAMM: He's white, isn't he?

CLOV: Nearly.

HAMM: What do you mean, nearly? Is he white or isn't he?

CLOV: He isn't.

(Pause.)

HAMM: You've forgotten the sex.

CLOV (vexed): But he isn't finished. The sex goes at the end.

(Pause.)

HAMM: You haven't put on his ribbon.

CLOV (angrily): But he isn't finished, I tell you! First you finish your dog and then you put on his ribbon!

(Pause.)

HAMM: Can he stand?

CLOV: I don't know.

HAMM: Try.

(He hands the dog to CLOV who places it on the ground.)

Well?

CLOV: Wait!

(He squats down and tries to get the dog to stand on its three legs, fails, lets it go. The dog falls on its side.)

HAMM (impatiently): Well?

CLOV: He's standing.

HAMM (groping for the dog): Where? Where is he?

(CLOV holds up the dog in a standing position.)

CLOV: There.

(He takes HAMM's hand and guides it towards the dog's head.)

HAMM (his hand on the dog's head): Is he gazing at me?

CLOV: Yes.

HAMM (proudly): As if he were asking me to take him for a walk?

CLOV: If you like.

HAMM (as before): Or as if he were begging me for a bone.

(He withdraws his hand.)

Leave him like that, standing there imploring me.

(CLOV straightens up. The dog falls on its side.)

CLOV: I'll leave you.

HAMM: Have you had your visions?

CLOV: Less.

HAMM: Is Mother Pegg's light on?

CLOV: Light! How could anyone's light be on?

HAMM: Extinguished!

CLOV: Naturally it's extinguished. If it's not on it's extinguished.

HAMM: No, I mean Mother Pegg.

CLOV: But naturally she's extinguished!

(Pause.)

What's the matter with you today?

HAMM: I'm taking my course.

(Pause.)

Is she buried?

CLOV: Buried! Who would have buried her?

HAMM: You.

CLOV: Me! Haven't I enough to do without burying people?

HAMM: But you'll bury me.

CLOV: No I won't bury you.

(Pause.)

HAMM: She was bonny once, like a flower of the field.

(With reminiscent leer.)

And a great one for the men!

CLOV: We too were bonny—once. It's a rare thing not to have been bonny—once.

(Pause.)

HAMM: Go and get the gaff.

(CLOV goes to door, halts.)

CLOV: Do this, do that, and I do it. I never refuse. Why?
HAMM: You're not able to.
CLOV: Soon I won't do it any more.
HAMM: You won't be able to any more.

(Exit CLOV.)

Ah the creatures, the creatures, everything has to be explained to them.

(Enter CLOV with gaff.)

CLOV: Here's your gaff. Stick it up.

(He gives the gaff to HAMM who, wielding it like a punt-pole, tries to move his chair.)

HAMM: Did I move?
CLOV: No.

(HAMM throws down the gaff.)

HAMM: Go and get the oilcan.
CLOV: What for?
HAMM: To oil the castors.
CLOV: I oiled them yesterday.
HAMM: Yesterday! What does that mean? Yesterday!
CLOV *(violently)*: That means that bloody awful day long ago, before this bloody awful day. I use the words you taught me. If they don't mean anything any more, teach me others. Or let me be silent.

(Pause.)

HAMM: I once knew a madman who thought the end of the world had come. He was a painter—and engraver. I had a great fondness for him. I used to go and see him, in the asylum. I'd take him by the hand and drag him to the window. Look! There! All that rising corn! And there! Look! The sails of the herring fleet! All that loveliness!

(Pause.)

He'd snatch away his hand and go back into his corner. Appalled. All he had seen was ashes.

(Pause.)

He alone had been spared.

(Pause.)

Forgotten.

(Pause.)

It appears the case is . . . was not so . . . so unusual.
CLOV: A madman? When was that?

HAMM: Oh way back, way back, you weren't in the land of the living.
CLOV: God be with the days!

(Pause. HAMM raises his toque.)

HAMM: I had a great fondness for him.

(Pause. He puts on his toque again.)

He was a painter—and engraver.
CLOV: There are so many terrible things.
HAMM No, no, there are not so many now.

(Pause.)

Clov!
CLOV: Yes.
HAMM: Do you not think this has gone on long enough?
CLOV: Yes!

(Pause.)

What?
HAMM: This . . . this . . . thing.
CLOV: I've always thought so.

(Pause.)

You not?
HAMM *(gloomily)*: Then it's a day like any other day.
CLOV: As long as it lasts.

(Pause.)

All life long the same inanities.
HAMM: I can't leave you.
CLOV: I know. And you can't follow me.

(Pause.)

HAMM: If you leave me how shall I know?
CLOV *(briskly)*: Well you simply whistle me and if I don't come running it means I've left you.

(Pause.)

HAMM: You won't come and kiss me goodbye?
CLOV: Oh I shouldn't think so.

(Pause.)

HAMM: But you might be merely dead in your kitchen.
CLOV: The result would be the same.
HAMM: Yes, but how would I know, if you were merely dead in your kitchen?
CLOV: Well . . . sooner or later I'd start to stink.
HAMM: You stink already. The whole place stinks of corpses.
CLOV: The whole universe.
HAMM *(angrily)*: To hell with the universe.

(Pause.)

Think of something.
CLOV: What?
HAMM: An idea, have an idea.

(Angrily.)

A bright idea!

CLOV: Ah good.

(*He starts pacing to and fro, his eyes fixed on the ground, his hands behind his back. He halts.*)

The pains in my legs! It's unbelievable! Soon I won't be able to think any more.

HAMM: You won't be able to leave me.

(CLOV *resumes his pacing.*)

What are you doing?

CLOV: Having an idea.

(*He paces.*)

Ah!

(*He halts.*)

HAMM: What a brain!

(*Pause.*)

Well?

CLOV: Wait!

(*He meditates. Not very convinced.*)

Yes . . .

(*Pause. More convinced.*)

Yes!

(*He raises his head.*)

I have it! I set the alarm.

(*Pause.*)

HAMM: This is perhaps not one of my bright days, but frankly—

CLOV: You whistle me. I don't come. The alarm rings. I'm gone. It doesn't ring. I'm dead.

(*Pause.*)

HAMM: Is it working?

(*Pause. Impatiently.*)

The alarm, is it working?

CLOV: Why wouldn't it be working?

HAMM: Because it's worked too much.

CLOV: But it's hardly worked at all.

HAMM (*angrily*): Then because it's worked too little!

CLOV: I'll go and see.

(*Exit* CLOV. *Brief ring of alarm off. Enter* CLOV *with alarm-clock. He holds it against* HAMM*'s ear and releases alarm. They listen to it ringing to the end. Pause.*)

Fit to wake the dead! Did you hear it?

HAMM: Vaguely.

CLOV: The end is terrific!

HAMM: I prefer the middle.

(*Pause.*)

Is it not time for my pain-killer?

CLOV: No!

(*He goes to door, turns.*)

I'll leave you.

HAMM: It's time for my story. Do you want to listen to my story.

CLOV: No.

HAMM: Ask my father if he wants to listen to my story.

(CLOV *goes to bins, raises the lid of* NAGG*'s, stoops, looks into it. Pause. He straightens up.*)

CLOV: He's asleep.

HAMM: Wake him.

(CLOV *stoops, wakes* NAGG *with the alarm. Unintelligible words.* CLOV *straightens up.*)

CLOV: He doesn't want to listen to your story.

HAMM: I'll give him a bon-bon.

(CLOV *stoops. As before.*)

CLOV: He wants a sugar-plum.

HAMM: He'll get a sugar-plum.

(CLOV *stoops. As before.*)

CLOV: It's a deal.

(*He goes toward door.* NAGG*'s hands appear, gripping the rim. Then the head emerges.* CLOV *reaches door, turns.*)

Do you believe in the life to come?

HAMM: Mine was always that.

(*Exit* CLOV.)

Got him that time!

NAGG: I'm listening.

HAMM: Scoundrel! Why did you engender me?

NAGG: I didn't know.

HAMM: What? What didn't you know?

NAGG: That it'd be you.

(*Pause.*)

You'll give me a sugar-plum?

HAMM: After the audition.

NAGG: You swear?

HAMM: Yes.

NAGG: On what?

HAMM: My honor.

(*Pause. They laugh heartily.*)

NAGG: Two.

HAMM: One.

NAGG: One for me and one for—

HAMM: One! Silence!

(*Pause.*)

Where was I?

(*Pause. Gloomily.*)

It's finished, we're finished.

(Pause.)

Nearly finished.

(Pause.)

There'll be no more speech.

(Pause.)

Something dripping in my head, ever since the fontanelles.

(Stifled hilarity of NAGG.)

Splash, splash, always on the same spot.

(Pause.)

Perhaps it's a little vein.

(Pause.)

A little artery.

(Pause. More animated.)

Enough of that, it's story time, where was I?

(Pause. Narrative tone.)

The man came crawling towards me, on his belly. Pale, wonderfully pale and thin, he seemed on the point of—

(Pause. Normal tone.)

No, I've done that bit.

(Pause. Narrative tone.)

I calmly filled my pipe—the meerschaum, lit it with . . . let us say a vesta, drew a few puffs. Aah!

(Pause.)

Well, what is it you want?

(Pause.)

It was an extra-ordinarily bitter day, I remember, zero by the thermometer. But considering it was Christmas Eve there was nothing . . . extra-ordinary about that. Seasonable weather, for once in a way.

(Pause.)

Well, what ill wind blows you my way? He raised his face to me, black with mingled dirt and tears.

(Pause. Normal tone.)

That should do it.

(Narrative tone.)

No, no, don't look at me, don't look at me. He dropped his eyes and mumbled something, apologies I presume.

(Pause.)

I'm a busy man, you know, the final touches, before the festivities. You know what it is.

(Pause. Forcibly.)

Come on now, what is the object of this invasion?

(Pause.)

It was a glorious bright day, I remember, fifty by the heliometer, but already the sun was sinking down into the . . . down among the dead.

(Normal tone.)

Nicely put, that.

(Narrative tone.)

Come on now, come on, present your petition and let me resume my labors.

(Pause. Normal tone.)

There's English for you. Ah well . . .

(Narrative tone.)

It was then he took the plunge. It's my little one, he said. Tsstss, a little one, that's bad. My little boy, he said, as if the sex mattered. Where did he come from? He named the hole. A good half-day, on horse. What are you insinuating? That the place is still inhabited? No, no, not a soul except himself and the child—assuming he existed. Good. I enquired about the situation at Kov, beyond the gulf. Not a sinner. Good. And you expect me to believe you have left your little one back there, all alone, and alive into the bargain? Come now!

(Pause.)

It was a howling wild day, I remember, a hundred by the anenometer. The wind was tearing up the dead pines and sweeping them . . . away.

(Pause. Normal tone.)

A bit feeble, that.

(Narrative tone.)

Come on, man, speak up, what is it you want from me. I have to put up my holly.

(Pause.)

Well to make it short it finally transpired that what he wanted from me was . . . bread for his brat? Bread? But I have no bread, it doesn't agree with me. Good. Then perhaps a little corn?

(Pause. Normal tone.)

That should do it.

(Narrative tone.)

Corn, yes, I have corn, it's true, in my granaries. But use your head. I give you some corn, a pound, a pound and a half, you bring it back to your child and you make him—if he's still alive—a nice pot of porridge,

(NAGG *reacts.*)

a nice pot and a half of porridge, full of nourishment. Good. The colors come back into his little cheeks—perhaps. And then?

(*Pause.*)

I lost patience.

(*Violently.*)

Use your head, can't you, use your head, you're on earth, there's no cure for that!

(*Pause.*)

It was an exceedingly dry day, I remember, zero by the hygrometer. Ideal weather, for my lumbago.

(*Pause. Violently.*)

But what in God's name do you imagine? That the earth will awake in spring? That the rivers and seas will run with fish again? That there's manna in heaven still for imbeciles like you?

(*Pause.*)

Gradually I cooled down, sufficiently at least to ask him how long he had taken on the way. Three whole days. Good. In what condition he had left the child. Deep in sleep.

(*Forcibly.*)

But deep in what sleep, deep in what sleep already?

(*Pause.*)

Well to make it short I finally offered to take him into my service. He had touched a chord. And then I imagined already that I wasn't much longer for this world.

(*He laughs. Pause.*)

Well?

(*Pause.*)

Well? Here if you were careful you might die a nice natural death, in peace and comfort.

(*Pause.*)

Well?

(*Pause.*)

In the end he asked me would I consent to take in the child as well—if he were still alive.

(*Pause.*)

It was the moment I was waiting for.

(*Pause.*)

Would I consent to take the child . . .

(*Pause.*)

I can see him still, down on his knees, his hands flat on the ground, glaring at me with his mad eyes, in defiance of my wishes.

(*Pause. Normal tone.*)

I'll soon have finished with this story.

(*Pause.*)

Unless I bring in other characters.

(*Pause.*)

But where would I find them?

(*Pause.*)

Where would I look for them?

(*Pause. He whistles. Enter* CLOV.)

Let us pray to God.

NAGG: Me sugar-plum!

CLOV: There's a rat in the kitchen!

HAMM: A rat! Are there still rats?

CLOV: In the kitchen there's one.

HAMM: And you haven't exterminated him?

CLOV: Half. You disturbed us.

HAMM: He can't get away?

CLOV: No.

HAMM: You'll finish him later. Let us pray to God.

CLOV: Again!

NAGG: Me sugar-plum!

HAMM: God first!

(*Pause.*)

Are you right?

CLOV (*resigned*): Off we go.

HAMM (*to* NAGG): And you?

NAGG (*clasping his hands, closing his eyes, in a gabble*): Our Father which art—

HAMM: Silence! In silence! Where are your manners?

(*Pause.*)

Off we go.

(*Attitudes of prayer. Silence. Abandoning his attitude, discouraged.*)

Well?

CLOV (*abandoning his attitude*): What a hope! And you?

HAMM: Sweet damn all! (*to* NAGG) And you?

NAGG: Wait!

(*Pause. Abandoning his attitude.*)

Nothing doing!

HAMM: The bastard! He doesn't exist!

CLOV: Not yet.

NAGG: Me sugar-plum!

HAMM: There are no more sugar-plums!

(Pause.)

NAGG: It's natural. After all I'm your father. It's true if it hadn't been me it would have been someone else. But that's no excuse.

(Pause.)

Turkish Delight, for example, which no longer exists, we all know that, there is nothing in the world I love more. And one day I'll ask you for some, in return for a kindness, and you'll promise it to me. One must live with the times.

(Pause.)

Whom did you call when you were a tiny boy, and were frightened, in the dark? Your mother? No. Me. We let you cry. Then we moved you out of earshot, so that we might sleep in peace.

(Pause.)

I was asleep, as happy as a king, and you woke me up to have me listen to you. It wasn't indispensable, you didn't really need to have me listen to you.

(Pause.)

I hope the day will come when you'll really need to have me listen to you, and need to hear my voice, any voice.

(Pause.)

Yes, I hope I'll live till then, to hear you calling me like when you were a tiny boy, and were frightened, in the dark, and I was your only hope.

(Pause. NAGG knocks on lid of NELL's bin. Pause.)

Nell!

(Pause. He knocks louder. Pause. Louder.)

Nell!

(Pause. NAGG sinks back into his bin, closes the lid behind him. Pause.)

HAMM: Our revels now are ended.

(He gropes for the dog.)

The dog's gone.

CLOV: He's not a real dog, he can't go.

HAMM *(groping)*: He's not there.

CLOV: He's lain down.

HAMM: Give him to me.

(CLOV picks up the dog and gives it to HAMM. HAMM holds it in his arms. Pause. HAMM throws away the dog.)

Dirty brute!

(CLOV begins to pick up the objects lying on the ground.)

What are you doing?

CLOV: Putting things in order.

(He straightens up. Fervently.)

I'm going to clear everything away!

(He starts picking up again.)

HAMM: Order!

CLOV *(straightening up)*: I love order. It's my dream. A world where all would be silent and still and each thing in its last place, under the last dust.

(He starts picking up again.)

HAMM *(exasperated)*: What in God's name do you think you are doing?

CLOV *(straightening up)*: I'm doing my best to create a little order.

HAMM: Drop it!

(CLOV drops the objects he has picked up.)

CLOV: After all, there or elsewhere.

(He goes towards door.)

HAMM *(irritably)*: What's wrong with your feet?

CLOV: My feet?

HAMM: Tramp! Tramp!

CLOV: I must have put on my boots.

HAMM: Your slippers were hurting you?

(Pause.)

CLOV: I'll leave you.

HAMM: No!

CLOV: What is there to keep me here?

HAMM: The dialogue.

(Pause.)

I've got on with my story.

(Pause.)

I've got on with it well.

(Pause. Irritably.)

Ask me where I've got to.

CLOV: Oh, by the way, your story?

HAMM *(surprised)*: What story?

CLOV: The one you've been telling yourself all your days.

HAMM: Ah you mean my chronicle?

CLOV: That's the one.

(Pause.)

HAMM *(angrily)*: Keep going, can't you, keep going!

CLOV: You've got on with it, I hope.

HAMM *(modestly)*: Oh not very far, not very far.

(He sighs.)

There are days like that, one isn't inspired.

(Pause.)

Nothing you can do about it, just wait for it to come.

(Pause.)

No forcing, no forcing, it's fatal.

(Pause.)

I've got on with it a little all the same.

(Pause.)

Technique, you know.

(Pause. Irritably.)

I say I've got on with it a little all the same.

CLOV *(admiringly)*: Well I never! In spite of everything you were able to get on with it!

HAMM *(modestly)*: Oh not very far, you know, not very far, but nevertheless, better than nothing.

CLOV: Better than nothing! Is it possible?

HAMM: I'll tell you how it goes. He comes crawling on his belly—

CLOV: Who?

HAMM: What?

CLOV: Who do you mean, he?

HAMM: Who do I mean! Yet another.

CLOV: Ah him! I wasn't sure.

HAMM: Crawling on his belly, whining for bread for his brat. He's offered a job as gardener. Before—

(CLOV bursts out laughing.)

What is there so funny about that?

CLOV: A job as gardener!

HAMM: Is that what tickles you?

CLOV: It must be that.

HAMM: It wouldn't be the bread?

CLOV: Or the brat.

(Pause.)

HAMM: The whole thing is comical, I grant you that. What about having a good guffaw the two of us together?

CLOV *(after reflection)*: I couldn't guffaw again today.

HAMM *(after reflection)*: Nor I.

(Pause.)

I continue then. Before accepting with gratitude he asks if he may have his little boy with him.

CLOV: What age?

HAMM: Oh tiny.

CLOV: He would have climbed the trees.

HAMM: All the little odd jobs.

CLOV: And then he would have grown up.

HAMM: Very likely.

(Pause.)

CLOV: Keep going, can't you, keep going!

HAMM: That's all. I stopped there.

(Pause.)

CLOV: Do you see how it goes on.

HAMM: More or less.

CLOV: Will it not soon be the end?

HAMM: I'm afraid it will.

CLOV: Pah! You'll make up another.

HAMM: I don't know.

(Pause.)

I feel rather drained.

(Pause.)

The prolonged creative effort.

(Pause.)

If I could drag myself down to the sea! I'd make a pillow of sand for my head and the tide would come.

CLOV: There's no more tide.

(Pause.)

HAMM: Go and see is she dead.

(CLOV goes to bins, raises the lid of NELL's, stoops, looks into it. Pause.)

CLOV: Looks like it.

(He closes the lid, straightens up. HAMM raises his toque. Pause. He puts it on again.)

HAMM *(with his hand to his toque)*: And Nagg?

(CLOV raises lid of NAGG's bin, stoops, looks into it. Pause.)

CLOV: Doesn't look like it.

(He closes the lid, straightens up.)

HAMM *(letting go his toque)*: What's he doing?

(CLOV raises lid of NAGG's bin, stoops, looks into it. Pause.)

CLOV: He's crying.

(He closes lid, straightens up.)

HAMM: Then he's living.

(Pause.)

Did you ever have an instant of happiness?

CLOV: Not to my knowledge.

(Pause.)

HAMM: Bring me under the window.

(CLOV goes towards chair.)

I want to feel the light on my face.

(CLOV *pushes chair.*)

Do you remember, in the beginning, when you took me for a turn? You used to hold the chair too high. At every step you nearly tipped me out.

(*With senile quaver.*)

Ah great fun, we had, the two of us, great fun.

(*Gloomily.*)

And then we got into the way of it.

(CLOV *stops the chair under window right.*)

There already?

(*Pause. He tilts back his head.*)

Is it light?
CLOV: It isn't dark.
HAMM (*angrily*): I'm asking you is it light.
CLOV: Yes.

(*Pause.*)

HAMM: The curtain isn't closed?
CLOV: No.
HAMM: What window is it?
CLOV: The earth.
HAMM: I knew it!

(*Angrily.*)

But there's no light there! The other!

(CLOV *pushes the chair towards window left.*)

The earth!

(CLOV *stops the chair under window left.* HAMM *tilts back his head.*)

That's what I call light!

(*Pause.*)

Feels like a ray of sunshine.

(*Pause.*)

No?
CLOV: No.
HAMM: It isn't a ray of sunshine I feel on my face?
CLOV: No.

(*Pause.*)

HAMM: Am I very white?

(*Pause. Angrily.*)

I'm asking you am I very white!
CLOV: Not more so than usual.

(*Pause.*)

HAMM: Open the window.
CLOV: What for?

HAMM: I want to hear the sea.
CLOV: You wouldn't hear it.
HAMM: Even if you opened the window?
CLOV: No.
HAMM: Then it's not worthwhile opening it?
CLOV: No.
HAMM (*violently*): Then open it!

(CLOV *gets up on the ladder, opens the window. Pause.*)

Have you opened it?
CLOV: Yes.

(*Pause.*)

HAMM: You swear you've opened it?
CLOV: Yes.

(*Pause.*)

HAMM: Well . . . !

(*Pause.*)

It must be very calm.

(*Pause. Violently.*)

I'm asking you is it very calm!
CLOV: Yes.
HAMM: It's because there are no more navigators.

(*Pause.*)

You haven't much conversation all of a sudden. Do you not feel well?
CLOV: I'm cold.
HAMM: What month are we?

(*Pause.*)

Close the window, we're going back.

(CLOV *closes the window, gets down, pushes the chair back to its place, remains standing behind it, head bowed.*)

Don't stay there, you give me the shivers!

(CLOV *returns to his place beside the chair.*)

Father!

(*Pause. Louder.*)

Father!

(*Pause.*)

Go and see did he hear me.

(CLOV *goes to* NAGG's *bin, raises the lid, stoops. Unintelligible words.* CLOV *straightens up.*)

CLOV: Yes.
HAMM: Both times?

(CLOV *stoops. As before.*)

CLOV: Once only.
HAMM: The first time or the second?

(CLOV *stoops. As before.*)

CLOV: He doesn't know.

HAMM: It must have been the second.

CLOV: We'll never know.

(*He closes lid.*)

HAMM: Is he still crying?

CLOV: No.

HAMM: The dead go fast.

(*Pause.*)

What's he doing?

CLOV: Sucking his biscuit.

HAMM: Life goes on.

(CLOV *returns to his place beside the chair.*)

Give me a rug, I'm freezing.

CLOV: There are no more rugs.

(*Pause.*)

HAMM: Kiss me.

(*Pause.*)

Will you not kiss me?

CLOV: No.

HAMM: On the forehead.

CLOV: I won't kiss you anywhere.

(*Pause.*)

HAMM (*holding out his hand*): Give me your hand at least.

(*Pause.*)

Will you not give me your hand?

CLOV: I won't touch you.

(*Pause.*)

HAMM: Give me the dog.

(CLOV *looks round for the dog.*)

No!

CLOV: Do you not want your dog?

HAMM: No.

CLOV: Then I'll leave you.

HAMM (*head bowed, absently*): That's right.

(CLOV *goes to door, turns.*)

CLOV: If I don't kill that rat he'll die.

HAMM (*as before*): That's right.

(*Exit* CLOV. *Pause.*)

Me to play.

(*He takes out his handkerchief, unfolds it, holds it spread out before him.*)

We're getting on.

(*Pause.*)

You weep, and weep, for nothing, so as not to laugh, and little by little . . . you begin to grieve.

(*He folds the handkerchief, he puts it back in his pocket, raises his head.*)

All those I might have helped.

(*Pause.*)

Helped!

(*Pause.*)

Saved.

(*Pause.*)

Saved!

(*Pause.*)

The place was crawling with them!

(*Pause. Violently.*)

Use your head, can't you, use your head, you're on earth, there's no cure for that!

(*Pause.*)

Get out of here and love one another! Lick your neighbor as yourself!

(*Pause. Calmer.*)

When it wasn't bread they wanted it was crumpets.

(*Pause. Violently.*)

Out of my sight and back to your petting parties!

(*Pause.*)

All that, all that!

(*Pause.*)

Not even a real dog!

(*Calmer.*)

The end is in the beginning and yet you go on.

(*Pause.*)

Perhaps I could go on with my story, end it and begin another.

(*Pause.*)

Perhaps I could throw myself out on the floor.

(*He pushes himself painfully off his seat, falls back again.*)

Dig my nails into the cracks and drag myself forward with my fingers.

(*Pause.*)

It will be the end and there I'll be, wondering what can have brought it on and wondering what can have . . . *(He hesitates.)* . . . why it was so long coming.

(Pause.)

There I'll be, in the old shelter, alone against the silence and . . . *(He hesitates.)* . . . the stillness. If I can hold my peace, and sit quiet, it will be all over with sound, and motion, all over and done with.

(Pause.)

I'll have called my father and I'll have called my . . . *(He hesitates.)* . . . my son. And even twice, or three times, in case they shouldn't have heard me, the first time, or the second.

(Pause.)

I'll say to myself. He'll come back.

(Pause.)

And then?

(Pause.)

And then?

(Pause.)

He couldn't, he has gone too far.

(Pause.)

And then?

(Pause. Very agitated.)

All kinds of fantasies! That I'm being watched! A rat! Steps! Breath held and then . . .

(He breathes out.)

Then babble, babble, words, like the solitary child who turns himself into children, two, three, so as to be together, and whisper together in the dark.

(Pause.)

Moment upon moment, pattering down, like the millet grains of . . . *(He hesitates.)* . . . that old Greek, and all life long you wait for that to mount up to a life.

(Pause. He opens his mouth to continue, renounces.)

Ah let's get it over!

(He whistles. Enter CLOV with alarm-clock. He halts beside the chair.)

What? Neither gone nor dead?

CLOV: In spirit only.
HAMM: Which?
CLOV: Both.
HAMM: Gone from me you'd be dead.

CLOV: And vice versa.
HAMM: Outside of here it's death!

(Pause.)

And the rat?
CLOV: He's got away.
HAMM: He can't go far.

(Pause. Anxious.)

Eh?
CLOV: He doesn't need to go far.

(Pause.)

HAMM: Is it not time for my pain-killer?
CLOV: Yes.
HAMM: Ah! At last! Give it to me! Quick!

(Pause.)

CLOV: There's no more pain-killer.

(Pause.)

HAMM *(appalled)*: Good . . . !

(Pause.)

No more pain-killer!
CLOV: No more pain-killer. You'll never get any more pain-killer.

(Pause.)

HAMM: But the little round box. It was full!
CLOV: Yes. But now it's empty.

(Pause. CLOV starts to move about the room. He is looking for a place to put down the alarm-clock.)

HAMM *(soft)*: What'll I do?

(Pause. In a scream.)

What'll I do?

(CLOV sees the picture, takes it down, stands it on the floor with its face to the wall, hangs up the alarm-clock in its place.)

What are you doing?
CLOV: Winding up.
HAMM: Look at the earth.
CLOV: Again!
HAMM: Since it's calling to you.
CLOV: Is your throat sore?

(Pause.)

Would you like a lozenge?

(Pause.)

No.

(Pause.)

Pity.

(CLOV *goes, humming, towards window right, halts before it, looks up at it.*)

HAMM: Don't sing.

CLOV (*turning towards* HAMM): One hasn't the right to sing any more?

HAMM: No.

CLOV: Then how can it end?

HAMM: You want it to end?

CLOV: I want to sing.

HAMM: I can't prevent you.

(*Pause.* CLOV *turns towards window right.*)

CLOV: What did I do with that steps?

(*He looks around for ladder.*)

You didn't see that steps?

(*He sees it.*)

Ah, about time.

(*He goes towards window left.*)

Sometimes I wonder if I'm in my right mind. Then it passes over and I'm as lucid as before.

(*He gets up on ladder, looks out of window.*)

Christ, she's under water!

(*He looks.*)

How can that be?

(*He pokes forward his head, his hand above his eyes.*)

It hasn't rained.

(*He wipes the pane, looks. Pause.*)

Ah what a fool I am! I'm on the wrong side!

(*He gets down, takes a few steps towards window right.*)

Under water!

(*He goes back for ladder.*)

What a fool I am!

(*He carries ladder towards window right.*)

Sometimes I wonder if I'm in my right senses. Then it passes off and I'm as intelligent as ever.

(*He sets down ladder under window right, gets up on it, looks out of window. He turns towards* HAMM.)

Any particular sector you fancy? Or merely the whole thing?

HAMM: Whole thing.

CLOV: The general effect? Just a moment.

(*He looks out of window. Pause.*)

HAMM: Clov.

CLOV (*absorbed*): Mmm.

HAMM: Do you know what it is?

CLOV (*as before*): Mmm.

HAMM: I was never there.

(*Pause.*)

Clov!

CLOV (*turning towards* HAMM, *exasperated*): What is it?

HAMM: I was never there.

CLOV: Lucky for you.

(*He looks out of window.*)

HAMM: Absent, always. It all happened without me. I don't know what's happened.

(*Pause.*)

Do you know what's happened?

(*Pause.*)

Clov!

CLOV (*turning towards* HAMM, *exasperated*): Do you want me to look at this muckheap, yes or no?

HAMM: Answer me first.

CLOV: What?

HAMM: Do you know what's happened?

CLOV: When? Where?

HAMM (*violently*): When! What's happened? Use your head, can't you? What has happened?

CLOV: What for Christ's sake does it matter?

(*He looks out of window.*)

HAMM: I don't know.

(*Pause.* CLOV *turns towards* HAMM.)

CLOV (*harshly*): When old Mother Pegg asked you for oil for her lamp and you told her to get out to hell, you knew what was happening then, no?

(*Pause.*)

You know what she died of, Mother Pegg? Of darkness.

HAMM (*feebly*): I hadn't any.

CLOV (*as before*): Yes, you had.

(*Pause.*)

HAMM: Have you the glass?

CLOV: No, it's clear enough as it is.

HAMM: Go and get it.

(*Pause.* CLOV *casts up his eyes, brandishes his fists. He loses balance, clutches on to the ladder. He starts to get down, halts.*)

CLOV: There's one thing I'll never understand.

(*He gets down.*)

Why I always obey you. Can you explain that to me?

HAMM: No. . . . Perhaps it's compassion.

(*Pause.*)

A kind of compassion.

(Pause.)

Oh you won't find it easy, you won't find it easy.

(Pause. CLOV begins to move about the room in search of the telescope.)

CLOV: I'm tired of our goings on, very tired.

(He searches.)

You're not sitting on it?

(He moves the chair, looks at the place where it stood, resumes his search.)

HAMM (anguished): Don't leave me there!

(Angrily CLOV restores the chair to its place.)

Am I right in the center?

CLOV: You'd need a microscope to find this—

(He sees the telescope.)

Ah, about time.

(He picks up the telescope, gets up on the ladder, turns the telescope on the without.)

HAMM: Give me the dog.

CLOV (looking): Quiet!

HAMM (angrily): Give me the dog!

(CLOV drops the telescope, clasps his hands to his head. Pause. He gets down precipitately, looks for the dog, sees it, picks it up, hastens towards HAMM and strikes him violently on the head with the dog.)

CLOV: There's your dog for you!

(The dog falls to the ground. Pause.)

HAMM: He hit me!

CLOV: You drive me mad, I'm mad!

HAMM: If you must hit me, hit me with the axe.

(Pause.)

Or with the gaff, hit me with the gaff. Not with the dog. With the gaff. Or with the axe.

(CLOV picks up the dog and gives it to HAMM who takes it in his arms.)

CLOV (imploringly): Let's stop playing!

HAMM: Never!

(Pause.)

Put me in my coffin.

CLOV: There are no more coffins.

HAMM: Then let it end!

(CLOV goes towards ladder.)

With a bang!

(CLOV gets up on ladder, gets down again, looks for telescope, sees it, picks it up, gets up on ladder, raises telescope.)

Of darkness! And me? Did anyone ever have pity on me?

CLOV (lowering the telescope, turning towards HAMM): What?

(Pause.)

Is it me you're referring to?

HAMM (angrily): An aside, ape! Did you never hear an aside before?

(Pause.)

I'm warming up for my last soliloquy.

CLOV: I warn you. I'm going to look at this filth since it's an order. But it's the last time.

(He turns the telescope on the without.)

Let's see.

(He moves the telescope.)

Nothing . . . nothing . . . good . . . good . . . nothing . . . goo—

(He starts, lowers the telescope, examines it, turns it again on the without. Pause.)

Bad luck to it!

HAMM: More complications!

(CLOV gets down.)

Not an underplot, I trust.

(CLOV moves ladder nearer window, gets up on it, turns telescope on the without.)

CLOV (dismayed): Looks like a small boy!

HAMM (sarcastic): A small . . . boy!

CLOV: I'll go and see.

(He gets down, drops the telescope, goes towards door, turns.)

I'll take the gaff.

(He looks for the gaff, sees it, picks it up, hastens towards door.)

HAMM: No!

(CLOV halts.)

CLOV: No? A potential procreator?

HAMM: If he exists he'll die there or he'll come here. And if he doesn't . . .

(Pause.)

CLOV: You don't believe me? You think I'm inventing?

(Pause.)

HAMM: It's the end, Clov, we've come to the end. I don't need you any more.

(Pause.)

CLOV: Lucky for you.

(He goes towards door.)

HAMM: Leave me the gaff.

(CLOV gives him the gaff, goes towards door, halts, looks at alarm-clock, takes it down, looks round for a better place to put it, goes to bins, puts it on lid of NAGG's bin. Pause.)

CLOV: I'll leave you.

(He goes towards door.)

HAMM: Before you go . . .

(CLOV halts near door.)

. . . say something.

CLOV: There is nothing to say.

HAMM: A few words . . . to ponder . . . in my heart.

CLOV: Your heart!

HAMM: Yes.

(Pause. Forcibly.)

Yes!

(Pause.)

With the rest, in the end, the shadows, the murmurs, all the trouble, to end up with.

(Pause.)

Clov. . . . He never spoke to me. Then, in the end, before he went, without my having asked him, he spoke to me. He said . . .

CLOV *(despairingly)*: Ah . . . !

HAMM: Something . . . from your heart.

CLOV: My heart!

HAMM: A few words . . . from your heart.

(Pause.)

CLOV *(fixed gaze, tonelessly, towards auditorium)*: They said to me, That's love, yes, yes, not a doubt, now you see how—

HAMM: Articulate!

CLOV *(as before)*: How easy it is. They said to me, That's friendship, yes, yes, no question, you've found it. They said to me, Here's the place, stop, raise your head and look at all that beauty. That order! They said to me, Come now, you're not a brute beast, think upon these things and you'll see how all becomes clear. And simple! They said to me, What skilled attention they get, all these dying of their wounds.

HAMM: Enough!

CLOV *(as before)*: I say to myself—sometimes, Clov, you must learn to suffer better than that if you want them to weary of punishing you—one day. I say to myself—sometimes, Clov, you must be there better than that if you want them to let you go—one

day. But I feel too old, and too far, to form new habits. Good, it'll never end, I'll never go.

(Pause.)

Then one day, suddenly, it ends, it changes, I don't understand, it dies, or it's me, I don't understand that either. I ask the words that remain—sleeping, waking, morning, evening. They have nothing to say.

(Pause.)

I open the door of the cell and go. I am so bowed I only see my feet, if I open my eyes, and between my legs a little trail of black dust. I say to myself that the earth is extinguished, though I never saw it lit.

(Pause.)

It's easy going.

(Pause.)

When I fall I'll weep for happiness.

(Pause. He goes towards door.)

HAMM: Clov!

(CLOV halts, without turning.)

Nothing.

(CLOV moves on.)

Clov!

(CLOV halts, without turning.)

CLOV: This is what we call making an exit.

HAMM: I'm obliged to you, Clov. For your services.

CLOV *(turning, sharply)*: Ah pardon, it's I am obliged to you.

HAMM: It's we are obliged to each other.

(Pause. CLOV goes towards door.)

One thing more.

(CLOV halts.)

A last favor.

(Exit CLOV.)

Cover me with the sheet.

(Long pause.)

No? Good.

(Pause.)

Me to play.

(Pause. Wearily.)

Old endgame lost of old, play and lose and have done with losing.

(*Pause. More animated.*)

    Let me see.

(*Pause.*)

    Ah yes!

(*He tries to move the chair, using the gaff as before. Enter* CLOV, *dressed for the road. Panama hat, tweed coat, raincoat over his arm, umbrella, bag. He halts by the door and stands there, impassive and motionless, his eyes are fixed on* HAMM, *till the end.* HAMM *gives up.*)

    Good.

(*Pause.*)

    Discard.

(*He throws away the gaff, makes to throw away the dog, thinks better of it.*)

    Take it easy.

(*Pause.*)

    And now?

(*Pause.*)

    Raise hat.

(*He raises his toque.*)

    Peace to our . . . arses.

(*Pause.*)

    And put on again.

(*He puts on his toque.*)

    Deuce.

(*Pauses. He takes off his glasses.*)

    Wipe.

(*He takes out his handkerchief and, without unfolding it, wipes his glasses.*)

    And put on again.

(*He puts on his glasses, puts back the handkerchief in his pocket.*)

    We're coming. A few more squirms like that and I'll call.

(*Pause.*)

    A little poetry.

(*Pause.*)

    You prayed—

(*Pause. He corrects himself.*)

    You CRIED for night; it comes—

(*Pause. He corrects himself.*)

    It FALLS: now cry in darkness.

(*He repeats, chanting.*)

    You cried for night; it falls: now cry in darkness.

(*Pause.*)

    Nicely put, that.

(*Pause.*)

    And now?

(*Pause.*)

    Moments for nothing, now as always, time was never and time is over, reckoning closed and story ended.

(*Pause. Narrative tone.*)

    If he could have his child with him. . . .

(*Pause.*)

    It was the moment I was waiting for.

(*Pause.*)

    You don't want to abandon him? You want him to bloom while you are withering? Be there to solace your last million last moments?

(*Pause.*)

    He doesn't realize, all he knows is hunger, and cold, and death to crown it all. But you! You ought to know what the earth is like, nowadays. Oh I put him before his responsibilities!

(*Pause. Normal tone.*)

    Well, there we are, there I am, that's enough.

(*He raises the whistle to his lips, hesitates, drops it. Pause.*)

    Yes, truly!

(*He whistles. Pause. Louder. Pause.*)

    Good.

(*Pause.*)

    Father!

(*Pause. Louder.*)

    Father!

(*Pause.*)

    Good.

(*Pause.*)

    We're coming.

(*Pause.*)

    And to end up with?

(Pause.)

Discard.

(He throws away the dog. He tears the whistle from his neck.)

With my compliments.

(He throws whistle towards auditorium. Pause. He sniffs. Soft.)

Clov!

(Long pause.)

No? Good.

(He takes out the handkerchief.)

Since that's the way we're playing it . . . *(He unfolds handkerchief.)* . . . let's play it that way . . . *(He unfolds.)* . . . and speak no more about it . . . *(He finishes unfolding.)* . . . speak no more.

(He holds handkerchief spread out before him.)

Old stancher!

(Pause.)

You . . . remain.

(Pause. He covers his face with handkerchief, lowers his arms to armrests, remains motionless.)

(Brief tableau.)

CURTAIN

Figure 1. Seated on his makeshift throne, Hamm (Ben Halley Jr.) pets the dog that Clov (John Bottoms, *standing*) has made for him. Behind them is a derelict subway car, part of Douglas Stein's set for the 1984 American Repertory Theatre production, directed by JoAnne Akalaitis. (Photograph: Richard Feldman.)

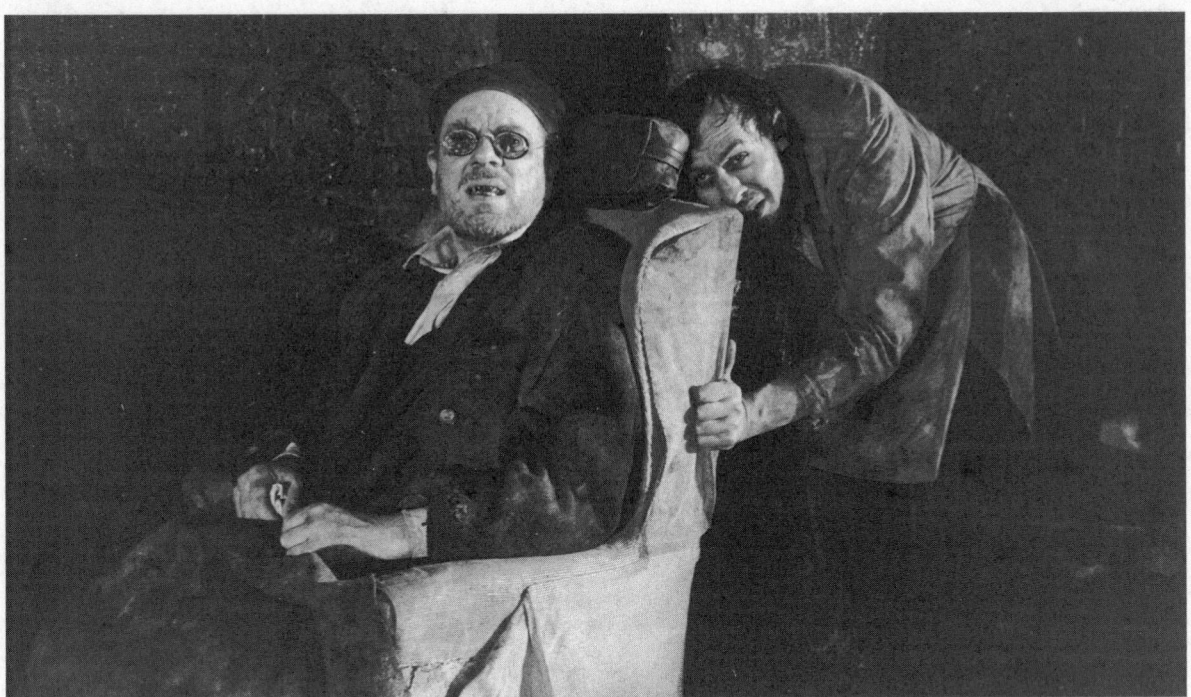

Figure 2. "Take me for a little turn," commands Hamm (Alun Armstrong), and the hunchbacked Clov (Stephen Dillane) laboriously complies, in the 1996 Donmar Warehouse production. (Photograph: Ivan Kyncl.)

Figure 3. Nagg (Harry Jones) and Nell (Eileen Nicholas) pop out of their trash cans to talk to each other, while Hamm (Alun Armstrong, *foreground*) listens. The 1996 production at the Donmar Warehouse, London, was directed by Katie Mitchell. (Photograph: Ivan Kyncl.)

Staging of *Endgame*

**REVIEW OF THE AMERICAN REPERTORY
THEATRE PRODUCTION, 1984,
BY MEL GUSSOW**

In absentia, Samuel Beckett has objected to JoAnne Akalaitis's production of "Endgame" at the American Repertory Theater on the grounds that it disregards his published stage directions. As Beckett writes in a note inserted in the program, "My play requires an empty room and two small windows."

That requirement is certainly the author's prerogative, but there is a problem in his evaluation of a production by proxy. For one thing, it overlooks Miss Akalaitis's reputation as a theater artist of intelligence and integrity, as she has demonstrated in productions of her own plays as well as adaptations of Beckett.

While keeping the author's objections in mind, one can appreciate Miss Akalaitis's production for its own Beckettian values. Through the screen of her imaginative impulses, "Endgame" speaks clearly and provocatively.

Though we can perceive two small windows in the distant reaches of the wide proscenium stage, Douglas Stein's set is the opposite of an empty room. It is an abandoned subway station, layered with trash as well as a derelict train, figuratively a subway car named despair. One could consider the set a visualization of what Clov refers to in the play as a "muckheap."

If we accept the metaphorical setting of the play to be a bunker in a world after the nuclear holocaust—a view that is supported in the text—then Miss Akalaitis could be credited with having made a defensible scenic interpretation. One man's cell could be another's graveyard.

Once having chosen her setting, the director uses it as prescribed by the author. Hamm sits still in a makeshift wheelchair—in this case, a platform on casters—and Clov scurries up and down ladders, peering out of the windows, describing the remains of civilization. To one side of the stage, in twin garbage cans, are Hamm's parents, Nagg and Nell, reduced to remnants of humanity.

The author has also objected to the use of music in the production, or in any production of one of his plays. Philip Glass, as eminent in the field of modern music as Miss Akalaitis is in modern theater, has written an overture rather than an orchestral score. It is played before the play begins, and occasionally reasserts itself in bursts of music to underline dramatic moments. The music is peripheral but support-

ive, a fierce scraping, like the sound—to extend the underground imagery—of a subway car careening off the track at high speed.

In other respects, the alterations are minimal. Briefly, Hamm and Clov freeze in their positions and we hear their voices on tape as from the subconscious. In another instance, a single order from Hamm is repeated three times. The director has not only respected the meaning of the dialogue, she has been attentive to the author's pauses, silences and intonations. While some other productions of "Endgame" have been freely elaborative, Americanizing Beckett or interrupting speeches for strobe-lighting effects, this is a valid representation of the spirit of the original work.

Hamm and Clov, master and servant, have been variously interpreted as Prospero and Caliban, or as an aged equivalent of Estragon and Vladimir. In Miss Akalaitis's production, it is two other characters from "Waiting for Godot" who are evoked—Pozzo and Lucky.

Ben Halley Jr.'s Hamm, a blind, immovable object, is every inch a dictator, and John Bottoms is a cringing slave, a bearer attached to his keeper by an invisible leash. He delivers some of his lines in a Lucky-like, stop-start style, a man brainwashed into subjugation. Mr. Halley falls short of Hamm's tragic dimension, but he does fill some lines with remembered passion. Dizzily obeying his master's whims, the bedraggled Mr. Bottoms is one of the most persuasive Clovs within my memory.

Rodney Hudson, as Nagg, affects a mocking drawl in response to his son's autocratic airs. This could be regarded as a variation on Hamm's description of his cast-off parents as "the old folks at home." Complementing Nagg, Shirley Wilber is a congenial Nell.

Clov, acting as commentator, suggests, "Something is taking its course," and that something is the end of the world. It is Hamm's decision to clamp a lid on his progenitors and to put an end to procreation. The view is bleak but tragicomic, as exemplified by Nell's famous line, "Nothing is funnier than unhappiness, I grant you that." Miss Akalaitis's approach to this contemporary masterwork is volatile. In her hands, "Endgame" has an intense dramatic drive as well as profundity.

REVIEW OF THE DONMAR WAREHOUSE
PRODUCTION, 1996, BY PAUL TAYLOR

Ever since the Beckett estate fell with punitive pedantry on Deborah Warner's staging of *Footfalls*,° I've found myself fantasising about ways you could produce his plays that would liberate them from the strait-jacket of his stage directions while not being untrue to the spirit or the significance of the works. How about *Happy Days* where the mound of earth in which Winnie is embedded had a different spatial relationship with the audience (brought right into its midst, say) in Act 2, by which time the mound has risen from waist to neck level? Or how about a version of *Endgame* that took place not in that dingy skull of a room, but on a plush, bourgeois stage set, thereby suggesting that the characters' bleakly terminal vision of external reality is a neurotically subjective one?

Too crude, perhaps. For, as Katie Mitchell's lovely, moving and strangely heartening Donmar Warehouse staging of *Endgame* establishes, you can sound different notes in this drama without altering the structure of the keyboard. Performed on a cellar-like set that is a veritable tone poem in greyness and grime, this is a production that finds a profound, pained humanity in a play Beckett called "more inhuman than *Godot*" and which he himself directed with the imagery of chess to the fore.

Mitchell does not undersell the music-hall-meets-the-Absurd comedy of the play nor its self-reflexive knowingness that it is a time-killing theatre event with a real-life audience. I've never seen the old running gag of Clov's having repeatedly to limp back for his

forgotten ladder performed with such hilarity as it is by Stephen Dillane who is an amazing humpbacked, effortfully shuffling Caliban to Alun Armstrong's paralysed, balefully Northern Prospero of a Hamm.

What the production ensures you notice, though, are the feelings each of these men keeps banked down in their deathly mutual dependency. There's an undertow of guilty self-disgust in Armstrong's wilful, snarling heartlessness and it's the terror of isolation, not the abject inconsistency, that hits you, when he asks Clov for a few words from the heart before he leaves. As Dillane demonstrated when he played Hamlet, he is a master at signalling a passionately sensitive, suffering soul through a barbedly ironic mildness of manner and a sort of stricken whimsy. He delivers Clov's lines in a light, soft, sometimes almost throwaway tone; it's as though he's so annoyed with Hamm he can hardly bear to address him and so depressed that words have come to seem a waste of breath. Yet you feel there's an enormous blighted potential for love and intimacy in this figure, though the blocking is such that the left hand side of the audience gets an enviably clearer view of him.

Harry Jones and Eileen Nicholas are the most affecting Nagg and Nell I have yet seen, playing this dust-binned duo as a pair of shrivelled senile Scots, who need one another to act as audience for rusty jokes and unreliable memories. "Nothing is funnier than unhappiness," opines Nell, but the laughter this raises, you feel here, need not be superior or heartless.

Deborah Warner, British director whose 1994 production of Beckett's *Footfalls* was stopped by the Beckett estate because she did not follow the text exactly.

EDWARD ALBEE

Twice in *The Zoo Story*, Jerry claims that "sometimes a person has to go a very long distance out of his way to come back a short distance correctly." In those two remarks, Jerry might well be speaking for his creator, Edward Albee, whose first theatrical success, *The Zoo Story*, which he wrote in 1958, was turned down by several New York producers. After circulating among friends, the play was first performed in Berlin in 1959, and only after its German success was finally produced in New York in January 1960. A strange theatrical beginning for someone who has subsequently come to be recognized as one of the most productive, compelling, and distinguished American dramatists of the twentieth century. Albee's early life also seems to have been marked by a complex blend of privilege and insecurity, of opportunity and failure, beginning with his adoption at two weeks old—he was thus a child both unwanted and wanted, a paradox he has returned to in several of his plays. Young Albee attended, and was dismissed from, three different prep schools before settling down at Choate, a prestigious Connecticut private school, where he published short stories, poems, and essays in the school literary magazine. He entered Trinity College in Connecticut in 1946 and took part in amateur theatrical groups, but was dismissed three semesters later. By 1948, Albee was living in New York City, working in a variety of jobs—office boy, sales clerk, luncheonette counterperson, and Western Union messenger. Yet because he was supported by a trust fund from his grandmother, he was able to travel to Italy in 1952, take time to write several unpublished plays, visit the McDowell Colony for writers, and study briefly at Columbia University.

Beginning with the world premiere of *The Zoo Story*, which won the Berlin Festival Award, Albee's theatrical career moved swiftly from one striking success to another, resulting in the production of four new plays in a single year, 1960. A double bill of *The Zoo Story* and Beckett's *Krapp's Last Tape* opened in January at the Provincetown Playhouse in New York's Greenwich Village and ran for 582 performances; in April, Albee had another premiere in Berlin, this time for *The Death of Bessie Smith*; in May, his 14-minute play, *The Sandbox*, opened at the Jazz Gallery in New York; and by the end of May, Albee received both the Obie (Off-Broadway) and Virginia Rice awards for *The Zoo Story*; in August, a sketch called *FAM and YAM*, a dialogue between a new playwright and a more established one, opened in Connecticut, and later was produced Off-Broadway. Then, just a year after the New York opening of *The Zoo Story*, Albee's *The American Dream*, a bitterly funny attack on the American family and its cruelty toward young and old, began a run of 360 performances at the York Theatre.

The capstone to this amazing record of successful new plays came with Albee's first full-length work, *Who's Afraid of Virginia Woolf?*, which opened on Broadway on October 13, 1962. The savage marital battles that Albee dramatizes in this major work compel his four characters, hosts George and Martha, as well as guests Nick and Honey, to spend the early hours of the morning drinking themselves into a frightening recognition of the truths about themselves and their marriages. Thus an evening that begins with "Fun and Games" (the title of the first act) turns into a "Walpurgisnacht" (the title of the second act, which refers to the orgiastic and nightmarish celebrations that once took place the evening before May Day), and concludes with "The Exorcism" (the title of the third and final act—an exorcism fraught with social and psychological significance). No matter how one interprets it—as a study in illusion and reality, as an uncompromising analysis of the psychological and social games people play, or as a veiled attack on American values (George and Martha bear the names of the first U.S. president and his wife)—the play's power derives from its combination of biting humor and unforgettably searing and often vicious dialogue. In 1963, it won almost every award possible with the exception of the Pulitzer Prize, which led two members of the award committee to resign in protest against the Pulitzer committee's refusal to give the prize to Albee because of the play's subject and language. But in London, the play won the Evening Standard Award in 1964, and in 1966, the film version starred a couple already famous for their own offstage brawls, Richard Burton and Elizabeth Taylor.

Though two of his later plays did win the Pulitzer Prize—*A Delicate Balance* (1966) and *Seascape* (1975)—and though Albee continued to turn out a series of full-length and one-act plays, most notably *Tiny Alice* (1964), *All Over* (1971), *Counting the Ways and Listening* (1976), and *The Man Who Had Three Arms* (1983), the popular success that he enjoyed with his early plays seemed to elude him until 1994, when the Vineyard Theatre produced *Three Tall Women,* a play Albee had initially directed himself in Vienna in 1991. Suddenly Albee was not only visible again but emphatically so, especially when *Three Tall Women* won both the Pulitzer Prize and the New York Drama Critics Circle Award. Audiences in New York, then in London, flocked to the play, lured not only by the acting challenges it offers for three women playing the same person at different stages of her life, but also by Albee's sometimes abrasive, sometimes poignant study of an aged person facing her death and remembering her life. Recently, by contrast, in *The Play about the Baby* (2001) and *The Goat* (2001, winner of the 2002 Pulitzer Prize for drama), Albee has returned to the grim yet comic familial explorations that marked *The American Dream* and *Who's Afraid of Virginia Woolf?*

Given the range of Albee's work during a career that spans some forty-five years, it might seem remarkable that his first successful piece, *The Zoo Story,* continues to be one of his most frequently performed plays. Still produced throughout the world by college and professional groups alike, its spare theatrical requirements— a park bench and two men in conversation—has led to some highly innovative productions, such as a 1994 North Hollywood staging in which the actors simultaneously spoke and used sign language for a combination of hearing and hearing-impaired audiences. And recently it was produced on a series of twenty-one different park benches, one for each of the twenty-one days of the 1999 Edinburgh Fringe Festival. But no matter how it is produced, *The Zoo Story* relentlessly probes some of the most complex social and psychological tensions in contemporary culture.

As Henry Hewes points out in his review following the text, the play begins with a very simple situation—one man, Jerry, approaching another, Peter, who is sitting on a park bench. At first, Jerry's questions to Peter may seem merely annoying and only slightly threatening. The audience, like Peter, may think that perhaps Jerry is planning to rob Peter, or, given the number of references to homosexuals, attempt a sexual pickup or hostile assault. But while the continuing questions and the hesitant answers reveal Peter's life of compromise, it is Jerry's desperate longing to make contact that drives the play forward: "Every once in a while I like to talk to somebody, know all about him." Peter, sitting alone on a "sun-drenched Sunday afternoon," may not know that he is escaping from his conventional existence as a husband, father of two girls, and publishing executive, but Jerry, a "permanent transient," recognizes in him another lonely figure, a recognition that inexorably leads to the violent climax of the play—a climax embodying Albee's intense awareness that human relationships may be both mutually sustaining and mutually destructive.

When *The Zoo Story* was first performed, its violent conclusion was variously interpreted. Henry Hewes in the review following the play interpreted it as the mark of Jerry's success in rousing Peter out of his "deep modern lethargy," whereas Harold Clurman, a noted director and critic, regarded the ending as Jerry's achievement of connection, albeit in death. No matter how one interprets the ending, the dramatic energy of the play arises out of the psychological tensions, the fascination and repulsion, that flow back and forth between Jerry and Peter (see Figure 1). Whether Jerry is shocking Peter with a description of his "laughably small room" or tickling him into hysterical laughter (see Figure 2), he is always compelling and disturbing. He may be the nightmare of the middle class brought to life as a nonstop talker, or he may be a parodic savior, or a demonic version of life imitating the violence reported on television news. Gradually he invades Peter's physical space and in doing so invades the audience's mental space. Peter's bench is no longer a refuge, and the theater is not a safe place; the animals have left their cages.

THE ZOO STORY
A Play in One Scene

BY EDWARD ALBEE

For William Flanagan

THE PLAYERS

PETER, *a man in his early forties, neither fat nor gaunt, neither handsome nor homely. He wears tweeds, smokes a pipe, carries horn-rimmed glasses. Although he is moving into middle age, his dress and his manner would suggest a man younger.*

JERRY, *a man in his late thirties, not poorly dressed, but carelessly. What was once a trim and lightly muscled body has begun to go to fat; and while he is no longer* handsome, it is evident that he once was. His fall from physical grace should not suggest debauchery; he has, to come closest to it, a great weariness.

SCENE

It is Central Park; a Sunday afternoon in summer; the present. There are two park benches, one toward either side of the stage; they both face the audience. Behind them: foliage, trees, sky. At the beginning, Peter is seated on one of the benches.

(As the curtain rises, PETER is seated on the bench stage-right. He is reading a book. He stops reading, cleans his glasses, goes back to reading. JERRY enters.)

JERRY: I've been to the zoo. *(PETER doesn't notice.)* I said, I've been to the zoo. MISTER, I'VE BEEN TO THE ZOO!

PETER: Hm? . . . What? . . . I'm sorry, were you talking to me?

JERRY: I went to the zoo, and then I walked until I came here. Have I been walking north?

PETER *(Puzzled)*: North? Why . . . I . . . I think so. Let me see.

JERRY *(Pointing past the audience)*: Is that Fifth Avenue?

PETER: Why yes; yes, it is.

JERRY: And what is that cross street there; that one, to the right?

PETER: That? Oh, that's Seventy-fourth Street.

JERRY: And the zoo is around Sixty-fifth Street; so, I've been walking north.

PETER *(Anxious to get back to his reading)*: Yes; it would seem so.

JERRY: Good old north.

PETER *(Lightly, by reflex)*: Ha, ha.

JERRY *(After a slight pause)*: But not due north.

PETER: I . . . well, no, not due north; but, we . . . call it north. It's northerly.

JERRY *(Watches as PETER, anxious to dismiss him, prepares his pipe)*: Well, boy; *you're* not going to get lung cancer, are you?

PETER *(Looks up, a little annoyed, then smiles)*: No, sir. Not from this.

JERRY: No, sir. What you'll probably get is cancer of the mouth, and then you'll have to wear one of those things Freud wore after they took one whole side of his jaw away. What do they call those things?

PETER *(Uncomfortable)*: A prosthesis?

JERRY: The very thing! A prosthesis. You're an educated man, aren't you? Are you a doctor?

PETER: Oh, no; no. I read about it somewhere; *Time* magazine, I think. *(He turns to his book.)*

JERRY: Well, *Time* magazine isn't for blockheads.

PETER: No, I suppose not.

JERRY *(After a pause)*: Boy, I'm glad that's Fifth Avenue there.

PETER *(Vaguely)*: Yes.

JERRY: I don't like the west side of the park much.

PETER: Oh? *(Then, slightly wary, but interested)* Why?

JERRY *(Offhand)*: I don't know.

PETER: Oh. *(He returns to his book.)*

JERRY *(He stands for a few seconds, looking at PETER, who finally looks up again, puzzled)*: Do you mind if we talk?

PETER *(Obviously minding)*: Why . . . no, no.

JERRY: Yes you do; you do.

PETER *(Puts his book down, his pipe out and away, smiling)*: No, really; I don't mind.

JERRY: Yes you do.

PETER *(Finally decided)*: No; I don't mind at all, really.

JERRY: It's . . . it's a nice day.

PETER *(Stares unnecessarily at the sky)*: Yes. Yes, it is; lovely.

JERRY: I've been to the zoo.

PETER: Yes, I think you said so . . . didn't you?

JERRY: You'll read about it in the papers tomorrow, if you don't see it on your TV tonight. You have TV, haven't you?

PETER: Why yes, we have two; one for the children.

JERRY: You're married!

PETER *(With pleased emphasis)*: Why, certainly.

JERRY: It isn't a law, for God's sake.

PETER: No . . . no, of course not.

JERRY: And you have a wife.

PETER *(Bewildered by the seeming lack of communication)*: Yes!

JERRY: And you have children.

PETER: Yes; two.

JERRY: Boys?

PETER: No, girls . . . both girls.

JERRY: But you wanted boys.

PETER: Well . . . naturally, every man wants a son, but . . .

JERRY *(Lightly mocking)*: But that's the way the cookie crumbles?

PETER *(Annoyed)*: I wasn't going to say that.

JERRY: And you're not going to have any more kids, are you?

PETER *(A bit distantly)*: No. No more. *(Then back, and irksome)* Why did you say that? How would you know about that?

JERRY: The way you cross your legs, perhaps; something in the voice. Or maybe I'm just guessing. Is it your wife?

PETER *(Furious)*: That's none of your business! *(A silence)* Do you understand? *(JERRY nods. PETER is quiet now.)* Well, you're right. We'll have no more children.

JERRY *(Softly)*: That *is* the way the cookie crumbles.

PETER *(Forgiving)*: Yes . . . I guess so.

JERRY: Well, now; what else?

PETER: What were you saying about the zoo . . . that I'd read about it, or see . . . ?

JERRY: I'll tell you about it, soon. Do you mind if I ask you questions?

PETER: Oh, not really.

JERRY: I'll tell you why I do it; I don't talk to many people—except to say like: give me a beer, or where's the john, or what time does the feature go on, or keep your hands to yourself, buddy. You know—things like that.

PETER: I must say I don't . . .

JERRY: But every once in a while I like to talk to somebody, really *talk;* like to get to know somebody, know all about him.

PETER *(Lightly laughing, still a little uncomfortable)*: And am I the guinea pig for today?

JERRY: On a sun-drenched Sunday afternoon like this? Who better than a nice married man with two daughters and . . . uh . . . a dog? *(PETER shakes his head.)* No? Two dogs. *(PETER shakes his head again.)* Hm. No dogs? *(PETER shakes his head, sadly.)* Oh, that's a shame. But you look like an animal man. CATS? *(PETER nods his head, ruefully.)* Cats! But, that can't be your idea. No, sir. Your wife and daughters? *(PETER nods his head.)* Is there anything else I should know?

PETER *(He has to clear his throat)*: There are . . . there are two parakeets. One . . . uh . . . one for each of my daughters.

JERRY: Birds.

PETER: My daughters keep them in a cage in their bedroom.

JERRY: Do they carry disease? The birds.

PETER: I don't believe so.

JERRY: That's too bad. If they did you could set them loose in the house and the cats could eat them and die, maybe. *(PETER looks blank for a moment, then laughs.)* And what else? What do you do to support your enormous household?

PETER: I . . . uh . . . I have an executive position with a . . . a small publishing house. We . . . uh . . . we publish textbooks.

JERRY: That sounds nice; very nice. What do you make?

PETER *(Still cheerful)*: Now look here!

JERRY: Oh, come on.

PETER: Well, I make around eighteen thousand a year, but I don't carry more than forty dollars at any one time . . . in case you're a . . . a holdup man . . . ha, ha, ha.

JERRY *(Ignoring the above)*: Where do you live? *(PETER is reluctant.)* Oh, look; I'm not going to rob you, and I'm not going to kidnap your parakeets, your cats, or your daughters.

PETER *(Too loud)*: I live between Lexington and Third Avenue, on Seventy-fourth Street.

JERRY: That wasn't so hard, was it?

PETER: I didn't mean to seem . . . ah . . . it's that you don't really carry on a conversation; you just ask questions. And I'm . . . I'm normally . . . uh . . . reticent. Why do you just stand there?

JERRY: I'll start walking around in a little while, and eventually I'll sit down. *(Recalling)* Wait until you see the expression on his face.

PETER: What? Whose face? Look here; is this something about the zoo?

JERRY *(Distantly)*: The what?

PETER: The zoo; the zoo. Something about the zoo.

JERRY: The zoo?

PETER: You've mentioned it several times.

JERRY *(Still distant, but returning abruptly)*: The zoo? Oh, yes; the zoo. I was there before I cam here. I told you that. Say, what's the dividing line between upper-middle-middle-class and lower-upper-middle-class?

PETER: My dear fellow, I . . .

JERRY: Don't my dear fellow me.

PETER *(Unhappily)*: Was I patronizing? I believe I was; I'm sorry. But, you see, your question about the classes bewildered me.

JERRY: And when you're bewildered you become patronizing?

PETER: I . . . I don't express myself too well, sometimes. *(He attempts a joke on himself.)* I'm in publishing, not writing.

JERRY *(Amused, but not at the humor)*: So be it. The truth *is: I* was being patronizing.

PETER: Oh, now; you needn't say that.

(It is at this point that JERRY *may begin to move about the stage with slowly increasing determination and authority, but pacing himself, so that the long speech about the dog comes at the high point of the arc.)*

JERRY: All right. Who are your favorite writers? Baudelaire° and J. P. Marquand°?

PETER *(Wary)*: Well, I like a great many writers; I have a considerable . . . catholicity of taste, if I may say so. Those two men are fine, each in his way. *(Warming up)* Baudelaire, of course . . . uh . . . is by far the finer of the two, but Marquand has a place . . . in our . . . uh . . . national . . .

JERRY: Skip it.

PETER: I . . . sorry.

JERRY: Do you know what I did before I went to the zoo today? I walked all the way up Fifth Avenue from Washington Square; all the way.

PETER: Oh; you live in the Village! *(This seems to enlighten* PETER.*)*

JERRY: No, I don't. I took the subway down to the Village so I could walk all the way up Fifth Avenue to the zoo. It's one of those things a person has to do; sometimes a person has to go a very long distance out of his way to come back a short distance correctly.

PETER *(Almost pouting)*: Oh, I thought you lived in the Village.

JERRY: What were you trying to do? Make sense out of things? Bring order? The old pigeonhole bit? Well, that's easy; I'll tell you. I live in a four-story brownstone roominghouse on the upper West Side between Columbus Avenue and Central Park West. I live on the top floor; rear; west. It's a laughably small room, and one of my walls is made of beaverboard; this beaverboard separates my room from another laughably small room, so I assume that the two rooms were once one room, a small room, but not necessarily laughable. The room beyond my beaverboard wall is occupied by a colored queen who always keeps his door open; well, not always, but *always* when he's plucking his eyebrows, which he does with Buddhist concentration. This colored queen has rotten teeth, which is rare, and he has a Japanese kimono, which is also pretty rare; and he wears this kimono to and from the john in the hall, which is pretty frequent. I mean, he goes to the john a lot. He never bothers me, and he never brings anyone up to his room. All he does is pluck his eyebrows, wear his kimono and go to the john. Now, the two front rooms on my floor are a little larger, I guess; but they're pretty small, too. There's a Puerto Rican family in one of them, a husband, a wife, and some kids; I don't know how many. These people entertain a lot. And in the other front room, there's somebody living there, but I don't know who it is. I've never seen who it is. Never. Never ever.

PETER *(Embarrassed)*: Why . . . why do you live there?

JERRY *(From a distance again)*: I don't know.

PETER: It doesn't sound like a very nice place . . . where you live.

JERRY: Well, no; it isn't an apartment in the East Seventies. But, then again, I don't have one wife, two daughters, two cats and two parakeets. What I do have, I have toilet articles, a few clothes, a hot plate that I'm not supposed to have, a can opener, one that works with a key, you know; a knife, two forks, and two spoons, one small, one large; three plates, a cup, a saucer, a drinking glass, two picture frames, both empty, eight or nine books, a pack of pornographic playing cards, regular deck, an old Western Union typewriter that prints nothing but capital letters, and a small strongbox without a lock which has in it . . . what? Rocks! Some rocks . . . sea-rounded rocks I picked up on the beach when I was a kid. Under which . . . weighed down . . . are some letters . . . please letters . . . please why don't you do this, and please when will you do that letters. And when letters, too. When will you write? When will you come? When? These letters are from more recent years.

PETER *(Stares glumly at his shoes, then)*: About those two empty picture frames . . . ?

JERRY: I don't see why they need any explanation at all. Isn't it clear? I don't have pictures of anyone to put in them.

PETER: Your parents . . . perhaps . . . a girl friend . . .

JERRY: You're a very sweet man, and you're possessed of a truly enviable innocence. But good old Mom and good old Pop are dead . . . you know? . . . I'm broken up about it, too . . . I mean really. BUT. That particular vaudeville act is playing the cloud circuit now, so I don't see how I can look at them, all neat and framed. Besides, or, rather, to be pointed about it, good old Mom walked out on good old Pop when I was ten and a half years old; she embarked on an adulterous turn of our southern states . . . a journey of a year's duration . . . and her most constant companion . . . among others, among many others . . . was a Mr. Barleycorn. At least, that's what good old Pop told me after he went down . . . came back . . . brought her body north. We'd received the news between Christmas and New Year's, you see, that good old Mom had parted with the ghost in some dump in

---

Baudelaire, Charles Baudelaire (1821–67), French symbolist poet known for his fascination with decadence and beauty. *J. P. Marquand*, 1893–1960, American author of novels satirizing middle-class affluence.

Alabama. And, without the ghost . . . she was less welcome. I mean, what was she? A stiff . . . a northern stiff. At any rate, good old Pop celebrated the New Year for an even two weeks and then slapped into the front of a somewhat moving city omnibus, which sort of cleaned things out family-wise. Well no; then there was Mom's sister, who was given neither to sin nor the consolations of the bottle. I moved in on her, and my memory of her is slight excepting I remember still that she did all things dourly: sleeping, eating, working, praying. She dropped dead on the stairs to her apartment, my apartment then, too, on the afternoon of my high school graduation. A terribly middle-European joke, if you ask me.

PETER: Oh, my; oh, my.

JERRY: Oh, your what? But that was a long time ago, and I have no feeling about any of it that I care to admit to myself. Perhaps you can see, though, why good old Mom and good old Pop are frameless. What's your name? Your first name?

PETER: I'm Peter.

JERRY: I'd forgotten to ask you. I'm Jerry.

PETER (*With a slight, nervous laugh*): Hello, Jerry.

JERRY (*Nods his hello*): And let's see now; what's the point of having a girl's picture, especially in two frames? I have two picture frames, you remember. I never see the pretty little ladies more than once, and most of them wouldn't be caught in the same room with a camera. It's odd, and I wonder if it's sad.

PETER: The girls?

JERRY: No. I wonder if it's sad that I never see the little ladies more than once. I've never been able to have sex with, or, how is it put? . . . make love to anybody more than once. Once; that's it. . . . Oh, wait; for a week and a half, when I was fifteen . . . and I hang my head in shame that puberty was late . . . I was a h-o-m-o-s-e-x-u-a-l. I mean, I was queer . . . (*Very fast*) . . . queer, queer, queer . . . with bells ringing, banners snapping in the wind. And for those eleven days, I met at least twice a day with the park superintendent's son . . . a Greek boy, whose birthday was the same as mine, except he was a year older. I think I was very much in love . . . maybe just with sex. But that was the jazz of a very special hotel, wasn't it? And now; oh, do I love the little ladies; really, I love them. For about an hour.

PETER: Well, it seems perfectly simple to me. . . .

JERRY (*Angry*): Look! Are you going to tell me to get married and have parakeets?

PETER (*Angry himself*): Forget the parakeets! And stay single if you want to. It's no business of mine. I didn't start this conversation in the . . .

JERRY: All right, all right. I'm sorry. All right? You're not angry?

PETER (*Laughing*): No, I'm not angry.

JERRY (*Relieved*): Good. (*Now back to his previous tone*) Interesting that you asked me about the picture frames. I would have thought that you would have asked me about the pornographic playing cards.

PETER (*With a knowing smile*): Oh, I've seen those cards.

JERRY: That's not the point. (*Laughs*) I suppose when you were a kid you and your pals passed them around, or you had a pack of your own.

PETER: Well, I guess a lot of us did.

JERRY: And you threw them away just before you got married.

PETER: Oh, now; look here. I didn't *need* anything like that when I got older.

JERRY: No?

PETER (*Embarrassed*): I'd rather not talk about these things.

JERRY: So? Don't. Besides, I wasn't trying to plumb your post-adolescent sexual life and hard times; what I wanted to get at is the value difference between pornographic playing cards when you're a kid, and pornographic playing cards when you're older. It's that when you're a kid you use the cards as a substitute for a real experience, and when you're older you use real experience as a substitute for the fantasy. But I imagine you'd rather hear about what happened at the zoo.

PETER (*Enthusiastic*): Oh, yes; the zoo. (*Then, awkward*) That is . . . if you . . .

JERRY: Let me tell you about why I went . . . well, let me tell you some things. I've told you about the fourth floor of the roominghouse where I live. I think the rooms are better as you go down, floor by floor. I guess they are; I don't know. I don't know any of the people on the third and second floors. Oh, wait! I do know that there's a lady living on the third floor, in the front. I know because she cries all the time. Whenever I go out or come back in, whenever I pass her door, I always hear her crying, muffled, but . . . very determined. Very determined indeed. But the one I'm getting to, and all about the dog, is the landlady. I don't like to use words that are too harsh in describing people. I don't like to. But the landlady is a fat, ugly, mean, stupid, unwashed, misanthropic, cheap, drunken bag of garbage. And you may have noticed that I very seldom use profanity, so I can't describe her as well as I might.

PETER: You describe her . . . vividly.

JERRY: Well, thanks. Anyway, she has a dog, and I will tell you about the dog, and she and her dog are the gatekeepers of my dwelling. The woman is bad enough; she leans around in the entrance hall, spying to see that I don't bring in things or people, and when she's had her mid-afternoon pint of lemon-flavored gin she always stops me in the hall, and grabs ahold of my coat or my arm, and she presses her disgusting body up against me to keep me in a corner so she can talk to me. The smell of her body and her breath . . . you can't imagine it . . . and somewhere, somewhere in the back of that pea-sized brain of hers, an organ developed just enough to let her eat, drink, and emit, she has some foul parody of sexual desire. And I, Peter, I am the object of her sweaty lust.

PETER: That's disgusting. That's . . . horrible.

JERRY: But I have found a way to keep her off. When she talks to me, when she presses herself to my body and mumbles about her room and how I should come there, I merely say: but, Love; wasn't yesterday enough for you, and the day before? Then she puzzles, she makes slits of her tiny eyes, she sways a little, and then, Peter . . . and it is at this moment that I think I might be doing some good in that tormented house . . . a simple-minded smile begins to form on her unthinkable face, and she giggles and groans as she thinks about yesterday and the day before; as she believes and relives what never happened. Then, she motions to that black monster of a dog she has, and she goes back to her room. And I am safe until our next meeting.

PETER: It's so . . . unthinkable. I find it hard to believe that people such as that really *are*.

JERRY (*Lightly mocking*): It's for reading about, isn't it?

PETER (*Seriously*): Yes.

JERRY: And fact is better left to fiction. You're right, Peter. Well, what I have been meaning to tell you about is the dog; I shall, now.

PETER (*Nervously*): Oh, yes; the dog.

JERRY: Don't go. You're not thinking of going, are you?

PETER: Well . . . no, I don't think so.

JERRY (*As if to a child*): Because after I tell you about the dog, do you know what then? Then . . . then I'll tell you about what happened at the zoo.

PETER (*Laughing faintly*): You're . . . you're full of stories, aren't you?

JERRY: You don't *have* to listen. Nobody is holding you here; remember that. Keep that in your mind.

PETER (*Irritably*): I know that.

JERRY: You do? Good.

(*The following long speech, it seems to me, should be done with a great deal of action, to achieve a hypnotic effect on* PETER, *and on the audience, too. Some specific actions have been suggested, but the director and the actor playing* JERRY *might best work it out for themselves.*)

ALL RIGHT. (*As if reading from a huge billboard*) THE STORY OF JERRY AND THE DOG! (*Natural again*) What I am going to tell you has something to do with how sometimes it's necessary to go a long distance out of the way in order to come back a short distance correctly; or, maybe I only think that it has something to do with that. But, it's why I went to the zoo today, and why I walked north . . . northerly, rather . . . until I came here. All right. The dog, I think I told you, is a black monster of a beast: an oversized head, tiny, tiny ears, and eyes . . . bloodshot, infected, maybe; and a body you can see the ribs through the skin. The dog is black, all black; all black except for the bloodshot eyes, and . . . yes . . . and an open sore on its . . . *right* forepaw; that is red, too. And, oh yes; the poor monster, and I do believe it's an old dog . . . it's certainly a misused one . . . almost always has an erection . . . of sorts. That's red, too. And . . . what else? . . . oh, yes; there's a gray-yellow-white color, too, when he bares his fangs. Like this: Grrrrrr! Which is what he did when he saw me for the first time . . . the day I moved in. I worried about that animal the very first minute I met him. Now, animals don't take to me like Saint Francis had birds hanging off him all the time. What I mean is: animals are indifferent to me . . . like people (*He smiles slightly*) . . . most of the time. But this dog wasn't indifferent. From the very beginning he'd snarl and then go for me, to get one of my legs. Not like he was rabid, you know; he was sort of a stumbly dog, but he wasn't half-assed, either. It was a good, stumbly run; but I always got away. He got a piece of my trouser leg, look, you can see right here, where it's mended; he got that the second day I lived there; but, I kicked free and got upstairs fast, so that was that. (*Puzzles*) I still don't know to this day how the other roomers manage it, but you know what I *think*: I think it had to do only with me. Cozy. So. Anyway, this went on for over a week, whenever I came in; but never when I went out. That's funny. Or, it *was* funny. I could pack up and live in the street for all the dog cared. Well, I thought about it up in my room one day, one of the times after I'd bolted upstairs, and I made up my mind. I decided: First, I'll kill the dog with kindness, and if that doesn't work . . . I'll just kill him. (PETER *winces.*) Don't react, Peter; just listen. So, the next day I went out and bought a bag of hamburgers, medium rare, no catsup, no onion; and on the way home I threw away all the rolls and kept just the meat.

(*Action for the following, perhaps*)

When I got back to the roominghouse the dog was waiting for me. I half opened the door that led into the entrance hall, and there he was; waiting for me. It figured. I went in, very cautiously, and I had the hamburgers, you remember; I opened the bag, and I set the meat down about twelve feet from where the dog was snarling at me. Like so! He snarled; stopped snarling;

sniffed; moved slowly; then faster; then faster toward the meat. Well, when he got to it he stopped, and he looked at me. I smiled; but tentatively, you understand. He turned his face back to the hamburgers, smelled, sniffed some more, and then . . . RRRAAAAGGGGGHHHH, like that . . . he tore into them. It was as if he had never eaten anything in his life before, except like garbage. Which might very well have been the truth. I don't think the landlady ever eats anything but garbage. But. He ate all the hamburgers, almost all at once, making sounds in his throat like a woman. *Then,* when he'd finished the meat, the hamburger, and tried to eat the paper, too, he sat down and smiled. I think he smiled; I know cats do. It was a very gratifying few moments. Then, BAM, he snarled and made for me again. He didn't get me this time, either. So, I got upstairs, and I lay down on my bed and started to think about the dog again. To be truthful, I was offended, and I was damn mad, too. It was six perfectly good hamburgers with not enough pork in them to make it disgusting. I was offended. But, after a while, I decided to try it for a few more days. If you think about it, this dog had what amounted to an antipathy toward me; really. And, I wondered if I mightn't overcome this antipathy. So, I tried it for five more days, but it was always the same: snarl, sniff; move; faster; stare; gobble; RAAGGGHHH; smile; snarl; BAM. Well, now; by this time Columbus Avenue was strewn with hamburger rolls and I was less offended than disgusted. So, I decided to kill the dog.

(PETER *raises a hand in protest.*)

Oh, don't be so alarmed, Peter; I didn't succeed. The day I tried to kill the dog I bought only one hamburger and what I thought was a murderous portion of rat poison. When I bought the hamburger I asked the man not to bother with the roll, all I wanted was the meat. I expected some reaction from him, like: we don't sell no hamburgers without rolls; or, wha' d'ya wanna do, eat it out'a ya han's? But no; he smiled benignly, wrapped up the hamburger in waxed paper, and said: A bite for ya pussy-cat? I wanted to say: No, not really; it's part of a plan to poison a dog I know. But, you can't say "a dog I know" without sounding funny; so I said, a little too loud, I'm afraid, and too formally: YES, A BITE FOR MY PUSSY-CAT. People looked up. It always happens when I try to simplify things; people look up. But that's neither hither nor thither. So. On my way back to the roominghouse, I kneaded the hamburger and the rat poison together between my hands, at that point feeling as much sadness as disgust. I opened the door to the entrance hall,

and there the monster was, waiting to take the offering and then jump me. Poor bastard; he never learned that the moment he took to smile before he went for me gave me time enough to get out of range. BUT, there he was; malevolence with an erection, waiting. I put the poison patty down, moved toward the stairs and watched. The poor animal gobbled the food down as usual, smiled, which made me almost sick, and then, BAM. But, I sprinted up the stairs, as usual, and the dog didn't get me, as usual. AND IT CAME TO PASS THAT THE BEAST WAS DEATHLY ILL. I knew this because he no longer attended me, and because the landlady sobered up. She stopped me in the hall the same evening of the attempted murder and confided the information that God had struck her puppy-dog a surely fatal blow. She had forgotten her bewildered lust, and her eyes were wide open for the first time. They looked like the dog's eyes. She sniveled and implored me to pray for the animal. I wanted to say to her: Madam, I have myself to pray for, the colored queen, the Puerto Rican family, the person in the front room whom I've never seen, the woman who cries deliberately behind her closed door, and the rest of the people in all roominghouses, everywhere; besides, Madam, I don't understand how to pray. But . . . to simplify things . . . I told her I would pray. She looked up. She said that I was a liar, and that I probably wanted the dog to die. I told her, and there was so much truth here, that I didn't want the dog to die. I didn't, and not just because I'd poisoned him. I'm afraid that I must tell you I wanted the dog to live so that I could see what our new relationship might come to.

(PETER *indicates his increasing displeasure and slowly growing antagonism.*)

Please understand, Peter; that sort of thing is important. You must believe me; it *is* important. We have to know the effect of our actions. *(Another deep sigh)* Well, anyway; the dog recovered. I have no idea why, unless he was a descendant of the puppy that guarded the gates of hell or some such resort. I'm not up on my mythology. *(He pronounces the word myth-o-*logy.*)* Are you?

(PETER *sets to thinking, but* JERRY *goes on.*)

At any rate, and you've missed the eight-thousand-dollar question, Peter; at any rate, the dog recovered his health and the landlady recovered her thirst, in no way altered by the bow-wow's deliverance. When I came home from a movie that was playing on Forty-second Street, a movie I'd seen, or one that was very much like one or several I'd seen, after the landlady told me puppykins was better, I was so hoping for the dog to be waiting for me. I was . . . well, how would you put it . . . enticed? . . . fascinated? . . . no, I don't think so . . . heart-shatteringly anxious, that's it; I was heart-shatteringly anxious to confront my friend again.

(PETER *reacts scoffingly.*)

Yes, Peter; friend. That's the only word for it. I was heart-shatteringly et cetera to confront my doggy friend again. I came in the door and advanced, unafraid, to the center of the entrance hall. The beast was there . . . looking at me. And, you know, he looked better for his scrape with the never-mind. I stopped; I looked at him; he looked at me. I think . . . I think we stayed a long time that way . . . still, stone-statue . . . just looking at one another. I looked more into his face than he looked into mine. I mean, I can concentrate longer at looking into a dog's face than a dog can concentrate at looking into mine, or into anybody else's face, for that matter. But during that twenty seconds or two hours that we looked into each other's face, we made contact. Now, here is what I had wanted to happen: I loved the dog now, and I wanted him to love me. I had tried to love, and I had tried to kill, and both had been unsuccessful by themselves. I hoped . . . and I don't really know why I expected the dog to understand anything, much less my motivations . . . I hoped that the dog would understand.

(PETER *seems to be hypnotized.*)

It's just . . . it's just that . . . (JERRY *is abnormally tense, now*) . . . it's just that if you can't deal with people, you have to make a start somewhere. WITH ANIMALS! (*Much faster now, and like a conspirator*) Don't you see? A person has to have some way of dealing with SOMETHING. If not with people . . . if not with people . . . SOMETHING. With a bed, with a cockroach, with a mirror . . . no, that's too hard, that's one of the last steps. With a cockroach, with a . . . with a . . . with a carpet, a roll of toilet paper . . . no, not that, either . . . that's a mirror, too; always check bleeding. You see how hard it is to find things? With a street corner, and too many lights, all colors reflecting on the oily-wet streets . . . with a wisp of smoke, a wisp . . . of smoke . . . with . . . with pornographic playing cards, with a strongbox . . . WITHOUT A LOCK . . . with love, with vomiting, with crying, with fury because the pretty little ladies aren't pretty little ladies, with making money with your body which is an act of love and I could prove it, with howling because you're alive; with God. How about that? WITH GOD WHO IS A COLORED QUEEN WHO WEARS A KIMONO AND PLUCKS HIS EYEBROWS, WHO IS A WOMAN WHO CRIES WITH DETERMINATION BEHIND HER CLOSED DOOR . . . with God who, I'm told, turned his back on the whole thing some time ago . . . with . . . some day, with people. (JERRY *sighs the next word heavily.*) People. With an idea; a concept. And where better, where ever better in this humiliating excuse for a jail, where better to communicate one single, simple-minded idea than in an entrance hall? Where? It would be A START! Where better to make a beginning . . . to understand and just possibly be understood . . . a beginning of an understanding, than with . . .

(Here JERRY *seems to fall into almost grotesque fatigue.*)

. . . than with A DOG. Just that; a dog.

(Here there is a silence that might be prolonged for a moment or so; then JERRY *wearily finishes his story.*)

A dog. It seemed like a perfectly sensible idea. Man is a dog's best friend, remember. So: the dog and I looked at each other. I longer than the dog. And what I saw then has been the same ever since. Whenever the dog and I see each other we both stop where we are. We regard each other with a mixture of sadness and suspicion, and then we feign indifference. We walk past each other safely; we have an understanding. It's very sad, but you'll have to admit that it is an understanding. We had made many attempts at contact, and we had failed. The dog has returned to garbage, and I to solitary but free passage. I have not returned. I mean to say, I have *gained* solitary free passage, if that much further loss can be said to be gain. I have learned that neither kindness nor cruelty by themselves, independent of each other, creates any effect beyond themselves; and I have learned that the two combined, together, at the same time, are the teaching emotion. And what is gained is loss. And what has been the result: the dog and I have attained a compromise; more of a bargain, really. We neither love nor hurt because we do not try to reach each other. And, *was* trying to feed the dog an act of love? And, perhaps, was the dog's attempt to bite me *not* an act of love? If we can so misunderstand, well then, why have we invented the word love in the first place?

(There is silence. JERRY *moves to* PETER'*s bench and sits down beside him. This is the first time* JERRY *has sat down during the play.*)

The Story of Jerry and the Dog: the end.

(PETER *is silent.*)

Well, Peter? (JERRY *is suddenly cheerful.*) Well, Peter? Do you think I could sell that story to the *Reader's Digest* and make a couple of hundred bucks for *The Most Unforgettable Character I've Ever Met*? Huh?

(JERRY is animated, but PETER is disturbed.)

Oh, come on now, Peter; tell me what you think.

PETER *(Numb)*: I . . . I don't understand what . . . I don't think I . . . *(Now, almost tearfully)* Why did you tell me all of this?

JERRY: Why not?

PETER: I DON'T UNDERSTAND!

JERRY *(Furious, but whispering)*: That's a lie.

PETER: No. No, it's not.

JERRY *(Quietly)*: I tried to explain it to you as I went along. I went slowly; it all has to do with . . .

PETER: I DON'T WANT TO HEAR ANY MORE. I don't understand you, or your landlady, or her dog . . .

JERRY: *Her* dog! I thought it was my . . . No. No, you're right. It *is* her dog. *(Looks at PETER intently, shaking his head)* I don't know what I was thinking about; of course you don't understand. *(In a monotone, wearily)* I don't live in your block; I'm not married to two parakeets, or whatever your setup is. I am a *permanent transient,* and my home is the sickening roominghouses on the West Side of New York City, which is the greatest city in the world. Amen.

PETER: I'm . . . I'm sorry; I didn't mean to . . .

JERRY: Forget it. I suppose you don't quite know what to make of me, eh?

PETER *(A joke)*: We get all kinds in publishing. *(Chuckles)*

JERRY: You're a funny man. *(He forces a laugh.)* You know that? You're a very . . . a richly comic person.

PETER *(Modestly, but amused)*: Oh, now, not really. *(Still chuckling)*

JERRY: Peter, do I annoy you, or confuse you?

PETER *(Lightly)*: Well, I must confess that this wasn't the kind of afternoon I'd anticipated.

JERRY: You mean, I'm not the gentleman you were expecting.

PETER: I wasn't expecting anybody.

JERRY: No, I don't imagine you were. But I'm here, and I'm not leaving.

PETER *(Consulting his watch)*: Well, you may not be, but I must be getting home soon.

JERRY: Oh, come on; stay a while longer.

PETER: I really should get home; you see . . .

JERRY *(Tickles PETER's ribs with his fingers)*: Oh, come on.

PETER *(He is very ticklish; as JERRY continues to tickle him his voice becomes falsetto)*: No, I . . . OHHHHH! Don't do that. Stop, Stop. Ohhh, no, no.

JERRY: Oh, come on.

PETER *(As JERRY tickles)*: Oh, hee, hee, hee. I must go. I . . . hee, hee, hee. After all, stop, stop, hee, hee, hee, after all, the parakeets will be getting dinner ready soon. Hee, hee. And the cats are setting the table. Stop, stop, and, and . . . *(PETER is beside himself now)* . . . and we're having . . . hee, hee . . . uh . . . ho, ho, ho.

(JERRY stops tickling PETER, but the combination of the tickling and his own mad whimsy has PETER laughing

almost hysterically. As his laughter continues, then subsides, JERRY watches him, with a curious fixed smile.)

JERRY: Peter?

PETER: Oh, ha, ha, ha, ha, ha, ha. What? What?

JERRY: Listen, now.

PETER: Oh, ho, ho. What . . . what is it, Jerry? Oh, my.

JERRY *(Mysteriously)*: Peter, do you want to know what happened at the zoo?

PETER: Ah, ha, ha. The what? Oh, yes; the zoo. Oh, ho, ho. Well, I had my own zoo there for a moment with . . . hee, hee, the parakeets getting dinner ready, and the . . . ha, ha, whatever it was, the . . .

JERRY *(Calmly)*: Yes, that was very funny, Peter. I wouldn't have expected it. But do you want to hear about what happened at the zoo, or not?

PETER: Yes. Yes, by all means; tell me what happened at the zoo. Oh, my. I don't know what happened to me.

JERRY: Now I'll let you in on what happened at the zoo; but first, I should tell you why I went to the zoo. I went to the zoo to find out more about the way people exist with animals, and the way animals exist with each other, and with people too. It probably wasn't a fair test, what with everyone separated by bars from everyone else, the animals for the most part from each other, and always the people from the animals. But, if it's a zoo, that's the way it is. *(He pokes PETER on the arm.)* Move over.

PETER *(Friendly)*: I'm sorry, haven't you enough room? *(He shifts a little.)*

JERRY *(Smiling slightly)*: Well, all the animals are there, and all the people are there, and it's Sunday and all the children are there. *(He pokes PETER again.)* Move over.

PETER *(Patiently, still friendly)*: All right.

(He moves some more, and JERRY has all the room he might need.)

JERRY: And it's a hot day, so all the stench is there, too, and all the balloon sellers, and all the ice cream sellers, and all the seals are barking, and all the birds are screaming. *(Pokes PETER harder.)* Move over!

PETER *(Beginning to be annoyed)*: Look here, you have more than enough room! *(But he moves more, and is now fairly cramped at one end of the bench.)*

JERRY: And I am there, and it's feeding time at the lions' house, and the lion keeper comes into the lion cage, one of the lion cages, to feed one of the lions. *(Punches PETER on the arm, hard)* MOVE OVER!

PETER *(Very annoyed)*: I can't move over any more, and stop hitting me. What's the matter with you?

JERRY: Do you want to hear the story? *(Punches PETER's arm again)*

PETER *(Flabbergasted)*: I'm not so sure! I certainly don't want to be punched in the arm.

JERRY (*Punches* PETER*'s arm again*): Like that?

PETER: Stop it! What's the matter with you?

JERRY: I'm crazy, you bastard.

PETER: That isn't funny.

JERRY: Listen to me, Peter. I want this bench. You go sit on the bench over there, and if you're good I'll tell you the rest of the story.

PETER (*Flustered*): But . . . whatever for? What *is* the matter with you? Besides, I see no reason why I should give up this bench. I sit on this bench almost every Sunday afternoon, in good weather. It's secluded here; there's never anyone sitting here, so I have it all to myself.

JERRY (*Softly*): Get off this bench, Peter; I want it.

PETER (*Almost whining*): No.

JERRY: I said I want this bench, and I'm going to have it. Now get over there.

PETER: People can't have everything they want. You should know that; it's a rule; people can have some of the things they want, but they can't have everything.

JERRY (*Laughs*): Imbecile! You're slow-witted!

PETER: Stop that!

JERRY: You're a vegetable! Go lie down on the ground.

PETER (*Intense*): Now *you* listen to me. I've put up with you all afternoon.

JERRY: Not really.

PETER: LONG ENOUGH. I've put up with you long enough. I've listened to you because you seemed . . . well, because I thought you wanted to talk to somebody.

JERRY: You put things well; economically, and, yet . . . oh, what is the word I want to put justice to your . . . JESUS, you make me sick . . . get off here and give me my bench.

PETER: MY BENCH!

JERRY (*Pushes* PETER *almost, but not quite, off the bench*): Get out of my sight.

PETER (*Regaining his position*): God da . . . mn you. That's enough! I've had enough of you. I will not give up this bench; you can't have it, and that's that. Now, go away. (JERRY *snorts but does not move.*) Go away, I said. (JERRY *does not move.*) Get away from here. If you don't move on . . . you're a bum . . . that's what you are. . . . If you don't move on, I'll get a policeman here and make you go. (JERRY *laughs, stays.*) I warn you, I'll call a policeman.

JERRY (*Softly*): You won't find a policeman around here; they're all over on the west side of the park chasing fairies down from trees or out of the bushes. That's all they do. That's their function. So scream your head off; it won't do you any good.

PETER: POLICE! I warn you, I'll have you arrested. POLICE! (*Pause*) I said POLICE! (*Pause*) I feel ridiculous.

JERRY: You look ridiculous: a grown man screaming for the police on a bright Sunday afternoon in the park with nobody harming you. If a policeman *did* fill his quota and come sludging over this way he'd probably take you in as a nut.

PETER (*With disgust and impotence*): Great God, I just came here to read, and now you want me to give up the bench. You're mad.

JERRY: Hey, I got news for you, as they say. I'm on your precious bench, and you're never going to have it for yourself again.

PETER (*Furious*): Look, you; get off my bench. I don't care if it makes any sense or not. I want this bench to myself; I want you OFF IT!

JERRY (*Mocking*): Aw . . . look who's mad.

PETER: GET OUT!

JERRY: No.

PETER: I WARN YOU!

JERRY: Do you know how ridiculous you look *now*?

PETER (*His fury and self-consciousness have possessed him*): It doesn't matter. (*He is almost crying.*) GET AWAY FROM MY BENCH!

JERRY: Why? You have everything in the world you want; you've told me about your home, and your family, and *your own* little zoo. You have everything, and now you want this bench. Are these the things men fight for? Tell me, Peter, is this bench, this iron and this wood, is this your honor? Is this the thing in the world you'd fight for? Can you think of anything more absurd?

PETER: Absurd? Look, I'm not going to talk to you about honor, or even try to explain it to you. Besides, it isn't a question of honor; but even if it were, you wouldn't understand.

JERRY (*Contemptuously*): You don't even know what you're saying, do you? This is probably the first time in your life you've had anything more trying to face than changing your cats' toilet box. Stupid! Don't you have any idea, not even the slightest what other people *need*?

PETER: Oh, boy, listen to you; well, you don't need this bench. That's for sure.

JERRY: Yes; yes, I do.

PETER (*Quivering*): I've come here for years; I have hours of great pleasure, great satisfaction, right here. And that's important to a man. I'm a responsible person, and I'm a GROWNUP. This is my bench, and you have no right to take it away from me.

JERRY: Fight for it, then. Defend yourself; defend your bench.

PETER: You've *pushed* me to it. Get up and fight.

JERRY: Like a man?

PETER (*Still angry*): Yes, like a man, if you insist on mocking me even further.

JERRY: I'll have to give you credit for one thing: you *are* a vegetable, and a slightly nearsighted one, I think . . .

PETER: THAT'S ENOUGH. . . .

JERRY: . . . but, you know, as they say on TV all the time—you know—and I mean this, Peter, you have a certain dignity; it surprises me. . . .

PETER: STOP!

JERRY (*Rises lazily*): Very well, Peter, we'll battle for the bench, but we're not evenly matched.

(*He takes out and clicks open an ugly-looking knife.*)

PETER (*Suddenly awakening to the reality of the situation*): You *are* mad! You're stark raving mad! YOU'RE GOING TO KILL ME!

(*But before* PETER *has time to think what to do,* JERRY *tosses the knife at* PETER'*s feet.*)

JERRY: There you go. Pick it up. You have the knife and we'll be more evenly matched.

PETER (*Horrified*): No!

JERRY (*Rushes over to* PETER, *grabs him by the collar;* PETER *rises; their faces almost touch*): Now you pick up that knife and you fight with me. You fight for your self-respect; you fight for that goddamned bench.

PETER (*Struggling*): No! Let . . . let go of me! He . . . Help!

JERRY (*Slaps* PETER *on each "fight"*): You fight, you miserable bastard; fight for that bench; fight for your parakeets; fight for your cats; fight for your two daughters; fight for your wife; fight for your manhood, you pathetic little vegetable. (*Spits in* PETER'*s face*) You couldn't even get your wife with a male child.

PETER (*Breaks away, enraged*): It's a matter of genetics, not manhood, you . . . you monster. (*He darts down, picks up the knife and backs off a little; he is breathing heavily.*) I'll give you one last chance; get out of here and leave me alone!

(*He holds the knife with a firm arm, but far in front of him, not to attack, but to defend.*)

JERRY (*Sighs heavily*): So be it!

(*With a rush he charges* PETER *and impales himself on the knife. Tableau: For just a moment, complete silence,* JERRY *impaled on the knife at the end of* PETER'*s still firm arm. Then* PETER *screams, pulls away, leaving the knife in* JERRY. JERRY *is motionless, on point. Then he, too, screams, and it must be the sound of an infuriated and fatally wounded animal. With the knife in him, he stumbles back to the bench that* PETER *had vacated. He crumbles there, sitting, facing* PETER, *his eyes wide in agony, his mouth open.*)

PETER (*Whispering*): Oh my God, oh my God, oh my God. . . .

(*He repeats these words many times, very rapidly.*)

JERRY (JERRY *is dying; but now his expression seems to change. His features relax, and while his voice varies, sometimes wrenched with pain, for the most part he seems removed from his dying. He smiles*): Thank you, Peter. I mean that, now; thank you very much. (PETER'*s mouth drops open. He cannot move; he is transfixed.*) Oh, Peter, I was so afraid I'd drive you away. (*He laughs as best he can.*) You don't know how afraid I was you'd go away and leave me. And now I'll tell you what happened at the zoo. I think . . . I think this is what happened at the zoo . . . I think. I think that while I was at the zoo I decided that I would walk north . . . northerly, rather . . . until I found you . . . or somebody . . . and decided that I would talk to you . . . I would tell you things . . . and things that I would tell you would . . . Well, here we are. You see? Here we *are*. But . . . I don't know . . . could I have planned all this? No . . . no, I couldn't have. But I think I did. And now I've told you what you wanted to know, haven't I? And now you know all about what happened at the zoo. And now you know what you'll see in your TV, and the face I told you about . . . you remember . . . the face I told you about . . . my face, the face you see right now. Peter . . . Peter? . . . Peter . . . thank you. I came unto you (*He laughs, so faintly*) and you have comforted me. Dear Peter.

PETER (*Almost fainting*): Oh my God!

JERRY: You'd better go now. Somebody might come by, and you don't want to be here when anyone comes.

PETER (*Does not move, but begins to weep*): Oh my God, oh my God.

JERRY (*Most faintly, now; he is very near death*): You won't be coming back here any more, Peter; you've been dispossessed. You've lost your bench, but you've defended your honor. And Peter, I'll tell you something now; you're not really a vegetable; it's all right, you're an animal. You're an animal, too. But you'd better hurry now, Peter. Hurry, you'd better go . . . see? (JERRY *takes a handkerchief and with great effort and pain wipes the knife handle clean of fingerprints.*) Hurry away, Peter. (PETER *begins to stagger away.*) Wait . . . wait, Peter. Take your book . . . book. Right here . . . beside me . . . on your bench . . . my bench, rather. Come . . . take your book. (PETER *starts for the book, but retreats.*) Hurry . . . Peter. (PETER *rushes to the bench, grabs the book, retreats.*) Very good, Peter . . . very good. Now . . . hurry away. (PETER *hesitates for a moment, then flees, stage-left.*) Hurry away. . . . (*His eyes are closed now.*) Hurry away, your parakeets are making the dinner . . . the cats . . . are setting the table . . .

PETER (*Off stage*): (*A pitiful howl*) OH MY GOD!

JERRY (*His eyes still closed, he shakes his head and speaks; a combination of scornful mimicry and supplication*): Oh . . . my . . . God.

(*He is dead.*)

CURTAIN

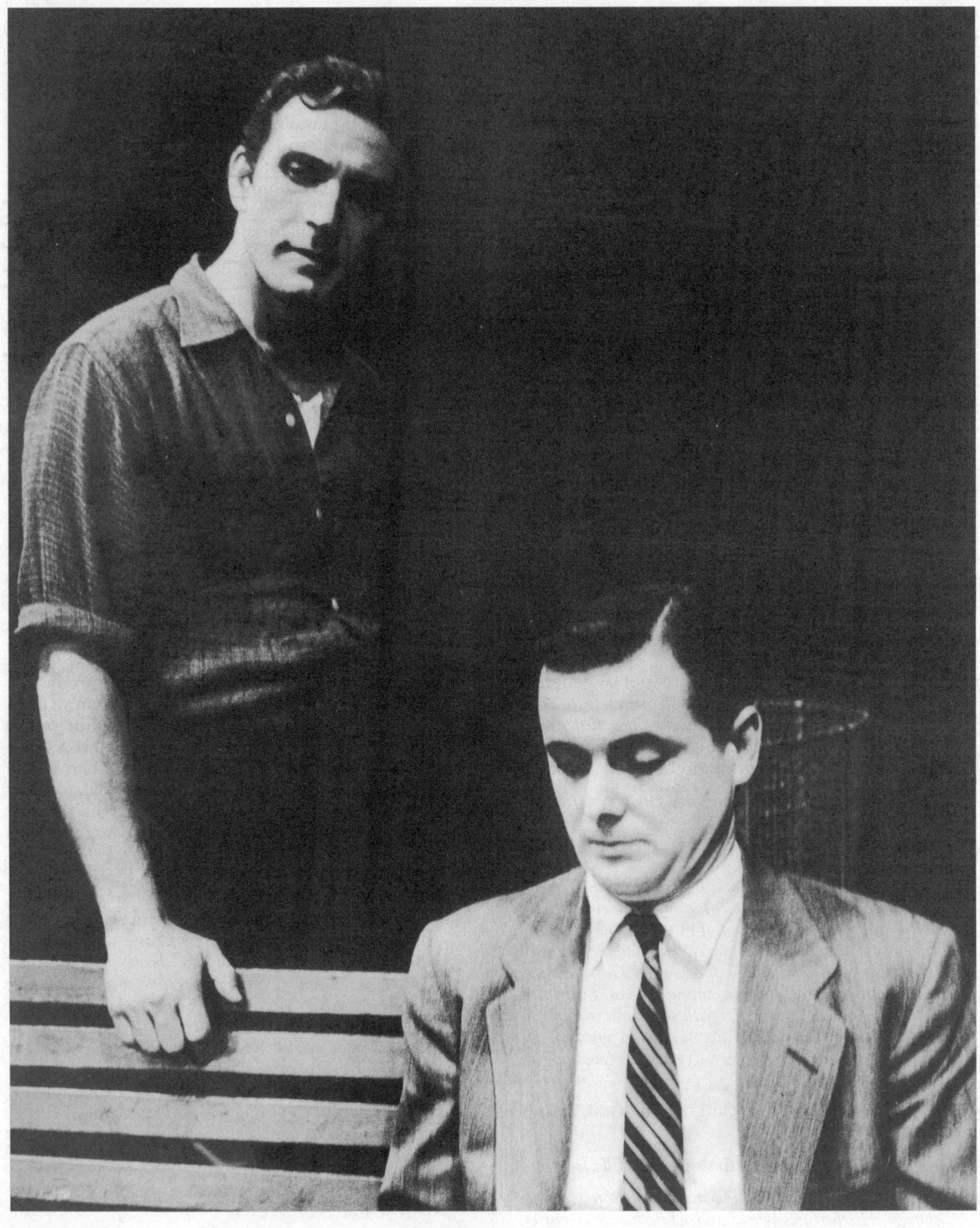

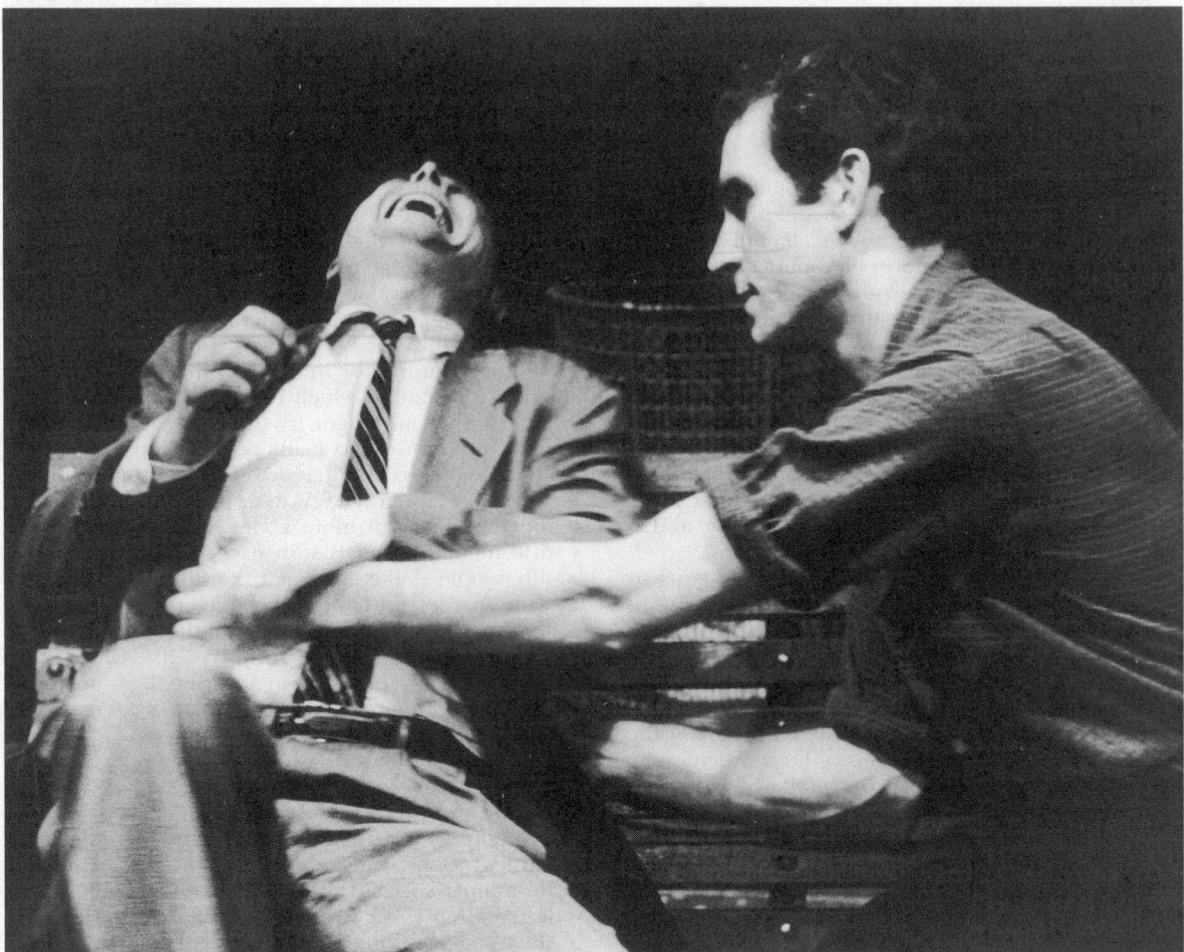

Figure 1. (facing page) Jerry (Mark Richman, who took over the role from George Maharis) questions a wary and reserved Peter (William Daniels) in the Provincetown Playhouse production of *The Zoo Story* in 1960, directed by Milton Katselas. (Photograph: Billy Rose Theatre Collection. The New York Public Library for the Performinng Arts. Astor, Lenox and Tilden Foundations.)

Figure 2. (above) Peter (William Daniels) responds with hysterical laughter as Jerry (Mark Richman) calmly tickles him in the 1960 Provincetown Playhouse production of *The Zoo Story*. (Photograph: Billy Rose Theatre Collection. The New York Public Library for the Performing Arts. Astor, Lenox, and Tilden Foundations.)

Staging of *The Zoo Story*

REVIEW OF THE PROVINCETOWN PLAYHOUSE
PRODUCTION, 1960, BY HENRY HEWES

Last week these columns were devoted mainly to a discussion of Samuel Beckett's rich and poetic playlet, *Krapp's Last Tape*. This play is the first half of a twin bill currently at the Provincetown Playhouse. The second play there, titled *The Zoo Story*, is equally exciting, not only because it is compelling theatre, but also because it introduces Edward Albee, a young (circa thirty) playwright of considerable potentiality.

Mr. Albee's play is quite simple in form. A dull, respectable man with that upper-middle-middle expression on his face is reading on a park bench when an obnoxious stranger approaches him with irritating personal questions and remarks. The stranger has a desperate need to make contact with someone, and as a last resort pushes his listener to violence.

The details of these events are made fascinating by the actors George Maharis and William Daniels. To the role of Jerry, the beatnick, Mr. Maharis brings a quietly hypnotic rhythm that comes across as theatrically colorful yet integrated with his own personality. And as Peter, the square, Mr. Daniels provides a genuine humor. He is at his best in the early part of the play where the tone *is* humorous, as Jerry ridicules the clichés he is able to smoke out of Peter's Madison Avenue existence. Of course, this ridicule has itself become a cliché, and if unimaginatively played would seem merely tired and predicable satire. But director Milton Katselas has permitted each actor an awareness of the situation and of what the dialogue means to one who speaks it. Jerry tends to have this awareness at the precise moment he speaks. And Peter has it a second or two after he has said his line. Even an ordinary interchange (JERRY: "Well, *Time* magazine isn't for blockheads." PETER: "No, I suppose not.") becomes subtly hilarious when given this particular treatment. And it is not just funny, for as he considers each random question, Peter becomes more and more aware of inadequacies not really faced before.

Jerry, on the other hand, seems compelled by an inner, not quite understood drive, an unwillingness to stop short of scraping out the last layer of truth. And even when he is using such colorful language as "But that was the jazz of a very special hotel," it is not done for effect, but rather because that is the best way he knows to express his nostalgia without oversentimentalization. The high point of his performance is reached when he tells "The Story of Jerry and the Dog." In the parable Jerry attempts first kindness and then cruelty to a dog that tries to bite him every time he comes into his boarding house. The result is an eventual compromise in which both Jerry and the dog arrive at a state in which they neither love nor hurt because they no longer try to reach each other. This state—the basis of so many relationships in modern adult society—is what has driven Jerry into his present pilgrimage up Fifth Avenue to the zoo where he had hoped to find out more about the way people exist with animals, animals with each other, and animals with people. As he tells Peter the story of what he saw at the zoo, Jerry attempts, through cruelty, to provoke some animal feeling in Peter, and though the ending is melodramatic and violent, Jerry—like Christ—succeeds at the cost of his life in arousing the human soul out of its deep modern lethargy to an awareness of its animal self.

The Zoo Story is done so well that we can afford to point out that Mr. Katselas might have made this production even more effective if he had been able to highlight some of the author's points more distinctly and had found a more interesting way of expressing the animal stirring within Peter at the play's melodramatic end. We can also afford to wonder if Mr. Albee's suggestion that Jerry's boarding house is a West Side purgatory in which God is a queen who plucks his eyebrows and goes to the john is not one that needs the fuller development he might give it in a longer play. And doesn't his description of Jerry's deceased mother ("She embarked on an adulterous turn of our southern states . . . and her most constant companion among others, among many others, was a Mr. Barleycorn") owe something to Tennessee Williams? No matter. Mr. Albee has written an extraordinary first play, which, next to Jack Gelber's *The Connection,* constitutes the finest new achievement in the theatre this season. Thank God for Off-Broadway, and, I guess, thank God for beatniks.

LORRAINE HANSBERRY

1930–1965

"To be young, gifted and black" is the phrase ringingly associated with Lorraine Hansberry—the first black woman to have a play produced on Broadway, as well as the first woman, the first black person, and the youngest American to win the New York Drama Critics Circle Award for Best Play of the Year. And she won it for her first play, *A Raisin in the Sun* (1959), though competing with works by Tennessee Williams, Archibald MacLeish, and Eugene O'Neill. But Hansberry's self-description, taken from the collection of autobiographical pieces and dramatic works that her ex-husband, Robert Nemiroff, put together after her death (*To Be Young, Gifted and Black*), reveals the difficulties behind that glowing appraisal:

> I was born on the Southside of Chicago. I was born black and female. I was born in a depression after one world war, and came into my adolescence during another.

Hansberry's early childhood abounds with contradictions. Living in a poor, predominantly black neighborhood, her parents were nonetheless wealthy enough to give her a white fur coat when she was just five years old—a coat that drew hostile attacks when she wore it to school. When Hansberry was eight, the family moved to a predominantly white neighborhood where a group of neighbors once threw a brick through the living-room window. The incident may well have been the germ for *A Raisin in the Sun*, the story of a Chicago family who try to move from their cramped Southside apartment to a house in a white neighborhood. Hansberry's parents—her father was a successful businessman who founded a bank and invested in real estate, her mother a bank teller with a college degree—introduced her to prominent black Americans: W.E.B. Du Bois, author of *The Souls of Black Folk;* poet and playwright Langston Hughes, whose words would furnish the title for *A Raisin in the Sun;* and actor-singer Paul Robeson, internationally acclaimed for his portrayals of O'Neill's Emperor Jones and Shakespeare's Othello but later kept from performing in America because of his political views.

Hansberry attended the University of Wisconsin for two years, and then, in 1950, moved to New York City, where she took classes at the New School for Social Research. But her real education came from her work as a writer and editor for Paul Robeson's *Freedom* magazine, a black activist publication dealing with, among other things, African politics (particularly the imprisonment of Jomo Kenyatta) and McCarthyism in the United States. During the early fifties, Hansberry met and married Nemiroff, a politically and socially conscious writer like herself. Though their daring interracial marriage ended in 1964, Nemiroff remained Hansberry's chief supporter. In fact, when her second play, *The Sign in Sidney Brustein's Window* (1964), met with reviews that varied from hostile to enthusiastic, Nemiroff helped keep the production alive. After Hansberry's death from cancer, barely three months after the play opened, he served not only as her literary executor but as her surrogate, putting together *To Be Young, Gifted and Black* (1969), editing her play *Les Blancs* (1970), and producing the musical *Raisin* in 1974.

Hansberry's experiences as a political activist and writer are crucial to her plays, but theatrical influences are equally important. A rich tradition of African American drama lies behind her work, although few black playwrights before Hansberry achieved success with predominantly white audiences on Broadway. And even fewer black playwrights were women, though the plays of Alice Childress, an actress with the American Negro Theatre, form a notable exception: *Trouble in Mind* (1955), which won an Off-Broadway award; *Wedding Band* (1966), an interracial love story; and *Wine in the Wilderness* (1969). Hansberry's stunning success with *A Raisin in the Sun* became the example for others to follow; Childress continued to write, and the last three decades have seen the work of Ntozake Shange, Adrienne Kennedy, Julie Ann Mason, Pearl Cleage, Kathleen Collins, and Suzan-Lori Parks.

Another important theatrical source for Hansberry came, somewhat surprisingly, from Irish playwright Sean O'Casey. Hansberry was just eighteen and a freshman at the University of Wisconsin when she saw a production of O'Casey's *Juno and the Paycock*. Years later, Juno's cry of pain as she realizes that her son Johnny has been killed for betraying an Irish Republican would become part of *To Be Young, Gifted and Black*, a testament to the power of this play on Hansberry's imagination. Though the struggles of the Boyles in Dublin of the twenties and the Youngers in Chicago of the fifties seem far distant, both plays focus on the family, and both family conflicts reflect political ones.

One of the distinctive strengths of Hansberry's play is its striking portrayal of characters who represent a wide range of personal histories and social constructs. From Lena (Mama) Younger, the sternly Christian matriarch, to Ruth, working as domestic help, to Beneatha, who hopes to be a doctor, the female characters in the play present a broad spectrum of black women who cope with unpleasant reality yet dream of better things. And in the play's male characters, Hansberry offers a similar range: Walter Lee Younger is a chauffeur, working for a white man; George Murchison is a fellow student of Beneatha's, but aspires to fit into the white world; and Joseph Asagai, from Nigeria, is proud of his African heritage. To the extent that these characters are "representative," they may seem stereotypical, and indeed, George C. Wolfe's 1986 play *The Colored Museum* contains a section—"The Last Mama-on-the-Couch Play"—satirizing *A Raisin in the Sun* with direct echoes of Hansberry's lines and a description of "Walter-Lee-Beau-Willie-Jones" as "Mama's thirty-year-old son. His brow is heavy from three hundred years of oppression." But the satire testifies to the power of *A Raisin in the Sun*—a play powerful enough both to provoke and to withstand parody.

In part, Wolfe's parody arises from a sense that Hansberry's work is comfortable and nonmilitant. It seems worlds away from Amiri Baraka's angry and expressionistic *Dutchman*, with its explicit violence and disturbing sexuality, yet it preceded that explosive play by just two years. But when Baraka himself looked back on Hansberry's play in 1986, he called attention first to his own misunderstanding and labeling of her work as "middle class" and then to his sense that these "middle class" concerns "are actually reflective of the essence of black people's striving and the will to defeat segregation, discrimination, and national oppression." For him, as for many audiences who flocked to the play when it celebrated its twenty-fifth anniversary in 1983, Hansberry's ideas and characters did not date but endured.

The play's twenty-fifth anniversary also reminded audiences and critics of the enormous influence of this play. The only "known" actors from the 1959 production were Sidney Poitier (Walter Lee) and Claudia McNeil (Mama), but in the cast were names that would become familiar in American theater as playwrights, directors, and major actors: Douglas Turner Ward, Lonne Elder III, Louis Gossett Jr., Ruby Dee, Diana Sands, and Glynn Turman. In addition, director Lloyd Richards would go on to become one of the most important forces in American drama. Further testament to the play's power comes from the playwright Adrienne Kennedy, who had in her words "abandoned playwriting" but then "felt reawakened" by Hansberry's stunning success. Brooks Atkinson's review identifies the source of Hansberry's power as "the honesty of the writing" and found the production's power in "the rousing honesty of the stage work"—honesty which seems to have survived the backstage conflicts discussed by Sidney Poitier and Lloyd Richards (see "Staging" section following the text of the play). That honesty grows out of Hansberry's perception that conflict and love may coexist. Though Mama loves Walter Lee, and wishes to help him (see Figure 1), she is equally determined to use the insurance check to get the family out of their crowded tenement. And though Hansberry shows us clearly the pain and pride that push Walter Lee to appropriate the insurance money for his own use, she also reveals the growth of the man for whom individual freedom lies not in money but in acting freely. In the play's final scene, both the characters on stage and the watching audience expect Walter Lee to capitulate to the white man who tries to bribe the family to keep them out of the neighborhood; the tension in his face fights the tenderness of his hands (Figure 2) as Walter Lee hugs his young son, and finally, painfully, announces: "We have decided to move into our house because my father—my father—he earned it for us brick by brick." The moment is powerful as a social and political statement, but it gains that power from the strength of the human relationships it embodies.

A RAISIN IN THE SUN

BY LORRAINE HANSBERRY

HARLEM (A Dream Deferred)

What happens to a dream deferred?

Does it dry up
like a raisin in the sun?
Or fester like a sore—
And then run?
Does it stink like rotten meat?
Or crust and sugar over—
like a syrupy sweet?

Maybe it just sags
like a heavy load.

Or does it explode? —LANGSTON HUGHES

CHARACTERS

RUTH YOUNGER
TRAVIS YOUNGER
WALTER LEE YOUNGER (*Brother*)
BENEATHA YOUNGER
LENA YOUNGER (*Mama*)
JOSEPH ASAGAI
GEORGE MURCHISON
KARL LINDNER
BOBO
MOVING MEN

SCENE

The action of the play is set in Chicago's Southside, sometime between World War II and the present.

ACT 1

Scene 1: *Friday morning.*
Scene 2: *The following morning.*

ACT 2

Scene 1: *Later, the same day.*
Scene 2: *Friday night, a few weeks later.*
Scene 3: *Moving day, one week later.*

ACT 3

An hour later.

ACT 1 / SCENE 1

(*The Younger living room would be a comfortable and well-ordered room if it were not for a number of indestructible contradictions to this state of being. Its furnishings are typical and undistinguished and their primary feature now is that they have clearly had to accommodate the living of too many people for too many years—and they are tired. Still, we can see that at some time, a time probably no longer remembered by the family [except perhaps for* MAMA*], the furnishings of this room were actually selected with care and love and even hope—and brought to this apartment and arranged with taste and pride.*)

(*That was a long time ago. Now the once loved pattern of the couch upholstery has to fight to show itself from under acres of crocheted doilies and couch covers which* have themselves finally come to be more important than the upholstery. And here a table or a chair has been moved to disguise the worn places in the carpet; but the carpet has fought back by showing its weariness, with depressing uniformity, elsewhere on its surface.*)

(*Weariness has, in fact, won in this room. Everything has been polished, washed, sat on, used, scrubbed too often. All pretenses but living itself have long since vanished from the very atmosphere of this room.*)

(*Moreover, a section of this room, for it is not really a room unto itself, though the landlord's lease would make it seem so, slopes backward to provide a small kitchen area, where the family prepares the meals that are eaten in the living room proper, which must also serve as dining room. The single window that has been provided for these "two" rooms is located in this kitchen area. The sole natural light the family may enjoy in the course of a day is only that which fights its way through this little window.)*

(At left, a door leads to a bedroom which is shared by MAMA *and her daughter,* BENEATHA. *At right, opposite, is a second room [which in the beginning of the life of this apartment was probably a breakfast room] which serves as a bedroom for* WALTER *and his wife,* RUTH.)

(Time: Sometime between World War II and the present.)

(Place: Chicago's Southside.)

(At rise: It is morning dark in the living room. TRAVIS *is asleep on the make-down bed at center. An alarm clock sounds from within the bedroom at right, and presently* RUTH *enters from that room and closes the door behind her. She crosses sleepily toward the window. As she passes her sleeping son she reaches down and shakes him a little. At the window she raises the shade and a dusky Southside morning light comes in feebly. She fills a pot with water and puts it on to boil. She calls to the boy, between yawns, in a slightly muffled voice.)*

(RUTH is about thirty. We can see that she was a pretty girl, even exceptionally so, but now it is apparent that life has been little that she expected, and disappointment has already begun to hang in her face. In a few years, before thirty-five even, she will be known among her people as a "settled woman.")

(She crosses to her son and gives him a good, final, rousing shake.)

RUTH: Come on now, boy, it's seven thirty! *(Her son sits up at last, in a stupor of sleepiness.)* I say hurry up, Travis! You ain't the only person in the world got to use a bathroom! *(The child, a sturdy, handsome little boy of ten or eleven, drags himself out of the bed and almost blindly takes his towels and "today's clothes" from drawers and a closet and goes out to the bathroom, which is in an outside hall and which is shared by another family or families on the same floor.* RUTH *crosses to the bedroom door at right and opens it and calls in to her husband.)* Walter Lee! . . . It's after seven thirty! Lemme see you do some waking up in there now! *(She waits.)* You better get up from there, man! It's after seven thirty I tell you. *(She waits again.)* All right, you just go ahead and lay there and next thing you know Travis be finished and Mr. Johnson'll be in there and you'll be fussing and cussing round here like a madman! And be late too! *(She waits, at the end of patience.)* Walter Lee—it's time for you to GET UP!

*(She waits another second and then starts to go into the bedroom, but is apparently satisfied that her husband has begun to get up. She stops, pulls the door to, and returns to the kitchen area. She wipes her face with a moist cloth and runs her fingers through her sleep-disheveled hair in a vain effort and ties an apron around her housecoat. The bedroom door at right opens and her husband stands in the doorway in his pajamas, which are rumpled and mis-*mated. *He is a lean, intense young man in his middle thirties, inclined to quick nervous movements and erratic speech habits—and always in his voice there is a quality of indictment.)*

WALTER: Is he out yet?

RUTH: What you mean *out*? He ain't hardly got in there good yet.

WALTER *(wandering in, still more oriented to sleep than to a new day)*: Well, what was you doing all that yelling for if I can't even get in there yet? *(Stopping and thinking.)* Check coming today?

RUTH: They *said* Saturday and this is just Friday and I hopes to God you ain't going to get up here first thing this morning and start talking to me 'bout no money—'cause I 'bout don't want to hear it.

WALTER: Something the matter with you this morning?

RUTH: No—I'm just sleepy as the devil. What kind of eggs you want?

WALTER: Not scrambled. *(RUTH starts to scramble eggs.)* Paper come? *(RUTH points impatiently to the rolled up* Tribune *on the table, and he gets it and spreads it out and vaguely reads the front page.)* Set off another bomb yesterday.

RUTH *(maximum indifference)*: Did they?

WALTER *(looking up)*: What's the matter with you?

RUTH: Ain't nothing the matter with me. And don't keep asking me that this morning.

WALTER: Ain't nobody bothering you. *(Reading the news of the day absently again.)* Say Colonel McCormick is sick.

RUTH *(affecting tea-party interest)*: Is he now? Poor thing.

WALTER *(sighing and looking at his watch)*: Oh, me. *(He waits.)* Now what is that boy doing in that bathroom all this time? He just going to have to start getting up earlier. I can't be being late to work on account of him fooling around in there.

RUTH *(turning on him)*: Oh, no he ain't going to be getting up no earlier no such thing! It ain't his fault that he can't get to bed no earlier nights 'cause he got a bunch of crazy good-for-nothing clowns sitting up running their mouths in what is supposed to be his bedroom after ten o'clock at night . . .

WALTER: That's what you mad about, ain't it? The things I want to talk about with my friends just couldn't be important in your mind, could they?

(He rises and finds a cigarette in her handbag on the table and crosses to the little window and looks out, smoking and deeply enjoying this first one.)

RUTH *(almost matter of factly, a complaint too automatic to deserve emphasis)*: Why you always got to smoke before you eat in the morning?

WALTER (*at the window*): Just look at 'em down there . . . Running and racing to work . . . (*He turns and faces his wife and watches her a moment at the stove, and then, suddenly.*) You look young this morning, baby.

RUTH (*indifferently*): Yeah?

WALTER: Just for a second—stirring them eggs. Just for a second it was—you looked real young again. (*He reaches for her; she crosses away. Then, drily.*) It's gone now—you look like yourself again!

RUTH: Man, if you don't shut up and leave me alone.

WALTER (*looking out to the street again*): First thing a man ought to learn in life is not to make love to no colored woman first thing in the morning. You all some eeeevil people at eight o'clock in the morning.

(TRAVIS *appears in the hall doorway, almost fully dressed and quite wide awake now, his towels and pajamas across his shoulders. He opens the door and signals for his father to make the bathroom in a hurry.*)

TRAVIS (*watching the bathroom*): Daddy, come on!

(*Walter gets his bathroom utensils and flies out to the bathroom.*)

RUTH: Sit down and have your breakfast, Travis.

TRAVIS: Mama, this is Friday. (*Gleefully.*) Check coming tomorrow, huh?

RUTH: You get your mind off money and eat your breakfast.

TRAVIS (*eating*): This is the morning we supposed to bring the fifty cents to school.

RUTH: Well, I ain't got no fifty cents this morning.

TRAVIS: Teacher say we have to.

RUTH: I don't care what teacher say. I ain't got it. Eat your breakfast, Travis.

TRAVIS: I *am* eating.

RUTH: Hush up now and just eat!

(*The boy gives her an exasperated look for her lack of understanding and eats grudgingly.*)

TRAVIS: You think Grandmama would have it?

RUTH: No! And I want you to stop asking your grandmother for money, you hear me?

TRAVIS (*outraged*): Gaaaleee! I don't ask her, she just gimme it sometimes!

RUTH: Travis Willard Younger—I got too much on me this morning to be—

TRAVIS: Maybe Daddy—

RUTH: *Travis!*

(*The boy hushes abruptly. They are both quiet and tense for several seconds.*)

TRAVIS (*presently*): Could I maybe go carry some groceries in front of the supermarket for a little while after school then?

RUTH: Just hush, I said. (TRAVIS *jabs his spoon into his cereal bowl viciously and rests his head in anger upon his fists.*) If you through eating, you can get over there and make up your bed.

(*The boy obeys stiffly and crosses the room, almost mechanically, to the bed and more or less folds the bedding into a heap, then angrily gets his books and cap.*)

TRAVIS (*sulking and standing apart from her unnaturally*): I'm gone.

RUTH (*looking up from the stove to inspect him automatically*): Come here. (*He crosses to her and she studies his head.*) If you don't take this comb and fix this here head, you better! (TRAVIS *puts down his books with a great sigh of oppression and crosses to the mirror. His mother mutters under her breath about his "slubbornness.*") 'Bout to march out of here with that head looking just like chickens slept in it! I just don't know where you get your slubborn ways . . . And get your jacket, too. Looks chilly out this morning.

TRAVIS (*with conspicuously brushed hair and jacket*): I'm gone.

RUTH: Get carfare and milk money—(*waving one finger*)—and not a single penny for no caps, you hear me?

TRAVIS (*with sullen politeness*): Yes'm.

(*He turns in outrage to leave. His mother watches after him as in his frustration he approaches the door almost comically. When she speaks to him, her voice has become a very gentle tease.*)

RUTH (*mocking; as she thinks he would say it*): Oh, Mama makes me so mad sometimes, I don't know what to do! (*She waits and continues to his back as he stands stock-still in front of the door.*) I wouldn't kiss that woman good-bye for nothing in this world this morning! (*The boy finally turns around and rolls his eyes at her, knowing the mood has changed and he is vindicated; he does not, however, move toward her yet.*) Not for nothing in this world! (*She finally laughs aloud at him and holds out her arms to him and we see that it is a way between them, very old and practiced. He crosses to her and allows her to embrace him warmly but keeps his face fixed with masculine rigidity. She holds him back from her presently and looks at him and runs her fingers over the features of his face. With utter gentleness—*) Now—whose little old angry man are you?

TRAVIS (*the masculinity and gruffness start to fade at last*): Aw gaalee—Mama . . .

RUTH (*mimicking*): Aw—gaaaaalleeeee, Mama! (*She pushes him, with rough playfulness and finality, toward the door.*) Get on out of here or you going to be late.

TRAVIS (*in the face of love, new aggressiveness*): Mama, could I *please* go carry groceries?

RUTH: Honey, it's starting to get so cold evenings.

WALTER (*coming in from the bathroom and drawing a make-*

believe gun from a make-believe holster and shooting at his son): What is it he wants to do?

RUTH: Go carry groceries after school at the supermarket.

WALTER: Well, let him go . . .

TRAVIS *(quickly, to the ally):* I *have* to—she won't gimme the fifty cents . . .

WALTER *(to his wife only):* Why not?

RUTH *(simply, and with flavor):* 'Cause we don't have it.

WALTER *(to* RUTH *only):* What you tell the boy things like that for? *(Reaching down into his pants with a rather important gesture.)* Here, son—

(He hands the boy the coin, but his eyes are directed to his wife's. TRAVIS *takes the money happily.)*

TRAVIS: Thanks, Daddy.

(He starts out. RUTH *watches both of them with murder in her eyes.* WALTER *stands and stares back at her with defiance and suddenly reaches into his pocket again on an afterthought.)*

WALTER *(without even looking at his son, still staring hard at his wife):* In fact, here's another fifty cents . . . Buy yourself some fruit today—or take a taxicab to school or something!

TRAVIS: Whoopee—

(He leaps up and clasps his father around the middle with his legs, and they face each other in mutual appreciation; slowly WALTER LEE *peeks around the boy to catch the violent rays from his wife's eyes and draws his head back as if shot.)*

WALTER: You better get down now—and get to school, man.

TRAVIS *(at the door):* O.K. Good-bye.

(He exits.)

WALTER *(after him, pointing with pride):* That's my boy. *(She looks at him in disgust and turns back to her work.)* You know what I was thinking 'bout in the bathroom this morning?

RUTH: No.

WALTER: How come you always try to be so pleasant!

RUTH: What is there to be pleasant 'bout!

WALTER: You want to know what I was thinking 'bout in the bathroom or not!

RUTH: I know what you thinking 'bout.

WALTER *(ignoring her):* 'Bout what me and Willy Harris was talking about last night.

RUTH *(immediately—a refrain):* Willy Harris is a good-for-nothing loudmouth.

WALTER: Anybody who talks to me has got to be a good-for-nothing loudmouth, ain't he? And what you know about who is just a good-for-nothing loudmouth? Charlie Atkins was just a "good-for-nothing loudmouth" too, wasn't he! When he wanted me to go in the dry-cleaning business with

him. And now—he's grossing a hundred thousand a year. A hundred thousand dollars a year! You still call *him* a loudmouth!

RUTH *(bitterly):* Oh, Walter Lee . . .

(She folds her head on her arms over the table.)

WALTER *(rising and coming to her and standing over her):* You tired, ain't you? Tired of everything. Me, the boy, the way we live—this beat-up hole—everything. Ain't you? *(She doesn't look up, doesn't answer.)* So tired—moaning and groaning all the time, but you wouldn't do nothing to help, would you? You couldn't be on my side that long for nothing, could you?

RUTH: Walter, please leave me alone.

WALTER: A man needs for a woman to back him up . . .

RUTH: Walter—

WALTER: Mama would listen to you. You know she listen to you more than she do me and Bennie. She think more of you. All you have to do is just sit down with her when you drinking your coffee one morning and talking 'bout things like you do and—*(He sits down beside her and demonstrates graphically what he thinks her methods and tone should be.)*—you just sip your coffee, see, and say easy like that you been thinking 'bout that deal Walter Lee is so interested in, 'bout the store and all, and sip some more coffee, like what you saying ain't really that important to you—And the next thing you know, she be listening good and asking you questions and when I come home—I can tell her the details. This ain't no fly-by-night proposition, baby. I mean we figured it out, me and Willy and Bobo.

RUTH *(with a frown):* Bobo?

WALTER: Yeah. You see, this little liquor store we got in mind cost seventy-five thousand and we figured the initial investment on the place be 'bout thirty thousand, see. That be ten thousand each. Course, there's a couple of hundred you got to pay so's you don't spend your life just waiting for them clowns to let your license get approved—

RUTH: You mean graft?

WALTER *(frowning impatiently):* Don't call it that. See there, that just goes to show you what women understand about the world. Baby, don't *nothing* happen for you in this world 'less you pay *somebody* off!

RUTH: Walter, leave me alone! *(She raises her head and stares at him vigorously—then says, more quietly.)* Eat your eggs, they gonna be cold.

WALTER *(straightening up from her and looking off):* That's it. There you are. Man say to his woman: I got me a dream. His woman say: Eat your eggs. *(Sadly, but gaining in power.)* Man say: I got to take hold of this here world, baby! And a woman will say: Eat your eggs and go to work. (*Passionately now.*) Man say: I got to change my life, I'm choking to death, baby! And his woman say—(*in utter anguish as he brings his fists down on his thighs*)— Your eggs is getting cold!

RUTH (*softly*): Walter, that ain't none of our money.

WALTER (*not listening at all or even looking at her*): This morning, I was lookin' in the mirror and thinking about it . . . I'm thirty-five years old; I been married eleven years and I got a boy who sleeps in the living room—(*very, very quietly*)—and all I got to give him is stories about how rich white people live . . .

RUTH: Eat your eggs, Walter.

WALTER (*slams the table and jumps up*): —DAMN MY EGGS—DAMN ALL THE EGGS THAT EVER WAS!

RUTH: Then go to work.

WALTER (*looking up at her*): See—I'm trying to talk to you 'bout myself— (*shaking his head with the repetition*)—and all you can say is eat them eggs and go to work.

RUTH (*wearily*): Honey, you never say nothing new. I listen to you every day, every night and every morning, and you never say nothing new. (*Shrugging.*) So you would rather *be* Mr. Arnold than be his chauffeur. So—I would *rather* be living in Buckingham Palace.

WALTER: That is just what is wrong with the colored woman in this world . . . Don't understand about building their men up and making 'em feel like they somebody. Like they can do something.

RUTH (*drily, but to hurt*): There *are* colored men who do things.

WALTER: No thanks to the colored woman.

RUTH: Well, being a colored woman, I guess I can't help myself none.

(*She rises and gets the ironing board and sets it up and attacks a huge pile of rough-dried clothes, sprinkling them in preparation for the ironing and then rolling them into tight fat balls.*)

WALTER (*mumbling*): We one group of men tied to a race of women with small minds!

(*His sister* BENEATHA *enters. She is about twenty, as slim and intense as her brother. She is not as pretty as her sister-in-law, but her lean, almost intellectual face has a handsomeness of its own. She wears a bright red flannel nightie, and her thick hair stands wildly about her head. Her speech is a mixture of many things; it is different from the rest of the family's insofar as education has permeated her sense of English—and perhaps the Midwest rather than the South has finally—at last—won out in her inflection; but not altogether, because over all of it is a soft slurring and transformed use of vowels which is the decided influence of the Southside. She passes through the room without looking at either* RUTH *or* WALTER *and goes to the outside door and looks, a little blindly, out to the bathroom. She*

sees that it has been lost to the Johnsons. She closes the door with a sleepy vengeance and crosses to the table and sits down a little defeated.*)

BENEATHA: I am going to start timing those people.

WALTER: You should get up earlier.

BENEATHA (*Her face in her hands. She is still fighting the urge to go back to bed*): Really—would you suggest dawn? Where's the paper?

WALTER (*pushing the paper across the table to her as he studies her almost clinically, as though he has never seen her before*): You a horrible-looking chick at this hour.

BENEATHA (*drily*): Good morning, everybody.

WALTER (*senselessly*): How is school coming?

BENEATHA (*in the same spirit*): Lovely. Lovely. And you know, biology is the greatest. (*Looking up at him.*) I dissected something that looked just like you yesterday.

WALTER: I just wondered if you've made up your mind and everything.

BENEATHA (*gaining in sharpness and impatience*): And what did I answer yesterday morning—and the day before that?

RUTH (*from the ironing board, like someone disinterested and old*): Don't be so nasty, Bennie.

BENEATHA (*still to her brother*): And the day before that and the day before that!

WALTER (*defensively*): I'm interested in you. Something wrong with that? Ain't many girls who decide—

WALTER AND BENEATHA (*in unison*): —"to be a doctor."

(*Silence.*)

WALTER: Have we figured out yet just exactly how much medical school is going to cost?

RUTH: Walter Lee, why don't you leave that girl alone and get out of here to work?

BENEATHA (*exits to the bathroom and bangs on the door*): Come on out of there, please!

(*She comes back into the room.*)

WALTER (*looking at his sister intently*): You know the check is coming tomorrow.

BENEATHA (*turning on him with a sharpness all her own*): That money belongs to Mama, Walter, and it's for her to decide how she wants to use it. I don't care if she wants to buy a house or a rocket ship or just nail it up somewhere and look at it. It's hers. Not ours—*hers*.

WALTER (*bitterly*): Now ain't that fine! You just got your mother's interest at heart, ain't you, girl? You such a nice girl—but if Mama got that money she can always take a few thousand and help you through school too—can't she?

BENEATHA: I have never asked anyone around here to do anything for me!

WALTER: No! And the line between asking and just

accepting when the time comes is big and wide—ain't it!

BENEATHA *(with fury)*: What do you want from me, Brother—that I quit school or just drop dead, which!

WALTER: I don't want nothing but for you to stop acting holy 'round here. Me and Ruth done made some sacrifices for you—why can't you do something for the family?

RUTH: Walter, don't be dragging me in it.

WALTER: You are in it—Don't you get up and go work in somebody's kitchen for the last three years to help put clothes on her back?

RUTH: Oh, Walter—that's not fair . . .

WALTER: It ain't that nobody expects you to get on your knees and say thank you, Brother; thank you, Ruth; thank you, Mama—and thank you, Travis, for wearing the same pair of shoes for two semesters—

BENEATHA *(dropping to her knees)*: Well—I *do*—all right?—thank everybody! And forgive me for ever wanting to be anything at all! *(Pursuing him on her knees across the floor.)* FORGIVE ME, FORGIVE ME, FORGIVE ME!

RUTH: Please stop it! Your mama'll hear you.

WALTER: Who the hell told you you had to be a doctor? If you so crazy 'bout messing 'round with sick people—then go be a nurse like other women—or just get married and be quiet . . .

BENEATHA: Well—you finally got it said . . . It took you three years but you finally got it said. Walter, give up; leave me alone—it's Mama's money.

WALTER: *He was my father, too!*

BENEATHA: So what? He was mine, too—and Travis' grandfather—but the insurance money belongs to Mama. Picking on me is not going to make her give it to you to invest in any liquor stores—*(under breath, dropping into a chair)*—and I for one say, God bless Mama for that!

WALTER *(to RUTH)*: See—did you hear? Did you hear!

RUTH: Honey, please go to work.

WALTER: Nobody in this house is ever going to understand me.

BENEATHA: Because you're a nut.

WALTER: Who's a nut?

BENEATHA: You—you are a nut. Thee is mad, boy.

WALTER *(looking at his wife and his sister from the door, very sadly)*: The world's most backward race of people, and that's a fact.

BENEATHA *(turning slowly in her chair)*: And then there are all those prophets who would lead us out of the wilderness—*(WALTER slams out of the house)*—into the swamps!

RUTH: Bennie, why you always gotta be pickin' on your brother? Can't you be a little sweeter sometimes? *(Door opens. WALTER walks in. He fumbles*

with his cap, starts to speak, clears throat, looks everywhere but at RUTH. Finally.)

WALTER *(to RUTH)*: I need some money for carfare.

RUTH *(looks at him, then warms; teasing, but tenderly)*: Fifty cents? *(She goes to her bag and gets money.)* Here—take a taxi!

(WALTER exits. MAMA enters. She is a woman in her early sixties, full-bodied and strong. She is one of those women of a certain grace and beauty who wear it so unobtrusively that it takes a while to notice. Her dark brown face is surrounded by the total whiteness of her hair, and, being a woman who has adjusted to many things in life and overcome many more, her face is full of strength. She has, we can see, wit and faith of a kind that keep her eyes lit and full of interest and expectancy. She is, in a word, a beautiful woman. Her bearing is perhaps most like the noble bearing of the women of the Hereros of Southwest Africa—rather as if she imagines that as she walks she still bears a basket or a vessel upon her head. Her speech, on the other hand, is as careless as her carriage is precise—she is inclined to slur everything—but her voice is perhaps not so much quiet as simply soft.)

MAMA: Who that 'round here slamming doors at this hour?

(She crosses through the room, goes to the window, opens it, and brings in a feeble little plant growing doggedly in a small pot on the window sill. She feels the dirt and puts it back out.)

RUTH: That was Walter Lee. He and Bennie was at it again.

MAMA: My children and they tempers. Lord, if this little old plant don't get more sun than it's been getting it ain't never going to see spring again. *(She turns from the window.)* What's the matter with you this morning, Ruth? You looks right peaked. You aiming to iron all them things? Leave some for me. I'll get to 'em this afternoon. Bennie honey, it's too drafty for you to be sitting 'round half dressed. Where's your robe?

BENEATHA: In the cleaners.

MAMA: Well, go get mine and put it on.

BENEATHA: I'm not cold, Mama, honest.

MAMA: I know—but you so thin . . .

BENEATHA *(irritably)*: Mama, I'm not cold.

MAMA *(seeing the make-down bed as TRAVIS has left it)*: Lord have mercy, look at that poor bed. Bless his heart—he tries, don't he?

(She moves to the bed TRAVIS has sloppily made up.)

RUTH: No—he don't half try at all 'cause he knows you going to come along behind him and fix everything. That's just how come he don't know how to do nothing right now—you done spoiled that boy so.

MAMA *(folding bedding)*: Well—he's a little boy. Ain't

supposed to know 'bout housekeeping. My baby, that's what he is. What you fix for his breakfast this morning?

RUTH (*angrily*): I feed my son, Lena!

MAMA: I ain't meddling—(*Under breath; busybodyish.*) I just noticed all last week he had cold cereal, and when it starts getting this chilly in the fall a child ought to have some hot grits or something when he goes out in the cold—

RUTH (*furious*): I gave him hot oats—is that all right!

MAMA: I ain't meddling. (*Pause.*) Put a lot of nice butter on it? (RUTH *shoots her an angry look and does not reply.*) He likes lots of butter.

RUTH (*exasperated*): Lena—

MAMA (*to* BENEATHA. MAMA *is inclined to wander conversationally sometimes*): What was you and your brother fussing 'bout this morning?

BENEATHA: It's not important, Mama.

(*She gets up and goes to look out at the bathroom, which is apparently free, and she picks up her towels and rushes out.*)

MAMA: What was they fighting about?

RUTH: Now you know as well as I do.

MAMA (*shaking her head*): Brother still worrying hisself sick about that money?

RUTH: You know he is.

MAMA: You had breakfast?

RUTH: Some coffee.

MAMA: Girl, you better start eating and looking after yourself better. You almost thin as Travis.

RUTH: Lena—

MAMA: Un-hunh?

RUTH: What are you going to do with it?

MAMA: Now don't you start, child. It's too early in the morning to be talking about money. It ain't Christian.

RUTH: It's just that he got his heart set on that store—

MAMA: You mean that liquor store that Willy Harris want him to invest in?

RUTH: Yes—

MAMA: We ain't no business people, Ruth. We just plain working folks.

RUTH: Ain't nobody business people till they go into business. Walter Lee say colored people ain't never going to start getting ahead till they start gambling on some different kinds of things in the world—investments and things.

MAMA: What done got into you, girl? Walter Lee done finally sold you on investing.

RUTH: No. Mama, something is happening between Walter and me. I don't know what it is—but he needs something—something I can't give him anymore. He needs this chance, Lena.

MAMA (*frowning deeply*): But liquor, honey—

RUTH: Well—like Walter say—I spec people going to always be drinking themselves some liquor.

MAMA: Well—whether they drinks it or not ain't none of my business. But whether I go into business selling it to 'em *is*, and I don't want that on my ledger this late in life. (*Stopping suddenly and studying her daughter-in-law.*) Ruth Younger, what's the matter with you today? You look like you could fall over right there.

RUTH: I'm tired.

MAMA: Then you better stay home from work today.

RUTH: I can't stay home. She'd be calling up the agency and screaming at them, "My girl didn't come in today—send me somebody! My girl didn't come in!" Oh, she just have a fit . . .

MAMA: Well, let her have it. I'll just call her up and say you got the flu—

RUTH (*laughing*): Why the flu?

MAMA: 'Cause it sounds respectable to 'em. Something white people get, too. They know 'bout the flu. Otherwise they think you been cut up or something when you tell 'em you sick.

RUTH: I got to go in. We need the money.

MAMA: Somebody would of thought my children done all but starved to death the way they talk about money here late. Child, we got a great big old check coming tomorrow.

RUTH (*sincerely, but also self-righteously*): Now that's your money. It ain't got nothing to do with me. We all feel like that—Walter and Bennie and me—even Travis.

MAMA (*thoughtfully, and suddenly very far away*): Ten thousand dollars—

RUTH: Sure is wonderful.

MAMA: Ten thousand dollars.

RUTH: You know what you should do, Miss Lena? You should take yourself a trip somewhere. To Europe or South America or someplace—

MAMA (*throwing up her hands at the thought*): Oh, child!

RUTH: I'm serious. Just pack up and leave! Go on away and enjoy yourself some. Forget about the family and have yourself a ball for once in your life—

MAMA (*drily*): You sound like I'm just about ready to die. Who'd go with me? What I look like wandering 'round Europe by myself?

RUTH: Shoot—these here rich white women do it all the time. They don't think nothing of packing up they suitcases and piling on one of them big steamships and—swoosh!—they gone, child.

MAMA: Something always told me I wasn't no rich white woman.

RUTH: Well—what are you going to do with it then?

MAMA: I ain't rightly decided. (*Thinking. She speaks now with emphasis.*) Some of it got to be put away for Beneatha and her schoolin'—and ain't nothing going to touch that part of it. Nothing. (*She waits several seconds, trying to make up her mind about something, and looks at* RUTH *a little tentatively before going on.*) Been thinking that we maybe could meet the notes on a little old two-story some-where, with a yard where Travis could play in the summertime, if we use part of the insurance for a down payment and everybody kind of pitch in. I could maybe take on a little day work again, few days a week—

RUTH (*studying her mother-in-law furtively and concentrating on her ironing, anxious to encourage without seeming to*): Well, Lord knows, we've put enough rent into this here rat trap to pay for four houses by now . . .

MAMA (*looking up at the words "rat trap" and then looking around and leaning back and sighing—in a suddenly reflective mood*): "Rat trap"—yes, that's all it is. (*Smiling.*) I remember just as well the day me and Big Walter moved in here. Hadn't been married but two weeks and wasn't planning on living here no more than a year. (*She shakes her head at the dissolved dream.*) We was going to set away, little by little, don't you know, and buy a little place out in Morgan Park. We had even picked out the house. (*Chuckling a little.*) Looks right dumpy today. But Lord, child, you should know all the dreams I had 'bout buying that house and fixing it up and making me a little garden in the back—(*She waits and stops smiling.*) And didn't none of it happen.

(*Dropping her hands in a futile gesture.*)

RUTH (*keeps her head down, ironing*): Yes, life can be a barrel of disappointments, sometimes.

MAMA: Honey, Big Walter would come in here some nights back then and slump down on that couch there and just look at the rug, and look at me and look at the rug and then back at me—and I'd know he was down then . . . really down. (*After a second very long and thoughtful pause; she is seeing back to times that only she can see.*) And then, Lord, when I lost that baby—little Claude—I almost thought I was going to lose Big Walter too. Oh, that man grieved hisself! He was one man to love his children.

RUTH: Ain't nothin' can tear at you like losin' your baby.

MAMA: I guess that's how come that man finally worked hisself to death like he done. Like he was fighting his own war with this here world that took his baby from him.

RUTH: He sure was a fine man, all right. I always liked Mr. Younger.

MAMA: Crazy 'bout his children! God knows there was plenty wrong with Walter Younger—hardheaded, mean, kind of wild with women—plenty wrong with him. But he sure loved his children. Always wanted them to have something—be something. That's where Brother gets all these notions, I reckon. Big Walter used to say, he'd get right wet in the eyes sometimes, lean his head back with the water standing in his eyes and say, "Seem like God didn't see fit to give the black man nothing but dreams—but He did give us children to make them dreams seem worthwhile." (*She smiles.*) He could talk like that, don't you know.

RUTH: Yes, he sure could. He was a good man, Mr. Younger.

MAMA: Yes, a fine man—just couldn't never catch up with his dreams, that's all.

(BENEATHA *comes in, brushing her hair and looking up to the ceiling, where the sound of a vacuum cleaner has started up.*)

BENEATHA: What could be so dirty on that woman's rugs that she has to vacuum them every single day?

RUTH: I wish certain young women 'round here who I could name would take inspiration about certain rugs in a certain apartment I could also mention.

BENEATHA (*shrugging*): How much cleaning can a house need, for Christ's sakes.

MAMA (*not liking the Lord's name used thus*): Bennie!

RUTH: Just listen to her—just listen!

BENEATHA: Oh, God!

MAMA: If you use the Lord's name just one more time—

BENEATHA (*a bit of a whine*): Oh, Mama—

RUTH: Fresh—just fresh as salt, this girl!

BENEATHA (*drily*): Well—if the salt loses its savor—

MAMA: Now that will do. I just ain't going to have you 'round here reciting the scriptures in vain—you hear me?

BENEATHA: How did I manage to get on everybody's wrong side by just walking into a room?

RUTH: If you weren't so fresh—

BENEATHA: Ruth, I'm twenty years old.

MAMA: What time you be home from school today?

BENEATHA: Kind of late. (*With enthusiasm.*) Madeline is going to start my guitar lessons today.

(MAMA *and* RUTH *look up with the same expression.*)

MAMA: Your *what* kind of lessons?

BENEATHA: Guitar.

RUTH: Oh, Father!

MAMA: How come you done taken it in your mind to learn to play the guitar?

BENEATHA: I just want to, that's all.

MAMA (*smiling*): Lord, child, don't you know what to do with yourself? How long it going to be before you get tired of this now—like you got tired of that little play-acting group you joined last year? (*Looking at* RUTH.) And what was it the year before that?

RUTH: The horseback-riding club for which she bought that fifty-five-dollar riding habit that's been hanging in the closet ever since!

MAMA (*to* BENEATHA): Why you got to flit so from one thing to another, baby?

BENEATHA (*sharply*): I just want to learn to play the guitar. Is there anything wrong with that?

MAMA: Ain't nobody trying to stop you. I just wonders sometimes why you has to flit so from one thing to another all the time. You ain't never done nothing with all that camera equipment you brought home—

BENEATHA: I don't flit! I—I experiment with different forms of expression—

RUTH: Like riding a horse?

BENEATHA: —People have to express themselves one way or another.

MAMA: What is it you want to express?

BENEATHA (*angrily*): Me! (MAMA *and* RUTH *look at each other and burst into raucous laughter.*) Don't worry—I don't expect you to understand.

MAMA (*to change the subject*): Who you going out with tomorrow night?

BENEATHA (*with displeasure*): George Murchison again.

MAMA (*pleased*): Oh—you getting a little sweet on him?

RUTH: You ask me, this child ain't sweet on nobody but herself—(*Under breath.*) Express herself!

(*They laugh.*)

BENEATHA: Oh—I like George all right, Mama. I mean I like him enough to go out with him and stuff, but—

RUTH (*for devilment*): What does *and stuff* mean?

BENEATHA: Mind your own business.

MAMA: Stop picking at her now, Ruth. (*She chuckles—then a suspicious sudden look at her daughter as she turns in her chair for emphasis.*) What DOES it mean?

BENEATHA (*wearily*): Oh, I just mean I couldn't ever really be serious about George. He's—he's so shallow.

RUTH: Shallow—what do you mean he's shallow? He's *rich!*

MAMA: Hush, Ruth.

BENEATHA: I know he's rich. He knows he's rich, too.

RUTH: Well—what other qualities a man got to have to satisfy you, little girl?

BENEATHA: You wouldn't even begin to understand. Anybody who married Walter could not possibly understand.

MAMA (*outraged*): What kind of way is that to talk about your brother?

BENEATHA: Brother is a flip—let's face it.

MAMA (*to* RUTH, *helplessly*): What's a flip?

RUTH (*glad to add kindling*): She's saying he's crazy.

BENEATHA: Not crazy. Brother isn't really crazy yet—he—he's an elaborate neurotic.

MAMA: Hush your mouth!

BENEATHA: As for George. Well. George looks good—he's got a beautiful car and he takes me to nice places and, as my sister-in-law says, he is probably the richest boy I will ever get to know and I even like him sometimes—but if the Youngers are sitting around waiting to see if their little Bennie is going to tie up the family with the Murchisons, they are wasting their time.

RUTH: You mean you wouldn't marry George Murchison if he asked you someday? That pretty, rich thing? Honey, I knew you was odd—

BENEATHA: No I would not marry him if all I felt for him was what I feel now. Besides, George's family wouldn't really like it.

MAMA: Why not?

BENEATHA: Oh, Mama—The Murchisons are honest-to-God-real-*live*-rich colored people, and the only people in the world who are more snobbish than rich white people are rich colored people. I thought everybody knew that. I've met Mrs. Murchison. She's a scene!

MAMA: You must not dislike people 'cause they well off, honey.

BENEATHA: Why not? It makes just as much sense as disliking people 'cause they are poor, and lots of people do that.

RUTH (*A wisdom-of-the-ages manner. To* MAMA): Well, she'll get over some of this—

BENEATHA: Get over it? What are you talking about, Ruth? Listen, I'm going to be a doctor. I'm not worried about who I'm going to marry yet—if I ever get married.

MAMA AND RUTH: *If!*

MAMA: Now, Bennie—

BENEATHA: Oh, I probably will . . . but first I'm going to be a doctor, and George, for one, still thinks that's pretty funny. I couldn't be bothered with that. I am going to be a doctor and everybody around here better understand that!

MAMA (*kindly*): 'Course you going to be a doctor, honey, God willing.

BENEATHA (*drily*): God hasn't got a thing to do with it.

MAMA: Beneatha—that just wasn't necessary.

BENEATHA: Well—neither is God. I get sick of hearing about God.

MAMA: Beneatha!

BENEATHA: I mean it! I'm just tired of hearing about God all the time. What has He got to do with anything? Does He pay tuition?

MAMA: You 'bout to get your fresh little jaw slapped!

RUTH: That's just what she needs, all right!

BENEATHA: Why? Why can't I say what I want to around here, like everybody else?

MAMA: It don't sound nice for a young girl to say things like that—you wasn't brought up that way. Me and your father went to trouble to get you and Brother to church every Sunday.

BENEATHA: Mama, you don't understand. It's all a matter of ideas, and God is just one idea I don't accept. It's not important. I am not going out and be immoral or commit crimes because I don't believe in God. I don't even think about it. It's just that I get tired of Him getting credit for all the things the human race achieves through its own stubborn effort. There simply is no blasted God— there is only man and it is *he* who makes miracles!

(MAMA *absorbs this speech, studies her daughter and rises slowly and crosses to* BENEATHA *and slaps her powerfully across the face. After, there is only silence and the daughter drops her eyes from her mother's face, and* MAMA *is very tall before her.*)

MAMA: Now—you say after me, in my mother's house there is still God. (*There is a long pause and* BENEATHA *stares at the floor wordlessly.* MAMA *repeats the phrase with precision and cool emotion.*) In my mother's house there is still God.

BENEATHA: In my mother's house there is still God.

(*A long pause.*)

MAMA (*Walking away from* BENEATHA, *too disturbed for triumphant posture. Stopping and turning back to her daughter*): There are some ideas we ain't going to have in this house. Not long as I am at the head of this family.

BENEATHA: Yes, ma'am.

(MAMA *walks out of the room.*)

RUTH (*almost gently, with profound understanding*): You think you a woman, Bennie—but you still a little girl. What you did was childish—so you got treated like a child.

BENEATHA: I see. (*Quietly.*) I also see that everybody thinks it's all right for Mama to be a tyrant. But all the tyranny in the world will never put a God in the heavens!

(*She picks up her books and goes out. Pause.*)

RUTH (*goes to* MAMA'*s door*): She said she was sorry.

MAMA (*coming out, going to her plant*): They frightens me, Ruth. My children.

RUTH: You got good children, Lena. They just a little off sometimes—but they're good.

MAMA: No—there's something come down between me and them that don't let us understand each other and I don't know what it is. One done almost lost his mind thinking 'bout money all the time and the other done commence to talk about things I can't seem to understand in no form or fashion. What is it that's changing, Ruth.

RUTH (*soothingly, older than her years*): Now . . . you taking it all too seriously. You just got strong-willed children and it takes a strong woman like you to keep 'em in hand.

MAMA (*looking at her plant and sprinkling a little water on it*): They spirited all right, my children. Got to admit they got spirit—Bennie and Walter. Like

this little old plant that ain't never had enough sunshine or nothing—and look at it . . .

(*She has her back to* RUTH, *who has had to stop ironing and lean against something and put the back of her hand to her forehead.*)

RUTH (*trying to keep* MAMA *from noticing*): You . . . sure . . . loves that little old thing, don't you? . . .

MAMA: Well, I always wanted me a garden like I used to see sometimes at the back of the houses down home. This plant is close as I ever got to having one. (*She looks out of the window as she replaces the plant.*) Lord, ain't nothing as dreary as the view from this window on a dreary day, is there? Why ain't you singing this morning, Ruth? Sing that "No Ways Tired." That song always lifts me up so—(*She turns at last to see that* RUTH *has slipped quietly to the floor, in a state of semiconsciousness.*) Ruth! Ruth honey—what's the matter with you . . . Ruth!

ACT 1 / SCENE 2

(*It is the following morning; a Saturday morning, and house cleaning is in progress at the Youngers'. Furniture has been shoved hither and yon and* MAMA *is giving the kitchen-area walls a washing down.* BENEATHA, *in dungarees, with a handkerchief tied around her face, is spraying insecticide into the cracks in the walls. As they work, the radio is on and a Southside disk jockey program is inappropriately filling the house with a rather exotic saxophone blues.* TRAVIS, *the sole idle one, is leaning on his arms, looking out of the window.*)

TRAVIS: Grandmama, that stuff Bennie is using smells awful. Can I go downstairs, please?

MAMA: Did you get all them chores done already? I ain't seen you doing much.

TRAVIS: Yes'm—finished early. Where did Mama go this morning?

MAMA (*looking at* BENEATHA): She had to go on a little errand.

(*The phone rings.* BENEATHA *runs to answer it and reaches it before* WALTER, *who has entered from bedroom.*)

TRAVIS: Where?

MAMA: To tend to her business.

BENEATHA: Haylo . . . (*Disappointed.*) Yes, he is. (*She tosses the phone to* WALTER, *who barely catches it.*) It's Willie Harris again.

WALTER (*as privately as possible under* MAMA'*s gaze*): Hello, Willie. Did you get the papers from the lawyer? . . . No, not yet. I told you the mailman doesn't get here till ten-thirty . . . No, I'll come there . . . Yeah! Right away. (*He hangs up and goes for his coat.*)

BENEATHA: Brother, where did Ruth go?

WALTER (*as he exits*): How should I know!

TRAVIS: Aw come on, Grandma. Can I go outside?

MAMA: Oh, I guess so. You stay right in front of the house, though, and keep a good lookout for the postman.

TRAVIS: Yes'm. (*He darts into bedroom for stickball and bat, reenters, and sees* BENEATHA *on her knees spraying under sofa with behind upraised. He edges closer to the target, takes aim, and lets her have it. She screams.*) Leave them poor little cockroaches alone, they ain't bothering you none! (*He runs as she swings the spraygun at him viciously and playfully.*) Grandma! Grandma!

MAMA: Look out there, girl, before you be spilling some of that stuff on that child!

TRAVIS (*safely behind the bastion of* MAMA): That's right—look out, now! (*He exits.*)

BENEATHA (*drily*): I can't imagine that it would hurt him—it has never hurt the roaches.

MAMA: Well, little boys' hides ain't as tough as South-side roaches. You better get over there behind the bureau. I seen one marching out of there like Napoleon yesterday.

BENEATHA: There's really only one way to get rid of them, Mama—

MAMA: How?

BENEATHA: Set fire to this building! Mama, where did Ruth go?

MAMA (*looking at her with meaning*): To the doctor, I think.

BENEATHA: The doctor? What's the matter? (*They exchange glances.*) You don't think—

MAMA (*with her sense of drama*): Now I ain't saying what I think. But I ain't never been wrong 'bout a woman neither.

(*The phone rings.*)

BENEATHA (*at the phone*): Hay-lo . . . (*Pause, and a moment of recognition.*) Well—when did you get back! . . . And how was it? . . . Of course I've missed you—in my way . . . This morning? No . . . house cleaning and all that and Mama hates it if I let people come over when the house is like this . . . You *have*? Well, that's different . . . What is it—Oh, what the hell, come on over . . . Right, see you then. *Arrivederci.*

(*She hangs up.*)

MAMA (*who has listened vigorously, as is her habit*): Who is that you inviting over here with this house looking like this? You ain't got the pride you was born with!

BENEATHA: Asagai doesn't care how houses look, Mama—he's an intellectual.

MAMA: *Who?*

BENEATHA: Asagai—Joseph Asagai. He's an African

boy I met on campus. He's been studying in Canada all summer.

MAMA: What's his name?

BENEATHA: Asagai, Joseph. Ah-sah-guy . . . He's from Nigeria.

MAMA: Oh, that's the little country that was founded by slaves way back . . .

BENEATHA: No, Mama—that's Liberia.

MAMA: I don't think I never met no African before.

BENEATHA: Well, do me a favor and don't ask him a whole lot of ignorant questions about Africans. I mean, do they wear clothes and all that—

MAMA: Well, now, I guess if you think we so ignorant 'round here maybe you shouldn't bring your friends here—

BENEATHA: It's just that people ask such crazy things. All anyone seems to know about when it comes to Africa is Tarzan—

MAMA (*indignantly*): Why should I know anything about Africa?

BENEATHA: Why do you give money at church for the missionary work?

MAMA: Well, that's to help save people.

BENEATHA: You mean save them from *heathenism*—

MAMA (*innocently*): Yes.

BENEATHA: I'm afraid they need more salvation from the British and the French.

(RUTH *comes in forlornly and pulls off her coat with dejection. They both turn to look at her.*)

RUTH (*dispiritedly*): Well, I guess from all the happy faces—everybody knows.

BENEATHA: You pregnant?

MAMA: Lord have mercy, I sure hope it's a little old girl. Travis ought to have a sister.

(BENEATHA *and* RUTH *give her a hopeless look for this grandmotherly enthusiasm.*)

BENEATHA: How far along are you?

RUTH: Two months.

BENEATHA: Did you mean to? I mean did you plan it or was it an accident?

MAMA: What do you know about planning or not planning?

BENEATHA: Oh, Mama.

RUTH (*wearily*): She's twenty years old, Lena.

BENEATHA: Did you plan it, Ruth?

RUTH: Mind your own business.

BENEATHA: It is my business—where is he going to live, on the *roof*? (*There is silence following the remark as the three women react to the sense of it.*) Gee—I didn't mean that, Ruth, honest. Gee, I don't feel like that at all. I—I think it is wonderful.

RUTH (*dully*): Wonderful.

BENEATHA: Yes—really.

MAMA (*looking at Ruth, worried*): Doctor say everything going to be all right?

RUTH (*far away*): Yes—she says everything is going to be fine . . .

MAMA (*immediately suspicious*): "She"—What doctor you went to?

(RUTH *folds over, near hysteria.*)

MAMA (*worriedly hovering over* RUTH): Ruth honey— what's the matter with you—you sick?

(RUTH *has her fists clenched on her thighs and is fighting hard to suppress a scream that seems to be rising in her.*)

BENEATHA: What's the matter with her, Mama?

MAMA (*working her fingers in* RUTH*'s shoulders to relax her*): She be all right. Women gets right depressed sometimes when they get her way. (*Speaking softly, expertly, rapidly.*) Now you just relax. That's right . . . just lean back, don't think 'bout nothing at all . . . nothing at all—

RUTH: I'm all right . . .

(*The glassy-eyed look melts and then she collapses into a fit of heavy sobbing. The bell rings.*)

BENEATHA: Oh, my God—that must be Asagai.

MAMA (*to* RUTH): Come on now, honey. You need to lie down and rest awhile . . . then have some nice hot food.

(*They exit,* RUTH*'s weight on her mother-in-law.* BENEATHA, *herself profoundly disturbed, opens the door to admit a rather dramatic-looking young man with a large package.*)

ASAGAI: Hello, Alaiyo—

BENEATHA (*holding the door open and regarding him with pleasure*): Hello . . . (*Long pause.*) Well—come in. And please excuse everything. My mother was very upset about my letting anyone come here with the place like this.

ASAGAI (*coming into the room*): You look disturbed too . . . Is something wrong?

BENEATHA (*still at the door, absently*): Yes . . . we've all got acute ghetto-itus. (*She smiles and comes toward him, finding a cigarette and sitting.*) So—sit down! No! Wait! (*She whips the spraygun off sofa where she had left it and puts the cushions back. At last perches on arm of sofa. He sits.*) So, how was Canada?

ASAGAI (*a sophisticate*): Canadian.

BENEATHA (*looking at him*): Asagai, I'm very glad you are back.

ASAGAI (*looking back at her in turn*): Are you really?

BENEATHA: Yes—very.

ASAGAI: Why?—you were quite glad when I went away. What happened?

BENEATHA: You went away.

ASAGAI: Ahhhhhhhh.

BENEATHA: Before—you wanted to be so serious before there was time.

ASAGAI: How much time must there be before one knows what one feels?

BENEATHA (*Stalling this particular conversation. Her hands pressed together, in a deliberately childish gesture*): What did you bring me?

ASAGAI (*handing her the package*): Open it and see.

BENEATHA (*eagerly opening the package and drawing out some records and the colorful robes of a Nigerian woman*): Oh Asagai! . . . You got them for me! . . . How beautiful . . . and the records too! (*She lifts out the robes and runs to the mirror with them and holds the drapery up in front of herself.*)

ASAGAI (*coming to her at the mirror*): I shall have to teach you how to drape it properly. (*He flings the material about her for the moment and stands back to look at her.*) Ah—*Oh-pay-gay-day, oh-gbah-mu-shay.* (*A Yoruba exclamation for admiration.*) You wear it well . . . very well . . . mutilated hair and all.

BENEATHA (*turning suddenly*): My hair—what's wrong with my hair?

ASAGAI (*shrugging*): Were you born with it like that?

BENEATHA (*reaching up to touch it*): No . . . of course not.

(*She looks back to the mirror, disturbed.*)

ASAGAI (*smiling*): How then?

BENEATHA: You know perfectly well how . . . as crinkly as yours . . . that's how.

ASAGAI: And it is ugly to you that way?

BENEATHA (*quickly*): Oh, no—not ugly . . . (*More slowly, apologetically.*) But it's so hard to manage when it's, well—raw.

ASAGAI: And so to accommodate that—you mutilate it every week?

BENEATHA: It's not mutilation!

ASAGAI (*laughing aloud at her seriousness*): Oh . . . please! I am only teasing you because you are so very serious about these things. (*He stands back from her and folds his arms across his chest as he watches her pulling at her hair and frowning in the mirror.*) Do you remember the first time you met me at school? . . . (*He laughs.*) You came up to me and you said—and I thought you were the most serious little thing I had ever seen—you said: (*He imitates her.*) "Mr. Asagai—I want very much to talk with you. About Africa. You see, Mr. Asagai, I am looking for my *identity*!"

(*He laughs.*)

BENEATHA (*turning to him, not laughing*): Yes—

(*Her face is quizzical, profoundly disturbed.*)

ASAGAI (*still teasing and reaching out and taking her face in his hands and turning her profile to him*): Well . . . it is true that this is not so much a profile of a Hollywood queen as perhaps a queen of the Nile— (*A mock dismissal of the importance of the question.*)

But what does it matter? Assimilationism is so popular in your country.

BENEATHA (*wheeling, passionately, sharply*): I am not an assimilationist!

ASAGAI (*the protest hangs in the room for a moment and* ASAGAI *studies her, his laughter fading*): Such a serious one. (*There is a pause.*) So—you like the robes? You must take excellent care of them—they are from my sister's personal wardrobe.

BENEATHA (*with incredulity*): You—you sent all the way home—for me?

ASAGAI (*with charm*): For you—I would do much more . . . Well, that is what I came for. I must go.

BENEATHA: Will you call me Monday?

ASAGAI: Yes . . . We have a great deal to talk about. I mean about identity and time and all that.

BENEATHA: Time?

ASAGAI: Yes. About how much time one needs to know what one feels.

BENEATHA: You never understood that there is more than one kind of feeling which can exist between a man and a woman—or, at least, there should be.

ASAGAI (*shaking his head negatively but gently*): No. Between a man and a woman there need be only one kind of feeling. I have that for you . . . Now even . . . right this moment . . .

BENEATHA: I know—and by itself—it won't do. I can find that anywhere.

ASAGAI: For a woman it should be enough.

BENEATHA: I know—because that's what it says in all the novels that men write. But it isn't. Go ahead and laugh—but I'm not interested in being someone's little episode in America or—(*with feminine vengeance*)—one of them! (ASAGAI *has burst into laughter again.*) That's funny as hell, huh!

ASAGAI: It's just that every American girl I have known has said that to me. White—black—in this you are all the same. And the same speech, too!

BENEATHA (*angrily*): Yuk, yuk, yuk!

ASAGAI: It's how you can be sure that the world's most liberated women are not liberated at all. You all talk about it too much!

(MAMA *enters and is immediately all social charm because of the presence of a guest.*)

BENEATHA: Oh—Mama—this is Mr. Asagai.

MAMA: How do you do?

ASAGAI (*total politeness to an elder*): How do you do, Mrs. Younger. Please forgive me for coming at such an outrageous hour on a Saturday.

MAMA: Well, you are quite welcome. I just hope you understand that our house don't always look like this. (*Chatterish.*) You must come again. I would love to hear all about—(*not sure of the name*)—your country. I think it's so sad the way our American Negroes don't know nothing about Africa 'cept Tarzan and all that. And all that money they pour into these churches when they ought to be helping you people over there drive out them French and Englishmen done taken away your land.

(*The mother flashes a slightly superior look at her daughter upon completion of the recitation.*)

ASAGAI (*taken aback by this sudden and acutely unrelated expression of sympathy*): Yes . . . yes . . .

MAMA (*smiling at him suddenly and relaxing and looking him over*): How many miles is it from here to where you come from?

ASAGAI: Many thousands.

MAMA (*looking at him as she would* WALTER): I bet you don't half look after yourself, being away from your mama either. I spec you better come 'round here from time to time to get yourself some decent home-cooked meals . . .

ASAGAI (*moved*): Thank you. Thank you very much. (*They are all quiet, then*—) Well . . . I must go. I will call you Monday, Alaiyo.

MAMA: What's that he call you?

ASAGAI: Oh—"Alaiyo." I hope you don't mind. It is what you would call a nickname, I think. It is a Yoruba word. I am a Yoruba.

MAMA (*looking at* BENEATHA): I—I thought he was from—(*Uncertain.*)

ASAGAI (*understanding*): Nigeria is my country. Yoruba is my tribal origin—

BENEATHA: You didn't tell us what Alaiyo means . . . for all I know, you might be calling me Little Idiot or something . . .

ASAGAI: Well . . . let me see . . . I do not know how just to explain it . . . The sense of a thing can be so different when it changes languages.

BENEATHA: You're evading.

ASAGAI: No—really it is difficult . . . (*Thinking.*) It means . . . it means One for Whom Bread—Food—Is Not Enough. (*He looks at her.*) Is that all right?

BENEATHA (*understanding, softly*): Thank you.

MAMA (*looking from one to the other and not understanding any of it*): Well . . . that's nice . . . You must come see us again—Mr.—

ASAGAI: Ah-sah-guy . . .

MAMA: Yes . . . Do come again.

ASAGAI: Good-bye.

(*He exits.*)

MAMA (*after him*): Lord, that's a pretty thing just went out here! (*Insinuatingly, to her daughter.*) Yes, I guess I see why we done commence to get so interested in Africa 'round here. Missionaries my aunt Jenny!

(*She exits.*)

BENEATHA: Oh, Mama! . . .

(She picks up the Nigerian dress and holds it up to her in front of the mirror again. She sets the headdress on haphazardly and then notices her hair again and clutches at it and then replaces the headdress and frowns at herself. Then she starts to wriggle in front of the mirror as she thinks a Nigerian woman might. TRAVIS *enters and stands regarding her.)*

TRAVIS: What's the matter, girl, you cracking up?

BENEATHA: Shut up.

(She pulls the headdress off and looks at herself in the mirror and clutches at her hair again and squinches her eyes as if trying to imagine something. Then, suddenly, she gets her raincoat and kerchief and hurriedly prepares for going out.)

MAMA *(coming back into the room)*: She's resting now. Travis, baby, run next door and ask Miss Johnson to please let me have a little kitchen cleanser. This here can is empty as Jacob's kettle.

TRAVIS: I just came in.

MAMA: Do as you told. *(He exits and she looks at her daughter.)* Where you going?

BENEATHA *(halting at the door)*: To become a queen of the Nile!

(She exits in a breathless blaze of glory. RUTH *appears in the bedroom doorway.)*

MAMA: Who told you to get up?

RUTH: Ain't nothing wrong with me to be lying in no bed for. Where did Bennie go?

MAMA *(drumming her fingers)*: Far as I could make out—to Egypt. *(*RUTH *just looks at her.)* What time is it getting to?

RUTH: Ten twenty. And the mailman going to ring that bell this morning just like he done every morning for the last umpteen years.

*(*TRAVIS *comes in with the cleanser can.)*

TRAVIS: She say to tell you that she don't have much.

MAMA *(angrily)*: Lord, some people I could name sure is tight-fisted! *(Directing her grandson.)* Mark two cans of cleanser down on the list there. If she that hard up for kitchen cleanser, I sure don't want to forget to get her none!

RUTH: Lena—maybe the woman is just short on cleanser—

MAMA *(not listening)*: —Much baking powder as she done borrowed from me all these years, she could of done gone into the baking business!

(The bell sounds suddenly and sharply and all three are stunned—serious and silent—mid-speech. In spite of all the other conversations and distractions of the morning, this is what they have been waiting for, even TRAVIS, *who looks helplessly from his mother to his grandmother.* RUTH *is the first to come to life again.)*

RUTH *(to* TRAVIS*)*: Get down them steps, boy!

*(*TRAVIS *snaps to life and flies out to get the mail.)*

MAMA *(her eyes wide, her hand to her breast)*: You mean it done really come?

RUTH *(excited)*: Oh, Miss Lena!

MAMA *(collecting herself)*: Well . . . I don't know what we all so excited about 'round here for. We known it was coming for months.

RUTH: That's a whole lot different from having it come and being able to hold it in your hands . . . a piece of paper worth ten thousand dollars . . . *(*TRAVIS *bursts back into the room. He holds the envelope high above his head, like a little dancer, his face is radiant and he is breathless. He moves to his grandmother with sudden slow ceremony and puts the envelope into her hands. She accepts it, and then merely holds it and looks at it.)* Come on! Open it . . . Lord have mercy, I wish Walter Lee was here!

TRAVIS: Open it, Grandmama!

MAMA *(staring at it)*: Now you all be quiet. It's just a check.

RUTH: Open it . . .

MAMA *(still staring at it)*: Now don't act silly . . . We ain't never been no people to act silly 'bout no money—

RUTH *(swiftly)*: We ain't never had none before— OPEN IT!

*(*MAMA *finally makes a good strong tear and pulls out the thin blue slice of paper and inspects it closely. The boy and his mother study it raptly over* MAMA*'s shoulders.)*

MAMA: Travis! *(She is counting off with doubt.)* Is that the right number of zeros?

TRAVIS: Yes'm . . . ten thousand dollars. Gaalee, Grandmama, you rich.

MAMA *(She holds the check away from her, still looking at it. Slowly her face sobers into a mask of unhappiness)*: Ten thousand dollars. *(She hands it to* RUTH.*)* Put it away somewhere, Ruth. *(She does not look at* RUTH; *her eyes seem to be seeing something somewhere very far off.)* Ten thousand dollars they give you. Ten thousand dollars.

TRAVIS *(to his mother, sincerely)*: What's the matter with Grandmama—don't she want to be rich?

RUTH *(distractedly)*: You go on out and play now, baby. *(*TRAVIS *exits.* MAMA *starts wiping dishes absently, humming intently to herself.* RUTH *turns to her, with kind exasperation.)* You've gone and got yourself upset.

MAMA *(not looking at her)*: I spec if it wasn't for you all . . . I would just put that money away or give it to the church or something.

RUTH: Now what kind of talk is that. Mr. Younger would just be plain mad if he could hear you talking foolish like that.

MAMA *(stopping and staring off)*: Yes . . . he sure would.

(Sighing.) We got enough to do with that money, all right. *(She halts then, and turns and looks at her daughter-in-law hard;* RUTH *avoids her eyes and* MAMA *wipes her hands with finality and starts to speak firmly to* RUTH.*)* Where did you go today, girl?

RUTH: To the doctor.

MAMA *(impatiently)*: Now, Ruth . . . you know better than that. Old Doctor Jones is strange enough in his way but there ain't nothing 'bout him make somebody slip and call him "she"—like you done this morning.

RUTH: Well, that's what happened—my tongue slipped.

MAMA: You went to see that woman, didn't you?

RUTH *(defensively, giving herself away)*: What woman you talking about?

MAMA *(angrily)*: That woman who—

*(*WALTER *enters in great excitement.)*

WALTER: Did it come?

MAMA *(quietly)*: Can't you give people a Christian greeting before you start asking about money?

WALTER *(to* RUTH*)*: Did it come? *(*RUTH *unfolds the check and lays it quietly before him, watching him intently with thoughts of her own.* WALTER *sits down and grasps it close and counts off the zeros.)* Ten thousand dollars—*(He turns suddenly, frantically to his mother and draws some papers out of his breast pocket.)* Mama—look. Old Willy Harris put everything on paper—

MAMA: Son—I think you ought to talk to your wife . . . I'll go on out and leave you alone if you want—

WALTER: I can talk to her later—Mama, look—

MAMA: Son—

WALTER: WILL SOMEBODY PLEASE LISTEN TO ME TODAY!

MAMA *(quietly)*: I don't 'low no yellin' in this house, Walter Lee, and you know it—*(*WALTER *stares at them in frustration and starts to speak several times.)* And there ain't going to be no investing in no liquor stores.

WALTER: But, Mama, you ain't even looked at it.

MAMA: I don't aim to have to speak on that again.

(A long pause.)

WALTER: You ain't looked at it and you don't aim to have to speak on that again? You ain't even looked at it and *you* have decided—*(Crumpling his papers.)* Well, *you* tell that to my boy tonight when you put him to sleep on the living room couch . . . *(Turning to* MAMA *and speaking directly to her.)* Yeah—and tell it to my wife, Mama, tomorrow when she has to go out of here to look after somebody else's kids. And tell it to *me*, Mama, every time we need a new pair of curtains and I have to watch *you* go out and work in somebody's kitchen. Yeah, you tell me then!

*(*WALTER *starts out.)*

RUTH: Where you going?

WALTER: I'm going out!

RUTH: Where?

WALTER: Just out of this house somewhere—

RUTH *(getting her coat)*: I'll come too.

WALTER: I don't want you to come!

RUTH: I got something to talk to you about, Walter.

WALTER: That's too bad.

MAMA *(still quietly)*: Walter Lee—*(She waits and he finally turns and looks at her.)* Sit down.

WALTER: I'm a grown man, Mama.

MAMA: Ain't nobody said you wasn't grown. But you still in my house and my presence. And as long as you are—you'll talk to your wife civil. Now sit down.

RUTH *(suddenly)*: Oh, let him go on out and drink himself to death! He makes me sick to my stomach! *(She flings her coat against him and exits to bedroom.)*

WALTER *(violently flinging the coat after her)*: And you turn mine too, baby! *(The door slams behind her.)* That was my biggest mistake—

MAMA *(still quietly)*: Walter, what is the matter with you?

WALTER: Matter with me? Ain't nothing the matter with *me*!

MAMA: Yes there is. Something eating you up like a crazy man. Something more than me not giving you this money. The past few years I been watching it happen to you. You get all nervous acting and kind of wild in the eyes—*(*WALTER *jumps up impatiently at her words.)* I said sit there now, I'm talking to you!

WALTER: Mama—I don't need no nagging at me today.

MAMA: Seem like you getting to a place where you always tied up in some kind of knot about something. But if anybody ask you 'bout it you just yell at 'em and bust out the house and go out and drink somewheres. Walter Lee, people can't live with that. Ruth's a good, patient girl in her way—but you getting to be too much. Boy, don't make the mistake of driving that girl away from you.

WALTER: Why—what she do for me?

MAMA: She loves you.

WALTER: Mama—I'm going out. I want to go off somewhere and be by myself for a while.

MAMA: I'm sorry 'bout your liquor store, son. It just wasn't the thing for us to do. That's what I want to tell you about—

WALTER: I got to go out, Mama—

(He rises.)

MAMA: It's dangerous, son.

WALTER: What's dangerous?

MAMA: When a man goes outside his home to look for peace.

WALTER (*beseechingly*): Then why can't there never be no peace in this house then?

MAMA: You done found it in some other house?

WALTER: No—there ain't no woman! Why do women always think there's a woman somewhere when a man gets restless. (*Picks up the check.*) Do you know what this money means to me? Do you know what this money can do for us? (*Puts it back.*) Mama—Mama—I want so many things . . .

MAMA: Yes, son—

WALTER: I want so many things that they are driving me kind of crazy . . . Mama—look at me.

MAMA: I'm looking at you. You a good-looking boy. You got a job, a nice wife, a fine boy and—

WALTER: A job. (*Looks at her.*) Mama, a job? I open and close car doors all day long. I drive a man around in his limousine and I say, "Yes, sir, no, sir; very good, sir; shall I take the Drive, sir?" Mama, that ain't no kind of job . . . that ain't nothing at all. (*Very quietly.*) Mama, I don't know if I can make you understand.

MAMA: Understand what, baby?

WALTER (*quietly*): Sometimes it's like I can see the future stretched out in front of me—just plain as day. The future, Mama. Hanging over there at the edge of my days. Just waiting for me—a big, looming blank space—full of *nothing*. Just waiting for *me*. But it don't have to be. (*Pause. Kneeling beside her chair.*) Mama—sometimes when I'm downtown and I pass them cool, quiet-looking restaurants where them white boys are sitting back and talking 'bout things . . . sitting there turning deals worth millions of dollars . . . sometimes I see guys don't look much older than me—

MAMA: Son—how come you talk so much 'bout money?

WALTER (*with immense passion*): Because it is life, Mama!

MAMA (*quietly*): Oh—(*Very quietly.*) So now it's life. Money is life. Once upon a time freedom used to be life—now it's money. I guess the world really do change . . .

WALTER: No—it was always money, Mama. We just didn't know about it.

MAMA: No . . . something has changed. (*She looks at him.*) You something new, boy. In my time we was worried about not being lynched and getting to the North if we could and how to stay alive and still have a pinch of dignity too . . . Now here come you and Beneatha—talking 'bout things we ain't never even thought about hardly, me and your daddy. You ain't satisfied or proud of nothing we done. I mean that you had a home, that we kept you out of trouble till you was grown, that you don't have to ride to work on the back of nobody's streetcar—You my children—but how different we done become.

WALTER (*A long beat. He pats her hand and gets up*): You just don't understand, Mama, you just don't understand.

MAMA: Son—do you know your wife is expecting another baby? (*WALTER stands, stunned, and absorbs what his mother has said.*) That's what she wanted to talk to you about. (*WALTER sinks down into a chair.*) This ain't for me to be telling—but you ought to know. (*She waits.*) I think Ruth is thinking 'bout getting rid of that child.

WALTER (*slowly understanding*): —No—no—Ruth wouldn't do that.

MAMA: When the world gets ugly enough—a woman will do anything for her family. *The part that's already living.*

WALTER: You don't know Ruth, Mama, if you think she would do that.

(RUTH *opens the bedroom door and stands there a little limp.*)

RUTH (*beaten*): Yes I would too, Walter. (*Pause.*) I gave her a five-dollar down payment.

(*There is total silence as the man stares at his wife and the mother stares at her son.*)

MAMA (*presently*): Well—(*Tightly.*) Well—son, I'm waiting to hear you say something . . . (*She waits.*) I'm waiting to hear how you be your father's son. Be the man he was . . . (*Pause. The silence shouts.*) Your wife says she going to destroy your child. And I'm waiting to hear you talk like him and say we a people who give children life, not who destroys them—(*She rises.*) I'm waiting to see you stand up and look like your daddy and say we done give up one baby to poverty and that we ain't going to give up nary another one . . . I'm waiting.

WALTER: Ruth—(*He can say nothing.*)

MAMA: If you a son of mine, tell her! (*WALTER picks up his keys and his coat and walks out. She continues, bitterly.*) You . . . you are a disgrace to your father's memory. Somebody get me my hat!

ACT 2 / SCENE 1

(*Time: Later the same day.*)

(*At rise:* RUTH *is ironing again. She has the radio going. Presently* BENEATHA's *bedroom door opens and* RUTH's *mouth falls and she puts down the iron in fascination.*)

RUTH: What have we got on tonight!

BENEATHA (*emerging grandly from the doorway so that we can see her thoroughly robed in the costume* ASAGAI *brought*): You are looking at what a well-dressed Nigerian woman wears—(*She parades for* RUTH, *her hair completely hidden by the headdress; she is coquettishly fanning herself with an ornate oriental fan, mistakenly more like Butterfly° than any Nigerian that ever was.)* Isn't it beautiful? *(She promenades to the radio and, with an arrogant flourish, turns off the good loud blues that is playing.)* Enough of this assimilationist junk! *(RUTH follows her with her eyes as she goes to the phonograph and puts on a record and turns and waits ceremoniously for the music to come up. Then, with a shout—)* OCOMOGOSIAY!

(RUTH jumps. The music comes up, a lovely Nigerian melody. BENEATHA listens, enraptured, her eyes far away—"back to the past." She begins to dance. RUTH is dumfounded.)

RUTH: What kind of dance is that?

BENEATHA: A folk dance.

RUTH *(Pearl Bailey°)*: What kind of folks do that, honey?

BENEATHA: It's from Nigeria. It's a dance of welcome.

RUTH: Who you welcoming?

BENEATHA: The men back to the village.

RUTH: Where they been?

BENEATHA: How should I know—out hunting or something. Anyway, they are coming back now . . .

RUTH: Well, that's good.

BENEATHA *(with the record)*:

*Alundi, alundi
Alundi alunya
Jop pu a jeepua
Ang gu soooooooooo*

*Ai yai yue . . .
Ayehaye—alundi . . .*

(WALTER comes in during this performance; he has obviously been drinking. He leans against the door heavily and watches his sister, at first with distaste. Then his eyes look off—"back to the past"—as he lifts both his fists to the roof, screaming.)

WALTER: YEAH . . . AND ETHIOPIA STRETCH FORTH HER HANDS AGAIN! . . .

RUTH *(drily, looking at him)*: Yes—and Africa sure is claiming her own tonight. *(She gives them both up and starts ironing again.)*

WALTER *(all in a drunken, dramatic shout)*: Shut up! . . . I'm digging them drums . . . them drums move me! . . . *(He makes his weaving way to his wife's face and leans in close to her.)* In my *heart of hearts*—(he thumps his chest)—I am much warrior!

RUTH *(without even looking up)*: In your heart of hearts you are much drunkard.

WALTER *(coming away from her and starting to wander around the room, shouting)*: Me and Jomo° . . . *(Intently, in his sister's face. She has stopped dancing to watch him in this unknown mood.)* That's my man, Kenyatta. *(Shouting and thumping his chest.)* FLAMING SPEAR! HOT DAMN! *(He is suddenly in possession of an imaginary spear and actively spearing enemies all over the room.)* OCOMOGOSIAY . . .

BENEATHA *(to encourage Walter, thoroughly caught up with this side of him)*: OCOMOGOSIAY, FLAMING SPEAR!

WALTER: THE LION IS WAKING . . . OWIMOWEH! *(He pulls his shirt open and leaps up on the table and gestures with his spear.)*

BENEATHA: OWIMOWEH!

WALTER *(On the table, very far gone, his eyes pure glass sheets. He sees what we cannot, that he is a leader of his people, a great chief, a descendant of Chaka, and that the hour to march has come)*: Listen, my black brothers—

BENEATHA: OCOMOGOSIAY!

WALTER: —Do you hear the waters rushing against the shores of the coastlands—

BENEATHA: OCOMOGOSIAY!

WALTER: —Do you hear the screeching of the cocks in yonder hills beyond where the chiefs meet in council for the coming of the mighty war—

BENEATHA: OCOMOGOSIAY!

(And now the lighting shifts subtly to suggest the world of WALTER's imagination, and the mood shifts from pure comedy. It is the inner WALTER speaking: the Southside chauffeur has assumed an unexpected majesty.)

WALTER: —Do you hear the beating of the wings of the birds flying low over the mountains and the low places of our land—

BENEATHA: OCOMOGOSIAY!

WALTER: —Do you hear the singing of the women singing the war songs of our fathers to the babies in the great houses? Singing the sweet war songs! *(The doorbell rings.)* OH, DO YOU HEAR, MY BLACK BROTHERS!

BENEATHA *(completely gone)*: We hear you, Flaming Spear—

(RUTH shuts off the phonograph and opens the door. GEORGE MURCHISON enters.)

WALTER: Telling us to prepare for the GREATNESS OF THE TIME! *(Lights back to normal. He turns and sees GEORGE.)* Black Brother!

(He extends his hand for the fraternal clasp.)

Butterfly, the title character of Puccini's 1904 opera, *Madame Butterfly,* set in Japan. **Pearl Bailey,** popular black entertainer (1918–90) known for her sly delivery.

Jomo, Jomo Kenyatta (1893?–1978), African revolutionary and later first president of independent Kenya (1964–78).

GEORGE: Black Brother, hell!

RUTH (*having had enough, and embarrassed for the family*): Beneatha, you got company—what's the matter with you? Walter Lee Younger, get down off that table and stop acting like a fool . . .

(WALTER *comes down off the table suddenly and makes a quick exit to the bathroom.*)

RUTH: He's had a little to drink . . . I don't know what her excuse is.

GEORGE (*to* BENEATHA): Look honey, we're going *to* the theater—we're not going to be *in* it . . . so go change, huh?

(BENEATHA *looks at him and slowly, ceremoniously, lifts her hands and pulls off the headdress. Her hair is close-cropped and unstraightened.* GEORGE *freezes mid-sentence and* RUTH*'s eyes all but fall out of her head.*)

GEORGE: What in the name of—

RUTH (*touching* BENEATHA*'s hair*): Girl, you done lost your natural mind? Look at your head!

GEORGE: What have you done to your head—I mean your hair!

BENEATHA: Nothing—except cut it off.

RUTH: Now that's the truth—it's what ain't been done to it! You expect this boy to go out with you with your head all nappy like that?

BENEATHA (*looking at* GEORGE): That's up to George. If he's ashamed of his heritage—

GEORGE: Oh, don't be so proud of yourself, Bennie—just because you look eccentric.

BENEATHA: How can something that's natural be eccentric?

GEORGE: That's what being eccentric means—being natural. Get dressed.

BENEATHA: I don't like that, George.

RUTH: Why must you and your brother make an argument out of everything people say?

BENEATHA: Because I hate assimilationist Negroes!

RUTH: Will somebody please tell me what assimila-whoever means!

GEORGE: Oh, it's just a college girl's way of calling people Uncle Toms—but that isn't what it means at all.

RUTH: Well, what does it mean?

BENEATHA (*cutting* GEORGE *off and staring at him as she replies to* RUTH): It means someone who is willing to give up his own culture and submerge himself completely in the dominant, and in this case *oppressive* culture!

GEORGE: Oh, dear, dear, dear! Here we go! A lecture on the African past! On our Great West African Heritage! In one second we will hear all about the great Ashanti empires; the great Songhay civilizations; and the great sculpture of Bénin—and then some poetry in the Bantu—and the whole monologue will end with the word *heritage*! (*Nas-*

tily.) Let's face it, baby, your heritage is nothing but a bunch of raggedy-assed spirituals and some grass huts!

BENEATHA: GRASS HUTS! (RUTH *crosses to her and forcibly pushes her toward the bedroom.*) See there . . . you are standing there in your splendid ignorance talking about people who were the first to smelt iron on the face of the earth! (RUTH *is pushing her through the door.*) The Ashanti were performing surgical operations when the English— (RUTH *pulls the door to, with* BENEATHA *on the other side, and smiles graciously at* GEORGE. BENEATHA *opens the door and shouts the end of the sentence defiantly at* GEORGE)—were still tattooing themselves with blue dragons! (*She goes back inside.*)

RUTH: Have a seat, George. (*They both sit.* RUTH *folds her hands rather primly on her lap, determined to demonstrate the civilization of the family.*) Warm, ain't it? I mean for September. (*Pause.*) Just like they always say about Chicago weather: If it's too hot or cold for you, just wait a minute and it'll change. (*She smiles happily at this cliché of clichés.*) Everybody say it's got to do with them bombs and things they keep setting off. (*Pause.*) Would you like a nice cold beer?

GEORGE: No, thank you. I don't care for beer. (*He looks at his watch.*) I hope she hurries up.

RUTH: What time is the show?

GEORGE: It's an eight-thirty curtain. That's just Chicago, though. In New York standard curtain time is eight forty.

(*He is rather proud of this knowledge.*)

RUTH (*properly appreciating it*): You get to New York a lot?

GEORGE (*offhand*): Few times a year.

RUTH: Oh—that's nice. I've never been to New York.

(WALTER *enters. We feel he has relieved himself, but the edge of unreality is still with him.*)

WALTER: New York ain't got nothing Chicago ain't. Just a bunch of hustling people all squeezed up together—being "Eastern."

(*He turns his face into a screw of displeasure.*)

GEORGE: Oh—you've been?

WALTER: Plenty of times.

RUTH (*shocked at the lie*): Walter Lee Younger!

WALTER (*staring her down*): Plenty! (*Pause.*) What we got to drink in this house? Why don't you offer this man some refreshment. (*To* GEORGE.) They don't know how to entertain people in this house, man.

GEORGE: Thank you—I don't really care for anything.

WALTER (*feeling his head; sobriety coming*): Where's Mama?

RUTH: She ain't come back yet.

WALTER (*looking* MURCHISON *over from head to toe, scrutinizing his carefully casual tweed sports jacket over cashmere V-neck sweater over soft eyelet shirt and tie, and soft slacks, finished off with white buckskin shoes*): Why all you college boys wear them faggoty-looking white shoes?

RUTH: Walter Lee!

(GEORGE MURCHISON *ignores the remark.*)

WALTER (*to* RUTH): Well, they look crazy as hell—white shoes, cold as it is.

RUTH (*crushed*): You have to excuse him—

WALTER: No he don't! Excuse me for what? What you always excusing me for! I'll excuse myself when I needs to be excused! (*A pause.*) They look as funny as them black knee socks Beneatha wears out of here all the time.

RUTH: It's the college *style,* Walter.

WALTER: Style, hell. She looks like she got burnt legs or something!

RUTH: Oh, Walter—

WALTER (*an irritable mimic*): Oh, Walter! Oh, Walter! (*To* MURCHISON.) How's your old man making out? I understand you all going to buy that big hotel on the Drive? (*He finds a beer in the refrigerator, wanders over to* MURCHISON, *sipping and wiping his lips with the back of his hand, and straddling a chair backward to talk to the other man.*) Shrewd move. Your old man is all right, man. (*Tapping his head and half winking for emphasis.*) I mean he knows how to operate. I mean he thinks *big,* you know what I mean, I mean for a *home,* you know? But I think he's kind of running out of ideas now. I'd like to talk to him. Listen, man, I got some plans that could turn this city upside down. I mean think like he does. *Big.* Invest big, gamble big, hell, lose *big* if you have to, you know what I mean. It's hard to find a man on this whole Southside who understands my kind of thinking—you dig? (*He scrutinizes* MURCHISON *again, drinks his beer, squints his eyes, and leans in close, confidential, man to man.*) Me and you ought to sit down and talk sometimes, man. Man, I got me some ideas . . .

MURCHISON (*with boredom*): Yeah—sometimes we'll have to do that, Walter.

WALTER (*understanding the indifference, and offended*): Yeah—well, when you get the time, man. I know you a busy little boy.

RUTH: Walter, please—

WALTER (*bitterly, hurt*): I know ain't nothing in this world as busy as you colored college boys with your fraternity pins and white shoes . . .

RUTH (*covering her face with humiliation*): Oh, Walter Lee—

WALTER: I see you all all the time—with the books tucked under your arms—going to your (*British*

A—a mimic) "clahsses." And for what! What the hell you learning over there? Filling up your heads—(*counting off on his fingers*)—with the sociology and the psychology—but they teaching you how to be a man? How to take over and run the world? They teaching you how to run a rubber plantation or a steel mill? Naw—just to talk proper and read books and wear them faggoty-looking white shoes . . .

GEORGE (*looking at him with distaste, a little above it all*): You're all wacked up with bitterness, man.

WALTER (*intently, almost quietly, between the teeth, glaring at the boy*): And you—ain't you bitter, man? Ain't you just about had it yet? Don't you see no stars gleaming that you can't reach out and grab? You happy?—You contented son-of-a-bitch—you happy? You got it made? Bitter? Man, I'm a volcano. Bitter? Here I am a giant—surrounded by ants! Ants who can't even understand what it is the giant is talking about.

RUTH (*passionately and suddenly*): Oh, Walter—ain't you with nobody!

WALTER (*violently*): No! 'Cause ain't nobody with me! Not even my own mother!

RUTH: Walter, that's a terrible thing to say!

(BENEATHA *enters, dressed for the evening in a cocktail dress and earrings, hair natural.*)

GEORGE: Well—hey—(*Crosses to* BENEATHA; *thoughtful, with emphasis, since this is a reversal.*) You look great!

WALTER (*seeing his sister's hair for the first time*): What's the matter with your head?

BENEATHA (*tired of the jokes now*): I cut it off, Brother.

WALTER (*coming close to inspect it and walking around her*): Well, I'll be damned. So that's what they mean by the African bush . . .

BENEATHA: Ha ha. Let's go, George.

GEORGE (*looking at her*): You know something? I like it. It's sharp. I mean it really is. (*Helps her into her wrap.*)

RUTH: Yes—I think so, too. (*She goes to the mirror and starts to clutch at her hair.*)

WALTER: Oh no! You leave yours alone, baby. You might turn out to have a pin-shaped head or something!

BENEATHA: See you all later.

RUTH: Have a nice time.

GEORGE: Thanks. Good night. (*Half out the door, he reopens it. To* WALTER.) Good night, Prometheus!°

(BENEATHA *and* GEORGE *exit.*)

Prometheus, Greek god, one of the Titans, who challenged divine power by stealing fire from the gods.

WALTER (*to* RUTH): Who is Prometheus?

RUTH: I don't know. Don't worry about it.

WALTER (*in fury, pointing after* GEORGE): See there— they get to a point where they can't insult you man to man—they got to go talk about something ain't nobody never heard of!

RUTH: How do you know it was an insult? (*To humor him.*) Maybe Prometheus is a nice fellow.

WALTER: Prometheus! I bet there ain't even no such thing! I bet that simple-minded clown—

RUTH: Walter—

(*She stops what she is doing and looks at him.*)

WALTER (*yelling*): Don't start!

RUTH: Start what?

WALTER: Your nagging! Where was I? Who was I with? How much money did I spend?

RUTH (*plaintively*): Walter Lee—why don't we just try to talk about it . . .

WALTER (*not listening*): I been out talking with people who understand me. People who care about the things I got on my mind.

RUTH (*wearily*): I guess that means people like Willy Harris.

WALTER: Yes, people like Willy Harris.

RUTH (*with a sudden flash of impatience*): Why don't you all just hurry up and go into the banking business and stop talking about it!

WALTER: Why? You want to know why? 'Cause we all tied up in a race of people that don't know how to do nothing but moan, pray, and have babies!

(*The line is too bitter even for him and he looks at her and sits down.*)

RUTH: Oh, Walter . . . (*Softly.*) Honey, why can't you stop fighting me?

WALTER (*without thinking*): Who's fighting you? Who even cares about you?

(*This line begins the retardation of his mood.*)

RUTH: Well—(*She waits a long time, and then with resignation starts to put away her things.*) I guess I might as well go on to bed . . . (*More or less to herself.*) I don't know where we lost it . . . but we have . . . (*Then, to him.*) I—I'm sorry about this new baby, Walter. I guess maybe I better go on and do what I started . . . I guess I just didn't realize how bad things was with us . . . I guess I just didn't really realize—(*She starts out to the bedroom and stops.*) You want some hot milk?

WALTER: Hot milk?

RUTH: Yes—hot milk.

WALTER: Why hot milk?

RUTH: 'Cause after all that liquor you come home with you ought to have something hot in your stomach.

WALTER: I don't want no milk.

RUTH: You want some coffee then?

WALTER: No, I don't want no coffee. I don't want nothing hot to drink. (*Almost plaintively.*) Why you always trying to give me something to eat?

RUTH (*standing and looking at him helplessly*): What *else* can I give you, Walter Lee Younger?

(*She stands and looks at him and presently turns to go out again. He lifts his head and watches her going away from him in a new mood which began to emerge when he asked her "Who even cares about you?"*)

WALTER: It's been rough, ain't it, baby? (*She hears and stops but does not turn around and he continues to her back.*) I guess between two people there ain't never as much understood as folks generally thinks there is. I mean like between me and you—(*She turns to face him.*) How we gets to the place where we scared to talk softness to each other. (*He waits, thinking hard himself.*) Why you think it got to be like that? (*He is thoughtful, almost as a child would be.*) Ruth, what is it gets into people ought to be close?

RUTH: I don't know, honey. I think about it a lot.

WALTER: On account of you and me, you mean? The way things are with us. The way something done come down between us.

RUTH: There ain't so much between us, Walter . . . Not when you come to me and try to talk to me. Try to be with me . . . a little even.

WALTER (*total honesty*): Sometimes . . . sometimes . . . I don't even know how to try.

RUTH: Walter—

WALTER: Yes?

RUTH (*coming to him, gently and with misgiving, but coming to him*): Honey . . . life don't have to be like this. I mean sometimes people can do things so that things are better . . . You remember how we used to talk when Travis was born . . . about the way we were going to live . . . the kind of house . . . (*She is stroking his head.*) Well, it's all starting to slip away from us . . .

(*He turns her to him and they look at each other and kiss, tenderly and hungrily. The door opens and* MAMA *enters—*WALTER *breaks away and jumps up. A beat.*)

WALTER: Mama, where have you been?

MAMA: My—them steps is longer than they used to be. Whew! (*She sits down and ignores him.*) How you feeling this evening, Ruth?

(RUTH *shrugs, disturbed at having been interrupted and watching her husband knowingly.*)

WALTER: Mama, where have you been all day?

MAMA (*still ignoring him and leaning on the table and changing to more comfortable shoes*): Where's Travis?

RUTH: I let him go out earlier and he ain't come back yet. Boy, is he going to get it!

WALTER: Mama!

MAMA (*as if she has heard him for the first time*): Yes, son?

WALTER: Where did you go this afternoon?

MAMA: I went downtown to tend to some business that I had to tend to.

WALTER: What kind of business?

MAMA: You know better than to question me like a child, Brother.

WALTER (*rising and bending over the table*): Where were you, Mama? (*Bringing his fists down and shouting.*) Mama, you didn't go do something with that insurance money, something crazy?

(*The front door opens slowly, interrupting him, and* TRAVIS *peeks his head in, less than hopefully.*)

TRAVIS (*to his mother*): Mama, I—

RUTH: "Mama I" nothing! You're going to get it, boy! Get on in that bedroom and get yourself ready!

TRAVIS: But I—

MAMA: Why don't you all never let the child explain hisself.

RUTH: Keep out of it now, Lena.

(MAMA *clamps her lips together, and* RUTH *advances toward her son menacingly.*)

RUTH: A thousand times I have told you not to go off like that—

MAMA (*holding out her arms to her grandson*): Well—at least let me tell him something. I want him to be the first one to hear . . . Come here, Travis. (*The boy obeys, gladly.*) Travis—(*she takes him by the shoulder and looks into his face*)—you know that money we got in the mail this morning?

TRAVIS: Yes'm—

MAMA: Well—what you think your grandmama gone and done with that money?

TRAVIS: I don't know, Grandmama.

MAMA (*putting her finger on his nose for emphasis*): She went out and she bought you a house! (*The explosion comes from* WALTER *at the end of the revelation and he jumps up and turns away from all of them in a fury.* MAMA *continues, to* TRAVIS.) You glad about the house? It's going to be yours when you get to be a man.

TRAVIS: Yeah—I always wanted to live in a house.

MAMA: All right, gimme some sugar then—(TRAVIS *puts his arms around her neck as she watches her son over the boy's shoulder. Then, to* TRAVIS, *after the embrace.*) Now when you say your prayers tonight, you thank God and your grandfather—'cause it was him who give you the house—in his way.

RUTH (*taking the boy from* MAMA *and pushing him toward the bedroom*): Now you get out of here and get ready for your beating.

TRAVIS: Aw, Mama—

RUTH: Get on in there—(*Closing the door behind him*

and turning radiantly to her mother-in-law.) So you went and did it!

MAMA (*quietly, looking at her son with pain*): Yes, I did.

RUTH (*raising both arms classically*): PRAISE GOD! (*Looks at* WALTER *a moment, who says nothing. She crosses rapidly to her husband.*) Please, honey—let me be glad . . . you be glad too. (*She has laid her hands on his shoulders, but he shakes himself free of her roughly, without turning to face her.*) Oh, Walter . . . a home . . . a home. (*She comes back to* MAMA.) Well—where is it? How big is it? How much it going to cost?

MAMA: Well—

RUTH: When we moving?

MAMA (*smiling at her*): First of the month.

RUTH (*throwing back her head with jubilance*): Praise God!

MAMA (*tentatively, still looking at her son's back turned against her and* RUTH): It's—it's a nice house too . . . (*She cannot help speaking directly to him. An imploring quality in her voice, her manner, makes her almost like a girl now.*) Three bedrooms—nice big one for you and Ruth . . . Me and Beneatha still have to share our room, but Travis have one of his own and (*with difficulty*) I figure if the—new baby—is a boy, we could get one of them double-decker outfits . . . And there's a yard with a little patch of dirt where I could maybe get to grow me a few flowers . . . And a nice big basement . . .

RUTH: Walter honey, be glad—

MAMA (*still to his back, fingering things on the table*): 'Course I don't want to make it sound fancier than it is . . . It's just a plain little old house—but it's made good and solid—and it will be *ours*. Walter Lee—it makes a difference in a man when he can walk on floors that belong to *him* . . .

RUTH: Where is it?

MAMA (*frightened at this telling*): Well—well—it's out there in Clybourne Park—

(RUTH's *radiance fades abruptly, and* WALTER *finally turns slowly to face his mother with incredulity and hostility.*)

RUTH: Where?

MAMA (*matter-of-factly*): Four o six Clybourne Street, Clybourne Park.

RUTH: Clybourne Park? Mama, there ain't no colored people living in Clybourne Park.

MAMA (*almost idiotically*): Well, I guess there's going to be some now.

WALTER (*bitterly*): So that's the peace and comfort you went out and bought for us today!

MAMA (*raising her eyes to meet his finally*): Son—I just tried to find the nicest place for the least amount of money for my family.

RUTH (*trying to recover from the shock*): Well—well—'course I ain't one never been 'fraid of no crackers, mind you—but—well, wasn't there no other houses nowhere?

MAMA: Them houses they put up for colored in them areas way out all seem to cost twice as much as other houses. I did the best I could.

RUTH (*struck senseless with the news, in its various degrees of goodness and trouble, she sits a moment, her fists propping her chin in thought, and then she starts to rise, bringing her fists down with vigor, the radiance spreading from cheek to cheek again*): Well—well— All I can say is—if this is my time in life—MY TIME—to say good-bye—(*and she builds with momentum as she starts to circle the room with an exuberant, almost tearfully happy release*)—to these Goddamned cracking walls!—(*she pounds the walls*)—and these marching roaches!—(*she wipes at an imaginary army of marching roaches*)—and this cramped little closet which ain't now or never was no kitchen! . . . then I say it loud and good, HAL-LELUJAH! AND GOOD-BYE MISERY . . . I DON'T NEVER WANT TO SEE YOUR UGLY FACE AGAIN! (*She laughs joyously, having practically destroyed the apart-ment, and flings her arms up and lets them come down happily, slowly, reflectively, over her abdomen, aware for the first time perhaps that the life therein pulses with happiness and not despair.*) Lena?

MAMA (*moved, watching her happiness*): Yes, honey?

RUTH (*looking off*): Is there—is there a whole lot of sunlight?

MAMA (*understanding*): Yes, child, there's a whole lot of sunlight.

(*Long pause.*)

RUTH (*collecting herself and going to the door of the room TRAVIS is in*): Well—I guess I better see 'bout Travis. (*To* MAMA.) Lord, I sure don't feel like whipping nobody today!

(*She exits.*)

MAMA (*the mother and son are left alone now and the mother waits a long time, considering deeply, before she speaks*): Son—you—you understand what I done, don't you? (WALTER *is silent and sullen.*) I—I just seen my family falling apart today . . . just falling to pieces in front of my eyes . . . We couldn't of gone on like we was today. We was going backwards 'stead of forwards—talking 'bout killing babies and wishing each other was dead . . . When it gets like that in life—you just got to do something differ-ent, push on out and do something bigger . . . (*She waits.*) I wish you say something, son . . . I wish you'd say how deep inside you you think I done the right thing—

WALTER (*crossing slowly to his bedroom door and finally turning there and speaking measuredly*): What you need me to say you done right for? *You* the head of this family. You run our lives like you want to. It was your money and you did what you wanted with it. So what you need for me to say it was all

right for? (*Bitterly, to hurt her as deeply as he knows is possible.*) So you butchered up a dream of mine— you—who always talking 'bout your children's dreams . . .

MAMA: Walter Lee—

(*He just closes the door behind him.* MAMA *sits alone, thinking heavily.*)

ACT 2 / SCENE 2

(*Time: Friday night. A few weeks later.*)

(*At rise: Packing crates mark the intention of the family to move.* BENEATHA *and* GEORGE *come in, presumably from an evening out again.*)

GEORGE: O.K. . . . O.K., whatever you say . . . (*They both sit on the couch. He tries to kiss her. She moves away.*) Look, we've had a nice evening; let's not spoil it, huh? . . .

(*He again turns her head and tries to nuzzle in and she turns away from him, not with distaste but with momen-tary lack of interest; in a mood to pursue what they were talking about.*)

BENEATHA: I'm *trying* to talk to you.

GEORGE: We always talk.

BENEATHA: Yes—and I love to talk.

GEORGE (*exasperated; rising*): I know it and I don't mind it sometimes . . . I want you to cut it out, see—The moody stuff, I mean. I don't like it. You're a nice-looking girl . . . all over. That's all you need, honey, forget the atmosphere. Guys aren't going to go for the atmosphere—they're going to go for what they see. Be glad for that. Drop the Garbo° routine. It doesn't go with you. As for myself, I want a nice—(*groping*)—simple (*thoughtfully*)—sophisticated girl . . . not a poet— O.K.?

(*He starts to kiss her, she rebuffs him again, and he jumps up.*)

BENEATHA: Why are you angry, George?

GEORGE: Because this is stupid! I don't go out with you to discuss the nature of "quiet desperation" or to hear all about your thoughts—because the world will go on thinking what it thinks regard-less—

BENEATHA: Then why read books? Why go to school?

GEORGE (*with artificial patience, counting on his fingers*): It's simple. You read books—to learn facts—to get grades—to pass the course—to get a degree. That's all—it has nothing to do with thoughts.

Garbo, Greta Garbo (1905–90), a film actress known for her cool intensity.

(A long pause.)

BENEATHA: I see. *(He starts to sit.)* Good night, George.

(GEORGE looks at her a little oddly, and starts to exit. He meets MAMA coming in.)

GEORGE: Oh—hello, Mrs. Younger.

MAMA: Hello, George, how you feeling?

GEORGE: Fine—fine, how are you?

MAMA: Oh, a little tired. You know them steps can get you after a day's work. You all have a nice time tonight?

GEORGE: Yes—a fine time. A fine time.

MAMA: Well, good night.

GEORGE: Good night. *(He exits. MAMA closes the door behind her.)*

MAMA: Hello, honey. What you sitting like that for?

BENEATHA: I'm just sitting.

MAMA: Didn't you have a nice time?

BENEATHA: No.

MAMA: No? What's the matter?

BENEATHA: Mama, George is a fool—honest. *(She rises.)*

MAMA *(Hustling around unloading the packages she has entered with. She stops)*: Is he, baby?

BENEATHA: Yes.

(BENEATHA makes up TRAVIS's bed as she talks.)

MAMA: You sure?

BENEATHA: Yes.

MAMA: Well—I guess you better not waste your time with no fools.

(BENEATHA looks up at her mother, watching her put groceries in the refrigerator. Finally she gathers up her things and starts into the bedroom. At the door she stops and looks back at her mother.)

BENEATHA: Mama—

MAMA: Yes, baby—

BENEATHA: Thank you.

MAMA: For what?

BENEATHA: For understanding me this time.

(She exits quickly and the mother stands, smiling a little, looking at the place where BENEATHA just stood. RUTH enters.)

RUTH: Now don't you fool with any of this stuff, Lena—

MAMA: Oh, I just thought I'd sort a few things out. Is Brother here?

RUTH: Yes.

MAMA *(with concern)*: Is he—

RUTH *(reading her eyes)*: Yes.

(The phone rings. RUTH answers.)

RUTH *(at the phone)*: Hello—Just a minute. *(Goes to door.)* Walter, it's Mrs. Arnold. *(Waits. Goes back to the phone. Tense.)* Hello. Yes, this is his wife speaking . . . He's lying down now. Yes . . . well, he'll be in tomorrow. He's been very sick. Yes—I know we should have called, but we were so sure he'd be able to come in today. Yes—yes, I'm very sorry. Yes . . . Thank you very much. *(She hangs up. WALTER is standing in the doorway of the bedroom behind her.)* That was Mrs. Arnold.

WALTER *(indifferently)*: Was it?

RUTH: She said if you don't come in tomorrow that they are getting a new man . . .

WALTER: Ain't that sad—ain't that crying sad.

RUTH: She said Mr. Arnold has had to take a cab for three days . . . Walter, you ain't been to work for three days! *(This is a revelation to her.)* Where you been, Walter Lee Younger? *(WALTER looks at her and starts to laugh.)* You're going to lose your job.

WALTER: That's right . . . *(He turns on the radio.)*

RUTH: Oh, Walter, and with your mother working like a dog every day—

(A steamy, deep blues pours into the room.)

WALTER: That's sad too—Everything is sad.

MAMA: What you been doing for these three days, son?

WALTER: Mama—you don't know all the things a man what got leisure can find to do in this city . . . What's this—Friday night? Well—Wednesday I borrowed Willy Harris' car and I went for a drive . . . just me and myself and I drove and drove . . . Way out . . . way past South Chicago, and I parked the car and I sat and looked at the steel mills all day long. I just sat in the car and looked at them big black chimneys for hours. Then I drove back and I went to the Green Hat. *(Pause.)* And Thursday—Thursday I borrowed the car again and I got in it and I pointed it the other way and I drove the other way—for hours—way, way up to Wisconsin, and I looked at the farms. I just drove and looked at the farms. Then I drove back and I went to the Green Hat. *(Pause.)* And today—today I didn't get the car. Today I just walked. All over the Southside. And I looked at the Negroes and they looked at me and finally I just sat down on the curb at Thirty-ninth and South Parkway and I just sat there and watched the Negroes go by. And then I went to the Green Hat. You all sad? You all depressed? And you know where I am going right now—

(RUTH goes out quietly.)

MAMA: Oh, Big Walter, is this the harvest of our days?

WALTER: You know what I like about the Green Hat? I like this little cat they got there who blows a sax . . . He blows. He talks to me. He ain't but 'bout five feet tall and he's got a conked head and his eyes is always closed and he's all music—

MAMA (*rising and getting some papers out of her handbag*): Walter—

WALTER: And there's this other guy who plays the piano . . . and they got a sound. I mean they can work on some music . . . They got the best little combo in the world in the Green Hat . . . You can just sit there and drink and listen to them three men play and you realize that don't nothing matter worth a damn, but just being there—

MAMA: I've helped do it to you, haven't I, son? Walter I been wrong.

WALTER: Naw—you ain't never been wrong about nothing, Mama.

MAMA: Listen to me, now. I say I been wrong, son. That I been doing to you what the rest of the world been doing to you. (*She turns off the radio.*) Walter—(*She stops and he looks up slowly at her and she meets his eyes pleadingly.*) What you ain't never understood is that I ain't got nothing, don't own nothing, ain't never really wanted nothing that wasn't for you. There ain't nothing as precious to me . . . There ain't nothing worth holding on to, money, dreams, nothing else—if it means—if it means it's going to destroy my boy. (*She takes an envelope out of her handbag and puts it in front of him and he watches her without speaking or moving.*) I paid the man thirty-five hundred dollars down on the house. That leaves sixty-five hundred dollars. Monday morning I want you to take this money and take three thousand dollars and put it in a savings account for Beneatha's medical schooling. The rest you put in a checking account—with your name on it. And from now on any penny that come out of it or that go in it is for you to look after. For you to decide. (*She drops her hands a little helplessly.*) It ain't much, but it's all I got in the world and I'm putting it in your hands. I'm telling you to be the head of this family from now on like you supposed to be.

WALTER (*stares at the money*): You trust me like that, Mama?

MAMA: I ain't never stop trusting you. Like I ain't never stop loving you.

(*She goes out, and* WALTER *sits looking at the money on the table. Finally, in a decisive gesture, he gets up and, in mingled joy and desperation, picks up the money. At the same moment,* TRAVIS *enters for bed.*)

TRAVIS: What's the matter, Daddy? You drunk?

WALTER (*sweetly, more sweetly than we have ever known him*): No, Daddy ain't drunk. Daddy ain't going to never be drunk again . . .

TRAVIS: Well, good night, Daddy.

(*The father has come from behind the couch and leans over, embracing his son.*)

WALTER: Son, I feel like talking to you tonight.

TRAVIS: About what?

WALTER: Oh, about a lot of things. About you and what kind of man you going to be when you grow up . . . Son—son, what do you want to be when you grow up?

TRAVIS: A bus driver.

WALTER (*laughing a little*): A what? Man, that ain't nothing to want to be!

TRAVIS: Why not?

WALTER: 'Cause, man—it ain't big enough—you know what I mean.

TRAVIS: I don't know then. I can't make up my mind. Sometimes Mama asks me that too. And sometimes when I tell her I just want to be like you—she says she don't want me to be like that and sometimes she says she does. . . .

WALTER (*gathering him up in his arms*): You know what, Travis? In seven years you going to be seventeen years old. And things is going to be very different with us in seven years Travis. . . . One day when you are seventeen I'll come home—home from my office downtown somewhere—

TRAVIS: You don't work in no office, Daddy.

WALTER: No—but after tonight. After what your daddy gonna do tonight, there's going to be offices—a whole lot of offices. . . .

TRAVIS: What you gonna do tonight, Daddy?

WALTER: You wouldn't understand yet, son, but your daddy's gonna make a transaction . . . a business transaction that's going to change our lives. . . . That's how come one day when you 'bout seventeen years old I'll come home and I'll be pretty tired, you know what I mean, after a day of conferences and secretaries getting things wrong the way they do . . . 'cause an executive's life is hell man—(*The more he talks the farther away he gets.*) And I'll pull the car up on the driveway . . . just a plain black Chrysler, I think, with white walls—no—black tires. More elegant. Rich people don't have to be flashy . . . though I'll have to get something a little sportier for Ruth—maybe a Cadillac convertible to do her shopping in. . . . And I'll come up the steps to the house and the gardener will be clipping away at the hedges and he'll say, "Good evening, Mr. Younger." And I'll say, "Hello, Jefferson, how are you this evening?" And I'll go inside and Ruth will come downstairs and meet me at the door and we'll kiss each other and she'll take my arm and we'll go up to your room to see you sitting on the floor with the catalogues of all the great schools in America around you. . . . All the great schools in the world! And—and I'll say, all right son—it's your seventeenth birthday, what is it you've decided? . . . Just tell me where you want to go to school and you'll *go*. Just tell me, what it is you want to be—and you'll *be* it. . . . Whatever you want to be—Yessir! (*He holds his arms open for* TRAVIS.*)* You just name it, son . . . *(*TRAVIS *leaps into them)* and I hand you the world!

*(*WALTER*'s voice has risen in pitch and hysterical promise and on the last line he lifts* TRAVIS *high.)*

ACT 2 / SCENE 3

(Time: Saturday, moving day, one week later.)

(Before the curtain rises, RUTH*'s voice, a strident, dramatic church alto, cuts through the silence.)*

(It is, in the darkness, a triumphant surge, a penetrating statement of expectation: "Oh, Lord, I don't feel no ways tired! Children, oh, glory hallelujah!")

(As the curtain rises we see that RUTH *is alone in the living room, finishing up the family's packing. It is moving day. She is nailing crates and tying cartons.* BENEATHA *enters, carrying a guitar case, and watches her exuberant sister-in-law.)*

RUTH: Hey!

BENEATHA *(putting away the case)*: Hi.

RUTH *(pointing at a package)*: Honey—look in that package there and see what I found on sale this morning at the South Center. *(*RUTH *gets up and moves to the package and draws out some curtains.)* Lookahere—hand-turned hems!

BENEATHA: How do you know the window size out there?

RUTH *(who hadn't thought of that)*: Oh—Well, they bound to fit something in the whole house. Anyhow, they was too good a bargain to pass up. *(*RUTH *slaps her head, suddenly remembering something.)* Oh, Bennie—I meant to put a special note on that carton over there. That's your mama's good china and she wants 'em to be very careful with it.

BENEATHA: I'll do it.

*(*BENEATHA *finds a piece of paper and starts to draw large letters on it.)*

RUTH: You know what I'm going to do soon as I get in that new house?

BENEATHA: What?

RUTH: Honey—I'm going to run me a tub of water up to here . . . *(With her fingers practically up to her nostrils.)* And I'm going to get in it—and I am going to sit . . . and sit . . . and sit in that hot water and the first person who knocks to tell *me* to hurry up and come out—

BENEATHA: Gets shot at sunrise.

RUTH *(laughing happily)*: You said it, sister! *(Noticing how large* BENEATHA *is absent-mindedly making the note.)* Honey, they ain't going to read that from no airplane.

BENEATHA *(laughing herself)*: I guess I always think things have more emphasis if they are big, somehow.

RUTH *(looking up at her and smiling)*: You and your brother seem to have that as a philosophy of life. Lord, that man—done changed so 'round here. You know—you know what we did last night? Me and Walter Lee?

BENEATHA: What?

RUTH *(smiling to herself)*: We went to the movies. *(Looking at* BENEATHA *to see if she understands.)* We went to the movies. You know the last time me and Walter went to the movies together?

BENEATHA: No.

RUTH: Me neither. That's how long it been. *(Smiling again.)* But we went last night. The picture wasn't much good, but that didn't seem to matter. We went—and we held hands.

BENEATHA: Oh, Lord!

RUTH: We held hands—and you know what?

BENEATHA: What?

RUTH: When we come out of the show it was late and dark and all the stores and things was closed up . . . and it was kind of chilly and there wasn't many people on the streets . . . and we was still holding hands, me and Walter.

BENEATHA: You're killing me.

*(*WALTER *enters with a large package. His happiness is deep in him; he cannot keep still with his newfound exuberance. He is singing and wiggling and snapping his fingers. He puts his package in a corner and puts a phonograph record which he has brought in with him, on the record player. As the music, soulful and sensuous, comes up he dances over to* RUTH *and tries to get her to dance with him. She gives in at last to his raunchiness and in a fit of giggling allows herself to be drawn into his mood. They dip and she melts into his arms in a classic, body-melding "slow drag.")*

BENEATHA *(regarding them a long time as they dance, then drawing in her breath for a deeply exaggerated comment which she does not particularly mean)*: Talk about—olddddddddddd—fashionedddddddd—Negroes!

WALTER *(stopping momentarily)*: What kind of Negroes?

(He says this in fun. He is not angry with her today, nor with anyone. He starts to dance with his wife again.)

BENEATHA: Old-fashioned.

WALTER *(as he dances with* RUTH*)*: You know, when these *New Negroes* have their convention—*(pointing at his sister)*—that is going to be the chairman of the Committee on Unending Agitation. *(He goes on dancing, then stops.)* Race, race, race! . . . Girl, I do believe you are the first person in the history of the entire human race to successfully brainwash yourself. *(*BENEATHA *breaks up and he goes on dancing. He stops again, enjoying his tease.)* Damn, even the N double A C P takes a holiday sometimes! *(*BENEATHA *and* RUTH *laugh. He dances with* RUTH *some more and starts to laugh and stops* and pantomimes someone over an operating table.) I can just see that chick someday looking down at some poor cat on an operating table and before she starts to slice him, she says . . . (pulling his sleeves back maliciously) "By the way, what are your views on civil rights down there? . . ."

(He laughs at her again and starts to dance happily. The bell sounds.)

BENEATHA: Sticks and stones may break my bones but . . . words will never hurt me!

(BENEATHA goes to the door and opens it as WALTER and RUTH go on with the clowning. BENEATHA is somewhat surprised to see a quiet-looking middle-aged white man in a business suit holding his hat and a briefcase in his hand and consulting a small piece of paper.)

MAN: Uh—how do you do, miss. I am looking for a Mrs.—(he looks at the slip of paper) Mrs. Lena Younger? (He stops short, struck dumb at the sight of the oblivious WALTER and RUTH.)

BENEATHA (smoothing her hair with slight embarrassment): Oh—yes, that's my mother. Excuse me. (She closes the door and turns to quiet the other two.) Ruth! Brother! (Enunciating precisely but soundlessly: "There's a white man at the door!" They stop dancing, RUTH cuts off the phonograph, BENEATHA opens the door. The man casts a curious quick glance at all of them.) Uh—come in please.

MAN (coming in): Thank you.

BENEATHA: My mother isn't here just now. Is it business?

MAN: Yes . . . well, of a sort.

WALTER (freely, the Man of the House): Have a seat. I'm Mrs. Younger's son. I look after most of her business matters.

(RUTH and BENEATHA exchange amused glances.)

MAN (regarding WALTER, and sitting): Well—My name is Karl Lindner . . .

WALTER (stretching out his hand): Walter Younger. This is my wife—(RUTH nods politely)—and my sister.

LINDNER: How do you do.

WALTER (amiably, as he sits himself easily on a chair, leaning forward on his knees with interest and looking expectantly into the newcomer's face): What can we do for you, Mr. Lindner!

LINDNER (some minor shuffling of the hat and briefcase on his knees): Well—I am a representative of the Clybourne Park Improvement Association—

WALTER (pointing): Why don't you sit your things on the floor?

LINDNER: Oh—yes. Thank you. (He slides the briefcase and hat under the chair.) And as I was saying—I am from the Clybourne Park Improvement Association and we have had it brought to our attention at the last meeting that you people—or at least

your mother—has bought a piece of residential property at—(he digs for the slip of paper again)—four o six Clybourne Street . . .

WALTER: That's right. Care for something to drink? Ruth, get Mr. Lindner a beer.

LINDNER (upset for some reason): Oh—no, really. I mean thank you very much, but no thank you.

RUTH (innocently): Some coffee?

LINDNER: Thank you, nothing at all.

(BENEATHA is watching the man carefully.)

LINDNER: Well, I don't know how much you folks know about our organization. (He is a gentle man; thoughtful and somewhat labored in his manner.) It is one of these community organizations set up to look after—oh, you know, things like block upkeep and special projects and we also have what we call our New Neighbors Orientation Committee . . .

BENEATHA (drily): Yes—and what do they do?

LINDNER (turning a little to her and then returning the main force to WALTER): Well—it's what you might call a sort of welcoming committee, I guess. I mean they, we—I'm the chairman of the committee—go around and see the new people who move into the neighborhood and sort of give them the lowdown on the way we do things out in Clybourne Park.

BENEATHA (with appreciation of the two meanings, which escape RUTH and WALTER): Un-huh.

LINDNER: And we also have the category of what the association calls—(he looks elsewhere)—uh—special community problems . . .

BENEATHA: Yes—and what are some of those?

WALTER: Girl, let the man talk.

LINDNER (with understood relief): Thank you. I would sort of like to explain this thing in my own way. I mean I want to explain to you in a certain way.

WALTER: Go ahead.

LINDNER: Yes. Well. I'm going to try to get right to the point. I'm sure we'll all appreciate that in the long run.

BENEATHA: Yes.

WALTER: Be still now!

LINDNER: Well—

RUTH (still innocently): Would you like another chair—you don't look comfortable.

LINDNER (more frustrated than annoyed): No, thank you very much. Please. Well—to get right to the point, I—(a great breath, and he is off at last) I am sure you people must be aware of some of the incidents which have happened in various parts of the city when colored people have moved into certain areas—(BENEATHA exhales heavily and starts tossing a piece of fruit up and down in the air.) Well—because we have what I think is going to be a unique type of organization in American community life—not only do we deplore that kind of thing—but we are trying to do something about it. (BENEATHA *stops tossing and turns with a new and quizzical interest to the man.*) We feel—(*gaining confidence in his mission because of the interest in the faces of the people he is talking to*)—we feel that most of the trouble in this world, when you come right down to it—(*he hits his knee for emphasis*)—most of the trouble exists because people just don't sit down and talk to each other.

RUTH (*nodding as she might in church, pleased with the remark*): You can say that again, mister.

LINDNER (*more encouraged by such affirmation*): That we don't try hard enough in this world to understand the other fellow's problem. The other guy's point of view.

RUTH: Now that's right.

(BENEATHA *and* WALTER *merely watch and listen with genuine interest.*)

LINDNER: Yes—that's the way we feel out in Clybourne Park. And that's why I was elected to come here this afternoon and talk to you people. Friendly like, you know, the way people should talk to each other and see if we couldn't find some way to work this thing out. As I say, the whole business is a matter of *caring* about the other fellow. Anybody can see that you are a nice family of folks, hard-working and honest I'm sure. (BENEATHA *frowns slightly, quizzically, her head tilted regarding him.*) Today everybody knows what it means to be on the outside of *something.* And of course, there is always somebody who is out to take advantage of people who don't always understand.

WALTER: What do you mean?

LINDNER: Well—you see our community is made up of people who've worked hard as the dickens for years to build up that little community. They're not rich and fancy people; just hard-working, honest people who don't really have much but those little homes and a dream of the kind of community they want to raise their children in. Now, I don't say we are perfect and there is a lot wrong in some of the things they want. But you've got to admit that a man, right or wrong, has the right to want to have the neighborhood he lives in a certain kind of way. And at the moment the overwhelming majority of our people out there feel that people get along better, take more of a common interest in the life of the community, when they share a common background. I want you to believe me when I tell you that race prejudice simply doesn't enter into it. It is a matter of the people of Clybourne Park believing, rightly or wrongly, as I say, that for the happiness of all concerned that our Negro families are happier when they live in their *own* communities.

BENEATHA (*with a grand and bitter gesture*): This, friends, is the Welcoming Committee!

WALTER (*dumfounded, looking at* LINDNER): Is this what you came marching all the way over here to tell us?

LINDNER: Well, now we've been having a fine conversation. I hope you'll hear me all the way through.

WALTER (*tightly*): Go ahead, man.

LINDNER: You see—in the face of all the things I have said, we are prepared to make your family a very generous offer . . .

BENEATHA: Thirty pieces and not a coin less!

WALTER: Yeah?

LINDNER (*putting on his glasses and drawing a form out of the briefcase*): Our association is prepared, through the collective effort of our people, to buy the house from you at a financial gain to your family.

RUTH: Lord have mercy, ain't this the living gall!

WALTER: All right, you through?

LINDNER: Well, I want to give you the exact terms of the financial arrangement—

WALTER: We don't want to hear no exact terms of no arrangements. I want to know if you got any more to tell us 'bout getting together?

LINDNER (*taking off his glasses*): Well—I don't suppose that you feel . . .

WALTER: Never mind how I feel—you got any more to say 'bout how people ought to sit down and talk to each other? . . . Get out of my house, man.

(*He turns his back and walks to the door.*)

LINDNER (*looking around at the hostile faces and reaching and assembling his hat and briefcase*): Well—I don't understand why you people are reacting this way. What do you think you are going to gain by moving into a neighborhood where you just aren't wanted and where some elements—well—people can get awful worked up when they feel that their whole way of life and everything they've ever worked for is threatened.

WALTER: Get out.

LINDNER (*at the door, holding a small card*): Well—I'm sorry it went like this.

WALTER: Get out.

LINDNER (*almost sadly regarding* WALTER): You just can't force people to change their hearts, son.

(*He turns and puts his card on a table and exits.* WALTER *pushes the door to with stinging hatred, and stands looking at it.* RUTH *just sits and* BENEATHA *just stands. They say nothing.* MAMA *and* TRAVIS *enter.*)

MAMA: Well—this all the packing got done since I left out of here this morning. I testify before God that my children got all the energy of the *dead!* What time the moving men due?

BENEATHA: Four o'clock. You had a caller, Mama.

(*She is smiling, teasingly.*)

MAMA: Sure enough—who?

BENEATHA (*her arms folded saucily*): The Welcoming Committee.

(WALTER *and* RUTH *giggle.*)

MAMA (*innocently*): Who?

BENEATHA: The Welcoming Committee. They said they're sure going to be glad to see you when you get there.

WALTER (*devilishly*): Yeah, they said they can't hardly wait to see your face.

(*Laughter.*)

MAMA (*sensing their facetiousness*): What's the matter with you all?

WALTER: Ain't nothing the matter with us. We just telling you 'bout the gentleman who came to see you this afternoon. From the Clybourne Park Improvement Association.

MAMA: What he want?

RUTH (*in the same mood as* BENEATHA *and* WALTER): To welcome you, honey.

WALTER: He said they can't hardly wait. He said the one thing they don't have, that they just *dying* to have out there is a fine family of fine colored people! (*To* RUTH *and* BENEATHA.) Ain't that right!

RUTH (*mockingly*): Yeah! He left his card—

BENEATHA (*handing card to* MAMA): In case.

(MAMA *reads and throws it on the floor—understanding and looking off as she draws her chair up to the table on which she has put her plant and some sticks and some cord.*)

MAMA: Father, give us strength. (*Knowingly—and without fun.*) Did he threaten us?

BENEATHA: Oh—Mama—they don't do it like that anymore. He talked Brotherhood. He said everybody ought to learn how to sit down and hate each other with good Christian fellowship.

(*She and* WALTER *shake hands to ridicule the remark.*)

MAMA (*sadly*): Lord, protect us . . .

RUTH: You should hear the money those folks raised to buy the house from us. All we paid and then some.

BENEATHA: What they think we going to do—eat 'em?

RUTH: No, honey, marry 'em.

MAMA (*shaking her head*): Lord, Lord, Lord . . .

RUTH: Well—that's the way the crackers crumble. (*A beat.*) Joke.

BENEATHA (*laughingly noticing what her mother is doing*): Mama, what are you doing?

MAMA: Fixing my plant so it won't get hurt none on the way . . .

BENEATHA: Mama, you going to take *that* to the new house?

MAMA: Un-huh—

BENEATHA: That raggedy-looking old thing?

MAMA (*stopping and looking at her*): It expresses ME!

RUTH (*with delight, to* BENEATHA): So there, Miss Thing!

(WALTER *comes to* MAMA *suddenly and bends down behind her and squeezes her in his arms with all his strength. She is overwhelmed by the suddenness of it and, though delighted, her manner is like that of* RUTH *and* TRAVIS.)

MAMA: Look out now, boy! You make me mess up my thing here!

WALTER (*his face lit, he slips down on his knees beside her, his arms still about her*): Mama . . . you know what it means to climb up in the chariot?

MAMA (*gruffly, very happy*): Get on away from me now . . .

RUTH (*near the gift-wrapped package, trying to catch* WALTER'S *eye*): Psst—

WALTER: What the old song say, Mama . . .

RUTH: Walter—Now?

(*She is pointing at the package.*)

WALTER (*speaking the lines, sweetly, playfully, in his mother's face*): I got wings . . . you got wings . . . All God's Children got wings . . .

MAMA: Boy—get out of my face and do some work . . .

WALTER: When I get to heaven gonna put on my wings, Gonna fly all over God's heaven . . .

BENEATHA (*teasingly, from across the room*): Everybody talking 'bout heaven ain't going there!

WALTER (*to* RUTH, *who is carrying the box across to them*): I don't know, you think we ought to give her that . . . Seems to me she ain't been very appreciative around here.

MAMA (*eyeing the box, which is obviously a gift*): What is that?

WALTER (*taking it from* RUTH *and putting it on the table in front of* MAMA): Well—what you all think? Should we give it to her?

RUTH: Oh—she was pretty good today.

MAMA: I'll good you—

(*She turns her eyes to the box again.*)

BENEATHA: Open it, Mama.

(*She stands up, looks at it, turns, and looks at all of them, and then presses her hands together and does not open the package.*)

WALTER (*sweetly*): Open it, Mama. It's for you. (MAMA *looks in his eyes. It is the first present in her life without its being Christmas. Slowly she opens her package and lifts out, one by one, a brand-new sparkling set of gardening tools.* WALTER *continues, prodding.*) Ruth made up the note—read it . . .

MAMA (*picking up the card and adjusting her glasses*): "To

our own Mrs. Miniver°—Love from Brother, Ruth, and Beneatha." Ain't that lovely . . .

TRAVIS (*tugging at his father's sleeve*): Daddy, can I give her mine now?

WALTER: All right, son. (TRAVIS *flies to get his gift.*)

MAMA: Now I don't have to use my knives and forks no more . . .

WALTER: Travis didn't want to go in with the rest of us, Mama. He got his own. (*Somewhat amused.*) We don't know what it is . . .

TRAVIS (*racing back in the room with a large hatbox and putting it in front of his grandmother*): Here!

MAMA: Lord have mercy, baby. You done gone and bought your grandmother a hat?

TRAVIS (*very proud*): Open it!

(*She does and lifts out an elaborate, but very elaborate, wide gardening hat, and all the adults break up at the sight of it.*)

RUTH: Travis, honey, what is that?

TRAVIS (*who thinks it is beautiful and appropriate*): It's a gardening hat! Like the ladies always have on in the magazines when they work in their gardens.

BENEATHA (*giggling fiercely*): Travis—we were trying to make Mama Mrs. Miniver—not Scarlett O'Hara!

MAMA (*indignantly*): What's the matter with you all! This here is a beautiful hat! (*Absurdly.*) I always wanted me one just like it!

(*She pops it on her head to prove it to her grandson, and the hat is ludicrous and considerably oversized.*)

RUTH: Hot dog! Go, Mama!

WALTER (*doubled over with laughter*): I'm sorry, Mama— but you look like you ready to go out and chop you some cotton sure enough!

(*They all laugh except* MAMA, *out of deference to* TRAVIS's *feelings.*)

MAMA (*gathering the boy up to her*): Bless your heart— this is the prettiest hat I ever owned—(WALTER, RUTH, *and* BENEATHA *chime in—noisily, festively, and insincerely congratulating* TRAVIS *on his gift.*) What are we all standing around here for? We ain't finished packin' yet. Bennie, you ain't packed one book.

(*The bell rings.*)

BENEATHA: That couldn't be the movers . . . it's not hardly two good yet—

(BENEATHA *goes into her room.* MAMA *starts for door.*)

WALTER (*turning, stiffening*): Wait—wait—I'll get it.

(*He stands and looks at the door.*)

MAMA: You expecting company, son?

WALTER (*just looking at the door*): Yeah—yeah . . .

(MAMA *looks at* RUTH, *and they exchange innocent and unfrightened glances.*)

MAMA (*not understanding*): Well, let them in, son.

BENEATHA (*from her room*): We need some more string.

MAMA: Travis—you run to the hardware and get me some string cord.

(MAMA *goes out and* WALTER *turns and looks at* RUTH. TRAVIS *goes to a dish for money.*)

RUTH: Why don't you answer the door, man?

WALTER (*suddenly bounding across the floor to embrace her*): 'Cause sometimes it hard to let the future begin! (*Stooping down in her face.*) I got wings! You got wings! All God's children got wings!

(*He crosses to the door and throws it open. Standing there is a very slight little man in a not too prosperous business suit and with haunted frightened eyes and a hat pulled down tightly, brim up, around his forehead.* TRAVIS *passes between the men and exits.* WALTER *leans deep in the man's face, still in his jubilance.*) When I get to heaven gonna put on my wings, Gonna fly all over God's heaven . . .

(*The little man just stares at him.*) Heaven—

(*Suddenly he stops and looks past the little man into the empty hallway.*) Where's Willy, man?

BOBO: He ain't with me.

WALTER (*not disturbed*): Oh—come on in. You know my wife.

BOBO (*dumbly, taking off his hat*): Yes—h'you, Miss Ruth.

RUTH (*quietly, a mood apart from her husband already, seeing* BOBO): Hello, Bobo.

WALTER: You right on time today . . . Right on time. That's the way! (*He slaps* BOBO *on his back.*) Sit down . . . lemme hear.

(RUTH *stands stiffly and quietly in back of them, as though somehow she senses death, her eyes fixed on her husband.*)

BOBO (*his frightened eyes on the floor, his hat in his hands*): Could I please get a drink of water, before I tell you about it, Walter Lee?

(WALTER *does not take his eyes off the man.* RUTH *goes blindly to the tap and gets a glass of water and brings it to* BOBO.)

WALTER: There ain't nothing wrong, is there?

BOBO: Lemme tell you—

Mrs. Miniver, suburban British housewife in a 1942 film of the same name.

WALTER: Man—didn't nothing go wrong?

BOBO: Lemme tell you—Walter Lee. (*Looking at* RUTH *and talking to her more than to* WALTER.) You know how it was. I got to tell you how it was. I mean first I got to tell you how it was all the way . . . I mean about the money I put in, Walter Lee . . .

WALTER (*with taut agitation now*): What about the money you put in?

BOBO: Well—it wasn't much as we told you—me and Willy—(*He stops.*) I'm sorry, Walter. I got a bad feeling about it. I got a real bad feeling about it . . .

WALTER: Man, what you telling me about all this for? . . . Tell me what happened in Springfield . . .

BOBO: Springfield.

RUTH (*like a dead woman*): What was supposed to happen in Springfield?

BOBO (*to her*): This deal that me and Walter went into with Willy—Me and Willy was going to go down to Springfield and spread some money 'round so's we wouldn't have to wait so long for the liquor license . . . That's what we were going to do. Everybody said that was the way you had to do, you understand, Miss Ruth?

WALTER: Man—what happened down there?

BOBO (*a pitiful man, near tears*): I'm trying to tell you, Walter.

WALTER (*screaming at him suddenly*): THEN TELL ME, GODDAMMIT . . . WHAT'S THE MATTER WITH YOU?

BOBO: Man . . . I didn't go to no Springfield, yesterday.

WALTER (*halted, life hanging in the moment*): Why not?

BOBO (*the long way, the hard way to tell*): 'Cause I didn't have no reasons to . . .

WALTER: Man, what are you talking about!

BOBO: I'm talking about the fact that when I got to the train station yesterday morning—eight o'clock like we planned . . . Man—*Willy didn't never show up.*

WALTER: Why . . . where was he . . . where is he?

BOBO: That's what I'm trying to tell you . . . I don't know . . . I waited six hours . . . I called his house . . . and I waited . . . six hours . . . I waited in that train station six hours . . . (*Breaking into tears.*) That was all the extra money I had in the world . . . (*Looking up at* WALTER *with the tears running down his face.*) Man, *Willy is gone.*

WALTER: Gone, what you mean Willy is gone? Gone where? You mean he went by himself. You mean he went off to Springfield by himself—to take care of getting the license—(*Turns and looks anxiously at* RUTH.) You mean maybe he didn't want too many people in on the business down there? (*Looks to* RUTH *again, as before.*) You know Willy got his own ways. (*Looks back to* BOBO.) Maybe you was late yesterday and he just went on down there without you. Maybe—maybe—he's been callin'

you at home tryin' to tell you what happened or something. Maybe—maybe—he just got sick. He's somewhere—he's got to be somewhere. We just got to find him—me and you got to find him. (*Grabs* BOBO *senselessly by the collar and starts to shake him.*) We got to!

BOBO (*in sudden angry, frightened agony*): What's the matter with you, Walter! *When a cat take off with your money he don't leave you no road maps!*

WALTER (*turning madly, as though he is looking for Willy in the very room*): Willy! . . . Willy . . . don't do it . . . Please don't do it . . . Man, not with that money . . . Man, please, not with that money . . . Oh, God . . . Don't let it be true . . . (*He is wandering around, crying out for Willy and looking for him or perhaps for help from God.*) Man . . . I trusted you . . . Man, I put my life in your hands . . . (*He starts to crumple down on the floor as* RUTH *just covers her face in horror.* MAMA *opens the door and comes into the room, with* BENEATHA *behind her.*) Man . . . (*He starts to pound the floor with his fists, sobbing wildly.*) THAT MONEY IS MADE OUT OF MY FATHER'S FLESH—

BOBO (*standing over him helplessly*): I'm sorry, Walter . . . (*only* WALTER's *sobs reply.* BOBO *puts on his hat.*) I had my life staked on this deal, too . . .

(*He exits.*)

MAMA (*to* WALTER): Son—(*She goes to him, bends down to him, talks to his bent head.*) Son . . . Is it gone? Son, I gave you sixty-five hundred dollars. Is it gone? All of it? Beneatha's money too?

WALTER (*lifting his head slowly*): Mama . . . I never . . . went to the bank at all . . .

MAMA (*not wanting to believe him*): You mean . . . your sister's school money . . . you used that too . . . Walter? . . .

WALTER: Yessss! All of it . . . It's all gone . . .

(*There is total silence.* RUTH *stands with her face covered with her hands;* BENEATHA *leans forlornly against a wall, fingering a piece of red ribbon from the mother's gift.* MAMA *stops and looks at her son without recognition and then, quite without thinking about it, starts to beat him senselessly in the face.* BENEATHA *goes to them and stops it.*)

BENEATHA: Mama!

(MAMA *stops and looks at both of her children and rises slowly and wanders vaguely, aimlessly away from them.*)

MAMA: I seen . . . him . . . night after night . . . come in . . . and look at that rug . . . and then look at me . . . the red showing in his eyes . . . the veins moving in his head . . . I seen him grow thin and old before he was forty . . . working and working and working like somebody's old horse . . . killing himself . . . and you—you give it all away in a day—(*She raises her arms to strike him again.*)

BENEATHA: Mama—

MAMA: Oh, God . . . *(She looks up to Him.)* Look down here—and show me the strength.

BENEATHA: Mama—

MAMA *(folding over)*: Strength . . .

BENEATHA *(plaintively)*: Mama . . .

MAMA: Strength!

ACT 3

(An hour later.)

(At curtain, there is a sullen light of gloom in the living room, gray light not unlike that which began the first scene of Act 1. At left we can see WALTER *within his room, alone with himself. He is stretched out on the bed, his shirt out and open, his arms under his head. He does not smoke, he does not cry out, he merely lies there, looking up at the ceiling, much as if he were alone in the world.)*

(In the living room BENEATHA *sits at the table, still surrounded by the now almost ominous packing crates. She sits looking off. We feel that this is a mood struck perhaps an hour before, and it lingers now, full of the empty sound of profound disappointment. We see on a line from her brother's bedroom the sameness of their attitudes. Presently the bell rings and* BENEATHA *rises without ambition or interest in answering. It is* ASAGAI, *smiling broadly, striding into the room with energy and happy expectation and conversation.)*

ASAGAI: I came over . . . I had some free time. I thought I might help with the packing. Ah, I like the look of packing crates! A household in preparation for a journey! It depresses some people . . . but for me . . . it is another feeling. Something full of the flow of life, do you understand? Movement, progress . . . It makes me think of Africa.

BENEATHA: Africa!

ASAGAI: What kind of a mood is this? Have I told you how deeply you move me?

BENEATHA: He gave away the money, Asagai . . .

ASAGAI: Who gave away what money?

BENEATHA: The insurance money. My brother gave it away.

ASAGAI: Gave it away?

BENEATHA: He made an investment! With a man even Travis wouldn't have trusted with his most worn-out marbles.

ASAGAI: And it's gone?

BENEATHA: Gone!

ASAGAI: I'm very sorry . . . And you, now?

BENEATHA: Me? . . . Me? . . . Me, I'm nothing . . . Me. When I was very small . . . we used to take our sleds out in the wintertime and the only hills we had were the ice-covered stone steps of some houses down the street. And we used to fill them in with snow and make them smooth and slide down them all day . . . and it was very dangerous,

you know . . . far too steep . . . and sure enough one day a kid named Rufus came down too fast and hit the sidewalk and we saw his face just split open right there in front of us . . . And I remember standing there looking at his bloody open face thinking that was the end of Rufus. But the ambulance came and they took him to the hospital and they fixed the broken bones and they sewed it all up . . . and the next time I saw Rufus he just had a little line down the middle of his face . . . I never got over that . . .

ASAGAI: What?

BENEATHA: That that was what one person could do for another, fix him up—sew up the problem, make him all right again. That was the most marvelous thing in the world . . . I wanted to do that. I always thought it was the one concrete thing in the world that a human being could do. Fix up the sick, you know—and make them whole again. This was truly being God . . .

ASAGAI: You wanted to be God?

BENEATHA: No—I wanted to cure. It used to be so important to me. I wanted to cure. It used to matter. I used to care. I mean about people and how their bodies hurt . . .

ASAGAI: And you've stopped caring?

BENEATHA: Yes—I think so.

ASAGAI: Why?

BENEATHA *(bitterly)*: Because it doesn't seem deep enough, close enough to what ails mankind! It was a child's way of seeing things—or an idealist's.

ASAGAI: Children see things very well sometimes—and idealists even better.

BENEATHA: I know that's what you think. Because you are still where I left off. You with all your talk and dreams about Africa! You still think you can patch up the world. Cure the Great Sore of Colonialism—*(loftily, mocking it)* with the Penicillin of Independence—!

ASAGAI: Yes!

BENEATHA: Independence *and then what?* What about all the crooks and thieves and just plain idiots who will come into power and steal and plunder the same as before—only now they will be black and do it in the name of the new Independence—WHAT ABOUT THEM?!

ASAGAI: That will be the problem for another time. First we must get there.

BENEATHA: And where does it end?

ASAGAI: End? Who even spoke of an end? To life? To living?

BENEATHA: An end to misery! To stupidity! Don't you see there isn't any real progress, Asagai, there is only one large circle that we march in, around and around, each of us with our own little picture in front of us—our own little mirage that we think is the future.

ASAGAI: That is the mistake.

BENEATHA: What?

ASAGAI: What you just said—about the circle. It isn't a circle—it is simply a long line—as in geometry, you know, one that reaches into infinity. And because we cannot see the end—we also cannot see how it changes. And it is very odd but those who see the changes—who dream, who will not give up—are called idealists . . . and those who see only the circle—we call *them* the "realists"!

BENEATHA: Asagai, while I was sleeping in that bed in there, people went out and took the future right out of my hands! And nobody asked me, nobody consulted me—they just went out and changed my life!

ASAGAI: Was it your money?

BENEATHA: What?

ASAGAI: Was it your money he gave away?

BENEATHA: It belonged to all of us.

ASAGAI: But did you earn it? Would you have had it at all if your father had not died?

BENEATHA: No.

ASAGAI: Then isn't there something wrong in a house—in a world—where all dreams, good or bad, must depend on the death of a man? I never thought to see *you* like this, Alaiyo. You! Your brother made a mistake and you are grateful to him so that now you can give up the ailing human race on account of it! You talk about what good is struggle, what good is anything! Where are we all going and why are we bothering!

BENEATHA: AND YOU CANNOT ANSWER IT!

ASAGAI (*shouting over her*): I LIVE THE ANSWER! (*Pause.*) In my village at home it is the exceptional man who can even read a newspaper . . . or who ever sees a book at all. I will go home and much of what I will have to say will seem strange to the people of my village. But I will teach and work and things will happen, slowly and swiftly. At times it will seem that nothing changes at all . . . and then again the sudden dramatic events which make history leap into the future. And then quiet again. Retrogression even. Guns, murder, revolution. And I even will have moments when I wonder if the quiet was not better than all that death and hatred. But I will look about my village at the illiteracy and disease and ignorance and I will not wonder long. And perhaps . . . perhaps I will be a great man . . . I mean perhaps I will hold on to the substance of truth and find my way always with the right course . . . and perhaps for it I will be butchered in my bed some night by the servants of empire . . .

BENEATHA: *The martyr!*

ASAGAI (*he smiles*): . . . or perhaps I shall live to be a very old man, respected and esteemed in my new nation . . . And perhaps I shall hold office and this is what I'm trying to tell you, Alaiyo: Perhaps the things I believe now for my country will be wrong and outmoded, and I will not understand and do terrible things to have things my way or merely to keep my power. Don't you see that there will be young men and women—not British soldiers then, but my own black countrymen—to step out of the shadows some evening and slit my then useless throat? Don't you see they have always been there . . . that they always will be. And that such a thing as my own death will be an advance? They who might kill me even . . . actually replenish all that I was.

BENEATHA: Oh, Asagai, I know all that.

ASAGAI: Good! Then stop moaning and groaning and tell me what you plan to do.

BENEATHA: Do?

ASAGAI: I have a bit of a suggestion.

BENEATHA: What?

ASAGAI (*rather quietly for him*): That when it is all over—that you come home with me—

BENEATHA (*staring at him and crossing away with exasperation*): Oh—Asagai—at this moment you decide to be romantic!

ASAGAI (*quickly understanding the misunderstanding*): My dear, young creature of the New World—I do not mean across the city—I mean across the ocean: home—to Africa.

BENEATHA (*slowly understanding and turning to him with murmured amazement*): To Africa?

ASAGAI: Yes! . . . (*Smiling and lifting his arms playfully.*) Three hundred years later the African Prince rose up out of the seas and swept the maiden back across the middle passage over which her ancestors had come—

BENEATHA (*unable to play*): To—to Nigeria?

ASAGAI: Nigeria. Home. (*Coming to her with genuine romantic flippancy.*) I will show you our mountains and our stars; and give you cool drinks from gourds and teach you the old songs and the ways of our people—and, in time, we will pretend that—(*very softly*)—you have only been away for a day. Say that you'll come—(*He swings her around and takes her full in his arms in a kiss which proceeds to passion.*)

BENEATHA (*pulling away suddenly*): You're getting me all mixed up—

ASAGAI: Why?

BENEATHA: Too many things—too many things have happened today. I must sit down and think. I don't know what I feel about anything right this minute.

(*She promptly sits down and props her chin on her fist.*)

ASAGAI (*charmed*): All right, I shall leave you. No—don't get up. (*Touching her, gently, sweetly.*) Just sit awhile and think . . . Never be afraid to sit awhile and think. (*He goes to door and looks at her.*) How often I have looked at you and said, "Ah—so this is what the New World hath finally wrought . . ."

(He exits. BENEATHA *sits on alone. Presently* WALTER *enters from his room and starts to rummage through things, feverishly looking for something. She looks up and turns in her seat.)*

BENEATHA *(hissingly)*: Yes—just look at what the New World hath wrought! . . . Just look! *(She gestures with bitter disgust.)* There he is! *Monsieur le petit bourgeois noir°*—himself! There he is—Symbol of a Rising Class! Entrepreneur! Titan of the system! (WALTER *ignores her completely and continues frantically and destructively looking for something and hurling things to floor and tearing things out of their place in his search.* BENEATHA *ignores the eccentricity of his actions and goes on with the monologue of insult.)* Did you dream of yachts on Lake Michigan, Brother? Did you see yourself on that Great Day sitting down at the Conference Table, surrounded by all the mighty bald-headed men in America? All halted, waiting, breathless, waiting for your pronouncements on industry? Waiting for you—Chairman of the Board! (WALTER *finds what he is looking for—a small piece of white paper—and pushes it in his pocket and puts on his coat and rushes out without ever having looked at her. She shouts after him.)* I look at you and I see the final triumph of stupidity in the world!

(The door slams and she returns to just sitting again. RUTH *comes quickly out of* MAMA*'s room.)*

RUTH: Who was that?

BENEATHA: Your husband.

RUTH: Where did he go?

BENEATHA: Who knows—maybe he has an appointment at U.S. Steel.

RUTH *(anxiously, with frightened eyes)*: You didn't say nothing bad to him, did you?

BENEATHA: Bad? Say anything bad to him? No—I told him he was a sweet boy and full of dreams and everything is strictly peachy keen, as the ofay° kids say!

*(*MAMA *enters from her bedroom. She is lost, vague, trying to catch hold, to make some sense of her former command of the world, but it still eludes her. A sense of waste overwhelms her gait; a measure of apology rides on her shoulders. She goes to her plant, which has remained on the table, looks at it, picks it up and takes it to the window sill and sits it outside, and she stands and looks at it a long moment. Then she closes the window, straightens her body with effort, and turns around to her children.)*

Monsieur . . . noir, Mr. Black Middle Class.   *ofay,* white (slang).

MAMA: Well—ain't it a mess in here, though? *(A false cheerfulness, a beginning of something.)* I guess we all better stop moping around and get some work done. All this unpacking and everything we got to do. (RUTH *raises her head slowly in response to the sense of the line; and* BENEATHA *in similar manner turns very slowly to look at her mother.)* One of you all better call the moving people and tell 'em not to come.

RUTH: Tell 'em not to come?

MAMA: Of course, baby. Ain't no need in 'em coming all the way here and having to go back. They charges for that too. *(She sits down, fingers to her brow, thinking.)* Lord, ever since I was a little girl, I always remembers people saying, "Lena—Lena Eggleston, you aims too high all the time. You needs to slow down and see life a little more like it is. Just slow down some." That's what they always used to say down home—"Lord, that Lena Eggleston is a high-minded thing. She'll get her due one day!"

RUTH: No, Lena . . .

MAMA: Me and Big Walter just didn't never learn right.

RUTH: Lena, no! We gotta go. Bennie—tell her . . . *(She rises and crosses to* BENEATHA *with her arms outstretched.* BENEATHA *doesn't respond.)* Tell her we can still move . . . the notes ain't but a hundred and twenty-five a month. We got four grown people in this house—we can work . . .

MAMA *(to herself)*: Just aimed too high all the time—

RUTH *(turning and going to* MAMA *fast—the words pouring out with urgency and desperation)*: Lena—I'll work . . . I'll work twenty hours a day in all the kitchens in Chicago . . . I'll strap my baby on my back if I have to and scrub all the floors in America and wash all the sheets in America if I have to—but we got to MOVE! We got to get OUT OF HERE!!

*(*MAMA *reaches out absently and pats* RUTH*'s hand.)*

MAMA: No—I sees things differently now. Been thinking 'bout some of the things we could do to fix this place up some. I seen a second-hand bureau over on Maxwell Street just the other day that could fit right there. *(She points to where the new furniture might go.* RUTH *wanders away from her.)* Would need some new handles on it and then a little varnish and it look like something brand-new. And—we can put up them new curtains in the kitchen . . . Why this place be looking fine. Cheer us all up so that we forget trouble ever come . . . *(To* RUTH.*)* And you could get some nice screens to put up in your room round the baby's bassinet . . . *(She looks at both of them pleadingly.)* Sometimes you just got to know when to give up some things . . . and hold on to what you got. . . .

(WALTER *enters from the outside, looking spent and leaning against the door, his coat hanging from him.*)

MAMA: Where you been, son?

WALTER (*breathing hard*): Made a call.

MAMA: To who, son?

WALTER: To The Man. (*He heads for his room.*)

MAMA: What man, baby?

WALTER (*stops in the door*): The Man, Mama. Don't you know who The Man is?

RUTH: Walter Lee?

WALTER: *The Man.* Like the guys in the streets say— The Man. Captain Boss—Mistuh Charley . . . Old Cap'n Please Mr. Bossman . . .

BENEATHA (*suddenly*): Lindner!

WALTER: That's right! That's good. I told him to come right over.

BENEATHA (*fiercely, understanding*): For what? What do you want to see him for!

WALTER (*looking at his sister*): We going to do business with him.

MAMA: What you talking 'bout, son?

WALTER: Talking 'bout life, Mama. You all always telling me to see life like it is. Well—I laid in there on my back today . . . and I figured it out. Life just like it is. Who gets and who don't get. (*He sits down with his coat on and laughs.*) Mama, you know it's all divided up. Life is. Sure enough. Between the takers and the "tooken." (*He laughs.*) I've figured it out finally. (*He looks around at them.*) Yeah. Some of us always getting "tooken." (*He laughs.*) People like Willy Harris, they don't never get "tooken." And you know why the rest of us do? 'Cause we all mixed up. Mixed up bad. We get to looking 'round for the right and the wrong; and we worry about it and cry about it and stay up nights trying to figure out 'bout the wrong and the right of things all the time . . . And all the time, man, them takers is out there operating, just taking and taking. Willy Harris? Shoot—Willy Harris don't even count. He don't even count in the big scheme of things. But I'll say one thing for old Willy Harris . . . he's taught me something. He's taught me to keep my eye on what counts in this world. Yeah—(*Shouting out a little.*) Thanks, Willy!

RUTH: What did you call that man for, Walter Lee?

WALTER: Called him to tell him to come on over to the show. Gonna put on a show for the man. Just what he wants to see. You see, Mama, the man came here today and he told us that them people out there where you want us to move—well they so upset they willing to pay us *not* to move! (*He laughs again.*) And—and oh, Mama—you would of been proud of the way me and Ruth and Bennie acted. We told him to get out . . . Lord have mercy! We told the man to get out! Oh, we was some proud folks this afternoon, yeah. (*He lights a cigarette.*) We were still full of that old-time stuff . . .

RUTH (*coming toward him slowly*): You talking 'bout taking them people's money to keep us from moving in that house?

WALTER: I ain't just talking 'bout it, baby—I'm telling you that's what's going to happen!

BENEATHA: Oh, God! Where is the bottom! Where is the real honest-to-God bottom so he can't go any farther!

WALTER: See—that's the old stuff. You and that boy that was here today. You all want everybody to carry a flag and a spear and sing some marching songs, huh? You wanna spend your life looking into things and trying to find the right and the wrong part, huh? Yeah. You know what's going to happen to that boy someday—he'll find himself sitting in a dungeon, locked in forever—and the takers will have the key! Forget it, baby! There ain't no causes—there ain't nothing but taking in this world, and he who takes most is smartest— and it don't make a damn bit of difference *how.*

MAMA: You making something inside me cry, son. Some awful pain inside me.

WALTER: Don't cry, Mama. Understand. That white man is going to walk in that door able to write checks for more money than we ever had. It's important to him and I'm going to help him . . . I'm going to put on the show, Mama.

MAMA: Son—I come from five generations of people who was slaves and sharecroppers—but ain't nobody in my family never let nobody pay 'em no money that was a way of telling us we wasn't fit to walk the earth. We ain't never been that poor. (*Raising her eyes and looking at him.*) We ain't never been that—dead inside.

BENEATHA: Well—we are dead now. All the talk about dreams and sunlight that goes on in this house. It's all dead now.

WALTER: What's the matter with you all! I didn't make this world! It was give to me this way! Hell, yes, I want me some yachts someday! Yes, I want to hang some real pearls 'round my wife's neck. Ain't she supposed to wear no pearls? Somebody tell me— tell me, who decides which women is suppose to wear pearls in this world. I tell you I am a *man*— and I think my wife should wear some pearls in this world!

(*This last line hangs a good while and* WALTER *begins to move about the room. The word "Man" has penetrated his consciousness; he mumbles it to himself repeatedly between strange agitated pauses as he moves about.*)

MAMA: Baby, how you going to feel on the inside?

WALTER: Fine! . . . Going to feel fine . . . a man . . .

MAMA: You won't have nothing left then, Walter Lee.

WALTER (*coming to her*): I'm going to feel fine, Mama.

I'm going to look that son-of-a-bitch in the eyes and say—(*he falters*)—and say, "All right, Mr. Lindner—(*he falters even more*)—that's *your* neighborhood out there! You got the right to keep it like you want! You got the right to have it like you want! Just write the check and—the house is yours." And—and I am going to say—(*His voice almost breaks.*) "And you—you people just put the money in my hand and you won't have to live next to this bunch of stinking niggers! . . ." (*He straightens up and moves away from his mother, walking around the room.*) And maybe—maybe I'll just get down on my black knees . . . (*He does so;* RUTH *and* BENNIE *and* MAMA *watch him in frozen horror.*) "Captain, Mistuh, Bossman—(*Groveling and grinning and wringing his hands in profoundly anguished imitation of the slow-witted movie stereotype.*) A-hee-hee-hee! Oh, yassuh boss! Yasssssuh! Great white—(*voice breaking, he forces himself to go on*)—Father, just gi' ussen de money, fo' God's sake, and we's—we's ain't gwine come out deh and dirty up yo' white folks neighborhood . . ." (*He breaks down completely.*) And I'll feel fine! Fine! FINE! (*He gets up and goes into the bedroom.*)

BENEATHA: That is not a man. That is nothing but a toothless rat.

MAMA: Yes—death done come in this here house. (*She is nodding, slowly, reflectively.*) Done come walking in my house on the lips of my children. You what supposed to be my beginning again. You—what supposed to be my harvest. (*To* BENEATHA.) You—you mourning your brother?

BENEATHA: He's no brother of mine.

MAMA: What you say?

BENEATHA: I said that that individual in that room is no brother of mine.

MAMA: That's what I thought you said. You feeling like you better than he is today? (BENEATHA *does not answer.*) Yes? What you tell him a minute ago? That he wasn't a man? Yes? You give him up for me? You done wrote his epitaph too—like the rest of the world? Well, who give you the privilege?

BENEATHA: Be on my side for once! You saw what he just did, Mama! You saw him—down on his knees. Wasn't it you who taught me to despise any man who would do that? Do what he's going to do?

MAMA: Yes—I taught you that. Me and your daddy. But I thought I taught you something else too . . . I thought I taught you to love him.

BENEATHA: Love him? There is nothing left to love.

MAMA: There is *always* something left to love. And if you ain't learned that, you ain't learned nothing. (*Looking at her.*) Have you cried for that boy today? I don't mean for yourself and for the family 'cause we lost the money. I mean for him: what he been through and what it done to him. Child, when do you think is the time to love somebody the most? When they done good and made things easy for everybody? Well then, you ain't through learning—because that ain't the time at all. It's when he's at his lowest and can't believe in hisself 'cause the world done whipped him so! When you starts measuring somebody, measure him right, child, measure him right. Make sure you done taken into account what hills and valleys he come through before he got to wherever he is.

(TRAVIS *bursts into the room at the end of the speech, leaving the door open.*)

TRAVIS: Grandmama—the moving men are downstairs! The truck just pulled up.

MAMA (*turning and looking at him*): Are they, baby? They downstairs?

(*She sighs and sits.* LINDNER *appears in the doorway. He peers in and knocks lightly, to gain attention, and comes in. All turn to look at him.*)

LINDNER (*hat and briefcase in hand*): Uh—hello . . .

(RUTH *crosses mechanically to the bedroom door and opens it and lets it swing open freely and slowly as the lights come up on* WALTER *within, still in his coat, sitting at the far corner of the room. He looks up and out through the room to* LINDNER.)

RUTH: He's here.

(*A long minute passes and* WALTER *slowly gets up.*)

LINDNER (*coming to the table with efficiency, putting his briefcase on the table and starting to unfold papers and unscrew fountain pens*): Well, I certainly was glad to hear from you people. (WALTER *has begun the trek out of the room, slowly and awkwardly, rather like a small boy, passing the back of his sleeve across his mouth from time to time.*) Life can really be so much simpler than people let it be most of the time. Well—with whom do I negotiate? You, Mrs. Younger, or your son here? (MAMA *sits with her hands folded on her lap and her eyes closed as* WALTER *advances.* TRAVIS *goes closer to* LINDNER *and looks at the papers curiously.*) Just some official papers, sonny.

RUTH: Travis, you go downstairs—

MAMA (*opening her eyes and looking into* WALTER's): No. Travis, you stay right here. And you make him understand what you doing, Walter Lee. You teach him good. Like Willy Harris taught you. You show where our five generations done come to. (WALTER *looks from her to the boy, who grins at him innocently.*) Go ahead, son—(*She folds her hands and closes her eyes.*) Go ahead.

WALTER (*at last crosses to* LINDNER, *who is reviewing the contract*): Well, Mr. Lindner. (BENEATHA *turns away.*) We called you—(*there is a profound, simple groping quality in his speech*)—because, well, me and my family (*he looks around and shifts from one foot to the other*) Well—we are very plain people . . .

LINDNER: Yes—

WALTER: I mean—I have worked as a chauffeur most of my life—and my wife here, she does domestic work in people's kitchens. So does my mother. I mean—we are plain people . . .

LINDNER: Yes, Mr. Younger—

WALTER (*really like a small boy, looking down at his shoes and then up at the man*): And—uh—well, my father, well, he was a laborer most of his life. . . .

LINDNER (*absolutely confused*): Uh, yes—yes, I understand. (*He turns back to the contract.*)

WALTER (*A beat; staring at him*): And my father—(*With sudden intensity.*) My father almost *beat a man to death* once because this man called him a bad name or something, you know what I mean?

LINDNER (*looking up, frozen*): No, no, I'm afraid I don't—

WALTER (*A beat. The tension hangs; then* WALTER *steps back from it*): Yeah. Well—what I mean is that we come from people who had a lot of *pride.* I mean—we are very proud people. And that's my sister over there and she's going to be a doctor—and we are very proud—

LINDNER: Well—I am sure that is very nice, but—

WALTER: What I am telling you is that we called you over here to tell you that we are very proud and that this—(*Signaling to* TRAVIS.) Travis, come here. (*TRAVIS crosses and* WALTER *draws him before him facing the man.*) This is my son, and he makes the sixth generation of our family in this country. And we have all thought about your offer—

LINDNER: Well, good . . . good—

WALTER: And we have decided to move into our house because my father—my father—he earned it for us brick by brick. (MAMA *has her eyes closed and is rocking back and forth as though she were in church, with her head nodding the Amen yes.*) We don't want to make no trouble for nobody or fight no causes, and we will try to be good neighbors. And that's *all* we got to say about that. (*He looks the man absolutely in the eyes.*) We don't want your money. (*He turns and walks away.*)

LINDNER (*looking around at all of them*): I take it then—that you have decided to occupy . . .

BENEATHA: That's what the man said.

LINDNER (*to* MAMA *in her reverie*): Then I would like to appeal to you, Mrs. Younger. You are older and wiser and understand things better I am sure . . .

MAMA: I am afraid you don't understand. My son said we was going to move and there ain't nothing left for me to say. (*Briskly.*) You know how these young folks is nowadays, mister. Can't do a thing with 'em! (*As he opens his mouth, she rises.*) Good-bye.

LINDNER (*folding up his materials*): Well—if you are that final about it . . . there is nothing left for me to say. (*He finishes, almost ignored by the family, who are concentrating on* WALTER LEE. *At the door* LIND-NER *halts and looks around.*) I sure hope you people know what you're getting into.

(*He shakes his head and exits.*)

RUTH (*looking around and coming to life*): Well, for God's sake—if the moving men are here—LET'S GET THE HELL OUT OF HERE!

MAMA (*into action*): Ain't it the truth! Look at all this here mess. Ruth, put Travis's good jacket on him . . . Walter Lee, fix your tie and tuck your shirt in, you look like somebody's hoodlum! Lord have mercy, where is my plant? (*She flies to get it amid the general bustling of the family, who are deliberately trying to ignore the nobility of the past moment.*) You all start on down . . . Travis child, don't go empty-handed . . . Ruth, where did I put that box with my skillets in it? I want to be in charge of it myself . . . I'm going to make us the biggest dinner we ever ate tonight . . . Beneatha, what's the matter with them stockings? Pull them things up, girl . . .

(*The family starts to file out as two moving men appear and begin to carry out the heavier pieces of furniture, bumping into the family as they move about.*)

BENEATHA: Mama, Asagai asked me to marry him today and go to Africa—

MAMA (*in the middle of her getting-ready activity*): He did? You ain't old enough to marry nobody—(*Seeing the moving men lifting one of her chairs precariously.*) Darling, that ain't no bale of cotton, please handle it so we can sit in it again! I had that chair twenty-five years . . .

(*The movers sigh with exasperation and go on with their work.*)

BENEATHA (*girlishly and unreasonably trying to pursue the conversation*): To go to Africa, Mama—be a doctor in Africa . . .

MAMA (*distracted*): Yes, baby—

WALTER: *Africa!* What he want you to go to Africa for?

BENEATHA: To practice there . . .

WALTER: Girl, if you don't get all them silly ideas out your head! You better marry yourself a man with some loot . . .

BENEATHA (*angrily, precisely as in the first scene of the play*): What have you got to do with who I marry!

WALTER: Plenty. Now I think George Murchison—

BENEATHA: *George Murchison!* I wouldn't marry him if he was Adam and I was Eve!

(WALTER *and* BENEATHA *go out yelling at each other vigorously and the anger is loud and real till their voices diminish.* RUTH *stands at the door and turns to* MAMA *and smiles knowingly.*)

MAMA (*fixing her hat at last*): Yeah—they something all right, my children . . .

RUTH: Yeah—they're something. Let's go, Lena.

MAMA (*stalling, starting to look around at the house*): Yes—I'm coming. Ruth—

RUTH: Yes?

MAMA (*quietly, woman to woman*): He finally come into his manhood today, didn't he? Kind of like a rainbow after the rain . . .

RUTH (*biting her lip lest her own pride explode in front of* MAMA): Yes, Lena.

(WALTER's *voice calls for them raucously.*)

WALTER (*offstage*): Y'all come on! These people charges by the hour, you know!

MAMA (*waving* RUTH *out vaguely*): All right, honey—go on down. I be down directly.

(RUTH *hesitates, then exits.* MAMA *stands, at last alone in the living room, her plant on the table before her as the lights start to come down. She looks around at all the walls and ceilings and suddenly, despite herself, while the children call below, a great heaving thing rises in her and she puts her fist to her mouth to stifle it, takes a final desperate look, pulls her coat about her, pats her hat, and goes out. The lights dim down. The door opens and she comes back in, grabs her plant, and goes out for the last time.*)

Figure 1. Mama (Claudia McNeil) hands the insurance check to Walter Lee (Sidney Poitier), trusting him to be "the head of the family" in the second act of *A Raisin in the Sun,* staged at the Ethel Barrymore Theatre, New York, 1959, and directed by Lloyd Richards. (Photograph: Gordon Parks.)

Figure 2. Walter Lee (Sidney Poitier) hugs his son Travis (Glynn Turman), as a puzzled Karl Lindner (John Fiedler) waits to hear what he will say in the 1959 production. (Photograph: Gordon Parks.)

Staging of *A Raisin in the Sun*

SIDNEY POITIER ON PLAYING WALTER LEE YOUNGER IN THE ETHEL BARRYMORE THEATRE PRODUCTION, NEW YORK, 1959

Philip Rose, an old and dear friend, was smitten by a play written by a friend of his and an acquaintance of mine named Lorraine Hansberry. I had heard talk of her being a gifted writer who was in the process of writing a play, but I knew her only as a politically aware, contemporary black American who was fairly close to Paul Robeson—one of those young people very much in his camp. Robeson was an enormous inspiration to us all. Philip Rose's enthusiasm over her gifts and his eagerness to produce her play were well founded. I was overwhelmed by the power of the material and told Mr. Rose I would be happy to play in it. Set in the 1950s, the drama concerned a black family on Chicago's South Side, headed by a very strong matriarchal figure who, widowed by an industrial accident that replaced her husband with a ten-thousand-dollar insurance check, struggles to hold her family together in the face of her son's fierce desire for recognition in a white man's society, her daughter's identity crisis, her daughter-in-law's unwanted pregnancy, and the problem of her grandson's future. The playwright's fix on the black experience was truly uncanny. She designed a plot structure and characters so refreshingly real that just reading her play, *A Raisin in the Sun,* was an uplifting experience. Philip Rose's production went into rehearsal on December 27, 1958, under the direction of Lloyd Richards with a cast that included Claudia McNeil, Diana Sands, Lou Gossett, Lonnie Elder, Ivan Dixon, Ruby Dee, and Glynn Turman. We rehearsed in New York, then went on the road for our first performance in New Haven. That evening, after a ten-year absence, I stepped out on a stage in the company of some heavyweight actors and actresses with material of substance in front of at least a thousand people. The immediate raw nakedness of being on a stage is very different from standing in front of a 35-millimeter Mitchell camera. A camera hums softly while it's watching you; an audience breathes, it coughs, it shifts about in its seat and whispers to itself while it is watching you. I had forgotten how unpredictable that classic one-on-one between audience and performer can sometimes be. At the end of the first act I took stock and to my surprise found that while I was very nervous, I was not intimidated, nor was I encumbered by the awkward tightness that ten years before used to interfere with the full use of my body. By the time the curtain came down on the third act, I had discovered that, one, we were on to something very special with that play, and, two, that I

had learned some useful things about my craft in the long absence. It seemed the additional ten years of life had left me a little wiser in the use of my tools. From New Haven we moved on to Philadelphia, where we were an instant success. In the light of our excellent reviews there, the management wanted to go directly into New York, but there were no theaters available. I, alas, didn't think the play was being performed as effectively as it could have been, which got me into a lot of trouble with Lorraine, Phil, and Lloyd Richards, who were happy with the production the way it was and were quite prepared to "lock it in" at the level of the Philadelphia appearance. I honestly thought the play wasn't yet working as well as it should be before we bared ourselves to New York in that "do or die" performance in front of the critics.

We had to go into Chicago for some weeks before a theater loosened up in New York, and opening night in Chicago turned out to be phenomenal for everyone, but especially for Claudia McNeil, who played the mother. In Chicago I was not on speaking terms with Lorraine, who was understandably happy because her play was doing so well and couldn't grasp why I was dissatisfied. The reason was complicated. I believed from the first day I went into rehearsal that the play should not unfold from the mother's point of view. I still believe that. I think that for maximum effect, *A Raisin in the Sun* should unfold from the point of view of the son, Walter Lee Younger. (Yes, I played Walter Lee.) Because Claudia registered so powerfully in the play and because the audience responded so wonderfully to her *and* the play, the producer, director, and author were all satisfied. And yet I kept insisting that the mother shouldn't be the focus of the play.

They accused me of "star" behavior. Of wanting to be the top dog on stage. The simple truth of the matter was that if the play is told from the point of view of the mother, and you don't have an actor playing the part of Walter Lee strongly, then the end result may very well be a negative comment on the black male. They didn't agree, and before we stopped speaking to each other over the issue, they argued with me for hours. They professed to be at a loss as to the underlying reasons for my feelings about the image of the black male. But I was in the dark every bit as much as they were. My feelings were real and strong, but I had no idea where they sprang from. Were they a reflection of my parents? My self? Were they political? Yes? No? Maybe? With no adequate response at my fingertips that would dispel their confusion, or arrest their suspicions, they went on to accuse me of (among other things) being unreasonably sensitive to this issue for unattractive and selfish personal reasons. But I still saw it that way, and I had an ally—the talented, highly intelligent Ruby Dee. We decided on an approach, and conspired to keep the strength in the character of Walter Lee Younger, which meant my playing *against* Claudia McNeil, who is a tower of strength as a stage personality. I had to change my whole performance to prevent the mother character from so dominating the stage that it would cast a negative focus on the black male. But the excellent reviews in Chicago hardened management's resolve to "put it to bed." After all, what strange kind of nut must I be to keep quarreling with success? By the end of the run in Chicago, management's position was: All Poitier is thinking of is that he's the star of the play and Claudia McNeil is getting all the audience's response.

But how could that have been? Wasn't I more secure than that? Didn't I receive marvelous reviews everywhere we went? Didn't I get terrific responses from the audiences too? Indeed I did! Then their stinging accusations were obviously not true—unless, God forbid, I was miles and miles off base, completely out of touch with my ego and therefore blinded to the merit of their argument. Heavenly Father! Could I be that far out of touch? You're damn right I could. I wasn't exactly what you could call a Rock of Gibraltar at that time in my life, and besides, they were very bright people, Lorraine, Phil, and Lloyd. Yes, they might be right—even then I recognized that there could be honest differences of opinion and judgment. But however much I leaned in the direction of objectivity, trying to give them the benefit of every doubt, I still was aware of the whiff of gold in the air. That intoxicating element was quietly orchestrating management's sharp responses to my specific challenge, as if it were an unholy threat to a bonanza whose aroma was already creeping over the horizon. And to management's not unreasonable desire to keep the play running forever had to be added the fact that I was committed to remain in the play no more than six months. Claudia McNeil had a "run of the play" contract, and they had seen by Chicago that she was going to be a big part of the future commerciality of the play, whereas I was leaving in six months to fulfill motion picture commitments.

One night before we left Chicago, Ruby Dee and I sat over drinks and analyzed the way the Walter Lee character should appear to the audience. He could appear as a weak man overwhelmed by his mother—incapable of engineering his own life, which he has based on dreams that exceed his skills; in other words, a weakling who doesn't deserve very much attention. Or he could appear as the average man with an average potential and average dreams, who fails to achieve them only through a combination of misunderstandings in his own family

and the racism of his environment—a man who winds up bested not because he is incapable but because circumstances conspire against him—a far cry from a weakling who is reaching beyond his grasp.

Anyway, the play opened in New York with me playing it the way I wanted to play it, and it was an enormous success.

The Barrymore Theatre was a place of magic that opening night. As the curtain fell at the end of the third act, the audience came to its feet in a standing ovation that brought tears to the eyes of our cast. That audience, many of them with tears streaming down their faces, stomped, howled, and screamed with joy. Finally, the thunderous applause took on a rhythmic clapping and they began shouting, "Author, author, author." Lorraine Hansberry was standing in the audience with members of her family, and Ruby Dee told me to go and get her. I jumped from the stage into the audience, took her by the hand, and led her up onto the stage, where the audience and her actors continued to pay her the tribute she so very much deserved.

The experience of being a big hit on Broadway is so thrilling it can never, even from this distance, be fully captured in words. We were an event! We were *the* play to see that season. Night after night people from all walks of life came to pack the Barrymore and get caught up in a powerful evening, laughing and crying and being moved before springing to their feet at the final curtain for that soul-satisfying standing ovation that has to number high among the best moments in an actor's life. Black people for the first time came to Broadway in unprecedented numbers; the majority of them had never seen a play before. Blue-collar workers from Harlem and Brooklyn; sleep-in domestics from the suburbs; professors; doctors; numbers runners; hairdressers—they all came to see Lorraine Hansberry's black family from the South Side of Chicago.

The breach between me and the management continued unrelieved for a number of reasons, not the least of which were my complaints about the unprofessional behavior on stage during performances of one actor who, for reasons that remained a mystery, would make subtle changes in performance style that would weaken the effectiveness of others' performances. Management, still suspecting that ego was the root cause of my earlier complaint, concluded that the new charges probably had no basis beyond my ego's addiction to the occasional stroking.

Lorraine and I barely spoke for years after, until, with her health failing, the time came for us to put aside petty things. When guards are down and weapons laid aside, the distance between argument and gentle discussion can be a short and simple step, and so it was with us in that New York City hospital room where she was confined during the advanced stages of her illness. We talked about her work in progress, my activities, politics, racism, Africa, and the general state of the arts from our people's point of view. She spoke simply but touchingly about the direction her life would take if circumstances were other-

wise. Even before her illness, it was clear that Lorraine Hansberry was orchestrating her life toward more involvement, more activism. The only subject we did not touch on was death. There was no need to.

INTERVIEW WITH LLOYD RICHARDS ON DIRECTING THE NEW YORK PRODUCTION, 1959, BY ARTHUR BARTOW

BARTOW: *How did* Raisin in the Sun *come about?*

RICHARDS: Sidney Poitier and I were out-of-work actors together. He knew that I had directed some stock, and he said to me—it was one of those strange things that two broke people say to one another in the middle of the night—"You know, if I ever get a major show, I'd like you to direct it." You respond, "Yeah, and if I get a show I'd like you to be in it." Those kinds of things. And then I got a call from Sidney. He said that he had been offered a play and he wanted to submit me as the director. I read *A Raisin in the Sun* and fell in love with it. He set up a meeting with Philip Rose, who produced it. We hit it off and he arranged a meeting with Lorraine Hansberry. And we also hit it off. Together, we worked on the play for a year before we went into rehearsal.

BARTOW: *Were there a lot of changes made during that year?*

RICHARDS: When the play was first written (and that was a draft that I was not involved with), by the second act the family was already in their new house and the play was about that and about Mama. It was suggested to Lorraine that the real play was in the first act, and that she should review that, which is what she did. I wasn't there, so I can't say who said what to whom. But then, the problem was that it became a play about the son, Walter. The original play had been about Mama. If you look very carefully at the first act, it still has those elements of a play about Mama. So the demands on the actor who plays Walter are tough because he gets up in the first scene, in the first five minutes, and goes out of the house. He doesn't come back until the end of the act, and then he's got to carry the play. It was a really tough struggle to bring what had been the third act of the play back into the first act. We did a lot of rewriting and reworking, took forty-five minutes out of it in rehearsal and lost one character, the woman upstairs, which was very painful. That role later reappeared in the musical version, *Raisin*. It's a wonderful character, a wonderful scene. Beah Richards, an

actress for whom I have great respect, was playing it in rehearsal. One day Lorraine came in and watched while we were in the run-through stage and said, "That character should go." "Why?" I said. "The scene is great and it works." She said, "It's redundant. That character takes something away from the later scene with Lindner." She was absolutely right. The character went out, the scene went out, and there were a lot of changes made on the road. We did a lot of reworking in Chicago. Lorraine wasn't there at the time, because of a legal problem she had involving real estate interests in New York and Chicago. She was in Chicago for opening night and then she had to get out of town or they were going to serve her with all kinds of subpoenas about her properties. So the changes were all made over the phone, and I would write them down for her every night and make suggestions. She didn't see the play for seven weeks, until we got back to New York.

BARTOW: *It had an extraordinary cast with Claudia McNeil, Ruby Dee, Diana Sands, Douglas Turner Ward, Lonne Elder 3rd and Louis Gossett in addition to Poitier. Its run of 530 performances was some kind of record for a serious play.*

RICHARDS: *Raisin* was a wonderful experience, a fantastic, tough experience—a play that almost never got on. Money. In 1959, who was going to invest in a play about a black family? Finally, it had more investors than any other play that had appeared on Broadway at that time. The money was raised in dribs and drabs, little $50, $100, $200 investments. Broadway is not that receptive to a serious play, but *Raisin* had a great deal of humor in it, a great deal of very warm feeling in it, familial feeling that transcended any ethnic concepts, just leaped over them.

BARTOW: *Do you ever have a sense of the play that conflicts with the playwright's original vision?*

RICHARDS: Sometimes you discover how different those things are as you proceed. I remember the first day of rehearsal for *A Raisin in the Sun,* when I was talking to the cast about the play after the first read-through. I delineated a history for every character in the family and how they arrived at where they were. It was the first time I'd said it aloud. Afterward, Lorraine came to me and said, "Well, you know, that's very interesting. I hadn't thought of it that way, but it's true." We never discussed how her history of the characters differed from mine, but the consequence was that my description worked for the actors, it was a right place for us to begin the play and it encompassed the elements that we wanted to affect the characters as they moved through the play.

REVIEW OF THE NEW YORK PRODUCTION, 1959, BY BROOKS ATKINSON

In "A Raisin in the Sun," which opened at the Ethel Barrymore last evening, Lorraine Hansberry touches on some serious problems. No doubt, her feelings about them are as strong as anyone's.

But she has not tipped her play to prove one thing or another. The play is honest. She has told the inner as well as the outer truth about a Negro family in the south-side of Chicago at the present time. Since the performance is also honest and since Sidney Poitier is a candid actor, "A Raisin in the Sun" has vigor as well as veracity and is likely to destroy the complacency of anyone who sees it.

The family consists of a firm-minded widow, her daughter, her restless son and his wife and son. The mother has brought up her family in a tenement that is small, battered but personable. All the mother wants is that her children adhere to the code of honor and self-respect that she inherited from her parents.

The son is dreaming of success in a business deal. And the daughter, who is race-conscious, wants to become a physician and heal the wounds of her people. After a long delay the widow receives $10,000 as the premium on her husband's life insurance. The money projects the family into a series of situations that test their individual characters.

What the situations are does not matter at the moment. For "A Raisin in the Sun" is a play about human beings who want, on the one hand, to preserve their family pride and, on the other hand, to break out of the poverty that seems to be their fate. Not having any axe to grind, Miss Hansberry has a wide range of topics to write about—some of them hilarious, some of them painful in the extreme.

You might, in fact, regard "A Raisin in the Sun" as a Negro "The Cherry Orchard." Although the social scale of the characters is different, the knowledge of how character is controlled by environment is much the same, and the alternation of humor and pathos is similar.

If there are occasional crudities in the craftsmanship, they are redeemed by the honesty of the writing. And also by the rousing honesty of the stage work. For Lloyd Richards has selected an admirable cast and directed a bold and stirring performance.

Mr. Poitier is a remarkable actor with enormous power that is always under control. Cast as the restless son, he vividly communicates the tumult of a high-strung young man. He is as eloquent when he has nothing to say as when he has a pungent line to speak. He can convey devious processes of thought as graphically as he can clown and dance.

As the matriarch, Claudia McNeil gives a heroic performance. Although the character is simple, Miss McNeil gives it nobility of spirit. Diana Sands' amusing portrait of the overintellectualized daughter; Ivan Dixon's quiet, sagacious student from Nigeria; Ruby Dee's young wife burdened with problems; Louis Gossett's supercilious suitor; John Fiedler's timid white man, who speaks sanctimonious platitudes—bring variety and excitement to a first-rate performance.

All the crises and comic sequences take place inside Ralph Alswang's set, which depicts both the poverty and the taste of the family. Like the play, it is honest. That is Miss Hansberry's personal contribution to an explosive situation in which simple honesty is the most difficult thing in the world. And also the most illuminating.

AMIRI BARAKA

1934–

Between March and December 1964, Baraka, who was then still writing under his original name of LeRoi Jones, had four one-act plays produced Off-Broadway, one of which, *Dutchman,* won the Obie Award for the best Off-Broadway play of 1963–64. That production record would be considered astonishing for any playwright, particularly for a young African American who until then was known only as a writer of essays and poems. Baraka was born in Newark, New Jersey, where he attended public school and then began college at Rutgers University, later transferring to Howard University, one of America's historically black colleges. Subsequently, he served in the United States Air Force, from 1954 to 1957, and then settled in New York City where, with Hettie Cohen, whom he married in 1958, he edited a literary magazine, publishing avant-garde writers such as William Burroughs, Gregory Corso, Allen Ginsberg, Jack Kerouac, Charles Olson, and himself. His sudden fame after the success of *Dutchman* led him to teaching positions at Columbia University and the New School for Social Research, as well as to the award of a Guggenheim Fellowship in 1965. It was also in 1965 that he changed his name to Imamu Amiri Baraka, roughly translatable as Priest-Warrior-Blessing, and wrote his well-known manifesto, "The Revolutionary Theater." In it he asserted that theater "should force change, it should be change," that it "must EXPOSE! Show up the insides of these humans, look into black skulls. White men will cower before this theater because it hates them." And in his subsequent plays, as well as in a major interview, "What Is Black Theater?" (see Ideas of Drama), Baraka followed up on his manifesto, developing the idea of black theater as "an act of liberation" that, by "providing consciousness," would stir African American audiences to radical action.

Although *Dutchman* was written before Baraka became explicitly associated with "revolutionary theater," it is clearly a revolutionary play, particularly when it is seen in the context of the African American drama that had preceded it. African Americans had written plays during the nineteenth century, yet their works did not achieve prominence until the 1920s with the plays of Garland Anderson, Wallace Thurman, and Willis Richardson. The Federal Theater project of the 1930s gave special encouragement to African American dramatists and led, in particular, to the plays of Langston Hughes, one of the leading figures of the Harlem Renaissance, whose works include *Mulatto* (1935); *Don't You Want to Be Free* (1936), a long-running historical panorama; and *Emperor of Haiti* (1938). In Chicago, the Federal Theater Unit sponsored the first production of Theodore Ward's *Big White Fog* (1938), a play that shows a family's struggle to attain a new life in the context of urban society through the political movement known as "back-to-Africa." Ward's later play, *Our Lan'* (1941), was even more successful with its depiction of newly freed blacks trying to live on an island off the Georgia coast. At the end of the 1950s, Lorraine Hansberry's *A Raisin in the Sun* (1959) became a major Broadway success by taking up once again the theme of the "new life," this time by showing a protagonist who maintains his individual and racial pride by moving out of the slums and into a white middle-class neighborhood, a neighborhood that had tried to buy him off to keep him from moving in.

All these plays concerned themselves with the social and political problems of African Americans, yet most concentrated almost exclusively on issues within that community, with only a few venturing to deal directly with confrontations between black and white characters. Not until the plays of Baraka did such confrontations become insistently—and violently—central. In *The Slave* (1964), Baraka shows a black leader, Walker Vessels, engaged in a long argument with two white liberals, Grace and Bradford Easley, about their conflicting ideologies. In *The Toilet* (1964), a group of African American boys beat up a white boy, a Puerto Rican, who has sent a "love letter" to the leader of their group. And in *Dutchman*, Baraka dramatizes the ultimate confrontation in a sexual encounter between a black man and a white woman, a confrontation that leads to a violent conclusion, in which the black man becomes the victim. In *Dutchman,* too, Baraka moved away from the realistic style that had prevailed in earlier African American plays toward a symbolic style, immediately announced by its title.

This title is meant to evoke the legend of the Flying Dutchman, the man doomed to sail the seas forever until he found a woman who would be faithful to him, and the subway in which the play is set reflects that ceaseless and meaningless voyaging. The title also alludes to the Dutch ships that brought black slaves to North America, and in this context Lula may be seen as a relentless traveler and destroyer, embodying the way that whites have always treated blacks. Baraka himself claimed that the situation rather than the characters was meant to be symbolic, an interpretation stressing the ceaselessness of racial violence. Apart from the title, the play's mythic quality is emphasized by Baraka's stage direction "The subway heaped in modern myth," by the appearance of Lula eating an apple, by her later remark that "Eating apples together is always the first step," and by Clay's name, which echoes Adam's formation "out of the dust of the ground." The interweaving of the realistic and the symbolic can also be seen in the dialogue of the play, which begins essentially with everyday conversation but quickly turns into metaphor, when Lula tells Clay that "You look like death eating a soda cracker." Lula then turns into a mock prophet in her litany at the end of the first scene, and finally a chanter of vicious and obscene litanies, meant to goad Clay into action.

When she does finally arouse him to the violent action and speech audiences yearn for after her relentless taunting, the effect is devastating, for he destroys any myths that whites may have about blacks, ending as he does with an explicit threat about what will happen when blacks are "accepted" by whites:

> They'll murder you, and have very rational explanations. Very much like your own. They'll cut your throats, and drag you out to the edge of your cities so the flesh can fall away from your bones, in sanitary isolation.

But instead of the physical assault that might be expected from Clay after this speech, Baraka creates an even more frightening conclusion in Lula's stabbing of him, an act that grotesquely inverts and parodies the sexual act they have been discussing. Her comment, "Get this man off me!" continues the sexual subtext. And when a young African American of twenty next enters the subway car, her act of turning and giving him a long, slow look clearly indicates that the destructive cycle will begin again, repeating itself endlessly like the travels of the subway and the Flying Dutchman.

When the play was first produced, critics were both impressed and defensive, as revealed in the two reviews reprinted following the text. But they also noted the symbolic significance of the play, as indicated by Harold Clurman's remarks about Lula: "She is our neurosis. Not a neurosis in regard to the Negro, but the absolute neurosis of American society." Jennifer West's performance conveyed that neurosis in her move from demure sexuality (see Figure 1) to uncontrollable aggression. When the play was turned into a film in 1967, critics found it stagey and dull, for the real subway car seemed much less effective as a frame for the play's violence than the make-believe one. On stage, the play still shocks, still continues to explode, precisely because the subway car is only a set while the anger, the cruelty, and the hatred are real.

DUTCHMAN

BY AMIRI BARAKA

CHARACTERS

CLAY, *twenty-year-old Negro*
LULA, *thirty-year-old white woman*
RIDERS OF COACH, *white and black*
YOUNG NEGRO
CONDUCTOR

SCENE

In the flying underbelly of the city. Steaming hot, and summer on top, outside. Underground. The subway heaped in modern myth.

Opening scene is a man sitting in a subway seat, holding a magazine but looking vacantly just above its wilting pages. Occasionally he looks blankly toward the window on his right. Dim lights and darkness whistling by against the glass. (Or paste the lights, as admitted props, right on the subway windows. Have them move, even dim and flicker. But give the sense of speed. Also stations, whether the train is stopped or the glitter and activity of these stations merely flashes by the windows.)

The man is sitting alone. That is, only his seat is visible, though the rest of the car is outfitted as a complete subway car. But only his seat is shown. There might be, for a time, as the play begins, a loud scream of the actual train. And it can recur throughout the play, or continue on a lower key once the dialogue starts.

The train slows after a time, pulling to a brief stop at one of the stations. The man looks idly up, until he sees a woman's face staring at him through the window; when it realizes that the man has noticed the face, it begins very premeditatedly to smile. The man smiles too, for a moment, without a trace of self-consciousness. Almost an instinctive though undesirable response. Then a kind of awkwardness or embarrassment sets in, and the man makes to look away, is further embarrassed, so he brings back his eyes to where the face was, but by now the train is moving again, and the face would seem to be left behind by the way the man turns his head to look back through the other windows at the slowly fading platform. He smiles then; more comfortably confident, hoping perhaps that his memory of this brief encounter will be pleasant. And then he is idle again.

SCENE 1

(Train roars. Lights flash outside the windows.

LULA *enters from the rear of the car in bright, skimpy summer clothes and sandals. She carries a net bag full of paper books, fruit, and other anonymous articles. She is wearing sunglasses, which she pushes up on her forehead from time to time.* LULA *is a tall, slender, beautiful woman with long red hair hanging straight down her back, wearing only loud lipstick in somebody's good taste. She is eating an apple, very daintily. Coming down the car toward* CLAY.

She stops beside CLAY's *seat and hangs languidly from the strap, still managing to eat the apple. It is apparent that she is going to sit in the seat next to* CLAY, *and that she is only waiting for him to notice her before she sits.*

CLAY *sits as before, looking just beyond his magazine, now and again pulling the magazine slowly back and forth in front of his face in a hopeless effort to fan himself. Then he sees the woman hanging there beside him and he looks up into her face, smiling quizzically.)*

LULA: Hello.
CLAY: Uh, hi're you?
LULA: I'm going to sit down. . . . O.K.?
CLAY: Sure.
LULA *(swings down onto the seat, pushing her legs straight out as if she is very weary)*: Ooof! Too much weight.
CLAY: Ha, doesn't look like much to me.

(Leaning back against the window, a little surprised and maybe stiff.)

LULA: It's so anyway.

(And she moves her toes in the sandals, then pulls her right leg up on the left knee, better to inspect the bottoms of the sandals and the back of her heel. She appears for a second not to notice that CLAY *is sitting next to her or that she has spoken to him just a second before.* CLAY *looks at the magazine, then out the black window. As he does this, she turns very quickly toward him.)*

Weren't you staring at me through the window?
CLAY *(wheeling around and very much stiffened)*: What?
LULA: Weren't you staring at me through the window? At the last stop?
CLAY: Staring at you? What do you mean?
LULA: Don't you know what staring means?
CLAY: I saw you through the window . . . if that's what it means. I don't know if I was staring. Seems to me you were staring through the window at me.
LULA: I was. But only after I'd turned around and saw you staring through that window down in the vicinity of my ass and legs.
CLAY: Really?
LULA: Really. I guess you were just taking those idle potshots. Nothing else to do. Run your mind over people's flesh.
CLAY: Oh boy. Wow, now I admit I was looking in your direction. But the rest of that weight is yours.

LULA: I suppose.

CLAY: Staring through train windows is weird business. Much weirder than staring very sedately at abstract asses.

LULA: That's why I came looking through the window . . . so you'd have more than that to go on. I even smiled at you.

CLAY: That's right.

LULA: I even got into this train, going some other way than mine. Walked down the aisle . . . searching you out.

CLAY: Really? That's pretty funny.

LULA: That's pretty funny. . . . God, you're dull.

CLAY: Well, I'm sorry, lady, but I really wasn't prepared for party talk.

LULA: No, you're not. What are you prepared for?

(Wrapping the apple core in a Kleenex and dropping it on the floor.)

CLAY *(takes her conversation as pure sex talk. He turns to confront her squarely with this idea)*: I'm prepared for anything. How about you?

LULA *(laughing loudly and cutting it off abruptly)*: What do you think you're doing?

CLAY: What?

LULA: You think I want to pick you up, get you to take me somewhere and screw me, huh?

CLAY: Is that the way I look?

LULA: You look like you been trying to grow a beard. That's exactly what you look like. You look like you live in New Jersey with your parents and are trying to grow a beard. That's what. You look like you've been reading Chinese poetry and drinking lukewarm sugarless tea. *(Laughs, uncrossing and recrossing her legs.)* You look like death eating a soda cracker.

CLAY *(cocking his head from one side to the other, embarrassed and trying to make some comeback, but also intrigued by what the woman is saying . . . even the sharp city coarseness of her voice, which is still a kind of gentle sidewalk throb)*: Really? I look like all that?

LULA: Not all of it.

(She feints a seriousness to cover an actual somber tone.)

I lie a lot. *(Smiling.)* It helps me control the world.

CLAY *(relieved and laughing louder than the humor)*: Yeah, I bet.

LULA: But it's true, most of it, right? Jersey? Your bumpy neck?

CLAY: How'd you know all that? Huh? Really, I mean about Jersey . . . and even the beard. I met you before? You know Warren Enright?

LULA: You tried to make it with your sister when you were ten. *(CLAY leans back hard against the back of the seat, his eyes opening now, still trying to look amused.)* But I succeeded a few weeks ago. *(She starts to laugh again.)*

CLAY: What're you talking about? Warren tell you that? You're a friend of Georgia's?

LULA: I told you I lie. I don't know your sister. I don't know Warren Enright.

CLAY: You mean you're just picking these things out of the air?

LULA: Is Warren Enright a tall skinny black black boy with a phony English accent?

CLAY: I figured you knew him.

LULA: But I don't. I just figured you would know somebody like that. *(Laughs.)*

CLAY: Yeah, yeah.

LULA: You're probably on your way to his house now.

CLAY: That's right.

LULA *(putting her hand on CLAY's closest knee, drawing it from the knee up to the thigh's hinge, then removing it, watching his face very closely, and continuing to laugh, perhaps more gently than before)*: Dull, dull, dull. I bet you think I'm exciting.

CLAY: You're O.K.

LULA: Am I exciting you now?

CLAY: Right. That's not what's supposed to happen?

LULA: How do I know? *(She returns her hand, without moving it, then takes it away and plunges it in her bag to draw out an apple.)* You want this?

CLAY: Sure.

LULA *(she gets one out of the bag for herself)*: Eating apples together is always the first step. Or walking up uninhabited Seventh Avenue in the twenties on weekends. *(Bites and giggles, glancing at CLAY and speaking in loose sing-song.)* Can get you involved . . . boy! Get us involved. Um-huh. *(Mock seriousness.)* Would you like to get involved with me, Mister Man?

CLAY *(trying to be as flippant as LULA, whacking happily at the apple)*: Sure. Why not? A beautiful woman like you. Huh, I'd be a fool not to.

LULA: And I bet you're sure you know what you're talking about. *(Taking him a little roughly by the wrist, so he cannot eat the apple, then shaking the wrist.)* I bet you're sure of almost everything anybody ever asked you . . . right? *(Shakes his wrist harder.)* Right?

CLAY: Yeah, right. . . . Wow, you're pretty strong, you know? Whatta you, a lady wrestler or something?

LULA: What's wrong with lady wrestlers? And don't answer because you never knew any. Huh. *(Cynically.)* That's for sure. They don't have any lady wrestlers in that part of Jersey. That's for sure.

CLAY: Hey, you still haven't told me how you know so much about me.

LULA: I told you I didn't know anything about *you* . . . you're a well-known type.

CLAY: Really?

LULA: Or at least I know the type very well. And your skinny English friend too.

CLAY: Anonymously?

LULA (*settles back in seat, single-mindedly finishing her apple and humming snatches of rhythm and blues song*): What?

CLAY: Without knowing us specifically?

LULA: Oh boy. (*Looking quickly at* CLAY.) What a face. You know, you could be a handsome man.

CLAY: I can't argue with you.

LULA (*vague, off-center response*): What?

CLAY (*raising his voice, thinking the train noise has drowned part of his sentence*): I can't argue with you.

LULA: My hair is turning gray. A gray hair for each year and type I've come through.

CLAY: Why do you want to sound so old?

LULA: But it's always gentle when it starts. (*Attention drifting.*) Hugged against tenements, day or night.

CLAY: What?

LULA (*refocusing*): Hey, why don't you take me to that party you're going to?

CLAY: You must be a friend of Warren's to know about the party.

LULA: Wouldn't you like to take me to the party? (*Imitates clinging vine.*) Oh, come on, ask me to your party.

CLAY: Of course I'll ask you to come with me to the party. And I'll bet you're a friend of Warren's.

LULA: Why not be a friend of Warren's? Why not? (*Taking his arm.*) Have you asked me yet?

CLAY: How can I ask you when I don't know your name?

LULA: Are you talking to my name?

CLAY: What is it, a secret?

LULA: I'm Lena the Hyena.

CLAY: The famous woman poet?

LULA: Poetess! the same!

CLAY: Well, you know so much about me . . . what's my name?

LULA: Morris the Hyena.

CLAY: The famous woman poet?

LULA: The same. (*Laughing and going into her bag.*) You want another apple?

CLAY: Can't make it, lady. I only have to keep one doctor away a day.

LULA: I bet your name is . . . something like . . . uh, Gerald or Walter. Huh?

CLAY: God, no.

LULA: Lloyd, Norman? One of those hopeless colored names creeping out of New Jersey. Leonard? Gag. . . .

CLAY: Like Warren?

LULA: Definitely. Just exactly like Warren. Or Everett.

CLAY: Gag. . . .

LULA: Well, for sure, it's not Willie.

CLAY: It's Clay.

LULA: Clay? Really? Clay what?

CLAY: Take your pick. Jackson, Johnson, or Williams.

LULA: Oh, really? Good for you. But it's got to be Williams. You're too pretentious to be a Jackson or Johnson.

CLAY: Thass right.

LULA: But Clay's O.K.

CLAY: So's Lena.

LULA: It's Lula.

CLAY: Oh?

LULA: Lula the Hyena.

CLAY: Very good.

LULA (*starts laughing again*): Now you say to me, "Lula, Lula, why don't you go to this party with me tonight?" It's your turn, and let those be your lines.

CLAY: Lula, why don't you go to this party with me tonight, Huh?

LULA: Say my name twice before you ask, and no huh's.

CLAY: Lula, Lula, why don't you go to this party with me tonight?

LULA: I'd like to go, Clay, but how can you ask me to go when you barely know me?

CLAY: That is strange, isn't it?

LULA: What kind of reaction is that? You're supposed to say, "Aw, come on, we'll get to know each other better at the party."

CLAY: That's pretty corny.

LULA: What are you into anyway? (*Looking at him half sullenly but still amused.*) What thing are you playing at, Mister? Mister Clay Williams? (*Grabs his thigh, up near the crotch.*) What are *you* thinking about?

CLAY: Watch it now, you're gonna excite me for real.

LULA (*taking her hand away and throwing her apple core through the window*): I bet. (*She slumps in the seat and is heavily silent.*)

CLAY: I thought you knew everything about me? What happened? (LULA *looks at him, then looks slowly away, then over where the other aisle would be. Noise of the train. She reaches in her bag and pulls out one of the paper books. She puts it on her leg and thumbs the pages listlessly.* CLAY *cocks his head to see the title of the book. Noise of the train.* LULA *flips pages and her eyes drift. Both remain silent.*) Are you going to the party with me, Lula?

LULA (*bored and not even looking*): I don't even know you.

CLAY: You said you know my type.

LULA (*strangely irritated*): Don't get smart with me, Buster. I know you like the palm of my hand.

CLAY: The one you eat the apples with?

LULA: Yeh. And the one I open doors late Saturday evening with. That's my door. Up at the top of the stairs. Five flights. Above a lot of Italians and lying Americans. And scrape carrots with. Also . . . (*Looks at him.*) the same hand I unbutton my dress with, or let my skirt fall down. Same hand. Lover.

CLAY: Are you angry about something? Did I say something wrong?

LULA: Everything you say is wrong. *(Mock smile.)* That's what makes you so attractive. Ha. In that funny-book jacket with all the buttons. *(More animate, taking hold of his jacket.)* What've you got that jacket and tie on in all this heat for? And why're you wearing a jacket and tie like that? Did your people ever burn witches or start revolutions over the price of tea? Boy, those narrow-shoulder clothes come from a tradition you ought to feel oppressed by. A three-button suit. What right do you have to be wearing a three-button suit and striped tie? Your father was a slave, he didn't go to Harvard.

CLAY: My grandfather was a night watchman.

LULA: And you went to a colored college where everybody thought they were Averell Harriman.

CLAY: All except me.

LULA: And who did you think you were? Who do you think you are now?

CLAY *(laughs as if to make light of the whole trend of the conversation)*: Well, in college I thought I was Baudelaire. But I've slowed down since.

LULA: I bet you never once thought you were a black nigger. *(Mock serious, then she howls with laughter. CLAY is stunned but after initial reaction, he quickly tries to appreciate the humor. LULA almost shrieks.)* A black Baudelaire.

CLAY: That's right.

LULA: Boy, are you corny. I take back what I said before. Everything you say is not wrong. It's perfect. You should be on television.

CLAY: You act like you're on television already.

LULA: That's because I'm an actress.

CLAY: I thought so.

LULA: Well, you're wrong. I'm no actress. I told you I always lie. I'm nothing, honey, and don't you ever forget it. *(Lighter.)* Although my mother was a Communist. The only person in my family ever to amount to anything.

CLAY: My mother was a Republican.

LULA: And your father voted for the man rather than the party.

CLAY: Right!

LULA: Yea for him. Yea, yea for him.

CLAY: Yea!

LULA: And yea for America where he is free to vote for the mediocrity of his choice! Yea!

CLAY: Yea!

LULA: And yea for both your parents who even though they differ about so crucial a matter as the body politic still forged a union of love and sacrifice that was destined to flower at the birth of the noble Clay . . . what's your middle name?

CLAY: Clay.

LULA: A union of love and sacrifice that was destined to flower at the birth of the noble Clay Clay Williams. Yea! And most of all yea yea for you, Clay Clay. The Black Baudelaire! Yes! *(And with knifelike cynicism.)* My Christ. My Christ.

CLAY: Thank you, ma'am.

LULA: May the people accept you as a ghost of the future. And love you, that you might not kill them when you can.

CLAY: What?

LULA: You're a murderer, Clay, and you know it. *(Her voice darkening with significance.)* You know god-damn well what I mean.

CLAY: I do?

LULA: So we'll pretend the air is light and full of perfume.

CLAY *(sniffing at her blouse)*: It is.

LULA: And we'll pretend the people cannot see you. That is, the citizens. And that you are free of your own history. And I am free of my history. We'll pretend that we are both anonymous beauties smashing along through the city's entrails. *(She yells as loud as she can.)* GROOVE!

SCENE 2

(Scene is the same as before, though now there are other seats visible in the car. And throughout the scene other people get on the subway. There are maybe one or two seated in the car as the scene opens, though neither CLAY or LULA notices them. CLAY's tie is open. LULA is hugging his arm.)

CLAY: The party!

LULA: I know it'll be something good. You can come in with me, looking casual and significant. I'll be strange, haughty, and silent, and walk with long slow strides.

CLAY: Right.

LULA: When you get drunk, pat me once, very lovingly on the flanks, and I'll look at you cryptically, licking my lips.

CLAY: It sounds like something we can do.

LULA: You'll go around talking to young men about your mind, and to old men about your plans. If you meet a very close friend who is also with someone like me, we can stand together, sipping our drinks and exchanging codes of lust. The atmosphere will be slithering in love and half-love and very open moral decision.

CLAY: Great. Great.

LULA: And everyone will pretend they don't know your name, and then . . . *(She pauses heavily.)* later, when they have to, they'll claim a friendship that denies your sterling character.

CLAY *(kissing her neck and fingers)*: And then what?

LULA: Then? Well, then we'll go down the street, late night, eating apples and winding very deliberately toward my house.

CLAY: Deliberately?

LULA: I mean, we'll look in all the shopwindows, and make fun of the queers. Maybe we'll meet a Jewish Buddhist and flatten his conceits over some very pretentious coffee.

CLAY: In honor of whose God?

LULA: Mine.

CLAY: Who is . . . ?

LULA: Me . . . and you?

CLAY: A corporate Godhead.

LULA: Exactly. Exactly. (*Notices one of the other people entering.*)

CLAY: Go on with the chronicle. Then what happens to us?

LULA (*a mild depression, but she still makes her description triumphant and increasingly direct*): To my house, of course.

CLAY: Of course.

LULA: And up the narrow steps of the tenement.

CLAY: You live in a tenement?

LULA: Wouldn't live anywhere else. Reminds me specifically of my novel form of insanity.

CLAY: Up the tenement stairs.

LULA: And with my apple-eating hand I push open the door and lead you, my tender big-eyed prey, into my . . . God, what can I call it . . . into my hovel.

CLAY: Then what happens?

LULA: After the dancing and games, after the long drinks and long walks, the real fun begins.

CLAY: Ah, the real fun. (*Embarrassed, in spite of himself.*) Which is . . . ?

LULA (*laughs at him*): Real fun in the dark house. Hah! Real fun in the dark house, high up above the street and the ignorant cowboys. I lead you in, holding your wet hand gently in my hand . . .

CLAY: Which is not wet?

LULA: Which is dry as ashes.

CLAY: And cold?

LULA: Don't think you'll get out of your responsibility that way. It's not cold at all. You Fascist! Into my dark living room. Where we'll sit and talk endlessly, endlessly.

CLAY: About what?

LULA: About what? About your manhood, what do you think? What do you think we've been talking about all this time?

CLAY: Well, I didn't know it was that. That's for sure. Every other thing in the world but that. (*Notices another person entering, looks quickly, almost involuntarily up and down the car, seeing the other people in the car.*) Hey, I didn't even notice when those people got on.

LULA: Yeah, I know.

CLAY: Man, this subway is slow.

LULA: Yeah, I know.

CLAY: Well, go on. We were talking about my manhood.

LULA: We still are. All the time.

CLAY: We were in your living room.

LULA: My dark living room. Talking endlessly.

CLAY: About my manhood.

LULA: I'll make you a map of it. Just as soon as we get to my house.

CLAY: Well, that's great.

LULA: One of the things we do while we talk. And screw.

CLAY (*trying to make his smile broader and less shaky*): We finally got there.

LULA: And you'll call my rooms black as a grave. You'll say, "This place is like Juliet's tomb."

CLAY (*laughs*): I might.

LULA: I know. You've probably said it before.

CLAY: And is that all? The whole grand tour?

LULA: Not all. You'll say to me very close to my face, many, many times, you'll say, even whisper, that you love me.

CLAY: Maybe I will.

LULA: And you'll be lying.

CLAY: I wouldn't lie about something like that.

LULA: Hah. It's the only kind of thing you will lie about. Especially if you think it'll keep me alive.

CLAY: Keep you alive? I don't understand.

LULA (*bursting out laughing, but too shrilly*): Don't understand? Well, don't look at me. It's the path I take, that's all. Where both feet take me when I set them down. One in front of the other.

CLAY: Morbid. Morbid. You sure you're not an actress? All that self-aggrandizement.

LULA: Well, I told you I wasn't an actress . . . but I also told you I lie all the time. Draw your own conclusions.

CLAY: And is that all of our lives together you've described? There's no more?

LULA: I've told you all I know. Or almost all.

CLAY: There's no funny parts?

LULA: I thought it was all funny.

CLAY: But you mean peculiar, not ha-ha.

LULA: You don't know what I mean.

CLAY: Well, tell me the almost part then. You said almost all. What else? I want the whole story.

LULA (*searching aimlessly through her bag. She begins to talk breathlessly, with a light and silly tone*): All stories are whole stories. All of 'em. Our whole story . . . nothing but change. How could things go on like that forever? Huh? (*Slaps him on the shoulder, begins finding things in her bag, taking them out and throwing them over her shoulder into the aisle.*) Except I do go on as I do. Apples and long walks with deathless intelligent lovers. But you mix it up. Look out the window, all the time. Turning pages. Change change change. Till, shit, I don't know you. Wouldn't, for that matter. You're too serious. I bet you're even too serious to be psychoanalyzed. Like all those Jewish poets from Yonkers, who leave their mothers looking for other mothers, or others' mothers, on whose baggy tits they lay their fumbling heads. Their poems are always funny, and all about sex.

CLAY: They sound great. Like movies.

LULA: But you change. *(Blankly.)* And things work on you till you hate them.

(More people come into the train. They come closer to the couple, some of them not sitting, but swinging drearily on the straps, staring at the two with uncertain interest.)

CLAY: Wow. All these people, so suddenly. They must all come from the same place.

LULA: Right. That they do.

CLAY: Oh? You know about them too?

LULA: Oh yeah. About them more than I know about you. Do they frighten you?

CLAY: Frighten me? Why should they frighten me?

LULA: 'Cause you're an escaped nigger.

CLAY: Yeah?

LULA: 'Cause you crawled through the wire and made tracks to my side.

CLAY: Wire?

LULA: Don't they have wire around plantations?

CLAY: You must be Jewish. All you can think about is wire. Plantations didn't have any wire. Plantations were big open whitewashed places like heaven, and everybody on 'em was grooved to be there. Just strummin' and hummin' all day.

LULA: Yes, yes.

CLAY: And that's how the blues was born.

LULA: Yes, yes. And that's how the blues was born. *(Begins to make up a song that becomes quickly hysterical. As she sings she rises from her seat, still throwing things out of her bag into the aisle, beginning a rhythmical shudder and twistlike wiggle, which she continues up and down the aisle, bumping into many of the standing people and tripping over the feet of those sitting. Each time she runs into a person she lets out a very vicious piece of profanity, wiggling and stepping all the time.)* And that's how the blues was born. Yes. Yes. Son of a bitch, get out of the way. Yes. Quack. Yes. Yes. And that's how the blues was born. Ten little niggers sitting on a limb, but none of them ever looked like him. *(Points to CLAY, returns toward the seat, with her hands extended for him to rise and dance with her.)* And that's how the blues was born. Yes. Come on, Clay. Let's do the nasty. Rub bellies. Rub bellies.

CLAY *(waves his hands to refuse. He is embarrassed, but determined to get a kick out of the proceedings)*: Hey, what was in those apples? Mirror, mirror on the wall, who's the fairest one of all? Snow White, baby, and don't you forget it.

LULA *(grabbing for his hands, which he draws away)*: Come on, Clay. Let's rub bellies on the train. The nasty. The nasty. Do the gritty grind, like your ol' raghead mammy. Grind till you lose your mind. Shake it, shake it, shake it, shake it! OOOOweeee!

Come on, Clay. Let's do the choo-choo train shuffle, the navel scratcher.

CLAY: Hey, you coming on like the lady who smoked up her grass skirt.

LULA *(becoming annoyed that he will not dance, and becoming more animated as if to embarrass him still further)*: Come on, Clay . . . let's do the thing. Uhh! Uhh! Clay! Clay! You middle-class black bastard. Forget your social-working mother for a few seconds and let's knock stomachs. Clay, you liver-lipped white man. You would-be Christian. You ain't no nigger, you're just a dirty white man. Get up, Clay. Dance with me, Clay.

CLAY: Lula! Sit down, now. Be cool.

LULA *(mocking him, in wild dance)*: Be cool. Be cool. That's all you know . . . shaking that wildroot cream-oil on your knotty head, jackets buttoning up to your chin, so full of white man's words. Christ. God. Get up and scream at these people. Like scream meaningless shit in these hopeless faces. *(She screams at people in train, still dancing.)* Red trains cough Jewish underwear for keeps! Expanding smells of silence. Gravy snot whistling like sea birds. Clay, Clay, you got to break out. Don't sit there dying the way they want you to die. Get up.

CLAY: Oh, sit the fuck down. *(He moves to restrain her.)* Sit down, goddamn it.

LULA *(twisting out of his reach)*: Screw yourself, Uncle Tom. Thomas Woolly-Head. *(Begins to dance a kind of jig, mocking CLAY with loud forced humor.)* There is Uncle Tom . . . I mean, Uncle Thomas Woolly-Head. With old white matted mane. He hobbles on his wooden cane. Old Tom. Old Tom. Let the white man hump his ol' mama and he jes' shuffle off in the woods and hide his gentle gray head. Ol' Thomas Woolly-Head.

(Some of the other riders are laughing now. A drunk gets up and joins LULA in her dance, singing, as best he can, her "song." CLAY gets up out of his seat and visibly scans the faces of the other riders.)

CLAY: Lula! Lula! *(She is dancing and turning, still shouting as loud as she can. The drunk too is shouting, and waving his hands wildly.)* Lula . . . you dumb bitch. Why don't you stop it? *(He rushes half stumbling from his seat, and grabs one of her flailing arms.)*

LULA: Let me go! You black son of a bitch. *(She struggles against him.)* Let me go! Help!

(CLAY is dragging her toward her seat, and the drunk seeks to interfere. He grabs CLAY around the shoulders and begins wrestling with him. CLAY clubs the drunk to the floor without releasing LULA, who is still screaming. CLAY finally gets her to the seat and throws her into it.)

CLAY: Now you shut the hell up. *(Grabbing her shoulders.)* Just shut up. You don't know what you're talking about. You don't know anything. So just keep your stupid mouth closed.

LULA: You're afraid of white people. And your father was. Uncle Tom Big Lip!

CLAY (*slaps her as hard as he can, across the mouth. LULA's head bangs against the back of the seat. When she raises it again, CLAY slaps her again*): Now shut up and let me talk. (*He turns toward the other riders, some of whom are sitting on the edge of their seats. The drunk is on one knee, rubbing his head, and singing softly the same song. He shuts up too when he sees CLAY watching him. The others go back to newspapers or stare out the window.*) Shit, you don't have any sense, Lula, nor feelings either. I could murder you now. Such a tiny ugly throat. I could squeeze it flat, and watch you turn blue, on a humble. For dull kicks. And all these weak-faced ofays squatting around here, staring over their papers at me. Murder them too. Even if they expected it. That man there . . . (*Points to well-dressed man.*) I could rip that *Times* right out of his hand, as skinny and middle-classed as I am, I could rip that paper out of his hand and just as easily rip out his throat. It takes no great effort. For what? To kill you soft idiots? You don't understand anything but luxury.

LULA: You fool!

CLAY (*pushing her against the seat*): I'm not telling you again, Tallulah Bankhead! Luxury. In your face and your fingers. You telling me what I ought to do. (*Sudden scream frightening the whole coach.*) Well, don't! Don't you tell me anything! If I'm a middle-class fake white man . . . let me be. And let me be in the way I want. (*Through his teeth.*) I'll rip your lousy breasts off! Let me be who I feel like being. Uncle Tom. Thomas. Whoever. It's none of your business. You don't know anything except what's there for you to see. An act. Lies. Device. Not the pure heart, the pumping black heart. You don't ever know that. And I sit here, in this buttoned-up suit, to keep myself from cutting all your throats. I mean wantonly. You great liberated whore! You fuck some black man and right away you're an expert on black people. What a lotta shit that is. The only thing you know is that you come if he bangs you hard enough. And that's all. The belly rub? You wanted me to do the belly rub? Shit, you don't even know how. You don't know that. That ol' dipty-dip shit you do, rolling your ass like an elephant. That's not my kind of belly rub. Belly rub is not Queens. Belly rub is dark places, with big hats and overcoats held up with one arm. Belly rub hates you. Old bald-headed four-eyed ofays popping their fingers . . . and don't know yet what they're doing. They say, "I love Bessie Smith." And don't even understand that Bessie Smith is saying, "Kiss my ass, kiss my black unruly ass." Before love, suffering, desire, anything you

can explain, she's saying, and very plainly, "Kiss my black ass." And if you don't know that, it's you that's doing the kissing.

Charlie Parker? Charlie Parker. All the hip white boys scream for Bird. And Bird saying, "Up your ass, feeble-minded ofay! Up your ass." And they sit there talking about the tortured genius of Charlie Parker. Bird would've played not a note of music if he just walked up to East Sixty-seventh Street and killed the first ten white people he saw. Not a note! And I'm the great would-be poet. Yes. That's right! Poet. Some kind of bastard litera-ture . . . all it needs is a simple knife thrust. Just let me bleed you, you loud whore, and one poem vanished. A whole people of neurotics, struggling to keep from being sane. And the only thing that would cure the neurosis would be your murder. Simple as that. I mean if I murdered you, then other white people would begin to understand me. You understand? No. I guess not. If Bessie Smith had killed some white people she wouldn't have needed that music. She could have talked very straight and plain about the world. No metaphors. No grunts. No wiggles in the dark of her soul. Just straight two and two are four. Money. Power. Luxury. Like that. All of them. Crazy niggers turning their backs on sanity. When all it needs is that simple act. Murder. Just mur-der! Would make us all sane. (*Suddenly weary.*) Ahhh. Shit. But who needs it? I'd rather be a fool. Insane. Safe with my words, and no deaths, and clean, hard thoughts, urging me to new con-quests. My people's madness. Hah! That's a laugh. My people. They don't need me to claim them. They got legs and arms of their own. Per-sonal insanities. Mirrors. They don't need all those words. They don't need any defense. But lis-ten, though, one more thing. And you tell this to your father, who's probably the kind of man who needs to know at once. So he can plan ahead. Tell him not to preach so much rationalism and cold logic to these niggers. Let them alone. Let them sing curses at you in code and see your filth as simple lack of style. Don't make the mistake, through some irresponsible surge of Christian charity, of talking too much about the advantages of Western rationalism, or the great intellectual legacy of the white man, or maybe they'll begin to listen. And then, maybe one day, you'll find they actually do understand exactly what you are talk-ing about, all these fantasy people. All these blues people. And on that day, as sure as shit, when you really believe you can "accept" them into your fold, as half-white trusties late of the subject peoples. With no more blues, except the very old ones, and not a watermelon in sight, the great missionary heart will have triumphed, and all of those ex-coons will be stand-up Western men, with eyes for clean hard useful lives, sober, pious and sane, and they'll murder you. They'll murder you, and have very rational explanations. Very much like your own. They'll cut your throats, and drag you out to the edge of your cities so the flesh can fall away from your bones, in sanitary isolation.

LULA (*her voice takes on a different, more businesslike quality*): I've heard enough.

CLAY (*reaching for his books*): I bet you have. I guess I better collect my stuff and get off this train. Looks like we won't be acting out that little pageant you outlined before.

LULA: No. We won't. You're right about that, at least. (*She turns to look quickly around the rest of the car.*) All right! (*The others respond.*)

CLAY (*bending across the girl to retrieve his belongings*): Sorry, baby, I don't think we could make it.

(*As he is bending over her, the girl brings up a small knife and plunges it into* CLAY*'s chest. Twice. He slumps across her knees, his mouth working stupidly.*)

LULA: Sorry is right. (*Turning to the others in the car who have already gotten up from their seats.*) Sorry is the rightest thing you've said. Get this man off me!

Hurry, now! (*The others come and drag* CLAY*'s body down the aisle.*) Open the door and throw his body out. (*They throw him off.*) And all of you get off at the next stop.

(LULA *busies herself straightening her things. Getting everything in order. She takes out a notebook and makes a quick scribbling note. Drops it in her bag. The train apparently stops and all the others get off, leaving her alone in the coach. Very soon a young Negro of about twenty comes into the coach, with a couple of books under his arms. He sits a few seats in back of* LULA. *When he is seated she turns and gives him a long slow look. He looks up from his book and drops the book on his lap. Then an old Negro conductor comes into the car, doing a sort of restrained soft shoe, and half mumbling the words of some song. He looks at the young man, briefly, with a quick greeting.*)

CONDUCTOR: Hey, brother!

YOUNG MAN: Hey.

(*The conductor continues down the aisle with his little dance and the mumbled song.* LULA *turns to stare at him and follows his movements down the aisle. The conductor tips his hat when he reaches her seat, and continues out the car.*)

CURTAIN

Figure 1. Lula (Jennifer West) munches her apple and provocatively crosses her legs while Clay (Robert Hooks) looks at his magazine in the opening moments of the Cherry Lane Theatre production of *Dutchman*, directed by Edward Parone, New York, 1964. (Photograph: Alix Jeffry. Billy Rose Theatre Collection. The New York Public Library for the Performing Arts. Astor, Lenox, and Tilden Foundations.)

Staging of *Dutchman*

REVIEW OF THE CHERRY LANE THEATRE
PRODUCTION, 1964, BY HAROLD CLURMAN

It is altogether likely that the folk who go down to the Cherry Lane Theatre to see the three one-act plays now being given there are witnesses to a signal event: the emergence of an outstanding dramatist—LeRoi Jones.

His is a turbulent talent. While turbulence is not always a sign of power or of valuable meaning, I have a hunch that LeRoi Jones's fire will burn ever higher and clearer if our theatre can furnish an adequate vessel to harbor his flame. We need it.

He is very angry. Anger alone may merely make a loud noise, confuse, sputter and die. For anger to burn to useful effect, it must be guided by an idea. With the "angry young men" of England one was not always certain of the source of dissatisfaction nor of its goal. With LeRoi Jones it is easy to say that the plight of the Negro ignited the initial rage—justification enough—and that the rage will not be appeased until there is no more black and white, no more color except as differences in hue and accent are part of the world's splendid spectacle. But there is more to his ferocity than a protest against the horrors of racism.

Dutchman, the first of Jones's plays to reach the professional stage, is a stylized account of a subway episode. A white girl picks up a young Negro who at first is rather embarrassed and later piqued by her advances. There is a perversity in her approach which finally provokes him to a hymn of hate. With lyrical obscenity he declares that murder is in his and every Negro's heart and were it to reach the point of action there would be less "singin' of the blues," less of that delightful folk music and hot jazz which beguile the white man's fancy, more calm in the Negro soul. Meanwhile, it is the black man who is murdered.

What we must not overlook in seeing the play is that, while this explosion of fury is its rhetorical and emotional climax, the crux of its significance resides in the depiction of the white girl whose relevance to the play's situation does not lie in her whiteness but in her representative value as a token of our civilization. She is our neurosis. Not a neurosis in regard to the Negro, but the absolute neurosis of American society.

She is "hep": she has heard about everything, understands and feels nothing. She twitches, jangles, jitters with a thin but inexhaustible energy, propelled by the vibrations from millions of ads, television quiz programs, newspaper columns, intellectual jargon culled from countless digests, panel discussions, illustrated summaries, smatterings of gossip on every conceivable subject (respectable and illicit), epithets, wisecracks, formulas, slogans, cynicisms, cures and solutions. She is the most "informed" person in the world and the most ignorant. (The information feeds the ignorance.) She is the bubbling, boiling garbage cauldron newly produced by our progress. She is a calculating machine gone berserk; she is the real killer. What she destroys is not men of a certain race but mankind. She is the compendium in little of the universal mess.

If *Dutchman* (a title I don't understand) has a fault, it is its completeness. Its ending is somewhat too pat, too pointed in its symbolism. If one has caught the drift of the play's meaning before its final moment, the ending is supererogatory; if one has failed to do so, it is probably useless.

Dutchman is very well played by Jennifer West and Robert Hooks.

REVIEW OF THE CHERRY LANE THEATRE
PRODUCTION, 1964, BY HOWARD TAUBMAN

Everything about LeRoi Jones's "Dutchman" is designed to shock—its basic idea, its language and its murderous rage.

This half-hour-long piece, the last of three one-act plays being performed at the Cherry Lane Theatre, is an explosion of hatred rather than a play. It puts into the mouth of its principal Negro character a scathing denunciation of all the white man's good works, pretensions and condescensions.

If this is the way the Negroes really feel about the

white world around them, there's more rancor buried in the breasts of colored conformists than anyone can imagine. If this is the way even one Negro feels, there is ample cause for guilt as well as alarm, and for a hastening of change.

As an extended metaphor of bitterness and fury, "Dutchman" is transparently simple in structure. Clay, a Negro who wears a three-button suit and is reserved and well-spoken, is accosted by a white female on a train. Lula is a liar, a slut, essentially an agent provocateur of a Caucasian society.

After she disarms Clay with her wild outbursts and sinuous attentions, she turns on him in challenging contempt. His answer is to drop the mask of conformity and to spew out all the anger that has built up in him and his fellow Negroes. When this outburst of violent resentment has finished and Clay has left the train, Lula notices that another Negro has boarded and she sets her slinky charms for him.

Mr. Jones writes with a kind of sustained frenzy. His little work is a mélange of sardonic images and undisciplined filth. The impact of his ferocity would be stronger if he did not work so hard and persistently to be shocking.

Jennifer West in a straight, tight-fitting dress striped like a prisoner's suit plays Lula with a rousing mixture of sultriness and insolence. Robert Hooks as Clay is impressive as he shifts from patient tolerance to savage wrath. Edward Parone's staging is mordant, and intense.

HAROLD PINTER

1930–

Harold Pinter is now so well known for his spare, elliptical dialogue about disturbing and menacing situations that his name has been transformed into a widely used adjective—Pinteresque—to describe his influential dramatic style. The grandson of Russian and Polish immigrants, the son of a Jewish tailor, a boy born and raised in London's hard-bitten East End, Pinter attended the local grammar school and during his teens began writing poems, short stories, and dialogues for little magazines, as well as taking part in school theatrical productions. During the late 1940s, he spent a couple of terms at London's Royal Academy of Dramatic Art, but he was put off by the insular theatricality of his fellow students and withdrew to start a professional career in acting—first in radio work during 1950, then with a professional company touring Ireland during 1951 and 1952. After returning to England, he continued to act in London and the provinces under the pseudonym David Baron until 1957, when he wrote his first play, *The Room*—a one-act piece he did at the suggestion of a friend who was then studying drama at Bristol University. This eerie little play, which depicts an old couple suddenly beset by menacing visits and messages, clearly foreshadowed the inexplicably threatening situations that Pinter has dramatized repeatedly in his subsequent plays. During 1957 Pinter also wrote his first full-length work for the stage, *The Birthday Party*. This time the menacing situation took the form of humiliating physical and verbal games inflicted on a retired pianist by two sinister men who turn up at his room, subject him to interrogation and then "birthday party games," and finally carry him off with them the next morning.

When *The Birthday Party* opened in London in 1958, most critics found it "opaque" (at best) and charged that the characters spoke "in nonsequiturs, half-gibberish, and lunatic ravings." Although it closed after one week, *The Birthday Party* was revived six years later by the Royal Shakespeare Company in a highly successful production directed by Pinter himself. By then, Pinter had already achieved his first popular success with *The Caretaker* (1960), which dramatizes the comic but convulsive quarrels and competition that develop in a run-down house among the owner, his brain-damaged brother, and a devious tramp whom the brother has befriended. Pinter's output in the 1960s was prolific. He wrote a series of short plays—*A Slight Ache* and *The Collection* in 1961, *The Lover* in 1963, *The Basement* in 1966, *Landscape* in 1967, and *Silence* in 1969—as well as the full-length *The Homecoming* (1965). At the same time, he began writing screenplays—first adapting his own work (*The Caretaker,* 1963), but then creating a series of memorable scripts for Joseph Losey (*The Servant,* 1963, *Accident,* 1965, and *The Go-Between,* 1969). By 1966, Pinter was sufficiently well known—and accepted—that he was awarded the C.B.E. (Commander of the Order of the British Empire) by the Queen.

Though the pace of Pinter's writing for the stage slowed somewhat during the 1970s and the 1980s, he continued to explore and develop his major dramatic concerns. Having once said that he was fascinated by "two people sitting in a room," he expanded the possibilities of that idea in his later plays, such as *Old Times* (1970) and *No Man's Land* (1974), where tension arises when a stranger comes into a seemingly fixed and stable relationship. In *Old Times,* Anna comes to visit her old friend and roommate, Kate, and in *No Man's Land,* the indigent poet Spooner is picked up at a pub by Hirst, a wealthy writer. The struggles in these plays are often about fleeting and uncertain memories: Did Kate see the film *Odd Man Out* with Anna, or is that where she met Deeley, who became her husband? Did Hirst ever know Spooner, whom he suddenly starts addressing as Charles Wetherby, or are Hirst's detailed recollections of their past history an elaborate mind game?

The questions are perhaps unanswerable but years of discerning criticism about other absurdist playwrights such as Samuel Beckett, Jean Genet, and Eugène Ionesco have helped audiences to recognize Pinter's work as part of a widespread movement in contemporary drama. The work of these playwrights moves away from clearly motivated characters and plots, as well as from entirely logical dialogue and events, to a theater in which the actions and utterances of characters, however preposterous or alarming, are interesting, even fascinating, because they can and do take place on stage, and because they bear a provocative relationship to life itself. Pinter himself has also talked openly and helpfully about this aspect of his plays. For the audiences who came to the Royal Court Theatre in 1960 to see *The Room* and *The Dumb Waiter,* he offered this brief statement revealing his approach to characterization:

> A character on the stage who can present no convincing argument or information as to his past experience, his present behaviour or his aspirations, nor give a comprehensive analysis of his motives is as legitimate and as worthy of attention as one who, alarmingly, can do all these things.

Pinter's program notes also illuminate his view of dialogue: "The more acute the experience, the less articulate its expression." Given this concept of inarticulateness in the theater, Pinter was naturally led to his famous statement about "the two silences," which he formulated in a 1962 speech to a student drama festival in Bristol:

> There are two silences. One when no word is spoken. The other when perhaps a torrent of language is employed. This speech is speaking of a language locked beneath it. That is its continual reference. The speech we hear is an indication of that which we don't hear. It is a necessary avoidance, a violent, shy, anguished, or mocking smoke-screen which keeps the other in its place. When true silence falls we are still left with echo but are nearer nakedness. One way of looking at speech is to say it is a constant stratagem to cover nakedness.

Both these kinds of silence are, of course, true to general human experience, as Chekhov had clearly exemplified in the dialogue of his plays seventy years earlier, but only in drama of the absurd—and particularly in the plays of Pinter—have they become a pervasive theatrical element.

Pinter's fascination with language has also shaped his short political plays, stemming primarily from the mid- to late 1980s. *Mountain Language* (1988), set in a prison camp where the guards forbid the use of the prisoners' own language, lasts for only twenty minutes but is an unforgettable and frightening portrayal of power turned into brutality. It harks back to Pinter's *One for the Road* (1984), whose chief character is a government interrogator, much as it looks forward to *Party Time* (1991), where party goers talk of health clubs, sex, and sports while ignoring the questions of a woman asking about her missing brother—a character revealed at the end as a victim of state oppression.

But whether Pinter's plays dramatize a world echoing political oppression or personal tensions, he consistently shows us human beings whose language both empowers them and isolates them. Characters who wish to seem important or assert their power often speak about particular subjects, using specialized terms to show off their knowledge. Mick, in *The Caretaker*, tries to intimidate Davies, the tramp, by talking about interior decoration; Briggs, in *No Man's Land*, describes a complicated one-way system and in so doing, implicitly lets Spooner know that Spooner is trapped; and Duff, in *Landscape*, describes the science of handling beer kegs, while Beth, his wife, seems lost in her memories of a romantic encounter. The distance between Beth's language and Duff's is a striking example of the distances that often separate characters in a Pinteresque world:

> Beth: I wore my blue dress.
> Duff: Let it stand for three days. Keep wet sacks over the barrels. Hose the cellar floor daily. Hose the barrels daily.
> Beth: It was a beautiful autumn morning.
> Duff: Run water through the pipes to the bar pumps daily.

Pinter emphasizes their separation in a brief note after the opening stage direction: "Duff refers normally to Beth, but does not appear to hear her voice. Beth never looks at Duff, and does not appear to hear his voice." Pinter never explains why this situation exists; indeed, as his comments in 1960 suggest, he would think such an explanation unnecessary. Instead, the audience will first take in the fact of noncommunication and will then listen to the two speakers in hopes of finding out why this strange couple sit in a kitchen, talking past each other.

Most reviewers of the 1994 revival of this play—produced in May at the Pinter Festival in Dublin, then in London at the Royal National Theatre—found the brief play mesmerizing, even while they disagreed on the life evoked by the two intersecting monologues. For some critics, Beth's memories of the man on the beach refer to their employer, Mr. Sykes; for others, Beth is speaking of Duff himself, but in earlier and happier times. We cannot know for sure, and indeed, for many critics and audience members, that is part of the play's fascination. Because Pinter has imposed such a rigorous separation on the couple—spatially, aurally, emotionally—he repeatedly lures the audience into trying to make the connections that they will not and cannot make, though resistant audience members, such as the critic Nick Curtis, have found this approach stifling. The 1994 production was made more powerful by the presence of a husband-and-wife team, Ian Holm and Penelope Wilton, in the roles of Duff and Beth (see Figures 1 and 2). As they sit in the same room (see Figure 3), they are clearly isolated from each other, yet just as clearly locked into remaining where they are.

LANDSCAPE

BY HAROLD PINTER

CHARACTERS

DUFF: *a man in his early fifties.*
BETH: *a woman in her late forties.*
The kitchen of a country house.
A long kitchen table.
BETH *sits in an armchair, which stands away from the table, to its left.*
DUFF *sits in a chair at the right corner of the table. The background, of a sink, stove, etc., and a window, is dim. Evening.*

NOTE

DUFF *refers normally to* BETH, *but does not appear to hear her voice.*
BETH *never looks at* DUFF, *and does not appear to hear his voice.*
Both characters are relaxed, in no sense rigid.

BETH: I would like to stand by the sea. It is there.

(Pause)

I have. Many times. It's something I cared for. I've done it.

(Pause)

I'll stand on the beach. On the beach. Well . . . it was very fresh. But it was hot, in the dunes. But it was so fresh, on the shore. I loved it very much.

(Pause)

Lots of people . . .

(Pause)

People move so easily. Men. Men move.

(Pause)

I walked from the dune to the shore. My man slept in the dune. He turned over as I stood. His eyelids. Belly button. Snoozing how lovely.

(Pause)

Would you like a baby? I said. Children? Babies? Of our own? Would be nice.

(Pause)

Women turn, look at me.

(Pause)

Our own child? Would you like that?

(Pause)

Two women looked at me, turned and stared. No. I was walking, they were still. I turned.

(Pause)

Why do you look?

(Pause)

I didn't say that, I stared. Then I was looking at them.

(Pause)

I am beautiful.

(Pause)

I walked back over the sand. He had turned. Toes under sand, head buried in his arms.

DUFF: The dog's gone. I didn't tell you.

(Pause)

I had to shelter under a tree for twenty minutes yesterday. Because of the rain. I meant to tell you. With some youngsters. I didn't know them.

(Pause)

Then it eased. A downfall.° I walked up as far as the pond. Then I felt a couple of big drops. Luckily I was only a few yards from the shelter. I sat down in there. I meant to tell you.

(Pause)

Do you remember the weather yesterday? That downfall?

BETH: He felt my shadow. He looked up at me standing above him.

DUFF: I should have had some bread with me. I could have fed the birds.

BETH: Sand on his arms.

DUFF: They were hopping about. Making a racket.

BETH: I lay down by him, not touching.

---

downfall, sudden or heavy rainfall.

DUFF: There wasn't anyone else in the shelter. There was a man and woman, under the trees, on the other side of the pond. I didn't feel like getting wet. I stayed where I was.

(Pause)

Yes, I've forgotten something. The dog was with me.

(Pause)

BETH: Did those women know me? I didn't remember their faces. I'd never seen their faces before. I'd never seen those women before. I'm certain of it. Why were they looking at me? There's nothing strange about me. There's nothing strange about the way I look. I look like anyone.

DUFF: The dog wouldn't have minded me feeding the birds. Anyway, as soon as we got in the shelter he fell asleep. But even if he'd been awake . . .

(Pause)

BETH: They all held my arm lightly, as I stepped out of the car, or out of the door, or down the steps. Without exception. If they touched the back of my neck, or my hand, it was done so lightly. Without exception. With one exception.

DUFF: Mind you, there was a lot of shit all over the place, all along the paths, by the pond. Dogshit, duckshit . . . all kinds of shit . . . all over the paths. The rain didn't clean it up. It made it even more treacherous.

(Pause)

The ducks were well away, right over on their island. But I wouldn't have fed them, anyway. I would have fed the sparrows.

BETH: I could stand now. I could be the same. I dress differently, but I am beautiful.

(Silence)

DUFF: You should have a walk with me one day down to the pond, bring some bread. There's nothing to stop you.

(Pause)

I sometimes run into one or two people I know. You might remember them.

(Pause)

BETH: When I watered the flowers he stood, watching me, and watched me arrange them. My gravity, he said. I was so grave, attending to the flowers, I'm going to water and arrange the flowers, I said. He followed me and watched, standing at a distance from me. When the arrangement was done I stayed still. I heard him moving. He didn't touch me. I listened. I looked at the flowers, blue and white, in the bowl.

(Pause)

Then he touched me.

(Pause)

He touched the back of my neck. His fingers, lightly, touching, lightly, touching, the back, of my neck.

DUFF: The funny thing was, when I looked, when the shower was over, the man and woman under the trees on the other side of the pond had gone. There wasn't a soul in the park.

BETH: I wore a white beach robe. Underneath I was naked.

(Pause)

There wasn't a soul on the beach. Very far away a man was sitting, on a breakwater.° But even so he was only a pinpoint, in the sun. And even so I could only see him when I was standing, or on my way from the shore to the dune. When I lay down I could no longer see him, therefore he couldn't see me.

(Pause)

I may have been mistaken. Perhaps the beach was empty. Perhaps there was no-one there.

(Pause)

He couldn't see . . . my man . . . anyway. He never stood up.

(Pause)

Snoozing how lovely I said to him. But I wasn't a fool, on that occasion. I lay quiet, by his side.

(Silence)

DUFF: Anyway . . .
BETH: My skin . . .
DUFF: I'm sleeping all right these days.
BETH: Was stinging.
DUFF: Right through the night, every night.
BETH: I'd been in the sea.
DUFF: Maybe it's something to do with the fishing. Getting to learn more about fish.
BETH: Stinging in the sea by myself.
DUFF: They're very shy creatures. You've got to woo them. You must never get excited with them. Or flurried. Never.
BETH: I knew there must be a hotel near, where we could get some tea.

(Silence)

---

breakwater, offshore structure to break the force of incoming waves.

DUFF: Anyway . . . luck was on my side for a change. By the time I got out of the park the pubs were open.

(Pause)

So I thought I might as well pop in and have a pint.° I wanted to tell you. I met some nut in there. First of all I had a word with the landlord. He knows me. Then this nut came in. He ordered a pint and he made a criticism of the beer. I had no patience with it.

BETH: But then I thought perhaps the hotel bar will be open. We'll sit in the bar. He'll buy me a drink. What will I order? But what will he order? What will he want? I shall hear him say it. I shall hear his voice. He will ask me what I would like first. Then he'll order the two drinks. I shall hear him do it.

DUFF: This beer is piss, he said. Undrinkable. There's nothing wrong with the beer, I said. Yes there is, he said, I just told you what was wrong with it. It's the best beer in the area, I said. No it isn't, this chap said, it's piss. The landlord picked up the mug and had a sip. Good beer, he said. Someone's made a mistake, this fellow said, someone's used this pintpot° instead of the boghole.°

(Pause)

The landlord threw a half a crown° on the bar and told him to take *it*. The pint's only two and three,° the man said, I owe you threepence, but I haven't got any change. Give the threepence to your son, the landlord said, with my compliments. I haven't got a son, the man said, I've never had any children. I bet you're not even married, the landlord said. This man said: I'm not married. No-one'll marry me.

(Pause)

Then the man asked the landlord and me if we would have a drink with him. The landlord said he'd have a pint. I didn't answer at first, but the man came over to me and said: Have one with *me*. Have one with *me*.

(Pause)

He put down a ten bob note° and said he'd have a pint as well.

(Silence)

BETH: Suddenly I stood. I walked to the shore and into the water. I didn't swim. I don't swim. I let the

---

pint, standard measure for beer in England. *pintpot,* glass or mug for beer. *boghole,* slang for "toilet." *half a crown,* coin (no longer in use) worth two shillings and six-pence (approximately 45 cents). *two and three,* two shillings and threepence. *ten bob note,* ten shillings (no longer in use), worth approximately $1.25.

---

water billow me. I rested in the water. The waves were very light, delicate. They touched the back of my neck.

(Silence)

DUFF: One day when the weather's good you could go out into the garden and sit down. You'd like that. The open air. I'm often out there. The dog liked it.

(Pause)

I've put in some flowers. You'd find it pleasant. Looking at the flowers. You could cut a few if you liked. Bring them in. No-one would see you. There's no-one there.

(Pause)

That's where we're lucky, in my opinion. To live in Mr Sykes' house in peace, no-one to bother us. I've thought of inviting one or two people I know from the village in here for a bit of a drink once or twice but I decided against it. It's not necessary.

(Pause)

You know what you get quite a lot of out in the garden? Butterflies.

BETH: I slipped out of my costume and put on my beachrobe. Underneath I was naked. There wasn't a soul on the beach. Except for an elderly man, far away on a breakwater. I lay down beside him and whispered. Would you like a baby? A child? Of our own? Would be nice.

(Pause)

DUFF: What did you think of that downfall?

(Pause)

Of course the youngsters I met under the first tree, during the first shower, they were larking about and laughing. I tried to listen, to find out what they were laughing about, but I couldn't work it out. They were whispering. I tried to listen, to find out what the joke was.

(Pause)

Anyway I didn't find out.

(Pause)

I was thinking . . . when you were young . . . you didn't laugh much. You were . . . grave.

(Silence)

BETH: That's why he'd picked such a desolate place. So that I could draw in peace. I had my sketch book with me. I took it out. I took my drawing pencil out. But there was nothing to draw. Only the beach, the sea.

(Pause)

Could have drawn him. He didn't want it. He laughed.

(Pause)

I laughed, with him.

(Pause)

I waited for him to laugh, then I would smile, turn away, he would touch my back, turn me, to him. My nose . . . creased. I would laugh with him, a little.

(Pause)

He laughed. I'm sure of it. So I didn't draw him.

(Silence)

DUFF: You were a first-rate housekeeper when you were young. Weren't you? I was very proud. You never made a fuss, you never got into a state, you went about your work. He could rely on you. He did. He trusted you, to run his house, to keep the house up to the mark, no panic.

(Pause)

Do you remember when I took him on that trip to the north? That long trip. When we got back he thanked you for looking after the place so well, everything running like clockwork.

(Pause)

You'd missed me. When I came into this room you stopped still. I had to walk all the way over the floor towards you.

(Pause)

I touched you.

(Pause)

But I had something to say to you, didn't I? I waited, I didn't say it then, but I'd made up my mind to say it, I'd decided I would say it, and I did say it, the next morning. Didn't I?

(Pause)

I told you that I'd let you down. I'd been unfaithful to you.

(Pause)

You didn't cry. We had a few hours off. We walked up to the pond, with the dog. We stood under the trees for a bit. I didn't know why you'd brought that carrier bag with you. I asked you. I said what's in that bag? It turned out to be bread. You fed the ducks. Then we stood under the trees and looked across the pond.

(Pause)

When we got back into this room you put your hands on my face and you kissed me.

BETH: But I didn't really want a drink.

(Pause)

I drew a face in the sand, then a body. The body of a woman. Then the body of a man, close to her, not touching. But they didn't look like anything. They didn't look like human figures. The sand kept on slipping, mixing the contours. I crept close to him and put my head on his arm, and closed my eyes. All those darting red and black flecks, under my eyelid. I moved my cheek on his skin. And all those darting red and black flecks, moving about under my eyelid. I buried my face in his side and shut the light out.

(Silence)

DUFF: Mr Sykes took to us from the very first interview, didn't he?

(Pause)

He said I've got the feeling you'll make a very good team. Do you remember? And that's what we proved to be. No question. I could drive well, I could polish his shoes well, I earned my keep. Turn my hand to anything. He never lacked for anything, in the way of being looked after. Mind you, he was a gloomy bugger.

(Pause)

I was never sorry for him, at any time, for his lonely life.

(Pause)

That nice blue dress he chose for you, for the house, that was very nice of him. Of course it was in his own interests for you to look good about the house, for guests.

BETH: He moved in the sand and put his arm around me.

(Silence)

DUFF: Do you like me to talk to you?

(Pause)

Do you like me to tell you about all the things I've been doing?

(Pause)

About all the things I've been thinking?

(Pause)

Mmmnn?

(Pause)

I think you do.

BETH: And cuddled me.

(Silence)

DUFF: Of course it was in his own interests to see that you were attractively dressed about the house, to give a good impression to his guests.

BETH: I caught a bus to the crossroads and then walked down the lane by the old church. It was very quiet, except for birds. There was an old man fiddling about on the cricket pitch, bending. I stood out of the sun, under a tree.

(Pause)

I heard the car. He saw me and stopped me. I stayed still. Then the car moved again, came towards me slowly. I moved round the front of it, in the dust. I couldn't see him for the sun, but he was watching me. When I got to the door it was locked. I looked through at him. He leaned over and opened the door. I got in and sat beside him. He smiled at me. Then he reversed, all in one movement, very quickly, quite straight, up the lane to the crossroads, and we drove to the sea.

(Pause)

DUFF: We're the envy of a lot of people, you know, living in this house, having this house all to ourselves. It's too big for two people.

BETH: He said he knew a very desolate beach, that no-one else in the world knew, and that's where we are going.

DUFF: I was very gentle to you. I was kind to you, that day. I knew you'd had a shock, so I was gentle with you. I held your arm on the way back from the pond. You put your hands on my face and kissed me.

BETH: All the food I had in my bag I had cooked myself, or prepared myself. I had baked the bread myself.

DUFF: The girl herself I considered unimportant. I didn't think it necessary to go into details. I decided against it.

BETH: The windows were open but we kept the hood up.

(Pause)

DUFF: Mr Sykes gave a little dinner party that Friday. He complimented you on your cooking and the service.

(Pause)

Two women. That was all. Never seen them before. Probably his mother and sister.

(Pause)

They wanted coffee late. I was in bed. I fell asleep. I would have come down to the kitchen to give you a hand but I was too tired.

(Pause)

But I woke up when you got into bed. You were out on your feet. You were asleep as soon as you hit the pillow. Your body . . . just fell back.

BETH: He was right. It was desolate. There wasn't a soul on the beach.

(Silence)

DUFF: I had a look over the house the other day. I meant to tell you. The dust is bad. We'll have to polish it up.

(Pause)

We could go up to the drawing room, open the windows. I could wash the old decanters. We could have a drink up there one evening, if it's a pleasant evening.

(Pause)

I think there's moths. I moved the curtain and they flew out.

(Pause)

BETH: Of course when I'm older I won't be the same as I am, I won't be what I am, my skirts, my long legs, I'll be older, I won't be the same.

DUFF: At least now . . . at least now, I can walk down to the pub in peace and up to the pond in peace, with no-one to nag the shit out of me.

(Silence)

BETH: All it is, you see . . . I said . . . is the lightness of your touch, the lightness of your look, my neck, your eyes, the silence, that is my meaning, the loveliness of my flowers, my hands touching my flowers, that is my meaning.

(Pause)

I've watched other people. I've seen them.

(Pause)

All the cars zooming by. Men with girls at their sides. Bouncing up and down. They're dolls. They squeak.

(Pause)

All the people were squeaking in the hotel bar. The girls had long hair. They were smiling.

DUFF: That's what matters, anyway. We're together. That's what matters.

(Silence)

BETH: But I was up early. There was still plenty to be done and cleared up. I had put the plates in the sink to soak. They had soaked overnight. They were easy to wash. The dog was up. He followed me. Misty morning. Comes from the river.

DUFF: This fellow knew bugger all about beer. He didn't know I'd been trained as a cellarman. That's why I could speak with authority.

BETH: I opened the door and went out. There was no-one about. The sun was shining. Wet, I mean wetness, all over the ground.

DUFF: A cellarman is the man responsible. He's the earliest up in the morning. Give the drayman° a hand with the barrels. Down the slide through the cellarflaps. Lower them by rope to the racks. Rock them on the belly, put a rim up them, use balance and leverage, hike them up onto the racks.

BETH: Still misty, but thinner, thinning.

DUFF: The bung° is on the vertical, in the bunghole. Spile° the bung. Hammer the spile through the centre of the bung. That lets the air through the bung, down the bunghole, lets the beer breathe.

BETH: Wetness all over the air. Sunny. Trees like feathers.

DUFF: Then you hammer the tap in.

BETH: I wore my blue dress.

DUFF: Let it stand for three days. Keep wet sacks over the barrels. Hose the cellar floor daily. Hose the barrels daily.

BETH: It was a beautiful autumn morning.

DUFF: Run water through the pipes to the bar pumps daily.

BETH: I stood in the mist.

DUFF: Pull off. Pull off. Stop pulling just before you get to the dregs. The dregs'll give you the shits. You've got an ullage barrel.° Feed the slops back to the ullage barrel, send them back to the brewery.

BETH: In the sun.

DUFF: Dip the barrels daily with a brass rod. Know your gallonage. Chalk it up. Then you're tidy. Then you never get caught short.

BETH: Then I went back to the kitchen and sat down.

(Pause)

DUFF: This chap in the pub said he was surprised to hear it. He said he was surprised to hear about hosing the cellar floor. He said he thought most cellars had a thermostatically controlled cooling system. He said he thought keg beer was fed with oxygen through a cylinder. I said I wasn't talking about keg beer, I was talking about normal draught beer. He said he thought they piped the beer from a tanker into metal containers. I said they may do, but he wasn't talking about the quality of beer I was. He accepted that point.

(Pause)

BETH: The dog sat down by me. I stroked him. Through the window I could see down into the valley. I saw children in the valley. They were running through the grass. They ran up the hill.

(Long silence)

DUFF: I never saw your face. You were standing by the windows. One of those black nights. A downfall. All I could hear was the rain on the glass, smacking on the glass. You knew I'd come in but you didn't move. I stood close to you. What were you looking at? It was black outside. I could just see your shape in the window, your reflection. There must have been some kind of light somewhere. Perhaps just your face reflected, lighter than all the rest. I stood close to you. Perhaps you were just thinking, in a dream. Without touching you, I could feel your bottom.

(Silence)

BETH: I remembered always, in drawing, the basic principles of shadow and light. Objects intercepting the light cast shadows. Shadow is deprivation of light. The shape of the shadow is determined by that of the object. But not always. Not always directly. Sometimes it is only indirectly affected by it. Sometimes the cause of the shadow cannot be found.

(Pause)

But I always bore in mind the basic principles of drawing.

(Pause)

So that I never lost track. Or heart.

(Pause)

DUFF: You used to wear a chain round your waist. On the chain you carried your keys, your thimble, your notebook, your pencil, your scissors.

(Pause)

You stood in the hall and banged the gong.°

(Pause)

What the bloody hell are you doing banging that bloody gong?

(Pause)

It's bullshit. Standing in an empty hall banging a bloody gong. There's no one to listen. No one'll hear. There's not a soul in the house. Except me. There's nothing for lunch. There's nothing

---

drayman, carrier. *bung*, plug for beer keg. *spile*, vent for beer keg. *ullage barrel*, barrel for dregs.

banged the gong, large houses sometimes had large metal gongs that were struck to summon the family to meals.

cooked. No stew. No pie. No greens. No joint.
Fuck all.

(Pause)

BETH: So that I never lost track. Even though, even
when, I asked him to turn, to look at me, but he
turned to look at me but I couldn't see his look.

(Pause)

I couldn't see whether he was looking at me.

(Pause)

Although he had turned. And appeared to be
looking at me.

DUFF: I took the chain off and the thimble, the keys,
the scissors slid off it and clattered down. I booted
the gong down the hall. The dog came in. I
thought you would come to me, I thought you
would come into my arms and kiss me, even . . .
offer yourself to me. I would have had you in
front of the dog, like a man, in the hall, on the
stone, banging the gong, mind you don't get the
scissors up your arse, or the thimble, don't worry,
I'll throw them for the dog to chase, the thimble
will keep the dog happy, he'll play with it with his
paws, you'll plead with me like a woman, I'll bang
the gong on the floor, if the sound is too flat,

lacks resonance, I'll hang it back on its hook,
bang you against it swinging, gonging, waking the
place up, calling them all for dinner, lunch is up,
bring out the bacon, bang your lovely head, mind
the dog doesn't swallow the thimble, slam—

(Silence)

BETH: He lay above me and looked down at me. He
supported my shoulder.

(Pause)

So tender his touch on my neck. So softly his kiss
on my cheek.

(Pause)

My hand on his rib.

(Pause)

So sweetly the sand over me. Tiny the sand on my
skin.

(Pause)

So silent the sky in my eyes. Gently the sound of
the tide.

(Pause)

Oh my true love I said.

Figure 1. Ian Holm as Duff in the Royal National Theatre production of *Landscape,* written and directed by Harold Pinter, 1994. (Photograph: Donald Cooper/Photostage.)

Figure 2. Penelope Wilton as Beth in *Landscape.* (Photograph: Donald Cooper/Photostage.)

Figure 3. Duff (Ian Holm) and Beth (Penelope Wilton), occupying the same theatrical space, but different mental worlds, in *Landscape*. (Photograph: Donald Cooper/Photostage.)

Staging of *Landscape*

REVIEW OF THE NATIONAL THEATRE PRODUCTION, LONDON, 1994, BY NICK CURTIS

LENGTH: 38 minutes, says the programme with Pinteresque precision of this slow, solemn, slender two-hander, glorified by the acting team of husband and wife Ian Holm and Penelope Wilton and the presence of Harold Pinter himself as director.

Landscape was first performed in 1980. Its theme is his old favourite, non-communication, expressed in the baldest, briefest terms possible. As an exercise in theatrical technique it's interesting: as a play, far from it.

Although *Landscape* features two characters, they never converse. Holm's battened-down Duff lobs comments which escalate from everyday banality to desperately brutal fantasy at Wilton's rhapsodising Beth, only to see them sail over her unhearing head. For her part, Beth keeps her gaze unfocused on the audience, locked in a vaguely sensual dream-world of past loves.

With grim inevitability we uncover a version of their lives, but this being Pinter, it's an unreliable one, refracted solely through Duff's biased perspective. It seems the pair are manservant and housekeeper, living in the master's house long after the master has gone. They may have been lovers, but now she refuses to acknowledge him.

Wilton and Holm perform with impeccable focus, but they are wasted. It's beautifully done, but these are artless devices. Holm and Wilton sketch the couple's life in air, but it evaporates before an audience can grasp it. There are longer, better Pinter plays which would flower with these actors at the helm, but this play is a stunted growth which stifles them. Pinter, presumably, is directing it for his own benefit, not the audience's.

REVIEW OF THE NATIONAL THEATRE PRODUCTION, LONDON, 1994, BY ALASTAIR MACAULAY

In his poetic, haunting, and seldom seen masterwork *Landscape*, Harold Pinter strips drama to its most enigmatic essence. The two characters, Duff and Beth, sit at either ends of a kitchen table, without ever rising. Nothing happens but talk; they seem never to hear each other, she never addresses him. The play, new in 1968, lasts only 40 minutes. We, listening, are baffled—and, finally, heartbroken. For heartbreak is part of the subject of this beautiful play.

Duff sits mainly in profile to us, leaning forwards to keep his hands on the table, like a Cézanne card-player. Beth sits facing us, hands folded in her lap, like Cézanne's mother. Man and woman: Pinter has distilled the age-old tensions between the two sexes so potently that the tragic division of gender has never seemed less bridgeable. The mysteries of the play lie in the dichotomies between what she says and what he says.

Beth sits there motionless. It is possible that she is in a coma or trance; certainly Duff addresses her as such. Yet the wonderful irony of the play is that her thoughts dwell entirely in sensuous contemplation of the lyrical past, while his thoughts ramble tensely. He is prose, she poetry. He talks of mundane facts, she of delicate feeling. He thinks about only home and work, she about would-be children and art. He speaks of sex as struggle, she as intimacy.

And, though she speaks frequently of "he" and "him," it is by no means clear if she is referring to Duff; we wonder about their (ex-?)employer Mr. Sykes. It is Duff who gives us most clues: we learn that he once told her of his infidelity to her, we learn that she once, at some other time, broke down by hammering at the gong. The clinching clue, I believe, to the identity of her lover lies in the word "grave."

More important, however, and nearest to the play's title, are her words on the principles of light and shade in drawing. Or, rather, light and *shadow*. Pinter extracts beautiful nuance from the latter word. "Shadow is deprivation of light . . . Sometimes the cause of the shadow cannot be found. But I always bore in mind the basic principles of drawing. So that I never lost track. Or heart."

Much more deserves to be said not only about this play but also about the performance it is being given, under Pinter's own direction, by Penelope Wilton and

Ian Holm at the Cottesloe. This is the staging that was the greatest revelation of the Pinter Festival at Dublin's Gate Theatre in May; even without the festival's other five plays, it is marvellous to have it here. I am now more aware of the moments when Beth and Duff seem to draw near to each other in thought, and of the weight of grief that hangs over him. But the slightest nuance here—the slightest turn of a head, the connection of two consonants, the beat of her eyelids, the silence in the air—is full of meaning.

ALAN AYCKBOURN

1939–

When Alan Ayckbourn's *Absent Friends* opened in London in July 1975, it became his fifth play to run simultaneously in the West End, joining his trilogy, *The Norman Conquests* (London, 1974), and his long-running play, *Absurd Person Singular* (London, 1973)—a remarkable achievement in contemporary commercial theater, yet not entirely surprising for England's most prolific dramatist, who has written sixty full-length plays. Ayckbourn began writing as a young boy, using a typewriter given to him by his mother, an author of stories for women's magazines. His interest in theater was kindled by Edgar Matthews, a teacher, who directed Shakespeare productions for the schoolboys at Haileybury, toured with them during the summer, and used his theatrical contacts to get the seventeen-year-old Ayckbourn his first job in professional theater, playing small roles and serving as an assistant stage manager. In 1957, after spending a year with different repertory companies, Ayckbourn moved to Scarborough, a resort town on England's northeast coast, to work with Stephen Joseph, the pioneer of theater-in-the-round in England and a supporter of young playwrights. In Scarborough, Ayckbourn became not only a skilled actor but started writing plays as well. In 1970, following Joseph's death, Ayckbourn took over as artistic director in Scarborough. By that time he had already spent five years working with the BBC in Leeds and already had two major successes, *Relatively Speaking* (1965) and *How the Other Half Loves* (1969), plays that had opened originally in Scarborough and then transferred to London. Ayckbourn continues to write and direct his own scripts in Scarborough, usually staging a new play each year. Over half of those plays have been successful enough to transfer to London, often with an entirely new cast and a new director. When Ayckbourn isn't writing—and he allots approximately a month each year for each new play—he directs, both in Scarborough and elsewhere. Knighted in 1997 for "services to theater," Ayckbourn has created a highly successful body of work that combines comedy and pain. Talking to Michael Billington, drama critic for the *Guardian,* Ayckbourn emphasized the necessity of entertaining the audience: "In the end we say that if your message is an empty theatre it is useless. Let's see how clever we can be at saying unpalatable things in a palatable manner."

Ayckbourn's social comedies rely on crucial misunderstandings that are amusing and compelling, and that usually reveal and explore problematic human relationships, especially between men and women. In *Relatively Speaking,* the character Greg thinks that his girlfriend Ginny is going away to visit her parents, Philip and Sheila. However, Philip is actually Ginny's ex-lover. Philip, meanwhile, believes that Sheila is having an affair and assumes that Greg, who has come to propose to Ginny, is Sheila's lover. In *Round and Round the Garden* (one of the three plays in *The Norman Conquests*), Norman's wife, Ruth, tries to persuade Tom, the rather dense local veterinarian, to pay more attention to her younger sister, Annie; Ruth ends up convincing Tom that she is madly in love with him, a situation that not only embarrasses Tom and Ruth but hurts Annie further. And in *Absurd Person Singular,* Eva spends the entire second act trying to commit suicide, only to have each of her attempts foiled by someone who has no idea of what she is really trying to do. As each of these examples suggests—and one could find many more in Ayckbourn's plays—misunderstanding can stem from personal frustration or unhappiness, and yet create comedy on stage.

Frequently such misunderstanding is the result not only of a lack of awareness or intelligence, but of the persistence with which his characters cling to social rituals. Ayckbourn is fascinated with the power of such rituals, as can be seen by the number of plays set at particular holidays, such as the three Christmas Eve parties of *Absurd Person Singular,* the four birthday parties of *Just Between Ourselves* (1976), and the family Christmas gathering of *Season's Greetings* (1980). Even more extraordinary is the comic mileage Ayckbourn gets from smaller social occasions, especially those that involve food. Two unforgettable family picnics provide a major source of comedy in *Sisterly Feelings* (1979) as the sandwiches prepared for eight characters, one of whom is a vegetarian, are repeatedly handed out, tallied, and then reshuffled. In *Table Manners* (part of *The Norman Conquests*), Ayckbourn stages a dinner scene where characters who do not wish to be together must nonetheless pretend that they are enjoying a totally inadequate meal. And in *How the Other Half Loves,* two very different couples, in different houses, occupy the stage at the same time with overlapping set pieces, thus making possible the scene in which a third couple has dinner simultaneously on Thursday and Friday night, swivelling in their chairs to address their respective hosts.

The technical tour-de-force of staging and acting represented in the dual dinner scene is but one example of the clever experimentation that is a major feature of Ayckbourn's playwriting. Following *How the Other Half Loves,* Ayckbourn turned to writing plays built around the same group of characters. In *The Norman Conquests,* Ayckbourn sets all three plays on the same weekend, and structures them so that when a character exits, say, the dining room of *Table Manners,* he or she may then walk into the living room of the same house (in *Living Together*) or into the garden *(Round and Round the Garden).* Each play is complete in itself, but is also intertwined with the other two, forming, in Michael Billington's words "a rueful, eight-hour comedy." The logical extension of the premise behind *The Norman Conquests*—that two other plays were going on simultaneously—came in 1999 with *House & Garden,* two plays written to be performed simultaneously in two connected auditoria. In these plays the same actors must dash between the two locations while stage managers communicate constantly by telephone so that music and lighting cues can be extended or shortened as needed.

Though Ayckbourn sets elaborate challenges for himself and his actors, his main goal of dramatizing "unpalatable things in a palatable manner" is fully evident in *Absurd Person Singular,* the play Michael Billington calls "the Big One. The one that shows his fascination with the desperation behind English social rituals interlocking with his well-oiled comic craft." Ayckbourn's emphasis on that craft is evident in his comments on the first production (see his commentary following the play), especially his sense that "It seemed an interesting solution to set the scene apparently in the wrong room, i.e. their kitchen." And each kitchen reflects a different social class: the clean and modern kitchen of the upwardly mobile

Sidney and Jane, the "trendy homespun" look favored by Geoffrey and Eva, and the old Victorian kitchen, somewhat modernized, of Ronald and Marion. Ayckbourn develops the changing personal and social relationships not only through setting, but through actions that may seem trivial at first, but point to deeper problems. For example, Eva's pill-taking in Act 1 is, we later realize, a warning of her suicide attempts in Act 2; and Marion's search for a stronger drink at Sidney and Jane's presages her descent into full alcoholism in Act 3. The ever-darkening tone of the play reportedly led its American producer to ask Ayckbourn to shift the second and third acts around so that audiences would leave the theater laughing. But Ayckbourn's structure cleverly escalates the notion of despair: Jane's panic at being caught without her party shoes is funny (Figure 1); Eva's attempts to kill herself are not funny, but the fact that her guests both fail to notice what she's doing and repeatedly thwart her efforts generates the play's most hilarious moments (Figure 2); Sidney's preparation of party games when he is the host seems silly in Act 1, but in the play's final moments, his insistence that the other two couples join in a version of musical chairs, dancing around a cold and cheerless kitchen (Figure 3), becomes almost demonic. Thus, in Ayckbourn's world, social rituals become exercises in power, their cruelty underlined by the laughter they generate.

ABSURD PERSON SINGULAR

BY ALAN AYCKBOURN

CHARACTERS

SIDNEY
JANE
RONALD
MARION
GEOFFREY
EVA

SCENE

Act 1 Sidney and Jane's kitchen. Last Christmas
Act 2 Geoffrey and Eva's kitchen. This Christmas
Act 3 Ronald and Marion's kitchen. Next Christmas

ACT 1

(SIDNEY *and* JANE HOPCROFT's *kitchen of their small suburban house. Last Christmas. Although on a modest scale, it is a model kitchen. Whilst not containing all the gadgetry, it does have an automatic washing machine, a fridge, an electric cooker° and a gleaming sink unit. All these are contained or surrounded by smart formica-topped working surfaces with the usual drawers and cupboards. The room also contains a small table, also formica-topped, and matching chairs.*

When the curtain rises, JANE, *a woman in her thirties, is discovered bustling round wiping the floor, cupboard doors, working surfaces—in fact, anything in sight—with a cloth. She sings happily as she works. She wears a pinafore° and bedroom slippers, but, under this, a smart new party dress. She is unimaginatively made up and her hair is tightly permed. She wears rubber gloves to protect her hands.*

As JANE *works,* SIDNEY *enters, a small dapper man of about the same age. He has a small trimmed moustache and a cheery, unflappable manner. He wears his best, rather old-fashioned, sober suit. A dark tie, polished hair and shoes complete the picture.*)

SIDNEY: Hallo, hallo. What are we up to out here, eh?

JANE (*without pausing in her work*): Just giving it a wipe.

SIDNEY: Dear oh dear. Good gracious me. Does it need it? Like a battleship. Just like a battleship. They need you in the Royal Navy.

JANE (*giggling*): Silly . . .

SIDNEY: No—the Royal Navy.

JANE: Silly . . .

(SIDNEY *goes to the back door, turns the yale knob, opens it and sticks his hand out.*)

SIDNEY: Still raining, I see.

JANE: Shut the door, it's coming in.

SIDNEY: Cats and dogs. Dogs and cats. (*He shuts the door, wiping his wet hand on his handkerchief. Striding to the centre of the room and staring up at his digital clock*) Eighteen-twenty-three.° (*Consulting his watch*) Eighteen-twenty-three. Getting on. Seven minutes—they'll be here.

JANE: Oh. (*She straightens up and looks round the kitchen for somewhere she's missed.*)

SIDNEY: I've got a few games lined up.

JANE: Games?

SIDNEY: Just in case.

JANE: Oh good.

SIDNEY: I've made a parcel for "Pass the Parcel," sorted out a bit of music for musical bumps and thought out a few forfeits.

JANE: Good.

SIDNEY: I've thought up some real devils. (*He puts his leg on the table.*)

JANE: I bet. (*She knocks his leg off, and wipes.*)

SIDNEY: Just in case. Just in case things need jollying up. (*Seeing* JANE *still wiping*) I don't want to disappoint you but we're not going to be out here for our drinks, you know.

JANE: Yes, I know.

SIDNEY: The way you're going . . .

JANE: They might want to look . . .

SIDNEY: I doubt it.

JANE: The ladies might.

SIDNEY (*chuckling knowingly*): I don't imagine the wife of a banker will particularly choose to spend her evening in our kitchen. Smart as it is.

JANE: No?

SIDNEY: I doubt if she spends very much time in her own kitchen. Let alone ours.

JANE: Still . . .

---

cooker, stove.   *pinafore*, apron.

Eighteen-twenty-three, 6:23 P.M. (24-hour clock system).

SIDNEY: Very much the lady of leisure, Mrs Brewster-Wright. Or so I would imagine.

JANE: What about Mrs Jackson?

SIDNEY *(doubtfully)*: Well—again, not a woman you think of in the same breath as you would a kitchen.

JANE: All women are interested in kitchens. *(She turns to the sink.)*

SIDNEY *(ironically)*: Oh, if you're looking for a little job . . .

JANE: What's that?

SIDNEY: A small spillage. My fault.

JANE *(very alarmed)*: Where?

SIDNEY: In there. On the sideboard.

JANE: Oh, Sidney. *(She snatches up an assortment of cloths, wet and dry.)*

SIDNEY: Nothing serious.

JANE: Honestly.

(SIDNEY goes to the back door, opens it, sticks a hand out.)

SIDNEY: Dear oh dear. *(He closes the door and dries his hand on his handkerchief.)*

JANE *(returning)*: Honestly.

SIDNEY: Could you see it?

JANE: You spoil that surface if you leave it. You leave a ring. *(She returns her dish cloth to the sink, her dry cloths to the drawer and now takes out a duster and a tin of polish.)* Now that room's going to smell of polish. I had the windows open all day so it wouldn't.

SIDNEY: Well then, don't polish.

JANE: I have to polish. There's a mark. *(She goes to the door and then pauses.)* I know, bring the air freshener.

SIDNEY: Air freshener?

JANE: Under the sink.

(JANE exits.)

SIDNEY: Ay, ay, Admiral. *(He whistles a sailor's horn-pipe, amused.)* Dear oh dear. *(He opens the cupboard under the sink, rummages and brings out an aerosol tin. He is one of those men who like to read all small print. This he does, holding the tin at arm's length to do so. Reading)* "Shake can before use." *(He does so. Reading)* "Remove cap." *(He does so. Reading)* "Hold away from body and spray into air by depressing button." *(He holds the can away from his body, points it in the air and depresses the button. The spray hisses out over his shirt front.)* Dear oh dear *(He puts down the tin, wipes his shift-front with a dishcloth.)*

(JANE enters.)

JANE: What are you doing?

SIDNEY: Just getting this to rights. Just coming to terms with your air freshener.

JANE: That's the fly spray.

SIDNEY: Ah.

JANE: Honestly. *(She takes the canister from him and puts it on top of the washing machine.)*

SIDNEY: My mistake.

JANE: For someone who's good at some things you're hopeless.

SIDNEY: Beg your pardon, Admiral, beg your pardon.

(JANE puts away the duster and polish.)

(Checking his watch with the clock) Four and a half minutes to go.

JANE: And you've been at those nuts, haven't you?

SIDNEY: Nuts?

JANE: In there. In the bowl. On the table. Those nuts. You know the ones I mean.

SIDNEY: I may have had a little dip. Anyway, how did you know I'd been at those nuts? Eh? How did you know, old eagle-eye?

JANE: Because I know how I left them. Now come on, out of my way. Don't start that. I've got things to do.

SIDNEY *(closing with her)*: What about a kiss then?

JANE *(trying to struggle free)*: Sidney . . .

SIDNEY: Come on. Christmas kiss.

JANE: Sidney. No, not now. What's the matter with you? Sidney . . . *(She pauses, sniffing)*

SIDNEY: What's the matter now?

JANE: What's that smell?

SIDNEY: Eh?

JANE: It's on your tie. What's this smell on your tie?

(They both sniff his tie.)

There. Can you smell?

SIDNEY: Oh, that'll be the fly spray.

JANE: Fly spray?

SIDNEY: Had a bit of a backfire.

JANE: It's killed off your after-shave.

SIDNEY *(jovially)*: As long as it hasn't killed off my flies, eh.

(He laughs.)
(JANE laughs.)

(Suddenly cutting through this) Eighteen-twenty-eight. Two minutes.

JANE *(nervous again)*: I hope everything's all right.

SIDNEY: When?

JANE: For them. I want it to be right.

SIDNEY: Of course it's right.

JANE: I mean. I don't want you to be let down. Not by me. I want it to look good for you. I don't want to let you down . . .

SIDNEY: You never have yet . . .

JANE: No, but it's special tonight, isn't it? I mean, with Mr and Mrs Brewster-Wright and Mr and Mrs Jackson. It's important.

SIDNEY: Don't forget Dick and Lottie Potter. They're coming, too.

JANE: Oh, well, I don't count Dick and Lottie. They're friends.

SIDNEY: I trust by the end of this evening, we shall all

be friends. Just don't get nervous. That's all. Don't get nervous. (*He consults the clock and checks it with his watch.*) One minute to go.

(*A slight pause. The front door chimes sound.*)

What was that?

JANE: The front door.

SIDNEY: They're early. Lucky we're ready for them.

JANE: Yes. (*In a sudden panic*) I haven't sprayed the room.

SIDNEY: All right, all right. You can do it whilst I'm letting them in. Plenty of time.

JANE: It doesn't take a second.

(JANE *snatches up the air freshener and follows* SIDNEY *out into the sitting-room. A silence.* JANE *comes hurrying back into the kitchen.*)

(JANE *puts away the air freshener, removes her pinny, straightens her clothing and hair in the mirror, creeps back to the kitchen door and opens it a chink. Voices are heard—*SIDNEY*'s and two others. One is a jolly hearty male voice and one a jolly hearty female voice. They are* DICK *and* LOTTIE POTTER, *whom we have the good fortune never to meet in person, but quite frequently hear whenever the door to the kitchen is open. Both have loud, braying distinctive laughs.* JANE *closes the door, cutting off the voices, straightens her hair and dress for the last time, looks at a mirror on the wall, grips the door handle, takes a deep breath, is about to make her entrance into the room when she sees she is still wearing her bedroom slippers.*)

Oh.

(*She takes off her slippers, puts them on the table and scuttles round the kitchen looking for her shoes. She cannot find them. She picks up the slippers and wipes the table with their fluffy side, where they have made a mark.*)

Oh.

(*She hurries back to the door, opens it a fraction. Jolly chatter and laughter is heard.* JANE *stands for a long time, peeping through the crack in the door, trying to catch sight of her shoes. She sees them. She closes the door again. She stands lost.*)

Oh. Oh. Oh.

(*The door opens. Loud laughter from off.* SIDNEY *comes in laughing. He closes the door. The laughter cuts off abruptly.*)

SIDNEY (*fiercely, in a low voice*): Come on. What are you doing?

JANE: I can't.

SIDNEY: What?

JANE: I've got no shoes.

SIDNEY: What do you mean, no shoes?

JANE: They're in there.

SIDNEY: Where?

JANE: By the fireplace. I left them so I could slip them on.

SIDNEY: Well, then, why didn't you?

JANE: I didn't have time. I forgot.

SIDNEY: Well, come and get them.

JANE: No . . .

SIDNEY: It's only Dick and Lottie Potter.

JANE: You fetch them.

SIDNEY: I can't fetch them.

JANE: Yes, you can. Pick them up and bring them in here.

SIDNEY: But I . . .

JANE: Sidney, please.

SIDNEY: Dear oh dear. What a start. I say, what a start. (*He opens the door cautiously and listens. Silence*) They've stopped talking.

JANE: Have they?

SIDNEY: Wondering where we are, no doubt.

JANE: Well, go in. Here.

SIDNEY: What?

JANE (*handing him her slippers*): Take these.

SIDNEY: What do I do with these?

JANE: The hall cupboard.

SIDNEY: You're really expecting rather a lot tonight, aren't you?

JANE: I'm sorry.

SIDNEY: Yes, well it's got to stop. It's got to stop. I have to entertain out there, you know. (*He opens the door and starts laughing heartily as he does so.*)

(SIDNEY *goes out, closing the door.*)

(JANE *hurries about nervously, making still more adjustments to her person and checking her appearance in the mirror.*)

(*At length the door opens, letting in a bellow of laughter.* SIDNEY *returns, carrying* JANE*'s shoes.*)

(*Behind him*) Yes, I will. I will. I'll tell her that, Dick . . . (*He laughs until he's shut the door. His laugh cuts off abruptly. Thrusting* JANE*'s shoes at her, ungraciously*) Here.

JANE: Oh, thank goodness.

SIDNEY: Now for heaven's sake, come in.

JANE (*struggling into her shoes*): Yes, I'm sorry. What did Dick say?

SIDNEY: When?

JANE: Just now? That you told him you'd tell me.

SIDNEY: I really can't remember. Now then, are you ready?

JANE: Yes, yes.

SIDNEY: It's a good job it's only Dick and Lottie out there. It might have been the Brewster-Wrights. I'd have had a job explaining this to them. Walking in and out like a shoe salesman. All right?

JANE: Yes.

SIDNEY: Right. (*He throws open the door, jovially.*) Here she is. (*Pushing* JANE *ahead of him*) Here she is at last.

(Heart cries of "Ah ha" from DICK *and* LOTTIE*)*

JANE *(going in):* Here I am.

(JANE *and* SIDNEY *exit.*)

SIDNEY *(closing the door behind him):* At last.

(A silence. A long one)
        (SIDNEY *returns to the kitchen. Conversation is heard as he opens and closes the door. He starts hunting round the kitchen opening drawers and not bothering to shut them. After a second, the door opens again, and* JANE *comes in.*)

JANE *(as she enters):* Yes, well you say that to Lottie, not to me. I don't want to know that . . . *(She closes the door.)* What are you doing? Oh, Sidney, what are you doing? *(She hurries round after him, closing the drawers.)*
SIDNEY: Bottle-opener. I'm trying to find the bottle-opener. I can't get the top off Lottie's bitter lemon.°
JANE: It's in there.
SIDNEY: In there?
JANE: Why didn't you ask me?
SIDNEY: Where in there?
JANE: On the mantelpiece.
SIDNEY: The mantelpiece?
JANE: It looks nice on the mantelpiece.
SIDNEY: It's no use having a bottle-opener on a mantelpiece, is it? I mean, how am I. . . ?

(The door chimes sound.)

JANE: Somebody else.
SIDNEY: All right, I'll go. You open the bitter lemon. With gin.
JANE: Gin and bitter lemon.
SIDNEY: And shake the bottle first.

(SIDNEY *opens the door. Silence from the room. He goes out, closing it.*)

JANE *(to herself):* Gin and bitter lemon—shake the bottle first—gin and bitter lemon—shake the bottle first . . . *(She returns to the door and opens it very slightly. There can now be heard the chatter of five voices. She closes the door and feverishly straightens herself.)*

(The door opens a crack and SIDNEY's *nose appears. Voices are heard behind him.)*

SIDNEY *(hissing):* It's them.
JANE: Mr and Mrs Brewster-Wright?
SIDNEY: Yes, Ronald and Marion. Come in.
JANE: Ronald and Marion.

---

bitter lemon, soft drink, mixture of lemon soda and tonic.

SIDNEY: Come in.

(SIDNEY *opens the door wider, grabs her arm, jerks her through the door and closes it.*)

JANE *(as she is dragged in):* Gin and bitter lemon—shake the bottle first . . .

(Silence. Another fairly long one. The door bursts open and JANE *comes rushing out.*)
(Murmur of voices)

(Over her shoulder) Wait there! Just wait there! *(She dashes to the sink and finds a tea towel and two dish cloths.)*

(RONALD, *a man in his mid-forties, enters. Impressive without being distinguished. He is followed by an anxious* SIDNEY. RONALD *is holding one leg of his trousers away from his body. He has evidently got drenched.*)

SIDNEY: Oh dear oh dear. I'm terribly sorry.
RONALD: That's all right. Can't be helped.
JANE: Here's a cloth.
RONALD: Oh, thank you—yes, yes. *(He takes the tea towel.)* I'll just use this one, if you don't mind.
SIDNEY: Well, what a start, eh? What a grand start to the evening. *(With a laugh)* Really, Jane.
JANE: I'm terribly sorry. I didn't realize it was going to splash like that.
RONALD: Well, tricky things, soda siphons. You either get a splash or a dry gurgle. Never a happy medium.
JANE: Your nice suit.
RONALD: Good God, it's only soda water. Probably do it good, eh?
JANE: I don't know about that.
RONALD *(returning the tea towel):* Thanks very much. Well, it's wet enough outside there. I didn't expect to get wet inside as well.
SIDNEY: No, no . . .
JANE: Terribly sorry.
RONALD: Accidents happen. Soon dry out. I'll run around for a bit.
SIDNEY: I'll tell you what. I could let you have a pair of my trousers from upstairs just while yours dry.
JANE: Oh, yes.
RONALD: No, no. That's all right. I'll stick with these. Hate to break up the suit, eh? *(He laughs.)*

(So do SIDNEY *and* JANE.*)*
*(MARION, *a well-groomed woman, a little younger than* RONALD *and decidedly better preserved, comes in.*)*

MARION: All right, darling?
RONALD: Yes, yes.
MARION: Oh! *(She stops short in the doorway.)* Isn't this gorgeous? Isn't this enchanting.
JANE: Oh.
MARION: What a simply dishy kitchen. *(To* JANE*)* Aren't you lucky.

JANE: Well . . .

MARION: It's so beautifully arranged. Ronnie, don't you agree? Isn't this splendid.

RONALD: Ah.

MARION: Just look at these working surfaces and you must have a gorgeous view from that window, I imagine.

SIDNEY: Well . . .

MARION: It must be stunning. You must look right over the fields at the back.

SIDNEY: No—no.

JANE: No, we just look into next door's fence.

MARION: Well, which way are the fields?

JANE: I've no idea.

MARION: How extraordinary. I must be thinking of somewhere else.

SIDNEY: Mind you, we've got a good ten yards to the fence . . .

RONALD: On a clear day, eh?

SIDNEY: Beg pardon?

MARION: Oh look, Ronnie, do come and look at these cupboards.

RONALD: Eh?

MARION: Look at these, Ronnie. (*Opening and shutting the cupboard doors*) They're so easy to open and shut.

JANE: Drawers—here, you see . . .

MARION: Drawers! (*Opening them*) Oh, lovely deep drawers. Put all sorts of things in these, can't you? And then just shut if up and forget them.

SIDNEY: Yes, yes, they're handy for that . . .

MARION: No, it's these cupboards. I'm afraid I really do envy you these. Don't you envy them, Ronnie?

RONALD: I thought we had cupboards.

MARION: Yes, darling, but they're nothing like these. Just open and shut that door. It's heaven.

RONALD (*picking up a booklet from the counter*): Cupboard's a cupboard. (*He sits and reads.*)

JANE (*proudly*): Look. (*Going to the washing machine*) Sidney's Christmas present to me . . .

MARION (*picking up the air freshener from the top of the washing machine*): Oh lovely. What is it? Hair spray?

SIDNEY: No, no. That's the fly spray, no. My wife meant the machine. (*He takes the spray from her and puts it down.*)

MARION: Machine?

JANE: Washing machine. Here . . .

MARION: Oh, that's a washing machine. Tucked under there. How thrilling. What a marvellous Christmas present.

JANE: Well, yes.

MARION: Do tell me, how did you manage to keep it a surprise from her?

SIDNEY: Well . . .

MARION: I mean, don't tell me he hid it or wrapped it up. I don't believe it.

SIDNEY: No, I just arranged for the men to deliver it and plumb it in.

JANE: They flooded the kitchen.

MARION: Super.

JANE: You see, it's the automatic. It's got—all the programmes° and then spin-drying and soak.

MARION: Oh, good heavens. Ronnie, come here at once and see this.

RONALD (*reading avidly*): Just coming . . .

MARION (*bending to read the dial*): What's this? Whites—coloureds—my God, it's apartheid.

JANE: Beg pardon?

MARION: What's this? Minimum icon? What on earth is that?

JANE: No, minimum iron.

MARION: Don't tell me it does the ironing too.

JANE: Oh, no, it . . .

MARION: Ronnie, have you seen this extraordinary machine?

RONALD: Yes. Yes . . .

MARION: It not only does your washing and your whites and your blacks and your coloureds and so on, it does your ironing.

SIDNEY: No, no . . .

JANE: No . . .

MARION (*to* JANE): We shall soon be totally redundant. (*She picks up the spray and fires it into the air and inhales.*) What a poignant smell. It's almost too good to waste on flies, isn't it. Now where. . . ? It's a little like your husband's gorgeous cologne, surely?

JANE: Oh, well . . .

(*The doorbell chimes.*)

MARION: Oh, good gracious. What was that? Does that mean your shirts are cooked or something.

SIDNEY: No, front doorbell.

MARION: Oh, I see. How pretty.

SIDNEY: Somebody else arrived.

JANE: Yes, I'd better . . .

SIDNEY: Won't be a minute.

JANE: No, I'll go.

SIDNEY: No . . .

JANE: No, I'll go.

(JANE *hurries out, closing the door.*)

MARION: I do hope your Mr and Mrs Potter don't feel terribly abandoned in there. They're splendidly jolly, blooming people, aren't they?

SIDNEY: Yes, Dick's a bit of a laugh.

MARION: Enormous. Now, you must tell me one thing, Mr Hopcraft. How on earth did you squeeze that machine so perfectly under the shelf? Did you try them for size or were you terribly lucky?

---

programmes, cycles on the washing machine.

SIDNEY: No, I went out and measured the machine in the shop.

MARION: Oh, I see.

SIDNEY: And then I made the shelf, you see. So it was the right height.

MARION: No, I mean how on earth did you know it was going to be right?

SIDNEY: Well, that's the way I built it.

MARION: No. You don't mean this is you?

SIDNEY: Yes, yes. Well, the shelf is.

MARION: Ronnie!

RONALD: Um?

MARION: Ronnie, darling, what are you reading?

RONALD (*vaguely consulting the cover of his book*): Er . . .

SIDNEY: Ah, that'll be the instruction book for the stove.

RONALD: Oh, is that what it is. I was just trying to work out what I was reading. Couldn't make head or tail.

MARION: Darling, did you hear what Mr Hop—er . . .

SIDNEY: Hopcroft.

MARION: Sidney, isn't it? Sidney was saying. . . ?

RONALD: What?

MARION: Darling, Sidney built this shelf on his own. He went out and measured the machine, got all his screws and nails and heaven knows what and built this shelf himself.

RONALD: Good Lord.

SIDNEY: I've got some more shelves upstairs. For the bedside. And also, I've partitioned off part of the spare bedroom as a walk-in cupboard for the wife. And I'm just about to panel the landing with those knotty pine units, have you seen them?

MARION: Those curtains are really the most insistent colour I've ever seen. They must just simply cry out to be drawn in the morning.

(JANE *sticks her head round the door.*)

JANE: Dear—it's Mr and Mrs Jackson.

SIDNEY: Oh. Geoff and Eva, is it? Right, I'll be in to say hallo.

MARION: Geoff and Eva Jackson?

SIDNEY: Yes. Do you know them?

MARION: Oh yes. Rather. Darling, it's Geoff and Eva Jackson.

RONALD: Geoff and Eva who?

MARION: The Jacksons.

RONALD: Oh, Geoff and Eva Jackson. (*He goes and studies the washing machine.*)

MARION: That's nice, isn't it?

RONALD: Yes?

JANE: Are you coming in?

SIDNEY: Yes, yes.

MARION: Haven't seen them for ages.

JANE: They've left the dog in the car.

SIDNEY: Oh, good.

MARION: Have they a dog?

JANE: Yes.

MARION: Oh, how lovely. We must see him.

JANE: He's—very big . . .

SIDNEY: Yes, well, lead on, dear.

(JANE *opens the door. A burst of conversation from the sitting room.* JANE *goes out.* SIDNEY *holds the door open for* MARION, *sees she is not following him and torn between his duties as a host, follows* JANE *off.*)

We'll be in here. (*He closes the door.*)

MARION: Ronnie . . .

RONALD (*studying the washing machine*): Mm?

MARION: Come along, darling.

RONALD: I was just trying to work out how this thing does the ironing. Don't see it at all. Just rolls it into a ball.

MARION: Darling, do come on.

RONALD: I think that woman's got it wrong.

MARION: Darling . . .

RONALD: Um?

MARION: Make our excuses quite shortly, please.

RONALD: Had enough, have you?

MARION: We've left the boys . . .

RONALD: They'll be all right.

MARION: What's that man's name?

RONALD: Hopcraft, do you mean?

MARION: No, the other one.

RONALD: Oh, Potter, isn't it?

MARION: Well, I honestly don't think I can sit through many more of his jokes.

RONALD: I thought they were quite funny.

MARION: And I've never had quite such a small gin in my life. Completely drowned.

RONALD: Really? My scotch was pretty strong.

MARION: That's only because she missed the glass with the soda water. Consider yourself lucky.

RONALD: I don't know about lucky. I shall probably have bloody° rheumatism in the morning.

(SIDNEY *sticks his head round the door. Laughter and chatter behind him.*)

SIDNEY: Er—Mrs Brewster-Wright, I wonder if you'd both . . .

MARION: Oh, yes, we're just coming. We can't tear ourselves away from your divine kitchen, can we, Ronnie? (*Turning to* RONALD, *holding up the fingers of one hand and mouthing.*) Five minutes.

RONALD: Righto.

(*They all go out, closing the door.*)
(*Silence*)
(JANE *enters with an empty bowl. She hurries to the cupboard and takes out a jumbo bag of crisps° and pours them into the bowl. She is turning to leave when the door opens again and* SIDNEY *hurries in, looking a little fraught.*)

---

bloody, familiar British swear word.   **crisps,** potato chips.

SIDNEY: Tonic water. We've run out.

JANE: Tonic water. Down there in the cupboard.

SIDNEY: Right.

JANE: Do you think it's going all right?

SIDNEY: Fine, fine. Now get back, get back there.

JANE (*as she goes*): Will you ask Lottie to stop eating all these crisps? Nobody else has had any.

(JANE *goes out closing the door behind her.*)
(SIDNEY *searches first one cupboard, then another, but cannot find any tonic.*)

SIDNEY: Oh dear, oh dear.

(SIDNEY *hurries back to the party closing the door behind him. After a second* JANE *enters looking worried, closing the door behind her.*)
(*She searches where* SIDNEY *has already searched. She finds nothing.*)

JANE: Oh. (*She wanders in rather aimless circles round the kitchen.*)

(SIDNEY *enters with a glass with gin and a slice of lemon in it. He closes the door.*)

SIDNEY: Is it there?

JANE: Yes, yes. Somewhere . . .

SIDNEY: Well, come along. She's waiting.

JANE: I've just—got to find it. . . .

SIDNEY: Oh dear, oh dear.

JANE: I tidied them away somewhere.

SIDNEY: Well, there was no point in tidying them away, was there? We're having a party.

JANE: Well—it just looked—tidier. You go back in, I'll bring them.

SIDNEY: Now that was your responsibility. We agreed buying the beverages was your department. I hope you haven't let us down.

JANE: No. I'm sure I haven't.

SIDNEY: Well, it's very embarrassing for me in the meanwhile, isn't it? Mrs Brewster-Wright is beginning to give me anxious looks.

JANE: Oh.

SIDNEY: Well then.

(SIDNEY *goes back in.*)
(JANE *stands helplessly. She gives a little whimper of dismay. She is on the verge of tears. Then a sudden decision. She goes to a drawer. Reaches to the back and brings out her housekeeping purse. She opens it and takes out some coins. She runs to the centre of the room and looks at the clock.*)

JANE: Nineteen-twenty-one. (*Hurried calculation*) Thirteen—fourteen—fifteen—sixteen—seventeen—eighteen—nineteen . . . seven-twenty-two. (*She hurries to the back door and opens it. She holds out her hand, takes a tentative step out and then a hasty step back again. She is again in a dilemma. She closes the back door. She goes to the cupboard just inside the door and, after rummaging about, she emerges holding a*

pair of men's large wellington boots in one hand and a pair of plimsolls° in the other. Mentally tossing up between them, she returns the plimsolls to the cupboard. She slips off her own shoes and steps easily into the wellingtons. She puts her own shoes neatly in the cupboard and rummages again. She pulls out a large man's gardening raincoat. She holds it up, realizes it's better than nothing and puts it on. She hurries back to the centre of the room buttoning it as she does so.*) Nineteen-twenty-four. (*She returns to the back door, opens it and steps out. It is evidently pelting down. She stands in the doorway holding up the collar of the coat and ineffectually trying to protect her hairdo from the rain with the other hand. Frantically*) Oh . . . (*She dives back into the cupboard and re-emerges with an old trilby° hat. She looks at it in dismay. After a moment's struggle she puts it on and hurries back to the centre of the room.*) Twenty-five.

(JANE *returns to the back door, hesitates for a second and then plunges out into the night, leaving the door only very slightly ajar. After a moment,* SIDNEY *returns still clutching the glass.*)

SIDNEY: Jane? Jane! (*He looks round, puzzled.*) Good gracious me. (*He peers around for her.*)

(EVA *comes in. In her thirties, she makes no concessions in either manner or appearance.*)

EVA: May I have a glass of water?

SIDNEY: Beg your pardon?

EVA: I have to take these. (*She holds out a couple of tablets enclosed in a sheet of tinfoil. She crosses to the back door and stands taking deep breaths of fresh air.*)

SIDNEY: Oh, yes. There's a glass here somewhere, I think.

EVA: Thanks.

SIDNEY (*finding a tumbler*): Here we are. (*He puts it down on the washing machine.*)

(EVA *stands abstractedly staring ahead of her, tearing at the paper round the pills without any effort to open them. A pause.* SIDNEY *looks at her.*)

Er . . .

EVA: What? Oh, thanks. (*She closes the back door and picks up the glass.*)

SIDNEY: Not ill, I hope?

EVA: What?

SIDNEY: The pills. Not ill?

EVA: It depends what you mean by ill, doesn't it?

SIDNEY: Ah.

EVA: If you mean do they prevent me from turning into a raving lunatic, the answer's probably yes. (*She laughs somewhat bitterly.*)

---

plimsolls, cheap rubber-soled canvas shoes.   **trilby,** soft felt hat.

SIDNEY *(laughing, too)*: Raving lunatic, yes—*(he is none too certain of this lady)*—but then I always say, it helps to be a bit mad, doesn't it? I mean, we're all a bit mad. I'm a bit mad. *(Pause)* Yes. *(Pause)* It's a mad world, as they say.

EVA *(surveying the pills in her hand which she has now opened)*: Extraordinary to think that one's sanity can depend on these. Frightening, isn't it? *(She puts them both in her mouth and swallows the glass of water in one gulp.)* Yuck. Alarming. Do you know I've been taking pills of one sort or another since I was eight years old. What chance does your body have? My husband tells me that even if I didn't need them, I'd still have to take them. My whole mentality is geared round swallowing tablets every three hours, twenty-four hours a day. I even have to set the alarm at night. You're looking at a mess. A wreck. *(She still holds the glass and is searching round absently as she speaks, for somewhere to put it.)* Don't you sometimes long to be out of your body and free? Free just to float? I know I do. *(She opens the pedal bin with her foot and tosses the empty glass into it.)* Thanks.

(She puts the screwed up tinfoil into SIDNEY's hand and starts for the door. SIDNEY gawps at her. EVA pauses.)

My God, was that our car horn?

SIDNEY: When?

EVA: Just now.

SIDNEY: No, I don't think so.

EVA: If you do hear it, it's George.

SIDNEY: George?

EVA: Our dog.

SIDNEY: Oh, yes, of course.

EVA: We left him in the car, you see. We have to leave him in the car these days, he's just impossible. He's all right there, usually, but lately he's been getting bored and he's learnt to push the horn button with his nose. He just rests his nose on the steering-wheel, you see.

SIDNEY: That's clever.

EVA: Not all that clever. We've had the police out twice.

SIDNEY: A bit like children, dogs.

EVA: What makes you say that?

SIDNEY: Need a bit of a firm hand now and again. Smack if they're naughty.

EVA: You don't smack George, you negotiate terms.

SIDNEY: Ah. *(He retrieves the glass from the waste-bin.)*

EVA: He was only this big when we bought him, now he's grown into a sort of yak. When we took him in, he—my God was that me?

SIDNEY: What?

EVA: Did I put the glass in there?

SIDNEY: Er—yes.

EVA: My God, I knew it, I'm going mad. I am finally going mad.

(She goes to the door and opens it.)
(Chatter is heard.)

Will you please tell my husband, if he drinks any more, I'm walking home.

SIDNEY: Well, I think that might be better coming from you as his wife.

EVA *(laughing)*: You really think he'd listen to me? He doesn't even know I'm here. As far as he's concerned, my existence ended the day he married me. I'm just an embarrassing smudge on a marriage licence.

(EVA goes out, closing the door.)

SIDNEY: Ah. *(He puts the glass on the washing machine and finds JANE's discarded shoes on the floor. He picks them up, stares at them and places them on the draining-board. Puzzled, he crosses to the back door and calls out into the night.)* Jane!

(He listens. No reply)
(MARION comes in.)

Jane!

MARION: I say . . .

SIDNEY: Rain . . . *(He holds out his hand by way of demonstration, then closes the back door.)*

MARION: Oh, yes, dreadful. I say, I think you dashed way with my glass.

SIDNEY: Oh, I'm so sorry. *(Handing it to her)* Here.

MARION: Thank you. I was getting terribly apprehensive in case it had gone into your washing machine. *(She sips the drink.)* Oh, that's lovely. Just that teeny bit stronger. You know what I mean. Not too much tonic . . .

SIDNEY: No, well . . .

MARION: Perfect.

SIDNEY: Actually, that's neat gin, that is.

MARION: Oh, good heavens! So it is. What are you trying to do to me? I can see we're going to have to keep an eye on you, Mr—er . . .

SIDNEY: No, no. You're safe enough with me.

MARION: Yes, I'm sure . . .

SIDNEY: The mistletoe's in there.

MARION: Well, what are we waiting for? Lead on, Mr—er . . . *(She ushers him in front of her.)*

SIDNEY: Follow me.

(SIDNEY goes through the door.)

MARION *(as she turns to close it, looking at her watch)*: My God.

(MARION goes out and closes the door.)
(A pause)
(JANE arrives at the back door still in her hat, coat and boots. She is soaking wet. She carries a carton of tonic waters. She rattles the back door knob but she has locked herself out. She knocks gently then louder, but no-one hears her. She rattles the knob again, pressing her face up

against the glass. We see her mouth opening and shouting but no sound. Eventually, she gives up and hurries away. After a second, SIDNEY *returns. He has the crisp bowl which is again empty. He is about to refill it when he pauses and looks round the kitchen, puzzled and slightly annoyed. He goes to the back door and opens it.)*

SIDNEY: Jane! Jane!

(SIDNEY *turns up his jacket collar and runs out, leaving the door ajar.)*

(*As soon as* SIDNEY *has gone, the doorbell chimes. There is a pause, then it chimes again, several times.)*

(RONALD *enters from the sitting-room.)*

RONALD: I say, old boy, I think someone's at your front—oh. *(He sees the empty room and the open back door.)*

(RONALD *turns and goes back into the room.)*

No, he seems to have gone out. I suppose we'd better . . . *(His voice cuts off as he closes the door.)*

(The doorbell chimes once more.)

(SIDNEY *returns, closing the back door. He finds a towel and dabs his face and hair.)*

SIDNEY: Dear oh dear. *(He shakes his head and returns to his crisps. Suddenly, the living-room door bursts open and* JANE *enters hurriedly in her strange garb, her boots squelching. She shuts the door behind her and stands against it, shaking and exhausted.)*

(SIDNEY *turns and throws the bag of crisps into the air in his astonishment.)*

JANE: Oh, my goodness.
SIDNEY: What are you doing?
JANE: Oh.
SIDNEY *(utterly incredulous)*: What do you think you're doing?
JANE *(still breathless)*: I went—I went out—to get the tonic. *(She puts a carton of tonic waters on the table.)*
SIDNEY: Like that?
JANE: I couldn't find—I didn't want . . .
SIDNEY: You went out—and came in again, like that?
JANE: I thought I'd just slip out the back to the off-licence° and slip in again. But I locked myself out. I had to come in the front.
SIDNEY: But who let you in?
JANE *(in a whisper)*: Mr Brewster-Wright.
SIDNEY: Mr Brewster-Wright? Mr Brewster-Wright let you in like that?

(JANE *nods.)*

What did he say?

---

off-licence, store permitted to sell liquor to take away.

JANE: I don't think he recognized me.
SIDNEY: I'm not surprised.
JANE: I couldn't look at him. I just ran straight past him and right through all of them and into here.
SIDNEY: Like that?
JANE: Yes.
SIDNEY: But what did they say?
JANE: They didn't say anything. They just stopped talking and stared and I ran through them. I couldn't very well . . .
SIDNEY: You'll have to go back in there and explain.
JANE: No, I couldn't.
SIDNEY: Of course you must.
JANE: Sidney, I don't think I can face them.
SIDNEY: You can't walk through a respectable cocktail party, the hostess, dressed like that without an apology.
JANE *(on the verge of tears again)*: I couldn't.
SIDNEY *(furious)*: You take off all that—and you go back in there and explain.
JANE *(with a wail)*: I just want to go to bed.
SIDNEY: Well, you cannot go to bed. Not at nineteen-forty-seven. Now, take off that coat.

(JANE *squelches to the cupboard.)*

(RONALD *opens the kitchen door. He is talking over his shoulder as he comes in, carrying a glass of scotch.)*

RONALD: Well I think I'd better, I mean . . .
JANE: Oh, no.

(JANE *has had no time to unbutton her coat. Rather than face* RONALD, *she rushes out of the back door hatless, abandoning her headgear in the middle of the kitchen table.)*

(SIDNEY, *trying to stop* JANE, *lunges after her vainly. The door slams behind her.* SIDNEY *stands with his back to it.)*

RONALD *(in the doorway, having caught a glimpse of violent activity, but unsure what)*: Ah, there you are, old chap.
SIDNEY: Oh, hallo. Hallo.
RONALD: Just popped out, did you?
SIDNEY: Yes, just popped out.
RONALD: Well—something rather odd. Someone at the door just now. Little short chap. Hat, coat, boots and bottles. Just stamped straight through. You catch a glimpse of him?
SIDNEY: Oh, him.
RONALD: Belong here, does he? I mean . . .
SIDNEY: Oh, yes.
RONALD: Ah. Well, as long as you know about him. Might have been after your silver. I mean, you never know. Not these days.
SIDNEY: No, indeed. No, he—he was from the off-licence. *(He shows* RONALD *the carton.)*
RONALD: Really?

SIDNEY: Brought round our order of tonic, you see.

(RONALD *stares at the hat on the table.* SIDNEY *notices and picks it up.*)

Silly fellow. Left his hat. *(He picks up the hat, walks to the back door, opens it and throws out the hat. He closes the door.)*

RONALD: Not the night to forget your hat.

SIDNEY: No, indeed.

RONALD *(Sitting at the table)*: Mind you, frankly, he didn't look all there to me. Wild eyed. That's what made me think . . .

SIDNEY: Quite right.

RONALD: Ought to get him to come round the back, you know. Take a tip from me. Once you let tradesmen into the habit of using your front door, you might as well move out, there and then.

SIDNEY: Well, quite. In my own particular business, I always insist that my staff . . .

RONALD: Oh, yes, of course. I was forgetting you're a—you're in business yourself, aren't you?

SIDNEY: Well, in a small way at the moment. My wife and I. I think I explained . . .

RONALD: Yes, of course. And doing very well.

SIDNEY: Well, for a little general stores, you know. Mustn't grumble.

RONALD: Good to hear someone's making the grade.

SIDNEY: These days.

RONALD: Quite. *(He picks up the booklet and looks at it.)*

(A pause)

SIDNEY: I know this isn't perhaps the moment, I mean it probably isn't the right moment, but none the less, I hope you've been giving a little bit of thought to our chat. The other day. If you've had a moment.

RONALD: Chat? Oh, yes—chat. At the bank? Well, yes, it's—probably not, as you say, the moment but, as I said then—and this is still off the cuff you understand—I think the bank could probably see their way to helping you out.

SIDNEY: Ah well, that's wonderful news. You see, as I envisage it, once I can get the necessary loan, that means I can put in a definite bid for the adjoining site—which hasn't incidentally come on to the market. I mean, as I said, this is all purely through personal contacts.

RONALD: Quite so, yes.

SIDNEY: I mean the site value alone—just taking it as a site—you follow me?

RONALD: Oh, yes.

SIDNEY: But it is a matter of striking while the iron's hot—before it goes off the boil . . .

RONALD: Mmm . . .

SIDNEY: I mean, in this world it's dog eat dog, isn't it? No place for sentiment. Not in business. I mean,

all right, so on occasions you can scratch mine. I'll scratch yours . . .

RONALD: Beg your pardon?

SIDNEY: Tit for tat. But when the chips are down° it's every man for himself and blow you Jack,° I regret to say . . .

RONALD: Exactly.

(The sitting-room door opens. GEOFFREY *enters. Mid-thirties. Good-looking, confident, easy-going. He carries a glass of scotch.)*

GEOFFREY: Ah. Is there a chance of sanctuary here?

RONALD: Hallo.

GEOFFREY: Like Dick Potter's harem in there.

SIDNEY: Dick still at it?

GEOFFREY: Yes. Keeping the ladies amused with jokes . . .

RONALD: Is he? Oh, dear. I'd better—in a minute . . .

GEOFFREY: You'll never stop him. Is he always like that? Or does he just break out at Christmas?

SIDNEY: Oh, no. Dick's a great laugh all the year round . . .

GEOFFREY: Is he?

RONALD: You don't say.

SIDNEY: He's a very fascinating character, is Dick. I thought you'd be interested to meet him. I mean, so's she. In her way. Very colourful. They're both teachers, you know. But he's very involved with youth work of all types. He takes these expeditions off to the mountains. A party of lads. Walks in Scotland. That sort of thing. Wonderful man with youngsters . . .

RONALD: Really?

SIDNEY: Got a lot of facets.

RONALD: Got a good-looking wife . . .

SIDNEY: Lottie? Yes, she's a fine-looking woman. Always very well turned out . . .

GEOFFREY: Yes, she seems to have turned out quite well.

SIDNEY: She does the same as him with girls . . .

RONALD: I beg your pardon?

SIDNEY: Hiking and so on. With the brownies, mainly.

RONALD: Oh, I see.

GEOFFREY: Oh.

(Pause)

RONALD: Better join the brownies, then, hadn't we? *(He laughs.)*

SIDNEY *(at length; laughing)*: Yes, I like that. Better join the brownies. *(He laughs.)* You must tell that to Dick. That would tickle Dick no end.

---

the chips are down, catchphrase, things are final. **blow you, Jack,** catchphrase, I'm done with you.

GEOFFREY *(after a pause)*: Nice pair of legs.

RONALD: Yes.

SIDNEY: Dick?

GEOFFREY: His wife.

SIDNEY: Lottie? Oh, yes. Mind you, I don't think I've really noticed them . . .

GEOFFREY: Usually, when they get to about that age, they tend to go a bit flabby round here. *(He pats his thigh.)* But she's very trim . . .

RONALD: Trim, oh yes.

GEOFFREY: Nice neat little bum . . .

SIDNEY: Ah.

RONALD: Has she? Hadn't seen that.

GEOFFREY: I was watching her, getting up and stretching out for the crisps. Very nice indeed.

RONALD: Oh, well, I'll keep an eye out.

(Pause)

SIDNEY: That'll be the hiking . . .

GEOFFREY: What?

SIDNEY *(tapping his thighs; somewhat self-consciously)*: This—you know. That'll be the hiking . . .

RONALD: Yes. *(After a pause)* How did you happen to see those?

GEOFFREY: What?

RONALD: Her . . . *(He slaps his thighs.)* I mean when I saw her just now she had a great big woolly—thing on. Down to here.

GEOFFREY: Oh, you can get around that.

RONALD: Really?

GEOFFREY: I've been picking imaginary peanuts off the floor round her feet all evening.

(RONALD laughs uproariously. SIDNEY joins in, a little out of his depth.)

RONALD: You'll have to watch this fellow, you know.

SIDNEY: Oh, yes?

RONALD: Don't leave your wife unattended if he's around.

SIDNEY: Oh, no?

RONALD: Lock her away . . .

SIDNEY *(getting the joke at last and laughing)*: Ah-ha! Yes . . .

(JANE suddenly appears outside the back door, peering in.)
(SIDNEY waves her away with urgent gestures.)

GEOFFREY: Still raining, is it?

SIDNEY *(holding out his hand)*: Yes. Yes.

RONALD: I'll tell you what I've been meaning to ask you . . .

GEOFFREY: What's that?

RONALD: Remember that party we were both at—during the summer—Malcolm Freebody's. . . ?

GEOFFREY: When was this?

RONALD: Eva—your wife was off sick . . .

GEOFFREY: That's nothing unusual.

RONALD: I remember it because you were making

tremendous headway with some woman that Freebody was using on his public relations thing. . . .

GEOFFREY: Was I?

RONALD: Blonde. Sort of blonde.

GEOFFREY *(a short thought)*: Binnie.

RONALD: Binnie, was it?

GEOFFREY: Binnie something. I think . . .

RONALD: Make out all right, did you?

GEOFFREY: Well—you know . . .

RONALD: Really?

GEOFFREY: You have no idea. Absolute little cracker.° Married to a steward on P. and O.° Hadn't seen him for eight months . . .

RONALD *(chuckling)*: Good Lord . . .

SIDNEY: Ah—ha—oh—ha—ha-ha. *(And other noises of sexual approval)*

(The others look at him.)

GEOFFREY: What have you done with yours? Buried her in the garden?

SIDNEY *(guiltily)*: What? No, no. She's about. Somewhere.

GEOFFREY: Wish I could lose mine, sometimes. Her and that dog. There's hardly room for me in the flat—I mean between the two of them, they have completely reduced that flat to rubble. I mean I'm very fond of her, bless her, she's a lovely girl—but she just doesn't know what it's all about. She really doesn't.

RONALD: Maybe. I still think you're pretty lucky with Eva . . .

GEOFFREY: Why's that?

RONALD: Well, she must have a jolly good idea by now about your—er . . .

GEOFFREY: Yes. I should imagine she probably has . . .

RONALD: Well, there you are . . .

GEOFFREY: Oh now, come off it. Nonsense. She chooses to live with me, she lives by my rules. I mean we've always made that perfectly clear. She lives her life to a certain extent; I live mine, do what I like within reason. It's the only way to do it . . .

SIDNEY: Good gracious.

RONALD: I wish you'd have a chat with Marion. Convince her.

GEOFFREY: Any time. Pleasure.

RONALD: Yes, well, perhaps not—on second thoughts.

GEOFFREY: No, seriously. Any man, it doesn't matter who he is—you, me, anyone—*(pointing at SIDNEY)*—him. They've just got to get it organized. I mean face it, there's just too much good stuff wandering around simply crying out for it for you not . . .

---

cracker, as in firecracker, i.e., "hot stuff."   ***P. and O.,*** ship company.

(The living-room door opens. EVA *appears. Behind,* DICK POTTER *still in full flow, laughing)*

    (To SIDNEY, *altering his tone immediately)* Anyway, I think that would be a good idea. Don't you?

EVA *(coolly)*: Are you all proposing to stay out here all night?

SIDNEY: Oh, dear. We seem to have neglected the ladies.

EVA: Neglected? We thought we'd been bloody well abandoned.

GEOFFREY: Can't manage without us, you see.

EVA: We can manage perfectly well, thank you. It just seemed to us terribly rude, that's all.

GEOFFREY: Oh, good God . . .

EVA: Anyway. Your jolly friends are leaving.

SIDNEY: Oh, really. Dick and Lottie? I'd better pop out and see them off, then. Excuse me . . .

*(*SIDNEY *goes off to the sitting-room.)*

EVA: And, darling, unless you want to see our car towed away again, horn blazing—we'd better get our coats.

GEOFFREY: He's not at it again . . .

EVA: Past his supper time . . .

GEOFFREY: Oh, honestly, Eva . . .

EVA: Don't honestly Eva me, darling. He's your dog.

GEOFFREY: What do you mean, he's my dog?

EVA *(sweetly)*: Your house, your dog, your car, your wife—we all belong to you, darling—we all expect to be provided for. Now are you coming, please?

*(*RONALD *smiles.)*

    And your wife is looking slightly less than pleased, I might tell you.

*(*RONALD*'s smile fades.)*
*(*EVA *goes out.)*

RONALD: Oh. *(He looks at his watch.)* I suppose I'd better, er . . .

GEOFFREY: Oh. Ronnie. By the way . . .

RONALD: Mmmm?

GEOFFREY: I wondered if you heard anything on the grapevine about the new building Harrison's having put up . . .

RONALD: Oh, this new shopping complex of his.

GEOFFREY: Has he got anyone yet?

RONALD: What, you mean in your line?

GEOFFREY: Yes. Has he settled on an architect? Or is it still open?

RONALD: Well, as far as I know, it's still wide open. I mean, it's still a gleam in his eye as far as I know.

GEOFFREY: Well. If you get a chance to put in a word. I know you're fairly thick with him.

RONALD: Yes, of course, I'll mention it, if the topic comes up. I mean, I'm sure you could do as good a job as anyone.

GEOFFREY: Look, I can design, standing on my head, any building that Harrison's likely to want.

RONALD: Yes, well, as I say, I'll mention it.

GEOFFREY: I'd be grateful . . .

*(*MARION *comes in.)*

RONALD: Ah.

MARION: All right, darling, we're off . . .

RONALD: Right.

MARION: Had a nice time out there?

RONALD: Oh, yes, grand.

MARION: Good. As long as you have . . .

*(*RONALD *goes off into the living-room.)*

    This really is a simply loathsome little house. I mean how can people live in them. I mean, Geoff, you're an architect, you must be able to tell me. How do people come to design these sort of monstrosities in the first place, let alone persuade people to live in them?

GEOFFREY: Well . . .

MARION: Oh, God. Now he's going to tell me he designed it.

GEOFFREY: No. I didn't do it. They're designed like this mainly because of cost and people who are desperate for somewhere to live aren't particularly choosey.

MARION: Oh, come. Nobody can be this desperate.

GEOFFREY: You'd be surprised.

MARION: Anyway, it's been lovely to see you. It's been ages. You must come up and see us . . .

*(*SIDNEY *and* RONALD, *now in his overcoat and carrying* MARION*'s coat, return.)*

RONALD: Darling . . .

MARION: Sidney, we've had a simply lovely time. Now some time you must come up and see us—and your wife, that's if you ever find her . . .

SIDNEY: Yes, yes, indeed . . .

(They all go out, chattering, closing the door.)
(Silence)
(After a pause, SIDNEY *returns. He closes the door.)*

(Rubbing his hands together) Hah! *(He smiles. Quite pleased. He takes up his drink and sips it. He munches a crisp.)*

(There is a knock at the back door—rather tentative. It is JANE.*)*
*(*SIDNEY *frowns. His concentration is disturbed.)*

    Just a minute. *(He opens the back door.)*

*(*JANE *falls in—a sodden mass.)*

(Recoiling) My word.

JANE: I saw them leaving.

SIDNEY: Yes. All gone now. They said for me to say good-bye to you.

JANE: Oh.

SIDNEY: Where have you been?

JANE: In the garden. Where else? Where do you think?

SIDNEY: Oh—I don't know. You might have been for a stroll.

JANE: In this?

SIDNEY: Oh. Still raining, is it?

JANE: Yes. *(Pause)* Sidney, if you'd only explained to them—I could've—I mean I've been out there for ages. I'm soaking. . . .

SIDNEY: Yes, well, your behaviour made things very difficult. Explanations, that is. What could I say?

JANE: You could have explained.

SIDNEY: So could you. It was really up to you, wasn't it?

JANE: Yes, I know but—I just thought that you might have—that you would've been . . . *(She gives up.)*

(JANE starts to peel off her things.)

SIDNEY: All went off rather satisfactorily, anyway . . .

JANE *(emptying a wellington boot into the sink)*: Good—I'm glad . . .

SIDNEY: So am I. I mean these people just weren't anybody. They are people in the future who can be very, very useful to us. . . .

JANE *(emptying the other boot)*: Yes . . .

SIDNEY: Now, you mustn't do that, Jane. You really mustn't. You see, you get yourself all worked up, and then what happens?

JANE: Yes.

SIDNEY: Right. Enough said. All forgotten, eh? *(Pause)* Oh dear . . .

JANE: What?

SIDNEY: We never got round to playing any of our games, did we?

JANE: No.

SIDNEY: In all the excitement. Never mind. Another year. Well, I think I'll have a look at television. Should be something. Christmas Eve. Usually is. Coming in, are you?

JANE: In a minute.

SIDNEY: Right then.

(SIDNEY goes out closing the door.)

(JANE stands. She sniffs. She has finished putting away her things. Her eye lights on the dirty things scattered about. She picks up a glass or so and puts them in the sink. She picks up the damp cloth and wipes first where the glasses were standing and then slowly, in wider and wider circles, till she has turned it, once more, into a full-scale cleaning operation. As she cleans she seems to relax. Softly at first, then louder, she is heard to sing happily to herself, and—

the CURTAIN falls)

ACT 2

(GEOFFREY and EVA JACKSON's kitchen in their fourth-floor flat. This Christmas.

One door leads to the sitting-room, another into a walk-in cupboard. The room gives an immediate impression of untidiness. It is a room continually lived in, unlike the HOPCROFT's immaculate ship's bridge. While it gives signs that the owners have a certain taste for the trendy homespuns in both equipment and furnishings, some of the equipment, particularly the gas stove, has seen better days. Besides the stove, the room contains a table [natural scrubbed wood], kitchen chairs [natural scrubbed wood], a chest of drawers [natural scrubbed wood] and a fridge and sink.

When the curtain rises EVA, unmade, unkempt and baggy-eyed, sits at the table in her dressing-gown. She is writing with a stub of pencil in a notepad. Whatever it is, it is difficult to word. She and the floor around her are ringed with screwed-up pieces of paper. In front of her is an open scotch bottle. After a minute she tears out the page she has been working on, screws that up as well, and tosses it on the floor to join the others. She starts again.

A door slams. From the sitting-room comes the sound of a large dog barking. EVA looks up alarmed, consults her watch, gives a moan, and quickly closes the notepad to cover up what she has been writing. GEOFFREY's voice is heard off.)

GEOFFREY *(off)*: Darling? Eva—Eva! Quiet, George!

(GEOFFREY backs in from the sitting-room.)
(GEORGE is still barking with wild glee.)

George! That's enough, George! Don't be silly, boy. Sit, George. Sit, boy. At once. That's a good boy. Sit. Good George. Good . . .

(GEORGE has quietened. GEOFFREY goes to close the door. GEORGE barks with fresh vigour.)

George. . . ! *(Giving up)* Oh, all right, suit yourself. *(He closes the door, turning to face EVA for the first time.)* Hallo, darling. *(He gives her a kiss as he passes.)*

(EVA hardly seems to notice. Instead, she sits fiddling with one of her pieces of screwed-up paper. Her face is a tense blank.)

God, I need a drink. You want a drink? *(Without waiting for a reply, he takes the scotch, finds a glass and pours himself a drink.)* You want one? No? *(He puts the bottle back on the table and drinks.)* Cheers. I think we're running into some sort of trouble with the Harrison job. Helluva day. Would you believe I could spend two months explaining to them exactly how to assemble that central-dome. I go along this morning, they're trying to put a bloody great pillar up the middle, straight through the fountain. I said to them, "Listen, you promise to put it up as you're told to—I promise it'll stay up, all right?" I now have to tell Harrison that his super Shopperdrome that he thought was only going to cost so much is going to finish up at twice that. He is not going to be pleased. No, I think I'm in trouble unless I can . . . Oh well, what the hell, it's Christmas. *(Going to the window)* You know, I think it's going to snow. By Boxing Day,° that site'll be under six foot of slush, mark my words. That'll put us another six months behind. *(Returning from the window)* Why didn't I pick something simple? *(Seeing the screwed-up paper)* What've you been up to? *(He tries to take* EVA*'s writing pad.)*

*(*EVA *clings to the pad.* GEOFFREY *shrugs, moves away, then turns and looks at her.)*

You all right? You're still in your dressing-gown,° did you know? Eva? Are you still thinking about this morning? I phoned you at lunch, you know. Were you out? Eva? Oh, come on, darling, we talked it over, didn't we? We were up till four o'clock this morning talking it over. You agreed. You did more than agree. I mean, it was your idea. And you're right. Believe me, darling, you were right. We can't go on. Sooner or later one of us has got to do something really positive for once in our lives—for both our sakes. And it's absolutely true that the best thing that could happen to you and me, at this point in our lives, is for me to go and live with Sally. You were absolutely right. You know, I was thinking on the way home—I nipped in for a quick one, that's why I'm a bit late—I was thinking, this could actually work out terribly well. If we're adult about it, I mean. Don't behave like lovesick kids or something. Sally and I will probably get somewhere together—and by that time you'll probably have got yourself fixed up— we could still see each other, you know. What I'm really saying is, let's not go through all that non-sense—all that good-bye, I never want to see you again bit. Because I do want to see you again. I always will. I mean, five years. We're not going to throw away five years, are we? Eva? Eva, if you're sitting there blaming yourself for this in any way, don't. It's me, love, it's all me. It's just I'm—okay, I'm weak, as you put it. I'm unstable. It's some-thing lacking in me, I know. I mean, other men don't have this trouble. Other men can settle down and be perfectly happy with one woman for the rest of their lives. And that's a wonderful thing. Do you think I don't envy that? *(Banging the*

table) God, how I envy them that. I mean, do you really think I enjoy living out my life like some sexual Flying Dutchman?° Eva, please—please try and see my side just a little, will you? Look, it's Christmas Eve. The day after Boxing Day, I prom-ise—I'll just clear everything of mine that you don't need out of the flat. That way, you can for-get I even existed, if that's what you want. But can't we try, between us to make the next couple of days . . . *(He breaks off.)* Did I say it's Christmas Eve? Haven't we got some people coming round? Yes, surely we . . . What time did we ask them for? *(He looks at his watch.)* Oh, my God. You didn't remember to put them off by any chance, did you? No. Well then . . . Have we got anything to drink in the house? Apart from this? *(He holds up the bottle of scotch.)* Oh well, we'll have that for a start. Now then . . . *(He finds a tray, puts it on the table and puts the scotch bottle on the table.)* What else have we got? *(He rummages in the cupboards.)* Brandy. That'll do. Bottle of coke. Aha, what's this? Tonic wine?° Who's been drinking tonic wine? Is that you? Eva? Oh, for heaven's sake, Eva—you've made your point, now snap out of it, will you? We have lots of people coming round who were due five minutes ago. Now come on . . . *(He looks at her and sighs.)* O.K. I get the message. O.K. There is no help or co-operation to be expected from you tonight, is that it? All systems shut down again, have they? All right. All right. It won't be the first time—don't worry. *(He returns to his hunt for bottles.)* I mean it's not as if you're par-ticularly famous as a gracious hostess, is it? It hasn't been unheard of for you to disappear to bed in the middle of a party and be found later reading a book. *(Producing a couple more bottles— gin and sherry)* I should think our friends will be a little disappointed if you do put in an appear-ance. *(Finding an assortment of glasses)* When, I say our friends, perhaps I should say yours. I will remind you that, so far as I can remember, all the people coming tonight come under the heading of your friends and not mine. And if I'm left to entertain them tonight because you choose to opt out, I shall probably finish up being very, very rude to them. Is that clear? Right. You have been warned. Yes, I know. You're very anxious, aren't you, that I should go and work for the up and coming Mr. Hopcroft? So is up and coming Mr. Hopcroft. But I can tell you both, here and now, I have no intention of helping to perpetuate his

---

Boxing Day, December 26th, a traditional day off in England. **dressing-gown,** bathrobe.

Flying Dutchman, legendary sea captain condemned to sail forever after cursing God. **tonic wine,** wine fortified with herbs, primarily for medicinal purposes.

squalid little developments. What I lack in morals—I make up in ethics.

(GEOFFREY *stamps out into the sitting-room with the tray.*)

(Off, as GEORGE *starts barking again)* George—no, this is not for you. Get down, I said get down. *(There is a crash as of a bottle coming off the tray.)* Oh, really—this damn dog—get out of it . . .

(GEOFFREY *returns with a couple of old coffee-cups which he puts in the sink.*)

That room is like a very untidy cesspit. *(He finds a dish cloth.)* One quick drink, that's all they're getting. Then it's happy Christmas and out they bloody well go.

(GEOFFREY *goes out again. He takes with him the dish cloth.*)
(EVA *opens her notepad and continues with her note.*)
(GEOFFREY *returns. He still has the cloth. In the other hand he has a pile of bits of broken dog biscuit.*)

Half-chewed biscuit. Why does he only chew half of them, can you tell me that? *(He deposits the bits in the waste bin. He is about to exit again, then pauses.)* Eva? Eva—I'm being very patient. Very patient indeed. But in a minute I really do believe I'm going to lose my temper. And we know what happens then, don't we? I will take a swing at you and then you will feel hard done by, and by way of reprisal, will systematically go round and smash everything in the flat. And come tomorrow breakfast time, there will be the familiar sight of the three of us, you, me and George, trying to eat our meals off our one surviving plate. Now, Eva, *please . . .*

(*The doorbell rings.* GEORGE *starts barking.*)

Oh, my God. Here's the first of them. *(Calling)* George. Now, Eva, go to bed now, please. Don't make things any more embarrassing. *(As he goes out)* George, will you be quiet.

(GEOFFREY *goes out. The door closes. Silence)*
(EVA *opens her notepad, finishes her note and tears it out. She pushes the clutter on the table to one side slightly. She goes to a drawer and produces a kitchen knife. She returns to the table and pins the note forcibly to it with the knife. She goes to the window.*)
(GEOFFREY *returns.*)
(*Barking and chattering are heard in the background—two voices.* EVA *stands motionless, looking out.*)

(Calling back) He's all right. He's quite harmless. Bark's worse than his bite. *(He closes the door.)* It would be the bloody Hopcrofts, wouldn't it. Didn't think they'd miss out. And that lift's broken down, would you believe it. *(Finding a bottle-*

opener in a drawer) Every Christmas. Every Christmas, isn't it? Eva, come on, love, for heaven's sake.

(GEOFFREY *goes out, closing the door.*)
(EVA *opens the window. She inhales the cold fresh air. After a second, she climbs uncertainly on to the window ledge. She stands giddily, staring down and clutching on to the frame.*)
(*The door opens, chatter,* GEOFFREY *returns, carrying a glass.*)

(Calling behind him) I'll get you a clean one, I'm terribly sorry. I'm afraid the cook's on holiday. *(He laughs.)*

(*The Hopcrofts' laughter is heard.* GEOFFREY *closes the door.*)

Don't think we can have washed these glasses since the last party. This one certainly didn't pass the Jane Hopcroft Good Housekeeping Test, anyway. *(He takes a dish cloth from the sink and wipes the glass rather casually.)* I sometimes think that woman must spend . . . Eva! What are you doing?

(EVA, *who is now feeling sick with vertigo, moans.*)

Eva! Eva—that's a good girl. Down. Come down—come down—that's a good girl—down. Come on . . . *(He reaches Eva.)* That's it. Come on, I've got you. Down you come. That's it.

(*He eases* EVA *gently back into the room. She stands limply. He guides her inert body to a chair.*)

Come on, sit down here. That's it. Darling, darling, what were you trying to do? What on earth made you want to. . . ? What was the point of that, what were you trying to prove? I mean . . . *(He sees the note and the knife for the first time.)* What on earth's this? *(He reads it.)* Oh, no. Eva, you mustn't think of . . . I mean, what do you mean, a burden to everyone? Who said you were a burden? I never said you were a burden . . . *(During the above,* EVA *picks up the bread-knife, looks at it, then at one of the kitchen drawers. She rises, unseen by* GEOFFREY, *crosses to the drawer and, half opening it, wedges the knife inside so the point sticks out. She measures out a run and turns to face the knife.* GEOFFREY, *still talking, is now watching her absently.* EVA *works up speed and then takes a desperate run at the point of the knife.* GEOFFREY, *belatedly realizing what she's up to, rushes forward, intercepts her and re-seats her.*)

Eva, now, for heaven's sake! Come on . . . *(He studies her nervously.)* Look, I'm going to phone the doctor. I'll tell him you're very upset and overwrought. *(He backs away and nearly impales himself on the knife. He grabs it.)* He can probably give you something to calm you down a bit.

(The doorbell rings.)

Oh God, somebody else. Now, I'm going to phone the doctor. I'll just be two minutes, all right? Now, you sit there. Don't move, just sit there like a good girl. *(Opening the door and calling off)* Would you mind helping yourselves? I just have to make one phone call . . .

(GEOFFREY goes out.)

(Silence. EVA finishes another note. A brief one. She tears it out and weights it down, this time with a tin of dog food which happens to be on the table. She gazes round, surveying the kitchen. She stares at the oven. She goes to it and opens it, looking inside thoughtfully. She reaches inside and removes a casserole dish, opens the lid, wrinkles her nose and carries the dish to the draining-board. Returning to the oven, she removes three shelves and various other odds and ends that seem to have accumulated in there. It is a very dirty oven. She looks at her hands, now grimy, goes to the kitchen drawer and fetches a nearly clean tea towel. Folding it carefully, she lays it on the floor of the oven. She lies down and sticks her head inside, as if trying it for size. She is apparently dreadfully uncomfortable. She wriggles about to find a satisfactory position.)

(The door opens quietly and JANE enters.)

(The hubbub outside has now died down to a gentle murmur so not much noise filters through. JANE carries rather carefully two more glasses she considers dirty. She closes the door. She looks round the kitchen but sees no-one. She crosses, rather furtively, to the sink and rinses the glasses. EVA throws an oven tray on to the floor with a clatter. JANE, startled, takes a step back and gives a little squeak. EVA, equally startled, tries to sit up in the oven and hits her head with a clang on the remaining top shelf.)

JANE: Mrs Jackson, are you all right? You shouldn't be on the cold floor in your condition, you know. You should be in bed. Surely? Here . . .

(She helps EVA to her feet and steers her back to the table.)

Now, you sit down here. Don't you worry about that oven now. That oven can wait. You clean it later. No point in damaging your health for an oven, is there? Mind you, I know just what you feel like, though. You suddenly get that urge, don't you? You say, I must clean that oven if it kills me. I shan't sleep, I shan't eat till I've cleaned that oven. It haunts you. I know just that feeling. I'll tell you what I'll do. Never say I'm not a good neighbour—shall I have a go at it for you? How would that be? Would you mind? I mean, it's no trouble for me. I quite enjoy it, actually—and you'd do the same for me, wouldn't you? Right. That's settled. No point in wasting time, let's get down to it. Now then, what are we going to need? Bowl of water, got any oven cleaner, have you? Never mind, we'll find it—I hope you're not get-

ting cold, you look very peaky.° *(Hunting under the sink)* Now then, oven cleaner? Have we got any? Well, if we haven't, we'll just have to use our old friend Mr. Vim, won't we? *(She rummages.)*

(The door opens. GEOFFREY enters and goes to EVA. Conversation is heard in the background.)

GEOFFREY: Darling, listen, it looks as if I've got . . . *(Seeing JANE)* Oh.

JANE: Hallo, there.

GEOFFREY: Oh, hallo—anything you—want?

JANE: I'm just being a good neighbour, that's all. Have you by any chance got an apron I could borrow?

GEOFFREY *(rather bewildered, pointing to the chair)*: Er— yes—there.

JANE: Oh, yes. *(Putting it on)* Couldn't see it for looking.

GEOFFREY: Er—what are you doing?

JANE: Getting your oven ready for tomorrow, that's what I'm doing.

GEOFFREY: For what?

JANE: For your Christmas dinner. What else do you think for what?

GEOFFREY: Yes, well, are you sure. . . ?

JANE: Don't you worry about me. *(She bustles around singing loudly, collecting cleaning things and a bowl of water.)*

GEOFFREY *(over this, irritated)*: Oh. Darling—Eva, look I've phoned the doctor but he's not there. He's apparently out on a call somewhere and the fool of a woman I spoke to has got the address and no number. It'll be quicker for me to try and catch him there than sitting here waiting for him to come back. Now, I'll be about ten minutes, that's all. You'll be all right, will you?

JANE: Don't you fret. I'll keep an eye on her. *(She puts on a rubber glove.)*

GEOFFREY: Thank you. *(He studies the immobile EVA. On a sudden inspiration, crosses to the kitchen drawer and starts taking out the knives. He scours the kitchen, gathering up the sharp implements.)*

(JANE watches him puzzled.)

(By way of explanation) People downstairs are having a big dinner party. Promised to lend them some stuff.

JANE: Won't they need forks?

GEOFFREY: No. No forks. They're Muslims. *(As he goes to the door)* Ten minutes.

(The doorbell rings.)

JANE: There's somebody.

GEOFFREY: The Brewster-Wrights, probably.

JANE: Oh . . .

---

peaky, sickly.

(GEOFFREY goes out, the dog barking as he does so, until the door is closed.)

Hark at that dog of yours. Huge, isn't he? Like a donkey—huge. Do you know what Dick's bought him? Dick Potter? He's bought George a Christmas present. One of those rubber rings. You know the ones you throw in the air. One of those. He loves it. He's been running up and down your hallway out there—Dick throwing it, him trying to catch it. But he's really wonderful with dogs, Dick. He really understands them. Do you know he nearly became a dog handler only he didn't have his proper eyesight. But he knows how to treat them. Doesn't matter what sort of dog it is . . . He knows all their ways. *(Turning to the oven)* Now then—oh, this is going to be a big one, isn't it? Dear oh dear. Never mind. Where there's a will. *(Removing the tea towel from the oven)* You haven't been trying to clean it with this, have you? You'll never clean it with this. Good old elbow grease—that's the way. *(She sets to work, her head almost inside the oven.)* Shall I tell you something—Sidney would get so angry if he heard me saying this—but I'd far sooner be down here on the floor, on my knees in the oven—than out there, talking. Isn't that terrible. But I'm never at ease, really, at parties. I don't enjoy drinking, you see. I'd just as soon be out here, having a natter° with you. *(She starts to sing cheerily as she works, her voice booming round the oven.)*

(During this, EVA rises, opens the cupboard, pulls out a tin box filled with first-aid things and searches through the contents. Eventually, she finds a white cylindrical cardboard pill box which is what she's looking for. She goes to the sink with it and runs herself a glass of water. She opens the box, takes out a couple of small tablets and puts the box back on the draining-board. She swallows one tablet with a great deal of difficulty and water. The same with the second. She leaves the tap running, pulls the cotton-wool out of the box—and the rest of the pills rattle down the drain. EVA tries desperately to save some with her finger before they can disappear, turning off the tap. This proving ineffective, she tries with a fork.)

(The door opens. Barking and chatter are heard. SIDNEY enters.)

SIDNEY: Hallo, hallo. Where's everyone gone then . . . *(Seeing JANE)* Dear oh dear. I just can't believe it. I just can't believe my eyes. You can't be at it again. What are you doing?

JANE: She's under the weather. She needs a hand.

SIDNEY: Do you realize that's your best dress?

JANE: Oh, bother my best dress.

SIDNEY: Mr and Mrs Brewster-Wright have arrived, you know. Ron and Marion. I hope they don't chance to see you down there. *(Turning to EVA who is still fishing rather half-heartedly with the fork)* And what's the trouble over here, eh? Can I help—since it seems to be in fashion this evening? *(SIDNEY takes the fork from EVA and seats her in her chair.)* Now. I'll give you a little tip, if you like. You'll never get a sink unblocked that way. Not by wiggling a fork about in it, like that. That's not the way to unblock a sink, now, is it? All you'll do that way, is to eventually take the chrome off your fork and possibly scratch the plug hole. Not the way. Let's see now . . . *(He runs the tap for a second and watches the water running away.)* Yes. It's a little on the sluggish side. Just a little. But it'll get worse. Probably a few tea-leaves, nothing more. Let's have a look, shall we? *(He opens the cupboard under the sink.)* Ten to one, this is where your troubles lie. Ah-ha. It's a good old-fashioned one, isn't it? Need the wrench for that one.

JANE: He'll soon fix that for you, won't you, Sidney?

SIDNEY: Brace of shakes.° Shake of braces as we used to say in the Navy. I've got the tools. Down in the car. No trouble at all. *(He turns to EVA.)* Nothing serious. All it is, you see—where the pipe bends under the sink there—they call that the trap. Now then. *(He takes out a pencil.)* I'll show you. Always useful to know. Paper? *(He picks up EVA's latest suicide note.)* This is nothing vital, is it. . . ? Now then *(He glances curiously at it, then turns it over and starts to draw his diagram on the back.)* Now—here's your plug hole, do you see, here—if I can draw it—and this is your pipe coming straight down and then almost doubling back on itself like that, for a second, you see? Then it runs away here, to the drain . . .

JANE: You want to know anything, you ask Sidney . . .

SIDNEY: And this little bit here's the actual drain trap. And all you have to do is get it open and out it all comes. Easy when you know. Now I suppose I'll have to walk down four flights for my tools. *(He screws up the paper and throws it away. At the door.)* Now, don't worry. Lottie's keeping them entertained at the moment and Dick's busy with George, so everybody's happy, aren't they?

(SIDNEY opens the door and goes out. We hear LOTTIE's laughter and the dog barking distantly for a moment before the door closes.)

JANE: It's at times like this you're glad of your friends, aren't you? *(She goes at the oven with fresh vigour, singing cheerily.)*

---

natter, chat.

brace of shakes, slang for "in no time at all."

(During the above EVA *writes another brief note and places it in a prominent position on the table. She now rises and goes to a chair where there is a plastic washing basket filled with clean but unironed clothes. Coiled on top is a washing line. She returns to the table.* JANE, *emerging for fresh water, catches sight of her.)*

Sorting out your laundry? You're a terror, aren't you? You're worse than me. *(She returns to her oven and resumes her song.)*

*(*EVA *begins to pull the washing line from the basket. She finds one end and ties it in a crude noose. She tests the effectiveness of this on one wrist and, satisfied, pulls the rest of the rope from the basket. Every foot or so is a plastic clothes peg which she removes.)*

I think I'm beginning to win through. I think I'm down to the metal, anyway, that's something. There's about eight layers on here.

*(*EVA *comes across a pair of knickers and two pairs of socks still pegged to the line. She removes these and replaces them in the basket.)*

There's something stuck on the bottom here like cement. You haven't had cement for dinner lately, have you? *(She laughs.)*

*(*EVA *now stands with her clothes line gazing at the ceiling. There are two light fittings and her eyes rest on the one immediately above the table. She crosses to the door, clicks a switch and just this one goes out.)*

Whooo! Where was Moses°. . . ? What's happened? Bulb gone, has it? We'll get Sidney to fix that when he comes back. Keep him on the go. *(She returns to the oven again, changing her tune to something suitable like "Dancing in the Dark.")*

*(*EVA *climbs first on to a chair then on to the table holding her rope. She removes the bulb and shade in one from the socket and places them on the table at her feet. She is beginning to yawn more and more frequently and is obviously beginning to feel the effect of the sleeping pills. Swaying slightly she starts to tie the rope round the flex above the holder. This proves a difficult operation since she has far too much rope for the job. She finally manages a knot which loosely encircles the flex.° She gives the rope a gentle tug—it holds. She tries again. It still remains in position. She gives it a third tug for luck. The rope slides down the flex as far as the bulb-holder and promptly pulls this away from the wires. The holder clatters on to the table and she is left clutching the rope. She stands swaying more pronouncedly now, a faint look of desperation on her face.)*

Where was Moses, a nineteenth-century popular song. "Where was Moses when the lights went out?" *flex,* insulated electrical wire.

*(*RONALD *enters. Behind him we hear* LOTTIE POTTER'*s laughter and, more distant, a dog barking.)*

RONALD: Now then, how's our little invalid getting . . . *(Seeing* EVA*)* Oh, good God. *(He dashes forward and steadies* EVA*.)* My dear girl, what on earth are you doing up there?

JANE *(emerging from her oven)*: Oh, no. She's a real terror, you know. *(She goes to assist* RONALD *in helping* EVA *off the table and back on to a chair.)* She can't keep still for a minute. *(Reprovingly to* EVA*)* You could have hurt yourself up there, you silly thing.

*(*RONALD *folds up the rope, which is looped round* EVA'*s wrist, and leaves it in her hand.)*

RONALD: Lucky I . . .

JANE: Yes, it was.

RONALD: I mean. What was she trying to do?

JANE: Bulb's gone.

RONALD *(looking up)*: Yes, so it has. Well, you could have asked me to do that, you know. I'm no handyman but even I can change a bulb.

*(*SIDNEY *enters with a large bag of tools. Behind him we hear* LOTTIE'*s laughter and a dog barking.)*

SIDNEY: Here we are, back again. I've brought everything, just in case. Everything except the kitchen sink and that's already here, eh? *(He laughs.)*

RONALD: What? Oh, yes, Very good.

JANE *(amused)*: Except the kitchen sink. Honestly.

SIDNEY *(noticing the light)*: Hallo, hallo. More trouble? *(He puts the tool back by the sink.)*

RONALD: Nothing much. Just a bulb gone.

SIDNEY: You've lost more than a bulb, by the look of it. You've lost the whole fitting.

RONALD: Good gracious me. So we have. Look at that.

SIDNEY: Just the bare wires, you see.

RONALD: Yes. There's no thingummyjig.

JANE: Just the wires, aren't there?

SIDNEY: Don't like the look of that.

RONALD: No.

JANE: No.

SIDNEY: I mean, if that was to short across like it is . . .

RONALD: Yes.

JANE: Yes.

SIDNEY: You could finish up with a fuse, or a fire . . .

RONALD: Or worse.

JANE: Worse.

SIDNEY: I mean, you've only got to be carrying, say, for instance, a pair of aluminum steps across the room and you happen accidentally to knock against the wires, electricity would be conducted down the steps and straight into you. Natural earth, you see. Finish.

RONALD: I suppose that would go for a very tall man in, say, a tin hat, eh? *(He laughs.)*

SIDNEY: True, true. Not so probable. But true.

JANE: Lucky it's not the war time.

SIDNEY: Oh, yes. In certain cases, one touch could be fatal.

RONALD: Better fix it, I suppose.

SIDNEY: I'd advise it. Going to have a go, are you?

RONALD: Well—I don't know. Looks a bit technical for me.

SIDNEY: Oh, no. Very simple. Nothing to it. Look, you've got your two wires coming down . . . Look, I'll draw it for you. (*He whips out his pencil again and, searching for a piece of paper, picks up* EVA'*s suicide note. With a casual glance at it*) Nothing important, is it? (*Without waiting for a reply, he turns it over and starts to sketch.*)

(EVA *stares—fascinated.*)

You've got your two wires coming down here, you see—like that. They go through the top of the plug, here—excuse the drawing, and then they just screw in to the little holes on the prongs, you see? Tighten your grubs. Screw your top to your bottom and away you go.

RONALD: Let there be light.

SIDNEY: Exactly.

(EVA *scrawls another note.*)

RONALD: Oh, well, that looks—simple enough. (*He still seems doubtful.*)

SIDNEY: Right. I'll get you a screwdriver and I'll get going on the sink. (*Opening his tool bag*) Now then, let's get you fixed up. What've we got here? (*He rummages through his tools, taking out a screwdriver and a spare fitting.*)

RONALD: Good gracious. What a collection.

SIDNEY: This is just the set I keep in the car.

RONALD: Really? Get a lot of trouble with it, do you?

(*During the above* EVA *climbs slowly on to her chair, steps on to the table and reaches out with both hands towards the bare wires.* JANE, *who has returned to her oven, turns in time to see her.*)

JANE: Watch her!

SIDNEY: Hey-hey . . .

RONALD: Hoy . . .

(*All three of them run, grab* EVA *and pull her back in the chair.*)

SIDNEY: They might have been live.

RONALD: Yes. (*A thought*) Might they?

SIDNEY: Yes.

RONALD: Well, how do we know they're not?

SIDNEY: Check the switches first.

RONALD: Yes, well, don't you think we'd better? I mean, I'm going to be the one who . . .

SIDNEY (*striding to the door*): Check the switches, by all means. (SIDNEY *plays with both switches, plunging the room into darkness a couple of times.*)

JANE (*During this, still with* EVA): She's got a charmed life, honestly. The sooner that doctor gets here . . .

RONALD: He'll fix her up.

JANE: He'd better.

SIDNEY (*completing his check*): Yes, all safe. (*He takes off his jacket and puts it over the back of a chair.*)

RONALD: Ah.

SIDNEY: Should be, anyway. Unless they've put this switch on upside down, of course.

RONALD: How do we know they haven't?

SIDNEY: Well, you'll be the first to find out, won't you? (*He roars with mirth.*)

JANE (*equally tickled*): You'll be the first . . .

(RONALD *is less amused.*)

SIDNEY: Well, let's get down to it, shall we?

RONALD (*gazing at the light*): Yes.

SIDNEY: Each to his own. (*He starts work under the sink.*)

JANE: Each to his own. (*She returns to the oven.*)

(*They prepare for their various tasks.*)

This is coming up a treat.

SIDNEY: Ought to get—er—Marion out here, eh? Find her something to do.

RONALD (*clearing the things off the table*): No—no. I don't think she'd contribute very much. Probably better off with the Potters. Matter of fact, she's just a bit—on her pins.° You know what I mean.

SIDNEY: Ah, well. Christmas.

JANE: If you can't do it at Christmas . . .

SIDNEY: Once a year, eh?

RONALD: Not in my wife's case. Festive season recurs rather more frequently. Every three or four days.

SIDNEY (*under the sink*): Ah-ha! You're going to be a tricky little fellow, aren't you? Nobody's opened you since you were last painted.

(SIDNEY *clatters under the sink.* JANE *scrubs cheerfully on.* RONALD *sets to work, standing on the table and on* EVA'*s latest note. He tackles his own particular job extremely slowly and with many false starts. He is not particularly electrically-minded.* EVA *attempts, under the following, to rescue her note from under* RONALD'*s feet. It rips. She scrawls another rapidly.*)

RONALD: Must be pretty pleased with your year, I should imagine.

SIDNEY: Beg pardon?

RONALD: Had a good year. Must be pretty pleased.

SIDNEY: Oh, yes. Had a few lucky hunches. Seemed to pay off.

RONALD: I should say so.

SIDNEY: Mustn't complain, anyway.

---

on her pins, literally "on her legs," but colloquially "feeling well." Ronald actually means the opposite, shaky.

JANE: No. Mustn't complain.

SIDNEY: As long as you're looking after our money. Eh?

(He laughs.)

RONALD: Oh, yes. Yes.

(They work. SIDNEY whistles. RONALD hums. JANE sings. Occasionally, the workers break off their respective melodies to make those sounds that people make when wrestling with inanimate objects. "Come on, you little . . . Just one more . . . get in, get in, etc." During this EVA, having finished her note, sees SIDNEY's bag of tools. Unseen by the others, she goes to the bag and removes a lethal-looking tin of paint stripper. Also a hammer and a nail. She nails her latest note to the table with the hammer which she leaves on the table. Turning her attention to the paint stripper, she tries to get the top off. It is very stiff. She struggles vainly, then goes to the room door, intending to use it as a vice.)

(At this moment MARION enters.)

(EVA is pushed behind the door, and, as it swings shut, she clings to the handle and falls across the floor. While the door is open the dog barks and raised voices are heard.)

MARION *(holding a gin bottle and glass)*: I say—something rather ghastly's happened.

RONALD *(concentrating hard)*: Oh, yes?

MARION: Goodness! Don't you all look busy? Darling, what are you doing up there?

(EVA tries to open the bottle with the walk-in cupboard door.)

RONALD: Oh, just a little light electrical work or should I say a little electrical light work? *(He laughs.)*

SIDNEY: Electrical light work. *(He laughs.)*

JANE: Electrical light work. *(She laughs.)*

SIDNEY: I like that—yes . . .

MARION: Yes, very funny, darling. Now do come down, please, before you blow us all up. You know absolutely nothing about that sort of thing at all.

RONALD: I don't know . . .

MARION: Absolutely nothing.

RONALD: I fixed that bottle lamp with a cork in it, didn't I?

MARION: Yes, darling, and we all had to sit around admiring it while the lampshade burst into flames.

(EVA goes to the toolbag for a screwdriver.)

RONALD *(irritably)*: That was entirely the fault of the bloody lampshade.

MARION: I was terrified. The whole thing was an absolute death trap. I had to give it to the Scouts for jumble.°

---

jumble, items sold off at cheap prices.

SIDNEY: What was the trouble?

MARION: It was like modern sculpture. Bare wires sticking out at extraordinary angles.

(EVA goes and sits down in a corner.)

SIDNEY: No. I meant when you came in.

MARION: Oh, yes. What was it? Something awful. *(She remembers.)* Oh, yes. I came for help, that's right. That dog . . .

JANE: George?

MARION: Is that his name—George—yes. Well, he's just bitten that Potter man in the leg.

JANE: Oh, dear.

MARION: Terribly nasty. Right through his trousers. Of course, it was entirely his fault. I mean, he was leaping about being desperately hearty with the poor animal till it had froth simply foaming from its jowls and didn't know where it was.

JANE: Oh, dear, are they . . .

SIDNEY: Yes, what are they. . . ?

MARION: Well, I think they were thinking of going. If they haven't gone. They seem to think he might need an anti-something.

SIDNEY: Rabies.

MARION: Probably. I'll see. *(She opens the door.)*

(Silence)

(Calling) I say, hallo. Hallo there.

(There is a low growl.)

Oh, dear.

RONALD: What's the matter?

MARION: It's sort of crouching in the doorway chewing a shoe and looking terribly threatening.

RONALD: Really?

MARION: I don't think it's going to let us through, you know.

RONALD *(picking up the tin of dog meat and moving tentatively to the sitting-room)*: He's probably all right, he just needs calming down. Here, boy, boy, good boy. Hallo, boy, good boy.

(A growl. RONALD returns, closes the door, and goes back to his work.)

No, well, best to leave them when they're like that. Just a bit excited.

SIDNEY: Mind you, once they've drawn blood, you know . . .

JANE: Old Mr Allsop's Alsatian . . .

SIDNEY: Yes.

MARION: Yes. Well, it's lucky I brought the drink. Keep the workers going. And the invalid. How is she?

RONALD: Very groggy.

MARION *(peering at her)*: Golly, yes. She's a dreadful colour. How are you feeling?

JANE: I don't think she really knows we're here.

MARION: Hallo. Hallo, there . . . *(No response)* No,

you're right. She's completely gone. Poor thing. Oh well, drink, everyone?

JANE: Not just at the moment. Nearly finished.

MARION: Jolly good. (*Nudging* SIDNEY *with her leg*) What about you?

SIDNEY: In a moment. In just a moment.

RONALD: Darling, I wouldn't drink too much more of that.

MARION: Oh, Ronnie, don't be such a misery. Honestly, he's such a misery. He's totally incapable of enjoying a party.

RONALD: No, all I'm saying is . . .

MARION: Well, Eva and I'll have one, won't we, Eva?

(MARION *pours out two glasses.*)

SIDNEY (*from under the sink*): Ah!

JANE: All right?

SIDNEY: Got it off.

JANE: Oh, well done.

MARION: What's he got off?

(EVA *finally gets the lid off the paint stripper and is about to drink it.*)

SIDNEY: That was a wrestle and no mistake. But I got it off. The big question now is, can I get it on again.

MARION: Eva, dear, now you drink that. (*She puts the glass in* EVA's *hand, removing the tin of stripper.*) That'll do you far more good than all the pills and patent medicines put together. (*She puts the paint stripper on the draining-board.*)

RONALD: Marion, seriously, I wouldn't advise . . .

MARION (*hitting him on the foot with the gin bottle*): Oh, Ronnie, just shut up!

RONALD: Ah!

MARION (*to* EVA; *confidentially*): You'd never think it but he was a really vital young man, Eva. You'd never think it to look at him, would you?

(MARION *fills* EVA's *glass of gin so that she is forced in her inert state to drink some.*)

SIDNEY (*emerging from his sink*): Well, time for a break. Now then, did somebody promise a drink?

MARION (*pushing the bottle towards him*): Help yourself.

SIDNEY: Thank you.

JANE: I think that's as much as I can do. It's a bit better.

MARION (*going to the stove*): Oh, look, isn't that marvellous. Look at that splendid oven.

SIDNEY: Well done. Well done.

JANE: Bit of a difference. (*She picks up her bowl of water and carries it to the sink.*)

RONALD (*having difficulty*): Ah . . .

SIDNEY: How's the electrical department?

RONALD (*muttering*): Damn fiddly thing.

SIDNEY (*seeing* JANE): Hey! Don't pour that down now!

JANE: Oh. Nearly forgot.

SIDNEY: You'd have been popular. (*He puts the gin bottle on the table.*)

JANE: I'd have been popular.

MARION: Well, I'm just going to sit here all night and admire that oven. I think she's honestly better than our Mrs Minns, isn't she, darling?

RONALD: Anyone's better than our Mrs Minns.

MARION: Oh, she means well. We have our Mrs Minns. She's a dear old soul. She can hardly see and she only comes in for two hours a day and when she's gone we spend the rest of the time cleaning up after her. But she's got an absolute heart of gold.

RONALD: Largely paid for by us.

SIDNEY: Good health. Happy Christmas to all.

MARION: Happy New Year.

JANE: Yes.

SIDNEY: Get this lot finished, maybe there'll be time for a game . . .

JANE: Oh, yes . . .

MARION: What sort of game do you mean?

SIDNEY: You know. Some good party game. Get everyone jumping about.

MARION: What an obscene idea.

SIDNEY: Oh, they're great fun. We've had some laughs, haven't we?

JANE: Talk about laughs . . .

RONALD: Blast.

SIDNEY: What's the matter?

RONALD: Dropped the little thing. Could you see if you can see it. I've got to keep holding on to this or it'll drop off. Little thing about so big.

MARION: What little thing?

RONALD: A whajamacallit.

JANE: Small was it?

RONALD: Lord, yes. Tiny little thingy.

SIDNEY: Oh dear oh dear.

(*They hunt,* SIDNEY *crawls on hands and knees.*)

JANE: Might have rolled anywhere.

MARION: What are we looking for?

RONALD: Little whosit. Goes in here.

MARION: Darling, do be more precise. What's a whosit?

JANE: You know, one of those—one of those—isn't that silly, I can't think of the word.

MARION: Well, I refuse to look till I know what we're looking for. We could be here all night. I mean, from the look of this floor it's simply littered with little whosits.

SIDNEY (*under the table*): Can't see it.

JANE: It's on the tip of my tongue . . . that's it, a nut. Little nut.

MARION (*searching by the sink*): Oh, well then, a nut. Now we know. Everyone hunt for a little nut.

(EVA *goes and sits at the table.*)

SIDNEY: I didn't know we were looking for a nut.

JANE: Aren't we?

RONALD: No. A screw. That's what I'm after, a screw.

SIDNEY: A screw, yes.

JANE: Oh, a screw.

MARION: All right, everybody, stop looking for nuts. Ronnie's now decided he wants a screw. I can't see a thing. And I think it would be terribly sensible if we put the light on, wouldn't it?

RONALD: Good idea.

(MARION *goes to the light switch.*)

SIDNEY (*realizing far too late.*): No, I wouldn't turn that on . . .

(MARION *presses the switch.*)

MARION: There.

(RONALD, *on the table, starts vibrating, emitting a low moan.*)

SIDNEY (*rising*): Turn it off.

JANE: Get him away.

MARION: Darling, what on earth are you doing?

JANE (*reaching out to pull* RONALD *away*): Get him away.

SIDNEY: No, don't touch him, he's live. (*He goes to the switch.*)

(JANE *touches him and recoils, with a squeak.*)

RONALD (*through gritted teeth*): Somebody turn it off.

(SIDNEY *turns it off.*)

SIDNEY: All right. Panic over.

(RONALD *continues to vibrate.*)

JANE: Turn him off, Sidney.

SIDNEY: I have.

JANE: Turn him off!

SIDNEY: He is off. (*Calming* JANE) Now, pull yourself together. Help me get him down. Get him down.

(SIDNEY *and* JANE *guide* RONALD *down from the table and to a chair.* MARION *watches them.*)

MARION: Good lord. Wasn't that extraordinary?

SIDNEY: Easy now.

JANE: Take it slowly.

(EVA *pours herself another drink.*)

MARION: Whenever he fiddles about with anything electrical it always ends in disaster. This always happens. Is he all right?

SIDNEY: He's in a state of shock.

JANE: He would be.

SIDNEY: Sit him down and keep him warm—that's the way. Pass me my jacket. Jacket. Jacket.

MARION: He looks frightfully odd.

JANE (*bringing* SIDNEY's *jacket*): Here.

SIDNEY: He needs more. He really needs to be wrapped up, otherwise . . .

JANE (*Looking round*): There's nothing much here.

SIDNEY: Well, find something. In the other room. We need blankets.

JANE: Right.

(JANE *goes to the door whilst* MARION *looks vaguely round the kitchen.*)

SIDNEY: Now easy, old chap. Just keep breathing . . .

(JANE *opens the door. There is a fierce growling. She withdraws swiftly and closes it.*)

JANE: He's still there.

SIDNEY: Who?

JANE: The dog.

SIDNEY: Well, step over him. This is an emergency.

JANE: I'm not stepping over him. You step over him.

SIDNEY: Oh dear oh dear.

MARION (*who has found the washing basket*): What about these bits and bobs? (*She picks up an article of clothing.*)

SIDNEY: What's that?

MARION: Last week's washing, I think. (*Sniffing it*) It seems fairly clean. Might be better than nothing.

SIDNEY: Yes, well, better than nothing.

MARION: It seems dry.

JANE: Better than nothing.

(*Between them, during the following, they cover* RONALD *in an assortment of laundry, both male and female. He finishes up more or less encased in it but still quivering.*)

SIDNEY: Quick as you can. Come along, quick as you can.

JANE (*examining a shirt*): She hasn't got this collar very clean.

SIDNEY: Jane, come along.

MARION (*holding up a petticoat*): Oh, that's rather pretty. I wonder where she got this.

SIDNEY: Not the time for that now. That the lot?

MARION: Yes. Only socks left. And you-know-whats.

SIDNEY: Well, it'll keep his temperature up.

MARION: Oh, my God, what does he look like? Ronnie! You know I've got a terrible temptation to phone up his chief cashier. If he could see him now . . . (*She starts to laugh.*)

JANE: I don't think he's very well, you know.

MARION: Yes, I'm sorry. It's just that I've never seen anything quite so ludicrous.

SIDNEY (*moving a stool up beside* RONALD): Might I suggest that Marion sits down with her husband just until the doctor gets here for Mrs Jackson . . .

JANE: Then he can look at them both.

SIDNEY: Precisely.

JANE: Lucky he was coming.

SIDNEY: Yes, well, we'd better just finish off and clear up, hadn't we?

MARION (*sitting beside* RONALD): Would you like a drink, darling? You look dreadful!

JANE: I'd better just go over the floor.

SIDNEY (*preparing to go under the sink again*): No, dear,

we don't want you to go over the floor. Not now . . .

JANE: Just where we've been tramping about. If Doctor's coming. It won't take a minute.

SIDNEY: All right. Carry on, Sister.° Sorry I spoke.

JANE (*going to the walk-in cupboard*): Now where does she keep her broom?

RONALD (*strained tone*): You know, I feel very peculiar.

(JANE *finds the broom and starts clearing the immediate vicinity around the table.*)

MARION: Well, I hope you won't be like this all over Christmas, darling. I mean we've got your mother over tomorrow for lunch and Edith and the twins on Boxing Day—I just couldn't face them alone. I just couldn't.

JANE (*to EVA*): Excuse me, dear. I wonder if you could just . . . (*She winds up the rope, still looped to EVA's wrist, and puts it in EVA's hand.*) Tell you what, why don't you sit up here? Just for a second. Then I won't get in the way of your feet. (*She assists EVA to sit on the edge of the table.*) Upsidaisy.

SIDNEY (*sliding under the sink*): She all right still?

JANE: I think so.

(EVA *yawns.*)

Just a bit tired. Neglected you in all the excitement, haven't we? Never mind. Just sit there. Doctor'll be here soon. (*She sweeps under the table.*)

MARION: You know, I believe I'm beginning to feel dizzy as well. I hope I haven't caught it from her.

JANE: I hope not. What a Christmas, eh?

SIDNEY (*from under the sink*): We'll be laughing about this.

JANE (*going to the sink and lifting SIDNEY's feet*): Excuse me, dear. What's that?

SIDNEY: I say, in about two weeks' time, we'll—(JANE *pours the water away in the sink*)—all be sitting down and laughing about—aaaah!

JANE: Oh, no.

SIDNEY: Put the plug in.

JANE (*feverishly following the plug chain*): I can't find the end.

SIDNEY: Put the plug in!

JANE (*putting the plug in*): I'm sorry.

SIDNEY (*emerging from under the sink, his top half drenched in dirty water*): Look what you've done.

JANE: I'm terribly sorry. (*She picks up a dish cloth.*)

SIDNEY: Look what you have done! You silly woman!

(*She tries to mop him down with the dish cloth.*)

(*Beating her away*) Don't do that! Don't do that! It's too late for that. Look at this shirt. This is a new shirt.

JANE: Well, it'll wash. It'll wash. I'll wash it. It's only oven grease.

SIDNEY: I told you, didn't I? I said, whatever you do—don't pour water down there, didn't I?

JANE: I didn't think . . .

SIDNEY: Obviously.

JANE: Well, take the shirt off now and I'll . . .

SIDNEY: And I'll go home in my singlet,° I suppose?

JANE: Nobody'll notice.

SIDNEY: Of course they'll notice. Otherwise, there'd be no point in wearing a shirt in the first place, would there? If nobody noticed, we'd all be walking around in our singlets.

JANE: It's dark.

SIDNEY: Don't change the subject. It would really teach you a lesson if I caught pneumonia.

JANE (*tearfully*): Don't say that.

SIDNEY: Teach you, that would.

(JANE *sniffs.* SIDNEY *strides to the door.*)

Dear oh dear.

JANE (*following him*): Where are you going?

SIDNEY: To get my overcoat before I freeze. Where else do you think I'm going?

JANE: But, Sidney . . .

(SIDNEY *ignores her, flinging open the door and striding out, making a dignified exit. There is a burst of furious barking.* SIDNEY *reappears very swiftly and closes the door behind him.*)

SIDNEY (*to EVA, furiously*): That dog of yours is a liability. You ought to keep that animal under control. I can't even get to my overcoat. It's not good enough.

(EVA *slowly lies down on the kitchen table, oblivious.*)

JANE: Come and sit down.

SIDNEY: Sit down? What's the point of sitting down?

JANE: Geoff should be back soon.

SIDNEY: I should hope so. This isn't what you expect at all. Not when you come round for a quiet drink and a chat. (*Almost screaming in EVA's ear*) This is the last time I accept hospitality in this household.

JANE: Ssh.

SIDNEY: What?

JANE: She'll hear you.

SIDNEY: I don't care who hears me. (*He sits.*)

JANE: Ssh. (*She sits.*)

(*A pause. The four of them are sitting.* EVA *lies.* RONALD *continues to look glassy, quivering slightly.* MARION's *drinking has caught up with her.* JANE *looks abjectly miserable.* SIDNEY *shivers in his vest.*)

Sister, British title for nurse.

singlet, undershirt.

SIDNEY: And we're missing the television.

JANE: Ssh.

(A silence. Then, from apparently nowhere, a sleepy voice begins to sing dreamily. It is EVA.)

EVA *(singing)*: "On the first day of Christmas my true love sent to me a partridge in a pear tree. On the second day of Christmas my true love sent to me, two turtle doves—

MARION *(joining her)*: —and a partridge in a pear tree. On the third day of Christmas my true love sent to me, three French hens—

JANE *(joining her)*: —two turtle doves and a partridge in a pear tree. On the fourth day of Christmas my true love sent to me, four calling birds—

RONALD *(joining them)*: —three French hens, two turtle doves and a partridge in a pear tree.

ALL: On the fifth day of Christmas my true love sent to me, five gold rings, etc.

(As the bedraggled quintet begin to open up, the singing gets bolder and more confident. Somewhere in the distance GEORGE begins to howl. EVA, still lying on her back, conducts them dreamily with both hands and then finally with the hammer.)

(The door bursts open. GEOFFREY enters hurriedly, calling behind him.)

GEOFFREY: Through here, Doctor. Please hurry, I . . .

(GEOFFREY is suddenly aware of the sound behind him. He turns, still breathless from his run up four flights. His mouth drops further open as he surveys the scene. The singing continues unabated, as the Lights black-out and—

the CURTAIN *falls)*

ACT 3

(The Brewster-Wrights' kitchen. Next Christmas.

They live in a big old Victorian house, and the kitchen, though modernized to some extent, still retains a lot of the flavour of the original room. A sink, an electric stove [or even an Aga range°], a fridge, a dark wood sideboard, a round table and chairs form the substantial furnishings for the room. On the table is an elderly radio set. There is a door, half of opaque glass, to the hall, and a garden door.

When the curtain rises, RONALD is discovered sitting in an armchair near the table. He wears a scarf and a green eye-shade.° Beside him is a lighted portable oil stove. At his elbow is an empty teacup. The radio is on, playing very quietly a very jolly carol. RONALD is reading a book. He is

---

obviously enjoying it, for every two or three seconds he chuckles to himself out loud. This continues for some seconds, until the door from the hall opens and EVA enters. She wears a winter coat and carries an empty teacup and a plate, which she puts down on the draining-board.)

RONALD: Oh. Hallo there.

EVA: All right?

RONALD: Oh, yes. *(He switches off the radio.)*

EVA: Are you warm enough in here?

RONALD: Oh, yes. It's fine in here. Well, not too bad.

EVA: The rest of the house is freezing. I don't envy you going to bed.

RONALD: Her room's all right though, is it?

EVA: Oh, she's got three electric fires° blazing away.

RONALD: My God. That'll be the second power station I've paid for this winter.

EVA: She seems to be rather dug in up there. Almost in a state of hibernation. Doesn't she ever come out?

RONALD: Not if she can help it. Heating system went on the blink, you see—usual thing and we had a few frosty words over it and—the outcome was, she said she wasn't setting foot outside her room until I got it fixed.

EVA *(putting on a pair of gloves)*: Well, how long's it been like this?

RONALD *(vaguely)*: Oh, I don't know. Two or three weeks, I suppose.

EVA: Well, that's disgusting. Can't you get the men round to fix it?

RONALD: Yes, yes. I have phoned them several times. But I've been a bit unlucky up to now. They always seem to be at lunch . . .

EVA *(taking off her coat and putting it on the back of a chair)*: Well, I wouldn't put up with it. I'd scream the place down till Geoffrey got it fixed. *(She hunts in the cupboards.)*

RONALD: Yes, we've had a packet of trouble with this central heating. Always goes on the blink. Either the day before Christmas, the day before Easter or the day before Whitsun.° Always seems to manage it. Don't understand the principle it works on but whatever it is, seems to be very closely tied in with the Church calendar. *(He laughs.)* Can I help you at all?

EVA: She said she'd like a sandwich. *(She puts a plate, knife, bread and a pot of peanut butter on a bread board.)*

RONALD *(looking at his watch)*: Oh, yes. She's about due for a sandwich.

EVA: I'm looking for the butter.

RONALD: Oh, don't you bother to do that, I'll . . .

Aga range, old-fashioned stove, now an expensive indication of social status.   *green eyeshade,* worn by old-fashioned accountants.

electric fires, electric space heaters.   *Whitsun,* seventh Sunday after Easter, a traditional holiday weekend.

EVA: It's all right. Where do you keep your butter?

RONALD: Do you know, that's very interesting. I have absolutely no idea. A closely guarded secret kept by Mrs Minns. I suppose we could hazard a guess. Now then, butter. Try the fridge.

EVA: Fridge?

RONALD: Keeps it soft. It's warmer in there than it is outside.

EVA (looking in the fridge): Right first time. (She sets about making a sandwich, taking off one glove.)

RONALD: What's she want? Peanut butter?

EVA: Apparently.

RONALD: Good grief. She's got an absolute craving for that stuff lately. That and cheese footballs. All most alarming. She's not up there knitting little blue bootees, by any chance?

EVA: Not that I noticed.

RONALD: Thank God for that.

EVA: She looks a lot better than when I last saw her, anyway.

RONALD: Really? Yes, yes. Well, she got a bit overtired, I think. Principally.

EVA: Geoff'll be here in a minute to pick me up. I'll get out of your way. I just heard Marion was—I hope you didn't mind . . .

RONALD: No, very good of you to look round. Sure she appreciated it. She doesn't get many visitors. Lottie Potter looked in briefly. That set her back a couple of weeks. No, the trouble with Marion you see, is she lives on her nerves. Far too much.

EVA: Marion does?

RONALD: Oh, yes. Very nervous, insecure sort of person basically, you know.

EVA: Really?

RONALD: That surprises you, does it? Well, I've got a pretty thorough working knowledge of her now, you know. I mean, she's calmer than she was. When I first met her she was really one of the jumpiest girls you could ever hope to meet. Still, as I say, she's much calmer since she's been with me. If I've done nothing else for her, I've acted as a sort of sedative.

EVA: You don't think that a lot of her trouble may be—drink?

RONALD: Drink? No, I don't honestly think so. She's always liked a—I mean, the doctor did say she should lay off. But that was only because it was acting as a stimulant. She hasn't touched it lately.

EVA: She has this evening.

RONALD: Really?

EVA: Yes.

RONALD: Well, you do surprise me.

EVA: She's got quite a collection up there.

RONALD: Oh, has she? Has she now?

EVA: Didn't you know?

RONALD: Well, I don't often have much cause to go into her room these days. She likes her privacy,

you see. And I respect that. Not that it's not a mutual arrangement, you understand. I mean, she doesn't particularly choose to come into my room either. So it works out rather conveniently. On the whole.

EVA: Do you ever see each other at all?

RONALD: Good Lord, it's not as if we aren't in the same house. We bang into each other quite frequently. It's not always as quiet as this, believe me. In the holidays we've got the boys here. They thump about. No end of a racket. Boys, of course. Mind you, they're no trouble—they're usually out, too, most of the time—with their friends.

EVA: Pity they're not with you for Christmas.

RONALD: Oh well, it's greatly over-estimated, this Christmas business. That reminds me, would you like a drink? Seeing as it's Christmas.

EVA: No, I don't think so.

RONALD: Oh, go on. Just one. With me, for Christmas.

EVA: Well—all right, a little one.

RONALD: Right. (He rises.) Good. I'll brave the elements then and try and make it as far as the sitting-room° . . .

(The doorbell rings.)

EVA: That's probably Geoff.

RONALD (opening the door): I'll let him in, then. (Stopping short) Good Lord, is that dust on the hall table or frost? Won't be a minute.

(RONALD goes out.)
(EVA, alone, looks round the room rather sadly. She leaves the sandwich and plate on the table, puts the other things back on the sideboard, returns to the table, sits and starts to eat the sandwich.)
(GEOFFREY enters in his overcoat.)

GEOFFREY: Blimey.° Why aren't you sitting in the garden, it's warmer.

EVA: Hullo.

GEOFFREY: Ready then?

EVA: I'm just going to have a drink with Ronnie.

GEOFFREY: Oh. And how is she?

EVA: Drunk.

GEOFFREY: God.

(Pause. EVA munches.)

EVA: How did you get on?

GEOFFREY: Well . . .

EVA: Did you ask him?

GEOFFREY: Well . . .

EVA: You didn't.

(GEOFFREY does not reply.)

---

sitting-room, living room. ***Blimey,*** mild swear word (short for Gorblimey, God blind me).

You didn't damn well ask him.

GEOFFREY: It's no good. I find it impossible to ask people for money.

(EVA *gives a short laugh.*)

I'm sorry.

EVA: He owes it you. You're not asking him a favour, you know. He owes it you.

GEOFFREY: I know.

EVA: Well then.

GEOFFREY: It doesn't matter.

EVA: Oh, my . . . Oh well I'll have to get in touch with him then. After Christmas. I don't mind doing it.

GEOFFREY: You don't have to do that.

EVA: Well, somebody has to, darling. Don't they?

(*The door opens. A drinks trolley° enters followed by* RONALD.)

RONALD: Here we come. The Trans-Siberian Express. Thank you so much. We seem to be a bit depleted on the old alcohol stakes. Odd, thought I'd stocked up only recently. Probably old Mrs Minns been knocking them off, eh? The woman must have some vices. She hasn't got much else to recommend her. Now what are we having, Eva?

EVA: Could I have just a bitter lemon?

RONALD: Good gracious, nothing stronger?

EVA: Not just now.

RONALD: Well, if that's what you want . . . Geoff, what about you?

GEOFFREY: I think I'd like the same, actually.

RONALD: What? A bitter lemon?

GEOFFREY: Just what I feel like.

RONALD: You won't last through Christmas at that rate. (*Inspecting his trolley*) Well, that seems to be the only thing I haven't brought.

EVA: Oh well, it doesn't matter. Something else.

RONALD: No, no. I'll get it, I'll get it. We've got some somewhere.

(RONALD *goes out, closing the door.*)

EVA: I mean, either you want me to help you or you don't.

GEOFFREY: Yes.

EVA: I mean, if you don't, just say so. I don't particularly enjoy working in that dark little office of yours. You're a terrible employer. You come in late even when I drive you to work. You take four-hour lunch breaks and then expect me to do all your damn typing at five o'clock in the evening.

GEOFFREY: That's the way I do business.

EVA: Not with me you don't.

GEOFFREY: That's what you're paid for.

EVA: That's what I'm what?

---

trolley, small wheeled cart.

GEOFFREY: Look, if you don't like the job . . .

EVA: You asked me to help you. Now, if you didn't mean that, that's a different matter.

GEOFFREY: Well yes, I did, but . . .

EVA: All right, then. That's settled. You asked me to help you. I am bloody well going to help you.

GEOFFREY: O.K. O.K., thanks.

EVA: Not at all. (*A slight pause*) And you're not going to ask for that money?

GEOFFREY: No.

EVA: Even though we're owed it?

GEOFFREY: No.

EVA: And you won't let me ask?

GEOFFREY: No.

EVA: All right. Then we'll have to think of something else.

GEOFFREY: Exactly.

EVA: I'll phone Sidney Hopcroft after Christmas and talk to him.

GEOFFREY: Sidney Hopcroft.

EVA: He's always asking if you're interested.

GEOFFREY: If you think I'm going to get myself involved in his seedy little schemes . . .

EVA: Why not?

GEOFFREY: Have you seen the buildings he's putting up? Half his tenants are asking to be re-housed and they haven't even moved in yet.

EVA: Darling, I hate to remind you but ever since the ceiling of the Harrison building caved in and nearly killed the Manager, Sidney Hopcroft is about your only hope of surviving as an architect in this city.

GEOFFREY: I can do without Sidney Hopcroft, thank you very much.

(*The door opens.* RONALD *enters with two bottles of bitter lemon.*)

RONALD: Here we are. Two very bitter lemons. (*He pours out two bitter lemons and a scotch.*)

EVA: Thank you.

RONALD: I think I'm going to have something more than that, if you'll excuse me. Bit quieter than last Christmas, eh?

GEOFFREY: What?

RONALD: Last Christmas. Remember that? Round at your place?

GEOFFREY: Yes.

EVA: Yes.

RONALD: Good gracious me. You have to laugh now. Old Hopcroft. (*He laughs*) Always remember old Hopcroft. Doing very well. Did you know that? Doing frightfully well. Seems to have a flair for it. Wouldn't think so to look at him. Always found him a bit unprepossessing. Still—the chap to keep in with. The rate he's going.

EVA: Yes.

GEOFFREY (*picking up* RONALD'*s book*): Is this good?

RONALD: Oh, yes. Yes, quite good. Very amusing. Bit—saucy, in parts. Mrs Minns found it under one of the boys' mattresses. Nearly finished her there and then, poor old thing. Bitter lemon.

EVA: Thanks.

RONALD: Bitter lemon.

GEOFFREY: Thank you.

RONALD (*raising his glass of scotch*): Well, Happy Christmas. Good health. God bless.

EVA: Happy Christmas.

GEOFFREY: Happy Christmas.

RONALD (*after a pause*): Sorry to hear about your problems, Geoff.

GEOFFREY: How do you mean?

RONALD: I meant, the Harrison thing. Hear it fell through . . . Oh, I'm sorry, perhaps that's the wrong expression to use—bit unfortunate.

GEOFFREY: That's all right.

EVA: It wasn't actually Geoff's fault.

RONALD: No, no, I'm sure—knowing Geoff. Unthinkable. I mean, that local paper's as biased as hell. I refused to read that particular article. So did all my friends.

EVA (*after a pause*): Just because Geoffrey was doing something totally new for a change . . .

GEOFFREY: How's the bank doing, then?

RONALD: Oh, well. We're not in the red, yet. No thanks to me, mind you.

(*A bell rings.*)

GEOFFREY: Is that the front door?

RONALD: No. It's the—er—bedroom bell, actually. We've never bothered to have them taken out. They always come in useful. Boys with measles and so on.

EVA: Shall I go up to her?

RONALD: No, no, I'll . . .

EVA: No, it's all right. I don't mind . . .

RONALD: Well, that's very good of you. Probably nothing important. Wants the page of her magazine turning over or something.

EVA: I hope not.

RONALD: What's the harm, I say. As long as it keeps her happy.

EVA: Yes.

(*EVA goes out, closing the door.*)

RONALD: I mean, who are we to argue with a woman, eh? You can never win. Hopeless. Mind you, I'm talking to the wrong chap, aren't I?

GEOFFREY: What?

RONALD: I mean you seem to do better than most of us.

GEOFFREY: Oh, yes. (*He sits in the armchair.*)

RONALD: You seem to have got things pretty well organized on the home front. (*He laughs.*)

GEOFFREY: Well, it's just a matter of knowing . . .

RONALD: Ah yes, that's the point. I never really have. Not really. I mean, take my first wife. Distinguished-looking woman. Very charming. Seemed pretty happy on the whole. Then one day, she suddenly ups and offs and goes. Quite amazing. I mean, I had literally no idea she was going to. I mean, we had the flat° over the bank at the time, so it wasn't as if I was even very far away and on this particular day, I came up for lunch and she'd laid on her usual splendid meal. I mean, I had absolutely no complaints about that. I think my very words were something like, jolly nice that, see you this evening. And when we knocked off for tea, I came upstairs and she'd just taken off. Well, I hunted about for a bit in case she'd got knocked down or gone shopping and lost her memory or something and then she wrote, some time later, and said she'd had enough. So I was forced to call it a day. Some time later again, I took up tennis to forget her and married Marion. Of course, that's all forgotten now. All the same, sometimes in the evening I can't help sitting here and trying to work it all out. I mean, something happened. Something must have happened. I'm just not sure what. Anyway. Under the bridge, eh? All I'm saying really, is some people seem to have the hang of it and some of us just aren't so lucky.

GEOFFREY: Hang of what?

RONALD: Well—this whole women business, really. I mean, this may sound ridiculous, but I've never to this day really known what most women think about anything. Completely closed book to me. I mean, God bless them, what would we do without them? But I've never understood them. I mean, damn it all, one minute you're having a perfectly good time and the next, you suddenly see them there like—some old sports jacket or something—literally beginning to come apart at the seams. Floods of tears, smashing your pots, banging the furniture about. God knows what. Both my wives, God bless them, they've given me a great deal of pleasure over the years but, by God, they've cost me a fortune in fixtures and fittings. All the same. Couldn't do without them, could we? I suppose. Want another one of those?

GEOFFREY: No, thanks.

(*The door opens. EVA enters.*)
(*GEOFFREY rises and sits again.*)

EVA (*coming in swiftly and closing the door*): Brrr.

RONALD: Ah.

EVA: Forgot to put my coat on. (*She puts her coat on.*)

RONALD: Anything serious?

---

flat, apartment.

EVA: No. (*Kneeling by the stove to warm herself.*) She says she wants to come down.

RONALD: Here? Is that wise?

EVA: She says she wants a Christmas drink with us since we're all here.

RONALD: Oh well. Sort of thing she does. Calls you all the way upstairs to tell you she's coming all the way downstairs. Your drink there.

EVA: Thanks.

RONALD: And how's that mad dog of yours? Still chewing up your guests?

GEOFFREY: Er—no . . .

EVA: No, we had to—give him away.

RONALD: No, really?

EVA: Yes—he got a bit much. He was really getting so expensive to keep. And then these people we know who've got a farm—they said they'd have him.

RONALD: Oh, dear. I didn't know that. That's a shame.

EVA: Yes, it was an awful decision to make. We just felt—well . . .

GEOFFREY: You did, you mean.

EVA: Darling, we couldn't afford to keep him.

RONALD: Well, old Dick Potter will be relieved, anyway. What did he have to have? Three stitches or something, wasn't it?

EVA: Something like that.

RONALD: Doesn't seem to have done him any harm, anyway. He should be half-way up some Swiss mountain by now. Hopefully, those two lads of ours are safely roped to him.

EVA: Oh, is that where they've gone?

RONALD: Yes. Something I always meant to take them on myself. Anyway, we'll have to do without old Dick to jolly us up this year, I suppose.

GEOFFREY: That's a pity.

(*The door opens.* MARION *sweeps in. She wears a negligée. She stands dramatically and flings out her arms.*)

MARION: Geoff, darling, it's sweet of you and Eva to come round to see me.

GEOFFREY (*rising*): Oh, that's O.K.

MARION: No, you don't know how much it means to me. It really is terribly, terribly sweet of you.

GEOFFREY: That's all right, we were . . .

MARION: And at Christmas, particularly. Bless you for remembering Christmas. (*She collapses into the armchair.*)

RONALD: Look, Marion, you're going to freeze to death. For goodness' sake, put something on, woman.

MARION: I'm all right.

RONALD: Let me get you your coat. You've only just got out of bed.

MARION: Darling, I am quite all right. And I am not sitting in my kitchen in a coat. Nobody sits in a kitchen in a coat. Except tradesmen. It's unheard of. Now, offer me a drink.

RONALD: Look, dear, you know the doctor said very plainly . . .

MARION (*snapping fiercely*): Oh, for the love of God, Ronnie, it's Christmas. Don't be such an utter misery. (*To the others*) He's Scrooge, you know. He's Scrooge in person. Have you noticed, he's turned all the heating off.

(RONALD, *dignified, goes to the trolley and pours* MARION *a drink.* GEOFFREY *sits by the table.*)

Oh, it's heavenly to be up. When you've lain in bed for any length of time, on your own, no-one to talk to, with just your thoughts, don't you find your whole world just begins to crowd in on you. Till it becomes almost unbearable. You just lie there thinking, oh God, it could've been so much better if only I'd had the sense to do so and so—you finish up lying there utterly filled with self-loathing.

EVA: I know the feeling.

RONALD (*handing* MARION *a glass*): Here you are, dear.

MARION: Heavens! I can hardly see it. Is there anything in here? No it's all right. I'll just sit here and inhale it. (*Turning to* GEOFFREY *and* EVA) How are you, anyway?

EVA: Well, as I told you we're—pretty well—

MARION: I don't know what it is about Christmas but—I know it's supposed to be a festive thing and we're all supposed to be enjoying ourselves—I just find myself remembering all the dreadful things—the dreadful things I've said—the dreadful things I've done and all those awful hurtful things I didn't mean—oh God, I didn't mean them. Forgive me, I didn't mean them. (*She starts to cry.*)

RONALD: Look, darling do try and jolly up just for a bit, for heaven's sake.

MARION (*savagely*): Jolly up? How the hell can—I—jolly—up?

EVA: Marion, dear . . .

MARION: Do you know what I saw in the hall just now? In the mirror. My face. My God, I saw my face. It was like seeing my face for the first time.

RONALD: Oh, come on. It's not a bad face, old sausage.

MARION: How could anything be so cruel? How could anything be so unutterably cruel?

RONALD (*to* GEOFFREY): Now, you see, this is a case in point. What am I supposed to do? I mean, something I've said has obviously upset her, but you tell me—you tell me.

MARION (*pulling* GEOFFREY *to her*): Geoff—Geoff—Geoff—did you know, Geoff, I used to be a very beautiful woman? I was a very, very beautiful woman. People used to stare at me in the street and say, "My God, what a beautiful, beautiful woman she is." People used to come from miles and miles just to take my picture . . .

RONALD: Marion.

MARION: I mean, who'd want my photograph now? Do you want my photograph now? No, of course you don't. Nobody wants my photograph now. Can anybody think of anyone who'd want a photograph of me now? Please, someone. Someone, please want my photograph.

RONALD *(bellowing)*: Marion! Nobody wants your damn picture, now shut up.

(A silence. GEOFFREY and EVA are stunned. RONALD removes his eyeshade and adjusts his scarf.)

(The first to recover) Now then, what were we saying?

(The doorbell rings.)

EVA *(after a pause)*: Doorbell.

RONALD: Bit late for a doorbell, isn't it?

(They sit. The doorbell rings again.)

EVA: Shall I see who it is?

RONALD: Yes, do. Have a look through the little glass window. If you don't like the look of them, don't open the door.

EVA: Right.

(EVA goes into the hall.)

RONALD: Can't think who'd be ringing doorbells at this time of night.

GEOFFREY: Carol singers?

RONALD: Not at this time. Anyway, we don't get many of them. Marion always asks them in. Insists on filling them up with hot soup and chocolate biscuits as if they were all starving. Had a great row with the chap next door. She made his children as sick as pigs.

(EVA enters. As she does so the doorbell rings. She closes the door behind her.)

EVA: I couldn't be sure but it looks suspiciously like the Hopcrofts. Do you want them in?

RONALD: Oh, good grief, hardly.

GEOFFREY: Heaven forbid.

RONALD: If we sit quiet, they'll go away.

EVA: Well, there's the hall light.

RONALD: That doesn't mean anything. People always leave their hall lights on for burglars. I don't know why they bother. I mean, there must be very few households who actually choose to spend their evenings sitting in the hall with the rest of the house in darkness.

GEOFFREY: If I know the Hopcrofts, they won't give up easily. They'll come round the side.

MARION: Why don't you just go in the hall and shout "Go away" through the letter-box?

RONALD: Because he happens to have a very large deposit account with my bank.

(The doorbell rings.)

EVA: They can smell us.

RONALD: I think we'll compromise and turn off the lights in here. Just to be on the safe side. *(Going to the door)* Everybody sit down and sit tight. *(By the switch)* Ready? Here we go.

(The room plunges into darkness. Just two streams of light—one from the door and one from the window.)

Now if we all keep absolutely quiet, there's no chance of them—ow! *(He cannons into EVA who gives a cry.)* I'm terribly sorry. I do beg your pardon. Was that your. . . ?

EVA: That's all right.

GEOFFREY: Ssh.

RONALD: I wish I knew where I was.

GEOFFREY: Well, stand still. I think someone's coming round the side.

EVA: Ssh.

(MARION starts to giggle.)

RONALD: Marion. Quiet.

MARION: I'm sorry I've just seen the funny side . . .

GEOFFREY: Ssh.

(SIDNEY and JANE appear at the back door. They wear party hats, are decked with the odd streamer, have had more drinks than they are used to and have a carrier bag full of goodies. They both press their faces against the back door, straining to see in.)

MARION: It's them.

GEOFFREY: Ssh.

(Pause)

RONALD: I say . . .

EVA: What?

RONALD: I've got a nasty feeling I didn't lock the back door.

MARION: Oh, no . . .

(GEOFFREY and EVA hide in front of the table. RONALD steps up into a corner by the window. The back door opens slowly.)

SIDNEY: Hallo?

JANE *(unwilling to enter)*: Sidney . . .

SIDNEY: Come on.

JANE: But there's nobody . . .

SIDNEY: The door was open, wasn't it? Of course there's somebody. They're probably upstairs.

JANE: But, Sidney, they might . . .

SIDNEY: Look, would you kindly not argue with me any more tonight, Jane. I haven't yet forgiven you for that business at the party. How did you manage to drop a whole plate of trifle?°

JANE: I didn't clean it up, Sidney, I didn't clean it up.

---

trifle, traditional dessert with fruit, cake, custard, and whipped cream.

SIDNEY: No. You just stood there with the mess at your feet. For all the world to see.

JANE: Well, what . . .

SIDNEY: I have told you before. If you drop something like that at a stand-up party, you move away and keep moving. Now come along.

JANE: I can't see.

SIDNEY: Then wait there and I'll find the light.

(A pause. SIDNEY crosses the room. GEOFFREY and EVA creep to the sideboard. The light goes on. SIDNEY and JANE are by the separate doors. The other four are in various absurd frozen postures obviously caught in the act of trying to find a hiding-place. JANE gives a short squeak of alarm. A long pause.)

MARION *(eventually)*: Boo.

SIDNEY: Good gracious.

RONALD *(as if seeing them for the first time)*: Ah, hallo there. It's you.

SIDNEY: Well, you had us fooled. They had us fooled there, didn't they?

JANE: Yes, they had us fooled.

SIDNEY: Playing a game on us, weren't you?

ALL: Yes.

EVA: Yes, we were playing a game.

SIDNEY: Completely fooled. Walked straight into that. Well, Happy Christmas, all.

ALL *(lamely, variously)*: Happy Christmas.

SIDNEY *(after a pause)*: Well.

JANE: Well.

(A pause)

RONALD: Would you like a drink? Now you're here.

SIDNEY: Oh, thank you.

JANE: Thank you very much.

SIDNEY: Since we're here.

RONALD: Well. What'll it be? *(He goes to the trolley.)*

SIDNEY: Sherry, please.

JANE: Yes, a sherry.

SIDNEY: Yes. We'd better stick to sherry.

RONALD: Sherry . . . *(He starts to pour.)*

SIDNEY: Sorry if we surprised you.

MARION: Quite all right.

SIDNEY: We knew you were here.

RONALD: How?

SIDNEY: We saw the car.

JANE: Saw your car.

RONALD: Oh. Yes.

(A pause. SIDNEY blows a party "blower.")

EVA: Been to a party?

SIDNEY: Yes.

JANE: Yes.

GEOFFREY: You look as if you have.

SIDNEY: Yes. Up at Walter's place. Walter Harrison.

RONALD: Oh—old Harrison's.

SIDNEY: Oh of course, you'll know him, won't you.

RONALD: Oh, yes.

GEOFFREY: Yes.

SIDNEY *(to GEOFFREY)*: Oh, yes, of course. Asking you if you know old Harrison. I should think you do know old Harrison. He certainly remembers you. In fact he was saying this evening . . .

RONALD: Two sherries.

SIDNEY: Oh, thank you.

JANE: Thank you very much.

SIDNEY: Compliments of the season.

JANE: Of the season.

RONALD: Yes. Indeed.

(A pause)

SIDNEY: What a house . Beautiful.

MARION: Oh, do you like it? Thank you.

SIDNEY: No. Old Harrison's. What a place.

JANE: Lovely.

RONALD: Didn't know you knew him.

SIDNEY: Well, I won't pretend. The reason we went was half pleasure and half—well, 'nuff said. Follow me? You scratch my back, I'll scratch yours.

RONALD: Ah.

(A pause)

JANE: It's a nice kitchen . . .

MARION: At the Harrisons'?

JANE: No. Here.

MARION: Oh. Glad you approve.

(A pause)

JANE *(very, very quietly)*: Sidney.

SIDNEY: Eh?

JANE *(mouthing and gesticulating towards the carrier bag)*: Their presents.

SIDNEY: What's that? *(He looks at his flies.)*

JANE *(still mouthing and miming)*: Shall we give them their presents now?

SIDNEY: Yes, yes, of course. That's why we've brought them.

JANE: We brought you a present.

SIDNEY: Just a little seasonal something.

RONALD: Oh.

MARION: Ah.

EVA: Thank you.

JANE *(to EVA)*: No, I'm afraid we didn't bring you and your husband anything. We didn't know you'd be here, you see.

SIDNEY: Sorry about that.

EVA: Oh, never mind.

GEOFFREY: Not to worry.

JANE: We could give them the hm-mm. You know, that we got given this evening.

SIDNEY: The what?

JANE: You know, the hm-mm. That we got in the thing.

SIDNEY: What, that? They don't want that.

JANE: No, I meant for hm-mm, you know. Hm-mm.

SIDNEY: Well, if you want to. Now, come on. Give Ron

and Marion their presents. They're dying to open them.

RONALD: Rather.

MARION: Thrilling.

JANE (*delving into her carrier and consulting the labels on various parcels*): Now this is for Ron. (*Reading*) To Ron with love from Sidney and Jane.

SIDNEY (*handing* RONALD *the present*): That's for you.

RONALD: Thank you. (*He unwraps it.*)

JANE: Now then, what's this?

SIDNEY: Is that Marion's?

JANE: No, that's from you and me to Auntie Gloria. (*Rummaging again*) Here we are. To Marion with love from Sidney and Jane.

SIDNEY: This is for you. (*He gives* MARION *her present.*)

MARION: Oh, super . . . (*To* RONALD) What've you got, darling?

RONALD (*gazing at his present mystified*): Oh, yes. This is very useful. Thank you very much.

MARION: What on earth is it?

RONALD: Well, it's—er—(*taking a stab at it*)—looks like a very nice set of pipe cleaners.

JANE: Oh, no.

SIDNEY: No, those aren't pipe cleaners.

RONALD: Oh, aren't they?

SIDNEY: Good gracious, no.

RONALD: Oh, no. Silly of me. Just looked terribly like them for a minute. From a certain angle.

SIDNEY: You should know those. It's a set of screwdrivers.

JANE: Set of screwdrivers.

SIDNEY: Electrical screwdrivers.

JANE: You should know those, shouldn't you?

(SIDNEY *and* JANE *laugh.* MARION *opens her present.*)

MARION (*with a joyous cry*): Oh, look! It's a lovely bottle of gin. Isn't that kind?

RONALD: Oh, my God.

SIDNEY: Bit of Christmas spirit.

MARION: Lovely. I'll think of you when I'm drinking it.

JANE (*still rummaging*): To the boys with love from Sidney and Jane. (*She produces two rather ghastly woolly toys—obviously unsuitable.*)

SIDNEY: That's just a little something.

JANE: Just for their stockings in the morning.

MARION: Oh, how nice.

RONALD: They'll love these . . .

SIDNEY: That the lot?

JANE: No, I'm just trying to find the hm-mm.

SIDNEY: Well, it'll be at the bottom somewhere, I should think.

JANE: I've got it. It's nothing very much. We just got it this evening out of a cracker° actually. We were

going to keep it for our budgie,° but we thought your George might like it. For his collar. (*She holds up a little bell on a ribbon.*)

EVA: Oh.

SIDNEY: So you'll know where he is.

JANE: As if you couldn't guess.

(SIDNEY *barks genially and hands them the bell.*)

SIDNEY: Woof woof!

EVA: Thank you.

SIDNEY (*to* GEOFFREY): Woof woof. (*No response*) Woof woof.

GEOFFREY (*flatly*): Thanks a lot.

SIDNEY: That's your lot. No more.

RONALD: I'm terribly sorry. I'm afraid we haven't got you anything at all. Not really much of ones for present buying.

SIDNEY: Oh, we didn't expect it.

JANE: No, no.

(*A pause.* SIDNEY *puts on a nose mask.* JANE *laughs. The others look horrified.* MARION *pours herself a gin.*)

SIDNEY: Well—(*he pauses*)—you know who ought to be here? now?

JANE: Who?

SIDNEY: Dick Potter. He'd start it off.

JANE: With a bit of help from Lottie.

SIDNEY: True. True.

RONALD: Yes, well, for some odd reason we're all feeling a bit low this evening. Don't know why. But we were just all saying how we felt a bit down.

JANE: Oh . . .

SIDNEY: Oh dear oh dear.

RONALD: Just one of those evenings, you know. The point is you'll have to excuse us if we're not our usual cheery selves.

MARION: I'm perfectly cheery. I don't know about anybody else.

RONALD: That is apart from my wife who is perfectly cheery.

SIDNEY: Oh, that's quite understood.

JANE: I have those sometimes, don't I?

SIDNEY: You certainly do. You can say that again. Well, that's a shame.

RONALD: Yes.

EVA (*after a slight pause*): My husband was saying to me just now, Sidney, that he feels terribly guilty that you keep on asking him to do jobs for you and he just hasn't been able to manage them.

SIDNEY: Yes. Well, he's a busy man.

EVA: Sometimes. But he really is dying to do something for you before long.

GEOFFREY: Eh?

EVA: He's really longing to.

---

cracker, Christmas "firecracker" with small gifts and a party hat inside.

budgie, parakeet.

SIDNEY: Oh, well in that case, we'll see.

EVA: If you could keep him in mind.

SIDNEY: Yes, I'll certainly keep him in mind. Really rather depends.

GEOFFREY: Yes, it does rather.

EVA: He'd love to.

SIDNEY (*after a pause*): Well now, what shall we do? Anyone got any ideas? We can't all sit round like this, can we? Not on Christmas Eve.

JANE: No, not on Christmas Eve.

SIDNEY: Spot of carpentry, spot of plumbing, eh? I know, what about a spot of electrical work? (*At the radio*) Well, we can have a bit of music to start off with, anyway. (*To* RONALD) This work all right, does it?

RONALD: Yes, yes, but I wouldn't . . .

SIDNEY: Get the party going, bit of music . . . (*He switches on the radio and begins to dance a little.*)

JANE: Bit of music'll get it going.

SIDNEY: Hey . . .

JANE: What?

SIDNEY: You know what we ought to do now?

JANE: What?

SIDNEY: We ought to move all the chairs back and clear the floor and . . .

(*The radio warms up and the room is filled with the sound of an interminable Scottish reel which plays continually. Like most Scottish reels, without a break. This effectively drowns the rest of* SIDNEY *and* JANE's *discussion. He continues to describe with graphic gestures his idea to* JANE. JANE *claps her hands with excitement. They move the table, stove and chairs out of the way.* SIDNEY *then wheels the trolley away past* MARION's *armchair. She grabs a bottle as it goes by.*)

RONALD (*yelling above the noise*): What the hell's going on?

SIDNEY (*yelling back*): You'll see. Just a minute. (*He turns the radio down a little.*) Now then. We can't have this. We can't have all these glum faces, not at Christmas time.

JANE (*scurrying about collecting a bowl of fruit, a spoon, a tea-cosy,° colander° and tea towel from the dresser and draining-board*): Not at Christmas time. (*She opens the gin bottle and puts a glass near it on the trolley.*)

SIDNEY: So we're going to get you all jumping about. Get you cheerful.

RONALD: No, well, I don't think we really . . .

SIDNEY: No arguments please.

RONALD: Yes, but all the same . . .

SIDNEY: Come on then, Eva, up you get.

EVA (*uncertainly*): Well . . .

SIDNEY: Come on. Don't you let me down.

---

tea-cosy, quilted or knitted cover for a teapot.   **colander,** strainer.

EVA: No . . . (*She rises.*)

GEOFFREY: I'm afraid we both have to . . .

EVA: No, we don't. We'll play.

GEOFFREY: What do you mean, we'll . . .

EVA: If he wants to play, we'll play, darling.

(JANE *begins to roll up the carpet.*)

SIDNEY: That's grand. That's marvellous. That's two—come on—any more?

MARION: What are we all doing? Is she going to be terribly sweet and wash our floor?

JANE: No, we're playing a game.

SIDNEY: A game.

MARION: Oh, what fun . . .

RONALD: Marion, I really don't think we should . . .

MARION: Oh, don't be such a misery, Ronnie. Come on.

RONALD: Oh . . .

SIDNEY: That's telling him, that's telling him. Now then, listen very carefully, everyone. This is a version of musical chairs called Musical Dancing.

JANE: Musical Forfeits.

SIDNEY: Musical Dancing. It's called Musical Dancing.

JANE: Oh, I thought it was called Musical Forfeits.

SIDNEY: Musical Dancing. It's very simple. All you do—you start dancing round the room and when I stop the music you all have to freeze in the position you were last in . . .

(GEOFFREY *sits on the high stool.*)

Don't let him sit down. (*To* GEOFFREY) Come on, get up.

EVA (*sharply*): Get up.

(GEOFFREY *gets up.*)

SIDNEY: Only to make it more difficult, the last person caught moving each time gets a forfeit. At the end, the person with the least forfeits gets the prize. (*To* JANE) What's the prize going to be?

JANE (*producing it from the carrier*): A chocolate Father Christmas.

SIDNEY: A chocolate Father Christmas, right. Everything ready your end?

JANE: I think so.

SIDNEY: Got the list?

JANE (*waving a scrap of paper*): Yes .

SIDNEY: Right. You take charge of the forfeits. I'll do the music. Ready, everybody? Right. Off we go.

(SIDNEY *turns up the music loud. The four stand looking faintly uneasy.* JANE *and* SIDNEY *dance about to demonstrate.*)

Well, come on then. Come on. I don't call that dancing. Everybody dance. Come on, dance about. Keep dancing till the music stops.

(MARION *starts to dance, in what she imagines to be a classical ballet style. She is extremely shaky.*)

That's it. She's doing it. That's it. Look at her. Everybody do what she's doing. Lovely.

(*The others begin sheepishly and reluctantly to hop about.*)

And—stop! (*He cuts off the music.*) Right. Who was the last?

JANE: Ron.

SIDNEY: Right. It's Ron. Ron has a forfeit. What's the first one?

JANE (*consulting her list*): Apple under the chin.

SIDNEY: Apple under his chin, right. Put an apple under his chin.

RONALD: Eh? What are you doing?

(JANE *puts the apple under his chin.*)

JANE: Here. Hold it. Go on, hold it.

RONALD: Oh, don't be so ridiculous, I can't possibly . . .

MARION: Oh, for heaven's sake, darling, do join in. We're all waiting for you. Don't be tedious.

RONALD (*talking with difficulty*): This is absolutely absurd. I mean how am I to be . . .

SIDNEY (*over this*): And off we go again. (*He turns up the music.*)

(*They resume dancing.* MARION *is the only one who moves around: the others jig about on one spot.* SIDNEY *shouts encouragement.*)

And—stop! (*He stops the music.*)

JANE: Eva!

SIDNEY: Right, Eva. What's Eva got?

JANE (*consulting list*): Orange between the knees.

SIDNEY: Orange between the knees, right. If you drop it you get another forfeit automatically.

(JANE *gives* EVA *her orange.*)

And off we go again.

(*Music. From now on the forfeits come quick and fast.* JANE *reading them out,* SIDNEY *repeating them.* RONALD *gets the next* [*spoon in mouth*]. *The music continues.* GEOFFREY *gets the next* [*tea-cosy on head*]. *They dance on.* MARION *gets the next* [*ironically, swallowing a gin in one*]. RONALD *opens his mouth to protest at this last forfeit of* MARION*'s. In doing so he drops his spoon.*)

(*Gleefully*) Another one for Ron!

JANE: Another one for Ron . . .

RONALD: What?

JANE: Pear on spoon in mouth . . .

SIDNEY: Pear on spoon in mouth . . . (*He gets up on the table and conducts.*)

RONALD: Now listen I . . .

(JANE *rams the spoon handle back in* RONALD*'s mouth. She balances a pear on the other end.*)

SIDNEY: And off we go. . . . !

(*The permutations to this game are endless and* SIDNEY*'s list covers them all. Under his increasingly strident commands, the dancers whirl faster and faster whilst accumulating bizarre appendages.* JANE, *the acolyte, darts in and out of the dancers with a dedicated frenzy.* GEOFFREY *throws his tea-cosy to the floor.* JANE *picks it up and wraps a tea towel round his leg. She then pours another gin for* MARION. SIDNEY, *at the finish, has abandoned the idea of stopping the music. He screams at the dancers in mounting exhortation bordering on the hysterical.*)

That's it. Dance. Come on. Dance. Dance. Come on. Dance. Dance. Dance. Keep dancing. Dance . . .

It is on this scene that—

the CURTAIN *falls*)

Figure 1. In the clean and modern Hopcroft kitchen, Jane Hopcroft (Bridget Turner) pauses to collect herself just before going into the living room to meet her guests, and is just about to realize that she is still wearing her bedroom slippers. The 1973 production of *Absurd Person Singular* at the Criterion Theatre, London, was directed by Eric Thompson. (Photograph: John Haynes.)

Figure 2. In the "trendy homespun" kitchen of the Jacksons, Eva Jackson (Anna Calder-Marshall, *on table*), reaches for the bare wires of the light fixture, while a length of electrical cord and rope dangle from her wrist. Jane and Sidney Hopcroft (Bridget Turner, Richard Briers, *left*) and Ronald Brewster-Wright (Michael Aldridge, *right*), stop her from touching the fixture, in the 1973 London production of *Absurd Person Singular.* (Photograph: John Haynes.)

Figure 3. In the old-fashioned kitchen of the Brewster-Wrights, Sidney Hopcroft (Richard Briers, *standing on table*) directs the game of "Musical Dancing," with comic forfeits, in the 1973 London production of *Absurd Person Singular*. Ronald Brewster-Wright (Michael Aldridge, *left*) balances a pear on a spoon in his mouth, while his alcoholic wife Marion (Sheila Hancock) dances happily in front of the table. Eva Jackson (Anna Calder-Marshall) bends over, trying to keep an orange between her knees, while her husband Geoffrey (David Burke) wears a tea cozy on his head and holds one leg up. (Photograph: John Haynes.)

Staging of *Absurd Person Singular*

ALAN AYCKBOURN, ON *ABSURD PERSON SINGULAR*

This was the fourth of my plays to be played in the West End although, like its predecessors, it started life in Scarborough in a modest 250 seat theatre-in-the-round. It was a makeshift auditorium. Borrowed seats on rickety rostra in a small airless room of the public library. On hot evenings, senior citizens would be supported from the theatre gasping for fresh sea air. Small children would, when carried away by the action, occasionally slip through the gaps in the seating and require rescuing. The stage floor was parquet and treacherously polished; the walls covered in untouchable, light green flock wallpaper. All in all an unpromising venue to present—as we saw it at the time—new work in new ways to new audiences.

For, despite the fact that the company—the brainchild initially of its founder, Stephen Joseph—had been running for fifteen years, theatre in the early seventies was still thought of largely as a proscenium arch affair. Heaven knows why. It was, as Stephen pointed out at the time, a comparatively recent invention in the overall scheme of things. Certainly the Greeks or the Elizabethans would have looked on it with some amazement.

Here we were, then, in the unlikeliest of towns in the most improbable of buildings presenting plays with young unfamiliar casts to largely non-theatrical audiences.

I can't pretend it wasn't a challenge. When we produced some particularly dark play—a verse drama about a young girl's journey to suicide was such a one, I seem to remember—on an especially bright seaside day, it was not uncommon to find yourself performing to crowds of eight or nine.

The problem was that on top of all the other disadvantages we were saddled with, our policy was wherever possible to present new work by new authors.

It was against this makeshift, hand to mouth, improvised theatrical background that I was encouraged to write. First, during the late fifties and early sixties until his premature death in 1967, by Stephen Joseph himself and then, as I gathered confidence, through my own volition.

By 1970, with seven or eight plays behind me—three of them international successes—I took over the Artistic Directorship of the Scarborough theatre. As a director I was enjoying myself enormously, playing with this new toy I had somewhat fortuitously inherited. As a writer though I was anxious, whilst still working under the general heading of comedy, to explore fresh territory. I'd established through my earlier work (especially *Relatively Speaking* and *How The Other Half Loves*) that I could construct plays and that I could make audiences laugh. More important, they were coming back and what's more bringing their friends. Which meant that the tiny Library Theatre was now beginning to fill—not only for my plays but, as people got to hear about the company, other newer writers as well.

I wrote *Absurd Person Singular*, I remember, as I tend to write most of my plays, in a great hurry. It was due to be the second production of the Scarborough 1972 season. Before that, for two weeks in London we rehearsed, with me directing, a new version by David Campton of the classic vampire tale, *Carmilla*. During the evenings, throughout that fortnight, I wrote *Absurd Person Singular* for the rehearsing company. We opened *Carmilla* at the end of the fortnight for a one week pre-Scarborough 'tour' in the studio of the newly opened Sheffield Crucible Theatre. There we also started rehearsals for *Absurd* before moving on to Scarborough where, a week or so later, we finally opened the play to goodish, if not universally good, reviews.

I confess it was, when it opened, half an hour too long. By the second night that had been remedied with some quite severe cutting. As it played in, too, it also gathered confidence and speed as the cast began to sense that they had a success. Audiences increased and nightly response became increasingly enthusiastic.

Yet in rehearsal we had had our doubts—me most of all. The first Act, at Sidney and Jane's, seemed safe enough. I was pleased to have discovered the idea of 'offstage-action,' to be sure. It seemed an interesting solution to set the scene apparently in the wrong room i.e. their kitchen. In what appeared strictly speaking to be a 'backstage' area. Where we should have been, surely, was in the sitting room. That's where the main action (apparently) was happening. Of course, it rarely was. The really interesting things, the things people want to say to each other in private were said in here by the sink. Besides, given that the other room contained Dick and Lottie Potter it seemed an audience would only thank me for keeping us all out here, away from his jokes. Nonetheless, although the Act had one or two original constructional notions, it departed very little from the conventional lines of the comedy I had attempted earlier.

Relating the play over three Christmases gave the play a progression and, at the same time, a unity. I also liked the idea, following our glimpse of Jane's shiny, new-pin culinary unit in Act I, of setting all the Acts in various kitchens. It appealed to my sense of symmetry besides observing further dramatic unity. In addition, it was an ideal way to indicate the three differing social levels that each couple inhabited. Nowhere in a house says more about a person's habit and background, the nature of their day to day existence, than their kitchen. All well and good, so far.

It was in Act II that the unknown, untried elements were introduced and the fears began to arise. The idea of having the second act of a comedy centring round a woman committing suicide (echoes of earlier verse dramas) seemed a potentially dangerous notion. Would we be accused of insensitivity and bad taste? Would the audience on the first night be filled with people trying to recover from their own unsuccessful suicide bids?

To counteract any charge that I was using human tragedy as a cheap way to get laughs (which was never my intention, of course), I resolved that whatever happened the humor would never be directed against the luckless Eva herself. The comedy would spring from a genuine, unmalicious misunderstanding; it would arise from the other misguided blunderers who had totally misread her intentions.

Indeed, as performances went by, I was to learn a vital comic lesson. Namely that a single, truthful, serious event can become funny when set alongside a parallel series of equally serious, contrasting events. The secret of the comedy in the second act (though I don't lay claim to having invented it!) is that everyone, Eva, Sidney, Jane, Ronald, even the inebriated Marion are behaving in a truthful, logical manner. All are unaware of the comedic possibilities of their plight. In order to appreciate it, they would need to be standing well back from it all, indeed to be where we, the audience are.

More important, by taking their own situations totally seriously, they present us with a choice of whether to laugh or sympathise, recognise and relish or identify and anguish. During the London run, Richard Briers who played the ultimately crowing, revengeful Sidney with such demonic glee, told me that for every two visitors who came backstage to his dressing room wet-eyed from seeing a performance, one blamed it on laughing and the other from the shock of recognising either a close relative, or worse still, themselves. The second act became, despite our fears, the comic high point of the play.

In Act III, I was again moving into fresh territory. The tone here is much more muted. A cold, bleak, ice-box of a kitchen. A dead central heating boiler and a dead marriage. Ronald, ironically, having lost any feelings he ever had, mournfully reads a soft porn novel with little sign of pleasure. Dick and Lottie have taken his children away for Christmas; the sons he and Marion have never understood or bothered to communicate with much.

The underdogs are baying outside. Sidney and Jane are soon to arrive and demand that the others dance, literally, to the Hopcroft tune. Geoff and Eva have, meantime, fought each other to a standstill. Eva, now withdrawn, no longer presents anyone most especially Geoff with a vulnerable emotional target—or conversely the smallest glimmer of warmth. Geoff, for his part is emasculated by the failure of his work and the ultimate hollowness of his sexual infidelities.

Not perhaps the most promising of material upon which to build the last act of a comedy. Yet there is laughter, if of a more salutary kind. By now, we can no longer hide the fact entirely that we are not heading for the happiest of endings. Marion's emergence like a drunken spectre at a wake provides the final bleak-comic moment. All have been brought down by a weakness in their character. Marion through her vanity, Ronald his remoteness and indifference, Geoff his sexual and professional arrogance and Eva her self-centred, self-obsession.

Only Sidney and Jane survive—but at what cost? Through an increasingly loveless, unfeeling, social climbing partnership where the pursuit of material success is everything.

And the moral? Not that the Hopcrofts of this world will always rise and conquer. They needn't. But given the world we have where materialism does often seem to matter most, given what flawed emotional muddles most of us are anyway, the odds seem stacked heavily in favour of those with the least feelings or scruples and those with the strongest, most uncaring ambitions. I wheel and deal, therefore I am. Beware. The kingdom of the Hopcroft is at hand!

"I mean, in this world it's dog eat dog, isn't it? No place for sentiment . . . when the chips are down it's every man for himself and blow you Jack, I regret to say."

WOLE SOYINKA

1934–

Awarded the Nobel Prize for literature in 1986, the first African writer to be so honored, Nigeria's Wole Soyinka began his Nobel lecture with an arresting anecdote about an actor in an improvisational performance refusing to come on stage for his part. The actor was, it turned out, Soyinka himself, and the improvisational theater piece dealt with the death of black Kenyans at the hands of their white warders. Soyinka's refusal to play his assigned role—as one of the killers—was, he explained, produced by his concern that acting out such a reality might not stir an audience to action but lull them into soporific acceptance. Soyinka's own career as playwright, poet, novelist, actor, director, and professor bears witness to his spacious awareness of such difficult political issues. Asked in 1983 about the possible contradiction between his call for a single black African language and his continued use of English, the language of a major colonial power, in his writing, Soyinka admitted that he did not write in Kiswahili, and then explained:

> English of course continues to be my medium of expression as it is the medium of expression for millions of people in Nigeria, Ghana, Sierra Leone, Gambia, Kenya, who I want to talk to, if possible. And I want to talk also to our black brothers in the United States, in the West Indies. I want to talk *also* even to Europeans, if they are interested in listening. . . . I do know that I enjoy works of literature from the European world—I'd be a liar if I said I didn't. And I also enjoy literary works from the Asian world. . . . I find no contradiction, no sense of guilt, in the fact that I write and communicate in English.

Soyinka's multicultural heritage reflects his education in Nigeria, where he was born and where he attended University College, Ibadan (to which he would return in 1967 as head of the Department of Theatre Arts), as well as his immersion in English literature at the University of Leeds, where he studied with two gifted literary scholars and critics, G. Wilson Knight and Arnold Kettle. In 1957, Soyinka became a play reader at London's Royal Court Theatre—the center for new writing in England, and also the place where he refused to come on stage for the experimental collective production *Eleven Men Dead at Hola,* even though he had participated in creating both words and music for that occasion. Subsequently, the Royal Court produced his first play, *The Invention* (1959). His second play, *The Swamp Dwellers* (1959), was produced at a student drama festival, and his poems were published in *African Treasury* (1960), edited by the American poet Langston Hughes.

Since that breakthrough period in England, Soyinka's playwriting career has embraced a wide range of subjects and moods. *The Lion and the Jewel* (1959), set in a small remote village, focuses on the familiar comic theme of an old man wanting a young wife, but ends up celebrating the cunning and vitality of the old man. *The Trials of Brother Jero* (1964) farcically depicts a "beach preacher" who escapes retribution from one of his followers and, in so doing, creates a "miracle" for a new worshiper. Two satirical revues, *The Republican* (1963) and *Before the Blackout*

(1965), offer an entertaining and topical look at political issues. And his refashioning of Brecht's *Threepenny Opera* into *Opera Wonyosi* (1977) is in part an attack on African dictators such as Idi Amin and Jean-Bedel Bokassa. After the takeover of Nigeria's government by a military and reactionary group, Soyinka was detained, often in solitary confinement, from August 1967 to October 1969. He left Nigeria in the summer of 1970, intending a "brief exile," but stayed away for almost five years.

During his years in exile, Soyinka continued to explore cultural, political, and religious themes—and in much deeper and more challenging ways than before. In *Jero's Metamorphosis* (written in 1973, first performed in 1974), Soyinka returned to the title character of his 1964 play, but portrayed him not as a farcical beach preacher but as a power-seeking bureaucrat, seeking to organize a whole group of hypocritical "prophets." The year 1973 also brought Soyinka a commission from the National Theatre of Great Britain, for whom he created a strikingly new version of *The Bacchae* of Euripides by ending it with the severed head of Pentheus, the repressive king, spurting not blood but wine, as if his death has become a force for regeneration. And in *Death and the King's Horseman* (1976), Soyinka returns explicitly to the Yoruba culture of his early years—a culture steeped in religious beliefs that include gods and spirits, ceremonial worship and celebrations, and community involvement through song and dance.

The specific source for *Death and the King's Horseman* was an incident from 1945 (Soyinka seems to be slightly mistaken about the date in his author's note), in which the ritual suicide of the Master of the Horse for the Alafin (or king) of Oyo was interrupted by a British colonial officer. Soyinka moved the play from post–World War II to a time during the war and added a visit by the Prince of Wales. The latter event, implicitly juxtaposing a future Western monarch against the dead African king, deepens the play's seemingly insoluble conflict—the conflict that arises when an ancient ritual from one culture seems strange, even perverse, to people who have grown up in quite a different culture. A reader or audience member for whom the Yoruba world is foreign may thus feel at a loss, not knowing why Elesin, the Horseman, is to die, or what to think about that death. Such a response may even lead one to welcome with relief the appearance of Simon Pilkings, the District Officer, and his wife, Jane—representatives of a more familiar world. Yet Soyinka immediately destabilizes that reaction as well, since Pilkings and Jane are wearing African costumes for a fancy-dress ball. Their costumes are radically inappropriate—not only because they are Westerners but because the African dress belongs, as the policeman Amusa points out, "to dead cult, not for human being." One might think back to Aeschylus in the *Agamemnon* when the victorious Greek general, Agamemnon, steps out of his chariot onto the rich purple tapestries that Clytemnestra has laid on the ground, and thus appears to be a proud man, trampling on the emblem of power. So, too, Pilkings and Jane are trampling on a hallowed system of belief.

And it is the system of belief—in Soyinka's words, "the world of the living, the dead and the unborn, and the numinous passage which links all: transition"—that the play asks us to experience. Elesin's love of all sensory pleasures, from the words of the Praise-Singer to the beauty of his new clothes to the youth and sexual appeal of his young bride, is easily understandable. But that vitality is also connected to his resolve to die and to the trance-dance he performs in Scene 3, as he begins his willed and willing passage to another realm. He explains to Pilkings: "I shed all thoughts of earth. I began to follow the moon to the abode of the gods . . . servant of the white king, that was when you entered my chosen place of departure on feet of desecration." The play enacts the force of Elesin's belief through two deaths—first that of his son, Olunde, and then that of his own sudden and violent suicide. Yet the last lines of the play, spoken by the "mother" of the market women to Elesin's young bride, signal that the deaths are indeed part of life, and a prelude to the new life that is to come: "Now forget the dead, forget even the living. Turn your mind only to the unborn."

Soyinka's blend of styles—satiric commentary, tense confrontations, and heightened ritualistic moments—challenges not only audiences but production teams as well. The 1979 production at Chicago's Goodman Theatre, which then moved to the Kennedy Center's Terrace Theatre in Washington, D.C., was directed by Soyinka himself, and included American actors who threw themselves energetically into learning the African dances and songs. Figure 1 shows the Praise-Singer leaping into the air as he sings to Elesin, while Figure 2 makes evident the warmth and communal spirit of the marketplace, as seen in the laughing and smiling faces of the women who surround the richly dressed Elesin. From these moments of shared excitement and friendship, the play moves through a series of increasingly painful confrontations, ending finally with the once-powerful Elesin imprisoned, manacled, and seemingly humiliated by seeing the body of the son who died so that his father's duty might be fulfilled. The challenge of staging the play, whether on stage or in the mind's theater, is to encompass the whole range of experience that Soyinka poetically and unflinchingly puts before us.

DEATH AND THE KING'S HORSEMAN

BY WOLE SOYINKA

*Dedicated
In Affectionate Greeting
to
My Father, Ayodele
who lately danced, and joined the Ancestors.*

AUTHOR'S NOTE

This play is based on events which took place in Oyo, ancient Yoruba city of Nigeria, in 1946. That year, the lives of Elesin (Olori Elesin), his son, and the Colonial District Officer intertwined with the disastrous results set out in the play. The changes I have made are in matters of detail, sequence and of course characterisation. The action has also been set back two or three years to while the war was still on, for minor reasons of dramaturgy.

The factual account still exists in the archives of the British Colonial Administration. It has already inspired a fine play in Yoruba (Oba Wàjà) by Duro Ladipo. It has also misbegotten a film by some German television company.

The bane of themes of this genre is that they are no sooner employed creatively than they acquire the facile tag of "clash of cultures," a prejudicial label which, quite apart from its frequent misapplication, presupposes a potential equality *in every given situation* of the alien culture and the indigenous, on the actual soil of the latter. (In the area of misapplication, the overseas prize for illiteracy and mental conditioning undoubtedly goes to the blurb-writer for the American edition of my novel

Season of Anomy who unblushingly declares that this work portrays the "clash between old values and new ways, between western methods and African traditions"!) It is thanks to this kind of perverse mentality that I find it necessary to caution the would-be producer of this play against a sadly familiar reductionist tendency, and to direct his vision instead to the far more difficult and risky task of eliciting the play's threnodic° essence.

One of the more obvious alternative structures of the play would be to make the District Officer the victim of a cruel dilemma. This is not to my taste and it is not by chance that I have avoided dialogue or situation which would encourage this. No attempt should be made in production to suggest it. The Colonial Factor is an incident, a catalytic incident merely. The confrontation in the play is largely metaphysical, contained in the human vehicle which is Elesin and the universe of the Yoruba mind—the world of the living, the dead and the unborn, and the numinous° passage which links all: transition. *Death and the King's Horseman* can be fully realised only through an evocation of music from the abyss of transition.

—W.S.

CHARACTERS

PRAISE-SINGER°
ELESIN, *Horseman of the King*
IYALOJA, *"Mother" of the market*
SIMON PILKINGS, *District Officer*
JANE PILKINGS, *his wife*
SERGEANT AMUSA
JOSEPH, *houseboy to the Pilkingses*
BRIDE

H.R.H. THE PRINCE
THE RESIDENT
AIDE-DE-CAMP
OLUNDE, *eldest son of Elesin*
DRUMMERS, WOMEN, YOUNG GIRLS, DANCERS AT THE
   BALL

The play should run without an interval. For rapid scene changes, one adjustable outline set is very appropriate.

Praise-Singer, professional giver of compliments.

threnodic, having to do with a funeral song.   *numinous,* associated with the divine or supernatural.

SCENE 1

(A passage through a market in its closing stages. The stalls are being emptied, mats folded. A few women pass through on their way home, loaded with baskets. On a cloth-stand, bolts of cloth are taken down, display pieces folded and piled on a tray. ELESIN OBA *enters along a passage before the market, pursued by his drummers and praise-singers. He is a man of enormous vitality, speaks, dances and sings with that infectious enjoyment of life which accompanies all his actions.)*

PRAISE-SINGER: Elesin o! Elesin Oba! Howu! What tryst is this the cockerel goes to keep with such haste that he must leave his tail behind?

ELESIN *(slows down a bit, laughing)*: A tryst where the cockerel needs no adornment.

PRAISE-SINGER: O-oh, you hear that my companions? That's the way the world goes. Because the man approaches a brand new bride he forgets the long faithful mother of his children.

ELESIN: When the horse sniffs the stable does he not strain at the bridle? The market is the long-suffering home of my spirit and the women are packing up to go. That Esu-harassed° day slipped into the stewpot while we feasted. We ate it up with the rest of the meat. I have neglected my women.

PRAISE-SINGER: We know all that. Still it's no reason for shedding your tail on this day of all days. I know the women will cover you in damask and alari° but when the wind blows cold from behind, that's when the fowl knows his true friends.

ELESIN: Olohun-iyo!°

PRAISE-SINGER: Are you sure there will be one like me on the other side?

ELESIN: Olohun-iyo!

PRAISE-SINGER: Far be it for me to belittle the dwellers of that place but, a man is either born to his art or he isn't. And I don't know for certain that you'll meet my father, so who is going to sing these deeds in accents that will pierce the deafness of the ancient ones. I have prepared my going—just tell me: Olohun-iyo, I need you on this journey and I shall be behind you.

ELESIN: You're like a jealous wife. Stay close to me, but only on this side. My fame, my honour are legacies to the living; stay behind and let the world sip its honey from your lips.

PRAISE-SINGER: Your name will be like the sweet berry a child places under his tongue to sweeten the passage of food. The world will never spit it out.

ELESIN: Come then. This market is my roost. When I come among the women I am a chicken with a hundred mothers. I become a monarch whose palace is built with tenderness and beauty.

PRAISE-SINGER: They love to spoil you but beware. The hands of women also weaken the unwary.

ELESIN: This night I'll lay my head upon their lap and go to sleep. This night I'll touch feet with their feet in a dance that is no longer of this earth. But the smell of their flesh, their sweat, the smell of indigo on their cloth, this is the last air I wish to breathe as I go to meet my great forebears.

PRAISE-SINGER: In their time the world was never tilted from its groove, it shall not be in yours.

ELESIN: The gods have said No.

PRAISE-SINGER: In their time the great wars came and went, the little wars came and went; the white slavers came and went, they took away the heart of our race, they bore away the mind and muscle of our race. The city fell and was rebuilt; the city fell and our people trudged through mountain and forest to find a new home but—Elesin Oba do you hear me?

ELESIN: I hear your voice Olohun-iyo.

PRAISE-SINGER: Our world was never wrenched from its true course.

ELESIN: The gods have said No.

PRAISE-SINGER: There is only one home to the life of a river-mussel; there is only one home to the life of a tortoise; there is only one shell to the soul of man; there is only one world to the spirit of our race. If that world leaves its course and smashes on boulders of the great void, whose world will give us shelter?

ELESIN: It did not in the time of my forebears, it shall not in mine.

PRAISE-SINGER: The cockerel must not be seen without his feathers.

ELESIN: Nor will the Not-I bird be much longer without his nest.

PRAISE-SINGER *(stopped in his lyric stride)*: The Not-I bird, Elesin?

ELESIN: I said, the Not-I bird.

PRAISE-SINGER: All respect to our elders but, is there really such a bird?

ELESIN: What! Could it be that he failed to knock on your door?

PRAISE-SINGER *(smiling)*: Elesin's riddles are not merely the nut in the kernel that breaks human teeth; he also buries the kernel in hot embers and dares a man's fingers to draw it out.

ELESIN: I am sure he called on you, Olohun-iyo. Did you hide in the loft and push out the servant to tell him you were out?

*(*ELESIN *executes a brief, half-taunting dance. The* DRUMMER *moves in and draws a rhythm out of his steps.* ELESIN *dances towards the market-place as he chants the story of the Not-I bird, his voice changing dexterously to mimic his*

Esu-harassed, beset by the devil. **alari,** a rich, woven cloth, brightly colored. **Olohun-iyo,** literally, "voice of salt," but used to mean "sweet voice"—an honorific for the Praise-Singer.

*characters. He performs like a born raconteur,° infecting
his retinue with his humour and energy. More* WOMEN
arrive during his recital, including IYALOJA.)

Death came calling
Who does not know his rasp of reeds?
A twilight whisper in the leaves before
The great araba° falls? Did you hear it?
Not I! swears the farmer. He snaps
His fingers round his head, abandons
A hard-worn harvest and begins
A rapid dialogue with his legs.

"Not I," shouts the fearless hunter, "but—
It's getting dark, and this night-lamp
Has leaked out all its oil. I think
It's best to go home and resume my hunt
Another day." But now he pauses, suddenly
Lets out a wail: "Oh foolish mouth, calling
Down a curse on your own head! Your lamp
Has leaked out all its oil, has it?"
Forwards or backwards now he dare not move.
To search for leaves and make etutu°
On that spot? Or race home to the safety
Of his hearth? Ten market-days have passed
My friends, and still he's rooted there
Rigid as the plinth of Orayan.°

The mouth of the courtesan barely
Opened wide enough to take a ha'penny robo°
When she wailed: "Not I." All dressed she was
To call upon my friend the Chief Tax Officer.
But now she sends her go-between instead:
"Tell him I'm ill: my period has come suddenly
But not—I hope—my time."

Why is the pupil crying?
His hapless head was made to taste
The knuckles of my friend the Mallam:
"If you were then reciting the Koran
Would you have ears for idle noises
Darkening the trees, you child of ill omen?"
He shuts down school before its time
Runs home and rings himself with amulets.
And take my good kinsman Ifawomi.
His hands were like a carver's, strong
And true. I saw them
Tremble like wet wings of a fowl.
One day he cast his time-smoothed opele°
Across the divination board. And all because
The suppliant looked him in the eye and asked,

"Did you hear that whisper in the leaves?"
"Not I," was his reply; "perhaps I'm growing deaf—
Good-day." And Ifa spoke no more that day
The priest locked fast his doors,
Sealed up his leaking roof—but wait!
This sudden care was not for Fawomi
But for Osanyin, a courier-bird of Ifa's
Heart of wisdom. I did not know a kite
Was hovering in the sky
And Ifa now a twittering chicken in
The brood of Fawomi the Mother Hen.

Ah, but I must not forget my evening
Courier from the abundant palm, whose groan
Became Not I, as he constipated down
A wayside bush. He wonders if Elegbara
Has tricked his buttocks to discharge
Against a sacred grove. Hear him
Mutter spells to ward off penalties
For an abomination he did not intend.
If any here
Stumbles on a gourd of wine, fermenting
Near the road, and nearby hears a stream
Of spells issuing from a crouching form.
Brother to a sigidi,° bring home my wine,
Tell my tapper I have ejected
Fear from home and farm. Assure him,
All is well.

PRAISE-SINGER: In your time we do not doubt the peace
    of farmstead and home, the peace of road and
    hearth, we do not doubt the peace of the forest.
ELESIN: There was fear in the forest too.
    Not-I was lately heard even in the lair
    Of beasts. The hyena cackled loud. Not I,
    The civet twitched his fiery tail and glared:
    Not I. Not-I became the answering-name
    Of the restless bird, that little one
    Whom Death found nesting in the leaves
    When whisper of his coming ran
    Before him on the wind. Not-I
    Has long abandoned home. This same dawn
    I heard him twitter in the gods' abode.
    Ah, companions of this living world
    What a thing this is, that even those
    We call immortal
    Should fear to die.
IYALOJA: But you, husband of multitudes?
ELESIN: I, when that Not-I bird perched
    Upon my roof, bade him seek his nest again.
    Safe, without care or fear. I unrolled
    My welcome mat for him to see. Not-I
    Flew happily away, you'll hear his voice

---

raconteur, storyteller.   *araba,* baobab tree, known for its
great size.   *etutu,* placatory rites or medicine.   *Orayan,* seventh son of the founder of the Yoruba tribe.   *robo,* a delicacy
made from crushed melon seeds, fried in tiny balls.   *opele,*
string of beads used in Ifa divination.

---

sigidi, a squat, carved figure, endowed with the powers
of an incubus.

No more in this lifetime—You all know
What I am.

PRAISE-SINGER: That rock which turns its open lodes
Into the path of lightning. A gay
Thoroughbred whose stride disdains
To falter though an adder reared
Suddenly in his path.

ELESIN: My rein is loosened.
I am master of my Fate. When the hour comes
Watch me dance along the narrowing path
Glazed by the soles of my great precursors.
My soul is eager. I shall not turn aside.

WOMEN: You will not delay?

ELESIN: Where the storm pleases, and when, it directs
The giants of the forest. When friendship summons
Is when the true comrade goes.

WOMEN: Nothing will hold you back?

ELESIN: Nothing. What! Has no one told you yet
I go to keep my friend and master company.
Who says the mouth does not believe in
"No, I have chewed all that before?" I say I have.
The world is not a constant honey-pot.
Where I found little I made do with little.
Where there was plenty I gorged myself.
My master's hands and mine have always
Dipped together and, home or sacred feast,
The bowl was beaten bronze, the meats
So succulent our teeth accused us of neglect.
We shared the choicest of the season's
Harvest of yams. How my friend would read
Desire in my eyes before I knew the cause—
However rare, however precious, it was mine.

WOMEN: The town, the very land was yours.

ELESIN: The world was mine. Our joint hands
Raised housepots of trust that withstood
The siege of envy and the termites of time.
But the twilight hour brings bats and rodents—
Shall I yield them cause to foul the rafters?

PRAISE-SINGER: Elesin Oba! Are you not that man
who
Looked out of doors that stormy day
The god of luck limped by, drenched
To the very lice that held
His rags together? You took pity upon
His sores and wished him fortune.
Fortune was footloose this dawn, he replied,
Till you trapped him in a heartfelt wish
That now returns to you. Elesin Oba!
I say you are that man who
Chanced upon the calabash° of honour
You thought it was palm wine and
Drained its contents to the final drop.

ELESIN: Life has an end. A life that will outlive

---

calabash, large gourd from the calabash tree, used when
dried and split as a drinking vessel.

Fame and friendship begs another name.
What elder takes his tongue to his plate,
Licks it clean of every crumb? He will encounter
Silence when he calls on children to fulfill
The smallest errand! Life is honour.
It ends when honour ends.

WOMEN: We know you for a man of honour.

ELESIN: Stop! Enough of that!

WOMEN (*puzzled, they whisper among themselves, turning
mostly to* IYALOJA): What is it? Did we say something to give offence? Have we slighted him in
some way?

ELESIN: Enough of that sound I say. Let me hear no
more in that vein. I've heard enough.

IYALOJA: We must have said something wrong. (*Comes
forward a little.*) Elesin Oba, we ask forgiveness
before you speak.

ELESIN: I am bitterly offended.

IYALOJA: Our unworthiness has betrayed us. All we
can do is ask your forgiveness. Correct us like a
kind father.

ELESIN: This day of all days . . .

IYALOJA: It does not bear thinking. If we offend you
now we have mortified the gods. We offend heaven
itself. Father of us all, tell us where we went astray.
(*She kneels, the other women follow.*)

ELESIN: Are you not ashamed? Even a tear-veiled
Eye preserves its function of sight.
Because my mind was raised to horizons
Even the boldest man lowers his gaze
In thinking of, must my body here
Be taken for a vagrant's?

IYALOJA: Horseman of the King, I am more baffled
than ever.

PRAISE-SINGER: The strictest father unbends his brow
when the child is penitent, Elesin. When time is
short, we do not spend it prolonging the riddle.
Their shoulders are bowed with the weight of fear
lest they have marred your day beyond repair.
Speak now in plain words and let us pursue the
ailment to the home of remedies.

ELESIN: Words are cheap. "We know you for
A man of honour." Well tell me, is this how
A man of honour should be seen?
Are these not the same clothes in which
I came among you a full half-hour ago?

(*He roars with laughter and the women, relieved, rise and
rush into stalls to fetch rich clothes.*)

WOMEN: The gods are kind. A fault soon remedied is
soon forgiven. Elesin Oba, even as we match our
words with deed, let your heart forgive us completely.

ELESIN: You who are breath and giver of my being
How shall I dare refuse you forgiveness
Even if the offence was real.

IYALOJA (*dancing round him. Sings*):

He forgives us. He forgives us.
What a fearful thing it is when
The voyager sets forth
But a curse remains behind.

WOMEN: For a while we truly feared
Our hands had wrenched the world adrift
In emptiness.

IYALOJA: Richly, richly, robe him richly
The cloth of honour is alari
Sanyan° is the band of friendship
Boa-skin makes slippers of esteem.

WOMEN: For a while we truly feared
Our hands had wrenched the world adrift
In emptiness.

PRAISE-SINGER: He who must, must voyage forth
The world will not roll backwards
It is he who must, with one
Great gesture overtake the world.

WOMEN: For a while we truly feared
Our hands had wrenched the world adrift
In emptiness.

PRAISE-SINGER: The gourd you bear is not for shirking.
The gourd is not for setting down
At the first crossroad or wayside grove.
Only one river may know its contents.

WOMEN: We shall all meet at the great market
We shall all meet at the great market
He who goes early takes the best bargains
   But we shall meet, and resume our banter.

(ELESIN *stands resplendent in rich clothes, cap, shawl, etc.
His sash is of a bright red alari cloth. The* WOMEN *dance
round him. Suddenly, his attention is caught by an object
off-stage.*)

ELESIN: The world I know is good.

WOMEN: We know you'll leave it so.

ELESIN: The world I know is the bounty
Of hives after bees have swarmed.
No goodness teems with such open hands
Even in the dreams of deities.

WOMEN: And we know you'll leave it so.

ELESIN: I was born to keep it so. A hive
Is never known to wander. An anthill
Does not desert its roots. We cannot see
The still great womb of the world—
No man beholds his mother's womb—
Yet who denies it's there? Coiled
To the navel of the world is that
Endless cord that links us all
To the great origin. If I lose my way
The trailing cord will bring me to the roots.

WOMEN: The world is in your hands.

(*The earlier distraction, a beautiful young girl, comes along
the passage through which* ELESIN *first made his entry.*)

ELESIN: I embrace it. And let me tell you, women—
I like this farewell that the world designed,
Unless my eyes deceive me, unless
We are already parted, the world and I,
And all that breeds desire is lodged
Among our tireless ancestors. Tell me friends,
Am I still earthed in that beloved market
Of my youth? Or could it be my will
Has outleapt the conscious act and I have come
Among the great departed?

PRAISE-SINGER: Elesin Oba why do your eyes roll like
a bush-rat who sees his fate like his father's spirit,
mirrored in the eye of a snake? And all those questions! You're standing on the same earth you've
always stood upon. This voice you hear is mine,
Olohun-iyo, not that of an acolyte° in heaven.

ELESIN: How can that be? In all my life
As Horseman of the King, the juiciest
Fruit on every tree was mine. I saw,
I touched, I wooed, rarely was the answer No.
The honour of my place, the veneration I
Received in the eye of man or woman
Prospered my suit and
Played havoc with my sleeping hours.
And they tell me my eyes were a hawk
In perpetual hunger. Split an iroko° tree
In two, hide a woman's beauty in its heartwood
And seal it up again—Elesin, journeying by,
Would make his camp beside that tree
Of all the shades in the forest.

PRAISE-SINGER: Who would deny your reputation,
snake-on-the-loose in dark passages of the market!
Bed-bug who wages war on the mat and receives
the thanks of the vanquished! When caught with
his bride's own sister he protested—but I was only
prostrating myself to her as becomes a grateful in-
law. Hunter who carries his powder-horn on the
hips and fires crouching or standing! Warrior who
never makes that excuse of the whining coward—
but how can I go to battle without my trousers?—
trouserless or shirtless it's all one to him. Oka-
rearing-from-a-camouflage-of-leaves, before he
strikes the victim is already prone! Once they told
me, Howu, a stallion does not feed on the grass
beneath him: he replied, true, but surely he can
roll on it!

WOMEN: Ba-a-a-ba O!

PRAISE-SINGER: Ah, but listen yet. You know there is the
leaf-nibbling grub and there is the cola-chewing
beetle; the leaf-nibbling grub lives on the leaf, the
cola-chewing beetle lives in the colanut. Don't we
know what our man feeds on when we find him
cocooned in a woman's wrapper?

---

sanyan, a richly valued woven cloth.

acolyte, attendant who assists with religious services.
iroko, oak.

ELESIN: Enough, enough, you all have cause
  To know me well. But, if you say this earth
  Is still the same as gave birth to those songs,
  Tell me who was that goddess through whose lips
  I saw the ivory pebbles of Oya's river-bed.
  Iyaloja, who is she? I saw her enter
  Your stall; all your daughters I know well.
  No, not even Ogun-of-the-farm toiling
  Dawn till dusk on his tuber patch
  Not even Ogun with the finest hoe he ever
  Forged at the anvil could have shaped
  That rise of buttocks, not though he had
  The richest earth between his fingers.
  Her wrapper was no disguise
  For thighs whose ripples shamed the river's
  Coils around the hills of Ilesi. Her eyes
  Were new-laid eggs glowing in the dark.
  Her skin . . .

IYALOJA: Elesin Oba . . .

ELESIN: What! Where do you all say I am?

IYALOJA: Still among the living.

ELESIN: And that radiance which so suddenly
  Lit up this market I could boast
  I knew so well?

IYALOJA: Has one step already in her husband's
  home. She is betrothed.

ELESIN (irritated): Why do you tell me that?

(IYALOJA falls silent. The WOMEN shuffle uneasily.)

IYALOJA: Not because we dare give you offence Elesin.
   Today is your day and the whole world is yours.
   Still, even those who leave town to make a new
   dwelling elsewhere like to be remembered by
   what they leave behind.

ELESIN: Who does not seek to be remembered?
  Memory is Master of Death, the chink
  In his armour of conceit. I shall leave
  That which makes my going the sheerest
  Dream of an afternoon. Should voyagers
  Not travel light? Let the considerate traveller
  Shed, of his excessive load, all
  That may benefit the living.

WOMEN (relieved): Ah Elesin Oba, we knew you for a
  man of honour.

ELESIN: Then honour me. I deserve a bed of honour
  to lie upon.

IYALOJA: The best is yours. We know you for a man of
  honour. You are not one who eats and leaves
  nothing on his plate for children. Did you not say
  it yourself? Not one who blights the happiness of
  others for a moment's pleasure.

ELESIN: Who speaks of pleasure? O women, listen!
  Pleasure palls. Our acts should have meaning.
  The sap of the plantain° never dries.

---

plantain, tropical fruit (similar to a banana).

  You have seen the young shoot swelling
  Even as the parent stalks begins to wither.
  Women, let my going be likened to
  The twilight hour of the plantain.

WOMEN: What does he mean Iyaloja? This language
  is the language of our elders, we do not fully
  grasp it.

IYALOJA: I dare not understand you yet Elesin.

ELESIN: All you who stand before the spirit that dares
  The opening of the last door of passage,
  Dare to rid my going of regrets! My wish
  Transcends the blotting out of thought
  In one mere moment's tremor of the senses.
  Do me credit. And do me honour.
  I am girded for the route beyond
  Burdens of waste and longing.
  Then let me travel light. Let
  Seed that will not serve the stomach
  On the way remain behind. Let it take root
  In the earth of my choice, in this earth
  I leave behind.

IYALOJA (turns to WOMEN): The voice I hear is already
  touched by the waiting fingers of our departed. I
  dare not refuse.

WOMAN: But Iyaloja . . .

IYALOJA: The matter is no longer in our hands.

WOMAN: But she is betrothed to your own son. Tell him.

IYALOJA: My son's wish is mine. I did the asking for
  him, the loss can be remedied. But who will remedy the blight of closed hands on the day when all
  should be openness and light? Tell him, you say!
  You wish that I burden him with knowledge that
  will sour his wish and lay regrets on the last moments of his mind. You pray to him who is your
  intercessor to the world—don't set this world
  adrift in your own time; would you rather it was
  my hand whose sacrilege wrenched it loose?

WOMAN: Not many men will brave the curse of a dispossessed husband.

IYALOJA: Only the curses of the departed are to be
  feared. The claims of one whose foot is on the
  threshold of their abode surpasses even the
  claims of blood. It is impiety even to place hin-
  drances in their ways.

ELESIN: What do my mothers say? Shall I step
  Burdened into the unknown?

IYALOJA: Not we, but the very earth says No. The sap in
  the plantain does not dry. Let grain that will not
  feed the voyager at his passage drop here and take
  root as he steps beyond this earth and us. Oh you
  who fill the home from hearth to threshold with
  the voices of children, you who now bestride the
  hidden gulf and pause to draw the right foot across
  and into the resting-home of the great forebears,
  it is good that your loins be drained into the earth
  we know, that your last strength be ploughed back
  into the womb that gave you being.

PRAISE-SINGER: Iyaloja, mother of multitudes in the teeming market of the world, how your wisdom transfigures you!

IYALOJA (*smiling broadly, completely reconciled*): Elesin, even at the narrow end of the passage I know you will look back and sigh a last regret for the flesh that flashed past your spirit in flight. You always had a restless eye. Your choice has my blessing. (*To the* WOMEN.) Take the good news to our daughter and make her ready. (*Some* WOMEN *go off.*)

ELESIN: Your eyes were clouded at first.

IYALOJA: Not for long. It is those who stand at the gateway of the great change to whose cry we must pay heed. And then, think of this—it makes the mind tremble. The fruit of such a union is rare. It will be neither of this world nor of the next. Nor of the one behind us. As if the timelessness of the ancestor world and the unborn have joined spirits to wring an issue of the elusive being of passage . . . Elesin!

ELESIN: I am here. What is it?

IYALOJA: Did you hear all I said just now?

ELESIN: Yes.

IYALOJA: The living must eat and drink. When the moment comes, don't turn the food to rodents' droppings in their mouth. Don't let them taste the ashes of the world when they step out at dawn to breathe the morning dew.

ELESIN: This doubt is unworthy of you Iyaloja.

IYALOJA: Eating the awusa° nut is not so difficult as drinking water afterwards.

ELESIN: The waters of the bitter stream are honey to a man
Whose tongue has savoured all.

IYALOJA: No one knows when the ants desert their home; they leave the mound intact. The swallow is never seen to peck holes in its nest when it is time to move with the season. There are always throngs of humanity behind the leave-taker. The rain should not come through the roof for them, the wind must not blow through the walls at night.

ELESIN: I refuse to take offence.

IYALOJA: You wish to travel light. Well, the earth is yours. But be sure the seed you leave in it attracts no curse.

ELESIN: You really mistake my person Iyaloja.

IYALOJA: I said nothing. Now we must go prepare your bridal chamber. Then these same hands will lay your shrouds.

ELESIN (*exasperated*): Must you be so blunt? (*Recovers.*) Well, weave your shrouds, but let the fingers of my bride seal my eyelids with earth and wash my body.

IYALOJA: Prepare yourself Elesin.

(*She gets up to leave. At that moment the* WOMEN *return, leading the* BRIDE. ELESIN'*s face glows with pleasure. He flicks the sleeves of his agbada° with renewed confidence and steps forward to meet the group. As the girl kneels before* IYALOJA, *lights fade out on the scene.*)

SCENE 2

(*The verandah of the District Officer's bungalow. A tango is playing from an old hand-cranked gramophone and, glimpsed through the wide windows and doors which open onto the forestage verandah are the shapes of* SIMON PILKINGS *and his wife,* JANE, *tangoing in and out of shadows in the living-room. They are wearing what is immediately apparent as some form of fancy-dress. The dance goes on for some moments and then the figure of a "Native Administration"* POLICEMAN *emerges and climbs up the steps onto the verandah. He peeps through and observes the dancing couple, reacting with what is obviously a long-standing bewilderment. He stiffens suddenly, his expression changes to one of disbelief and horror. In his excitement he upsets a flower-pot and attracts the attention of the couple. They stop dancing.*)

PILKINGS: Is there anyone out there?

JANE: I'll turn off the gramophone.

PILKINGS (*approaching the verandah*): I'm sure I heard something fall over. (*The* CONSTABLE *retreats slowly, open-mouthed as* PILKINGS *approaches the verandah.*) Oh it's you Amusa. Why didn't you just knock instead of knocking things over?

AMUSA (*stammers badly and points a shaky finger at his dress*): Mista Pirinkin . . . Mista Pirinkin . . .

PILKINGS: What is the matter with you?

JANE (*emerging*): Who is it dear? Oh, Amusa . . .

PILKINGS: Yes it's Amusa, and acting most strangely.

AMUSA (*his attention now transferred to* MRS PILKINGS): Mammadam . . . you too!

PILKINGS: What the hell is the matter with you man!

JANE: Your costume darling. Our fancy dress.

PILKINGS: Oh hell, I'd forgotten all about that. (*Lifts the face mask over his head showing his face. His* WIFE *follows suit.*)

JANE: I think you've shocked his big pagan heart bless him.

PILKINGS: Nonsense, he's a Moslem. Come on Amusa, you don't believe in all that nonsense do you? I thought you were a good Moslem.

AMUSA: Mista Pirinkin, I beg you sir, what you think you do with that dress? It belong to dead cult, not for human being.

PILKINGS: Oh Amusa, what a let down you are. I swear by you at the club you know—thank God for

---

awusa, nut that must be chewed up carefully, otherwise it sticks in the throat and thus makes drinking difficult.

agbada, traditional Yoruba robe, with long flowing sleeves.

Amusa, he doesn't believe in any mumbo-jumbo. And now look at you!

AMUSA: Mista Pirinkin, I beg you, take it off. Is not good for man like you to touch that cloth.

PILKINGS: Well, I've got it on. And what's more Jane and I have bet on it we're taking first prize at the ball. Now, if you can just pull yourself together and tell me what you wanted to see me about . . .

AMUSA: Sir, I cannot talk this matter to you in that dress. I no fit.

PILKINGS: What's that rubbish again?

JANE: He is dead earnest too Simon. I think you'll have to handle this delicately.

PILKINGS: Delicately my . . . ! Look here Amusa, I think this little joke has gone far enough hm? Let's have some sense. You seem to forget that you are a police officer in the service of His Majesty's Government. I order you to report your business at once or face disciplinary action.

AMUSA: Sir, it is a matter of death. How can man talk against death to person in uniform of death? Is like talking against government to person in uniform of police. Please sir, I go and come back.

PILKINGS (roars): Now! (AMUSA switches his gaze to the ceiling suddenly, remains mute.)

JANE: Oh Amusa, what is there to be scared of in the costume? You saw it confiscated last month from those egungun° men who were creating trouble in town. You helped arrest the cult leaders yourself—if the juju° didn't harm you at the time how could it possibly harm you now? And merely by looking at it?

AMUSA (without looking down): Madam, I arrest the ringleaders who make trouble but me I no touch egungun. That egungun inself, I no touch. And I no abuse 'am. I arrest ringleader but I treat egungun with respect.

PILKINGS: It's hopeless. We'll merely end up missing the best part of the ball. When they get this way there is nothing you can do. It's simply hammering against a brick wall. Write your report or whatever it is on that pad Amusa and take yourself out of here. Come on Jane. We only upset his delicate sensibilities by remaining here.

(AMUSA waits for them to leave, then writes in the notebook, somewhat laboriously. Drumming from the direction of the town wells up. AMUSA listens, makes a movement as if he wants to recall PILKINGS but changes his mind. Completes his note and goes. A few moments later PILKINGS emerges, picks up the pad and reads.)

Jane!

JANE (from the bedroom): Coming darling. Nearly ready.

_____

egungun, ancestral masquerade.   juju, magic charm or medicine.

PILKINGS: Never mind being ready, just listen to this.

JANE: What is it?

PILKINGS: Amusa's report. Listen. "I have to report that it come to my information that one prominent chief, namely, the Elesin Oba, is to commit death tonight as a result of native custom. Because this is criminal offence I await further instruction at charge office. Sergeant Amusa."

(JANE comes out onto the verandah while he is reading.)

JANE: Did I hear you say commit death?

PILKINGS: Obviously he means murder.

JANE: You mean a ritual murder?

PILKINGS: Must be. You think you've stamped it all out but it's always lurking under the surface somewhere.

JANE: Oh. Does it mean we are not getting to the ball at all?

PILKINGS: No-o. I'll have the man arrested. Everyone remotely involved. In any case there may be nothing to it. Just rumours.

JANE: Really? I thought you found Amusa's rumours generally reliable.

PILKINGS: That's true enough. But who knows what may have been giving him the scare lately. Look at his conduct tonight.

JANE (laughing): You have to admit he had his own peculiar logic. (Deepens her voice.) How can man talk against death to person in uniform of death? (Laughs.) Anyway, you can't go into the police station dressed like that.

PILKINGS: I'll send Joseph with instructions. Damn it, what a confounded nuisance!

JANE: But don't you think you should talk first to the man, Simon?

PILKINGS: Do you want to go to the ball or not?

JANE: Darling, why are you getting rattled? I was only trying to be intelligent. It seems hardly fair just to lock up a man—and a chief at that—simply on the er . . . what is the legal word again?—uncorroborated word of a sergeant.

PILKINGS: Well, that's easily decided. Joseph!

JOSEPH (from within): Yes master.

PILKINGS: You're quite right of course, I am getting rattled. Probably the effect of those bloody drums. Do you hear how they go on and on?

JANE: I wondered when you'd notice. Do you suppose it has something to do with this affair?

PILKINGS: Who knows? They always find an excuse for making a noise . . . (Thoughtfully.) Even so . . .

JANE: Yes Simon?

PILKINGS: It's different Jane. I don't think I've heard this particular—sound—before. Something unsettling about it.

JANE: I thought all bush drumming sounded the same.

PILKINGS: Don't tease me now Jane. This may be serious.

JANE: I'm sorry. (*Gets up and throws her arms around his neck. Kisses him. The houseboy enters, retreats and knocks.*)

PILKINGS (*wearily*): Oh, come in Joseph! I don't know where you pick up all these elephantine notions of tact. Come over here.

JOSEPH: Sir?

PILKINGS: Joseph, are you a Christian or not?

JOSEPH: Yessir.

PILKINGS: Does seeing me in this outfit bother you?

JOSEPH: No sir, it has no power.

PILKINGS: Thank God for some sanity at last. Now Joseph, answer me on the honour of a Christian— what is supposed to be going on in town tonight?

JOSEPH: Tonight sir? You mean the chief who is going to kill himself?

PILKINGS: What?

JANE: What do you mean, kill himself?

PILKINGS: You do mean he is going to kill somebody don't you?

JOSEPH: No master. He will not kill anybody and no one will kill him. He will simply die.

JANE: But why Joseph?

JOSEPH: It is native law and custom. The King die last month. Tonight is his burial. But before they can bury him, the Elesin must die so as to accompany him to heaven.

PILKINGS: I seem to be fated to clash more often with that man than with any of the other chiefs.

JOSEPH: He is the King's Chief Horseman.

PILKINGS (*in a resigned way*): I know.

JANE: Simon, what's the matter?

PILKINGS: It would have to be him!

JANE: Who is he?

PILKINGS: Don't you remember? He's that chief with whom I had a scrap some three or four years ago. I helped his son get to a medical school in England, remember? He fought tooth and nail to prevent it.

JANE: Oh now I remember. He was that very sensitive young man. What was his name again?

PILKINGS: Olunde. Haven't replied to his last letter come to think of it. The old pagan wanted him to stay and carry on some family tradition or the other. Honestly I couldn't understand the fuss he made. I literally had to help the boy escape from close confinement and load him onto the next boat. A most intelligent boy, really bright.

JANE: I rather thought he was much too sensitive you know. The kind of person you feel should be a poet munching rose petals in Bloomsbury.

PILKINGS: Well, he's going to make a first-class doctor. His mind is set on that. And as long as he wants my help he is welcome to it.

JANE (*after a pause*): Simon.

PILKINGS: Yes?

JANE: This boy, he was the eldest son wasn't he?

PILKINGS: I'm not sure. Who could tell with that old ram?

JANE: Do you know, Joseph?

JOSEPH: Oh yes Madam. He was the eldest son. That's why Elesin cursed master good and proper. The eldest son is not supposed to travel away from the land.

JANE (*giggling*): Is that true Simon? Did he really curse you good and proper?

PILKINGS: By all accounts I should be dead by now.

JOSEPH: Oh no, master is white man. And good Christian. Black man juju can't touch master.

JANE: If he was his eldest, it means that he would be the Elesin to the next king. It's a family thing isn't it Joseph?

JOSEPH: Yes madam. And if this Elesin had died before the King, his eldest son must take his place.

JANE: That would explain why the old chief was so mad you took the boy away.

PILKINGS: Well it makes me all the more happy I did.

JANE: I wonder if he knew.

PILKINGS: Who? Oh, you mean Olunde?

JANE: Yes. Was that why he was so determined to get away? I wouldn't stay if I knew I was trapped in such a horrible custom.

PILKINGS (*thoughtfully*): No, I don't think he knew. At least he gave no indication. But you couldn't really tell with him. He was rather close you know, quite unlike most of them. Didn't give much away, not even to me.

JANE: Aren't they all rather close, Simon?

PILKINGS: These natives here? Good gracious. They'll open their mouths and yap with you about their family secrets before you can stop them. Only the other day . . .

JANE: But Simon, do they really give anything away? I mean, anything that really counts. This affair for instance, we didn't know they still practised that custom did we?

PILKINGS: Ye-e-es, I suppose you're right there. Sly, devious bastards.

JOSEPH (*stiffly*): Can I go now master? I have to clean the kitchen.

PILKINGS: What? Oh, you can go. Forgot you were still here.

(JOSEPH *goes.*)

JANE: Simon, you really must watch your language. Bastard isn't just a simple swear-word in these parts, you know.

PILKINGS: Look, just when did you become a social anthropologist, that's what I'd like to know.

JANE: I'm not claiming to know anything. I just happen to have overheard quarrels among the servants. That's how I know they consider it a smear.

PILKINGS: I thought the extended family system took care of all that. Elastic family, no bastards.

JANE *(shrugs)*: Have it your own way.

(Awkward silence. The drumming increases in volume. JANE gets up suddenly, restless.)

That drumming Simon, do you think it might really be connected with this ritual? It's been going on all evening.

PILKINGS: Let's ask our native guide. Joseph! Just a minute Joseph. *(JOSEPH re-enters.)* What's the drumming about?

JOSEPH: I don't know master.

PILKINGS: What do you mean you don't know? It's only two years since your conversion. Don't tell me all that holy water nonsense also wiped out your tribal memory.

JOSEPH *(visibly shocked)*: Master!

JANE: Now you've done it.

PILKINGS: What have I done now?

JANE: Never mind. Listen Joseph, just tell me this. Is that drumming connected with dying or anything of that nature?

JOSEPH: Madam, this is what I am trying to say: I am not sure. It sounds like the death of a great chief and then, it sounds like the wedding of a great chief. It really mix me up.

PILKINGS: Oh get back to the kitchen. A fat lot of help you are.

JOSEPH: Yes master. *(Goes.)*

JANE: Simon . . .

PILKINGS: All right, all right. I'm in no mood for preaching.

JANE: It isn't my preaching you have to worry about, it's the preaching of the missionaries who preceded you here. When they make converts they really convert them. Calling holy water nonsense to our Joseph is really like insulting the Virgin Mary before a Roman Catholic. He's going to hand in his notice tomorrow you mark my word.

PILKINGS: Now you're being ridiculous.

JANE: Am I? What are you willing to bet that tomorrow we are going to be without a steward-boy? Did you see his face?

PILKINGS: I am more concerned about whether or not we will be one native chief short by tomorrow. Christ! Just listen to those drums. *(He strides up and down, undecided.)*

JANE *(getting up)*: I'll change and make up some supper.

PILKINGS: What's that?

JANE: Simon, it's obvious we have to miss this ball.

PILKINGS: Nonsense. It's the first bit of real fun the European club has managed to organise for over a year, I'm damned if I'm going to miss it. And it is a rather special occasion. Doesn't happen every day.

JANE: You know this business has to be stopped Simon. And you are the only man who can do it.

PILKINGS: I don't have to stop anything. If they want to throw themselves off the top of a cliff or poison themselves for the sake of some barbaric custom what is that to me? If it were ritual murder or something like that I'd be duty-bound to do something. I can't keep an eye on all the potential suicides in this province. And as for that man—believe me it's good riddance.

JANE *(laughs)*: I know you better than that Simon. You are going to have to do something to stop it—after you've finished blustering.

PILKINGS *(shouts after her)*: And suppose after all it's only a wedding? I'd look a proper fool if I interrupted a chief on his honeymoon, wouldn't I? *(Resumes his angry stride, slows down.)* Ah well, who can tell what those chiefs actually do on their honeymoon anyway? *(He takes up the pad and scribbles rapidly on it.)* Joseph! Joseph! Joseph! *(Some moments later JOSEPH puts in a sulky appearance.)* Did you hear me call you? Why the hell didn't you answer?

JOSEPH: I didn't hear master.

PILKINGS: You didn't hear me! How come you are here then?

JOSEPH *(stubbornly)*: I didn't hear master.

PILKINGS *(controls himself with an effort)*: We'll talk about it in the morning. I want you to take this note directly to Sergeant Amusa. You'll find him at the charge office. Get on your bicycle and race there with it. I expect you back in twenty minutes exactly. Twenty minutes, is that clear?

JOSEPH: Yes master. *(Going.)*

PILKINGS: Oh er . . . Joseph.

JOSEPH: Yes Master?

PILKINGS *(between gritted teeth)*: Er . . . forget what I said just now. The holy water is not nonsense. *I* was talking nonsense.

JOSEPH: Yes master. *(Goes.)*

JANE *(pokes her head round the door)*: Have you found him?

PILKINGS: Found who?

JANE: Joseph. Weren't you shouting for him?

PILKINGS: Oh yes, he turned up finally.

JANE: You sounded desperate. What was it all about?

PILKINGS: Oh nothing. I just wanted to apologise to him. Assure him that the holy water isn't really nonsense.

JANE: Oh? And how did he take it?

PILKINGS: Who the hell gives a damn! I had a sudden vision of our Very Reverend Macfarlane drafting another letter of complaint to the Resident about my unchristian language towards his parishioners.

JANE: Oh I think he's given up on you by now.

PILKINGS: Don't be too sure. And anyway, I wanted to

make sure Joseph didn't "lose" my note on the way. He looked sufficiently full of the holy crusade to do some such thing.

JANE: If you've finished exaggerating, come and have something to eat.

PILKINGS: No, put it all away. We can still get to the ball.

JANE: Simon . . .

PILKINGS: Get your costume back on. Nothing to worry about. I've instructed Amusa to arrest the man and lock him up.

JANE: But that station is hardly secure Simon. He'll soon get his friends to help him escape.

PILKINGS: A-ah, that's where I have out-thought you. I'm not having him put in the station cell. Amusa will bring him right here and lock him up in my study. And he'll stay with him till we get back. No one will dare come here to incite him to anything.

JANE: How clever of you darling. I'll get ready.

PILKINGS: Hey.

JANE: Yes darling.

PILKINGS: I have a surprise for you. I was going to keep it until we actually got to the ball.

JANE: What is it?

PILKINGS: You know the Prince is on a tour of the colonies don't you? Well, he docked in the capital only this morning but he is already at the Residency. He is going to grace the ball with his presence later tonight.

JANE: Simon! Not really.

PILKINGS: Yes he is. He's been invited to give away the prizes and he has agreed. You must admit old Engleton is the best Club Secretary we ever had. Quick off the mark that lad.

JANE: But how thrilling.

PILKINGS: The other provincials are going to be damned envious.

JANE: I wonder what he'll come as.

PILKINGS: Oh I don't know. As a coat-of-arms perhaps. Anyway it won't be anything to touch this.

JANE: Well that's lucky. If we are to be presented I won't have to start looking for a pair of gloves. It's all sewn on.

PILKINGS (laughing): Quite right. Trust a woman to think of that. Come on, let's get going.

JANE (rushing off): Won't be a second. (Stops.) Now I see why you've been so edgy all evening. I thought you weren't handling this affair with your usual brilliance—to begin with that is.

PILKINGS (his mood is much improved): Shut up woman and get your things on.

JANE: All right boss, coming.

(PILKINGS suddenly begins to hum the tango to which they were dancing before. Starts to execute a few practice steps. Lights fade.)

SCENE 3

(A swelling, agitated hum of women's voices rises immediately in the background. The lights come on and we see the frontage of a converted cloth stall in the market. The floor leading up to the entrance is covered in rich velvets and woven cloth. The WOMEN come on stage, borne backwards by the determined progress of Sergeant AMUSA and his two CONSTABLES who already have their batons out and use them as a pressure against the WOMEN. At the edge of the cloth-covered floor however the WOMEN take a determined stand and block all further progress of the MEN. They begin to tease them mercilessly.)

AMUSA: I am tell you women for last time to commot° my road. I am here on official business.

WOMAN: Official business you white man's eunuch? Official business is taking place where you want to go and it's a business you wouldn't understand.

WOMAN (makes a quick tug at the CONSTABLE's baton): That doesn't fool anyone you know. It's the one you carry under your government knickers that counts. (She bends low as if to peep under the baggy shorts. The embarrassed CONSTABLE quickly puts his knees together. The WOMEN roar.)

WOMAN: You mean there is nothing there at all?

WOMAN: Oh there was something. You know that handbell which the white man uses to summon his servants . . . ?

AMUSA (he manages to preserve some dignity throughout): I hope you women know that interfering with officer in execution of his duty is criminal offence.

WOMAN: Interfere? He says we're interfering with him. You foolish man we're telling you there's nothing to interfere with.

AMUSA: I am order you now to clear the road.

WOMAN: What road? The one your father built?

WOMAN: You are a policeman not so? Then you know what they call trespassing in court. Or—(Pointing to the cloth-lined steps.)—do you think that kind of road is built for every kind of feet?

WOMAN: Go back and tell the white man who sent you to come himself.

AMUSA: If I go I will come back with reinforcement. And we will all return carrying weapons.

WOMAN: Oh, now I understand. Before they can put on those knickers the white man first cuts off their weapons.

WOMAN: What a cheek! You mean you come here to show power to women and you don't even have a weapon.

AMUSA (shouting above the laughter): For the last time I warn you women to clear the road.

WOMAN: To where?

---

commot, come out, get out of.

AMUSA: To that hut. I know he dey dere.

WOMAN: Who?

AMUSA: The chief who call himself Elesin Oba.

WOMAN: You ignorant man. It is not he who calls himself Elesin Oba, it is his blood that says it. As it called out to his father before him and will to his son after him. And that is in spite of everything your white man can do.

WOMAN: Is it not the same ocean that washes this land and the white man's land? Tell your white man he can hide our son away as long as he likes. When the time comes for him, the same ocean will bring him back.

AMUSA: The government say dat kin' ting must stop.

WOMAN: Who will stop it? You? Tonight our husband and father will prove himself greater than the laws of strangers.

AMUSA: I tell you nobody go prove anyting tonight or anytime. Is ignorant and criminal to prove dat kin' prove.

IYALOJA (*entering from the hut. She is accompanied by a group of young girls who have been attending the* BRIDE): What is it Amusa? Why do you come here to disturb the happiness of others?

AMUSA: Madame Iyaloja, I glad you come. You know me, I no like trouble but duty is duty. I am here to arrest Elesin for criminal intent. Tell these women to stop obstructing me in the performance of my duty.

IYALOJA: And you? What gives you the right to obstruct our leader of men in the performance of his duty?

AMUSA: What kin' duty be dat one Iyaloja?

IYALOJA: What kin' duty? What kin' duty does a man have to his new bride?

AMUSA (*bewildered, looks at the women and at the entrance to the hut*): Iyaloja, is it wedding you call dis kin' ting?

IYALOJA: You have wives haven't you? Whatever the white man has done to you he hasn't stopped you having wives. And if he has, at least he is married. If you don't know what a marriage is, go and ask him to tell you.

AMUSA: This no to wedding.

IYALOJA: And ask him at the same time what he would have done if anyone had come to disturb him on his wedding night.

AMUSA: Iyaloja, I say dis no to wedding.

IYALOJA: You want to look inside the bridal chamber? You want to see for yourself how a man cuts the virgin knot?

AMUSA: Madam . . .

WOMAN: Perhaps his wives are still waiting for him to learn.

AMUSA: Iyaloja, make you tell dese women make den no insult me again. If I hear dat kin' insult once more . . .

GIRL (*pushing her way through*): You will do what?

GIRL: He's out of his mind. It's our mothers you're talking to, do you know that? Not to any illiterate villager you can bully and terrorise. How dare you intrude here anyway?

GIRL: What a cheek, what impertinence!

GIRL: You've treated them too gently. Now let them see what it is to tamper with the mothers of this market.

GIRL: Your betters dare not enter the market when the women say no!

GIRL: Haven't you learnt that yet, you jester in khaki and starch?

IYALOJA: Daughters . . .

GIRL: No no Iyaloja, leave us to deal with him. He no longer knows his mother, we'll teach him.

(*With a sudden movement they snatch the batons of the two* CONSTABLES. *They begin to hem them in.*)

GIRL: What next? We have your batons? What next? What are you going to do?

(*With equally swift movements they knock off their hats.*)

GIRL: Move if you dare. We have your hats, what will you do about it? Didn't the white man teach you to take off your hats before women?

IYALOJA: It's a wedding night. It's a night of joy for us. Peace . . .

GIRL: Not for him. Who asked him here?

GIRL: Does he dare go to the Residency without an invitation?

GIRL: Not even where the servants eat the left-overs.

GIRLS (*in turn. In an "English" accent*): Well well it's Mister Amusa. Were you invited? (*Play-acting to one another. The older women encourage them with their titters.*)

—Your invitation card please?

—Who are you? Have we been introduced?

—And who did you say you were?

—Sorry, I didn't quite catch your name.

—May I take your hat?

—If you insist. May I take yours? (*Exchanging the* POLICEMEN's *hats.*)

—How very kind of you.

—Not at all. Won't you sit down?

—After you.

—Oh no.

—I insist.

—You're most gracious.

—And how do you find the place?

—The natives are all right.

—Friendly?

—Tractable.

—Not a teeny-weeny bit restless?

—Well, a teeny-weeny bit restless.

—One might even say, difficult?

—Indeed one might be tempted to say, difficult.

—But you do manage to cope?

—Yes indeed I do. I have a rather faithful ox called Amusa.

—He's loyal?

—Absolutely.

—Lay down his life for you what?

—Without a moment's thought.

—Had one like that once. Trust him with my life.

—Mostly of course they are liars.

—Never known a native to tell the truth.

—Does it get rather close around here?

—It's mild for this time of the year.

—But the rains may still come.

—They are late this year aren't they?

—They are keeping African time.

—Ha ha ha ha

—Ha ha ha ha

—The humidity is what gets me.

—It used to be whisky.

—Ha ha ha ha

—Ha ha ha ha

—What's your handicap old chap?

—Is there racing by golly?

—Splendid golf course, you'll like it.

—I'm beginning to like it already.

—And a European club, exclusive.

—You've kept the flag flying.

—We do our best for the old country.

—It's a pleasure to serve.

—Another whisky old chap?

—You are indeed too too kind.

—Not at all sir. Where is that boy? *(With a sudden bellow.)* Sergeant!

AMUSA *(snaps to attention)*: Yessir!

(The WOMEN *collapse with laughter.)*

GIRL: Take your men out of here.

AMUSA *(realising the trick, he rages from loss of face)*: I'm give you warning . . .

GIRL: All right then. Off with his knickers! *(They surge slowly forward.)*

IYALOJA: Daughters, please.

AMUSA *(squaring himself for defence)*: The first woman wey touch me . . .

IYALOJA: My children, I beg of you . . .

GIRL: Then tell him to leave this market. This is the home of our mothers. We don't want the eater of white left-overs at the feast their hands have prepared.

IYALOJA: You heard them Amusa. You had better go.

GIRL: Now!

AMUSA *(commencing his retreat)*: We dey go now, but make you no say we no warn you.

GIRL: Now!

GIRLS: Before we read the riot act—you should know all about that.

AMUSA: Make we go. *(They depart, more precipitately.)*

(The WOMEN *strike their palms across in the gesture of wonder.)*

WOMAN: Do they teach you all that at school?

WOMAN: And to think I nearly kept Apinke away from the place.

WOMAN: Did you hear them? Did you see how they mimicked the white man?

WOMAN: The voices exactly. Hey, there are wonders in this world!

IYALOJA: Well, our elders have said it: Dada may be weak, but he has a younger sibling who is truly fearless.

WOMAN: The next time the white man shows his face in this market I will set Wuraola on his tail.

(A WOMAN *bursts into song and dance of euphoria—"Tani l'awa o l'ogbeja? Kayi! A l'ogbeja. Omo Kekere l'ogbeja."° The rest of the* WOMEN *join in, some placing the* GIRLS *on their back like infants, others dancing round them. The dance becomes general, mounting in excitement.* ELESIN *appears, in wrapper only. In his hands a white velvet cloth folded loosely as if it held some delicate object. He cries out.)*

ELESIN: Oh you mothers of beautiful brides! *(The dancing stops. They turn and see him, and the object in his hands.* IYALOJA *approaches and gently takes the cloth from him.)* Take it. It is no mere virgin stain, but the union of life and the seeds of passage. My vital flow, the last from this flesh is intermingled with the promise of future life. All is prepared. Listen! *(A steady drumbeat from the distance.)* Yes. It is nearly time. The King's dog has been killed. The King's favourite horse is about to follow his master. My brother chiefs know their task and perform it well. *(He listens again.)*

(The BRIDE *emerges, stands shyly by the door. He turns to her.)*

Our marriage is not yet wholly fulfilled. When earth and passage wed, the consummation is complete only when there are grains of earth on the eyelids of passage. Stay by me till then. My faithful drummers, do me your last service. This is where I have chosen to do my leave-taking, in this heart of life, this hive which contains the swarm of the world in its small compass. This is where I have known love and laughter away from the palace. Even the richest food cloys when eaten days on end; in the market, nothing ever cloys. Listen. *(They listen to the drums.)* They have begun to seek out the heart of the King's favourite horse.

Tani l'awa o l'ogbeja . . . l'ogbeja, "Who says we haven't a defender? Silence! We have our defenders. Little children are our champions."

Soon it will ride in its bolt of raffia° with the dog at its feet. Together they will ride on the shoulders of the King's grooms through the pulse centres of the town. They know it is here I shall await them. I have told them. (*His eyes appear to cloud. He passes his hand over them as if to clear his sight. He gives a faint smile.*) It promises well; just then I felt my spirit's eagerness. The kite makes for wide spaces and the wind creeps up behind its tail; can the kite say less than—thank you, the quicker the better? But wait a while my spirit. Wait. Wait for the coming of the courier of the King. Do you know friends, the horse is born to this one destiny, to bear the burden that is man upon its back. Except for this night, this night alone when the spotless stallion will ride in triumph on the back of man. In the time of my father I witnessed the strange sight. Perhaps tonight also I shall see it for the last time. If they arrive before the drums beat for me, I shall tell him to let the Alafin° know I follow swiftly. If they come after the drums have sounded, why then, all is well for I have gone ahead. Our spirits shall fall in step along the great passage. (*He listens to the drums. He seems again to be falling into a state of semi-hypnosis; his eyes scan the sky but it is in a kind of daze. His voice is a little breathless.*) The moon has fed, a glow from its full stomach fills the sky and air, but I cannot tell where is that gateway through which I must pass. My faithful friends, let our feet touch together this last time, lead me into the other market with sounds that cover my skin with down yet make my limbs strike earth like a thoroughbred. Dear mothers, let me dance into the passage even as I have lived beneath your roofs.

(*He comes down progressively among them. They make way for him, the drummers playing. His dance is one of solemn, regal motions, each gesture of the body is made with a solemn finality. The* WOMEN *join him, their steps a somewhat more fluid version of his. Beneath the* PRAISE-SINGER's *exhortations the* WOMEN *dirge "Ale le le, awo mi lo."*)

PRAISE-SINGER: Elesin Alafin, can you hear my voice?
ELESIN: Faintly, my friend, faintly.
PRAISE-SINGER: Elesin Alafin, can you hear my call?
ELESIN: Faintly my king, faintly.
PRAISE-SINGER: Is your memory sound Elesin?
  Shall my voice be a blade of grass and
  Tickle the armpit of the past?
ELESIN: My memory needs no prodding but
  What do you wish to say to me?

PRAISE-SINGER: Only what has been spoken. Only what concerns
  The dying wish of the father of all.
ELESIN: It is buried like seed-yam in my mind
  This is the season of quick rains, the harvest
  Is this moment due for gathering.
PRAISE-SINGER: If you cannot come, I said, swear
  You'll tell my favourite horse. I shall
  Ride on through the gates alone.
ELESIN: Elesin's message will be read
  Only when his loyal heart no longer beats.
PRAISE-SINGER: If you cannot come Elesin, tell my dog.
  I cannot stay the keeper too long
  At the gate.
ELESIN: A dog does not outrun the hand
  That feeds it meat. A horse that throws its rider
  Slows down to a stop. Elesin Alafin
  Trusts no beasts with messages between
  A king and his companion.
PRAISE-SINGER: If you get lost my dog will track
  The hidden path to me.
ELESIN: The seven-way crossroads confuses
  Only the stranger. The Horseman of the King
  Was born in the recesses of the house.
PRAISE-SINGER: I know the wickedness of men. If there is
  Weight on the loose end of your sash, such weight
  As no mere man can shift; if your sash is earthed
  By evil minds who mean to part us at the last . . .
ELESIN: My sash is of the deep purple alari;
  It is no tethering-rope. The elephant
  Trails no tethering-rope; that king
  Is not yet crowned who will peg an elephant—
  Not even you my friend and King.
PRAISE-SINGER: And yet this fear will not depart from me
  The darkness of this new abode is deep
  Will your human eyes suffice?
ELESIN: In a night which falls before our eyes
  However deep, we do not miss our way.
PRAISE-SINGER: Shall I now not acknowledge I have stood
  Where wonders met their end? The elephant deserves
  Better than that we say "I have caught
  A glimpse of something." If we see the tamer
  Of the forest let us say plainly, we have seen
  An elephant.
ELESIN (*his voice is drowsy*):
  I have freed myself of earth and now
  It's getting dark. Strange voices guide my feet.
PRAISE-SINGER: The river is never so high that the eyes
  Of a fish are covered. The night is not so dark
  That the albino fails to find his way. A child
  Returning homewards craves no leading by the hand.

---

raffia, palm tree fiber.   **Alafin**, title for King of Oyo, an ancient (and still existing) city in Nigeria.

Gracefully does the mask regain his grove at the
    end of the day . . .
Gracefully. Gracefully does the mask dance
Homeward at the end of the day, gracefully . . .

(ELESIN's *trance appears to be deepening, his steps heavier.*)

IYALOJA: It is the death of war that kills the valiant,
Death of water is how the swimmer goes
It is the death of markets that kills the trader
And death of indecision takes the idle away
The trade of the cutlass blunts its edge
And the beautiful die the death of beauty.
It takes an Elesin to die the death of death . . .
Only Elesin . . . dies the unknowable death of
    death . . .
Gracefully, gracefully does the horseman regain
The stables at the end of day, gracefully . . .

PRAISE-SINGER: How shall I tell what my eyes have
    seen? The Horseman gallops on before the
    courier, how shall I tell what my eyes have seen?
    He says a dog may be confused by new scents of
    beings he never dreamt of, so he must precede
    the dog to heaven. He says a horse may stumble
    on strange boulders and be lamed, so he races on
    before the horse to heaven. It is best, he says, to
    trust no messenger who may falter at the outer
    gate; oh how shall I tell what my ears have heard?
    But do you hear me still Elesin, do you hear your
    faithful one?

(ELESIN *in his motions appears to feel for a direction of
sound, subtly, but he only sinks deeper into his trance-
dance.*)

Elesin Alafin, I no longer sense your flesh. The
drums are changing now but you have gone far
ahead of the world. It is not yet noon in heaven;
let those who claim it is begin their own journey
home. So why must you rush like an impatient
bride: why do you race to desert your Olohun-iyo?

(ELESIN *is now sunk fully deep in his trance, there is no
longer sign of any awareness of his surroundings.*)

Does the deep voice of gbedu° cover you then,
like the passage of royal elephants? Those drums
that brook no rivals, have they blocked the passage to your ears that my voice passes into wind, a
mere leaf floating in the night? Is your flesh light-
ened Elesin, is that lump of earth I slid between
your slippers to keep you longer slowly sifting
from your feet? Are the drums on the other side
now tuning skin to skin with ours in osugbo?° Are
there sounds there I cannot hear, do footsteps

surround you which pound the earth like gbedu,
roll like thunder round the dome of the world? Is
the darkness gathering in your head Elesin? Is
there now a streak of light at the end of the passage, a light I dare not look upon? Does it reveal
whose voices we often heard, whose touches we
often felt, whose wisdoms come suddenly into the
mind when the wisest have shaken their heads
and murmured: It cannot be done? Elesin Alafin,
don't think I do not know why your lips are heavy,
why your limbs are drowsy as palm oil in the cold
of harmattan.° I would call you back but when the
elephant heads for the jungle, the tail is too small
a handhold for the hunter that would pull him
back. The sun that heads for the sea no longer
heeds the prayers of the farmer. When the river
begins to taste the salt of the ocean, we no longer
know what deity to call on, the river-god or
Olokun.° No arrow flies back to the string, the
child does not return through the same passage
that gave it birth. Elesin Oba, can you hear me at
all? Your eyelids are glazed like a courtesan's, is it
that you see the dark groom and master of life?
And will you see my father? Will you tell him that I
stayed with you to the last? Will my voice ring in
your ears awhile, will you remember Olohun-iyo
even if the music on the other side surpasses his
mortal craft? But will they know you over there?
Have they eyes to gauge your worth, have they the
heart to love you, will they know what thoroughbred prances towards them in caparisons of honour? If they do not Elesin, if any there cuts your
yam with a small knife, or pours you wine in a
small calabash, turn back and return to welcoming hands. If the world were not greater than the
wishes of Olohun-iyo, I would not let you go . . .

(He *appears to break down.* ELESIN *dances on, completely
in a trance. The dirge wells up louder and stronger.*
ELESIN's *dance does not lose its elasticity but his gestures
become, if possible, even more weighty. Lights fade slowly
on the scene.*)

SCENE 4

(A Masque. *The front side of the stage is part of a wide corridor around the great hall of the Residency extending
beyond vision into the rear and wings. It is redolent of the
tawdry decadence of a far-flung but key imperial frontier.
The* COUPLES *in a variety of fancy-dress are ranged
around the walls, gazing in the same direction. The guest-
of-honour is about to make an appearance. A portion of
the local police brass band with its white* CONDUCTOR *is*

---

gbedu, a deep-timbred royal drum. **osugbo,** secret
"executive" cult of the Yoruba; its meeting place.

harmattan, cold and dry season, usually in December or
January. **Olokun,** the sea god.

just visible. At last, the entrance of ROYALTY. *The band plays "Rule Britannia," badly, beginning long before he is visible. The couples bow and curtsey as he passes by them. Both he and his companions are dressed in seventeenth century European costume. Following behind are the* RESIDENT *and his* PARTNER *similarly attired. As they gain the end of the hall where the orchestra dais begins the music comes to an end. The* PRINCE *bows to the guests. The* BAND *strikes up a Viennese waltz and the* PRINCE *formally opens the floor. Several bars later the* RESIDENT *and his companion follow suit. Others follow in appropriate pecking order. The orchestra's waltz rendition is not of the highest musical standard.*

Some time later the PRINCE *dances again into view and is settled into a corner by the* RESIDENT *who then proceeds to select* COUPLES *as they dance past for introduction, sometimes threading his way through the dancers to tap the lucky* COUPLE *on the shoulder. Desperate efforts from many to ensure that they are recognised in spite of, perhaps, their costume. The ritual of introductions soon takes in* PILKINGS *and his* WIFE. *The* PRINCE *is quite fascinated by their costume and they demonstrate the adaptations they have made to it, pulling down the mask to demonstrate how the egungun normally appears, then showing the various press-button controls they have innovated for the face flaps, the sleeves, etc. They demonstrate the dance steps and the guttural sounds made by the* egungun, *harass other dancers in the hall,* MRS PILKINGS *playing the "restrainer" to* PILKINGS' *manic darts. Everyone is highly entertained, the Royal Party especially who lead the applause.*

At this point a liveried FOOTMAN *comes in with a note on a salver and is intercepted almost absent-mindedly by the* RESIDENT *who takes the note and reads it. After polite coughs he succeeds in excusing the* PILKINGS *from the* PRINCE *and takes them aside. The* PRINCE *considerately offers the* RESIDENT'S WIFE *his hand and dancing is resumed.*

On their way out the RESIDENT *gives an order to his* AIDE-DE-CAMP. *They come into the side corridor where the* RESIDENT *hands the note to* PILKINGS.*)*

RESIDENT: As you see it says "emergency" on the outside. I took the liberty of opening it because His Highness was obviously enjoying the entertainment. I didn't want to interrupt unless really necessary.

PILKINGS: Yes, yes of course, Sir.

RESIDENT: Is it really as bad as it says? What's it all about?

PILKINGS: Some strange custom they have, sir. It seems because the King is dead some important chief has to commit suicide.

RESIDENT: The King? Isn't it the same one who died nearly a month ago?

PILKINGS: Yes, sir.

RESIDENT: Haven't they buried him yet?

PILKINGS: They take their time about these things, sir. The pre-burial ceremonies last nearly thirty days. It seems tonight is the final night.

RESIDENT: But what has it got to do with the market women? Why are they rioting? We've waived that troublesome tax haven't we?

PILKINGS: We don't quite know that they are exactly rioting yet, sir. Sergeant Amusa is sometimes prone to exaggerations.

RESIDENT: He sounds desperate enough. That comes out even in his rather quaint grammar. Where is the man anyway? I asked my aide-de-camp to bring him here.

PILKINGS: They are probably looking in the wrong verandah. I'll fetch him myself.

RESIDENT: No no you stay here. Let your wife go and look for them. Do you mind my dear . . . ?

JANE: Certainly not, your Excellency. (*Goes.*)

RESIDENT: You should have kept me informed, Pilkings. You realise how disastrous it would have been if things had erupted while His Highness was here.

PILKINGS: I wasn't aware of the whole business until tonight, sir.

RESIDENT: Nose to the ground Pilkings, nose to the ground. If we all let these little things slip past us where would the empire be eh? Tell me that. Where would we all be?

PILKINGS (*low voice*): Sleeping peacefully at home I bet.

RESIDENT: What did you say, Pilkings?

PILKINGS: It won't happen again, sir.

RESIDENT: It mustn't, Pilkings. It mustn't. Where is that damned sergeant? I ought to get back to His Highness as quickly as possible and offer him some plausible explanation for my rather abrupt conduct. Can you think of one, Pilkings?

PILKINGS: You could tell him the truth, sir.

RESIDENT: I could? No no no no Pilkings, that would never do. What! Go and tell him there is a riot just two miles away from him? This is supposed to be a secure colony of His Majesty, Pilkings.

PILKINGS: Yes, sir.

RESIDENT: Ah, there they are. No, these are not our native police. Are these the ring-leaders of the riot?

PILKINGS: Sir, these are my police officers.

RESIDENT: Oh, I beg your pardon officers. You do look a little . . . I say, isn't there something missing in their uniform? I think they used to have some rather colourful sashes. If I remember rightly I recommended them myself in my young days in the service. A bit of colour always appeals to the natives, yes, I remember putting that in my report. Well well well, where are we? Make your report man.

PILKINGS (*moves close to* AMUSA, *between his teeth*): And let's have no more superstitious nonsense from you Amusa or I'll throw you in the guardroom for a month and feed you pork!

RESIDENT: What's that? What has pork to do with it?

PILKINGS: Sir, I was just warning him to be brief. I'm sure you are most anxious to hear his report.

RESIDENT: Yes yes yes of course. Come on man, speak up. Hey, didn't we give them some colourful fez hats with all those wavy things, yes, pink tassels . . .

PILKINGS: Sir, I think if he was permitted to make his report we might find that he lost his hat in the riot.

RESIDENT: Ah yes indeed. I'd better tell His Highness that. Lost his hat in the riot, ha ha. He'll probably say well, as long as he didn't lose his head. (*Chuckles to himself.*) Don't forget to send me a report first thing in the morning young Pilkings.

PILKINGS: No, sir.

RESIDENT: And whatever you do, don't let things get out of hand. Keep a cool head and—nose to the ground Pilkings. (*Wanders off in the general direction of the hall.*)

PILKINGS: Yes, sir.

AIDE-DE-CAMP: Would you be needing me, sir?

PILKINGS: No thanks, Bob. I think His Excellency's need of you is greater than ours.

AIDE-DE-CAMP: We have a detachment of soldiers from the capital, sir. They accompanied His Highness up here.

PILKINGS: I doubt if it will come to that but, thanks, I'll bear it in mind. Oh, could you send an orderly with my cloak.

AIDE-DE-CAMP: Very good, sir. (*Goes.*)

PILKINGS: Now, sergeant.

AMUSA: Sir . . . (*Makes an effort, stops dead. Eyes to the ceiling.*)

PILKINGS: Oh, not again.

AMUSA: I cannot against death to dead cult. This dress get power of dead.

PILKINGS: All right, let's go. You are relieved of all further duty Amusa. Report to me first thing in the morning.

JANE: Shall I come, Simon?

PILKINGS: No, there's no need for that. If I can get back later I will. Otherwise get Bob to bring you home.

JANE: Be careful Simon . . . I mean, be clever.

PILKINGS: Sure I will. You two, come with me. (*As he turns to go, the clock in the Residency begins to chime.* PILKINGS *looks at his watch then turns, horror-stricken, to stare at his* WIFE. *The same thought clearly occurs to her. He swallows hard. An* ORDERLY *brings his cloak.*) It's midnight. I had no idea it was that late.

JANE: But surely . . . they don't count the hours the way we do. The moon, or something . . .

PILKINGS: I am . . . not so sure.

(*He turns and breaks into a sudden run. The two* CONSTABLES *follow, also at a run.* AMUSA, *who has kept his eyes on the ceiling throughout waits until the last of the* footsteps has faded out of hearing. He salutes suddenly, but without once looking in the direction of the WOMAN.)

AMUSA: Goodnight, madam.

JANE: Oh. (*She hesitates.*) Amusa . . . (*He goes off without seeming to have heard.*) Poor Simon . . . (*A figure emerges from the shadows, a young black MAN dressed in a sober western suit. He peeps into the hall, trying to make out the figures of the dancers.*) Who is that?

OLUNDE (*emerges into the light*): I didn't mean to startle you madam. I am looking for the District Officer.

JANE: Wait a minute . . . don't I know you? Yes, you are Olunde, the young man who . . .

OLUNDE: Mrs Pilkings! How fortunate. I came here to look for your husband.

JANE: Olunde! Let's look at you. What a fine young man you've become. Grand but solemn. Good God, when did you return? Simon never said a word. But you do look well Olunde. Really!

OLUNDE: You are . . . well, you look quite well yourself Mrs Pilkings. From what little I can see of you.

JANE: Oh, this. It's caused quite a stir I assure you, and not all of it very pleasant. You are not shocked I hope?

OLUNDE: Why should I be? But don't you find it rather hot in there? Your skin must find it difficult to breathe.

JANE: Well, it is a little hot I must confess, but it's all in a good cause.

OLUNDE: What cause Mrs Pilkings?

JANE: All this. The ball. And His Highness being here in person and all that.

OLUNDE (*mildly*): And that is the good cause for which you desecrate an ancestral mask?

JANE: Oh, so you are shocked after all. How disappointing.

OLUNDE: No I am not shocked, Mrs Pilkings. You forget that I have now spent four years among your people. I discovered that you have no respect for what you do not understand.

JANE: Oh. So you've returned with a chip on your shoulder. That's a pity Olunde. I am sorry.

(*An uncomfortable silence follows.*)

I take it then that you did not find your stay in England altogether edifying.

OLUNDE: I don't say that. I found your people quite admirable in many ways, their conduct and courage in this war for instance.

JANE: Ah yes, the war. Here of course it is all rather remote. From time to time we have a black-out drill just to remind us that there is a war on. And the rare convoy passes through on its way somewhere or on manoeuvres. Mind you there is the occasional bit of excitement like that ship that was blown up in the harbour.

OLUNDE: Here? Do you mean through enemy action?

JANE: Oh no, the war hasn't come that close. The captain did it himself. I don't quite understand it really. Simon tried to explain. The ship had to be blown up because it had become dangerous to the other ships, even to the city itself. Hundreds of the coastal population would have died.

OLUNDE: Maybe it was loaded with ammunition and had caught fire. Or some of those lethal gases they've been experimenting on.

JANE: Something like that. The captain blew himself up with it. Deliberately. Simon said someone had to remain on board to light the fuse.

OLUNDE: It must have been a very short fuse.

JANE (shrugs): I don't know much about it. Only that there was no other way to save lives. No time to devise anything else. The captain took the decision and carried it out.

OLUNDE: Yes . . . I quite believe it. I met men like that in England.

JANE: Oh just look at me! Fancy welcoming you back with such morbid news. Stale too. It was at least six months ago.

OLUNDE: I don't find it morbid at all. I find it rather inspiring. It is an affirmative commentary on life.

JANE: What is?

OLUNDE: That captain's self-sacrifice.

JANE: Nonsense. Life should never be thrown deliberately away.

OLUNDE: And the innocent people around the harbour?

JANE: Oh, how does one know? The whole thing was probably exaggerated anyway.

OLUNDE: That was a risk the captain couldn't take. But please Mrs Pilkings, do you think you could find your husband for me? I have to talk to him.

JANE: Simon? (As she recollects for the first time the full significance of OLUNDE's presence.) Simon is . . . there is a little problem in town. He was sent for. But . . . when did you arrive? Does Simon know you're here?

OLUNDE (suddenly earnest): I need your help Mrs Pilkings. I've always found you somewhat more understanding than your husband. Please find him for me and when you do, you must help me talk to him.

JANE: I'm afraid I don't quite . . . follow you. Have you seen my husband already?

OLUNDE: I went to your house. Your houseboy told me you were here. (He smiles.) He even told me how I would recognise you and Mr Pilkings.

JANE: Then you must know what my husband is trying to do for you.

OLUNDE: For me?

JANE: For you. For your people. And to think he didn't even know you were coming back! But how do you happen to be here? Only this evening we were talking about you. We thought you were still four thousand miles away.

OLUNDE: I was sent a cable.

JANE: A cable? Who did? Simon? The business of your father didn't begin till tonight.

OLUNDE: A relation sent it weeks ago, and it said nothing about my father. All it said was, Our King is dead. But I knew I had to return home at once so as to bury my father. I understood that.

JANE: Well, thank God you don't have to go through that agony. Simon is going to stop it.

OLUNDE: That's why I want to see him. He's wasting his time. And since he has been so helpful to me I don't want him to incur the enmity of our people. Especially over nothing.

JANE (sits down open-mouthed): You . . . you Olunde!

OLUNDE: Mrs Pilkings, I came home to bury my father. As soon as I heard the news I booked my passage home. In fact we were fortunate. We travelled in the same convoy as your Prince, so we had excellent protection.

JANE: But you don't think your father is also entitled to whatever protection is available to him?

OLUNDE: How can I make you understand? He *has* protection. No one can undertake what he does tonight without the deepest protection the mind can conceive. What can you offer him in place of his peace of mind, in place of the honour and veneration of his own people? What would you think of your Prince if he refused to accept the risk of losing his life on this voyage? This . . . showing-the-flag tour of colonial possessions.

JANE: I see. So it isn't just medicine you studied in England.

OLUNDE: Yet another error into which your people fall. You believe that everything which appears to make sense was learnt from you.

JANE: Not so fast Olunde. You have learnt to argue I can tell that, but I never said you made sense. However clearly you try to put it, it is still a barbaric custom. It is even worse—it's feudal! The king dies and a chieftain must be buried with him. How feudalistic can you get!

OLUNDE (waves his hand towards the background. The PRINCE is dancing past again—to a different step—and all the guests are bowing and curtseying as he passes): And this? Even in the midst of a devastating war, look at that. What name would you give to that?

JANE: Therapy, British style. The preservation of sanity in the midst of chaos.

OLUNDE: Others would call it decadence. However, it doesn't really interest me. You white races know how to survive; I've seen proof of that. By all logical and natural laws this war should end with all the white races wiping out one another, wiping out their so-called civilisation for all time and reverting to a state of primitivism the like of which has so far only existed in your imagination when you thought of us. I thought all that at the beginning. Then I slowly realised that your greatest art is the art of survival. But at least have the humility to let others survive in their own way.

JANE: Through ritual suicide?

OLUNDE: Is that worse than mass suicide? Mrs Pilkings, what do you call what those young men are sent to do by their generals in this war? Of course you have also mastered the art of calling things by names which don't remotely describe them.

JANE: You talk! You people with your long-winded, roundabout way of making conversation.

OLUNDE: Mrs Pilkings, whatever we do, we never suggest that a thing is the opposite of what it really is. In your newsreels I heard defeats, thorough, murderous defeats described as strategic victories. No wait, it wasn't just on your newsreels. Don't forget I was attached to hospitals all the time. Hordes of your wounded passed through those wards. I spoke to them. I spent long evenings by their bedsides while they spoke terrible truths of the realities of that war. I know now how history is made.

JANE: But surely, in a war of this nature, for the morale of the nation you must expect . . .

OLUNDE: That a disaster beyond human reckoning be spoken of as a triumph? No. I mean, is there no mourning in the home of the bereaved that such blasphemy is permitted?

JANE (after a moment's pause): Perhaps I can understand you now. The time we picked for you was not really one for seeing us at our best.

OLUNDE: Don't think it was just the war. Before that even started I had plenty of time to study your people. I saw nothing, finally, that gave you the right to pass judgement on other peoples and their ways. Nothing at all.

JANE (hesitantly): Was it the . . . colour thing? I know there is some discrimination.

OLUNDE: Don't make it so simple, Mrs Pilkings. You make it sound as if when I left, I took nothing at all with me.

JANE: Yes . . . and to tell the truth, only this evening, Simon and I agreed that we never really knew what you left with.

OLUNDE: Neither did I. But I found out over there. I am grateful to your country for that. And I will never give it up.

JANE: Olunde, please . . . promise me something. Whatever you do, don't throw away what you have started to do. You want to be a doctor. My husband and I believe you will make an excellent one, sympathetic and competent. Don't let anything make you throw away your training.

OLUNDE (genuinely surprised): Of course not. What a strange idea. I intend to return and complete my training. Once the burial of my father is over.

JANE: Oh, please . . . !

OLUNDE: Listen! Come outside. You can't hear anything against that music.

JANE: What is it?

OLUNDE: The drums. Can you hear the drums? Listen.

(The drums come over, still distant but more distinct. There is a change of rhythm, it rises to a crescendo and then, suddenly, it is cut off. After a silence, a new beat begins, slow and resonant.)

There, it's all over.

JANE: You mean he's . . .

OLUNDE: Yes, Mrs Pilkings, my father is dead. His willpower has always been enormous; I know he is dead.

JANE (screams): How can you be so callous! So unfeeling! You announce your father's own death like a surgeon looking down on some strange . . . stranger's body! You're just a savage like all the rest.

AIDE-DE-CAMP (rushing out): Mrs Pilkings. Mrs Pilkings. (She breaks down, sobbing.) Are you all right, Mrs Pilkings?

OLUNDE: She'll be all right. (Turns to go.)

AIDE-DE-CAMP: Who are you? And who the hell asked your opinion?

OLUNDE: You're quite right, nobody. (Going.)

AIDE-DE-CAMP: What the hell! Did you hear me ask you who you were?

OLUNDE: I have business to attend to.

AIDE-DE-CAMP: I'll give you business in a moment you impudent nigger. Answer my question!

OLUNDE: I have a funeral to arrange. Excuse me. (Going.)

AIDE-DE-CAMP: I said stop! Orderly!

JANE: No, no, don't do that. I'm all right. And for heaven's sake don't act so foolishly. He's a family friend.

AIDE-DE-CAMP: Well he'd better learn to answer civil questions when he's asked them. These natives put a suit on and they get high opinions of themselves.

OLUNDE: Can I go now?

JANE: No, no, don't go. I must talk to you. I'm sorry about what I said.

OLUNDE: It's nothing, Mrs Pilkings. And I'm really anxious to go. I couldn't see my father before, it's forbidden for me, his heir and successor to set eyes on him from the moment of the King's death. But now . . . I would like to touch his body while it is still warm.

JANE: You will. I promise I shan't keep you long. Only, I couldn't possibly let you go like that. Bob, please excuse us.

AIDE-DE-CAMP: If you're sure . . .

JANE: Of course I'm sure. Something happened to upset me just then, but I'm all right now. Really.

(The AIDE-DE-CAMP *goes, somewhat reluctantly.)*

OLUNDE: I mustn't stay long.

JANE: Please, I promise not to keep you. It's just that . . . oh you saw yourself what happens to one in this place. The Resident's man thought he was being helpful, that's the way we all react. But I can't go in among that crowd just now and if I stay by myself somebody will come looking for me. Please, just say something for a few moments and then you can go. Just so I can recover myself.

OLUNDE: What do you want me to say?

JANE: Your calm acceptance for instance, can you explain that? It was so unnatural. I don't understand that at all. I feel a need to understand all I can.

OLUNDE: But you explained it yourself. My medical training perhaps. I have seen death too often. And the soldiers who returned from the front, they died on our hands all the time.

JANE: No. It has to be more than that. I feel it has to do with the many things we don't really grasp about your people. At least you can explain.

OLUNDE: All these things are part of it. And anyway, my father has been dead in my mind for nearly a month. Ever since I learnt of the King's death. I've lived with my bereavement so long now that I cannot think of him alive. On that journey on the boat, I kept my mind on my duties as the one who must perform the rites over his body. I went through it all again and again in my mind as he himself had taught me. I didn't want to do anything wrong, something which might jeopardise the welfare of my people.

JANE: But he had disowned you. When you left he swore publicly you were no longer his son.

OLUNDE: I told you, he was a man of tremendous will. Sometimes that's another way of saying stubborn. But among our people, you don't disown a child just like that. Even if I had died before him I would still be buried like his eldest son. But it's time for me to go.

JANE: Thank you. I feel calmer. Don't let me keep you from your duties.

OLUNDE: Goodnight, Mrs Pilkings.

JANE: Welcome home.

(She holds out her hand. As he takes it footsteps are heard approaching the drive. A short while later a woman's sobbing is also heard.)

PILKINGS *(off)*: Keep them here till I get back. *(He strides into view, reacts at the sight of* OLUNDE *but turns to his* WIFE.*)* Thank goodness you're still here.

JANE: Simon, what happened?

PILKINGS: Later Jane, please. Is Bob still here?

JANE: Yes, I think so. I'm sure he must be.

PILKINGS: Try and get him out here as quickly as you can. Tell him it's urgent.

JANE: Of course. Oh Simon, you remember . . .

PILKINGS: Yes yes. I can see who it is. Get Bob out here. *(She runs off.)* At first I thought I was seeing a ghost.

OLUNDE: Mr Pilkings, I appreciate what you tried to do. I want you to believe that. I can tell you it would have been a terrible calamity if you'd succeeded.

PILKINGS *(opens his mouth several times, shuts it)*: You . . . said what?

OLUNDE: A calamity for us, the entire people.

PILKINGS *(sighs)*: I see. Hm.

OLUNDE: And now I must go. I must see him before he turns cold.

PILKINGS: Oh ah . . . em . . . but this is a shock to see you. I mean er thinking all this while you were in England and thanking God for that.

OLUNDE: I came on the mail boat. We travelled in the Prince's convoy.

PILKINGS: Ah yes, a-ah, hm . . . er well . . .

OLUNDE: Goodnight. I can see you are shocked by the whole business. But you must know by now there are things you cannot understand—or help.

PILKINGS: Yes. Just a minute. There are armed policemen that way and they have instructions to let no one pass. I suggest you wait a little. I'll er . . . give you an escort.

OLUNDE: That's very kind of you. But do you think it could be quickly arranged.

PILKINGS: Of course. In fact, yes, what I'll do is send Bob over with some men to the er . . . place. You can go with them. Here he comes now. Excuse me a minute.

AIDE-DE-CAMP: Anything wrong sir?

PILKINGS *(takes him to one side)*: Listen Bob, that cellar in the disused annexe of the Residency, you know, where the slaves were stored before being taken down to the coast . . .

AIDE-DE-CAMP: Oh yes, we use it as a storeroom for broken furniture.

PILKINGS: But it's still got the bars on it?

AIDE-DE-CAMP: Oh yes, they are quite intact.

PILKINGS: Get the keys please. I'll explain later. And I want a strong guard over the Residency tonight.

AIDE-DE-CAMP: We have that already. The detachment from the coast . . .

PILKINGS: No, I don't want them at the gates of the Residency. I want you to deploy them at the bottom of the hill, a long way from the main hall so they can deal with any situation long before the sound carries to the house.

AIDE-DE-CAMP: Yes of course.

PILKINGS: I don't want His Highness alarmed.

AIDE-DE-CAMP: You think the riot will spread here?

PILKINGS: It's unlikely but I don't want to take a

chance. I made them believe I was going to lock the man up in my house, which was what I had planned to do in the first place. They are probably assailing it by now. I took a roundabout route here so I don't think there is any danger at all. At least not before dawn. Nobody is to leave the premises of course—the native employees I mean. They'll soon smell something is up and they can't keep their mouths shut.

AIDE-DE-CAMP: I'll give instructions at once.

PILKINGS: I'll take the prisoner down myself. Two policemen will stay with him throughout the night. Inside the cell.

AIDE-DE-CAMP: Right sir. (*Salutes and goes off at the double.*)

PILKINGS: Jane. Bob is coming back in a moment with a detachment. Until he gets back please stay with Olunde. (*He makes an extra warning gesture with his eyes.*)

OLUNDE: Please, Mr Pilkings . . .

PILKINGS: I hate to be stuffy old son, but we have a crisis on our hands. It has to do with your father's affair if you must know. And it happens also at a time when we have His Highness here. I am responsible for security so you'll simply have to do as I say. I hope that's understood. (*Marches off quickly, in the direction from which he made his first appearance.*)

OLUNDE: What's going on? All this can't be just because he failed to stop my father killing himself.

JANE: I honestly don't know. Could it have sparked off a riot?

OLUNDE: No. If he'd succeeded that would be more likely to start the riot. Perhaps there were other factors involved. Was there a chieftaincy dispute?

JANE: None that I know of.

ELESIN (*an animal bellow from off*): Leave me alone! Is it not enough that you have covered me in shame! White man, take your hand from my body!

(OLUNDE *stands frozen to the spot.* JANE *understanding at last, tries to move him.*)

JANE: Let's go in. It's getting chilly out here.

PILKINGS (*off*): Carry him.

ELESIN: Give me back the name you have taken away from me you ghost from the land of the nameless!

PILKINGS: Carry him! I can't have a disturbance here. Quickly! Stuff up his mouth.

JANE: Oh God! Let's go in. Please Olunde.

(OLUNDE *does not move.*)

ELESIN: Take your albino's hand from me you . . .

(*Sounds of a struggle. His voice chokes as he is gagged.*)

OLUNDE (*quietly*): That was my father's voice.

JANE: Oh you poor orphan, what have you come home to?

(*There is a sudden explosion of rage from off-stage and powerful steps come running up the drive.*)

PILKINGS: You bloody fools, after him!

(*Immediately* ELESIN, *in handcuffs, comes pounding in the direction of* JANE *and* OLUNDE, *followed some moments afterwards by* PILKINGS *and the* CONSTABLES. ELESIN *confronted by the seeming statue of his son, stops dead.* OLUNDE *stares above his head into the distance. The* CONSTABLES *try to grab him.* JANE *screams at them.*)

JANE: Leave him alone! Simon, tell them to leave him alone.

PILKINGS: All right, stand aside you. (*Shrugs.*) Maybe just as well. It might help to calm him down.

(*For several moments they hold the same position.* ELESIN *moves a step forward, almost as if he's still in doubt.*)

ELESIN: Olunde? (*He moves his head, inspecting him from side to side.*) Olunde! (*He collapses slowly at* OLUNDE*'s feet.*) Oh son, don't let the sight of your father turn you blind!

OLUNDE (*he moves for the first time since he heard his voice, brings his head slowly down to look on him*): I have no father, eater of left-overs.

(*He walks slowly down the way his father had run. Light fades out on* ELESIN, *sobbing into the ground.*)

SCENE 5

(*A wide iron-barred gate stretches almost the whole width of the cell in which* ELESIN *is imprisoned. His wrists are encased in thick iron bracelets, chained together; he stands against the bars, looking out. Seated on the ground to one side on the outside is his recent* BRIDE, *her eyes bent perpetually to the ground. Figures of the two* GUARDS *can be seen deeper inside the cell, alert to every movement* ELESIN *makes.* PILKINGS *now in a police officer's uniform enters noiselessly, observes him a while. Then he coughs ostentatiously and approaches. Leans against the bars near a corner, his back to* ELESIN. *He is obviously trying to fall in mood with him. Some moments' silence.*)

PILKINGS: You seem fascinated by the moon.

ELESIN (*after a pause*): Yes, ghostly one. Your twin-brother up there engages my thoughts.

PILKINGS: It is a beautiful night.

ELESIN: Is that so?

PILKINGS: The light on the leaves, the peace of the night . . .

ELESIN: The night is not at peace, District Officer.

PILKINGS: No? I would have said it was. You know, quiet . . .

ELESIN: And does quiet mean peace for you?

PILKINGS: Well, nearly the same thing. Naturally there is a subtle difference . . .

ELESIN: The night is not at peace, ghostly one. The

world is not at peace. You have shattered the peace of the world for ever. There is no sleep in the world tonight.

PILKINGS: It is still a good bargain if the world should lose one night's sleep as the price of saving a man's life.

ELESIN: You did not save my life, District Officer. You destroyed it.

PILKINGS: Now come on . . .

ELESIN: And not merely my life but the lives of many. The end of the night's work is not over. Neither this year nor the next will see it. If I wished you well, I would pray that you do not stay long enough on our land to see the disaster you have brought upon us.

PILKINGS: Well, I did my duty as I saw it. I have no regrets.

ELESIN: No. The regrets of life always come later.

(Some moments' pause.)

You are waiting for dawn, white man. I hear you saying to yourself: only so many hours until dawn and then the danger is over. All I must do is to keep him alive tonight. You don't quite understand it all but you know that tonight is when what ought to be must be brought about. I shall ease your mind even more, ghostly one. It is not an entire night but a moment of the night, and that moment is past. The moon was my messenger and guide. When it reached a certain gateway in the sky, it touched that moment for which my whole life has been spent in blessings. Even I do not know the gateway. I have stood here and scanned the sky for a glimpse of that door but, I cannot see it. Human eyes are useless for a search of this nature. But in the house of osugbo, those who keep watch through the spirit recognised the moment, they sent word to me through the voice of our sacred drums to prepare myself. I heard them and I shed all thoughts of earth. I began to follow the moon to the abode of the gods . . . servant of the white king, that was when you entered my chosen place of departure on feet of desecration.

PILKINGS: I'm sorry, but we all see our duty differently.

ELESIN: I no longer blame you. You stole from me my first-born, sent him to your country so you could turn him into something in your own image. Did you plan it all beforehand? There are moments when it seems part of a larger plan. He who must follow my footsteps is taken from me, sent across the ocean. Then, in my turn, I am stopped from fulfilling my destiny. Did you think it all out before, this plan to push our world from its course and sever the cord that links us to the great origin?

PILKINGS: You don't really believe that. Anyway, if that was my intention with your son, I appear to have failed.

ELESIN: You did not fail in the main, ghostly one. We know the roof covers the rafters, the cloth covers blemishes; who would have known that the white skin covered our future, preventing us from seeing the death our enemies had prepared for us. The world is set adrift and its inhabitants are lost. Around them, there is nothing but emptiness.

PILKINGS: Your son does not take so gloomy a view.

ELESIN: Are you dreaming now, white man? Were you not present at my reunion of shame? Did you not see when the world reversed itself and the father fell before his son, asking forgiveness?

PILKINGS: That was in the heat of the moment. I spoke to him and . . . if you want to know, he wishes he could cut out his tongue for uttering the words he did.

ELESIN: No. What he said must never be unsaid. The contempt of my own son rescued something of my shame at your hands. You have stopped me in my duty but I know now that I did give birth to a son. Once I mistrusted him for seeking the companionship of those my spirit knew as enemies of our race. Now I understand. One should seek to obtain the secrets of his enemies. He will avenge my shame, white one. His spirit will destroy you and yours.

PILKINGS: That kind of talk is hardly called for. If you don't want my consolation . . .

ELESIN: No white man, I do not want your consolation.

PILKINGS: As you wish. Your son anyway, sends his consolation. He asks your forgiveness. When I asked him not to despise you his reply was: I cannot judge him, and if I cannot judge him, I cannot despise him. He wants to come to you and say goodbye and to receive your blessing.

ELESIN: Goodbye? Is he returning to your land?

PILKINGS: Don't you think that's the most sensible thing for him to do? I advised him to leave at once, before dawn, and he agrees that is the right course of action.

ELESIN: Yes, it is best. And even if I did not think so, I have lost the father's place of honour. My voice is broken.

PILKINGS: Your son honours you. If he didn't he would not ask your blessing.

ELESIN: No. Even a thoroughbred is not without pity for the turf he strikes with his hoof. When is he coming?

PILKINGS: As soon as the town is a little quieter. I advised it.

ELESIN: Yes, white man, I am sure you advised it. You

advise all our lives although on the authority of what gods, I do not know.

PILKINGS (*opens his mouth to reply, then appears to change his mind. Turns to go. Hesitates and stops again*): Before I leave you, may I ask just one thing of you?

ELESIN: I am listening.

PILKINGS: I wish to ask you to search the quiet of your heart and tell me—do you not find great contradictions in the wisdom of your own race?

ELESIN: Make yourself clear, white one.

PILKINGS: I have lived among you long enough to learn a saying or two. One came to my mind tonight when I stepped into the market and saw what was going on. You were surrounded by those who egged you on with song and praises. I thought, are these not the same people who say: the elder grimly approaches heaven and you ask him to bear your greetings yonder; do you really think he makes the journey willingly? After that, I did not hesitate.

(*A pause.* ELESIN *sighs. Before he can speak a sound of running feet is heard.*)

JANE (*off*): Simon! Simon!

PILKINGS: What on earth . . . ! (*Runs off.*)

(ELESIN *turns to his new* WIFE, *gazes on her for some moments.*

ELESIN: My young bride, did you hear the ghostly one? You sit and sob in your silent heart but say nothing to all this. First I blamed the white man, then I blamed my gods for deserting me. Now I feel I want to blame you for the mystery of the sapping of my will. But blame is a strange peace offering for a man to bring a world he has deeply wronged, and to its innocent dwellers. Oh little mother, I have taken countless women in my life but you were more than a desire of the flesh. I needed you as the abyss across which my body must be drawn, I filled it with earth and dropped my seed in it at the moment of preparedness for my crossing. You were the final gift of the living to their emissary to the land of the ancestors, and perhaps your warmth and youth brought new insights of this world to me and turned my feet leaden on this side of the abyss. For I confess to you, daughter, my weakness came not merely from the abomination of the white man who came violently into my fading presence, there was also a weight of longing on my earth-held limbs. I would have shaken it off, already my foot had begun to lift but then, the white ghost entered and all was defiled.

(*Approaching voices of* PILKINGS *and his* WIFE.)

JANE: Oh Simon, you will let her in won't you?

PILKINGS: I really wish you'd stop interfering.

(*They come into view.* JANE *is in a dressing-gown.* PILKINGS *is holding a note to which he refers from time to time.*)

JANE: Good gracious, I didn't initiate this. I was sleeping quietly, or trying to anyway, when the servant brought it. It's not my fault if one can't sleep undisturbed even in the Residency.

PILKINGS: He'd have done the same thing if we were sleeping at home so don't sidetrack the issue. He knows he can get round you or he wouldn't send you the petition in the first place.

JANE: Be fair Simon. After all he was thinking of your own interests. He is grateful you know, you seem to forget that. He feels he owes you something.

PILKINGS: I just wish they'd leave this man alone tonight, that's all.

JANE: Trust him Simon. He's pledged his word it will all go peacefully.

PILKINGS: Yes, and that's the other thing. I don't like being threatened.

JANE: Threatened? (*Takes the note.*) I didn't spot any threat.

PILKINGS: It's there. Veiled, but it's there. The only way to prevent serious rioting tomorrow—what a cheek!°

JANE: I don't think he's threatening you Simon.

PILKINGS: He's picked up the idiom all right. Wouldn't surprise me if he's been mixing with commies or anarchists over there. The phrasing sounds too good to be true. Damn! If only the Prince hadn't picked this time for his visit.

JANE: Well, even so Simon, what have you got to lose? You don't want a riot on your hands, not with the Prince here.

PILKINGS (*going up to* ELESIN): Let's see what he has to say. Chief Elesin, there is yet another person who wants to see you. As she is not a next-of-kin I don't really feel obliged to let her in. But your son sent a note with her, so it's up to you.

ELESIN: I know who that must be. So she found out your hiding-place. Well, it was not difficult. My stench of shame is so strong, it requires no hunter's dog to follow it.

PILKINGS: If you don't want to see her, just say so and I'll send her packing.

ELESIN: Why should I not want to see her? Let her come. I have no more holes in my rag of shame. All is laid bare.

PILKINGS: I'll bring her in. (*Goes off.*)

JANE (*hesitates, then goes to* ELESIN): Please, try and understand. Everything my husband did was for the best.

ELESIN (*he gives her a long strange stare, as if he is trying to

---

what a cheek, British slang for "what nerve."

understand who she is): You are the wife of the District Officer?

JANE: Yes. My name is Jane.

ELESIN: That is my wife sitting down there. You notice how still and silent she sits? My business is with your husband.

(PILKINGS *returns with* IYALOJA.)

PILKINGS: Here she is. Now first I want your word of honour that you will try nothing foolish.

ELESIN: Honour? White one, did you say you wanted my word of honour?

PILKINGS: I know you to be an honourable man. Give me your word of honour you will receive nothing from her.

ELESIN: But I am sure you have searched her clothing as you would never dare touch your own mother. And there are these two lizards of yours who roll their eyes even when I scratch.

PILKINGS: And I shall be sitting on that tree trunk watching even how you blink. Just the same I want your word that you will not let her pass anything to you.

ELESIN: You have my honour already. It is locked up in that desk in which you will put away your report of this night's events. Even the honour of my people you have taken already; it is tied together with those papers of treachery which make you masters in this land.

PILKINGS: All right. I am trying to make things easy but if you must bring in politics we'll have to do it the hard way. Madam, I want you to remain along this line and move no nearer to the cell door. Guards! (*They spring to attention.*) If she moves beyond this point, blow your whistle. Come on Jane. (*They go off.*)

IYALOJA: How boldly the lizard struts before the pigeon when it was the eagle itself he promised us he would confront.

ELESIN: I don't ask you to take pity on me Iyaloja. You have a message for me or you would not have come. Even if it is the curses of the world, I shall listen.

IYALOJA: You made so bold with the servant of the white king who took your side against death. I must tell your brother chiefs when I return how bravely you waged war against him. Especially with words.

ELESIN: I more than deserve your scorn.

IYALOJA (*with sudden anger*): I warned you, if you must leave a seed behind, be sure it is not tainted with the curses of the world. Who are you to open a new life when you dared not open the door to a new existence? I say who are you to make so bold? (*The* BRIDE *sobs and* IYALOJA *notices her. Her contempt noticeably increases as she turns back to* ELESIN.) Oh you self-vaunted stem of the plantain, how

hollow it all proves. The pith is gone in the parent stem, so how will it prove with the new shoot? How will it go with that earth that bears it? Who are you to bring this abomination on us!

ELESIN: My powers deserted me. My charms, my spells, even my voice lacked strength when I made to summon the powers that would lead me over the last measure of earth into the land of the fleshless. You saw it, Iyaloja. You saw me struggle to retrieve my will from the power of the stranger whose shadow fell across the doorway and left me floundering and blundering in a maze I had never before encountered. My senses were numbed when the touch of cold iron came upon my wrists. I could do nothing to save myself.

IYALOJA: You have betrayed us. We fed you sweetmeats such as we hoped awaited you on the other side. But you said No, I must eat the world's leftovers. We said you were the hunter who brought the quarry down; to you belonged the vital portions of the game. No, you said, I am the hunter's dog and I shall eat the entrails of the game and the faeces of the hunter. We said you were the hunter returning home in triumph, a slain buffalo pressing down on his neck; you said wait, I first must turn up this cricket hole with my toes. We said yours was the doorway at which we first spy the tapper° when he comes down from the tree, yours was the blessing of the twilight wine, the purl that brings night spirits out of doors to steal their portion before the light of day. We said yours was the body of wine whose burden shakes the tapper like a sudden gust on his perch. You said, No, I am content to lick the dregs from each calabash when the drinkers are done. We said, the dew on earth's surface was for you to wash your feet along the slopes of honour. You said No, I shall step in the vomit of cats and the droppings of mice; I shall fight them for the left-overs of the world.

ELESIN: Enough Iyaloja, enough.

IYALOJA: We called you leader and oh, how you led us on. What we have no intention of eating should not be held to the nose.

ELESIN: Enough, enough. My shame is heavy enough.

IYALOJA: Wait. I came with a burden.

ELESIN: You have more than discharged it.

IYALOJA: I wish I could pity you.

ELESIN: I need neither pity nor the pity of the world. I need understanding. Even I need to understand. You were present at my defeat. You were part of the beginnings. You brought about the renewal of my tie to earth, you helped in the binding of the cord.

---

tapper, person who taps the palm tree for liquor.

IYALOJA: I gave you warning. The river which fills up before our eyes does not sweep us away in its flood.

ELESIN: What were warnings beside the moist contact of living earth between my fingers? What were warnings beside the renewal of famished embers lodged eternally in the heart of man. But even that, even if it overwhelmed one with a thousand-fold temptations to linger a little while, a man could overcome it. It is when the alien hand pollutes the source of will, when a stranger force of violence shatters the mind's calm resolution, this is when a man is made to commit the awful treachery of relief, commit in his thought the unspeakable blasphemy of seeing the hand of the gods in this alien rupture of his world. I know it was this thought that killed me, sapped my powers and turned me into an infant in the hands of unnamable strangers. I made to utter my spells anew but my tongue merely rattled in my mouth. I fingered hidden charms and the contact was damp; there was no spark left to sever the life-strings that should stretch from every fingertip. My will was squelched in the spittle of an alien race, and all because I had committed this blasphemy of thought—that there might be the hand of the gods in a stranger's intervention.

IYALOJA: Explain it how you will, I hope it brings you peace of mind. The bush-rat fled his rightful cause, reached the market and set up a lamentation. "Please save me!"—are these fitting words to hear from an ancestral mask? "There's a wild beast at my heels" is not becoming language from a hunter.

ELESIN: May the world forgive me.

IYALOJA: I came with a burden I said. It approaches the gates which are so well guarded by those jackals whose spittle will from this day be on your food and drink. But first, tell me, you who were once Elesin Oba, tell me, you who know so well the cycle of the plantain: is it the parent shoot which withers to give sap to the younger or, does your wisdom see it running the other way?

ELESIN: I don't see your meaning Iyaloja.

IYALOJA: Did I ask you for a meaning? I asked a question. Whose trunk withers to give sap to the other? The parent shoot or the younger?

ELESIN: The parent.

IYALOJA: Ah. So you do know that. There are sights in this world which say different Elesin. There are some who choose to reverse the cycle of our being. Oh you emptied bark that the world once saluted for a pith-laden being, shall I tell you what the gods have claimed of you?

(In her agitation she steps beyond the line indicated by PILKINGS *and the air is rent by piercing whistles. The two*

GUARDS *also leap forward and place safe-guarding hands on* ELESIN. IYALOJA *stops, astonished.* PILKINGS *comes racing in, followed by* JANE.*)*

PILKINGS: What is it? Did they try something?

GUARD: She stepped beyond the line.

ELESIN *(in a broken voice)*: Let her alone. She meant no harm.

IYALOJA: Oh Elesin, see what you've become. Once you had no need to open your mouth in explanation because evil-smelling goats, itchy of hand and foot had lost their senses. And it was a brave man indeed who dared lay hands on you because Iyaloja stepped from one side of the earth onto another. Now look at the spectacle of your life. I grieve for you.

PILKINGS: I think you'd better leave. I doubt you have done him much good by coming here. I shall make sure you are not allowed to see him again. In any case we are moving him to a different place before dawn, so don't bother to come back.

IYALOJA: We foresaw that. Hence the burden I trudged here to lay beside your gates.

PILKINGS: What was that you said?

IYALOJA: Didn't our son explain? Ask that one. He knows what it is. At least we hope the man we once knew as Elesin remembers the lesser oaths he need not break.

PILKINGS: Do you know what she is talking about?

ELESIN: Go to the gates, ghostly one. Whatever you find there, bring it to me.

IYALOJA: Not yet. It drags behind me on the slow, weary feet of women. Slow as it is Elesin, it has long overtaken you. It rides ahead of your laggard will.

PILKINGS: What is she saying now? Christ! Must your people forever speak in riddles?

ELESIN: It will come white man, it will come. Tell your men at the gates to let it through.

PILKINGS *(dubiously)*: I'll have to see what it is.

IYALOJA: You will. *(Passionately.)* But this is one oath he cannot shirk. White one, you have a king here, a visitor from your land. We know of his presence here. Tell me, were he to die would you leave his spirit roaming restlessly on the surface of earth? Would you bury him here among those you consider less than human? In your land have you no ceremonies of the dead?

PILKINGS: Yes. But we don't make our chiefs commit suicide to keep him company.

IYALOJA: Child, I have not come to help your understanding. *(Points to* ELESIN.*)* This is the man whose weakened understanding holds us in bondage to you. But ask him if you wish. He knows the meaning of a king's passage; he was not born yesterday. He knows the peril to the race when our dead father, who goes as intermediary, waits and waits and knows he is betrayed. He knows when the narrow gate was opened and he knows it will not stay for laggards who drag their feet in dung and vomit, whose lips are reeking of the left-overs of lesser men. He knows he has condemned our King to wander in the void of evil with beings who are enemies of life.

PILKINGS: Yes er . . . but look here . . .

IYALOJA: What we ask is little enough. Let him release our King so he can ride on homewards alone. The messenger is on his way on the backs of women. Let him send word through the heart that is folded up within the bolt. It is the least of all his oaths, it is the easiest fulfilled.

(The AIDE-DE-CAMP *runs in.)*

PILKINGS: Bob?

AIDE-DE-CAMP: Sir, there's a group of women chanting up the hill.

PILKINGS *(rounding on* IYALOJA*)*: If you people want trouble . . .

JANE: Simon, I think that's what Olunde referred to in his letter.

PILKINGS: He knows damned well I can't have a crowd here! Damn it, I explained the delicacy of my position to him. I think it's about time I got him out of town. Bob, send a car and two or three soldiers to bring him in. I think the sooner he takes his leave of his father and gets out the better.

IYALOJA: Save your labour white one. If it is the father of your prisoner you want, Olunde, he who until this night we knew as Elesin's son, he comes soon himself to take his leave. He has sent the women ahead, so let them in.

*(*PILKINGS *remains undecided.)*

AIDE-DE-CAMP: What do we do about the invasion? We can still stop them far from here.

PILKINGS: What do they look like?

AIDE-DE-CAMP: They're not many. And they seem quite peaceful.

PILKINGS: No men?

AIDE-DE-CAMP: Mm, two or three at the most.

JANE: Honestly, Simon, I'd trust Olunde. I don't think he'll deceive you about their intentions.

PILKINGS: He'd better not. All right then, let them in Bob. Warn them to control themselves. Then hurry Olunde here. Make sure he brings his baggage because I'm not returning him into town.

AIDE-DE-CAMP: Very good, sir. *(Goes.)*

PILKINGS *(to* IYALOJA*)*: I hope you understand that if anything goes wrong it will be on your head. My men have orders to shoot at the first sign of trouble.

IYALOJA: To prevent one death you will actually make other deaths? Ah, great is the wisdom of the white race. But have no fear. Your Prince will sleep peacefully. So at long last will ours. We will disturb you no further, servant of the white king. Just let

Elesin fulfill his oath and we will retire home and pay homage to our King.

JANE: I believe her Simon, don't you?

PILKINGS: Maybe.

ELESIN: Have no fear ghostly one. I have a message to send my King and then you have nothing more to fear.

IYALOJA: Olunde would have done it. The chiefs asked him to speak the words but he said no, not while you lived.

ELESIN: Even from the depths to which my spirit has sunk, I find some joy that this little has been left to me.

(The WOMEN *enter, intoning the dirge "Ale le le" and swaying from side to side. On their shoulders is borne a longish object roughly like a cylindrical bolt, covered in cloth. They set it down on the spot where* IYALOJA *had stood earlier, and form a semi-circle round it. The* PRAISE-SINGER *and* DRUMMER *stand on the inside of the semi-circle but the drum is not used at all. The* DRUMMER *intones under the* PRAISE-SINGER*'s invocations.)*

PILKINGS *(as they enter)*: What is *that*?

IYALOJA: The burden you have made white one, but we bring it in peace.

PILKINGS: I said *what* is it?

ELESIN: White man, you must let me out. I have a duty to perform.

PILKINGS: I most certainly will not.

ELESIN: There lies the courier of my King. Let me out so I can perform what is demanded of me.

PILKINGS: You'll do what you need to do from inside there or not at all. I've gone as far as I intend to with this business.

ELESIN: The worshipper who lights a candle in your church to bear a message to his god bows his head and speaks in a whisper to the flame. Have I not seen it ghostly one? His voice does not ring out to the world. Mine are not words for anyone's ears. They are not words even for the bearers of this load. They are words I must speak secretly, even as my father whispered them in my ears and I in the ears of my first-born. I cannot shout them to the wind and the open night-sky.

JANE: Simon . . .

PILKINGS: Don't interfere. Please!

IYALOJA: They have slain the favourite horse of the king and slain his dog. They have borne them from pulse to pulse centre of the land receiving prayers for their king. But the rider has chosen to stay behind. Is it too much to ask that he speak his heart to heart of the waiting courier? *(*PILKINGS *turns his back on her.)* So be it. Elesin Oba, you see how even the mere leavings are denied you. *(She gestures to the* PRAISE-SINGER*.)*

PRAISE-SINGER: Elesin Oba! I call you by that name only this last time. Remember when I said, if you cannot come, tell my horse. *(Pause.)* What? I cannot hear you? I said, if you cannot come, whisper in the ears of my horse. Is your tongue severed from the roots? Elesin? I can hear no response. I said, if there are boulders you cannot climb, mount my horse's back, this spotless black stallion, he'll bring you over them. *(Pauses.)* Elesin Oba, once you had a tongue that darted like a drummer's stick. I said, if you get lost my dog will track a path to me. My memory fails me but I think you replied: My feet have found the path, Alafin.

(The dirge rises and falls.)

I said at the last, if evil hands hold you back, just tell my horse there is weight on the hem of your smock. I dare not wait too long.

(The dirge rises and falls.)

There lies the swiftest ever messenger of a king, so set me free with the errand of your heart. There lie the head and heart of the favourite of the gods, whisper in his ears. Oh my companion, if you had followed when you should, we would not say that the horse preceded its rider. If you had followed when it was time, we would not say the dog has raced beyond and left his master behind. If you had raised your will to cut the thread of life at the summons of the drums, we would not say your mere shadow fell across the gateway and took its owner's place at the banquet. But the hunter, laden with slain buffalo, stayed to root in the cricket's hole with his toes. What now is left? If there is a dearth of bats, the pigeon must serve us for the offering. Speak the words over your shadow which must now serve in your place.

ELESIN: I cannot approach. Take off the cloth. I shall speak my message from heart to heart of silence.

IYALOJA *(moves forward and removes the covering)*: Your courier Elesin, cast your eyes on the favoured companion of the King.

(Rolled up in the mat, his head and feet showing at either end, is the body of OLUNDE.*)*

There lies the honour of your household and of our race. Because he could not bear to let honour fly out of doors, he stopped it with his life. The son has proved the father Elesin, and there is nothing left in your mouth to gnash but infant gums.

PRAISE-SINGER: Elesin, we placed the reins of the world in your hands yet you watched it plunge over the edge of the bitter precipice. You sat with folded arms while evil strangers tilted the world from its course and crashed it beyond the edge of emptiness—you muttered, there is little that one man can do, you left us floundering in a blind future. Your heir has taken the burden on himself. What the end will be, we are not gods to tell.

But this young shoot has poured its sap into the parent stalk, and we know this is not the way of life. Our world is tumbling in the void of strangers, Elesin.

*(*ELESIN *has stood rock-still, his knuckles taut on the bars, his eyes glued to the body of his son. The stillness seizes and paralyses everyone, including* PILKINGS *who has turned to look. Suddenly* ELESIN *flings one arm round his neck, once, and with the loop of the chain, strangles himself in a swift, decisive pull. The* GUARDS *rush forward to stop him but they are only in time to let his body down.* PILKINGS *has leapt to the door at the same time and struggles with the lock. He rushes within, fumbles with the handcuffs and unlocks them, raises the body to a sitting position while he tries to give resuscitation. The* WOMEN *continue their dirge, unmoved by the sudden event.)*

IYALOJA: Why do you strain yourself? Why do you labour at tasks for which no one, not even the man lying there, would give you thanks? He is gone at last into the passage but oh, how late it all is. His son will feast on the meat and throw him bones. The passage is clogged with droppings from the King's stallion; he will arrive all stained in dung.

PILKINGS *(in a tired voice)*: Was this what you wanted?

IYALOJA: No child, it is what you brought to be, you who play with strangers' lives, who even usurp the vestments of our dead, yet believe that the stain of death will not cling to you. The gods demanded only the old expired plantain but you cut down the sap-laden shoot to feed your pride. There is your board, filled to overflowing. Feast on it. *(She screams at him suddenly, seeing that* PILKINGS *is about to close* ELESIN*'s staring eyes.)* Let him alone! However sunk he was in debt he is no pauper's carrion abandoned on the road. Since when have strangers donned clothes of indigo° before the bereaved cries out his loss?

(She turns to the BRIDE *who has remained motionless throughout.)*

Child.

(The girl takes up a little earth, walks calmly into the cell and closes ELESIN*'s eyes. She then pours some earth over each eyelid and comes out again.)*

Now forget the dead, forget even the living. Turn your mind only to the unborn.

(She goes off, accompanied by the BRIDE. *The dirge rises in volume and the* WOMEN *continue their sway. Lights fade to a black-out.)*

---

indigo, dark blue color, indicative of mourning.

Figure 1. The Praise-Singer (Ben Halley Jr.) leaps into the air while Elesin (Norman Matlock, *left*) begins to dance in the 1979 Terrace Theatre production of Wole Soyinka's *Death and the King's Horseman*. (Photograph: Harry Naltchayan.)

Figure 2. Elesin (Norman Matlock), arrayed in rich clothes, is surrounded by the women of the marketplace in the first scene of *Death and the King's Horseman*. (Photograph: James C. Clark/The Goodman Theatre.)

Staging of *Death and the King's Horseman*

**REVIEW OF THE TERRACE THEATRE
PRODUCTION, 1979, BY JAMES LARDNER**

Something extraordinary arrived at the Terrace Theater last night—from Nigeria by way of Chicago.

The something is Wole Soyinka's "Death and the King's Horseman," a physically spectacular, intellectually stimulating, stylistically eccentric play that mixes motifs from an assortment of cultures and centuries. Far less ambitious pieces of theatrical cargo have suffered terrible damage crossing the Atlantic, but this elaborate package seems to have been handled with care all the way.

Based on real events in post-war Nigeria (post-Second-World-War, that is), "Death and the King's Horseman" opens amid verse, music and spectacle as Elesin Oba, the late king's chief horseman, prepares to commit ritual suicide so he can join his king in heaven. On his last day among the living, Elesin spies a beautiful girl and asks the women of the marketplace—who serve as an ongoing chorus—to send her to him.

But the girl is engaged, Elesin is curtly informed. Would he "blight the happiness of others for a moment's pleasure?"

"Who speaks of pleasure?" he asks. He wants to make his departure free of all regrets—to "travel light" into the beyond, he says. And he would like to leave the seed of a child to "take root in the earth of my choice." To this the elders yield, guided by Iyaloja, the "mother of the marketplace" whose own son was to have married the girl Elesin has selected.

Then the action shifts to the colonial district officer's bungalow, and the style turns suddenly brittle and comic. The district officer, archly named "Simon Pilkings," ridicules tribal ritual while making his own elaborate plans to attend a costume ball at the local European Club.

Learning of Elesin's suicidal intent, Pilkings arranges to have him locked up, and heads off to the ball (where the guest of honor is a visiting English prince, on tour in the colonies). Elesin's English-educated son, a protege of the Pilkings, also shows up, having returned to Nigeria to be with his father at his death.

From here, the play acquires the rolling momentum of classical tragedy; but while the conclusion is true to the grim course of preceding events, it has a 20th-century twist.

Soyinka is fascinated with the "irrationality" in all cultures—the need for it when addressing issues of life, death and birth, and the pretense of earth-shaking importance to which we give clashes between one culture's irrational tenets and another's.

The Goodman Theatre of Chicago fought for two years to bring this play to the United States, and they wisely brought the author along to direct it. So with due allowance for the adjustment problems of American actors learning African attitudes and inflections, we are probably entitled to assume that the Chicago/ Washington-version of the play bears at least a strong resemblance to the work that premiered at Nigeria's University of Ife in 1976.

However authentic, it is a compelling production. The scenery works inventive and colorful variations on a slate-gray foundation. The costumes are a feast for the eye. And the cast—while the accents may waver now and again—performs with an air of authority throughout.

As Elesin, Norman Matlock has some difficulty with the play's tragic resolution, but otherwise he makes impressive use of his rich voice and athletic grace.

As Iyaloja, Celestine Heard also possesses an awesome voice and bearing. And as Pilkings, Alan Coates manages to make a convincing whole of the contrary sides of this initially absurd but later more complicated character.

To an American viewer, Soyinka's play has confusing passages, and the imagery gets a bit crowded at times. How valuable is it for example, to compare a son's pity for his dishonored father with the pity of a thoroughbred horse "for the turf he strikes with his hoof"? And Soyinka hits some of his points too squarely, reducing the character of Elesin's son to little more than author's mouthpiece.

The most serious problem of all is the final scene, where the impact of classical tragedy is usually best measured. As rendered at the Terrace, "Death and the King's Horseman" ends with all the right tragic rhythms and, strangely, a good deal less than expected emotional force.

But the task Soyinka set for himself was so ambitious that even partial fulfillment makes exciting theater.

DEREK WALCOTT

"The Divided Child," Derek Walcott's title for the first section of his 1973 autobiography, *Another Life,* aptly describes this Nobel Prize–winning writer both literally and figuratively. A twin, a descendant of white grandfathers and black grandmothers, a Methodist in the predominantly Catholic community of St. Lucia, a native of the Caribbean educated in the language, literature, and cultural traditions of England and America, Walcott is acutely aware of his different identities. In an introductory essay to four of his plays, "What the Twilight Says" (1970), Walcott speaks of himself in the third person as "this neither proud nor ashamed bastard, this hybrid, this West Indian" and indicates that his choice was to make "creative use of his schizophrenia, an electric fusion of the old and the new." That fusion can be seen in Walcott's first play, *Henri Christophe* (1950), written when he was only nineteen. Though its subject and title character are unquestionably West Indian, centering on one of the men who helped liberate Haiti from French rule, the play's style seemed to listeners, and to Walcott himself, to echo Shakespeare and his contemporaries.

Honored in 1992 by the Nobel Committee as "the great poet of West Indian culture," Walcott has also been a major force in West Indian theater, both as a dramatist and as a theatrical producer. An amateur group cofounded by Walcott, the St. Lucia Arts Guild, produced *Henri Christophe* and then, under the direction of Roderick Walcott (Derek's twin brother), became a more professional repertory group, producing Marlowe, Shakespeare, Chekhov, and plays by both of the Walcott brothers. After a Rockefeller Foundation grant enabled Walcott to visit professional theaters in New York and Canada, he settled in Trinidad, first to produce a historical pageant-play (*Drums and Colours,* 1958) for the West Indian Festival of the Arts, and then to train West Indian actors. In 1959, with a group of both actors and dancers, he created the Little Carib Theatre Workshop to provide opportunities for performers, directors, and writers to work together and practice their craft, which led in turn to public performances of both European and West Indian plays. In 1966, Walcott split from the original workshop and created the Trinidad Theatre Workshop, which remains active today. It was this company that produced in 1966 the double bill of Albee's *The Zoo Story* (see p. 1024) and Walcott's *The Sea at Dauphin* (1954). This combination embodies Walcott's perennial interest in fusing imported and native traditions as does *The Sea at Dauphin* itself, which is unquestionably indebted to J. M. Synge's one-act play, *Riders to the Sea* (1902), echoing the harsh realities of Irish fishing life in a Caribbean setting. In a similar spirit, Walcott produced plays not only by well-known European playwrights (Samuel Beckett, Jean Genet), but also by the then lesser known Nigerian playwright Wole Soyinka (whose *Death and the King's Horseman* is included in this volume) as well as by other West Indian writers.

Walcott's sustained involvement in West Indian theater from 1958 to 1976 not only enabled him to work with a variety of talented actors and writers, but led him back to the folk legends of the West Indies. Thus, *Ti-Jean and His Brothers,* first produced at the Little Carib Theatre in 1958, draws on familiar folktale elements: three brothers, a challenge from the devil, and talking animals. Enlivened with music and dance, written in both prose and poetry, *Ti-Jean* is an exuberant and humorous presentation of the contest between the devil and three brothers (Gros-Jean, Mi-Jean, Ti-Jean) as well as an allegorical play about the human struggle to survive. At the play's end, Ti-Jean's victory over the devil allows him to bring to life a new brother, the Bolom, an aborted fetus who wishes to live; though coming to life inevitably means dying, and though the final chorus calls Ti-Jean "a fool like all heroes," the play celebrates the will to live. A later play, *Dream on Monkey Mountain* (1967), dedicated to "Errol Jones and the Trinidad Theatre Workshop" and written for the company's first international tour, presents a series of personal and social conflicts within the phantasmagoric dreams of Makak, the protagonist, who at moments seems like Jesus healing the sick, while at others appears to be a madman.

Though "the divided child" is one metaphor for Walcott's struggle to bridge different cultures, another is the castaway, as he made clear in his 1965 lecture, "The Figure of Crusoe":

An image may do better. It is that of a lonely man on a beach who has heaped a pile of dead bush, twigs, etc., to make a bonfire. The bonfire may be purposeless. Or it may be a signal of his loneliness, his desperation, his isolation, his symbol of need for another. Or the bonfire may be lit from some atavistic need, for contemplation. Fire mesmerizes us. We dissolve in burning. The man sits before the fire, its glow warming his face, watching it leap, gesticulate, and lessen, and he keeps throwing twigs, dead thoughts, fragments of memory, all the used parts of his life to keep his contemplation pure and bright. When he is tired and returns into himself, then he has performed some sort of sacrifice, some ritual. . . . The metaphor of the bonfire, in the case of the West Indian poet, may be the metaphor of tradition and the colonial talent.

Walcott has evoked mythical wanderers and castaways in his 1992 dramatization of Homer's *Odyssey* and in his book-length poem, *Omeros* (1990), using Caribbean figures with names drawn from Homer's epics and a series of journeys ranging over past and present, Europe and the West Indies. Even more central to Walcott's thinking is Robinson Crusoe, the titular hero of Daniel Defoe's 1719 novel. In his lecture on Crusoe and in his poem from *The Castaway,* "Crusoe's Journal," Walcott turned the fictional figure into a series of metaphoric figures: "My Crusoe, then, is Adam, Christopher Columbus, God, a missionary, a beachcomber, and his interpreter, Daniel Defoe." So rich are the possible shapes that this Protean figure has taken for Walcott that he finally focused an entire play on the Crusoe myth, but in a contemporary West Indian setting.

Thus, *Pantomime* (1980) embodies Walcott's sense of the never-ending struggle between Western tradition and West Indian culture, between white man and black man, between the colonizing master and the colonized servant, by focusing on the complex relationship between Harry Trewe—"English, mid-forties, owner of the Castaways Guest House, retired actor"—and Jackson Phillip—"Trinidadian, forty, his factotum, retired calypsonian." These brief character descriptions and the name of the guest house make clear the symbolic nature of the relationship; they are differentiated by ethnic backgrounds and by roles (owner and the handyman), but drawn together by age and by their performance backgrounds (actor and singer). Trewe's fascination with the story of Crusoe extends well beyond a simple reenactment where he would play Crusoe and Jackson would play the native Friday, who becomes Crusoe's servant. Instead, he fancies himself an enlightened liberal by choosing to perform the role of Friday, while Jackson plays Crusoe (see Figure 1), and blithely imagines that such a reversal would be hilarious, though Jackson offers the frank opinion, "I think it is shit." In fact, the more Trewe tries to tell Jackson how to act as "Crusoe," the more he reasserts his position as the white imperialist.

Although *Pantomime* embodies a series of haunting scenes and intriguing questions that focus on how white and black men see each other and react to each other, it is also a play celebrating the energy and mystery of theater itself. Like other rehearsal plays, its characters repeatedly concern themselves with the problematics of acting and staging a play. And Walcott's long theatrical experience in working with actors is evident in the bravura roles he creates here, in his comments about the comedy created by the competition between Trewe and Jackson (see the interview with Walcott following the play), and in his striking transformation of the traditional British entertainment, the Christmas pantomime. In naming his play *Pantomime,* Walcott clearly invokes the popular English tradition of rowdy comedies, often based on fairy tales or legends, featuring songs, familiar comic figures, and traditional cross-dressed roles, including the Principal Boy, played by a woman wearing tights to show off her legs, and the Dame, played by a man, often a very large man, dressed in elaborate costumes, wigs, and jewelry. Clearly the "pantomime" that Trewe imagines and that Walcott writes is subtler, but the basic elements are still present though transformed. Both Trewe and Jackson sing; both act as Crusoe (see Figures 2 and 3); Jackson "performs" as the wife, holding her photograph (see Figure 4); and Trewe, taking the role of Friday, kneels down next to Jackson in the role of Crusoe (see Figure 1). But just as Walcott uses role-playing and folktale figures to interrogate problems of West Indian identity, he uses comic dialogue, costumes, and songs to examine the deeper power of theater. As Trewe and Jackson play various roles, they uncover deeply repressed feelings and discover a new partnership. In the words of the final song, they recognize the difference between "one classical actor and one Creole" but still affirm a shared humanity: "It go be man to man, and we go do it fine."

PANTOMIME

BY DEREK WALCOTT

For Wilbert Holder°

CHARACTERS

HARRY TREWE, *English, mid-forties, owner of the Castaways Guest House, retired actor*

JACKSON PHILLIP, *Trinidadian, forty, his factotum,*° *retired calypsonian*°

SCENE

The action takes place in a gazebo on the edge of a cliff, part of a guest house on the island of Tobago, West Indies.

ACT 1

(A small summerhouse or gazebo, painted white, with a few plants and a table set for breakfast. HARRY TREWE *enters—in white, carrying a tape recorder, which he rests on the table. He starts the machine.)*

HARRY *(Sings and dances)*:

> It's our Christmas panto,°
> it's called: Robinson Crusoe.
> We're awfully glad that you've shown up,
> it's for kiddies as well as for grown-ups.
> Our purpose is to please:
> so now with our magic wand . . .

(Dissatisfied with the routine, he switches off the machine. Rehearses his dance. Then presses the machine again.)

> Just picture a lonely island
> and a beach with its golden sand.
> There walks a single man
> in the beautiful West Indies!

(He turns off the machine. Stands, staring out to sea. Then exits with the tape recorder. Stage empty for a few beats, then JACKSON, *in an open, white waiter's jacket and black trousers, but barefoot, enters with a breakfast tray. He puts the tray down, looks around.)*

JACKSON: Mr. Trewe? *(English accent)* Mr. Trewe, your scramble eggs is here! *are* here! *(Creole accent)* You hear, Mr. Trewe? I here wid your eggs! *(English accent)* Are you in there? *(To himself)* And when his eggs get cold, is I to catch. *(He fans the eggs with one*

Wilbert Holder, actor working with Walcott in the Trinidad Theatre Workshop. The role of Jackson was written specifically for Holder. **factotum,** man of all work (servant). **calypsonian,** performer of original West Indian music, marked by lively duple meter and improvised lyrics. **panto,** short for pantomime, in England a traditional Christmastime show, often based on a fairy tale.

hand.) What the hell I doing? That ain't go heat them. It go make them more cold. Well, he must be leap off the ledge. At long last. Well, if he ain't dead, he could call.

(He exits with tray. Stage bare. HARRY *returns, carrying a hat made of goatskin and a goatskin parasol. He puts on the hat, shoulders the parasol, and circles the table. Then he recoils, looking down at the floor.)*

HARRY *(Sings and dances)*:

> Is this the footprint of a naked man,
> or is it the naked footprint of a man,
> that startles me this morning on this bright
>   and golden sand.

(To audience)

> There's no one here but I,
> just the sea and lonely sky . . .

(Pauses)

> Yes . . . and how the hell did it go on?

*(*JACKSON *enters, without the tray. Studies* HARRY*)*

JACKSON: Morning, Mr. Trewe. Your breakfast ready.

HARRY: So how're you this morning, Jackson?

JACKSON: Oh, fair to fine, with seas moderate, with waves three to four feet in open water, and you, sir?

HARRY: Overcast with sunny periods, with the possibility of heavy showers by mid-afternoon, I'd say, Jackson.

JACKSON: Heavy showers, Mr. Trewe?

HARRY: Heavy showers. I'm so bloody bored I could burst into tears.

JACKSON: I bringing in breakfast.

HARRY: You do that, Friday.

JACKSON: Friday? It ain't go keep.

HARRY *(Gesturing)*: Friday, you, bring Crusoe, me, breakfast now. Crusoe hungry.

JACKSON: Mr. Trewe, you come back with that same

rake° again? I tell you, I ain't no actor, and I ain't walking in front a set of tourists naked playing cannibal. Carnival, but not canni-bal.

HARRY: What tourists? We're closed for repairs. We're the only ones in the guest house. Apart from the carpenter, if he ever shows up.

JACKSON: Well, you ain't seeing him today, because he was out on a heavy lime° last night . . . Saturday, you know? And with the peanuts you does pay him for overtime.

HARRY: All right, then. It's goodbye!

(He climbs onto the ledge between the uprights, teetering, walking slowly.)

JACKSON: Get offa that ledge, Mr. Trewe! Is a straight drop to them rocks!

(HARRY kneels, arms extended, Jolson-style.°)

HARRY: Hold on below there, sonny boooy! Daddy's a-coming. Your papa's a-coming, Sonnnnneee Boooooooy! *(To* JACKSON*)* You're watching the great Harry Trewe and his high-wire act.

JACKSON: You watching Jackson Phillip and his disappearing act.

(Turning to leave)

HARRY *(Jumping down)*: I'm not a suicide, Jackson. It's a good act, but you never read the reviews. It would be too exasperating, anyway.

JACKSON: What, sir?

HARRY: Attempted suicide in a Third World country. You can't leave a note because the pencils break, you can't cut your wrist with the local blades . . .

JACKSON: We trying we best, sir, since all you gone.

HARRY: Doesn't matter if we're a minority group. Suicides are taxpayers, too, you know, Jackson.

JACKSON: Except it ain't going be suicide. They go say I push you. So, now the fun and dance done, sir, breakfast now?

HARRY: I'm rotting from insomnia, Jackson. I've been up since three, hearing imaginary guests arriving in the rooms, and I haven't slept since. I nearly came around the back to have a little talk. I started thinking about the same bloody problem, which is, What entertainment can we give the guests?

JACKSON: They ain't guests, Mr. Trewe. They's casualties.

HARRY: How do you mean?

JACKSON: This hotel like a hospital. The toilet catch asthma, the air-condition got ague,° the front-balcony rail missing four teet', and every minute

the fridge like it dancing the Shango° . . . brrgudup . . . jukjuk . . . brrugudup. Is no wonder that the carpenter collapse. Termites jumping like steel band in the foundations.

HARRY: For fifty dollars a day they want Acapulco?

JACKSON: Try giving them the basics: Food. Water. Shelter. They ain't shipwrecked, they pay in advance for their vacation.

HARRY: Very funny. But the ad says, "Tours" and "Nightly Entertainment." Well, Christ, after they've seen the molting parrot in the lobby and the faded sea fans, they'll be pretty livid if there's no "nightly entertainment," and so would you, right? So, Mr. Jackson, it's your neck and mine. We open next Friday.

JACKSON: Breakfast, sir. Or else is overtime.

HARRY: I kept thinking about this panto I co-authored, man. *Robinson Crusoe,* and I picked up this old script. I can bring it all down to your level, with just two characters. Crusoe, Man Friday, maybe even the parrot, if that horny old bugger will remember his lines . . .

JACKSON: Since we on the subject, Mr. Trewe, I am compelled to report that parrot again.

HARRY: No, not again, Jackson?

JACKSON: Yes.

HARRY *(Imitating parrot)*: Heinegger, Heinegger. *(In his own voice)* Correct?

JACKSON: Wait, wait! I know your explanation: that a old German called Herr Heinegger used to own this place, and that when that maquereau° of a macaw keep cracking: "Heinegger, Heinegger," he remembering the Nazi and not heckling me, but it playing a little havoc with me nerves. This is my fifth report. I am marking them down. Language is ideas, Mr. Trewe. And I think that this pre-colonial parrot have the wrong idea.

HARRY: It's his accent, Jackson. He's a Creole parrot. What can I do?

JACKSON: Well, I am not saying not to give the bird a fair trial, but I see nothing wrong in taking him out the cage at dawn, blindfolding the bitch, giving him a last cigarette if he want it, lining him up against the garden wall, and perforating his arse by firing squad.

HARRY: The war's over, Jackson! And how can a bloody parrot be prejudiced?

JACKSON: The same damn way they corrupt a child. By their upbringing. That parrot survive from a pre-colonial epoch, Mr. Trewe, and if it want to last in Trinidad and Tobago, then it go have to adjust.

(Long pause)

---

rake, annoying request. *lime,* drinking binge. **Jolson-style,** Al Jolson (1886–1950), popular U.S. singer, blackface comedian, and movie star. *ague,* shivering fever.

Shango, African dance for the god of thunder. **maquereau,** French slang for pimp.

HARRY (*Leaping up*): Do you think we could work him into the panto? Give him something to do? Crusoe had a parrot, didn't he? You're right, Jackson, let's drop him from the show.

JACKSON: Mr. Trewe, you are a truly, truly stubborn man. I am *not* putting that old goatskin hat on my head and making an ass of myself for a million dollars, and I have said so already.

HARRY: You got it wrong. I put the hat on, I'm . . . Wait, wait a minute. *Cut! Cut!* You know what would be a heavy twist, heavy with irony?

JACKSON: What, Mr. Trewe?

HARRY: We reverse it.

(*Pause*)

JACKSON: You mean you prepared to walk round naked as your mother make you, in your jockstrap, playing a white cannibal in front of your own people? You're a real actor! And you got balls, too, excuse me, Mr. Trewe, to even consider doing a thing like that! Good. Joke finish. Breakfast now, eh? Because I ha' to fix the sun deck since the carpenter ain't reach.

HARRY: All right, breakfast. Just heat it a little.

JACKSON: Right, sir. The coffee must be warm still. But I best do some brand-new scramble eggs.

HARRY: Never mind the eggs, then. Slip in some toast, butter, and jam.

JACKSON: How long you in this hotel business, sir? No butter. Marge.° No sugar. Big strike. Island-wide shortage. We down to half a bag.

HARRY: Don't forget I've heard you sing calypsos, Jackson. Right back there in the kitchen.

JACKSON: Mr. Trewe, every day I keep begging you to stop trying to make an entertainer out of me. I finish with show business. I finish with Trinidad. I come to Tobago for peace and quiet. I quite satisfy. If you ain't want me to resign, best drop the topic.

(*Exits.* HARRY *sits at the table, staring out to sea. He is reciting softly to himself, then more audibly.*)

HARRY: *"Alone, alone, all, all alone,*
   Alone on a wide wide sea . . .
   I bit my arm, I sucked the blood,
   And cried, A sail! a sail!"°

(*He removes the hat, then his shirt, rolls up his trousers, removes them, puts them back on, removes them again.*)

Mastah . . . Mastah . . . Friday sorry. Friday never do it again. Master.

(JACKSON *enters with breakfast tray, groans, turns to leave. Returns.*)

JACKSON: Mr. Trewe, what it is going on on this blessed Sunday morning, if I may ask?

HARRY: I was feeling what it was like to be Friday.

JACKSON: Well, Mr. Trewe, you ain't mind putting back on your pants?

HARRY: Why can't I eat breakfast like this?

JACKSON: Because I am here. I happen to be here. I am the one serving you, Mr. Trewe.

HARRY: There's nobody here.

JACKSON: Mr. Harry, you putting on back your pants?

HARRY: You're frightened of something?

JACKSON: You putting on back your pants?

HARRY: What're you afraid of? Think I'm bent?° That's such a corny interpretation of the Crusoe-Friday relationship, boy. My son's been dead three years, Jackson, and I'vn't had much interest in women since, but I haven't gone queer, either. And to be a flasher, you need an audience.

JACKSON: Mr. Trewe, I am trying to explain that I myself feel like a ass holding this tray in my hand while you standing up there naked, and that if anybody should happen to pass, my name is immediately mud. So, when you put back on your pants, I will serve your breakfast.

HARRY: Actors do this sort of thing. I'm getting into a part.

JACKSON: Don't bother getting into the part, get into the pants. Please.

HARRY: Why? You've got me worried now, Jackson.

JACKSON (*Exploding*): *Put on your blasted pants, man! You like a blasted child, you know!*

(*Silence.* HARRY *puts on his pants.*)

HARRY: Shirt, too? (JACKSON *sucks his teeth.*) There. (HARRY *puts on his shirt.*) You people are such prudes, you know that? What's it in you, Jackson, that gets so Victorian about a man in his own hotel deciding to have breakfast in his own underwear, on a totally deserted Sunday morning?

JACKSON: Manners, sir. Manners.

(*He puts down the tray.*)

HARRY: Sit.

JACKSON: Sit? Sit where? How you mean, sit?

HARRY: Sit, and I'll serve breakfast. You can teach me manners. There's more manners in serving than in being served.

JACKSON: I ain't know what it is eating you this Sunday morning, you hear, Mr. Trewe, but I don't feel you have any right to mama-guy me, because I is a big man with three children, all outside. Now, being

---

Marge, margarine. ***"Alone . . . a sail,"*** from Samuel Taylor Coleridge's poem "The Rime of the Ancient Mariner."

---

bent, homosexual.

served by a white man ain't no big deal for me. It happen to me every day in New York, so it's not going to be any particularly thrilling experience. I would like to get breakfast finish with, wash up, finish my work, and go for my sea bath. Now I have worked here six months and never lost my temper, but it wouldn't take much more for me to fling this whole fucking tray out in that sea and get somebody more to your sexual taste.

HARRY (*Laughs*): Aha!

JACKSON: Not aha, oho!

HARRY (*Drawing out a chair*): Mr. Phillips . . .

JACKSON: Phillip. What?

HARRY: Your reservation.

JACKSON: You want me play this game, eh? (*He walks around, goes to a corner of the gazebo.*) I'll tell you something, you hear, Mr. Trewe? And listen to me good, good. Once and for all. My sense of humor can stretch so far. Then it does snap. You see that sea out there? You know where I born? I born over there. Trinidad. I was a very serious steel-band man, too. And where I come from is a very serious place. I used to get into some serious trouble. A man keep bugging my arse once. A bad john called Boysie. Indian fellow, want to play nigger. Every day in that panyard° he would come making joke with nigger boy this, and so on, and I used to just laugh and tell him stop, but he keep laughing and I keep laughing and he going on and I begging him to stop and two of us laughing, until . . . (*He turns, goes to the tray, and picks up a fork*) one day, just out of the blue, I pick up a ice pick and walk over to where he and two fellers was playing card, and I nail that ice pick through his hand to the table, and I laugh, and I walk away.

HARRY: Your table, Mr. Phillip.

(*Silence.* JACKSON *shrugs, sits at the table.*)

JACKSON: Okay, then. Until.

HARRY: You know, if you want to exchange war experiences, lad, I could bore you with a couple of mine. Want to hear?

JACKSON: My shift is seven-thirty to one. (*He folds his arms.* HARRY *offers him a cigarette.*) I don't smoke on duty.

HARRY: We put on a show in the army once. Ground crew. RAF.° In what used to be Palestine. A Christmas panto. Another one. And yours truly here was the dame. The dame in a panto is played by a man. Well, I got the part. Wrote the music, the book, everything, whatever original music there was. *Aladdin and His Wonderful Vamp.* Very obscene, of course. I was the Wonderful Vamp. Ter-

rific reaction all around. Thanks to me music-hall background. Went down great. Well, there was a party afterward. Then a big sergeant in charge of maintenance started this very boring business of confusing my genius with my life. Kept pinching my arse and so on. It got kind of boring after a while. Well, he was the size of a truck, mate. And there wasn't much I could do but keep blushing and pretending to be liking it. But the Wonderful Vamp was waiting outside for him, the Wonderful Vamp and a wrench this big, and after that, laddie, it took all of maintenance to put him back again.

JACKSON: That is white-man fighting. Anyway, Mr. Trewe, I feel the fun finish; I would like, with your permission, to get up now and fix up the sun deck. 'Cause when rain fall . . .

HARRY: Forget the sun deck. I'd say, Jackson, that we've come closer to a mutual respect, and that things need not get that hostile. Sit, and let me explain what I had in mind.

JACKSON: I take it that's an order?

HARRY: You want it to be an order? Okay, it's an order.

JACKSON: It didn't sound like no order.

HARRY: Look, I'm a liberal, Jackson. I've done the whole routine. Aldermaston,° Suez,° Ban the Bomb, Burn the Bra, Pity the Poor Pakis, et cetera. I've even tried jumping up to the steel band at Notting Hill Gate,° and I'd no idea I'd wind up in this ironic position of giving orders, but if the new script I've been given says: HARRY TREWE, HOTEL MANAGER, then I'm going to play Harry Trewe, Hotel Manager, to the hilt, damnit. So *sit* down! Please. Oh, goddamnit, *sit . . . down . . .* (JACKSON *sits. Nods*) Good. Relax. Smoke. Have a cup of tepid coffee. I sat up from about three this morning, working out this whole skit in my head. (*Pause*) Mind putting that hat on for a second, it will help my point. Come on. It'll make things clearer.

(*He gives* JACKSON *the goatskin hat.* JACKSON, *after a pause, puts it on.*)

JACKSON: I'll take that cigarette.

(HARRY *hands over a cigarette.*)

HARRY: They've seen that stuff, time after time. Limbo, dancing girls, fire-eating . . .

---

panyard, practice area for a steel band.   **RAF,** Royal Air Force.

Aldermaston, British site where atomic bombs were tested and protested.   **Suez,** 1956 conflict between Israel and Egypt prompted protests in Great Britain over the country's military involvement.   **Notting Hill Gate,** London area known for its large population of Caribbean immigrants, specifically those from Trinidad.

JACKSON: Light.

HARRY: Oh, sorry.

(*He lights* JACKSON's *cigarette.*)

JACKSON: I listening.

HARRY: We could turn this little place right here into a little cabaret, with some very witty acts. Build up the right audience. Get an edge on the others. So, I thought, Suppose I get this material down to two people. Me and . . . well, me and somebody else. Robinson Crusoe and Man Friday. We could work up a good satire, you know, on the master-servant—no offense—relationship. Labor-management, white-black, and so on . . . Making some trenchant points about topical things, you know. Add that show to the special dinner for the price of one ticket . . .

JACKSON: You have to have music.

HARRY: Pardon?

JACKSON: A show like that should have music. Just a lot of talk is very boring.

HARRY: Right. But I'd have to have somebody help me, and that's where I thought . . . Want to take the hat off?

JACKSON: It ain't bothering me. When you going make your point?

HARRY: We had that little Carnival contest with the staff and you knocked them out improvising, remember that? You had the bloody guests in stitches . . .

JACKSON: You ain't start to talk money yet, Mr. Harry.

HARRY: Just improvising with the quatro.° And not the usual welcome to Port of Spain, I am glad to see you again, but I'll tell you, artist to artist, I recognized a real pro, and this is the point of the hat. I want to make a point about the hotel industry, about manners, conduct, to generally improve relations all around. So, whoever it is, you or whoever, plays Crusoe, and I, or whoever it is, get to play Friday, and imagine first of all the humor and then the impact of that. What you think?

JACKSON: You want my honest, professional opinion?

HARRY: Fire away.

JACKSON: I think is shit.

HARRY: I've never been in shit in my life, my boy.

JACKSON: It sound like shit to me, but I could be wrong.

HARRY: You could say things in fun about this place, about the whole Caribbean, that would hurt while people laughed. You get half the gate.°

JACKSON: Half?

HARRY: What do you want?

JACKSON: I want you to come to your senses, let me fix the sun deck and get down to the beach for my sea bath. So, I put on this hat, I pick up this parasol, and I walk like a mama-poule° up and down this stage and you have a black man playing Robinson Crusoe and then a half-naked, white, fish-belly man playing Friday, and you want to tell me it ain't shit?

HARRY: It could be hilarious!

JACKSON: Hilarious, Mr. Trewe? Supposing I wasn't a waiter, and instead of breakfast I was serving you communion, this Sunday morning on this tropical island, and I turn to you, Friday, to teach you my faith, and I tell you, kneel down and eat this man. Well, kneel, nuh! What you think you would say, eh? (*Pause*) You, this white savage?

HARRY: No, that's cannibalism.

JACKSON: Is no more cannibalism than to eat a god. Suppose I make you tell me: For three hundred years I have made you my servant. For three hundred years . . .

HARRY: It's pantomime, Jackson, just keep it light . . . Make them laugh.

JACKSON: Okay. (*Giggling*) For three hundred years I served you. Three hundred years I served you breakfast in . . . in my white jacket on a white veranda, boss, bwana,° effendi,° bacra,° sahib° . . . in that sun that never set on your empire I was your shadow, I did what you did, boss, bwana, effendi, bacra, sahib . . . that was my pantomime. Every movement you made, your shadow copied . . . (*Stops giggling*) and you smiled at me as a child does smile at his shadow's helpless obedience, boss, bwana, effendi, bacra, sahib, Mr. Crusoe. Now . . .

HARRY: Now?

(JACKSON's *speech is enacted in a trance-like drone, a zombie.*)

JACKSON: But after a while the child does get frighten of the shadow he make. He say to himself, That is too much obedience, I better hads stop. But the shadow don't stop, no matter if the child stop playing that pantomime, and the shadow does follow the child everywhere; when he praying, the shadow pray too, when he turn round frighten, the shadow turn round too, when he hide under the sheet, the shadow hiding too. He cannot get rid of it, no matter what, and that is the power and black magic of the shadow, boss, bwana, effendi, bacra, sahib, until it is the shadow that start dominating the child, it is the servant that start dominating the master . . . (*Laughs mania-*

---

quatro, small four-stringed guitar. **gate,** money received. **mama-poule,** a weakling. **bwana,** Swahili for ruler. **effendi,** Turkish title of respect. **bacra,** Caribbean for slavemaster. **sahib,** Indian term of respect for British master.

cally, like The Shadow°) and that is the victory of the shadow, boss. *(Normally)* And that is why all them Pakistani and West Indians in England, all them immigrant Fridays driving all you so crazy. And they go keep driving you crazy till you go mad. In that sun that never set, they's your shadow, you can't shake them off.

HARRY: Got really carried away that time, didn't you? It's pantomime, Jackson, keep it light. Improvise!

JACKSON: You mean we making it up as we go along?

HARRY: Right!

JACKSON: Right! I in dat! *(He assumes a stern stance and points stiffly.)* Robinson obey Thursday now. Speak Thursday language. Obey Thursday gods.

HARRY: Jesus Christ!

JACKSON *(Inventing language)*: Amaka nobo sakamaka khaki pants kamaluma Jesus Christ! Jesus Christ kamalogo! *(Pause. Then with a violent gesture)* Kamalongo kaba!

(Meaning: Jesus is dead!)

HARRY: Sure. *(Pause. Peers forward. Then speaks to an imaginary projectionist, while JACKSON stands, feet apart, arms folded, frowning, in the usual stance of the Noble Savage.)* Now, could you run it with the subtitles, please? *(He walks over to JACKSON, who remains rigid. Like a movie director)* Let's have another take, Big Chief. *(To imaginary camera)* Roll it. Sound!

(JACKSON shoves HARRY aside and strides to the table. He bangs the heel of his palm on the tabletop.)

JACKSON: Patamba! Patamba! Yes?

HARRY: You want us to strike the prop? The patamba? *(To cameraman)* Cut!

JACKSON *(To cameraman)*: Rogoongo! Rogoongo!

(Meaning: Keep it rolling.)

HARRY: Cut!

JACKSON: *Rogoongo, damnit! (Defiantly, furiously, JACKSON moves around, first signaling the camera to follow him, then pointing out the objects which he rechristens, shaking or hitting them violently. Slams table)* Patamba! *(Rattles beach chair)* Backaraka! Backaraka! *(Holds up cup, points with other hand)* Banda! *(Drops cup)* Banda karan! *(Puts his arm around HARRY; points at him)* Subu! *(Faster, pointing)* Masz! *(Stamping the floor)* Zohgooooor! *(Rests his snoring head on his closed palms)* Oma! Omaaaa! *(Kneels, looking skyward. Pauses; eyes closed)* Booora! Booora! *(Meaning the world. Silence. He rises.)* Cut! And dat is what it was like, before you come here with your table this and cup that.

HARRY: All right. Good audition. You get twenty dollars a day without dialogue.

JACKSON: But why?

HARRY: You never called anything by the same name twice. What's a table?

JACKSON: I forget.

HARRY: I remember: patamba!

JACKSON: Patamba?

HARRY: Right. You fake.

JACKSON: That's a breakfast table. *Ogushi.* That's a dressing table. *Amanga ogushi.* I remember now.

HARRY: I'll tell you one thing, friend. If you want me to learn your language, you'd better have a gun.

JACKSON: You best play Crusoe, chief. I surrender. All you win. *(Points wearily)* Table. Chair. Cup. Man. Jesus. I accept. I accept. All you win. Long time.

(Smiles)

HARRY: All right, then. Improvise, then. Sing us a song. In your new language, mate. In English. Go ahead. I challenge you.

JACKSON: You what? *(Rises, takes up parasol, handling it like a guitar, and strolls around the front row of the audience)*

(Sings)

> *I want to tell you 'bout Robinson Crusoe.*
> *He tell Friday, when I do so, do so.*
> *Whatever I do, you must do like me.*
> *He make Friday a Good Friday Bohbolee;°*
> *That was the first example of slavery,*
> *'Cause I am still Friday and you ain't me.*
> *Now Crusoe he was this Christian and all,*
> *And Friday, his slave, was a cannibal,*
> *But one day things bound to go in reverse,*
> *With Crusoe the slave and Friday the boss.*

HARRY: Then comes this part where Crusoe sings to the goat. Little hint of animal husbandry *(Kneels, embraces an imaginary goat, to the melody of "Swanee"):*

(Sings)

> *Nanny, how I love you,*
> *How I love you,*
> *My dear old nanny . . .*

JACKSON: Is a li'l obscene.

HARRY *(Music-hall style)*: Me wife thought so. Know what I used to tell her? Obscene? Well, better to be obscene than not heard. How's that? Harry Trewe, I'm telling you again, the music hall's loss is calypso's gain.

The Shadow, popular radio mystery show (1930–54). Each episode began with "Who knows what evil lurks in the hearts of men? The Shadow knows!"

Good Friday Bohbolee, a Judas effigy beaten at Easter in Trinidad and Tobago.

(Stops)

(JACKSON pauses. Stares upward, muttering to himself. HARRY turns. JACKSON is signaling in the air with a self-congratulatory smile.)

HARRY: What is it? What've we stopped for? *(JACKSON hisses for silence from HARRY, then returns to his reverie. Miming)* Are you feeling all right, Jackson? *(JACKSON walks some distance away from HARRY. An imaginary guitar suddenly appears in his hand. HARRY circles him. Lifts one eyelid, listens to his heartbeat. JACKSON revolves, HARRY revolves with him. JACKSON's whole body is now silently rocking in rhythm. He is laughing to himself. We hear, very loud, a calypso rhythm.)* Two can play this game, Jackson.

(He strides around in imaginary straw hat, twirling a cane. We hear, very loud, music hall. It stops. HARRY peers at JACKSON.)

JACKSON: You see what you start?

(Sings)

> Well, a Limey° name Trewe came to Tobago.
> He was in show business but he had no show,
> so in desperation he turn to me
> and said: "Mister Phillip" is the two o' we,
> one classical actor, and one Creole . . .

HARRY: Wait! Hold it, hold it, man! Don't waste that. Try and remember it. I'll be right back.
JACKSON: Where you going?
HARRY: Tape. Repeat it, and try and keep it. That's what I meant, you see?
JACKSON: You start to exploit me already?
HARRY: That's right. Memorize it. *(Exits quickly. JACKSON removes his shirt and jacket, rolls up his pants above the knee, clears the breakfast tray to one side of the floor, overturns the table, and sits in it, as if it were a boat, as HARRY returns with the machine.)* What's all this? I'm ready to tape. What're you up to? *(JACKSON sits in the upturned table, rowing calmly, and from time to time surveying the horizon. He looks up toward the sky, shielding his face from the glare with one hand; then he gestures to HARRY.)* What? *(JACKSON flaps his arms around leisurely, like a large sea bird, indicating that HARRY should do the same.)* What? What about the song? You'll forget the bloody song. It was a fluke.
JACKSON *(Steps out from the table, crosses to HARRY, irritated)*: If I suppose to help you with this stupidness, we will have to cool it and collaborate a little bit. Now, I was in that boat, rowing, and I was looking up to the sky to see a storm gathering,

---

Limey, slang for British sailor.

and I wanted a big white sea bird beating inland from a storm. So what's the trouble, Mr. Trewe?
HARRY: Sea bird? What sea bird? I'm not going to play a fekking sea bird.
JACKSON: Mr. Trewe, I'm only asking you to play a white sea bird because I am supposed to play a black explorer.
HARRY: Well, I don't want to do it. Anyway, that's the silliest acting I've seen in a long time. And Robinson Crusoe wasn't *rowing* when he got shipwrecked; he was on a huge boat. I didn't come here to play a sea bird, I came to tape the song.
JACKSON: Well, then, is either the sea bird or the song. And I don't see any reason why you have to call my acting silly. We suppose to improvise.
HARRY: All right, Jackson, all right. After I do this part, I hope you can remember the song. Now you just tell me, before we keep stopping, what I am supposed to do, how many animals I'm supposed to play, and . . . you know, and so on, and so on, and then when we get all that part fixed up, we'll tape the song, all right?
JACKSON: That suits me. Now, the way I see it here: whether Robinson Crusoe was on a big boat or not, the idea is that he got . . . *(Pause)* shipwrecked. So I . . . if I am supposed to play Robinson Crusoe my way, then I will choose the way in which I will get shipwrecked. Now, as Robinson Crusoe is rowing, he looks up and he sees this huge white sea bird, which is making loud sea-bird noises, because a storm is coming. And Robinson Crusoe looks up toward the sky and sees that there is this storm. Then, there is a large wave, and Robinson Crusoe finds himself on the beach.
HARRY: Am I supposed to play the beach? Because that's white . . .
JACKSON: Hilarious! Mr. Trewe. Now look, you know, I am doing *you* a favor. On this beach, right? Then he sees a lot of goats. And, because he is naked and he needs clothes, he kills a goat, he takes off the skin, and he makes this parasol here and this hat, so he doesn't go around naked for everybody to see. Now I *know* that there is nobody there, but there is an audience, so the sooner Robinson Crusoe puts on his clothes, then the better and happier we will all be. I am going to go back in the boat. I am going to look up toward the sky. You will, *please*, make the sea-bird noises. I will do the wave, I will crash onto the sand, you will come down like a goat, I will kill you, take off your skin, make a parasol *and* a hat, and after that, then I promise you that I will remember the song. And I will sing it to the best of my ability. *(Pause)* However shitty that is.
HARRY: I said "silly." Now listen . . .
JACKSON: Yes, Mr. Trewe?

HARRY: Okay, if you're a black explorer . . . Wait a minute . . . wait a minute. If you're really a white explorer but you're black, shouldn't I play a black sea bird because I'm white?

JACKSON: Are you . . . going to extend . . . the limits of prejudice to include . . . the flora and fauna of this island? I am entering the boat.

(He is stepping into the upturned table or boat, as HARRY *halfheartedly imitates a bird, waving his arms.)*

HARRY: Kekkkk, kekkkk, kekkk, kekkkk! *(Stops)* What's wrong?

JACKSON: What's wrong? Mr. Trewe, that is not a sea gull . . . that is some kind of . . . well, I don't know what it is . . . some kind of *jumbie* bird° or something. *(Pause)* I am returning to the boat.

(He carefully enters the boat, expecting an interrupting bird cry from HARRY, *but there is none, so he begins to row.)*

HARRY: Kekk! Kekkk. *(He hangs his arms down. Pause)* Er, Jackson, wait a minute. Hold it a second. Come here a minute. (JACKSON *patiently gets out of the boat, elaborately pantomiming lowering his body into shallow water, releasing his hold on the boat, swimming a little distance toward shore, getting up from the shallows, shaking out his hair and hands, wiping his hands on his trousers, jumping up and down on one foot to unplug water from his clogged ear, seeing* HARRY, *then walking wearily, like a man who has swum a tremendous distance, and collapsing at* HARRY*'s feet.)* Er, Jackson. This is too humiliating. Now, let's just forget it and please don't continue, or you're fired.

*(*JACKSON *leisurely wipes his face with his hands.)*

JACKSON: It don't go so, Mr. Trewe. You know me to be a meticulous man. I didn't want to do this job. I didn't even want to work here. You convinced me to work here. I have worked as meticulously as I can, until I have been promoted. This morning I had no intention of doing what I am doing now; you have always admired the fact that whatever I begin, I finish. Now, I will accept my resignation, if you want me to, *after* we have finished this thing. But I am not leaving in the middle of a job, that has never been my policy. So you can sit down, as usual, and watch me work, but until I have finished this whole business of Robinson Crusoe being in the boat *(He rises and repeats the pantomime)* looking at an imaginary sea bird, being shipwrecked, killing a goat, making this hat *and* this parasol, walking up the beach and finding a naked footprint, which should take me into

about another ten or twelve minutes, at the most, I will pack my things and I will leave, and you can play *Robinson Crusoe* all by yourself. My plans were, after this, to take the table like this . . . *(He goes to the table, puts it upright.)* Let me show you: take the table, turn it all around, go under the table . . . *He goes under the table)* and this would now have become Robinson Crusoe's hut. *(Emerges from under the table and, without looking at* HARRY, *continues to talk)* Now, you just tell me if you think I am overdoing it, or if you think it's more or less what we agreed on? *(Pause)* Okay? But I am not resigning. *(Turns to* HARRY *slowly)* You see, it's your people who introduced us to this culture: Shakespeare, *Robinson Crusoe*, the classics, and so on, and when we start getting as good as them, you can't leave halfway. So, I will continue? Please?

HARRY: No, Jackson. You will *not* continue. You will straighten this table, put back the tablecloth, take away the breakfast things, give me back the hat, put your jacket back on, and we will continue as normal and forget the whole matter. Now, I'm very serious, I've had enough of this farce. I would like to stop.

JACKSON: May I say what I think, Mr. Trewe? I think it's a matter of prejudice. I think that you cannot believe: one: that I can act, and two: that any black man should play Robinson Crusoe. A little while aback, I came out here quite calmly and normally with the breakfast thins and find you almost stark naked, kneeling down, and you told me you were getting into your part. Here am I getting into *my* part and you object. This is the story . . . this is history. This moment that we are now acting here is the history of imperialism; it's nothing less than that. And I don't think that I can—should—concede my getting into a part halfway and abandoning things, just because you, as my superior, give me orders. People become independent. Now, I could go down to that beach by myself with this hat, and I could play Robinson Crusoe, I could play Columbus, I could play Sir Francis Drake, I could play anybody discovering anywhere, but I don't want you to tell me when and where to draw the line! *(Pause)* Or what to discover and when to discover it. All right?

HARRY: Look, I'm sorry to interrupt you again, Jackson, but as I—you know—was watching you, I realized it's much more profound than that; that it could get offensive. We're trying to do something light, just a little pantomime, a little satire, a little picong. But if you take this thing seriously, we might commit Art, which is a kind of crime in this society . . . I mean, there'd be a lot of things there that people . . . well, it would make them think too much, and well, we don't want that . . . we just want a little . . . entertainment.

---

jumbie bird, a small owl, or "spirit bird," superstitiously thought to foretell death.

JACKSON: How do you mean, Mr. Trewe?

HARRY: Well, I mean if you . . . well, I mean. If you did the whole thing in reverse . . . I mean, okay, well, all right . . . you've got this black man . . . no, no . . . all right. You've got this man who is black, Robinson Crusoe, and he discovers this island on which there is this white cannibal, all right?

JACKSON: Yes. That is, after he has killed the goat . . .

HARRY: Yes, I know, I know. After he has killed the goat and made a . . . the hat, the parasol, and all of that . . . and, anyway, he comes across this man called Friday.

JACKSON: How do you know I mightn't choose to call him Thursday? Do I have to copy every . . . I mean, are we improvising?

HARRY: All right, so it's Thursday. He comes across this naked white cannibal called Thursday, you know. And then look at what would happen. He would have to start to . . . well, he'd have to, sorry . . . This cannibal, who is a Christian, would have to start unlearning his Christianity. He would have to be taught . . . I mean . . . he'd have to be taught by this—African . . . that everything was wrong, that what he was doing . . . I mean, for nearly two thousand years . . . was wrong. That his civilization, his culture, his whatever, was . . . *horrible*. Was all . . . wrong. Barbarous, I mean, you know. And Crusoe would then have to teach him things like, you know, about . . . Africa, his gods, patamba, and so on . . . and it would get very, very complicated, and I suppose ultimately it would be very boring, and what we'd have on our hands would be . . . would be a play and not a little pantomime . . .

JACKSON: I'm too ambitious?

HARRY: No, no, the whole thing would have to be reversed; white would become black, you know . . .

JACKSON (*Smiling*): You see, Mr. Trewe, I don't see anything wrong with that, up to now.

HARRY: Well, I do. It's not the sort of thing I want, and I think you'd better clean up, and I'm going inside, and when I come back I'd like this whole place just as it was. I mean, just before everything started.

JACKSON: You mean you'd like it returned to its primal state? Natural? Before Crusoe finds Thursday? But, you see, that is not history. That is not the world.

HARRY: No, no, I don't give an Eskimo's fart about the world, Jackson. I just want this little place here *cleaned up*, and I'd like you to get back to fixing the sun deck. Let's forget the whole matter. Righto. Excuse me.

(*He is leaving.* JACKSON*'s tone will stop him.*)

JACKSON: Very well. So I take it you don't want to hear the song, neither?

HARRY: No, no, I'm afraid not. I think really it was a silly idea, it's all my fault, and I'd like things to return to where they were.

JACKSON: The story of the British Empire, Mr. Trewe. However, it is too late. The history of the British Empire.

HARRY: Now, how do you get that?

JACKSON: Well, you come to a place, you find that place as God make it; like Robinson Crusoe, you civilize the natives; they try to do something, you turn around and you say to them: "You are not good enough, let's call the whole thing off, return things to normal, you go back to your position as slave or servant, I will keep mine as master, and we'll forget the whole thing ever happened." Correct? You would like me to accept this.

HARRY: You're really making this very difficult, Jackson. Are you hurt? Have I offended you?

JACKSON: Hurt? No, no, no. I didn't expect any less. I am not hurt. (*Pause*) I am just . . .

(*Pause*)

HARRY: You're just what?

JACKSON: I am just ashamed . . . of making such a fool of myself. (*Pause*) I expected . . . a little respect. That is all.

HARRY: I respect you . . . I just, I . . .

JACKSON: No. It's perfectly all right. (HARRY *goes to the table, straightens it.*) I . . . no . . . I'll fix the table myself. (*He doesn't move.*) I am all right, thank you. Sir. (HARRY *stops fixing the table.*) (*With the hint of a British accent*) Thank you very much.

HARRY (*Sighs*): I . . . am sorry . . . er . . .

(JACKSON *moves toward the table.*)

JACKSON: It's perfectly all right, sir. It's perfectly all . . . right. (*Almost inaudibly*) Thank you. (HARRY *begins to straighten the table again.*) No, thank you very much, don't touch anything. (JACKSON *is up against the table.* HARRY *continues to straighten the table.*) Don't touch anything . . . Mr. Trewe. Please. (JACKSON *rests one arm on the table, fist closed. They watch each other for three beats.*) Now that . . . is MY order . . .

(*They watch each other for several beats as the lights fade.*)

ACT 2

(*Noon. White glare.* HARRY, *with shirt unbuttoned, in a deck chair reading a paperback thriller. Sound of intermittent hammering from stage left, where* JACKSON *is repairing the sun-deck slats.* HARRY *rises, decides he should talk to* JACKSON *about the noise, decides against it, and leans back in the deck chair, eyes closed. Hammering has stopped for a long while.* HARRY *opens his eyes, senses* JACKSON's *presence, turns suddenly, to see him standing quite close, shirtless, holding a hammer.* HARRY *bolts from his chair.*)

JACKSON: You know something, sir? While I was up there nailing the sun deck, I just stay so and start giggling all by myself.

HARRY: Oh, yes? Why?

JACKSON: No, I was remembering a feller, you know . . . ahhh, he went for audition once for a play, you know, and the way he, you know, the way he prop . . . present himself to the people, said . . . ahmm, "You know, I am an actor, you know. I do all kind of acting, classical acting, *Creole* acting." That's when I laugh, you know? *(Pause)* I going back and fix the deck, then. *(Moves off. Stops, turns)* The . . . the hammering not disturbing you?

HARRY: No, no, it's fine. You have to do it, right? I mean, you volunteered, the carpenter didn't come, right?

JACKSON: Yes. Creole acting. I wonder what kind o' acting dat is. *(Spins the hammer in the air and does or does not catch it)* Yul Brynner.° *Magnificent Seven.*° Picture, papa! A kind of Western Creole acting. It ain't have no English cowboys, eh, Mr. Harry? Something wrong, boy, something wrong. *(He exits.* HARRY *lies back in the deck chair, the book on his chest, arms locked behind his head. Silence. Hammering violently resumes.) (Off)* Kekkk, kekkkekk, kekk! Kekkekk, kekkkekk, ekkek!

*(*HARRY *rises, moves from the deck chair toward the sun deck.)*

HARRY: *Jackson!* What the hell are you doing? What's that noise?

JACKSON *(Off; loud)*: I doing like a black sea gull, suh!

HARRY: Well, it's very distracting.

JACKSON *(Off)*: Sorry, sir. *(*HARRY *returns. Sits down on the deck chair. Waits for the hammering. Hammering resumes. Then stops. Silence. Then we hear)*

(Singing loudly)

I want to tell you 'bout Robinson Crusoe.
He tell Friday, when I do so, do so.
Whatever I do, you must do like me,
He make Friday a Good Friday Bohbolee

(Spoken)

And the chorus:

(Sings)

Laide-die
Laidie, lay-day, de-day-de-die,

Laidee-doo-day-dee-day-dee-die
Laidee-day-doh-dee-day-dee-die

Now that was the first example of slavery,
'Cause I am still Friday and you ain't me,
Now Crusoe he was this Christian and all,
Friday, his slave, was a cannibal,
But one day things bound to go in reverse,
With Crusoe the slave and Friday the boss . . .
Caiso,° boy! Caiso!

*(*HARRY *rises, goes toward the sun deck.)*

HARRY: Jackson, man! Jesus!

(He returns to the deck chair, is about to sit.)

JACKSON *(Off)*: Two more lash and the sun deck finish, sir! *(*HARRY *waits.)* Stand by . . . here they come . . . First lash . . . *(Sound)* Pow! Second lash: *(Two sounds)* Pataow! Job complete! Lunch, Mr. Trewe? You want your lunch now? Couple sandwich or what?

HARRY *(Shouts without turning)*: Just bring a couple beers from the icebox, Jackson. And the Scotch. *(To himself)* What the hell, let's all get drunk. *(To* JACKSON*)* Bring some beer for yourself, too, Jackson!

JACKSON *(Off)*: Thank you, Mr. Robinson . . . Thank you, Mr. Trewe, sir! *Cru-soe, Trewe-so! (Faster)* Crusoe-Truesoe, Robinson Trewe-so!

HARRY: Jesus, Jackson; cut that out and just bring the bloody beer!

JACKSON *(Off)*: Right! A beer for you and a beer for me! Now, what else is it going to be? A sandwich for you, but none for me. *(*HARRY *picks up the paperback and opens it, removing a folded sheet of paper. He opens it and is reading it carefully, sometimes lifting his head, closing his eyes, as if remembering its contents, then reading again. He puts it into a pocket quickly as* JACKSON *returns, carrying a tray with two beers, a bottle of Scotch, a pitcher of water, and two glasses.* JACKSON *sets them down on the table.)* I'm here, sir. At your command.

HARRY: Sit down. Forget the sandwiches, I don't want to eat. Let's sit down, man to man, and have a drink. That was the most sarcastic hammering I've ever heard, and I know you were trying to get back at me with all those noises and that Uncle Tom crap. So let's have a drink, man to man, and try and work out what happened this morning, all right?

JACKSON: I've forgotten about this morning, sir.

HARRY: No, no, no, I mean, the rest of the day it's going to bother me, you know?

JACKSON: Well, I'm leaving at half-past one.

Yul Brynner, Russian-born stage and film star (1915–85), known primarily for his performance as the Siamese monarch in *The King and I.* **Magnificent Seven,** classic Western film (1960) starring Yul Brynner.

caiso, a variant of calypso.

HARRY: No, but still . . . Let's . . . Okay. Scotch?

JACKSON: I'll stick to beer, sir, thank you.

(HARRY *pours a Scotch and water,* JACKSON *serves himself a beer. Both are still standing.*)

HARRY: Sit over there, please, Mr. Phillip. On the deck chair. (JACKSON *sits on the deck chair, facing* HARRY.) Cheers?

JACKSON: Cheers. Cheers. Deck chair and all.

(*They toast and drink.*)

HARRY: All right. Look, I think you misunderstood me this morning.

JACKSON: Why don't we forget the whole thing, sir? Let me finish this beer and go for my sea bath, and you can spend the rest of the day all by yourself. (*Pause*) Well. What's wrong? What happen, sir? I said something wrong just now?

HARRY: This place isn't going to drive me crazy, Jackson. Not if I have to go mad preventing it. Not physically crazy; but you just start to think crazy thoughts, you know? At the beginning it's fine; there's the sea, the palm trees, monarch of all I survey and so on, all that postcard stuff. And then it just becomes another back yard. God, is there anything deadlier than Sunday afternoons in the tropics when you can't sleep? The horror and stillness of the heat, the shining, godforsaken sea, the bored and boring clouds? Especially in an empty boarding house. You sit by the stagnant pool counting the dead leaves drifting to the edge. I daresay the terror of emptiness made me want to act. I wasn't trying to humiliate you. I meant nothing by it. Now, I don't usually apologize to people. I don't do things to apologize for. When I do them, I mean them, but, in your case, I'd like to apologize.

JACKSON: Well, if you find here boring, go back home. Do something else, nuh?

HARRY: It's not that simple. It's a little more complicated than that. I mean, everything I own is sunk here, you see? There's a little matter of a brilliant actress who drank too much, and a car crash at Brighton after a panto . . . Well. That's neither here nor there now. Right? But I'm determined to make this place work. I gave up the theater for it.

JACKSON: Why?

HARRY: Why? I wanted to be the best. Well, among other things; oh, well, that's neither here nor there. Flopped at too many things, though. Including classical and Creole acting. I just want to make this place work, you know. And a desperate man'll try anything. Even at the cost of his sanity, maybe. I mean, I'd hate to believe that under everything else I was also prejudiced, as well. I wouldn't have any right here, right?

JACKSON: 'Tain't prejudice that bothering you, Mr. Trewe; you ain't no parrot to repeat opinion. No, is loneliness that sucking your soul as dry as the sun suck a crab shell. On a Sunday like this, I does watch you. The whole staff does study you. Walking round restless, staring at the sea. You remembering your wife and your son, not right? You ain't get over that yet?

HARRY: Jackson . . .

JACKSON: Is none of my business. But it really lonely here out of season. Is summer, and your own people gone, but come winter they go flock like sandpipers all down that beach. So you lonely, but I could make you forget all o' that. I could make H. Trewe, Esquire, a brand-new man. You come like a challenge.

HARRY: Think I keep to myself too much?

JACKSON: If! You would get your hair cut by phone. You drive so careful you make your car nervous. If you was in charge of the British Empire, you wouldn'ta lose it, you'da misplace it.

HARRY: I see, Jackson.

JACKSON: But all that could change if you do what I tell you.

HARRY: I don't want a new life, thanks.

JACKSON: Same life. Different man. But that stiff upper lip goin' have to quiver a little.

HARRY: What's all this? Obeah?° "That old black magic"?

JACKSON: Nothing. I could have the next beer?

HARRY: Go ahead. I'm drinking Scotch.

(JACKSON *takes the other beer, swallows deep, smacks his lips, grins at* HARRY.)

JACKSON: Nothing. We will have to continue from where we stop this morning. You will have to be Thursday.

HARRY: Aha, you bastard! It's a thrill giving orders, hey? But I'm not going through all that rubbish again.

JACKSON: All right. Stay as you want. But if you say yes, it go have to be man to man, and none of this boss-and-Jackson business, you see, Trewe . . . I mean, I just call you plain Trewe, for example, and I notice that give you a slight shock. Just a little twitch of the lip, but a shock all the same, eh, Trewe? You see? You twitch again. It would be just me and you, all right? You see, two of we both acting a role here we ain't really really believe in, you know. I ent think you strong enough to give people orders, and I *know* I ain't the kind who like taking *them*. So both of we doesn't have to *improvise* so much as *exaggerate*. We faking, faking all the

---

Obeah, traditional African "science" related to matters of the spirit and healing.

time. But, man to man, I mean . . . *(Pause)* that could be something else. Right, Mr. Trewe?

HARRY: Aren't we man to man now?

JACKSON: No, no. We having one of them "playing man-to-man" talks, where a feller does look a next feller in the eye and say, "Le' we settle this thing, man to man," and this time the feller who smiling and saying it, his whole honest intention is to take that feller by the crotch and rip out he stones, and dig out he eye and leave him for corbeaux° to pick.

(Silence)

HARRY: You know, that thing this morning had an effect on me, man to man now. I didn't think so much about the comedy of *Robinson Crusoe*, I thought what we were getting into was a little sad. So, when I went back to the room, I tried to rest before lunch, before you began all that vindictive hammering . . .

JACKSON: Vindictive?

HARRY: Man to man: that vindictive hammering and singing, and I thought, Well, maybe we could do it straight. Make a real straight thing out of it.

JACKSON: You mean like a tradegy. With one joke?

HARRY: Or a codemy, with none. You mispronounce words on purpose, don't you, Jackson? *(JACKSON smiles.)* Don't think for one second that I'm not up on your game, Jackson. You're playing the stage nigger with me. I'm an actor, you know. It's a smile in front and a dagger behind your back, right? Or the smile itself is the bloody dagger. I'm aware, chum. I'm aware.

JACKSON: The smile kinda rusty, sir, but it goes with the job. Just like the water in this hotel: *(Demonstrates)* I turn it on at seven and lock it off at one.

HARRY: Didn't hire you for the smile; I hired you for your voice. We've the same background. Old-time calypso, old-fashioned music hall:

(Sings)

Oh, me wife can't cook and she looks like a horse
And the way she makes coffee is grounds for divorce . . .

(Does a few steps)

But when love is at stake she's my Worcester sauce . . .

(Stops)

Used to wow them with that. All me own work. Ah, the lost glories of the old music hall, the old provincials, grimy brocade, the old stars faded one by one. The brassy pantomimes! Come from

an old music-hall family, you know, Jackson. Me mum had this place she ran for broken-down actors. Had tea with the greats as a tot.°

(Sings softly, hums)

Oh, me wife can't cook . . .

(Silence)

You married, Jackson?

JACKSON: I not too sure, sir.

HARRY: You're not sure?

JACKSON: That's what I said.

HARRY: I know what you mean. I wasn't sure I was when I was. My wife's remarried.

JACKSON: You showed me her photo. And the little boy own.

HARRY: But I'm not. Married. So there's absolutely no hearth for Crusoe to go home to. While you were up there, I rehearsed this thing. *(Presents a folded piece of paper)* Want to read it?

JACKSON: What . . . er . . . what is it . . . a poetry?

HARRY: No, no, not a poetry. A thing I wrote. Just a speech in the play . . . that if . . .

JACKSON: Oho, we back in the play again?

HARRY: Almost. You want to read it?

(He offers the paper.)

JACKSON: All right.

HARRY: I thought—no offense, now. Man to man. If you were doing Robinson Crusoe, this is what you'd read.

JACKSON: You want me to read this, right?

HARRY: Yeah.

JACKSON *(Reads slowly)*: "O silent sea, O wondrous sunset that I've gazed on ten thousand times, who will rescue me from this complete desolation? . . ." *(Breaking)* All o' this?

HARRY: If you don't mind. Don't act it. Just read it. *(JACKSON looks at him.)* No offense.

JACKSON *(Reads)*: "Yes, this is paradise, I know. For I see around me the splendors of nature . . ."

HARRY: Don't act it . . .

JACKSON *(Pauses; then continues)*: "How I'd like to fuflee this desolate rock." *(Pauses)* Fuflee? Pardon, but what is a fuflee, Mr. Trewe?

HARRY: A fuflee? I've got "fuflee" written there?

JACKSON *(Extends paper, points at word)*: So, how you does fuflee, Mr Harry? Is Anglo-Saxon English?

(HARRY kneels down and peers at the word. He rises.)

HARRY: It's F . . . then F-L-E-E—flee to express his hesitation. It's my own note as an actor. He quivers, he hesitates . . .

---

corbeaux, ravens (French).

tot, small child.

JACKSON: He quivers, he hesitates, but he still can't fuflee?

HARRY: Just leave that line out, Jackson.

JACKSON: I like it.

HARRY: *Leave it out!*

JACKSON: No fuflee?

HARRY: I said no.

JACKSON: Just because I read it wrong. I know the word "flee," you know. Like to take off. Flee. Faster than run. Is the extra *F* you put in there so close to flee that had me saying fuflee like a damn ass, but le' we leave it in, nuh? One fuflee ain't go kill anybody. Much less bite them. *(Silence)* Get it?

HARRY: Don't take this personally . . .

JACKSON: No fuflees on old Crusoe, boy . . .

HARRY: But, if you're going to do professional theater, Jackson, don't take this personally, more discipline is required. All right?

JACKSON: You write it. Why you don't read it?

HARRY: I wanted to hear it. Okay, give it back . . .

JACKSON *(Loudly, defiantly)*: "The ferns, the palms like silent sentinels, the wide and silent lagoons that briefly hold my passing, solitary reflection. The volcano . . ." *(Stops)* "The volcano." What?

HARRY: . . . "wreathed" . . .

JACKSON: Oho, oho . . . like a wreath? "The volcano *wreathed* in mist. But what is paradise without a woman? Adam in paradise!"

HARRY: Go ahead.

JACKSON *(Restrained)*: "Adam in paradise had his woman to share his loneliness, but I miss the voice of even one consoling creature, the touch of a hand, the look of kind eyes. Where is the wife from whom I vowed never to be sundered? How old is my little son? If he could see his father like this, mad with memories of them . . . Even Job had his family. But I am alone, alone, I am all alone." *(Pause)* Oho. You write this?

HARRY: Yeah.

JACKSON: Is good. Very good.

HARRY: Thank you.

JACKSON: Touching. Very sad. But something missing.

HARRY: What?

JACKSON: Goats. You leave out the goats.

HARRY: The goats. So what? What've you got with goats, anyway?

JACKSON: Very funny. Very funny, sir.

HARRY: Try calling me Trewe.

JACKSON: Not yet. That will come. Stick to the point. You ask for my opinion and I *gave* you my opinion. No doubt I don't have the brains. But *my* point is that this man ain't facing reality. *There are goats* all around him.

HARRY: You're full of shit.

JACKSON: The man is not facing reality. He is not a practical man *shipwrecked.*

HARRY: I suppose that's the difference between classical and Creole acting?

(He pours a drink and downs it furiously.)

JACKSON: If he is not practical, he is not Robinson Crusoe. And yes, is Creole acting, yes. Because years afterward his little son could look at the parasol and the hat and look at a picture of Daddy and boast: "My daddy smart, boy. He get shipwreck and first thing he do is he build a hut, then he kill a goat or two and make clothes, a parasol and a hat." That way Crusoe *achieve* something, and his son could boast . . .

HARRY: Only his son is dead.

JACKSON: Whose son dead?

HARRY: Crusoe's.

JACKSON: No, pardner. *Your* son dead. Crusoe wife and child waiting for him, and he is a practical man and he know somebody go come and save him . . .

HARRY *(Almost inaudibly)*:

*"I bit my arm, I sucked the blood,
And cried, 'A sail! a sail!'"*

How the hell does he know "somebody go come and save him"? That's shit. That's not in his character at that moment. How the hell can he know? You're a cruel bastard . . .

JACKSON *(Enraged)*: *Because, you fucking ass, he has faith!*

HARRY *(Laughing)*: Faith? What faith?

JACKSON: He not sitting on his shipwrecked arse bawling out . . . what it is you have here? *(Reads)* "O . . ." Where is it? *(Reads)* "O silent sea, O wondrous sunset," and all that shit. No. He shipwrecked. He desperate, he hungry. He look up and he see this fucking goat with its fucking beard watching him and smiling, this goat with its forked fucking beard and square yellow eye just like the fucking devil, standing up there . . . *(Pantomimes the goat and Crusoe in turn)* smiling at him, and putting out its tongue and letting go one fucking *bleeeeeh!* And Robbie ent thinking 'bout his wife and son and O silent sea and O wondrous sunset; no, Robbie is the First True Creole, so he watching the goat with his eyes narrow, narrow, and he say: *blehhh*, eh? You muther-fucker, I go show you *blehhh* in your goat-ass, and vam, vam, next thing is Robbie and the goat, *mano a mano,*° man to man, man to goat, goat to man, wrestling on the sand, and next thing we know we hearing one last faint, feeble *bleeeeeehhhhhhhhhhhhhh*, and Robbie is next seen walking up the beach with a goatskin hat and a goatskin umbrella, feeling like a million dollars because *he have faith!*

---

mano a mano, Spanish, hand to hand, or one-on-one.

HARRY (*Applauds*): Bravo! You're the Christian. I am the cannibal. Bravo!

JACKSON: If I does hammer sarcastic, you does clap sarcastic. Now I want to pee.

HARRY: I think I'll join you.

JACKSON: So because I go and pee, you must pee, too?

HARRY: Subliminal suggestion.

JACKSON: Monkey see, monkey do.

HARRY: You're the bloody ape, mate. You people just came down from the trees.

JACKSON: Say that again, please.

HARRY: I'm going to keep that line.

JACKSON: Oho! Rehearse you rehearsing? I thought you was serious.

HARRY: You go have your pee. I'll run over my monologue.

JACKSON: No, you best do it now, sir. Or it going to be on my mind while we rehearsing that what you really want to do is take a break and pee. We best go together, then.

HARRY: We'll call it the pee break. Off we go, then. How long will you be, then? You people take forever.

JACKSON: Maybe you should hold up a sign, sir, or give some sort of signal when you serious or when you joking, so I can know not to react. I would say five minutes.

HARRY: Five minutes? What is this, my friend, Niagara Falls?

JACKSON: It will take me . . . look, you want me to time it? I treat it like a ritual, I don't just pee for peeing's sake. It will take me about forty to fifty seconds to walk to the servants' toilets . . .

HARRY: Wait a second . . .

JACKSON: No, you wait, please, sir. That's almost one minute, take another fifty seconds to walk back, or even more, because after a good pee a man does be in a mood, both ruminative and grateful that the earth has received his libation, so that makes . . .

HARRY: Hold on, please.

JACKSON (*Voice rising*): Jesus, sir, give me a break, nuh? That is almost two minutes, and in between those two minutes it have such solemn and ruminative behavior as opening the fly, looking upward or downward, the ease and relief, the tender shaking, the solemn tucking in, like you putting a little baby back to sleep, the reverse zipping or buttoning, depending on the pants, then, with the self-congratulating washing of the hands, looking at yourself for at least half a minute in the mirror, then the drying of hands as if you were a master surgeon just finish a major operation, and the walk back . . .

HARRY: You said that. Any way you look at it, it's under five minutes, and I interrupted you because . . .

JACKSON: I could go and you could time me, to see if I

on a go-slow, or wasting up my employer's precious time, but I know it will take at least five, unless, like most white people, you either don't flush it, a part I forgot, or just wipe your hands fast fast or not at all . . .

HARRY: Which white people, Jackson?

JACKSON: I was bathroom attendant at the Hilton, and I know men and races from their urinary habits, and most Englishmen . . .

HARRY: Most Englishmen . . . Look, I was trying to tell you, instead of going all the way round to the servants' lavatories, pop into my place, have a quick one, and that'll be under five bloody minutes in any circumstances and regardless of the capacity. Go on. I'm all right.

JACKSON: Use your bathroom, Mr. Harry?

HARRY: Go on, will you?

JACKSON: I want to get this. You giving me permission to go through your living room, with all your valuables lying about, with the picture of your wife watching me in case I should leave the bathroom open, and you are granting me the privilege of taking out my thing, doing my thing right there among all those lotions and expensive soaps, and . . . after I finish, wiping my hands on a clean towel?

HARRY: Since you make it so vividly horrible, why don't you just walk around to the servants' quarters and take as much time as you like? Five minutes won't kill me.

JACKSON: I mean, equality is equality and art is art, Mr. Harry, but to use those clean, rough Cannon towels . . . You mustn't rush things, people have to slide into independence. They give these islands independence so fast that people still ain't recover from the shock, so they pissing and wiping their hands indiscriminately. You don't want that to happen in this guest house, Mr. Harry. Let me take my little five minutes, as usual, and if you have to go, you go to your place, and I'll go to mine, and let's keep things that way until I can feel I can use your towels without a profound sense of gratitude, and you could, if you wanted, a little later maybe, walk round the guest house in the dark, put your foot in the squelch of those who missed the pit by the outhouse, that charming old-fashioned outhouse so many tourists take Polaroids of, without feeling degraded, and we can then respect each other as artists. So, I appreciate the offer, but I'll be back in five. Kindly excuse me.

(*He exits.*)

HARRY: You've got logorrhea,° Jackson. You've been

---

logorrhea, verbal profusion, talking too much.

running your mouth like a parrot's arse. But don't get sarcastic with me, boy!

(JACKSON *returns.*)

JACKSON: You don't understand, Mr. Harry. My problem is, I really mean what I say.

HARRY: You've been pretending indifference to this game, Jackson, but you've manipulated it your way, haven't you? Now you can spew out all that bitterness in fun, can't you? Well, we'd better get things straight around here, friend. You're still on duty. And if you stay out there too long, your job is at stake. It's . . . (*Consulting his watch*) five minutes to one now. You've got exactly three minutes to get in there and back, and two minutes left to finish straightening this place. It's a bloody mess.

(*Silence*)

JACKSON: Bloody mess, eh?

HARRY: That's correct.

JACKSON (*In exaggerated British accent*): I go try and make it back in five, bwana. If I don't, the mess could be bloodier. I saw a sign once in a lavatory in Mobile, Alabama. COLORED. But it didn't have no time limit. Funny, eh?

HARRY: Ape! Mimic! Three bloody minutes!

(JACKSON *exits, shaking his head.* HARRY *recovers the sheet of paper from the floor and puts it back in his pants pocket. He pours a large drink, swallows it all in two large gulps, then puts the glass down. He looks around the gazebo, wipes his hands briskly. He removes the drinks tray with Scotch, the two beer bottles, glasses, water pitcher, and sets them in a corner of the gazebo. He lifts up the deck chair and sets it, sideways, in another corner. He turns the table carefully over on its side; then, when it is on its back, he looks at it. He changes his mind and carefully tilts the table back upright. He removes his shirt and folds it and places it in another corner of the gazebo. He rolls up his trouser cuffs almost to the knee. He is now half-naked. He goes over to the drinks tray and pours the bowl of melted ice, now tepid water, over his head. He ruffles his hair, his face dripping; then he sees an ice pick. He picks it up.*)

JACKSON'S VOICE: "One day, just out of the blue, I pick up a ice pick and walk over to where he and two fellers was playing cards, and I nail that ice pick through his hand to the table, and I laugh . . ."

(HARRY *drives the ice pick hard into the tabletop, steps back, looking at it. Then he moves up to it, wrenches it out, and gets under the table, the ice pick at his feet. A few beats, then* JACKSON *enters, pauses.*)

JACKSON (*Laughs*): What you doing under the table, Mr. Trewe? (*Silence.* JACKSON *steps nearer the table.*) Trewe? You all right? (*Silence.* JACKSON *crouches close to* HARRY.) Harry, boy, you cool? (JACKSON

rises. Moves away some distance. He takes in the space. An arena. Then he crouches again.) Ice-pick time, then? Okay. "Fee fi fo fum, I smell the blood of an Englishman . . ." (JACKSON *exits quickly.* HARRY *waits a while, then crawls from under the table, straightens up, and places the ice pick gently on the tabletop. He goes to the drinks tray and has a sip from the Scotch; then replaces the bottle and takes up a position behind the table.* JACKSON *returns dressed as Crusoe—goatskin hat, open umbrella, the hammer stuck in the waistband of his rolled-up trousers. He throws something across the room to* HARRY'S *feet. The dead parrot, in a carry-away box.* HARRY *opens it.*) One parrot, to go! Or you eating it here?

HARRY: You son of a bitch.

JACKSON: Sure. (HARRY *picks up the parrot and hurls it into the sea.*) First bath in five years.

(JACKSON *moves toward the table, very calmly.*)

HARRY: You're a bloody savage. Why'd you strangle him?

JACKSON (*As Friday*): Me na strangle him, bwana. Him choke from prejudice.

HARRY: Prejudice? A bloody parrot. The bloody thing can't reason. (*Pause. They stare at each other.* HARRY *crouches, tilts his head, shifts on his perch, flutters his wings like the parrot, squawks.*) Heinegger. Heinegger. (JACKSON *stands over the table and folds the umbrella.*) You people create nothing. You imitate everything. It's all been done before, you see, Jackson. The parrot. Think that's something? It's from *The Seagull.* It's from *Miss Julie.* You can't ever be original, boy. That's the trouble with shadows, right? They can't think for themselves. (JACKSON *shrugs, looking away from him.*) So you take it out on a parrot. Is that one of your African sacrifices, eh?

JACKSON: Run your mouth, Harry, run your mouth.

HARRY (*Squawks*): Heinegger . . . Heinegger . . . (JACKSON *folds the parasol and moves to enter the upturned table.*) I wouldn't go under there if I were you, Jackson.

(JACKSON *reaches into the back of his waistband and removes a hammer.*)

JACKSON: The first English cowboy.

(*He turns and faces* HARRY.)

HARRY: It's my property. Don't get in there.

JACKSON: The hut. That was my idea.

HARRY: The table's mine.

JACKSON: What else is yours, Harry? (*Gestures*) This whole fucking island? Dem days gone, boy.

HARRY: The costume's mine, too. (*He crosses over, almost nudging* JACKSON, *and picks up the ice pick.*) I'd like them back.

JACKSON: Suit yourself.

(HARRY *crosses to the other side, sits on the edge of the wall or leans against a post.* JACKSON *removes the hat and throws it into the arena, then the parasol.*)

HARRY: The hammer's mine.
JACKSON: I feel I go need it.
HARRY: If you keep it, you're a bloody thief.

(JACKSON *suddenly drops to the floor on his knees, letting go of the hammer, weeping and cringing, and advancing on his knees toward* HARRY.)

JACKSON: Pardon, master, pardon! Friday bad boy! Friday wicked nigger. Sorry. Friday nah t'ief again. Mercy, master. Mercy. (*He rolls around on the floor, laughing.*) Oh, Jesus, I go dead! I go dead. Ay-ay.

(*Silence.* JACKSON *on the floor, gasping, lying on his back.* HARRY *crosses over, picks up the parasol, opens it, after a little difficulty, then puts on the goatskin hat.* JACKSON *lies on the floor, silent.*)

HARRY: I never hit any goddamned maintenance sergeant on the head in the service. I've never hit anybody in my life. Violence makes me sick. I don't believe in ownership. If I'd been more possessive, more authoritative, I don't think she'd have left me. I don't think you ever drove an ice pick through anybody's hand, either. That was just the two of us acting.
JACKSON: Creole acting? (*He is still lying on the floor.*) Don't be too sure about the ice pick.
HARRY: I'm sure. You're a fake. You're a kind man and you think you have to hide it. A lot of other people could have used that to their own advantage. That's the difference between master and servant.
JACKSON: That master-and-servant shit finish. Bring a beer for me.

(*He is still on his back.*)

HARRY: There's no more beer. You want a sip of Scotch?
JACKSON: Anything.

(HARRY *goes to the Scotch, brings over the bottle, stands over* JACKSON.)

HARRY: Here. To me bloody wife! (JACKSON *sits up, begins to move off.*) What's wrong, you forget to flush it?
JACKSON: I don't think you should bad-talk her behind her back.

(*He exits.*)

HARRY: Behind her back? She's in England. She's a star. Star? She's a bloody planet.

(JACKSON *returns, holding the photograph of* HARRY's *wife.*)

JACKSON: If you going bad-talk, I think she should hear what you going to say, you don't think so, darling? (*Addressing the photograph, which he puts down*) If you have to tell somebody something, tell them to their face. (*Addressing the photograph*) Now, you know all you women, eh? Let the man talk his talk and don't interrupt.
HARRY: You're fucking bonkers,° you know that? Before I hired you, I should have asked for a medical report.
JACKSON: Please tell your ex-wife good afternoon or something. The dame in the pantomime is always played by a man, right?
HARRY: Bullshit.

(JACKSON *sits close to the photograph, wiggling as he ventriloquizes.*)

JACKSON (*In an Englishwoman's voice*): Is not bullshit at all, Harold. Everything I say you always saying bullshit, bullshit. How can we conduct a civilized conversation if you don't give me a chance? What have I done, Harold, oh, Harold, for you to treat me so?
HARRY: Because you're a silly selfish bitch and you *killed our son!*
JACKSON (*Crying*): There, there, you see. . . ? (*He wipes the eyes of the photograph.*) You're calling me names, it wasn't my fault, and you're calling me names. Can't you ever forgive me for that, Harold?
HARRY: Ha! You never told him that, did you? You neglected to mention that little matter, didn't you, love?
JACKSON (*Weeping*): I love you, Harold. I love you, and I loved him, too. Forgive me, O God, please, please forgive me . . . (*As himself*) So how it happen? Murder? A accident?
HARRY (*To the photograph*): Love me? You loved me so much you get drunk and you . . . ah, ah, what's the use? What's the bloody use?

(*Wipes his eyes. Pause*)

JACKSON (*As wife*): I'm crying too, Harold. Let bygones be bygones . . . (HARRY *lunges for the photograph, but* JACKSON *whips it away.*) (*As himself*) You miss, Harold. (*Pause; as wife*) Harold . . . (*Silence*) Harold . . . speak to me . . . please. (*Silence*) What do you plan to do next? (*Sniffs*) What'll you do now?
HARRY: What difference does it make? . . . All right. I'll tell you what I'm going to do next, Ellen: you're such a big star, you're such a luminary, I'm

---

bonkers, crazy.

going to leave you to shine by yourself. I'm giving up this bloody rat race and I'm going to take up Mike's offer. I'm leaving "the theatuh," which destroyed my confidence, screwed up my marriage, and made you a star. I'm going somewhere where I can get pissed every day and watch the sun set, like Robinson bloody Crusoe. That's what I'm going to bloody do. You always said it's the only part I could play.

JACKSON (*As wife*): Take me with you, then. Let's get away together. I always wanted to see the tropics, the palm trees, the lagoons . . .

(HARRY *grabs the photograph from* JACKSON; *he picks up the ice pick and puts the photograph on the table, pressing it down with one palm.*)

HARRY: All right, Ellen, I'm going to . . . You can scream all you like, but I'm going to . . .

(*He raises the ice pick.*)

JACKSON (*As wife*): My face is my fortune.

(*He snakes up behind* HARRY, *whips the photograph away while* HARRY *is poised with the ice pick.*)

HARRY: Your face is your fortune, eh? I'll kill her, Jackson, I'll maim that smirking bitch . . .

(*He lunges toward* JACKSON, *who leaps away, holding the photograph before his face, and runs around the gazebo, shrieking.*)

JACKSON (*As wife*): Help! Help! British police! My husband trying to kill me! Help, somebody, help! (HARRY *chases* JACKSON *with the ice pick, but* JACKSON *nimbly avoids him.*) (*As wife*) Harry! Have you gone mad?

(*He scrambles onto the ledge of the gazebo. He no longer holds the photograph to his face, but his voice is the wife's.*)

HARRY: Get down off there, you melodramatic bitch. You're too bloody conceited to kill yourself. Get down from there, Ellen! Ellen, it's a straight drop to the sea!

JACKSON (*As wife*): Push me, then! Push me, Harry! You hate me so much, why you don't come and push me?

HARRY: Push yourself, then. You never needed my help. Jump!

JACKSON (*As wife*): Will you forgive me now, or after I jump?

HARRY: Forgive you? . . .

JACKSON (*As wife*): All right, then. Goodbye!

(*He turns, teetering, about to jump.*)

HARRY (*Shouts*): Ellen! Stop! I forgive you! (JACKSON *turns on the ledge. Silence.* HARRY *is now sitting on the floor.*) That's the real reason I wanted to do the panto. To do it better than you ever did. You

played Crusoe in the panto, Ellen. I was Friday. Black bloody greasepaint that made you howl. You wiped the stage with me . . . Ellen . . . well. Why not? I was no bloody good.

JACKSON (*As himself*): Come back to the play, Mr. Trewe. Is Jackson. We was playing Robinson Crusoe, remember? (*Silence*) Master, Friday here . . . (*Silence*) You finish with the play? The panto? Crusoe must get up, he must make himself get up. He have to face a next day again. (*Shouts*) I tell you: man must live! Then, after many years, he see this naked footprint that is the mark of his salvation . . .

HARRY (*Recites*):

"The self-same moment I could pray;
and . . . tata tee-tum-tum
The Albatross fell off and sank
Like lead into the sea."

God, my memory . . .

JACKSON: That ain't Crusoe, that is "The Rime of the Ancient Mariner."

(*He pronounces it "Marina."*)

HARRY: Mariner.
JACKSON: Marina.
HARRY: Mariner.
JACKSON: "The Rime of the Ancient Marina." So I learn it in Fourth Standard.
HARRY: It's your country, mate.
JACKSON: Is your language, pardner. I stand corrected. Now, you ain't see English crazy? I could sit down right next to you and tell you I *stand* corrected.
HARRY: Sorry. Where were we, Mr. Phillip?
JACKSON: Tobago. Where are you? It was your cue, Mr. Trewe.
HARRY: Where was I, then?
JACKSON: Ahhhm . . . That speech you was reading . . . that speech . . .
HARRY: Speech?
JACKSON: "O silent sea and so on . . . wreathed in mist . . ." Shall we take it from there, then? The paper.
HARRY: I should know it. After all, I wrote it. But prompt . . . (HARRY *gives* JACKSON *his copy of the paper, rises, walks around, looks toward the sea.*) Creole or classical?
JACKSON: Don't make joke.

(*Silence. Sea-gull cries.*)

HARRY: Then Crusoe, in his desolation, looks out to the sea, for the ten thousandth time, and remembers England, his wife, his little son, and speaks to himself: (*As Crusoe*) "O silent sea, O wondrous sunset that I've gazed on ten thousand times, who will rescue me from this complete desolation?

Yes, this is paradise, I know. For I see around me the splendors of nature. The ferns, the palms like silent sentinels, the wide and silent lagoons that briefly hold my passing, solitary reflection. The volcano wreathed in mist. But what is paradise without a woman? Adam in paradise had his woman to share his loneliness . . . loneliness . . .

JACKSON (*Prompts*): . . . but I miss the voice . . .

HARRY (*Remembering*): "But I miss the voice . . . (*Weeping, but speaking clearly*) of even one consoling creature, the touch . . . of a hand . . . the look of kind eyes . . . Where is the wife from whom I vowed . . . never to be sundered? How old is my little son? If he could see his father like this . . . dressed in goatskins and mad with memories of them?"

(*He breaks down, quietly sobbing. A long pause*)

JACKSON: You crying or you acting?

HARRY: Acting.

JACKSON: I think you crying. Nobody could act that good.

HARRY: How would you know? You an actor?

JACKSON: Maybe not. But I cry a'ready.

HARRY: Okay, I was crying.

JACKSON: For what?

HARRY (*Laughs*): For what? I got carried away. I'm okay now.

JACKSON: But you laughing now.

HARRY: It's the same sound. You can't tell the difference if I turn my back.

JACKSON: Don't make joke.

HARRY: It's an old actor's trick. I'm going to cry now, all right?

(*He turns, then sobs with laughter, covering and uncovering his face with his hands.* JACKSON *stalks around, peers at him, then begins to giggle. They are now both laughing.*)

JACKSON (*Through laughter*): So . . . so . . . next Friday . . . when the tourists come . . . Crusoe . . . Crusoe go be ready for them . . . Goat race . . .

HARRY (*Laughing*): Goat-roti!°

JACKSON (*Laughing*): Gambling.

HARRY (*Baffled*): Gambling?

JACKSON: Goat-to-pack. Every night . . .

HARRY (*Laughing*): Before they goat-to-bed!

JACKSON (*Laughing*): So he striding up the beach with his little goat-ee . . .

HARRY (*Laughing*): E-goat-istical, again.

(*Pause*)

JACKSON: You get the idea. So, you okay, Mr. Trewe?

HARRY: I'm fine, Mr. Phillip. You know . . . (*He wipes his eyes.*) An angel passes through a house and leaves no imprint of his shadow on its wall. A man's life slowly changes and he does not understand the change. Things like this have happened before, and they can happen again. You understand, Jackson? You see what it is I'm saying?

JACKSON: You making a mole hill out of a mountain, sir. But I think I follow you. You know what all this make me decide, pardner?

HARRY: What?

(JACKSON *picks up the umbrella, puts on the goatskin hat.*)

JACKSON: I going back to the gift that's my God-given calling. I benignly resign, you fire me. With inspiration. Caiso is my true work, caiso is my true life.

(*Sings*)

Well, a Limey name Trewe come to Tobago.
He was in show business but he had no show,
so in desperation he turn to me
and said: "Mr. Phillip" is the two o' we,
one classical actor and one Creole,
let we act together with we heart and soul.
It go be man to man, and we go do it fine,
and we go give it the title of pantomime.
La da dee da da da
dee da da da da da . . .

(*He is singing as if in a spotlight. Music, audience applause.* HARRY *joins in.*)

Wait! Wait! Hold it! (*Silence: walks over to* HARRY) Starting from Friday, Robinson, we could talk 'bout a raise?

FADEOUT

Goat-roti, slow-cooked curried goat meat, scooped up with roti, a fried flatbread.

Figure 1. In the first act of the 1981 Arena Stage production of *Pantomime,* directed by Martin Fried, Harry Trewe (Richard Bauer, *right*) pretends to be Friday, kneeling down in obedience to the command of Jackson Phillip (Avery Brooks, *left*), pretending to be Crusoe. (Photograph: Arena Stage Collection, George Mason University Libraries.)

Figure 2. Harry Trewe (Michael Tolaydo), wearing a goatskin cap and carrying a goatskin umbrella, pretends to be Robinson Crusoe, while Jackson Phillip (Doug Brown) watches him. *Pantomime*, at the Round House Theatre, Washington, D.C., 1998, was directed by Scot Reese. (Photograph: Stan Barouh.)

Figure 3. Taking his turn to play Crusoe, Jackson Phillip (Doug Brown) pretends to row his small boat (the upturned table), while Harry Trewe (Michael Tolaydo) looks on, in the 1998 Round House Theatre production. (Photograph: Stan Barouh.)

Figure 4. In the 1998 Round House Theatre production, at the play's emotional climax, Harry Trewe (Michael Tolaydo) reaches for the framed picture of his wife held by Jackson Phillip (Doug Brown). The ice pick, which Trewe will use to attack the "wife," is visible on the table. (Photograph: Stan Barouh.)

Staging of *Pantomime*

INTERVIEW WITH DEREK WALCOTT, 2002, BY ANDREW WILSON

WILSON: *Pantomime* is set in the West Indies but it's been produced throughout the whole English-speaking world. In fact I read in one of the reviews that it's your most produced play. So that suggests it speaks to a lot of people. What are the challenges of producing it in one place rather than in another, say in Scotland rather than in New England?

WALCOTT: I think one of the dangers of [producing the play in] America is that [the conflict of the play] is looked at as a racial conflict, which it is not. It is really a matter of cultural temperament, which has to do with race I guess eventually. But it is also about a man who is very tight-lipped and tight-assed—who is reduced to being more human and not so self-punishing. So that's the core of the thing. It's not a matter of black and white.

WILSON: So you think people get it better in the West Indies, then?

WALCOTT: I think so. I think they may get the comedy of it in terms of watching an Englishman break down that wall, that is part of what we are going through in a way. You see, the guy [Jackson Phillip] wants to help him [Harry Trewe], you know? So Jackson does everything he can do to help. But what one wants to avoid, which is hard to avoid in America, is [the interpretation] that it's a racial conflict about territory. That's not what the core of the play is.

WILSON: Did you become aware of a specific American perspective at the first U.S. staging, at the Arena Stage theater in 1981? Or did you anticipate such a response beforehand?

WALCOTT: I think in America or in England, you know, you put a black guy and a white guy up there and at some point, someone's going to say nigger or something, and that's not what I was after, obviously. It's very hard to avoid that. Also what tends to be overlooked is that Jackson can be an irritating person too, you know . . . I mean, he can be *irritating*. He's overvolatile. However, I think it's the Englishman, Trewe, who is sometimes looked at unsympathetically. So you have to have a very very good English actor, I think, to play up against the black actor. The black actor has the advantage of being dispossessed and disadvantaged when he's playing the role. Therefore the white guy looks like he's penitential about being a slave-owner or master you know—but that's not the point of it. You need an English actor who has a good sense of how his actions can be irritating.

WILSON: Do you have any English actor in mind who's done a particularly good job with this role?

WALCOTT: I've seen quite a few. I can't pinpoint one particular actor. The play has been produced a lot in America, and the Americans . . . It's very hard, without criticism, to get an American actor to get this temperamental thing about Englishmen. Also it's very difficult for [an American] black actor not to have the belligerence that I think a West Indian actor would not have—a sort of bitter belligerence. So to make that balance happen . . . I would give the edge to the English actor rather than the predictable black comic or embittered actor. He [the English actor playing Trewe] is not embittered.

WILSON: You dedicated the role to Wilbert Holder who created the role of Jackson. Could you say a little bit about the actor and how he helped you to imagine the role?

WALCOTT: Well he is a superb actor, an excellent comic—his timing, his diction, very inventive. I've seen him play when he was masterful, a really good actor. And I'm not making provincial comparisons. I've seen very fine actors in my plays in England and America, and Wilbert was certainly equal to the best of them.

WILSON: Can you think of any moments in the play that have seemed particularly challenging for actors? Moments that have caused some kind of difficulty in the productions you've been associated with?

WALCOTT: Well, I think it's very hard sometimes to believe the whole scene where he [Jackson Phillip] uses a photograph and acts the role of [Harry Trewe's ex-] wife. How it's done, it takes a very delicate balance I think between the actor [playing Jackson] getting into the role of the English wife, and the belief on [Trewe's] part. I mean they're attacking the photograph more than the performance in a sense, but I have seen it succeed. Where it hasn't succeeded it's disastrous.*

WILSON: Why is it disastrous?

WALCOTT: Because you don't believe it. Unless it's done right, you don't believe that Harry Trewe would go to such lengths to do what he's doing. You know the hatred of his wife, the confrontation with the photograph, to crack up that much . . . It has to be a kind of role playing thing that has to be very very finely tuned between both actors. I think that's a very hard part.

WILSON: Given the fact that pantomime, role playing, rehearsal, and play acting are the central activities

---

*See Act 2, pp. 1203–4.

of *Pantomime* and the persistent focus of the dialogue in the play between Harry and Jackson, is it fair to say that your play is as much concerned with theater in its potentially transforming power as it is with colonialism, subjugation, etc.?

WALCOTT: Oh definitely. I mean it has to do with these two people being performers. I mean one says "come back into the theater. Perform" And the other guy says "No." And it changes around. Then the other guy says, "*You* come back into the theater." Two actors are on either side saying "Listen, the theater is a purifying thing." Yes, that's the psychodrama part of it.

WILSON: So it's theater as a way of bringing out emotional truth?

WALCOTT: Yes. And of course the ambiguity of acting, which is artificial, becoming real, and reality becoming artifice.

WILSON: What about the role of the literal pantomime? I'm thinking of when Jackson turns the table over, and he's rowing, and he gets shipwrecked. How does that work within the overall play?

WALCOTT: Well, he gets too carried away with performing. He's being challenged as an actor, and the competition is, "Oh you think you're an actor, I'll show you what acting is." But again, you see, if that's taken on an almost absurd level of competition, as two actors competing, that becomes funnier than if it were presented historically or sociologically. I mean he [Jackson] gets so caught up in the part that his vanity makes him take it to absurd lengths. That's what's exasperating to Trewe. Trewe is saying there's a limit to acting, and Jackson is saying "No, I have no limits, I just go on." Trewe is saying "You have to stop," and Jackson says "No, I just go on. Why should I stop? You started me."

WILSON: Do you see the actual pantomime as an ultra-pure form of theater?

WALCOTT: Well, a calypso competition in an arena would be the equivalent of English pantomime. You know there's a dame, and there are songs, and it's corny and funny and so on. That's the English tradition—the music hall thing. We have our own tradition, and the two traditions confront each other. But they're the same. That's the ultimate point. They're the same thing.

WILSON: You once said in an interview that you heard the characters in your head while you were writing *Pantomime,* and that writing the play was like taking dictation.

WALCOTT: That's true. I remember when I was working on it, I could hardly keep up with what I was writing because of the voices . . . Some of this I did directly onto tape, in two voices. I did both voices and then transcribed it.

WILSON: Do you sympathize more with Harry or with Jackson?

WALCOTT: No. I try to create a balance. I take the extremes of either cliché. The given cliché is that the Englishman is tight-lipped and non-confessional, and the black guy is exuberant and shallow. You try to take two extremes and reverse them, so in a sense Harry becomes very very voluble and very talkative, and they change roles. So Jackson behaves like an Englishman sometimes, and Trewe tries to behave like a Calypsonian sometimes. That's the reversal that happens. The roles change.

WILSON: When you were staging the play for the first time, how did you deal with the role of humor? Was the performance meant to be funny in some sections, to make the audience laugh?

WALCOTT: Well the whole intention of a comedy is to make the audience laugh. I hope it's a comedy. What may happen is that what the audience may laugh at in the Caribbean, they may not laugh at in England or in America. Because comedy can be very provincial, you know. Somebody talks in Brooklynese, and that's hilarious to someone from America. Or somebody talks Cockney and that's hilarious. . . . It varies. Ultimately the result is the same if the actors are excellent. But I consider my plays as coming out of the Caribbean. They're not aimed at an international audience as such. They're not trying to be international.

WILSON: Are there any passages that almost always make the audience laugh?

WALCOTT: You know how hard comedy is? That long part with the expletives, about the goat, "fucking goat" and all that—if it doesn't work, it sounds obscene. When it does work, you know . . . the President of Boston University used to crack up. He loved it.

BRIAN FRIEL

1929–

Whether one calls the mythical setting of Brian Friel's major plays Baile Beag or its Anglicized version, Ballybeg, the name still means "small town." And just as a small town can be both comfortable yet stifling, the place to which one returns and the place from which one tries to escape, so Friel's plays repeatedly explore the contradictions of home and family, particularly families confronting their own personal difficulties within the larger sphere of Irish political and social divisions. Though Friel's early schooling was in Derry, the birthplace of his father and the second largest city in Northern Ireland, he often spent holidays in the Donegal countryside—the birthplace of his mother and the locale of his mythical small town Ballybeg. Friel's education took him from Derry to Dublin, where he studied at Ireland's national seminary, and then back to Northern Ireland for a teacher-training course in Belfast. Like his father, Friel became a schoolteacher but also started writing short stories, many of which were published in *The New Yorker*. So successful was his writing that he gave up teaching in 1960, by which time he had also written two radio plays, broadcast in 1958, and a play for the theater.

Friel's first big theatrical success, *Philadelphia, Here I Come!*, opened in Dublin in 1964 and quickly became a hit in New York in 1965. Not only did this play establish Friel as a major talent, but it embodied many of the concerns to which he would return in later plays. Focusing on the last night spent in Ballybeg by the protagonist, Gareth (Gar) O'Donnell, before he leaves for the United States, *Philadelphia, Here I Come!* dramatizes Gar's conflicting feelings by literally splitting him into two separate figures—Public Gar and Private Gar, who are played by two different actors. Though they appear on stage together, Private Gar remains invisible to everyone but the audience; even Public Gar "never sees him and *never looks at him*" for, as Friel makes clear, "One cannot look at one's *alter ego*." This theatrical device exposes Gar's shifting and contradictory feelings about Ballybeg, which Public Gar condemns—"I hate the place, and every stone, and every rock, and every piece of heather around it!"—while Private Gar asks softly, at the play's end, "God, Boy, why do you have to leave? Why? Why?" Though the play presents plenty of answers to that question—a failed romance, a cold and loveless father, a group of friends who seem only too ready to forget Gar—the play's final line from Public Gar reflects his unresolved conflict: "I don't know. I-I-I don't know."

While Friel's use of two actors is central to dramatizing Gar's internal conflict, it also anticipates Friel's later manipulations of character as a means of providing theatrical commentary. In *The Freedom of the City* (1973), for example, Dr. Dodds, a pompous American sociologist, directly addresses the audience with talk about "the subculture of poverty," while the play itself focuses on three victims of that subculture who have accidentally come together in the mayor's office in Derry during a political demonstration. *Living Quarters* (1977) also features a character who stands outside the action—in this case with a ledger-book in which is recorded every event that occurred during the traumatic day when Commandant Frank Butler shot himself. By choosing particular moments to replay, this special commentator, named Sir, represents the mind's power to organize events and make sense of them, in contrast to the emotional turmoil producing the events. And in *Dancing at Lughnasa* (1993), the narrator-commentator is Michael, present both as a seven-year-old child and as his adult self remembering the time during his childhood when his mother was living with her four sisters in a small house near Ballybeg.

Friel's varied theatrical commentators ultimately enable him to explore his conflicting thoughts about Ballybeg itself. While *Philadelphia, Here I Come!* centers around the question of leaving Ballybeg and the sort of small-minded, insular, and stultifying atmosphere represented most clearly by Gar's father, Friel's later plays show Ballybeg as a place to which people return, clinging to their memories of a past that was often happier than the present. Nowhere is that wistful sense of Ballybeg more powerful than in *Dancing at Lughnasa,* whose central characters, the Mundy sisters, seem to lead an unbearably confined existence; their link to a larger world, and their only source of entertainment, is a radio with a battery that keeps failing. But in the middle of the first act, when their radio finally starts working properly, the stage erupts in a spontaneous dance. First Maggie turns from bread-making to dancing, then three of her sisters join in one by one, and finally Kate, the one most tied to "proper" behavior, starts dancing too. Their dancing celebrates the bond between the sisters, as well as the passion and love that support their marginalized existence. Later in the play, in fact, dancing comes to represent "the very heart of life and all its hopes" in a world where "language no longer existed because words were no longer necessary."

But if *Dancing at Lughnasa* presents a world where words finally are not necessary, Friel's *Translations* (1980) centers directly on language and on the significance of language in Ballybeg. Moving back to 1833, a hundred years before the family so lovingly evoked in *Dancing at Lughnasa,* Friel shows us Baile Beag being transformed, or translated, into Ballybeg. Instead of the kinship families who usually inhabit Friel's dramatic worlds, we see a group of people united by their love of learning. These Irish-speaking peasants study in a hedge-school, an independent community-run enterprise that would, by the middle of the nineteenth century, be replaced by state-run, English-only schools. The hedge-school in *Translations* includes an unusual group of adult students, ranging from Jimmy Jack, the Infant Prodigy (actually a man in his sixties) who speaks of the goddess Athene as if she actually existed, to Maire, who dreams of escaping to America, to Sarah, who can barely speak at all. Presenting such a strange group of students together with a teacher, Hugh, who is often drunk and pompous, Friel forces us to ask the question, Why are these people studying classical Greek and Latin?

The language question presented so forcefully at the beginning of the play admits of sharply contrasting answers. Friel may be suggesting that classical languages, though dead, represent the splendid heritage of the past, and that by learning these languages, the early-nineteenth-century figures of the play tacitly associate themselves with the heroic deeds of characters from the *Odyssey* and the *Aeneid.* Or he could be implying that these people are helplessly trapped in their veneration of the past, that they refuse to look toward the future, just as their teacher, Hugh, scoffs at the idea of state-run schools with teachers speaking English. The issue of language is clearly central to the play's action, given the invasion of this small Irish village by English soldiers who come armed not only with weapons but with maps and surveying instruments. As they map the country, they also rename it and thereby dominate it with their own language. No wonder, then, that Friel wrote in a diary, "the naming-taming process is what the play is about." Even Owen, the Irishman who is helping the British, exists for them in his Anglicized name, Roland. While Owen jokes that "it's only a name" and that he is "the same me" anyhow, the play suggests that names constitute identity, whether of individuals or of nations. Complicating the haunting array of questions about whether personal, political, and romantic relationships can transcend the divisiveness of linguistic and cultural differences is Friel's choice to write in English even though many of the characters speak no English at all. Thus, in the play's first scene, all of the natives of Baile Beag are to be understood as speaking Gaelic except when Jimmy reads Greek or Hugh greets his students in Latin or Maire speaks English, but with a "strange" accent. Similarly, the love scene between Maire and Yolland is written as if both are speaking English, but the disconnected lines reveal that Maire is, until she tries Latin, speaking Gaelic and Yolland is speaking English until he tries to communicate through the Irish names he has been writing down.

Produced originally in 1980 by the newly formed Field Day Theatre Company, a company created by Friel and actor Stephen Rea (best known to American audiences for his film work, especially in *The Crying Game*), *Translations* has continued to speak to audiences. When it was revived in London in 1993 at the Donmar Warehouse, critics hailed it as a "modern classic." Recognizing Friel's political and social concerns, they also saw his ability to embody those concerns in human relationships: in the way that Manus, Hugh's older son and assistant teacher, helps Sarah to speak her name (see Figure 1); in the concentration of Jimmy Jack as he expounds Horace to the plodding Doalty who pretends to be interested (Figure 2); and in the shared conviviality of Manus and Owen—the brother who has stayed at home, speaking Irish, and the brother who has left home only to return as assistant to the English (see Figure 3). Such moments of connection are moments to treasure, especially in contrast to the last scene of the play, which reveals the brutality of which both Irish and English are capable. Though Hugh normally evades reality through drink and classical quotations, his stricken disbelief (see Figure 4) reveals the pain that has engulfed the little community. His final lines mourn the downfall of an ancient city, as words from the past hauntingly mourn the destruction of the Irish civilization he, and the playwright, cherish so deeply.

TRANSLATIONS

BY BRIAN FRIEL

for Stephen Rea

CHARACTERS

MANUS
SARAH
JIMMY JACK
MAIRE
DOALTY
BRIDGET
HUGH
OWEN
CAPTAIN LANCEY
LIEUTENANT YOLLAND

SCENE

The action takes place in a hedge-school in the townland of Baile Beag/Ballybeg, an Irish-speaking community in County Donegal.
ACT 1: An afternoon in late August 1833.
ACT 2: A few days later.
ACT 3: The evening of the following day.
One interval—between the two scenes in Act 2.

ACT 1

(The hedge-school is held in a disused barn or hay-shed or byre. Along the back wall are the remains of five or six stalls—wooden posts and chains—where cows were once milked and bedded. A double door left, large enough to allow a cart to enter. A window right. A wooden stairway without a banister leads to the upstairs living-quarters (off) of the schoolmaster and his son. Around the room are broken and forgotten implements: a cart-wheel, some lobster-pots, farming tools, a battle of hay, a churn, etc. There are also the stools and bench-seats which the pupils use and a table and chair for the master. At the door a pail of water and a soiled towel. The room is comfortless and dusty and functional—there is no trace of a woman's hand.

When the play opens, MANUS is teaching SARAH to speak. He kneels beside her. She is sitting on a low stool, her head down, very tense, clutching a slate on her knees. He is coaxing her gently and firmly and—as with everything he does—with a kind of zeal.

MANUS is in his late twenties/early thirties; the master's older son. He is pale-faced, lightly built, intense, and works as an unpaid assistant—a monitor—to his father. His clothes are shabby; and when he moves we see that he is lame.

SARAH's speech defect is so bad that all her life she has been considered locally to be dumb and she has accepted this: when she wishes to communicate, she grunts and makes unintelligible nasal sounds. She has a waiflike appearance and could be any age from seventeen to thirty-five.

JIMMY JACK CASSIE—known as the Infant Prodigy—sits by himself, contentedly reading Homer in Greek and smiling to himself. He is a bachelor in his sixties, lives alone, and comes to these evening classes partly for the company and partly for the intellectual stimulation. He is fluent in Latin and Greek but is in no way pedantic—to him it is perfectly normal to speak these tongues. He never washes. His clothes—heavy top coat, hat, mittens, which he wears now—are filthy and he lives in them summer and winter, day and night. He now reads in a quiet voice and smiles in profound satisfaction. For JIMMY the world of the gods and the ancient myths is as real and as immediate as everyday life in the townland of Baile Beag.

MANUS holds SARAH's hands in his and he articulates slowly and distinctly into her face.)

MANUS: We're doing very well. And we're going to try it once more—just once more. Now—relax and breathe in . . . deep . . . and out . . . in . . . and out . . .

(SARAH shakes her head vigorously and stubbornly.)

Come on, Sarah. This is our secret.

(Again vigorous and stubborn shaking of SARAH's head.)

Nobody's listening. Nobody hears you.

JIMMY: *"Ton d'emeibet epeita thea glaukopis Athene . . ."*°

MANUS: Get your tongue and your lips working. "My name—" Come on. One more try. "My name is—" Good girl.

SARAH: My . . .

MANUS: Great. "My name—"

SARAH: My . . . my . . .

MANUS: Raise your head. Shout it out. Nobody's listening.

JIMMY: *". . . alla hekelos estai en Atreidao domois . . ."*°

MANUS: Jimmy, please! Once more—just once more— "My name—" Good girl. Come on now. Head up. Mouth open.

Ton d'emeibet epeita thea glaukopis Athene, (Lit.) "But the grey-eyed goddess Athene then replied to him" (Homer, *Odyssey*, XIII, 420). **alla hekelos estai en Atreidao domois,** (Lit.) ". . . but he sits at ease in the halls of the Sons of Athens . . ." (Homer, *Odyssey*, XIII, 423–4).

SARAH: My . . .

MANUS: Good.

SARAH: My . . .

MANUS: Great.

SARAH: My name . . .

MANUS: Yes?

SARAH: My name is . . .

MANUS: Yes?

(SARAH *pauses. Then in a rush.*)

SARAH: My name is Sarah.

MANUS: Marvellous! Bloody marvellous!

(MANUS *hugs* SARAH. *She smiles in shy, embarrassed pleasure.*)

Did you hear that, Jimmy?—"My name is Sarah"—clear as a bell.

(*To* SARAH) The Infant Prodigy doesn't know what we're at.

(SARAH *laughs at this.* MANUS *hugs her again and stands up.*)

Now we're really started! Nothing'll stop us now! Nothing in the wide world!

(JIMMY, *chuckling at his text, comes over to them.*)

JIMMY: Listen to this, Manus.

MANUS: Soon you'll be telling me all the secrets that have been in that head of yours all these years. Certainly, James—what is it? (*To* SARAH) Maybe you'd set out the stools?

(MANUS *runs up the stairs.*)

JIMMY: Wait till you hear this, Manus.

MANUS: Go ahead. I'll be straight down.

JIMMY: *"Hos ara min phamene rabdo epemassat Athene—"*° "After Athene had said this, she touched Ulysses with her wand. She withered the fair skin of his supple limbs and destroyed the flaxen hair from off his head and about his limbs she put the skin of an old man . . ."! The divil! The divil!

(MANUS *has emerged again with a bowl of milk and a piece of bread.*)

And wait till you hear! She's not finished with him yet!

(*As* MANUS *descends the stairs he toasts* SARAH *with his bowl.*)

"Knuzosen de oi osse—"° "She dimmed his two eyes that were so beautiful and clothed him in a vile ragged cloak begrimed with filthy smoke . . ."! D'you see! Smoke! Smoke! D'you see! Sure look at what the same turf-smoke has done to myself!

Hos ara min phamene rabdo epemassat Athene, (Lit.) "As she spoke Athene touched him with her wand" (Homer, *Odyssey*, XIII, 429). *Knuzosen de oi osse,* "She dimmed his eyes" (Homer, *Odyssey*, XIII, 433).

(*He rapidly removes his hat to display his bald head.*) Would you call that flaxen hair?

MANUS: Of course I would.

JIMMY: "And about him she cast the great skin of a filthy hind, stripped of the hair, and into his hand she thrust a staff and a wallet"! Ha-ha-ha! Athene did that to Ulysses! Made him into a tramp! Isn't she the tight one?

MANUS: You couldn't watch her, Jimmy.

JIMMY: You know what they call her?

MANUS: *"Glaukopis Athene."*°

JIMMY: That's it! The flashing-eyed Athene! By God, Manus, sir, if you had a woman like that about the house, it's not stripping a turf-bank you'd be thinking about—eh?

MANUS: She was a goddess, Jimmy.

JIMMY: Better still. Sure isn't our own Grania a class of a goddess and—

MANUS: Who?

JIMMY: Grania—Grania—Diarmuid's Grania.

MANUS: Ah.

JIMMY: And sure she can't get her fill of men.

MANUS: Jimmy, you're impossible.

JIMMY: I was just thinking to myself last night: if you had the choosing between Athene and Artemis and Helen of Troy—all three of them Zeus's girls—imagine three powerful-looking daughters like that all in the one parish of Athens!—now, if you had the picking between them, which would you take?

MANUS (*To* SARAH): Which should I take, Sarah?

JIMMY: No harm to Helen; and no harm to Artemis; and indeed no harm to our own Grania, Manus. But I think I've no choice but to go bull-straight for Athene. By God, sir, them flashing eyes would fair keep a man jigged up constant!

(*Suddenly and momentarily, as if in spasm,* JIMMY *stands to attention and salutes, his face raised in pained ecstasy.* MANUS *laughs. So does* SARAH. JIMMY *goes back to his seat, and his reading.*)

MANUS: You're a dangerous bloody man, Jimmy Jack.

JIMMY: "Flashing-eyed"! Hah! Sure Homer knows it all, boy. Homer knows it all.

(MANUS *goes to the window and looks out.*)

MANUS: Where the hell has he got to?

(SARAH *goes to* MANUS *and touches his elbow. She mimes rocking a baby.*)

Yes, I know he's at the christening; but it doesn't take them all day to put a name on a baby, does it?

Glaukopis Athene, (Lit.) flashing-eyed Athena.

(SARAH *mimes pouring drinks and tossing them back quickly.*)

You may be sure. Which pub?

(SARAH *indicates.*)

Gracie's?

(*No. Further away.*)

Con Connie Tim's?

(*No. To the right of there.*)

Anna na mBreag's?

(*Yes. That's it.*)

Great. She'll fill him up. I suppose I may take the class then.

(MANUS *begins to distribute some books, slates and chalk, texts, etc., beside the seats.* SARAH *goes over to the straw and produces a bunch of flowers she has hidden there. During this:*)

JIMMY: "*Autar o ek limenos prosebe*—"° "But Ulysses went forth from the harbour and through the woodland to the place where Athene had shown him he could find the good swineherd who— "*o oi biotoio malista kedeto*"°—what's that, Manus?

MANUS: "Who cared most for his substance."

JIMMY: That's it! "The good swineherd who cared most for his substance above all the slaves that Ulysses possessed . . ."

(SARAH *presents the flowers to* MANUS.)

MANUS: Those are lovely, Sarah.

(*But* SARAH *has fled in embarrassment to her seat and has her head buried in a book.* MANUS *goes to her.*)

Flow-ers.

(*Pause.* SARAH *does not look up.*)

Say the word: flow-ers. Come on—flow-ers.

SARAH: Flowers.

MANUS: You see?—you're off!

(MANUS *leans down and kisses the top of* SARAH*'s head.*)

And they're beautiful flowers. Thank you.

(MAIRE *enters, a strong-minded, strong-bodied woman in her twenties with a head of curly hair. She is carrying a small can of milk.*)

MAIRE: Is this all's here? Is there no school this evening?

MANUS: If my father's not back, I'll take it.

Autar o ek limenos prosebe, (Lit.) "But he went forth from the harbour . . ." (Homer, *Odyssey*, XIV, 1). o oi biotoio mal-ista kedeto, (Lit.) ". . . he cared very much for his substance . . ." (Homer, *Odyssey*, XIV, 3–4).

(MANUS *stands awkwardly, having been caught kissing* SARAH *and with the flowers almost formally at his chest.*)

MAIRE: Well now, isn't that a pretty sight. There's your milk. How's Sarah?

(SARAH *grunts a reply.*)

MANUS: I saw you out at the hay.

(MAIRE *ignores this and goes to* JIMMY.)

MAIRE: And how's Jimmy Jack Cassie?

JIMMY: Sit down beside me, Maire.

MAIRE: Would I be safe?

JIMMY: No safer man in Donegal.

(MAIRE *flops on a stool beside* JIMMY.)

MAIRE: Ooooh. The best harvest in living memory, they say; but I don't want to see another like it. (*Showing* JIMMY *her hands*) Look at the blisters.

JIMMY: *Esne fatigata?*°

MAIRE: *Sum fatigatissima.*°

JIMMY: *Bene! Optime!*°

MAIRE: That's the height of my Latin. Fit me better if I had even that much English.

JIMMY: English? I thought you had some English?

MAIRE: Three words. Wait—there was a spake I used to have off by heart. What's this it was? (*Her accent is strange because she is speaking a foreign language and because she does not understand what she is saying.*) "In Norfolk we besport ourselves around the maypoll." What about that!

MANUS: Maypole.

(*Again* MAIRE *ignores* MANUS.)

MAIRE: God have mercy on my Aunt Mary—she taught me that when I was about four, whatever it means. Do you know what it means, Jimmy?

JIMMY: Sure you know I have only Irish like yourself.

MAIRE: And Latin. And Greek.

JIMMY: I'm telling you a lie: I know one English word.

MAIRE: What?

JIMMY: Bo-som.

MAIRE: What's a bo-som?

JIMMY: You know—(*He illustrates with his hands*)—bo-som—bo-som—you know—Diana, the huntress, she has two powerful bosom.

MAIRE: You may be sure that's the one English word you would know. (*Rises*) Is there a drop of water about?

(MANUS *gives* MAIRE *his bowl of milk.*)

MANUS: I'm sorry I couldn't get up last night.

MAIRE: Doesn't matter.

Esne fatigata? Are you tired? Sum fatigatissima, I am very tired. Bene! Optime! Good! Excellent!

MANUS: Biddy Hanna sent for me to write a letter to her sister in Nova Scotia. All the gossip of the parish. "I brought the cow to the bull three times last week but no good. There's nothing for it now but Big Ned Frank."

MAIRE *(Drinking)*: That's better.

MANUS: And she got so engrossed in it that she forgot who she was dictating to: "The aul drunken schoolmaster and that lame son of his are still footering about in the hedge-school, wasting people's good time and money."

(MAIRE has to laugh at this.)

MAIRE: She did not!

MANUS: And me taking it all down. "Thank God one of them new national schools is being built above at Poll na gCaorach." It was after midnight by the time I got back.

MAIRE: Great to be a busy man.

(MAIRE moves away. MANUS follows.)

MANUS: I could hear music on my way past but I thought it was too late to call.

MAIRE *(To SARAH)*: Wasn't your father in great voice last night?

(SARAH nods and smiles.)

It must have been near three o'clock by the time you got home?

(SARAH holds up four fingers.)

Was it four? No wonder we're in pieces.

MANUS: I can give you a hand at the hay tomorrow.

MAIRE: That's the name of a hornpipe, isn't it?—"The Scholar In The Hayfield"—or is it a reel?

MANUS: If the day's good.

MAIRE: Suit yourself. The English soldiers below in the tents, them sapper fellas, they're coming up to give us a hand. I don't know a word they're saying, nor they me; but sure that doesn't matter, does it?

MANUS: What the hell are you so crabbed about?!

(DOALTY and BRIDGET enter noisily. Both are in their twenties. DOALTY is brandishing a surveyor's pole. He is an open-minded, open-hearted, generous and slightly thick young man. BRIDGET is a plump, fresh young girl, ready to laugh, vain, and with a countrywoman's instinctive cunning. DOALTY enters doing his imitation of the master.)

DOALTY: Vesperal salutations to you all.

BRIDGET: He's coming down past Carraig na Ri and he's as full as a pig!

DOALTY: *Ignari, stulti, rustici°*—pot-boys and peasant whelps—semi-literates and illegitimates.

BRIDGET: He's been on the batter since this morning; he sent the wee ones home at eleven o'clock.

DOALTY: Three questions. Question A—Am I drunk? Question B—Am I sober? *(Into MAIRE's face) Responde—responde!°*

BRIDGET: Question C, Master—When were you last sober?

MAIRE: What's the weapon, Doalty?

BRIDGET: I warned him. He'll be arrested one of these days.

DOALTY: Up in the bog with Bridget and her aul fella, and the Red Coats were just across at the foot of Croc na Mona, dragging them aul chains and peeping through that big machine they lug about everywhere with them—you know the name of it, Manus?

MAIRE: Theodolite.

BRIDGET: How do you know?

MAIRE: They leave it in our byre at night sometimes if it's raining.

JIMMY: Theodolite—what's the etymology of that word, Manus?

MANUS: No idea.

BRIDGET: Get on with the story.

JIMMY: *Theo—theos°*—something to do with a god. Maybe *thea°*—a goddess! What shape's the yoke?

DOALTY: "Shape!" Will you shut up, you aul eejit you! Anyway, every time they'd stick one of these poles into the ground and move across the bog, I'd creep up and shift it twenty or thirty paces to the side.

BRIDGET: God!

DOALTY: Then they'd come back and stare at it and look at their calculations and stare at it again and scratch their heads. And cripes, d'you know what they ended up doing?

BRIDGET: Wait till you hear!

DOALTY: They took the bloody machine apart!

(And immediately he speaks in gibberish—an imitation of two very agitated and confused sappers in rapid conversation.)

BRIDGET: That's the image of them!

MAIRE: You must be proud of yourself, Doalty.

DOALTY: What d'you mean?

MAIRE: That was a very clever piece of work.

MANUS: It was a gesture.

MAIRE: What sort of gesture?

MANUS: Just to indicate . . . a presence.

MAIRE: Hah!

BRIDGET: I'm telling you—you'll be arrested.

(When DOALTY is embarrassed—or pleased—he reacts physically. He now grabs BRIDGET around the waist.)

Ignari, stulti, rustici, Ignoramuses, fools, peasants.

Responde—responde! Answer—answer! **Theo—theos,** a god. **thea,** a goddess.

DOALTY: What d'you make of that for an implement, Bridget? Wouldn't that make a great aul shaft for your churn?

BRIDGET: Let go of me, you dirty brute! I've a head-line to do before Big Hughie comes.

MANUS: I don't think we'll wait for him. Let's get started.

(Slowly, reluctantly they begin to move to their seats and specific tasks. DOALTY *goes to the bucket of water at the door and washes his hands.* BRIDGET *sets up a hand-mirror and combs her hair.)*

BRIDGET: Nellie Ruadh's baby was to be christened this morning. Did any of yous hear what she called it? Did you, Sarah?

*(*SARAH *grunts: No.)*

Did you, Maire?

MAIRE: No.

BRIDGET: Our Seamus says she was threatening she was going to call it after its father.

DOALTY: Who's the father?

BRIDGET: That's the point, you donkey you!

DOALTY: Ah.

BRIDGET: So there's a lot of uneasy bucks about Baile Beag this day.

DOALTY: She told me last Sunday she was going to call it Jimmy.

BRIDGET: You're a liar, Doalty.

DOALTY: Would I tell you a lie? Hi, Jimmy, Nellie Ruadh's aul fella's looking for you.

JIMMY: For me?

MAIRE: Come on, Doalty.

DOALTY: Someone told him . . .

MAIRE: Doalty!

DOALTY: He heard you know the first book of the Satires of Horace off by heart . . .

JIMMY: That's true.

DOALTY: . . . and he wants you to recite it for him.

JIMMY: I'll do that for him certainly, certainly.

DOALTY: He's busting to hear it.

*(*JIMMY *fumbles in his pockets.)*

JIMMY: I came across this last night—this'll interest you—in Book Two of Virgil's *Georgics.*

DOALTY: Be God, that's my territory alright.

BRIDGET: You clown you! *(To* SARAH*)* Hold this for me, would you? *(her mirror)*

JIMMY: Listen to this, Manus. *"Nigra fere et presso pinguis sub vomere terra . . ."*°

DOALTY: Steady on now—easy, boys, easy—don't rush me, boys—

Nigra fere et presso pinguis sub vomere terra, Land that is black and rich beneath the pressure of the plough.

(He mimes great concentration.)

JIMMY: Manus?

MANUS: "Land that is black and rich beneath the pressure of the plough . . ."

DOALTY: Give *me* a chance!

JIMMY: "And with *cui putre*—with crumbly soil—is in the main best for corn." There you are!

DOALTY: There you are.

JIMMY: "From no other land will you see more wagons wending homeward behind slow bullocks." Virgil! There!

DOALTY: "Slow bullocks"!

JIMMY: Isn't that what I'm always telling you? Black soil for corn. *That's* what you should have in that upper field of yours—corn, not spuds.

DOALTY: Would you listen to that fella! Too lazy be Jasus to wash himself and he's lecturing me on agriculture! Would you go and take a running race at yourself, Jimmy Jack Cassie! *(Grabs* SARAH*)* Come away out of this with me, Sarah, and we'll plant some corn together.

MANUS: All right—all right. Let's settle down and get some work done. I know Sean Beag isn't com-ing—he's at the salmon. What about the Don-nelly twins? *(To* DOALTY*)* Are the Donnelly twins not coming any more?

*(*DOALTY *shrugs and turns away.)*

Did you ask them?

DOALTY: Haven't seen them. Not about these days.

*(*DOALTY *begins whistling through his teeth. Suddenly the atmosphere is silent and alert.)*

MANUS: Aren't they at home?

DOALTY: No.

MANUS: Where are they then?

DOALTY: How would I know?

BRIDGET: Our Seamus says two of the soldiers' horses were found last night at the foot of the cliffs at Machaire Buidhe and . . . *(She stops suddenly and begins writing with chalk on her slate.)* D'you hear the whistles of this aul slate? Sure nobody could write on an aul slippery thing like that.

MANUS: What headline did my father set you?

BRIDGET: "It's easier to stamp out learning than to recall it."

JIMMY: Book Three, the *Agricola* of Tacitus.

BRIDGET: God but you're a dose.

MANUS: Can you do it?

BRIDGET: There. Is it bad? Will he ate me?

MANUS: It's very good. Keep your elbow in closer to your side. Doalty?

DOALTY: I'm at the seven-times table. I'm perfect, skipper.

*(*MANUS *moves to* SARAH*.)*

MANUS: Do you understand those sums?

(SARAH *nods: Yes.* MANUS *leans down to her ear.*)

My name is Sarah.

(MANUS *goes to* MAIRE. *While he is talking to her the others swop books, talk quietly, etc.*)

MANUS: Can I help you? What are you at?

MAIRE: Map of America. (*Pause*) The passage money came last Friday.

MANUS: You never told me that.

MAIRE: Because I haven't seen you since, have I?

MANUS: You don't want to go. You said that yourself.

MAIRE: There's ten below me to be raised and no man in the house. What do you suggest?

MANUS: Do you want to go?

MAIRE: Did you apply for that job in the new national school?

MANUS: No.

MAIRE: You said you would.

MANUS: I said I might.

MAIRE: When it opens, this is finished: nobody's going to pay to go to a hedge-school.

MANUS: I know that and I . . . (*He breaks off because he sees* SARAH, *obviously listening, at his shoulder. She moves away again.*) I was thinking that maybe I could . . .

MAIRE: It's £56 a year you're throwing away.

MANUS: I can't apply for it.

MAIRE: You *promised* me you would.

MANUS: My father has applied for it.

MAIRE: He has not!

MANUS: Day before yesterday.

MAIRE: For God's sake, sure you know he'd never—

MANUS: I couldn't—I can't go in against him.

(MAIRE *looks at him for a second. Then:—*)

MAIRE: Suit yourself. (*To* BRIDGET) I saw your Seamus heading off to the Port fair early this morning.

BRIDGET: And wait till you hear this—I forgot to tell you this. He said that as soon as he crossed over the gap at Cnoc na Mona—just beyond where the soldiers are making the maps—the sweet smell was everywhere.

DOALTY: You never told me that.

BRIDGET: It went out of my head.

DOALTY: He saw the crops in Port?

BRIDGET: Some.

MANUS: How did the tops look?

BRIDGET: Fine—I think.

DOALTY: In flower?

BRIDGET: I don't know. I think so. He didn't say.

MANUS: Just the sweet smell—that's all?

BRIDGET: They say that's the way it snakes in, don't they? First the smell; and then one morning the stalks are all black and limp.

DOALTY: Are you stupid? It's the rotting stalks makes the sweet smell for God's sake. That's what the smell is—rotting stalks.

MAIRE: Sweet smell! Sweet smell! Every year at this time somebody comes back with stories of the sweet smell. Sweet God, did the potatoes ever fail in Baile Beag? Well, did they ever—ever? Never! There was never blight here. Never. Never. But we're always sniffing about for it, aren't we?—looking for disaster. The rents are going to go up again—the harvest's going to be lost—the herring have gone away for ever—there's going to be evictions. Honest to God, some of you people aren't happy unless you're miserable and you'll not be right content until you're dead!

DOALTY: Bloody right, Maire. And sure St Colmcille prophesied there'd never be blight here. He said:

The spuds will bloom in Baile Beag
Till rabbits grow an extra lug.

And sure that'll never be. So we're all right. Seven threes are twenty-one; seven fours are twenty-eight; seven fives are forty-nine—Hi, Jimmy, do you fancy my chances as boss of the new national school?

JIMMY: What's that?—what's that?

DOALTY: Agh, g'way back home to Greece, son.

MAIRE: You ought to apply, Doalty.

DOALTY: D'you think so? Cripes, maybe I will. Hah!

BRIDGET: Did you know that you start at the age of six and you have to stick at it until you're twelve at least—no matter how smart you are or how much you know.

DOALTY: Who told you that yarn?

BRIDGET: And every child from every house has to go all day, every day, summer or winter. That's the law.

DOALTY: I'll tell you something—nobody's going to go near them—they're not going to take on—law or no law.

BRIDGET: And everything's free in them. You pay for nothing except the books you use; that's what our Seamus says.

DOALTY: "Our Seamus." Sure your Seamus wouldn't pay anyway. She's making this all up.

BRIDGET: Isn't that right, Manus?

MANUS: I think so.

BRIDGET: And from the very first day you go, you'll not hear one word of Irish spoken. You'll be taught to speak English and every subject will be taught through English and everyone'll end up as cute as the Buncrana people.

(SARAH *suddenly grunts and mimes a warning that the master is coming. The atmosphere changes. Sudden business. Heads down.*)

DOALTY: He's here, boys. Cripes, he'll make yella meal out of me for those bloody tables.

BRIDGET: Have you any extra chalk, Manus?

MAIRE: And the atlas for me.

(DOALTY *goes to* MAIRE *who is sitting on a stool at the back.*)

DOALTY: Swop you seats.

MAIRE: Why?

DOALTY: There's an empty one beside the Infant Prodigy.

MAIRE: I'm fine here.

DOALTY: Please, Maire. I want to jouk in the back here.

(MAIRE *rises.*)

God love you. (*Aloud*) Anyone got a bloody table-book? Cripes, I'm wrecked.

(SARAH *gives him one.*)

God, I'm dying about you.

(*In his haste to get to the back seat,* DOALTY *bumps into* BRIDGET *who is kneeling on the floor and writing laboriously on a slate resting on top of a bench-seat.*)

BRIDGET: Watch where you're going, Doalty!

(DOALTY *gooses* BRIDGET. *She squeals. Now the quiet hum of work:* JIMMY *reading Homer in a low voice;* BRIDGET *copying her headline;* MAIRE *studying the atlas;* DOALTY, *his eyes shut tight, mouthing his tables;* SARAH *doing sums. After a few seconds:—*)

Is this "g" right, Manus? How do you put a tail on it?

DOALTY: Will you shut up! I can't concentrate!

(*A few more seconds of work. Then* DOALTY *opens his eyes and looks around.*)

False alarm, boys. The bugger's not coming at all. Sure the bugger's hardly fit to walk.

(*And immediately* HUGH *enters. A large man, with residual dignity, shabbily dressed, carrying a stick. He has, as always, a large quantity of drink taken, but he is by no means drunk. He is in his early sixties.*)

HUGH: *Adsum,*° Doalty, *adsum.* Perhaps not in *sobrietate perfecta*° but adequately *sobrius*° to overhear your quip. Vesperal salutations to you all.

(*Various responses.*)

JIMMY: *Ave,*° Hugh.

HUGH: James. (*He removes his hat and coat and hands them and his stick to* MANUS, *as if to a footman.*) Apologies for my late arrival: we were celebrating the baptism of Nellie Ruadh's baby.

BRIDGET (*Innocently*): What name did she put on it, Master?

HUGH: Was it Eamon? Yes, it was Eamon.

BRIDGET: Eamon Donal from Tor! Cripes!

HUGH: And after the *caerimonia nominationis*°—Maire?

MAIRE: The ritual of naming.

HUGH: Indeed—we then had a few libations to mark the occasion. Altogether very pleasant. The derivation of the word "baptize"?—where are my Greek scholars? Doalty?

DOALTY: Would it be—ah—ah—

HUGH: Too slow. James?

JIMMY: "*Baptizein*"°—to dip or immerse.

HUGH: Indeed—our friend Pliny Minor speaks of the "*baptisterium*"—the cold bath.

DOALTY: Master.

HUGH: Doalty?

DOALTY: I suppose you could talk then about baptizing a sheep at sheep-dipping, could you?

(*Laughter. Comments.*)

HUGH: Indeed—the precedent is there—the day you were appropriately named Doalty—seven nines?

DOALTY: What's that, Master?

HUGH: Seven times nine?

DOALTY: Seven nines—seven nines—seven times nine—seven times nine are—cripes, it's on the tip of my tongue, Master—I knew it for sure this morning—funny that's the only one that foxes me—

BRIDGET (*Prompt*): Sixty-three.

DOALTY: What's wrong with me: sure seven nines are fifty-three, Master.

HUGH: Sophocles from Colonus would agree with Doalty Dan Doalty from Tulach Alainn: "To know nothing is the sweetest life." Where's Sean Beag?

MANUS: He's at the salmon.

HUGH: And Nora Dan?

MAIRE: She says she's not coming back any more.

HUGH: Ah. Nora Dan can now write her name—Nora Dan's education is complete. And the Donnelly twins?

(*Brief pause. Then:—*)

BRIDGET: They're probably at the turf. (*She goes to* HUGH.) There's the one-and-eight I owe you for last quarter's arithmetic and there's my one-and-six for this quarter's writing.

HUGH: *Gratias tibi ago.*° (*He sits at his table.*) Before we commence our *studia*° I have three items of infor-

---

Adsum, I am present.   *sobrietate perfecta,* with complete sobriety.   *sobrius,* sober.   *ave,* hail.

caerimonia nominationis, ceremony of naming. *Baptizein,* to dip or immerse. *baptisterium,* a cold bath, swimming-pool. *Gratias tibi ago,* I thank you. *studia,* studies.

mation to impart to you—*(To* MANUS*)* A bowl of tea, strong tea, black—

*(*MANUS *leaves.)*

Item A: on my perambulations today—Bridget? Too slow. Maire?

MAIRE: *Perambulare°*—to walk about.

HUGH: Indeed—I encountered Captain Lancey of the Royal Engineers who is engaged in the ordnance survey of this area. He tells me that in the past few days two of his horses have strayed and some of his equipment seems to be mislaid. I expressed my regret and suggested he address you himself on these matters. He then explained that he does not speak Irish. Latin? I asked. None. Greek? Not a syllable. He speaks—on his own admission—only English; and to his credit he seemed suitably verecund—James?

JIMMY: *Verecundus°*—humble.

HUGH: Indeed—he voiced some surprise that we did not speak his language. I explained that a few of us did, on occasion—outside the parish of course—and then usually for the purposes of commerce, a use to which his tongue seemed particularly suited—*(Shouts)* and a slice of soda bread—and I went on to propose that our own culture and the classical tongues made a happier conjugation—Doalty?

DOALTY: *Conjugo°*—I join together.

*(*DOALTY *is so pleased with himself that he prods and winks at* BRIDGET.*)*

HUGH: Indeed—English, I suggested, couldn't really express us. And again to his credit he acquiesced to my logic. Acquiesced—Maire?

*(*MAIRE *turns away impatiently.* HUGH *is unaware of the gesture.)*

Too slow. Bridget?

BRIDGET: *Acquiesco.°*

HUGH: *Procede.°*

BRIDGET: *Acquiesco, acquiescere, acquievi, acquietum.*

HUGH: Indeed—and Item B . . .

MAIRE: Master.

HUGH: Yes?

*(*MAIRE *gets to her feet uneasily but determinedly. Pause.)*

Well, girl?

MAIRE: We should all be learning to speak English. That's what my mother says. That's what I say. That's what Dan O'Connell said last month in Ennis. He said the sooner we all learn to speak English the better. *(Suddenly several speak together.)*

JIMMY: What's she saying? What? What?

DOALTY: It's Irish he uses when he's travelling around scrounging votes.

BRIDGET: And sleeping with married women. Sure no woman's safe from that fella.

JIMMY: Who-who-who? Who's this? Who's this?

HUGH: *Silentium!°* *(Pause)* Who is she talking about?

MAIRE: I'm talking about Daniel O'Connell.

HUGH: Does she mean that little Kerry politician?

MAIRE: I'm talking about the Liberator, Master, as you well know. And what he said was this: "The old language is a barrier to modern progress." He said that last month. And he's right. I don't want Greek. I don't want Latin. I want English.

*(*MANUS *reappears on the platform above.)*

I want to be able to speak English because I'm going to America as soon as the harvest's all saved.

*(*MAIRE *remains standing.* HUGH *puts his hand into his pocket and produces a flask of whiskey. He removes the cap, pours a drink into it, tosses it back, replaces the cap, puts the flask back into his pocket. Then:—)*

HUGH: We have been diverted—*diverto—divertere°*—Where were we?

DOALTY: Three items of information, Master. You're at Item B.

HUGH: Indeed—Item B—Item B—yes—On my way to the christening this morning I chanced to meet Mr George Alexander, Justice of the Peace. We discussed the new national school. Mr Alexander invited me to take charge of it when it opens. I thanked him and explained that I could do that only if I were free to run it as I have run this hedge-school for the past thirty-five years—filling what our friend Euripides calls the *"aplestos pithos"°*—James?

JIMMY: "The cask that cannot be filled."

HUGH: Indeed, and Mr Alexander retorted courteously and emphatically that he hopes that is how it will be run.

*(*MAIRE *now sits.)*

Indeed. I have had a strenuous day and I am weary of you all. *(He rises.)* Manus will take care of you.

*(*HUGH *goes towards the steps.* OWEN *enters.* OWEN *is the younger son, a handsome, attractive young man in his twenties. He is dressed smartly—a city man. His manner is easy and charming: everything he does is invested with consideration and enthusiasm. He now stands framed in the doorway, a travelling bag across his shoulder.)*

Perambulare, to walk through. *Verecundus,* shamefaced, modest. *Conjugo,* I join together. *Acquiesco,* to rest, to find comfort in. *Procede,* proceed.

Silentium! Silence! *diverto—divertere,* to turn away. *aplestos pithos,* unfillable cask.

OWEN: Could anybody tell me is this where Hugh Mor O'Donnell holds his hedge-school?

DOALTY: It's Owen—Owen Hugh! Look, boys—it's Owen Hugh!

(OWEN *enters. As he crosses the room he touches and has a word for each person.*)

OWEN: Doalty! *(Playful punch)* How are you, boy? *Jacobe, quid agis?*° Are you well?

JIMMY: Fine. Fine.

OWEN: And Bridget! Give us a kiss. Aaaaaah!

BRIDGET: You're welcome, Owen.

OWEN: It's not—? Yes, it *is* Maire Chatach! God! A young woman!

MAIRE: How are you, Owen?

(OWEN *is now in front of* HUGH. *He puts his two hands on his* FATHER's *shoulders.*)

OWEN: And how's the old man himself?

HUGH: Fair—fair.

OWEN: Fair? For God's sake you never looked better! Come here to me. *(He embraces* HUGH *warmly and genuinely.)* Great to see you, Father. Great to be back.

(HUGH's *eyes are moist—partly joy, partly the drink.*)

HUGH: I—I'm—I'm—pay no attention to—

OWEN: Come on—come on—come on—*(He gives* HUGH *his handkerchief.)* Do you know what you and I are going to do tonight? We are going to go up to Anna na mBreag's . . .

DOALTY: Not there, Owen.

OWEN: Why not?

DOALTY: Her poteen's worse than ever.

BRIDGET: They say she puts frogs in it!

OWEN: All the better. *(To* HUGH*)* And you and I are going to get footless drunk. That's arranged.

(OWEN *sees* MANUS *coming down the steps with tea and soda bread. They meet at the bottom.*)

And Manus!

MANUS: You're welcome, Owen.

OWEN: I know I am. And it's great to be here. *(He turns round, arms outstretched.)* I can't believe it. I come back after six years and everything's just as it was! Nothing's changed! Not a thing! *(Sniffs)* Even that smell—that's the same smell this place always had. What is it anyway? Is it the straw?

DOALTY: Jimmy Jack's feet.

(*General laughter. It opens little pockets of conversation round the room.*)

OWEN: And Doalty Dan Doalty hasn't changed either!

DOALTY: Bloody right, Owen.

OWEN: Jimmy, are you well?

JIMMY: Dodging about.

OWEN: Any word of the big day?

(*This is greeted with "ohs" and "ahs."*)

Time enough, Jimmy. Homer's easier to live with, isn't he?

MAIRE: We heard stories that you own ten big shops in Dublin—is it true?

OWEN: Only nine.

BRIDGET: And you've twelve horses and six servants.

OWEN: Yes—that's true. God Almighty, would you listen to them—taking a hand at me!

MANUS: When did you arrive?

OWEN: We left Dublin yesterday morning, spent last night in Omagh and got here half an hour ago.

MANUS: You're hungry then.

HUGH: Indeed—get him food—get him a drink.

OWEN: Not now, thanks; later. Listen—am I interrupting you all?

HUGH: By no means. We're finished for the day.

OWEN: Wonderful. I'll tell you why. Two friends of mine are waiting outside the door. They'd like to meet you and I'd like you to meet them. May I bring them in?

HUGH: Certainly. You'll all eat and have . . .

OWEN: Not just yet, Father. You've seen the sappers working in this area for the past fortnight, haven't you? Well, the older man is Captain Lancey . . .

HUGH: I've met Captain Lancey.

OWEN: Great. He's the cartographer in charge of this whole area. Cartographer—James?

(OWEN *begins to play this game—his father's game—partly to involve his classroom audience, partly to show he has not forgotten it, and indeed partly because he enjoys it.*)

JIMMY: A maker of maps.

OWEN: Indeed—and the younger man that I travelled with from Dublin, his name is Lieutenant Yolland and he is attached to the toponymic department—Father?—*responde—responde!*

HUGH: He gives names to places.

OWEN: Indeed—although he is in fact an orthographer—Doalty?—too slow—Manus?

MANUS: The correct spelling of those names.

OWEN: Indeed—indeed!

(OWEN *laughs and claps his hands. Some of the others join in.*)

Beautiful! Beautiful! Honest to God, it's such a delight to be back here with you all again—"civilized" people. Anyhow—may I bring them in?

HUGH: Your friends are our friends.

OWEN: I'll be straight back.

(*There is general talk as* OWEN *goes towards the door. He stops beside* SARAH.)

OWEN: That's a new face. Who are you? *(A very brief hesitation. Then:—)*

Jacobe, quid agis? James, how are you?

SARAH: My name is Sarah.

OWEN: Sarah who?

SARAH: Sarah Johnny Sally.

OWEN: Of course! From Bun na hAbhann! I'm Owen—Owen Hugh Mor. From Baile Beag. Good to see you.

(*During this* OWEN–SARAH *exchange.*)

HUGH: Come on now. Let's tidy this place up. (*He rubs the top of his table with his sleeve.*) Move, Doalty—lift those books off the floor.

DOALTY: Right, Master; certainly, Master; I'm doing my best, Master.

(OWEN *stops at the door.*)

OWEN: One small thing, Father.

HUGH: *Silentium!*

OWEN: I'm on their pay-roll.

(SARAH, *very elated at her success, is beside* MANUS.)

SARAH: I said it, Manus!

(MANUS *ignores* SARAH. *He is much more interested in* OWEN *now.*)

MANUS: You haven't enlisted, have you?!

(SARAH *moves away.*)

OWEN: Me a soldier? I'm employed as a part-time, underpaid, civilian interpreter. My job is to translate the quaint, archaic tongue you people persist in speaking into the King's good English. (*He goes out.*)

HUGH: Move—move—move! Put some order on things! Come on, Sarah—hide that bucket. Whose are these slates? Somebody take these dishes away. *Festinate!*° *Festinate!*

(MANUS *goes to* MAIRE *who is busy tidying.*)

MANUS: You didn't tell me you were definitely leaving.

MAIRE: Not now.

HUGH: Good girl, Bridget. That's the style.

MANUS: You might at least have told me.

HUGH: Are these your books, James?

JIMMY: Thank you.

MANUS: Fine! Fine! Go ahead! Go ahead!

MAIRE: You talk to me about getting married—with neither a roof over your head nor a sod of ground under your foot. I suggest you go for the new school; but no—"My father's in for that." Well now he's got it and now this is finished and now you've nothing.

MANUS: I can always . . .

MAIRE: What? Teach classics to the cows? Agh—

(MAIRE *moves away from* MANUS. OWEN *enters with* LANCEY *and* YOLLAND. CAPTAIN LANCEY *is middle-aged; a small, crisp officer, expert in his field as cartographer but uneasy with people—especially civilians, especially these foreign civilians. His skill is with deeds, not words.* LIEUTENANT YOLLAND *is in his late twenties/early thirties. He is tall and thin and gangling, blond hair, a shy, awkward manner. A soldier by accident.*)

OWEN: Here we are. Captain Lancey—my father.

LANCEY: Good evening.

(HUGH *becomes expansive, almost courtly, with his visitors.*)

HUGH: You and I have already met, sir.

LANCEY: Yes.

OWEN: And Lieutenant Yolland—both Royal Engineers—my father.

HUGH: You're very welcome, gentlemen.

YOLLAND: How do you do.

HUGH: *Gaudeo vos hic adesse.*°

OWEN: And I'll make no other introductions except that these are some of the people of Baile Beag and—what?—well you're among the best people in Ireland now. (*He pauses to allow* LANCEY *to speak.* LANCEY *does not.*) Would you like to say a few words, Captain?

HUGH: What about a drop, sir?

LANCEY: A what?

HUGH: Perhaps a modest refreshment? A little sampling of our *aqua vitae?*

LANCEY: No, no.

HUGH: Later perhaps when—

LANCEY: I'll say what I have to say, if I may, and as briefly as possible. Do they speak *any* English, Roland?

OWEN: Don't worry. I'll translate.

LANCEY: I see. (*He clears his throat. He speaks as if he were addressing children—a shade too loudly and enunciating excessively.*) You may have seen me—seen me—working in this section—section?—working. We are here—here—in this place—you understand?—to make a map—a map—a map and—

JIMMY: *Nonne Latine loquitur?*°

(HUGH *holds up a restraining hand.*)

HUGH: James.

LANCEY (*To* JIMMY): I do not speak Gaelic, sir. (*He looks at* OWEN.)

OWEN: Carry on.

LANCEY: A map is a representation on paper—a picture—you understand picture?—a paper picture—showing, representing this country—yes?—showing your country in miniature—a scaled drawing on paper of—of—of—

Festinate! Hurry!   ***Gaudeo vos hic adesse,*** Welcome.   ***Nonne Latine loquitur?*** Does he not speak Latin?

(Suddenly DOALTY *sniggers. Then* BRIDGET. *Then* SARAH. OWEN *leaps in quickly.)*

OWEN: It might be better if you *assume* they understand you—

LANCEY: Yes?

OWEN: And I'll translate as you go along.

LANCEY: I see. Yes. Very well. Perhaps you're right. Well. What we are doing is this. *(He looks at* OWEN. OWEN *nods reassuringly.)* His Majesty's government has ordered the first ever comprehensive survey of this entire country—a general triangulation which will embrace detailed hydrographic and topographic information and which will be executed to a scale of six inches to the English mile.

HUGH *(Pouring a drink)*: Excellent—excellent.

*(*LANCEY *looks at* OWEN.*)*

OWEN: A new map is being made of the whole country.

*(*LANCEY *looks to* OWEN: *Is that all?* OWEN *smiles reassuringly and indicates to proceed.)*

LANCEY: This enormous task has been embarked on so that the military authorities will be equipped with up-to-date and accurate information on every corner of this part of the Empire.

OWEN: The job is being done by soldiers because they are skilled in this work.

LANCEY: And also so that the entire basis of land valuation can be reassessed for purposes of more equitable taxation.

OWEN: This new map will take the place of the estate agent's map so that from now on you will know exactly what is yours in law.

LANCEY: In conclusion I wish to quote two brief extracts from the white paper which is our governing charter: *(Reads)* "All former surveys of Ireland originated in forfeiture and violent transfer of property; the present survey has for its object the relief which can be afforded to the proprietors and occupiers of land from unequal taxation."

OWEN: The captain hopes that the public will cooperate with the sappers and that the new map will mean that taxes are reduced.

HUGH: A worthy enterprise—*opus honestum!*° And Extract B?

LANCEY: "Ireland is privileged. No such survey is being undertaken in England. So this survey cannot but be received as proof of the disposition of this government to advance the interests of Ireland." My sentiments, too.

OWEN: This survey demonstrates the government's interest in Ireland and the captain thanks you for listening so attentively to him.

---

opus honestum! an honourable task.

HUGH: Our pleasure, Captain.

LANCEY: Lieutenant Yolland?

YOLLAND: I—I—I've nothing to say—really—

OWEN: The captain is the man who actually makes the new map. George's task is to see that the place-names on this map are . . . correct. *(To* YOLLAND*)* Just a few words—they'd like to hear you. *(To class)* Don't you want to hear George, too?

MAIRE: Has he anything to say?

YOLLAND *(To* MAIRE*)*: Sorry—sorry?

OWEN: She says she's dying to hear you.

YOLLAND *(To* MAIRE*)*: Very kind of you—thank you . . . *(To class)* I can only say that I feel—I feel very foolish to—to—to be working here and not to speak your language. But I intend to rectify that—with Roland's help—indeed I do.

OWEN: He wants me to teach him Irish!

HUGH: You are doubly welcome, sir.

YOLLAND: I think your countryside is—is—is—is very beautiful. I've fallen in love with it already. I hope we're not too—too crude an intrusion on your lives. And I know that I'm going to be happy, very happy, here.

OWEN: He is already a committed Hibernophile—

JIMMY: He loves—

OWEN: All right, Jimmy—we know—he loves Baile Beag; and he loves you all.

HUGH: Please . . . May I . . . ?

*(*HUGH *is now drunk. He holds on to the edge of the table.)*

OWEN: Go ahead, Father. *(Hands up for quiet)* Please—please.

HUGH: And we, gentlemen, we in turn are happy to offer you our friendship, our hospitality, and every assistance that you may require. Gentlemen—welcome!

(A few desultory claps. The formalities are over. General conversation. The soldiers meet the locals. MANUS *and* OWEN *meet down stage.)*

OWEN: Lancey's a bloody ramrod but George's all right. How are you anyway?

MANUS: What sort of a translation was that, Owen?

OWEN: Did I make a mess of it?

MANUS: You weren't saying what Lancey was saying!

OWEN: "Uncertainty in meaning is incipient poetry"—who said that?

MANUS: There was nothing uncertain about what Lancey said: it's a bloody military operation, Owen! And what's Yolland's function? What's "incorrect" about the place-names we have here?

OWEN: Nothing at all. They're just going to be standardized.

MANUS: You mean changed into English?

OWEN: Where there's ambiguity, they'll be Anglicized.

MANUS: And they call you Roland! They both call you Roland!

OWEN: Shhhhh. Isn't it ridiculous? They seemed to get it wrong from the very beginning—or else they can't pronounce Owen. I was afraid some of you bastards would laugh.

MANUS: Aren't you going to tell them?

OWEN: Yes—yes—soon—soon.

MANUS: But they . . .

OWEN: Easy, man, easy. Owen—Roland—what the hell. It's only a name. It's the same me, isn't it? Well, isn't it?

MANUS: Indeed it is. It's the same Owen.

OWEN: And the same Manus. And in a way we complement each other. (*He punches* MANUS *lightly, playfully and turns to join the others. As he goes*) All right—who has met whom? Isn't this a job for the go-between?

(MANUS *watches* OWEN *move confidently across the floor, taking* MAIRE *by the hand and introducing her to* YOLLAND. HUGH *is trying to negotiate the steps.* JIMMY *is lost in a text.* DOALTY *and* BRIDGET *are reliving their giggling.* SARAH *is staring at* MANUS.)

ACT 2 / SCENE 1

(*The sappers have already mapped most of the area.* YOLLAND*'s official task, which* OWEN *is now doing, is to take each of the Gaelic names—every hill, stream, rock, even every patch of ground which possessed its own distinctive Irish name—and Anglicize it, either by changing it into its approximate English sound or by translating it into English words. For example, a Gaelic name like Cnoc Ban could become Knockban or—directly translated—Fair Hill. These new standardized names were entered into the Name-Book, and when the new maps appeared they contained all these new Anglicized names.* OWEN*'s official function as translator is to pronounce each name in Irish and then provide the English translation.*

The hot weather continues. It is late afternoon some days later.

Stage right: an improvised clothes-line strung between the shafts of the cart and a nail in the wall; on it are some shirts and socks.

A large map—one of the new blank maps—is spread out on the floor. OWEN *is on his hands and knees, consulting it. He is totally engrossed in his task which he pursues with great energy and efficiency.*

YOLLAND*'s hesitancy has vanished—he is at home here now. He is sitting on the floor, his long legs stretched out before him, his back resting against a creel, his eyes closed. His mind is elsewhere. One of the reference books—a church registry—lies open on his lap.*

Around them are various reference books, the Name-Book, a bottle of poteen, some cups, etc.

OWEN *completes an entry in the Name-Book and returns to the map on the floor.*)

OWEN: Now. Where have we got to? Yes—the point where that stream enters the sea—that tiny little beach there. George!

YOLLAND: Yes. I'm listening. What do you call it? Say the Irish name again?

OWEN: Bun na hAbhann.

YOLLAND: Again.

OWEN: Bun na hAbhann.

YOLLAND: Bun na hAbhann.

OWEN: That's terrible, George.

YOLLAND: I know. I'm sorry. Say it again.

OWEN: Bun na hAbhann.

YOLLAND: Bun na hAbhann.

OWEN: That's better. Bun is the Irish word for bottom. And Abha means river. So it's literally the mouth of the river.

YOLLAND: Let's leave it alone. There's no English equivalent for a sound like that.

OWEN: What is it called in the church registry?

(*Only now does* YOLLAND *open his eyes.*)

YOLLAND: Let's see . . . Banowen.

OWEN: That's wrong. (*Consults text*) The list of freeholders calls it Owenmore—that's completely wrong: Owenmore's the big river at the west end of the parish. (*Another text*) And in the grand jury lists it's called—God!—Binhone!—wherever they got that. I suppose we could Anglicize it to Bunowen; but somehow that's neither fish nor flesh.

(YOLLAND *closes his eyes again.*)

YOLLAND: I give up.

OWEN (*At map*): Back to first principles. What are we trying to do?

YOLLAND: Good question.

OWEN: We are trying to denominate and at the same time describe that tiny area of soggy, rocky, sandy ground where that little stream enters the sea, an area known locally as Bun na hAbhann . . . Burnfoot! What about Burnfoot?

YOLLAND (*Indifferently*): Good, Roland, Burnfoot's good.

OWEN: George, my name isn't . . .

YOLLAND: B-u-r-n-f-o-o-t?

OWEN: Are you happy with that?

YOLLAND: Yes.

OWEN: Burnfoot it is then. (*He makes the entry into the Name-Book.*) Bun na hAbhann—B-u-r-n-

YOLLAND: You're becoming very skilled at this.

OWEN: We're not moving fast enough.

YOLLAND (*Opens eyes again*): Lancey lectured me again last night.

OWEN: When does he finish here?

YOLLAND: The sappers are pulling out at the end of the week. The trouble is, the maps they've completed can't be printed without these names. So London screams at Lancey and Lancey screams at me. But I wasn't intimidated.

(MANUS *emerges from upstairs and descends.*)

"I'm sorry, sir," I said, "But certain tasks demand their own tempo. You cannot rename a whole country overnight." Your Irish air has made me bold. *(To* MANUS*)* Do you want us to leave?

MANUS: Time enough. Class won't begin for another half-hour.

YOLLAND: Sorry—sorry?

OWEN: Can't you speak English?

(MANUS *gathers the things off the clothes-line.* OWEN *returns to the map.*)

OWEN: We now come across that beach . . .

YOLLAND: Tra—that's the Irish for beach. *(To* MANUS*)* I'm picking up the odd word, Manus.

MANUS: So.

OWEN: . . . on past Burnfoot; and there's nothing around here that has any name that I know of until we come down here to the south end, just about here . . . and there should be a ridge of rocks there . . . Have the sappers marked it? They have. Look, George.

YOLLAND: Where are we?

OWEN: There.

YOLLAND: I'm lost.

OWEN: Here. And the name of that ridge is Druim Dubh. Put English on that, Lieutenant.

YOLLAND: Say it again.

OWEN: Druim Dubh.

YOLLAND: Dubh means black.

OWEN: Yes.

YOLLAND: And Druim means . . . what? a fort?

OWEN: We met it yesterday in Druim Luachra.

YOLLAND: A ridge! The Black Ridge! *(To* MANUS*)* You see, Manus?

OWEN: We'll have you fluent at the Irish before the summer's over.

YOLLAND: Oh, I wish I were. *(To* MANUS *as he crosses to go back upstairs)* We got a crate of oranges from Dublin today. I'll send some up to you.

MANUS: Thanks. *(To* OWEN*)* Better hide that bottle. Father's just up and he'd be better without it.

OWEN: Can't you speak English before your man?

MANUS: Why?

OWEN: Out of courtesy.

MANUS: Doesn't he want to learn Irish? *(To* YOLLAND*)* Don't you want to learn Irish?

YOLLAND: Sorry—sorry? I—I—

MANUS: I understand the Lanceys perfectly but people like you puzzle me.

OWEN: Manus, for God's sake!

MANUS *(Still to* YOLLAND*)*: How's the work going?

YOLLAND: The work?—the work? Oh, it's—it's staggering along—I think—*(To* OWEN*)*—isn't it? But we'd be lost without Roland.

MANUS *(Leaving)*: I'm sure. But there are always the Rolands, aren't there?

(*He goes upstairs and exits.*)

YOLLAND: What was that he said?—something about Lancey, was it?

OWEN: He said we should hide that bottle before Father gets his hands on it.

YOLLAND: Ah.

OWEN: He's always trying to protect him.

YOLLAND: Was he lame from birth?

OWEN: An accident when he was a baby: Father fell across his cradle. That's why Manus feels so responsible for him.

YOLLAND: Why doesn't he marry?

OWEN: Can't afford to, I suppose.

YOLLAND: Hasn't he a salary?

OWEN: What salary? All he gets is the odd shilling Father throws him—and that's seldom enough. I got out in time, didn't I?

(YOLLAND *is pouring a drink.*)

Easy with that stuff—it'll hit you suddenly.

YOLLAND: I like it.

OWEN: Let's get back to the job. Druim Dubh—what's it called in the jury lists? *(Consults texts)*

YOLLAND: Some people here resent us.

OWEN: Dramduff—wrong as usual.

YOLLAND: I was passing a little girl yesterday and she spat at me.

OWEN: And it's Drimdoo here. What's it called in the registry?

YOLLAND: Do you know the Donnelly twins?

OWEN: Who?

YOLLAND: The Donnelly twins.

OWEN: Yes. Best fishermen about here. What about them?

YOLLAND: Lancey's looking for them.

OWEN: What for?

YOLLAND: He wants them for questioning.

OWEN: Probably stolen somebody's nets. Dramduffy! Nobody ever called it Dramduffy. Take your pick of those three.

YOLLAND: My head's addled. Let's take a rest. Do you want a drink?

OWEN: Thanks. Now, every Dubh we've come across we've changed to Duff. So if we're to be consistent, I suppose Druim Dubh has to become Dromduff.

(YOLLAND *is now looking out the window.*)

You can see the end of the ridge from where you're standing. But D-r-u-m- or D-r-o-m-? *(Name-Book)* Do you remember—which did we agree on for Druim Luachra?

YOLLAND: That house immediately above where we're camped—

OWEN: Mm?

YOLLAND: The house where Maire lives.

OWEN: Maire? Oh, Maire Chatach.

YOLLAND: What does that mean?

OWEN: Curly-haired; the whole family are called the Chatachs. What about it?

YOLLAND: I hear music coming from that house almost every night.

OWEN: Why don't you drop in?

YOLLAND: Could I?

OWEN: Why not? We used D-r-o-m then. So we've got to call it D-r-o-m-d-u-f-f—all right?

YOLLAND: Go back up to where the new school is being built and just say the names again for me, would you?

OWEN: That's a good idea. Poolkerry, Ballybeg—

YOLLAND: No, no; as they still are—in your own language.

OWEN: Poll na gCaorach,

(YOLLAND *repeats the names silently after him.*)

Baile Beag, Ceann Balor, Lis Maol, Machaire Buidhe, Baile na gGall, Carraig na Ri, Mullach Dearg—

YOLLAND: Do you think I could live here?

OWEN: What are you talking about?—

YOLLAND: Settle down here—live here.

OWEN: Come on, George.

YOLLAND: I mean it.

OWEN: Live on what? Potatoes? Buttermilk?

YOLLAND: It's really heavenly.

OWEN: For God's sake! The first hot summer in fifty years and you think it's Eden. Don't be such a bloody romantic. You wouldn't survive a mild winter here.

YOLLAND: Do you think not? Maybe you're right.

(DOALTY *enters in a rush.*)

DOALTY: Hi, boys, is Manus about?

OWEN: He's upstairs. Give him a shout.

DOALTY: Manus! The cattle's going mad in that heat—Cripes, running wild all over the place. (*To* YOLLAND) How are you doing, skipper?

(MANUS *appears.*)

YOLLAND: Thank you for—I—I'm very grateful to you for—

DOALTY: Wasting your time. I don't know a word you're saying. Hi, Manus, there's two bucks down the road there asking for you.

MANUS (*Descending*): Who are they?

DOALTY: Never clapped eyes on them. They want to talk to you.

MANUS: What about?

DOALTY: They wouldn't say. Come on. The bloody beasts'll end up in Loch an Iubhair if they're not capped. Good luck, boys!

(DOALTY *rushes off.* MANUS *follows him.*)

OWEN: Good luck! What were you thanking Doalty for?

YOLLAND: I was washing outside my tent this morning and he was passing with a scythe across his shoulder and he came up to me and pointed to the long grass and then cut a pathway round my tent and from the tent down to the road—so that my feet won't get wet with the dew. Wasn't that kind of him? And I have no words to thank him . . . I suppose you're right: I suppose I couldn't live here . . . Just before Doalty came up to me this morning, I was thinking that at that moment I might have been in Bombay instead of Ballybeg. You see, my father was at his wits end with me and finally he got me a job with the East India Company—some kind of a clerkship. This was ten, eleven months ago. So I set off for London. Unfortunately I—I—I missed the boat. Literally. And since I couldn't face Father and hadn't enough money to hang about until the next sailing, I joined the army. And they stuck me into the Engineers and posted me to Dublin. And Dublin sent me here. And while I was washing this morning and looking across the Tra Bhan, I was thinking how very, very lucky I am to be here and not in Bombay.

OWEN: Do you believe in fate?

YOLLAND: Lancey's so like my father. I was watching him last night. He met every group of sappers as they reported in. He checked the field kitchens. He examined the horses. He inspected every single report—even examining the texture of the paper and commenting on the neatness of the handwriting. The perfect colonial servant: not only must the job be done—it must be done with excellence. Father has that drive, too; that dedication; that indefatigable energy. He builds roads—hopping from one end of the Empire to the other. Can't sit still for five minutes. He says himself the longest time he ever sat still was the night before Waterloo when they were waiting for Wellington to make up his mind to attack.

OWEN: What age is he?

YOLLAND: Born in 1789—the very day the Bastille fell. I've often thought maybe that gave his whole life its character. Do you think it could? He inherited a new world the day he was born—The Year One. Ancient time was at an end. The world had cast off its old skin. There were no longer any frontiers to man's potential. Possibilities were endless and exciting. He still believes that. The Apocalypse is just about to happen . . . I'm afraid I'm a great disappointment to him. I've neither his energy, nor his coherence, nor his belief. Do I believe in fate? The day I arrived in Ballybeg—no, Baile Beag—the moment you brought me in here, I had a curious sensation. It's difficult to describe. It was a momentary sense of discovery; no—not quite a sense of discovery—a sense of recognition, of confirmation of something I half knew instinctively; as if I had stepped . . .

OWEN: Back into ancient time?

YOLLAND: No, no. It wasn't an awareness of *direction* being changed but of experience being of a totally different order. I had moved into a consciousness that wasn't striving nor agitated, but at its ease and with its own conviction and assurance. And when I heard Jimmy Jack and your father swapping stories about Apollo and Cuchulainn and Paris and Ferdia—as if they lived down the road—it was then that I thought—I knew—perhaps I could live here . . . (*Now embarrassed*) Where's the pot-een?

OWEN: Poteen.

YOLLAND: Poteen—poteen—poteen. Even if I did speak Irish I'd always be an outsider here, wouldn't I? I may learn the password but the language of the tribe will always elude me, won't it? The private core will always be . . . hermetic, won't it?

OWEN: You can learn to decode us.

(*HUGH emerges from upstairs and descends. He is dressed for the road. Today he is physically and mentally jaunty and alert—almost self-consciously jaunty and alert. Indeed, as the scene progresses, one has the sense that he is deliberately parodying himself. The moment HUGH gets to the bottom of the steps YOLLAND leaps respectfully to his feet.*)

HUGH (*As he descends*):

Quantumvis cursum longum fessumque moratur
Sol, sacro tandem carmine vesper adest.°

I dabble in verse, Lieutenant, after the style of Ovid. (*To OWEN*) A drop of that to fortify me.

YOLLAND: You'll have to translate it for me.

HUGH: Let's see—

No matter how long the sun may linger on his long and weary journey
At length evening comes with its sacred song.

YOLLAND: Very nice, sir.

HUGH: English succeeds in making it sound . . . plebeian.

OWEN: Where are you off to, Father?

HUGH: An *expeditio*° with three purposes. Purpose A: to acquire a testimonial from our parish priest— (*To YOLLAND*) a worthy man but barely literate; and since he'll ask me to write it myself, how in all modesty can I do myself justice? (*To OWEN*) Where did this (*drink*) come from?

OWEN: Anna na mBreag's.

HUGH (*To YOLLAND*): In that case address yourself to it with circumspection. (*And HUGH instantly tosses the drink back in one gulp and grimaces.*) Aaaaaaagh! (*Holds out his glass for a refill*) Anna na mBreag means Anna of the Lies. And Purpose B: to talk to the builders of the new school about the kind of living accommodation I will require there. I have lived too long like a journeyman tailor.

YOLLAND: Some years ago we lived fairly close to a poet—well, about three miles away.

HUGH: His name?

YOLLAND: Wordsworth—William Wordsworth.

HUGH: Did he speak of me to you?

YOLLAND: Actually I never talked to him. I just saw him out walking—in the distance.

HUGH: Wordsworth? . . . No. I'm afraid we're not familiar with your literature, Lieutenant. We feel closer to the warm Mediterranean. We tend to overlook your island.

YOLLAND: I'm learning to speak Irish, sir.

HUGH: Good.

YOLLAND: Roland's teaching me.

HUGH: Splendid.

YOLLAND: I mean—I feel so cut off from the people here. And I was trying to explain a few minutes ago how remarkable a community this is. To meet people like yourself and Jimmy Jack who actually converse in Greek and Latin. And your place names—what was the one we came across this morning?—Termon, from Terminus, the god of boundaries. It—it—it's really astonishing.

HUGH: We like to think we endure around truths immemorially posited.

YOLLAND: And your Gaelic literature—you're a poet yourself—

HUGH: Only in Latin, I'm afraid.

YOLLAND: I understand it's enormously rich and ornate.

HUGH: Indeed, Lieutenant. A rich language. A rich literature. You'll find, sir, that certain cultures expend on their vocabularies and syntax acquisitive energies and ostentations entirely lacking in their material lives. I suppose you could call us a spiritual people.

OWEN (*Not unkindly; more out of embarrassment before YOLLAND*): Will you stop that nonsense, Father.

HUGH: Nonsense? What nonsense?

OWEN: Do you know where the priest lives?

HUGH: At Lis na Muc, over near . . .

OWEN: No, he doesn't. Lis na Muc, the Fort of the Pigs, has become Swinefort. (*Now turning the pages of the Name-Book—a page per name*) And to get to Swinefort you pass through Greencastle and Fair Head and Strandhill and Gort and Whiteplains. And the new school isn't at Poll na gCaorach— it's at Sheepsrock. Will you be able to find your way?

Quantumvis cursum longum fessumque moratur/Sol, sacro tandem carmine vesper adest, No matter how long the sun delays on his long weary course/At length evening comes with its sacred song. *expeditio,* an expedition.

(HUGH *pours himself another drink. Then:—*)

HUGH: Yes, it is a rich language, Lieutenant, full of the mythologies of fantasy and hope and self-deception—a syntax opulent with tomorrows. It is our response to mud cabins and a diet of potatoes; our only method of replying to . . . inevitabilities. (*To* OWEN) Can you give me the loan of half-a-crown? I'll repay you out of the subscriptions I'm collecting for the publication of my new book. (*To* YOLLAND) It is entitled: "The Pentaglot Preceptor or Elementary Institute of the English, Greek, Hebrew, Latin and Irish Languages; Particularly Calculated for the Instruction of Such Ladies and Gentlemen as may Wish to Learn without the Help of a Master."

YOLLAND (*Laughs*): That's a wonderful title!

HUGH: Between ourselves—the best part of the enterprise. Nor do I, in fact, speak Hebrew. And that last phrase—"without the Help of a Master"—that was written before the new national school was thrust upon me—do you think I ought to drop it now? After all you don't dispose of the cow just because it has produced a magnificent calf, do you?

YOLLAND: You certainly do not.

HUGH: The phrase goes. And I'm interrupting work of moment. (*He goes to the door and stops there.*) To return briefly to that other matter, Lieutenant. I understand your sense of exclusion, of being cut off from a life here; and I trust you will find access to us with my son's help. But remember that words are signals, counters. They are not immortal. And it can happen—to use an image you'll understand—it can happen that a civilization can be imprisoned in a linguistic contour which no longer matches the landscape of . . . fact. Gentlemen. (*He leaves.*)

OWEN: "An *expeditio* with three purposes": the children laugh at him: he always promises three points and he never gets beyond A and B.

MANUS: He's an astute man.

OWEN: He's bloody pompous.

YOLLAND: But so astute.

OWEN: And he drinks too much. Is it astute not to be able to adjust for survival? Enduring around truths immemorially posited—hah!

YOLLAND: He knows what's happening.

OWEN: What is happening?

YOLLAND: I'm not sure. But I'm concerned about my part in it. It's an eviction of sorts.

OWEN: We're making a six-inch map of the country. Is there something sinister in that?

YOLLAND: Not in—

OWEN: And we're taking place-names that are riddled with confusion and—

YOLLAND: Who's confused? Are the people confused?

OWEN: —and we're standardizing those names as accurately and as sensitively as we can.

YOLLAND: Something is being eroded.

OWEN: Back to the romance again. All right! Fine! Fine! Look where we've got to. (*He drops on his hands and knees and stabs a finger at the map.*) We've come to this crossroads. Come here and look at it, man! Look at it! And we call that crossroads Tobair Vree. And why do we call it Tobair Vree? I'll tell you why. Tobair means a well. But what does Vree mean? It's a corruption of Brian—(*Gaelic pronunciation*) Brian—an erosion of Tobair Bhriain. Because a hundred-and-fifty years ago there used to be a well there, not at the crossroads, mind you—that would be too simple—but in a field close to the crossroads. And an old man called Brian, whose face was disfigured by an enormous growth, got it into his head that the water in that well was blessed; and every day for seven months he went there and bathed his face in it. But the growth didn't go away; and one morning Brian was found drowned in that well. And ever since that crossroads is known as Tobair Vree—even though that well has long since dried up. I know the story because my grandfather told it to me. But ask Doalty—or Maire—or Bridget—even my father—even Manus—why it's called Tobair Vree; and do you think they'll know? I know they don't know. So the question I put to you, Lieutenant, is this: what do we do with a name like that? Do we scrap Tobair Vree altogether and call it—what?—The Cross? Crossroads? Or do we keep piety with a man long dead, long forgotten, his name "eroded" beyond recognition, whose trivial little story nobody in the parish remembers?

YOLLAND: Except you.

OWEN: I've left here.

YOLLAND: You remember it.

OWEN: I'm asking you: what do we write in the Name-Book?

YOLLAND: Tobair Vree.

OWEN: Even though the well is a hundred yards from the actual crossroads—and there's no well anyway—and what the hell does Vree mean?

YOLLAND: Tobair Vree.

OWEN: That's what you want?

YOLLAND: Yes.

OWEN: You're certain?

YOLLAND: Yes.

OWEN: Fine. Fine. That's what you'll get.

YOLLAND: That's what you want, too, Roland.

(*Pause.*)

OWEN (*Explodes*): George! For God's sake! *My name is not Roland!*

YOLLAND: What?

OWEN (*Softly*): My name is Owen.

(*Pause.*)

YOLLAND: Not Roland?

OWEN: Owen.

YOLLAND: You mean to say—?

OWEN: Owen.

YOLLAND: But I've been—

OWEN: O-w-e-n.

YOLLAND: Where did Roland come from?

OWEN: I don't know.

YOLLAND: It was never Roland?

OWEN: Never.

YOLLAND: O my God!

(*Pause. They stare at one another. Then the absurdity of the situation strikes them suddenly. They explode with laughter.* OWEN *pours drinks. As they roll about, their lines overlap.*)

YOLLAND: Why didn't you tell me?

OWEN: Do I look like a Roland?

YOLLAND: Spell Owen again.

OWEN: I was getting fond of Roland.

YOLLAND: O my God!

OWEN: O-w-e-n.

YOLLAND: What'll we write—

OWEN: —in the Name-Book?!

YOLLAND: R-o-w-e-n!

OWEN: Or what about Ol—

YOLLAND: Ol- what?

OWEN: Oland!

(*And again they explode.* MANUS *enters. He is very elated.*)

MANUS: What's the celebration?

OWEN: A christening!

YOLLAND: A baptism!

OWEN: A hundred christenings!

YOLLAND: A thousand baptisms! Welcome to Eden!

OWEN: Eden's right! We name a thing and—bang!—it leaps into existence!

YOLLAND: Each name a perfect equation with its roots.

OWEN: A perfect congruence with its reality. (*To* MANUS) Take a drink.

YOLLAND: Poteen—beautiful.

OWEN: Lying Anna's poteen.

YOLLAND: Anna na mBreag's poteen.

OWEN: Excellent, George.

YOLLAND: I'll decode you yet.

OWEN (*Offers drink*): Manus?

MANUS: Not if that's what it does to you.

OWEN: You're right. Steady—steady—sober up—sober up.

YOLLAND: Sober as a judge, Owen.

(MANUS *moves beside* OWEN.)

MANUS: I've got good news! Where's Father?

OWEN: He's gone out. What's the good news?

MANUS: I've been offered a job.

OWEN: Where? (*Now aware of* YOLLAND) Come on, man—speak in English.

MANUS: For the benefit of the colonist?

OWEN: He's a decent man.

MANUS: Aren't they all at some level?

OWEN: Please.

(MANUS *shrugs.*)

He's been offered a job.

YOLLAND: Where?

OWEN: Well—tell us!

MANUS: I've just had a meeting with two men from Inis Meadhon. They want me to go there and start a hedge-school. They're giving me a free house, free turf, and free milk; a rood of standing corn; twelve drills of potatoes; and—

(*He stops.*)

OWEN: And what?

MANUS: A salary of £42 a year!

OWEN: Manus, that's wonderful!

MANUS: You're talking to a man of substance.

OWEN: I'm delighted.

YOLLAND: Where's Inis Meadhon?

OWEN: An island south of here. And they came looking for you?

MANUS: Well, I mean to say . . .

(OWEN *punches* MANUS.)

OWEN: Aaaaagh! This calls for a real celebration.

YOLLAND: Congratulations.

MANUS: Thank you.

OWEN: Where are you, Anna?

YOLLAND: When do you start?

MANUS: Next Monday.

OWEN: We'll stay with you when we're there. (*To* YOLLAND) How long will it be before we reach Inis Meadhon?

YOLLAND: How far south is it?

MANUS: About fifty miles.

YOLLAND: Could we make it by December?

OWEN: We'll have Christmas together. (*Sings*) "Christmas Day on Inis Meadhon . . ."

YOLLAND (*Toast*): I hope you're very content there, Manus.

MANUS: Thank you.

(YOLLAND *holds out his hand.* MANUS *takes it. They shake warmly.*)

OWEN (*Toast*): Manus.

MANUS (*Toast*): To Inis Meadhon.

(*He drinks quickly and turns to leave.*)

OWEN: Hold on—hold on—refills coming up.

MANUS: I've got to go.

OWEN: Come on, man; this is an occasion. Where are you rushing to?

MANUS: I've got to tell Maire.

(MAIRE *enters with her can of milk.*)

MAIRE: You've got to tell Maire what?

OWEN: He's got a job!

MAIRE: Manus?

OWEN: He's been invited to start a hedge-school in Inis Meadhon.

MAIRE: Where?

MANUS: Inis Meadhon—the island! They're giving me £42 a year and . . .

OWEN: A house, fuel, milk, potatoes, corn, pupils, what-not!

MANUS: I start on Monday.

OWEN: You'll take a drink. Isn't it great?

MANUS: I want to talk to you for—

MAIRE: There's your milk. I need the can back.

(MANUS *takes the can and runs up the steps.*)

MANUS (*As he goes*): How will you like living on an island?

OWEN: You know George, don't you?

MAIRE: We wave to each other across the fields.

YOLLAND: Sorry-sorry?

OWEN: She says you wave to each other across the fields.

YOLLAND: Yes, we do; oh, yes; indeed we do.

MAIRE: What's he saying?

OWEN: He says you wave to each other across the fields.

MAIRE: That's right. So we do.

YOLLAND: What's she saying?

OWEN: Nothing—nothing—nothing. (*To* MAIRE) What's the news?

(MAIRE *moves away, touching the text books with her toe.*)

MAIRE: Not a thing. You're busy, the two of you.

OWEN: We think we are.

MAIRE: I hear the Fiddler O'Shea's about. There's some talk of a dance tomorrow night.

OWEN: Where will it be?

MAIRE: Maybe over the road. Maybe at Tobair Vree.

YOLLAND: Tobair Vree!

MAIRE: Yes.

YOLLAND: Tobair Vree! Tobair Vree!

MAIRE: Does he know what I'm saying?

OWEN: Not a word.

MAIRE: Tell him then.

OWEN: Tell him what?

MAIRE: About the dance.

OWEN: Maire says there may be a dance tomorrow night.

YOLLAND (*To* OWEN): Yes? May I come? (*To* MAIRE) Would anybody object if I came?

MAIRE (*To* OWEN): What's he saying?

OWEN (*To* YOLLAND): Who would object?

MAIRE (*To* OWEN): Did you tell him?

YOLLAND (*To* MAIRE): Sorry-sorry?

OWEN (*To* MAIRE): He says may he come?

MAIRE (*To* YOLLAND): That's up to you.

YOLLAND (*To* OWEN): What does she say?

OWEN (*To* YOLLAND): She says—

YOLLAND (*To* MAIRE): What-what?

MAIRE (*To* OWEN): Well?

YOLLAND (*To* OWEN): Sorry-sorry?

OWEN (*To* YOLLAND): Will you go?

YOLLAND (*To* MAIRE): Yes, yes, if I may.

MAIRE (*To* OWEN): What does he say?

YOLLAND (*To* OWEN): What is she saying?

OWEN: Oh for God's sake! (*To* MANUS *who is descending with the empty can*) You take on this job, Manus.

MANUS: I'll walk you up to the house. Is your mother at home? I want to talk to her.

MAIRE: What's the rush? (*To* OWEN) Didn't you offer me a drink?

OWEN: Will you risk Anna na mBreag?

MAIRE: Why not.

(YOLLAND *is suddenly intoxicated. He leaps up on a stool, raises his glass and shouts.*)

YOLLAND: Anna na mBreag! Baile Beag! Inis Meadhon! Bombay! Tobair Vree! Eden! And poteen—correct, Owen?

OWEN: Perfect.

YOLLAND: And bloody marvellous stuff it is, too. I love it! Bloody, bloody, bloody marvellous!

(*Simultaneously with his final "bloody marvellous" bring up very loud the introductory music of the reel. Then immediately go to black. Retain the music throughout the very brief interval.*)

ACT 2 / SCENE 2

(*The following night.*

This scene may be played in the schoolroom, but it would be preferable to lose—by lighting—as much of the schoolroom as possible, and to play the scene down front in a vaguely "outside" area.

The music rises to a crescendo. Then in the distance we hear MAIRE *and* YOLLAND *approach—laughing and running. They run on, hand-in-hand. They have just left the dance. Fade the music to distant background. Then after a time it is lost and replaced by guitar music.* MAIRE *and* YOLLAND *are now down front, still holding hands and excited by their sudden and impetuous escape from the dance.*)

MAIRE: O my God, that leap across the ditch nearly killed me.

YOLLAND: I could scarcely keep up with you.

MAIRE: Wait till I get my breath back.

YOLLAND: We must have looked as if we were being chased.

(They now realize they are alone and holding hands—the beginnings of embarrassment. The hands disengage. They begin to drift apart. Pause.)

MAIRE: Manus'll wonder where I've got to.
YOLLAND: I wonder did anyone notice us leave.

(Pause. Slightly further apart.)

MAIRE: The grass must be wet. My feet are soaking.
YOLLAND: Your feet must be wet. The grass is soaking.

(Another pause. Another few paces apart. They are now a long distance from one another.)

YOLLAND *(Indicating himself)*: George.

(MAIRE nods: Yes-yes. Then:—)

MAIRE: Lieutenant George.
YOLLAND: Don't call me that. I never think of myself as Lieutenant.
MAIRE: What-what?
YOLLAND: Sorry-Sorry? *(He points to himself again.)* George.

(MAIRE nods: Yes-yes. Then points to herself.)

MAIRE: Maire.
YOLLAND: Yes, I know you're Maire. Of course I know you're Maire. I mean I've been watching you night and day for the past—
MAIRE *(Eagerly)*: What-what?
YOLLAND *(Points)*: Maire. *(Points)* George. *(Points both)* Maire and George.

(MAIRE nods: Yes-yes-yes.)

I—I—I—
MAIRE: Say anything at all. I love the sound of your speech.
YOLLAND *(Eagerly)*: Sorry-sorry?

(In acute frustration he looks around, hoping for some inspiration that will provide him with communicative means. Now he has a thought: he tries raising his voice and articulating in a staccato style and with equal and absurd emphasis on each word.)

Every-morning-I-see-you-feeding-brown-hens-and-giving-meal-to-black-calf—*(The futility of it)*—O my God.

(MAIRE smiles. She moves towards him. She will try to communicate in Latin.)

MAIRE: Tu es centurio in—in—in exercitu Britannico°—
YOLLAND: Yes-yes? Go on—go on—say anything at all—I love the sound of your speech.

MAIRE: —et es in castris quae—quae—quae sunt in agro°—*(The futility of it)*—O my God.

(YOLLAND smiles. He moves towards her. Now for her English words.)

George—water.
YOLLAND: "Water"? Water! Oh yes—water—water—very good—water—good—good.
MAIRE: Fire.
YOLLAND: Fire—indeed—wonderful—fire, fire, fire—splendid—splendid!
MAIRE: Ah . . . ah . . .
YOLLAND: Yes? Go on.
MAIRE: Earth.
YOLLAND: "Earth"?
MAIRE: Earth. Earth.

(YOLLAND still does not understand. MAIRE stoops down and picks up a handful of clay. Holding it out.) Earth.

YOLLAND: Earth! Of course—earth! Earth. Earth. Good Lord, Maire, your English is perfect!
MAIRE *(Eagerly)*: What-what?
YOLLAND: Perfect English. English perfect.
MAIRE: George—
YOLLAND: That's beautiful—oh, that's really beautiful.
MAIRE: George—
YOLLAND: Say it again—say it again—
MAIRE: Shhh. *(She holds her hand up for silence—she is trying to remember her one line of English. Now she remembers it and she delivers the line as if English were her language—easily, fluidly, conversationally.)* George, "In Norfolk we besport ourselves around the maypoll."
YOLLAND: Good God, do you? That's where my mother comes from—Norfolk. Norwich actually. Not exactly Norwich town but a small village called Little Walsingham close beside it. But in our own village of Winfarthing we have a maypole too and every year on the first of May—*(He stops abruptly, only now realizing. He stares at her. She in turn misunderstands his excitement.)*
MAIRE *(To herself)*: Mother of God, my Aunt Mary wouldn't have taught me something dirty, would she?

(Pause. YOLLAND extends his hand to MAIRE. She turns away from him and moves slowly across the stage.)

YOLLAND: Maire.

(She still moves away.)

Maire Chatach.

(She still moves away.)

Tu es centurio in exercitu Britannico, You are a centurion in the British Army.

et es in castris quae sunt in agro, And you are in the camp in the field.

Bun na hAbhann? (*He says the name softly, almost privately, very tentatively, as if he were searching for a sound she might respond to. He tries again.*) Druim Dubh?

(MAIRE *stops. She is listening.* YOLLAND *is encouraged.*)

Poll na gCaorach. Lis Maol.

(MAIRE *turns towards him.*)

Lis na nGall.

MAIRE: Lis na nGradh.

(*They are now facing each other and begin moving—almost imperceptibly—towards one another.*)

MAIRE: Carraig an Phoill.
YOLLAND: Carraig na Ri. Loch na nEan.
MAIRE: Loch an Iubhair. Machaire Buidhe.
YOLLAND: Machaire Mor. Cnoc na Mona.
MAIRE: Cnoc na nGabhar.
YOLLAND: Mullach.
MAIRE: Port.
YOLLAND: Tor.
MAIRE: Lag.

(*She holds out her hands to* YOLLAND. *He takes them. Each now speaks almost to himself/herself.*)

YOLLAND: I wish to God you could understand me.
MAIRE: Soft hands; a gentleman's hands.
YOLLAND: Because if you could understand me I could tell you how I spend my days either thinking of you or gazing up at your house in the hope that you'll appear even for a second.
MAIRE: Every evening you walk by yourself along the Tra Bhan and every morning you wash yourself in front of your tent.
YOLLAND: I would tell you how beautiful you are, curly-headed Maire. I would so like to tell you how beautiful you are.
MAIRE: Your arms are long and thin and the skin on your shoulders is very white.
YOLLAND: I would tell you . . .
MAIRE: Don't stop—I know what you're saying.
YOLLAND: I would tell you how I want to be here—to live here—always—with you—always, always.
MAIRE: "Always"? What is that word—"always"?
YOLLAND: Yes-yes; always.
MAIRE: You're trembling.
YOLLAND: Yes, I'm trembling because of you.
MAIRE: I'm trembling, too.

(*She holds his face in her hand.*)

YOLLAND: I've made up my mind . . .
MAIRE: Shhhh.
YOLLAND: I'm not going to leave here . . .
MAIRE: Shhh—listen to me. I want you, too, soldier.
YOLLAND: Don't stop—I know what you're saying.

MAIRE: I want to live with you—anywhere—anywhere at all—always—always.
YOLLAND: "Always"? What is that word—"always"?
MAIRE: Take me away with you, George.

(*Pause. Suddenly they kiss.* SARAH *enters. She sees them. She stands shocked, staring at them. Her mouth works. Then almost to herself.*)

SARAH: Manus . . . Manus!

(SARAH *runs off. Music to crescendo.*)

ACT 3

(*The following evening. It is raining.*
    SARAH *and* OWEN *alone in the schoolroom.* SARAH, *more waiflike than ever, is sitting very still on a stool, an open book across her knee. She is pretending to read but her eyes keep going up to the room upstairs.* OWEN *is working on the floor as before, surrounded by his reference books, map, Name-Book, etc. But he has neither concentration nor interest; and like* SARAH *he glances up at the upstairs room.*
    After a few seconds MANUS *emerges and descends, carrying a large paper bag which already contains his clothes. His movements are determined and urgent. He moves around the classroom, picking up books, examining each title carefully, and choosing about six of them which he puts into his bag. As he selects these books:—*)

OWEN: You know that old limekiln beyond Con Connie Tim's pub, the place we call The Murren?—do you know why it's called The Murren?

(MANUS *does not answer.*)

I've only just discovered: it's a corruption of Saint Muranus. It seems Saint Muranus had a monastery somewhere about there at the beginning of the seventh century. And over the years the name became shortened to the Murren. Very unattractive name, isn't it? I think we should go back to the original—Saint Muranus, What do you think? The original's Saint Muranus. Don't you think we should go back to that?

(*No response.* OWEN *begins writing the name into the Name-Book.* MANUS *is now rooting about among the forgotten implements for a piece of rope. He finds a piece. He begins to tie the mouth of the flimsy, overloaded bag—and it bursts, the contents spilling out on the floor.*)

MANUS: Bloody, bloody, bloody hell!

(*His voice breaks in exasperation: he is about to cry.* OWEN *leaps to his feet.*)

OWEN: Hold on. I've a bag upstairs.

(*He runs upstairs.* SARAH *waits until* OWEN *is off. Then:—*)

SARAH: Manus . . . Manus, I . . .

(MANUS *hears* SARAH *but makes no acknowledgement. He gathers up his belongings.* OWEN *reappears with the bag he had on his arrival.*)

OWEN: Take this one—I'm finished with it anyway. And it's supposed to keep out the rain.

(MANUS *transfers his few belongings.* OWEN *drifts back to his task. The packing is now complete.*)

MANUS: You'll be here for a while? For a week or two anyhow?

OWEN: Yes.

MANUS: You're not leaving with the army?

OWEN: I haven't made up my mind. Why?

MANUS: Those Inis Meadhon men will be back to see why I haven't turned up. Tell them—tell them I'll write to them as soon as I can. Tell them I still want the job but that it might be three or four months before I'm free to go.

OWEN: You're being damned stupid, Manus.

MANUS: Will you do that for me?

OWEN: Clear out now and Lancey'll think you're involved somehow.

MANUS: Will you do that for me?

OWEN: Wait a couple of days even. You know George—he's a bloody romantic—maybe he's gone out to one of the islands and he'll suddenly reappear tomorrow morning. Or maybe the search party'll find him this evening lying drunk somewhere in the sandhills. You've seen him drinking that poteen—doesn't know how to handle it. Had he drink on him last night at the dance?

MANUS: I had a stone in my hand when I went out looking for him—I was going to fell him. The lame scholar turned violent.

OWEN: Did anybody see you?

MANUS (*Again close to tears*): But when I saw him standing there at the side of the road—smiling—and her face buried in his shoulder—I couldn't even go close to them. I just shouted something stupid—something like, "You're a bastard, Yolland." If I'd even said it in English . . . 'cos he kept saying "Sorry-sorry?" The wrong gesture in the wrong language.

OWEN: And you didn't see him again?

MANUS: "Sorry?"

OWEN: Before you leave tell Lancey that—just to clear yourself.

MANUS: What have I to say to Lancey? You'll give that message to the islandmen?

OWEN: I'm warning you: run away now and you're bound to be—

MANUS (*To* SARAH): Will you give that message to the Inis Meadhon men?

SARAH: I will.

(MANUS *picks up an old sack and throws it across his shoulders.*)

OWEN: Have you any idea where you're going?

MANUS: Mayo, maybe. I remember Mother saying she had cousins somewhere away out in the Erris Peninsula. (*He picks up his bag.*) Tell Father I took only the Virgil and the Caesar and the Aeschylus because they're mine anyway—I bought them with the money I got for that pet lamb I reared—do you remember that pet lamb? And tell him that Nora Dan never returned the dictionary and that she still owes him two-and-six for last quarter's reading—he always forgets those things.

OWEN: Yes.

MANUS: And his good shirt's ironed and hanging up in the press and his clean socks are in the butter-box under the bed.

OWEN: All right.

MANUS: And tell him I'll write.

OWEN: If Maire asks where you've gone . . . ?

MANUS: He'll need only half the amount of milk now, won't he? Even less than half—he usually takes his tea black. (*Pause*) And when he comes in at night—you'll hear him; he makes a lot of noise—I usually come down and give him a hand up. Those stairs are dangerous without a banister. Maybe before you leave you'd get Big Ned Frank to put up some sort of a handrail. (*Pause*) And if you can bake, he's very fond of soda bread.

OWEN: I can give you money. I'm wealthy. Do you know what they pay me? Two shillings a day for this—this—this—

(MANUS *rejects the offer by holding out his hand.*)

Goodbye, Manus.

(MANUS *and* OWEN *shake hands. Then* MANUS *picks up his bag briskly and goes towards the door. He stops a few paces beyond* SARAH, *turns, comes back to her. He addresses her as he did in Act 1 but now without warmth or concern for her.*)

MANUS: What is your name? (*Pause*) Come on. What is your name?

SARAH: My name is Sarah.

MANUS: Just Sarah? Sarah what? (*Pause*) Well?

SARAH: Sarah Johnny Sally.

MANUS: And where do you live? Come on.

SARAH: I live in Bun na hAbhann.

(*She is now crying quietly.*)

MANUS: Very good, Sarah Johnny Sally. There's nothing to stop you now—nothing in the wide world. (*Pause. He looks down at her.*) It's all right—it's all right—you did no harm—you did no harm at all.

(*He stoops over her and kisses the top of her head—as if in absolution. Then briskly to the door and off.*)

OWEN: Good luck, Manus!

SARAH *(Quietly)*: I'm sorry . . . I'm sorry . . . I'm so sorry, Manus . . .

(OWEN tries to work but cannot concentrate. He begins folding up the map. As he does:—)

OWEN: Is there a class this evening?

(SARAH nods: yes.)

I suppose Father knows. Where is he anyhow?

(SARAH points.)

Where?

(SARAH mimes rocking a baby.)

I don't understand—where?

(SARAH repeats the mime and wipes away tears. OWEN is still puzzled.)

It doesn't matter. He'll probably turn up.

(BRIDGET and DOALTY enter, sacks over their heads against the rain. They are self-consciously noisier, more ebullient, more garrulous than ever—brimming over with excitement and gossip and brio.)

DOALTY: You're missing the crack, boys! Cripes, you're missing the crack! Fifty more soldiers arrived an hour ago!

BRIDGET: And they're spread out in a big line from Sean Neal's over to Lag and they're moving straight across the fields towards Cnoc na nGabhar!

DOALTY: Prodding every inch of the ground in front of them with their bayonets and scattering animals and hens in all directions!

BRIDGET: And tumbling everything before them—fences, ditches, haystacks, turf-stacks!

DOALTY: They came to Barney Petey's field of corn—straight through it be God as if it was heather!

BRIDGET: Not a blade of it left standing!

DOALTY: And Barney Petey just out of his bed and running after them in his drawers: "You hoors you! Get out of my corn, you hoors you!"

BRIDGET: First time he ever ran in his life.

DOALTY: Too lazy, the wee get, to cut it when the weather was good.

(SARAH begins putting out the seats.)

BRIDGET: Tell them about Big Hughie.

DOALTY: Cripes, if you'd seen your aul fella, Owen.

BRIDGET: They were all inside in Anna na mBreag's pub—all the crowd from the wake—

DOALTY: And they hear the commotion and they all come out to the street—

BRIDGET: Your father in front; the Infant Prodigy footless behind him!

DOALTY: And your aul fella, he sees the army stretched across the countryside—

BRIDGET: O my God!

DOALTY: And Cripes he starts roaring at them!

BRIDGET: "Visigoths! Huns! Vandals!"

DOALTY: *"Ignari! Stulti! Rustici!"*°

BRIDGET: And wee Jimmy Jack jumping up and down and shouting, "Thermopylae! Thermopylae!"

DOALTY: You never saw crack like it in your life, boys. Come away on out with me, Sarah, and you'll see it all.

BRIDGET: Big Hughie's fit to take no class. Is Manus about?

OWEN: Manus is gone.

BRIDGET: Gone where?

OWEN: He's left—gone away.

DOALTY: Where to?

OWEN: He doesn't know. Mayo, maybe.

DOALTY: What's on in Mayo?

OWEN *(To BRIDGET)*: Did you see George and Maire Chatach leave the dance last night?

BRIDGET: We did. Didn't we, Doalty?

OWEN: Did you see Manus following them out?

BRIDGET: I didn't see him going out but I saw him coming in by himself later.

OWEN: Did George and Maire come back to the dance?

BRIDGET: No.

OWEN: Did you see them again?

BRIDGET: He left her home. We passed them going up the back road—didn't we, Doalty?

OWEN: And Manus stayed till the end of the dance?

DOALTY: We know nothing. What are you asking us for?

OWEN: Because Lancey'll question me when he hears Manus's gone. *(Back to BRIDGET)* That's the way George went home? By the back road? That's where you saw him?

BRIDGET: Leave me alone, Owen. I know nothing about Yolland. If you want to know about Yolland, ask the Donnelly twins.

(Silence. DOALTY moves over to the window.)

(To SARAH) He's a powerful fiddler, O'Shea, isn't he? He told our Seamus he'll come back for a night at Hallowe'en.

(OWEN goes to DOALTY who looks resolutely out the window.)

OWEN: What's this about the Donnellys? *(Pause)* Were they about last night?

DOALTY: Didn't see them if they were.

(Begins whistling through his teeth.)

OWEN: George is a friend of mine.

DOALTY: So.

Ignari! Stulti! Rustici! Ignoramuses! Fools! Peasants!

OWEN: I want to know what's happened to him.

DOALTY: Couldn't tell you.

OWEN: What have the Donnelly twins to do with it? *(Pause.)* Doalty!

DOALTY: I know nothing, Owen—nothing at all—I swear to God. All I know is this: on my way to the dance I saw their boat beached at Port. It wasn't there on my way home, after I left Bridget. And that's all I know. As God's my judge. The half-dozen times I met him I didn't know a word he said to me; but he seemed a right enough sort . . . *(With sudden excessive interest in the scene outside)* Cripes, they're crawling all over the place! Cripes, there's millions of them! Cripes, they're levelling the whole land!

(OWEN moves away. MAIRE enters. She is bareheaded and wet from the rain; her hair in disarray. She attempts to appear normal but she is in acute distress, on the verge of being distraught. She is carrying the milk-can.)

MAIRE: Honest to God, I must be going off my head. I'm half-way here and I think to myself, "Isn't this can very light?" and I look into it and isn't it empty.

OWEN: It doesn't matter.

MAIRE: How will you manage for tonight?

OWEN: We have enough.

MAIRE: Are you sure?

OWEN: Plenty, thanks.

MAIRE: It'll take me no time at all to go back up for some.

OWEN: Honestly, Maire.

MAIRE: Sure it's better you have it than that black calf that's . . . that . . . *(She looks around.)* Have you heard anything?

OWEN: Nothing.

MAIRE: What does Lancey say?

OWEN: I haven't seen him since this morning.

MAIRE: What does he *think?*

OWEN: We really didn't talk. He was here for only a few seconds.

MAIRE: He left me home, Owen. And the last thing he said to me—he tried to speak in Irish—he said, "I'll see you yesterday"—he meant to say "I'll see you tomorrow." And I laughed that much he pretended to get cross and he said "Maypoll! Maypoll!" because I said that word wrong. And off he went, laughing—laughing, Owen! Do you think he's all right? What do *you* think?

OWEN: I'm sure he'll turn up. Maire.

MAIRE: He comes from a tiny wee place called Winfarthing. *(She suddenly drops on her hands and knees on the floor—where OWEN had his map a few minutes ago—and with her finger traces out an outline map.)* Come here till you see. Look. There's Winfarthing. And there's two other wee villages right beside it; one of them's called Barton Bendish—it's there; and the other's called Saxingham Nethergate—it's about there. And there's Little Walsingham—that's his mother's townland. Aren't they odd names? Sure they make no sense to me at all. And Winfarthing's near a big town called Norwich. And Norwich is in a county called Norfolk. And Norfolk is in the east of England. He drew a map for me on the wet strand and wrote the names on it. I have it all in my head now: Winfarthing—Barton Bendish—Saxingham Nethergate—Little Walsingham—Norwich—Norfolk. Strange sounds, aren't they? But nice sounds; like Jimmy Jack reciting his Homer. *(She gets to her feet and looks around; she is almost serene now. To SARAH)* You were looking lovely last night, Sarah. Is that the dress you got from Boston? Green suits you. *(To OWEN)* Something very bad's happened to him, Owen. I know. He wouldn't go away without telling me. Where is he, Owen? You're his friend—where is he? *(Again she looks around the room; then sits on a stool.)* I didn't get a chance to do my geography last night. The master'll be angry with me. *(She rises again.)* I think I'll go home now. The wee ones have to be washed and put to bed and that black calf has to be fed . . . My hands are that rough; they're still blistered from the hay. I'm ashamed of them. I hope to God there's no hay to be saved in Brooklyn. *(She stops at the door.)* Did you hear? Nellie Ruadh's baby died in the middle of the night. I must go up to the wake. It didn't last long, did it?

(MAIRE leaves. Silence. Then:—)

OWEN: I don't think there'll be any class. Maybe you should . . .

(OWEN begins picking up his texts. DOALTY goes to him.)

DOALTY: Is he long gone?—Manus.

OWEN: Half an hour.

DOALTY: Stupid bloody fool.

OWEN: I told him that.

DOALTY: Do they know he's gone?

OWEN: Who?

DOALTY: The army.

OWEN: Not yet.

DOALTY: They'll be after him like bloody beagles. Bloody, bloody fool, limping along the coast. They'll overtake him before night for Christ's sake.

(DOALTY returns to the window. LANCEY enters—now the commanding officer.)

OWEN: Any news? Any word?

(LANCEY moves into the centre of the room, looking around as he does.)

LANCEY: I understood there was a class. Where are the others?

OWEN: There was to be a class but my father—

LANCEY: This will suffice. I will address them and it will be their responsibility to pass on what I have to say to every family in this section.

(LANCEY *indicates to* OWEN *to translate.* OWEN *hesitates, trying to assess the change in* LANCEY*'s manner and attitude.*)

I'm in a hurry, O'Donnell.

OWEN: The captain has an announcement to make.

LANCEY: Lieutenant Yolland is missing. We are searching for him. If we don't find him, or if we receive no information as to where he is to be found, I will pursue the following course of action. (*He indicates to* OWEN *to translate.*)

OWEN: They are searching for George. If they don't find him—

LANCEY: Commencing twenty-four hours from now we will shoot all livestock in Ballybeg.

(OWEN *stares at* LANCEY.)

At once.

OWEN: Beginning this time tomorrow they'll kill every animal in Baile Beag—unless they're told where George is.

LANCEY: If that doesn't bear results, commencing forty-eight hours from now we will embark on a series of evictions and levelling of every abode in the following selected areas—

OWEN: You're not—!

LANCEY: Do your job. Translate.

OWEN: If they still haven't found him in two days time they'll begin evicting and levelling every house starting with these townlands.

(LANCEY *reads from his list.*)

LANCEY: Swinefort.

OWEN: Lis na Muc.

LANCEY: Burnfoot.

OWEN: Bun na hAbhann.

LANCEY: Dromduff.

OWEN: Druim Dubh.

LANCEY: Whiteplains.

OWEN: Machaire Ban.

LANCEY: Kings Head.

OWEN: Cnoc na Ri.

LANCEY: If by then the lieutenant hasn't been found, we will proceed until a complete clearance is made of this entire section.

OWEN: If Yolland hasn't been got by then, they will ravish the whole parish.

LANCEY: I trust they know exactly what they've got to do. (*Pointing to* BRIDGET) I know you. I know where you live. (*Pointing to* SARAH) Who are you? Name!

(SARAH*'s mouth opens and shuts, opens and shuts. Her face becomes contorted.*)

What's your name?

(*Again* SARAH *tries frantically.*)

OWEN: Go on, Sarah. You can tell him.

(*But* SARAH *cannot. And she knows she cannot. She closes her mouth. Her head goes down.*)

Her name is Sarah Johnny Sally.

LANCEY: Where does she live?

OWEN: Bun na hAbhann.

LANCEY: Where?

OWEN: Burnfoot.

LANCEY: I want to talk to your brother—is he here?

OWEN: Not at the moment.

LANCEY: Where is he?

OWEN: He's at a wake.

LANCEY: What wake?

(DOALTY, *who has been looking out the window all through* LANCEY*'s announcements, now speaks—calmly, almost casually.*)

DOALTY: Tell him his whole camp's on fire.

LANCEY: What's your name? (*To* OWEN) Who's that lout?

OWEN: Doalty Dan Doalty.

LANCEY: Where does he live?

OWEN: Tulach Alainn.

LANCEY: What do we call it?

OWEN: Fair Hill. He says your whole camp is on fire.

(LANCEY *rushes to the window and looks out. Then he wheels on* DOALTY.)

LANCEY: I'll remember you, Mr. Doalty. (*To* OWEN) You carry a big responsibility in all this.

(*He goes off.*)

BRIDGET: Mother of God, does he mean it, Owen?

OWEN: Yes, he does.

BRIDGET: We'll have to hide the beasts somewhere—our Seamus'll know where. Maybe at the back of Lis na nGradh—or in the caves at the far end of the Tra Bhan. Come on, Doalty! Come on! Don't be standing about there!

(DOALTY *does not move.* BRIDGET *runs to the door and stops suddenly. She sniffs the air. Panic.*)

The sweet smell! Smell it! It's the sweet smell! Jesus, it's the potato blight!

DOALTY: It's the army tents burning, Bridget.

BRIDGET: Is it? Are you sure? Is that what it is? God, I thought we were destroyed altogether. Come on! Come on!

(*She runs off.* OWEN *goes to* SARAH *who is preparing to leave.*)

OWEN: How are you? Are you all right?

(SARAH *nods: Yes.*)

Don't worry. It will come back to you again.

(SARAH *shakes her head.*)

It will. You're upset now. He frightened you. That's all's wrong.

(*Again* SARAH *shakes her head, slowly, emphatically, and smiles at* OWEN. *Then she leaves.* OWEN *busies himself gathering his belongings.* DOALTY *leaves the window and goes to him.*)

DOALTY: He'll do it, too.

OWEN: Unless Yolland's found.

DOALTY: Hah!

OWEN: Then he'll certainly do it.

DOALTY: When my grandfather was a boy they did the same thing.
(*Simply, altogether without irony*) And after all the trouble you went to, mapping the place and thinking up new names for it.
(OWEN *busies himself. Pause.* DOALTY *almost dreamily*) I've damned little to defend but he'll not put me out without a fight. And there'll be others who think the same as me.

OWEN: That's a matter for you.

DOALTY: If we'd all stick together. If we knew how to defend ourselves.

OWEN: Against a trained army.

DOALTY: The Donnelly twins know how.

OWEN: If they could be found.

DOALTY: If they could be found. (*He goes to the door.*) Give me a shout after you've finished with Lancey. I might know something then.

(*He leaves.*)

(OWEN *picks up the Name-Book. He looks at it momentarily, then puts it on top of the pile he is carrying. It falls to the floor. He stoops to pick it up—hesitates—leaves it. He goes upstairs. As* OWEN *ascends,* HUGH *and* JIMMY JACK *enter. Both wet and drunk.* JIMMY *is very unsteady. He is trotting behind* HUGH, *trying to break in on* HUGH*'s declamation.* HUGH *is equally drunk but more experienced in drunkenness: there is a portion of his mind which retains its clarity.*)

HUGH: There I was, appropriately dispositioned to proffer my condolences to the bereaved mother . . .

JIMMY: Hugh—

HUGH: . . . and about to enter the *domus lugubris*°— Maire Chatach?

JIMMY: The wake house.

HUGH: Indeed—when I experience a plucking at my

elbow: Mister George Alexander, Justice of the Peace. "My tidings are infelicitous," said he— Bridget? Too slow. Doalty?

JIMMY: *Infelix*°—unhappy.

HUGH: Unhappy indeed. "Master Bartley Timlin has been appointed to the new national school." "Timlin? Who is Timlin?" "A schoolmaster from Cork. And he will be a major asset to the community: he is also a very skilled bacon-curer!"

JIMMY: Hugh—

HUGH: Ha-ha-ha-ha-ha! The Cork bacon-curer! *Barbarus hic ego sum quia non intelligor ulli*°—James?

JIMMY: Ovid.

HUGH: *Procede.*°

JIMMY: "I am a barbarian in this place because I am not understood by anyone."

HUGH: Indeed—(*Shouts*) Manus! Tea! I will compose a satire on Master Bartley Timlin, schoolmaster and bacon-curer. But it will be too easy, won't it? (*Shouts*) Strong tea! Black!

(*The only way* JIMMY *can get* HUGH*'s attention is by standing in front of him and holding his arms.*)

JIMMY: Will you listen to me, Hugh!

HUGH: James. (*Shouts*) And a slice of soda bread.

JIMMY: I'm going to get married.

HUGH: Well!

JIMMY: At Christmas.

HUGH: Splendid.

JIMMY: To Athene.

HUGH: Who?

JIMMY: Pallas Athene.

HUGH: *Glaukopis Athene?*

JIMMY: Flashing-eyed, Hugh, flashing-eyed!

(*He attempts the gesture he has made before: standing to attention, the momentary spasm, the salute, the face raised in pained ecstasy—but the body does not respond efficiently this time. The gesture is grotesque.*)

HUGH: The lady has assented?

JIMMY: She asked *me*—I assented.

HUGH: Ah. When was this?

JIMMY: Last night.

HUGH: What does her mother say?

JIMMY: Metis from Hellespont? Decent people—good stock.

HUGH: And her father?

JIMMY: I'm meeting Zeus tomorrow. Hugh, will you be my best man?

HUGH: Honoured, James; profoundly honoured.

JIMMY: You know what I'm looking for, Hugh, don't

---

domus lugubris, house of mourning.

Infelix, unlucky, unhappy. *Barbarus hic ego sum quia non intelligor ulli,* I am a barbarian here because I am not understood by anyone. *Procede,* proceed.

you? I mean to say—you know—I—I—I joke like the rest of them—you know?—*(Again he attempts the pathetic routine but abandons it instantly.)* You know yourself, Hugh—don't you?—you know all that. But what I'm really looking for, Hugh—what I really want—companionship, Hugh—at my time of life, companionship, company, someone to talk to. Away up in Beann na Gaoithe—you've no idea how lonely it is. Companionship—correct, Hugh? Correct?

HUGH: Correct.

JIMMY: And I always liked her, Hugh. Correct?

HUGH: Correct, James.

JIMMY: Someone to talk to.

HUGH: Indeed.

JIMMY: That's all, Hugh. The whole story. You know it all now, Hugh. You know it all.

(As JIMMY says those last lines he is crying, shaking his head, trying to keep his balance, and holding a finger up to his lips in absurd gestures of secrecy and intimacy. Now he staggers away, tries to sit on a stool, misses it, slides to the floor, his feet in front of him, his back against the broken cart. Almost at once he is asleep. HUGH watches all of this. Then he produces his flask and is about to pour a drink when he sees the Name-Book on the floor. He picks it up and leafs through it, pronouncing the strange names as he does. Just as he begins, OWEN emerges and descends with two bowls of tea.)

HUGH: Ballybeg. Burnfoot. King's Head. Whiteplains. Fair Hill. Dunboy. Green Bank.

(OWEN snatches the book from HUGH.)

OWEN: I'll take that. *(In apology)* It's only a catalogue of names.

HUGH: I know what it is.

OWEN: A mistake—my mistake—nothing to do with us. I hope that's strong enough *(tea)*. *(He throws the book on the table and crosses over to JIMMY.)* Jimmy. Wake up, Jimmy. Wake up, man.

JIMMY: What—what-what?

OWEN: Here. Drink this. Then go on away home. There may be trouble. Do you hear me, Jimmy? There may be trouble.

HUGH *(Indicating Name-Book)*: We must learn those new names.

OWEN *(Searching around)*: Did you see a sack lying about?

HUGH: We must learn where we live. We must learn to make them our own. We must make them our new home.

(OWEN finds a sack and throws it across his shoulders.)

OWEN: I know where I live.

HUGH: James thinks he knows, too. I look at James and three thoughts occur to me: A—that it is not the literal past, the "facts" of history, that shape us, but images of the past embodied in language. James has ceased to make that discrimination.

OWEN: Don't lecture me, Father.

HUGH: B—we must never cease renewing those images; because once we do, we fossilize. Is there no soda bread?

OWEN: And C, Father—one single, unalterable "fact": if Yolland is not found, we are all going to be evicted. Lancey has issued the order.

HUGH: Ah. *Edictum imperatoris.*°

OWEN: You should change out of those wet clothes. I've got to go. I've got to see Doalty Dan Doalty.

HUGH: What about?

OWEN: I'll be back soon.

(As OWEN exits.)

HUGH: Take care, Owen. To remember everything is a form of madness.

(He looks around the room, carefully, as if he were about to leave it forever. Then he looks at Jimmy, asleep again.)

The road to Sligo. A spring morning. 1798. Going into battle. Do you remember, James? Two young gallants with pikes across their shoulders and the *Aeneid* in their pockets. Everything seemed to find definition that spring—a congruence, a miraculous matching of hope and past and present and possibility. Striding across the fresh, green land. The rhythms of perception heightened. The whole enterprise of consciousness accelerated. We were gods that morning, James; and I had recently married *my* goddess, Caitlin Dubh Nic Reactainn, may she rest in peace. And to leave her and my infant son in his cradle—that was heroic, too. By God, sir, we were magnificent. We marched as far as—where was it?—Glenties! All of twenty-three miles in one day. And it was there, in Phelan's pub, that we got homesick for Athens, just like Ulysses. The *desiderium nostrorum*°—the need for our own. Our *pietas,*° James, was for older, quieter things. And that was the longest twenty-three miles back I ever made. *(Toasts JIMMY)* My friend, confusion is not an ignoble condition.

(MAIRE enters.)

MAIRE: I'm back again. I set out for somewhere but I couldn't remember where. So I came back here.

HUGH: Yes, I will teach you English, Maire Chatach.

MAIRE: Will you, Master? I must learn it. I need to learn it.

HUGH: Indeed you may well be my only pupil.

Edictum imperatoris, the decree of the commander. ***desiderium nostrorum,*** longing/need for our things/people. ***pietas,*** piety.

(He goes towards the steps and begins to ascend.)

MAIRE: When can we start?

HUGH: Not today. Tomorrow, perhaps. After the funeral. We'll begin tomorrow. *(Ascending)* But don't expect too much. I will provide you with the available words and the available grammar. But will that help you to interpret between privacies? I have no idea. But it's all we have. I have no idea at all.

(He is now at the top.)

MAIRE: Master, what does the English word "always" mean?

HUGH: *Semper—per omnia saecula.*° The Greeks called it *"aei."*° It's not a word I'd start with. It's a silly word, girl.

(He sits. JIMMY *is awake. He gets to his feet.* MAIRE *sees the Name-Book, picks it up, and sits with it on her knee.)*

MAIRE: When he comes back, this is where he'll come to. He told me this is where he was happiest.

*(*JIMMY *sits beside* MAIRE.*)*

JIMMY: Do you know the Greek word *endogamein?*° It means to marry within the tribe. And the word *exogamein*° means to marry outside the tribe. And you don't cross those borders casually—both sides get very angry. Now, the problem is this: Is Athene sufficiently mortal or am I sufficiently godlike for the marriage to be acceptable to her people and to my people? You think about that.

HUGH: *Urbs antiqua fuit*°—there was an ancient city which, 'tis said, Juno loved above all the lands. And it was the goddess's aim and cherished hope that here should be the capital of all nations—should the fates perchance allow that. Yet in truth she discovered that a race was springing from Trojan blood to overthrow some day these Tyrian towers—a people *late regem belloque superbum*°—kings of broad realms and proud in war who would come forth for Lybia's downfall—such was—such was the course—such was the course ordained—ordained by fate . . . What the hell's wrong with me? Sure I know it backways. I'll begin again. *Urbs antiqua fuit*—there was an ancient city which, 'tis said, Juno loved above all the lands.

(Begin to bring down the lights.)

And it was the goddess's aim and cherished hope that here should be the capital of all nations—should the fates perchance allow that. Yet in truth she discovered that a race was springing from Trojan blood to overthrow some day these Tyrian towers—a people kings of broad realms and proud in war who would come forth for Lybia's downfall . . .

BLACK

Semper—per omnia saecula, Always—for all time. *aei,* always. *endogamein,* to marry within the tribe. *exogamein,* to marry outside the tribe.

Urbs antiqua fuit, There was an ancient city. *late regem belloque superbum,* kings of broad realms and proud in war.

Figure 1. Manus (Barry Lynch) encourages a delighted Sarah (Cara Kelly) to speak in the Donmar Warehouse production of *Translations*, directed by Sam Mendes, 1993. (Photograph: Mark Douet.)

Figure 2. Jimmy Jack (Tony Rohr) explains a passage from Horace to Doalty (Daniel Flynn), who adopts an expression of intense interest. (Photograph: Mark Douet.)

Figure 3. Owen (Robert Patterson, *right*) offers a bottle of locally made liquor (poteen) to his brother, Manus (Barry Lynch). (Photograph: Mark Douet.)

Figure 4. Hugh (Norman Rodway) reacts with anger and disbelief to the news that they will all be evicted if the British lieutenant, Yolland, is not found. (Photograph: Mark Douet.)

Staging of *Translations*

REVIEW OF THE DONMAR WAREHOUSE
PRODUCTION, 1993, BY NICHOLAS DE JONGH

Brian Friel's plays are often messages written in code. At first they seem as clear as Californian swimming pools. Then you glimpse something sinister lurking beneath the surface calm.

Friel's *Translations,* which has acquired near classic status since its first performance in 1980, memorably reveals the playwright's subtle reticence. He leaves us to gather clues, to decipher the cryptic signals, to catch the great meaning in the little action.

At first Friel seems to conjure up a sentimental vision of long-lost rural Ireland. His scene is a hedge school in the hot Irish summer of 1833. These schools, flourishing in disused barns, were informal peasant institutions which satisfied a hunger for knowledge and learning.

Here almost everything and everybody happens, presided over by Hugh, an elderly slight drunken old classicist: Tony Rohr's sexagenarian Jimmy Jack, looking like a tramp lifted from Samuel Beckett, declaims Homer and is clearly more at home with Greek goddesses than Irish peasants. Hugh's son Manus, vainly waiting for his own hedge school, teaches Sarah, a girl with an overwhelming speech defect, to speak her own name.

Sam Mendes's production, with Johan Engels's earthy set design and romantic lighting, revels in this eccentric atmosphere. But then a change begins to steal across the stage.

Owen, Hugh's younger son, appears after six years away, bringing two Royal Engineers from England. The engineers, with a contingent of sappers in this outpost of empire, are on a mission of generosity: they will make the first Ordnance Survey of Ireland, putting Irish names into English. Of course Captain Lancey, in scarlet, plume and well-heeled English courtesy, accompanied by young Lieutenant Yolland, has to have his explanatory speech translated into Irish by Owen. But it is not long before this useful go-between and the Lieutenant, played with the right impetuous eagerness by James Larkin, are putting an English gloss upon Irish names.

Meanwhile Friel makes ample mock of the way in which the Lieutenant, and Manus's girl, Maire (an inhibited Zara Turner), find it so hard to leap the language gap to whisper sweet somethings to each other. The process is so gently amused, so lyrical, you begin to regret the lack of dramatic momentum, though already there is a strange sense of unease which Mendes fails to stress.

Translations does not just deal with English empire building. This little peasant enclave becomes a microcosm of Ireland. It is a scene of loss, strangeness and change. Ireland is losing its tongue, its individualising essence. Retaliation comes on. As Manus, all brooding, watchful intensity in Barry Lynch's enigmatic performance, loses his girl, so Yolland disappears. And a terrible vengeance is threatened by Lancey.

In the final darkening scene, which Mendes turns into a lament for a vanishing world, Jimmy and Norman Rodway's over-flamboyant Hugh are left like two old relics retreating into their classical dreams.

An illuminated map of Ireland appears behind Hugh. The sense is of a country doomed to division, warfare and wild fanaticism. The echoes sound down the years and reach us in the here and now.

ATHOL FUGARD

1932–

Although Fugard's plays deal almost exclusively with the world of South African experience, they have engaged and challenged audiences throughout the world, for in bearing witness to the inhumanity of his country's long-standing racist policy of *apartheid* (literally, "separateness"), Fugard persistently creates characters and situations that lamentably reflect an international condition. Even with the legal dismantling of apartheid, South Africa is still a country divided, often violently, between the white minority and the black majority, as well as between political factions on both sides. Fugard himself grew up in a family that was sharply divided in its view of racial affairs: his father, a hard-drinking jazz pianist of English and Irish descent, was, as Fugard remembers him, "full of pointless, unthought-out prejudices," whereas his mother, an Afrikaner of Dutch colonial stock, had a limitless "capacity for rising above the South African situation and seeing people as people." Thus he speaks of his mother as having "paced my emancipation from prejudice and bigotry."

Fugard was born in Middleburg, a village in the semidesert region of South Africa where his father once led a small band called the Orchestral Jazzonians. Fugard's father became so alcoholic and indolent that his mother was compelled to support the family, first by running a small boardinghouse, the Jubilee Hotel, then by operating a café, the St. George's Park Tea Room, which is the setting for Fugard's highly autobiographical play, *"MASTER HAROLD"... and the Boys* (1982). In his childhood, Fugard, like the character Hally who is modeled on him (indeed, who bears his childhood nickname), developed a close friendship with one of his mother's black waiters, a man named Sam Semela. Despite the racial gulf and the difference of some twenty years in their ages, they became so close that Fugard thinks of Semela as "the most significant—the only—friend of my boyhood years." Like Hally in the play, Fugard vividly remembers a kite-flying experience with Sam as one of his most precious boyhood experiences. Similarly, Fugard shared his reading and academic learning with Sam, and Sam shared his worldly experience and wisdom with Fugard. And when he was ten years old, Fugard had an argument with his friend (the cause of which he does not remember), and as he bicycled past Sam shortly after the argument, he "spat in his face." Looking back upon that event years later in his notebooks, Fugard did not imagine he would "ever deal with the shame that overwhelmed me the second after I had done that."

Though the play reflects Fugard's overwhelming sense of shame about that incident, it does not show another prominent side of his adolescence, namely the fact that he was, like his friend Sam, a highly accomplished ballroom dancer. Indeed, he and his sister Glenda were junior ballroom dancing champions several times during his teenage years. As a teenager, he also attended the equivalent of technical high school, evidently planning to become a mechanic, but was so academically gifted that he won a scholarship to the University of Cape Town, where he majored in philosophy and did some lightweight boxing on the side. By the time of his senior year, however, he "had a sense of horizons *shrinking,*" so he quit school before graduation and started hitchhiking north in the hopes of eventually reaching Cairo. But after running out of money in Port Sudan, he took a job as the only white seaman on a ship bound for Japan, and during the next two years developed several friendships with blacks and Asians that called into question the racial prejudices of his native land. In his spare time aboard ship, Fugard spent hundreds of hours working on a novel based on his mother's life—he "wanted to write the great South African novel"—but eventually became discouraged with the manuscript and threw it overboard. When he returned to South Africa, however, he could not imagine any other line of work than writing, so his mother bought him a typewriter, and he began writing articles for the local paper and then news bulletins for the national radio in Cape Town.

As a journalist, Fugard was evidently impatient with the task of objective reporting—"my work was always too colored by emotion." So, when in 1956 he met and married an actress, Sheila Meiring, he was naturally inclined to become "more and more involved in theater." He turned out a few highly artificial one-acts, but after witnessing the rebellious drama of the English playwright John Osborne, as well as reading the "*unashamedly* regional" fiction of William Faulkner, Fugard came to realize "how many bloody good South African stories there were to be told." Fugard's decision to focus his plays on South African life was also fueled by his dismaying experience as a clerk in the Johannesburg office of the Native Commissioner's Court, where he witnessed firsthand the impersonal and oppressive imposition of South Africa's passbook laws, which severely restricted the lives and livelihood of black South Africans. Out of this experience and his encounters with several black South African writers in their segregated shantytowns, Fugard wrote his first full-length play, *No-Good Friday* (1958), which bears witness to both the idealistic impulses and the oppressed lives of black South Africans in the townships. As with many of his subsequent works, Fugard directed *No-Good Friday* and acted in it together with a cast of nonprofessional black actors, including Zakes Mokae, who has since come to assume a leading role in many of Fugard's plays.

After a brief and frustrating period in London, where Fugard and his wife had gone seeking further theatrical experience, they decided to return home in 1960, to be among friends and to lend support to the antiapartheid movement after a massacre of peacefully protesting blacks took place in Sharpesville, South Africa. During 1961, drawing on a notebook of literary quotations, personal observations, and theatrical ideas that he had begun keeping in London, Fugard wrote his first highly successful play, *Blood Knot*, which explores the psychologically complex love-hate relationship between two "coloured" (the South African term for people of mixed race) half brothers—the light-skinned and guilt-ridden Morrie (performed by Fugard himself) and the dark-skinned, envious, and bitter Zach (performed by Zakes Mokae). Following their performance of the play for an enthusiastic audience of invited friends, critics, writers, and actors, Fugard and Mokae took the play throughout South Africa, segregated while on trains but together on stage. A London production of *Blood Knot* did not fare so well, but in 1964 an Off-Broadway production starring James Earl Jones as Zach ran for seven months and established Fugard's reputation in America.

Like *Blood Knot*, most of Fugard's subsequent plays have focused on two or three characters complexly related to each other not only by blood, friendship, or marriage but also by the racially divided world of South African life. Among the most successful of these highly concentrated works are *Boesman and Lena* (1968), which details the wretched life and abusive marriage of a coloured husband and wife wandering across the veld; *The Island* (1972), which dramatizes the heroic effort of two black political prisoners to transcend the brutality of the prison by producing the Greek play *Antigone* in an adaptation that applies the civil disobedience of its heroine to the state of affairs in South Africa; *Sizwe Bansi Is Dead* (1972), which focuses on an unemployed black man whose fear of being arrested because his passbook is not in order drives him to steal the passbook, and thus the identity, of a dead man; *Statements after an Arrest under the Immorality Act* (1974), which explores the multifaceted relationship between a white female librarian and a coloured teacher to whom she first lends books secretly and with whom she then falls in love; *A Lesson from Aloes* (1978), which tells the story of an activist white bus driver suspected of being a political informer, his emotionally distressed wife, and the inspiration he draws from the endurance of his aloe plants to remain true to his own moral convictions; and *The Road to Mecca* (1984), which centers on several days in the life of an eccentric white sculptress as she faces the terror both of losing her artistic inspiration and of being committed to an old folks' rest home.

In the years since the dismantling of apartheid in South Africa, Fugard has continued to explore the knotty relationships between whites and blacks there. In his 1992 *Playland*—set on New Year's Eve in a traveling amusement park—two men, one black and one white, talk about their lives and share some of their deepest secrets, including the fact that each has killed a person of the other race. *Valley Song* (1995) is another play for two actors, in which Fugard himself performed the dual role of "The Author" and the coloured grandfather of a fourteen-year-old girl. Fugard's most recent play, *Sorrows and Rejoicings* (2001), explores the life of an exiled white South African writer whose relationship to his native land is complicated by his personal relationships to his white wife and black mistress.

"MASTER HAROLD" . . . *and the Boys,* widely regarded as Fugard's finest play, also focuses intensely on just a few characters. But in this case, the focal relationship of the play does not involve racially identical persons—blacks, coloureds, or whites—as do most of Fugard's earlier works. Instead *"MASTER HAROLD,"* like *Statements after an Arrest,* centers on a relationship involving racially different persons, in particular the long-standing friendship between a black waiter and the white son of his employer. In this respect, it depicts a special relationship that seems to transcend the racial tension and conflict engendered by the South African policy of apartheid. But as the play unfolds, we discover that loving relationship to be painfully, indeed shockingly, subverted by the complex familial and cultural situation within which it is deeply rooted. For just as Fugard drew on Sam Semela to create the play's Sam, so too he made Hally's offstage father, like his own father, an alcoholic and a cripple. Hally's rejection of his natural father, his turning to a black "father-figure," and his attack on both when he spits on Sam thus come not only out of Fugard's life but also out of his understanding that racial hatred can be seen, in part, as each individual's own psychological choice. In this fundamental sense, *"MASTER HAROLD,"* as Frank Rich notes in the review following the text, is concerned not just with South African apartheid but with the capacity for cruelty that divides human beings everywhere.

The two major insults of the play—Sam baring his rump to Hally and Hally spitting at Sam—are so arresting and intense, especially following upon the earlier warmth and camaraderie between the two characters (see Figure 1), that one can readily understand how difficult it is for actors to perform them, even in rehearsal. Indeed when Fugard was directing his play for the Yale Repertory Theatre premiere, he had to shock the actors into these insulting gestures by performing them himself, first baring his own backside to Zakes Mokae, the actor playing Sam, and then repeatedly spitting at him. The risk Fugard took in reenacting the moment of shame—a moment that he thought he would never deal with—was ultimately liberating both for himself and for the actors. Political theater can ask for no greater success, and Fugard's plays, though written out of a specific political reality, nonetheless speak to audiences everywhere. Perhaps they do so because they root the political in the personal, as Sam eloquently displays when he sternly rebukes Hally for mocking his father (see Figure 2), or when he says to Hally, late in the play, "I've got no right to tell you what being a man means if I don't behave like one myself, and I'm not doing so well at that this afternoon. Should we try again, Hally?" Though Hally can't give him a positive answer, Sam's willingness to try again reflects Fugard's hope that solutions, both personal and political, may yet be found.

"MASTER HAROLD"...
AND THE BOYS

BY ATHOL FUGARD

CHARACTERS

WILLIE

SAM

HALLY

SCENE

The St. George's Park Tea Room on a wet and windy Port Elizabeth afternoon.

Tables and chairs have been cleared and are stacked on one side except for one which stands apart with a single chair. On this table a knife, fork, spoon and side plate in anticipation of a simple meal, together with a pile of comic books.

Other elements: a serving counter with a few stale cakes under glass and a not very impressive display of sweets, cigarettes and cool drinks, etc.; a few cardboard advertising handouts—Cadbury's Chocolate, Coca-Cola—and a blackboard on which an untrained hand has chalked up the prices of Tea, Coffee, Scones, Milkshakes—all flavors—and Cool Drinks; a few sad ferns in pots; a telephone; an old-style jukebox.

There is an entrance on one side and an exit into a kitchen on the other.

Leaning on the solitary table, his head cupped in one hand as he pages through one of the comic books, is Sam. A black man in his mid-forties. He wears the white coat of a waiter. Behind him on his knees, mopping down the floor with a bucket of water and a rag, is Willie. Also black and about the same age as Sam. He has his sleeves and trousers rolled up.

The year: 1950.

WILLIE (Singing as he works):

> "She was scandalizin' my name,
> She took my money
> She called me honey
> But she was scandalizin' my name.
> Called it love but was playin' a game. . . ."

(He gets up and moves the bucket. Stands thinking for a moment, then, raising his arms to hold an imaginary partner, he launches into an intricate ballroom dance step. Although a mildly comic figure, he reveals a reasonable degree of accomplishment.)

Hey, Sam.

(SAM, absorbed in the comic book, does not respond.)

Hey, Boet° Sam!

(SAM looks up.)

I'm getting it. The quickstep. Look now and tell me. (He repeats the step.) Well?

SAM (Encouragingly): Show me again.

WILLIE: Okay, count for me.

SAM: Ready?

WILLIE: Ready.

Boet, Brother.

SAM: Five, six, seven, eight. . . . (WILLIE starts to dance.) A-n-d one two three four . . . and one two three four. . . . (Ad libbing as WILLIE dances.) Your shoulders, Willie . . . your shoulders! Don't look down! Look happy, Willie! Relax, Willie!

WILLIE (Desperate but still dancing): I am relax.

SAM: No, you're not.

WILLIE (He falters): Ag no man, Sam! Mustn't talk. You make me make mistakes.

SAM: But you're stiff.

WILLIE: Yesterday I'm not straight . . . today I'm too stiff!

SAM: Well, you are. You asked me and I'm telling you.

WILLIE: Where?

SAM: Everywhere. Try to glide through it.

WILLIE: Glide?

SAM: Ja, make it smooth. And give it more style. It must look like you're enjoying yourself.

WILLIE (Emphatically): I wasn't.

SAM: Exactly.

WILLIE: How can I enjoy myself? Not straight, too stiff and now it's also glide, give it more style, make it smooth. . . . Haai! Is hard to remember all those things, Boet Sam.

SAM: That's your trouble. You're trying too hard.

WILLIE: I try hard because it is hard.

SAM: But don't let me see it. The secret is to make it look easy. Ballroom must look happy, Willie, not

1251

like hard work. It must. . . . Ja! . . . it must look like romance.

WILLIE: Now another one! What's romance?

SAM: Love story with happy ending. A handsome man in tails, and in his arms, smiling at him, a beautiful lady in evening dress!

WILLIE: Fred Astaire, Ginger Rogers.

SAM: You got it. Tapdance or ballroom, it's the same. Romance. In two weeks' time when the judges look at you and Hilda, they must see a man and a woman who are dancing their way to a happy ending. What I saw was you holding her like you were frightened she was going to run away.

WILLIE: Ja! Because that is what she wants to do! I got no romance left for Hilda anymore, Boet Sam.

SAM: Then pretend. When you put your arms around Hilda, imagine she is Ginger Rogers.

WILLIE: With no teeth? You try.

SAM: Well, just remember, there's only two weeks left.

WILLIE: I know, I know! (To the jukebox.) I do it better with music. You got sixpence for Sarah Vaughan?

SAM: That's a slow foxtrot. You're practicing the quickstep.

WILLIE: I'll practice slow foxtrot.

SAM (Shaking his head): It's your turn to put money in the jukebox.

WILLIE: I only got bus fare to go home. (He returns disconsolately to his work.) Love story and happy ending! She's doing it all right, Boet Sam, but is not me she's giving happy endings. Fuckin' whore! Three nights now she doesn't come practice. I wind up gramophone, I get record ready and I sit and wait. What happens? Nothing. Ten o'clock I start dancing with my pillow. You try and practice romance by yourself, Boet Sam. Struesgod,° she doesn't come tonight I take back my dress and ballroom shoes and I find me new partner. Size twenty-six. Shoes size seven. And now she's also making trouble for me with the baby again. Reports me to Child Wellfed, that I'm not giving her money. She lies! Every week I am giving her money for milk. And how do I know is my baby? Only his hair looks like me. She's fucking around all the time I turn my back. Hilda Samuels is a bitch! (Pause.) Hey, Sam!

SAM: Ja.

WILLIE: You listening?

SAM: Ja.

WILLIE: So what you say?

SAM: About Hilda?

WILLIE: Ja.

SAM: When did you last give her a hiding?

WILLIE (Reluctantly): Sunday night.

SAM: And today is Thursday.

WILLIE (He knows what's coming): Okay.

SAM: Hiding on Sunday night, then Monday, Tuesday, and Wednesday she doesn't come to practice . . . and you are asking me why?

WILLIE: I said okay, Boet Sam!

SAM: You hit her too much. One day she's going to leave you for good.

WILLIE: So? She makes me the hell-in too much.

SAM (Emphasizing his point): Too much and too hard. You had the same trouble with Eunice.

WILLIE: Because she also make the hell-in, Boet Sam. She never got the steps right. Even the waltz.

SAM: Beating her up every time she makes a mistake in the waltz? (Shaking his head.) No, Willie! That takes the pleasure out of ballroom dancing.

WILLIE: Hilda is not too bad with the waltz, Boet Sam. Is the quickstep where the trouble starts.

SAM (Teasing him gently): How's your pillow with the quickstep?

WILLIE (Ignoring the tease): Good! And why? Because it got no legs. That's her trouble. She can't move them quick enough, Boet Sam. I start the record and before halfway Count Basie is already winning. Only time we catch up with him is when gramophone runs down. (SAM laughs.) Haaikona, Boet Sam, is not funny.

SAM (Snapping his fingers): I got it! Give her a handicap.

WILLIE: What's that?

SAM: Give her a ten-second start and then let Count Basie go. Then I put my money on her. Hot favorite in the Ballroom Stakes: Hilda Samuels ridden by Willie Malopo.

WILLIE (Turning away): I'm not talking to you no more.

SAM (Relenting): Sorry, Willie. . . .

WILLIE: It's finish between us.

SAM: Okay, okay . . . I'll stop.

WILLIE: You can also fuck off.

SAM: Willie, listen! I want to help you!

WILLIE: No more jokes?

SAM: I promise.

WILLIE: Okay. Help me.

SAM (His turn to hold an imaginary partner): Look and learn. Feet together. Back straight. Body relaxed. Right hand placed gently in the small of her back and wait for the music. Don't start worrying about making mistakes or the judges or the other competitors. It's just you, Hilda and the music, and you're going to have a good time. What Count Basie do you play?

WILLIE: "You the cream in my coffee, you the salt in my stew."

SAM: Right. Give it to me in strict tempo.

WILLIE: Ready?

SAM: Ready.

WILLIE: A-n-d . . . (Singing.)

Struesgod, As true as God (exclamation).

"You the cream in my coffee.
You the salt in my stew.
You will always be my necessity.
I'd be lost without you. . . ." (etc.)

(SAM *launches into the quickstep. He is obviously a much more accomplished dancer than* WILLIE. HALLY *enters. A seventeen-year-old white boy. Wet raincoat and school case. He stops and watches* SAM. *The demonstration comes to an end with a flourish. Applause from* HALLY *and* WILLIE.)

HALLY: Bravo! No question about it. First place goes to Mr. Sam Semela.

WILLIE *(In total agreement):* You was gliding with style, Boet Sam.

HALLY *(Cheerfully):* How's it, chaps?

SAM: Okay, Hally.

WILLIE *(Springing to attention like a soldier and saluting):* At your service, Master Harold!

HALLY: Not long to the big event, hey!

SAM: Two weeks.

HALLY: You nervous?

SAM: No.

HALLY: Think you stand a chance?

SAM: Let's just say I'm ready to go out there and dance.

HALLY: It looked like it. What about you, Willie?

(WILLIE *groans.*)

What's the matter?

SAM: He's got leg trouble.

HALLY *(Innocently):* Oh, sorry to hear that, Willie.

WILLIE: Boet Sam! You promised. (WILLIE *returns to his work.*)

(HALLY *deposits his school case and takes off his raincoat. His clothes are a little neglected and untidy: black blazer with school badge, gray flannel trousers in need of an ironing, khaki shirt and tie, black shoes.* SAM *has fetched a towel for* HALLY *to dry his hair.*)

HALLY: God, what a lousy bloody day. It's coming down cats and dogs out there. Bad for business, chaps. . . . *(Conspiratorial whisper)* . . . but it also means we're in for a nice quiet afternoon.

SAM: You can speak loud. Your Mom's not here.

HALLY: Out shopping?

SAM: No. The hospital.

HALLY: But it's Thursday. There's no visiting on Thursday afternoons. Is my Dad okay?

SAM: Sounds like it. In fact, I think he's going home.

HALLY *(Stopped short by* SAM's *remark):* What do you mean?

SAM: The hospital phoned.

HALLY: To say what?

SAM: I don't know. I just heard your Mom talking.

HALLY: So what makes you say he's going home?

SAM: It sounded as if they were telling her to come and fetch him.

(HALLY *thinks about what* SAM *has said for a few seconds.*)

HALLY: When did she leave?

SAM: About an hour ago. She said she would phone you. Want to eat?

(HALLY *doesn't respond.*)

Hally, want your lunch?

HALLY: I suppose so. *(His mood has changed.)* What's on the menu? . . . as if I don't know.

SAM: Soup, followed by meat pie and gravy.

HALLY: Today's?

SAM: No.

HALLY: And the soup?

SAM: Nourishing pea soup.

HALLY: Just the soup. *(The pile of comic books on the table.)* And these?

SAM: For your Dad. Mr. Kempston brought them.

HALLY: You haven't been reading them, have you?

SAM: Just looking.

HALLY *(Examining the comics):* Jungle Jim . . . Batman and Robin . . . Tarzan . . . God, what rubbish! Mental pollution. Take them away.

(SAM *exits waltzing into the kitchen.* HALLY *turns to* WILLIE.)

HALLY: Did you hear my Mom talking on the telephone, Willie?

WILLIE: No, Master Hally. I was at the back.

HALLY: And she didn't say anything to you before she left?

WILLIE: She said I must clean the floors.

HALLY: I mean about my Dad.

WILLIE: She didn't say nothing to me about him, Master Hally.

HALLY *(With conviction):* No! It can't be. They said he needed at least another three weeks of treatment. Sam's definitely made a mistake. *(Rummages through his school case, finds a book and settles down at the table to read.)* So, Willie!

WILLIE: Yes, Master Hally! Schooling okay today?

HALLY: Yes, okay. . . . *(He thinks about it)* . . . No, not really. Ag, what's the difference? I don't care. And Sam says you've got problems.

WILLIE: Big problems.

HALLY: Which leg is sore?

(WILLIE *groans.*)

Both legs.

WILLIE: There is nothing wrong with my legs. Sam is just making jokes.

HALLY: So then you *will* be in the competition.

WILLIE: Only if I can find a partner.

HALLY: But what about Hilda?

SAM (*Returning with a bowl of soup*): She's the one who's got trouble with her legs.

HALLY: What sort of trouble, Willie?

SAM: From the way he describes it, I think the lady has gone a bit lame.

HALLY: Good God! Have you taken her to see a doctor?

SAM: I think a vet would be better.

HALLY: What do you mean?

SAM: What do you call it again when a racehorse goes very fast?

HALLY: Gallop?

SAM: That's it!

WILLIE: Boet Sam!

HALLY: "A gallop down the homestretch to the winning post." But what's that got to do with Hilda?

SAM: Count Basie always gets there first.

(WILLIE *lets fly with his slop rag. It misses* SAM *and hits* HALLY.)

HALLY (*Furious*): For Christ's sake, Willie! What the hell do you think you're doing?

WILLIE: Sorry, Master Hally, but it's him. . . .

HALLY: Act your bloody age! (*Hurls the rag back at* WILLIE.) Cut out the nonsense now and get on with your work. And you too, Sam. Stop fooling around.

(SAM *moves away.*)

No. Hang on. I haven't finished! Tell me exactly what my Mom said.

SAM: I have. "When Hally comes, tell him I've gone to the hospital and I'll phone him."

HALLY: She didn't say anything about taking my Dad home?

SAM: No. It's just that when she was talking on the phone. . . .

HALLY (*Interrupting him*): No, Sam. They can't be discharging him. She would have said so if they were. In any case, we saw him last night and he wasn't in good shape at all. Staff nurse even said there was talk about taking more X-rays. And now suddenly today he's better? If anything, it sounds more like a bad turn to me . . . which I sincerely hope it isn't. Hang on . . . how long ago did you say she left?

SAM: Just before two . . . (*His wrist watch*) . . . hour and a half.

HALLY: I know how to settle it. (*Behind the counter to the telephone. Talking as he dials.*) Let's give her ten minutes to get to the hospital, ten minutes to load him up, another ten, at the most, to get home, and another ten to get him inside. Forty minutes. They should have been home for at least half an hour already. (*Pause—he waits with the receiver to his ear.*) No reply, chaps. And you know why? Because she's at his bedside in hospital helping him pull through a bad turn. You definitely heard wrong.

SAM: Okay.

(*As far as* HALLY *is concerned, the matter is settled. He returns to his table, sits down, and divides his attention between the book and his soup.* SAM *is at his school case and picks up a textbook.*)

Modern Graded Mathematics for Standards Nine and Ten.

(*Opens it at random and laughs at something he sees.*)

Who is this supposed to be?

HALLY: Old fart-face Prentice.

SAM: Teacher?

HALLY: Thinks he is. And believe me, that is not a bad likeness.

SAM: Has he seen it?

HALLY: Yes.

SAM: What did he say?

HALLY: Tried to be clever, as usual. Said I was no Leonardo da Vinci and that bad art had to be punished. So, six of the best, and his are bloody good.

SAM: On your bum?

HALLY: Where else? The days when I got them on my hands are gone forever, Sam.

SAM: With your trousers down!

HALLY: No. He's not quite that barbaric.

SAM: That's the way they do it in jail.

HALLY (*Flicker of morbid interest*): Really?

SAM: Ja. When the magistrate sentences you to "strokes with a light cane."

HALLY: Go on.

SAM: They make you lie down on a bench. One policeman pulls down your trousers and holds your ankles, another one pulls your shirt over your head and holds your arms. . . .

HALLY: Thank you! That's enough.

SAM: . . . and the one that gives you the strokes talks to you gently and for a long time between each one. (*He laughs.*)

HALLY: I've heard enough. Sam! Jesus! It's a bloody awful world when you come to think of it. People can be real bastards.

SAM: That's the way it is, Hally.

HALLY: It doesn't *have* to be that way. There is something called progress, you know. We don't exactly burn people at the stake anymore.

SAM: Like Joan of Arc.

HALLY: Correct. If she was captured today, she'd be given a fair trial.

SAM: And then the death sentence.

HALLY (*A world-weary sigh*): I know, I know! I oscillate between hope and despair for this world as well, Sam. But things will change, you wait and see. One day somebody is going to get up and give history a kick up the backside and get it going again.

SAM: Like who?

HALLY (*After thought*): They're called social reformers. Every age, Sam, has got its social reformer. My history book is full of them.

SAM: So where's ours?

HALLY: Good question. And I hate to say it, but the answer is: I don't know. Maybe he hasn't even been born yet. Or is still only a babe in arms at his mother's breast. God, what a thought.

SAM: So we just go on waiting.

HALLY: Ja, looks like it. (*Back to his soup and the book.*)

SAM (*Reading from the textbook*): "Introduction: In some mathematical problems only the magnitude. . . ." (*He mispronounces the word "magnitude."*)

HALLY (*Correcting him without looking up*): Magnitude.

SAM: What's it mean?

HALLY: How big it is. The size of the thing.

SAM (*Reading*): " . . . magnitude of the quantities is of importance. In other problems we need to know whether these quantities are negative or positive. For example, whether there is a debit or credit bank balance . . ."

HALLY: Whether you're broke or not.

SAM: " . . . whether the temperature is above or below Zero. . . ."

HALLY: Naught degrees. Cheerful state of affairs! No cash and you're freezing to death. Mathematics won't get you out of that one.

SAM: "All these quantities are called . . ." (*Spelling the word*) . . . s-c-a-l. . . .

HALLY: Scalars.

SAM: Scalars! (*Shaking his head with a laugh.*) You understand all that?

HALLY (*Turning a page*): No. And I don't intend to try.

SAM: So what happens when the exams come?

HALLY: Failing a maths exam isn't the end of the world, Sam. How many times have I told you that examination results don't measure intelligence?

SAM: I would say about as many times as you've failed one of them.

HALLY (*Mirthlessly*): Ha, ha, ha.

SAM (*Simultaneously*): Ha, ha, ha.

HALLY: Just remember Winston Churchill didn't do particularly well at school.

SAM: You've also told me that one many times.

HALLY: Well, it just so happens to be the truth.

SAM (*Enjoying the word*): Magnitude! Magnitude! Show me how to use it.

HALLY (*After thought*): An intrepid social reformer will not be daunted by the magnitude of the task he has undertaken.

SAM (*Impressed*): Couple of jaw-breakers in there!

HALLY: I gave you three for the price of one. Intrepid, daunted, and magnitude. I did that once in an exam. Put five of the words I had to explain in one sentence. It was half a page long.

SAM: Well, I'll put my money on you in the English exam.

HALLY: Piece of cake. Eighty percent without even trying.

SAM (*Another textbook from* HALLY's *case*): And history?

HALLY: So-so. I'll scrape through. In the fifties if I'm lucky.

SAM: You didn't do too badly last year.

HALLY: Because we had World War One. That at least has some action. You try to find that in the South African Parliamentary system.

SAM (*Reading from the history textbook*): "Napoleon and the principle of equality." Hey! This sounds interesting. "After concluding peace with Britain in 1802, Napoleon used a brief period of calm to in-sti-tute . . ."

HALLY: Introduce.

SAM: " . . . many reforms. Napoleon regarded all people as equal before the law and wanted them to have equal opportunities for advancement. All ves-ti-ges of the feu-dal sys-tem with its oppression of the poor were abol-ished." Vestiges, feudal system, and abolished. I'm all right on oppression.

HALLY: I'm thinking. He swept away . . . abolished . . . the last remains . . . vestiges . . . of the bad old days . . . feudal system.

SAM: Ha! There's the social reformer we're waiting for. He sounds like a man of some magnitude.

HALLY: I'm not so sure about that. It's a damn good title for a book, though. A man of magnitude!

SAM: He sounds pretty big to me, Hally.

HALLY: Don't confuse historical significance with greatness. But maybe I'm being a bit prejudiced. Have a look in there and you'll see he's two chapters long. And hell! . . . has he only got dates, Sam, all of which you've got to remember! This campaign and that campaign, and then, because of all the fighting, the next thing is we get Peace Treaties all over the place. And what's the end of the story? Battle of Waterloo, which he loses. Wasn't worth it. No, I don't know about him as a man of magnitude.

SAM: Then who would you say was?

HALLY: To answer that, we need a definition of greatness, and I suppose that would be somebody who . . . somebody who benefited all mankind.

SAM: Right. But like who?

HALLY (*He speaks with total conviction*): Charles Darwin. Remember him? That big book from the library. *The Origin of the Species.*

SAM: Him?

HALLY: Yes. For his Theory of Evolution.

SAM: You didn't finish it.

HALLY: I ran out of time. I didn't finish it because my two weeks was up. But I'm going to take it out again after I've digested what I read. It's safe. I've hidden it away in the Theology section. Nobody ever goes in there. And anyway who are you to talk? You hardly even looked at it.

SAM: I tried. I looked at the chapters in the beginning and I saw one called "The Struggle for an Existence." Ah ha, I thought. At last! But what did I get? Something called the mistiltoe which needs the apple tree and there's too many seeds and all are going to die except one . . . ! No, Hally.

HALLY (*Intellectually outraged*): What do you mean, No! The poor man had to start somewhere. For God's sake, Sam, he revolutionized science. Now we know.

SAM: What?

HALLY: Where we come from and what it all means.

SAM: And that's a benefit to mankind? Anyway, I still don't believe it.

HALLY: God, you're impossible. I showed it to you in black and white.

SAM: Doesn't mean I got to believe it.

HALLY: It's the likes of you that kept the Inquisition in business. It's called bigotry. Anyway, that's my man of magnitude. Charles Darwin! Who's yours?

SAM (*Without hesitation*): Abraham Lincoln.

HALLY: I might have guessed as much. Don't get sentimental, Sam. You've never been a slave, you know. And anyway we freed your ancestors here in South Africa long before the Americans. But if you want to thank somebody on their behalf, do it to Mr. William Wilberforce.° Come on. Try again. I want a real genius.

(*Now enjoying himself, and so is* SAM. HALLY *goes behind the counter and helps himself to a chocolate.*)

SAM: William Shakespeare.

HALLY (*No enthusiasm*): Oh. So you're also one of them, are you? You're basing that opinion on only one play, you know. You've only read my *Julius Caesar* and even I don't understand half of what they're talking about. They should do what they did with the old Bible: bring the language up to date.

SAM: That's all you've got. It's also the only one *you've* read.

HALLY: I know. I admit it. That's why I suggest we reserve our judgment until we've checked up on a few others. I've got a feeling, though, that by the end of this year one is going to be enough for me, and I can give you the names of twenty-nine other chaps in the Standard Nine class of the Port Elizabeth Technical College who feel the same. But if you want him, you can have him. My turn now. (*Pacing.*) This is a damned good exercise, you know! It started off looking like a simple question and here it's got us really probing into the intellectual heritage of our civilization.

SAM: So who is it going to be?

HALLY: My next man . . . and he gets the title on two scores: social reform and literary genius . . . is Leo Nikolaevich Tolstoy.

SAM: That Russian.

HALLY: Correct. Remember the picture of him I showed you?

SAM: With the long beard.

HALLY (*Trying to look like Tolstoy*): And those burning, visionary eyes. My God, the face of a social prophet if ever I saw one! And remember my words when I showed it to you? Here's a *man*, Sam!

SAM: Those were words, Hally.

HALLY: Not many intellectuals are prepared to shovel manure with the peasants and then go home and write a "little book" called *War and Peace*. Incidentally, Sam, he was somebody else who, to quote, ". . . did not distinguish himself scholastically."

SAM: Meaning?

HALLY: He was also no good at school.

SAM: Like you and Winston Churchill.

HALLY (*Mirthlessly*): Ha, ha, ha.

SAM (*Simultaneously*): Ha, ha, ha.

HALLY: Don't get clever, Sam. That man freed his serfs of his own free will.

SAM: No argument. He was somebody, all right. I accept him.

HALLY: I'm sure Count Tolstoy will be very pleased to hear that. Your turn. Shoot. (*Another chocolate from behind the counter.*) I'm waiting, Sam.

SAM: I've got him.

HALLY: Good. Submit your candidate for examination.

SAM: Jesus.

HALLY (*Stopped dead in his tracks*): Who?

SAM: Jesus Christ.

HALLY: Oh, come on, Sam!

SAM: The Messiah.

HALLY: Ja, but still . . . No, Sam. Don't let's get started on religion. We'll just spend the whole afternoon arguing again. Suppose I turn around and say Mohammed?

SAM: All right.

HALLY: You can't have them both on the same list!

SAM: Why not? You like Mohammed, I like Jesus.

HALLY: I *don't* like Mohammed. I never have. I was merely being hypothetical. As far as I'm concerned, the Koran is as bad as the Bible. No. Religion is out! I'm not going to waste my time again arguing with you about the existence of God. You know perfectly well I'm an atheist . . . and I've got homework to do.

SAM: Okay, I take him back.

HALLY: You've got time for one more name.

SAM (*After thought*): I've got one I know we'll agree on. A simple straightforward great Man of Magnitude . . . and no arguments. And *he* really *did* benefit all mankind.

William Wilberforce, British politician (1759–1833), ardent supporter of the abolition of slavery.

HALLY: I wonder. After your last contribution I'm beginning to doubt whether anything in the way of an intellectual agreement is possible between the two of us. Who is he?

SAM: Guess.

HALLY: Socrates? Alexandre Dumas? Karl Marx, Dostoevsky? Nietzsche?

(SAM *shakes his head after each name.*)

Give me a clue.

SAM: The letter *P* is important. . . .

HALLY: Plato!

SAM: . . . and his name begins with an *F.*

HALLY: I've got it. Freud and Psychology.

SAM: No. I didn't understand him.

HALLY: That makes two of us.

SAM: Think of moldy apricot jam.

HALLY (*After a delighted laugh*): Penicillin and Sir Alexander Fleming! And the title of the book: *The Microbe Hunters.* (*Delighted.*) Splendid, Sam! Splendid. For once we are in total agreement. The major breakthrough in medical science in the Twentieth Century. If it wasn't for him, we might have lost the Second World War. It's deeply gratifying, Sam, to know that I haven't been wasting my time in talking to you. (*Strutting around proudly.*) Tolstoy may have educated his peasants, but I've educated you.

SAM: Standard Four to Standard Nine.

HALLY: Have we been at it as long as that?

SAM: Yep. And my first lesson was geography.

HALLY (*Intrigued*): Really? I don't remember.

SAM: My room there at the back of the old Jubilee Boarding House. I had just started working for your Mom. Little boy in short trousers walks in one afternoon and asks me seriously: "Sam, do you want to see South Africa?" Hey man! Sure I wanted to see South Africa!

HALLY: Was that me?

SAM: . . . So the next thing I'm looking at a map you had just done for homework. It was your first one and you were very proud of yourself.

HALLY: Go on.

SAM: Then came my first lesson. "Repeat after me, Sam: Gold in the Transvaal, mealies° in the Free State, sugar in Natal, and grapes in the Cape." I still know it!

HALLY: Well, I'll be buggered. So that's how it all started.

SAM: And your next map was one with all the rivers and the mountains they came from. The Orange, the Vaal, the Limpopo, the Zambezi. . . .

HALLY: You've got a phenomenal memory!

SAM: You should be grateful. That is why you started passing your exams. You tried to be better than me.

(*They laugh together.* WILLIE *is attracted by the laughter and joins them.*)

HALLY: The old Jubilee Boarding House. Sixteen rooms with board and lodging, rent in advance and one week's notice. I haven't thought about it for donkey's years . . . and I don't think that's an accident. God, was I glad when we sold it and moved out. Those years are not remembered as the happiest ones of an unhappy childhood.

WILLIE (*Knocking on the table and trying to imitate a woman's voice*): "Hally, are you there?"

HALLY: Who's that supposed to be?

WILLIE: "What you doing in there, Hally? Come out at once!"

HALLY (*To* SAM): What's he talking about?

SAM: Don't you remember?

WILLIE: "Sam, Willie . . . is he in there with you boys?"

SAM: Hiding away in our room when your mother was looking for you.

HALLY (*Another good laugh*): Of course! I used to crawl and hide under your bed! But finish the story, Willie. Then what used to happen? You chaps would give the game away by telling her I was in there with you. So much for friendship.

SAM: We couldn't lie to her. She knew.

HALLY: Which meant I got another rowing° for hanging around the "servants' quarters." I think I spent more time in there with you chaps than anywhere else in that dump. And do you blame me? Nothing but bloody misery wherever you went. Somebody was always complaining about the food, or my mother was having a fight with Micky Nash because she'd caught her with a petty officer in her room. Maud Meiring was another one. Remember those two? They were prostitutes, you know. Soldiers and sailors from the troopships. Bottom fell out of the business when the war ended. God, the flotsam and jetsam that life washed up on our shores! No joking, if it wasn't for your room, I would have been the first certified ten-year-old in medical history. Ja, the memories are coming back now. Walking home from school and thinking: "What can I do this afternoon?" Try out a few ideas, but sooner or later I'd end up in there with you fellows. I bet you I could still find my way to your room with my eyes closed. (*He does exactly that.*) Down the corridor . . . telephone on the right, which my Mom keeps locked because somebody is using it on the sly and not paying . . . past the kitchen and unappetizing cooking smells . . . around the corner into the backyard, hold my breath again because there are more smells coming when I pass your lavatory,

---

mealies, South African for maize (corn).

rowing, reprimand.

then into that little passageway, first door on the right and into your room. How's that?

SAM: Good. But, as usual, you forgot to knock.

HALLY: Like that time I barged in and caught you and Cynthia . . . at it. Remember? God, was I embarrassed! I didn't know what was going on at first.

SAM: Ja, that taught you a lesson.

HALLY: And about a lot more than knocking on doors, I'll have you know, and I don't mean geography either. Hell, Sam, couldn't you have waited until it was dark?

SAM: No.

HALLY: Was it that urgent?

SAM: Yes, and if you don't believe me, wait until your time comes.

HALLY: No, thank you. I am not interested in girls. (*Back to his memories. . . . Using a few chairs he re-creates the room as he lists the items.*) A gray little room with a cold cement floor. Your bed against that wall . . . and I now know why the mattress sags so much! . . . Willie's bed . . . it's propped up on bricks because one leg is broken . . . that wobbly little table with the washbasin and jug of water . . . Yes! . . . stuck to the wall above it are some pin-up pictures from magazines. Joe Louis. . . .°

WILLIE: Brown Bomber. World Title. (*Boxing pose.*) Three rounds and knockout.

HALLY: Against who?

SAM: Max Schmeling.

HALLY: Correct. I can also remember Fred Astaire and Ginger Rogers, and Rita Hayworth in a bathing costume which always made me hot and bothered when I looked at it. Under Willie's bed is an old suitcase with all his clothes in a mess, which is why I never hide there. Your things are neat and tidy in a trunk next to your bed, and on it there is a picture of you and Cynthia in your ballroom clothes, your first silver cup for third place in a competition and an old radio which doesn't work anymore. Have I left out anything?

SAM: No.

HALLY: Right, so much for the stage directions. Now the characters. (SAM *and* WILLIE *move to their appropriate positions in the bedroom.*) Willie is in bed, under his blankets with his clothes on, complaining nonstop about something, but we can't make out a word of what he's saying because he's got his head under the blankets as well. You're on your bed trimming your toenails with a knife—not a very edifying sight—and as for me. . . . What am I doing?

SAM: You're sitting on the floor giving Willie a lecture about being a good loser while you get the

_____

Joe Louis, boxer (1914–81), world heavyweight champion (1937–49).

checkerboard and pieces ready for a game. Then you go to Willie's bed, pull off the blankets and make him play with you first because you know you're going to win, and that gives you the second game with me.

HALLY: And you certainly were a bad loser, Willie!

WILLIE: Haai!

HALLY: Wasn't he, Sam? And so slow! A game with you almost took the whole afternoon. Thank God I gave up trying to teach you how to play chess.

WILLIE: You and Sam cheated.

HALLY: I never saw Sam cheat, and mine were mostly the mistakes of youth.

WILLIE: Then how is it you two was always winning?

HALLY: Have you ever considered the possibility, Willie, that it was because we were better than you?

WILLIE: Every time better?

HALLY: Not every time. There were occasions when we deliberately let you win a game so that you would stop sulking and go on playing with us. Sam used to wink at me when you weren't looking to show me it was time to let you win.

WILLIE: So then you two didn't play fair.

HALLY: It was for your benefit, Mr. Malopo, which is more than being fair. It was an act of self-sacrifice. (*To* SAM.) But you know what my best memory is, don't you?

SAM: No.

HALLY: Come on, guess. If your memory is so good, you must remember it as well.

SAM: We got up to a lot of tricks in there, Hally.

HALLY: This one was special, Sam.

SAM: I'm listening.

HALLY: It started off looking like another of those useless nothing-to-do afternoons. I'd already been down to Main Street looking for adventure, but nothing had happened. I didn't feel like climbing trees in the Donkin Park or pretending I was a private eye and following a stranger . . . so as usual: See what's cooking in Sam's room. This time it was you on the floor. You had two thin pieces of wood and you were smoothing them down with a knife. It didn't look particularly interesting, but when I asked you what you were doing, you just said, "Wait and see, Hally. Wait . . . and see" . . . in that secret sort of way of yours, so I knew there was a surprise coming. You teased me, you bugger, by being deliberately slow and not answering my questions!

(SAM *laughs.*)

And whistling while you worked away! God, it was infuriating! I could have brained you! It was only when you tied them together in a cross and put that down on the brown paper that I realized what you were doing. "Sam is making a kite?" And when I asked you and you said "Yes" . . . ! *(Shaking his head with disbelief.)* The sheer audacity of it took my breath away. I mean, seriously, what the hell does a black man know about flying a kite? I'll be honest with you, Sam, I had no hopes for it. If you think I was excited and happy, you got another guess coming. In fact, I was shit-scared that we were going to make fools of ourselves. When we left the boarding house to go up onto the hill, I was praying quietly that there wouldn't be any other kids around to laugh at us.

SAM *(Enjoying the memory as much as* HALLY*)*: Ja, I could see that.

HALLY: I made it obvious, did I?

SAM: Ja. You refused to carry it.

HALLY: Do you blame me? Can you remember what the poor thing looked like? Tomato-box wood and brown paper! Flour and water for glue! Two of my mother's old stockings for a tail, and then all those bits and pieces of string you made me tie together so that we could fly it! Hell, no, that was now only asking for a miracle to happen.

SAM: Then the big argument when I told you to hold the string and run with it when I let go.

HALLY: I was prepared to run, all right, but straight back to the boarding house.

SAM *(Knowing what's coming)*: So what happened?

HALLY: Come on, Sam, you remember as well as I do.

SAM: I want to hear it from you.

*(*HALLY *pauses. He wants to be as accurate as possible.)*

HALLY: You went a little distance from me down the hill, you held it up ready to let it go. . . . "This is it," I thought. "Like everything else in my life, here comes another fiasco." Then you shouted, "Go, Hally!" and I started to run. *(Another pause.)* I don't know how to describe it, Sam. Ja! The miracle happened! I was running, waiting for it to crash to the ground, but instead suddenly there was something alive behind me at the end of the string, tugging at it as if it wanted to be free. I looked back . . . *(Shakes his head)* . . . I still can't believe my eyes. It was flying! Looping around and trying to climb even higher into the sky. You shouted to me to let it have more string. I did, until there was none left and I was just holding that piece of wood we had tied it to. You came up and joined me. You were laughing.

SAM: So were you. And shouting, "It works, Sam! We've done it!"

HALLY: And we had! I was so proud of us! It was the most splendid thing I had ever seen. I wished there were hundreds of kids around to watch us. The part that scared me, though, was when you showed me how to make it dive down to the ground and then just when it was on the point of crashing, swoop up again!

SAM: You didn't want to try yourself.

HALLY: Of course not! I would have been suicidal if anything had happened to it. Watching you do it made me nervous enough. I was quite happy just to see it up there with its tail fluttering behind it. You left me after that, didn't you? You explained how to get it down, we tied it to the bench so that I could sit and watch it, and you went away. I wanted you to stay, you know. I was a little scared of having to look after it by myself.

SAM *(Quietly)*: I had work to do, Hally.

HALLY: It was sort of sad bringing it down, Sam. And it looked sad again when it was lying there on the ground. Like something that had lost its soul. Just tomato-box wood, brown paper and two of my mother's old stockings! But, hell, I'll never forget that first moment when I saw it up there. I had a stiff neck the next day from looking up so much.

*(*SAM *laughs.* HALLY *turns to him with a question he never thought of asking before.)*

Why did you make that kite, Sam?

SAM *(Evenly)*: I can't remember.

HALLY: Truly?

SAM: Too long ago, Hally.

HALLY: Ja, I suppose it was. It's time for another one, you know.

SAM: Why do you say that?

HALLY: Because it feels like that. Wouldn't be a good day to fly it, though.

SAM: No. You can't fly kites on rainy days.

HALLY *(He studies* SAM. *Their memories have made him conscious of the man's presence in his life.)*

How old are you, Sam?

SAM: Two score and five.

HALLY: Strange, isn't it?

SAM: What?

HALLY: Me and you.

SAM: What's strange about it?

HALLY: Little white boy in short trousers and a black man old enough to be his father flying a kite. It's not every day you see that.

SAM: But why strange? Because the one is white and the other black?

HALLY: I don't know. Would have been just as strange, I suppose, if it had been me and my Dad . . . cripple man and a little boy! Nope! There's no chance of me flying a kite without it being strange. *(Simple statement of fact—no self-pity.)* There's a nice little short story there. "The Kite-Flyers." But we'd have to find a twist in the ending.

SAM: Twist?

HALLY: Yes. Something unexpected. The way it ended with us was too straightforward . . . me on the bench and you going back to work. There's no drama in that.

WILLIE: And me?

HALLY: You?

WILLIE: Yes me.

HALLY: You want to get into the story as well, do you? I got it! Change the title: "Afternoons in Sam's Room" . . . expand it and tell all the stories. It's on its way to being a novel. Our days in the old Jubilee. Sad in a way that they're over. I almost wish we were still in that little room.

SAM: We're still together.

HALLY: That's true. It's just that life felt the right size in there . . . not too big and not too small. Wasn't so hard to work up a bit of courage. It's got so bloody complicated since then.

(The telephone rings. SAM answers it.)

SAM: St. George's Park Tea Room . . . Hello, Madam . . . Yes, Madam, he's here. . . . Hally, it's your mother.

HALLY: Where is she phoning from?

SAM: Sounds like the hospital. It's a public telephone.

HALLY *(Relieved)*: You see! I told you. *(The telephone.)* Hello, Mom . . . Yes . . . Yes no fine. Everything's under control here. How's things with poor old Dad? . . . Has he had a bad turn? . . . What? . . . Oh, God! . . . Yes, Sam told me, but I was sure he'd made a mistake. But what's this all about, Mom? He didn't look at all good last night. How can he get better so quickly? . . . Then very obviously you must say no. Be firm with him. You're the boss. . . . You know what it's going to be like if he comes home. . . . Well then, don't blame me when I fail my exams at the end of the year. . . . Yes! How am I expected to be fresh for school when I spend half the night massaging his gammy leg? . . . So am I! . . . So tell him a white lie. Say Dr. Colley wants more X-rays of his stump. Or bribe him. We'll sneak in double tots of brandy in future. . . . What? . . . Order him to get back into bed at once! If he's going to behave like a child, treat him like one. . . . All right, Mom! I was just trying to . . . I'm sorry. . . . I said I'm sorry. . . . Quick, give me your number. I'll phone you back. *(He hangs up and waits a few seconds.)* Here we go again! *(He dials.)* I'm sorry, Mom. . . . Okay. . . . But now listen to me carefully. All it needs is for you to put your foot down. Don't take no for an answer. . . . Did you hear me? And whatever you do, don't discuss it with him. . . . Because I'm frightened you'll give in to him. . . . Yes, Sam gave me lunch. . . . I ate all of it! . . . No, Mom, not a soul. It's still raining here. . . . Right, I'll tell them. I'll just do some homework and then lock up. . . . But remember now, Mom. Don't listen to anything he says. And phone me back and let me know what happens. . . . Okay. Bye, Mom. *(He hangs up. The men are staring at him.)* My Mom says that when you're finished with the floors you must do the windows. *(Pause.)* Don't misunderstand me, chaps. All I want is for him to get better. And if he was, I'd be the first person to say: "Bring him home." But he's not, and we can't give him the medical care and attention he needs at home. That's what hospitals are there for. *(Brusquely.)* So don't just stand there! Get on with it!

(SAM clears HALLY's table.)

You heard right. My Dad wants to go home.

SAM: Is he better?

HALLY *(Sharply)*: No! How the hell can he be better when last night he was groaning with pain? This is not an age of miracles!

SAM: Then he should stay in hospital.

HALLY *(Seething with irritation and frustration)*: Tell me something I don't know, Sam. What the hell do you think I was saying to my Mom? All I can say is fuck-it-all.

SAM: I'm sure he'll listen to your Mom.

HALLY: You don't know what she's up against. He's already packed his shaving kit and pajamas and is sitting on his bed with his crutches, dressed and ready to go. I know him when he gets in that mood. If she tries to reason with him, we've had it. She's no match for him when it comes to a battle of words. He'll tie her up in knots. *(Trying to hide his true feelings.)*

SAM: I suppose it gets lonely for him in there.

HALLY: With all the patients and nurses around? Regular visits from the Salvation Army? Balls! It's ten times worse for him at home. I'm at school and my mother is here in the business all day.

SAM: He's at least got you at night.

HALLY *(Before he can stop himself)*: And we've got him! Please! I don't want to talk about it anymore. *(Unpacks his school case, slamming down books on the table.)* Life is just a plain bloody mess, that's all. And people are fools.

SAM: Come on, Hally.

HALLY: Yes, they are! They bloody well deserve what they get.

SAM: Then don't complain.

HALLY: Don't try to be clever, Sam. It doesn't suit you. Anybody who thinks there's nothing wrong with this world needs to have his head examined. Just when things are going along all right, without fail someone or something will come along and spoil everything. Somebody should write that down as a fundamental law of the Universe. The principle of perpetual disappointment. If there is a God who created this world, he should scrap it and try again.

SAM: All right, Hally, all right. What you got for homework?

HALLY: Bullshit, as usual. *(Opens an exercise book and reads.)* "Write five hundred words describing an annual event of cultural or historical significance."

SAM: That should be easy enough for you.

HALLY: And also plain bloody boring. You know what he wants, don't you? One of their useless old ceremonies. The commemoration of the landing of the 1820 Settlers, or if it's going to be culture, Carols by Candlelight every Christmas.

SAM: It's an impressive sight. Make a good description, Hally. All those candles glowing in the dark and the people singing hymns.

HALLY: And it's called religious hysteria. (*Intense irritation.*) Please, Sam! Just leave me alone and let me get on with it. I'm not in the mood for games this afternoon. And remember my Mom's orders . . . you're to help Willie with the windows. Come on now, I don't want any more nonsense in here.

SAM: Okay, Hally, okay.

(HALLY *settles down to his homework; determined preparations . . . pen, ruler, exercise book, dictionary, another cake . . . all of which will lead to nothing.*)

(SAM *waltzes over to* WILLIE *and starts to replace tables and chairs. He practices a ballroom step while doing so.* WILLIE *watches. When* SAM *is finished,* WILLIE *tries.*)

Good! But just a little bit quicker on the turn and only move in to her after she's crossed over. What about this one?

(*Another step. When* SAM *is finished,* WILLIE *again has a go.*)

Much better. See what happens when you just relax and enjoy yourself? Remember that in two weeks' time and you'll be all right.

WILLIE: But I haven't got partner, Boet Sam.

SAM: Maybe Hilda will turn up tonight.

WILLIE: No, Boet Sam. (*Reluctantly.*) I gave her a good hiding.

SAM: You mean a bad one.

WILLIE: Good bad one.

SAM: Then you mustn't complain either. Now you pay the price for losing your temper.

WILLIE: I also pay two pounds ten shilling entrance fee.

SAM: They'll refund you if you withdraw now.

WILLIE (*Appalled*): You mean, don't dance?

SAM: Yes.

WILLIE: No! I wait too long and I practice too hard. If I find me new partner, you think I can be ready in two weeks? I ask Madam for my leave now and we practice every day.

SAM: Quickstep nonstop for two weeks. World record, Willie, but you'll be mad at the end.

WILLIE: No jokes, Boet Sam.

SAM: I'm not joking.

WILLIE: So then what?

SAM: Find Hilda. Say you're sorry and promise you won't beat her again.

WILLIE: No.

SAM: Then withdraw. Try again next year.

WILLIE: No.

SAM: Then I give up.

WILLIE: Haaikona,° Boet Sam, you can't.

SAM: What do you mean, I can't? I'm telling you: I give up.

WILLIE (*Adamant*): No! (*Accusingly.*) It was you who start me ballroom dancing.

SAM: So?

WILLIE: Before that I use to be happy. And is you and Miriam who bring me to Hilda and say here's partner for you.

SAM: What are you saying, Willie?

WILLIE: You!

SAM: But me what? To blame?

WILLIE: Yes.

SAM: Willie . . . ? (*Bursts into laughter.*)

WILLIE: And now all you do is make jokes at me. You wait. When Miriam leaves you is my turn to laugh. Ha! Ha! Ha!

SAM (*He can't take* WILLIE *seriously any longer*): She can leave me tonight! I know what to do. (*Bowing before an imaginary partner.*) May I have the pleasure? (*He dances and sings.*)

"Just a fellow with his pillow . . .
Dancin' like a willow . . .
In an autumn breeze. . . ."

WILLIE: There you go again! (SAM *goes on dancing and singing.*) Boet Sam!

SAM: There's the answer to your problem! Judges' announcement in two weeks' time: "Ladies and gentlemen, the winner in the open section . . . Mr. Willie Malopo and his pillow!"

(*This is too much for a now really angry* WILLIE. *He goes for* SAM, *but the latter is too quick for him and puts* HALLY*'s table between the two of them.*)

HALLY (*Exploding*): For Christ's sake, you two!

WILLIE (*Still trying to get at* SAM): I donner° you, Sam! Struesgod!

SAM (*Still laughing*): Sorry, Willie . . . Sorry. . . .

HALLY: Sam! Willie! (*Grabs his ruler and gives* WILLIE *a vicious whack on the bum.*) How the hell am I supposed to concentrate with the two of you behaving like bloody children!

WILLIE: Hit him too!

HALLY: Shut up, Willie.

Haaikona, colloquialism of emphatic denial, "not on your life." **donner,** beat up.

WILLIE: He started jokes again.

HALLY: Get back to your work. You too, Sam. *(His ruler.)* Do you want another one, Willie?

(SAM and WILLIE return to their work. HALLY uses the opportunity to escape from his unsuccessful attempt at homework. He struts around like a little despot, ruler in hand, giving vent to his anger and frustration.)

Suppose a customer had walked in then? Or the Park Superintendent. And seen the two of you behaving like a pair of hooligans. That would have been the end of my mother's license, you know. And your jobs? Well, this is the end of it. From now on there will be no more of your ballroom nonsense in here. This is a business establishment, not a bloody New Brighton dancing school. I've been far too lenient with the two of you. *(Behind the counter for a green cool drink and a dollop of ice cream. He keeps up his tirade as he prepares it.)* But what really makes me bitter is that I allow you chaps a little freedom in here when business is bad and what do you do with it? The foxtrot! Specially you, Sam. There's more to life than trotting around a dance floor and I thought at least you knew it.

SAM: It's a harmless pleasure, Hally. It doesn't hurt anybody.

HALLY: It's also a rather simple one, you know.

SAM: You reckon so? Have you ever tried?

HALLY: Of course not.

SAM: Why don't you? Now.

HALLY: What do you mean? Me dance?

SAM: Yes. I'll show you a simple step—the waltz—then you try it.

HALLY: What will that prove?

SAM: That it might not be as easy as you think.

HALLY: I didn't say it was easy. I said it was simple—like in simple-minded, meaning mentally retarded. You can't exactly say it challenges the intellect.

SAM: It does other things.

HALLY: Such as?

SAM: Make people happy.

HALLY *(The glass in his hand)*: So do American cream sodas with ice cream. For God's sake, Sam, you're not asking me to take ballroom dancing serious, are you?

SAM: Yes.

HALLY *(Sigh of defeat)*: Oh, well, so much for trying to give you a decent education. I've obviously achieved nothing.

SAM: You still haven't told me what's wrong with admiring something that's beautiful and then trying to do it yourself.

HALLY: Nothing. But we happen to be talking about a foxtrot, not a thing of beauty.

SAM: But that is just what I'm saying. If you were to see two champions doing, two masters of the art . . . !

HALLY: Oh God, I give up. So now it's also art!

SAM: Ja.

HALLY: There's a limit, Sam. Don't confuse art and entertainment.

SAM: So then what is art?

HALLY: You want a definition?

SAM: Ja.

HALLY *(He realizes he has got to be careful. He gives the matter a lot of thought before answering)*: Philosophers have been trying to do that for centuries. What is Art? What is Life? But basically I suppose it's . . . the giving of meaning to matter.

SAM: Nothing to do with beautiful?

HALLY: It goes beyond that. It's the giving of form to the formless.

SAM: Ja, well, maybe it's not art, then. But I still say it's beautiful.

HALLY: I'm sure the word you mean to use is entertaining.

SAM *(Adamant)*: No. Beautiful. And if you want proof come along to the Centenary Hall in New Brighton in two weeks' time.

(The mention of the Centenary Hall draws WILLIE over to them.)

HALLY: What for? I've seen the two of you prancing around in here often enough.

SAM *(He laughs)*: This isn't the real thing, Hally. We're just playing around in here.

HALLY: So? I can use my imagination.

SAM: And what do you get?

HALLY: A lot of people dancing around and having a so-called good time.

SAM: That all?

HALLY: Well, basically, it is that, surely.

SAM: No, it isn't. Your imagination hasn't helped you at all. There's a lot more to it than that. We're getting ready for the championships, Hally, not just another dance. There's going to be a lot of people, all right, and they're going to have a good time, but they'll only be spectators, sitting around and watching. It's just the competitors out there on the dance floor. Party decorations and fancy lights all around the walls! The ladies in beautiful evening dresses!

HALLY: My mother's got one of those, Sam, and, quite frankly, it's an embarrassment every time she wears it.

SAM *(Undeterred)*: Your imagination left out the excitement.

(HALLY scoffs.)

Oh, yes. The finalists are not going to be out there just to have a good time. One of those couples will be the 1950 Eastern Province Champions. And your imagination left out the music.

WILLIE: Mr. Elijah Gladman Guzana and his Orchestral Jazzonions.

SAM: The sound of the big band, Hally. Trombone, trumpet, tenor and alto sax. And then, finally, your imagination also left out the climax of the evening when the dancing is finished, the judges have stopped whispering among themselves and the Master of Ceremonies collects their scorecards and goes up onto the stage to announce the winners.

HALLY: All right. So you make it sound like a bit of a do. It's an occasion. Satisfied?

SAM *(Victory)*: So you admit that!

HALLY: Emotionally yes, intellectually no.

SAM: Well, I don't know what you mean by that, all I'm telling you is that it is going to be *the* event of the year in New Brighton. It's been sold out for two weeks already. There's only standing room left. We've got competitors coming from Kingwilliamstown, East London, Port Alfred.

(HALLY starts pacing thoughtfully.)

HALLY: Tell me a bit more.

SAM: I thought you weren't interested . . . intellectually.

HALLY *(Mysteriously)*: I've got my reasons.

SAM: What do you want to know?

HALLY: It takes place every year?

SAM: Yes. But only every third year in New Brighton. It's East London's turn to have the championships next year.

HALLY: Which, I suppose, makes it an even more significant event.

SAM: Ah ha! We're getting somewhere. Our "occasion" is now a "significant event."

HALLY: I wonder.

SAM: What?

HALLY: I wonder if I would get away with it.

SAM: But what?

HALLY *(To the table and his exercise book)*: "Write five hundred words describing an annual event of cultural or historical significance." Would I be stretching poetic license a little too far if I called your ballroom championships a cultural event?

SAM: You mean . . . ?

HALLY: You think we could get five hundred words out of it, Sam?

SAM: Victor Sylvester has written a whole book on ballroom dancing.

WILLIE: You going to write about it, Master Hally?

HALLY: Yes, gentlemen, that is precisely what I am considering doing. Old Doc Bromely—he's my English teacher—is going to argue with me, of course. He doesn't like natives. But I'll point out to him that in strict anthropological terms the culture of a primitive black society includes its dancing and singing. To put my thesis in a nutshell: The war-dance has been replaced by the waltz. But it still amounts to the same thing: the release of primitive emotions through movement. Shall we give it a go?

SAM: I'm ready.

WILLIE: Me also.

HALLY: Ha! This will teach the old bugger a lesson. *(Decision taken.)* Right. Let's get ourselves organized. *(This means another cake on the table. He sits.)* I think you've given me enough general atmosphere, Sam, but to build the tension and suspense I need facts. *(Pen poised.)*

WILLIE: Give him facts, Boet Sam.

HALLY: What you called the climax . . . how many finalists?

SAM: Six couples.

HALLY *(Making notes)*: Go on. Give me the picture.

SAM: Spectators seated right around the hall. (WILLIE *becomes a spectator.)*

HALLY: . . . and it's a full house.

SAM: At one end, on the stage, Gladman and his Orchestral Jazzonions. At the other end is a long table with the three judges. The six finalists go onto the dance floor and take up their positions. When they are ready and the spectators have settled down, the Master of Ceremonies goes to the microphone. To start with, he makes some jokes to get people laughing. . . .

HALLY: Good touch. *(As he writes.)* ". . . creating a relaxed atmosphere which will change to one of tension and drama as the climax is approached."

SAM *(Onto a chair to act out the M.C.)*: "Ladies and gentlemen, we come now to the great moment you have all been waiting for this evening. . . . The finals of the 1950 Eastern Province Open Ballroom Dancing Championships. But first let me introduce the finalists! Mr. and Mrs. Welcome Tchabalala from Kingwilliamstown . . ."

WILLIE *(He applauds after every name)*: Is when the people clap their hands and whistle and make a lot of noise, Master Hally.

SAM: "Mr. Mulligan Njikelane and Miss Nomhle Nkonyeni of Grahamstown; Mr. and Mrs. Norman Nchinga from Port Alfred; Mr. Fats Bokolane and Miss Dina Plaatjies from East London; Mr. Sipho Dugu and Mrs. Mable Magada from Peddie; and from New Brighton our very own Mr. Willie Malopo and Miss Hilda Samuels."

(WILLIE can't believe his ears. He abandons his role as spectator and scrambles into position as a finalist.)

WILLIE: Relaxed and ready to romance!

SAM: The applause dies down. When everybody is silent, Gladman lifts up his sax, nods at the Orchestral Jazzonions. . . .

WILLIE: Play the jukebox please, Boet Sam!

SAM: I also only got bus fare, Willie.

HALLY: Hold it, everybody. (*Heads for the cash register behind the counter.*) How much is in the till, Sam?

SAM: Three shillings. Hally . . . Your Mom counted it before she left.

(HALLY *hesitates.*)

HALLY: Sorry, Willie. You know how she carried on the last time I did it. We'll just have to pool our combined imaginations and hope for the best. (*Returns to the table.*) Back to work. How are the points scored, Sam?

SAM: Maximum of ten points each for individual style, deportment, rhythm, and general appearance.

WILLIE: Must I start?

HALLY: Hold it for a second, Willie. And penalties?

SAM: For what?

HALLY: For doing something wrong. Say you stumble or bump into somebody . . . do they take off any points?

SAM (*Aghast*): Hally . . . !

HALLY: When you're dancing. If you and your partner collide into another couple.

(HALLY *can get no further.* SAM *has collapsed with laughter. He explains to* WILLIE.)

SAM: If me and Miriam bump into you and Hilda. . . .

(WILLIE *joins him in another good laugh.*)

Hally, Hally . . . !

HALLY (*Perplexed*): Why? What did I say?

SAM: There's no collisions out there, Hally. Nobody trips or stumbles or bumps into anybody else. That's what that moment is all about. To be one of those finalists on that dance floor is like . . . like being in a dream about a world in which accidents don't happen.

HALLY (*Genuinely moved by* SAM'*s image*): Jesus, Sam! That's beautiful!

WILLIE (*Can endure waiting no longer*): I'm starting!

(WILLIE *dances while* SAM *talks.*)

SAM: Of course it is. That's what I've been trying to say to you all afternoon. And it's beautiful because that is what we want life to be like. But instead, like you said, Hally, we're bumping into each other all the time. Look at the three of us this afternoon: I've bumped into Willie, the two of us have bumped into you, you've bumped into your mother, she bumping into your Dad. . . . None of us knows the steps and there's no music playing. And it doesn't stop with us. The whole world is doing it all the time. Open a newspaper and what do you read? America has bumped into Russia, England is bumping into India, rich man bumps into poor man. Those are big collisions, Hally. They make for a lot of bruises. People get hurt in all that bumping, and we're sick and tired of it now. It's been going on for too long. Are we never going to get it right? . . . Learn to dance life like champions instead of always being just a bunch of beginners at it?

HALLY (*Deep and sincere admiration of the man*): You've got a vision, Sam!

SAM: Not just me. What I'm saying to you is that everybody's got it. That's why there's only standing room left for the Centenary Hall in two weeks' time. For as long as the music lasts, we are going to see six couples get it right, the way we want life to be.

HALLY: But is that the best we can do, Sam . . . watch six finalists dreaming about the way it should be?

SAM: I don't know. But it starts with that. Without the dream we won't know what we're going for. And anyway I reckon there are a few people who have got past just dreaming about it and are trying for something real. Remember that thing we read once in the paper about the Mahatma Gandhi? Going without food to stop those riots in India?

HALLY: You're right. He certainly was trying to teach people to get the steps right.

SAM: And the Pope.

HALLY: Yes, he's another one. Our old General Smuts° as well, you know. He's also out there dancing. You know, Sam, when you come to think of it, that's what the United Nations boils down to . . . a dancing school for politicians!

SAM: And let's hope they learn.

HALLY (*A little surge of hope*): You're right. We mustn't despair. Maybe there's some hope for mankind after all. Keep it up, Willie. (*Back to his table with determination.*) This is a lot bigger than I thought. So what have we got? Yes, our title: "A World Without Collisions."

SAM: That sounds good! "A World Without Collisions."

HALLY: Subtitle: "Global Politics on the Dance Floor." No. A bit too heavy, hey? What about "Ballroom Dancing as a Political Vision"?

(*The telephone rings.* SAM *answers it.*)

SAM: St. George's Park Tea Room . . . Yes, Madam . . . Hally, it's your Mom.

HALLY (*Back to reality*): Oh, God, yes! I'd forgotten all about that. Shit! Remember my words, Sam? Just when you're enjoying yourself, someone or something will come along and wreck everything.

SAM: You haven't heard what she's got to say yet.

HALLY: Public telephone?

SAM: No.

Jan Smuts, South African general and later prime minister (1870–1950).

HALLY: Does she sound happy or unhappy?

SAM: I couldn't tell. *(Pause.)* She's waiting, Hally.

HALLY *(To the telephone)*: Hello, Mom . . . No, everything is okay here. Just doing my homework. . . . What's your news? . . . You've what? . . . *(Pause. He takes the receiver away from his ear for a few seconds. In the course of* HALLY's *telephone conversation,* SAM *and* WILLIE *discreetly position the stacked tables and chairs.* HALLY *places the receiver back to his ear.)* Yes, I'm still here. Oh, well, I give up now. Why did you do it, Mom? . . . Well, I just hope you know what you've let us in for. . . . *(Loudly.)* I said I hope you know what you've let us in for! It's the end of the peace and quiet we've been having. *(Softly.)* Where is he? *(Normal voice.)* He can't hear us from in there. But for God's sake, Mom, what happened? I told you to be firm with him. . . . Then you and the nurses should have held him down, taken his crutches away. . . . I know only too well he's my father! . . . I'm not being disrespectful, but I'm sick and tired of emptying stinking chamber pots full of phlegm and piss. . . . Yes, I do! When you're not there, he asks *me* to do it. . . . If you really want to know the truth, that's why I've got no appetite for my food. . . . Yes! There's a lot of things you don't know about. For your information, I still haven't got that science textbook I need. And you know why? He borrowed the money you gave me for it. . . . Because I didn't want to start another fight between you two. . . . He says that every time. . . . All right, Mom! *(Viciously.)* Then just remember to start hiding your bag away again, because he'll be at your purse before long for money for booze. And when he's well enough to come down here, you better keep an eye on the till as well, because that is also going to develop a leak. . . . Then don't complain to me when he starts his old tricks. . . . Yes, you do. I get it from you on one side and from him on the other, and it makes life hell for me. I'm not going to be the peacemaker anymore. I'm warning you now: when the two of you start fighting again, I'm leaving home. . . . Mom, if you start crying, I'm going to put down the receiver. . . . Okay. . . . *(Lowering his voice to a vicious whisper.)* Okay, Mom. I heard you. *(Desperate.)* No. . . . Because I don't want to. I'll see him when I get home! Mom! . . . *(Pause. When he speaks again, his tone changes completely. It is not simply pretense. We sense a genuine emotional conflict.)* Welcome home, chum! . . . What's that? . . . Don't be silly, Dad. You being home is just about the best news in the world. . . . I bet you are. Bloody depressing there with everybody going on about their ailments, hey! . . . How you feeling? . . . Good. . . . Here as well, pal. Coming down cats and dogs. . . . That's right. Just the day for a kip and a toss in your old Uncle Ned. . . . Everything's just hunky-dory on my side, Dad. . . . Well, to start with, there's a nice pile of comics for you on the counter. . . . Yes, old Kemple brought them in. *Batman and Robin, Submariner* . . . just your cup of tea. . . . I will. . . . Yes, we'll spin a few yarns tonight. . . . Okay, chum, see you in a little while. . . . No, I promise. I'll come straight home. . . . *(Pause—his mother comes back on the phone.)* Mom? Okay. I'll lock up now. . . . What? . . . Oh, the brandy . . . Yes, I'll remember! . . . I'll put it in my suitcase now, for God's sake. I know well enough what will happen if he doesn't get it. . . . *(Places a bottle of brandy on the counter.)* I *was* kind to him, Mom. I didn't say anything nasty! . . . All right. Bye. *(End of telephone conversation. A desolate* HALLY *doesn't move. A strained silence.)*

SAM *(Quietly)*: That sounded like a bad bump, Hally.

HALLY *(Having a hard time controlling his emotions. He speaks carefully)*: Mind your own business, Sam.

SAM: Sorry, I wasn't trying to interfere. Shall we carry on? Hally? *(He indicates the exercise book. No response from* HALLY.*)*

WILLIE *(Also trying)*: Tell him about when they give out the cups, Boet Sam.

SAM: Ja! That's another big moment. The presentation of the cups after the winners have been announced. You've got to put that in.

(Still no response from HALLY.*)*

WILLIE: A big silver one, Master Hally, called floating trophy for the champions.

SAM: We always invite some big-shot personality to hand them over. Guest of honor this year is going to be His Holiness Bishop Jabulani of the All African Free Zionist Church.

*(*HALLY *gets up abruptly, goes to his table, and tears up the page he was writing on.)*

HALLY: So much for a bloody world without collisions.

SAM: Too bad. It was on its way to being a good composition.

HALLY: Let's stop bullshitting ourselves, Sam.

SAM: Have we been doing that?

HALLY: Yes! That's what all our talk about a decent world has been . . . just so much bullshit.

SAM: We did say it was still only a dream.

HALLY: And a bloody useless one at that. Life's a fuckup and it's never going to change.

SAM: Ja, maybe that's true.

HALLY: There's no maybe about it. It's a blunt and brutal fact. All we've done this afternoon is waste our time.

SAM: Not if we'd got your homework done.

HALLY: I don't give a shit about my homework, so, for Christ's sake, just shut up about it. *(Slamming books viciously into his school case.)* Hurry up now and finish your work. I want to lock up and get out of here. *(Pause.)* And then go where? Home-sweet-fucking-home. Jesus, I hate that word.

(HALLY goes to the counter to put the brandy bottle and comics in his school case. After a moment's hesitation, he smashes the bottle of brandy. He abandons all further attempts to hide his feelings. SAM *and* WILLIE *work away as unobtrusively as possible.)*

Do you want to know what is really wrong with your lovely little dream, Sam? It's not just that we are all bad dancers. That does happen to be perfectly true, but there's more to it than just that. You left out the cripples.

SAM: Hally!

HALLY *(Now totally reckless)*: Ja! Can't leave them out, Sam. That's why we always end up on our backsides on the dance floor. They're also out there dancing . . . like a bunch of broken spiders trying to do the quickstep! *(An ugly attempt at laughter.)* When you come to think of it, it's a bloody comical sight. I mean, it's bad enough on two legs . . . but one and a pair of crutches! Hell, no, Sam. That's guaranteed to turn that dance floor into a shambles. Why you shaking your head? Picture it, man. For once this afternoon let's use our imaginations sensibly.

SAM: Be careful, Hally.

HALLY: Of what? The truth? I seem to be the only one around here who is prepared to face it. We've had the pretty dream, it's time now to wake up and have a good long look at the way things really are. Nobody knows the steps, there's no music, the cripples are also out there tripping up everybody and trying to get into the act, and it's all called the All-Comers-How-to-Make-a-Fuckup-of-Life Championships. *(Another ugly laugh.)* Hang on, Sam! The best bit is still coming. Do you know what the winner's trophy is? A beautiful big chamber pot with roses on the side, and it's full to the brim with piss. And guess who I think is going to be this year's winner.

SAM *(Almost shouting)*: Stop now!

HALLY *(Suddenly appalled by how far he has gone)*: Why?

SAM: Hally? It's your father you're talking about.

HALLY: So?

SAM: Do you know what you've been saying?

(HALLY can't answer. He is rigid with shame. SAM *speaks to him sternly.)*

No, Hally, you mustn't do it. Take back those words and ask for forgiveness! It's a terrible sin for a son to mock his father with jokes like that. You'll be punished if you carry on. Your father is your father, even if he is a . . . cripple man.

WILLIE: Yes, Master Hally. Is true what Sam say.

SAM: I understand how you are feeling, Hally, but even so. . . .

HALLY: No, you don't!

SAM: I think I do.

HALLY: And I'm telling you you don't. Nobody does. *(Speaking carefully as his shame turns to rage at* SAM.*)* It's your turn to be careful, Sam. Very careful! You're treading on dangerous ground. Leave me and my father alone.

SAM: I'm not the one who's been saying things about him.

HALLY: What goes on between me and my Dad is none of your business!

SAM: Then don't tell me about it. If that's all you've got to say about him, I don't want to hear.

(For a moment HALLY is at a loss for a response.)

HALLY: Just get on with your bloody work and shut up.

SAM: Swearing at me won't help you.

HALLY: Yes, it does! Mind your own fucking business and shut up!

SAM: Okay. If that's the way you want it, I'll stop trying.

(He turns away. This infuriates HALLY even more.)

HALLY: Good. Because what you've been trying to do is meddle in something you know nothing about. All that concerns you in here, Sam, is to try and do what you get paid for—keep the place clean and serve the customers. In plain words, just get on with your job. My mother is right. She's always warning me about allowing you to get too familiar. Well, this time you've gone too far. It's going to stop right now.

(No response from SAM.*)*

You're only a servant in here, and don't forget it.

(Still no response. HALLY *is trying hard to get one.)*

And as far as my father is concerned, all you need to remember is that he is your boss.

SAM *(Needled at last)*: No, he isn't. I get paid by your mother.

HALLY: Don't argue with me, Sam!

SAM: Then don't say he's my boss.

HALLY: He's a white man and that's good enough for you.

SAM: I'll try to forget you said that.

HALLY: Don't! Because you won't be doing me a favor if you do. I'm telling you to remember it.

(A pause. SAM *pulls himself together and makes one last effort.)*

SAM: Hally, Hally . . . ! Come on now. Let's stop before it's too late. You're right. We *are* on dangerous ground. If we're not careful, somebody is going to get hurt.

HALLY: It won't be me.

SAM: Don't be so sure.

HALLY: I don't know what you're talking about, Sam.

SAM: Yes, you do.

HALLY *(Furious)*: Jesus, I wish you would stop trying to tell me what I do and what I don't know.

(SAM gives up. He turns to WILLIE.)

SAM: Let's finish up.

HALLY: Don't turn your back on me! I haven't finished talking.

(He grabs SAM by the arm and tries to make him turn around. SAM reacts with a flash of anger.)

SAM: Don't do that, Hally! *(Facing the boy.)* All right, I'm listening. Well? What do you want to say to me?

HALLY *(Pause as HALLY looks for something to say)*: To begin with, why don't you also start calling me Master Harold, like Willie.

SAM: Do you mean that?

HALLY: Why the hell do you think I said it?

SAM: And if I don't?

HALLY: You might just lose your job.

SAM *(Quietly and very carefully)*: If you make me say it once, I'll never call you anything else again.

HALLY: So? *(The boy confronts the man.)* Is that meant to be a threat?

SAM: Just telling you what will happen if you make me do that. You must decide what it means to you.

HALLY: Well, I have. It's good news. Because that is exactly what Master Harold wants from now on. Think of it as a little lesson in respect, Sam, that's long overdue, and I hope you remember it as well as you do your geography. I can tell you now that somebody who will be glad to hear I've finally given it to you will be my Dad. Yes! He agrees with my Mom. He's always going on about it as well. "You must teach the boys to show you more respect, my son."

SAM: So now you can stop complaining about going home. Everybody is going to be happy tonight.

HALLY: That's perfectly correct. You see, you mustn't get the wrong idea about me and my Dad, Sam. We also have our good times together. Some bloody good laughs. He's got a marvelous sense of humor. Want to know what our favorite joke is? He gives out a big groan, you see, and says: "It's not fair, is it, Hally?" Then I have to ask: "What, chum?" And then he says: "A nigger's arse" . . . and we both have a good laugh.

(The men stare at him with disbelief.)

What's the matter, Willie? Don't you catch the joke? You always were a bit slow on the uptake. It's what is called a pun. You see, fair means both light in color and to be just and decent. *(He turns to SAM.)* I thought *you* would catch it, Sam.

SAM: Oh ja, I catch it all right.

HALLY: But it doesn't appeal to your sense of humor.

SAM: Do you really laugh?

HALLY: Of course.

SAM: To please him? Make him feel good?

HALLY: No, for heaven's sake! I laugh because I think it's a bloody good joke.

SAM: You're really trying hard to be ugly, aren't you? And why drag poor old Willie into it? He's done nothing to you except show you the respect you want so badly. That's also not being fair, you know . . . and *I* mean just or decent.

WILLIE: It's all right, Sam. Leave it now.

SAM: It's me you're after. You should just have said "Sam's arse" . . . because that's the one you're trying to kick. Anyway, how do you know it's not fair? You've never seen it. Do you want to? *(He drops his trousers and underpants and presents his backside for HALLY's inspection.)* Have a good look. A real Basuto arse . . . which is about as nigger as they can come. Satisfied? *(Trousers up.)* Now you can make your Dad even happier when you go home tonight. Tell him I showed you my arse and he is quite right. It's not fair. And if it will give him an even better laugh next time, I'll also let *him* have a look. Come, Willie, let's finish up and go.

(SAM and WILLIE start to tidy up the tea room. HALLY doesn't move. He waits for a moment when SAM passes him.)

HALLY *(Quietly)*: Sam . . .

(SAM stops and looks expectantly at the boy. HALLY spits in his face. A long and heartfelt groan from WILLIE. For a few seconds SAM doesn't move.)

SAM *(Taking out a handkerchief and wiping his face)*: It's all right, Willie.

(To HALLY.)

Ja, well, you've done it . . . Master Harold. Yes, I'll start calling you that from now on. It won't be difficult anymore. You've hurt yourself, Master Harold. I saw it coming. I warned you, but you wouldn't listen. You've just hurt yourself *bad*. And you're a coward, Master Harold. The face you should be spitting in is your father's . . . but you used mine, because you think you're safe inside your fair skin . . . and this time I don't mean just or decent. *(Pause, then moving violently toward HALLY.)* Should I hit him, Willie?

WILLIE *(Stopping SAM)*: No, Boet Sam.

SAM *(Violently)*: Why not?

WILLIE: It won't help, Boet Sam.

SAM: I don't want to help! I want to hurt him.

WILLIE: You also hurt yourself.

SAM: And if he had done it to you, Willie?

WILLIE: Me? Spit at me like I was a dog? *(A thought that had not occurred to him before. He looks at HALLY.)* Ja. Then I want to hit him. I want to hit him hard!

(A dangerous few seconds as the men stand staring at the boy. WILLIE *turns away, shaking his head.)*

But maybe all I do is go cry at the back. He's little boy, Boet Sam. Little *white* boy. Long trousers now, but he's still little boy.

SAM *(His violence ebbing away into defeat as quickly as it flooded)*: You're right. So go on, then: groan again, Willie. You do it better than me. *(To* HALLY.*)* You don't know all of what you've just done . . . Master Harold. It's not just that you've made me feel dirtier than I've ever been in my life . . . I mean, how do I wash off yours and your father's filth? . . . I've also failed. A long time ago I promised myself I was going to try and do something, but you've just shown me . . . Master Harold . . . that I've failed. *(Pause.)* I've also got a memory of a little white boy when he was still wearing short trousers and a black man, but they're not flying a kite. It was the old Jubilee days, after dinner one night. I was in my room. You came in and just stood against the wall, looking down at the ground, and only after I'd asked you what you wanted, what was wrong, I don't know how many times, did you speak and even then so softly I almost didn't hear you. "Sam, please help me to go and fetch my Dad." Remember? He was dead drunk on the floor of the Central Hotel Bar. They'd phoned for your Mom, but you were the only one at home. And do you remember how we did it? You went in first by yourself to ask permission for me to go into the bar. Then I loaded him onto my back like a baby and carried him back to the boarding house with you following behind carrying his crutches. *(Shaking his head as he remembers.)* A crowded Main Street with all the people watching a little white boy following his drunk father on a nigger's back! I felt for that little boy . . . Master Harold. I felt for him. After that we still had to clean him up, remember? He'd messed in his trousers, so we had to clean him up and get him into bed.

HALLY *(Great pain)*: I love him, Sam.

SAM: I know you do. That's why I tried to stop you from saying these things about him. It would have been so simple if you could have just despised him for being a weak man. But he's your father. You love him and you're ashamed of him. You're ashamed of so much! . . . And now that's going to include yourself. That was the promise I made to myself: to try and stop that happening. *(Pause.)* After we got him to bed you came back with me to my room and sat in a corner and carried on just looking down at the ground. And for two days after that! You hadn't done anything wrong, but you went around as if you owed the world an apology for being alive. I didn't like seeing that! That's not the way a boy grows up to be a man! . . . But the one person who should have been teaching you what that means was the cause of your shame. If you really want to know, that's why I made you that kite. I wanted you to look up, be proud of something, of yourself . . . *(Bitter smile at the memory)* . . . and you certainly were that when I left you with it up there on the hill. Oh, ja . . . something else! . . . If you ever do write it as a short story, there *was* a twist in our ending. I couldn't sit down there and stay with you. It was a "Whites Only" bench. You were too young, too excited to notice then. But not anymore. If you're not careful . . . Master Harold . . . you're going to be sitting up there by yourself for a long time to come, and there won't be a kite in the sky. *(SAM *has got nothing more to say. He exits into the kitchen, taking off his waiter's jacket.)*

WILLIE: Is bad. Is all bad in here now.

HALLY *(Books into his school case, raincoat on)*: Willie . . . *(It is difficult to speak.)* Will you lock up for me and look after the keys?

WILLIE: Okay.

*(SAM *returns.* HALLY *goes behind the counter and collects the few coins in the cash register. As he starts to leave. . . .)*

SAM: Don't forget the comic books.

*(HALLY *returns to the counter and puts them in his case. He starts to leave again.)*

SAM *(To the retreating back of the boy)*: Stop . . . Hally. . . .

*(HALLY *stops, but doesn't turn to face him.)*

Hally . . . I've got no right to tell you what being a man means if I don't behave like one myself, and I'm not doing so well at that this afternoon. Should we try again, Hally?

HALLY: Try what?

SAM: Fly another kite, I suppose. It worked once, and this time I need it as much as you do.

HALLY: It's still raining, Sam. You can't fly kites on rainy days, remember.

SAM: So what do we do? Hope for better weather tomorrow?

HALLY *(Helpless gesture)*: I don't know. I don't know anything anymore.

SAM: You sure of that, Hally? Because it would be pretty hopeless if that was true. It would mean nothing has been learnt in here this afternoon, and there was a hell of a lot of teaching going on . . . one way or the other. But anyway, I don't believe you. I reckon there's one thing you know. You don't *have* to sit up there by yourself. You know what that bench means now, and you can leave it any time you choose. All you've got to do is stand up and walk away from it.

(HALLY *leaves.* WILLIE *goes up quietly to* SAM.)

WILLIE: Is okay, Boet Sam. You see. Is . . . *(He can't find any better words)* . . . is going to be okay tomorrow. *(Changing his tone.)* Hey, Boet Sam! *(He is trying hard.)* You right. I think about it and you right. Tonight I find Hilda and say sorry. And make promise I won't beat her no more. You hear me, Boet Sam?

SAM: I hear you, Willie.

WILLIE: And when we practice I relax and romance with her from beginning to end. Nonstop! You watch! Two weeks' time: "First prize for promising newcomers: Mr. Willie Malopo and Miss Hilda Samuels." *(Sudden impulse.)* To hell with it! I walk home. *(He goes to the jukebox, puts in a coin and selects a record. The machine comes to life in the gray twilight, blushing its way through a spectrum of soft, romantic colors.)* How did you say it, Boet Sam?

Let's dream. *(*WILLIE *sways with the music and gestures for* SAM *to dance.)*

(Sarah Vaughan sings.)

> *"Little man you're crying,*
> *I know why you're blue,*
> *Someone took your kiddy car away;*
> *Better go to sleep now,*
> *Little man you've had a busy day."* (etc., etc.)

You lead. I follow.

(The men dance together.)

> *"Johnny won your marbles,*
> *Tell you what we'll do;*
> *Dad will get you new ones right away;*
> *Better go to sleep now,*
> *Little man you've had a busy day."*

Figure 1. Hally (Lonny Price) and Willie (Danny Glover) listen to Sam (Zakes Mokae) describe the dancing championships in the Yale Repertory Theatre production of *"MASTER HAROLD"* . . . *and the Boys,* directed by Athol Fugard, 1982. (Photograph: Martha Swope © Time Inc.)

Figure 2. Sam (Zakes Mokae) rebukes Hally (Lonny Price) for mocking his father, while Willie (Danny Glover) looks on in surprise in the 1982 Yale Repertory Theatre production. (Photograph: Martha Swope © Time Inc.)

Staging of *"MASTER HAROLD"* . . . and the Boys

**REVIEW OF THE YALE REPERTORY THEATRE
PRODUCTION, 1982, BY FRANK RICH**

There may be two or three living playwrights in the world who can write as well as Athol Fugard, but I'm not sure that any of them has written a recent play that can match *"MASTER HAROLD"* . . . *and the Boys.* Mr. Fugard's drama—lyrical in design, shattering in impact—is likely to be an enduring part of the theater long after most of this Broadway season has turned to dust.

"MASTER HAROLD," which opened at the Lyceum last night following its March premiere at the Yale Repertory Theatre, may even outlast the society that spawned it—the racially divided South Africa of apartheid. Though Mr. Fugard's play is set there in 1950, it could take place nearly anywhere at any time. The word "apartheid" is never mentioned; the South African references are minimal. The question that Mr. Fugard raises—how can men of all kinds find the courage to love one another?—is dealt with at such a profound level that *"MASTER HAROLD"* sweeps quickly beyond the transitory specifics of any one nation. It's not for nothing that this is the first play Mr. Fugard has chosen to open away from home.

What's more, the author deals with his issue without attitudinizing, without sentimentality, without lecturing the audience. *"MASTER HAROLD"* isn't another problem play in which people stand for ideological positions. By turns funny and tragic, it uncovers its moral imperatives by burrowing deeply into the small, intimately observed details of its three characters' lives.

We meet those characters on a rainy afternoon, as they josh and chat in a fading tea room. Two of them, Sam (Zakes Mokae) and Willie (Danny Glover), are black waiters who rehearse for a coming ballroom dancing contest while tidying up the restaurant. Because they only have enough money for bus fare home, they can't put Sarah Vaughan on the jukebox: they imagine the music, as well as their Ginger Rogers–like partners, as they twirl about. Eventually they are joined by Hally (Lonny Price), who is the son of the tea room's owner. A precocious white prep-school student on the verge of manhood, Hally has stopped by to eat lunch and work on an English essay.

The black servants are the boy's second family: they have been employed by his parents since Hally was in short trousers. But, for all the easy camaraderie and tender memories that unite master and servants, there's a slight distance in their relationship, too. As the waiters practice their steps, Hally playfully but condescendingly calls them "a pair of hooligans." To the

boy, such dancing is a "simple-minded" reflection of "the culture of primitive black society"—only now "the war dance has been replaced by the waltz."

But the articulate Sam, an unacknowledged mentor to Hally since childhood, patiently sets the boy to thinking otherwise. Dancing, Sam contends, "is like being in a dream about a world where accidents don't happen"— where white and black, rich and poor, men and women don't bump into one another. Hally is so taken with this theory that he decides to write his essay about it. Maybe, he postulates, "the United Nations is a dancing school for politicians." Maybe "there is hope for mankind after all."

It's a lovely, idyllic metaphor, and there is much joy in *"MASTER HAROLD"* as the characters imagine their utopian "world without collisions." Yet the joy soon dissipates. Mr. Fugard has structured his intermissionless 100-minute play much as Sam describes a dance contest: "a relaxed atmosphere changes to one of tension and drama as the climax approaches." When the tension erupts in *"MASTER HAROLD,"* it rips through the audience so mercilessly that the Lyceum falls into an almost deathly hush.

The drama is catalyzed by a series of phone calls Hally receives from his real-life family offstage. Hally's father, we learn, is a drunk, a cripple and a racist; his mother is his long-suffering victim. Hally is caught between them, and, as old wounds are ripped open, the bitterness of his entire childhood comes raging to the surface. The boy is soon awash in tearful self-pity and, in the absence of his real father, takes out his anger on his surrogate father, Sam. What follows is an unstoppable, almost unwatchable outpouring of ugliness, in which Hally humiliates the black man he loves by insisting that he call him "Master Harold," by mocking their years of shared secrets, by spitting in his face.

Mr. Fugard's point is simple enough: Before we can practice compassion—before we can, as Sam says, "dance life like champions"—we must learn to respect ourselves. It is Hally's self-hatred that leads him to strike at the black man and his crippled Dad and, in this sense, the boy is typical of anyone who attacks the defenseless to bolster his own self-esteem.

But *"MASTER HAROLD,"* unlike many works that deal with the genesis of hatred, forces us to identify with the character who inflicts the cruelty. We like Hally so much in the play's early stages, and empathize with his familial sorrow so keenly later on, that it's impossible to pull back once he lashes out. And because we can't sever ourselves from Hally, we're forced to confront our own capacity for cruelty—and to see all too clearly just who it is we really hurt when we give in to it.

Mr. Fugard can achieve this effect because he has the guts to face his own shame: Hally, a fledgling artist who believes in social reform, is too richly drawn not to be a ruthlessly honest portrait of the playwright as a young man. But if Mr. Fugard's relentless conscience gives *"MASTER HAROLD"* its remarkable moral center, his brilliance as an artist gives the play its classic esthetic simplicity.

This work is totally without pretension. As Sam says that the trick of dancing is to "make it look easy," so Mr. Fugard understands that the same is true in the theater. The dialogue is light and easy, full of lilting images that gradually warp as the darkness descends. After Hally relives the exultant childhood experience of flying his first kite with Sam, the kite comes down to the ground, "like something that has lost its soul." Sam's description of graceful waltzers is usurped by the boy's vision of "cripples dancing like a bunch of broken spiders."

Like the script, the production has been deftly choreographed by the author: you don't know you're entering the center of a storm until you're there. The one newcomer to the cast since Yale, Mr. Price, will be at the level of his predecessor, Zeljko Ivanek, as soon as he tones down his overly cute youthful friskiness in Hally's early scenes. Once the protagonist falls apart, Mr. Price takes the audience right with him on his bottomless descent to self-immolation.

As the easygoing Willie, Mr. Glover is a paragon of sweet kindliness—until events leave him whipped and sobbing in a chair, his low moans serving as forlorn counterpoint to the play's main confrontation. Mr. Mokae's Sam is a transcendental force—an avuncular, hearty figure who slowly withdraws into dignified serenity as Hally taunts him. Though the boy has repaid the servant's lifelong instruction in tolerance by making him feel "dirty," Mr. Mokae still glows with his dream of a world of perfect dancers—one that's like "a love story with a happy ending."

The author doesn't provide that happy ending, of course—it's not his to confer. But if *"MASTER HAROLD"* finally lifts us all the way from pain to hope, it's because Mr. Fugard insists that that ending can be—must be—ours to write.

CARYL CHURCHILL

When asked if she thought there was a "female aesthetic," Caryl Churchill responded: "I don't see how you can tell until there are so many plays by women that you can begin to see what they have in common that's different from the way men have written, and there are still relatively so few." But among those "relatively few," the more than thirty dramas of Caryl Churchill, ranging from radio and television scripts to stage plays, have put her unquestionably into the ranks of major contemporary playwrights.

An only child, Churchill began writing stories at an early age, attended school in London and then in Montreal, and returned to England to study at Oxford University where she started writing plays for student productions. Marriage in 1961 to David Harter, a lawyer, took her to London and to her initial work on radio and television plays. As Churchill put it, she turned to radio plays in part because she liked radio but also because the process of bearing and raising children made it virtually impossible to do anything but shorter pieces. After her third child was born, Churchill felt she needed more time for her writing and briefly hired a nanny to care for her youngest child. That "a woman must have money and a room of her own if she is to write fiction" seems just as true for Churchill as it was when Virginia Woolf issued her famous manifesto in 1929.

Churchill has said that her 1972 play *Owners* was the beginning of the second part of her career, since it marked the start of her almost total commitment to theater, rather than radio and television. That play, like *Objections to Sex and Violence* (1975) and *Traps* (1977), opened originally at London's Royal Court Theatre—the home since 1956 for many new British plays. Churchill's plays show men and women caught in social, political, gender-based, and personal "traps" from which they try to escape in a variety of ways, including through terrorism and suicide. Perhaps the major influence on Churchill's work came in 1976 when she began working with experimental theater groups in the process of conceiving and drafting her plays. For *Light Shining in Buckinghamshire* (1976), which she developed in collaboration with Joint Stock, Churchill and her director first decided on their subject—the millennial movement during the English Civil War, an essentially working-class movement based on the belief that fighting the king (Charles I) would lead to the second coming of Christ. Then the crucial part of the creative process was, according to Churchill, a three-week workshop with the Joint Stock actors where, "through talk, reading, games, and improvisation, we tried to get closer to the issues and the people." She next spent nine weeks writing a script and worked with the company for another six weeks of rehearsal. Given such extensive collaboration, she acknowledges that, while the actors did not write the lines, "many of the characters and scenes were based on ideas that came from improvisation at the workshop and during rehearsal."

Churchill's reading in seventeenth-century material also fostered her work with Monstrous Regiment, a feminist/socialist theater group with whom she had agreed to do a play about witches. Her research convinced her that she "wanted to write a play about witches with no witches in it; a play not about evil, hysteria, and possession by the devil but about poverty, humiliation, and prejudice, and how the women accused of witchcraft saw themselves." For this play, *Vinegar Tom* (1976), she first talked with the group, drafted the play in three days, went off to work with Joint Stock, came back to Monstrous Regiment in the autumn, and expanded the play to create a new character, in part because a new actress had joined the company, and in part because discussion with the actors indicated that a certain kind of character was needed. Not only did both of these plays come out of similar working conditions and deal with (roughly) the same historical period, but both show Churchill's move into a less realistic kind of drama than she had previously written. The plays call for large casts, yet each production uses only a small group of actors: twenty-five roles in *Light Shining in Buckinghamshire* were played by six actors, while fourteen roles in *Vinegar Tom* were played by nine actors. What may have started as a financial necessity—a limit on the number of actors the group could support— turns into a highly suggestive mode of staging, since, as Churchill points out, "When different actors play the parts what comes over is a large event involving many people, whose characters resonate in a way they wouldn't if they were more clearly defined." The events and their political significance become central rather than the psychology of the characters or the star quality of the actors.

Most of Churchill's major plays since the 1976 collaborative ventures show the influence of that experience, for *Cloud Nine* (1979), *Fen* (1983), and *Serious Money* (1987) have also been developed out of workshops with the original actors. These plays, as well as *Top Girls* (1982) and *Softcops* (1984), call for actors to play multiple roles, and increasingly Churchill stresses the connection of the actor with the role. Thus, in *Cloud Nine,* a black farce that examines the similarities between colonial and sexual repression, the casting of a man in the role of Betty, the wife of the white colonial administrator in Africa, represents for Churchill the idea that Betty "wants to be what men want her to be." Similarly, the black servant, Joshua, is played by a white man, and Edward, the young son whose homosexual tendencies are both repressed and revealed, is played by a woman. In the second act—which moves forward 100 years to contemporary London, with the characters only twenty-five years older—Churchill asks for different gender castings, again to make points about the changing self-perceptions of men and women; thus Betty "is now played by a woman, as she gradually becomes real to herself," but Cathy, a child of five, is to be played by a man, "partly, as with Edward, to show more clearly the issues involved in learning what is considered correct behavior for a girl."

In later plays, Churchill has continued to juxtapose past and present as she does in *Cloud Nine. Mad Forest* (1990), which traces the lives of two Romanian families before, during, and after the overthrow of dictator Nicolae Ceaușescu, suggests that its characters are incapable of casting off the past and creating a new future. In *The Skriker* (1994) an ancient, shape-shifting demon and assorted otherworldly beings out of some grim fairy tale haunt two contemporary London women. And in the first scene of *Top Girls,* Church dazzlingly dramatizes the interpenetration of past and present. In a contemporary London restaurant, Marlene, the new managing director of the "Top Girls" Employment Agency, hosts a dinner to celebrate her promotion, and her dinner guests, who span centuries and continents, include both real women and women imagined by men. Thus, the Victorian traveler Isabella Bird, the Japanese-courtesan-turned-nun Lady Nijo, and the Italian pope Joan join Marlene along with Dull Gret, a woman in apron and armor from Brueghel's painting *Dulle Griet*, and Patient Griselda, the much-abused heroine of Chaucer's "The Clerk's Tale" (see Figure 1). Not only does Churchill blend the real and the imaginary with the medieval, Renaissance, Victorian, and modern worlds, but she invents an overlapping style, so that characters speak over each other, or continue their speeches without noticing that another character has spoken on a seemingly different topic. Although these women from the past look unrelated, their stories link together in that they show the painful experiences women suffer in dealing with men, with children, and with their own sexual identity. Even Dull Gret, who speaks in monosyllables for most of the scene, suddenly bursts into a long speech that recounts the Brueghel painting from her own point of view, showing that her anger springs from a mother's outrage rather than from the plundering instincts of an unwomanly woman.

Churchill devotes the rest of the play to Marlene's story, gradually detailing what she has become in order to run "Top Girls," and the price she has paid for her success. Marlene is the only role not switched or shared, a theatrical choice that may also suggest that she can't escape into another life. The fifteen other characters are played by only six actresses, often with ironic juxtapositions. The intrepid traveler Isabella Bird turns into Marlene's sister Joyce, who, unlike Marlene and Isabella, is trapped at home, visiting their sick mother once a week and taking care of Angie, a "slow" sixteen-year-old, who turns out to be Marlene's daughter rather than her niece. Angie, less surprisingly, is played by the actress who played Dull Gret, both characters who seem to have little to say. And Patient Griselda, who has taken so much abuse from her husband, becomes a client interviewed by Marlene, showing the same vacuous adaptability as the character from the past.

When the play opened in 1982, reviews commented extensively on the play's elaborate dinner scene (see Figure 1), but also on the quality of the acting of the seven women taking the sixteen roles. While reactions to the play ranged widely ("articulate, eloquent, alive" or "predictable and, at times, rather trite" or "a strange play, disturbing and intriguing"), most reviewers agreed that Churchill had created a feast of acting opportunities, fully realized in performance. Though all of the actresses received praise, frequent attention went most often to Carole Hayman's "lovely, humane performance" of Angie, who is "a bit thick." Angie's existence, and Marlene's attempt to hide from her true relationship to the girl, posed the question for one reviewer: "What use is female emancipation, Churchill asks, if it transforms the clever women into predators and does nothing for the stupid, weak, and helpless?" Thus it seems especially appropriate that the exotic worlds conjured up in the play's first scene shrink to the rooms of the employment agency and Joyce's backyard, where Angie and her friend Kit play "squashed together" in "a shelter made of junk" (see Figure 2). No matter what dreams women have had, have enacted, or have yet to dream, Churchill reminds us in the play's final lines of today's reality. Marlene comforts Angie, who has suddenly awakened: "Did you have a bad dream? What happened in it? Well you're awake now, aren't you, pet?" Angie's answer may reflect Churchill's: "Frightening."

TOP GIRLS

BY CARYL CHURCHILL

CHARACTERS

MARLENE
WAITRESS/KIT/SHONA
ISABELLA BIRD/JOYCE/MRS. KIDD
LADY NIJO/WIN
DULL GRET/ANGIE
POPE JOAN/LOUISE
PATIENT GRISELDA/NELL/JEANINE

ACT 1

Scene 1: *A Restaurant.*
Scene 2: *"Top Girls" Employment Agency, London.*
Scene 3: *Joyce's backyard in Suffolk.*

ACT 2

Scene 1: *"Top Girls" Employment Agency.*
Scene 2: *A Year Earlier. Joyce's kitchen.*

Production Note: *The seating order for Act 1, Scene 1 in the original production at the Royal Court was (from right) Gret, Nijo, Marlene, Joan, Griselda, Isabella.*

THE CHARACTERS

ISABELLA BIRD (1831–1904): Lived in Edinburgh, traveled extensively between the ages of forty and seventy.
LADY NIJO (b. 1258): Japanese, was an Emperor's courtesan and later a Buddhist nun who traveled on foot through Japan.
DULL GRET: Is the subject of the Brueghel painting *Dulle Griet*, in which a woman in an apron and armor leads a crowd of women charging through hell and fighting the devils.
POPE JOAN: Disguised as a man, is thought to have been pope between 854 and 856.
PATIENT GRISELDA: Is the obedient wife whose story is told by Chaucer in "The Clerk's Tale" of *The Canterbury Tales.*

THE LAYOUT: *A speech usually follows the one immediately before it but: (1) When one character starts speaking before the other has finished, the point of interruption is marked /. E.g.,*

ISABELLA: This is the Emperor of Japan? / I once met the Emperor of Morocco.
NIJO: In fact he was the ex-Emperor.

(2) A character sometimes continues speaking right through another's speech. E.g.,

ISABELLA: When I was forty I thought my life was over. / Oh I was pitiful. I was
NIJO: I didn't say I felt it for twenty years. Not every minute.
ISABELLA: sent on a cruise for my health and felt even worse. Pains in my bones, pins and needles . . . etc.

*(3) Sometimes a speech follows on from a speech earlier than the one immediately before it, and continuity is marked *. E.g.,*

GRISELDA: I'd seen him riding by, we all had. And he'd seen me in the fields with the sheep.*
ISABELLA: I would have been well suited to minding sheep.
NIJO: And Mr. Nugent went riding by.
ISABELLA: Of course not, Nijo, I mean a healthy life in the open air.
JOAN: *He just rode up while you were minding the sheep and asked you to marry him?

where "in the fields with the sheep" is the cue to both "I would have been" and "He just rode up."

ACT 1 / SCENE 1

(Restaurant. Saturday night. There is a table with a white cloth set for dinner with six places. The lights come up on MARLENE *and the* WAITRESS.)

MARLENE: Excellent, yes, table for six. One of them's going to be late but we won't wait. I'd like a bottle of Frascati straight away if you've got one really cold. *(The* WAITRESS *goes.* ISABELLA BIRD *arrives.)* Here we are. Isabella.

ISABELLA: Congratulations, my dear.
MARLENE: Well, it's a step. It makes for a party. I haven't time for a holiday. I'd like to go somewhere exotic like you but I can't get away. I don't know how you could bear to leave Hawaii. / I'd like to lie
ISABELLA: I did think of settling.
MARLENE: in the sun forever, except of course I can't bear sitting still.
ISABELLA: I sent for my sister Hennie to come and join me. I said, Hennie we'll live here forever and

1276

help the natives. You can buy two sirloins of beef for what a pound of chops cost in Edinburgh. And Hennie wrote back, the dear, that yes, she would come to Hawaii if I wished, but I said she had far better stay where she was. Hennie was suited to life in Tobermory.

MARLENE: Poor Hennie.

ISABELLA: Do you have a sister?

MARLENE: Yes in fact.

ISABELLA: Hennie was happy. She was good. I did miss its face, my own pet. But I couldn't stay in Scotland. I loathed the constant murk.

(LADY NIJO arrives.)

MARLENE *(Seeing her)*: Ah! Nijo! *(The WAITRESS enters with the wine.)*

NIJO: Marlene! *(To ISABELLA.)* So excited when Marlene told me / you were coming.

ISABELLA: I'm delighted / to meet you.

MARLENE: I think a drink while we wait for the others. I think a drink anyway. What a week. *(MARLENE seats NIJO. The WAITRESS pours the wine.)*

NIJO: It was always the men who used to get so drunk. I'd be one of the maidens, passing the sake.

ISABELLA: I've had sake. Small hot drink. Quite fortifying after a day in the wet.

NIJO: One night my father proposed three rounds of three cups, which was normal, and then the Emperor should have said three rounds of three cups, but he said three rounds of nine cups, so you can imagine. Then the Emperor passed his sake cup to my father and said, "Let the wild goose come to me this spring."

MARLENE: Let the what?

NIJO: It's a literary allusion to a tenth-century epic, / His Majesty was very cultured.

ISABELLA: This is the Emperor of Japan? / I once met the Emperor of Morocco.

NIJO: In fact he was the ex-Emperor.

MARLENE: But he wasn't old? / Did you, Isabella?

NIJO: Twenty-nine.

ISABELLA: Oh it's a long story.

MARLENE: Twenty-nine's an excellent age.

NIJO: Well I was only fourteen and I knew he meant something but I didn't know what. He sent me an eight-layered gown and I sent it back. So when the time came I did nothing but cry. My thin gowns were badly ripped. But even that morning when he left / he'd a green

MARLENE: Are you saying he raped you?

NIJO: robe with a scarlet lining and very heavily embroidered trousers, I already felt different about him. It made me uneasy. No, of course not, Marlene, I belonged to him, it was what I was brought up for from a baby. I soon found I was sad if he stayed away. It was depressing day after day not knowing when he would come. I never enjoyed taking other women to him.

ISABELLA: I certainly never saw my father drunk. He was a clergyman. / And I didn't get married till I was fifty. *(The WAITRESS brings the menus.)*

NIJO: Oh, my father was a very religious man. Just before he died he said to me, "Serve His Majesty, be respectful, if you lose his favor enter holy orders."

MARLENE: But he meant stay in a convent, not go wandering round the country.

NIJO: Priests were often vagrants, so why not a nun? You think I shouldn't. / I still did what my father wanted.

MARLENE: No no, I think you should. / I think it was wonderful.

(DULL GRET arrives.)

ISABELLA: I tried to do what my father wanted.

MARLENE: Gret, good. Nijo. Gret / I know Griselda's going to be late, but should we wait for Joan? / Let's get you a drink.

ISABELLA: Hello, Gret! *(She continues to NIJO.)* I tried to be a clergyman's daughter. Needlework, music, charitable schemes. I had a tumor removed from my spine and spent a great deal of time on the sofa. I studied the metaphysical poets and hymnology. / I thought I enjoyed intellectual pursuits.

NIJO: Ah, you like poetry. I come of a line of eight generations of poets. Father had a poem / in the anthology.

ISABELLA: My father taught me Latin although I was a girl. / But really I was

MARLENE: They didn't have Latin at my school.

ISABELLA: more suited to manual work. Cooking, washing, mending, riding horses. / Better than reading

NIJO: Oh but I'm sure you're very clever.

ISABELLA: books, eh Gret? A rough life in the open air.

NIJO: I can't say I enjoyed my rough life. What I enjoyed most was being the Emperor's favorite / and wearing thin silk.

ISABELLA: Did you have any horses, Gret?

GRET: Pig.

(POPE JOAN arrives.)

MARLENE: Oh Joan, thank God, we can order. Do you know everyone? We were just talking about learning Latin and being clever girls. Joan was by way of an infant prodigy. Of course you were. What excited you when you were ten?

JOAN: Because angels are without matter they are not individuals. Every angel is a species.

MARLENE: There you are. *(They laugh. They look at the menus.)*

ISABELLA: Yes, I forgot all my Latin. But my father was the mainspring of my life and when he died I was so grieved. I'll have the chicken, please, / and the soup.

NIJO: Of course you were grieved. My father was saying his prayers and he dozed off in the sun. So I touched his knee to rouse him. "I wonder what will happen," he said, and then he was dead before he finished the sentence. / If he'd

MARLENE: What a shock.

NIJO: died saying his prayers he would have gone straight to heaven. / Waldorf salad.

JOAN: Death is the return of all creatures to God.

NIJO: I shouldn't have woken him.

JOAN: Damnation only means ignorance of the truth. I was always attracted by the teachings of John the Scot, though he was inclined to confuse / God and the world.

ISABELLA: Grief always overwhelmed me at the time.

MARLENE: What I fancy is a rare steak. Gret?

ISABELLA: I am of course a member of the / Church of England.

MARLENE: Gret?

GRET: Potatoes.

MARLENE: I haven't been to church for years. / I like Christmas carols.

ISABELLA: Good works matter more than church attendance.

MARLENE: Make that two steaks and a lot of potatoes. Rare. But I don't do good works either.

JOAN: Cannelloni, please, / and a salad.

ISABELLA: Well, I tried, but oh dear. Hennie did good works.

NIJO: The first half of my life was all sin and the second / all repentance.*

MARLENE: Oh what about starters?

GRET: Soup.

JOAN: *And which did you like best?

MARLENE: Were your travels just a penance? Avocado vinaigrette. Didn't you / enjoy yourself?

JOAN: Nothing to start with for me, thank you.

NIJO: Yes, but I was very unhappy. / It hurt to remember the past.

MARLENE: And the wine list.

NIJO: I think that was repentance.

MARLENE: Well I wonder.

NIJO: I might have just been homesick.

MARLENE: Or angry.

NIJO: Not angry, no, / why angry?

GRET: Can we have some more bread?

MARLENE: Don't you get angry? I get angry.

NIJO: But what about?

MARLENE: Yes let's have two more Frascati. And some more bread, please. (The WAITRESS exits.)

ISABELLA: I tried to understand Buddhism when I was in Japan but all this birth and death succeeding each other through eternities just filled me with the most profound melancholy. I do like something more active.

NIJO: You couldn't say I was inactive. I walked every day for twenty years.

ISABELLA: I don't mean walking. / I mean in the head.

NIJO: I vowed to copy five Mahayana sutras.° / Do you know how long they are?

MARLENE: I don't think religious beliefs are something we have in common. Activity yes. (GRET empties the bread basket into her apron.)

NIJO: My head was active. / My head ached.

JOAN: It's no good being active in heresy.

ISABELLA: What heresy? She's calling the Church of England / a heresy.

JOAN: There are some very attractive / heresies.

NIJO: I had never heard of Christianity. Never / heard of it. Barbarians.

MARLENE: Well I'm not a Christian. / And I'm not a Buddhist.

ISABELLA: You have heard of it?

MARLENE: We don't all have to believe the same.

ISABELLA: I knew coming to dinner with a Pope we should keep off religion.

JOAN: I always enjoy a theological argument. But I won't try to convert you, I'm not a missionary. Anyway I'm a heresy myself.

ISABELLA: There are some barbaric practices in the east.

NIJO: Barbaric?

ISABELLA: Among the lower classes.

NIJO: I wouldn't know.

ISABELLA: Well theology always made my head ache.

MARLENE: Oh good, some food. (The WAITRESS brings the first course, serves it during the following, then exits.)

NIJO: How else could I have left the court if I wasn't a nun? When father died I had only His Majesty. So when I fell out of favor I had nothing. Religion is a kind of nothing / and I dedicated what was left of me to nothing.

ISABELLA: That's what I mean about Buddhism. It doesn't brace.

MARLENE: Come on, Nijo, have some wine.

NIJO: Haven't you ever felt like that? You've all felt / like that. Nothing will ever happen again. I am dead already.

ISABELLA: You thought your life was over but it wasn't.

JOAN: You wish it was over.

GRET: Sad.

MARLENE: Yes, when I first came to London I sometimes . . . and when I got back from America I did. But only for a few hours. Not twenty years.

ISABELLA: When I was forty I thought my life was over. / Oh I was pitiful. I was sent

NIJO: I didn't say I felt it for twenty years. Not every minute.

Mahayana sutras, Buddhist religious texts.

ISABELLA: on a cruise for my health and I felt even worse. Pains in my bones, pins and needles in my hands, swelling behind the ears, and—oh, stupidity. I shook all over, indefinable terror. And Australia seemed to me a hideous country, the acacias stank like drains. / I

NIJO: You were homesick. (GRET *steals a bottle of wine.*)

ISABELLA: had a photograph taken for Hennie but I told her I wouldn't send it, my hair had fallen out and my clothes were crooked, I looked completely insane and suicidal.

NIJO: So did I, exactly, dressed as a nun. / I was wearing walking shoes for the first time.

ISABELLA: I longed to go home, / but home to what? Houses are so perfectly dismal.*

NIJO: I longed to go back ten years.

MARLENE: *I thought traveling cheered you both up.

ISABELLA: Oh it did / of course. It was on

NIJO: I'm not a cheerful person, Marlene. I just laugh a lot.

ISABELLA: the trip from Australia to the Sandwich Isles, I fell in love with the sea. There were rats in the cabin and ants in the food but suddenly it was like a new world. I woke up every morning happy, knowing there would be nothing to annoy me. No nervousness. No dressing.

NIJO: Don't you like getting dressed? I adored my clothes. / When I was chosen

MARLENE: You had prettier colors than Isabella.

NIJO: to give sake to His Majesty's brother, the Emperor Kameyana, on his formal visit, I wore raw silk pleated trousers and a seven-layered gown in shades of red, and two outer garments, / yellow lined with green

MARLENE: Yes, all that silk must have been very—(*The* WAITRESS *enters, clears the first course and exits.*)

JOAN: I dressed as a boy when I left home.*

NIJO: and a light green jacket. Lady Betto had a five-layered gown in shades of green and purple.

ISABELLA: *You dressed as a boy?

MARLENE: Of course, / for safety.

JOAN: It was easy, I was only twelve. / Also women weren't allowed in the library. We wanted to study in Athens.

MARLENE: You ran away alone?

JOAN: No, not alone, I went with my friend. / He was

NIJO: Ah, an elopement.

JOAN: sixteen but I thought I knew more science than he did and almost as much philosophy.

ISABELLA: Well I always traveled as a lady and I repudiated strongly any suggestion in the press that I was other than feminine.

MARLENE: I don't wear trousers in the office. / I could but I don't.

ISABELLA: There was no great danger to a woman of my age and appearance.

MARLENE: And you got away with it, Joan?

JOAN: I did then. (*The* WAITRESS *brings in the main course.*)

MARLENE: And nobody noticed anything?

JOAN: They noticed I was a very clever boy. / And

MARLENE: I couldn't have kept pretending for so long.

JOAN: when I shared a bed with my friend, that was ordinary—two poor students in a lodging house. I think I forgot I was pretending.

ISABELLA: Rocky Mountain Jim, Mr. Nugent, showed me no disrespect. He found it interesting, I think, that I could make scones and also lasso cattle. Indeed he declared his love for me, which was most distressing.

NIJO: What did he say? / We always sent poems first.

MARLENE: What did you say?

ISABELLA: I urged him to give up whiskey, / but he said it was too late.

MARLENE: Oh Isabella.

ISABELLA: He had lived alone in the mountains for many years.

MARLENE: But did you—? (*The* WAITRESS *goes.*)

ISABELLA: Mr. Nugent was a man that any woman might love but none could marry. I came back to England.

NIJO: Did you write him a poem when you left? / Snow on the mountains. My sleeves

MARLENE: Did you never see him again?

ISABELLA: No, never.

NIJO: are wet with tears. In England no tears, no snow.

ISABELLA: Well, I say never. One morning very early in Switzerland, it was a year later, I had a vision of him as I last saw him / in his trapper's clothes with his

NIJO: A ghost!

ISABELLA: hair round his face, and that was the day, / I learned later, he died with a

NIJO: Ah!

ISABELLA: bullet in his brain. / He just bowed to me and vanished.

MARLENE: Oh Isabella.

NIJO: When your lover dies—One of my lovers died. / The priest Ariake.

JOAN: My friend died. Have we all got dead lovers?

MARLENE: Not me, sorry.

NIJO (*To* ISABELLA): I wasn't a nun, I was still at court, but he was a priest, and when he came to me he dedicated his whole life to hell. / He knew that when he died he would fall into one of the three lower realms. And he died, he did die.

JOAN (*To* MARLENE): I'd quarreled with him over the teachings of John the Scot,° who held that our ignorance of God is the same as his ignorance of

---

John the Scot, John Scotus Erigena (c. 810–866), Irish scholastic philosopher.

himself. He only knows what he creates because he creates everything he knows but he himself is above being—do you follow?

MARLENE: No, but go on.

NIJO: I couldn't bear to think / in what shape would he be reborn.*

JOAN: St. Augustine maintained that the Neo-Platonic Ideas are indivisible

ISABELLA: *Buddhism is really most uncomfortable.

JOAN: from God, but I agreed with John that the created world is essences derived from Ideas which derived from God. As Denys the Areopagite° said—the pseudo-Denys—first we give God a name, then deny it, / then reconcile the contradiction

NIJO: In what shape would he return?

JOAN: by looking beyond / those terms—

MARLENE: Sorry, what? Denys said what?

JOAN: Well we disagreed about it, we quarreled. And next day he was ill, / I was so annoyed with him

NIJO: Misery in this life and worse in the next, all because of me.

JOAN: all the time I was nursing him I kept going over the arguments in my mind. Matter is not a means of knowing the essence. The source of the species is the Idea. But then I realized he'd never understand my arguments again, and that night he died. John the Scot held that the individual disintegrates / and there is no personal immortality.

ISABELLA: I wouldn't have you think I was in love with Jim Nugent. It was yearning to save him that I felt.

MARLENE (To JOAN): So what did you do?

JOAN: First I decided to stay a man. I was used to it. And I wanted to devote my life to learning. Do you know why I went to Rome? Italian men didn't have beards.

ISABELLA: The loves of my life were Hennie, my own pet, and my dear husband the doctor, who nursed Hennie in her last illness. I knew it would be terrible when Hennie died but I didn't know how terrible. I felt half of myself had gone. How could I go on my travels without that sweet soul waiting at home for my letters? It was Doctor Bishop's devotion to her in her last illness that made me decide to marry him. He and Hennie had the same sweet character. I had not.

NIJO: I thought His Majesty had sweet character because when he found out about Ariake he was so kind. But really it was because he no longer cared for me. One night he even sent me out to a man who had been pursuing me. / He lay awake on the other side of the screens and listened.

Denys the Areopagite, the "pseudo-Denys" is the author of influential Neo-Platonic philosophical texts dating from the late fifth or early sixth century.

ISABELLA: I did wish marriage had seemed more of a step. I tried very hard to cope with the ordinary drudgery of life. I was ill again with carbuncles on the spine and nervous prostration. I ordered a tricycle, that was my idea of adventure then. And John himself fell ill, with erysipelas and anemia. I began to love him with my whole heart but it was too late. He was a skeleton with transparent white hands. I wheeled him on various seafronts in a bathchair. And he faded and left me. There was nothing in my life. The doctors said I had gout / and my heart was much affected.

NIJO: There was nothing in my life, nothing, without the Emperor's favor. The Empress had always been my enemy, Marlene, she said I had no right to wear three-layered gowns. / But I was the adopted daughter of my grandfather the Prime Minister. I had been publicly granted permission to wear thin silk.

JOAN: There was nothing in my life except my studies. I was obsessed with pursuit of the truth. I taught at the Greek School in Rome, which St. Augustine had made famous. I was poor, I worked hard, I spoke apparently brilliantly, I was still very young, I was a stranger, suddenly I was quite famous, I was everyone's favorite. Huge crowds came to hear me. The day after they made me cardinal I fell ill and lay two weeks without speaking, full of terror and regret. / But then I got up determined to

MARLENE: Yes, success is very . . .

JOAN: go on. I was seized again / with a desperate longing for the absolute.

ISABELLA: Yes, yes, to go on. I sat in Tobermory among Hennie's flowers and sewed a complete outfit in Jaeger flannel. / I was fifty-six years old.

NIJO: Out of favor but I didn't die. I left on foot, nobody saw me go. For the next twenty years I walked through Japan.

GRET: Walking is good. (Meanwhile, the WAITRESS enters, pours lots of wine, then shows MARLENE the empty bottle.)

JOAN: Pope Leo died and I was chosen. All right then. I would be Pope. I would know God. I would know everything.

ISABELLA: I determined to leave my grief behind and set off for Tibet.

MARLENE: Magnificent all of you. We need some more wine, please, two bottles I think, Griselda isn't even here yet, and I want to drink a toast to you all. (The WAITRESS exits.)

ISABELLA: To yourself surely, / we're here to celebrate your success.

NIJO: Yes, Marlene.

JOAN: Yes, what is it exactly, Marlene?

MARLENE: Well it's not Pope but it is managing director.*

JOAN: And you find work for people.

MARLENE: Yes, an employment agency.

NIJO: *Over all the women you work with. And the men.

ISABELLA: And very well deserved too. I'm sure it's just the beginning of something extraordinary.

MARLENE: Well it's worth a party.

ISABELLA: To Marlene.*

MARLENE: And all of us.

JOAN: *Marlene.

NIJO: Marlene.

GRET: Marlene.

MARLENE: We've all come a long way. To our courage and the way we changed our lives and our extraordinary achievements. (*They laugh and drink a toast.*)

ISABELLA: Such adventures. We were crossing a mountain pass at seven thousand feet, the cook was all to pieces, the muleteers suffered fever and snow blindness. But even though my spine was agony I managed very well.*

MARLENE: Wonderful.

NIJO: *Once I was ill for four months lying alone at an inn. Nobody to offer a horse to Buddha. I had to live for myself, and I did live.

ISABELLA: Of course you did. It was far worse returning to Tobermory. I always felt dull when I was stationary. / That's why I could never stay anywhere.

NIJO: Yes, that's it exactly. New sights. The shrine by the beach, the moon shining on the sea. The goddess had vowed to save all living things. / She would even save the fishes. I was full of hope.

JOAN: I had thought the Pope would know everything. I thought God would speak to me directly. But of course he knew I was a woman.

MARLENE: But nobody else even suspected? (*The WAITRESS brings more wine and then exits.*)

JOAN: In the end I did take a lover again.*

ISABELLA: In the Vatican?

GRET: *Keep you warm.

NIJO: *Ah, lover.

MARLENE: *Good for you.

JOAN: He was one of my chamberlains. There are such a lot of servants when you're Pope. The food's very good. And I realized I did know the truth. Because whatever the Pope says, that's true.

NIJO: What was he like, the chamberlain?*

GRET: Big cock.

ISABELLA: Oh, Gret.

MARLENE: *Did he fancy you when he thought you were a fella?

NIJO: What was he like?

JOAN: He could keep a secret.

MARLENE: So you did know everything.

JOAN: Yes, I enjoyed being Pope. I consecrated bishops and let people kiss my feet. I received the King of England when he came to submit to the church. Unfortunately there were earthquakes, and some village reported it had rained blood,

and in France there was a plague of giant grasshoppers, but I don't think that can have been my fault, do you?* (*Laughter.*) The grasshoppers fell on the English Channel / and were washed up on shore.

NIJO: I once went to sea. It was very lonely. I realized it made very little difference where I went.

JOAN: and their bodies rotted and poisoned the air and everyone in those parts died. (*Laughter.*)

ISABELLA: *Such superstition! I was nearly murdered in China by a howling mob. They thought the barbarians ate babies and put them under railway sleepers to make the tracks steady, and ground up their eyes to make the lenses of cameras. / So they were shouting,

MARLENE: And you had a camera!

ISABELLA: "Child-eater, child-eater." Some people tried to sell girl babies to Europeans for cameras or stew! (*Laughter.*)

MARLENE: So apart from the grasshoppers it was a great success.

JOAN: Yes, if it hadn't been for the baby I expect I'd have lived to an old age like Theodora of Alexandria, who lived as a monk. She was accused by a girl / who fell in love with her of being the father of her child and—

NIJO: But tell us what happened to your baby. I had some babies.

MARLENE: Didn't you think of getting rid of it?

JOAN: Wouldn't that be a worse sin than having it? / But a Pope with a child was about as bad as possible.

MARLENE: I don't know, you're the Pope.

JOAN: But I wouldn't have known how to get rid of it.

MARLENE: Other Popes had children, surely.

JOAN: They didn't give birth to them.

NIJO: Well you were a woman.

JOAN: Exactly and I shouldn't have been a woman. Women, children, and lunatics can't be Pope.

MARLENE: So the only thing to do / was to get rid of it somehow.

NIJO: You had to have it adopted secretly.

JOAN: But I didn't know what was happening. I thought I was getting fatter, but then I was eating more and sitting about, the life of a Pope is quite luxurious. I don't think I'd spoken to a woman since I was twelve. The chamberlain was the one who realized.

MARLENE: And by then it was too late.

JOAN: Oh I didn't want to pay attention. It was easier to do nothing.

NIJO: But you had to plan for having it. You had to say you were ill and go away.

JOAN: That's what I should have done I suppose.

MARLENE: Did you want them to find out?

NIJO: I too was often in embarrassing situations, there's no need for a scandal. My first child was

His Majesty's, which unfortunately died, but my second was Akebono's. I was seventeen. He was in love with me when I was thirteen, he was very upset when I had to go to the Emperor, it was very romantic, a lot of poems. Now His Majesty hadn't been near me for two months so he thought I was four months pregnant when I was really six, so when I reached the ninth month /I announced I was seriously ill,

JOAN: I never knew what month it was.

NIJO: and Akebono announced he had gone on a religious retreat. He held me round the waist and lifted me up as the baby was born. He cut the cord with a short sword, wrapped the baby in white and took it away. It was only a girl but I was sorry to lose it. Then I told the Emperor that the baby had miscarried because of my illness, and there you are. The danger was past.

JOAN: But, Nijo, I wasn't used to having a woman's body.

ISABELLA: So what happened?

JOAN: I didn't know of course that it was near the time. It was Rogation Day,° there was always a procession. I was on the horse dressed in my robes and a cross was carried in front of me, and all the cardinals were following, and all the clergy of Rome, and a huge crowd of people. / We set off from St. Peter's° to go

MARLENE: Total Pope. (GRET *pours the wine and steals the bottle.*)

JOAN: to St. John's.° I had felt a slight pain earlier, I thought it was something I'd eaten, and then it came back, and came back more often. I thought when this is over I'll go to bed. There were still long gaps when I felt perfectly all right and I didn't want to attract attention to myself and spoil the ceremony. Then I suddenly realized what it must be. I had to last out till I could get home and hide. Then something changed, my breath started to catch. I couldn't plan things properly anymore. We were in a little street that goes between St. Clement's° and the Colosseum, and I just had to get off the horse and sit down for a minute. Great waves of pressure were going through my body, I heard sounds like a cow lowing, they came out of my mouth. Far away I heard people screaming, "The Pope is ill, the Pope is dying." And the baby just slid out on to the road.*

MARLENE: The cardinals / won't have known where to put themselves.

NIJO: Oh dear, Joan, what a thing to do! In the street!

Rogation Day, day set aside for solemn procession to invoke God's mercy; the major Rogation Day was April 25. *St. Peter's, St. John's,* major churches in Rome.   *St. Clement's,* church in Rome.

ISABELLA: *How embarrassing.

GRET: In a field, yah. (*They are laughing.*)

JOAN: One of the cardinals said, "The Antichrist!" and fell over in a faint. (*They all laugh.*)

MARLENE: So what did they do? They weren't best pleased.

JOAN: They took me by the feet and dragged me out of town and stoned me to death. (*They stop laughing.*)

MARLENE: Joan, how horrible.

JOAN: I don't really remember.

NIJO: And the child died too?

JOAN: Oh yes, I think so, yes. (*The WAITRESS enters to clear the plates. Pause. They start talking very quietly.*)

ISABELLA (*To JOAN*): I never had any children. I was very fond of horses.

NIJO (*To MARLENE*): I saw my daughter once. She was three years old. She wore a plum-red / small sleeved gown. Akebono's wife

ISABELLA: Birdie was my favorite. A little Indian bay mare I rode in the Rocky Mountains.

NIJO: had taken the child because she had her own died. Everyone thought I was just a visitor. She was being brought up carefully so she could be sent to the palace like I was. (GRET *steals her empty plate.*)

ISABELLA: Legs of iron and always cheerful, and such a pretty face. If a stranger led her she reared up like a bronco.

NIJO: I never saw my third child after he was born, the son of Ariake the priest. Ariake held him on his lap the day he was born and talked to him as if he could understand, and cried. My fourth child was Ariake's too. Ariake died before he was born. I didn't want to see anyone, I stayed alone in the hills. It was a boy again, my third son. But oddly enough I felt nothing for him.

MARLENE: How many children did you have, Gret?

GRET: Ten.

ISABELLA: Whenever I came back to England I felt I had so much to atone for. Hennie and John were so good. I did no good in my life. I spent years in self-gratification. So I hurled myself into committees, I nursed the people of Tobermory in the epidemic of influenza, I lectured the Young Women's Christian Association on Thrift. I talked and talked explaining how the East was corrupt and vicious. My travels must do good to someone besides myself. I wore myself out with good causes.

MARLENE (*Pause*): Oh god, why are we all so miserable?

JOAN (*Pause*): The procession never went down that street again.

MARLENE: They rerouted it specially?

JOAN: Yes, they had to go all round to avoid it. And they introduced a pierced chair.

MARLENE: A pierced chair?

JOAN: Yes, a chair made out of solid marble with a hole in the seat / and it was

MARLENE: You're not serious.

JOAN: in the Chapel of the Savior, and after he was elected the Pope had to sit in it.

MARLENE: And someone looked up his skirts? / Not really!

ISABELLA: What an extraordinary thing.

JOAN: Two of the clergy / made sure he was a man.

NIJO: On their hands and knees!

MARLENE: A pierced chair!

GRET: Balls!

(GRISELDA *arrives unnoticed.*)

NIJO: Why couldn't he just pull up his robe?

JOAN: He had to sit there and look dignified.

MARLENE: You could have made all your chamberlains sit in it.*

GRET: Big one. Small one.

NIJO: Very useful chair at court.

ISABELLA: *Or the Laird of Tobermory in his kilt.

(*They are quite drunk. They get the giggles.* MARLENE *notices* GRISELDA *and gets up to welcome her. The others go on talking and laughing.* GRET *crosses to* JOAN *and* ISABELLA *and pours them wine from her stolen bottles. The* WAITRESS *gives out the menus.*)

MARLENE: Griselda! / There you are. Do you want to eat?

GRISELDA: I'm sorry I'm so late. No, no, don't bother.

MARLENE: Of course it's no bother. / Have you eaten?

GRISELDA: No really, I'm not hungry.

MARLENE: Well have some pudding.

GRISELDA: I never eat pudding.

MARLENE: Griselda, I hope you're not anorexic. We're having pudding, I am, and getting nice and fat.

GRISELDA: Oh if everyone is. I don't mind.

MARLENE: Now who do you know? This is Joan who was Pope in the ninth century, and Isabella Bird, the Victorian traveler, and Lady Nijo from Japan, Emperor's concubine and Buddhist nun, thirteenth century, nearer your own time, and Gret who was painted by Brueghel. Griselda's in Boccaccio and Petrarch and Chaucer because of her extraordinary marriage. I'd like profiteroles because they're disgusting.

JOAN: Zabaglione,° please.

ISABELLA: Apple pie / and cream.

NIJO: What's this?

MARLENE: Zabaglione, it's Italian, it's what Joan's having, / it's delicious.

NIJO: A Roman Catholic / dessert? Yes please.

MARLENE: Gret?

GRET: Cake.

GRISELDA: Just cheese and biscuits, thank you. (*The* WAITRESS *exits.*)

Zabaglione, frothy dessert of beaten eggs, sugar, wine.

MARLENE: Yes, Griselda's life is like a fairy story, except it starts with marrying the prince.

GRISELDA: He's only a marquis, Marlene.

MARLENE: Well everyone for miles around is his liege and he's absolute lord of life and death and you were the poor but beautiful peasant girl and he whisked you off. / Near enough a prince.

NIJO: How old were you?

GRISELDA: Fifteen.

NIJO: I was brought up in court circles and it was still a shock. Had you ever seen him before?

GRISELDA: I'd seen him riding by, we all had. And he'd seen me in the fields with the sheep.*

ISABELLA: I would have been well suited to minding sheep.

NIJO: And Mr. Nugent riding by.

ISABELLA: Of course not, Nijo, I mean a healthy life in the open air.

JOAN: *He just rode up while you were minding the sheep and asked you to marry him?

GRISELDA: No, no, it was on the wedding day. I was waiting outside the door to see the procession. Everyone wanted him to get married so there'd be an heir to look after us when he died, / and at last he

MARLENE: I don't think Walter wanted to get married. It is Walter? Yes.

GRISELDA: announced a day for the wedding but nobody knew who the bride was, we thought it must be a foreign princess, we were longing to see her. Then the carriage stopped outside our cottage and we couldn't see the bride anywhere. And he came and spoke to my father.

NIJO: And your father told you to serve the Prince.

GRISELDA: My father could hardly speak. The Marquis said it wasn't an order, I could say no, but if I said yes I must always obey him in everything.

MARLENE: That's when you should have suspected.

GRISELDA: But of course a wife must obey her husband. / And of course I must obey the Marquis.*

ISABELLA: I swore to obey dear John, of course, but it didn't seem to arise. Naturally I wouldn't have wanted to go abroad while I was married.

MARLENE: *Then why bother to mention it at all? He'd got a thing about it, that's why.

GRISELDA: I'd rather obey the Marquis than a boy from the village.

MARLENE: Yes, that's a point.

JOAN: I never obeyed anyone. They all obeyed me.

NIJO: And what did you wear? He didn't make you get married in your own clothes? That would be perverse.*

MARLENE: Oh, you wait.

GRISELDA: *He had ladies with him who undressed me and they had a white silk dress and jewels for my hair.

MARLENE: And at first he seemed perfectly normal?

GRISELDA: Marlene, you're always so critical of him. / Of course he was normal, he was very kind.

MARLENE: But, Griselda, come on, he took your baby.

GRISELDA: Walter found it hard to believe I loved him. He couldn't believe I would always obey him. He had to prove it.

MARLENE: I don't think Walter likes women.

GRISELDA: I'm sure he loved me, Marlene, all the time.

MARLENE: He just had a funny way / of showing it.

GRISELDA: It was hard for him too.

JOAN: How do you mean he took away your baby?

NIJO: Was it a boy?

GRISELDA: No, the first one was a girl.

NIJO: Even so it's hard when they take it away. Did you see it at all?

GRISELDA: Oh yes, she was six weeks old.

NIJO: Much better to do it straight away.

ISABELLA: But why did your husband take the child?

GRISELDA: He said all the people hated me because I was just one of them. And now I had a child they were restless. So he had to get rid of the child to keep them quiet. But he said he wouldn't snatch her, I had to agree and obey and give her up. So when I was feeding her a man came in and took her away. I thought he was going to kill her even before he was out of the room.

MARLENE: But you let him take her? You didn't struggle?

GRISELDA: I asked him to give her back so I could kiss her. And I asked him to bury her where no animals could dig her up. / It was Walter's child to do what he

ISABELLA: Oh, my dear.

GRISELDA: liked with.*

MARLENE: Walter was bonkers.°

GRET: Bastard.

ISABELLA: *But surely, murder.

GRISELDA: I had promised.

MARLENE: I can't stand this. I'm going for a pee.

(MARLENE *goes out. The* WAITRESS *brings the dessert, serves it during the following, then exits.*)

NIJO: No, I understand. Of course you had to, he was your life. And were you in favor after that?

GRISELDA: Oh yes, we were very happy together. We never spoke about what had happened.

ISABELLA: I can see you were doing what you thought was your duty. But didn't it make you ill?

GRISELDA: No, I was very well, thank you.

NIJO: And you had another child?

GRISELDA: Not for four years, but then I did, yes, a boy.

NIJO: Ah a boy. / So it all ended happily.

GRISELDA: Yes he was pleased. I kept my son till he was two years old. A peasant's grandson. It made the people angry. Walter explained.

ISABELLA: But surely he wouldn't kill his children /just because—

GRISELDA: Oh it wasn't true. Walter would never give in to the people. He wanted to see if I loved him enough.

JOAN: He killed his children / to see if you loved him enough?

NIJO: Was it easier the second time or harder?

GRISELDA: It was always easy because I always knew I would do what he said. (*Pause. They start to eat.*)

ISABELLA: I hope you didn't have any more children.

GRISELDA: Oh no, no more. It was twelve years till he tested me again.

ISABELLA: So whatever did he do this time? / My poor John, I never loved him enough, and he would never have dreamt . . .

GRISELDA: He sent me away. He said the people wanted him to marry someone else who'd give him an heir and he'd got special permission from the Pope. So I said I'd go home to my father. I came with nothing / so I went with nothing. I took

NIJO: Better to leave if your master doesn't want you.

GRISELDA: off my clothes. He let me keep a slip so he wouldn't be shamed. And I walked home barefoot. My father came out in tears. Everyone was crying except me.

NIJO: At least your father wasn't dead. / I had nobody.

ISABELLA: Well it can be a relief to come home. I loved to see Hennie's sweet face again.

GRISELDA: Oh yes, I was perfectly content. And quite soon he sent for me again.

JOAN: I don't think I would have gone.

GRISELDA: But he told me to come. I had to obey him. He wanted me to help prepare his wedding. He was getting married to a young girl from France / and nobody except me knew how to arrange things the way he liked them.

NIJO: It's always hard taking him another woman. (MARLENE *comes back.*)

JOAN: I didn't live a woman's life. I don't understand it.

GRISELDA: The girl was sixteen and far more beautiful than me. I could see why he loved her. / She had her younger brother with her as a page. (*The* WAITRESS *enters.*)

MARLENE: Oh God, I can't bear it. I want some coffee. Six coffees. Six brandies. / Double brandies. Straightaway. (*The* WAITRESS *exits.*)

GRISELDA: They all went into the feast I'd prepared. And he stayed behind and put his arms round me and kissed me. / I felt half asleep with the shock.

NIJO: Oh, like a dream.

MARLENE: And he said, "This is your daughter and your son."

___

bonkers, crazy.

GRISELDA: Yes.

JOAN: What?

NIJO: Oh. Oh I see. You got them back.

ISABELLA: I did think it was remarkably barbaric to kill them but you learn not to say anything. / So he had them brought up secretly I suppose.

MARLENE: Walter's a monster. Weren't you angry? What did you do?

GRISELDA: Well I fainted. Then I cried and kissed the children. / Everyone was making a fuss of me.

NIJO: But did you feel anything for them?

GRISELDA: What?

NIJO: Did you feel anything for the children?

GRISELDA: Of course, I loved them.

JOAN: So you forgave him and lived with him?

GRISELDA: He suffered so much all those years.

ISABELLA: Hennie had the same sweet nature.

NIJO: So they dressed you again?

GRISELDA: Cloth of gold.

JOAN: I can't forgive anything.

MARLENE: You really are exceptional, Griselda.

NIJO: Nobody gave me back my children. *(She cries.)*

(The WAITRESS *brings the brandies and then exits. During the following,* JOAN *goes to* NIJO.*)*

ISABELLA: I can never be like Hennie. I was always so busy in England, a kind of business I detested. The very presence of people exhausted my emotional reserves. I could not be like Hennie however I tried. I tried and was as ill as could be. The doctor suggested a steel net to support my head, the weight of my own head was too much for my diseased spine. It is dangerous to put oneself in depressing circumstances. Why should I do it?

JOAN *(To* NIJO): Don't cry.

NIJO: My father and the Emperor both died in the autumn. So much pain.

JOAN: Yes, but don't cry.

NIJO: They wouldn't let me into the palace when he was dying. I hid in the room with his coffin, then I couldn't find where I'd left my shoes, I ran after the funeral procession in bare feet, I couldn't keep up. When I got there it was over, a few wisps of smoke in the sky, that's all that was left of him. What I want to know is, if I'd still been at court, would I have been allowed to wear full mourning?

MARLENE: I'm sure you would.

NIJO: Why do you say that? You don't know anything about it. Would I have been allowed to wear full mourning?

ISABELLA: How can people live in this dim pale island and wear our hideous clothes? I cannot and will not live the life of a lady.

NIJO: I'll tell you something that made me angry. I was eighteen, at the Full Moon Ceremony. They make a special rice gruel and stir it with their sticks, and then they beat their women across the loins so they'll have sons and not daughters. So the Emperor beat us all / very hard as

MARLENE: What a sod. *(The* WAITRESS *enters with the coffees.)*

NIJO: usual—that's not it, Marlene, that's normal, what made us angry he told his attendants they could beat us too. Well they had a wonderful time. / So Lady Genki and I made a plan, and the ladies

MARLENE: I'd like another brandy, please. Better make it six. *(The* WAITRESS *exits.)*

NIJO: all hid in his rooms, and Lady Mashimizu stood guard with a stick at the door, and when His Majesty came in Genki seized him and I beat him till he cried out and promised he would never order anyone to hit us again. Afterward there was a terrible fuss. The nobles were horrified. "We wouldn't even dream of stepping on Your Majesty's shadow." And I had hit him with a stick. Yes, I hit him with a stick.

(The WAITRESS *brings the brandy bottle and tops up the glasses.* JOAN *crosses in front of the table and back to her place while drunkenly reciting:)*

JOAN:

> *Suave, mari magno turantibus aequora ventis,*
> *e terra magnum alterius spectare laborem;*
> *non quia vexari quemquamst iucunda voluptas,*
> *sed quibus ipse malis careas quia cernere suave est.*
> *Suave etiam belli certamina magna tueri*
> *per campos instructa tua sine parte pericli.*
> *Sed nil dulcius est, bene quam munita tenere*
> *edita doctrina sapientum templa serena, /*
> *despicere unde queas alios passimque videre*
> *errare atque viam palantis quaerere vitae,°*

GRISELDA: I do think—I do wonder—it would have been nicer if Walter hadn't had to.

ISABELLA: Why should I? Why should I?

MARLENE: Of course not.

Suave, . . . quaerere vitae, This passage opens the second book of the long poem *De Rerum Natura* (On the Nature of Things) by the Roman stoic philosopher Lucretius (97?–54 B.C.E.). The speaker begins by contrasting the privilege of calm observation with the turmoil of dangerous involvement. Translation by Rolfe Humphries. "How sweet it is, when whirlwinds roil great ocean, / To watch, from land, the danger of another, / Not that to see some other person suffer / Brings great enjoyment, but the sweetness lies / In watching evils you yourself are free from. / How sweet, again, to see the clash of battle / Across the plains, yourself immune to danger. / But nothing is more sweet than full possession / Of those calm heights, well built, well fortified / By wise men's teaching, to look down from here / At others wandering below, men lost, / Confused, in hectic search for the right road."

NIJO: I hit him with a stick.
JOAN:

certare ingenio, contendere nobilitate,
noctes atque dies niti praestante labore
ad summas emergere opes rerumque potiri.
O miseras hominum mentis, / o pectora caeca!°

ISABELLA: O miseras!
NIJO: *Pectora caeca!
JOAN:

qualibus in tenebris vitae quantisque periclis
degitur hoc aevi quodcumquest! / nonne videre
nil aliud sibi naturam latrare, nisi utqui
corpore seiunctus dolor absit, mente fruatur . . .°
(She subsides.)

GRET: We come to hell through a big mouth. Hell's black and red. / It's
MARLENE *(To JOAN)*: Shut up, pet.
GRISELDA: Hush, please.
ISABELLA: Listen, she's been to hell.
GRET: like the village where I come from. There's a river and a bridge and houses. There's places on fire like when the soldiers come. There's a big devil sat on a roof with a big hole in his arse and he's scooping stuff out of it with a big ladle and it's falling down on us, and it's money, so a lot of the women stop and get some. But most of us is fighting the devils. There's lots of little devils, our size, and we get them down all right and give them a beating. There's lots of funny creatures round your feet, you don't like to look, like rats and lizards, and nasty things, a bum° with a face, and fish with legs, and faces on things that don't have faces on. But they don't hurt, you just keep going. Well we'd had worse, you see, we'd had the Spanish. We'd all had family killed. My big son die on a wheel. Birds eat him. My baby, a soldier run her through with a sword. I'd had enough, I was mad, I hate the bastards. I come out of my front door that morning and shout till my neighbors come out and I said, "Come on, we're going where the evil come from and pay the bastards out." And they all come out just as they was / from baking or

NIJO: All the ladies come.
GRET: washing in their aprons, and we push down the street and the ground opens up and we go through a big mouth into a street just like ours but in hell. I've got a sword in my hand from somewhere and I fill a basket with gold cups they drink out of down there. You just keep running on and fighting, / you didn't stop for nothing. Oh we give them devils such a beating.*
NIJO: Take that, take that.
JOAN:

Something something something mortisque timores
tum vacuum pectus—damn.
Quod si ridicula—
something something on and on and on
and something splendorem purpureai.°

ISABELLA: I thought I would have a last jaunt up the west river in China. Why not? But the doctors were so very grave I just went to Morocco. The sea was so wild I had to be landed by ship's crane in a coal bucket. / My horse was a terror to me, a powerful black charger.
GRET: Coal bucket good.
JOAN:

nos in luce timemus
something
terrorem°

(NIJO is laughing and crying. JOAN gets up and is sick. GRISELDA looks after her.)

GRISELDA: Can I have some water, please? *(The WAITRESS exits.)*

---

certare . . . caeca! Lucretius continues: "The strife of wits, the wars for precedence / The everlasting struggle, night and day, / To win towards heights of wealth and power. O wretched, / O wretched minds of men! O hearts in darkness!" *qualibus . . . mente fruatur. . . ,* "Under what shadows and among what dangers / Your lives are spent, such as they are. But look—/ Your nature snarls, yaps, barks for nothing, really, / Except that pain be absent from the body / And mind enjoy delight. . . ." *bum,* buttocks.

Something . . . splendorem purpureai, Joan is still quoting from Lucretius, this time in fragments. The passage she is attempting to remember is this: "And does all this frighten religious terror / In panic from your heart? does the great fear / Of death depart, and leave you comforted? / What vanity, what nonsense! If men's fears, / Anxieties, pursuing horrors, move, / Indifferent to any clash of arms, / Untroubled among lords and monarchs, bow / Before no gleam of gold, no crimson robe [*splendorem purpureai*], / Why do you hesitate, why doubt that reason / Alone has absolute power?" *nos in luce . . . terrorem,* The passage Joan is trying to remember ends with an appeal to reason, though she gets only to the notion of "terrors": "As children tremble and fear everything / In their dark shadows, we, in the full light, / Fear things that really are not one bit more awful / Than what poor babies shudder at in darkness, / The horrors they imagine to be coming. / Our terrors and our darknesses of mind / Must be dispelled, then, not by sunshine's rays, / . . . / But by insight into nature, and a scheme / of systematic contemplation."

ISABELLA: So off I went to visit the Berber sheikhs in full blue trousers and great brass spurs. I was the only European woman ever to have seen the Emperor of Morocco. I was *(The* WAITRESS *brings the water)* seventy years old. What lengths to go to for a last chance of joy. I knew my return of vigor was only temporary, but how marvelous while it lasted.

ACT 1 / SCENE 2

("Top Girls" Employment Agency. Monday morning. The lights come up on MARLENE *and* JEANINE.*)*

MARLENE: Right, Jeanine, you are Jeanine aren't you? Let's have a look. O's and A's.° / No A's, all those

JEANINE: Six O's.

MARLENE: O's you probably could have got an A. / Speeds, not brilliant, not too bad.

JEANINE: I wanted to go to work.

MARLENE: Well, Jeanine, what's your present job like?

JEANINE: I'm a secretary.

MARLENE: Secretary or typist?

JEANINE: I did start as a typist but the last six months I've been a secretary.

MARLENE: To?

JEANINE: To three of them, really, they share me. There's Mr. Ashford, he's the office manager, and Mr. Philby / is sales, and—

MARLENE: Quite a small place?

JEANINE: A bit small.

MARLENE: Friendly?

JEANINE: Oh it's friendly enough.

MARLENE: Prospects?

JEANINE: I don't think so, that's the trouble. Miss Lewis is secretary to the managing director and she's been there forever, and Mrs. Bradford / is—

MARLENE: So you want a job with better prospects?

JEANINE: I want a change.

MARLENE: So you'll take anything comparable?

JEANINE: No, I do want prospects. I want more money.

MARLENE: You're getting—?

JEANINE: Hundred.

MARLENE: It's not bad you know. You're what? Twenty?

JEANINE: I'm saving to get married.

MARLENE: Does that mean you don't want a long-term job, Jeanine?

JEANINE: I might do.

MARLENE: Because where do the prospects come in? No kids for a bit?

JEANINE: Oh no, not kids, not yet.

MARLENE: So you won't tell them you're getting married?

JEANINE: Had I better not?

MARLENE: It would probably help.

JEANINE: I'm not wearing a ring. We thought we wouldn't spend on a ring.

MARLENE: Saves taking it off.

JEANINE: I wouldn't take it off.

MARLENE: There's no need to mention it when you go for an interview. / Now, Jeanine, do you have a feel

JEANINE: But what if they ask?

MARLENE: for any particular kind of company?

JEANINE: I thought advertising.

MARLENE: People often do think advertising. I have got a few vacancies but I think they're looking for something glossier.

JEANINE: You mean how I dress? / I can

MARLENE: I mean experience.

JEANINE: dress different. I dress like this on purpose for where I am now.

MARLENE: I have a marketing department here of a knitwear manufacturer. / Marketing is near enough

JEANINE: Knitwear?

MARLENE: advertising. Secretary to the marketing manager, he's thirty-five, married, I've sent him a girl before and she was happy, left to have a baby, you won't want to mention marriage there. He's very fair I think, good at his job, you won't have to nurse him along. Hundred and ten, so that's better than you're doing now.

JEANINE: I don't know.

MARLENE: I've a fairly small concern here, father and two sons, you'd have more say potentially, secretarial and reception duties, only a hundred but the job's going to grow with the concern and then you'll be in at the top with new girls coming in underneath you.

JEANINE: What is it they do?

MARLENE: Lampshades. / This would be my first choice for you.

JEANINE: Just lampshades?

MARLENE: There's plenty of different kinds of lampshade. So we'll send you there, shall we, and the knitwear second choice. Are you free to go for an interview any day they call you?

JEANINE: I'd like to travel.

MARLENE: We don't have any foreign clients. You'd have to go elsewhere.

JEANINE: Yes I know. I don't really . . . I just mean . . .

MARLENE: Does your fiancé want to travel?

JEANINE: I'd like a job where I was here in London and with him and everything but now and then— I expect it's silly. Are there jobs like that?

MARLENE: There's personal assistant to a top executive in a multinational. If that's the idea you need to be planning ahead. Is that where you want to be in ten years?

JEANINE: I might not be alive in ten years.

O's and A's, former standardized exams in the British educational system. O-levels (Ordinary) were usually taken at sixteen and A-levels (Advanced) were usually taken at eighteen.

MARLENE: Yes but you will be. You'll have children.

JEANINE: I can't think about ten years.

MARLENE: You haven't got the speeds anyway. So I'll send you to these two shall I? You haven't been to any other agency? Just so we don't get crossed wires. Now, Jeanine, I want you to get one of these jobs, all right? If I send you that means I'm putting myself on the line for you. Your presentation's OK, you look fine, just be confident and go in there convinced that this is the best job for you and you're the best person for the job. If you don't believe it they won't believe it.

JEANINE: Do you believe it?

MARLENE: I think you could make me believe it if you put your mind to it.

JEANINE: Yes, all right.

ACT 1 / SCENE 3

(JOYCE's backyard. Sunday afternoon. The house with a back door is upstage. Downstage is a shelter made of junk, made by children. The lights come up on two girls, ANGIE and KIT, who are squashed together in the shelter. ANGIE is sixteen, KIT is twelve. They cannot be seen from the house.)

JOYCE (Off, calling from the house): Angie. Angie, are you out there?

(Silence. They keep still and wait. When nothing else happens they relax.)

ANGIE: Wish she was dead.

KIT: Wanna watch The Exterminator?

ANGIE: You're sitting on my leg.

KIT: There's nothing on telly. We can have an ice cream. Angie?

ANGIE: Shall I tell you something?

KIT: Do you wanna watch The Exterminator?

ANGIE: It's X, innit?

KIT: I can get into Xs.

ANGIE: Shall I tell you something?

KIT: We'll go to something else. We'll go to Ipswich. What's on the Odeon?°

ANGIE: She won't let me, will she?

KIT: Don't tell her.

ANGIE: I've no money.

KIT: I'll pay.

ANGIE: She'll moan though, won't she?

KIT: I'll ask her for you if you like.

ANGIE: I've no money, I don't want you to pay.

KIT: I'll ask her.

ANGIE: She don't like you.

KIT: I still got three pounds birthday money. Did she say she don't like me? I'll go by myself then.

°Odeon, popular chain of cinemas.

ANGIE: Your mum don't let you. I got to take you.

KIT: She won't know.

ANGIE: You'd be scared who'd sit next to you.

KIT: No I wouldn't. She does like me anyway. Tell me then.

ANGIE: Tell you what?

KIT: It's you she doesn't like.

ANGIE: Well I don't like her so tough shit.

JOYCE (Off): Angie. Angie. Angie. I know you're out there. I'm not coming out after you. You come in here. (Silence. Nothing happens.)

ANGIE: Last night when I was in bed. I been thinking yesterday could I make things move. You know, make things move by thinking about them without touching them. Last night I was in bed and suddenly a picture fell down off the wall.

KIT: What picture?

ANGIE: My gran, that picture. Not the poster. The photograph in the frame.

KIT: Had you done something to make it fall down?

ANGIE: I must have done.

KIT: But were you thinking about it?

ANGIE: Not about it, but about something.

KIT: I don't think that's very good.

ANGIE: You know the kitten?

KIT: Which one?

ANGIE: There only is one. The dead one.

KIT: What about it?

ANGIE: I heard it last night.

KIT: Where?

ANGIE: Out here. In the dark. What if I left you here in the dark all night?

KIT: You couldn't. I'd go home.

ANGIE: You couldn't.

KIT: I'd / go home.

ANGIE: No you couldn't, not if I said.

KIT: I could.

ANGIE: Then you wouldn't see anything. You'd just be ignorant.

KIT: I can see in the daytime.

ANGIE: No you can't. You can't hear it in the daytime.

KIT: I don't want to hear it.

ANGIE: You're scared that's all.

KIT: I'm not scared of anything.

ANGIE: You're scared of blood.

KIT: It's not the same kitten anyway. You just heard an old cat, / you just heard some old cat.

ANGIE: You don't know what I heard. Or what I saw. You don't know nothing because you're a baby.

KIT: You're sitting on me.

ANGIE: Mind my hair / you silly cunt.

KIT: Stupid fucking cow, I hate you.

ANGIE: I don't care if you do.

KIT: You're horrible.

ANGIE: I'm going to kill my mother and you're going to watch.

KIT: I'm not playing.

ANGIE: You're scared of blood. (KIT *puts her hand under dress, brings it out with blood on her finger.*)

KIT: There, see, I got my own blood, so. (ANGIE *takes* KIT's *hand and licks her finger.*)

ANGIE: Now I'm a cannibal. I might turn into a vampire now.

KIT: That picture wasn't nailed up right.

ANGIE: You'll have to do that when I get mine.

KIT: I don't have to.

ANGIE: You're scared.

KIT: I'll do it, I might do it. I don't have to just because you say. I'll be sick on you.

ANGIE: I don't care if you are sick on me, I don't mind sick. I don't mind blood. If I don't get away from here I'm going to die.

KIT: I'm going home.

ANGIE: You can't go through the house. She'll see you.

KIT: I won't tell her.

ANGIE: Oh great, fine.

KIT: I'll say I was by myself. I'll tell her you're at my house and I'm going there to get you.

ANGIE: She knows I'm here, stupid.

KIT: Then why can't I go through the house?

ANGIE: Because I said not.

KIT: My mum don't like you anyway.

ANGIE: I don't want her to like me. She's a slag.°

KIT: She is not.

ANGIE: She does it with everyone.

KIT: She does not.

ANGIE: You don't even know what it is.

KIT: Yes I do.

ANGIE: Tell me then.

KIT: We get it all at school, cleverclogs. It's on television. You haven't done it.

ANGIE: How do you know?

KIT: Because I know you haven't.

ANGIE: You know wrong then because I have.

KIT: Who with?

ANGIE: I'm not telling you / who with.

KIT: You haven't anyway.

ANGIE: How do you know?

KIT: Who with?

ANGIE: I'm not telling you.

KIT: You said you told me everything.

ANGIE: I was lying wasn't I.

KIT: Who with? You can't tell me who with because / you never—

ANGIE: Sh.

(JOYCE *has come out of the house. She stops halfway across the yard and listens. They listen.*)

JOYCE: You there Angie? Kit? You there Kitty? Want a cup of tea? I've got some chocolate biscuits. Come

---

°*slag,* slut.

on now I'll put the kettle on. Want a choccy biccy, Angie? (*They all listen and wait.*) Fucking rotten little cunt. You can stay there and die. I'll lock the door.

(*They all wait.* JOYCE *goes back to the house.* ANGIE *and* KIT *sit in silence for a while.*)

KIT: When there's a war, where's the safest place?

ANGIE: Nowhere.

KIT: New Zealand is, my mum said. Your skin's burned right off. Shall we go to New Zealand?

ANGIE: I'm not staying here.

KIT: Shall we go to New Zealand?

ANGIE: You're not old enough.

KIT: You're not old enough.

ANGIE: I'm old enough to get married.

KIT: You don't want to get married.

ANGIE: No but I'm old enough.

KIT: I'd find out where they were going to drop it and stand right in the place.

ANGIE: You couldn't find out.

KIT: Better than walking round with your skin dragging on the ground. Eugh. / Would you like walking round with your skin dragging on the ground?

ANGIE: You couldn't find out, stupid, it's a secret.

KIT: Where are you going?

ANGIE: I'm not telling you.

KIT: Why?

ANGIE: It's a secret.

KIT: But you tell me all your secrets.

ANGIE: Not the true secrets.

KIT: Yes you do.

ANGIE: No I don't.

KIT: I want to go somewhere away from the war.

ANGIE: Just forget the war.

KIT: I can't.

ANGIE: You have to. It's so boring.

KIT: I'll remember it at night.

ANGIE: I'm going to do something else anyway.

KIT: What? Angie, come on. Angie.

ANGIE: It's a true secret.

KIT: It can't be worse than the kitten. And killing your mother. And the war.

ANGIE: Well I'm not telling you so you can die for all I care.

KIT: My mother says there's something wrong with you playing with someone my age. She says why haven't you got friends your own age. People your own age know there's something funny about you. She says you're a bad influence. She says she's going to speak to your mother. (ANGIE *twists* KIT's *arm till she cries out.*)

ANGIE: Say you're a liar.

KIT: She said it not me.

ANGIE: Say you eat shit.

KIT: You can't make me. (ANGIE *lets go.*)

ANGIE: I don't care anyway. I'm leaving.

KIT: Go on then.

ANGIE: You'll all wake up one morning and find I've gone.

KIT: Good.

ANGIE: I'm not telling you when.

KIT: Go on then.

ANGIE: I'm sorry I hurt you.

KIT: I'm tired.

ANGIE: Do you like me?

KIT: I don't know.

ANGIE: You do like me.

KIT: I'm going home. *(She gets up.)*

ANGIE: No you're not.

KIT: I'm tired.

ANGIE: She'll see you.

KIT: She'll give me a chocolate biscuit.

ANGIE: Kitty.

KIT: Tell me where you're going.

ANGIE: Sit down.

KIT: *(Sitting down again)* Go on then.

ANGIE: Swear?

KIT: Swear.

ANGIE: I'm going to London. To see my aunt.

KIT: And what?

ANGIE: That's it.

KIT: I see my aunt all the time.

ANGIE: I don't see my aunt.

KIT: What's so special?

ANGIE: It is special. She's special.

KIT: Why?

ANGIE: She is.

KIT: Why?

ANGIE: She is.

KIT: Why?

ANGIE: My mother hates her.

KIT: Why?

ANGIE: Because she does.

KIT: Perhaps she's not very nice.

ANGIE: She is nice.

KIT: How do you know?

ANGIE: Because I know her.

KIT: You said you never see her.

ANGIE: I saw her last year. You saw her.

KIT: Did I?

ANGIE: Never mind.

KIT: I remember her. That aunt. What's so special?

ANGIE: She gets people jobs.

KIT: What's so special?

ANGIE: I think I'm my aunt's child. I think my mother's really my aunt.

KIT: Why?

ANGIE: Because she goes to America, now shut up.

KIT: I've been to London.

ANGIE: Now give us a cuddle and shut up because I'm sick.

KIT: You're sitting on my arm.

(They curl up in each other's arms. Silence. JOYCE *comes out of the house and comes up to them quietly.)*

JOYCE: Come on.

KIT: Oh hello.

JOYCE: Time you went home.

KIT: We want to go to the Odeon.

JOYCE: What time?

KIT: Don't know.

JOYCE: What's on?

KIT: Don't know.

JOYCE: Don't know much do you?

KIT: That all right then?

JOYCE: Angie's got to clean her room first.

ANGIE: No I don't.

JOYCE: Yes you do, it's a pigsty.

ANGIE: Well I'm not.

JOYCE: Then you're not going. I don't care.

ANGIE: Well I am going.

JOYCE: You've no money, have you?

ANGIE: Kit's paying anyway.

JOYCE: No she's not.

KIT: I'll help you with your room.

JOYCE: That's nice.

ANGIE: No you won't. You wait here.

KIT: Hurry then.

ANGIE: I'm not hurrying. You just wait. (ANGIE *goes slowly into the house. Silence.)*

JOYCE: I don't know. *(Silence.)* How's school then?

KIT: All right.

JOYCE: What are you now? Third year?

KIT: Second year.

JOYCE: Your mum says you're good at English. *(Silence.)* Maybe Angie should've stayed on.

KIT: She didn't like it.

JOYCE: I didn't like it. And look at me. If your face fits at school it's going to fit other places too. It wouldn't make no difference to Angie. She's not going to get a job when jobs are hard to get. I'd be sorry for anyone in charge of her. She'd better get married. I don't know who'd have her, mind. She's one of those girls might never leave home. What do you want to be when you grow up, Kit?

KIT: Physicist.

JOYCE: What?

KIT: Nuclear physicist.

JOYCE: Whatever for?

KIT: I could, I'm clever.

JOYCE: I know you're clever, pet. *(Silence.)* I'll make a cup of tea. *(Silence.)* Looks like it's going to rain. *(Silence.)* Don't you have friends your own age?

KIT: Yes.

JOYCE: Well then.

KIT: I'm old for my age.

JOYCE: And Angie's simple is she? She's not simple.

KIT: I love Angie.

JOYCE: She's clever in her own way.

KIT: You can't stop me.

JOYCE: I don't want to.

KIT: You can't, so.

JOYCE: Don't be cheeky, Kitty. She's always kind to little children.

KIT: She's coming so you better leave me alone.

(ANGIE *comes out. She has changed into an old best dress, slightly small for her.*)

JOYCE: What you put that on for? Have you done your room? You can't clean your room in that.

ANGIE: I looked in the cupboard and it was there.

JOYCE: Of course it was there, it's meant to be there. Is that why it was a surprise, finding something in the right place? I should think she's surprised, wouldn't you, Kit, to find something in her room in the right place.

ANGIE: I decided to wear it.

JOYCE: Not today, why? To clean your room? You're not going to the pictures till you've done your room. You can put your dress on after if you like. (ANGIE *picks up a brick.*) Have you done your room? You're not getting out of it, you know.

KIT: Angie, let's go.

JOYCE: She's not going till she's done her room.

KIT: It's starting to rain.

JOYCE: Come on, come on then. Hurry and do your room, Angie, and then you can go to the cinema with Kit. Oh it's wet, come on. We'll look up the time in the paper. Does your mother know, Kit, it's going to be a late night for you, isn't it? Hurry up, Angie. You'll spoil your dress. You make me sick. (JOYCE *and* KIT *run into the house.* ANGIE *stays where she is. There is the sound of rain.* KIT *comes out of the house.*)

KIT (*Shouting*): Angie. Angie, come on, you'll get wet.

(*She comes back to* ANGIE.)

ANGIE: I put on this dress to kill my mother.

KIT: I suppose you thought you'd do it with a brick.

ANGIE: You can kill people with a brick. (*She puts the brick down.*)

KIT: Well you didn't, so.

ACT 2 / SCENE 1

(*"Top Girls" Employment Agency. Monday morning. There are three desks in the main office and a separate small interviewing area. The lights come up in the main office on* WIN *and* NELL *who have just arrived for work.*)

NELL: Coffee coffee coffee coffee / coffee.

WIN: The roses were smashing. / Mermaid.

NELL: Ohhh.

WIN: Iceberg. He taught me all their names. (NELL *has some coffee now.*)

NELL: Ah. Now then.

WIN: He has one of the finest rose gardens in West Sussex. He exhibits.

NELL: He what?

WIN: His wife was visiting her mother. It was like living together.

NELL: Crafty, you never said.

WIN: He rang on Saturday morning.

NELL: Lucky you were free.

WIN: That's what I told him.

NELL: Did you hell.

WIN: Have you ever seen a really beautiful rose garden?

NELL: I don't like flowers. /I like swimming pools.

WIN: Marilyn. Esther's Baby. They're all called after birds.

NELL: Our friend's late. Celebrating all weekend I bet you.

WIN: I'd call a rose Elvis. Or John Conteh.°

NELL: Is Howard in yet?

WIN: If he is he'll be bleeping us with a problem.

NELL: Howard can just hang on to himself.

WIN: Howard's really cut up.

NELL: Howard thinks because he's a fella the job was his as of right. Our Marlene's got far more balls than Howard and that's that.

WIN: Poor little bugger.

NELL: He'll live.

WIN: He'll move on.

NELL: I wouldn't mind a change of air myself.

WIN: Serious?

NELL: I've never been a staying-put lady. Pastures new.

WIN: So who's the pirate?

NELL: There's nothing definite.

WIN: Inquiries?

NELL: There's always inquiries. I'd think I'd got bad breath if there stopped being inquiries. Most of them can't afford me. Or you.

WIN: I'm all right for the time being. Unless I go to Australia.

NELL: There's not a lot of room upward.

WIN: Marlene's filled it up.

NELL: Good luck to her. Unless there's some prospects moneywise.

WIN: You can but ask.

NELL: Can always but ask.

WIN: So what have we got? I've got a Mr. Holden I saw last week.

NELL: Any use?

WIN: Pushy. Bit of a cowboy.

NELL: Goodlooker?

WIN: Good dresser.

NELL: High flyer?°

WIN: That's his general idea certainly but I'm not sure he's got it up there.

John Conteh, popular boxer and model. *High flyer*, someone who is succeeding by moving up in a chosen field.

NELL: Prestel° wants six flyers and I've only seen two and a half.

WIN: He's making a bomb on the road but he thinks it's time for an office. I sent him to IBM but he didn't get it.

NELL: Prestel's on the road.

WIN: He's not overbright.

NELL: Can he handle an office?

WIN: Provided his secretary can punctuate he should go far.

NELL: Bear Prestel in mind then, I might put my head round the door. I've got that poor little nerd I should never have said I could help. Tender heart me.

WIN: Tender like old boots. How old?

NELL: Yes well forty-five.

WIN: Say no more.

NELL: He knows his place, he's not after calling himself a manager, he's just a poor little bod wants a better commission and a bit of sunshine.

WIN: Don't we all.

NELL: He's just got to relocate. He's got a bungalow in Dymchurch.

WIN: And his wife says.

NELL: The lady wife wouldn't care to relocate. She's going through the change.

WIN: It's his funeral, don't waste your time.

NELL: I don't waste a lot.

WIN: Good weekend you?

NELL: You could say.

WIN: Which one?

NELL: One Friday, one Saturday.

WIN: Aye—aye.

NELL: Sunday night I watched telly.

WIN: Which of them do you like best really?

NELL: Sunday was best, I like the Ovaltine.°

WIN: Holden, Barker, Gardner, Duke.

NELL: I've a lady here thinks she can sell.

WIN: Taking her on?

NELL: She's had some jobs.

WIN: Services?

NELL: No, quite heavy stuff, electric.

WIN: Tough bird like us.

NELL: We could do with a few more here.

WIN: There's nothing going here.

NELL: No but I always want the tough ones when I see them. Hang on to them.

WIN: I think we're plenty.

NELL: Derek asked me to marry him again.

WIN: He doesn't know when he's beaten.

NELL: I told him I'm not going to play house, not even in Ascot.

WIN: Mind you, you could play house.

NELL: If I chose to play house I would play house ace.°

WIN: You could marry him and go on working.

NELL: I could go on working and not marry him.

(MARLENE arrives.)

MARLENE: Morning ladies. (WIN *and* NELL *cheer and whistle.*) Mind my head.

NELL: Coffee coffee coffee.

WIN: We're tactfully not mentioning you're late.

MARLENE: Fucking tube.°

WIN: We've heard that one.

NELL: We've used that one.

WIN: It's the top executive doesn't come in as early as the poor working girl.

MARLENE: Pass the sugar and shut your face, pet.

WIN: Well I'm delighted.

NELL: Howard's looking sick.

WIN: Howard is sick. He's got ulcers and heart. He told me.

NELL: He'll have to stop then, won't he?

WIN: Stop what?

NELL: Smoking, drinking, shouting. Working.

WIN: Well, working.

NELL: We're just looking through the day.

MARLENE: I'm doing some of Pam's ladies. They've been piling up while she's away.

NELL: Half a dozen little girls and an arts graduate who can't type.

WIN: I spent the whole weekend at his place in Sussex.

NELL: She fancies his rose garden.

WIN: I had to lie down in the back of the car so the neighbors wouldn't see me go in.

NELL: You're kidding.

WIN: It was funny.

NELL: Fuck that for a joke.

WIN: It was funny.

MARLENE: Anyway they'd see you in the garden.

WIN: The garden has extremely high walls.

NELL: I think I'll tell the wife.

WIN: Like hell.

NELL: She might leave him and you could have the rose garden.

WIN: The minute it's not a secret I'm out on my ear.

NELL: Don't know why you bother.

WIN: Bit of fun.

NELL: I think it's time you went to Australia.

WIN: I think it's pushy Mr. Holden time.

NELL: If you've any really pretty bastards, Marlene, I want some for Prestel.

MARLENE: I might have one this afternoon. This morning it's all Pam's secretarial.

NELL: Not long now and you'll be upstairs watching over us all.

MARLENE: Do you feel bad about it?

Prestel, television and computer stock market information service. *Ovaltine,* hot chocolate malt drink.

ace, slang for "first-class." *tube,* London subway.

NELL: I don't like coming second.

MARLENE: Who does?

WIN: We'd rather it was you than Howard. We're glad for you, aren't we, Nell?

NELL: Oh yes. Aces.

(LOUISE enters the interviewing area. The lights crossfade to WIN and LOUISE in the interviewing area. NELL exits.)

WIN: Now, Louise, hello, I have your details here. You've been very loyal to the one job I see.

LOUISE: Yes I have.

WIN: Twenty-one years is a long time in one place.

LOUISE: I feel it is. I feel it's time to move on.

WIN: And you are what age now?

LOUISE: I'm in my early forties.

WIN: Exactly?

LOUISE: Forty-six.

WIN: It's not necessarily a handicap, well it is of course we have to face that, but it's not necessarily a disabling handicap, experience does count for something.

LOUISE: I hope so.

WIN: Now between ourselves is there any trouble, any reason why you're leaving that wouldn't appear on the form?

LOUISE: Nothing like that.

WIN: Like what?

LOUISE: Nothing at all.

WIN: No long-term understandings come to a sudden end, making for an insupportable atmosphere?

LOUISE: I've always completely avoided anything like that at all.

WIN: No personality clashes with your immediate superiors or inferiors?

LOUISE: I've always taken care to get on very well with everyone.

WIN: I only ask because it can affect the reference and it also affects your motivation. I want to be quite clear why you're moving on. So I take it the job itself no longer satisfies you. Is it the money?

LOUISE: It's partly the money. It's not so much the money.

WIN: Nine thousand is very respectable. Have you dependants?

LOUISE: No, no dependants. My mother died.

WIN: So why are you making a change?

LOUISE: Other people make changes.

WIN: But why are you, now, after spending most of your life in the one place?

LOUISE: There you are, I've lived for that company, I've given my life really you could say because I haven't had a great deal of social life, I've worked in the evenings. I haven't had office entanglements for the very reason you just mentioned and if you are committed to your work you don't move in many other circles. I had management status from the age of twenty-seven and you'll appreci-ate what that means. I've built up a department. And there it is, it works extremely well, and I feel I'm stuck there. I've spent twenty years in middle management. I've seen young men who I trained go on, in my own company or elsewhere, to higher things. Nobody notices me, I don't expect it, I don't attract attention by making mistakes, everybody takes it for granted that my work is perfect. They will notice me when I go, they will be sorry I think to lose me, they will offer me more money of course, I will refuse. They will see when I've gone what I was doing for them.

WIN: If they offer you more money you won't stay?

LOUISE: No I won't.

WIN: Are you the only woman?

LOUISE: Apart from the girls of course, yes. There was one, she was my assistant, it was the only time I took on a young woman assistant, I always had my doubts. I don't care greatly for working with women, I think I pass as a man at work. But I did take on this young woman, her qualifications were excellent, and she did well, she got a department of her own, and left the company for a competitor where she's now on the board and good luck to her. She has a different style, she's a new kind of attractive well dressed—I don't mean I don't dress properly. But there is a kind of woman who is thirty now who grew up in a different climate. They are not so careful. They take themselves for granted. I have had to justify my existence every minute, and I have done so, I have proved—well.

WIN: Let's face it, vacancies are ones where you'll be in competition with younger men. And there are companies that will value your experience enough that you'll be in with a chance. There are also fields that are easier for a woman, there is a cosmetic company here where your experience might be relevant. It's eight and a half, I don't know if that appeals.

LOUISE: I've proved I can earn money. It's more important to get away. I feel it's now or never. I sometimes / think—

WIN: You shouldn't talk too much at an interview.

LOUISE: I don't. I don't normally talk about myself. I know very well how to handle myself in an office situation. I only talk to you because it seems to me this is different, it's your job to understand me, surely. You asked the questions.

WIN: I think I understand you sufficiently.

LOUISE: Well good, that's good.

WIN: Do you drink?

LOUISE: Certainly not. I'm not a teetotaler, I think that's very suspect, it's seen as being an alcoholic if you're teetotal. What do you mean? I don't drink. Why?

WIN: I drink.

LOUISE: I don't.

WIN: Good for you.

(The lights crossfade to the main office with MARLENE *sitting at her desk.* WIN *and* LOUISE *exit.* ANGIE *arrives in the main office.)*

ANGIE: Hello.

MARLENE: Have you an appointment?

ANGIE: It's me. I've come.

MARLENE: What? It's not Angie?

ANGIE: It was hard to find this place. I got lost.

MARLENE: How did you get past the receptionist? The girl on the desk, didn't she try to stop you?

ANGIE: What desk?

MARLENE: Never mind.

ANGIE: I just walked in. I was looking for you.

MARLENE: Well you found me.

ANGIE: Yes.

MARLENE: So where's your mum? Are you up in town for the day?

ANGIE: Not really.

MARLENE: Sit down. Do you feel all right?

ANGIE: Yes thank you.

MARLENE: So where's Joyce?

ANGIE: She's at home.

MARLENE: Did you come up on a school trip then?

ANGIE: I've left school.

MARLENE: Did you come up with a friend?

ANGIE: No. There's just me.

MARLENE: You came up by yourself, that's fun. What have you been doing? Shopping? Tower of London?

ANGIE: No, I just come here. I come to you.

MARLENE: That's very nice of you to think of paying your aunty a visit. There's not many nieces make that the first port of call. Would you like a cup of coffee?

ANGIE: No thank you.

MARLENE: Tea, orange?

ANGIE: No thank you.

MARLENE: Do you feel all right?

ANGIE: Yes thank you.

MARLENE: Are you tired from the journey?

ANGIE: Yes, I'm tired from the journey.

MARLENE: You sit there for a bit then. How's Joyce?

ANGIE: She's all right.

MARLENE: Same as ever.

ANGIE: Oh yes.

MARLENE: Unfortunately you've picked a day when I'm rather busy, if there's ever a day when I'm not, or I'd take you out to lunch and we'd go to Madame Tussaud's.° We could go shopping. What time do you have to be back? Have you got a day return?

ANGIE: No.

Madame Tussaud's, London waxworks museum.

MARLENE: So what train are you going back on?

ANGIE: I came on the bus.

MARLENE: So what bus are you going back on? Are you staying the night?

ANGIE: Yes.

MARLENE: Who are you staying with? Do you want me to put you up for the night, is that it?

ANGIE: Yes please.

MARLENE: I haven't got a spare bed.

ANGIE: I can sleep on the floor.

MARLENE: You can sleep on the sofa.

ANGIE: Yes please.

MARLENE: I do think Joyce might have phoned me. It's like her.

ANGIE: This is where you work is it?

MARLENE: It's where I have been working the last two years but I'm going to move into another office.

ANGIE: It's lovely.

MARLENE: My new office is nicer than this. There's just the one big desk in it for me.

ANGIE: Can I see it?

MARLENE: Not now, no, there's someone else in it now. But he's leaving at the end of next week and I'm going to do his job.

ANGIE: Is that good?

MARLENE: Yes, it's very good.

ANGIE: Are you going to be in charge?

MARLENE: Yes I am.

ANGIE: I knew you would be.

MARLENE: How did you know?

ANGIE: I knew you'd be in charge of everything.

MARLENE: Not quite everything.

ANGIE: You will be.

MARLENE: Well we'll see.

ANGIE: Can I see it next week then?

MARLENE: Will you still be here next week?

ANGIE: Yes.

MARLENE: Don't you have to go home?

ANGIE: No.

MARLENE: Why not?

ANGIE: It's all right.

MARLENE: Is it all right?

ANGIE: Yes, don't worry about it.

MARLENE: Does Joyce know where you are?

ANGIE: Yes of course she does.

MARLENE: Well does she?

ANGIE: Don't worry about it.

MARLENE: How long are you planning to stay with me then?

ANGIE: You know when you came to see us last year?

MARLENE: Yes, that was nice wasn't it.

ANGIE: That was the best day of my whole life.

MARLENE: So how long are you planning to stay?

ANGIE: Don't you want me?

MARLENE: Yes yes, I just wondered.

ANGIE: I won't stay if you don't want me.

MARLENE: No, of course you can stay.

ANGIE: I'll sleep on the floor. I won't be any bother.

MARLENE: Don't get upset.

ANGIE: I'm not, I'm not. Don't worry about it.

(MRS. KIDD *comes in.*)

MRS. KIDD: Excuse me.

MARLENE: Yes.

MRS. KIDD: Excuse me.

MARLENE: Can I help you?

MRS. KIDD: Excuse me bursting in on you like this but I have to talk to you.

MARLENE: I am engaged at the moment. / If you could go to reception—

MRS. KIDD: I'm Rosemary Kidd, Howard's wife, you don't recognize me but we did meet, I remember you of course / but you wouldn't—

MARLENE: Yes of course, Mrs. Kidd, I'm sorry, we did meet. Howard's about somewhere I expect, have you looked in his office?

MRS. KIDD: Howard's not about, no. I'm afraid it's you I've come to see if I could have a minute or two.

MARLENE: I do have an appointment in five minutes.

MRS. KIDD: This won't take five minutes. I'm very sorry. It is a matter of some urgency.

MARLENE: Well of course. What can I do for you?

MRS. KIDD: I just wanted a chat, an informal chat. It's not something I can simply—I'm sorry if I'm interrupting your work. I know office work isn't like housework / which is all interruptions.

MARLENE: No no, this is my niece. Angie. Mrs. Kidd.

MRS. KIDD: Very pleased to meet you.

ANGIE: Very well thank you.

MRS. KIDD: Howard's not in today.

MARLENE: Isn't he?

MRS. KIDD: He's feeling poorly.

MARLENE: I didn't know. I'm sorry to hear that.

MRS. KIDD: The fact is he's in a state of shock. About what's happened.

MARLENE: What has happened?

MRS. KIDD: You should know if anyone. I'm referring to you being appointed managing director instead of Howard. He hasn't been at all well all weekend. He hasn't slept for three nights. I haven't slept.

MARLENE: I'm sorry to hear that, Mrs. Kidd. Has he thought of taking sleeping pills?

MRS. KIDD: It's very hard when someone has worked all these years.

MARLENE: Business life is full of little setbacks. I'm sure Howard knows that. He'll bounce back in a day or two. We all bounce back.

MRS. KIDD: If you could see him you'd know what I'm talking about. What's it going to do to him working for a woman? I think if it was a man he'd get over it as something normal.

MARLENE: I think he's going to have to get over it.

MRS. KIDD: It's me that bears the brunt. I'm not the one that's been promoted. I put him first every inch of the way. And now what do I get? You women this, you women that. It's not my fault. You're going to have to be very careful how you handle him. He's very hurt.

MARLENE: Naturally I'll be tactful and pleasant to him, you don't start pushing someone around. I'll consult him over any decisions affecting his department. But that's no different, Mrs. Kidd, from any of my other colleagues.

MRS. KIDD: I think it is different, because he's a man.

MARLENE: I'm not quite sure why you came to see me.

MRS. KIDD: I had to do something.

MARLENE: Well you've done it, you've seen me. I think that's probably all we've time for. I'm sorry he's been taking it out on you. He really is a shit, Howard.

MRS. KIDD: But he's got a family to support. He's got three children. It's only fair.

MARLENE: Are you suggesting I give up the job to him then?

MRS. KIDD: It had crossed my mind if you were unavailable after all for some reason, he would be the natural second choice I think, don't you? I'm not asking.

MARLENE: Good.

MRS. KIDD: You mustn't tell him I came. He's very proud.

MARLENE: If he doesn't like what's happening here he can go and work somewhere else.

MRS. KIDD: Is that a threat?

MARLENE: I'm sorry but I do have some work to do.

MRS. KIDD: It's not that easy, a man of Howard's age. You don't care. I thought he was going too far but he's right. You're one of these ballbreakers, / that's what you

MARLENE: I'm sorry but I do have some work to do.

MRS. KIDD: are. You'll end up miserable and lonely. You're not natural.

MARLENE: Could you please piss off?

MRS. KIDD: I thought if I saw you at least I'd be doing something. (MRS. KIDD *goes.*)

MARLENE: I've got to go and do some work now. Will you come back later?

ANGIE: I think you were wonderful.

MARLENE: I've got to go and do some work now.

ANGIE: You told her to piss off.

MARLENE: Will you come back later?

ANGIE: Can't I stay here?

MARLENE: Don't you want to go sightseeing?

ANGIE: I'd rather stay here.

MARLENE: You can stay here I suppose, if it's not boring.

ANGIE: It's where I most want to be in the world.

MARLENE: I'll see you later then.

(MARLENE *goes.* SHONA *and* NELL *enter the interviewing area.* ANGIE *sits at* WIN's *desk. The lights crossfade to* NELL *and* SHONA *in the interviewing area.*)

NELL: Is this right? You are Shona?

SHONA: Yeh.

NELL: It says here you're twenty-nine.

SHONA: Yeh.

NELL: Too many late nights, me. So you've been where you are for four years, Shona, you're earning six basic and three commission. So what's the problem?

SHONA: No problem.

NELL: Why do you want a change?

SHONA: Just a change.

NELL: Change of product, change of area?

SHONA: Both.

NELL: But you're happy on the road?

SHONA: I like driving.

NELL: You're not after management status?

SHONA: I would like management status.

NELL: You'd be interested in titular management status but not come off the road?

SHONA: I want to be on the road, yeh.

NELL: So how many calls have you been making a day?

SHONA: Six.

NELL: And what proportion of those are successful?

SHONA: Six.

NELL: That's hard to believe.

SHONA: Four.

NELL: You find it easy to get the initial interest do you?

SHONA: Oh yeh, I get plenty of initial interest.

NELL: And what about closing?

SHONA: I close, don't I?

NELL: Because that's what an employer is going to have doubts about with a lady as I needn't tell you, whether she's got the guts to push through to a closing situation. They think we're too nice. They think we listen to the buyer's doubts. They think we consider his needs and his feelings.

SHONA: I never consider people's feelings.

NELL: I was selling for six years, I can sell anything, I've sold in three continents, and I'm jolly as they come but I'm not very nice.

SHONA: I'm not very nice.

NELL: What sort of time do you have on the road with the other reps? Get on all right? Handle the chat?

SHONA: I get on. Keep myself to myself.

NELL: Fairly much of a loner are you?

SHONA: Sometimes.

NELL: So what field are you interested in?

SHONA: Computers.

NELL: That's a top field as you know and you'll be up against some very slick fellas there, there's some very pretty boys in computers, it's an American-style field.

SHONA: That's why I want to do it.

NELL: Video systems appeal? That's a high-flying situation.

SHONA: Video systems appeal OK.

NELL: Because Prestel have half a dozen vacancies I'm looking to fill at the moment. We're talking in the area of ten to fifteen thousand here and upwards.

SHONA: Sounds OK.

NELL: I've half a mind to go for it myself. But it's good money here if you've got the top clients. Could you fancy it do you think?

SHONA: Work here?

NELL: I'm not in a position to offer, there's nothing officially going just now, but we're always on the lookout. There's not that many of us. We could keep in touch.

SHONA: I like driving.

NELL: So the Prestel appeals?

SHONA: Yeh.

NELL: What about ties?

SHONA: No ties.

NELL: So relocation wouldn't be a problem.

SHONA: No problem.

NELL: So just fill me in a bit more could you about what you've been doing.

SHONA: What I've been doing. It's all down there.

NELL: The bare facts are down here but I've got to present you to an employer.

SHONA: I'm twenty-nine years old.

NELL: So it says here.

SHONA: We look young. Youngness runs in the family in our family.

NELL: So just describe your present job for me.

SHONA: My present job at present. I have a car. I have a Porsche. I go up the M1° a lot. Burn up the M1 a lot. Straight up the M1 in the fast lane to where the clients are, Staffordshire, Yorkshire, I do a lot in Yorkshire. I'm selling electric things. Like dishwashers, washing machines, stainless steel tubs are a feature and the reliability of the program. After sales service, we offer a very good after sales service, spare parts, plenty of spare parts. And fridges, I sell a lot of fridges specially in the summer. People want to buy fridges in the summer because of the heat melting the butter and you get fed up standing the milk in a basin of cold water with a cloth over, stands to reason people don't want to do that in this day and age. So I sell a lot of them. Big ones with big freezers. Big freezers. And I stay in hotels at night when I'm away from home. On my expense account. I stay in various hotels. They know me, the ones I go to. I check in, have a bath, have a shower. Then I go

---

M1, expressway running from London to Yorkshire.

down to the bar, have a gin and tonic, have a chat.
Then I go into the dining room and have dinner.
I usually have fillet steak and mushrooms, I like
mushrooms. I like smoked salmon very much. I
like having a salad on the side. Green salad. I
don't like tomatoes.
NELL: Christ what a waste of time.
SHONA: Beg your pardon?
NELL: Not a word of this is true, is it?
SHONA: How do you mean?
NELL: You just filled in the form with a pack of lies.
SHONA: Not exactly.
NELL: How old are you?
SHONA: Twenty-nine.
NELL: Nineteen?
SHONA: Twenty-one.
NELL: And what jobs have you done? Have you done
any?
SHONA: I could though, I bet you.

(The lights crossfade to the main office with ANGIE *sitting
as before.* WIN *comes in to the main office.* SHONA *and*
NELL *exit.)*

WIN: Who's sitting in my chair?
ANGIE: What? Sorry.
WIN: Who's been eating my porridge?
ANGIE: What?
WIN: It's all right, I saw Marlene. Angie, isn't it? I'm
Win. And I'm not going out for lunch because
I'm knackered. I'm going to set me down here
and have a yogurt. Do you like yogurt?
ANGIE: No.
WIN: That's good because I've only got one. Are you
hungry?
ANGIE: No.
WIN: There's a café on the corner.
ANGIE: No thank you. Do you work here?
WIN: How did you guess?
ANGIE: Because you look as if you might work here
and you're sitting at the desk. Have you always
worked here?
WIN: No I was headhunted. That means I was work-
ing for another outfit like this and this lot came
and offered me more money. I broke my con-
tract, there was a hell of a stink. There's not
many top ladies about. Your aunty's a smashing
bird.
ANGIE: Yes I know.
WIN: Fan are you? Fan of your aunty's?
ANGIE: Do you think I could work here?
WIN: Not at the moment.
ANGIE: How do I start?
WIN: What can you do?
ANGIE: I don't know. Nothing.
WIN: Type?
ANGIE: Not very well. The letters jump up when I do

capitals. I was going to do a CSE° in commerce
but I didn't.
WIN: What have you got?
ANGIE: What?
WIN: CSE's, O's.
ANGIE: Nothing, none of that. Did you do all that?
WIN: Oh yes, all that, and a science degree funnily
enough. I started out doing medical research but
there's no money in it. I thought I'd go abroad.
Did you know they sell Coca Cola in Russia and
Pepsi-Cola in China? You don't have to be qualified as much as you might think. Men are awful
bullshitters, they like to make out jobs are harder
than they are. Any job I ever did I started doing it
better than the rest of the crowd and they didn't
like it. So I'd get unpopular and I'd have a drink
to cheer myself up. I lived with a fella and supported him for four years, he couldn't get work.
After that I went to California. I like the sunshine.
Americans know how to live. This country's too
slow. Then I went to Mexico, still in sales, but it's
no country for a single lady. I came home, went
bonkers for a bit, thought I was five different
people, got over that all right, the psychiatrist said
I was perfectly sane and highly intelligent. Got
married in a moment of weakness and he's inside°
now, he's been inside four years, and I've not
been to see him too much this last year. I like this
better than sales, I'm not really that aggressive. I
started thinking sales was a good job if you want
to meet people, but you're meeting people that
don't want to meet you. It's no good if you like
being liked. Here your clients want to meet you
because you're the one doing them some good.
They hope. (ANGIE *has fallen asleep.* NELL *comes in.)*
NELL: You're talking to yourself, sunshine.
WIN: So what's new?
NELL: Who is this?
WIN: Marlene's little niece.
NELL: What's she got, brother, sister? She never talks
about her family.
WIN: I was telling her my life story.
NELL: Violins?
WIN: No, success story.
NELL: You've heard Howard's had a heart attack?
WIN: No, when?
NELL: I heard just now. He hadn't come in, he was at
home, he's gone to hospital. He's not dead. His
wife was here, she rushed off in a cab.
WIN: Too much butter, too much smoke. We must send
him some flowers. (MARLENE *comes in.)* You've
heard about Howard?

CSE, Certificate of Secondary Education, similar to
O-levels, but less prestigious.   *inside,* in jail.

MARLENE: Poor sod.

NELL: Lucky he didn't get the job if that's what his health's like.

MARLENE: Is she asleep?

WIN: She wants to work here.

MARLENE: Packer in Tesco° more like.

WIN: She's a nice kid. Isn't she?

MARLENE: She's a bit thick. She's a bit funny.

WIN: She thinks you're wonderful.

MARLENE: She's not going to make it.

ACT 2 / SCENE 2

(JOYCE's *kitchen. Sunday evening, a year earlier. The lights come up on* JOYCE, ANGIE, *and* MARLENE. MARLENE *is taking presents out of a bright carrier bag.* ANGIE *has already opened a box of chocolates.*)

MARLENE: Just a few little things. / I've

JOYCE: There's no need.

MARLENE: no memory for birthdays have I, and Christmas seems to slip by. So I think I owe Angie a few presents.

JOYCE: What do you say?

ANGIE: Thank you very much. Thank you very much, Aunty Marlene. (*She opens a present. It is the dress from Act 1, new.*) Oh look, Mum, isn't it lovely?

MARLENE: I don't know if it's the right size. She's grown up since I saw her. / I knew she was always

ANGIE: Isn't it lovely?

MARLENE: tall for her age.

JOYCE: She's a big lump.

MARLENE: Hold it up, Angie, let's see.

ANGIE: I'll put it on, shall I?

MARLENE: Yes, try it on.

JOYCE: Go on to your room then, we don't want / a strip show thank you.

ANGIE: Of course I'm going to my room, what do you think. Look, Mum, here's something for you. Open it, go on. What is it? Can I open it for you?

JOYCE: Yes, you open it, pet.

ANGIE: Don't you want to open it yourself? / Go on.

JOYCE: I don't mind, you can do it.

ANGIE: It's something hard. It's—what is it? A bottle. Drink is it? No, it's what? Perfume, look. What a lot. Open it, look, let's smell it. Oh it's strong. It's lovely. Put it on me. How do you do it? Put it on me.

JOYCE: You're too young.

ANGIE: I can play wearing it like dressing up.

JOYCE: And you're too old for that. Here, give it here, I'll do it, you'll tip the whole bottle over yourself / and we'll have you smelling all summer.

ANGIE: Put it on you. Do I smell? Put it on Aunty too. Put it on Aunty too. Let's all smell.

MARLENE: I didn't know what you'd like.

°**Packer in Tesco,** shelf stocker in major grocery store.

JOYCE: There's no danger I'd have it already, / that's one thing.

ANGIE: Now we all smell the same.

MARLENE: It's a bit of nonsense.

JOYCE: It's very kind of you Marlene, you shouldn't.

ANGIE: Now I'll put on the dress and then we'll see. (ANGIE *goes.*)

JOYCE: You've caught me on the hop with the place in a mess. / If you'd let me

MARLENE: That doesn't matter.

JOYCE: know you was coming I'd have got something in to eat. We had our dinner dinnertime. We're just going to have a cup of tea. You could have an egg.

MARLENE: No, I'm not hungry. Tea's fine.

JOYCE: I don't expect you take sugar.

MARLENE: Why not?

JOYCE: You take care of yourself.

MARLENE: How do you mean you didn't know I was coming?

JOYCE: You could have written. I know we're not on the phone but we're not completely in the dark ages, / we do have a postman.

MARLENE: But you asked me to come.

JOYCE: How did I ask you to come?

MARLENE: Angie said when she phoned up.

JOYCE: Angie phoned up, did she.

MARLENE: Was it just Angie's idea?

JOYCE: What did she say?

MARLENE: She said you wanted me to come and see you. / It was a couple of

JOYCE: Ha.

MARLENE: weeks ago. How was I to know that's a ridiculous idea? My diary's always full a couple of weeks ahead so we fixed it for this weekend. I was meant to get here earlier but I was held up. She gave me messages from you.

JOYCE: Didn't you wonder why I didn't phone you myself?

MARLENE: She said you didn't like using the phone. You're shy on the phone and can't use it. I don't know what you're like, do I?

JOYCE: Are there people who can't use the phone?

MARLENE: I expect so.

JOYCE: I haven't met any.

MARLENE: Why should I think she was lying?

JOYCE: Because she's like what she's like.

MARLENE: How do I know / what she's like?

JOYCE: It's not my fault you don't know what she's like. You never come and see her.

MARLENE: Well I have now / and you don't seem over the moon.*

JOYCE: Good. *Well I'd have got a cake if she'd told me. (*Pause.*)

MARLENE: I did wonder why you wanted to see me.

JOYCE: I didn't want to see you.

MARLENE: Yes, I know. Shall I go?

JOYCE: I don't mind seeing you.

MARLENE: Great, I feel really welcome.

JOYCE: You can come and see Angie any time you like, I'm not stopping you. / You

MARLENE: Ta ever so.°

JOYCE: know where we are. You're the one went away, not me. I'm right here where I was. And will be a few years yet I shouldn't wonder.

MARLENE: All right. All right. (JOYCE gives MARLENE a cup of tea.)

JOYCE: Tea.

MARLENE: Sugar? (JOYCE passes MARLENE the sugar.) It's very quiet down here.

JOYCE: I expect you'd notice it.

MARLENE: The air smells different too.

JOYCE: That's the scent.

MARLENE: No, I mean walking down the lane.

JOYCE: What sort of air you get in London then?

(ANGIE comes in, wearing the dress. It fits.)

MARLENE: Oh, very pretty. / You do look pretty, Angie.

JOYCE: That fits all right.

MARLENE: Do you like the color?

ANGIE: Beautiful. Beautiful.

JOYCE: You better take it off, / you'll get it dirty.

ANGIE: I want to wear it. I want to wear it.

MARLENE: It is for wearing after all. You can't just hang it up and look at it.

ANGIE: I love it.

JOYCE: Well if you must you must.

ANGIE: If someone asks me what's my favorite color I'll tell them it's this. Thank you very much, Aunty Marlene.

MARLENE: You didn't tell your mum you asked me down.

ANGIE: I wanted it to be a surprise.

JOYCE: I'll give you a surprise / one of these days.

ANGIE: I thought you'd like to see her. She hasn't been here since I was nine. People do see their aunts.

MARLENE: Is it that long? Doesn't time fly.

ANGIE: I wanted to.

JOYCE: I'm not cross.

ANGIE: Are you glad?

JOYCE: I smell nicer anyhow, don't I?

(KIT comes in without saying anything, as if she lived there.)

MARLENE: I think it was a good idea, Angie, about time. We are sisters after all. It's a pity to let that go.

JOYCE: This is Kitty, / who lives up the road. This is Angie's Aunty Marlene.

KIT: What's that?

ANGIE: It's a present. Do you like it?

KIT: It's all right. / Are you coming out?*

MARLENE: Hello, Kitty.

ANGIE: *No.

KIT: What's that smell?

ANGIE: It's a present.

KIT: It's horrible. Come on.*

MARLENE: Have a chocolate.

ANGIE: *No, I'm busy.

KIT: Coming out later?

ANGIE: No.

KIT (To MARLENE): Hello. (KIT goes without a chocolate.)

JOYCE: She's a little girl Angie sometimes plays with because she's the only child lives really close. She's like a little sister to her really. Angie's good with little children.

MARLENE: Do you want to work with children, Angie? / Be a teacher or a nursery nurse?

JOYCE: I don't think she's ever thought of it.

MARLENE: What do you want to do?

JOYCE: She hasn't an idea in her head what she wants to do. / Lucky to get anything.

MARLENE: Angie?

JOYCE: She's not clever like you. (Pause.)

MARLENE: I'm not clever, just pushy.

JOYCE: True enough. (MARLENE takes a bottle of whiskey out of the bag.) I don't drink spirits.

ANGIE: You do at Christmas.

JOYCE: It's not Christmas, is it?

ANGIE: It's better than Christmas.

MARLENE: Glasses?

JOYCE: Just a small one then.

MARLENE: Do you want some, Angie?

ANGIE: I can't, can I?

JOYCE: Taste it if you want. You won't like it. (ANGIE tastes it.)

ANGIE: Mmm.

MARLENE: We got drunk together the night your grandfather died.

JOYCE: We did not get drunk.

MARLENE: I got drunk. You were just overcome with grief.

JOYCE: I still keep up the grave with flowers.

MARLENE: Do you really?

JOYCE: Why wouldn't I?

MARLENE: Have you seen Mother?

JOYCE: Of course I've seen Mother.

MARLENE: I mean lately.

JOYCE: Of course I've seen her lately, I go every Thursday.

MARLENE (To ANGIE): Do you remember your grandfather?

ANGIE: He got me out of the bath one night in a towel.

MARLENE: Did he? I don't think he ever gave me a bath. Did he give you a bath, Joyce? He probably got soft in his old age. Did you like him?

ANGIE: Yes of course.

MARLENE: Why?

ANGIE: What?

MARLENE: So what's the news? How's Mrs. Paisley?

Ta ever so, Thanks ever so much.

Still going crazily? / And Dorothy. What happened to Dorothy?*

ANGIE: Who's Mrs. Paisley?

JOYCE: *She went to Canada.

MARLENE: Did she? What to do?

JOYCE: I don't know. She just went to Canada.

MARLENE: Well / good for her.

ANGIE: Mr. Connolly killed his wife.

MARLENE: What, Connolly at Whitegates?

ANGIE: They found her body in the garden. / Under the cabbages.

MARLENE: He was always so proper.

JOYCE: Stuck up git,° Connolly. Best lawyer money could buy but he couldn't get out of it. She was carrying on with Matthew.

MARLENE: How old's Matthew then?

JOYCE: Twenty-one. / He's got a motorbike.

MARLENE: I think he's about six.

ANGIE: How can he be six? He's six years older than me. / If he was six I'd be nothing, I'd be just born this minute.

JOYCE: Your aunty knows that, she's just being silly. She means it's so long since she's been here she's forgotten about Matthew.

ANGIE: You were here for my birthday when I was nine. I had a pink cake. Kit was only five then, she was four, she hadn't started school yet. She could read already when she went to school. You remember my birthday? / You remember me?

MARLENE: Yes, I remember the cake.

ANGIE: You remember me?

MARLENE: Yes, I remember you.

ANGIE: And Mum and Dad was there, and Kit was.

MARLENE: Yes, how is your dad? Where is he tonight? Up the pub?

JOYCE: No, he's not here.

MARLENE: I can see he's not here.

JOYCE: He moved out.

MARLENE: What? When did he? /Just recently?*

ANGIE: Didn't you know that? You don't know much.

JOYCE: *No, it must be three years ago. Don't be rude, Angie.

ANGIE: I'm not, am I, Aunty? What else don't you know?

JOYCE: You was in America or somewhere. You sent a postcard.

ANGIE: I've got that in my room. It's the Grand Canyon. Do you want to see it? Shall I get it? I can get it for you.

MARLENE: Yes, all right. (ANGIE goes.)

JOYCE: You could be married with twins for all I know. You must have affairs and break up and I don't need to know about any of that so I don't see what the fuss is about.

°git, idiot.

MARLENE: What fuss? (ANGIE comes back with the postcard.)

ANGIE: "Driving across the states for a new job in L.A. It's a long way but the car goes very fast. It's very hot. Wish you were here. Love from Aunty Marlene."

JOYCE: Did you make a lot of money?

MARLENE: I spent a lot.

ANGIE: I want to go to America. Will you take me?

JOYCE: She's not going to America, she's been to America, stupid.

ANGIE: She might go again, stupid. It's not something you do once. People who go keep going all the time, back and forth on jets. They go on Concorde and Laker and get jet lag. Will you take me?

MARLENE: I'm not planning a trip.

ANGIE: Will you let me know?

JOYCE: Angie, / you're getting silly.

ANGIE: I want to be American.

JOYCE: It's time you were in bed.

ANGIE: No it's not. / I don't have to go to bed at all tonight.

JOYCE: School in the morning.

ANGIE: I'll wake up.

JOYCE: Come on now, you know how you get.

ANGIE: How do I get? / I don't get anyhow.*

JOYCE: Angie. *Are you staying the night?

MARLENE: Yes, if that's all right. / I'll see you in the morning.

ANGIE: You can have my bed. I'll sleep on the sofa.

JOYCE: You will not, you'll sleep in your bed. / Think

ANGIE: Mum.

JOYCE: I can't see through that? I can just see you going to sleep / with us talking.

ANGIE: I would, I would go to sleep, I'd love that.

JOYCE: I'm going to get cross, Angie.

ANGIE: I want to show her something.

JOYCE: Then bed.

ANGIE: It's a secret.

JOYCE: Then I expect it's in your room so off you go. Give us a shout when you're ready for bed and your aunty'll be up and see you.

ANGIE: Will you?

MARLENE: Yes of course. (ANGIE goes. Silence.) It's cold tonight.

JOYCE: Will you be all right on the sofa? You can / have my bed.

MARLENE: The sofa's fine.

JOYCE: Yes the forecast said rain tonight but it's held off.

MARLENE: I was going to walk down to the estuary but I've left it a bit late. Is it just the same?

JOYCE: They cut down the hedges a few years back. Is that since you were here?

MARLENE: But it's not changed down the end, all the mud? And the reeds? We used to pick them up when they were bigger than us. Are there still lapwings?

JOYCE: You get strangers walking there on a Sunday. I expect they're looking at the mud and the lap-wings, yes.

MARLENE: You could have left.

JOYCE: Who says I wanted to leave?

MARLENE: Stop getting at me then, you're really bor-ing.

JOYCE: How could I have left?

MARLENE: Did you want to?

JOYCE: I said how, / how could I?

MARLENE: If you'd wanted to you'd have done it.

JOYCE: Christ.

MARLENE: Are we getting drunk?

JOYCE: Do you want something to eat?

MARLENE: No, I'm getting drunk.

JOYCE: Funny time to visit, Sunday evening.

MARLENE: I came this morning. I spent the day—

ANGIE (Off): Aunty! Aunty Marlene!

MARLENE: I'd better go.

JOYCE: Go on then.

MARLENE: All right.

ANGIE (Off): Aunty! Can you hear me? I'm ready.

(MARLENE goes. JOYCE goes on sitting, clears up, sits again. MARLENE comes back.)

JOYCE: So what's the secret?

MARLENE: It's a secret.

JOYCE: I know what it is anyway.

MARLENE: I bet you don't. You always said that.

JOYCE: It's her exercise book.

MARLENE: Yes, but you don't know what's in it.

JOYCE: It's some game, some secret society she has with Kit.

MARLENE: You don't know the password. You don't know the code.

JOYCE: You're really in it, aren't you. Can you do the handshake?

MARLENE: She didn't mention a handshake.

JOYCE: I thought they'd have a special handshake. She spends hours writing that but she's useless at school. She copies things out of books about black magic, and politicians out of the paper. It's a bit childish.

MARLENE: I think it's a plot to take over the world.

JOYCE: She's been in the remedial class the last two years.

MARLENE: I came up this morning and spent the day in Ipswich. I went to see Mother.

JOYCE: Did she recognize you?

MARLENE: Are you trying to be funny?

JOYCE: No, she does wander.

MARLENE: She wasn't wandering at all, she was very lucid thank you.

JOYCE: You were very lucky then.

MARLENE: Fucking awful life she's had.

JOYCE: Don't tell me.

MARLENE: Fucking waste.

JOYCE: Don't talk to me.

MARLENE: Why shouldn't I talk? Why shouldn't I talk to you? / Isn't she my mother too?

JOYCE: Look, you've left, you've gone away, / we can do without you.

MARLENE: I left home, so what, I left home. People do leave home / it is normal.

JOYCE: We understand that, we can do without you.

MARLENE: We weren't happy. Were you happy?

JOYCE: Don't come back.

MARLENE: So it's just your mother is it, your child, you never wanted me round, / you were jealous

JOYCE: Here we go.

MARLENE: of me because I was the little one and I was clever.

JOYCE: I'm not clever enough for all this psychology / if that's what it is.

MARLENE: Why can't I visit my own family / without

JOYCE: Aah.

MARLENE: all this?

JOYCE: Just don't go on about Mum's life when you haven't been to see her for how many years. / I go

MARLENE: It's up to me.

JOYCE: and see her every week.

MARLENE: Then don't go and see her every week.

JOYCE: Somebody has to.

MARLENE: No they don't. / Why do they?

JOYCE: How would I feel if I didn't go?

MARLENE: A lot better.

JOYCE: I hope you feel better.

MARLENE: It's up to me.

JOYCE: You couldn't get out of here fast enough. (Pause.)

MARLENE: Of course I couldn't get out of here fast enough. What was I going to do? Marry a dairy-man who'd come home pissed? / Don't you fuck-ing this

JOYCE: Christ.

MARLENE: fucking that fucking bitch fucking tell me what to fucking do fucking.

JOYCE: I don't know how you could leave your own child.

MARLENE: You were quick enough to take her.

JOYCE: What does that mean?

MARLENE: You were quick enough to take her.

JOYCE: Or what? Have her put in a home? Have some stranger / take her would you rather?

MARLENE: You couldn't have one so you took mine.

JOYCE: I didn't know that then.

MARLENE: Like hell, / married three years.

JOYCE: I didn't know that. Plenty of people / take that long.

MARLENE: Well it turned out lucky for you, didn't it?

JOYCE: Turned out all right for you by the look of you. You'd be getting a few less thousand a year.

MARLENE: Not necessarily.

JOYCE: You'd be stuck here / like you said.

MARLENE: I could have taken her with me.

JOYCE: You didn't want to take her with you. It's no good coming back now, Marlene, / and saying—

MARLENE: I know a managing director who's got two children, she breastfeeds in the board room, she pays a hundred pounds a week on domestic help alone and she can afford that because she's an extremely high-powered lady earning a great deal of money.

JOYCE: So what's that got to do with you at the age of seventeen?

MARLENE: Just because you were married and had somewhere to live—

JOYCE: You could have lived at home. / Or live

MARLENE: Don't be stupid.

JOYCE: with me and Frank. / You

MARLENE: You never suggested.

JOYCE: said you weren't keeping it. You shouldn't have had it / if you wasn't

MARLENE: Here we go.

JOYCE: going to keep it. You was the most stupid, / for someone so clever you was the most stupid, get yourself pregnant, not go to the doctor, not tell.

MARLENE: You wanted it, you said you were glad, I remember the day, you said I'm glad you never got rid of it, I'll look after it, you said that down by the river. So what are you saying, sunshine, you don't want her?

JOYCE: Course I'm not saying that.

MARLENE: Because I'll take her, / wake her up and pack now.

JOYCE: You wouldn't know how to begin to look after her.

MARLENE: Don't you want her?

JOYCE: Course I do, she's my child.

MARLENE: Then what are you going on about / why did I have her?

JOYCE: You said I got her off you / when you didn't—

MARLENE: I said you were lucky / the way it—

JOYCE: Have a child now if you want one. You're not old.

MARLENE: I might do.

JOYCE: Good. (Pause.)

MARLENE: I've been on the pill so long / I'm probably sterile.

JOYCE: Listen when Angie was six months I did get pregnant and I lost it because I was so tired looking after your fucking baby / because she cried so

MARLENE: You never told me.

JOYCE: much—yes I did tell you—/ and the doctor

MARLENE: Well I forgot.

JOYCE: said if I'd sat down all day with my feet up I'd've kept it / and that's the only chance I ever had because after that—

MARLENE: I've had two abortions, are you interested? Shall I tell you about them? Well I won't, it's boring, it wasn't a problem. I don't like messy talk about blood / and what a bad time we all had. I

JOYCE: If I hadn't had your baby. The doctor said.

MARLENE: don't want a baby. I don't want to talk about gynecology.

JOYCE: Then stop trying to get Angie off of me.

MARLENE: I come down here after six years. All night you've been saying I don't come often enough. If I don't come for another six years she'll be twenty-one, will that be OK?

JOYCE: That'll be fine, yes, six years would suit me fine. (Pause.)

MARLENE: I was afraid of this. I only came because I thought you wanted . . . I just want . . . (She cries.)

JOYCE: Don't grizzle,° Marlene, for God's sake. Marly? Come on, pet. Love you really. Fucking stop it, will you? (She goes to MARLENE.)

MARLENE: No, let me cry. I like it. (They laugh, MARLENE begins to stop crying.) I knew I'd cry if I wasn't careful.

JOYCE: Everyone's always crying in this house. Nobody takes any notice.

MARLENE: You've been wonderful looking after Angie.

JOYCE: Don't get carried away.

MARLENE: I can't write letters but I do think of you.

JOYCE: You're getting drunk. I'm going to make some tea.

MARLENE: Love you. (JOYCE goes to make tea.)

JOYCE: I can see why you'd want to leave. It's a dump here.

MARLENE: So what's this about you and Frank?

JOYCE: He was always carrying on, wasn't he. And if I wanted to go out in the evening he'd go mad, even if it was nothing, a class, I was going to go to an evening class. So he had this girlfriend, only twenty-two poor cow, and I said go on, off you go, hoppit. I don't think he even likes her.

MARLENE: So what about money?

JOYCE: I've always said I don't want your money.

MARLENE: No, does he send you money?

JOYCE: I've got four different cleaning jobs. Adds up. There's not a lot round here.

MARLENE: Does Angie miss him?

JOYCE: She doesn't say.

MARLENE: Does she see him?

JOYCE: He was never that fond of her to be honest.

MARLENE: He tried to kiss me once. When you were engaged.

JOYCE: Did you fancy him?

MARLENE: No, he looked like a fish.

JOYCE: He was lovely then.

MARLENE: Ugh.

JOYCE: Well I fancied him. For about three years.

MARLENE: Have you got someone else?

JOYCE: There's not a lot round here. Mind you, the minute you're on your own, you'd be amazed

---

grizzle, whine.

how your friends' husbands drop by. I'd sooner do without.

MARLENE: I don't see why you couldn't take my money.

JOYCE: I do, so don't bother about it.

MARLENE: Only got to ask.

JOYCE: So what about you? Good job?

MARLENE: Good for a laugh. / Got back

JOYCE: Good for more than a laugh I should think.

MARLENE: from the US of A a bit wiped out and slotted into this speedy employment agency and still there.

JOYCE: You can always find yourself work then?

MARLENE: That's right.

JOYCE: And men?

MARLENE: Oh there's always men.

JOYCE: No one special?

MARLENE: There's fellas who like to be seen with a high-flying lady. Shows they've got something really good in their pants. But they can't take the day to day. They're waiting for me to turn into the little woman. Or maybe I'm just horrible of course.

JOYCE: Who needs them.

MARLENE: Who needs them. Well I do. But I need adventures more. So on on into the sunset. I think the eighties are going to be stupendous.

JOYCE: Who for?

MARLENE: For me. / I think I'm going up up up.

JOYCE: Oh for you. Yes, I'm sure they will.

MARLENE: And for the country, come to that. Get the economy back on its feet and whoosh. She's a tough lady, Maggie.° I'd give her a job. / She just needs to hang

JOYCE: You voted for them, did you?

MARLENE: in there. This country needs to stop whining. / Monetarism is not

JOYCE: Drink your tea and shut up, pet.

MARLENE: stupid. It takes time, determination. No more slop. / And

JOYCE: Well I think they're filthy bastards.

MARLENE: who's got to drive it on? First woman prime minister. Terrifico. Aces. Right on. / You must admit. Certainly gets my vote.

JOYCE: What good's first woman if it's her? I suppose you'd have liked Hitler if he was a woman. Ms. Hitler. Got a lot done, Hitlerina. / Great adventures.

MARLENE: Bosses still walking on the workers' faces? Still dadda's little parrot? Haven't you learned to think for yourself? I believe in the individual. Look at me.

JOYCE: I am looking at you.

MARLENE: Come on, Joyce, we're not going to quarrel over politics.

JOYCE: We are though.

Maggie, Margaret Thatcher, former prime minister (1979–91).

MARLENE: Forget I mentioned it. Not a word about the slimy unions will cross my lips. (Pause.)

JOYCE: You say Mother had a wasted life.

MARLENE: Yes I do. Married to that bastard.

JOYCE: What sort of life did he have? /

MARLENE: Violent life?

JOYCE: Working in the fields like an animal. / Why

MARLENE: Come off it.

JOYCE: wouldn't he want a drink? You want a drink. He couldn't afford whiskey.

MARLENE: I don't want to talk about him.

JOYCE: You started, I was talking about her. She had a rotten life because she had nothing. She went hungry.

MARLENE: She was hungry because he drank the money. / He used to hit her.

JOYCE: It's not all down to him. / Their

MARLENE: She didn't hit him.

JOYCE: lives were rubbish. They were treated like rubbish. He's dead and she'll die soon and what sort of life / did they have?

MARLENE: I saw him one night. I came down.

JOYCE: Do you think I didn't? / They

MARLENE: I still have dreams.

JOYCE: didn't get to America and drive across it in a fast car. / Bad nights, they had bad days.

MARLENE: America, America, you're jealous. / I had to get out, I knew when I

JOYCE: Jealous?

MARLENE: was thirteen, out of their house, out of them, never let that happen to me, / never let him, make my own way, out.

JOYCE: Jealous of what you've done, you'd be ashamed of me if I came to your office, your smart friends, wouldn't you, I'm ashamed of you, think of nothing but yourself, you've got on, nothing's changed for most people, / has it?

MARLENE: I hate the working class / which is what

JOYCE: Yes you do.

MARLENE: you're going to go on about now, it doesn't exist any more, it means lazy and stupid. / I don't

JOYCE: Come on, now we're getting it.

MARLENE: like the way they talk. I don't like beer guts and football vomit and saucy tits / and brothers and sisters—

JOYCE: I spit when I see a Rolls Royce, scratch it with my ring / Mercedes it was.

MARLENE: Oh very mature—

JOYCE: I hate the cows I work for / and their dirty dishes with blanquette of fucking veau.

MARLENE: and I will not be pulled down to their level by a flying picket and I won't be sent to Siberia / or a loony bin just because I'm original. And I support

JOYCE: No, you'll be on a yacht, you'll be head of Coca Cola and you wait, the eighties is going to be stupendous all right because we'll get you lot off our backs—

MARLENE: Reagan even if he is a lousy movie star because the reds are swarming up his map and I want to be free in a free world—

JOYCE: What? / What?

MARLENE: I know what I mean / by that—not shut up here.

JOYCE: So don't be round here when it happens because if someone's kicking you I'll just laugh. (*Silence.*)

MARLENE: I don't mean anything personal. I don't believe in class. Anyone can do anything if they've got what it takes.

JOYCE: And if they haven't?

MARLENE: If they're stupid or lazy or frightened, I'm not going to help them get a job, why should I?

JOYCE: What about Angie?

MARLENE: What about Angie?

JOYCE: She's stupid, lazy, and frightened, so what about her?

MARLENE: You run her down too much. She'll be all right.

JOYCE: I don't expect so, no. I expect her children will say what a wasted life she had. If she has children. Because nothing's changed and it won't with them in.

MARLENE: Them, them. / Us and them?

JOYCE: And you're one of them.

MARLENE: And you're us, wonderful us, and Angie's us / and Mum and Dad's us.

JOYCE: Yes, that's right, and you're them.

MARLENE: Come on, Joyce, what a night. You've got what it takes.

JOYCE: I know I have.

MARLENE: I didn't really mean all that.

JOYCE: I did.

MARLENE: But we're friends anyway.

JOYCE: I don't think so, no.

MARLENE: Well it's lovely to be out in the country. I really must make the effort to come more often. I want to go to sleep. I want to go to sleep. (*JOYCE gets blankets for the sofa.*)

JOYCE: Goodnight then. I hope you'll be warm enough.

MARLENE: Goodnight. Joyce—

JOYCE: No, pet. Sorry. (*JOYCE goes. MARLENE sits wrapped in a blanket and has another drink. ANGIE comes in.*)

ANGIE: Mum?

MARLENE: Angie? What's the matter?

ANGIE: Mum?

MARLENE: No, she's gone to bed. It's Aunty Marlene.

ANGIE: Frightening.

MARLENE: Did you have a bad dream? What happened in it? Well you're awake now, aren't you, pet?

ANGIE: Frightening.

Figure 1. Marlene (Gwen Taylor, *seated center*) hosts a dinner for her guests (*left to right*): Lady Nijo (Lindsay Duncan), Dull Gret (Carole Hayman), Pope Joan (Selina Cadell), Patient Griselda (Lesley Manville), and Isabella Bird (Deborah Findlay) in the Royal Court production of *Top Girls* directed by Max Stafford-Clark, 1982. (Photograph: Donald Cooper/ Photostage.)

Figure 2. Kit (Lou Wakefield) and Angie (Carole Hayman) share confidences in "a shelter made of junk, made by children," in the 1982 Royal Court production. (Photograph: Donald Cooper/Photostage.)

Staging of *Top Girls*

**REVIEW OF THE ROYAL COURT THEATRE
PRODUCTION, 1982, BY ROBERT CUSHMAN**

Last week Caryl Churchill's *Top Girls* opened on the Royal Court's main stage, while Louise Page's *Salonika* ended its run upstairs. For a short time the Court housed the two most interesting new plays of the year, both of them written by women. A chap has to take notice.

Miss Churchill's last play, *Cloud Nine,* had a complicated time-scheme, simplicity itself compared to what happens in *Top Girls.* In the first scene Marlene, who has just been made managing director of an employment agency, hosts a dinner party at a London restaurant called La Prima Donna. Her guests are various historical prima donnas: Isabella Bird, Scots Victorian lady traveler; Lady Nijo, thirteenth-century Japanese courtesan turned Buddhist nun, and also a traveler; Dull Gret, kitchenmaid in armor, centerpiece of a Bruegel painting depicting a female invasion of Hell; Pope Joan; Patient Griselda.

These are all ladies who have suffered. Joan, for example, may have been Pope, but she ended up stoned to death, having ill-advisedly given birth. On the other hand they are all, in some sense, successes. Even Griselda, as Marlene points out, made it into three bestsellers through the terrible psychological battering she took from her husband.

They all profess devotion to the men in their lives: fathers, emperors, lovers actual or platonic, even husbands. This shocks Marlene; she wants them all as her patron saints, but she can't stomach Griselda, who typically arrives late and will only order cheese and biscuits. At first we share her irritation; after all, she's modern and they're archaic. Then our feelings slide.

Dull Gret doesn't say much. She's the real subversive. She—if you except an even more silent waitress—is the only person present not, by birth or adoption, upper class. She is played by Carole Hayman, who appears in the rest of the play as a modern girl similarly disinherited: someone who has dreams but no prospects.

This girl is presented to us as Marlene's niece. The bulk of the play is split between Marlene's London office and her East Anglian roots. The office is revealing, since not only is Marlene a success herself, but she is in the business of sniffing out success in other people, and of mercilessly weeding out failure. The play here goes down intriguing side-turnings, showing us two of Marlene's juniors, both self-consciously tough, and a variety of their clients.

One of them is nervous and middle-aging, aware of having suppressed her sexuality to survive on men's terms in their world. She is played by Selina Cadell, who has already scored a booming success as Pope Joan. Another is differently androgynous, with salesman fantasies.

Meanwhile there is Marlene's sister, who stayed at home. (Isabella Bird's sister also stayed home, though I confess I failed to pick up this thread at the time.) She points out that Marlene's upward mobility has changed nothing for most women, or indeed most men. Marlene declares herself a Thatcherite, which we might have deduced for ourselves. Her sister's political stance comes as a surprise, and seems manufactured for the occasion.

But the play runs thin nowhere else. Thoroughly personal in tone and structure, it manages to be an amazingly full polygonal presentation of a feminist predicament: career women behaving like career men. The situation is (mostly) deplored, but sympathy is withheld from no one. Miss Churchill also does for overlapping dialogue on stage what Robert Altman has done in the movies.

The seven actresses are terrific. Gwen Taylor, in her third play on socially sundered sisters (she's also played Mrs. Thatcher), is Marlene; Lindsay Duncan is gorgeous as Lady Nijo, wrestling simultaneously with the ways of Western woman and her first zabaglione. Max Stafford-Clark directed; I congratulate him, and wonder how he felt at rehearsals.

MARSHA NORMAN

1947–

Like Caryl Churchill, Marsha Norman is among the many women who have energized contemporary theater with plays that embody and explore female experience. Indeed, her best-known plays, *Getting Out* (1977) and *'night, Mother* (1983), focus on the psychic crises of women whose lives have been vexed by a complex array of disturbing and thwarting personal relationships, particularly their relationships with their mothers. In works such as these, Norman expresses her commitment "to a full, rich, and self-controlled life for the women on this planet." Her concern with the self-control of women is evidently rooted at least in part in her childhood experience of growing up in a highly repressive home, dominated by the moral strictures of her mother, who did not allow her to watch television, did not permit her to play with the neighborhood children because they were not "good enough," and did not let her "say anything that was in the least angry or that had any conflict in it at all."

Born and raised in a middle-class neighborhood in Louisville, Kentucky, Norman sought to escape the loneliness and solitude of her childhood through reading, through playing with an imaginary friend, and through writing stories. After graduating from high school, she attended Agnes Scott College in Decatur, Georgia, a liberal arts college for women, where she majored in philosophy and received her B.A. degree in 1969. Having returned to Louisville after graduation, she married one of her former English teachers (whom she divorced in 1974); studied for an M.A., which she received in 1971; and then went to work at the Kentucky Central State Hospital as a teacher of disturbed adolescents. In her work at the hospital, she found herself confronted by "children who never talked at all," by others "who would just as soon stab you in the back as talk to you," but most of all by "violent kids," one of whom was so vicious that the memory of the terror she aroused in Norman provided the seminal idea for Norman's first play, *Getting Out*, which focuses on the psychic life of a recently rehabilitated woman parolee.

But Norman's work at the hospital school did not immediately lead her into playwriting. From 1973 to 1976, she worked at a school for gifted children, teaching filmmaking and developing a curriculum in the arts and humanities. It was during this period, evidently influenced by her creatively talented students, that she began to try her own hand at writing—mostly pieces for the local newspapers but also a children's musical and scripts for a children's television program. During this time she met Jon Jory, artistic director of the Actors Theater of Louisville—one of several regional American theaters that has been particularly influential in the development of new plays and playwrights. Though she went to Jory seeking his advice about an arts program she was then developing to stimulate the interest of young people in the performing arts, he instead encouraged her to think about writing a play herself—in particular, a docudrama about busing, which had recently hit Louisville and thus was a prominent local issue. But the subject of busing interested her less than Jory's subsequent suggestion that she think of writing a play about "a painful subject"—a suggestion that led her to think about the violent thirteen-year-old girl who had terrified her several years earlier at the hospital school.

Stimulated by that memory, Norman decided to write a play that would in some way incorporate a convulsively disturbed and disturbing young adolescent woman. But Norman was not content to focus just on someone like the violent young prisoner she had known, for in *Getting Out* she portrays two sides of a woman who has just been released from prison and is trying to make a new life for herself. In order to dramatize two sides of a single person, Norman created two distinctly different but clearly interrelated characters: Arlene Holsclaw, the protagonist, who, having served eight years in prison for robbery, kidnapping, and manslaughter, is shown during her first day out of prison, trying to fix up her apartment and in the process trying to deal with her past; and Arlie, the embodiment of her younger, vicious self, who suddenly appears at moments when Arlene's memory calls her into being, or when Arlene is cruelly reminded of her past by visits she receives from her former pimp, her former prison guard, and her mother. In working out the complex psychic drama of Arlene/Arlie, Norman drew not only on her memory of the vicious adolescent she had encountered in the hospital school but also on extensive interviews with fifteen women prisoners who told her at length "exactly what it was like to be in prison and exactly what it was like to be out." She also drew on her own personal experience of feeling emotionally imprisoned, as she made clear in her forthright acknowledgment that "that person locked up was me" and that "the writing of *Getting Out* for me was my own opening of the door." And years later, writing "Ten Golden Rules for Playwrights" (see Ideas of Drama), Norman counseled new playwrights: "Write about your past. Write about something that terrified you, something that you *still* think is unfair, something that you have not been able to forget in all the time that's passed since it happened."

Though it was her first professionally staged play, *Getting Out* was produced not only at the Actors Theater of Louisville in 1977 but also at the Mark Taper Forum in Los Angeles in 1978 and at the Phoenix Theatre in Manhattan in 1978, where critics and audiences responded so enthusiastically that it was revived in 1979 for an eight-month run at the Theatre de Lys. *Getting Out* brought Norman several awards for the best new play by a new American playwright, and it evidently stimulated her to devote herself entirely to playwriting. During 1978 and 1979, she continued to work with the Actors Theater of Louisville, though she moved to New York City at the end of 1978 with her new husband. As a playwright-in-residence during 1978, she completed a highly successful pair of one-acts: *The Laundromat,* which depicts the encounter of a widow and a woman involved in a failed marriage; and *The Pool Hall,* which portrays the owner of the hall in conversation with the son of a notorious pool shark. In these short naturalistic pieces, as in the less successful *Circus Valentine* (1979), which portrays the attempt of a woman aerialist to save a failing family circus, Norman continued to focus on the painful experience of "folks you wouldn't even notice in life."

While in recent years she has turned her attention away from such everyday characters—writing instead the book and lyrics for two Broadway musicals, one a well-received adaptation of Frances Hodgson Burnett's 1911 novel *The Secret Garden* (1991), the other based on the 1948 ballet film *The Red Shoes* (1993)—certainly

Norman's most successful play focuses precisely on this lower-middle-class milieu. The Pulitzer Prize–winning 'night, Mother offers a spare and relentlessly worked-out study of a woman's decision to commit suicide. Here Norman creates a challengingly different kind of protagonist from the Arlene of Getting Out, for Jessie Cates in 'night, Mother is by no means passive or emotionally imprisoned. In contrast to Arlene, she is vocally and actively concerned with regaining a significant measure of self-control in her life, so much so that she is willing to put an end to it, since she cannot imagine a tolerable future, afflicted as she is by the painful circumstances of her past. Given Jessie's clear-cut and reiterated announcement of her intention to commit suicide, the energy of 'night Mother inevitably arises not out of whether (or when, or even how) she will go through with her decision, but rather out of how she attempts to make sense of such a momentous decision both for herself and for her mother.

Making sense of Jessie's decision is the work of the play for both characters and audience, and Norman deliberately chooses to emphasize the realistic world of the characters so as to contrast the abnormality of Jessie's decision, at first, with the setting in which it takes place. Her stage directions stress the "ordinary" quality of the house, and insist that "under no circumstances should the set and its dressing make a judgment about the intelligence or taste of Jessie and Mama. It should simply indicate that they are very specific real people who happen to live in a particular part of the country." Thus the kitchen so realistically presented in Heidi Landesman's set for the New York production at the John Golden Theater (see Figure 1) and the many details of stage properties create a world which seems familiar and "real" to the audience. At the same time, Jessie's list-making and deliberate handling of all the props, from the gun which she carefully cleans (see Figure 2) to the seemingly endless supply of candy for her mother, represent her attempt to control this world from which she feels alienated and which she can finally control only by "getting out" of it. The laughter which the play evokes in performance similarly functions as both protective and horrifying; the audience may laugh at familiar mother-daughter routines as well as at telling comments about the absent family members, and yet recoil from the laughter because it is inappropriate to the subject and situation.

Norman's combination of the ordinary and the extraordinary, of laughter and horror, has provoked equally contradictory reactions in critics, as suggested by the two reviews of the New York production reprinted following the text. Some reviewers, such as Douglas Watt, found the basic situation of the play to be "alien, pat, and unlikely," while others, such as Frank Rich, found themselves gradually drawn into Jessie's "inexorable logic." A further complication of the play is that it addresses not just the question of suicide but the larger questions concerning a woman's identity in a world dominated by men. Though no men appear in the play, Jessie and Mama do, after all, talk constantly about Jessie's dead father, her brother, her husband, and her delinquent son. And shortly after the pistol shot, Mama seeks the counsel not of another woman but of a man—"Loretta, let me talk to Dawson, honey." Norman's vision of the prison in which women find themselves, and put themselves, is unsparing. Readers and audiences will have to decide if it is also hopeless.

'NIGHT, MOTHER

BY MARSHA NORMAN

CHARACTERS

JESSIE CATES, *in her late thirties or early forties, is pale and vaguely unsteady physically. It is only in the last year that* JESSIE *has gained control of her mind and body, and tonight she is determined to hold on to that control. She wears pants and a long black sweater with deep pockets, which contain scraps of paper, and there may be a pencil behind her ear or a pen clipped to one of the pockets of the sweater.*

As a rule, JESSIE *doesn't feel much like talking. Other people have rarely found her quirky sense of humor amusing. She has a peaceful energy on this night, a sense of purpose, but is clearly aware of the time passing moment by moment. Oddly enough,* JESSIE *has never been as communicative or as enjoyable as she is on this evening, but we must know she has not always been this way. There is a familiarity between these two women that comes from having lived together for a long time. There is a shorthand to the talk and a sense of routine comfort in the way they relate to each other physically. Naturally, there are also routine aggravations.*

THELMA CATES, *"MAMA," is* JESSIE's *mother, in her late fifties or early sixties. She has begun to feel her age and so takes it easy when she can, or when it serves her purpose to let someone help her. But she speaks quickly and enjoys talking. She believes that things are what she says they are. Her sturdiness is more a mental quality than a physical one, finally. She is chatty and nosy, and this is her house.*

SCENE

The play takes place in a relatively new house built way out on a country road, with a living room and connecting kitchen, and a center hall that leads off to the bedrooms. A pull cord in the hall ceiling releases a ladder which leads to the attic. One of these bedrooms opens directly onto the hall, and its entry should be visible to everyone in the audience. It should be, in fact, the focal point of the entire set, and the lighting should make it disappear completely at times and draw the entire set into it at others. It is a point of both threat and promise. It is an ordinary door that opens onto absolute nothingness. That door is the point of all the action, and the utmost care should be given to its design and construction.

The living room is cluttered with magazines and needle-work catalogues, ashtrays and candy dishes. Examples of MAMA's *needlework are everywhere—pillows, afghans, and quilts, doilies and rugs, and they are quite nice examples. The house is more comfortable than messy, but there is quite a lot to keep in place here. It is more personal than charming. It is not quaint. Under no circumstances should the set and its dressing make a judgment about the intelligence or taste of* JESSIE *and* MAMA. *It should simply indicate that they are very specific real people who happen to live in a particular part of the country. Heavy accents, which would further distance the audience from* JESSIE *and* MAMA, *are also wrong.*

The time is the present, with the action beginning about 8:15. Clocks onstage in the kitchen and on a table in the living room should run throughout the performance and be visible to the audience.

MAMA *stretches to reach the cupcakes in a cabinet in the kitchen. She can't see them, but she can feel around for them, and she's eager to have one, so she's working pretty hard at it. This may be the most serious exercise* MAMA *ever gets. She finds a cupcake, the coconut-covered, raspberry-and-marshmallow-filled kind known as a snowball, but sees that there's one missing from the package. She calls to* JESSIE, *who is apparently somewhere else in the house.*

MAMA (*Unwrapping the cupcake*): Jessie, it's the last snowball, sugar. Put it on the list, O.K.? And we're out of Hershey bars, and where's that peanut brittle? I think maybe Dawson's been in it again. I ought to put a big mirror on the refrigerator door. That'll keep him out of my treats, won't it? You hear me, honey? (*Then more to herself.*) I hate it when the coconut falls off. Why does the coconut fall off?

(JESSIE *enters from her bedroom, carrying a stack of newspapers.*)

JESSIE: We got any old towels?

MAMA: There you are!

JESSIE (*Holding a towel that was on the stack of newspapers*): Towels you don't want anymore. (*Picking up* MAMA'S *snowball wrapper.*) How about this swimming towel Loretta gave us? Beach towel, that's the name of it. You want it? (MAMA *shakes her head no.*)

MAMA: What have you been doing in there?

JESSIE: And a big piece of plastic like a rubber sheet or something. Garbage bags would do if there's enough.

MAMA: Don't go making a big mess, Jessie. It's eight o'clock already.

JESSIE: Maybe an old blanket or towels we got in a soap box sometime?

MAMA: I said don't make a mess. Your hair is black enough, hon.

JESSIE (*Continuing to search the kitchen cabinets, finding two or three more towels to add to her stack*): It's not for my hair, Mama. What about some old pillows anywhere, or a foam cushion out of a yard chair would be real good.

MAMA: You haven't forgot what night it is, have you? (*Holding up her fingernails.*) They're all chipped, see? I've been waiting all week, Jess. It's Saturday night, sugar.

JESSIE: I know. I got it on the schedule.

MAMA (*Crossing to the living room*): You want me to wash 'em now or are you making your mess first? (*Looking at the snowball.*) We're out of these. Did I say that already?

JESSIE: There's more coming tomorrow. I ordered you a whole case.

MAMA (*Checking the* TV Guide): A whole case will go stale, Jessie.

JESSIE: They can go in the freezer till you're ready for them. Where's Daddy's gun?

MAMA: In the attic.

JESSIE: Where in the attic? I looked your whole nap and couldn't find it anywhere.

MAMA: One of his shoeboxes, I think.

JESSIE: Full of shoes. I looked already.

MAMA: Well, you didn't look good enough, then. There's that box from the ones he wore to the hospital. When he died, they told me I could have them back, but I never did like those shoes.

JESSIE (*Pulling them out of her pocket*): I found the bullets. They were in an old milk can.

MAMA (*As* JESSIE *starts for the hall*): Dawson took the shotgun, didn't he? Hand me that basket, hon.

JESSIE (*Getting the basket for her*): Dawson better not've taken that pistol.

MAMA (*Stopping her again*): Now my glasses, please. (JESSIE *returns to get the glasses.*) I told him to take those rubber boots, too, but he said they were for fishing. I told him to take up fishing.

(JESSIE *reaches for the cleaning spray and cleans* MAMA'S *glasses for her.*)

JESSIE: He's just too lazy to climb up there, Mama. Or maybe he's just being smart. That floor's not very steady.

MAMA (*Getting out a piece of knitting*): It's not a floor at all, hon, it's a board now and then. Measure this for me. I need six inches.

JESSIE (*As she measures*): Dawson could probably use some of those clothes up there. Somebody should have them. You ought to call the Salvation Army before the whole thing falls in on you. Six inches exactly.

MAMA: It's plenty safe! As long as you don't go up there.

JESSIE (*Turning to go again*): I'm careful.

MAMA: What do you want the gun for, Jess?

JESSIE (*Not returning this time. Opening the ladder in the hall*): Protection. (*She steadies the ladder as* MAMA *talks.*)

MAMA: You take the TV way too serious, hon. I've never seen a criminal in my life. This is way too far to come for what's out here to steal. Never seen a one.

JESSIE (*Taking her first step up*): Except for Ricky.

MAMA: Ricky is mixed up. That's not a crime.

JESSIE: Get your hands washed. I'll be right back. And get 'em real dry. You dry your hands till I get back or it's no go, all right?

MAMA: I thought Dawson told you not to go up those stairs.

JESSIE (*Going up*): He did.

MAMA: I don't like the idea of a gun, Jess.

JESSIE (*Calling down from the attic*): Which shoebox, do you remember?

MAMA: Black.

JESSIE: The box was black?

MAMA: The shoes were black.

JESSIE: That doesn't help much, Mother.

MAMA: I'm not trying to help, sugar. (*No answer.*) We don't have anything anybody'd want, Jessie. I mean, I don't even want what we got, Jessie.

JESSIE: Neither do I. Wash your hands. (MAMA *gets up and crosses to stand under the ladder.*)

MAMA: You come down from there before you have a fit. I can't come up and get you, you know.

JESSIE: I know.

MAMA: We'll just hand it over to them when they come, how's that? Whatever they want, the criminals.

JESSIE: That's a good idea, Mama.

MAMA: Ricky will grow out of this and be a real fine boy, Jess. But I have to tell you, I wouldn't want Ricky to know we had a gun in the house.

JESSIE: Here it is. I found it.

MAMA: It's just something Ricky's going through. Maybe he's in with some bad people. He just needs some time, sugar. He'll get back in school or get a job or one day you'll get a call and he'll say he's sorry for all the trouble he's caused and invite you out for supper someplace dress-up.

JESSIE (Coming back down the steps): Don't worry. It's not for him, it's for me.

MAMA: I didn't think you would shoot your own boy, Jessie. I know you've felt like it, well, we've all felt like shooting somebody, but we don't do it. I just don't think we need . . .

JESSIE (Interrupting): Your hands aren't washed. Do you want a manicure or not?

MAMA: Yes, I do, but . . .

JESSIE (Crossing to the chair): Then wash your hands and don't talk to me any more about Ricky. Those two rings he took were the last valuable things I had, so now he's started in on other people, door to door. I hope they put him away sometime. I'd turn him in myself if I knew where he was.

MAMA: You don't mean that.

JESSIE: Every word. Wash your hands and that's the last time I'm telling you.

(JESSIE sits down with the gun and starts cleaning it, pushing the cylinder out, checking to see that the chambers and barrel are empty, then putting some oil on a small patch of cloth and pushing it through the barrel with the push rod that was in the box. MAMA goes to the kitchen and washes her hands, as instructed, trying not to show her concern about the gun.)

MAMA: I shoulda got you to bring down that milk can. Agnes Fletcher sold hers to somebody with a flea market for forty dollars apiece.

JESSIE: I'll go back and get it in a minute. There's a wagon wheel up there, too. There's even a churn. I'll get it all if you want.

MAMA (Coming over, now, taking over now): What are you doing?

JESSIE: The barrel has to be clean, Mama. Old powder, dust gets in it . . .

MAMA: What for?

JESSIE: I told you.

MAMA (Reaching for the gun): And I told you, we don't get criminals out here.

JESSIE (Quickly pulling it to her): And I told you . . . (Then trying to be calm.) The gun is for me.

MAMA: Well, you can have it if you want. When I die, you'll get it all, anyway.

JESSIE: I'm going to kill myself, Mama.

MAMA (Returning to the sofa): Very funny. Very funny.

JESSIE: I am.

MAMA: You are not! Don't even say such a thing, Jessie.

JESSIE: How would you know if I didn't say it? You want it to be a surprise? You're lying there in your bed or maybe you're just brushing your teeth and you hear this . . . noise down the hall?

MAMA: Kill yourself.

JESSIE: Shoot myself. In a couple of hours.

MAMA: It must be time for your medicine.

JESSIE: Took it already.

MAMA: What's the matter with you?

JESSIE: Not a thing. Feel fine.

MAMA: You feel fine. You're just going to kill yourself.

JESSIE: Waited until I felt good enough, in fact.

MAMA: Don't make jokes, Jessie. I'm too old for jokes.

JESSIE: It's not a joke, Mama.

(MAMA watches for a moment in silence.)

MAMA: That gun's no good, you know. He broke it right before he died. He dropped it in the mud one day.

JESSIE: Seems O.K. (She spins the chamber, cocks the pistol, and pulls the trigger. The gun is not yet loaded, so all we hear is the click, but it will definitely work. It's also obvious that JESSIE knows her way around a gun. MAMA cannot speak.) I had Cecil's all ready in there, just in case I couldn't find this one, but I'd rather use Daddy's.

MAMA: Those bullets are at least fifteen years old.

JESSIE (Pulling out another box): These are from last week.

MAMA: Where did you get those?

JESSIE: Feed store Dawson told me about.

MAMA: Dawson!

JESSIE: I told him I was worried about prowlers. He said he thought it was a good idea. He told me what kind to ask for.

MAMA: If he had any idea . . .

JESSIE: He took it as a compliment. He thought I might be taking an interest in things. He got through telling me all about the bullets and then he said we ought to talk like this more often.

MAMA: And where was I while this was going on?

JESSIE: On the phone with Agnes. About the milk can, I guess. Anyway, I asked Dawson if he thought they'd send me some bullets and he said he'd just call for me, because he knew they'd send them if he told them to. And he was absolutely right. Here they are.

MAMA: How could he do that?

JESSIE: Just trying to help, Mama.

MAMA: And then I told you where the gun was.

JESSIE (Smiling, enjoying this joke): See? Everybody's doing what they can.

MAMA: You told me it was for protection!

JESSIE: It *is*! I'm still doing your nails, though. Want to try that new Chinaberry color?

MAMA: Well, I'm calling Dawson right now. We'll just see what he has to say about this little stunt.

JESSIE: Dawson doesn't have any more to do with this.

MAMA: He's your brother.

JESSIE: And that's all.

MAMA (*Stands up, moves toward the phone*): Dawson will put a stop to this. Yes he will. He'll take the gun away.

JESSIE: If you call him, I'll just have to do it before he gets here. Soon as you hang up the phone, I'll just walk in the bedroom and lock the door. Dawson will get here just in time to help you clean up. Go ahead, call him. Then call the police. Then call the funeral home. Then call Loretta and see if *she'll* do your nails.

MAMA: You will not! This is crazy talk, Jessie!

(MAMA *goes directly to the telephone and starts to dial, but* JESSIE *is fast, coming up behind her and taking the receiver out of her hand, putting it back down.*)

JESSIE (*Firm and quiet*): I said no. This is private. Dawson is not invited.

MAMA: Just me.

JESSIE: I don't want anybody else over here. Just you and me. If Dawson comes over, it'll make me feel stupid for not doing it ten years ago.

MAMA: I think we better call the doctor. Or how about the ambulance. You like that one driver, I know. What's his name, Timmy? Get you somebody to talk to.

JESSIE (*Going back to her chair*): I'm through talking, Mama. You're it. No more.

MAMA: We're just going to sit around like every other night in the world and then you're going to kill yourself? (JESSIE *doesn't answer.*) You'll miss. (*Again there is no response.*) You'll just wind up a vegetable. How would you like that? Shoot your ear off? You know what the doctor said about getting excited. You'll cock the pistol and have a fit.

JESSIE: I think I can kill myself, Mama.

MAMA: You're not going to kill yourself, Jessie. You're not even upset! (JESSIE *smiles, or laughs quietly, and* MAMA *tries a different approach.*) People don't really kill themselves, Jessie. No, mam, doesn't make sense, unless you're retarded or deranged, and you're as normal as they come, Jessie, for the most part. We're all *afraid* to die.

JESSIE: I'm not, Mama. I'm cold all the time, anyway.

MAMA: That's ridiculous.

JESSIE: It's exactly what I want. It's dark and quiet.

MAMA: So is the back yard, Jessie! Close your eyes. Stuff cotton in your ears. Take a nap! It's quiet in your room. I'll leave the TV off all night.

JESSIE: So quiet I don't know it's quiet. So nobody can get me.

MAMA: You don't know what dead is like. It might not be quiet at all. What if it's like an alarm clock and you can't wake up so you can't shut it off. Ever.

JESSIE: Dead is everybody and everything I ever knew, gone. Dead is dead quiet.

MAMA: It's a sin. You'll go to hell.

JESSIE: Uh-huh.

MAMA: You will!

JESSIE: Jesus was a suicide, if you ask me.

MAMA: You'll go to hell just for saying that. Jessie!

JESSIE (*With genuine surprise*): I didn't know I thought that.

MAMA: Jessie!

(JESSIE *doesn't answer. She puts the now-loaded gun back in the box and crosses to the kitchen. But* MAMA *is afraid she's headed for the bedroom.*)

MAMA (*In a panic*): You can't use my towels! They're my towels. I've had them for a long time. I like my towels.

JESSIE: I asked you if you wanted that swimming towel and you said you didn't.

MAMA: And you can't use your father's gun, either. It's mine now, too. And you can't do it in my house.

JESSIE: Oh, come on.

MAMA: No. You can't do it. I won't let you. The house is in my name.

JESSIE: I have to go in the bedroom and lock the door behind me so they won't arrest you for killing me. They'll probably test your hands for gunpowder, anyway, but you'll pass.

MAMA: Not in my house!

JESSIE: If I'd known you were going to act like this, I wouldn't have told you.

MAMA: How am I supposed to act? Tell you to go ahead? O.K. by me, sugar? Might try it myself. What took you so long?

JESSIE: There's just no point in fighting me over it, that's all. Want some coffee?

MAMA: Your birthday's coming up, Jessie. Don't you want to know what we got you?

JESSIE: You got me dusting powder, Loretta got me a new housecoat, pink probably, and Dawson got me new slippers, too small, but they go with the robe, he'll say. (MAMA *cannot speak.*) Right? (*Apparently* JESSIE *is right.*) Be back in a minute.

(JESSIE *takes the gun box, puts it on top of the stack of towels and garbage bags, and takes them into her bedroom.* MAMA, *alone for a moment, goes to the phone, picks up the receiver, looks toward the bedroom, starts to dial, and then replaces the receiver in its cradle as* JESSIE *walks back into the room.* JESSIE *wonders, silently. They have lived together for so long there is very rarely any reason for one to ask what the other was about to do.*)

MAMA: I started to, but I didn't. I didn't call him.

JESSIE: Good. Thank you.

MAMA (*Starting over, a new approach*): What's this all about, Jessie?

JESSIE: About?

(JESSIE *now begins the next task she had "on the schedule," which is refilling all the candy jars, taking the empty papers out of the boxes of chocolates, etc.* MAMA *generally snitches when* JESSIE *does this. Not tonight, though. Nevertheless,* JESSIE *offers.*)

MAMA: What did I do?

JESSIE: Nothing. Want a caramel?

MAMA (*Ignoring the candy*): You're mad at me.

JESSIE: Not a bit. I am worried about you, but I'm going to do what I can before I go. We're not just going to sit around tonight. I made a list of things.

MAMA: What things?

JESSIE: How the washer works. Things like that.

MAMA: I know how the washer works. You put the clothes in. You put the soap in. You turn it on. You wait.

JESSIE: You do something else. You don't just wait.

MAMA: Whatever else you find to do, you're still mainly waiting. The waiting's the worst part of it. The waiting's what you pay somebody else to do, if you can.

JESSIE (*Nodding*): O.K. Where do we keep the soap?

MAMA: I could find it.

JESSIE: See?

MAMA: If you're mad about doing the wash, we can get Loretta to do it.

JESSIE: Oh now, that might be worth staying to see.

MAMA: She'd never in her life, would she?

JESSIE: Nope.

MAMA: What's the matter with her?

JESSIE: She thinks she's better than we are. She's not.

MAMA: Maybe if she didn't wear that yellow all the time.

JESSIE: The washer repair number is on a little card taped to the side of the machine.

MAMA: Loretta doesn't ever have to come over here again. Dawson can just leave her at home when he comes. And we don't ever have to see Dawson either if he bothers you. Does he bother you?

JESSIE: Sure he does. Be sure you clean out the lint tray every time you use the dryer. But don't ever put your house shoes in, it'll melt the soles.

MAMA: What does Dawson do, that bothers you?

JESSIE: He just calls me Jess like he knows who he's talking to. He's always wondering what I do all day. I mean, I wonder that myself, but it's my day, so it's mine to wonder about, not his.

MAMA: Family is just accident, Jessie. It's nothing personal, hon. They don't mean to get on your nerves. They don't even mean to be your family, they just are.

JESSIE: They know too much.

MAMA: About what?

JESSIE: They know things about you, and they learned it before you had a chance to say whether you wanted them to know it or not. They were there when it happened and it don't belong to them, it belongs to you, only they got it. Like my mail-order bra got delivered to their house.

MAMA: By accident!

JESSIE: All the same . . . they opened it. They saw the little rosebuds on it. (*Offering her another candy.*) Chewy mint?

MAMA (*Shaking her head no*): What do they know about you? I'll tell them never to talk about it again. Is it Ricky or Cecil or your fits or your hair is falling out or you drink too much coffee or you never go out of the house or what?

JESSIE: I just don't like their talk. The account at the grocery is in Dawson's name when you call. The number's on a whole list of numbers on the back cover of the phone book.

MAMA: Well! Now we're getting somewhere. They're none of them ever setting foot in this house again.

JESSIE: It's not them, Mother. I wouldn't kill myself just to get away from them.

MAMA: You leave the room when they come over, anyway.

JESSIE: I stay as long as I can. Besides, it's you they come to see.

MAMA: That's because I stay in the room when they come.

JESSIE: It's not them.

MAMA: Then what is it?

JESSIE (*Checking the list on her note pad*): The grocery won't deliver on Saturday anymore. And if you want your order the same day, you have to call before ten. And they won't deliver less than fifteen dollars' worth. What I do is tell them what we need and tell them to add on cigarettes until it gets to fifteen dollars.

MAMA: It's Ricky. You're trying to get through to him.

JESSIE: If I thought I could do that, I would stay.

MAMA: Make him sorry he hurt you, then. That's it, isn't it?

JESSIE: He's hurt me, I've hurt him. We're about even.

MAMA: You'll be telling him killing is O.K. with you, you know. Want him to start killing next? Nothing wrong with it. Mom did it.

JESSIE: Only a matter of time, anyway, Mama. When the call comes, you let Dawson handle it.

MAMA: Honey, nothing says those calls are always going to be some new trouble he's into. You could get one that he's got a job, that he's getting married, or how about he's joined the army, wouldn't that be nice?

JESSIE: If you call the Sweet Tooth before you call the grocery, that Susie will take your fudge next door to the grocery and it'll all come out together. Be sure you talk to Susie, though. She won't let them put it in the bottom of a sack like that one time, remember?

MAMA: Ricky could come over, you know. What if he calls us?

JESSIE: It's not Ricky, Mama.

MAMA: Or anybody could call us, Jessie.

JESSIE: Not on Saturday night, Mama.

MAMA: Then what is it? Are you sick? If your gums are swelling again, we can get you to the dentist in the morning.

JESSIE: No. Can you order your medicine or do you want Dawson to? I've got a note to him. I'll add that to it if you want.

MAMA: Your eyes don't look right. I thought so yesterday.

JESSIE: That was just the ragweed. I'm not sick.

MAMA: Epilepsy is sick, Jessie.

JESSIE: It won't kill me. (A pause.) If it would, I wouldn't have to.

MAMA: You don't *have* to.

JESSIE: No, I don't. That's what I like about it.

MAMA: Well, I won't let you!

JESSIE: It's not up to you.

MAMA: Jessie!

JESSIE: I want to hang a big sign around my neck, like Daddy's on the barn. GONE FISHING.

MAMA: You don't like it here.

JESSIE (Smiling): Exactly.

MAMA: I meant here in my house.

JESSIE: I know you did.

MAMA: You never should have moved back in here with me. If you'd kept your little house or found another place when Cecil left you, you'd have made some new friends at least. Had a life to lead. Had your own things around you. Give Ricky a place to come see you. You never should've come here.

JESSIE: Maybe.

MAMA: But I didn't force you, did I?

JESSIE: If it was a mistake, we made it together. You took me in. I appreciate that.

MAMA: You didn't have any business being by yourself right then, but I can see how you might want a place of your own. A grown woman should . . .

JESSIE: Mama . . . I'm just not having a very good time and I don't have any reason to think it'll get anything but worse. I'm tired. I'm hurt. I'm sad. I feel used.

MAMA: Tired of what?

JESSIE: It all.

MAMA: What does that mean?

JESSIE: I can't say it any better.

MAMA: Well, you'll have to say it better because I'm not letting you alone till you do. What were those other things? Hurt . . . (Before JESSIE can answer.) You had this all ready to say to me, didn't you?

Did you write this down? How long have you been thinking about this?

JESSIE: Off and on, ten years. On all the time, since Christmas.

MAMA: What happened at Christmas?

JESSIE: Nothing.

MAMA: So why Christmas?

JESSIE: That's it. On the nose.

(A pause. MAMA knows exactly what JESSIE means. She was there, too, after all.)

JESSIE (Putting the candy sacks away): See where all this is? Red hots up front, sour balls and horehound mixed together in this one sack. New packages of toffee and licorice right in back there.

MAMA: Go back to your list. You're hurt by what?

JESSIE (MAMA knows perfectly well): Mama . . .

MAMA: O.K. Sad about what? There's nothing real sad going on right now. If it was after your divorce or something, that would make sense.

JESSIE (Looking at her list, then opening the drawer): Now, this drawer has everything in it that there's no better place for. Extension cords, batteries for the radio, extra lighters, sandpaper, masking tape, Elmer's glue, thumbtacks, that kind of stuff. The mousetraps are under the sink, but you call Dawson if you've got one and let him do it.

MAMA: Sad about what?

JESSIE: The way things are.

MAMA: Not good enough. What things?

JESSIE: Oh, everything from you and me to Red China.

MAMA: I think we can leave the Chinese out of this.

JESSIE (Crosses back into the living room): There's extra light bulbs in a box in the hall closet. And we've got a couple of packages of fuses in the fuse box. There's candles and matches in the top of the broom closet, but if the lights go out, just call Dawson and sit tight. But don't open the refrigerator door. Things will stay cool in there as long as you keep the door shut.

MAMA: I asked you a question.

JESSIE: I read the paper. I don't like how things are. And they're not any better out there than they are in here.

MAMA: If you're doing this because of the newspapers, I can sure fix that!

JESSIE: There's just more of it on TV.

MAMA (Kicking the television set): Take it out, then!

JESSIE: You wouldn't do that.

MAMA: Watch me.

JESSIE: What would you do all day?

MAMA (Desperately): Sing. (JESSIE laughs.) I would, too. You want to watch? I'll sing till morning to keep you alive, Jessie, please!

JESSIE: No. (Then affectionately.) It's a funny idea, though. What do you sing?

MAMA (*Has no idea how to answer this*): We've got a good life here!

JESSIE (*Going back into the kitchen*): I called this morning and canceled the papers, except for Sunday, for your puzzles; you'll still get that one.

MAMA: Let's get another dog, Jessie! You liked a big dog, now, didn't you? That King dog, didn't you?

JESSIE (*Washing her hands*): I did like that King dog, yes.

MAMA: I'm so dumb. He's the one run under the tractor.

JESSIE: That makes him dumb, not you.

MAMA: For bringing it up.

JESSIE: It's O.K. Handi-Wipes and sponges under the sink.

MAMA: We could get a new dog and keep him in the house. Dogs are cheap!

JESSIE (*Getting big pill jars out of the cabinet*): No.

MAMA: Something for you to take care of.

JESSIE: I've had you, Mama.

MAMA (*Frantically starting to fill pill bottles*): You do too much for me. I can fill pill bottles all day, Jessie, and change the shelf paper and wash the floor when I get through. You just watch me. You don't have to do another thing in this house if you don't want to. You don't have to take care of me, Jessie.

JESSIE: I know that. You've just been letting me do it so I'll have something to do, haven't you?

MAMA (*Realizing this was a mistake*): I don't do it as well as you. I just meant if it tires you out or makes you feel used . . .

JESSIE: Mama, I know you used to ride the bus. Riding the bus and it's hot and bumpy and crowded and too noisy and more than anything in the world you want to get off and the only reason in the world you don't get off is it's still fifty blocks from where you're going? Well, I can get off right now if I want to, because even if I ride fifty more years and get off then, it's the same place when I step down to it. Whenever I feel like it, I can get off. As soon as I've had enough, it's my stop. I've had enough.

MAMA: You're feeling sorry for yourself!

JESSIE: The plumber's helper is under the sink, too.

MAMA: You're not having a good time! Whoever promised you a good time? Do you think I've had a good time?

JESSIE: I think you're pretty happy, yeah. You have things you like to do.

MAMA: Like what?

JESSIE: Like crochet.

MAMA: I'll teach you to crochet.

JESSIE: I can't do any of that nice work, Mama.

MAMA: Good time don't come looking for you, Jessie. You could work some puzzles or put in a garden or go to the store. Let's call a taxi and go to the A&P!

JESSIE: I shopped you up for about two weeks already.

You're not going to need toilet paper till Thanksgiving.

MAMA (*Interrupting*): You're acting like some little brat, Jessie. You're mad and everybody's boring and you don't have anything to do and you don't like me and you don't like going out and you don't like staying in and you never talk on the phone and you don't watch TV and you're miserable and it's your own sweet fault.

JESSIE: And it's time I did something about it.

MAMA: Not something like killing yourself. Something like . . . buying us all new dishes! I'd like that. Or maybe the doctor would let you get a driver's license now, or I know what let's do right this minute, let's rearrange the furniture.

JESSIE: I'll do that. If you want. I always thought if the TV was somewhere else, you wouldn't get such a glare on it during the day. I'll do whatever you want before I go.

MAMA (*Badly frightened by those words*): You could get a job!

JESSIE: I took that telephone sales job and I didn't even make enough money to pay the phone bill, and I tried to work at the gift shop at the hospital and they said I made people real uncomfortable smiling at them the way I did.

MAMA: You could keep books. You kept your dad's books.

JESSIE: But nobody ever checked them.

MAMA: When he died, they checked them.

JESSIE: And that's when they took the books away from me.

MAMA: That's because without him there wasn't any business, Jessie!

JESSIE (*Putting the pill bottles away*): You know I couldn't work. I can't do anything. I've never been around people my whole life except when I went to the hospital. I could have a seizure any time. What good would a job do? The kind of job I could get would make me feel worse.

MAMA: Jessie!

JESSIE: It's true!

MAMA: It's what you think is true!

JESSIE (*Struck by the clarity of that*): That's right. It's what I think is true.

MAMA (*Hysterically*): But I can't do anything about that!

JESSIE (*Quietly*): No. You can't. (MAMA *slumps, if not physically, at least emotionally.*) And I can't do anything either, about my life, to change it, make it better, make me feel better about it. Like it better, make it work. But I can stop it. Shut it down, turn it off like the radio when there's nothing on I want to listen to. It's all I really have that belongs to me and I'm going to say what happens to it. And it's going to stop. And I'm going to stop it. So. Let's just have a good time.

MAMA: Have a good time.

JESSIE: We can't go on fussing all night. I mean, I could ask you things I always wanted to know and you could make me some hot chocolate. The old way.

MAMA (*In despair*): It takes cocoa, Jessie.

JESSIE (*Gets it out of the cabinet*): I bought cocoa, Mama. And I'd like to have a caramel apple and do your nails.

MAMA: You didn't eat a bite of supper.

JESSIE: Does that mean I can't have a caramel apple?

MAMA: Of course not. I mean . . . (*Smiling a little.*) Of course you can have a caramel apple.

JESSIE: I thought I could.

MAMA: I make the best caramel apples in the world.

JESSIE: I know you do.

MAMA: Or used to. And you don't get cocoa like mine anywhere anymore.

JESSIE: It takes time, I know, but . . .

MAMA: The salt is the trick.

JESSIE: Trouble and everything.

MAMA (*Backing away toward the stove*): It's no trouble. What trouble? You put it in the pan and stir it up. All right. Fine. Caramel apples. Cocoa. O.K.

(JESSIE *walks to the counter to retrieve her cigarettes as* MAMA *looks for the right pan. There are brief near-smiles, and maybe* MAMA *clears her throat. We have a truce, for the moment. A genuine but nevertheless uneasy one.* JESSIE, *who has been in constant motion since the beginning, now seems content to sit.*)

(MAMA *starts looking for a pan to make the cocoa, getting out all the pans in the cabinets in the process. It looks like she's making a mess on purpose so* JESSIE *will have to put them all away again.* MAMA *is buying time, or trying to, and entertaining.*)

JESSIE: You talk to Agnes today?

MAMA: She's calling me from a pay phone this week. God only knows why. She has a perfectly good Trimline at home.

JESSIE (*Laughing*): Well, how is she?

MAMA: How is she every day, Jessie? Nuts.

JESSIE: Is she really crazy or just silly?

MAMA: No, she's really crazy. She was probably using the pay phone because she had another little fire problem at home.

JESSIE: Mother . . .

MAMA: I'm serious! Agnes Fletcher's burned down every house she ever lived in. Eight fires, and she's due for a new one any day now.

JESSIE (*Laughing*): No!

MAMA: Wouldn't surprise me a bit.

JESSIE (*Laughing*): Why didn't you tell me this before? Why isn't she locked up somewhere?

MAMA: 'Cause nobody ever got hurt, I guess. Agnes woke everybody up to watch the fires as soon as she set 'em. One time she set out porch chairs and served lemonade.

JESSIE (*Shaking her head*): Real lemonade?

MAMA: The houses they lived in, you knew they were going to fall down anyway, so why wait for it, is all I could ever make out about it. Agnes likes a feeling of accomplishment.

JESSIE: Good for her.

MAMA (*Finding the pan she wants*): Why are you asking about Agnes? One cup or two?

JESSIE: One. She's your friend. No marshmallows.

MAMA (*Getting the milk, etc.*): You have to have marshmallows. That's the old way, Jess. Two or three? Three is better.

JESSIE: Three, then. Her whole house burns up? Her clothes and pillows and everything? I'm not sure I believe this.

MAMA: When she was a girl, Jess, not now. Long time ago. But she's still got it in her, I'm sure of it.

JESSIE: She wouldn't burn her house down now. Where would she go? She can't get Buster to build her a new one, he's dead. How could she burn it up?

MAMA: Be exciting, though, if she did. You never know.

JESSIE: You do too know, Mama. She wouldn't do it.

MAMA (*Forced to admit, but reluctant*): I guess not.

JESSIE: What else? Why does she wear all those whistles around her neck?

MAMA: Why does she have a house full of birds?

JESSIE: I didn't know she had a house full of birds!

MAMA: Well, she does. And she says they just follow her home. Well, I know for a fact she's still paying on the last parrot she bought. You gotta keep your life filled up, she says. She says a lot of stupid things. (JESSIE *laughs*, MAMA *continues, convinced she's getting somewhere.*) It's all that okra she eats. You can't just willy-nilly eat okra two meals a day and expect to get away with it. Made her crazy.

JESSIE: She really eats okra twice a day? Where does she get it in the winter?

MAMA: Well, she eats it a lot. Maybe not two meals, but . . .

JESSIE: More than the average person.

MAMA (*Beginning to get irritated*): I don't know how much okra the average person eats.

JESSIE: Do you know how much okra Agnes eats?

MAMA: No.

JESSIE: How many birds does she have?

MAMA: Two.

JESSIE: Then what are the whistles for?

MAMA: They're not real whistles. Just little plastic ones on a necklace she won playing Bingo, and I only told you about it because I thought I might get a laugh out of you for once even if it wasn't the truth, Jessie. Things don't have to be true to talk about 'em, you know.

JESSIE: Why won't she come over here?

(MAMA *is suddenly quiet, but the cocoa and milk are in the pan now, so she lights the stove and starts stirring.*)

MAMA: Well now, what a good idea. We should've had more cocoa. Cocoa is perfect.

JESSIE: Except you don't like milk.

MAMA (*Another attempt, but not as energetic*): I hate milk. Coats your throat as bad as okra. Something just downright disgusting about it.

JESSIE: It's because of me, isn't it?

MAMA: No, Jess.

JESSIE: Yes, Mama.

MAMA: O.K. Yes, then, but she's crazy. She's as crazy as they come. She's a lunatic.

JESSIE: What is it exactly? Did I say something, sometime? Or did she see me have a fit and's afraid I might have another one if she came over, or what?

MAMA: I guess.

JESSIE: You guess what? What's she ever said? She must've given you some reason.

MAMA: Your hands are cold.

JESSIE: What difference does that make?

MAMA: "Like a corpse," she says, "and I'm gonna be one soon enough as it is."

JESSIE: That's crazy.

MAMA: That's Agnes. "Jessie's shook the hand of death and I can't take the chance it's catching, Thelma, so I ain't comin' over, and you can understand or no, but I ain't comin'. I'll come up the driveway, but that's as far as I go."

JESSIE (*Laughing, relieved*): I thought she didn't like me! She's scared of me! How about that! Scared of me.

MAMA: I could make her come over here, Jessie. I could call her up right now and she could bring the birds and come visit. I didn't know you ever thought about her at all. I'll tell her she just has to come and she'll come, all right. She owes me one.

JESSIE: No, that's all right. I just wondered about it. When I'm in the hospital, does she come over here?

MAMA: Her kitchen is just a tiny thing. When she comes over here, she feels like . . . (*Toning it down a little.*) Well, we all like a change of scene, don't we?

JESSIE (*Playing along*): Sure we do. Plus there's no birds diving around.

MAMA: I hate those birds. She says I don't understand them. What's there to understand about birds?

JESSIE: Why Agnes likes them, for one thing. Why they stay with her when they could be outside with the other birds. What their singing means. How they fly. What they think Agnes is.

MAMA: Why do you have to know so much about things, Jessie? There's just not that much *to* things that I could ever see.

JESSIE: That you could ever *tell*, you mean. You didn't have to lie to me about Agnes.

MAMA: I didn't lie. You never asked before!

JESSIE: You lied about setting fire to all those houses and about how many birds she has and how much okra she eats and why she won't come over here. If I have to keep dragging the truth out of you, this is going to take all night.

MAMA: That's fine with me. I'm not a bit sleepy.

JESSIE: Mama . . .

MAMA: All right. Ask me whatever you want. Here.

(*They come to an awkward stop, as the cocoa is ready and* MAMA *pours it into the cups* JESSIE *has set on the table.*)

JESSIE (*As* MAMA *takes her first sip*): Did you love Daddy?

MAMA: No.

JESSIE (*Pleased that* MAMA *understands the rules better now*): I didn't think so. Were you really fifteen when you married him?

MAMA: The way he told it? I'm sitting in the mud, he comes along, drags me in the kitchen, "She's been there ever since"?

JESSIE: Yes.

MAMA: No. It was a big fat lie, the whole thing. He just thought it was funnier that way. God, this milk in here.

JESSIE: The cocoa helps.

MAMA (*Pleased that they agree on this, at least*): Not enough, though, does it? You can still taste it, can't you?

JESSIE: Yeah, it's pretty bad. I thought it was my memory that was bad, but it's not. It's the milk, all right.

MAMA: It's a real waste of chocolate. You don't have to finish it.

JESSIE (*Putting her cup down*): Thanks, though.

MAMA: I should've known not to make it. I knew you wouldn't like it. You never did like it.

JESSIE: You didn't ever love him, or he did something and you stopped loving him, or what?

MAMA: He felt sorry for me. He wanted a plain country woman and that's what he married, and then he held it against me the rest of my life like I was supposed to change and surprise him somehow. Like I remember this one day he was standing on the porch and I told him to get a shirt on and he went in and got one and then he said, real peaceful, but to the point, "You're right, Thelma. If God had meant for people to go around without any clothes on, they'd have been born that way."

JESSIE (*Sees* MAMA's *hurt*): He didn't mean anything by that, Mama.

MAMA: He never said a word he didn't have to, Jessie. That was probably all he'd said to me all day, Jessie. So if he said it, there was something to it, but I never did figure that one out. What did that mean?

JESSIE: I don't know. I liked him better than you did, but I didn't know him any better.

MAMA: How could I love him, Jessie. I didn't have a thing he wanted. (JESSIE *doesn't answer.*) He got his share, though. You loved him enough for both of us. You followed him around like some . . . Jessie, all the man ever did was farm and sit . . . and try to think of somebody to sell the farm to.

JESSIE: Or make me a boyfriend out of pipe cleaners and sit back and smile like the stick man was about to dance and wasn't I going to get a kick out of that. Or sit up with a sick cow all night and leave me a chain of sleepy stick elephants on my bed in the morning.

MAMA: Or just sit.

JESSIE: I liked him sitting. Big old faded blue man in the chair. Quiet.

MAMA: Agnes gets more talk out of her birds than I got from the two of you. He could've had that GONE FISHING sign around his neck in that chair. I saw him stare off at the water. I saw him look at the weather rolling in. I got where I could practically see the boat myself. But you, you knew what he was thinking about and you're going to tell me.

JESSIE: I don't know, Mama! His life, I guess. His corn. His boots. Us. Things. You know.

MAMA: No, I don't know, Jessie! You had those quiet little conversations after supper every night. What were you whispering about?

JESSIE: We weren't whispering, you were just across the room.

MAMA: What did you talk about?

JESSIE: We talked about why black socks are warmer than blue socks. Is that something to go tell Mother? You were just jealous because I'd rather talk to him than wash the dishes with you.

MAMA: I was jealous because you'd rather talk to him than anything! (JESSIE *reaches across the table for the small clock and stars to wind it.*) If I had died instead of him, he wouldn't have taken you in like I did.

JESSIE: I wouldn't have expected him to.

MAMA: Then what would you have done?

JESSIE: Come visit.

MAMA: Oh, I see. He died and left you stuck with me and you're mad about it.

JESSIE (*Getting up from the table*): Not anymore. He didn't mean to. I didn't have to come here. We've been through this.

MAMA: He felt sorry for you, too, Jessie, don't kid yourself about that. He said you were a runt and he said it from the day you were born and he said you didn't have a chance.

JESSIE (*Getting the canister of sugar and starting to refill the sugar bowl*): I know he loved me.

MAMA: What if he did? It didn't change anything.

JESSIE: It didn't have to. I miss him.

MAMA: He never really went fishing, you know. Never once. His tackle box was full of chewing tobacco and all he ever did was drive out to the lake and sit in his car. Dawson told me. And Bennie at the bait shop, he told Dawson. They all laughed about it. And he'd come back from fishing and all he'd have to show for it was . . . a whole pipe-cleaner *family*—chickens, pigs, a dog with a bad leg—it was creepy strange. It made me sick to look at them and I hid his pipe cleaners a couple of times but he always had more somewhere.

JESSIE: I thought it might be better for you after he died. You'd get interested in things. Breathe better. Change somehow.

MAMA: Into what? The Queen? A clerk in a shoe store? Why should I? Because he said to? Because you said to? (JESSIE *shakes her head.*) Well I wasn't here for his entertainment and I'm not here for yours either, Jessie. I don't know what I'm here for, but then I don't think about it. (*Realizing what all this means.*) But I bet you wouldn't be killing yourself if he were still alive. That's a fine thing to figure out, isn't it?

JESSIE (*Filling the honey jar now*): That's not true.

MAMA: Oh no? Then what were you asking about him for? Why did you want to know if I loved him?

JESSIE: I didn't think you did, that's all.

MAMA: Fine then. You were right. Do you feel better now?

JESSIE (*Cleaning the honey jar carefully*): It feels good to be right about it.

MAMA: It didn't matter whether I loved him. It didn't matter to me and it didn't matter to him. And it didn't mean we didn't get along. It wasn't important. We didn't talk about it. (*Sweeping the pots off the cabinet.*) Take all these pots out to the porch!

JESSIE: What for?

MAMA: Just leave me this one pan. (*She jerks the silverware drawer open.*) Get me one knife, one fork, one big spoon, and the can opener, and put them out where I can get them. (*Starts throwing knives and forks in one of the pans.*)

JESSIE: Don't do that! I just straightened that drawer!

MAMA (*Throwing the pan in the sink*): And throw out all the plates and cups. I'll use paper. Loretta can have what she wants and Dawson can sell the rest.

JESSIE (*Calmly*): What are you doing?

MAMA: I'm not going to cook. I never liked it, anyway. I like candy. Wrapped in plastic or coming in sacks. And tuna. I like tuna. I'll eat tuna, thank you.

JESSIE (*Taking the pan out of the sink*): What if you want to make apple butter? You can't make apple butter in that little pan. What if you leave carrots on cooking and burn up that pan?

MAMA: I don't like carrots.

JESSIE: What if the strawberries are good this year and you want to go picking with Agnes?

MAMA: I'll tell her to bring a pan. You said you would do whatever I wanted! I don't want a bunch of pans cluttering up my cabinets I can't get down to, anyway. Throw them out. Every last one.

JESSIE (*Gathering up the pots*): I'm putting them all back in. I'm not taking them to the porch. If you want them, they'll be here. You'll bend down and get them, like you got the one for the cocoa. And if somebody else comes over here to cook, they'll have something to cook in, and that's the end of it!

MAMA: Who's going to come cook here?

JESSIE: Agnes.

MAMA: In my pots. Not on your life.

JESSIE: There's no reason why the two of you couldn't just live here together. Be cheaper for both of you and somebody to talk to. And if the birds bothered you, well, one day when Agnes is out getting her hair done, you could take them all for a walk!

MAMA (*As* JESSIE *straightens the silverware*): So that's why you're pestering me about Agnes. You think you can rest easy if you get me a new babysitter? Well, I don't want to live with Agnes. I barely want to talk with Agnes. She's just around. We go back, that's all. I'm not letting Agnes near this place. You don't get off as easy as that, child.

JESSIE: O.K., then. It's just something to think about.

MAMA: I don't like things to think about. I like things to go on.

JESSIE (*Closing the silverware drawer*): I want to know what Daddy said to you the night he died. You came storming out of his room and said I could wait it out with him if I wanted to, but you were going to watch *Gunsmoke*. What did he say to you?

MAMA: He didn't have *anything* to say to me, Jessie. That's why I left. He didn't say a thing. It was his last chance not to talk to me and he took full advantage of it.

JESSIE (*After a moment*): I'm sorry you didn't love him. Sorry for you, I mean. He seemed like a nice man.

MAMA (*As* JESSIE *walks to the refrigerator*): Ready for your apple now?

JESSIE: Soon as I'm through here, Mama.

MAMA: You won't like the apple, either. It'll be just like the cocoa. You never liked eating at all, did you? Any of it! What have you been living on all these years, toothpaste?

JESSIE (*As she starts to clean out the refrigerator*): Now, you know the milkman comes on Wednesdays and Saturdays, and he leaves the order blank in an egg box, and you give the bills to Dawson once a month.

MAMA: Do they still make that orangeade?

JESSIE: It's not orangeade, it's just orange.

MAMA: I'm going to get some. I thought they stopped making it. You just stopped ordering it.

JESSIE: You should drink milk.

MAMA: Not anymore, I'm not. That hot chocolate was the last. Hooray.

JESSIE (*Getting the garbage can from under the sink*): I told them to keep delivering a quart a week no matter what you said. I told them you'd run out of Cokes and you'd have to drink it. I told them I knew you wouldn't pour it on the ground . . .

MAMA (*Finishing her sentence*): And you told them you weren't going to be ordering anymore?

JESSIE: I told them I was taking a little holiday and to look after you.

MAMA: And they didn't think something was funny about that? You who doesn't go to the front steps? You, who only sees the driveway looking down from a stretcher passed out cold?

JESSIE (*Enjoying this, but not laughing*): They said it was about time, but why didn't I take you with me? And I said I didn't think you'd want to go, and they said, "Yeah, everybody's got their own idea of vacation."

MAMA: I guess you think that's funny.

JESSIE (*Pulling jars out of the refrigerator*): You know there never was any reason to call the ambulance for me. All they ever did for me in the emergency room was let me wake up. I could've done that here. Now, I'll just call them out and you say yes or no. I know you like pickles. Ketchup?

MAMA: Keep it.

JESSIE: We've had this since last Fourth of July.

MAMA: Keep the ketchup. Keep it all.

JESSIE: Are you going to drink ketchup from the bottle or what? How can you want your food and not want your pots to cook it in? This stuff will all spoil in here, Mother.

MAMA: Nothing I ever did was good enough for you and I want to know why.

JESSIE: That's not true.

MAMA: And I want to know why you've lived here this long feeling the way you do.

JESSIE: You have no earthly idea how I feel.

MAMA: Well, how could I? You're real far back there, Jessie.

JESSIE: Back where?

MAMA: What's it like over there, where you are? Do people always say the right thing or get whatever they want, or what?

JESSIE: What are you talking about?

MAMA: Why do you read the newspaper? Why don't you wear that sweater I made for you? Do you remember how I used to look, or am I just any old woman now? When you have a fit, do you see stars or what? How did you fall off the horse, really? Why did Cecil leave you? Where did you put my old glasses?

JESSIE (*Stunned by* MAMA's *intensity*): They're in the bottom drawer of your dresser in an old Milk of

Magnesia box. Cecil left me because he made me choose between him and smoking.

MAMA: Jessie, I know he wasn't that dumb.

JESSIE: I never understood why he hated it so much when it's so good. Smoking is the only thing I know that's always just what you think it's going to be. Just like it was the last time, right there when you want it and real quiet.

MAMA: Your fits made him sick and you know it.

JESSIE: Say seizures, not fits. Seizures.

MAMA: It's the same thing. A seizure in the hospital is a fit at home.

JESSIE: They didn't bother him at all. Except he did feel responsible for it. It *was* his idea to go horseback riding that day. It was his idea I could do *anything* if I just made up my mind to. I fell off the horse because I didn't know how to hold on. Cecil left for pretty much the same reason.

MAMA: He had a girl, Jessie. I walked right in on them in the toolshed.

JESSIE (*After a moment*): O.K. That's fair. (*Lighting another cigarette.*) Was she very pretty?

MAMA: She was Agnes's girl, Carlene. Judge for yourself.

JESSIE (*As she walks to the living room*): I guess you and Agnes had a good talk about that, huh?

MAMA: I never thought he was good enough for you. They moved here from Tennessee, you know.

JESSIE: What are you talking about? You liked him better than I did. You flirted him out here to build your porch or I'd never even met him at all. You thought maybe he'd help you out around the place, come in and get some coffee and talk to you. God knows what you thought. All that curly hair.

MAMA: He's the best carpenter I ever saw. That little house of yours will still be standing at the end of the world, Jessie.

JESSIE: You didn't need a porch, Mama.

MAMA: All right! I wanted you to have a husband.

JESSIE: And I couldn't get one on my own, of course.

MAMA: How were you going to get a husband never opening your mouth to a living soul?

JESSIE: So I was quiet about it, so what?

MAMA: So I should have let you just sit here? Sit like your daddy? Sit here?

JESSIE: Maybe.

MAMA: Well, I didn't think so.

JESSIE: Well, what did you know?

MAMA: I never said I knew much. How was I supposed to learn anything living out here? I didn't know enough to do half the things I did in my life. Things happen. You do what you can about them and you see what happens next. I married you off to the wrong man, I admit that. So I took you in when he left. I'm sorry

JESSIE: He wasn't the wrong man.

MAMA: He didn't love you, Jessie, or he wouldn't have left.

JESSIE: He wasn't the wrong man, Mama. I loved Cecil so much. And I tried to get more exercise and I tried to stay awake. I tried to learn to ride a horse. And I tried to stay outside with him, but he always knew I was trying, so it didn't work.

MAMA: He was a selfish man. He told me once he hated to see people move into his houses after he built them. He knew they'd mess them up.

JESSIE: I loved that bridge he built over the creek in back of the house. It didn't have to be anything special, a couple of boards would have been just fine, but he used that yellow pine and rubbed it so smooth . . .

MAMA: He had responsibilities here. He had a wife and son here and he failed you.

JESSIE: Or that baby bed he built for Ricky. I told him he didn't have to spend so much time on it, but he said it had to last, and the thing ended up weighing two hundred pounds and I couldn't move it. I said, "How long does a baby bed have to last, anyway?" But maybe he thought if it was strong enough, it might keep Ricky a baby.

MAMA: Ricky is too much like Cecil.

JESSIE: He is not. Ricky is as much like me as it's possible for any human to be. We even wear the same size pants. These are his, I think.

MAMA: That's just the same size. That's not you're the same person.

JESSIE: I see it on his face. I hear it when he talks. We look out at the world and we see the same thing: Not Fair. And the only difference between us is Ricky's out there trying to get even. And he knows not to trust anybody and he got it straight from me. And he knows not to try to get work, and guess where he got that. He walks around like there's loose boards in the floor, and you know who laid that floor, I did.

MAMA: Ricky isn't through yet. You don't know how he'll turn out!

JESSIE (*Going back to the kitchen*): Yes I do and so did Cecil. Ricky is the two of us together for all time in too small a space. And we're tearing each other apart, like always, inside that boy, and if you don't see it, then you're just blind.

MAMA: Give him time, Jess.

JESSIE: Oh, he'll have plenty of that. Five years for forgery, ten years for armed assault . . .

MAMA (*Furious*): Stop that! (*Then pleading.*) Jessie, Cecil might be ready to try it again, honey, that happens sometimes. Go downtown. Find him. Talk to him. He didn't know what he had in you. Maybe he sees things different now, but you're not going to know that till you go see him. Or call him up! Right now! He might be home.

JESSIE: And say what? Nothing's changed, Cecil, I'd just like to look at you, if you don't mind? No. He loved me, Mama. He just didn't know how things fall down around me like they do. I think he did the right thing. He gave himself another chance, that's all. But I did beg him to take me with him. I did tell him I would leave Ricky and you and everything I loved out here if only he would take me with him, but he couldn't and I understood that. *(Pause.)* I wrote that note I showed you. I wrote it. Not Cecil. I said "I'm sorry, Jessie, I can't fix it all for you." I said I'd always love me, not Cecil. But that's how he felt.

MAMA: Then he should've taken you with him!

JESSIE *(Picking up the garbage bag she has filled)*: Mama, you don't pack your garbage when you move.

MAMA: You will not call yourself garbage, Jessie.

JESSIE *(Taking the bag to the big garbage can near the back door)*: Just a way of saying it, Mama. Thinking about my list, that's all. *(Opening the can, putting the garbage in, then securing the lid.)* Well, a little more than that. I was trying to say it's all right that Cecil left. It was . . . a relief in a way. I never was what he wanted to see, so it was better when he wasn't looking at me all the time.

MAMA: I'll make your apple now.

JESSIE: No thanks. You get the manicure stuff and I'll be right there.

(JESSIE ties up the big garbage bag in the can and replaces the small garbage bag under the sink, all the time trying desperately to regain her calm. MAMA watches, from a distance, her hand reaching unconsciously for the phone. Then she has a better idea. Or rather she thinks of the only other thing left and is willing to try it. Maybe she is even convinced it will work.)

MAMA: Jessie, I think your daddy had little . . .

JESSIE *(Interrupting her)*: Garbage night is Tuesday. Put it out as late as you can. The Davis's dogs get in it if you don't. *(Replacing the garbage bag in the can under the sink.)* And keep ordering the heavy black bags. It doesn't pay to buy the cheap ones. And I've got all the ties here with the hammers and all. Take them out of the box as soon as you open a new one and put them in this drawer. They'll get lost if you don't, and rubber bands or something else won't work.

MAMA: I think your daddy had fits, too. I think he sat in his chair and had little fits. I read this a long time ago in a magazine, how little fits go, just little blackouts where maybe their eyes don't even close and people just call them "thinking spells."

JESSIE *(Getting the slipcover out of the laundry basket)*: I don't think you want this manicure we've been looking forward to. I washed this cover for the sofa, but it'll take both of us to get it back on.

MAMA: I watched his eyes. I know that's what it was. The magazine said some people don't even know they've had one.

JESSIE: Daddy would've known if he'd had fits, Mama.

MAMA: The lady in this story had kept track of hers and she'd had eighty thousand of them in the last eleven years.

JESSIE: Next time you wash this cover, it'll dry better if you put it on wet.

MAMA: Jessie, listen to what I'm telling you. This lady had anywhere between five and five hundred fits a day and they lasted maybe fifteen seconds apiece, so that out of her life, she'd only lost about two weeks altogether, and she had a full-time secretary job and an IQ of 120.

JESSIE *(Amused by MAMA's approach)*: You want to talk about fits, is that it?

MAMA: Yes. I do. I want to say . . .

JESSIE *(Interrupting)*: Most of the time I wouldn't even know I'd had one, except I wake up with different clothes on, feeling like I've been run over. Sometimes I feel my head start to turn around or hear myself scream. And sometimes there *is* this dizzy stupid feeling a little before it, but if the TV's on, well, it's easy to miss.

(As JESSIE and MAMA replace the slipcover on the sofa and the afghan on the chair, the physical struggle somehow mirrors the emotional one in the conversation.)

MAMA: I can tell when you're about to have one. Your eyes get this big! But, Jessie, you haven't . . .

JESSIE *(Taking charge of this)*: What do they look like? The seizures.

MAMA *(Reluctant)*: Different each time, Jess.

JESSIE: O.K. Pick one, then. A good one. I think I want to know now.

MAMA: There's not much to tell. You just . . . crumple, in a heap, like a puppet and somebody cut the strings all at once, or like the firing squad in some Mexican movie, you just slide down the wall, you know. You don't know what happens? How can you not know what happens?

JESSIE: I'm busy.

MAMA: That's not funny.

JESSIE: I'm not laughing. My head turns around and I fall down and then what?

MAMA: Well, your chest squeezes in and out, and you sound like you're gagging, sucking air in and out like you can't breathe.

JESSIE: Do it for me. Make the sound for me.

MAMA: I will not. It's awful-sounding.

JESSIE: Yeah. It felt like it might be. What's next?

MAMA: Your mouth bites down and I have to get your tongue out of the way fast, so you don't bite yourself.

JESSIE: Or you. I bite you, too, don't I?

MAMA: You got me once real good. I had to get a tetanus! But I know what to watch for now. And then you turn blue and the jerks start up. Like I'm standing there poking you with a cattle prod or you're sticking your finger in a light socket as fast as you can . . .

JESSIE: Foaming like a mad dog the whole time.

MAMA: It's bubbling, Jess, not foam like the washer overflowed, for God's sake; it's bubbling like a baby spitting up. I go get a wet washcloth, that's all. And then the jerks slow down and you wet yourself and it's over. Two minutes tops.

JESSIE: How do I get to the bed?

MAMA: How do you think?

JESSIE: I'm too heavy for you now. How do you do it?

MAMA: I call Dawson. But I get you cleaned up before he gets here and I make him leave before you wake up.

JESSIE: You could just leave me on the floor.

MAMA: I want you to wake up someplace nice, O.K.? (Then making a real effort.) But, Jessie, and this is the reason I even brought this up! You haven't had a seizure for a solid year. A whole year, do you realize that?

JESSIE: Yeah, the phenobarb's about right now, I guess.

MAMA: You bet it is. You might never have another one, ever! You might be through with it for all time!

JESSIE: Could be.

MAMA: You are. I know you are!

JESSIE: I sure am feeling good. I really am. The double vision's gone and my gums aren't swelling. No rashes or anything. I'm feeling as good as I ever felt in my life. I'm even feeling like worrying or getting mad and I'm not afraid it will start a fit if I do, I just go ahead.

MAMA: Of course you do! You can even scream at me, if you want to. I can take it. You don't have to act like you're just visiting here, Jessie. This is your house, too.

JESSIE: The best part is, my memory's back.

MAMA: Your memory's always been good. When couldn't you remember things? You're always reminding me what . . .

JESSIE: Because I've made lists for everything. But now I remember what things mean on my lists. I see "dish towels," and I used to wonder whether I was supposed to wash them, buy them, or look for them because I wouldn't remember where I put them after I washed them, but now I know it means wrap them up, they're a present for Loretta's birthday.

MAMA (Finished with the sofa now): You used to go looking for your lists, too, I've noticed that. You always know where they are now! (Then suddenly worried.) Loretta's birthday isn't coming up, is it?

JESSIE: I made a list of all the birthdays for you. I even put yours on it. (A small smile.) So you can call Loretta and remind her.

MAMA: Let's take Loretta to Howard Johnson's and have those fried clams. I know you love that clam roll.

JESSIE (Slight pause): I won't be here, Mama.

MAMA: What have we just been talking about? You'll be here. You're well, Jessie. You're starting all over. You said it yourself. You're remembering things and . . .

JESSIE: I won't be here. If I'd ever had a year like this, to think straight and all, before now, I'd be gone already.

MAMA (Not pleading, commanding): No, Jessie.

JESSIE (Folding the rest of the laundry): Yes, Mama. Once I started remembering, I could see what it all added up to.

MAMA: The fits are over!

JESSIE: It's not the fits, Mama.

MAMA: Then it's me for giving them to you, but I didn't do it!

JESSIE: It's not the fits! You said it yourself, the medicine takes care of the fits.

MAMA (Interrupting): Your daddy gave you those fits, Jessie. He passed it down to you like your green eyes and your straight hair. It's not my fault!

JESSIE: So what if he had little fits? It's not inherited. I fell off the horse. It was an accident.

MAMA: The horse wasn't the first time, Jessie. You had a fit when you were five years old.

JESSIE: I did not.

MAMA: You did! You were eating a popsicle and down you went. He gave it to you. It's his fault, not mine.

JESSIE: Well, you took your time telling me.

MAMA: How do you tell that to a five-year-old?

JESSIE: What did the doctor say?

MAMA: He said kids have them all the time. He said there wasn't anything to do but wait for another one.

JESSIE: But I didn't have another one.

(Now there is a real silence.)

JESSIE: You mean to tell me I had fits all the time as a kid and you just told me I fell down or something and it wasn't till I had the fit when Cecil was looking that anybody bothered to find out what was the matter with me?

MAMA: It wasn't all the time, Jessie. And they changed when you started to school. More like your daddy's. Oh, that was some swell time, sitting here with the two of you turning off and on like light bulbs some nights.

JESSIE: How many fits did I have?

MAMA: You never hurt yourself. I never let you out of my sight. I caught you every time.

JESSIE: But you didn't tell anybody.

MAMA: It was none of their business.

JESSIE: You were ashamed.

MAMA: I didn't want anybody to know. Least of all you.

JESSIE: Least of all me. Oh, right. That was mine to know, Mama, not yours. Did Daddy know?

MAMA: He thought you were . . . you fell down a lot. That's what he thought. You were careless. Or maybe he thought I beat you. I don't know what he thought. He didn't think about it.

JESSIE: Because you didn't tell him!

MAMA: If I told him about you, I'd have to tell him about him!

JESSIE: I don't like this. I don't like this one bit.

MAMA: I didn't think you'd like it. That's why I didn't tell you.

JESSIE: If I'd known I was an epileptic, Mama, I wouldn't have ridden any horses.

MAMA: Make you feel like a freak, is that what I should have done?

JESSIE: Just get the manicure tray and sit down!

MAMA (*Throwing it to the floor*): I don't want a manicure!

JESSIE: Doesn't look like you do, no.

MAMA: Maybe I did drop you, you don't know.

JESSIE: If you say you didn't, you didn't.

MAMA (*Beginning to break down*): Maybe I fed you the wrong thing. Maybe you had a fever sometime and I didn't know it soon enough. Maybe it's a punishment.

JESSIE: For what?

MAMA: I don't know. Because of how I felt about your father. Because I didn't want any more children. Because I smoked too much or didn't eat right when I was carrying you. It has to be something I did.

JESSIE: It does not. It's just a sickness, not a curse. Epilepsy doesn't mean anything. It just is.

MAMA: I'm not talking about the fits here, Jessie! I'm talking about this killing yourself. It has to be me that's the matter here. You wouldn't be doing this if it wasn't. I didn't tell you things or I married you off to the wrong man or I took you in and let your life get away from you or all of it put together. I don't know what I did, but I did it, I know. This is all my fault, Jessie, but I don't know what to do about it now!

JESSIE (*Exasperated at having to say this again*): It doesn't have anything to do with you!

MAMA: Everything you do has to do with me, Jessie. You can't do *anything*, wash your face or cut your finger, without doing it to me. That's right! You might as well kill me as you, Jessie, it's the same thing. This has to do with me, Jessie.

JESSIE: Then what if it does! What if it has everything to do with you! What if you are all I have and you're not enough? What if I could take all the rest of it if only I didn't have you here? What if the only way I can get away from you for good is to kill myself? What if it is? I can *still* do it!

MAMA (*In desperate tears*): Don't leave me, Jessie! (JESSIE *stands for a moment, then turns for the bedroom.*) No! (*She grabs* JESSIE'S *arm.*)

JESSIE (*Carefully taking her arm away*): I have a box of things I want people to have. I'm just going to go get it for you. You . . . just rest a minute.

(JESSIE *is gone.* MAMA *heads for the telephone, but she can't even pick up the receiver this time and, instead, stoops to clean up the bottles that have spilled out of the manicure tray.*)

(JESSIE *returns, carrying a box that groceries were delivered in. It probably says Hershey Kisses or Starkist Tuna.* MAMA *is still down on the floor cleaning up, hoping that maybe if she just makes it look nice enough,* JESSIE *will stay.*)

MAMA: Jessie, how can I live here without you? I need you! You're supposed to tell me to stand up straight and say how nice I look in my pink dress, and drink my milk. You're supposed to go around and lock up so I know we're safe for the night, and when I wake up, you're supposed to be out there making the coffee and watching me get older every day, and you're supposed to help me die when the time comes. I can't do that by myself, Jessie. I'm not like you, Jessie. I hate the quiet and I don't want to die and I don't want you to go, Jessie. How can I . . . (*Has to stop a moment.*) How can I get up every day knowing you had to kill yourself to make it stop hurting and I was here all the time and I never even saw it. And then you gave me this chance to make it better, convince you to stay alive, and I couldn't do it. How can I live with myself after this, Jessie?

JESSIE: I only told you so I could explain it, so you wouldn't blame yourself, so you wouldn't feel bad. There wasn't anything you could say to change my mind. I didn't want you to save me. I just wanted you to know.

MAMA: Stay with me just a little longer. Just a few more years. I don't have that many more to go, Jessie. And as soon as I'm dead, you can do whatever you want. Maybe with me gone, you'll have all the quiet you want, right here in the house. And maybe one day you'll put in some begonias up the walk and get just the right rain for them all summer. And Ricky will be married by then and he'll bring your grandbabies over and you can sneak them a piece of candy when their daddy's not looking and then be real glad when they've gone home and left you to your quiet again.

JESSIE: Don't you see, Mama, everything I do winds up like this. How could I think you would understand? How could I think you would want a manicure? We could hold hands for an hour and then I could go shoot myself? I'm sorry about tonight, Mama, but it's exactly why I'm doing it.

MAMA: If you've got the guts to kill yourself, Jessie, you've got the guts to stay alive.

JESSIE: I know that. So it's really just a matter of where I'd rather be.

MAMA: Look, maybe I can't think of what you should do, but that doesn't mean there isn't something that would help. *You* find it. *You* think of it. You can keep trying. You can get brave and try some more. You don't have to give up!

JESSIE: I'm *not* giving up! This *is* the other thing I'm trying. And I'm sure there are some other things that *might* work, but *might* isn't good enough anymore. I need something that *will* work. *This* will work. That's why I picked it.

MAMA: But something might happen. Something that could change everything. Who knows what it might be, but it might be worth waiting for! (JESSIE *doesn't respond.*) Try it for two more weeks. We could have more talks like tonight.

JESSIE: No, Mama.

MAMA: I'll pay more attention to you. Tell the truth when you ask me. Let you have your say.

JESSIE: No, Mama! We wouldn't have more talks like tonight, because it's this next part that's made this last part so good, Mama. No, Mama. *This* is how I have my say. This is how I say what I thought about it *all* and I say no. To Dawson and Loretta and the Red Chinese and epilepsy and Ricky and Cecil and you. And me. And hope. I say no! (*Then going to* MAMA *on the sofa.*) Just let me go easy, Mama.

MAMA: How can I let you go?

JESSIE: You can because you have to. It's what you've always done.

MAMA: You are my child!

JESSIE: I am what became of your child. (MAMA *cannot answer.*) I found an old baby picture of me. And it was somebody else, not me. It was somebody pink and fat who never heard of sick or lonely, somebody who cried and got fed, and reached up and got held and kicked but didn't hurt anybody, and slept whenever she wanted to, just by closing her eyes. Somebody who mainly just laid there and laughed at the colors waving around over her head and chewed on a polka-dot whale and woke up knowing some new trick nearly every day, and rolled over and drooled on the sheet and felt your hand pulling my quilt back up over me. That's who I started out and this is who is left. (*There is no self-pity here.*) That's what this is about. It's somebody I lost, all right, it's my own self. Who I never was. Or who I tried to be and never got there. Somebody I waited for who never came. And never will. So, see, it doesn't much matter what else happens in the world or in this house, even. I'm what was worth waiting for and I didn't make it. Me . . . who might have made a difference to me . . . I'm not going to show up, so

there's no reason to stay, except to keep you company, and that's . . . not reason enough because I'm not . . . very good company. (*Pause.*) Am I.

MAMA (*Knowing she must tell the truth*): No. And neither am I.

JESSIE: I had this strange little thought, well, maybe it's not so strange. Anyway, after Christmas, after I decided to do this, I would wonder, sometimes, what might keep me here, what might be worth staying for, and you know what it was? It was maybe if there was something I really liked, like maybe if I really liked rice pudding or cornflakes for breakfast or something, that might be enough.

MAMA: Rice pudding is good.

JESSIE: Not to me.

MAMA: And you're not afraid?

JESSIE: Afraid of what?

MAMA: I'm afraid of it, for me, I mean. When my time comes. I know it's coming, but . . .

JESSIE: You don't know when. Like in a scary movie.

MAMA: Yeah, sneaking up on me like some killer on the loose, hiding out in the back yard just waiting for me to have my hands full someday and how am I supposed to protect myself anyhow when I don't know what he looks like and I don't know how he sounds coming up behind me like that or if it will hurt or take very long or what I don't get done before it happens.

JESSIE: You've got plenty of time left.

MAMA: I forget what for, right now.

JESSIE: For whatever happens, I don't know. For the rest of your life. For Agnes burning down one more house or Dawson losing his hair or . . .

MAMA (*Quickly*): Jessie, I can't just sit here and say O.K., kill yourself if you want to.

JESSIE: Sure you can. You just did. Say it again.

MAMA (*Really startled*): Jessie! (*Quiet horror.*) How dare you! (*Furious.*) How dare you! You think you can just leave whenever you want, like you're watching television here? No, you can't, Jessie. You make me feel like a fool for being alive, child, and you are so wrong! I like it here, and I will stay here until they make me go, until they drag me screaming and I mean screeching into my grave, and you're real smart to get away before then because, I mean, honey, you've never heard noise like that in your life. (JESSIE *turns away.*) Who am I talking to? You're gone already, aren't you? I'm looking right through you! I can't stop you because you're already gone! I guess you think they'll all have to talk about you now! I guess you think this will really confuse them. Oh yes, ever since Christmas you've been laughing to yourself and thinking, "Boy, are they all in for a surprise." Well, nobody's going to be a bit surprised, sweetheart. This is just like you. Do it the hard way, that's my girl, all right. (JESSIE *gets up and goes into the kitchen, but* MAMA *follows her.*) You know who they're going to feel sorry for? Me! How about that! Not you, me! They're going to be *ashamed* of you. Yes. *Ashamed!* If somebody asks Dawson about it, he'll change the subject as fast as he can. He'll talk about how much he has to pay to park his car these days.

JESSIE: Leave me alone.

MAMA: It's the truth!

JESSIE: I should've just left you a note!

MAMA (*Screaming*): Yes! (*Then suddenly understanding what she has said, nearly paralyzed by the thought of it, she turns slowly to face* JESSIE, *nearly whispering.*) No. No. I . . . might not have thought of all the things you've said.

JESSIE: It's O.K., Mama.

(MAMA *is nearly unconscious from the emotional devastation of these last few moments. She sits down at the kitchen table, hurt and angry and desperately afraid. But she looks almost numb. She is so far beyond what is known as pain that she is virtually unreachable and* JESSIE *knows this, and talks quietly, watching for signs of recovery.*)

JESSIE (*Washes her hands in the sink*): I remember you liked that preacher who did Daddy's, so if you want to ask him to do the service, that's O.K. with me.

MAMA (*Not an answer, just a word*): What.

JESSIE (*Putting on hand lotion as she talks*): And pick some songs you like or let Agnes pick, she'll know exactly which ones. Oh, and I had your dress cleaned that you wore to Daddy's. You looked real good in that.

MAMA: I don't remember, hon.

JESSIE: And it won't be so bad once your friends start coming to the funeral home. You'll probably see people you haven't seen for years, but I thought about what you should say to get you over that nervous part when they first come in.

MAMA (*Simply repeating*): Come in.

JESSIE: Take them up to see their flowers, they'd like that. And when they say, "I'm so sorry, Thelma," you just say, "I appreciate your coming, Connie." And then ask how their garden was this summer or what they're doing for Thanksgiving or how their children . . .

MAMA: I don't think I should ask about their children. I'll talk about what they have on, that's always good. And I'll have some crochet work with me.

JESSIE: And Agnes will be there, so you might not have to talk at all.

MAMA: Maybe if Connie Richards does come, I can get her to tell me where she gets that Irish yarn, she calls it. I know it doesn't come from Ireland. I think it just comes with a green wrapper.

JESSIE: And be sure to invite enough people home afterward so you get enough food to feed them all and have some left for you. But don't let anybody take anything home, especially Loretta.

MAMA: Loretta will get all the food set up, honey. It's only fair to let her have some macaroni or something.

JESSIE: No, Mama. You have to be more selfish from now on. (*Sitting at the table with* MAMA.) Now, somebody's bound to ask you why I did it and you just say you don't know. That you loved me and you know I loved you and we just sat around tonight like every other night of our lives, and then I came over and kissed you and said, " 'night, Mother," and you heard me close my bedroom door and the next thing you heard was the shot. And whatever reasons I had, well, you guess I just took them with me.

MAMA (*Quietly*): It was something personal.

JESSIE: Good. That's good, Mama.

MAMA: That's what I'll say, then.

JESSIE: Personal. Yeah.

MAMA: Is that what I tell Dawson and Loretta, too? We sat around, you kissed me, " 'night, Mother"? They'll want to know more, Jessie. They won't believe it.

JESSIE: Well, then, tell them what we did. I filled up the candy jars. I cleaned out the refrigerator. We made some hot chocolate and put the cover back on the sofa. You had no idea. All right? I really think it's better that way. If they know we talked about it, they really won't understand how you let me go.

MAMA: I guess not.

JESSIE: It's private. Tonight is private, yours and mine, and I don't want anybody else to have any of it.

MAMA: O.K., then.

JESSIE (*Standing behind* MAMA *now, holding her shoulders*): Now, when you hear the shot, I don't want you to come in. First of all, you won't be able to get in by yourself, but I don't want you trying. Call Dawson, then call the police, and then call Agnes. And then you'll need something to do till somebody gets here, so wash the hot-chocolate pan. You wash that pan till you hear the doorbell ring and I don't care if it's an hour, you keep washing that pan.

MAMA: I'll make my calls and then I'll just sit. I won't need something to do. What will the police say?

JESSIE: They'll do that gunpowder test, I guess, and ask you what happened, and by that time, the ambulance will be here and they'll come in and get me and you know how that goes. You stay out here with Dawson and Loretta. You keep Dawson out here. I want the police in the room first, not Dawson, O.K.?

MAMA: What if Dawson and Loretta want me to go home with them?

JESSIE (*Returning to the living room*): That's up to you.

MAMA: I think I'll stay here. All they've got is Sanka.

JESSIE: Maybe Agnes could come stay with you for a few days.

MAMA (*Standing up, looking into the living room*): I'd rather be by myself, I think. (*Walking toward the box* JESSIE *brought in earlier.*) You want me to give people those things?

JESSIE (*They sit down on the sofa,* JESSIE *holding the box on her lap*): I want Loretta to have my little calculator. Dawson bought it for himself, you know, but then he saw one he liked better and he couldn't bring both of them home with Loretta counting every penny the way she does, so he gave the first one to me. Be funny for her to have it now, don't you think? And all my house slippers are in a sack for her in my closet. Tell her I know they'll fit and I've never worn any of them, and make sure Dawson hears you tell her that. I'm glad he loves Loretta so much, but I wish he knew not everybody has her size feet.

MAMA (*Taking the calculator*): O.K.

JESSIE (*Reaching into the box again*): This letter is for Dawson, but it's mostly about you, so read it if you want. There's a list of presents for you for at least twenty more Christmases and birthdays, so if you want anything special you better add it to this list before you give it to him. Or if you want to be surprised, just don't read that page. This Christmas, you're getting mostly stuff for the house, like a new rug in your bathroom and needlework, but next Christmas, you're really going to cost him next Christmas. I think you'll like it a lot and you'd never think of it.

MAMA: And you think he'll go for it?

JESSIE: I think he'll feel like a real jerk if he doesn't. Me telling him to, like this and all. Now, this number's where you call Cecil. I called it last week and he answered, so I know he still lives there.

MAMA: What do you want me to tell him?

JESSIE: Tell him we talked about him and I only had good things to say about him, but mainly tell him to find Ricky and tell him what I did, and tell Ricky you have something for him, out here, from me, and to come get it. (*Pulls a sack out of the box.*)

MAMA (*The sack feels empty*): What is it?

JESSIE (*Taking it off*): My watch. (*Putting it in the sack and taking a ribbon out of the sack to tie around the top of it.*)

MAMA: He'll sell it!

JESSIE: That's the idea. I appreciate him not stealing it already. I'd like to buy him a good meal.

MAMA: He'll buy dope with it!

JESSIE: Well, then, I hope he gets some good dope with it, Mama. And the rest of this is for you. (*Handing* MAMA *the box now.* MAMA *picks up the things and looks at them.*)

MAMA (*Surprised and pleased*): When did you do all this? During my naps, I guess.

JESSIE: I guess. I tried to be quiet about it. (*As* MAMA *is puzzled by the presents.*) Those are just little presents. For whenever you need one. They're not bought presents, just things I thought you might like to look at, pictures or things you think you've lost. Things you didn't know you had, even. You'll see.

MAMA: I'm not sure I want them. They'll make me think of you.

JESSIE: No they won't. They're just things, like a free tube of toothpaste I found hanging on the door one day.

MAMA: Oh. All right, then.

JESSIE: Well, maybe there's one present in there somewhere. It's Granny's ring she gave me and I thought you might like to have it, but I didn't think you'd wear it if I gave it to you right now.

MAMA (*Taking the box to a table nearby*): No. Probably not. (*Turning back to face her.*) I'm ready for my manicure, I guess. Want me to wash my hands again?

JESSIE (*Standing up*): It's time for me to go, Mama.

MAMA (*Starting for her*): No, Jessie, you've got all night!

JESSIE (*As* MAMA *grabs her*): No, Mama.

MAMA: It's not even ten o'clock.

JESSIE (*Very calm*): Let me go, Mama.

MAMA: I can't. You can't go. You can't do this. You didn't say it would be so soon, Jessie. I'm scared. I love you.

JESSIE (*Takes her hands away*): Let go of me, Mama. I've said everything I had to say.

MAMA (*Standing still a minute*): You said you wanted to do my nails.

JESSIE (*Taking a small step backward*): I can't. It's too late.

MAMA: It's not too late!

JESSIE: I don't want you to wake Dawson and Loretta when you call. I want them to still be up and dressed so they can get right over.

MAMA (*As* JESSIE *backs up,* MAMA *moves in on her, but carefully*): They wake up fast, Jessie, if they have to. They don't matter here, Jessie. You do. I do. We're not through yet. We've got a lot of things to take care of here. I don't know where my prescriptions are and you didn't tell me what to tell Dr. Davis when he calls or how much you want me to tell Ricky or who I call to rake the leaves or . . .

JESSIE: Don't try and stop me, Mama, you can't do it.

MAMA (*Grabbing her again, this time hard*): I can too! I'll stand in front of this hall and you can't get past me. (*They struggle.*) You'll have to knock me down to get away from me, Jessie. I'm not about to let you . . .

(MAMA *struggles with* JESSIE *at the door and in the struggle* JESSIE *gets away from her and—*)

JESSIE (*Almost a whisper*): 'night, Mother. (*She vanishes into her bedroom and we hear the door lock just as* MAMA *gets to it.*)

MAMA (*Screams*): Jessie! (*Pounding on the door.*) Jessie, you let me in there. Don't you do this, Jessie. I'm not going to stop screaming until you open this door, Jessie. Jessie! Jessie! What if I don't do any of the things you told me to do! I'll tell Cecil what a miserable man he was to make you feel the way he did and I'll give Ricky's watch to Dawson if I feel like it and the only way you can make sure I do what you want is you come out here and make me, Jessie! (*Pounding again.*) Jessie! Stop this! I didn't know! I was here with you all the time. How could I know you were so alone?

(*And* MAMA *stops for a moment, breathless and frantic, putting her ear to the door, and when she doesn't hear anything, she stands up straight again and screams once more.*)

Jessie! Please!

(*And we hear the shot, and it sounds like an answer, it sounds like No.*)

(MAMA *collapses against the door, tears streaming down her face, but not screaming anymore. In shock now.*)

Jessie, Jessie, child . . . Forgive me. (*Pause.*) I thought you were mine.

(*And she leaves the door and makes her way through the living room, around the furniture, as though she didn't know where it was, not knowing what to do. Finally, she goes to the stove in the kitchen and picks up the hot-chocolate pan and carries it with her to the telephone and holds on to it while she dials the number. She looks down at the pan, holding it tight like her life depended on it. She hears Loretta answer.*)

MAMA: Loretta, let me talk to Dawson, honey.

Figure 1. Mama (Anne Pitoniak) shares her memories of Daddy with Jessie (Kathy Bates) in the John Golden Theater production of *'night, Mother,* directed by Tom Moore, 1983. (Photograph: Richard M. Feldman.)

Figure 2. In the 1983 production, Jessie (Kathy Bates) examines Daddy's gun, while Mama (Anne Pitoniak) tries to convince her that it's broken. (Photograph: Richard M. Feldman.)

Staging of 'night, Mother

**REVIEW OF THE JOHN GOLDEN THEATER
PRODUCTION, 1983, BY DOUGLAS WATT**

Marsha Norman doesn't fool around. In 'night, Mother, which came to the Golden last night, the author of the schizophrenic *Getting Out* of a few seasons back offers a clinical study of a suicide—of the last 85 minutes (the play's exact length) in the life of a hopeless young woman. It's a spellbinding idea, and one held in tight control by the playwright's spare, effective dialogue; but it is less involving than one might expect, even with that final offstage gunshot.

There are several reasons for this, not the least of them the fact that the act of suicide is, in its most profound sense, as mysterious as life itself. But then, there is the troublesome situation Norman has posed.

Jessie Cates lives with her mother, Thelma, in the latter's "relatively new house, built way out on a country road," someplace in the South, judging from speech patterns and the author's Louisville background. At the very start, Jessie asks where her late father's gun has been kept, then retrieves it from a shoebox in the storage space above the ceiling, starts cleaning and oiling it and, pushing bullets into the chambers, announces her intention of killing herself this very evening.

But not until she's polished her mother's fingernails (she never gets around to this, though), given instructions about milk and other deliveries, specified people to phone, bagged the garbage and relined the pail, attended to countless other details with cool efficiency, tidied up in general and resisted any attempt on Thelma's part to dissuade her from taking her life.

The way Jessie feels about it is that her life and her disposal of it is the one thing she has complete control over. The lonely and, until now, uncommunicative child of a loveless marriage (a married brother lives nearby), she has been divorced by her husband and has given up on a son who is already a common thief and who, she is certain, will end up in prison as a result of the coming together in him of the worst aspects of herself and her former husband.

That's not all, though. Jessie, as she learns now for the first time, has been subject to epileptic fits since childhood, manifestations that have been explained away by her mother as dizzy spells or "seizures." What with one thing and another, Jessie has decided that wherever her life might end (she compares it to riding on a bus and either getting off at will or continuing to a known and undesirable destination), it will never improve, so why not make a decisive move and end it right here instead of going on sinking deeper and deeper within herself in these tacky surroundings while looking after a mother who apparently is capable of caring for herself and, worse, listening to her endlessly foolish chatter.

So the evening is spent in watching the homely preparations made for the inevitable act and listening to the mundane, often joking, conversation. Norman's intent, somewhat akin to Hitchcock's frequent juxtaposition, is to build horror—though with much more deadly intensity than the film maker sought—within the familiar, commonplace, everyday world.

The troubling aspect of the play is that Jessie is not a truly tragic figure. Her self-containment as she busily sets things to order about the house suggests one dedicated to her awful purpose, true, but also suggests a congenitally deranged woman. And Thelma's actual acceptance of the situation, having at last given up arguing against it, has a surreal air about it, as strange in its way as Jessie's early announcement of her purpose and subsequent behavior, including a break to share cocoa with her mother. The final cap-pistol report from behind a bedroom door is as weak as the play's premise. The mother's faltering steps to the kitchen area following the gunshot and her near-blind dialing of the phone to call the brother is the evening's most real moment.

Kathy Bates holds our interest as the plump, tight-lipped, bustling Jessie, who breaks down briefly just once or twice, and Anne Pitoniak is a lanky flibberti-gibbet of a vacant mother whose speech, sometimes a bit hard to understand, should have been cleared up by the director, Tom Moore, who otherwise has done a serviceable job. Heidi Landesman's set is, indeed, neat, new-looking and impersonal enough to drive any occupant to suicide sooner or later, given that secret urge to begin with.

Norman's writing is diamond-sharp and expressive, under the circumstances. It's just the circumstances that struck me as alien, pat, and unlikely.

REVIEW OF THE JOHN GOLDEN THEATER
PRODUCTION, 1983, BY FRANK RICH

"We've got a good life here," says Thelma Cates to her daughter, Jessie, in Marsha Norman's new play, *'night, Mother.* Many would agree. Thelma, who is a widow, and Jessie, who is divorced, live together in a spick-and-span house on a country road somewhere in the New South. There are no money problems. Nights are spent in such relaxed pursuits as crocheting and watching television.

But on the particular, ordinary Saturday night that we meet Thelma (Anne Pitoniak) and Jessie (Kathy Bates), we learn that the good life may not be so good after all. As the daughter prepares to perform her weekly ritual of giving her mother a manicure, she says calmly, almost as a throwaway line, "I'm going to kill myself, Mama." And, over the next 90 minutes, Mama—and the rest of us—must face the fact that Jessie is not kidding.

'night, Mother, which has traveled to Broadway's John Golden Theater from Harvard's American Repertory Theater, is a shattering evening, but it looks like simplicity itself. A totally realistic play, set in real time counted by onstage clocks, it shows us what happens after Jessie makes her announcement. What happens, unsurprisingly, is that the first skeptical and then terrified mother tries to cajole and talk her child out of suicide. "People don't really kill themselves," argues Thelma, "unless they're retarded or deranged."

But Jessie isn't deranged—she's never felt better in her life—and that's why *'night, Mother* is more complex than it looks, more harrowing than even its plot suggests. Miss Norman's play is simple only in the way that an Edward Hopper painting is simple. As she perfectly captures the intimate details of two individual, ordinary women, this playwright locates the emptiness that fills too many ordinary homes on too many faceless streets in the vast country we live in now.

Why does Jessie want to kill herself? There are many conceivable motives. She's a fat, lumpy, anonymous-looking woman in her thirties who spends her days indoors, eating junk food. Her son is a hoodlum. Her last job, working at a gift shop in a hospital, didn't work out. She misses her dead father, as well as the husband who left her. She suffers from epilepsy, though it's now been brought under control by medication.

As the play progresses, her mother enumerates all these disappointments, desperately offering to solve any of them she can. But Jessie will have none of it. She instead wants to use her last hours to help her mother get the house in order and to sit around chatting "like every other night of our lives." The daughter insists that they make cocoa, re-cover the couch and clean out the refrigerator.

Jessie is at peace about her decision because she has decided that nothing can change it. "It doesn't really matter what else happens in the world or in this house," she says, for the real problem is "nobody out there, but my own self." In Jessie's opinion, that self—her interior life—is something that she "lost" and that will "never show up." It is also the only "real" possession she has, and she claims the right to "stop it, shut it down, turn it off."

Although it is likely to kindle many debates about the subject, *'night, Mother* is not a message play about the choice to commit suicide. It's about contemporary life and what gives it—or fails to give it—value. We first get a sense of the Cates's existence before *'night, Mother* begins. Heidi Landesman's disturbing set, in view as we enter the theater, is an all-American living room and kitchen, right out of a television sitcom: homey, appointed with the right appliances, conventionally tasteful. But, when James F. Ingalls's cruelly bright lighting comes up, we see the house is colorless and dead—a pair of antiseptic model rooms, framed like a department-store window.

Miss Norman's dialogue maps the rest of the vacuum. When Thelma at first mistakes Jessie's preoccupation with guns for a fear of burglars, she says, "We don't have anything people would want." And we come to see that neither mother nor daughter do. Their lives are built on neighborhood gossip, ritualized familial obligations and housekeeping. Before tonight—when a gun is literally to their heads—they've never expressed their real feelings to one another or to anybody else. The more loneliness that is exposed the more we realize that the most horrifying aspect of *'night, Mother* is not Jessie's decision to end her life but her mother's gradual awakening—and ours—to the inexorable logic of that decision.

The play would never work, never make that logic real, if Miss Norman for a second condescended to her characters by painting them as fools—or if she stuck in authorial speeches that commented on or judged their predicament. As previously demonstrated in *Getting Out*, Miss Norman is far too honest a writer to fall into those traps.

Jessie and Thelma are not caricatured as stupid yokels. They are not without wit. When the mother begs the daughter to stay around "for a few more years" until her own death, she uses every argument that the smartest member of the audience might muster. Jessie, meanwhile, knocks those arguments down with brutal, eloquent force.

The strongest argument, of course, is the blood tie. Miss Norman draws the mother-daughter relationship painfully, with all the guilt and anger and twisted passion it can contain. During the course of the play, Thelma and Jessie ask each other every question they've ever wanted to ask—from "Why did your husband leave you?" to "Why did you never wear the sweater I made you?" As they do, the women often switch roles, to the excruciating point at which Thelma becomes a tantrum-throwing infant, lashing out at Jessie any way she can.

At more tender times, we see the love between these women, but we also see that it's not enough to make a difference to Jessie, who has no self-love. "You are my child!" cries the mother, in a primal plea. "No," says the daughter. "I am what became of your child."

Under the brilliant, unerring choreographic hand of the director Tom Moore—who follows the playwright by refusing to gild or theatricalize any moment—the superb actresses, both veterans of Louisville's Actors Theater, circle each other in a grueling dance of death that ebbs and flows so naturally that every violent transition catches us by surprise. There are pockets of humor—the mother even gets a laugh describing her daughter's youthful epileptic fits—and there is warmth.

But there is also the sight of Miss Pitoniak's Thelma, a gabby "plain country woman," turning white and dumb with fear as she realizes that the daughter through whom she's lived by proxy is beyond her reach—"already gone," even though still alive. And there is the moment when the otherwise deliberate Miss Bates turns away from her whimpering mother to wail defiantly, "I say *no* to hope."

Does *'night, Mother* say no to hope? It's easy to feel that way after reeling from this play's crushing blow. But there *can* be hope if there is understanding, and it is Marsha Norman's profound achievement that she brings both understanding and dignity to forgotten and tragic American lives.

AUGUST WILSON

1945–

Though he has been preceded in the American theater by several well-known black playwrights and plays—Langston Hughes (*Don't You Want to Be Free*, 1936), Theodore Ward (*Our Lan'*, 1941), Lorraine Hansberry (*A Raisin in the Sun*, 1959), Amiri Baraka (*Dutchman*, 1963), and Charles Fuller (*A Soldier's Story*, 1981)—August Wilson is unquestionably the most ambitious and likely to be the most widely produced and highly regarded black dramatist of the twentieth century. His ambition may be seen in his intention to write a cycle of ten plays about the experience of African Americans—one for each decade of the twentieth century, each one focused on a distinctively different but emblematic set of characters and situations. The quality of his accomplishments thus far may be judged from the fact that four of the plays in the cycle have been widely produced and enthusiastically received: *Ma Rainey's Black Bottom* (1984), *Fences* (1985), and *Joe Turner's Come and Gone* (1986), all of which have won the prestigious New York Drama Critics Circle Award, and *The Piano Lesson* (1989), which, like *Fences*, won the Pulitzer Prize. Almost as highly praised were Wilson's later additions to the cycle: *Two Trains Running* (1992), *Seven Guitars* (1996), and *King Hedley II* (2001).

Wilson's probing drama of African American experience is deeply rooted in his own quite complex personal experience of growing up in the Hill district of Pittsburgh—a black slum community where he was raised in a two-room cold-water flat by his mother, after she had been abandoned by the white man who fathered all of her six children. Although he bears the name of his natural father, who died in 1965, Wilson knew him only from occasional visits and remembers him largely as a hard-drinking German baker who turned up intermittently with a bag of rolls in his hand. And though he acquired a stepfather, David Bedford, during his early adolescent years, Wilson found himself at odds with Bedford when, at the age of fifteen, he decided to quit his high school football team and drop out of school. Wilson's decision to quit school, as it turns out, was provoked largely by the racial harassment he suffered after his family moved into the heavily white community of Hazlewood, Pennsylvania.

Out of school, Wilson continued his education in the local library, where he discovered and read his way through a small section of some thirty "Negro" books by such eminent writers as Ralph Ellison, Langston Hughes, and Richard Wright—a discovery that he remembers as having been especially significant for him. "Those books were a comfort. Just the idea black people would write books. I wanted my book up there, too." From that point on, Wilson evidently read voraciously in the fiction, poetry, and drama of black and white writers alike, and then began to try his own hand at fiction and poetry writing. Looking back on that time, he recalls himself as having been heavily influenced by the theatricality of Dylan Thomas's verse, by the "psychic shorthand" of John Berryman's poetry, and by the jazzy street style of Baraka's poetry and plays.

But Wilson primarily describes himself as having been influenced by the extraordinary diversity of African American culture—by the street talk and the street violence that he witnessed growing up in the black ghetto of Pittsburgh, by the Black Power movement that he became involved in during the late 1960s and early 1970s, and by the blues, which he regards as "a book of literature" that contains the "blacks' cultural response to the world" and which "influences everything I do." The Black Power movement initially attracted Wilson to the theater, for it led him to see drama as a powerful means to "politicize the community and raise consciousness." Indeed, during the 1960s, he cofounded a black activist theater in Pittsburgh—the Black Horizon on the Hill—which staged his earliest plays.

Paradoxically, however, Wilson did not really develop his unique talents as a dramatist of black experience until he moved away from the familiar world of his roots in Pittsburgh to the strikingly different community of St. Paul, Minnesota. There he became involved with the Playwrights Center of Minneapolis, and there, too, he began to remember in vivid detail the language and experience of the black ghetto, as well as to see the rich dramatic potentialities in the experience of that world. Thus during the late 1970s and early 1980s, Wilson began to write plays that aimed at a realistic evocation of African American life as he had come to know it through his past experience in Pittsburgh. In *Jitney* (1982), for example, he focused attention on the lives that intersect in a Pittsburgh gypsy-cab station.

A similarly high degree of concentration is evident in his three best-known plays. *Ma Rainey's Black Bottom* is set in a Chicago recording studio in 1927, *Fences* in the front yard of a two-story brick house in Pittsburgh in 1957, and *The Piano Lesson* in a tidy Pittsburgh apartment in 1936. Such highly localized settings enable Wilson to develop in each case an intensely focused human situation. *Ma Rainey's Black Bottom* relentlessly explores the tensions within an African American musical group as well as between the musicians and the white men who manage the talent and own the musical business. *Fences* documents the discord within a single family, in particular among Troy Maxson, the fifty-three-year-old protagonist; his wife Rose, whose love he betrays during the course of the play; and their son Cory, whose desire for fatherly affection Troy cannot fulfill. *The Piano Lesson* revolves around the struggle between an adult brother and sister over whether or not to sell an heirloom piano that represents both their grandfather's slave heritage and the ghosts of their own past.

Typically, Wilson expands the particular human predicament and the larger social context through highly evocative imagery both verbal and visual. *Ma Rainey's Black Bottom* draws its central image from the world of popular music, in particular from "singing the blues." Through its focus on this distinctive aspect of African American culture, the play bears witness to the white exploitation of black performers in the racist world of Sturdyvant's recording studio. Ma Rainey, the African American singer known as "the Mother of the Blues" (1886–1939), never forgets that her manager is "always talking about sticking together," always treating her solicitously in public, but "the only time he had me in his house was to sing for some of his friends." The play's tension, however, is not just between white and black people but among blacks as well, a tension that is epitomized by the difference between the old-fashioned "jug-band music" favored by Ma, as opposed to the newer "jazz" on which Levee, the youngest of the four instrumentalists, hopes to make his name. Much of the first act, in fact, concerns which version of Ma's signature song the band will play—Levee's, with an instrumental introduction, or Ma's, with a spoken one. But the real issue that fuels this conflict is what kind of identity and thus what kind of power is possible for an African American person in the America of the 1920s.

That same question is posed in *Fences,* although Wilson here switches his attention to the 1950s, and his central image to baseball. Baseball functions mythically as the all-American game and the game through which the color barrier was broken in professional sports—although too late for the play's protagonist, Troy Maxson, who thinks constantly of his batting record in the Negro Leagues. For Troy, baseball provides a rich source of metaphors to express the frustrating conditions of his world, a world where "you born with two strikes on you before you come to the plate," and where cheating on his wife is like wanting "to steal second." While baseball shapes Troy's language and his dreams of the man he might have been, other images comment ironically on those dreams: his first name reminds us of the great but doomed city of classical legend; he works as a garbage collector; and the fence he keeps planning to build, but never finishes, is his figurative defense against death.

At the heart of *Fences* is a drama of family conflict, a drama that sets father against son, husband against wife, brother against brother. Like Willy Loman in *Death of a Salesman* and like Walter Lee Younger in *A Raisin in the Sun,* Troy is a man struggling to achieve stature both in his home and in the world. And, like both of these men, he hurts the people he loves most. He claims to love his wife Rose "so much it hurts" (see Figure 1) but he fathers a child with another woman and then, when that woman dies in childbirth, awkwardly comes home with the baby, begging Rose to take care of his new daughter (see Figure 2). Though he cherishes his memories as a baseball player, he becomes fiercely antagonistic when his son Cory wants to play football (see Figure 3), determined that Cory won't be hurt by professional sports, as he thinks he was. So, in the play's climactic moment, he challenges Cory to attack him, and, after wresting the bat away from his son, then "assumes a batting posture and begins to taunt Death, the fastball in the outside corner" (see Figure 4).

To play such a complex figure, repeatedly described by Wilson as "large," Wilson and director Lloyd Richards turned to one of the great African American actors of the twentieth century, James Earl Jones. Though perhaps best known to millions as the voice of Darth Vader in *Star Wars* and of King Mufasa in *The Lion King,* Jones made his theatrical reputation as another sports hero, the black boxer Jack Johnson (in *The Great White Hope,* 1968), as King Lear in a multiracial production in New York's Central Park, and as Othello, a role he has played repeatedly over three decades. Jones's richly varied theatrical and film experience gave him Troy's assurance, while his personal background informed his sense of Troy's relationship with his family and friends (see interview following the play). Similarly, Mary Alice, who played Troy's wife, Rose, though admitting that she had been able, unlike Rose, to follow her dreams, brought her experience of attending a predominantly white school to bear on her understanding of the racism that the characters face. But as both actors make clear in the interview following the play, the racial discrimination felt by the play's characters transcends both time and place, just as Troy's dreams and failures ultimately transcend race. Rose's epitaph for Troy, "I do know he meant to do more good than he meant to do harm," bears witness to the timeless conflict in human existence between what we dream and what we accomplish.

FENCES

BY AUGUST WILSON

CHARACTERS

TROY MAXSON
JIM BONO, TROY's friend
ROSE, TROY's wife
LYONS, TROY's oldest son by previous marriage
GABRIEL, TROY's brother
CORY, TROY and ROSE's son
RAYNELL, TROY's daughter

When the sins of our fathers visit us
We do not have to play host.
We can banish them with forgiveness
As God, in His Largeness and Laws.

—August Wilson

SCENE

The setting is the yard which fronts the only entrance to the MAXSON household, an ancient two-story brick house set back off a small alley in a big-city neighborhood. The entrance to the house is gained by two or three steps leading to a wooden porch badly in need of paint.

A relatively recent addition to the house and running its full width, the porch lacks congruence. It is a sturdy porch with a flat roof. One or two chairs of dubious value sit at one end where the kitchen window opens onto the porch. An old-fashioned icebox stands silent guard at the opposite end.

The yard is a small dirt yard, partially fenced, except for the last scene, with a wooden sawhorse, a pile of lumber, and other fence-building equipment set off to the side. Opposite is a tree from which hangs a ball made of rags. A baseball bat leans against the tree. Two oil drums serve as garbage receptacles and sit near the house at right to complete the setting.

THE PLAY

Near the turn of the century, the destitute of Europe sprang on the city with tenacious claws and an honest and solid dream. The city devoured them. They swelled its belly until it burst into a thousand furnaces and sewing machines, a thousand butcher shops and bakers' ovens, a thousand churches and hospitals and funeral parlors and money-lenders. The city grew. It nourished itself and offered each man a partnership limited only by his talent, his guile, and his willingness and capacity for hard work. For the immigrants of Europe, a dream dared and won true.

The descendants of African slaves were offered no such welcome or participation. They came from places called the Carolinas and the Virginias, Georgia, Alabama, Mississippi, and Tennessee. They came strong, eager, searching. The city rejected them and they fled and settled along the riverbanks and under bridges in shallow, ramshackle houses made of sticks and tar-paper. They collected rags and wood. They sold the use of their muscles and their bodies. They cleaned houses and washed clothes, they shined shoes, and in quiet desperation and vengeful pride, they stole, and lived in pursuit of their own dream. That they could breathe free, finally, and stand to meet life with the force of dignity and whatever eloquence the heart could call upon.

By 1957, the hard-won victories of the European immigrants had solidified the industrial might of America. War had been confronted and won with new energies that used loyalty and patriotism as its fuel. Life was rich, full, and flourishing. The Milwaukee Braves won the World Series, and the hot winds of change that would make the sixties a turbulent, racing, dangerous, and provocative decade had not yet begun to blow full.

ACT 1 / SCENE 1

(It is 1957. TROY and BONO enter the yard, engaged in conversation. TROY is fifty-three years old, a large man with thick, heavy hands; it is this largeness that he strives to fill out and make an accommodation with. Together with his blackness, his largeness informs his sensibilities and the choices he has made in his life.)

(Of the two men, BONO is obviously the follower. His commitment to their friendship of thirty-odd years is rooted in his admiration of TROY's honesty, capacity for hard work, and his strength, which BONO seeks to emulate.)

(It is Friday night, payday, and the one night of the week the two men engage in a ritual of talk and drink. TROY is usually the most talkative and at times he can be crude and almost vulgar, though he is capable of rising to profound heights of expression. The men carry lunch buckets and wear or carry burlap aprons and are dressed in clothes suitable to their jobs as garbage collectors.)

BONO: Troy, you ought to stop that lying!

TROY: I ain't lying! The nigger had a watermelon this big.

(He indicates with his hands.)

Talking about . . . "What watermelon, Mr. Rand?" I liked to fell out! "What watermelon, Mr. Rand?". . . And it sitting there big as life.

BONO: What did Mr. Rand say?

TROY: Ain't said nothing. Figure if the nigger too dumb to know he carrying a watermelon, he wasn't gonna get much sense out of him. Trying to hide that great big old watermelon under his coat. Afraid to let the white man see him carry it home.

BONO: I'm like you . . . I ain't got no time for them kind of people.

TROY: Now what he look like getting mad cause he see the man from the union talking to Mr. Rand?

BONO: He come to me talking about . . . "Maxson gonna get us fired." I told him to get away from me with that. He walked away from me calling you a troublemaker. What Mr. Rand say?

TROY: Ain't said nothing. He told me to go down the Commissioner's office next Friday. They called me down there to see them.

BONO: Well, as long as you got your complaint filed, they can't fire you. That's what one of them white fellows tell me.

TROY: I ain't worried about them firing me. They gonna fire me cause I asked a question? That's all I did. I went to Mr. Rand and asked him, "Why? Why you got the white mens driving and the colored lifting?" Told him "what's the matter, don't I count? You think only white fellows got sense enough to drive a truck. That ain't no paper job! Hell, anybody can drive a truck. How come you got all whites driving and the colored lifting? He told me "take it to the union." Well, hell, that's what I done! Now they wanna come up with this pack of lies.

BONO: I told Brownie if the man come and ask him any questions . . . just tell the truth! It ain't nothing but something they done trumped up on you cause you filed a complaint on them.

TROY: Brownie don't understand nothing. All I want them to do is change the job description. Give everybody a chance to drive the truck. Brownie can't see that. He ain't got that much sense.

BONO: How you figure he be making out with that gal be up at Taylors' all the time . . . that Alberta gal?

TROY: Same as you and me. Getting just as much as we is. Which is to say nothing.

BONO: It is, huh? I figure you doing a little better than me . . . and I ain't saying what I'm doing.

TROY: Aw, nigger, look here . . . I know you. If you had got anywhere near that gal, twenty minutes later you be looking to tell somebody. And the first one you gonna tell . . . that you gonna want to brag to . . . is gonna be me.

BONO: I ain't saying that. I see where you be eyeing her.

TROY: I eye all the women. I don't miss nothing. Don't never let nobody tell you Troy Maxson don't eye the women.

BONO: You been doing more than eyeing her. You done bought her a drink or two.

TROY: Hell yeah, I bought her a drink! What that mean? I bought you one, too. What that mean cause I buy her a drink? I'm just being polite.

BONO: It's alright to buy her one drink. That's what you call being polite. But when you wanna be buying two or three . . . that's what you call eyeing her.

TROY: Look here, as long as you known me . . . you ever known me to chase after women?

BONO: Hell yeah! Long as I done known you. You forgetting I knew you when.

TROY: Naw, I'm talking about since I been married to Rose?

BONO: Oh, not since you been married to Rose. Now, that's the truth, there. I can say that.

TROY: All right then! Case closed.

BONO: I see you be walking up around Alberta's house. You supposed to be at Taylors' and you be walking up around there.

TROY: What you watching where I'm walking for? I ain't watching after you.

BONO: I seen you walking around there more than once.

TROY: Hell, you liable to see me walking anywhere! That don't mean nothing cause you see me walking around there.

BONO: Where she come from anyway? She just kinda showed up one day.

TROY: Tallahassee. You can look at her and tell she one of them Florida gals. They got some big healthy women down there. Grow them right up out the ground. Got a little bit of Indian in her. Most of them niggers down in Florida got some Indian in them.

BONO: I don't know about that Indian part. But she damn sure big and healthy. Woman wear some big stockings. Got them great big old legs and hips as wide as the Mississippi River.

TROY: Legs don't mean nothing. You don't do nothing but push them out of the way. But them hips cushion the ride!

BONO: Troy, you ain't got no sense.

TROY: It's the truth! Like you riding on Goodyears!

(ROSE *enters from the house. She is ten years younger than* TROY, *her devotion to him stems from her recognition of the possibilities of her life without him: a succession of abusive men and their babies, a life of partying and running the streets, the Church, or aloneness with its attendant pain and frustration. She recognizes* TROY*'s spirit as a fine and illuminating one and she either ignores or forgives his faults, only some of which she recognizes. Though she doesn't drink, her presence is an integral part of the Friday night rituals. She alternates between the porch and the kitchen, where supper preparations are under way.*)

ROSE: What you all out here getting into?

TROY: What you worried about what we getting into for? This is men talk, woman.

ROSE: What I care what you all talking about? Bono, you gonna stay for supper?

BONO: No, I thank you, Rose. But Lucille say she cooking up a pot of pigfeet.

TROY: Pigfeet! Hell, I'm going home with you! Might even stay the night if you got some pigfeet. You got something in there to top them pigfeet, Rose?

ROSE: I'm cooking up some chicken. I got some chicken and collard greens.

TROY: Well, go on back in the house and let me and Bono finish what we was talking about. This is men talk. I got some talk for you later. You know what kind of talk I mean. You go on and powder it up.

ROSE: Troy Maxson, don't you start that now!

TROY (*Puts his arm around her*): Aw, woman . . . come here. Look here, Bono . . . when I met this woman . . . I got out that place, say, "Hitch up my pony, saddle up my mare . . . there's a woman out there for me somewhere. I looked here. Looked there. Saw Rose and latched on to her." I latched on to her and told her—I'm gonna tell you the truth—I told her, "Baby, I don't wanna marry, I just wanna be your man." Rose told me . . . tell him what you told me, Rose.

ROSE: I told him if he wasn't the marrying kind, then move out the way so the marrying kind could find me.

TROY: That's what she told me. "Nigger, you in my way. You blocking the view! Move out the way so I can find me a husband." I thought it over two or three days. Come back—

ROSE: Ain't no two or three days nothing. You was back the same night.

TROY: Come back, told her . . . "Okay, baby . . . but I'm gonna buy me a banty rooster and put him out there in the backyard . . . and when he see a stranger come, he'll flap his wings and crow . . ." Look here, Bono, I could watch the front door by myself . . . it was that back door I was worried about.

ROSE: Troy, you ought not talk like that. Troy ain't doing nothing but telling a lie.

TROY: Only thing is . . . when we first got married . . . forget the rooster . . . we ain't had no yard!

BONO: I hear you tell it. Me and Lucille was staying down there on Logan Street. Had two rooms with the outhouse in the back. I ain't mind the outhouse none. But when that goddamn wind blow through there in the winter . . . that's what I'm talking about! To this day I wonder why in the hell I ever stayed down there for six long years. But see, I didn't know I could do no better. I thought only white folks had inside toilets and things.

ROSE: There's a lot of people don't know they can do no better than they doing now. That's just something you got to learn. A lot of folks still shop at Bella's.

TROY: Ain't nothing wrong with shopping at Bella's. She got fresh food.

ROSE: I ain't said nothing about if she got fresh food. I'm talking about what she charge. She charge ten cents more than the A&P.°

TROY: The A&P ain't never done nothing for me. I spends my money where I'm treated right. I go down to Bella, say, "I need a loaf of bread, I'll pay you Friday." She give it to me. What sense that make when I got money to go and spend it somewhere else and ignore the person who done right by me? That ain't in the Bible.

ROSE: We ain't talking about what's in the Bible. What sense it make to shop there when she overcharge?

TROY: You shop where you want to. I'll do my shopping where the people been good to me.

ROSE: Well, I don't think it's right for her to overcharge. That's all I was saying.

BONO: Look here . . . I got to get on. Lucille going be raising all kind of hell.

TROY: Where you going, nigger? We ain't finished this pint. Come here, finish this pint.

BONO: Well, hell, I am . . . if you ever turn the bottle loose.

TROY (*Hands him the bottle*): The only thing I say about the A&P is I'm glad Cory got that job down there. Help him take care of his school clothes and things. Gabe done moved out and things getting tight around here. He got that job. . . . He can start to look out for himself.

ROSE: Cory done went and got recruited by a college football team.

TROY: I told that boy about that football stuff. The white man ain't gonna let him get nowhere with that football. I told him when he first come to me with it. Now you come telling me he done went and got more tied up in it. He ought to go and get recruited in how to fix cars or something where he can make a living.

ROSE: He ain't talking about making no living playing football. It's just something the boys in school do. They gonna send a recruiter by to talk to you. He'll tell you he ain't talking about making no living playing football. It's a honor to be recruited.

TROY: It ain't gonna get him nowhere. Bono'll tell you that.

BONO: If he be like you in the sports . . . he's gonna be alright. Ain't but two men ever played baseball as good as you. That's Babe Ruth° and Josh Gibson.° Them's the only two men ever hit more home runs than you.

A&P, chain of supermarkets. **Babe Ruth,** George Herman Ruth (1895–1948), New York Yankee ballplayer, and for many years, holder of the record for most home runs hit in a major-league season. *Josh Gibson,* nicknamed the "Black Babe Ruth," Gibson (1911–47) played in the Negro Leagues and once hit 84 home runs in a single season.

TROY: What it ever get me? Ain't got a pot to piss in or a window to throw it out of.

ROSE: Times have changed since you was playing baseball, Troy. That was before the war. Times have changed a lot since then.

TROY: How in hell they done changed?

ROSE: They got lots of colored boys playing ball now. Baseball and football.

BONO: You right about that, Rose. Times have changed, Troy. You just come along too early.

TROY: There ought not never have been no time called too early! Now you take that fellow . . . what's that fellow they had playing right field for the Yankees back then? You know who I'm talking about, Bono. Used to play right field for the Yankees.

ROSE: Selkirk?°

TROY: Selkirk! That's it! Man batting .269, understand? .269. What kind of sense that make? I was hitting .432 with thirty-seven home runs! Man batting .269 and playing right field for the Yankees! I saw Josh Gibson's daughter yesterday. She walking around with raggedy shoes on her feet. Now I bet you Selkirk's daughter ain't walking around with raggedy shoes on her feet! I bet you that!

ROSE: They got a lot of colored baseball players now. Jackie Robinson° was the first. Folks had to wait for Jackie Robinson.

TROY: I done seen a hundred niggers play baseball better than Jackie Robinson. Hell, I know some teams Jackie Robinson couldn't even make! What you talking about Jackie Robinson. Jackie Robinson wasn't nobody. I'm talking about if you could play ball then they ought to have let you play. Don't care what color you were. Come telling me I come along too early. If you could play . . . then they ought to have let you play.

(TROY *takes a long drink from the bottle.*)

ROSE: You gonna drink yourself to death. You don't need to be drinking like that.

TROY: Death ain't nothing. I done seen him. Done wrassled with him. You can't tell me nothing about death. Death ain't nothing but a fastball on the outside corner. And you know what I'll do to that! Lookee here, Bono . . . am I lying? You get one of them fastballs, about waist high, over the outside corner of the plate where you can get the meat of the bat on it . . . and good god! You can kiss it goodbye. Now, am I lying?

Selkirk, George Selkirk (1934–87), replaced Babe Ruth in the Yankee outfield. *Jackie Robinson*, 1919–72, first African American to play in the major leagues, starting in 1947 for the Brooklyn Dodgers.

BONO: Naw, you telling the truth there. I seen you do it.

TROY: If I'm lying . . . that 450 feet worth of lying!

(*Pause.*)

That's all death is to me. A fastball on the outside corner.

ROSE: I don't know why you want to get on talking about death.

TROY: Ain't nothing wrong with talking about death. That's part of life. Everybody gonna die. You gonna die, I'm gonna die. Bono's gonna die. Hell, we all gonna die.

ROSE: But you ain't got to talk about it. I don't like to talk about it.

TROY: You the one brought it up. Me and Bono was talking about baseball . . . you tell me I'm gonna drink myself to death. Ain't that right, Bono? You know I don't drink this but one night out of the week. That's Friday night. I'm gonna drink just enough to where I can handle it. Then I cuts it loose. I leave it alone. So don't you worry about me drinking myself to death. 'Cause I ain't worried about Death. I done seen him. I done wrestled with him.

Look here, Bono . . . I looked up one day and Death was marching straight at me. Like Soldiers on Parade! The Army of Death was marching straight at me. The middle of July, 1941. It got real cold just like it be winter. It seem like Death himself reached out and touched me on the shoulder. He touch me just like I touch you. I got cold as ice and Death standing there grinning at me.

ROSE: Troy, why don't you hush that talk.

TROY: I say . . . What you want, Mr. Death? You be wanting me? You done brought your army to be getting me? I looked him dead in the eye. I wasn't fearing nothing. I was ready to tangle. Just like I'm ready to tangle now. The Bible say be ever vigilant. That's why I don't get but so drunk. I got to keep watch.

ROSE: Troy was right down there in Mercy Hospital. You remember he had pneumonia? Laying there with a fever talking plumb out of his head.

TROY: Death standing there staring at me . . . carrying that sickle in his hand. Finally he say, "You want bound over for another year?" See, just like that . . . "You want bound over for another year?" I told him, "Bound over hell! Let's settle this now!"

It seem like he kinda fell back when I said that, and all the cold went out of me. I reached down and grabbed that sickle and threw it just as far as I could throw it . . . and me and him commenced to wrestling.

We wrestled for three days and three nights. I can't say where I found the strength from. Every time it seemed like he was gonna get the best of me, I'd reach way down deep inside myself and find the strength to do him one better.

ROSE: Every time Troy tell that story he find different ways to tell it. Different things to make up about it.

TROY: I ain't making up nothing. I'm telling you the facts of what happened. I wrestled with Death for three days and three nights and I'm standing here to tell you about it.

(Pause.)

Alright. At the end of the third night we done weakened each other to where we can't hardly move. Death stood up, throwed on his robe . . . had him a white robe with a hood on it. He throwed on that robe and went off to look for his sickle. Say, "I'll be back." Just like that. "I'll be back." I told him, say, "Yeah, but . . . you gonna have to find me!" I wasn't no fool. I wasn't going looking for him. Death ain't nothing to play with. And I know he's gonna get me. I know I got to join his army . . . his camp followers. But as long as I keep my strength and see him coming . . . as long as I keep up my vigilance . . . he's gonna have to fight to get me. I ain't going easy.

BONO: Well, look here, since you got to keep up your vigilance . . . let me have the bottle.

TROY: Aw hell, I shouldn't have told you that part. I should have left out that part.

ROSE: Troy be talking that stuff and half the time don't even know what he be talking about.

TROY: Bono know me better than that.

BONO: That's right. I know you. I know you got some Uncle Remus in your blood. You got more stories than the devil got sinners.

TROY: Aw hell, I done seen him too! Done talked with the devil.

ROSE: Troy, don't nobody wanna be hearing all that stuff.

(LYONS enters the yard from the street. Thirty-four years old, TROY's son by a previous marriage, he sports a neatly trimmed goatee, sport coat, white shirt, tieless and buttoned at the collar. Though he fancies himself a musician, he is more caught up in the rituals and "idea" of being a musician than in the actual practice of the music. He has come to borrow money from TROY, and while he knows he will be successful, he is uncertain as to what extent his lifestyle will be held up to scrutiny and ridicule.)

LYONS: Hey, Pop.

TROY: What you come "Hey, Popping" me for?

LYONS: How you doing, Rose?

(He kisses her.)

Mr. Bono. How you doing?

BONO: Hey, Lyons . . . how you been?

TROY: He must have been doing alright. I ain't seen him around here last week.

ROSE: Troy, leave your boy alone. He come by to see you and you wanna start all that nonsense.

TROY: I ain't bothering Lyons.

(Offers him the bottle.)

Here . . . get you a drink. We got an understanding. I know why he come by to see me and he know I know.

LYONS: Come on, Pop . . . I just stopped by to say hi . . . see how you was doing.

TROY: You ain't stopped by yesterday.

ROSE: You gonna stay for supper, Lyons? I got some chicken cooking in the oven.

LYONS: No, Rose . . . thanks. I was just in the neighborhood and thought I'd stop by for a minute.

TROY: You was in the neighborhood alright, nigger. You telling the truth there. You was in the neighborhood cause it's my payday.

LYONS: Well, hell, since you mentioned it . . . let me have ten dollars.

TROY: I'll be damned! I'll die and go to hell and play blackjack with the devil before I give you ten dollars.

BONO: That's what I wanna know about . . . that devil you done seen.

LYONS: What . . . Pop done seen the devil? You too much, Pops.

TROY: Yeah, I done seen him. Talked to him too!

ROSE: You ain't seen no devil. I done told you that man ain't had nothing to do with the devil. Anything you can't understand, you want to call it the devil.

TROY: Look here, Bono . . . I went down to see Hertzberger about some furniture. Got three rooms for two-ninety-eight. That what it say on the radio. "Three rooms . . . two-ninety-eight." Even made up a little song about it. Go down there . . . man tell me I can't get no credit. I'm working every day and can't get no credit. What to do? I got an empty house with some raggedy furniture in it. Cory ain't got no bed. He's sleeping on a pile of rags on the floor. Working every day and can't get no credit. Come back here—Rose'll tell you—madder than hell. Sit down . . . try to figure what I'm gonna do. Come a knock on the door. Ain't been living here but three days. Who know I'm here? Open the door . . . devil standing there bigger than life. White fellow . . . got on good clothes and everything. Standing there with a clipboard in his hand. I ain't had to say nothing. First words come out of his mouth was . . . "I understand you need some furniture and can't get no credit." I liked to fell over. He say, "I'll give you all the credit you want, but you got to pay the interest on it." I told him, "Give me three rooms worth and charge whatever you want." Next day a truck pulled up here and two men unloaded them three rooms. Man what drove the truck give me a book. Say send ten dollars, first of every month to the address in the book and everything will be alright. Say if I miss a payment the devil was coming back and it'll be hell to pay. That was fifteen years ago. To this day . . . the first of the month I send my ten dollars, Rose'll tell you.

ROSE: Troy lying.

TROY: I ain't never seen that man since. Now you tell me who else that could have been but the devil? I ain't sold my soul or nothing like that, you understand. Naw, I wouldn't have truck with the devil about nothing like that. I got my furniture and pays my ten dollars the first of the month just like clockwork.

BONO: How long you say you been paying this ten dollars a month?

TROY: Fifteen years!

BONO: Hell, ain't you finished paying for it yet? How much the man done charged you.

TROY: Ah hell, I done paid for it. I done paid for it ten times over! The fact is I'm scared to stop paying it.

ROSE: Troy lying. We got that furniture from Mr. Glickman. He ain't paying no ten dollars a month to nobody.

TROY: Aw hell, woman. Bono know I ain't that big a fool.

LYONS: I was just getting ready to say . . . I know where there's a bridge for sale.

TROY: Look here, I'll tell you this . . . it don't matter to me if he was the devil. It don't matter if the devil give credit. Somebody has got to give it.

ROSE: It ought to matter. You going around talking about having truck with the devil . . . God's the one you gonna have to answer to. He's the one gonna be at the Judgment.

LYONS: Yeah, well, look here, Pop . . . let me have that ten dollars. I'll give it back to you. Bonnie got a job working at the hospital.

TROY: What I tell you, Bono? The only time I see this nigger is when he wants something. That's the only time I see him.

LYONS: Come on, Pop, Mr. Bono don't want to hear all that. Let me have the ten dollars. I told you Bonnie working.

TROY: What that mean to me? "Bonnie working." I don't care if she working. Go ask her for the ten dollars if she working. Talking about "Bonnie working." Why ain't you working?

LYONS: Aw, Pop, you know I can't find no decent job. Where am I gonna get a job at? You know I can't get no job.

TROY: I told you I know some people down there. I can get you on the rubbish if you want to work. I told you that the last time you came by here asking me for something.

LYONS: Naw, Pop . . . thanks. That ain't for me. I don't wanna be carrying nobody's rubbish. I don't wanna be punching nobody's time clock.

TROY: What's the matter, you too good to carry people's rubbish? Where you think that ten dollars you talking about come from? I'm just supposed to haul people's rubbish and give my money to you cause you too lazy to work. You too lazy to work and wanna know why you ain't got what I got.

ROSE: What hospital Bonnie working at? Mercy?

LYONS: She's down at Passavant working in the laundry.

TROY: I ain't got nothing as it is. I give you that ten dollars and I got to eat beans the rest of the week. Naw . . . you ain't getting no ten dollars here.

LYONS: You ain't got to be eating no beans. I don't know why you wanna say that.

TROY: I ain't got no extra money. Gabe done moved over to Miss Pearl's paying her the rent and things done got tight around here. I can't afford to be giving you every payday.

LYONS: I ain't asked you to give me nothing. I asked you to loan me ten dollars. I know you got ten dollars.

TROY: Yeah, I got it. You know why I got it? Cause I don't throw my money away out there in the streets. You living the fast life . . . wanna be a musician . . . running around in them clubs and things . . . then, you learn to take care of yourself. You ain't gonna find me going and asking nobody for nothing. I done spent too many years without.

LYONS: You and me is two different people, Pop.

TROY: I done learned my mistake and learned to do what's right by it. You still trying to get something for nothing. Life don't owe you nothing. You owe it to yourself. Ask Bono. He'll tell you I'm right.

LYONS: You got your way of dealing with the world . . . I got mine. The only thing that matters to me is the music.

TROY: Yeah, I can see that! It don't matter how you gonna eat . . . where your next dollar is coming from. You telling the truth there.

LYONS: I know I got to eat. But I got to live too. I need something that gonna help me to get out of the bed in the morning. Make me feel like I belong in the world. I don't bother nobody. I just stay with my music cause that's the only way I can find to live in the world. Otherwise there ain't no telling what I might do. Now I don't come criticizing you and how you live. I just come by to ask you for ten dollars. I don't wanna hear all that about how I live.

TROY: Boy, your mamma did a hell of a job raising you.

LYONS: You can't change me, Pop. I'm thirty-four years old. If you wanted to change me, you should have been there when I was growing up. I come by to see you . . . ask for ten dollars and you want to talk about how I was raised. You don't know nothing about how I was raised.

ROSE: Let the boy have ten dollars, Troy.

TROY (*To* LYONS): What the hell you looking at me for? I ain't got no ten dollars. You know what I do with my money. (*To* ROSE.) Give him ten dollars if you want him to have it.

ROSE: I will. Just as soon as you turn it loose.

TROY (*Handing* ROSE *the money*): There it is. Seventy-six dollars and forty-two cents. You see this, Bono? Now, I ain't gonna get but six of that back.

ROSE: You ought to stop telling that lie. Here, Lyons.

(*She hands him the money.*)

LYONS: Thanks, Rose. Look . . . I got to run . . . I'll see you later.

TROY: Wait a minute. You gonna say, "thanks, Rose" and ain't gonna look to see where she got that ten dollars from? See how they do me, Bono?

LYONS: I know she got it from you, Pop. Thanks. I'll give it back to you.

TROY: There he go telling another lie. Time I see that ten dollars . . . he'll be owing me thirty more.

LYONS: See you, Mr. Bono.

BONO: Take care, Lyons!

LYONS: Thanks, Pop. I'll see you again.

(LYONS *exits the yard.*)

TROY: I don't know why he don't go and get him a decent job and take care of that woman he got.

BONO: He'll be alright, Troy. The boy is still young.

TROY: The *boy* is thirty-four years old.

ROSE: Let's not get off into all that.

BONO: Look here . . . I got to be going. I got to be getting on. Lucille gonna be waiting.

TROY (*Puts his arm around* ROSE): See this woman, Bono? I love this woman. I love this woman so much it hurts. I love her so much . . . I done run out of ways of loving her. So I got to go back to basics. Don't you come by my house Monday morning talking about time to go to work . . . 'cause I'm still gonna be stroking!

ROSE: Troy! Stop it now!

BONO: I ain't paying him no mind, Rose. That ain't nothing but gin-talk. Go on, Troy. I'll see you Monday.

TROY: Don't you come by my house, nigger! I done told you what I'm gonna be doing.

(*The lights go down to black.*)

ACT 1 / SCENE 2

(*The lights come up on* ROSE *hanging up clothes. She hums and sings softly to herself. It is the following morning.*)

ROSE (*Sings*):

Jesus, be a fence all around me every day.
Jesus, I want you to protect me as I travel on my way.
Jesus, be a fence all around me every day.

(TROY *enters from the house.*)

ROSE (*continued*):

Jesus, I want you to protect me
As I travel on my way.

(*To* TROY) 'Morning. You ready for breakfast? I can fix it soon as I finish hanging up these clothes?

TROY: I got the coffee on. That'll be alright. I'll just drink some of that this morning.

ROSE: That 651 hit yesterday. That's the second time this month. Miss Pearl hit for a dollar . . . seem like those that need the least always get lucky. Poor folks can't get nothing.

TROY: Them numbers don't know nobody. I don't know why you fool with them. You and Lyons both.

ROSE: It's something to do.

TROY: You ain't doing nothing but throwing your money away.

ROSE: Troy, you know I don't play foolishly. I just play a nickel here and a nickel there.

TROY: That's two nickels you done thrown away.

ROSE: Now I hit sometimes . . . that makes up for it. It always comes in handy when I do hit. I don't hear you complaining then.

TROY: I ain't complaining now. I just say it's foolish. Trying to guess out of six hundred ways which way the number gonna come. If I had all the money niggers, these Negroes, throw away on numbers for one week—just one week—I'd be a rich man.

ROSE: Well, you wishing and calling it foolish ain't gonna stop folks from playing numbers. That's one thing for sure. Besides . . . some good things come from playing numbers. Look where Pope done bought him that restaurant off of numbers.

TROY: I can't stand niggers like that. Man ain't had two dimes to rub together. He walking around with his shoes all run over bumming money for cigarettes. Alright. Got lucky there and hit the numbers . . .

ROSE: Troy, I know all about it.

TROY: Had good sense, I'll say that for him. He ain't throwed his money away. I seen niggers hit the numbers and go through two thousand dollars in four days. Man bought him that restaurant down there . . . fixed it up real nice . . . and then didn't want nobody to come in it! A Negro go in there and can't get no kind of service. I seen a white fellow come in there and order a bowl of stew. Pope picked all the meat out the pot for him. Man ain't had nothing but a bowl of meat! Negro come behind him and ain't got nothing but the potatoes and carrots. Talking about what numbers do for people, you picked a wrong example. Ain't done nothing but make a worser fool out of him than he was before.

ROSE: Troy, you ought to stop worrying about what happened at work yesterday.

TROY: I ain't worried. Just told me to be down there at the Commissioner's office on Friday. Everybody think they gonna fire me. I ain't worried about them firing me. You ain't got to worry about that.

(Pause.)

Where's Cory? Cory in the house? *(Calls)* Cory?

ROSE: He gone out.

TROY: Out, huh? He gone out 'cause he know I want him to help me with this fence. I know how he is. That boy scared of work.

(GABRIEL enters. He comes halfway down the alley and, hearing TROY's voice, stops.)

TROY *(continues)*: He ain't done a lick of work in his life.

ROSE: He had to go to football practice. Coach wanted them to get in a little extra practice before the season start.

TROY: I got his practice . . . running out of here before he get his chores done.

ROSE: Troy, what is wrong with you this morning? Don't nothing set right with you. Go on back in there and go to bed . . . get up on the other side.

TROY: Why something got to be wrong with me? I ain't said nothing wrong with me.

ROSE: You got something to say about everything. First it's the numbers . . . then it's the way the man runs his restaurant . . . then you done got on Cory. What's it gonna be next? Take a look up there and see if the weather suits you . . . or is it gonna be how you gonna put up the fence with the clothes hanging in the yard.

TROY: You hit the nail on the head then.

ROSE: I know you like I know the back of my hand. Go on in there and get you some coffee . . . see if that straighten you up. 'Cause you ain't right this morning.

(TROY starts into the house and sees GABRIEL. GABRIEL starts singing. TROY's brother, he is seven years younger than TROY. Injured in World War II, he has a metal plate in his head. He carries an old trumpet tied around his waist and believes with every fiber of his being that he is the Archangel Gabriel. He carries a chipped basket with an assortment of discarded fruits and vegetables he has picked up in the strip district and which he attempts to sell.)

GABRIEL *(Singing)*:

Yes, ma'am, I got plums
You ask me how I sell them
Oh ten cents apiece
Three for a quarter
Come and buy now
'Cause I'm here today
And tomorrow I'll be gone

(GABRIEL enters.)

Hey, Rose!

ROSE: How you doing, Gabe?

GABRIEL: There's Troy . . . Hey, Troy!

TROY: Hey, Gabe.

(Exit into kitchen.)

ROSE *(To GABRIEL)*: What you got there?

GABRIEL: You know what I got, Rose. I got fruits and vegetables.

ROSE *(Looking in basket)*: Where's all these plums you talking about?

GABRIEL: I ain't got no plums today, Rose. I was just singing that. Have some tomorrow. Put me in a big order for plums. Have enough plums tomorrow for St. Peter and everybody.

(TROY reenters from kitchen, crosses to steps.)

(To ROSE) Troy's mad at me.

TROY: I ain't mad at you. What I got to be mad at you about? You ain't done nothing to me.

GABRIEL: I just moved over to Miss Pearl's to keep out from in your way. I ain't mean no harm by it.

TROY: Who said anything about that? I ain't said anything about that.

GABRIEL: You ain't mad at me, is you?

TROY: Naw . . . I ain't mad at you, Gabe. If I was mad at you I'd tell you about it.

GABRIEL: Got me two rooms. In the basement. Got my own door too. Wanna see my key?

(He holds up a key.)

That's my own key! Ain't nobody else got a key like that. That's my key! My two rooms!

TROY: Well, that's good, Gabe. You got your own key . . . that's good.

ROSE: You hungry, Gabe? I was just fixing to cook Troy his breakfast.

GABRIEL: I'll take some biscuits. You got some biscuits? Did you know when I was in heaven . . . every morning me and St. Peter would sit down by the gate and eat some big fat biscuits? Oh, yeah! We had us a good time. We'd sit there and eat us them biscuits and then St. Peter would go off to sleep and tell me to wake him up when it's time to open the gates for the judgment.

ROSE: Well, come on . . . I'll make up a batch of biscuits.

(ROSE exits into the house.)

GABRIEL: Troy . . . St. Peter got your name in the book. I seen it. It say . . . Troy Maxson. I say . . . I know him! He got the same name like what I got. That's my brother!

TROY: How many times you gonna tell me that, Gabe?

GABRIEL: Ain't got my name in the book. Don't have

to have my name. I done died and went to heaven. He got your name though. One morning St. Peter was looking at his book . . . marking it up for the judgment . . . and he let me see your name. Got it in there under M. Got Rose's name . . . I ain't seen it like I seen yours . . . but I know it's in there. He got a great big book. Got everybody's name what was ever been born. That's what he told me. But I seen your name. Seen it with my own eyes.

TROY: Go on in the house there. Rose going to fix you something to eat.

GABRIEL: Oh, I ain't hungry. I done had breakfast with Aunt Jemimah. She come by and cooked me up a whole mess of flapjacks. Remember how we used to eat them flapjacks?

TROY: Go on in the house and get you something to eat now.

GABRIEL: I got to go sell my plums. I done sold some tomatoes. Got me two quarters. Wanna see?

(He shows TROY *his quarters.)*

I'm gonna save them and buy me a new horn so St. Peter can hear me when it's time to open the gates.

(GABRIEL stops suddenly. Listens.)

Hear that? That's the hellhounds. I got to chase them out of here. Go on get out of here! Get out!

(GABRIEL exits singing.)

Better get ready for the judgment
Better get ready for the judgment
My Lord is coming down

(ROSE enters from the house.)

TROY: He gone off somewhere.
GABRIEL *(Offstage)*:

Better get ready for the judgment
Better get ready for the judgment morning
Better get ready for the judgment
My God is coming down

ROSE: He ain't eating right. Miss Pearl say she can't get him to eat nothing.

TROY: What you want me to do about it, Rose? I done did everything I can for the man. I can't make him get well. Man got half his head blown away . . . what you expect?

ROSE: Seem like something ought to be done to help him.

TROY: Man don't bother nobody. He just mixed up from that metal plate he got in his head. Ain't no sense for him to go back into the hospital.

ROSE: Least he be eating right. They can help him take care of himself.

TROY: Don't nobody wanna be locked up, Rose. What you wanna lock him up for? Man go over there and fight the war . . . messin' around with them Japs, get half his head blown off . . . and they give him a lousy three thousand dollars. And I had to swoop down on that.

ROSE: Is you fixing to go into that again?

TROY: That's the only way I got a roof over my head . . . cause of that metal plate.

ROSE: Ain't no sense you blaming yourself for nothing. Gabe wasn't in no condition to manage that money. You done what was right by him. Can't nobody say you ain't done what was right by him. Look how long you took care of him . . . till he wanted to have his own place and moved over there with Miss Pearl.

TROY: That ain't what I'm saying, woman! I'm just stating the facts. If my brother didn't have that metal plate in his head . . . I wouldn't have a pot to piss in or a window to throw it out of. And I'm fifty-three years old. Now see if you can understand that!

(TROY gets up from the porch and starts to exit the yard.)

ROSE: Where you going off to? You been running out of here every Saturday for weeks. I thought you was gonna work on this fence.

TROY: I'm gonna walk down to Taylors'. Listen to the ball game. I'll be back in a bit. I'll work on it when I get back.

(He exits the yard. The lights go to black.)

ACT 1 / SCENE 3

(The lights come up on the yard. It is four hours later. ROSE *is taking down the clothes from the line.* CORY *enters carrying his football equipment.)*

ROSE: Your daddy like to had a fit with you running out of here this morning without doing your chores.

CORY: I told you I had to go to practice.

ROSE: He say you were supposed to help him with this fence.

CORY: He been saying that the last four or five Saturdays, and then he don't never do nothing but go down to Taylors'. Did you tell him about the recruiter?

ROSE: Yeah, I told him.

CORY: What he say?

ROSE: He ain't said nothing too much. You get in there and get started on your chores before he gets back. Go on and scrub down them steps before he gets back here hollering and carrying on.

CORY: I'm hungry. What you got to eat, Mama?

ROSE: Go on and get started on your chores. I got some meat loaf in there. Go on and make you a sandwich . . . and don't leave no mess in there.

(CORY *exits into the house.* ROSE *continues to take down the clothes.* TROY *enters the yard and sneaks up and grabs her from behind.*)

Troy! Go on, now. You liked to scared me to death. What was the score of the game? Lucille had me on the phone and I couldn't keep up with it.

TROY: What I care about the game? Come here, woman.

(*He tries to kiss her.*)

ROSE: I thought you went down Taylors' to listen to the game. Go on, Troy! You supposed to be putting up this fence.

TROY (*Attempting to kiss her again*): I'll put it up when I finish with what is at hand.

ROSE: Go on, Troy. I ain't studying you.

TROY (*Chasing after her*): I'm studying you . . . fixing to do my homework!

ROSE: Troy, you better leave me alone.

TROY: Where's Cory? That boy brought his butt home yet?

ROSE: He's in the house doing his chores.

TROY (*Calling*): Cory! Get your butt out here, boy!

(ROSE *exits into the house with the laundry.* TROY *goes over to the pile of wood, picks up a board, and starts sawing.* CORY *enters from the house.*)

TROY: You just now coming in here from leaving this morning?

CORY: Yeah, I had to go to football practice.

TROY: Yeah, what?

CORY: Yessir.

TROY: I ain't but two seconds off you noway. The garbage sitting in there overflowing . . . you ain't done none of your chores . . . and you come in here talking about "Yeah."

CORY: I was just getting ready to do my chores now, Pop . . .

TROY: Your first chore is to help me with this fence on Saturday. Everything else come after that. Now get that saw and cut them boards.

(CORY *takes the saw and begins cutting the boards.* TROY *continues working. There is a long pause.*)

CORY: Hey, Pop . . . why don't you buy a TV?

TROY: What I want with a TV? What I want one of them for?

CORY: Everybody got one. Earl, Ba Bra . . . Jesse!

TROY: I ain't asked you who had one. I say what I want with one?

CORY: So you can watch it. They got lots of things on TV. Baseball games and everything. We could watch the World Series.

TROY: Yeah . . . and how much this TV cost?

CORY: I don't know. They got them on sale for around two hundred dollars.

TROY: Two hundred dollars, huh?

CORY: That ain't that much, Pop.

TROY: Naw, it's just two hundred dollars. See that roof you got over your head at night? Let me tell you something about that roof. It's been over ten years since that roof was last tarred. See now . . . the snow come this winter and sit up there on that roof like it is . . . and it's gonna seep inside. It's just gonna be a little bit . . . ain't gonna hardly notice it. Then the next thing you know, it's gonna be leaking all over the house. Then the wood rot from all that water and you gonna need a whole new roof. Now, how much you think it cost to get that roof tarred?

CORY: I don't know.

TROY: Two hundred and sixty-four dollars . . . cash money. While you thinking about a TV, I got to be thinking about the roof . . . and whatever else go wrong around here. Now if you had two hundred dollars, what would you do . . . fix the roof or buy a TV?

CORY: I'd buy a TV. Then when the roof started to leak . . . when it needed fixing . . . I'd fix it.

TROY: Where you gonna get the money from? You done spent it for a TV. You gonna sit up and watch the water run all over your brand new TV.

CORY: Aw, Pop. You got money. I know you do.

TROY: Where I got it at, huh?

CORY: You got it in the bank.

TROY: You wanna see my bankbook? You wanna see that seventy-three dollars and twenty-two cents I got sitting up in there.

CORY: You ain't got to pay for it all at one time. You can put a down payment on it and carry it on home with you.

TROY: Not me. I ain't gonna owe nobody nothing if I can help it. Miss a payment and they come and snatch it right out your house. Then what you got? Now, soon as I get two hundred dollars clear, then I'll buy a TV. Right now, as soon as I get two hundred and sixty-four dollars, I'm gonna have this roof tarred.

CORY: Aw . . . Pop!

TROY: You go on and get you two hundred dollars and buy one if ya want it. I got better things to do with my money.

CORY: I can't get no two hundred dollars. I ain't never seen two hundred dollars.

TROY: I'll tell you what . . . you get you a hundred dollars and I'll put the other hundred with it.

CORY: Alright, I'm gonna show you.

TROY: You gonna show me how you can cut them boards right now.

(CORY *begins to cut the boards. There is a long pause.*)

CORY: The Pirates won today. That makes five in a row.

TROY: I ain't thinking about the Pirates. Got an all-white team. Got that boy . . . that Puerto Rican boy . . . Clemente.° Don't even half-play him. That boy could be something if they give him a chance. Play him one day and sit him on the bench the next.

CORY: He gets a lot of chances to play.

TROY: I'm talking about playing regular. Playing every day so you can get your timing. That's what I'm talking about.

CORY: They got some white guys on the team that don't play every day. You can't play everybody at the same time.

TROY: If they got a white fellow sitting on the bench . . . you can bet your last dollar he can't play! The colored guy got to be twice as good before he get on the team. That's why I don't want you to get all tied up in them sports. Man on the team and what it get him? They got colored on the team and don't use them. Same as not having them. All them teams the same.

CORY: The Braves got Hank Aaron° and Wes Covington.° Hank Aaron hit two home runs today. That makes forty-three.

TROY: Hank Aaron ain't nobody. That's what you supposed to do. That's how you supposed to play the game. Ain't nothing to it. It's just a matter of timing . . . getting the right follow-through. Hell, I can hit forty-three home runs right now!

CORY: Not off no major-league pitching, you couldn't.

TROY: We had better pitching in the Negro leagues. I hit seven home runs off of Satchel Paige.° You can't get no better than that!

CORY: Sandy Koufax.° He's leading the league in strikeouts.

TROY: I ain't thinking of no Sandy Koufax.

Clemente, Roberto Clemente (1934–72), first Hispanic player selected for the Baseball Hall of Fame, right fielder for the Pittsburgh Pirates (1955–71). ***Hank Aaron,*** 1934–, African American player (Milwaukee and Atlanta), broke Babe Ruth's career home run record. ***Wes Covington,*** 1932–, African American player, played for the Milwaukee Braves in the 1957 World Series. ***Satchel Paige,*** famed African American pitcher (1906–82), played primarily in the Negro Leagues, but became a major league player at the age of 42 for the Cleveland Indians. ***Sandy Koufax,*** 1935–, pitcher for the Brooklyn and Los Angeles Dodgers.

CORY: You got Warren Spahn° and Lew Burdette.° I bet you couldn't hit no home runs off of Warren Spahn.

TROY: I'm through with it now. You go on and cut them boards.

(*Pause.*)

Your mama tell me you done got recruited by a college football team? Is that right?

CORY: Yeah. Coach Zellman say the recruiter gonna be coming by to talk to you. Get you to sign the permission papers.

TROY: I thought you supposed to be working down there at the A&P. Ain't you suppose to be working down there after school?

CORY: Mr. Stawicki say he gonna hold my job for me until after the football season. Say starting next week I can work weekends.

TROY: I thought we had an understanding about this football stuff? You suppose to keep up with your chores and hold that job down at the A&P. Ain't been around here all day on a Saturday. Ain't none of your chores done . . . and now you telling me you done quit your job.

CORY: I'm gonna be working weekends.

TROY: You damn right you are! And ain't no need for nobody coming around here to talk to me about signing nothing.

CORY: Hey, Pop . . . you can't do that. He's coming all the way from North Carolina.

TROY: I don't care where he coming from. The white man ain't gonna let you get nowhere with that football noway. You go on and get your book-learning so you can work yourself up in that A&P or learn how to fix cars or build houses or something, get you a trade. That way you have something can't nobody take away from you. You go on and learn how to put your hands to some good use. Besides hauling people's garbage.

CORY: I get good grades, Pop. That's why the recruiter wants to talk with you. You got to keep up your grades to get recruited. This way I'll be going to college. I'll get a chance . . .

TROY: First you gonna get your butt down there to the A&P and get your job back.

CORY: Mr. Stawicki done already hired somebody else 'cause I told him I was playing football.

TROY: You a bigger fool than I thought . . . to let somebody take away your job so you can play

---

Warren Spahn, 1921–, pitcher, Milwaukee Braves. ***Lew Burdette,*** 1926–, pitcher for six major league teams, including Milwaukee.

some football. Where you gonna get your money to take out your girlfriend and whatnot? What kind of foolishness is that to let somebody take away your job?

CORY: I'm still gonna be working weekends.

TROY: Naw . . . naw. You getting your butt out of here and finding you another job.

CORY: Come on, Pop! I got to practice. I can't work after school and play football too. The team needs me. That's what Coach Zellman say . . .

TROY: I don't care what nobody else say. I'm the boss . . . you understand? I'm the boss around here. I do the only saying what counts.

CORY: Come on, Pop!

TROY: I asked you . . . did you understand?

CORY: Yeah . . .

TROY: What?!

CORY: Yessir.

TROY: You go on down there to that A&P and see if you can get your job back. If you can't do both . . . then you quit the football team. You've got to take the crookeds with the straights.

CORY: Yessir.

(Pause.)

Can I ask you a question?

TROY: What the hell you wanna ask me? Mr. Stawicki the one you got the questions for.

CORY: How come you ain't never liked me?

TROY: Liked you? Who the hell say I got to like you? What law is there say I got to like you? Wanna stand up in my face and ask a damn fool-ass question like that. Talking about liking somebody. Come here, boy, when I talk to you.

(CORY comes over to where TROY is working. He stands slouched over and TROY shoves him on his shoulder.)

Straighten up, goddammit! I asked you a question . . . what law is there say I got to like you?

CORY: None.

TROY: Well, alright then! Don't you eat every day?

(Pause.)

Answer me when I talk to you! Don't you eat every day?

CORY: Yeah.

TROY: Nigger, as long as you in my house, you put that sir on the end of it when you talk to me!

CORY: Yes . . . sir.

TROY: You eat every day.

CORY: Yessir!

TROY: Got a roof over your head.

CORY: Yessir!

TROY: Got clothes on your back.

CORY: Yessir.

TROY: Why you think that is?

CORY: Cause of you.

TROY: Ah, hell I know it's 'cause of me . . . but why do you think that is?

CORY *(Hesitant)*: Cause you like me.

TROY: Like you? I go out of here every morning . . . bust my butt . . . putting up with them crackers every day . . . cause I like you? You about the biggest fool I ever saw.

(Pause.)

It's my job. It's my responsibility! You understand that? A man got to take care of his family. You live in my house . . . sleep you behind on my bedclothes . . . fill you belly up with my food . . . cause you my son. You my flesh and blood. Not 'cause I like you! Cause it's my duty to take care of you. I owe a responsibility to you! Let's get this straight right here . . . before it go along any further . . . I ain't got to like you. Mr. Rand don't give me my money come payday cause he likes me. He gives me cause he owe me. I done give you everything I had to give you. I gave you your life! Me and your mama worked that out between us. And liking your black ass wasn't part of the bargain. Don't you try and go through life worrying about if somebody like you or not. You best be making sure they doing right by you. You understand what I'm saying, boy?

CORY: Yessir.

TROY: Then get the hell out of my face, and get on down to that A&P.

(ROSE has been standing behind the screen door for much of the scene. She enters as CORY exits.)

ROSE: Why don't you let the boy go ahead and play football, Troy? Ain't no harm in that. He's just trying to be like you with the sports.

TROY: I don't want him to be like me! I want him to move as far away from my life as he can get. You the only decent thing that ever happened to me. I wish him that. But I don't wish him a thing else from my life. I decided seventeen years ago that boy wasn't getting involved in no sports. Not after what they did to me in the sports.

ROSE: Troy, why don't you admit you was too old to play in the major leagues? For once . . . why don't you admit that?

TROY: What do you mean too old? Don't come telling me I was too old. I just wasn't the right color. Hell, I'm fifty-three years old and can do better than Selkirk's .269 right now!

ROSE: How's was you gonna play ball when you were over forty? Sometimes I can't get no sense out of you.

TROY: I got good sense, woman. I got sense enough not to let my boy get hurt over playing no sports.

You been mothering that boy too much. Worried about if people like him.

ROSE: Everything that boy do . . . he do for you. He wants you to say "Good job, son." That's all.

TROY: Rose, I ain't got time for that. He's alive. He's healthy. He's got to make his own way. I made mine. Ain't nobody gonna hold his hand when he get out there in that world.

ROSE: Times have changed from when you was young, Troy. People change. The world's changing around you and you can't even see it.

TROY (Slow, methodical): Woman . . . I do the best I can do. I come in here every Friday. I carry a sack of potatoes and a bucket of lard. You all line up at the door with your hands out. I give you the lint from my pockets. I give you my sweat and my blood. I ain't got no tears. I done spent them. We go upstairs in that room at night . . . and I fall down on you and try to blast a hole into forever. I get up Monday morning . . . find my lunch on the table. I go out. Make my way. Find my strength to carry me through to the next Friday.

(Pause.)

That's all I got, Rose. That's all I got to give. I can't give nothing else.

(TROY exits into the house. The lights go down to black.)

ACT 1 / SCENE 4

(It is Friday. Two weeks later. CORY starts out of the house with his football equipment. The phone rings.)

CORY (Calling): I got it!

(He answers the phone and stands in the screen door talking.)

Hello? Hey, Jesse. Naw . . . I was just getting ready to leave now.

ROSE (Calling): Cory!

CORY: I told you, man, them spikes is all tore up. You can use them if you want, but they ain't no good. Earl got some spikes.

ROSE (Calling): Cory!

CORY (Calling to ROSE): Mam? I'm talking to Jesse. (Into phone) When she say that? (Pause.) Aw, you lying, man. I'm gonna tell her you said that.

ROSE (Calling): Cory, don't you go nowhere!

CORY: I got to go to the game, Ma! (Into the phone) Yeah, hey, look, I'll talk to you later. Yeah, I'll meet you over Earl's house. Later. Bye, Ma.

(CORY exits the house and starts out the yard.)

ROSE: Cory, where you going off to? You got that stuff all pulled out and thrown all over your room.

CORY (In the yard): I was looking for my spikes. Jesse wanted to borrow my spikes.

ROSE: Get up there and get that cleaned up before your daddy get back in here.

CORY: I got to go to the game! I'll clean it up when I get back.

(CORY exits.)

ROSE: That's all he need to do is see that room all messed up.

(ROSE exits into the house. TROY and BONO enter the yard. TROY is dressed in clothes other than his work clothes.)

BONO: He told him the same thing he told you. Take it to the union.

TROY: Brownie ain't got that much sense. Man wasn't thinking about nothing. He wait until I confront them on it . . . then he wanna come crying seniority. (Calls) Hey, Rose!

BONO: I wish I could have seen Mr. Rand's face when he told you.

TROY: He couldn't get it out of his mouth! Liked to bit his tongue! When they called me down there to the Commissioner's office . . . he thought they was gonna fire me. Like everybody else.

BONO: I didn't think they was gonna fire you. I thought they was gonna put you on the warning paper.

TROY: Hey, Rose! (To BONO) Yeah, Mr. Rand like to bit his tongue.

(TROY breaks the seal on the bottle, takes a drink, and hands it to BONO.)

BONO: I see you run right down to Taylors' and told that Alberta gal.

TROY (Calling): Hey, Rose! (To BONO) I told everybody. Hey, Rose! I went down there to cash my check.

ROSE (Entering from the house): Hush all that hollering, man! I know you out here. What they say down there at the Commissioner's office?

TROY: You supposed to come when I call you, woman. Bono'll tell you that. (To BONO) Don't Lucille come when you call her?

ROSE: Man, hush your mouth. I ain't no dog . . . talk about "come when you call me."

TROY (Puts his arm around ROSE): You hear this, Bono? I had me an old dog used to get uppity like that. You say, "C'mere, Blue!". . . and he just lay there and look at you. End up getting a stick and chasing him away trying to make him come.

ROSE: I ain't studying you and your dog. I remember you used to sing that old song.

TROY (He sings): Hear it ring! Hear it ring! I had a dog his name was Blue.

ROSE: Don't nobody wanna hear you sing that old song.

TROY (Sings): You know Blue was mighty true.

ROSE: Used to have Cory running around here singing that song.

BONO: Hell, I remember that song myself.

TROY *(Sings)*:

> *You know Blue was a good old dog.*
> *Blue treed a possum in a hollow log.*

That was my daddy's song. My daddy made up that song.

ROSE: I don't care who made it up. Don't nobody wanna hear you sing it.

TROY *(Makes a song like calling a dog)*: Come here, woman.

ROSE: You come in here carrying on, I reckon they ain't fired you. What they say down there at the Commissioner's office?

TROY: Look here, Rose . . . Mr. Rand called me into his office today when I got back from talking to them people down there . . . it come from up top . . . he called me in and told me they was making me a driver.

ROSE: Troy, you kidding!

TROY: No I ain't. Ask Bono.

ROSE: Well, that's great, Troy. Now you don't have to hassle them people no more.

(LYONS enters from the street.)

TROY: Aw hell, I wasn't looking to see you today. I thought you was in jail. Got it all over the front page of the *Courier* about them raiding Sefus' place . . . where you be hanging out with all them thugs.

LYONS: Hey, Pop . . . that ain't got nothing to do with me. I don't go down there gambling. I go down there to sit in with the band. I ain't got nothing to do with the gambling part. They got some good music down there.

TROY: They got some rogues . . . is what they got.

LYONS: How you been, Mr. Bono? Hi, Rose.

BONO: I see where you playing down at the Crawford Grill tonight.

ROSE: How come you ain't brought Bonnie like I told you. You should have brought Bonnie with you, she ain't been over in a month of Sundays.

LYONS: I was just in the neighborhood . . . thought I'd stop by.

TROY: Here he come . . .

BONO: Your daddy got a promotion on the rubbish. He's gonna be the first colored driver. Ain't got to do nothing but sit up there and read the paper like them white fellows.

LYONS: Hey, Pop . . . if you knew how to read you'd be alright.

BONO: Naw . . . naw . . . you mean if the nigger knew how to *drive* he'd be alright. Been fighting with them people about driving and ain't even got a license. Mr. Rand know you ain't got no driver's license?

TROY: Driving ain't nothing. All you do is point the truck where you want it to go. Driving ain't nothing.

BONO: Do Mr. Rand know you ain't got no driver's license? That's what I'm talking about. I ain't asked if driving was easy. I asked if Mr. Rand know you ain't got no driver's license.

TROY: He ain't got to know. The man ain't got to know my business. Time he find out, I have two or three driver's licenses.

LYONS *(Going into his pocket)*: Say, look here, Pop . . .

TROY: I knew it was coming. Didn't I tell you, Bono? I know what kind of "Look here, Pop" that was. The nigger fixing to ask me for some money. It's Friday night. It's my payday. All them rogues down there on the avenue . . . the ones that ain't in jail . . . and Lyons is hopping in his shoes to get down there with them.

LYONS: See, Pop . . . if you give somebody else a chance to talk sometime, you'd see that I was fixing to pay you back your ten dollars like I told you. Here . . . I told you I'd pay you when Bonnie got paid.

TROY: Naw . . . you go ahead and keep that ten dollars. Put it in the bank. The next time you feel like you wanna come by here and ask me for something . . . you go on down there and get that.

LYONS: Here's your ten dollars, Pop. I told you I don't want you to give me nothing. I just wanted to borrow ten dollars.

TROY: Naw . . . you go on and keep that for the next time you want to ask me.

LYONS: Come on, Pop . . . here go your ten dollars.

ROSE: Why don't you go on and let the boy pay you back, Troy?

LYONS: Here you go, Rose. If you don't take it I'm gonna have to hear about it for the next six months.

(He hands her the money.)

ROSE: You can hand yours over here too, Troy.

TROY: You see this, Bono. You see how they do me.

BONO: Yeah, Lucille do me the same way.

(GABRIEL is heard singing offstage. He enters.)

GABRIEL: Better get ready for the Judgment! Better get ready for . . . Hey! . . . Hey! . . . There's Troy's boy!

LYONS: How are you doing, Uncle Gabe?

GABRIEL: Lyons . . . The King of the Jungle! Rose . . . hey, Rose. Got a flower for you.

(He takes a rose from his pocket.)

Picked it myself. That's the same rose like you is!

ROSE: That's right nice of you, Gabe.

LYONS: What you been doing, Uncle Gabe?

GABRIEL: Oh, I been chasing hellhounds and waiting on the time to tell St. Peter to open the gates.

LYONS: You been chasing hellhounds, huh? Well . . . you doing the right thing, Uncle Gabe. Somebody got to chase them.

GABRIEL: Oh, yeah . . . I know it. The devil's strong. The devil ain't no pushover. Hellhounds snipping at everybody's heels. But I got my trumpet waiting on the judgment time.

LYONS: Waiting on the Battle of Armageddon, huh?

GABRIEL: Ain't gonna be too much of a battle when God get to waving that Judgment sword. But the people's gonna have a hell of a time trying to get into heaven if them gates ain't open.

LYONS (*Putting his arm around* GABRIEL): You hear this, Pop. Uncle Gabe, you alright!

GABRIEL (*Laughing with* LYONS): Lyons! King of the Jungle.

ROSE: You gonna stay for supper, Gabe. Want me to fix you a plate?

GABRIEL: I'll take a sandwich, Rose. Don't want no plate. Just wanna eat with my hands. I'll take a sandwich.

ROSE: How about you, Lyons? You staying? Got some short ribs cooking.

LYONS: Naw, I won't eat nothing till after we finished playing.

(*Pause.*)

You ought to come down and listen to me play, Pop.

TROY: I don't like that Chinese music. All that noise.

ROSE: Go on in the house and wash up, Gabe . . . I'll fix you a sandwich.

GABRIEL (*To* LYONS, *as he exits*): Troy's mad at me.

LYONS: What you mad at Uncle Gabe for, Pop.

ROSE: He thinks Troy's mad at him cause he moved over to Miss Pearl's.

TROY: I ain't mad at the man. He can live where he want to live at.

LYONS: What he move over there for? Miss Pearl don't like nobody.

ROSE: She don't mind him none. She treats him real nice. She just don't allow all that singing.

TROY: She don't mind that rent he be paying . . . that's what she don't mind.

ROSE: Troy, I ain't going through that with you no more. He's over there cause he want to have his own place. He can come and go as he please.

TROY: Hell, he could come and go as he please here. I wasn't stopping him. I ain't put no rules on him.

ROSE: It ain't the same thing, Troy. And you know it.

(GABRIEL *comes to the door.*)

Now, that's the last I wanna hear about that. I don't wanna hear nothing else about Gabe and Miss Pearl. And next week . . .

GABRIEL: I'm ready for my sandwich, Rose.

ROSE: And next week . . . when that recruiter come from that school . . . I want you to sign that paper and go on and let Cory play football. Then that'll be the last I have to hear about that.

TROY (*To* ROSE *as she exits into the house*): I ain't thinking about Cory nothing.

LYONS: What . . . Cory got recruited? What school he going to?

TROY: That boy walking around here smelling his piss . . . thinking he's grown. Thinking he's gonna do what he want, irrespective of what I say. Look here, Bono . . . I left the Commissioner's office and went down to the A&P . . . that boy ain't working down there. He lying to me. Telling me he got his job back . . . telling me he working weekends . . . telling me he working after school . . . Mr. Stawicki tell me he ain't working down there at all!

LYONS: Cory just growing up. He's just busting at the seams trying to fill out your shoes.

TROY: I don't care what he's doing. When he get to the point where he wanna disobey me . . . then it's time for him to move on. Bono'll tell you that. I bet he ain't never disobeyed his daddy without paying the consequences.

BONO: I ain't never had a chance. My daddy came on through . . . but I ain't never knew him to see him . . . or what he had on his mind or where he went. Just moving on through. Searching out the New Land. That's what the old folks used to call it. See a fellow moving around from place to place . . . woman to woman . . . called it searching out the New Land. I can't say if he ever found it. I come along, didn't want no kids. Didn't know if I was gonna be in one place long enough to fix on them right as their daddy. I figured I was going searching too. As it turned out I been hooked up with Lucille near about as long as your daddy been with Rose. Going on sixteen years.

TROY: Sometimes I wish I hadn't known my daddy. He ain't cared nothing about no kids. A kid to him wasn't nothing. All he wanted was for you to learn how to walk so he could start you to working. When it come time for eating . . . he ate first. If there was anything left over, that's what you got. Man would sit down and eat two chickens and give you the wing.

LYONS: You ought to stop that, Pop. Everybody feed their kids. No matter how hard times is . . . everybody care about their kids. Make sure they have something to eat.

TROY: The only thing my daddy cared about was getting them bales of cotton in to Mr. Lubin. That's the only thing that mattered to him. Sometimes I used to wonder why he was living. Wonder why the devil hadn't come and got him. "Get them bales of cotton in to Mr. Lubin" and find out he owe him money . . .

LYONS: He should have just went on and left when he saw he couldn't get nowhere. That's what I would have done.

TROY: How he gonna leave with eleven kids? And where he gonna go? He ain't knew how to do nothing but farm. No, he was trapped and I think he knew it. But I'll say this for him . . . he felt a responsibility toward us. Maybe he ain't treated us the way I felt he should have . . . but without that responsibility he could have walked off and left us . . . made his own way.

BONO: A lot of them did. Back in those days what you talking about . . . they walk out their front door and just take on down one road or another and keep on walking.

LYONS: There you go! That's what I'm talking about.

BONO: Just keep on walking till you come to something else. Ain't you never heard of nobody having the walking blues? Well, that's what you call it when you just take off like that.

TROY: My daddy ain't had them walking blues! What you talking about? He stayed right there with his family. But he was just as evil as he could be. My mama couldn't stand him. Couldn't stand that evilness. She run off when I was about eight. She sneaked off one night after he had gone to sleep. Told me she was coming back for me. I ain't never seen her no more. All his women run off and left him. He wasn't good for nobody.

When my turn come to head out, I was fourteen and got to sniffing around Joe Canewell's daughter. Had us an old mule we called Greyboy. My daddy sent me out to do some plowing and I tied up Greyboy and went to fooling around with Joe Canewell's daughter. We done found us a nice little spot, got real cozy with each other. She about thirteen and we done figured we was grown anyway . . . so we down there enjoying ourselves . . . ain't thinking about nothing. We didn't know Greyboy had got loose and wandered back to the house and my daddy was looking for me. We down there by the creek enjoying ourselves when my daddy come up on us. Surprised us. He had them leather straps off the mule and commenced to whupping me like there was no tomorrow. I jumped up, mad and embarrassed. I was scared of my daddy. When he commenced to whupping on me . . . quite naturally I run to get out of the way.

(Pause.)

Now I thought he was mad cause I ain't done my work. But I see where he was chasing me off so he could have the gal for himself. When I see what the matter of it was, I lost all fear of my daddy. Right there is where I become a man . . . at fourteen years of age.

(Pause.)

Now it was my turn to run him off. I picked up them same reins that he had used on me. I picked up them reins and commenced to whupping on him. The gal jumped up and run off . . . and when my daddy turned to face me, I could see why the devil had never come to get him . . . cause he was the devil himself. I don't know what happened. When I woke up, I was laying right there by the creek, and Blue . . . this old dog we had . . . was licking my face. I thought I was blind. I couldn't see nothing. Both my eyes were swollen shut. I layed there and cried. I didn't know what I was gonna do. The only thing I knew was the time had come for me to leave my daddy's house. And right there the world suddenly got big. And it was a long time before I could cut it down to where I could handle it.

Part of that cutting down was when I got to the place where I could feel him kicking in my blood and knew that the only thing that separated us was the matter of a few years.

(GABRIEL enters from the house with a sandwich.)

LYONS: What you got there, Uncle Gabe?

GABRIEL: Got me a ham sandwich. Rose gave me a ham sandwich.

TROY: I don't know what happened to him. I done lost touch with everybody except Gabriel. But I hope he's dead. I hope he found some peace.

LYONS: That's a heavy story, Pop. I didn't know you left home when you was fourteen.

TROY: And didn't know nothing. The only part of the world I knew was the forty-two acres of Mr. Lubin's land. That's all I knew about life.

LYONS: Fourteen's kinda young to be out on your own. *(Phone rings.)* I don't even think I was ready to be out on my own at fourteen. I don't know what I would have done.

TROY: I got up from the creek and walked on down to Mobile. I was through with farming. Figured I could do better in the city. So I walked the two hundred miles to Mobile.

LYONS: Wait a minute . . . you ain't walked no two hundred miles, Pop. Ain't nobody gonna walk no two hundred miles. You talking about some walking there.

BONO: That's the only way you got anywhere back in them days.

LYONS: Shhh. Damn if I wouldn't have hitched a ride with somebody!

TROY: Who you gonna hitch it with? They ain't had no

cars and things like they got now. We talking about 1918.

ROSE (*Entering*): What you all out here getting into?

TROY (*To* ROSE): I'm telling Lyons how good he got it. He don't know nothing about this I'm talking.

ROSE: Lyons, that was Bonnie on the phone. She say you supposed to pick her up.

LYONS: Yeah, okay, Rose.

TROY: I walked on down to Mobile and hitched up with some of them fellows that was heading this way. Got up here and found out . . . not only couldn't you get a job . . . you couldn't find no place to live. I thought I was in freedom. Shhh. Colored folks living down there on the riverbanks in whatever kind of shelter they could find for themselves. Right down there under the Brady Street Bridge. Living in shacks made of sticks and tarpaper. Messed around there and went from bad to worse. Started stealing. First it was food. Then I figured, hell, if I steal money I can buy me some food. Buy me some shoes too! One thing led to another. Met your mama. I was young and anxious to be a man. Met your mama and had you. What I do that for? Now I got to worry about feeding you and her. Got to steal three times as much. Went out one day looking for somebody to rob . . . that's what I was, a robber. I'll tell you the truth. I'm ashamed of it today. But it's the truth. Went to rob this fellow . . . pulled out my knife . . . and he pulled out a gun. Shot me in the chest. It felt just like somebody had taken a hot branding iron and laid it on me. When he shot me I jumped at him with my knife. They told me I killed him and they put me in the penitentiary and locked me up for fifteen years. That's where I met Bono. That's where I learned how to play baseball. Got out that place and your mama had taken you and went on to make life without me. Fifteen years was a long time for her to wait. But that fifteen years cured me of that robbing stuff. Rose'll tell you. She asked me when I met her if I had gotten all that foolishness out of my system. And I told her, "Baby, it's you and baseball all what count with me." You hear me, Bono? I meant it too. She say "Which one comes first?" I told her, "Baby, ain't no doubt it's baseball . . . but you stick and get old with me and we'll both outlive this baseball." Am I right, Rose? And it's true.

ROSE: Man, hush your mouth. You ain't said no such thing. Talking about, "Baby, you know you'll always be number one with me." That's what you was talking.

TROY: You hear that, Bono. That's why I love her.

BONO: Rose'll keep you straight. You get off the track, she'll straighten you up.

ROSE: Lyons, you better get on up and get Bonnie. She waiting on you.

LYONS (*Gets up to go*): Hey, Pop, why don't you come on down to the Grill and hear me play?

TROY: I ain't going down there. I'm too old to be sitting around in them clubs.

BONO: You got to be good to play down at the Grill.

LYONS: Come on, Pop . . .

TROY: I got to get up in the morning.

LYONS: You ain't got to stay long.

TROY: Naw, I'm gonna get my supper and go on to bed.

LYONS: Well, I got to go. I'll see you again.

TROY: Don't you come around my house on my payday.

ROSE: Pick up the phone and let somebody know you coming. And bring Bonnie with you. You know I'm always glad to see her.

LYONS: Yeah, I'll do that, Rose. You take care now. See you, Pop. See you, Mr. Bono. See you, Uncle Gabe.

GABRIEL: Lyons! King of the Jungle!

(LYONS *exits.*)

TROY: Is supper ready, woman? Me and you got some business to take care of. I'm gonna tear it up too.

ROSE: Troy, I done told you now!

TROY (*Puts his arm around* BONO): Aw hell, woman . . . this is Bono. Bono like family. I done known this nigger since . . . how long I done know you?

BONO: It's been a long time.

TROY: I done known this nigger since Skippy was a pup. Me and him done been through some times.

BONO: You sure right about that.

TROY: Hell, I done know him longer than I known you. And we still standing shoulder to shoulder. Hey, look here, Bono . . . a man can't ask for no more than that. (*Drinks to him*) I love you, nigger.

BONO: Hell, I love you too . . . but I got to get home see my woman. You got yours in hand. I got to go get mine.

(BONO *starts to exit as* CORY *enters the yard, dressed in his football uniform. He gives* TROY *a hard, uncompromising look.*)

CORY: What you do that for, Pop?

(*He throws his helmet down in the direction of* TROY.)

ROSE: What's the matter? Cory . . . what's the matter?

CORY: Papa done went up to the school and told Coach Zellman I can't play football no more. Wouldn't even let me play the game. Told him to tell the recruiter not to come.

ROSE: Troy . . .

TROY: What you Troying me for. Yeah, I did it. And the boy know why I did it.

CORY: Why you wanna do that to me? That was the one chance I had.

ROSE: Ain't nothing wrong with Cory playing football, Troy.

TROY: The boy lied to me. I told the nigger if he wanna play football . . . to keep up his chores and hold down that job at the A&P. That was the conditions. Stopped down there to see Mr. Stawicki . . .

CORY: I can't work after school during the football season, Pop! I tried to tell you that Mr. Stawicki's holding my job for me. You don't never want to listen to nobody. And then you wanna go and do this to me!

TROY: I ain't done nothing to you. You done it to yourself.

CORY: Just cause you didn't have a chance! You just scared I'm gonna be better than you, that's all.

TROY: Come here.

ROSE: Troy . . .

(CORY *reluctantly crosses over to* TROY.)

TROY: Alright! See. You done made a mistake.

CORY: I didn't even do nothing!

TROY: I'm gonna tell you what your mistake was. See . . . you swung at the ball and didn't hit it. That's strike one. See, you in the batter's box now. You swung and you missed. That's strike one. Don't you strike out!

(*Lights fade to black.*)

ACT 2 / SCENE 1

(*The following morning.* CORY *is at the tree hitting the ball with the bat. He tries to mimic* TROY, *but his swing is awkward, less sure.* ROSE *enters from the house.*)

ROSE: Cory, I want you to help me with this cupboard.

CORY: I ain't quitting the team. I don't care what Poppa say.

ROSE: I'll talk to him when he gets back. He had to go see about your Uncle Gabe. The police done arrested him. Say he was disturbing the peace. He'll be back directly. Come on in here and help me clean out the top of this cupboard.

(CORY *exits into the house.* ROSE *sees* TROY *and* BONO *coming down the alley.*)

Troy . . . what they say down there?

TROY: Ain't said nothing. I give them fifty dollars and they let him go. I'll talk to you about it. Where's Cory?

ROSE: He's in there helping me clean out these cupboards.

TROY: Tell him to get his butt out here.

(TROY *and* BONO *go over to the pile of wood.* BONO *picks up the saw and begins sawing.*)

TROY (*To* BONO): All they want is the money. That makes six or seven times I done went down there and got him. See me coming they stick out their *hands.*

BONO: Yeah. I know what you mean. That's all they care about . . . that money. They don't care about what's right.

(*Pause.*)

Nigger, why you got to go and get some hard wood? You ain't doing nothing but building a little old fence. Get you some soft pine wood. That's all you need.

TROY: I know what I'm doing. This is outside wood. You put pine wood inside the house. Pine wood is inside wood. This here is outside wood. Now you tell me where the fence is gonna be?

BONO: You don't need this wood. You can put it up with pine wood and it'll stand as long as you gonna be here looking at it.

TROY: How you know how long I'm gonna be here, nigger? Hell, I might just live forever. Live longer than old man Horsely.

BONO: That's what Magee used to say.

TROY: Magee's a damn fool. Now you tell me who you ever heard of gonna pull their own teeth with a pair of rusty pliers.

BONO: The old folks . . . my granddaddy used to pull his teeth with pliers. They ain't had no dentists for the colored folks back then.

TROY: Get clean pliers! You understand? Clean pliers! Sterilize them! Besides we ain't living back then. All Magee had to do was walk over to Doc Goldblum's.

BONO: I see where you and that Tallahassee gal . . . that Alberta . . . I see where you all done got tight.

TROY: What you mean "got tight"?

BONO: I see where you be laughing and joking with her all the time.

TROY: I laughs and jokes with all of them, Bono. You know me.

BONO: That ain't the kind of laughing and joking I'm talking about.

(CORY *enters from the house.*)

CORY: How you doing, Mr. Bono?

TROY: Cory? Get that saw from Bono and cut some wood. He talking about the wood's too hard to cut. Stand back there, Jim, and let that young boy show you how it's done.

BONO: He's sure welcome to it.

(CORY *takes the saw and begins to cut the wood.*)

Whew-e-e! Look at that. Big old strong boy. Look like Joe Louis.° Hell, must be getting old the way I'm watching that boy whip through that wood.

Joe Louis, 1914–81, African American boxer, known as the "Brown Bomber," held the world heavyweight title for almost twelve years.

CORY: I don't see why Mama want a fence around the yard noways.

TROY: Damn if I know either. What the hell she keeping out with it? She ain't got nothing nobody want.

BONO: Some people build fences to keep people out . . . and other people build fences to keep people in. Rose wants to hold on to you all. She loves you.

TROY: Hell, nigger, I don't need nobody to tell me my wife loves me, Cory . . . go on in the house and see if you can find that other saw.

CORY: Where's it at?

TROY: I said find it! Look for it till you find it!

(CORY exits into the house.)

What's that supposed to mean? Wanna keep us in?

BONO: Troy . . . I done known you seem like damn near my whole life. You and Rose both. I done know both of you all for a long time. I remember when you met Rose. When you was hitting them baseball out the park. A lot of them old gals was after you then. You had the pick of the litter. When you picked Rose, I was happy for you. That was the first time I knew you had any sense. I said . . . My man Troy knows what he's doing . . . I'm gonna follow this nigger . . . he might take me somewhere. I been following you too. I done learned a whole heap of things about life watching you. I done learned how to tell where the shit lies. How to tell it from the alfalfa. You done learned me a lot of things. You showed me how to not make the same mistakes . . . to take life as it comes along and keep putting one foot in front of the other.

(Pause.)

Rose a good woman, Troy.

TROY: Hell, nigger, I know she a good woman. I been married to her for eighteen years. What you got on your mind, Bono?

BONO: I just say she a good woman. Just like I say anything. I ain't got to have nothing on my mind.

TROY: You just gonna say she a good woman and leave it hanging out there like that? Why you telling me she a good woman?

BONO: She loves you, Troy. Rose loves you.

TROY: You saying I don't measure up. That's what you trying to say. I don't measure up cause I'm seeing this other gal. I know what you trying to say.

BONO: I know what Rose means to you, Troy. I'm just trying to say I don't want to see you mess up.

TROY: Yeah, I appreciate that, Bono. If you was messing around on Lucille I'd be telling you the same thing.

BONO: Well, that's all I got to say. I just say that because I love you both.

TROY: Hell, you know me . . . I wasn't out there looking for nothing. You can't find a better woman than Rose. I know that. But seems like this woman just stuck onto me where I can't shake her loose. I done wrestled with it, tried to throw her off me . . . but she just stuck on tighter. Now she's stuck on for good.

BONO: You's in control . . . that's what you tell me all the time. You responsible for what you do.

TROY: I ain't ducking the responsibility of it. As long as it sets right in my heart . . . then I'm okay. Cause that's all I listen to. It'll tell me right from wrong every time. And I ain't talking about doing Rose no bad turn. I love Rose. She done carried me a long ways and I love and respect her for that.

BONO: I know you do. That's why I don't want to see you hurt her. But what you gonna do when she find out? What you got then? If you try and juggle both of them . . . sooner or later you gonna drop one of them. That's common sense.

TROY: Yeah, I hear what you saying, Bono. I been trying to figure a way to work it out.

BONO: Work it out right, Troy. I don't want to be getting all up between you and Rose's business . . . but work it so it come out right.

TROY: Ah hell, I get all up between you and Lucille's business. When you gonna get that woman that refrigerator she been wanting? Don't tell me you ain't got no money now. I know who your banker is. Mellon don't need that money bad as Lucille want that refrigerator. I'll tell you that.

BONO: Tell you what I'll do . . . when you finish building this fence for Rose . . . I'll buy Lucille that refrigerator.

TROY: You done stuck your foot in your mouth now!

(TROY grabs up a board and begins to saw. BONO starts to walk out the yard.)

Hey, nigger . . . where you going?

BONO: I'm going home. I know you don't expect me to help you now. I'm protecting my money. I wanna see you put that fence up by yourself. That's what I want to see. You'll be here another six months without me.

TROY: Nigger, you ain't right.

BONO: When it comes to my money . . . I'm right as fireworks on the Fourth of July.

TROY: Alright, we gonna see now. You better get out your bankbook.

(BONO exits, and TROY continues to work. ROSE enters from the house.)

ROSE: What they say down there? What's happening with Gabe?

TROY: I went down there and got him out. Cost me fifty dollars. Say he was disturbing the peace. Judge set up a hearing for him in three weeks. Say to show cause why he shouldn't be re-committed.

ROSE: What was he doing that cause them to arrest him?

TROY: Some kids was teasing him and he run them off home. Say he was howling and carrying on. Some folks seen him and called the police. That's all it was.

ROSE: Well, what's you say? What'd you tell the judge?

TROY: Told him I'd look after him. It didn't make no sense to recommit the man. He stuck out his big greasy palm and told me to give him fifty dollars and take him on home.

ROSE: Where's he at now? Where'd he go off to?

TROY: He's gone on about his business. He don't need nobody to hold his hand.

ROSE: Well, I don't know. Seem like that would be the best place for him if they did put him into the hospital. I know what you're gonna say. But that's what I think would be best.

TROY: The man done had his life ruined fighting for what? And they wanna take and lock him up. Let him be free. He don't bother nobody.

ROSE: Well, everybody got their own way of looking at it I guess. Come on and get your lunch. I got a bowl of lima beans and some cornbread in the oven. Come on get something to eat. Ain't no sense you fretting over Gabe.

(ROSE *turns to go into the house.*)

TROY: Rose . . . got something to tell you.

ROSE: Well, come on . . . wait till I get this food on the table.

TROY: Rose!

(*She stops and turns around.*)

I don't know how to say this.

(*Pause.*)

I can't explain it none. It just sort of grows on you till it gets out of hand. It starts out like a little bush . . . and the next thing you know it's a whole forest.

ROSE: Troy . . . what is you talking about?

TROY: I'm talking, woman, let me talk. I'm trying to find a way to tell you . . . I'm gonna be a daddy. I'm gonna be somebody's daddy.

ROSE: Troy . . . you're not telling me this? You're gonna be . . . what?

TROY: Rose . . . now . . . see . . .

ROSE: You telling me you gonna be somebody's daddy? You telling your *wife* this?

(GABRIEL *enters from the street. He carries a rose in his hand.*)

GABRIEL: Hey, Troy! Hey, Rose!

ROSE: I have to wait eighteen years to hear something like this.

GABRIEL: Hey, Rose . . . I got a flower for you.

(*He hands it to her.*)

That's a rose. Same rose like you is.

ROSE: Thanks, Gabe.

GABRIEL: Troy, you ain't mad at me is you? Them bad mens come and put me away. You ain't mad at me is you?

TROY: Naw, Gabe, I ain't mad at you.

ROSE: Eighteen years and you wanna come with this.

GABRIEL (*Takes a quarter out of his pocket*): See what I got? Got a brand new quarter.

TROY: Rose . . . it's just . . .

ROSE: Ain't nothing you can say, Troy. Ain't no way of explaining that.

GABRIEL: Fellow that give me this quarter had a whole mess of them. I'm gonna keep this quarter till it stop shining.

ROSE: Gabe, go on in the house there. I got some watermelon in the frigidaire. Go on and get you a piece.

GABRIEL: Say, Rose . . . you know I was chasing hellhounds and them bad mens come and get me and take me away. Troy helped me. He come down there and told them they better let me go before he beat them up. Yeah, he did!

ROSE: You go on and get you a piece of watermelon, Gabe. Them bad mens is gone now.

GABRIEL: Okay, Rose . . . gonna get me some watermelon. The kind with the stripes on it.

(GABRIEL *exits into the house.*)

ROSE: Why, Troy? Why? After all these years to come dragging this in to me now. It don't make no sense at your age. I could have expected this ten or fifteen years ago, but not now.

TROY: Age ain't got nothing to do with it, Rose.

ROSE: I done tried to be everything a wife should be. Everything a wife could be. Been married eighteen years and I got to live to see the day you tell me you been seeing another woman and done fathered a child by her. And you know I ain't never wanted no half nothing in my family. My whole family is half. Everybody got different fathers and mothers . . . my two sisters and my brother. Can't hardly tell who's who. Can't never sit down and talk about Papa and Mama. It's your papa and your mama and my papa and my mama . . .

TROY: Rose . . . stop it now.

ROSE: I ain't never wanted that for none of my children. And now you wanna drag your behind in here and tell me something like this.

TROY: You ought to know. It's time for you to know.

ROSE: Well, I don't want to know, goddamn it!

TROY: I can't just make it go away. It's done now. I can't wish the circumstance of the thing away.

ROSE: And you don't want to either. Maybe you want to wish me and my boy away. Maybe that's what you want? Well, you can't wish us away. I've got eighteen years of my life invested in you. You ought to have stayed upstairs in my bed where you belong.

TROY: Rose . . . now listen to me . . . we can get a handle on this thing. We can talk this out . . . come to an understanding.

ROSE: All of a sudden it's "we." Where was "we" at when you was down there rolling around with some godforsaken woman? "We" should have come to an understanding before you started making a damn fool of yourself. You're a day late and a dollar short when it comes to an understanding with me.

TROY: It's just . . . She gives me a different idea . . . a different understanding about myself. I can step out of this house and get away from the pressures and problems . . . be a different man. I ain't got to wonder how I'm gonna pay the bills or get the roof fixed. I can just be a part of myself that I ain't never been.

ROSE: What I want to know . . . is do you plan to continue seeing her. That's all you can say to me.

TROY: I can sit up in her house and laugh. Do you understand what I'm saying. I can laugh out loud . . . and it feels good. It reaches all the way down to the bottom of my shoes.

(*Pause.*)

Rose, I can't give that up.

ROSE: Maybe you ought to go on and stay down there with her . . . if she's a better woman than me.

TROY: It ain't about nobody being a better woman or nothing. Rose, you ain't the blame. A man couldn't ask for no woman to be a better wife than you've been. I'm responsible for it. I done locked myself into a pattern trying to take care of you all that I forgot about myself.

ROSE: What the hell was I there for? That was my job, not somebody else's.

TROY: Rose, I done tried all my life to live decent . . . to live a clean . . . hard . . . useful life. I tried to be a good husband to you. In every way I knew how. Maybe I come into the world backwards, I don't know. But . . . you born with two strikes on you before you come to the plate. You got to guard it closely . . . always looking for the curve ball on the inside corner. You can't afford to let none get past you. You can't afford a call strike. If you going down . . . you going down swinging. Everything lined up against you. What you gonna do. I fooled them, Rose. I bunted. When I found you and Cory and a halfway decent job . . . I was safe. Couldn't nothing touch me. I wasn't gonna strike out no more. I wasn't going back to the penitentiary. I wasn't gonna lay in the streets with a bottle of wine. I was safe. I had me a family. A job. I

wasn't gonna get that last strike. I was on first looking for one of them boys to knock me in. To get me home.

ROSE: You should have stayed in my bed, Troy.

TROY: Then when I saw that gal . . . she firmed up my backbone. And I got to thinking that if I tried . . . I just might be able to steal second. Do you understand after eighteen years I wanted to steal second.

ROSE: You should have held me tight. You should have grabbed me and held on.

TROY: I stood on first base for eighteen years and I thought . . . well, goddamn it . . . go on for it!

ROSE: We're not talking about baseball! We're talking about you going off to lay in bed with another woman . . . and then bring it home to me. That's what we're talking about. We ain't talking about no baseball.

TROY: Rose, you're not listening to me. I'm trying the best I can to explain it to you. It's not easy for me to admit that I been standing in the same place for eighteen years.

ROSE: I been standing with you! I been right here with you, Troy. I got a life too. I gave eighteen years of my life to stand in the same spot with you. Don't you think I ever wanted other things? Don't you think I had dreams and hopes? What about my life? What about me. Don't you think it ever crossed my mind to want to know other men? That I wanted to lay up somewhere and forget about my responsibilities? That I wanted someone to make me laugh so I could feel good? You not the only one who's got wants and needs. But I held on to you, Troy. I took all my feelings, my wants and needs, my dreams . . . and I buried them inside you. I planted a seed and watched and prayed over it. I planted myself inside you and waited to bloom. And it didn't take me no eighteen years to find out the soil was hard and rocky and it wasn't never gonna bloom.

But I held on to you, Troy. I held you tighter. You was my husband. I owed you everything I had. Every part of me I could find to give you. And upstairs in that room . . . with the darkness falling in on me . . . I gave everything I had to try and erase the doubt that you wasn't the finest man in the world. And wherever you was going . . . I wanted to be there with you. Cause you was my husband. Cause that's the only way I was gonna survive as your wife. You always talking about what you give . . . and what you don't have to give. But you take too. You take . . . and don't even know nobody's giving!

(ROSE *turns to exit into the house;* TROY *grabs her arm.*)

TROY: You say I take and don't give!

ROSE: Troy! You're hurting me!

TROY: You say I take and don't give.

ROSE: Troy . . . you're hurting my arm! Let go!

TROY: I done give you everything I got. Don't you tell that lie on me.

ROSE: Troy!

TROY: Don't you tell that lie on me!

(CORY enters from the house.)

CORY: Mama!

ROSE: Troy. You're hurting me.

TROY: Don't you tell me about no taking and giving.

(CORY comes up behind TROY and grabs him. TROY, surprised, is thrown off balance just as CORY throws a glancing blow that catches him on the chest and knocks him down. TROY is stunned, as is CORY.)

ROSE: Troy. Troy. No!

(TROY gets to his feet and starts at CORY.)

Troy . . . no. Please! Troy!

(ROSE pulls on TROY to hold him back. TROY stops himself.)

TROY *(To CORY)*: Alright. That's strike two. You stay away from around me, boy. Don't you strike out. You living with a full count. Don't you strike out.

(TROY exits out the yard as the lights go down.)

ACT 2 / SCENE 2

(It is six months later, early afternoon. TROY enters from the house and starts to exit the yard. ROSE enters from the house.)

ROSE: Troy, I want to talk to you.

TROY: All of a sudden, after all this time, you want to talk to me, huh? You ain't wanted to talk to me for months. You ain't wanted to talk to me last night. You ain't wanted no part of me then. What you wanna talk to me about now?

ROSE: Tomorrow's Friday.

TROY: I know what day tomorrow is. You think I don't know tomorrow's Friday? My whole life I ain't done nothing but look to see Friday coming and you got to tell me it's Friday.

ROSE: I want to know if you're coming home.

TROY: I always come home, Rose. You know that. There ain't never been a night I ain't come home.

ROSE: That ain't what I mean . . . and you know it. I want to know if you're coming straight home after work.

TROY: I figure I'd cash my check . . . hang out at Taylors' with the boys . . . maybe play a game of checkers . . .

ROSE: Troy, I can't live like this. I won't live like this. You livin' on borrowed time with me. It's been going on six months now you ain't been coming home.

TROY: I be here every night. Every night of the year. That's 365 days.

ROSE: I want you to come home tomorrow after work.

TROY: Rose . . . I don't mess up my pay. You know that now. I take my pay and I give it to you. I don't have no money but what you give me back. I just want to have a little time to myself . . . a little time to enjoy life.

ROSE: What about me? When's my time to enjoy life?

TROY: I don't know what to tell you, Rose. I'm doing the best I can.

ROSE: You ain't been home from work but time enough to change your clothes and run out . . . and you wanna call that the best you can do?

TROY: I'm going over to the hospital to see Alberta. She went into the hospital this afternoon. Look like she might have the baby early. I won't be gone long.

ROSE: Well, you ought to know. They went over to Miss Pearl's and got Gabe today. She said you told them to go ahead and lock him up.

TROY: I ain't said no such thing. Whoever told you that is telling a lie. Pearl ain't doing nothing but telling a big fat lie.

ROSE: She ain't had to tell me. I read it on the papers.

TROY: I ain't told them nothing of the kind.

ROSE: I saw it right there on the papers.

TROY: What it say, huh?

ROSE: It said you told them to take him.

TROY: Then they screwed that up, just the way they screw up everything. I ain't worried about what they got on the paper.

ROSE: Say the government send part of his check to the hospital and the other part to you.

TROY: I ain't got nothing to do with that if that's the way it works. I ain't made up the rules about how it work.

ROSE: You did Gabe just like you did Cory. You wouldn't sign the paper for Cory . . . but you signed for Gabe. You signed that paper.

(The telephone is heard ringing inside the house.)

TROY: I told you I ain't signed nothing, woman! The only thing I signed was the release form. Hell, I can't read, I don't know what they had on that paper! I ain't signed nothing about sending Gabe away.

ROSE: I said send him to the hospital . . . you said let him be free . . . now you done went down there and signed him to the hospital for half his money. You went back on yourself, Troy. You gonna have to answer for that.

TROY: See now . . . you been over there talking to Miss Pearl. She done got mad cause she ain't getting Gabe's rent money. That's all it is. She's liable to say anything.

ROSE: Troy, I seen where you signed the paper.

TROY: You ain't seen nothing I signed. What she doing got papers on my brother anyway? Miss Pearl telling a big fat lie. And I'm gonna tell her about it too! You ain't seen nothing I signed. Say . . . you ain't seen nothing I signed.

(ROSE *exits into the house to answer the telephone. Presently she returns.*)

ROSE: Troy . . . that was the hospital. Alberta had the baby.

TROY: What she have? What is it?

ROSE: It's a girl.

TROY: I better get on down to the hospital to see her.

ROSE: Troy . . .

TROY: Rose . . . I got to go see her now. That's only right . . . what's the matter . . . the baby's alright, ain't it?

ROSE: Alberta died having the baby.

TROY: Died . . . you say she's dead? Alberta's dead?

ROSE: They said they done all they could. They couldn't do nothing for her.

TROY: The baby? How's the baby?

ROSE: They say it's healthy. I wonder who's gonna bury her.

TROY: She had family, Rose. She wasn't living in the world by herself.

ROSE: I know she wasn't living in the world by herself.

TROY: Next thing you gonna want to know if she had any insurance.

ROSE: Troy, you ain't got to talk like that.

TROY: That's the first thing that jumped out your mouth. "Who's gonna bury her?" Like I'm fixing to take on that task for myself.

ROSE: I am your wife. Don't push me away.

TROY: I ain't pushing nobody away. Just give me some space. That's all. Just give me some room to breathe.

(ROSE *exits into the house.* TROY *walks about the yard.*)

TROY (*With a quiet rage that threatens to consume him*): Alright . . . Mr. Death. See now . . . I'm gonna tell you what I'm gonna do. I'm gonna take and build me a fence around this yard. See? I'm gonna build me a fence around what belongs to me. And then I want you to stay on the other side. See? You stay over there until you're ready for me. Then you come on. Bring your army. Bring your sickle. Bring your wrestling clothes. I ain't gonna fall down on my vigilance this time. You ain't gonna sneak up on me no more. When you ready for me . . . when the top of your list say Troy Maxson . . . that's when you come around here. You come up and knock on the front door. Ain't nobody else got nothing to do with this. This is between you and me. Man to man. You stay on the other side of that fence until you ready for

me. Then you come up and knock on the front door. Anytime you want. I'll be ready for you.

(*The lights go down to black.*)

ACT 2 / SCENE 3

(*The lights come up on the porch. It is late evening three days later.* ROSE *sits listening to the ball game waiting for* TROY. *The final out of the game is made and* ROSE *switches off the radio.* TROY *enters the yard carrying an infant wrapped in blankets. He stands back from the house and calls.*)

(ROSE *enters and stands on the porch. There is a long, awkward silence, the weight of which grows heavier with each passing second.*)

TROY: Rose . . . I'm standing here with my daughter in my arms. She ain't but a wee bittie little old thing. She don't know nothing about grownups' business. She innocent . . . and she ain't got no mama.

ROSE: What you telling me for, Troy?

(*She turns and exits into the house.*)

TROY: Well . . . I guess we'll just sit out here on the porch.

(*He sits down on the porch. There is an awkward indelicateness about the way he handles the baby. His largeness engulfs and seems to swallow it. He speaks loud enough for* ROSE *to hear.*)

A man's got to do what's right for him. I ain't sorry for nothing I done. It felt right in my heart. (*To the baby*) What you smiling at? Your daddy's a big man. Got these great big old hands. But sometimes he's scared. And right now your daddy's scared cause we sitting out here and ain't got no home. Oh, I been homeless before. I ain't had no little baby with me. But I been homeless. You just be out on the road by your lonesome and you see one of them trains coming and you just kinda go like this . . .

(*He sings as a lullaby.*)

Please, Mr. Engineer let a man ride the line
Please, Mr. Engineer let a man ride the line
I ain't got no ticket please let me ride the blinds

(ROSE *enters from the house.* TROY *hearing her steps behind him, stands and faces her.*)

She's my daughter, Rose. My own flesh and blood. I can't deny her no more than I can deny them boys.

(*Pause.*)

You and them boys is my family. You and them and this child is all I got in the world. So I guess what I'm saying is . . . I'd appreciate it if you'd help me take care of her.

ROSE: Okay, Troy . . . you're right. I'll take care of your baby for you . . . cause . . . like you say . . . she's innocent . . . and you can't visit the sins of the father upon the child. A motherless child has got a hard time.

(She takes the baby from him.)

From right now . . . this child got a mother. But you a womanless man.

(ROSE turns and exits into the house with the baby. Lights go down to black.)

ACT 2 / SCENE 4

(It is two months later. LYONS *enters from the street. He knocks on the door and calls.)*

LYONS: Hey, Rose! *(Pause.)* Rose!

ROSE *(From inside the house)*: Stop that yelling. You gonna wake up Raynell. I just got her to sleep.

LYONS: I just stopped by to pay Papa this twenty dollars I owe him. Where's Papa at?

ROSE: He should be here in a minute. I'm getting ready to go down to the church. Sit down and wait on him.

LYONS: I got to go pick up Bonnie over her mother's house.

ROSE: Well, sit it down there on the table. He'll get it.

LYONS *(Enters the house and sets the money on the table)*: Tell Papa I said thanks. I'll see you again.

ROSE: Alright, Lyons. We'll see you.

(LYONS starts to exit as CORY enters.)

CORY: Hey, Lyons.

LYONS: What's happening, Cory. Say man, I'm sorry I missed your graduation. You know I had a gig and couldn't get away. Otherwise, I would have been there, man. So what you doing?

CORY: I'm trying to find a job.

LYONS: Yeah I know how that go, man. It's rough out here. Jobs are scarce.

CORY: Yeah, I know.

LYONS: Look here, I got to run. Talk to Papa . . . he know some people. He'll be able to help get you a job. Talk to him . . . see what he say.

CORY: Yeah . . . alright, Lyons.

LYONS: You take care. I'll talk to you soon. We'll find some time to talk.

(LYONS exits the yard. CORY *wanders over to the tree, picks up the bat, and assumes a batting stance. He studies an imaginary pitcher and swings. Dissatisfied with the result,*

he tries again. TROY *enters. They eye each other for a beat.* CORY *puts the bat down and exits the yard.* TROY *starts into the house as* ROSE *exits with Raynell. She is carrying a cake.)*

TROY: I'm coming in and everybody's going out.

ROSE: I'm taking this cake down to the church for the bakesale. Lyons was by to see you. He stopped by to pay you your twenty dollars. It's laying in there on the table.

TROY *(Going into his pocket)*: Well . . . here go this money.

ROSE: Put it in there on the table, Troy. I'll get it.

TROY: What time you coming back?

ROSE: Ain't no use in you studying me. It don't matter what time I come back.

TROY: I just asked you a question, woman. What's the matter . . . can't I ask you a question?

ROSE: Troy, I don't want to go into it. Your dinner's in there on the stove. All you got to do is heat it up. And don't you be eating the rest of them cakes in there. I'm coming back for them. We having a bakesale at the church tomorrow.

(ROSE exits the yard. TROY *sits down on the steps, takes a pint bottle from his pocket, opens it, and drinks. He begins to sing.)*

TROY:

Hear it ring! Hear it ring!
Had an old dog his name was Blue
You know Blue was mighty true
You know Blue as a good old dog
Blue trees a possum in a hollow log
You know from that he was a good old dog

(BONO enters the yard.)

BONO: Hey, Troy.

TROY: Hey, what's happening, Bono?

BONO: I just thought I'd stop by to see you.

TROY: What you stop by and see me for? You ain't stopped by in a month of Sundays. Hell, I must owe you money or something.

BONO: Since you got your promotion I can't keep up with you. Used to see you every day. Now I don't even know what route you working.

TROY: They keep switching me around. Got me out in Greentree now . . . hauling white folks' garbage.

BONO: Greentree, huh? You lucky, at least you ain't got to be lifting them barrels. Damn if they ain't getting heavier. I'm gonna put in my two years and call it quits.

TROY: I'm thinking about retiring myself.

BONO: You got it easy. You can *drive* for another five years.

TROY: It ain't the same, Bono. It ain't like working the back of the truck. Ain't got nobody to talk to . . .

feel like you working by yourself. Naw, I'm thinking about retiring. How's Lucille?

BONO: She alright. Her arthritis get to acting up on her sometime. Saw Rose on my way in. She going down to the church, huh?

TROY: Yeah, she took up going down there. All them preachers looking for somebody to fatten their pockets.

(Pause.)

Got some gin here.

BONO: Naw, thanks. I just stopped by to say hello.

TROY: Hell, nigger . . . you can take a drink. I ain't never known you to say no to a drink. You ain't got to work tomorrow.

BONO: I just stopped by. I'm fixing to go over to Skinner's. We got us a domino game going over his house every Friday.

TROY: Nigger, you can't play no dominoes. I used to whup you four games out of five.

BONO: Well, that learned me. I'm getting better.

TROY: Yeah? Well, that's alright.

BONO: Look here . . . I got to be getting on. Stop by sometime, huh?

TROY: Yeah, I'll do that, Bono. Lucille told Rose you bought her a new refrigerator.

BONO: Yeah, Rose told Lucille you had finally built your fence . . . so I figured we'd call it even.

TROY: I knew you would.

BONO: Yeah . . . okay. I'll be talking to you.

TROY: Yeah, take care, Bono. Good to see you. I'm gonna stop over.

BONO: Yeah. Okay, Troy.

(BONO exits. TROY drinks from the bottle.)

TROY:

Old Blue died and I dig his grave
Let him down with a golden chain
Every night when I hear old Blue bark
I know Blue treed a possum in Noah's Ark.
Hear it ring! Hear it ring!

(CORY enters the yard. They eye each other for a beat. TROY is sitting in the middle of the steps. CORY walks over.)

CORY: I got to get by.

TROY: Say what? What's you say?

CORY: You in my way. I got to get by.

TROY: You got to get by where? This is my house. Bought and paid for. In full. Took me fifteen years. And if you wanna go in my house and I'm sitting on the steps . . . you say excuse me. Like your mama taught you.

CORY: Come on, Pop . . . I got to get by.

(CORY starts to maneuver his way past TROY. TROY grabs his leg and shoves him back.)

TROY: You just gonna walk over top of me?

CORY: I live here too!

TROY (Advancing toward him): You just gonna walk over top of me in my own house?

CORY: I ain't scared of you.

TROY: I ain't asked if you was scared of me. I asked you if you was fixing to walk over top of me in my own house? That's the question. You ain't gonna say excuse me? You just gonna walk over top of me?

CORY: If you wanna put it like that.

TROY: How else am I gonna put it?

CORY: I was walking by you to go into the house cause you sitting on the steps drunk, singing to yourself. You can put it like that.

TROY: Without saying excuse me???

(CORY doesn't respond.)

I asked you a question. Without saying excuse me???

CORY: I ain't got to say excuse me to you. You don't count around here no more.

TROY: Oh, I see . . . I don't count around here no more. You ain't got to say excuse me to your daddy. All of a sudden you done got so grown that your daddy don't count around here no more . . . Around here in his own house and yard that he done paid for with the sweat of his brow. You done got so grown to where you gonna take over. You gonna take over my house. Is that right? You gonna wear my pants. You gonna go in there and stretch out on my bed. You ain't got to say excuse me cause I don't count around here no more. Is that right?

CORY: That's right. You always talking this dumb stuff. Now, why don't you just get out my way.

TROY: I guess you got someplace to sleep and something to put in your belly. You got that, huh? You got that? That's what you need. You got that, huh?

CORY: You don't know what I got. You ain't got to worry about what I got.

TROY: You right! You one hundred percent right! I done spent the last seventeen years worrying about what you got. Now it's your turn, see? I'll tell you what to do. You grown . . . we done established that. You a man. Now, let's see you act like one. Turn your behind around and walk out this yard. And when you get out there in the alley . . . you can forget about this house. See? Cause this is my house. You go on and be a man and get your own house. You can forget about this. 'Cause this is mine. You go on and get yours cause I'm through with doing for you.

CORY: You talking about what you did for me . . . what'd you ever give me?

TROY: Them feet and bones! That pumping heart, nigger! I give you more than anybody else is ever gonna give you.

CORY: You ain't never gave me nothing! You ain't never done nothing but hold me back. Afraid I was gonna be better than you. All you ever did was try and make me scared of you. I used to tremble every time you called my name. Every time I heard your footsteps in the house. Wondering all the time . . . what's Papa gonna say if I do this? . . . What's he gonna say if I do that? . . . What's Papa gonna say if I turn on the radio? And Mama, too . . . she tries . . . but she's scared of you.

TROY: You leave your mama out of this. She ain't got nothing to do with this.

CORY: I don't know how she stand you . . . after what you did to her.

TROY: I told you to leave your mama out of this!

(He advances toward CORY.*)*

CORY: What you gonna do . . . give me a whupping? You can't whup me no more. You're too old. You just an old man.

TROY *(Shoves him on his shoulder)*: Nigger! That's what you are. You just another nigger on the street to me!

CORY: You crazy! You know that?

TROY: Go on now! You got the devil in you. Get on away from me!

CORY: You just a crazy old man . . . talking about I got the devil in me.

TROY: Yeah, I'm crazy! If you don't get on the other side of that yard . . . I'm gonna show you how crazy I am! Go on . . . get the hell out of my yard.

CORY: It ain't your yard. You took Uncle Gabe's money he got from the army to buy this house and then you put him out.

TROY *(*TROY *advances on* CORY*)*: Get your black ass out of my yard!

*(*TROY*'s advance backs* CORY *up against the tree.* CORY *grabs up the bat.)*

CORY: I ain't going nowhere! Come on . . . put me out! I ain't scared of you.

TROY: That's my bat!

CORY: Come on!

TROY: Put my bat down!

CORY: Come on, put me out.

*(*CORY *swings at* TROY, *who backs across the yard.)*

What's the matter? You so bad . . . put me out!

*(*TROY *advances toward* CORY.*)*

CORY *(Backing up)*: Come on! Come on!

TROY: You're gonna have to use it! You wanna draw that bat back on me . . . you're gonna have to use it.

CORY: Come on! . . . Come on!

*(*CORY *swings the bat at* TROY *a second time. He misses.* TROY *continues to advance toward him.)*

TROY: You're gonna have to kill me! You wanna draw that bat back on me. You're gonna have to kill me.

*(*CORY, *backed up against the tree, can go no farther.* TROY *taunts him. He sticks out his head and offers him a target.)*

Come on! Come on!

*(*CORY *is unable to swing the bat.* TROY *grabs it.)*

TROY: Then I'll show you.

*(*CORY *and* TROY *struggle over the bat. The struggle is fierce and fully engaged.* TROY *ultimately is the stronger and takes the bat from* CORY *and stands over him ready to swing. He stops himself.)*

Go on and get away from around my house.

*(*CORY, *stung by his defeat, picks himself up, walks slowly out of the yard and up the alley.)*

CORY: Tell Mama I'll be back for my things.

TROY: They'll be on the other side of that fence.

*(*CORY *exits.)*

TROY: I can't taste nothing. Helluljah! I can't taste nothing no more. (*TROY assumes a batting posture and begins to taunt Death, the fastball on the outside corner.*) Come on! It's between you and me now! Come on! Anytime you want! Come on! I be ready for you . . . but I ain't gonna be easy.

(The lights go down on the scene.)

ACT 2 / SCENE 5

(The time is 1965. The lights come up in the yard. It is the morning of TROY*'s funeral. A funeral plaque with a light hangs beside the door. There is a small garden plot off to the side. There is noise and activity in the house as* ROSE, GABRIEL *and* BONO *have gathered. The door opens and* RAYNELL, *seven years old, enters dressed in a flannel nightgown. She crosses to the garden and pokes around with a stick.* ROSE *calls from the house.)*

ROSE: Raynell!

RAYNELL: Mam?

ROSE: What you doing out there?

RAYNELL: Nothing.

*(*ROSE *comes to the door.)*

ROSE: Girl, get in here and get dressed. What you doing?

RAYNELL: Seeing if my garden growed.

ROSE: I told you it ain't gonna grow overnight. You got to wait.

RAYNELL: It don't look like it never gonna grow. Dag!

ROSE: I told you a watched pot never boils. Get in here and get dressed.

RAYNELL: This ain't even no pot, Mama.

ROSE: You just have to give it a chance. It'll grow. Now you come on and do what I told you. We got to be getting ready. This ain't no morning to be playing around. You hear me?

RAYNELL: Yes, mam.

(ROSE *exits into the house.* RAYNELL *continues to poke at her garden with a stick.* CORY *enters. He is dressed in a Marine corporal's uniform, and carries a duffel bag. His posture is that of a military man, and his speech has a clipped sternness.*)

CORY (*To* RAYNELL): Hi.

(*Pause.*)

I bet your name is Raynell.

RAYNELL: Uh huh.

CORY: Is your mama home?

(RAYNELL *runs up on the porch and calls through the screendoor.*)

RAYNELL: Mama . . . there's some man out here. Mama?

(ROSE *comes to the door.*)

ROSE: Cory? Lord have mercy! Look here, you all!

(ROSE *and* CORY *embrace in a tearful reunion as* BONO *and* LYONS *enter from the house dressed in funeral clothes.*)

BONO: Aw, looka here . . .

ROSE: Done got all grown up!

CORY: Don't cry, Mama. What you crying about?

ROSE: I'm just so glad you made it.

CORY: Hey Lyons. How you doing, Mr. Bono.

(LYONS *goes to embrace* CORY.)

LYONS: Look at you, man. Look at you. Don't he look good, Rose. Got them Corporal stripes.

ROSE: What took you so long.

CORY: You know how the Marines are, Mama. They got to get all their paperwork straight before they let you do anything.

ROSE: Well, I'm sure glad you made it. They let Lyons come. Your Uncle Gabe's still in the hospital. They don't know if they gonna let him out or not. I just talked to them a little while ago.

LYONS: A Corporal in the United States Marines.

BONO: Your daddy knew you had it in you. He used to tell me all the time.

LYONS: Don't he look good, Mr. Bono?

BONO: Yeah, he remind me of Troy when I first met him.

(*Pause.*)

Say, Rose, Lucille's down at the church with the choir. I'm gonna go down and get the pallbearers lined up. I'll be back to get you all.

ROSE: Thanks, Jim.

CORY: See you, Mr. Bono.

LYONS (*With his arm around* RAYNELL): Cory . . . look at Raynell. Ain't she precious? She gonna break a whole lot of hearts.

ROSE: Raynell, come and say hello to your brother. This is your brother, Cory. You remember Cory.

RAYNELL: No, Mam.

CORY: She don't remember me, Mama.

ROSE: Well, we talk about you. She heard us talk about you. (*To* RAYNELL) This is your brother, Cory. Come on and say hello.

RAYNELL: Hi.

CORY: Hi. So you're Raynell. Mama told me a lot about you.

ROSE: You all come on into the house and let me fix you some breakfast. Keep up your strength.

CORY: I ain't hungry, Mama.

LYONS: You can fix me something, Rose. I'll be in there in a minute.

ROSE: Cory, you sure you don't want nothing. I know they ain't feeding you right.

CORY: No, Mama . . . thanks. I don't feel like eating. I'll get something later.

ROSE: Raynell . . . get on upstairs and get that dress on like I told you.

(ROSE *and* RAYNELL *exit into the house.*)

LYONS: So . . . I hear you thinking about getting married.

CORY: Yeah, I done found the right one, Lyons. It's about time.

LYONS: Me and Bonnie been split up about four years now. About the time Papa retired. I guess she just got tired of all them changes I was putting her through.

(*Pause.*)

I always knew you was gonna make something out yourself. Your head was always in the right direction. So . . . you gonna stay in . . . make it a career . . . put in your twenty years?

CORY: I don't know. I got six already, I think that's enough.

LYONS: Stick with Uncle Sam and retire early. Ain't nothing out here. I guess Rose told you what happened with me. They got me down the work-house. I thought I was being slick cashing other people's checks.

CORY: How much time you doing?

LYONS: They give me three years. I got that beat now. I ain't got but nine more months. It ain't so bad. You learn to deal with it like anything else. You got to take the crookeds with the straights. That's what Papa used to say. He used to say that when he struck out. I seen him strike out three times in a row . . . and the next time up he hit the ball over the grandstand. Right out there in Homestead Field. He wasn't satisfied hitting in the seats . . . he want to hit it over everything! After the game he had two hundred people standing around waiting to shake his hand. You got to take the crookeds with the straights. Yeah, Papa was something else.

CORY: You still playing?

LYONS: Cory . . . you know I'm gonna do that. There's some fellows down there we got us a band . . . we gonna try and stay together when we get out . . . but yeah, I'm still playing. It still helps me to get out of bed in the morning. As long as it do that I'm gonna be right there playing and trying to make some sense out of it.

ROSE (*Calling*): Lyons, I got these eggs in the pan.

LYONS: Let me go on and get these eggs, man. Get ready to go bury Papa.

(*Pause.*)

How you doing? You doing alright?

(CORY *nods.* LYONS *touches him on the shoulder and they share a moment of silent grief.* LYONS *exits into the house.* CORY *wanders about the yard.* RAYNELL *enters.*)

RAYNELL: Hi.

CORY: Hi.

RAYNELL: Did you used to sleep in my room?

CORY: Yeah . . . that used to be my room.

RAYNELL: That's what Papa call it. "Cory's room." It got your football in the closet.

(ROSE *comes to the door.*)

ROSE: Raynell, get in there and get them good shoes on.

RAYNELL: Mama, can't I wear these. Them other one hurt my feet.

ROSE: Well, they just gonna have to hurt your feet for a while. You ain't said they hurt your feet when you went down to the store and got them.

RAYNELL: They didn't hurt then. My feet done got bigger.

ROSE: Don't you give me no backtalk now. You get in there and get them shoes on.

(RAYNELL *exits into the house.*)

Ain't too much changed. He still got that piece of rag tied to that tree. He was out here swinging that bat. I was just ready to go back in the house. He swung that bat and then he just fell over. Seem like he swung it and stood there with this grin on his face . . . and then he just fell over. They carried him on down to the hospital, but I knew there wasn't no need . . . why don't you come on in the house?

CORY: Mama . . . I got something to tell you. I don't know how to tell you this . . . but I've got to tell you . . . I'm not going to Papa's funeral.

ROSE: Boy, hush your mouth. That's your daddy you talking about. I don't want hear that kind of talk this morning. I done raised you to come to this? You standing there all healthy and grown talking about you ain't going to your daddy's funeral?

CORY: Mama . . . listen . . .

ROSE: I don't want to hear it, Cory. You just get that thought out of your head.

CORY: I can't drag Papa with me everywhere I go. I've got to say no to him. One time in my life I've got to say no.

ROSE: Don't nobody have to listen to nothing like that. I know you and your daddy ain't seen eye to eye, but I ain't got to listen to that kind of talk this morning. Whatever was between you and your daddy . . . the time has come to put it aside. Just take it and set it over there on the shelf and forget about it. Disrespecting your daddy ain't gonna make you a man, Cory. You got to find a way to come to that on your own. Not going to your daddy's funeral ain't gonna make you a man.

CORY: The whole time I was growing up . . . living in his house . . . Papa was like a shadow that followed you everywhere. It weighed on you and sunk into your flesh. It would wrap around you and lay there until you couldn't tell which one was you anymore. That shadow digging in your flesh. Trying to crawl in. Trying to live through you. Everywhere I looked, Troy Maxson was staring back at me . . . hiding under the bed . . . in the closet. I'm just saying I've got to find a way to get rid of that shadow, Mama.

ROSE: You just like him. You got him in you good.

CORY: Don't tell me that, Mama.

ROSE: You Troy Maxson all over again.

CORY: I don't want to be Troy Maxson. I want to be me.

ROSE: You can't be nobody but who you are, Cory. That shadow wasn't nothing but you growing into yourself. You either got to grow into it or cut it down to fit you. But that's all you got to make life with. That's all you got to measure yourself against that world out there. Your daddy wanted you to be everything he wasn't . . . and at the same time he tried to make you into everything he was. I don't know if he was right or wrong . . . but I do know he meant to do more good than he meant to do harm. He wasn't always right. Sometimes when he touched he bruised. And sometimes when he took me in his arms he cut.

When I first met your daddy I thought . . . Here is a man I can lay down with and make a baby. That's the first thing I thought when I seen him. I was thirty years old and had done seen my share of men. But when he walked up to me and said "I can dance a waltz that'll make you dizzy," I thought, Rose Lee, here is a man that you can open yourself up to and be filled to bursting. Here is a man that can fill all them empty spaces you been tipping around the edges of. One of them empty spaces was being somebody's mother.

I married your daddy and settled down to cooking his supper and keeping clean sheets on the bed. When your daddy walked through the house he was so big he filled it up. That was my first mistake. Not to make him leave some room for me. For my part in the matter. But at that time I wanted that. I wanted a house that I could sing in. And that's what your daddy gave me. I didn't know to keep up his strength I had to give up little pieces of mine. I did that. I took on his life as mine and mixed up the pieces so that you couldn't hardly tell which was which anymore. It was my choice. It was my life and I didn't have to live it like that. But that's what life offered me in the way of being a woman and I took it. I grabbed hold of it with both hands.

By the time Raynell came into the house, me and your daddy had done lost touch with one another. I didn't want to make my blessing off of nobody's misfortune . . . but I took on to Raynell like she was all them babies I had wanted and never had.

(The phone rings.)

Like I'd been blessed to relive a part of my life. And if the Lord see fit to keep up my strength . . . I'm gonna do her just like your daddy did you . . . I'm gonna give her the best of what's in me.

RAYNELL *(Entering, still with her old shoes)*: Mama . . . Reverend Tollivier on the phone.

(ROSE exits into the house.)

RAYNELL: Hi.
CORY: Hi.
RAYNELL: You in the Army or the Marines?
CORY: Marines.
RAYNELL: Papa said it was the Army. Did you know Blue?
CORY: Blue? Who's Blue?
RAYNELL: Papa's dog what he sing about all the time.
CORY *(Singing)*:

> Hear it ring! Hear it ring!
> I had a dog his name was Blue
> You know Blue was mighty true
> You know Blue was a good old dog
> Blue treed a possum in a hollow log
> You know from that he was a good old dog.
> Hear it ring! Hear it ring!

(RAYNELL joins in singing.)

CORY and RAYNELL:

> Blue treed a possum out on a limb
> Blue looked at me and I looked at him
> Grabbed that possum and put him in a sack
> Blue stayed there till I came back
> Old Blue's feets was big and round
> Never allowed a possum to touch the ground.

> Old Blue died and I dug his grave
> I dug his grave with a silver spade
> Let him down with a golden chain
> And every night I call his name
> Go on Blue, you good dog you
> Go on Blue, you good dog you

RAYNELL:

> Blue laid down and died like a man
> Blue laid down and died . . .

BOTH:

> Blue laid down and died like a man
> Now he's treeing possums in the Promised Land
> I'm gonna tell you this to let you know
> Blue's gone where the good dogs go
> When I hear old Blue bark
> When I hear old Blue bark
> Blue treed a possum in Noah's Ark
> Blue treed a possum in Noah's Ark.

(ROSE comes to the screen door.)

ROSE: Cory, we gonna be ready to go in a minute.
CORY *(To RAYNELL)*: You go on in the house and change them shoes like Mama told you so we can go to Papa's funeral.
RAYNELL: Okay, I'll be back.

(RAYNELL exits into the house. CORY gets up and crosses over to the tree. ROSE stands in the screen door watching him. GABRIEL enters from the alley.)

GABRIEL *(Calling)*: Hey, Rose!
ROSE: Gabe?
GABRIEL: I'm here, Rose. Hey Rose, I'm here!

(ROSE enters from the house.)

ROSE: Lord . . . Look here, Lyons!
LYONS: See, I told you, Rose . . . I told you they'd let him come.
CORY: How you doing, Uncle Gabe?
LYONS: How you doing, Uncle Gabe?
GABRIEL: Hey, Rose. It's time. It's time to tell St. Peter to open the gates. Troy, you ready? You ready,

Troy. I'm gonna tell St. Peter to open the gates. You get ready now.

(GABRIEL, *with great fanfare, braces himself to blow. The trumpet is without a mouthpiece. He puts the end of it into his mouth and blows with great force, like a man who has been waiting some twenty-odd years for this single moment. No sound comes out of the trumpet. He braces himself and blows again with the same result. A third time he blows. There is a weight of impossible description that falls away and leaves him bare and exposed to a frightful realization.*

It is a trauma that a sane and normal mind would be unable to withstand. He begins to dance. A slow, strange dance, eerie and life-giving. A dance of atavistic signature and ritual. LYONS *attempts to embrace him.* GABRIEL *pushes* LYONS *away. He begins to howl in what is an attempt at song, or perhaps a song turning back into itself in an attempt at speech. He finishes his dance and the gates of heaven stand open as wide as God's closet.*)

That's the way that go!

BLACKOUT.

Figure 1. Troy (James Earl Jones) embraces Rose (Mary Alice) in the first scene of *Fences*. The 1987 New York production was directed by Lloyd Richards. (Photograph: Ron Scherl.)

Figure 2. Awkwardly holding his baby daughter, Troy (James Earl Jones) brings her home to Rose, hoping that Rose will take care of her. (Photograph: Ron Scherl.)

Figure 3. At the end of the first act, Troy (James Earl Jones) angrily confronts Cory (Courtney B. Vance), who is dressed for the football practice
Troy has forbidden him to attend, in the 1987 New York production. (Photograph: Ron Scherl.)

Figure 4. Challenging death, "the fastball in the corner," Troy (James Earl Jones) assumes his batting stance. (Photograph: Ron Scherl.)

Staging of *Fences*

INTERVIEW WITH MARY ALICE
AND JAMES EARL JONES, 1985,
BY HEATHER HENDERSON

HENDERSON: What has it been like to work in an August Wilson play?

JONES: A dear friend of mine, a director, came backstage today and said that the play is unusual, and I agreed. You don't often find this kind of play. Steinbeck used to write about this stratum of life, but among American playwrights, it is rare. Few writers can capture dialect as dialogue in a manner as interesting and accurate as August's. My first experience with a play with the black sound was by a white writer, Howard Sackler—in *The Great White Hope*. That dialogue was not identifiable as Galveston, Texas; it was a poetic rendering of an *idea* of Southern dialect. August's dialogue is less "invented." Howard's dialogue was invented totally out of his imagination, which I admired. But August's language has a certain root—I've *heard* other people speak with the same kind of inarticulateness. You find it in other cultures—the uneducated Irish too sometimes speak with great floweriness, they use language very richly—and I think August is catching this sort of speech.

My dad, who was a Mississippian before I was, said don't ever lose touch with that sound; don't let your children lose touch with it. People do get educated out of it.

ALICE: I have found this with other writers, too—Charles Gordone, who wrote *No Place to Be Somebody,* Lorraine Hansberry, Charles Fuller—the wonderful thing is that because they are writing about material they're very familiar with, they can create the proper language, which is very important. Also—and August has admitted this—they love actors. So they write interesting characters. No matter how small the roles are, the characters are always complete.

HENDERSON: Was Troy's character difficult for you to realize, James?

JONES: There are certain things that I find very difficult to achieve, and certain things in Troy that I haven't yet resolved. But overall, I love the person. I have known men similar to him, although their characters were not as rich.

It's been hard to modulate Troy's levels of energy, to measure the extent to which he is deeply angry and the extent to which he is just loud-mouthing. I have not found yet where his depths and his highs are. He's like a manic-depressive; he's up and he's down. His relationship to his son is the most complicated one—I don't believe I have yet solved that. The love relationships he has with Rose, with Bono, and even with the older son are a lot easier to achieve than those he has with his younger son and his daughter. That is probably because an actor draws from his own experience, and unless you have things in your own life that can enlighten you, you have to search and search until you understand it.

HENDERSON (*To* JONES): Your two-year old hasn't quite reached Cory's age yet?

ALICE: In fifteen years.

JONES (*laughing*): Maybe it is all sitting there and I haven't found the connection yet. I'll share something with you. When I was thirteen, I was being raised by my maternal grandfather. We lived in the country, in both Mississippi and Michigan. In Michigan, my folks were church people—Southern Methodists, but they'd shout and holler and roll on the floor—they invented their own churches, or they would engage circuit preachers, black ministers who would ride by horse or car to a different church every Sunday. The preacher we had engaged that season was attending the chicken dinner one Sunday, and I overheard a conversation between him and my grandfather about men in one household. The preacher was saying, "Now, the boy's thirteen, and he's going to be fourteen." He didn't use the expression "smelling his piss," but he might well have used what August uses in this play. He said, "Sooner or later he's got to go, because two men in one house don't cut it." I was devastated to hear this; I loved my grandfather more than anybody. I couldn't imagine that there would be a conflict between him and me that would force me to leave or force him to make that decision. I read this play and I see there it is again. Is it inevitable?

HENDERSON: Did it happen to you and your grandfather?

JONES: No, but I assumed that it would be inevitable. And of course in the animal kingdom it *is* inevitable that young males are driven away, unless they prove themselves strong enough. I'm haunted by that: by the past and by the prospects of it in the future. Will I have a conflict with my own son? I guess it is so prevalent in the animal kingdom that it is certainly worth holding up as a prototype of a conflict.

HENDERSON: And not just the animal kingdom—it's in the Bible. You're supposed to leave your parents' house or—put away childish things . . .

ALICE: "When I was a child I behaved as a child, but

when I became a man I put away childish things." It's from *Corinthians*.

JONES: You know the Bible, don't you?

HENDERSON: What about you, Mary? How did you approach your role in this play?

ALICE: In terms of how I approached the work, it was not too different from most characters that I have played. I tried to come to it very openly, and I also came to this one willingly, because it's a play I love. Then, of course, I looked forward to being the wife of James, unlike sometimes when I am playing the wife of actors and they're difficult. Not necessarily interpersonally difficult, but when you have to work at making the other actor your husband. I didn't have this difficulty with James at all. But basically I just started with what had been given by the writer, what Rose says, what is said about her. I suppose I somehow used women that I knew, women I knew in 1957. Pittsburgh is not too far removed from Chicago, where I grew up. I didn't have any real difficulty creating her in the atmosphere of rehearsals and in Lloyd's direction. I just trusted Lloyd, which is very important; whatever he said I accepted.

A lot of who *I* am is also Rose. I know many women who are waiting, as she says, to bloom, and many will never bloom. I have bloomed as a person, more than Rose, I feel, because I have at least to some degree been able to follow my dreams. So there are little petals sticking up somewhere. Rose is not unhappy being the wife and the mother. She is contented, but this is something that people do; they say, this is my place in life, and they accept it. She is able to be happy with this until she finds out that her husband has betrayed her. And it's only then that she begins to deal with what she really wants, with the sacrifices she made in giving all, putting everything into her marriage. There was so much there, already in the script, and given a good director, it was very, very clear.

HENDERSON: Some audience members seeing *Fences* have said they see their own lives portrayed by it. You remember the audience member who told us that her parents were Portuguese immigrants and saw her own life on the stage. What of *your* lives did you find in the play, if you found any of your life there?

ALICE: Having to deal with the racism, like the way Troy is trying to break into baseball. When I grew up, I attended an all-girls school that was predominantly white, and I began to see that there are at least two cultures in America. I can also relate to the oral tradition: my grandfather, my father, even my mother were always telling stories. That is a very African tradition. Dark people did not write it; it was passed on orally. That's very much a part of what I heard in the play.

HENDERSON (*To* JONES): You have said you've known men like Troy.

JONES: Yes. My summer nights in Michigan were very similar to this play's situation. I don't remember who *wouldn't* take it upon himself to entertain or tell a story. On summer nights the gatherings would happen on a porch. Somebody would end up telling a story, and someone else—visitors, guests—would counter with another story.

ALICE: I remember we used to sit out in front of the house a lot—every night, especially in summer. Everybody would sit out there. People don't do that anymore. I guess they're more afraid now.

HENDERSON: Within the limits of blocking and specific direction in *Fences,* I've enjoyed the spontaneity that you bring to your roles—from rehearsal right into performance. How have you found that freshness in this play?

ALICE: In rehearsals, Lloyd had a firm hand on the direction, but it was like you didn't feel it. It was always there, shaping the play, but within that, within whatever he wanted, there was so much freedom allowed to the actors. I still feel that.

JONES: Lloyd has a word he used to me and one or two other actors; he said it as an admonition. He would tell us, "Don't *manage* it. Let it happen to you." Then we relaxed enough so we developed a certain energy, and that got built into the production. Lloyd would make directorial choices by reminding us of things that we had done and saying he still wanted them. But a lot of his directorial choices were the things that he got us free and spontaneous enough to find. So he didn't have to say, "Do it this way, do it that way."

The greatest reward to come out of our spontaneity was after I had found the extent to which I thought I could take Troy's exposing himself when he says, "I'm going to be a daddy." I made it quite large, and Mary was engaging at quite a full level, too. And then one day in rehearsal, Russell [who played Gabriel] suddenly came in holding a real rose when he said his line about having a flower for Rose. Whatever was happening to Mary, in response to what I had just said to her, stopped. The flower filled the void. I don't know how a director could have managed that.

HENDERSON: Has August's play affected you emotionally in any special way? Do you invest more or less emotional energy than is usual in your performances?

JONES: I feel a fatigue that does not occur in a play where the character resolves his situation before the end. Here Troy dies before the last scene, so he does not resolve things onstage. I bring a lot of stuff offstage with me after my last scene, and then I don't know what to do with it. In serious plays, especially tragedies, the actor undergoes a resolution, and he can go home. I can't quite feel that. It helps when I sit backstage and listen to the last scene when they sort things out about me before my funeral. Then I feel better about going home. For a long time in the rehearsal period I did not watch the last scene, and I was missing something: that resolve. For an audience there has to be a kind of catharsis, but an actor has to have it, too.

HENDERSON: In a "conventional" tragedy, as the actor, you would go through that catharsis with the audience.

JONES: Yes. The first time I watched the rehearsal of the last scene, I was crying—not just for what I should have been crying about. I was crying for all the times that I should have been watching it and hadn't. There are three moments that trigger the ending catharsis: the moment when Rose acknowledges Troy has died, Cory's tribute, and Gabe's blowing the trumpet.

ALICE: Unlike Jimmy, I think I *have* a catharsis. I have mine at the top of the second act. I don't feel it in the evening, but more when I wake up the next morning—then I feel drained. I usually don't feel like being with people after the show, because all of that stuff that is set up from the first scene onward is still operating. The play requires such concentration and takes such energy. Not effort—but it *is* draining. After the play is over there is a residue; the character does not leave me right away. Regardless of what Mary Alice's behavior is after the show, inside, Rose is still there.

JONES: Is it possible that most plays or their stories demand only an aspect of the character, whereas this play demands the total character? There is not much more to Troy than what we are given, in spite of this private life he has with another woman. Troy speaks of her as something new—he thinks he has discovered something new. He says he laughs at home, but then he talks about another kind of laughter, another part of himself that he never knew before. I think that may just be a fantasy on his part. I think this play, this story, demands all of what this man is, and it asks its actors to make a commitment larger than you would make even in a Shakespeare play.

ALICE: There was a moment in the show today when I was looking at Troy sitting on the sawhorse—you know, when Lyons comes in and Bono tells him Troy has been promoted. Jimmy was just sitting there, and I thought, "Troy is really a great man." He doesn't think of himself as a great man.

JONES: No.

ALICE: But he has been trying to do something. Not just for himself. He is trying to make it better for others working. And he is sitting there modestly, kind of laughing about it. And I just looked at him and thought, "This is really a great man."

JONES: That's curious, because that is the one moment he is not shooting his mouth off.

ALICE: Yes; he is just sitting there, having gotten the promotion, and they're teasing him and he takes the teasing.

JONES: There isn't much subtext or many hidden parts to these people; they are all out there. They have private thoughts, but not as you would have them in most modern plays.

ALICE: They are very open. The subtext is there, but you don't have to play that. You don't have to worry about it. You know who you are, what you want, what your relationship is, and before you know it the moment changes; you're laughing at one moment, and the next moment it's serious. It's so real; that's how people are. That's what is so beautiful about this play: the moments. And no matter how many times we have done it, it's still fresh.

DAVID HENRY HWANG

1957–

"Study your face and you will see—the shape of your face is the shape of faces back many generations—across an ocean, in another soil. You must become one with your family before you can hope to live away from it." In these haunting lines from David Henry Hwang's third play, a native Chinese character speaking to his Chinese American great-nephew defines one of the central problems of identity that have perennially vexed immigrants and children of immigrants—the problem of how to honor one's ethnic heritage while at the same time making a new life in a new land. Hwang (pronounced "Wong"), a first-generation Chinese American, has explored such problems in a series of plays, each offering a slightly different perspective on the central question of constructing and maintaining one's identity, culminating in the award-winning *M. Butterfly* (1988). Hwang's parents were both born in China, his father immigrating to Los Angeles in the late 1940s to study business at the University of Southern California, his mother arriving in 1952 to study music. His father worked first as an accountant and then went into business for himself, eventually founding the first federally chartered Asian American bank in the United States. Such notable business success led to almost complete assimilation for the children, all born in America, who studied Chinese for a while but were then withdrawn from those classes. Hwang took violin lessons, participated in debate competition at his private school, and entered Stanford University with plans to study law.

While at Stanford, Hwang became interested in writing plays, despite minimal theatrical experience, and switched his major to English. He saw Sam Shepard's new plays as they were produced at the San Francisco Magic Theatre, spent the summer of 1977 working odd jobs in a theater, and in 1978 signed up for a playwriting workshop run by Sam Shepard. As a result, he drafted his first play, *FOB*, which was then produced by his Stanford dormitory as part of a campus festival of student-written plays. He also sent *FOB* to the 1979 Playwrights' Conference at the O'Neill Theater Center in Waterford, Connecticut, where it became one of the twelve selected for development. A year later, in June 1980, Joseph Papp produced *FOB* at the New York Shakespeare Festival Public Theater, thus beginning an association that would last for three years, during which Hwang saw five of his plays produced in New York.

FOB (the initials stand for "Fresh Off the Boat" in Hwang's play, as well as "Free on Board" in standard shipping terminology) embodies many of the issues that dominate Hwang's writing. Most centrally, the play dramatizes the question of how Chinese-Americans cope with their various "faces." Each of the play's three characters represents a different stage in the process of cultural mixing and therefore a different balance of the dual heritage: Steve, the FOB, son of a wealthy Hong Kong souvenir manufacturer, has just arrived in Los Angeles; Grace, a first-generation Chinese-American, works in a Chinese restaurant; and Dale, Grace's cousin, a second-generation American of Chinese descent, calls himself an ABC ("American

Born Chinese") and despises all FOBs. Yet Hwang asks the audience to see that Dale's verbal attack on Steve is part of his desperate attempt to assimilate—"To not be a Chinese, a yellow, a slant, a gook." Faced with a heritage he cannot escape, in a world he wishes to join, Dale mocks Steve's accent, dumps a bottle of hot sauce all over Steve's food, and competes with Steve for Grace's attention. But in addition to the rivalry over Grace, which is depicted primarily in realistic confrontations, Hwang also presents a symbolic conflict between Grace and Steve, staged as a ritual battle. Grace takes on the persona of Fa Mu Lan, the Chinese woman warrior, while Steve assumes the persona of Gwan Gung, the god of fighters and writers. Grace follows her victory over Steve with a peace offering of Chinese food, the same food Steve asked for at the play's beginning, and then, in a swift return to the play's more realistic mode, invites Steve out for an evening of dancing.

While *FOB* ends with a staged battle, Hwang's second play, *The Dance and the Railroad* (1981), is concerned with performance as a way of accepting one's heritage. Set in 1867, on a mountaintop near the transcontinental railroad, the play presents just two characters: Lone, a dancer from the Chinese Opera who is working as a railroad builder, and Ma, who has been in the country for four weeks and is also working on the railroad. By juxtaposing the highly disciplined and ritualistic world of Chinese opera with the unlikely setting of the American West, Hwang underscores Lone's intense commitment to his Chinese heritage. Ma, at first a naïve newcomer (another FOB), gradually wins Lone's respect, and in the play's final scene the two men stage their own "opera," with Ma as the hero.

Though Hwang's third play, *Family Devotions* (1981), also explores issues of Chinese and American identity, it draws much more directly on details from Hwang's own life: a prosperous Southern California setting, a Chinese-American banker, his violinist son, and elderly relations who, like Hwang's own family, are "born-again Christians." In a world defined by an opulent California lifestyle—complete with sunroom, barbecue grill, and tennis courts—comes Di-Gou, a resident of the People's Republic of China, who has come to California to bring his older sisters back to China. By exposing an unpleasant truth about their aunt See-Goh-Poh—a legend through her status as a Christian missionary—Di-Gou tries to pull his sisters back to their common Chinese heritage, but the shock kills them. Hwang's most recent play, *Golden Child* (1996, revised 1998), again deals with Chinese heritage and Christianity, but this time set in the China of 1912. The protagonist, Eng Tien-Bin, is a wealthy businessman who decides to convert to Christianity. Complicating matters is the fact that he is the husband of three wives—the traditional Siu-Yong, the scheming Luan, and the naïve Elin—two of whom will have to go, in accordance with Christian doctrine. While Hwang doesn't paint Westernization as simply a threat to these Chinese characters, he nonetheless shows how the resulting tensions lead to tragedy.

Hwang's plays not only probe his own life as a Chinese American but celebrate his rediscovery of the traditions of Oriental theater. While creating *The Dance and the Railroad*, Hwang drew on the extensive background in traditional Chinese dance and theater of his actors, John Lone (who appeared as Steve in the New York production of *FOB*) and Tzi Ma; so crucial was their special training that he named the characters for these actors. Likewise, in *The Sound of a Voice*, a one-act play about "a warrior who goes into the woods to kill a witch and winds up falling in love with her," Hwang originally imagined the Woman as an *onnagata* role, that is, to be played, as in Kabuki theater, by a man who specializes in playing women's roles. Although eventually an actress played the Woman, Hwang's intention creates double meanings throughout the text; the warrior's first line is "You are very kind to take me in" while near the end of the play the Woman demonstrates her ability to handle a sword and then apologizes by saying, "My skills—they're so— inappropriate. I look like a man."

So when Hwang heard what one might call a real-life *onnagata* story, involving a French diplomat and a performer from the Peking Opera, he found a situation that poignantly embodied many of his long-standing preoccupations with identity. In the afterword to *M. Butterfly* (reprinted following the play), Hwang wonders "What did Bouriscot [the diplomat] think he was getting in this Chinese actress?" And his answer is "He probably thought he had found Madame Butterfly," or, as Hwang explains, "the submissive Oriental number." In deconstructing the story that Puccini's opera has made world famous—the story of the ill-fated romance between Pinkerton, an American naval officer, and Butterfly, a young Japanese woman whom Pinkerton buys as a wife, impregnates, and then deserts—Hwang investigates yet again the question, What is the relationship between the Oriental and the Westerner? But instead of working from the point of view of the Asian American, who feels split between two worlds, Hwang suggests that the image of the Oriental is actually a deeply held cultural construction that reveals Western desires and fears. Gallimard (the renamed Bouriscot) falls in love with Song Liling as Butterfly—their first meeting comes after a performance of Butterfly's death scene—and tells his story to the audience in a desperate wish to rewrite the story, "always searching for a new ending . . . where she returns at last to my arms."

The unique theatricality of the play and its constant juxtaposing of "performance" and "reality" in the story of Gallimard were stunningly realized on stage in the original production directed by John Dexter. Eiko Ishioka's design surrounded the black rectangular central acting area with a curved ramp, swirling across and around the stage (see Figure 1 and Ishioka's commentary following the play). Clive Barnes, writing in the *New York Post*, called it "a runway equally fit for an Oriental queen or even Hollywood's Rita Hayworth," and indeed to many viewers, the ramp recalled the Japanese *hanamichi* (a long entrance platform in Kabuki theater) as well as the more Western version often used by strippers. The ornate costumes associated with Oriental theater and with Western opera (see Figure 2) made Song Liling a striking figure. In fact, even when not performing Butterfly, Song's attire seems to recall the suave elegance of Anna May Wong, a Chinese American actress familiar to thousands of Americans through her appearance in Hollywood films (see Figure 3). By emphasizing the appealing exoticism of Song Liling's world, Hwang, Dexter, and Ishioka put the audience in the position of the protagonist, Gallimard. The gorgeous costumes, the choreographed movement, the music (both Oriental and Western) all work to seduce the audience so that Gallimard's surprising betrayal is ultimately ours as well.

M. BUTTERFLY

BY DAVID HENRY HWANG

CHARACTERS

RENE GALLIMARD
SONG LILING
MARC/MAN #2/CONSUL SHARPLESS
RENEE/WOMAN AT PARTY/GIRL IN MAGAZINE
COMRADE CHIN/SUZUKI/SHU FANG
HELGA
M. TOULON/MAN #1/JUDGE
KUROGO [*dancers/stagehands*]

PLAYWRIGHT'S NOTES

A former French diplomat and a Chinese opera singer have been sentenced to six years in jail for spying for China after a two-day trial that traced a story of clandestine love and mistaken sexual identity. . . . Mr. Bouriscot was accused of passing information to China after he fell in love with Mr. Shi, whom he believed for twenty years to be a woman.

—*The New York Times*, May 11, 1986

This play was suggested by international newspaper accounts of a recent espionage trial. For purposes of dramatization, names have been changed, characters created, and incidents devised or altered, and this play does not purport to be a factual record of real events or real people.

I could escape this feeling
With my China girl . . .

—David Bowie & Iggy Pop

SETTING

The action of the play takes place in a Paris prison in the present, and in recall, during the decade 1960 to 1970 in Beijing, and from 1966 to the present in Paris.

ACT 1 / SCENE 1

(M. GALLIMARD's *prison cell. Paris. Present.*)

(*Lights fade up to reveal* RENE GALLIMARD, *65, in a prison cell. He wears a comfortable bathrobe, and looks old and tired. The sparsely furnished cell contains a wooden crate upon which sits a hot plate with a kettle, and a portable tape recorder.* GALLIMARD *sits on the crate staring at the recorder, a sad smile on his face.*

Upstage SONG, *who appears as a beautiful woman in traditional Chinese garb, dances a traditional piece from the Peking Opera, surrounded by the percussive clatter of Chinese music.*

Then, slowly, lights and sound cross-fade; the Chinese opera music dissolves into a Western opera, the "Love Duet" from Puccini's Madame Butterfly. SONG *continues dancing, now to the Western accompaniment. Though her movements are the same, the difference in music now gives them a balletic quality.*

GALLIMARD *rises, and turns upstage towards the figure of* SONG, *who dances without acknowledging him.*)

GALLIMARD: Butterfly, Butterfly . . .

(*He forces himself to turn away, as the image of* SONG *fades out, and talks to us.*)

GALLIMARD: The limits of my cell are as such: four-and-a-half meters by five. There's one window against the far wall; a door, very strong, to protect me from autograph hounds. I'm responsible for the tape recorder, the hot plate, and this charming coffee table.

When I want to eat, I'm marched off to the dining room—hot, steaming slop appears on my plate. When I want to sleep, the light bulb turns itself off—the work of fairies. It's an enchanted space I occupy. The French—we know how to run a prison.

But, to be honest, I'm not treated like an ordinary prisoner. Why? Because I'm a celebrity. You see, I make people laugh.

I never dreamed this day would arrive. I've never been considered witty or clever. In fact, as a young boy, in an informal poll among my grammar school classmates, I was voted "least likely to be invited to a party." It's a title I managed to hold on to for many years. Despite some stiff competition.

But now, how the tables turn! Look at me: the life of every social function in Paris. Paris? Why be modest? My fame has spread to Amsterdam, London, New York. Listen to them! In the world's smartest parlors. I'm the one who lifts their spirits!

(With a flourish, GALLIMARD *directs our attention to another part of the stage.)*

ACT 1 / SCENE 2

(A party. Present.)

(Lights go up on a chic-looking parlor, where a well-dressed trio, two men and one woman, make conversation. GALLIMARD *also remains lit; he observes them from his cell.)*

WOMAN: And what of Gallimard?

MAN 1: Gallimard?

MAN 2: Gallimard!

GALLIMARD *(To us)*: You see? They're all determined to say my name, as if it were some new dance.

WOMAN: He still claims not to believe the truth.

MAN 1: What? Still? Even since the trial?

WOMAN: Yes. Isn't it mad?

MAN 2 *(Laughing)*: He says . . . it was dark . . . and she was very modest!

(The trio break into laughter.)

MAN 1: So—what? He never touched her with his hands?

MAN 2: Perhaps he did, and simply misidentified the equipment. A compelling case for sex education in the schools.

WOMAN: To protect the National Security—the Church can't argue with that.

MAN 1: That's impossible! How could he not know?

MAN 2: Simple ignorance.

MAN 1: For twenty years?

MAN 2: Time flies when you're being stupid.

WOMAN: Well, I thought the French were ladies' men.

MAN 2: It seems Monsieur Gallimard was overly anxious to live up to his national reputation.

WOMAN: Well, he's not very good-looking.

MAN 1: No, he's not.

MAN 2: Certainly not.

WOMAN: Actually, I feel sorry for him.

MAN 2: A toast! To Monsieur Gallimard!

WOMAN: Yes! To Gallimard!

MAN 1: To Gallimard!

MAN 2: Vive la différence!

(They toast, laughing. Lights down on them.)

ACT 1 / SCENE 3

(M. GALLIMARD*'s cell.)*

GALLIMARD *(Smiling)*: You see? They toast me. I've become patron saint of the socially inept. Can they really be so foolish? Men like that—they should be scratching at my door, begging to learn my secrets! For I, Rene Gallimard, you see, I have known, and been loved by . . . the Perfect Woman.

Alone in this cell, I sit night after night, watching our story play through my head, always searching for a new ending, one which redeems my honor, where she returns at last to my arms. And I imagine you—my ideal audience—who come to understand and even, perhaps just a little, to envy me.

(He turns on his tape recorder. Over the house speakers, we hear the opening phrases of Madame Butterfly.*)*

GALLIMARD: In order for you to understand what I did and why, I must introduce you to my favorite opera: *Madame Butterfly.* By Giacomo Puccini. First produced at La Scala, Milan, in 1904, it is now beloved throughout the Western world.

(As GALLIMARD *describes the opera, the tape segues in and out to sections he may be describing.)*

GALLIMARD: And why not? Its heroine, Cio-Cio-San, also known as Butterfly, is a feminine ideal, beautiful and brave. And its hero, the man for whom she gives up everything, is—*(He pulls out a naval officer's cap from under his crate, pops it on his head, and struts about)*—not very good-looking, not too bright, and pretty much a wimp: Benjamin Franklin Pinkerton of the U.S. Navy. As the curtain rises, he's just closed on two great bargains: one on a house, the other on a woman—call it a package deal.

Pinkerton purchased the rights to Butterfly for one hundred yen—in modern currency, equivalent to about . . . sixty-six cents. So, he's feeling pretty pleased with himself as Sharpless, the American consul, arrives to witness the marriage.

*(*MARC, *wearing an official cap to designate* SHARPLESS, *enters and plays the character.)*

SHARPLESS/MARC: Pinkerton!

PINKERTON/GALLIMARD: Sharpless! How's it hangin'? It's a great day, just great. Between my house, my wife, and the rickshaw ride in from town, I've saved nineteen cents just this morning.

SHARPLESS: Wonderful. I can see the inscription on your tombstone already: "I saved a dollar, here I lie." *(He looks around)* Nice house.

PINKERTON: It's artistic. Artistic, don't you think? Like the way the shoji screens slide open to reveal the wet bar and disco mirror ball? Classy, huh? Great for impressing the chicks.

SHARPLESS: "Chicks"? Pinkerton, you're going to be a married man!

PINKERTON: Well, sort of.

SHARPLESS: What do you mean?

PINKERTON: This country—Sharpless, it is okay. You got all these geisha girls running around—

SHARPLESS: I know! I live here!

PINKERTON: Then, you know the marriage laws, right? I split for one month, it's annulled!

SHARPLESS: Leave it to you to read the fine print. Who's the lucky girl?

PINKERTON: Cio-Cio-San. Her friends call her Butterfly. Sharpless, she eats out of my hand!

SHARPLESS: She's probably very hungry.

PINKERTON: Not like American girls. It's true what they say about Oriental girls. They want to be treated bad!

SHARPLESS: Oh, please!

PINKERTON: It's true!

SHARPLESS: Are you serious about this girl?

PINKERTON: I'm marrying her, aren't I?

SHARPLESS: Yes—with generous trade-in terms.

PINKERTON: When I leave, she'll know what it's like to have loved a real man. And I'll even buy her a few nylons.

SHARPLESS: You aren't planning to take her with you?

PINKERTON: Huh? Where?

SHARPLESS: Home!

PINKERTON: You mean, America? Are you crazy? Can you see her trying to buy rice in St. Louis?

SHARPLESS: So, you're not serious.

(Pause.)

PINKERTON/GALLIMARD *(As* PINKERTON*)*: Consul, I am a sailor in port. *(As* GALLIMARD*)* They then proceed to sing the famous duet, "The Whole World Over."

(The duet plays on the speakers. GALLIMARD, *as* PINKERTON, *lip-syncs his lines from the opera.)*

GALLIMARD: To give a rough translation: "The whole world over, the Yankee travels, casting his anchor wherever he wants. Life's not worth living unless he can win the hearts of the fairest maidens, then hotfoot it off the premises ASAP." *(He turns towards* MARC*)* In the preceding scene, I played Pinkerton, the womanizing cad, and my friend Marc from school . . . *(*MARC *bows grandly for our benefit)* played Sharpless, the sensitive soul of reason. In life, however, our positions were usually—no, always—reversed.

ACT 1 / SCENE 4

(Ecole Nationale. Aix-en-Provence. 1947.)

GALLIMARD: No, Marc, I think I'd rather stay home.

MARC: Are you crazy?! We are going to Dad's condo in Marseilles! You know what happened last time?

GALLIMARD: Of course I do.

MARC: Of course you don't! You never know. . . . They stripped, Rene!

GALLIMARD: Who stripped?

MARC: The girls!

GALLIMARD: Girls? Who said anything about girls?

MARC: Rene, we're a buncha university guys goin' up

to the woods. What are we gonna do—talk philosophy?

GALLIMARD: What girls? Where do you get them?

MARC: Who cares? The point is, they come. On trucks. Packed in like sardines. The back flips open, babes hop out, we're ready to—roll.

GALLIMARD: You mean, they just—?

MARC: Before you know it, every last one of them—they're stripped and splashing around my pool. There's no moon out, they can't see what's going on, their boobs are flapping, right? You close your eyes, reach out—it's grab bag, get it? Doesn't matter whose ass is between whose legs, whose teeth are sinking into who. You're just in there, going at it, eyes closed, on and on for as long as you can stand. *(Pause)* Some fun, huh?

GALLIMARD: What happens in the morning?

MARC: In the morning, you're ready to talk some philosophy. *(Beat)* So how 'bout it?

GALLIMARD: Marc, I can't . . . I'm afraid they'll say no—the girls. So I never ask.

MARC: You don't have to ask! That's the beauty—don't you see? They don't have to say yes. It's perfect for a guy like you, really.

GALLIMARD: You go ahead . . . I may come later.

MARC: Hey, Rene—it doesn't matter that you're clumsy and got zits—they're not looking!

GALLIMARD: Thank you very much.

MARC: Wimp.

*(*MARC *walks over to the other side of the stage, and starts waving and smiling at women in the audience.)*

GALLIMARD *(To us)*: We now return to my version of *Madame Butterfly* and the events leading to my recent conviction for treason.

*(*GALLIMARD *notices* MARC *making lewd gestures.)*

GALLIMARD: Marc, what are you doing?

MARC: Huh? *(Sotto voce)* Rene, there're a lotta great babes out there. They're probably lookin' at me and thinking, "What a dangerous guy."

GALLIMARD: Yes—how could they help but be impressed by your cool sophistication?

*(*GALLIMARD *pops the* SHARPLESS *cap on* MARC*'s head, and points him offstage.* MARC *exits, leering.)*

ACT 1 / SCENE 5

(M. GALLIMARD*'s cell.)*

GALLIMARD: Next, Butterfly makes her entrance. We learn her age—fifteen . . . but very mature for her years.

(Lights come up on the area where we saw SONG *dancing at the top of the play. She appears there again, now dressed as Madame Butterfly, moving to the "Love Duet."* GALLIMARD *turns upstage slightly to watch, transfixed.)*

GALLIMARD: But as she glides past him, beautiful, laughing softly behind her fan, don't we who are men sigh with hope? We, who are not handsome, nor brave, nor powerful, yet somehow believe, like Pinkerton, that we deserve a Butterfly. She arrives with all her possessions in the folds of her sleeves, lays them all out, for her man to do with as he pleases. Even her life itself—she bows her head as she whispers that she's not even worth the hundred yen he paid for her. He's already given too much, when we know he's really had to give nothing at all.

(*Music and lights on* SONG *out.* GALLIMARD *sits at his crate.*)

GALLIMARD: In real life, women who put their total worth at less than sixty-six cents are quite hard to find. The closest we come is in the pages of these magazines. (*He reaches into his crate, pulls out a stack of girlie magazines, and begins flipping through them*) Quite a necessity in prison. For three or four dollars, you get seven or eight women.

I first discovered these magazines at my uncle's house. One day, as a boy of twelve. The first time I saw them in his closet . . . all lined up—my body shook. Not with lust—no, with power. Here were women—a shelfful—who would do exactly as I wanted.

(*The "Love Duet" creeps in over the speakers. Special comes up, revealing, not* SONG *this time, but a pinup girl in a sexy negligee, her back to us.* GALLIMARD *turns upstage and looks at her.*)

GIRL: I know you're watching me.
GALLIMARD: My throat . . . it's dry.
GIRL: I leave my blinds open every night before I go to bed.
GALLIMARD: I can't move.
GIRL: I leave my blinds open and the lights on.
GALLIMARD: I'm shaking. My skin is hot, but my penis is soft. Why?
GIRL: I stand in front of the window.
GALLIMARD: What is she going to do?
GIRL: I toss my hair, and I let my lips part . . . barely.
GALLIMARD: I shouldn't be seeing this. It's so dirty. I'm so bad.
GIRL: Then, slowly, I lift off my nightdress.
GALLIMARD: Oh, god. I can't believe it. I can't—
GIRL: I toss it to the ground.
GALLIMARD: Now, she's going to walk away. She's going to—
GIRL: I stand there, in the light, displaying myself.
GALLIMARD: No. She's—why is she naked?
GIRL: To you.
GALLIMARD: In front of a window? This is wrong. No—
GIRL: Without shame.

GALLIMARD: No, she must . . . like it.
GIRL: I like it.
GALLIMARD: She . . . she wants me to see.
GIRL: I want you to see.
GALLIMARD: I can't believe it! She's getting excited!
GIRL: I can't see you. You can do whatever you want.
GALLIMARD: I can't do a thing. Why?
GIRL: What would you like me to do . . . next?

(*Lights go down on her. Music off. Silence, as* GALLIMARD *puts away his magazines. Then he resumes talking to us.*)

GALLIMARD: Act Two begins with Butterfly staring at the ocean. Pinkerton's been called back to the U.S., and he's given his wife a detailed schedule of his plans. In the column marked "return date," he's written "when the robins nest." This failed to ignite her suspicions. Now, three years have passed without a peep from him. Which brings a response from her faithful servant, Suzuki.

(COMRADE CHIN *enters, playing* SUZUKI.)

SUZUKI: Girl, he's a loser. What'd he ever give you? Nineteen cents and those ugly Day-Glo stockings? Look, it's finished! Kaput! Done! And you should be glad! I mean, the guy was a woofer! He tried before, you know—before he met you, he went down to geisha central and plunked down his spare change in front of the usual candidates—everyone else gagged! These are hungry prostitutes, and they were not interested, get the picture? Now, stop slathering when an American ship sails in, and let's make some bucks—I mean, yen! We are broke!

Now, what about Yamadori? Hey, hey—don't look away—the man is a prince—figuratively, and, what's even better, literally. He's rich, he's handsome, he says he'll die if you don't marry him—and he's even willing to overlook the little fact that you've been deflowered all over the place by a foreign devil. What do you mean, "But he's Japanese?" You're Japanese! You think you've been touched by the whitey god? He was a sailor with dirty hands!

(SUZUKI *stalks offstage.*)

GALLIMARD: She's also visited by Consul Sharpless, sent by Pinkerton on a minor errand.

(MARC *enters, as* SHARPLESS.)

SHARPLESS: I hate this job.
GALLIMARD: This Pinkerton—he doesn't show up personally to tell his wife he's abandoning her. No, he sends a government diplomat . . . at taxpayer's expense.
SHARPLESS: Butterfly? Butterfly? I have some bad— I'm going to be ill. Butterfly, I came to tell you—

GALLIMARD: Butterfly says she knows he'll return and if he doesn't she'll kill herself rather than go back to her own people. (*Beat*) This causes a lull in the conversation.

SHARPLESS: Let's put it this way . . .

GALLIMARD: Butterfly runs into the next room, and returns holding—

(*Sound cue: a baby crying.* SHARPLESS, *"seeing" this, backs away.*)

SHARPLESS: Well, good. Happy to see things going so well. I suppose I'll be going now. Ta ta. Ciao. (*He turns away. Sound cue out*) I hate this job. (*He exits*)

GALLIMARD: At that moment, Butterfly spots in the harbor an American ship—the *Abramo Lincoln!*

(*Music cue: "The Flower Duet."* SONG, *still dressed as Butterfly, changes into a wedding kimono, moving to the music.*)

GALLIMARD: This is the moment that redeems her years of waiting. With Suzuki's help, they cover the room with flowers—

(CHIN, *as* SUZUKI, *trudges onstage and drops a lone flower without much enthusiasm.*)

GALLIMARD: —and she changes into her wedding dress to prepare for Pinkerton's arrival.

(SUZUKI *helps Butterfly change.* HELGA *enters, and helps* GALLIMARD *change into a tuxedo.*)

GALLIMARD: I married a woman older than myself— Helga.

HELGA: My father was ambassador to Australia. I grew up among criminals and kangaroos.

GALLIMARD: Hearing that brought me to the altar—

(HELGA *exits.*)

GALLIMARD: —where I took a vow renouncing love. No fantasy woman would ever want me, so, yes, I would settle for a quick leap up the career ladder. Passion, I banish, and in its place—practicality!

But my vows had long since lost their charm by the time we arrived in China. The sad truth is that all men want a beautiful woman, and the uglier the man, the greater the want.

(SUZUKI *makes final adjustments of Butterfly's costume, as does* GALLIMARD *of his tuxedo.*)

GALLIMARD: I married late, at age thirty-one. I was faithful to my marriage for eight years. Until the day when, as a junior-level diplomat in puritanical Peking, in a parlor at the German ambassador's house, during the "Reign of a Hundred Flowers," I first saw her . . . singing the death scene from *Madame Butterfly*.

(SUZUKI *runs offstage.*)

ACT 1 / SCENE 6

(*German ambassador's house. Beijing. 1960.*)

(*The upstage special area now becomes a stage. Several chairs face upstage, representing seating for some twenty guests in the parlor. A few "diplomats"—*RENEE, MARC, TOULON—*in formal dress enter and take seats.*

GALLIMARD *also sits down, but turns towards us and continues to talk. Orchestral accompaniment on the tape is now replaced by a simple piano.* SONG *picks up the death scene from the point where Butterfly uncovers the hara-kiri knife.*)

GALLIMARD: The ending is pitiful. Pinkerton, in an act of great courage, stays home and sends his American wife to pick up Butterfly's child. The truth, long deferred, has come up to her door.

(SONG, *playing Butterfly, sings the lines from the opera in her own voice—which, though not classical, should be decent.*)

SONG: "Con onor muore/ chi non puo serbar/ vita con onore."

GALLIMARD (*Simultaneously*): "Death with honor/ Is better than life/ Life with dishonor."

(*The stage is illuminated; we are now completely within an elegant diplomat's residence.* SONG *proceeds to play out an abbreviated death scene. Everyone in the room applauds.* SONG, *shyly, takes her bows. Others in the room rush to congratulate her.* GALLIMARD *remains with us.*)

GALLIMARD: They say in opera the voice is everything. That's probably why I'd never before enjoyed opera. Here . . . here was a Butterfly with little or no voice—but she had the grace, the delicacy . . . I believed this girl. I believed her suffering. I wanted to take her in my arms—so delicate, even I could protect her, take her home, pamper her until she smiled.

(*Over the course of the preceding speech,* SONG *has broken from the upstage crowd and moved directly upstage of* GALLIMARD.)

SONG: Excuse me. Monsieur . . . ?

(GALLIMARD *turns upstage, shocked.*)

GALLIMARD: Oh! Gallimard. Mademoiselle . . . ? A beautiful . . .

SONG: Song Liling.

GALLIMARD: A beautiful performance.

SONG: Oh, please.

GALLIMARD: I usually—

SONG: You make me blush. I'm no opera singer at all.

GALLIMARD: I usually don't like *Butterfly*.

SONG: I can't blame you in the least.

GALLIMARD: I mean, the story—

SONG: Ridiculous.

GALLIMARD: I like the story, but . . . what?

SONG: Oh, you like it?

GALLIMARD: I . . . what I mean is, I've always seen it played by huge women in so much bad makeup.

SONG: Bad makeup is not unique to the West.

GALLIMARD: But, who can believe them?

SONG: And you believe me?

GALLIMARD: Absolutely. You were utterly convincing. It's the first time—

SONG: Convincing? As a Japanese woman? The Japa–nese used hundreds of our people for medical experiments during the war, you know. But I gather such an irony is lost on you.

GALLIMARD: No! I was about to say, it's the first time I've seen the beauty of the story.

SONG: Really?

GALLIMARD: Of her death. It's a . . . a pure sacrifice. He's unworthy, but what can she do? She loves him . . . so much. It's a very beautiful story.

SONG: Well, yes, to a Westerner.

GALLIMARD: Excuse me?

SONG: It's one of your favorite fantasies, isn't it? The submissive Oriental woman and the cruel white man.

GALLIMARD: Well, I didn't quite mean . . .

SONG: Consider it this way: what would you say if a blonde homecoming queen fell in love with a short Japanese businessman? He treats her cru–elly, then goes home for three years, during which time she prays to his picture and turns down marriage from a young Kennedy. Then, when she learns he has remarried, she kills her–self. Now, I believe you would consider this girl to be a deranged idiot, correct? But because it's an Oriental who kills herself for a Westerner—ah!—you find it beautiful.

(Silence.)

GALLIMARD: Yes . . . well . . . I see your point . . .

SONG: I will never do Butterfly again, Monsieur Galli–mard. If you wish to see some real theatre come to the Peking Opera sometime. Expand your mind.

(SONG walks offstage.)

GALLIMARD *(To us)*: So much for protecting her in my big Western arms.

ACT 1 / SCENE 7

(M. GALLIMARD's apartment. Beijing. 1960.)

(GALLIMARD changes from his tux into a casual suit. HELGA enters.)

GALLIMARD: The Chinese are an incredibly arrogant people.

HELGA: They warned us about that in Paris, remember?

GALLIMARD: Even Parisians consider them arrogant. That's a switch.

HELGA: What is it that Madame Su says? "We are a very old civilization." I never know if she's talking about her country or herself.

GALLIMARD: I walk around here, all I hear every day, everywhere is how *old* this culture is. The fact that "old" may be synonymous with "senile" doesn't occur to them.

HELGA: You're not going to change them. "East is east, west is west, and . . ." whatever that guy said.

GALLIMARD: It's just that—silly. I met . . . at Ambas–sador Koening's tonight—you should've been there.

HELGA: Koening? Oh god, no. Did he enchant you all again with the history of Bavaria?

GALLIMARD: No. I met, I suppose, the Chinese equiva–lent of a diva. She's a singer in the Chinese opera.

HELGA: They have an opera, too? Do they sing in Chi–nese? Or maybe—in Italian?

GALLIMARD: Tonight, she did sing in Italian.

HELGA: How'd she manage that?

GALLIMARD: She must've been educated in the West before the Revolution. Her French is very good also. Anyway, she sang the death scene from *Madame Butterfly.*

HELGA: *Madame Butterfly!* Then I should have come. *(She begins humming, floating around the room as if dragging long kimono sleeves)* Did she have a nice costume? I think it's a classic piece of music.

GALLIMARD: That's what *I* thought, too. Don't let her hear you say that.

HELGA: What's wrong?

GALLIMARD: Evidently the Chinese hate it.

HELGA: She hated it, but she performed it anyway? Is she perverse?

GALLIMARD: They hate it because the white man gets the girl. Sour grapes if you ask me.

HELGA: Politics again? Why can't they just hear it as a piece of beautiful music? So, what's in their opera?

GALLIMARD: I don't know. But, whatever it is, I'm sure it must be *old.*

(HELGA exits.)

ACT 1 / SCENE 8

(Chinese opera house and the streets of Beijing. 1960.)
(The sound of gongs clanging fills the stage.)

GALLIMARD: My wife's innocent question kept ringing in my ears. I asked around, but no one knew any–thing about the Chinese opera. It took four weeks, but my curiosity overcame my cowardice. This Chinese diva—this unwilling Butterfly—what did she do to make her so proud?

The room was hot, and full of smoke. Wrinkled faces, old women, teeth missing—a man with a growth on his neck, like a human toad. All smiling, pipes falling from their mouths, cracking nuts between their teeth, a live chicken pecking at my foot—all looking, screaming, gawking . . . at her.

(The upstage area is suddenly hit with a harsh white light. It has become the stage for the Chinese opera performance. Two dancers enter, along with SONG. GALLIMARD *stands apart, watching.* SONG *glides gracefully amidst the two dancers. Drums suddenly slam to a halt.* SONG *strikes a pose, looking straight at* GALLIMARD. *Dancers exit. Light change. Pause, then* SONG *walks right off the stage and straight up to* GALLIMARD.*)*

SONG: Yes. You. White man. I'm looking straight at you.

GALLIMARD: Me?

SONG: You see any other white men? It was too easy to spot you. How often does a man in my audience come in a tie?

*(*SONG *starts to remove her costume. Underneath, she wears simple baggy clothes. They are now backstage. The show is over.)*

SONG: So, you are an adventurous imperialist?

GALLIMARD: I . . . thought it would further my education.

SONG: It took you four weeks. Why?

GALLIMARD: I've been busy.

SONG: Well, education has always been undervalued in the West, hasn't it?

GALLIMARD *(Laughing)*: I don't think that's true.

SONG: No, you wouldn't. You're a Westerner. How can you objectively judge your own values?

GALLIMARD: I think it's possible to achieve some distance.

SONG: Do you? *(Pause)* It stinks in here. Let's go.

GALLIMARD: These are the smells of your loyal fans.

SONG: I love them for being my fans, I hate the smell they leave behind. I too can distance myself from my people. *(She looks around, then whispers in his ear)* "Art for the masses" is a shitty excuse to keep artists poor. *(She pops a cigarette in her mouth)* Be a gentleman, will you? And light my cigarette.

*(*GALLIMARD *fumbles for a match.)*

GALLIMARD: I don't . . . smoke.

SONG *(Lighting her own)*: Your loss. Had you lit my cigarette, I might have blown a puff of smoke right between your eyes. Come.

(They start to walk about the stage. It is a summer night on the Beijing streets. Sounds of the city play on the house speakers.)

SONG: How I wish there were even a tiny cafe to sit in. With cappuccinos, and men in tuxedos and bad expatriate jazz.

GALLIMARD: If my history serves me correctly, you weren't even allowed into the clubs in Shanghai before the Revolution.

SONG: Your history serves you poorly, Monsieur Gallimard. True, there were signs reading "No dogs and Chinamen." But a woman, especially a delicate Oriental woman—we always go where we please. Could you imagine it otherwise? Clubs in China filled with pasty, big-thighed white women, while thousands of slender lotus blossoms wait just outside the door? Never. The clubs would be empty. *(Beat)* We have always held a certain fascination for you Caucasian men, have we not?

GALLIMARD: But . . . that fascination is imperialist, or so you tell me.

SONG: Do you believe everything I tell you? Yes. It is always imperialist. But sometimes . . . sometimes, it is also mutual. Oh—this is my flat.

GALLIMARD: I didn't even—

SONG: Thank you. Come another time and we will further expand your mind.

*(*SONG *exits.* GALLIMARD *continues roaming the streets as he speaks to us.)*

GALLIMARD: What was that? What did she mean, "Sometimes . . . it is mutual"? Women do not flirt with me. And I normally can't talk to them. But tonight, I held up my end of the conversation.

ACT 1 / SCENE 9

*(*GALLIMARD*'s bedroom. Beijing. 1960.)*

*(*HELGA *enters.)*

HELGA: You didn't tell me you'd be home late.

GALLIMARD: I didn't intend to. Something came up.

HELGA: Oh? Like what?

GALLIMARD: I went to the . . . to the Dutch ambassador's home.

HELGA: Again?

GALLIMARD: There was a reception for a visiting scholar. He's writing a six-volume treatise on the Chinese revolution. We all gathered that meant he'd have to live here long enough to actually write six volumes, and we all expressed our deepest sympathies.

HELGA: Well, I had a good night too. I went with the ladies to a martial arts demonstration. Some of those men—when they break those thick boards— *(She mimes fanning herself)* whoo-whoo!

*(*HELGA *exits. Lights dim.)*

GALLIMARD: I lied to my wife. Why? I've never had any reason to lie before. But what reason did I have tonight? I didn't do anything wrong. That night, I had a dream. Other people, I've been told, have dreams where angels appear. Or dragons, or Sophia Loren in a towel. In my dream, Marc from school appeared.

(MARC enters, in a nightshirt and cap.)

MARC: Rene! You met a girl!

(GALLIMARD and MARC stumble down the Beijing streets. Night sounds over the speakers.)

GALLIMARD: It's not that amazing, thank you.

MARC: No! It's so monumental, I heard about it halfway around the world in my sleep!

GALLIMARD: I've met girls before, you know.

MARC: Name one. I've come across time and space to congratulate you. *(He hands GALLIMARD a bottle of wine)*

GALLIMARD: Marc, this is expensive.

MARC: On those rare occasions when you become a formless spirit, why not steal the best?

(MARC pops open the bottle, begins to share it with GALLI-MARD.)

GALLIMARD: You embarrass me. She . . . there's no reason to think she likes me.

MARC: "Sometimes, it is mutual"?

GALLIMARD: Oh.

MARC: "Mutual"? "Mutual"? What does that mean?

GALLIMARD: You heard?

MARC: It means the money is in the bank, you only have to write the check!

GALLIMARD: I am a married man!

MARC: And an excellent one too. I cheated after . . . six months. Then again and again, until now—three hundred girls in twelve years.

GALLIMARD: I don't think we should hold that up as a model.

MARC: Of course not! My life—it is disgusting! Phooey! Phooey! But, you—you are the model husband.

GALLIMARD: Anyway, it's impossible. I'm a foreigner.

MARC: Ah, yes. She cannot love you, it is taboo, but something deep inside her heart . . . she cannot help herself . . . she must surrender to you. It is her destiny.

GALLIMARD: How do you imagine all this?

MARC: The same way you do. It's an old story. It's in our blood. They fear us, Rene. Their women fear us. And their men—their men hate us. And, you know something? They are all correct.

(They spot a light in a window.)

MARC: There! There, Rene!

GALLIMARD: It's her window.

MARC: Late at night—it burns. The light—it burns for you.

GALLIMARD: I won't look. It's not respectful.

MARC: We don't have to be respectful. We're foreign devils.

(Enter SONG, in a sheer robe. The "One Fine Day"° aria creeps in over the speakers. With her back to us, SONG mimes attending to her toilette. Her robe comes loose, revealing her white shoulders.)

MARC: All your life you've waited for a beautiful girl who would lay down for you. All your life you've smiled like a saint when it's happened to every other man you know. And you see them in magazines and you see them in movies. And you wonder, what's wrong with me? Will anyone beautiful ever want me? As the years pass, your hair thins and you struggle to hold onto even your hopes. Stop struggling, Rene. The wait is over. *(He exits)*

GALLIMARD: Marc? Marc?

(At that moment, SONG, her back still towards us, drops her robe. A second of her naked back, then a sound cue: a phone ringing, very loud. Blackout, followed in the next beat by a special up on the bedroom area, where a phone now sits. GALLIMARD stumbles across the stage and picks up the phone. Sound cue out. Over the course of his conversation, area lights fill in the vicinity of his bed. It is the following morning.)

GALLIMARD: Yes? Hello?

SONG *(Offstage)*: Is it very early?

GALLIMARD: Why, yes.

SONG *(Offstage)*: How early?

GALLIMARD: It's . . . it's 5:30. Why are you—?

SONG *(Offstage)*: But it's light outside. Already.

GALLIMARD: It is. The sun must be in confusion today.

(Over the course of SONG's next speech, her upstage special comes up again. She sits in a chair, legs crossed, in a robe, telephone to her ear.)

SONG: I waited until I saw the sun. That was as much discipline as I could manage for one night. Do you forgive me?

GALLIMARD: Of course . . . for what?

SONG: Then I'll ask you quickly. Are you really interested in the opera?

GALLIMARD: Why, yes. Yes I am.

SONG: Then come again next Thursday. I am playing *The Drunken Beauty.* May I count on you?

GALLIMARD: Yes. You may.

SONG: Perfect. Well, I must be getting to bed. I'm exhausted. It's been a very long night for me.

(SONG hangs up; special on her goes off. GALLIMARD begins to dress for work.)

"One Fine Day," the opera's most famous aria, "Un bel di" ("One Fine Day"), in which Madame Butterfly rapturously describes the imagined return of Pinkerton.

ACT 1 / SCENE 10

(SONG LILING's *apartment. Beijing. 1960.*)

GALLIMARD: I returned to the opera that next week, and the week after that . . . she keeps our meetings so short—perhaps fifteen, twenty minutes at most. So I am left each week with a thirst which is intensified. In this way, fifteen weeks have gone by. I am starting to doubt the words of my friend Marc. But no, not really. In my heart, I know she has . . . an interest in me. I suspect this is her way. She is outwardly bold and outspoken, yet her heart is shy and afraid. It is the Oriental in her at war with her Western education.

SONG (*Offstage*): I will be out in an instant. Ask the servant for anything you want.

GALLIMARD: Tonight, I have finally been invited to enter her apartment. Though the idea is almost beyond belief, I believe she is afraid of me.

(GALLIMARD *looks around the room. He picks up a picture in a frame, studies it. Without his noticing,* SONG *enters, dressed elegantly in a black gown from the twenties. She stands in the doorway looking like Anna May Wong.°*)

SONG: That is my father.

GALLIMARD (*Surprised*): Mademoiselle Song . . .

(*She glides up to him, snatches away the picture.*)

SONG: It is very good that he did not live to see the Revolution. They would, no doubt, have made him kneel on broken glass. Not that he didn't deserve such a punishment. But he is my father. I would've hated to see it happen.

GALLIMARD: I'm very honored that you've allowed me to visit your home.

(SONG *curtseys.*)

SONG: Thank you. Oh! Haven't you been poured any tea?

GALLIMARD: I'm really not—

SONG (*To her offstage servant*): Shu-Fang! Cha! Kwai-lah! (*To* GALLIMARD) I'm sorry. You want everything to be perfect—

GALLIMARD: Please.

SONG: —and before the evening even begins—

GALLIMARD: I'm really not thirsty.

SONG: —it's ruined.

GALLIMARD (*Sharply*): Mademoiselle Song!

(SONG *sits down.*)

SONG: I'm sorry.

GALLIMARD: What are you apologizing for now?

Anna May Wong (1907–61), Chinese American actress, stereotyped as the "Oriental enchantress."

(*Pause;* SONG *starts to giggle.*)

SONG: I don't know!

(GALLIMARD *laughs.*)

GALLIMARD: Exactly my point.

SONG: Oh, I am silly. Lightheaded. I promise not to apologize for anything else tonight, do you hear me?

GALLIMARD: That's a good girl.

(SHU-FANG, *a servant girl, comes out with a tea tray and starts to pour.*)

SONG (*To* SHU-FANG): No! I'll pour myself for the gentleman!

(SHU-FANG, *staring at* GALLIMARD, *exits.*)

SONG: No, I . . . I don't even know why I invited you up.

GALLIMARD: Well, I'm glad you did.

(SONG *looks around the room.*)

SONG: There is an element of danger to your presence.

GALLIMARD: Oh?

SONG: You must know.

GALLIMARD: It doesn't concern me. We both know why I'm here.

SONG: It doesn't concern me either. No . . . well perhaps . . .

GALLIMARD: What?

SONG: Perhaps I am slightly afraid of scandal.

GALLIMARD: What are we doing?

SONG: I'm entertaining you. In my parlor.

GALLIMARD: In France, that would hardly—

SONG: France. France is a country living in the modern era. Perhaps even ahead of it. China is a nation whose soul is firmly rooted two thousand years in the past. What I do, even pouring the tea for you now . . . it has . . . implications. The walls and windows say so. Even my own heart, strapped inside this Western dress . . . even it says things—things I don't care to hear.

(SONG *hands* GALLIMARD *a cup of tea.* GALLIMARD *puts his hand over both the teacup and* SONG's *hand.*)

GALLIMARD: This is a beautiful dress.

SONG: Don't.

GALLIMARD: What?

SONG: I don't even know if it looks right on me.

GALLIMARD: Believe me—

SONG: You are from France. You see so many beautiful women.

GALLIMARD: France? Since when are the European women—?

SONG: Oh! What am I trying to do, anyway?!

(SONG *runs to the door, composes herself, then turns towards* GALLIMARD.)

SONG: Monsieur Gallimard, perhaps you should go.

GALLIMARD: But . . . why?

SONG: There's something wrong about this.

GALLIMARD: I don't see what.

SONG: I feel . . . I am not myself.

GALLIMARD: No. You're nervous.

SONG: Please. Hard as I try to be modern, to speak like a man, to hold a Western woman's strong face up to my own . . . in the end, I fail. A small, frightened heart beats too quickly and gives me away. Monsieur Gallimard, I'm a Chinese girl. I've never . . . never invited a man up to my flat before. The forwardness of my actions makes my skin burn.

GALLIMARD: What are you afraid of? Certainly not me, I hope.

SONG: I'm a modest girl.

GALLIMARD: I know. And very beautiful. (He touches her hair)

SONG: Please—go now. The next time you see me, I shall again be myself.

GALLIMARD: I like you the way you are right now.

SONG: You are a cad.

GALLIMARD: What do you expect? I'm a foreign devil.

(GALLIMARD walks downstage. SONG exits.)

GALLIMARD (To us): Did you hear the way she talked about Western women? Much differently than the first night. She does—she feels inferior to them—and to me.

ACT 1 / SCENE 11

(The French embassy. Beijing. 1960.)

(GALLIMARD moves towards a desk.)

GALLIMARD: I determined to try an experiment. In Madame Butterfly, Cio-Cio-San fears that the Western man who catches a butterfly will pierce its heart with a needle, then leave it to perish. I began to wonder: had I, too, caught a butterfly who would writhe on a needle?

(MARC enters, dressed as a bureaucrat, holding a stack of papers. As GALLIMARD speaks, MARC hands papers to him. He peruses, then signs, stamps, or rejects them.)

GALLIMARD: Over the next five weeks, I worked like a dynamo. I stopped going to the opera, I didn't phone or write her. I knew this little flower was waiting for me to call, and, as I wickedly refused to do so, I felt for the first time that rush of power—the absolute power of a man.

(MARC continues acting as the bureaucrat, but he now speaks as himself.)

MARC: Rene! It's me!

GALLIMARD: Marc—I hear your voice everywhere now. Even in the midst of work.

MARC: That's because I'm watching you—all the time.

GALLIMARD: You were always the most popular guy in school.

MARC: Well, there's no guarantee of failure in life like happiness in high school. Somehow I knew I'd end up in the suburbs working for Renault and you'd be in the Orient picking exotic women off the trees. And they say there's no justice.

GALLIMARD: That's why you were my friend?

MARC: I gave you a little of my life, so that now you can give me some of yours. (Pause) Remember Isabelle?

GALLIMARD: Of course I remember! She was my first experience.

MARC: We all wanted to ball her. But she only wanted me.

GALLIMARD: I had her.

MARC: Right. You balled her.

GALLIMARD: You were the only one who ever believed me.

MARC: Well, there's a good reason for that. (Beat) C'mon. You must've guessed.

GALLIMARD: You told me to wait in the bushes by the cafeteria that night. The next thing I knew, she was on me. Dress up in the air.

MARC: She never wore underwear.

GALLIMARD: My arms were pinned to the dirt.

MARC: She loved the superior position. A girl ahead of her time.

GALLIMARD: I looked up, and there was this woman . . . bouncing up and down on my loins.

MARC: Screaming, right?

GALLIMARD: Screaming, and breaking off the branches all around me, and pounding my butt up and down into the dirt.

MARC: Huffing and puffing like a locomotive.

GALLIMARD: And in the middle of all this, the leaves were getting into my mouth, my legs were losing circulation, I thought, "God. So this is it?"

MARC: You thought that?

GALLIMARD: Well, I was worried about my legs falling off.

MARC: You didn't have a good time?

GALLIMARD: No, that's not what I—I had a great time!

MARC: You're sure?

GALLIMARD: Yeah. Really.

MARC: 'Cuz I wanted you to have a good time.

GALLIMARD: I did.

(Pause.)

MARC: Shit. (Pause) When all is said and done, she was kind of a lousy lay, wasn't she? I mean, there was a lot of energy there, but you never knew what she was doing with it. Like when she yelled "I'm coming!"—hell, it was so loud, you wanted to go, "Look, it's not that big a deal."

GALLIMARD: I got scared. I thought she meant someone was actually coming. (Pause) But, Marc?

MARC: What?

GALLIMARD: Thanks.

MARC: Oh, don't mention it.

GALLIMARD: It was my first experience.

MARC: Yeah. You got her.

GALLIMARD: I got her.

MARC: Wait! Look at that letter again!

(GALLIMARD *picks up one of the papers he's been stamping, and rereads it.*)

GALLIMARD (*To us*): After six weeks, they began to arrive. The letters.

(*Upstage special on* SONG, *as Madame Butterfly. The scene is underscored by the "Love Duet."*)

SONG: Did we fight? I do not know. Is the opera no longer of interest to you? Please come—my audiences miss the white devil in their midst.

(GALLIMARD *looks up from the letter, towards us.*)

GALLIMARD (*To us*): A concession, but much too dignified. (*Beat; he discards the letter*) I skipped the opera again that week to complete a position paper on trade.

(*The bureaucrat hands him another letter.*)

SONG: Six weeks have passed since last we met. Is this your practice—to leave friends in the lurch? Sometimes I hate you, sometimes I hate myself, but always I miss you.

GALLIMARD (*To us*): Better, but I don't like the way she calls me "friend." When a woman calls a man her "friend," she's calling him a eunuch or a homosexual. (*Beat; he discards the letter*) I was absent from the opera for the seventh week, feeling a sudden urge to clean out my files.

(*Bureaucrat hands him another letter.*)

SONG: Your rudeness is beyond belief. I don't deserve this cruelty. Don't bother to call. I'll have you turned away at the door.

GALLIMARD (*To us*): I didn't. (*He discards the letter; bureaucrat hands him another*) And then finally, the letter that concluded my experiment.

SONG: I am out of words. I can hide behind dignity no longer. What do you want? I have already given you my shame.

(GALLIMARD *gives the letter back to* MARC, *slowly. Special on* SONG *fades out.*)

GALLIMARD (*To us*): Reading it, I became suddenly ashamed. Yes, my experiment had been a success. She was turning on my needle. But the victory seemed hollow.

MARC: Hollow?! Are you crazy?

GALLIMARD: Nothing, Marc. Please go away.

MARC (*Exiting, with papers*): Haven't I taught you anything?

GALLIMARD: "I have already given you my shame." I had to attend a reception that evening. On the way, I felt sick. If there is a God, surely he would punish me now. I had finally gained power over a beautiful woman, only to abuse it cruelly. There must be justice in the world. I had the strange feeling that the ax would fall this very evening.

ACT 1 / SCENE 12

(AMBASSADOR TOULON's *residence. Beijing. 1960.*)

(*Sound cue: party noises. Light change. We are now in a spacious residence.* TOULON, *the French ambassador, enters and taps* GALLIMARD *on the shoulder.*)

TOULON: Gallimard? Can I have a word? Over here.

GALLIMARD (*To us*): Manuel Toulon. French ambassador to China. He likes to think of us all as his children. Rather like God.

TOULON: Look, Gallimard, there's not much to say. I've liked you. From the day you walked in. You were no leader, but you were tidy and efficient.

GALLIMARD: Thank you, sir.

TOULON: Don't jump the gun. Okay, our needs in China are changing. It's embarrassing that we lost Indochina. Someone just wasn't on the ball there. I don't mean you personally, of course.

GALLIMARD: Thank you, sir.

TOULON: We're going to be doing a lot more information-gathering in the future. The nature of our work here is changing. Some people are just going to have to go. It's nothing personal.

GALLIMARD: Oh.

TOULON: Want to know a secret? Vice-Consul LeBon is being transferred.

GALLIMARD (*To us*): My immediate superior!

TOULON: And most of his department.

GALLIMARD (*To us*): Just as I feared! God has seen my evil heart—

TOULON: But not you.

GALLIMARD (*To us*): —and he's taking her away just as . . . (*To* TOULON) Excuse me, sir?

TOULON: Scare you? I think I did. Cheer up, Gallimard. I want you to replace LeBon as vice-consul.

GALLIMARD: You—? Yes, well, thank you, sir.

TOULON: Anytime.

GALLIMARD: I . . . accept with great humility.

TOULON: Humility won't be part of the job. You're going to coordinate the revamped intelligence division. Want to know a secret? A year ago, you would've been out. But the past few months, I don't know how it happened, you've become this new aggressive confident . . . thing. And they also tell me you get along with the Chinese. So I think you're a lucky man, Gallimard. Congratulations.

(*They shake hands.* TOULON *exits. Party noises out.* GALLIMARD *stumbles across a darkened stage.*)

GALLIMARD: Vice-consul? Impossible! As I stumbled out of the party, I saw it written across the sky: There is no God. Or, no—say that there is a God. But that God . . . understands. Of course! God who creates Eve to serve Adam, who blesses Solomon with his harem but ties Jezebel to a burning bed—that God is a man. And he understands! At age thirty-nine, I was suddenly initiated into the way of the world.

ACT 1 / SCENE 13

(SONG LILING's apartment. Beijing. 1960.)

(SONG enters, in a sheer dressing gown.)

SONG: Are you crazy?

GALLIMARD: Mademoiselle Song—

SONG: To come here—at this hour? After . . . after eight weeks?

GALLIMARD: It's the most amazing—

SONG: You bang on my door? Scare my servants, scandalize the neighbors?

GALLIMARD: I've been promoted. To vice-consul.

(Pause.)

SONG: And what is that supposed to mean to me?

GALLIMARD: Are you my Butterfly?

SONG: What are you saying?

GALLIMARD: I've come tonight for an answer: are you my Butterfly?

SONG: Don't you know already?

GALLIMARD: I want you to say it.

SONG: I don't want to say it.

GALLIMARD: So, that is your answer?

SONG: You know how I feel about—

GALLIMARD: I do remember one thing.

SONG: What?

GALLIMARD: In the letter I received today.

SONG: Don't.

GALLIMARD: "I have already given you my shame."

SONG: It's enough that I even wrote it.

GALLIMARD: Well, then—

SONG: I shouldn't have it splashed across my face.

GALLIMARD: —if that's all true—

SONG: Stop!

GALLIMARD: Then what is one more short answer?

SONG: I don't want to!

GALLIMARD: Are you my Butterfly? (Silence; he crosses the room and begins to touch her hair) I want from you honesty. There should be nothing false between us. No false pride.

(Pause.)

SONG: Yes, I am. I am your Butterfly.

GALLIMARD: Then let me be honest with you. It is because of you that I was promoted tonight. You have changed my life forever. My little Butterfly, there should be no more secrets: I love you.

(He starts to kiss her roughly. She resists slightly.)

SONG: No . . . no . . . gently . . . please, I've never . . .

GALLIMARD: No?

SONG: I've tried to appear experienced, but . . . the truth is . . . no.

GALLIMARD: Are you cold?

SONG: Yes. Cold.

GALLIMARD: Then we will go very, very slowly.

(He starts to caress her; her gown begins to open.)

SONG: No . . . let me . . . keep my clothes . . .

GALLIMARD: But . . .

SONG: Please . . . it all frightens me. I'm a modest Chinese girl.

GALLIMARD: My poor little treasure.

SONG: I am your treasure. Though inexperienced, I am not . . . ignorant. They teach us things, our mothers, about pleasing a man.

GALLIMARD: Yes?

SONG: I'll do my best to make you happy. Turn off the lights.

(GALLIMARD gets up and heads for a lamp. SONG, propped up on one elbow, tosses her hair back and smiles.)

SONG: Monsieur Gallimard?

GALLIMARD: Yes, Butterfly?

SONG: "Vieni, vieni!"°

GALLIMARD: "Come, darling."

SONG: "Ah! Dolce notte!"

GALLIMARD: "Beautiful night."

SONG: "Tutto estatico d'amor ride il ciel!"

GALLIMARD: "All ecstatic with love, the heavens are filled with laughter."

(He turns off the lamp. Blackout.)

ACT 2 / SCENE 1

(M. GALLIMARD's cell. Paris. Present.)

(Lights up on GALLIMARD. He sits in his cell, reading from a leaflet.)

GALLIMARD: This, from a contemporary critic's commentary on Madame Butterfly: "Pinkerton suffers from . . . being an obnoxious bounder whom every man in the audience itches to kick." Bully for us men in the audience! Then, in the same note: "Butterfly is the most irresistibly appealing of Puccini's 'Little Women.' Watching the succession of her humiliations is like watching a child under torture." (He tosses the pamphlet over his shoulder) I suggest that, while we men may all want to kick Pinkerton, very few of us would pass up the opportunity to be Pinkerton.

(GALLIMARD moves out of his cell.)

"Vieni, vieni," the words are from the love duet at the end of Madame Butterfly's first act.

ACT 2 / SCENE 2

(GALLIMARD *and Butterfly's flat. Beijing. 1960.*)

(*We are in a simple but well-decorated parlor.* GALLIMARD *moves to sit on a sofa, while* SONG, *dressed in a chong sam, enters and curls up at his feet.*)

GALLIMARD (*To us*): We secured a flat on the outskirts of Peking. Butterfly, as I was calling her now, decorated our "home" with Western furniture and Chinese antiques. And there, on a few stolen afternoons or evenings each week, Butterfly commenced her education.

SONG: The Chinese men—they keep us down.

GALLIMARD: Even in the "New Society"?

SONG: In the "New Society," we are all kept ignorant equally. That's one of the exciting things about loving a Western man. I know you are not threatened by a woman's education.

GALLIMARD: I'm no saint, Butterfly.

SONG: But you come from a progressive society.

GALLIMARD: We're not always reminding each other how "old" we are, if that's what you mean.

SONG: Exactly. We Chinese—once, I suppose, it is true, we ruled the world. But so what? How much more exciting to be part of the society ruling the world today. Tell me—what's happening in Vietnam?

GALLIMARD: Oh, Butterfly—you want me to bring my work home?

SONG: I want to know what you know. To be impressed by my man. It's not the particulars so much as the fact that you're making decisions which change the shape of the world.

GALLIMARD: Not the world. At best, a small corner.

(TOULON *enters, and sits at a desk upstage.*)

ACT 2 / SCENE 3

(*French embassy. Beijing. 1961.*)

(GALLIMARD *moves downstage, to* TOULON*'s desk.* SONG *remains upstage, watching.*)

TOULON: And a more troublesome corner is hard to imagine.

GALLIMARD: So, the Americans plan to begin bombing?

TOULON: This is very secret, Gallimard: yes. The Americans don't have an embassy here. They're asking us to be their eyes and ears. Say Jack Kennedy signed an order to bomb North Vietnam, Laos. How would the Chinese react?

GALLIMARD: I think the Chinese will squawk—

TOULON: Uh-huh.

GALLIMARD: —but, in their hearts, they don't even like Ho Chi Minh.

(*Pause.*)

TOULON: What a bunch of jerks. Vietnam was *our* colony. Not only didn't the Americans help us fight to keep them, but now, seven years later, they've come back to grab the territory for themselves. It's very irritating.

GALLIMARD: With all due respect, sir, why should the Americans have won our war for us back in '54 if we didn't have the will to win it ourselves?

TOULON: You're kidding, aren't you?

(*Pause.*)

GALLIMARD: The Orientals simply want to be associated with whoever shows the most strength and power. You live with the Chinese, sir. Do you think they like Communism?

TOULON: I live in China. Not with the Chinese.

GALLIMARD: Well, I—

TOULON: *You* live with the Chinese.

GALLIMARD: Excuse me?

TOULON: I can't keep a secret.

GALLIMARD: What are you saying?

TOULON: Only that I'm not immune to gossip. So, you're keeping a native mistress? Don't answer. It's none of my business. (*Pause*) I'm sure she must be gorgeous.

GALLIMARD: Well . . .

TOULON: I'm impressed. You have the stamina to go out into the streets and hunt one down. Some of us have to be content with the wives of the expatriate community.

GALLIMARD: I do feel . . . fortunate.

TOULON: So, Gallimard, you've got the inside knowledge—what *do* the Chinese think?

GALLIMARD: Deep down, they miss the old days. You know, cappuccinos, men in tuxedos—

TOULON: So what do we tell the Americans about Vietnam?

GALLIMARD: Tell them there's a natural affinity between the West and the Orient.

TOULON: And that you speak from experience?

GALLIMARD: The Orientals are people too. They want the good things we can give them. If the Americans demonstrate the will to win, the Vietnamese will welcome them into a mutually beneficial union.

TOULON: I don't see how the Vietnamese can stand up to American firepower.

GALLIMARD: Orientals will always submit to a greater force.

TOULON: I'll note your opinions in my report. The Americans always love to hear how "welcome" they'll be. (*He starts to exit*)

GALLIMARD: Sir?

TOULON: Mmmm?

GALLIMARD: This . . . rumor you've heard.

TOULON: Uh-huh?

GALLIMARD: How . . . widespread do you think it is?

TOULON: It's only widespread within this embassy. Where nobody talks because everybody is guilty. We were worried about you, Gallimard. We thought you were the only one here without a secret. Now you go and find a lotus blossom . . . and top us all. *(He exits)*

GALLIMARD *(To us)*: Toulon knows! And he approves! I was learning the benefits of being a man. We form our own clubs, sit behind thick doors, smoke—and celebrate the fact that we're still boys. *(He starts to move downstage, towards* SONG*)* So, over the—

(Suddenly COMRADE CHIN *enters.* GALLIMARD *backs away.)*

GALLIMARD *(To* SONG*)*: No! Why does she have to come in?

SONG: Rene, be sensible. How can they understand the story without her? Now, don't embarrass yourself.

*(*GALLIMARD *moves down center.)*

GALLIMARD *(To us)*: Now, you will see why my story is so amusing to so many people. Why they snicker at parties in disbelief. Please—try to understand it from my point of view. We are all prisoners of our time and place. *(He exits)*

ACT 2 / SCENE 4

*(*GALLIMARD *and Butterfly's flat. Beijing. 1961.)*

SONG *(To us)*: 1961. The flat Monsieur Gallimard rented for us. An evening after he has gone.

CHIN: Okay, see if you can find out when the Americans plan to start bombing Vietnam. If you can find out what cities, even better.

SONG: I'll do my best, but I don't want to arouse his suspicions.

CHIN: Yeah, sure, of course. So, what else?

SONG: The Americans will increase troops in Vietnam to 170,000 soldiers with 120,000 militia and 11,000 American advisors.

CHIN *(Writing)*: Wait, wait. 120,000 militia and—

SONG: —11,000 American—

CHIN: —American advisors. *(Beat)* How do you remember so much?

SONG: I'm an actor.

CHIN: Yeah. *(Beat)* Is that how come you dress like that?

SONG: Like what, Miss Chin?

CHIN: Like that dress! You're wearing a dress. And every time I come here, you're wearing a dress. Is that because you're an actor? Or what?

SONG: It's a . . . disguise, Miss Chin.

CHIN: Actors, I think they're all weirdos. My mother tells me actors are like gamblers or prostitutes or—

SONG: It helps me in my assignment.

(Pause.)

CHIN: You're not gathering information in any way that violates Communist Party principles, are you?

SONG: Why would I do that?

CHIN: Just checking. Remember: when working for the Great Proletarian State, you represent our Chairman Mao in every position you take.

SONG: I'll try to imagine the Chairman taking my positions.

CHIN: We all think of him this way. Good-bye, comrade. *(She starts to exit)* Comrade?

SONG: Yes?

CHIN: Don't forget: there is no homosexuality in China!

SONG: Yes, I've heard.

CHIN: Just checking. *(She exits)*

SONG *(To us)*: What passes for a woman in modern China.

*(*GALLIMARD *sticks his head out from the wings.)*

GALLIMARD: Is she gone?

SONG: Yes, Rene. Please continue in your own fashion.

ACT 2 / SCENE 5

(Beijing. 1961–63.)

*(*GALLIMARD *moves to the couch where* SONG *still sits. He lies down in her lap, and she strokes his forehead.)*

GALLIMARD *(To us)*: And so, over the years 1961, '62, '63, we settled into our routine, Butterfly and I. She would always have prepared a light snack and then, ever so delicately, and only if I agreed, she would start to pleasure me. With her hands, her mouth . . . too many ways to explain, and too sad, given my present situation. But mostly we would talk. About my life. Perhaps there is nothing more rare than to find a woman who passionately listens.

*(*SONG *remains upstage, listening, as* HELGA *enters and plays a scene downstage with* GALLIMARD*.)*

HELGA: Rene, I visited Dr. Bolleart this morning.

GALLIMARD: Why? Are you ill?

HELGA: No, no. You see, I wanted to ask him . . . that question we've been discussing.

GALLIMARD: And I told you, it's only a matter of time. Why did you bring a doctor into this? We just have to keep trying—like a crapshoot, actually.

HELGA: I went, I'm sorry. But listen: he says there's nothing wrong with me.

GALLIMARD: You see? Now, will you stop—?

HELGA: Rene, he says he'd like you to go in and take some tests.

GALLIMARD: Why? So he can find there's nothing wrong with both of us?

HELGA: Rene, I don't ask for much. One trip! One

visit! And then, whatever you want to do about it—you decide.

GALLIMARD: You're assuming he'll find something defective!

HELGA: No! Of course not! Whatever he finds—if he finds nothing, we decide what to do about nothing! But go!

GALLIMARD: If he finds nothing, we keep trying. Just like we do now.

HELGA: But at least we'll know! (Pause) I'm sorry. (She starts to exit)

GALLIMARD: Do you really want me to see Dr. Bolleart?

HELGA: Only if you want a child, Rene. We have to face the fact that time is running out. Only if you want a child. (She exits)

GALLIMARD (To SONG): I'm a modern man, Butterfly. And yet, I don't want to go. It's the same old voodoo. I feel like God himself is laughing at me if I can't produce a child.

SONG: You men of the West—you're obsessed by your odd desire for equality. Your wife can't give you a child, and you're going to the doctor?

GALLIMARD: Well, you see, she's already gone.

SONG: And because this incompetent can't find the defect, you now have to subject yourself to him? It's unnatural.

GALLIMARD: Well, what is the "natural" solution?

SONG: In Imperial China, when a man found that one wife was inadequate, he turned to another—to give him his son.

GALLIMARD: What do you—? I can't . . . marry you, yet.

SONG: Please. I'm not asking you to be my husband. But I am already your wife.

GALLIMARD: Do you want to . . . have my child?

SONG: I thought you'd never ask.

GALLIMARD: But, your career . . . your—

SONG: Phooey on my career! That's your Western mind, twisting itself into strange shapes again. Of course I love my career. But what would I love most of all? To feel something inside me—day and night—something I know is yours. (Pause) Promise me . . . you won't go to this doctor. Who is this Western quack to set himself as judge over the man I love? I know who is a man, and who is not. (She exits)

GALLIMARD (To us): Dr. Bolleart? Of course I didn't go. What man would?

ACT 2 / SCENE 6

(Beijing. 1963.)

(Part noises over the house speakers. RENEE enters, wearing a revealing gown.)

GALLIMARD: 1963. A party at the Austrian embassy. None of us could remember the Austrian ambas-sador's name, which seemed somehow appropriate. (To RENEE) So, I tell the Americans, Diem must go. The U.S. wants to be respected by the Vietnamese, and yet they're propping up this nobody seminarian as her president. A man whose claim to fame is his sister-in-law imposing fanatic "moral order" campaigns? Oriental women—when they're good, they're very good, but when they're bad, they're Christians.

RENEE: Yeah.

GALLIMARD: And what do you do?

RENEE: I'm a student. My father exports a lot of use-less stuff to the Third World.

GALLIMARD: How useless?

RENEE: You know. Squirt guns, confectioner's sugar, hula hoops . . .

GALLIMARD: I'm sure they appreciate the sugar.

RENEE: I'm here for two years to study Chinese.

GALLIMARD: Two years?

RENEE: That's what everybody says.

GALLIMARD: When did you arrive?

RENEE: Three weeks ago.

GALLIMARD: And?

RENEE: I like it. It's primitive, but . . . well, this is the place to learn Chinese, so here I am.

GALLIMARD: Why Chinese?

RENEE: I think it'll be important someday.

GALLIMARD: You do?

RENEE: Don't ask me when, but . . . that's what I think.

GALLIMARD: Well, I agree with you. One hundred per-cent. That's very farsighted.

RENEE: Yeah. Well of course, my father thinks I'm a complete weirdo.

GALLIMARD: He'll thank you someday.

RENEE: Like when the Chinese start buying hula hoops?

GALLIMARD: There're a billion bellies out there.

RENEE: And if they end up taking over the world—well, then I'll be lucky to know Chinese too, right?

(Pause.)

GALLIMARD: At this point, I don't see how the Chinese can possibly take—

RENEE: You know what I don't like about China?

GALLIMARD: Excuse me? No—what?

RENEE: Nothing to do at night.

GALLIMARD: You come to parties at embassies like everyone else.

RENEE: Yeah, but they get out at ten. And then what?

GALLIMARD: I'm afraid the Chinese idea of a dance hall is a dirt floor and a man with a flute.

RENEE: Are you married?

GALLIMARD: Yes. Why?

RENEE: You wanna . . . fool around?

(Pause.)

GALLIMARD: Sure.

RENEE: I'll wait for you outside. What's your name?

GALLIMARD: Gallimard. Rene.

RENEE: Weird. I'm Renee too. *(She exits)*

GALLIMARD *(To us)*: And so, I embarked on my first extra-extramarital affair. Renee was picture perfect. With a body like those girls in the magazines. If I put a tissue paper over my eyes, I wouldn't have been able to tell the difference. And it was exciting to be with someone who wasn't afraid to be seen completely naked. But is it possible for a woman to be *too* uninhibited, *too* willing, so as to seem almost too . . . masculine?

(Chuck Berry blares from the house speakers, then comes down in volume as RENEE *enters, toweling her hair.)*

RENEE: You have a nice weenie.

GALLIMARD: What?

RENEE: Penis. You have a nice penis.

GALLIMARD: Oh. Well, thank you. That's very . . .

RENEE: What—can't take a compliment?

GALLIMARD: No, it's very . . . reassuring.

RENEE: But most girls don't come out and say it, huh?

GALLIMARD: And also . . . what did you call it?

RENEE: Oh. Most girls don't call it a "weenie," huh?

GALLIMARD: It sounds very—

RENEE: Small, I know.

GALLIMARD: I was going to say, "young."

RENEE: Yeah. Young, small, same thing. Most guys are pretty, uh, sensitive about that. Like, you know, I had a boyfriend back home in Denmark. I got mad at him once and called him a little weeniehead. He got so mad! He said at least I should call him a great big weeniehead.

GALLIMARD: I suppose I just say "penis."

RENEE: Yeah. That's pretty clinical. There's "cock," but that sounds like a chicken. And "prick" is painful, and "dick" is like you're talking about someone who's not in the room.

GALLIMARD: Yes. It's a . . . bigger problem than I imagined.

RENEE: I—I think maybe it's because I really don't know what to do with them—that's why I call them "weenies."

GALLIMARD: Well, you did quite well with . . . mine.

RENEE: Thanks, but I mean, really *do* with them. Like, okay, have you ever looked at one? I mean, really?

GALLIMARD: No, I suppose when it's part of you, you sort of take it for granted.

RENEE: I guess. But, like, it just hangs there. This little . . . flap of flesh. And there's so much fuss that we make about it. Like, I think the reason we fight wars is because we wear clothes. Because no one knows—between the men, I mean—who has the bigger . . . weenie. So, if I'm a guy with a small one, I'm going to build a really big building or take over a really big piece of land or write a really long book so the other men don't know, right?

But, see, it never really works, that's the problem. I mean, you conquer the country, or whatever, but you're still wearing clothes, so there's no way to prove absolutely whose is bigger or smaller. And that's what we call a civilized society. The whole world run by a bunch of men with pricks the size of pins. *(She exits)*

GALLIMARD *(To us)*: This was simply not acceptable.

(A high-pitched chime rings through the air. SONG, *dressed as Butterfly, appears in the upstage special. She is obviously distressed. Her body swoons as she attempts to clip the stems of flowers she's arranging in a vase.)*

GALLIMARD: But I kept up our affair, wildly, for several months. Why? I believe because of Butterfly. She knew the secret I was trying to hide. But, unlike a Western woman, she didn't confront me, threaten, even pout. I remembered the words of Puccini's *Butterfly:*

SONG: "Noi siamo gente avvezza/ alle piccole cose/ umili e silenziose."

GALLIMARD: "I come from a people/ Who are accustomed to little/ Humble and silent." I saw Pinkerton and Butterfly, and what she would say if he were unfaithful . . . nothing. She would cry, alone, into those wildly soft sleeves, once full of possessions, now empty to collect her tears. It was her tears and her silence that excited me, every time I visited Renee.

TOULON *(Offstage)*: Gallimard!

*(*TOULON *enters.* GALLIMARD *turns towards him. During the next section,* SONG, *up center, begins to dance with the flowers. It is a drunken dance, where she breaks small pieces off the stems.)*

TOULON: They're killing him.

GALLIMARD: Who? I'm sorry? What?

TOULON: Bother you to come over at this late hour?

GALLIMARD: No . . . of course not.

TOULON: Not after you hear my secret. Champagne?

GALLIMARD: Um . . . thank you.

TOULON: You're surprised. There's something that you've wanted, Gallimard. No, not a promotion. Next time. Something in the world. You're not aware of this, but there's an informal gossip circle among intelligence agents. And some of ours heard from some of the Americans—

GALLIMARD: Yes?

TOULON: That the U.S. will allow the Vietnamese generals to stage a coup . . . and assassinate President Diem.

(The chime rings again. TOULON *freezes.* GALLIMARD *turns upstage and looks at Butterfly, who slowly and deliberately clips a flower off its stem.* GALLIMARD *turns back towards* TOULON.*)*

GALLIMARD: I think . . . that's a very wise move!

(TOULON unfreezes.)

TOULON: It's what you've been advocating. A toast?

GALLIMARD: Sure. I consider this a vindication.

TOULON: Not exactly. "To the test. Let's hope you pass."

(They drink. The chime rings again. TOULON *freezes.* GALLIMARD *turns upstage, and* SONG *clips another flower.)*

GALLIMARD *(To* TOULON*)*: The test?

TOULON *(Unfreezing)*: It's a test of everything you've been saying. I personally think the generals probably will stop the Communists. And you'll be a hero. But if anything goes wrong, then your opinions won't be worth a pig's ear. I'm sure that won't happen. But sometimes it's easier when they don't listen to you.

GALLIMARD: They're your opinions too, aren't they?

TOULON: Personally, yes.

GALLIMARD: So we agree.

TOULON: But my opinions aren't on that report. Yours are. Cheers.

(TOULON turns away from GALLIMARD and raises his glass. At that instant SONG picks up the vase and hurls it to the ground. It shatters. SONG sinks down amidst the shards of the vase, in a calm, childlike trance. She sings softly, as if reciting a child's nursery rhyme.)

SONG *(Repeat as necessary)*: "The whole world over, the white man travels, setting anchor, wherever he likes. Life's not worth living, unless he finds, the finest maidens, of every land . . ."

(GALLIMARD turns downstage towards us. SONG continues singing.)

GALLIMARD: I shook as I left his house. That coward! That worm! To put the burden for his decisions on my shoulders!

I started for Renee's. But no, that was all I needed. A schoolgirl who would question the role of the penis in modern society. What I wanted was revenge. A vessel to contain my humiliation. Though I hadn't seen her in several weeks, I headed for Butterfly's.

(GALLIMARD enters SONG's apartment.)

SONG: Oh! Rene . . . I was dreaming!

GALLIMARD: You've been drinking?

SONG: If I can't sleep, then yes, I drink. But then, it gives me these dreams which—Rene, it's been almost three weeks since you visited me last.

GALLIMARD: I know. There's been a lot going on in the world.

SONG: Fortunately I am drunk. So I can speak freely. It's not the world, it's you and me. And an old problem. Even the softest skin becomes like leather to a man who's touched it too often. I con-

fess I don't know how to stop it. I don't know how to become another woman.

GALLIMARD: I have a request.

SONG: Is this a solution? Or are you ready to give up the flat?

GALLIMARD: It may be a solution. But I'm sure you won't like it.

SONG: Oh well, that's very important. "Like it?" Do you think I "like" lying here alone, waiting, always waiting for your return? Please—don't worry about what I may not "like."

GALLIMARD: I want to see you . . . naked.

(Silence.)

SONG: I thought you understood my modesty. So you want me to—what—strip? Like a big cowboy girl? Shiny pasties on my breasts? Shall I fling my kimono over my head and yell "ya-hoo" in the process? I thought you respected my shame!

GALLIMARD: I believe you gave me your shame many years ago.

SONG: Yes—and it is just like a white devil to use it against me. I can't believe it. I thought myself so repulsed by the passive Oriental and the cruel white man. Now I see—we are always most revolted by the things hidden within us.

GALLIMARD: I just mean—

SONG: Yes?

GALLIMARD: —that it will remove the only barrier left between us.

SONG: No, Rene. Don't couch your request in sweet words. Be yourself—a cad—and know that my love is enough, that I submit—submit to the worst you can give me. *(Pause)* Well, come. Strip me. Whatever happens, know that you have willed it. Our love, in your hands. I'm helpless before my man.

(GALLIMARD starts to cross the room.)

GALLIMARD: Did I not undress her because I knew, somewhere deep down, what I would find? Perhaps. Happiness is so rare that our mind can turn somersaults to protect it.

At the time, I only knew that I was seeing Pinkerton stalking towards his Butterfly, ready to reward her love with his lecherous hands. The image sickened me, pulled me to my knees, so I was crawling towards her like a worm. By the time I reached her, Pinkerton . . . had vanished from my heart. To be replaced by something new, something unnatural, that flew in the face of all I'd learned in the world—something very close to love.

(He grabs her around the waist; she strokes his hair.)

GALLIMARD: Butterfly, forgive me.

SONG: Rene . . .

GALLIMARD: For everything. From the start.

SONG: I'm . . .

GALLIMARD: I want to—

SONG: I'm pregnant. (Beat) I'm pregnant. (Beat) I'm pregnant.

(Beat.)

GALLIMARD: I want to marry you!

ACT 2 / SCENE 7

(GALLIMARD and Butterfly's flat. Beijing. 1963.)

(Downstage, SONG paces as COMRADE CHIN reads from her notepad. Upstage, GALLIMARD is still kneeling. He remains on his knees throughout the scene, watching it.)

SONG: I need a baby.

CHIN (From pad): He's been spotted going to a dorm.

SONG: I need a baby.

CHIN: At the Foreign Language Institute.

SONG: I need a baby.

CHIN: The room of a Danish girl . . . What do you mean, you need a baby?!

SONG: Tell Comrade Kang—last night, the entire mission, it could've ended.

CHIN: What do you mean?

SONG: Tell Kang—he told me to strip.

CHIN: Strip?!

SONG: Write!

CHIN: I tell you, I don't understand nothing about this case anymore. Nothing.

SONG: He told me to strip, and I took a chance. Oh, we Chinese, we know how to gamble.

CHIN (Writing): ". . . told him to strip."

SONG: My palms were wet, I had to make a split-second decision.

CHIN: Hey! Can you slow down?!

(Pause.)

SONG: You write faster, I'm the artist here. Suddenly, it hit me—"All he wants is for her to submit. Once a woman submits, a man is always ready to become 'generous.'"

CHIN: You're just gonna end up with rough notes.

SONG: And it worked! He gave in! Now, if I can just present him with a baby. A Chinese baby with blond hair—he'll be mine for life!

CHIN: Kang will never agree! The trading of babies has to be a counterrevolutionary act!

SONG: Sometimes, a counterrevolutionary act is necessary to counter a counterrevolutionary act.

(Pause.)

CHIN: Wait.

SONG: I need one . . . in seven months. Make sure it's a boy.

CHIN: This doesn't sound like something the Chairman would do. Maybe you'd better talk to Comrade Kang yourself.

SONG: Good. I will.

(CHIN gets up to leave.)

SONG: Miss Chin? Why, in the Peking Opera, are women's roles played by men?

CHIN: I don't know. Maybe, a reactionary remnant of male—

SONG: No. (Beat) Because only a man knows how a woman is supposed to act.

(CHIN exits. SONG turns upstage, towards GALLIMARD.)

GALLIMARD (Calling after CHIN): Good riddance! (To SONG) I could forget all that betrayal in an instant, you know. If you'd just come back and become Butterfly again.

SONG: Fat chance. You're here in prison, rotting in a cell. And I'm on a plane, winging my way back to China. Your President pardoned me of our treason, you know.

GALLIMARD: Yes, I read about that.

SONG: Must make you feel . . . lower than shit.

GALLIMARD: But don't you, even a little bit, wish you were here with me?

SONG: I'm an artist, Rene. You were my greatest . . . acting challenge. (She laughs) It doesn't matter how rotten I answer, does it? You still adore me. That's why I love you, Rene. (She points to us) So— you were telling your audience about the night I announced I was pregnant.

(GALLIMARD puts his arms around SONG's waist. He and SONG are in the positions they were in at the end of Scene 6.)

ACT 2 / SCENE 8

(Same.)

GALLIMARD: I'll divorce my wife. We'll live together here, and then later in France.

SONG: I feel so . . . ashamed.

GALLIMARD: Why?

SONG: I had begun to lose faith. And now, you shame me with your generosity.

GALLIMARD: Generosity? No, I'm proposing for very selfish reasons.

SONG: Your apologies only make me feel more ashamed. My outburst a moment ago!

GALLIMARD: Your outburst? What about my request?!

SONG: You've been very patient dealing with my . . . eccentricities. A Western man, used to women freer with their bodies—

GALLIMARD: It was sick! Don't make excuses for me.

SONG: I have to. You don't seem willing to make them for yourself.

(Pause.)

GALLIMARD: You're crazy.

SONG: I'm happy. Which often looks like crazy.

GALLIMARD: Then make me crazy. Marry me.

(Pause.)

SONG: No.

GALLIMARD: What?

SONG: Do I sound silly, a slave, if I say I'm not worthy?

GALLIMARD: Yes. In fact you do. No one has loved me like you.

SONG: Thank you. And no one ever will. I'll see to that.

GALLIMARD: So what is the problem?

SONG: Rene, we Chinese are realists. We understand rice, gold, and guns. You are a diplomat. Your career is skyrocketing. Now, what would happen if you divorced your wife to marry a Communist Chinese actress?

GALLIMARD: That's not being realistic. That's defeating yourself before you begin.

SONG: We conserve our strength for the battles we can win.

GALLIMARD: That sounds like a fortune cookie!

SONG: Where do you think fortune cookies come from!

GALLIMARD: I don't care.

SONG: You do. So do I. And we should. That is why I say I'm not worthy. I'm worthy to love and even to be loved by you. But I am not worthy to end the career of one of the West's most promising diplomats.

GALLIMARD: It's not that great a career! I made it sound like more than it is!

SONG: Modesty will get you nowhere. Flatter yourself, and you flatter me. I'm flattered to decline your offer. *(She exits)*

GALLIMARD *(To us)*: Butterfly and I argued all night. And, in the end, I left, knowing I would never be her husband. She went away for several months— to the countryside, like a small animal. Until the night I received her call.

(A baby's cry from offstage. SONG *enters, carrying a child.)*

SONG: He looks like you.

GALLIMARD: Oh! *(Beat; he approaches the baby)* Well, babies are never very attractive at birth.

SONG: Stop!

GALLIMARD: I'm sure he'll grow more beautiful with age. More like his mother.

SONG: "Chi vide mai/ a bimbo del Giappon . . ."

GALLIMARD: "What baby, I wonder, was ever born in Japan"—or China, for that matter—

SONG: ". . . occhi azzurrini?"

GALLIMARD: "With azure eyes"—they're actually sort of brown, wouldn't you say?

SONG: "E il labbro."

GALLIMARD: "And such lips!" *(He kisses* SONG*)* And such lips.

SONG: "E i ricciolini d'oro schietto?"

GALLIMARD: "And such a head of golden"—if slightly patchy—"curls?"

SONG: I'm going to call him "Peepee."

GALLIMARD: Darling, could you repeat that because I'm sure a rickshaw just flew by overhead.

SONG: You heard me.

GALLIMARD: "Song Peepee"? May I suggest Michael, or Stephan, or Adolph?

SONG: You may, but I won't listen.

GALLIMARD: You can't be serious. Can you imagine the time this child will have in school?

SONG: In the West, yes.

GALLIMARD: It's worse than naming him Ping Pong or Long Dong or—

SONG: But he's never going to live in the West, is he?

(Pause.)

GALLIMARD: That wasn't my choice.

SONG: It is mine. And this is my promise to you: I will raise him, he will be our child, but he will never burden you outside of China.

GALLIMARD: Why do you make these promises? I want to be burdened! I want a scandal to cover the papers!

SONG *(To us)*: Prophetic.

GALLIMARD: I'm serious.

SONG: So am I. His name is as I registered it. And he will never live in the West.

*(*SONG *exits with the child.)*

GALLIMARD *(To us)*: It is possible that her stubbornness only made me want her more. That drawing back at the moment of my capitulation was the most brilliant strategy she could have chosen. It is possible. But it is also possible that by this point she could have said, could have done . . . anything, and I would have adored her still.

ACT 2 / SCENE 9

(Beijing. 1966.)

(A driving rhythm of Chinese percussion fills the stage.)

GALLIMARD: And then, China began to change. Mao became very old, and his cult became very strong. And, like many old men, he entered his second childhood. So he handed over the reins of state to those with minds like his own. And children ruled the Middle Kingdom with complete caprice. The doctrine of the Cultural Revolution implied continuous anarchy. Contact between Chinese and foreigners became impossible. Our flat was confiscated. Her fame and my money now counted against us.

(Two dancers in Mao suits and red-starred caps enter, and begin crudely mimicking revolutionary violence, in an agitprop fashion.)

GALLIMARD: And somehow the American war went wrong too. Four hundred thousand dollars were being spent for every Viet Cong killed; so General Westmoreland's remark that the Oriental does not value life the way Americans do was oddly accurate. Why weren't the Vietnamese people giving in? Why were they content instead to die and die and die again?

(TOULON enters.)

TOULON: Congratulations, Gallimard.

GALLIMARD: Excuse me, sir?

TOULON: Not a promotion. That was last time. You're going home.

GALLIMARD: What?

TOULON: Don't say I didn't warn you.

GALLIMARD: I'm being transferred . . . because I was wrong about the American war?

TOULON: Of course not. We don't care about the Americans. We care about your mind. The quality of your analysis. In general, everything you've predicted here in the Orient . . . just hasn't happened.

GALLIMARD: I think that's premature.

TOULON: Don't force me to be blunt. Okay, you said China was ready to open to Western trade. The only thing they're trading out there are Western heads. And, yes, you said the Americans would succeed in Indochina. You were kidding, right?

GALLIMARD: I think the end is in sight.

TOULON: Don't be pathetic. And don't take this personally. You were wrong. It's not your fault.

GALLIMARD: But I'm going home.

TOULON: Right. Could I have the number of your mistress? *(Beat)* Joke! Joke! Eat a croissant for me.

(TOULON exits. SONG, wearing a Mao suit, is dragged in from the wings as part of the upstage dance. They "beat" her, then lampoon the acrobatics of the Chinese opera, as she is made to kneel onstage.)

GALLIMARD *(Simultaneously)*: I don't care to recall how Butterfly and I said our hurried farewell. Perhaps it was better to end our affair before it killed her.

(GALLIMARD exits. COMRADE CHIN walks across the stage with a banner reading: "The Actor Renounces His Decadent Profession!" She reaches the kneeling SONG. Percussion stops with a thud. Dancers strike poses.)

CHIN: Actor-oppressor, for years you have lived above the common people and looked down on their labor. While the farmer ate millet—

SONG: I ate pastries from France and sweetmeats from silver trays.

CHIN: And how did you come to live in such an exalted position?

SONG: I was a plaything for the imperialists!

CHIN: What did you do?

SONG: I shamed China by allowing myself to be corrupted by a foreigner . . .

CHIN: What does this mean? The People demand a full confession!

SONG: I engaged in the lowest perversions with China's enemies!

CHIN: What perversions? Be more clear!

SONG: I let him put it up my ass!

(Dancers look over, disgusted.)

CHIN: Aaaa-ya! How can you use such sickening language?!

SONG: My language . . . is only as foul as the crimes I committed . . .

CHIN: Yeah. That's better. So—what do you want to do now?

SONG: I want to serve the people.

(Percussion starts up, with Chinese strings.)

CHIN: What?

SONG: I want to serve the people!

(Dancers regain their revolutionary smiles, and begin a dance of victory.)

CHIN: What?!

SONG: I want to serve the people!!

(Dancers unveil a banner: "The Actor Is Rehabilitated!" SONG remains kneeling before CHIN, as the dancers bounce around them, then exit. Music out.)

ACT 2 / SCENE 10

(A commune. Hunan Province. 1970.)

CHIN: How you planning to do that?

SONG: I've already worked four years in the fields of Hunan, Comrade Chin.

CHIN: So? Farmers work all their lives. Let me see your hands.

(SONG holds them out for her inspection.)

CHIN: Goddamn! Still so smooth! How long does it take to turn you actors into good anythings? Hunh. You've just spent too many years in luxury to be any good to the Revolution.

SONG: I served the Revolution.

CHIN: Served the Revolution? Bullshit! You wore dresses! Don't tell me—I was there. I saw you! You and your white vice-consul! Stuck up there in your flat, living off the People's Treasury! Yeah, I knew what was going on! You two . . . homos! Homos! Homos! *(Pause; she composes herself)* Ah! Well . . . you will serve the people, all right. But not with the Revolution's money. This time, you use your own money.

SONG: I have no money.

CHIN: Shut up! And you won't stink up China anymore with your pervert stuff. You'll pollute the place where pollution begins—the West.

SONG: What do you mean?

CHIN: Shut up! You're going to France. Without a cent in your pocket. You find your consul's house, you make him pay your expenses—

SONG: No.

CHIN: And you give us weekly reports! Useful information!

SONG: That's crazy. It's been four years.

CHIN: Either that, or back to rehabilitation center!

SONG: Comrade Chin, he's not going to support me! Not in France! He's a white man! I was just his plaything—

CHIN: Oh yuck! Again with the sickening language? Where's my stick?

SONG: You don't understand the mind of a man.

(Pause.)

CHIN: Oh no? No I don't? Then how come I'm married, huh? How come I got a man? Five, six years ago, you always tell me those kind of things, I felt very bad. But not now! Because what does the Chairman say? He tells us *I'm* now the smart one, you're now the nincompoop! *You're* the blockhead, the harebrain, the nitwit! You think you're so smart? You understand "The Mind of a Man"? Good! Then *you* go to France and be a pervert for Chairman Mao!

(CHIN and SONG exit in opposite directions.)

ACT 2 / SCENE 11

(Paris. 1968–70.)

(GALLIMARD enters.)

GALLIMARD: And what was waiting for me back in Paris? Well, better Chinese food than I'd eaten in China. Friends and relatives. A little accounting, regular schedule, keeping track of traffic violations in the suburbs. . . . And the indignity of students shouting the slogans of Chairman Mao at me—in French.

HELGA: Rene? Rene? *(She enters, soaking wet)* I've had a . . . a problem. *(She sneezes)*

GALLIMARD: You're wet.

HELGA: Yes, I . . . coming back from the grocer's. A group of students, waving red flags, they—

(GALLIMARD fetches a towel.)

HELGA: —they ran by, I was caught up along with them. Before I knew what was happening—

(GALLIMARD gives her the towel.)

HELGA: Thank you. The police started firing water cannons at us. I tried to shout, to tell them I was the wife of a diplomat, but—you know how it is . . . *(Pause)* Needless to say, I lost the groceries. Rene, what's happening to France?

GALLIMARD: What's—? Well, nothing, really.

HELGA: Nothing?! The storefronts are in flames, there's glass in the streets, buildings are toppling—and I'm wet!

GALLIMARD: Nothing! . . . that I care to think about.

HELGA: And is that why you stay in this room?

GALLIMARD: Yes, in fact.

HELGA: With the incense burning? You know something. I hate incense. It smells so sickly sweet.

GALLIMARD: Well, I hate the French. Who just smell—period!

HELGA: And the Chinese were better?

GALLIMARD: Please—don't start.

HELGA: When we left, this exact same thing, the riots—

GALLIMARD: No, no . . .

HELGA: Students screaming slogans, smashing down doors—

GALLIMARD: Helga—

HELGA: It was all going on in China, too. Don't you remember?!

GALLIMARD: Helga! Please! *(Pause)* You have never understood China, have you? You walk in here with these ridiculous ideas, that the West is falling apart, that China was spitting in our faces. You come in, dripping of the streets, and you leave water all over my floor. *(He grabs HELGA's towel, begins mopping up the floor)*

HELGA: But it's the truth!

GALLIMARD: Helga, I want a divorce.

(Pause; GALLIMARD continues mopping the floor.)

HELGA: I take it back. China is . . . beautiful. Incense, I like incense.

GALLIMARD: I've had a mistress.

HELGA: So?

GALLIMARD: For eight years.

HELGA: I knew you would. I knew you would the day I married you. And now what? You want to marry her?

GALLIMARD: I can't. She's in China.

HELGA: I see. You want to leave. For someone who's not here, is that right?

GALLIMARD: That's right.

HELGA: You can't live with her, but still you don't want to live with me.

GALLIMARD: That's right.

(Pause.)

HELGA: Shit. How terrible that I can figure that out. *(Pause)* I never thought I'd say it. But, in China, I was happy. I knew, in my own way, I knew that you were not everything you pretended to be. But the pretense—going on your arm to the embassy ball, visiting your office and the guards saying, "Good morning, good morning, Madame Gallimard"—the pretense . . . was very good indeed. *(Pause)* I hope everyone is mean to you for the rest of your life. *(She exits)*

GALLIMARD *(To us):* Prophetic.

(MARC enters with two drinks.)

GALLIMARD *(To MARC):* In China, I was different from all other men.

MARC: Sure. You were white. Here's your drink.

GALLIMARD: I felt . . . touched.

MARC: In the head? Rene, I don't want to hear about the Oriental love goddess. Okay? One night—can we just drink and throw up without a lot of conversation?

GALLIMARD: You still don't believe me, do you?

MARC: Sure I do. She was the most beautiful, et cetera, et cetera, blasé blasé.

(Pause.)

GALLIMARD: My life in the West has been such a disappointment.

MARC: Life in the West is like that. You'll get used to it. Look, you're driving me away. I'm leaving. Happy, now? *(He exits, then returns)* Look, I have a date tomorrow night. You wanna come? I can fix you up with—

GALLIMARD: Of course. I would love to come.

(Pause.)

MARC: Uh—on second thought, no. You'd better get ahold of yourself first.

(He exits; GALLIMARD nurses his drink.)

GALLIMARD *(To us):* This is the ultimate cruelty, isn't it? That I can talk and talk and to anyone listening, it's only air—too rich a diet to be swallowed by a mundane world. Why can't anyone understand? That in China, I once loved, and was loved by, very simply, the Perfect Woman.

(SONG enters, dressed as Butterfly in wedding dress.)

GALLIMARD *(To SONG):* Not again. My imagination is hell. Am I asleep this time? Or did I drink too much?

SONG: Rene?

GALLIMARD: God, it's too painful! That you speak?

SONG: What are you talking about? Rene—touch me.

GALLIMARD: Why?

SONG: I'm real. Take my hand.

GALLIMARD: Why? So you can disappear again and leave me clutching at the air? For the entertainment of my neighbors who—?

(SONG touches GALLIMARD.)

SONG: Rene?

(GALLIMARD takes SONG's hand. Silence.)

GALLIMARD: Butterfly? I never doubted you'd return.

SONG: You hadn't . . . forgotten—?

GALLIMARD: Yes, actually, I've forgotten everything. My mind, you see—there wasn't enough room in this hard head—not for the world *and* for you. No, there was only room for one. *(Beat)* Come, look. See? Your bed has been waiting, with the Klimt poster you like, and—see? The xiang lu° you gave me?

SONG: I . . . I don't know what to say.

GALLIMARD: There's nothing to say. Not at the end of a long trip. Can I make you some tea?

SONG: But where's your wife?

GALLIMARD: She's by my side. She's by my side at last.

(GALLIMARD reaches to embrace SONG. SONG sidesteps, dodging him.)

GALLIMARD: Why?

SONG *(To us):* So I did return to Rene in Paris. Where I found—

GALLIMARD: Why do you run away? Can't we show them how we embraced that evening?

SONG: Please. I'm talking.

GALLIMARD: You have to do what I say! I'm conjuring you up in *my* mind!

SONG: Rene, I've never done what you've said. Why should it be any different in your mind? Now split—the story moves on, and I must change.

GALLIMARD: I welcomed you into my home! I didn't have to, you know! I could've left you penniless on the streets of Paris! But I took you in!

SONG: Thank you.

GALLIMARD: So . . . please . . . don't change.

SONG: You know I have to. You know I will. And anyway, what difference does it make? No matter what your eyes tell you, you can't ignore the truth. You already know too much.

(GALLIMARD exits. SONG turns to us.)

SONG: The change I'm going to make requires about five minutes. So I thought you might want to take this opportunity to stretch your legs, enjoy a drink, or listen to the musicians. I'll be here, when you return, right where you left me.

(SONG goes to a mirror in front of which is a wash basin of water. She starts to remove her makeup as stagelights go to half and houselights come up.)

---

xiang lu, incense burner.

ACT 3 / SCENE 1

(A courthouse in Paris. 1986.)

(As he promised, SONG *has completed the bulk of his transformation, onstage by the time the houselights go down and the stagelights come up full. He removes his wig and kimono, leaving them on the floor. Underneath, he wears a well-cut suit.)*

SONG: So I'd done my job better than I had a right to expect. Well, give him some credit, too. He's right—I was in a fix when I arrived in Paris. I walked from the airport into town, then I located, by blind groping, the Chinatown district. Let me make one thing clear: whatever else may be said about the Chinese, they are stingy! I slept in doorways three days until I could find a tailor who would make me this kimono on credit. As it turns out, maybe I didn't even need it. Maybe he would've been happy to see me in a simple shift and mascara. But . . . better safe than sorry.

That was 1970, when I arrived in Paris. For the next fifteen years, yes, I lived a very comfy life. Some relief, believe me, after four years on a fucking commune in Nowheresville, China. Rene supported the boy and me, and I did some demonstrations around the country as part of my "cultural exchange" cover. And then there was the spying.

*(*SONG *moves upstage, to a chair.* TOULON *enters as a judge, wearing the appropriate wig and robes. He sits near* SONG*. It's 1986, and* SONG *is testifying in a courtroom.)*

SONG: Not much at first. Rene had lost all his high-level contacts. Comrade Chin wasn't very interested in parking-ticket statistics. But finally, at my urging, Rene got a job as a courier, handling sensitive documents. He'd photograph them for me, and I'd pass them on to the Chinese embassy.

JUDGE: Did he understand the extent of his activity?

SONG: He didn't ask. He knew that I needed those documents, and that was enough.

JUDGE: But he must've known he was passing classified information.

SONG: I can't say.

JUDGE: He never asked what you were going to do with them?

SONG: Nope.

(Pause.)

JUDGE: There is one thing that the court—indeed, that all of France—would like to know.

SONG: Fire away.

JUDGE: Did Monsieur Gallimard know you were a man?

SONG: Well, he never saw me completely naked. Ever.

JUDGE: But surely, he must've . . . how can I put this?

SONG: Put it however you like. I'm not shy. He must've felt around?

JUDGE: Mmmmm.

SONG: Not really. I did all the work. He just laid back. Of course we did enjoy more . . . complete union, and I suppose he *might* have wondered why I was always on my stomach, but. . . . But what you're thinking is, "Of course a wrist must've brushed . . . a hand hit . . . over twenty years!" Yeah. Well, Your Honor, it was my job to make him think I was a woman. And chew on this: it wasn't all that hard. See, my mother was a prostitute along the Bundt before the Revolution. And, uh, I think it's fair to say she learned a few things about Western men. So I borrowed her knowledge. In service to my country.

JUDGE: Would you care to enlighten the court with this secret knowledge? I'm sure we're all very curious.

SONG: I'm sure you are. *(Pause)* Okay, Rule One is: Men always believe what they want to hear. So a girl can tell the most obnoxious lies and the guys will believe them every time—"This is my first time"—"That's the biggest I've ever seen"—or *both,* which, if you really think about it, is not possible in a single lifetime. You've maybe heard those phrases a few times in your own life, yes, Your Honor?

JUDGE: It's not my life, Monsieur Song, which is on trial today.

SONG: Okay, okay, just trying to lighten up the proceedings. Tough room.

JUDGE: Go on.

SONG: Rule Two: As soon as a Western man comes into contact with the East—he's already confused. The West has sort of an international rape mentality towards the East. Do you know rape mentality?

JUDGE: Give us your definition, please.

SONG: Basically, "Her mouth says no, but her eyes say yes."

The West thinks of itself as masculine—big guns, big industry, big money—so the East is feminine—weak, delicate, poor . . . but good at art, and full of inscrutable wisdom—the feminine mystique.

Her mouth says no, but her eyes say yes. The West believes the East, deep down, *wants* to be dominated—because a woman can't think for herself.

JUDGE: What does this have to do with my question?

SONG: You expect Oriental countries to submit to your guns, and you expect Oriental women to be submissive to your men. That's why you say they make the best wives.

JUDGE: But why would that make it possible for you to fool Monsieur Gallimard? Please—get to the point.

SONG: One, because when he finally met his fantasy woman, he wanted more than anything to believe that she was, in fact, a woman. And second, I am an Oriental. And being an Oriental, I could never be completely a man.

(Pause.)

JUDGE: Your armchair political theory is tenuous, Monsieur Song.

SONG: You think so? That's why you'll lose in all your dealings with the East.

JUDGE: Just answer my question: did he know you were a man?

(Pause.)

SONG: You know, Your Honor, I never asked.

ACT 3 / SCENE 2

(Same.)

(Music from the "Death Scene" from Butterfly *blares over the house speakers. It is the loudest thing we've heard in this play.*
GALLIMARD *enters, crawling towards* SONG's *wig and kimono.)*

GALLIMARD: Butterfly? Butterfly?

*(*SONG *remains a man, in the witness box, delivering a testimony we do not hear.)*

GALLIMARD *(To us)*: In my moment of greatest shame, here, in this courtroom—with that . . . person up there, telling the world. . . . What strikes me especially is how shallow he is, how glib and obsequious . . . completely . . . without substance! The type that prowls around discos with a gold medallion stinking of garlic. So little like my Butterfly.

Yet even in this moment my mind remains agile, flip-flopping like a man on a trampoline. Even now, my picture dissolves, and I see that . . . witness . . . talking to me.

*(*SONG *suddenly stands straight up in his witness box, and looks at* GALLIMARD.*)*

SONG: Yes. You. White man.

*(*SONG *steps out of the witness box, and moves downstage towards* GALLIMARD. *Light change.)*

GALLIMARD *(To* SONG*)*: Who? Me?

SONG: Do you see any other white men?

GALLIMARD: Yes. There're white men all around. This is a French courtroom.

SONG: So you are an adventurous imperialist. Tell me, why did it take you so long? To come back to this place?

GALLIMARD: What place?

SONG: This theatre in China. Where we met many years ago.

GALLIMARD *(To us)*: And once again, against my will, I am transported.

(Chinese opera music comes up on the speakers. SONG *begins to do opera moves, as he did the night they met.)*

SONG: Do you remember? The night you gave your heart?

GALLIMARD: It was a long time ago.

SONG: Not long enough. A night that turned your world upside down.

GALLIMARD: Perhaps.

SONG: Oh, be honest with me. What's another bit of flattery when you've already given me twenty years' worth? It's a wonder my head hasn't swollen to the size of China.

GALLIMARD: Who's to say it hasn't?

SONG: Who's to say? And what's the shame? In pride? You think I could've pulled this off if I wasn't already full of pride when we met? No, not just pride. Arrogance. It takes arrogance, really—to believe you can will, with your eyes and your lips, the destiny of another. *(He dances)* C'mon. Admit it. You still want me. Even in slacks and a button-down collar.

GALLIMARD: I don't see what the point of—

SONG: You don't? Well maybe, Rene, just maybe—I want you.

GALLIMARD: You do?

SONG: Then again, maybe I'm just playing with you. How can you tell? *(Reprising his feminine character, he sidles up to* GALLIMARD*)* "How I wish there were even a small cafe to sit in. With men in tuxedos, and cappuccinos, and bad expatriate jazz." Now you want to kiss me, don't you?

GALLIMARD *(Pulling away)*: What makes you—?

SONG: —so sure? See? I take the words from your mouth. Then I wait for you to come and retrieve them. *(He reclines on the floor)*

GALLIMARD: Why?! Why do you treat me so cruelly?

SONG: Perhaps I *was* treating you cruelly. But now—I'm being nice. Come here, my little one.

GALLIMARD: I'm not your little one!

SONG: My mistake. It's I who am *your* little one, right?

GALLIMARD: Yes, I—

SONG: So come get your little one. If you like. I may even let you strip me.

GALLIMARD: I mean, you were! Before . . . but not like this!

SONG: I was? Then perhaps I still am. If you look hard enough. *(He starts to remove his clothes)*

GALLIMARD: What—what are you doing?

SONG: Helping you to see through my act.

GALLIMARD: Stop that! I don't want to! I don't—

SONG: Oh, but you asked me to strip, remember?

GALLIMARD: What? That was years ago! And I took it back!

SONG: No. You postponed it. Postponed the inevitable. Today, the inevitable has come calling.

(From the speakers, cacophony: Butterfly *mixed in with Chinese gongs.)*

GALLIMARD: No! Stop! I don't want to see!

SONG: Then look away.

GALLIMARD: You're only in my mind! All this is in my mind! I order you! To stop!

SONG: To what? To strip? That's just what I'm—

GALLIMARD: No! Stop! I want you—!

SONG: You want me?

GALLIMARD: To stop!

SONG: You know something, Rene? Your mouth says no, but your eyes say yes. Turn them away. I dare you.

GALLIMARD: I don't have to! Every night, you say you're going to strip, but then I beg you and you stop!

SONG: I guess tonight is different.

GALLIMARD: Why? Why should that be?

SONG: Maybe I've become frustrated. Maybe I'm saying "Look at me, you fool!" Or maybe I'm just feeling . . . sexy. *(He is down to his briefs)*

GALLIMARD: Please. This is unnecessary. I know what you are.

SONG: You do? What am I?

GALLIMARD: A—a man.

SONG: You don't really believe that.

GALLIMARD: Yes I do! I knew all the time somewhere that my happiness was temporary, my love a deception. But my mind kept the knowledge at bay. To make the wait bearable.

SONG: Monsieur Gallimard—the wait is over.

(SONG drops his briefs. He is naked. Sound cue out. Slowly, we and SONG come to the realization that what we had thought to be GALLIMARD's sobbing is actually his laughter.)

GALLIMARD: Oh god! What an idiot! Of course!

SONG: Rene—what?

GALLIMARD: Look at you! You're a man! *(He bursts into laughter again)*

SONG: I fail to see what's so funny!

GALLIMARD: "You fail to see—!" I mean, you never did have much of a sense of humor, did you? I just think it's ridiculously funny that I've wasted so much time on just a man!

SONG: Wait. I'm not "just a man."

GALLIMARD: No? Isn't that what you've been trying to convince me of?

SONG: Yes, but what I mean—

GALLIMARD: And now, I finally believe you, and you tell me it's not true? I think you must have some kind of identity problem.

SONG: Will you listen to me?

GALLIMARD: Why?! I've been listening to you for twenty years. Don't I deserve a vacation?

SONG: I'm not just any man!

GALLIMARD: Then, what exactly are you?

SONG: Rene, how can you ask—? Okay, what about this?

(He picks up Butterfly's robes, starts to dance around. No music.)

GALLIMARD: Yes, that's very nice. I have to admit.

(SONG holds out his arm to GALLIMARD.)

SONG: It's the same skin you've worshiped for years. Touch it.

GALLIMARD: Yes, it does feel the same.

SONG: Now—close your eyes.

(SONG covers GALLIMARD's eyes with one hand. With the other, SONG draws GALLIMARD's hand up to his face. GALLIMARD, like a blind man, lets his hands run over SONG's face.)

GALLIMARD: This skin, I remember. The curve of her face, the softness of her cheek, her hair against the back of my hand . . .

SONG: I'm your Butterfly. Under the robes, beneath everything, it was always me. Now, open your eyes and admit it—you adore me. *(He removes his hand from GALLIMARD's eyes)*

GALLIMARD: You, who knew every inch of my desires—how could you, of all people, have made such a mistake?

SONG: What?

GALLIMARD: You showed me your true self. When all I loved was the lie. A perfect lie, which you let fall to the ground—and now, it's old and soiled.

SONG: So—you never really loved me? Only when I was playing a part?

GALLIMARD: I'm a man who loved a woman created by a man. Everything else—simply falls short.

(Pause.)

SONG: What am I supposed to do now?

GALLIMARD: You were a fine spy, Monsieur Song, with an even finer accomplice. But now I believe you should go. Get out of my life!

SONG: Go where? Rene, you can't live without me. Not after twenty years.

GALLIMARD: I certainly can't live with you—not after twenty years of betrayal.

SONG: Don't be stubborn! Where will you go?

GALLIMARD: I have a date . . . with my Butterfly.

SONG: So, throw away your pride. And come . . .

GALLIMARD: Get away from me! Tonight, I've finally learned to tell fantasy from reality. And, knowing the difference, I choose fantasy.

SONG: *I'm* your fantasy!

GALLIMARD: You? You're as real as hamburger. Now get out! I have a date with my Butterfly and I don't want your body polluting the room! *(He tosses SONG's suit at him)* Look at these—you dress like a pimp.

SONG: Hey! These are Armani slacks and—! *(He puts on his briefs and slacks)* Let's just say . . . I'm disappointed in you, Rene. In the crush of your adoration, I thought you'd become something more. More like . . . a woman.

But no. Men. You're like the rest of them. It's all in the way we dress, and make up our faces, and bat our eyelashes. You really have so little imagination!

GALLIMARD: You, Monsieur Song? Accuse me of too little imagination? You, if anyone, should know— I am pure imagination. And in imagination I will remain. Now get out!

(GALLIMARD *bodily removes* SONG *from the stage, taking his kimono.*)

SONG: Rene! I'll never put on those robes again! You'll be sorry!

GALLIMARD (*To* SONG): I'm already sorry! (*Looking at the kimono in his hands*) Exactly as sorry . . . as a Butterfly.

ACT 3 / SCENE 3

(M. GALLIMARD*'s prison cell. Paris. Present.*)

GALLIMARD: I've played out the events of my life night after night, always searching for a new ending to my story, one where I leave this cell and return forever to my Butterfly's arms.

Tonight I realize my search is over. That I've looked all along in the wrong place. And now, to you, I will prove that my love was not in vain— by returning to the world of fantasy where I first met her.

(*He picks up the kimono; dancers enter.*)

GALLIMARD: There is a vision of the Orient that I have. Of slender women in chong sams and kimonos who die for the love of unworthy foreign devils. Who are born and raised to be the perfect women. Who take whatever punishment we give them, and bounce back, strengthened by love, unconditionally. It is a vision that has become my life.

(*Dancers bring the wash basin to him and help him make up his face.*)

GALLIMARD: In public, I have continued to deny that Song Liling is a man. This brings me headlines, and is a source of great embarrassment to my French colleagues, who can now be sent into a coughing fit by the mere mention of Chinese food. But alone, in my cell, I have long since faced the truth.

And the truth demands a sacrifice. For mistakes made over the course of a lifetime. My mistakes were simple and absolute—the man I loved was a cad, a bounder. He deserved nothing but a kick in the behind, and instead I gave him . . . all my love.

Yes—love. Why not admit it all? That was my undoing, wasn't it? Love warped my judgment, blinded my eyes, rearranged the very lines on my face . . . until I could look in the mirror and see nothing but . . . a woman.

(*Dancers help him put on the Butterfly wig.*)

GALLIMARD: I have a vision. Of the Orient. That, deep within its almond eyes, there are still women. Women willing to sacrifice themselves for the love of a man. Even a man whose love is completely without worth.

(*Dancers assist* GALLIMARD *in donning the kimono. They hand him a knife.*)

GALLIMARD: Death with honor is better than life . . . life with dishonor. (*He sets himself center stage, in a seppuku position*) The love of a Butterfly can withstand many things—unfaithfulness, loss, even abandonment. But how can it face the one sin that implies all others? The devastating knowledge that, underneath it all, the object of her love was nothing more, nothing less than . . . a man. (*He sets the tip of the knife against his body*) It is 19——. And I have found her at last. In a prison on the outskirts of Paris. My name is Rene Gallimard— also known as Madame Butterfly.

(GALLIMARD *turns upstage and plunges the knife into his body, as music from the "Love Duet" blares over the speakers. He collapses into the arms of the dancers, who lay him reverently on the floor. The image holds for several beats. Then a tight special up on* SONG, *who stands as a man, staring at the dead* GALLIMARD. *He smokes a cigarette; the smoke filters up through the lights. Two words leave his lips.*)

SONG: Butterfly? Butterfly?

(*Smoke rises as lights fade slowly to black.*)

AFTERWORD

It all started in May of 1986, over casual dinner conversation. A friend asked, had I heard about the French diplomat who'd fallen in love with a Chinese actress, who subsequently turned out to be not only a spy, but a man? I later found a two-paragraph story in *The New York Times*. The diplomat, Bernard Bouriscot, attempting to account for the fact that he had never seen his "girlfriend" naked, was quoted as saying, "I thought she was very modest. I thought it was a Chinese custom."

Now, I am aware that this is *not* a Chinese custom, that Asian women are no more shy with their lovers than are women of the West. I am also aware, however, that Bouriscot's assumption was consistent with a certain stereotyped view of Asians as bowing, blushing flowers. I therefore concluded that the diplomat must have fallen in love, not with a person, but with a fantasy stereotype. I also inferred that, to the extent the Chinese spy encouraged these misperceptions, he must have played up to and exploited this image of the Oriental woman as demure and submissive. (In general, by the way, we prefer the term "Asian" to "Oriental," in the same way "Black" is superior to "Negro." I use the term "Oriental" specifically to denote an exotic or imperialistic view of the East.)

I suspected there was a play here. I purposely refrained from further research, for I was not interested in writing docudrama. Frankly, I didn't want the "truth" to interfere with my own speculations. I told Stuart Ostrow, a producer with whom I'd worked before, that I envisioned the story as a musical. I remember going so far as to speculate that it could be some "great *Madame Butterfly*–like tragedy." Stuart was very intrigued, and encouraged me with some early funding.

Before I can begin writing, I must "break the back of the story," and find some angle which compels me to set pen to paper. I was driving down Santa Monica Boulevard one afternoon, and asked myself, "What did Bouriscot think he was getting in this Chinese actress?" The answer came to me clearly: "He probably thought he had found Madame Butterfly."

The idea of doing a deconstructivist *Madame Butterfly* immediately appealed to me. This, despite the fact that I didn't even know the plot of the opera! I knew Butterfly only as a cultural stereotype; speaking of an Asian woman, we would sometimes say, "She's pulling a Butterfly," which meant playing the submissive Oriental number. Yet, I felt convinced that the libretto would include yet another lotus blossom pining away for a cruel Caucasian man, and dying for her love. Such a story has become too much of a cliché not to be included in the archetypal East-West romance that started it all. Sure enough, when I purchased the record, I discovered it contained a wealth of sexist and racist clichés, reaffirming my faith in Western culture.

Very soon after, I came up with the basic "arc" of my play: the Frenchman fantasizes that he is Pinkerton and his lover is Butterfly. By the end of the piece, he realizes that it is he who has been Butterfly, in that the Frenchman has been duped by love; the Chinese spy, who exploited that love, is therefore the real Pinkerton. I wrote a proposal to Stuart Ostrow, who found it very exciting. (On the night of the Tony Awards, Stuart produced my original two-page treatment, and we were gratified to see that it was, indeed, the play I eventually wrote.)

I wrote a play, rather than a musical, because, having "broken the back" of the story, I wanted to start immediately and not be hampered by the lengthy process of collaboration. I would like to think, however, that the play has retained many of its musical roots. So *Monsieur Butterfly* was completed in six weeks between September and mid-October, 1986. My wife, Ophelia, thought *Monsieur Butterfly* too obvious a title, and suggested I abbreviate it in the French fashion. Hence, *M. Butterfly*, far more mysterious and ambiguous, was the result.

I sent the play to Stuart Ostrow as a courtesy, assuming he would not be interested in producing what had become a straight play. Instead, he flew out to Los Angeles immediately for script conferences. Coming from a background in the not-for-profit theater, I suggested that we develop the work at a regional institution. Stuart, nothing if not bold, argued for bringing it directly to Broadway.

It was also Stuart who suggested John Dexter to direct. I had known Dexter's work only by its formidable reputation. Stuart sent the script to John, who called back the next day, saying it was the best play he'd read in twenty years. Naturally, this predisposed me to like him a great deal. We met in December in New York. Not long after, we persuaded Eiko Ishioka to design our sets and costumes. I had admired her work from afar ever since, as a college student, I had seen her poster for *Apocalypse Now* in Japan. By January, 1987, Stuart had optioned *M. Butterfly*, Dexter was signed to direct, and the normally sloth-like pace of commercial theater had been given a considerable prod.

On January 4, 1988, we commenced rehearsals. I was very pleased that John Lithgow had agreed to play the French diplomat, whom I named Rene Gallimard. Throughout his tenure with us, Lithgow was every inch the center of our company, intelligent and professional, passionate and generous. B. D. Wong was forced to endure a five-month audition period before we selected him to play Song Liling. Watching B. D.'s growth was one of the joys of the rehearsal process, as he constantly attained higher levels of performance. It became clear that we had been fortunate enough to put together a company with not only great talent, but also wonderful camaraderie.

As for Dexter, I have never worked with a director more respectful of text and bold in the uses of theatricality. On the first day of rehearsal, the actors were given movement and speech drills. Then Dexter asked that everyone not required at rehearsal leave the room. A week later, we returned for an amazingly thorough run-through. It was not until that day that I first heard my play read, a note I direct at many regional theaters who "develop" a script to death.

We opened in Washington, D.C., at the National Theatre, where *West Side Story* and *Amadeus* had premiered. On the morning after opening night, most of the reviews were glowing, except for *The Washington Post*. Throughout our run in Washington, Stuart never pressured us to make the play more "commercial" in reaction to that review. We all simply concluded that the gentleman was possibly insecure about his own sexual orientation and therefore found the play threatening. And we continued our work.

Once we opened in New York, the play found a life of its own. I suppose the most gratifying thing for me is that we had never compromised to be more "Broadway"; we simply did the work we thought best. That our endeavor should be rewarded to the degree it has is one of those all-too-rare instances when one's own perception and that of the world are in agreement.

Many people have subsequently asked me about the "ideas" behind the play. From our first preview in Washington, I have been pleased that people leaving the theater were talking not only about the sexual, but also the political, issues raised by the work.

From my point of view, the "impossible" story of a Frenchman duped by a Chinese man masquerading as a woman always seemed perfectly explicable; given the degree of misunderstanding between men and women and also between East and West, it seemed inevitable that a mistake of this magnitude would one day take place.

Gay friends have told me of a derogatory term used in their community: "Rice Queen"—a gay Caucasian man primarily attracted to Asians. In these relationships, the Asian virtually always plays the role of the "woman"; the Rice Queen, culturally and sexually, is the "man." This pattern of relationships had become so codified that, until recently, it was considered unnatural for gay Asians to date one another. Such men would be taunted with a phrase which implied they were lesbians.

Similarly, heterosexual Asians have long been aware of "Yellow Fever"—Caucasian men with a fetish for exotic Oriental women. I have often heard it said that "Oriental women make the best wives." (Rarely is this heard from the mouths of Asian men, incidentally.)

This mythology is exploited by the Oriental mail-order bride trade which has flourished over the past decade. American men can now send away for catalogues of "obedient, domesticated" Asian women looking for husbands. Anyone who believes such stereotypes are a thing of the past need look no further than Manhattan cable television, which advertises call girls from "the exotic east, where men are king; obedient girls, trained in the art of pleasure."

In these appeals, we see issues of racism and sexism intersect. The catalogues and TV spots appeal to a strain in men which desires to reject Western women for what they have become—independent, assertive, self-possessed—in favor of a more reactionary model—the prefeminist, domesticated geisha girl.

That the Oriental woman is penultimately feminine does not of course imply that she is always "good." For every Madonna there is a whore; for every lotus blossom there is also a dragon lady. In popular culture, "good" Asian women are those who serve the White protagonist in his battle against her own people, often sleeping with him in the process. Stallone's *Rambo II,* Cimino's *Year of the Dragon,* Clavell's *Shogun,* Van Lustbader's *The Ninja* are all familiar examples.

Now our considerations of race and sex intersect the issue of imperialism. For this formula—good natives serve Whites, bad natives rebel—is consistent with the mentality of colonialism. Because they are submissive and obedient, good natives of both sexes necessarily take on "feminine" characteristics in a colonialist world. Gunga Din's unfailing devotion to his British master, for instance, is not so far removed from Butterfly's slavish faith in Pinkerton.

It is reasonable to assume that influences and attitudes so pervasively displayed in popular culture might also influence our policymakers as they consider the world. The neo-Colonialist notion that good elements of a native society, like a good woman, desire submission to the masculine West speaks precisely to the heart of our foreign policy blunders in Asia and elsewhere.

For instance, Frances Fitzgerald wrote in *Fire in the Lake,* "The idea that the United States could not master the problems of a country as small and underdeveloped as Vietnam did not occur to Johnson as a possibility." Here, as in so many other cases, by dehumanizing the enemy, we dehumanize ourselves. We become the Rice Queens of *realpolitik.*

M. Butterfly has sometimes been regarded as an anti-American play, a diatribe against the stereotyping of the East by the West, of women by men. Quite to the contrary, I consider it a plea to all sides to cut through our respective layers of cultural and sexual misperception, to deal with one another truthfully for our mutual good, from the common and equal ground we share as human beings.

For the myths of the East, the myths of the West, the myths of men, and the myths of women—these have so saturated our consciousness that truthful contact between nations and lovers can only be the result of heroic effort. Those who prefer to bypass the work involved will remain in a world of surfaces, misperceptions running rampant. This is, to me, the convenient world in which the French diplomat and the Chinese spy lived. This is why, after twenty years, he had learned nothing at all about his lover, not even the truth of his sex.

D. H. H.

New York City
September, 1988

Figure 1. At the opening of the play, Gallimard (John Lithgow) sits in his prison cell while Song Liling (B. D. Wong) poses above. The swirling ramp was designed by Eiko Ishioka for the 1988 production of *M. Butterfly* at the Eugene O'Neill Theatre, New York, directed by John Dexter. (Photograph: Martha Swope © Time Inc.)

Figure 2. Song Liling (B. D. Wong) as Butterfly in the 1988 New York production. (Photograph: Martha Swope © Time Inc.)

Figure 3. Gallimard (John Lithgow) and Song Liling (B. D. Wong) in her Beijing apartment, from the 1988 New York production. (Photograph: Martha Swope © Time Inc.)

Staging of *M. Butterfly*

EIKO ISHIOKA ON DESIGNING THE 1988 NEW YORK PRODUCTION

In terms of the play's visuals, Dexter gave me only two specific guidelines: first, that the set should have three levels of interplay (top, middle, and bottom); second, that the mechanics should be kept simple. He hated the way technology was used on Broadway—the flashing laser beams and motor-driven revolving stages. "To me," he explained, "the *kurogo* idea of Kabuki theater is the most sophisticated technology I've seen on stage. Keep that in mind." (*Kurogo* are stagehands. Dressed in black with their faces covered, they are meant to move like shadows across the stage as they move props or help with wardrobe changes.) In fact, Dexter ended up reinterpreting *kurogo* for *M. Butterfly;* it was probably the first time anyone on Broadway had done it. He used Asian actors as *kurogo*, only instead of being silent shadows they played roles in the story. I had thought Dexter was just using *kurogo* as an abstract point of reference, but in fact he was serious about using traditional methods.

I was delighted to be given such free rein, but a bit scared by it, too. To get started, I tried to dissect what the *M. Butterfly* story means to me. At its center seems to be the issue of human fantasy that lies within us all, and how it propels human behavior. For the French diplomat, *M. Butterfly* was the ultimate fantasy. In his case it was the cause of some serious scandal, but not all fantasies create havoc. Often they help smooth over difficulties in relationships or make one blind to reality. Sometimes it's necessary to live in fantasy as a means of survival. Then there is the subcategory of fantasies about foreigners. The West has long held false preconceptions about the East, and vice versa. When it comes to China, Westerners know so little that they tend to fill in the gaps with their imagination. Even to me—a Japanese-born woman—China is a big question mark. This ignorance can serve as a screen that protects us from the truth, but it can also be dangerous. The play takes full advantage of how fantasy can be a source of both joy and danger. The script deftly weaves together real events and elements of Puccini's opera around this central element of fantasy, with very powerful results.

I knew I had to take this double-edged nature of fantasy and translate it to the stage somehow. The way I work is to put as many ideas as possible on the table

initially, then hone in on the best ones. There are times when the right idea strikes you from the get-go, but still I like to consider all the possibilities first. In terms of the three levels, I knew that I wanted the set to be minimalistic, and at first I thought it should be symmetrical as well. The highest point of the middle level would be the focal point of the stage, and from there a curved slope would fan out to either side. But once Durfee had made two models, one of the symmetrical set and one with the sloped portion on one side only, it was clear that the asymmetrical stage had much more impact. Dexter agreed and we went from there.

The essential idea was to create a continuous flow of movement from the highest point on the set to the lowest point. The action would wind downward from the top of the ramp. The actors would exit the stage below the orchestra pit (there was no orchestra there in this production) at the base of the slope and return to the top of the slope using a staircase backstage. The design would encourage the audience to imagine what was happening in the areas it couldn't see. This aspect of the set would be the central connection to the fantasy theme. To highlight it we would install a gauzy scrim covering the space at the bottom of the ramp. When lit from behind, any action on the other side would be visible. When lit from the front, however, the scrim would become completely opaque, a true wall. Instead of a full orchestra, there was a seven-musician group that would sometimes sit and play in this room beneath the ramp; actors would also come in and out of this room for certain scenes. Perhaps the only drawback of this overall ramp design was the fact that the actors would have to run up the backstage steps very quickly, over and over again. The set would definitely require great physical strength.

Next, we calculated the ramp's height and curvature using computer simulation. We tried different angles, keeping in mind the safety of the actors and structural concerns. Once we hit the right combination, the computer did the drawing for us. Even so, the ramp was terribly high and steep, so much so that I experienced a sense of vertigo when I first stood at the top. Made entirely of wood, with small interlocking panels creating the curve, the ramp was only six feet wide and without edges. It was quite dangerous for the actors. We had to make sure they wouldn't slide off; at the same time, they had to be able to move naturally. With practice, all of the actors became adept at running up and down, but I imagine it was especially scary

Note: This material is reprinted from Eiko Ishioka and Francis Ford Coppola, *Eiko on Stage* (New York: Callaway Editions, 2000, 54–66).

for someone as tall as John Lithgow, who played Galli-mard, the French diplomat. There was one scene that required a lot from him in particular: when he discovers the true identity of his lover, in a state of shock he falls down and rolls all the way to the bottom of the ramp.

In fact, Lithgow's height served him well in another regard. On Broadway, the title role of Song Liling was played by B. D. Wong, who is quite short. The contrast created when the huge Westerner encounters the diminutive, feminine Asian came through beautifully. In particular, the moment when Lithgow knelt down and cried, "Butterfly!" captured the ironic frailty of an almighty West, another element of the script's underlying theme of illusion and reality.

Although I wanted the set to reflect themes like these, I did not want it to be just the humble underling of the script or the acting, or to be mere visual wallpaper. Theater sets should be powerfully expressive. At our first design presentation I suggested black, red, and white as our thematic colors. I also said I wanted to use a semicircular red cyclorama as a backdrop that would remain in place throughout the play. I didn't know if Dexter would go for it. A strong color like red on a minimalist set tends to dominate the view, and a less confident director might have felt upstaged by such aggressive visuals. But Dexter accepted the idea without question. In combination with such a powerful script and assured direction, I imagined that the set would create an impact like static electricity. In addition I wanted the runway to be totally white, even though I realized it would be difficult to keep clean. With the ramp's support system draped in black velvet, we could create a stunning effect with a white slope floating in space. I was given the green light to put this color scheme into effect.

There wasn't a single shop in the United States that could create the curved, semicircular—and most important, seamless—red cloth I wanted for the backdrop, so we ordered it from Europe. I sent samples of "Eiko Red" cloth, dyed to my specifications, so that there would be no question across the Atlantic. My methods may have seemed a little over-the-top to the Broadway veterans I was working with, but this was an extremely important element of the show and it had to be just right.

The stagehands tried to dissuade me with comments like, "Nobody is going to see the seam in the cloth anyway, so what's the difference?" I wouldn't budge. For all I know they probably suspected that this was a manifestation of some mysterious Eastern philosophy. I'm sure they thought I was nuts when I asked them to work delicately on a part of the wall not visible to the audience. It was an uphill battle, but when the carpenters and stagehands saw how powerful the final product was, I think they appreciated where I was coming from. When I entered the theater to view the completed set for the first time, they shouted a chorus of "Eiko! Eiko! Eiko!" Though, I wasn't completely sure if their chorus was one of celebration or of relief.

Despite our total lack of computers and motors, several people who saw the show commented that the stage seemed to be moving. One critic said that the curved ramp and the lighting design created a "world of light and shadow" with a "yin-yang element." This particular example of symbolism was certainly not intentional; it's not as if we Asians are always thinking about things like how we can incorporate yin and yang into everything! Nevertheless, I was pleased by the effect the stage had on people.

When it came to the costumes, Dexter was extremely hands-off as he had been with the set design. I started out with the Butterfly character, for whom I wanted the design motif to be—what else?—butterflies. I applied the same principle that guided the set design: the seemingly invisible details of the costumes were, counterintuitively, just as important as the overall look. Accordingly, I had Song Liling's gown richly embroidered. It was my belief that doing this would get the actor in the mood, so to speak. Someone playing a beggar doesn't need an authentic costume, but someone playing an aristocratic or elaborately dressed character must wear an outfit that is as close as possible to the real thing. Just as you feel different when you put on a nice, expensive piece of clothing, so an actor feels different when he or she wears an expertly made costume. From a distance you couldn't tell that the gown was actually embroidered, but you could definitely sense the sumptuousness that only embroidery conveys. More important, since the actor wearing the gown could sense its richness at all times, the audience in turn could feel the actor's confidence in the role. You can trace the roots of this idea to the Japanese tradition of wearing a kimono. According to custom, a guest entering a home will take off his *haori* (an outer kimono), and just for a split second the hostess waiting to take the *haori* will get a flash of its beautifully rich inner lining, which at all other times is out of view. It's this hidden detail that makes all the difference, both to the wearer and to the hostess. It says, I am so rich that I don't have to expose it to the world. This sentiment is an essential difference between the American and Japanese aesthetic sensibility.

To make the embroidery, I looked back to the Peking Opera and its incredibly intricate craft of costume embroidery, which was sadly destroyed during the Cultural Revolution. I once saw *The Monkey King*, a Chinese opera brought by the Peking Opera to Tokyo, and was overwhelmed by the beauty of the craftwork. I really wanted to employ this tradition and the Chinese spirit it expresses. The fabric I chose for Song Liling's wedding gown was embossed with a traditional, figured-satin pattern of a single pair of golden butterfly wings extended on white silk. Over thirty different shades of gold thread were used to create the design. Of course the audience couldn't see those thirty individual shades, but collectively they convey a sense of beauty. I'll never forget the detailed, labor-intensive work of the craftspeople in the town of Kiryu, which is just outside of Tokyo, who helped me execute what even now seems a crazy idea for a costume.

I had wanted to have the wigs made in Japan. Sending Wong there for fittings was out of the question budget-wise, so Ostrow asked me to work with a New York–based wigmaker. It turned out to be an extremely trying process. The woman in charge of hair design had researched the style of the time period in which the play is set, but had no innate sense of what it should look like. What's more, the wigs were constructed by union craftspeople unfamiliar with Asian hair design. When I saw the final product, I knew we were in trouble. I called upon the expertise of Kiharu Nakamura, a former geisha who has consulted on many similar productions in America. Nakamura came over, took one look at the wigs resting on their stands, and with several swats of her cane tore them apart. "When you make Japanese wigs, you must pay careful attention to the correct order in which they are constructed—more attention, in fact, than to how they look from the outside," she said. "Otherwise, they'll end up falling apart like these wigs." Despite some valuable advice from her, the craftspeople were only able to patch together something that still left me anxious about how it might hold up during the performances. I knew they had tried their best, but my heart was heavy at the thought of even one Japanese sitting at the front of the house and seeing those wigs.

Transforming B. D. Wong into a character the audience would view as a beautiful woman was a challenge, too, but I think the look we (B. D. Wong, costume assistant John Donn, and I) ended up with was a great success. We went out of our way to create the illusion of femininity. We had him wear false breasts when he was dressed in Western clothing, and Wong and I studied various types and styles of makeup together. Our efforts paid off: when Wong took off his clothes in the play, many people were truly shocked to discover that he was a man. For this dramatic moment in which Song Liling reveals his sex to Gallimard, I felt that the most effective action would be for him to quickly drop his drawers. Finding myself embroiled in devising ways for a guy's underwear to fall to the floor in one fell swoop, I began to wonder, "What am I doing? What is this job, anyway?" Costume design is definitely a strange business. After much experimentation, it was a pair of silk boxer shorts that slid off the easiest.

The play was controversial in many ways, not least in that for many Western audience members it was the first time they saw an Asian man naked, on stage or off. Of course, the facts of the real story are even more shocking: the French diplomat had never seen his lover of twenty years naked. He apparently believed her when she explained that Asian women don't show their bodies out of modesty. But how could he carry on sexual relations for twenty years and never see the body of his lover? Now that is unfathomable, even to a modest Asian woman like myself! I mean, this was the twentieth century!

I'm certainly not your typical Asian woman, but I got my fair share of questions about how one has sex without taking one's clothes off. So I called my mother and asked her if she knew the answer. At first she acted offended and said, how would she know such a thing? She had heard that in the old days a prostitute would employ all manner of tools and techniques to give men pleasure, without ever being touched herself. Song Liling's mother was a prostitute, so I guess she learned the tricks of the trade from her. If she was able to satisfy the diplomat, and if the man made no special effort to explore her body, then everything could go along smoothly.

M. Butterfly, happily, turned out to be a success, with a three-year run in New York. When Anthony Hopkins played the lead in London, tickets sold out immediately six months in advance. To be sure, the success of *M. Butterfly* owes much to Hwang's script and Dexter's direction, but I think the element of scandal played a large part as well. When the reviews first came out, I got word that the positive ones were generally quite long, while—thankfully—the bad ones were short. But I was disappointed to realize that for the most part critics all but ignore the design of a show. If you have a bad script, it makes little difference whether the design is good or bad, because it is likely not to be discussed at any length. Despite the fact that a play is obviously the product of many different artistic disciplines, it is equally true that even on Broadway, scenic and costume design are often overlooked. I was reminded of this again when I attended the Tony Awards ceremony, where design is most definitely at the bottom of the totem pole. I suppose this situation will improve gradually, but I feel a bit frustrated because naturally I don't have the power to change it on my own.

CHERRÍE MORAGA

1952–

"I admit I am one of those writers shamelessly committed to change. . . . I am not not ashamed to affirm that I write to right a wrong, a distorted picture of our mexiana/americana selves." So it is that Cherríe Moraga, the Chicana author of poems, essays, stories, and plays, openly declares the cultural and political purposes of her writing, in which she persistently explores what it means to be female, lesbian, and bilingual in America at the end of the twentieth century. Born in California, Moraga retains the name of her Mexican mother rather than that of her Anglo father. Educated at San Francisco State University, she has taught both at Stanford University and at the University of California at Berkeley. Moraga first staked out her cultural and political interests in *This Bridge Called My Back: Writings by Radical Women of Color* (1981), an anthology of essays, short stories, poems, and letters that she coedited with Gloria Anzaldua. Widely praised for highlighting difficult issues of race, class, and sexual orientation, *This Bridge Called My Back* led in turn to *Tongues of Fire*, a theatrical adaptation of some poems from that anthology, presented at Mills College, Oakland, that same year, which helped to stimulate interest both in the anthology and in the possibility of producing works by Chicana playwrights.

Before the 1980s, most of the prominent Chicano playwrights were male, and their plays focused primarily on political issues. So, when Luis Valdez founded El Teatro Campesino (The Farmworkers' Theater) in 1965, he used touring actors to support César Chávez's farmworkers' union, and to educate the workers. Within two years, El Teatro Campesino became an independent theater group, committed to developing and producing plays about the full range of the Chicano experience, and by 1971, had established a home base near Santa Cruz, California. The influence both of Chávez as a political force and of Valdez as a theatrical one can be seen in Moraga's *Heroes and Saints* (first performed as a staged reading in 1989 and then fully staged in 1992), a play that deals with the environmental hazards of pesticide poisoning. Moraga dedicated the play to Chávez and explicitly acknowledged her debt to Luis Valdez's first play, *The Shrunken Head of Pancho Villa* (1964). Valdez's play celebrates the Mexican revolutionary by creating a symbolic character out of the supposedly decapitated head of Pancho Villa, who incites a new revolution. Moraga, after watching a documentary that showed a child born without limbs because her mother had been working in pesticide-sprayed fields, created a female character, Cerezita. Cerezita is just a head, but a powerfully articulate one who calls for the burning of the town and the poisoned vineyards as well. By changing the "head" from a male revolutionary to a female martyr, Moraga underscored a major change in Chicano/a drama—the shift from plays written by men, with male protagonists, to plays by and about women.

This shift, supported by the formation in the late 1970s of all-women theater groups in California, and by the work of Maria Irene Fornes, in New York, led to new opportunities for Latina performers and playwrights. In the 1980s, the Cuban-born Fornes—who began her career as a costume designer at the Judson Poets Theatre in New York, and then became a playwright and director—offered a series of writing workshops that both supported and guided Latina writers such as Josefina López, Migdalia Cruz, and Caridad Svich, all of whom worked with Fornes. During 1983 and 1984, Moraga was in New York and first drafted *Shadow of a Man* for one of Fornes's workshops, although she would not finish the play until 1990. Fittingly, Fornes went to San Francisco to direct the play's premiere, and in interviews commented on her contribution to Moraga's work: "When I met Cherríe, I could see she had talent and obvious potential, and I wanted to help her make the shift from poet to playwright."

Moraga's first play, *Giving Up the Ghost* (1986), is artistically daring, and not just because its three characters speak as often in monologue as in dialogue. Two characters are actually the same, Marisa, a Chicana in her late twenties, and Corky, who is Marisa as a teenager. As the play portrays Marisa's affair with Amalia, a mature Mexican woman, Corky's monologues reveal the young girl's questions about sexual roles and stereotypes—and her rape when she was just twelve years old. In addition to the vocal music of the characters' speeches, Moraga constantly uses instrumental music—contemporary urban popular music, traditional Mexican folk music, and even "the more ancient indigenous sounds of the flauta, concha, and tambor"—to create the various moods and worlds of the play. And she moves the audience from a barrio in Los Angeles, to a mental institution, to a dream-like ancient Mexico. These dreams are meant to remind the audience that, as Amalia says, "Nothing remains buried forever. Not even memory. Especially not memory."

The power of memory is likewise a central issue in Moraga's *Shadow of a Man*, in which the character Manuel Rodríguez is obsessed with his past relationship with Conrado, the compadre (godfather) of his children. Moraga defines this relationship between godfather and the parents as "a very special bond, akin to that of blood ties, sometimes stronger," as she explores an essentially male/male bond that is complicated by the triangular relationship between Manuel, Conrado, and Hortensia, Manuel's wife (see Figure 3). Though this past relationship shadows Manuel's present, it is balanced dramatically by the variety and power of the women in the play, each of whom represents a different choice for Latinas. The mother, Hortensia, is torn between resentment of and love for her husband. Hortensia's older daughter, Leticia, seems determined to break out of the restrictive life she sees her mother living and Lupe, the younger daughter, is becoming aware of her own sexuality. Rosario, Hortensia's sister, was once married but now lives alone by choice. The play begins with Lupe looking into a mirror worrying "I think there's somethin' wrong with me" and ends with Lupe again at the mirror (see Figure 1), but now much more secure about her future life and her feelings.

Like *The House of Bernada Alba*, Federico García Lorca's chilling depiction of the tyranny of male sexuality, Moraga's *Shadow of a Man* repeatedly suggests the extent to which the women of the Rodríguez family are oppressed by male desires and demands. But unlike Lorca, Moraga questions that oppression, explicitly in the words of Leticia, "Es hombre. I'm sick of hearing that. It's not fair" and implicitly in the creation of Manuel, described by Peter Haugen (in his review following the play) as "emotionally crippled by stubbornness, snagged on an enforced idea of manhood." More important, Moraga creates a world in which women can talk openly to each other (see Figure 2), bridging differences in age and behavior through a shared sense of love and sorrow. Their conversation moves back and forth casually between English and Spanish, reflecting, as Haugen puts it, "the everyday language, the kitchen-table talk" of women who have grown up with two cultures. But monolingual audiences and readers are not excluded, since characters often restate seemingly foreign phrases; moreover, as the play continues, the audience becomes familiar both with the characters and with their blend of English and Spanish. Moraga's bold choices—to write in two languages, to question the male-centered values of Chicano nationalism, to affirm the right of women's sexual desires whether homosexual or heterosexual—place her in a continuing dialogue with many cultures, a dialogue she finds both exhilarating and optimistic.

SHADOW OF A MAN

BY CHERRÍE MORAGA / WITH TRANSLATIONS BY MARÍA ELENA GAITÁN

CHARACTERS

LUPE, *the younger daughter, 12*
ROSARIO, *the aunt, mid-50s*
HORTENSIA, *the mother, mid-40s*
LETICIA, *the older daughter, 17*
MANUEL, *the father, early 50s*
CONRADO, *the compadre, early 50s*

(Compadre *refers to the relationship of a godfather to the parents of his god-child. In Mexican culture, it is a very special bond, akin to that of blood ties, sometimes stronger.*)

SCENE

1969. The action takes place in the home of the Rodríguez family in Los Ange-les over a period of about a year.

The play opens into the interior of the house to the places chiefly inhabited by mothers and daughters. The kitchen is the central feature with the bathroom (stage right) and daughters' bedroom (stage left). Downstage is the porch, sur-rounded by the family garden of chiles, nopales, *and roses. Props and set pieces have been kept to a minimum, only what is essential to the action. Rooms are divided by representative walls that rise about sixteen inches from the floor, yet still give the impression of providing some minimal privacy for secrets both shared and concealed. There is an exit upstage center.*

The backdrop to the house is a Mexican painting of a Los Angeles sunset. As the light descends into garden, the smoggy sky takes on a faint mixture of orange and lavender, a pastel rose against the stark silhouette of cactus and palm trees; multiple plant life abounds.

nopales prickly pear

ACT 1 / SCENE 1

(At rise, spot on LUPE, *staring with deep intensity into the bathroom mirror. She wears a Catholic school uniform. She holds a lit votive candle under her chin and a rosary with crucifix in her hand. Her face is a circle of light in the darkness. The shadow of the crucifix looms over the back wall.)*

LUPE: I think there's somethin' wrong with me. I have ex-ray eyes. *(Star-ing.)* I can see through Sister Genevieve's habit, through her thick black belt with the rosary hanging from it, through her scapular and cotton slip. She has a naked body under there. I try not to see Sister Genevieve this way, but I can't stop. *(Pause.)* I look at other kids' faces. Their eyes are smart like Frankie Pacheco or sleepy like Chela La Bembona, but they seem to be seeing things purty much as they are. Not ex-ray or nuthin'. *(Pause.)* Sometimes I think I should tell somebody about myself. It's a sin to have secrets. A'least the priest is apose to find out everything that's insida you. I try. I really do try, but no matter how many times I make confession, no matter how many times I try to tell the priest what I hold insida me, I know I'm still lying. Sinning. Keeping secrets. *(She pauses before the reflection, then blows out the candle.)*

*(*ROSARIO *appears in the garden. She wears a bandana around her head and an apron around her thick middle. She picks a few chiles, tastes them. Moments later,* LUPE *enters.)*

ROSARIO (*chewing on a chile*): I still say *que los chiles no saben buenos aquí.* I think it's the smog. They don' taste like nut'ing. *Aquí en Los Angeles* the sun has to fight its way down to the *plantas* . . . and to the peepo, too. (*Takes another bite. To* LUPE:) *No sabe a nada.* Try one.

LUPE: No, these things are like fire.

ROSARIO: *Pruébalo, gallina.*

LUPE (*taking the chile and very gingerly taking a bite off the top*): Hmm. Not so bad. (*Swallows.*) ¡*Ay, tía!* You tricked me. (*Fans her mouth.*)

ROSARIO: ¡*Eres gringuita!*

LUPE: I swear I dunno how you can eat them like they were nuthin'.

ROSARIO: *Vas a ver when your tía* is kicked the bucket and is gone, you'll be there in your big Hollywood mansion *haciendo tortillas y el chile, nomás* to remember me. Or maybe you'll get *la criada mexicana* to do it.

LUPE: I won't have a maid. I don't believe in that.

ROSARIO: *Es trabajo* like any other work. There will always be *ricos,* an' the rich peepo always need someone to clean up after them. ¿*Sabes qué? En México,* half the woman got criadas. *Allá* you don' have to be *rico* to have one.

LUPE: That's why it's better here.

ROSARIO: ¿*Por qué?*

LUPE: People don't have to be maids.

ROSARIO: *Bueno, pero la tierra no me da ni un chile verdadero.* (ROSARIO *crosses to the rose bushes.*) *Mijita, ¿me traes el agua? Tienen tanta sed estas rosas.* I don't know why I let them go so long *sin agua.* (LUPE *brings her the watering can.*) *Gracias, mija.* Make sure you cut a few of these *para la mesa. Mañana es sábado.*

LUPE: Flowers won't make this Saturday any better.

ROSARIO: It's your brother's wedding.

LUPE: I'm never leaving home like Rigo.

ROSARIO: Never say never, *hija.* (*She continues watering.*) *Ya, ya. No 'stén eno-jaditas conmigo.* You're thirsty ¿*no, mis rositas? Tomen el agua. Ya, ya* . . .

LUPE: Why do you talk to them, tía?

ROSARIO: To who, *las plantas?*

LUPE: Yeah.

ROSARIO: Because they got souls, the same as you and me.

LUPE: You believe that?

ROSARIO: It's true.

LUPE: The nuns don't say that.

ROSARIO: And you think the nuns are always right?

LUPE: I guess so.

ROSARIO: God is always right, not the Church. The Church is made by men. Men make mistakes, I oughta know. (*To the roses:*) ¡*Ay, pobrecitas! ¡Qué mala madre soy, mis pobres rositas! Tomen, tomen el agua. Ya, mis hijitas* . . . *mis rositas.*

LUPE: Tía, you know how they say that . . . that when you get that chill that goes through your body—

ROSARIO: *Es el diablo que te toca.*

LUPE: Yeah, the devil. He comes up and kinda brushes past you, touching you on the shoulder or somethin', right?

ROSARIO: *Sí, pero es un dicho nomás.*

LUPE: *Pero ¿sabe qué, tía? A veces* I do feel him. *El diablo me entra a mí.* He's like a shadow. I can barely tell he's there, jus' kinda get a glimpse of him outta the corner of my eye, like he's following me or some-thin', but when I turn my head, he's gone. I jus' feel the brush of his tail as he goes by me.

ROSARIO: ¿*Tiene cola?*

---

que los chiles no saben buenos aquí that the chiles don't taste good here

Aquí en Los Angeles Here in Los Angeles

plantas plants

No sabe a nada. It has no taste.

Pruébalo, gallina. Taste it, chicken.

¡**Ay, tía!** Ay, auntie!

¡**Eres gringuita!** You're a little gringa!

Vas a ver when your tía You'll see when your auntie

haciendo tortillas y el chile, nomás making tortillas and chile just

la criada mexicana the Mexican maid

Es trabajo It's work

ricos rich people

¿**Sabes qué? En México** You know what? In Mexico

Allá Over there

rico rich

¿**Por qué?** Why?

Bueno, pero la tierra no me da ni un chile verdadero. Well fine, but the earth won't even give me a real chile.

Mijita . . . estas rosas. My little child, will you bring me water? These roses are so thirsty.

sin agua without water

Gracias, mija. Thank you, my child.

para la mesa for the table

Mañana es sábado. Tomorrow is Saturday.

hija child

Ya, ya . . . conmigo. There, there. Don't be angry with me.

¿**no, mis rositas? Tomen el agua. Ya, ya.** aren't you, my little roses? Drink the water. There, there.

¡**Ay, pobrecitas! . . . mis rositas.** Oh poor little things! What a bad mother I am, my poor little roses! Drink, drink the water. There, my little daughters . . . my little roses.

Es el diablo que te toca. It's the devil that touches you.

Sí, pero es un dicho nomás. Yes, but it's a saying—that's all.

Pero ¿sabe qué, tía? A veces But you know what, auntie? Sometimes

El diablo me entra a mí. The devil gets into me.

¿**Tiene cola?** Does he have a tail?

Sí. Yes.
El diablo. The devil.
No hables así, hija. Don't talk that
    way, child.
monjas nuns

con tanto miedo with so much fear
pero la voz no me sale but my voice
    won't come out
Tu mamá y yo Your mom and I
el diablo y la religión y todo eso the
    devil and religion and all of that
Se volvió loca, hija. She went crazy,
    child.

No sé, mija. I don't know, my child.

¿Quiéres saber la verdad, Lupita? Do
    you want to know the truth,
    Lupita?
los estúpidos stupid people
con nuestros diablitos. Tanto que with
    our little devils. So much so that
Vente. Come here.
las rosas. . . . cuando the roses.
    Sundee [Sunday], when

La gringa The gringa
Ni lo conozco. I don't even know
    him.

para darle un abrazo to give him a
    hug

LUPE: *Sí.*

ROSARIO: *El diablo.*

LUPE: I tole you and I get a chill all over.

ROSARIO: *No hables así, hija.* I don' know what those *monjas* teach you at tha' school sometimes.

LUPE: The nuns never tole me this.

ROSARIO: Well, take it out of your head. It's not good for you.

LUPE: It's not like I'm making myself think about it, it jus' keeps popping up in my head. It's like the more I try not to think about somethin', the more it stays in my head. I mean your mind jus' thinks what it wants to, doesn't it?

ROSARIO: No, you gottu train it. If you don', it could make you a very unhappy girl.

LUPE: I try, but I can't. At night, I try to stay awake cuz when I fall asleep that's when he sneaks inside me. I wake up *con tanto miedo.* It's like my whole body's on fire and I can hardly breathe. I try to call Lettie *pero la voz no me sale.* Nuthin' comes out of my mouth.

ROSARIO: You gottu stop thinking like tha'. *Tu mamá y yo,* we had a cousin, Fina, a very good-looking girl, but she thought about *el diablo y la religión y todo eso* so much that she went crazy. *Se volvió loca, hija.*

LUPE: You think I'm going to go crazy, *tía?*

ROSARIO: No, *mija.*

LUPE: Is it a sin to think like this?

ROSARIO: *No sé, mija.* I don' think so. Not if you can't help it.

LUPE: Sometimes I jus' feel like my eyes are too open. It's like the more you see, the more you got to be afraid of.

ROSARIO: *¿Quiéres saber la verdad, Lupita?*

LUPE: What?

ROSARIO: Only *los estúpidos* don' know enough to be afraid. The rest of us, we learn to live *con nuestros diablitos. Tanto que* if those little devils wernt around, we woont even know who we were. *(Collecting the roses.) Vente.* Today we think about *las rosas. Sundee, cuando* we go to church, there's plenty a time to think about el diablo.

ACT 1 / SCENE 2

(Crossfade to the kitchen, where a "telenovela" (a Mexican soap opera) plays on the TV. HORTENSIA, *wearing a house dress and apron, is rolling out tortillas onto a chopping block. There is a kind of grace to her movements as she alternately crosses to the stove, where she heats the tortillas on the comal, then back to the board again.* LUPE *and* ROSARIO *are seated next to each other at the kitchen table, engrossed in the novela. For a few moments all that is heard are the muted voices coming from the TV and the steady beat of the rolling pin.)*

HORTENSIA: She can go to hell as far as I'm concern.

ROSARIO: Who, Hortensia?

HORTENSIA: *La gringa.* They didn't even get married yet, and she's already got my son where she wants him. *Ni lo conozco.* He's a stranger. *(She puts the tortilla on the comal, watches it rise.)* The other day, Rigo comes home from the college. Manuel sees him in the door, and of course he jumps up from the chair *para darle un abrazo.* And you know what Rigo does?

ROSARIO: What?

HORTENSIA: He pushes Manuel away.

ROSARIO: No!

HORTENSIA: And you know what he says?

ROSARIO: *¿Qué?*

HORTENSIA: He says, "No, Dad. I'm a man now. We shake hands."

ROSARIO: *No me digas.*

HORTENSIA: *Te digo.* Does that sound like my son to you?

ROSARIO: No.

HORTENSIA: And to see the look on Manuel's face. . . . *Y la* girl standing there with a smile *en la cara.*

ROSARIO: *¡Qué barbaridad!*

HORTENSIA: It's eating Manuel up. (*She gestures that* MANUEL *has been drinking.*)

ROSARIO: Tha's not so good, Tencha.

HORTENSIA (*intimately*): *Claro que no. Pero ¿qué puedo hacer yo?*

LUPE: *Miren.* María's telling Enrique she's pregnant.

ROSARIO: No! *¿de veras?*

(*They all stop and watch, mesmerized. Muffled voices emerge from the TV, then commercial.*)

LUPE: ¡Ay, wait til he finds out *quién es el padre!*

ROSARIO: *¡Híjole!*

HORTENSIA (*resuming her work*): But, I tell you one of this days I'm gointu tell *esa gringuita* everything I think of her. She thinks she gointu keep my son, holding him all to herself? But, they're a difernt kina peepo, *los gringos,* . . . *gente fría.* I try to tell Rigo this before they were *novios que iba tener problemas con ella pero no me quiso escuchar.* They might fool you with their *pecas y ojos azules,* but the women are cold.

ROSARIO: I bet her thing down there is already frozen up.

HORTENSIA (*loving it*): ¡Ay, Rosario, *no digas eso!*

ROSARIO: I may be old . . . but my thing is still good 'n' hot *¿verdad, mija?* Us *mexicanas* keep our things *muy caliente* . . . as hot as tha' *comal allí ¿no?*

LUPE: I dunno, *tía.*

ROSARIO: *¿No sabes? ¿Tú no sabes, eh?* (*Snatches playfully at* LUPE *between the legs.*) Is your fuchi fachi hot down there, too?

LUPE (*jumping away*): Stop, *tía!*

HORTENSIA: *Chayo!*

ROSARIO: *¡Ay, tú eres pura gallina!*

(LUPE *comes up behind* HORTENSIA *and takes a warm tortilla from the stack.* HORTENSIA *slaps her hand lightly.*)

HORTENSIA: With you around, the stack never gets any bigger.

LUPE: But my *panza* does. (*She sticks out her stomach.*)

ROSARIO: Now you look like María on the novela.

(LUPE *begins to enact "la desesperada" role as* LETICIA *enters. She is wearing late '60s Chicana "radical" attire: tight jeans, large looped earrings, an army jacket with a UFW [United Farm Workers] insignia on it.*)

HORTENSIA: *Allí viene la política.* (*To* LETICIA:) I tole you I don' wan' you to wear *esa chaqueta.*

ROSARIO: *Es el estilo,* Tencha.

LETICIA (*stealing a warm tortilla from the stack*): Yeah.

HORTENSIA: *¡Tú también!*

LETICIA (*putting butter on the tortilla*): How can you stand watching those things? Those *novelas* are so phony. I mean, c'mon. What do you think the percentage of blondes is in Méxicó?

ROSARIO: *No sé.*

¿Qué? What?

No me digas. You don't say.
Te digo. I'm telling you.

Y la And the
en la cara on her face
¡Qué barbaridad! That's too much!

Claro . . . hacer yo? Of course not. But what can I do?
Miren. Look.
¿de veras? really?

quién es el padre who the father is
¡Híjole! Damn!
esa gringuita that little gringa
los gringos . . . gente fría the gringos . . . cold people
novios que . . . escuchar [before they were] engaged that he was going to have problems with her but he didn't want to listen to me
pecas y ojos azules freckles and blue eyes
¡no digas eso! don't say that!
¿verdad, mija? right, my child?
mexicanas Mexican women
muy caliente real hot
comal allí, ¿no? [as that] griddle there, no?
¿No sabes? ¿Tú no sabes, eh? You don't know? You don't know, eh?
Chayo! [the word *child,* pronounced with an accent]
¡Ay, tú eres pura gallina! Ay, you're just such a chicken!

panza belly

"la desesperada" "the desperate"

Allí viene la política. Here comes the politics.
esa chaqueta that jacket
Es el estilo It's the style
¡Tú también! You too!

novelas soap operas

No sé. I don't know.

güeras blondes
patrón boss

Ni modo Too bad
Es pura fantasía. Pero mija It's all fantasy. But my child
problemas problems

Y si te pide cigarros And if he asks you for cigarettes
¿Todavía 'sta fumando? Is he still smoking?

Es otro día que no trabaja. It's another day he doesn't work.

que that
que le duele mucho that it hurts a lot

y sus piyamas and his pajamas

Pero vas a ver But you'll see
Pues, ay te watcho. Well, I'll see you around.
¿A dónde vas? Where are you going?
¿Qué vas a hacer con ésa? What are you going to do with her?

Déjala Let her
Pero no la conoces, es callejera. But you don't know her, she's always on the street.
una mujer? Eres mujer cuando te cases. a woman? You're a woman when you get married.
Claro. Es hombre. Of course. He's a man.

Te digo I tell you

LETICIA: I mean in relation to the whole population.

ROSARIO: No sé.

LETICIA: One percent? But no, the novelas make it look like half the population is Swedish or something. Even the maids are *güeras.* But, of course, the son of the *patrón* falls madly in love with one and they live happily ever after in luxury. Give me a break!

HORTENSIA: *Ni modo,* I enjoy them.

ROSARIO: *Es pura fantasía. Pero mija,* they got so many *problemas,* it gets your mind off your own.

LETICIA: I guess that's the idea.

(Offstage, a man's heavy, labored steps.)

MANUEL: Hortensia! Hortensia!

HORTENSIA: ¡Ay, that man's gointu make me crazy! Lupita, go see what your papi wan's.

LUPE: Sí, mami.

HORTENSIA: *Y si te pide cigarros,* don' give him none.

LUPE: Okay. *(She exits.)*

ROSARIO: *¿Todavía 'stá fumando?*

LETICIA: Like a chimney.

HORTENSIA: Sure! He wants to kill himself. He's not suppose to smoke. *Es otro día que no trabaja.* I don' know what we're gointu do if he keep missing work.

ROSARIO: He dint see el doctor?

LETICIA: Are you kidding?

HORTENSIA: He's scare to death of them. He complain *que* he pull something in his arm on the job, *que le duele mucho.* But I don' believe it. I think it's his heart. The other night he woke up in the middle of the night and he could har'ly breathe. He was burning up. I had to get up to change all the sheets *y sus piyamas* . . . they were completely soak. Now he's gottu take the sleeping pills jus' to close his eyes for a few hours. *Pero vas a ver,* tonight he'll go out again.

LETICIA *(kissing* HORTENSIA *on the cheek):* *Pues, ay te watcho.*

HORTENSIA: *¿A dónde vas?*

LETICIA: To Irma's.

HORTENSIA: *¿Qué vas a hacer con ésa?*

LETICIA: Oh, we're jus' gonna hang out for a while.

HORTENSIA: Well, not on the street, do you hear me?

LETICIA: Aw, Mom!

HORTENSIA: Aw, Mom!

ROSARIO: *Déjala,* Tencha.

HORTENSIA: *Pero no la conoces, es callejera.*

LETICIA: Shoot, I'll be graduating in a month.

HORTENSIA: You think graduating makes you *una mujer? Eres mujer cuando te cases.* Then your husband can worry about you, not me.

LETICIA: Yeah, but Rigo can come and go as he pleases whether he's married or not.

HORTENSIA: *Claro. Es hombre.*

LETICIA: Es hombre. Es hombre. I'm sick of hearing that. It's not fair.

HORTENSIA: Well, you better get usetu things not being fair. Whoever said the world was gointu be fair?

LETICIA: Well my world's going to be fair!

(LETICIA exits upstage. ROSARIO and HORTENSIA stare at the air in silence.)

HORTENSIA: *Te digo* the girl scares me sometimes.

LUPE (*entering*): Papi wants his cigarettes.

(*A beat, then all three simultaneously turn their attention back to the novela. The lights fade to black while the novela continues playing in the darkness. It gradually fades out.*)

ACT 1 / SCENE 3

(*Late that night. Offstage, a car pulls up, then a door slams. The sound of keys being tossed and a man's heavy steps.* MANUEL *enters, drunk. He wears a hat and a light jacket. From the point of his entrance, the scene assumes a stylized, surreal quality. Characters' actions seem to slow down into almost ritualized movement. This scenario has replayed itself many times in the lives of the Rodríguez family.*)

MANUEL: Rigo, mijo. I can't touch you no more. I have to tie my hands down to keep them from reaching for you. Cuz it goes against my nature, not to touch the face of my son. (*He sits, takes off his hat.*) You usetu sit and converse with me. Your eyes were so black, I forgot myself in there sometimes. I watched the little fold of *indio* skin above your eyes, and felt those eyes hold me to the ground. They saw. I know they saw *lo que sabía mi compadre*, that I am a weak man, but they did not judge me. Why do you judge me now, *hijo*? How does the eye turn like that so suddenly?

HORTENSIA (*entering*): ¿A quién 'stás hablando?

MANUEL (*as if snapping out of a trance*): He doesn't got a mind no more.

HORTENSIA: Who?

MANUEL: Who do you think? (*He looks at her.*) She's took his mind.

(HORTENSIA *goes to* MANUEL, *begins to undress him.*)

HORTENSIA: And who's took your mind, talking to yourself *como un loco*?

MANUEL (*rising*): What was my son given *huevos* for? Tell me. For some spoiled *gabachita* to come along and squeeze the blood white from them?

HORTENSIA: *No hables cochino. Siéntate.* (MANUEL *sits; she removes his shoes.*)

MANUEL: You know what they call men like that que let the women do their thinking for 'em? Pussywhipped, that's what they call 'em.

HORTENSIA: *No seas grosero.* The girls are gointu hear you.

MANUEL: My son is a pussywhipped!

HORTENSIA: *Estás borracho.* I dunno how you gointu get up for the wedding tomorrow. (*She unbuttons his shirt.*)

MANUEL: *Ni modo.* I'm not going.

HORTENSIA: *No empieces.*

MANUEL: *No voy.*

HORTENSIA: *Quítate la camisa.*

MANUEL: We're not good enough for them, that's what they think! *Y tú eres igual que Rigo.* You jus' want to put on the face in front a those gringos. (*Digging at her.*) They don' even let your sister come.

HORTENSIA: They said it's gointu be a small ceremony.

MANUEL: *¡A la chingada!* A small ceremony.

HORTENSIA (*unbuckling his pants*): How you think Rigo's gointu feel without his *padre* there?

MANUEL: He's gonna feel nothing. Rigo's got no feelings no more.

HORTENSIA: You're not gointu do this to me ¿*m'oyes*?

MANUEL: Where's my baby? (*He rises, hoists up his pants.*)

HORTENSIA: Manuel.

---

indio Indian

lo que sabía mi compadre what my compadre knew

hijo son

¿A quién 'stás hablando? Who you talkin' to?

como un loco? like a mad man?

huevos balls

gabachita little white girl

No hables cochino. Siéntate. Don't talk dirty. Sit down.

no seas grosero. Don't be vulgar.

Estás borracho. You're drunk.

Ni modo. No way.

No empieces. Don't start.

No voy. I'm not going.

Quítate la camisa. Take off your shirt.

Y tú eres igual que Rigo. And you're just like Rigo.

¡A la chingada! Fuck it!

padre father

¿m'oyes? do you hear me?

Quiero verla.   I want to see her.
solitas   all alone

¡Mija! ¡Mijiiita!   My child! My little
   daughter!

gabachero   gringo lover
de los bars   of the bars

con el cheque en la mano   with the
   check in my hand
Tiene ojos.   He has eyes.
¡Soy hombre!   I'm a man!
¡Pégame! Es lo único que sabes.   Hit
   me! That's all you know.
te molesta   it bothers you

Pero sigues tomando.   But you keep
   drinking.
¡No, no necesito nada!   No, I don't
   need anything.

Y ¿qué quieres tú?   And what do you
   want?

metiche   nosey
Déjala.   Leave her alone.

viejas   broads

Eres fría, ¿sabes?   You're cold, you
   know that?

la chiquita   the little one
mi niñita   my little girl
papacito   dear daddy
¿ 'Stás durmiendo, hijita?   Are you
   sleeping, my little child?
mijita   my little child
papi   Daddy
Eres mi preferida ¿sabes?   You're my
   favorite, you know?
Sí, papi.   Yes, daddy.

MANUEL: *Quiero verla.*

HORTENSIA: You're not gointu leave us *solitas* to go into the church
   tomorrow.

MANUEL: *¡Mija! ¡Mijiiita!*

HORTENSIA: Leave the girls alone.

MANUEL: *¡Mija! (He tries to fasten his pants, fumbling.)*

HORTENSIA: Why do you think your son lef' this house?

MANUEL: Because he's a *gabachero!*

HORTENSIA: Because you make him ashame, coming home smelling *de
   los bars.*

MANUEL: Coming home *con el cheque en la mano* to feed you.

HORTENSIA *(severely)*: *Tiene ojos.* He can see what you are.

MANUEL: *¡Soy hombre! (He takes a feeble swing at her, misses.)*

HORTENSIA: *¡Pégame! Es lo único que sabes.*

(A shot of pain rushes through MANUEL*'s arm. He doubles over.)*

HORTENSIA: Your heart, *te molesta.*

MANUEL: No.

HORTENSIA: *Pero sigues tomando.* I'm gointu get your pills. *(She starts for
   the bathroom.)*

MANUEL: *¡No, no necesito nada!*

HORTENSIA *(with disdain)*: I should let you die.

*(*LETICIA *appears at the doorway.)*

MANUEL: *Y ¿qué quieres tú?*

LETICIA: What did you do to her?

MANUEL: I didn't touch her.

LETICIA: Did he hit you?

MANUEL: What I say is not good enough for you, *metiche?*

HORTENSIA: *Déjala.*

MANUEL: You wanna defend your mother? You think cuz your brother's
   gone, que you're the macho around this house now?

LETICIA: No.

MANUEL: I'm sick of this house full of *viejas.*

LETICIA: Why don't you leave then?

HORTENSIA: Leticia!

MANUEL: If my compadre could see how you and Rigo turned out . . .

HORTENSIA: That's enough!

MANUEL: *Eres fría ¿sabes?* You're cold as a piece of ice . . . jus' like your
   mother.

HORTENSIA *(glaring at* MANUEL*)*: I wish I had a heart of stone.

*(*HORTENSIA *goes out to the porch, takes out a cigarette and lights it.* MANUEL
   crosses to the girls' bedroom. LETICIA *remains in the kitchen. Lights rise on
   *LUPE *in bed, the covers pulled up tight around her. She clutches a rosary in
   one hand.* MANUEL *stands at the doorway, his shadow filling it.)*

MANUEL: I know *la chiquita* is waiting for me. She's got a soft heart, *mi
   niñita.* She makes sure her *papacito* comes home safe.

HORTENSIA: If he doesn't give a damn about himself, why should I care?

MANUEL *(going to* LUPE*)*: Lupita! *¿ 'Stás durmiendo, hijita? (He lays his
   huge man's head on* LUPE*'s small shoulder.)* You'll never leave me *¿no,
   mijita?*

LUPE: No, *papi.*

MANUEL: *Eres mi preferida ¿sabes?*

LUPE: *Sí, papi.*

MANUEL: You're different from the rest. You got a heart that was made
   to love. Don't ever leave me, baby.

LUPE: No, papi. I won't.

(He begins to weep softly. Her thin arm mechanically caresses his broad back. A muted tension falls over the scene. A few moments later, LETICIA *enters the bedroom, brings* MANUEL *to his feet.)*

LETICIA: C'mon, Dad. Let's get you to bed now.

(He gets up without resistance. LETICIA *holds him up as they exit. Fade out.)*

ACT 1 / SCENE 4

(The next morning. LETICIA *is standing in front of the bathroom mirror fixing her hair, while* LUPE *polishes a pair of white dress shoes. They are wearing bathrobes.* MANUEL *sits on the porch, drinking a beer, a six-pack next to him. It is cloudy out. Lucha Villa's "Que me lleve el tren" is playing on the radio.)*

RADIO:

> *'Estoy al punto de volver contigo.*
> *Estoy al punto de subirme al tren . . .'*

LUPE: I liked Teresa better.

LETICIA: I liked Teresa, too, but Rigo thought he was too good for a Chicana, so he's gonna marry a gringa.

LUPE: Well, he mus' love Karen.

LETICIA: Right.

LUPE: Doesn't he?

LETICIA *(holding a bang in place)*: I can never get these bangs to lay right.

LUPE: Well, does he?

LETICIA: Does he what?

LUPE: Love her. Does he love Karen?

LETICIA: Who knows what he feels, man. Jus' forget it. Do you hear me? Don't think about him no more. He's gone. In a couple of hours he'll be married and that's it. We'll never see him again. *(Beat.)* Hand me the Dippity Do.

*(*LUPE *gets up, gives* LETICIA *the styling gel.* LETICIA *begins applying it her bangs.* LUPE *moves in front of* LETICIA *into the face of the mirror. She stretches open her eyelids with her fingertips.)*

LETICIA: Lupe, get out the way.

LUPE: You can see yourself in there . . . in the darkest part.

LETICIA: What?

LUPE: Two little faces, one in each eye. It's like you got other people living inside you. Maybe you're not really you. Maybe they're the real you and the big you is just a dream you.

LETICIA: I swear you give me the creeps when you talk about this stuff. You're gonna make yourself nuts.

LUPE: But I'm not kidding. I mean how d'you know? How do you really know what's regular life and what's a *sueño*?

LETICIA: You're talking to me, aren't you? That's no dream. *(Holds her hand up to* LUPE.*)* How many fingers do you see?

LUPE: Five.

LETICIA: Right! *(Grabs* LUPE's *face.)* Five fingers around your fat little face. You feel this?

LUPE: Yeah. Yeah.

LETICIA: That's what's real, *'manita*. What you can see, taste, and touch . . . that's real.

"Que me lleve el tren" "Let the train take me"

'Estoy al punto . . . al tren . . .' 'I'm about to return to you. I'm about to get on the train . . .'

sueño dream.

'manita 'lil sis

lonche lunch

huevón lazy guy
cholo gang member or "wannabe" gang member

gatos cats
colas tails
grito scream

lengua así [with its] tongue like this

¡Bruta! You animal!

'Voy a tratar . . . el tren.' "I'm going to try to be happy like before, and if I can't then let the train take me away."

¿Qué dices? What are you saying?

Siéntate. Sit down.
la boda the wedding

LUPE: I still say you can't know for sure.

LETICIA: Say something else. You're boring me.

LUPE *(putting her shoes on)*: I went over to Cholo Park yesterday.

LETICIA: You better not tell Mom. Some chick jus' got her *lonche* down there the other day. They found her naked, man, all chopped up.

LUPE: Oooh. Shaddup.

LETICIA: Well, it's true. What were you doing down there?

LUPE: Nuthin'. Jus' hanging out with Frankie and her brother, Nacho.

LETICIA: God, I hate that *huevón*. Stupid *cholo*. He jus' hangs out with you girls cuz nobody his own age will have anything to do with him. So, what were you guys up to?

LUPE: Nuthin'.

LETICIA: C'mon. Fess up! Out with it!

LUPE: Nuthin'. The boys were jus' throwing cats.

LETICIA: What?

LUPE: They was throwing cats off the hill.

LETICIA: Whadda you mean?

LUPE: Well, they stand up there, grab the *gatos* by the *colas* and swing 'em above their heads and let 'em go. ¡Ay! They let out such a *grito*! It's horrible! It sounds like a baby being killed!

LETICIA: And you watch that shit?

LUPE: They was the ones doing it! Most of the time the gatos land on their feet. But this one time this one got caught on these telephone wires. It jus' hung there in shock with its *lengua así*. *(She sticks out her tongue dramatically.)*

LETICIA: ¡Ay! Stop it! I swear you're really sick. How can you stand to see 'em do that?

LUPE: It's hard to take your eyes off it.

LETICIA: Si-ick. *(Holding her hair in place.)* Here, Lupe. Stick the bobby pin in for me.

LUPE: Where?

LETICIA: Back here. C'mon, my arm's getting tired. *(LUPE does it.)* Ouch! *¡Bruta!* You want to draw blood or what?

(HORTENSIA walks through the kitchen toward the porch. Her hair and face are done. She wears dress shoes and a house robe. She carries MANUEL's suit.)

HORTENSIA: I hear too much talking in there!

LUPE: We'll be right out, mami!

HORTENSIA: We're gointu be late for the wedding!

LETICIA *(muttering)*: Ask me if I care.

(Crossfade to HORTENSIA at the screen door of the porch.)

HORTENSIA *(to MANUEL)*: I got your clothes ready.

(He ignores her, turns up the volume on the radio.)

RADIO:

> *'Voy a tratar de ser feliz como antes*
> *y si no puedo que me lleva el tren.'*

(ROSARIO enters from the garden.)

ROSARIO: If you listen too much to that music, you start to believe there's something good about suffering.

MANUEL: *¿Qué dices?*

ROSARIO: I don' believe in suffering . . . for nobody.

MANUEL: *Siéntate.*

ROSARIO: You're gointu be late for *la boda*, Manuel.

MANUEL (*cracking open a beer for her*): *Toma.*

(ROSARIO *sits as* HORTENSIA *turns away. They watch her exit.*)

MANUEL (*lowering the volume on the radio*): *Salud.* (*They toast, clinking bottles.*) One of these days, I'm gonna get in the car, buy me a coupla six-packs and hit the road and I'm not gonna stop until I reach the desert. They got the road paved now all the way to my *pueblito.* I'll stop off and see my compadre in Phoenix. Conrado's got a real nice life there. He's getting rich, I bet, pouring cement holes in the ground. He's making swimming pools. Everybody's got a swimming pool out there. (*There's a slight rumbling in the sky.*)

ROSARIO: It's gointu rain.

MANUEL (*observing the sky for a moment*): In Arizona, it rains when you least expect it. You got thunder and lightning and the whole sky lights up. (*Thunder is heard. He takes a swig of beer.*) I remember when I was a little *esquincle,* riding in the back of my *tío's troque.* We was coming back from digging ditches or something, me and a buncha *primos* all piled up in back, jus' watching the sky get darker and darker. Suddenly the lightning flashed and the whole desert lit up and you could see the mountain with the camel back clear as noontime. Then, crack! The thunder came and it started raining cats and dogs. In minutes the water soaked up all the dust of the road and it smelled real clean. Then right there in the open back of the troque, we tore off our clothes and took our showers in the rain. (*Another swig.*) Sometimes, you know, you want to be a boy like that again. The rain was better then, it cleaned something.

LUPE (*standing at the screen door, dressed for the wedding*): Papi?

(MANUEL *turns to* LUPE. *They all freeze. The lights and music fade.*)

ACT 1 / SCENE 5

(*Days later. Afternoon.* HORTENSIA *is sorting beans at the table while* LETICIA *shows* ROSARIO *snapshots from Rodrigo's wedding.*)

LETICIA: *Mira, tía.* Look at all the stiffs lined up in a row.

ROSARIO: ¡Ay, Leticia!

LETICIA: You didn't miss much, tía. All they gave you was a little drop of lousy champagne and this white cake that stuck to the roof of your mouth. (*Shows her a picture.*) Don't we look miserable?

ROSARIO: I haftu admit you look like a buncha sourpusses.

LUPE (*entering*): What bothered me was the stupid dress I had to wear.

HORTENSIA: You look purty, mija.

ROSARIO: Wasn' tha' the dress you wore for Easter?

LUPE: Yeah.

LETICIA (*taking out another photo*): Look. Karen's mother is spose to be younger than my mom and she already looks like she's ready for the grave!

HORTENSIA (*to* ROSARIO): You know how *güeras'* skin gets *arrugas* so young.

ROSARIO: It's true.

LETICIA: Well, I feel sorry for Rigo cuz his wife is gonna be a has-been in no time. It runs in their genes, you can tell.

ROSARIO: Don' you have anyt'ing nice to say about the wedding?

HORTENSIA: Rigo looked real handsome. He smelled good, too. I got to say it, I got a good-looking boy. He had on a beautiful white . . . *como lino* . . . suit and a kina grey tie with a tiny design in it, *muy fino.* I think *era de seda.*

Toma. Here.

Salud. Cheers.

pueblito little town

esquincle kid
tío's troque uncle's truck
primos cousins

Mira, tía. Look, auntie.

güeras' blondes'
arrugas wrinkles

como lino like linen
muy fino very classy
era de seda it was silk

la vieja   the old lady

Tu hermano   Your brother

Déjame ver otra   Let me look at
another one

cacahuates   peanuts
platitos   little plates

"caca"   "poop"

el marido   the husband

Y ¿qué pasó?   And what happened?

¿Había mucha gente?   Were there a
lot of people?
¡Montones!   Bunches!
Sí. Mucha.   Yes. A lot.

No importa.   It doesn't matter.
Y   And
tampoco   either
Ni una palabra.   Not a word.
¡Válgame Dios!   Dear God!
me besó en la cara   he kissed my face
muy formal . . . y nada más   real formal . . . and that's all
¡No me digas!   You don't say!
Te digo . . . y la   I'm telling you . . .
and the

LETICIA: Probably *la vieja* bought it for him, so he'd look classy enough for them.

HORTENSIA: *Tu hermano* has more class than all those peepo put together.

LETICIA: You don't have to tell me that! Tell him. He's the one trying to get over.

ROSARIO: *Déjame ver otra*, Lupita.

LETICIA *(sarcastically)*: Oh, that's us standing by the "horn of plenty," the big banquet table.

HORTENSIA: Chayo, you could of died of starvation there. We didn't eat before cuz I thought they'd feed us at the wedding. Pero you know, the peepo that got the most are the tightest with their money.

ROSARIO: Tha's why they got it.

LETICIA: I dunno. The *cacahuates* they had in the little *platitos* really filled me up.

LUPE *(sing-songy)*: Ca-ca-huates. Ca-ca-huates. I like that word!

LETICIA: You just like the *"caca"* part.

LUPE: Shad-dup.

(HORTENSIA shows ROSARIO another photo. LUPE and LETICIA start exploring a packet of old photos.)

HORTENSIA: This is *el marido*. Not a bad-looking man, really. *(Almost proud.)* He's a doctor.

ROSARIO: ¿De veras?

HORTENSIA: I think for the babies.

LETICIA: A pediatrician.

ROSARIO: Uh huh. *Y ¿qué pasó* when they saw que Manuel wasn' with you?

HORTENSIA: When we came in, the mother—

LETICIA: She knew something was up.

HORTENSIA: I guess she could tell from our faces. I felt so ashame to walk in there without my husband, and I sure wasn't gointu tell her que he refuse to come. But she didn't give me a chance to say nothing. She jus' grab me by the arm and, right away like she har'ly notice, says to me, "Oh, I'm so sorry Mr. Rodríguez couldn't make it, I hope it's nothing serious." *Pero muy suave.*

LETICIA: And then she took us into this big room, introducing us to all these stiffs, going *(very upper-class WASP)*, "Isn't it a pity that Mr. Road-ree-gays had to be ill today . . . of all days!" It got me ill!

ROSARIO: ¿Había mucha gente?

LETICIA: ¡Montones!

HORTENSIA: *Sí. Mucha.* It was a lie that there was no room for our family.

LETICIA: They were afraid that if too many Mexicans got together, we'd take over the joint. Bring out the mariachi, spill guacamole over everything . . .

HORTENSIA: They jus' didn't want us.

LUPE: You should've been there, tía.

ROSARIO *(a bit martyred)*: *No importa. Y* Rigo dint say nut'ing *tampoco* about his papá?

HORTENSIA: *Ni una palabra.*

ROSARIO: ¡Válgame Dios!

HORTENSIA: When we came into the church, *me besó en la cara.* "Hello, Mother," he says to me, *muy formal . . . y nada más.*

ROSARIO: ¡No me digas!

HORTENSIA: *Te digo . . . y la* girl had nothing to say to me neither. She hug me—

LETICIA: Cold enough to freeze the dead.

LUPE *(taking out another photo)*: Oooh! I like this picture of you, Lettie. What grade were you in?

(MANUEL enters unnoticed. He stands behind the women.)

LETICIA: What grade, mamá?

HORTENSIA *(examining the photo)*: Kinnergarten.

LUPE: I like your little curly top. *(They pass it around, amused.)*

ROSARIO: *Se parece a Chirlee Temple ¿no?*

HORTENSIA *(tossing LETICIA's hair)*: Un poco.

LUPE *(with another photo)*: Who's this, mami? *(Passes it on to HORTENSIA.)*

HORTENSIA: Este . . . that's . . . Conrado.

LUPE: Who's that?

ROSARIO: A friend of your *papi's, mija.*

HORTENSIA: His compadre.

LUPE: He's really handsome. Where's he at?

HORTENSIA *(nervously)*: No sé. I don' know where he is. Don' talk about him.

LUPE: Why? Is he dead or something?

HORTENSIA: No, he's not dead!

LUPE: God, I jus' asked.

HORTENSIA: *Pues, no seas tan preguntona. It makes tu papi* . . . *(MANUEL comes up from behind and takes the photo from HORTENSIA's hand.)* . . . *nervioso.*

MANUEL: I've been looking for this.

HORTENSIA *(gathering up the photos, to the girls)*: Mira. You messed up all my pictures. Next time I wannu find somethinjg, I won' be able to. Put them away now. I can't pass the whole day here *contando los chismes.* Put all these fotos away now!

(As the rest of the lights fade, a spot remains on MANUEL staring at the picture. A look of nostalgia passes over his face as "Sombras" by Javier Solis rises. Fade out.)

'*Sombras nada más, acariciando mis manos,*
sombras nada más, en el temblor de mi voz . . .'

ACT 1 / SCENE 6

(Many months later. A Saturday afternoon. HORTENSIA is changing Rodrigo's baby on top of the kitchen table, making the usual exclamations a grandmother does over her first grandchild.)

HORTENSIA: *¡Ay, mi chulito! ¡Riguito! ¡Qué precioso!* . . .

LETICIA *(offstage)*: Mom, I got the car!

HORTENSIA: Is that you, hijas?

LUPE *(entering with LETICIA)*: It's so tuff, mami!

HORTENSIA: *Miren lo que tengo aquí.*

LETICIA: It's jus' an old jalopy, but I can fix it up.

LUPE: Hey! When'd Sean come?

HORTENSIA: ¡Ay, don' call him that! It sounds like a girl's name.

LETICIA: That's what they called him.

HORTENSIA: Well, I call him Riguito, *como su papá*, not . . . Shawn!

LETICIA: Yeah, well jus' don't try calling him that in front of Karen. What's he doing here anyway?

HORTENSIA: She left me the baby to watch. *Qué milagro ¿eh?*

LUPE: That's for sure.

HORTENSIA: Una 'mergency came up. She tole me would I mind

Se parece a Chirlee Temple ¿no? She looks like Shirley Temple, no?

papi's, mija [your] daddy's, my child

Pues, no seas . . . nervioso. Well don't ask so many questions. It makes your daddy . . . nervous.

contando los chismes gossiping

'*Sombras nada . . . mi voz . . .*'
'Nothing but shadows, caressing my hands, Nothing but shadows, in the trembling of my voice . . .'

¡Ay, mi chulito! ¡Riguito! ¡Qué precioso! . . . Oh, my pretty baby boy! Riguito! How precious! . . .

Miren lo que tengo aquí. Look what I have here.

como su papá like his dad

Qué milagro ¿eh? What a miracle, huh?

Raza's   Chicano race is

Es mejor que . . .   It would have been
better if he had gone to Vietnam?

No te entiendo.   I don't understand
you.

Es para ir al trabajo, nomás.   It's just
for going to work.

chola   rough girl, female gang
member

¡Fuchi! Apestas.   Yuk! You stink!
¡Ay, Dios! Miren.   Oh, God! Look.
mijito   my little boy
tu pajarito   your little birdie

pipis   pee-pees

Mi güerito   My little blondie
Miren, su pajarito es igual al de Rigo
Look, his little birdie is the same
as Rigo's
Igualito.   It's just the same.
Dicen que esta parte siempre es   They
say that part is always
del hombre, el color de su . . . nature.
the man's true color, the color of
his . . . nature.
Mira, qué lindo es . . .   Look, how
lovely it is . . .
Mi machito.   My little man.
Somos las creadoras.   We are the cre-
ators.
Tú no entiendes.   You don't under-
stand.
Adió.   Don't give me that.

panza   tripe
menudo   tripe stew

watching the baby. I said of course not. Even though they only call me when they need me.

LETICIA: Where's Rigo?

HORTENSIA: He has the army this weekend. ¡Ay! You should of seen how handsome he look in that uniform! He remind me of your papá.

LETICIA: The entire *Raza's* on the streets protesting the war and my brother's got to be strutting around in a uniform.

HORTENSIA: *Es mejor que* he should of gone to Vietnam?

LETICIA: No, but he doesn't have to go around parading it. God, I hope nobody I know saw him.

HORTENSIA: *No te entiendo.*

LUPE: Lettie got the car, Mom.

HORTENSIA: I know, mija. *(To* LETICIA:*)* But don' think this means you are free to go wherever you please now. *Es para ir al trabajo, nomás.*

LETICIA: I paid for it.

HORTENSIA: And who's paid for you for the las' eighteen years of your life?

LETICIA *(doesn't respond; she dangles her car keys over the baby; then, with a thick "chola" accent):* Hey, little guy. You wannu go cruising with me, ése?

HORTENSIA *(taking out various articles from the diaper bag):* She brought enough things for a week. And she gave me a long list of instruc- tions. You think I dint already have three babies of my own. *(Chang- ing the diaper, to the baby:)* ¡Fuchi! Apestas. *(The baby sprays her.)* ¡Ay, Dios! Miren. He soak me. *(Wiping herself.)* No *mijito,* you haftu learn not to shoot *tu pajarito* in the air. I forgot since I had you girls, Rigu- ito usetu do the same thing. I'd get it right in the face sometimes.

LUPE: Ugh!

HORTENSIA: They don' know yet to control their little *pipis.*

LUPE: Let me have the keys, Lettie. *(*LETICIA *gives them to her.)*

LETICIA: He is a little cutie, but I don't know about that blond hair.

LUPE *(dangling the keys over the baby):* The rest of him is brown.

HORTENSIA: *Mi güerito.* He's as purty as they get to be. *Miren, su pajarito es igual al de Rigo* when he was a baby.

LETICIA: Please, spare me.

LUPE: Really?

HORTENSIA: *Igualito. (To the baby:)* You got your papi's thing, mi Riguito. *(To her daughters:)* Dicen que esta parte siempre es the true color *del hom- bre, el color de su . . . nature.*

LETICIA: Does that make him a real Mexican then?

HORTENSIA: *Mira, qué lindo es . . .* like a little jewel. *Mi machito.* That's one thing you know, the men can never take from us. The birth of a son. *Somos las creadoras.* Without us women, they'd be nothing but a dream.

LETICIA: Well, I don't see you getting so much credit.

HORTENSIA: But the woman knows. *Tú no entiendes.* Wait until you have your own son.

LETICIA: Who knows? Maybe I won't kave kids.

HORTENSIA: *Adió.* Then you should of been born a man. *(She finishes changing the baby.)*

LETICIA: I'm gonna go wash the car. You want to help, Lupe?

LUPE *(dangling the keys):* I'll be there in a second.

LETICIA: Well, give me the keys then. *(*LUPE *does.* LETICIA *starts to exit.)*

HORTENSIA: When you're done, you can go pick up the *panza* from Pedro's Place. I wannu make *menudo* for the morning.

LETICIA: All right. All right. *(She exits.)*

HORTENSIA: ¡Ay! They grow up so fast, Lupita. In only minutes, *los muchachitos* are already standing at the toilet, their legs straight like a man's. I remember sometimes being in the kitchen and hearing little Riguito, he must of been only three or so, going to the toilet by himself. The toilet seat flipped back. Bang! it would go. Then the stream from his baby's body. But the sound was like a man's, full . . . *y fuerte*. It gives you a kind of comfort, that sound. And I knew the time would fly so fast. In minutes, he would be a man. *(To the baby:)* You, too ¿no, *mijito*? You got your papi's thing. *El color de la tierra.* A sleeping mountain, with a little worm of life in it. *Una joya. Ya ya, duérmete, mi chulito.*

LUPE: *Duérmete.*

(Fade out.)

ACT 1 / SCENE 7

(LETICIA is practicing dance steps in the kitchen to the tune of "I Heard It through the Grapevine." She sings along. LUPE sits on the front porch, drawing.)

LETICIA: 'Oh I heard it through the grapevine . . . And I'm just about to looooose my mind.'

MANUEL *(entering, carrying a lunch pail):* *Apaga la música.*

LETICIA *(turning down the radio):* You're home early.

MANUEL: *Apágala.* (LETICIA *turns it off, glaring at him.)* Don't look at me in the eyes like that. You look at your father *con respeto ¿m'oyes?*

LETICIA: I hear you.

MANUEL *(muttering as he passes):* If my compadre could see you now, it'd break his heart.

LETICIA: I don't even remember him, Dad.

(MANUEL stops, looks at her absently, then exits.)

LETICIA *(going out onto the porch):* I bet they're gonna fire him.

LUPE: You think so, Lettie?

LETICIA: Yeah.

LUPE: He's sick.

LETICIA: He's not sick. He's drunk. *(She sits on the step.)*

LUPE *(after a pause):* I wish Rigo'd come home and take me down to the cañón like he usetu cuz everything would be better there.

LETICIA: I'll take you, . . . soon as I get the car running again.

LUPE: I never told mami pero sometimes Rigo'd leave me there by myself.

LETICIA: I bet when he took Carmen along.

LUPE: Yeah, *(Pause.)* but it was jus' fine with me. I'd pack a little *lonche, una manzana, un taco de papas* and fill a jar up with chocolate. Then I'd find my special spot by the stream and sit myself down to eat. *(Pause.)* Funny, being alone by that *riyito* makes everything different. It's like the *cañón* is a cathedral greater than any church you've ever seen. *Más grande que even la misión* and there you can really feel God in the incense, the *viejitas* kissing their rosaries . . . and just the oldness of the place. It echoes *con las voces de los ancianos.* But the cañón is different, even older . . . and God, a lot kinder. *(Pause.)* I can never put a face to Him out there. I just feel Him in a way that makes my whole body disappear. Not like I'm a ghost or somethin', but just that my body doesn't matter. I mean it doesn't matter any more than the little *pajarito* landing on the *ramita* or the tiny stream of water that cools my toes. And I feel so light, like an

---

los muchachitos the little boys

y fuerte and strong

mijito my little son
El color de la tierra. The color of earth.
Una joya . . . chulito. A jewel. There, there, go to sleep my lovely baby boy.
Duérmete. Go to sleep.

Apaga la música. Turn off the music.
Apágala. Turn it off.
con respeto ¿m'oyes? with respect, you hear me?

lonche . . . de papas lunch, an apple, a potato taco

riyito stream or small river
cañón canyon
Más grande que even la misión Even bigger than the mission
viejitas old ladies
con las voces de los ancianos with the voices of the elders

pajarito little bird
ramita little branch

astronaut or somethin, weightless, with no worries holding me down to the ground.

LETICIA: You feel free there.

LUPE: Yeah, that's how it feels, Lettie. It feels free.

(The lights fade to black.)

ACT 1 / SCENE 8

(HORTENSIA and ROSARIO are just finishing folding clothes on the kitchen table. It is a humid evening. HORTENSIA wears a light robe.)

HORTENSIA: For weeks now, I walk around the house and hold my breath. Conrado is the only name on Manuel's lips. He don' talk about nothing else.

ROSARIO: *¿Qué dice, Hortensia?*

HORTENSIA: *Estupideces.* Half the time, I can't understand him. I see him sitting on the toilet, crying. I go to him, "Manuel *¿qué tienes?*" *Pero no responde.* His heart is as closed as this. *(Makes a fist.)* I can't make him open up to me. *No puedo.* He miss work already two times this week. And the week before, another two days. El patrón call him this morning. He wouldn't go to the phone.

ROSARIO: You're going to make yourself sick, worrying so much about him.

HORTENSIA: How often does he have anything to do with me? Once in a blue moon. I touch his feet in bed and he freezes. *No soy tan vieja.* I don' wannu give up, Chayo. If I give up, I might as well put on the black dress and say I'm a dead man's wife.

ROSARIO: Then don' give up, sister. Make your husband see you. Grab his face and make him see you. It's not that men don' love. They jus' don' stop to see a woman. Us women do all the seeing for them. If a man sighs for no reason, we already know the reason. We watch their faces *y sabemos cuando se vuelvan máscaras.* What they hide from us, we smell on their clothes and hear *en sus sueños.* We know better than them what they feel . . . and tha's enough to make us believe it's love. Tha's a marriage.

HORTENSIA: *Pues para mí, ya no.* It's not a marriage for me.

ROSARIO *(after a pause):* Tencha, sooner or later, we choose.

HORTENSIA: *¿Qué quiere decir eso?*

ROSARIO: Bueno, I know sometimes you look at me and think there's somet'ing wrong with me becuz I coont stay with a husband.

HORTENSIA: That's not true, *hermana.*

ROSARIO: But after you see the other side of a man, your heart changes. It's harder to love. I've seen tha' side too many times, *mija. (Pause.) Ahora tengo me casita, mi jardín,* my kids are grown. What more do I need?

HORTENSIA: I need more, Chayo. *(She carries the basket of clothes upstage.)* I think about Conrado sometimes . . . the way he walked into a room . . . like a warrior, *un gallo.* His *plumas bien planchadas.* His shoes shined, the crease in his *pantalones* sharp like swords . . . *y tan perfumado,* you could smell him before you saw him. I remember how when Conrado touch me . . . jus' to grab my hand *nomás, and los vellitos* on my arm would stand straight up. *(Pause.)* I've never felt that with Manuel.

ROSARIO: Conrado was not the kina man you marry, hija.

HORTENSIA: He never ask me.

ROSARIO: *Yo sé.*

¿Qué dice, Hortensia? What does he say, Hortensia?

Estupideces. Stupid things.

"¿que tienes?" Pero no responde. What do you have? But he doesn't answer.

No puedo. I can't.

No soy tan vieja. I'm not so old.

y sabemos cuando se vuelven máscaras and we know when they turn into masks

en sus sueños in their dreams

Pues para mí, ya no. Well for me, not anymore.

¿Qué quiere decir eso? What does that mean?

hermana sister

mija my child

Ahora tengo mi casita, mi jardín Now I have my little house, my garden

un gallo a cock

plumas bien planchadas his plumes well pressed

pantalones pants

y tan perfumado and so full of cologne

nomás, and los vellitos [to grab my hand] is all, and the little hairs

Yo sé. I know.

(MANUEL *can be seen coming up the porch steps from the garden. He carries a caged canary.*)

ROSARIO: *Allí viene.*

(MANUEL *sets the cage on the porch, removes his jacket. He wears a sleeveless undershirt, sits and stares at the canary.*)

MANUEL: Lupita's lying to me. She knows. I know she knows. She puts her little hand on my back and pats me real softly. "It's okay, papi," she says. "It's okay." But I know she's just waiting for the day she can get away from me.

ROSARIO: *Me voy, hermana. Nos vemos mañana.*

HORTENSIA: *'Stá bien. Buenas noches.*

(*They embrace.* ROSARIO *exits upstage.* MANUEL *enters, still mumbling to himself. He doesn't notice* HORTENSIA *until she speaks.*)

HORTENSIA: Manuel. (*He stops.*) Touch me. (*Pause.*) *Yo existo.* (*Pause.*) Manuel, *yo existo. Existo yo.* (*He walks past her.*) Nothing's changed, has it? I look at your back and it tells me nothing's changed. A back doesn't cry, *ni tiene sonrisa, ni sabe gemir, gritar.* But this is what I look at day in and day out.

(*He doesn't move. She approaches him.*)

HORTENSIA (*tenderly*): You know how good I know this back? (*Lightly touching him, he stiffens.*) I know it *mejor que tú. ¿Sabes que tienes* a scar right there? (*Touching it.*) *¿Y un lunar allí?* (*Touching*). *¿Y otro acá?* (*Pounding his back.*) *¡Mírame, cabrón!* Why don't you look at me? *¡Mírame!*

MANUEL (*spinning around, grabbing her by the wrists*): No, you take a good look at me!

HORTENSIA: Manuel!

MANUEL: Everywhere I go, everybody's laughing at me. The girls, they're laughing at me all the time. The people I work with, the patrón . . . he's laughing, too. Nobody knows our secret, but they all know and they're all laughing at what they see inside my head.

HORTENSIA: *¡No es cierto!*

MANUEL: You don' think I hear you laughing every day at the big joke? (*Pushes her away violently.*)

HORTENSIA: No!

MANUEL: I don' need this! I got friends. I don' need to suffer no more on account a you!

HORTENSIA (*going to him*): *¡Manuel, por favor!*

(*He slaps her, throws her to the floor, then pulls her up by the hair.*)

MANUEL: You make me sick *¿sabes?* I can't stand for you to touch me!

(*He drops her to the floor, grabs his jacket and the bird and exits.* HORTENSIA *sobs, starts crawling on the floor to the bathroom. Her face is bruised.* LUPE *enters.*)

LUPE (*running to her*): *Mami, ¿qué pasó?* Did papi hurt you, mami?

HORTENSIA: *Estoy sucia.*

LUPE: No, mami.

HORTENSIA: *Me tengo que bañar.* (*Looks up at* LUPE *with glazed eyes.*) Oh, eres tú, hija. Vente, mi bebita. I haftu give you a bath.

LUPE: What, mami? I don't need a bath.

Allí viene.　Here he comes.

Me voy, hermana. Nos vemos mañana.　I'm going, sister. See you tomorrow.

'Stá bien. Buenas noches.　Okay. Good night.

Yo existo　I exist.

Yo existo. Existo yo.　I exist. I *exist.*

ni tiene sonrisa, ni sabe gemir, gritar　it doesn't smile, it doesn't know how to groan, how to scream

mejor que tú. ¿Sabes que tienes　I know it better than you. Do you know you have

¿Y un lunar allí?　And a mole there?

¿Y otro acá?　and another one over here?

¡Mírame, cabrón!　Look at me, you bastard!

¡No es cierto!　It's not true!

¡Manuel, por favor!　Manuel, please!

¿sabes?　you know?

Mami, ¿qué pasó?　Mommy, what happened?

Estoy sucia.　I'm dirty.

Me tengo que bañar.　I have to take a bath.

Oh, eres tú, hija. Vente, mi bebita.　Oh, it's you, child. Come here, my baby girl.

piyamita   little pajamas

¿Qué 'stás diciendo, mamá?   What are you saying, mom?
con el dedito   with my baby finger

¡No puedo soportarlo!   I can't stand it!

No llores más, bebita.   Don't cry anymore, baby girl.

piernitas   little legs
Sí. Eso.   Yes. That's it.

¡Dios mío! ¿Qué he hecho?   My God! What have I done?
¿Para qué?   For what?

¡Estoy cochina!   I'm filthy!
¡Me tengo que lavar! ¡Me voy a bañar!   I have to wash myself! I'm going to take a bath!
No mamá. ¡Dámela!   No mom. Give it to me!
¡Déjame sola! ¡'Stoy sucia! ¡Desgraciada!   Leave me alone! I'm dirty! I'm disgraced!
Tu padre   Your father
pues   well
¿Por qué no me mata tu papá? ¿Por qué no?   Why doesn't your dad kill me? Why not?
No llores, mami.   Don't cry, mommy.
No me toques. 'Stoy sucia.   Don't touch me. I'm dirty.

¡Dile que se vaya!   Tell her to leave!

bata   housecoat
¡No quiero que me vea!   I don't want her to see me!
me así, mija   me this way, my child

HORTENSIA (*pulling at* LUPE*'s clothes*): I haftu take off your *piyamita* and your little diaper.
LUPE: No, mami.
HORTENSIA: I'll put you in the water.
LUPE: *¿Qué 'stás diciendo, mamá?*
HORTENSIA (*trying to drag* LUPE *to the bathroom*): Don' worry. I'm gointu test the water first *con el dedito*. (*Pulls her.*)
LUPE: Stop, mami. You're hurting me.
HORTENSIA (*catching the fear in* LUPE*'s eyes*): Don' look at me like that! (*Covering* LUPE*'s eyes.*) *¡No puedo soportarlo!* (LUPE *begins to cry.*) Conrado. . . . You got his eyes. Why you gottu have his eyes?

(HORTENSIA *buries* LUPE*'s face into her lap, holds* LUPE *down, covering her face and mouth.* LUPE *struggles, cries out.*)

HORTENSIA: I have to turn off the sound. *No llores más, bebita.* (*Smothering* LUPE*'s cries, she pushes her head onto the floor.*) I cover your little head with my hand and push it down into the water. (LUPE *stiffens.*) Your *piernitas* stop kicking. Your skin turns white and your little hands float up like a toy baby. *Sí. Eso.* Everything is quiet.

(LUPE *passes out. She lies limp on the floor. There is a pause, then* HORTENSIA *suddenly realizes what she has done.*)

HORTENSIA: *iDios mío! ¿Qué he hecho?* I killed her. *¿Para qué?* For him? *¿Qué he hecho? ¿Qué he hecho?*

(LUPE *stirs, sits up.* HORTENSIA, *hysterical, rushes to the bathroom. She grabs a douche bag and a bottle of vinegar.* LETICIA *enters.* LUPE *runs to her.*)

LUPE: Lettie, it's mami.

(HORTENSIA *climbs into the tub, starts to pour the vinegar into the bag, her hands shaking.* LUPE *stands back, horrified.* LETICIA *goes to* HORTENSIA.)

LETICIA: Mamá, what are you doing?
HORTENSIA: *¡Estoy cochina!* Filthy!
LETICIA: Did he hit you, mamá?
HORTENSIA: *¡Me tengo que lavar! ¡Me voy a bañar!* (*She abandons the bag, pouring vinegar directly all over herself.* LETICIA *tries to get the bottle from her.*)
LETICIA: *No, mamá. ¡Dámela!*
HORTENSIA: *¡Dejame sola! i'Stoy sucia! ¡Desgraciada!*
LETICIA: Mamá, you're gonna hurt yourself, let it go!
HORTENSIA: *Tu padre* thinks I stink, *pues* now I stink for sure!
LETICIA: Give me it! (*She grabs the bottle.* HORTENSIA *slumps into the tub, holding her bruised face.*)
HORTENSIA: *¿Por qué no me mata tu papá? ¿Por qué no?* It'd be better if he kill me!
LUPE (*softly*): No llores, mami.
LETICIA: Let me see your eye.
HORTENSIA: *No me toques. 'Stoy sucia.*
LETICIA (*putting a washcloth to the bruise*): C'mon, mamá. Now, hold it there. (*Removes* HORTENSIA*'s robe.*) God, you're drenched in the stuff.
HORTENSIA (*seeing* LUPE, *to* LETICIA): *¡Dile que se vaya!* I don' want her to see me!
LETICIA: Lupe, go get another *bata*. (LUPE *doesn't move.*)
HORTENSIA: *¡No quiero que me vea!*
LETICIA: Now! (LUPE *runs out.*)
HORTENSIA: I'm sorry you gottu see *me así, mija.*

LETICIA (*drying* HORTENSIA's *shoulders*): It's okay, mamá. It's not your fault.

HORTENSIA: I guess all my girls are grown up now.

LETICIA: Yeah.

(LETICIA *unties* HORTENSIA's *hair.* LUPE *enters with the robe.* LETICIA *puts it over* HORTENSIA's *shoulders, dries her hair.*)

HORTENSIA: *¿Sabes qué, Leticia? Tu hermanita es una señorita* now.

LUPE: *¡Ay, mami!*

LETICIA: I know, mamá.

HORTENSIA (*to* LUPE): No, *ya no eres baby.* You gottu behave a little difernt now, *mija. Tú sabes,* . . . *con más vergüenza.* You can't go jumping around all over the place *con los chavos* like before.

LUPE (*soberly*): *Sí, mami.*

HORTENSIA: I got no more babies. (*To* LUPE:) *Vente.*

(LUPE *goes to her. They embrace.* LUPE *massages* HORTENSIA's *shoulders.* LETICIA *sits on the edge of the tub, watching.*)

HORTENSIA: You got good hands, hija. Now, I'm your baby *¿no, mija?* Now you have to clean my nalguitas jus' like I wipe yours when you was a baby.

LUPE: *¡Ay, mami!*

HORTENSIA: You girls are all I got in the world, you know.

LUPE: *Sí, mami. Sí.*

("Sombras" *rises as the lights gradually fade to black.*)

'Sombras nada más, entre tu vida y mi vida.
Sombras nada más, entre tu amor y mi amor.'

ACT 2 / SCENE 1

(*Sunset. A few months have passed.* ROSARIO *sits on the porch. She fans herself.* LUPE *sits on the step below her.* LETICIA *lies on top of the bed.* "Evil Ways" *by Santana plays in the background.*)

'Oh you got to change your evil ways, baby . . .' (*The music gradually fades.*)

LUPE: Papi keeps talking to himself all the time. Maybe he's a saint.

ROSARIO: *Tu papá no es un santo, mija.*

LUPE: He could be. He suffers inside like the saints.

ROSARIO: Alotta peepo suffer. It doesn' make them saints.

LUPE: Maybe he'll die and it'll be our sin because we didn't know he was a saint.

ROSARIO: Don' say that. Some peepo suffer because they wannu.

LUPE: I don't wannu.

ROSARIO: So don'. But your papi wan's to suffer.

LUPE: He doesn't. He has something inside . . . that hurts him.

ROSARIO: What?

LUPE: I dunno.

LETICIA (*from the bedroom*): Lupe!

LUPE: What?

LETICIA: Are you gonna do my toenails?

LUPE: Yeah!

(MANUEL *enters the kitchen from upstage center, talking silently to himself. An orange color washes over the scene.* ROSARIO *looks to the horizon.*)

¿Sabes qué, Leticia? Tu hermanita es una señorita now. You know what, Leticia? Your little sister is a young lady now.

¡Ay, mami! Oh, mommy!

ya no eres baby you aren't a baby anymore

mija. Tú sabes, . . . con más vergüenza. my child. You know . . . with more modesty.

con los chavos with the boys

Sí, mami. Yes, mommy.

Vente. Come here

Sí, mami. Sí. Yes, mommy. Yes.

"Sombras" "Shadows"

'Sombras nada más . . . mi amor.' 'Nothing more than shadows, between your life and my life. Nothing more than shadows, between your love and my love.'

Tu papá no es un santo, mija. Your dad is not a saint, my child.

Mira. Ya se pone el sol. Look. The
  sun is setting.
¿Ves las sombras? You see the shadows?
En esta hora At this hour

ROSARIO: *Mira. Ya se pone el sol. (They all observe the sunset for a moment.)*
  This is the bes' time of the day. *¿Ves las sombras?*
LUPE: They're so clear.
ROSARIO: *En esta hora,* jus' before the sun sets, you see the shadows
  more clear than any time of the day.

(*The sunset colors deepen, then fade as the sun descends into the horizon.*
LUPE *goes to the kitchen, pulls a chair out for her father to sit.* ROSARIO *exits
upstage.* LUPE *sits at* MANUEL's *feet, rubs some dirt off his shoe.* MANUEL
*takes out the photo of Conrado from the breast pocket of his shirt. He stares at
it, then puts it on the table.*)

MANUEL: When my compadre Conrado was a little boy, he usetu shine
  shoes for a living. He was never ashamed of it because, like he said,
  it was about making a buck any way you could. He built the little
  shoeshine box with his own hands. I watched him do it. He sawed
  six perfectly even rectangles of wood and hammered them
  together. He made the top piece so it could flip open and shut.
  Like this. (*He demonstrates.*) And then he sanded it *con una piedra.*

con una piedra with a stone

polvo dust

  He painted the box black because most of the shoes he shined
  were black, he said, and that way the box would never look dirty.
  But the Tucson streets were very dusty in those days and the *polvo*
  would seep into the cracks of the box anyway. (*Pause.*) You don't
  know him, Lupita. But my compadre is an American success story.
  He usetu live here . . . near us. But then he went back to Arizona to
  make it big.
LETICIA: Lupe!
LUPE: Yeah! . . . I'm coming! (*She starts to go.*)
MANUEL: Lupita. (LUPE *stops.* MANUEL *stares at her absently.*)
LUPE: ¿Sí, papi?

(MANUEL *walks out mumbling to himself. He has left the photo on the table.*
LUPE *picks it up, studies it.*)

LETICIA: Lupe!
LUPE: Okay!

(*She stuffs the photo into her pocket and crosses to the bedroom.* LETICIA
hands her a bottle of nail polish. LUPE *sits by the foot of the bed and starts
applying polish to* LETICIA's *toes.* LETICIA *keeps reading.*)

LUPE: What name did you choose for your confirmation, Lettie?
LETICIA: Cecilia.
LUPE: Why Cecilia? Saint Cecilia was burned at the stake.
LETICIA: I liked the name.
LUPE: I was thinking of Magdalena for me. . . . Naw, cuz then people call
  you Maggie. That's Maggie O'Connell's name. I can't stand her.
LETICIA: They could call you Lena. Anyway, nobody calls anybody by
  their confirmation name. It's just on paper.
LUPE: Yeah, but I love the story about her.
LETICIA: Who?
LUPE: Mary Magdalene. (*She rises, begins to dramatize the story.*) I love how
  she jus' walked right through all those phony baloney pharisees,
  right up to the face of Jesus. And there they were all looking down
  their noses at her like she was nuthin' but a . . . *tú sabes,* a fallen
  woman.

tú sabes you know

LETICIA: Well, she was a prostitute.
LUPE: She doesn't look to the right or to the left, jus' keeps staring
  straight ahead. The pharisees try to stop her, but Jesus tells them,
  "Let her come forward" (*Returns to the toes.*)

LETICIA: Make sure you get it all the way down to the cuticle.

LUPE: I am. (*She paints one toe, then goes back to her story.*) So the crowd opens up and makes a path for her. And then she kneels down in front of Jesus and jus' starts crying and crying for all the sins she's done. (*Sobs dramatically at the feet of "Jesus."*) And y'see his feet are dusty from all those long walks in the desert. She's crying up a storm. It's coming down in buckets all over Jesus' feet. (*Sob, sob, sob.*)

LETICIA: Are you finished?

LUPE: In a minute. But suddenly the tears become like bath water, real soft and warm and soothing-like. She's got this hair, y'see, this long beautiful dark hair and it's so thick she can make a towel out of it. It's so soft, it's almost like velvet as she spreads it all over Jesus' feet. (*She pours her hair over "Jesus'" feet, then returns to* LETICIA's *toes.*)

LETICIA: Blow on 'em a little, will you? So they can dry faster. (LUPE *does.*)

LUPE: Can you imagine what it musta felt like to have this woman with such beautiful hair *wiping* it on you? It's jus' too much to think about. And then Jesus says . . . (*She grabs* LETICIA's *hand as if* LETICIA *were Mary Magdalene.*) "Rise woman and go and sin no more." Now that's what I call forgiveness. That's . . . relief.

HORTENSIA (*offstage*): Lupita! Lupe!

ROSARIO (*offstage*): Lupe! ¡Tu mamá te 'stá llamando!

LUPE: God, I'm everybody's slave around here.

(LUPE *exits. "Evil Ways" rises in the background. The light and the music gradually fade out.*)

ACT 2 / SCENE 2

(MANUEL *is talking to the caged canary in the garden. He drinks from a bottle of tequila. It is dusk.*)

MANUEL: I am a lonely man. I bring the bottle to my lips and feel the tequila pour down behind my tongue, *remojando* the back of my throat. *Corre* down *la espina*, until it hits my belly and burns *como madre* in there. For a minute, I am filled up, *contento . . . satisfecho.* (*Pause.*) I look across the table and my compadre's there *y me siento bien.* All I gotta do is sit in my own skin in that chair. (*Pause.*) But he was leaving. I could smell it coming. I tried to make him stay. How did I let myself disappear like that? I became nothing, a ghost. I asked him, "Do you want her, compa?" And he said, "Yes." So, I told him, "What's mine is yours, compadre. Take her." (*Pause.*) I floated into the room with him. In my mind, I was him. And then, I was her too. In my mind, I imagined their pleasure, and I turned into nothing.

(*Black out.*)

ACT 2 / SCENE 3

(MANUEL, LETICIA *and* LUPE *are seated at the kitchen table.* LUPE *wears a Catholic school uniform.* HORTENSIA *is making breakfast.* LUPE *and* LETICIA *are eating.* LETICIA *puts the food to her mouth without lifting her eyes from the college textbook she is reading.* MANUEL *is writing a letter.*)

HORTENSIA: Leticia, if you read while you eat, the food doesn't set right in your stomach.

LETICIA: I'm all right.

¡Tú mamá te 'stá llamando! Your mom's calling you!

remojando wetting
Corre It runs
la espina my spine
como madre like a mother
contento . . . satisfecho content . . . satisfied
y me siento bien and I feel good

hija. Tiene que estudiar.   child. She
    has to study.

LUPE: You got a test, Lettie?
LETICIA: A mid-term.
LUPE: Is college hard?
LETICIA: Uh-huh.
HORTENSIA: Don't bother your sister, *hija. Tiene que estudiar.*
LUPE: I wanna go to college, too.
LETICIA: You should try to get a scholarship. Go to Harvard or some-
    thing.
LUPE: What's Harvard?
LETICIA: The best.

(HORTENSIA *puts a plate of food down for* MANUEL. *He ignores it.*)

HORTENSIA: What are you doing?
MANUEL: Writing a letter.
HORTENSIA: You're not gointu eat?

(*He doesn't respond. They all look at him. After a beat,* LUPE *takes a slip of paper and a pen from her book bag, goes to* HORTENSIA.)

Dásela a tu padre.   Give it to your
    father.

LUPE: Mami, I need my confirmation form signed.
HORTENSIA: *Dásela a tu padre.*
LUPE: Will you sign this for me, papi? (MANUEL *ignores her.* LUPE *points to the signature line.*) Right here. (*He continues writing the letter.* HORTEN-SIA *signs the form.*) Thanks, mami.
LETICIA: You ready, Lupe?
LUPE: Yeah.

(*They gather their things to leave, kiss their mother, then their father.* MANUEL *does not respond.*)

LETICIA: See ya, Dad.
LUPE: Bye, papi.
LETICIA (*exiting*): 'Bout the time you're in college, lots of Chicanos will
    be going to Harvard. You'll see.
LUPE: Where's it at?
LETICIA: Cambridge, Massachusetts.
LUPE: Too far.
LETICIA (*calling out*): I'll be home late! Gotta work tonight!
HORTENSIA: Okay, mija!
LUPE: Bye, mami!

¡Que les vaya bien!   Hope everything
    goes well.

HORTENSIA: *¡Que les vaya bien!*

(HORTENSIA *clears off the table.* MANUEL *is addressing an envelope. She brings him a cup of coffee. He pushes it away very slowly the full length of his arm.*)

HORTENSIA (*after a pause*): Why are you writing him?
MANUEL: Because he's my compadre.

Y ¿quién soy yo?   And who am I?

HORTENSIA: *Y ¿quién soy yo?*
MANUEL: You're my wife.

Sí, soy tu esposa. Cuando tienes hambre
    Yes, I'm your wife. When you're
    hungry
pantalones   pants
piyamas   pajamas

HORTENSIA: *Sí, soy tu esposa. Cuando tienes hambre,* I put the food in front
    of you. When you're sick, I force the medicine into your mouth. I
    iron your *pantalones* and put out clean *piyamas* for you each night.
    Every time you take a bath, I wash out the ring in the tub.

(MANUEL *tears the page from the writing tablet.* HORTENSIA *takes an envelope from her apron and tosses it onto the table.*)

HORTENSIA: You asked him to come back.
MANUEL (*grabbing the envelope*): You read this? . . . You read my com-
    padre's letter?

HORTENSIA: *Sí, la leí.*

MANUEL: You had no right. Do you see your name on this *sobre*?

HORTENSIA: No.

MANUEL: *Pues,* until my compadre puts your name here, you got no right to read what he writes to me.

HORTENSIA: Why, Manuel? Why you want that man back in our lives?

MANUEL: *No te importa a tí.* My compadre's coming back cuz I ask him to. And when he does, we aint never even gonna talk about you. *Ni una palabra.* We're gonna talk about the track or the weather or my new grandson or *cualquiera chingada cosa que queremos,* but we aint gonna talk about you. Ard we aint gonna talk about my son neither. I had a *compadre* before you went and mess it all up. So you can forget any other ideas you got, cuz everything's gonna go back to normal. *Todo está bien arreglado. Y cuando te digo que my compadre's* coming for dinner, you're gonna make his favorite chile verde. I don't care what you feel *¿m'entiendes? Me vas a obedecer.* And you'll put the plate of food in front of his face and you'll pretend that you feel nothing, *menos que antes.* Becuz if I see you give him even a little sign, like your face gets a little red *o demasiada pálida* or your hand shakes a little when you pour *el café into la taza, recuerdas que te estoy watchando, mujer.* And it's gonna be like old times and you're not going to mess it up again.

(*He stuffs the letter he has written into an envelope and seals it. He puts both letters into his pocket and exits.* HORTENSIA *sits, drops her face into her hands. Fade out.*)

ACT 2 / SCENE 4

(LUPE *is on the porch, shining* MANUEL's *shoes.* ROSARIO *approaches, sits on the step.*)

ROSARIO: Tu papi's getting all spruced up, eh?

LUPE: Really.

ROSARIO: *Dáme uno. Yo te auyudo.*

LUPE: Thanks, *tía.* (ROSARIO *hands* LUPE *a shoe to polish.*)

ROSARIO: He's going out?

LUPE: Uh-huh.

ROSARIO: *¿A dónde?*

LUPE: To see that man.

ROSARIO: Who?

LUPE: Conrado.

ROSARIO: How do you know?

LUPE: I heard papi telling mami. She's getting his clothes ready. She's been singing all day, so she won't say nuthin' mean to him.

ROSARIO: She's singing?

LUPE: She's mad inside, so she sings. That way only nice things come out of her mouth.

ROSARIO: *Tu mamá es una buena mujer.*

LUPE: I know.

(HORTENSIA *enters the kitchen singing to herself. She puts a pair of* MANUEL's *dress pants and a suit coat over the back of a chair. She crosses to the ironing board, begins pressing his dress shirt.*)

MANUEL (*offstage*): Lupe! *¡Los zapatos!*

LUPE: I'm coming! (ROSARIO *and* LUPE *rise, go into the kitchen.*)

ROSARIO: If they dint take the license from me we could all go out and paint the town ourselves tonight.

Sí, la leí.   Yes, I read it.

No te importa a tí.   None of your business.

Ni una palabra.   Not a word.

cualquiera chingada cosa que queremos   the weather or any fucking thing we want

Todo está bien . . . my compadre's   Everything's all arranged. And when I tell you that my compadre's

¿m'entiendes? Me vas a obedecer.   you understand me? You're going to obey me.

menos que antes   less than before

o demasiada pálida   or too pale

el café . . . watchando, mujer   the coffee into the cup, you remember I'm watching you, woman

Dáme uno. Yo te ayudo.   Give me one, I'll help you.

¿A dónde?   Where?

Tu mamá es una buena mujer.   Your mom is a good woman.

¡Los zapatos!   The shoes!

herida wound

La azul The blue one

ni su madre ni los children or his mother, or the children

No 'stoy jugando. I'm not kidding.

No puedo aguantarlo. No puedo. I can't stand it. I can't.

Adiós, mujer. Good-bye, woman.

Sí, hermana. Yes, sister.

LUPE: In that car! Forget it, tía! It's got fins sharp enough to kill somebody.

ROSARIO: Pues, we got pertection then.

(LUPE *exits with the shoes.* ROSARIO *pours herself a cup of coffee and sits at the table.*)

ROSARIO: Conrado's back?

HORTENSIA: Sí. *(Pause.)* It's like he wants to jump right into the heart of the *herida* and bury himself in there. I'm his wife, but I'm not gointu jump in there with him.

(MANUEL *enters in boxer shorts and T-shirt, talking to himself softly. He wears a hat and holds his shoes and two ties.* HORTENSIA *hands him the shirt and he puts it on. The two women watch him dress in silence. He puts on the pants, examining its crease. He licks his fingers and runs them down the crease's edge. He sits down, then stands up, checking the crease again.*)

MANUEL: The crease doesn't stay in them. *(He looks distraught, holds up the two ties.)* La azul *or the yellow one?*

HORTENSIA: La azul.

(MANUEL *chooses the yellow one instead, stuffing the blue one into his pant pocket. He sits down and puts on his shoes with a shoehorn. The women continue watching him dress, their eyes never leaving him.*)

ROSARIO: Sometimes a man thinks of another man before he thinks of nobody else. He don' think about his woman *ni su madre ni los children,* jus' what he gots in his head about tha' man. He closes his eyes and dreams, "If I could get inside tha' man, then I'd really be somebody!" But when he opens his eyes and sees that he's as empty as he was before, he curls his fingers into fists and knocks down whatever he thinks is standing in his way.

(MANUEL *stands, buttons his coat, looks at* HORTENSIA.)

HORTENSIA: If you go, Manuel, you won't find me here when you get back. I don't know where you'll find me, but I won't be here.

MANUEL: Fine. *(He starts for the door.)*

HORTENSIA: I'll take the girls, Manuel. You'll have a empty house to come home to. *No 'stoy jugando.* The minute you walk out that door.

(MANUEL *turns around, crosses to her and kisses her on the cheek. She stares back at him.*)

HORTENSIA: *No puedo aguantarlo. No puedo.*

MANUEL: You'll do as I say. Things will get better now. You'll see.

(*He goes to the door, dips his hat slightly over one eye and runs his fingers over the rim of it. He imagines himself a different man, in Conrado's image.*)

MANUEL: *Adiós, mujer.*

(*He exits. The women stare at the door in silence.*)

HORTENSIA: I don't want Lupita here when Manuel comes home tonight.

ROSARIO: *Sí, hermana.* I'll take her.

LUPE *(reentering, suddenly frightened)*: Tía?

HORTENSIA: You're gointu go with your tía tonight, mija.

LUPE: But . . .

HORTENSIA: Lettie will bring your piyamas later.

(ROSARIO *puts her arm around* LUPE *to escort her out of the house.*)

LUPE: Is it papi's friend, mami?

HORTENSIA: No. Everything's fine. You be a good girl now. Help your tía.

LUPE: Sí, mami.

ROSARIO: Good night, hermana. *(They go to the door.)*

HORTENSIA: Good night.

LUPE: Mami? . . .

HORTENSIA *(goes to* LUPE, *kisses her)*: *Nos vemos por la mañana, mija . . . muy tempranito.*

*(*LUPE *and* ROSARIO *exit. After a few moments,* HORTENSIA *goes out onto the porch, lights a cigarette, waits.)*

Nos vemos . . . tempranito.   I'll see you in the morning, my child . . . real early.

ACT 2 / SCENE 5

(It is the wee hours of the morning. HORTENSIA *sits out on the porch.* LETICIA *enters wearing a miniskirt and boots.* LETICIA *doesn't notice* HORTENSIA *until she speaks.)*

HORTENSIA: It's two o'clock in the morning.

LETICIA: I know. *(*LETICIA *goes into the kitchen.* HORTENSIA *follows her.)*

HORTENSIA: *¿Crees que eres mujer ya?*

LETICIA: No.

HORTENSIA: *Eres hombre, entonces.* That's what you want, isn't it? To be free like a man.

LETICIA: That wouldn't be so bad.

HORTENSIA: *Pues, no naciste varón.* If God had wanted you to be a man, he would of given you something between your legs.

LETICIA: I have something between my legs.

HORTENSIA: *Está bien.* Then go wipe the streets with it if that's what you want!

LETICIA: Why do you gotta talk to me like that?

HORTENSIA: *¡Lárgate de esta casa! ¡Si no tienes respeto a tus padres, lárgate!* There's the door, *señorita.*

LETICIA: I can see it. *(She goes tg the cupboard, finds a shopping bag.)*

HORTENSIA: *¿A dónde vas?*

LETICIA: Just obeying you, mamá.

HORTENSIA: Go 'head. You think your *pachuco* boyfriend loves you so much?

LETICIA: No.

HORTENSIA: Pues, go to him. But he'll kick you out in the street, too. He knows what you are.

LETICIA: And what am I, mamá? *Dime.* What am I?

HORTENSIA: *¡Desgraciada!*

LETICIA: *¿Como tú?*

HORTENSIA *(grabbing the bag from her)*: Maybe better I should of cut Lupita out from me! That would of made all you *santos* happy . . . that I would cut your sister from me and nobody had to know the difernce.

LETICIA: Mamá.

HORTENSIA: Well, I can tell you one thing, mujer, I don' give a damn who sticks their thing inside me, that doesn't make a father. What comes out of me is my own flesh and blood! The father is the one who puts the food on the table, *nomás.*

LETICIA *(softly)*: I know that.

*(*HORTENSIA *lights up another cigarette, sits at the table and for a few moments smokes in silence.)*

¿Crees que eres mujer ya?   You think you're a woman already?

Eres hombre, entonces?   Are you a man, then?

Pues, no naciste varón.   Well you weren't born a male.

Está bien.   That's fine.

¡Lárgate de esta casa! ¡Si no tienes respeto a tus padres, lárgate!   Get out of this house! If you don't respect your parents, get out!
señorita   young lady
¿A dónde vas?   Where are you going?
pachuco   hoodlum

Dime.   Tell me.
¡Desgraciada!   Worthless!
¿Cómo tú?   Like you?

santos   saints

nomás   that's it

LETICIA: Mamá?

HORTENSIA: Do you think I was never young? I know what you're feeling and I can't stop you. You walk in that door and I can smell the woman coming out of you.

LETICIA: What's wrong with that?

HORTENSIA: Maybe there's nothing wrong with that. I don' know what to tell you no more. What *consejo* can I give you? I marry *un hombre tranquilo*, a good man. And I watch his back bend, his belly blow up with beer and I see my own daughter grow to look at him *con desprecio* and . . . contempt.

consejo   advice
un hombre tranquilo   a quiet man
con desprecio   with scorn

LETICIA: It's not contempt, mamá. It's pity.

HORTENSIA: That's worse.

(There is a pause. LETICIA goes downstage, stands with her back to HORTENSIA.)

LETICIA: I thought of you tonight. I thought of no longer being your daughter, that what I was gonna do would turn you away from me.

HORTENSIA: I don' wannu know.

LETICIA: There they were, the Raza gods with their legs spread, popping beers, talking revolución and those things, each with its own life, its own personality and I wanted to taste them all. Each and every *fruta*. *"Una joya,"* you would say. *(Pause.)* So, I opened my legs to one of them, mamá. The way a person opens her arms to take the whole world in, I opened my legs.

fruta   fruit
"una joya"   "a jewel"

HORTENSIA: Is that what you call love?

LETICIA *(turning to her)*: It's not about love. It's power. Power we get to hold and caress and protect. Power they drop into our hands, so fragile the slightest pressure makes them weak with pain.

HORTENSIA: Why, mija? Why you give your *virginidad* away for nothing?

virginidad   virginity

LETICIA: I was tired of carrying it around, that weight of being a woman with a prize. Walking around with that special secret, that valuable commodity, waiting for some lucky guy to put his name on it. I wanted it to be worthless, mamá. Don't you see? Not for me to be worthless, but to know that my worth had nothing to do with it.

HORTENSIA *(after a pause)*: You protect yourself, hija?

LETICIA: Yeah. I'll be all right.

(After a pause, HORTENSIA goes to her. They embrace. HORTENSIA's anguished face can be seen over LETICIA's shoulder. LETICIA exits upstage.)

ACT 2 / SCENE 6

(Crossfade to CONRADO entering the garden. The lighting assumes a dreamlike, surreal quality. Action seems to occur outside of time. CONRADO is well dressed in a double-breasted, '40s-style suit and wears a hat dipped over one eye. HORTENSIA sits in the kitchen, still waiting or MANUEL's return. As CONRADO goes up the porch steps, he removes his hat, combs his hair with his fingers, replaces the hat. At the same moment, HORTENSIA takes off her bathrobe. She wears a dark evening dress. She goes to the door.)

HORTENSIA: *¿Dónde 'stá Manuel?*

CONRADO: He told me to go on ahead. He's not here yet?

HORTENSIA: No. *(Pause.) Pásale.* (CONRADO *enters.*)

CONRADO: *Te ves igual.*

HORTENSIA: After thirteen years?

CONRADO: You look the same.

HORTENSIA: *¿Y tú?* Are you the same?

CONRADO: *Pues, dime.* Am I?

¿Dónde 'stá Manuel?   Where's Manuel?
Pásale.   Come in.
Te ves igual.   You look the same.

¿Y tú?   And you?
Pues, dime.   Well tell me.

HORTENSIA: You've changed.
CONRADO: I'm older. *(He laughs.)*

(They both sit.)

HORTENSIA *(after a pause)*: Why did you come back?
CONRADO: To see Manuel. *(Pause.)* He wrote me.
HORTENSIA: *Ya lo sé.*   **Ya lo sé.**   I already know.
CONRADO: He told you?
HORTENSIA: Sí.
CONRADO: He said you wanted me to come back.
HORTENSIA: And you believe that?
CONRADO: *No sé.* (Pause.) I'm broke.   **No sé.**   I don't know.
HORTENSIA: That's why you came back?
CONRADO: Pues . . .
HORTENSIA: So, you didn't make it so big?
CONRADO: *No, 'mana.*   **No, 'mana.**   No, sis.

(They both smile.)

HORTENSIA: So, here you are.
CONRADO: Here I am. *(Pause.)* You remember one morning, I was
    standing on the corner of First and Figueroa. I was with a woman,
    una güera, muy alta. I was talking to her when I heard the streetcar   **una güera, muy alta**   a real tall
    go pass behind me. I turned around and I saw you looking at me   blonde
    through the window. The sun was just coming up into our eyes.   **la güera y la besé en la boca**   the
    And I turned to *la güera y la besé en la boca.*   blonde and kissed her on the
HORTENSIA: *Yo recuerdo.*   mouth
CONRADO: I did that to let you go, so that you would go to him. Barely a   **Yo recuerdo.**   I remember.
    month later and you married Manuel. *(Pause.)* He never knew what
    he had.
HORTENSIA: He's been good to me.
CONRADO *(after a pause)*: In those early days I used to watch Riguito and
    Leticia circling around you in the kitchen. Two little satellites in
    your orbit. I watched the way you moved inside your apron. I
    wanted you, Tencha.
HORTENSIA: *No me digas más. (She stands. "Sunrise Serenade" by Glenn*   **No me digas más.**   Don't tell me any-
    Miller rises in the background.) When we first met, you and Manuel   more.
    and me . . . we had a good time, the three of us. He was the one I
    was with, but I was proud of you both, *tan guapos en sus uniformes.*   **tan guapos en sus uniformes**   so hand-
    Manuel would dance a few numbers with me and then he'd say,   some in your uniforms
    "This one's for you, *'mano.* Dance with Tencha."   **'mano**   brother

*(CONRADO goes to HORTENSIA, takes her into his arms and they dance.
MANUEL appears upstage in shadow, watching. CONRADO dips HORTENSIA
and is about to kiss her, she turns her face away. CONRADO spies MANUEL.)*

CONRADO: Compadre.

(HORTENSIA backs away.)

MANUEL *(to CONRADO)*: You never have enough. What I gave you was
    never enough.
CONRADO: Nothing happened.
MANUEL: *¿Ahora quieres más, compadre?* It's not enough you come back   **¿Ahora quiéres más, compadre?**   Now
    to pick my pocket without a dime in your own?   you want more, compadre?
CONRADO: Manuel, I didn't—
MANUEL: "There she is waiting for you, compadre." Isn't that what I
    said? "I'll give you the shirt off my back." You want my shirt? *(He
    starts unbuttoning his shirt.)*
CONRADO: Stop it, compa.

la waifa   the wife

como un trapo en la cama   like a rag
  on the bed

que no es tuyo   that's not yours

hasta mi propia mujer   I even gave
  you my own woman
cabrón   you bastard

a mí no me puedes echar la culpa   you
  can't blame me

está bien quieto y veo esta sombra   is
  real still and I see this shadow

sin decir nada   without saying any-
  thing
Pones la mano   You put your hand
Hablas   You speak

que te vayas   to go
Y me respondes   And you answer me
No te apures.   Don't worry.
Y cierro los ojos   And I close my eyes

MANUEL: You want my hat? (*He shoves* CONRADO *into a chair, removes* CON-RADO*'s hat and sticks his own hat on him.*) How about *la waifa*?

(MANUEL *grabs* HORTENSIA *and throws her onto* CONRADO*'s lap. She crawls away.*)

MANUEL: After you left her *como un trapo en la cama*, how was I suppose to go to her? Wipe up the little that you left of her. She walked around the house like she was something special, like she (*He grabs* CONRADO *by the balls.*) got a piece of you. You know what that feels like? To have your own wife hold something inside her *que no es tuyo*? She made me feel like I was nothing. (*Pause.*) I loved you, man. I gave you *hasta mi propia mujer*, but that didn't mean nothing to me. You just went and left. I gave you my fucking wife, *cabrón*. What does that make me? (*Pause.*) And all these years she looks at me like she knows something I don't know, like she's got something I don't got.

HORTENSIA: Manuel, *a mí no me puedes echar la culpa*. You were there that night. I heard you both coming in, laughing and crying. Conrado was leaving. And then I fell off to sleep, but when I open my eyes again, the whole house *está bien bien quieto y veo esta sombra* in the doorway.

(CONRADO *slowly moves toward* HORTENSIA. *He comes up behind her.*)

HORTENSIA: You stand there in the dark *sin decir nada*, jus' staring at me. You come and lay down next to me. (CONRADO *puts his arms around her.*) *Pones la mano* around my waist and your touch is difernt. *Hablas* . . .

CONRADO: Hortensia.

HORTENSIA: And it's not your voice. I tell you *que te vayas*, that we can't do what you're thinking. *Y me respondes* . . .

CONRADO: *No te apures.* Manuel knows. This is what he wants.

HORTENSIA: *Y cierro los ojos*, and I wrap myself around you, and nothing is the same after that. (*Pause.*) Leave us alone now, compadre.

(CONRADO *hesitates, looking at them each for a moment, then grabs his hat and exits. There is a pause.* HORTENSIA *reaches her arms out to* MANUEL *in a final gesture to him. He turns his face away. She exits.*

MANUEL *sits in a stupor alone in the room. He slowly rises, takes out a fresh fifth of tequila and a bottle of pills. He swallows half the pills, washing them down with the tequila.*)

MANUEL: Lupita! (*He goes toward the bedroom.*) She's waiting for me. (*He enters the bedroom. When he doesn't see her, he begins to panic.*) Lupe? Lupita! (*He rushes back into the kitchen.*) She's gone! ¡Miji-i-i-ta!

(*He slumps into the chair and begins to cry. It is a kind of labored sobbing of a man unable to reach the core of his despair.*)

MANUEL: She took from me everything I ever loved.

(*Moments later, he composes himself, his face hardened, impassive. He grabs the bottle of tequila and goes out onto the porch. The sun is beginning to rise. He sits, a silhouette against the dawn's light, swallows the remainder of the pills and raises the bottle to his lips. He drinks the entire bottle down, his head thrown back. Black out. In the dark, there is the sound of his body hitting the floor.*

Moments later; the lights rise to reveal MANUEL *in a heap on the floor.* HORTENSIA *enters, rushes to him, puts her ear to his heart. She looks up in horror. Black out.*)

ACT 2 / SCENE 7

(LUPE *stands in her robe in front of the bathroom mirror, a rosary with cruci-fix in her hand. She lights a candle as at the beginning of the play, then takes out the photo of Conrado her father had left. She studies the image for a moment, measuring it against her own reflection in the mirror. Then she tears the small photo into pieces and drops it into the mouth of the burning candle. The shadow of the crucifix goes up in flames. Fade out.)*

ACT 2 / SCENE 8

(*The day of* MANUEL's *funeral. The women are gathered in the Rodríguez kitchen.* HORTENSIA *is ironing a black dress.* ROSARIO *mends a black* rebozo. LETICIA *is painting her fingernails.* LUPE *enters, joins her sister and aunt at the table.*)

ROSARIO: *Bueno, somos puras hembras now.* A house full of women *nomás.* (*They look at one another, as if noticing for the first time.*)
HORTENSIA: I wish it were all over already. (*She hands* LETICIA *the dress.*)
LETICIA (*blowing on her nails*): Thanks, Mom.
HORTENSIA (*with affection*): And do something about your hair. I don' wan' it wild *como una india.*
ROSARIO: *Ven, mija. Te hago una trenza.* I got a nice *cinta* for it.
LETICIA: All right.

(LETICIA *and* ROSARIO *exit upstage.* HORTENSIA *begins to iron* LUPITA's *dress.*)

LUPE (*after a pause*): Did you love papi, mami?
HORTENSIA (*after a pause*): *No sé.* To be with a man so long, day in and day out, it's hard to know. Your head on the pillow next to his. You feel his body, his weight, *su aliento.* I could know *tu padre's* breath-ing anywhere *porque lo oigo hasta en mis sueños. Entra en el alma cuando uno duerme.* (*Pause.*) Funny, when a man is asleep, that's when you really get to know him. You see the child's look on his face, before he wakes up and remembers he's a man again. *¿Sabes qué, mija? Tu papi siempre se despertaba con la voz de un niño.*
LUPE: *¿Un niño?*
HORTENSIA: He sound jus' like a little boy. (*Pause.*) *Después de tantos años, es difícil decir,* "He dug his own grave, let him lie in it." I know I could never do that with you children. No matter what you did, you would always be my children.
LUPE: Even Rigo, mami?
HORTENSIA: Of course, even Rigo. With a husband, it's difernt. You see, this man did not come from your body. No matter *cuántas veces le das la chichi, tu marido no es tu hijo.* Your blood never mixes. He stays a stranger in his own home. (*She gives* LUPE *the dress.*) *Ándale, mijita.* You better get dressed. Rigo will be here *para llevarnos* purty soon.
LUPE: All right, mami.

(LUPE *exits to the bathroom. She dresses.* LETICIA *enters with a suitcase as* CONRADO *approaches the porch. He holds a note in his hand. He removes his hat, combs his hair back with his fingers.* LETICIA *gives* HORTENSIA *the suit-case.*)

LETICIA: It's Conrado.
HORTENSIA: Did I kill him? When you let go your child's hand and they go off to meet *la Muerte* in the street, *es tu culpa? Or es el destino?*

(LETICIA *exits.* HORTENSIA *goes to the door.*)

Glossary (right column):

rebozo shawl

Bueno, somos puras hembras now . . . nomás Well, we're all females now. . . . Just a house full of women.
Como una india like an Indian [woman]
Ven, mija. Te hago una trenza. Come, my child. I'll make you a braid.
cinta ribbon

No sé. I don't know.

su aliento his breath
tu padre's your father's
porque lo oigo . . . duerme because I hear it even in my dreams. It gets into your soul when you sleep.
¿Sabes qué . . . la voz de un niño. You know what, my child? Your daddy would always wake up sounding like a child.
¿Un niño? A child?
Después de tantos años, es difícil decir After so many years it's hard to say
cuántas veces le das la chichi, tu marido no es tu hijo. [No matter] how many times you give him your tit-tie, your husband is not your son.
Ándale, mijita. Hurry, my little child.
para llevarnos to take us

la Muerte Death
es tu culpa? Or es el destino? is it your fault? Or is it destiny?

Aquí 'stá su ropa. Here's his clothes.

Ya es hora. Ha llegado Rigo. It's time. Rigo's here.

ese espejo that mirror

Sí, señora. Yes, ma'am.

Ya voy. I'm coming.

CONRADO (*referring to the note*): You wanted me to get his things?
HORTENSIA: *Aquí 'stá su ropa.* (*She gives him the suitcase.*)
CONRADO: What should I do with them?
HORTENSIA: Wear them. Burn them.

(CONRADO *exits. Sound of car pulling up.* ROSARIO *enters.*)

ROSARIO: *Ya es hora. Ha llegado Rigo.*
HORTENSIA: Lupe!
LUPE: I'm coming.

(*The three women begin to file out.* ROSARIO *stops, crosses to the table, picks up the rebozo, and goes to* LUPE.)

ROSARIO (*handing her the rebozo*): Lupita, cover up *ese espejo.* We don' wan' your papi to come back and try and take us with him.
LUPE: *Sí, señora.*

(*The women exit in procession.* LUPE *starts to cover the mirror, then pauses for a moment before her reflection.*)

LUPE: I've decided my confirmation name will be Frances cuz that's what Frankie Pacheco's name is and I wannu be in her body. When she sits, she doesn't hold her knees together like my mom and the nuns are always telling me to. She jus' lets them fly and fall wherever they want, real natural-like, like they was wings instead of knees. (*Pause.*) And she's got a laugh, a laugh that seems to come from way deep inside herself, from the bottom of her heart or something. (*Pause.*) If I could, I'd like to jus' unzip her chest and climb right inside there, next to her heart, to feel everything she's feeling and I could forget about me. (*Pause.*) It's okay if she doesn't feel the same way, . . . it's my secret.
HORTENSIA (*offstage*): Lupe!
LUPE: *Ya voy.*

(*She covers the mirror with the rebozo. The lights fade to black.*)

END

Figure 1. Lupe (Jade Power) gazes at herself in her mirror at the end of *Shadow of a Man*. A moment later, she will tear up the photograph of Conrado in the 1990 production directed by Maria Irene Fornes for Brava! For Women in the Arts and the Eureka Theatre Company. (Photograph: Courtesy of Brava! For Women in the Arts/James McCaffey.)

Figure 2. The women of the household gather around the kitchen table, as Hortensia (Alma Martínez, *center*) makes tortillas, flanked by Rosario (Jennifer L. Proctor, *left*), and Lupe (Jade Power, *right*). Leticia (Raquel Haro), stands behind her mother in the 1990 production of *Shadow of a Man*. (Photograph: Courtesy of Brava! For Women in the Arts/ James McCaffey.)

Figure 3. In a dream-like reenactment of the past, Manuel (Carlos Baron, *right*) throws Hortensia (Alma Martínez) onto the lap of Conrado (Luis Saguar) in the 1990 production of *Shadow of a Man*. (Photograph: Courtesy of Brava! For Women in the Arts/ James McCaffey.)

Staging of *Shadow of a Man*

REVIEW OF THE EUREKA THEATRE/BRAVA!
PRODUCTION, 1990, BY PETER HAUGEN

To find the heart of the working-class family, pull up a chair in the heart of the working-class household.

Some critic in 1950s Britain dismissed the bleak vision of John Osborne and other angry, young postwar playwrights as "kitchen-sink drama." The insult backfired. A genre wasn't exactly born, but named. When the theater's new voices, especially minority voices, look for a realistic emotional footing in their own families, their own subcultures, their own anger, like as not they return to kitchen, back porch, front stoop. So it is with August Wilson and so it is with Cherríe Moraga, whose "Shadow of a Man" opened to hyperbolic fanfare Saturday in an ambitious collaborative production by the Eureka Theatre Company and Brava! For Women in the Arts.

Wilson comes to mind because like him, Los Angeles-born Moraga was a poet before playwright. Like him, she crafts a euphonious, musical medium out of the everyday language, the kitchen-table talk of her people, although in her case it's a skillful, barrio blend of English and Spanish. "Shadow of a Man" even resembles "Fences" in that it shows the male head of a working-class household in self-imposed isolation, emotionally crippled by stubbornness, snagged on an enforced idea of manhood.

But in keeping with Moraga's hailed status as a feminist Chicana writer, she focuses on the women of the Rodriguez family in 1969 Los Angeles. She seems less interested in a Wilson-style, grand cultural metaphor than in the intricacies of sorrow that shape individuals, and thus a people. It is at close emotional range that her work resonates beyond a single Latino kitchen, beyond any single culture's experience.

The kitchen-centered set, designed by director Maria Irene Fornes, also features a garden with peppers and citrus trees, a child's bedroom, a bathroom. In the yard we meet Tia Rosario (Jennifer L. Proctor), mentor and confidante to her adolescent niece Lupe (Jade Power). They are at opposite ends of the female experience—the young one full of fear and wonder at a budding sexual-spiritual awareness, her elder armed with hard-won wisdom and resignation. They serve as a frame for the story of Lupe's mother, Hortensia, who is still invested with the first, not yet ready to surrender to the other. Alma Martinez (TV's "Adam 12"—1990) plays her with harrowing power.

Hortensia suffers from the close-quarters estrangement of her husband, Manuel (Carlos Baron), who fits the title description. Bloated with beer and tequila, racked with a bad heart (in more than one sense), he has been destroying himself and his marriage for 13 years over an incident that we learn about only in fragments. Moraga's storytelling style, which withholds the details of that crucial event until the play's overly melodramatic climax, is too coy, but the pain and the performances ring with authenticity.

Paunchy Baron at first shows us a clown, as viewed through the eyes of the imminently more reasonable women of his family, then we see him as tortured tyrant and finally tragic hulk. Martinez shows a woman loyal beyond a fault, burdened by a mistake that she cannot be forgiven because her husband cannot forgive himself.

Director Fornes is herself a feminist-Latina playwright of longstanding note. (Her "Mud" is playing at San Francisco's Magic Theatre.) Her participation in this two-company production, with major funding from the Kennedy Center's Fund for New American Plays, has been made much of. She invests "Shadow of a Man" with a style that accents Moraga's playful, poetic wit without slighting depth of thought. It stumbles only in the dark melodrama of the final scenes.

Performances are sharp—Power's seeking little girl, feeling the devil's hot tail, Proctor's chorus-like tia. Raquel Haro rings true as the college-age daughter Leticia, tentatively rebelling against a male-dominant culture. She's especially fine as Leticia tells her mother how she "gave away" her virginity so that it would no longer define her value.

Luis Saguar does a smooth, cryptic turn of late in the action as Conrado, who is also, perhaps, the shadow of a man. He is the specter that has haunted both Manuel and Hortensia, once his best friends. Moraga's play hides at its center a classic love triangle, complicated by a macho bond between a pair of compadres, seen from the perspective of a woman torn by passion on the one hand and dogged loyalty on the other. It's an emotion-charged package, as kitchen-sink drama is wont to be, and a worthy addition to the genre.

DAVID MAMET

1947–

Though he "kind of stumbled upon a career as a playwright," David Mamet during the past thirty years has clearly regained his footing—some ten full-length plays, over a dozen one-acts, more than twenty screenplays, two Academy Award nominations, and a Pulitzer Prize. He grew up in Chicago and its suburbs, living first with his mother (his parents divorced when he was ten), then with his father. He got his first taste of theater through Chicago's famed center of improvisational sketches—Second City—where he worked as a busboy. As an undergraduate at Vermont's Goddard College, he spent his "junior year abroad" studying acting in New York City and then returned to Goddard where his senior thesis was the script of a revue. After graduation he worked in a variety of theatrical jobs (as an actor in Toronto, as a stage manager in New York) before moving back to Vermont as a teacher and director—first at Marlboro College, then at Goddard. At Marlboro, his students performed an early version of his first play, *Lakeboat* (1970), and at Goddard, he formed the St. Nicholas Theater Company, together with two students for whom he wrote *Duck Variations* (1972) and an early draft of *Sexual Perversity in Chicago* (1974). The memory of those early plays and student actors evidently gave rise to Mamet's deceptively simple explanation of his motive for playwriting: "I started writing because I was working with very young actors and there was nothing for them to do."

In 1972 Mamet returned to Chicago, and his hometown became the base of his artistic support. In 1974, the two student actors of the St. Nicholas Theater Company also moved to Chicago, and one of them, William H. Macy, continued to work with Mamet for years, appearing in the first production of *American Buffalo* (1975), then in *The Water Engine* (1977), *Bobby Gould in Hell* (1989), and *Oleanna* (1992). Gregory Mosher, another Chicago friend, has directed most of Mamet's full-length plays, beginning with *American Buffalo* and continuing through the Pulitzer Prize–winning *Glengarry Glen Ross* (1984) and *Speed-the-Plow* (1988). With Macy and Mosher, as well as other close associates—stage designer Michael Merritt, actress Lindsay Crouse (Mamet's first wife), actor Joe Mantegna, and Rebecca Pidgeon (Mamet's current wife)—Mamet has created a body of work marked by a uniquely harsh theatrical language and peopled by characters whose viciousness commands attention even as it repels.

Though Mamet's plays resound with his harsh voice and vision of experience, they also embody distinctive aspects of American life and drama. His early play, *Duck Variations*, came, as Mamet said, "from listening to a lot of old Jewish men all my life, particularly my grandfather," but it is also a cousin to Edward Albee's *The Zoo Story*, a kinship reflected in Mamet's comment, "You can count the playwrights who haven't written about two men sitting in a park on one hand. This is just another one." *A Life in the Theatre* (1977) extends and complicates the basic two-person conversation by having it take place between men of different ages (Robert, the older actor, and John, the younger one) and by alternating their backstage conversations with snippets from the plays they are performing. The set of *American Buffalo* is a junk shop, recalling the junkyard of Sam Shepard's *The Unseen Hand*. And *Glengarry Glen Ross* boldly takes up the commercial world of Arthur Miller's *Death of a Salesman* but populates it with a cast of tawdry and corrupt real estate salesmen, ready to steal, lie, and cheat in order to "win."

Equally influential in Mamet's career is the playwright to whom he is most often compared—Harold Pinter. Both playwrights frequently dramatize enigmatic relationships and the sudden violence that can erupt in those relationships. Both playwrights also tend to create marginalized characters who speak in language that is simultaneously realistic yet poetic in its economy and spareness. And both playwrights are known for dialogue that often reveals character through what is *not* said or *not* acknowledged.

Yet what first attracted attention about Mamet's language was not just its fragmentary and elusive style but its obscenity and comic rhythms. Jack Kroll, writing in *Newsweek,* called Mamet "the Aristophanes of the inarticulate" because of his "antiphonal exchanges, which dwindle to single words or even fragments of words and then explode into a crossfire of scatological buckshot." The repetition of phrases, the rush to finish other people's sentences or even to interrupt the speaker's own thoughts, and the limited vocabulary reflect the corrupted state of the characters' worlds, from the macho posturing of Dan and Bernie in *Sexual Perversity* to the fake camaraderie of Hollywood producers in *Speed-the-Plow*. In such contexts, people who use polysyllabic words, such as the older actor Robert in *A Life in the Theatre* or the college professor John in *Oleanna,* seem pretentious and out of touch with their actual situations. Their language becomes defensive, covering up insecurity or unhappiness.

Though it shares similarities of language and structure with Mamet's preceding work, *Oleanna,* which opened Off-Broadway in 1992, is the first of his plays to echo a specific contemporary event. Its central conflict between a female college student and her male professor seemed at the time to reflect the confirmation hearings of Clarence Thomas, when his former assistant, Anita Hill, accused him of sexual harassment. The extensive media coverage of the hearings in the fall of 1991 for a prospective Supreme Court justice inevitably raised the question of who was really telling the truth. Mamet had, as he makes clear in the interview following the play, started *Oleanna* before the hearings, and then "stuck it in a drawer," feeling that "it seemed a little farfetched." But the Thomas/Hill hearings sent him back to the play that makes the question of truth-telling even more intriguing by giving the audience direct access to the moments *before* the accusation has been made. Thus, when Carol first appears in John's office, she seems nervous and afraid, worried about her inability to understand John's lectures. John, trying to deal both with Carol's problems and with an impending house-closure, including repeated phone calls from his wife and their lawyer, alternates between irritation with Carol's presence and sympathetic attempts to allay her distress. The bombshell comes in the play's second act when John asks Carol to explain why she has filed a sexual harassment complaint against him with the committee reviewing him for tenure.

At this point, the audience must rethink the long first scene. Were John's actions indeed "sexist" and "elitist"? Did he really tell "a rambling, sexually explicit story"? Did he "embrace" Carol? The audience has seen everything, but now the question becomes, What did we actually see? And the more accusing Carol becomes, the more the audience must consider not only John's conscious motives but his unconscious ones as well. Is he, without realizing it, not merely pompous but condescending and invasive? Are his frequent interruptions of Carol genuine signs of his desire to help or indications of his unwillingness to actually listen to her? Most important, is the violence with which he attacks her in the play's final moments (see Figure 3) a quality that has always been part of him and his attitude toward women or is it a response that her own accusation has created? Audience reaction to the attack has been audible and varied—expressions of shock but also applause.

Thus Mamet plays yet another variation on the theme of the domineering teacher and the submissive student, a theme explored in Shaw's *Pygmalion* and Ionesco's *The Lesson*. But Mamet complicates the problems of power and gender by relating them to recent discussions of feminism, censorship, and political correctness. The New York production, directed by Mamet, clearly portrayed the changing power relationships. In Figure 1, John is carefully dressed in suit and tie, his hair neatly combed, and he stands by his symbol of power, his desk; in Figure 2, Carol stands while *he* sits, his disheveled appearance reflecting how much power he has lost. Though the difference in the teacher/student relationship is clear, how one understands the motives and actions of the characters is still a matter for discussion. The folk song that gives the play its title suggests a bountiful, if imaginary world, while the world that Mamet evokes is spare, contradictory, and all too real, a world that forces audiences to confront their own prejudices and beliefs.

OLEANNA

BY DAVID MAMET

This play is dedicated to the memory of Michael Merritt.

The want of fresh air does not seem much to affect the happiness of children in a London alley: the greater part of them sing and play as though they were on a moor in Scotland. So the absence of a genial mental atmosphere is not commonly recognized by children who have never known it. Young people have a marvelous faculty of either dying or adapting themselves to circumstances. Even if they are unhappy—very unhappy—it is astonishing how easily they can be prevented from finding it out, or at any rate from attributing it to any other cause than their own sinfulness.

The Way of All Flesh, SAMUEL BUTLER

Oh, to be in *Oleanna,*
That's where I would rather be.
Than be bound in Norway
And drag the chains of slavery.

—folk song°

CHARACTERS

CAROL, A woman of twenty
JOHN, A man in his forties

The play takes place in John's office.

ACT 1

(JOHN *is talking on the phone.* CAROL *is seated across the desk from him.*)

JOHN *(on phone)*: And what about the land. *(Pause)* The land. And what about the land? *(Pause)* What about it? *(Pause)* No. I don't understand. Well, yes, I'm I'm . . . no, I'm *sure* it's signif . . . I'm sure it's significant. *(Pause)* Because it's significant to mmmmmm . . . did you call Jerry? *(Pause)* Because . . . no, no, no, no, no. What did they say . . . ? Did you speak to the *real* estate . . . where *is* she . . . ? Well, well, all right. Where are her notes? Where are the notes we took with her. *(Pause)* I thought you were? No. No, I'm sorry, I didn't mean that, I just thought that I saw you, when we were there . . . what . . . ? I thought I saw you with a *pencil.* WHY NOW? is what I'm say . . . well, that's why I say "call Jerry." Well, I can't right now, be . . . no, I *didn't* schedule any . . . Grace: I *didn't* . . . I'm well aware . . . Look: Look. Did you call Jerry? Will you call Jerry . . . ? Because I can't now. I'll be there, I'm sure I'll be there in fifteen, in twenty. I intend to. No, we aren't *going* to lose the, we aren't *going* to lose the house. Look: Look, I'm not minimizing it. The "easement." Did she say "easement"? *(Pause)* What did she *say; is* it a "term of art," are we *bound* by it . . . I'm sorry . . . *(Pause)* are: we: yes. *Bound* by . . . Look: *(He checks his watch.)* before the other side *goes home,* all right? "a term of art." Because: that's right *(Pause)* The yard for the boy. Well, that's the whole . . .

Look: I'm going to meet you there . . . *(He checks his watch.)* Is the realtor there? All right, tell her to show you the basement again. Look at the *this* because . . . Bec . . . I'm leaving in, I'm leaving in ten or fifteen . . . Yes. No, no, I'll meet you at the new . . . That's a good. If he thinks it's nec . . . you tell Jerry to meet . . . All right? We *aren't* going to lose the deposit. All right? I'm sure it's going to be . . . *(Pause)* I hope so. *(Pause)* I love you, too. *(Pause)* I love you, too. As soon as . . . I will.

(He hangs up. He bends over the desk and makes a note. He looks up.) (To CAROL:) I'm sorry . . .

CAROL: *(Pause)* What is a "term of art"?

JOHN: *(Pause)* I'm sorry . . . ?

CAROL: *(Pause)* What is a "term of art"?

JOHN: Is that what you want to talk about?

CAROL: . . . to talk about . . . ?

JOHN: Let's take the mysticism out of it, shall we? Carol? *(Pause)* Don't you think? I'll tell you: when you have some "thing." Which must be broached. *(Pause)* Don't you think . . . ? *(Pause)*

CAROL: . . . don't I think . . . ?

---

folk song, The Norwegian song, in a translation popularized by the folksinger Pete Seeger, refers to a nineteenth-century Norwegian colony founded in Pennsylvania by the violinist Ole Bull. But since Ole Bull mistakenly bought stony soil, the first colonists could plant no crops and the colony failed. The song's evocation of a place so bountiful that "the wheat and corn just plant themselves" and "the cows all like to milk themselves and hens lay eggs ten times a day" is thus simultaneously Utopian and satiric.

JOHN: Mmm?

CAROL: . . . did I . . . ?

JOHN: . . . what?

CAROL: Did . . . did I . . . did I say something wr . . .

JOHN: *(Pause)* No. I'm sorry. No. You're right. I'm very sorry. I'm somewhat rushed. As you see. I'm sorry. You're right. *(Pause)* What is a "term of art"? It seems to mean a *term*, which has come, through its use, to mean something *more specific* than the words would, to someone *not acquainted* with them . . . indicate. That, I believe, is what a "term of art," would mean. *(Pause)*

CAROL: You don't know what it means . . . ?

JOHN: I'm not sure that I know what it means. It's one of those things, perhaps you've had them, that, you look them up, or have someone explain them to you, and you say "aha," and, you immediately *forget* what . . .

CAROL: You don't do that.

JOHN: . . . I . . . ?

CAROL: You don't do . . .

JOHN: . . . I don't, what . . . ?

CAROL: . . . for . . .

JOHN: . . . I don't for . . .

CAROL: . . . no . . .

JOHN: . . . forget things? Everybody does that.

CAROL: No, they don't.

JOHN: They don't . . .

CAROL: No.

JOHN: *(Pause)* No. Everybody does that.

CAROL: Why would they do that . . . ?

JOHN: Because. I don't know. Because it doesn't interest them.

CAROL: No.

JOHN: I think so, though. *(Pause)* I'm sorry that I was distracted.

CAROL: You don't have to say that to me.

JOHN: You paid me the compliment, or the "obeisance"—all right—of coming in here . . . All right. *Carol.* I find that I am at a *standstill.* I find that I . . .

CAROL: . . . what . . .

JOHN: . . . one moment. In regard to your . . . to your . . .

CAROL: Oh, oh. You're buying a new house!

JOHN: No, let's get on with it.

CAROL: "get on"? *(Pause)*

JOHN: I know how . . . *believe* me. I know how . . . potentially *humiliating* these . . . I have no desire to . . . I have no desire other than to help you. But: *(He picks up some papers on his desk.)* I won't even say "but." I'll say that as I go back over the . . .

CAROL: I'm just, I'm just trying to . . .

JOHN: . . . no, it will not do.

CAROL: . . . what? What will . . . ?

JOHN: No. I see, I see what you, it . . . *(He gestures to the papers.)* but your work . . .

CAROL: I'm just: I sit in class I . . . *(She holds up her notebook.)* I take notes . . .

JOHN *(simultaneously with* "notes"*)*: Yes. I understand. What I am trying to *tell* you is that some, some basic . . .

CAROL: . . . I . . .

JOHN: . . . one moment: some basic missed communi . . .

CAROL: I'm doing what I'm told. I bought your book, I read your . . .

JOHN: No, I'm sure you . . .

CAROL: No, no, no. I'm doing what I'm told. It's *difficult* for me. It's *difficult* . . .

JOHN: . . . but . . .

CAROL: I don't . . . lots of the *language* . . .

JOHN: . . . please . . .

CAROL: The *language,* the "things" that you say . . .

JOHN: I'm sorry. No. I don't think that that's true.

CAROL: It *is* true. I . . .

JOHN: I think . . .

CAROL: It *is* true.

JOHN: . . . I . . .

CAROL: Why would I . . . ?

JOHN: I'll tell you why: you're an incredibly bright girl.

CAROL: . . . I . . .

JOHN: You're an incredibly . . . you have no problem with the . . . Who's kidding who?

CAROL: . . . I . . .

JOHN: No. No. I'll tell you why. I'll tell. . . . I think you're *angry,* I . . .

CAROL: . . . why would I . . .

JOHN: . . . wait one moment. I . . .

CAROL: It *is* true. I have *problems* . . .

JOHN: . . . every . . .

CAROL: . . . I come from a different *social* . . .

JOHN: . . . ev . . .

CAROL: a different economic . . .

JOHN: . . . Look:

CAROL: No. I: when I *came* to this school:

JOHN: Yes. Quite . . . *(Pause)*

CAROL: . . . does that mean nothing . . . ?

JOHN: . . . but look: look . . .

CAROL: . . . I . . .

JOHN: *(Picks up paper.)* Here: Please: Sit down. *(Pause)* Sit down. *(Reads from her paper.)* "I think that the ideas contained in this work express the author's feelings in a way that he intended, based on his results." What can that mean? Do you see? What . . .

CAROL: I, the best that I . . .

JOHN: I'm saying, that perhaps this course . . .

CAROL: No, no, no, you can't, you can't . . . I have to . . .

JOHN: . . . how . . .

CAROL: . . . I have to pass it . . .

JOHN: Carol, I:

CAROL: I *have* to pass this course, I . . .

JOHN: Well.

CAROL: . . . don't you . . .

JOHN: Either the . . .

CAROL: . . . I . . .

JOHN: . . . either the, I . . . either the *criteria* for judging progress in the class are . . .

CAROL: No, no, no, no, I have to pass it.

JOHN: Now, look: I'm a human being, I . . .

CAROL: I did what you told me. I did, I did everything that, I read your *book,* you told me to buy your book and read it. Everything you *say* I . . . *(She gestures to her notebook.) (The phone rings.)* I do. . . . Ev . . .

JOHN: . . . look:

CAROL: . . . everything I'm told . . .

JOHN: Look. Look. I'm not your *father. (Pause)*

CAROL: What?

JOHN: I'm.

CAROL: Did I say you were my father?

JOHN: . . . no . . .

CAROL: Why did you say that . . . ?

JOHN: I . . .

CAROL: . . . why . . . ?

JOHN: . . . in class I . . . *(He picks up the phone.) (Into phone:)* Hello. I can't talk now. Jerry? Yes? I underst . . . I can't talk now. I know . . . I know . . . Jerry. I can't *talk* now. Yes, I. Call me back in . . . Thank you. *(He hangs up.) (To* CAROL:*)* What do you want me to do? We are two people, all right? Both of whom have subscribed to . . .

CAROL: No, no . . .

JOHN: . . . certain arbitrary . . .

CAROL: No. You have to help me.

JOHN: Certain institutional . . . you tell me what you want me to do. . . . You tell me what you want me to . . .

CAROL: How can I go back and tell them the *grades* that I . . .

JOHN: . . . what can I do . . . ?

CAROL: *Teach* me. *Teach* me.

JOHN: . . . I'm trying to teach you.

CAROL: I read your book. I read it. I don't under . . .

JOHN: . . . you don't understand it.

CAROL: No.

JOHN: Well, perhaps it's not well *written* . . .

CAROL *(simultaneously with* "written"*)*: No. No. No. I want to *understand* it.

JOHN: What don't you understand? *(Pause)*

CAROL: *Any* of it. What you're trying to say. When you talk about . . .

JOHN: . . . yes . . . ? *(She consults her notes.)*

CAROL: "Virtual warehousing of the young" . . .

JOHN: "Virtual warehousing of the young." If we artificially prolong adolescence . . .

CAROL: . . . and about "The Curse of Modern Education."

JOHN: . . . well . . .

CAROL: I don't . . .

JOHN: Look. It's just a *course,* it's just a *book,* it's just a . . .

CAROL: No. No. There are *people* out there. People who came *here.* To know something they didn't *know.* Who *came* here. To be *helped.* To be *helped.* So someone would *help* them. To *do* something. To *know* something. To get, what do they say? "To get on in the world." How can I do that if I don't, if I fail? But I don't *understand.* I don't *understand.* I don't understand what anything means . . . and I walk around. From morning 'til night: with this one thought in my head. I'm *stupid.*

JOHN: No one thinks you're stupid.

CAROL: No? What am I . . . ?

JOHN: I . . .

CAROL: . . . what am I, then?

JOHN: I think you're angry. Many people are. I have a *telephone* call that I have to make. And an *appointment,* which is rather *pressing;* though I sympathize with your concerns, and though I wish I had the time, this was not a previously scheduled meeting and I . . .

CAROL: . . . you think I'm nothing . . .

JOHN: . . . have an appointment with a *realtor,* and with my wife and . . .

CAROL: You think that I'm stupid.

JOHN: No. I certainly don't.

CAROL: You said it.

JOHN: No. I did not.

CAROL: You did.

JOHN: When?

CAROL: . . . you . . .

JOHN: No. I never did, or never would say that to a student, and . . .

CAROL: You said, "What can that mean?" *(Pause)* "What can that mean?" . . . *(Pause)*

JOHN: . . . and what did that mean to you . . . ?

CAROL: That meant I'm stupid. And I'll never learn. That's what that meant. And you're right.

JOHN: . . . I . . .

CAROL: But then. But then, what am I doing here . . . ?

JOHN: . . . if you thought that I . . .

CAROL: . . . when nobody wants me, and . . .

JOHN: . . . if you interpreted . . .

CAROL: Nobody *tells* me anything. And I *sit* there . . . in the *corner.* In the *back.* And everybody's talking about "this" all the time. And "concepts," and "precepts" and, and, and, and, and, WHAT IN THE WORLD ARE YOU *TALKING* ABOUT? And I read your book. And they said, "Fine, go in that class." Because you talked about responsibility to the young. I DON'T KNOW WHAT IT MEANS AND I'M *FAILING* . . .

JOHN: May . . .

CAROL: No, you're right. "Oh, hell." I failed. Flunk me out of it. It's garbage. Everything I do. "The ideas contained in this work express the author's feel-

ings." That's right. That's right. I know I'm stupid. I know what I am. *(Pause)* I know what I am,
Professor. You don't have to tell me. *(Pause)* It's
pathetic. Isn't it?

JOHN: . . . Aha . . . *(Pause)* Sit down. Sit down. Please.
(Pause) Please sit down.

CAROL: Why?

JOHN: I want to talk to you.

CAROL: Why?

JOHN: Just sit down. *(Pause)* Please. Sit down. Will you,
please . . . ? *(Pause. She does so.)* Thank you.

CAROL: What?

JOHN: I want to tell you something.

CAROL: *(Pause)* What?

JOHN: Well, I know what you're talking about.

CAROL: No. You don't.

JOHN: I think I do. *(Pause)*

CAROL: How can you?

JOHN: I'll tell you a story about myself. *(Pause)* Do you
mind? *(Pause)* I was raised to think myself stupid.
That's what I want to tell you. *(Pause)*

CAROL: What do you mean?

JOHN: Just what I said. I was brought up, and my earliest, and most persistent memories are of being
told that I was stupid. "You have such *intelligence.*
Why must you behave so *stupidly*?" Or, "Can't you
understand? Can't you *understand*?" And I could
not understand. I could *not* understand.

CAROL: What?

JOHN: The simplest problem. Was beyond me. It was a
mystery.

CAROL: What was a mystery?

JOHN: How people learn. How *I* could learn. Which is
what I've been speaking of in class. And of *course*
you can't hear it. Carol. Of *course* you can't.
(Pause) I used to speak of "real people," and wonder what the *real* people did. The *real* people.
Who were they? *They* were the people other than
myself. The *good* people. The *capable* people. The
people who could do the things, I could not do:
learn, study, retain . . . all that *garbage*—which is
what I have been talking of in class, and that's
exactly what I have been talking of—If you are
told. . . . Listen to this. If the young child is told
he cannot understand. Then he takes it as a
description of himself. What am I? I am *that which
cannot understand.* And I saw you out there, when
we were speaking of the concepts of . . .

CAROL: I can't understand any of them.

JOHN: Well, then, that's *my* fault. That's not your fault.
And that is not verbiage. That's what I firmly hold
to be the truth. And I am sorry, and I owe you an
apology.

CAROL: Why?

JOHN: And I suppose that I have had some *things* on
my mind. . . . We're buying a *house,* and . . .

CAROL: People said that you were stupid . . . ?

JOHN: Yes.

CAROL: When?

JOHN: I'll tell you when. Through my life. In my childhood; and, perhaps, they stopped. But I heard
them continue.

CAROL: And what did they say?

JOHN: They said I was incompetent. Do you see? And
when I'm tested the, the, the *feelings* of my youth
about the *very subject of learning* come up. And
I . . . I become, I feel "unworthy," and "unprepared." . . .

CAROL: . . . yes.

JOHN: . . . eh?

CAROL: . . . yes.

JOHN: And I feel that I must fail. *(Pause)*

CAROL: . . . but then you *do* fail. *(Pause)* You have to.
(Pause) Don't you?

JOHN: *A pilot.* Flying a plane. The pilot is flying the
plane. He thinks: Oh, my *God,* my mind's been
drifting! Oh, my God! What kind of a cursed
imbecile am I, that I, with this so precious cargo
of *Life* in my charge, would allow my attention to
wander. Why was I born? How deluded are those
who put their trust in me, . . . et cetera, so on, and
he crashes the plane.

CAROL: *(Pause)* He could just . . .

JOHN: That's right.

CAROL: He could say:

JOHN: My attention *wandered* for a moment . . .

CAROL: . . . uh huh . . .

JOHN: I had a *thought* I did not like . . . but now:

CAROL: . . . but now it's . . .

JOHN: That's what I'm telling you. It's time to put my
attention . . . see: it is not: this is what I learned. It
is Not Magic. Yes. Yes. *You.* You are going to be
frightened. When faced with what may or may not
be but which you are going to perceive as a test.
You will become frightened. And you will say: "I
am incapable of . . ." and everything *in* you will
think these two things. "I must. But I can't." And
you will think: Why was I born to be the laughing-
stock of a world in which everyone is better than
I? In which I am entitled to nothing. Where I can
not learn.

(Pause)

CAROL: Is that . . . *(Pause)* Is that what I have . . . ?

JOHN: Well. I don't know if I'd put it that way. Listen:
I'm talking to you as I'd talk to my son. Because
that's what I'd like him to have that I never had.
I'm talking to you the way I wish that someone
had talked to me. I don't know how to do it, other
than to be *personal,* . . . but . . .

CAROL: Why would you want to be personal with me?

JOHN: Well, you see? That's what I'm saying. We can
only interpret the behavior of others through the
screen we . . . *(The phone rings.)* Through . . . *(To*

phone:) Hello . . . ? *(To* CAROL:*)* Through the screen we create. *(To phone:)* Hello. *(To* CAROL:*)* Excuse me a moment. *(To phone:)* Hello? No, I can't talk nnn . . . I know I did. In a few . . . I'm . . . is he coming to the . . . yes. I talked to him. We'll meet you at the No, because I'm with a *student.* It's going to be fff . . . This is important, too. I'm with a *student,* Jerry's going to . . . Listen: the sooner I get off, the sooner I'll be down, all right. I love you. Listen, listen, I said "I love you," it's going to work *out* with the, because I feel that it is, I'll be right down. All right? Well, then it's going to take as long as it takes. *(He hangs up.)* *(To* CAROL:*)* I'm sorry.

CAROL: What was that?

JOHN: There are some problems, as there usually are, about the final agreements for the new house.

CAROL: You're buying a new house.

JOHN: That's right.

CAROL: Because of your promotion.

JOHN: Well, I suppose that that's right.

CAROL: Why did you stay here with me?

JOHN: Stay here.

CAROL: Yes. When you should have gone.

JOHN: Because I like you.

CAROL: You like me.

JOHN: Yes.

CAROL: Why?

JOHN: Why? Well? Perhaps we're similar. *(Pause)* Yes. *(Pause)*

CAROL: You said "everyone has problems."

JOHN: Everyone has problems.

CAROL: Do they?

JOHN: Certainly.

CAROL: You do?

JOHN: Yes.

CAROL: What are they?

JOHN: Well. *(Pause)* Well, you're perfectly right. *(Pause)* If we're going to take off the Artificial *Stricture,* of "Teacher," and "Student," why should *my* problems be any more a mystery than your own? Of *course* I have problems. As you saw.

CAROL: . . . with what?

JOHN: With my *wife* . . . with *work* . . .

CAROL: With work?

JOHN: Yes. And, and, perhaps my problems are, do you see? *Similar* to yours.

CAROL: Would you tell me?

JOHN: All right. *(Pause)* I came *late* to teaching. And I found it Artificial. The notion of "I know and you do not"; and I saw an *exploitation* in the education process. I told you. I hated school, I hated teachers. I hated everyone who was in the position of a "boss" because I *knew*—I didn't *think,* mind you, I *knew* I was going to fail. Because I was a fuckup. I was just no goddamned good. When I . . . late in life . . . *(Pause)* When I *got out from under* . . . when

I worked my way out of the need to fail. When I . . .

CAROL: How do you do that? *(Pause)*

JOHN: You have to look at what you are, and what you feel, and how you act. And, finally, you have to look at how you act. And say: If that's what I *did,* that must be how I think of myself.

CAROL: I don't understand.

JOHN: If I fail all the time, it must be that I think of myself as a failure. If I do not want to think of myself as a failure, perhaps I should begin by *succeeding* now and again. Look. The tests, you see, which you encounter, in school, in college, in life, were designed, in the most part, for idiots. *By* idiots. There is no need to fail at them. They are not a test of your worth. They are a test of your ability to retain and spout back misinformation. Of *course* you fail them. They're *nonsense.* And I . . .

CAROL: . . . no . . .

JOHN: Yes. They're *garbage.* They're a *joke.* Look at me. Look at me. The Tenure Committee. The Tenure Committee. Come to judge me. The Bad Tenure Committee.

The "Test." Do you see? They put me to the test. Why, they had people voting on me I wouldn't employ to wax my car. And yet, I go before the Great Tenure Committee, and I have an urge, to *vomit,* to, to, to puke my *badness* on the table, to show them: "I'm no good. Why would you pick *me?*"

CAROL: They granted you tenure.

JOHN: Oh no, they announced it, but they haven't *signed.* Do you see? "At any moment . . .

CAROL: . . . mmm . . .

JOHN: "They might not *sign*" . . . I might not . . . the *house* might not go through . . . Eh? Eh? They'll find out my "dark secret." *(Pause)*

CAROL: . . . what is it . . . ?

JOHN: There *isn't* one. But *they* will find an index of my badness . . .

CAROL: Index?

JOHN: A " . . . pointer." A "Pointer." You see? Do you see? I *understand* you. I. Know. That. Feeling. Am I entitled to my job, and my nice *home,* and my *wife,* and my *family,* and so on. This is what I'm saying: That theory of education which, that *theory:*

CAROL: I . . . I . . . *(Pause)*

JOHN: What?

CAROL: I . . .

JOHN: What?

CAROL: I want to know about my grade. *(Long pause)*

JOHN: Of course you do.

CAROL: Is that bad?

JOHN: No.

CAROL: Is it bad that I asked you that?

JOHN: No.

CAROL: Did I upset you?

JOHN: No. And I apologize. Of *course* you want to know about your grade. And, of course, you can't concentrate on anyth . . . *(The telephone starts to ring.)* Wait a moment.

CAROL: I should go.

JOHN: I'll make you a deal.

CAROL: No, you have to . . .

JOHN: Let it ring. I'll make you a deal. You stay here. We'll start the whole course over. I'm going to say it was not you, it was I who was not paying attention. We'll start the whole course over. Your grade is an "A." Your final grade is an "A." *(The phone stops ringing.)*

CAROL: But the class is only half over . . .

JOHN *(simultaneously with* "over"*)*: Your grade for the whole term is an "A." If you will come back and meet with me. A few more times. Your grade's an "A." Forget about the paper. You didn't like it, you didn't like writing it. It's not important. What's important is that I awake your interest, if I can, and that I answer your questions. Let's start over. *(Pause)*

CAROL: Over. With what?

JOHN: Say this is the beginning.

CAROL: The beginning.

JOHN: Yes.

CAROL: Of what?

JOHN: Of the class.

CAROL: But we can't start over.

JOHN: I say we can. *(Pause)* I say we can.

CAROL: But I don't believe it.

JOHN: Yes, I know that. But it's true. What is The Class but you and me? *(Pause)*

CAROL: There are rules.

JOHN: Well. We'll break them.

CAROL: How can we?

JOHN: We won't tell anybody.

CAROL: Is that all right?

JOHN: I say that it's fine.

CAROL: Why would you do this for me?

JOHN: I like you. Is that so difficult for you to . . .

CAROL: Um . . .

JOHN: There's no one here but you and me. *(Pause)*

CAROL: All right. I did not understand. When you referred . . .

JOHN: All right, yes?

CAROL: When you referred to hazing.

JOHN: Hazing.

CAROL: You wrote, in your book. About the comparative . . . the comparative . . . *(She checks her notes.)*

JOHN: Are you checking your notes . . . ?

CAROL: Yes.

JOHN: Tell me in your own . . .

CAROL: I want to make sure that I have it right.

JOHN: No. Of course. You want to be exact.

CAROL: I want to know everything that went on.

JOHN: . . . that's good.

CAROL: . . . so I . . .

JOHN: That's very good. But I was suggesting, many times, that that which we wish to retain is retained oftentimes, I think, *better* with less expenditure of effort.

CAROL: *(Of notes)* Here it is: you wrote of *hazing*.

JOHN: . . . that's correct. Now: I said "hazing." It means ritualized annoyance. We shove this book at you, we say read it. Now, you say you've read it? I think that you're *lying*. I'll *grill* you, and when I find you've lied, you'll be disgraced, and your life will be ruined. It's a sick game. Why do we do it? Does it educate? In no sense. Well, then, what is higher education? It is something-other-than-useful.

CAROL: What is "something-other-than-useful?"

JOHN: It has become a ritual, it has become an article of faith. That all must be subjected to, or to put it differently, that all are entitled to Higher Education. And my point . . .

CAROL: You disagree with that?

JOHN: Well, let's address that. What do you think?

CAROL: I don't know.

JOHN: What do you think, though? *(Pause)*

CAROL: I don't know.

JOHN: I spoke of it in class. Do you remember my example?

CAROL: Justice.

JOHN: Yes. Can you repeat it to me? *(She looks down at her notebook.)* Without your notes? I ask you as a favor to me, so that I can see if my idea was interesting.

CAROL: You said "justice" . . .

JOHN: Yes?

CAROL: . . . that all are entitled . . . *(Pause)* I . . . I . . . I . . .

JOHN: Yes. To a speedy trial. To a fair trial. But they needn't be given a trial *at all* unless they stand accused. Eh? Justice is their right, should they choose to avail themselves of it, they should have a fair trial. It does not follow, of necessity, a person's life is incomplete without a trial in it. Do you see?

My point is a confusion between equity and *utility* arose. So we confound the *usefulness* of higher education with our, granted, right to equal access to the same. We, in effect, create a *prejudice* toward it, completely independent of . . .

CAROL: . . . that it is prejudice that we should go to school?

JOHN: Exactly. *(Pause)*

CAROL: How can you say that? How . . .

JOHN: Good. Good. *Good.* That's right! Speak up! What is a prejudice? An unreasoned belief. We are all subject to it. None of us is not. When it is threatened, or opposed, we feel anger, and feel, do we not? As you do now. Do you not? Good.

CAROL: . . . but how can you . . .

JOHN: . . . let us examine. Good.

CAROL: How . . .
JOHN: Good. Good. When . . .
CAROL: I'M SPEAKING . . . *(Pause)*
JOHN: I'm sorry.
CAROL: How can you . . .
JOHN: . . . I beg your pardon.
CAROL: That's all right.
JOHN: I beg your pardon.
CAROL: That's all right.
JOHN: I'm sorry I interrupted you.
CAROL: That's all right.
JOHN: You were saying?
CAROL: I was saying . . . I was saying . . . *(She checks her notes.)* How can you say in a class. Say in a college class, that college education is prejudice?
JOHN: I said that our predilection for it . . .
CAROL: Predilection . . .
JOHN: . . . you know what that means.
CAROL: Does it mean "liking"?
JOHN: Yes.
CAROL: But how can you say that? That College . . .
JOHN: . . . that's my *job,* don't you know.
CAROL: What is?
JOHN: To provoke you.
CAROL: No.
JOHN: Oh. Yes, though.
CAROL: To provoke me?
JOHN: That's right.
CAROL: To make me mad?
JOHN: That's right. To force you . . .
CAROL: . . . to make me mad is your job?
JOHN: To force you to . . . listen: *(Pause)* Ah. *(Pause)* When I was young somebody told me, are you ready, the rich copulate less often than the poor. But when they do, they take more of their clothes off. Years. Years, mind you, I would compare experiences of my own to this dictum, saying, aha, this fits the norm, or ah, this is a variation from it. What did it mean? Nothing. It was some jerk thing, some school kid told me that took up room inside my head. *(Pause)*
   Somebody told *you,* and you hold it as an article of faith, that higher education is an unassailable good. This notion is so dear to you that when I question it you become angry. Good. Good, I say. Are not those the very things which we should question? I say college education, since the war, has become so a matter of course, and such a fashionable necessity, for those either of or aspiring *to* to the new vast middle class, that we *espouse* it, as a matter of right, and have ceased to ask, "What is it good for?" *(Pause)*
   What might be some reasons for pursuit of higher education?
One: A love of learning.
Two: The wish for mastery of a skill.
Three: For economic betterment.

(Stops. Makes a note.)

CAROL: I'm keeping you.
JOHN: One moment. I have to make a note . . .
CAROL: It's something that I said?
JOHN: No, we're buying a house.
CAROL: You're buying the new house.
JOHN: To go with the tenure. That's right. Nice *house,* close to the *private school . . . (He continues making his note.) . . .* We were talking of economic *betterment* (CAROL *writes in her notebook.) . . .* I was thinking of the School Tax. *(He continues writing.) (To himself:) . . . where is it written* that I have to send my child to public school. . . . Is it a law that I have to improve the City Schools at the expense of my own interest? And, is this not simply *The White Man's Burden?* Good. And *(Looks up to* CAROL*) . . .* does this interest you?
CAROL: No. I'm taking notes . . .
JOHN: You don't have to take notes, you know, you can just listen.
CAROL: I want to make sure I remember it. *(Pause)*
JOHN: I'm not lecturing you, I'm just trying to tell you some things I think.
CAROL: What do you think?
JOHN: Should all kids go to college? *Why* . . .
CAROL: *(Pause)* To learn.
JOHN: But if he does not learn.
CAROL: If the child does not learn?
JOHN: Then why is he in college? Because he was told it was his "right"?
CAROL: Some might find college instructive.
JOHN: I would hope so.
CAROL: But how do they feel? Being told they are wasting their time?
JOHN: I don't think I'm telling them that.
CAROL: You said that education was "prolonged and systematic hazing."
JOHN: Yes. It can be so.
CAROL: . . . if education is so *bad,* why do you do it?
JOHN: I do it because I love it. *(Pause)* Let's. . . . I suggest you look at the demographics, wage-earning capacity, college- and non-college-educated men and women, 1855 to 1980, and let's see if we can wring some worth from the statistics. Eh? And . . .
CAROL: No.
JOHN: What?
CAROL: I can't understand them.
JOHN: . . . you . . . ?
CAROL: . . . the "charts." The *Concepts,* the . . .
JOHN: "Charts" are simply . . .
CAROL: When I leave here . . .
JOHN: Charts, do you see . . .
CAROL: No, I can't . . .
JOHN: You can, though.
CAROL: NO, NO—I DON'T UNDERSTAND. DO YOU SEE??? I DON'T *UNDERSTAND* . . .

JOHN: What?

CAROL: *Any* of it. *Any* of it. I'm *smiling* in class, I'm *smiling*, the whole time. What are you *talking* about? What is everyone *talking* about? I don't *understand*. I don't know what it *means*. I don't know what it means to *be* here . . . you tell me I'm intelligent, and then you tell me I should not be *here*, what do you *want* with me? What does it *mean*? Who should I *listen* to . . . I . . .

(He goes over to her and puts his arm around her shoulder.)

No! *(She walks away from him.)*

JOHN: Sshhhh.

CAROL: No, I don't under . . .

JOHN: Sshhhhh.

CAROL: I don't know what you're *saying* . . .

JOHN: Sshhhhh. It's all right.

CAROL: . . . I have no . . .

JOHN: Sshhhhh. Sshhhhh. Let it go a moment. *(Pause)* Sshhhhh . . . let it go. *(Pause)* Just let it go. *(Pause)* Just let it go. It's all right. *(Pause)* Sshhhhh. *(Pause)* I understand . . . *(Pause)* What do you feel?

CAROL: I feel bad.

JOHN: I know. It's all right.

CAROL: I . . . *(Pause)*

JOHN: What?

CAROL: I . . .

JOHN: What? Tell me.

CAROL: I don't understand you.

JOHN: I know. It's all right.

CAROL: I . . .

JOHN: What? *(Pause)* What? *Tell* me.

CAROL: I can't tell you.

JOHN: No, you must.

CAROL: I can't.

JOHN: No. Tell me. *(Pause)*

CAROL: I'm bad. *(Pause)* Oh, God. *(Pause)*

JOHN: It's all right.

CAROL: I'm . . .

JOHN: It's all right.

CAROL: I can't talk about this.

JOHN: It's all right. Tell me.

CAROL: Why do you want to know this?

JOHN: I don't want to know. I want to know whatever you . . .

CAROL: I always . . .

JOHN: . . . good . . .

CAROL: I always . . . all my life . . . I have never told anyone this . . .

JOHN: Yes. Go on. *(Pause)* Go on.

CAROL: All of my life . . . *(The phone rings.)* *(Pause.* JOHN *goes to the phone and picks it up.)*

JOHN *(into phone)*: I can't talk now. *(Pause)* What? *(Pause)* Hmm. *(Pause)* All right, I . . . I. Can't. Talk. Now. No, no, no, I *know* I did, but . . . What? Hello. What? She *what*? She *can't*, she said the

agreement is void? How, how is the agreement *void? That's Our House.*

I have the *paper;* when we come down, next week, with the payment, and the paper, that house is . . . wait, wait, wait, wait, wait, wait, wait: Did Jerry . . . is Jerry there? *(Pause)* Is *she* there . . . ? Does she have a *lawyer* . . . ? How the *hell,* how the *Hell.* That is . . . it's a question, you said, of the *easement.* I don't underst . . . it's not the *whole agreement.* It's just the *easement,* why would she? Put, put, put, *Jerry* on. *(Pause)* Jer, *Jerry:* What the *Hell* . . . that's my *house.* That's . . . Well, I'm, no, no, no, I'm *not* coming ddd . . . List, *Listen, screw* her. You *tell* her. You, listen: I want you to take *Grace,* you take Grace, and get out of that house. You *leave* her there. Her and her lawyer, and you *tell* them, we'll see them in court next . . . no. No. leave her there, leave her to *stew* in it: You tell her, we're *getting* that house, and we are going to . . . No. I'm *not* coming down. I'll be damned if I'll sit in the same rrr . . . the next, you tell her the next time I *see* her is in court . . . I . . . *(Pause)* What? *(Pause)* What? I don't understand. *(Pause)* Well, what about the house? *(Pause)* There isn't any problem with the hhh . . . *(Pause)* No, no, no, that's all right. All ri . . . All right . . . *(Pause)* Of course. Tha . . . Thank you. No, I will. Right away. *(He hangs up.)* *(Pause)*

CAROL: What is it? *(Pause)*

JOHN: It's a surprise party.

CAROL: It is.

JOHN: Yes.

CAROL: A party for you.

JOHN: Yes.

CAROL: Is it your birthday?

JOHN: No.

CAROL: What is it?

JOHN: The tenure announcement.

CAROL: The tenure announcement.

JOHN: They're throwing a party for us in our new house.

CAROL: Your new house.

JOHN: The house that we're buying.

CAROL: You have to go.

JOHN: It seems that I do.

CAROL: *(Pause)* They're proud of you.

JOHN: Well, there are those who would say it's a form of aggression.

CAROL: What is?

JOHN: A surprise.

ACT 2

*(*JOHN *and* CAROL *seated across the desk from each other.)*

JOHN: You see, *(pause)* I love to teach. And flatter myself I am *skilled* at it. And I love the, the aspect of *performance.* I think I must confess that.

When I found I loved to teach I swore that I would not become that cold, rigid automaton of an instructor which I had encountered as a child.

Now, I was not unconscious that it was given me to err upon the other side. And, so, I asked and *ask* myself if I engaged in heterodoxy, I will not say "gratuitously" for I do not care to posit orthodoxy as a given good—but, "to the detriment of, of my students." *(Pause)*

As I said. When the possibility of tenure opened, and, of course, I'd long pursued it, I was, of course *happy,* and *covetous* of it.

I asked myself if I was wrong to covet it. And thought about it long, and, I hope, truthfully, and saw in myself several things in, I think, no particular order. *(Pause)*

That I *would* pursue it. That I *desired* it, that I was not pure of longing for security, and that that, perhaps, was not reprehensible in me. That I had duties *beyond* the school, and that my duty to my home, for instance, was, or should be, if it were not, of an equal weight. That tenure, and security, and yes, *comfort,* were not, of themselves, to be scorned; and were even worthy of honorable pursuit. And that it was given me. Here, in this place, which I enjoy, and in which I find comfort, to assure myself of—as far as it rests in The Material—a continuation of that joy and comfort. In exchange for what? Teaching. Which I love.

What was the price of this security? To obtain *tenure.* Which tenure the committee is in the process of granting me. And on the basis of which I contracted to purchase a house. Now, as you don't have your own family, at this point, you may not know what that means. But to me it is important. A home. A Good Home. To raise my family. Now: The Tenure Committee will meet. This is the process, and a *good* process. Under which the school has functioned for quite a long time. They will meet, and hear your complaint—which you have the right to make; and they will dismiss it. They will *dismiss* your complaint; and, in the intervening period, I will lose my house. I will not be able to close on my house. I will lose my *deposit,* and the home I'd picked out for my wife and son will go by the boards. Now: I see I have angered you. I understand your anger at teachers. I was angry with mine. I felt hurt and humiliated by them. Which is one of the reasons that I went into education.

CAROL: What do you want of me?

JOHN: *(Pause)* I was hurt. When I received the report. Of the tenure committee. I was shocked. And I was hurt. No, I don't mean to subject you to my weak sensibilities. All right. Finally, I didn't understand. Then I thought: is it not always at those points at which we reckon ourselves unassailable that we are most vulnerable and . . . *(Pause)* Yes.

All right. You find me pedantic. Yes. I am. By nature, by *birth,* by profession, I don't know . . . I'm always looking for a *paradigm* for . . .

CAROL: I don't know what a paradigm is.

JOHN: It's a model.

CAROL: Then why can't you use that word? *(Pause)*

JOHN: If it is important to you. Yes, all right. I was looking for a model. To continue: I feel that one point . . .

CAROL: I . . .

JOHN: One second . . . upon which I am unassailable is my unflinching concern for my students' dignity. I asked you here to . . . in the spirit of *investigation,* to ask you . . . to ask . . . *(Pause)* What have I done to you? *(Pause)* And, and, I suppose, how I can make amends. Can we not settle this now? It's pointless, really, and I want to know.

CAROL: What you can do to force me to retract?

JOHN: That is not what I meant at all.

CAROL: To bribe me, to convince me . . .

JOHN: . . . No.

CAROL: To retract . . .

JOHN: That is not what I meant at all. I think that you know it is not.

CAROL: That is not what I know. I *wish* I . . .

JOHN: I do not want to . . . you wish what?

CAROL: No, you said what amends can you make. To force me to retract.

JOHN: That is not what I said.

CAROL: I have my notes.

JOHN: Look. Look. The Stoics say . . .

CAROL: The Stoics?

JOHN: The Stoical Philosophers say if you remove the phrase "I have been injured," you have removed the injury. Now: Think: I know that you're upset. Just tell me. Literally. Literally: what wrong have I done you?

CAROL: Whatever you have done to me—to the extent that you've done it to *me,* do you know, rather than to me as a *student,* and, so, to the student body, is contained in my report. To the tenure committee.

JOHN: Well, all right. *(Pause)* Let's see. *(He reads.)* I find that I am sexist. That I am *elitist.* I'm not sure I know what that means, other than it's a derogatory word, meaning "bad." That I . . . That I insist on wasting time, in nonprescribed, in self-aggrandizing and theatrical *diversions* from the prescribed *text* . . . that these have taken both sexist and pornographic forms . . . here we find listed . . . *(Pause)* Here we find listed . . . instances " . . . closeted with a student" . . . "Told a rambling, sexually explicit story, in which the frequency and attitudes of fornication of the poor and rich are, it would seem, the central point . . . moved to *embrace* said student and . . . all part of a pattern . . ." *(Pause)*

(He reads.) That I used the phrase "The White Man's Burden" . . . that I told you how I'd asked you to my room because I quote like you. *(Pause)* *(He reads.)* "He said he 'liked' me. That he 'liked being with me.' He'd let me write my examination paper over, if I could come back oftener to see him in his office." *(Pause)* *(To* CAROL:*)* It's *ludicrous.* Don't you know that? It's not *necessary.* It's going to *humiliate* you, and it's going to cost me my *house,* and . . .

CAROL: It's *"ludicrous . . ."?*

*(*JOHN *picks up the report and reads again.)*

JOHN: "He told me he had problems with his wife; and that he wanted to take off the artificial stricture of Teacher and Student. He put his arm around me . . ."

CAROL: Do you deny it? Can you deny it . . . ? Do you see? *(Pause)* Don't you see? You don't see, do you?

JOHN: I don't see . . .

CAROL: You think, you think you can deny that these things happened; or, if they *did,* if they *did,* that they meant what you *said* they meant. Don't you see? You drag me in here, you drag us, to listen to you "go on"; and "go on" about this, or that, or we don't "express" ourselves very well. We don't say what we mean. Don't we? Don't we? We *do* say what we mean. And you say that "I don't understand you . . .": Then *you . . . (Points.)*

JOHN: "Consult the Report"?

CAROL: . . . that's right.

JOHN: You see. You see. Can't you. . . . You see what I'm saying? Can't you tell me in your own words?

CAROL: Those are my own words. *(Pause)*

JOHN: *(He reads.)* "He told me that if I would stay alone with him in his office, he would change my grade to an A." *(To* CAROL:*)* What have I done to you? Oh. My God, are you so hurt?

CAROL: What I "feel" is irrelevant. *(Pause)*

JOHN: Do you know that I tried to help you?

CAROL: What I know I have reported.

JOHN: I would like to help you now. I would. Before this escalates.

CAROL *(simultaneously with* "escalates"*)*: You see. I don't think that I need your help. I don't think I need anything you have.

JOHN: I feel . . .

CAROL: I don't *care* what you feel. Do you see? DO YOU SEE? You can't *do* that anymore. You. Do. Not. Have. The. Power. Did you misuse it? *Someone* did. Are you part of that group? *Yes. Yes.* You Are. You've *done* these things. And to say, and to say, "Oh. Let me help you with your problem . . ."

JOHN: Yes. I understand. I understand. You're *hurt.* You're *angry.* Yes. I think your *anger* is *betraying* you. Down a path which helps no one.

CAROL: I don't *care* what you think.

JOHN: You don't? *(Pause)* But you talk of *rights.* Don't you see? *I* have rights too. Do you see? I have a *house . . .* part of the *real* world; and The Tenure Committee, Good Men and True . . .

CAROL: . . . Professor . . .

JOHN: . . . Please: *Also* part of that world: you understand? This is my *life.* I'm not a *bogeyman.* I don't "stand" for something, I . . .

CAROL: . . . Professor . . .

JOHN: . . . I . . .

CAROL: Professor. I came here as a *favor.* At your personal request. Perhaps I should not have done so. But I did. On my behalf, and on behalf of my group. And you speak of the tenure committee, one of whose members is a woman, as you know. And though you might call it Good Fun, or An Historical Phrase, or An Oversight, or, All of the Above, to refer to the committee as Good Men and True, it is a demeaning remark. It is a sexist remark, and to overlook it is to countenance continuation of that method of thought. It's a remark . . .

JOHN: OH COME ON. Come on. . . . Sufficient to deprive a family of . . .

CAROL: Sufficient? Sufficient? Sufficient? Yes. It is a *fact . . .* and that story, which I quote, is *vile* and *classist,* and *manipulative* and *pornographic.* It . . .

JOHN: . . . it's pornographic . . . ?

CAROL: What gives you the *right.* Yes. To speak to a *woman* in your private . . . Yes. Yes. I'm sorry. I'm sorry. You feel yourself empowered . . . you say so yourself. To *strut.* To *posture.* To "perform." To "Call me in here . . ." Eh? You say that higher education is a joke. And treat it as such, you *treat* it as such. And *confess* to a taste to play the *patriarch* in your class. To grant *this.* To deny *that.* To embrace your students.

JOHN: How can you assert. How can you stand there and . . .

CAROL: How can you *deny* it. You did it to me. *Here.* You *did. . . .* You *confess.* You love the Power. To *deviate.* To *invent,* to transgress . . . to *transgress* whatever norms have been established for us. And you think it's charming to "question" in yourself this taste to mock and destroy. But you should question it, Professor. And you pick those things which you feel *advance* you: publication, *tenure,* and the steps to get them you call "harmless rituals." And you perform those steps. Although you say it is hypocrisy. But to the aspirations of your students. Of *hardworking students,* who come here, who *slave* to come here—you have no idea what it cost me to come to this school—you *mock* us. You call education "hazing," and from your so-protected, so-elitist seat you hold our confusion as a *joke,* and our hopes and efforts with it. Then you sit there and say "what have I done?" And ask me to understand that *you* have aspirations too. But I tell you. I tell you. That you are vile. And that you are exploitative. And if you possess one ounce of that inner honesty you describe in your book, you can look in yourself and see those things that I see. And you can find revulsion equal to my own. Good day. *(She prepares to leave the room.)*

JOHN: Wait a second, will you, just one moment. *(Pause)* Nice day today.

CAROL: What?

JOHN: You said "Good day." I think that it is a nice day today.

CAROL: *Is* it?

JOHN: Yes, I think it is.

CAROL: And why is that important?

JOHN: Because it is the essence of all human communication. I say something conventional, you respond, and the information we exchange is not about the "weather," but that we both agree to converse. In effect, we agree that we are both human. *(Pause)*

I'm not a . . . "exploiter," and you're not a . . . "deranged," what? *Revolutionary* . . . that we may, that we may have . . . positions, and that we may have . . . desires, which are in *conflict,* but that we're just human. *(Pause)* That means that sometimes we're *imperfect.* *(Pause)* Often we're in conflict . . . *(Pause)* *Much* of what we do, you're right, in the name of "principles" is *self-serving* . . . much of what we do is *conventional.* *(Pause)* You're right. *(Pause)* You said you came in the class because you wanted to learn about *education.* I don't know what I can teach you about education. But I know that I can tell you what I *think* about education, and then *you* decide. And you don't have to fight with me. *I'm* not the subject. *(Pause)* And where I'm *wrong* . . . perhaps it's not your job to "fix" me. I don't want to fix *you.* I would like to tell you what I *think,* because that *is* my job, conventional as it is, and flawed as I may be. And then, if you can show me some better *form,* then we can proceed from there. But, just like "nice day, isn't it . . . ?" I don't think we can proceed until we accept that each of us is human. *(Pause)* And we still can have difficulties. We *will* have them . . . that's all right too. *(Pause)* Now:

CAROL: . . . wait . . .

JOHN: Yes. I want to hear it.

CAROL: . . . the . . .

JOHN: Yes. Tell me frankly.

CAROL: . . . my position . . .

JOHN: I want to hear it. In your own words. What you want. And what you feel.

CAROL: . . . I . . .

JOHN: . . . yes . . .

CAROL: My Group.

JOHN: Your "Group" . . . ? *(Pause)*

CAROL: The people I've been talking to . . .

JOHN: There's no shame in that. Everybody needs advisers. Everyone needs to expose themselves. To various points of view. It's not wrong. It's essential. Good. Good. Good. Now: You and I . . . *(The phone rings.)* You and I . . .

(He hesitates for a moment, and then picks it up.) *(Into phone)* Hello. *(Pause)* Um . . . no, I know they do. *(Pause)* I know she does. Tell her that I . . . can I call you back? . . . Then tell her that I think it's going to be fine. *(Pause)* Tell her just, just hold on, I'll . . . can I get back to you? . . . Well . . . no, no, no, we're *taking* the house . . . we're . . . no, no, nn . . . no, she will nnn, it's not a *question* of refunding the dep . . . no . . . it's not a *question* of the deposit . . . will you call Jerry? Babe, baby, will you just call Jerry? Tell him, nnn . . . tell him they, well, they're to keep the deposit, because the deal, be . . . because the deal is going to go *through* . . . because I know . . . be . . . will you please? Just *trust* me. Be . . . well, I'm dealing with the complaint. Yes. Right *Now.* Which is why I . . . yes, no, no, it's really, I can't *talk* about it now. Call Jerry, and I can't talk now. Ff . . . fine. Gg . . . good-bye. *(Hangs up.)* *(Pause)* I'm sorry we were interrupted.

CAROL: No . . .

JOHN: I . . . I was saying:

CAROL: You said that we should agree to talk about my complaint.

JOHN: That's correct.

CAROL: But we *are* talking about it.

JOHN: Well, that's correct too. You see? This is the *gist* of education.

CAROL: No, no. I mean, we're talking about it at the Tenure Committee Hearing. *(Pause)*

JOHN: Yes, but I'm saying: we can talk about it *now,* as easily as . . .

CAROL: No. I think that we should stick to the process . . .

JOHN: . . . wait a . . .

CAROL: . . . the "conventional" process. As you said. *(She gets up.)* And you're right, I'm sorry if I was, um, if I was "discourteous" to you. You're right.

JOHN: Wait, wait a . . .

CAROL: I really should go.

JOHN: Now, look, granted. I have an interest. In the status quo. All right? Everyone does. But what I'm saying is that the *committee* . . .

CAROL: Professor, you're right. Just don't impinge on me. We'll take our differences, and . . .

JOHN: You're going to make a . . . look, look, look, you're going to . . .

CAROL: I shouldn't have come here. They told me . . .

JOHN: One moment. No. No. There are *norms,* here, and there's no reason. Look: I'm trying to *save* you . . .

CAROL: No one *asked* you to . . . you're trying to save *me?* Do me the courtesy to . . .

JOHN: I *am* doing you the courtesy. I'm talking *straight* to you. We can settle this *now.* And I want you to sit *down* and . . .

CAROL: You must excuse me . . . *(She starts to leave the room.)*

JOHN: Sit down, it seems we each have a. . . . Wait one moment. Wait one moment . . . just do me the courtesy to . . .

(He restrains her from leaving.)

CAROL: LET ME GO.

JOHN: I have no desire to *hold* you, I just want to *talk* to you . . .

CAROL: LET ME GO. LET ME GO. WOULD SOMEBODY *HELP* ME? WOULD SOMEBODY *HELP* ME PLEASE . . . ?

ACT 3

(At rise, CAROL *and* JOHN *are seated.)*

JOHN: I have asked you here. *(Pause)* I have asked you here against, against my . . .

CAROL: I was most surprised you asked me.

JOHN: . . . against my better *judgment,* against . . .

CAROL: I was most surprised . . .

JOHN: . . . against the . . . yes. I'm sure.

CAROL: . . . If you would like me to leave, I'll leave. I'll go right now . . . *(She rises.)*

JOHN: Let us begin *correctly,* may we? I feel . . .

CAROL: That is what I wished to do. That's why I came here, but now . . .

JOHN: . . . I feel . . .

CAROL: But now perhaps you'd like me to leave . . .

JOHN: I don't want you to leave. I asked you to come . . .

CAROL: I didn't have to come here.

JOHN: No. *(Pause)* Thank you.

CAROL: All right. *(Pause) (She sits down.)*

JOHN: Although I feel that it *profits,* it would *profit* you something to . . .

CAROL: . . . what I . . .

JOHN: If you would hear me out, if you would hear me out.

CAROL: I came here to, the court officers told me not to come.

JOHN: . . . the "court" officers . . . ?

CAROL: I was shocked that you asked.

JOHN: . . . wait . . .

CAROL: Yes. But I did *not* come here to hear what it "profits" me.

JOHN: The "court" officers . . .

CAROL: . . . no, no, perhaps I should leave . . . *(She gets up.)*

JOHN: Wait.

CAROL: No. I shouldn't have . . .

JOHN: . . . wait. Wait. Wait a moment.

CAROL: Yes? What is it you want? *(Pause)* What is it you want?

JOHN: I'd like you to stay.

CAROL: You want me to stay.

JOHN: Yes.

CAROL: You do.

JOHN: Yes. *(Pause)* Yes. I would like to have you hear me out. If you would. *(Pause)* Would you please? If you would do that I would be in your debt. *(Pause) (She sits.)* Thank you. *(Pause)*

CAROL: What is it you wish to tell me?

JOHN: All right. I cannot . . . *(Pause)* I cannot help but feel you are owed an apology. *(Pause) (Of papers in his hands)* I have read. *(Pause)* And reread these accusations.

CAROL: What "accusations"?

JOHN: The, the tenure comm . . . what other accusations . . ."

CAROL: The tenure committee . . . ?

JOHN: Yes.

CAROL: Excuse me, but those are not accusations. They have been *proved.* They are facts.

JOHN: . . . I . . .

CAROL: No. Those are not "accusations."

JOHN: . . . those?

CAROL: . . . the committee *(The phone starts to ring.)* the committee has . . .

JOHN: . . . All right . . .

CAROL: . . . those are not accusations. The Tenure Committee.

JOHN: ALL RIGHT, ALL RIGHT. ALL RIGHT. *(He picks up the phone.)* Hello. Yes. No. I'm here. Tell Mister . . . No, I can't talk to him now . . . I'm sure he has, but I'm fff . . . I know . . . No, I have no time t . . . tell Mister . . . tell Mist . . . tell Jerry that I'm *fine* and that I'll call him right aw . . . *(Pause)* My wife . . . Yes. I'm sure she has. Yes, thank you. Yes, I'll call her too. I cannot talk to you now. *(He hangs up.) (Pause)* All right. It was good of you to come. Thank you. I have studied. I have spent some time studying the indictment.

CAROL: You will have to explain that word to me.

JOHN: An "indictment". . .

CAROL: Yes.

JOHN: Is a "bill of particulars." A . . .

CAROL: All right. Yes.

JOHN: In which is alleged . . .

CAROL: No. I cannot allow that. I cannot allow that. Nothing is alleged. Everything is proved . . .

JOHN: Please, wait a sec . . .

CAROL: I cannot *come* to allow . . .

JOHN: If I may . . . If I may, from whatever you feel is "established," by . . .

CAROL: The issue here is not what I "feel." It is not my "feelings," but the feelings of women. And men. Your superiors, who've been "polled," do you see? To whom *evidence* has been presented, who have *ruled*, do you see? Who have weighed the testimony and the evidence, and have *ruled*, do you see? That you are *negligent*. That you are *guilty*, that you are found *wanting*, and in *error*; and are *not*, for the reasons so-told, to be given tenure. That you are to be disciplined. For facts. For *facts*. Not "alleged," what is the word? But *proved*. Do you see? *By your own actions.*

That is what the tenure committee has said. That is what my lawyer said. For what you did in class. For what you did *in this office*.

JOHN: They're going to discharge me.

CAROL: As full well they should. You don't understand? You're angry? What has *led* you to this place? Not your sex. Not your race. Not your class. YOUR OWN ACTIONS. And you're *angry*. You *ask* me here. What *do* you want? You want to "charm" me. You want to "convince" me. You want me to recant. I will *not* recant. Why should I . . . ? What I say is right. You tell me, you are going to tell me that you have a wife and child. You are going to say that you have a career and that you've worked for twenty years for this. Do you know what you've *worked* for? *Power*. For *power*. Do you understand? And you sit there, and you tell me *stories*. About your *house*, about all the private *schools*, and about *privilege*, and how you are entitled. To *buy*, to *spend*, to *mock*, to *summon*. All your stories. All your silly weak *guilt*, it's all about *privilege*; and you won't know it. Don't you see? You worked twenty years for the right to *insult* me. And you feel entitled to be *paid* for it. Your Home. Your Wife . . . Your sweet "deposit" on your house.

JOHN: Don't you have feelings?

CAROL: That's my point. You see? Don't you have feelings? Your final argument. What is it that has no feelings. *Animals*. I don't take your side, you question if I'm Human.

JOHN: Don't you have feelings?

CAROL: I have a responsibility. I . . .

JOHN: . . . to . . . ?

CAROL: To? This institution. To the *students*. To my *group*.

JOHN: . . . your "group." . . .

CAROL: Because I speak, yes, not for myself. But for the group; for those who suffer what I suffer. On behalf of whom, even if I, were, inclined, to what, forgive? Forget? What? Overlook your . . .

JOHN: . . . my behavior?

CAROL: . . . it would be wrong.

JOHN: Even if you were inclined to "forgive" me.

CAROL: It would be wrong.

JOHN: And what would transpire.

CAROL: Transpire?

JOHN: Yes.

CAROL: "Happen?"

JOHN: Yes.

CAROL: Then *say* it. For Christ's sake. Who the *hell* do you think that you are? You want a post. You want unlimited power. To do and to say what you want. As it pleases you—Testing, Questioning, Flirting . . .

JOHN: I never . . .

CAROL: Excuse me, one moment, will you?

(She reads from her notes.)

The twelfth: "Have a good day, dear."
The fifteenth: "Now, don't *you* look fetching . . ."
April seventeenth: "If you girls would come over here . . ." I saw you. I saw you, Professor. For two semesters sit there, stand there and exploit our, as you thought, "paternal prerogative," and what is that but rape; I swear to God. You asked me in here to explain something to me, as a child, that I did not understand. But I came to explain something to you. You Are Not God. You ask me why I came? I came here to instruct you.

(She produces his book.)

And your book? You think you're going to show me some "light"? You *"maverick."* Outside of tradition. No, no, *(She reads from the book's liner notes.)* *"Of* that fine tradition of *inquiry.* Of Polite *skepticism"* . . . and you say you believe in free intellectual discourse. YOU BELIEVE IN NOTHING. YOU BELIEVE IN NOTHING AT ALL.

JOHN: I believe in freedom of thought.

CAROL: Isn't that fine. *Do* you?

JOHN: Yes. I do.

CAROL: Then why do you question, for one moment, the committee's decision refusing your tenure? Why do you question your suspension? You believe in what *you call* freedom of thought. Then, fine. *You* believe in freedom-of-thought *and* a home, and, *and* prerogatives for your kid, *and* tenure. And I'm going to tell you. You believe *not* in "freedom of thought," but in an elitist, in, in a protected hierarchy which rewards you. And for whom you are the clown. And you mock and exploit the system which pays your rent. You're wrong. I'm not wrong. You're wrong. You think that I'm full of hatred. I know what you think I am.

JOHN: Do you?

CAROL: You think I'm a, of course I do. You think I am a frightened, repressed, confused, I don't know, abandoned young thing of some doubtful sexuality, who wants, power and revenge. *(Pause)* Don't you? *(Pause)*

JOHN: Yes. I do. *(Pause)*

CAROL: Isn't that better? And I feel that that is the first moment which you've treated me with respect. For you told me the truth. *(Pause)* I did not come here, as you are assured, to gloat. Why would I want to gloat? I've profited nothing from your, your, as you say, your "misfortune." I came here, as you did me the honor to *ask* me here, I came here to *tell* you something.

(Pause) That I think . . . that I think you've been wrong. That I think you've been terribly wrong. Do you hate me now? *(Pause)*

JOHN: Yes.

CAROL: Why do you hate me? Because you think me wrong? No. Because I have, you think, *power* over you. Listen to me. Listen to me, Professor. *(Pause)* It is the power that you hate. So deeply that, that any atmosphere of free discussion is impossible. It's not "unlikely." It's *impossible.* Isn't it?

JOHN: Yes.

CAROL: *Isn't* it . . . ?

JOHN: Yes. I suppose.

CAROL: Now. The thing which you find so cruel is the selfsame process of selection I, and my group, go through *every day of our lives.* In admittance to school. In our tests, in our class rankings. . . . Is it unfair? I can't tell you. But, if it is fair. Or even if it is "unfortunate but necessary" for us, then, by God, so must it be for you. *(Pause)* You write of your "responsibility to the young." Treat us with respect, and that will *show* you your responsibility. You write that education is just hazing. *(Pause)* But we worked to get to this school. *(Pause)* And some of us. *(Pause)* Overcame prejudices. Economic, sexual, you cannot begin to imagine. And endured humiliations I *pray* that you and those you love never will encounter. *(Pause)* To gain admittance here. To pursue that same dream of security *you* pursue. We, who, who are, at any moment, in danger of being deprived of it. By . . .

JOHN: . . . by . . . ?

CAROL: By the administration. By the teachers. By *you.* By, say, one low grade, that keeps us out of graduate school; by one, say, one capricious or inventive answer on our parts, which, perhaps, you don't find amusing. Now you *know,* do you see? What it is to be subject to that power. *(Pause)*

JOHN: I don't understand. *(Pause)*

CAROL: My charges are not trivial. You see that in the haste, I think, with which they were accepted. A *joke* you have told, with a sexist tinge. The language you use, a verbal or physical caress, yes, yes, I know, you say that it is meaningless. I understand. I differ from you. To lay a hand on someone's shoulder.

JOHN: It was devoid of sexual content.

CAROL: I say it was not. I SAY IT WAS NOT. Don't you begin to *see* . . . ? Don't you begin to understand? IT'S NOT FOR YOU TO SAY.

JOHN: I take your point, and I see there is much good in what you refer to.

CAROL: . . . do you think so . . . ?

JOHN: . . . but, and this is not to say that I cannot change, in those things in which I am deficient . . . But, the . . .

CAROL: Do you hold yourself harmless from the charge of sexual exploitativeness . . . ? *(Pause)*

JOHN: Well, I . . . I . . . I . . . You know I, as I said. I . . . think I am not too old to *learn,* and I *can* learn, I . . .

CAROL: Do you hold yourself innocent of the charge of . . .

JOHN: . . . wait, wait, wait . . . All right, let's go back to . . .

CAROL: YOU FOOL. Who do you think I am? To come here and be taken in by a *smile.* You little yapping fool. You think I want "revenge." I don't want revenge. I WANT UNDERSTANDING.

JOHN: . . . *do* you?

CAROL: I do. *(Pause)*

JOHN: What's the use. It's over.

CAROL: Is it? What is?

JOHN: My job.

CAROL: Oh. Your job. That's what you want to talk about. *(Pause) (She starts to leave the room. She steps and turns back to him.)* All right. *(Pause)* What if it were possible that my Group withdraws its complaint. *(Pause)*

JOHN: What?

CAROL: That's right. *(Pause)*

JOHN: Why.

CAROL: Well, let's say as an act of friendship.

JOHN: An act of friendship.

CAROL: Yes. *(Pause)*

JOHN: In exchange for what.

CAROL: Yes. But I don't think, "exchange." Not "in exchange." For what do we derive from it? *(Pause)*

JOHN: "Derive."

CAROL: Yes.

JOHN: *(Pause)* Nothing. *(Pause)*

CAROL: That's right. We derive nothing. *(Pause)* Do you see that?

JOHN: Yes.

CAROL: That is a little word, Professor. "Yes." "I see that." But you will.

JOHN: And you might speak to the committee . . . ?

CAROL: To the committee?

JOHN: Yes.

CAROL: Well. Of course. That's on your mind. We might.

JOHN: "If" what?

CAROL: "Given" what. Perhaps. I think that that is more friendly.

JOHN: GIVEN WHAT?

CAROL: And, believe me, I understand your rage. It is not that I don't feel it. But I do not see that it is deserved, so I do not resent it. . . . All right. I have a list.

JOHN: . . . a list.

CAROL: Here is a list of books, which we . . .

JOHN: . . . a list of books . . . ?

CAROL: That's right. Which we find questionable.

JOHN: What?

CAROL: Is this so bizarre . . . ?

JOHN: I can't believe . . .

CAROL: It's not necessary you believe it.

JOHN: Academic freedom . . .

CAROL: Someone chooses the books. If you can choose them, others can. What are you, "God"?

JOHN: . . . no, no, the "dangerous." . . .

CAROL: You have an agenda, we have an agenda. I am not interested in your feelings or your motivation, but your actions. If you would like me to speak to the Tenure Committee, here is my list. You are a Free Person, you decide. (*Pause*)

JOHN: Give me the list. (*She does so. He reads.*)

CAROL: I think you'll find . . .

JOHN: I'm capable of reading it. Thank you.

CAROL: We have a number of *texts* we need re . . .

JOHN: I see that.

CAROL: We're amenable to . . .

JOHN: Aha. Well, let me look over the . . . (*He reads.*)

CAROL: I think that . . .

JOHN: LOOK. I'm reading your demands. All right?! (*He reads*) (*Pause*) You want to ban my book?

CAROL: We do not . . .

JOHN (*Of list*): It says here . . .

CAROL: . . . We want it removed from inclusion as a representative example of the university.

JOHN: Get out of here.

CAROL: If you put aside the issues of personalities.

JOHN: Get the fuck out of my office.

CAROL: No, I think I would reconsider.

JOHN: . . . you think you can.

CAROL: We can and we *will*. Do you want our support? That is the only quest . . .

JOHN: . . . to ban my *book* . . . ?

CAROL: . . . that is correct . . .

JOHN: . . . this . . . this is a *university* . . . we . . .

CAROL: . . . and we have a statement . . . which we need you to . . . (*She hands him a sheet of paper.*)

JOHN: No, no. It's out of the question. I'm sorry. I don't know what I was thinking of. I want to tell you something. I'm a teacher. I am a teacher. Eh? It's my *name* on the door, and *I* teach the class, and that's what I do. I've got a book with my name on it. And my son will *see* that *book* someday. And I have a respon . . . No, I'm sorry I have a *responsibility* . . . to *myself*, to my *son*, to my *profession*. . . . I haven't been *home* for two days, do you know that? Thinking this out.

CAROL: . . . you haven't?

JOHN: I've been, no. If it's of interest to you. I've been in a *hotel. Thinking.* (*The phone starts ringing.*) *Thinking* . . .

CAROL: . . . you haven't been home?

JOHN: . . . *thinking*, do you see.

CAROL: Oh.

JOHN: And, and, I owe you a debt, I see that now. (*Pause*) You're *dangerous*, you're *wrong* and it's my *job* . . . to say no to you. That's my job. You are absolutely right. You want to ban my book? Go to *hell*, and they can do whatever they want to me.

CAROL: . . . you haven't been home in two days . . .

JOHN: I think I told you that.

CAROL: . . . you'd better get that phone. (*Pause*) I think that you should pick up the phone. (*Pause*)

(JOHN *picks up the phone.*)

JOHN (*on phone*): Yes. (*Pause*) Yes. Wh . . . I. I. I had to be away. All ri . . . did they wor . . . did they worry ab . . . No. I'm all right, now, Jerry. I'm f . . . I got a little turned *around*, but I'm *sitting* here and . . . I've got it figured out. I'm fine. I'm fine don't worry about me. I got a little bit mixed up. But I am not sure that it's not a blessing. It cost me my job? Fine. Then the job was not worth having. Tell Grace that I'm coming home and everything is fff . . . (*Pause*) What? (*Pause*) *What?* (*Pause*) What do you *mean?* WHAT? Jerry . . . Jerry. They . . . Who, who, what can they do . . . ? (*Pause*) NO. (*Pause*) NO. They can't do th . . . What do you mean? (*Pause*) But how . . . (*Pause*) She's, she's, she's *here* with me. To . . . Jerry. I don't underst . . . (*Pause*) (*He hangs up.*) (*To* CAROL:) What does this mean?

CAROL: I thought you knew.

JOHN: What. (*Pause*) What does it mean. (*Pause*)

CAROL: You tried to rape me. (*Pause*) According to the law. (*Pause*)

JOHN: . . . what . . . ?

CAROL: You tried to rape me. I was leaving this office, you "pressed" yourself into me. You "pressed" your body into me.

JOHN: . . . I . . .

CAROL: My Group has told your lawyer that we may pursue criminal charges.

JOHN: . . . no . . .

CAROL: . . . under the statute. I am told. It was battery.

JOHN: . . . no . . .

CAROL: Yes. And attempted rape. That's right. (*Pause*)

JOHN: I think that you should go.

CAROL: Of course. I thought you knew.

JOHN: I have to talk to my lawyer.

CAROL: Yes. Perhaps you should.

(*The phone rings again.*) (*Pause*)

JOHN: *(Picks up phone. Into phone:)* Hello? I . . . Hello . . . ? I . . . Yes, he just called. No . . . I. I can't talk to you now, Baby. *(To* CAROL:*)* Get out.

CAROL: . . . your wife . . . ?

JOHN: . . . who it is is no concern of yours. Get out. *(To phone:)* No, no, it's going to be all right. I. I can't talk now, Baby. *(To* CAROL:*)* Get out of here.

CAROL: I'm going.

JOHN: Good.

CAROL *(exiting)*: . . . and don't call your wife "baby."

JOHN: What?

CAROL: Don't call your wife baby. You heard what I said.

*(*CAROL *starts to leave the room.* JOHN *grabs her and begins to beat her.)*

JOHN: You vicious little bitch. You think you can come in here with your political correctness and destroy my life?

(He knocks her to the floor.)

   After how I treated you . . . ? You should be . . . *Rape you* . . . ? Are you kidding me . . . ?

(He picks up a chair, raises it above his head, and advances on her.)

   I wouldn't touch you with a ten-foot pole. You little *cunt* . . .

(She cowers on the floor below him. Pause. He looks down at her. He lowers the chair. He moves to his desk, and arranges the papers on it. Pause. He looks over at her.)

. . . well . . .

(Pause. She looks at him.)

CAROL: Yes. That's right.

(She looks away from him, and lowers her head. To herself:) . . . yes. That's right.

Figure 1. In the first scene of *Oleanna,* John (William H. Macy) looks quizzically at Carol (Rebecca Pidgeon) as she explains her confusion to him. The 1992 New York premiere was directed by David Mamet. (Photograph: Brigitte Lacombe, New York.)

Figure 2. In the last scene of *Oleanna,* Carol (Rebecca Pidgeon) demands that John (William H. Macy) accede to a list of demands, including removing his book from the reading list in the 1992 New York premiere. (Photograph: Brigitte Lacombe, New York.)

Figure 3. In the last moments of *Oleanna,* John (William H. Macy) attacks Carol (Rebecca Pidgeon) both verbally and physically in the 1992 New York premiere. (Photograph: Brigitte Lacombe, New York.)

Staging of *Oleanna*

**REVIEW OF THE ORPHEUM THEATRE
PRODUCTION, 1992, BY JOHN LAHR**

David Mamet understands that envy is the gasoline on which a competitive society runs, and no modern American playwright has been bolder or more brilliant in analyzing its corrosive social effects. In his most recent play, "Oleanna," at the Orpheum, Mamet returns to this theme but stages it in the upwardly mobile arena of university life. Here a sense of shaming humiliation at ignorance becomes the subtext of Mamet's powerful dissection of political correctness. John, a teacher with bona-fide intellectual credentials, tries to help Carol, a student who is paralyzed by her sense of inadequacy. "I don't *understand*. I don't *understand*. I don't understand what anything means. . . . I'm stupid," she says. Mamet is shrewdly setting the stage for the bracingly unfashionable notion of a woman harassing a man. What finally humiliates Carol is not so much her ignorance as his prowess. The battle that ensues brings the audience up against the awful spoiling power of envy disguised as political ideology. Carol ends up trashing the professor's life. To offer a story that risks the hue and cry of underclass ideologues is typical of Mamet's curmudgeonly brilliance. It's the theatrical equivalent of pulling to an inside straight, and Mamet, with his great narrative gifts, accomplishes it deftly, with a competent assist from two of his ever-expanding family of performers, William H. Macy and his new wife, the British-born Rebecca Pidgeon.

Mamet likes to jump the audience into the middle of a dramatic situation, and let it piece together the jigsaw of the story from the tantalizing chunks of speech his characters scatter around the stage. Here we encounter the professor on the phone, trying to close on the new house that is the first fruit of his tenure (newly granted but not yet confirmed). Across the stage, Carol, turned away from him, sits morosely on a bench. John is all orders and authority; Carol is subservience in a schmatte. Carol has arrived for an unscheduled appointment, and her professor is obviously in a rush. "Words are acts," Mamet has written, and when John and Carol finally talk to each other the authority both of John's position and of his knowledge makes the gap between them almost unbridgeable. John brusquely cuts through Carol's tentative opening questions. "Let's take the mysticism out of it," he says, sternly trying to teach Carol how to negotiate and to think like an adult. The line haunts the evening. Mystification of power is precisely the point on which John will be shafted. Carol has no apparent powers of analysis—something John demonstrates by reading a snatch of her failing essay. "'I think that the ideas con-

tained in this work express the author's feelings in a way that he intended, based on his results,'" he says, and breaks off in understandable professorial frustration. "What can that mean?" Carol asks the same question, not just about his lectures but about his language. Carol continually interrupts the discourse for definitions of John's educated vocabulary. Words like "predilection," "paradigm," "transpire" throw her. She demands meaning but hasn't the language to define her feelings to herself or to the world. Her adamant dimness is rightly interpreted by John as anger. In their stutter-speech, which Mamet orchestrates with overlapping rhythms, interjected phrases, emotional retreats, and attempted advances, the drama of their missed communication is made transparent and startling. No American playwright is more expert than Mamet at externalizing the sludge of consciousness and dramatizing both the meaning and the music in our stammerings:

CAROL: I'm just: I sit in class I . . . I take notes . . .
JOHN (*simultaneously with "notes"*): Yes. I understand. What I am trying to *tell* you is that some, some basic . . .
CAROL: . . . I . . .
JOHN: . . . one moment: some basic missed communi . . .
CAROL: No, no, no. I'm doing what I'm told. It's *difficult* . . .
JOHN: . . . but . . .
CAROL: I don't . . . lots of the *language* . . .
JOHN: . . . please . . .
CAROL: The *language,* the "things" that you say . . .
JOHN: I'm sorry. No. I don't think that that's true.
CAROL: It *is* true. I . . .
JOHN: I think . . .
CAROL: It *is* true.

By making Carol's situation so immediately poignant, Mamet sets a cunning trap for the sympathies of the audience. "*Teach* me. *Teach* me," she pleads, with that combination of fierce vacancy and ambition which distinguishes the American undergraduate. "I'm not your *father,*" says John, who is nonetheless put in a parental role by her show of powerlessness. Carol literally calls out John's power. She has no command of language, no knowledge, no psychological understanding. But she has the pedigree of the underprivileged:

CAROL: It *is* true. I have problems.
JOHN: . . . every . . .
CAROL: . . . I come from a different *social* . . .
JOHN: . . . ev . . .

CAROL: a different . . .
JOHN: . . . Look:
CAROL: No. I: when I *came* to this school:
JOHN: Yes. quite . . .
CAROL: . . . does that mean nothing . . . ?

The issue of class does mean something to John. From their different positions in the pecking order, he has arrived at the secure place Carol wants a university education to get her to. After twenty years on the tenure track, John is now set to move into the upper middle class and to shift his son from public to private school. He interrupts their talk to make a note to himself about the school tax. "Is it a law that I have to improve the city schools at the expense of my own interest?" says John, whose liberality is confined to the classroom, and doesn't extend to society. "Is this not simply 'The White Man's Burden'?" John recognizes in Carol not only the same class struggle he underwent but the same educational struggle. His career in academe and his iconoclastic views on education are his revenge on early learning difficulties, which he spells out to Carol to assuage her panic. He immediately names her feeling of humiliation, and later shows her the dynamic of her terror, saying, "Why was I born to be the laughingstock of a world in which everyone is better than I? In which I am entitled to nothing. Where I can not learn." He is pedantic but decent. "Men are the puppydogs of the universe," Mamet wrote in his essay collection, "Some Freaks." And so John seems. He takes Carol's failure as his own, and in a rush of pedagogic vainglory he throws away the offending essay, takes up her educational challenge, and gives her a comradely hug. John becomes a latter-day Professor Higgins, offering to recap the course for her in private tutorials, and easing her anxiety about grades by promising her an A. When Carol asks why he's doing this for her, he replies, "I like you."

John, like Mamet, is a self-styled provocateur; he holds to the antique notion that education should encourage thought, and argues that the job of a teacher is to provoke. "To make me mad is your job?" says his incredulous, pragmatic pupil. John is a bit of a wag. He swaggers in speech, and the idioms that Carol finds impenetrable are metaphoric turns of phrase that intelligently tease received opinion about higher education. He talks of college as "warehousing of the young," as something that prolongs adolescence; refers to tests as "hazing"; and, like the American sociologist Thorstein Veblen, whose argument about higher learning Mamet cunningly glosses, characterizes university education as a "ritual" of "something-other-than-useful"—what Veblen called "a by-product of the priestly vicarious leisure class." Carol is a zealot who, having got educational religion, can't comprehend backsliders. As the audience soon discovers, John's skepticism about education marks him as a heretic.

When John and Carol square off in Act 2, John is no longer the master, although at first he fondly thinks he is. His power and his blocking have changed. He sits face to face with Carol, who is now dressed in greens and blacks that hint at the paramilitary, and tries to shortcut procedure by reasoning her out of her accusations of sexism, racism, and élitism before the Tenure Committee reconvenes, by which time he will have lost his new house and his deposit. "You think, you think you can deny that these things happened; or, if they *did,* if they *did,* that they meant what you *said* they meant," Carol says. Every gesture in Act 1, every exchange, every idea has been taken out of context and turned into an indictment. "What gives you the *right,*" she says, in highest dudgeon, "to speak to a woman in your private, yes. Yes. I'm sorry. I'm sorry. You feel yourself empowered. . . . To *strut.* To *posture.* . . . And *confess* to a taste to play the *Patriarch* in your class. To grant *this.* To deny *that.* To embrace—your students." Mamet puts the audience exactly where John sits: up against it. Such is the power of Mamet's storytelling that the audience receives each willful misinterpretation like a body blow, audibly catching its breath at Carol's argument. Carol, who lacked words before, has got educated in a hurry by what she refers to as her Group, and she speaks now with the righteous fervor of a woman whose day has come. This transition is jarring but intentional. She has acquired a new voice and a new vocabulary, whose authority precludes ambiguity. She adopts political correctness as an intellectual carapace that substitutes dogma for thought, mission for mastery. Naming is claiming, and since Carol won't work to master a world she can't comprehend, she changes the frame of reference to a world she can. She advocates a kind of linguistic affirmative action, forcing John to define "paradigm," for example. "It's a model," he says. Carol counters, sharpish, "Then why can't you use that word?" And later, when she requires a simpler definition for the word "transpire," she rounds on John with the full malice of her envy, offering "happen" as an alternative. "Then *say* it. For Christ's sake. Who the *hell* do you think that you are? You want a post. You want unlimited power. To do and to say what you want. As it pleases you—Testing, Questioning, Flirting." This policing of language leads inevitably to a policing of the curriculum. Carol holds out the possibility of reprieve from the Tenure Committee if he'll agree to a new reading list, from which his book, among many, has been banned. "If you can choose them, others can," Carol tells him. "What are you, God?" Here, in a series of exchanges, Mamet exposes the central paradox of political correctness, which demands diversity in everything but thought.

Carol remains staunch. She is the embodiment of Mamet's mischievous assertion that "women don't give a tinker's damn about being well-liked, which means they don't know how to compromise." Carol's rigidity is a sign of her insecurity. Her ruthless orthodoxy is skillfully shown as her means of controlling her enormous anxiety of ignorance. In this production, the intelligence of Rebecca Pidgeon, who plays Carol, makes it hard to suspend disbelief in her academic ineptness but also makes her puritan willfulness powerfully credible. Dressed now, in the last of their three encounters, in a loose-fitting black jacket, green chinos, and sensible black shoes, and peering out from behind wire-rimmed glasses, Carol stands above John like some Maoist enforcer. By this last scene, it is the student who is dishing out the humiliation to the professor, calling him a "little yapping fool." William H. Macy plays John with droll liberal long-suffering. He's slow to kindle, but when Carol interprets as rape his attempt to keep her in the room to settle their disagreement ("I was leaving this office, you 'pressed' yourself into me. You 'pressed' your body into me") he finally ignites. A telephone call from his wife interrupts the final argument. "I can't talk now, baby," John says, and then orders Carol out of the office. "Don't call your wife 'baby,'" she says. It is Mamet's shrewdly placed parting shot. The throw-away line turns out to be the last straw. John belts Carol around the room. The explosion of violence sends both Carol and John's academic career crashing.

Because of the limits of the scope and intention in this short polemical play, "Oleanna" may not belong to the major part of Mamet's canon, but it's a powerful, exciting play that shows off his enormous skills as a writer. The production, however, reveals his limitations as a director. The actors' job, according to Mamet, "is to accomplish *beat by beat,* as simply as possible, the specific action set out for them by the script and the director." Both Mr. Macy and Ms. Pidgeon are a bit under wraps here, at once awed and cowed by Mamet's authority, which takes some of the acting oxygen out

of the air. In this, Mamet joins the likes of Samuel Beckett and Harold Pinter, whose literary touch was always much surer than their directorial hand. Mamet keeps his show clean and crisp, but leaves a lot of production values still to be explored in the many other versions that "Oleanna" will certainly have.

On the night I saw it, the play was already doing its work in the world as the audience filed out of the theatre; it was a drizzly evening, and people clustered under the Orpheum Theatre marquee to keep talking.

"Too bad he had to have a woman be the heavy," one matron said.

"He's a bit of a misogynist," her friend said, and then turned to a stooped man who was obviously her husband. "What do you think?"

"No one escaped sin in the Garden of Eden," the man said—an acid thought, in keeping with the even-handed skepticism of the play, and one that echoed something Mamet had written elsewhere about corruption. "The corrupted person, politician, parent, doctor, and artist offer us two choices," he said in "Some Freaks." "To accept them and their presumption of power *totally,* or to reject them *totally* and, so, realize that we have been cruelly duped and accept the humiliation, anger, and despair that realization entails." "Oleanna" bravely makes the audience own the ambiguity of its idealism.

My friend Liz and I walked away talking about the play's title, which is never mentioned. Liz remembered the old Pete Seeger/Alan Lomax song about a world turned upside down—a song as oblique, and as knowing, as the play. The last stanza goes:

So if you'd like a happy life,
To Oleanna you must go,
The poorest man from the old country
Becomes a king in a year or so.

INTERVIEW WITH DAVID MAMET
BY GEOFFREY NORMAN AND JOHN REZEK
FOR *PLAYBOY*, 1995

PLAYBOY: Your film *Oleanna*—and the play—pushed the culture's hot buttons, with a man and woman winding up, literally, each at the other's throat. Why is there such tension between the sexes?

MAMET: This has always been a puritan country, and we've always been terrified of sex. That terror takes

different forms. Sometimes it is overindulgence, and, of course, at other times it's the opposite.

PLAYBOY: Why should this be a time of repression?

MAMET: For one thing, there is economic scarcity. People tend to get cranky when there aren't so many jobs to go around. Also, I think our expectations are scrambled. Sexual drive is designed to make sure the species will survive, as much as we fight the fact. But for young people today it is very difficult to say, "Fine, either with you this year or with someone else next year, I'm going to get married, buy a house, get a job, settle down and raise kids." It's terrifying for them to say that. They can't get married. There aren't any jobs. They can't buy the house and have the dog named Randy. Our expectations have become greater than our ability to meet them.

PLAYBOY: So the alternative is the kind of antagonism we see between the sexes?

MAMET: Alternatives are going to emerge. In the Seventies and Eighties, there was the notion of continual romantic involvement. You said, "I don't want to get married; I just want to go out there and have a good time." That worked for a while and then, suddenly, it didn't seem like such a good idea anymore. Back in the Sixties or Seventies, *National Lampoon* published a story of a rumor about a new strain of the clap that guys brought back from Vietnam. If you got it, you died. Very funny.

So now you can't become committed to somebody because you can't support a family, and recreational sex is out because AIDS might kill you. As a result, society is going to bring us to some sort of intermediary mechanism, something to keep people wary about getting involved with each other. Here it comes—sexual harassment. The culture has to supersede. Alternatives will emerge to take the problem off our shoulders.

"Gee, what does she want of me?" It's a rhetorical question. It means, "I don't understand, better back off." On the other hand, "I need him to be more sensitive to me." That's poetry. It doesn't mean anything. It means, "I'd better back off because of my fear."

PLAYBOY: Your timing with *Oleanna* was perfect. When the play was first performed, sexual harassment was probably the most incendiary issue around. Were you influenced by the Clarence Thomas hearings?

MAMET: No. I didn't follow those hearings, actually. It was weird. I wrote the play before the hearings and I stuck it in a drawer.

PLAYBOY: Why?

MAMET: Two reasons. First, I didn't have a last act. Second, when I wrote the play, it seemed a little far-fetched to me. And then the Thomas hearings began and I took the play out of the drawer and started working on it again. One of the first people to see the play was a headmaster at a very good school here in Cambridge. He said to me, "Eighteen months ago, I would have said this play was fantasy. But now, when all the headmasters get together at conferences, we whisper to one another, 'You know, all of us are only one dime away from the end of a career.'"

PLAYBOY: Was that a typical response?

MAMET: There was a great deal of controversy at a level I've never encountered in the theater. In the audience, people got into shouting matches and fistfights. People stood up and screamed, "Oh bullshit" at the stage before they realized they'd done it. A couple of people got a little crazy and lost their composure.

PLAYBOY: So it isn't a good date play?

MAMET: It is a terrible date play. But I never really saw it as a play about sexual harassment. I think the issue was, to a large extent, a flag of convenience for a play that's structured as a tragedy. Just like the issues of race relations and xenophobia are flags of convenience for *Othello*. It doesn't have anything to do with race. This play—and the film—is a tragedy about power. These are two people with a lot to say to each other, with legitimate affection for each other. But protecting their positions becomes more important than pursuing their own best interests. And that leads them down the slippery slope to a point where, at the end of the play, they tear each other's throat out. My plays are not political. They're dramatic. I don't believe that the theater is a good venue for political argument. Not because it is wrong, but because it doesn't work very well.

PLAYBOY: Do you think you can understand and empathize with the female point of view in this hostile climate? Your critics would say your point of view is almost exclusively male. Cheap shot?

MAMET: Not cheap, but inaccurate. Take *Oleanna*, for instance, the points she makes about power and privilege—I believe them all. If I didn't believe them, the play wouldn't work as well. It is a play about two people, and each person's point of view is correct. Yet they end up destroying each other.

PLAYBOY: So it is possible, then, that Anita Hill and Clarence Thomas were both telling the truth?

MAMET: Yeah, sure. You know, the whole notion of American jurisprudence is that you can't determine who is telling the truth. That's not the job of the jury. The jury is supposed to decide which side has made the best case. Polls—which are replacing the judicial system as the way we settle disputes—are no better.

PLAYBOY: But they do provide clarity, which some critics find lacking in your work. They find your dialogue almost intentionally obscure. What do you say to them?

MAMET: First of all, I'd like to thank them for their interest in my work.

PLAYBOY: Then?

MAMET: Then, I suppose, I'd like them to think about *Oleanna*. They say the play is "unclear," and it occurs to me that what they mean is "provocative." That rather than sending the audience out whistling over the tidy moral of the play, it leaves them unsettled. I've noticed over the past 30 years that a lot of what passes in the theater is not drama but rather a morality tale. "Go thou now and do likewise." That's very comforting to someone who is concerned or upset. When you leave the theater and you say, "Oh, now I get it. Women are people, too." Or, "Now I get it, handicapped people have rights," then you feel very soothed for the amount of time it takes you to get to your car. Then you forget about the play. If, on the other hand, you leave the theater upset, you might have seen a rotten play. Or you might be provoked because something was suggested that you could not have known when you came into the theater. Aristotle said we should see something at the end of tragedy that is surprising and inevitable.

PLAYBOY: But while your structure is classical, the speech is entirely modern and urban, and, some critics have said, free of content. How do you get your characters to convey anything?

MAMET: There is always content in what's being said. That content is not necessarily carried by the context of the words. There has never been a conversation without content. If you're in a room where a lot of people are talking with one another and you can't hear a word of what's being said, you can still tell what the people are saying because their intent communicates itself.

One of the things I learned when I studied acting is that the content of what is being said is rarely carried by the connotation of the words. It is carried by the rhythm of the speech and the posture of the speaker and a lot of other things. All conversations have meaning.

TONY KUSHNER

Tony Kushner has never been modest in his theatrical ambitions, nor has he been modest in writing about them, as he makes clear in his afterword to *Perestroika,* the second part of his seven-hour play *Angels in America:* "Given the bloody opulence of this country's great and terrible history, given its newness and its grand improbability, its artists are bound to be tempted toward large gestures and big embraces." Admitting his determination "to attempt something of ambition and size, even if that meant being vulnerable to accusations of having strayed too close to ambition's ugly twin, pretentiousness," Kushner places himself firmly in the American tradition of writers who reach for "large gestures and big embraces," mentioning Herman Melville, his favorite American writer, and invoking Walt Whitman as a spiritual father.

Kushner's reach is large indeed, for *Angels in America,* though set in 1985–86, attempts a whole national and spiritual history, both for the immigrant (as represented by Louis Ironson and his grandmother) and for the gay man in America, whether in power (Roy Cohn) or out of power (Prior Walter). Kushner's achievement is similarly large, as *Angels in America* has become one of the most honored plays in contemporary American theater: in 1993, *Millennium Approaches (Part I)* won the Pulitzer Prize, the Tony Award for best play, the Drama Desk Award, and the New York Drama Critics Circle Award, after winning London's Evening Standard Award in 1992; in addition, in 1994, *Perestroika (Part II)* also won the Tony Award and the Drama Desk Award. Kushner's most recent play, *Homebody/Kabul* (2001), which contrasts a British woman's romanticized look at Afghanistan, gleaned from an old guidebook, with the reality of contemporary Afghanistan under the Taliban, seems not only political but even prophetic. Though conceived and written before the terrorist attacks of September 11, 2001, Kushner's play stunned New York audiences when one of its characters, an Afghan woman rejected by her husband, screamed: "We must suffer under the Taliban so that the U.S. might settle a twenty-year-old score with Iran! You love the Taliban so much, bring them to New York! Well, don't worry, they're coming to New York!"

When *Millennium Approaches* opened in New York in 1993, Kushner felt that the play, after productions elsewhere, had finally arrived at its setting and his home. Born in New York City, Kushner nonetheless grew up in Louisiana where his parents moved when he was just a year old. He returned to the city for his undergraduate education at Columbia University, though he still spent summers in Louisiana, directing a children's theater group. He moved back to New York to get an MFA in directing at New York University, but soon turned his full attention to playwriting, supported by a series of fellowships. His first full-length play, *A Brigh[t] Room Called Day* (1985, produced in New York in 1991), clearly displayed his [politi]cal interests, as Kushner juxtaposed his portrayal of liberal Germans in p[...]

Germany with commentary by a contemporary American woman who insists on parallels between Hitler and Presidents Reagan and Bush. Based in part on Brecht's *Fear and Misery of the Third Reich,* Kushner intended it as a tribute to Brecht's plays and theories, to which he is profoundly indebted, as well as a way of finding his own theatrical voice.

Angels in America is likewise a deeply political and profoundly personal play, born out of Kushner's experience as a Jew, a gay man, and the grandchild of immigrants. Indeed, his grandmother's death, which occurred just as he was beginning to work on *Millennium Approaches,* influenced the beginning of the play, since the rabbi who spoke at her funeral emphasized—as does the rabbi in the play—her essential foreignness. Kushner's early days in Louisiana in a community with only a hundred Jewish families also contributed to his own sense of being a stranger. "Had I grown up in New York, being a Jew might not have been necessarily as immediate an instructive experience, in terms of feeling marginal." And of course the most "marginalizing" experience of all—and the most crucial—is Kushner's awareness of his homosexuality: "The reason that *Angels* is the best thing I have ever written is because I decided to write about being gay. That was tremendously liberating and it made me a better writer than I was before."

Kushner's ability to write openly about homosexuality may owe something to the time at which he became a serious playwright. Unlike Tennessee Williams in the 1940s and 1950s, or Edward Albee and Joe Orton in the 1960s—playwrights who often alluded to homosexual relationships but in veiled and guarded ways—Kushner inherited a rich tradition of plays by gay writers and about openly gay characters. Charles Ludlam's multifaceted career as an actor, director, adaptor, and drag performer with the Ridiculous Theatrical Company was influential. Plays that radically altered the theatrical portrayal of homosexuals and the gay experience include Mart Crowley's *The Boys in the Band* (1968), Harvey Fierstein's *Torch Song Trilogy* (1983) as well as his book for the hit musical *La Cage aux Folles* (1983), and Larry Kramer's *The Normal Heart* (1985). In these and other contemporary plays by gay writers about the gay experience, homosexuals are no longer presented as shameful and ashamed figures, but as complex human beings. Moreover, AIDS, once seen as a "gay plague," had by the early 1990s been recognized as a disease that could attack anyone.

Still, what makes *Angels in America* so remarkable is not simply Kushner's deep personal commitment but the extraordinary theatrical imagination that animates this "gay fantasia on national themes." When Kushner began working on it, he knew "it was going to be a play about AIDS, gay men, Reagan, and Roy Cohn, and Mormons, and angels"—and as the list expands, from the expected (AIDS and gay men) to the unexpected (Mormons and angels), the play moves from realism to surrealism. In one scene, for example, we watch Roy Cohn offer a job to Joe Pitt at the same time that he is holding a series of phone conversations that display his profane power-broking; in the following scene, Harper Pitt, Joe's wife, muses to herself, "I'd like to go traveling," whereupon Mr. Lies, a travel agent, suddenly appears and just as suddenly disappears. Later, Harper and Prior Walter appear in each other's dream, and the stage direction admits: *"It is bewildering."* Later still, ghosts mingle with "real" characters, as two ancestors of Prior Walter (prior Priors), each from a time associated with major outbreaks of plague, appear to the contemporary Prior, dying of the twentieth-century "plague"—AIDS. And near the end of the play, the ghost of Ethel Rosenberg, executed in 1953 for procuring atomic research for the Russians, appears to Roy Cohn, through whose intervention her execution was assured. Such interplay between characters who are alive and characters who are ghostly or figures in a dream is a counterpoint to the play's focus on a series of couples—especially the homosexual pair, Louis and Prior, and the seemingly straight couple, Joe and Harper. In each case, homosexuality—whether acknowledged and painful, as with Louis's inability to stay with the dying Prior, or hidden, as with Joe's increasingly futile attempts to deny who he is—is central to the relationship. And each relationship blends the personal and the cultural/historical, asking us to consider people as both individual and representative.

The multiple casting called for by the play—there are twenty characters but only eight actors—reinforces the play's thematic and theatrical concern with the ambiguous nature of gender and identity. So it is especially appropriate that the actress who plays the Angel, the play's most "unrealistic" character, performs a variety of roles, including a homeless woman in the South Bronx and a nurse, while the actress who plays Hannah, Joe's mother, appears as a series of male characters, including an Orthodox rabbi. Such overlapping of roles and disregard for conventional gender distinctions force audiences to consider their own inclinations to label and restrict people in one way or another. Indeed, the very sweep of the play—embracing characters from the Middle Ages to the present, figures both real and mythical, moments of clinically painful reality and moments of hallucination—is immensely liberating. Kushner calls the play a "fantasia," a term referring to a musical composition that brings together a number of themes and motifs, but is without a fixed form. This is appropriate, as *Millennium Approaches* and its sequel, *Perestroika* (meaning "restructuring"), are free-form pieces, held together by characters and ideas rather than by story.

The performance history of these two extraordinary plays has been as long and complex as the plays themselves, for both works went through a series of workshops and productions over a three-year period. When *Millennium Approaches* opened in New York in 1993, it had already been produced in London and Los Angeles, and was one of the season's most highly anticipated openings. Nominated for nine Tony Awards, more nominations than any nonmusical play had ever received, it was an event that reflected American society's interest in and acceptance of controversial, challenging drama. Stefan Kanfer is but one of many reviewers who saw the play as genuinely challenging the fundamental conventions of New York theater (his review is reprinted following the text). George C. Wolfe's production for the New York Public Theater was both praised and criticized, as was Ron Leibman's blistering Roy Cohn (see Figure 1). Leibman recognized, as did many critics, the demonic side to Kushner's characterization of Roy Cohn, but pointed to the complexity of the character when he called him "a man struggling to stay alive" and "a multicolored villain." The play's magical and spiritual dimension is evident in its final moments when the Angel appears and Prior Walter, with defensive mockery, reacts with "*Very* Steven Spielberg" (see Figure 2). Kushner's prefatory note speaks of such a moment as "wonderful *theatrical* illusion—which means it's OK if the wires show, and maybe it's good that they do." But, he adds, "the magic should at the same time be thoroughly amazing." So the special challenge of producing this long and amazing play is to find both its reality and magic.

ANGELS IN AMERICA
A Gay Fantasia on National Themes
Part One:
Millennium Approaches

BY TONY KUSHNER

CHARACTERS

ROY M. COHN, *a successful New York lawyer and unofficial power broker.*

JOSEPH PORTER PITT, *chief clerk for Justice Theodore Wilson of the Federal Court of Appeals, Second Circuit.*

HARPER AMATY PITT, JOE's *wife, an agoraphobic with a mild Valium addiction.*

LOUIS IRONSON, *a word processor working for the Second Circuit Court of Appeals.*

PRIOR WALTER, LOUIS's *boyfriend. Occasionally works as a club designer or caterer, otherwise lives very modestly but with great style off a small trust fund.*

HANNAH PORTER PITT, JOE's *mother, currently residing in Salt Lake City, living off her deceased husband's army pension.*

BELIZE, *a former drag queen and former lover of* PRIOR's. *A registered nurse.* BELIZE's *name was originally Norman Arriaga;* BELIZE *is a drag name that stuck.*

THE ANGEL, *four divine emanations, Fluor, Phosphor, Lumen and Candle; manifest in One: the Continental Principality of America. She has magnificent steel-gray wings.*

RABBI ISIDOR CHEMELWITZ, *an orthodox Jewish rabbi, played by the actor playing* HANNAH.

MR. LIES, HARPER's *imaginary friend, a travel agent, who in style of dress and speech suggests a jazz musician; he always wears a large lapel badge emblazoned "IOTA" (The International Order of Travel Agents). He is played by the actor playing* BELIZE.

THE MAN IN THE PARK, *played by the actor playing* PRIOR.

THE VOICE, *the voice of* THE ANGEL.

HENRY, ROY's *doctor, played by the actor playing* [text obscured]

...yed by the actor playing THE ANGEL.

... Reagan Administration Justice ...nan, played by the actor playing

...ER, a Salt Lake City real-estate ...d by the actor playing THE ANGEL.

PRIOR 1, *the ghost of a dead Prior Walter from the 13th century, played by the actor playing* JOE. *He is a blunt, gloomy medieval farmer with a guttural Yorkshire accent.*

PRIOR 2, *the ghost of a dead Prior Walter from the 17th century, played by the actor playing* ROY. *He is a Londoner, sophisticated, with a High British accent.*

THE ESKIMO, *played by the actor playing* JOE.

THE WOMAN IN THE SOUTH BRONX, *played by the actor playing* THE ANGEL.

ETHEL ROSENBERG, *played by the actor playing* HANNAH.

PLAYWRIGHT'S NOTES

A DISCLAIMER: Roy M. Cohn,° the character, is based on the late Roy M. Cohn (1927–1986), who was all too real; for the most part the acts attributed to the character Roy, such as his illegal conferences with Judge Kaufmann during the trial of Ethel Rosenberg,° are to be found in the historical record. But this Roy is a work of dramatic fiction; his words are my invention, and liberties have been taken.

A NOTE ABOUT THE STAGING: The play benefits from a pared-down style of presentation, with minimal scenery and scene shifts done rapidly (no blackouts!), employing the cast as well as stagehands—which makes for an actor-driven event, as this must

---

Roy M. Cohn, American lawyer, who served as chief counsel to Senator Joseph McCarthy's committee investigating communist sympathizers in the government; he became nationally visible in 1954 during the Army-McCarthy hearings, brought on in part by Cohn's efforts to secure preferential treatment in the army for his close friend David Schine. He died, probably of AIDS, in 1986. **Ethel Rosenberg,** Ethel and Julius Rosenberg were arrested for wartime espionage and charged with passing information about atomic research to the Soviet Union; she and her husband were executed in 1953.

be. The moments of magic—the appearance and disappearance of Mr. Lies and the ghosts, the Book hallucination, and the ending—are to be fully realized, as bits of wonderful *theatrical* illusion—which means it's OK if the wires show, and maybe it's good that they do, but the magic should at the same time be thoroughly amazing.

In a murderous time
  the heart breaks and breaks
    and lives by breaking.
          —Stanley Kunitz
          "The Testing-Tree"

ACT 1 / BAD NEWS

October–November 1985

ACT 1 / SCENE 1

(The last days of October. RABBI ISIDOR CHEMELWITZ *alone onstage with a small coffin. It is a rough pine box with two wooden pegs, one at the foot and one at the head, holding the lid in place. A prayer shawl embroidered with a Star of David is draped over the lid, and by the head a yarzheit candle is burning.)*

RABBI ISIDOR CHEMELWITZ *(He speaks sonorously, with a heavy Eastern European accent, unapologetically consulting a sheet of notes for the family names)*: Hello and good morning. I am Rabbi Isidor Chemelwitz of the Bronx Home for Aged Hebrews. We are here this morning to pay respects at the passing of Sarah Ironson, devoted wife of Benjamin Ironson, also deceased, loving and caring mother of her sons Morris, Abraham, and Samuel, and her daughters Esther and Rachel; beloved grandmother of Max, Mark, Louis, Lisa, Maria . . . uh . . . Lesley, Angela, Doris, Luke and Eric. *(Looks more closely at paper)* Eric? This is a Jewish name? *(Shrugs)* Eric. A large and loving family. We assemble that we may mourn collectively this good and righteous woman.
    (He looks at the coffin)
    This woman. I did not know this woman. I cannot accurately describe her attributes, nor do justice to her dimensions. She was. . . . Well, in the Bronx Home of Aged Hebrews are many like this, the old, and to many I speak but not to be frank with this one. She preferred silence. So I do not know her and yet I know her. She was . . .
    (He touches the coffin)
    . . . not a person but a whole kind of person, the ones who crossed the ocean, who brought with us to America the villages of Russia and Lithuania—and how we struggled, and how we fought, for the family, for the Jewish home, so that you would not grow up *here*, in this strange place, in the melting pot where nothing melted. Descendants of this immigrant woman, you do not grow up in America, you and your children and their children with the goyische° names. You do not live in America. No such place exists. Your clay is the clay of some Litvak shtetl,° your air the air of the steppes—because she carried the old world on her back across the ocean, in a boat, and she put it down on Grand Concourse Avenue, or in Flatbush, and she worked that earth into your bones, and you pass it to your children, this ancient, ancient culture and home.
    (Little pause)
    You can never make that crossing that she made, for such Great Voyages in this world do not any more exist. But every day of your lives the miles that voyage between that place and this one you cross. Every day. You understand me? In you that journey is.
    So . . .
    She was the last of the Mohicans, this one was. Pretty soon . . . all the old will be dead.

ACT 1 / SCENE 2

(Same day. ROY *and* JOE *in* ROY*'s office.* ROY *at an impressive desk, bare except for a very elaborate phone system, rows and rows of flashing buttons which bleep and beep and whistle incessantly, making chaotic music underneath* ROY*'s conversations.* JOE *is sitting, waiting.* ROY *conducts business with great energy, impatience and sensual abandon: gesticulating, shouting, cajoling, crooning, playing the phone, receiver and hold button with virtuosity and love.)*

ROY *(Hitting a button)*: Hold. *(To* JOE*)* I wish I was an octopus, a fucking octopus. Eight loving arms and all those suckers. Know what I mean?
JOE: No, I . . .
ROY *(Gesturing to a deli platter of little sandwiches on his desk)*: You want lunch?
JOE: No, that's OK really I just . . .
ROY *(Hitting a button)*: Ailene? Roy Cohn. Now what

---

    goyische, Yiddish for non-Jewish, especially Christia[n]
Litvak shtetl, Yiddish for Lithuanian Jewish small commun[ity]

kind of a greeting is. . . . I thought we were friends, Ai. . . . Look Mrs. Soffer you don't have to get. . . . You're upset. You're yelling. You'll aggravate your condition, you shouldn't yell, you'll pop little blood vessels in your face if you yell. . . . No that was a joke, Mrs. Soffer, I was joking. . . . I already apologized sixteen times for that, Mrs. Soffer, you . . . *(While she's fulminating,* ROY *covers the mouthpiece with his hand and talks to* JOE*)* This'll take a minute, *eat* already, what is this tasty sandwich here it's—*(He takes a bite of a sandwich)* Mmmmm, liver or some. . . . Here.

(He pitches the sandwich to JOE*, who catches it and returns it to the platter.)*

ROY *(Back to Mrs. Soffer)*: Uh huh, uh huh. . . . No, I already told you, it wasn't a vacation, it was business, Mrs. Soffer, I have clients in Haiti, Mrs. Soffer, I. . . . Listen, Ailene, YOU THINK I'M THE ONLY GODDAM LAWYER IN HISTORY EVER MISSED A COURT DATE? Don't make such a big fucking. . . . Hold. *(He hits the hold button)* You HAG!

JOE: If this is a bad time . . .

ROY: *Bad* time? This is a *good* time! *(Button)* Baby doll, get me. . . . Oh fuck, wait . . . *(Button, button)* Hello? Yah. Sorry to keep you holding, Judge Hollins, I. . . . Oh *Mrs.* Hollins, sorry dear deep voice you got. Enjoying your visit? *(Hand over mouthpiece again, to* JOE*)* She sounds like a truckdriver and he sounds like Kate Smith, very confusing. Nixon appointed him, all the geeks are Nixon appointees . . . *(To Mrs. Hollins)* Yeah yeah right good so how many tickets dear? Seven. For what, *Cats, 42nd Street,* what? No you wouldn't like *La Cage,* trust me, I know. Oh for godsake. . . . Hold. *(Button, button)* Baby doll, seven for *Cats* or something, anything hard to get, I don't give a fuck what and neither will they. *(Button; to* JOE*)* You see *La Cage?*

JOE: No, I . . .

ROY: Fabulous. Best thing on Broadway. Maybe ever. *(Button)* Who? Aw, Jesus H. Christ, Harry, *no,* Harry, Judge John Francis Grimes, Manhattan Family Court. Do I have to do every goddam thing myself? *Touch* the bastard, Harry, and don't call me on this line again, I told you not to . . .

JOE *(Starting to get up)*: Roy, uh, should I wait outside or . . .

t. *(To Harry)* You hold. I pay you to Harry you jerk. *(Button)* Half-wit tantly *philosophical)* I see the uni-kind of sandstorm in outer space ga-hurricane velocity, but instead it's shards and splinters of glass. way? Ever have one of those days?

ROY: So how's life in Appeals? How's the Judge?

JOE: He sends his best.

ROY: He's a good man. Loyal. Not the brightest man on the bench, but he has manners. And a nice head of silver hair.

JOE: He gives me a lot of responsibility.

ROY: Yeah, like writing his decisions and signing his name.

JOE: Well . . .

ROY: He's a nice guy. And you cover admirably.

JOE: Well, thanks, Roy, I . . .

ROY *(Button)*: Yah? Who is *this?* Well who the fuck are *you?* Hold—*(Button)* Harry? Eighty-seven grand, something like that. Fuck him. Eat me. New Jersey, chain of porno film stores in, uh, Weehawken. That's—Harry, that's the beauty of the law. *(Button)* So, baby doll, what? *Cats?* Bleah. *(Button) Cats!* It's about cats. Singing cats, you'll love it. Eight o'clock, the theatre's always at eight. *(Button)* Fucking tourists. *(Button, then to* JOE*)* Oh live a little, Joe, *eat* something for Christ sake—

JOE: Um, Roy, could you . . .

ROY: What? *(To Harry)* Hold a minute. *(Button)* Mrs. Soffer? Mrs. . . . *(Button)* God-fucking-dammit to hell, where is . . .

JOE *(Overlapping)*: Roy, I'd really appreciate it if . . .

ROY *(Overlapping)*: Well she was here a minute ago, baby doll, see if . . .

(The phone starts making three different beeping sounds, all at once.)

ROY *(Smashing buttons)*: Jesus fuck this goddam thing . . .

JOE *(Overlapping)*: I really wish you wouldn't . . .

ROY *(Overlapping)*: Baby doll? Ring the *Post* get me Suzy see if . . .

(The phone starts whistling loudly.)

ROY: CHRIST!

JOE: *Roy.*

ROY *(Into receiver)*: Hold. *(Button; to* JOE*) What?*

JOE: Could you please not take the Lord's name in vain?

(Pause)

I'm sorry. But please. At least while I'm . . .

ROY *(Laughs, then)*: Right. Sorry. Fuck.

Only in America. *(Punches a button)* Baby doll, tell 'em all to fuck off. Tell 'em I died. You handle Mrs. Soffer. Tell her it's on the way. Tell her I'm schtupping° the judge. I'll call her back. I *will* call her. I *know* how much I borrowed. She's got four hundred times that stuffed up her. . . . Yeah, tell her I said that. *(Button. The phone is silent)*

So, Joe.

JOE: I'm sorry Roy, I just . . .

---

schtupping, Yiddish slang for having sexual intercourse.

ROY: No no no no, principles count, I respect principles, I'm not religious but I like God and God likes me. Baptist, Catholic?

JOE: Mormon.

ROY: Mormon. Delectable. Absolutely. Only in America. So, Joe. Whattya think?

JOE: It's . . . well . . .

ROY: Crazy life.

JOE: Chaotic.

ROY: Well but God bless chaos. Right?

JOE: Ummm . . .

ROY: Huh. Mormons. I knew Mormons, in, um, Nevada.

JOE: Utah, mostly.

ROY: No, these Mormons were in Vegas.

So. So, how'd you like to go to Washington and work for the Justice Department?

JOE: Sorry?

ROY: How'd you like to go to Washington and work for the Justice Department? All I gotta do is pick up the phone, talk to Ed, and you're in.

JOE: In . . . what, exactly?

ROY: Associate Assistant Something Big. Internal Affairs, heart of the woods, something nice with clout.

JOE: Ed . . . ?

ROY: Meese.° The Attorney General.

JOE: Oh.

ROY: I just have to pick up the phone . . .

JOE: I have to think.

ROY: Of course.

(Pause)

It's a great time to be in Washington, Joe.

JOE: Roy, it's incredibly exciting . . .

ROY: And it would mean something to me. You understand?

(Little pause.)

JOE: I . . . can't say how much I appreciate this Roy, I'm sort of . . . well, stunned, I mean. . . . Thanks, Roy. But I have to give it some thought. I have to ask my wife.

ROY: Your wife. Of course.

JOE: But I really appreciate . . .

ROY: Of course. Talk to your wife.

ACT 1 / SCENE 3

(Later that day. HARPER *at home, alone. She is listening to the radio and talking to herself, as she often does. She speaks to the audience.)*

HARPER: People who are lonely, people left alone, sit talking nonsense to the air, imagining . . . beautiful systems dying, old fixed orders spiraling apart . . .

Meese, Ed Meese, attorney general during President Reagan's administration.

When you look at the ozone layer, from outside, from a spaceship, it looks like a pale blue halo, a gentle, shimmering aureole encircling the atmosphere encircling the earth. Thirty miles above our heads, a thin layer of three-atom oxygen molecules, product of photosynthesis, which explains the fussy vegetable preference for visible light, its rejection of darker rays and emanations. Danger from without. It's a kind of gift, from God, the crowning touch to the creation of the world: guardian angels, hands linked, make a spherical net, a blue-green nesting orb, a shell of safety for life itself. But everywhere, things are collapsing, lies surfacing, systems of defense giving way. . . . This is why, Joe, this is why I shouldn't be left alone.

(Little pause)

I'd like to go traveling. Leave you behind to worry. I'll send postcards with strange stamps and tantalizing messages on the back. "Later maybe." "Nevermore . . ."

*(*MR. LIES, *a travel agent, appears.)*

HARPER: Oh! You startled me!

MR. LIES: Cash, check or credit card?

HARPER: I remember you. You're from Salt Lake. You sold us the plane tickets when we flew here. What are you doing in Brooklyn?

MR. LIES: You said you wanted to travel . . .

HARPER: And here you are. How thoughtful.

MR. LIES: Mr. Lies. Of the International Order of Travel Agents. We mobilize the globe, we set people adrift, we stir the populace and send nomads eddying across the planet. We are adepts of motion, acolytes of the flux. Cash, check or credit card. Name your destination.

HARPER: Antarctica, maybe. I want to see the hole in the ozone. I heard on the radio . . .

MR. LIES *(He has a computer terminal in his briefcase)*: I can arrange a guided tour. Now?

HARPER: Soon. Maybe soon. I'm not safe here you see. Things aren't right with me. Weird stuff happens . . .

MR. LIES: Like?

HARPER: Well, like you, for instance. Just appearing. Or last week . . . well never mind.

People are like planets, you need a thick skin. Things get to me, Joe stays away and now. . . . Well look. My dreams are talking back to me.

MR. LIES: It's the price of rootlessness. Motion sickness. The only cure: to keep moving.

HARPER: I'm undecided. I feel . . . that something's going to give. It's 1985. Fifteen years till the third millennium. Maybe Christ will come again. Maybe seeds will be planted, maybe there'll be harvests then, maybe early figs to eat, maybe new life, maybe fresh blood, maybe companionship and love and protection, safety from what's outside, maybe the door will hold, or maybe . . . maybe the troubles will come, and the end will come, and the sky will collapse and there will be terrible rains and showers of poison light, or maybe my life is really fine, maybe Joe loves me and I'm only crazy thinking otherwise, or maybe not, maybe it's even worse than I know, maybe . . . I want to know, maybe I don't. The suspense, Mr. Lies, it's killing me.

MR. LIES: I suggest a vacation.

HARPER (*Hearing something*): That was the elevator. Oh God, I should fix myself up, I. . . . You have to go, you shouldn't be here . . . you aren't even real.

MR. LIES: Call me when you decide . . .

HARPER: Go!

(*The* TRAVEL AGENT *vanishes as* JOE *enters.*)

JOE: Buddy?
     Buddy? Sorry I'm late. I was just . . . out. Walking. Are you mad?

HARPER: I got a little anxious.

JOE: Buddy kiss.

(*They kiss.*)

JOE: Nothing to get anxious about.
     So. So how'd you like to move to Washington?

ACT 1 / SCENE 4

(*Same day.* LOUIS *and* PRIOR *outside the funeral home, sitting on a bench, both dressed in funereal finery, talking. The funeral service for Sarah Ironson has just concluded and* LOUIS *is about to leave for the cemetery.*)

LOUIS: My grandmother actually saw Emma Goldman° speak. In Yiddish. But all Grandma could remember was that she spoke well and wore a hat.
     What a weird service. That rabbi . . .

PRIOR: A definite find. Get his number when you go to the graveyard. I want him to bury me.

LOUIS: Better head out there. Everyone gets to put dirt on the coffin once it's lowered in.

PRIOR: Oooh. Cemetery fun. Don't want to miss that.

LOUIS: It's an old Jewish custom to express love. Here, Grandma, have a shovelful. Latecomers run the risk of finding the grave completely filled.
     She was pretty crazy. She was up there in that home for ten years, talking to herself. I never visited. She looked too much like my mother.

PRIOR (*Hugs him*): Poor Louis. I'm sorry your grandma is dead.

LOUIS: Tiny little coffin, huh?
     Sorry I didn't introduce you to. . . . I always get so closety at these family things.

PRIOR: Butch. You get butch. (*Imitating*) "Hi Cousin Doris, you don't remember me I'm Lou, Rachel's boy." Lou, not Louis, because if you say Louis they'll hear the sibilant S.

LOUIS: I don't have a . . .

PRIOR: I don't blame you, hiding. Bloodlines. Jewish curses are the worst. I personally would dissolve if anyone ever looked me in the eye and said "Feh." Fortunately WASPs don't say "Feh." Oh and by the way, darling, cousin Doris is a dyke.

LOUIS: No.
     Really?

PRIOR: You don't notice anything. If I hadn't spent the last four years fellating you I'd swear you were straight.

LOUIS: You're in a pissy mood. Cat still missing?

(*Little pause.*)

PRIOR: Not a furball in sight. It's your fault.

LOUIS: It is?

PRIOR: I warned you, Louis. Names are important. Call an animal "Little Sheba"° and you can't expect it to stick around. Besides, it's a dog's name.

LOUIS: I wanted a dog in the first place, not a cat. He sprayed my books.

PRIOR: He was a female cat.

LOUIS: Cats are stupid, high-strung predators. Babylonians sealed them up in bricks. Dogs have brains.

PRIOR: Cats have intuition.

LOUIS: A sharp dog is as smart as a really dull two-year-old child.

PRIOR: Cats know when something's wrong.

LOUIS: Only if you stop feeding them.

PRIOR: They know. That's why Sheba left, because she knew.

LOUIS: Knew what?

(*Pause.*)

PRIOR: I did my best Shirley Booth this morning, floppy slippers, housecoat, curlers, can of Little Friskies; "Come back, Little Sheba, come back. . . ." To no avail. Le chat, elle ne reviendra jamais, jamais . . .
     (*He removes his jacket, rolls up his sleeve, shows* LOUIS *a dark-purple spot on the underside of his arm near the shoulder*)
     See.

LOUIS: That's just a burst blood vessel.

PRIOR: Not according to the best medical authorities.

LOUIS: What?
     (*Pause*)
     Tell me.

Emma Goldman, Goldman (1869–1940) immigrated to the United States from Lithuania and was a well-known early feminist and anarchist.

Little Sheba, William Inge's play *Come Back, Little Sheba* was produced in 1950 and became a film in 1953; both play and film starred Shirley Booth.

PRIOR: K.S., baby. Lesion number one. Lookit. The wine-dark kiss of the angel of death.

LOUIS (*Very softly, holding* PRIOR*'s arm*): Oh please . . .

PRIOR: I'm a lesionnaire. The Foreign Lesion. The American Lesion. Lesionnaire's disease.

LOUIS: Stop.

PRIOR: My troubles are lesion.

LOUIS: Will you *stop*.

PRIOR: Don't you think I'm handling this well?
     I'm going to die.

LOUIS: Bullshit.

PRIOR: Let go of my arm.

LOUIS: No.

PRIOR: Let go.

LOUIS (*Grabbing* PRIOR, *embracing him ferociously*): No.

PRIOR: I can't find a way to spare you baby. No wall like the wall of hard scientific fact. K.S. Wham. Bang your head on that.

LOUIS: Fuck you. (*Letting go*) Fuck you fuck you fuck you.

PRIOR: Now that's what I like to hear. A mature reaction.
     Let's go see if the cat's come home.
     Louis?

LOUIS: When did you find this?

PRIOR: I couldn't tell you.

LOUIS: Why?

PRIOR: I was scared, Lou.

LOUIS: Of what?

PRIOR: That you'll leave me.

LOUIS: Oh.

(*Little pause.*)

PRIOR: Bad timing, funeral and all, but I figured as long as we're on the subject of death . . .

LOUIS: I have to go bury my grandma.

PRIOR: Lou?
     (*Pause*)
     Then you'll come home?

LOUIS: Then I'll come home.

ACT 1 / SCENE 5

(*Same day, later on. Split scene:* JOE *and* HARPER *at home;* LOUIS *at the cemetery with* RABBI ISIDOR CHEMELWITZ *and the little coffin.*)

HARPER: Washington?

JOE: It's an incredible honor, buddy, and . . .

HARPER: I have to think.

JOE: Of course.

HARPER: Say no.

JOE: You said you were going to think about it.

HARPER: I don't want to move to Washington.

JOE: Well I do.

HARPER: It's a giant cemetery, huge white graves and mausoleums everywhere.

JOE: We could live in Maryland. Or Georgetown.

HARPER: We're happy here.

JOE: That's not really true, buddy, we . . .

HARPER: Well happy enough! Pretend-happy. That's better than nothing.

JOE: It's time to make some changes, Harper.

HARPER: No changes. Why?

JOE: I've been chief clerk for four years. I make twenty-nine thousand dollars a year. That's ridiculous. I graduated fourth in my class and I make less than anyone I know. And I'm . . . I'm tired of being a clerk, I want to go where something good is happening.

HARPER: Nothing good happens in Washington. We'll forget church teachings and buy furniture at . . . at *Conran's* and become yuppies. I have too much to do here.

JOE: Like what?

HARPER: I *do* have things . . .

JOE: What things?

HARPER: I have to finish painting the bedroom.

JOE: You've been painting in there for over a year.

HARPER: I know, I. . . . It just isn't done because I never get time to finish it.

JOE: Oh that's . . . that doesn't make sense. You have all the time in the world. You could finish it when I'm at work.

HARPER: I'm afraid to go in there alone.

JOE: Afraid of what?

HARPER: I heard someone in there. Metal scraping on the wall. A man with a knife, maybe.

JOE: There's no one in the bedroom, Harper.

HARPER: Not now.

JOE: Not this morning either.

HARPER: How do you know? You were at work this morning. There's something creepy about this place. Remember *Rosemary's Baby*?°

JOE: *Rosemary's Baby*?

HARPER: Our apartment looks like that one. Wasn't that apartment in Brooklyn?

JOE: No, it was . . .

HARPER: Well, it looked like this. It did.

JOE: Then let's move.

HARPER: Georgetown's worse. *The Exorcist*° was in Georgetown.

JOE: The devil, everywhere you turn, huh, buddy.

HARPER: Yeah. Everywhere.

JOE: How many pills today, buddy?

HARPER: None. One. Three. Only three.

LOUIS (*Pointing at the coffin*): Why are there just two little wooden pegs holding the lid down?

Rosemary's Baby, 1968 film by Roman Polanski about a young couple involved with black magic. *The Exorcist*, 1971 novel by William Peter Blatty and 1973 film.

RABBI ISIDOR CHEMELWITZ: So she can get out easier if she wants to.

LOUIS: I hope she stays put.

I pretended for years that she was already dead. When they called to say she had died it was a surprise. I abandoned her.

RABBI ISIDOR CHEMELWITZ: "Sharfer vi di tson fun a shlang iz an umdankbar kind!"

LOUIS: I don't speak Yiddish.

RABBI ISIDOR CHEMELWITZ: Sharper than the serpent's tooth is the ingratitude of children. Shakespeare. *Kenig Lear.*°

LOUIS: Rabbi, what does the Holy Writ say about someone who abandons someone he loves at a time of great need?

RABBI ISIDOR CHEMELWITZ: Why would a person do such a thing?

LOUIS: Because he has to.

Maybe because this person's sense of the world, that it will change for the better with struggle, maybe a person who has this neo-Hegelian positivist sense of constant historical progress towards happiness or perfection or something, who feels very powerful because he feels connected to these forces, moving uphill all the time . . . maybe that person can't, um, incorporate sickness into his sense of how things are supposed to go. Maybe vomit . . . and sores and disease . . . really frighten him, maybe . . . he isn't so good with death.

RABBI ISIDOR CHEMELWITZ: The Holy Scriptures have nothing to say about such a person.

LOUIS: Rabbi, I'm afraid of the crimes I may commit.

RABBI ISIDOR CHEMELWITZ: Please, mister. I'm a sick old rabbi facing a long drive home to the Bronx. You want to confess, better you should find a priest.

LOUIS: But I'm not a Catholic, I'm a Jew.

RABBI ISIDOR CHEMELWITZ: Worse luck for you, bubbulah. Catholics believe in forgiveness. Jews believe in Guilt. (*He pats the coffin tenderly*)

LOUIS: You just make sure those pegs are in good and tight.

RABBI ISIDOR CHEMELWITZ: Don't worry, mister. The life she had, she'll stay put. She's better off.

JOE: Look, I know this is scary for you. But try to understand what it means to me. Will you try?

HARPER: Yes.

JOE: Good. Really try.

I think things are starting to change in the world.

HARPER: But I don't want . . .

JOE: Wait. For the good. Change for the good. Amer-

ica has rediscovered itself. Its sacred position among nations. And people aren't ashamed of that like they used to be. This is a great thing. The truth restored. Law restored. That's what President Reagan's done, Harper. He says "Truth exists and can be spoken proudly." And the country responds to him. We become better. More good. I need to be a part of that, I need something big to lift me up. I mean, six years ago the world seemed in decline, horrible, hopeless, full of unsolvable problems and crime and confusion and hunger and . . .

HARPER: But it still seems that way. More now than before. They say the ozone layer is . . .

JOE: Harper . . .

HARPER: And today out the window on Atlantic Avenue there was a schizophrenic traffic cop who was making these . . .

JOE: Stop it! I'm trying to make a point.

HARPER: So am I.

JOE: You aren't even making sense, you . . .

HARPER: My point is the world seems just as . . .

JOE: It only seems that way to you because you never go out in the world, Harper, and you have emotional problems.

HARPER: I do so get out in the world.

JOE: You don't. You stay in all day, fretting about imaginary . . .

HARPER: I get out. I do. You don't know what I do.

JOE: You don't stay in all day.

HARPER: No.

JOE: Well. . . . Yes you do.

HARPER: That's what you think.

JOE: Where do you go?

HARPER: Where do *you* go? When you walk.

(*Pause, then angrily*) And I DO NOT have emotional problems.

JOE: I'm sorry.

HARPER: And if I do have emotional problems it's from living with you. Or . . .

JOE: I'm sorry buddy, I didn't mean to . . .

HARPER: Or if you do think I do then you should never have married me. You have all these secrets and lies.

JOE: I want to be married to you, Harper.

HARPER: You shouldn't. You never should.

(*Pause*)

Hey buddy. Hey buddy.

JOE: Buddy kiss . . .

(*They kiss.*)

HARPER: I heard on the radio how to give a blowjob.

JOE: What?

HARPER: You want to try?

JOE: You really shouldn't listen to stuff like that.

HARPER: Mormons can give blowjobs.

JOE: *Harper.*

HARPER (*Imitating his tone*): *Joe.*

Kenig Lear, Yiddish for *"King Lear."* The rabbi alludes to Lear's line, "How sharper than a serpent's tooth it is / To have a thankless child" (1.4.265–66).

It was a little Jewish lady with a German accent. This is a good time. For me to make a baby.

(Little pause. JOE *turns away.)*

HARPER: Then they went on to a program about holes in the ozone layer. Over Antarctica. Skin burns, birds go blind, icebergs melt. The world's coming to an end.

ACT 1 / SCENE 6

(First week of November. In the men's room of the offices of the Brooklyn Federal Court of Appeals; LOUIS *is crying over the sink;* JOE *enters.)*

JOE: Oh, um. . . . Morning.

LOUIS: Good morning, counselor.

JOE *(He watches* LOUIS *cry)*: Sorry, I . . . I don't know your name.

LOUIS: Don't bother. Word processor. The lowest of the low.

JOE *(Holding out hand)*: Joe Pitt. I'm with Justice Wilson . . .

LOUIS: Oh, I know that. Counselor Pitt. Chief Clerk.

JOE: Were you . . . are you OK?

LOUIS: Oh, yeah. Thanks. What a nice man.

JOE: Not so nice.

LOUIS: What?

JOE: Not so nice. Nothing. You sure you're . . .

LOUIS: Life sucks shit. Life . . . just sucks shit.

JOE: What's wrong?

LOUIS: Run in my nylons.

JOE: Sorry . . . ?

LOUIS: Forget it. Look, thanks for asking.

JOE: Well . . .

LOUIS: I mean it really is nice of you.
    (He starts crying again)
    Sorry, sorry, sick friend . . .

JOE: Oh, I'm sorry.

LOUIS: Yeah, yeah, well, that's sweet.
    Three of your colleagues have preceded you to this baleful sight and you're the first one to ask. The others just opened the door, saw me, and fled. I hope they had to pee real bad.

JOE *(Handing him a wad of toilet paper)*: They just didn't want to intrude.

LOUIS: Hah. Reaganite heartless macho asshole lawyers.

JOE: Oh, that's unfair.

LOUIS: What is? Heartless? Macho? Reaganite? Lawyer?

JOE: I voted for Reagan.

LOUIS: You did?

JOE: Twice.

LOUIS: Twice? Well, oh boy. A Gay Republican.

JOE: Excuse me?

LOUIS: Nothing.

JOE: I'm not . . .
    Forget it.

LOUIS: Republican? Not Republican? Or . . .

JOE: What?

LOUIS: What?

JOE: Not gay. I'm not gay.

LOUIS: Oh. Sorry.
    (Blows his nose loudly) It's just . . .

JOE: Yes?

LOUIS: Well, sometimes you can tell from the way a person sounds that . . . I mean you *sound* like a . . .

JOE: No I don't. Like what?

LOUIS: Like a Republican.

(Little pause. JOE *knows he's being teased;* LOUIS *knows he knows.* JOE *decides to be a little brave.)*

JOE *(Making sure no one else is around)*: Do I? Sound like a . . . ?

LOUIS: What? Like a . . . ? Republican, or. . . ? Do *I*?

JOE: Do you what?

LOUIS: Sound like a . . . ?

JOE: Like a . . . ?
    I'm . . . confused.

LOUIS: Yes.
    My name is Louis. But all my friends call me Louise. I work in Word Processing. Thanks for the toilet paper.

*(*LOUIS *offers* JOE *his hand,* JOE *reaches,* LOUIS *feints and pecks* JOE *on the cheek, then exits.)*

ACT 1 / SCENE 7

(A week later. Mutual dream scene. PRIOR *is at a fantastic makeup table, having a dream, applying the face.* HARPER *is having a pill-induced hallucination. She has these from time to time. For some reason,* PRIOR *has appeared in this one. Or* HARPER *has appeared in* PRIOR's *dream. It is bewildering.)*

PRIOR *(Alone, putting on makeup, then examining the results in the mirror; to the audience)*: "I'm ready for my closeup, Mr. DeMille."°
    One wants to move through life with elegance and grace, blossoming infrequently but with exquisite taste, and perfect timing, like a rare bloom, a zebra orchid. . . . One wants. . . . But one so seldom gets what one wants, does one? No. One does not. One gets fucked. Over. One . . . dies at thirty, robbed of . . . decades of majesty.
    Fuck this shit. Fuck this shit.
    (He almost crumbles; he pulls himself together; he studies his handiwork in the mirror)
    I look like a corpse. A corpsette. Oh my queen;

"I'm ready for my closeup, Mr. DeMille," famous line from the 1950 film *Sunset Boulevard,* spoken by Gloria Swanson as the aging ex-star Norma Desmond.

you know you've hit rock-bottom when even drag is a drag.

(HARPER *appears.*)

HARPER: Are you. . . . Who are you?

PRIOR: Who are you?

HARPER: What are you doing in my hallucination?

PRIOR: I'm not in your hallucination. You're in my dream.

HARPER: You're wearing makeup.

PRIOR: So are you.

HARPER: But you're a man.

PRIOR (*Feigning dismay, shock, he mimes slashing his throat with his lipstick and dies, fabulously tragic. Then*): The hands and feet give it away.

HARPER: There must be some mistake here. I don't recognize you. You're not. . . . Are you my . . . some sort of imaginary friend?

PRIOR: No. Aren't you too old to have imaginary friends?

HARPER: I have emotional problems. I took too many pills. Why are you wearing makeup?

PRIOR: I was in the process of applying the face, trying to make myself feel better—I swiped the new fall colors at the Clinique counter at Macy's. (*Showing her*)

HARPER: You stole these?

PRIOR: I was out of cash; it was an emotional emergency!

HARPER: Joe will be so angry. I promised him. No more pills.

PRIOR: These pills you keep alluding to?

HARPER: Valium. I take Valium. Lots of Valium.

PRIOR: And you're dancing as fast as you can.

HARPER: I'm not *addicted*. I don't believe in addiction, and I never . . . well, I *never* drink. And I *never* take drugs.

PRIOR: Well, smell *you*, Nancy Drew.

HARPER: Except Valium.

PRIOR: Except Valium; in wee fistfuls.

HARPER: It's terrible. Mormons are not supposed to be addicted to anything. I'm a Mormon.

PRIOR: I'm a homosexual.

HARPER: Oh! In my church we don't believe in homosexuals.

PRIOR: In my church we don't believe in Mormons.

HARPER: What church do . . . oh! (*She laughs*) I get it.

I don't understand this. If I didn't ever see you before and I don't think I did then I don't think you should be here, in this hallucination, because in my experience the mind, which is where hallucinations come from, shouldn't be able to make up anything that wasn't there to start with, that didn't enter it from experience, from the real world. Imagination can't create anything new, can it? It only recycles bits and pieces from the world and reassembles them into visions. . . . Am I making sense right now?

PRIOR: Given the circumstances, yes.

HARPER: So when we think we've escaped the unbearable ordinariness and, well, untruthfulness of our lives, it's really only the same old ordinariness and falseness rearranged into the appearance of novelty and truth. Nothing unknown is knowable. Don't you think it's depressing?

PRIOR: The limitations of the imagination?

HARPER: Yes.

PRIOR: It's something you learn after your second theme party: It's All Been Done Before.

HARPER: The world. Finite. Terribly, terribly. . . . Well. . . .

This is the most depressing hallucination I've ever had.

PRIOR: Apologies. I do try to be amusing.

HARPER: Oh, well, don't apologize, you. . . . I can't expect someone who's really sick to entertain me.

PRIOR: How on earth did you know . . .

HARPER: Oh that happens. This is the very threshold of revelation sometimes. You can see things . . . how sick you are. Do you see anything about me?

PRIOR: Yes.

HARPER: What?

PRIOR: You are amazingly unhappy.

HARPER: Oh big deal. You meet a Valium addict and you figure out she's unhappy. That doesn't count. Of course I. . . . Something else. Something surprising.

PRIOR: Something surprising.

HARPER: Yes.

PRIOR: Your husband's a homo.

(*Pause.*)

HARPER: Oh, ridiculous.
(*Pause, then very quietly*)
Really?

PRIOR (*Shrugs*): Threshold of revelation.

HARPER: Well I don't like your revelations. I don't think you intuit well at all. Joe's a very normal man, he . . .

Oh God. Oh God. He. . . . Do homos take, like, lots of long walks?

PRIOR: Yes. We do. In stretch pants with lavender coifs. I just looked at you, and there was . . .

HARPER: A sort of blue streak of recognition.

PRIOR: Yes.

HARPER: Like you knew me incredibly well.

PRIOR: Yes.

HARPER: Yes.

I have to go now, get back, something just . . . fell apart.

Oh God, I feel so sad . . .

PRIOR: I . . . I'm sorry. I usually say, "Fuck the truth," but mostly, the truth fucks you.

HARPER: I see something else about you . . .

PRIOR: Oh?

HARPER: Deep inside you, there's a part of you, the

most inner part, entirely free of disease. I can see that.

PRIOR: Is that. . . . That isn't true.

HARPER: Threshold of revelation.

Home . . .

(She vanishes.)

PRIOR: People come and go so quickly here . . .

(To himself in the mirror) I don't think there's any uninfected part of me. My heart is pumping polluted blood. I feel dirty.

(He begins to wipe makeup off with his hands, smearing it around. A large gray feather falls from up above. PRIOR stops smearing the makeup and looks at the feather. He goes to it and picks it up.)

A VOICE *(It is an incredibly beautiful voice)*: Look up!

PRIOR *(Looking up, not seeing anyone)*: Hello?

A VOICE: Look up!

PRIOR: Who is that?

A VOICE: Prepare the way!

PRIOR: I don't see any . . .

(There is a dramatic change in lighting, from above.)

A VOICE:

Look up, look up,
prepare the way
the infinite descent
A breath in air
floating down
Glory to . . .

(Silence.)

PRIOR: Hello? Is that it? Helloooo!

What the fuck . . . ? *(He holds himself)*

Poor me. Poor poor me. Why me? Why poor poor me? Oh I don't feel good right now. I really don't.

ACT 1 / SCENE 8

(That night. Split scene: HARPER and JOE at home; PRIOR and LOUIS in bed.)

HARPER: Where were you?

JOE: Out.

HARPER: Where?

JOE: Just out. Thinking.

HARPER: It's late.

JOE: I had a lot to think about.

HARPER: I burned dinner.

JOE: Sorry.

HARPER: Not my dinner. My dinner was fine. Your dinner. I put it back in the oven and turned everything up as high as it could go and I watched till it burned black. It's still hot. Very hot. Want it?

JOE: You didn't have to do that.

HARPER: I know. It just seemed like the kind of thing a mentally deranged sex-starved pill-popping housewife would do.

JOE: Uh huh.

HARPER: So I did it. Who knows anymore what I have to do?

JOE: How many pills?

HARPER: A bunch. Don't change the subject.

JOE: I won't talk to you when you . . .

HARPER: No. No. Don't do that! I'm . . . I'm fine, pills are not the problem, not our problem, I WANT TO KNOW WHERE YOU'VE BEEN! I WANT TO KNOW WHAT'S GOING ON!

JOE: Going on with what? The job?

HARPER: Not the job.

JOE: I said I need more time.

HARPER: Not the job!

JOE: Mr. Cohn, I talked to him on the phone, he said I had to hurry . . .

HARPER: Not the . . .

JOE: But I can't get you to talk sensibly about anything so . . .

HARPER: SHUT UP!

JOE: Then what?

HARPER: Stick to the subject.

JOE: I don't know what that is. You have something you want to ask me? Ask me. Go.

HARPER: I . . . can't. I'm scared of you.

JOE: I'm tired, I'm going to bed.

HARPER: Tell me without making me ask. Please.

JOE: This is crazy, I'm not . . .

HARPER: When you come through the door at night your face is never exactly the way I remembered it. I get surprised by something . . . mean and hard about the way you look. Even the weight of you in the bed at night, the way you breathe in your sleep seems unfamiliar.

You terrify me.

JOE *(Cold)*: I know who you are.

HARPER: Yes. I'm the enemy. That's easy. That doesn't change.

You think you're the only one who hates sex; I do; I hate it with you; I do. I dream that you batter away at me till all my joints come apart, like wax, and I fall into pieces. It's like a punishment. It was wrong of me to marry you. I knew you . . . *(She stops herself)* It's a sin, and it's killing us both.

JOE: I can always tell when you've taken pills because it makes you red-faced and sweaty and frankly that's very often why I don't want to . . .

HARPER: Because . . .

JOE: Well, you aren't pretty. Not like this.

HARPER: I have something to ask you.

JOE: Then ASK! ASK! What in hell are you . . .

HARPER: Are you a homo?

(Pause)

Are you? If you try to walk out right now I'll put your dinner back in the oven and turn it up so high the whole building will fill with smoke and everyone in it will asphyxiate. So help me God I will.

Now answer the question.

JOE: What if I . . .

(Small pause.)

HARPER: Then tell me, please. And we'll see.

JOE: No. I'm not.

I don't see what difference it makes.

LOUIS: Jews don't have any clear textual guide to the afterlife; even that it exists. I don't think much about it. I see it as a perpetual rainy Thursday afternoon in March. Dead leaves.

PRIOR: Eeeugh. Very Greco-Roman.

LOUIS: Well for us it's not the verdict that counts, it's the act of judgment. That's why I could never be a lawyer. In court all that matters is the verdict.

PRIOR: You could never be a lawyer because you are oversexed. You're too distracted.

LOUIS: Not distracted; *ab*stracted. I'm trying to make a point:

PRIOR: Namely:

LOUIS: It's the judge in his or her chambers, weighing, books open, pondering the evidence, ranging freely over categories: good, evil, innocent, guilty; the judge in the chamber of circumspection, not the judge on the bench with the gavel. The shaping of the law, not its execution.

PRIOR: The point, dear, the point . . .

LOUIS: That it should be the questions and shape of a life, its total complexity gathered, arranged and considered, which matters in the end, not some stamp of salvation or damnation which disperses all the complexity in some unsatisfying little decision—the balancing of the scales . . .

PRIOR: I like this; very zen; it's . . . reassuringly incomprehensible and useless. We who are about to die thank you.

LOUIS: You are not about to die.

PRIOR: It's not going well, really . . . two new lesions. My leg hurts. There's protein in my urine, the doctor says, but who knows what the fuck that portends. Anyway it shouldn't be there, the protein. My butt is chapped from diarrhea and yesterday I shat blood.

LOUIS: I really hate this. You don't tell me . . .

PRIOR: You get too upset, I wind up comforting you. It's easier . . .

LOUIS: Oh thanks.

PRIOR: If it's bad I'll tell you.

LOUIS: Shitting blood sounds bad to me.

PRIOR: And I'm telling you.

LOUIS: And I'm handling it.

PRIOR: Tell me some more about justice.

LOUIS: I *am* handling it.

PRIOR: Well Louis you win Trooper of the Month.

(LOUIS starts to cry.)

PRIOR: I take it back. You aren't Trooper of the Month. This isn't working . . .

Tell me some more about justice.

LOUIS: You are not about to die.

PRIOR: Justice . . .

LOUIS: . . . is an immensity, a confusing vastness. Justice is God.

Prior?

PRIOR: Hmmm?

LOUIS: You love me.

PRIOR: Yes.

LOUIS: What if I walked out on this? Would you hate me forever?

(PRIOR kisses LOUIS on the forehead.)

PRIOR: Yes.

JOE: I think we ought to pray. Ask God for help. Ask him together . . .

HARPER: God won't talk to me. I have to make up people to talk to me.

JOE: You have to keep asking.

HARPER: I forgot the question.

Oh yeah. God, is my husband a . . .

JOE *(Scary)*: Stop it. Stop it. I'm warning you.

Does it make any difference? That I might be one thing deep within, no matter how wrong or ugly that thing is, so long as I have fought, with everything I have, to kill it. What do you want from me? What do you want from me, Harper? More than that? For God's sake, there's nothing left, I'm a shell. There's nothing left to kill.

As long as my behavior is what I know it has to be. Decent. Correct. That alone in the eyes of God.

HARPER: No, no, not that, that's Utah talk, Mormon talk, I hate it, Joe, tell me, say it . . .

JOE: All I will say is that I am a very good man who has worked very hard to become good and you want to destroy that. You want to destroy me, but I am not going to let you do that.

(Pause.)

HARPER: I'm going to have a baby.

JOE: Liar.

HARPER: You liar.

A baby born addicted to pills. A baby who does not dream but who hallucinates, who stares up at us with big mirror eyes and who does not know who we are.

(Pause.)

JOE: Are you really . . .

HARPER: No. Yes. No. Yes. Get away from me.

Now we both have a secret.

PRIOR: One of my ancestors was a ship's captain who made money bringing whale oil to Europe and returning with immigrants—Irish mostly, packed in tight, so many dollars per head. The last ship he captained foundered off the coast of Nova Scotia in a winter tempest and sank to the bottom. He went down with the ship—la Grande Geste°—but his crew took seventy women and kids in the ship's only longboat, this big, open rowboat, and when the weather got too rough, and they thought the boat was overcrowded, the crew started lifting people up and hurling them into the sea. Until they got the ballast right. They walked up and down the longboat, eyes to the waterline, and when the boat rode low in the water they'd grab the nearest passenger and throw them into the sea. The boat was leaky, see; seventy people; they arrived in Halifax with nine people on board.

LOUIS: Jesus.

PRIOR: I think about that story a lot now. People in a boat, waiting, terrified, while implacable, unsmiling men, irresistibly strong, seize . . . maybe the person next to you, maybe you, and with no warning at all, with time only for a quick intake of air you are pitched into freezing, turbulent water and salt and darkness to drown.

I like your cosmology, baby. While time is running out I find myself drawn to anything that's suspended, that lacks an ending—but it seems to me that it lets you off scot-free.

LOUIS: What do you mean?

PRIOR: No judgment, no guilt or responsibility.

LOUIS: For me.

PRIOR: For anyone. It was an editorial "you."

LOUIS: Please get better. Please.

Please don't get any sicker.

ACT 1 / SCENE 9

(Third week in November. ROY *and* HENRY, *his doctor, in* HENRY'S *office.)*

HENRY: Nobody knows what causes it. And nobody knows how to cure it. The best theory is that we blame a retrovirus, the Human Immuno-deficiency Virus. Its presence is made known to us by the useless antibodies which appear in reaction to its entrance into the bloodstream through a cut, or an orifice. The antibodies are powerless to protect the body against it. Why, we don't know. The body's immune system ceases to function. Sometimes the body even attacks itself. At

any rate it's left open to a whole horror house of infections from microbes which it usually defends against.

Like Kaposi's sarcomas. These lesions. Or your throat problem. Or the glands.

We think it may also be able to slip past the blood-brain barrier into the brain. Which is of course very bad news.

And it's fatal in we don't know what percent of people with suppressed immune responses.

(Pause.)

ROY: This is very interesting, Mr. Wizard, but why the fuck are you telling me this?

(Pause.)

HENRY: Well, I have just removed one of three lesions which biopsy results will probably tell us is a Kaposi's sarcoma lesion. And you have a pronounced swelling of glands in your neck, groin, and armpits—lymphadenopathy is another sign. And you have oral candidiasis and maybe a little more fungus under the fingernails of two digits on your right hand. So that's why . . .

ROY: This disease . . .

HENRY: Syndrome.

ROY: Whatever. It afflicts mostly homosexuals and drug addicts.

HENRY: Mostly. Hemophiliacs are also at risk.

ROY: Homosexuals and drug addicts. So why are you implying that I . . .

(Pause)

What are you implying, Henry?

HENRY: I don't . . .

ROY: I'm not a drug addict.

HENRY: Oh come on Roy.

ROY: What, what, come on Roy what? Do you think I'm a junkie, Henry, do you see tracks?

HENRY: This is absurd.

ROY: Say it.

HENRY: Say what?

ROY: Say, "Roy Cohn, you are a . . ."

HENRY: Roy.

ROY: "You are a. . . ." Go on. Not "Roy Cohn you are a drug fiend." "Roy Marcus Cohn, you are a . . ."

Go on, Henry, it starts with an "H."

HENRY: Oh I'm not going to . . .

ROY: *With an "H,"* Henry, and it isn't "Hemophiliac." Come on . . .

HENRY: What are you doing, Roy?

ROY: No, say it. I mean it. Say: "Roy Cohn, you are a homosexual."

(Pause)

And I will proceed, systematically, to destroy your reputation and your practice and your career in New York State, Henry. Which you know I can do.

---

la Grande Geste, French for "the noble act."

(Pause.)

HENRY: Roy, you have been seeing me since 1958. Apart from the facelifts I have treated you for everything from syphilis . . .

ROY: From a whore in Dallas.

HENRY: From syphilis to venereal warts. In your rectum. Which you may have gotten from a whore in Dallas, but it wasn't a female whore.

(Pause.)

ROY: So say it.

HENRY: Roy Cohn, you are . . .
   You have had sex with men, many many times, Roy, and one of them, or any number of them, has made you very sick. You have AIDS.

ROY: AIDS.
   Your problem, Henry, is that you are hung up on words, on labels, that you believe they mean what they seem to mean. AIDS. Homosexual. Gay. Lesbian. You think these are names that tell you who someone sleeps with, but they don't tell you that.

HENRY: No?

ROY: No. Like all labels they tell you one thing and one thing only: where does an individual so identified fit in the food chain, in the pecking order? Not ideology, or sexual taste, but something much simpler: clout. Not who I fuck or who fucks me, but who will pick up the phone when I call, who owes me favors. This is what a label refers to. Now to someone who does not understand this, homosexual is what I am because I have sex with men. But really this is wrong. Homosexuals are not men who sleep with other men. Homosexuals are men who in fifteen years of trying cannot get a pissant antidiscrimination bill through City Council. Homosexuals are men who know nobody and who nobody knows. Who have zero clout. Does this sound like me, Henry?

HENRY: No.

ROY: No. I have clout. A lot. I can pick up this phone, punch fifteen numbers, and you know who will be on the other end in under five minutes, Henry?

HENRY: The President.

ROY: Even better, Henry. His wife.

HENRY: I'm impressed.

ROY: I don't want you to be impressed. I want you to understand. This is not sophistry. And this is not hypocrisy. This is reality. I have sex with men. But unlike nearly every other man of whom this is true, I bring the guy I'm screwing to the White House and President Reagan smiles at us and shakes his hand. Because *what* I am is defined entirely by *who* I am. Roy Cohn is not a homosexual. Roy Cohn is a heterosexual man, Henry, who fucks around with guys.

HENRY: OK, Roy.

ROY: And what is my diagnosis, Henry?

HENRY: You have AIDS, Roy.

ROY: No, Henry, no. AIDS is what homosexuals have. I have liver cancer.

(Pause.)

HENRY: Well, whatever the fuck you have, Roy, it's very serious, and I haven't got a damn thing for you. The NIH in Bethesda has a new drug called AZT with a two-year waiting list that not even I can get you onto. So get on the phone, Roy, and dial the fifteen numbers, and tell the First Lady you need in on an experimental treatment for liver cancer, because you can call it any damn thing you want, Roy, but what it boils down to is very bad news.

ACT 2 / IN VITRO

December 1985–January 1986

ACT 2 / SCENE 1

(Night, the third week in December. PRIOR *alone on the floor of his bedroom; he is much worse.)*

PRIOR: Louis, Louis, please wake up, oh God.

*(*LOUIS *runs in.)*

PRIOR: I think something horrible is wrong with me I can't breathe . . .

LOUIS *(Starting to exit)*: I'm calling the ambulance.

PRIOR: No, wait, I . . .

LOUIS: *Wait?* Are you fucking crazy? Oh God you're on fire, your head is on fire.

PRIOR: It hurts, it hurts . . .

LOUIS: I'm calling the ambulance.

PRIOR: I don't want to go to the hospital, I don't want to go to the hospital please let me lie here, just . . .

LOUIS: No, no, God, Prior, stand up . . .

PRIOR: DON'T TOUCH MY LEG!

LOUIS: We have to . . . oh God this is so crazy.

PRIOR: I'll be OK if I just lie here Lou, really, if I can only sleep a little . . .

*(*LOUIS *exits.)*

PRIOR: Louis?
   NO! NO! Don't call, you'll send me there and I won't come back, please, please Louis I'm begging, baby, please . . .
   (Screams) LOUIS!!

LOUIS *(From off; hysterical)*: WILL YOU SHUT THE FUCK UP!

PRIOR *(Trying to stand)*: Aaaah. I have . . . to go to the bathroom. Wait. Wait, just . . . oh. Oh God. *(He shits himself)*

LOUIS *(Entering)*: Prior? They'll be here in . . .
   Oh my God.

PRIOR: I'm sorry, I'm sorry.

LOUIS: What did . . . ? What?

PRIOR: I had an accident.

(LOUIS goes to him.)

LOUIS: This is blood.

PRIOR: Maybe you shouldn't touch it . . . me. . . . I . . .
(He faints)

LOUIS *(Quietly)*: Oh help. Oh help. Oh God oh God
oh God help me I can't I can't I can't.

ACT 2 / SCENE 2

*(Same night. HARPER is sitting at home, all alone, with no
lights on. We can barely see her. JOE enters, but he doesn't
turn on the lights.)*

JOE: Why are you sitting in the dark? Turn on the light.

HARPER: *No.* I heard the sounds in the bedroom
again. I know someone was in there.

JOE: No one was.

HARPER: Maybe actually in the bed, under the covers
with a knife.
  Oh, boy. Joe. I, um, I'm thinking of going away.
By which I mean: I think I'm going off again.
You . . . you know what I mean?

JOE: Please don't. Stay. We can fix it. I pray for that.
This is my fault, but I can correct it. You have to
try too . . .

(He turns on the light. She turns it off again.)

HARPER: When you pray, what do you pray for?

JOE: I pray for God to crush me, break me up into
little pieces and start all over again.

HARPER: Oh. Please. Don't pray for that.

JOE: I had a book of Bible stories when I was a kid.
There was a picture I'd look at twenty times every
day: Jacob wrestles with the angel. I don't really
remember the story, or why the wrestling—just
the picture. Jacob is young and very strong. The
angel is . . . a beautiful man, with golden hair and
wings, of course. I still dream about it. Many
nights. I'm. . . . It's me. In that struggle. Fierce,
and unfair. The angel is not human, and it holds
nothing back, so how could anyone human win,
what kind of a fight is that? It's not just. Losing
means your soul thrown down in the dust, your
heart torn out from God's. But you can't not lose.

HARPER: In the whole entire world, you are the only
person, the only person I love or have ever loved.
And I love you terribly. Terribly. That's what's so
awfully, irreducibly real. I can make up anything
but I can't dream that away.

JOE: Are you . . . are you really going to have a baby?

HARPER: It's my time, and there's no blood. I don't
really know. I suppose it wouldn't be a great
thing. Maybe I'm just not bleeding because I take
too many pills. Maybe I'll give birth to a pill. That
would give a new meaning to pill-popping, huh?
  I think you should go to Washington. Alone.
Change, like you said.

JOE: I'm not going to leave you, Harper.

HARPER: Well maybe not. But I'm going to leave you.

ACT 2 / SCENE 3

*(One AM, the next morning. LOUIS and a nurse, EMILY,
are sitting in PRIOR's room in the hospital.)*

EMILY: He'll be all right now.

LOUIS: No he won't.

EMILY: No. I guess not. I gave him something that
makes him sleep.

LOUIS: Deep asleep?

EMILY: Orbiting the moons of Jupiter.

LOUIS: A good place to be.

EMILY: Anyplace better than here. You his . . . uh?

LOUIS: Yes. I'm his uh.

EMILY: This must be hell for you.

LOUIS: It is. Hell. The After Life. Which is not at all like
a rainy afternoon in March, by the way, Prior. A lot
more vivid than I'd expected. Dead leaves, but the
crunchy kind. Sharp, dry air. The kind of long,
luxurious dying feeling that breaks your heart.

EMILY: Yeah, well we all get to break our hearts on this
one.
  He seems like a nice guy. Cute.

LOUIS: Not like this.
  Yes, he is. Was. Whatever.

EMILY: Weird name. Prior Walter. Like, "The Walter
before this one."

LOUIS: Lots of Walters before this one. Prior is an old
old family name in an old old family. The Walters
go back to the Mayflower and beyond. Back to the
Norman Conquest. He says there's a Prior Walter
stitched into the Bayeux tapestry.

EMILY: Is that impressive?

LOUIS: Well, it's old. Very old. Which in some circles
equals impressive.

EMILY: Not in my circle. What's the name of the tapestry?

LOUIS: The Bayeux tapestry. Embroidered by La
Reine Mathilde.

EMILY: I'll tell my mother. She embroiders. Drives me
nuts.

LOUIS: Manual therapy for anxious hands.

EMILY: Maybe you should try it.

LOUIS: Mathilde stitched while William the Conqueror was off to war. She was capable of . . .
more than loyalty. Devotion.
  She waited for him, she stitched for years. And
if he had come back broken and defeated from
war, she would have loved him even more. And if
he had returned mutilated, ugly, full of infection

and horror, she would still have loved him; fed by pity, by a sharing of pain, she would love him even more, and even more, and she would never, never have prayed to God, please let him die if he can't return to me whole and healthy and able to live a normal life. . . . If he had died, she would have buried her heart with him.

So what the fuck is the matter with me?

(Little pause)

Will he sleep through the night?

EMILY: At least.

LOUIS: I'm going.

EMILY: It's one AM. Where do you have to go at . . .

LOUIS: I know what time it is. A walk. Night air, good for the. . . . The park.

EMILY: Be careful.

LOUIS: Yeah. Danger.

Tell him, if he wakes up and you're still on, tell him goodbye, tell him I had to go.

ACT 2 / SCENE 4

(An hour later. Split scene: JOE *and* ROY *in a fancy [straight] bar;* LOUIS *and a* MAN IN THE RAMBLES *in Central Park.* JOE *and* ROY *are sitting at the bar; the place is brightly lit.* JOE *has a plate of food in front of him but he isn't eating.* ROY *occasionally reaches over the table and forks small bites off* JOE'S *plate.* ROY *is drinking heavily,* JOE *not at all.* LOUIS *and the* MAN *are eyeing each other, each alternating interest and indifference.)*

JOE: The pills were something she started when she miscarried or . . . no, she took some before that. She had a really bad time at home, when she was a kid, her home was really bad. I think a lot of drinking and physical stuff. She doesn't talk about that, instead she talks about . . . the sky falling down, people with knives hiding under sofas. Monsters. Mormons. Everyone thinks Mormons don't come from homes like that, we aren't supposed to behave that way, but we do. It's not lying, or being two-faced. Everyone tries very hard to live up to God's strictures, which are very . . . um . . .

ROY: Strict.

JOE: I shouldn't be bothering you with this.

ROY: No, please. Heart to heart. Want another. . . . What is that, seltzer?

JOE: The failure to measure up hits people very hard. From such a strong desire to be good they feel very far from goodness when they fail.

What scares me is that maybe what I really love in her is the part of her that's farthest from the light, from God's love; maybe I was drawn to that in the first place. And I'm keeping it alive because I need it.

ROY: Why would you need it?

JOE: There are things. . . . I don't know how well we know ourselves. I mean, what if? I know I married her because she . . . because I loved it that she was always wrong, always doing something wrong, like one step out of step. In Salt Lake City that stands out. I never stood out, on the outside, but inside, it was hard for me. To pass.

ROY: Pass?

JOE: Yeah.

ROY: Pass as what?

JOE: Oh. Well. . . . As someone cheerful and strong. Those who love God with an open heart unclouded by secrets and struggles are cheerful; God's easy simple love for them shows in how strong and happy they are. The saints.

ROY: But you had secrets? Secret struggles . . .

JOE: I wanted to be one of the elect, one of the Blessed. You feel you ought to be, that the blemishes are yours by choice, which of course they aren't. Harper's sorrow, that really deep sorrow, she didn't choose that. But it's there.

ROY: You didn't put it there.

JOE: No.

ROY: You sound like you think you did.

JOE: I am responsible for her.

ROY: Because she's your wife.

JOE: That. And I do love her.

ROY: Whatever. She's your wife. And so there are obligations. To her. But also to yourself.

JOE: She'd fall apart in Washington.

ROY: Then let her stay here.

JOE: She'll fall apart if I leave her.

ROY: Then bring her to Washington.

JOE: I just can't, Roy. She needs me.

ROY: Listen, Joe. I'm the best divorce lawyer in the business.

(Little pause.)

JOE: Can't Washington wait?

ROY: You do what you need to do, Joe. What *you* need. *You.* Let her life go where it wants to go. You'll both be better for that. *Somebody* should get what they want.

MAN: What do you want?

LOUIS: I want you to fuck me, hurt me, make me bleed.

MAN: I want to.

LOUIS: Yeah?

MAN: I want to hurt you.

LOUIS: Fuck me.

MAN: Yeah?

LOUIS: Hard.

MAN: Yeah? You been a bad boy?

(Pause. LOUIS *laughs, softly.)*

LOUIS: Very bad. Very bad.

MAN: You need to be punished, boy?

LOUIS: Yes. I do.

MAN: Yes what?

(Little pause.)

LOUIS: Um, I . . .

MAN: Yes *what*, boy?

LOUIS: Oh. Yes sir.

MAN: I want you to take me to your place, boy.

LOUIS: No, I can't do that.

MAN: No *what*?

LOUIS: No sir, I can't, I . . .
     I don't live alone, sir.

MAN: Your lover know you're out with a man tonight, boy?

LOUIS: No sir, he . . .
     My lover doesn't know.

MAN: Your lover know you . . .

LOUIS: Let's change the subject, OK? Can we go to your place?

MAN: I live with my parents.

LOUIS: Oh.

ROY: Everyone who makes it in this world makes it because somebody older and more powerful takes an interest. The most precious asset in life, I think, is the ability to be a good son. You have that, Joe. Somebody who can be a good son to a father who pushes them farther than they would otherwise go. I've had many fathers, I owe my life to them, powerful, powerful men. Walter Winchell,° Edgar Hoover.° Joe McCarthy° most of all. He valued me because I am a good lawyer, but he loved me because I was and am a good son. He was a very difficult man, very guarded and cagey; I brought out something tender in him. He would have died for me. And me for him. Does this embarrass you?

JOE: I had a hard time with my father.

ROY: Well sometimes that's the way. Then you have to find other fathers, substitutes, I don't know. The father-son relationship is central to life. Women are for birth, beginning, but the father is continuance. The son offers the father his life as a vessel for carrying forth his father's dream. Your father's living?

JOE: Um, dead.

ROY: He was . . . what? A difficult man?

JOE: He was in the military. He could be very unfair. And cold.

ROY: But he loved you.

Walter Winchell, American journalist and broadcaster, 1897–1972. *Edgar Hoover,* J. Edgar Hoover (1895–72) was an American lawyer, best known as director of the FBI from 1924 until his death. *Joe McCarthy,* Joseph McCarthy (1908–57) was a Republican senator from Wisconsin, chairman of the Senate Committee on Government Operations, and dogged investigator of suspected communists.

JOE: I don't know.

ROY: No, no, Joe, he did, I know this. Sometimes a father's love has to be very, very hard, unfair even, cold to make his son grow strong in a world like this. This isn't a good world.

MAN: Here, then.

LOUIS: I. . . . Do you have a rubber?

MAN: I don't use rubbers.

LOUIS: You should. *(He takes one from his coat pocket)* Here.

MAN: I don't use them.

LOUIS: Forget it, then. *(He starts to leave)*

MAN: No, wait.
     Put it on me. Boy.

LOUIS: Forget it, I have to get back. Home. I must be going crazy.

MAN: Oh come on please he won't find out.

LOUIS: It's cold. Too cold.

MAN: It's never too cold, let me warm you up. Please?

(They begin to fuck.)

MAN: Relax.

LOUIS *(A small laugh)*: Not a chance.

MAN: It . . .

LOUIS: What?

MAN: I think it broke. The rubber. You want me to keep going?
(Little pause) Pull out? Should I . . .

LOUIS: Keep going.
     Infect me.
     I don't care. I don't care.

(Pause. THE MAN *pulls out.)*

MAN: I . . . um, look, I'm sorry, but I think I want to go.

LOUIS: Yeah.
     Give my best to mom and dad.

*(*THE MAN *slaps him.)*

LOUIS: Ow!

(They stare at each other.)

LOUIS: It was a joke.

*(*THE MAN *leaves.)*

ROY: How long have we known each other?

JOE: Since 1980.

ROY: Right. A long time. I feel close to you, Joe. Do I advise you well?

JOE: You've been an incredible friend, Roy, I . . .

ROY: I want to be family. Familia, as my Italian friends call it. La Familia. A lovely word. It's important for me to help you, like I was helped.

JOE: I owe practically everything to you, Roy.

ROY: I'm dying, Joe. Cancer.

JOE: Oh my God.

ROY: Please. Let me finish.

Few people know this and I'm telling you this only because.... I'm not afraid of death. What can death bring that I haven't faced? I've lived; life is the worst. (*Gently mocking himself*) Listen to me, I'm a philosopher.

Joe. You must do this. You must must must. Love; that's a trap. Responsibility; that's a trap too. Like a father to a son I tell you this: Life is full of horror; nobody escapes, nobody; save yourself. Whatever pulls on you, whatever needs from you, threatens you. Don't be afraid; people are so afraid; don't be afraid to live in the raw wind, naked, alone.... Learn at least this: What you are capable of. Let nothing stand in your way.

ACT 2 / SCENE 5

(*Three days later.* PRIOR *and* BELIZE *in* PRIOR*'s hospital room.* PRIOR *is very sick but improving.* BELIZE *has just arrived.*)

PRIOR: Miss Thing.
BELIZE: Ma cherie bichette.°
PRIOR: Stella.
BELIZE: Stella for star.° Let me see. (*Scrutinizing Prior*) You look like shit, why yes indeed you do, comme la merde!
PRIOR: Merci.
BELIZE (*Taking little plastic bottles from his bag, handing them to* PRIOR): Not to despair, Belle Reeve. Lookie! Magic goop!
PRIOR (*Opening a bottle, sniffing*): Pooh! What kinda crap is that?
BELIZE: Beats me. Let's rub it on your poor blistered body and see what it does.
PRIOR: This is not Western medicine, these bottles . . .
BELIZE: Voodoo cream. From the botanica 'round the block.
PRIOR: And you a registered nurse.
BELIZE (*Sniffing it*): Beeswax and cheap perfume. Cut with Jergen's Lotion. Full of good vibes and love from some little black Cubana witch in Miami.
PRIOR: Get that trash away from me, I am immune-suppressed.
BELIZE: I *am* a health professional. I *know* what I'm doing.
PRIOR: It stinks. Any word from Louis?

(*Pause.* BELIZE *starts giving* PRIOR *a gentle massage.*)

PRIOR: Gone.
BELIZE: He'll be back. I know the type. Likes to keep a girl on edge.

PRIOR: It's been . . .

(*Pause.*)

BELIZE (*Trying to jog his memory*): How long?
PRIOR: I don't remember.
BELIZE: How long have you been here?
PRIOR (*Getting suddenly upset*): I don't remember, I don't give a fuck. I want Louis. I want my fucking boyfriend, where the fuck is he? I'm dying, I'm dying, where's Louis?
BELIZE: Shhhh, shhh . . .
PRIOR: This is a very strange drug, this drug. Emotional lability, for starters.
BELIZE: Save a tab or two for me.
PRIOR: Oh no, not this drug, ce n'est pas pour la joyeux noël et la bonne année,° this drug she is serious poisonous chemistry, ma pauvre bichette.
And not just disorienting. I hear things. Voices.
BELIZE: Voices.
PRIOR: A voice.
BELIZE: Saying what?

(*Pause.*)

PRIOR: I'm not supposed to tell.
BELIZE: You better tell the doctor. Or I will.
PRIOR: No no don't. Please. I want the voice; it's wonderful. It's all that's keeping me alive. I don't want to talk to some intern about it.
You know what happens? When I hear it, I get hard.
BELIZE: Oh my.
PRIOR: Comme ça.° (*He uses his arm to demonstrate*) And you know I am slow to rise.
BELIZE: My jaw aches at the memory.
PRIOR: And would you deny me this little solace—betray my concupiscence to Florence Nightingale's storm troopers?
BELIZE: Perish the thought, ma bébé.°
PRIOR: They'd change the drug just to spoil the fun.
BELIZE: You and your boner can depend on me.
PRIOR: Je t'adore, ma belle nègre.°
BELIZE: All this girl-talk shit is politically incorrect, you know. We should have dropped it back when we gave up drag.
PRIOR: I'm sick, I get to be politically incorrect if it makes me feel better. You sound like Lou.
(*Little pause*)
Well, at least I have the satisfaction of knowing he's in anguish somewhere. I loved his anguish. Watching him stick his head up his asshole and eat his guts out over some relatively minor moral

---

Ma cherie bichette, French for "my dear pet." *Stella for star,* "Stella" is Latin for star; the line is also a quotation from Tennessee Williams's *A Streetcar Named Desire* (1947).

ce n'est pas pour la joyeux noël et la bonne année, French, "it is not for celebrating Christmas or New Year's." *comme ça,* French, "like that." *ma bébé,* French, "my baby." *Je t'adore, ma belle nègre,* French, "I adore you, my beautiful Negro."

conundrum—it was the best show in town. But Mother warned me: if they get overwhelmed by the little things . . .

BELIZE: They'll be belly-up bustville when something big comes along.

PRIOR: Mother warned me.

BELIZE: And they do come along.

PRIOR: But I didn't listen.

BELIZE: No. (*Doing Hepburn°*) Men are beasts.

PRIOR (*Also Hepburn*): The absolute lowest.

BELIZE: I have to go. If I want to spend my whole lonely life looking after white people I can get underpaid to do it.

PRIOR: You're just a Christian martyr.

BELIZE: Whatever happens, baby, I will be here for you.

PRIOR: Je t'aime.

BELIZE: Je t'aime. Don't go crazy on me, girlfriend, I already got enough crazy queens for one lifetime. For two. I can't be bothering with dementia.

PRIOR: I promise.

BELIZE (*Touching him; softly*): Ouch.

PRIOR: Ouch. Indeed.

BELIZE: Why'd they have to pick on you?

And eat more, girlfriend, you really do look like shit.

(BELIZE *leaves.*)

PRIOR (*After waiting a beat*): He's gone.

Are you still . . .

VOICE: I can't stay. I will return.

PRIOR: Are you one of those "Follow me to the other side" voices?

VOICE: No. I am no nightbird. I am a messenger . . .

PRIOR: You have a beautiful voice, it sounds . . . like a viola, like a perfectly tuned, tight string, balanced, the truth. . . . Stay with me.

VOICE: Not now. Soon I will return, I will reveal myself to you; I am glorious, glorious; my heart, my countenance and my message. You must prepare.

PRIOR: For what? I don't want to . . .

VOICE: No death, no:

A marvelous work and a wonder we undertake, an edifice awry we sink plumb and straighten, a great Lie we abolish, a great error correct, with the rule, sword and broom of Truth!

PRIOR: What are you talking about, I . . .

VOICE:

I am on my way; when I am manifest, our Work begins:

Prepare for the parting of the air,

The breath, the ascent,

Glory to . . .

Hepburn, Katharine Hepburn (1909–), stage actress and film star.

ACT 2 / SCENE 6

(*The second week of January.* MARTIN, ROY *and* JOE *in a fancy Manhattan restaurant.*)

MARTIN: It's a revolution in Washington, Joe. We have a new agenda and finally a real leader. They got back the Senate but we have the courts. By the nineties the Supreme Court will be block-solid Republican appointees, and the Federal bench— Republican judges like land mines, everywhere, everywhere they turn. Affirmative action? Take it to court. Boom! Land mine. And we'll get our way on just about everything: abortion, defense, Central America, family values, a live investment climate. We have the White House locked till the year 2000. And beyond. A permanent fix on the Oval Office? It's possible. By '92 we'll get the Senate back, and in ten years the South is going to give us the House. It's really the end of Liberalism. The end of New Deal Socialism. The end of ipso facto secular humanism. The dawning of a genuinely American political personality. Modeled on Ronald Wilson Reagan.

JOE: It sounds great, Mr. Heller.

MARTIN: Martin. And Justice is the hub. Especially since Ed Meese took over. He doesn't specialize in Fine Points of the Law. He's a flatfoot, a cop. He reminds me of Teddy Roosevelt.

JOE: I can't wait to meet him.

MARTIN: Too bad, Joe, he's been dead for sixty years!

(*There is a little awkwardness.* JOE *doesn't respond.*)

MARTIN: Teddy Roosevelt. You said you wanted to. . . . Little joke. It reminds me of the story about the . . .

ROY (*Smiling, but nasty*): Aw shut the fuck up Martin.

(*To* JOE) You see that? Mr. Heller here is one of the mighty, Joseph, in D.C. he sitteth on the right hand of the man who sitteth on the right hand of The Man. And yet I can say "shut the fuck up" and he will take no offense. Loyalty. He . . . Martin?

MARTIN: Yes, Roy?

ROY: Rub my back.

MARTIN: Roy . . .

ROY: No no really, a sore spot, I get them all the time now, these. . . . Rub it for me darling, would you do that for me?

(MARTIN *rubs* ROY*'s back. They both look at* JOE.)

ROY (*To* JOE): How do you think a handful of Bolsheviks turned St. Petersburg into Leningrad in one afternoon? *Comrades.* Who do for each other. Marx and Engels. Lenin and Trotsky. Josef Stalin and Franklin Delano Roosevelt.

(MARTIN *laughs.*)

ROY: *Comrades*, right Martin?

MARTIN: This man, Joe, is a Saint of the Right.

JOE: I know, Mr. Heller, I . . .

ROY: And you see what I mean, Martin? He's special, right?

MARTIN: Don't embarrass him, Roy.

ROY: Gravity, decency, smarts! His strength is as the strength of ten because his heart is pure! *And* he's a Royboy, one hundred percent.

MARTIN: We're on the move, Joe. On the move.

JOE: Mr. Heller, I . . .

MARTIN *(Ending backrub)*: We can't wait any longer for an answer.

(Little pause.)

JOE: Oh. Um, I . . .

ROY: Joe's a married man, Martin.

MARTIN: Aha.

ROY: With a wife. She doesn't care to go to D.C., and so Joe cannot go. And keeps us dangling. We've seen that kind of thing before, haven't we? These men and their wives.

MARTIN: Oh yes. Beware.

JOE: I really can't discuss this under . . .

MARTIN: Then *don't* discuss. Say yes, Joe.

ROY: Now.

MARTIN: Say yes I will.

ROY: Now.

Now. I'll hold my breath till you do, I'm turning blue waiting. . . . *Now,* goddammit!

MARTIN: Roy, calm down, it's not . . .

ROY: Aw, fuck it. *(He takes a letter from his jacket pocket, hands it to* JOE*)*

Read. Came today.

*(*JOE *reads the first paragraph, then looks up.)*

JOE: Roy. This is . . . Roy, this is terrible.

ROY: You're telling me.

A letter from the New York State Bar Association, Martin.

They're gonna try and disbar me.

MARTIN: Oh my.

JOE: Why?

ROY: Why, Martin?

MARTIN: Revenge.

ROY: The whole Establishment. Their little rules. Because I know no rules. Because I don't see the Law as a dead and arbitrary collection of antiquated dictums, thou shall, thou shalt not, because, because I know the Law's a pliable, breathing, sweating . . . *organ,* because, because . . .

MARTIN: Because he borrowed half a million from one of his clients.

ROY: Yeah, well, there's that.

MARTIN: *And* he forgot to *return* it.

JOE: Roy, that's. . . . You borrowed money from a client?

ROY: I'm deeply ashamed.

(Little pause.)

JOE *(Very sympathetic)*: Roy, you know how much I admire you. Well I mean I know you have unorthodox ways, but I'm sure you only did what you thought at the time you needed to do. And I have faith that . . .

ROY: Not so damp, please. I'll deny it was a loan. She's got no paperwork. Can't prove a fucking thing.

(Little pause. MARTIN *studies the menu.)*

JOE *(Handing back the letter, more official in tone)*: Roy I really appreciate your telling me this, and I'll do whatever I can to help.

ROY *(Holding up a hand, then, carefully)*: I'll tell you what you can do.

I'm about to be tried, Joe, by a jury that is not a jury of my peers. The disbarment committee: genteel gentleman Brahmin lawyers, country-club men. I offend them, to these men . . . I'm what, Martin, some sort of filthy little Jewish troll?

MARTIN: Oh well, I wouldn't go so far as . . .

ROY: Oh well I would.

Very fancy lawyers, these disbarment committee lawyers, fancy lawyers with fancy corporate clients and complicated cases. Antitrust suits. Deregulation. Environmental control. Complex cases like these need Justice Department cooperation like flowers need the sun. Wouldn't you say that's an accurate assessment, Martin?

MARTIN: I'm not here, Roy. I'm not hearing any of this.

ROY: No. Of course not.

Without the light of the sun, Joe, these cases, and the fancy lawyers who represent them, will wither and die.

A well-placed friend, someone in the Justice Department, say, can turn off the sun. Cast a deep shadow on my behalf. Make them shiver in the cold. If they overstep. They would fear that.

(Pause.)

JOE: Roy. I don't understand.

ROY: You do.

(Pause.)

JOE: You're not asking me to . . .

ROY: Sssshhhh. Careful.

JOE *(A beat, then)*: Even if I said yes to the job, it would be illegal to interfere. With the hearings. It's unethical. No. I can't.

ROY: Un-ethical.

Would you excuse us, Martin?

MARTIN: Excuse you?

ROY: Take a walk, Martin. For real.

*(*MARTIN *leaves.)*

ROY: Un-ethical. Are you trying to embarrass me in front of my friend?

JOE: Well it is unethical, I can't . . .

ROY: Boy, you are really something. What the fuck do you think this is, Sunday School?

JOE: No, but Roy this is . . .

ROY: This is . . . this is gastric juices churning, this is enzymes and acids, this is intestinal is what this is, bowel movement and blood-red meat—this stinks, this is *politics,* Joe, the game of being alive. And you think you're. . . . What? Above that? Above alive is what? Dead! In the clouds! You're on earth, goddammit! Plant a foot, stay a while.

    I'm sick. They smell I'm weak. They want blood this time. I must have eyes in Justice. In Justice you will protect me.

JOE: Why can't Mr. Heller . . .

ROY: Grow up, Joe. The administration can't get involved.

JOE: But I'd be part of the administration. The same as him.

ROY: Not the same. Martin's Ed's man. And Ed's Reagan's man. So Martin's Reagan's man.

    And you're mine.

    (*Little pause. He holds up the letter*)

    This will never be. Understand me?

    (*He tears the letter up*)

    I'm gonna be a lawyer, Joe, I'm gonna be a lawyer, Joe, I'm gonna be a goddam motherfucking legally licensed member of the bar lawyer, just like my daddy was, till my last bitter day on earth, Joseph, until the day I die.

(MARTIN *returns.*)

ROY: Ah, Martin's back.

MARTIN: So are we agreed?

ROY: Joe?

(*Little pause.*)

JOE: I will think about it.

    (*To* ROY) I will.

ROY: Huh.

MARTIN: It's the fear of what comes after the doing that makes the doing hard to do.

ROY: Amen.

MARTIN: But you can almost always live with the consequences.

ACT 2 / SCENE 7

(*That afternoon. On the granite steps outside the Hall of Justice, Brooklyn. It is cold and sunny. A Sabrett wagon is selling hot dogs.* LOUIS, *in a shabby overcoat, is sitting on the steps contemplatively eating one.* JOE *enters with three hot dogs and a can of Coke.*)

JOE: Can I . . . ?

LOUIS: Oh sure. Sure. Crazy cold sun.

JOE (*Sitting*): Have to make the best of it.
    How's your friend?

LOUIS: My . . . ? Oh. He's worse. My friend is worse.

JOE: I'm sorry.

LOUIS: Yeah, well. Thanks for asking. It's nice. You're nice. I can't believe you voted for Reagan.

JOE: I hope he gets better.

LOUIS: Reagan?

JOE: Your friend.

LOUIS: He won't. Neither will Reagan.

JOE: Let's not talk politics, OK?

LOUIS (*Pointing to* JOE'*s lunch*): You're eating *three* of those?

JOE: Well . . . I'm . . . hungry.

LOUIS: They're really terrible for you. Full of rat-poo and beetle legs and wood shavings 'n' shit.

JOE: Huh.

LOUIS: And . . . um . . . iridium, I think. Something toxic.

JOE: You're eating one.

LOUIS: Yeah, well, the shape, I can't help myself, plus I'm *trying* to commit suicide, what's your excuse?

JOE: I don't have an excuse. I just have Pepto-Bismol.

(JOE *takes a bottle of Pepto-Bismol and chugs it.* LOUIS *shudders audibly.*)

JOE: Yeah I know but then I wash it down with Coke.

(*He does this.* LOUIS *mimes barfing in* JOE'*s lap.* JOE *pushes* LOUIS'*s head away.*)

JOE: Are you *always* like this?

LOUIS: I've been worrying a lot about his kids.

JOE: Whose?

LOUIS: Reagan's. Maureen and Mike and little orphan Patti and Miss Ron Reagan Jr., the you-should-pardon-the-expression heterosexual.

JOE: Ron Reagan Jr. is *not.* . . . You shouldn't just make these assumptions about people. How do you know? About him? What he is? You don't know.

LOUIS (*Doing Tallulah°*): Well darling he never sucked *my* cock but . . .

JOE: Look, if you're going to get vulgar . . .

LOUIS: No no really I mean. . . . What's it like to be the child of the Zeitgeist? To have the American Animus as your dad? It's not really a *family,* the Reagans, I read *People,* there aren't any connections there, no love, they don't ever even speak to each other except through their agents. So what's it like to be Reagan's kid? Enquiring minds want to know.

JOE: You can't believe everything you . . .

LOUIS (*Looking away*): But . . . I think we all know what that's like. Nowadays. No connections. No responsibilities. All of us . . . falling through the

---

Tallulah, Tallulah Bankhead (1902–68), deep-voiced actress of stage and screen.

cracks that separate what we owe to our selves and . . . and what we owe to love.

JOE: You just. . . . Whatever you feel like saying or doing, you don't care, you just . . . do it.

LOUIS: Do what?

JOE: It. Whatever. Whatever it is you want to do.

LOUIS: Are you trying to tell me something?

(Little pause, sexual. They stare at each other. joe looks away.)

JOE: No, I'm just observing that you . . .

LOUIS: Impulsive.

JOE: Yes, I mean it must be scary, you . . .

LOUIS *(Shrugs)*: Land of the free. Home of the brave. Call me irresponsible.

JOE: It's kind of terrifying.

LOUIS: Yeah, well, freedom is. Heartless, too.

JOE: Oh you're not heartless.

LOUIS: You don't know.
Finish your weenie.

(He pats JOE *on the knee, starts to leave.)*

JOE: Um . . .

*(*LOUIS *turns, looks at him.* JOE *searches for something to say.)*

JOE: Yesterday was Sunday but I've been a little unfocused recently and I thought it was Monday. So I came here like I was going to work. And the whole place was empty. And at first I couldn't figure out why, and I had this moment of incredible . . . fear and also. . . . It just flashed through my mind: The whole Hall of Justice, it's empty, it's deserted, it's gone out of business. Forever. The people that make it run have up and abandoned it.

LOUIS *(Looking at the building)*: Creepy.

JOE: Well yes but. I felt that I was going to scream. Not because it was creepy, but because the emptiness felt so *fast*.
And . . . well, good. A . . . happy scream.
I just wondered what a thing it would be . . . if overnight everything you owe anything to, justice, or love, had really gone away. Free.
It would be . . . heartless terror. Yes. Terrible, and . . .
Very great. To shed your skin, every old skin, one by one and then walk away, unencumbered, into the morning.

(Little pause. He looks at the building)

I can't go in there today.

LOUIS: Then don't.

JOE *(Not really hearing* LOUIS*)*: I can't go in, I need . . .

(He looks for what he needs. He takes a swig of Pepto-Bismol)

I can't *be* this anymore. I need . . . a change, I should just . . .

LOUIS *(Not a come-on, necessarily; he doesn't want to be alone)*: Want some company? For whatever?

(Pause. JOE *looks at* LOUIS *and looks away, afraid.* LOUIS *shrugs.)*

LOUIS: Sometimes, even if it scares you to death, you have to be willing to break the law. Know what I mean?

(Another little pause.)

JOE: Yes.

(Another little pause.)

LOUIS: I moved out. I moved out on my . . .
I haven't been sleeping well.

JOE: Me neither.

*(*LOUIS *goes up to* JOE*, licks his napkin and dabs at* JOE's *mouth.)*

LOUIS: Antacid moustache.
(Points to the building) Maybe the court won't convene. Ever again. Maybe we are free. To do whatever.
Children of the new morning, criminal minds. Selfish and greedy and loveless and blind. Reagan's children.
You're scared. So am I. Everybody is in the land of the free. God help us all.

ACT 2 / SCENE 8

(Late that night. Joe at a payphone phoning HANNAH *at home in Salt Lake City.)*

JOE: Mom?

HANNAH: Joe?

JOE: Hi.

HANNAH: You're calling from the street. It's . . . it must be four in the morning. What's happened?

JOE: Nothing, nothing, I . . .

HANNAH: It's Harper. Is Harper. . . . Joe? Joe?

JOE: Yeah, hi. No, Harper's fine. Well, no, she's . . . not fine. How are you, Mom?

HANNAH: What's happened?

JOE: I just wanted to talk to you. I, uh, wanted to try something out on you.

HANNAH: Joe, you haven't . . . have you been drinking, Joe?

JOE: Yes ma'am. I'm drunk.

HANNAH: That isn't like you.

JOE: No. I mean, who's to say?

HANNAH: Why are you out on the street at four AM? In that crazy city. It's dangerous.

JOE: Actually, Mom, I'm not on the street. I'm near the boathouse in the park.

HANNAH: What park?

JOE: Central Park.

HANNAH: CENTRAL PARK! Oh my Lord. What on earth are you doing in Central Park at this time of night? Are you . . .

Joe, I think you ought to go home right now. Call me from home.
(Little pause)
Joe?

JOE: I come here to watch, Mom. Sometimes. Just to watch.

HANNAH: Watch what? What's there to watch at four in the . . .

JOE: Mom, did Dad love me?

HANNAH: What?

JOE: Did he?

HANNAH: You ought to go home and call from there.

JOE: Answer.

HANNAH: Oh now really. This is maudlin. I don't like this conversation.

JOE: Yeah, well, it gets worse from here on.

(Pause.)

HANNAH: Joe?

JOE: Mom. Momma. I'm a homosexual, Momma.
Boy, did that come out awkward.
(Pause)
Hello? Hello?
I'm a homosexual.
(Pause)
Please, Momma. Say something.

HANNAH: You're old enough to understand that your father didn't love you without being ridiculous about it.

JOE: What?

HANNAH: You're ridiculous. You're being ridiculous.

JOE: I'm . . .
What?

HANNAH: You really ought to go home now to your wife. I need to go to bed. This phone call. . . . We will just forget this phone call.

JOE: Mom.

HANNAH: No more talk. Tonight. This . . .
(Suddenly very angry) Drinking is a sin! A sin! I raised you better than that. *(She hangs up)*

ACT 2 / SCENE 9

(The following morning, early. Split scene: HARPER and JOE at home; LOUIS and PRIOR in PRIOR's hospital room. JOE and LOUIS have just entered. This should be fast and obviously furious; overlapping is fine; the proceedings may be a little confusing but not the final results.)

HARPER: Oh God. Home. The moment of truth has arrived.

JOE: Harper.

LOUIS: I'm going to move out.

PRIOR: The fuck you are.

JOE: Harper. Please listen. I still love you very much. You're still my best buddy; I'm not going to leave you.

HARPER: No, I don't like the sound of this. I'm leaving.

LOUIS: I'm leaving.
I already have.

JOE: Please listen. Stay. This is really hard. We have to talk.

HARPER: We are talking. Aren't we. Now please shut up. OK?

PRIOR: Bastard. Sneaking off while I'm flat out here, that's low. If I could get up now I'd beat the holy shit out of you.

JOE: Did you take pills? How many?

HARPER: No pills. Bad for the . . . *(Pats stomach)*

JOE: You aren't pregnant. I called your gynecologist.

HARPER: I'm seeing a new gynecologist.

PRIOR: You have no right to do this.

LOUIS: Oh, that's ridiculous.

PRIOR: No right. It's criminal.

JOE: Forget about that. Just listen. You want the truth. This is the truth.
I knew this when I married you. I've known this I guess for as long as I've known anything, but . . . I don't know, I thought maybe that with enough effort and will I could change myself . . . but I can't . . .

PRIOR: Criminal.

LOUIS: There oughta be a law.

PRIOR: There is a law. You'll see.

JOE: I'm losing ground here, I go walking, you want to know where I walk, I . . . go to the park, or up and down 53rd Street, or places where. . . . And I keep swearing I won't go walking again, but I just can't.

LOUIS: I need some privacy.

PRIOR: That's new.

LOUIS: Everything's new, Prior.

JOE: I try to tighten my heart into a knot, a snarl, I try to learn to live dead, just numb, but then I see someone I want, and it's like a nail, like a hot spike right through my chest, and I know I'm losing.

PRIOR: Apartment too small for three? Louis and Prior comfy but not Louis and Prior and Prior's disease?

LOUIS: Something like that.
I won't be judged by you. This isn't a crime, just—the inevitable consequence of people who run out of—whose limitations . . .

PRIOR: Bang bang bang. The court will come to order.

LOUIS: I mean let's talk practicalities, schedules; I'll come over if you want, spend nights with you when I can, I can . . .

PRIOR: Has the jury reached a verdict?

LOUIS: I'm doing the best I can.

PRIOR: Pathetic. Who cares?

JOE: My whole life has conspired to bring me to this place, and I can't despise my whole life. I think I believed when I met you I could save you, you at least if not myself, but . . .
I don't have any sexual feelings for you, Harper. And I don't think I ever did.

(Little pause.)

HARPER: I think you should go.

JOE: Where?

HARPER: Washington. Doesn't matter.

JOE: What are you talking about?

HARPER: Without me.

Without me, Joe. Isn't that what you want to hear?

(Little pause.)

JOE: Yes.

LOUIS: You can love someone and fail them. You can love someone and not be able to . . .

PRIOR: You *can*, theoretically, yes. A person can, maybe an editorial "you" can love, Louis, but not *you*, specifically you, I don't know, I think you are excluded from that general category.

HARPER: You were going to save me, but the whole time you were spinning a lie. I just don't understand that.

PRIOR: A person could theoretically love and maybe many do but we both know now you can't.

LOUIS: I do.

PRIOR: You can't even say it.

LOUIS: I love you, Prior.

PRIOR: I repeat. Who cares?

HARPER: This is so scary, I want this to stop, to go back . . .

PRIOR: We have reached a verdict, your honor. This man's heart is deficient. He loves, but his love is worth nothing.

JOE: Harper . . .

HARPER: Mr. Lies, I want to get away from here. Far away. Right now. Before he starts talking again. Please, please . . .

JOE: As long as I've known you Harper you've been afraid of . . . of men hiding under the bed, men hiding under the sofa, men with knives.

PRIOR *(Shattered; almost pleading; trying to reach him)*: I'm dying! You stupid fuck! Do you know what that is! Love! Do you know what love means? We lived together four-and-a-half years, you animal, you idiot.

LOUIS: I have to find some way to save myself.

JOE: Who are these men? I never understood it. Now I know.

HARPER: What?

JOE: It's me.

HARPER: It is?

PRIOR: GET OUT OF MY ROOM!

JOE: I'm the man with the knives.

HARPER: You are?

PRIOR: If I could get up now I'd kill you. I would. Go away. Go away or I'll scream.

HARPER: Oh God . . .

JOE: I'm sorry . . .

HARPER: It is you.

LOUIS: Please don't scream.

PRIOR: Go.

HARPER: I recognize you now.

LOUIS: Please . . .

JOE: Oh. Wait, I. . . . Oh!

(He covers his mouth with his hand, gags, and removes his hand, red with blood)

I'm bleeding.

(PRIOR screams.)

HARPER: Mr. Lies.

MR. LIES *(Appearing, dressed in antarctic explorer's apparel)*: Right here.

HARPER: I want to go away. I can't see him anymore.

MR. LIES: Where?

HARPER: Anywhere. Far away.

MR. LIES: Absolutamento.

(HARPER and MR. LIES vanish. JOE looks up, sees that she's gone.)

PRIOR *(Closing his eyes)*: When I open my eyes you'll be gone.

(LOUIS leaves.)

JOE: Harper?

PRIOR *(Opening his eyes)*: Huh. It worked.

JOE *(Calling)*: Harper?

PRIOR: I hurt all over. I wish I was dead.

ACT 2 / SCENE 10

(The same day, sunset. HANNAH *and* SISTER ELLA CHAPTER, *a real-estate saleswoman,* HANNAH PITT's *closest friend, in front of* HANNAH's *house in Salt Lake City.)*

SISTER ELLA CHAPTER: Look at that view! A view of heaven. Like the living city of heaven, isn't it, it just fairly glimmers in the sun.

HANNAH: Glimmers.

SISTER ELLA CHAPTER: Even the stone and brick it just glimmers and glitters like heaven in the sunshine. Such a nice view you get, perched up on a canyon rim. Some kind of beautiful place.

HANNAH: It's just Salt Lake, and you're selling the house *for* me, not *to* me.

SISTER ELLA CHAPTER: I like to work up an enthusiasm for my properties.

HANNAH: Just get me a good price.

SISTER ELLA CHAPTER: Well, the market's off.

HANNAH: At least fifty.

SISTER ELLA CHAPTER: Forty'd be more like it.

HANNAH: Fifty.

SISTER ELLA CHAPTER: Wish you'd wait a bit.

HANNAH: Well I can't.

SISTER ELLA CHAPTER: Wish you would. You're about the only friend I got.

HANNAH: Oh well now.

SISTER ELLA CHAPTER: Know why I decided to like you? I decided to like you 'cause you're the only unfriendly Mormon I ever met.

HANNAH: Your wig is crooked.
SISTER ELLA CHAPTER: Fix it.

(HANNAH straightens SISTER ELLA's wig.)

SISTER ELLA CHAPTER: New York City. All they got
  there is tiny rooms.
    I always thought: People ought to stay put.
  That's why I got my license to sell real estate. It's a
  way of saying: Have a house! Stay put! It's a way of
  saying traveling's no good. Plus I needed the
  cash. (She takes a pack of cigarettes out of her purse,
  lights one, offers pack to HANNAH)
HANNAH: Not out here, anyone could come by.
    There's been days I've stood at this ledge and
  thought about stepping over.
    It's a hard place, Salt Lake: baked dry. Abun-
  dant energy; not much intelligence. That's a combination that can wear a body out. No harm
  looking someplace else. I don't need much room.
    My sister-in-law Libby thinks there's radon gas
  in the basement.
SISTER ELLA CHAPTER: Is there gas in the . . .
HANNAH: Of course not. Libby's a fool.
SISTER ELLA CHAPTER: 'Cause I'd have to include that
  in the description.
HANNAH: There's no gas, Ella. (Little pause) Give a
  puff. (She takes a furtive drag of ELLA's cigarette) Put it
  away now.
SISTER ELLA CHAPTER: So I guess it's goodbye.
HANNAH: You'll be all right, Ella, I wasn't ever much
  of a friend.
SISTER ELLA CHAPTER: I'll say something but don't
  laugh, OK?
    This is the home of saints, the godliest place on
  earth, they say, and I think they're right. That
  mean there's no evil here? No. Evil's everywhere.
  Sin's everywhere. But this . . . is the spring of
  sweet water in the desert, the desert flower. Every
  step a Believer takes away from here is a step
  fraught with peril. I fear for you, Hannah Pitt,
  because you are my friend. Stay put. This is the
  right home of saints.
HANNAH: Latter-day saints.
SISTER ELLA CHAPTER: Only kind left.
HANNAH: But still. Late in the day . . . for saints and
  everyone. That's all. That's all.
    Fifty thousand dollars for the house, Sister Ella
  Chapter; don't undersell. It's an impressive view.

ACT 3 / NOT-YET-CONSCIOUS,
FORWARD DAWNING

January 1986

ACT 3 / SCENE 1

(Late night, three days after the end of Act Two. The stage
is completely dark. PRIOR is in bed in his apartment, having a nightmare. He wakes up, sits up and switches on a
nightlight. He looks at his clock. Seated by the table near
the bed is a man dressed in the clothing of a 13th-century
British squire.)

PRIOR (Terrified): Who are you?
PRIOR 1: My name is Prior Walter.

(Pause.)

PRIOR: My name is Prior Walter.
PRIOR 1: I know that.
PRIOR: Explain.
PRIOR 1: You're alive. I'm not. We have the same
  name. What do you want me to explain?
PRIOR: A ghost?
PRIOR 1: An ancestor.
PRIOR: Not the Prior Walter? The Bayeux tapestry
  Prior Walter?
PRIOR 1: His great-great grandson. The fifth of the
  name.
PRIOR: I'm the thirty-fourth, I think.
PRIOR 1: Actually the thirty-second.
PRIOR: Not according to Mother.
PRIOR 1: She's including the two bastards, then; I say
  leave them out. I say no room for bastards. The
  little things you swallow . . .
PRIOR: Pills.
PRIOR 1: Pills. For the pestilence. I too . . .
PRIOR: Pestilence. . . . You too what?
PRIOR 1: The pestilence in my time was much worse
  than now. Whole villages of empty houses. You
  could look outdoors and see Death walking in the
  morning, dew dampening the ragged hem of his
  black robe. Plain as I see you now.
PRIOR: You died of the plague.
PRIOR 1: The spotty monster. Like you, alone.
PRIOR: I'm not alone.
PRIOR 1: You have no wife, no children.
PRIOR: I'm gay.
PRIOR 1: So? Be gay, dance in your altogether for all I
  care, what's that to do with not having children?
PRIOR: Gay homosexual, not bonny, blithe and . . .
  never mind.
PRIOR 1: I had twelve. When I died.

(The second ghost appears, this one dressed in the clothing
of an elegant 17th-century Londoner.)

PRIOR 1 (Pointing to PRIOR 2): And I was three years
  younger than him.

(PRIOR sees the new ghost, screams.)

PRIOR: Oh God another one.
PRIOR 2: Prior Walter. Prior to you by some seventeen
  others.
PRIOR 1: He's counting the bastards.
PRIOR: Are we having a convention?
PRIOR 2: We've been sent to declare her fabulous
  incipience. They love a well-paved entrance with
  lots of heralds, and . . .

PRIOR 1: The messenger come. Prepare the way. The infinite descent, a breath in air . . .

PRIOR 2: They chose us, I suspect, because of the mortal affinities. In a family as long-descended as the Walters there are bound to be a few carried off by plague.

PRIOR 1: The spotty monster.

PRIOR 2: Black Jack. Came from a water pump, half the city of London, can you imagine? His came from fleas. Yours, I understand, is the lamentable consequence of venery° . . .

PRIOR 1: Fleas on rats, but who knew that?

PRIOR: Am I going to die?

PRIOR 2: We aren't allowed to discuss . . .

PRIOR 1: When you do, you don't get ancestors to help you through it. You may be surrounded by children but you die alone.

PRIOR: I'm afraid.

PRIOR 1: You should be. There aren't even torches, and the path's rocky, dark and steep.

PRIOR 2: Don't alarm him. There's good news before there's bad.

We two come to strew rose petal and palm leaf before the triumphal procession. Prophet. Seer. Revelator. It's a great honor for the family.

PRIOR 1: He hasn't got a family.

PRIOR 2: I meant for the Walters, for the family in the larger sense.

PRIOR (Singing):
All I want is a room somewhere,
Far away from the cold night air . . .

PRIOR 2 (Putting a hand on PRIOR's forehead): Calm, calm, this is no brain fever . . .

(PRIOR calms down, but keeps his eyes closed. The lights begin to change. Distant Glorious Music.)

PRIOR 1 (Low chant):
Adonai, Adonai,
Olam ha-yichud,
Zefirot, Zazahot,
Ha-adam, ha-gadol°
Daughter of Light,
Daughter of Splendors,
Fluor! Phosphor!
Lumen! Candle!°

PRIOR 2 (Simultaneously):
Even now,
From the mirror-bright halls of heaven,
Across the cold and lifeless infinity of space,
The Messenger comes
Trailing orbs of light,
Fabulous, incipient,
Oh Prophet,
To you . . .

PRIOR 1 and PRIOR 2:
Prepare, prepare,
The Infinite Descent,
A breath, a feather,
Glory to . . .

(They vanish.)

ACT 3 / SCENE 2

(The next day. Split scene: LOUIS and BELIZE in a coffee shop. PRIOR is at the outpatient clinic at the hospital with EMILY, the nurse; she has him on a pentamidine IV drip.)

LOUIS: Why has democracy succeeded in America? Of course by succeeded I mean comparatively, not literally, not in the present, but what makes for the prospect of some sort of radical democracy spreading outward and growing up? Why does the power that was once so carefully preserved at the top of the pyramid by the original framers of the Constitution seem drawn inexorably downward and outward in spite of the best effort of the Right to stop this? I mean it's the really hard thing about being Left in this country, the American Left can't help but trip over all these petrified little fetishes: freedom, that's the worst; you know, *Jeane Kirkpatrick*° for God's sake will go on and on about freedom and so what does that mean, the word freedom, when she talks about it, or human rights; you have Bush talking about human rights, and so what are these people talking about, they might as well be talking about the mating habits of Venusians, these people don't begin to know what, ontologically, freedom is or human rights, like they see these bourgeois property-based Rights-of-Man-type rights but that's not enfranchisement, not democracy, not what's implicit, what's potential within the idea, not the idea with blood in it. That's just liberalism, the worst kind of liberalism, really, bourgeois tolerance, and what I think is that what AIDS shows us is the limits of tolerance, that it's not enough to be tolerated, because when the shit hits the fan you find

---

venery, sexual intercourse (from the Latin *Veneris,* of Venus, goddess of love). ***Adonai, Adonai . . . Ha-adam, ha-gadol,*** The phrases are drawn from traditions of Jewish mysticism, although not from a single source. The Hebrew translates as: Lord, Lord / The world of unity / Emanations of God, Despoilers / The man, the great one [possibly a reference to the primordial man whose shape becomes the shape for all future men]. ***Fluor! Phosphor! Lumen! Candle!,*** Many mythologies have names for bringers of light. Fluor and Phosphor refer to qualities of light, Lumen is Latin for light, and Candle is self-explanatory.

Jeane Kirkpatrick, political scientist and professor, appointed by Reagan as representative to the United Nations, 1981–85.

out how much tolerance is worth. Nothing. And underneath all the tolerance is intense, passionate hatred.

BELIZE: Uh huh.

LOUIS: Well don't you think that's true?

BELIZE: Uh huh. It is.

LOUIS: *Power* is the object, not being tolerated. Fuck assimilation. But I mean in spite of all this the thing about America, I think, is that ultimately we're different from every other nation on earth, in that, with people here of every race, we can't. . . . Ultimately what defines us isn't race, but politics. Not like any European country where there's an insurmountable fact of a kind of racial, or ethnic, monopoly, or monolith, like all Dutchmen, I mean Dutch people, are well, Dutch, and the Jews of Europe were never Europeans, just a small problem. Facing the monolith. But here there are so many small problems, it's really just a collection of small problems, the monolith is missing. Oh, I mean, of course I suppose there's the monolith of White America. White Straight Male America.

BELIZE: Which is not unimpressive, even among monoliths.

LOUIS: Well, no, but when the race thing gets taken care of, and I don't mean to minimalize how major it is, I mean I know it is, this is a really, really incredibly racist country but it's like, well, the British. I mean, all these blue-eyed pink people. And it's just weird, you know, I mean I'm not all that Jewish-looking, or . . . well, maybe I am but, you know, in New York, everyone is . . . well, not everyone, but so many are but so but in England, in London I walk into bars and I feel like Sid the Yid, you know I mean like Woody Allen in *Annie Hall*,° with the payess and the gabardine coat, like never, never anywhere so much—I mean, not actively despised, not like they're Germans, who I think are still terribly anti-Semitic, and racist too, I mean black-racist, they pretend otherwise but, anyway, in London, there's just . . . and at one point I met this black gay guy from Jamaica who talked with a lilt but he said his family'd been living in London since before the Civil War—the American one—and how the English never let him forget for a minute that he wasn't blue-eyed and pink and I said yeah, me too, these people are anti-Semites and he said yeah but the British Jews have the clothing business all sewed up and blacks there can't get a foothold. And it was an incredibly awkward moment of just. . . . I mean here we were, in this bar that was gay but it was a

pub, you know, the beams and the plaster and those horrible little, like, two-day-old fish and egg sandwiches—and just so British, so *old,* and I felt, well, there's no way out of this because both of us are, right now, too much immersed in this history, hope is dissolved in the sheer age of this place, where race is what counts and there's no real hope of change—it's the racial destiny of the Brits that matters to them, not their political destiny, whereas in America . . .

BELIZE: Here in America race doesn't count.

LOUIS: No, no, that's not. . . . I mean you *can't* be hearing that . . .

BELIZE: I . . .

LOUIS: It's—look, race, yes, but ultimately race here is a political question, right? Racists just try to use race here as a tool in a political struggle. It's not really about race. Like the spiritualists try to use that stuff, are you enlightened, are you centered, channeled, whatever, this reaching out for a spiritual past in a country where no indigenous spirits exist—only the Indians, I mean Native American spirits and we killed them off so now, there are no gods here, no ghosts and spirits in America, there are no angels in America, no spiritual past, no racial past, there's only the political, and the decoys and the ploys to maneuver around the inescapable battle of politics, the shifting downwards and outwards of political power to the people . . .

BELIZE: POWER to the People! AMEN! *(Looking at his watch) OH MY GOODNESS!* Will you look at the time, I gotta . . .

LOUIS: Do you. . . . You think this is, what, racist or naive or something?

BELIZE: Well it's certainly *something.* Look, I just remembered I have an appointment . . .

LOUIS: What? I mean I really don't want to, like, speak from some position of privilege and . . .

BELIZE: I'm sitting here, thinking, eventually he's *got* to run out of steam, so I let you rattle on and on saying about maybe seven or eight things I find really offensive.

LOUIS: What?

BELIZE: But I know you, Louis, and I know the guilt fueling this peculiar tirade is obviously already swollen bigger than your hemorrhoids.

LOUIS: I don't have hemorrhoids.

BELIZE: I hear different. May I finish?

LOUIS: Yes, but I don't have hemorrhoids.

BELIZE: So finally, when I . . .

LOUIS: Prior told you, he's an asshole, he shouldn't have . . .

BELIZE: You promised, Louis. Prior is not a subject.

LOUIS: You brought him up.

BELIZE: I brought up hemorrhoids.

LOUIS: So it's indirect. Passive-aggressive.

Annie Hall, 1977 film, written and directed by, and starring Woody Allen.

BELIZE: Unlike, I suppose, banging me over the head with your theory that America doesn't have a race problem.

LOUIS: Oh be fair I never said that.

BELIZE: Not exactly, but . . .

LOUIS: I said . . .

BELIZE: . . . but it was close enough, because if it'd been that blunt I'd've just walked out and . . .

LOUIS: You deliberately misinterpreted! I . . .

BELIZE: Stop interrupting! I haven't been able to . . .

LOUIS: Just let me . . .

BELIZE: NO! What, *talk?* You've been running your mouth nonstop since I got here, yaddadda yaddadda blah blah blah, up the hill, down the hill, playing with your MONOLITH . . .

LOUIS (*Overlapping*): Well, you could have joined in at any time instead of . . .

BELIZE (*Continuing over* LOUIS): . . . and girlfriend it is truly an *awesome* spectacle but I got better things to do with my time than sit here listening to this racist bullshit just because I feel sorry for you that . . .

LOUIS: I am not a racist!

BELIZE: Oh come on . . .

LOUIS: So maybe I am a racist but . . .

BELIZE: Oh I really hate that! It's no fun picking on you Louis; you're so guilty, it's like throwing darts at a glob of jello, there's no satisfying hits, just quivering, the darts just blop in and vanish.

LOUIS: I just think when you are discussing lines of oppression it gets very complicated and . . .

BELIZE: Oh is that a fact? You know, we black drag queens have a rather intimate knowledge of the complexity of the lines of . . .

LOUIS: *Ex*-black drag queen.

BELIZE: Actually ex-ex.

LOUIS: You're doing drag again?

BELIZE: I don't. . . . Maybe. I don't have to tell you. Maybe.

LOUIS: I think it's sexist.

BELIZE: I didn't ask you.

LOUIS: Well it is. The gay community, I think, has to adopt the same attitude towards drag as black women have to take towards black women blues singers.

BELIZE: Oh my we *are* walking dangerous tonight.

LOUIS: Well, it's all internalized oppression, right, I mean the masochism, the stereotypes, the . . .

BELIZE: Louis, are you deliberately trying to make me hate you?

LOUIS: No, I . . .

BELIZE: I mean, are you deliberately transforming yourself into an arrogant, sexual-political Stalinist-slash-racist flag-waving thug for my benefit?

(*Pause.*)

LOUIS: You know what I think?

BELIZE: What?

LOUIS: You hate me because I'm a Jew.

BELIZE: I'm leaving.

LOUIS: It's true.

BELIZE: You have no basis except your . . .

Louis, it's good to know you haven't changed; you are still an honorary citizen of the Twilight Zone, and after your pale, pale white polemics on behalf of racial insensitivity you have a flaming *fuck* of a lot of nerve calling me an anti-Semite. Now I really gotta go.

LOUIS: You called me Lou the Jew.

BELIZE: That was a joke.

LOUIS: I didn't think it was funny. It was hostile.

BELIZE: It was three years ago.

LOUIS: So?

BELIZE: You just called yourself Sid the Yid.

LOUIS: That's not the same thing.

BELIZE: Sid the Yid is different from Lou the Jew.

LOUIS: Yes.

BELIZE: Someday you'll have to explain that to me, but right now . . .

You hate me because you hate black people.

LOUIS: I do not. But I do think most black people are anti-Semitic.

BELIZE: "Most black people." *That's* racist, Louis, and *I* think most Jews . . .

LOUIS: Louis Farrakhan.

BELIZE: Ed Koch.

LOUIS: Jesse Jackson.

BELIZE: Jackson. Oh really, Louis, this is . . .

LOUIS: Hymietown! Hymietown!

BELIZE: Louis, you voted for Jesse Jackson. You send checks to the Rainbow Coalition.

LOUIS: I'm ambivalent. The checks bounced.

BELIZE: All your checks bounce, Louis; you're ambivalent about everything.

LOUIS: What's that supposed to mean?

BELIZE: You may be dumber than shit but I refuse to believe you can't figure it out. Try.

LOUIS: I was never ambivalent about Prior. I love him. I do. I really do.

BELIZE: Nobody said different.

LOUIS: Love and ambivalence are. . . . Real love isn't ambivalent.

BELIZE: "Real love isn't ambivalent." I'd swear that's a line from my favorite bestselling paperback novel, *In Love with the Night Mysterious,* except I don't think you ever read it.

(*Pause.*)

LOUIS: I never read it, no.

BELIZE: You ought to. Instead of spending the rest of your life trying to get through *Democracy in America.* It's about this white woman whose Daddy owns a plantation in the Deep South in the years before the Civil War—the American one—and her name is Margaret, and she's in love with her Daddy's number-one slave, and his name is Thaddeus, and she's married but her white slave-owner husband has AIDS: Antebellum Insufficiently Developed Sexorgans. And there's a lot of hot stuff going down when Margaret and Thaddeus can catch a spare torrid ten under the cotton-picking moon, and then of course the Yankees come, and they set the slaves free, and the slaves string up old Daddy, and so on. Historical fiction. Somewhere in there I recall Margaret and Thaddeus find the time to discuss the nature of love; her face is reflecting the flames of the burning plantation—you know, the way white people do—and his black face is dark in the night and she says to him, "Thaddeus, real love isn't ever ambivalent."

(Little pause. EMILY *enters and turns off IV drip.)*

BELIZE: Thaddeus looks at her; he's contemplating her thesis; and he isn't sure he agrees.

EMILY *(Removing IV drip from* PRIOR's *arm)*: Treatment number . . . *(Consulting chart)* four.

PRIOR: Pharmaceutical miracle. Lazarus breathes again.

LOUIS: Is he. . . . How bad is he?

BELIZE: You want the laundry list?

EMILY: Shirt off, let's check the . . .

*(*PRIOR *takes his shirt off. She examines his lesions.)*

BELIZE: There's the weight problem and the shit problem and the morale problem.

EMILY: Only six. That's good. Pants.

(He drops his pants. He's naked. She examines.)

BELIZE: And. He thinks he's going crazy.

EMILY: Looking good. What else?

PRIOR: Ankles sore and swollen, but the leg's better. The nausea's mostly gone with the little orange pills. BM's pure liquid but not bloody anymore, for now, my eye doctor says everything's OK, for now, my dentist says "Yuck!" when he sees my fuzzy tongue, and now he wears little condoms on his thumb and forefinger. And a mask. So what? My dermatologist is in Hawaii and my mother . . . well leave my mother out of it. Which is usually where my mother is, out of it. My glands are like walnuts, my weight's holding steady for week two, and a friend died two days ago of bird tuberculosis; bird tuberculosis; that scared me and I didn't go to the funeral today because he was an Irish Catholic and it's probably open casket and I'm afraid of . . . something, the bird TB or seeing him or. . . . So I guess I'm doing OK. Except for of course I'm going nuts.

EMILY: We ran the toxoplasmosis series and there's no indication . . .

PRIOR: I know, I know, but I feel like something terri-

fying is on its way, you know, like a missile from outer space, and it's plummeting down towards the earth, and I'm ground zero, and . . . I am generally known where I am known as one cool, collected queen. And I am ruffled.

EMILY: There's really nothing to worry about. I think that shochen bamromim hamtzeh menucho nechono al kanfey haschino.°

PRIOR: What?

EMILY: Everything's fine. Bemaalos k'doshim ut'horim kezohar horokeea mazhirim.°

PRIOR: Oh I don't understand what you're . . .

EMILY: Es nishmas Prior sheholoch leolomoh, baavur shenodvoo z'dokoh b'ad hazkoras nishmosoh.°

PRIOR: Why are you doing that?! Stop it! Stop it!

EMILY: Stop what?

PRIOR: You were just . . . weren't you just speaking in Hebrew or something.

EMILY: *Hebrew? (Laughs)* I'm basically Italian-American. No. I didn't speak in Hebrew.

PRIOR: Oh no, oh God please I really think I . . .

EMILY: Look, I'm sorry, I have a waiting room full of. . . . I think you're one of the lucky ones, you'll live for years, probably—you're pretty healthy for someone with no immune system. Are you seeing someone? Loneliness is a danger. A therapist?

PRIOR: No, I don't need to see anyone, I just . . .

EMILY: Well think about it. You aren't going crazy. You're just under a lot of stress. No wonder . . .

(She starts to write in his chart)

(Suddenly there is an astonishing blaze of light, a huge chord sounded by a gigantic choir, and a great book with steel pages mounted atop a molten-red pillar pops up from the stage floor. The book opens; there is a large Aleph° inscribed on its pages, which bursts into flames. Immediately the book slams shut and disappears instantly under the floor as the lights become normal again. EMILY *notices none of this, writing.* PRIOR *is agog.)*

EMILY *(Laughing, exiting)*: Hebrew . . .

*(*PRIOR *flees.)*

LOUIS: Help me.

BELIZE: I beg your pardon?

LOUIS: You're a nurse, give me something, I . . . don't know what to do anymore, I. . . . Last week at

---

shochen bamromim . . . haschino, Transliteration of the Hebrew prayer spoken at a funeral service after the body has been interred. "Thou who dwellest on high! Grant perfect rest beneath the sheltering wings of Thy presence." **Bemaalos k'doshim . . . mazhirim,** The prayer continues, "among the holy and pure who shine as the brightness of the firmament." **Es nishmas . . . nishmosoh,** The prayer continues, "unto the soul of Prior, who has gone into eternity, and in whose memory charity is offered. May his repose be in Paradise." **Aleph,** first letter of the Hebrew alphabet.

work I screwed up the Xerox machine like permanently and so I . . . then I tripped on the subway steps and my glasses broke and I cut my forehead, here, see, and now I can't see much and my forehead . . . it's like the Mark of Cain, stupid, right, but it won't heal and every morning I see it and I think, Biblical things, Mark of Cain, Judas Iscariot and his silver and his noose, people who . . . in betraying what they love betray what's truest in themselves, I feel . . . nothing but cold for myself, just cold, and every night I miss him, I miss him so much but then . . . those sores, and the smell and . . . where I thought it was going. . . . I could be . . . I could be sick too, maybe I'm sick too. I don't know.

Belize. Tell him I love him. Can you do that?

BELIZE: I've thought about it for a very long time, and I still don't understand what love is. Justice is simple. Democracy is simple. Those things are unambivalent. But love is very hard. And it goes bad for you if you violate the hard law of love.

LOUIS: I'm dying.

BELIZE: He's dying. You just wish you were.

Oh cheer up, Louis. Look at that heavy sky out there.

LOUIS: Purple.

BELIZE: *Purple?* Boy, what kind of a homosexual are you, anyway? That's not purple, Mary, that color up there is *(Very grand)* mauve.

All day today it's felt like Thanksgiving. Soon, this . . . ruination will be blanketed white. You can smell it—can you smell it?

LOUIS: Smell what?

BELIZE: Softness, compliance, forgiveness, grace.

LOUIS: No . . .

BELIZE: I can't help you learn that. I can't help you, Louis. You're not my business. *(He exits)*

(LOUIS *puts his head in his hands, inadvertently touching his cut forehead.*)

LOUIS: Ow FUCK! *(He stands slowly, looks towards where* BELIZE *exited)* Smell what?

(He looks both ways to be sure no one is watching, then inhales deeply, and is surprised) Huh. Snow.

ACT 3 / SCENE 3

(Same day. HARPER *in a very white, cold place, with a brilliant blue sky above; a delicate snowfall. She is dressed in a beautiful snowsuit. The sound of the sea, faint.)*

HARPER: Snow! Ice! Mountains of ice! Where am I? I . . . I feel better, I do, I . . . feel better. There are ice crystals in my lungs, wonderful and sharp. And the snow smells like cold, crushed peaches. And there's something . . . some current of blood in the wind, how strange, it has that iron taste.

MR. LIES: Ozone.

HARPER: Ozone! Wow! Where am I?

MR. LIES: The Kingdom of Ice, the bottommost part of the world.

HARPER *(Looking around, then realizing):* Antarctica. This is Antarctica!

MR. LIES: Cold shelter for the shattered. No sorrow here, tears freeze.

HARPER: Antarctica, Antarctica, oh boy oh boy, LOOK at this, I. . . . Wow, I must've really snapped the tether, huh?

MR. LIES: Apparently . . .

HARPER: That's great. I want to stay here forever. Set up camp. Build things. Build a city, an enormous city made up of frontier forts, dark wood and green roofs and high gates made of pointed logs and bonfires burning on every street corner. I should build by a river. Where are the forests?

MR. LIES: No timber here. Too cold. Ice, no trees.

HARPER: Oh details! I'm sick of details! I'll plant them and grow them. I'll live off caribou fat, I'll melt it over the bonfires and drink it from long, curved goat-horn cups. It'll be great. I want to make a new world here. So that I never have to go home again.

MR. LIES: As long as it lasts. Ice has a way of melting . . .

HARPER: No. Forever. I can have anything I want here— maybe even companionship, someone who has . . . desire for me. You, maybe.

MR. LIES: It's against the by-laws of the International Order of Travel Agents to get involved with clients. Rules are rules. Anyway, I'm not the one you really want.

HARPER: There isn't anyone . . . maybe an Eskimo. Who could ice-fish for food. And help me build a nest for when the baby comes.

MR. LIES: There are no Eskimo in Antarctica. And you're not really pregnant. You made that up.

HARPER: Well all of this is made up. So if the snow feels cold I'm pregnant. Right? Here, I can be pregnant. And I can have any kind of a baby I want.

MR. LIES: This is a retreat, a vacuum, its virtue is that it lacks everything; deep-freeze for feelings. You can be numb and safe here, that's what you came for. Respect the delicate ecology of your delusions.

HARPER: You mean like no Eskimo in Antarctica.

MR. LIES: Correcto. Ice and snow, no Eskimo. Even hallucinations have laws.

HARPER: Well then who's that?

(The Eskimo appears.)

MR. LIES: An Eskimo.

HARPER: An antarctic Eskimo. A fisher of the polar deep.

MR. LIES: There's something wrong with this picture.

(The Eskimo beckons.)

HARPER: I'm going to like this place. It's my own National Geographic Special! Oh! Oh! *(She holds her stomach)* I think . . . I think I felt her kicking. Maybe I'll give birth to a baby covered with thick white fur, and that way she won't be cold. My breasts will be full of hot cocoa so she doesn't get chilly. And if it gets really cold, she'll have a pouch I can crawl into. Like a marsupial. We'll mend together. That's what we'll do; we'll mend.

ACT 3 / SCENE 4

(Same day. An abandoned lot in the South Bronx. A homeless WOMAN *is standing near an oil drum in which a fire is burning. Snowfall. Trash around.* HANNAH *enters dragging two heavy suitcases.)*

HANNAH: Excuse me? I said excuse me? Can you tell me where I am? Is this Brooklyn? Do you know a Pineapple Street? Is there some sort of bus or train or . . . ?

   I'm lost, I just arrived from Salt Lake. City. Utah? I took the bus that I was told to take and I got off—well it was the very last stop, so I had to get off, and I *asked* the driver was this Brooklyn, and he nodded yes but he was from one of those foreign countries where they think it's good manners to nod at everything even if you have no idea what it is you're nodding at, and in truth I think he spoke no English at all, which I think would make him ineligible for employment on public transportation. The public being English-speaking, mostly. Do you speak English?

(The WOMAN *nods.)*

HANNAH: I was supposed to be met at the airport by my son. He didn't show and I don't wait more than three and three-quarters hours for *anyone*. I should have been patient, I guess, I. . . . Is this . . .

WOMAN: Bronx.

HANNAH: Is that. . . . The *Bronx?* Well how in the name of Heaven did I get to the Bronx when the bus driver said . . .

WOMAN *(Talking to herself)*: Slurp slurp slurp will you STOP that disgusting slurping! YOU DISGUSTING SLURPING FEEDING ANIMAL! Feeding yourself, just feeding yourself, what would it matter, to you or to ANYONE, if you just stopped. Feeding. And DIED?

(Pause.)

HANNAH: Can you just tell me where I . . .

WOMAN: Why was the Kosciusko Bridge named after a Polack?

HANNAH: I don't know what you're . . .

WOMAN: That was a joke.

HANNAH: Well what's the punchline?

WOMAN: I don't know.

HANNAH *(Looking around desperately)*: Oh for pete's sake, is there anyone else who . . .

WOMAN *(Again, to herself)*: Stand further off you fat loathsome whore, you can't have any more of this soup, slurp slurp slurp you animal, and the—I know you'll just go pee it all away and where will you do that? Behind what bush? It's FUCKING COLD out here and I . . .

   Oh that's right, because it was supposed to have been a tunnel!

   That's not very funny.

   Have you read the prophecies of Nostradamus?°

HANNAH: Who?

WOMAN: Some guy I went out with once somewhere, Nostradamus. Prophet, outcast, eyes like. . . . Scary shit, he . . .

HANNAH: Shut up. Please. Now I want you to stop jabbering for a minute and pull your wits together and tell me how to get to Brooklyn. Because you know! And you are going to tell me! Because there is no one else around to tell me and I am wet and cold and I am very angry! So I am sorry you're psychotic but just make the effort—take a deep breath—DO IT!

(HANNAH and the WOMAN *breathe together.)*

HANNAH: That's good. Now exhale.

(They do.)

HANNAH: Good. Now how do I get to Brooklyn?

WOMAN: Don't know. Never been. Sorry. Want some soup?

HANNAH: Manhattan? Maybe you know . . . I don't suppose you know the location of the Mormon Visitor's . . .

WOMAN: 65th and Broadway.

HANNAH: How do you . . .

WOMAN: Go there all the time. Free movies. Boring, but you can stay all day.

HANNAH: Well. . . . So how do I . . .

WOMAN: Take the D Train. Next block make a right.

HANNAH: Thank you.

WOMAN: Oh yeah. In the new century I think we will all be insane.

ACT 3 / SCENE 5

(Same day. JOE *and* ROY *in the study of* ROY*'s brownstone.* ROY *is wearing an elegant bathrobe. He has made a considerable effort to look well. He isn't well, and he hasn't succeeded much in looking it.)*

JOE: I can't. The answer's no. I'm sorry.

ROY: Oh, well, apologies . . .

   I can't see that there's anyone asking for apologies.

Nostradamus, Latin name for Michel de Notre Dame, French physician and astrologer (1503–66), known for his predictions.

(Pause.)

JOE: I'm sorry, Roy.

ROY: Oh, well, apologies.

JOE: My wife is missing, Roy. My mother's coming from Salt Lake to . . . to help look, I guess. I'm supposed to be at the airport now, picking her up but. . . . I just spent two days in a hospital, Roy, with a bleeding ulcer, I was spitting up blood.

ROY: Blood, huh? Look, I'm very busy here and . . .

JOE: It's just a job.

ROY: A job? *A job? Washington!* Dumb Utah Mormon hick shit!

JOE: Roy . . .

ROY: *WASHINGTON!* When Washington called me I was younger than you, you think I said "Aw fuck no I can't go I got two fingers up my asshole and a little moral nosebleed to boot!" When Washington calls you my pretty young punk friend you go or you can go fuck yourself sideways 'cause the train has pulled out of the station, and you are *out,* nowhere, out in the cold. Fuck you, Mary Jane, get outta here.

JOE: Just let me . . .

ROY: Explain? Ephemera. You broke my heart. Explain that. Explain that.

JOE: I love you. Roy.

    There's so much that I want, to be . . . what you see in me, I want to be a participant in the world, in your world, Roy, I want to be capable of that, I've tried, really I have but . . . I can't do this. Not because I don't believe in you, but because I believe in you so much, in what you stand for, at heart, the order, the decency. I would give anything to protect you, but. . . . There are laws I can't break. It's too ingrained. It's not me. There's enough damage I've already done.

    Maybe you were right, maybe I'm dead.

ROY: You're not dead, boy, you're a sissy.

    You love me; that's moving, I'm moved. It's nice to be loved. I warned you about her, didn't I, Joe? But you don't listen to me, why, because you say Roy is smart and Roy's a friend but Roy . . . well, he isn't nice, and you wanna be nice. Right? A nice, nice man!

    (Little pause)

    You know what my greatest accomplishment was, Joe, in my life, what I am able to look back on and be proudest of? And I have helped make Presidents and unmake them and mayors and more goddam judges than anyone in NYC ever— AND several million dollars, tax-free—and what do you think means the most to me?

    You ever hear of Ethel Rosenberg? Huh, Joe, huh?

JOE: Well, yeah, I guess I. . . . Yes.

ROY: Yes. Yes. You have heard of Ethel Rosenberg. Yes.

Maybe you even read about her in the history books.

    If it wasn't for me, Joe, Ethel Rosenberg would be alive today, writing some personal-advice column for *Ms.* magazine. She isn't. Because during the trial, Joe, I was on the phone every day, talking with the judge . . .

JOE: Roy . . .

ROY: Every day, doing what I do best, talking on the telephone, making sure that timid Yid nebbish on the bench did his duty to America, to history. That sweet unprepossessing woman, two kids, boo-hoo-hoo, reminded us all of our little Jewish mamas—she came this close to getting life; I pleaded till I wept to put her in the chair. Me. I did that. I would have fucking pulled the switch if they'd have let me. Why? Because I fucking hate traitors. Because I fucking hate communists. Was it legal? Fuck legal. Am I a nice man? Fuck nice. They say terrible things about me in the *Nation.* Fuck the *Nation.* You want to be Nice, or you want to be Effective? Make the law, or subject to it. Choose. Your wife chose. A week from today, she'll be back. SHE knows how to get what SHE wants. Maybe I ought to send *her* to Washington.

JOE: I don't believe you.

ROY: Gospel.

JOE: You can't possibly mean what you're saying.

    Roy, you were the Assistant United States Attorney on the Rosenberg case, ex-parte communication with the judge during the trial would be . . . censurable, at least, probably conspiracy and . . . in a case that resulted in execution, it's . . .

ROY: What? Murder?

JOE: You're not well is all.

ROY: What do you mean, not well? Who's not well?

(Pause.)

JOE: You said . . .

ROY: No I didn't. I said what?

JOE: Roy, you have cancer.

ROY: No I don't.

(Pause.)

JOE: You told me you were dying.

ROY: What the fuck are you talking about, Joe? I never said that. I'm in perfect health. There's not a goddam thing wrong with me.

    (He smiles)

    Shake?

(JOE hesitates. He holds out his hand to ROY. ROY *pulls* JOE *into a close, strong clinch.)*

ROY *(More to himself than to* JOE): It's OK that you hurt me because I love you, baby Joe. That's why I'm so rough on you.

(ROY releases JOE. JOE backs away a step or two.)

ROY: Prodigal son. The world will wipe its dirty hands all over you.

JOE: It already has, Roy.

ROY: Now go.

(ROY shoves JOE, hard. JOE turns to leave. ROY stops him, turns him around.)

ROY *(Smoothing JOE's lapels, tenderly)*: I'll always be here, waiting for you . . .
> *(Then again, with sudden violence, he pulls JOE close, violently)*
> What did you want from me, what was all this, what do you want, treacherous ungrateful little . . .

(JOE, very close to belting ROY, grabs him by the front of his robe, and propels him across the length of the room. He holds ROY at arm's length, the other arm ready to hit.)

ROY *(Laughing softly, almost pleading to be hit)*: Transgress a little, Joseph.

(JOE releases ROY.)

ROY: There are so many laws; find one you can break.

(JOE hesitates, then leaves, backing out. When JOE has gone, ROY doubles over in great pain, which he's been hiding throughout the scene with JOE.)

ROY: Ah, Christ . . .
> Andy! Andy! Get in here! Andy!

(The door opens, but it isn't Andy. A small Jewish WOMAN dressed modestly in a fifties hat and coat stands in the doorway. The room darkens.)

ROY: Who the fuck are you? The new nurse?

(The figure in the doorway says nothing. She stares at ROY. A pause. ROY looks at her carefully, gets up, crosses to her. He crosses back to the chair, sits heavily.)

ROY: Aw, fuck. Ethel.

ETHEL ROSENBERG *(Her manner is friendly, her voice is ice-cold)*: You don't look good, Roy.

ROY: Well, Ethel. I don't feel good.

ETHEL ROSENBERG: But you lost a lot of weight. That suits you. You were heavy back then. Zaftig,° mit hips.

ROY: I haven't been that heavy since 1960. We were all heavier back then, before the body thing started. Now I look like a skeleton. They stare.

ETHEL ROSENBERG: The shit's really hit the fan, huh, Roy?

(Little pause. ROY nods.)

ETHEL ROSENBERG: Well the fun's just started.

Zaftig, Yiddish for curvaceous and plump.

ROY: What is this, Ethel, Halloween? You trying to scare me?

(ETHEL says nothing.)

ROY: Well you're wasting your time! I'm scarier than you any day of the week! So beat it, Ethel! BOOO! BETTER DEAD THAN RED! Somebody trying to shake me up? HAH HAH! From the throne of God in heaven to the belly of hell, you can all fuck yourselves and then go jump in the lake because I'M NOT AFRAID OF YOU OR DEATH OR HELL OR ANYTHING!

ETHEL ROSENBERG: Be seeing you soon, Roy. Julius sends his regards.

ROY: Yeah, well send this to Julius!

(He flips the bird in her direction, stands and moves towards her. Halfway across the room he slumps to the floor, breathing laboriously, in pain.)

ETHEL ROSENBERG: You're a very sick man, Roy.

ROY: Oh God . . . ANDY!

ETHEL ROSENBERG: Hmmm. He doesn't hear you, I guess. We should call the ambulance.
> *(She goes to the phone)*
> Hah! Buttons! Such things they got now. What do I dial, Roy?

(Pause. ROY looks at her, then:)

ROY: 911.

ETHEL ROSENBERG *(Dials the phone)*: It sings!
> *(Imitating dial tones)* La la la . . .
> Huh.
> Yes, you should please send an ambulance to the home of Mister Roy Cohn, the famous lawyer. What's the address, Roy?

ROY *(A beat, then)*: 244 East 87th.

ETHEL ROSENBERG: 244 East 87th Street. No apartment number, he's got the whole building.
> My name? *(A beat)* Ethel Greenglass Rosenberg.
> *(Small smile)* Me? No I'm not related to Mr. Cohn. An old friend.
> *(She hangs up)*
> They said a minute.

ROY: I have all the time in the world.

ETHEL ROSENBERG: You're immortal.

ROY: I'm immortal. Ethel. *(He forces himself to stand)*
> I have *forced* my way into history. I ain't never gonna die.

ETHEL ROSENBERG *(A little laugh, then)*: History is about to crack wide open. Millennium approaches.

ACT 3 / SCENE 6

(Late that night. PRIOR's bedroom. PRIOR 1 watching PRIOR in bed, who is staring back at him, terrified. Tonight PRIOR 1 is dressed in weird alchemical robes and

hat over his historical clothing and he carries a long palm-leaf bundle.)

PRIOR 1: Tonight's the night! Aren't you excited? Tonight she arrives! Right through the roof! Ha-adam, Ha-gadol . . .

PRIOR 2 *(Appearing, similarly attired)*: Lumen! Phosphor! Fluor! Candle! An unending billowing of scarlet and . . .

PRIOR: Look. Garlic. A mirror. Holy water. A crucifix. FUCK OFF! Get the fuck out of my room! GO!

PRIOR 1 *(To PRIOR 2)*: Hard as a hickory knob, I'll bet.

PRIOR 2: We all tumesce when they approach. We wax full, like moons.

PRIOR 1: Dance.

PRIOR: Dance?

PRIOR 1: Stand up, dammit, give us your hands, dance!

PRIOR 2: Listen . . .

(A lone oboe begins to play a little dance tune.)

PRIOR 2: Delightful sound. Care to dance?

PRIOR: Please leave me alone, please just let me sleep . . .

PRIOR 2: Ah, he wants someone familiar. A partner who knows his steps. *(To PRIOR)* Close your eyes. Imagine . . .

PRIOR: I don't . . .

PRIOR 2: Hush. Close your eyes.

(PRIOR does.)

PRIOR 2: Now open them.

(PRIOR does. LOUIS appears. He looks gorgeous. The music builds gradually into a full-blooded, romantic dance tune.)

PRIOR: Lou.

LOUIS: Dance with me.

PRIOR: I can't, my leg, it hurts at night . . .
Are you . . . a ghost, Lou?

LOUIS: No. Just spectral. Lost to myself. Sitting all day on cold park benches. Wishing I could be with you. Dance with me, babe . . .

(PRIOR stands up. The leg stops hurting. They begin to dance. The music is beautiful.)

PRIOR 1 *(To PRIOR 2)*: Hah. Now I see why he's got no children. He's a sodomite.

PRIOR 2: Oh be quiet, you medieval gnome, and let them dance.

PRIOR 1: I'm not interfering, I've done my bit. Hooray, hooray, the messenger's come, now I'm blowing off. I don't like it here.

(PRIOR 1 vanishes.)

PRIOR 2: The twentieth century. Oh dear, the world has gotten so terribly, terribly old.

(PRIOR 2 vanishes. LOUIS and PRIOR waltz happily. Lights fade back to normal. LOUIS vanishes.
PRIOR dances alone.
Then suddenly, the sound of wings fills the room.)

ACT 3 / SCENE 7

(Split scene: PRIOR alone in his apartment; LOUIS alone in the park.

Again, a sound of beating wings.)

PRIOR: Oh don't come in here don't come in . . . LOUIS!!
No. My name is Prior Walter, I am . . . the scion of an ancient line, I am . . . abandoned I . . . no, my name is . . . is . . . Prior and I live . . . *here and now,* and . . . in the dark, in the dark, the Recording Angel opens its hundred eyes and snaps the spine of the Book of Life and . . . hush! Hush!
I'm talking nonsense, I . . .
No more mad scene, hush, hush . . .

(LOUIS in the park on a bench. JOE approaches, stands at a distance. They stare at each other, then LOUIS turns away.)

LOUIS: Do you know the story of Lazarus?°

JOE: Lazarus?

LOUIS: Lazarus. I can't remember what happens, exactly.

JOE: I don't . . . Well, he was dead, Lazarus, and Jesus breathed life into him. He brought him back from death.

LOUIS: Come here often?

JOE: No. Yes. Yes.

LOUIS: Back from the dead. You believe that really happened?

JOE: I don't know anymore what I believe.

LOUIS: This is quite a coincidence. Us meeting.

JOE: I followed you.
From work. I . . . followed you here.

(Pause.)

LOUIS: You followed me.
You probably saw me that day in the washroom and thought: there's a sweet guy, sensitive, cries for friends in trouble.

JOE: Yes.

LOUIS: You thought maybe I'll cry for you.

JOE: Yes.

LOUIS: Well I fooled you. Crocodile tears. Nothing . . .
(He touches his heart, shrugs)

(JOE reaches tentatively to touch LOUIS's face.)

LOUIS *(Pulling back)*: What are you doing? Don't do that.

JOE *(Withdrawing his hand)*: Sorry. I'm sorry.

LOUIS: I'm . . . just not . . . I think, if you touch me, your hand might fall off or something. Worse things have happened to people who have touched me.

Lazarus, Cf. The Gospel of John, 11.

JOE: Please.
>   Oh, boy . . .
>   Can I . . .
>   I . . . want . . . to touch you. Can I please just touch you . . . um, here?
>   *(He puts his hand on one side of* LOUIS's *face. He holds it there)*
>   I'm going to hell for doing this.

LOUIS: Big deal. You think it could be any worse than New York City?
>   *(He puts his hand on* JOE's *hand. He takes* JOE's *hand away from his face, holds it for a moment, then)*
>   Come on.

JOE: Where?

LOUIS: Home. With me.

JOE: This makes no sense. I mean I don't know you.

LOUIS: Likewise.

JOE: And what you do know about me you don't like.

LOUIS: The Republican stuff?

JOE: Yeah, well for starters.

LOUIS: I don't not like that. I *hate* that.

JOE: So why on earth should we . . .

*(*LOUIS *goes to* JOE *and kisses him.)*

LOUIS: Strange bedfellows. I don't know. I never made it with one of the damned before.
>   I would really rather not have to spend tonight alone.

JOE: I'm a pretty terrible person, Louis.

LOUIS: Lou.

JOE: No, I really really am. I don't think I deserve being loved.

LOUIS: There? See? We already have a lot in common.

*(*LOUIS *stands, begins to walk away. He turns, looks back at* JOE. JOE *follows. They exit.)*

*(*PRIOR *listens. At first no sound, then once again, the sound of beating wings, frighteningly near.)*

PRIOR: That sound, that sound, it. . . . What is that, like birds or something, like a *really* big bird, I'm frightened, I . . . no, no fear, find the anger, find the . . . anger, my blood is clean, my brain is fine, I can handle pressure, I am a gay man and I am used to pressure, to trouble, I am tough and strong and. . . . Oh. Oh my goodness. I . . . *(He is washed over by an intense sexual feeling)* Ooohhhh. . . . I'm hot, I'm . . . so . . . aw Jeez what is going on here I . . . must have a fever I . . .

(The bedside lamp flickers wildly as the bed begins to roll forward and back. There is a deep bass creaking and groaning from the bedroom ceiling, like the timbers of a ship under immense stress, and from above a fine rain of plaster dust.)

PRIOR: OH!
>   PLEASE, OH PLEASE! Something's coming in here, I'm scared, I don't like this at all, something's approaching and I. . . . OH!

(There is a great blaze of triumphal music, heralding. The light turns an extraordinary harsh, cold, pale blue, then a rich, brilliant warm golden color, then a hot, bilious green, and then finally a spectacular royal purple. Then silence.)

PRIOR *(An awestruck whisper)*: God almighty . . .
>   *Very* Steven Spielberg.

(A sound, like a plummeting meteor, tears down from very, very far above the earth, hurtling at an incredible velocity towards the bedroom; the light seems to be sucked out of the room as the projectile approaches; as the room reaches darkness, we hear a terrifying CRASH as something immense strikes earth; the whole building shudders and a part of the bedroom ceiling, lots of plaster and lathe and wiring, crashes to the floor. And then in a shower of unearthly white light, spreading great opalescent gray-silver wings, THE ANGEL *descends into the room and floats above the bed.)*

ANGEL:
>   Greetings, Prophet;
>   The Great Work begins:
>   The Messenger has arrived.

(Blackout.)

END OF PART ONE

Figure 1. Roy Cohn (Ron Leibman) on the phone in the second scene of *Angels in America*. The New York production was directed by George C. Wolfe, 1993. (Photograph: Joan Marcus.)

Figure 2. The Angel (Ellen McLaughlin) appears to Prior Walter (Stephen Spinella) in the final moments of *Angels in America* in the 1993 New York production. (Photograph: Joan Marcus.)

Staging of *Angels in America: Millennium Approaches*

**REVIEW OF THE WALTER KERR THEATER
PRODUCTION, 1993, BY STEFAN KANFER**

When *Angels in America* received the Pulitzer Prize *before* its New York debut, the results were inevitable. Ever since opening night, a majority of ticketholders have obediently greeted the finale with standing ovations. But a handful of people stomping up the aisles can be heard muttering that they paid good money to see The Emperor's New Play. As it happens, both groups are mistaken. Tony Kushner's work, subtitled *Millennium Approaches,* has indeed been overhyped: *Angels* is pocked with flaws and disfigured with excesses. It is also one of the most imaginative productions in Broadway history.

Essentially, what takes place at the Walter Kerr Theater is a tragic circus, unfurling in '80s New York. In the right ring is Roy Cohn (Ron Leibman), one of the most execrated power brokers of his time. Shakespeare's line, "The first thing we do, let's kill all the lawyers," was invoked by Cohn's enemies almost every time he appeared in court. It was always said *sotto voce,* though. For Cohn had outlived his mentor, Senator Joe McCarthy, to become the friend of mayors, congressmen and cardinals.

In middle age, the unrepentant Red-hunter amused himself by making reputations and destroying careers. He also amused himself by sleeping with young men, something no one dared to mention—including Cohn. A champion of denial, he once denounced homosexuality at a Republican fund-raiser while a male prostitute sat waiting for him in a limousine. Leibman, in the role of a lifetime, catches every nuance and hypocrisy of Citizen Cohn. Using the phone as a flame-thrower or a firehose, slipping easily from plaintiff to defendant, from bully to charmer, he brings dimension to a character who might easily have been a caricature.

In the center ring, a four-year relationship is about to dissolve. A WASP drag queen, Prior Walter (Stephen Spinella), has not been feeling well. A spot has developed on his arm—the first sign of Kaposi's sarcoma. The mere mention of AIDS is enough to chill his Jewish lover, Louis Ironson (Joe Mantello). No nobility here, no long-lasting loyal gay marriage. A few bad scenes of illness and Louis is out the door, afflicted with guilt but unable to return.

In the third ring there is an early thirty-something Mormon couple, Joe Pitt (David Marshall Grant) and his wife Harper (Marcia Gay Harden). By the time we meet them their marriage is in extremis. Joe is cold and remote. Harper has become addicted to Valium and fantasies. They are her response to a suspicion she simply cannot confront: The righteous lawyer who shares her bed may not be as straight as he seems.

As the evening progresses, these rings become concentric circles. Cohn, in the course of business, takes an avuncular liking to Joe. He offers to get the young man a big job in Ed Meese's Justice Department. But Harper is too catatonic to leave New York, and Joe is too confused and frightened to leave his wife He becomes a taker of long, ruminative walks on the city streets. On more than one occasion Joe runs into Louis, with suggestive results.

Through, around and outside the rings a tumultuous side show goes on. At the funeral of an old woman, a rabbi lectures his parishioners about "The last of the Mohicans," the generation that trekked from the Pale to the New World. Joe's mother (Kathleen Chalfant) decides to pull up stakes in Utah to save her son from the fleshpots of New York. Harper's apparitions include a black travel agent, Mr. Lies (Jeffrey Wright), who entices her to Antarctica. Prior's visions are even more bizarre: As his malady advances, he is attended by distant ancestors dressed in medieval and Georgian costumes.

At the same time Cohn, suffering from the Acquired Immune Deficiency Syndrome he refuses to acknowledge, has his own hallucinations. In one of them Ethel Rosenberg materializes. Cohn snaps at her. How dare this woman enter his precincts? Why, he was the one who bullied the judge into giving Ethel and her husband Julius the death penalty for treason. She coolly accepts his boast, dials 911 and gets Roy an ambulance. Topping all this is the celebrated wide-winged seraph of the title, bursting through the roof as Prior breathes his last.

In this swirl of events and figments, one vital ingredient is missing: coherence. Lacking a strong "through line"—except for homosexuality in and out of the closet—*Angels in America* relies on Kushner's vivid expressionistic scenes, and director George C. Wolfe's extraordinary use of space and personae. If they never add up to a well-made play, that may be because *Millennium* is the first half of a theatrical statement. The second half, *Perestroika,* is to be presented next season. Only then will we know whether Kushner can relate his disparate themes.

But even if he turns out to be more of a scenewright than a playwright, he has shaken the New York theater to its foundations. The long file of AIDS plays (*Falset-*

tos, The Destiny of Me, Jeffrey, Lips Together, Teeth Apart, etc.) suddenly seems to be covered with dust—the plaster that came down when the angel burst through Prior's ceiling. The relation of religion, power, sex, and politics has never been so audaciously displayed. Cohn, for example, regards gays as men with "zero clout." He sees himself as a "straight man who happens to sleep with men." Yet it is the flamboyant Prior who turns out to be the stoic: "I am a gay man, and I am used to pressure." The rabbi and the Mormon mother take journeys—one physical, to the West, one emotional, to the East; in the process, they redefine the immigrant experience.

Although *Angels* could have used an editor, its principal weakness lies not in the writing but in the playing. Every man in the cast is distinctive and memorable. Spinella's bone-thin appearance gives him the aspect of a gothic Christ, yet his comic timing is impeccable. In his death throes, Prior stares at one of his elaborate visions and remarks, "*Very* Steven Spielberg." It brings down the house. Mantello is Spinella's psychological mirror image, matching him laugh for laugh, tear for tear. In a variety of lesser roles (everybody except Spinella plays at least two parts)

Grant and Wright are alternately sympathetic, irritating or funny, as the script demands.

Unhappily, the women range from adequate to ineffective. Playwright and director have points to make about gender, and from time to time Chalfant and Harden are required to double as men. Harden, who has enough trouble establishing the character of a pill freak, is wholly at sea impersonating a harrumphing Reaganite. Chalfant manages her upright Christian roles, but cannot bring off the rabbi's Yiddish accent or Ethel Rosenberg's urban intonations. Portraying a nurse in one act and a homeless woman in another, Ellen McLaughlin is brassy and unconvincing. She does make a smashing angel, ingeniously suspended from the flies. That, however, is due to Toni-Leslie James' costuming and Jules Fisher's lighting, both brilliant in every sense of the word.

Still, the play remains a true original. There has been nothing like it before, and there may be nothing like it again—unless *Perestroika* makes good on *Millennium*'s promises. In that case, Kushner's career will take wing without any special effects, except for the ones he creates on his typewriter.

TOM STOPPARD

1937–

When Tom Stoppard told critic Ronald Hayman "the only useful metaphor I can think of for the way I think I write my plays is convergences of different threads," he chose a metaphor that also describes his complex personal heritage. Born in Czechoslovakia as Tomás Straüssler, he was taken in 1939 to Singapore when his family fled the Nazi invasion, and then, when four years old, to Darjeeling, India, to escape the Japanese. His father, a doctor, stayed in Singapore and was killed in 1942, and his mother remarried in 1945. Adopted by his stepfather, Kenneth Stoppard, and moving to England in 1946, he became Tom Stoppard: public school student, reporter (after leaving school at 17), drama critic, internationally acclaimed playwright, and, in 1997, Sir Tom Stoppard. In 1999, Stoppard's characteristic blend of intellectual wit received international recognition when he won an Academy Award for his contributions to the screenplay of *Shakespeare in Love*, a script filled with deftly comic allusions to Shakespeare's plays.

The success of *Shakespeare in Love* looks back some twenty years to Stoppard's first professionally produced play, *Rosencrantz and Guildenstern Are Dead* (1967). Irreverently retelling the events of *Hamlet* from the perspective of two minor characters, Stoppard emphasizes what *Hamlet* only implies, namely, that the two characters are indistinguishable, even to themselves. But at the same time that he rewrites past literature, Stoppard places himself within the main currents of twentieth-century theater and its persistent concern with problematic issues of existence. Rosencrantz and Guildenstern's verbal game-playing and anxious waiting for Hamlet to appear make them cousins to Samuel Beckett's tramps, Vladimir and Estragon, in *Waiting for Godot*. Their bantering comments on the relationship between life and art recall Luigi Pirandello's obsessive treatment of that subject. The epigrammatic thrust of Stoppard's lines that echo Oscar Wilde's elegantly witty prose reflects Stoppard's debt to nineteenth-century British drama, particularly farce.

Stoppard's device in *Rosencrantz and Guildenstern Are Dead* of taking minor figures from literature and making them protagonists takes a new direction in *Travesties* (1974), where he transforms historical figures into characters on stage. Having discovered that the novelist James Joyce, the Dadaist artist Tristan Tzara, and the Russian revolutionary Vladimir Lenin all lived in Zurich in 1918, Stoppard decided to bring them together. Characteristically, his approach to these major figures of art and politics is oblique, for the central character in *Travesties* is a fictionalized Henry Carr, a young clerk in the British Consul's office with whom Joyce quarreled violently because of the money he spent for his costume in an amateur production of *The Importance of Being Earnest*. Like *Rosencrantz and Guildenstern Are Dead* (and *The Real Inspector Hound*, Stoppard's 1968 parody of stage murder mysteries), *Travesties* offers a feast of allusions for literate playgoers. But it also raises uncomfortable questions about the role of the artist and the meaning, if any, of art itself. Carr and Tzara debate the subject; Lenin (perhaps predictably) attacks bourgeois art; and Carr ends the play with a speech implying that art and politics are opposed and yet interchangeable:

> I learned three things in Zurich during the war. I wrote them down. Firstly, you're either a revolutionary or you're not, and if you're not, you might as well be an artist as anything else. Secondly, if you can't be an artist, you might as well be a revolutionary . . . I forget the third thing.

That "third thing"—the joining of artistic endeavor and revolutionary zeal—becomes the key to the next phase of Stoppard's work. Though he previously had denied any interest in writing "political" drama, Stoppard's 1977 visit to Russia and his native Czechoslovakia, and his meeting with the dissident playwright Václav Havel (who would later become president of the Czech Republic), made him painfully aware of political repression. Two short plays from 1977 mark a distinct shift in his dramatic intentions: *Every Good Boy Deserves Favor,* written for actors and orchestra, centering on the imprisonment of Russian dissenters in mental hospitals, and *Professional Foul,* a television play about a philosophy professor visiting Prague who personally encounters the ugly political reality of the repressive government. From 1978 on, questions that are political and deeply moral become increasingly central to Stoppard's plays. *Night and Day* (1978), set in an imaginary African country in the midst of a revolution, takes on the issue of the freedom of the press, while *The Real Thing* (1982) centers on a playwright who finds the cozy intellectual world of his plays destroyed by the messiness of a real-life love affair. The character Henry's confession in *The Real Thing,* "I don't know how to write love. I try to write it properly and it just comes out embarrassing," sounds faintly autobiographical; indeed, when Mel Gussow asked him in 1983 if *The Real Thing* was "the closest you've come to writing about love," Stoppard declared: "Yes. As far as I'm concerned, this is all I'll do. For better or worse, that's it—the love play!"

Fortunately, Stoppard did not follow his own resolve, and, in fact, made love increasingly central not only to his screenplay for *Shakespeare in Love* (first written in 1992) but to two of his later plays, *Arcadia* (1993) and *The Invention of Love* (1997). Both plays deal with literary figures—Lord Byron, absent from the stage but central to the plot, in *Arcadia,* and the poet A. E. Housman, also a renowned professor of classical literature, in *The Invention of Love.* What unites all of these works is Stoppard's perception that creativity and love are interdependent; young William Shakespeare writes *Romeo and Juliet* because he falls headlong in love; Housman, stifling his homosexual impulses toward a fellow undergraduate, becomes first a classical scholar but then writes his true feelings in the poems collected as *A Shropshire Lad;* and young Thomasina Coverly, the precocious but charming thirteen-year-old girl at the center of *Arcadia,* discovers love and the solution to a famous mathematical problem at the same time.

Stoppard's love of witty paradoxes is on full display in *Arcadia,* which portrays two different time periods in the same space, "a room on the garden front of a very large country house in Derbyshire," a room existing both in 1809 and then in "the present" (i.e., 1993). The large table dominating the room, is, by turns, the desk at which Thomasina and her tutor, Septimus Hodge, study; the research space for Hannah Jarvis, the twentieth-century author looking for information about the "hermit of Sidley Park"; and the place where characters from both centuries leave books, drawings, papers, pens, and so on. Stoppard points out at the beginning of the second scene that the props need not be changed: "During the course of the play the table collects this and that, and where an object from one scene would be an anachronism in another (say a coffee mug) it is simply deemed to have become invisible. By the end of the play the table has collected an inventory of objects."

The physical overlapping of two historical periods is at first confined to objects, although in a stage direction, Stoppard does ask for books in both "old" and "new" versions. The characters, however, seem to remain separate, both in physical appearance and behavior. In the nineteenth century, we watch an upper-class family, complete with a tutor for the young daughter, a butler, and even a landscape architect, while in the twentieth century, we watch two researchers, Hannah Jarvis and Bernard Nightingale, as each tries to decipher the events of 1809. While Hannah searches for the mysterious hermit (originally a figure that Thomasina whimsically sketched into a landscape design), Bernard is convinced that events at Sidley Park contributed to Lord Byron's sudden departure from England in 1809. Positing a duel between Byron and Chater, Bernard delivers a pompous lecture on his theory about Lord Byron (see Figure 2), only to be frequently interrupted by Hannah's objections. The audience shares her scorn, but from an even more informed perspective, since the events set in 1809 make clear that the quarrel is between Chater and Septimus. But gradually the parallels between the two periods become so prominent and numerous that they envelop the characters themselves, and thus in the last moments of the play, both centuries are visible simultaneously. Thomasina asks Septimus to teach her to walk and as they do so, "fluently"; young Gus bows to Hannah and the two of them begin to dance "rather awkwardly." What makes this moment particularly moving is our awareness that Thomasina will die later that night in a fire. Indeed, her candlestick is on the table, and Septimus even warns her, "Be careful with the flame."

Stoppard's blend of literate comedy, mathematical theory, sexual double-entendre, and gentle pathos evoked a variety of responses from London's theater critics, sometimes within the same review; Nicholas de Jongh was both "irritated and exhilarated, bemused and challenged," while John Gross felt that the play was "three plays rolled into one." But a number of reviews—including Paul Taylor's, reprinted following the play—responded to the emotional power of *Arcadia,* even while noting its wit and inventiveness. The production's juxtaposition of two time periods is illustrated in Figures 1 and 2, where the same table, loaded with the same books, appears first to separate Ezra Chater and Septimus Hodge, and then to furnish a background for Nightingale's lecture on Byron. The comic extravagance of some of the nineteenth-century characters is clear when Lady Croom objects to the plans for the remodeled Sidley Park (see Figure 3). But the pain and tenderness that underlies the play is similarly part of the nineteenth-century story, as when Septimus comforts Thomasina (see Figure 4) by asserting that all of the lost works of the past, whether literary or scientific, will eventually be reimagined or rediscovered. In this respect, Stoppard's play bears witness to his own effort to understand both past and present, and connects thoughts and feelings that span the centuries.

ARCADIA°

TOM STOPPARD

CHARACTERS

THOMASINA COVERLY, *aged thirteen, later sixteen*
SEPTIMUS HODGE, *her tutor, aged twenty-two, later twenty-five*
JELLABY, *a butler, middle-aged*
EZRA CHATER, *a poet, aged thirty-one*
RICHARD NOAKES, *a landscape architect, middle-aged*
LADY CROOM, *middle thirties*

CAPT. BRICE, RN, *middle thirties*
HANNAH JARVIS, *an author, late thirties*
CHLOË COVERLY, *aged eighteen*
BERNARD NIGHTINGALE, *a don, late thirties*
VALENTINE COVERLY, *aged twenty-five to thirty*
GUS COVERLY, *aged fifteen*
AUGUSTUS COVERLY, *aged fifteen*

ACT 1 / SCENE 1

(A room on the garden front of a very large country house in Derbyshire in April 1809. Nowadays, the house would be called a stately home. The upstage wall is mainly tall, shapely, uncurtained windows, one or more of which work as doors. Nothing much need be said or seen of the exterior beyond. We come to learn that the house stands in the typical English park of the time. Perhaps we see an indication of this, perhaps only light and air and sky.

The room looks bare despite the large table which occupies the centre of it. The table, the straight-backed chairs and, the only other item of furniture, the architect's stand or reading stand, would all be collectable pieces now but here, on an uncarpeted wood floor, they have no more pretension than a schoolroom, which is indeed the main use of this room at this time. What elegance there is, is architectural, and nothing is impressive but the scale. There is a door in each of the side walls. These are closed, but one of the french windows is open to a bright but sunless morning.

There are two people, each busy with books and paper and pen and ink, separately occupied. The pupil is THOMASINA COVERLY, *aged 13. The tutor is* SEPTIMUS HODGE, *aged 22. Each has an open book. Hers is a slim mathematics primer. His is a handsome thick quarto,° brand new, a vanity production, with little tapes to tie when the book is closed. His loose papers, etc, are kept in a stiff-backed portfolio which also ties up with tapes.*

SEPTIMUS *has a tortoise which is sleepy enough to serve as a paperweight. Elsewhere on the table there is an old-fashioned theodolite° and also some other books stacked up.)*

THOMASINA: Septimus, what is carnal embrace?
SEPTIMUS: Carnal embrace is the practice of throwing one's arms around a side of beef.
THOMASINA: Is that all?
SEPTIMUS: No . . . a shoulder of mutton, a haunch of venison well hugged, an embrace of grouse . . . *caro, carnis;* feminine; flesh.
THOMASINA: Is it a sin?
SEPTIMUS: Not necessarily, my lady, but when carnal embrace is sinful it is a sin of the flesh, QED. We had *caro* in our Gallic Wars°—'The Britons live on milk and meat'—'*lacte et carne vivunt.*' I am sorry that the seed fell on stony ground.
THOMASINA: That was the sin of Onan,° wasn't it, Septimus?
SEPTIMUS: Yes. He was giving his brother's wife a Latin lesson and she was hardly the wiser after it than before. I thought you were finding a proof for Fermat's last theorem.°
THOMASINA: It is very difficult, Septimus. You will have to show me how.
SEPTIMUS: If I knew how, there would be no need to ask *you.* Fermat's last theorem has kept people busy for a hundred and fifty years, and I hoped it would keep *you* busy long enough for me to read Mr Chater's poem in praise of love with only the distraction of its own absurdities.
THOMASINA: Our Mr Chater has written a poem?
SEPTIMUS: He believes he has written a poem, yes. I can see that there might be more carnality in your algebra than in Mr Chater's 'Couch of Eros.'

Arcadia, ancient Greek region, idealized in poetry as a place of innocence and simplicity. *quarto,* size of book, roughly comparable to a modern novel. *theodolite,* surveyor's measuring instrument, a telescope mounted between poles.

Gallic Wars, Julius Caesar's account of his military campaigns in Gaul (France, England, and Germany), frequently used as a Latin textbook. *Onan,* Genesis 38:9. *Fermat's last theorem,* famous problem proposed by Pierre de Fermat (1601–65), French mathematician, and proved in the 1990s by Andrew Wiles.

THOMASINA: Oh, it was not my algebra. I heard Jellaby telling cook that Mrs Chater was discovered in carnal embrace in the gazebo.°

SEPTIMUS: *(Pause)* Really? With whom, did Jellaby happen to say?

(THOMASINA considers this with a puzzled frown.)

THOMASINA: What do you mean, with whom?

SEPTIMUS: With what? Exactly so. The idea is absurd. Where did this story come from?

THOMASINA: Mr Noakes.

SEPTIMUS: Mr Noakes!

THOMASINA: Papa's landskip° architect. He was taking bearings in the garden when he saw—through his spyglass—Mrs Chater in the gazebo in carnal embrace.

SEPTIMUS: And do you mean to tell me that Mr Noakes told the butler?

THOMASINA: No. Mr Noakes told Mr Chater. *Jellaby* was told by the groom, who overheard Mr Noakes telling Mr Chater, in the stable yard.

SEPTIMUS: Mr Chater being engaged in closing the stable door.

THOMASINA: What do you mean, Septimus?

SEPTIMUS: So, thus far, the only people who know about this are Mr Noakes the landskip architect, the groom, the butler, the cook and, of course, Mrs Chater's husband, the poet.

THOMASINA: And Arthur who was cleaning the silver, and the bootboy. And now you.

SEPTIMUS: Of course. What else did he say?

THOMASINA: Mr Noakes?

SEPTIMUS: No, not Mr Noakes. Jellaby. You heard Jellaby telling the cook.

THOMASINA: Cook hushed him almost as soon as he started. Jellaby did not see that I was being allowed to finish yesterday's upstairs' rabbit pie before I came to my lesson. I think you have not been candid with me, Septimus. A gazebo is not, after all, a meat larder.

SEPTIMUS: I never said my definition was complete.

THOMASINA: Is carnal embrace kissing?

SEPTIMUS: Yes.

THOMASINA: And throwing one's arms around Mrs Chater?

SEPTIMUS: Yes. Now, Fermat's last theorem—

THOMASINA: I thought as much. I hope you are ashamed.

SEPTIMUS: I, my lady?

THOMASINA: If *you* do not teach me the true meaning of things, who will?

SEPTIMUS: Ah. Yes, I am ashamed. Carnal embrace is sexual congress, which is the insertion of the male genital organ into the female genital organ for purposes of procreation and pleasure. Fermat's last theorem, by contrast, asserts that when x, y and z are whole numbers each raised to power of n, the sum of the first two can never equal the third when n is greater than 2.

(Pause.)

THOMASINA: Eurghhh!

SEPTIMUS: Nevertheless, that is the theorem.

THOMASINA: It is disgusting and incomprehensible. Now when I am grown to practise it myself I shall never do so without thinking of you.

SEPTIMUS: Thank you very much, my lady. Was Mrs Chater down this morning?

THOMASINA: No. Tell me more about sexual congress.

SEPTIMUS: There is nothing more to be said about sexual congress.

THOMASINA: Is it the same as love?

SEPTIMUS: Oh no, it is much nicer than that.

(One of the side doors leads to the music room. It is the other side door which now opens to admit JELLABY, *the butler.)*

JELLABY: Beg your pardon, Mr Hodge, Mr Chater said it was urgent you receive his letter.

SEPTIMUS: Oh, very well. (SEPTIMUS *takes the letter.)* Thank you. *(And to dismiss* JELLABY*)* Thank you.

JELLABY *(Holding his ground)*: Mr Chater asked me to bring him your answer.

SEPTIMUS: My answer?

(He opens the letter. There is no envelope as such, but there is a 'cover' which, folded and sealed, does the same service. SEPTIMUS *tosses the cover negligently aside and reads.)*

Well, my answer is that as is my custom and my duty to his lordship I am engaged until a quarter to twelve in the education of his daughter. When I am done, and if Mr, Chater is still there, I will be happy to wait upon him in—*(he checks the letter)*—in the gunroom.

JELLABY: I will tell him so, thank you, sir.

(SEPTIMUS folds the letter and places it between the pages of 'The Couch of Eros.')

THOMASINA: What is for dinner, Jellaby?

JELLABY: Boiled ham and cabbages, my lady, and a rice pudding.

THOMASINA: Oh, goody.

(JELLABY leaves.)

SEPTIMUS: Well, so much for Mr Noakes. He puts himself forward as a gentleman, a philosopher of the picturesque, a visionary who can move mountains and cause lakes, but in the scheme of the garden he is as the serpent.

THOMASINA: When you stir your rice pudding, Septimus, the spoonful of jam spreads itself round

---

gazebo, decorative building in garden.   **landskip,** landscape.

making red trails like the picture of a meteor in my astronomical atlas. But if you stir backward, the jam will not come together again. Indeed, the pudding does not notice and continues to turn pink just as before. Do you think this is odd?

SEPTIMUS: No.

THOMASINA: Well, I do. You cannot stir things apart.

SEPTIMUS: No more you can, time must needs run backward, and since it will not, we must stir our way onward mixing as we go, disorder out of disorder into disorder until pink is complete, unchanging and unchangeable, and we are done with it for ever. This is known as free will or self-determination.

(He picks up the tortoise and moves it a few inches as though it had strayed, on top of some loose papers, and admonishes it.)

Sit!

THOMASINA: Septimus, do you think God is a Newtonian?

SEPTIMUS: An Etonian?° Almost certainly, I'm afraid. We must ask your brother to make it his first enquiry.

THOMASINA: No, Septimus, a Newtonian. Septimus! Am I the first person to have thought of this?

SEPTIMUS: No.

THOMASINA: I have not said yet.

SEPTIMUS: 'If everything from the furthest planet to the smallest atom of our brain acts according to Newton's law of motion, what becomes of free will?'

THOMASINA: No.

SEPTIMUS: God's will.

THOMASINA: No.

SEPTIMUS: Sin.

THOMASINA *(Derisively)*: No!

SEPTIMUS: Very well.

THOMASINA: If you could stop every atom in its position and direction, and if your mind could comprehend all the actions thus suspended, then if you were really, *really* good at algebra you could write the formula for all the future; and although nobody can be so clever to do it, the formula must exist just as if one could.

SEPTIMUS: *(Pause)* Yes. *(Pause)* Yes, as far as I know, you are the first person to have thought of this. *(Pause. With an effort)* In the margin of his copy of *Arithmetica*, Fermat wrote that he had discovered a wonderful proof of his theorem but, the margin being too narrow for his purpose, did not have

room to write it down. The note was found after his death, and from that day to this—

THOMASINA: Oh! I see now! The answer is perfectly obvious.

SEPTIMUS: This time you may have overreached yourself.

(The door is opened, somewhat violently. CHATER enters.)

Mr Chater! Perhaps my message miscarried. I will be at liberty at a quarter to twelve, if that is convenient.

CHATER: It is not convenient, sir. My business will not wait.

SEPTIMUS: Then I suppose you have Lord Croom's opinion that your business is more important than his daughter's lesson.

CHATER: I do not, but, if you like, I will ask his lordship to settle the point.

SEPTIMUS: *(Pause)* My lady, take Fermat into the music room. There will be an extra spoonful of jam if you find his proof.

THOMASINA: There is no proof, Septimus. The thing that is perfectly obvious is that the note in the margin was a joke to make you all mad.

(THOMASINA leaves.)

SEPTIMUS: Now, sir, what is this business that cannot wait?

CHATER: I think you know it, sir. You have insulted my wife.

SEPTIMUS: Insulted her? That would deny my nature, my conduct, and the admiration in which I hold Mrs Chater.

CHATER: I have heard of your admiration, sir! You insulted my wife in the gazebo yesterday evening!

SEPTIMUS: You are mistaken. I made love to your wife in the gazebo. She asked me to meet her there, I have her note somewhere, I dare say I could find it for you, and if someone is putting it about that I did not turn up, by God, sir, it is a slander.

CHATER: You damned lecher! You would drag down a lady's reputation to make a refuge for your cowardice. It will not do! I am calling you out!

SEPTIMUS: Chater! Chater, Chater, Chater! My dear friend!

CHATER: You dare to call me that. I demand satisfaction!

SEPTIMUS: Mrs Chater demanded satisfaction and now you are demanding satisfaction. I cannot spend my time day and night satisfying the demands of the Chater family. As for your wife's reputation, it stands where it ever stood.

CHATER: You blackguard!

SEPTIMUS: I assure you. Mrs Chater is charming and spirited, with a pleasing voice and a dainty step, she is the epitome of all the qualities society applauds in her sex—and yet her chief renown is

---

Etonian, student at Eton, one of England's most prestigious private schools for boys.

for a readiness that keeps her in a state of tropical humidity as would grow orchids in her drawers in January.

CHATER: Damn you, Hodge, I will not listen to this! Will you fight or not?

SEPTIMUS (*Definitively*): Not! There are no more than two or three poets of the first rank now living, and I will not shoot one of them dead over a perpendicular poke in a gazebo with a woman whose reputation could not be adequately defended with a platoon of musketry deployed by rota.

CHATER: Ha! You say so! Who are the others? In your opinion?—no—no—!—this goes very ill, Hodge. I will not be flattered out of my course. You say so, do you?

SEPTIMUS: I do. And I would say the same to Milton° were he not already dead. Not the part about his wife, of course—

CHATER: But among the living? Mr Southey?°

SEPTIMUS: Southey I would have shot on sight.

CHATER (*Shaking his head sadly*): Yes, he has fallen off. I admired 'Thalaba' *quite*, but 'Madoc,' (*he chuckles*) oh dear me!—but we are straying from the business here—you took advantage of Mrs Chater, and if that were not bad enough, it appears every stableboy and scullery maid on the strength—

SEPTIMUS: Damn me! Have you not listened to a word I said?

CHATER: I have heard you, sir, and I will not deny I welcome your regard, God knows one is little appreciated if one stands outside the coterie of hacks and placemen who surround Jeffrey° and the *Edinburgh*—

SEPTIMUS: My dear Chater, they judge a poet by the seating plan of Lord Holland's table!

CHATER: By heaven, you are right! And I would very much like to know the name of the scoundrel who slandered my verse drama 'Maid of Turkey' in the *Piccadilly Recreation,*° too!

SEPTIMUS: 'The Maid of Turkey'! I have it by my bedside! When I cannot sleep I take up 'The Maid of Turkey' like an old friend!

CHATER (*Gratified*): There you are! And the scoundrel wrote he would not give it to his dog for dinner were it covered in bread sauce and stuffed with chestnuts. When Mrs Chater read that, she wept,

sir, and would not give herself to me for a fortnight—which recalls me to my purpose—

SEPTIMUS: The new poem, however, will make your name perpetual—

CHATER: Whether it do or not—

SEPTIMUS: It is not a question, sir. No coterie can oppose the acclamation of the reading public. 'The Couch of Eros' will take the town.

CHATER: Is that your estimation?

SEPTIMUS: It is my intent.

CHATER: Is it, is it? Well, well! I do not understand you.

SEPTIMUS: You see I have an early copy—sent to me for review. I say review, but I speak of an extensive appreciation of your gifts and your rightful place in English literature.

CHATER: Well, I must say. That is certainly . . . You have written it?

SEPTIMUS (*Crisply*): Not yet.

CHATER: Ah. And how long does. . . ?

SEPTIMUS: To be done right, it first requires a careful re-reading of your book, of both your books, several readings, together with outlying works for an exhibition of deference or disdain as the case merits. I make notes, of course, I order my thoughts, and finally, when all is ready and I am *calm in my mind* . . .

CHATER (*Shrewdly*): Did Mrs Chater know of this before she—before you—

SEPTIMUS: I think she very likely did.

CHATER (*Triumphantly*): There is nothing that woman would not do for me! Now you have an insight to her character. Yes, by God, she is a wife to me, sir!

SEPTIMUS: For that alone, I would not make her a widow.

CHATER: Captain Brice once made the same observation!

SEPTIMUS: Captain Brice did?

CHATER: Mr Hodge, allow me to inscribe your copy in happy anticipation. Lady Thomasina's pen will serve us.

SEPTIMUS: Your connection with Lord and Lady Croom you owe to your fighting her ladyship's brother?

CHATER: No! It was all nonsense, sir—a canard! But a fortunate mistake, sir. It brought me the patronage of a captain of His Majesty's Navy and the brother of a countess. I do not think Mr Walter Scott° can say as much, and here I am, a respected guest at Sidley Park.

SEPTIMUS: Well, sir, you can say you have received satisfaction.

(CHATER *is already inscribing the book, using the pen and ink-pot on the table.* NOAKES *enters through the door used*

Milton, John Milton (1608–74), English poet, author of *Paradise Lost.* *Southey,* Robert Southey (1774–1843), English poet. "Thalaba" and "Madoc" are two of his longer poems. *Jeffrey,* Francis Jeffrey (1773–1850), editor and cofounder of the *Edinburgh Review,* a new journal that first appeared in 1802. His outspoken criticism of many poets, including Byron, occasioned Byron's satire "English Bards and Scotch Reviewers." *Piccadilly Recreation,* an imaginary literary review.

Walter Scott, 1771–1832, Scots novelist and poet.

by CHATER. *He carries rolled-up plans.* CHATER, *inscribing, ignores* NOAKES. NOAKES *on seeing the occupants, panics.*)

NOAKES: Oh!

SEPTIMUS: Ah, Mr Noakes!—my muddy-mettled rascal! Where's your spyglass?

NOAKES: I beg your leave—I thought her ladyship—excuse me—

(*He is beating an embarrassed retreat when he becomes rooted by* CHATER's *voice.* CHATER *reads his inscription in ringing tones.*)

CHATER: 'To my friend Septimus Hodge, who stood up and gave his best on behalf of the Author—Ezra Chater, at Sidley Park, Derbyshire, April 10th, 1809.' (*Giving the book to* SEPTIMUS) There, sir—something to show your grandchildren!

SEPTIMUS: This is more than I deserve, this is handsome, what do you say, Noakes?

(*They are interrupted by the appearance, outside the windows, of* LADY CROOM *and* CAPTAIN EDWARD BRICE, RN. *Her first words arrive through the open door.*)

LADY CROOM: Oh, no! Not the gazebo!

(*She enters, followed by* BRICE *who carries a leatherbound sketch book.*)

Mr Noakes! What is this I hear?

BRICE: Not only the gazebo, but the boat-house, the Chinese bridge, the shrubbery—

CHATER: By God, sir! Not possible!

BRICE: Mr Noakes will have it so.

SEPTIMUS: Mr Noakes, this is monstrous!

LADY CROOM: I am glad to hear it from *you*, Mr Hodge.

THOMASINA (*Opening the door from the music room*): May I return now?

SEPTIMUS (*Attempting to close the door*): Not just yet—

LADY CROOM: Yes, let her stay. A lesson in folly is worth two in wisdom.

(BRICE *takes the sketch book to the reading stand, where he lays it open. The sketch book is the work of* MR NOAKES, *who is obviously an admirer of Humphry Repton's 'Red Books.'° The pages, drawn in watercolours, show 'before' and 'after' views of the landscape, and the pages are cunningly cut to allow the latter to be superimposed over portions of the former, though Repton did it the other way round.*)

BRICE: Is Sidley Park to be an Englishman's garden or the haunt of Corsican brigands?

SEPTIMUS: Let us not hyperbolize, sir.

BRICE: It is rape, sir!

Humphry Repton, 1752–1818, landscape architect who presented his designs in books with "before" and "after" pictures.

NOAKES (*Defending himself*): It is the modern style.

CHATER (*Under the same misapprehension as* SEPTIMUS): Regrettable, of course, but so it is.

(THOMASINA *has gone to examine the sketch book.*)

LADY CROOM: Mr Chater, you show too much submission. Mr Hodge, I appeal to you.

SEPTIMUS: Madam, I regret the gazebo, I sincerely regret the gazebo—and the boat-house up to a point—but the Chinese bridge, fantasy!—and the shrubbery I reject with contempt! Mr Chater!—would you take the word of a jumped-up jobbing gardener who sees carnal embrace in every nook and cranny of the landskip!

THOMASINA: Septimus, they are not speaking of carnal embrace, are you, Mama?

LADY CROOM: Certainly not. What do you know of carnal embrace?

THOMASINA: Everything, thanks to Septimus. In my opinion, Mr Noakes's scheme for the garden is perfect. It is a Salvator!

LADY CROOM: What does she mean?

NOAKES (*Answering the wrong question*): Salvator Rosa,° your ladyship, the painter. He is indeed the very exemplar of the picturesque style.

BRICE: Hodge, what is this?

SEPTIMUS: She speaks from innocence not from experience.

BRICE: You call it innocence? Has he ruined you, child?

(*Pause.*)

SEPTIMUS: Answer your uncle!

THOMASINA (*To* SEPTIMUS): How is a ruined child different from a ruined castle?

SEPTIMUS: On such questions I defer to Mr Noakes.

NOAKES (*Out of his depth*): A ruined castle is picturesque, certainly.

SEPTIMUS: That is the main difference. (*To* BRICE) I teach the classical authors. If I do not elucidate their meaning, who will?

BRICE: As her tutor you have a duty to keep her in ignorance.

LADY CROOM: Do not dabble in paradox, Edward, it puts you in danger of fortuitous wit. Thomasina, wait in your bedroom.

THOMASINA (*Retiring*): Yes, mama. I did not intend to get you into trouble, Septimus. I am very sorry for it. It is plain that there are some things a girl is allowed to understand, and these include the whole of algebra, but there are others, such as embracing a side of beef, that must be kept from her until she is old enough to have a carcass of her own.

Salvator Rosa, 1615–73, Italian painter specializing in romantic, wild landscapes.

LADY CROOM: One moment.

BRICE: What is she talking about?

LADY CROOM: Meat.

BRICE: Meat?

LADY CROOM: Thomasina, you had better remain. Your knowledge of the picturesque obviously exceeds anything the rest of us can offer. Mr Hodge, ignorance should be like an empty vessel waiting to be filled at the well of truth—not a cabinet of vulgar curios. Mr Noakes—now at last it is your turn—

NOAKES: Thank you, your ladyship—

LADY CROOM: Your drawing is a very wonderful transformation. I would not have recognized my own garden but for your ingenious book—is it not?—look! Here is the Park as it appears to us now, and here as it might be when Mr Noakes has done with it. Where there is the familiar pastoral refinement of an Englishman's garden, here is an eruption of gloomy forest and towering crag, of ruins where there was never a house, of water dashing against rocks where there was neither spring nor a stone I could not throw the length of a cricket pitch. My hyacinth dell is become a haunt for hobgoblins, my Chinese bridge, which I am assured is superior to the one at Kew,° and for all I know at Peking, is usurped by a fallen obelisk overgrown with briars—

NOAKES (Bleating): Lord Little has one very similar—

LADY CROOM: I cannot relieve Lord Little's misfortunes by adding to my own. Pray, what is this rustic hovel that presumes to superpose itself on my gazebo?

NOAKES: That is the hermitage, madam.

LADY CROOM: I am bewildered.

BRICE: It is all irregular, Mr Noakes.

NOAKES: It is, sir. Irregularity is one of the chiefest principles of the picturesque style—

LADY CROOM: But Sidley Park is already a picture, and a most amiable picture too. The slopes are green and gentle. The trees are companionably grouped at intervals that show them to advantage. The rill is a serpentine ribbon unwound from the lake peaceably contained by meadows on which the right amount of sheep are tastefully arranged—in short, it is nature as God intended, and I can say with the painter, 'Et in Arcadia ego!'° 'Here I am in Arcadia,' Thomasina.

THOMASINA: Yes, mama, if you would have it so.

LADY CROOM: Is she correcting my taste or my translation?

THOMASINA: Neither are beyond correction, mama, but it was your geography caused the doubt.

LADY CROOM: Something has occurred with the girl since I saw her last, and surely that was yesterday. How old are you this morning?

THOMASINA: Thirteen years and ten months, mama.

LADY CROOM: Thirteen years and ten months. She is not due to be pert for six months at the earliest, or to have notions of taste for much longer. Mr Hodge, I hold you accountable. Mr Noakes, back to you—

NOAKES: Thank you, my—

LADY CROOM: You have been reading too many novels by Mrs Radcliffe,° that is my opinion. This is a garden for *The Castle of Otranto or The Mysteries of Udolpho*—

CHATER: *The Castle of Otranto,* my lady, is by Horace Walpole.°

NOAKES (Thrilled): Mr Walpole the gardener?

LADY CROOM: Mr Chater, you are a welcome guest at Sidley Park but while you are one, *The Castle of Otranto* was written by whomsoever I say it was, otherwise what is the point of being a guest or having one?

(*The distant popping of guns heard.*)

Well, the guns have reached the brow—I will speak to his lordship on the subject, and we will see by and by—(*She stands looking out.*) Ah!—your friend has got down a pigeon, Mr Hodge. (*Calls out*) Bravo, sir!

SEPTIMUS: The pigeon, I am sure, fell to your husband or to your son, your ladyship—my schoolfriend was never a sportsman.

BRICE (Looking out): Yes, to Augustus!—bravo, lad!

LADY CROOM (Outside): Well, come along! Where are my troops?

(BRICE, NOAKES *and* CHATER *obediently follow her,* CHATER *making a detour to shake* SEPTIMUS *'s hand fervently.*)

CHATER: My dear Mr Hodge!

(CHATER *leaves also. The guns are heard again, a little closer.*)

THOMASINA: Pop, pop, pop . . . I have grown up in the sound of guns like the child of a siege. Pigeons and rooks in the close season, grouse on the

---

Kew, site in west London of the Royal Botanic Gardens. **Et in Arcadia ego,** Latin phrase appearing on a tomb in a famous painting (1623) by Guercino, and then in a painting by Poussin (1627). Lady Croom's translation, "Here am I in Arcadia," misses the line's ironic meaning, "Even in Arcadia, here am I (Death)."

Mrs Radcliffe, Ann Radcliffe (1764–1823), author of gothic novels, including *The Mysteries of Udolpho.* **Horace Walpole,** 1717–97, author of the gothic novel *The Castle of Otranto* (1765), known also for popularizing the picturesque approach to landscape design.

heights from August, and the pheasants to follow—partridge, snipe, woodcock, and teal—
pop—pop—pop, and the culling of the herd.
Papa has no need of the recording angel, his life
is written in the game book.

SEPTIMUS: A calendar of slaughter. 'Even in Arcadia,
there am I!'

THOMASINA: Oh, phooey to Death!

(She dips a pen and takes it to the reading stand.)

I will put in a hermit, for what is a hermitage without a hermit? Are you in love with my mother,
Septimus?

SEPTIMUS: You must not be cleverer than your elders.
It is not polite.

THOMASINA: Am I cleverer?

SEPTIMUS: Yes. Much.

THOMASINA: Well, I am sorry, Septimus. *(She pauses in
her drawing and produces a small envelope from her
pocket.)* Mrs Chater came to the music room with a
note for you. She said it was of scant importance,
and that therefore I should carry it to you with
the utmost safety, urgency and discretion. Does
carnal embrace addle the brain?

SEPTIMUS *(Taking the letter)*: Invariably. Thank you.
That is enough education for today.

THOMASINA: There. I have made him like the Baptist°
in the wilderness.

SEPTIMUS: How picturesque.

*(LADY CROOM is heard calling distantly for THOMASINA
who runs off into the garden, cheerfully, an uncomplicated
girl. SEPTIMUS opens Mrs Chater's note. He crumples the
envelope and throws it away. He reads the note, folds it and
inserts it into the pages of 'The Couch of Eros.')*

ACT 1 / SCENE 2

*(The lights come up on the same room, on the same sort
of morning, in the present day, as is instantly clear from
the appearance of HANNAH JARVIS; and from nothing
else.*

*Something needs to be said about this. The action of the
play shuttles back and forth between the early nineteenth
century and the present day, always in this same room.
Both periods must share the state of the room, without the
additions and subtractions which would normally be
expected. The general appearance of the room should
offend neither period. In the case of props—books, paper,
flowers, etc., there is no absolute need to remove the evidence of one period to make way for another. However,
books, etc., used in both periods should exist in both old
and new versions. The landscape outside, we are told, has*

Baptist, John the Baptist, who lived many years in the
desert.

*undergone changes. Again, what we see should neither
change nor contradict.*

*On the above principle, the ink and pens etc., of the first
scene can remain. Books and papers associated with Hannah's research, in Scene 2, can have been on the table from
the beginning of the play. And so on. During the course of
the play the table collects this and that, and where an object
from one scene would be an anachronism in another (say a
coffee mug) it is simply deemed to have become invisible. By
the end of the play the table has collected an inventory of
objects.*

*HANNAH is leafing through the pages of Mr Noakes's
sketch book. Also to hand, opened and closed, are a number of small volumes like diaries [these turn out to be Lady
Croom's 'garden books']. After a few moments, HANNAH
takes the sketch book to the windows, comparing the view
with what has been drawn, and then she replaces the
sketch book on the reading stand.*

*She wears nothing frivolous. Her shoes are suitable for
the garden, which is where she goes now after picking up
the theodolite from the table. The room is empty for a few
moments.*

*One of the other doors opens to admit CHLOË and
BERNARD. She is the daughter of the house and is dressed
casually. BERNARD, the visitor, wears a suit and a tie. His
tendency is to dress flamboyantly, but he has damped it
down for the occasion, slightly. A peacock-coloured display
handkerchief boils over in his breast pocket. He carries a
capacious leather bag which serves as a briefcase.)*

CHLOË: Oh! Well, she *was* here . . .

BERNARD: Ah . . . the french window . . .

CHLOË: Yes. Hang on.

*(CHLOË steps out through the garden door and disappears
from view. BERNARD hangs on. The second door opens
and VALENTINE looks in.)*

VALENTINE: Sod.°

*(VALENTINE goes out again, closing the door. CHLOË
returns, carrying a pair of rubber boots. She comes in and
sits down and starts exchanging her shoes for the boots,
while she talks.)*

CHLOË: The best thing is, you wait here, save you
tramping around. She spends a good deal of time
in the garden, as you may imagine.

BERNARD: Yes. Why?

CHLOË: Well, she's writing a history of the garden,
didn't you know?

BERNARD: No, I knew she was working on the Croom
papers but . . .

CHLOË: Well, it's not exactly a history of the garden
either. I'll let Hannah explain it. The trench you
nearly drove into is all to do with it. I was going to

---

sod, expletive (derived from sodomist).

say make yourself comfortable but that's hardly possible, everything's been cleared out, it's en route to the nearest lavatory.

BERNARD: Everything is?

CHLOË: No, this room is. They drew the line at chemical 'Ladies.'

BERNARD: Yes, I see. Did you say Hannah?

CHLOË: Hannah, yes. Will you be all right?

(She stands up wearing the boots.)

I won't be . . . *(But she has lost him.)* Mr Nightingale?

BERNARD *(Waking up)*: Yes. Thank you. Miss Jarvis is Hannah Jarvis the author?

CHLOË: Yes. Have you read her book?

BERNARD: Oh, yes. Yes.

CHLOË: I bet she's in the hermitage, can't see from here with the marquee . . .

BERNARD: Are you having a garden party?

CHLOË: A dance for the district, our annual dressing up and general drunkenness. The wrinklies won't have it in the house, there was a teapot we once had to bag back from Christie's in the nick of time, so anything that can be destroyed, stolen or vomited on has been tactfully removed; tactlessly, I should say—

(She is about to leave.)

BERNARD: Um—look—would you tell her—would you mind not mentioning my name just yet?

CHLOË: Oh. All right.

BERNARD *(Smiling)*: More fun to surprise her. Would you mind?

CHLOË: No. But she's bound to ask . . . Should I give you another name, just for the moment?

BERNARD: Yes, why not?

CHLOË: Perhaps another bird, you're not really a Nightingale.

(She leaves again. BERNARD *glances over the books on the table. He puts his briefcase down. There is the distant pop-pop of a shotgun. It takes* BERNARD *vaguely to the window. He looks out. The door he entered by now opens and* GUS *looks into the room.* BERNARD *turns and sees him.)*

BERNARD: Hello.

*(*GUS *doesn't speak. He never speaks. Perhaps he cannot speak. He has no composure, and faced with a stranger, he caves in and leaves again. A moment later the other door opens again and* VALENTINE *crosses the room, not exactly ignoring* BERNARD *and yet ignoring him.)*

VALENTINE: Sod, sod, sod, sod, sod, sod . . . *(As many times as it takes him to leave by the opposite door, which he closes behind him. Beyond it, he can be heard shouting.* Chlo! Chlo! BERNARD*'s discomfort increases. The same door opens and* VALENTINE *returns. He looks at* BERNARD.*)*

BERNARD: She's in the garden looking for Miss Jarvis.

VALENTINE: Where is everything?

BERNARD: It's been removed for the, er . . .

VALENTINE: The dance is all in the tent, isn't it?

BERNARD: Yes, but this is the way to the nearest toilet.

VALENTINE: I need the commode.°

BERNARD: Oh. Can't you use the toilet?

VALENTINE: It's got all the game books in it.

BERNARD: Ah. The toilet has or the commode has?

VALENTINE: Is anyone looking after you?

BERNARD: Yes. Thank you. I'm Bernard Nigh—I've come to see Miss Jarvis. I wrote to Lord Croom but unfortunately I never received a reply, so I—

VALENTINE: Did you type it?

BERNARD: Type it?

VALENTINE: Was your letter typewritten?

BERNARD: Yes.

VALENTINE: My father never replies to typewritten letters.

(He spots a tortoise which has been half-hidden on the table.)

Oh! Where have you been hiding, Lightning? *(He picks up the tortoise.)*

BERNARD: So I telephoned yesterday and I think I spoke to you—

VALENTINE: To me? Ah! Yes! Sorry! You're doing a talk about—someone—and you wanted to ask Hannah—something—

BERNARD: Yes. As it turns out. I'm hoping Miss Jarvis will look kindly on me.

VALENTINE: I doubt it.

BERNARD: Ah, you know about research?

VALENTINE: I know Hannah.

BERNARD: Has she been here long?

VALENTINE: Well in possession, I'm afraid. My mother had read her book, you see. Have you?

BERNARD: No. Yes. Her book. Indeed.

VALENTINE: She's terrifically pleased with herself.

BERNARD: Well, I dare say if I wrote a bestseller—

VALENTINE: No, for reading it. My mother basically reads gardening books.

BERNARD: She must be delighted to have Hannah Jarvis writing a book about her garden.

VALENTINE: Actually it's about hermits.

*(*GUS *returns through the same door, and turns to leave again.)*

It's all right, Gus—what do you want?—

(But GUS *has gone again.)*

Well . . . I'll take Lightning for his run.

BERNARD: Actually, we've met before. At Sussex, a couple of years ago, a seminar . . .

---

commode, toilet (also a cabinet/chest of drawers).

VALENTINE: Oh. Was I there?

BERNARD: Yes. One of my colleagues believed he had found an unattributed short story by D. H. Lawrence, and he analysed it on his home computer, most interesting, perhaps you remember the paper?

VALENTINE: Not really. But I often sit with my eyes closed and it doesn't necessarily mean I'm awake.

BERNARD: Well, by comparing sentence structures and so forth, this chap showed that there was a ninety per cent chance that the story had indeed been written by the same person as *Women in Love.* To my inexpressible joy, one of your maths mob was able to show that on the same statistical basis there was a ninety per cent chance that Lawrence also, wrote the *Just William* books° and much of the previous day's *Brighton and Hove Argus.*

VALENTINE: *(Pause)* Oh, Brighton. Yes. I was there. *(And looking out)* Oh—here she comes, I'll leave you to talk. By the way, is yours the red Mazda?

BERNARD: Yes.

VALENTINE: If you want a tip I'd put it out of sight through the stable arch before my father comes in. He won't have anyone in the house with a Japanese car. Are you queer?

BERNARD: No, actually.

VALENTINE: Well, even so.

(VALENTINE leaves, closing the door. BERNARD keeps staring at the closed door. Behind him, HANNAH comes to the garden door.)

HANNAH: Mr Peacock?

(BERNARD looks round vaguely then checks over his shoulder for the missing Peacock, then recovers himself and turns on the Nightingale bonhomie.)

BERNARD: Oh . . . hello! Hello. Miss Jarvis, of course. Such a pleasure. I was thrown for a moment—the photograph doesn't do you justice.

HANNAH: Photograph?

(Her shoes have got muddy and she is taking them off.)

BERNARD: On the book. I'm sorry to have brought you indoors, but Lady Chloë kindly insisted she—

HANNAH: No matter—you would have muddied your shoes.

BERNARD: How thoughtful. And how kind of you to spare me a little of your time.

(He is overdoing it. She shoots him a glance.)

HANNAH: Are you a journalist?

BERNARD *(Shocked)*: No!

HANNAH *(Resuming)*: I've been in the ha-ha,° very squelchy.

BERNARD *(Unexpectedly)*: Ha-*hah*!

HANNAH: What?

BERNARD: A theory of mine. Ha-*hah*, not ha-ha. If you were strolling down the garden and all of a sudden the ground gave way at your feet, you're not going to go 'ha-ha', you're going to jump back and go 'ha-hah!', or more probably, 'Bloody 'ell!'. . . though personally I think old Murray was up the pole on that one—in France, you know, 'ha-ha' is used to denote a strikingly ugly woman, a much more likely bet for something that keeps the cows off the lawn.

(This is not going well for BERNARD but he seems blithely unaware. HANNAH stares at him for a moment.)

HANNAH: Mr Peacock, what can I do for you?

BERNARD: Well, to begin with, you can call me Bernard, which is my name.

HANNAH: Thank you.

(She goes to the garden door to bang her shoes together and scrape off the worst of the mud.)

BERNARD: The book!—the book is a revelation! To see Caroline Lamb° through your eyes is really like seeing her for the first time. I'm ashamed to say I never read her fiction, and how right you are, it's extraordinary stuff—Early Nineteenth is my period as much as anything is.

HANNAH: You teach?

BERNARD: Yes. And write, like you, like we all, though I've never done anything which has sold like *Caro.*

HANNAH: I don't teach.

BERNARD: No. All the more credit to you. To rehabilitate a forgotten writer, I suppose you could say that's the main reason for an English don.

HANNAH: Not to teach?

BERNARD: Good God, no, let the brats sort it out for themselves. Anyway, many congratulations. I expect someone will be bringing out Caroline Lamb's oeuvre now?

HANNAH: Yes, I expect so.

BERNARD: How wonderful! Bravo! Simply as a document shedding reflected light on the character of Lord Byron,° it's bound to be—

HANNAH: Bernard. You did say Bernard, didn't you?

BERNARD: I did.

Just William *books,* well-known series of children's books.

ha-ha, dirt wall used in landscaping; from the lawn, the view is unobstructed, but from the "pasture" side, there is a wall, keeping animals from the lawn. *Caroline Lamb,* 1785–1828, mistress of Lord Byron and an author in her own right. *Lord Byron,* 1788–1824, English romantic poet known for both his poetry and his love affairs.

HANNAH: I'm putting my shoes on again.

BERNARD: Oh. You're not going to go out?

HANNAH: No, I'm going to kick you in the balls.

BERNARD: Right. Point taken. Ezra Chater.

HANNAH: Ezra Chater.

BERNARD: Born Twickenham, Middlesex, 1778, author of two verse narratives, 'The Maid of Turkey,' 1808, and 'The Couch of Eros,' 1809. Nothing known after 1809, disappears from view.

HANNAH: I see. And?

BERNARD *(Reaching for his bag)*: There is a Sidley Park connection.

(He produces 'The Couch of Eros' from the bag. He reads the inscription.)

'To my friend Septimus Hodge, who stood up and gave his best on behalf of the Author—Ezra Chater, at Sidley Park, Derbyshire, April 10th 1809.'

(He gives her the book.)

I am in your hands.

HANNAH: 'The Couch of Eros.' Is it any good?

BERNARD: Quite surprising.

HANNAH: You think there's a book in him?

BERNARD: No, no—a monograph perhaps for the *Journal of English Studies.* There's almost nothing on Chater, not a word in the *DNB,*° of course—by that time he'd been completely forgotten.

HANNAH: Family?

BERNARD: Zilch. There's only one other Chater in the British Library database.

HANNAH: Same period?

BERNARD: Yes, but he wasn't a poet like our Ezra, he was a botanist who described a dwarf dahlia in Martinique and died there after being bitten by a monkey.

HANNAH: And Ezra Chater?

BERNARD: He gets two references in the periodical index, one for each book, in both cases a substantial review in the *Piccadilly Recreation,* a thrice weekly folio sheet, but giving no personal details.

HANNAH: And where was this *(the book)*?

BERNARD: Private collection. I've got a talk to give next week, in London, and I think Chater is interesting, so anything on him, or this Septimus Hodge, Sidley Park, any leads at all . . . I'd be most grateful.

(Pause.)

HANNAH: Well! This is a new experience for me. A grovelling academic.

BERNARD: Oh, I say.

HANNAH: Oh, but it is. All the academics who reviewed my book patronized it.

BERNARD: Surely not.

HANNAH: Surely yes. The Byron gang unzipped their flies and patronized all over it. Where is it you don't bother to teach, by the way?

BERNARD: Oh, well, Sussex, actually.

HANNAH: Sussex. *(She thinks a moment.)* Nightingale. Yes; a thousand words in the *Observer*° to see me off the premises with a pat on the bottom. You must know him.

BERNARD: As I say, I'm in your hands.

HANNAH: Quite. Say please, then.

BERNARD: Please.

HANNAH: Sit down, do.

BERNARD: Thank you.

(He takes a chair. She remains standing. Possibly she smokes; if so, perhaps now. A short cigarette-holder sounds right, too. Or brown-paper cigarillos.)

HANNAH: How did you know I was here?

BERNARD: Oh, I didn't. I spoke to the son on the phone but he didn't mention you by name . . . and then he forgot to mention me.

HANNAH: Valentine. He's at Oxford, technically.

BERNARD: Yes, I met him. Brideshead Regurgitated.°

HANNAH: My fiancé.

(She holds his look.)

BERNARD: *(Pause)* I'll take a chance. You're lying.

HANNAH: *(Pause)* Well done, Bernard.

BERNARD: Christ.

HANNAH: He calls me his fiancée.

BERNARD: Why?

HANNAH: It's a joke.

BERNARD: You turned him down?

HANNAH: Don't be silly, do I look like the next Countess of—

BERNARD: No, no—a freebie. The joke that consoles. My tortoise Lightning, my fiancée Hannah.

HANNAH: Oh. Yes. You have a way with you, Bernard. I'm not sure I like it.

BERNARD: What's he doing, Valentine?

HANNAH: He's a postgrad. Biology.

BERNARD: No, he's a mathematician.

HANNAH: Well, he's doing grouse.

BERNARD: Grouse?

HANNAH: Not actual grouse. Computer grouse.

BERNARD: Who's the one who doesn't speak?

HANNAH: Gus.

DNB, Dictionary of National Biography (British).

Observer, English Sunday paper. **Brideshead Regurgitated,** Evelyn Waugh's 1945 novel, *Brideshead Revisited,* focuses on an upper-class family, and especially the Oxford-educated Sebastian.

BERNARD: What's the matter with him?

HANNAH: I didn't ask.

BERNARD: And the father sounds like a lot of fun.

HANNAH: Ah yes.

BERNARD: And the mother is the gardener. What's going on here?

HANNAH: What do you mean?

BERNARD: I nearly took her head off—she was standing in a trench at the time.

HANNAH: Archaeology. The house had a formal Italian garden until about 1740. Lady Croom is interested in garden history. I sent her my book—it contains, as you know if you've read it—which I'm not assuming, by the way—a rather good description of Caroline's garden at Brocket Hall. I'm here now helping Hermione.

BERNARD (Impressed): Hermione.

HANNAH: The records are unusually complete and they have never been worked on.

BERNARD: I'm beginning to admire you.

HANNAH: Before was bullshit?

BERNARD: Completely. Your photograph does you justice, I'm not sure the book does.

(She considers him. He waits, confident.)

HANNAH: Septimus Hodge was the tutor.

BERNARD (Quietly): Attagirl.

HANNAH: His pupil was the Croom daughter. There was a son at Eton. Septimus lived in the house: the pay book specifies allowances for wine and candles. So, not quite a guest but rather more than a steward. His letter of self-recommendation is preserved among the papers. I'll dig it out for you. As far as I remember he studied mathematics and natural philosophy at Cambridge. A scientist, therefore, as much as anything.

BERNARD: I'm impressed. Thank you. And Chater?

HANNAH: Nothing.

BERNARD: Oh. Nothing at all?

HANNAH: I'm afraid not.

BERNARD: How about the library?

HANNAH: The catalogue was done in the 1880s. I've been through the lot.

BERNARD: Books or catalogue?

HANNAH: Catalogue.

BERNARD: Ah. Pity.

HANNAH: I'm sorry.

BERNARD: What about the letters? No mention?

HANNAH: I'm afraid not. I've been very thorough in your period because, of course, it's my period too.

BERNARD: Is it? Actually, I don't quite know what it is you're . . .

HANNAH: The Sidley hermit.

BERNARD: Ah. Who's he?

HANNAH: He's my peg for the nervous breakdown of the Romantic Imagination. I'm doing landscape and literature 1750 to 1834.

BERNARD: What happened in 1834?

HANNAH: My hermit died.

BERNARD: Of course.

HANNAH: What do you mean, of course?

BERNARD: Nothing.

HANNAH: Yes, you do.

BERNARD: No, no . . . However, Coleridge° also died in 1834.

HANNAH: So he did. What a stroke of luck. (Softening) Thank you, Bernard.

(She goes to the reading stand and opens Noakes's sketch book.)

Look—there he is.

(BERNARD goes to look.)

BERNARD: Mmm.

HANNAH: The only known likeness of the Sidley hermit.

BERNARD: Very biblical.

HANNAH: Drawn in by a later hand, of course. The hermitage didn't yet exist when Noakes did the drawings.

BERNARD: Noakes . . . the painter?

HANNAH: Landscape gardener. He'd do these books for his clients, as a sort of prospectus. (She demonstrates.) Before, and after, you see. This is how it all looked until, say, 1810—smooth, undulating, serpentine—open water, clumps of trees, classical boat-house—

BERNARD: Lovely. The real England.

HANNAH: You can stop being silly now, Bernard. English landscape was invented by gardeners imitating foreign painters who were evoking classical authors. The whole thing was brought home in the luggage from the grand tour. Here, look—Capability Brown° doing Claude,° who was doing Virgil.° Arcadia! And here, superimposed by Richard Noakes, untamed nature in the style of Salvator Rosa. It's the Gothic novel expressed in landscape. Everything but vampires. There's an account of my hermit in a letter by your illustrious namesake.

BERNARD: Florence?

HANNAH: What?

BERNARD: No. You go on.

Coleridge, Samuel Taylor Coleridge (1722–1834), English romantic poet. *Capability Brown,* Lancelot Brown (1715–83), probably England's most famous landscape designer; he designed Kew Gardens and the grounds at Blenheim Palace. *Claude,* Claude Lorrain (1600–82), French landscape painter. *Virgil,* Roman poet (70–19 B.C.), author of the *Aeneid,* but also many poems describing and celebrating the pastoral life.

HANNAH: Thomas Love Peacock.°

BERNARD: Ah yes.

HANNAH: I found it in an essay on hermits and anchorites published in the *Cornhill Magazine* in the 1860s . . . *(She fishes for the magazine itself among the books on the table, and finds it.)* . . . 1862 . . . Peacock calls him *(She quotes from memory.)* 'Not one of your village simpletons to frighten the ladies, but a savant among idiots, a sage of lunacy.'

BERNARD: An oxy-moron, so to speak.

HANNAH *(Busy)*: Yes. What?

BERNARD: Nothing.

HANNAH *(Having found the place)*: Here we are. 'A letter we have seen, written by the author of *Heading Hall* nearly thirty years ago, tells of a visit to the Earl of Croom's estate, Sidley Park—'

BERNARD: Was the letter to Thackeray?°

HANNAH *(Brought up short)*: I don't know. Does it matter?

BERNARD: No. Sorry.

(But the gaps he leaves for her are false promises—and she is not quick enough. That's how it goes.)

Only, Thackeray edited the *Cornhill* until '63 when, as you know, he died. His father had been with the East India Company where Peacock, of course, had held the position of Examiner, so it's quite possible that if the essay were by Thackeray, the *letter* . . . Sorry. Go on.

Of course, the East India Library in Blackfriars has most of Peacock's letters, so it would be quite easy to . . . Sorry. Can I look?

(Silently she hands him the Cornhill.)

Yes, it's been topped and tailed, of course. It might be worth . . . Go on. I'm listening . . .

(Leafing through the essay, he suddenly chuckles.) Oh yes, it's Thackeray all right . . .

(He slaps the book shut.) Unbearable . . .

(He hands it back to her.) What were you saying?

HANNAH: Are you always like this?

BERNARD: Like what?

HANNAH: The point is, the Crooms, of course, had the hermit under their noses for twenty years so hardly thought him worth remarking. As I'm finding out. The Peacock letter is still the main source, unfortunately. When I read this *(the magazine in her hand)* well, it was one of those moments that tell you what your next book is going to be. The hermit of Sidley Park was my . . .

Thomas Love Peacock, 1785–1866, English novelist and poet, author of *Heading Hall.* **Thackeray,** William Makepeace Thackery (1811–63), English novelist and satirist. He also edited the *Cornhill Magazine.*

BERNARD: Peg.

HANNAH: Epiphany.

BERNARD: Epiphany, that's it.

HANNAH: The hermit was *placed* in the landscape exactly as one might place a pottery gnome. And there he lived out his life as a garden ornament.

BERNARD: Did he do anything?

HANNAH: Oh, he was very busy. When he died, the cottage was stacked solid with paper. Hundreds of pages. Thousands. Peacock says he was suspected of genius. It turned out, of course, he was off his head. He'd covered every sheet with cabalistic proofs that the world was coming to an end. It's perfect, isn't it? A perfect symbol, I mean.

BERNARD: Oh, yes. Of what?

HANNAH: The whole Romantic sham, Bernard! It's what happened to the Enlightenment, isn't it? A century of intellectual rigour turned in on itself. A mind in chaos suspected of genius. In a setting of cheap thrills and false emotion. The history of the garden says it all, beautifully. There's an engraving of Sidley Park in 1730 that makes you want to weep. Paradise in the age of reason. By 1760 everything had gone—the topiary, pools and terraces, fountains, an avenue of limes—the whole sublime geometry was ploughed under by Capability Brown. The grass went from the doorstep to the horizon and the best box hedge in Derbyshire was dug up for the ha-ha so that the fools could pretend they were living in God's countryside. And then Richard Noakes came in to bring God up to date. By the time he'd finished it looked like this *(the sketch book).* The decline from thinking to feeling, you see.

BERNARD *(A judgement)*: That's awfully good.

(HANNAH looks at him in case of irony but he is professional.)

No, that'll stand up.

HANNAH: Thank you.

BERNARD: Personally I like the ha-ha. Do you like hedges?

HANNAH: I don't like sentimentality.

BERNARD: Yes, I see. Are you sure? You seem quite sentimental over geometry. But the hermit is very very good. The genius of the place.

HANNAH *(Pleased)*: That's my title!

BERNARD: Of course.

HANNAH *(Less pleased)*: Of course?

BERNARD: Of course. Who was he when he wasn't being a symbol?

HANNAH: I don't know.

BERNARD: Ah.

HANNAH: I mean, yet.

BERNARD: Absolutely. What did they do with all the paper? Does Peacock say?

HANNAH: Made a bonfire.

BERNARD: Ah, well.

HANNAH: I've still got Lady Croom's garden books to go through.

BERNARD: Account books or journals?

HANNAH: A bit of both. They're gappy but they span the period.

HANNAH: Really? Have you come across Byron at all? As a matter of interest.

HANNAH: A first edition of 'Childe Harold'° in the library, and *English Bards*, I think.

BERNARD: Inscribed?

HANNAH: No.

BERNARD: And he doesn't pop up in the letters at all?

HANNAH: Why should he? The Crooms don't pop up in his.

BERNARD (*Casually*): That's true, of course. But Newstead isn't so far away. Would you mind terribly if I poked about a bit? Only in the papers you've done with, of course.

(HANNAH *twigs something.*)

HANNAH: Are you looking into Byron or Chater?

(CHLOË *enters in stockinged feet through one of the side doors, laden with an armful of generally similar leather-covered ledgers. She detours to collect her shoes.*)

CHLOË: Sorry—just cutting through—there's tea in the pantry if you don't mind mugs—

BERNARD: How kind.

CHLOË: Hannah will show you.

BERNARD: Let me help you.

CHLOË: No, it's all right—

(BERNARD *opens the opposite door for her.*)

Thank you—I've been saving Val's game books. Thanks.

(BERNARD *closes the door.*)

BERNARD: Sweet girl.

HANNAH: Mmm.

BERNARD: Oh, really?

HANNAH: Oh really what?

(CHLOË's *door opens again and she puts her head round it.*)

CHLOË: Meant to say, don't worry if father makes remarks about your car, Mr Nightingale, he's got a thing about—(*and the Nightingale now being out of the bag*) ooh—ah, how was the surprise?—not yet, eh? Oh, well—sorry—tea, anyway—so sorry if I—(*Embarrassed, she leaves again, closing the door. Pause.*)

HANNAH: You absolute shit.

°**'Childe Harold,'** "Childe Harold's Pilgrimage," a long narrative poem (1812) by Lord Byron.

(*She heads off to leave.*)

BERNARD: The thing is, there's a Byron connection too.

(HANNAH *stops and faces him.*)

HANNAH: I don't care.

BERNARD: You should. The Byron gang are going to get their dicks caught in their zip.

HANNAH: (*Pause*) Oh really?

BERNARD: If we collaborate.

HANNAH: On what?

BERNARD: Sit down, I'll tell you.

HANNAH: I'll stand for the moment.

BERNARD: This copy of 'The Couch of Eros' belonged to Lord Byron.

HANNAH: It belonged to Septimus Hodge.

BERNARD: Originally, yes. But it was in Byron's library which was sold to pay his debts when he left England for good in 1816. The sales catalogue is in the British Library. 'Eros' was lot 74A and was bought by the bookseller and publisher John Nightingale of Opera Court, Pall Mall . . . whose name survives in the firm of Nightingale and Matlock, the present Nightingale being my cousin.

(*He pauses.* HANNAH *hesitates and then sits down at the table.*)

I'll just give you the headlines. 1939, stock removed to Nightingale country house in Kent. 1945, stock returned to bookshop. Meanwhile, overlooked box of early nineteenth-century books languish in country house cellar until house sold to make way for the Channel Tunnel rail-link. 'Eros' discovered with sales slip from 1816 attached—photocopy available for inspection.

(*He brings this from his bag and gives it to* HANNAH *who inspects it.*)

HANNAH: All right. It was in Byron's library.

BERNARD: A number of passages have been underlined.

(HANNAH *picks up the book and leafs through it.*)

All of them, and only them—no, no, look at me, not at the book—all the underlined passages, word for word, were used as quotations in the review of 'The Couch of Eros' in the *Piccadilly Recreation* of April 30th 1809. The reviewer begins by drawing attention to his previous notice in the same periodical of 'The Maid of Turkey.'

HANNAH: The reviewer is obviously Hodge. 'My friend Septimus Hodge who stood up and gave his best on behalf of the Author.'

BERNARD: That's the point. The *Piccadilly* ridiculed both books.

HANNAH: (*Pause*) Do the reviews read like Byron?

BERNARD (*Producing two photocopies from his case*): They read a damn sight more like Byron than Byron's review of Wordsworth the previous year.

(HANNAH *glances over the photocopies.*)

HANNAH: I see. Well, congratulations. Possibly. Two previously unknown book reviews by the young Byron. Is that it?

BERNARD: No. Because of the tapes, three documents survived undisturbed in the book.

(*He has been carefully opening a package produced from his bag. He has the originals. He holds them carefully one by one.*)

'Sir—we have a matter to settle. I wait on you in the gun room. E. Chater, Esq.'

'My husband has sent to town for pistols. Deny what cannot be proven—for Charity's sake—I keep my room this day.' Unsigned.

'Sidley Park, April 11th 1809. Sir—I call you a liar, a lecher, a slanderer in the press and a thief of my honour. I wait upon your arrangements for giving me satisfaction as a man and a poet. E. Chater, Esq.'

(*Pause.*)

HANNAH: Superb. But inconclusive. The book had seven years to find its way into Byron's possession. It doesn't connect Byron with Chater, or with Sidley Park. Or with Hodge for that matter. Furthermore, there isn't a hint in Byron's letters and this kind of scrape is the last thing he would have kept quiet about.

BERNARD: *Scrape?*

HANNAH: He would have made a comic turn out of it.

BERNARD: Comic turn, fiddlesticks! (*He pauses for effect.*) He killed Chater!

HANNAH (*A raspberry*): Oh, really!

BERNARD: Chater was thirty-one years old. The author of two books. Nothing more is heard from him after 'Eros.' He disappears completely after April 1809. And Byron—Byron had just published his satire, *English Bards and Scotch Reviewers,* in March. He was just getting a name. Yet he sailed for Lisbon as soon as he could find a ship, and stayed abroad for two years. Hannah, *this is* fame. Somewhere in the Croom papers there will be *something—*

HANNAH: There isn't, I've looked.

BERNARD: But you were looking for something else! It's not going to jump out at you like 'Lord Byron remarked wittily at breakfast!'

HANNAH: Nevertheless his presence would be unlikely to have gone unremarked. But there is nothing to suggest that Byron was here, and I don't believe he ever was.

BERNARD: All right, but let me have a look.

HANNAH: You'll queer my pitch.

BERNARD: Dear girl, I know how to handle myself—

HANNAH: And don't call me dear girl. If I find anything on Byron, or Chater, or Hodge, I'll pass it on. Nightingale, Sussex.

(*Pause. She stands up.*)

BERNARD: Thank you. I'm sorry about that business with my name.

HANNAH: Don't mention it . . .

BERNARD: What was Hodge's college, by the way?

HANNAH: Trinity.°

BERNARD: Trinity?

HANNAH: Yes. (*She hesitates.*) Yes. Byron's old college.

BERNARD: How old was Hodge?

HANNAH: I'd have to look it up but a year or two older than Byron. Twenty-two . . .

BERNARD: Contemporaries at Trinity?

HANNAH (*Wearily*): Yes, Bernard, and no doubt they were both in the cricket eleven when Harrow° played Eton at Lords!

(BERNARD *approaches her and stands close to her.*)

BERNARD (*Evenly*): Do you mean that Septimus Hodge was at school with Byron?

HANNAH (*Falters slightly*): Yes . . . he must have been . . . as a matter of fact.

BERNARD: Well, you silly cow.

(*With a large gesture of pure happiness,* BERNARD *throws his arms around* HANNAH *and gives her a great smacking kiss on the cheek.* CHLOË *enters to witness the end of this.*)

CHLOË: Oh—erm . . . I thought I'd bring it to you.

(*She is carrying a small tray with two mugs on it.*)

BERNARD: I have to go and see about my car.

HANNAH: Going to hide it?

BERNARD: Hide it? I'm going to sell it! Is there a pub I can put up at in the village?

(*He turns back to them as he is about to leave through the garden.*)

Aren't you glad I'm here?

(*He leaves.*)

CHLOË: He said he knew you.

HANNAH: He couldn't have.

CHLOË: No, perhaps not. He said he wanted to be a surprise, but I suppose that's different. I thought there was a lot of sexual energy there, didn't you?

HANNAH: What?

CHLOË: Bouncy on his feet, you see, a sure sign. Should I invite him for you?

Trinity, Trinity College, Cambridge University. *Harrow,* prestigious private school for boys.

HANNAH: To what? No.

CHLOË: You can invite him—that's better. He can come as your partner.

HANNAH: Stop it. Thank you for the tea.

CHLOË: If you don't want him, I'll have him. Is he married?

HANNAH: I haven't the slightest idea. Aren't you supposed to have a pony?

CHLOË: I'm just trying to fix you up, Hannah.

HANNAH: Believe me, it gets less important.

CHLOË: I mean for the dancing. He can come as Beau Brummel.°

HANNAH: I don't want to dress up and I don't want a dancing partner, least of all Mr Nightingale. I don't dance.

CHLOË: Don't be such a prune. You were kissing him, anyway.

HANNAH: He was kissing me, and only out of general enthusiasm.

CHLOË: Well, don't say I didn't give you first chance. My genius brother will be much relieved. He's in love with you, I suppose you know.

HANNAH (*Angry*): That's a joke!

CHLOË: It's not a joke to him.

HANNAH: Of course it is—not even a joke—how can you be so ridiculous?

(GUS *enters from the garden, in his customary silent awkwardness.*)

CHLOË: Hello, Gus, what have you got?

(GUS *has an apple, just picked, with a leaf or two still attached. He offers the apple to* HANNAH.)

HANNAH (*Surprised*): Oh! . . . Thank you!

CHLOË (*Leaving*): Told you.

(CHLOË *closes the door on herself.*)

HANNAH: Thank you. Oh dear.

ACT 1 / SCENE 3

(*The schoolroom. The next morning. Present are:* THOMASINA, SEPTIMUS, JELLABY. *We have seen this composition before:* THOMASINA *at her place at the table;* SEPTIMUS *reading a letter which has just arrived;* JELLABY *waiting, having just delivered the letter.*
'The Couch of Eros' *is in front of* SEPTIMUS, *open, together with sheets of paper on which he has been writing. His portfolio is on the table.* Plautus [*the tortoise*] *is the paperweight. There is also an apple on the table now, the same apple from all appearances.*)

SEPTIMUS (*With his eyes on the letter*): Why have you stopped?

(THOMASINA *is studying a sheet of paper, a 'Latin unseen' lesson. She is having some difficulty.*)

THOMASINA: *Solio insessa . . . in igne . . .* seated on a throne . . . in the fire . . . and also on a ship . . . *sedebat regina . . .* sat the queen . . .

SEPTIMUS: There is no reply, Jellaby. Thank you.

(*He folds the letter up and places it between the leaves of 'The Couch of Eros.'*)

JELLABY: I will say so, sir.

THOMASINA: . . . the wind smelling sweetly . . . *purpureis vilis . . .* by, with or from purple sails—

SEPTIMUS (*To* JELLABY): I will have something for the post, if you would be so kind.

JELLABY (*Leaving*): Yes, sir.

THOMASINA: . . . was like as to—something—by, with or from lovers—oh, Septimus!—*musica tibiarum imperabat . . .* music of pipes commanded . . .

SEPTIMUS: 'Ruled' is better.

THOMASINA: . . . the silver oars—exciting the ocean—as if—as if—amorous—

SEPTIMUS: That is very good.

(*He picks up the apple. He picks off the twig and leaves, placing these on the table. With a pocket knife he cuts a slice of apple, and while he eats it, cuts another slice which he offers to Plautus.*)

THOMASINA: *Regina reclinabat . . .* the queen—was reclining—*praeter descriptionem*—indescribably—in a golden tent . . . like Venus and yet more—

SEPTIMUS: Try to put some poetry into it.

THOMASINA: How can I if there is none in the Latin?

SEPTIMUS: Oh, a critic!

THOMASINA: Is it Queen Dido?°

SEPTIMUS: No.

THOMASINA: Who is the poet?

SEPTIMUS: Known to you.

THOMASINA: Known to me?

SEPTIMUS: Not a Roman.

THOMASINA: Mr Chater?

SEPTIMUS: Your translation is quite like Chater.

(SEPTIMUS *picks up his pen and continues with his own writing.*)

THOMASINA: I know who it is, it is your friend Byron.

SEPTIMUS: Lord Byron, if you please.

THOMASINA: Mama is in love with Lord Byron.

SEPTIMUS (*Absorbed*): Yes. Nonsense.

Beau Brummel, George Bryan Brummel (1778–1840), known as "Beau" for his elegant attire.

Queen Dido, legendary queen of Carthage, and figure in Virgil's *Aeneid.* When her lover, Aeneas, leaves her, she commits suicide by burning herself to death.

THOMASINA: It is not nonsense. I saw them together in the gazebo.

(SEPTIMUS's *pen stops moving, he raises his eyes to her at last.*)

Lord Byron was reading to her from his satire, and mama was laughing, with her head in her best position.

SEPTIMUS: She did not understand the satire, and was showing politeness to a guest.

THOMASINA: She is vexed with papa for his determination to alter the park, but that alone cannot account for her politeness to a guest. She came downstairs hours before her custom. Lord Byron was amusing at breakfast. He paid you a tribute, Septimus.

SEPTIMUS: Did he?

THOMASINA: He said you were a witty fellow, and he had almost by heart an article you wrote about— well, I forget what, but it concerned a book called 'The Maid of Turkey' and how you would not give it to your dog for dinner.

SEPTIMUS: Ah. Mr Chater was at breakfast, of course.

THOMASINA: He was, not like certain lazybones.

SEPTIMUS: He does not have Latin to set and mathematics to correct.

(*He takes Thomasina's lesson book from underneath Plautus and tosses it down the table to her.*)

THOMASINA: Correct? What was incorrect in it? (*She looks into the book.*) Alpha minus? Pooh! What is the minus for?

SEPTIMUS: For doing more than was asked.

THOMASINA: You did not like my discovery?

SEPTIMUS: A fancy is not a discovery.

THOMASINA: A gibe is not a rebuttal.

(SEPTIMUS *finishes what he is writing. He folds the pages into a letter. He has sealing wax and the means to melt it. He seals the letter and writes on the cover. Meanwhile—*)

You are churlish with me because mama is paying attention to your friend. Well, let them elope, they cannot turn back the advancement of knowledge. I think it is an excellent discovery. Each week I plot your equations dot for dot, xs against ys in all manner of algebraical relation, and every week they draw themselves as commonplace geometry, as if the world of forms were nothing but arcs and angles. God's truth, Septimus, if there is an equation for a curve like a bell, there must be an equation for one like a bluebell, and if a bluebell, why not a rose? Do we believe nature is written in numbers?

SEPTIMUS: We do.

THOMASINA: Then why do your equations only describe the shapes of manufacture?

SEPTIMUS: I do not know.

THOMASINA: Armed thus, God could only make a cabinet.

SEPTIMUS: He has mastery of equations which lead into infinities where we cannot follow.

THOMASINA: What a faint-heart! We must work outward from the middle of the maze. We will start with something simple. (*She picks up the apple leaf.*) I will plot this leaf and deduce its equation. You will be famous for being my tutor when Lord Byron is dead and forgotten.

(SEPTIMUS *completes the business with his letter. He puts the letter in his pocket.*)

SEPTIMUS (*Firmly*): Back to Cleopatra.°

THOMASINA: Is it Cleopatra?—I hate Cleopatra!

SEPTIMUS: You hate her? Why?

THOMASINA: Everything is turned to love with her. New love, absent love, lost love—I never knew a heroine that makes such noodles of our sex. It only needs a Roman general to drop anchor outside the window and away goes the empire like a christening mug into a pawn shop. If Queen Elizabeth° had been a Ptolemy° history would have been quite different—we would be admiring the pyramids of Rome and the great Sphinx of Verona.

SEPTIMUS: God save us.

THOMASINA: But instead, the Egyptian noodle made carnal embrace with the enemy who burned the great library of Alexandria without so much as a fine for all that is overdue. Oh, Septimus!—can you bear it? All the lost plays of the Athenians! Two hundred at least by Aeschylus, Sophocles, Euripides—thousands of poems—Aristotle's own library brought to Egypt by the noodle's ancestors! How can we sleep for grief?

SEPTIMUS: By counting our stock. Seven plays from Aeschylus, seven from Sophocles, *nineteen* from Euripides, my lady! You should no more grieve for the rest than for a buckle lost from your first shoe, or for your lesson book which will be lost when you are old. We shed as we pick up, like travellers who must carry everything in their arms, and what we let fall will be picked up by those behind. The procession is very long and life is very short. We die on the march. But there is nothing outside the march so nothing can be lost to it. The missing plays of Sophocles will turn up piece by piece, or be written again in another

---

Cleopatra, 69–30 B.C., Queen of Egypt, mistress of both Julius Caesar and Marc Antony. **Queen Elizabeth,** Elizabeth I (1533–1603). ***Ptolemy,*** name of the ruling Egyptian dynasty from 323 to 30 B.C. Cleopatra's son, Ptolemy, was the last ruler in this family.

language. Ancient cures for diseases will reveal themselves once more. Mathematical discoveries glimpsed and lost to view will have their time again. You do not suppose, my lady, that if all of Archimedes had been hiding in the great library of Alexandria, we would be at a loss for a corkscrew? I have no doubt that the improved steam-driven heat-engine which puts Mr Noakes into an ecstasy that he and it and the modern age should all coincide, was described on papyrus. Steam and brass were not invented in Glasgow. Now, where are we? Let me see if I can attempt a free translation for you. At Harrow I was better at this than Lord Byron.

(He takes the piece of paper from her and scrutinizes it, testing one or two Latin phrases speculatively before committing himself.)

Yes—'The barge she sat in, like a burnished throne° . . . burned on the water . . . the—something—the poop was beaten gold, purple the sails, and—what's this?—oh yes,—so perfumed that—'

THOMASINA *(Catching on and furious)*: Cheat!

SEPTIMUS *(Imperturbably)*: '—the winds were lovesick with them . . .'

THOMASINA: Cheat!

SEPTIMUS: '. . . the oars were silver which to the tune of flutes kept stroke . . .'

THOMASINA *(Jumping to her feet)*: Cheat! Cheat! Cheat!

SEPTIMUS *(As though it were too easy to make the effort worthwhile)*: '. . . and made the water which they beat to follow faster, as *amorous* of their strokes. For her own person, it beggared all description— she did lie in her pavilion—'

(THOMASINA, in tears of rage, is hurrying out through the garden.)

THOMASINA: I hope you die!

(She nearly bumps into BRICE who is entering. She runs out of sight. BRICE enters.)

BRICE: Good God, man, what have you told her?

SEPTIMUS: Told her? Told her what?

BRICE: Hodge!

(SEPTIMUS looks outside the door, slightly contrite about THOMASINA, and sees that CHATER is skulking out of view.)

The barge she sat in . . . she did lie in her pavilion, the Latin passage that Thomasina has been struggling over is actually a Latinized version of Enobarbus' description of Cleopatra, from Shakespeare's *Antony and Cleopatra,* 2.2.

SEPTIMUS: Chater! My dear fellow! Don't hang back— come in, sir!

(CHATER allows himself to be drawn sheepishly into the room, where BRICE stands on his dignity.)

CHATER: Captain Brice does me the honour—I mean to say, sir, whatever you have to say to me, sir, address yourself to Captain Brice.

SEPTIMUS: How unusual. *(To BRICE)* Your wife did not appear yesterday, sir. I trust she is not sick?

BRICE: My wife? I have no wife. What the devil do you mean, sir? *(SEPTIMUS makes to reply, but hesitates, puzzled. He turns back to CHATER.)*

SEPTIMUS: I do not understand the scheme, Chater. Whom do I address when I want to speak to Captain Brice?

BRICE: Oh, slippery, Hodge—slippery!

SEPTIMUS *(To CHATER)*: By the way, Chater—*(he interrupts himself and turns back to BRICE, and continues as before)* by the way, Chater, I have amazing news to tell you. Someone has taken to writing wild and whirling letters in your name. I received one not half an hour ago.

BRICE *(Angrily)*: Mr Hodge! Look to your honour, sir! If you cannot attend to me without this foolery, nominate your second who might settle the business as between gentlemen. No doubt your friend Byron would do you the service.

(SEPTIMUS gives up the game.)

SEPTIMUS: Oh yes, he would do me the service. *(His mood changes, he turns to CHATER.)* Sir—I repent your injury. You are an honest fellow with no more malice in you than poetry.

CHATER *(Happily)*: Ah well!—that is more like the thing! *(Overtaken by doubt)* Is he apologizing?

BRICE: There is still the injury to his conjugal property, Mrs Chater's—

CHATER: Tush, sir!

BRICE: As you will—her tush. Nevertheless—

(But they are interrupted by LADY CROOM, also entering from the garden.)

LADY CROOM: Oh—excellently found! Mr Chater, this will please you very much. Lord Byron begs a copy of your new book. He dies to read it and intends to include your name in the second edition of his *English Bards and Scotch Reviewers.*

CHATER: *English Bards and Scotch Reviewers,* your ladyship, is a doggerel aimed at Lord Byron's seniors and betters. If he intends to include me, he intends to insult me.

LADY CROOM: Well, of course he does, Mr Chater. Would you rather be thought not worth insulting? You should be proud to be in the company of

Rogers° and Moore° and Wordsworth°—ah! 'The Couch of Eros!' *(For she has spotted Septimus's copy of the book on the table.)*

SEPTIMUS: That is my copy, madam.

LADY CROOM: So much the better—what are a friend's books for if not to be borrowed?

(Note: 'The Couch of Eros' now contains the three letters, and it must do so without advertising the fact. This is why the volume has been described as a substantial quarto.)

Mr Hodge, you must speak to your friend and put him out of his affectation of pretending to quit us. I will not have it. He says he is determined on the Malta packet sailing out of Falmouth! His head is full of Lisbon and Lesbos, and his portmanteau of pistols, and I have told him it is not to be thought of. The whole of Europe is in a Napoleonic fit, all the best ruins will be closed, the roads entirely occupied with the movement of armies, the lodgings turned to billets and the fashion for godless republicanism not yet arrived at its natural reversion. He says his aim is poetry. One does not aim at poetry with pistols. At poets, perhaps. I charge you to take command of his pistols, Mr Hodge! He is not safe with them. His lameness, he confessed to me, is entirely the result of his habit from boyhood of shooting himself in the foot. What is that *noise*?

(The noise is a badly played piano in the next room. It has been going on for some time since THOMASINA *left.)*

SEPTIMUS: The new Broadwood pianoforte, madam. Our music lessons are at an early stage.

LADY CROOM: Well, restrict your lessons to the *piano* side of the instrument and let her loose on the *forte* when she has learned something.

*(*LADY CROOM, *holding the book, sails out back into the garden.)*

BRICE: Now! If that was not God speaking through Lady Croom, he never spoke through anyone!

CHATER *(Awed)*: Take command of Lord Byron's pistols!

BRICE: You hear Mr Chater, sir—how will you answer him?

*(*SEPTIMUS *has been watching* LADY CROOM's *progress up the garden. He turns back.)*

SEPTIMUS: By killing him. I am tired of him.

Rogers, Samuel Rogers (1763–1855), minor English poet. *Moore*, Thomas Moore (1779–1852), Irish poet who also wrote a biography of Byron. *Wordsworth*, William Wordsworth (1770–1850), English romantic poet, later Poet Laureate.

CHATER *(Startled)*: Eh?

BRICE *(Pleased)*: Ah!

SEPTIMUS: Oh, damn your soul, Chater! Ovid° would have stayed a lawyer and Virgil a farmer if they had known the bathos to which love would descend in your sportive satyrs and noodle nymphs! I am at your service with a half-ounce ball in your brain. May it satisfy you—behind the boat-house at daybreak—shall we say five o'clock? My compliments to Mrs Chater—have no fear for her, she will not want for protection while Captain Brice has a guinea in his pocket, he told her so himself.

BRICE: You lie, sir!

SEPTIMUS: No, sir. Mrs Chater, perhaps.

BRICE: You lie, or you will answer to me!

SEPTIMUS *(Wearily)*: Oh, very well—I can fit you in at five minutes after five. And then it's off to the Malta packet out of Falmouth. You two will be dead, my penurious schoolfriend will remain to tutor Lady Thomasina, and I trust everybody including Lady Croom will be satisfied!

*(*SEPTIMUS *slams the door behind him.)*

BRICE: He is all bluster and bladder. Rest assured, Chater, I will let the air out of him.

*(*BRICE *leaves by the other door.* CHATER's *assurance lasts only a moment. When he spots the flaw . . .)*

CHATER: Oh! But . . .

(He hurries out after BRICE.*)*

ACT 1 / SCENE 4

*(*HANNAH *and* VALENTINE. *She is reading aloud. He is listening. Lightning, the tortoise, is on the table and is not readily distinguishable from Plautus. In front of* VALENTINE *is Septimus's portfolio, recognizably so but naturally somewhat faded. It is open. Principally associated with the portfolio [although it may contain sheets of blank paper also] are three items: a slim maths primer; a sheet of drawing paper on which there is a scrawled diagram and some mathematical notations, arrow marks, etc.; and Thomasina's mathematics lesson book, i.e. the one she writes in, which* VALENTINE *is leafing through as he listens to* HANNAH *reading from the primer.)*

HANNAH: 'I, Thomasina Coverly, have found a truly wonderful method whereby all the forms of nature must give up their numerical secrets and draw themselves through number alone. This

---

Ovid, Roman poet (43 B.C.–17 A.D.), known for erotic poems and mythological stories.

margin being too mean for my purpose, the reader must look elsewhere for the New Geometry of Irregular Forms discovered by Thomasina Coverly.'

(Pause. She hands VALENTINE *the text book.* VALENTINE *looks at what she has been reading. From the next room, a piano is heard, beginning to play quietly, unintrusively, improvisationally.)*

Does it mean anything?

VALENTINE: I don't know. I don't know what it means, except mathematically.

HANNAH: I meant mathematically.

VALENTINE *(Now with the lesson book again)*: It's an iterated algorithm.°

HANNAH: What's that?

VALENTINE: Well, it's . . . Jesus . . . it's an algorithm that's been . . . iterated. How'm I supposed to . . . ? *(He makes an effort.)* The left-hand pages are graphs of what the numbers are doing on the right-hand pages. But all on different scales. Each graph is a small section of the previous one, blown up. Like you'd blow up a detail of a photograph, and then a detail of the detail, and so on, forever. Or in her case, till she ran out of pages.

HANNAH: Is it difficult?

VALENTINE: The maths isn't difficult. It's what you did at school. You have some *x*-and-*y* equation. Any value for *x* gives you a value for *y*. So you put a dot where it's right for both *x* and *y*. Then you take the next value for *x* which gives you another value for *y*, and when you've done that a few times you join up the dots and that's your graph of whatever the equation is.

HANNAH: And is that what she's doing?

VALENTINE: No. Not exactly. Not at all. What she's doing is, every time she works out a value for *y*, she's using *that* as her next value for *x*. And so on. Like a feedback. She's feeding the solution back into the equation, and then solving it again. Iteration, you see.

HANNAH: And that's surprising, is it?

VALENTINE: Well, it is a bit. It's the technique I'm using on my grouse numbers, and it hasn't been around for much longer than, well, call it twenty years.

(Pause.)

HANNAH: Why would she be doing it?

VALENTINE: I have no idea.

(Pause.)

---

iterated algorithm, mathematical process for computing results through a series of repeated operations.

I thought you were doing the hermit.

HANNAH: I am. I still am. But Bernard, damn him . . . Thomasina's tutor turns out to have interesting connections. Bernard is going through the library like a bloodhound. The portfolio was in a cupboard.

VALENTINE: There's a lot of stuff around. Gus loves going through it. No old masters or anything . . .

HANNAH: The maths primer she was using belonged to him—the tutor; he wrote his name in it.

VALENTINE *(Reading)*: 'Septimus Hodge.'

HANNAH: Why were these things saved, do you think?

VALENTINE: Why should there be a reason?

HANNAH: And the diagram, what's it of?

VALENTINE: How would I know?

HANNAH: Why are you cross?

VALENTINE: I'm not cross. *(Pause)* When your Thomasina was doing maths it had been the same maths for a couple of thousand years. Classical. And for a century after Thomasina. Then maths left the real world behind, just like modern art, really. Nature was classical, maths was suddenly Picassos. But now nature is having the last laugh. The freaky stuff is turning out to be the mathematics of the natural world.

HANNAH: This feedback thing?

VALENTINE: For example.

HANNAH: Well, could Thomasina have—

VALENTINE *(Snaps)*: No, of course she bloody couldn't!

HANNAH: All right, you're not cross. What did you mean you were doing the same thing she was doing? *(Pause)* What *are* you doing?

VALENTINE: Actually I'm doing it from the other end. She started with an equation and turned it into a graph. I've got a graph—real data—and I'm trying to find the equation which would give you the graph if you used it the way she's used hers. Iterated it.

HANNAH: What for?

VALENTINE: It's how you look at population changes in biology. Goldfish in a pond, say. This year there are *x* goldfish. Next year there'll be *y* goldfish. Some get born, some get eaten by herons, whatever. Nature manipulates the *x* and turns it into *y*. Then *y* goldfish is your starting population for the following year. Just like Thomasina. Your value for *y* becomes your next value for *x*. The question is: what is being done to *x*? What is the manipulation? Whatever it is, it can be written down as mathematics. It's called an algorithm.

HANNAH: It can't be the same every year.

VALENTINE: The details change, you can't keep tabs on everything, it's not nature in a box. But it isn't necessary to know the details. When they are all put together, it turns out the population is obeying a mathematical rule.

HANNAH: The goldfish are?

VALENTINE: Yes. No. The numbers. It's not about the behaviour of fish. It's about the behaviour of numbers. This thing works for any phenomenon which eats its own numbers—measles epidemics, rainfall averages, cotton prices, it's a natural phenomenon in itself. Spooky.

HANNAH: Does it work for grouse?

VALENTINE: I don't know yet. I mean, it does undoubtedly, but it's hard to show. There's more noise with grouse.

HANNAH: Noise?

VALENTINE: Distortions. Interference. Real data is messy. There's a thousand acres of moorland that had grouse on it, always did till about 1930. But nobody counted the grouse. They shot them. So you count the grouse they shot. But burning the heather interferes, it improves the food supply. A good year for foxes interferes the other way, they eat the chicks. And then there's the weather. It's all very, very noisy out there. Very hard to spot the tune. Like a piano in the next room, it's playing your song, but unfortunately it's out of whack, some of the strings are missing, and the pianist is tone deaf and drunk—I mean, the *noise*! Impossible!

HANNAH: What do you do?

VALENTINE: You start guessing what the tune might be. You try to pick it out of the noise. You try this, you try that, you start to get something—it's half-baked but you start putting in notes which are missing or not quite the right notes . . . and bit by bit . . . (*He starts to dumdi-da to the tune of 'Happy Birthday.'*) Dumdi-dum-dum, dear Val-en-tine, dumdi-dum-dum to you—the lost algorithm!

HANNAH (*Soberly*): Yes, I see. And then what?

VALENTINE: I publish.

HANNAH: Of course. Sorry. Jolly good.

VALENTINE: That's the theory. Grouse are bastards compared to goldfish.

HANNAH: Why did you choose them?

VALENTINE: The game books. My true inheritance. Two hundred years of real data on a plate.

HANNAH: Somebody wrote down everything that's shot?

VALENTINE: Well, that's what a game book is. I'm only using from 1870, when butts and beaters came in.

HANNAH: You mean the game books go back to Thomasina's time?

VALENTINE: Oh yes. Further. (*And then getting ahead of her thought*) No—really. I promise you. I *promise* you. Not a schoolgirl living in a country house in Derbyshire in eighteen-something!

HANNAH: Well, what was she doing?

VALENTINE: She was just playing with the numbers. The truth is, she wasn't doing anything.

HANNAH: She must have been doing something.

VALENTINE: Doodling. Nothing she understood.

HANNAH: A monkey at a typewriter?

VALENTINE: Yes. Well, a piano.

(*HANNAH picks up the algebra book and reads from it.*)

HANNAH: '. . . a method of whereby all the forms of nature must give up their numerical secrets and draw themselves through number alone.' This feedback, is it a way of making pictures of forms in nature? Just tell me if it is or it isn't.

VALENTINE (*Irritated*): To *me* it is. Pictures of turbulence—growth—change—creation—it's not a way of drawing an elephant, for God's sake!

HANNAH: I'm sorry.

(*She picks up an apple leaf from the table. She is timid about pushing the point.*)

So you couldn't make a picture of this leaf by iterating a whatsit?

VALENTINE (*Off-hand*): Oh yes, you could do that.

HANNAH (*Furiously*): Well, tell me! Honestly, I could kill you!

VALENTINE: If you knew the algorithm and fed it back say ten thousand times, each time there'd be a dot somewhere on the screen. You'd never know where to expect the next dot. But gradually you'd start to see this shape, because every dot will be inside the shape of this leaf. It wouldn't *be* a leaf, it would be a mathematical object. But yes. The unpredictable and the predetermined unfold together to make everything the way it is. It's how nature creates itself, on every scale, the snowflake and the snowstorm. It makes me so happy. To be at the beginning again, knowing almost nothing. People were talking about the end of physics. Relativity and quantum looked as if they were going to clean out the whole problem between them. A theory of everything. But they only explained the very big and the very small. The universe, the elementary particles. The ordinary-sized stuff which is our lives, the things people write poetry about—clouds—daffodils—waterfalls—and what happens in a cup of coffee when the cream goes in—these things are full of mystery, as mysterious to us as the heavens were to the Greeks. We're better at predicting events at the edge of the galaxy or inside the nucleus of an atom than whether it'll rain on auntie's garden party three Sundays from now. Because the problem turns out to be different. We can't even predict the next drip from a dripping tap when it gets irregular. Each drip sets up the conditions for the next, the smallest variation blows prediction apart, and the weather is unpredictable the same way, will always be unpredictable. When you push the numbers through the computer you can see it on the screen. The future is disorder. A door like this has cracked open five or six times since we got up on our hind legs. It's the best possible time to be alive, when almost everything you thought you knew is wrong.

(Pause.)

HANNAH: The weather is fairly predictable in the Sahara.

VALENTINE: The scale is different but the graph goes up and down the same way. Six thousand years in the Sahara looks like six months in Manchester, I bet you.

HANNAH: How much?

VALENTINE: Everything you have to lose.

HANNAH: *(Pause)* No.

VALENTINE: Quite right. That's why there was corn in Egypt.

(Hiatus. The piano is heard again.)

HANNAH: What is he playing?

VALENTINE: I don't know. He makes it up.

HANNAH: Chloë called him 'genius.'

VALENTINE: It's what my mother calls him—only *she* means it. Last year some expert had her digging in the wrong place for months to find something or other—the foundations of Capability Brown's boat-house—and Gus put her right first go.

HANNAH: Did he ever speak?

VALENTINE: Oh yes. Until he was five. You've never asked about him. You get high marks here for good breeding.

HANNAH: Yes, I know. I've always been given credit for my unconcern.

(BERNARD enters in high excitement and triumph.)

BERNARD: *English Bards and Scotch Reviewers.* A pencilled superscription. Listen and kiss my cycle-clips!

(He is carrying the book. He reads from it.)

'O harbinger of Sleep, who missed the press
And hoped his drone might thus escape redress!
The wretched Chater, bard of Eros' Couch,
For his narcotic let my pencil vouch!'

You see, *you have to turn over every page.*

HANNAH: Is it his handwriting?

BERNARD: Oh, come *on.*

HANNAH: Obviously not.

BERNARD: Christ, what do you want?

HANNAH: Proof.

VALENTINE: Quite right. Who are you talking about?

BERNARD: Proof? *Proof*? You'd have to be there, you silly bitch!

VALENTINE *(Mildly)*: I say, you're speaking of my fiancée.

HANNAH: Especially when I have a present for you. Guess what I found. *(Producing the present for BERNARD)* Lady Croom writing from London to her husband. Her brother, Captain Brice, married a Mrs Chater. In other words, one might assume, a widow.

(BERNARD looks at the letter.)

BERNARD: I *said* he was dead. What year? 1810! Oh my God, 1810! Well *done*, Hannah! Are you going to tell me it's a different Mrs Chater?

HANNAH: Oh no. It's her all right. Note her Christian name.

BERNARD: Charity. Charity . . .'Deny what cannot be proven for Charity's sake!'

HANNAH: Don't kiss me!

VALENTINE: She won't let anyone kiss her.

BERNARD: You see! They wrote—they scribbled—they put it on paper. It was their employment. Their diversion. Paper is what they had. And there'll be more. There is always more. We can find it!

HANNAH: Such passion. First Valentine, now you. It's moving.

BERNARD: The aristocratic friend of the tutor—under the same roof as the poor sod whose book he savaged—the first thing he does is seduce Chater's wife. All is discovered. There is a duel. Chater dead, Byron fled! P.S. guess what?, the widow married her ladyship's brother! Do you honestly think no one wrote a word? How could they not! It dropped from sight but we will write it again!

HANNAH: You can, Bernard. I'm not going to take any credit, I haven't done anything.

(The same thought has clearly occurred to BERNARD. He becomes instantly po-faced.°)

BERNARD: Well, that's—very fair—generous—

HANNAH: Prudent. Chater could have died of anything, anywhere.

(The po-face is forgotten.)

BERNARD: But he fought a duel with Byron!

HANNAH: You haven't established it was fought. You haven't established it was Byron. For God's sake, Bernard, you haven't established Byron was even here!

BERNARD: I'll tell you your problem. No guts.

HANNAH: Really?

BERNARD: By which I mean a visceral belief in yourself. Gut instinct. The part of you which doesn't

---

po-faced, blank, humorless look.

reason. The certainty for which there is no back-reference. Because time is reversed. Tock, tick goes the universe and then recovers itself, but it was enough, you were in there and you bloody *know*.

VALENTINE: Are you talking about Lord Byron, the poet?

BERNARD: No, you fucking idiot, we're talking about Lord Byron the chartered accountant.

VALENTINE *(Unoffended)*: Oh well, *he* was here all right, the poet.

(Silence.)

HANNAH: How do you know?

VALENTINE: He's in the game book. I think he shot a hare. I read through the whole lot once when I had mumps—some quite interesting people—

HANNAH: Where's the book?

VALENTINE: It's not one I'm using—too early, of course—

HANNAH: 1809.

VALENTINE: They've always been in the commode. Ask Chloë.

(HANNAH looks to BERNARD. BERNARD has been silent because he has been incapable of speech. He seems to have gone into a trance, in which only his mouth tries to work. HANNAH steps over to him and gives him a demure kiss on the cheek. It works. BERNARD lurches out into the garden and can be heard croaking for 'Chloë . . . Chloë!')

VALENTINE: My mother's lent him her bicycle. Lending one's bicycle is a form of safe sex, possibly the safest there is. My mother is in a flutter about Bernard, and he's no fool. He gave her a first edition of Horace Walpole, and now she's lent him her bicycle.

(He gathers up the three items [the primer, the lesson book and the diagram] and puts them into the portfolio.)

Can I keep these for a while?

HANNAH: Yes, of course.

(The piano stops. GUS enters hesitantly from the music room.)

VALENTINE *(To GUS)*: Yes, finished . . . coming now. *(To HANNAH)* I'm trying to work out the diagram.

(GUS nods and smiles, at HANNAH too, but she is preoccupied.)

HANNAH: What I don't understand is . . . why nobody did this feedback thing before—it's not like relativity, you don't have to be Einstein.

VALENTINE: You couldn't see to look before. The electronic calculator was what the telescope was for Galileo.

HANNAH: Calculator?

VALENTINE: There wasn't enough time before. There weren't enough *pencils!* *(He flourishes Thomasina's lesson book.)* This took her I don't know how many days and she hasn't scratched the paintwork. Now she'd only have to press a button, the same button over and over. Iteration. A few minutes. And what I've done in a couple of months, with only a *pencil* the calculations would take me the rest of my life to do again—thousands of pages—tens of thousands! And so boring!

HANNAH: Do you mean—?

(She stops because GUS is plucking VALENTINE's sleeve.)

Do you mean—?

VALENTINE: All right, Gus, I'm coming.

HANNAH: Do you mean that was the only problem? Enough time? And paper? And the boredom?

VALENTINE: We're going to get out the dressing-up box.

HANNAH *(Driven to raising her voice)*: *Val!* Is that what you're saying?

VALENTINE *(Surprised by her. Mildly)*: No, I'm saying you'd have to have a reason for doing it.

(GUS runs out of the room, upset.)

(Apologetically) He hates people shouting.

HANNAH: I'm sorry.

(VALENTINE starts to follow GUS.)

But anything else?

VALENTINE: Well, the other thing is, you'd have to be insane.

(VALENTINE leaves. HANNAH stays, thoughtful. After a moment, she turns to the table and picks up the Cornhill Magazine. *She looks into it briefly, then closes it, and leaves the room, taking the magazine with her. The empty room. The light changes to early morning. From a long way off, there is a pistol shot. A moment later there is the cry of dozens of crows disturbed from the unseen trees.)*

ACT 2 / SCENE 1

(BERNARD is pacing around, reading aloud from a handful of typed sheets. VALENTINE, CHLOË and GUS are his audience. GUS sits somewhat apart, perhaps less attentive. VALENTINE has his tortoise and is eating a sandwich from which he extracts shreds of lettuce to offer the tortoise.)

BERNARD: 'Did it happen? could it happen?'
Undoubtedly it could. Only three years earlier the Irish poet Tom Moore appeared on the field of combat to avenge a review by Jeffrey of the *Edinburgh*. These affairs were seldom fatal and sometimes farcical but, potentially, the duellist stood in respect to the law no differently from a murderer. As for the murderee, a minor poet like

Ezra Chater could go to his death in a Derbyshire glade as unmissed and unremembered as his contemporary and namesake, the minor botanist who died in the forests of the West Indies, lost to history like the monkey that bit him. On April 16th 1809, a few days after he left Sidley Park, Byron wrote to his solicitor John Hanson: 'If the consequences of my leaving England were ten times as ruinous as you describe, I have no alternative; there are circumstances which render it absolutely indispensable, and quit the country I must immediately.' To which, the editor's note in the Collected Letters reads as follows: 'What Byron's urgent reasons for leaving England were at this time has never been revealed.' The letter was written from the family seat, Newstead Abbey, Nottinghamshire. A long day's ride to the northwest lay Sidley Park, the estate of the Coverlys—a far grander family, raised by Charles II to the Earldom of Croom . . .'

(HANNAH enters briskly, a piece of paper in her hand.)

HANNAH: Bernard. . . ! Val . . .

BERNARD: Do you mind?

(HANNAH puts her piece of paper down in front of VALENTINE.)

CHLOË *(Angrily)*: *Hannah!*

HANNAH: What?

CHLOË: She's so *rude!*

HANNAH *(Taken aback)*: What? Am I?

VALENTINE: Bernard's reading us his lecture.

HANNAH: Yes, I know. *(Then recollecting herself)* Yes—yes—that *was* rude. I'm sorry, Bernard.

VALENTINE *(With the piece of paper)*: What is this?

HANNAH *(To BERNARD)*: Spot on—the India Office Library. *(To VALENTINE)* Peacock's letter in holograph,° I got a copy sent—

CHLOË: *Hannah!* Shut up!

HANNAH *(Sitting down)*: Yes, sorry.

BERNARD: It's all right, I'll read it to myself.

CHLOË: *No.*

(HANNAH reaches for the Peacock letter and takes it back.)

HANNAH: Go on, Bernard. Have I missed anything? Sorry.

(BERNARD stares at her balefully but then continues to read.)

BERNARD: 'The Byrons of Newstead in 1809 comprised an eccentric widow and her undistinguished son, the "lame brat," who until the age of ten when he came into the title, had been carted about the

---

holograph, in the original handwriting.

country from lodging to lodging by his vulgar hectoring monster of a mother—' *(HANNAH's hand has gone up)*—overruled—'and who four months past his twenty-first birthday was master of nothing but his debts and his genius. Between the Byrons and the Coverlys there was no social equality and none to be expected. The connection, undisclosed to posterity until now, was with Septimus Hodge, Byron's friend at Harrow and Trinity College—' *(HANNAH's hand goes up again)*—sustained—*(He makes an instant correction with a silver pencil.)* 'Byron's contemporary at Harrow and Trinity College, and now tutor in residence to the Croom daughter, Thomasina Coverly. Byron's letters tell us where he was on April 8th and on April 12th. He was at Newstead. But on the 10th he was at Sidley Park, as attested by the game book preserved there: "April 10th 1809—forenoon. High cloud, dry, and sun between times, wind southeasterly. Self—Augustus—Lord Byron. Fourteen pigeon, one hare (Lord B.)." But, as we know now, the drama of life and death at Sidley Park was not about pigeons but about sex and literature.'

VALENTINE: Unless you were the pigeon.

BERNARD: I don't have to do this. I'm paying you a compliment.

CHLOË: Ignore him, Bernard—go on, get to the duel.

BERNARD: Hannah's not even paying attention.

HANNAH: Yes I am, it's all going in. I often work with the radio on.

BERNARD: Oh thanks!

HANNAH: Is there much more?

CHLOË: *Hannah!*

HANNAH: No, it's fascinating. I just wondered how much more there was. I need to ask Valentine about this *(letter)*—sorry, Bernard, go on, this will keep.

VALENTINE: Yes—sorry, Bernard.

CHLOË: Please, Bernard!

BERNARD: Where was I?

VALENTINE: Pigeons.

CHLOË: Sex.

HANNAH: Literature.

BERNARD: Life and death. Right. 'Nothing could be more eloquent of that than the three documents I have quoted: the terse demand to settle a matter in private; the desperate scribble of "my husband has sent for pistols"; and on April 11th, the gauntlet thrown down by the aggrieved and cuckolded author Ezra Chater. The covers have not survived. What is certain is that all three letters were in Byron's possession when his books were sold in 1816—preserved in the pages of "The Couch of Eros" which seven years earlier at Sidley Park Byron had borrowed from Septimus Hodge.'

HANNAH: Borrowed?

BERNARD: I will be taking questions at the end. Constructive comments will be welcome. Which is indeed my reason for trying out in the provinces before my London opening under the auspices of the Byron Society prior to publication. By the way, Valentine, do you want a credit?—'the game book recently discovered by'?

VALENTINE: It was never lost, Bernard.

BERNARD: 'As recently pointed out by.' I don't normally like giving credit where it's due, but with scholarly articles as with divorce, there is a certain cachet in citing a member of the aristocracy. I'll pop it in ad lib for the lecture, and give you a mention in the press release. How's that?

VALENTINE: Very kind.

HANNAH: Press release? What happened to the *Journal of English Studies*?

BERNARD: That comes later with the apparatus, and in the recognized tone—very dry, very modest, absolutely gloat-free, and yet unmistakably 'Eat your heart out, you dozy bastards.' But first, it's 'Media Don, book early to avoid disappointment.' Where was I?

VALENTINE: Game book.

CHLOË: Eros.

HANNAH: Borrowed.

BERNARD: Right. '—borrowed from Septimus Hodge. Is it conceivable that the letters were already in the book when Byron borrowed it?'

VALENTINE: Yes.

CHLOË: Shut up, Val.

VALENTINE: Well, it's conceivable.

BERNARD: 'Is it *likely* that Hodge would have lent Byron the book without first removing the three private letters?'

VALENTINE: Look, sorry—I only meant, Byron could have borrowed the book without asking.

HANNAH: That's true.

BERNARD: Then why wouldn't Hodge get them back?

HANNAH: I don't know, I wasn't there.

BERNARD: That's right, you bloody weren't.

CHLOË: Go on, Bernard.

BERNARD: 'It is the third document, the challenge itself, that convinces. Chater "as a man and a poet," points the finger at his "slanderer in the press." Neither as a man nor a poet did Ezra Chater cut such a figure as to be habitually slandered or even mentioned in the press. It is surely indisputable that the slander was the review of "The Maid of Turkey" in the *Piccadilly Recreation*. Did Septimus Hodge have any connection with the London periodicals? No. Did Byron? Yes! He had reviewed Wordsworth two years earlier, he was to review Spencer two years later. And do we have any clue as to Byron's opinion of Chater the poet? Yes! Who but Byron could have written the four lines pencilled into Lady Croom's copy of *English Bards and Scotch Reviewers*'—

HANNAH: Almost anybody.

BERNARD: Darling—

HANNAH: Don't call me darling.

BERNARD: Dickhead, then, is it likely that the man Chater calls his friend Septimus Hodge is the same man who screwed his wife and kicked the shit out of his last book?

HANNAH: Put it like that, almost certain.

CHLOË *(Earnestly)*: You've been deeply wounded in the past, haven't you, Hannah?

HANNAH: Nothing compared to listening to this. Why is there nothing in Byron's letters about the *Piccadilly* reviews?

BERNARD: Exactly. Because he killed the author.

HANNAH: But the first one, 'The Maid of Turkey,' was the year before. Was he clairvoyant?

CHLOË: Letters get lost.

BERNARD: Thank you! Exactly! There is a platonic letter which confirms everything—lost but ineradicable, like radio voices rippling through the universe for all eternity. 'My dear Hodge—here I am in Albania and you're the only person in the whole world who knows why. Poor C! I never wished him any harm—except in the *Piccadilly*, of course—it was the woman who bade me eat, dear Hodge!—what a tragic business, but thank God it ended well for poetry. Yours ever, B.—P.S. Burn this.'

VALENTINE: How did Chater find out the reviewer was Byron?

BERNARD *(Irritated)*: I don't know, I wasn't there, was I? *(Pause. To* HANNAH*)* You wish to say something?

HANNAH: Moi?

CHLOË: I know. Byron told Mrs Chater in bed. Next day he dumped her so she grassed on him, and pleaded date rape.

BERNARD *(Fastidiously)*: Date rape? What do you mean, date rape?

HANNAH: April the tenth.

*(*BERNARD *cracks. Everything becomes loud and overlapped as* BERNARD *threatens to walk out and is cajoled into continuing.)*

BERNARD: Right!—forget it!

HANNAH: Sorry—

BERNARD: No—I've had nothing but sarcasm and childish interruptions—

VALENTINE: What did I do?

BERNARD: No credit for probably the most sensational literary discovery of the century—

CHLOË: I think you're jolly unfair—they're jealous, Bernard—

HANNAH: I won't say another word—

VALENTINE: Yes, go on, Bernard—we promise.

BERNARD *(Finally)*: Well, only if you stop *feeding tortoises*!

VALENTINE: Well, it's his lunch time.

BERNARD: And on condition that I am afforded the common courtesy of a scholar among scholars—

HANNAH: Absolutely mum till you're finished—

BERNARD: After which, any comments are to be couched in terms of accepted academic—

HANNAH: Dignity—you're right, Bernard.

BERNARD: —respect.

HANNAH: Respect. Absolutely. The language of scholars. Count on it.

(Having made a great show of putting his pages away, BERNARD *reassembles then and finds his place, glancing suspiciously at the other three for signs of levity.)*

BERNARD: Last paragraph. 'Without question, Ezra Chater issued a challenge to *somebody*. If a duel was fought in the dawn mist of Sidley Park in April 1809, his opponent, on the evidence, was a critic with a gift for ridicule and a taste for seduction. Do we need to look far? Without question, Mrs Chater was a widow by 1810. If we seek the occasion of Ezra Chater's early and unrecorded death, do we need to look far? Without question, Lord Byron, in the very season of his emergence as a literary figure, quit the country in a cloud of panic and mystery, and stayed abroad for two years at a time when Continental travel was unusual and dangerous. If we seek his reason—*do we need to look far?*

(No mean performer, he is pleased with the effect of his peroration. There is a significant silence.)

HANNAH: Bollocks.°

CHLOË: Well, I think it's true.

HANNAH: You've left out everything which doesn't fit. Byron had been banging on for months about leaving England—there's a letter in *February*—

BERNARD: But he didn't go, did he?

HANNAH: And then he didn't sail until the beginning of July!

BERNARD: Everything moved more slowly then. Time was different. He was two weeks in Falmouth waiting for wind or something—

HANNAH: Bernard, I don't know why I'm bothering—you're arrogant, greedy and reckless. You've gone from a glint in your eye to a sure thing in a hop, skip and a jump. You deserve what you get and I think you're mad. But I can't help myself, you're like some exasperating child pedalling its tricycle towards the edge of a cliff, and I have to do something. So listen to me. If Byron killed Chater in a duel I'm Marie of Romania. You'll end up with so much *fame* you won't leave the house without a paper bag over your head.

Bollocks, nonsense (originally referred to bull testicles).

VALENTINE: Actually, Bernard, as a scientist, your theory is incomplete.

BERNARD: But I'm not a scientist.

VALENTINE *(Patiently)*: No, *as a scientist*—

BERNARD *(Beginning to shout)*: I have yet to hear a proper argument.

HANNAH: Nobody would kill a man and then pan his book. I mean, not in that order. So he must have borrowed the book, written the review, *posted it,* seduced Mrs Chater, fought a duel and departed, all in the space of two or three days. Who would do that?

BERNARD: Byron.

HANNAH: It's hopeless.

BERNARD: You've never understood him, as you've shown in your novelette.

HANNAH: In my what?

BERNARD: Oh, sorry—did you think it was a work of historical revisionism? Byron the spoilt child promoted beyond his gifts by the spirit of the age! And Caroline the closet intellectual shafted by a male society!

VALENTINE: I read that somewhere—

HANNAH: It's his review.

BERNARD: And bloody well said, too!

(Things are turning a little ugly and BERNARD *seems in a mood to push them that way.)*

You got them backwards, darling. Caroline was Romantic waffle on wheels with no talent, and Byron was an eighteenth-century Rationalist touched by genius. And he killed Chater.

HANNAH: *(Pause)* If it's not too late to change my mind, I'd like you to go ahead.

BERNARD: I intend to. Look to the mote in your own eye!—you even had the wrong bloke on the dust-jacket!

HANNAH: Dust-jacket?

VALENTINE: What about my computer model? Aren't you going to mention it?

BERNARD: It's inconclusive.

VALENTINE *(To* HANNAH*)*: The *Piccadilly* reviews aren't a very good fit with Byron's other reviews, you see.

HANNAH *(To* BERNARD*)*: What do you mean, the wrong bloke?

BERNARD *(Ignoring her)*: The other reviews aren't a very good fit for each other, are they?

VALENTINE: No, but differently. The parameters—

BERNARD *(Jeering)*: Parameters! You can't stick Byron's head in your laptop! Genius isn't like your average grouse.

VALENTINE *(Casually)*: Well, it's all trivial anyway.

BERNARD: What is?

VALENTINE: Who wrote what when . . .

BERNARD: Trivial?

VALENTINE: Personalities.

BERNARD: I'm sorry—did you say trivial?

VALENTINE: It's a technical term.

BERNARD: Not where I come from, it isn't.

VALENTINE: The questions you're asking don't matter, you see. It's like arguing who got there first with the calculus. The English say Newton, the Germans say Leibnitz. But it doesn't *matter*. Personalities. What matters is the calculus. Scientific progress. Knowledge.

BERNARD: Really? Why?

VALENTINE: Why what?

BERNARD: Why does scientific progress matter more than personalities?

VALENTINE: Is he serious?

HANNAH: No, he's trivial. Bernard—

VALENTINE *(Interrupting, to* BERNARD*)*: Do yourself a favour, you're on a loser.

BERNARD: Oh, you're going to zap me with penicillin and pesticides. Spare me that and I'll spare you the bomb and aerosols. But don't confuse progress with perfectibility. A great poet is always timely. A great philosopher is an urgent need. There's no rush for Isaac Newton. We were quite happy with Aristotle's cosmos. Personally, I preferred it. Fifty-five crystal spheres geared to God's crankshaft is my idea of a satisfying universe. I can't think of anything more trivial than the speed of light. Quarks, quasars—big bangs, black holes—who gives a shit? How did you people con us out of all that status? All that money? And why are you so pleased with yourselves?

CHLOË: Are you against penicillin, Bernard?

BERNARD: Don't feed the animals. *(Back to* VALENTINE*)* I'd push the lot of you over a cliff myself. Except the one in the wheelchair, I think I'd lose the sympathy vote before people had time to think it through.

HANNAH *(Loudly)*: What the hell do you mean, the dust-jacket?

BERNARD *(Ignoring her)*: If knowledge isn't self-knowledge it isn't doing much, mate. Is the universe expanding? Is it contracting? Is it standing on one leg and singing 'When Father Painted the Parlour'? Leave me out. I can expand my universe without you. 'She walks in beauty, like the night of cloudless climes and starry skies, and all that's best of dark and bright meet in her aspect and her eyes.'° There you are, he wrote it after coming home from a party. *(With offensive politeness)* What is it that you're doing with grouse, Valentine, I'd love to know?

*(*VALENTINE *stands up and it is suddenly apparent that he is shaking and close to tears.)*

VALENTINE *(To* CHLOË*)*: He's not against penicillin, and he knows I'm not against poetry. *(To* BERNARD*)* I've given up on the grouse.

HANNAH: You haven't, Valentine!

VALENTINE *(Leaving)*: I can't do it.

HANNAH: *Why?*

VALENTINE: Too much noise. There's just too much *bloody noise!*

(On which, VALENTINE *leaves the room.* CHLOË, *upset and in tears, jumps up and briefly pummels* BERNARD *ineffectually with her fists.)*

CHLOË: You bastard, Bernard!

(She follows VALENTINE *out.* GUS *watches all this, upset by it, and follows* CHLOË *out. Pause.)*

HANNAH: Well, I think that's everybody. You can leave now, give Lightning a kick on your way out.

BERNARD: Yes, I m sorry about that. It s no fun when it's not among pros, is it?

HANNAH: No.

BERNARD: Oh, well . . . *(he begins to put his lecture sheets away in his briefcase, and is thus reminded . . .)* do you want to know about your book jacket? 'Lord Byron and Caroline Lamb at the Royal Academy'? Ink study by Henry Fuseli?°

HANNAH: What about it?

BERNARD: It's not them.

HANNAH *(She explodes)*: Who says!?

*(*BERNARD *brings the* Byron Society Journal *from his briefcase.)*

BERNARD: This Fuseli expert in the *Byron Society Journal*. They sent me the latest . . . as a distinguished guest speaker.

HANNAH: But of course it's them! Everyone knows—

BERNARD: Popular tradition only. *(He is finding the place in the journal.)* Here we are. 'No earlier than 1820.' He's analysed it. *(Offers it to her)* Read at your leisure.

HANNAH *(She sounds like* BERNARD *jeering)*: Analysed it?

BERNARD: Charming sketch, of course, but Byron was in Italy . . .

HANNAH: But, Bernard—I *know* it's them.

BERNARD: How?

HANNAH: How? It just *is*. 'Analysed it,' my big toe!

BERNARD: Language!

HANNAH: He's wrong.

BERNARD: Oh, gut instinct, you mean?

HANNAH *(Flatly)*: He's wrong.

*(*BERNARD *snaps shut his briefcase.)*

"She walks in beauty . . . her eyes," from Byron's poem "Hebrew Melodies."

Fuseli, Henry Fuseli (1741–1825), Swiss-born painter, living in England.

BERNARD: Well, it's all trivial, isn't it? Why don't you come?

HANNAH: Where?

BERNARD: With me.

HANNAH: To London? What for?

BERNARD: What for.

HANNAH: Oh, your lecture.

BERNARD: No, no, bugger that. Sex.

HANNAH: Oh . . . No. Thanks . . . *(then, protesting)* Bernard!

BERNARD: You should try it. It's very underrated.

HANNAH: Nothing against it.

BERNARD: Yes, you have. You should let yourself go a bit. You might have written a better book. Or at any rate the right book.

HANNAH: Sex and literature. Literature and sex. Your conversation, left to itself, doesn't have many places to go. Like two marbles rolling around a pudding basin. One of them is always sex.

BERNARD: Ah well, yes. Men all over.

HANNAH: No doubt. Einstein—relativity and sex. Chippendale—sex and furniture. Galileo—'Did the earth move?' What the hell is it with you people? Chaps sometimes wanted to marry me, and I don't know a worse bargain. Available sex against not being allowed to fart in bed. What do you mean the right book?

BERNARD: It takes a romantic to make a heroine of Caroline Lamb. You were cut out for Byron.

(Pause.)

HANNAH: So, cheerio.

BERNARD: Oh, I'm coming back for the dance, you know. Chloë asked me.

HANNAH: She meant well, but I don't dance.

BERNARD: No, no—I'm going with her.

HANNAH: Oh, I see. I don't, actually.

BERNARD: I'm her date. Sub rosa.° Don't tell Mother.

HANNAH: She doesn't want her mother to know?

BERNARD: No—*I* don't want her mother to know. This is my first experience of the landed aristocracy. I tell you, I'm boggle-eyed.

HANNAH: Bernard!—you haven't seduced that girl?

BERNARD: Seduced her? Every time I turned round she was up a library ladder. In the end I gave in. That reminds me—I spotted something between her legs that made me think of you.

(He instantly receives a sharp stinging slap on the face but manages to remain completely unperturbed by it. He is already producing from his pocket a small book. His voice has hardly hesitated.)

The Peaks Traveller and Gazetteer—James Godolphin 1832—unillustrated, I'm afraid. *(He has opened the book to a marked place.)* 'Sidley Park in Derbyshire, property of the Earl of Croom . . .'

HANNAH *(Numbly)*: The world is going to hell in a handcart.

BERNARD: 'Five hundred acres including forty of lake—the Park by Brown and Noakes has pleasing features in the horrid style—viaduct, grotto, etc—a hermitage occupied by a lunatic since twenty years without discourse or companion save for a pet tortoise, Plautus by name, which he suffers children to touch on request.' *(He holds out the book for her.)* A tortoise. They must be a feature.

(After a moment HANNAH takes the book.)

HANNAH: Thank you.

(VALENTINE comes to the door.)

VALENTINE: The station taxi is at the front . . .

BERNARD: Yes . . . thanks . . . Oh—did Peacock come up trumps?

HANNAH: For some.

BERNARD: Hermit's name and cv?

(He picks up and glances at the Peacock letter.)

'My dear Thackeray . . .' God, I'm good.

(He puts the letter down.)

Well, wish me luck—*(Vaguely to VALENTINE)* Sorry about . . . you know . . . *(and to HANNAH)* and about your . . .

VALENTINE: Piss off, Bernard.

BERNARD: Right.

(BERNARD goes.)

HANNAH: Don't let Bernard get to you. It's only performance art, you know. Rhetoric. They used to teach it in ancient times, like PT.° It's not about being right, they had philosophy for that. Rhetoric was their chat show. Bernard's indignation is a sort of aerobics for when he gets on television.

VALENTINE: I don't care to be rubbished by the dustbin man. *(He has been looking at the letter.)* The what of the lunatic?

(HANNAH reclaims the letter and reads it for him.)

HANNAH: 'The testament of the lunatic serves as a caution against French fashion . . . for it was Frenchified mathematick that brought him to the melancholy certitude of a world without light or life . . . as a wooden stove that must consume itself until ash and stove are as one, and heat is gone from the earth.'

VALENTINE *(Amused, surprised)*: Huh!

HANNAH: 'He died aged two score years and seven,

---

sub rosa, Latin phrase meaning "confidentially."

PT, physical training (gym class).

hoary as Job and meagre as a cabbage-stalk, the proof of his prediction even yet unyielding to his labours for the restitution of hope through good English algebra.'

VALENTINE: That's it?

HANNAH *(Nods)*: Is there anything in it?

VALENTINE: In what? We are all doomed? *(Casually)* Oh yes, sure—it's called the second law of thermo-dynamics.°

HANNAH: Was it known about?

VALENTINE: By poets and lunatics from time imme-morial.

HANNAH: Seriously.

VALENTINE: No.

HANNAH: Is it anything to do with . . . you know, Thomasina's discovery?

VALENTINE: She didn't discover anything.

HANNAH: Her lesson book.

VALENTINE: No.

HANNAH: A coincidence, then?

VALENTINE: What is?

HANNAH *(Reading)*: 'He died aged two score years and seven.' That was in 1834. So he was born in 1787. So was the tutor. He says so in his letter to Lord Croom when he recommended himself for the job: 'Date of birth—1787.' The hermit was born in the same year as Septimus Hodge.

VALENTINE: *(Pause)* Did Bernard bite you in the leg?

HANNAH: Don't you see? I thought my hermit was a perfect symbol. An idiot in the landscape. But this is better. The Age of Enlightenment banished into the Romantic wilderness! The genius of Sidley Park living on in a hermit's hut!

VALENTINE: You don't *know* that.

HANNAH: Oh, but I do. I do. Somewhere there will be *something* . . . if only I can find it.

ACT 2 / SCENE 2

(The room is empty. A reprise: early morning—a distant pistol shot—the sound of the crows.

JELLABY enters the dawn-dark room with a lamp. He goes to the windows and looks out. He sees something. He returns to put the lamp on the table, and then opens one of the french windows and steps outside.)

JELLABY *(Outside)*: Mr Hodge!

(SEPTIMUS comes in, followed by JELLABY, who closes the garden door. SEPTIMUS is wearing a greatcoat.)

SEPTIMUS: Thank you, Jellaby. I was expecting to be locked out. What time is it?

---

second law of thermodynamics, the familiar example is that heat will move from a warmer body to a cooler body, but not the other way around.

JELLABY: Half past five.

SEPTIMUS: That is what I have. Well!—what a bracing experience!

(He produces two pistols from inside his coat and places them on the table.)

The dawn, you know. Unexpectedly lively. Fishes, birds, frogs . . . rabbits . . . *(he produces a dead rabbit from inside his coat)* and very beautiful. If only it did not occur so early in the day. I have brought Lady Thomasina a rabbit. Will you take it?

JELLABY: It's dead.

SEPTIMUS: Yes. Lady Thomasina loves a rabbit pie.

(JELLABY takes the rabbit without enthusiasm. There is a little blood on it.)

JELLABY: You were missed, Mr Hodge.

SEPTIMUS: I decided to sleep last night in the boat-house. Did I see a carriage leaving the Park?

JELLABY: Captain Brice's carriage, with Mr and Mrs Chater also.

SEPTIMUS: Gone?!

JELLABY: Yes, sir. And Lord Byron's horse was brought round at four o'clock.

SEPTIMUS: Lord Byron too!

JELLABY: Yes, sir. The house has been up and hop-ping.

SEPTIMUS: But I have his rabbit pistols! What am I to do with his rabbit pistols?

JELLABY: You were looked for in your room.

SEPTIMUS: By whom?

JELLABY: By her ladyship.

SEPTIMUS: In my room?

JELLABY: I will tell her ladyship you are returned.

(He starts to leave.)

SEPTIMUS: Jellaby! Did Lord Byron leave a book for me?

JELLABY: A book?

SEPTIMUS: He had the loan of a book from me.

JELLABY: His lordship left nothing in his room, sir, not a coin.

SEPTIMUS: Oh. Well, I'm sure he would have left a coin if he'd had one. Jellaby—here is a half-guinea for you.

JELLABY: Thank you very much, sir.

SEPTIMUS: What has occurred?

JELLABY: The servants are told nothing, sir.

SEPTIMUS: Come, come, does a half-guinea buy nothing any more?

JELLABY *(Sighs)*: Her ladyship encountered Mrs Chater during the night.

SEPTIMUS: Where?

JELLABY: On the threshold of Lord Byron's room.

SEPTIMUS: Ah. Which one was leaving and which entering?

JELLABY: Mrs Chater was leaving Lord Byron's room.

SEPTIMUS: And where was Mr Chater?

JELLABY: Mr Chater and Captain Brice were drinking cherry brandy. They had the footman to keep the fire up until three o'clock. There was a loud altercation upstairs, and—

(LADY CROOM *enters the room.*)

LADY CROOM: Well, Mr Hodge.

SEPTIMUS: My lady.

LADY CROOM: All this to shoot a hare?

SEPTIMUS: A rabbit. (*She gives him one of her looks.*) No, indeed, a hare, though very rabbit-like—

(JELLABY *is about to leave.*)

LADY CROOM: My infusion.

JELLABY: Yes, my lady.

(*He leaves.* LADY CROOM *is carrying two letters. We have not seen them before. Each has an envelope which has been opened. She flings them on the table.*)

LADY CROOM: How dare you!

SEPTIMUS: I cannot be called to account for what was written in private and read without regard to propriety.

LADY CROOM: Addressed to me!

SEPTIMUS: Left in my room, in the event of my death—

LADY CROOM: Pah!—what earthly use is a love letter from beyond the grave?

SEPTIMUS: As much, surely, as from this side of it. The second letter, however, was not addressed to your ladyship.

LADY CROOM: I have a mother's right to open a letter addressed by you to my daughter, whether in the event of your life, your death, or your imbecility. What do you mean by writing to her of rice pudding when she has just suffered the shock of violent death in our midst?

SEPTIMUS: Whose death?

LADY CROOM: Yours, you wretch!

SEPTIMUS: Yes, I see.

LADY CROOM: I do not know which is the madder of your ravings. One envelope full of rice pudding, the other of the most insolent familiarities regarding several parts of my body, but have no doubt which is the more intolerable to me.

SEPTIMUS: Which?

LADY CROOM: Oh, aren't we saucy when our bags are packed! Your friend has gone before you, and I have despatched the harlot Chater and her husband—and also my brother for bringing them here. Such is the sentence, you see, for choosing unwisely in your acquaintance. Banishment. Lord Byron is a rake and a hypocrite, and the sooner he sails for the Levant the sooner he will find society congenial to his character.

SEPTIMUS: It has been a night of reckoning.

LADY CROOM: Indeed I wish it had passed unevent-

fully with you and Mr Chater shooting each other with the decorum due to a civilized house. You have no secrets left, Mr Hodge. They spilled out between shrieks and oaths and tears. It is fortunate that a lifetime's devotion to the sporting gun has halved my husband's hearing to the ear he sleeps on.

SEPTIMUS: I'm afraid I have no knowledge of what has occurred.

LADY CROOM: Your trollop was discovered in Lord Byron's room.

SEPTIMUS: Ah. Discovered by Mr Chater?

LADY CROOM: Who else?

SEPTIMUS: I am very sorry, madam, for having used your kindness to bring my unworthy friend to your notice. He will have to give an account of himself to me, you may be sure.

(*Before* LADY CROOM *can respond to this threat,* JELLABY *enters the room with her 'infusion.' This is quite an elaborate affair: a pewter tray on small feet on which there is a kettle suspended over a spirit lamp. There is a cup and saucer and the silver 'basket' containing the dry leaves for the tea.* JELLABY *places the tray on the table and is about to offer further assistance with it.*)

LADY CROOM: I will do it.

JELLABY: Yes, my lady. (*To* SEPTIMUS) Lord Byron left a letter for you with the valet, sir.

SEPTIMUS: Thank you.

(SEPTIMUS *takes the letter off the tray.* JELLABY *prepares to leave.* LADY CROOM *eyes the letter.*)

LADY CROOM: When did he do so?

JELLABY: As he was leaving, your ladyship.

(JELLABY *leaves.* SEPTIMUS *puts the letter into his pocket.*)

SEPTIMUS: Allow me.

(*Since she does not object, he pours a cup of tea for her. She accepts it.*)

LADY CROOM: I do not know if it is proper for you to receive a letter written in my house from someone not welcome in it.

SEPTIMUS: Very improper, I agree. Lord Byron's want of delicacy is a grief to his friends, among whom I no longer count myself. I will not read his letter until I have followed him through the gates.

(*She considers that for a moment.*)

LADY CROOM: That may excuse the reading but not the writing.

SEPTIMUS: Your ladyship should have lived in the Athens of Pericles! The philosophers would have fought the sculptors for your idle hour!

LADY CROOM (*Protesting*): Oh, really! . . . (*Protesting less*) Oh really . . .

(SEPTIMUS *has taken Byron's letter from his pocket and is now setting fire to a corner of it using the little flame from the spirit lamp.*)

Oh . . . really . . .

(*The paper blazes in* SEPTIMUS*'s hand and he drops it and lets it burn out on the metal tray.*)

SEPTIMUS: Now there's a thing—a letter from Lord Byron never to be read by a living soul. I will take my leave, madam, at the time of your desiring it.

LADY CROOM: To the Indies?

SEPTIMUS: The Indies! Why?

LADY CROOM: To follow the Chater, of course. She did not tell you?

SEPTIMUS: She did not exchange half-a-dozen words with me.

LADY CROOM: I expect she did not like to waste the time. The Chater sails with Captain Brice.

SEPTIMUS: Ah. As a member of the crew?

LADY CROOM: No, as wife to Mr Chater, plant-gatherer to my brother's expedition.

SEPTIMUS: I knew he was no poet. I did not know it was botany under the false colours.

LADY CROOM: He is no more a botanist. My brother paid fifty pounds to have him published, and he will pay a hundred and fifty to have Mr Chater picking flowers in the Indies for a year while the wife plays mistress of the Captain's quarters. Captain Brice has fixed his passion on Mrs Chater, and to take her on voyage he has not scrupled to deceive the Admiralty, the Linnean Society° and Sir Joseph Banks, botanist to His Majesty at Kew.

SEPTIMUS: Her passion is not as fixed as his.

LADY CROOM: It is a defect of God's humour that he directs our hearts everywhere but to those who have a right to them.

SEPTIMUS: Indeed, madam. (*Pause*) But is Mr Chater deceived?

LADY CROOM: He insists on it, and finds the proof of his wife's virtue in his eagerness to defend it. Captain Brice is *not* deceived but cannot help himself. He would die for her.

SEPTIMUS: I think, my lady, he would have Mr Chater die for her.

LADY CROOM: Indeed, I never knew a woman worth the duel, or the other way about. Your letter to me goes very ill with your conduct to Mrs Chater, Mr Hodge. I have had experience of being betrayed before the ink is dry, but to be betrayed before the pen is even dipped, and with the village notice-board, what am I to think of such a performance?

SEPTIMUS: My lady, I was alone with my thoughts in the gazebo, when Mrs Chater ran me to ground, and I being in such a passion, in an agony of unrelieved desire—

LADY CROOM: Oh. . . !

SEPTIMUS: —I thought in my madness that the Chater with her skirts over her head would give me the momentary illusion of the happiness to which I dared not put a face.

(*Pause.*)

LADY CROOM: I do not know when I have received a more unusual compliment, Mr Hodge. I hope I am more than a match for Mrs Chater with her head in a bucket. Does she wear drawers?

SEPTIMUS: She does.

LADY CROOM: Yes, I have heard that drawers are being worn now. It is unnatural for women to be got up like jockeys. I cannot approve.

(*She turns with a whirl of skirts and moves to leave.*)

I know nothing of Pericles or the Athenian philosophers. I can spare them an hour, in my sitting room when I have bathed. Seven o'clock. Bring a book.

(*She goes out.* SEPTIMUS *picks up the two letters, the ones he wrote, and starts to burn them in the flame of the spirit lamp.*)

ACT 2 / SCENE 3

(VALENTINE *and* CHLOË *are at the table.* GUS *is in the room.* CHLOË *is reading from two Saturday newspapers. She is wearing workaday period clothes, a Regency° dress, no hat.* VALENTINE *is pecking at a portable computer. He is wearing unkempt Regency clothes, too. The clothes have evidently come from a large wicker laundry hamper, from which* GUS *is producing more clothes to try on himself. He finds a Regency coat and starts putting it on.*

The objects on the table now include two geometrical solids, pyramid and cone, about twenty inches high, of the type used in a drawing lesson; and a pot of dwarf dahlias [which do not look like modern dahlias].)

CHLOË: 'Even in Arcadia—Sex, Literature and Death at Sidley Park.' Picture of Byron.

VALENTINE: Not of Bernard?

CHLOË: 'Byron Fought Fatal Duel, Says Don' . . . Valentine, do you think I'm the first person to think of this?

VALENTINE: No.

Linnean Society, London nature society studying plants and animals.

Regency, fashions in clothing and buildings popular during 1811 to 1820, when George, Prince of Wales, was the Regent (i.e., ruled during the reign of his father, George III, who was judged too insane to serve as king).

CHLOË: I haven't said yet. The future is all programmed like a computer—that's a proper theory, isn't it?

VALENTINE: The deterministic universe, yes.

CHLOË: Right. Because everything including us is just a lot of atoms bouncing off each other like billiard balls.

VALENTINE: Yes. There was someone, forget his name, 1820s, who pointed out that from Newton's laws you could predict everything to come—I mean, you'd need a computer as big as the universe but the formula would exist.

CHLOË: But it doesn't work, does it?

VALENTINE: No. It turns out the maths is different.

CHLOË: No, it's all because of sex.

VALENTINE: Really?

CHLOË: That's what I think. The universe is deterministic all right, just like Newton said, I mean it's trying to be, but the only thing going wrong is people fancying people who aren't supposed to be in that part of the plan.

VALENTINE: Ah. The attraction that Newton left out. All the way back to the apple in the garden. Yes. *(Pause)* Yes, I think you're the first person to think of this.

(HANNAH enters, carrying a tabloid paper, and a mug of tea.)

HANNAH: Have you seen this? 'Bonking Byron Shot Poet.'

CHLOË *(Pleased)*: Let's see.

(HANNAH gives her the paper, smiles at GUS.)

VALENTINE: He's done awfully well, hasn't he? How did they all know?

HANNAH: Don't be ridiculous. *(To CHLOË)* Your father wants it back.

CHLOË: All right.

HANNAH: What a fool.

CHLOË: Jealous. I think it's brilliant. *(She gets up to go. To GUS)* Yes, that's perfect, but not with trainers.° Come on, I'll lend you a pair of flatties, they'll look period on you—

HANNAH: Hello, Gus. You all look so romantic.

(GUS following CHLOË out, hesitates, smiles at her.)

CHLOË *(Pointedly)*: Are you coming?

(She holds the door for GUS and follows him out, leaving a sense of her disapproval behind her.)

HANNAH: The important thing is not to give two monkeys for what young people think about you.

(She goes to look at the other newspapers.)

---

trainers, sneakers.

VALENTINE *(Anxiously)*: You don't think she's getting a thing about Bernard, do you?

HANNAH: I wouldn't worry about Chloë, she's old enough to vote on her back. 'Byron Fought Fatal Duel, Says Don.' Or rather—*(sceptically)* 'Says Don!'

VALENTINE: It may all prove to be true.

HANNAH: It can't prove to be true, it can only not prove to be false yet.

VALENTINE *(Pleased)*: Just like science.

HANNAH: If Bernard can stay ahead of getting the rug pulled till he's dead, he'll be a success.

VALENTINE: *Just* like science . . . The ultimate fear is of posterity . . .

HANNAH: Personally I don't think it'll take that long.

VALENTINE: . . . and then there's the afterlife. An afterlife would be a mixed blessing. 'Ah— Bernard Nightingale, I don't believe you know Lord Byron.' It must be heaven up there.

HANNAH: You can't believe in an afterlife, Valentine.

VALENTINE: Oh, you're going to disappoint me at last.

HANNAH: Am I? Why?

VALENTINE: Science and religion.

HANNAH: No, no, been there, done that, boring.

VALENTINE: Oh, Hannah. Fiancée. Have pity. Can't we have a trial marriage and I'll call it off in the morning?

HANNAH *(Amused)*: I don't know when I've received a more unusual proposal.

VALENTINE *(Interested)*: Have you had many?

HANNAH: That would be telling.

VALENTINE: Well, why not? Your classical reserve is only a mannerism; and neurotic.

HANNAH: Do you want the room?

VALENTINE: You get nothing if you give nothing.

HANNAH: I ask nothing.

VALENTINE: No, stay.

(VALENTINE resumes work at his computer. HANNAH establishes herself among her references at 'her' end of the table. She has a stack of pocket-sized volumes, Lady Croom's 'garden books.')

HANNAH: What are you doing? Valentine?

VALENTINE: The set of points on a complex plane made by—

HANNAH: Is it the grouse?

VALENTINE: Oh, the grouse. The damned grouse.

HANNAH: You mustn't give up.

VALENTINE: Why? Didn't you agree with Bernard?

HANNAH: Oh, that. It's *all* trivial—your grouse, my hermit, Bernard's Byron. Comparing what we're looking for misses the point. It's wanting to know that makes us matter. Otherwise we're going out the way we came in. That's why you can't believe in the afterlife, Valentine. Believe in the after, by all means, but not the life. Believe in God, the soul, the spirit, the infinite, believe in angels if you like, but not in the great celestial get-together for an exchange of views. If the answers are in the back of the book I can wait, but what a drag. Better to struggle on knowing that failure is final. *(She looks over* VALENTINE's *shoulder at the computer screen. Reacting)* Oh!, but . . . how beautiful!

VALENTINE: The Coverly set.

HANNAH: The Coverly set! My goodness, Valentine!

VALENTINE: Lend me a finger.

(He takes her finger and presses one of the computer keys several times.)

See? In an ocean of ashes, islands of order. Patterns making themselves out of nothing.
I can't show you how deep it goes. Each picture is a detail of the previous one, blown up. And so on. For ever. Pretty nice, eh?

HANNAH: Is it important?

VALENTINE: Interesting. Publishable.

HANNAH: Well done!

VALENTINE: Not me. It's Thomasina's. I just pushed her equations through the computer a few million times further than she managed to do with her pencil.

(From the old portfolio he takes Thomasina's lesson book and gives it to HANNAH. *The piano starts to be heard.)*

You can have it back now.

HANNAH: What does it mean?

VALENTINE: Not what you'd like it to.

HANNAH: Why not?

VALENTINE: Well, for one thing, she'd be famous.

HANNAH: No, she wouldn't. She was dead before she had time to be famous . . .

VALENTINE: She died?

HANNAH: . . . burned to death.

VALENTINE *(Realizing)*: Oh . . . the girl who died in the fire!

HANNAH: The night before her seventeenth birthday. You can see where the dormer doesn't match. That was her bedroom under the roof. There's a memorial in the Park.

VALENTINE *(Irritated)*: I know—it's my house.

*(*VALENTINE *turns his attention back to his computer.* HANNAH *goes back to her chair. She looks through the lesson book.)*

HANNAH: Val, Septimus was her tutor—he and Thomasina would have—

VALENTINE: You do yours.

(Pause. Two researchers. LORD AUGUSTUS, *fifteen years old, wearing clothes of 1812, bursts in through the non-music room door. He is laughing. He dives under the table. He is chased into the room by* THOMASINA, *aged sixteen and furious. She spots* AUGUSTUS *immediately.)*

THOMASINA: You swore! You crossed your heart!

*(*AUGUSTUS *scampers out from under the table and* THOMASINA *chases him around it.)*

AUGUSTUS: I'll tell mama! I'll tell mama!

THOMASINA: You beast!

(She catches AUGUSTUS *as* SEPTIMUS *enters from the other door, carrying a book, a decanter and a glass, and his portfolio.)*

SEPTIMUS: Hush! What is this? My lord! Order, order!

*(*THOMASINA *and* AUGUSTUS *separate.)*

I am obliged.

*(*SEPTIMUS *goes to his place at the table. He pours himself a glass of wine.)*

AUGUSTUS: Well, good day to you, Mr Hodge!

(He is smirking about something. THOMASINA *dutifully picks up a drawing book and settles down to draw the geometrical solids.* SEPTIMUS *opens his portfolio.)*

SEPTIMUS: Will you join us this morning, Lord Augustus? We have our drawing lesson.

AUGUSTUS: I am a master of it at Eton, Mr Hodge, but we only draw naked women.

SEPTIMUS: You may work from memory.

THOMASINA: Disgusting!

SEPTIMUS: We will have silence now, if you please.

(From the portfolio SEPTIMUS *takes Thomasina's lesson book and tosses it to her; returning homework. She snatches it and opens it.)*

THOMASINA: No marks?! Did you not like my rabbit equation?

SEPTIMUS: I saw no resemblance to a rabbit.

THOMASINA: It eats its own progeny.

SEPTIMUS: *(Pause)* I did not see that.

(He extends his hand for the lesson book. She returns it to him.)

THOMASINA: I have not room to extend it.

*(*SEPTIMUS *and* HANNAH *turn the pages doubled by time.* AUGUSTUS *indolently starts to draw the models.)*

HANNAH: Do you mean the world is saved after all?

VALENTINE: No, it's still doomed. But if this is how it started, perhaps it's how the next one will come.

HANNAH: From good English algebra?

SEPTIMUS: It will go to infinity or zero, or nonsense.

THOMASINA: No, if you set apart the minus roots they square back to sense.

*(*SEPTIMUS *turns the pages.* THOMASINA *starts drawing the models.* HANNAH *closes the lesson book and turns her attention to her stack of 'garden books.')*

VALENTINE: Listen—you know your tea's getting cold.

HANNAH: I like it cold.

VALENTINE (*Ignoring that*): I'm telling you something. Your tea gets cold by itself, it doesn't get hot by itself. Do you think that's odd?

HANNAH: No.

VALENTINE: Well, it is odd. Heat goes to cold. It's a one-way street. Your tea will end up at room temperature. What's happening to your tea is happening to everything everywhere. The sun and the stars. It'll take a while but we're all going to end up at room temperature. When your hermit set up shop nobody understood this. But let's say you're right, in 18-whatever nobody knew more about heat than this scribbling nutter living in a hovel in Derbyshire.

HANNAH: He was at Cambridge—a scientist.

VALENTINE: Say he was. I'm not arguing. And the girl was his pupil, she had a genius for her tutor.

HANNAH: Or the other way round.

VALENTINE: Anything you like. But not *this*! Whatever he thought he was doing to save the world with good English algebra it wasn't this!

HANNAH: Why? Because they didn't have calculators?

VALENTINE: No. Yes. Because there's an order things can't happen in. You can't open a door till there's a house.

HANNAH: I thought that's what genius was.

VALENTINE: Only for lunatics and poets.

(*Pause.*)

HANNAH: 'I had a dream which was not all a dream.
The bright sun was extinguished, and the stars
Did wander darkling in the eternal space,
Rayless, and pathless, and the icy earth
Swung blind and blackening in the moonless
air . . .'°

VALENTINE: Your own?

HANNAH: Byron.

(*Pause. Two researchers again.*)

THOMASINA: Septimus, do you think that I will marry Lord Byron?

AUGUSTUS: Who is he?

THOMASINA: He is the author of 'Childe Harold's Pilgrimage,' the most poetical and pathetic and bravest hero of any book I ever read before, and the most modern and the handsomest, for Harold is Lord Byron himself to those who know him, like myself and Septimus. Well, Septimus?

SEPTIMUS (*Absorbed*): No.

(*Then he puts her lesson book away into the portfolio and picks up his own book to read.*)

"*I had a dream . . . moonless air,*" from "Darkness," by Byron.

THOMASINA: Why not?

SEPTIMUS: For one thing, he is not aware of your existence.

THOMASINA: We exchanged many significant glances when he was at Sidley Park. I do wonder that he has been home almost a year from his adventures and has not written to me once.

SEPTIMUS: It is indeed improbable, my lady.

AUGUSTUS: Lord Byron?!—he claimed my hare, although my shot was the earlier! He said I missed by a hare's breadth. His conversation was very facetious. But I think Lord Byron will not marry you, Thom, for he was only lame and not blind.

SEPTIMUS: Peace! Peace until a quarter to twelve. It is intolerable for a tutor to have his thoughts interrupted by his pupils.

AUGUSTUS: You are not *my* tutor, sir. I am visiting your lesson by my free will.

SEPTIMUS: If you are so determined, my lord.

(THOMASINA *laughs at that, the joke is for her.* AUGUSTUS, *not included, becomes angry.*)

AUGUSTUS: Your peace is nothing to me, sir. You do not rule over me.

THOMASINA (*Admonishing*): Augustus!

SEPTIMUS: I do not rule here, my lord. I inspire by reverence for learning and the exaltation of knowledge whereby man may approach God. There will be a shilling for the best cone and pyramid drawn in silence by a quarter to twelve *at the earliest*.

AUGUSTUS: You will not buy my silence for a shilling, sir. What I know to tell is worth much more than that.

(*And throwing down his drawing book and pencil, he leaves the room on his dignity, closing the door sharply. Pause.* SEPTIMUS *looks enquiringly at* THOMASINA.)

THOMASINA: I told him you kissed me. But he will not tell.

SEPTIMUS: When did I kiss you?

THOMASINA: What! Yesterday!

SEPTIMUS: Where?

THOMASINA: On the lips!

SEPTIMUS: In which county?

THOMASINA: In the hermitage, Septimus!

SEPTIMUS: On the lips in the hermitage! That? That was not a shilling kiss! I would not give sixpence to have it back. I had almost forgot it already.

THOMASINA: Oh, cruel! Have you forgotten our compact?

SEPTIMUS: God save me! Our compact?

THOMASINA: To teach me to waltz! Sealed with a kiss, and a second kiss due when I can dance like mama!

SEPTIMUS: Ah yes. Indeed. We were all waltzing like mice in London.

THOMASINA: I must waltz, Septimus! I will be despised if I do not waltz! It is the most fashionable and gayest and boldest invention conceivable—started in Germany!

SEPTIMUS: Let them have the waltz, they cannot have the calculus.

THOMASINA: Mama has brought from town a whole book of waltzes for the Broadwood, to play with Count Zelinsky.

SEPTIMUS: I need not be told what I cannot but suffer. Count Zelinsky banging on the Broadwood without relief has me reading in waltz time.

THOMASINA: Oh, stuff! What is your book?

SEPTIMUS: A prize essay of the Scientific Academy in Paris. The author deserves your indulgence, my lady, for you are his prophet.

THOMASINA: I? What does he write about? The waltz?

SEPTIMUS: Yes. He demonstrates the equation of the propagation of heat in a solid body. But in doing so he has discovered heresy—a natural contradiction of Sir Isaac Newton.

THOMASINA: Oh!—he contradicts determinism?

SEPTIMUS: No! . . . Well, perhaps. He shows that the atoms do not go according to Newton.

(Her interest has switched in the mercurial way characteristic of her—she has crossed to take the book.)

THOMASINA: Let me see—oh! In French?

SEPTIMUS: Yes. Paris is the capital of France.

THOMASINA: Show me where to read.

(He takes the book back from her and finds the page for her. Meanwhile, the piano music from the next room has doubled its notes and its emotion.)

THOMASINA: Four-handed now! Mama is in love with the Count.

SEPTIMUS: He is a Count in Poland. In Derbyshire he is a piano tuner.

(She has taken the book and is already immersed in it. The piano music becomes rapidly more passionate, and then breaks off suddenly in mid-phrase. There is an expressive silence next door which makes SEPTIMUS *raise his eyes. It does not register with* THOMASINA. *The silence allows us to hear the distant regular thump of the steam engine which is to be a topic. A few moments later* LADY CROOM *enters from the music room, seeming surprised and slightly flustered to find the schoolroom occupied. She collects herself, closing the door behind her. And remains watching, aimless and discreet, as though not wanting to interrupt the lesson.* SEPTIMUS *has stood, and she nods him back into his chair.* CHLOË, *in Regency dress, enters from the door opposite the music room. She takes in* VALENTINE *and* HANNAH *but crosses without pausing to the music room door.)*

CHLOË: Oh!—where's Gus?

VALENTINE: Dunno.

(CHLOË goes into the music room.)

LADY CROOM *(Annoyed)*: Oh!—Mr Noakes's engine!

(She goes to the garden door and steps outside. CHLOË *re-enters.)*

CHLOË: Damn.

LADY CROOM *(Calls out)*: Mr Noakes!

VALENTINE: He was there not long ago . . .

LADY CROOM: Halloo!

CHLOË: Well, he has to be in the photograph—is he dressed?

HANNAH: Is Bernard back?

CHLOË: No—he's late!

(The piano is heard again under the noise of the steam engine. LADY CROOM *steps back into the room.* CHLOË *steps outside the garden door. Shouts)*

Gus!

LADY CROOM: I wonder you can teach against such a disturbance and I am sorry for it, Mr Hodge.

(CHLOË comes back inside.)

VALENTINE *(Getting up)*: Stop ordering everybody about.

LADY CROOM: It is an unendurable noise.

VALENTINE: The photographer will wait.

(But grumbling, he follows CHLOË *out of the door she came in by, and closes the door behind them.* HANNAH *remains absorbed. In the silence, the rhythmic thump can be heard again.)*

LADY CROOM: The ceaseless dull overbearing monotony of it! It will drive me distracted. I may have to return to town to escape it.

SEPTIMUS: Your ladyship could remain in the country and let Count Zelinsky return to town where you would not hear him.

LADY CROOM: I mean Mr Noakes's engine! *(Semi-aside to* SEPTIMUS*)* Would you sulk? I will not have my daughter study sulking.

THOMASINA *(Not listening)*: What, mama?

(THOMASINA remains lost in her book. LADY CROOM *returns to close the garden door and the noise of the steam engine subsides.* HANNAH *closes one of the 'garden books,' and opens the next. She is making occasional notes. The piano ceases.)*

LADY CROOM *(To* THOMASINA*)*: What are we learning today? *(Pause)* Well, not manners.

SEPTIMUS: We are drawing today.

(LADY CROOM negligently examines what THOMASINA *had started to draw.)*

LADY CROOM: Geometry. I approve of geometry.

SEPTIMUS: Your ladyship's approval is my constant object.

LADY CROOM: Well, do not despair of it. *(Returning to the window impatiently.)* Where is 'Culpability' Noakes?° *(She looks out and is annoyed.)* Oh!—he has gone for his hat so that he may remove it.

(She returns to the table and touches the bowl of dahlias. HANNAH *sits back in her chair, caught by what she is reading.)*

For the widow's dowry of dahlias I can almost forgive my brother's marriage. We must be thankful the monkey bit the husband. If it had bit the wife the monkey would be dead and we would not be first in the kingdom to show a dahlia. *(*HANNAH, *still reading the garden book, stands up.)* I sent one potted to Chatsworth. The Duchess was most satisfactorily put out by it when I called at Devonshire House. Your friend was there lording it as a poet.

*(*HANNAH *leaves through the door, following* VALENTINE *and* CHLOË. *Meanwhile,* THOMASINA *thumps the book down on the table.)*

THOMASINA: Well! Just as I said! Newton's machine which would knock our atoms from cradle to grave by the laws of motion is incomplete! Determinism leaves the road at every corner, as I knew all along, and the cause is very likely hidden in this gentleman's observation.

LADY CROOM: Of what?

THOMASINA: The action of bodies in heat.

LADY CROOM: Is this geometry?

THOMASINA: This? No, I despise geometry! *(Touching the dahlias she adds almost to herself)* The Chater would overthrow the Newtonian system in a weekend.

SEPTIMUS: Geometry, Hobbes assures us in the *Leviathan,*° is the only science God has been pleased to bestow on mankind.

LADY CROOM: And what does he mean by it?

SEPTIMUS: Mr Hobbes or God?

LADY CROOM: I am sure I do not know what either means by it.

THOMASINA: Oh, pooh to Hobbes! Mountains are not pyramids and trees are not cones. God must love gunnery and architecture if Euclid is his only geometry. There is another geometry which I am engaged in discovering by trial and error, am I not, Septimus?

SEPTIMUS: Trial and error perfectly describes your enthusiasm, my lady.

LADY CROOM: How old are you today?

THOMASINA: Sixteen years and eleven months, mama, and three weeks.

LADY CROOM: Sixteen years and eleven months. We must have you married before you are educated beyond eligibility.

THOMASINA: I am going to marry Lord Byron.

LADY CROOM: Are you? He did not have the manners to mention it.

THOMASINA: You have spoken to him?!

LADY CROOM: Certainly not.

THOMASINA: Where did you see him?

LADY CROOM *(With some bitterness)*: Everywhere.

THOMASINA: Did you, Septimus?

SEPTIMUS: At the Royal Academy where I had the honour to accompany your mother and Count Zelinsky.

THOMASINA: What was Lord Byron doing?

LADY CROOM: Posing.

SEPTIMUS *(Tactfully)*: He was being sketched during his visit . . . by the Professor of Painting . . . Mr Fuseli.

LADY CROOM: There was more posing *at* the pictures than *in* them. His companion likewise reversed the custom of the Academy that the ladies viewing wear more than the ladies viewed—well, enough! Let him be hanged there for a Lamb. I have enough with Mr Noakes, who is to a garden what a bull is to a china shop.

(This as NOAKES *enters.)*

THOMASINA: The Emperor of Irregularity!

(She settles down to drawing the diagram which is to be the third item in the surviving portfolio.)

LADY CROOM: Mr Noakes!

NOAKES: Your ladyship—

LADY CROOM: What have you done to me!

NOAKES: Everything is satisfactory, I assure you. A little behind, to be sure, but my dam will be repaired within the month—

LADY CROOM *(Banging the table)*: Hush!

(In the silence, the steam engine thumps in the distance.)

Can you hear, Mr Noakes?

NOAKES *(Pleased and proud)*: The Improved Newcomen steam pump°—the only one in England!

LADY CROOM: That is what I object to. If everybody had his own I would bear my portion of the agony without complaint. But to have been singled out by the only Improved Newcomen steam pump in England, this is hard, sir, this is not to be borne.

'Culpability' Noakes, playing off the name of Capability Brown. **Leviathan,** 1651 philosophical treatise by Thomas Hobbes (1588–1679).

Improved Newcomen steam pump, an engine used to pump water (1711), predating James Watt's steam engine (1769).

NOAKES: Your lady—

LADY CROOM: And for what? My lake is drained to a ditch for no purpose I can understand, unless it be that snipe and curlew have deserted three counties so that they may be shot in our swamp. What you painted as forest is a mean plantation, your greenery is mud, your waterfall is wet mud, and your mount is an opencast mine for the mud that was lacking in the dell. *(Pointing through the window)* What is that cowshed?

NOAKES: The hermitage, my lady?

LADY CROOM: It is a cowshed.

NOAKES: Madam, it is, I assure you, a very habitable cottage, properly founded and drained, two rooms and a closet under a slate roof and a stone chimney—

LADY CROOM: And who is to live in it?

NOAKES: Why, the hermit.

LADY CROOM: Where is he?

NOAKES: Madam?

LADY CROOM: You surely do not supply a hermitage without a hermit?

NOAKES: Indeed, madam—

LADY CROOM: Come, come, Mr Noakes. If I am promised a fountain I expect it to come with water. What hermits do you have?

NOAKES: I have no hermits, my lady.

LADY CROOM: Not one? I am speechless.

NOAKES: I am sure a hermit can be found. One could advertise.

LADY CROOM: Advertise?

NOAKES: In the newspapers.

LADY CROOM: But surely a hermit who takes a newspaper is not a hermit in whom one can have complete confidence.

NOAKES: I do not know what to suggest, my lady.

SEPTIMUS: Is there room for a piano?

NOAKES *(Baffled)*: A piano?

LADY CROOM: We are intruding here—this will not do, Mr Hodge. Evidently, nothing is being learned. *(To NOAKES)* Come along, sir!

THOMASINA: Mr Noakes—bad news from Paris!

NOAKES: Is it the Emperor Napoleon?

THOMASINA: No. *(She tears the page off her drawing block, with her 'diagram' on it.)* It concerns your heat engine. Improve it as you will, you can never get out of it what you put in. It repays eleven pence in the shilling at most. The penny is for this author's thoughts.

(She gives the diagram to SEPTIMUS who looks at it.)

NOAKES *(Baffled again)*: Thank you, my lady.

(NOAKES goes out into the garden.)

LADY CROOM *(To SEPTIMUS)*: Do you understand her?

SEPTIMUS: No.

LADY CROOM: Then this business is over. I was married

at seventeen. *Ce soir il faut qu'on parle français, je te demande,°* Thomasina, as a courtesy to the Count. Wear your green velvet, please, I will send Briggs to do your hair. Sixteen and eleven months. . . !

(She follows NOAKES out of view.)

THOMASINA: Lord Byron was with a lady?

SEPTIMUS: Yes.

THOMASINA: Huh!

(Now SEPTIMUS retrieves his book from THOMASINA. He turns the pages, and also continues to study Thomasina's diagram. He strokes the tortoise absently as he reads. THOMASINA takes up pencil and paper and starts to draw SEPTIMUS with Plautus.)

SEPTIMUS: Why does it mean Mr Noakes's engine pays eleven pence in the shilling? Where does he say it?

THOMASINA: Nowhere. I noticed it by the way. I cannot remember now.

SEPTIMUS: Nor is he interested by determinism—

THOMASINA: Oh . . . yes. Newton's equations go forwards and backwards, they do not care which way. But the heat equation cares very much, it goes only one way. That is the reason Mr Noakes's engine cannot give the power to drive Mr Noakes's engine.

SEPTIMUS: Everybody knows that.

THOMASINA: Yes, Septimus, they know it about engines!

SEPTIMUS: *(Pause. He looks at his watch.)* A quarter to twelve. For your essay this week, explicate your diagram.

THOMASINA: I cannot. I do not know the mathematics.

SEPTIMUS: Without mathematics, then.

(THOMASINA has continued to draw. She tears the top page from her drawing pad and gives it to SEPTIMUS.)

THOMASINA: There. I have made a drawing of you and Plautus.

SEPTIMUS *(Looking at it)*: Excellent likeness. Not so good of me.

(THOMASINA laughs, and leaves the room. AUGUSTUS appears at the garden door. His manner cautious and diffident. SEPTIMUS does not notice him for a moment. SEPTIMUS gathers his papers together.)

AUGUSTUS: Sir . . .

SEPTIMUS: My lord. . . ?

AUGUSTUS: I gave you offence, sir, and I am sorry for it.

SEPTIMUS: I took none, my lord, but you are kind to mention it.

Ce soir . . . demande, French, "This evening I ask that you speak French."

AUGUSTUS: I would like to ask you a question, Mr Hodge. (*Pause*) You have an elder brother, I dare say, being a Septimus?

SEPTIMUS: Yes, my lord. He lives in London. He is the editor of a newspaper, the *Piccadilly Recreation*. (*Pause*) Was that your question?

(AUGUSTUS, *evidently embarrassed about something, picks up the drawing of Septimus.*)

AUGUSTUS: No. Oh . . . it is you? . . . I would like to keep it. (SEPTIMUS *inclines his head in assent.*) There are things a fellow cannot ask his friends. Carnal things. My sister has told me . . . my sister believes such things as I cannot, I assure you, bring myself to repeat.

SEPTIMUS: You must not repeat them, then. The walk between here and dinner will suffice to put us straight, if we stroll by the garden. It is an easy business. And then I must rely on you to correct your sister's state of ignorance.

(*A commotion is heard outside*—BERNARD'*s loud voice in a sort of agony.*)

BERNARD (*Outside the door*): Oh no—no—no—oh, bloody hell!—

AUGUSTUS: Thank you, Mr Hodge, I will.

(*Taking the drawing with him* AUGUSTUS *allows himself to be shown out through the garden door, and* SEPTIMUS *follows him.* BERNARD *enters the room, through the door* HANNAH *left by.* VALENTINE *comes in with him, leaving the door open and they are followed by* HANNAH *who is holding the 'garden book.'*)

BERNARD: Oh, no—no—

HANNAH: I'm sorry, Bernard.

BERNARD: Fucked by a dahlia! Do you think? Is it open and shut? Am I fucked? What does it really amount to? When all's said and done? Am I fucked? What do *you* think, Valentine? Tell me the truth.

VALENTINE: You're fucked.

BERNARD: Oh God! Does it mean that?

HANNAH: Yes, Bernard, it does.

BERNARD: I'm not sure. Show me where it says. I want to see it. No—read it—no, wait . . .

(BERNARD *sits at the table. He prepares to listen as though listening were an oriental art.*)

Right.

HANNAH (*Reading*): 'October 1st, 1810. Today under the direction of Mr Noakes, a parterre° was dug on the south lawn and will be a handsome show

---

parterre, ornamental patterned garden.

next year, a consolation for the picturesque catastrophe of the second and third distances. The dahlia having propagated under glass with no ill effect from the sea voyage, is named by Captain Brice 'Charity' for his bride, though the honour properly belongs to the husband who exchanged beds with my dahlia, and an English summer for everlasting night in the Indies.'

(*Pause.*)

BERNARD: Well it's so round the houses, isn't it? Who's to say what it means?

HANNAH (*Patiently*): It means that Ezra Chater of the Sidley Park connection is the same Chater who described a dwarf dahlia in Martinique in 1810 and died there, of a monkey bite.

BERNARD (*Wildly*): Ezra wasn't a botanist! He was a poet!

HANNAH: He was not much of either, but he was both.

VALENTINE: It's not a disaster.

BERNARD: Of course it's a disaster! I was on 'The Breakfast Hour'!

VALENTINE: It doesn't mean Byron didn't fight a duel, it only means Chater wasn't killed in it.

BERNARD: Oh, pull yourself together!—do you think I'd have been on 'The Breakfast Hour' if Byron had *missed*!

HANNAH: Calm down, Bernard. Valentine's right.

BERNARD (*Grasping at straws*): Do you think so? You mean the *Piccadilly* reviews? Yes, two completely unknown Byron essays—and my discovery of the lines he added to 'English Bards.' That counts for something.

HANNAH (*Tactfully*): Very possible—persuasive, indeed.

BERNARD: Oh, bugger persuasive! I've proved Byron was here and as far as I'm concerned he wrote those lines as sure as he shot that hare. If only I hadn't somehow . . . made it all about *killing Chater.* Why didn't you stop me?! It's bound to get out, you know—I mean this—this *gloss* on my discovery—I mean how long do you think it'll be before some botanical pedant blows the whistle on me?

HANNAH: The day after tomorrow. A letter in *The Times.*

BERNARD: You wouldn't.

HANNAH: It's a dirty job but somebody—

BERNARD: Darling. Sorry. Hannah—

HANNAH: —and, after all, it is my discovery.

BERNARD: Hannah.

HANNAH: Bernard.

BERNARD: Hannah.

HANNAH: Oh, shut up. It'll be very short, very dry, absolutely gloat-free. Would you rather it were one of your friends?

BERNARD (*Fervently*): Oh God, no!

HANNAH: And then in *your* letter to *The Times*—

BERNARD: Mine?

HANNAH: Well, of course. Dignified congratulations to a colleague, in the language of scholars, I trust.

BERNARD: Oh, eat shit, you mean?

HANNAH: Think of it as a breakthrough in dahlia studies.

(CHLOË *hurries in from the garden.*)

CHLOË: Why aren't you coming?!—Bernard! And you're not dressed! How long have you been back?

(BERNARD *looks at her and then at* VALENTINE *and realizes for the first time that* VALENTINE *is unusually dressed.*)

BERNARD: Why are you wearing those clothes?

CHLOË: Do be quick!

(*She is already digging into the basket and producing odd garments for* BERNARD.)

Just put anything on. We're all being photographed. Except Hannah.

HANNAH: I'll come and watch.

(VALENTINE *and* CHLOË *help* BERNARD *into a decorative coat and fix a lace collar round his neck.*)

CHLOË (*To* HANNAH): Mummy says have you got the theodolite?

VALENTINE: What are you supposed to be, Chlo? Bo-Peep?

CHLOË: Jane Austen!

VALENTINE: Of course.

HANNAH (*To* CHLOË): Oh—it's in the hermitage! Sorry.

BERNARD: I thought it wasn't till this evening. What photograph?

CHLOË: The local paper of course—they always come before we start. We want a good crowd of us—Gus looks gorgeous—

BERNARD (*Aghast*): The newspaper! (*He grabs something like a bishop's mitre from the basket and pulls it down completely over his face. Muffled*) I'm ready!

(*And he staggers out with* VALENTINE *and* CHLOË, *followed by* HANNAH. *A light change to evening. The paper lanterns outside begin to glow. Piano music from the next room.* SEPTIMUS *enters with an oil lamp. He carries Thomasina's algebra primer, and also her essay on loose sheets. He settles down to read at the table. It is nearly dark outside, despite the lanterns.* THOMASINA *enters, in a nightgown and barefoot, holding a candlestick. Her manner is secretive and excited.*)

SEPTIMUS: My lady! What is it?

THOMASINA: Septimus! Shush!

(*She closes the door quietly.*)

Now is our chance!

SEPTIMUS: For what, dear God?

(*She blows out the candle and puts the candlestick on the table.*)

THOMASINA: Do not act the innocent! Tomorrow I will be seventeen!

(*She kisses* SEPTIMUS *full on the mouth.*)

There!

SEPTIMUS: Dear Christ!

THOMASINA: Now you must show me, you are paid in advance.

SEPTIMUS (*Understanding*): Oh!

THOMASINA: The Count plays for us, it is God-given! I cannot be seventeen and not waltz.

SEPTIMUS: But your mother—

THOMASINA: While she swoons, we can dance. The house is all abed. I heard the Broadwood. Oh, Septimus, teach me now!

SEPTIMUS: Hush! I cannot now!

THOMASINA: Indeed you can, and I am come barefoot so mind my toes.

SEPTIMUS: I cannot because it is not a waltz.

THOMASINA: It is not?

SEPTIMUS: No, it is too quick for waltzing.

THOMASINA: Oh! Then we will wait for him to play slow.

SEPTIMUS: My lady—

THOMASINA: Mr Hodge!

(*She takes a chair next to him and looks at his work.*)

Are you reading my essay? Why do you work here so late?

SEPTIMUS: To save my candles.

THOMASINA: You have my old primer.

SEPTIMUS: It is mine again. You should not have written in it.

(*She takes it, looks at the open page.*)

THOMASINA: It was a joke.

SEPTIMUS: It will make me mad as you promised. Sit over there. You will have us in disgrace.

(THOMASINA *gets up and goes to the furthest chair.*)

THOMASINA: If mama comes I will tell her we only met to kiss, not to waltz.

SEPTIMUS: Silence or bed.

THOMASINA: Silence!

(SEPTIMUS *pours himself some more wine. He continues to read her essay. The music changes to party music from the marquee. And there are fireworks—small against the sky, distant flares of light like exploding meteors.* HANNAH *enters. She has dressed for the party. The difference is not, however, dramatic. She closes the door and crosses to leave by the garden door. But as she gets there,* VALENTINE *is entering. He has a glass of wine in his hand.*)

HANNAH: Oh . . .

(But VALENTINE *merely brushes past her, intent on something, and half-drunk.)*

VALENTINE *(To her)*: Got it!

(He goes straight to the table and roots about in what is now a considerable mess of papers, books and objects. HANNAH *turns back, puzzled by his manner. He finds what he has been looking for—the 'diagram.' Meanwhile,* SEPTIMUS *reading Thomasina's essay, also studies the diagram.* SEPTIMUS *and* VALENTINE *study the diagram doubled by time.)*

VALENTINE: It's heat.

HANNAH: Are you tight, Val?

VALENTINE: It's a diagram of heat exchange.

SEPTIMUS: So, we are all doomed!

THOMASINA *(Cheerfully)*: Yes.

VALENTINE: Like a steam engine, you see—

*(*HANNAH *fills Septimus's glass from the same decanter, and sips from it.)*

She didn't have the maths, not remotely. She saw what things meant, way ahead, like seeing a picture.

SEPTIMUS: This is not science. This is story-telling.

THOMASINA: Is it a waltz now?

SEPTIMUS: No.

(The music is still modern.)

VALENTINE: Like a film.

HANNAH: What did she see?

VALENTINE: That you can't run the film backwards. Heat was the first thing which didn't work that way. Not like Newton. A film of a pendulum, or a ball falling through the air—backwards, it looks the same.

HANNAH: The ball would be going the wrong way.

VALENTINE: You'd have to know that. But with heat— friction—a ball breaking a window—

HANNAH: Yes.

VALENTINE: It won't work backwards.

HANNAH: Who thought it did?

VALENTINE: She saw why. You can put back the bits of glass but you can't collect up the heat of the smash. It's gone.

SEPTIMUS: So the Improved Newtonian Universe must cease and grow cold. Dear me.

VALENTINE: The heat goes into the mix.

(He gestures to indicate the air in the room, in the universe.)

THOMASINA: Yes, we must hurry if we are going to dance.

VALENTINE: And everything is mixing the same way, all the time, irreversibly . . .

SEPTIMUS: Oh, we have time, I think.

VALENTINE: . . . till there's no time left. That's what time means.

SEPTIMUS: When we have found all the mysteries and lost all the meaning, we will be alone, on an empty shore.

THOMASINA: Then we will dance. Is this a waltz?

SEPTIMUS: It will serve.

(He stands up.)

THOMASINA *(Jumping up)*: Goody!

*(*SEPTIMUS *takes her in his arms carefully and the waltz lesson, to the music from the marquee, begins.* BERNARD, *in unconvincing Regency dress, enters carrying a bottle.)*

BERNARD: Don't mind me, I left my jacket . . .

(He heads for the area of the wicker basket.)

VALENTINE: Are you leaving?

*(*BERNARD *is stripping off his period coat. He is wearing his own trousers, tucked into knee socks and his own shirt.)*

BERNARD: Yes, I'm afraid so.

HANNAH: What's up, Bernard?

BERNARD: Nothing I can go into—

VALENTINE: Should I go?

BERNARD: No, *I'm* going!

*(*VALENTINE *and* HANNAH *watch* BERNARD *struggling into his jacket and adjusting his clothes.* SEPTIMUS, *holding* THOMASINA, *kisses her on the mouth. The waltz lesson pauses. She looks at him. He kisses her again, in earnest. She puts her arms round him.)*

THOMASINA: Septimus . . .

*(*SEPTIMUS *hushes her. They start to dance again, with the slight awkwardness of a lesson.* CHLOË *bursts in from the garden.)*

CHLOË: I'll kill her! I'll *kill* her!

BERNARD: Oh dear.

VALENTINE: What the hell is it, Chlo?

CHLOË *(Venomously)*: Mummy!

BERNARD *(To* VALENTINE*)*: Your mother caught us in that cottage.

CHLOË: She snooped!

BERNARD: I don't think so. She was rescuing a theodolite.

CHLOË: I'll come with you, Bernard.

BERNARD: No, you bloody won't.

CHLOË: Don't you want me to?

BERNARD: Of course not. What for? *(To* VALENTINE*)* I'm sorry.

CHLOË *(In furious tears)*: What are you saying sorry to *him* for?

BERNARD: Sorry to you too. Sorry one and all. Sorry, Hannah—sorry, Hermione—sorry, Byron—sorry, sorry, sorry, now can I go?

(CHLOË *stands stiffly, tearfully.*)

CHLOË: Well . . .

(THOMASINA *and* SEPTIMUS *dance.*)

HANNAH: What a bastard you are, Bernard.

(CHLOË *rounds on her.*)

CHLOË: And you mind your own business! What do you know about anything?

HANNAH: Nothing.

CHLOË (*to* BERNARD): It *was* worth it, though, wasn't it?

BERNARD: It was wonderful.

(CHLOË *goes out, through the garden door, towards the party.*)

HANNAH (*An echo*): Nothing.

VALENTINE: Well, you shit. I'd drive you but I'm a bit sloshed.

(VALENTINE *follows* CHLOË *out and can be heard outside calling 'Chlo! Chlo!'*)

BERNARD: A scrape.

HANNAH: Oh . . . (*she gives up*) Bernard!

BERNARD: I look forward to *The Genius of the Place.* I hope you find your hermit. I think out front is the safest.

(*He opens the door cautiously and looks out.*)

HANNAH: Actually, I've got a good idea who he was, but I can't prove it.

BERNARD (*With a carefree expansive gesture*) Publish!

(*He goes out closing the door.* SEPTIMUS *and* THOMASINA *are now waltzing freely. She is delighted with herself.*)

THOMASINA: Am I waltzing?

SEPTIMUS: Yes my lady.

(*He gives her a final twirl bringing them to the table where he bows to her. He lights her candlestick.* HANNAH *goes to sit at the table, playing truant from the party. She pours herself more wine. The table contains the geometrical solids, the computer, decanter, glasses, tea mug, Hannah's research books, Septimus's books, the two portfolios,* Thomasina's candlestick, the oil lamp, the dahlia, the Sunday papers . . . GUS *appears in the doorway. It takes a moment to realize that he is not Lord Augustus; perhaps not until* HANNAH *sees him.*)

SEPTIMUS: Take your essay, I have given it an alpha in blind faith. Be careful with the flame.

THOMASINA: I will wait for you to come.

SEPTIMUS: I cannot.

THOMASINA: You may.

SEPTIMUS: I may not.

THOMASINA: You must.

SEPTIMUS: I will not.

(*She puts the candlestick and the essay on the table.*)

THOMASINA: Then I will not go. Once more, for my birthday.

(SEPTIMUS *and* THOMASINA *start to waltz together.* GUS *comes forward, startling* HANNAH.)

HANNAH: Oh!—you made me jump.

(GUS *looks resplendent. He is carrying an old and somewhat tattered stiff-backed folio fastened with a tape tied in a bow. He comes to* HANNAH *and thrusts this present at her.*)

Oh . . .

(*She lays the folio down on the table and starts to open it. It consists only of two boards hinged, containing Thomasina's drawing.*)

'Septimus with Plautus'. (*To* GUS) I was looking for that. Thank you.

(GUS *nods several times. Then, rather awkwardly, he bows to her. A Regency bow, an invitation to dance.*)

Oh, dear, I don't really . . .

(*After a moment's hesitation, she gets up and they hold each other, keeping a decorous distance between them, and start to dance, rather awkwardly.* SEPTIMUS *and* THOMASINA *continue to dance, fluently, to the piano.*)

END

Figure 1. Ezra Chater (Derek Hutchinson, *standing*), satisfied by the explanation Septimus Hodge (Rufus Sewell) gives of the encounter between Mrs Chater and Hodge, prepares to inscribe his book of poetry to Hodge. The Royal National Theatre production of *Arcadia*, 1993, was directed by Trevor Nunn. (Photograph: Donald Cooper/Photostage.)

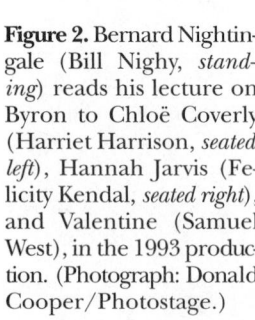

Figure 2. Bernard Nightingale (Bill Nighy, *standing*) reads his lecture on Byron to Chloë Coverly (Harriet Harrison, *seated left*), Hannah Jarvis (Felicity Kendal, *seated right*), and Valentine (Samuel West), in the 1993 production. (Photograph: Donald Cooper/Photostage.)

Figure 3. Lady Croom (Harriet Walter) gestures disdainfully toward the landscape designs for Sidley Park, while her brother, Captain Brice (Graham Sinclair) displays the offending page in the 1993 production. (Photograph: Donald Cooper/Photostage.)

Figure 4. Septimus Hodge (Rufus Sewell) tries to comfort a troubled Thomasina Coverly (Emma Fielding) in the 1993 production. (Photograph: Donald Cooper/Photostage.)

Staging of *Arcadia*

REVIEW OF THE ROYAL NATIONAL THEATRE PRODUCTION, 1993, BY PAUL TAYLOR

A couple of years back, Louise Page wrote a play called *Adam Was A Gardener*, that shuttled back and forth between the present and the early-19th century. It used changing fashions in landscape gardening—from the modified classical vistas of Capability Brown to the new picturesque Gothic style, replete with false ruins and optional live-in hermit—as a metaphor for broader emotional and cultural divisions. In *Arcadia* (his first full-length stage play for five years), Tom Stoppard gets up to strikingly similar tricks, only—as you might imagine—things don't remain anything like as simple.

Undaunted by the comparative failure of *Hapgood*, his last theatrical venture, which brought spy pastiche and quantum physics into stubbornly sterile union, Stoppard once again strives to give scientific theory dramatic life and make it part of the play's imaginative pulse and its thematic patterns. *Arcadia*'s concern with the links between the regular and irregular on the aesthetic/social plane finds its scientific counterpart in the mathematical endeavours of two of its key characters.

In the 19th-century scenes, we see Thomasina Coverly, a brilliant adolescent beautifully played by Emma Fielding, as she anticipates modern discoveries about iterated algorithms, the simple mathematical equations that can generate behaviour at once unpredictable and not random. Working from equations outwards, Thomasina hopes to find the geometry of irregular forms. Without a computer, this would have taken her several lifetimes, we're notified by Val (excellent Samuel West), her opposite number in the present-day scenes, who, better equipped, is working in the other direction.

As Val wittily puts it, the second law of thermodynamics (also foreseen by Thomasina) means roughly that "We're all going to end up at room temperature." You could be forgiven for thinking that a play full of maths would also produce a fairly steady state of torpidity. What is impressive about *Arcadia*, though, is the haunting mix of playfulness and poignancy to which, thanks to the author's skills and Trevor Nunn's fine production, the ideas constantly give rise.

Crucial to this effect is the structure. At its simplest, the play is a story of literary detection in which a pair of present-day sleuths, Hannah (Felicity Kendal), a no-nonsense popular historian of classical temperament, and Bernard Nightingale (Bill Nighy), an ambitious, vulgar, far-from-rigorous don of Romantic kidney—lock antlers over Nightingale's theory about the house's unsung place in English letters. While staying at Sidley Park in 1809, he maintains, Lord Byron first cuckolded and then killed in a duel a minor versifier and so was forced to flee the country. Set in the same large room of this Derbyshire country house, the action keeps shifting between then and now so that the audience can enjoy, from a position of superior awareness, the contemporary misinterpretations of the past and its evidence. Having seen Thomasina, as a joke, scrawl a picture of a hermit on to the landscape gardener's sketch of the projected hermitage, we derive a certain smug delight from watching Hannah present this as the only extant likeness of the actual Sidley hermit, the figure who is to be her peg for a study of the nervous breakdown of the Romantic Imagination.

The play is often very funny, but the easy superiority of the structural gags would pall if, alongside this comic demonstration of the past's irrecoverability, Stoppard didn't also give you a wistful sense that the back-and-forth motion is art's attempt to belie the bleak conclusion to which Thomasina's science eventually leads: that all equations are not reversible as in the "timeless" Newtonian universe and that time moves in only one direction. So when the past and present merge in the dream-like final sequence, it feels like the temporal counterpart to the play's artful blurring of a whole set of distinctions and antitheses.

The play shows how evidence, left partly as a harmless prank, can drive the people who find it mad. This may have been the fate of Thomasina's tutor (sensitively played by Rufus Sewell). Before her premature death, she had granted him a glimpse of a universe consuming itself and he seems to have declined into a career as Sidley's mad hermit, though Stoppard leaves a frisson of mystery. But in its very form, *Arcadia* lends support to the tutor's earlier optimism about man's endless capacity for self-renewal: "Mathematical discoveries glimpsed and lost to view will have their time again." To the idea of entropy, this entertaining and intriguing play puts up a pocket of imaginative resistance.

YASMINA REZA

1960–

Three men, three chairs, a coffee table, and an all-white painting might seem unlikely to draw crowds of theatergoers in Berlin, Paris, London, and New York, but Yasmina Reza's *"Art,"* which features such a spare set of elements, has been drawing enthusiastic audiences ever since it opened in Berlin in 1994. In Paris, it won the Molière Award for best play, best production, and best author. Then it became a long-running hit in London's West End, where it won the Evening Standard Award for best new play and the Olivier Award for best comedy—an unusual achievement for a play by a heretofore little-known French playwright. And it triumphed again in New York, winning the Tony Award for best new play of the 1997–98 theatrical season.

Yasmina Reza's background actually combines central and eastern Europe with the Middle East, since her Iranian father was born in Russia but later moved to France with his Hungarian wife. Reza herself first studied drama at the University of Nanterre and then entered the prestigious Jacques Lecocq school to train as an actress. After appearing in a series of contemporary plays, as well as in works by the classic French playwrights Molière and Marivaux, she turned her hand to playwriting. Her first work, *Conversations after a Burial* (1986), won two major awards in France—the Best Author Molière Award and the New Writer Award—and attracted offers for screenplays as well as a stage adaptation in French of Kafka's *Metamorphosis.* But not until 1994, with the French production of *"Art,"* did Reza's career take its giant step forward.

Her next play, *The Unexpected Man* (1995), was produced in the spring of 1998 by the Royal Shakespeare Company, with Sir Michael Gambon and Eileen Atkins starring in the two-character drama. At moments, the 80-minute play, consisting of two characters—a famous novelist and an unknown woman—thinking to themselves in a train compartment, is highly self-reflective. One of the novelist's musings aptly describes the play's central situation: "A famous author goes on a journey and sits opposite an unknown woman who's reading his latest book." And one of the woman's internal monologues aptly describes the very same situation from her radically different point of view: "A woman who travels from Paris to Frankfurt with nothing else to read but *The Unexpected Man* is a deeply depressed woman." But just as the disparate monologues of Pinter's *Landscape* reveal a past of intersecting memories, so too the monologues in *The Unexpected Man* show us two quite disparate people connected by their loneliness: the novelist who complains of everything from his bowel movements to the possibility of his daughter's unsuitable marriage, and the quietly elegant woman whose generous heart finds in the novelist's writing all the feeling that he is at pains to deny. So it seems especially touching that in the play's final moments, the novelist says of himself, "Paul Parsky has never known how to weep for everything that is," and Martha counters by citing "moments like eternity" from his novels, "All these things and so many others you've described, Mr. Parsky, have made me weep."

Like *The Unexpected Man, "Art"* focuses on questions of artistic merit and value,

1565

but it does so even more directly, more provocatively—and with a great deal of humor as well. Here the characters do not avoid confrontation but actually seem to seek it out. And in the first half of the play, Reza skillfully maneuvers the three friends through a series of complexly interrelated duologues: Serge proudly shows Marc his newly acquired "white" painting; Marc tells Yvan how appalled he is that Serge should so waste his money; Yvan visits Serge to see the painting; Yvan reports to Marc, "I didn't like the painting . . . but I didn't actually hate it." But by mid-play, Marc decides that he's behaved badly: "Even if it makes me physically ill that my best friend has bought a white painting, all the same I ought to avoid attacking him about it." So he returns to Serge's apartment, trying to stay polite, and, as one might expect, fails utterly in his attempted diplomacy.

What emerges in the rest of the play, which features all three men on stage together, is less a discussion of art and painting than it is an exploration of the relationships, both onstage and off, of these three friends and of their friendship itself. Marc's use of the word "masterpiece"—referring not to the disputed artwork but to Seneca's treatise on living a happy and fulfilled life—starts an argument that seems way out of proportion to his lightly sarcastic twist to the word. But as Marc and Serge squabble over whether or not the book is a masterpiece, their conversation reveals that they are really talking not about a book or even a philosophy but about the extent to which they do or don't understand each other. It seems that each had taken the other's friendship for granted until the painting and their drastically different reactions to it exposed a gap that frightened them. As Marc puts it, "I can't love the Serge who's capable of buying that painting." For a while, they both turn on Yvan, who, as a friend of both but without the deep emotional attachment that Marc's comments reveal, tries to find a middle ground. But middle ground is exactly what neither Serge nor Marc can inhabit. Serge's resentment of Paula, Marc's girlfriend (unseen, as are all the women mentioned in the play), is clear, despite his denial of it. And Marc finally admits that he resents the painting because it seems to have replaced him in Serge's affections.

The gradual exposure of what really concerns all three men depends not only on the play's dialogue but on the skill of the three actors who must each create an individual character and then suggest the webs of offstage relationships which underlie the onstage ones. Though reviewers of the London production—produced by Sean Connery and translated into English by the British playwright Christopher Hampton—disagreed about the quality of Reza's play, some finding it banal, others applauding its wit and invention, almost all of them cheered the performances of Albert Finney, Tom Courtenay, and Ken Stott. On a stage set only with white flats, a coffee table, three chairs (each of a different style), and, at moments, the "white" painting (see Figure 1), the contrasting personalities of the three men emerge vividly. The emotional dilemma of Yvan, trapped between Marc and Serge, becomes physical when he tries to stop a fight and ends up the unintended recipient of Marc's fist (see Figure 2). And at the play's climax, when Serge hands a felt-tip pen to Marc (Figure 3), an audience that might have begun the play laughing at the pretentiousness of the painting now holds its breath, waiting to see what will happen. We recognize, as do Yvan, Serge, and Marc in the three monologues at the play's end, that the painting has revealed them, exposing through its whiteness the varied colors of their lives.

"ART"

BY YASMINA REZA / TRANSLATED BY CHRISTOPHER HAMPTON

CHARACTERS

MARC
SERGE
YVAN

SCENE

The main room of a flat.
A single set. As stripped-down and neutral as possible.
The scenes unfold, successively, at SERGE*'s,* YVAN*'s and*
MARC*'s.*
Nothing changes, except for the painting on the wall.

---

*(*MARC*, alone.)*

MARC: My friend Serge has bought a painting. It's a canvas about five foot by four: white. The background is white and if you screw up your eyes, you can make out some fine white diagonal lines.

Serge is one of my oldest friends.

He's done very well for himself, he's a dermatologist and he's keen on *art*.

On Monday, I went to see the painting; Serge had actually got hold of it on the Saturday, but he'd been lusting after it for several months.

This white painting with white lines.

(At SERGE*'s.*
At floor level, a white canvas with fine white diagonal scars. SERGE *looks at his painting, thrilled.* MARC *looks at the painting.* SERGE *looks at* MARC *looking at the painting.*
Long silence: from both of them, a whole range of wordless emotions.)

MARC: Expensive?
SERGE: Two hundred thousand.
MARC: Two hundred thousand?
SERGE: Huntingdon would take it off my hands for two hundred and twenty.
MARC: Who's that?
SERGE: Huntingdon?
MARC: Never heard of him.
SERGE: Huntingdon! The Huntingdon Gallery!
MARC: The Huntingdon Gallery would take it off your hands for two hundred and twenty?
SERGE: No, not the Gallery. Him. Huntingdon himself. For his own collection.
MARC: Then why didn't Huntingdon buy it?
SERGE: It's important for them to sell to private clients. That's how the market circulates.
MARC: Mm hm . . .
SERGE: Well?
MARC: . . .

SERGE: You're not in the right place. Look at it from this angle.
　　　Can you see the lines?
MARC: What's the name of the . . . ?
SERGE: Painter. Antrios.
MARC: Well-known?
SERGE: Very. Very!

(Pause.)

MARC: Serge, you haven't bought this painting for two hundred thousand francs?
SERGE: You don't understand, that's what it costs. It's an Antrios.
MARC: You haven't bought this painting for two hundred thousand francs?
SERGE: I might have known you'd miss the point.
MARC: You paid two hundred thousand francs for this shit?

*(*SERGE*, as if alone.)*

SERGE: My friend Marc's an intelligent enough fellow, I've always valued our relationship, he has a good job, he's an aeronautical engineer, but he's one of those new-style intellectuals, who are not only enemies of modernism, but seem to take some sort of incomprehensible pride in running it down . . .

In recent years these nostalgia-merchants have become quite breathtakingly arrogant.

(Same pair. Same place. Same painting.
Pause.)

SERGE: What do you mean, 'this shit'?
MARC: Serge, where's your sense of humour? Why aren't you laughing? . . . It's fantastic, you buying this painting.

*(*MARC *laughs.* SERGE *remains stony.)*

SERGE: I don't care how fantastic you think it is, I don't mind if you laugh, but I would like to know what you mean by 'this shit.'

MARC: You're taking the piss!

SERGE: No, I'm not. By whose standards is it shit? If you call something shit, you need to have some criterion to judge it by.

MARC: Who are you talking to? Who do you think you're talking to? Hello! . . .

SERGE: You have no interest whatsoever in contemporary painting, you never have had. This is a field about which you know absolutely nothing, so how can you assert that any given object, which conforms to laws you don't understand, is shit?

MARC: Because it is. It's shit. I'm sorry.

(SERGE, *alone.*)

SERGE: He doesn't like the painting.
　　Fine . . .
　　But there was no warmth in the way he reacted.
　　No attempt.
　　No warmth when he dismissed it out of hand.
　　Just that vile, pretentious laugh.
　　A real know-all laugh.
　　I hated that laugh.

(MARC, *alone.*)

MARC: It's a complete mystery to me, Serge buying this painting. It's unsettled me, it's filled me with some indefinable unease.
　　When I left his place, I had to take three capsules of Gelsemium 9X which Paula recommended—Gelsemium or Ignatia, she said, Gelsemium or Ignatia, which do you prefer, I mean, how the hell should I know?—because I couldn't begin to understand how Serge, my friend, could have bought that picture.
　　Two hundred thousand francs!
　　He's comfortably off, but he's hardly rolling in money.
　　Comfortable, no more, just comfortable. And he spends two hundred grand on a white painting.
　　I must go and see Yvan, he's a friend of ours, I have to discuss this with Yvan. Mind you, Yvan's a very tolerant bloke, which of course, when it comes to relationships, is the worst thing you can be.
　　Yvan's very tolerant because he couldn't care less.
　　If Yvan tolerates the fact that Serge has spent two hundred grand on some piece of white shit, it's because he couldn't care less about Serge. Obviously.

(*At* YVAN's.
On the wall, some daub.
YVAN *is on all fours with his back to us. He seems to be looking for something underneath a piece of furniture. As he does so, he turns to introduce himself.*)

YVAN: I'm Yvan.
　　I'm a bit tense at the moment, because, having spent my life in textiles, I've just found a new job as a sales agent for a wholesale stationery business.
　　People like me. My professional life has always been a failure and I'm getting married in a couple of weeks. She's a lovely intelligent girl from a good family.

(MARC *enters.* YVAN *has resumed his search and has his back to him.*)

MARC: What are you doing?

YVAN: I'm looking for the top of my pen.

(*Time passes.*)

MARC: All right, that's enough.

YVAN: I had it five minutes ago.

MARC: It doesn't matter.

YVAN: Yes, it does.

(MARC *gets down on his knees to help him look. Both of them spend some time looking.* MARC *straightens up.*)

MARC: Stop it. Buy another one.

YVAN: It's a felt-tip, they're special, they'll write on any surface . . . It's just infuriating. Objects, I can't tell you how much they infuriate me. I had it in my hand five minutes ago.

MARC: Are you going to live here?

YVAN: Do you think it's suitable for a young couple?

MARC: Young couple! Ha, ha . . .

YVAN: Try not to laugh like that in front of Catherine.

MARC: How's the stationery business?

YVAN: All right. I'm learning.

MARC: You've lost weight.

YVAN: A bit. I'm pissed off about that top. It'll all dry up. Sit down.

MARC: If you go on looking for that top, I'm leaving.

YVAN: OK, I'll stop. You want something to drink?

MARC: A Perrier, if you have one.
　　Have you seen Serge lately?

YVAN: No. Have you?

MARC: Yesterday.

YVAN: Is he well?

MARC: Very.
　　He's just bought a painting.

YVAN: Oh yes?

MARC: Mm.

YVAN: Nice?

MARC: White.

YVAN: White?

MARC: White.
　　Imagine a canvas about five foot by four . . . with a white background . . . completely white in fact . . . with fine white diagonal stripes . . . you know . . . and maybe another horizontal white line, towards the bottom . . .

YVAN: How can you see them?

MARC: What?

YVAN: These white lines. If the background's white, how can you see the lines?

MARC: You just do. Because I suppose the lines are slightly grey, or vice versa, or anyway there are degrees of white! There's more than one kind of white!

YVAN: Don't get upset. Why are you getting upset?

MARC: You immediately start quibbling. Why can't you let me finish?

YVAN: All right. Go on.

MARC: Right. So, you have an idea of what the painting looks like.

YVAN: I think so, yes.

MARC: Now you have to guess how much Serge paid for it.

YVAN: Who's the painter?

MARC: Antrios. Have you heard of him?

YVAN: No. Is he fashionable?

MARC: I knew you were going to ask me that!

YVAN: Well, it's logical . . .

MARC: No, it isn't logical . . .

YVAN: Of course it's logical, you ask me to guess the price, you know very well the price depends on how fashionable the painter might be . . .

MARC: I'm not asking you to apply a whole set of critical standards, I'm not asking you for a professional valuation, I'm asking you what you, Yvan, would give for a white painting tarted up with a few off-white stripes.

YVAN: Bugger all.

MARC: Right. And what about Serge? Pick a figure at random.

YVAN: Ten thousand francs.

MARC: Ha!

YVAN: Fifty thousand.

MARC: Ha!

YVAN: A hundred thousand.

MARC: Keep going.

YVAN: A hundred and fifty? Two hundred?!

MARC: Two hundred. Two hundred grand.

YVAN: No!

MARC: Yes.

YVAN: Two hundred grand?

MARC: Two hundred grand.

YVAN: Has he gone crazy?

MARC: Looks like it.

(Slight pause.)

YVAN: All the same . . .

MARC: What do you mean, all the same?

YVAN: If it makes him happy . . . he can afford it . . .

MARC: So that's what you think, is it?

YVAN: Why? What do you think?

MARC: You don't understand the seriousness of this, do you?

YVAN: Er . . . no.

MARC: It's strange how you're missing the basic point of this story. All you can see is externals. You don't understand the seriousness of it.

YVAN: What is the seriousness of it?

MARC: Don't you understand what this means?

YVAN: Would you like a cashew nut?

MARC: Don't you see that suddenly, in some grotesque way, Serge fancies himself as a 'collector.'

YVAN: Well . . .

MARC: From now on, our friend Serge is one of the great connoisseurs.

YVAN: Bollocks.

MARC: Well of course it's bollocks. You can't buy your way in that cheap. But that's what *he* thinks.

YVAN: Oh, I see.

MARC: Doesn't that upset you?

YVAN: No. Not if it makes him happy.

MARC: If it makes him happy. What's that supposed to mean?

What sort of a philosophy is that, if it makes him happy?

YVAN: As long as it's not doing any harm to anyone else . . .

MARC: But it is. It's doing harm to me! I'm disturbed, I'm disturbed, more than that, I'm hurt, yes, I am, I'm fond of Serge, and to see him let himself be ripped off and lose every ounce of discernment through sheer snobbery . . .

YVAN: I don't know why you're so surprised. He's always haunted galleries in the most absurd way, he's always been an exhibition freak.

MARC: He's always been a freak, but a freak with a sense of humour. You see, basically, what really upsets me is that you can't have a laugh with him any more.

YVAN: I'm sure you can.

MARC: You can't!

YVAN: Have you tried?

MARC: Of course I've tried. I laughed. Heartily. What do you think I did? He didn't crack a smile.

Mind you, two hundred grand, I suppose it might be hard to see the funny side.

YVAN: Yes.

(They laugh.)

I'll make him laugh.

MARC: I'd be amazed. Any more nuts?

YVAN: He'll laugh, you just wait.

(At SERGE's.

SERGE *is with Yvan. The painting isn't there.)*

SERGE: . . . and you get on with the in-laws?

YVAN: Wonderfully. As far as they're concerned, I'm some berk tottering from one dodgy job to another and now I'm groping my way into the world of vellum . . . This thing on my hand, what is it?

(SERGE *examines it.*)

Is it serious?

SERGE: No.

YVAN: Oh, good. How are things?

SERGE: Nothing. Lot of work. Exhausted.
It's nice to see you. You never phone.

YVAN: I don't like to disturb you.

SERGE: You're joking. You just speak to my secretary
and I'll call you back right away.

YVAN: I suppose so.
Your place gets more and more monastic . . .

(SERGE *laughs.*)

SERGE: Yes!
Seen Marc recently?

YVAN: Not recently, no.
Have you?

SERGE: Two or three days ago.

YVAN: Is he all right?

SERGE: Yes. More or less.

YVAN: Oh?

SERGE: No, he's all right.

YVAN: I talked to him on the phone last week, he
seemed all right.

SERGE: Well, he is. He's all right.

YVAN: You seemed to be implying he wasn't all right.

SERGE: On the contrary, I said, he was all right.

YVAN: More or less, you said.

SERGE: Yes, more or less. More or less all right.

(*Long silence.* YVAN *wanders around the room.*)

YVAN: You been out? Seen anything?

SERGE: No. I can't afford to go out.

YVAN: Oh?

SERGE (*cheerfully*): I'm ruined.

YVAN: Oh?

SERGE: You want to see something special? Would you
like to?

YVAN: Of course I would. Show me.

(SERGE *exits and returns with the Antrios, which he turns
round and sets down in front of* YVAN.
YVAN *looks at the painting and, strangely enough,
doesn't manage the hearty laugh he'd predicted.
A long pause, while* YVAN *studies the painting
and* SERGE *studies* YVAN.)

Oh, yes. Yes, yes.

SERGE: Antrios.

YVAN: Yes, yes.

SERGE: It's a seventies Antrios. Worth mentioning.
He's going through a similar phase now, but this
one's from the seventies.

YVAN: Yes, yes.
Expensive?

SERGE: In absolute terms, yes. In fact, no.
You like it?

YVAN: Oh, yes, yes, yes.

SERGE: Plain.

YVAN: Plain, yes . . . Yes . . . And at the same time . . .

SERGE: Magnetic.

YVAN: Mm . . . yes . . .

SERGE: You don't really get the resonance just at the
moment.

YVAN: Well, a bit . . .

SERGE: No, you don't. You have to come back in the
middle of the day. That resonance you get from
something monochromatic, it doesn't really happen under artificial light.

YVAN: Mm hm.

SERGE: Not that it is actually monochromatic.

YVAN: No! . . .
How much was it?

SERGE: Two hundred thousand.

YVAN: Very reasonable.

SERGE: Very.

(*Silence. Suddenly* SERGE *bursts out laughing, immediately followed by* YVAN. *Both of them roar with laughter.*)

Crazy, or what?

YVAN: Crazy!

SERGE: Two hundred grand!

(*Hearty laughter. They stop. They look at each other. They
start again. Then stop.
They've calmed down.*)

SERGE: You know Marc's seen this painting.

YVAN: Oh?

SERGE: Devastated.

YVAN: Oh?

SERGE: He told me it was shit. A completely inappropriate description.

YVAN: Absolutely.

SERGE: You can't call this shit.

YVAN: No.

SERGE: You can say, I don't get it, I can't grasp it, you
can't say 'it's shit.'

YVAN: You've seen his place.

SERGE: Nothing to see.
It's like yours, it's . . . what I mean is, you
couldn't care less.

YVAN: His taste is classical, he likes things classical,
what do you expect . . .

SERGE: He started in with this sardonic laugh . . . Not
a trace of charm . . . Not a trace of humour.

YVAN: You know Marc is moody, there's nothing new
about that . . .

SERGE: He has no sense of humour. With you, I can
laugh. With him, I'm like a block of ice.

YVAN: It's true he's a bit gloomy at the moment.

SERGE: I don't blame him for not responding to this
painting, he hasn't the training, there's a whole
apprenticeship you have to go through, which he
hasn't, either because he's never wanted to or
because he has no particular instinct for it, none

of that matters, no, what I blame him for is his tone of voice, his complacency, his tactlessness.

I blame him for his insensitivity. I don't blame him for not being interested in modern Art, I couldn't give a toss about that, I like him for other reasons . . .

YVAN: And he likes you!

SERGE: No, no, no, no, I felt it the other day, a kind of . . . a kind of condescension . . . contempt with a really bitter edge . . .

YVAN: No, surely not!

SERGE: Oh, yes! Don't keep trying to smooth things over. Where d'you get this urge to be the great reconciler of the human race? Why don't you admit that Marc is atrophying? If he hasn't already atrophied.

(Silence.)

(At MARC's.
On the wall, a figurative painting: a landscape seen through a window.)

YVAN: We had a laugh.

MARC: You had a laugh?

YVAN: We had a laugh. Both of us. We had a laugh. I promise you on Catherine's life, we had a good laugh, both of us, together.

MARC: You told him it was shit and you had a good laugh.

YVAN: No, I didn't tell him it was shit, we laughed spontaneously.

MARC: You arrived, you looked at the painting and you laughed. And then he laughed.

YVAN: Yes. If you like. We talked a bit, then it was more or less as you described.

MARC: A genuine laugh, was it?

YVAN: Perfectly genuine.

MARC: Well, then, I've made a mistake. Good. I'm really pleased to hear it.

YVAN: It was even better than you think. It was Serge who laughed first.

MARC: It was Serge who laughed first . . .

YVAN: Yes.

MARC: He laughed first and you joined in.

YVAN: Yes.

MARC: But what made him laugh?

YVAN: He laughed because he sensed I was about to laugh. If you like, he laughed to put me at my ease.

MARC: It doesn't count if he laughed first.

If he laughed first, it was to defuse your laughter.

It means it wasn't a genuine laugh.

YVAN: It was a genuine laugh.

MARC: It may have been a genuine laugh, but it wasn't for the right reason.

YVAN: What is the right reason? I'm confused.

MARC: He wasn't laughing because his painting is ridiculous, you and he weren't laughing for the same reasons, you were laughing at the painting and he was laughing to ingratiate himself, to put himself on your wavelength, to show you that on top of being an aesthete who can spend more on a painting than you earn in a year, he's still your same old subversive mate who likes a good laugh.

YVAN: Mm hm . . .

(A brief silence.)

You know . . .

MARC: Yes . . .

YVAN: This is going to amaze you . . .

MARC: Go on . . .

YVAN: I didn't like the painting . . . but I didn't actually hate it.

MARC: Well, of course. You can't hate what's invisible, you can't hate nothing.

YVAN: No, no, it has something . . .

MARC: What do you mean?

YVAN: It has something. It's not nothing.

MARC: You're joking.

YVAN: I'm not as harsh as you. It's a work of art, there's a system behind it.

MARC: A system?

YVAN: A system.

MARC: What system?

YVAN: It's the completion of a journey . . .

MARC: Ha, ha, ha!

YVAN: It wasn't painted by accident, it's a work of art which stakes its claim as part of a trajectory . . .

MARC: Ha, ha, ha!

YVAN: All right, laugh.

MARC: You're parroting out all Serge's nonsense. From him, it's heart-breaking, from you it's just comical!

YVAN: You know, Marc, this complacency, you want to watch out for it. You're getting bitter, it's not very attractive.

MARC: Good. The older I get, the more offensive I hope to become.

YVAN: Great.

MARC: A system!

YVAN: You're impossible to talk to.

MARC: There's a system behind it! . . . You look at this piece of shit, but never mind, never mind, there's a system behind it! . . . You reckon there's a system behind this landscape? *(He indicates the painting on his wall.)* . . . No, uh? Too evocative. Too expressive. Everything's on the canvas! No scope for a system! . . .

YVAN: I'm glad you're enjoying yourself.

MARC: Yvan, look, speak for yourself. Describe your feelings to me.

YVAN: I felt a resonance.

MARC: You felt a resonance? . . .

YVAN: You're denying that I'm capable of appreciating this painting on my own account.

MARC: Of course I am.

YVAN: Well, why?

MARC: Because I know you. Because apart from your disastrous indulgence, you're quite sane.

YVAN: I wish I could say the same for you.

MARC: Yvan, look me in the eye.

YVAN: I'm looking at you.

MARC: Were you moved by Serge's painting?

YVAN: No.

MARC: Answer me this. You're getting married tomorrow and you and Catherine get this painting as a wedding present. Does it make you happy? . . .

Does it make you happy? . . .

(YVAN, alone.)

YVAN: Of course it doesn't make me happy.

It doesn't make me happy, but, generally speaking, I'm not the sort of person who can say I'm happy, just like that.

I'm trying to . . . I'm trying to think of an occasion when I could have said yes, I'm happy . . . Are you happy to be getting married, my mother stupidly asked me one day, are you at least happy to be getting married? . . . Why wouldn't I be, mother?

What do you mean, why wouldn't I be? You're either happy or you're not happy, what's why wouldn't I be got to do with it? . . .

(SERGE, alone.)

SERGE: As far as I'm concerned, it's not white.

When I say as far as I'm concerned, I mean objectively.

Objectively speaking, it's not white.

It has a white background, with a whole range of greys . . .

There's even some red in it.

You could say it's very pale.

I wouldn't like it if it was white.

Marc thinks it's white . . . that's his limit . . .

Marc thinks it's white because he's got hung up on the idea that it's white.

Unlike Yvan. Yvan can see it isn't white.

Marc can think what he likes, what do I care?

(MARC, alone.)

MARC: Obviously I should have taken the Ignatia.

Why do I have to be so categorical?

What possible difference can it make to me, if Serge lets himself be taken in by modern Art?

I mean, it is a serious matter. But I could have found some other way to put it to him.

I could have taken a less aggressive tone.

Even if it makes me physically ill that my best friend has bought a white painting, all the same I ought to avoid attacking him about it.

I ought to be nice to him.

From now on, I'm on my best behaviour.

(At SERGE's.)

SERGE: Feel like a laugh?

MARC: Go on.

SERGE: Yvan liked the Antrios.

MARC: Where is it? . . .

SERGE: You want another look?

MARC: Fetch it out.

SERGE: I knew you'd come round to it! . . .

(He exits and returns with the painting. A moment of contemplation.)

Yvan got the hang of it. Right away.

MARC: Mm.

SERGE: All right, listen, it's just a picture, we don't have to get bogged down with it, life's too short . . . By the way, have you read this? *(He picks up* De Vita Beata *by Seneca° and throws it on to the low table just in front of* MARC.) Read it, it's a masterpiece.

(MARC picks up the book, opens it and leafs through it.)

Incredibly modern. Read that, you don't need to read anything else. What with the office, the hospital, Françoise, who's now decreed that I'm to see the children every weekend—which is something new for Françoise, the notion that children need a father—I don't have time to read any more, I'm obliged to go straight for the essentials.

MARC: . . . As in painting . . . Where you've ingeniously eliminated form and colour. Those old chestnuts.

SERGE: Yes . . . Although I'm still capable of appreciating more figurative work. Like your Flemish job. Very restful.

MARC: What's Flemish about it? It's a view of Carcassonne.

SERGE: Yes, but I mean . . . it's slightly Flemish in style . . . the window, the view, the . . . in any case, it's very pretty.

MARC: It's not worth anything, you know that.

SERGE: What difference does that make? . . . Anyway, in a few years God knows if the Antrios will be worth anything! . . .

MARC: . . . You know, I've been thinking. I've been thinking and I've changed my mind. The other day, driving across Paris, I was thinking about you and I said to myself: isn't there, deep down, some-

---

De Vita Beata *by Seneca,* "On Happy Life," Latin treatise by the Roman philosopher Seneca (c. 4 B.C.–A.D. 65).

thing really poetic about what Serge has done? . . . Isn't surrendering to this incoherent urge to buy in fact an authentically poetic impulse?

SERGE: You're very conciliatory today. Unrecognizable. What's this bland, submissive tone of voice? It doesn't suit you at all, by the way.

MARC: No, no, I'm trying to explain, I'm apologizing.

SERGE: Apologizing? What for?

MARC: I'm too thin-skinned, I'm too highly strung, I overreact . . . You could say, I lack judgement.

SERGE: Read Seneca.

MARC: That's it. See, for instance, you say 'read Seneca' and I could easily have got annoyed. I'm quite capable of being really annoyed by your saying to me, in the course of our conversation, 'read Seneca'. Which is absurd!

SERGE: No. It's not absurd.

MARC: Really?

SERGE: No, because you thought you could identify . . .

MARC: I didn't say I *was* annoyed . . .

SERGE: You said you could easily . . .

MARC: Yes, yes. I could easily . . .

SERGE: Get annoyed, and I understand that. Because when I said 'read Seneca', you thought you could identify a kind of superiority. You tell me you lack judgement and my answer is 'read Seneca', well, it's obnoxious!

MARC: It is, rather.

SERGE: Having said that, it's true you lack judgement, because I didn't say 'read Seneca', I said 'read Seneca!'

MARC: You're right. You're right.

SERGE: The fact of the matter is, you've quite simply lost your sense of humour.

MARC: Probably.

SERGE: You've lost your sense of humour, Marc. You really have lost your sense of humour, old chap. When I was talking to Yvan the other day, we agreed you'd lost your sense of humour. Where the hell is he? He's incapable of being on time, it's infuriating! We'll miss the beginning!

MARC: . . . Yvan thinks I've lost my sense of humour? . . .

SERGE: Yvan agrees with me that recently you've somewhat lost your sense of humour.

MARC: The last time you saw each other, Yvan said he liked your painting very much and I'd lost my sense of humour . . .

SERGE: Oh, yes, that, yes, the painting, really, very much. And he meant it . . . What's that you're eating?

MARC: Ignatia.

SERGE: Oh, you believe in homeopathy now?

MARC: I don't believe in anything.

SERGE: Didn't you think Yvan had lost a lot of weight?

MARC: So's she.

SERGE: It's the wedding, eating away at them.

MARC: Yes.

(They laugh.)

SERGE: How's Paula?

MARC: All right. *(He indicates the Antrios.)* Where are you going to put it?

SERGE: Haven't decided. There. Or there? . . . Too ostentatious.

MARC: Are you going to have it framed?

(SERGE laughs discreetly.)

SERGE: No! . . . No, no . . .

MARC: Why not?

SERGE: It's not supposed to be framed.

MARC: Is that right?

SERGE: The artist doesn't want it to be. It mustn't be interrupted. It's already in its setting. *(He signals MARC over to examine the edge.)* Look . . . you see . . .

MARC: What is it, Elastoplast?°

SERGE: No, it's a kind of Kraft paper . . . Made up by the artist.

MARC: It's funny the way you say the artist.

SERGE: What else am I supposed to say?

MARC: You say the artist when you could say the painter or . . . whatever his name is . . . Antrios . . .

SERGE: So? . . .

MARC: But you say the artist, as if he's a sort of . . . well, anyway, doesn't matter. What are we seeing? Let's try and see something with a bit of substance for once.

SERGE: It's eight o'clock. Everything will have started. I can't imagine how this man, who has nothing whatsoever to do—am I right?—manages to be late every single time. Where the fuck is he?

MARC: Let's just have dinner.

SERGE: All right. It's five past eight. We said we'd meet between seven and half-past . . . What d'you mean, the way I say the artist?

MARC: Nothing. I was going to say something stupid.

SERGE: Well, go on.

MARC: You say the artist as if . . . as if he's some unattainable being. The artist . . . some sort of god . . .

(SERGE laughs.)

SERGE: Well, for me, he is a god! You don't think I'd have forked out a fortune for a mere mortal! . . .

MARC: I see.

SERGE: I went to the Pompidou° on Monday, you know how many Antrioses they have at the Pompidou? . . . Three! Three Antrioses! . . . At the Pompidou!

Elastoplast, adhesive tape. **Pompidou,** Paris museum, devoted to contemporary art.

MARC: Amazing.

SERGE: And mine's as good as any of them! If not better! . . .

Listen, I have a suggestion, let's give Yvan exactly three more minutes and then bugger off. I've found a very good new place. Lyonnaise.°

MARC: Why are you so jumpy?

SERGE: I'm not jumpy.

MARC: Yes, you are jumpy.

SERGE: I am not jumpy, well, I am, I'm jumpy because this slackness is intolerable, this inability to practise any kind of self-discipline!

MARC: The fact is, I'm getting on your nerves and you're taking it out on poor Yvan.

SERGE: What do you mean, poor Yvan, are you taking the piss? You're not getting on my nerves, why should you be getting on my nerves?

SERGE: He is getting on my nerves. It's true.

He's getting on my nerves.

It's this ingratiating tone of voice. A little smile behind every word.

It's as if he's forcing himself to be pleasant.

Don't be pleasant, whatever you do, don't be pleasant!

Could it be buying the Antrios? . . . Could buying the Antrios have triggered off this feeling of constraint between us?

Buying something . . . without his backing? . . .

Well, bugger his backing! Bugger your backing, Marc!

MARC: Could it be the Antrios, buying the Antrios?

No—

It started some time ago . . .

To be precise, it started on the day we were discussing some work of art and you uttered, quite seriously, the word *deconstruction*.

It wasn't so much the word *deconstruction* which upset me, it was the air of solemnity you imbued it with.

You said, humourlessly, unapologetically, without a trace of irony, the word *deconstruction*, you, my friend.

I wasn't sure how best to deal with the situation, so I made this throwaway remark, I said I think I must be getting intolerant in my old age, and you answered, who do you think you are? What makes you so high and mighty? . . .

What gives you the right to set yourself apart, Serge answered in the bloodiest possible way. And quite unexpectedly.

You're just Marc, what makes you think you're so special?

Lyonnaise, in the style of Lyons.

That day, I should have punched him in the mouth.

And when he was lying there on the ground, half-dead, I should have said to him, you're supposed to be my friend, what sort of a friend are you, Serge, if you don't think your friends are special?

(*At* SERGE'*s*.
MARC *and* SERGE, *as we left them.*)

MARC: Lyonnaise, did you say? Bit heavy, isn't it? Bit fatty, all those sausages . . . what do you think?

(*The doorbell rings.*)

SERGE: Twelve minutes past eight.

(SERGE *goes to open the door to* YVAN. YVAN *walks into the room, already talking.*)

YVAN: So, a crisis, insoluble problem, major crisis, both step-mothers want their names on the wedding invitation. Catherine adores her step-mother, who more or less brought her up, she wants her name on the invitation, she wants it and her step-mother is not anticipating, which is understandable, since the mother is dead, not appearing next to Catherine's father, whereas my step-mother, whom I detest, it's out of the question her name should appear on the invitation, but my father won't have his name on it if hers isn't, unless Catherine's step-mother's is left off, which is completely unacceptable, I suggested none of the parents' names should be on it, after all we're not adolescents, we can announce our wedding and invite people ourselves, so Catherine screamed her head off, arguing that would be a slap in the face for her parents who were paying through the nose for the reception, and particularly for her step-mother, who's gone to so much trouble when she isn't even her daughter and I finally let myself be persuaded, totally against my better judgement, because she wore me down, I finally agreed that my step-mother, whom I detest, who's a complete bitch, will have her name on the invitation, so I telephoned my mother to warn her, mother, I said, I've done everything I can to avoid this, but we have absolutely no choice, Yvonne's name has to be on the invitation, she said, if Yvonne's name is on the invitation, take mine off it, mother, I said, please, I beg you, don't make things even more difficult, and she said, how dare you suggest my name is left to float around the card on its own, as if I was some abandoned woman, below Yvonne, who'll be clamped on to your father's surname, like a limpet, I said to her, mother, I have friends waiting for me, I'm going to hang up and we'll discuss all this tomorrow after a good night's sleep, she said, why is it I'm always an afterthought, what are you talking about, mother, you're not always an afterthought, of course I am and when you say don't make things even more difficult, what you mean is, everything's already been decided, everything's been organized without me, everything's been cooked up behind my back, good old Huguette, she'll agree to anything and all this, she said—to put the old tin lid on it—in aid of an event, the importance of which I'm having some trouble grasping, mother, I have friends waiting for me, that's right, there's always something better to do, anything's more important than I am, good-bye and she hung up, Catherine, who was next to me, but who hadn't heard her side of the conversation, said, what did she say, I said, she doesn't want her name on the invitation with Yvonne, which is understandable, I'm not talking about that, what was it she said about the wedding, nothing, you're lying, I'm not, Cathy, I promise you, she just doesn't want her name on the invitation with Yvonne, call her back and tell her when your son's getting married, you rise above your vanity, you could say the same thing to your step-mother, that's got nothing to do with it, Catherine shouted, it's me, I'm the one who's insisting her name's on it, it's not her, poor thing, she's tact personified, if she had any idea of the problem this is causing, she'd be down on her knees, begging for her name to be taken off the invitation, now call your mother, so I called her again, by now I'm in shreds, Catherine's listening on the extension, Yvan, my mother says, up to now you've conducted your affairs in the most chaotic way imaginable and just because, out of the blue, you've decided to embark on matrimony, I find myself obliged to spend all afternoon and evening with your father, a man I haven't seen for seventeen years and to whom I was not expecting to have to reveal my hip-size and my puffy cheeks, not to mention Yvonne who incidentally, I may tell you, according to Félix Perolari, has now taken up bridge—my mother also plays bridge—I can see none of this can be helped, but on the invitation, the one item everyone is going to receive and examine, I insist on making a solo appearance, Catherine, listening on the extension, shakes her head and screws up her face in disgust, mother, I say, why are you so selfish, I'm not selfish, I'm not selfish, Yvan, you're not going to start as well, you're not going to be like Mme Roméro this morning and tell me I have a heart of stone, that everybody in our family has a heart of stone, that's what Mme Roméro said this morning when I refused to raise her wages—she's gone completely mad, by the way—to sixty francs an hour tax-free, she had the gall to

say everyone in the family had a heart of stone, when she knows very well about poor André's pacemaker, you haven't even bothered to drop him a line, yes, that's right, very funny, everything's a joke to you, it's not me who's the selfish one, Yvan, you've still got a lot to learn about life, off you go, my boy, go on, go on, go and see your precious friends . . .

(Silence.)

SERGE: Then what? . . .

YVAN: Then nothing. Nothing's been resolved. I hung up. Mini-drama with Catherine. Cut short, because I was late.

MARC: Why do you let yourself be buggered around by all these women?

YVAN: Why do I let myself be buggered around, I don't know! They're all insane.

SERGE: You've lost weight.

YVAN: Of course I have. Half a stone. Purely through stress.

MARC: Read Seneca . . .

YVAN: *De Vita Beata,* just what I need! What's he suggest?

MARC: It's a masterpiece.

YVAN: Oh?

SERGE: He hasn't read it.

YVAN: Oh.

MARC: No, but Serge just told me it was a masterpiece.

SERGE: I said it was a masterpiece because it is a masterpiece.

MARC: Quite.

SERGE: It is a masterpiece.

MARC: Why are you getting annoyed?

SERGE: You seem to be insinuating I use the word masterpiece at the slightest excuse.

MARC: Not at all . . .

SERGE: You said the word in a kind of sarcastic way . . .

MARC: Not at all!

SERGE: Yes, yes, the word masterpiece in a kind of . . .

MARC: Is he crazy? Not at all! . . . However, when you used the word, you qualified it by saying 'incredibly modern.'

SERGE: Yes. So?

MARC: You said 'incredibly modern,' as if modern was the highest compliment you could give. As if, when describing something, you couldn't think of anything more admirable, more profoundly admirable, than modern.

SERGE: So?

MARC: So nothing.
And please note I made no mention of the word incredibly . . . Incredibly modern!

SERGE: You're really needling me today.

MARC: No, I'm not . . .

YVAN: You're not going to quarrel all evening, that would just about finish me!

SERGE: You don't think it's extraordinary that a man who wrote nearly two thousand years ago should still be bang up to date?

MARC: No. Of course not. That's the definition of a classic.

SERGE: You're just playing with words.

YVAN: So, what are we going to do? I suppose the cinema's up the spout, sorry. Shall we eat?

MARC: Serge tells me you're very taken with his painting.

YVAN: Yes . . . I am quite . . . taken with it, yes . . .
You're not, I gather.

MARC: No.
Let's go and eat. Serge knows a tasty spot. Lyonnaise.

SERGE: You think the food's too fatty.

MARC: I think the food's a bit on the fatty side, but I don't mind giving it a whirl.

SERGE: No, if you think the food's too fatty, we'll find somewhere else.

MARC: No, I don't mind giving it a whirl.

SERGE: We'll go to the restaurant if you think you'll like it. If not, we won't.
(to YVAN*)* You like Lyonnaise food?

YVAN: I'll do whatever you like.

MARC: He'll do whatever you like. Whatever you like, he'll always do.

YVAN: What's the matter with you? You're both behaving very strangely.

SERGE: He's right, you might once in a while have an opinion of your own.

YVAN: Listen, if you think you're going to use me as a coconut shy, I'm out of here! I've put up with enough today.

MARC: Where's your sense of humour, Yvan?

YVAN: What?

MARC: Where's your sense of humour, old chap?

YVAN: Where's my sense of humour? I don't see anything to laugh at. Where's my sense of humour, are you trying to be funny?

MARC: I think recently you've somewhat lost your sense of humour. You want to watch out, believe me!

YVAN: What's the matter with you?

MARC: Don't you think recently I've also somewhat lost my sense of humour?

YVAN: Oh, I see!

SERGE: All right, that's enough, let's make a decision. Tell you the truth, I'm not even hungry.

YVAN: You're both really sinister this evening.

SERGE: You want my opinion about your women problems?

YVAN: Go on.

SERGE: In my view, the most hysterical of them all is Catherine. By far.

MARC: No question.

SERGE: And if you're already letting yourself be buggered around by her, you're in for a hideous future.

YVAN: What can I do?

MARC: Cancel it.

YVAN: Cancel the wedding?

SERGE: He's right.

YVAN: But I can't, are you crazy?

MARC: Why not?

YVAN: Well, because I can't, that's all! It's all arranged. I've only been working at the stationery business for a month . . .

MARC: What's that got to do with it?

YVAN: It's her uncle's stationery business, he had absolutely no need to take on anyone, least of all someone who's only ever worked in textiles.

SERGE: You must do what you like. I've told you what I think.

YVAN: I'm sorry, Serge, I don't mean to be rude, but you're not necessarily the person I'd come to for matrimonial advice. You can't claim to have been a great success in that field . . .

SERGE: Precisely.

YVAN: I can't back out of the wedding. I know Catherine is hysterical but she has her good points. There are certain crucial qualities you need when you're marrying someone like me . . . *(He indicates the Antrios.)* Where are you going to put it?

SERGE: I don't know yet.

YVAN: Why don't you put it there?

SERGE: Because there, it'd be wiped out by the sunlight.

YVAN: Oh, yes.
I thought of you today at the shop, we ran off five hundred posters by this bloke who paints white flowers, totally white, on a white background.

SERGE: The Antrios is not white.

YVAN: No, of course not. I was just saying.

MARC: You think this painting is not white, Yvan?

YVAN: Not entirely, no . . .

MARC: Ah. Then what colour is it?

YVAN: Various colours . . . There's yellow, there's grey, some slightly ochrish lines.

MARC: And you're moved by these colours?

YVAN: Yes . . . I'm moved by these colours.

MARC: You have no substance, Yvan. You're flabby, you're an amoeba.

SERGE: Why are you attacking Yvan like this?

MARC: Because he's a little arse-licker, he's obsequious, dazzled by money, dazzled by what he believes to be culture, and as you know culture is something I absolutely piss on.

(Brief silence.)

SERGE: . . . What's got into you?

MARC *(to* YVAN*)*: How could you, Yvan? . . . And in front of me. In front of me, Yvan.

YVAN: What d'you mean, in front of you? . . . What d'you mean, in front of you?

I find these colours touching. Yes. If it's all the same to you.

Stop wanting to control everything.

MARC: How could you say, in front of me, that you find these colours touching?

YVAN: Because it's the truth.

MARC: The truth? You find these colours touching?

YVAN: Yes. I find these colours touching.

MARC: You find these colours touching, Yvan?!

SERGE: He finds these colours touching! He's perfectly entitled to!

MARC: No, he's not entitled to.

SERGE: What do you mean, he's not entitled to?

MARC: He's not entitled to.

YVAN: I'm not entitled to? . . .

MARC: No.

SERGE: Why is he not entitled to? I don't think you're very well, perhaps you ought to go and see someone.

MARC: He's not entitled to say he finds these colours touching, because he doesn't.

YVAN: I don't find these colours touching?

MARC: There are no colours. You can't see them. And you don't find them touching.

YVAN: Speak for yourself!

MARC: This is really demeaning, Yvan! . . .

SERGE: Who do you think you are, Marc? . . .

Who are you to legislate? You don't like anything, you despise everyone. You take pride in not being a man of your time . . .

MARC: What's that supposed to mean, a man of my time?

YVAN: Right. I'm off.

SERGE: Where are you going?

YVAN: I'm off. I don't see why I have to put up with your tantrums.

SERGE: Don't go! You're not going to start taking offence, are you? . . . If you go, you're giving in to him.

(YVAN *stands there, hesitating, caught between two possibilities.*)

A man of his time is a man who lives in his own time.

MARC: Balls. How can a man live in any other time but his own? Answer me that.

SERGE: A man of his time is someone of whom it can be said in twenty years' or in a hundred years' time, he was representative of his era.

MARC: Hm.

To what end?

SERGE: What do you mean, to what end?

MARC: What use is it to me if one day somebody says, I was representative of my era?

SERGE: Listen, old fruit, we're not talking about you, if

you can imagine such a thing! We don't give a fuck about you! A man of his time, I'm trying to explain to you, like most people you admire, is someone who makes some contribution to the human race . . . A man of his time doesn't assume the history of Art has come to an end with a pseudo-Flemish view of Cavaillon . . .

MARC: Carcassonne.

SERGE: Same thing. A man of his time plays his part in the fundamental dynamic of evolution . . .

MARC: And that's a good thing, in your view.

SERGE: It's not good or bad, why do you always have to moralize, it's just the way things are.

MARC: And you, for example, you play your part in the fundamental dynamic of evolution.

SERGE: I do.

MARC: What about Yvan? . . .

YVAN: Surely not. What sort of part can an amoeba play?

SERGE: In his way, Yvan is a man of his time.

MARC: How can you tell? Not from that daub hanging over his mantelpiece!

YVAN: That is not a daub!

SERGE: It is a daub.

YVAN: It is not!

SERGE: What's the difference? Yvan represents a certain way of life, a way of thinking which is completely modern. And so do you. I'm sorry, but you're a typical man of your time. And in fact, the harder you try not to be, the more you are.

MARC: Well, that's all right then. So what's the problem?

SERGE: There's no problem, except for you, because you take pride in your desire to shut yourself off from humanity. And you'll never manage it. It's like you're in a quicksand, the more you struggle to get out of it, the deeper you sink. Now apologize to Yvan.

MARC: Yvan is a coward.

(*At this point,* YVAN *makes his decision, and exits in a rush. Slight pause.*)

SERGE: Well done.

(*Silence.*)

MARC: It wasn't a good idea to meet this evening . . . was it? . . . I'd better go as well . . .

SERGE: Maybe . . .

MARC: Right.

SERGE: You're the coward . . . attacking someone who's incapable of defending himself . . . as you well know.

MARC: You're right . . . you're right and when you put it like that, it makes me feel even worse . . . the thing is, all of a sudden, I can't understand, I have no idea what Yvan and I have in common . . . I have no idea what my relationship with him consists of.

SERGE: Yvan's always been as he is.

MARC: No. He used to be eccentric, kind of absurd . . . he was always unstable, but his eccentricity was disarming . . .

SERGE: What about me?

MARC: What about you?

SERGE: Have you any idea what you and I have in common? . . .

MARC: That's a question that could take us down a very long road . . .

SERGE: Lead on.

(Short silence.)

MARC: . . . I'm sorry I upset Yvan.

SERGE: Ah! At last you've said something approximately human . . . What makes it worse is that the daub he has hanging over his mantelpiece was I'm afraid painted by his father.

MARC: Was it? Shit.

SERGE: Yes . . .

MARC: But you said . . .

SERGE: Yes, yes, but I remembered as soon as I'd said it.

MARC: Oh, shit . . .

SERGE: Mm . . .

(Slight pause.
        The doorbell rings. SERGE *goes to answer it.* YVAN *enters immediately, talking as he arrives, as before.)*

YVAN: Yvan returns! The lift was full, I plunged off down the stairs, clattering all the way down thinking, a coward, an amoeba, no substance, I thought I'll come back with a gun and blow his head off, then he'll see how flabby and obsequious I am, I got to the ground floor and I said to myself, listen, mate, you haven't been in therapy for six years to finish up shooting your best friend and you haven't been in therapy for six years without learning that some deep malaise must lie behind his insane aggression, so I relaunch myself, telling myself as I mount the penitential stair, this is a cry for help. I have to help Marc if it's the last thing I do . . . In fact the other day I discussed you both with Finkelzohn . . .

SERGE: You discussed us with Finkelzohn?

YVAN: I discuss everything with Finkelzohn.

SERGE: And why exactly were you discussing us?

MARC: I forbid you to discuss me with that arsehole.

YVAN: You're in no position to forbid me anything.

SERGE: Why were you discussing us?

YVAN: I knew your relationship was under strain and I wanted Finkelzohn to explain . . .

SERGE: And what did the bastard say?

YVAN: He said something rather amusing . . .

MARC: They're allowed to give their opinions?

YVAN: No, they never give their opinions, but this time he did give his opinion, he even made a ges-

ture and he never makes a gesture, he's always rigid, I sometimes say to him, for God's sake, move about a bit! . . .

SERGE: All right, what did he say?

MARC: Who gives a fuck what he said?

SERGE: What did he say?

MARC: What possible interest could we have in what he said?

SERGE: I want to know what the bastard said, all right? Shit!

(YVAN reaches into his jacket pocket.)

YVAN: You want to know? . . .

(He fetches out a piece of folded paper.)

MARC: You took notes?

YVAN *(unfolding it)*: I wrote it down because it was complicated . . . Shall I read it to you?

SERGE: Go on.

YVAN: . . . 'If I'm who I am because I'm who I am and you're who you are because you're who you are, then I'm who I am and you're who you are. If, on the other hand, I'm who I am because you're who you are, and if you're who you are because I'm who I am, then I'm not who I am and you're not who you are . . .'
        You see why I had to write it down.

(Short silence.)

MARC: How much do you pay this man?

YVAN: Four hundred francs a session, twice a week.

MARC: Great.

SERGE: And in cash. I found something out, they don't allow you to pay by cheque. Freud said you have to feel the banknotes as they slip through your fingers.

MARC: What a lucky man you are, to be getting the benefit of this fellow's experience.

SERGE: Absolutely! . . . We'd really appreciate it if you'd copy that out for us.

MARC: Yes. It's bound to come in handy.

(YVAN carefully refolds the piece of paper.)

YVAN: You're wrong. It's very profound.

MARC: If it's because of him you've come back to turn the other cheek, you should be grateful to him. He's turned you into a pudding, but you're happy, that's all that counts.

YVAN: *(to* SERGE*)* And all this because he doesn't want to believe I like your Antrios.

SERGE: I don't give a fuck what you think of it. Either of you.

YVAN: The more I see it, the more I like it, honestly.

SERGE: Let's stop talking about the painting, shall we; once and for all. I have no interest in discussing it further.

MARC: Why are you so touchy?

SERGE: I am not touchy, Marc. You've told us what you think. Fine. The subject is closed.

MARC: You're getting upset.

SERGE: I am not getting upset. I'm exhausted.

MARC: See, if you're touchy about it, it means you're too caught up in other people's opinions . . .

SERGE: I'm exhausted, Marc. This is completely pointless . . . To tell you the truth, I'm quite close to getting bored with the pair of you.

YVAN: Let's go and eat.

SERGE: You go, why don't you go off together?

YVAN: No! It's so rare the three of us are together.

SERGE: Just as well, by the look of it.

YVAN: I don't understand what's going on. Can't we just calm down? There's no reason to insult each other, especially over a painting.

SERGE: You realize all this 'calm down' and behaving like the vicar is just adding fuel to the fire! Is this something new?

YVAN: I will not be undermined.

MARC: This is most impressive. Perhaps I should go to Finkelzohn! . . .

YVAN: You can't. There are no vacancies.
What's that you're eating?

MARC: Gelsemium.

YVAN: I've given in to the logic of events, marriage, children, death. Stationery. What can go wrong?

(Moved by a sudden impulse, SERGE *picks up the Antrios and takes it back where he found it, in the next room. He returns immediately.)*

MARC: We're not worthy to look at it . . .

SERGE: Exactly.

MARC: Or are you afraid, if it stays in my presence, you'll finish up looking at it through my eyes? . . .

SERGE: No. You know what Paul Valéry° says? And I'd go quite a bit further.

MARC: I don't give a fuck what Paul Valéry says.

SERGE: You've gone off Paul Valéry?

MARC: Don't quote Paul Valéry at me.

SERGE: But you used to love Paul Valéry.

MARC: I don't give a fuck what Paul Valéry says.

SERGE: But I discovered him through you. You're the one who put me on to Paul Valéry.

MARC: Don't quote Paul Valéry at me, I don't give a fuck what Paul Valéry says.

SERGE: What do you give a fuck about?

MARC: I give a fuck about you buying that painting.
I give a fuck about you spending two hundred grand on that piece of shit.

YVAN: Don't start again, Marc!

SERGE: I'm going to tell you what I give a fuck about— since everyone is coming clean—I give a fuck

about your sniggering and insinuations, your suggestion that I also think this picture is a grotesque joke. You've denied that I could feel a genuine attachment to it. You've tried to set up some kind of loathsome complicity between us. And that's what's made me feel, Marc, to repeat your expression, that we have less and less in common recently, your perpetual display of suspicion.

MARC: It's true I can't imagine you genuinely loving that painting.

YVAN: But why?

MARC: Because I love Serge and I can't love the Serge who's capable of buying that painting.

SERGE: Why do you say, buying, why don't you say, loving?

MARC: Because I can't say loving, I can't believe loving.

SERGE: So why would I buy it, if I didn't love it?

MARC: That's the nub of the question.

SERGE *(to* YVAN*):* See how smug he is! All I'm doing is teasing him, and his answer is this serenely pompous heavy hint! . . . *(to* MARC*)* And it never crossed your mind for a second, however improbable it might seem, that I might really love it and that your vicious, inflexible opinions and your disgusting assumption of complicity might be hurtful to me?

MARC: No.

SERGE: When you asked me what I thought of Paula— a girl who once spent an entire dinner party maintaining Elhers Danlos's syndrome could be cured homeopathically—did I say I found her ugly, repellent and charmless? I could have done.

MARC: Is that what you think of Paula?

SERGE: What's your theory?

YVAN: No, of course he doesn't think that! You couldn't possibly think that of Paula!

MARC: Answer me.

SERGE: You see the effect you can have!

MARC: Do you think what you just said about Paula?

SERGE: Worse, actually.

YVAN: No!

MARC: Worse, Serge? Worse than repellent? Will you explain how someone can be worse than repellent?

SERGE: Aha! When it's something that concerns you personally, I see words can bite a little deeper! . . .

MARC: Serge, will you explain how someone can be worse than repellent . . .

SERGE: No need to take that frosty tone. Perhaps it's— let me try and answer you—perhaps it's the way she waves away cigarette smoke.

MARC: The way she waves away cigarette smoke . . .

SERGE: Yes. The way she waves away cigarette smoke. What appears to you a gesture of no significance, what you think of as a harmless gesture is in fact the opposite, and the way she waves away cigarette smoke sits right at the heart of her repellentness.

Paul Valéry, French symbolist poet (1871–1945).

MARC: You're speaking to me of Paula, the woman who shares my life, in these intolerable terms, because you disapprove of her method of waving away cigarette smoke? . . .

SERGE: That's right. Her method of waving away cigarette smoke condemns her out of hand.

MARC: Serge, before I completely lose control, you'd better explain yourself. This is very serious, what you're doing.

SERGE: A normal woman would say, I'm sorry, I find the smoke a bit uncomfortable, would you mind moving your ashtray, but not her, she doesn't deign to speak, she describes her contempt in the air with this calculated gesture, wearily malicious, this hand movement she imagines is imperceptible, the implication of which is to say, go on, smoke, smoke, it's pathetic but what's the point of calling attention to it, which means you can't tell if it's you or your cigarette that's getting up her nose.

YVAN: You're exaggerating!

SERGE: You notice he doesn't say I'm wrong, he says I'm exaggerating, but he doesn't say I'm wrong. Her method of waving away cigarette smoke reveals a cold, condescending and narrow-minded nature. Just what you're in the process of acquiring yourself. It's a shame, Marc, it's a real shame you've taken up with such a life-denying woman . . .

YVAN: Paula is not life-denying! . . .

MARC: Take back everything you've just said, Serge.

SERGE: No.

YVAN: Yes, you must!

MARC: Take back what you've just said . . .

YVAN: Take it back, take it back! This is ridiculous!

MARC: Serge, for the last time, I demand you take back what you've just said.

SERGE: In my view, the two of you are an aberration. A pair of fossils.

(MARC *throws himself at* SERGE. YVAN *rushes forward to get between them.*)

MARC *(to* YVAN*)*: Get off! . . .

SERGE *(to* YVAN*)*: Mind your own business! . . .

(*A kind of bizarre struggle ensues, very short, which ends with a blow mistakenly landing on* YVAN.)

YVAN: Oh, shit! . . . Oh, shit! . . .

SERGE: Show me, show me . . .

(YVAN *is groaning. More than is necessary, it would seem.*)

Come on, show me! . . . That's all right . . . it's nothing . . . Wait a minute . . .

(*He goes out and comes back with a compress.*)

There you are, hold that on it for a while.

YVAN: . . . You're complete freaks, both of you. Two normal men gone completely insane!

SERGE: Don't get excited.

YVAN: That really hurt! . . . If I find out you've burst my eardrum! . . .

SERGE: Of course not.

YVAN: How do you know? You're not ear, nose and throat! . . . Two old friends, educated people! . . .

SERGE: Go on, calm down.

YVAN: You can't demolish someone because you don't like her method of waving away cigarette smoke! . . .

SERGE: Yes, you can.

YVAN: But it doesn't make any sense!

SERGE: What do you know about sense?

YVAN: That's right, attack me, keep attacking me! . . . I could be haemorrhaging internally, I've just seen a mouse running past! . . .

SERGE: It's a rat.

YVAN: A rat?

SERGE: He comes and goes.

YVAN: You have a rat?!

SERGE: Don't take the compress away, leave it where it is.

YVAN: What's the matter with you? . . . What's happened between you? Something must have happened for you to go this demented.

SERGE: I've bought a work of art which makes Marc uncomfortable.

YVAN: You're starting again! . . . You're in a downward spiral, both of you, you can't stop yourselves . . . It's like me and Yvonne. The most pathological relationship you can imagine!

SERGE: Who's Yvonne?

YVAN: My step-mother!

SERGE: It's a long time since you mentioned her.

(*Brief silence.*)

MARC: Why didn't you tell me right away what you thought about Paula?

SERGE: I didn't want to upset you.

MARC: No, no, no . . .

SERGE: What do you mean, no, no, no? . . .

MARC: No.
When I asked you what you thought of Paula, what you said was: she's a perfect match for you.

SERGE: Yes . . .

MARC: Which sounded quite positive, coming from you.

SERGE: Sure. . . .

MARC: Given the state you were in at the time.

SERGE: All right, what are you trying to prove?

MARC: But today, your assessment of Paula, or in other words me, is far harsher.

SERGE: . . . I don't understand.

MARC: Of course you understand.

SERGE: I don't.

MARC: Since I can no longer support you in your frenzied, though recent, craving for novelty, I've become 'condescending,' 'narrow-minded' . . . 'fossilized'. . .

YVAN: I'm in agony! It's like a corkscrew drilling through my brain!

SERGE: Have a drop of brandy.

YVAN: What do you think? . . . If something's shaken loose in my brain, don't you think alcohol's a bit of a risk?

SERGE: Would you like an aspirin?

YVAN: I'm not sure aspirin agrees with me . . .

SERGE: Then what the hell do you want?

YVAN: Don't worry about me. Carry on with your preposterous conversation, don't pay any attention to me.

MARC: Easier said than done.

YVAN: You might squeeze out a drop of compassion. But no.

SERGE: I don't mind your spending time with Paula. I don't resent you being with Paula.

MARC: You've no reason to resent it.

SERGE: But you . . . you resent me . . . well, I was about to say, for being with the Antrios!

MARC: Yes!

SERGE: I'm missing something here.

MARC: I didn't replace you with Paula.

SERGE: Are you saying, I replaced you with the Antrios?

MARC: Yes.

SERGE: . . . I replaced you with the Antrios?

MARC: Yes. With the Antrios . . . and all it implies.

SERGE (to YVAN): Do you understand what he's talking about?

YVAN: I couldn't care less, you're both insane.

MARC: In my time, you'd never have bought that picture.

SERGE: What's that supposed to mean, in your time?

MARC: The time you made a distinction between me and other people, when you judged things by my standards.

SERGE: Was there such a time?

MARC: That's just cruel. And petty.

SERGE: No, I assure you, I'm staggered.

MARC: And if Yvan hadn't turned into such a sponge, he'd back me up.

YVAN: Go on, that's right, I've told you, it's water off a duck's back.

MARC (to SERGE): There was a time you were proud to be my friend . . . You congratulated yourself on my peculiarity, on my taste for standing apart. You enjoyed exhibiting me untamed to your circle, you, whose life was so normal. I was your alibi. But . . . eventually, I suppose, that sort of affection dries up . . . Belatedly, you claim your independence.

SERGE: 'Belatedly' is nice.

MARC: But I detest your independence. Its violence. You've abandoned me. I've been betrayed. As far as I'm concerned, you're a traitor.

(Silence.)

SERGE (to YVAN): . . . If I understand correctly, he was my mentor! . . .

(YVAN doesn't respond. MARC stares at him contemptuously. Slight pause.)

. . . And if I loved you as my mentor . . . what was the nature of your feelings?

MARC: You can guess.

SERGE: Yes, yes, but I want to hear you say it.

MARC: . . . I enjoyed your admiration. I was flattered. I was always grateful to you for thinking of me as a man apart. I even thought being a man apart was a somehow superior condition, until one day you pointed out to me that it wasn't.

SERGE: This is very alarming.

MARC: It's the truth.

SERGE: What a disaster . . . !

MARC: Yes, what a disaster!

SERGE: What a disaster!

MARC: Especially for me . . . Whereas you've found a new family. Your penchant for idolatry has unearthed new objects of worship. The Artist! . . . Deconstruction!

(Short silence.)

YVAN: What is deconstruction? . . .

MARC: You don't know about deconstruction? . . . Ask Serge, he's very much on top of the subject . . . (to SERGE) To convince me some ridiculous artwork is comprehensible, you pick a phrase from Builders' Weekly . . . Oh, you're smiling! You see, when you smile like that, I think there's still some hope, like an idiot . . .

YVAN: Why don't you make up? And let's spend an enjoyable evening, all this is ludicrous!

MARC: . . . It's my fault. We haven't seen much of one another recently. I've been away and you started mixing with the great and the good . . . the Ropses . . . the Desprez-Couderts . . . that dentist, Guy Hallié . . . he's the one who . . .

SERGE: No, no, no, no, not at all, he's from another world, he only likes conceptual Art . . .

MARC: It's all the same thing.

SERGE: No, it's not all the same thing.

MARC: You see, more evidence of how I let you slip away . . . now when we talk we can't even make ourselves understood.

SERGE: I had no idea whatsoever—really, it's come as a complete surprise—the extent to which I was under your influence and in your control.

MARC: Not in my control, as it turns out . . . You

should never leave your friends unchaperoned. Your friends need to be chaperoned, otherwise they'll get away . . .

Look at poor Yvan, whose chaotic behaviour used to delight us, we've allowed him to become this timid stationer . . . Practically married . . . He brought us his originality and now he's making every effort to piss it away.

SERGE: Us! He brought us! Do you realize what you're saying? Everything has to revolve around you! Why can't you learn to love people for themselves, Marc?

MARC: What does that mean, for themselves?

SERGE: For what they are.

MARC: But what are they?! What are they?! . . .
Apart from my faith in them? . . .

I'm desperate to find a friend who has some kind of prior existence. So far, I've had no luck. I've had to mould you . . . But you see, it never works. There comes a day when your creature has dinner with the Desprez-Couderts and, to confirm his new status, goes off and buys a white painting.

(Silence.)

SERGE: So here we are at the end of a fifteen-year friendship . . .

MARC: Yes . . .

YVAN: Pathetic . . .

MARC: You see, if we'd only managed to have a normal discussion, that is, if I'd have been able to put my point of view without losing my temper . . .

SERGE: Well? . . .

MARC: Nothing . . .

SERGE: Yes. Go on. Why can't we exchange one single dispassionate word?

MARC: . . . I don't believe in the values which dominate contemporary Art. The rule of novelty. The rule of surprise.

Surprise is dead meat, Serge. No sooner conceived than dead.

SERGE: All right. So?

MARC: That's all.

Except that my appeal to you has always been my surprise value.

SERGE: What are you talking about?

MARC: A surprise which has lasted quite some time, I'll admit.

YVAN: Finkelzohn is a genius.

I told you he'd understood the whole thing!

MARC: I'd prefer it if you stopped refereeing, Yvan, and stopped imagining you're not fully implicated in this conversation.

YVAN: You want to implicate me, I refuse, what's it to do with me? I've already got a burst eardrum, you work things out for yourselves!

MARC: Perhaps he does have a burst eardrum. I hit him very hard.

(SERGE sniggers.)

SERGE: Please, stop boasting.

MARC: See, Yvan, what I can't bear about you at the moment—quite apart from what I've already told you—is your urge to put Serge and me on the same level. You would like us to be equal. To indulge your cowardice. Talking on an equal footing, equal the way you thought of us when we were friends. But we never were equal, Yvan. You have to choose.

YVAN: I have chosen.

MARC: Excellent.

SERGE: I don't need a supporter.

MARC: You're not going to turn the poor boy down?

YVAN: Why do we see each other, if we hate each other? It's obvious we do hate each other! Or rather, I don't hate you, but you hate each other! And you hate me! So why do we see each other? . . . I was looking forward to a relaxing evening after a ridiculously fraught week, meeting my two best friends, going to the cinema, having a laugh, getting away from all these dramas . . .

SERGE: Are you aware that you've talked about nothing but yourself?

YVAN: Well, who are you talking about? Everybody talks about themselves!

SERGE: You fuck up our evening, you . . .

YVAN: I fuck up your evening?! . . .

SERGE: Yes.

YVAN: I fuck up your evening?! I?! I fuck up your evening?!

MARC: All right, don't get excited!

YVAN: You're saying it's me who's fucked up your evening?! . . .

SERGE: How many more times are you going to say it?

YVAN: Just answer the question, are you saying it's me who's fucked up your evening?! . . .

MARC: You arrive three-quarters of an hour late, you don't apologize, you deluge us with your domestic woes . . .

SERGE: And your inertia, your sheer neutral spectator's inertia has lured Marc and me into the worst excesses.

YVAN: You as well! You're starting as well?

SERGE: Yes, because on this subject I'm entirely in agreement with him. You create the conditions of conflict.

MARC: You've been piping up with this finicky, subservient voice of reason ever since you arrived, it's intolerable.

YVAN: You know I could burst into tears . . . I could start crying right now . . . I'm very close to tears.

MARC: Cry.

SERGE: Cry.

YVAN: Cry! You're telling me to cry!

MARC: You've every reason to cry, you're marrying a gorgon, you're losing your two best friends . . .

YVAN: That's it then, is it, it's all over!

MARC: You said it yourself, what's the point of seeing each other, if we hate each other?

YVAN: What about my wedding?! You're my witnesses, remember?

SERGE: Find someone else.

YVAN: I can't! You're on the invitation!

MARC: You can choose someone else at the last minute.

YVAN: You're not allowed to!

SERGE: Of course you are!

YVAN: You're not! . . .

MARC: Don't panic, we'll come.

SERGE: But what you ought to do is cancel the wedding.

MARC: He's right.

YVAN: Oh, shit! What have I ever done to you? Shit!

(*He bursts into tears.*
Time passes.)

It's brutal what you're doing! You could have had your fight after the 12th, but no, you're determined to ruin my wedding, a wedding which is already a catastrophe, which has made me lose half a stone and now you're completely buggering it up! The only two people whose presence guaranteed some spark of satisfaction are determined to destroy one another, just my luck! . . . (*to* MARC) You think I like packs of filofax paper or rolls of sellotape,° you think any normal man wakes up one day desperate to sell expandable document wallets? . . . What am I supposed to do? I pissed around for forty years, I made you laugh, oh, yes, wonderful, I made all my friends laugh their heads off playing the fool, but come the evening, who was left solitary as a rat? Who crawled back into his hole every evening all on his own? This buffoon, dying of loneliness, who'd switch on anything that talks and who does he find on the answering machine? His mother. His mother. And his mother.

(*A short silence.*)

MARC: Don't get yourself in such a state.

YVAN: Don't get yourself in such a state! Who got me in this state in the first place? Look at me—I don't have your refined sensibilities. I'm a lightweight. I have no opinions.

---

sellotape, cellophane tape, Scotch tape.

MARC: Calm down . . .

YVAN: Don't tell me to calm down! What possible reason do I have to calm down, are you trying to drive me demented, telling me to calm down? Calm down's the worst thing you can say to someone who's lost his calm! I'm not like you, I don't want to be an authority figure, I don't want to be a point of reference, I don't want to be self-sufficient, I just want to be your friend Yvan the joker! Yvan the joker!

(*Silence.*)

SERGE: Could we try to steer clear of pathos? . . .

YVAN: I've finished.
     Haven't you got any nibbles? Anything, just to stop from passing out.

SERGE: I have some olives.

YVAN: Hand them over.

(SERGE *reaches for a little bowl of olives and hands it to him.*)

SERGE (*to* MARC): Want some?

(MARC *nods.* YVAN *hands him the bowl. They eat olives.*)

YVAN: Is there somewhere to put the . . .

SERGE: Yes.

(*He fetches a saucer and puts it on the table.*
Pause.)

YVAN (*still eating olives*): . . . To think we've reached these extremes . . . Apocalypse because of a white square . . .

SERGE: It is not white.

YVAN: A piece of white shit! . . .

(*He's seized by uncontrollable laughter.*)

That's what it is, a piece of white shit! . . . Let's face it, mate . . . What you've bought is insane! . . .

(MARC *laughs, caught up by* YVAN'*s extravagance.* SERGE *leaves the room. He returns immediately with the Antrios.*)

SERGE: Do you have one of your famous felt-tips? . . .

YVAN: What for? . . . You're not going to draw on the painting.

SERGE: Do you or don't you?

YVAN: Just a minute . . . (*He goes through the pockets of his jacket.*) Yes . . . A blue one . . .

SERGE: Give it to me.

(YVAN *hands the felt-tip to* SERGE.
     SERGE *takes the felt-tip, pulls the top off it, examines the tip for a moment, puts the top back on.*
     He looks up at MARC *and throws him the felt-tip.* MARC *catches it.*
     Slight pause.)

(*to* MARC) Go on.

(Silence.)

Go on!

(MARC approaches the painting . . .
He looks at SERGE . . .
Then he takes the top off the felt-tip.)

YVAN: You're not going to do it! . . .

(MARC is looking at SERGE.)

SERGE: Come on.

YVAN: You're raving mad, both of you!

(MARC leans towards the painting.
Under YVAN's horrified gaze, he draws the felt-tip along
one of the diagonal scars. SERGE remains impassive.
Then, carefully, on this slope, MARC draws a little skier
with a woolly hat.
When he's finished, he straightens up and contemplates
his work.
SERGE remains adamantine.°
YVAN is as if turned to stone.
Silence.)

SERGE: Well, I'm starving.
Shall we eat?

(MARC tries a smile. He puts the top back on and playfully
throws the pen to YVAN, who catches it.)

(At SERGE's.
At the back, hanging on the wall, the Antrios. Standing
in front of the canvas, MARC is holding a basin of water,
into which SERGE is dipping a little piece of cloth. MARC
has rolled up his sleeves and SERGE is wearing a little
builder's apron which is too short for him. Round about are
various cleaning products, bottles of white spirit and stain
remover, rags and sponges. Moving very delicately, SERGE
puts the finishing touch to the cleaning of the painting.
The Antrios is as white as ever. MARC puts down the
basin and looks at the painting. SERGE turns to YVAN,
who's sitting off to one side. YVAN nods approvingly.
SERGE steps back and contemplates the picture in his turn.
Silence.)

YVAN *(as if alone, speaking in a slightly muffled voice):* . . .
The day after the wedding, at the Montparnasse
cemetery Catherine put her wedding bouquet
and a little bag of sugared almonds on her mother's
grave. I slipped away to cry behind a monument
and in the evening, thinking again about this
touching tribute, I started silently sobbing in my
bed. I absolutely must speak to Finkelzohn about
my tendency to cry, I cry all the time, it's not normal for someone my age. It started, or at least

clearly revealed itself at Serge's, the evening of
the white painting. After Serge, in an act of pure
madness, had demonstrated to Marc that he
cared more about him than he did about his
painting, we went and had dinner, chez Emile.
Over dinner, Serge and Marc took the decision to
try to rebuild a relationship destroyed by word
and deed. At a certain moment, one of them used
the expression 'trial period' and I burst into tears.

This expression, 'trial period,' applied to our
friendship, set off in me an uncontrollable and
ridiculous convulsion.

In fact I can no longer bear any kind of rational
argument, nothing formative in the world, nothing great or beautiful in the world has ever been
born of rational argument.

(Pause.
SERGE dries his hands. He goes to empty the basin of
water then puts away all the cleaning products, until
there's no sign left of domestic activity. Once again he looks
at his painting. Then he turns and advances towards the
audience.)

SERGE: When Marc and I succeeded in obliterating
the skier, with the aid of Swiss soap with added ox
gall, recommended by Paula, I looked at the
Antrios and turned to Marc:
'Did you know ink from felt-tips was washable?'
'No,' Marc said . . . 'No . . . did you?'
'No,' I said, very fast, lying. I came within an
inch of saying, yes, I did know. But how could I
have launched our trial period with such a disappointing admission? . . . On the other hand, was
it right to start with a lie? . . . A lie! Let's be reasonable. Why am I so absurdly virtuous? Why does
my relationship with Marc have to be so complicated? . . .

(Gradually, the light begins to narrow down on the Antrios.
MARC approaches the painting.)

MARC: Under the white clouds, the snow is falling.
You can't see the white clouds, or the snow.
Or the cold, or the white glow of the earth.
A solitary man glides downhill on his skis.
The snow is falling.
It falls until the man disappears back into the
landscape.
My friend Serge, who's one of my oldest
friends, has bought a painting.
It's a canvas about five foot by four.
It represents a man who moves across a space
and disappears.

---

adamantine, unyielding.

Figure 1. Yvan (Ken Stott, *left*) and Marc (Albert Finney, *seated right*) look at the painting that Serge (Tom Courtenay, *center*) has purchased in the Wyndham's Theatre production of *"Art,"* directed by Matthew Warchus, 1996. (Photograph: Donald Cooper/Photostage.)

Figure 2. Yvan's attempt to stop a fight between Serge and Marc ends up with Yvan (Ken Stott, *towel to ear*) getting hit by mistake. Marc (Albert Finney, *right*) extends an apologetic hand while Serge (Tom Courtenay, *left*) remains aloof in the 1996 production. (Photograph: Donald Cooper/ Photostage.)

Figure 3. Yvan (Ken Stott) stares in amazement at Serge (Tom Courtenay), who has just handed a felt-tip pen to Marc (Albert Finney, *in front of painting*) in the 1996 production. (Photograph: Donald Cooper/Photostage.)

Staging of *"Art"*

How pleasing it is to welcome a play about ideas into the West End. For Yasmina Reza's *"Art"* not only brings to the stage a topical debate, it makes it invigorating, touching and finally disturbing.

This dark comedy, translated from the French by Christopher Hampton in sparkling form, explores its themes through a rift between friends. Battle commences when Marc tells us that his friend, Serge, has bought a piece of modern art: a plain white square by a fashionable artist for which he has forked out 200,000 francs. Marc is surprisingly incensed by his purchase—taken aback by his friend's folly, but even more astonished at his own vehement response. A feud develops between the two, initially purely about art, opposing those two adversaries, the traditionalists and the modernists. Marc, who favours classical, figurative paintings, foams at the very word "deconstruction" and pours ridicule on Serge's attachment to his picture and all things modern.

But, like the painting, the play is deceptive. Starting out as a comedy, raising easy laughs at the expense of abstract art, it gradually becomes darker and darker. Serge and Marc move into murkier territory and start hacking at the very roots of their friendship—to the consternation of their mutual friend Yvan, who is buffeted to and fro by the floods of bitterness and contempt that the two unleash on one another. Stealthily Reza shifts the ground until she is exploring the price, not of paintings, but of companionship, and the value of telling the truth.

Since it features only three characters and never wanders from its precipitous path, the play demands an expert production. It is served here by three masterly performances from Albert Finney, Tom Courtenay and Ken Stott.

The three play off each other like a jazz trio; their different styles are beautifully counterpointed in Matthew Warchus's production.

Finney, as the sceptical Marc, fills the stage as only Finney can. He plants himself before Serge's painting, squaring up to this assault on his values like a bull sizing up an opponent. It is in the detail that his performance is most enjoyable, twitching with effort as he tries to control his temper and digs in his pockets for homeopathic calming remedies. Courtenay, meanwhile, is suave and urbane as Serge, but with a capricious streak that is first delightful and then menacing. His enthusiasm for his artwork, which bursts out as sudden boyish bouts of dancing on the spot, gives way to a cold determination as he realises that he and his friend have painted themselves into a corner.

But it is to Ken Stott as Yvan that the highest honours go. Playing the henpecked little loser, squeezed into a career selling stationery and heading for a meaningless marriage, he is initially very funny. His big speech, when he describes the nightmare of compiling his wedding invitations, is a tour de force, but as his friends' destructive behaviour reveals to him the emptiness of his own life, he seems to cave in before your eyes, becoming the real casualty of the evening. It is a beautifully controlled and compact performance that matches the play's journey from light to dark and back.

Modern art, right? Load of rubbish, right? Emperor's new clothes, right? Conspiracy of affectation, right? Heard all that before? On and off, since about 1900? So hear it again. *"Art"* is a prize-winning new play by Yasmina Reza (on at Wyndham's) translated from the French by Christopher Hampton. In it a respectable bourgeois buys a picture. But here's the thing: it's just white. White on white. With some streaks of off-white. And he paid 200,000 francs for it. And he actually claims to like it.

Thus the fun begins—and so it pretty much continues. Tom Courtenay is the earnest buyer and Albert

Finney his friend, a man of downright common sense. Many's the moment they stand before the offending object, one in absorbed appreciation, the other in stark disbelief—and wait for the laughs to roll. If this sort of painting is, to you, the most risible thing in the world, then *"Art"* is your kind of comedy. If, though, you feel the joke has lost some of its sparkle in the course of the century, then the play's unstinting incitements to guffaw at the picture, and anyone who could admire it, make this 90 minute one-acter into a weary while.

There are of course things to be said in favour of minimalist abstraction, and things to be said against it. We don't hear either. We never learn why Courtenay's character likes the work. We have only the Finney fellow's blunt certainty that it is "shit," and his conviction that an old mate has "let himself be ripped off by modern art." When a third old friend (Ken Stott) gets roped in as uneasy mediator, you begin to wonder why it is such a bone of contention anyway. And will the white canvas jokes never end?

About half-way, *"Art"* takes stock and suddenly decides that, more than a skit on "modern art," it's going to get a bit serious and become a play about the death of friendship. It then finds it has established no characters or relationships, and hastily fits out the threesome with some background life (e.g., they all dislike each other's wives/fiancées), so they can have The Big Row. A neat visual gag ties things up. Curtain.

This quite arbitrary procedure must account for the weird detachment of the performances. Courtenay does an unpunctuated sing-song throughout (think of Derek Nimmo in *Just a Minute*), while Finney enjoys himself heartily with a bluff and burly read-through. Stott, the diffident, appeasing man-in-the-middle, corners any comedy that happens to be around. This is heavy casting for a dramatic idea whose ideal home is half an hour of *Seinfeld*. Mark Thompson's set, by contrast, is a noble thing, a soaring off-white interior, very minimal, very abstract, and deserving much more substantial business.

PAULA VOGEL

Writing in 1995 about the pornography and violence in her play *Hot 'N' Throbbing*, Paula Vogel noted that the term *obscene* originates from the Greek word meaning *offstage* and that violence in Greek theater happened offstage: "Platforms on wheels brought the bodies onstage to show the outcome, rather than the act." Vogel's plays bring the "obscene" back to the stage, not for the sake of violence or sexual titillation, but, in her words, "to confront the disturbing questions of our time. I remain scared of the dark—scared of our darkness—and I seek a communal light in the darkness of our theatres." Thus her plays focus on problems ranging from AIDS to prostitution to dysfunctional families to pedophilia. Though her subject matter is serious, the tone of her plays is far from grim. Vogel's sharp ear for the clichés of contemporary culture lures an audience into laughter, even as she reveals alarming realities behind the seemingly respectable surfaces of her characters. *Desdemona: A Play about a Handkerchief* (1977) rewrites *Othello* to portray Desdemona as a snobbish, swearing, and sexually transgressive woman; the five elderly women sitting on a bench in *The Oldest Profession* (1981) turn out to be prostitutes; and *The Mineola Twins* (1995) presents almost identical twins who are completely opposite in terms of personal and political values.

Paula Vogel's background is likewise full of contrasts. Her father was Jewish, her mother Catholic. The marriage broke up when Paula was eleven, and her mother moved the family from one apartment to another. Vogel received a B.A. from Catholic University (1974) and spent three years at Cornell University, where she worked on, but did not complete, a Ph.D. in theater, although she would later return to teach at Cornell (1979–82). In 1985, she became head of the M.F.A. writing program at Brown University, where she still teaches. Yet she felt just then that her "playwriting career was going nowhere," although her first play, *Meg*, had received the American College Theater Festival Award for best new play (1977), and two other plays had been produced Off-Broadway in 1981. Vogel generously credits her students with inspiring her. "Because I wasn't being produced, I wasn't being listened to. But my students listened, and I listened to them."

Listening to her students and to her own theatrical convictions evidently led her toward a very imaginative form of drama in *And Baby Makes Seven* (1984), a play that also had its roots in her personal experience: "I went through planning having a baby with my best friend and my lover at the time, and when it fell through I wrote this play." It turned out to be a wildly comic tour-de-force for three actors, two of whom play adult women, Anna and Ruth, who in turn have created three imaginary young male children. The play centers on a lesbian couple who have created imaginary children but—once they are able to have a real child—decide that they must get rid of their imaginary offspring. The play raises a series of provocative questions about parents and children, lesbian lovers, lesbian women and gay men, and the very thin, perhaps porous, barrier between illusion and reality. In a series of harrowing scenes, each child is "killed"; one dies from rabies, one is thrown from a fire escape, and the last commits suicide by running onto his sword, as if in a Shakespeare play. Only when the imaginary children are dead can the real one be born.

Vogel's haunting transformation of personal experience into highly imaginative drama is even more strikingly evident in *The Baltimore Waltz* (1992), a play inspired by her late brother Carl, who died of pneumonia (and AIDS) in 1988. Carl had invited her to go to Europe with him in 1986, but she refused. So in the aftermath of his death she took that journey "to a Europe that exists only in the imagination," a Europe consisting of scraps of basic phrases in Dutch, French, and German, and highly indebted to the 1950 film, *The Third Man,* a thriller set in postwar Vienna. Vogel transforms what might have been a sentimental story into a surrealist fantasy. She does so in part by creating a nonrealistic world, and by switching the characters so that not Carl but his sister Anna (Vogel's middle name is Anne) is the patient. As Anna and Carl travel to Vienna to find a strange doctor and a strange cure, all of the other characters are played by a single actor (the third man). The play's thirty short scenes are often introduced either by a phrase from a language lesson or by a musical introduction, and characters talk directly to the audience, as well as to each other. Vogel's production notes emphasize the play's presentational style, calling for lighting that is "highly stylized, lush, dark and imaginative" and music that reflects "every cliché of the European experience as imagined by Hollywood. Only in the last scene do the stage lights become "for the first time, harsh, stark and white," as Anna confronts the fact that Carl has died.

Vogel's openness about her personal experience and her sexuality is clearly part of her identity, both politically and professionally. When her 1997 play *How I Learned to Drive* won the Pulitzer Prize, one headline ran "Lesbian wins Pulitzer," since Vogel was the first openly lesbian writer so honored. But, as Vogel makes clear in the interview with Arthur Holmberg (reprinted following the play), her personal sexuality in no way limits her awareness that both men and women are responsible for behavior that can be called misogynistic or homophobic. Indeed, Vogel admits that she "was taught to hate gays" and "taught to hate women." Out of her awareness of labels and stereotypes, an awareness perhaps made more vivid by being gay and having a gay brother, she moves to a larger cultural reality—"how this culture sexualizes children." Her achievement in *How I Learned to Drive* is to make that reality specific through the mosaic of scenes that depict the complex relationship between Li'l Bit, the narrator and central character, and her Uncle Peck, the man who teaches her to drive, the man who held her in his hand when she was a baby and who has loved her ever since, and the man who seduces her. Indeed, as reviewers and Vogel herself have noted, the inspiration for the play is Vladimir Nabokov's novel *Lolita,* except that the play is told from the point of view of the girl. Li'l Bit controls the play as narrator, and the scenes take place at different stages of her life, beginning when she is seventeen, and moving back to the first sexual encounter with Uncle Peck when she is just eleven. Though she is Peck's victim, she is equally the product of the highly sexualized world in which she lives, since people both at home and at school comment frequently on her body, especially her noticeable breasts. As her defense strategies include not only flight but flirtation, she becomes complicit in the relationship with Uncle Peck.

Thus the play, and its performance, involve a series of delicate balances. Vogel's description of Peck suggests that "he should be played by an actor one might cast in the role of Atticus in *To Kill a Mockingbird*," the gentle, soft-spoken Southern lawyer who defends a black man, a role that earned Gregory Peck an Academy Award in the 1962 film version. David Morse, who created the role in the New York production, brought with him another positive role model, the good-hearted doctor he had played for six years in television's *St. Elsewhere* series. His tenderness is evident even when he is unbuttoning Li'l Bit's sweater (Figure 1) or positioning her body for the photographs he's taking of her (Figure 2). The role of Li'l Bit is written for an adult actress, not a little girl, so that when the audience sees Li'l Bit and Peck together, it sees simultaneously the consensual and the abusive qualities of the relationship. The expressions on Li'l Bit's face are the key: Mary-Louise Parker, who created the role, can be wary (Figure 1), quietly smiling (Figure 2), or enigmatically sad as she lies in bed, fully clothed, embraced by Peck (Figure 3). Vogel has commented often on her sense that the play shows not only the harm done to Li'l Bit but the gifts she receives as well: "It's abuse simultaneously with a kind of affirmation and reassurance." Such a vision may be difficult to accept, but Vogel presents the abuser and the abused with generosity, so that ultimately we recognize the pain on both sides.

HOW I LEARNED TO DRIVE

BY PAULA VOGEL

This play is dedicated to Peter Franklin.

CHARACTERS

LI'L BIT *A woman who ages forty-something to eleven years old. (See Notes on the New York Production.)*

PECK *Attractive man in his forties. Despite a few problems, he should be played by an actor one might cast in the role of Atticus in* To Kill A Mockingbird.

THE GREEK CHORUS *If possible, these three members should be able to sing three-part harmony.*

MALE GREEK CHORUS *Plays Grandfather, Waiter, High School Boys. Thirties–forties. (See Notes on the New York Production.)*

FEMALE GREEK CHORUS *Plays Mother, Aunt Mary, High School Girls. Thirty–fifty. (See Notes on the New York Production.)*

TEENAGE GREEK CHORUS *Plays Grandmother, high school girls and the voice of eleven-year-old* LI'L BIT. *Note on the casting of this actor: I would strongly recommend casting a young woman who is "of legal age," that is, twenty-one to twenty-five years old, who can look as close to eleven as possible. The contrast with the other cast members will help. If the actor is too young, the audience may feel uncomfortable. (See Notes on the New York Production.)*

PRODUCTION NOTES

I urge directors to use the Greek Chorus in staging as environment and, well, part of the family—with the exception of the Teenage Greek Chorus member who, after the last time she appears onstage, should perhaps disappear.

As For Music: Please have fun. I wrote sections of the play listening to music like Roy Orbison's "Dream Baby" and The Mamas and the Papas' "Dedicated to the One I Love." The vaudeville sections go well to the Tijuana Brass or any music that sounds like a Laugh-In *soundtrack. Other sixties music is rife with pedophilish (?) reference: the "You're Sixteen" genre hits; The Beach Boys' "Little Surfer Girl"; Gary Puckett and the Union Gap's "This Girl Is a Woman Now"; "Come Back When You Grow Up," etc.*

And whenever possible, please feel free to punctuate the action with traffic signs: "No Passing," "Slow Children," "Dangerous Curves," "One Way," and the visual signs for children, deer crossings, hills, school buses, etc. (See Notes on the New York Production.)

This script uses the notion of slides and projections, which were not used in the New York production of the play.

On Titles: Throughout the script there are bold-faced titles. In production these should be spoken in a neutral voice (the type of voice that driver education films employ). In the New York production these titles were assigned to various members of the Greek Chorus and were done live.

NOTES ON THE NEW YORK PRODUCTION

The role of Li'l Bit was originally written as a character who is forty-something. When we cast Mary-Louise Parker in the role of Li'l Bit, we cast the Greek Chorus members with younger actors as the Female Greek and the Male Greek, and cast the Teenage Greek with an older (that is, mid-twenties) actor as well. There is a great deal of flexibility in age. Directors should change the age in the last monologue for Li'l Bit ("And before you know it, I'll be thirty-five. . . .") to reflect the actor's age who is playing Li'l Bit.

(As the house lights dim, a Voice announces:)

Safety First—You and Driver Education.

(Then the sound of a key turning the ignition of a car. LI'L BIT *steps into a spotlight on the stage; "well-endowed," she is a softer-looking woman in the present time than she was at seventeen.)*

LI'L BIT: Sometimes to tell a secret, you first have to teach a lesson. We're going to start our lesson tonight on an early, warm summer evening.

In a parking lot overlooking the Beltsville Agricultural Farms in suburban Maryland.

Less than a mile away, the crumbling concrete of U.S. One wends its way past one-room revival churches, the porno drive-in, and boarded up motels with For Sale signs tumbling down.

Like I said, it's a warm summer evening.

Here on the land the Department of Agriculture owns, the smell of sleeping farm animal is thick on the air. The smells of clover and hay mix in with the smells of the leather dashboard. You can still imagine how Maryland used to be, before the malls took over. This countryside was once dotted with farmhouses—from their porches you could have witnessed the Civil War raging in the front fields.

Oh yes. There's a moon over Maryland tonight, that spills into the car where I sit beside a man old enough to be—did I mention how still the night is? Damp soil and tranquil air. It's the kind of night that makes a middle-aged man with a mortgage feel like a country boy again.

It's 1969. And I am very old, very cynical of the world, and I know it all. In short, I am seventeen years old, parking off a dark lane with a married man on an early summer night.

(Lights up on two chairs facing front—or a Buick Riviera, if you will. Waiting patiently, with a smile on his face, PECK sits sniffing the night air. LI'L BIT climbs in beside him, seventeen years old and tense. Throughout the following, the two sit facing directly front. They do not touch. Their bodies remain passive. Only their facial expressions emote.)

PECK: Ummm. I love the smell of your hair.

LI'L BIT: Uh-huh.

PECK: Oh, Lord. Ummmm. *(Beat)* A man could die happy like this.

LI'L BIT: Well, *don't.*

PECK: What shampoo is this?

LI'L BIT: Herbal Essence.

PECK: Herbal Essence. I'm gonna buy me some. Herbal Essence. And when I'm all alone in the house, I'm going to get into the bathtub, and uncap the bottle and—

LI'L BIT: —Be good.

PECK: What?

LI'L BIT: Stop being . . . bad.

PECK: What did you think I was going to say? What do you think I'm going to do with the shampoo?

LI'L BIT: I don't want to know. I don't want to hear it.

PECK: I'm going to wash my hair. That's all.

LI'L BIT: Oh.

PECK: What did you think I was going to do?

LI'L BIT: Nothing . . . I don't know. Something . . . nasty.

PECK: With shampoo? Lord, gal—your mind!

LI'L BIT: And whose fault is it?

PECK: Not mine. I've got the mind of a boy scout.

LI'L BIT: Right. A horny boy scout.

PECK: Boy scouts are always horny. What do you think the first Merit Badge is for?

LI'L BIT: There. You're going to be nasty again.

PECK: Oh, no. I'm good. Very good.

LI'L BIT: It's getting late.

PECK: Don't change the subject. I was talking about how good I am. *(Beat)* Are you ever gonna let me show you how good I am?

LI'L BIT: Don't go over the line now.

PECK: I won't. I'm not gonna do anything you don't want me to do.

LI'L BIT: That's right.

PECK: And I've been good all week.

LI'L BIT: You have?

PECK: Yes. All week. Not a single drink.

LI'L BIT: Good boy.

PECK: Do I get a reward? For not drinking?

LI'L BIT: A small one. It's getting late.

PECK: Just let me undo you. I'll do you back up.

LI'L BIT: All right. But be quick about it. *(PECK pantomimes undoing LI'L BIT's brassiere with one hand)* You know, that's amazing. The way you can undo the hooks through my blouse with one hand.

PECK: Years of practice.

LI'L BIT: You would make an incredible brain surgeon with that dexterity.

PECK: I'll bet Clyde—what's the name of the boy taking you to the prom?

LI'L BIT: Claude Souders.

PECK: Claude Souders. I'll bet it takes him two hands, lights on, and you helping him on to get to first base.

LI'L BIT: Maybe.

(Beat.)

PECK: Can I . . . kiss them? Please?

LI'L BIT: I don't know.

PECK: Don't make a grown man beg.

LI'L BIT: Just one kiss.

PECK: I'm going to lift your blouse.

LI'L BIT: It's a little cold.

(PECK laughs gently.)

PECK: That's not why you're shivering. *(They sit, perfectly still, for a long moment of silence. PECK makes gentle, concentric circles with his thumbs in the air in front of him)* How does that feel?

(LI'L BIT closes her eyes, carefully keeps her voice calm:)

LI'L BIT: It's . . . okay.

(Sacred music, organ music or a boy's choir swells beneath the following.)

PECK: I tell you, you can keep all the cathedrals of Europe. Just give me a second with these—these celestial orbs—

(PECK bows his head as if praying. But he is kissing her nipple. LI'L BIT, eyes still closed, rears back her head on the leather Buick car seat.)

LI'L BIT: Uncle Peck—we've got to go. I've got graduation rehearsal at school tomorrow morning. And you should get on home to Aunt Mary—

PECK: —All right, Li'l Bit.

LI'L BIT: —Don't call me that no more. *(Calmer)* Any more. I'm a big girl now, Uncle Peck. As you know.

(LI'L BIT *pantomimes refastening her bra behind her back.*)

PECK: That you are. Going on eighteen. Kittens will turn into cats. *(Sighs)* I live all week long for these few minutes with you—you know that?

LI'L BIT: I'll drive.

(A Voice cuts in with:)

Idling in the Neutral Gear.

(Sound of car revving cuts off the sacred music; LI'L BIT, *now an adult, rises out of the car and comes to us.)*

LI'L BIT: In most families, relatives get names like "Junior," or "Brother," or "Bubba." In my family, if we call someone "Big Papa," it's not because he's tall. In my family, folks tend to get nicknamed for their genitalia. Uncle Peck, for example. My mama's adage was "the titless wonder," and my cousin Bobby got branded for life as "B.B."

(In unison with GREEK CHORUS:*)*

LI'L BIT: For blue balls.	GREEK CHORUS: For blue balls.

FEMALE GREEK CHORUS *(As Mother)*: And of course, we were so excited to have a baby girl that when the nurse brought you in and said, "It's a girl! It's a baby girl!" I just had to see for myself. So we whipped your diapers down and parted your chubby little legs—and right between your legs there was—

*(*PECK *has come over during the above and chimes along:)*

PECK: Just a little bit.	GREEK CHORUS: Just a little bit.

FEMALE GREEK CHORUS *(As Mother)*: And when you were born, you were so tiny that you fit in Uncle Peck's outstretched hand.

*(*PECK *stretches his hand out.)*

PECK: Now that's a fact. I held you, one day old, right in this hand.

(A traffic signal is projected of a bicycle in a circle with a diagonal red slash.)

LI'L BIT: Even with my family background, I was sixteen or so before I realized that pedophilia did not mean people who loved to bicycle. . . .

(A Voice intrudes:)

Driving in First Gear.

LI'L BIT: 1969. A typical family dinner.

FEMALE GREEK CHORUS *(As Mother)*: Look, Grandma. Li'l Bit's getting to be as big in the bust as you are.

LI'L BIT: Mother! Could we please change the subject?

TEENAGE GREEK CHORUS *(As Grandmother)*: Well, I hope you are buying her some decent bras. I never had a decent bra, growing up in the Depression, and now my shoulders are just crippled—crippled from the weight hanging on my shoulders—the dents from my bra straps are big enough to put your finger in.—Here, let me show you—

(As Grandmother starts to open her blouse:)

LI'L BIT: Grandma! Please don't undress at the dinner table.

PECK: I thought the entertainment came *after* the dinner.

LI'L BIT *(To the audience)*: This is how it always starts. My grandfather, Big Papa, will chime in next with—

MALE GREEK CHORUS *(As Grandfather)*: Yup. If Li'l Bit gets any bigger, we're gonna haveta buy her a wheelbarrow to carry in front of her—

LI'L BIT: —Damn it—

PECK: —How about those Redskins on Sunday, Big Papa?

LI'L BIT *(To the audience)*: The only sport Big Papa followed was chasing Grandma around the house—

MALE GREEK CHORUS *(As Grandfather)*: —Or we could write to Kate Smith.° Ask her for somma her used brassieres she don't want anymore—she could maybe give to Li'l Bit here—

LI'L BIT: —I can't stand it. I can't.

PECK: Now, honey, that's just their way—

FEMALE GREEK CHORUS *(As Mother)*: I tell you, Grandma, Li'l Bit's at that age. She's so sensitive, you can't say boo—

LI'L BIT: I'd like some privacy, that's all. Okay? Some goddamn privacy—

PECK: —Well, at least she didn't use the savior's name—

LI'L BIT *(To the audience)*: And Big Papa wouldn't let a dead dog lie. No sirree.

MALE GREEK CHORUS *(As Grandfather)*: Well, she'd better stop being so sensitive. 'Cause five minutes before Li'l Bit turns the corner, her tits turn first—

LI'L BIT *(Starting to rise from the table)*: —That's it. That's it.

PECK: Li'l Bit, you can't let him get to you. Then he wins.

LI'L BIT: I hate him. *Hate* him.

PECK: That's fine. But hate him and eat a good dinner at the same time.

*(*LI'L BIT *calms down and sits with perfect dignity.)*

LI'L BIT: The gumbo is really good, Grandma.

MALE GREEK CHORUS *(As Grandfather)*: A'course, Li'l

Kate Smith, American popular singer, large both in voice and size, best known for her version of "God Bless America."

Bit's got a big surprise coming for her when she goes to that fancy college this fall—

PECK: Big Papa—let it go.

MALE GREEK CHORUS (*As Grandfather*): What does she need a college degree for? She's got all the credentials she'll need on her chest—

LI'L BIT: —Maybe I want to learn things. Read. Rise above my cracker background—

PECK: —Whoa, now, Li'l Bit—

MALE GREEK CHORUS (*As Grandfather*): What kind of things do you want to read?

LI'L BIT: There's a whole semester course, for example, on Shakespeare—

(GREEK CHORUS, *as Grandfather, laughs until he weeps.*)

MALE GREEK CHORUS (*As Grandfather*): Shakespeare. That's a good one. Shakespeare is really going to help you in life.

PECK: I think it's wonderful. And on scholarship!

MALE GREEK CHORUS (*As Grandfather*): How is Shakespeare going to help her lie on her back in the dark?

(LI'L BIT *is on her feet.*)

LI'L BIT: You're getting old, Big Papa. You are going to die—very very soon. Maybe even *tonight*. And when you get to heaven, God's going to be a beautiful black woman in a long white robe. She's gonna look at your chart and say: Uh-oh. Fornication. Dog-ugly mean with blood relatives. Oh. Uh-oh. Voted for George Wallace. Well, one last chance: If you can name the play, all will be forgiven. And then she'll quote: "The quality of mercy is not strained."° Your answer? Oh, too bad—*Merchant of Venice:* Act IV, Scene iii. And then she'll send your ass to fry in hell with all the other crackers. Excuse me, please.

(*To the audience*) And as I left the house, I would always hear Big Papa say:

MALE GREEK CHORUS (*As Grandfather*): Lucy, your daughter's got a mouth on her. Well, no sense in wasting good gumbo. Pass me her plate, Mama.

LI'L BIT: And Aunt Mary would come up to Uncle Peck:

FEMALE GREEK CHORUS (*As Aunt Mary*): Peck, go after her, will you? You're the only one she'll listen to when she gets like this.

PECK: She just needs to cool off.

FEMALE GREEK CHORUS (*As Aunt Mary*): Please, honey—Grandma's been on her feet cooking all day.

PECK: All right.

LI'L BIT: And as he left the room, Aunt Mary would say:

°"*The quality of mercy is not strained,*" *The Merchant of Venice,* Act 4, Scene i. Li'l Bit has the right play, but not the right scene.

FEMALE GREEK CHORUS (*As Aunt Mary*): Peck's so good with them when they get to be this age.

(LI'L BIT *has stormed to another part of the stage, her back turned, weeping with a teenage fury.* PECK, *cautiously, as if stalking a deer, comes to her. She turns away even more. He waits a bit.*)

PECK: I don't suppose you're talking to family. (*No response*) Does it help that I'm in-law?

LI'L BIT: Don't you dare make fun of this.

PECK: I'm not. There's nothing funny about this. (*Beat*) Although I'll bet when Big Papa is about to meet his maker, he'll remember *The Merchant of Venice.*

LI'L BIT: I've got to get away from here.

PECK: You're going away. Soon. Here, take this.

(PECK *hands her his folded handkerchief.* LI'L BIT *uses it, noisily. Hands it back. Without her seeing, he reverently puts it back.*)

LI'L BIT: I hate this family.

PECK: Your grandfather's ignorant. And you're right—he's going to die soon. But he's family. Family is . . . family.

LI'L BIT: Grown-ups are always saying that. Family.

PECK: Well, when you get a little older, you'll see what we're saying.

LI'L BIT: Uh-huh. So family is another acquired taste, like French kissing?

PECK: Come again?

LI'L BIT: You know, at first it really grosses you out, but in time you grow to like it?

PECK: Girl, you are . . . a handful.

LI'L BIT: Uncle Peck—you have the keys to your car?

PECK: Where do you want to go?

LI'L BIT: Just up the road.

PECK: I'll come with you.

LI'L BIT: No—please? I just need to . . . to drive for a little bit. Alone.

(PECK *tosses her the keys.*)

PECK: When can I see you alone again?

LI'L BIT: Tonight.

(LI'L BIT *crosses to center stage while the lights dim around her. A Voice directs:*)

Shifting Forward from First to Second Gear.

LI'L BIT: There were a lot of rumors about why I got kicked out of that fancy school in 1970. Some say I got caught with a man in my room. Some say as a kid on scholarship I fooled around with a rich man's daughter.

(LI'L BIT *smiles innocently at the audience*) I'm not talking.

But the real truth was I had a constant companion in my dorm room—who was less than discreet. Canadian V.O. A fifth a day.

1970. A Nixon recession. I slept on the floors of friends who were out of work themselves. Took factory work when I could find it. A string of dead-end jobs that didn't last very long.

What I did, most nights, was cruise the Beltway and the back roads of Maryland, where there was still country, past the battlefields and farm houses. Racing in a 1965 Mustang—and as long as I had gasoline for my car and whiskey for me, the nights would pass. Full tanked, I would speed past the churches and the trees on the bend, thinking just one notch of the steering wheel would be all it would take, and yet some . . . reflex took over. My hands on the wheel in the nine and three o'clock position—I never so much as got a ticket. He taught me well.

(A Voice announces:)

You and the Reverse Gear.

LI'L BIT: Back up. 1968. On the Eastern Shore. A celebration dinner.

(LI'L BIT joins PECK at a table in a restaurant.)

PECK: Feeling better, missy?

LI'L BIT: The bathroom's really amazing here, Uncle Peck! They have these little soaps—instead of borax or something—and they're in the shape of shells.

PECK: I'll have to take a trip to the gentleman's room just to see.

LI'L BIT: How did you know about this place?

PECK: This inn is famous on the Eastern Shore—it's been open since the seventeenth century. And I know how you like history. . . .

(LI'L BIT is shy and pleased.)

LI'L BIT: It's great.

PECK: And you've just done your first, legal, long-distance drive. You must be hungry.

LI'L BIT: I'm starved.

PECK: I would suggest a dozen oysters to start, and the crab imperial. . . . *(LI'L BIT is genuinely agog)* You might be interested to know the town history. When the British sailed up this very river in the dead of night—see outside where I'm pointing?—they were going to bombard the heck out of this town. But the town fathers were ready for them. They crept up all the trees with lanterns so that the British would think they saw the town lights and they aimed their cannons too high. And that's why the inn is still here for business today.

LI'L BIT: That's a great story.

PECK *(Casually)*: Would you like to start with a cocktail?

LI'L BIT: You're not . . . you're not going to start drinking, are you, Uncle Peck?

PECK: Not me. I told you, as long as you're with me, I'll never drink. I asked you if *you'd* like a cocktail before dinner. It's nice to have a little something with the oysters.

LI'L BIT: But . . . I'm not . . . legal. We could get arrested. Uncle Peck, they'll never believe I'm twenty-one!

PECK: So? Today we celebrate your driver's license— on the first try. This establishment reminds me a lot of places back home.

LI'L BIT: What does that mean?

PECK: In South Carolina, like here on the Eastern Shore, they're . . . *(Searches for the right euphemism)* . . . "European." Not so puritanical. And very understanding if gentlemen wish to escort very attractive young ladies who might want a before-dinner cocktail. If you want one, I'll order one.

LI'L BIT: Well—sure. Just . . . one.

(The FEMALE GREEK CHORUS appears in a spot.)

FEMALE GREEK CHORUS *(As Mother)*: A Mother's Guide to Social Drinking:

A lady never gets sloppy—she may, however, get tipsy and a little gay.

Never drink on an empty stomach. Avail yourself of the bread basket and generous portions of butter. *Slather* the butter on your bread.

Sip your drink, slowly, let the beverage linger in your mouth—interspersed with interesting, fascinating conversation. Sip, never . . . slurp or gulp. Your glass should always be three-quarters full when his glass is empty.

Stay away from *ladies'* drinks: drinks like pink ladies, slow gin fizzes, daiquiris, gold cadillacs, Long Island iced teas, margaritas, piña coladas, mai tais, planters punch, white Russians, black Russians, red Russians, melon balls, blue balls, hummingbirds, hemorrhages, and hurricanes. In short, avoid anything with sugar, or anything with an umbrella. Get your vitamin C from *fruit*. Don't order anything with Voodoo or Vixen in the title or sexual positions in the name like Dead Man Screw or the Missionary. *(She sort of titters)*

Believe me, they are lethal. . . . I think you were conceived after one of those.

Drink, instead, like a man: straight up or on the rocks, with plenty of water in between.

Oh, yes. And never mix your drinks. Stay with one all night long, like the man you came in with: bourbon, gin, or tequila till dawn, damn the torpedoes, full speed ahead!

(As the FEMALE GREEK CHORUS retreats, the MALE GREEK CHORUS approaches the table as a Waiter.)

MALE GREEK CHORUS *(As Waiter)*: I hope you all are having a pleasant evening. Is there something I can bring you, sir, before you order?

(LI'L BIT *waits in anxious fear. Carefully,* UNCLE PECK *says with command:*)

PECK: I'll have a plain iced tea. The lady would like a drink, I believe.

(*The* MALE GREEK CHORUS *does a double take; there is a moment when* UNCLE PECK *and he are in silent communication.*)

MALE GREEK CHORUS (*As Waiter*): Very good. What would the . . . lady like?

LI'L BIT (*A bit flushed*): Is there . . . is there any sugar in a martini?

PECK: None that I know of.

LI'L BIT: That's what I'd like then—a dry martini. And could we maybe have some bread?

PECK: A drink fit for a woman of the world.—Please bring the lady a dry martini, be generous with the olives, straight up.

(*The* MALE GREEK CHORUS *anticipates a large tip.*)

MALE GREEK CHORUS (*As Waiter*): Right away. Very good, sir.

(*The* MALE GREEK CHORUS *returns with an empty martini glass which he puts in front of* LI'L BIT.)

PECK: Your glass is empty. Another martini, madam?

LI'L BIT: Yes, thank you.
    (PECK *signals the* MALE GREEK CHORUS, *who nods*)
So why did you leave South Carolina, Uncle Peck?

PECK: I was stationed in D.C. after the war, and decided to stay. Go North, Young Man, someone might have said.

LI'L BIT: What did you do in the service anyway?

PECK (*Suddenly taciturn*): I . . . I did just this and that. Nothing heroic or spectacular.

LI'L BIT: But did you see fighting? Or go to Europe?

PECK: I served in the Pacific Theater. It's really nothing interesting to talk about.

LI'L BIT: It is to me. (*The Waiter has brought another empty glass*) Oh, goody. I love the color of the swizzle sticks. What were we talking about?

PECK: Swizzle sticks.

LI'L BIT: Do you ever think of going back?

PECK: To the Marines?

LI'L BIT: No—to South Carolina.

PECK: Well, we do go back. To visit.

LI'L BIT: No, I mean to live.

PECK: Not very likely. I think it's better if my mother doesn't have a daily reminder of her disappointment.

LI'L BIT: Are these floorboards slanted?

PECK: Yes, the floor is very slanted. I think this is the original floor.

LI'L BIT: Oh, good.

(*The* FEMALE GREEK CHORUS *as Mother enters swaying a little, a little past tipsy.*)

FEMALE GREEK CHORUS (*As Mother*): Don't leave your drink unattended when you visit the ladies' room. There is such a thing as white slavery; the modus operandi is to spike an unsuspecting young girl's drink with a "mickey" when she's left the room to powder her nose.

But if you feel you have had more than your sufficiency in liquor, do go to the ladies' room—often. Pop your head out of doors for a refreshing breath of the night air. If you must, wet your face and head with tap water. Don't be afraid to dunk your head if necessary. A wet woman is still less conspicuous than a drunk woman.

(*The* FEMALE GREEK CHORUS *stumbles a little; conspiratorially*) When in the course of human events it becomes necessary, go to a corner stall and insert the index and middle finger down the throat almost to the epiglottis. Divulge your stomach contents by such persuasion, and then wait a few moments before rejoining your beau waiting for you at your table.

Oh, no. Don't be shy or embarrassed. In the very best of establishments, there's always one or two debutantes crouched in the corner stalls, their beaded purses tossed willy-nilly, sounding like cats in heat, heaving up the contents of their stomachs.

(*The* FEMALE GREEK CHORUS *begins to wander off*) I wonder what is it they do in the men's rooms. . . .

LI'L BIT: So why is your mother disappointed in you, Uncle Peck?

LI'L BIT: Every mother in Horry County has Great Expectations.

LI'L BIT: —Could I have another mar-ti-ni, please?

PECK: I think this is your last one.

(PECK *signals the Waiter. The Waiter looks at* LI'L BIT *and shakes his head no.* PECK *raises his eyebrow, raises his finger to indicate one more, and then rubs his fingers together. It looks like a secret code. The Waiter sighs, shakes his head sadly, and brings over another empty martini glass. He glares at* PECK.)

LI'L BIT: The name of the county where you grew up is "Horry?" (LI'L BIT, *plastered, begins to laugh. Then she stops*) I think your mother should be proud of you.

(PECK *signals for the check.*)

PECK: Well, missy, she wanted me to do—to *be* everything my father was not. She wanted me to amount to something.

LI'L BIT: But you have! You've amounted a lot. . . .

PECK: I'm just a very ordinary man.

(*The Waiter has brought the check and waits.* PECK *draws out a large bill and hands it to the Waiter.* LI'L BIT *is in the soppy stage.*)

LI'L BIT: I'll bet your mother loves you, Uncle Peck.

(PECK *freezes a bit. To* MALE GREEK CHORUS *as Waiter:*)

PECK: Thank you. The service was exceptional. Please keep the change.

MALE GREEK CHORUS (*As Waiter, in a tone that could freeze*): Thank you, sir. Will you be needing any help?

PECK: I think we can manage, thank you.

(*Just then, the* FEMALE GREEK CHORUS *as Mother lurches on stage; the* MALE GREEK CHORUS *as Waiter escorts her off as she delivers:*)

FEMALE GREEK CHORUS (*as Mother*): Thanks to judicious planning and several trips to the ladies' loo, your mother once out-drank an entire regiment of British officers on a good-will visit to Washington! Every last man of them! Milquetoasts! How'd they ever kick Hitler's cahones, huh? No match for an American lady—I could drink every man in here under the table.
    (*She delivers one last crucial hint before she is gently "bounced"*) As a last resort, when going out for an evening on the town, be sure to wear a skin-tight girdle—so tight that only a surgical knife or acetylene torch can get it off you—so that if you do pass out in the arms of your escort, he'll end up with rubber burns on his fingers before he can steal your virtue—

(*A Voice punctures the interlude with:*)

Vehicle Failure.
Even with careful maintenance and preventive operation of your automobile, it is all too common for us to experience an unexpected breakdown. If you are driving at any speed when a breakdown occurs, you must slow down and guide the automobile to the side of the road.

(PECK *is slowly propping up* LI'L BIT *as they work their way to his car in the parking lot of the inn.*)

PECK: How are you doing, missy?

LI'L BIT: It's so far to the car, Uncle Peck. Like the lanterns in the trees the British fired on . . .

(LI'L BIT *stumbles.* PECK *swoops her up in his arms.*)

PECK: Okay, I think we're going to take a more direct route.
    (LI'L BIT *closes her eyes*) Dizzy? (*She nods her head*) Don't look at the ground. Almost there—do you feel sick to your stomach? (LI'L BIT *nods. They reach the "car."* PECK *gently deposits her on the front seat*) Just settle here a little while until things stop spinning. (LI'L BIT *opens her eyes*)

LI'L BIT: What are we doing?

PECK: We're just going to sit here until your tummy settles down.

LI'L BIT: It's such nice upholst'ry—

PECK: Think you can go for a ride, now?

LI'L BIT: Where are you taking me?

PECK: Home.

LI'L BIT: You're not taking me—upstairs? There's no room at the inn? (LI'L BIT *giggles*)

PECK: Do you want to go upstairs? (LI'L BIT *doesn't answer*) Or home?

LI'L BIT: —This isn't right, Uncle Peck.

PECK: What isn't right?

LI'L BIT: What we're doing. It's wrong. It's very wrong.

PECK: What are we doing? (LI'L BIT *does not answer*) We're just going out to dinner.

LI'L BIT: You know. It's not nice to Aunt Mary.

PECK: You let me be the judge of what's nice and not nice to my wife.

(*Beat.*)

LI'L BIT: Now you're mad.

PECK: I'm not mad. It's just that I thought you . . . understood me, Li'l Bit. I think you're the only one who does.

LI'L BIT: Someone will get hurt.

PECK: Have I forced you to do anything?

(*There is a long pause as* LI'L BIT *tries to get sober enough to think this through.*)

LI'L BIT: . . . I guess not.

PECK: We are just enjoying each other's company. I've told you, nothing is going to happen between us until you want it to. Do you know that?

LI'L BIT: Yes.

PECK: Nothing is going to happen until you want it to. (*A second more, with* PECK *staring ahead at the river while seated at the wheel of his car. Then, softly:*) Do you want something to happen?

(PECK *reaches over and strokes her face, very gently.* LI'L BIT *softens, reaches for him, and buries her head in his neck. Then she kisses him. Then she moves away, dizzy again.*)

LI'L BIT: . . . I don't know.

(PECK *smiles; this has been good news for him—it hasn't been a "no."*)

PECK: Then I'll wait. I'm a very patient man. I've been waiting for a long time. I don't mind waiting.

LI'L BIT: Someone is going to get hurt.

PECK: No one is going to get hurt. (LI'L BIT *closes her eyes*) Are you feeling sick?

LI'L BIT: Sleepy.

(*Carefully,* PECK *props* LI'L BIT *up on the seat.*)

PECK: Stay here a second.

LI'L BIT: Where're you going?

PECK: I'm getting something from the back seat.

LI'L BIT (*Scared; too loud*): What? What are you going to do?

(PECK reappears in the front seat with a lap rug.)

PECK: Shhh. *(PECK covers* LI'L BIT. *She calms down)* There. Think you can sleep?

*(*LI'L BIT *nods. She slides over to rest on his shoulder. With a look of happiness,* PECK *turns the ignition key. Beat.* PECK *leaves* LI'L BIT *sleeping in the car and strolls down to the audience. Wagner's* Flying Dutchman° *comes up faintly.)*

(A Voice interjects:)

Idling in the Neutral Gear.

TEENAGE GREEK CHORUS: Uncle Peck Teaches Cousin Bobby How to Fish.

PECK: I get back once or twice a year—supposedly to visit Mama and the family, but the real truth is to fish. I miss this the most of all. There's a smell in the Low Country—where the swamp and fresh inlet join the saltwater—a scent of sand and cypress, that I haven't found anywhere yet.

I don't say this very often up North because it will just play into the stereotype everyone has, but I will tell you: I didn't wear shoes in the summertime until I was sixteen. It's unnatural down here to pen up your feet in leather. Go ahead—take 'em off. Let yourself breathe—it really will make you feel better.

We're going to aim for some pompano today—and I have to tell you, they're a very shy, mercurial fish. Takes patience, and psychology. You have to believe it doesn't matter if you catch one or not.

Sky's pretty spectacular—there's some beer in the cooler next to the crab salad I packed, so help yourself if you get hungry. Are you hungry? Thirsty? Holler if you are.

Okay. You don't want to lean over the bridge like that—pompano feed in shallow water, and you don't want to get too close—they're frisky and shy little things—wait, check your line. Yep, something's been munching while we were talking.

Okay, look: We take the sand flea and you take the hook like this—right through his little sand flea rump. Sand fleas should always keep their backs to the wall. Okay. Cast it in, like I showed you. That's great! I can taste that pompano now, sautéed with some pecans and butter, a little bourbon—now—let it lie on the bottom—now, reel, jerk, reel, jerk—

Look—look at your line. There's something calling, all right. Okay, tip the rod up—not too sharp—hook it—all right, now easy, reel and then

---

Wagner's **Flying Dutchman,** opera (1843) based on the legend of a sea-captain who must sail endlessly until he finds a woman who will love and be true to him.

rest—let it play. And reel—play it out, that's right—really good! I can't believe it! It's a pompano.—Good work! Way to go! You are an official fisherman now. Pompano are hard to catch. We are going to have a delicious little—

What? Well, I don't know how much pain a fish feels—you can't think of that. Oh, no, don't cry, come on now, it's just a fish—the other guys are going to see you.—No, no, you're just real sensitive, and I think that's wonderful at your age—look, do you want me to cut it free? You do?

Okay, hand me those pliers—look—I'm cutting the hook—okay? And we're just going to drop it in—no I'm not mad. It's just for fun, okay? There—it's going to swim back to its lady friend and tell her what a terrible day it had and she's going to stroke him with her fins until he feels better, and then they'll do something alone together that will make them both feel good and sleepy. . . .

*(*PECK *bends down, very earnest)* I don't want you to feel ashamed about crying. I'm not going to tell anyone, okay? I can keep secrets. You know, men cry all the time. They just don't tell anybody, and they don't let anybody catch them. There's nothing you could do that would make me feel ashamed of you. Do you know that? Okay. *(*PECK *straightens up, smiles)*

Do you want to pack up and call it a day? I tell you what—I think I can still remember—there's a really neat tree house where I used to stay for days. I think it's still here—it was the last time I looked. But it's a secret place—you can't tell anybody we've gone there—least of all your mom or your sisters.—This is something special just between you and me. Sound good? We'll climb up there and have a beer and some crab salad—okay, B.B.? Bobby? Robert. . . .

*(*LI'L BIT *sits at a kitchen table with the two* FEMALE GREEK CHORUS *members.)*

LI'L BIT *(To the audience)*: Three women, three generations, sit at the kitchen table.
On Men, Sex, and Women: Part I:

FEMALE GREEK CHORUS *(As Mother)*: Men only want one thing.

LI'L BIT *(Wide-eyed)*: But what? What is it they want?

FEMALE GREEK CHORUS *(As Mother)*: And once they have it, they lose all interest. So Don't Give It to Them.

TEENAGE GREEK CHORUS *(As Grandmother)*: I never had the luxury of the rhythm method. Your grandfather is just a big bull. A big bull. Every morning, every evening.

FEMALE GREEK CHORUS *(As Mother, whispers to* LI'L BIT*)*: And he used to come home for lunch every day.

LI'L BIT: My god, Grandma!

TEENAGE GREEK CHORUS (*As Grandmother*): Your grandfather only cares that I do two things: have the table set and the bed turned down.

FEMALE GREEK CHORUS (*As Mother*): And in all that time, Mother, you never have experienced—?

LI'L BIT (*To the audience*): —Now my grandmother believed in all the sacraments of the church, to the day she died. She believed in Santa Claus and the Easter Bunny until she was fifteen. But she didn't believe in—

TEENAGE GREEK CHORUS (*As Grandmother*): —Orgasm! That's just something you and Mary have made up! I don't believe you.

FEMALE GREEK CHORUS (*As Mother*): Mother, it happens to women all the time—

TEENAGE GREEK CHORUS (*As Grandmother*): —Oh, now you're going to tell me about the G force!

LI'L BIT: No, Grandma, I think that's astronauts—

FEMALE GREEK CHORUS (*As Mother*): Well, Mama, after all, you were a child bride when Big Papa came and got you—you were a married woman and you still believed in Santa Claus.

TEENAGE GREEK CHORUS (*As Grandmother*): It was legal, what Daddy and I did! I was fourteen and in those days, fourteen was a grown-up woman—

(BIG PAPA *shuffles in the kitchen for a cookie.*)

MALE GREEK CHORUS (*As Grandfather*): —Oh, now we're off on Grandma and the Rape of the Sabean Women!°

TEENAGE GREEK CHORUS (*As Grandmother*): Well, you were the one in such a big hurry—

MALE GREEK CHORUS (*As Grandfather to* LI'L BIT): —I picked your grandmother out of that herd of sisters just like a lion chooses the gazelle—the plump, slow, flaky gazelle dawdling at the edge of the herd—your sisters were too smart and too fast and too scrawny—

LI'L BIT (*To the audience*): —The family story is that when Big Papa came for Grandma, my Aunt Lily was waiting for him with a broom—and she beat him over the head all the way down the stairs as he was carrying out Grandma's hope chest—

MALE GREEK CHORUS (*As Grandfather*): —And they were *mean.* 'Specially Lily.

FEMALE GREEK CHORUS (*As Mother*): Well, you were robbing the baby of the family!

TEENAGE GREEK CHORUS (*As Grandmother*): I still keep a broom handy in the kitchen! And I know how to use it! So get your hand out of the cookie jar and don't you spoil your appetite for dinner—out of the kitchen!

Rape of the Sa-bean Women, the Sabine women were, according to legend, abducted by early settlers of Rome.

(MALE GREEK CHORUS *as Grandfather leaves chuckling with a cookie.*)

FEMALE GREEK CHORUS (*As Mother*): Just one thing a married woman needs to know how to use—the rolling pin or the broom. I prefer a heavy, cast-iron fry pan—they're great on a man's head, no matter how thick the skull is.

TEENAGE GREEK CHORUS (*As Grandmother*): Yes, sir, your father is ruled by only two bosses! Mr. Gut and Mr. Peter! And sometimes, first thing in the morning, Mr. Sphincter Muscle!

FEMALE GREEK CHORUS (*As Mother*): It's true. Men are like children. Just like little boys.

TEENAGE GREEK CHORUS (*As Grandmother*): Men are bulls! Big bulls!

(*The* GREEK CHORUS *is getting aroused.*)

FEMALE GREEK CHORUS (*As Mother*): They'd still be crouched on their haunches over a fire in a cave if we hadn't cleaned them up!

TEENAGE GREEK CHORUS (*As Grandmother, flushed*): Coming in smelling of sweat—

FEMALE GREEK CHORUS (*As Mother*): —Looking at those naughty pictures like boys in a dime store with a dollar in their pockets!

TEENAGE GREEK CHORUS (*As Grandmother; raucous*): No matter to them what they smell like! They've got to have it, right then, on the spot, right there! Nasty!—

FEMALE GREEK CHORUS (*As Mother*): —Vulgar!

TEENAGE GREEK CHORUS (*As Grandmother*): Primitive!—

FEMALE GREEK CHORUS (*As Mother*): —Hot!—

LI'L BIT: And just about then, Big Papa would shuffle in with—

MALE GREEK CHORUS (*As Grandfather*): —What are you all cackling about in here?

TEENAGE GREEK CHORUS (*As Grandmother*): Stay out of the kitchen! This is just for girls!

(*As Grandfather leaves:*)

MALE GREEK CHORUS (*As Grandfather*): Lucy, you'd better not be filling Mama's head with sex! Every time you and Mary come over and start in about sex, when I ask a simple question like, "What time is dinner going to be ready?," Mama snaps my head off!

TEENAGE GREEK CHORUS (*As Grandmother*): Dinner will be ready when I'm good and ready! Stay out of this kitchen!

(LI'L BIT *steps out.*
A Voice directs:*)

When Making a Left Turn, You Must Downshift While Going Forward.

LI'L BIT: 1979. A long bus trip to Upstate New York. I settled in to read, when a young man sat beside me.

MALE GREEK CHORUS (*As Young Man; voice cracking*): "What are you reading?"

LI'L BIT: He asked. His voice broke into that miserable equivalent of vocal acne, not quite falsetto and not tenor, either. I glanced a side view. He was appealing in an odd way, huge ears at a defiant angle springing forward at ninety degrees. He must have been shaving, because his face, with a peach sheen, was speckled with nicks and styptic. "I have a class tomorrow," I told him.

MALE GREEK CHORUS (*As Young Man*): "You're taking a class?"

LI'L BIT: "I'm teaching a class." He concentrated on lowering his voice.

MALE GREEK CHORUS (*As Young Man*): "I'm a senior. Walt Whitman High."

LI'L BIT: The light was fading outside, so perhaps he was—with a very high voice.

    I felt his "interest" quicken. Five steps ahead of the hopes in his head, I slowed down, waited, pretended surprise, acted at listening, all the while knowing we would get off the bus, he would just then seem to think to ask me to dinner, he would chivalrously insist on walking me home, he would continue to converse in the street until I would casually invite him up to my room—and—I was only into the second moment of conversation and I could see the whole evening before me.

    And dramaturgically speaking, after the faltering and slightly comical "first act," there was the very briefest of intermissions, and an extremely capable and forceful and *sustained* second act. And after the second act climax and a gentle denouement—before the post-play discussion—I lay on my back in the dark and I thought about you, Uncle Peck. Oh. Oh—this is the allure. Being older. Being the first. Being the translator, the teacher, the epicure, the already jaded. This is how the giver gets taken.

    (LI'L BIT *changes her tone*) On Men, Sex, and Women: Part II:

(LI'L BIT *steps back into the scene as a fifteen-year-old, gawky and quiet, as the gazelle at the edge of the herd.*)

TEENAGE GREEK CHORUS (*As Grandmother, to* LI'L BIT): You're being mighty quiet, missy. Cat Got Your Tongue?

LI'L BIT: I'm just listening. Just thinking.

TEENAGE GREEK CHORUS (*As Grandmother*): Oh, yes, Little Miss Radar Ears? Soaking it all in? Little Miss Sponge? Penny for your thoughts?

(LI'L BIT *hesitates to ask but she really wants to know.*)

LI'L BIT: Does it—when you do it—you know, theoretically when I do it and I haven't done it before—I mean—does it hurt?

FEMALE GREEK CHORUS (*As Mother*): Does what hurt, honey?

LI'L BIT: When a . . . when a girl does it for the first time—with a man—does it hurt?

TEENAGE GREEK CHORUS (*As Grandmother; horrified*): That's what you're thinking about?

FEMALE GREEK CHORUS (*As Mother, calm*): Well, just a little bit. Like a pinch. And there's a little blood.

TEENAGE GREEK CHORUS (*As Grandmother*): Don't tell her that! She's too young to be thinking those things!

FEMALE GREEK CHORUS (*As Mother*): Well, if she doesn't find out from me, where is she going to find out? In the street?

TEENAGE GREEK CHORUS (*As Grandmother*): Tell her it hurts! It's agony! You think you're going to die! Especially if you do it before marriage!

FEMALE GREEK CHORUS (*As Mother*): Mama! I'm going to tell her the truth! Unlike you, you left me and Mary completely in the dark with fairy tales and told us to go to the priest! What does an eighty-year-old priest know about love-making with girls!

LI'L BIT (*Getting upset*): It's not fair!

FEMALE GREEK CHORUS (*As Mother*): Now, see, she's getting upset—you're scaring her.

TEENAGE GREEK CHORUS (*As Grandmother*): Good! Let her be good and scared! It hurts! You bleed like a stuck pig! And you lay there and say, "Why, O Lord, have you forsaken me?!"

LI'L BIT: It's not fair! Why does everything have to hurt for girls? Why is there always blood?

FEMALE GREEK CHORUS (*As Mother*): It's not a lot of blood—and it feels wonderful after the pain subsides . . .

TEENAGE GREEK CHORUS (*As Grandmother*): You're encouraging her to just go out and find out with the first drugstore joe who buys her a milk shake!

FEMALE GREEK CHORUS (*As Mother*): Don't be scared. It won't hurt you—if the man you go to bed with really loves you. It's important that he loves you.

TEENAGE GREEK CHORUS (*As Grandmother*): —Why don't you just go out and rent a motel room for her, Lucy?

FEMALE GREEK CHORUS (*As Mother*): I believe in telling my daughter the truth! We have a very close relationship! I want her to be able to ask me anything—I'm not scaring her with stories about Eve's sin and snakes crawling on their bellies for eternity and women bearing children in mortal pain—

TEENAGE GREEK CHORUS (*As Grandmother*): —If she stops and thinks before she takes her knickers off, maybe someone in this family will finish high school!

(LI'L BIT *knows what is about to happen and starts to retreat from the scene at this point.*)

FEMALE GREEK CHORUS *(As Mother)*: Mother! If you and Daddy had helped me—I wouldn't have had to marry that—that no-good-son-of-a—

TEENAGE GREEK CHORUS *(As Grandmother)*: —He was good enough for you on a full moon! I hold you responsible!

FEMALE GREEK CHORUS *(As Mother)*: —You could have helped me! You could have told me something about the facts of life!

TEENAGE GREEK CHORUS *(As Grandmother)*: —I told you what my mother told me! A girl with her skirt up can outrun a man with his pants down!

(The MALE GREEK CHORUS *enters the fray;* LI'L BIT *edges farther downstage.)*

FEMALE GREEK CHORUS *(As Mother)*: And when I turned to you for a little help, all I got afterwards was—

MALE GREEK CHORUS *(As Grandfather)*: You Made Your Bed; Now Lie On It!

(The GREEK CHORUS *freezes, mouths open, argumentatively.)*

LI'L BIT *(To the audience)*: Oh, please! I still can't bear to listen to it, after all these years—

(The MALE GREEK CHORUS *"unfreezes," but out of his open mouth, as if to his surprise, comes a bass refrain from a Motown song.)*

MALE GREEK CHORUS: "Do-Bee-Do-Wah!"

(The FEMALE GREEK CHORUS *member is also surprised; but she, too, unfreezes.)*

FEMALE GREEK CHORUS: "Shoo-doo-be-doo-be-doo; shoo-doo-be-doo-be-doo."

(The MALE *and* FEMALE GREEK CHORUS *members continue with their harmony, until the Teenage member of the Chorus starts in with Motown lyrics such as "Dedicated to the One I Love," or "In the Still of the Night," or "Hold Me"—any Sam Cooke will do. The three modulate down into three-part harmony, softly, until they are submerged by the actual recording playing over the radio in the car in which* UNCLE PECK *sits in the driver's seat, waiting.* LI'L BIT *sits in the passenger's seat.)*

LI'L BIT: Ahh. That's better.

*(*UNCLE PECK *reaches over and turns the volume down; to* LI'L BIT:*)*

PECK: How can you hear yourself think?

*(*LI'L BIT *does not answer.*
A Voice insinuates itself in the pause:)

Before You Drive.
Always check under your car for obstructions—broken bottles, fallen tree branches, and the bodies of small children. Each year hundreds of children are crushed beneath the wheels of unwary drivers in

their own driveways. Children depend on you to watch them.

(Pause.
The Voice continues:)

You and the Reverse Gear.

(In the following section, it would be nice to have slides of erotic photographs of women and cars: women posed over the hood; women draped along the sideboards; women with water hoses spraying the car; and the actress playing LI'L BIT *with a Bel Air or any 1950s car one can find for the finale.)*

LI'L BIT: 1967. In a parking lot of the Beltsville Agricultural Farms. The Initiation into a Boy's First Love.

PECK *(With a soft look on his face)*: Of course, my favorite car will always be the '56 Bel Air Sports Coupe. Chevy sold more '55s, but the '56!—a V-8 with Corvette option, 225 horsepower; went from zero to sixty miles per hour in 8.9 seconds.

LI'L BIT *(To the audience)*: Long after a mother's tits, but before a woman's breasts:

PECK: Super-Turbo-Fire! What a Power Pack—mechanical lifters, twin four-barrel carbs, lightweight valves, dual exhausts—

LI'L BIT *(To the audience)*: After the milk but before the beer:

PECK: A specific intake manifold, higher-lift camshaft, and the tightest squeeze Chevy had ever made—

LI'L BIT *(To the audience)*: Long after he's squeezed down the birth canal but before he's pushed his way back in: The boy falls in love with the thing that bears his weight with speed.

PECK: I want you to know your automobile inside and out. —Are you there? Li'l Bit?

(Slides end here.)

LI'L BIT: —What?

PECK: You're drifting. I need you to concentrate.

LI'L BIT: Sorry.

PECK: Okay. Get into the driver's seat. *(*LI'L BIT *does)* Okay. Now. Show me what you're going to do before you start the car.

*(*LI'L BIT *sits, with her hands in her lap. She starts to giggle.)*

LI'L BIT: I don't know, Uncle Peck.

PECK: Now, come on. What's the first thing you're going to adjust?

LI'L BIT: My bra strap?—

PECK: —Li'l Bit. What's the most important thing to have control of on the inside of the car?

LI'L BIT: That's easy. The radio. I tune the radio from Mama's old fart tunes to—

*(*LI'L BIT *turns the radio up so we can hear a 1960s tune. With surprising firmness,* PECK *commands:)*

PECK: —Radio off. Right now. (LI'L BIT *turns the radio off*) When you are driving your car, with your license, you can fiddle with the stations all you want. But when you are driving with a learner's permit in my car, I want all your attention to be on the road.

LI'L BIT: Yes, sir.

PECK: Okay. Now the seat—forward and up. (LI'L BIT *pushes it forward*) Do you want a cushion?

LI'L BIT: No—I'm good.

PECK: You should be able to reach all the switches and controls. Your feet should be able to push the accelerator, brake and clutch all the way down. Can you do that?

LI'L BIT: Yes.

PECK: Okay, the side mirrors. You want to be able to see just a bit of the right side of the car in the right mirror—can you?

LI'L BIT: Turn it out more.

PECK: Okay. How's that?

LI'L BIT: A little more. . . . Okay, that's good.

PECK: Now the left—again, you want to be able to see behind you—but the left lane—adjust it until you feel comfortable. (LI'L BIT *does so*) Next. I want you to check the rearview mirror. Angle it so you have a clear vision of the back. (LI'L BIT *does so*) Okay. Lock your door. Make sure all the doors are locked.

LI'L BIT (*Making a joke of it*): But then I'm locked in with you.

PECK: Don't fool.

LI'L BIT: All right. We're locked in.

PECK: We'll deal with the air vents and defroster later. I'm teaching you on a manual—once you learn manual, you can drive anything. I want you to be able to drive any car, any machine. Manual gives you *control*. In ice, if your brakes fail, if you need more power—okay? It's a little harder at first, but then it becomes like breathing. Now. Put your hands on the wheel. I never want to see you driving with one hand. Always two hands. (LI'L BIT *hesitates*) What? What is it now?

LI'L BIT: If I put my hands on the wheel—how do I defend myself?

PECK (*Softly*): Now listen. Listen up close. We're not going to fool around with this. This is serious business. I will never touch you when you are driving a car. Understand?

LI'L BIT: Okay.

PECK: Hands on the nine o'clock and three o'clock position gives you maximum control and turn.

(PECK *goes silent for a while.* LI'L BIT *waits for more instruction.*)

Okay. Just relax and listen to me, Li'l Bit, okay? I want you to lift your hands for a second and look at them. (LI'L BIT *feels a bit silly, but does it*)

Those are your two hands. When you are driving, your life is in your own two hands. Understand? (LI'L BIT *nods*)

I don't have any sons. You're the nearest to a son I'll ever have—and I want to give you something. Something that really matters to me.

There's something about driving—when you're in control of the car, just you and the machine and the road—that nobody can take from you. A power. I feel more myself in my car than anywhere else. And that's what I want to give to you.

There's a lot of assholes out there. Crazy men, arrogant idiots, drunks, angry kids, geezers who are blind—and you have to be ready for them. I want to teach you to drive like a man.

LI'L BIT: What does that mean?

PECK: Men are taught to drive with confidence—with aggression. The road belongs to them. They drive defensively—always looking out for the other guy. Women tend to be polite—to hesitate. And that can be fatal.

You're going to learn to think what the other guy is going to do before he does it. If there's an accident, and ten cars pile up, and people get killed, you're the one who's gonna steer through it, put your foot on the gas if you have to, and be the only one to walk away. I don't know how long you or I are going to live, but we're for damned sure not going to die in a car.

So if you're going to drive with me, I want you to take this very seriously.

LI'L BIT: I will, Uncle Peck. I want you to teach me to drive.

PECK: Good. You're going to pass your test on the first try. Perfect score. Before the next four weeks are over, you're going to know this baby inside and out. Treat her with respect.

LI'L BIT: Why is it a "she?"

PECK: Good question. It doesn't have to be a "she"—but when you close your eyes and think of someone who responds to your touch—someone who performs just for you and gives you what you ask for—I guess I always see a "she." You can call her what you like.

LI'L BIT (*To the audience*): I closed my eyes—and decided not to change the gender.

(*A Voice:*)

Defensive driving involves defending yourself from hazardous and sudden changes in your automotive environment. By thinking ahead, the defensive driver can adjust to weather, road conditions, and road kill. Good defensive driving involves mental and physical preparation. Are you prepared?

(*Another Voice chimes in:*)

You and the Reverse Gear.

LI'L BIT: 1966. The Anthropology of the Female Body in Ninth Grade—Or A Walk Down Mammary Lane.

(*Throughout the following, there is occasional rhythmic beeping, like a transmitter signalling.* LI'L BIT *is aware of it, but can't figure out where it is coming from. No one else seems to hear it.*)

MALE GREEK CHORUS: In the hallway of Francis Scott Key Middle School.

(*A bell rings; the* GREEK CHORUS *is changing classes and meets in the hall, conspiratorially.*)

TEENAGE GREEK CHORUS: She's coming!

(LI'L BIT *enters the scene; the* MALE GREEK CHORUS *member has a sudden, violent sneezing and lethal allergy attack.*)

FEMALE GREEK CHORUS: Jerome? Jerome? Are you all right?
MALE GREEK CHORUS: I—don't—know. I can't breathe—get Li'l Bit—
TEENAGE GREEK CHORUS: —He needs oxygen!—
FEMALE GREEK CHORUS: —Can you help us here?
LI'L BIT: What's wrong? Do you want me to get the school nurse—

(*The* MALE GREEK CHORUS *member wheezes, grabs his throat and sniffs at* LI'L BIT'S *chest, which is beeping away.*)

MALE GREEK CHORUS: No—it's okay—I only get this way when I'm around an allergy trigger—
LI'L BIT: Golly. What are you allergic to?
MALE GREEK CHORUS (*With a sudden grab of her breast*): Foam rubber.

(*The* GREEK CHORUS *members break up with hilarity; Jerome leaps away from* LI'L BIT'S *kicking rage with agility; as he retreats:*)

LI'L BIT: Jerome! Creep! Cretin! Cro-Magnon!
TEENAGE GREEK CHORUS: Rage is not attractive in a girl.
FEMALE GREEK CHORUS: Really. Get a Sense of Humor.

(*A Voice echoes:*)

Good defensive driving involves mental and physical preparation. Were You Prepared?

FEMALE GREEK CHORUS: Gym Class: In the showers.

(*The sudden sound of water; the* FEMALE GREEK CHORUS *members and* LI'L BIT, *while fully clothed, drape towels across their fronts, miming nudity. They stand, hesitate, at an imaginary shower's edge.*)

LI'L BIT: Water looks hot.
FEMALE GREEK CHORUS: Yesss. . . .

(FEMALE GREEK CHORUS *members are not going to make the first move. One dips a tentative toe under the water, clutching the towel around her.*)

LI'L BIT: Well, I guess we'd better shower and get out of here.
FEMALE GREEK CHORUS: Yep. You go ahead. I'm still cooling off.
LI'L BIT: Okay.—Sally? Are you gonna shower?
TEENAGE GREEK CHORUS: After you—

(LI'L BIT *takes a deep breath for courage, drops the towel and plunges in: The two* FEMALE GREEK CHORUS *members look at* LI'L BIT *in the all together, laugh, gasp and high-five each other.*)

TEENAGE GREEK CHORUS: Oh my god! Can you believe—
FEMALE GREEK CHORUS: Told you! It's not foam rubber! I win! Jerome owes me fifty cents!

(*A Voice editorializes:*)

Were You Prepared?

(LI'L BIT *tries to cover up; she is exposed, as suddenly 1960s Motown fills the room and we segue into:*)

FEMALE GREEK CHORUS: The Sock Hop.

(LI'L BIT *stands up against the wall with her female classmates.* TEENAGE GREEK CHORUS *is mesmerized by the music and just sways alone, lip-synching the lyrics.*)

LI'L BIT: I don't know. Maybe it's just me—but—do you ever feel like you're just a walking Mary Jane joke?
FEMALE GREEK CHORUS: I don't know what you mean.
LI'L BIT: You haven't heard the Mary Jane jokes? (FEMALE GREEK CHORUS *member shakes her head no*) Okay. "Little Mary Jane is walking through the woods, when all of a sudden this man who was hiding behind a tree *jumps* out, *rips* open Mary Jane's blouse, and *plunges* his hands on her breasts. And Little Mary Jane just laughed and laughed because she knew her money was in her shoes."

(LI'L BIT *laughs; the* FEMALE GREEK CHORUS *does not.*)

FEMALE GREEK CHORUS: You're weird.

(*In another space, in a strange light,* UNCLE PECK *stands and stares at* LI'L BIT*'s body. He is setting up a tripod, but he just stands, appreciative, watching her.*)

LI'L BIT: Well, don't you ever feel . . . self-conscious? Like you're being looked at all the time?
FEMALE GREEK CHORUS: That's not a problem for me.—Oh—look—Greg's coming over to ask you to dance.

(TEENAGE GREEK CHORUS *becomes attentive, flustered.* MALE GREEK CHORUS *member, as Greg, bends slightly as a very short young man, whose head is at* LI'L BIT*'s chest level. Ardent, sincere, and socially inept, Greg will become a successful gynecologist.*)

TEENAGE GREEK CHORUS (*Softly*): Hi, Greg.

(Greg does not hear. He is intent on only one thing.)

MALE GREEK CHORUS *(As Greg, to* LI'L BIT*)*: Good
Evening. Would you care to dance?

LI'L BIT *(Gently)*: Thank you very much, Greg—but
I'm going to sit this one out.

MALE GREEK CHORUS *(As Greg)*: Oh. Okay. I'll try my
luck later.

(He disappears.)

TEENAGE GREEK CHORUS: Oohhh.

*(*LI'L BIT *relaxes. Then she tenses, aware of* PECK*'s gaze.)*

FEMALE GREEK CHORUS: Take pity on him. Someone
should.

LI'L BIT: But he's so short.

TEENAGE GREEK CHORUS: He can't help it.

LI'L BIT: But his head comes up to *(*LI'L BIT *gestures)*
here. And I think he asks me on the fast dances so
he can watch me—you know—jiggle.

FEMALE GREEK CHORUS: I wish I had your problems.

(The tune changes; Greg is across the room in a flash.)

MALE GREEK CHORUS *(As Greg)*: Evening again. May I
ask you for the honor of a spin on the floor?

LI'L BIT: I'm . . . very complimented, Greg. But I . . . I
just don't do fast dances.

MALE GREEK CHORUS *(As Greg)*: Oh. No problem.
That's okay.

(He disappears. TEENAGE GREEK CHORUS *watches him
go.)*

TEENAGE GREEK CHORUS: That is just so—*sad.*

*(*LI'L BIT *becomes aware of* PECK *waiting.)*

FEMALE GREEK CHORUS: You know, you should take it
as a compliment that the guys want to watch you
jiggle. They're guys. That's what they're supposed
to do.

LI'L BIT: I guess you're right. But sometimes I feel like
these alien life forces, these two mounds of flesh
have grafted themselves onto my chest, and
they're using me until they can "propagate" and
take over the world and they'll just keep growing,
with a mind of their own until I collapse under
their weight and they suck all the nourishment
out of my body and I finally just waste away while
they get bigger and bigger and—*(*LI'L BIT*'s classmates are just staring at her in disbelief)*

FEMALE GREEK CHORUS: —You are the strangest girl I
have ever met.

*(*LI'L BIT*'s trying to joke but feels on the verge of tears.)*

LI'L BIT: Or maybe someone's implanted radio transmitters in my chest at a frequency I can't hear, that
girls can't detect, but they're sending out these signals to men who get mesmerized, like sirens, calling them to dash themselves on these "rocks"—

*(Just then, the music segues into a slow dance, perhaps a
Beach Boys tune like "Little Surfer," but over the music
there's a rhythmic, hypnotic beeping transmitted, which
both Greg and* PECK *hear.* LI'L BIT *hears it too, and in
horror she stares at her chest. She, too, is almost hypnotized. In a trance, Greg responds to the signals and is
called to her side—actually, her front. Like a zombie, he
stands in front of her, his eyes planted on her two orbs.)*

MALE GREEK CHORUS *(As Greg)*: This one's a slow
dance. I hope your dance card isn't . . . filled?

*(*LI'L BIT *is aware of* PECK*; but the signals are calling her
to him. The signals are no longer transmitters, but an elec-
tromagnetic force, pulling* LI'L BIT *to his side, where he
again waits for her to join him. She must get away from the
dance floor.)*

LI'L BIT: Greg—you really are a nice boy. But I don't
like to dance.

MALE GREEK CHORUS *(As Greg)*: That's okay. We don't
have to move or anything. I could just hold you
and we could just *sway* a little—

LI'L BIT: —No! I'm sorry—but I think I have to leave;
I hear someone calling me—

*(*LI'L BIT *starts across the dance floor, leaving Greg
behind. The beeping stops. The lights change, although the
music does not. As* LI'L BIT *talks to the audience, she continues to change and prepare for the coming session. She
should be wearing a tight tank top or a sheer blouse and
very tight pants. To the audience:)*

In every man's home some small room, some
zone in his house, is set aside. It might be the
attic, or the study, or a den. And there's an invisible sign as if from the old treehouse: Girls Keep
Out.

Here, away from female eyes, lace doilies and
crochet, he keeps his manly toys: the Vargas pin-
ups, the tackle. A scent of tobacco and WD-40.
(She inhales deeply) A dash of his Bay Rum. Ahhh . . .
*(*LI'L BIT *savors it for just a moment more)*

Here he keeps his secrets: a violin or saxophone, drum set or darkroom, and the stacks of
Playboy. (In a whisper) Here, in my aunt's home, it
was the basement. Uncle Peck's turf.

(A Voice commands:)

You and the Reverse Gear.

LI'L BIT: 1965. The Photo Shoot.

*(*LI'L BIT *steps into the scene as a nervous but curious
thirteen-year-old. Music, from the previous scene, continues to play, changing into something like Roy Orbison
later—something seductive with a beat.* PECK *fiddles, all
business, with his camera. As in the driving lesson, he is
all competency and concentration.* LI'L BIT *stands awkwardly. He looks through the Leica camera on the tripod,
adjusts the back lighting, etc.)*

PECK: Are you cold? The lights should heat up some in a few minutes—

LI'L BIT: —Aunt Mary is?

PECK: At the National Theatre matinee. With your mother. We have time.

LI'L BIT: But—what if—

PECK: —And so what if they return? I told them you and I were going to be working with my camera. They won't come down. (LI'L BIT *is quiet, apprehensive*)—Look, are you sure you want to do this?

LI'L BIT: I said I'd do it. But—

PECK: —I know. You've drawn the line.

LI'L BIT (*Reassured*): That's right. No frontal nudity.

PECK: Good heavens, girl, where did you pick that up?

LI'L BIT (*Defensive*): I read.

(PECK *tries not to laugh.*)

PECK: And I read *Playboy* for the interviews. Okay. Let's try some different music.

(PECK *goes to an expensive reel-to-reel and forwards. Something like "Sweet Dreams" begins to play.*)

LI'L BIT: I didn't know you listened to this.

PECK: I'm not dead, you know, I try to keep up. Do you like this song? (LI'L BIT *nods with pleasure*) Good. Now listen—at professional photo shoots, they always play music for the models. Okay? I want you to just enjoy the music. Listen to it with your body, and just—respond.

LI'L BIT: Respond to the music with my . . . body?

PECK: Right. Almost like dancing. Here—let's get you on the stool, first. (PECK *comes over and helps her up*)

LI'L BIT: But nothing showing—

(PECK *firmly, with his large capable hands, brushes back her hair, angles her face.* LI'L BIT *turns to him like a plant to the sun.*)

PECK: Nothing showing. Just a peek.

(*He holds her by the shoulders, looking at her critically. Then he unbuttons her blouse to the midpoint, and runs his hands over the flesh of her exposed sternum, arranging the fabric, just touching her. Deliberately, calmly. Asexually.* LI'L BIT *quiets, sits perfectly still, and closes her eyes.*)

  Okay?

LI'L BIT: Yes.

(PECK *goes back to his camera.*)

PECK: I'm going to keep talking to you. Listen without responding to what I'm saying; you want to *listen* to the music. Sway, move just your torso or your head—I've got to check the light meter.

LI'L BIT: But—you'll be watching.

PECK: No—I'm not here—just my voice. Pretend you're in your room all alone on a Friday night with your mirror—and the music feels good—just move for me, Li'l Bit—

(LI'L BIT *closes her eyes. At first self-conscious; then she gets more into the music and begins to sway. We hear the camera start to whir. Throughout the shoot, there can be a slide montage of actual shots of the actor playing* LI'L BIT—*interspersed with other models à la* Playboy, *Calvin Klein, and Victoriana/Lewis Carroll's Alice Liddell)°*

  That's it. That looks great. Okay. Just keep doing that. Lift your head up a bit more, good, good, just keep moving, that a girl—you're a very beautiful young woman. Do you know that? (LI'L BIT *looks up, blushes.* PECK *shoots the camera. The audience should see this shot on the screen*)

LI'L BIT: No. I don't know that.

PECK: Listen to the music. (LI'L BIT *closes her eyes again*) Well you are. For a thirteen year old, you have a body a twenty-year-old woman would die for.

LI'L BIT: The boys in school don't think so.

PECK: The boys in school are little Neanderthals in short pants. You're ten years ahead of them in maturity; it's gonna take a while for them to catch up.

(PECK *clicks another shot; we see a faint smile on* LI'L BIT *on the screen.*)

  Girls turn into women long before boys turn into men.

LI'L BIT: Why is that?

PECK: I don't know, Li'l Bit. But it's a blessing for men.

  (LI'L BIT *turns silent*) Keep moving. Try arching your back on the stool, hands behind you, and throw your head back. (*The slide shows a* Playboy *model in this pose*) Oohh, great. That one was great. Turn your head away, same position. (*Whir*) Beautiful.

(LI'L BIT *looks at him a bit defiantly.*)

LI'L BIT: I think Aunt Mary is beautiful.

(PECK *stands still.*)

PECK: My wife is a very beautiful woman. Her beauty doesn't cancel yours out. (*More casually; he returns to the camera*) All the women in your family are beautiful. In fact, I think all women are. You're not listening to the music. (PECK *shoots some more film in silence*) All right, turn your head to the left. Good. Now take the back of your right hand and put it on your right cheek—your elbow angled up—now slowly, slowly, stroke your cheek, draw back your hair with the back of your hand. (*Another classic* Playboy *or Vargas*) Good. One hand above and behind your head; stretch your body; smile. (*Another pose*)

Alice Liddell, the young girl for whom Charles Dodgson (Lewis Carroll) wrote *Alice in Wonderland;* she also posed for photographs for Dodgson.

Li'l Bit. I want you to think of something that makes you laugh—

LI'L BIT: I can't think of anything.

PECK: Okay. Think of Big Papa chasing Grandma around the living room. (LI'L BIT *lifts her head and laughs. Click. We should see this shot*) Good. Both hands behind your head. Great! Hold that. *(From behind his camera)* You're doing great work. If we keep this up, in five years we'll have a really professional portfolio.

(LI'L BIT stops.)

LI'L BIT: What do you mean in five years?

PECK: You can't submit work to *Playboy* until you're eighteen.—

(PECK continues to shoot; he knows he's made a mistake.)

LI'L BIT: —Wait a minute. You're joking, aren't you, Uncle Peck?

PECK: Heck, no. You can't get into *Playboy* unless you're the very best. And you are the very best.

LI'L BIT: I would never do that!

(PECK stops shooting. He turns off the music.)

PECK: Why? There's nothing wrong with *Playboy*—it's a very classy maga—

LI'L BIT *(More upset)*: But I thought you said I should go to college!

PECK: Wait—Li'l Bit—it's nothing like that. Very respectable women model for *Playboy*—actresses with major careers—women in college—there's an Ivy League issue every—

LI'L BIT: —I'm never doing anything like that! You'd show other people these—other *men*—these— what I'm doing.—Why would you do that?! Any *boy* around here could just pick up, just go into The Stop & Go and *buy*—Why would you ever want to—to share—

PECK: —Whoa, whoa. Just stop a second and listen to me. Li'l Bit. Listen. There's nothing wrong in what we're doing. I'm very proud of you. I think you have a wonderful body and an even more wonderful mind. And of course I want other people to *appreciate* it. It's not anything shameful.

LI'L BIT *(Hurt)*: But this is something—that I'm only doing for you. This is something—that you said was just between us.

PECK: It is. And if that's how you feel, five years from now, it will remain that way. Okay? I know you're not going to do anything you don't feel like doing.
    (He walks back to the camera) Do you want to stop now? I've got just a few more shots on this roll—

LI'L BIT: I don't want anyone seeing this.

PECK: I swear to you. No one will. I'll treasure this— that you're doing this only for me.

(LI'L BIT, still shaken, sits on the stool. She closes her eyes) Li'l Bit? Open your eyes and look at me. (LI'L BIT *shakes her head no*) Come on. Just open your eyes, honey.

LI'L BIT: If I look at you—if I look at the camera: You're gonna know what I'm thinking. You'll see right through me—

PECK: —No, I won't. I want you to look at me. All right, then. I just want you to listen. Li'l Bit. *(She waits)* I love you. (LI'L BIT *opens her eyes; she is startled.* PECK *captures the shot. On the screen we see right through her.* PECK *says softly*) Do you know that? (LI'L BIT *nods her head yes*) I have loved you every day since the day you were born.

LI'L BIT: Yes.

*(LI'L BIT and PECK just look at each other. Beat. Beneath the shot of herself on the screen, LI'L BIT, still looking at her uncle, begins to unbutton her blouse.
A neutral Voice cuts off the above scene with:)*

Implied Consent.
As an individual operating a motor vehicle in the state of Maryland, you must abide by "Implied Consent." If you do not consent to take the blood alcohol content test, there may be severe penalties: a suspension of license, a fine, community service and a possible *jail* sentence.

(The Voice shifts tone:)

Idling in the Neutral Gear.

MALE GREEK CHORUS *(Announcing)*: Aunt Mary on behalf of her husband.

*(FEMALE GREEK CHORUS *checks her appearance, and with dignity comes to the front of the stage and sits down to talk to the audience.)*

FEMALE GREEK CHORUS *(As Aunt Mary)*: My husband was such a good man—is. Is such a good man. Every night, he does the dishes. The second he comes home, he's taking out the garbage, or doing yard work, lifting the heavy things I can't. Everyone in the neighborhood borrows Peck— it's true—women with husbands of their own, men who just don't have Peck's abilities—there's always a knock on our door for a jump start on cold mornings, when anyone needs a ride, or help shoveling the sidewalk—I look out, and there Peck is, without a coat, pitching in.

I know I'm lucky. The man works from dawn to dusk. And the overtime he does every year—my poor sister. She sits every Christmas when I come to dinner with a new stole, or diamonds, or with the tickets to Bermuda.

I know he has troubles. And we don't talk about them. I wonder, sometimes, what happened to him during the war. The men who fought World War II didn't have "rap sessions" to talk about their feelings. Men in his generation were expected to be quiet about it and get on with their lives. And sometimes I can feel him just fighting the trouble—whatever has burrowed deeper than the scar tissue—and we don't talk about it. I know he's having a bad spell because he comes looking for me in the house, and just hangs around me until it passes. And I keep my banter light—I discuss a new recipe, or sales, or gossip—because I think domesticity can be a balm for men when they're lost. We sit in the house and listen to the peace of the clock ticking in his well-ordered living room, until it passes.

(Sharply) I'm not a fool. I know what's going on. I wish you could feel how hard Peck fights against it—he's swimming against the tide, and what he needs is to see me on the shore, believing in him, knowing he won't go under, he won't give up—

And I want to say this about my niece. She's a sly one, that one is. She knows exactly what she's doing; she's twisted Peck around her little finger and thinks it's all a big secret. Yet another one who's borrowing my husband until it doesn't suit her anymore.

Well. I'm counting the days until she goes away to school. And she manipulates someone else. And then he'll come back again, and sit in the kitchen while I bake, or beside me on the sofa when I sew in the evenings. I'm a very patient woman. But I'd like my husband back.

I am counting the days.

(A Voice repeats:)

You and the Reverse Gear.

MALE GREEK CHORUS: Li'l Bit's Thirteenth Christmas. Uncle Peck Does the Dishes. Christmas 1964.

(PECK stands in a dress shirt and tie, nice pants, with an apron. He is washing dishes. He's in a mood we haven't seen. Quiet, brooding. LI'L BIT watches him a moment before seeking him out.)

LI'L BIT: Uncle Peck? *(He does not answer. He continues to work on the pots)* I didn't know where you'd gone to. *(He nods. She takes this as a sign to come in)* Don't you want to sit with us for a while?

PECK: No. I'd rather do the dishes.

(Pause. LI'L BIT watches him.)

LI'L BIT: You're the only man I know who does dishes. *(PECK says nothing)* I think it's really nice.

PECK: My wife has been on her feet all day. So's your grandmother and your mother.

LI'L BIT: I know. *(Beat)* Do you want some help?

PECK: No. *(He softens a bit towards her)* You can help by just talking to me.

LI'L BIT: Big Papa never does the dishes. I think it's nice.

PECK: I think men should be nice to women. Women are always working for us. There's nothing particularly manly in wolfing down food and then sitting around in a stupor while the women clean up.

LI'L BIT: That looks like a really neat camera that Aunt Mary got you.

PECK: It is. It's a very nice one.

(Pause, as PECK works on the dishes and some demon that LI'L BIT intuits.)

LI'L BIT: Did Big Papa hurt your feelings?

PECK *(Tired)*: What? Oh, no—it doesn't hurt me. Family is family. I'd rather have him picking on me than—I don't pay him any mind, Li'l Bit.

LI'L BIT: Are you angry with us?

PECK: No, Li'l Bit. I'm not angry.

(Another pause.)

LI'L BIT: We missed you at Thanksgiving. . . . I did. I missed you.

PECK: Well, there were . . . "things" going on. I didn't want to spoil anyone's Thanksgiving.

LI'L BIT: Uncle Peck? *(Very carefully)* Please don't drink anymore tonight.

PECK: I'm not . . . overdoing it.

LI'L BIT: I know. *(Beat)* Why do you drink so much?

(PECK stops and thinks, carefully.)

PECK: Well, Li'l Bit—let me explain it this way. There are some people who have a . . . a "fire" in the belly. I think they go to work on Wall Street or they run for office. And then there are people who have a "fire" in their heads—and they become writers or scientists or historians. *(He smiles a little at her)* You. You've got a "fire" in the head. And then there are people like me.

LI'L BIT: Where do you have . . . a fire?

PECK: I have a fire in my heart. And sometimes the drinking helps.

LI'L BIT: There's got to be other things that can help.

PECK: I suppose there are.

LI'L BIT: Does it help—to talk to me?

PECK: Yes. It does. *(Quiet)* I don't get to see you very much.

LI'L BIT: I know. *(LI'L BIT thinks)* You could talk to me more.

PECK: Oh?

LI'L BIT: I could make a deal with you, Uncle Peck.

PECK: I'm listening.

LI'L BIT: We could meet and talk—once a week. You could just store up whatever's bothering you during the week—and then we could talk.

PECK: Would you like that?

LI'L BIT: As long as you don't drink. I'd meet you

somewhere for lunch or for a walk—on the week-ends—as long as you stop drinking. And we could talk about whatever you want.

PECK: You would do that for me?

LI'L BIT: I don't think I'd want Mom to know. Or Aunt Mary. I wouldn't want them to think—

PECK: —No. It would just be us talking.

LI'L BIT: I'll tell Mom I'm going to a girlfriend's. To study. Mom doesn't get home until six, so you can call me after school and tell me where to meet you.

PECK: You get home at four?

LI'L BIT: We can meet once a week. But only in public. You've got to let me—draw the line. And once it's drawn, you mustn't cross it.

PECK: Understood.

LI'L BIT: Would that help?

(PECK *is very moved.*)

PECK: Yes. Very much.

LI'L BIT: I'm going to join the others in the living room now. (LI'L BIT *turns to go*)

PECK: Merry Christmas, Li'l Bit.

(LI'L BIT *bestows a very warm smile on him.*)

LI'L BIT: Merry Christmas, Uncle Peck.

(*A Voice dictates:*)

Shifting Forward from Second to Third Gear.

(*The* MALE AND FEMALE GREEK CHORUS *members come forward.*)

MALE GREEK CHORUS: 1969. Days and Gifts: A Count-down:

FEMALE GREEK CHORUS: A note. "September 3, 1969. Li'l Bit: You've only been away two days and it feels like months. Hope your dorm room is cozy. I'm sending you this tape cassette—it's a new model—so you'll have some music in your room. Also that music you're reading about for class— *Carmina Burana.*° Hope you enjoy. Only ninety days to go!—Peck."

MALE GREEK CHORUS: September 22. A bouquet of roses. A note: "Miss you like crazy. Sixty-nine days . . ."

TEENAGE GREEK CHORUS: September 25. A box of chocolates. A card: "Don't worry about the weight gain. You still look great. Got a post office box— write to me there. Sixty-six days.—Love, your candy man."

MALE GREEK CHORUS: October 16. A note: "Am trying to get through the Jane Austen you're reading—

Emma°—here's a book in return: *Liaisons Dan-gereuses.*° Hope you're saving time for me." Scrawled in the margin the number: "47."

FEMALE GREEK CHORUS: November 16. "Sixteen days to go!—Hope you like the perfume.—Having a hard time reaching you on the dorm phone. You must be in the library a lot. Won't you think about me getting you your own phone so we can talk?"

TEENAGE GREEK CHORUS: November 18. "Li'l Bit—got a package returned to the P.O. Box. Have you changed dorms? Call me at work or write to the P.O. Am still on the wagon. Waiting to see you. Only two weeks more!"

MALE GREEK CHORUS: November 23. A letter. "Li'l Bit. So disappointed you couldn't come home for the turkey. Sending you some money for a nice din-ner out—nine days and counting!"

GREEK CHORUS (*In unison*): November 25th. A letter:

LI'L BIT: "Dear Uncle Peck: I am sending this to you at work. Don't come up next weekend for my birth-day. I will not be here—"

(*A Voice directs:*)

Shifting Forward from Third to Fourth Gear.

MALE GREEK CHORUS: December 10, 1969. A hotel room. Philadelphia. There is no moon tonight.

(PECK *sits on the side of the bed while* LI'L BIT *paces. He can't believe she's in his room, but there's a desperate edge to his happiness.* LI'L BIT *is furious, edgy. There is a bottle of champagne in an ice bucket in a very nice hotel room.*)

PECK: Why don't you sit?

LI'L BIT: I don't want to.—What's the champagne for?

PECK: I thought we might toast your birthday—

LI'L BIT: —I am so pissed off at you, Uncle Peck.

PECK: Why?

LI'L BIT: I mean, are you crazy?

PECK: What did I do?

LI'L BIT: You scared the holy crap out of me—sending me that stuff in the mail—

PECK: —They were gifts! I just wanted to give you some little perks your first semester—

LI'L BIT: —Well, what the hell were those numbers all about! Forty-four days to go—only two more weeks.—And then just numbers—69—68—67— like some serial killer!

PECK: Li'l Bit! Whoa! This is me you're talking to—I was just trying to pick up your spirits, trying to cel-ebrate your birthday.

LI'L BIT: My *eighteenth* birthday. I'm not a child, Uncle

Carmina Burana, literally "profane songs," Carl Orff's 1937 setting of medieval Latin songs about wine, women, and love.

Emma, 1816 novel by Jane Austen. ***Les Liaisons Dan-gereuses,*** 1782 epistolary novel by Choderlos de Laclos detail-ing a series of seductions, including one of a fifteen-year-old girl by an older man.

Peck. You were counting down to my eighteenth birthday.

PECK: So?

LI'L BIT: So? So statutory rape is not in effect when a young woman turns eighteen. And you and I both know it.

(PECK *is walking on ice.*)

PECK: I think you misunderstand.

LI'L BIT: I think I understand all too well. I know what you want to do five steps ahead of you doing it. Defensive Driving 101.

PECK: Then why did you suggest we meet here instead of the restaurant?

LI'L BIT: I don't want to have this conversation in public.

PECK: Fine. Fine. We have a lot to talk about.

LI'L BIT: Yeah. We do.
(LI'L BIT *doesn't want to do what she has to do*) Could I . . . have some of that champagne?

PECK: Of course, madam! (PECK *makes a big show of it*) Let me do the honors. I wasn't sure which you might prefer—Taittingers or Veuve Clicquot—so I thought we'd start out with an old standard— Perrier Jouet. (*The bottle is popped*)
Quick—Li'l Bit—your glass! (UNCLE PECK *fills* LI'L BIT*'s glass. He puts the bottle back in the ice and goes for a can of ginger ale*) Let me get some of this ginger ale—my bubbly—and toast you.

(*He turns and sees that* LI'L BIT *has not waited for him.*)

LI'L BIT: Oh—sorry, Uncle Peck. Let me have another.
(PECK *fills her glass and reaches for his ginger ale; she stops him*) Uncle Peck—maybe you should join me in the champagne.

PECK: You want me to—drink?

LI'L BIT: It's not polite to let a lady drink alone.

PECK: Well, missy, if you insist. . . . (PECK *hesitates*)— Just one. It's been a while. (PECK *fills another flute for himself*) There. I'd like to propose a toast to you and your birthday! (PECK *sips it tentatively*) I'm not used to this anymore.

LI'L BIT: You don't have anywhere to go tonight, do you?

(PECK *hopes this is a good sign.*)

PECK: I'm all yours.—God, it's good to see you! I've gotten so used to . . . to . . . talking to you in my head. I'm used to seeing you every week—there's so much—I don't quite know where to begin. How's school, Li'l Bit?

LI'L BIT: I—it's hard. Uncle Peck. Harder than I thought it would be. I'm in the middle of exams and papers and—I don't know.

PECK: You'll pull through. You always do.

LI'L BIT: Maybe. I . . . might be flunking out.

PECK: You always think the worst, Li'l Bit, but when

the going gets tough—(LI'L BIT *shrugs and pours herself another glass*)—Hey, honey, go easy on that stuff, okay?

LI'L BIT: Is it very expensive?

PECK: Only the best for you. But the cost doesn't matter—champagne should be "sipped." (LI'L BIT *is quiet*) Look—if you're in trouble in school—you can always come back home for a while.

LI'L BIT: No—(LI'L BIT *tries not to be so harsh*)—Thanks, Uncle Peck, but I'll figure some way out of this.

PECK: You're supposed to get in scrapes, your first year away from home.

LI'L BIT: Right. How's Aunt Mary?

PECK: She's fine. (*Pause*) Well—how about the new car?

LI'L BIT: It's real nice. What is it, again?

PECK: It's a Cadillac El Dorado.

LI'L BIT: Oh. Well, I'm real happy for you, Uncle Peck.

PECK: I got it for you.

LI'L BIT: What?

PECK: I always wanted to get a Cadillac—but I thought, Peck, wait until Li'l Bit's old enough— and thought maybe you'd like to drive it, too.

LI'L BIT (*Confused*): Why would I want to drive your car?

PECK: Just because it's the best—I want you to have the best.

(*They are running out of "gas"; small talk.*)

LI'L BIT: Listen, Uncle Peck, I don't know how to begin this, but—

PECK: I have been thinking of how to say this in my head, over and over—

PECK: Sorry.

LI'L BIT: You first.

PECK: Well, your going away—has just made me realize how much I miss you. Talking to you and being alone with you. I've really come to depend on you, Li'l Bit. And it's been so hard to get in touch with you lately—the distance and—and you're never in when I call—I guess you've been living in the library—

LI'L BIT: —No—the problem is, I haven't been in the library—

PECK: —Well, it doesn't matter—I hope you've been missing me as much.

LI'L BIT: Uncle Peck—I've been thinking a lot about this—and I came here tonight to tell you that— I'm not doing very well. I'm getting very confused—I can't concentrate on my work—and now that I'm away—I've been going over and over it in my mind—and I don't want us to "see" each other anymore. Other than with the rest of the family.

PECK (*Quiet*): Are you seeing other men?

LI'L BIT (*Getting agitated*): I—no, that's not the reason—I—well, yes, I am seeing other—listen, it's not really anybody's business!

PECK: Are you in love with anyone else?

LI'L BIT: That's not what this is about.

PECK: Li'l Bit—you're scared. Your mother and your grandparents have filled your head with all kinds of nonsense about men—I hear them working on you all the time—and you're scared. It won't hurt you—if the man you go to bed with really loves you. (LI'L BIT *is scared. She starts to tremble*) And I have loved you since the day I held you in my hand. And I think everyone's just gotten you frightened to death about something that is just like breathing—

LI'L BIT: Oh, my god—(*She takes a breath*) I can't see you anymore, Uncle Peck.

(PECK *downs the rest of his champagne.*)

PECK: Li'l Bit. Listen. Listen. Open your eyes and look at me. Come on. Just open your eyes, honey. (LI'L BIT, *eyes squeezed shut, refuses*) All right then. I just want you to listen. Li'l Bit—I'm going to ask you just this once. Of your own free will. Just lie down on the bed with me—our clothes on—just lie down with me, a man and a woman . . . and let's . . . hold one another. Nothing else. Before you say anything else. I want the chance to . . . hold you. Because sometimes the body knows things that the mind isn't listening to . . . and after I've held you, then I want you to tell me what you feel.

LI'L BIT: You'll just . . . hold me?

PECK: Yes. And then you can tell me what you're feeling.

(LI'L BIT—*half wanting to run, half wanting to get it over with, half wanting to be held by him:*)

LI'L BIT: Yes. All right. Just hold. Nothing else.

(PECK *lies down on the bed and holds his arms out to her.* LI'L BIT *lies beside him, putting her head on his chest. He looks as if he's trying to soak her into his pores by osmosis. He strokes her hair, and she lies very still. The* MALE GREEK CHORUS *member and the* FEMALE GREEK CHORUS *member as Aunt Mary come into the room.*)

MALE GREEK CHORUS: Recipe for a Southern Boy:

FEMALE GREEK CHORUS (*As Aunt Mary*): A drawl of molasses in the way he speaks.

MALE GREEK CHORUS: A gumbo of red and brown mixed in the cream of his skin.

(*While* PECK *lies, his eyes closed,* LI'L BIT *rises in the bed and responds to her aunt.*)

LI'L BIT: Warm brown eyes—

FEMALE GREEK CHORUS (*As Aunt Mary*): Bedroom eyes—

MALE GREEK CHORUS: A dash of Southern Baptist Fire and Brimstone—

LI'L BIT: A curl of Elvis on his forehead—

FEMALE GREEK CHORUS (*As Aunt Mary*): A splash of Bay Rum—

MALE GREEK CHORUS: A closely shaven beard that he razors just for you—

FEMALE GREEK CHORUS (*As Aunt Mary*): Large hands—rough hands—

LI'L BIT: Warm hands—

MALE GREEK CHORUS: The steel of the military in his walk—

LI'L BIT: The slouch of the fishing skiff in his walk—

MALE GREEK CHORUS: Neatly pressed khakis—

FEMALE GREEK CHORUS (*As Aunt Mary*): And under the wide leather of the belt—

LI'L BIT: Sweat of cypress and sand—

MALE GREEK CHORUS: Neatly pressed khakis—

LI'L BIT: His heart beating Dixie—

FEMALE GREEK CHORUS (*As Aunt Mary*): The whisper of the zipper—you could reach out with your hand and—

LI'L BIT: His mouth—

FEMALE GREEK CHORUS (*As Aunt Mary*): You could just reach out and—

LI'L BIT: Hold him in your hand—

FEMALE GREEK CHORUS (*As Aunt Mary*): And his mouth—

(LI'L BIT *rises above her uncle and looks at his mouth; she starts to lower herself to kiss him—and wrenches herself free. She gets up from the bed.*)

LI'L BIT: —I've got to get back.

PECK: Wait—Li'l Bit. Did you . . . feel nothing?

LI'L BIT (*Lying*): No. Nothing.

PECK: Do you—do you think of me?

(*The* GREEK CHORUS *whispers:*)

FEMALE GREEK CHORUS: Khakis—

MALE GREEK CHORUS: Bay Rum—

FEMALE GREEK CHORUS: The whisper of the—

LI'L BIT: —No.

(PECK, *in a rush, trembling, gets something out of his pocket.*)

PECK: I'm forty-five. That's not old for a man. And I haven't been able to do anything else but think of you. I can't concentrate on my work—Li'l Bit. You've got to—I want you to think about what I am about to ask you.

LI'L BIT: I'm listening.

(PECK *opens a small ring box.*)

PECK: I want you to be my wife.

LI'L BIT: This isn't happening.

PECK: I'll tell Mary I want a divorce. We're not blood-related. It would be legal—

LI'L BIT: —What have you been thinking! You are married to my aunt, Uncle Peck. She's my family.

You have—you have gone way over the line. Family is family.

(*Quickly,* LI'L BIT *flies through the room, gets her coat*) I'm leaving. Now. I am not seeing you. Again.

(PECK *lies down on the bed for a moment, trying to absorb the terrible news. For a moment, he almost curls into a fetal position.*)

I'm not coming home for Christmas. You should go home to Aunt Mary. Go home now, Uncle Peck.

(PECK *gets control, and sits, rigid.*)

Uncle Peck?—I'm sorry but I have to go.

(*Pause*)

Are you all right?

(*With a discipline that comes from being told that boys don't cry,* PECK *stands upright.*)

PECK: I'm fine. I just think—I need a real drink.

(*The* MALE GREEK CHORUS *has become a bartender. At a small counter, he is lining up shots for* PECK. *As* LI'L BIT *narrates, we see* PECK *sitting, carefully and calmly downing shot glasses.*)

LI'L BIT (*To the audience*): I never saw him again. I stayed away from Christmas and Thanksgiving for years after.

It took my uncle seven years to drink himself to death. First he lost his job, then his wife, and finally his driver's license. He retreated to his house, and had his bottles delivered.

(PECK *stands, and puts his hands in front of him—almost like Superman flying*)

One night he tried to go downstairs to the basement—and he flew down the steep basement stairs. My aunt came by weekly to put food on the porch, and she noticed the mail and the papers stacked up, uncollected.

They found him at the bottom of the stairs. Just steps away from his dark room.

Now that I'm old enough, there are some questions I would have liked to have asked him. Who did it to you, Uncle Peck? How old were you? Were you eleven?

(PECK *moves to the driver's seat of the car and waits*)

Sometimes I think of my uncle as a kind of Flying Dutchman. In the opera, the Dutchman is doomed to wander the sea; but every seven years he can come ashore, and if he finds a maiden who will love him of her own free will—he will be released.

And I see Uncle Peck in my mind, in his Chevy '56, a spirit driving up and down the back roads of Carolina—looking for a young girl who, of her own free will, will love him. Release him.

(*A Voice states:*)

You and the Reverse Gear.

LI'L BIT: The summer of 1962. On Men, Sex, and Women: Part III:

(LI'L BIT *steps, as an eleven-year-old, into:*)

FEMALE GREEK CHORUS (*As Mother*): It is out of the question. End of Discussion.

LI'L BIT: But why?

FEMALE GREEK CHORUS (*As Mother*): Li'l Bit—we are not discussing this. I said no.

LI'L BIT: But I could spend an extra week at the beach! You're not telling me why!

FEMALE GREEK CHORUS (*As Mother*): Your uncle pays entirely too much attention to you.

LI'L BIT: He listens to me when I talk. And—and he talks to me. He teaches me about things. Mama—he knows an awful lot.

FEMALE GREEK CHORUS (*As Mother*): He's a small town hick who's learned how to mix drinks from Hugh Hefner.°

LI'L BIT: Who's Hugh Hefner?

(*Beat.*)

FEMALE GREEK CHORUS (*As Mother*): I am not letting an eleven-year-old girl spend seven hours alone in the car with a man. . . . I don't like the way your uncle looks at you.

LI'L BIT: For god's sake, mother! Just because you've gone through a bad time with my father—you think every man is evil!

FEMALE GREEK CHORUS (*As Mother*): Oh no, Li'l Bit—not all men. . . . We . . . we just haven't been very lucky with the men in our family.

LI'L BIT: Just because you lost your husband—I still deserve a chance at having a father! Someone! A man who will look out for me! Don't I get a chance?

FEMALE GREEK CHORUS (*As Mother*): I will feel terrible if something happens.

LI'L BIT: Mother! It's in your head! Nothing will happen! I can take care of myself. And I can certainly handle Uncle Peck.

FEMALE GREEK CHORUS (*As Mother*): All right. But I'm warning you—if anything happens, I hold you responsible.

(LI'L BIT *moves out of this scene and toward the car.*)

LI'L BIT: 1962. On the Back Roads of Carolina: The First Driving Lesson.

(*The* TEENAGE GREEK CHORUS *member stands apart on stage. She will speak all of* LI'L BIT*'s lines.* LI'L BIT *sits*

Hugh Hefner, publisher of *Playboy* magazine.

beside PECK *in the front seat. She looks at him closely, remembering.*)

PECK: Li'l Bit? Are you getting tired?

TEENAGE GREEK CHORUS: A little.

PECK: It's a long drive. But we're making really good time. We can take the back road from here and see . . . a little scenery. Say—I've got an idea— (PECK *checks his rearview mirror*)

TEENAGE GREEK CHORUS: Are we stopping, Uncle Peck?

PECK: There's no traffic here. Do you want to drive?

TEENAGE GREEK CHORUS: I can't drive.

PECK: It's easy. I'll show you how. I started driving when I was your age. Don't you want to?—

TEENAGE GREEK CHORUS: —But it's against the law at my age!

PECK: And that's why you can't tell anyone I'm letting you do this—

TEENAGE GREEK CHORUS: —But—I can't reach the pedals.

PECK: You can sit in my lap and steer. I'll push the pedals for you. Did your father ever let you drive his car?

TEENAGE GREEK CHORUS: No way.

PECK: Want to try?

TEENAGE GREEK CHORUS: Okay. (LI'L BIT *moves into* PECK's *lap. She leans against him, closing her eyes*)

PECK: You're just a little thing, aren't you? Okay—now think of the wheel as a big clock—I want you to put your right hand on the clock where three o'clock would be; and your left hand on the nine—

(LI'L BIT *puts one hand to* PECK's *face, to stroke him. Then, she takes the wheel.*)

TEENAGE GREEK CHORUS: Am I doing it right?

PECK: That's right. Now, whatever you do, don't let go of the wheel. You tell me whether to go faster or slower—

TEENAGE GREEK CHORUS: Not so fast, Uncle Peck!

PECK: Li'l Bit—I need you to watch the road—

(PECK *puts his hands on* LI'L BIT's *breasts. She relaxes against him, silent, accepting his touch.*)

TEENAGE GREEK CHORUS: Uncle Peck—what are you doing?

PECK: Keep driving. (*He slips his hands under her blouse.*)

TEENAGE GREEK CHORUS: Uncle Peck—please don't do this—

PECK: —Just a moment longer . . . (PECK *tenses against* LI'L BIT)

TEENAGE GREEK CHORUS (*Trying not to cry*): This isn't happening.

(PECK *tenses more, sharply. He buries his face in* LI'L BIT's *neck, and moans softly. The* TEENAGE GREEK CHORUS *exits, and* LI'L BIT *steps out of the car.* PECK, *too, disappears.*

A Voice reflects:)

Driving in Today's World.

LI'L BIT: That day was the last day I lived in my body. I retreated above the neck, and I've lived inside the "fire" in my head ever since.

And now that seems like a long, long time ago. When we were both very young.

And before you know it, I'll be thirty-five. That's getting up there for a woman. And I find myself believing in things that a younger self vowed never to believe in. Things like family and forgiveness.

I know I'm lucky. Although I still have never known what it feels like to jog or dance. Any thing that . . . "jiggles." I do like to watch people on the dance floor, or out on the running paths, just jiggling away. And I say—good for them. (LI'L BIT *moves to the car with pleasure*)

The nearest sensation I feel—of flight in the body—I guess I feel when I'm driving. On a day like today. It's five A.M. The radio says it's going to be clear and crisp. I've got five hundred miles of highway ahead of me—and some back roads too. I filled the tank last night, and had the oil checked. Checked the tires, too. You've got to treat her . . . with respect.

First thing I do is: Check under the car. To see if any two year olds or household cats have crawled beneath, and strategically placed their skulls behind my back tires. (LI'L BIT *crouches*)

Nope. Then I get in the car. (LI'L BIT *does so*)

I lock the doors. And turn the key. Then I adjust the most important control on the dashboard—the radio—(LI'L BIT *turns the radio on: We hear all of the* GREEK CHORUS *overlapping, and static:*)

FEMALE GREEK CHORUS (*Overlapping*): —"You were so tiny you fit in his hand—"

MALE GREEK CHORUS (*Overlapping*): —"How is Shakespeare gonna help her lie on her back in the—"

TEENAGE GREEK CHORUS (*Overlapping*): —"Am I doing it right?"

(LI'L BIT *fine-tunes the radio station. A song like "Dedicated to the One I Love" or Orbison's "Sweet Dreams" comes on, and cuts off the* GREEK CHORUS.)

LI'L BIT: Ahh . . . (*Beat*) I adjust my seat. Fasten my seat belt. Then I check the right side mirror—check the left side. (*She does*) Finally, I adjust the rearview mirror. (*As* LI'L BIT *adjusts the rearview mirror, a faint light strikes the spirit of* UNCLE PECK, *who is sitting in the back seat of the car. She sees him in the mirror. She smiles at him, and he nods at her. They are happy to be going for a long ride together.* LI'L BIT *slips the car into first gear; to the audience:*) And then—I floor it. (*Sound of a car taking off. Blackout*)

END OF PLAY

Figure 1. Peck (David Morse) starts to unbutton Li'l Bit's (Mary-Louise Parker) sweater as he gets her ready for a series of photographs. The 1997 premiere of *How I Learned to Drive,* at the Vineyard Theatre, New York City, was directed by Mark Brokaw. (Photograph: Carol Rosegg.)

Figure 2. Li'l Bit (Mary-Louise Parker) smiles as Peck (David Morse) arranges her position in front of the camera, in the 1997 production of *How I Learned to Drive*. (Photograph: Carol Rosegg.)

Figure 3. Yielding to Peck's (David Morse) plea, "Just lie down on the bed with me—our clothes on—just lie down with me," Li'l Bit (Mary-Louise Parker) stares sadly into space, while Peck's face reflects his satisfaction, in the 1997 production of *How I Learned to Drive*. (Photograph: Carol Rosegg.)

Staging of *How I Learned to Drive*

INTERVIEW WITH PAULA VOGEL, 1998, BY
ARTHUR HOLMBERG

HOLMBERG: Your plays frequently deal with taboos. If I had to explain your theatrical signature to someone unfamiliar with your work, I would say that you trespass into forbidden territory with a smile on your face. You disturb the bones of forbidden topics, then make the audience laugh. What is the function of humor in your vision?

VOGEL: I actually describe *Drive* as a comedy. Of course it's not, but the first half very much functions as comedy. At some elemental level, it is who I am. My family had the most inappropriate moments of humor at funerals. Maybe it's a survival strategy. Some people say that this comes from Jewish genes. At the beginning of the *Baltimore Waltz* [a play about her brother's death from AIDS] I used a real letter my brother wrote me with instructions for his funeral that included directions on how to lay him out in the coffin in drag. For me combining sadness and comedy heightens both. The collision of tones makes both more extreme. One of my favorite movies is Roman Polanski's *The Fearless Vampire Killers*. I've seen it sixteen times, and the reason I watch it so often is the combination of terror and comedy. You're scared to the point of screaming, then he cracks a joke. It doesn't defuse the terror, it defuses the guarding against the terror. We don't want to be taken by surprise, so we keep our guard up. Comedy defuses that vigilance so in the next moment we are unprepared for the explosion. I'll give you an example. There is a little Jewish hotel keeper who lusts after voluptuous young women in the village, but his wife keeps him on a tight leash. One night he stays out too late, and vampires kill him. In the grave he is finally beyond his wife's reach. So he comes back that night to get a buxom virgin. She screams and screams, and it's a horrifying moment. He starts to attack, she reaches for a cross, and he says, "Boy, have you got the wrong vampire," then lunges for the kill. The comedy dismantles any protective covering. Hitchcock uses comedy and terror the same way. So that's why I think I do it.

HOLMBERG: Humor is also a form of seduction. In one of the play's funniest speeches, "A Mother's Guide to Social Drinking," an older woman tells a young girl how not to get drunk. She advises her never to touch a drink with a sexual position in the name like Dead Man Screw or The Missionary and to learn to drink like a man: straight up. The speech makes the audience laugh, but then you hit hard with an emotionally devastating scene.

VOGEL: Li'l Bit's drunk and can't defend herself.

HOLMBERG: A double seduction, Li'l Bit and the audience.

VOGEL: Comedy is complicity. If you make an audience laugh . . .

HOLMBERG: They are your friends.

VOGEL: Not only your friends, but also in alliance with the play world. They're on the side of the play now because they laughed.

HOLMBERG: Many of your plays deal with families. European critics often say American drama does not achieve greatness because our playwrights, obsessed by petty family melodramas, never look through the living room window to see the larger world and the problems outside.

VOGEL: Rubbish. The Greeks dealt with the family. Aristotle describes domestic violence among kings as tragedy. British critics often throw that complaint at me, but Pinter and David Hare also deal with families. It's important that the family be put in its social context, that there is a world beyond. The family remains the structure at the heart of most drama because the family, after all, reflects its community's values and the politics of their time.

HOLMBERG: *King Lear* and *The Oresteia* are family dramas.

VOGEL: So is *Hamlet* and *Mother Courage*. The great American playwrights, like the great European playwrights, like the great global playwrights, deal with the family as a unit within a greater body politic.

HOLMBERG: So how do you see *Drive* as political?

VOGEL: A lot of people are trying to turn this into a drama about an individual family. To me it is not. It is a way of looking on a microcosmic level at how this culture sexualizes children. How we are taught at an extremely early age to look at female bodies. One of the tag lines I had in my head when I was writing this play was, it takes a whole village to molest a child. Jon Benet Ramsey was not a fluke. When we Americans saw the video tape of her at the beauty contest when she was five, a chill went up our collective spines. At what age are we sexualizing our children in a consumer culture to sell blue jeans and underwear? So children's bodies are sexualized all the way down from Madison Avenue to the wealthy suburb of Denver where the Ramseys lived. I would call that political and

Arthur Holmberg is Literary Director of the American Repertory Theatre and Associate Professor of Theater at Brandeis University.

not specifically the psychopathology of an individual family. I would say that's cultural. And now we are starting to see a sexualized gaze toward young boys. Leonardo DiCaprio enjoys cult status because he looks prepubescent. Wherever there is confusion or double, triple, and quadruple standards, that is the realm of theatre. Drama lives in paradoxes and contradictions. If you look at the structure of my play, all I'm doing is asking how do you feel about this? We see a girl of seventeen and an older man in a car seat. You think you know how you feel about this relationship? Alright, fine. Now, let's go back a year earlier. Do you still think you know what you feel about this situation? Great. Now let's change the situation a little bit more. He's married to her aunt. How do you feel about that? The play allows me this kind of slippage because we have these contradictory feelings about the sexuality of boys and girls. So I tease out those contradictions. The play is a reverse syllogism. It constantly pulls the rug out from under our emotional responses by going back earlier and earlier in time. The play moves in reverse.

HOLMBERG: Earlier you said we are starting to see a sexual gaze turned towards young boys. *Drive* eroticizes the male. American playwrights have generally shied away from the eroticized male, even overtly homosexual playwrights like Tennessee Williams or William Inge. In Williams and Inge the sexualized male is dangerous or dysfunctional. So even gay playwrights are terrified of eroticized men.

VOGEL: I'm not. Here I am the "out" lesbian, but my pronounced subject position as a lesbian does not mean that I do not love the male of the species. In my plays, I want to present women as desiring subjects, which means that men sometimes become the object of the female gaze. But this also goes back to *Baltimore Waltz,* in which I wanted to pay homage to my brother's desire for men. In order to do that I used a woman subject desiring the male body. I wanted the audience to appreciate how beautiful the male body is. Some women automatically do that, so I used a woman, and through a female subject, straight men who are homophobic would go, yeah, I can see how she finds him beautiful. And if I've got them there, I've got the entire audience understanding that the male body can be a desired object. And then I am halfway there in terms of overcoming our homophobia towards men on stage. The two male actors in *Baltimore Waltz* were so beautiful—Richard Thompson and Joe Mantello. They took my breath away. How could you not want to touch that? How could you judge anyone for desiring those men? It was initially something that I worked with to embrace my brother's gaze as a gay man.

HOLMBERG: *Drive* eroticizes the female as well as the male, but in different ways. Whereas you eroticize the

male verbally in "Recipe for a Southern Boy," you eroticize the female visually.

VOGEL: Yes, Li'l Bit's eroticized through the photo shoots, through the visual presentation of the body. When I was doing research for *Hot 'n' Throbbing* [a play about female pornography that premiered at the A.R.T.], I discovered that women tend to eroticize through words and narration as much or more than through the eyes. So for me "Recipe for a Southern Boy" was the way to really present the desiring female subject and the desired male object.

HOLMBERG: *Drive* dramatizes in a disturbing way how we receive great harm from the people who love us.

VOGEL: I would reverse that. I would say that we can receive great love from the people who harm us.

HOLMBERG: Why is it significant to reverse it?

VOGEL: We are now living in a culture of victimization, and great harm can be inflicted by well-intentioned therapists, social workers, and talk show hosts who encourage people to dwell in their identity as victim. Without denying or forgetting the original pain, I wanted to write about the great gifts that can also be inside that box of abuse. My play dramatizes the gifts we receive from the people who hurt us.

HOLMBERG: So what does Li'l Bit receive?

VOGEL: She received the gift of how to survive.

HOLMBERG: From her Uncle?

VOGEL: Absolutely. I am going to teach you to drive like a man, he says. He becomes her mentor and shows her a way of thinking ahead ten steps down the road before anyone else to figure out what the other guy is going to do before he does it. That not only enables her to survive but actually enables her, I think, to reject him and destroy him.

HOLMBERG: And she does destroy him.

VOGEL: He gives her the gifts to do that. He gives her the training. He gives her the ego formation. You, he says, you've got a fire in the head. He gives her gifts in just about every scene. He teaches her the importance of herself as an individual and the ability to strategize to protect that. It's all there in the driving lessons. It's abuse simultaneously with a kind of affirmation and reassurance.

HOLMBERG: In *Drive*, Li'l Bit looks at her painful memories, processes the experiences, and then moves on. Why is it important to forgive the harm?

VOGEL: Many people stay rooted in anger against transgressions that occurred in childhood, and this rage will be directed to other people in their adult lives and toward themselves. Whether we call it forgiveness or understanding, there comes a moment when the past has to be processed, and we have to find some control. There are two forgivenesses in the play. One forgiveness for Peck, but the most crucial forgiveness would be Li'l Bit's forgiving Li'l Bit. Li'l Bit as an adult looking at and understanding her complicity . . .

HOLMBERG: Her destructiveness. You once said that it was important to give the audience a catharsis.

VOGEL: Catharsis purges the pity and the terror and enables the audience to transcend them. So you have her memories of the final confrontation with Peck in the hotel room and afterwards the flashback to the first driving lesson. And then the last scene, which brings us up to the present. This is a movement forward. For me, purgation means a forward movement.

HOLMBERG: In *Drive,* as in many of your plays, music is a crucial element.

VOGEL: Music contains a subliminal message that I will never be able to accomplish with words because words always involve the cognitive. Music speaks directly to the emotions. So for me as a playwright, music is an important ally. It is also important as a way of saying this was gender in 1960.

HOLMBERG: Gender? You gender music?

VOGEL: Yes. It has messages about being a man and being a woman. When you listen to the Beach Boys what comes back is a code of the 1960s. Just like disco music brings back the entire culture of the seventies. So I used music to get to the culture of the 60s. Music is a time capsule.

HOLMBERG: You're a feminist, but some critics have called your plays misogynistic.

VOGEL: In the 70s a lot of people at the Women's Project [an important theatre company in N.Y.] thought I was misogynistic. And Julia Miles always commented that my work was so negative about women, that it was so dark and distressing. For me being a feminist does not mean showing a positive image of women. For me being a feminist means looking at things that disturb me, looking at things that hurt me as a woman. We live in a misogynist world, and I want to see why. And I want to look and see why not just men are the enemy but how I as a woman participate in the system. To say that men are the enemy is patronizing. It makes me a victim, and I am not confortable as a victim. It's a mistake to attribute goodness, pure abstract goodness, to either sex. I don't recognize that, so maybe I'm not extremely feminist. To me a play doesn't need to make me feel good. It can be a view of the world that is so upsetting

that when I leave the theatre, I want to say no to that play, I will not allow that to happen in my life.

HOLMBERG: *Desdemona* [a play in which Vogel explores the secret lives of the women in Shakespeare's tragedy] may not have positive female role models, but it most certainly is a feminist play.

VOGEL: *Desdemona* shows how women participate in a social system that does not allow them to bond. We bond with our husbands and our class structure rather than with each other. I don't know how you can get more feminist than that. Does it make me feel good? No. Does it worry me? Yes. Does it call on me to act? Absolutely. At the moment, we women are colluding with the patriarchal system and with the class structure. You can't deport the enemy, the enemy is inside us. The really dangerous enemy is that we have internalized misogyny and homophobia. There were a lot of headlines, "Lesbian wins Pulitzer, blah, blah, blah . . ." I am the first person to say, hey wait, I'm not here to make every one else feel homophobic, I'm homophobic. I was brought up in this country. I was taught to hate gays. I was taught to hate women. What we are taught to hate unifies us as a society. Our communal bond is that we are all racist, not just whites. Blacks are racist, Latinos are racist. We're taught racism the way we're taught homophobia and misogyny. It's all internalized. So it's not clear-cut to me, here is the good guy and here is the bad guy. I understand Strindberg. Strindberg is an extremely powerfully ally for me as a woman dramatist because in his plays there is a fear and a power of woman not approached by any other dramatist. In grad school, I steeped myself in Strindberg. He is a remarkable dramatist. But in the sixties and seventies, feminist theatre did not produce plays of negative empathy. Like Hollywood, they only wanted positive role models—feel-good role models. There is nothing wrong with that. It is necessary, and I am finally about to write my first play with a positive role model. It takes place on the last Christmas Eve of the Civil War in Washington DC. The kids in my family—my nephews and godchildren—keep asking, "When can we see one of your plays," and I go, "Oh, maybe in another ten years when you're old enough." So now I'm writing a Christmas play with positive role models for the kids.

SUZAN-LORI PARKS

1964–

> As a Black person writing for theatre, what is theatre good for? What can theatre do for us? We can "tell it like it is"; "tell it as it was"; "tell it as it could be." In my plays I do all 3; and the writing is rich because we are not an impoverished people, but a wealthy people fallen on hard times.

Suzan-Lori Parks not only makes bold claims for her writing (and her heritage), but she matches her claims with substantial achievements: two Obie Awards for the best Off-Broadway play (in 1990 and 1996), a Guggenheim fellowship, a MacArthur Foundation "genius" grant, and, in May 2002, the Pulitzer Prize for her play *Topdog/Underdog*, the first Pulitzer Prize in drama awarded to an African American woman. Her plays have been produced at the Yale Repertory Theater, and at the Joseph Papp Public Theater/New York Shakespeare Festival, and film director Spike Lee asked her to write the screenplay for *Girl 6* (1996). And fellow playwright Tony Kushner, interviewed in 1994 (soon after he had won every award in sight for *Angels in America*), called her "the best playwright in the country today," adding, "She's completely extraordinary. I'm insanely jealous of her, and I think people should see her work."

Parks brings to her playwriting the multiple perspectives gained from being both an outsider and a privileged insider. Her father was a colonel in the U.S. Army, his career requiring him to move his family from state to state, and, while Parks was in junior high school, to West Germany, an experience that made her an outsider not because she was black but because she was a foreigner. As an undergraduate at Mt. Holyoke College, she studied with James Baldwin, the African American novelist and playwright who had, like Parks, lived abroad—and who encouraged her to write not just short stories but plays. Influenced by the experimental fiction of James Joyce, Samuel Beckett, and Virginia Woolf, and by the nontraditional approach to drama of Adrienne Kennedy and Ntozake Shange, Parks's first plays were bold attempts to explore the history of African Americans through a series of extraordinary characters and situations. In one section of *Imperceptible Mutabilities in the Third Kingdom* (1989, winner of an Obie), Parks portrays the slave trade through Aretha Saxon, a black woman who first speaks about herself as if she is a slave ship greeting the people packed on board, then undergoes a series of painful victimizations, including the removal of all her teeth. *The Death of the Last Black Man in the Whole Entire World* (1990), using characters named after "soul food" stereotypes (Black Man with Watermelon, Black Woman with Fried Drumstick, Lots of Grease and Lots of Pork), portrays the violence announced in the title, as the Black Man with Watermelon describes his death in the electric chair, his death by drowning after being chased by dogs, and his death by lynching, yet suggests his ability to survive by reappearing. One of Parks's most haunting situations emerges in *The America Play* (1994), in which a black man who resembles Abraham Lincoln makes a living by reenacting Lincoln's death, sitting in a rocking chair, and allowing people to "shoot" him. And in *Venus* (1996, winner of an Obie),

Parks dramatized the historical case of a South African woman exhibited in England in 1810 who was called the "Venus Hottentot."

All of these plays reflect Parks's interest in working with stories from the past as well as with her personal tradition (see her essay "Tradition and the Individual Talent" in Ideas of Drama). Thus while using historical characters or symbolic stereotypes, she also creates a structure based, as she puts it, on "Repetition and Revision . . . a concept integral to the Jazz esthetic in which the composer or performer will write or play a musical phrase once and again and again; etc.—with each revisit the phrase is slightly revised." In *The America Play,* for example, the "shooting" of Lincoln happens eight times in the first act, and the repetition underscores not only the horror but also the irony of turning Lincoln's murder into a carnival sideshow. Just as Parks invents a surreal and repetitive structure, so too she invents her own rules for language and pauses. She often avoids conventional punctuation (no apostrophes, for instance), or uses numbers instead of writing out the word, or spells words phonetically. Silence is also an important part of her writing, and she signals different lengths for silence through the "rest" or the "spell" as described in the "Author's Elements of Style" printed at the beginning of her most recent plays.

Yet Parks's most recent plays embody a more straightforward and realistic style, as she takes symbolic characters and reworks them into complex human beings. The two brothers in *Topdog/Underdog* (2001) exemplify the process, since they are called Booth and Lincoln, and Lincoln does indeed work as a Lincoln impersonator who sits in an arcade and gets "shot." But Parks goes beyond the stereotypes of *The America Play* by creating a detailed and complicated relationship between the brothers, built around their mutual need for each other, as well as their never-ending competition. The historical names they bear mark them as enemies—even if those names were their father's idea of a joke—but the play, like the con game of three-card monte that Booth and Lincoln play, explores the seemingly endless possibilities of winning and losing, of knowing where the right card is or of being repeatedly fooled.

A similar process of turning from the symbolic toward the realistic can be seen in her two recent plays known collectively as *The Red Letter Plays.* Both are influenced by Nathaniel Hawthorne's *The Scarlet Letter,* the American novel of guilt and adultery set in Puritan New England, whose central character, Hester Prynne, wears a red *A* embroidered on her dress. Parks began with a Brechtian-style satire, *Fucking A* (2000), set in a dystopian society in which Hester Smith's *A,* branded on her skin rather than embroidered on her dress, marks her as an abortionist. But as she wrote, Parks found herself so fascinated by Hester that she began a second play, *In the Blood* (1999). Here Parks transforms Hester into La Negrita, a single mother with five children, each by a different father. The scarlet letter is now an *A* that Hester keeps trying to write in the dirt, hoping to learn how to read and write as a way of bettering her situation. And while the play is framed by a prologue in which the characters join in a chorus of attack on Hester and is punctuated by a series of "Confessions" in which the adults reveal their sexual fantasies about Hester, most of the play is essentially a realistic story that revolves around Hester's efforts to feed her children and survive in a painful and threatening world.

The story of Hester—and of Hester's abuse—reaches back not only to Hawthorne but to Greek tragedy, as slowly, relentlessly, the character's love for her children and her insistence on her own dignity lead to the final catastrophe. Hester's imprisonment extends to the audience, since, as Margo Jefferson notes in the review following the play, we are implicated in the culture that produces and punishes Hester. Moreover, the theatrical choice to use only six actors—one actor plays Hester and each of the other five actors play both a child and an adult—creates, in Jefferson's words, "the potent and terrible sense of being closed in with the characters." That same choice creates additional ironies for the play, particularly when we see Hester and her family together—as in Scene 1 (Figure 1), in which the adult actors pretend to be children as Hester tells them a fairy tale. Later, when Hester's lover Chilli returns and proposes to her in Scene 7 (Figure 2), but is clearly appalled by seeing four children, she pretends that they are the neighbors' kids. Of course the one child not present is Jabber, Chilli's son, since the same actor plays both roles. Hester's greatest frustration grows out of her repeated confrontations with Reverend D., her most recent lover and the father of Baby. Early in the play, Hester persistently asks that he help her and the children (Figure 3); midway through the play she tries again; and in the penultimate scene, following his rejection she attacks him physically (Figure 4). But Reverend D. escapes unscathed, and the frustrated Hester takes out her violence on another victim. The bleakness of *In the Blood* from beginning to end reflects Parks's ability to "tell it like it is" but her repeated evocation of Hester's dignity and power also suggest that this playwright may one day "tell it as it could be."

IN THE BLOOD

BY SUZAN-LORI PARKS

CHARACTERS

HESTER, LA NEGRITA
CHILLI/JABBER, *her oldest son*
REVEREND D./BABY, *her youngest son*
THE WELFARE LADY/BULLY, *her oldest daughter*
THE DOCTOR/TROUBLE, *her middle son*
AMIGA GRINGA/BEAUTY, *her youngest daughter*

SCENE

Here

TIME

Now

AUTHOR'S NOTE

This play requires a cast of six adult actors, five of whom double as adults and children. The setting should be spare, to reflect the poverty of the world of the play.

AUTHOR'S ELEMENTS OF STYLE

I'm continuing the use of my slightly unconventional theatrical elements. Here's a road map.

- *(Rest)*
  Take a little time, a pause, a breather; make a transition.
- A Spell
  An elongated and heightened *(Rest)*. Denoted by repetition of figures' names with no dialogue. Has sort of an architectural look:

  REVEREND D.

  HESTER

  REVEREND D.

  HESTER

  This is a place where the figures experience their pure true simple state. While no action or stage business is necessary, directors should fill this moment as they best see fit.
- [Brackets in the text indicate optional cuts for production.]
- (Parentheses around dialogue indicate softly spoken passages ((asides; sotto voce)).

PROLOGUE

(All clustered together.)

ALL: THERE SHE IS!
WHO DOES SHE THINK
SHE IS
THE NERVE SOME PEOPLE HAVE
SHOULDNT HAVE IT IF YOU CANT AFFORD IT
AND YOU KNOW SHE CANT
SHE DONT GOT NO SKILLS
CEPT ONE
CANT READ CANT WRITE
SHE MARRIED?
WHAT DO YOU THINK?
SHE OUGHTA BE MARRIED
THATS WHY THINGS ARE BAD LIKE THEY ARE
CAUSE OF
GIRLS LIKE THAT
THAT EVER HAPPEN TO ME YOU WOULDNT SEE ME
   HAVING IT
YOU WOULDNT SEE THAT HAPPENING TO ME
WHO THE HELL SHE THINK SHE IS
AND NOW WE GOT TO PAY FOR IT
THE NERVE
SOME PEOPLE HAVE

BAD LUCK
SHE OUGHTA GET MARRIED
TO WHO?
THIS AINT THE FIRST TIME THIS HAS HAPPENED TO
   HER
NO?
THIS IS HER FIFTH
FIFTH?
SHE GOT FIVE OF THEM
FIVE BRATS
AND NOT ONE OF THEM GOT A DADDY
PAH!

(They spit.)

WHOS THE DADDY?
SHE WONT TELL
SHE WONT TELL CAUSE SHE DONT KNOW
SHE KNOWS
NO SHE DONT
HOW COULD A GIRL NOT KNOW
WHEN YOU HAD SO MUCH ACTION YOU LOSE A
   FRACTION
OF YR GOOD SENSE
THE PART OF MEN SHE SEES ALL LOOK THE SAME
   ANYWAY

WATCH YR MOUTH
I DIDNT SAY NOTHING
YOU TALKING ALL NASTY AND THAT AINT RIGHT
THERES CHILDREN HERE
WHERES THE CHILDREN I DONT SEE NO CHILDREN
SHE MARRIED?
SHE AINT MARRIED
SHE DONT GOT NO SKILLS
CEPT ONE
CANT READ CANT WRITE
SHE MARRIED?
WHAT DO YOU THINK?

ALL
ALL
ALL
SHE KNOWS SHES A NO COUNT
SHIFTLESS
HOPELESS
BAD NEWS
BURDEN TO SOCIETY
HUSSY
SLUT
PAH!

(They spit.)

JUST PLAIN STUPID IF YOU ASK ME AINT NO SMART
    WOMAN GOT 5 BASTARDS
AND NOT A PENNY TO HER NAME
SOMETHINGS GOTTA BE DONE TO STOP THIS SORT
    OF THING
CAUSE I'LL BE DAMNED IF SHE GONNA LIVE OFF ME
HERE SHE COMES
MOVE ASIDE
WHAT SHE GOTS CATCHY
LET HER PASS
DONT GET CLOSE
YOU DONT WANNA LOOK LIKE YOU KNOW HER
STEP OFF!

(They part like the Red Sea would. HESTER, LA NEGRITA *passes through them. She holds a Newborn Baby in her arms.)*

ALL: IT WONT END WELL FOR HER
    HOW YOU KNOW?
    I GOT EYES DON'T I
    BAD NEWS IN HER BLOOD
    PLAIN AS DAY.
ALL
HESTER
ALL

*(*HESTER *lifts the child up, raising it toward the sky.)*

HESTER: My treasure. My joy.
ALL: PAH!

(They spit.)

SCENE 1

Under the Bridge

*(Home under the bridge. The word "*SLUT*" scrawled on a wall.* HESTER's *oldest child* JABBER, *13, studies that scrawl.* HESTER *lines up soda cans as her youngest child* BABY, *2 years old, watches.)*

HESTER: Zit uh good word or a bad word?
JABBER
JABBER
HESTER: Aint like you to have yr mouth shut, Jabber.
    Say it to me and we can figure out the meaning
    together.
JABBER: Naaaa—
HESTER: What I tell you bout saying "Naa" when you
    mean "no"? You talk like that people wont think
    you got no brains and Jabbers got brains. All my
    kids got brains, now.

(Rest)

    Lookie here, Baby. Mamma set the cans for you.
    Mamma gonna show you how to make some
    money. Watch.
JABBER: Im slow.
HESTER: Slow aint never stopped nothing, Jabber. You
    bring yr foot down on it and smash it flat.
    Howabout that, Baby? Put it in the pile and thats
    that. Now you try.

*(*BABY *jumps on the can smashing it flat, hollering as he smashes.)*

BABY: Ha!
HESTER: Yr a natural! Jabber, yr little baby brothers a
    natural. We gonna come out on top this month, I
    can feel it. Try another one, Baby.
JABBER: They wrote it in yr practice place.
HESTER: Yes they did.
JABBER: They wrote in yr practice place so you didnt
    practice today.
HESTER: I practiced. In my head. In the air. In the dirt
    underfoot.
JABBER: Lets see.

(With great difficulty HESTER *makes an "A" in the dirt.)*

HESTER: The letter A.
JABBER: Almost.
HESTER: You gonna disparage me I aint gonna prac-
    tice.
BABY: Mommmmieee!
HESTER: Gimmieuhminute, Baby-child.
JABBER: Legs apart hands crost the chest like I showd
    you. Try again.
BABY: Mommieee!
HESTER: See the pretty can, Baby?
BABY: Ha!
JABBER: Try again.

BABY: Mommmieee!

HESTER: Later. Read that word out to me, huh? I like it when you read to me.

JABBER: Dont wanna read it.

HESTER: Cant or wont?

JABBER: —Cant.

HESTER

JABBER

(He knows what the word says, but he wont say it.)

HESTER: I was sick when I was carrying you. Damn you, slow fool. Aaah, my treasure, cmmeer. My oldest treasure.

(HESTER gives him a quick hug. She looks at the word, its letters mysterious to her. BABY smashes can after can.)

HESTER: Go scrub it off, then. I like my place clean.

(JABBER dutifully scrubs the wall.)

HESTER: We know who writ it up there. It was them bad boys writing on my home. And in my practice place. Do they write on they own homes? I dont think so. They come under the bridge and write things they dont write nowhere else. A mean ugly word, I'll bet. A word to hurt our feelings. And because we aint lucky we gotta live with it. 5 children I got. 5 treasures. 5 joys. But we aint got our leg up, just yet. So we gotta live with mean words and hurt feelings.

JABBER: Words dont hurt my feelings, Mamma.

HESTER: Dont disagree with me.

JABBER: Sticks and stones, Mamma.

HESTER: Yeah. I guess.

(Rest)

Too late for yr sisters and brothers to still be out. Yr little brother Babys gonna make us rich. He learns quick. Look at him go.

(HESTER lines up more cans and BABY jumps on them, smashing them all. BULLY, her 12-year-old girl, runs in.)

BULLY: Mommieeeeeeeeee! Mommie, Trouble he has really done it this time. I told him he was gonna be doing life and he laughed and then I said he was gonna get the electric chair and you know what he said?

HESTER: Help me sack the cans.

BULLY: He said a bad word!

HESTER: Sack the cans.

(They sack the crushed cans.)

BULLY: Trouble he said something really bad but Im not saying it cause if I do yll wash my mouth. What he said was bad but what he did, what he did was worse.

HESTER: Whatd he do?

BULLY: Stole something.

HESTER: Food?

BULLY: No.

HESTER: Toys?

BULLY: No.

HESTER: I dont like youall stealing toys and I dont like youall stealing food but it happens. I wont punish you for it. Yr just kids. Trouble thinks with his stomach. He hungry he takes, sees a toy, gotta have it.

BULLY: A policeman saw him steal and ran after him but Trouble ran faster cause the policeman was fat.

HESTER: Policeman chased him?

BULLY: He had a big stomach. Like he was pregnant. He was jiggling and running and yelling and red in the face.

HESTER: What he steal?

BULLY: —Nothing.

HESTER: You talk that much and you better keep talking, Miss.

(BULLY buttons her lips. HESTER pops her upside the head.)

BULLY: Owwww!

HESTER: Get outa my sight. Worse than a thief is a snitch that dont snitch.

(TROUBLE, age 10, and BEAUTY, age 7, run in, breathless. They see HESTER eyeing them and stop running; they walk nonchalantly.)

HESTER: What you got behind you?

TROUBLE: Nothing. Jabber, what you doing?

JABBER: Cleaning the wall.

BEAUTY: My hair needs a ribbon.

HESTER: Not right now it dont. You steal something?

TROUBLE: Me? Whats cookin?

HESTER: Soup of the day.

TROUBLE: We had soup the day yesterday.

HESTER: Todays a new day.

BEAUTY: Is it a new soup?

HESTER: Wait and see. You gonna end up in the penitentiary and embarrass your mother?

TROUBLE: No.

HESTER: If you do I'll kill you. Set the table.

JABBER: Thats girls work.

TROUBLE: Mommiee—

BULLY: Troubles doing girls work Troubles doing girls work.

HESTER: Set the damn table or Ima make a girl outa you!

TROUBLE: You cant make a girl outa me.

HESTER: Dont push me!

(Rest)

Look, Baby. See the soup? Mommies stirring it. Dont come close, its hot.

BEAUTY: I want a ribbon.

HESTER: Get one I'll tie it in.

(BEAUTY *gets a ribbon.* TROUBLE *gets bowls, wipes them clean, hands them out.* HESTER *follows behind him and, out of the back of his pants, yanks a policemans club.*)

HESTER: Whered you get this?

TROUBLE

HESTER

TROUBLE

HESTER: I said—

TROUBLE: I found it. On the street. It was just lying there.

BULLY: You stole it.

TROUBLE: Did not!

HESTER: Dont lie to me.

TROUBLE: I found it. I did. It was just lying on the street. I was minding my own business.

HESTER: That why the cops was chasing you?

TROUBLE: Snitch!

BULLY: Jailbait!

(BULLY *hits* TROUBLE *hard. They fight. Pandemonium.*)

HESTER: Suppertime!

(*Order is restored.* HESTER *slips the club into the belt of her dress; it hangs there like a sword. She wears it like this for most of the play. Her children sit in a row holding their bowls. She ladles out the soup.*)

HESTER: Todays soup the day, ladies and gents, is a very special blend of herbs and spices. The broth is chef Mommies worldwide famous "whathaveyou" stock. Theres carrots in there. Theres meat. Theres oranges. Theres pie.

TROUBLE: What kinda pie?

HESTER: What kind you like?

TROUBLE: Apple.

HESTER: Theres apple pie.

JABBER: Pumpkin.

BULLY: And cherry!

HESTER: Theres pumpkin and cherry too. And steak. And mash potatoes for Beauty. And milk for Baby.

BEAUTY: And diamonds.

JABBER: You cant eat diamonds.

HESTER: So when you find one in yr soup whatll you do?

BEAUTY: Put it on my finger.

(*They slurp down their soup quickly. As soon as she fills their bowls, theyre empty again. The kids eat.* HESTER *doesnt.*)

JABBER: You aint hungry?

HESTER: I'll eat later.

JABBER: You always eating later.

HESTER: You did a good job with the wall, Jabber. Whatd that word say anyway?

JABBER: —Nothing.

(*The soup pot is empty.*)

HESTER
JABBER/BULLY/TROUBLE/BEAUTY/BABY

(*Rest*)

HESTER: Bedtime.

BULLY: Can we have a story?

(*Rest*)

HESTER: All right.

(*Rest*)

There were once these five brothers and they were all big and strong and handsome and didnt have a care in the world. One was known for his brains so they called him Smarts and one was known for his muscles, so they called him Toughguy, the third one was a rascal so they called him Wild, the fourth one was as goodlooking as all get out and they called him Looker and the fifth was the youngest and they called him Honeychild cause he was as young as he was sweet. And they was always together these five brothers. Everywhere they went they always went together. No matter what they was always together cause they was best friends and wasnt nothing could divide them. And there was this Princess. And she lived in a castle and she was lonesome. She was lonesome and looking for love but she couldnt leave her castle so she couldnt look very far so every day she would stick her head out her window and sing to the sun and every night she would stick her head out and sing to the moon and the stars: "Where are you?" And one day the five brothers heard her and came calling and she looked upon them and she said: "There are five of you, and each one is wonderful and special in his own way. But the law of my country doesnt allow a princess to have more than one husband." And that was such bad news and they were all so in love that they all cried. Until the Princess had an idea. She was after all the Princess, so she changed the law of the land and married them all.

(*Rest*)

And with Bro Smarts she had a baby named Jabber. And with Bro Toughguy she had Bully. With Bro Wild came Trouble. With Bro Looker she had Beauty. With Bro Honeychild came Baby. And they was all happy.

JABBER: Until the bad news came.

HESTER: No bad news came.

JABBER: Theres always bad news.

HESTER: Bedtime.

BEAUTY: Where did the daddys go?

HESTER: They went to bed.

TROUBLE: They ran off.

JABBER: The war came and the brothers went off to fight and they all died.

BEAUTY: They all died?

JABBER: And they fell into the ground and the dirt covered up they heads.

HESTER: Its bedtime. Now!

BEAUTY: Im scared.

TROUBLE: I aint scared. Jabber, you a spook.

BULLY: Yr the spook.

TROUBLE: Yr a bastard.

BULLY: Yr a bastard.

HESTER: Yr all bastards!

(The children burst into tears.)

HESTER: Cmmeer. Cmmeer. Mama loves you. Shes just tired is all. Lemmie hug you.

(They nestle around her and she hugs them.)

HESTER: My 5 treasures. My 5 joys.

HESTER

JABBER/BULLY/TROUBLE/BEAUTY/BABY

HESTER

HESTER: Lets hit the sack! And leave yr shoes for polish and yr shirts and blouses for press. You dont wanna look like you dont got nobody.

(They take off their shoes and tops and go inside leaving HESTER *outside alone.)*

HESTER

HESTER

HESTER

(Rest)

*(*HESTER *examines the empty soup pot, shines the kids shoes, "presses" their clothes. A wave of pain shoots through her.)*

HESTER: You didnt eat, Hester. And the pain in yr gut comes from having nothing in it.

(Rest)

Kids ate good though. Ate their soup all up. They wont starve.

(Rest)

None of these shoes shine. Never did no matter how hard you spit on em, Hester. You get a leg up the first thing you do is get shoes. New shoes for yr 5 treasures. You got yrself a good pair of shoes already.

(From underneath a pile of junk she takes a shoebox. Inside is a pair of white pumps. She looks them over then puts them away.)

HESTER: Dont know where yr going but yll look good when you get there.

[HESTER *takes out a small tape player. Pops in a tape. She takes a piece of chalk from her pocket and, on the freshly scrubbed wall, practices her letters: she writes the letter A over and over and over. The cassette tape plays as she writes. On tape:*

REVEREND D.: If you cant always do right then you got to admit that some times, some times my friends you are going to do wrong and you are going to have to *live* with that. Somehow work that into the fabric of your life. Because there aint a soul out there that is spot free. There aint a soul out there that has walked but hasnt stumbled. Aint a single solitary soul out there that has said "hello" and not "goodbye," has said "yes" to the lord and "yes" to the devil too, has drunk water and drunk wine, loved and hated, experienced the good side of the tracks and the bad. That is what they call "Livin," friends. L-I-V-I-N, friends. Life on earth is full of confusion. Life on earth is full of misunderstandings, reprimandings, and we focus on the trouble, friends, when it is the solution to those troubles we oughta be looking at. "I have fallen and I cant get up!" How many times have you heard that, friends? The fellow on the street with his whisky breath and his outstretched hand, the banker scraping the money off the top, the runaway child turned criminal all cry out "I have fallen, and I cant get up!" "I have fallen, and I cant get up!" "I have fallen—"

HESTER *hears someone coming and turns the tape off.]*
(She goes back to polishing the shoes. AMIGA GRINGA *comes in.)*

AMIGA GRINGA: Look at old Mother Hubbard or whatever.

HESTER: Keep quiet. Theyre sleeping.

AMIGA GRINGA: The old woman and the shoe. Thats who you are.

HESTER: I get my leg up thats what Im getting. New shoes for my treasures.

AMIGA GRINGA: Thatll be some leg up.

HESTER: You got my money?

AMIGA GRINGA: Is that a way to greet a friend? "You got my money?" What world is this?

HESTER: You got my money, Amiga?

AMIGA GRINGA: I got *news* for you, Hester. News thats better than gold. But first—heads up.

*(*THE DOCTOR *comes in. He wears a sandwich board and carries all his office paraphernalia on his back.)*

DOCTOR: Hester! Yr due for a checkup.

HESTER: My guts been hurting me.

DOCTOR: Im on my way home just now. Catch up with me tomorrow. We'll have a look at it then.

(He goes on his way.)

AMIGA GRINGA: Doc! I am in pain like you would not believe. My hips, Doc. When I move them—blinding flashes of light and then—down I go, flat on my back, like Im dead, Doc.

DOCTOR: I gave you something for that yesterday.

DOCTOR

AMIGA GRINGA

(He slips AMIGA *a few pills. He goes on his way.)*

AMIGA GRINGA: Hes a saint.

HESTER: Sometimes.

AMIGA GRINGA: Want some?

HESTER: I want my money?

AMIGA GRINGA: Patience, girl. All good things are on their way. Do you know what the word is?

HESTER: What word?

AMIGA GRINGA: Word is that yr first love is back in town, doing well and looking for you.

HESTER: Chilli? Jabbers daddy? Looking for me?

AMIGA GRINGA: Thats the word.

HESTER

HESTER

HESTER: Bullshit. Gimmie my money, Miga. I promised the kids cake and ice cream. How much you get?

AMIGA GRINGA: First, an explanation of the economic environment.

HESTER: Just gimmie my money—

AMIGA GRINGA: The Stock Market, The Bond Market, Wall Street, Grain Futures, Bulls and Bears and Pork Bellies. They all impact the price a woman such as myself can get for a piece of "found" jewelry.

HESTER: That werent jewelry I gived you that was a watch. A Mans watch. Name brand. And it was working.

AMIGA GRINGA: Do you know what the Dow did today, Hester? The Dow was up twelve points. And that prize fighter, the one everyone is talking about, the one with the pretty wife and the heavyweight crown, he rang the opening bell. She wore a dress cut down to here. And the Dow shot up 43 points in the first minutes of trading, Hester. Up like a rocket. And men glanced up at the faces of clocks on the walls of their offices and women around the country glanced into the faces of their children and time passed. [And someone looks at their watch because its lunchtime, Hester. And theyre having—lunch. And they wish it would last forever. Cause when they get back to their office where they—work, when they get back the Dow has plummeted. And theres a lot of racing around and time is brief and something must be done before the closing bell. Phone calls are made, marriages dissolve, promises lost in the shuffle, Hester, and all this time your Amiga Gringa is going from fence to fence trying to get the best price on this piece of "found" jewelry. Numbers racing on lightboards, Hester, telling those that are in the know, the value of who knows what. One man, broken down in tears in the middle of the avenue, "Oh my mutual funds" he was saying.] The market was hot, and me, a suspicious looking mother, very much like yrself, with no real address and no valid forms of identification, walking the streets with a hot watch.

(Rest)

Here.

(She gives HESTER *$.)*

HESTER: Wheres the rest?

AMIGA GRINGA: Thats it.

HESTER: 5 bucks?

AMIGA GRINGA: It wasnt a good day. Some days are good some days are bad. I kept a buck for myself.

HESTER: You stole from me.

AMIGA GRINGA: Dont be silly. We're friends, Hester.

HESTER: I shoulda sold it myself.

AMIGA GRINGA: But you had the baby to watch.

HESTER: And no ones gonna give money to me with me carrying Baby around. Still I coulda got more than 5.

AMIGA GRINGA: Go nextime yrself then. The dangers I incur, working with you. You oughta send yr kids away. Like me. I got 3 kids. All under the age of 3. And do you see me looking all baggy eyed, up all night shining little shoes and flattening little shirts and going without food? Theres plenty of places that you can send them. Homes. Theres plenty of peoples, rich ones especially, that cant have kids. The rich spend days looking through the newspaper for ads where they can buy one. Or they go to the bastard homes and pick one out. Youd have some freedom. Youd have a chance at life. Like me.

HESTER: My kids is mine. I get rid of em what do I got? Nothing. I got nothing now, but if I lose them I got less than nothing.

AMIGA GRINGA: Suit yrself. You wouldnt have to send them all away, just one or two or three.

HESTER: All I need is a leg up. I get my leg up I'll be ok.

*(*BULLY *comes outside and stands there watching them. She wears pink, one-piece, flame-retardant pajamas.)*

HESTER: What.

BULLY: My hands stuck.

HESTER: Why you sleep with yr hands in fists?

AMIGA GRINGA: Yr an angry girl, arentcha, Bully.

BULLY: Idunno. This ones stuck too.

HESTER: Maybe yll grow up to be a boxer, huh? We can watch you ringside, huh? *Wide World of Sports.*

AMIGA GRINGA: Presenting in this corner weighing 82 pounds the challenger: Bully!

BULLY: Ima good girl.

HESTER: Course you are. There. You shouldnt sleep with yr hands balled up. The good fairies come by in the night with treats for little girls and they put them in yr hands. How you gonna get any treats if yr hands are all balled up?

BULLY: Jabber is bad and Trouble is bad and Beauty is bad and Baby is bad but I'm good. Bullys a good girl.

HESTER: Go on back to bed now.

BULLY: Miga. Smell.

AMIGA GRINGA: You got bad breath.

BULLY: I forgot to brush my teeth.

HESTER: Go head.

(BULLY *squats off in the "bathroom" and rubs her teeth with her finger.*)

AMIGA GRINGA: Babys daddy, that Reverend, he ever give you money?

HESTER: No.

AMIGA GRINGA: Hes a gold mine. I seen the collection plate going around. Its a full plate.

HESTER: I aint seen him since before Baby was born.

AMIGA GRINGA: Thats two years.

HESTER: He didn't want nothing to do with me. His heart went hard.

AMIGA GRINGA: My second kids daddy had a hard heart at first. But time mushed him up. Remember when he comed around crying about his lineage and asking whered the baby go? And I'd already gived it up.

HESTER: Reverend D., his heart is real hard. Like a rock.

AMIGA GRINGA: Worth a try all the same.

HESTER: Yeah.

(*Rest*)

Who told you Chilli was looking for me?

AMIGA GRINGA: Word on the street, thats all.

(TROUBLE, *dressed in superhero pajamas, comes in. He holds a box of matches. He lights one.*)

HESTER: What the hell you doing?

TROUBLE: Sleepwalking.

HESTER: You sleepwalk yrself back over here and gimmie them matches or Ima kill you.

(TROUBLE *gives her the matches.* BULLY *has finished with her teeth.*)

BULLY: You wanna smell?

HESTER: Thats ok.

BULLY: Dont you wanna smell?

(HESTER *leans in and* BULLY *opens her mouth.*)

BULLY: I only did one side cause I only ate with one side today.

HESTER: Go on to bed.

(BULLY *passes* TROUBLE *and hits him hard.*)

TROUBLE: Aaaaah!

BULLY: Yr a bad person!

(BULLY *hits him again.*)

TROUBLE: Aaaaaaaaah!

HESTER: Who made you policewoman?

TROUBLE: Ima blow you sky high one day you bully bitch!

(BULLY *goes to hit him again.*)

HESTER: Trouble I thought you said you was sleep. Go inside and lie down and shut up or you wont see tomorrow.

(TROUBLE *goes back to sleepwalking and goes inside.*)

HESTER: Bully. Go over there. Close yr eyes and yr mouth and not a word, hear?

(BULLY *goes a distance off curling up to sleep without a word.*)

HESTER: I used to wash Troubles mouth out with soap when he used bad words. Found out he likes the taste of soap. Sometimes you cant win. No matter what you do.

(*Rest*)

Im gonna talk to Welfare and get an upgrade. The worldll take care of the women and children.

AMIGA GRINGA: Theyre gonna give you the test. See what skills you got. Make you write stuff.

HESTER: Like what?

AMIGA GRINGA: Like yr name.

HESTER: I can write my damn name. Im not such a fool that I cant write my own goddamn name. I can write my goddamn name.

(*Inside,* BABY *starts crying.*)

HESTER: HUSH!

(BABY *hushes.*)

AMIGA GRINGA: You should pay yrself a visit to Babys daddy. Dont take along the kid in the flesh thatll be too much. For a buck I'll get someone to take a snapshot.

(JABBER *comes in. He wears mismatched pajamas. He doesnt come too close, keeps his distance.*)

JABBER: I was in a rowboat and the sea was flat like a blue plate and you was rowing me and it was fun.

HESTER: Go back to bed.

JABBER: It was a good day but then Bad News and the sea started rolling and the boat tipped and I felt out and—

HESTER: You wet the bed.

JABBER: I fell out the boat.

HESTER: You wet the bed.

JABBER: I wet the bed.

HESTER: 13 years old still peeing in the bed.

JABBER: It was uh accident.

HESTER: Whats wrong with you?

JABBER: Accidents happen.

HESTER: Yeah you should know cause yr uh damn accident. Shit. Take that off.

(JABBER *strips.*)

AMIGA GRINGA: He aint bad looking, Hester. A little slow, but some women like that.

HESTER: Wear my coat. Gimmie a kiss.

(JABBER *puts on* HESTER*'s coat and kisses her on the cheek.*)

JABBER: Mommie?

HESTER: Bed.

JABBER: All our daddys died, right? All our daddys died in the war, right?

HESTER: Yeah, Jabber.

JABBER: They went to war and they died and you cried. They went to war and died but whered they go when they died?

HESTER: They into other things now.

JABBER: Like what?

HESTER: —. Worms. They all turned into worms, honey. They crawling around in the dirt happy as larks, eating the world up, never hungry. Go to bed.

(JABBER *goes in.*)

(*Rest*)

AMIGA GRINGA: Worms?

HESTER: Whatever.

AMIGA GRINGA: Hes yr favorite. You like him the best.

HESTER: Hes my first.

AMIGA GRINGA: Hes yr favorite.

HESTER: I dont got no *favorite.*

(*Rest*)

5 bucks. 3 for their treats. And one for that photo. Reverend D. aint the man I knew. Hes got money now. A salvation business and all. Maybe his stone-heart is mush, though. Maybe.

AMIGA GRINGA: Cant hurt to try.

SCENE 2

Street Practice

(HESTER *walks alone down the street. She has a framed picture of* BABY.)

HESTER: Picture, it comed out pretty good. Got him sitting on a chair, and dont he look like he got

everything one could want in life? Hes 2 years old. Andll be growd up with a life of his own before I blink.

(*Rest*)

Picture comed out good. Thought Amiga was cheating me but it comed out good.

(HESTER *meets the* DOCTOR, *coming the other way. As before he carries all of his office paraphernalia on his back. He wears a sandwich board, the words written on it are hidden.*)

DOCTOR: Hester. Dont move a muscle, I'll be set up in a jiffy.

HESTER: I dont got more than a minute.

DOCTOR: Hows yr gut?

HESTER: Not great.

DOCTOR: Say "Aaaah!"

HESTER: Aaaah!

(*As* HESTER *stands there with her mouth open, he sets up his roadside office: a thin curtain, his doctors shingle, his instruments, his black bag.*)

DOCTOR: Good good good good good. Lets take yr temperature. Do you know what it takes to keep my road-side practice running? Do you know how much The Higher Ups would like to shut me down? Every blemish on your record is a blemish on mine. Take yr guts for instance. Yr pain could be nothing or it could be the end of the road—a cyst or a tumor, a lump or a virus or an infected sore. Or cancer, Hester. Undetected. There youd be, lying in yr coffin with all yr little ones gathered around motherlessly weeping and The Higher Ups pointing their fingers at me, saying I should of saved the day, but instead stood idly by. You and yr children live as you please and Im the one The Higher Ups hold responsible. Would you like a pill?

HESTER: No thanks.

(HESTER *doubles over in pain.*)

HESTER: My gut hurts.

(THE DOCTOR *takes a pill.*)

DOCTOR: In a minute. We'll get to that in a minute. How are yr children?

HESTER: Theyre all right.

DOCTOR: All 5?

HESTER: All 5.

DOCTOR: Havent had any more have you?

HESTER: No.

DOCTOR: But you could. But you might.

HESTER: —Maybe.

DOCTOR: Word from The Higher Ups is that one more kid outa the likes of you and theyre on the likes of me like white on rice. I'd like to propose something—. Yr running a temperature. Bit of a fever. Whats this?

HESTER: Its a club. For protection.

DOCTOR: Good thinking.

(*The* DOCTOR *examines her quickly and thoroughly.*)

DOCTOR: The Higher Ups are breathing down my back, Hester. They want answers! They want results! Solutions! Solutions! Solutions! Thats what they want.

(*He goes to take another pill, but doesnt.*)

DOCTOR: I only take one a day. I only allow myself one a day.

(*Rest*)

(*He goes back to examining her.*)

DOCTOR: Breathe in deep. Lungs are clear. Yr heart sounds good. Strong as an ox.

HESTER: This falls been cold. The wind under the bridge is colder than the wind on the streets.

DOCTOR: Exercise. Thats what I suggest. When the temperature drops, I run in place. Hold yr hands out. Shaky. Experiencing any stress and tension?

HESTER: Not really.

DOCTOR: Howre yr meals?

HESTER: The kids come first.

DOCTOR: Course they do. Howre yr bowels. Regular?

HESTER: I dunno.

DOCTOR: Once a day?

HESTER: Sometimes. My gut—

DOCTOR: In a minute. Gimmie the Spread & Squat right quick. Lets have a look under the hood.

(*Standing,* HESTER *spreads her legs and squats. Like an otter, he slides between her legs on a dolly and looks up into her privates with a flashlight.*)

DOCTOR: Last sexual encounter?

HESTER: Thats been a while, now.

DOCTOR: Yve healed up well from yr last birth.

HESTER: Its been 2 years. His names Baby.

DOCTOR: Any pain, swelling, off-color discharge, strange smells?

HESTER: No.

DOCTOR: L.M.P.?

HESTER: About a week ago.

(*Rest*)

How *you* been feeling, Doc?

DOCTOR: Sometimes Im up, sometimes Im down.

HESTER: You said you was lonesome once. I came for a checkup and you said you was lonesome. You lonesome today, Doc?

DOCTOR: No.

HESTER: Oh.

(*Far away,* CHILLI *walks by with his picnic basket on his arm. He pauses, checks his pocket watch, then continues on.*)

DOCTOR: Yr intelligent. Attractive enough. You could of made something of yrself.

HESTER: Im doing all right.

DOCTOR: The Higher Ups say yr in a skid. I agree.

HESTER: Oh, I coulda been the Queen of Sheba, it just werent in the cards, Doc.

DOCTOR: Yr kids are 5 strikes against you.

HESTER: I dont need no lecture. Gimmie something for my gut so I can go.

DOCTOR: The Higher Ups, they say Im not making an impact. But what do you care.

HESTER: My gut—

DOCTOR: Stand right here.

(*The* DOCTOR *draws a line in the dirt, positions her behind it and walks a few steps away. He reveals the writing on his sandwich board. It is an eye exam chart. The letters on the first line spell "SPAY."*)

DOCTOR: Read.

HESTER: —. A.

DOCTOR: Good.

(*He takes a step closer decreasing the distance between them.*)

DOCTOR: Read.

HESTER: —. —. —.

(*Rest*)

I need glasses for that.

DOCTOR: Uh huhn.

(*He steps closer.*)

DOCTOR: How about now?

HESTER: I need glasses I guess.

DOCTOR: I guess you do.

(*He steps even closer.*)

HESTER: ((somethin-somethin-A-somethin.))

(*Rest*)

I need glasses.

DOCTOR: You cant read this?

HESTER: I gotta go.

(HESTER *turns to go and he grabs her hand, holding her fast.*)

DOCTOR: When I say removal of your "womanly parts" do you know what parts Im talking about?

HESTER: Yr gonna take my womans parts?

DOCTOR: My hands are tied. The Higher Ups are calling the shots now.

(*Rest*)

You have 5 healthy children, itll be for the best, considering.

HESTER: My womans parts.

DOCTOR: Ive forwarded my recommendation to yr caseworker. Its out of my hands. Im sorry.

HESTER: I gotta go.

(But she doesnt move. She stands there numbly.)

DOCTOR: Yr gut. Lets have a listen.

(He puts his ear to her stomach and listens.)

DOCTOR: Growling hungry stomach. Heres a dollar.
Go get yrself a sandwich.

(HESTER takes the money and goes.)

DOCTOR
DOCTOR
DOCTOR

FIRST CONFESSION: THE DOCTOR

"Times Are Tough: What Can We Do?"

DOCTOR: Times are tough:
What can we do?
When I see a woman begging on the streets I
guess I could
bring her in my house
sit her at my table
make her a member of my family, sure.
But there are hundreds and thousands of them
and my house cant hold them all.
Maybe we should all take in just one.
Except they wouldnt really fit.
They wouldnt really fit in with us.
Theres such a gulf between us. What can we do?
I am a man of the people, from way back my
streetside practice
is a testament to that
so dont get me wrong
do not for a moment think that I am one of those
people haters who does not understand who
does not experience—compassion.

(Rest)

Shes been one of my neediest cases for several
years now.
What can I do?
Each time she comes to me
looking more and more forlorn
and more and more in need
of affection.
At first I wouldnt touch her without gloves on, but
then—

(Rest)

we did it once
in that alley there,
she was
phenomenal.

(Rest)

I was
lonesome and

she gave herself to me in a way that I had never
experienced
even with women Ive paid
she was, like she was giving me something that was
not hers to give me but something that was mine
that I'd lent her
and she was returning it to me.
Sucked me off for what seemed like hours
but I was very insistent. And held back
and she understood that I wanted her in the traditional way.
And she was very giving very motherly very obliging very understanding
very phenomenal.
Let me cumm inside her. Like I needed to.
What could I do?
I couldnt help it.

SCENE 3

The Reverend on His Soapbox

*(Late at night. The REVEREND D. on his soapbox preach-
ing to no one in particular. There are audio recordings of
his sermons for sale.)*

REVEREND D.: You all know me. You all know this face.
These arms. These legs. This body of mine is
known to you. To all of you. There isnt a person on
the street tonight that hasnt passed me by at some
point. Maybe when I was low, many years ago, with
a bottle in my hand and the cold hard unforgiving
pavement for my dwelling place. Perhaps you know
me from that. Or perhaps you know me from my
more recent incarnation. The man on the soapbox, telling you of a better life thats available to
you, not after the demise of your physical being,
not in some heaven where we all gonna be robed
in satin sheets and wearing gossamer wings, but
right here on earth, my friends. Right here right
now. Let the man on the soapbox tell you how to
pick yourself up. Let the man on the soapbox tell
you how all yr dreams can come true. Let the man
on the soapbox tell you that you dont have to be
down and dirty, you dont have to be ripped off
and renounced, you dont have to be black and
blue, your neck dont have to be red, your clothes
dont have to be torn, your head dont have to be
hanging, you dont have to *hate* yourself, you dont
have to hate yr neighbor. You can pull yrself up.

*(HESTER comes in with a framed picture of BABY. She
stands a ways off. REVEREND D. keeps on talking.)*

REVEREND D.: And I am an example of that. I am a
man who has crawled out of the quicksand of
despair. I am a man who has pulled himself out of
that never ending gutter—and you notice friends
that every city and every towns got a gutter. Aint
no place in the world that dont have some little

trench for its waste. And the gutter, is endless, and deep and wide and if you think you gonna crawl out of the gutter by crawling along the gutter you gonna be in the gutter for the rest of your life. You gotta step out of it, friends and I am here to tell you that you can.

(Rest)

(He sees HESTER *but doesnt recognize her.)*

REVEREND D.: What can I do for you tonight, my sister.
HESTER: I been good.
REVEREND D.: But yr life is weighing heavy on you tonight.
HESTER: I havent bothered you.
REVEREND D.: Reverend D. likes to be bothered. Reverend D. enjoys having the tired, the deprived and the depraved come knocking on his door. Come gathering around his soapbox. Come closer. Come on.

*(*HESTER *holds the picture of* BABY *in front of her face, hiding her face from view.)*

HESTER: This child here dont know his daddy.
REVEREND D.: The ultimate disaster of modern times. Sweet child. Yours?
HESTER: Yes.
REVEREND D.: Do you know the father?
HESTER: Yes.
REVEREND D.: You must go to him and say, "Mister, here is your child!"
HESTER: Mister here is your child!
REVEREND D.: "You are wrong to deny what God has made!"
HESTER: You are wrong to deny what God has made!
REVEREND D.: "He has nothing but love for you and reaches out his hands every day crying wheres daddy?"
HESTER: Wheres daddy?
REVEREND D.: "Wont you answer those cries?"
HESTER: Wont you answer those cries?
REVEREND D.: If he dont respond to that then hes a good-for-nothing deadbeat, and you report him to the authorities. Theyll garnish his wages so at least you all wont starve. I have a motivational cassette which speaks to that very subject. I'll give it to you free of charge.
HESTER: I got all yr tapes. I send my eldest up here to get them.
REVEREND D.: Wonderful. Thats wonderful. You should go to yr childs father and demand to be recognized.
HESTER: Its been years since I seen him. He didnt want me bothering him so I been good.
REVEREND D.: Go to him. Plead with him. Show him this sweet face and yours. He cannot deny you.

*(*HESTER *lowers the picture, revealing her face.)*

HESTER
REVEREND D.
HESTER
REVEREND D.

(Rest)

HESTER: You know me?
REVEREND D.: No. God.
HESTER: I aint bothered you for 2 years.
REVEREND D.: You should go. Home. Let me call you a taxi. *Taxi!* You shouldnt be out this time of night. Young mother like you. In a neighborhood like this. We'll get you home in a jiff. Where ya live? East? West? North I bet, am I right? *TAXI!* God.
HESTER: hes talking now. Not much but some. hes a good boy.
REVEREND D.: I am going to send one of my people over to your home tomorrow. Theyre marvelous, the people who work with me. Theyll put you in touch with all sorts of agencies that can help you. Get some food in that stomach of yours. Get you some sleep.
HESTER: Doctor says I got a fever. We aint doing so good. We been slipping. I been good. I dont complain. They breaking my back is all. 5 kids. My treasures, breaking my back.
REVEREND D.: We'll take up a collection for you.
HESTER: You know me.
REVEREND D.: You are under the impression that—. Your mind, having nothing better to fix itself on, has fixed on me. Me, someone youve never even met.
HESTER: There aint no one here but you and me. Say it. You know me. You know my name. You know my—. You know me and I know you.
HESTER
REVEREND D.

(Rest)

REVEREND D.: Here is a card. My lawyer. He'll call you.
HESTER: We dont got no phone.
REVEREND D.: He'll visit. Write yr address on—. Tell me yr address. I'll write it down. I'll give it to him in the morning and he'll visit you.

(Rest)

Do the authorities know the name of the father?
HESTER: I dont tell them nothing.
REVEREND D.: They would garnish his wages if you did. That would provide you with a small income. If you agree not to ever notify the authorities, we could, through my institution, arrange for you to get a much larger amount of money.
HESTER: How much more?
REVEREND D.: Twice as much.
HESTER: 3 times.
REVEREND D.: Fine.

HESTER: Theres so many things we need. Food. New shoes. A regular dinner with meat and salad and bread.

REVEREND D.: I should give you some money right now. As a promise to you that I'll keep my word. But Im short of cash.

HESTER: Oh.

REVEREND D.: Come back in 2 days. Late. I'll have some then.

HESTER: You dont got no food or nothing do ya?

REVEREND D.: Come back in 2 days. Not early. Late. And not a word to no one. Okay?

HESTER: —. K.

REVEREND D.

HESTER

REVEREND D.

HESTER

(Rest)

REVEREND D.: You better go.

(HESTER goes.)

SCENE 4

With the Welfare

(Outside, JABBER, TROUBLE *and* BEAUTY *sit in the dirt playing with toy cars.)*

TROUBLE: Red light. Green light. Red light. Green light.

JABBER: Look, a worm.

(They all study the worm as it writhes in the dirt. WELFARE *enters.)*

WELFARE: Wheres your mommie?

BEAUTY: Inside.

JABBER: Mommie! Welfares here.

WELFARE: Thank you.

(HESTER enters.)

HESTER: You all go inside.

(The kids go inside.)

WELFARE: Hands clean?

HESTER: Yes, Maam.

WELFARE: Wash them again.

(HESTER washes her hands again. Dries them.)

WELFARE: The welfare of the world.

HESTER: Maam?

WELFARE: Come on over, come on.

(HESTER stands behind WELFARE, giving her a shoulder rub.)

WELFARE: The welfare of the world weighs on these shoulders, Hester.

(Rest)

We at Welfare are at the end of our rope with you. We put you in a job and you quit. We put you in a shelter and you walk. We put you in school and you drop out. Yr children are also truant. Word is they steal. Stealing is a gateway crime, Hester. Perhaps your young daughter is pregnant. Who knows. We build bridges you burn them. We sew safety nets, rub harder, good strong safety nets and you slip through the weave.

HESTER: We was getting by all right, then I dunno, I been tired lately. Like something in me broke.

WELFARE: You and yr children live, who knows where.

HESTER: Here, Maam, under the Main Bridge.

WELFARE: This is not the country, Hester. You cannot simply—live off the land. If yr hungry you go to the shelter and get a hot meal.

HESTER: The shelter hassles me. Always prying in my business. Stealing my shit. Touching my kids. We was making ends meet all right then—ends got further apart.

WELFARE: "Ends got further apart." God!

(Rest)

I care because it is my job to care. I am paid to stretch out these hands, Hester. Stretch out these hands. To you.

HESTER: I gived you the names of 4 daddys: Jabbers and Bullys and Troubles and Beautys. You was gonna find them. Garnish they wages.

WELFARE: No luck as yet but we're looking. Sometimes these searches take years.

HESTER: Its been years.

WELFARE: Lifetimes then. Sometimes they take that long. These men of yours, theyre deadbeats. They dont want to be found. Theyre probably all in Mexico wearing false mustaches. Ha ha ha.

(Rest)

What about the newest child?

HESTER: Baby.

WELFARE: What about "Babys" father?

HESTER: —. I dunno.

WELFARE: Dont know or dont remember?

HESTER: You think Im doing it with mens I dont know?

WELFARE: No need to raise your voice no need of that at all. You have to help me help you, Hester.

(Rest)

Run yr fingers through my hair. Go on. Feel it. Silky isnt it?

HESTER: Yes, Maam.

WELFARE: Comes from a balanced diet. Three meals a day. Strict adherence to the food pyramid. Money in my pocket, clothes on my back, teeth in my mouth, womanly parts where they should be, hair on my head, husband in my bed.

(HESTER *combs* WELFARE*'s hair.*)

WELFARE: Yr doctor recommends that you get a hysterectomy. Take out yr womans parts. A spay.

HESTER: Spay.

WELFARE: I hope things wont come to that. I will do what I can. But you have to help me, Hester.

HESTER: ((Dont *make* me hurt you.))

WELFARE: What?

HESTER: I didnt mean it. Just slipped out.

WELFARE: Remember yr manners. We worked good and hard on yr manners. Remember? Remember that afternoon over at my house? That afternoon with the teacups?

HESTER: *Manners,* Maam?

WELFARE: Yes. Manners.

HESTER

WELFARE

WELFARE: Babys daddy. Whats his name?

HESTER: You wont find him no how.

WELFARE: We could get lucky. He could be right around the corner and I could walk out and there he would be and then we at Welfare would wrestle him to the ground and turn him upside down and let you and yr Baby grab all the money that falls from Deadbeat Daddys pockets. I speak metaphorically. We would garnish his wages.

HESTER: How much would that put in my pocket?

WELFARE: Depends how much he earns. Maybe 100. Maybe. We take our finders fee. Whats his name?

HESTER: I dunno.

WELFARE: You dont have to say it out loud. Write it down.

(*She gives* HESTER *pencil and paper.* HESTER *writes.* WELFARE *looks at the paper.*)

WELFARE: "A."

(Rest)

Adam, Andrew, Archie, Arthur, Aloysius, "A" what?

HESTER: Looks good dont it?

WELFARE: You havent learned yr letters yet, have you?

HESTER: I want my leg up is all.

WELFARE: You wont get something for nothing.

HESTER: I been good.

WELFARE: 5 bastards is not good. 5 bastards is bad.

HESTER: Dont make me hurt you!

(HESTER *raises her club to strike* WELFARE.)

WELFARE: You hurt me and, kids or no kids, I'll have you locked up. We'll take yr kids away and yll never see them again.

HESTER: My lifes my own fault. I know that. But the world dont help, Maam.

WELFARE: The world is not here to help us, Hester. The world is simply here. We must help ourselves.

(Rest)

I know just the job for you. It doesnt pay well, but the work is very rewarding. Hard honest work. Unless yr afraid of hard honest work.

HESTER: I aint afraid of hard work.

WELFARE: Its sewing. You can do it at home. No work no pay but thats yr decision.

(Rest)

Heres the fabric. Make sure you dont get it dirty.

HESTER: Can I express myself?

WELFARE: Needles, thread and the pattern, in this bag. Take the cloth. Sew it. If you do a good job therell be more work. Have it sewn by tomorrow morning, yll get a bonus.

(HESTER *takes the cloth and notions.*)

HESTER: I dont think the world likes women much.

WELFARE: Dont be silly.

HESTER: I was just thinking.

WELFARE: Im a woman too! And a black woman too just like you. Dont be silly.

HESTER

WELFARE

(Rest)

(HESTER *puts her hand out, waiting.*)

HESTER: Yr shoulders. Plus I did yr hair.

WELFARE: Is a buck all right?

HESTER

WELFARE

WELFARE: Unless yll change a 50.

HESTER: I could go get change—

WELFARE: Take the buck, K? And the cloth. And go.

(WELFARE *owes* HESTER *more $, but after a beat,* HESTER *just leaves.*)

SECOND CONFESSION: THE WELFARE

"I Walk the Line"

WELFARE: I walk the line
   between us and them
   between our kind and their kind.
   The balance of the system depends on a well-
      drawn boundary line
   and all parties respecting that boundary.
   I am
   I am a married woman.
   I dont—that is have never
   never in the past or even in the recent present or
      even when I look
   look out into the future of my life I do not see any
      interest
   any *sexual* interest
   in anyone
   other than my husband.

(Rest)

My dear husband.
The hours he keeps.
The money he brings home.
Our wonderful children.
The vacations we go on.
My dear husband he needed
a little spice.
And I agreed. We both needed spice.
We both hold very demanding jobs.
We put an ad in the paper: "Husband and Bi-Curi-
    ous Wife, seeking—"
But the women we got:
Hookers. Neurotics. Gold diggers!
"Bring one of those gals home from work,"
    Hubby said. And
Hester,
she came to tea.

(Rest)

She came over and we had tea.
From my mothers china.
And marzipan on matching china plates.
Hubby sat opposite in the recliner
hard as Gibralter. He told us what he wanted and
    we did it.
We were his little puppets.
She was surprised, but consented.
Her body is better than mine.
Not a single stretchmark on her.
Im a looker too dont get me wrong just in a differ-
    ent way and
Hubby liked the contrast.
Just light petting at first.
Running our hands on each other
then Hubby joined in
and while she and I kissed
Hubby did her and me alternately.
The thrill of it—.

(Rest)

I was so afraid I'd catch something
but I was swept away and couldnt stop.
She stuck her tongue down my throat
and Hubby doing his thing on top
my skin shivered.
She let me slap her across the face
and I crossed the line.

(Rest)

It was my first threesome
and it wont happen again.
And I should emphasize that
she is a low-class person.
What I mean by that is that we have absolutely
    nothing in common.

As her caseworker I realize that maintenance of
    the system depends on a well-drawn bound-
    ary line
and all parties respecting that boundary.
And I am, after all,
I am a married woman.

(WELFARE exits. HESTER reenters, watches WELFARE exit.)

HESTER: Bitch.

(HESTER, alone on stage, examines the cloth WELFARE gave her.)

HESTER: Sure is pretty cloth. Sewing cant be that hard. Thread the needle stick it in and pull it through. Pretty cloth. Lets see what we making. Oooooh. Uh evening dress. Go to a party in. Drink champagne and shit. Uh huh, "Dont mind if I do," and shit and la de *dah* and come up in a limo and everbody wants a picture. So many lights Im blinded. Wear dark glasses. Strut my stuff.

(HESTER has another painful stomach attack which knocks the wind out of her and doubles her over. Far away, CHILLI walks by with his picnic basket on his arm. He pauses, checks his pocket watch, then continues on. HESTER, recovering from her attack, sees him just before he disappears.)

HESTER: Chilli!

INTERMISSION

SCENE 5
Small Change and Sandwiches

(Late at night. The children inside, all sleeping. Lots of "A's" written in HESTER's practice place. HESTER, working on her sewing, tries to thread the needle.)

HESTER: Damn needle eyes too damn small. Howmy supposed to get the thread through. Theres a catch to everything, Hester. No easy money nowheres. Wet the thread good. Damn.

(She squeezes her eyes shut and opens them, trying to focus. Having difficulty threading the needle, she takes out an object wrapped in brown paper. Looks cautiously around. Begins to unwrap it. A sandwich.)

HESTER: Put something in my stomach maybe my eyesll work.

(AMIGA GRINGA comes in. HESTER stashes the package, picks up her sewing.)

AMIGA GRINGA: Mother Hubbard sewing by street lamp. Very moving.

HESTER: I got me uh job. This here is work.

AMIGA GRINGA: From Welfare?

HESTER: Shes getting me back in the workforce. I do good on this she'll give me more.

AMIGA GRINGA: Whats the pay?

HESTER: Its by the piece.

AMIGA GRINGA: How much?

HESTER: 10 bucks maybe.

AMIGA GRINGA: Maybe?

HESTER: I get a bonus for working fast.

AMIGA GRINGA: Very nice fabric. Very pretty. Very expensive. And oooh, look at what yr making.

HESTER: You good with needles? Thread this. My eyes aint good.

(AMIGA *tries halfheartedly to thread the needle. Quits.*)

AMIGA GRINGA: Sorry.

(HESTER *continues trying to thread the needle.*)

HESTER: Today we had uh E-clipse. You seen it?

AMIGA GRINGA: Cant say I did. Good yr working. Getting some money in yr pocket. Making a good example for the kids. Pulling yrself up by yr bootstraps. Getting with the program. Taking responsibility for yr life. I envy you.

HESTER: Me?

AMIGA GRINGA: Yr working, Im—looking for work.

HESTER: I bet I could get you some sewing.

AMIGA GRINGA: Oh no. Thats not for me. If I work, Hester, I would want to be paid a living wage. You have agreed to work for less than a living wage. May as well be a slave. Or an animal.

HESTER: Its a start. She said if I do well—

AMIGA GRINGA: If you do well shes gonna let you be her slave *for life.* Wouldnt catch me doing that. Chump work. No no no. But its a good thing you are. Example to the kids.

HESTER: I aint no chump.

AMIGA GRINGA: Course you arent. Yr just doing chump work is all.

HESTER: Its a leg up. Cant start from the top.

AMIGA GRINGA: Why not? Plenty of people start from the top. Why not you? Sure is pretty fabric.

HESTER: All I gotta do is sew along the lines.

AMIGA GRINGA: Bet the fabric cost a lot. I wonder how much we could get for it—on the open market.

HESTER: Aint mine to sell. Its gonna make a nice dress. Im gonna sew it up and try it on before I give it to her. Just for fun.

(But HESTER *still hasnt been able to thread the needle.*)

AMIGA GRINGA: Bet we could get 100 bucks. For the fabric. A lot more than youd get for sewing it. And you wouldnt have to lift a finger. I'd sell it tonight. Have the money for you in the morning.

HESTER: No thanks.

AMIGA GRINGA: Suit yrself.

(HESTER *continues trying to thread that damn needle.*)

AMIGA GRINGA: Chump work.

HESTER: They make the eyes too small, thats the problem.

(*Rest*)

I seen Chilli right after I was with the Welfare. You said he was looking for me and there he was! Jabbers daddy walking right by with a big gold pocket watch. But did I tell? Did I run after Welfare and say, "Theres Jabbers daddy?" I did not. Can you imagine?

AMIGA GRINGA: I told ya he was looking for ya. Hes gonna find you too.

HESTER: Jabbers daddy, after all these years!

AMIGA GRINGA: Maybe yr lucks turning.

HESTER: You think?

AMIGA GRINGA: Maybe.

AMIGA GRINGA

HESTER

(*Rest*)

AMIGA GRINGA: I missed my period.

HESTER: Don't look at *me.*

(*Rest*)

Whatcha gonna do.

AMIGA GRINGA: Have it, I guess.

HESTER: You may not be knocked up.

AMIGA GRINGA: Theres something in here all right. I can feel it growing inside. Just my luck.

HESTER: You shoulda been careful.

AMIGA GRINGA: —Whatever.

HESTER: So get rid of it if you dont want it.

AMIGA GRINGA: Or birth it then sell it.

HESTER: You as crazy as they come.

AMIGA GRINGA

HESTER

AMIGA GRINGA

(AMIGA *leans toward* HESTER *to kiss her.* HESTER *pulls back a bit.*)

AMIGA GRINGA: Whassamatter?

HESTER: I don't got no love for nobody cept the kids.

(AMIGA *pulls back, takes up the fabric.*)

AMIGA GRINGA: I'll get you a lot of money for this.

HESTER: No.

AMIGA GRINGA: Whassis?

(AMIGA GRINGA *discovers the brown paper package.*)

HESTER: Nothing.

AMIGA GRINGA: Smells like something. Smells like food. Smells like egg salad.

HESTER: I was saving it.

AMIGA GRINGA: Lets celebrate! Come on itll be fun. Kids!

HESTER: They *sleep.* Let em sleep.

AMIGA GRINGA: Lets toast my new kid. Just you and me. A new life has begun. Am I showing? Not yet, right? Will be soon enough. Little Bastards in there living high on the hog, taking up space. Little Bastard, we toast you with: egg salad.

(AMIGA *takes a big bite out of the sandwich.* HESTER *grasps at it but* AMIGA *keeps it from her reach.* BULLY *comes outside.*)

BULLY: Mommie?
HESTER: Yes, Bully.
BULLY: My hands.
HESTER: Lemmie unlock em.

(BULLY *comes over.* HESTER *opens her hands.*)

BULLY: Egg salad?
AMIGA GRINGA: Yeah. Its yr mommies sandwich.

(AMIGA *gives the sandwich to* HESTER *who almost takes a bite but sees* BULLY *looking on hungrily.* HESTER *gives the sandwich to* BULLY. BULLY *eats.* HESTER *gives* AMIGA *the fabric.*)

HESTER: Cheat me and I'll kill you.
AMIGA GRINGA: Have a little faith, Hester. Amiga will sell this fabric for you. You will not be a chump. In the morning when the sun comes up yll be 100 bucks richer. Sleep tight.

(AMIGA *takes the fabric and leaves.* BULLY *sits with her mother, licking her fingers.*)

THIRD CONFESSION: AMIGA GRINGA

"In My Head I Got It Going On"

AMIGA GRINGA: In my head I got it going on.
    The triple X rated movie:
    Hester and Amiga get down and get dirty.
    Chocolate and Vanilla get into the ugly.
    We coulda done a sex show behind a curtain
    then make a movie and sell it
    for 3 bucks a peek.
    I had me some delicious schemes
    to get her out of that hole she calls home.
    Im doing well for myself
    working my money maker.
    Do you have any idea how much cash I'll get for
        the fruit of my white womb?!
    Grow it.
    Birth it.
    Sell it.
    And why shouldnt I?

(*Rest*)

    Funny how a woman like Hester
    driving her life all over the road
    most often chooses to walk the straight and
        narrow.
    Girl on girl action is a very lucrative business.
    And someones gotta do something for her.
    Im just trying to help her out.

And myself too, ok. They dont call it Capitalizm for nothing.

(*Rest*)

    She liked the idea of the sex
    at least she acted like it.
    Her looking at me with those eyes of hers.
    You looking like you want it, Hester.
    Shoot, Miga, she says thats just the way I look she
        says.
    It took a little cajoling to get her to do it with me
    for an invited audience.
    For a dime a look.
    Over at my place.
    Every cent was profit and no overhead to speak of.
    The guys in the neighborhood got their pleasure
    and we was our own boss so we didnt have to pay
        no joker off the top.
    We slipped right into a very profitable situation
    like sliding into warm water.
    Her breasts her bottom
    she let me touch her however I wanted
    I let her ride my knees.
    She made sounds like an animal.
    She put her hand between my legs.
    One day some of the guys took advantage.
    Ah, what do you expect in a society based on Cap-
        italizm.
    I tell you the plight of the worker these days—.
    Still one day Im gonna get her to make the movie
    cause her and me we had the moves down
    very sensual, very provocative, very scientific, very
        lucrative.
    In my head I got it going on.

SCENE 6

The Reverend on the Rock

(*Late at night. Down the road,* REVEREND D. *cleaning his cornerstone, a white block of granite bearing the date in Roman numerals, and practicing his preaching.*)

[REVEREND D.: "It is easier for a camel to go through the eye of a needle than for a rich man to enter the kingdom of God." And you hear that and you say, let me get a tax shelter and hide some of my riches so that when I stand up there in judgment God wont be none the wiser! And that is the problem with the way we see God. For most of us, God is like the IRS. God garnishes yr wages if you dont pay up. God withholds. The wages of sin, they lead to death, so you say, let me give to the poor. But not any poor, just those respectable charities. I want my poor looking good. I want my poor to know that it was me who bought the such and such. I want my poor on tv. I want famous poor, not miscellaneous poor. And I dont want local poor. Local poor dont look good. Gimmie foreign poor. Poverty exotica. Gimmie brown and yellow skins against a non-Western landscape, some savanna, some rain forest some rice paddy. Gimmie big sad eyes with the berri-berri belly and the outstretched hands struggling to say "Thank You" the only english they know, right into the camera. And put me up there with them, holding them, comforting them, telling them everythings gonna be alright, we gonna raise you up, we gonna get you on the bandwagon of our ways, put a smile in yr heart and a hamburger in yr belly, baby.

(Rest)

And that is how we like our poor. At arms length. Like a distant relation with no complication. But folks, we gotta—]

(HESTER *comes in and watches him. After a while, he notices her and stops talking.)*

HESTER: Nice rock.
REVEREND D.: Thank you.
HESTER: Theres writing on it.
REVEREND D.: Dont come close. Its the date its just the date. The date. Well, the year.
HESTER: Like a calendar.
REVEREND D.: Its a cornerstone. The first stone of my new church. My backers are building me a church and this is the first stone.
HESTER: Oh.

(Rest)

You told me to come back. Im back.
REVEREND D.: Theyll start building my church tomorrow. My church will be a beautiful place. Its not much of a neighborhood now but when my church gets built, oh therell be a turnaround. Lots of opportunity for everyone. I feel like one of the pilgrims. You know, they step out of their boats and on to that Plymouth rock. I step off my soapbox and on to my cornerstone.
HESTER: You said come back to get my money. Im back.
REVEREND D.: Do you know what a "backer" is?
HESTER: Uh-uhn.
REVEREND D.: Its a person who backs you. A person who believes in you. A person who looks you over and figures you just might make something of yrself. And they get behind you. With kinds words, connections to high places, money. But they want to make sure they havent been suckered, so they watch you real close, to make sure yr as good as they think you are. To make sure you wont screw up and shame them and waste their money.

(Rest)

My backers are building me a church. It will be beautiful. And to make sure theyre not wasting

their money on a man who was only recently a neerdowell, they watch me.
HESTER: They watching now?
REVEREND D.: Not now. Now theyre in their nice beds. Between the cool sheets. Fast asleep. I dont sleep. I have this feeling that if I sleep I will miss someone. Someone in desperate need of what I have to say.
HESTER: Someone like me.
REVEREND D.: I dont have your money yet but I will. I'll take up a collection for you on Sunday. I'll tell them yr story, that yr someone in need, and all the money will go to you. Every cent of it. We get good crowds on Sunday.

(Rest)

Ive got work to do.

(He waits for her to go but she stays. He goes back to cleaning his cornerstone.)

HESTER: Today we had uh *E*-clipse. You seen it?
REVEREND D.: You should go.
HESTER: A shadow passed over the sky. Evrything was dark. For a minute.
REVEREND D.: It was a cloud. Or an airplane. Happens all the time.
HESTER: No clouds out today. It was uh *E*-clipse.
REVEREND D.: I am taking a collection for you on Sunday. Youll have to wait until then. Good night.
HESTER: Uh *E*-clipse.
REVEREND D.: There was no eclipse today! No eclipse!

(Rest)

Good night.
HESTER: I was crossing the street with the kids. We had a walk sign. White is walk and red is dont walk. I know white from red. Aint colorblind, right? And we was crossing. And a shadow fell over, everything started going dark and, shoot I had to look up. They say when theres uh *E*-clipse you shouldnt look up cause then you go blind and alls I need is to go blind, thank you. But I couldnt help myself. And so I stopped right there in the street and looked up. Never seen nothing like it.

(Rest)

I dont know what I expected to see but.

(Rest)

It was a big dark thing. Blocking the sun out. Like the hand of fate. The hand of fate with its 5 fingers coming down on me.

(Rest)

(Rest)

And then the trumpets started blaring.

(Rest)

And then there was Jabber saying "Come on Mommie, Come on!" The trumpets was the taxi cabs. Wanting to run me over. Get out the road.

REVEREND D.

HESTER

REVEREND D.

HESTER

(REVEREND D. sits on his rock, his back hiding his behavior which has become unseemly.)

REVEREND D.: Comeer.

(HESTER slowly goes to him.)

REVEREND D.: Suck me off.

HESTER: No.

REVEREND D.: Itll only take a minute. Im halfway there. Please.

(She goes down on him. Briefly. He cumms. Mildly. Into his handkerchief. She stands there. Ashamed. Expectant.)

REVEREND D.: Go home. Put yr children to bed.

HESTER: Maybe we could get something regular going again—

REVEREND D.: Go home. Go home.

HESTER

REVEREND D.

(Rest)

REVEREND D.: Heres something. Its all I have.

(He offers her a crumpled bill which she takes.)

REVEREND D.: Next time you come by—. It would be better if you could come around to the *back*. My churchll be going up and—. If you want your money, it would be better if you come around to the back.

HESTER: Yeah.

(HESTER goes. REVEREND sits there, watching her leave.)

FOURTH CONFESSION: REVEREND D.

"Suffering Is an Enormous Turn-on"

REVEREND D.: Suffering is an enormous turn-on.

(Rest)

She had four kids and she came to me asking me
    what to do.
She had a look in her eye that invites liaisons
eyes that say red spandex.
She had four children four fatherless children
    four fatherless mouths to feed
fatherless mouths fatherless children.
Add insult to injury was what I was thinking.
There was a certain animal magnetism between us.

And she threw herself at me
like a baseball in the Minors
fast but not deadly
I coulda stepped aside but.
God made her
and her fatherless mouths.

(Rest)

I was lying in the never ending gutter of the street
    of the world.
You can crawl along it forever and never crawl out
praying for God to take my life
you can take it God
you can take my life back
you can have it
before I hurt myself somebody
before I do a damage that I cannot undo
before I do a crime that I can never pay for
in the never ending blistering heat
of the never ending gutter of the world
my skin hot against the pavement
but lying there I knew
that I had never hurt anybody in my life.

(Rest)

(Rest)

She was one of the multitude. She did not stand
    out.

(Rest)

The intercourse was not memorable.
And when she told me of her *predicament*
I gave her enough money to take care of it.

(Rest)

In all my days in the gutter I never hurt anyone.
I never held hate for anyone.
And now the hate I have for her
and her hunger
and the *hate* I have for her hunger.
God made me.
God pulled me up.
Now God, through her, wants to drag me down
and sit me at the table
at the head of the table of her fatherless house.

SCENE 7

My Song in the Street

(HESTER with the kids. They are all playing freeze tag. After a bit, HESTER is "it." She runs then stops, standing stock-still, looking up into the sky. BULLY gets tagged.)

BULLY: 1 Mississippi, 2 Mississippi, 3 Mississippi, 4 Mississippi, 5 Mississippi.

(JABBER gets tagged.)

JABBER: 1 Mississippi, 2 Mississippi, 3 Mississippi, 4 Mississippi, 5 Mississippi. Yr it.

(HESTER *gets tagged.*)

HESTER

HESTER

JABBER: Mommie?

HESTER: What.

BULLY: Whasswrong?

HESTER: You think I like you bothering me all day?

HESTER

JABBER/BULLY/TROUBLE/BEAUTY

(*Rest*)

HESTER: All yall. Leave Mommie be. She cant play right now. Shes tired.

(HESTER *stands there looking up into the sky. The kids play apart.*)

BULLY: Lemmie see it.

TROUBLE: What?

BULLY: Yr pee.

TROUBLE

BULLY

BULLY: Dont got no hair or nothing on it yet. I got hair on mines. Look.

TROUBLE

BULLY

TROUBLE: Jabber. Lets see yrs.

TROUBLE

JABBER

BULLY

BULLY: Its got hair. Not as much as mines though.

BEAUTY: I had hairs but they fell out.

TROUBLE: Like a bald man or something?

BEAUTY: Yeah.

TROUBLE

TROUBLE

BULLY: Dont be touching yrself like that, Trouble, dont be nasty.

TROUBLE

TROUBLE

JABBER: You keep playing with it ssgonna fall off. Yr pee be laying in the street like a dead worm.

TROUBLE: Mommieeee!

HESTER: Dont talk to Mommie just now.

BULLY: Shes having a nervous breakdown.

HESTER: Shut the fuck up, please.

(*Rest*)

(*Rest*)

JABBER: When I grow up I aint never gonna use mines.

TROUBLE: Not me. I be *using* mines.

JABBER: Im gonna keep mines in my pants.

BULLY: How you ever gonna get married?

JABBER: Im gonna get married but Im gonna keep it in my pants.

BULLY: When you get married you gonna have to get on top uh yr wife.

JABBER: I'll get on top of her all right but I'll keep it in my pants.

TROUBLE: Jabber, you uh tragedy.

BULLY: When I get married my husbands gonna get on top of me and—

HESTER: No ones getting on top of you, Bully.

BULLY: He'll put the ring on my finger and I'll have me uh white dress and he'll get on top of me—

HESTER: No ones getting on top of you, Bully, no ones getting on top of you, so shut yr mouth about it.

TROUBLE: How she gonna have babies if no one gets on top of her?

HESTER: Dont *make* me hurt you!

(HESTER *raises her hand to* TROUBLE *who runs off.* BULLY *starts crying.*)

HESTER: Shut the fuck up or I'll give you something to cry about!

(*The kids huddle together in a knot.*)

HESTER

JABBER/BULLY/BEAUTY

HESTER

JABBER/BULLY/BEAUTY

HESTER

(*Rest*)

HESTER: Bedtime.

BEAUTY: Its too early for bed—

HESTER: BEDTIME!

(*They hurry off.* HESTER *goes back to contemplating the sky.*)

HESTER

HESTER

HESTER

HESTER: Big dark thing. Gods hand. Coming down on me. Blocking the light out. 5-fingered hand of fate. Coming down on me.

(*The* DOCTOR *comes on wearing his "SPAY" sandwich board. He watches her looking up. After a bit he looks up too.*)

DOCTOR: We've scheduled you in for the day after tomorrow. First thing in the morning. You can send yr kids off to school then come on in. We'll have childcare for the baby. We'll give you good meals during yr recovery. Yll go to sleep. Yll go to sleep and when you wake up, whisk! Yll be all clean. No worries no troubles no trials no tribulations no more mistakes. Clean as a whistle. You wont feel a thing. Day after tomorrow. First thing in the morning. Free of charge. Itll be our pleasure. And yours. All for the best. In the long run, Hester. Congratulations.

(The DOCTOR *walks off.* HESTER *is still looking up.* CHILLI *walks in with his picnic basket on his arm. He pauses to check his pocket watch.* HESTER *lowers her head. The sight of him knocks the wind out of her.)*

HESTER: Oh.

CHILLI: Ive been looking for you.

HESTER: Oh.

CHILLI: Ssbeen a long time.

HESTER: I—I—.

CHILLI: No need to speak.

HESTER: I—

CHILLI: Yr glad to see me.

HESTER: Yeah.

CHILLI: I been looking for you. Like I said. Lifes been good to me. Hows life been to you?

HESTER: Ok. —. Hard.

CHILLI

HESTER

HESTER: I was with the Welfare and I seed you. I called out yr name.

CHILLI: I didnt hear you. Darn.

HESTER: Yeah.

(Rest)

I woulda run after you but—

CHILLI: But you were weak in the knees. And you couldnt move a muscle.

HESTER: Running after you woulda gived you away. And Welfares been after me to know the names of my mens.

CHILLI: Mens? More than one?

HESTER: I seed you and I called out yr name but I didnt run after you.

(Rest)

You look good. I mean you always looked good but now you look better.

(Rest)

I didnt run after you. I didnt give you away.

CHILLI: Thats my girl.

(Rest)

Welfare has my name on file, though, doesnt she?

HESTER: From years ago. I—

CHILLI: Not to worry couldnt be helped. I changed my name. Theyll never find me. Theres no trace of the old me left anywhere.

HESTER: Cept Jabber.

CHILLI: Who?

HESTER: Yr son.

HESTER

CHILLI

CHILLI: Guess what time it is?

HESTER: He takes after you.

CHILLI: Go on guess. Betcha cant guess. Go on.

HESTER: Noon?

CHILLI: Lets see. I love doing this. I love guessing the time and then pulling out my watch and seeing how close I am or how far off. I love it. I spend all day doing it. Doctor says its a tick. A sure sign of some disorder. But I cant help it. And it doesnt hurt anyone. You guessed?

HESTER: Noon.

CHILLI: Lets see. Ah! 3.

HESTER: Oh.

*(*HESTER *goes back to contemplating the sky.)*

CHILLI: Sorry.

(Rest)

Whats up there?

HESTER: Nothing.

CHILLI: I want you to look at me. I want you to take me in. Ive been searching for you for weeks now and now Ive found you. I wasnt much when you knew me. When we knew each other I was—I was a shit.

(Rest)

I was a shit, wasnt I?

HESTER

CHILLI

CHILLI: I was a shit, agree with me.

HESTER: We was young.

CHILLI: We was young. We had a romance. We had a love affair. We was young. We was in love. I was infatuated with narcotics. I got you knocked up then I split.

HESTER: Jabber, hes yr spitting image. Only hes a little slow, but—

CHILLI: Who?

HESTER: Jabber. Yr son.

CHILLI: Dont bring him into it just yet. I need time. Time to get to know you again. We need time alone together. Guess.

HESTER: 3:02.

CHILLI: Ah! 3:05. But better, yr getting better. Things move so fast these days. Ive seen the world Ive made some money Ive made a new name for myself and I have a loveless life. I dont have love in my life. Do you know what thats like? To be alone? Without love?

HESTER: I got my childr—I got Jabber. hes my treasure.

HESTER

CHILLI

(Rest)

CHILLI: Im looking for a wife.

HESTER: Oh.

CHILLI: I want you to try this on.

(CHILLI *takes a wedding dress out of his basket. He puts it on her, right over her old clothes.* HESTER *rearranges the club, still held in her belt, to get the dress on more securely.*)

HESTER: I seed you and I called out your name, but you didnt hear me, and I wanted to run after you but I was like, Hester, if Welfare finds out Chillis in town they gonna give him hell so I didnt run. I didnt move a muscle. I was mad at you. Years ago. Then I seed you and I was afraid I'd never see you again and now here you are.
CHILLI: What do you think?
HESTER: Its so clean.
CHILLI: It suits you.

(HESTER *gets her shoes.*)

HESTER: I got some special shoes. Theyd go good with this. Jabber, come meet yr daddy!
CHILLI: Not yet, kid!

(Rest)

Lets not bring him into this just yet, K?

(He fiddles with his watch.)

CHILLI: 14 years ago. Back in the old neighborhood. You and me and the moon and the stars. What was our song?
HESTER
CHILLI
HESTER: Huh?
CHILLI: What was our song?

(Rest)

Da dee dah, dah dah dee dee?
HESTER: Its been a long time.
CHILLI: Listen.

(CHILLI *plays their song, "The Looking Song," on a tinny tape recorder. He sings along as she stands there. After a bit he dances and gets her to dance with him. They sing as they dance and do a few moves from the old days.*)

CHILLI:
Im looking for someone
to lose my looks with
looking for someone
to lose my shape with
looking for someone
to-get-my-hip-replaced with
looking for someone
Could it be you?

Im looking for someone
to lose my teeth with
looking for someone
to go stone deef with
looking for someone

to-lie-6-feet-underneath with
looking for someone
Could it be you?

They say, "Seek and ye shall find"
so I will look until Im blind
through this big old universe
for rich or poor better or worse
Singing:
yuck up my tragedy
oh darling, marry me
let's walk on down the aisle, walk on
Down Down Down.

Cause Im looking for someone
to lose my looks with
looking for someone
to lose my teeth with
looking for someone
I'll-lie-6-feet-underneath with
looking for someone
Could it be you?

(Theyre breathless from dancing.)

CHILLI: This is real. The feelings I have for you, the feelings you are feeling for me, these are all real. Ive been fighting my feelings for years. With every dollar I made. Every hour I spent. I spent it fighting. Fighting my feelings. Maybe you did the same thing. Maybe you remembered me against yr will, maybe you carried a torch for me against yr better judgment.
HESTER: You were my first.
CHILLI: Likewise.

(Rest)

(He silently guesses the time and checks his guess against his watch. Is he right or wrong?)

CHILLI: "Yuck up my tragedy."
HESTER: Huh?
CHILLI: "Marry me."
HESTER
CHILLI
HESTER: K.
CHILLI: There are some conditions some things we have to agree on. They dont have anything to do with money. I understand your situation.
HESTER: And my—
CHILLI: And your child—ok. *Our* child—ok. These things have to do with you and me. You would be mine and I would be yrs and all that. But I would still retain my rights to my manhood. You understand.
HESTER: Sure. My—
CHILLI: Yr kid. We'll get to him. I would rule the roost. I would call the shots. The whole roost and

every single shot. Ive proven myself as a success. Youve not done that. It only makes sense that I would be in charge.

HESTER: —K.

(Rest)

I love you.

CHILLI: Would you like me to get down on my knees?

(CHILLI gets down on his knees, offering her a ring.)

CHILLI: Heres an engagement ring. Its rather expensive. With an adjustable band. If I didnt find you I would have had to, well—. Try it on, try it on.

(CHILLI checks his watch. As HESTER fiddles with the ring, BULLY and TROUBLE rush in. BEAUTY and BABY follow them.)

BULLY: Mommie!
HESTER: No.
TROUBLE: You look fine!
HESTER: No.
BEAUTY: Is that a diamond?
HESTER: No!
BABY: Mommie!

(HESTER recoils from her kids.)

HESTER
BULLY/TROUBLE/BEAUTY/BABY
BULLY: Mommie?
CHILLI: Who do we have here, honey?
HESTER
BULLY/TROUBLE/BEAUTY/BABY
CHILLI: Who do we have here?
HESTER: The neighbors kids.

(CHILLI goes to look at his watch, doesnt.)

CHILLI: Honey?
HESTER: Bully, wheres Jabber at?
CHILLI: Honey?
HESTER: Bully, Im asking you a question.
CHILLI: Honey?
TROUBLE: hes out with Miga.
CHILLI: So you all are the neighbors kids, huh?
TROUBLE: Who the fuck are you?
HESTER: Trouble—
CHILLI: Who the fuck are you?
BULLY: We the neighbors kids.
CHILLI
HESTER

(Rest)

CHILLI: Honey?
HESTER: Huh?
CHILLI: Im—. I'm thinking this through. I'm thinking this all the way through. And I think—I think—.

(Rest)

(Rest)

I carried around this picture of you. Sad and lonely with our child on yr hip. Stuggling to make do. Stuggling against all odds. And triumphant. Triumphant against everything. Like—hell, like Jesus and Mary. And if they could do it so could my Hester. My dear Hester. Or so I thought.

(Rest)

But I dont think so.

(CHILLI takes her ring and her veil. He takes her dress. He packs up his basket.)

(Rest)

HESTER: Please.
CHILLI: Im sorry.

(CHILLI looks at his watch, flipping it open and then snapping it shut. He leaves.)

FIFTH CONFESSION: CHILLI

"We Was Young"

CHILLI: We was young
and we didnt think
we didnt think that nothing we could do would hurt us
nothing we did would come back to haunt us
we was young and we knew all about gravity but gravity was a law that did not apply to those persons under the age of 18
gravity was something that came later
and we was young and we could
float
weightless
I was her first
and zoom to the moon if we wanted and couldnt nothing stop us
we would go
fast
and we were gonna live forever
and any mistakes we would shake off
we were Death Defying
we were Hot Lunatics
careless as all get out
and she needed to keep it and I needed to leave town.
People get old that way.

(Rest)

We didnt have a car and everything was pitched toward love in a car
and there was this car lot down from where we worked and
we were fearless

late nights go sneak in those rusted Buicks that
  hadnt moved in years
I would sit at the wheel and pretend to drive
and she would say she felt the wind in her face
surfing her hand out the window
then we'd park
without even moving
in the full light of the lot
making love—
She was my first.
We was young.
Times change.

SCENE 8

The Hand of Fate

(*Night. The back entrance to the* REVEREND*s new church.*
HESTER *comes in with the kids in tow.*)

HESTER: Sunday night. He had people in there listening to him this morning. He passed the plate in
  my name. Not in my name directly. Keeps me
  secret, cause, well, he has his image. I understand
  that. Dont want to step on everything hes made
  for himself. And he still wants me. I can tell. A
  woman can tell when a man eyes her and he eyed
  me all right.

(*Rest*)

Yr building this just from talking. Must be saying
the right things. Nobodyd ever give me nothing
like this for running my mouth. Gonna get me
something now. Get something or do something.
Fuck you up fuck you up! Hold on, girl, it wont
come to that.

(*Rest*)

[I'll only ask for 5 dollars. 5 dollars a week. That
way he cant say no. And hes got a church, so he
got 5 dollars. I'll say I need to buy something for
the kids. No. I'll say I need to—get my hair done.
There is this style, curls piled up on the head, I'll
say. Takes hours to do. I need to fix myself up, I'll
say. Need to get my looks back. Need to get my
teeth done. Caps, bridges, what they called,
fillers, whatever. New teeth, dentures. Dentures.
He dont cough up I'll go straight to Welfare.
Maybe.]

(*Rest*)

(JABBER *comes running around the building. He sees*
HESTER *and sneaks up on her, touching her arm.*)

JABBER: Yr it.
HESTER: I aint playing.
JABBER: K.
HESTER: Where you been.

JABBER: Out with Miga.
HESTER: Oh.

(*Rest*)

JABBER: Mommie?
HESTER: What.
JABBER
HESTER

(*Rest*)

JABBER: I don't like the moon.
HESTER: I'll cover it up for you.

(HESTER *holds her hand up to the sky, hiding the moon
from view.*)

JABBER: Whered it go?
HESTER: Its gone to bed. You too.

(HESTER *nudges him away from her. He curls up with the
others.*)

HESTER
HESTER

(REVEREND D. *comes outside. He carries a large neon
cross.*)

HESTER: Its Sunday.

(*He sees the children.*)

REVEREND D.: Oh God.
HESTER: Its Sunday. —. Yesterday was—Saturday.
REVEREND D.: Excuse me a minute?

(*He props the cross against a wall.*)

HESTER: Its Sunday.
REVEREND D.: I passed the plate and it came back
  empty.
HESTER: Oh.
REVEREND D.: But not to worry: I'll have some. Tomor-
  row morning—
HESTER: I was gonna—get myself fixed up.
REVEREND D.: —When the bank opens. 100 bucks. To-
  morrow morning. All for you. You have my word.
HESTER: I was thinking, you know, in my head, that
  there was something I can do to stop that hand
  coming down. Must be something—
REVEREND D.: I'll have my lawyer deliver the money.
  Its better if you dont come back. Its too danger-
  ous. My following are an angry bunch. They dont
  like the likes of you.
HESTER: But you do. You like me.
REVEREND D.: Youd better go.
HESTER: Why you dont like me? Why you dont like me
  no more?

(*He tries to go back inside.* HESTER *grabs ahold of him.*)

HESTER: Dont go.
REVEREND D.: Take yr hands off me.

HESTER: Why you dont like me?

(They struggle as he tries to shake her loose. Then, in a swift motion, HESTER *raises her club to strike him. He is much stronger than she. He brutally twists her hand. She recoils in pain and falls to the ground.* JABBER, *wide awake, watches.)*

REVEREND D.: Slut.

(Rest)

    Dont ever come back here again! Ever! Yll never get nothing from me! Common Slut. Tell on me! Go on! Tell the world! I'll crush you underfoot.

(He goes inside.)

HESTER

HESTER

HESTER

JABBER: Mommie.

HESTER

HESTER

JABBER: The moon came out again.

JABBER

HESTER

JABBER

(Rest)

JABBER: Them bad boys had writing. On our house. Remember the writing they had on our house and you told me to read it and I didnt wanna I said I couldnt but that wasnt really true I could I can read but I didnt wanna.

HESTER: Hush up now.

JABBER: I was reading it but I was only reading it in my head I wasnt reading it with my mouth I was reading it with my mouth but not with my tongue I was reading it only with my lips and I could hear the word outloud but only outloud in my head.

HESTER: Shhhh.

JABBER: I didnt wanna say the word outloud in your head.

HESTER

HESTER

JABBER: I didnt wanna say you the word. You wanna know why I didnt wanna say you the word? You wanna know why? Mommie?

HESTER

HESTER

(Rest)

HESTER: What.

JABBER: It was a bad word.

HESTER

HESTER

JABBER: Wanna know what it said? Wanna know what the word said?

HESTER: What.

JABBER

JABBER

HESTER: What?

JABBER: "Slut."

HESTER: Go to sleep, Jabber.

JABBER: It read "Slut." "Slut."

HESTER: Hush up.

JABBER: Whassa "slut"?

HESTER: Go sleep.

JABBER: You said if I read it youd say what it means. Slut. Whassit mean?

HESTER: I said I dont wanna hear that word. How slow are you? Slomo.

JABBER: Slut.

HESTER: You need to close yr mouth, Jabber.

JABBER: I know what it means. Slut.

HESTER: (Shut up.)

JABBER: Slut.

HESTER: (I said shut up, now.)

JABBER: I know what it means.

HESTER: (And I said shut up! Shut up.)

(Rest)

(Rest)

JABBER: Slut. Sorry.

(The word just popped out, a childs joke. He covers his mouth, sheepishly. They look at each other.)

HESTER

JABBER

HESTER

JABBER

*(*HESTER *quickly raises her club and hits him once. Brutally. He cries out and falls down dead. His cry wakes* BULLY, TROUBLE *and* BEAUTY. *They look on.* HESTER *beats* JABBERS *body again and again and again.* TROUBLE *and* BULLY *back away.* BEAUTY *stands there watching.* JABBER *is dead and bloody.* HESTER *looks up from her deed to see* BEAUTY *who runs off.* HESTER *stands there alone—wet with her sons blood. Grief-stricken, she cradles his body. Her hands wet with blood, she writes an "A" on the ground.)*

HESTER: Looks good, Jabber, dont it? Dont it, huh?

SIXTH CONFESSION: HESTER, LA NEGRITA

"I Shoulda Had a Hundred-Thousand"

HESTER, LA NEGRITA: Never shoulda had him.
    Never shoulda had none of em.
    Never was nothing but a pain to me:
    5 Mistakes!
    No, dont say that.
    —nnnnnnnn—
    Kids? Where you gone?
    Never shoulda haddem.

Me walking around big as a house
Knocked up and Showing
and always by myself.
Men come near me oh yeah but then
love never sticks longer than a quick minute
wanna see something last forever watch water
    boil, you know.
I never shoulda haddem!

(Rest)

(She places her hand in the pool of JABBERS *blood.)*

No:
I shoulda had a hundred
a hundred
I shoulda had a hundred-thousand
A hundred-thousand a whole *army* full I shoulda!
I shoulda.
One right after the other! Spitting em out with no
    years in between!
One after another:
Tail to head:
Spitting em out:
Bad mannered Bad mouthed Bad Bad *Bastards*!
A whole *army full* I shoulda!
I shoulda
—nnnnnnn—
I shoulda

*(*HESTER *sits there, crumpled, alone. The prison bars come down.)*

SCENE 9

The Prison Door.

(All circle around HESTER *as they speak.)*

ALL: LOOK AT HER!
    WHO DOES SHE THINK
    SHE IS
    THE ANIMAL
    NO SKILLS
    CEPT ONE
    CANT READ CANT WRITE

SHE MARRIED?
WHAT DO YOU THINK?
SHE OUGHTA BE MARRIED
SHE AINT MARRIED
THATS WHY THINGS ARE BAD LIKE THEY ARE
CAUSE OF
GIRLS LIKE THAT
THAT EVER HAPPEN TO ME YOU WOULDNT SEE ME
DOING THAT
YOU WOULDNT SEE THAT HAPPENING TO ME
WHO THE HELL SHE THINK SHE IS
AND NOW WE GOT TO PAY FOR IT
HAH!

(They spit.)

ALL: SHE DONT GOT NO SKILLS
    CEPT ONE
    CANT READ CANT WRITE
    SHE MARRIED?
    WHAT DO YOU THINK?
    JUST PLAIN STUPID IF YOU ASK ME AINT NO SMART
    WOMAN GOT ALL THEM BASTARDS
    AND NOT A PENNY TO HER NAME
    SOMETHINGS GOTTA BE DONE
    CAUSE I'LL BE DAMNED IF SHE GONNA LIVE OFF ME.

ALL

HESTER

ALL

WELFARE: Is she in any pain?

DOCTOR: She shouldnt be. She wont be having anymore children.

WELFARE: No more mistakes.

CHILLI: Whats that?

WELFARE: An "A."

AMIGA GRINGA: An "A."

DOCTOR: First letter of the alphabet.

WELFARE: Thats as far as she got.

*(*HESTER *holds up her hands—theyre covered with blood. She looks up with outstretched arms.)*

HESTER: Big hand coming down on me. Big hand coming down on me. Big hand coming down on me

END OF PLAY

Figure 1. Hester (Charlayne Woodard, *center*) ladles out soup to Trouble (Bruce MacVittie, *left*), while Jabber (Rob Campbell, *behind Hester*), Bully (Gail Grate, *seated left*), and Baby (Reggie Montgomery, *seated front*) clutch their soup bowls. Beauty (Deirdre O'Connell, *standing*) wears the hair ribbon that she has asked for. The 1999 production of *In the Blood* was directed by David Esbjornson at the Joseph Papp Public Theater/New York Shakespeare Festival. (Photograph: Michal Daniel.)

Figure 2. Hester (Charlayne Woodard), wearing the bridal veil and dress that Chilli (Rob Campbell) has put on her, listens to Chilli's proposal in the 1999 production of *In the Blood*. (Photograph: Michal Daniel.)

Figure 3. Reverend D. (Reggie Montgomery) tells Hester (Charlayne Woodard) that she only imagines he is the father of her baby in the 1999 production of *In the Blood*. (Photograph: Michal Daniel.)

Figure 4. Angered by Reverend D.'s rejection in the penultimate scene of the play, Hester (Charlayne Woodard) raises her club to attack him. The neon cross that Reverend D. has carried on stage stands as an emblem of his hypocrisy in the 1999 production of *In the Blood*. (Photograph: Michal Daniel.)

Staging of *In the Blood*

REVIEW OF THE JOSEPH PAPP PUBLIC THEATER PRODUCTION, 1999, BY MARGO JEFFERSON

Artists talk with one another across the centuries; they talk about their obsessions, their ancestors, the particulars of their time and place and about whatever can go beyond the particular to take on a new life.

Suzan-Lori Parks's extraordinary new play, "In the Blood," which opened last night at the Public Theater, is a conversation with—a revision of, a set of improvisations on—Nathaniel Hawthorne's "Scarlet Letter." Ms. Parks and Hawthorne share an obsession with American history and the large patterns of sin, cruelty, punishment and redemption that give it form and content.

Hawthorne was the descendant of Salem, Mass., Puritans who persecuted Quakers, denounced witches and had their deeds recorded in the annals of New England history. His fiction unveiled and sought to redeem those ancestral crimes; in his introduction to "The Scarlet Letter" he vowed: "I, the present writer, as their representative, hereby take shame upon myself for their sakes, and pray that any curse incurred by them . . . may be now and henceforth removed." Ms. Parks is the inheritor of an African-American history much of which has gone, in her words, "unrecorded, dismembered, washed out"; her task, she says in an essay called "Possession," is "to locate the ancestral burial ground, dig for bones, find bones, hear the bones sing, write it down."

This time around we are in New York, not Salem. The adulteress is Hester, La Negrita, played—no, embodied with stunning coherence—by Charlayne Woodard. She is a woman on welfare living under a bridge with her five children. Like Hester Prynne, she offers tortured assertions of her responsibility. ("My life's my own fault. I know that. But the world don't help. . . . I ain't afraid of hard work. It's a leg up. Can't start from the top.") But she, too, is being ground down by a society that wields power pitilessly and, when it sees fit, vengefully. (Hester Prynne longed to be the prophetess for a new truth that would "establish the whole relation between man and woman on a surer ground of mutual happiness.") Three centuries later Hester can only say bleakly, "I don't think the world likes women much." As for the people around her, they are just a little more powerful (therefore better at being selfish) or just a little more canny (therefore better at manipulating things).

"In the Blood" is about the way we live now, and it is truly harrowing. (What is "in" Hester's blood, as the world sees it? Sin, sluttishness, the lower-class racial weakness that leads to sloth and reckless procreation.) We cannot turn away, and we do not want to. The play strikes us as Hawthorne claimed his first glimpse of the scarlet letter struck him: with "a sensation not altogether physical yet almost so, as of burning heat, as if the letter were not of red cloth but red-hot iron."

This Hester can't read or write. Her oldest son, Jabber (Rob Campbell), is supposed to be teaching her, but she hasn't gotten past A. She certainly can't make out the word "slut" scrawled on a nearby wall, and Jabber won't read it for her.

They live on mean words and slim chances. Her son Trouble (Bruce MacVittie) steals a policeman's club, her daughter Bully (Gail Grate) sleeps with her hands in fists; her youngest, Baby (Reggie Montgomery), is learning how to smash the soda cans that earn them small change at the local supermarket.

Still, when we first see them all sitting around Hester as she ladles out a dinner of soup, there's a tenuous sweetness there; she is trying so hard to keep them together as a family. Then, when Hester makes up a bedtime story in which a princess changes the law of the land and gets to marry all five of the men who court her, we realize that those folk tales we love so would be narratives of misery and woe if poor and powerless storytellers hadn't invented supernatural forces to save the day.

Having no recourse to those forces, Hester's path leads no place but down. She is hungry all the time (the children get whatever food she has), and the world is eating her up. There is the doctor with the community street practice (Mr. MacVittie), her snappy drug-besotted white friend, The Amiga Gringa (Deirdre O'Connell), The Welfare Lady in the prim pink suit (Ms. Grate), the minister who is building his own church (Mr. Montgomery) and Chilli (Mr. Campbell), Jabber's father and her first love.

Every one of them has used her for sex. And they try or pretend they will try to do better by her, especially the Rev. D, who is the father of Baby and promises child support money if she keeps quiet.

These exchanges are taut and packed. Ms. Parks's writing has grown leaner and hungrier since plays like "The Death of the Last Black Man on Earth" and "Venus," with their layers of historical allusion and soliloquy-like dialogue. Here the dialogue alternates with beautifully timed and paced confessions from each character, delivered in a square of harsh white light.

The confessions strip these people down to their bare selves with an insistence that comes as much from the anguished intimacy of Adrienne Kennedy's plays as from Hawthorne: "Times are tough: what can we do?" asks the doctor. "There's a mamma dog running loose and her puppies are crying because there's not/there's not enough food for those poor little pups/and the pups grow into dogs unhousebroken and ill-mannered with families of their own." The caseworker is a black woman, too. "I walk the line/between us and them/between our kind and their kind" she reminds us.

The Amiga Gringa regrets the money they could have made together as Chocolate and Vanilla: "We coulda done a sex show behind a curtain/Then make a movie and sell it/for 3 bucks a peek." The Rev. D confides that suffering is an enormous turn-on, up to the moment when he realizes that through Hester, God "wants to drag me down/and sit me at the table/at the head of the table of her fatherless house." And Chilli, the long-gone lover who comes back to town looking for her, still remembers the days when they were so desperate to make love in a car, all-American-boy-and-girl style, they would go to a vacant lot and "sneak in those rusted Buicks that hadn't moved in years/and I would sit at the wheel and pretend to drive/and she would say she felt the wind in her face."

And finally there is Hester, moving toward tragedy, shadowed by "a big dark thing. Blocking the sun out. Like the hand of fate."

This potent and terrible sense of being closed in with the characters is heightened by the fact that, apart from Ms. Woodard, each actor plays both a child and an adult. The director, David Esbjornson, has made them into a real ensemble, though I think he could encourage them to bring out more of the humor—stark and dissonant, but humor nevertheless—in the text. This is especially true of Reggie Montgomery's performance. When it comes to characters who like to season corruption with wit, Mr. Montgomery is a master; but at the moment his Rev. D is in the grip of too many melodramatic flourishes.

Gail Grate is especially good as both the needy daughter and the repressive Welfare Lady, while Rob Campbell gives Jabber real sweetness and Chilli a languid, playful menace. The stage, with just the bare necessities, could easily be a street just blocks away from the theater; the lighting, clothing, sound (subways, harsh rhythmic music) intensify without showing off. (Kudos to Narelle Sissons, Elizabeth Hope Clancy, Jane Cox, Don DiNicola).

You will leave "In the Blood" feeling pity and terror. And because it is a work of art, you will leave thrilled, even comforted by its mastery.

IDEAS OF DRAMA
Classical to Contemporary

Ideas of drama—of its essential nature, its basic purposes, its various kinds, its distinctive elements—have been, and continue to be, as multifarious and changeable as the history of theater itself. So, in the collection that follows, we have reprinted fourteen pieces that reflect the wide range of classical to contemporary thinking about drama. Aristotle's discussion of tragedy constitutes the most fully developed and systematic body of ideas to appear during the classical period. Its influence has been so profound ever since then that in one sense, many other ideas of drama can be seen as a response to Aristotle's definition of plot and character in classical Greek tragedy. For example, Sir Philip Sidney's ideas about the fundamental difference between "right tragedies" and "right comedies"—ideas formulated during the English Renaissance—are clearly an extension of Aristotle's basic distinctions between tragedy and comedy, whereas Arthur Miller's modern American belief in the common man as "an apt subject for tragedy" is just as clearly a repudiation of Aristotle's idea of the tragic hero as a person who belongs "to the class of those who enjoy great esteem and prosperity." Likewise, the brevity, as well as the no-nonsense quality, of Marsha Norman's "Ten Golden Rules for Playwrights" might be seen as a witty put-down of the laborious theorizing and rule making that grew out of the Aristotelian tradition. But in another sense, changing ideas of drama inevitably take form in response to changing aspects of drama itself, as one can see in Oliver Goldsmith's reflections on developments that took place in English comedy from the late-seventeenth to the late-eighteenth century—from "laughing" to "weeping" comedy—or in George Bernard Shaw's essay on the changes that took place in nineteenth-century European drama from the "well-made play" of French theater to the "problem plays" of Henrik Ibsen, or in Martin Esslin's remarks on the absurdist drama that emerged during the mid-twentieth century. Sometimes, however, ideas of theater are deliberately formulated anew in order to provoke a change in the nature of drama, as Antonin Artaud clearly aimed to do in propounding "a theater of cruelty," or Amiri Baraka in expounding upon the essence of an authentically black theater, or Suzan-Lori Parks in advocating the "Tradition of the Next New Thing." Ultimately, of course, most ideas of theater arise out of a complex interaction among playwrights, plays, actors, directors, audiences, critics, and their immediate cultural situation, as can be seen in August Strindberg's comments on the "modern" way of looking at things that is reflected in the characters, plot, and setting of his play, or in William Butler Yeats's conception of an Irish national theater, or in Constantin Stanislavski's psychologically astute ideas about directing and acting, or Bertolt Brecht's explanation and defense of "epic theatre." So the pieces in this collection can fruitfully be studied in connection with each other or in relation to the plays themselves.

On the Nature and Elements of Tragedy

BY ARISTOTLE, ca. 355 B.C.,
translated by Stephen Halliwell

Aristotle (384–322 B.C.) was a Greek philosopher who wrote treatises on ethics, poetics, rhetoric, metaphysics, and natural history. Born near Macedonia, he was a student of Plato at the Academy in Athens, tutored Alexander the Great in Macedon, and later founded the Lyceum in Athens. His philosophical belief that the knowledge of something requires a systematic inquiry into its purpose or function can be seen in his discussion of tragedy from The Poetics, *reprinted below.*

The Nature of Tragedy and Its Basic Elements

I shall discuss epic mimesis and comedy later. But let us deal with tragedy by taking up the definition of its essential nature which arises out of what has so far been said.

Tragedy, then, is a representation of an action which is serious, complete, and of a certain magnitude—in language which is garnished in various forms in its different parts—in the mode of dramatic enactment, not narrative—and through the arousal of pity and fear effecting the *katharsis*° of such emotions.

By 'garnished' language I mean with rhythm and melody; and by the 'various forms' I mean that some parts use spoken metre, and others use lyric song. Since the mimesis is enacted by agents, we can deduce that one element of tragedy must be the adornment of visual spectacle, while others are lyric poetry and verbal style, for it is in these that the mimesis is presented. By 'style' I mean the composition of the spoken metres; the meaning of 'lyric poetry' is entirely evident.

Since tragedy is a representation of an action, and is enacted by agents, who must be characterised in both their character and their thought (for it is through these that we can also judge the qualities of their actions, and it is in their actions that all men either succeed or fail), we have the plot-structure as the mimesis of the action (for by this term 'plot-structure' I mean the organisation of the events) while characterisation is what allows us to judge the nature of the agents, and 'thought' represents the parts in which by their speech they put forward arguments or make statements.

So then, tragedy as a whole must have six elements which make it what it is: they are plot-structure, character, style, thought, spectacle, lyric poetry. Two of these are the media, one the mode, and three the objects, of the mimesis—and that embraces everything. Many poets have exploited these parts in order to produce certain types of play [. . .].

The most important of these elements is the structure of events, because tragedy is a representation not of people as such but of actions and life, and both happiness and unhappiness rest on action. The goal is a certain activity, not a qualitative state; and while men do have certain qualities by virtue of their character, it is in their actions that they achieve, or fail to achieve, happiness. It is not, therefore, the function of the agents' actions to allow the portrayal of their characters; it is, rather, for the sake of their actions that characterisation is included. So, the events and the plot-structure are the goal of tragedy, and the goal is what matters most of all.

Besides, without action you would not have a tragedy, but one without character would be feasible, for the tragedies of most recent poets are lacking in characterisation, and in general there are many such poets. Compare, among painters, the difference between Zeuxis and Polygnotus: while Polygnotus is a fine portrayer of character, Zeuxis' art has no characterisation. Furthermore, if a poet strings together speeches to illustrate character, even allowing he composes them well in style and thought, he will not achieve the stated aim of tragedy. Much more effective will be a play with a plot and structure of events, even if it is deficient in style and thought.

In addition to these considerations, tragedy's greatest means of emotional power are components of the plot-structure: namely, reversals and recognitions. Moreover, it is symptomatic that poetic novices can achieve precision in style and characterisation before they acquire it in plot-construction—as was the case with virtually all the early poets. And so, the plot-structure is the first principle and, so to speak, the soul of tragedy, while characterisation is the element of second importance. (An analogous point holds for painting: a random distribution of the most attractive colours would never yield as much pleasure as a definite image without colour.) Tragedy is a mimesis of action, and only for the sake of this is it mimesis of the agents themselves.

Third in importance is thought: this is the capacity to produce pertinent and appropriate arguments, which is the task in prose speeches of the arts of politics and rhetoric. The older poets used to make their characters speak in a political vein, whereas modern poets do so in a rhetorical vein. Character is the ele-

---

katharsis, purification or purgation.

ment which reveals the nature of a moral choice, in cases where it is not anyway clear what a person is choosing or avoiding (and so speeches in which the speaker chooses or avoids nothing at all do not possess character); while thought arises in passages where people show that something is or is not the case, or present some universal proposition.

The fourth element is style: as previously said, I mean by this term the verbal expression achieved through the choice of words, which has the same force whether in verse or in prose. Of the remaining elements, lyric poetry is the most important of garnishings, while spectacle is emotionally powerful but is the least integral of all to the poet's art: for the potential of tragedy does not depend upon public performance and actors; and, besides, the art of the mask-maker carries more weight than the poet's as regards the elaboration of visual effects.

Basic Principles of a Well-Designed Plot

Given these definitions, my next topic is to prescribe the form which the structure of events ought to take, since this is the first and foremost component of tragedy. We have already laid down that tragedy is a representation of an action which is complete, whole and of a certain magnitude (for something can be whole but of no magnitude).

By 'whole' I mean possessing a beginning, middle and end. By 'beginning' I mean that which does not have a necessary connection with a preceding event, but which can itself give rise naturally to some further fact or occurrence. An 'end,' by contrast, is something which naturally occurs after a preceding event, whether by necessity or as a general rule, but need not be followed by anything else. The 'middle' involves causal connections with both what precedes and what ensues. Consequently, well-designed plot-structures ought not to begin or finish at arbitrary points, but to follow the principles indicated.

Moreover, any beautiful object, whether a living creature or any other structure of parts, must possess not only ordered arrangement but also an appropriate scale (for beauty is grounded in both size and order). A creature could not be beautiful if it is either too small—for perception of it is practically instantaneous and so cannot be experienced—or too great, for contemplation of it cannot be a single experience, and it is not possible to derive a sense of unity and wholeness from our perception of it (imagine an animal a thousand miles long). Just, therefore, as a beautiful body or creature must have some size, but one which allows it to be perceived all together, so plot-structures should be of a length which can be easily held in the memory.

An artistic definition of length cannot be related to dramatic competitions and the spectators' concentra-tion. For if a hundred tragedies had to compete, they would measure them by the water-clock (as people say they once did). The limit which accords with the true nature of the matter is this: beauty of size favours as large a structure as possible, provided that coherence is maintained. A concise definition is to say that the sufficient limit of a poem's scale is the scope required for a probable or necessary succession of events which produce a transformation either from affliction to prosperity, or the reverse.

Unity in Plot-Structure

A plot-structure does not possess unity (as some believe) by virtue of centring on an individual. For just as a particular thing may have many random properties, some of which do not combine to make a single entity, so a particular character may perform many actions which do not yield a single 'action.' Consequently, all those poets who have written a *Heracleid*° or *Theseid*,° or the like, are evidently at fault: they believe that because Heracles was a single individual, a plot-structure about him ought thereby to have unity. As in other respects, Homer is exceptional by the fineness of his insight into this point, whether we regard this as an acquired ability or a natural endowment of his: although composing an *Odyssey*,° he did not include everything that happened to the hero (such as his wounding on Parnassus or his pretence of madness at the levy—events which involved no necessary or probable connection with one another). Instead, he constructed the *Odyssey* around a single action of the kind I mean, and likewise with the *Iliad*.

So then, just as in the other mimetic arts a unitary mimesis is a representation of a unitary object, so the plot-structure, as the mimesis of action, should be a representation of a unitary and complete action; and its parts, consisting of the events, should be so constructed that the displacement or removal of any one of them will disturb and disjoint the work's wholeness. For anything whose presence or absence has no clear effect cannot be counted an integral part of the whole.

Probability in Plot Structures

It is a further clear implication of what has been said that the poet's task is to speak not of events which have occurred, but of the kind of events which *could* occur, and are possible by the standards of probability or necessity. For it is not the use or absence of metre which distinguishes poet and historian (one could put

---

Heracleid, a dramatic or narrative work about the life of the hero Hercules. *Theseid*, a dramatic or narrative work about the life of the hero Theseus. *Odyssey*, a narrative work about the Greek hero Odysseus.

Herodotus'° work into verse, but it would be no less a sort of history with it than without it): the difference lies in the fact that the one speaks of events which have occurred, the other of the sort of events which could occur.

It is for this reason that poetry is both more philosophical and more serious than history, since poetry speaks more of universals, history of particulars. A 'universal' comprises the *kind* of speech or action which belongs by probability or necessity to a certain *kind* of character—something which poetry aims at *despite* its addition of particular names. A 'particular,' by contrast, is (for example) what Alcibiades° did or experienced.

This point has become clear in the case of comedy, where it is only after constructing a plot in terms of probable events that they give the characters ordinary names, so diverging from the iambic poets' practice of writing about individuals. In tragedy, on the other hand, the poets hold to the actual names. (The reason for this is that people are ready to believe in what is possible; and while we may not yet believe in the possibility of things that have not already happened, actual events are evidently possible, otherwise they would not have occurred.) Even so, there are some tragedies in which one or two of the familiar names are kept, while others are due to the poet; and some plays in which all are new, as in Agathon's *Antheus:* for in this play both the events and the names are equally the poet's work, yet the pleasure it gives is just as great. So, fidelity to the traditional plots which are the subject of tragedies is not to be sought at all costs. Indeed, to do this is absurd, since even familiar material is familiar only to a minority, but it can still afford pleasure to all.

It is clear, then, from what has been said that the poet should be a maker of plot-structures rather than of verses, in so far as his status as poet depends on mimesis, and the object of his mimesis is actions. And he is just as much a poet even if the material of his poetry comprises actual events, since there is no reason why *some* historical events should not be in conformity with probability, and it is with respect to probability that the poet can make his poetry from them.

Of simple plot-structures and actions the worst are episodic. I call an 'episodic' plot-structure one in which the episodes follow in a succession which is neither probable nor necessary. Such plays are produced by bad poets through their own fault, and by good poets because of their actors: for in composing declamatory set-pieces, and straining the plot-structure

to excess, they are often compelled to distort the dramatic sequence.

Since tragic mimesis° portrays not just a whole action, but events which are fearful and pitiful, this can best be achieved when things occur contrary to expectation yet still on account of one another. A sense of wonder will be more likely to be aroused in this way than as a result of the arbitrary or fortuitous, since even chance events make the greatest impact of wonder when they *appear* to have a purpose (as in the case where Mitys's statue at Argos fell on Mitys's murderer and killed him, while he was looking at it: such things do not *seem* to happen without reason). So then, plot-structures which embody this principle must be superior.

Simple and Complex Plots

Plot-structures can be divided into the simple and the complex, for the actions which they represent consist naturally of these types. By a 'simple' action I mean one which is, as earlier defined, continuous and unitary, but whose transformation occurs without reversal or recognition. A 'complex' action is one whose transformation involves recognition or reversal, or both. Reversal and recognition should arise from the intrinsic structure of the plot, so that what results follows by either necessity or probability from the preceding events: for it makes a great difference whether things happen because of one another, or only *after* one another.

Reversal and Recognition in Tragic Plots

Reversal, as indicated, is a complete swing in the direction of the action; but this, as we insist, must conform to probability or necessity. Take, for example, Sophocles' *Oedipus Tyrannus*, where the person comes to bring Oedipus happiness, and intends to free him from his fear about his mother; but he produces the opposite effect, by revealing Oedipus' identity. And in *Lynceus* the one person is led off to die, while Danaus follows to kill him; yet it comes about that the latter's death and the former's rescue result from the chain of events.

Recognition, as the very name shows, is a change from ignorance to knowledge, bringing the characters into either a close bond, or enmity, with one another, and concerning matters which bear on their prosperity or affliction. The finest recognition occurs in direct conjunction with reversal—as with the one in the *Oedipus*. There are, of course, other kinds of recognition, for recognition can relate to inanimate or fortu-

---

Herodotus, Greek historian (ca. 484–425 B.C.). **Alcibiades,** Athenian statesman and general (ca. 450–404 B.C.).

---

mimesis, literally, imitation; i.e., representation of human actions and events.

itous objects, or reveal that someone has, or has not, committed a deed. But the type I have mentioned is the one which is most integral to the plot-structure and its action: for such a combination of recognition and reversal will produce pity or fear (and it is events of this kind that tragedy, on our definition, is a mimesis of), since both affliction and prosperity will hinge on such circumstances. And since recognition involves people, there are cases where one person's recognition by another takes place (when this other's own identity is clear), and cases where the recognition must be reciprocal: for instance, Iphigeneia was recognised by Orestes through the sending of the letter, but another means of recognition was needed for Iphigeneia's identification of *him*.

Well then, reversal and recognition form two components of the plot-structure; the third is suffering. To the definitions of reversal and recognition already given we can add that of suffering: a destructive or painful action, such as visible deaths, torments, woundings, and other things of the same kind.

Quantitative Divisions of a Tragedy

Having earlier given the parts of tragedy which determine its qualities, the quantitative divisions of the genre can be listed as: prologue, episode, *exodos,* choral unit. The latter can be divided into the choral entry (*parodos*) and the choral ode (*stasimon*), which are common to all plays, while actors' songs and lyric exchanges (*kommoi*) are peculiar to only certain plays.

The prologue is the entire portion of a tragedy preceding the choral entry. An episode is an entire portion of a tragedy lying between complete choral odes. The *exodos* is the entire portion of a tragedy which follows the final choral ode. Of the choral elements, the *parodos* is the first entire choral utterance; a *stasimon* is a choral song in a metre other than anapaestic or trochaic; while a *kommos* is a lamentation shared between chorus and actors.

The parts of tragedy which determine its qualities were given earlier, while those above are the divisions of a quantitative analysis.

Guidelines for Construction of Tragic Plots

It follows on from my earlier argument that I should define what ought to be aimed at and avoided in plot-construction, as well as the source of tragedy's effect. Since, then, the structure of the finest tragedy should be complex, not simple, and, moreover, should portray fearful and pitiful events (for this is the distinctive feature of this type of mimesis), it is to begin with clear that:

(a) good men should not be shown passing from prosperity to affliction, for this is neither fearful nor pitiful but repulsive;

(b) wicked men should not be shown passing from affliction to prosperity, for this is the most untragic of all possible cases and is entirely defective (it is neither moving nor pitiful nor fearful);

(c) the extremely evil man should not fall from prosperity to affliction, for such a plot-structure might move us, but would not arouse pity or fear, since pity is felt towards one whose affliction is undeserved, fear towards one who is like ourselves (so what happens in such a case will be neither pitiful nor fearful).

We are left, then, with the figure who falls between these types. Such a man is one who is not preeminent in virtue and justice, and one who falls into affliction not because of evil and wickedness, but because of a certain fallibility (*hamartia*).° He will belong to the class of those who enjoy great esteem and prosperity, such as Oedipus, Thyestes, and outstanding men from such families.

It is imperative that a fine plot-structure be single and not double (as some assert), and involve a change from prosperity to affliction (rather than the reverse) caused not by wickedness but by a great fallibility on the part of the sort of agent stipulated, or one who is better, not worse, than indicated. Actual practice tends to confirm my thesis. For in the beginning the poets' choice of stories was arbitrary, whereas now the finest tragedies are constructed around a few families—Alcmaeon, for example, Oedipus, Orestes, Meleager, Thyestes, Telephus, and others who have suffered or committed terrible deeds.

This, then, is the plot-pattern for the tragedy which best fulfils the standards of poetic art. Those who fault Euripedes, for following this, and for ending many of his plays with affliction, make the same mistake as mentioned above. For such an ending is legitimate, as argued, and the greatest confirmation is that such plays make the most tragic impression in acted competition (provided they are staged effectively), and Euripides, whatever other faults of organisation he may have, at least makes the most tragic impression of all poets.

The second-best pattern (which some hold to be the best) is the kind which involves a double structure (like the *Odyssey*) and contrasting outcomes for good and bad characters. It is the weakness of audiences which produces the view of this type's superiority; poets are led to give the spectators what they want. But this is not the proper pleasure to be derived from

---

hamartia, defect of character; otherwise known as tragic flaw.

tragedy—more like that of comedy: for in that genre people who are outright foes in the plot (say, Orestes and Aegisthus) go off as friends at the end, and nobody is killed.

Fear, Pity, and the Experience of Tragedy

The effect of fear and pity can arise from theatrical spectacle, but it can also arise from the intrinsic structure of events, and it is this which matters more and is the task of a superior poet. For the plot-structure ought to be so composed that, even without seeing a performance, anyone who hears the events which occur will experience terror and pity as a result of the outcome; this is what someone would feel while hearing the plot of the *Oedipus*. To produce this effect through spectacle is not part of the poet's art, and calls for material resources; while those who use spectacle to produce an effect not of the fearful but only of the sensational fall quite outside the sphere of tragedy: for it is not every pleasure, but the appropriate one, which should be sought from tragedy. And since the poet ought to provide the pleasure which derives from pity and fear by means of mimesis, it is evident that this ought to be embodied in the events of the plot.

Let us, then, take up the question of what sort of circumstances make an impression of terror or pity. These are the only possibilities: such actions must involve dealings between those who are bonded by kinship or friendship; or between enemies; or between those who are neither. Well, if enemy faces enemy, neither the deed nor the prospect of it will be pitiful (except for the intrinsic potential of visible suffering); and the same is true of those whose relations are neutral. What must be sought are cases where suffering befalls bonded relations—when brother kills brother (or is about to, or to do something similar), son kills father, mother kills son, or son kills mother. Now, one cannot alter traditional plots (I mean, Clytemnestra's death at Orestes' hands, or Eriphyle's at Alcmaeon's) but the individual poet should find ways of handling even these to good effect.

I should explain more clearly what I mean by 'to good effect.' It is possible

(a) for the deed to be done with full knowledge and understanding, as the old poets used to arrange it, and in the way that Euripides too made Medea kill her children;
(b) for the deed to be done, but by agents who do not know the terrible thing they are doing, and who then later recognise their bond-relationship to the other, as with Sophocles' *Oedipus* (that is an instance where the deed occurs outside the drama, but Astydamas' *Alcmaeon,* and Telegonus in *Odysseus Wounded,* supply examples within the play itself);

(c) alternatively, for one who is on the point of committing an incurable deed in ignorance to come to a recognition before he has done it.

These are the only possibilities, for either the deed is done or it is not, and the agents must either know the facts or be ignorant of them. Of these cases, the worst is where the agent, in full knowledge, is on the point of acting, yet fails to do so: for this is repulsive and untragic (as it lacks suffering). Consequently, poets only rarely do this (for instance, Haemon's intention against Creon in *Antigone*). Not much better is for the deed to be executed in such a case. A superior arrangement is where the agent acts in ignorance, and discovers the truth after acting: for here there is nothing repulsive, and the recognition produces a powerful effect. But the best case is the last I have listed—for example, where Merope is about to kill her son in the *Cresphontes,* but does not do so because she recognises him; likewise with sister and brother in *Iphigeneia,* and in the *Helle,* where the son, on the point of handing her over, recognises his mother. Hence, as said before, tragedies concentrate on a few families. Luck not art led poets to find how to achieve such an effect in their plots; so they have to turn to the families in which such sufferings have occurred.

Enough, then, about the structure of events and the required qualities of plots.

Basic Elements of Tragic Characterization

Regarding characterisation, there should be four aims:

(a) first and foremost, that the characters be good. Characterisation will arise, as earlier explained (ch.6), where speech or action exhibits the nature of an ethical choice; and the character will be good when the choice is good. But this depends on each class of person: there can be a good woman and a good slave, even though perhaps the former is an inferior type, and the latter a wholly base one.
(b) that the characters be appropriate. For it is possible to have a woman manly in character, but it is not appropriate for a woman to be so manly or clever.
(c) likeness of character—for this is independent of making character good and appropriate, as described.
(d) consistency of character. For even where an inconsistent person is portrayed, and such a character is presupposed, there should still be consistency in the inconsistency.

An illustration of unnecessary wickedness of character is Menelaus in *Orestes;* of unbecoming and inappropriate character, the lament of Odysseus in *Scylla,* or Melanippe's speech; and of inconsistency, *Iphigeneia in Aulis* (for the girl who beseeches bears no resemblance to the later girl). In characterisation just as in plot-construction, one should always seek the principle of necessity or probability, so that a necessary or probable reason exists for a particular character's speech or action, and similarly for the sequence of events.

It is evident that the dénouements of plot-structures should arise from the plot itself, and not, as in *Medea,* from a *deus ex machina°* or in the episode of the departure in the *Iliad.* But the *deus ex machina* should be used for events outside the play, whether earlier events of which a human cannot have knowledge, or future events which call for a prospective narrative; for we attribute to the gods a vision of all things. No irrational element should have a part in the events, unless outside the tragedy (as, for example, in Sophocles' *Oedipus*).

Since tragedy is a mimesis of men better than ourselves, the example set by good portrait-painters should be followed: they, while rendering the individual physique realistically, improve on their subjects' beauty. Similarly, the poet, while portraying men who are irascible or lazy or who have other such faults, ought to give them, despite such traits, goodness of character. An example of this is Homer's presentation of Achilles as good, despite his harshness. In addition to observing these points, the poet must guard against contraventions of the perceptions which necessarily attach to poetic art, since there are many ways of making mistakes in relation to these. But I have discussed these matters adequately in my published writings.

Kinds of Tragic Recognition

I earlier defined the nature of recognition, but of the kinds of recognition there is, firstly, the least artistic and the one which is used most out of inadequacy: recognition through signs. These signs can be either congenital (as with [. . .] the starred birthmarks used by Carcinus in *Thyestes*) or acquired; and the latter can be subdivided into the physical (e.g., scars) and the external, such as necklaces or the use of the boat in *Tyro.* These means can be employed either well or badly: for instance, through his scar Odysseus was recognised in different ways by his nurse and by the swineherds. Those recognitions which occur for the sake of confirmation, and all similar sorts, are less artistic; while those which accompany a reversal,

like the one in the washing scene of the *Odyssey,* are superior.

The second kind are those contrived by the poet (and consequently inartistic). An example is the way in which Orestes makes himself known in *Iphigeneia,* for Iphigeneia is recognised through the letter, while Orestes himself says what the poet, but not the plot, requires: the result is close to the fault mentioned above, since producing tokens would be equivalent. Another instance is the voice of the shuttle in Sophocles' *Tereus.*

The third kind is recognition through memory. The experience may depend on the sight of something: for example, the case in Dicaeogenes' *Cyprians,* where the person wept on seeing the painting. Or there is the example in Odysseus' speech to Alcinous, where he heard the singer and wept at the memory. Recognition resulted in both instances.

The fourth kind of recognition results from reasoning: for example, in *Choephori* (someone like Electra has come, and there is no one like her other than Orestes, so it is he who has come). Also the example from Polyidus the sophist's work on Iphigeneia: he said it was plausible for Orestes to reason that he was to be sacrificed just as his sister had been. Another example in Theodectes' *Tydeus:* the character reasons that it is by coming to find his son that he is facing death. And the instance in the *Phineidai:* upon seeing the place, they reasoned that it was their destiny to die there, since it was also the place where they had been exposed.

It is also possible to make a recognition depend on the audience's false reasoning, as in *Odysseus the False Messenger:* the fact that he alone could bend the bow is a premise contrived by the poet, as is his statement that he would recognise the bow (which he had never seen); and it is false reasoning to suppose that he will reveal himself through this.

The best of all recognitions is the type which arises from the events themselves, where the emotional impact comes about through a probable sequence of action. There are examples in Sophocles' *Oedipus,* and in *Iphigeneia* (for it is in conformity with probability that she should want to entrust a letter). Such instances alone avoid contrived tokens. Next best are those resulting from reasoning.

Imagining a Plot and Developing It in Detail

A poet ought to imagine his material to the fullest possible extent while composing his plot-structures and elaborating them in language. By seeing them as vividly as possible in this way—as if present at the very occurrence of the events—he is likely to discover what is appropriate, and least likely to miss contradictions. (One can see this from the criticism brought against Carcinus: for Amphiaraus was returning from the shrine, but the poet missed the point by not visualising

---

deus ex machina, literally "god from a machine"; i.e., an unexpected, artificial, or improbable character, device, or event that is used in order to resolve or untangle a dramatic plot.

it, and the play failed in the theatre on account of the spectators' annoyance.) So far as possible, the poet should even include gestures in the process of composition: for, assuming the same natural talent, the most convincing effect comes from those who actually put themselves in the emotions; and the truest impression of distress or anger is given by the person who experiences these feelings. Consequently, it is the imaginative man, rather than the manic, who is the best composer of poetry: since, of these types, the former can mould their emotions, while the latter are carried away.

Whether it exists already or is his own invention, the poet should lay out the general structure of his story, and then proceed to work out episodes and enlarge it. What I mean by contemplating the general structure can be illustrated from *Iphigeneia.* A girl was sacrificed and mysteriously vanished from her sacrificers; she was planted in another land, where strangers were traditionally sacrificed to the goddess whose priesthood the girl came to hold. Subsequently, it happened that the priestess's brother came to the place (the fact that

a god's oracle sent him, and the reason for this, are outside the plot). Captured on his arrival, he was on the point of being sacrificed when he caused his own recognition (whether according to Euripides' version, or, as in Polyidus,' by saying—as was plausible—that it was his own as well as his sister's destiny to be sacrificed). The upshot was his rescue.

The next stage is to supply names and work out the episodes. But care must be taken to make the episodes integral—as with the fit of madness which occasions Orestes' capture, and his rescue through the purification-rite. Now, in drama the episodes are concise, while epic gains extra length from them. For the main story of the *Odyssey* is short: a man is abroad for many years, is persecuted by Poseidon, and is left desolate; further, circumstances at home mean that his property is consumed by suitors, and his son is a target for conspiracy; but the man survives shipwreck to reach home again, reveals his identity to certain people, and launches an attack—his own safety is restored, and he destroys his enemies. This much is essential; the rest consists of episodes.

On Time and Place, On Comedy and Tragedy

BY SIR PHILIP SIDNEY, 1595

Sir Philip Sidney (1554–1586) was an English Renaissance man—poet, scholar, courtier, diplomat, soldier, and gentleman par excellence—best known as a writer for his extended sonnet sequence, Astrophel and Stella; *his pastoral romance,* Arcadia; *and his critical essay,* The Defence of Poesy, *an excerpt from which is reprinted below.*

Our tragedies and comedies, not without cause cried out against, observing rules neither of honest civility nor skilful poetry. Excepting *Gorboduc*° (again I say of those that I have seen), which notwithstanding as it is full of stately speeches and well-sounding phrases, climbing to the height of Seneca° his style, and as full of notable morality, which it doeth most delightfully teach, and so obtain the very end of poesy;

Gorboduc, an English tragedy, published in 1565.
Seneca, Roman philosopher, poet, and tragic dramatist (ca. 4 B.C.–A.D. 65).

yet, in truth, it is very defectious in the circumstances, which grieves me, because it might not remain as an exact model of all tragedies. For it is faulty both in place and time, the two necessary companions of all corporal actions. For where the stage should always represent but one place, and the uttermost time presupposed in it should be, both by Aristotle's precept and common reason, but one day; there is both many days and many places inartificially imagined.

But if it be so in *Gorboduc,* how much more in all the rest? Where you shall have Asia of the one side, and Afric of the other, and so many other under kingdoms, that the player, when he comes in, must ever begin with telling where he is, or else the tale will not be conceived. Now shall you have three ladies walk to gather flowers, and then we must believe the stage to be a garden. By and by, we hear news of shipwreck in the same place, then we are to blame if we accept it not for a rock. Upon the back of that comes out a hideous monster with fire and smoke, and then the miserable beholders are bound to take it for a cave; while, in the meantime, two armies fly in, represented with four swords and bucklers, and then what hard heart will not receive it for a pitched field?

Now of time they are much more liberal; for ordinary it is, that two young princes fall in love, after many traverses she is got with child, delivered of a fair boy, he is lost, groweth a man, falleth in love, and is ready to get another child; and all this in two hours' space; which, how absurd it is in sense, even sense may imagine; and art hath taught, and all ancient examples justified, and at this day the ordinary players in Italy will not err in. Yet will some bring in an example of *Eunuchus*° in Terence,° that containeth matter of two days, yet far short of twenty years. True it is, and so was it to be played in two days, and so fitted to the time it set forth. And though Plautus have in one place done amiss, let us hit it with him, and not miss with him. But they will say, how then shall we set forth a story which contains both many places and many times? And do they not know that a tragedy is tied to the laws of poesy, and not of history; not bound to follow the story, but having liberty either to feign a quite new matter or to frame the history to the most tragical conveniency? Again, many things may be told which cannot be showed—if they know the difference betwixt reporting and representing. As for example, I may speak, though I am here, of Peru, and in speech digress from that to the description of Calicut;° but in action I cannot represent it without Pacolet's° horse. And so was the manner the ancients took, by some *Nuntius*° to recount things done in former time, or other place.

Lastly, if they will represent an history they must not (as Horace° saith) begin *ab ovo,*° but they must come to the principal point of that one action which they will represent. By example this will be best expressed. I have a story of young Polydorus, delivered, for safety's sake, with great riches, by his father Priamus to Polymnestor, King of Thrace, in the Trojan war time. He, after some years, hearing of the overthrow of Priamus, for to make the treasure his own, murthereth the child; the body of the child is taken up by Hecuba; she, the same day, findeth a sleight to be revenged most cruelly of the tyrant. Where, now, would one of our tragedy-writers begin, but with the delivery of the child? Then should he sail over into Thrace, and so spend I know not how many years, and travel numbers of places. But where doth Euripides? Even with the finding of the body; leaving the rest to be told by the spirit of Polydorus. This needs no further to be enlarged; the dullest wit may conceive it.

But, besides these gross absurdities, how all their plays be neither right tragedies nor right comedies, mingling kings and clowns, not because the matter so carrieth it, but thrust in the clown by head and shoulders to play a part in majestical matters, with neither decency nor discretion; so as neither the admiration and commiseration, nor the right sportfulness, is by their mongrel tragi-comedy obtained. I know Apuleius° did somewhat so, but that is a thing recounted with space of time, not represented in one moment; and I know the ancients have one or two examples of tragi-comedies as Plautus hath *Amphytrio.* But, if we mark them well, we shall find that they never, or very daintily, match hornpipes and funerals. So falleth it out, that having indeed no right comedy in that comical part of our tragedy, we have nothing but scurrility, unworthy of any chaste ears; or some extreme show of doltishness, indeed fit to lift up a loud laughter, and nothing else; where the whole tract of a comedy should be full of delight, as the tragedy should be still maintained in a well-raised admiration.

But our comedians think there is no delight without laughter, which is very wrong; for though laughter may come with delight, yet cometh it not of delight, as though delight should be the cause of laughter. But well may one thing breed both together. Nay, rather in themselves they have, as it were, a kind of contrariety. For delight we scarcely do, but in things that have a conveniency to ourselves, or to the general nature; laughter almost ever cometh of things most disproportioned to ourselves and nature. Delight hath a joy in it either permanent or present; laughter hath only a scornful tickling. For example, we are ravished with delight to see a fair woman, and yet are far from being moved to laughter. We laugh at deformed creatures, wherein certainly we cannot delight. We delight in good chances; we laugh at mischances. We delight to hear the happiness of our friends and country, at which he were worthy to be laughed at that would laugh; we shall, contrarily, sometimes laugh to find a matter quite mistaken, and go down the hill against the bias, in the mouth of some such men as, for the respect of them, one shall be heartily sorry he cannot choose but laugh, and so is rather pained than delighted with laughter. Yet deny I not but that they may go well together; for as in Alexander's picture well set out we delight without laughter, and in twenty mad antics we laugh without delight. So in Hercules painted,

Eunuchus, a Roman comedy, performed in 162 B.C. *Terence,* Roman comic playwright (ca. 190–159 B.C.). *Calicut,* seaport in India. *Pacolet,* a magic horse from a French romance of 1495. *Nuntius,* messenger. *Horace,* Roman poet (65–8 B.C.) *ab ovo,* literally "from the egg"; i.e., from the beginning

Apuleius, Roman author (born ca. A.D. 125).

with his great beard and furious countenance, in a woman's attire, spinning at Omphale's° commandment, it breeds both delight and laughter; for the representing of so strange a power in love procures delight, and the scornfulness of the action stirreth laughter.

But I speak to this purpose, that all the end of the comical part be not upon such scornful matters as stir laughter only, but mix with it that delightful teaching which is the end of poesy. And the great fault, even in that point of laughter, and forbidden plainly by Aristotle, is, that they stir laughter in sinful things, which are rather execrable than ridiculous; or in miserable, which are rather to be pitied than scorned. For what is it to make folks gape at a wretched beggar, and a beggarly clown; or against law of hospitality, to jest at

---

Omphale, Hercules' mistress.

strangers because they speak not English so well as we do? What do we learn? Since it is certain,

Nil habet infelix paupertas durius in se,
Quam quod ridiculos homines facit.°

But rather a busy loving courtier, and a heartless threatening Thraso;° a self-wise-seeming schoolmaster; a wry-transformed traveler—these, if we saw walk in stage-names, which we play naturally, therein were delightful laughter, and teaching delightfulness; as in the other, the tragedies of Buchanan do justly bring forth a divine admiration.

Nil habit . . . facit, "unhappy poverty has in it nothing worse than the fact that it makes men ridiculous." ***Thraso,*** a stock character of the braggart.

A Comparison between Sentimental and Laughing Comedy

BY OLIVER GOLDSMITH, 1772

Oliver Goldsmith (1728–1774), an Anglo-Irish writer and theatrical contemporary of George Sheridan, was a prolific essayist, widely known in his own time for a series of whimsical pieces, Citizen of the World. *But he is remembered today largely for his novel,* The Vicar of Wakefield, *and his play,* She Stoops to Conquer, *which is a deft mix of the laughing and sentimental comedy that he discusses in the following essay.*

The theatre, like all other amusements, has its fashions and its prejudices; and when satiated with its excellence, mankind begin to mistake change for improvement. For some years tragedy was the reigning entertainment; but of late it has entirely given way to comedy, and our best efforts are now exerted in these lighter kinds of composition. The pompous train, the swelling phrase, and the unnatural rant, are displaced for that natural portrait of human folly and frailty, of which all are judges, because all have sat for the picture.

But as in describing nature it is presented with a double face, either of mirth or sadness, our modern writers find themselves at a loss which chiefly to copy from; and it is now debated, whether the exhibition of

human distress is likely to afford the mind more entertainment than that of human absurdity.

Comedy is defined by Aristotle to be a picture of the frailties of the lower part of mankind to distinguish it from tragedy, which is an exhibition of the misfortunes of the great. When comedy therefore ascends to produce the characters of princes or generals upon the stage, it is out of its walk, since low life and middle life are entirely its object. The principal question therefore is, whether in describing low or middle life, an exhibition of its follies be not preferable to a detail of its calamities? Or, in other words, which deserves the preference—the weeping sentimental comedy, so much in fashion at present, or the laughing and even low comedy, which seems to have been last exhibited by Vanbrugh and Cibber?°

If we apply to authorities, all the great masters in the dramatic art have but one opinion. Their rule is, that

---

Vanbrugh and Cibber, English comic playwrights. John Vanbrugh (1664–1726) and Colley Cibber (1671–1757).

as tragedy displays the calamities of the great, so comedy should excite our laughter, by ridiculously exhibiting the follies of the lower part of mankind. Boileau, one of the best modern critics, asserts, that comedy will not admit of tragic distress:

Le comique, ennemi des soupirs et des pleurs,
N'admet point dans ses vers de tragiques douleurs.°

Nor is this rule without the strongest foundation in nature, as the distresses of the mean by no means affect us so strongly as the calamities of the great. When tragedy exhibits to us some great man fallen from his height, and struggling with want and adversity, we feel his situation in the same manner as we suppose he himself must feel, and our pity is increased in proportion to the height from which he fell. On the contrary, we do not so strongly sympathize with one born in humbler circumstances, and encountering accidental distress: so that while we melt for Belisarius,° we scarcely give halfpence to the beggar who accosts us in the street. The one has our pity; the other our contempt. Distress, therefore, is the proper object of tragedy, since the great excite our pity by their fall; but not equally so of comedy, since the actors employed in it are originally so mean, that they sink but little by their fall.

Since the first origin of the stage, tragedy and comedy have run in distinct channels, and never till of late encroached upon the provinces of each other. Terence, who seems to have made the nearest approaches, always judiciously stops short before he comes to the downright pathetic; and yet he is even reproached by Caesar for wanting the *vis comica*.° All other comic writers of antiquity aim only at rendering folly or vice ridiculous, but never exalt their characters into buskin pomp, or make what Voltaire humorously calls "a tradesman's tragedy."

Yet notwithstanding this weight of authority, and the universal practice of former ages, a new species of dramatic composition has been introduced under the name of *sentimental comedy*, in which the virtues of private life are exhibited, rather than the vices exposed; and the distresses rather than the faults of mankind make our interest in the piece. These comedies have had of late great success, perhaps from their novelty, and also from their flattering every man in his favourite foible. In these plays almost all the charac-

ters are good, and exceedingly generous; they are lavish enough of their tin money on the stage; and though they want humour, have abundance of sentiment and feeling. If they happen to have faults or foibles, the spectator is taught not only to pardon, but to applaud them, in consideration of the goodness of their hearts; so that folly, instead of being ridiculed, is commended, and the comedy aims at touching our passions, without the power of being truly pathetic. In this manner we are likely to lose one great source of entertainment on the stage; for while the comic poet is invading the province of the tragic muse, he leaves her lovely sister quite neglected. Of this, however, he is no way solicitous, as he measures his fame by his profits.

But it will be said, that the theatre is formed to amuse mankind, and that it matters little, if this end be answered, by what means it is obtained. If mankind find delight in weeping at comedy, it would be cruel to abridge them in that or any other innocent pleasure. If those pieces are denied the name of comedies, yet call them by any other name, and if they are delightful, they are good. Their success, it will be said, is a mark of their merit, and it is only abridging our happiness to deny us an inlet to amusement.

These objections, however, are rather specious than solid. It is true, that amusement is a great object at a theatre; and it will be allowed, that these sentimental pieces do often amuse us; but the question is, whether the true comedy would not amuse us more? The question is, whether a character supported throughout a piece, with its ridicule still attending, would not give us more delight than this species of bastard tragedy, which only is applauded because it is new.

A friend of mine who was sitting unmoved at one of the sentimental pieces, was asked how he could be so indifferent? "Why truly," says he, "as the hero is but a tradesman, it is indifferent to me whether he be turned out of his counting-house on Fishstreet Hill, since he will still have enough left to open shop at St. Giles's."

The other objection is as ill-grounded; for though we should give these pieces another name, it will not mend their efficacy. It will continue a kind of mulish production, with all the defects of its opposite parents, and marked with sterility. If we are permitted to make comedy weep, we have an equal right to make tragedy laugh, and to set down in blank verse the jests and repartees of all the attendants in a funeral procession.

But there is one argument in favor of sentimental comedy which will keep it on the stage, in spite of all that can be said against it. It is of all others the most easily written. Those abilities that can hammer out a novel, are fully sufficient for the production of a sentimental comedy. It is only sufficient to raise the characters a little; to deck out the hero with a riband, or give

---

Le comique . . . douleurs, "The comic muse, averse to tears and sighs, / From tragic sorrows with abhorrence flies" [Goldsmith's note]. *Belisarius,* a general under Emperor Justinian of Constantinople, Belisarius had successes that aroused Justinian's jealousy. He was disgraced and became a beggar. *vis comica,* comic spirit.

the heroine a title; then to put an insipid dialogue, without character or humour, into their mouths, give them mighty good hearts, very fine clothes, furnish a new set of scenes, make a pathetic scene or two, with a sprinkling of tender melancholy conversation through the whole, and there is no doubt but all the ladies will cry, and all the gentlemen applaud.

Humour at present seems to be departing from the stage; and it will soon happen that our comic players will have nothing left for it but a fine coat and a song. It depends upon the audience, whether they will actually drive those poor merry creatures from the stage, or sit at a play as gloomy as at the tabernacle. It is not easy to recover an art when once lost; and it will be but a just punishment, that when, by our being too fastidious, we have banished humour from the stage, we should ourselves be deprived of the art of laughing.

The Preface to *Miss Julie*

BY AUGUST STRINDBERG, 1888

August Strindberg (1849–1912). For biographical details, see pp. 589–91.

Like the arts in general, the theatre has for a long time seemed to me a *Biblia Pauperum,* a picture Bible for those who cannot read, and the playwright merely a lay preacher who hawks the latest ideas in popular form, so popular that the middle classes—the bulk of the audiences—can grasp them without racking their brains too much. That explains why the theatre has always been an elementary school for youngsters and the half-educated, and for women, who still retain a primitive capacity for deceiving themselves and for letting themselves be deceived, that is, for succumbing to illusions and responding hypnotically to the suggestions of the author. Consequently, now that the rudimentary and undeveloped mental processes that operate in the realm of fantasy appear to be evolving to the level of reflection, research, and experimentation, I believe that the theatre, like religion, is about to be replaced as a dying institution for whose enjoyment we lack the necessary qualifications. Support for my view is provided by the theatre crisis through which all of Europe is now passing, and still more by the fact that in those highly cultured lands which have produced the finest minds of our time—England and Germany—the drama is dead, as for the most part are the other fine arts.

Other countries, however, have thought to create a new drama by filling the old forms with new contents. But since there has not been enough time to popularize the new ideas, the public cannot understand them. And in the second place, controversy has so stirred up the public that they can no longer look on with a pure and dispassionate interest, especially when they see their most cherished ideals assailed or hear an applauding or booing majority openly exercise its tyrannical power, as can happen in the theatre. And in the third place, since the new forms for the new ideas have not been created, the new wine has burst the old bottles.

In the play that follows I have not tried to accomplish anything new—that is impossible. I have only tried to modernize the form to satisfy what I believe up-to-date people expect and demand of this art. And with that in mind I have seized upon—or let myself be seized by—a theme which may be said to lie outside current party strife, since the question of being on the way up or the way down the social ladder, of being on the top or on the bottom, superior or inferior, man or woman, is, has been, and will be of perennial interest. When I took this theme from real life—I heard about it a few years ago and it made a deep impression on me—I thought it would be a suitable subject for a tragedy, since it still strikes us as tragic to see a happily favored individual go down in defeat, and even more so to see an entire family line die out. But perhaps a time will come when we shall be so highly developed and so enlightened that we can look with indifference upon the brutal, cynical, and heartless spectacle that life offers us, a time when we shall have laid aside those inferior and unreliable instruments of thought called feelings, which will become superfluous and even harmful as our mental organs develop. The fact that my heroine wins sympathy is due entirely to the fact that we are still too weak to overcome the fear that the same fate might overtake us. The extremely sensitive viewer will of course not be satisfied with mere expressions of sympathy, and the man who believes in progress will demand that certain positive actions be taken for getting rid of the evil, a kind of program, in other words. But in the first place absolute evil does not exist. The decline of one family is the making of another, which now gets its chance to rise. This alternate rising and falling provides one of life's greatest pleasures, for happiness is, after all, relative. As for the man who has a program for changing the disagreeable circumstance that the eagle eats the dove and that lice eat up the eagle, I should like to ask him why it should be changed. Life is not prearranged with such idiotic mathematical precision that only the larger gets to eat the smaller. Just as frequently the little bee destroys the lion [in Aesop's fable]—or at least drives him wild.

If my tragedy makes most people feel sad, that is their fault. When we get to be as strong as the first French Revolutionists were, we shall be perfectly content and happy to watch the forests being cleared of rotting, superannuated trees that have stood too long in the way of others with just as much right to grow and flourish for a while—as content as we are when we see an incurably ill man finally die.

Recently my tragedy *The Father* was censured for being too unpleasant—as if one wanted amusing tragedies. "The joy of life" is now the slogan of the day. Theatre managers send out orders for nothing but farces, as if the joy of living lay in behaving like a clown and in depicting people as if they were afflicted with St. Vitus's dance or congenital idiocy. I find the joy of living in the fierce and ruthless battles of life, and my pleasure comes from learning something, from being taught something. That is why I have chosen for my play an unusual but instructive case, an exception, in other words—but an important exception of the kind that proves the rule—a choice of subject that I know will offend all lovers of the conventional. The next thing that will bother simple minds is that the motivation for the action is not simple and that the point of view is not single. Usually an event in life—and this is a fairly new discovery—is the result of a whole series of more or less deep-rooted causes. The spectator, however, generally chooses the one that puts the least strain on his mind or reflects most credit on his insight. Consider a case of suicide. "Business failure," says the merchant. "Unhappy love," say the women. "Physical illness," says the sick man. "Lost hopes," says the down-and-out. But it may be that the reason lay in all of these or in none of them, and that the suicide hid his real reason behind a completely different one that would reflect greater glory on his memory.

I have motivated the tragic fate of Miss Julie with an abundance of circumstances: her mother's basic instincts, her father's improper bringing-up of the girl, her own inborn nature, and her fiancé's sway over her weak and degenerate mind. Further and more immediately: the festive atmosphere of Midsummer Eve, her father's absence, her monthly illness, her preoccupation with animals, the erotic excitement of the dance, the long summer twilight, the highly aphrodisiac influence of flowers, and finally chance itself, which drives two people together in an out-of-the-way room, plus the boldness of the aroused man.

As one can see, I have not concerned myself solely with physiological causes, nor confined myself monomaniacally to psychological causes, nor traced everything to an inheritance from her mother, nor put the blame entirely on her monthly indisposition or exclusively on "immorality." Nor have I simply preached a sermon. Lacking a priest, I have let the cook take care of that.

I am proud to say that this complicated way of looking at things is in tune with the times. And if others have anticipated me in this, I am proud that I am not alone in my paradoxes, as all new discoveries are called. And no one can say this time that I am being one-sided.

As far as the drawing of characters is concerned, I have made the people in my play fairly "characterless" for the following reasons. In the course of time the word *character* has acquired many meanings. Originally it probably meant the dominant and fundamental trait in the soul complex and was confused with temperament. Later the middle class used it to mean an automation. An individual who once for all had found his own true nature or adapted himself to a certain role in life, who in fact had ceased to grow, was called a man of character, while the man who was constantly developing, who, like a skillful sailor on the currents of life, did not sail with close-tied sheets but who fell off before the wind in order to luff again, was called a man of no character—derogatorily of course, since he was so difficult to keep track of, to pin down and pigeonhole. This middle-class conception of a fixed character was transferred to the stage, where the middle class has always ruled. A character there came to mean someone who was always one and the same, always drunk, always joking, always moving, and who needed to be characterized only by some physical defect such as a club foot, a wooden leg, or a red nose, or by the repetition of some such phrase as, "That's capital," or "Barkis is willin'." This uncomplicated way of viewing people is still to be found in the great Molière. Harpagon is nothing but a miser, although Harpagon could have been both a miser and an exceptional financier, a fine father, and a good citizen. Worse still, his "defect" is extremely advantageous to his son-in-law and his daughter who will be his heirs and therefore should not find fault with him, even if they do have to wait a while to jump into bed together. So I do not believe in simple stage characters. And the summary judgments that writers pass on people—he is stupid, this one is brutal, that one is jealous, this one is stingy, and so on—should not pass unchallenged by the naturalists who know how complicated the soul is and who realize that vice has a reverse side very much like virtue.

Since the persons in my play are modern characters, living in a transitional era more hectic and hysterical than the previous one at least, I have depicted them as more unstable, as torn and divided, a mixture of the old and the new. Nor does it seem improbable to me that modern ideas might also have seeped down through newspapers and kitchen talk to the level of the servants. Consequently the valet may belch forth from his inherited slave soul certain modern ideas. And if there are those who find it wrong to allow people in a modern drama to talk Darwin and who recommend the practice of Shakespeare to our attention, may I remind them that the gravedigger in *Hamlet* talks the then fashionable philosophy of Giordano Bruno (Bacon's philosophy), which is even more improbable, seeing that the means of spreading ideas were fewer then than now. And besides, the fact of the matter is that Darwinism has always existed, ever since Moses' history of creation from the lower animals up to man, but it was not until recently that we discovered it and formulized it.

My souls—or characters—are conglomerations from various stages of culture, past and present, walking scrapbooks, shreds of human lives, tatters torn from former fancy dresses that are now old rags—hodge-podges just like the human soul. I have even supplied a little source history into the bargain by letting the weaker steal and repeat words of the stronger, letting them get ideas (suggestions as they are called) from one another, from the environment (the songbird's blood), and from objects (the razor). I have also arranged for *Gedankenübertragung*° through an inanimate medium to take place (the count's boots, the servant's bell). And I have even made use of "waking suggestion" (a variation of hypnotic suggestion), which have by now been so popularized that they cannot arouse ridicule or scepticism as they would have done in Mesmer's time.

I say Miss Julie is a modern character not because the man-hating half-woman has not always existed but because she has now been brought out into the open, has taken the stage, and is making noises. Victim of a superstition (one that has seized even stronger minds) that woman, that stunted form of human being, standing with man, the lord of creation, the creator of culture, is meant to be the equal of man or could ever possibly be, she involves herself in an absurd struggle with him in which she falls. Absurd because a stunted

form, subject to the laws of propagation, will always be born stunted and can never catch up with the one who has the lead. As follows: A (the man) and B (the woman) start from the same point C, A with a speed of let us say 100 and B with a speed of 60. When will B overtake A? Answer: never. Neither with the help of equal education or equal voting rights—nor by universal disarmament and temperance societies—any more than two parallel lines can never meet. The half-woman is a type that forces itself on others, selling itself for power, medals, recognition, diplomas, as formerly it sold itself for money. It represents degeneration. It is not a strong species for it does not maintain itself, but unfortunately it propagates its misery in the following generation. Degenerate men unconsciously select their mates from among these half-women, so that they breed and spread, producing creatures of indeterminate sex to whom life is a torture, but who fortunately are overcome eventually either by a hostile reality, or by the uncontrolled breaking loose of their repressed instincts, or else by their frustration in not being able to compete with the male sex. It is a tragic type, offering us the spectacle of a desperate fight against nature; a tragic legacy of romanticism that is now being dissipated by naturalism—a movement which seeks only happiness, and for that strong and healthy species are required.

But Miss Julie is also a vestige of the old warrior nobility that is now being superseded by a new nobility of nerve and brain. She is a victim of the disorder produced within a family by a mother's "crime," of the mistakes of a whole generation gone wrong, of circumstances, of her own defective constitution—all of which put together is equivalent to the fate or universal law of the ancients. The naturalists have banished guilt along with God, but the consequences of the act—punishment, imprisonment, or the fear of it—cannot be banished for the simple reason that they remain whether or not the naturalist dismisses the case from his court. Those sitting on the sidelines can easily afford to be lenient; but what of the injured parties? And even if her father were compelled to forgo taking his revenge, Miss Julie would take vengeance on herself, as she does in the play, because of that inherited or acquired sense of honor that has been transmitted to the upper classes from—well where does it come from? From the age of barbarism, from the first Aryans, from the chivalry of the Middle Ages. And a very fine code it was, but now inimical to the survival of the race. It is the aristocrat's form of hara-kiri, a law of conscience that bids the Japanese to slice his own stomach when someone else dishonors him. The same sort of thing survives, slightly modified, in that exclusive prerogative of the aristocracy, the duel. (Example: the husband challenges his wife's lover to a duel; the lover shoots the husband and runs off with

---

Gedankenübertragung, telepathy.

the wife. Result: the husband has saved his *honor* but lost his wife.) Hence the servant Jean lives on; but not Miss Julie, who cannot live without honor. The advantage that the slave has over his master is that he has not committed himself to this defeatist principle. In all of us Aryans there is enough of the nobleman, or of the Don Quixote, to make us sympathize with the man who takes his own life after having dishonored himself by shameful deeds. And we are all of us aristocrats enough to be distressed at the sight of a great man lying like a dead hulk ready for the scrap pile, even, I suppose, if he were to raise himself up again and redeem himself by honorable deeds.

The servant Jean is the beginning of a new species in which noticeable differentiation has already taken place. He began as the child of a poor worker and is now evolving through self-education into a future gentleman of the upper classes. He is quick to learn, has highly developed senses (smell, taste, sight), and a keen appreciation of beauty. He has already come up in the world, for he is strong enough not to hesitate to make use of other people. He is already a stranger to his old friends, whom he despises as reminders of past stages in his development, and whom he fears and avoids because they know his secrets, guess his intentions, look with envy on his rise and in joyful expectation toward his fall. Hence his character is unformed and divided. He wavers between an admiration of high positions and a hatred of the men who occupy them. He is an aristocrat—he says so himself—familiar with the ins and outs of good society. He is polished on the outside, but coarse underneath. He wears his frock coat with elegance but gives no assurance that he keeps his body clean.

He respects Miss Julie but he is afraid of Christine, for she knows his innermost secrets. Yet he is sufficiently hard-hearted not to let the events of the night upset his plans for the future. Possessing both the coarseness of the slave and the toughmindedness of the born ruler, he can look at blood without fainting, shake off bad luck like water, and take calamity by the horns. Consequently he will escape from the battle unwounded, probably ending up as proprietor of a hotel. And if he himself does not get to be a Rumanian count, his son will doubtless go to college and possibly end up as a government official.

Now his observations about life as the lower classes see it, from below, are well worth listening to—that is, they are whenever he is telling the truth, which is not too often, because he is more likely to say what is advantageous to him than what is true. When Miss Julie supposes that everyone in the lower classes must feel greatly oppressed by the weight of the classes above, Jean naturally agrees with her since he wants to win her sympathy. But he promptly takes it all back when he finds it advisable to separate himself from the mob.

Apart from the fact that Jean is coming up in the world, he is also superior to Miss Julie in that he is a man. In the sexual sphere, he is the aristocrat. He has the strength of the male, more highly developed senses, and the ability to take the initiative. His inferiority is merely the result of his social environment, which is only temporary and which he will probably slough off along with his livery.

His slave nature expresses itself in his awe of the Count (the boots) and in his religious superstitions. But he is awed by the Count mainly because the Count occupies the place he wants most in life; and this awe is still there even after he has won the daughter of the house and seen how hollow that beautiful shell was.

I do not believe that any love in the "higher" sense can be born from the union of two such different souls; so I have let Miss Julie's love be refashioned in her imagination as a love that protects and purifies, and I have let Jean imagine that even his love might have a chance to grow under other social circumstances. For I suppose love is very much like the hyacinth that must strike roots deep in the dark earth *before* it can produce a vigorous blossom. Here it shoots up, bursts into bloom, and turns to seed all at once; and that is why it dies so quickly.

Christine—finally to get to her—is a female slave, spineless and phlegmatic after years spent at the kitchen stove, bovinely unconscious of her own hypocrisy, and with a full quota of moral and religious notions that serve as scapegoats and cloaks for her sins—which a stronger soul does not require since he is able either to carry the burden of his own sins or to rationalize them out of existence. She attends church regularly where she deftly unloads unto Jesus—that straw man—her household thefts and picks up from him another load of innocence. She is only a secondary character, and I have deliberately done no more than sketch her in—just as I treated the country doctor and parish priest in *The Father* where I only wanted to draw ordinary everyday people such as most country doctors and parsons are. That some have found my minor characters one-dimensional is due to the fact that ordinary people while at work are to a certain extent one-dimensional and do lack an independent existence, showing only one side of themselves in the performance of their duties. And as long as the audience does not feel it needs to see them from different angles, my abstract sketches will pass muster.

Now as far as the dialogue is concerned, I have broken somewhat with tradition in refusing to make my characters into interlocutors who ask stupid questions to elicit witty answers. I have avoided the symmetrical and mathematical design of the artfully constructed French dialogue and have let minds work as irregularly as they do in real life, where no subject is quite exhausted before another mind engages at random some cog in the conversation and governs it for a while. My dialogue wanders here and there, gathers material in the first scenes which is later picked up, repeated, re-worked, developed, and expanded like the theme in a piece of music.

The action of the play poses no problems. Since it really involves only two people, I have limited myself to these two, introducing only one minor character, the cook, and keeping the unhappy spirit of the father brooding over the action as a whole. I have chosen this course because I have noticed that what interests people most nowadays is the psychological action. Our inveterately curious souls are no longer content to see a thing happen; we want to see how it happens. We want to see the strings, look at the machinery, examine the double-bottom drawer, put on the magic ring to find the hidden seam, look in the deck for the marked cards.

In treating the subject this way I have had in mind the case-history novels of the Goncourt brothers, which appeal to me more than anything else in modern literature.

As far as play construction is concerned, I have made a stab at getting rid of act divisions. I was afraid that the spectator's declining susceptibility to illusion might not carry him through the intermission, when he would have time to think about what he has seen and to escape the suggestive influence of the author-hypnotist. I figure my play lasts about ninety minutes. Since one can listen to a lecture, a sermon, or a political debate for that long or even longer, I have convinced myself that a play should not exhaust an audience in that length of time. As early as 1872 in one of my first attempts at the drama, *The Outlaw*, I tried out this concentrated form, although with little success. I had finished the work in five acts when I noticed the disjointed and disturbing effect it produced. I burned it, and from the ashes there arose a single, completely reworked act of fifty pages that would run for less than an hour. This play form is not completely new but seems to be my special property and has a good chance of gaining favor with the public when tastes change. My hope is to educate a public to sit through a full evening's show in one act. But this whole question must first be probed more deeply. In the meantime, in order to establish resting places for the audience and the actors without destroying the illusion, I have made use of three arts that belong to the drama: the monologue, the pantomime, and the ballet, all of which were part of classic tragedy, the monody having become the monologue and the choral dance, the ballet.

The realists have banished the monologue from the stage as implausible. But if I can motivate it, I make it plausible, and I can then use it to my advantage. Now it is certainly plausible for a speaker to pace the floor and read his speech aloud to himself. It is plausible for an actor to practice his part aloud, for a child to talk to her cat, a mother to babble to her baby, an old lady to chatter to her parrot, and a sleeping man to talk in his sleep. And in order to give the actor a chance to work on his own for once and for a moment not be obliged to follow the author's directions, I have not written out the monologues in detail but simply outlined them. Since it makes very little difference what is said while asleep, or to the parrot or the cat, inasmuch as it does not affect the main action, a gifted player who is in the midst of the situation and mood of the play can probably improvise the monologue better than the author, who cannot estimate ahead of time how much may be said and for how long before the illusion is broken.

Some theatres in Italy have, as we know, returned to the art of improvisation and have thereby trained actors who are truly inventive—without, however, violating the intentions of the author. This seems to be a step in the right direction and possibly the beginning of a new, fertile form of art that will be genuinely productive.

In places where the monologue cannot be properly motivated, I have resorted to pantomime. Here I have given the actor even more freedom to be creative and win honor on his own. Nevertheless, not to try the audience beyond its limits, I have relied on music—well motivated by the Midsummer Eve dance—to exercise its hypnotic powers during the pantomime scene. I beg the music director to select his tunes with great care, so that associations foreign to the mood of the play will not be produced by reminders of popular operettas or current dance numbers or by folk music of interest only to ethnologists.

The ballet that I have introduced cannot be replaced by a so-called crowd scene. Such scenes are always badly acted, with a pack of babbling fools taking advantage of the occasion to "gag it up," thereby destroying the illusion. Inasmuch as country people do not improvise their taunts but make use of material already to hand by giving it a double meaning, I have not composed an original lampoon but have made use of a little known round dance that I noted down in the Stockholm district. The words do not fit the situation exactly, which is what I intended, since the slave in his cunning (that is, weakness) never attacks directly. At any rate, let us have no comedians in this serious story and no obscene smirking over an affair that nails the lid on a family coffin.

As far as the scenery is concerned, I have borrowed from impressionistic painting the idea of asymmetrical and open composition, and I believe that I have thereby gained something in the way of greater illusion. Because the audience cannot see the whole room and all the furniture, they will have to surmise what's missing; that is, their imagination will be stimulated to fill in the rest of the picture. I have gained something else by this: I have avoided those tiresome exits through doors. Stage doors are made of canvas and rock at the slightest touch. They cannot even be used to indicate the wrath of an angry father who storms out of the house after a bad dinner, slamming the door behind him "so that the whole house shakes." (In the theatre it sways and billows.) Furthermore, I have confined the action to one set, both to give the characters a chance to become part and parcel of their environment and to cut down on scenic extravagance. If there is only one set, one has a right to expect it to be as realistic as possible. Yet nothing is more difficult than to make a room look like a room, however easy it may be for the scene painter to create waterfalls and erupting volcanos. I suppose we shall have to put up with walls made of canvas, but isn't it about time that we stopped painting shelves and pots and pans on the canvas? There are so many other conventions in the theater which we are told to accept in good faith that we should be spared the strain of believing in painted saucepans.

I have placed the backdrop and the table at an angle to force the actors to play face to face or in half profile when they are seated opposite each other at the table. In a production of *Aïda* I saw a flat placed at such an angle, which led the eye out in an unfamiliar perspective. Nor did it look as if it had been set that way simply to be different or to avoid those monotonous right angles.

Another desirable innovation would be the removal of the footlights. I understand that the purpose of lighting from below is to make the actors look more full in the face. But may I ask why all actors should have full faces? Doesn't this kind of lighting wipe out many of the finer features in the lower part of the face, especially around the jaws? Doesn't it distort the shape of nose and throw false shadows above the eyes? If not, it certainly does something else: it hurts the actor's eyes. The footlights hit the retina at an angle from which it is usually shielded (except in sailors who must look at the sunlight reflected in the water), and the result is the loss of any effective play of the eyes. All one ever sees on stage are goggle-eyed glances sideways at the boxes or upward at the balcony, with only the whites of the eyes being visible in the latter case. And this probably also accounts for that tiresome fluttering of the eyelashes that the female performers are particularly guilty of. If an actor nowadays wants to express something with his eyes, he can only do it looking right at the audience, in which case he makes direct contact with someone outside the proscenium arch—a bad habit known justifiably or not, as "saying hello to friends."°

I should think that the use of sufficiently strong side lights (through the use of reflectors or something like them) would provide the actor with a new asset: an increased range of expression made possible by the play of the eyes, the most expressive part of the face.

I have scarcely any illusions about getting actors to play for the audience and not directly at them, although this should be the goal. Nor do I dream of ever seeing an actor play through all of an important scene with his back to the audience. But is it too much to hope that crucial scenes could be played where the author indicated and not in front of the prompter's box as if they were duets demanding applause? I am not calling for a revolution, only for some small changes. I am well aware that transforming the stage into a real room with the fourth wall missing and with some of the furniture placed with backs to the auditorium would only upset the audience, at least for the present.

If I bring up the subject of make-up, it is not because I dare hope to be heeded by the ladies, who would rather be beautiful than truthful. But the male actor might do well to consider if it is an advantage to paint his face with character lines that remain there like a mask. Let us imagine an actor who pencils in with soot a few lines between his eyes to indicate great anger, and let us suppose that in that permanently enraged state he finds he has to smile on a certain line. Imagine the horrible grimace! And how can the old character actor wrinkle his brows in anger when his false bald pate is as smooth as a billiard ball?

In a modern psychological drama, in which every tremor of the soul should be reflected more by facial expressions than by gestures and grunts, it would probably be most sensible to experiment with strong side lighting on a small stage, using actors without any make-up or a minimum of it.

And then, if we could get rid of the visible orchestra with its disturbing lights and the faces turned toward the public; if the auditorium floor could be raised so that the spectator's eyes are not level with the actor's knees; if we could get rid of the proscenium boxes and their occupants, giggling diners and drinkers; and if we could have it dark in the auditorium during the performance, and if, above everything else, we could have a small stage and an intimate auditorium—then possibly a new drama might arise and at least one theatre become a refuge for cultured audiences. While we are waiting for such a theatre, we shall have to write for the dramatic stockpile and prepare the repertory that one day shall come.

Here is my attempt. If I have failed, there is still time to try again!

"saying hello to friends," the equivalent in American theatre slang would be "counting the house" [translator's note].

First Principles

BY WILLIAM BUTLER YEATS, 1904

William Butler Yeats (1865–1939) was an Irish poet and playwright, whose early work was inspired by his fascination with Irish legend and the occult. His commitment to fostering an indigenous Irish literature led to his cofounding of the Irish Literary Theatre in 1898 and The Abbey Theatre in 1902, which fostered the work of such distinguished Irish playwrights as John Millington Synge, Sean O'Casey, and Brendan Behan. Yeats explains his conception of a national Irish theater in the following excerpt from Samhain, *an occasional magazine that he edited for the Theatre.*

What attracts one to drama is that it is, in the most obvious way, what all the arts are upon a last analysis. A farce and a tragedy are alike in this that they are a moment of intense life. An action is taken out of all other actions; it is reduced to its simple form, or at any rate to as simple a form as it can be brought to without our losing the sense of its place in the world. The characters that are involved in it are freed from everything that is not a part of that action; and whether it is, as in the less important kinds of drama, a mere bodily activity, a hair-breadth escape or the like, or as it is in the more important kinds, an activity of the souls of the characters, it is an energy, an eddy of life purified from everything but itself. The dramatist must picture life in action, with an unpreoccupied mind, as the musician pictures her in sound and the sculptor in form.

But if this be true, has art nothing to do with moral judgments? Surely it has, and its judgments are those from which there is no appeal. The character, whose fortune we have been called in to see, or the personality of the writer, must keep our sympathy, and whether it be farce or tragedy, we must laugh and weep with him and call down blessings on his head. This character who delights us may commit murder like Macbeth, or fly the battle for his sweetheart as did Antony, or betray his country like Coriolanus, and yet we will rejoice in every happiness that comes to him and sorrow at his death as if it were our own. It is no use telling us that the murderer and the betrayer do not deserve our sympathy. We thought so yesterday, and we still know what crime is, but everything has been changed of a sudden; we are caught up into another code, we are in the presence of a higher court. Complain of us if you will, but it will be useless, for before the curtain falls a thousand ages, grown conscious in our sympathies, will have cried *Absolvo te*. Blame if you

will the codes, the philosophies, the experiences of all past ages that have made us what we are, as the soil under our feet has been made out of unknown vegetations: quarrel with the acorns of Eden if you will, but what has that to do with us? We understand the verdict and not the law; and yet there is some law, some code, some judgment. If the poet's hand had slipped, if Antony had railed at Cleopatra in the tower, if Coriolanus had abated that high pride of his in the presence of death, we might have gone away muttering the Ten Commandments. Yet may be we are wrong to speak of judgment, for we have but contemplated life, and what more is there to say when she that is all virtue, the gift and the giver, the fountain whither all flows again, has given all herself? If the subject of drama or any other art, were a man himself, an eddy of momentary breath, we might desire the contemplation of perfect characters; but the subject of all art is passion, the flame of life itself, and a passion can only be contemplated when separated by itself, purified of all but itself, and aroused into a perfect intensity by opposition with some other passion, or it may be with the law, that is the expression of the whole whether of Church or Nation or external nature. Had Coriolanus not been a law-breaker neither he nor we had ever discovered, it may be, that noble pride of his, and if we had not seen Cleopatra through the eyes of so many lovers, would we have known that soul of hers to be all flame, and wept at the quenching of it? If we were not certain of law we would not feel the struggle, the drama, but the subject of art is not law, which is a kind of death, but the praise of life, and it has no commandments that are not positive.

But if literature does not draw its substance from history, or anything about us in the world, what is a National literature[?] Our friends have already told us, writers for the Theatre in Abbey Street, that we have no right to the name, some because we do not write in Irish, and others because we do not plead the National cause in our plays, as if we were writers for the newspapers. I have not asked my fellow-workers what they mean by the words National literature, but though I have no great love for definitions, I would define it in some such way as this: It is the work of writers, who are moulded by influences that are moulding their country, and who write out of so deep a life that they are accepted there in the end. It leaves a good deal unsettled—was Rosetti° an Englishman, or Swift° an Irishman?—but it covers more kinds of National literature than any other I can think of. If one says a National literature must be in the language of the country, there are many difficulties. Should it be written in the language that one's country does speak or the language that it ought to speak? Was Milton an Englishman when he wrote in Latin or Italian, and had we no part in Columbanus° when he wrote in Latin the beautiful sermon comparing life to a highway and to a smoke? And then there is Beckford,° who is in every

---

Rosetti, Dante Gabriel Rosetti (1828–1882). *Swift,* Jonathan Swift (1667–1745), author and satirist, though born in Dublin, was active in English politics, as well as a cleric in the Anglican Church and returned to Dublin as dean of St. Patrick's Cathedral. *Columbanus,* St. Columban (543–615), who was indicted in 603 by a synod of French bishops for keeping Easter according to Celtic usage. *Beckford,* William Beckford (1760–1844). The book referred to is a novel, *Vathek* (1782).

---

history of English literature, and yet his one memorable book, a story of Persia, was written in French. . . .

I mean by deep life that men must put into their writing the emotions and experiences that have been most important to themselves. If they say, "I will write of Irish country people and make them charming and picturesque like those dear peasants my great grandmother used to put in the foreground of her watercolour paintings," then they had better be satisfied with the word "provincial." If one condescends to one's material, if it is only what a popular novelist would call local colour, it is certain that one's real soul is somewhere else. Mr. Synge, upon the other hand, who is able to express his own finest emotions in those curious ironical plays of his, where, for all that, by the illusion of admirable art, everyone seems to be thinking and feeling as only countrymen could think and feel, is truly a National writer, as Burns was when he wrote finely and as Burns was not when he wrote *Highland Mary* and *The Cotter's Saturday Night.*

A writer is not less National because he shows the influence of other countries and of the great writers of the world.

The Technical Novelty in Ibsen's Plays

BY GEORGE BERNARD SHAW, 1913

George Bernard Shaw (1856–1950). For biographical details, see pp. 693–96. The following is excerpted from The Quintessence of Ibsenism.

It is a striking and melancholy example of the preoccupation of critics with phrases and formulas to which they have given life by taking them into the tissue of their own living minds, and which therefore seem and feel vital and important to them whilst they are to everybody else the deadest and dreariest rubbish (this is the great secret of academic dryasdust) that to this day they remain blind to a new technical factor in the art of popular stage-play making which every considerable playwright has been thrusting under their noses night after night for a whole generation. This technical factor in the play is the discussion. Formerly you had in what was called a well made play an exposition in the first act, a situation in the second,

an unravelling in the third. Now you have exposition, situation, and discussion; and the discussion is the test of the playwright. The critics protest in vain. They declare that discussions are not dramatic, and that art should not be didactic. Neither the playwrights nor the public take the smallest notice of them. The discussion conquered Europe in Ibsen's *Doll's House;* and now the serious playwright recognizes in the discussion not only the main test of his highest powers, but also the real centre of his play's interest. Sometimes he even takes every possible step to assure the public beforehand that his play will be fitted with that newest improvement.

This was inevitable if the drama was ever again to be raised above the childish demand for fables without morals. Children have a settled arbitrary morality: therefore to them moralizing is nothing but an intolerable platitudinizing. The morality of the grown-ups is also very largely a settled morality, either purely conventional and of no ethical significance, like the rule of the road or the rule that when you ask for a yard of ribbon the shopkeeper shall give you thirty-six inches and not interpret the word yard as he pleases, or else too obvious in its ethics to leave any room for discussion: for instance, that if the boots keeps you waiting too long for your shaving water you must not plunge your razor into his throat in your irritation, no matter how great an effort of self-control your forbearance may cost you.

Now when a play is only a story of how a villain tries to separate an honest young pair of betrothed lovers; to gain the hand of the woman by calumny; and to ruin the man by forgery, murder, false witness, and other commonplaces of the *Newgate Calendar,*° the introduction of a discussion would clearly be ridiculous. There is nothing for sane people to discuss; and any attempt to Chadbandize° on the wickedness of such crimes is at once resented as, in Milton's phrase, "moral babble."°

But this sort of drama is soon exhausted by people who go often to the theatre. In twenty visits one can see every possible change rung on all the available plots and incidents out of which plays of this kind can be manufactured. The illusion of reality is soon lost: in fact it may be doubted whether any adult ever entertains it: it is only to very young children that the fairy queen is anything but an actress. But at the age when we cease to mistake the figures on the stage for dramatis personae, and know that they are actors and actresses, the charm of the performer begins to assert itself, and the child who would have been cruelly hurt by being told that the Fairy Queen was only Miss Smith dressed up to look like one, becomes the man who goes to the theatre expressly to see Miss Smith, and is fascinated by her skill or beauty to the point of delighting in plays which would be unendurable to him without her. Thus we get plays "written round" popular performers, and popular performers who give value to otherwise useless plays by investing them with their own attractiveness. But all these enterprises are, commercially speaking, desperately precarious. To begin with, the supply of performers whose attraction is so far independent of the play that their inclusion in the cast sometimes makes the difference between success and failure is too small to enable all our theatres, or even many of them, to depend on their

actors rather than on their plays. And to finish with, no actor can make bricks entirely without straw. From Grimaldi to Sothern, Jefferson, and Henry Irving° (not to mention living actors) we have had players succeeding once in a lifetime in grafting on to a play which would have perished without them some figure imagined wholly by themselves; but none of them has been able to repeat the feat, nor to save many of the plays in which he has appeared from failure. In the long run nothing can retain the interest of the playgoer after the theatre has lost its illusion for his childhood, and its glamor for his adolescence, but a constant supply of interesting plays; and this is specially true in London, where the expense and trouble of theatregoing have been raised to a point at which it is surprising that sensible people of middle age go to the theatre at all. As a matter of fact, they mostly stay at home.

Now an interesting play cannot in the nature of things mean anything but a play in which problems of conduct and character of personal importance to the audience are raised and suggestively discussed. People have a thrifty sense of taking away something from such plays: they not only have had something for their money, but they retain that something as a permanent possession. Consequently none of the commonplaces of the box office hold good of such plays. In vain does the experienced acting manager declare that people want to be amused and not preached at in the theatre; that they will not stand long speeches; that a play must not contain more than 18,000 words; that it must not begin before nine nor last beyond eleven; that there must be no politics and no religion in it; that breach of these golden rules will drive people to the variety theatres; that there must be a woman of bad character, played by a very attractive actress, in the piece; and so on and so forth. All these counsels are valid for plays in which there is nothing to discuss. They may be disregarded by the playwright who is a moralist and a debater as well as a dramatist. From him, within the inevitable limits set by the clock and by the physical endurance of the human frame, people will stand anything as soon as they are matured enough and cultivated enough to be susceptible to the appeal of his particular form of art. The difficulty at present is that mature and cultivated people do not go to the theatre, just as they do not read penny novelets; and when an attempt is made to cater for them they do not respond to it in time, partly because they have not the habit of playgoing, and partly because it takes too long for them to find out that the new theatre is not like all the

---

Newgate Calendar, also known as the *Malefactors' Bloody Register,* a series of sensationalized periodicals (eighteenth and nineteenth centuries), which listed notorious crimes. *Chadbandize,* to be hypocritical; after Chadband, a character in Dickens's *Bleak House.* *"moral babble,"* in Comus (1634), l. 807.

Grimaldi . . . Irving, Joseph Grimaldi (1778–1837), E. A. Sothern (1826–1881), Joseph Jefferson (1829–1905), Henry Irving (1838–1905)—well-known nineteenth century actors.

other theatres. But when they do at last find their way there, the attraction is not the firing of blank cartridges at one another by actors, nor the pretence of falling down dead that ends the stage combat, nor the simulation of erotic thrills by a pair of stage lovers, nor any of the other tomfooleries called action, but the exhibition and discussion of the character and conduct of stage figures who are made to appear real by the art of the playwright and the performers.

This, then, is the extension of the old dramatic form effected by Ibsen. Up to a certain point in the last act, *A Doll's House* is a play that might be turned into a very ordinary French drama by the excision of a few lines, and the substitution of a sentimental happy ending for the famous last scene: indeed the very first thing the theatrical wiseacres did with it was to effect exactly this transformation, with the result that the play thus pithed had no success and attracted no notice worth mentioning. But at just that point in the last act, the heroine very unexpectedly (by the wiseacres) stops her emotional acting and says: "We must sit down and discuss all this that has been happening between us." And it was by this new technical feature: this addition of a new movement, as musicians would say, to the dramatic form, that *A Doll's House* conquered Europe and founded a new school of dramatic art.

Since that time the discussion has expanded far beyond the limits of the last ten minutes of an otherwise "well-made" play. The disadvantage of putting the decision at the end was not only that it came when the audience was fatigued, but that it was necessary to see the play over again, so as to follow the earlier acts in the light of the final discussion, before it became fully intelligible. The practical utility of this book is due to the fact that unless the spectator at an Ibsen play has read the pages referring to it beforehand, it is hardly possible for him to get its bearings at a first hearing if he approaches it, as most spectators still do, with conventional idealist prepossessions. Accordingly, we now have plays, including some of my own, which begin with discussion and end with action, and others in which the discussion interpenetrates the action from beginning to end. When Ibsen invaded England discussion had vanished from the stage; and women could not write plays. Within twenty years women were writing better plays than men; and these plays were passionate arguments from beginning to end. The action of such plays consists of a case to be argued. If the case is uninteresting or stale or badly conducted or obviously trumped up, the play is a bad one. If it is important and novel and convincing, or at least disturbing, the play is a good one. But anyhow the play in which there is no argument and no case no longer counts as serious drama. It may still please the child in us as Punch and Judy does, but nobody nowadays pretends to regard the well-made play as anything

more than a commercial product which is not in question when modern schools of serious drama are under discussion. Indeed within ten years of the production of *A Doll's House* in London, audiences had become so derisive of the more obvious and hackneyed features of the methods of Sardou° that it became dangerous to resort to them; and playwrights who persisted in "constructing" plays in the old French manner lost ground not for lack of ideas, but because their technique was unbearably out of fashion.

In the new plays, the drama arises through a conflict of unsettled ideas rather than through vulgar attachments, rapacities, generosities, resentments, ambitions, misunderstandings, oddities and so forth as to which no moral question is raised. The conflict is not between clear right and wrong: the villain is as conscientious as the hero, if not more so: in fact, the question which makes the play interesting (when it *is* interesting) is which is the villain and which the hero. Or, to put it another way, there are no villains and no heroes. This strikes the critics mainly as departure from dramatic art; but it is really the inevitable return to nature which ends all the merely technical fashions. Now the natural is mainly the everyday; and its climaxes must be, if not everyday, at least everylife, if they are to have any importance for the spectator. Crimes, fights, big legacies, fires, shipwrecks, battles, and thunderbolts are mistakes in a play, even when they can be effectively simulated. No doubt they may acquire dramatic interest by putting a character through the test of an emergency; but the test is likely to be too obviously theatrical, because, as the playwright cannot in the nature of things have much experience of such catastrophes, he is forced to substitute a set of conventions or conjectures for the feelings they really produce.

In short, pure accidents are not dramatic: they are only anecdotic. They may be sensational, impressive, provocative, ruinous, curious, or a dozen other things; but they have no specifically dramatic interest. There is no drama in being knocked down or run over. The catastrophe in *Hamlet* would not be in the least dramatic had Polonius fallen downstairs and broken his neck, Claudius succumbed to delirium tremens, Hamlet forgotten to breathe in the intensity of his philosophic speculation, Ophelia died of Danish measles, Laertes been shot by the palace sentry, and Rosencrantz and Guildenstern drowned in the North Sea. Even as it is, the Queen, who poisons herself by accident, has an air of being polished off to get her out of the way: her death is the one dramatic failure of the piece. Bushels of good paper have been inked in vain by writers who imagined they could produce a tragedy by killing everyone in the last act accidentally. As a matter of fact no accident, however sanguinary, can produce a moment of real drama, though a difference of opinion between husband and wife as to living in town or country might be the beginning of an appalling tragedy or a capital comedy.

It may be said that everything is an accident: that Othello's character is an accident, Iago's character another accident, and the fact that they happened to come together in the Venetian service an even more accidental accident. Also that Torvald Helmer might just as likely have married Mrs Nickelby as Nora.° Granting this trifling for what it is worth, the fact remains that marriage is no more an accident than birth or death: that is, it is expected to happen to everybody. And if every man has a good deal of Torvald Helmer in him, and every woman a good deal of Nora, neither their characters nor their meeting and marrying are accidents. *Othello,* though entertaining, pitiful, and resonant with the thrills a master of language can produce by mere artistic sonority is certainly much more accidental than *A Doll's House;* but it is correspondingly less important and interesting to us. It has been kept alive, not by its manufactured misunderstandings and stolen handkerchiefs and the like, nor even by its orchestral verse, but by its exhibition and discussion of human nature, marriage, and jealousy; and it would be a prodigiously better play if it were a serious discussion of the highly interesting problem of how a simple Moorish soldier would get on with a "supersubtle" Venetian lady of fashion if he married her. As it is, the play turns on a mistake; and though a mistake can produce a murder, which is the vulgar substitute for a tragedy, it cannot produce a real tragedy in the modern sense. Reflective people are not more interested in the Chamber of Horrors than in their own homes, nor in murderers, victims, and villains than in themselves; and the moment a man has acquired sufficient reflective power to cease gaping at waxworks, he is on his way to losing interest in Othello, Desdemona, and Iago exactly to the extent to which they become interesting to the police. Cassio's weakness for drink comes much nearer home to most of us than Othello's strangling and throat cutting, or Iago's theatrical confidence trick. The proof is that Shakespear's professional colleagues, who exploited all his sensational devices, and piled up torture on murder and incest on adultery until they had far outHeroded Herod, are now unmemorable and unplayable. Shakespear survives because he cooly treated the sensational horrors of his borrowed plots as inorganic theatrical accessories, using them simply as pretexts for dramatizing human character as it exists in the normal world. In enjoying and discussing his plays we unconsciously discount the combats and murders: commentators are never so astray (and consequently so ingenious) as when they take Hamlet seriously as a madman, Macbeth as a homicidal Highlander, and impish humorists like Richard and Iago as lurid villains of the Renascence. The plays in which these figures appear could be changed into comedies without altering a hair of their beards. Shakespear, had anyone been intelligent enough to tax him with this, would perhaps have said that most crimes are accidents that happen to people exactly like ourselves, and that Macbeth, under propitious circumstances, would have made an exemplary rector of Stratford, a real criminal being a defective monster, a human accident, useful on the stage only for minor parts such as Don Johns, second murderers, and the like. Anyhow, the fact remains that Shakespear survives by what he has in common with Ibsen, and not by what he has in common with Webster and the rest. Hamlet's surprise at finding that he "lacks gall" to behave in the idealistically conventional manner, and that no extremity of rhetoric about the duty of revenging "a dear father slain" and exterminating the "bloody bawdy villain" who murdered him seems to make any difference in their domestic relations in the palace in Elsinore, still keeps us talking about him and going to the theatre to listen to him, whilst the older Hamlets, who never had any Ibsenist hesitations, and shammed madness, and entangled the courtiers in the arras and burnt them, and stuck hard to the theatrical school of the fat boy in *Pickwick*° ("I wants to make your flesh creep"), are as dead as John Shakespear's mutton.

We have progressed so rapidly on this point under the impulse given to the drama by Ibsen that it seems strange now to contrast him favorably with Shakespear on the ground that he avoided the old catastrophes which left the stage strewn with the dead at the end of an Elizabethan tragedy. For perhaps the most plausible reproach leveled at Ibsen by modern critics of his own school is just that survival of the old school in him which makes the death rate so high in his last acts. Do Oswald Alving, Hedvig Ekdal, Rosmer and Rebecca, Hedda Gabler, Solness, Eyolf, Borkman, Rubeck and Irene° die dramatically natural deaths, or are they

---

° *Torvald . . . Nora,* characters in Ibsen's *A Doll's House* (1879).

Pickwick, The Pickwick Papers (*The Posthumous Papers of the Pickwick Club*) by Charles Dickens.   *Oswald . . . Irene,* characters in (respectively) the following plays of Ibsen: *Ghosts* (1881), *The Wild Duck* (1884), *Rosmersholm* (1886), *Hedda Gabler* (1890), *The Master Builder* (1892), *Little Eyolf* (1894), *John Gabriel Borkman* (1896), *When We Dead Awaken* (1899).

slaughtered in the classic and Shakespearean manner, partly because the audience expects blood for its money, partly because it is difficult to make people attend seriously to anything except by startling them with some violent calamity? It is so easy to make out a case for either view that I shall not argue the point. The post-Ibsen playwrights apparently think that Ibsen's homicides and suicides were forced. In Tchekov's *Cherry Orchard,* for example, where the sentimental ideals of our amiable, cultured, Schumann playing propertied class are reduced to dust and ashes by a hand not less deadly than Ibsen's because it is so much more caressing, nothing more violent happens than that the family cannot afford to keep up its old house. In Granville-Barker's° plays, the campaign against our society is carried on with all Ibsen's implacability; but the one suicide (in *Waste*) is unhistorical; for neither Parnell nor Dilke, who were the actual cases in point of the waste which was the subject of the play, killed himself. I myself have been reproached because the characters in my plays "talk but do nothing," meaning that they do not commit felonies. As a matter of fact we have come to see that it is no true dénouement to cut the Gordian knot as Alexander did with a stroke of the sword. If people's souls are tied up by law and public opinion it is much more tragic to leave them to wither in these bonds than to end their misery and relieve the salutary compunction of the audience by outbreaks of violence. Judge Brack° was, on the whole, right when he said that people dont do such things. If they did, the idealists would be brought to their senses very quickly indeed.

But in Ibsen's play the catastrophe, even when it seems forced, and when the ending of the play would be more tragic without it, is never an accident; and the play never exists for its sake. His nearest to an accident is the death of little Eyolf, who falls off a pier and is drowned. But this instance only reminds us that there is one good dramatic use for an accident: it can awaken people. When England wept over the deaths of little Nell and Paul Dombey,° the strong soul of Ruskin° was moved to scorn: to novelists who were at a loss to make their books sell he offered the formula: When at a loss, kill a child. But Ibsen did not kill little Eyolf to manufacture pathos. The surest way to achieve a thoroughly bad performance of Little Eyolf is to conceive it is a sentimental tale of a drowned darling. Its drama lies in the awakening of Allmers and his wife to the despic-

able quality and detestable rancors of the life they had been idealizing as blissful and poetic. They are so sunk in their dream that the awakening can be effected only by a violent shock. And that is just the one dramatically useful thing an accident can do. It can shock. Hence the accident that befalls Eyolf.

As to the deaths in Ibsen's last acts, they are a sweeping up of the remains of dramatically finished people. Solness's fall from the tower is as obviously symbolic as Phaeton's fall from the chariot of the sun. Ibsen's dead bodies are those of the exhausted or destroyed: he does not kill Hilda, for instance, as Shakespear killed Juliet. He is ruthless enough with Hedvig and Eyolf because he wants to use their deaths to expose their parents; but if he had written *Hamlet* nobody would have been killed in the last act except perhaps Horatio, whose correct nullity might have provoked Fortinbras to let some of the moral sawdust out of him with his sword. For Shakespearean deaths in Ibsen you must go back to *Lady Inger* and the plays of his nonage, with which this book is not concerned.

The drama was born of old from the union of two desires: the desire to have a dance and the desire to hear a story. The dance became a rant: the story became a situation. When Ibsen began to make plays, the art of the dramatist had shrunk into the art of contriving a situation. And it was held that the stranger the situation, the better the play. Ibsen saw that, on the contrary, the more familiar the situation, the more interesting the play. Shakespear had put ourselves on the stage but not our situations. Our uncles seldom murder fathers, and cannot legally marry our mothers; we do not meet witches; our kings are not as a rule stabbed and succeeded by their stabbers; and when we raise money by bills we do not promise to pay pounds of our flesh. Ibsen supplies the want left by Shakespear. He gives us not only ourselves, but ourselves in our own situations. The things that happen to his stage figures are things that happen to us. One consequence is that his plays are much more important to us than Shakespear's. Another is that they are capable both of hurting us cruelly and of filling us with excited hopes of escape from idealistic tyrannies, and with visions of intenser life in the future.

Changes in technique follow inevitably from these changes in the subject matter of the play. When a dramatic poet can give you hopes and visions, such old maxims as that stage-craft is the art of preparation become boyish, and may be left to those unfortunate playwrights who, being unable to make anything really interesting happen on the stage, have to acquire the art of continually persuading the audience that it is going to happen presently. When he can stab people to the heart by shewing them the meanness or cruelty of something they did yesterday and intend to do tomorrow, all the old tricks to catch and hold their

---

Granville-Barker, Harley Granville-Barker (1877–1946), English actor, director, playwright, and critic. ***Judge Brack,*** character in Ibsen's *Hedda Gabler.* ***Paul Dombey,*** character in Dickens's *The Old Curiosity Shop* and *Dombey and Son.* ***Ruskin,*** John Ruskin (1819–1900); English artist, scientist, poet, philosopher, and art critic.

attention become the silliest of superfluities. The play called *The Murder of Gonzago,* which Hamlet makes the players act before his uncle, is artlessly constructed; but it produces a greater effect on Claudius than the Oedipus of Sophocles, because it is about himself. The writer who practises the art of Ibsen therefore discards all the old tricks of preparation, catastrophe, dénouement, and so forth without thinking about it, just as a modern rifleman never dreams of providing himself with powder horns, percussion caps, and wads: indeed he does not know the use of them. Ibsen substituted a terrible art of sharpshooting at the audience, trapping them, fencing with them, aiming always at the sorest spot in their consciences. Never mislead an audience, was an old rule. But the new school will trick the spectator into forming a meanly false judgment, and then convict him of it in the next act, often to his grievous mortification. When you despise something you ought to take off your hat to, or admire and imitate something you ought to loathe, you cannot resist the dramatist who knows how to touch these morbid spots in you and make you see that they are morbid. The dramatist knows that as long as he is teaching and saving his audience, he is as sure of their strained attention as a dentist is, or the Angel of the Annunciation. And though he may use all the magic of art to make you forget the pain he causes you or to enhance the joy of the hope and courage he awakens, he is never occupied in the old work of manufacturing interest and expectation with materials that have neither novelty, significance, nor relevance to the experience or prospects of the spectators.

Hence a cry has arisen that the post-Ibsen play is not a play, and that its technique, not being the technique described by Aristotle, is not a technique at all. I will not enlarge on this: the fun poked at my friend Mr A. B.

Walkley° in the prologue of *Fanny's First Play*° need not be repeated here. But I may remind him that the new technique is new only on the modern stage. It has been used by preachers and orators ever since speech was invented. It is the technique of playing upon the human conscience; and it has been practised by the playwright whenever the playwright has been capable of it. Rhetoric, irony, argument, paradox, epigram, parable, the rearrangement of haphazard facts into orderly and intelligent situations: these are both the oldest and the newest arts of the drama; and your plot construction and art of preparation are only the tricks of theatrical talent and the shifts of moral sterility, not the weapons of dramatic genius. In the theatre of Ibsen we are not flattered spectators killing an idle hour with an ingenious and amusing entertainment: we are "guilty creatures sitting at a play"; and the technique of pastime is no more applicable than at a murder trial.

The technical novelties of the Ibsen and post-Ibsen plays are, then: first, the introduction of the discussion and its development until it so overspreads and interpenetrates the action that it finally assimilates it, making play and discussion practically identical; and, second, as a consequence of making the spectators themselves the persons of the drama, and the incidents of their own lives its incidents, the disuse of the old stage tricks by which audiences had to be induced to take an interest in unreal people and improbable circumstances, and the substitution of a forensic technique of recrimination, disillusion, and penetration through ideals to the truth, with a free use of all the rhetorical and lyrical arts of the orator, the preacher, the pleader, and the rhapsodist.

A. B. Walkley, Arthur Bingham Walkley (1855–1926), English drama critic. *Fanny's First Play,* 1911 play by Shaw.

Direction and Acting

BY CONSTANTIN STANISLAVSKI, 1947

Constantin Stanislavski (1863–1938) was a Russian theatrical director, teacher, actor, and cofounder of the Moscow Art Theatre, a repertory company that was the first to produce Chekhov's plays. His innovative technique for actors, which he explains in the article that follows, revolutionized modern acting by emphasizing the emotional truth and inner motivation of characters.

Theatrical art has always been collective, arising only where poetical-dramatic talent was actively combined with the actor's. The basis of a play is always a dramatic conception; a general artistic sense is imparted to the theatrical action by the unifying, creative genius of the actor. Thus the actor's dramatic activity begins at the foundation of the play. In the first place, each actor, either independently or through the theatre manager, must probe for the fundamental motive in the finished play—the creative idea that is characteristic of the author and that reveals itself as the germ from which his work grows organically. The motive of the play always holds the character developing before the spectator; each personality in the work takes a part conforming to his own character; the work, then developing in the appointed direction, flows on to the final point conceived by the author. The first stage in the work of the actor and theatre manager is to probe for the germ of the play, investigating the fundamental line of action that traverses all of its episodes and is therefore called by the writer its transparent effect or action. In contrast to some theatrical directors, who consider every play only as material for theatrical repetition, the writer believes that in the production of every important drama the director and actor must go straight for the most exact and profound conception of the mind and ideal of the dramatist, and must not change that ideal for their own. The interpretation of the play and the character of its artistic incarnation inevitably appear in a certain measure subjective, and bear the mark of the individual peculiarities of the manager and actors; but only by profound attention to the artistic individuality of the author and to his ideal and mentality, which have been disclosed as the creative germ of the play, can the theatre realize all its artistic depth and transmit, as in a poetical production, completeness and harmony of composition. Every part of the future spectacle is then unified in it by its own artistic work; each part, in the measure of its own genius, will flow on to the artistic realization aimed at by the dramatist.

The actor's task, then, begins with the search for the play's artistic seed. All artistic action—organic action, as in every constructive operation of nature—starts from this seed at the moment when it is conveyed to the mind. On reaching the actor's mind, the seed must wander around, germinate, put out roots, drinking in the juices of the soil in which it is planted, grow and eventually bring forth a lively flowering plant. Artistic process must in all cases flow very rapidly, but usually, in order that it may preserve the character of the true organic action and may lead to the creation of life, of a clear truly artistic theatrical image, and not of a trade substitute, it demands much more time than is allotted to it in the best European theatres. That is why in the writer's theatre every dramatization passes through eight to ten revisions, as is also done in Germany by the famous theatre manager and theorist, K. Hagemann. Sometimes even more than ten revisions are needed, occasionally extending over several months. But even under these conditions, the creative genius of the actor does not appear so freely as does, for instance, the creative genius of the dramatist. Bound by the strict obligations of his *collectif*, the actor must not postpone his work to the moment when his physical and psychic condition appears propitious for creative genius. Meanwhile, his exacting and capricious artistic nature is prompted by aspirations of his artistic intuition, and in the absence of creative genius is not reached by any effort of his will. He is not aided in that respect by outward technique—his skill in making use of his body, his vocal equipment and his powers of speech.

The Artistic Condition.—But is it really impossible? Are there no means, no processes that sensibly would help us, and spontaneously lead to that artistic condition which is born of genius without any effort on its part? If that capacity is unattainable all at once, by some process or other, it may, perhaps, be acquired in parts, and through progressive stages may perfect those elements out of which the artistic condition is composed, and which are subject to our will. Of course the general run of acting does not come into being from this genius, but cannot such acting, in some measure, be brought by it near to what is evidence of genius? These are the problems which presented themselves to the writer about 20 years ago, when reflecting on the external obstacles that hamper actors' artistic genius, and partly compel substitution of the crude outward marks of the actor's profession for its results. They drove him to the rediscovery of processes of external technique, *i.e.*, methods proceeding from consciousness to sub-consciousness, in which domain flow nine-tenths of all real artistic processes. Observations both upon himself and other actors with whom he happened to rehearse, but chiefly upon growing theatrical skill in Russia and abroad, allowed him to do some generalizing, which thereupon he verified in practice.

The first is that, in an artistic condition, full freedom of body plays a principal rôle; *i.e.*, the freedom from that muscular strain which, without our knowing it, fetters us not only on the stage but also in ordinary life, hindering us from being obedient convictors of our psychic action. This muscular strain, reaching its maximum at those times when the actor is called upon to perform something especially difficult in his theatrical work, swallows up the bulk of this external energy, diverting him from activity of the higher centres. This teaches us the possibility of availing ourselves of the muscular energy of our limbs only as necessity demands, and in exact conformity with our creative efforts.

The second observation is that the flow of the actor's artistic force is considerably retarded by the visual auditorium and the public, whose presence may hamper his outward freedom of movement, and powerfully hinder his concentration on his own artistic taste. It is almost unnecessary to remark that the artistic achievement of great actors is always bound by the concentration of attention to the action of their own performance, and that when in that condition, *i.e.,* just when the actor's attention is taken away from the spectator, he gains a particular power over the audience, grips it, and compels it to take an active share in his artistic existence. This does not mean, of course, that the actor must altogether cease to feel the public; but the public is concerned only in so far as it neither exerts pressure on him nor diverts him unnecessarily from the artistic demands of the moment, which last might happen to him even while knowing how to regulate his attention. The actor suitably disciplined must automatically restrict the sphere of his attention, concentrating on what comes within this sphere, and only half consciously seizing on what comes within its aura. If need be, he must restrict that sphere to such an extent that it reaches a condition that may be called *public solitude.* But as a rule this sphere of attention is elastic, it expands or contracts for the actor, with regard to the course of his theatrical actions. Within the boundary of this sphere, as one of the actual aspects of the play, there is also the actor's immediate central *object of attention,* the object on which, somehow or other, his will is concentrated at the moment with which, in the course of the play, he is in inward communication. This theatrical sympathy with the object can only be complete when the actor has trained himself by long practice to surrender himself in his own impressions, and also in his reactions to those impressions, with maximum intensity: only so does theatrical action attain the necessary force, only so is created between the actual aspects of the play, *i.e.,* between the actors, that link, that living bond, which is essential for the carrying through of the play to its goal, with the general maintenance of the rhythm and time of each performance.

Concentration.—But whatever may be the sphere of the actor's attention, whether it confines him at some moments to public solitude, or whether it grips the faces of all those before the stage, dramatic artistic genius, as in the preparation of the part so in its repeated performance, requires a full concentration of all the mental and physical talents of the actor, and the participation of the whole of his physical and psychic capacity. It takes hold of his sight and hearing, all his external senses; it draws out not only the periphery but also the essential depth of his existence, and it evokes to activity his memory, imagination, emotions, intelligence and will. The whole mental and physical being of the actor must be directed to that which is derived from his facial expression. At the moment of inspiration, of the involuntary use of all the actor's qualities, at that moment he actually exists. On the other hand, in the absence of this employment of his qualities, the actor is gradually led astray along the road leading to time-honoured theatrical traditions;

he begins to "produce" wherever he sees them, or, glancing at his own image, imitates the inward manifestations of his emotions, or tries to draw from himself the emotions of the perfected part, to "inspire" them within himself. But when forcing such an image by his own psychic equipment, with its unchanging organic laws, he by no means attains that desired result of artistic genius; he must present only the rough counterfeit of emotion, because emotions do not come to order. By no effort of conscious will can one awake them in oneself at a moment, nor can they ever be of use for creative genius striving to bring this about by searching the depths of its mind. A fundamental axiom, therefore, for the actor who wishes to be a real artist on the stage, may be stated thus: he must not play to produce emotions, and he must not involuntarily evoke them in himself.

Activity of Imagination.—Considerations on the nature of artistically gifted people, however, inevitably open up the road to the possession of the emotion of the part. This road traverses activity of imagination, which in most of its stages is subject to the action of consciousness. One must not suddenly begin to operate on emotion; one must put oneself in motion in the direction of artistic imagination, but imagination—as is also shown by observations of scientific psychology—disturbs our aberrant memory, and, luring from the hidden recesses beyond the boundaries of its sense of harmony whatever elements there may be of proved emotions, organizes them afresh in sympathy with those that have arisen in our imagery. So surrounded within our figures of imagination, without effort on our part, the answer to our aberrant memory is found and the sounds of sympathetic emotion are called out from us. This is why the creative imagination presents itself afresh, the indispensable gift of the actor. Without a well developed, mobile imagination, creative faculty is by no means possible, not by instinct nor intuition nor the aid of external technique. In the acquiring of it, that which has lain dormant in the mind of the artist is, when immersed in his sphere of unconscious imagery and emotion, completely harmonized within him.

This practical method for the artistic education of the actor, directed by means of his imagination to the storing up of effective memory, is sufficiently enlarged upon; his individual emotional experience, by its limits, actually leads to the restriction of the sphere of his creative genius, and does not allow him to play parts dissimilar to those of his psychic harmony. This opinion is fundamental for the clearing away of misunderstandings of those elements of reality from which are produced fictitious creations of imagination; these are also derived from organic experience, but a wealth and variety of these creations are only obtained by combinations drawn from a trial of elements. The musical scale has only its basic notes, the solar spectrum its radical colours, but the combination of sounds in music and of colours in painting are infinite. One can in the same way speak of radical emotions preserved in imaginative memory, just as the reception in imagination of outward harmony remains in the intellectual memory; the sum of these radical emotions in the inner experience of each person is limited, but the shades and combinations are as infinite as the combinations that create activity of imagination out of the elements of inward experience.

Certainly, but the actor's outward experience—*i.e.,* his sphere of vital sensations and reflections—must always be elastic, for only in that condition can the actor enlarge the sphere of his creative faculty. On the other hand, he must judiciously develop his imagination, harnessing it again and again to new propositions. But, in order that that imaginary union which is the actor's very foundation, produced by the creative genius of the dramatist, should take hold of him emotionally and lead him on to theatrical action, it is necessary that the actor should "swing toward" that union, as toward something as real as the union of reality surrounding him.

The Emotion of Truth. —This does not mean that the actor must surrender himself on the stage to some such hallucination as that when playing he should lose the sense of reality around him, to take scenery for real trees, etc. On the contrary, some part of his senses must remain free from the grip of the play to control everything that he attempts and achieves as the performer of his part. He does not forget that surrounding him on the stage are decorations, scenery, etc., but they have no meaning for him. He says to himself, as it were: "I know that all around me on the stage is a rough counterfeit of reality. It is false. But if all should be real, see how I might be carried away to some such scene; then I would act." And at that instant, when there arises in his mind that artistic "suppose," encircling his real life, he loses interest in it, and is transported to another plane, created for him, of imaginary life. Restored to real life again, the actor must perforce modify the truth, as in the actual construction of his invention, so also in the survivals connected to it. His invention can be shown to be illogical, wide of the truth—and then he ceases to believe it. Emotion rises in him with invention; *i.e.,* his outward regard for imagined circumstances may be shown as "determined" without relation to the individual nature of a given emotion. Finally, in the expression of the outward life of his part, the actor, as a living complex emotion, never making use of sufficient perfection of all his bodily equipment, may give an untrue intonation, may not keep the artistic mean in gesticulation and may through the temptation of cheap effect drift into mannerism or awkwardness.

Only by a strongly developed sense of the truth may he achieve that, in order that every one of his poses, and every gesture may be outwardly realistic; *i.e.,* he may express the condition representing the character, and may not serve, like the conventional theatrical gestures and poses of every race, a single inward beauty.

Internal Technique.—The combination of all the above-named procedure and habits also composes the actor's external technique. Parallel with its development must go also the development of internal technique—the perfecting of that bodily equipment which serves for the incarnation of the theatrical image created by the actor, and the exact, clear expression of his external consciousness. With this aim in view the actor must work out within himself not only the ordinary flexibility and mobility of action, but also the particular consciousness that directs all his groups of muscles, and the ability to feel the energy transfused within him, which, arising from his highest creative centres, forms in a definite manner his mimicry and gestures, and, radiating from him, brings into the circle of its influence his partners on the stage and in the auditorium. The same growth of consciousness and fineness of internal feelings must be worked out by the actor in relation to his vocal equipment. Ordinary speech—in life, so on the stage—is prosaic and monotonous; in it words sound disjointed, without any harmonious stringing together in a vocal melody as continuous as that of a violin, which by the hand of a master violinist can become fuller, deeper, finer and more transparent, and can without difficulty run from the higher to the lower notes and vice versa, and can alternate from pianissimo to forte. To counteract the wearisome monotony of reading, actors often elaborate, especially when declaiming poetry, with those artificial vocal *fioritures,* cadences and sudden raising and lowering of the voice, which are so characteristic of the conventional, pompous declamation, and which are not influenced by the corresponding emotion of the part, and therefore impress the more sensitive auditors with a feeling of unreality.

But there exists another natural musical sonorousness of speech, which we may see in great actors at the moment of their own true artistic elation, and which is closely knit to the internal sonorousness of their rôle. The actor must develop within himself this natural musical speech by practising his voice with due regard to his sense of reality, almost as much as a singer. At the same time he must perfect his elocution. It is possible to have a strong, flexible, impressive voice, and still distort speech, on the one hand by incorrect pronunciation, on the other by neglect of those almost imperceptible pauses and emphases through which are attained the exact transmission of the sense of the sentence, and also its particular emotional colouring.

In the perfect production of the dramatist, every word, every letter, every punctuation mark has its part in transmitting his inward reality; the actor in his interpretation of the play, according to his intelligence, introduces into each sentence his individual nuances, which must be transmitted not only by the motions of his body, but also by artistically developed speech. He must bear this in mind, that every sound which goes to make a word appears as a separate note, which has its part in the harmonious sound of the word, and which is the expression of one or other particle of the soul drawn out through the word. The perfecting, therefore, of the phonetics of speech cannot be limited to mechanical exercise of the vocal equipment, but must also be directed in such a way that the actor learns to feel each separate sound in a word as an instrument of artistic expression. But in regard to the musical tone of the voice, freedom, elasticity, rhythm of movement and generally all external technique of dramatic art, to say nothing of internal technique, the present day actor is still on a low rung of the ladder of artistic culture, still far behind in this respect, from many causes, the masters of music, poetry and painting, with an almost infinite road of development to travel.

Production.—It is evident that under these conditions, the staging of a play, which will satisfy highly artistic demands, cannot be achieved at the speed that economic factors unfortunately make necessary in most theatres. This creative process, which every actor must go through, from his conception of the part to its artistic incarnation, is essentially very complicated, and is hampered by lack of perfection of outward and inward technique. It is also much hindered by the necessity of fitting in the actors one with another—the adjustment of their artistic individualities into an artistic whole.

Responsibility for bringing about this accord, and the artistic integrity and expression of the performance rests with the theatre manager. During the period when the manager exercised a despotic rule in the theatre, a period starting with the Meiningen players and still in force even in many of the foremost theatres, the manager worked out in advance all the plans for staging a play, and, while certainly having regard to the existing cast, indicated to the actors the general outlines of the scenic effects, and the *mise-en-scène*.° The writer also adhered to this system, but now he has come to the conclusion that the creative work of the manager must be done in collaboration with the actor's work, neither ignoring nor confirming it. To encourage the actor's creative genius, to control and adjust it, ensuring that this creative genius grows out of the unique artistic germ of the drama, as much as

---

mise-en-scène, stage setting.

the external building up of the performance—that in the opinion of the writer is the problem of the theatre director today.

The joint work of the director and actor begins with the analysis of the drama and the discovery of its artistic germ, and with the investigation of its *transparent effect*. The next step is the discovery of the transparent effect of individual parts—of that fundamental will direction of each individual actor, which, organically derived from his character, determines his place in the general action of the play. If the actor cannot at once secure this transparent effect, then it must be traced bit by bit with the manager's aid—by dividing the part into sections corresponding to the separate stages of the life of the particular actor—from the separate problems developing before him in his struggle for the attainment of his goal. Each such section of a part or each problem, can, if necessary, be subjected to further psychological analysis, and sub-divided into problems even more detailed, responding to those separate mind actions of the performer out of which stage life is summed up. The actor must catch the *mind axes* of the emotions and temperaments, but not the emotions and temperaments that give colour to these sections of the part. In other words, when studying each portion of his part, he must ask himself what he wants, what he requires as a performer of the play and which definite partial problem he is putting before himself at a given moment. The answer to this question should not be in the form of a noun, but rather of a verb: "I wish to obtain possession of the heart of this lady"—"I wish to enter her house"—"I wish to push aside the servants who are protecting her," etc. Formulated in this manner, the mind problem, of which the object and setting, thanks to the working of his creative imagination, are forming a brighter and clearer picture for the actor, begins to grip him and to excite him, extracting from the recesses of his working memory the combinations of emotions necessary to the part; of emotions that have an active character and mould themselves into dramatic action. In this way the different sections of the actor's part grow more lively and richer by degrees, owing to the involuntary play of the complicated organic survivals. By joining together and grafting these sections, the *score of the part* is formed; the scores of the separate parts, after the continual joint work of the actors during rehearsals and by the necessary adjustment of them one with another, are summed up in a single *score of the performance.*

The Score Condensed.—Nevertheless, the work of the actors and manager is still unfinished. The actor is studying and *living* in the part and the play deeper and deeper still, finding their deeper artistic motives; so he lives in the score of his part still more profoundly. But the score of the part itself and of the play are actually subject by degrees during the work to further alterations. As in a perfect poetical production there are no superfluous words but only those necessary to the poet's artistic scheme, so in a score of the part there must not be a single superfluous emotion but only emotions necessary for the *transparent effect.* The score of each part must be condensed, as also the form of its transmitting, and bright, simple and compelling forms of its incarnation must be found. Only then, when in each actor every part not only organically ripens and comes to life but also all emotions are stripped of the superfluous, when they all crystallize and sum up into a live contact, when they harmonize amongst themselves in the general tune, rhythm and time of the performance, then the play may be presented to the public.

During repeated presentations the theatrical score of the play and each part remains in general unaltered. But that does not mean that, from the moment the performance is shown to the public the actor's creative process is to be considered ended, and that there remains for him only the mechanical repetition of his achievement at the first presentation. On the contrary,

every performance imposes on him creative conditions; all his psychical forces must take part in it, because only in these conditions can they creatively adapt the score of the part to those capricious changes which may develop in them from hour to hour, as in all living nervous creatures influencing one another by their emotions, and only then can they transmit to the spectator that invisible something, inexpressible in words, which forms the spiritual content of the plays. And that is the whole origin of the substance of dramatic art.

As regards the outward arrangements of the play—scenery, theatrical properties, etc.—all are of value in so far as they correspond to the expression of dramatic action, *i.e.,* to the actors' talents; in no case may they claim to have an independent artistic importance in the theatre, although up to now they have been so considered by many great scene painters. The art of scene painting, as well as the music included in the play, is on the stage only an auxiliary art, and the manager's duty is to get from each what is necessary for the illumination of the play performed before an audience, while subordinating each to the problems of the actors.

Theatre for Pleasure or Theatre for Instruction

BY BERTOLT BRECHT, 1936

Bertolt Brecht (1898–1956). For biographical details, see pp. 833–35.

THE EPIC THEATRE

Many people imagine that the term 'epic theatre' is self-contradictory, as the epic and dramatic ways of narrating a story are held, following Aristotle, to be basically distinct. The difference between the two forms was never thought simply to lie in the fact that the one is performed by living beings while the other operates via the written word; epic works such as those of Homer and the medieval singers were at the same time theatrical performances, while dramas like Goethe's *Faust* and Byron's *Manfred*° are agreed to have been more effective as books. Thus even by Aris-

totle's definition the difference between the dramatic and epic forms was attributed to their different methods of construction, whose laws were dealt with by two different branches of aesthetics. The method of construction depended on the different way of presenting the work to the public, sometimes via the stage, sometimes through a book; and independently of that there was the 'dramatic element' in epic works and the 'epic element' in dramatic. The bourgeois novel in the last century developed much that was 'dramatic,' by which was meant the strong centralization of the story, a momentum that drew the separate parts into a common relationship. A particular passion of utterance, a certain emphasis on the clash of forces are hallmarks of the 'dramatic.' The epic writer Döblin° provided an excellent criterion when he said

---

Goethe's Faust and Byron's Manfred: nineteenth-century plays that were based on earlier narrative works.

Döblin, Alexander Döblin (1878–1957), German novelist.

that with an epic work, as opposed to a dramatic, one can as it were take a pair of scissors and cut it into individual pieces, which remain fully capable of life.

This is no place to explain how the opposition of epic and dramatic lost its rigidity after having long been held to be irreconcilable. Let us just point out that the technical advances alone were enough to permit the stage to incorporate an element of narrative in its dramatic productions. The possibility of projections, the greater adaptability of the stage due to mechanization, the film, all completed the theatre's equipment, and did so at a point where the most important transactions between people could no longer be shown simply by personifying the motive forces or subjecting the characters to invisible metaphysical powers.

To make these transactions intelligible the environment in which the people lived had to be brought to bear in a big and 'significant' way.

This environment had of course been shown in the existing drama, but only as seen from the central figure's point of view, and not as an independent element. It was defined by the hero's reactions to it. It was seen as a storm can be seen when one sees the ships on a sheet of water unfolding their sails, and the sails filling out. In the epic theatre it was to appear standing on its own.

The stage began to tell a story. The narrator was no longer missing, along with the fourth wall. Not only did the background adopt an attitude to the events on the stage—by big screens recalling other simultaneous events elsewhere, by projecting documents which confirmed or contradicted what the characters said, by concrete and intelligible figures to accompany abstract conversations, by figures and sentences to support mimed transactions whose sense was unclear—but the actors too refrained from going over wholly into their role, remaining detached from the character they were playing and clearly inviting criticism of him.

The spectator was no longer in any way allowed to submit to an experience uncritically (and without practical consequences) by means of simple empathy with the characters in a play. The production took the subject-matter and the incidents shown and put them through a process of alienation: the alienation that is necessary to all understanding. When something seems 'the most obvious thing in the world' it means that any attempt to understand the world has been given up.

What is 'natural' must have the force of what is startling. This is the only way to expose the laws of cause and effect. People's activity must simultaneously be so and be capable of being different.

It was all a great change.

The dramatic theatre's spectator says: Yes, I have felt like that too—Just like me—It's only natural—It'll never change—The sufferings of this man appal me, because they are inescapable—That's great art; it all seems the most obvious thing in the world—I weep when they weep, I laugh when they laugh.

The epic theatre's spectator says: I'd never have thought it—That's not the way—That's extraordinary, hardly believable—It's got to stop—The sufferings of this man appal me, because they are unnecessary—That's great art: nothing obvious in it—I laugh when they weep, I weep when they laugh.

THE INSTRUCTIVE THEATRE

The stage began to be instructive.

Oil, inflation, war, social struggles, the family, religion, wheat, the meat market, all became subjects for theatrical representation. Choruses enlightened the spectator about facts unknown to him. Films showed a montage of events from all over the world. Projections added statistical material. And as the 'background' came to the front of the stage so people's activity was subjected to criticism. Right and wrong courses of action were shown. People were shown who knew what they were doing, and others who did not. The theatre became an affair for philosophers, but only for such philosophers as wished not just to explain the world but also to change it. So we had philosophy, and we had instruction. And where was the amusement in all that? Were they sending us back to school, teaching us to read and write? Were we supposed to pass exams, work for diplomas?

Generally there is felt to be a very sharp distinction between learning and amusing oneself. The first may be useful, but only the second is pleasant. So we have to defend the epic theatre against the suspicion that it is a highly disagreeable, humourless, indeed strenuous affair.

Well: all that can be said is that the contrast between learning and amusing oneself is not laid down by divine rule; it is not one that has always been and must continue to be.

Undoubtedly there is much that is tedious about the kind of learning familiar to us from school, from our professional training, etc. But it must be remembered under what conditions and to what end that takes place.

It is really a commercial transaction. Knowledge is just a commodity. It is acquired in order to be resold. All those who have grown out of going to school have to do their learning virtually in secret, for anyone who admits that he still has something to learn devalues himself as a man whose knowledge is inadequate. Moreover the usefulness of learning is very much limited by factors outside the learner's control. There is unemployment, for instance, against which no knowledge can protect one. There is the division of labour, which makes generalized knowledge unnecessary and impossible. Learning is often among the concerns of those whom no amount of concern will get any forwarder. There is not much knowledge that leads to power, but plenty of knowledge to which only power can lead.

Learning has a very different function for different social strata. There are strata who cannot imagine any improvement in conditions: they find the conditions good enough for them. Whatever happens to oil they will benefit from it. And: they feel the years beginning to tell. There can't be all that many years more. What is the point of learning a lot now? They have said their final word: a grunt. But there are also strata 'waiting their turn' who are discontented with conditions, have a vast interest in the practical side of learning, want at all costs to find out where they stand, and know that they are lost without learning; these are the best and keenest learners. Similar differences apply to countries and peoples. Thus the pleasure of learning depends on all sorts of things; but none the less there is such a thing as pleasurable learning, cheerful and militant learning.

If there were not such amusement to be had from learning the theatre's whole structure would unfit it for teaching.

Theatre remains theatre even when it is instructive theatre, and in so far as it is good theatre it will amuse.

THEATRE AND KNOWLEDGE

But what has knowledge got to do with art? We know that knowledge can be amusing, but not everything that is amusing belongs in the theatre.

I have often been told, when pointing out the invaluable services that modern knowledge and science, if properly applied, can perform for art and specially for the theatre, that art and knowledge are two estimable but wholly distinct fields of human activity. This is a fearful truism, of course, and it is as well to agree quickly that, like most truisms, it is perfectly true. Art and science work in quite different ways: agreed. But, bad as it may sound, I have to admit that I cannot get along as an artist without the use of one or two sciences. This may well arouse serious doubts as to my artistic capacities. People are used to seeing poets as unique and slightly unnatural beings who reveal with a truly godlike assurance things that other people can only recognize after much sweat and toil. It is naturally distasteful to have to admit that one does not belong to this select band. All the same, it must be admitted. It must at the same time be made clear that the scientific occupations just confessed to are not pardonable side interests, pursued on days off after a good week's work. We all know how Goethe was interested in natural history,

Schiller° in history: as a kind of hobby, it is charitable to assume. I have no wish promptly to accuse these two of having needed these sciences for their poetic activity; I am not trying to shelter behind them; but I must say that I do need the sciences, I have to admit, however, that I look askance at all sorts of people who I know do not operate on the level of scientific understanding: that is to say, who, sing as the birds sing, or as people imagine the birds to sing. I don't mean by that that I would reject a charming poem about the taste of fried fish or the delights of a boating party just because the writer had not studied gastronomy or navigation. But in my view the great and complicated things that go on in the world cannot be adequately recognized by people who do not use every possible aid to understanding.

Let us suppose that great passions or great events have to be shown which influence the fate of nations. The lust for power is nowadays held to be such a passion. Given that a poet 'feels' this lust and wants to have someone strive for power, how is he to show the exceedingly complicated machinery within which the struggle for power nowadays takes place? If his hero is a politician, how do politics work? If he is a business man, how does business work? And yet there are writers who find business and politics nothing like so passionately interesting as the individual's lust for power. How are they to acquire the necessary knowledge? They are scarcely likely to learn enough by going round and keeping their eyes open, though even then it is more than they would get by just rolling their eyes in an exalted frenzy. The foundation of a paper like the *Völkischer Beobachter*° or a business like Standard Oil is a pretty complicated affair, and such things cannot be conveyed just like that. One important field for the playwright is psychology. It is taken for granted that a poet, if not an ordinary man, must be able without further instruction to discover the motives that lead a man to commit murder; he must be able to give a picture of a murderer's mental state 'from within himself.' It is taken for granted that one only has to look inside oneself in such a case; and then there's always one's imagination. . . . There are various reasons why I can no longer surrender to this agreeable hope of getting a result quite so simply. I can no longer find in myself all those motives which the press or scientific reports show to have been observed in people. Like the average judge when pronouncing

---

Schiller, Friedrich von Schiller (1759–1805), German dramatist, poet, and historian, best known for his plays based on historical figures and events. *Völkischer Beobachter,* literally "The People's Observer," a German newspaper that was the mouthpiece of the Nazi party.

sentence, I cannot without further ado conjure up an adequate picture of a murderer's mental state. Modern psychology, from psychoanalysis to behaviourism, acquaints me with facts that lead me to judge the case quite differently, especially if I bear in mind the findings of sociology and do not overlook economics and history. You will say: but that's getting complicated. I have to answer that it *is* complicated. Even if you let yourself be convinced, and agree with me that a large slice of literature is exceedingly primitive, you may still ask with profound concern: won't an evening in such a theatre be a most alarming affair? The answer to that is: no.

Whatever knowledge is embodied in a piece of poetic writing has to be wholly transmuted into poetry. Its utilization fulfils the very pleasure that the poetic element provokes. If it does not at the same time fulfil that which is fulfilled by the scientific element, none the less in an age of great discoveries and inventions one must have a certain inclination to penetrate deeper into things—a desire to make the world controllable—if one is to be sure of enjoying its poetry.

IS THE EPIC THEATRE SOME KIND OF 'MORAL INSTITUTION'?

According to Friedrich Schiller the theatre is supposed to be a moral institution. In making this demand it hardly occurred to Schiller that by moralizing from the stage he might drive the audience out of the theatre. Audiences had no objection to moralizing in his day. It was only later that Friedrich Nietzsche° attacked him for blowing a moral trumpet. To Nietzsche any concern with morality was a depressing affair; to Schiller it seemed thoroughly enjoyable. He knew of nothing that could give greater amusement and satisfaction than the propagation of ideas. The bourgeoisie was setting about forming the ideas of the nation.

Putting one's house in order, patting oneself on the back, submitting one's account, is something highly agreeable. But describing the collapse of one's house, having pains in the back, paying one's account, is indeed a depressing affair, and that was how Friedrich Nietzsche saw things a century later. He was poorly disposed towards morality, and thus towards the previous Friedrich too.

The epic theatre was likewise often objected to as moralizing too much. Yet in the epic theatre moral arguments only took second place. Its aim was less to

---

Friedrich Nietzsche (1844–1900), German philosopher who envisioned a breed of "supermen" that would create a new society.

moralize than to observe. That is to say it observed, and then the thick end of the wedge followed: the story's moral. Of course we cannot pretend that we started our observations out of a pure passion for observing and without any more practical motive, only to be completely staggered by their results. Undoubtedly there were some painful discrepancies in our environment, circumstances that were barely tolerable, and this not merely on account of moral considerations. It is not only moral considerations that make hunger, cold and oppression hard to bear. Similarly the object of our inquiries was not just to arouse moral objections to such circumstances (even though they could easily be felt—though not by all the audience alike; such objections were seldom for instance felt by those who profited by the circumstances in question) but to discover means for their elimination. We were not in fact speaking in the name of morality but in that of the victims. These truly are two distinct matters, for the victims are often told that they ought to be contented with their lot, for moral reasons. Moralists of this sort see man as existing for morality, not morality for man. At least it should be possible to gather from the above to what degree and in what sense the epic theatre is a moral institution.

CAN EPIC THEATRE BE PLAYED ANYWHERE?

Stylistically speaking, there is nothing all that new about the epic theatre. Its expository character and its emphasis on virtuosity bring it close to the old Asiatic theatre. Didactic tendencies are to be found in the medieval mystery plays and the classical Spanish theatre, and also in the Jesuits.

These theatrical forms corresponded to particular trends of theirs and vanished with them. Similarly the modern epic theatre is linked to certain trends. It cannot by any means be practised universally. Most of the great nations today are not disposed to use the theatre for venting their problems. London, Paris, Tokyo and Rome maintain theirs for quite different purposes. Up to now favourable circumstances for an epic and didactic theatre have only been found in a few places and for a short period of time. In Berlin Fascism put a very definite stop to the development of such a theatre.

It demands not only a certain technological level but a powerful movement in society which is interested to see vital questions freely aired with a view to their solution, and can defend this interest against every contrary trend.

The epic theatre is the broadest and most far-reaching attempt at larger scale modern theatre, and it has all those immense difficulties to overcome that always confront the vital forces in the sphere of politics, philosophy, science and art.

No More Masterpieces

BY ANTONIN ARTAUD, 1938–1945

Antonin Artaud (1896–1949), an avant-garde poet, essayist, playwright, actor, director, theorist, and philosopher was born in France and fought briefly in the first world war before being sent home because of a mental disturbance that would plague him through much of his life. During the 1920s, he had an illustrious acting career in Paris, where he became associated with the Surrealist movement and founded the Alfred Jarry Theatre. During the 1930s and 40s, though he was in and out of mental asylums, he wrote on a wide range of visionary, artistic, religious, and psychiatric subjects, including his major theatrical work, The Theatre and Its Double, *an essay from which is reprinted below.*

One of the reasons for the asphyxiating atmosphere in which we live without possible escape or remedy—and in which we all share, even the most revolutionary among us—is our respect for what has been written, formulated, or painted, what has been given form, as if all expression were not at last exhausted, were not at a point where things must break apart if they are to start anew and begin fresh.

We must have done with this idea of masterpieces reserved for a self-styled elite and not understood by the general public; the mind has no such restricted districts as those so often used for clandestine sexual encounters.

Masterpieces of the past are good for the past: they are not good for us. We have the right to say what has been said and even what has not been said in a way that belongs to us, a way that is immediate and direct, corresponding to present modes of feeling, and understandable to everyone.

It is idiotic to reproach the masses for having no sense of the sublime, when the sublime is confused with one or another of its formal manifestations, which are moreover always defunct manifestations. And if for example a contemporary public does not understand *Oedipus Rex,* I shall make bold to say that it is the fault of *Oedipus Rex* and not of the public.

In *Oedipus Rex* there is the theme of incest and the idea that nature mocks at morality and that there are certain unspecified powers at large which we would do well to beware of, call them *destiny* or anything you choose.

There is in addition the presence of a plague epidemic which is a physical incarnation of these powers. But the whole in a manner and language that have lost all touch with the rude and epileptic rhythm of our time. Sophocles speaks grandly perhaps, but in a style that is no longer timely. His language is too refined for this age, it is as if he were speaking beside the point.

However, a public that shudders at train wrecks, that is familiar with earthquakes, plagues, revolutions, wars; that is sensitive to the disordered anguish of love, can be affected by all these grand notions and asks only to become aware of them, but on condition that it is addressed in its own language, and that its knowledge of these things does not come to it through adulterated trappings and speech that belong to extinct eras which will never live again.

Today as yesterday, the public is greedy for mystery: it asks only to become aware of the laws according to which destiny manifests itself, and to divine perhaps the secret of its apparitions.

Let us leave textual criticism to graduate students, formal criticism to esthetes, and recognize that what has been said is not still to be said; that an expression does not have the same value twice, does not live two lives; that all words, once spoken, are dead and function only at the moment when they are uttered, that a form, once it has served, cannot be used again and asks only to be replaced by another, and that the theater is the only place in the world where a gesture, once made, can never be made the same way twice.

If the public does not frequent our literary masterpieces, it is because those masterpieces are literary, that is to say, fixed; and fixed in forms that no longer respond to the needs of the time.

Far from blaming the public, we ought to blame the formal screen we interpose between ourselves and the public, and this new form of idolatry, the idolatry of fixed masterpieces which is one of the aspects of bourgeois conformism.

This conformism makes us confuse sublimity, ideas, and things with the forms they have taken in time and in our minds—in our snobbish, precious, aesthetic mentalities which the public does not understand.

How pointless in such matters to accuse the public of bad taste because it relishes insanities, so long as the public is not shown a valid spectacle; and I defy anyone to show me *here* a spectacle valid—valid in the supreme sense of the theater—since the last great romantic melodramas, i.e., since a hundred years ago.

The public, which takes the false for the true, has

the sense of the true and always responds to it when it is manifested. However it is not upon the stage that the true is to be sought nowadays, but in the street; and if the crowd in the street is offered an occasion to show its human dignity, it will always do so.

If people are out of the habit of going to the theater, if we have all finally come to think of theater as an inferior art, a means of popular distraction, and to use it as an outlet for our worst instincts, it is because we have learned too well what the theater has been, namely, falsehood and illusion. It is because we have been accustomed for four hundred years, that is since the Renaissance, to a purely descriptive and narrative theater—storytelling psychology; it is because every possible ingenuity has been exerted in bringing to life on the stage plausible but detached beings, with the spectacle on one side, the public on the other—and because the public is no longer shown anything but the mirror of itself.

Shakespeare himself is responsible for this aberration and decline, this disinterested idea of the theater which wishes a theatrical performance to leave the public intact, without setting off one image that will shake the organism to its foundations and leave an ineffaceable scar.

If, in Shakespeare, a man is sometimes preoccupied with what transcends him, it is always in order to determine the ultimate consequences of this preoccupation within him, i.e., psychology.

Psychology, which works relentlessly to reduce the unknown to the known, to the quotidian and the ordinary, is the cause of the theater's abasement and its fearful loss of energy, which seems to me to have reached its lowest point. And I think both the theater and we ourselves have had enough of psychology.

I believe furthermore that we can all agree on this matter sufficiently so that there is no need to descend to the repugnant level of the modern and French theater to condemn the theater of psychology.

Stories about money, worry over money, social careerism, the pangs of love unspoiled by altruism, sexuality sugar-coated with an eroticism that has lost its mystery have nothing to do with the theater, even if they do belong to psychology. These torments, seductions, and lusts before which we are nothing but Peeping Toms gratifying our cravings, tend to go bad, and their rot turns to revolution: we must take this into account.

But this is not our most serious concern.

If Shakespeare and his imitators have gradually insinuated the idea of art for art's sake, with art on one side and life on the other, we can rest on this feeble and lazy idea only as long as the life outside endures. But there are too many signs that everything that used to sustain our lives no longer does so, that we are all mad, desperate, and sick. And I call for *us* to react.

This idea of a detached art, of poetry as a charm which exists only to distract our leisure, is a decadent idea and an unmistakable symptom of our power to castrate.

Our literary admiration for Rimbaud,° Jarry,° Lautréamont,° and a few others, which has driven two men to suicide, but turned into café gossip for the rest, belongs to this idea of literary poetry, of detached art, of neutral spiritual activity *which* creates nothing and produces nothing; and I can bear witness that at the very moment when that kind of personal poetry which involves only the man who creates it and only at the moment he creates it broke out in its most abusive fashion, the theater was scorned more than ever before by poets who have never had the sense of direct and concerted action, nor of efficacity, nor of danger.

We must get rid of our superstitious valuation of texts and *written* poetry. Written poetry is worth reading once, and then should be destroyed. Let the dead poets make way for others. Then we might even come to see that it is our veneration for what has already been created, however beautiful and valid it may be, that petrifies us, deadens our responses, and prevents us from making contact with that underlying power, call it thought-energy, the life force, the determinism of change, lunar menses, or anything you like. Beneath the poetry of the texts, there is the actual poetry, without form and without text. And just as the efficacity of masks in the magic practices of certain tribes is exhausted—and these masks are no longer good for anything except museums—so the poetic efficacity of a text is exhausted; yet the poetry and the efficacity of the theater are exhausted least quickly of all, since they permit the *action* of what is gesticulated and pronounced, and which is never made the same way twice.

It is a question of knowing what we want. If we are prepared for war, plague, famine, and slaughter we do not even need to say so, we have only to continue as we are; continue behaving like snobs, rushing en masse to hear such and such a singer, to see such and such an admirable performance which never transcends the realm of art (and even the Russian ballet at the height of its splendor never transcended the realm of art), to marvel at such and such an exhibition of painting in which exciting shapes explode here and there but at random and without any genuine consciousness of the forces they could rouse.

Rimbaud, Arthur Rimbaud (1854–1891), French poet known for his dreamlike and hallucinatory verse. **Jarry,** Alfred Jarry (1873–1907), French author known for his pre-dadaist, pre-absurdist play *Ubu Roi* (King Ubu). **Lautréamont,** Comte de Lautréamont (Isidore Ducasse), 1846–1870. French poet and precursor of surrealism.

This empiricism, randomness, individualism, and anarchy must cease.

Enough of personal poems, benefitting those who create them much more than those who read them.

Once and for all, enough of this closed, egoistic, and personal art.

Our spiritual anarchy and intellectual disorder is a function of the anarchy of everything else—or rather, everything else is a function of this anarchy.

I am not one of those who believe that civilization has to change in order for the theater to change; but I do believe that the theater, utilized in the highest and most difficult sense possible, has the power to influence the aspect and formation of things: and the encounter upon the stage of two passionate manifestations, two living centers, two nervous magnetisms is something as entire, true, even decisive, as, in life, the encounter of one epidermis with another in a timeless debauchery

That is why I propose a theater of cruelty.—With this mania we all have for depreciating everything, as soon as I have said "cruelty," everybody will at once take it to mean "blood." But *"theater of cruelty"* means a theater difficult and cruel for myself first of all. And, on the level of performance, it is not the cruelty we can exercise upon each other by hacking at each other's bodies, carving up our personal anatomies, or, like Assyrian emperors, sending parcels of human ears, noses, or neatly detached nostrils through the mail, but the much more terrible and necessary cruelty which things can exercise against us. We are not free. And the sky can still fall on our heads. And the theater has been created to teach us that first of all.

Either we will be capable of returning by present-day means to this superior idea of poetry and poetry-through-theater which underlies the Myths told by the great ancient tragedians, capable once more of entertaining a religious idea of the theater (without meditation, useless contemplation, and vague dreams), capable of attaining awareness and a possession of certain dominant forces, of certain notions that control all others, and (since ideas, when they are effective, carry their energy with them) capable of recovering within ourselves those energies which ultimately create order and increase the value of life, or else we might as well abandon ourselves now, without protest, and recognize that we are no longer good for anything but disorder, famine, blood, war, and epidemics.

Either we restore all the arts to a central attitude and necessity, finding an analogy between a gesture made in painting or the theater, and a gesture made by lava in a volcanic explosion, or we must stop painting, babbling, writing, or doing whatever it is we do.

I propose to bring back into the theater this elementary magical idea, taken up by modern psychoanalysis, which consists in effecting a patient's cure by making him assume the apparent and exterior attitudes of the desired condition.

I propose to renounce our empiricism of imagery, in which the unconscious furnishes images at random, and which the poet arranges at random too, calling them poetic and hence hermetic images, as if the kind of trance that poetry provides did not have its reverberations throughout the whole sensibility, in every nerve, and as if poetry were some vague force whose movements were invariable.

I propose to return through the theater to an idea of the physical knowledge of images and the means of inducing trances, as in Chinese medicine which knows, over the entire extent of the human anatomy, at what points to puncture in order to regulate the subtlest functions.

Those who have forgotten the communicative power and magical mimesis of a gesture, the theater can reinstruct, because a gesture carries its energy with it, and there are still human beings in the theater to manifest the force of the gesture made.

To create art is to deprive a gesture of its reverberation in the organism, whereas this reverberation, if the gesture is made in the conditions and with the force required, incites the organism and, through it, the entire individuality, to take attitudes in harmony with the gesture.

The theater is the only place in the world, the last general means we still possess of directly affecting the organism and, in periods of neurosis and petty sensuality like the one in which we are immersed, of attacking this sensuality by physical means it cannot withstand.

If music affects snakes, it is not on account of the spiritual notions it offers them, but because snakes are long and coil their length upon the earth, because their bodies touch the earth at almost every point; and because the musical vibrations which are communicated to the earth affect them like a very subtle, very long massage; and I propose to treat the spectators like the snakecharmer's subjects and conduct them *by means of their organisms* to an apprehension of the subtlest notions.

At first by crude means, which will gradually be refined. These immediate crude means will hold their attention at the start.

That is why in the "theater of cruelty" the spectator is in the center and the spectacle surrounds him.

In this spectacle the sonorisation is constant: sounds, noises, cries are chosen first for their vibratory quality, then for what they represent.

Among these gradually refined means light is interposed in its turn. Light which is not created merely to add color or to brighten, and which brings its power, influence, suggestions with it. And the light of a green cavern does not sensually dispose the organism like the light of a windy day.

After sound and light there is action, and the dynamism of action: here the theater, far from copying life, puts itself whenever possible in communication with pure forces. And whether you accept or deny them, there is nevertheless a way of speaking which gives the name of "forces" to whatever brings to birth images of energy in the unconscious, and gratuitous crime on the surface.

A violent and concentrated action is a kind of lyricism: it summons up supernatural images, a bloodstream of images, a bleeding spurt of images in the poet's head and in the spectator's as well.

Whatever the conflicts that haunt the mind of a given period, I defy any spectator to whom such violent scenes will have transferred their blood, who will have felt in himself the transit of a superior action, who will have seen the extraordinary and essential movements of his thought illuminated in extraordinary deeds—the violence and blood having been placed at the service of the violence of the thought—I defy that spectator to give himself up, once outside the theater, to ideas of war, riot, and blatant murder.

So expressed, this idea seems dangerous and sophomoric. It will be claimed that example breeds example, that if the attitude of cure induces cure, the attitude of murder will induce murder. Everything depends upon the manner and the purity with which the thing is done. There is a risk. But let it not be forgotten that though a theatrical gesture is violent, it is disinterested; and that the theater teaches precisely the uselessness of the action which, once done, is not to be done, and the superior use of the state unused by the action and which, *restored*, produces a purification.

I propose then a theater in which violent physical images crush and hypnotize the sensibility of the spectator seized by the theater as by a whirlwind of higher forces.

A theater which, abandoning psychology, recounts the extraordinary, stages natural conflicts, natural and subtle forces, and presents itself first of all as an exceptional power of redirection. A theater that induces trance, as the dances of Dervishes induce trance, and that addresses itself to the organism by precise instruments, by the same means as those of certain tribal music cures which we admire on records but are incapable of originating among ourselves.

There is a risk involved, but in the present circumstances I believe it is a risk worth running. I do not believe we have managed to revitalize the world we live in, and I do not believe it is worth the trouble of clinging to; but I do propose something to get us out of our marasmus, instead of continuing to complain about it, and about the boredom, inertia, and stupidity of everything.

Tragedy and the Common Man

BY ARTHUR MILLER, 1949

Arthur Miller (1915–). For biographical details, see pp. 865–67.

In this age few tragedies are written. It has often been held that the lack is due to a paucity of heroes among us, or else that modern man has had the blood drawn out of his organs of belief by the skepticism of science, and the heroic attack on life cannot feed on an attitude of reserve and circumspection. For one reason or another, we are often held to be below tragedy—or tragedy above us. The inevitable conclusion is, of course, that the tragic mode is archaic, fit only for the very highly placed, the kings or the kingly, and where this admission is not made in so many words it is most often implied.

I believe that the common man is as apt a subject for tragedy in its highest sense as kings were. On the face of it this ought to be obvious in the light of modern psychiatry, which bases its analysis upon classic formulations, such as the Oedipus and Orestes complexes, for instances, which were enacted by royal beings, but which apply to everyone in similar emotional situations.

More simply, when the question of tragedy in art is not at issue, we never hesitate to attribute to the well-placed and the exalted the very same mental processes as the lowly. And finally, if the exaltation of tragic action were truly a property of the high-bred character alone, it is inconceivable that the mass of mankind should cherish tragedy above all other forms, let alone be capable of understanding it.

As a general rule, to which there may be exceptions unknown to me, I think the tragic feeling is evoked in us when we are in the presence of a character who is ready to lay down his life, if need be, to secure one thing—his sense of personal dignity. From Orestes to Hamlet, Medea to Macbeth, the underlying struggle is that of the individual attempting to gain his "rightful" position in his society.

Sometimes he is one who has been displaced from it, sometimes one who seeks to attain it for the first time, but the fateful wound from which the inevitable events spiral is the wound of indignity, and its dominant force is indignation. Tragedy, then, is the consequence of a man's total compulsion to evaluate himself justly.

In the sense of having been initiated by the hero himself, the tale always reveals what has been called his "tragic flaw," a failing that is not peculiar to grand or elevated characters. Nor is it necessarily a weakness. The flaw, or crack in the character, is really nothing— and need be nothing—but his inherent unwillingness to remain passive in the face of what he conceives to be a challenge to his dignity, his image of his rightful status. Only the passive, only those who accept their lot without active retaliation, are "flawless." Most of us are in that category.

But there are among us today, as there always have been, those who act against the scheme of things that degrades them, and in the process of action everything we have accepted out of fear or insensitivity or ignorance is shaken before us and examined, and from this total onslaught by an individual against the seemingly stable cosmos surrounding us—from this total examination of the "unchangeable" environment—comes the terror and the fear that is classically associated with tragedy.

More important, from this total questioning of what has previously been unquestioned, we learn. And such a process is not beyond the common man. In revolutions around the world, these past thirty years, he has demonstrated again and again this inner dynamic of all tragedy.

Insistence upon the rank of the tragic hero, or the so-called nobility of his character, is really but a clinging to the outward forms of tragedy. If rank or nobility of character was indispensable, then it would follow that the problems of those with rank were the particular problems of tragedy. But surely the right of one monarch to capture the domain from another no longer raises our passions, nor are our concepts of justice what they were to the mind of an Elizabethan king.

The quality in such plays that does shake us, however, derives from the underlying fear of being displaced, the disaster inherent in being torn away from our chosen image of what and who we are in this world. Among us today this fear is as strong, and per-haps stronger, than it ever was, In fact, it is the common man who knows this fear best.

Now, if it is true that tragedy is the consequence of a man's total compulsion to evaluate himself justly, his destruction in the attempt posits a wrong or an evil in his environment. And this is precisely the morality of tragedy and its lesson. The discovery of the moral law, which is what the enlightenment of tragedy consists of, is not the discovery of some abstract or metaphysical quantity.

The tragic right is a condition of life, a condition in which the human personality is able to flower and realize itself. The wrong is the condition which suppresses man, perverts the flowing out of his love and creative instinct. Tragedy enlightens—and it must, in that it points the heroic finger at the enemy of man's freedom. The thrust for freedom is the quality in tragedy which exalts. The revolutionary questioning of the stable environment is what terrifies. In no way is the common man debarred from such thoughts or such actions.

Seen in this light, our lack of tragedy may be partially accounted for by the turn which modern literature has taken toward the purely psychiatric view of life, or the purely sociological. If all our miseries, our indignities, are born and bred within our minds, then all action, let alone the heroic action, is obviously impossible.

And if society alone is responsible for the cramping of our lives, then the protagonist must be so pure and faultless as to force us to deny his validity as a character. From neither of these views can tragedy derive, simply because neither represents a balanced concept of life. Above all else, tragedy requires the finest appreciation by the writer of cause and effect.

No tragedy can therefore come about when its author fears to question absolutely everything, when he regards any institution, habit or custom as being either everlasting, immutable or inevitable. In the tragic view the need of man to wholly realize himself is the only fixed star, and whatever it is that hedges his nature and lowers it is ripe for attack and examination. Which is not to say that tragedy must preach revolution.

The Greeks could probe the very heavenly origin of their ways and return to confirm the rightness of laws. And Job could face God in anger, demanding his right and end in submission. But for a moment everything is in suspension, nothing is accepted, and in this stretching and tearing apart of the cosmos, in the very action of so doing, the character gains "size," the tragic stature which is spuriously attached to the royal or the highborn in our minds. The commonest of men may take on that stature to the extent of his willingness to throw all he has into the contest, the battle to secure his rightful place in his world.

There is a misconception of tragedy with which I have been struck in review after review, and in many conversations with writers and readers alike. It is the idea that tragedy is of necessity allied to pessimism. Even the dictionary says nothing more about the word than that it means a story with a sad or unhappy ending. This impression is so firmly fixed that I almost hesitate to claim that in truth tragedy implies more optimism in its author than does comedy, and that its final result ought to be the reinforcement of the onlooker's brightest opinions of the human animal.

For, if it is true to say that in essence the tragic hero is intent upon claiming his whole due as a personality, and if this struggle must be total and without reservation, then it automatically demonstrates the indestructible will of man to achieve his humanity.

The possibility of victory must be there in tragedy.

Where pathos rules, where pathos is finally derived, a character has fought a battle he could not possibly have won. The pathetic is achieved when the protagonist is, by virtue of his witlessness, his insensitivity or the very air he gives off, incapable of grappling with a much superior force.

Pathos truly is the mode for the pessimist. But tragedy requires a nicer balance between what is possible and what is impossible. And it is curious, although edifying, that the plays we revere, century after century, are the tragedies. In them, and in them alone, lies the belief—optimistic, if you will, in the perfectibility of man.

It is time, I think, that we who are without kings, took up this bright thread of our history and followed it to the only place it can possibly lead in our time—the heart and spirit of the average man.

The Theatre of the Absurd

BY MARTIN ESSLIN, 1961

Martin Esslin (1918–2002) was born in Vienna, immigrated to England in 1939, and eventually became head of the BBC Radio Drama Department until he immigrated to the United States in 1977, where he became a professor in the Drama Department at Stanford University until his retirement in 1991. A widely published critic, historian, and theorist of drama, Esslin edited an encyclopedia of world drama, and wrote book-length studies of Artaud, Brecht, and Pinter, as well as other works on drama and television. But he is best known for his groundbreaking study, Theater of the Absurd, *an excerpt from which is reprinted below, explaining the phrase he devised to define a major dramatic phenomenon of the mid-twentieth century.*

The reception of *Waiting for Godot* at San Quentin,° and the wide acclaim given to plays by Ionesco, Adamov, Pinter,° and others, testify that these plays, which are so often superciliously dismissed as nonsense or mystification, *have* something to say and *can* be understood. Most of the incomprehension with which plays of this type are still being received by crit-

---

Waiting for Godot at San Quentin, given by the San Francisco Actor's Workshop in 1957. *Ionesco . . . Pinter,* Eugene Ionesco (1912–), Arthur Adamov (1908–), Harold Pinter (1930–).

ics and theatrical reviewers, most of the bewilderment they have caused and to which they still give rise, come from the fact that they are part of a new, and still developing stage convention that has not yet been generally understood and has hardly ever been defined. Inevitably, plays written in this new convention will, when judged by the standards and criteria of another, be regarded as impertinent and outrageous impostures. If a good play must have a cleverly constructed story, these have no story or plot to speak of; if a good play is judged by subtlety of characterization and motivation, these are often without recognizable characters and present the audience with almost mechanical puppets; if a good play has to have a fully explained theme, which is neatly exposed and finally solved, these often have neither a beginning nor an end; if a good play is to hold the mirror up to nature and portray the manners and mannerisms of the age in finely observed sketches, these seem often to be reflections of dreams and nightmares; if a good play relies on witty repartee and pointed dialogue, these often consist of incoherent babblings.

But the plays we are concerned with here pursue ends quite different from those of the conventional play and therefore use quite different methods. They can be judged only by the standards of the Theatre of the Absurd which it is the purpose of this book to define and clarify.

It must be stressed, however, that the dramatists whose work is here discussed do not form part of any self-proclaimed or self-conscious school or movement. On the contrary, each of the writers in question is an individual who regards himself as a lone outsider, cut off and isolated in his private world. Each has his own personal approach to both subject-matter and forms his own roots, sources, and background. If they also, very clearly and in spite of themselves, have a good deal in common, it is because their work most sensitively mirrors and reflects the preoccupations and anxieties, the emotions and thinking of many of their contemporaries in the Western world.

This is not to say that their works are representative of mass attitudes. It is an oversimplification to assume that any age presents a homogeneous pattern. Ours being, more than most others, an age of transition, it displays a bewildering stratified picture: medieval beliefs still held and overlaid by eighteenth-century rationalism and mid-nineteenth-century Marxism rocked by sudden volcanic eruptions of prehistoric fanaticisms and primitive tribal cults. Each of these components of the cultural pattern of the age finds its own artistic expression. The Theatre of the Absurd, however, can be seen as the reflection of what seems to be the attitude most genuinely representative of our own time.

The hallmark of this attitude is its sense that the certitudes and unshakable basic assumptions of former ages have been swept away, that they have been tested and found wanting, that they have been discredited as cheap and somewhat childish illusions. The decline of religious faith was masked until the end of the Second World War by the substitute religions of faith in progress, nationalism, and various totalitarian fallacies. All this was shattered by the war. By 1942, Albert Camus° was calmly putting the question why, since life had lost all meaning, man should not seek escape in suicide. In one of the great, seminal heart-searchings of our time, *The Myth of Sisyphus,* Camus tried to diagnose the human situation in a world of shattered beliefs:

A world that can be explained by reasoning, however faulty, is a familiar world. But in a universe that is suddenly deprived of illusions and of light, man feels a stranger. His is an irremediable exile, because he is deprived of memories of a lost homeland as much as he lacks the hope of a promised land to come. This divorce between man and his life, the actor and his setting, truly constitutes the feeling of Absurdity.°

"Absurd" originally means "out of harmony," in a musical context. Hence its dictionary definition: "out of harmony with reason or propriety; incongruous, unreasonable, illogical." In common usage, "absurd" may simply mean "ridiculous," but this is not the sense in which Camus uses the word, and in which it is used when we speak of the Theatre of the Absurd. In an essay on Kafka, Ionesco defined his understanding of the term as follows: "Absurd is that which is devoid of purpose.... Cut from his religious, metaphysical, and transcendental roots, man is lost; all his actions become senseless, absurd, useless."°

This sense of metaphysical anguish at the absurdity of the human condition is, broadly speaking, the theme of the plays of Beckett,° Adamov, Ionesco, Genet,° and the other writers discussed in this book. But it is not merely the subject matter that defines what is here called the Theatre of the Absurd. A similar sense of the senselessness of life, of the inevitable devaluation of ideals, purity, and purpose, is also the theme of much of the work of dramatists like Giraudoux, Anouilh, Salacrou, Sartre,° and Camus himself. Yet these writers differ from the dramatists of the Absurd in an important respect: they present their sense of the irrationality of the human condition in the form of highly lucid and logically constructed reasoning, while the Theatre of the Absurd strives to express its sense of the senselessness of the human condition and the inadequacy of the rational approach by the open abandonment of rational devices and discursive thought. While Sartre or Camus express the new content in the old convention, the Theatre of the Absurd goes a step further in trying to achieve a unity between its basic assumptions and the form in which these are expressed. In some senses, the *theatre* of Sartre and Camus is less adequate as an expression of the *philosophy* of Sartre and Camus—in artistic, as distinct from philosophic, terms—than the Theatre of the Absurd.

If Camus argued that in our disillusioned age the world has ceased to make sense, he did so in the elegantly rationalistic and discursive style of an eighteenth-century moralist, in well-constructed and polished plays. If Sartre argues that existence comes before essence and that human personality can be reduced to pure potentiality and the freedom to choose itself

---

Albert Camus, French existentialist playwright and author (1913–1960). *"A world . . . ," from Albert Camus's Le Mythe de Sisyphe* (Paris: Gallimard, 1942), p. 18 [Esslin's note].

"Absurd is . . . ," from Eugene Ionesco's "Dans les armes de la ville," Cahiers de la Compagnie Madeleine Renaud-Jean-Louis Barrault, Paris, no. 20, October 1957 [Esslin's note]. **Beckett,** Samuel Beckett, Irish existentialist playwright and author (1906–). **Genet,** Jean Genet, French avant-garde dramatist (1909–). **Giraudoux . . . Sartre,** Jean Giraudoux (1882–1944), Jean Anouilh (1910–), Armand Salacrou (1899–), Jean-Paul Sartre (1905–).

anew at any moment, he presents his ideas in plays based on brilliantly drawn characters who remain wholly consistent and thus reflect the old convention that each human being has a core of immutable, unchanging essence—in fact, an immortal soul. And the beautiful phrasing and argumentative brilliance of both Sartre and Camus in their relentless probing still, by implication, proclaim a tacit conviction that logical discourse can offer valid solutions, that the analysis of language will lead to the uncovering of basic concepts—Platonic ideas.

This is an inner contradiction that the dramatists of the Absurd are trying, by instinct and intuition rather than by conscious effort, to overcome and resolve. The Theatre of the Absurd has renounced arguing *about* the absurdity of the human condition; it merely *presents* it in being—that is, in terms of concrete stage images. This is the difference between the approach of the philosopher and that of the poet; the difference, to take an example from another sphere, between the *idea* of God in the works of Thomas Aquinas or Spinoza and the *intuition* of God in those of St. John of the Cross or Meister Eckhart—the difference between theory and experience.

It is this striving for an integration between the subject-matter and the form in which it is expressed that separates the Theatre of the Absurd from the Existentialist theatre.

It must also be distinguished from another important, and parallel, trend in the contemporary French theatre, which is equally preoccupied with the absurdity and uncertainty of the human condition; the "poetic avant-garde" theatre of dramatists like Michel de Ghelderode,° Jacques Audiberti,° Georges Neveux,° and, in the younger generation, Georges Schehadé,° Henri Pickette,° and Jean Vauthier,° to name only some of its most important exponents. This is an even more difficult dividing line to draw, for the two approaches overlap a good deal. The "poetic avant-garde" relies on fantasy and dream reality as much as the Theatre of the Absurd does; it also disregards such traditional axioms as that of the basic unity and consistency of each character or the need for a plot. Yet basically the "poetic avant-garde" represents a different mood; it is more lyrical, and far less violent and grotesque. Even more important is its different attitude toward language: the "poetic avant-garde" relies to a far greater extent on consciously "poetic" speech; it aspires to plays that are in effect poems, images composed of a rich web of verbal associations.

The Theatre of the Absurd, on the other hand, tends toward a radical devaluation of language, toward a poetry that is to emerge from the concrete and objectified images of the stage itself. The element of language still plays an important part in this conception, but what *happens* on the stage transcends, and often contradicts, the *words* spoken by the characters. In Ionesco's *The Chairs,* for example, the poetic content of a powerfully poetic play does not lie in the banal words that are uttered but in the fact that they are spoken to an ever-growing number of empty chairs.

Michel de Ghelderode (1898–1962). *Jacques Audiberti* (1899–1965). *Georges Neveux* (1900–). *Georges Schehadé* (1910–). *Henri Pichette* (1923–). *Jean Vauthier* (1910–).

What Is Black Theater?

**BY AMIRI BARAKA, INTERVIEWED
BY MIKE COLEMAN, 1971**

Amiri Baraka (1934–). For biographical details, see pp. 1083–85.

COLEMAN: My first question is, what is Black Theater?

BARAKA: Black Theater actually deals with the lives of Black people. It is a theater that actually functions to liberate Black people. It is a theater that will commit Black people to their own liberation and instruct them about what they should do and what they should be doing. It will involve them emotionally. It will also, hopefully, involve them programmatically in their liberation and should not only be utilizing the so-called Black lifestyle or the lifestyle of African people in America, but it should also be an act of liberation. Because you can show the lives of "Negroes" doesn't have anything to do with my definition of Black Theater. Black Theater has to be making a dynamic statement and be of itself an act of liberation.

COLEMAN: How can the community better understand it?

BARAKA: It is up to the so-called artists, artists/nationalists, to see that the theater is totally in tune with the people themselves. There can not be any separation because the artists themselves must be in tune first. Separation is usually caused by the fact that the artist is imposing an inorganic form on the people.

Theater should be as necessary to the people as anything else. For example, the people feel a lot of the music on the soul stations is necessary to themselves. They feel that they could not really conduct their lives correctly without it. Although we know a lot of it is poison—poisonous content—still, this is the point that we must arrive at, where the theater is as organic a part of the community as anything else and that the people need it because it is *in* the community. What he (the uncommitted artist) does is always outside the community, even though the theater may be physically in the Black community. If the concerns are not the same, it is still an alien kind of thing.

COLEMAN: As one of the leading black playwrights, what do you feel is the duty of the black playwright?

BARAKA: The duty of all Black people is to liberate themselves, to see that eventually Black people have political, economic, and social self-determination; that we become a politically powerful nation of people. This is the role of all Black men and women; to create a conscious people. And no matter how you are supposed to be doing it, it is supposed to be in tune with the totality of the struggle. There is no other road that we have except political liberation. Every act that we commit ourselves to should be about that.

COLEMAN: Where would you draw the line between Black Theater and show business?

BARAKA: Show Business is just that—show for business; you are making money, pure and simple. I am not saying that Black Theater should not be about making money. I wish that Black Theater could make money because, if it could, the community itself could make money; if the community could make money—in terms of its total cooperative use of it—this is what needs to be happening. The very fact that Black Theater, *Black Theater,* can not make money is because it has not systematized, formalized itself enough to utilize the resources of the community such as they are already.

When you say Show Biz, you usually mean materialistic, commercial sort of things as the goal. The intention is purely commerce, and it is usually dealing with the unconscious and providing them with something to keep them unconscious. Show Biz deals with the maintenance of unconsciousness.

Black Theater should be providing consciousness. Show Biz does not do anything to raise the level of consciousness. It does quite the contrary; it is antithetical to consciousness. Show Biz can exist right within the system. We are talking about theater that is part of a new system, part of a Black system.

COLEMAN: This theater that you speak of, do you see any room in it for critics? Will this theater, in the new system, produce theater critics like those that are produced in the Western sense?

BARAKA: The critic is all right if he shares the same value system as the artist.

When we say value system, we mean the morality that is supposed to inform and animate the work. If it does not hold with that, if it is not close to that value system, then those of us who hold with that value system can make criticism on that. But what is happening is that you have a critic who is practicing a totally different set of values. Usually what he is criticizing you on is your values and not on your technical capacity to exercise in a particular discipline. He is criticizing your values.

The white boy is usually criticizing you because you do not hold white values. Also white-minded Negro critics criticize you because you are not holding with white values. But with people who are in tune with the same value system, I think that honest criticism can be made in terms of how closely you are in tune with the particular value system, if we both ostensibly share the same values. If we create the Black Theater, which is no more than an extention of the Black nation, which practices a value system that is legitimized by that nation, then criticism must be made dealing with how far away from that value system a particular work of art may be. For instance, if we celebrate unity—*umoja*, the first principle of the value system—and say a work of a particular so-called Black artist raises disunity, then it seems to me criticism should be made on that.

If we are talking about unity and collectivity, and certain works by certain Africans in America celebrate individualism, then they should be criticized for that by the nation's artists in order to raise their consciousness to where they are in tune with unity and in tune with cooperative or collective work and responsibility, or cooperative economics, and so forth. The critic now usually means somebody in a totally alien value system, who is admonishing you because you are not white or are not in that value system.

COLEMAN: In your recently published play *Jello,* published by Third World Press, the prologue is a statement on the Negro Theater pimp. Could you give me an example of what would be considered a Negro Theater pimp?

BARAKA: I call Negro Theater a pimp because of the thrusts made by nationalists, because we have talked about Black Theater and we must have a Black Theater and Black Art. What the white boy did was to go to the integrationist Negro and put him in the spotlight as the Black artist so that, ostensibly, he was taking the pressure off.

We are talking about Black Theater, and the white boy creates the Negro Ensemble Company° as Black Theater, when actually it is a Negro Theater in the village, when actually people who were talking about Black art got out of the village because they saw the contradiction in trying to do Black Theater in the white community.

But what the white boy does is to utilize the integrationist as *the* Black face, when actually the so-called integrationist is carrying the same value system as the white boy. So that you get white theater in Black face. You can see it in the arts all the time, but not only in the arts. In politics, you say, "Black," and they will raise up a Negro who will say, "Black is invalid."

The white boy has actually recontrolled the theater in places like New York, just by restructuring it based on his approval and opinion. For instance, he sets up the Negro Ensemble Company and Charles Gordone° and Lonne Elder° and Douglas Turner Ward° by giving out awards and giving out grants. You have a blood who wins the Pulitzer Prize so, in terms of America, that is supposed to be the most honored Negro playwright, hence the most valuable one. Then you give somebody else under him, who might be a little more militant, you give him fewer awards. In other words, that is the next most valuable playwright. You go on down the line. What the white boy has done is recreated a Negro Theater at the same time saying, "Black."

Negro Ensemble Company, a theater company, created in 1965 by black actors and dramatists. *Charles Gordone* (1925–1995), black actor, playwright, and educator. *Lonne Elder* (1926–1996), black playwright. *Douglas Turner Ward* (1930–), black actor and cofounder of Negro Ensemble Company.

What he has done is recreate a Negro Theater structure which is dependent upon him just as it always was—it is not different.

COLEMAN: What definite changes will Black Theater have to undergo in order to improve its ability to communicate with the people?

BARAKA: First of all, the people who are dealing in theater have to understand that the theater (or the arts) has to be a total concept, that it can not exist just as art "separated from the need to develop institutions," that the Black artist must be engaged in creating institutions so that his art will be an organic manifestation of the community's need to develop itself; so that the Black Theater is an economic institution, it is a political institution, it is a creative institution, it is a religious institution, it is a place where social organization can be taught. It is not just artists who get together and perform and then go off and live in a totally different way. It has to be the creative aspect of the nationalist's lifestyle, or the nationalist's thrust for complete self-determination.

The people who are interested in creating Black art have got to come together and begin to create institutions, city institutions, state institutions, national institutions, and deal in such a way that they are not totally dependent on white people's approval and, finally, white people's money. We have got to create institutions that are not just based on receiving grants; institutions that can deal with the economy that is in the community, that talk to the needs of the community, that *actually* talk to the needs of the community. We need plays to be dealing with Urban Renewal and plays to be solving the problems of the community, or offering solutions, and not plays that are always talking from some kind of liberal "artistic" vantage point that do not take any stand on anything. The playwright is not supposed to be the invisible man.

Ten Golden Rules for Playwrights

BY MARSHA NORMAN, 1985

Marsha Norman (1947–). For biographical details, see pp. 1307–9.

Budding playwrights often write to ask me advice on getting started—and succeeding—in writing plays. The following are a few basics that I hope aspiring playwrights will find helpful.
                                                                    —M. N.

1. Read at least four hours every day, and don't let anybody ask you what you're doing just sitting there reading.
2. Don't write about your present life. You don't have a clue what it's about yet. Write about your past. Write about something that terrified you, something you *still* think is unfair, something that

you have not been able to forget in all the time that's passed since it happened.

3. Don't write in order to tell the audience how smart you are. The audience is not the least bit interested in the playwright. The audience only wants to know about the characters. If the audience begins to suspect that the thing onstage was actually written by some other person, they're going to quit listening. So keep yourself out of it!

4. If you have characters you cannot write fairly, cut them out. Grudges have no place in the theatre. Nobody cares about your grudges but you, and you are not enough to fill a house.

5. There must be one central character. One. Everybody write that down. Just one. And he or she must want something. And by the end of the play, he or she must either get it or not. Period. No exceptions.

6. You must tell the audience right away what is at stake in the evening, i.e. how they know when they can go home. They are, in a sense, the jury. You present the evidence, and then they say whether it seems true to them. If it does, it will run, because they will tell all their friends to come see this true thing, God bless them. If it does not seem true to them, try to find out why and don't do it any more.

7. If, while you are writing, thoughts of critics, audience members or family members occur to you, stop writing and go read until you have successfully forgotten them.

8. Don't talk about your play while you are writing it. Good plays are always the product of a single vision, a single point of view. Your friends will be helpful later, after the play's direction is established. A play is one thing you can get too much help with. If you must break this rule, try not to say what you have learned by talking. Or just let other people talk and you listen. Don't talk the play away.

9. Keep pads of paper near all your chairs. You will be in your chairs a good bit (see Rule 1), and you will have thoughts for your play. Write them down. But don't get up from reading to do it. Go right back to the reading once the thoughts are on the paper.

10. Never go to your typewriter until you know what that first sentence is that day. It is definitely unhealthy to sit in front of a silent typewriter for any length of time. If, after you have typed the first sentence, you can't think of a second one, go read. There is only one good reason to write a play, and that is that there is no other way to take care of it, whatever it is. There are too many made-up plays being written these days. So if it doesn't spill out faster than you can write it, don't write it at all. Or write about something that does spill out. Spilling out is what the theatre is about. Writing is for novels.

Tradition and the Individual Talent

BY SUZAN-LORI PARKS, 1999

Suzan-Lori Parks (1964–). For biographical details, see pp. 1621–23.

Three traditions are at work simultaneously inside each one of us: The Great Tradition, the Personal Tradition, and the Tradition of the Next New Thing. These three traditions work to shape us as we live our lives and work our jobs and raise our children and comfort our friends and create our art. While each is separate and distinct, one Tradition does not exist in isolation; never one without the others. Each tradition always has the sound of the others within its earshot, the color of the others within its light, the smell of the others within its own intoxicating scent. What I am writing about here is how these three traditions work within us, how they help and hinder our art making, and specifically, since I am a writer, how they help and hinder our writing. They are as natural to life as breathing and, like the breath, deserve some attention.

The Great Tradition is the tradition of the past, those millions of great writers and storysmiths all over the world throughout the ages, weaving their tales and enthralling their audiences. Some met with success in their own lifetimes, some not until long after their own deaths. Some were ridiculed and revered later, some revered then ridiculed later. However they were treated and whatever color or gender they happened to have been, God bless them, they're dead. But they haunt us, Writers, Scholar-Critics, Theater and Literary Professionals all. Their books fill the shelves of our stores and libraries; we writers read their words often when we do not have the courage to write our own. We talk about their writing, love their words, their plots, their characters, pilfer their turns of phrases, sometimes wishing we were them, those great dead writers.

Each artist, regardless of medium or genre, who has created before us should be of use. We each have a responsibility to read and see and hear as much as we can. One year a writer may find a certain style of writing most helpful and inspiring, the next year she will undoubtedly be embracing other styles and forsaking those she once found so necessary. Not to worry. What is important is that, as we work to develop our artistic muscles, we should embrace the Great Tradition warmly and thoroughly, reading Mr. Aristotle and Mr. Soyinka, enjoying Ms. Stein° along with Mr. Williams,° immersing ourselves in Mr. Shakespeare as well as Ms. Shange.° And cross-fertilize (or "cross-train," as they call it these days—there are more athletes today than farmers): novelists and those in the novel corner read the poets and the playwrights, playwrights and theater professionals read the novelists, and so on. Everyone, listen to the music! Mr. J. S. Bach and Ms. E. Fitzgerald° and countless others can teach us as much about phrasing, rhythm, rhyme, and the breath as Mr. Euripides can. No need to snub a writer because she is not similar to you in color, gender, or age: there is no such thing as an "old white fart," just as there is no such thing as a "marginal colored writer." Writing styled differently from my own can teach me too: there is no need to wrinkle my nose at a "kitchen-sink drama" or a potboiler novel just because its lines seem far from mine.

The Great Tradition is an enormous sledgehammer that comes with very few operating instructions. Many writers use the hammer incorrectly—grasping it firmly by the handle (we always get the first step right) and then—horror—hitting ourselves over the head with it. Or as a student of mine said once, "I don't write as well as Dostoyevsky, so what's the use?" The use! Literature has inside of it what was inside its creators, which means that literature holds all three traditions, Great, Personal, and Next New Thing. Inside every great work of literature, inside every theatrical production that has moved and amazed us, there we all were and are, conceived within its every line and gesture, as part of the Next New Thing. The Great Tradition is like your great-grandmother who was born with the seed

---

Ms. Stein, Gertrude Stein (1874–1946), avant garde American author. *Mr. Williams,* William Carlos Williams (1883–1963), major American poet. *Ms. Shange,* Ntozake Shange (1948–), African American dramatist and educator. *Mrs. E. Fitzgerald:* Ella Fitzgerald (1918–1996), African American jazz singer.

for you deep inside her. Be a John Henry° with the sledgehammer, build a railroad.

The Personal Tradition (a.k.a. the Individual Talent) springs from the writer's own life story, the sum of all her years on earth (through all her incarnations). The people she has seen, and not seen, and seen in her head, and all the things she has heard and felt, and all the things she has not heard and felt, everything she has ever done, longed to do, or has never done or longed for, the smells, the psychic experiences, all this is grist for the writer's personal mill.

The writer is alive, the time is now. What should she write? The writer writes what interests her. There is a rule that one should write only about "what one knows," which is often interpreted to mean that, if the writer has never been married, but has just broken up with her beau, broken beauing, and not marriage, is the suitable subject for her. Well. We "know" much more than our conscious minds think we know. We also have a gut and a reptilian brain, right at the axis, the gateway to the spine, oh, the grand knowing spine, the original information superhighway. The spine knows about all kinds of things, like back when the writer was little and had gills, so write about fish if that's where the gut takes you. There is no need to let a "lack" of personal experience keep the writing unwritten. There is a truth that undercurrents most writing, regardless of situation or subject matter. While there are many fine poets who fought a duel a day, many playwrights who slept with all the men in the state of Texas, many novelists who rode motorcycles helmetless at high speeds, remember too that Phillis Wheatley° was a slave, Anton Chekhov worked as a simple country doctor, and Marcel Proust and Emily Dickinson both hardly ever went out of the house.

So the writer writes a novel, or a play, or a bundle of poems and she is hardworking and smart enough to primarily associate with people whom she respects, and people who in turn respect her, and she is not in a rush to show her work to people whose only good point is that they may advance her career; rather, she shows her work mostly to people who care about her and have some intelligence. She may attend a specialized writing program and get a writing degree, but this is not necessary. And a degree never ensures anything. The writer works hard for several years and before long she has carved out her literary niche, carved it out of solid rock, and has what the world is beginning to refer to as a "body of work."

John Henry: 19th century slave and legendary hero of "The Steel Driver's Ballad." *Phillis Wheatley:* First African American to be published (1753–1784).

Now comes the second part of the Personal Tradition, the fruit of the Individual Talent: the writer's very own Body of Work. The Body of Work (let's call it "BOW," as in "Bow Wow Wow!") is as difficult to navigate as the literature of the Great Tradition. The writer is here now. Behind her, the succulent fruit of her talent—spanning fifty years or five—with all its accolades and maybe some cash and, yes, her public, those people who have come to know her BOW. Some of them adore her, some of them may not like her so much, but that doesn't matter. What matters is that she has a body of work and a public, and her New Work is being written. With any luck her public will surround her new work and look at it and read it and love and revere or hate and despise her all the more; yeah, they will come to know the writer all the more, that is what the writer's hopes are for the work that is growing inside her right now.

And say the writer's name is X.

And her Body of Work is referred to as "Xish," or better yet, "Xian." In write-ups in newspapers and in scholarly journals, in the mouths of her public, theater professionals, scholar-critics, editors, and fans, there is forming an idea of the kind of work that Miss X writes. "Do your thing so that I may know you," said Thoreau, and there is Miss X working and slaving and creating an "Xian use of language" or an "Xian type of character development." And her public is getting to know her work, and her public is thinking of X in terms of Y: The literature of Miss X in terms of the Great Tradition; the writings of Miss X alongside the writings of her contemporaries Mr. P and Ms. Q. And Miss X is invited to speak at conferences and expound the essentials of her Xian style, and her public studies her work and spreads the words unto the masses and her public grows, and people she does not know, know her and maybe even some stranger recognizes her on the street from the photo on her book jacket. The literary movement Miss X has helped to create is well under way. And she is on her way home to write, and she gets home and gets writing only to discover that her new writing doesn't seem to be "Xish" and doesn't seem to be "Xian."

Or as someone once told me, "*Venus* isn't really a Suzan-Lori Parks play." To which I responded: "There isn't any such thing as a Suzan-Lori Parks play."

What I mean is this. I don't discount the plays I've written but I do realize that I am growing and changing as I grow. Once Miss X starts thinking that she can/should/must only write Xian literature and anything that is not clearly Xian is a betrayal to the great Xian tradition, or a slap in the face to the traditions of all those who have kindly accepted Miss X into their folds—once Miss X buys into the existence of an Xian style of writing and once that purchase keeps her simply and stupidly repeating her last best hit, well, then

Miss X gets really stinky—no matter in what genre she writes or in what camp she parks, naturalists, realists, avant-gardists, or experimentalists. As a writer know that your work flows from the river of your spirit, your own private Mississippi. Get out of the way.

But the writer is also probably hearing the voices of critics, actors, editors, producers, dramaturgs, literary agents, parents, teachers, publishers, directors, fans—those people who can help the career along or squash it flat. They want the writer to listen to them, they tell the writer what to write, they tell the writer how to write. We should be careful who we listen to. There are very few people capable of giving a writer honest-to-god good feedback. We must learn to think for ourselves. For feedback on early drafts, I listen to my gut and then to my very close friends—people who care more about me than about any literature I may create, people who will continue to support me whether I take or forsake their advice—real friends. I don't have readings of my plays before I have a good idea of what the play is. Sometimes artistic directors will plan a reading when they hear the writer has completed a first draft. Appreciate their enthusiasm but the writer needn't air her work until she is ready. There are writers who enjoy thrashing out their plays in the workshop process. I do most of my writing at home, on my own. This has made me slightly unpopular on the workshop circuit.

The Writer's Body of Work can in times of great despair give her courage; yes, she can do it because she looks to her BOW and knows that she has done it. But she need not stick to what worked just because it worked once. Often a writer becomes terrified when her new work does not bear an easy resemblance to her work of old. She is afraid she is losing her voice and tosses out the new writing or changes it, forcing it into the old shape, thinking she is keeping her voice intact. The writer's voice is always inside her. With proper care and hard work, her voice may grow and change, but she needn't fear—she will never lose it.

Word is that young writers are experimental and then, as the writer grows up, she grows more conventional. Some writers, hungry for wider acceptance, do force their Talent into more conventional shapes, while other writers, not wanting to follow the Individual Talent wherever it leads, dig in their heels and take up permanent residence in their old camps. Both trying to write the next Broadway hit will not listening to the voice that wants to write that small, challenging downtown play, and steadfastly replowing those experimental fields, resisting all the new growth, lopping off the heads of flowers because one only grows corn, are dead ways of living, horrid dead ends of writing.

The Tradition of the Next New Thing. Like the Ghost of Christmas Future, or the Holy Spirit, this is the fun one and the frightening one; this is the shapeless one and the one that lights the way. With the tradition of the Next New Thing we are looking into a future we see in our mind's eye, in the faces of children, a future that's held in the past and present too but, for the most part, lives in Tomorrow—an actual, simple dawning of the day, which may or may not happen. It is an interest in this Tomorrow, and a love for it, that moves the writer to send things out, from the pages, futureward. Part of the joy of reading Virginia Woolf's diaries is that, as she wonders, "Who will read this?" she is imagining her future readers; with her words she conceives each one of us.

The Tradition of the Next New Thing can trip up the writer if she puts the cart before the horse, if she tries to second-guess the future, evaluating her work in the minds of the unborn. The future, and the writer's place in it, will take care of itself. The upside is that being forgotten isn't as painful as being ignored and, whether forgotten or ignored, there will very likely be some shining scholar to resurrect all worthy writers. In the future, if there is no shining scholar riding to the rescue, not to worry because we will all be dead and on to other things.

The Future. Worst-case scenario: a world that only allows sports, TV, sex shows, and politics. The Future Folk may not believe in literature and may not see the need to; literature may go the way of God—into amnesia. Best-case scenario (?): Artists rule the world (but will this make for a better art scene and a better world for writers????—think about it). Middle-of-the-road scenario: it is much like it is today, it is much like it has

been for hundreds of years—writing is hard work, quality writing rises to the surface along with some crap writing; some crap writing falls along the wayside, along with some quality writing. The future may be a theaterless one, the future may be one with a theater on every corner! What is our greatest fear? That we will be forgotten? That fiction will be outlawed in favor of the tabloid true story? That future generations will be stupid? That no one will read? There are some of us who have become fierce public advocates, fighting to ensure the existence of theater and literature for the future. One could take to the streets, overthrow the government, hold the corporate executives ransom for more money for the arts. But this course of action cannot ensure the future. Look at the Russian Revolution, look at the Berlin Wall. Tastes change, minds change, sensibilities change; this change is frightening and this change is also a part of life.

At this very moment I am writing and riding. Riding the subway home from a library in Harlem where I work with a bunch of schoolkids. Today they gave me an impromptu "present": an improvised historical theater piece involving Rosa Parks° and the back of the bus. Wow.

While we have a responsibility to the Great Tradition and our Personal Tradition, our greatest responsibility may be to the future, the Tradition of the Next New Thing. Our work conceives it. We are who they will know. They will turn to us for solace, humor, guidance, and grace. A great piece of writing is a revolutionary act. Do your best work and the rest will follow.

Rosa Parks, an African American woman from Birmingham, Alabama, whose refusal in December 1955 to give up her seat to a white man in a segregated bus ignited a bus boycott by Martin Luther King that eventually led to the end of institutionalized segregation in the South.

APPENDIX A
Analyzing a Play: Close Reading for Writing

Writing about a play, like reading a play, requires close attention to the words in the text—both in the stage directions and in the dialogue. The dialogue is especially important not only because it contains the fundamental source of drama, both on stage and on the page, but also because it constitutes a basic source of information for discovering, developing, and documenting any thoughts you have about any aspect of the play. While a playwright can offer interpretative comments in stage directions, the playwright's voice is never heard directly on stage. Instead, the dialogue is the primary means by which a play implies the total makeup of its imaginative world and describes the behavior of all the characters who populate that world. So, the more closely you examine the dialogue, the more ideas you will discover to write about and the more specific material you will have readily available to support your ideas when you begin to write. In the following section, we show how close reading and annotating is the preliminary "research" for any kind of writing about drama, whether that writing focuses on characters or scenes, in print or in production. We then discuss several different kinds of writing that can be developed from the process of questioning, analyzing, and annotating.

Analyzing and Annotating Dialogue

Whenever you annotate a passage of dialogue, the best way to proceed is by using a basic method of inquiry and discovery—that is, by asking yourself a series of key questions and jotting down your answers on a notepad, in a computer file, or in the margin next to the dialogue. These notes and annotations together with the dialogue become major source material for your writing.

What sections of the play might you choose for annotation? The obvious answer is "All of them" because the more information you gather, the more issues will present themselves as possible topics. Still, if you are trying to decide where to focus your attention first, we offer some suggestions. Opening sequences are often important because from the play's first moments the playwright sends signals about the characters and the world they inhabit. The first entrance of a major character is crucial because the changes that a character undergoes are measured against those first impressions. In addition to looking at scenes that are obviously central, it is often helpful to look carefully at scenes that at first glance might seem unimportant or even irrelevant. And if a scene creates problems for you and you find yourself asking, "What's going on here?" or "Why is this scene in the play?" you will want to work carefully with the scene so that its meaning becomes clear.

Once you've chosen a section of the play to annotate, you might ask the following questions.

- What happens during this dialogue and as a result of this dialogue?
- What does this passage reveal about the inner life and motives of each character?

- What does it reveal about the relationships of the characters to each other?
- What does it reveal about the plot or about any of the circumstances contributing to the complication or resolution of the plot?
- What are the most notable moments or statements in the passage?
- What implicit or unspoken matters are most important in the passage?

In addition to these questions, which focus on the imaginative world of the play, there are also questions pertaining to the play as a work meant to be acted and produced in a theater.

- How might each line be performed?
- What facial expressions, physical gestures, or bodily movements are implied by the dialogue?
- What props or set pieces are explicitly or implicitly called for in the dialogue?
- What vocal inflections or tone of voice does a line suggest?
- Where might the characters pause in delivering their lines?
- Where might the characters increase or decrease the volume or speed of their delivery?
- Where might the characters stand on stage and in relation to each other at the beginning of the passage and at later points in the passage?

As an example of how these questions can be applied to a particular piece of dialogue, we annotate a passage that occurs near the beginning of Eugène Ionesco's play *The Lesson,* namely the first meeting of a teacher and a young student who has come for a private tutoring session. The list of characters tells us that the professor is somewhere between fifty and sixty years old, and that the pupil is eighteen. We do not know their names and, although Ionesco does supply a description of each character in a stage direction, the theater audience doesn't read or hear the stage directions. Thus, as the professor and the pupil meet, their lines must reveal who they are.

The following annotation is deliberately suggestive in several ways. It represents the kind of thinking that actors and directors might engage in as they repeatedly comb every syllable for information about the characters—and thus it is more thorough than any single first reading would be. It is also suggestive in that it not only attempts to describe how the characters might respond to each other but also offers a range of possible choices. Thus, the annotation answers some of the questions we have raised and then poses more questions for further thought and exploration. We have put the dialogue of the characters in the left-hand column and our notes in the right-hand column.

PROFESSOR: Good morning, young lady.	Polite, but not very interested in her as an individual. Calling her "young lady" puts her in a role distinctly subservient to his.
You . . . I expect that you . . . that you are the new pupil?	He probably starts to say "You must be the new pupil" but evidently finds it difficult to get that sentence spoken. What do those ellipses mean?

PUPIL: Yes, Professor. Good morning, Professor.

As you see, I'm on time. I didn't want to be late.

PROFESSOR: That's fine, miss.

Thank you, you didn't really need to hurry. I am very sorry to have kept you waiting . . . I was just finishing up . . .

well . . . I'm sorry . . .

You will excuse me, won't you?

PUPIL: Oh, certainly, Professor.

It doesn't matter at all, Professor.

PROFESSOR: Please excuse me . . . Did you have any trouble finding the house?

PUPIL: No . . . Not at all. I just asked the way.

Everybody knows you around here.

Is he so absentminded that he can't remember what he was going to say? Or is he painfully shy?

She responds immediately, repeating his title twice. Is she flattering him by being so deferential? Does the repetition suggest nervousness? Her next lines similarly lend themselves to different readings.

Perhaps she's trying to impress him with her desire to learn and her punctuality. Or maybe she is one of those people who always explain every little thing.

Whatever her inflection, the professor may choose his response. He may wish to be equally polite, or he may try to cut off what could be a longer series of statements.

Here he seems genuinely reassuring and even moves into an apology of his own. Once again he doesn't quite finish the sentence. Does he feel that he somehow owes the pupil an explanation? That's what he seems to offer.

But then he decides not to continue the explanation. Perhaps she's not worth it. Perhaps the explanation would be too personal (was he in the bathroom?).

Still he apologizes. What is all this politeness about? "Why should he keep apologizing to me?" she may think. So she reassures him using his title, again repeating it. As before, she seems unable to say something only once.

Now he's apologizing yet *again*. So the choices above are narrowing down; he seems, though we don't know why, anxious or insecure.

And the pupil is eager to alleviate that insecurity. She thus throws in a reassuring and complimentary remark.

PROFESSOR: For thirty years I've lived in this town.

Her compliment seems to work. He responds with a personal statement, rather than a worried apology. Perhaps he feels that he ought to find out something about her.

You've not been here for long?

Polite small talk.

How do you find it?

PUPIL: It's all right.

Hardly an enthusiastic response. He may look at her quizzically, and so she shifts to more extended—and more complimentary—statements. Her list reveals the average quality of her mind. The adjective she uses is the innocuous "nice" and she uses it twice. We note her mention of the bishop, almost in passing, and that she seems to place him in the list as if he's just another town feature, along with the park, the school, and the shops.

The town is attractive and even agreeable, there's a nice park, a boarding school, a bishop, nice shops and streets . . .

Before she extends the list indefinitely, the professor hastily agrees with her.

PROFESSOR: That's very true, young lady.

Then, as if questioning what she's said, he adds reflectively, even wistfully— Bordeaux is a less exciting town, but at least, his tone implies, it would be more exciting than *this* town.

And yet, I'd just as soon live somewhere else. In Paris, or at least Bordeaux.

She is slightly surprised by the turn the conversation has taken, but responds to the implied put-down of Bordeaux.

PUPIL: Do you like Bordeaux?

Not the remark we're expecting. Normally, if someone prefers one place to another, we assume that he has seen both places.

PROFESSOR: I don't know. I've never seen it.

The pupil shares our surprise and hurries to get back to what she expects, the praise of Paris from one who knows it well.

PUPIL: But you know Paris?

Is he embarrassed to admit that he doesn't know Paris? How could anyone speaking French (the original language of the play) *not* know Paris? She gives him a ques-

PROFESSOR: No, I don't know it either, young lady,

but if you'll permit me,

can you tell me, Paris is
the capital city of . . .
miss?
PUPIL: Paris is the capital city of . . .

France?
PROFESSOR: Yes, young lady,
bravo, that's very good, that's perfect. My congratulations.

You have your French geography at your fingertips. You know your chief cities.

tioning look and he hastens
to take over the conversation.
He returns to the overly polite tone of the first few lines.
He phrases the question as a
request; can this be a serious
question? Is he testing her?
She repeats the question and
the pause indicated by the
ellipses tells us that she is thinking of the answer. If we were
surprised that the professor
didn't know Paris, we're even
more surprised that she hesitates over the capital of her
own country.
He acknowledges the correct
answer but *amazingly*, he
keeps on congratulating her.
Surely the pupil's trivial display of knowledge doesn't
demand such a response.
Perhaps, we wonder, he's
being ironic. Or is this just a
further manifestation of his
own insecurity, one so great
that he feels he has to compliment the student? Or do
we have a situation in which
neither the pupil (when she
mentions the bishop) nor the
professor (at this point) recognizes the incongruity of
their remarks?

As you can see from our sample annotations, the process of close reading and analyzing dialogue can lead to richly detailed information, insights, and ideas about the characters, the plot, and the staging of the play; it is also a way to raise further questions, to see how a single line may suggest several interpretative choices. In our annotations, for instance, we raise questions about the Professor's politeness and whether that implies shyness or nervousness. After seeing how the Professor behaves at the end of the play, we may want to come back to these questions and ask whether or not the nervousness is genuine. While the annotating process may help you to see certain patterns of behavior, it may also force you to realize that some moments are particularly problematic and do not fit easily into a consistent pattern. Don't ignore behaviors that don't seem to fit, but continue to look for other instances of such behavior.

Once you have used this process to examine a series of passages or scenes, you will then have an extensive body of material to draw on for any kind of piece you might wish to write about a play. You will have a wealth of material you can use to explain and support your ideas about the work, whether those ideas concern the play as it exists on the page or as it might be (or has been) produced on the stage.

Some Different Kinds of Writing: Staging Papers, Analyses of Character and/or Scene, and Analytical Reviews/Production-Based Writing

Once you've worked carefully on annotating a series of scenes, you may ask yourself "Where do I go from here?" The kinds of papers we suggest in this section are by no means the only possibilities, and obviously a particular class or assignment may dictate different approaches. But they do suggest some approaches to writing about drama that not only grow out of careful analysis and annotation but also reflect the stage-oriented approach that this anthology embodies. While a play script may exist solely on the page, the play itself is most fully alive when it is produced—either on an actual stage or in the theater of the mind. Thus, we stress that your writing about a play, like your reading of a play, needs to recognize, and even imitate, the multifaceted experience of a play in performance. The types of papers that we outline suggest particular stage-oriented strategies.

Staging Papers   Your annotations can readily be turned into a staging paper in which you imagine yourself as a director contemplating the production of a particular scene or segment of a scene, such as the one we considered from *The Lesson*. This kind of paper might begin with a brief discussion of the production problems and interpretative questions that you see as central to understanding the scene. In the annotated section of *The Lesson*, for example, one major interpretative question might be "What is the initial attitude of the pupil toward the professor?" Production questions might deal with physical descriptions of the characters, their costumes, and the set for the play. In many modern and contemporary plays, as in *The Lesson*, you often find stage directions for the characters provided by the playwright, but you will almost always need to be more detailed in your production notes. And even if the playwright provides a detailed set design, you may choose to create a different one to fit your own interpretation of the scene. At the beginning of *The Lesson*, for example, Ionesco's description of the professor's office calls for doors, a window, "ordinary potted plants," a buffet, a table, three chairs, and bookshelves, all of which suggest a fairly realistic setting against which the surprising behavior of the professor and pupil unfolds. But you might instead choose to design a setting that emphasizes the absurd world of these characters by showing a room with walls at strange angles (or no walls at all), decorated with unexpected colors and unusual furniture. Thus, one version of the staging paper would join questions about the play to annotations of the dialogue, together with notes on set design, costuming, props, and so on.

Another version of the staging paper, which focuses even more directly on visual and costume elements, might be built around the question "What does the audience see and hear *before* the first line of the play?" For many readers, a play seems to begin with the first line, but in fact a production offers a great deal of information to the audience before any words are spoken: the set, the lighting, the music (if any), and the physical appearance of the characters. In deciding what the audience will see, you will need to consider the set for the first scene (or, as in *The Lesson*, for the entire play), the clues for characterization that you have found in your annotations and how those might translate into casting and costume choices, as well as what the first speaking character is doing or has just done, which forms the basis for that character's first words.

A related paper might deal with the simple but challenging question "What does the audience see at the end of the play?" We often think of the ending as coming with a blackout on a tableau or perhaps a curtain falling, but the picture on which that curtain falls nonetheless tells a story. And if, as is often the case with earlier plays—plays written for theaters that didn't have artificial lighting or curtains—the characters must leave the stage, then how do they leave and in what order? What might their leaving indicate about how the audience could respond to the play? Look, for example, at the end of *Othello:* a production must decide how the characters leave (Is Iago dragged out by servants? Does he stop to look at the people whose lives he has destroyed? What is Cassio, the new governor, doing?) and, perhaps just as important, what characters are left on stage, and in what relationships? We know that Desdemona, Emilia, and Othello are dead, but where are they? Desdemona is probably on her bed, but where is Emilia, who requests after she's been stabbed, "lay me by my mistress' side"? And where is Othello, who dies kissing the wife he has killed? Is he too on the bed, thus giving the audience the picture that Iago conjured up in the first scene, of Othello and Desdemona in bed together? Or does he fall to the side of the bed after kissing her? Any of these choices—and other possible ones—offer slightly different conclusions to the story.

Since a staging paper is perhaps less familiar than others we discuss, we have included below an undergraduate student's staging paper. As you will see, this staging paper on David Mamet's *Oleanna* combines detailed commentary on character relationships with the problem of the play's violent but "open" ending. The author briefly introduces major issues of the play and then discusses the two characters separately, offering a variety of possible interpretations of their interaction. She recognizes that there are a number of questions that admit of more than one answer, and so demonstrates an awareness of the complex motivations that bring John and Carol into conflict. In the longer section of the paper, as she works through the dialogue from "All right. I have a list" (p. 1708) through the end of the play, she builds her interpretation of the scene carefully, using specific words and passages from the text to help support her readings. For example, when she argues that Carol "begins with a new tactic," she finds that idea coming out of Carol's use of "we" in "we have an agenda" and in her reference to the Tenure Committee; when she suggests that Carol is "flustered," she notes the shift into "big words to sound impressive." And, most important, she offers a reading of the scene in which the actions and reactions of one character come in response to those of the other.

Liz Lekas
Reading Plays
December 3, 1997

Staging *Oleanna*

The final scene of David Mamet's *Oleanna* brings the play's issues of power and political correctness to an uncertain conclusion. Because of the text's terseness and ambiguity, the points that the two characters are left at individually, as well as the dynamics of their relationship, are open to interpretation. Decisions made by the actors and the director about separate motivations behind both Carol's and John's actions ultimately come together to determine what exactly has happened. Therefore, the director not only has to create the way the scene should unfold, but also *why* the scene happens the way it does.

Carol's character is what drives the scene. It is her actions that move things forward, while John reacts to those actions. Although it is clear that her goal is to bring John down, the problem here is determining exactly how Carol feels about it. Does she want to ruin both his professional *and* personal lives? The depth her character is given is crucial in constructing the situation. An intelligent as well as conniving Carol creates a totally different scene than a Carol who is more one-dimensional, practically unaware of what she is doing. Depending on how strongly she believes in the mission of her "Group," the buildup from demanding that his book be banned to her attempted rape charge to his final attack on her can be seen as either a carefully calculated plot to drive him over the edge, or as the naive undertakings of a brainwashed girl who has gotten in way over her head.

John's reactions to Carol's blows also present staging options. Does his arrogance cause him to not take Carol's initial threats seriously? Is that the reason he has asked her to his office again, to reclaim control and charm his way out of his predicament? He can also be seen as a much more fragile character who fears Carol almost immediately and is desperate and scared. Portraying a professor with a God complex or an earnest man who fears losing everything works again to set up the direction the scene will take. After all, while it is Carol who creates the scene's momentum, it is John's reactions that bring it to a screeching halt with his physicality. The director must figure out where that aggressive physicality comes from.

To bring this scene to a close, a director must rely on choices made about several issues. Is the climax mental, as Carol delivers John's fate, or is it the physical action of John beating Carol? Most important, who wins? How is the audience to understand the outcome? The give and take power struggle between the two characters can be left in several ways. How far do the characters come over the course of the scene? What changes in John to push him that far? Does Carol change? These two push each other's buttons over and over, but to what extent their actions are seen as intentional depends on the staging. With this text, there are no clear-cut answers, and the director must take clues from the text to support fully and continuously the choices that are made.

CAROL: All right. I have a list.	They begin seated in a civilized manner. C* begins by producing list with a rehearsed-looking draw, like a gun. Stands tall and feels adult for first time ever. Confident that she will finally be listened to, now that she has something as grown-up as a list.

*Note: For the sake of saving space, abbreviations will be used for the characters' names. C=Carol, J=John.

JOHN: . . . a list.

J sighs this, mildly exasperated, because he knows she is wasting her time. Humors her, but C ignores this and musters up a breath to continue. She is scared to confront an authority figure, but

CAROL: Here is a list of books, which we . . .

finds a renewed burst of confidence with the word "we." C knows she is not alone in this situation.

JOHN: . . . a list of books . . . ?

Again, J is almost amused that she is worried about something as insignificant as books and is confused about what her point is. He interrupts her to make sure he heard right.

CAROL: That's right. Which we find questionable.

C is pleased that he is following her and uses this as a springboard to continue.

JOHN: What?

J chokes on this word when he realizes that this is about censorship. Now it is going too far. C realizes that he feels this way and immediately becomes defensive. She is hurt,

CAROL: Is this so bizarre . . . ?

but hides it with indignation. She will be taken seriously.

JOHN: I can't believe . . .

J begins to scold her like a child and is embarrassed for her, but C immediately interrupts and attempts to

CAROL: It's not necessary you believe it.

end her argument simply, as though this is enough.

JOHN: Academic freedom . . .

J begins a paternal speech to try and end this nonsense and intentionally uses a condescending tone. After all, she is getting out of hand and he needs to put her back in her place.

CAROL: Someone chooses the books. If you can choose them, others can. What are you, "God"?

C will not give up, but her response sounds like a child complaining about a parent's unfair rule.

JOHN: . . . no, no, the "dangerous." . . .

J continues to patronize with a chuckle, but C realizes she is losing and begins with

CAROL: You have an agenda, we have an agenda. I am not interested in your feelings or your motivation, but your actions. If you would like me to speak to the Tenure Committee, here is my list. You are a Free Person, you decide. *(Pause)*

a new tactic. She brings herself up to his level, again finding strength in "we" and her list. "Tenure Committee" is stressed to remind him that she is not playing around. The line is ended a bit sarcastically, as J is not the only one capable of

JOHN: Give me the list. *(She does so. He reads.)*

CAROL: I think you'll find . . .

JOHN: I'm capable of reading it. Thank you.

CAROL: We have a number of *texts* we need re . . .

JOHN: I see that.

CAROL: We're amenable to . . .

JOHN: Aha. Well, let me look over the . . . *(He reads.)*

CAROL: I think that . . .

JOHN: LOOK. I'm reading your demands. All right?! *(He reads) (Pause)* You want to ban my book?

CAROL: We do not . . .

JOHN *(Of list)*: It says here . . .

CAROL: . . . We want it removed from inclusion as a representative example of the university.

JOHN: Get out of here.

CAROL: If you put aside the issues of personalities.

demeaning the other. J sees this, and angrily asks for the list. She smiles, knowing she has won the battle. Her smirk fuels his annoyance as he quickly tears the sheet out of her hand.

This does not bother her, and she is gloating by "helping" him look it over.

Casually sarcastic, as he is involved in reading it. His eyes scan the titles lethargically, and he basically ignores her interjections by cutting her off so he will not have to listen to her voice.

C is frustrated that she cannot get a word in edgewise, reminding her of past visits with him. This makes her more determined to make him *listen.*

However, she gets a little nervous when she realizes that he is about to get to his own book, and even tries to warn him.

J snaps at her and elicits a frightened silence from C.

J speaks slowly and disbelievingly when he realizes his book is on the list, and looks up at her in shock.

C becomes flustered. She did not know what kind of a reaction to expect, and feels a twinge of guilt. J attempts to take advantage of her moment of weakness, but

C instantly remembers her purpose and pulls herself together, gaining confidence through using big words to sound impressive, just as he would do in this situation, right?

J now understands that he is dealing with something much bigger than he is, which infuriates him. How dare this nobody try to screw with him in his own office? C's mocking remark is just humiliation for J, because she has just about grabbed all the power.

JOHN: Get the fuck out of my office.

CAROL: No, I think I would reconsider.

JOHN: . . . you think you can.

CAROL: We can and we *will*. Do you want our support? That is the only quest . . .

JOHN: . . . to ban my *book* . . . ?

CAROL: . . . that is correct . . .

JOHN: . . . this . . . this is a *university* . . . we . . .

CAROL: . . . and we have a statement . . . which we need you to . . . *(She hands him a sheet of paper.)*

JOHN: No, no. It's out of the question. I'm sorry. I don't know what I was thinking of. I want to tell you something. I'm a teacher. I am a teacher. Eh? It's my *name* on the door, and *I* teach the class, and that's what I do. I've got a book with my name on it. And my son will *see* that *book* someday. And I have a respon . . . No, I'm sorry I have a *responsibility* . . . to *myself*, to my *son*, to my *profession*. . . . I haven't been *home* for two days, do you know that? Thinking this out.

CAROL: . . . you haven't?

J is enraged by the satisfaction she is obviously getting out of this. However, observing his anger and frustration just pleases her more. C likes being on top. J cannot let her leave with things this way. He is a *professor*, and she pathetic for even thinking about getting away with this. C is surprised by how well she is doing and by how easy it is to stand up to him. She is even confident enough to turn away from him, now that she is sure he is listening. J cannot believe how ridiculous this is and is beginning to feel like he is going crazy. Does C honestly believe what she is saying? It is like he is talking to himself, because she is going on about statements and signatures and not listening to one *word* of sense. C cannot believe the roll she is on! The Group would be so proud. Getting out the paper for him to sign, she is startled by the sound of an urgent "No." Everything was going the way it was supposed to . . . Finally, J grabs C's attention. Finally. He laughs at himself for letting this go so far and practically forgetting who he is. J sets the record straight. This is *his* show, not hers. He is older, smarter, and has worked his butt off to get to where he is now. Thank God she finally shut up, and did this girl stop for even one *second* and think about what this is doing to me? He lets her know exactly how it is affecting him. J still holds on to his practice of using personal stories to get through to a student. It is a habit. The thought that his personal life might be affected never crossed her mind. She is shy about asking, knowing it is none of her business.

JOHN: I've been, no. If it's of interest
to you. I've been in a *hotel. Thinking.*
(The phone starts ringing.)
Thinking . . .

CAROL: . . . you haven't been home?

JOHN: . . . *thinking,* do you see.

CAROL: Oh.
JOHN: And, and, I owe you a debt,
I see that now. *(Pause)* You're
dangerous, you're *wrong* and it's
my *job* . . . to say no to you.
That's my job. You are absolutely
right. You want to ban my book?
Go to *hell,* and they can do
whatever they want to me.

CAROL: . . . you haven't been home in two days . . .

JOHN: I think I told you that.
CAROL: . . . you'd better get that phone.
(Pause) I think that you should
pick up the phone. *(Pause)*

(JOHN *picks up the phone.)*

JOHN: *(on phone).* Yes. *(Pause)* Yes.
Wh . . . I. I. I had to be away.
All ri . . . did they wor . . . did they
worry ab . . . No. I'm all right, now,
Jerry. I'm f . . . I got a little turned
around, but I'm *sitting* here and . . .
I've got it figured out. I'm fine. I'm
fine don't worry about me. I got a
little bit mixed up. But I am not
sure that it's not a blessing. It
cost me my job? Fine. Then the
job was not worth having. Tell
Grace that I'm coming home and
everything is fff . . . *(Pause)* What?
(Pause) What? *(Pause)* What do you
mean? WHAT? Jerry . . . Jerry.

J is relieved that this is getting through to her, but is slightly irritated that this didn't occur to her earlier. He is so wrapped up in thinking about himself that he does not even notice the phone ringing.
C has still not gotten over the "home" issue and is wondering if he is fighting with his wife. She snaps back to the present and finds herself with nothing to say. She slumps in her chair.
Ha-ha! She's got nothing to say, so let's continue. J intends to make C fully understand what an idiot she is. She could never win against him. How could he have been so stupid as to have ever felt *threatened* by her? Who would listen to a whiny brat like her, anyway? J is not afraid. He is talking to himself, though. He is able to go on for so long because she is not even listening. While he paces and rambles, her gaze is aimed nowhere in particular. She sits and imagines what it would be like to not go home for two days.
Confused and unable to think straight because of the drone of his voice and the shriek of the phone, C tells J to answer it. He hesitates, wanting to answer it, but not wanting to seem like he is obeying her. He sits at his desk, across from her, keeping his eye on her. Not excited to hear from his lawyer again, but benefiting from getting to think out loud to him, J finally begins to relax a bit. He smiles as he watches C squirm in her seat, as she thinks about what she has done. Was it right? Yes, she knows it. They told her. After all, she didn't make anything up. They explained it to her. She read things in books. C glares at J when she hears him say the job wasn't worth it. What a liar he is. He hurt me. C thinks about how

They . . . Who, who, what can they do . . . ? *(Pause)* NO. *(Pause)* NO. They can't do th . . . What do you mean? *(Pause)* But how . . . *(Pause)* She's, she's, she's *here* with me. To . . . Jerry. I don't underst . . . *(Pause) (He hangs up.)* *(To* CAROL:*)* What does this mean?

CAROL: I thought you knew.

JOHN: What. *(Pause)* What does it mean. *(Pause)*

CAROL: You tried to rape me. *(Pause)* According to the law. *(Pause)*

JOHN: . . . what . . . ?

CAROL: You tried to rape me. I was leaving this office, you "pressed" yourself into me. You "pressed" your body into me.

JOHN: . . . I . . .

CAROL: My Group has told your lawyer that we may pursue criminal charges.

JOHN: . . . no . . .

CAROL: . . . under the statute. I am told. It was battery.

badly he deserves all of this. The blood drains out of J's face. I did *not* just hear . . . he asks over and over again, even though the questions are of no use when he does not wait for an answer. His heart pounds and he feels nauseous as he pictures losing the job, the house, his wife, his car, his friends, everything. What the hell has she done? His movement and words are so weak that C can barely hear him, especially with his head in his hands on the desk.

C snatches the ball back in her court, and it makes more sense to her why things were going so smoothly before. How could he not have known?

J is speaking slowly and trying to take deep breaths. Maybe he just misunderstood. Maybe this is just a bad dream.

Somehow, standing up to J now is not quite so rewarding as it was earlier. She is surprised by how calm he is, causing her to remain calm. She is apprehensive, and just sticks to the facts, staring intently at him, searching for some sort of reaction.

C confidently reminds him of what happened, secure that the law is on her side. She cannot allow him to get away with this anymore. It does not matter what happens to his life, because J is a criminal, practically a rapist.

J is confused. He wonders how far this has gone already without his knowing. For the first time in his life, he is scared.

C cannot believe that she has to to explain this to him. She wishes he already knew, because this is so awkward. But she must remain firm. He really did attempt rape . . . didn't he? God, look at his face. C silently scolds herself for hesitating. She is right.

No one is ever going to do that to me again. Not him, or

JOHN: . . . no . . .

CAROL: Yes. And attempted rape. That's right. *(Pause)*

JOHN: I think that you should go.

CAROL: Of course. I thought you knew.

JOHN: I have to talk to my lawyer.

CAROL: Yes. Perhaps you should.

(The phone rings again.) (Pause)

JOHN: *(Picks up phone. Into phone:)*

Hello? I . . . Hello . . . ? I . . . Yes, he just called. No . . . I. I can't talk to you now, Baby. *(To CAROL:)* Get out.

CAROL: . . . your wife . . . ?

JOHN: . . . who it is no concern of yours. Get out. *(To phone:)* No, no, it's going to be all right. I. I can't talk now, Baby.

(To CAROL:) Get out of here.
CAROL: I'm going.

JOHN: Good.

anybody. How can they put men like this in university positions? She was supposed to look to him for help; how could he betray her?

J's head is spinning. He hates the sight of her. How dare she accuse him of something so vile? He needs to be alone. To talk to his wife. Just get her out of here.

J mutters this through gritted teeth without looking at her. He is scared of what he might do if he actually looked into her ugly face. C accepts the calmness of the situation, mistakenly identifying it as "maturity." She thinks that once again, they are equals. She sure showed him. The Group probably never imagined how smoothly this would go!

Finding a renewed sense of pleasure from her smugness, C doesn't hurry this moment. She gets lost in the thought of all the things she can do now. What it will feel like to win in court. C is quickly getting used to winning.

J looks at C, realizes that she isn't leaving, and hears his wife's voice. He clears his throat, trying his best to disguise his state. She didn't marry a loser. His Baby married a brilliant professor, about to get tenure. He will not let C win. No one beats him, especially this bitch. Maybe she means it as a last sort of attempt to connect with him, but C is snide.

How can there be a woman who loves him? The way he looks at us? Speaks to us? C stares at him in disgust, which J notices. He returns the look. Rape her. In her dreams. It was completely obvious to him that she had a crush on him. His tone is icy cold. She gathers her things hastily. C cannot stand to be in this office a moment longer. This is the place where everything

CAROL: *(exiting)* . . . and don't call
your wife "baby."

JOHN: What?

CAROL: Don't call your wife
"baby." You heard what I said.

(CAROL starts to leave the room.
JOHN *grabs her and begins to*
beat her.)

JOHN: You vicious little bitch.
You think you can come
in here with your political
correctness and destroy
my life?
(He knocks her to the floor.)

After how I treated you . . . ?
You should be . . . *Rape*
you . . . ? Are you kidding me . . . ?

(He picks up a chair, raises it above
his head, and advances on her.)

I wouldn't touch you with a
ten-foot pole. You little *cunt* . . .

(She cowers on the floor below him.
Pause. He looks down at her. He
lowers the chair. He moves to his
desk, and arranges the papers on it.
Pause. He looks over at her.)

. . . well . . .
(Pause. She looks at him.)

CAROL: Yes. That's right.

happened. She is embarrassed
for ever feeling any sympathy
for him, and whether anything
really *did* happen or not, she
hates him.
From now on, C is going to hate
anyone who casts her aside.
Now, just one last thing to show
him, Mr. Bigshot Professor, that
C is strong.
J feels something snap inside him.
He had tried to stay calm, to
handle it. Who the hell does that
little whore think she is?
For C, it's all over. She succeeded. Nothing matters now.
C is too startled to fight back.
She realizes that she wouldn't
have a chance against him,
anyway.
J has never felt so good. If this is
the only way to show her who's
in charge, so be it.
He has nothing left to lose.

C is praying for life. Was this
worth it? Will it be worth it in
the end?
All J can think about is the way
it feels to see her on the floor
like that. Where she belongs.
Where I put her. J can do
whatever he wants.
The chair feels so good in his
hands, he feels so strong. C
wishes she were invisible.
She's nothing. NOTHING. J is
too crazed to even notice that
he never hung up the phone.
This is the climax of the scene.
Towering over her with chair in
hand, J has never been happier.
He grins as he puts it down.
Now she understands. C holds
back tears. This was NOT supposed to happen. She was so
sure . . . or were *they* the ones
who were sure? The Group is
okay. C is the one who is hurt.
C's mouth hangs open as she
stares up from the floor. *Had* he
been right? But now . . .
now he was wrong. Because she
had listened to them. All she

(She looks away from him, and lowers her head. To herself:)

. . . yes. That's right.

wanted was to be listened *to*, for once.
They had both betrayed her.
The Group and him. Could that be? Yes.
C slumps down, and realizes her *own* thoughts are right, for the first time, without anybody's help.

Analyses of Character and/or Scene   Many of the readings presented in the staging paper from *Oleanna* or in the annotations of *The Lesson* could also serve as a useful point of departure for an analysis of a character or a scene. The sample annotations of *The Lesson* might lead to a detailed study of either the professor or the pupil. Or, you might prefer instead to examine the behavior of the professor's maid, a third character who appears occasionally but who seems to have little if any influence on the behavior of the professor and the pupil. You might wonder if she is really necessary to the play. Using the annotation technique, you would look closely at the moments when she appears, considering her relationship to the professor and the pupil and noting in particular whom she speaks to and how she interacts with each. Then you might develop a paper beginning with a generalization or thesis statement something like this: "Though the professor's maid seems to be a colorless minor character, she actually turns out to dominate the professor, treating him at the end like a naughty child." The same kind of analysis can be done for an apparently minor scene in a play by studying the scene in detail, and then asking why and how it's useful in the play.

The staging paper on the closing section of *Oleanna* offers a reading of Carol's character and actions as those of a young woman who is both confused and hurt, and who finally recognizes that she has been used by the "group" that she trusted. It is a reading firmly based in the text, but it is not the only reading. Given the number of questions that the introductory section of the staging paper raises about Carol's and John's motivations, one could imagine not only a very different staging paper but a critical analysis that, while entertaining the notion of Carol's confusion and even sympathy for John's predicament, might end up with a very different approach to the play's ending. Similarly, a different staging paper or analytical paper might examine the scene more fully from John's perspective, raising the question of whether he fully realizes what he's done and exploring how he feels about his actions.

Analytical Reviews/Production-Based Writing   The process of annotating the text of a play in detail can lead not only to the discussion of your own "production" of the play, or to critical analyses of issues raised by the play, but to the critique of a fully staged production. By thinking through questions about staging the play and by searching for a range of answers, you will become much more aware of the choices that a particular production has made. You then need to ask thoughtful questions about a performance in the same way that you raise questions about a written text. If you watch a stage performance, which you will probably see only once, you might want to jot down quick notes immediately after the performance and then, as soon as possible, try to remember more details about what you saw. If you watch a videotaped or filmed performance, you will be able to look back at particular moments, just as you would go back to a written text to find individual details. Such preparation will then lead to an analytical review of a production, including as much specific detail as possible, so that you are both re-creating the performance for your reader and at the same time offering your reader a discriminating guide to the production.

Most of the reviews included in this anthology were written under the pressure of newspaper or magazine deadlines; most offer evaluative judgments of the performances and, especially with the new plays, of the play itself. But the most useful sections of the reviews are not the judgments but the specific descriptions of what the reviewer saw and heard on stage; in this respect, a review furnishes information that is relevant years later. Sometimes the reviewer is acutely aware of his or her responsibility as a theater historian. Look at the opening sentence of Ronald Bryden's review of the 1964 production of *Othello:* (p. 336) "All posterity will want to know is how he played." Here Bryden admits that what he thought of Olivier's Othello is not so much the point as the need to "record" the performance, and this he proceeds to do in paragraph after paragraph of closely observed detail. Even without such an explicit statement, reviewers frequently provide descriptions that make the performances visible. Claire Bloom's Nora comes alive in Walter Kerr's review of the 1971 *A Doll's House* (pp. 584–85), as does Janet McTeer's Nora in Ben Brantley's review of the 1997 production (pp. 586–87). Michael Billington's details about the set and costumes of *The House of Bernarda Alba* (p. 832) help to re-create the power of Nuria Espert's 1986 production. Often the reviewer will talk about a particular production in the context of other productions of the play; thus, Michael Billington contrasts the 1982 Peter Hall production of *The Importance of Being Earnest* with others he has seen, admiring Hall's ability to get rid of "the usual fussy accretions" and to find instead "recognisable passions like lust and greed" (p. 645).

Each of the reviews cited above is of a play already known to the reviewer. That previous knowledge creates a sharp awareness of the variety of interpretative choices that are possible and thus an understanding of the ones made. Obviously, not all reviews are written about familiar plays, but the more knowledgeable the reviewer is—about the play, the playwright, and other plays by the same writer—the more likely he or she is to offer a balanced and judicious analysis of the performance.

Another way to write about a play in production is to gather together as many different reviews as possible from as many different productions as possible. Look for the topics that recur: characters who seem susceptible to different interpretations; major scenes or confrontations; the design of the production; unusual casting choices; or the impact of a particular actor on a particular role. The more descriptive the review, the more useful information it will offer you. Conflicting reviews—such as those we reprint for *Landscape* (pp. 1109–10), and *"Art"* (pp. 1587–88)—may stimulate your thinking by suggesting how the same performance can evoke very different reactions. Background material, including comments by the director or actors, often indicates the intentions behind the production, although not necessarily the final result. Thus, it is possible to write intelligently about productions you have not seen, and to use those productions as points of reference and argument for your own interpretation of the play. Indeed, actors and directors who work on very familiar plays—Shakespeare is the obvious example—often define their own work by studying past productions. In addition to studying reviews and photographs, they look at textual cuts and rearrangements, finding in the details of the reconstructed past productions ideas that they may wish to borrow or, more often, argue with. As you read about productions—in reviews, in interviews, in memoirs, in surveys of performance—you will find a wide range of interpretations. Using this information and your own reading of the play, you can then develop arguments about those performance choices.

All of these suggestions represent approaches to writing about plays that call on you to be both creator and spectator, both actor and audience. Thinking with the specificity of actors who must find a way to make sense of every word they speak and who must respond to what others do and say on stage leads you to discover more possibilities for interpreting those words. Writing about a play develops your understanding of the play and then allows you to communicate that understanding to others.

APPENDIX B
Film and Video Productions of Plays in
Stages of Drama

NOTE: DISTRIBUTORS' ADDRESSES, TELEPHONE NUMBERS, FAX NUMBERS, AND E-MAIL ADDRESSES FOLLOW THIS LIST OF FILM AND VIDEO PRODUCTIONS.

Aeschylus, *Agamemnon*
90 min.
VHS
Directed by Peter Hall
Distributed by Films for the Humanities and
    Sciences, Insight Media

Aeschylus, *Agamemnon*
120 min., 1991
VHS
Directed by Peter Meineck
Distributed by Insight Media

Albee, *The Zoo Story*
Titled *Edward Albee*
52 min.
VHS
Biographical production with scenes from *Zoo Story*
    and a number of other plays
Distributed by Films for the Humanities and
    Sciences

Anonymous, *Everyman*
53 min., 1991
VHS
Produced in conjunction with Columbia
    University
Distributed by Insight Media

Aristophanes, *Lysistrata*
97 min., 1997
VHS
Greek with English subtitles
With Jenny Karezi and Costas Kazakos
Directed by Yiannis Negrepontis
Distributed by Insight Media

Beckett, *Endgame*
90 min., 1992
VHS
Directed by Tony Coe
Produced by the BBC
Distributed by Insight Media

Brecht, *Galileo*
Titled *Bertolt Brecht*
53 min.
VHS
Biographical production with excerpts from *Galileo*
    and other plays
Distributed by Films for the Humanities and Sciences

Büchner, *Woyzeck*
82 min., 1978
VHS, DVD
German with English subtitles
With Klaus Kinski, Eva Mattes, and Wolfgang
    Reichman
Directed by Werner Herzog
Distributed by Facets Multimedia, Inc., New Yorker
    Video

Büchner, *Woyzeck*
49 min., 1979
VHS
Distributed by Films for the Humanities and Sciences

Büchner, *Woyzeck*
93 min., B/W, 1994
VHS
Directed by Janos Szaz
Hungarian with subtitles
Distributed by Facets Multimedia, Inc.

Chekhov, *The Cherry Orchard*
44 min., 1968
VHS
Selected scenes
Distributed by Encyclopaedia Britannica Educational
    Corporation

Chekhov, *The Cherry Orchard*
Titled *Chekhov and the Moscow Art Theatre*
130 min., 1982
VHS
Uses archival footage from the Moscow Art Theatre
Distributed by Insight Media

Euripides, *The Bacchae*
78 min.
VHS
Distributed by Insight Media

Fugard, *"MASTER HAROLD" . . . and the Boys*
90 min., 1985
VHS
With Matthew Broderick
Directed by Michael Lindsay-Hogg
Distributed by Insight Media, Facets Multimedia,
    Inc., and Filmic Archives

Hansberry, *A Raisin in the Sun*
128 min., B/W, 1961
VHS, DVD
With Sidney Poitier, Claudia McNeil, Ruby Dee,
    Diana Sands, Ivan Dixon, and Louis Gossett Jr.
Directed by Daniel Petrie
Distributed by Columbia Tristar Home
    Entertainment, Teacher's Video Company,
    Facets Multimedia, Inc., and Filmic Archives

Hansberry, *A Raisin in the Sun*
171 min., 1988
VHS
With Danny Glover, Esther Rolle, and Starletta
    DuPois
Distributed by Insight Media, and Facets Multimedia,
    Inc.

Hwang, *M. Butterfly*
101 min., 1993
VHS
With Jeremy Irons
Directed by David Cronenberg
Distributed by Tower Records

Ibsen, *A Doll's House*
103 min., 1973
VHS
With Jane Fonda and Trevor Howard

Directed by Joseph Losey
Distributed by Anchor Bay Entertainment Inc.,
    Facets Multimedia, Inc., and Image
    Entertainment

Ibsen, *A Doll's House*
140 min., 1991
VHS
BBC Production
With Juliet Stevenson and Trevor Eve
Distributed by Insight Media

Ibsen, *A Doll's House*
95 min., 1975
VHS
With Claire Bloom, Anthony Hopkins, Ralph
    Richardson, and Anna Massey
Directed by Patrick Garland
Distributed by Facets Multimedia, Inc., MGM/
    United Artists Home Video and Tower
    Records

Johnson, *Volpone*
95 min., 1939
VHS
French with English subtitles
With Harry Sauer and Louis Jouvet
Directed by Maurice Tourneur
Distributed by Facets Multimedia, Inc.

Lorca, *The House of Bernarda Alba*
100 min., 1987
VHS
With Glenda Jackson, Joan Plowright,
    Patricia Hayes
Directed by Nuria Espert and Stuart Burge
Translated by Robert David MacDonald
Distributed by Films for the Humanities and the
    Sciences

Mamet, *Oleanna*
90 min., 1994
VHS
With William H. Macy and Debra Eisenstadt
Directed by David Mamet
Distributed by Facets Multimedia, Inc., and Insight
    Media

Marlowe, *Doctor Faustus*
93 min., 1968
VHS
With Richard Burton and Elizabeth Taylor
Directed by Richard Burton and Nevill Coghill
Distributed by Columbia Tristar Home Video,
    Teacher's Video Company, Critic's Choice, and
    Filmic Archives

Marlowe, *Marlowe's Faust Part 1 & 2*
24 min. each
VHS
With excerpts but not the entire play
Distributed by Films for the Humanities and Sciences

Miller, *Death of a Salesman*
120 min., 1967
With Lee J. Cobb, Mildred Dunnock, George Segal,
    James Ferentino, Gene Wilder
Distributed by Insight Media and Facets Multimedia,
    Inc.

Miller, *Death of a Salesman*
135 min., 1986
VHS
With Dustin Hoffman, Kate Reid, John Malkovich,
    and Charles Durning
Directed by Volker Schlondorff
Produced by Dustin Hoffman and Arthur Miller
Distributed by Facets Multimedia, Inc., Image
    Entertainment, and Insight Media

Molière, *The Misanthrope*
120 min.
VHS
French with English subtitles
Produced by the Comediens Français
Distributed by Films for the Humanities
    and Sciences

Norman, *'night Mother*
97 min., 1996
VHS
With Sissy Spacek and Anne Bancroft
Directed by Tom Moore
Distributed by Universal Studios Home Video, Inc.

O'Neill, *Homecoming* (from *Morning Becomes Electra*)
5 episodes, 58 min. each, 1979
VHS
With Bruce Davison, Joan Hackett, and Roberta
    Maxwell
Directed by Nick Havinga
Distributed by Insight Media and Facets
    Multimedia, Inc.

Pirandello, *Six Characters in Search of an Author*
60 min., 1977
VHS
Hosted by Jose Ferrer and Ossie Davis
Distributed by Insight Media

Pirandello, *Sir Characters in Search of an Author*
110 min., B/W, 1992
VHS

With John Hurt
Distributed by Insight Media

Pirandello, *Six Characters in Search of an Author*
90 min., 1976
VHS
With Andy Griffith, John Houseman, Julie Adams,
    Beverly Todd, and James Keach
Directed by Stacy Keach
Distributed by Insight Media

Pirandello, *Six Characters in Search of an Author*
96 min., B/W
VHS
With John Hurt
Distributed by Films for the Humanities and Sciences

Platus, *A Funny Thing Happened on the Way to the Forum*
100 min., 1966
VHS, DVD
With Zero Mostel, Phil Silvers, and Buster Keaton
Directed by Richard Lester
Distributed by Facets Multimedia, Inc.

Shakespeare, *Much Ado About Nothing*
120 min., 1984
VHS
With Robert Lindsay and Cherie Lunghi
Distributed by Ambrose Video Publishing, Inc.

Shakespeare, *Much Ado About Nothing*
25 min., 1984
VHS
With Eleanor Bron
Directed by Stuart Burge
Distributed by Films for the Humanities
    and Sciences

Shakespeare, *Much Ado About Nothing*
110 min., 1993
VHS, DVD
With Kenneth Branagh, Emma Thompson, Michael
    Keaton, Robert Sean Leonard, Keanu Reeves,
    and Denzel Washington
Directed by Kenneth Branagh
Distributed by Facets Multimedia, Inc., and Tower
    Records

Shakespeare, *Othello*
81 min., B/W, silent, 1922
VHS
With Emil Jannings and Werner Karuss
Directed by Dmitri Buschowetzki
Distributed by Discount Video Tapes,
    Inc./Hollywood's Attic, Facets Multimedia, Inc.,
    and Insight Media

Shakespeare, *Othello*
92 min., B/W, 1952
VHS, DVD
With Orson Welles, Suzanne Cloutier, Michael
    MacLiammoir, and Fay Compton
Directed by Orson Welles
Distributed by Facets Multimedia, Inc.

Shakespeare, *Othello*
108 min., 1955
VHS
Russian dubbed in English
Directed by Sergei Bondarchuk
Distributed by Facets Multimedia, Inc.

Shakespeare, *Othello*
167 min., 1965
PAL
With Laurence Olivier, Maggie Smith, Frank Finlay,
    and Derek Jacobi
Directed by Stuart Burge
Distributed by Blackstar

Shakespeare, *Othello*
195 min., 1983
DVD
With Jenny Agutter, Ron Moody, and
    William Marshall
Distributed by Tower Records and Image
    Entertainment

Shakespeare, *Othello*
208 min., 1982
VHS
With Anthony Hopkins, Bob Hoskins, and
    Penelope Wilton
Distributed by Ambrose Video Publishing, Inc.,
    and Filmic Archives

Shakespeare, *Othello*
193 min., 1987
VHS
With John Kani and Joanna Weinberg
Directed by Janet Suzman
Distributed by Films for the Humanities
    and Sciences

Shakespeare, *Othello*
210 min., 1990
VHS
With Ian McKellen and Willard White
Royal Shakespeare Company production
Directed by Trevor Nunn
Distributed by Films for the Humanities
    and Sciences

Shakespeare, *Othello*
125 min., 1996
VHS, DVD
With Laurence Fishburne, Kenneth Branagh, Irene
    Jacob, Nathaniel Parker, and Michael Maloney
Directed by Oliver Parker
Distributed by Columbia Tristar Home Video, Critic's
    Choice, Insight Media, and Facets
    Multimedia, Inc.

Shakespeare, *Othello*
CD-ROM
Provides select scenes of the play, the full text, and
    criticism
Distributed by Films for the Humanities and Sciences

Shakespeare, *Othello*
96 min., 2001
VHS, DVD
With Eamonn Walker and Christopher Eccleston
Directed by Geoffrey Sax
Distributed by Facets Multimedia, Inc., and Image
    Entertainment

Shakespeare, *Othello*
Titled *O*
94 min., 2001
VHS, DVD, With Julia Stiles, Mekhi Phifer, and Josh
    Hartnett
Directed by Tim Blake Nelson
Distributed by Facets Multimedia, Inc., and Tower
    Records

Shaw, *Pygmalion*
96 min., B/W, 1938
VHS, DVD
With Wendy Hiller and Leslie Howard
Directed by Anthony Asquith and Leslie Howard
Produced by Gabriel Pascal
Distributed by Critic's Choice, Monterey Home
    Video, Insight Media, Facets Multimedia, Inc.,
    and Teacher's Video Company

Sheridan, *The School for Scandal*
100 min., B/W, 1938
VHS
With Joan Plowright and Felix Aylmer
Distributed by Facets Multimedia, Inc., and Filmic
    Archives

Sheridan, *The School for Scandal*
118 min., 1975
VHS
With Blair Brown, Patricia Connolly, and Kenneth
    Walsh
Distributed by Insight Media

Sophocles, *Oedipus Rex*
90 min., B/W, 1957
VHS
With Douglas Rain and Douglas Campbell
Directed by Tyrone Guthrie
Distributed by Facets Multimedia, Inc., and Insight
    Media

Sophocles, *Oedipus Rex*
VHS
With Felicity Palmer
Distributed by Facets Multimedia, Inc.

Sophocles, *Oedipus Rex*
110 min., 1967
VHS
With Franco Citti, Silvana Mangano, and Alida Valli
Directed by Pier Paolo Pasolini
Distributed by Facets Multimedia, Inc.

Sophocles, *Oedipus Rex*
120 minutes
VHS
With Michael Pennington, John Gielgud, and Clare
    Bloom
Distributed by Films for the Humanities and Sciences

Strindberg, *Miss Julie*
90 min., B/W, 1950
VHS
Swedish with English subtitles
With Anita Björk, Ulf Palme, and Anders Henrikson
Directed by Alf Sjöberg
Distributed by Films for the Humanities and
    Sciences, Insight Media, Facets Multimedia, Inc.,
    and Columbia Tristar Home Entertainment

Strindberg, *Miss Julie*
105 min., 1977
VHS
Produced by the Royal Shakespeare Company
Distributed by Insight Media

Strindberg, *Miss Julie*
100 min., color, 1997
VHS
With Janet McTeer and Patrick Malahide
Directed by Michael Simpson
Distributed by Films for the Humanities and Sciences

Strindberg, *Miss Julie*
101 min., 1999
VHS, DVD

With Peter Mullan and Saffron Burrows
Directed by Mike Figgis
Distributed by Facets Multimedia, Inc.

Wakefield Master, *The Second Shepherd's Play*
Titled *Medieval Drama: From Sanctuary to Stage*
48 min.
VHS
Excerpts from *Second Shepherd's Play, Everyman, Ordo*
    Virtutum and the York Mystery Cycle
Distributed by Films for the Humanities and Sciences

Walcott, *Pantomime*
26 min.
VHS
Distributed by Films for the Humanities and Sciences

Wilde, *The Importance of Being Earnest*
95 min., 1952
VHS
With Michael Redgrave, Joan Greenwood, Margaret
    Rutherford, Michael Dennison, and Edith Evans
Directed by Anthony Asquith
Distributed by Facets Multimedia, Inc.

Williams, *Cat on a Hot Tin Roof*
108 min., 1958
VHS, DVD
With Elizabeth Taylor, Paul Newman, Burl Ives, and
    Jack Carson
Directed by Richard Brooks
Distributed by MGM/United Artists Home Video,
    Facets Multimedia, Inc., Teacher's Video
    Company, Critic's Choice, and Filmic Archives

Williams, *Cat on a Hot Tin Roof*
122 min., 1994
VHS
With Jessica Lange, Tommy Lee Jones, and Rip Torn
Directed by Jack Hofsiss
Distributed by MGM/United Artists Home Video,
    Facets Multimedia, Inc.

Wilson, *Fences*
52 min.
VHS
Contains interview footage and scenes from *Fences,*
    Ma Rainey's Black Bottom, etc.
Distributed by Films for the Humanities and Sciences

Directory of Film and Video Distributors

Ambrose Video Publishing Inc.
145 W. 45th Street
Suite 115
New York, NY 10036
Tel: (212) 768-7383
Toll-free: (800) 526-4663
http://www.ambrosevideo.com

Anchor Bay Entertainment, Inc.
500 Kirts Boulevard
Troy, MI 48084
Tel: (877) 709-1330
Toll-free: (800) 786-8777
http://www.anchorbayentertainment.com

BlackStar Video
19-21 Alfred Street
Beffast
BT@ 8ED
Northern Ireland
Tel: +44(0)28-9050-9050
Fax: +44(0)28-9050-9010
http://www.blackstar.co.uk

Columbia Tristar Home Entertainment
Sony Pictures Plaza
10202 W. Washington Boulevard
Culver City, CA 90232
Tel: (310) 244-1193
Fax: (310) 244-2462
http://www.sonypictures.com

Critic's Choice
900 N. Rohlwing Road
Itasca, IL 60067
Toll-free: (800) 993-6357
http://www.ccvideo.com

Encyclopaedia Britannica Educational
    Corporation
310 S. Michigan Avenue
Chicago, IL 60604
Tel: (312) 347-7000
Toll-free: (800) 323-1229
Fax: (312) 347-7996

Facets Multimedia, Inc.
1517 W. Fullerton Avenue
Chicago, IL 60614
Tel: (773) 281-9075
http://www.facets.org

Filmic Archives
The Cinema Center
Botsford, CT 06404
Toll-free: (800) 366-1920
Fax: (202) 268-1796
http://www.filmicarchives.com

Films for the Humanities and Sciences
P.O. Box 2053
Princeton, NJ 08543-2053
Tel: (609) 419-8000
Toll-free: (800) 257-5126
http://www.films.com

Hollywood's Attic/Discount Video Tapes, Inc.
P.O. Box 7122
Burbank, CA 91510
Tel: (818) 843-3366
http://www.hollywoodsattic.com

Image Entertainment
9333 Oso Avenue
Chatsworth, CA 91311
Tel: (818) 407-9100
http://www.image-entertainment.com

Insight Media
2162 Broadway
New York, NY 10024-0621
Toll-free: (800) 233-1920
http://www.insight-media.com

MGM/United Artists Home Video
MGM Plaza, 2500 Broadway
Santa Monica, CA 90404-3061
Tel: (310) 449-3000
Toll-free: (800) 562-3330
Fax: (212) 714-0871
http://www.mgm.com

Monterey Home Video
566 St. Charles Drive
Thousand Oaks, CA 91360
Tel: (805) 494-7199
Toll-free: (800) 424-2593
Fax: (805) 496-6061
http://www.teachersvideo.com

New Yorker Films
16 W. 61st Street
New York, NY 10023
Tel: (212) 247-6110
Toll-free: (800) 447-0196

Fax: (212) 307-7855
http://www.newyorkerfilms.com

Teacher's Video Company
P.O. Box ENF-4455
Scottsdale, AZ 85261
Toll-free: (800) 262-8837
Fax: (602) 860-8650
see *Monterey Home Video*

Tower Records
Toll-free: (800) ASK-TOWER
Fax: (800) 538-6938
http://www.towerrecords.com

Universal Studios Home Video, Inc.
70 Universal City Plaza, No. 435
Universal City, CA 91608
Tel: (818) 777-3367
Fax: (818) 866-1483
1755 Broadway
New York, NY 10019
Tel: (212) 759-7500
http://www.universalstudios.com

ACKNOWLEDGMENTS

Plays

Aeschylus. *The Agamemnon of Aeschylus,* translated by Louis MacNeice. Published by Faber & Faber Ltd. Reprinted by permission of David Higham Associates.

Edward Albee. *The Zoo Story,* copyright © 1960 by Edward Albee. Reprinted by permission of William Morris Agency, Inc. on behalf of the Author. CAUTION: Professionals and amateurs are hereby warned that *The Zoo Story* is subject to a royalty. It is fully protected under the copyright laws of the United States of America and of all countries covered by the International Copyright Union (including the Dominion of Canada and the rest of the British Commonwealth), the Berne Convention, the Pan American Copyright Convention and the Universal Copyright Convention as well as all countries with which the United States has reciprocal copyright relations. All rights, including professional/amateur stage rights, motion picture, recitation, lecturing, public reading, radio broadcasting, television, video or sound recording, all other forms of mechanical or electronic reproduction, such as CD-ROM, CD-I, information storage and retrieval systems and photocopying, and the rights of translation into foreign languages are strictly reserved. Particular emphasis is laid upon the matter of readings, permission for which must be secured from the Author's agent in writing. Inquiries concerning rights should be addressed to : William Morris Agency, Inc., 1325 Avenue of the Americas, New York, NY 10019, Attn: Owen Laster.

Anonymous. *Everyman,* edited by Kate Franks. Reprinted by permission of Kate Franks.

Aristophanes. *Lysistrata,* from *Greek Literature in Translation* by Whitney Jennings Oates and Charles Theophilus Murphy. Copyright © 1942 by Longman Publishing Group. Reprinted by permission of Pearson Education, Inc.

Alan Ayckbourn. *Absurd Person Singular,* from *Three Plays* by Alan Acykbourn. Copyright © 1975 by Alan Ayckbourn. Reprinted by permission of Grove/Atlantic, Inc., Chatto & Windus and The Random House Group Limited.

Amiri Baraka. *Dutchman,* published in *Dutchman and the Slave* by William Morrow & Company. Copyright © 1964 by Amiri Baraka. Reprinted by permission of Sterling Lord Literistic, Inc.

Samuel Beckett. *Endgame,* copyright © 1958 by Grove Press, Inc.; copyright renewed 1986 by Samuel Beckett. Used by permission of Grove/Atlantic, Inc.

Bertolt Brecht. *Galileo,* translated by Charles Laughton from Chapter 2 of *In the Modern Repertoire,* Volume 2, edited by Eric Bentley. Reprinted by permission of Indiana University Press.

Georg Büchner. *Woyzeck,* by Georg Büchner, translated by Henry J. Schmidt. Copyright © 1969 by Avon Books. Published by arrangement with Werner Lehmann, Wegner Verlag. Reprinted by permission of Avon Books, a division of the Hearst Corporation.

Anton Chekhov. *The Cherry Orchard,* from *Anton Chekhov: Four Plays* translated by David Magarshack. Translation copyright © 1969 by David Magarshack. Reprinted by permission of Hill and Wang, a division of Farrar, Straus and Giroux, LLC.

Caryl Churchill. *Top Girls,* copyright © 1982 by Caryl Churchill. Reprinted by permission of Methuen Publishing Ltd.

Euripides. *The Bacchae,* translated by Kenneth Cavander. Copyright © 1966 by Kenneth Cavander. Reprinted by permission of Kenneth Cavander. WARNING: For performance rights, please apply to Peregrine Whittlesey, 345 East 80th Street, New York, NY 10021.

Brian Friel. *Translations,* from *Selected Plays of Brian* by Brian Friel. Copyright © 1986 by Brian Friel. Reprinted by permission of The Catholic University of America.

Athol Fugard. From *"MASTER HAROLD"... and the Boys* by Athol Fugard. Copyright © 1982 by Athol Fugard. Used by permission of Alfred A. Knopf, a division of Random House, Inc.

Lorraine Hansberry. *A Raisin in the Sun,* copyright © 1958 by Robert Nemiroff, as an unpublished work. Copyright © 1959, 1966, 1984 by Robert Nemiroff. Reprinted by permission of Random House, Inc.

David Henry Hwang. *Fences,* from *M. Butterfly* by David Henry Hwang. Copyright © 1986, 1987, 1988 by David Henry Hwang. Used by permission of Dutton Signet, a division of Penguin Putnam Inc.

Henrik Ibsen. *A Doll's House,* from *Ghosts and Three Other Plays* by Henrik Ibsen, translated by Michael Meyer. Copyright renewed 1994 by Michael Meyer. Reprinted by permission of Harold Ober Associates Incorporated. CAUTION: These plays are fully protected, in whole, in part, or in any form under the copyright laws of the United States of America, the British Empire including the Dominion of Canada, and all other countries of the Copyright Union, and are subject to royalty. All rights, including motion picture, radio, television, recitation, public reading are strictly reserved. For professional rights and amateur rights all inquiries should be addressed to the Author's agent: Robert A. Freedman Dramatic Agency Inc., 1501 Broadway, New York, NY 10036.

Eugene Ionesco. *The Lesson,* from *The Bald Soprano and Other Plays* by Eugene Ionesco, translated by Donald M. Allen. Copyright © 1958 by Grove Press, Inc. Reprinted by permission of Grove/Atlantic, Inc.

Ben Johnson. *Volpone,* from *Volpone* by Ben Johnson, text and notes by Philip Brockbank. Copyright © 1968 by Ernest Benn, Ltd. Reprinted by permission of Hill and Wang, a division of Farrar, Straus and Giroux, LLC.

Tony Kushner. *Angels in America, Part One: Millennium,* copyright © 1993 by Tony Kushner. Reprinted by permission of Theatre Communications Group, Inc.

Federico García Lorca. *The House of Bernarda Alba,* translated by James Graham-Lujan and Richard L. O'Connell, from *Three Tragedies,* copyright © 1947 by New Directions Publishing Corp. Reprinted by permission of New Directions Publishing Corp.

David Mamet. *Oleanna,* from *Oleanna* by David Mamet, copyright © 1992 by David Mamet. Used by permission of Pantheon Books, a division of Random House, Inc.

Christopher Marlowe. *Doctor Faustus* translated by Irving Ribner. From *Doctor Faustus: Text and Criticism* by Irving Ribner. Copyright © 1985. Reprinted by permission of Pearson Education, Inc., Upper Saddle River, NJ.

Arthur Miller. *Death of a Salesman,* from *Death of a Salesman* by Arthur Miller. Copyright © 1949, renewed 1977 by Arthur Miller. Used by permission of Viking Penguin, a division of Penguin Putnam Inc.

Molière. *The Misanthrope,* from *The Misanthrope Comedy in Five Acts* by Jean-Baptiste Poquelin de Molière. Translation copyright © 1955 and renewed 1983 by Richard Wilbur, reprinted by permission of Harcourt, Inc.

Cherríe Moraga. *Shadow of a Man,* from *Heroes and Saints & Other Plays.* Copyright © 1994, 1989 by Cherríe Moraga. Reprinted with the permission of West End Press, Albuquerque, New Mexico.

Marsha Norman. *'night, Mother,* from *'night, Mother* by Marsha Norman. Copyright © 1983 by Marsha Norman. Reprinted by permission of Hill and Wang, a division of Farrar, Straus and Giroux, LLC.

Eugene O'Neill. *Homecoming,* from *Mourning Becomes Electra* by Eugene O'Neill. Copyright © 1931 by Eugene O'Neill. Copyright renewed 1959 by Carlotta Monterery O'Neill. From *Plays of Eugene O'Neill* by Eugene O'Neill. Used by permission of Random House, Inc.

Suzan-Lori Parks. *In the Blood,* from *Red Letter Plays* by Suzan-Lori Parks. Copyright © 1998, 2001 by Suzan-Lori Parks. Published by Theatre Communications Group. Used by permission of Theatre Communications Group.

Harold Pinter. *Landscape,* from *Complete Works: Three* by Harold Pinter. Copyright © 1968 by Harold Pinter Ltd. Used by permission of Grove/Atlantic, Inc. and Faber and Faber Ltd.

Plautus. *Casina,* translated by Richard Beacham. Pages 259–318 from *Plautus: The Comedies, Vol. 1.* The series title is *Complete Roman Drama in Translation,* ed. David R. Slavitt and Palmer Bovie. Copyright © 1995.

Reprinted by permission of The Johns Hopkins University Press.

Yasmina Reza. *"Art,"* by Yasmina Reza, translation by Christopher Hampton. Translation copyright © 1996 by Yasmina Reza and Christopher Hampton. Reprinted by permission of Faber and Faber, Inc., an affiliate of Farrar, Straus and Giroux, LLC.

William Shakespeare. *Much Ado About Nothing,* from *Much Ado About Nothing* by William Shakespeare, edited by David L. Stevenson. Copyright © 1964 by David L. Stevenson. Copyright © 1963, 1989, 1998 by Sylvan Barnet. Used by permission of Dutton Signet, a division of Penguin Putnam Inc.

William Shakespeare. *The Tragedy of Othello,* from *The Tragedy of Othello* by William Shakespeare, edited by Alvin Kernan. Copyright © 1963 by Alvin Kernan. Used by permission of Dutton Signet, a division of Penguin Putnam Inc.

George Bernard Shaw. *Pygmalion,* Copyright © 1913, 1914, 1916, 1930, 1941 by George Bernard Shaw. Copyright © 1957 by The Public Trustee as Executor of the Estate of George Bernard Shaw. Reprinted by permission of The Society of Authors on behalf of the Estate of Bernard Shaw.

Sophocles. *Oedipus Rex,* from *Sophocles, The Oedipus Cycle: An English Version* by Dudley Fitts and Robert Fitzgerald, copyright © 1949 by Harcourt, Inc. and renewed 1977 by Cornelia Fitts and Robert Fitzgerald. Reprinted by permission of the publisher. CAUTION: All rights, including professional, amateur, motion picture, recitation, lecturing, public reading, radio broadcasting and television are strictly reserved. Inquiries on all rights should be addressed to Harcourt, Inc., Permissions Department, Orlando, FL 32887-6777.

Wole Soyinka. *Death and the King's Horseman,* from *Death and the King's Horseman* by Wole Soyinka. Copyright © 1975 by Wole Soyinka. Used by permission of W.W. Norton & Company, Inc. and Melanie Jackson Agency, L.L.C.

Tom Stoppard. *Arcadia,* from *Arcadia* by Tom Stoppard. Copyright © 1993 by Tom Stoppard. Reprinted by permission of Faber and Faber, Inc., an affiliate of Farrar, Straus and Giroux, LLC.

August Strindberg. *Miss Julie,* from *Six Plays of August Strindberg,* translated by Elizabeth Sprigge. Copyright © 1960 by Elizabeth Sprigge. Reprinted by permission of Curtis Brown, Ltd.

J. M. Synge. *In the Shadow of the Glen,* by J. M. Synge, notes by T. R. Henn. Reprinted by permission of Methuen Rights.

Paula Vogel. *How I Learned to Drive,* from *The Mammary Plays* by Paula Vogel. Copyright © 1997, 1998 by Paula Vogel. Published by Theatre Communications Group. Used by permission of Theatre Communications Group.

The Wakefield Master. *The Second Shepherds' Play,* modernized and edited by Anthony Caputi, first published in *Masterworks of World Drama, Vol. 2,* 1968. Reprinted by permission of Anthony Caputi.

Derek Walcott. *Pantomime,* from *Remembrance and Pantomime* by Derek Walcott. Copyright © 1980 by Derek Walcott. Reprinted by permission of Farrar, Straus & Giroux, LLC.

Oscar Wilde. *The Importance of Being Earnest,* from the Routledge English Texts Series Edition, edited by Joseph Bristow. Reprinted by permission of Routledge and Joseph Bristow.

Tennessee Williams. *Cat on a Hot Tin Roof,* from *Cat on a Hot Tin Roof* by Tennessee Williams. Copyright © 1954, 1955, 1971, 1975 by University of the South. Reprinted by permission of New Directions Publishing Corp.

August Wilson. *Fences* from *Fences,* by August Wilson. Copyright © 1986 by August Wilson. Used by permission of Dutton Signet, a division of Penguin Putnam Inc.

Reviews, Interviews, and Essays

Norman Allen. "Lee and Greenwood on Collaborating with O'Neill" from *Asides,* 1997, published by The Shakespeare Theatre, Washington, DC.

Antonin Artaud. Excerpt from *The Theater and Its Double* by Antonin Artaud, copyright © 1958. Reprinted by permission of Grove/Atlantic.

Elizabeth Ashley. Excerpt from *Actress: Postcards from the Road* by Elizabeth Ashley and Ross Firestone. Copyright © 1978 by Elizabeth Ashley. Reprinted by permission of M. Evans & Company, Inc.

Brooks Atkinson. Review of *A Raisin in the Sun* from *The New York Times,* March 12, 1959. Copyright © 1959 by the New York Times Co. Reprinted by permission.

Alan Ayckbourn. Excerpt from *A Guided Tour Through Ayckbourn Country,* edited by Albert-Reiner Glaap and Nicholas P. Quaintmere. (WVT Wissenschaftlicher Verlag, Trier).

Amiri Baraka. Interview with Mike Coleman from *Black World* 20, no. 6 (April 1971) 32–36. Copyright © 1971 by Amiri Baraka. Reprinted by permission of Sterling Lord Literistic for the author and the Johnson Publishing Company, Chicago, Illinois.

David Barbour. "Molière à la Mode," Review of *The Misanthrope* from *Entertainment Design,* April 1999. Reprinted by permission of Primemedia Enterprises.

Arthur Bartow. Interview with Lloyd Richards from *The Director's Voice.* Reprinted with permission of Theatre Communications Group.

Clive Barnes. Review of *The Misanthrope* from *The New York Times,* October 10, 1968. Review of *Cat on a Hot Tin Roof* from *The New York Times,* September 25, 1974. Review of *The School for Scandal* from *The New York Times,* June 11, 1970. Copyright © 1968, 1970, 1974 by The New York Times Company. Reprinted by permission.

Michael Billington. Review of *The House of Bernarda Alba* from *The Guardian,* May 2, 1987. Copyright © 1987 by Michael Billington. Reprinted by permission of the author. Review of *The Importance of Being Earnest* from *The Guardian,* 1982. Copyright © 1982 by *The Guardian.* Reprinted by permission of Guardian News Services.

Ben Brantley. Review of *A Doll's House,* "A Nora Who Makes Ibsen's Rebellious Housewife New" from *The New York Times,* April 3, 1997. Copyright © 1997 by The New York Times Company. Reprinted by permission.

Bertolt Brecht. Excerpt from *Brecht on Theatre,* translated by John Willett. Copyright © 1964. Reprinted by permission of Farrar, Straus & Giroux and Suhrkamp Verlag.

Ronald Bryden. Review of *Othello* from *New Statesman & Society,* May 1, 1964. Copyright © 1964 by *New Statesman & Society.* Reprinted by permission of Guardian News Service Limited. Review of *Pygmalion* reprinted by permission of *Plays & Players.*

Anthony Burgess. Letters by Anthony Burgess from *Sophocles: Oedipus the King,* translated and adapted by Anthony Burgess, with Comments by Anthony Burgess, Michael Langham and Stanley Silverman. Copyright © 1972 by Anthony Burgess. Copyright © 1972 by the University of Minnesota. All Rights Reserved. Reprinted by permission.

Harold Clurman. Review of *Dutchman* from the April 13, 1964, issue of *The Nation.* Reprinted by permission.

Michael Coveney. Review of *Lysistrata* from *The Observer,* June 20, 1993. Copyright © 1993 by *The Observer.* Reprinted by permission of Guardian News Services.

Scott Cummings. "*The Bacchae:* American Repertory Theatre" from *InTheater,* January 23, 1998.

Nick Curtis. Review of *Landscape* from the *London Evening Standard,* November 24, 1994. Copyright © 1994 by the London Evening Standard. Reprinted by permission of Atlantic Syndication.

Robert Cushman. Review of *Top Girls* from *The Observer,* September 1982. Copyright © 1982 by Robert Cushman. Reprinted by permission of *The Observer.*

Martin Esslin. Excerpt from *The Theatre of the Absurd* by Martin Esslin. Copyright © 1961 by Martin Esslin. Reprinted by permission of Doubleday, a division of Random House, Inc.

Ann Fitzgerald. Review of the Royal Shakespeare Company's production of *The Second Shepherds' Play* from *The Stage,* 1978. Reprinted by permission of The Stage Newspaper Ltd.

Mel Gussow. Review of *Much Ado About Nothing* from *The New York Times,* August 18, 1972. Copyright © 1972 by The New York Times Company. Review of *Miss Julie* from *The New York Times*, June 12, 1991. Copyright © 1991 by The New York Times Company. Review of *Woyzeck* from *The New York Times*, December 7, 1992. Copyright © 1992 by The New York Times Company. Reprinted by permission. Review of *Endgame* from *The New York Times*, December 20, 1984. Copyright © 1984 by the New York Times Co. Reprinted by permission.

Peter Hall. Excerpt from *Exposed by the Mask: Form and Language in Drama* by Peter Hall. Copyright © 2000 by Peter Hall. Reprinted by permission of Theatre Communications Group.

Stephen Halliwell. Excerpt from "On the Nature and Elements of Tragedy" from *The Poetics* by Aristotle, translated by Stephen Halliwell (London: Duckworth, 1987). Reprinted by permission of Stephen Halliwell and Gerald Duckworth and Company Ltd.

Peter Haugen. Review of *Shadow of a Man* by Peter Haugen from *The Sacramento Bee*, November 12, 1990. Copyright, *The Sacramento Bee*, 2002.

Sarah Hemming. Review of *"Art"* from *Financial Times*, October 16, 1996. Review of *Volpone* from *Financial Times*, July 29, 1995. Reprinted by permission of Financial Times Syndication.

Heather Henderson. "Building Fences: An Interview with Mary Alice and James Earl Jones" from *Theater*, Summer/Fall 1985. Copyright © 1985 by *Theatre*. Reprinted by permission of Duke University Press.

Henry Hewes. Review of *The Zoo Story* from the *Saturday Review*, February 6, 1960. Reprinted by permission of The General Media Publishing Group.

Arthur Holmberg. "Through the Eyes of Lolita" an interview with Paula Vogel, is reprinted with permission of the American Repertory Theatre.

Eiko Ishioka. Excerpt from *Eiko on Stage* (New York: Callaway Editions, 2000, 54-56) is reprinted by permission of Callaway Editions.

Margo Jefferson. Review of *In the Blood* from *The New York Times*, November 23, 1999. Copyright © 1999 by The New York Times Company. Reprinted by permission.

Nicholas de Jongh. Review of *Translations* from the *London Evening Standard*, June 10, 1983. Copyright © 1993 by the London Evening Standard. Reprinted by permission of Atlantic Syndication.

Stefan Kanfer. Review of *Angels in America: Millennium Approaches* from *The New Leader*, June 14–28, 1993. pp. 22–23. Copyright © 1993 by the American Conference on International Affairs. Reprinted with permission from The New Leader, Inc.

Walter Kerr. Review of *A Doll's House* from *The New York Times*, January 24, 1971. Copyright © 1971 by The New York Times Company. Reprinted by permission. Review of *The Lesson* from *The New York Herald Tribune*, book review section, January 10, 1958.

Jack Kroll. Review of *The Bacchae* from *Newsweek*, March 2, 1969. Copyright © 1969, Newsweek, Inc. Reprinted by permission. All rights reserved.

John Lahr. "Making Willy Loman," copyright © 1999 by John Lahr. "Dogma Days," copyright © 1992 by John Lahr. Both originally appeared in *The New Yorker*. Reprinted by permission of Georges Borchardt, Inc.

James Lardner. Review of *Death and the King's Horseman* from *The Washington Post*, December 5, 1979. Reprinted by permission of the author.

Stuart Little. Excerpt from *Enter Joseph Papp* from *Enter Joseph Papp: In Search of a New American Theater* by Stuart W. Little (Coward, McCann & Geoghegan, Inc.). Copyright © 1974 by Stuart W. Little.

Tim Lubbock. Review of *"Art"* from *The Observer*, October 20, 1996. Copyright © 1996 by Tim Lubbock. Reprinted by permission of *The Observer*.

Alastair Macaulay. Review of *Landscape* from the *Financial Times*, November 24, 1994. Review of *Shadows* from the *Financial Times*, March 5, 1998. Both reprinted by permission of Financial Times Syndication.

Melvin Maddocks. Review of *Oedipus Rex*. From *The Christian Science Monitor*, November 6, 1972. Copyright © 1972 by The Christian Science Publishing Society. Reprinted by permission of *The Christian Science Monitor*.

Peter Marks. Review of *A Doll's House*, "A Nora Beyond All Pretense" from *The New York Times*, June 3, 1997. Copyright © 1997 by The New York Times Company. Reprinted by permission.

Arthur Miller. "Tragedy and the Common Man," excerpted from *The Theatre Essays of Arthur Miller* by Arthur Miller, edited by Robert A. Martin. Copyright © 1949, renewed 1977 by Arthur Miller. Used by permission of Viking Penguin, a division of Penguin Putnam Inc.

Gwyn Morgan. "Three Women in Othello" from *Plays & Players*, October 1989.

Benedict Nightingale. Review of *The Rover* from *The New Statesman*, July 18, 1996. Copyright © 1996 by the New Statesman. Reprinted by permission of Guardian News Services.

Roderick Nordell. Review of *Agamemnon*. From *The Christian Science Monitor*, September 22, 1967. Copyright © 1967 by The Christian Science Publishing Society. Reprinted by permission of *The Christian Science Monitor*. All rights reserved.

Geoffrey Norman and John Rezek. Interview with David Mamet. Copyright © 1995 by Playboy. From "The Playboy Interview: David Mamet," *Playboy Magazine* (April 1995). Reprinted with permission. All rights reserved.

Marsha Norman. "Ten Golden Rules for Playwrights" from *The Writer*, September, 1985, volume 98. Copyright © 1985 by Marsha Norman. Reprinted by permission of The Gersh Agency. All rights reserved.

Suzan-Lori Parks. "Tradition and the Individual Talent" from *Theater,* Summer 1999, Volume 29. Copyright 1999 by Yale School of Drama/Yale Repertory Theater. Reprinted by permission of Duke University Press.

John Peter. Review of *Six Characters in Search of an Author* from the *Sunday Times,* February 25, 2001. Reprinted by permission of Financial Times Syndication.

Sidney Poitier. Excerpt from *This Life* by Sidney Poitier, copyright © 1980 by Sidney Poitier. Used by permission of Alfred Knopf, a division of Random House, Inc.

Frank Rich. Review of *'night, Mother* from *The New York Times,* April 1, 1983. Copyright © 1983 by The New York Times Co. Review of *"MASTER HAROLD"... and the Boys* from *The New York Times,* May 5, 1982. Copyright © 1982 by The New York Times Co. Reprinted by permission.

G. B. Shand. Excerpt from "Directing Doctor Faustus" from *The Elizabethan Theatre XI.* Reprinted by permission of the author.

Irwin Shaw. "The Earth Stands Still" from *The New Republic,* December 29, 1947.

Don Shirley. Review of *Casina* from *The Los Angeles Times,* October 20, 1994. Copyright © 1994. Reprinted by permission of The Los Angeles Times Syndicate.

Charles Spencer. Review of *Everyman,* "Art: New Life in an Old Play about Death" from *The Daily Telegraph,* November 18, 1996. Copyright © 1996 by *The Daily Telegraph.* Reprinted by permission of Ewan Macnaughton Associates.

August Strindberg. "Preface" to *Miss Julie* by August Strindberg, translated by E. M. Sprinchorn. San Francisco: Chandler Publishing Company, 1961.

Howard Taubman. Review of *Dutchman* from *The New York Times,* March 25, 1964. Copyright © 1964 by The New York Times Co. Reprinted by permission.

Paul Taylor. "More than the Sum of Its Parts: Paul Taylor on Tom Stoppard's Arcadia" from *The Independent,* April 15, 1993. Copyright © 1993 by *The Independent.* "Endgame, Donmar Warehouse" by Paul Taylor from *The Independent,* April 19, 1996. Copyright © 1996 by *The Independent.* Reprinted by permission.

Kenneth Tynan. Interview with Laurence Olivier by Kenneth Tynan, from *Great Acting,* edited by Hal Burton. Copyright © The Authors and the British Broadcasting Corporation. All rights reserved. Excerpt from pages 6–8 in *Othello: The National Theatre Production* by Kenneth Tynan. Copyright © 1966 by The National Theatre Production. Rupert Hart-Davis Ltd., publisher. Reprinted by permission of International Creative Management, Ltd. for the estates of Laurence Olivier and Kenneth Tynan.

Douglas Watt. Review of *'night, Mother* from the *Daily News,* April 1, 1983. Copyright © 1983 by New York News, Inc. Reprinted with permission.

Penelope Wilton. "On Playing Madame Ranevskaya" from *In the Company of Actors* by Carole Zucker. Copyright © 1999 by Carole Zucker. Reproduced by permission of Routledge, Inc., part of The Taylor & Francis Group.